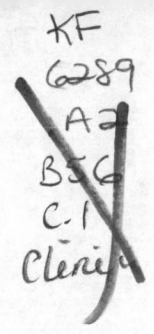

# Bloomberg BNA
# 2015 Federal Tax Guide

# PREFACE

> > > > > > > > > > > > > > > > > > > > > > > > > > >

Bloomberg BNA Tax and Accounting is pleased to publish this first annual edition of the Bloomberg BNA 2015 Federal Tax Guide. This book is designed as a quick reference tool for the preparation of 2014 individual and business tax returns.

Useful for both novices and experts, the Federal Tax Guide is written in easy-to-understand language, and is supported by numerous examples and citations to underlying authority, as well as cross-references to Bloomberg BNA Tax Management Portfolios and Tax Practice Series chapters. You will find the Federal Tax Guide a reliable and useful resource in the preparation of 2014 IRS Forms 1040, 1041, 1120, 1120S, 1065, 706 and 709, and accompanying schedules.

The Federal Tax Guide is organized by topics, such as income items and exclusions, deductions, credits, property transactions, tax computation, retirement plans, and transfer taxes. The Federal Tax Guide covers taxation of individuals, corporations, partnerships, and exempt organizations.

To aid practitioners in easily accessing tax rates, filing requirements and similar information, the Schedules & Tables section of the Federal Tax Guide includes tables, worksheets, charts, checklists, diagrams, and flowcharts. This book is one of a series of annual tax handbooks that include:

- 2015 State Tax Essentials; and
- 2015 U.S. International Tax Guide.

For more information on Bloomberg BNA tax publications, including the Bloomberg BNA Tax & Accounting Center, go to www.bna.com.

The Bloomberg BNA 2015 Federal Tax Guide includes coverage of a number of temporary tax breaks, known as "tax extenders," that expired on December 31, 2013. As of the date of publication, there are pending legislative proposals that would extend many of these temporary tax breaks or make them permanent. For updates on year-end tax legislation and other content updates affecting the Bloomberg BNA 2015 Federal Tax Guide, please visit www.bna.com/2015-federal-tax-update.

# TABLE OF CONTENTS

# 2015 Federal Tax Guide

## Table of Contents

# Table of Contents

# Table of Contents

# Table of Contents

**Table of Contents**

## Table of Contents

# Table of Contents

## Table of Contents

# Table of Contents

## Table of Contents

# Table of Contents

# Table of Contents

# Table of Contents

## Table of Contents

## Table of Contents

## Table of Contents

**Table of Contents**

# Table of Contents

## Table of Contents

## 2015 Federal Tax Guide

# 1. 2014 Tax Rate Schedules
(Source: Rev. Proc. 2013-35, 2013-47 I.R.B. 537)

### Section 1(a) - MARRIED INDIVIDUALS FILING JOINT RETURNS AND SURVIVING SPOUSES

| If Taxable Income Is: | The Tax Is: |
| --- | --- |
| Not Over $18,150 | 10% of the taxable income. |
| Over $18,150 but not over $73,800 | $1,815 plus 15% of the excess over $18,150. |
| Over $73,800 but not over $148,850 | $10,162.50 plus 25% of the excess over $73,800. |
| Over $148,850 but not over $226,850 | $28,925 plus 28% of the excess over $148,850. |
| Over $226,850 but not over $405,100 | $50,765 plus 33% of the excess over $226,850. |
| Over $405,100 but not over $457,600 | $109,587.50 plus 35% of the excess over $405,100. |
| Over $457,600 | $127,962.50 plus 39.6% of the excess over $457,600. |

### Section 1(b) - HEADS OF HOUSEHOLDS

| If Taxable Income Is: | The Tax Is: |
| --- | --- |
| Not Over $12,950 | 10% of the taxable income. |
| Over $12,950 but not over $49,400 | $1,295 plus 15% of the excess over $12,950. |
| Over $49,400 but not over $127,550 | $6,762.50 plus 25% of the excess over $49,400. |
| Over $127,550 but not over $206,600 | $26,300 plus 28% of the excess over $127,550. |
| Over $206,600 but not over $405,100 | $48,434 plus 33% of the excess over $206,600. |
| Over $405,100 but not over $432,200 | $113,939 plus 35% of the excess over $405,100. |
| Over $432,200 | $123,424 plus 39.6% of the excess over $432,200. |

### Section 1(c) - UNMARRIED INDIVIDUALS (OTHER THAN SURVIVING SPOUSES AND HEADS OF HOUSEHOLDS)

| If Taxable Income Is: | The Tax Is: |
| --- | --- |
| Not Over $9,075 | 10% of the taxable income. |
| Over $9,075 but not over $36,900 | $907.50 plus 15% of the excess over $9,075. |
| Over $36,900 but not over $89,350 | $5,081.25 plus 25% of the excess over $36,900. |
| Over $89,350 but not over $186,350 | $18,193.75 plus 28% of the excess over $89,350. |
| Over $186,350 but not over $405,100 | $45,353.75 plus 33% of the excess over $186,350. |
| Over $405,100 but not over $406,750 | $117,541.25 plus 35% of the excess over $405,100. |
| Over $406,750 | $118,118.75 plus 39.6% of the excess over $406,750. |

### Section 1(d) - MARRIED INDIVIDUALS FILING SEPARATE RETURNS

| If Taxable Income Is: | The Tax Is: |
| --- | --- |
| Not Over $9,075 | 10% of the taxable income. |
| Over $9,075 but not over $36,900 | $907.50 plus 15% of the excess over $9,075. |
| Over $36,900 but not over $74,425 | $5,081.25 plus 25% of the excess over $36,900. |
| Over $74,425 but not over $113,425 | $14,462.50 plus 28% of the excess over $74,425. |
| Over $113,425 but not over $202,550 | $25,382.50 plus 33% of the excess over $113,425. |
| Over $202,550 but not over $228,800 | $54,793.75 plus 35% of the excess over $202,550. |
| Over $228,800 | $63,981.25 plus 39.6% of the excess over $228,800. |

### Section 1(e) - ESTATES AND TRUSTS

| If Taxable Income Is: | The Tax Is: |
| --- | --- |
| Not Over $2,500 | 15% of the taxable income. |
| Over $2,500 but not over $5,800 | $375 plus 25% of the excess over $2,500. |
| Over $5,800 but not over $8,900 | $1,200 plus 28% of the excess over $5,800. |
| Over $8,900 but not over $12,150 | $2,068 plus 33% of the excess over $8,900. |
| Over $12,150 | $3,140.50 plus 39.6% of the excess over $12,150. |

## 2. 2015 Tax Rate Schedules
(Source: Rev. Proc. 2014-61, 2014-47 I.R.B. 860)

### Section 1(a) — MARRIED INDIVIDUALS FILING JOINT RETURNS AND SURVIVING SPOUSES

| If Taxable Income Is: | The Tax Is: |
| --- | --- |
| Not Over $18,450 | 10% of the taxable income. |
| Over $18,450 but not over $74,900 | $1,845 plus 15% of excess over $18,450. |
| Over $74,900 but not over $151,200 | $10,312.50 plus 25% of excess over $74,900. |
| Over $151,200 but not over $230,450 | $29,387.50 plus 28% of excess over $151,200. |
| Over $230,450 but not over $411,500 | $51,577.50 plus 33% of excess over $230,450. |
| Over $411,500 but not over $464,850 | $111,324 plus 35% of excess over $411,500. |
| Over $464,850 | $129,996.50 plus 39.6% of excess over $464,850. |

### Section 1(b) — HEADS OF HOUSEHOLDS

| If Taxable Income Is: | The Tax Is: |
| --- | --- |
| Not Over $13,150 | 10% of the taxable income. |
| Over $13,150 but not over $50,200 | $1,315 plus 15% of excess over $13,150. |
| Over $50,200 but not over $129,600 | $6,872.50 plus 25% of excess over $50,200. |
| Over $129,600 but not over $209,850 | $26,722.50 plus 28% of excess over $129,600. |
| Over $209,850 but not over $411,500 | $49,192.50 plus 33% of excess over $209,850. |
| Over $411,500 but not over $439,000 | $115,737 plus 35% of excess over $411,500. |
| Over $439,000 | $125,362 plus 39.6% of excess over $439,000. |

### Section 1(c) — UNMARRIED INDIVIDUALS (OTHER THAN SURVIVING SPOUSES AND HEADS OF HOUSEHOLDS)

| If Taxable Income Is: | The Tax Is: |
| --- | --- |
| Not Over $9,225 | 10% of the taxable income. |
| Over $9,225 but not over $37,450 | $922.50 plus 15% of excess over $9,225. |
| Over $37,450 but not over $90,750 | $5,156.25 plus 25% of excess over $37,450. |
| Over $90,750 but not over $189,300 | $18,481.25 plus 28% of excess over $90,750. |
| Over $189,300 but not over $411,500 | $46,075.25 plus 33% of excess over $189,300. |
| Over $411,500 but not over $413,200 | $119,401.25 plus 35% of excess over $411,500. |

Over $413,200         $119,996.25 plus 39.6% of excess over $413,200.

## Section 1(d) — MARRIED INDIVIDUALS FILING SEPARATE RETURNS

| If Taxable Income Is: | The Tax Is: |
| --- | --- |
| Not Over $9,225 | 10% of the taxable income. |
| Over $9,225 but not over $37,450 | $922.50 plus 15% of excess over $9,225. |
| Over $37,450 but not over $75,600 | $5,156.25 plus 25% of excess over $37,450. |
| Over $75,600 but not over $115,225 | $14,693.75 plus 28% of excess over $75,600. |
| Over $115,225 but not over $205,750 | $25,788.75 plus 33% of excess over $115,225. |
| Over $205,750 but not over $232,425 | $55,662 plus 35% of excess over $205,750. |
| Over $232,425 | $64,998.25 plus 39.6% of excess over $232,425. |

## Section 1(e) — ESTATES AND TRUSTS

| If Taxable Income Is: | The Tax Is: |
| --- | --- |
| Not Over $2,500 | 15% of the taxable income. |
| Over $2,500 but not over $5,900 | $375 plus 25% of excess over $2,500. |
| Over $5,900 but not over $9,050 | $1,225 plus 28% of excess over $5,900. |
| Over $9,050 but not over $12,300 | $2,107 plus 33% of excess over $9,050. |
| Over $12,300 | $3,179.50 plus 39.6% of excess over $12,300. |

# 3. 2014 Tax Computation Worksheet
### (Source: 2014 Form 1040 Draft Instructions)

## 2014 Tax Computation Worksheet—Line 44

 *See the instructions for line 44 to see if you must use the worksheet below to figure your tax.*

**Note.** If you are required to use this worksheet to figure the tax on an amount from another form or worksheet, such as the Qualified Dividends and Capital Gain Tax Worksheet, the Schedule D Tax Worksheet, Schedule J, Form 8615, or the Foreign Earned Income Tax Worksheet, enter the amount from that form or worksheet in column (a) of the row that applies to the amount you are looking up. Enter the result on the appropriate line of the form or worksheet that you are completing.

**Section A**—Use if your filing status is **Single**. Complete the row below that applies to you.

| Taxable income. If line 43 is— | (a) Enter the amount from line 43 | (b) Multiplication amount | (c) Multiply (a) by (b) | (d) Subtraction amount | Tax. Subtract (d) from (c). Enter the result here and on Form 1040, line 44 |
|---|---|---|---|---|---|
| At least $100,000 but not over $186,350 | $ | × 28% (.28) | $ | $ 6,824.25 | $ |
| Over $186,350 but not over $405,100 | $ | × 33% (.33) | $ | $ 16,141.75 | $ |
| Over $405,100 but not over $406,750 | $ | × 35% (.35) | $ | $ 24,243.75 | $ |
| Over $406,750 | $ | × 39.6% (.396) | $ | $ 42,954.25 | $ |

**Section B**—Use if your filing status is **Married filing jointly** or **Qualifying widow(er)**. Complete the row below that applies to you.

| Taxable income. If line 43 is— | (a) Enter the amount from line 43 | (b) Multiplication amount | (c) Multiply (a) by (b) | (d) Subtraction amount | Tax. Subtract (d) from (c). Enter the result here and on Form 1040, line 44 |
|---|---|---|---|---|---|
| At least $100,000 but not over $148,850 | $ | × 25% (.25) | $ | $ 8,287.50 | $ |
| Over $148,850 but not over $226,850 | $ | × 28% (.28) | $ | $ 12,753.00 | $ |
| Over $226,850 but not over $405,100 | $ | × 33% (.33) | $ | $ 24,095.50 | $ |
| Over $405,100 but not over $457,600 | $ | × 35% (.35) | $ | $ 32,197.50 | $ |
| Over $457,600 | $ | × 39.6% (.396) | $ | $ 53,247.10 | $ |

**Section C**—Use if your filing status is **Married filing separately**. Complete the row below that applies to you.

| Taxable income. If line 43 is— | (a) Enter the amount from line 43 | (b) Multiplication amount | (c) Multiply (a) by (b) | (d) Subtraction amount | Tax. Subtract (d) from (c). Enter the result here and on Form 1040, line 44 |
|---|---|---|---|---|---|
| At least $100,000 but not over $113,425 | $ | × 28% (.28) | $ | $ 6,376.50 | $ |
| Over $113,425 but not over $202,550 | $ | × 33% (.33) | $ | $ 12,047.75 | $ |
| Over $202,550 but not over $228,800 | $ | × 35% (.35) | $ | $ 16,098.75 | $ |
| Over $228,800 | $ | × 39.6% (.396) | $ | $ 26,623.55 | $ |

**Section D**—Use if your filing status is **Head of household**. Complete the row below that applies to you.

| Taxable income. If line 43 is— | (a) Enter the amount from line 43 | (b) Multiplication amount | (c) Multiply (a) by (b) | (d) Subtraction amount | Tax. Subtract (d) from (c). Enter the result here and on Form 1040, line 44 |
|---|---|---|---|---|---|
| At least $100,000 but not over $127,550 | $ | × 25% (.25) | $ | $ 5,587.50 | $ |
| Over $127,550 but not over $206,600 | $ | × 28% (.28) | $ | $ 9,414.00 | $ |
| Over $206,600 but not over $405,100 | $ | × 33% (.33) | $ | $ 19,744.00 | $ |
| Over $405,100 but not over $432,200 | $ | × 35% (.35) | $ | $ 27,846.00 | $ |
| Over $432,200 | $ | × 39.6% (.396) | $ | $ 47,727.20 | $ |

# 4. 2014 Tax Tables

(Source: 2014 Form 1040 Draft Instructions)

**2014 Tax Table**

See the instructions for line 44 to see if you must use the Tax Table below to figure your tax.

**Example.** Mr. and Mrs. Brown are filing a joint return. Their taxable income on Form 1040, line 43, is $25,300. First, they find the $25,300-25,350 taxable income line. Next, they find the column for married filing jointly and read down the column. The amount shown where the taxable income line and filing status column meet is $2,891. This is the tax amount they should enter on Form 1040, line 44.

**Sample Table**

| At Least | But Less Than | Single | Married filing jointly* | Married filing separately | Head of a household |
|---|---|---|---|---|---|
| | | | **Your tax is—** | | |
| 25,200 | 25,250 | 3,330 | 2,876 | 3,330 | 3,136 |
| 25,250 | 25,300 | 3,338 | 2,884 | 3,338 | 3,144 |
| 25,300 | 25,350 | 3,345 | (2,891) | 3,345 | 3,151 |
| 25,350 | 25,400 | 3,353 | 2,899 | 3,353 | 3,159 |

| If line 43 (taxable income) is— | | And you are— | | | | If line 43 (taxable income) is— | | And you are— | | | | If line 43 (taxable income) is— | | And you are— | | | |
|---|---|---|---|---|---|---|---|---|---|---|---|---|---|---|---|---|---|
| At least | But less than | Single | Married filing jointly * | Married filing separately | Head of a household | At least | But less than | Single | Married filing jointly * | Married filing separately | Head of a household | At least | But less than | Single | Married filing jointly * | Married filing separately | Head of a household |
| | | | **Your tax is—** | | | | | | **Your tax is—** | | | | | | **Your tax is—** | | |
| 0 | 5 | 0 | 0 | 0 | 0 | **1,000** | | | | | | **2,000** | | | | | |
| 5 | 15 | 1 | 1 | 1 | 1 | | | | | | | | | | | | |
| 15 | 25 | 2 | 2 | 2 | 2 | | | | | | | | | | | | |
| 25 | 50 | 4 | 4 | 4 | 4 | | | | | | | | | | | | |
| 50 | 75 | 6 | 6 | 6 | 6 | 1,000 | 1,025 | 101 | 101 | 101 | 101 | 2,000 | 2,025 | 201 | 201 | 201 | 201 |
| | | | | | | 1,025 | 1,050 | 104 | 104 | 104 | 104 | 2,025 | 2,050 | 204 | 204 | 204 | 204 |
| 75 | 100 | 9 | 9 | 9 | 9 | 1,050 | 1,075 | 106 | 106 | 106 | 106 | 2,050 | 2,075 | 206 | 206 | 206 | 206 |
| 100 | 125 | 11 | 11 | 11 | 11 | 1,075 | 1,100 | 109 | 109 | 109 | 109 | 2,075 | 2,100 | 209 | 209 | 209 | 209 |
| 125 | 150 | 14 | 14 | 14 | 14 | 1,100 | 1,125 | 111 | 111 | 111 | 111 | 2,100 | 2,125 | 211 | 211 | 211 | 211 |
| 150 | 175 | 16 | 16 | 16 | 16 | | | | | | | | | | | | |
| 175 | 200 | 19 | 19 | 19 | 19 | 1,125 | 1,150 | 114 | 114 | 114 | 114 | 2,125 | 2,150 | 214 | 214 | 214 | 214 |
| | | | | | | 1,150 | 1,175 | 116 | 116 | 116 | 116 | 2,150 | 2,175 | 216 | 216 | 216 | 216 |
| 200 | 225 | 21 | 21 | 21 | 21 | 1,175 | 1,200 | 119 | 119 | 119 | 119 | 2,175 | 2,200 | 219 | 219 | 219 | 219 |
| 225 | 250 | 24 | 24 | 24 | 24 | 1,200 | 1,225 | 121 | 121 | 121 | 121 | 2,200 | 2,225 | 221 | 221 | 221 | 221 |
| 250 | 275 | 26 | 26 | 26 | 26 | 1,225 | 1,250 | 124 | 124 | 124 | 124 | 2,225 | 2,250 | 224 | 224 | 224 | 224 |
| 275 | 300 | 29 | 29 | 29 | 29 | | | | | | | | | | | | |
| 300 | 325 | 31 | 31 | 31 | 31 | 1,250 | 1,275 | 126 | 126 | 126 | 126 | 2,250 | 2,275 | 226 | 226 | 226 | 226 |
| | | | | | | 1,275 | 1,300 | 129 | 129 | 129 | 129 | 2,275 | 2,300 | 229 | 229 | 229 | 229 |
| 325 | 350 | 34 | 34 | 34 | 34 | 1,300 | 1,325 | 131 | 131 | 131 | 131 | 2,300 | 2,325 | 231 | 231 | 231 | 231 |
| 350 | 375 | 36 | 36 | 36 | 36 | 1,325 | 1,350 | 134 | 134 | 134 | 134 | 2,325 | 2,350 | 234 | 234 | 234 | 234 |
| 375 | 400 | 39 | 39 | 39 | 39 | 1,350 | 1,375 | 136 | 136 | 136 | 136 | 2,350 | 2,375 | 236 | 236 | 236 | 236 |
| 400 | 425 | 41 | 41 | 41 | 41 | | | | | | | | | | | | |
| 425 | 450 | 44 | 44 | 44 | 44 | 1,375 | 1,400 | 139 | 139 | 139 | 139 | 2,375 | 2,400 | 239 | 239 | 239 | 239 |
| | | | | | | 1,400 | 1,425 | 141 | 141 | 141 | 141 | 2,400 | 2,425 | 241 | 241 | 241 | 241 |
| 450 | 475 | 46 | 46 | 46 | 46 | 1,425 | 1,450 | 144 | 144 | 144 | 144 | 2,425 | 2,450 | 244 | 244 | 244 | 244 |
| 475 | 500 | 49 | 49 | 49 | 49 | 1,450 | 1,475 | 146 | 146 | 146 | 146 | 2,450 | 2,475 | 246 | 246 | 246 | 246 |
| 500 | 525 | 51 | 51 | 51 | 51 | 1,475 | 1,500 | 149 | 149 | 149 | 149 | 2,475 | 2,500 | 249 | 249 | 249 | 249 |
| 525 | 550 | 54 | 54 | 54 | 54 | | | | | | | | | | | | |
| 550 | 575 | 56 | 56 | 56 | 56 | 1,500 | 1,525 | 151 | 151 | 151 | 151 | 2,500 | 2,525 | 251 | 251 | 251 | 251 |
| | | | | | | 1,525 | 1,550 | 154 | 154 | 154 | 154 | 2,525 | 2,550 | 254 | 254 | 254 | 254 |
| 575 | 600 | 59 | 59 | 59 | 59 | 1,550 | 1,575 | 156 | 156 | 156 | 156 | 2,550 | 2,575 | 256 | 256 | 256 | 256 |
| 600 | 625 | 61 | 61 | 61 | 61 | 1,575 | 1,600 | 159 | 159 | 159 | 159 | 2,575 | 2,600 | 259 | 259 | 259 | 259 |
| 625 | 650 | 64 | 64 | 64 | 64 | 1,600 | 1,625 | 161 | 161 | 161 | 161 | 2,600 | 2,625 | 261 | 261 | 261 | 261 |
| 650 | 675 | 66 | 66 | 66 | 66 | | | | | | | | | | | | |
| 675 | 700 | 69 | 69 | 69 | 69 | 1,625 | 1,650 | 164 | 164 | 164 | 164 | 2,625 | 2,650 | 264 | 264 | 264 | 264 |
| | | | | | | 1,650 | 1,675 | 166 | 166 | 166 | 166 | 2,650 | 2,675 | 266 | 266 | 266 | 266 |
| 700 | 725 | 71 | 71 | 71 | 71 | 1,675 | 1,700 | 169 | 169 | 169 | 169 | 2,675 | 2,700 | 269 | 269 | 269 | 269 |
| 725 | 750 | 74 | 74 | 74 | 74 | 1,700 | 1,725 | 171 | 171 | 171 | 171 | 2,700 | 2,725 | 271 | 271 | 271 | 271 |
| 750 | 775 | 76 | 76 | 76 | 76 | 1,725 | 1,750 | 174 | 174 | 174 | 174 | 2,725 | 2,750 | 274 | 274 | 274 | 274 |
| 775 | 800 | 79 | 79 | 79 | 79 | | | | | | | | | | | | |
| 800 | 825 | 81 | 81 | 81 | 81 | 1,750 | 1,775 | 176 | 176 | 176 | 176 | 2,750 | 2,775 | 276 | 276 | 276 | 276 |
| | | | | | | 1,775 | 1,800 | 179 | 179 | 179 | 179 | 2,775 | 2,800 | 279 | 279 | 279 | 279 |
| 825 | 850 | 84 | 84 | 84 | 84 | 1,800 | 1,825 | 181 | 181 | 181 | 181 | 2,800 | 2,825 | 281 | 281 | 281 | 281 |
| 850 | 875 | 86 | 86 | 86 | 86 | 1,825 | 1,850 | 184 | 184 | 184 | 184 | 2,825 | 2,850 | 284 | 284 | 284 | 284 |
| 875 | 900 | 89 | 89 | 89 | 89 | 1,850 | 1,875 | 186 | 186 | 186 | 186 | 2,850 | 2,875 | 286 | 286 | 286 | 286 |
| 900 | 925 | 91 | 91 | 91 | 91 | | | | | | | | | | | | |
| 925 | 950 | 94 | 94 | 94 | 94 | 1,875 | 1,900 | 189 | 189 | 189 | 189 | 2,875 | 2,900 | 289 | 289 | 289 | 289 |
| | | | | | | 1,900 | 1,925 | 191 | 191 | 191 | 191 | 2,900 | 2,925 | 291 | 291 | 291 | 291 |
| 950 | 975 | 96 | 96 | 96 | 96 | 1,925 | 1,950 | 194 | 194 | 194 | 194 | 2,925 | 2,950 | 294 | 294 | 294 | 294 |
| 975 | 1,000 | 99 | 99 | 99 | 99 | 1,950 | 1,975 | 196 | 196 | 196 | 196 | 2,950 | 2,975 | 296 | 296 | 296 | 296 |
| | | | | | | 1,975 | 2,000 | 199 | 199 | 199 | 199 | 2,975 | 3,000 | 299 | 299 | 299 | 299 |

*(Continued)*

* This column must also be used by a qualifying widow(er).

**2014 Tax Table** — *Continued*

## 3,000

| If line 43 (taxable income) is— At least | But less than | Single | Married filing jointly * | Married filing separately | Head of a household |
|---|---|---|---|---|---|
| | | | Your tax is— | | |
| 3,000 | 3,050 | 303 | 303 | 303 | 303 |
| 3,050 | 3,100 | 308 | 308 | 308 | 308 |
| 3,100 | 3,150 | 313 | 313 | 313 | 313 |
| 3,150 | 3,200 | 318 | 318 | 318 | 318 |
| 3,200 | 3,250 | 323 | 323 | 323 | 323 |
| 3,250 | 3,300 | 328 | 328 | 328 | 328 |
| 3,300 | 3,350 | 333 | 333 | 333 | 333 |
| 3,350 | 3,400 | 338 | 338 | 338 | 338 |
| 3,400 | 3,450 | 343 | 343 | 343 | 343 |
| 3,450 | 3,500 | 348 | 348 | 348 | 348 |
| 3,500 | 3,550 | 353 | 353 | 353 | 353 |
| 3,550 | 3,600 | 358 | 358 | 358 | 358 |
| 3,600 | 3,650 | 363 | 363 | 363 | 363 |
| 3,650 | 3,700 | 368 | 368 | 368 | 368 |
| 3,700 | 3,750 | 373 | 373 | 373 | 373 |
| 3,750 | 3,800 | 378 | 378 | 378 | 378 |
| 3,800 | 3,850 | 383 | 383 | 383 | 383 |
| 3,850 | 3,900 | 388 | 388 | 388 | 388 |
| 3,900 | 3,950 | 393 | 393 | 393 | 393 |
| 3,950 | 4,000 | 398 | 398 | 398 | 398 |

## 4,000

| At least | But less than | Single | Married filing jointly * | Married filing separately | Head of a household |
|---|---|---|---|---|---|
| 4,000 | 4,050 | 403 | 403 | 403 | 403 |
| 4,050 | 4,100 | 408 | 408 | 408 | 408 |
| 4,100 | 4,150 | 413 | 413 | 413 | 413 |
| 4,150 | 4,200 | 418 | 418 | 418 | 418 |
| 4,200 | 4,250 | 423 | 423 | 423 | 423 |
| 4,250 | 4,300 | 428 | 428 | 428 | 428 |
| 4,300 | 4,350 | 433 | 433 | 433 | 433 |
| 4,350 | 4,400 | 438 | 438 | 438 | 438 |
| 4,400 | 4,450 | 443 | 443 | 443 | 443 |
| 4,450 | 4,500 | 448 | 448 | 448 | 448 |
| 4,500 | 4,550 | 453 | 453 | 453 | 453 |
| 4,550 | 4,600 | 458 | 458 | 458 | 458 |
| 4,600 | 4,650 | 463 | 463 | 463 | 463 |
| 4,650 | 4,700 | 468 | 468 | 468 | 468 |
| 4,700 | 4,750 | 473 | 473 | 473 | 473 |
| 4,750 | 4,800 | 478 | 478 | 478 | 478 |
| 4,800 | 4,850 | 483 | 483 | 483 | 483 |
| 4,850 | 4,900 | 488 | 488 | 488 | 488 |
| 4,900 | 4,950 | 493 | 493 | 493 | 493 |
| 4,950 | 5,000 | 498 | 498 | 498 | 498 |

## 5,000

| At least | But less than | Single | Married filing jointly * | Married filing separately | Head of a household |
|---|---|---|---|---|---|
| 5,000 | 5,050 | 503 | 503 | 503 | 503 |
| 5,050 | 5,100 | 508 | 508 | 508 | 508 |
| 5,100 | 5,150 | 513 | 513 | 513 | 513 |
| 5,150 | 5,200 | 518 | 518 | 518 | 518 |
| 5,200 | 5,250 | 523 | 523 | 523 | 523 |
| 5,250 | 5,300 | 528 | 528 | 528 | 528 |
| 5,300 | 5,350 | 533 | 533 | 533 | 533 |
| 5,350 | 5,400 | 538 | 538 | 538 | 538 |
| 5,400 | 5,450 | 543 | 543 | 543 | 543 |
| 5,450 | 5,500 | 548 | 548 | 548 | 548 |
| 5,500 | 5,550 | 553 | 553 | 553 | 553 |
| 5,550 | 5,600 | 558 | 558 | 558 | 558 |
| 5,600 | 5,650 | 563 | 563 | 563 | 563 |
| 5,650 | 5,700 | 568 | 568 | 568 | 568 |
| 5,700 | 5,750 | 573 | 573 | 573 | 573 |
| 5,750 | 5,800 | 578 | 578 | 578 | 578 |
| 5,800 | 5,850 | 583 | 583 | 583 | 583 |
| 5,850 | 5,900 | 588 | 588 | 588 | 588 |
| 5,900 | 5,950 | 593 | 593 | 593 | 593 |
| 5,950 | 6,000 | 598 | 598 | 598 | 598 |

## 6,000

| At least | But less than | Single | Married filing jointly * | Married filing separately | Head of a household |
|---|---|---|---|---|---|
| 6,000 | 6,050 | 603 | 603 | 603 | 603 |
| 6,050 | 6,100 | 608 | 608 | 608 | 608 |
| 6,100 | 6,150 | 613 | 613 | 613 | 613 |
| 6,150 | 6,200 | 618 | 618 | 618 | 618 |
| 6,200 | 6,250 | 623 | 623 | 623 | 623 |
| 6,250 | 6,300 | 628 | 628 | 628 | 628 |
| 6,300 | 6,350 | 633 | 633 | 633 | 633 |
| 6,350 | 6,400 | 638 | 638 | 638 | 638 |
| 6,400 | 6,450 | 643 | 643 | 643 | 643 |
| 6,450 | 6,500 | 648 | 648 | 648 | 648 |
| 6,500 | 6,550 | 653 | 653 | 653 | 653 |
| 6,550 | 6,600 | 658 | 658 | 658 | 658 |
| 6,600 | 6,650 | 663 | 663 | 663 | 663 |
| 6,650 | 6,700 | 668 | 668 | 668 | 668 |
| 6,700 | 6,750 | 673 | 673 | 673 | 673 |
| 6,750 | 6,800 | 678 | 678 | 678 | 678 |
| 6,800 | 6,850 | 683 | 683 | 683 | 683 |
| 6,850 | 6,900 | 688 | 688 | 688 | 688 |
| 6,900 | 6,950 | 693 | 693 | 693 | 693 |
| 6,950 | 7,000 | 698 | 698 | 698 | 698 |

## 7,000

| At least | But less than | Single | Married filing jointly * | Married filing separately | Head of a household |
|---|---|---|---|---|---|
| 7,000 | 7,050 | 703 | 703 | 703 | 703 |
| 7,050 | 7,100 | 708 | 708 | 708 | 708 |
| 7,100 | 7,150 | 713 | 713 | 713 | 713 |
| 7,150 | 7,200 | 718 | 718 | 718 | 718 |
| 7,200 | 7,250 | 723 | 723 | 723 | 723 |
| 7,250 | 7,300 | 728 | 728 | 728 | 728 |
| 7,300 | 7,350 | 733 | 733 | 733 | 733 |
| 7,350 | 7,400 | 738 | 738 | 738 | 738 |
| 7,400 | 7,450 | 743 | 743 | 743 | 743 |
| 7,450 | 7,500 | 748 | 748 | 748 | 748 |
| 7,500 | 7,550 | 753 | 753 | 753 | 753 |
| 7,550 | 7,600 | 758 | 758 | 758 | 758 |
| 7,600 | 7,650 | 763 | 763 | 763 | 763 |
| 7,650 | 7,700 | 768 | 768 | 768 | 768 |
| 7,700 | 7,750 | 773 | 773 | 773 | 773 |
| 7,750 | 7,800 | 778 | 778 | 778 | 778 |
| 7,800 | 7,850 | 783 | 783 | 783 | 783 |
| 7,850 | 7,900 | 788 | 788 | 788 | 788 |
| 7,900 | 7,950 | 793 | 793 | 793 | 793 |
| 7,950 | 8,000 | 798 | 798 | 798 | 798 |

## 8,000

| At least | But less than | Single | Married filing jointly * | Married filing separately | Head of a household |
|---|---|---|---|---|---|
| 8,000 | 8,050 | 803 | 803 | 803 | 803 |
| 8,050 | 8,100 | 808 | 808 | 808 | 808 |
| 8,100 | 8,150 | 813 | 813 | 813 | 813 |
| 8,150 | 8,200 | 818 | 818 | 818 | 818 |
| 8,200 | 8,250 | 823 | 823 | 823 | 823 |
| 8,250 | 8,300 | 828 | 828 | 828 | 828 |
| 8,300 | 8,350 | 833 | 833 | 833 | 833 |
| 8,350 | 8,400 | 838 | 838 | 838 | 838 |
| 8,400 | 8,450 | 843 | 843 | 843 | 843 |
| 8,450 | 8,500 | 848 | 848 | 848 | 848 |
| 8,500 | 8,550 | 853 | 853 | 853 | 853 |
| 8,550 | 8,600 | 858 | 858 | 858 | 858 |
| 8,600 | 8,650 | 863 | 863 | 863 | 863 |
| 8,650 | 8,700 | 868 | 868 | 868 | 868 |
| 8,700 | 8,750 | 873 | 873 | 873 | 873 |
| 8,750 | 8,800 | 878 | 878 | 878 | 878 |
| 8,800 | 8,850 | 883 | 883 | 883 | 883 |
| 8,850 | 8,900 | 888 | 888 | 888 | 888 |
| 8,900 | 8,950 | 893 | 893 | 893 | 893 |
| 8,950 | 9,000 | 898 | 898 | 898 | 898 |

## 9,000

| At least | But less than | Single | Married filing jointly * | Married filing separately | Head of a household |
|---|---|---|---|---|---|
| 9,000 | 9,050 | 903 | 903 | 903 | 903 |
| 9,050 | 9,100 | 908 | 908 | 908 | 908 |
| 9,100 | 9,150 | 915 | 913 | 915 | 913 |
| 9,150 | 9,200 | 923 | 918 | 923 | 918 |
| 9,200 | 9,250 | 930 | 923 | 930 | 923 |
| 9,250 | 9,300 | 938 | 928 | 938 | 928 |
| 9,300 | 9,350 | 945 | 933 | 945 | 933 |
| 9,350 | 9,400 | 953 | 938 | 953 | 938 |
| 9,400 | 9,450 | 960 | 943 | 960 | 943 |
| 9,450 | 9,500 | 968 | 948 | 968 | 948 |
| 9,500 | 9,550 | 975 | 953 | 975 | 953 |
| 9,550 | 9,600 | 983 | 958 | 983 | 958 |
| 9,600 | 9,650 | 990 | 963 | 990 | 963 |
| 9,650 | 9,700 | 998 | 968 | 998 | 968 |
| 9,700 | 9,750 | 1,005 | 973 | 1,005 | 973 |
| 9,750 | 9,800 | 1,013 | 978 | 1,013 | 978 |
| 9,800 | 9,850 | 1,020 | 983 | 1,020 | 983 |
| 9,850 | 9,900 | 1,028 | 988 | 1,028 | 988 |
| 9,900 | 9,950 | 1,035 | 993 | 1,035 | 993 |
| 9,950 | 10,000 | 1,043 | 998 | 1,043 | 998 |

## 10,000

| At least | But less than | Single | Married filing jointly * | Married filing separately | Head of a household |
|---|---|---|---|---|---|
| 10,000 | 10,050 | 1,050 | 1,003 | 1,050 | 1,003 |
| 10,050 | 10,100 | 1,058 | 1,008 | 1,058 | 1,008 |
| 10,100 | 10,150 | 1,065 | 1,013 | 1,065 | 1,013 |
| 10,150 | 10,200 | 1,073 | 1,018 | 1,073 | 1,018 |
| 10,200 | 10,250 | 1,080 | 1,023 | 1,080 | 1,023 |
| 10,250 | 10,300 | 1,088 | 1,028 | 1,088 | 1,028 |
| 10,300 | 10,350 | 1,095 | 1,033 | 1,095 | 1,033 |
| 10,350 | 10,400 | 1,103 | 1,038 | 1,103 | 1,038 |
| 10,400 | 10,450 | 1,110 | 1,043 | 1,110 | 1,043 |
| 10,450 | 10,500 | 1,118 | 1,048 | 1,118 | 1,048 |
| 10,500 | 10,550 | 1,125 | 1,053 | 1,125 | 1,053 |
| 10,550 | 10,600 | 1,133 | 1,058 | 1,133 | 1,058 |
| 10,600 | 10,650 | 1,140 | 1,063 | 1,140 | 1,063 |
| 10,650 | 10,700 | 1,148 | 1,068 | 1,148 | 1,068 |
| 10,700 | 10,750 | 1,155 | 1,073 | 1,155 | 1,073 |
| 10,750 | 10,800 | 1,163 | 1,078 | 1,163 | 1,078 |
| 10,800 | 10,850 | 1,170 | 1,083 | 1,170 | 1,083 |
| 10,850 | 10,900 | 1,178 | 1,088 | 1,178 | 1,088 |
| 10,900 | 10,950 | 1,185 | 1,093 | 1,185 | 1,093 |
| 10,950 | 11,000 | 1,193 | 1,098 | 1,193 | 1,098 |

## 11,000

| At least | But less than | Single | Married filing jointly * | Married filing separately | Head of a household |
|---|---|---|---|---|---|
| 11,000 | 11,050 | 1,200 | 1,103 | 1,200 | 1,103 |
| 11,050 | 11,100 | 1,208 | 1,108 | 1,208 | 1,108 |
| 11,100 | 11,150 | 1,215 | 1,113 | 1,215 | 1,113 |
| 11,150 | 11,200 | 1,223 | 1,118 | 1,223 | 1,118 |
| 11,200 | 11,250 | 1,230 | 1,123 | 1,230 | 1,123 |
| 11,250 | 11,300 | 1,238 | 1,128 | 1,238 | 1,128 |
| 11,300 | 11,350 | 1,245 | 1,133 | 1,245 | 1,133 |
| 11,350 | 11,400 | 1,253 | 1,138 | 1,253 | 1,138 |
| 11,400 | 11,450 | 1,260 | 1,143 | 1,260 | 1,143 |
| 11,450 | 11,500 | 1,268 | 1,148 | 1,268 | 1,148 |
| 11,500 | 11,550 | 1,275 | 1,153 | 1,275 | 1,153 |
| 11,550 | 11,600 | 1,283 | 1,158 | 1,283 | 1,158 |
| 11,600 | 11,650 | 1,290 | 1,163 | 1,290 | 1,163 |
| 11,650 | 11,700 | 1,298 | 1,168 | 1,298 | 1,168 |
| 11,700 | 11,750 | 1,305 | 1,173 | 1,305 | 1,173 |
| 11,750 | 11,800 | 1,313 | 1,178 | 1,313 | 1,178 |
| 11,800 | 11,850 | 1,320 | 1,183 | 1,320 | 1,183 |
| 11,850 | 11,900 | 1,328 | 1,188 | 1,328 | 1,188 |
| 11,900 | 11,950 | 1,335 | 1,193 | 1,335 | 1,193 |
| 11,950 | 12,000 | 1,343 | 1,198 | 1,343 | 1,198 |

*(Continued)*

* This column must also be used by a qualifying widow(er).

# 2014 Tax Tables

## 12,000

| At least | But less than | Single | Married filing jointly * | Married filing separately | Head of a household |
|---|---|---|---|---|---|
| 12,000 | 12,050 | 1,350 | 1,203 | 1,350 | 1,203 |
| 12,050 | 12,100 | 1,358 | 1,208 | 1,358 | 1,208 |
| 12,100 | 12,150 | 1,365 | 1,213 | 1,365 | 1,213 |
| 12,150 | 12,200 | 1,373 | 1,218 | 1,373 | 1,218 |
| 12,200 | 12,250 | 1,380 | 1,223 | 1,380 | 1,223 |
| 12,250 | 12,300 | 1,388 | 1,228 | 1,388 | 1,228 |
| 12,300 | 12,350 | 1,395 | 1,233 | 1,395 | 1,233 |
| 12,350 | 12,400 | 1,403 | 1,238 | 1,403 | 1,238 |
| 12,400 | 12,450 | 1,410 | 1,243 | 1,410 | 1,243 |
| 12,450 | 12,500 | 1,418 | 1,248 | 1,418 | 1,248 |
| 12,500 | 12,550 | 1,425 | 1,253 | 1,425 | 1,253 |
| 12,550 | 12,600 | 1,433 | 1,258 | 1,433 | 1,258 |
| 12,600 | 12,650 | 1,440 | 1,263 | 1,440 | 1,263 |
| 12,650 | 12,700 | 1,448 | 1,268 | 1,448 | 1,268 |
| 12,700 | 12,750 | 1,455 | 1,273 | 1,455 | 1,273 |
| 12,750 | 12,800 | 1,463 | 1,278 | 1,463 | 1,278 |
| 12,800 | 12,850 | 1,470 | 1,283 | 1,470 | 1,283 |
| 12,850 | 12,900 | 1,478 | 1,288 | 1,478 | 1,288 |
| 12,900 | 12,950 | 1,485 | 1,293 | 1,485 | 1,293 |
| 12,950 | 13,000 | 1,493 | 1,298 | 1,493 | 1,299 |

## 13,000

| At least | But less than | Single | Married filing jointly * | Married filing separately | Head of a household |
|---|---|---|---|---|---|
| 13,000 | 13,050 | 1,500 | 1,303 | 1,500 | 1,306 |
| 13,050 | 13,100 | 1,508 | 1,308 | 1,508 | 1,314 |
| 13,100 | 13,150 | 1,515 | 1,313 | 1,515 | 1,321 |
| 13,150 | 13,200 | 1,523 | 1,318 | 1,523 | 1,329 |
| 13,200 | 13,250 | 1,530 | 1,323 | 1,530 | 1,336 |
| 13,250 | 13,300 | 1,538 | 1,328 | 1,538 | 1,344 |
| 13,300 | 13,350 | 1,545 | 1,333 | 1,545 | 1,351 |
| 13,350 | 13,400 | 1,553 | 1,338 | 1,553 | 1,359 |
| 13,400 | 13,450 | 1,560 | 1,343 | 1,560 | 1,366 |
| 13,450 | 13,500 | 1,568 | 1,348 | 1,568 | 1,374 |
| 13,500 | 13,550 | 1,575 | 1,353 | 1,575 | 1,381 |
| 13,550 | 13,600 | 1,583 | 1,358 | 1,583 | 1,389 |
| 13,600 | 13,650 | 1,590 | 1,363 | 1,590 | 1,396 |
| 13,650 | 13,700 | 1,598 | 1,368 | 1,598 | 1,404 |
| 13,700 | 13,750 | 1,605 | 1,373 | 1,605 | 1,411 |
| 13,750 | 13,800 | 1,613 | 1,378 | 1,613 | 1,419 |
| 13,800 | 13,850 | 1,620 | 1,383 | 1,620 | 1,426 |
| 13,850 | 13,900 | 1,628 | 1,388 | 1,628 | 1,434 |
| 13,900 | 13,950 | 1,635 | 1,393 | 1,635 | 1,441 |
| 13,950 | 14,000 | 1,643 | 1,398 | 1,643 | 1,449 |

## 14,000

| At least | But less than | Single | Married filing jointly * | Married filing separately | Head of a household |
|---|---|---|---|---|---|
| 14,000 | 14,050 | 1,650 | 1,403 | 1,650 | 1,456 |
| 14,050 | 14,100 | 1,658 | 1,408 | 1,658 | 1,464 |
| 14,100 | 14,150 | 1,665 | 1,413 | 1,665 | 1,471 |
| 14,150 | 14,200 | 1,673 | 1,418 | 1,673 | 1,479 |
| 14,200 | 14,250 | 1,680 | 1,423 | 1,680 | 1,486 |
| 14,250 | 14,300 | 1,688 | 1,428 | 1,688 | 1,494 |
| 14,300 | 14,350 | 1,695 | 1,433 | 1,695 | 1,501 |
| 14,350 | 14,400 | 1,703 | 1,438 | 1,703 | 1,509 |
| 14,400 | 14,450 | 1,710 | 1,443 | 1,710 | 1,516 |
| 14,450 | 14,500 | 1,718 | 1,448 | 1,718 | 1,524 |
| 14,500 | 14,550 | 1,725 | 1,453 | 1,725 | 1,531 |
| 14,550 | 14,600 | 1,733 | 1,458 | 1,733 | 1,539 |
| 14,600 | 14,650 | 1,740 | 1,463 | 1,740 | 1,546 |
| 14,650 | 14,700 | 1,748 | 1,468 | 1,748 | 1,554 |
| 14,700 | 14,750 | 1,755 | 1,473 | 1,755 | 1,561 |
| 14,750 | 14,800 | 1,763 | 1,478 | 1,763 | 1,569 |
| 14,800 | 14,850 | 1,770 | 1,483 | 1,770 | 1,576 |
| 14,850 | 14,900 | 1,778 | 1,488 | 1,778 | 1,584 |
| 14,900 | 14,950 | 1,785 | 1,493 | 1,785 | 1,591 |
| 14,950 | 15,000 | 1,793 | 1,498 | 1,793 | 1,599 |

## 15,000

| At least | But less than | Single | Married filing jointly * | Married filing separately | Head of a household |
|---|---|---|---|---|---|
| 15,000 | 15,050 | 1,800 | 1,503 | 1,800 | 1,606 |
| 15,050 | 15,100 | 1,808 | 1,508 | 1,808 | 1,614 |
| 15,100 | 15,150 | 1,815 | 1,513 | 1,815 | 1,621 |
| 15,150 | 15,200 | 1,823 | 1,518 | 1,823 | 1,629 |
| 15,200 | 15,250 | 1,830 | 1,523 | 1,830 | 1,636 |
| 15,250 | 15,300 | 1,838 | 1,528 | 1,838 | 1,644 |
| 15,300 | 15,350 | 1,845 | 1,533 | 1,845 | 1,651 |
| 15,350 | 15,400 | 1,853 | 1,538 | 1,853 | 1,659 |
| 15,400 | 15,450 | 1,860 | 1,543 | 1,860 | 1,666 |
| 15,450 | 15,500 | 1,868 | 1,548 | 1,868 | 1,674 |
| 15,500 | 15,550 | 1,875 | 1,553 | 1,875 | 1,681 |
| 15,550 | 15,600 | 1,883 | 1,558 | 1,883 | 1,689 |
| 15,600 | 15,650 | 1,890 | 1,563 | 1,890 | 1,696 |
| 15,650 | 15,700 | 1,898 | 1,568 | 1,898 | 1,704 |
| 15,700 | 15,750 | 1,905 | 1,573 | 1,905 | 1,711 |
| 15,750 | 15,800 | 1,913 | 1,578 | 1,913 | 1,719 |
| 15,800 | 15,850 | 1,920 | 1,583 | 1,920 | 1,726 |
| 15,850 | 15,900 | 1,928 | 1,588 | 1,928 | 1,734 |
| 15,900 | 15,950 | 1,935 | 1,593 | 1,935 | 1,741 |
| 15,950 | 16,000 | 1,943 | 1,598 | 1,943 | 1,749 |

## 16,000

| At least | But less than | Single | Married filing jointly * | Married filing separately | Head of a household |
|---|---|---|---|---|---|
| 16,000 | 16,050 | 1,950 | 1,603 | 1,950 | 1,756 |
| 16,050 | 16,100 | 1,958 | 1,608 | 1,958 | 1,764 |
| 16,100 | 16,150 | 1,965 | 1,613 | 1,965 | 1,771 |
| 16,150 | 16,200 | 1,973 | 1,618 | 1,973 | 1,779 |
| 16,200 | 16,250 | 1,980 | 1,623 | 1,980 | 1,786 |
| 16,250 | 16,300 | 1,988 | 1,628 | 1,988 | 1,794 |
| 16,300 | 16,350 | 1,995 | 1,633 | 1,995 | 1,801 |
| 16,350 | 16,400 | 2,003 | 1,638 | 2,003 | 1,809 |
| 16,400 | 16,450 | 2,010 | 1,643 | 2,010 | 1,816 |
| 16,450 | 16,500 | 2,018 | 1,648 | 2,018 | 1,824 |
| 16,500 | 16,550 | 2,025 | 1,653 | 2,025 | 1,831 |
| 16,550 | 16,600 | 2,033 | 1,658 | 2,033 | 1,839 |
| 16,600 | 16,650 | 2,040 | 1,663 | 2,040 | 1,846 |
| 16,650 | 16,700 | 2,048 | 1,668 | 2,048 | 1,854 |
| 16,700 | 16,750 | 2,055 | 1,673 | 2,055 | 1,861 |
| 16,750 | 16,800 | 2,063 | 1,678 | 2,063 | 1,869 |
| 16,800 | 16,850 | 2,070 | 1,683 | 2,070 | 1,876 |
| 16,850 | 16,900 | 2,078 | 1,688 | 2,078 | 1,884 |
| 16,900 | 16,950 | 2,085 | 1,693 | 2,085 | 1,891 |
| 16,950 | 17,000 | 2,093 | 1,698 | 2,093 | 1,899 |

## 17,000

| At least | But less than | Single | Married filing jointly * | Married filing separately | Head of a household |
|---|---|---|---|---|---|
| 17,000 | 17,050 | 2,100 | 1,703 | 2,100 | 1,906 |
| 17,050 | 17,100 | 2,108 | 1,708 | 2,108 | 1,914 |
| 17,100 | 17,150 | 2,115 | 1,713 | 2,115 | 1,921 |
| 17,150 | 17,200 | 2,123 | 1,718 | 2,123 | 1,929 |
| 17,200 | 17,250 | 2,130 | 1,723 | 2,130 | 1,936 |
| 17,250 | 17,300 | 2,138 | 1,728 | 2,138 | 1,944 |
| 17,300 | 17,350 | 2,145 | 1,733 | 2,145 | 1,951 |
| 17,350 | 17,400 | 2,153 | 1,738 | 2,153 | 1,959 |
| 17,400 | 17,450 | 2,160 | 1,743 | 2,160 | 1,966 |
| 17,450 | 17,500 | 2,168 | 1,748 | 2,168 | 1,974 |
| 17,500 | 17,550 | 2,175 | 1,753 | 2,175 | 1,981 |
| 17,550 | 17,600 | 2,183 | 1,758 | 2,183 | 1,989 |
| 17,600 | 17,650 | 2,190 | 1,763 | 2,190 | 1,996 |
| 17,650 | 17,700 | 2,198 | 1,768 | 2,198 | 2,004 |
| 17,700 | 17,750 | 2,205 | 1,773 | 2,205 | 2,011 |
| 17,750 | 17,800 | 2,213 | 1,778 | 2,213 | 2,019 |
| 17,800 | 17,850 | 2,220 | 1,783 | 2,220 | 2,026 |
| 17,850 | 17,900 | 2,228 | 1,788 | 2,228 | 2,034 |
| 17,900 | 17,950 | 2,235 | 1,793 | 2,235 | 2,041 |
| 17,950 | 18,000 | 2,243 | 1,798 | 2,243 | 2,049 |

## 18,000

| At least | But less than | Single | Married filing jointly * | Married filing separately | Head of a household |
|---|---|---|---|---|---|
| 18,000 | 18,050 | 2,250 | 1,803 | 2,250 | 2,056 |
| 18,050 | 18,100 | 2,258 | 1,808 | 2,258 | 2,064 |
| 18,100 | 18,150 | 2,265 | 1,813 | 2,265 | 2,071 |
| 18,150 | 18,200 | 2,273 | 1,819 | 2,273 | 2,079 |
| 18,200 | 18,250 | 2,280 | 1,826 | 2,280 | 2,086 |
| 18,250 | 18,300 | 2,288 | 1,834 | 2,288 | 2,094 |
| 18,300 | 18,350 | 2,295 | 1,841 | 2,295 | 2,101 |
| 18,350 | 18,400 | 2,303 | 1,849 | 2,303 | 2,109 |
| 18,400 | 18,450 | 2,310 | 1,856 | 2,310 | 2,116 |
| 18,450 | 18,500 | 2,318 | 1,864 | 2,318 | 2,124 |
| 18,500 | 18,550 | 2,325 | 1,871 | 2,325 | 2,131 |
| 18,550 | 18,600 | 2,333 | 1,879 | 2,333 | 2,139 |
| 18,600 | 18,650 | 2,340 | 1,886 | 2,340 | 2,146 |
| 18,650 | 18,700 | 2,348 | 1,894 | 2,348 | 2,154 |
| 18,700 | 18,750 | 2,355 | 1,901 | 2,355 | 2,161 |
| 18,750 | 18,800 | 2,363 | 1,909 | 2,363 | 2,169 |
| 18,800 | 18,850 | 2,370 | 1,916 | 2,370 | 2,176 |
| 18,850 | 18,900 | 2,378 | 1,924 | 2,378 | 2,184 |
| 18,900 | 18,950 | 2,385 | 1,931 | 2,385 | 2,191 |
| 18,950 | 19,000 | 2,393 | 1,939 | 2,393 | 2,199 |

## 19,000

| At least | But less than | Single | Married filing jointly * | Married filing separately | Head of a household |
|---|---|---|---|---|---|
| 19,000 | 19,050 | 2,400 | 1,946 | 2,400 | 2,206 |
| 19,050 | 19,100 | 2,408 | 1,954 | 2,408 | 2,214 |
| 19,100 | 19,150 | 2,415 | 1,961 | 2,415 | 2,221 |
| 19,150 | 19,200 | 2,423 | 1,969 | 2,423 | 2,229 |
| 19,200 | 19,250 | 2,430 | 1,976 | 2,430 | 2,236 |
| 19,250 | 19,300 | 2,438 | 1,984 | 2,438 | 2,244 |
| 19,300 | 19,350 | 2,445 | 1,991 | 2,445 | 2,251 |
| 19,350 | 19,400 | 2,453 | 1,999 | 2,453 | 2,259 |
| 19,400 | 19,450 | 2,460 | 2,006 | 2,460 | 2,266 |
| 19,450 | 19,500 | 2,468 | 2,014 | 2,468 | 2,274 |
| 19,500 | 19,550 | 2,475 | 2,021 | 2,475 | 2,281 |
| 19,550 | 19,600 | 2,483 | 2,029 | 2,483 | 2,289 |
| 19,600 | 19,650 | 2,490 | 2,036 | 2,490 | 2,296 |
| 19,650 | 19,700 | 2,498 | 2,044 | 2,498 | 2,304 |
| 19,700 | 19,750 | 2,505 | 2,051 | 2,505 | 2,311 |
| 19,750 | 19,800 | 2,513 | 2,059 | 2,513 | 2,319 |
| 19,800 | 19,850 | 2,520 | 2,066 | 2,520 | 2,326 |
| 19,850 | 19,900 | 2,528 | 2,074 | 2,528 | 2,334 |
| 19,900 | 19,950 | 2,535 | 2,081 | 2,535 | 2,341 |
| 19,950 | 20,000 | 2,543 | 2,089 | 2,543 | 2,349 |

## 20,000

| At least | But less than | Single | Married filing jointly * | Married filing separately | Head of a household |
|---|---|---|---|---|---|
| 20,000 | 20,050 | 2,550 | 2,096 | 2,550 | 2,356 |
| 20,050 | 20,100 | 2,558 | 2,104 | 2,558 | 2,364 |
| 20,100 | 20,150 | 2,565 | 2,111 | 2,565 | 2,371 |
| 20,150 | 20,200 | 2,573 | 2,119 | 2,573 | 2,379 |
| 20,200 | 20,250 | 2,580 | 2,126 | 2,580 | 2,386 |
| 20,250 | 20,300 | 2,588 | 2,134 | 2,588 | 2,394 |
| 20,300 | 20,350 | 2,595 | 2,141 | 2,595 | 2,401 |
| 20,350 | 20,400 | 2,603 | 2,149 | 2,603 | 2,409 |
| 20,400 | 20,450 | 2,610 | 2,156 | 2,610 | 2,416 |
| 20,450 | 20,500 | 2,618 | 2,164 | 2,618 | 2,424 |
| 20,500 | 20,550 | 2,625 | 2,171 | 2,625 | 2,431 |
| 20,550 | 20,600 | 2,633 | 2,179 | 2,633 | 2,439 |
| 20,600 | 20,650 | 2,640 | 2,186 | 2,640 | 2,446 |
| 20,650 | 20,700 | 2,648 | 2,194 | 2,648 | 2,454 |
| 20,700 | 20,750 | 2,655 | 2,201 | 2,655 | 2,461 |
| 20,750 | 20,800 | 2,663 | 2,209 | 2,663 | 2,469 |
| 20,800 | 20,850 | 2,670 | 2,216 | 2,670 | 2,476 |
| 20,850 | 20,900 | 2,678 | 2,224 | 2,678 | 2,484 |
| 20,900 | 20,950 | 2,685 | 2,231 | 2,685 | 2,491 |
| 20,950 | 21,000 | 2,693 | 2,239 | 2,693 | 2,499 |

*(Continued)*

\* This column must also be used by a qualifying widow(er).

## 21,000

| If line 43 (taxable income) is— At least | But less than | Single | Married filing jointly * | Married filing separately | Head of a household |
|---|---|---|---|---|---|
| 21,000 | 21,050 | 2,700 | 2,246 | 2,700 | 2,506 |
| 21,050 | 21,100 | 2,708 | 2,254 | 2,708 | 2,514 |
| 21,100 | 21,150 | 2,715 | 2,261 | 2,715 | 2,521 |
| 21,150 | 21,200 | 2,723 | 2,269 | 2,723 | 2,529 |
| 21,200 | 21,250 | 2,730 | 2,276 | 2,730 | 2,536 |
| 21,250 | 21,300 | 2,738 | 2,284 | 2,738 | 2,544 |
| 21,300 | 21,350 | 2,745 | 2,291 | 2,745 | 2,551 |
| 21,350 | 21,400 | 2,753 | 2,299 | 2,753 | 2,559 |
| 21,400 | 21,450 | 2,760 | 2,306 | 2,760 | 2,566 |
| 21,450 | 21,500 | 2,768 | 2,314 | 2,768 | 2,574 |
| 21,500 | 21,550 | 2,775 | 2,321 | 2,775 | 2,581 |
| 21,550 | 21,600 | 2,783 | 2,329 | 2,783 | 2,589 |
| 21,600 | 21,650 | 2,790 | 2,336 | 2,790 | 2,596 |
| 21,650 | 21,700 | 2,798 | 2,344 | 2,798 | 2,604 |
| 21,700 | 21,750 | 2,805 | 2,351 | 2,805 | 2,611 |
| 21,750 | 21,800 | 2,813 | 2,359 | 2,813 | 2,619 |
| 21,800 | 21,850 | 2,820 | 2,366 | 2,820 | 2,626 |
| 21,850 | 21,900 | 2,828 | 2,374 | 2,828 | 2,634 |
| 21,900 | 21,950 | 2,835 | 2,381 | 2,835 | 2,641 |
| 21,950 | 22,000 | 2,843 | 2,389 | 2,843 | 2,649 |

## 22,000

| At least | But less than | Single | Married filing jointly * | Married filing separately | Head of a household |
|---|---|---|---|---|---|
| 22,000 | 22,050 | 2,850 | 2,396 | 2,850 | 2,656 |
| 22,050 | 22,100 | 2,858 | 2,404 | 2,858 | 2,664 |
| 22,100 | 22,150 | 2,865 | 2,411 | 2,865 | 2,671 |
| 22,150 | 22,200 | 2,873 | 2,419 | 2,873 | 2,679 |
| 22,200 | 22,250 | 2,880 | 2,426 | 2,880 | 2,686 |
| 22,250 | 22,300 | 2,888 | 2,434 | 2,888 | 2,694 |
| 22,300 | 22,350 | 2,895 | 2,441 | 2,895 | 2,701 |
| 22,350 | 22,400 | 2,903 | 2,449 | 2,903 | 2,709 |
| 22,400 | 22,450 | 2,910 | 2,456 | 2,910 | 2,716 |
| 22,450 | 22,500 | 2,918 | 2,464 | 2,918 | 2,724 |
| 22,500 | 22,550 | 2,925 | 2,471 | 2,925 | 2,731 |
| 22,550 | 22,600 | 2,933 | 2,479 | 2,933 | 2,739 |
| 22,600 | 22,650 | 2,940 | 2,486 | 2,940 | 2,746 |
| 22,650 | 22,700 | 2,948 | 2,494 | 2,948 | 2,754 |
| 22,700 | 22,750 | 2,955 | 2,501 | 2,955 | 2,761 |
| 22,750 | 22,800 | 2,963 | 2,509 | 2,963 | 2,769 |
| 22,800 | 22,850 | 2,970 | 2,516 | 2,970 | 2,776 |
| 22,850 | 22,900 | 2,978 | 2,524 | 2,978 | 2,784 |
| 22,900 | 22,950 | 2,985 | 2,531 | 2,985 | 2,791 |
| 22,950 | 23,000 | 2,993 | 2,539 | 2,993 | 2,799 |

## 23,000

| At least | But less than | Single | Married filing jointly * | Married filing separately | Head of a household |
|---|---|---|---|---|---|
| 23,000 | 23,050 | 3,000 | 2,546 | 3,000 | 2,806 |
| 23,050 | 23,100 | 3,008 | 2,554 | 3,008 | 2,814 |
| 23,100 | 23,150 | 3,015 | 2,561 | 3,015 | 2,821 |
| 23,150 | 23,200 | 3,023 | 2,569 | 3,023 | 2,829 |
| 23,200 | 23,250 | 3,030 | 2,576 | 3,030 | 2,836 |
| 23,250 | 23,300 | 3,038 | 2,584 | 3,038 | 2,844 |
| 23,300 | 23,350 | 3,045 | 2,591 | 3,045 | 2,851 |
| 23,350 | 23,400 | 3,053 | 2,599 | 3,053 | 2,859 |
| 23,400 | 23,450 | 3,060 | 2,606 | 3,060 | 2,866 |
| 23,450 | 23,500 | 3,068 | 2,614 | 3,068 | 2,874 |
| 23,500 | 23,550 | 3,075 | 2,621 | 3,075 | 2,881 |
| 23,550 | 23,600 | 3,083 | 2,629 | 3,083 | 2,889 |
| 23,600 | 23,650 | 3,090 | 2,636 | 3,090 | 2,896 |
| 23,650 | 23,700 | 3,098 | 2,644 | 3,098 | 2,904 |
| 23,700 | 23,750 | 3,105 | 2,651 | 3,105 | 2,911 |
| 23,750 | 23,800 | 3,113 | 2,659 | 3,113 | 2,919 |
| 23,800 | 23,850 | 3,120 | 2,666 | 3,120 | 2,926 |
| 23,850 | 23,900 | 3,128 | 2,674 | 3,128 | 2,934 |
| 23,900 | 23,950 | 3,135 | 2,681 | 3,135 | 2,941 |
| 23,950 | 24,000 | 3,143 | 2,689 | 3,143 | 2,949 |

## 24,000

| At least | But less than | Single | Married filing jointly * | Married filing separately | Head of a household |
|---|---|---|---|---|---|
| 24,000 | 24,050 | 3,150 | 2,696 | 3,150 | 2,956 |
| 24,050 | 24,100 | 3,158 | 2,704 | 3,158 | 2,964 |
| 24,100 | 24,150 | 3,165 | 2,711 | 3,165 | 2,971 |
| 24,150 | 24,200 | 3,173 | 2,719 | 3,173 | 2,979 |
| 24,200 | 24,250 | 3,180 | 2,726 | 3,180 | 2,986 |
| 24,250 | 24,300 | 3,188 | 2,734 | 3,188 | 2,994 |
| 24,300 | 24,350 | 3,195 | 2,741 | 3,195 | 3,001 |
| 24,350 | 24,400 | 3,203 | 2,749 | 3,203 | 3,009 |
| 24,400 | 24,450 | 3,210 | 2,756 | 3,210 | 3,016 |
| 24,450 | 24,500 | 3,218 | 2,764 | 3,218 | 3,024 |
| 24,500 | 24,550 | 3,225 | 2,771 | 3,225 | 3,031 |
| 24,550 | 24,600 | 3,233 | 2,779 | 3,233 | 3,039 |
| 24,600 | 24,650 | 3,240 | 2,786 | 3,240 | 3,046 |
| 24,650 | 24,700 | 3,248 | 2,794 | 3,248 | 3,054 |
| 24,700 | 24,750 | 3,255 | 2,801 | 3,255 | 3,061 |
| 24,750 | 24,800 | 3,263 | 2,809 | 3,263 | 3,069 |
| 24,800 | 24,850 | 3,270 | 2,816 | 3,270 | 3,076 |
| 24,850 | 24,900 | 3,278 | 2,824 | 3,278 | 3,084 |
| 24,900 | 24,950 | 3,285 | 2,831 | 3,285 | 3,091 |
| 24,950 | 25,000 | 3,293 | 2,839 | 3,293 | 3,099 |

## 25,000

| At least | But less than | Single | Married filing jointly * | Married filing separately | Head of a household |
|---|---|---|---|---|---|
| 25,000 | 25,050 | 3,300 | 2,846 | 3,300 | 3,106 |
| 25,050 | 25,100 | 3,308 | 2,854 | 3,308 | 3,114 |
| 25,100 | 25,150 | 3,315 | 2,861 | 3,315 | 3,121 |
| 25,150 | 25,200 | 3,323 | 2,869 | 3,323 | 3,129 |
| 25,200 | 25,250 | 3,330 | 2,876 | 3,330 | 3,136 |
| 25,250 | 25,300 | 3,338 | 2,884 | 3,338 | 3,144 |
| 25,300 | 25,350 | 3,345 | 2,891 | 3,345 | 3,151 |
| 25,350 | 25,400 | 3,353 | 2,899 | 3,353 | 3,159 |
| 25,400 | 25,450 | 3,360 | 2,906 | 3,360 | 3,166 |
| 25,450 | 25,500 | 3,368 | 2,914 | 3,368 | 3,174 |
| 25,500 | 25,550 | 3,375 | 2,921 | 3,375 | 3,181 |
| 25,550 | 25,600 | 3,383 | 2,929 | 3,383 | 3,189 |
| 25,600 | 25,650 | 3,390 | 2,936 | 3,390 | 3,196 |
| 25,650 | 25,700 | 3,398 | 2,944 | 3,398 | 3,204 |
| 25,700 | 25,750 | 3,405 | 2,951 | 3,405 | 3,211 |
| 25,750 | 25,800 | 3,413 | 2,959 | 3,413 | 3,219 |
| 25,800 | 25,850 | 3,420 | 2,966 | 3,420 | 3,226 |
| 25,850 | 25,900 | 3,428 | 2,974 | 3,428 | 3,234 |
| 25,900 | 25,950 | 3,435 | 2,981 | 3,435 | 3,241 |
| 25,950 | 26,000 | 3,443 | 2,989 | 3,443 | 3,249 |

## 26,000

| At least | But less than | Single | Married filing jointly * | Married filing separately | Head of a household |
|---|---|---|---|---|---|
| 26,000 | 26,050 | 3,450 | 2,996 | 3,450 | 3,256 |
| 26,050 | 26,100 | 3,458 | 3,004 | 3,458 | 3,264 |
| 26,100 | 26,150 | 3,465 | 3,011 | 3,465 | 3,271 |
| 26,150 | 26,200 | 3,473 | 3,019 | 3,473 | 3,279 |
| 26,200 | 26,250 | 3,480 | 3,026 | 3,480 | 3,286 |
| 26,250 | 26,300 | 3,488 | 3,034 | 3,488 | 3,294 |
| 26,300 | 26,350 | 3,495 | 3,041 | 3,495 | 3,301 |
| 26,350 | 26,400 | 3,503 | 3,049 | 3,503 | 3,309 |
| 26,400 | 26,450 | 3,510 | 3,056 | 3,510 | 3,316 |
| 26,450 | 26,500 | 3,518 | 3,064 | 3,518 | 3,324 |
| 26,500 | 26,550 | 3,525 | 3,071 | 3,525 | 3,331 |
| 26,550 | 26,600 | 3,533 | 3,079 | 3,533 | 3,339 |
| 26,600 | 26,650 | 3,540 | 3,086 | 3,540 | 3,346 |
| 26,650 | 26,700 | 3,548 | 3,094 | 3,548 | 3,354 |
| 26,700 | 26,750 | 3,555 | 3,101 | 3,555 | 3,361 |
| 26,750 | 26,800 | 3,563 | 3,109 | 3,563 | 3,369 |
| 26,800 | 26,850 | 3,570 | 3,116 | 3,570 | 3,376 |
| 26,850 | 26,900 | 3,578 | 3,124 | 3,578 | 3,384 |
| 26,900 | 26,950 | 3,585 | 3,131 | 3,585 | 3,391 |
| 26,950 | 27,000 | 3,593 | 3,139 | 3,593 | 3,399 |

## 27,000

| At least | But less than | Single | Married filing jointly * | Married filing separately | Head of a household |
|---|---|---|---|---|---|
| 27,000 | 27,050 | 3,600 | 3,146 | 3,600 | 3,406 |
| 27,050 | 27,100 | 3,608 | 3,154 | 3,608 | 3,414 |
| 27,100 | 27,150 | 3,615 | 3,161 | 3,615 | 3,421 |
| 27,150 | 27,200 | 3,623 | 3,169 | 3,623 | 3,429 |
| 27,200 | 27,250 | 3,630 | 3,176 | 3,630 | 3,436 |
| 27,250 | 27,300 | 3,638 | 3,184 | 3,638 | 3,444 |
| 27,300 | 27,350 | 3,645 | 3,191 | 3,645 | 3,451 |
| 27,350 | 27,400 | 3,653 | 3,199 | 3,653 | 3,459 |
| 27,400 | 27,450 | 3,660 | 3,206 | 3,660 | 3,466 |
| 27,450 | 27,500 | 3,668 | 3,214 | 3,668 | 3,474 |
| 27,500 | 27,550 | 3,675 | 3,221 | 3,675 | 3,481 |
| 27,550 | 27,600 | 3,683 | 3,229 | 3,683 | 3,489 |
| 27,600 | 27,650 | 3,690 | 3,236 | 3,690 | 3,496 |
| 27,650 | 27,700 | 3,698 | 3,244 | 3,698 | 3,504 |
| 27,700 | 27,750 | 3,705 | 3,251 | 3,705 | 3,511 |
| 27,750 | 27,800 | 3,713 | 3,259 | 3,713 | 3,519 |
| 27,800 | 27,850 | 3,720 | 3,266 | 3,720 | 3,526 |
| 27,850 | 27,900 | 3,728 | 3,274 | 3,728 | 3,534 |
| 27,900 | 27,950 | 3,735 | 3,281 | 3,735 | 3,541 |
| 27,950 | 28,000 | 3,743 | 3,289 | 3,743 | 3,549 |

## 28,000

| At least | But less than | Single | Married filing jointly * | Married filing separately | Head of a household |
|---|---|---|---|---|---|
| 28,000 | 28,050 | 3,750 | 3,296 | 3,750 | 3,556 |
| 28,050 | 28,100 | 3,758 | 3,304 | 3,758 | 3,564 |
| 28,100 | 28,150 | 3,765 | 3,311 | 3,765 | 3,571 |
| 28,150 | 28,200 | 3,773 | 3,319 | 3,773 | 3,579 |
| 28,200 | 28,250 | 3,780 | 3,326 | 3,780 | 3,586 |
| 28,250 | 28,300 | 3,788 | 3,334 | 3,788 | 3,594 |
| 28,300 | 28,350 | 3,795 | 3,341 | 3,795 | 3,601 |
| 28,350 | 28,400 | 3,803 | 3,349 | 3,803 | 3,609 |
| 28,400 | 28,450 | 3,810 | 3,356 | 3,810 | 3,616 |
| 28,450 | 28,500 | 3,818 | 3,364 | 3,818 | 3,624 |
| 28,500 | 28,550 | 3,825 | 3,371 | 3,825 | 3,631 |
| 28,550 | 28,600 | 3,833 | 3,379 | 3,833 | 3,639 |
| 28,600 | 28,650 | 3,840 | 3,386 | 3,840 | 3,646 |
| 28,650 | 28,700 | 3,848 | 3,394 | 3,848 | 3,654 |
| 28,700 | 28,750 | 3,855 | 3,401 | 3,855 | 3,661 |
| 28,750 | 28,800 | 3,863 | 3,409 | 3,863 | 3,669 |
| 28,800 | 28,850 | 3,870 | 3,416 | 3,870 | 3,676 |
| 28,850 | 28,900 | 3,878 | 3,424 | 3,878 | 3,684 |
| 28,900 | 28,950 | 3,885 | 3,431 | 3,885 | 3,691 |
| 28,950 | 29,000 | 3,893 | 3,439 | 3,893 | 3,699 |

## 29,000

| At least | But less than | Single | Married filing jointly * | Married filing separately | Head of a household |
|---|---|---|---|---|---|
| 29,000 | 29,050 | 3,900 | 3,446 | 3,900 | 3,706 |
| 29,050 | 29,100 | 3,908 | 3,454 | 3,908 | 3,714 |
| 29,100 | 29,150 | 3,915 | 3,461 | 3,915 | 3,721 |
| 29,150 | 29,200 | 3,923 | 3,469 | 3,923 | 3,729 |
| 29,200 | 29,250 | 3,930 | 3,476 | 3,930 | 3,736 |
| 29,250 | 29,300 | 3,938 | 3,484 | 3,938 | 3,744 |
| 29,300 | 29,350 | 3,945 | 3,491 | 3,945 | 3,751 |
| 29,350 | 29,400 | 3,953 | 3,499 | 3,953 | 3,759 |
| 29,400 | 29,450 | 3,960 | 3,506 | 3,960 | 3,766 |
| 29,450 | 29,500 | 3,968 | 3,514 | 3,968 | 3,774 |
| 29,500 | 29,550 | 3,975 | 3,521 | 3,975 | 3,781 |
| 29,550 | 29,600 | 3,983 | 3,529 | 3,983 | 3,789 |
| 29,600 | 29,650 | 3,990 | 3,536 | 3,990 | 3,796 |
| 29,650 | 29,700 | 3,998 | 3,544 | 3,998 | 3,804 |
| 29,700 | 29,750 | 4,005 | 3,551 | 4,005 | 3,811 |
| 29,750 | 29,800 | 4,013 | 3,559 | 4,013 | 3,819 |
| 29,800 | 29,850 | 4,020 | 3,566 | 4,020 | 3,826 |
| 29,850 | 29,900 | 4,028 | 3,574 | 4,028 | 3,834 |
| 29,900 | 29,950 | 4,035 | 3,581 | 4,035 | 3,841 |
| 29,950 | 30,000 | 4,043 | 3,589 | 4,043 | 3,849 |

*(Continued)*

\* This column must also be used by a qualifying widow(er).

# 2014 Tax Tables

**If line 43 (taxable income) is— And you are—**

Columns: At least | But less than | Single | Married filing jointly * | Married filing separately | Head of a household

Your tax is—

## 30,000

| At least | But less than | Single | Married filing jointly * | Married filing separately | Head of a household |
|---|---|---|---|---|---|
| 30,000 | 30,050 | 4,050 | 3,596 | 4,050 | 3,856 |
| 30,050 | 30,100 | 4,058 | 3,604 | 4,058 | 3,864 |
| 30,100 | 30,150 | 4,065 | 3,611 | 4,065 | 3,871 |
| 30,150 | 30,200 | 4,073 | 3,619 | 4,073 | 3,879 |
| 30,200 | 30,250 | 4,080 | 3,626 | 4,080 | 3,886 |
| 30,250 | 30,300 | 4,088 | 3,634 | 4,088 | 3,894 |
| 30,300 | 30,350 | 4,095 | 3,641 | 4,095 | 3,901 |
| 30,350 | 30,400 | 4,103 | 3,649 | 4,103 | 3,909 |
| 30,400 | 30,450 | 4,110 | 3,656 | 4,110 | 3,916 |
| 30,450 | 30,500 | 4,118 | 3,664 | 4,118 | 3,924 |
| 30,500 | 30,550 | 4,125 | 3,671 | 4,125 | 3,931 |
| 30,550 | 30,600 | 4,133 | 3,679 | 4,133 | 3,939 |
| 30,600 | 30,650 | 4,140 | 3,686 | 4,140 | 3,946 |
| 30,650 | 30,700 | 4,148 | 3,694 | 4,148 | 3,954 |
| 30,700 | 30,750 | 4,155 | 3,701 | 4,155 | 3,961 |
| 30,750 | 30,800 | 4,163 | 3,709 | 4,163 | 3,969 |
| 30,800 | 30,850 | 4,170 | 3,716 | 4,170 | 3,976 |
| 30,850 | 30,900 | 4,178 | 3,724 | 4,178 | 3,984 |
| 30,900 | 30,950 | 4,185 | 3,731 | 4,185 | 3,991 |
| 30,950 | 31,000 | 4,193 | 3,739 | 4,193 | 3,999 |

## 31,000

| At least | But less than | Single | Married filing jointly * | Married filing separately | Head of a household |
|---|---|---|---|---|---|
| 31,000 | 31,050 | 4,200 | 3,746 | 4,200 | 4,006 |
| 31,050 | 31,100 | 4,208 | 3,754 | 4,208 | 4,014 |
| 31,100 | 31,150 | 4,215 | 3,761 | 4,215 | 4,021 |
| 31,150 | 31,200 | 4,223 | 3,769 | 4,223 | 4,029 |
| 31,200 | 31,250 | 4,230 | 3,776 | 4,230 | 4,036 |
| 31,250 | 31,300 | 4,238 | 3,784 | 4,238 | 4,044 |
| 31,300 | 31,350 | 4,245 | 3,791 | 4,245 | 4,051 |
| 31,350 | 31,400 | 4,253 | 3,799 | 4,253 | 4,059 |
| 31,400 | 31,450 | 4,260 | 3,806 | 4,260 | 4,066 |
| 31,450 | 31,500 | 4,268 | 3,814 | 4,268 | 4,074 |
| 31,500 | 31,550 | 4,275 | 3,821 | 4,275 | 4,081 |
| 31,550 | 31,600 | 4,283 | 3,829 | 4,283 | 4,089 |
| 31,600 | 31,650 | 4,290 | 3,836 | 4,290 | 4,096 |
| 31,650 | 31,700 | 4,298 | 3,844 | 4,298 | 4,104 |
| 31,700 | 31,750 | 4,305 | 3,851 | 4,305 | 4,111 |
| 31,750 | 31,800 | 4,313 | 3,859 | 4,313 | 4,119 |
| 31,800 | 31,850 | 4,320 | 3,866 | 4,320 | 4,126 |
| 31,850 | 31,900 | 4,328 | 3,874 | 4,328 | 4,134 |
| 31,900 | 31,950 | 4,335 | 3,881 | 4,335 | 4,141 |
| 31,950 | 32,000 | 4,343 | 3,889 | 4,343 | 4,149 |

## 32,000

| At least | But less than | Single | Married filing jointly * | Married filing separately | Head of a household |
|---|---|---|---|---|---|
| 32,000 | 32,050 | 4,350 | 3,896 | 4,350 | 4,156 |
| 32,050 | 32,100 | 4,358 | 3,904 | 4,358 | 4,164 |
| 32,100 | 32,150 | 4,365 | 3,911 | 4,365 | 4,171 |
| 32,150 | 32,200 | 4,373 | 3,919 | 4,373 | 4,179 |
| 32,200 | 32,250 | 4,380 | 3,926 | 4,380 | 4,186 |
| 32,250 | 32,300 | 4,388 | 3,934 | 4,388 | 4,194 |
| 32,300 | 32,350 | 4,395 | 3,941 | 4,395 | 4,201 |
| 32,350 | 32,400 | 4,403 | 3,949 | 4,403 | 4,209 |
| 32,400 | 32,450 | 4,410 | 3,956 | 4,410 | 4,216 |
| 32,450 | 32,500 | 4,418 | 3,964 | 4,418 | 4,224 |
| 32,500 | 32,550 | 4,425 | 3,971 | 4,425 | 4,231 |
| 32,550 | 32,600 | 4,433 | 3,979 | 4,433 | 4,239 |
| 32,600 | 32,650 | 4,440 | 3,986 | 4,440 | 4,246 |
| 32,650 | 32,700 | 4,448 | 3,994 | 4,448 | 4,254 |
| 32,700 | 32,750 | 4,455 | 4,001 | 4,455 | 4,261 |
| 32,750 | 32,800 | 4,463 | 4,009 | 4,463 | 4,269 |
| 32,800 | 32,850 | 4,470 | 4,016 | 4,470 | 4,276 |
| 32,850 | 32,900 | 4,478 | 4,024 | 4,478 | 4,284 |
| 32,900 | 32,950 | 4,485 | 4,031 | 4,485 | 4,291 |
| 32,950 | 33,000 | 4,493 | 4,039 | 4,493 | 4,299 |

## 33,000

| At least | But less than | Single | Married filing jointly * | Married filing separately | Head of a household |
|---|---|---|---|---|---|
| 33,000 | 33,050 | 4,500 | 4,046 | 4,500 | 4,306 |
| 33,050 | 33,100 | 4,508 | 4,054 | 4,508 | 4,314 |
| 33,100 | 33,150 | 4,515 | 4,061 | 4,515 | 4,321 |
| 33,150 | 33,200 | 4,523 | 4,069 | 4,523 | 4,329 |
| 33,200 | 33,250 | 4,530 | 4,076 | 4,530 | 4,336 |
| 33,250 | 33,300 | 4,538 | 4,084 | 4,538 | 4,344 |
| 33,300 | 33,350 | 4,545 | 4,091 | 4,545 | 4,351 |
| 33,350 | 33,400 | 4,553 | 4,099 | 4,553 | 4,359 |
| 33,400 | 33,450 | 4,560 | 4,106 | 4,560 | 4,366 |
| 33,450 | 33,500 | 4,568 | 4,114 | 4,568 | 4,374 |
| 33,500 | 33,550 | 4,575 | 4,121 | 4,575 | 4,381 |
| 33,550 | 33,600 | 4,583 | 4,129 | 4,583 | 4,389 |
| 33,600 | 33,650 | 4,590 | 4,136 | 4,590 | 4,396 |
| 33,650 | 33,700 | 4,598 | 4,144 | 4,598 | 4,404 |
| 33,700 | 33,750 | 4,605 | 4,151 | 4,605 | 4,411 |
| 33,750 | 33,800 | 4,613 | 4,159 | 4,613 | 4,419 |
| 33,800 | 33,850 | 4,620 | 4,166 | 4,620 | 4,426 |
| 33,850 | 33,900 | 4,628 | 4,174 | 4,628 | 4,434 |
| 33,900 | 33,950 | 4,635 | 4,181 | 4,635 | 4,441 |
| 33,950 | 34,000 | 4,643 | 4,189 | 4,643 | 4,449 |

## 34,000

| At least | But less than | Single | Married filing jointly * | Married filing separately | Head of a household |
|---|---|---|---|---|---|
| 34,000 | 34,050 | 4,650 | 4,196 | 4,650 | 4,456 |
| 34,050 | 34,100 | 4,658 | 4,204 | 4,658 | 4,464 |
| 34,100 | 34,150 | 4,665 | 4,211 | 4,665 | 4,471 |
| 34,150 | 34,200 | 4,673 | 4,219 | 4,673 | 4,479 |
| 34,200 | 34,250 | 4,680 | 4,226 | 4,680 | 4,486 |
| 34,250 | 34,300 | 4,688 | 4,234 | 4,688 | 4,494 |
| 34,300 | 34,350 | 4,695 | 4,241 | 4,695 | 4,501 |
| 34,350 | 34,400 | 4,703 | 4,249 | 4,703 | 4,509 |
| 34,400 | 34,450 | 4,710 | 4,256 | 4,710 | 4,516 |
| 34,450 | 34,500 | 4,718 | 4,264 | 4,718 | 4,524 |
| 34,500 | 34,550 | 4,725 | 4,271 | 4,725 | 4,531 |
| 34,550 | 34,600 | 4,733 | 4,279 | 4,733 | 4,539 |
| 34,600 | 34,650 | 4,740 | 4,286 | 4,740 | 4,546 |
| 34,650 | 34,700 | 4,748 | 4,294 | 4,748 | 4,554 |
| 34,700 | 34,750 | 4,755 | 4,301 | 4,755 | 4,561 |
| 34,750 | 34,800 | 4,763 | 4,309 | 4,763 | 4,569 |
| 34,800 | 34,850 | 4,770 | 4,316 | 4,770 | 4,576 |
| 34,850 | 34,900 | 4,778 | 4,324 | 4,778 | 4,584 |
| 34,900 | 34,950 | 4,785 | 4,331 | 4,785 | 4,591 |
| 34,950 | 35,000 | 4,793 | 4,339 | 4,793 | 4,599 |

## 35,000

| At least | But less than | Single | Married filing jointly * | Married filing separately | Head of a household |
|---|---|---|---|---|---|
| 35,000 | 35,050 | 4,800 | 4,346 | 4,800 | 4,606 |
| 35,050 | 35,100 | 4,808 | 4,354 | 4,808 | 4,614 |
| 35,100 | 35,150 | 4,815 | 4,361 | 4,815 | 4,621 |
| 35,150 | 35,200 | 4,823 | 4,369 | 4,823 | 4,629 |
| 35,200 | 35,250 | 4,830 | 4,376 | 4,830 | 4,636 |
| 35,250 | 35,300 | 4,838 | 4,384 | 4,838 | 4,644 |
| 35,300 | 35,350 | 4,845 | 4,391 | 4,845 | 4,651 |
| 35,350 | 35,400 | 4,853 | 4,399 | 4,853 | 4,659 |
| 35,400 | 35,450 | 4,860 | 4,406 | 4,860 | 4,666 |
| 35,450 | 35,500 | 4,868 | 4,414 | 4,868 | 4,674 |
| 35,500 | 35,550 | 4,875 | 4,421 | 4,875 | 4,681 |
| 35,550 | 35,600 | 4,883 | 4,429 | 4,883 | 4,689 |
| 35,600 | 35,650 | 4,890 | 4,436 | 4,890 | 4,696 |
| 35,650 | 35,700 | 4,898 | 4,444 | 4,898 | 4,704 |
| 35,700 | 35,750 | 4,905 | 4,451 | 4,905 | 4,711 |
| 35,750 | 35,800 | 4,913 | 4,459 | 4,913 | 4,719 |
| 35,800 | 35,850 | 4,920 | 4,466 | 4,920 | 4,726 |
| 35,850 | 35,900 | 4,928 | 4,474 | 4,928 | 4,734 |
| 35,900 | 35,950 | 4,935 | 4,481 | 4,935 | 4,741 |
| 35,950 | 36,000 | 4,943 | 4,489 | 4,943 | 4,749 |

## 36,000

| At least | But less than | Single | Married filing jointly * | Married filing separately | Head of a household |
|---|---|---|---|---|---|
| 36,000 | 36,050 | 4,950 | 4,496 | 4,950 | 4,756 |
| 36,050 | 36,100 | 4,958 | 4,504 | 4,958 | 4,764 |
| 36,100 | 36,150 | 4,965 | 4,511 | 4,965 | 4,771 |
| 36,150 | 36,200 | 4,973 | 4,519 | 4,973 | 4,779 |
| 36,200 | 36,250 | 4,980 | 4,526 | 4,980 | 4,786 |
| 36,250 | 36,300 | 4,988 | 4,534 | 4,988 | 4,794 |
| 36,300 | 36,350 | 4,995 | 4,541 | 4,995 | 4,801 |
| 36,350 | 36,400 | 5,003 | 4,549 | 5,003 | 4,809 |
| 36,400 | 36,450 | 5,010 | 4,556 | 5,010 | 4,816 |
| 36,450 | 36,500 | 5,018 | 4,564 | 5,018 | 4,824 |
| 36,500 | 36,550 | 5,025 | 4,571 | 5,025 | 4,831 |
| 36,550 | 36,600 | 5,033 | 4,579 | 5,033 | 4,839 |
| 36,600 | 36,650 | 5,040 | 4,586 | 5,040 | 4,846 |
| 36,650 | 36,700 | 5,048 | 4,594 | 5,048 | 4,854 |
| 36,700 | 36,750 | 5,055 | 4,601 | 5,055 | 4,861 |
| 36,750 | 36,800 | 5,063 | 4,609 | 5,063 | 4,869 |
| 36,800 | 36,850 | 5,070 | 4,616 | 5,070 | 4,876 |
| 36,850 | 36,900 | 5,078 | 4,624 | 5,078 | 4,884 |
| 36,900 | 36,950 | 5,088 | 4,631 | 5,088 | 4,891 |
| 36,950 | 37,000 | 5,100 | 4,639 | 5,100 | 4,899 |

## 37,000

| At least | But less than | Single | Married filing jointly * | Married filing separately | Head of a household |
|---|---|---|---|---|---|
| 37,000 | 37,050 | 5,113 | 4,646 | 5,113 | 4,906 |
| 37,050 | 37,100 | 5,125 | 4,654 | 5,125 | 4,914 |
| 37,100 | 37,150 | 5,138 | 4,661 | 5,138 | 4,921 |
| 37,150 | 37,200 | 5,150 | 4,669 | 5,150 | 4,929 |
| 37,200 | 37,250 | 5,163 | 4,676 | 5,163 | 4,936 |
| 37,250 | 37,300 | 5,175 | 4,684 | 5,175 | 4,944 |
| 37,300 | 37,350 | 5,188 | 4,691 | 5,188 | 4,951 |
| 37,350 | 37,400 | 5,200 | 4,699 | 5,200 | 4,959 |
| 37,400 | 37,450 | 5,213 | 4,706 | 5,213 | 4,966 |
| 37,450 | 37,500 | 5,225 | 4,714 | 5,225 | 4,974 |
| 37,500 | 37,550 | 5,238 | 4,721 | 5,238 | 4,981 |
| 37,550 | 37,600 | 5,250 | 4,729 | 5,250 | 4,989 |
| 37,600 | 37,650 | 5,263 | 4,736 | 5,263 | 4,996 |
| 37,650 | 37,700 | 5,275 | 4,744 | 5,275 | 5,004 |
| 37,700 | 37,750 | 5,288 | 4,751 | 5,288 | 5,011 |
| 37,750 | 37,800 | 5,300 | 4,759 | 5,300 | 5,019 |
| 37,800 | 37,850 | 5,313 | 4,766 | 5,313 | 5,026 |
| 37,850 | 37,900 | 5,325 | 4,774 | 5,325 | 5,034 |
| 37,900 | 37,950 | 5,338 | 4,781 | 5,338 | 5,041 |
| 37,950 | 38,000 | 5,350 | 4,789 | 5,350 | 5,049 |

## 38,000

| At least | But less than | Single | Married filing jointly * | Married filing separately | Head of a household |
|---|---|---|---|---|---|
| 38,000 | 38,050 | 5,363 | 4,796 | 5,363 | 5,056 |
| 38,050 | 38,100 | 5,375 | 4,804 | 5,375 | 5,064 |
| 38,100 | 38,150 | 5,388 | 4,811 | 5,388 | 5,071 |
| 38,150 | 38,200 | 5,400 | 4,819 | 5,400 | 5,079 |
| 38,200 | 38,250 | 5,413 | 4,826 | 5,413 | 5,086 |
| 38,250 | 38,300 | 5,425 | 4,834 | 5,425 | 5,094 |
| 38,300 | 38,350 | 5,438 | 4,841 | 5,438 | 5,101 |
| 38,350 | 38,400 | 5,450 | 4,849 | 5,450 | 5,109 |
| 38,400 | 38,450 | 5,463 | 4,856 | 5,463 | 5,116 |
| 38,450 | 38,500 | 5,475 | 4,864 | 5,475 | 5,124 |
| 38,500 | 38,550 | 5,488 | 4,871 | 5,488 | 5,131 |
| 38,550 | 38,600 | 5,500 | 4,879 | 5,500 | 5,139 |
| 38,600 | 38,650 | 5,513 | 4,886 | 5,513 | 5,146 |
| 38,650 | 38,700 | 5,525 | 4,894 | 5,525 | 5,154 |
| 38,700 | 38,750 | 5,538 | 4,901 | 5,538 | 5,161 |
| 38,750 | 38,800 | 5,550 | 4,909 | 5,550 | 5,169 |
| 38,800 | 38,850 | 5,563 | 4,916 | 5,563 | 5,176 |
| 38,850 | 38,900 | 5,575 | 4,924 | 5,575 | 5,184 |
| 38,900 | 38,950 | 5,588 | 4,931 | 5,588 | 5,191 |
| 38,950 | 39,000 | 5,600 | 4,939 | 5,600 | 5,199 |

*(Continued)*

* This column must also be used by a qualifying widow(er).

# 2015 Federal Tax Guide

DRAFT AS OF October 8, 2014

*The table below is divided into three income-bracket columns, each with the same header structure:*

| If line 43 (taxable income) is— At least | But less than | Single | Married filing jointly * | Married filing separately | Head of a household |
|---|---|---|---|---|---|
| | | | Your tax is— | | |

## 39,000

| At least | But less than | Single | Married filing jointly * | Married filing separately | Head of a household |
|---|---|---|---|---|---|
| 39,000 | 39,050 | 5,613 | 4,946 | 5,613 | 5,206 |
| 39,050 | 39,100 | 5,625 | 4,954 | 5,625 | 5,214 |
| 39,100 | 39,150 | 5,638 | 4,961 | 5,638 | 5,221 |
| 39,150 | 39,200 | 5,650 | 4,969 | 5,650 | 5,229 |
| 39,200 | 39,250 | 5,663 | 4,976 | 5,663 | 5,236 |
| 39,250 | 39,300 | 5,675 | 4,984 | 5,675 | 5,244 |
| 39,300 | 39,350 | 5,688 | 4,991 | 5,688 | 5,251 |
| 39,350 | 39,400 | 5,700 | 4,999 | 5,700 | 5,259 |
| 39,400 | 39,450 | 5,713 | 5,006 | 5,713 | 5,266 |
| 39,450 | 39,500 | 5,725 | 5,014 | 5,725 | 5,274 |
| 39,500 | 39,550 | 5,738 | 5,021 | 5,738 | 5,281 |
| 39,550 | 39,600 | 5,750 | 5,029 | 5,750 | 5,289 |
| 39,600 | 39,650 | 5,763 | 5,036 | 5,763 | 5,296 |
| 39,650 | 39,700 | 5,775 | 5,044 | 5,775 | 5,304 |
| 39,700 | 39,750 | 5,788 | 5,051 | 5,788 | 5,311 |
| 39,750 | 39,800 | 5,800 | 5,059 | 5,800 | 5,319 |
| 39,800 | 39,850 | 5,813 | 5,066 | 5,813 | 5,326 |
| 39,850 | 39,900 | 5,825 | 5,074 | 5,825 | 5,334 |
| 39,900 | 39,950 | 5,838 | 5,081 | 5,838 | 5,341 |
| 39,950 | 40,000 | 5,850 | 5,089 | 5,850 | 5,349 |

## 40,000

| At least | But less than | Single | Married filing jointly * | Married filing separately | Head of a household |
|---|---|---|---|---|---|
| 40,000 | 40,050 | 5,863 | 5,096 | 5,863 | 5,356 |
| 40,050 | 40,100 | 5,875 | 5,104 | 5,875 | 5,364 |
| 40,100 | 40,150 | 5,888 | 5,111 | 5,888 | 5,371 |
| 40,150 | 40,200 | 5,900 | 5,119 | 5,900 | 5,379 |
| 40,200 | 40,250 | 5,913 | 5,126 | 5,913 | 5,386 |
| 40,250 | 40,300 | 5,925 | 5,134 | 5,925 | 5,394 |
| 40,300 | 40,350 | 5,938 | 5,141 | 5,938 | 5,401 |
| 40,350 | 40,400 | 5,950 | 5,149 | 5,950 | 5,409 |
| 40,400 | 40,450 | 5,963 | 5,156 | 5,963 | 5,416 |
| 40,450 | 40,500 | 5,975 | 5,164 | 5,975 | 5,424 |
| 40,500 | 40,550 | 5,988 | 5,171 | 5,988 | 5,431 |
| 40,550 | 40,600 | 6,000 | 5,179 | 6,000 | 5,439 |
| 40,600 | 40,650 | 6,013 | 5,186 | 6,013 | 5,446 |
| 40,650 | 40,700 | 6,025 | 5,194 | 6,025 | 5,454 |
| 40,700 | 40,750 | 6,038 | 5,201 | 6,038 | 5,461 |
| 40,750 | 40,800 | 6,050 | 5,209 | 6,050 | 5,469 |
| 40,800 | 40,850 | 6,063 | 5,216 | 6,063 | 5,476 |
| 40,850 | 40,900 | 6,075 | 5,224 | 6,075 | 5,484 |
| 40,900 | 40,950 | 6,088 | 5,231 | 6,088 | 5,491 |
| 40,950 | 41,000 | 6,100 | 5,239 | 6,100 | 5,499 |

## 41,000

| At least | But less than | Single | Married filing jointly * | Married filing separately | Head of a household |
|---|---|---|---|---|---|
| 41,000 | 41,050 | 6,113 | 5,246 | 6,113 | 5,506 |
| 41,050 | 41,100 | 6,125 | 5,254 | 6,125 | 5,514 |
| 41,100 | 41,150 | 6,138 | 5,261 | 6,138 | 5,521 |
| 41,150 | 41,200 | 6,150 | 5,269 | 6,150 | 5,529 |
| 41,200 | 41,250 | 6,163 | 5,276 | 6,163 | 5,536 |
| 41,250 | 41,300 | 6,175 | 5,284 | 6,175 | 5,544 |
| 41,300 | 41,350 | 6,188 | 5,291 | 6,188 | 5,551 |
| 41,350 | 41,400 | 6,200 | 5,299 | 6,200 | 5,559 |
| 41,400 | 41,450 | 6,213 | 5,306 | 6,213 | 5,566 |
| 41,450 | 41,500 | 6,225 | 5,314 | 6,225 | 5,574 |
| 41,500 | 41,550 | 6,238 | 5,321 | 6,238 | 5,581 |
| 41,550 | 41,600 | 6,250 | 5,329 | 6,250 | 5,589 |
| 41,600 | 41,650 | 6,263 | 5,336 | 6,263 | 5,596 |
| 41,650 | 41,700 | 6,275 | 5,344 | 6,275 | 5,604 |
| 41,700 | 41,750 | 6,288 | 5,351 | 6,288 | 5,611 |
| 41,750 | 41,800 | 6,300 | 5,359 | 6,300 | 5,619 |
| 41,800 | 41,850 | 6,313 | 5,366 | 6,313 | 5,626 |
| 41,850 | 41,900 | 6,325 | 5,374 | 6,325 | 5,634 |
| 41,900 | 41,950 | 6,338 | 5,381 | 6,338 | 5,641 |
| 41,950 | 42,000 | 6,350 | 5,389 | 6,350 | 5,649 |

## 42,000

| At least | But less than | Single | Married filing jointly * | Married filing separately | Head of a household |
|---|---|---|---|---|---|
| 42,000 | 42,050 | 6,363 | 5,396 | 6,363 | 5,656 |
| 42,050 | 42,100 | 6,375 | 5,404 | 6,375 | 5,664 |
| 42,100 | 42,150 | 6,388 | 5,411 | 6,388 | 5,671 |
| 42,150 | 42,200 | 6,400 | 5,419 | 6,400 | 5,679 |
| 42,200 | 42,250 | 6,413 | 5,426 | 6,413 | 5,686 |
| 42,250 | 42,300 | 6,425 | 5,434 | 6,425 | 5,694 |
| 42,300 | 42,350 | 6,438 | 5,441 | 6,438 | 5,701 |
| 42,350 | 42,400 | 6,450 | 5,449 | 6,450 | 5,709 |
| 42,400 | 42,450 | 6,463 | 5,456 | 6,463 | 5,716 |
| 42,450 | 42,500 | 6,475 | 5,464 | 6,475 | 5,724 |
| 42,500 | 42,550 | 6,488 | 5,471 | 6,488 | 5,731 |
| 42,550 | 42,600 | 6,500 | 5,479 | 6,500 | 5,739 |
| 42,600 | 42,650 | 6,513 | 5,486 | 6,513 | 5,746 |
| 42,650 | 42,700 | 6,525 | 5,494 | 6,525 | 5,754 |
| 42,700 | 42,750 | 6,538 | 5,501 | 6,538 | 5,761 |
| 42,750 | 42,800 | 6,550 | 5,509 | 6,550 | 5,769 |
| 42,800 | 42,850 | 6,563 | 5,516 | 6,563 | 5,776 |
| 42,850 | 42,900 | 6,575 | 5,524 | 6,575 | 5,784 |
| 42,900 | 42,950 | 6,588 | 5,531 | 6,588 | 5,791 |
| 42,950 | 43,000 | 6,600 | 5,539 | 6,600 | 5,799 |

## 43,000

| At least | But less than | Single | Married filing jointly * | Married filing separately | Head of a household |
|---|---|---|---|---|---|
| 43,000 | 43,050 | 6,613 | 5,546 | 6,613 | 5,806 |
| 43,050 | 43,100 | 6,625 | 5,554 | 6,625 | 5,814 |
| 43,100 | 43,150 | 6,638 | 5,561 | 6,638 | 5,821 |
| 43,150 | 43,200 | 6,650 | 5,569 | 6,650 | 5,829 |
| 43,200 | 43,250 | 6,663 | 5,576 | 6,663 | 5,836 |
| 43,250 | 43,300 | 6,675 | 5,584 | 6,675 | 5,844 |
| 43,300 | 43,350 | 6,688 | 5,591 | 6,688 | 5,851 |
| 43,350 | 43,400 | 6,700 | 5,599 | 6,700 | 5,859 |
| 43,400 | 43,450 | 6,713 | 5,606 | 6,713 | 5,866 |
| 43,450 | 43,500 | 6,725 | 5,614 | 6,725 | 5,874 |
| 43,500 | 43,550 | 6,738 | 5,621 | 6,738 | 5,881 |
| 43,550 | 43,600 | 6,750 | 5,629 | 6,750 | 5,889 |
| 43,600 | 43,650 | 6,763 | 5,636 | 6,763 | 5,896 |
| 43,650 | 43,700 | 6,775 | 5,644 | 6,775 | 5,904 |
| 43,700 | 43,750 | 6,788 | 5,651 | 6,788 | 5,911 |
| 43,750 | 43,800 | 6,800 | 5,659 | 6,800 | 5,919 |
| 43,800 | 43,850 | 6,813 | 5,666 | 6,813 | 5,926 |
| 43,850 | 43,900 | 6,825 | 5,674 | 6,825 | 5,934 |
| 43,900 | 43,950 | 6,838 | 5,681 | 6,838 | 5,941 |
| 43,950 | 44,000 | 6,850 | 5,689 | 6,850 | 5,949 |

## 44,000

| At least | But less than | Single | Married filing jointly * | Married filing separately | Head of a household |
|---|---|---|---|---|---|
| 44,000 | 44,050 | 6,863 | 5,696 | 6,863 | 5,956 |
| 44,050 | 44,100 | 6,875 | 5,704 | 6,875 | 5,964 |
| 44,100 | 44,150 | 6,888 | 5,711 | 6,888 | 5,971 |
| 44,150 | 44,200 | 6,900 | 5,719 | 6,900 | 5,979 |
| 44,200 | 44,250 | 6,913 | 5,726 | 6,913 | 5,986 |
| 44,250 | 44,300 | 6,925 | 5,734 | 6,925 | 5,994 |
| 44,300 | 44,350 | 6,938 | 5,741 | 6,938 | 6,001 |
| 44,350 | 44,400 | 6,950 | 5,749 | 6,950 | 6,009 |
| 44,400 | 44,450 | 6,963 | 5,756 | 6,963 | 6,016 |
| 44,450 | 44,500 | 6,975 | 5,764 | 6,975 | 6,024 |
| 44,500 | 44,550 | 6,988 | 5,771 | 6,988 | 6,031 |
| 44,550 | 44,600 | 7,000 | 5,779 | 7,000 | 6,039 |
| 44,600 | 44,650 | 7,013 | 5,786 | 7,013 | 6,046 |
| 44,650 | 44,700 | 7,025 | 5,794 | 7,025 | 6,054 |
| 44,700 | 44,750 | 7,038 | 5,801 | 7,038 | 6,061 |
| 44,750 | 44,800 | 7,050 | 5,809 | 7,050 | 6,069 |
| 44,800 | 44,850 | 7,063 | 5,816 | 7,063 | 6,076 |
| 44,850 | 44,900 | 7,075 | 5,824 | 7,075 | 6,084 |
| 44,900 | 44,950 | 7,088 | 5,831 | 7,088 | 6,091 |
| 44,950 | 45,000 | 7,100 | 5,839 | 7,100 | 6,099 |

## 45,000

| At least | But less than | Single | Married filing jointly * | Married filing separately | Head of a household |
|---|---|---|---|---|---|
| 45,000 | 45,050 | 7,113 | 5,846 | 7,113 | 6,106 |
| 45,050 | 45,100 | 7,125 | 5,854 | 7,125 | 6,114 |
| 45,100 | 45,150 | 7,138 | 5,861 | 7,138 | 6,121 |
| 45,150 | 45,200 | 7,150 | 5,869 | 7,150 | 6,129 |
| 45,200 | 45,250 | 7,163 | 5,876 | 7,163 | 6,136 |
| 45,250 | 45,300 | 7,175 | 5,884 | 7,175 | 6,144 |
| 45,300 | 45,350 | 7,188 | 5,891 | 7,188 | 6,151 |
| 45,350 | 45,400 | 7,200 | 5,899 | 7,200 | 6,159 |
| 45,400 | 45,450 | 7,213 | 5,906 | 7,213 | 6,166 |
| 45,450 | 45,500 | 7,225 | 5,914 | 7,225 | 6,174 |
| 45,500 | 45,550 | 7,238 | 5,921 | 7,238 | 6,181 |
| 45,550 | 45,600 | 7,250 | 5,929 | 7,250 | 6,189 |
| 45,600 | 45,650 | 7,263 | 5,936 | 7,263 | 6,196 |
| 45,650 | 45,700 | 7,275 | 5,944 | 7,275 | 6,204 |
| 45,700 | 45,750 | 7,288 | 5,951 | 7,288 | 6,211 |
| 45,750 | 45,800 | 7,300 | 5,959 | 7,300 | 6,219 |
| 45,800 | 45,850 | 7,313 | 5,966 | 7,313 | 6,226 |
| 45,850 | 45,900 | 7,325 | 5,974 | 7,325 | 6,234 |
| 45,900 | 45,950 | 7,338 | 5,981 | 7,338 | 6,241 |
| 45,950 | 46,000 | 7,350 | 5,989 | 7,350 | 6,249 |

## 46,000

| At least | But less than | Single | Married filing jointly * | Married filing separately | Head of a household |
|---|---|---|---|---|---|
| 46,000 | 46,050 | 7,363 | 5,996 | 7,363 | 6,256 |
| 46,050 | 46,100 | 7,375 | 6,004 | 7,375 | 6,264 |
| 46,100 | 46,150 | 7,388 | 6,011 | 7,388 | 6,271 |
| 46,150 | 46,200 | 7,400 | 6,019 | 7,400 | 6,279 |
| 46,200 | 46,250 | 7,413 | 6,026 | 7,413 | 6,286 |
| 46,250 | 46,300 | 7,425 | 6,034 | 7,425 | 6,294 |
| 46,300 | 46,350 | 7,438 | 6,041 | 7,438 | 6,301 |
| 46,350 | 46,400 | 7,450 | 6,049 | 7,450 | 6,309 |
| 46,400 | 46,450 | 7,463 | 6,056 | 7,463 | 6,316 |
| 46,450 | 46,500 | 7,475 | 6,064 | 7,475 | 6,324 |
| 46,500 | 46,550 | 7,488 | 6,071 | 7,488 | 6,331 |
| 46,550 | 46,600 | 7,500 | 6,079 | 7,500 | 6,339 |
| 46,600 | 46,650 | 7,513 | 6,086 | 7,513 | 6,346 |
| 46,650 | 46,700 | 7,525 | 6,094 | 7,525 | 6,354 |
| 46,700 | 46,750 | 7,538 | 6,101 | 7,538 | 6,361 |
| 46,750 | 46,800 | 7,550 | 6,109 | 7,550 | 6,369 |
| 46,800 | 46,850 | 7,563 | 6,116 | 7,563 | 6,376 |
| 46,850 | 46,900 | 7,575 | 6,124 | 7,575 | 6,384 |
| 46,900 | 46,950 | 7,588 | 6,131 | 7,588 | 6,391 |
| 46,950 | 47,000 | 7,600 | 6,139 | 7,600 | 6,399 |

## 47,000

| At least | But less than | Single | Married filing jointly * | Married filing separately | Head of a household |
|---|---|---|---|---|---|
| 47,000 | 47,050 | 7,613 | 6,146 | 7,613 | 6,406 |
| 47,050 | 47,100 | 7,625 | 6,154 | 7,625 | 6,414 |
| 47,100 | 47,150 | 7,638 | 6,161 | 7,638 | 6,421 |
| 47,150 | 47,200 | 7,650 | 6,169 | 7,650 | 6,429 |
| 47,200 | 47,250 | 7,663 | 6,176 | 7,663 | 6,436 |
| 47,250 | 47,300 | 7,675 | 6,184 | 7,675 | 6,444 |
| 47,300 | 47,350 | 7,688 | 6,191 | 7,688 | 6,451 |
| 47,350 | 47,400 | 7,700 | 6,199 | 7,700 | 6,459 |
| 47,400 | 47,450 | 7,713 | 6,206 | 7,713 | 6,466 |
| 47,450 | 47,500 | 7,725 | 6,214 | 7,725 | 6,474 |
| 47,500 | 47,550 | 7,738 | 6,221 | 7,738 | 6,481 |
| 47,550 | 47,600 | 7,750 | 6,229 | 7,750 | 6,489 |
| 47,600 | 47,650 | 7,763 | 6,236 | 7,763 | 6,496 |
| 47,650 | 47,700 | 7,775 | 6,244 | 7,775 | 6,504 |
| 47,700 | 47,750 | 7,788 | 6,251 | 7,788 | 6,511 |
| 47,750 | 47,800 | 7,800 | 6,259 | 7,800 | 6,519 |
| 47,800 | 47,850 | 7,813 | 6,266 | 7,813 | 6,526 |
| 47,850 | 47,900 | 7,825 | 6,274 | 7,825 | 6,534 |
| 47,900 | 47,950 | 7,838 | 6,281 | 7,838 | 6,541 |
| 47,950 | 48,000 | 7,850 | 6,289 | 7,850 | 6,549 |

*(Continued)*

* This column must also be used by a qualifying widow(er).

# 2014 Tax Tables

| If line 43 (taxable income) is— | | And you are— | | | |
|---|---|---|---|---|---|
| At least | But less than | Single | Married filing jointly * | Married filing separately | Head of a household |
| | | Your tax is— | | | |

## 48,000

| At least | But less than | Single | Married filing jointly * | Married filing separately | Head of a household |
|---|---|---|---|---|---|
| 48,000 | 48,050 | 7,863 | 6,296 | 7,863 | 6,556 |
| 48,050 | 48,100 | 7,875 | 6,304 | 7,875 | 6,564 |
| 48,100 | 48,150 | 7,888 | 6,311 | 7,888 | 6,571 |
| 48,150 | 48,200 | 7,900 | 6,319 | 7,900 | 6,579 |
| 48,200 | 48,250 | 7,913 | 6,326 | 7,913 | 6,586 |
| 48,250 | 48,300 | 7,925 | 6,334 | 7,925 | 6,594 |
| 48,300 | 48,350 | 7,938 | 6,341 | 7,938 | 6,601 |
| 48,350 | 48,400 | 7,950 | 6,349 | 7,950 | 6,609 |
| 48,400 | 48,450 | 7,963 | 6,356 | 7,963 | 6,616 |
| 48,450 | 48,500 | 7,975 | 6,364 | 7,975 | 6,624 |
| 48,500 | 48,550 | 7,988 | 6,371 | 7,988 | 6,631 |
| 48,550 | 48,600 | 8,000 | 6,379 | 8,000 | 6,639 |
| 48,600 | 48,650 | 8,013 | 6,386 | 8,013 | 6,646 |
| 48,650 | 48,700 | 8,025 | 6,394 | 8,025 | 6,654 |
| 48,700 | 48,750 | 8,038 | 6,401 | 8,038 | 6,661 |
| 48,750 | 48,800 | 8,050 | 6,409 | 8,050 | 6,669 |
| 48,800 | 48,850 | 8,063 | 6,416 | 8,063 | 6,676 |
| 48,850 | 48,900 | 8,075 | 6,424 | 8,075 | 6,684 |
| 48,900 | 48,950 | 8,088 | 6,431 | 8,088 | 6,691 |
| 48,950 | 49,000 | 8,100 | 6,439 | 8,100 | 6,699 |

## 49,000

| At least | But less than | Single | Married filing jointly * | Married filing separately | Head of a household |
|---|---|---|---|---|---|
| 49,000 | 49,050 | 8,113 | 6,446 | 8,113 | 6,706 |
| 49,050 | 49,100 | 8,125 | 6,454 | 8,125 | 6,714 |
| 49,100 | 49,150 | 8,138 | 6,461 | 8,138 | 6,721 |
| 49,150 | 49,200 | 8,150 | 6,469 | 8,150 | 6,729 |
| 49,200 | 49,250 | 8,163 | 6,476 | 8,163 | 6,736 |
| 49,250 | 49,300 | 8,175 | 6,484 | 8,175 | 6,744 |
| 49,300 | 49,350 | 8,188 | 6,491 | 8,188 | 6,751 |
| 49,350 | 49,400 | 8,200 | 6,499 | 8,200 | 6,759 |
| 49,400 | 49,450 | 8,213 | 6,506 | 8,213 | 6,769 |
| 49,450 | 49,500 | 8,225 | 6,514 | 8,225 | 6,781 |
| 49,500 | 49,550 | 8,238 | 6,521 | 8,238 | 6,794 |
| 49,550 | 49,600 | 8,250 | 6,529 | 8,250 | 6,806 |
| 49,600 | 49,650 | 8,263 | 6,536 | 8,263 | 6,819 |
| 49,650 | 49,700 | 8,275 | 6,544 | 8,275 | 6,831 |
| 49,700 | 49,750 | 8,288 | 6,551 | 8,288 | 6,844 |
| 49,750 | 49,800 | 8,300 | 6,559 | 8,300 | 6,856 |
| 49,800 | 49,850 | 8,313 | 6,566 | 8,313 | 6,869 |
| 49,850 | 49,900 | 8,325 | 6,574 | 8,325 | 6,881 |
| 49,900 | 49,950 | 8,338 | 6,581 | 8,338 | 6,894 |
| 49,950 | 50,000 | 8,350 | 6,589 | 8,350 | 6,906 |

## 50,000

| At least | But less than | Single | Married filing jointly * | Married filing separately | Head of a household |
|---|---|---|---|---|---|
| 50,000 | 50,050 | 8,363 | 6,596 | 8,363 | 6,919 |
| 50,050 | 50,100 | 8,375 | 6,604 | 8,375 | 6,931 |
| 50,100 | 50,150 | 8,388 | 6,611 | 8,388 | 6,944 |
| 50,150 | 50,200 | 8,400 | 6,619 | 8,400 | 6,956 |
| 50,200 | 50,250 | 8,413 | 6,626 | 8,413 | 6,969 |
| 50,250 | 50,300 | 8,425 | 6,634 | 8,425 | 6,981 |
| 50,300 | 50,350 | 8,438 | 6,641 | 8,438 | 6,994 |
| 50,350 | 50,400 | 8,450 | 6,649 | 8,450 | 7,006 |
| 50,400 | 50,450 | 8,463 | 6,656 | 8,463 | 7,019 |
| 50,450 | 50,500 | 8,475 | 6,664 | 8,475 | 7,031 |
| 50,500 | 50,550 | 8,488 | 6,671 | 8,488 | 7,044 |
| 50,550 | 50,600 | 8,500 | 6,679 | 8,500 | 7,056 |
| 50,600 | 50,650 | 8,513 | 6,686 | 8,513 | 7,069 |
| 50,650 | 50,700 | 8,525 | 6,694 | 8,525 | 7,081 |
| 50,700 | 50,750 | 8,538 | 6,701 | 8,538 | 7,094 |
| 50,750 | 50,800 | 8,550 | 6,709 | 8,550 | 7,106 |
| 50,800 | 50,850 | 8,563 | 6,716 | 8,563 | 7,119 |
| 50,850 | 50,900 | 8,575 | 6,724 | 8,575 | 7,131 |
| 50,900 | 50,950 | 8,588 | 6,731 | 8,588 | 7,144 |
| 50,950 | 51,000 | 8,600 | 6,739 | 8,600 | 7,156 |

## 51,000

| At least | But less than | Single | Married filing jointly * | Married filing separately | Head of a household |
|---|---|---|---|---|---|
| 51,000 | 51,050 | 8,613 | 6,746 | 8,613 | 7,169 |
| 51,050 | 51,100 | 8,625 | 6,754 | 8,625 | 7,181 |
| 51,100 | 51,150 | 8,638 | 6,761 | 8,638 | 7,194 |
| 51,150 | 51,200 | 8,650 | 6,769 | 8,650 | 7,206 |
| 51,200 | 51,250 | 8,663 | 6,776 | 8,663 | 7,219 |
| 51,250 | 51,300 | 8,675 | 6,784 | 8,675 | 7,231 |
| 51,300 | 51,350 | 8,688 | 6,791 | 8,688 | 7,244 |
| 51,350 | 51,400 | 8,700 | 6,799 | 8,700 | 7,256 |
| 51,400 | 51,450 | 8,713 | 6,806 | 8,713 | 7,269 |
| 51,450 | 51,500 | 8,725 | 6,814 | 8,725 | 7,281 |
| 51,500 | 51,550 | 8,738 | 6,821 | 8,738 | 7,294 |
| 51,550 | 51,600 | 8,750 | 6,829 | 8,750 | 7,306 |
| 51,600 | 51,650 | 8,763 | 6,836 | 8,763 | 7,319 |
| 51,650 | 51,700 | 8,775 | 6,844 | 8,775 | 7,331 |
| 51,700 | 51,750 | 8,788 | 6,851 | 8,788 | 7,344 |
| 51,750 | 51,800 | 8,800 | 6,859 | 8,800 | 7,356 |
| 51,800 | 51,850 | 8,813 | 6,866 | 8,813 | 7,369 |
| 51,850 | 51,900 | 8,825 | 6,874 | 8,825 | 7,381 |
| 51,900 | 51,950 | 8,838 | 6,881 | 8,838 | 7,394 |
| 51,950 | 52,000 | 8,850 | 6,889 | 8,850 | 7,406 |

## 52,000

| At least | But less than | Single | Married filing jointly * | Married filing separately | Head of a household |
|---|---|---|---|---|---|
| 52,000 | 52,050 | 8,863 | 6,896 | 8,863 | 7,419 |
| 52,050 | 52,100 | 8,875 | 6,904 | 8,875 | 7,431 |
| 52,100 | 52,150 | 8,888 | 6,911 | 8,888 | 7,444 |
| 52,150 | 52,200 | 8,900 | 6,919 | 8,900 | 7,456 |
| 52,200 | 52,250 | 8,913 | 6,926 | 8,913 | 7,469 |
| 52,250 | 52,300 | 8,925 | 6,934 | 8,925 | 7,481 |
| 52,300 | 52,350 | 8,938 | 6,941 | 8,938 | 7,494 |
| 52,350 | 52,400 | 8,950 | 6,949 | 8,950 | 7,506 |
| 52,400 | 52,450 | 8,963 | 6,956 | 8,963 | 7,519 |
| 52,450 | 52,500 | 8,975 | 6,964 | 8,975 | 7,531 |
| 52,500 | 52,550 | 8,988 | 6,971 | 8,988 | 7,544 |
| 52,550 | 52,600 | 9,000 | 6,979 | 9,000 | 7,556 |
| 52,600 | 52,650 | 9,013 | 6,986 | 9,013 | 7,569 |
| 52,650 | 52,700 | 9,025 | 6,994 | 9,025 | 7,581 |
| 52,700 | 52,750 | 9,038 | 7,001 | 9,038 | 7,594 |
| 52,750 | 52,800 | 9,050 | 7,009 | 9,050 | 7,606 |
| 52,800 | 52,850 | 9,063 | 7,016 | 9,063 | 7,619 |
| 52,850 | 52,900 | 9,075 | 7,024 | 9,075 | 7,631 |
| 52,900 | 52,950 | 9,088 | 7,031 | 9,088 | 7,644 |
| 52,950 | 53,000 | 9,100 | 7,039 | 9,100 | 7,656 |

## 53,000

| At least | But less than | Single | Married filing jointly * | Married filing separately | Head of a household |
|---|---|---|---|---|---|
| 53,000 | 53,050 | 9,113 | 7,046 | 9,113 | 7,669 |
| 53,050 | 53,100 | 9,125 | 7,054 | 9,125 | 7,681 |
| 53,100 | 53,150 | 9,138 | 7,061 | 9,138 | 7,694 |
| 53,150 | 53,200 | 9,150 | 7,069 | 9,150 | 7,706 |
| 53,200 | 53,250 | 9,163 | 7,076 | 9,163 | 7,719 |
| 53,250 | 53,300 | 9,175 | 7,084 | 9,175 | 7,731 |
| 53,300 | 53,350 | 9,188 | 7,091 | 9,188 | 7,744 |
| 53,350 | 53,400 | 9,200 | 7,099 | 9,200 | 7,756 |
| 53,400 | 53,450 | 9,213 | 7,106 | 9,213 | 7,769 |
| 53,450 | 53,500 | 9,225 | 7,114 | 9,225 | 7,781 |
| 53,500 | 53,550 | 9,238 | 7,121 | 9,238 | 7,794 |
| 53,550 | 53,600 | 9,250 | 7,129 | 9,250 | 7,806 |
| 53,600 | 53,650 | 9,263 | 7,136 | 9,263 | 7,819 |
| 53,650 | 53,700 | 9,275 | 7,144 | 9,275 | 7,831 |
| 53,700 | 53,750 | 9,288 | 7,151 | 9,288 | 7,844 |
| 53,750 | 53,800 | 9,300 | 7,159 | 9,300 | 7,856 |
| 53,800 | 53,850 | 9,313 | 7,166 | 9,313 | 7,869 |
| 53,850 | 53,900 | 9,325 | 7,174 | 9,325 | 7,881 |
| 53,900 | 53,950 | 9,338 | 7,181 | 9,338 | 7,894 |
| 53,950 | 54,000 | 9,350 | 7,189 | 9,350 | 7,906 |

## 54,000

| At least | But less than | Single | Married filing jointly * | Married filing separately | Head of a household |
|---|---|---|---|---|---|
| 54,000 | 54,050 | 9,363 | 7,196 | 9,363 | 7,919 |
| 54,050 | 54,100 | 9,375 | 7,204 | 9,375 | 7,931 |
| 54,100 | 54,150 | 9,388 | 7,211 | 9,388 | 7,944 |
| 54,150 | 54,200 | 9,400 | 7,219 | 9,400 | 7,956 |
| 54,200 | 54,250 | 9,413 | 7,226 | 9,413 | 7,969 |
| 54,250 | 54,300 | 9,425 | 7,234 | 9,425 | 7,981 |
| 54,300 | 54,350 | 9,438 | 7,241 | 9,438 | 7,994 |
| 54,350 | 54,400 | 9,450 | 7,249 | 9,450 | 8,006 |
| 54,400 | 54,450 | 9,463 | 7,256 | 9,463 | 8,019 |
| 54,450 | 54,500 | 9,475 | 7,264 | 9,475 | 8,031 |
| 54,500 | 54,550 | 9,488 | 7,271 | 9,488 | 8,044 |
| 54,550 | 54,600 | 9,500 | 7,279 | 9,500 | 8,056 |
| 54,600 | 54,650 | 9,513 | 7,286 | 9,513 | 8,069 |
| 54,650 | 54,700 | 9,525 | 7,294 | 9,525 | 8,081 |
| 54,700 | 54,750 | 9,538 | 7,301 | 9,538 | 8,094 |
| 54,750 | 54,800 | 9,550 | 7,309 | 9,550 | 8,106 |
| 54,800 | 54,850 | 9,563 | 7,316 | 9,563 | 8,119 |
| 54,850 | 54,900 | 9,575 | 7,324 | 9,575 | 8,131 |
| 54,900 | 54,950 | 9,588 | 7,331 | 9,588 | 8,144 |
| 54,950 | 55,000 | 9,600 | 7,339 | 9,600 | 8,156 |

## 55,000

| At least | But less than | Single | Married filing jointly * | Married filing separately | Head of a household |
|---|---|---|---|---|---|
| 55,000 | 55,050 | 9,613 | 7,346 | 9,613 | 8,169 |
| 55,050 | 55,100 | 9,625 | 7,354 | 9,625 | 8,181 |
| 55,100 | 55,150 | 9,638 | 7,361 | 9,638 | 8,194 |
| 55,150 | 55,200 | 9,650 | 7,369 | 9,650 | 8,206 |
| 55,200 | 55,250 | 9,663 | 7,376 | 9,663 | 8,219 |
| 55,250 | 55,300 | 9,675 | 7,384 | 9,675 | 8,231 |
| 55,300 | 55,350 | 9,688 | 7,391 | 9,688 | 8,244 |
| 55,350 | 55,400 | 9,700 | 7,399 | 9,700 | 8,256 |
| 55,400 | 55,450 | 9,713 | 7,406 | 9,713 | 8,269 |
| 55,450 | 55,500 | 9,725 | 7,414 | 9,725 | 8,281 |
| 55,500 | 55,550 | 9,738 | 7,421 | 9,738 | 8,294 |
| 55,550 | 55,600 | 9,750 | 7,429 | 9,750 | 8,306 |
| 55,600 | 55,650 | 9,763 | 7,436 | 9,763 | 8,319 |
| 55,650 | 55,700 | 9,775 | 7,444 | 9,775 | 8,331 |
| 55,700 | 55,750 | 9,788 | 7,451 | 9,788 | 8,344 |
| 55,750 | 55,800 | 9,800 | 7,459 | 9,800 | 8,356 |
| 55,800 | 55,850 | 9,813 | 7,466 | 9,813 | 8,369 |
| 55,850 | 55,900 | 9,825 | 7,474 | 9,825 | 8,381 |
| 55,900 | 55,950 | 9,838 | 7,481 | 9,838 | 8,394 |
| 55,950 | 56,000 | 9,850 | 7,489 | 9,850 | 8,406 |

## 56,000

| At least | But less than | Single | Married filing jointly * | Married filing separately | Head of a household |
|---|---|---|---|---|---|
| 56,000 | 56,050 | 9,863 | 7,496 | 9,863 | 8,419 |
| 56,050 | 56,100 | 9,875 | 7,504 | 9,875 | 8,431 |
| 56,100 | 56,150 | 9,888 | 7,511 | 9,888 | 8,444 |
| 56,150 | 56,200 | 9,900 | 7,519 | 9,900 | 8,456 |
| 56,200 | 56,250 | 9,913 | 7,526 | 9,913 | 8,469 |
| 56,250 | 56,300 | 9,925 | 7,534 | 9,925 | 8,481 |
| 56,300 | 56,350 | 9,938 | 7,541 | 9,938 | 8,494 |
| 56,350 | 56,400 | 9,950 | 7,549 | 9,950 | 8,506 |
| 56,400 | 56,450 | 9,963 | 7,556 | 9,963 | 8,519 |
| 56,450 | 56,500 | 9,975 | 7,564 | 9,975 | 8,531 |
| 56,500 | 56,550 | 9,988 | 7,571 | 9,988 | 8,544 |
| 56,550 | 56,600 | 10,000 | 7,579 | 10,000 | 8,556 |
| 56,600 | 56,650 | 10,013 | 7,586 | 10,013 | 8,569 |
| 56,650 | 56,700 | 10,025 | 7,594 | 10,025 | 8,581 |
| 56,700 | 56,750 | 10,038 | 7,601 | 10,038 | 8,594 |
| 56,750 | 56,800 | 10,050 | 7,609 | 10,050 | 8,606 |
| 56,800 | 56,850 | 10,063 | 7,616 | 10,063 | 8,619 |
| 56,850 | 56,900 | 10,075 | 7,624 | 10,075 | 8,631 |
| 56,900 | 56,950 | 10,088 | 7,631 | 10,088 | 8,644 |
| 56,950 | 57,000 | 10,100 | 7,639 | 10,100 | 8,656 |

*(Continued)*

* This column must also be used by a qualifying widow(er).

# 2015 Federal Tax Guide

## 57,000

| If line 43 (taxable income) is— | | And you are— | | | |
| At least | But less than | Single | Married filing jointly * | Married filing separately | Head of a household |
|---|---|---|---|---|---|
| | | | | | Your tax is— |
| 57,000 | 57,050 | 10,113 | 7,646 | 10,113 | 8,669 |
| 57,050 | 57,100 | 10,125 | 7,654 | 10,125 | 8,681 |
| 57,100 | 57,150 | 10,138 | 7,661 | 10,138 | 8,694 |
| 57,150 | 57,200 | 10,150 | 7,669 | 10,150 | 8,706 |
| 57,200 | 57,250 | 10,163 | 7,676 | 10,163 | 8,719 |
| 57,250 | 57,300 | 10,175 | 7,684 | 10,175 | 8,731 |
| 57,300 | 57,350 | 10,188 | 7,691 | 10,188 | 8,744 |
| 57,350 | 57,400 | 10,200 | 7,699 | 10,200 | 8,756 |
| 57,400 | 57,450 | 10,213 | 7,706 | 10,213 | 8,769 |
| 57,450 | 57,500 | 10,225 | 7,714 | 10,225 | 8,781 |
| 57,500 | 57,550 | 10,238 | 7,721 | 10,238 | 8,794 |
| 57,550 | 57,600 | 10,250 | 7,729 | 10,250 | 8,806 |
| 57,600 | 57,650 | 10,263 | 7,736 | 10,263 | 8,819 |
| 57,650 | 57,700 | 10,275 | 7,744 | 10,275 | 8,831 |
| 57,700 | 57,750 | 10,288 | 7,751 | 10,288 | 8,844 |
| 57,750 | 57,800 | 10,300 | 7,759 | 10,300 | 8,856 |
| 57,800 | 57,850 | 10,313 | 7,766 | 10,313 | 8,869 |
| 57,850 | 57,900 | 10,325 | 7,774 | 10,325 | 8,881 |
| 57,900 | 57,950 | 10,338 | 7,781 | 10,338 | 8,894 |
| 57,950 | 58,000 | 10,350 | 7,789 | 10,350 | 8,906 |

## 58,000

| At least | But less than | Single | Married filing jointly * | Married filing separately | Head of a household |
|---|---|---|---|---|---|
| 58,000 | 58,050 | 10,363 | 7,796 | 10,363 | 8,919 |
| 58,050 | 58,100 | 10,375 | 7,804 | 10,375 | 8,931 |
| 58,100 | 58,150 | 10,388 | 7,811 | 10,388 | 8,944 |
| 58,150 | 58,200 | 10,400 | 7,819 | 10,400 | 8,956 |
| 58,200 | 58,250 | 10,413 | 7,826 | 10,413 | 8,969 |
| 58,250 | 58,300 | 10,425 | 7,834 | 10,425 | 8,981 |
| 58,300 | 58,350 | 10,438 | 7,841 | 10,438 | 8,994 |
| 58,350 | 58,400 | 10,450 | 7,849 | 10,450 | 9,006 |
| 58,400 | 58,450 | 10,463 | 7,856 | 10,463 | 9,019 |
| 58,450 | 58,500 | 10,475 | 7,864 | 10,475 | 9,031 |
| 58,500 | 58,550 | 10,488 | 7,871 | 10,488 | 9,044 |
| 58,550 | 58,600 | 10,500 | 7,879 | 10,500 | 9,056 |
| 58,600 | 58,650 | 10,513 | 7,886 | 10,513 | 9,069 |
| 58,650 | 58,700 | 10,525 | 7,894 | 10,525 | 9,081 |
| 58,700 | 58,750 | 10,538 | 7,901 | 10,538 | 9,094 |
| 58,750 | 58,800 | 10,550 | 7,909 | 10,550 | 9,106 |
| 58,800 | 58,850 | 10,563 | 7,916 | 10,563 | 9,119 |
| 58,850 | 58,900 | 10,575 | 7,924 | 10,575 | 9,131 |
| 58,900 | 58,950 | 10,588 | 7,931 | 10,588 | 9,144 |
| 58,950 | 59,000 | 10,600 | 7,939 | 10,600 | 9,156 |

## 59,000

| At least | But less than | Single | Married filing jointly * | Married filing separately | Head of a household |
|---|---|---|---|---|---|
| 59,000 | 59,050 | 10,613 | 7,946 | 10,613 | 9,169 |
| 59,050 | 59,100 | 10,625 | 7,954 | 10,625 | 9,181 |
| 59,100 | 59,150 | 10,638 | 7,961 | 10,638 | 9,194 |
| 59,150 | 59,200 | 10,650 | 7,969 | 10,650 | 9,206 |
| 59,200 | 59,250 | 10,663 | 7,976 | 10,663 | 9,219 |
| 59,250 | 59,300 | 10,675 | 7,984 | 10,675 | 9,231 |
| 59,300 | 59,350 | 10,688 | 7,991 | 10,688 | 9,244 |
| 59,350 | 59,400 | 10,700 | 7,999 | 10,700 | 9,256 |
| 59,400 | 59,450 | 10,713 | 8,006 | 10,713 | 9,269 |
| 59,450 | 59,500 | 10,725 | 8,014 | 10,725 | 9,281 |
| 59,500 | 59,550 | 10,738 | 8,021 | 10,738 | 9,294 |
| 59,550 | 59,600 | 10,750 | 8,029 | 10,750 | 9,306 |
| 59,600 | 59,650 | 10,763 | 8,036 | 10,763 | 9,319 |
| 59,650 | 59,700 | 10,775 | 8,044 | 10,775 | 9,331 |
| 59,700 | 59,750 | 10,788 | 8,051 | 10,788 | 9,344 |
| 59,750 | 59,800 | 10,800 | 8,059 | 10,800 | 9,356 |
| 59,800 | 59,850 | 10,813 | 8,066 | 10,813 | 9,369 |
| 59,850 | 59,900 | 10,825 | 8,074 | 10,825 | 9,381 |
| 59,900 | 59,950 | 10,838 | 8,081 | 10,838 | 9,394 |
| 59,950 | 60,000 | 10,850 | 8,089 | 10,850 | 9,406 |

## 60,000

| If line 43 (taxable income) is— | | And you are— | | | |
| At least | But less than | Single | Married filing jointly * | Married filing separately | Head of a household |
|---|---|---|---|---|---|
| 60,000 | 60,050 | 10,863 | 8,096 | 10,863 | 9,419 |
| 60,050 | 60,100 | 10,875 | 8,104 | 10,875 | 9,431 |
| 60,100 | 60,150 | 10,888 | 8,111 | 10,888 | 9,444 |
| 60,150 | 60,200 | 10,900 | 8,119 | 10,900 | 9,456 |
| 60,200 | 60,250 | 10,913 | 8,126 | 10,913 | 9,469 |
| 60,250 | 60,300 | 10,925 | 8,134 | 10,925 | 9,481 |
| 60,300 | 60,350 | 10,938 | 8,141 | 10,938 | 9,494 |
| 60,350 | 60,400 | 10,950 | 8,149 | 10,950 | 9,506 |
| 60,400 | 60,450 | 10,963 | 8,156 | 10,963 | 9,519 |
| 60,450 | 60,500 | 10,975 | 8,164 | 10,975 | 9,531 |
| 60,500 | 60,550 | 10,988 | 8,171 | 10,988 | 9,544 |
| 60,550 | 60,600 | 11,000 | 8,179 | 11,000 | 9,556 |
| 60,600 | 60,650 | 11,013 | 8,186 | 11,013 | 9,569 |
| 60,650 | 60,700 | 11,025 | 8,194 | 11,025 | 9,581 |
| 60,700 | 60,750 | 11,038 | 8,201 | 11,038 | 9,594 |
| 60,750 | 60,800 | 11,050 | 8,209 | 11,050 | 9,606 |
| 60,800 | 60,850 | 11,063 | 8,216 | 11,063 | 9,619 |
| 60,850 | 60,900 | 11,075 | 8,224 | 11,075 | 9,631 |
| 60,900 | 60,950 | 11,088 | 8,231 | 11,088 | 9,644 |
| 60,950 | 61,000 | 11,100 | 8,239 | 11,100 | 9,656 |

## 61,000

| At least | But less than | Single | Married filing jointly * | Married filing separately | Head of a household |
|---|---|---|---|---|---|
| 61,000 | 61,050 | 11,113 | 8,246 | 11,113 | 9,669 |
| 61,050 | 61,100 | 11,125 | 8,254 | 11,125 | 9,681 |
| 61,100 | 61,150 | 11,138 | 8,261 | 11,138 | 9,694 |
| 61,150 | 61,200 | 11,150 | 8,269 | 11,150 | 9,706 |
| 61,200 | 61,250 | 11,163 | 8,276 | 11,163 | 9,719 |
| 61,250 | 61,300 | 11,175 | 8,284 | 11,175 | 9,731 |
| 61,300 | 61,350 | 11,188 | 8,291 | 11,188 | 9,744 |
| 61,350 | 61,400 | 11,200 | 8,299 | 11,200 | 9,756 |
| 61,400 | 61,450 | 11,213 | 8,306 | 11,213 | 9,769 |
| 61,450 | 61,500 | 11,225 | 8,314 | 11,225 | 9,781 |
| 61,500 | 61,550 | 11,238 | 8,321 | 11,238 | 9,794 |
| 61,550 | 61,600 | 11,250 | 8,329 | 11,250 | 9,806 |
| 61,600 | 61,650 | 11,263 | 8,336 | 11,263 | 9,819 |
| 61,650 | 61,700 | 11,275 | 8,344 | 11,275 | 9,831 |
| 61,700 | 61,750 | 11,288 | 8,351 | 11,288 | 9,844 |
| 61,750 | 61,800 | 11,300 | 8,359 | 11,300 | 9,856 |
| 61,800 | 61,850 | 11,313 | 8,366 | 11,313 | 9,869 |
| 61,850 | 61,900 | 11,325 | 8,374 | 11,325 | 9,881 |
| 61,900 | 61,950 | 11,338 | 8,381 | 11,338 | 9,894 |
| 61,950 | 62,000 | 11,350 | 8,389 | 11,350 | 9,906 |

## 62,000

| At least | But less than | Single | Married filing jointly * | Married filing separately | Head of a household |
|---|---|---|---|---|---|
| 62,000 | 62,050 | 11,363 | 8,396 | 11,363 | 9,919 |
| 62,050 | 62,100 | 11,375 | 8,404 | 11,375 | 9,931 |
| 62,100 | 62,150 | 11,388 | 8,411 | 11,388 | 9,944 |
| 62,150 | 62,200 | 11,400 | 8,419 | 11,400 | 9,956 |
| 62,200 | 62,250 | 11,413 | 8,426 | 11,413 | 9,969 |
| 62,250 | 62,300 | 11,425 | 8,434 | 11,425 | 9,981 |
| 62,300 | 62,350 | 11,438 | 8,441 | 11,438 | 9,994 |
| 62,350 | 62,400 | 11,450 | 8,449 | 11,450 | 10,006 |
| 62,400 | 62,450 | 11,463 | 8,456 | 11,463 | 10,019 |
| 62,450 | 62,500 | 11,475 | 8,464 | 11,475 | 10,031 |
| 62,500 | 62,550 | 11,488 | 8,471 | 11,488 | 10,044 |
| 62,550 | 62,600 | 11,500 | 8,479 | 11,500 | 10,056 |
| 62,600 | 62,650 | 11,513 | 8,486 | 11,513 | 10,069 |
| 62,650 | 62,700 | 11,525 | 8,494 | 11,525 | 10,081 |
| 62,700 | 62,750 | 11,538 | 8,501 | 11,538 | 10,094 |
| 62,750 | 62,800 | 11,550 | 8,509 | 11,550 | 10,106 |
| 62,800 | 62,850 | 11,563 | 8,516 | 11,563 | 10,119 |
| 62,850 | 62,900 | 11,575 | 8,524 | 11,575 | 10,131 |
| 62,900 | 62,950 | 11,588 | 8,531 | 11,588 | 10,144 |
| 62,950 | 63,000 | 11,600 | 8,539 | 11,600 | 10,156 |

## 63,000

| If line 43 (taxable income) is— | | And you are— | | | |
| At least | But less than | Single | Married filing jointly * | Married filing separately | Head of a household |
|---|---|---|---|---|---|
| 63,000 | 63,050 | 11,613 | 8,546 | 11,613 | 10,169 |
| 63,050 | 63,100 | 11,625 | 8,554 | 11,625 | 10,181 |
| 63,100 | 63,150 | 11,638 | 8,561 | 11,638 | 10,194 |
| 63,150 | 63,200 | 11,650 | 8,569 | 11,650 | 10,206 |
| 63,200 | 63,250 | 11,663 | 8,576 | 11,663 | 10,219 |
| 63,250 | 63,300 | 11,675 | 8,584 | 11,675 | 10,231 |
| 63,300 | 63,350 | 11,688 | 8,591 | 11,688 | 10,244 |
| 63,350 | 63,400 | 11,700 | 8,599 | 11,700 | 10,256 |
| 63,400 | 63,450 | 11,713 | 8,606 | 11,713 | 10,269 |
| 63,450 | 63,500 | 11,725 | 8,614 | 11,725 | 10,281 |
| 63,500 | 63,550 | 11,738 | 8,621 | 11,738 | 10,294 |
| 63,550 | 63,600 | 11,750 | 8,629 | 11,750 | 10,306 |
| 63,600 | 63,650 | 11,763 | 8,636 | 11,763 | 10,319 |
| 63,650 | 63,700 | 11,775 | 8,644 | 11,775 | 10,331 |
| 63,700 | 63,750 | 11,788 | 8,651 | 11,788 | 10,344 |
| 63,750 | 63,800 | 11,800 | 8,659 | 11,800 | 10,356 |
| 63,800 | 63,850 | 11,813 | 8,666 | 11,813 | 10,369 |
| 63,850 | 63,900 | 11,825 | 8,674 | 11,825 | 10,381 |
| 63,900 | 63,950 | 11,838 | 8,681 | 11,838 | 10,394 |
| 63,950 | 64,000 | 11,850 | 8,689 | 11,850 | 10,406 |

## 64,000

| At least | But less than | Single | Married filing jointly * | Married filing separately | Head of a household |
|---|---|---|---|---|---|
| 64,000 | 64,050 | 11,863 | 8,696 | 11,863 | 10,419 |
| 64,050 | 64,100 | 11,875 | 8,704 | 11,875 | 10,431 |
| 64,100 | 64,150 | 11,888 | 8,711 | 11,888 | 10,444 |
| 64,150 | 64,200 | 11,900 | 8,719 | 11,900 | 10,456 |
| 64,200 | 64,250 | 11,913 | 8,726 | 11,913 | 10,469 |
| 64,250 | 64,300 | 11,925 | 8,734 | 11,925 | 10,481 |
| 64,300 | 64,350 | 11,938 | 8,741 | 11,938 | 10,494 |
| 64,350 | 64,400 | 11,950 | 8,749 | 11,950 | 10,506 |
| 64,400 | 64,450 | 11,963 | 8,756 | 11,963 | 10,519 |
| 64,450 | 64,500 | 11,975 | 8,764 | 11,975 | 10,531 |
| 64,500 | 64,550 | 11,988 | 8,771 | 11,988 | 10,544 |
| 64,550 | 64,600 | 12,000 | 8,779 | 12,000 | 10,556 |
| 64,600 | 64,650 | 12,013 | 8,786 | 12,013 | 10,569 |
| 64,650 | 64,700 | 12,025 | 8,794 | 12,025 | 10,581 |
| 64,700 | 64,750 | 12,038 | 8,801 | 12,038 | 10,594 |
| 64,750 | 64,800 | 12,050 | 8,809 | 12,050 | 10,606 |
| 64,800 | 64,850 | 12,063 | 8,816 | 12,063 | 10,619 |
| 64,850 | 64,900 | 12,075 | 8,824 | 12,075 | 10,631 |
| 64,900 | 64,950 | 12,088 | 8,831 | 12,088 | 10,644 |
| 64,950 | 65,000 | 12,100 | 8,839 | 12,100 | 10,656 |

## 65,000

| At least | But less than | Single | Married filing jointly * | Married filing separately | Head of a household |
|---|---|---|---|---|---|
| 65,000 | 65,050 | 12,113 | 8,846 | 12,113 | 10,669 |
| 65,050 | 65,100 | 12,125 | 8,854 | 12,125 | 10,681 |
| 65,100 | 65,150 | 12,138 | 8,861 | 12,138 | 10,694 |
| 65,150 | 65,200 | 12,150 | 8,869 | 12,150 | 10,706 |
| 65,200 | 65,250 | 12,163 | 8,876 | 12,163 | 10,719 |
| 65,250 | 65,300 | 12,175 | 8,884 | 12,175 | 10,731 |
| 65,300 | 65,350 | 12,188 | 8,891 | 12,188 | 10,744 |
| 65,350 | 65,400 | 12,200 | 8,899 | 12,200 | 10,756 |
| 65,400 | 65,450 | 12,213 | 8,906 | 12,213 | 10,769 |
| 65,450 | 65,500 | 12,225 | 8,914 | 12,225 | 10,781 |
| 65,500 | 65,550 | 12,238 | 8,921 | 12,238 | 10,794 |
| 65,550 | 65,600 | 12,250 | 8,929 | 12,250 | 10,806 |
| 65,600 | 65,650 | 12,263 | 8,936 | 12,263 | 10,819 |
| 65,650 | 65,700 | 12,275 | 8,944 | 12,275 | 10,831 |
| 65,700 | 65,750 | 12,288 | 8,951 | 12,288 | 10,844 |
| 65,750 | 65,800 | 12,300 | 8,959 | 12,300 | 10,856 |
| 65,800 | 65,850 | 12,313 | 8,966 | 12,313 | 10,869 |
| 65,850 | 65,900 | 12,325 | 8,974 | 12,325 | 10,881 |
| 65,900 | 65,950 | 12,338 | 8,981 | 12,338 | 10,894 |
| 65,950 | 66,000 | 12,350 | 8,989 | 12,350 | 10,906 |

*(Continued)*

* This column must also be used by a qualifying widow(er).

# 2014 Tax Tables

**2014 Tax Table** — *Continued*



| If line 43 (taxable income) is— | | And you are— | | | |
|---|---|---|---|---|---|
| At least | But less than | Single | Married filing jointly * | Married filing separately | Head of a household |
| | | Your tax is— | | | |
| **66,000** | | | | | |
| 66,000 | 66,050 | 12,363 | 8,996 | 12,363 | 10,919 |
| 66,050 | 66,100 | 12,375 | 9,004 | 12,375 | 10,931 |
| 66,100 | 66,150 | 12,388 | 9,011 | 12,388 | 10,944 |
| 66,150 | 66,200 | 12,400 | 9,019 | 12,400 | 10,956 |
| 66,200 | 66,250 | 12,413 | 9,026 | 12,413 | 10,969 |
| 66,250 | 66,300 | 12,425 | 9,034 | 12,425 | 10,981 |
| 66,300 | 66,350 | 12,438 | 9,041 | 12,438 | 10,994 |
| 66,350 | 66,400 | 12,450 | 9,049 | 12,450 | 11,006 |
| 66,400 | 66,450 | 12,463 | 9,056 | 12,463 | 11,019 |
| 66,450 | 66,500 | 12,475 | 9,064 | 12,475 | 11,031 |
| 66,500 | 66,550 | 12,488 | 9,071 | 12,488 | 11,044 |
| 66,550 | 66,600 | 12,500 | 9,079 | 12,500 | 11,056 |
| 66,600 | 66,650 | 12,513 | 9,086 | 12,513 | 11,069 |
| 66,650 | 66,700 | 12,525 | 9,094 | 12,525 | 11,081 |
| 66,700 | 66,750 | 12,538 | 9,101 | 12,538 | 11,094 |
| 66,750 | 66,800 | 12,550 | 9,109 | 12,550 | 11,106 |
| 66,800 | 66,850 | 12,563 | 9,116 | 12,563 | 11,119 |
| 66,850 | 66,900 | 12,575 | 9,124 | 12,575 | 11,131 |
| 66,900 | 66,950 | 12,588 | 9,131 | 12,588 | 11,144 |
| 66,950 | 67,000 | 12,600 | 9,139 | 12,600 | 11,156 |
| **67,000** | | | | | |
| 67,000 | 67,050 | 12,613 | 9,146 | 12,613 | 11,169 |
| 67,050 | 67,100 | 12,625 | 9,154 | 12,625 | 11,181 |
| 67,100 | 67,150 | 12,638 | 9,161 | 12,638 | 11,194 |
| 67,150 | 67,200 | 12,650 | 9,169 | 12,650 | 11,206 |
| 67,200 | 67,250 | 12,663 | 9,176 | 12,663 | 11,219 |
| 67,250 | 67,300 | 12,675 | 9,184 | 12,675 | 11,231 |
| 67,300 | 67,350 | 12,688 | 9,191 | 12,688 | 11,244 |
| 67,350 | 67,400 | 12,700 | 9,199 | 12,700 | 11,256 |
| 67,400 | 67,450 | 12,713 | 9,206 | 12,713 | 11,269 |
| 67,450 | 67,500 | 12,725 | 9,214 | 12,725 | 11,281 |
| 67,500 | 67,550 | 12,738 | 9,221 | 12,738 | 11,294 |
| 67,550 | 67,600 | 12,750 | 9,229 | 12,750 | 11,306 |
| 67,600 | 67,650 | 12,763 | 9,236 | 12,763 | 11,319 |
| 67,650 | 67,700 | 12,775 | 9,244 | 12,775 | 11,331 |
| 67,700 | 67,750 | 12,788 | 9,251 | 12,788 | 11,344 |
| 67,750 | 67,800 | 12,800 | 9,259 | 12,800 | 11,356 |
| 67,800 | 67,850 | 12,813 | 9,266 | 12,813 | 11,369 |
| 67,850 | 67,900 | 12,825 | 9,274 | 12,825 | 11,381 |
| 67,900 | 67,950 | 12,838 | 9,281 | 12,838 | 11,394 |
| 67,950 | 68,000 | 12,850 | 9,289 | 12,850 | 11,406 |
| **68,000** | | | | | |
| 68,000 | 68,050 | 12,863 | 9,296 | 12,863 | 11,419 |
| 68,050 | 68,100 | 12,875 | 9,304 | 12,875 | 11,431 |
| 68,100 | 68,150 | 12,888 | 9,311 | 12,888 | 11,444 |
| 68,150 | 68,200 | 12,900 | 9,319 | 12,900 | 11,456 |
| 68,200 | 68,250 | 12,913 | 9,326 | 12,913 | 11,469 |
| 68,250 | 68,300 | 12,925 | 9,334 | 12,925 | 11,481 |
| 68,300 | 68,350 | 12,938 | 9,341 | 12,938 | 11,494 |
| 68,350 | 68,400 | 12,950 | 9,349 | 12,950 | 11,506 |
| 68,400 | 68,450 | 12,963 | 9,356 | 12,963 | 11,519 |
| 68,450 | 68,500 | 12,975 | 9,364 | 12,975 | 11,531 |
| 68,500 | 68,550 | 12,988 | 9,371 | 12,988 | 11,544 |
| 68,550 | 68,600 | 13,000 | 9,379 | 13,000 | 11,556 |
| 68,600 | 68,650 | 13,013 | 9,386 | 13,013 | 11,569 |
| 68,650 | 68,700 | 13,025 | 9,394 | 13,025 | 11,581 |
| 68,700 | 68,750 | 13,038 | 9,401 | 13,038 | 11,594 |
| 68,750 | 68,800 | 13,050 | 9,409 | 13,050 | 11,606 |
| 68,800 | 68,850 | 13,063 | 9,416 | 13,063 | 11,619 |
| 68,850 | 68,900 | 13,075 | 9,424 | 13,075 | 11,631 |
| 68,900 | 68,950 | 13,088 | 9,431 | 13,088 | 11,644 |
| 68,950 | 69,000 | 13,100 | 9,439 | 13,100 | 11,656 |

| If line 43 (taxable income) is— | | And you are— | | | |
|---|---|---|---|---|---|
| At least | But less than | Single | Married filing jointly * | Married filing separately | Head of a household |
| | | Your tax is— | | | |
| **69,000** | | | | | |
| 69,000 | 69,050 | 13,113 | 9,446 | 13,113 | 11,669 |
| 69,050 | 69,100 | 13,125 | 9,454 | 13,125 | 11,681 |
| 69,100 | 69,150 | 13,138 | 9,461 | 13,138 | 11,694 |
| 69,150 | 69,200 | 13,150 | 9,469 | 13,150 | 11,706 |
| 69,200 | 69,250 | 13,163 | 9,476 | 13,163 | 11,719 |
| 69,250 | 69,300 | 13,175 | 9,484 | 13,175 | 11,731 |
| 69,300 | 69,350 | 13,188 | 9,491 | 13,188 | 11,744 |
| 69,350 | 69,400 | 13,200 | 9,499 | 13,200 | 11,756 |
| 69,400 | 69,450 | 13,213 | 9,506 | 13,213 | 11,769 |
| 69,450 | 69,500 | 13,225 | 9,514 | 13,225 | 11,781 |
| 69,500 | 69,550 | 13,238 | 9,521 | 13,238 | 11,794 |
| 69,550 | 69,600 | 13,250 | 9,529 | 13,250 | 11,806 |
| 69,600 | 69,650 | 13,263 | 9,536 | 13,263 | 11,819 |
| 69,650 | 69,700 | 13,275 | 9,544 | 13,275 | 11,831 |
| 69,700 | 69,750 | 13,288 | 9,551 | 13,288 | 11,844 |
| 69,750 | 69,800 | 13,300 | 9,559 | 13,300 | 11,856 |
| 69,800 | 69,850 | 13,313 | 9,566 | 13,313 | 11,869 |
| 69,850 | 69,900 | 13,325 | 9,574 | 13,325 | 11,881 |
| 69,900 | 69,950 | 13,338 | 9,581 | 13,338 | 11,894 |
| 69,950 | 70,000 | 13,350 | 9,589 | 13,350 | 11,906 |
| **70,000** | | | | | |
| 70,000 | 70,050 | 13,363 | 9,596 | 13,363 | 11,919 |
| 70,050 | 70,100 | 13,375 | 9,604 | 13,375 | 11,931 |
| 70,100 | 70,150 | 13,388 | 9,611 | 13,388 | 11,944 |
| 70,150 | 70,200 | 13,400 | 9,619 | 13,400 | 11,956 |
| 70,200 | 70,250 | 13,413 | 9,626 | 13,413 | 11,969 |
| 70,250 | 70,300 | 13,425 | 9,634 | 13,425 | 11,981 |
| 70,300 | 70,350 | 13,438 | 9,641 | 13,438 | 11,994 |
| 70,350 | 70,400 | 13,450 | 9,649 | 13,450 | 12,006 |
| 70,400 | 70,450 | 13,463 | 9,656 | 13,463 | 12,019 |
| 70,450 | 70,500 | 13,475 | 9,664 | 13,475 | 12,031 |
| 70,500 | 70,550 | 13,488 | 9,671 | 13,488 | 12,044 |
| 70,550 | 70,600 | 13,500 | 9,679 | 13,500 | 12,056 |
| 70,600 | 70,650 | 13,513 | 9,686 | 13,513 | 12,069 |
| 70,650 | 70,700 | 13,525 | 9,694 | 13,525 | 12,081 |
| 70,700 | 70,750 | 13,538 | 9,701 | 13,538 | 12,094 |
| 70,750 | 70,800 | 13,550 | 9,709 | 13,550 | 12,106 |
| 70,800 | 70,850 | 13,563 | 9,716 | 13,563 | 12,119 |
| 70,850 | 70,900 | 13,575 | 9,724 | 13,575 | 12,131 |
| 70,900 | 70,950 | 13,588 | 9,731 | 13,588 | 12,144 |
| 70,950 | 71,000 | 13,600 | 9,739 | 13,600 | 12,156 |
| **71,000** | | | | | |
| 71,000 | 71,050 | 13,613 | 9,746 | 13,613 | 12,169 |
| 71,050 | 71,100 | 13,625 | 9,754 | 13,625 | 12,181 |
| 71,100 | 71,150 | 13,638 | 9,761 | 13,638 | 12,194 |
| 71,150 | 71,200 | 13,650 | 9,769 | 13,650 | 12,206 |
| 71,200 | 71,250 | 13,663 | 9,776 | 13,663 | 12,219 |
| 71,250 | 71,300 | 13,675 | 9,784 | 13,675 | 12,231 |
| 71,300 | 71,350 | 13,688 | 9,791 | 13,688 | 12,244 |
| 71,350 | 71,400 | 13,700 | 9,799 | 13,700 | 12,256 |
| 71,400 | 71,450 | 13,713 | 9,806 | 13,713 | 12,269 |
| 71,450 | 71,500 | 13,725 | 9,814 | 13,725 | 12,281 |
| 71,500 | 71,550 | 13,738 | 9,821 | 13,738 | 12,294 |
| 71,550 | 71,600 | 13,750 | 9,829 | 13,750 | 12,306 |
| 71,600 | 71,650 | 13,763 | 9,836 | 13,763 | 12,319 |
| 71,650 | 71,700 | 13,775 | 9,844 | 13,775 | 12,331 |
| 71,700 | 71,750 | 13,788 | 9,851 | 13,788 | 12,344 |
| 71,750 | 71,800 | 13,800 | 9,859 | 13,800 | 12,356 |
| 71,800 | 71,850 | 13,813 | 9,866 | 13,813 | 12,369 |
| 71,850 | 71,900 | 13,825 | 9,874 | 13,825 | 12,381 |
| 71,900 | 71,950 | 13,838 | 9,881 | 13,838 | 12,394 |
| 71,950 | 72,000 | 13,850 | 9,889 | 13,850 | 12,406 |

| If line 43 (taxable income) is— | | And you are— | | | |
|---|---|---|---|---|---|
| At least | But less than | Single | Married filing jointly * | Married filing separately | Head of a household |
| | | Your tax is— | | | |
| **72,000** | | | | | |
| 72,000 | 72,050 | 13,863 | 9,896 | 13,863 | 12,419 |
| 72,050 | 72,100 | 13,875 | 9,904 | 13,875 | 12,431 |
| 72,100 | 72,150 | 13,888 | 9,911 | 13,888 | 12,444 |
| 72,150 | 72,200 | 13,900 | 9,919 | 13,900 | 12,456 |
| 72,200 | 72,250 | 13,913 | 9,926 | 13,913 | 12,469 |
| 72,250 | 72,300 | 13,925 | 9,934 | 13,925 | 12,481 |
| 72,300 | 72,350 | 13,938 | 9,941 | 13,938 | 12,494 |
| 72,350 | 72,400 | 13,950 | 9,949 | 13,950 | 12,506 |
| 72,400 | 72,450 | 13,963 | 9,956 | 13,963 | 12,519 |
| 72,450 | 72,500 | 13,975 | 9,964 | 13,975 | 12,531 |
| 72,500 | 72,550 | 13,988 | 9,971 | 13,988 | 12,544 |
| 72,550 | 72,600 | 14,000 | 9,979 | 14,000 | 12,556 |
| 72,600 | 72,650 | 14,013 | 9,986 | 14,013 | 12,569 |
| 72,650 | 72,700 | 14,025 | 9,994 | 14,025 | 12,581 |
| 72,700 | 72,750 | 14,038 | 10,001 | 14,038 | 12,594 |
| 72,750 | 72,800 | 14,050 | 10,009 | 14,050 | 12,606 |
| 72,800 | 72,850 | 14,063 | 10,016 | 14,063 | 12,619 |
| 72,850 | 72,900 | 14,075 | 10,024 | 14,075 | 12,631 |
| 72,900 | 72,950 | 14,088 | 10,031 | 14,088 | 12,644 |
| 72,950 | 73,000 | 14,100 | 10,039 | 14,100 | 12,656 |
| **73,000** | | | | | |
| 73,000 | 73,050 | 14,113 | 10,046 | 14,113 | 12,669 |
| 73,050 | 73,100 | 14,125 | 10,054 | 14,125 | 12,681 |
| 73,100 | 73,150 | 14,138 | 10,061 | 14,138 | 12,694 |
| 73,150 | 73,200 | 14,150 | 10,069 | 14,150 | 12,706 |
| 73,200 | 73,250 | 14,163 | 10,076 | 14,163 | 12,719 |
| 73,250 | 73,300 | 14,175 | 10,084 | 14,175 | 12,731 |
| 73,300 | 73,350 | 14,188 | 10,091 | 14,188 | 12,744 |
| 73,350 | 73,400 | 14,200 | 10,099 | 14,200 | 12,756 |
| 73,400 | 73,450 | 14,213 | 10,106 | 14,213 | 12,769 |
| 73,450 | 73,500 | 14,225 | 10,114 | 14,225 | 12,781 |
| 73,500 | 73,550 | 14,238 | 10,121 | 14,238 | 12,794 |
| 73,550 | 73,600 | 14,250 | 10,129 | 14,250 | 12,806 |
| 73,600 | 73,650 | 14,263 | 10,136 | 14,263 | 12,819 |
| 73,650 | 73,700 | 14,275 | 10,144 | 14,275 | 12,831 |
| 73,700 | 73,750 | 14,288 | 10,151 | 14,288 | 12,844 |
| 73,750 | 73,800 | 14,300 | 10,159 | 14,300 | 12,856 |
| 73,800 | 73,850 | 14,313 | 10,169 | 14,313 | 12,869 |
| 73,850 | 73,900 | 14,325 | 10,181 | 14,325 | 12,881 |
| 73,900 | 73,950 | 14,338 | 10,194 | 14,338 | 12,894 |
| 73,950 | 74,000 | 14,350 | 10,206 | 14,350 | 12,906 |
| **74,000** | | | | | |
| 74,000 | 74,050 | 14,363 | 10,219 | 14,363 | 12,919 |
| 74,050 | 74,100 | 14,375 | 10,231 | 14,375 | 12,931 |
| 74,100 | 74,150 | 14,388 | 10,244 | 14,388 | 12,944 |
| 74,150 | 74,200 | 14,400 | 10,256 | 14,400 | 12,956 |
| 74,200 | 74,250 | 14,413 | 10,269 | 14,413 | 12,969 |
| 74,250 | 74,300 | 14,425 | 10,281 | 14,425 | 12,981 |
| 74,300 | 74,350 | 14,438 | 10,294 | 14,438 | 12,994 |
| 74,350 | 74,400 | 14,450 | 10,306 | 14,450 | 13,006 |
| 74,400 | 74,450 | 14,463 | 10,319 | 14,463 | 13,019 |
| 74,450 | 74,500 | 14,475 | 10,331 | 14,477 | 13,031 |
| 74,500 | 74,550 | 14,488 | 10,344 | 14,491 | 13,044 |
| 74,550 | 74,600 | 14,500 | 10,356 | 14,505 | 13,056 |
| 74,600 | 74,650 | 14,513 | 10,369 | 14,519 | 13,069 |
| 74,650 | 74,700 | 14,525 | 10,381 | 14,533 | 13,081 |
| 74,700 | 74,750 | 14,538 | 10,394 | 14,547 | 13,094 |
| 74,750 | 74,800 | 14,550 | 10,406 | 14,561 | 13,106 |
| 74,800 | 74,850 | 14,563 | 10,419 | 14,575 | 13,119 |
| 74,850 | 74,900 | 14,575 | 10,431 | 14,589 | 13,131 |
| 74,900 | 74,950 | 14,588 | 10,444 | 14,603 | 13,144 |
| 74,950 | 75,000 | 14,600 | 10,456 | 14,617 | 13,156 |

*(Continued)*

* This column must also be used by a qualifying widow(er).

# 2015 Federal Tax Guide

*Sample header for each section:*

| If line 43 (taxable income) is— | | And you are— | | | |
|---|---|---|---|---|---|
| At least | But less than | Single | Married filing jointly * | Married filing separately | Head of a household |
| | | Your tax is— | | | |

## 75,000

| At least | But less than | Single | MFJ * | MFS | HoH |
|---|---|---|---|---|---|
| 75,000 | 75,050 | 14,613 | 10,469 | 14,631 | 13,169 |
| 75,050 | 75,100 | 14,625 | 10,481 | 14,645 | 13,181 |
| 75,100 | 75,150 | 14,638 | 10,494 | 14,659 | 13,194 |
| 75,150 | 75,200 | 14,650 | 10,506 | 14,673 | 13,206 |
| 75,200 | 75,250 | 14,663 | 10,519 | 14,687 | 13,219 |
| 75,250 | 75,300 | 14,675 | 10,531 | 14,701 | 13,231 |
| 75,300 | 75,350 | 14,688 | 10,544 | 14,715 | 13,244 |
| 75,350 | 75,400 | 14,700 | 10,556 | 14,729 | 13,256 |
| 75,400 | 75,450 | 14,713 | 10,569 | 14,743 | 13,269 |
| 75,450 | 75,500 | 14,725 | 10,581 | 14,757 | 13,281 |
| 75,500 | 75,550 | 14,738 | 10,594 | 14,771 | 13,294 |
| 75,550 | 75,600 | 14,750 | 10,606 | 14,785 | 13,306 |
| 75,600 | 75,650 | 14,763 | 10,619 | 14,799 | 13,319 |
| 75,650 | 75,700 | 14,775 | 10,631 | 14,813 | 13,331 |
| 75,700 | 75,750 | 14,788 | 10,644 | 14,827 | 13,344 |
| 75,750 | 75,800 | 14,800 | 10,656 | 14,841 | 13,356 |
| 75,800 | 75,850 | 14,813 | 10,669 | 14,855 | 13,369 |
| 75,850 | 75,900 | 14,825 | 10,681 | 14,869 | 13,381 |
| 75,900 | 75,950 | 14,838 | 10,694 | 14,883 | 13,394 |
| 75,950 | 76,000 | 14,850 | 10,706 | 14,897 | 13,406 |

## 76,000

| At least | But less than | Single | MFJ * | MFS | HoH |
|---|---|---|---|---|---|
| 76,000 | 76,050 | 14,863 | 10,719 | 14,911 | 13,419 |
| 76,050 | 76,100 | 14,875 | 10,731 | 14,925 | 13,431 |
| 76,100 | 76,150 | 14,888 | 10,744 | 14,939 | 13,444 |
| 76,150 | 76,200 | 14,900 | 10,756 | 14,953 | 13,456 |
| 76,200 | 76,250 | 14,913 | 10,769 | 14,967 | 13,469 |
| 76,250 | 76,300 | 14,925 | 10,781 | 14,981 | 13,481 |
| 76,300 | 76,350 | 14,938 | 10,794 | 14,995 | 13,494 |
| 76,350 | 76,400 | 14,950 | 10,806 | 15,009 | 13,506 |
| 76,400 | 76,450 | 14,963 | 10,819 | 15,023 | 13,519 |
| 76,450 | 76,500 | 14,975 | 10,831 | 15,037 | 13,531 |
| 76,500 | 76,550 | 14,988 | 10,844 | 15,051 | 13,544 |
| 76,550 | 76,600 | 15,000 | 10,856 | 15,065 | 13,556 |
| 76,600 | 76,650 | 15,013 | 10,869 | 15,079 | 13,569 |
| 76,650 | 76,700 | 15,025 | 10,881 | 15,093 | 13,581 |
| 76,700 | 76,750 | 15,038 | 10,894 | 15,107 | 13,594 |
| 76,750 | 76,800 | 15,050 | 10,906 | 15,121 | 13,606 |
| 76,800 | 76,850 | 15,063 | 10,919 | 15,135 | 13,619 |
| 76,850 | 76,900 | 15,075 | 10,931 | 15,149 | 13,631 |
| 76,900 | 76,950 | 15,088 | 10,944 | 15,163 | 13,644 |
| 76,950 | 77,000 | 15,100 | 10,956 | 15,177 | 13,656 |

## 77,000

| At least | But less than | Single | MFJ * | MFS | HoH |
|---|---|---|---|---|---|
| 77,000 | 77,050 | 15,113 | 10,969 | 15,191 | 13,669 |
| 77,050 | 77,100 | 15,125 | 10,981 | 15,205 | 13,681 |
| 77,100 | 77,150 | 15,138 | 10,994 | 15,219 | 13,694 |
| 77,150 | 77,200 | 15,150 | 11,006 | 15,233 | 13,706 |
| 77,200 | 77,250 | 15,163 | 11,019 | 15,247 | 13,719 |
| 77,250 | 77,300 | 15,175 | 11,031 | 15,261 | 13,731 |
| 77,300 | 77,350 | 15,188 | 11,044 | 15,275 | 13,744 |
| 77,350 | 77,400 | 15,200 | 11,056 | 15,289 | 13,756 |
| 77,400 | 77,450 | 15,213 | 11,069 | 15,303 | 13,769 |
| 77,450 | 77,500 | 15,225 | 11,081 | 15,317 | 13,781 |
| 77,500 | 77,550 | 15,238 | 11,094 | 15,331 | 13,794 |
| 77,550 | 77,600 | 15,250 | 11,106 | 15,345 | 13,806 |
| 77,600 | 77,650 | 15,263 | 11,119 | 15,359 | 13,819 |
| 77,650 | 77,700 | 15,275 | 11,131 | 15,373 | 13,831 |
| 77,700 | 77,750 | 15,288 | 11,144 | 15,387 | 13,844 |
| 77,750 | 77,800 | 15,300 | 11,156 | 15,401 | 13,856 |
| 77,800 | 77,850 | 15,313 | 11,169 | 15,415 | 13,869 |
| 77,850 | 77,900 | 15,325 | 11,181 | 15,429 | 13,881 |
| 77,900 | 77,950 | 15,338 | 11,194 | 15,443 | 13,894 |
| 77,950 | 78,000 | 15,350 | 11,206 | 15,457 | 13,906 |

## 78,000

| At least | But less than | Single | MFJ * | MFS | HoH |
|---|---|---|---|---|---|
| 78,000 | 78,050 | 15,363 | 11,219 | 15,471 | 13,919 |
| 78,050 | 78,100 | 15,375 | 11,231 | 15,485 | 13,931 |
| 78,100 | 78,150 | 15,388 | 11,244 | 15,499 | 13,944 |
| 78,150 | 78,200 | 15,400 | 11,256 | 15,513 | 13,956 |
| 78,200 | 78,250 | 15,413 | 11,269 | 15,527 | 13,969 |
| 78,250 | 78,300 | 15,425 | 11,281 | 15,541 | 13,981 |
| 78,300 | 78,350 | 15,438 | 11,294 | 15,555 | 13,994 |
| 78,350 | 78,400 | 15,450 | 11,306 | 15,569 | 14,006 |
| 78,400 | 78,450 | 15,463 | 11,319 | 15,583 | 14,019 |
| 78,450 | 78,500 | 15,475 | 11,331 | 15,597 | 14,031 |
| 78,500 | 78,550 | 15,488 | 11,344 | 15,611 | 14,044 |
| 78,550 | 78,600 | 15,500 | 11,356 | 15,625 | 14,056 |
| 78,600 | 78,650 | 15,513 | 11,369 | 15,639 | 14,069 |
| 78,650 | 78,700 | 15,525 | 11,381 | 15,653 | 14,081 |
| 78,700 | 78,750 | 15,538 | 11,394 | 15,667 | 14,094 |
| 78,750 | 78,800 | 15,550 | 11,406 | 15,681 | 14,106 |
| 78,800 | 78,850 | 15,563 | 11,419 | 15,695 | 14,119 |
| 78,850 | 78,900 | 15,575 | 11,431 | 15,709 | 14,131 |
| 78,900 | 78,950 | 15,588 | 11,444 | 15,723 | 14,144 |
| 78,950 | 79,000 | 15,600 | 11,456 | 15,737 | 14,156 |

## 79,000

| At least | But less than | Single | MFJ * | MFS | HoH |
|---|---|---|---|---|---|
| 79,000 | 79,050 | 15,613 | 11,469 | 15,751 | 14,169 |
| 79,050 | 79,100 | 15,625 | 11,481 | 15,765 | 14,181 |
| 79,100 | 79,150 | 15,638 | 11,494 | 15,779 | 14,194 |
| 79,150 | 79,200 | 15,650 | 11,506 | 15,793 | 14,206 |
| 79,200 | 79,250 | 15,663 | 11,519 | 15,807 | 14,219 |
| 79,250 | 79,300 | 15,675 | 11,531 | 15,821 | 14,231 |
| 79,300 | 79,350 | 15,688 | 11,544 | 15,835 | 14,244 |
| 79,350 | 79,400 | 15,700 | 11,556 | 15,849 | 14,256 |
| 79,400 | 79,450 | 15,713 | 11,569 | 15,863 | 14,269 |
| 79,450 | 79,500 | 15,725 | 11,581 | 15,877 | 14,281 |
| 79,500 | 79,550 | 15,738 | 11,594 | 15,891 | 14,294 |
| 79,550 | 79,600 | 15,750 | 11,606 | 15,905 | 14,306 |
| 79,600 | 79,650 | 15,763 | 11,619 | 15,919 | 14,319 |
| 79,650 | 79,700 | 15,775 | 11,631 | 15,933 | 14,331 |
| 79,700 | 79,750 | 15,788 | 11,644 | 15,947 | 14,344 |
| 79,750 | 79,800 | 15,800 | 11,656 | 15,961 | 14,356 |
| 79,800 | 79,850 | 15,813 | 11,669 | 15,975 | 14,369 |
| 79,850 | 79,900 | 15,825 | 11,681 | 15,989 | 14,381 |
| 79,900 | 79,950 | 15,838 | 11,694 | 16,003 | 14,394 |
| 79,950 | 80,000 | 15,850 | 11,706 | 16,017 | 14,406 |

## 80,000

| At least | But less than | Single | MFJ * | MFS | HoH |
|---|---|---|---|---|---|
| 80,000 | 80,050 | 15,863 | 11,719 | 16,031 | 14,419 |
| 80,050 | 80,100 | 15,875 | 11,731 | 16,045 | 14,431 |
| 80,100 | 80,150 | 15,888 | 11,744 | 16,059 | 14,444 |
| 80,150 | 80,200 | 15,900 | 11,756 | 16,073 | 14,456 |
| 80,200 | 80,250 | 15,913 | 11,769 | 16,087 | 14,469 |
| 80,250 | 80,300 | 15,925 | 11,781 | 16,101 | 14,481 |
| 80,300 | 80,350 | 15,938 | 11,794 | 16,115 | 14,494 |
| 80,350 | 80,400 | 15,950 | 11,806 | 16,129 | 14,506 |
| 80,400 | 80,450 | 15,963 | 11,819 | 16,143 | 14,519 |
| 80,450 | 80,500 | 15,975 | 11,831 | 16,157 | 14,531 |
| 80,500 | 80,550 | 15,988 | 11,844 | 16,171 | 14,544 |
| 80,550 | 80,600 | 16,000 | 11,856 | 16,185 | 14,556 |
| 80,600 | 80,650 | 16,013 | 11,869 | 16,199 | 14,569 |
| 80,650 | 80,700 | 16,025 | 11,881 | 16,213 | 14,581 |
| 80,700 | 80,750 | 16,038 | 11,894 | 16,227 | 14,594 |
| 80,750 | 80,800 | 16,050 | 11,906 | 16,241 | 14,606 |
| 80,800 | 80,850 | 16,063 | 11,919 | 16,255 | 14,619 |
| 80,850 | 80,900 | 16,075 | 11,931 | 16,269 | 14,631 |
| 80,900 | 80,950 | 16,088 | 11,944 | 16,283 | 14,644 |
| 80,950 | 81,000 | 16,100 | 11,956 | 16,297 | 14,656 |

## 81,000

| At least | But less than | Single | MFJ * | MFS | HoH |
|---|---|---|---|---|---|
| 81,000 | 81,050 | 16,113 | 11,969 | 16,311 | 14,669 |
| 81,050 | 81,100 | 16,125 | 11,981 | 16,325 | 14,681 |
| 81,100 | 81,150 | 16,138 | 11,994 | 16,339 | 14,694 |
| 81,150 | 81,200 | 16,150 | 12,006 | 16,353 | 14,706 |
| 81,200 | 81,250 | 16,163 | 12,019 | 16,367 | 14,719 |
| 81,250 | 81,300 | 16,175 | 12,031 | 16,381 | 14,731 |
| 81,300 | 81,350 | 16,188 | 12,044 | 16,395 | 14,744 |
| 81,350 | 81,400 | 16,200 | 12,056 | 16,409 | 14,756 |
| 81,400 | 81,450 | 16,213 | 12,069 | 16,423 | 14,769 |
| 81,450 | 81,500 | 16,225 | 12,081 | 16,437 | 14,781 |
| 81,500 | 81,550 | 16,238 | 12,094 | 16,451 | 14,794 |
| 81,550 | 81,600 | 16,250 | 12,106 | 16,465 | 14,806 |
| 81,600 | 81,650 | 16,263 | 12,119 | 16,479 | 14,819 |
| 81,650 | 81,700 | 16,275 | 12,131 | 16,493 | 14,831 |
| 81,700 | 81,750 | 16,288 | 12,144 | 16,507 | 14,844 |
| 81,750 | 81,800 | 16,300 | 12,156 | 16,521 | 14,856 |
| 81,800 | 81,850 | 16,313 | 12,169 | 16,535 | 14,869 |
| 81,850 | 81,900 | 16,325 | 12,181 | 16,549 | 14,881 |
| 81,900 | 81,950 | 16,338 | 12,194 | 16,563 | 14,894 |
| 81,950 | 82,000 | 16,350 | 12,206 | 16,577 | 14,906 |

## 82,000

| At least | But less than | Single | MFJ * | MFS | HoH |
|---|---|---|---|---|---|
| 82,000 | 82,050 | 16,363 | 12,219 | 16,591 | 14,919 |
| 82,050 | 82,100 | 16,375 | 12,231 | 16,605 | 14,931 |
| 82,100 | 82,150 | 16,388 | 12,244 | 16,619 | 14,944 |
| 82,150 | 82,200 | 16,400 | 12,256 | 16,633 | 14,956 |
| 82,200 | 82,250 | 16,413 | 12,269 | 16,647 | 14,969 |
| 82,250 | 82,300 | 16,425 | 12,281 | 16,661 | 14,981 |
| 82,300 | 82,350 | 16,438 | 12,294 | 16,675 | 14,994 |
| 82,350 | 82,400 | 16,450 | 12,306 | 16,689 | 15,006 |
| 82,400 | 82,450 | 16,463 | 12,319 | 16,703 | 15,019 |
| 82,450 | 82,500 | 16,475 | 12,331 | 16,717 | 15,031 |
| 82,500 | 82,550 | 16,488 | 12,344 | 16,731 | 15,044 |
| 82,550 | 82,600 | 16,500 | 12,356 | 16,745 | 15,056 |
| 82,600 | 82,650 | 16,513 | 12,369 | 16,759 | 15,069 |
| 82,650 | 82,700 | 16,525 | 12,381 | 16,773 | 15,081 |
| 82,700 | 82,750 | 16,538 | 12,394 | 16,787 | 15,094 |
| 82,750 | 82,800 | 16,550 | 12,406 | 16,801 | 15,106 |
| 82,800 | 82,850 | 16,563 | 12,419 | 16,815 | 15,119 |
| 82,850 | 82,900 | 16,575 | 12,431 | 16,829 | 15,131 |
| 82,900 | 82,950 | 16,588 | 12,444 | 16,843 | 15,144 |
| 82,950 | 83,000 | 16,600 | 12,456 | 16,857 | 15,156 |

## 83,000

| At least | But less than | Single | MFJ * | MFS | HoH |
|---|---|---|---|---|---|
| 83,000 | 83,050 | 16,613 | 12,469 | 16,871 | 15,169 |
| 83,050 | 83,100 | 16,625 | 12,481 | 16,885 | 15,181 |
| 83,100 | 83,150 | 16,638 | 12,494 | 16,899 | 15,194 |
| 83,150 | 83,200 | 16,650 | 12,506 | 16,913 | 15,206 |
| 83,200 | 83,250 | 16,663 | 12,519 | 16,927 | 15,219 |
| 83,250 | 83,300 | 16,675 | 12,531 | 16,941 | 15,231 |
| 83,300 | 83,350 | 16,688 | 12,544 | 16,955 | 15,244 |
| 83,350 | 83,400 | 16,700 | 12,556 | 16,969 | 15,256 |
| 83,400 | 83,450 | 16,713 | 12,569 | 16,983 | 15,269 |
| 83,450 | 83,500 | 16,725 | 12,581 | 16,997 | 15,281 |
| 83,500 | 83,550 | 16,738 | 12,594 | 17,011 | 15,294 |
| 83,550 | 83,600 | 16,750 | 12,606 | 17,025 | 15,306 |
| 83,600 | 83,650 | 16,763 | 12,619 | 17,039 | 15,319 |
| 83,650 | 83,700 | 16,775 | 12,631 | 17,053 | 15,331 |
| 83,700 | 83,750 | 16,788 | 12,644 | 17,067 | 15,344 |
| 83,750 | 83,800 | 16,800 | 12,656 | 17,081 | 15,356 |
| 83,800 | 83,850 | 16,813 | 12,669 | 17,095 | 15,369 |
| 83,850 | 83,900 | 16,825 | 12,681 | 17,109 | 15,381 |
| 83,900 | 83,950 | 16,838 | 12,694 | 17,123 | 15,394 |
| 83,950 | 84,000 | 16,850 | 12,706 | 17,137 | 15,406 |

*(Continued)*

* This column must also be used by a qualifying widow(er).

# 2014 Tax Tables

DRAFT AS OF

## 84,000

| At least | But less than | Single | Married filing jointly * | Married filing separately | Head of a household |
|---|---|---|---|---|---|
| 84,000 | 84,050 | 16,863 | 12,719 | 17,151 | 15,419 |
| 84,050 | 84,100 | 16,875 | 12,731 | 17,165 | 15,431 |
| 84,100 | 84,150 | 16,888 | 12,744 | 17,179 | 15,444 |
| 84,150 | 84,200 | 16,900 | 12,756 | 17,193 | 15,456 |
| 84,200 | 84,250 | 16,913 | 12,769 | 17,207 | 15,469 |
| 84,250 | 84,300 | 16,925 | 12,781 | 17,221 | 15,481 |
| 84,300 | 84,350 | 16,938 | 12,794 | 17,235 | 15,494 |
| 84,350 | 84,400 | 16,950 | 12,806 | 17,249 | 15,506 |
| 84,400 | 84,450 | 16,963 | 12,819 | 17,263 | 15,519 |
| 84,450 | 84,500 | 16,975 | 12,831 | 17,277 | 15,531 |
| 84,500 | 84,550 | 16,988 | 12,844 | 17,291 | 15,544 |
| 84,550 | 84,600 | 17,000 | 12,856 | 17,305 | 15,556 |
| 84,600 | 84,650 | 17,013 | 12,869 | 17,319 | 15,569 |
| 84,650 | 84,700 | 17,025 | 12,881 | 17,333 | 15,581 |
| 84,700 | 84,750 | 17,038 | 12,894 | 17,347 | 15,594 |
| 84,750 | 84,800 | 17,050 | 12,906 | 17,361 | 15,606 |
| 84,800 | 84,850 | 17,063 | 12,919 | 17,375 | 15,619 |
| 84,850 | 84,900 | 17,075 | 12,931 | 17,389 | 15,631 |
| 84,900 | 84,950 | 17,088 | 12,944 | 17,403 | 15,644 |
| 84,950 | 85,000 | 17,100 | 12,956 | 17,417 | 15,656 |

## 85,000

| At least | But less than | Single | Married filing jointly * | Married filing separately | Head of a household |
|---|---|---|---|---|---|
| 85,000 | 85,050 | 17,113 | 12,969 | 17,431 | 15,669 |
| 85,050 | 85,100 | 17,125 | 12,981 | 17,445 | 15,681 |
| 85,100 | 85,150 | 17,138 | 12,994 | 17,459 | 15,694 |
| 85,150 | 85,200 | 17,150 | 13,006 | 17,473 | 15,706 |
| 85,200 | 85,250 | 17,163 | 13,019 | 17,487 | 15,719 |
| 85,250 | 85,300 | 17,175 | 13,031 | 17,501 | 15,731 |
| 85,300 | 85,350 | 17,188 | 13,044 | 17,515 | 15,744 |
| 85,350 | 85,400 | 17,200 | 13,056 | 17,529 | 15,756 |
| 85,400 | 85,450 | 17,213 | 13,069 | 17,543 | 15,769 |
| 85,450 | 85,500 | 17,225 | 13,081 | 17,557 | 15,781 |
| 85,500 | 85,550 | 17,238 | 13,094 | 17,571 | 15,794 |
| 85,550 | 85,600 | 17,250 | 13,106 | 17,585 | 15,806 |
| 85,600 | 85,650 | 17,263 | 13,119 | 17,599 | 15,819 |
| 85,650 | 85,700 | 17,275 | 13,131 | 17,613 | 15,831 |
| 85,700 | 85,750 | 17,288 | 13,144 | 17,627 | 15,844 |
| 85,750 | 85,800 | 17,300 | 13,156 | 17,641 | 15,856 |
| 85,800 | 85,850 | 17,313 | 13,169 | 17,655 | 15,869 |
| 85,850 | 85,900 | 17,325 | 13,181 | 17,669 | 15,881 |
| 85,900 | 85,950 | 17,338 | 13,194 | 17,683 | 15,894 |
| 85,950 | 86,000 | 17,350 | 13,206 | 17,697 | 15,906 |

## 86,000

| At least | But less than | Single | Married filing jointly * | Married filing separately | Head of a household |
|---|---|---|---|---|---|
| 86,000 | 86,050 | 17,363 | 13,219 | 17,711 | 15,919 |
| 86,050 | 86,100 | 17,375 | 13,231 | 17,725 | 15,931 |
| 86,100 | 86,150 | 17,388 | 13,244 | 17,739 | 15,944 |
| 86,150 | 86,200 | 17,400 | 13,256 | 17,753 | 15,956 |
| 86,200 | 86,250 | 17,413 | 13,269 | 17,767 | 15,969 |
| 86,250 | 86,300 | 17,425 | 13,281 | 17,781 | 15,981 |
| 86,300 | 86,350 | 17,438 | 13,294 | 17,795 | 15,994 |
| 86,350 | 86,400 | 17,450 | 13,306 | 17,809 | 16,006 |
| 86,400 | 86,450 | 17,463 | 13,319 | 17,823 | 16,019 |
| 86,450 | 86,500 | 17,475 | 13,331 | 17,837 | 16,031 |
| 86,500 | 86,550 | 17,488 | 13,344 | 17,851 | 16,044 |
| 86,550 | 86,600 | 17,500 | 13,356 | 17,865 | 16,056 |
| 86,600 | 86,650 | 17,513 | 13,369 | 17,879 | 16,069 |
| 86,650 | 86,700 | 17,525 | 13,381 | 17,893 | 16,081 |
| 86,700 | 86,750 | 17,538 | 13,394 | 17,907 | 16,094 |
| 86,750 | 86,800 | 17,550 | 13,406 | 17,921 | 16,106 |
| 86,800 | 86,850 | 17,563 | 13,419 | 17,935 | 16,119 |
| 86,850 | 86,900 | 17,575 | 13,431 | 17,949 | 16,131 |
| 86,900 | 86,950 | 17,588 | 13,444 | 17,963 | 16,144 |
| 86,950 | 87,000 | 17,600 | 13,456 | 17,977 | 16,156 |

## 87,000

| At least | But less than | Single | Married filing jointly * | Married filing separately | Head of a household |
|---|---|---|---|---|---|
| 87,000 | 87,050 | 17,613 | 13,469 | 17,991 | 16,169 |
| 87,050 | 87,100 | 17,625 | 13,481 | 18,005 | 16,181 |
| 87,100 | 87,150 | 17,638 | 13,494 | 18,019 | 16,194 |
| 87,150 | 87,200 | 17,650 | 13,506 | 18,033 | 16,206 |
| 87,200 | 87,250 | 17,663 | 13,519 | 18,047 | 16,219 |
| 87,250 | 87,300 | 17,675 | 13,531 | 18,061 | 16,231 |
| 87,300 | 87,350 | 17,688 | 13,544 | 18,075 | 16,244 |
| 87,350 | 87,400 | 17,700 | 13,556 | 18,089 | 16,256 |
| 87,400 | 87,450 | 17,713 | 13,569 | 18,103 | 16,269 |
| 87,450 | 87,500 | 17,725 | 13,581 | 18,117 | 16,281 |
| 87,500 | 87,550 | 17,738 | 13,594 | 18,131 | 16,294 |
| 87,550 | 87,600 | 17,750 | 13,606 | 18,145 | 16,306 |
| 87,600 | 87,650 | 17,763 | 13,619 | 18,159 | 16,319 |
| 87,650 | 87,700 | 17,775 | 13,631 | 18,173 | 16,331 |
| 87,700 | 87,750 | 17,788 | 13,644 | 18,187 | 16,344 |
| 87,750 | 87,800 | 17,800 | 13,656 | 18,201 | 16,356 |
| 87,800 | 87,850 | 17,813 | 13,669 | 18,215 | 16,369 |
| 87,850 | 87,900 | 17,825 | 13,681 | 18,229 | 16,381 |
| 87,900 | 87,950 | 17,838 | 13,694 | 18,243 | 16,394 |
| 87,950 | 88,000 | 17,850 | 13,706 | 18,257 | 16,406 |

## 88,000

| At least | But less than | Single | Married filing jointly * | Married filing separately | Head of a household |
|---|---|---|---|---|---|
| 88,000 | 88,050 | 17,863 | 13,719 | 18,271 | 16,419 |
| 88,050 | 88,100 | 17,875 | 13,731 | 18,285 | 16,431 |
| 88,100 | 88,150 | 17,888 | 13,744 | 18,299 | 16,444 |
| 88,150 | 88,200 | 17,900 | 13,756 | 18,313 | 16,456 |
| 88,200 | 88,250 | 17,913 | 13,769 | 18,327 | 16,469 |
| 88,250 | 88,300 | 17,925 | 13,781 | 18,341 | 16,481 |
| 88,300 | 88,350 | 17,938 | 13,794 | 18,355 | 16,494 |
| 88,350 | 88,400 | 17,950 | 13,806 | 18,369 | 16,506 |
| 88,400 | 88,450 | 17,963 | 13,819 | 18,383 | 16,519 |
| 88,450 | 88,500 | 17,975 | 13,831 | 18,397 | 16,531 |
| 88,500 | 88,550 | 17,988 | 13,844 | 18,411 | 16,544 |
| 88,550 | 88,600 | 18,000 | 13,856 | 18,425 | 16,556 |
| 88,600 | 88,650 | 18,013 | 13,869 | 18,439 | 16,569 |
| 88,650 | 88,700 | 18,025 | 13,881 | 18,453 | 16,581 |
| 88,700 | 88,750 | 18,038 | 13,894 | 18,467 | 16,594 |
| 88,750 | 88,800 | 18,050 | 13,906 | 18,481 | 16,606 |
| 88,800 | 88,850 | 18,063 | 13,919 | 18,495 | 16,619 |
| 88,850 | 88,900 | 18,075 | 13,931 | 18,509 | 16,631 |
| 88,900 | 88,950 | 18,088 | 13,944 | 18,523 | 16,644 |
| 88,950 | 89,000 | 18,100 | 13,956 | 18,537 | 16,656 |

## 89,000

| At least | But less than | Single | Married filing jointly * | Married filing separately | Head of a household |
|---|---|---|---|---|---|
| 89,000 | 89,050 | 18,113 | 13,969 | 18,551 | 16,669 |
| 89,050 | 89,100 | 18,125 | 13,981 | 18,565 | 16,681 |
| 89,100 | 89,150 | 18,138 | 13,994 | 18,579 | 16,694 |
| 89,150 | 89,200 | 18,150 | 14,006 | 18,593 | 16,706 |
| 89,200 | 89,250 | 18,163 | 14,019 | 18,607 | 16,719 |
| 89,250 | 89,300 | 18,175 | 14,031 | 18,621 | 16,731 |
| 89,300 | 89,350 | 18,188 | 14,044 | 18,635 | 16,744 |
| 89,350 | 89,400 | 18,201 | 14,056 | 18,649 | 16,756 |
| 89,400 | 89,450 | 18,215 | 14,069 | 18,663 | 16,769 |
| 89,450 | 89,500 | 18,229 | 14,081 | 18,677 | 16,781 |
| 89,500 | 89,550 | 18,243 | 14,094 | 18,691 | 16,794 |
| 89,550 | 89,600 | 18,257 | 14,106 | 18,705 | 16,806 |
| 89,600 | 89,650 | 18,271 | 14,119 | 18,719 | 16,819 |
| 89,650 | 89,700 | 18,285 | 14,131 | 18,733 | 16,831 |
| 89,700 | 89,750 | 18,299 | 14,144 | 18,747 | 16,844 |
| 89,750 | 89,800 | 18,313 | 14,156 | 18,761 | 16,856 |
| 89,800 | 89,850 | 18,327 | 14,169 | 18,775 | 16,869 |
| 89,850 | 89,900 | 18,341 | 14,181 | 18,789 | 16,881 |
| 89,900 | 89,950 | 18,355 | 14,194 | 18,803 | 16,894 |
| 89,950 | 90,000 | 18,369 | 14,206 | 18,817 | 16,906 |

## 90,000

| At least | But less than | Single | Married filing jointly * | Married filing separately | Head of a household |
|---|---|---|---|---|---|
| 90,000 | 90,050 | 18,383 | 14,219 | 18,831 | 16,919 |
| 90,050 | 90,100 | 18,397 | 14,231 | 18,845 | 16,931 |
| 90,100 | 90,150 | 18,411 | 14,244 | 18,859 | 16,944 |
| 90,150 | 90,200 | 18,425 | 14,256 | 18,873 | 16,956 |
| 90,200 | 90,250 | 18,439 | 14,269 | 18,887 | 16,969 |
| 90,250 | 90,300 | 18,453 | 14,281 | 18,901 | 16,981 |
| 90,300 | 90,350 | 18,467 | 14,294 | 18,915 | 16,994 |
| 90,350 | 90,400 | 18,481 | 14,306 | 18,929 | 17,006 |
| 90,400 | 90,450 | 18,495 | 14,319 | 18,943 | 17,019 |
| 90,450 | 90,500 | 18,509 | 14,331 | 18,957 | 17,031 |
| 90,500 | 90,550 | 18,523 | 14,344 | 18,971 | 17,044 |
| 90,550 | 90,600 | 18,537 | 14,356 | 18,985 | 17,056 |
| 90,600 | 90,650 | 18,551 | 14,369 | 18,999 | 17,069 |
| 90,650 | 90,700 | 18,565 | 14,381 | 19,013 | 17,081 |
| 90,700 | 90,750 | 18,579 | 14,394 | 19,027 | 17,094 |
| 90,750 | 90,800 | 18,593 | 14,406 | 19,041 | 17,106 |
| 90,800 | 90,850 | 18,607 | 14,419 | 19,055 | 17,119 |
| 90,850 | 90,900 | 18,621 | 14,431 | 19,069 | 17,131 |
| 90,900 | 90,950 | 18,635 | 14,444 | 19,083 | 17,144 |
| 90,950 | 91,000 | 18,649 | 14,456 | 19,097 | 17,156 |

## 91,000

| At least | But less than | Single | Married filing jointly * | Married filing separately | Head of a household |
|---|---|---|---|---|---|
| 91,000 | 91,050 | 18,663 | 14,469 | 19,111 | 17,169 |
| 91,050 | 91,100 | 18,677 | 14,481 | 19,125 | 17,181 |
| 91,100 | 91,150 | 18,691 | 14,494 | 19,139 | 17,194 |
| 91,150 | 91,200 | 18,705 | 14,506 | 19,153 | 17,206 |
| 91,200 | 91,250 | 18,719 | 14,519 | 19,167 | 17,219 |
| 91,250 | 91,300 | 18,733 | 14,531 | 19,181 | 17,231 |
| 91,300 | 91,350 | 18,747 | 14,544 | 19,195 | 17,244 |
| 91,350 | 91,400 | 18,761 | 14,556 | 19,209 | 17,256 |
| 91,400 | 91,450 | 18,775 | 14,569 | 19,223 | 17,269 |
| 91,450 | 91,500 | 18,789 | 14,581 | 19,237 | 17,281 |
| 91,500 | 91,550 | 18,803 | 14,594 | 19,251 | 17,294 |
| 91,550 | 91,600 | 18,817 | 14,606 | 19,265 | 17,306 |
| 91,600 | 91,650 | 18,831 | 14,619 | 19,279 | 17,319 |
| 91,650 | 91,700 | 18,845 | 14,631 | 19,293 | 17,331 |
| 91,700 | 91,750 | 18,859 | 14,644 | 19,307 | 17,344 |
| 91,750 | 91,800 | 18,873 | 14,656 | 19,321 | 17,356 |
| 91,800 | 91,850 | 18,887 | 14,669 | 19,335 | 17,369 |
| 91,850 | 91,900 | 18,901 | 14,681 | 19,349 | 17,381 |
| 91,900 | 91,950 | 18,915 | 14,694 | 19,363 | 17,394 |
| 91,950 | 92,000 | 18,929 | 14,706 | 19,377 | 17,406 |

## 92,000

| At least | But less than | Single | Married filing jointly * | Married filing separately | Head of a household |
|---|---|---|---|---|---|
| 92,000 | 92,050 | 18,943 | 14,719 | 19,391 | 17,419 |
| 92,050 | 92,100 | 18,957 | 14,731 | 19,405 | 17,431 |
| 92,100 | 92,150 | 18,971 | 14,744 | 19,419 | 17,444 |
| 92,150 | 92,200 | 18,985 | 14,756 | 19,433 | 17,456 |
| 92,200 | 92,250 | 18,999 | 14,769 | 19,447 | 17,469 |
| 92,250 | 92,300 | 19,013 | 14,781 | 19,461 | 17,481 |
| 92,300 | 92,350 | 19,027 | 14,794 | 19,475 | 17,494 |
| 92,350 | 92,400 | 19,041 | 14,806 | 19,489 | 17,506 |
| 92,400 | 92,450 | 19,055 | 14,819 | 19,503 | 17,519 |
| 92,450 | 92,500 | 19,069 | 14,831 | 19,517 | 17,531 |
| 92,500 | 92,550 | 19,083 | 14,844 | 19,531 | 17,544 |
| 92,550 | 92,600 | 19,097 | 14,856 | 19,545 | 17,556 |
| 92,600 | 92,650 | 19,111 | 14,869 | 19,559 | 17,569 |
| 92,650 | 92,700 | 19,125 | 14,881 | 19,573 | 17,581 |
| 92,700 | 92,750 | 19,139 | 14,894 | 19,587 | 17,594 |
| 92,750 | 92,800 | 19,153 | 14,906 | 19,601 | 17,606 |
| 92,800 | 92,850 | 19,167 | 14,919 | 19,615 | 17,619 |
| 92,850 | 92,900 | 19,181 | 14,931 | 19,629 | 17,631 |
| 92,900 | 92,950 | 19,195 | 14,944 | 19,643 | 17,644 |
| 92,950 | 93,000 | 19,209 | 14,956 | 19,657 | 17,656 |

*(Continued)*

* This column must also be used by a qualifying widow(er).

# 2015 Federal Tax Guide

2014 Tax Table — *Continued*

## 93,000

| At least | But less than | Single | Married filing jointly * | Married filing separately | Head of a household |
|---|---|---|---|---|---|
| 93,000 | 93,050 | 19,223 | 14,969 | 19,671 | 17,669 |
| 93,050 | 93,100 | 19,237 | 14,981 | 19,685 | 17,681 |
| 93,100 | 93,150 | 19,251 | 14,994 | 19,699 | 17,694 |
| 93,150 | 93,200 | 19,265 | 15,006 | 19,713 | 17,706 |
| 93,200 | 93,250 | 19,279 | 15,019 | 19,727 | 17,719 |
| 93,250 | 93,300 | 19,293 | 15,031 | 19,741 | 17,731 |
| 93,300 | 93,350 | 19,307 | 15,044 | 19,755 | 17,744 |
| 93,350 | 93,400 | 19,321 | 15,056 | 19,769 | 17,756 |
| 93,400 | 93,450 | 19,335 | 15,069 | 19,783 | 17,769 |
| 93,450 | 93,500 | 19,349 | 15,081 | 19,797 | 17,781 |
| 93,500 | 93,550 | 19,363 | 15,094 | 19,811 | 17,794 |
| 93,550 | 93,600 | 19,377 | 15,106 | 19,825 | 17,806 |
| 93,600 | 93,650 | 19,391 | 15,119 | 19,839 | 17,819 |
| 93,650 | 93,700 | 19,405 | 15,131 | 19,853 | 17,831 |
| 93,700 | 93,750 | 19,419 | 15,144 | 19,867 | 17,844 |
| 93,750 | 93,800 | 19,433 | 15,156 | 19,881 | 17,856 |
| 93,800 | 93,850 | 19,447 | 15,169 | 19,895 | 17,869 |
| 93,850 | 93,900 | 19,461 | 15,181 | 19,909 | 17,881 |
| 93,900 | 93,950 | 19,475 | 15,194 | 19,923 | 17,894 |
| 93,950 | 94,000 | 19,489 | 15,206 | 19,937 | 17,906 |

## 94,000

| At least | But less than | Single | Married filing jointly * | Married filing separately | Head of a household |
|---|---|---|---|---|---|
| 94,000 | 94,050 | 19,503 | 15,219 | 19,951 | 17,919 |
| 94,050 | 94,100 | 19,517 | 15,231 | 19,965 | 17,931 |
| 94,100 | 94,150 | 19,531 | 15,244 | 19,979 | 17,944 |
| 94,150 | 94,200 | 19,545 | 15,256 | 19,993 | 17,956 |
| 94,200 | 94,250 | 19,559 | 15,269 | 20,007 | 17,969 |
| 94,250 | 94,300 | 19,573 | 15,281 | 20,021 | 17,981 |
| 94,300 | 94,350 | 19,587 | 15,294 | 20,035 | 17,994 |
| 94,350 | 94,400 | 19,601 | 15,306 | 20,049 | 18,006 |
| 94,400 | 94,450 | 19,615 | 15,319 | 20,063 | 18,019 |
| 94,450 | 94,500 | 19,629 | 15,331 | 20,077 | 18,031 |
| 94,500 | 94,550 | 19,643 | 15,344 | 20,091 | 18,044 |
| 94,550 | 94,600 | 19,657 | 15,356 | 20,105 | 18,056 |
| 94,600 | 94,650 | 19,671 | 15,369 | 20,119 | 18,069 |
| 94,650 | 94,700 | 19,685 | 15,381 | 20,133 | 18,081 |
| 94,700 | 94,750 | 19,699 | 15,394 | 20,147 | 18,094 |
| 94,750 | 94,800 | 19,713 | 15,406 | 20,161 | 18,106 |
| 94,800 | 94,850 | 19,727 | 15,419 | 20,175 | 18,119 |
| 94,850 | 94,900 | 19,741 | 15,431 | 20,189 | 18,131 |
| 94,900 | 94,950 | 19,755 | 15,444 | 20,203 | 18,144 |
| 94,950 | 95,000 | 19,769 | 15,456 | 20,217 | 18,156 |

## 95,000

| At least | But less than | Single | Married filing jointly * | Married filing separately | Head of a household |
|---|---|---|---|---|---|
| 95,000 | 95,050 | 19,783 | 15,469 | 20,231 | 18,169 |
| 95,050 | 95,100 | 19,797 | 15,481 | 20,245 | 18,181 |
| 95,100 | 95,150 | 19,811 | 15,494 | 20,259 | 18,194 |
| 95,150 | 95,200 | 19,825 | 15,506 | 20,273 | 18,206 |
| 95,200 | 95,250 | 19,839 | 15,519 | 20,287 | 18,219 |
| 95,250 | 95,300 | 19,853 | 15,531 | 20,301 | 18,231 |
| 95,300 | 95,350 | 19,867 | 15,544 | 20,315 | 18,244 |
| 95,350 | 95,400 | 19,881 | 15,556 | 20,329 | 18,256 |
| 95,400 | 95,450 | 19,895 | 15,569 | 20,343 | 18,269 |
| 95,450 | 95,500 | 19,909 | 15,581 | 20,357 | 18,281 |
| 95,500 | 95,550 | 19,923 | 15,594 | 20,371 | 18,294 |
| 95,550 | 95,600 | 19,937 | 15,606 | 20,385 | 18,306 |
| 95,600 | 95,650 | 19,951 | 15,619 | 20,399 | 18,319 |
| 95,650 | 95,700 | 19,965 | 15,631 | 20,413 | 18,331 |
| 95,700 | 95,750 | 19,979 | 15,644 | 20,427 | 18,344 |
| 95,750 | 95,800 | 19,993 | 15,656 | 20,441 | 18,356 |
| 95,800 | 95,850 | 20,007 | 15,669 | 20,455 | 18,369 |
| 95,850 | 95,900 | 20,021 | 15,681 | 20,469 | 18,381 |
| 95,900 | 95,950 | 20,035 | 15,694 | 20,483 | 18,394 |
| 95,950 | 96,000 | 20,049 | 15,706 | 20,497 | 18,406 |

## 96,000

| At least | But less than | Single | Married filing jointly * | Married filing separately | Head of a household |
|---|---|---|---|---|---|
| 96,000 | 96,050 | 20,063 | 15,719 | 20,511 | 18,419 |
| 96,050 | 96,100 | 20,077 | 15,731 | 20,525 | 18,431 |
| 96,100 | 96,150 | 20,091 | 15,744 | 20,539 | 18,444 |
| 96,150 | 96,200 | 20,105 | 15,756 | 20,553 | 18,456 |
| 96,200 | 96,250 | 20,119 | 15,769 | 20,567 | 18,469 |
| 96,250 | 96,300 | 20,133 | 15,781 | 20,581 | 18,481 |
| 96,300 | 96,350 | 20,147 | 15,794 | 20,595 | 18,494 |
| 96,350 | 96,400 | 20,161 | 15,806 | 20,609 | 18,506 |
| 96,400 | 96,450 | 20,175 | 15,819 | 20,623 | 18,519 |
| 96,450 | 96,500 | 20,189 | 15,831 | 20,637 | 18,531 |
| 96,500 | 96,550 | 20,203 | 15,844 | 20,651 | 18,544 |
| 96,550 | 96,600 | 20,217 | 15,856 | 20,665 | 18,556 |
| 96,600 | 96,650 | 20,231 | 15,869 | 20,679 | 18,569 |
| 96,650 | 96,700 | 20,245 | 15,881 | 20,693 | 18,581 |
| 96,700 | 96,750 | 20,259 | 15,894 | 20,707 | 18,594 |
| 96,750 | 96,800 | 20,273 | 15,906 | 20,721 | 18,606 |
| 96,800 | 96,850 | 20,287 | 15,919 | 20,735 | 18,619 |
| 96,850 | 96,900 | 20,301 | 15,931 | 20,749 | 18,631 |
| 96,900 | 96,950 | 20,315 | 15,944 | 20,763 | 18,644 |
| 96,950 | 97,000 | 20,329 | 15,956 | 20,777 | 18,656 |

## 97,000

| At least | But less than | Single | Married filing jointly * | Married filing separately | Head of a household |
|---|---|---|---|---|---|
| 97,000 | 97,050 | 20,343 | 15,969 | 20,791 | 18,669 |
| 97,050 | 97,100 | 20,357 | 15,981 | 20,805 | 18,681 |
| 97,100 | 97,150 | 20,371 | 15,994 | 20,819 | 18,694 |
| 97,150 | 97,200 | 20,385 | 16,006 | 20,833 | 18,706 |
| 97,200 | 97,250 | 20,399 | 16,019 | 20,847 | 18,719 |
| 97,250 | 97,300 | 20,413 | 16,031 | 20,861 | 18,731 |
| 97,300 | 97,350 | 20,427 | 16,044 | 20,875 | 18,744 |
| 97,350 | 97,400 | 20,441 | 16,056 | 20,889 | 18,756 |
| 97,400 | 97,450 | 20,455 | 16,069 | 20,903 | 18,769 |
| 97,450 | 97,500 | 20,469 | 16,081 | 20,917 | 18,781 |
| 97,500 | 97,550 | 20,483 | 16,094 | 20,931 | 18,794 |
| 97,550 | 97,600 | 20,497 | 16,106 | 20,945 | 18,806 |
| 97,600 | 97,650 | 20,511 | 16,119 | 20,959 | 18,819 |
| 97,650 | 97,700 | 20,525 | 16,131 | 20,973 | 18,831 |
| 97,700 | 97,750 | 20,539 | 16,144 | 20,987 | 18,844 |
| 97,750 | 97,800 | 20,553 | 16,156 | 21,001 | 18,856 |
| 97,800 | 97,850 | 20,567 | 16,169 | 21,015 | 18,869 |
| 97,850 | 97,900 | 20,581 | 16,181 | 21,029 | 18,881 |
| 97,900 | 97,950 | 20,595 | 16,194 | 21,043 | 18,894 |
| 97,950 | 98,000 | 20,609 | 16,206 | 21,057 | 18,906 |

## 98,000

| At least | But less than | Single | Married filing jointly * | Married filing separately | Head of a household |
|---|---|---|---|---|---|
| 98,000 | 98,050 | 20,623 | 16,219 | 21,071 | 18,919 |
| 98,050 | 98,100 | 20,637 | 16,231 | 21,085 | 18,931 |
| 98,100 | 98,150 | 20,651 | 16,244 | 21,099 | 18,944 |
| 98,150 | 98,200 | 20,665 | 16,256 | 21,113 | 18,956 |
| 98,200 | 98,250 | 20,679 | 16,269 | 21,127 | 18,969 |
| 98,250 | 98,300 | 20,693 | 16,281 | 21,141 | 18,981 |
| 98,300 | 98,350 | 20,707 | 16,294 | 21,155 | 18,994 |
| 98,350 | 98,400 | 20,721 | 16,306 | 21,169 | 19,006 |
| 98,400 | 98,450 | 20,735 | 16,319 | 21,183 | 19,019 |
| 98,450 | 98,500 | 20,749 | 16,331 | 21,197 | 19,031 |
| 98,500 | 98,550 | 20,763 | 16,344 | 21,211 | 19,044 |
| 98,550 | 98,600 | 20,777 | 16,356 | 21,225 | 19,056 |
| 98,600 | 98,650 | 20,791 | 16,369 | 21,239 | 19,069 |
| 98,650 | 98,700 | 20,805 | 16,381 | 21,253 | 19,081 |
| 98,700 | 98,750 | 20,819 | 16,394 | 21,267 | 19,094 |
| 98,750 | 98,800 | 20,833 | 16,406 | 21,281 | 19,106 |
| 98,800 | 98,850 | 20,847 | 16,419 | 21,295 | 19,119 |
| 98,850 | 98,900 | 20,861 | 16,431 | 21,309 | 19,131 |
| 98,900 | 98,950 | 20,875 | 16,444 | 21,323 | 19,144 |
| 98,950 | 99,000 | 20,889 | 16,456 | 21,337 | 19,156 |

## 99,000

| At least | But less than | Single | Married filing jointly * | Married filing separately | Head of a household |
|---|---|---|---|---|---|
| 99,000 | 99,050 | 20,903 | 16,469 | 21,351 | 19,169 |
| 99,050 | 99,100 | 20,917 | 16,481 | 21,365 | 19,181 |
| 99,100 | 99,150 | 20,931 | 16,494 | 21,379 | 19,194 |
| 99,150 | 99,200 | 20,945 | 16,506 | 21,393 | 19,206 |
| 99,200 | 99,250 | 20,959 | 16,519 | 21,407 | 19,219 |
| 99,250 | 99,300 | 20,973 | 16,531 | 21,421 | 19,231 |
| 99,300 | 99,350 | 20,987 | 16,544 | 21,435 | 19,244 |
| 99,350 | 99,400 | 21,001 | 16,556 | 21,449 | 19,256 |
| 99,400 | 99,450 | 21,015 | 16,569 | 21,463 | 19,269 |
| 99,450 | 99,500 | 21,029 | 16,581 | 21,477 | 19,281 |
| 99,500 | 99,550 | 21,043 | 16,594 | 21,491 | 19,294 |
| 99,550 | 99,600 | 21,057 | 16,606 | 21,505 | 19,306 |
| 99,600 | 99,650 | 21,071 | 16,619 | 21,519 | 19,319 |
| 99,650 | 99,700 | 21,085 | 16,631 | 21,533 | 19,331 |
| 99,700 | 99,750 | 21,099 | 16,644 | 21,547 | 19,344 |
| 99,750 | 99,800 | 21,113 | 16,656 | 21,561 | 19,356 |
| 99,800 | 99,850 | 21,127 | 16,669 | 21,575 | 19,369 |
| 99,850 | 99,900 | 21,141 | 16,681 | 21,589 | 19,381 |
| 99,900 | 99,950 | 21,155 | 16,694 | 21,603 | 19,394 |
| 99,950 | 100,000 | 21,169 | 16,706 | 21,617 | 19,406 |

$100,000 or over use the Tax Computation Worksheet

* This column must also be used by a qualifying widow(er).

# 5. 2014 Filing Requirement Charts

(Source: 2014 Form 1040 Draft Instructions)

**Chart A—For Most People**

| IF your filing status is . . . | AND at the end of 2014 you were* . . . | THEN file a return if your gross income** was at least . . . |
|---|---|---|
| Single (see the instructions for line 1) | under 65<br>65 or older | $10,150<br>11,700 |
| Married filing jointly*** (see the instructions for line 2) | under 65 (both spouses)<br>65 or older (one spouse)<br>65 or older (both spouses) | $20,300<br>21,500<br>22,700 |
| Married filing separately (see the instructions for line 3) | any age | $3,950 |
| Head of household (see the instructions for line 4) | under 65<br>65 or older | $13,050<br>14,600 |
| Qualifying widow(er) with dependent child (see the instructions for line 5) | under 65<br>65 or older | $16,350<br>17,550 |

*If you were born on January 1, 1950, you are considered to be age 65 at the end of 2014. (If your spouse died in 2014 or if you are preparing a return for someone who died in 2014, see Pub. 501.)

**Gross income** means all income you received in the form of money, goods, property, and services that is not exempt from tax, including any income from sources outside the United States or from the sale of your main home (even if you can exclude part or all of it). Do not include any social security benefits unless (a) you are married filing a separate return and you lived with your spouse at any time in 2014 or (b) one-half of your social security benefits plus your other gross income and any tax-exempt interest is more than $25,000 ($32,000 if married filing jointly). If (a) or (b) applies, see the instructions for lines 20a and 20b to figure the taxable part of social security benefits you must include in gross income. Gross income includes gains, but not losses, reported on Form 8949 or Schedule D. Gross income from a business means, for example, the amount on Schedule C, line 7, or Schedule F, line 9. But, in figuring gross income, do not reduce your income by any losses, including any loss on Schedule C, line 7, or Schedule F, line 9.

***If you did not live with your spouse at the end of 2014 (or on the date your spouse died) and your gross income was at least $3,950, you must file a return regardless of your age.

## Chart B—For Children and Other Dependents (See the instructions for line 6c to find out if someone can claim you as a dependent.)

If your parent (or someone else) can claim you as a dependent, use this chart to see if you must file a return.

In this chart, **unearned income** includes taxable interest, ordinary dividends, and capital gain distributions. It also includes unemployment compensation, taxable social security benefits, pensions, annuities, and distributions of unearned income from a trust. **Earned income** includes salaries, wages, tips, professional fees, and taxable scholarship and fellowship grants. **Gross income** is the total of your unearned and earned income.

**Single dependents.** Were you **either** age 65 or older **or** blind?

☐ **No.** You must file a return if **any** of the following apply.
- Your unearned income was over $1,000.
- Your earned income was over $6,200.
- Your gross income was more than the **larger** of—
  - $1,000, or
  - Your earned income (up to $5,850) plus $350.

☐ **Yes.** You must file a return if **any** of the following apply.
- Your unearned income was over $2,550 ($4,100 if 65 or older **and** blind).
- Your earned income was over $7,750 ($9,300 if 65 or older **and** blind).
- Your gross income was more than the **larger** of—
  - $2,550 ($4,100 if 65 or older **and** blind), or
  - Your earned income (up to $5,850) plus $1,900 ($3,450 if 65 or older **and** blind).

**Married dependents.** Were you **either** age 65 or older **or** blind?

☐ **No.** You must file a return if **any** of the following apply.
- Your unearned income was over $1,000.
- Your earned income was over $6,200.
- Your gross income was at least $5 and your spouse files a separate return and itemizes deductions.
- Your gross income was more than the **larger** of—
  - $1,000, or
  - Your earned income (up to $5,850) plus $350.

☐ **Yes.** You must file a return if **any** of the following apply.
- Your unearned income was over $2,200 ($3,400 if 65 or older **and** blind).
- Your earned income was over $7,400 ($8,600 if 65 or older **and** blind).
- Your gross income was at least $5 and your spouse files a separate return and itemizes deductions.
- Your gross income was more than the **larger** of—
  - $2,200 ($3,400 if 65 or older **and** blind), or
  - Your earned income (up to $5,850) plus $1,550 ($2,750 if 65 or older **and** blind).

## Chart C—Other Situations When You Must File

You must file a return if any of the five conditions below apply for 2014.

1. You owe any special taxes, including any of the following.
   a. Alternative minimum tax.
   b. Additional tax on a qualified plan, including an individual retirement arrangement (IRA), or other tax-favored account. But if you are filing a return only because you owe this tax, you can file **Form 5329** by itself.
   c. Household employment taxes. But if you are filing a return only because you owe this tax, you can file **Schedule H** by itself.
   d. Social security and Medicare tax on tips you did not report to your employer or on wages you received from an employer who did not withhold these taxes.
   e. Recapture of first-time homebuyer credit. See the instructions for line 60b.
   f. Write-in taxes, including uncollected social security and Medicare or RRTA tax on tips you reported to your employer or on group-term life insurance and additional taxes on health savings accounts. See the instructions for line 62.
   g. Recapture taxes. See the instructions for line 44 and line 62.
2. You (or your spouse, if filing jointly) received HSA, Archer MSA, or Medicare Advantage MSA distributions.
3. You had net earnings from self-employment of at least $400.
4. You had wages of $108.28 or more from a church or qualified church-controlled organization that is exempt from employer social security and Medicare taxes.
5. Advance payments of the premium tax credit were made for you, your spouse, or a dependent who enrolled in coverage through the Health Insurance Marketplace. You should have received Form(s) 1095-A showing the amount of the advance payments, if any.

# 6. Where to File Forms 1040 and 4868

**Where to File Forms 1040 and 4868 — 2014 Tax Year [As of October 9, 2014]**

| State of Residence | 1040, no payment enclosed | 1040, payment enclosed | 4868, payment enclosed | 4868, no payment enclosed |
|---|---|---|---|---|
| Florida, Louisiana, Mississippi, Texas | Internal Revenue Service, Austin, TX 73301-0002 | Internal Revenue Service, P.O. Box 1214, Charlotte, NC 28201-1214 | Internal Revenue Service, P.O. Box 1302, Charlotte, NC 28201-1302 | Internal Revenue Service, Austin, TX 73301-0045 |
| Alabama, Georgia, Kentucky, New Jersey, North Carolina, South Carolina, Tennessee, Virginia | Internal Revenue Service, Kansas City, MO 64999-0002 | Internal Revenue Service, P.O. Box 931000, Louisville, KY 40293-1000 | Internal Revenue Service, P.O. Box 931300, Louisville, KY 40293-1300 | Internal Revenue Service, Kansas City, MO 64999-0045 |
| Alaska, Arizona, California, Colorado, Hawaii, Idaho, Nevada, New Mexico, Oregon, Utah, Washington, Wyoming | Internal Revenue Service, Fresno, CA 93888-0002 | Internal Revenue Service, P.O. Box 7704, San Francisco, CA 94120-7704 | Internal Revenue Service, P.O. Box 7122, San Francisco, CA 94120-7122 | Internal Revenue Service, Fresno, CA 93888-0045 |
| Arkansas, Illinois, Indiana, Iowa, Kansas, Michigan, Minnesota, Montana, Nebraska, North Dakota, Ohio, Oklahoma, South Dakota, Wisconsin | Internal Revenue Service, Fresno, CA 93888-0002 | Internal Revenue Service, P.O. Box 802501, Cincinnati, OH 45280-2501 | Internal Revenue Service, P.O. Box 802503, Cincinnati, OH 45280-2503 | Internal Revenue Service, Fresno, CA 93888-0045 |

| State of Residence | 1040, no payment enclosed | 1040, payment enclosed | 4868, payment enclosed | 4868, no payment enclosed |
|---|---|---|---|---|
| Connecticut, Delaware, District of Columbia, Maine, Maryland, Massachusetts, New Hampshire, New York, Pennsylvania, Rhode Island, Vermont, West Virginia | Internal Revenue Service, Kansas City, MO 64999-0002 | Internal Revenue Service, P.O. Box 37008, Hartford, CT 06176-7008 | Internal Revenue Service, P.O. Box 37009, Hartford, CT 06176-7009 | Internal Revenue Service, Kansas City, MO 64999-0045 |
| Missouri | Internal Revenue Service, Kansas City, MO 64999-0002 | Internal Revenue Service, P.O. Box 37008, Hartford, CT 06176-7008 | Internal Revenue Service, P.O. Box 931300, Louisville, KY 40293-1300 | Internal Revenue Service, Kansas City, MO 64999-0045 |
| Any of the following applies: • Resident of a foreign country, American Samoa, or Puerto Rico • Income excluded under IRC § 933. • An APO or FPO address is used. • Form 2555 or Form 4563 is filed. • Taxpayer is a dual-status alien or nonpermanent resident of Guam or the Virgin Islands. | Internal Revenue Service, Austin, TX 73301-0215 USA | Internal Revenue Service, P.O. Box 1303, Charlotte, NC 28201-1303 USA | Internal Revenue Service, P.O. Box 1302, Charlotte, NC 28201-1302 USA | Internal Revenue Service, Austin, TX 73301-0215 USA |

# 7. 2014 Earned Income Credit Table

(Source: 2014 Form 1040 Draft Instructions)

## 2014 Earned Income Credit (EIC) Table
**Caution.** This is **not** a tax table.

**1.** To find your credit, read down the "At least - But less than" columns and find the line that includes the amount you were told to look up from your EIC Worksheet.

**2.** Then, go to the column that includes your filing status and the number of qualifying children you have. Enter the credit from that column on your EIC Worksheet.

**Example.** If your filing status is single, you have one qualifying child, and the amount you are looking up from your EIC Worksheet is $2,455, you would enter $842.

| If the amount you are looking up from the worksheet is— | | And your filing status is— | | | |
|---|---|---|---|---|---|
| | | Single, head of household, or qualifying widow(er) and the number of children you have is— | | | |
| | | 0 | 1 | 2 | 3 |
| At least | But less than | Your credit is— | | | |
| 2,400 | 2,450 | 186 | | 970 | 1,091 |
| 2,450 | 2,500 | 189 | 842 | 990 | 1,114 |

| If the amount you are looking up from the worksheet is— | | Single, head of household, or qualifying widow(er) and the number of children you have is— | | | | Married filing jointly and the number of children you have is— | | | |
|---|---|---|---|---|---|---|---|---|---|
| At least | But less than | 0 | 1 | 2 | 3 | 0 | 1 | 2 | 3 |
| | | Your credit is— | | | | Your credit is— | | | |
| $1 | $50 | 2 | 9 | 10 | 11 | 2 | 9 | 10 | 11 |
| 50 | 100 | 6 | 26 | 30 | 34 | 6 | 26 | 30 | 34 |
| 100 | 150 | 10 | 43 | 50 | 56 | 10 | 43 | 50 | 56 |
| 150 | 200 | 13 | 60 | 70 | 79 | 13 | 60 | 70 | 79 |
| 200 | 250 | 17 | 77 | 90 | 101 | 17 | 77 | 90 | 101 |
| 250 | 300 | 21 | 94 | 110 | 124 | 21 | 94 | 110 | 124 |
| 300 | 350 | 25 | 111 | 130 | 146 | 25 | 111 | 130 | 146 |
| 350 | 400 | 29 | 128 | 150 | 169 | 29 | 128 | 150 | 169 |
| 400 | 450 | 33 | 145 | 170 | 191 | 33 | 145 | 170 | 191 |
| 450 | 500 | 36 | 162 | 190 | 214 | 36 | 162 | 190 | 214 |
| 500 | 550 | 40 | 179 | 210 | 236 | 40 | 179 | 210 | 236 |
| 550 | 600 | 44 | 196 | 230 | 259 | 44 | 196 | 230 | 259 |
| 600 | 650 | 48 | 213 | 250 | 281 | 48 | 213 | 250 | 281 |
| 650 | 700 | 52 | 230 | 270 | 304 | 52 | 230 | 270 | 304 |
| 700 | 750 | 55 | 247 | 290 | 326 | 55 | 247 | 290 | 326 |
| 750 | 800 | 59 | 264 | 310 | 349 | 59 | 264 | 310 | 349 |
| 800 | 850 | 63 | 281 | 330 | 371 | 63 | 281 | 330 | 371 |
| 850 | 900 | 67 | 298 | 350 | 394 | 67 | 298 | 350 | 394 |
| 900 | 950 | 71 | 315 | 370 | 416 | 71 | 315 | 370 | 416 |
| 950 | 1,000 | 75 | 332 | 390 | 439 | 75 | 332 | 390 | 439 |
| 1,000 | 1,050 | 78 | 349 | 410 | 461 | 78 | 349 | 410 | 461 |
| 1,050 | 1,100 | 82 | 366 | 430 | 484 | 82 | 366 | 430 | 484 |
| 1,100 | 1,150 | 86 | 383 | 450 | 506 | 86 | 383 | 450 | 506 |
| 1,150 | 1,200 | 90 | 400 | 470 | 529 | 90 | 400 | 470 | 529 |
| 1,200 | 1,250 | 94 | 417 | 490 | 551 | 94 | 417 | 490 | 551 |
| 1,250 | 1,300 | 98 | 434 | 510 | 574 | 98 | 434 | 510 | 574 |
| 1,300 | 1,350 | 101 | 451 | 530 | 596 | 101 | 451 | 530 | 596 |
| 1,350 | 1,400 | 105 | 468 | 550 | 619 | 105 | 468 | 550 | 619 |
| 1,400 | 1,450 | 109 | 485 | 570 | 641 | 109 | 485 | 570 | 641 |
| 1,450 | 1,500 | 113 | 502 | 590 | 664 | 113 | 502 | 590 | 664 |
| 1,500 | 1,550 | 117 | 519 | 610 | 686 | 117 | 519 | 610 | 686 |
| 1,550 | 1,600 | 120 | 536 | 630 | 709 | 120 | 536 | 630 | 709 |
| 1,600 | 1,650 | 124 | 553 | 650 | 731 | 124 | 553 | 650 | 731 |
| 1,650 | 1,700 | 128 | 570 | 670 | 754 | 128 | 570 | 670 | 754 |
| 1,700 | 1,750 | 132 | 587 | 690 | 776 | 132 | 587 | 690 | 776 |
| 1,750 | 1,800 | 136 | 604 | 710 | 799 | 136 | 604 | 710 | 799 |
| 1,800 | 1,850 | 140 | 621 | 730 | 821 | 140 | 621 | 730 | 821 |
| 1,850 | 1,900 | 143 | 638 | 750 | 844 | 143 | 638 | 750 | 844 |
| 1,900 | 1,950 | 147 | 655 | 770 | 866 | 147 | 655 | 770 | 866 |
| 1,950 | 2,000 | 151 | 672 | 790 | 889 | 151 | 672 | 790 | 889 |
| 2,000 | 2,050 | 155 | 689 | 810 | 911 | 155 | 689 | 810 | 911 |
| 2,050 | 2,100 | 159 | 706 | 830 | 934 | 159 | 706 | 830 | 934 |
| 2,100 | 2,150 | 163 | 723 | 850 | 956 | 163 | 723 | 850 | 956 |
| 2,150 | 2,200 | 166 | 740 | 870 | 979 | 166 | 740 | 870 | 979 |
| 2,200 | 2,250 | 170 | 757 | 890 | 1,001 | 170 | 757 | 890 | 1,001 |
| 2,250 | 2,300 | 174 | 774 | 910 | 1,024 | 174 | 774 | 910 | 1,024 |
| 2,300 | 2,350 | 178 | 791 | 930 | 1,046 | 178 | 791 | 930 | 1,046 |
| 2,350 | 2,400 | 182 | 808 | 950 | 1,069 | 182 | 808 | 950 | 1,069 |
| 2,400 | 2,450 | 186 | 825 | 970 | 1,091 | 186 | 825 | 970 | 1,091 |
| 2,450 | 2,500 | 189 | 842 | 990 | 1,114 | 189 | 842 | 990 | 1,114 |
| 2,500 | 2,550 | 193 | 859 | 1,010 | 1,136 | 193 | 859 | 1,010 | 1,136 |
| 2,550 | 2,600 | 197 | 876 | 1,030 | 1,159 | 197 | 876 | 1,030 | 1,159 |
| 2,600 | 2,650 | 201 | 893 | 1,050 | 1,181 | 201 | 893 | 1,050 | 1,181 |
| 2,650 | 2,700 | 205 | 910 | 1,070 | 1,204 | 205 | 910 | 1,070 | 1,204 |
| 2,700 | 2,750 | 208 | 927 | 1,090 | 1,226 | 208 | 927 | 1,090 | 1,226 |
| 2,750 | 2,800 | 212 | 944 | 1,110 | 1,249 | 212 | 944 | 1,110 | 1,249 |

| If the amount you are looking up from the worksheet is— | | Single, head of household, or qualifying widow(er) and the number of children you have is— | | | | Married filing jointly and the number of children you have is— | | | |
|---|---|---|---|---|---|---|---|---|---|
| At least | But less than | 0 | 1 | 2 | 3 | 0 | 1 | 2 | 3 |
| | | Your credit is— | | | | Your credit is— | | | |
| 2,800 | 2,850 | 216 | 961 | 1,130 | 1,271 | 216 | 961 | 1,130 | 1,271 |
| 2,850 | 2,900 | 220 | 978 | 1,150 | 1,294 | 220 | 978 | 1,150 | 1,294 |
| 2,900 | 2,950 | 224 | 995 | 1,170 | 1,316 | 224 | 995 | 1,170 | 1,316 |
| 2,950 | 3,000 | 228 | 1,012 | 1,190 | 1,339 | 228 | 1,012 | 1,190 | 1,339 |
| 3,000 | 3,050 | 231 | 1,029 | 1,210 | 1,361 | 231 | 1,029 | 1,210 | 1,361 |
| 3,050 | 3,100 | 235 | 1,046 | 1,230 | 1,384 | 235 | 1,046 | 1,230 | 1,384 |
| 3,100 | 3,150 | 239 | 1,063 | 1,250 | 1,406 | 239 | 1,063 | 1,250 | 1,406 |
| 3,150 | 3,200 | 243 | 1,080 | 1,270 | 1,429 | 243 | 1,080 | 1,270 | 1,429 |
| 3,200 | 3,250 | 247 | 1,097 | 1,290 | 1,451 | 247 | 1,097 | 1,290 | 1,451 |
| 3,250 | 3,300 | 251 | 1,114 | 1,310 | 1,474 | 251 | 1,114 | 1,310 | 1,474 |
| 3,300 | 3,350 | 254 | 1,131 | 1,330 | 1,496 | 254 | 1,131 | 1,330 | 1,496 |
| 3,350 | 3,400 | 258 | 1,148 | 1,350 | 1,519 | 258 | 1,148 | 1,350 | 1,519 |
| 3,400 | 3,450 | 262 | 1,165 | 1,370 | 1,541 | 262 | 1,165 | 1,370 | 1,541 |
| 3,450 | 3,500 | 266 | 1,182 | 1,390 | 1,564 | 266 | 1,182 | 1,390 | 1,564 |
| 3,500 | 3,550 | 270 | 1,199 | 1,410 | 1,586 | 270 | 1,199 | 1,410 | 1,586 |
| 3,550 | 3,600 | 273 | 1,216 | 1,430 | 1,609 | 273 | 1,216 | 1,430 | 1,609 |
| 3,600 | 3,650 | 277 | 1,233 | 1,450 | 1,631 | 277 | 1,233 | 1,450 | 1,631 |
| 3,650 | 3,700 | 281 | 1,250 | 1,470 | 1,654 | 281 | 1,250 | 1,470 | 1,654 |
| 3,700 | 3,750 | 285 | 1,267 | 1,490 | 1,676 | 285 | 1,267 | 1,490 | 1,676 |
| 3,750 | 3,800 | 289 | 1,284 | 1,510 | 1,699 | 289 | 1,284 | 1,510 | 1,699 |
| 3,800 | 3,850 | 293 | 1,301 | 1,530 | 1,721 | 293 | 1,301 | 1,530 | 1,721 |
| 3,850 | 3,900 | 296 | 1,318 | 1,550 | 1,744 | 296 | 1,318 | 1,550 | 1,744 |
| 3,900 | 3,950 | 300 | 1,335 | 1,570 | 1,766 | 300 | 1,335 | 1,570 | 1,766 |
| 3,950 | 4,000 | 304 | 1,352 | 1,590 | 1,789 | 304 | 1,352 | 1,590 | 1,789 |
| 4,000 | 4,050 | 308 | 1,369 | 1,610 | 1,811 | 308 | 1,369 | 1,610 | 1,811 |
| 4,050 | 4,100 | 312 | 1,386 | 1,630 | 1,834 | 312 | 1,386 | 1,630 | 1,834 |
| 4,100 | 4,150 | 316 | 1,403 | 1,650 | 1,856 | 316 | 1,403 | 1,650 | 1,856 |
| 4,150 | 4,200 | 319 | 1,420 | 1,670 | 1,879 | 319 | 1,420 | 1,670 | 1,879 |
| 4,200 | 4,250 | 323 | 1,437 | 1,690 | 1,901 | 323 | 1,437 | 1,690 | 1,901 |
| 4,250 | 4,300 | 327 | 1,454 | 1,710 | 1,924 | 327 | 1,454 | 1,710 | 1,924 |
| 4,300 | 4,350 | 331 | 1,471 | 1,730 | 1,946 | 331 | 1,471 | 1,730 | 1,946 |
| 4,350 | 4,400 | 335 | 1,488 | 1,750 | 1,969 | 335 | 1,488 | 1,750 | 1,969 |
| 4,400 | 4,450 | 339 | 1,505 | 1,770 | 1,991 | 339 | 1,505 | 1,770 | 1,991 |
| 4,450 | 4,500 | 342 | 1,522 | 1,790 | 2,014 | 342 | 1,522 | 1,790 | 2,014 |
| 4,500 | 4,550 | 346 | 1,539 | 1,810 | 2,036 | 346 | 1,539 | 1,810 | 2,036 |
| 4,550 | 4,600 | 350 | 1,556 | 1,830 | 2,059 | 350 | 1,556 | 1,830 | 2,059 |
| 4,600 | 4,650 | 354 | 1,573 | 1,850 | 2,081 | 354 | 1,573 | 1,850 | 2,081 |
| 4,650 | 4,700 | 358 | 1,590 | 1,870 | 2,104 | 358 | 1,590 | 1,870 | 2,104 |
| 4,700 | 4,750 | 361 | 1,607 | 1,890 | 2,126 | 361 | 1,607 | 1,890 | 2,126 |
| 4,750 | 4,800 | 365 | 1,624 | 1,910 | 2,149 | 365 | 1,624 | 1,910 | 2,149 |
| 4,800 | 4,850 | 369 | 1,641 | 1,930 | 2,171 | 369 | 1,641 | 1,930 | 2,171 |
| 4,850 | 4,900 | 373 | 1,658 | 1,950 | 2,194 | 373 | 1,658 | 1,950 | 2,194 |
| 4,900 | 4,950 | 377 | 1,675 | 1,970 | 2,216 | 377 | 1,675 | 1,970 | 2,216 |
| 4,950 | 5,000 | 381 | 1,692 | 1,990 | 2,239 | 381 | 1,692 | 1,990 | 2,239 |
| 5,000 | 5,050 | 384 | 1,709 | 2,010 | 2,261 | 384 | 1,709 | 2,010 | 2,261 |
| 5,050 | 5,100 | 388 | 1,726 | 2,030 | 2,284 | 388 | 1,726 | 2,030 | 2,284 |
| 5,100 | 5,150 | 392 | 1,743 | 2,050 | 2,306 | 392 | 1,743 | 2,050 | 2,306 |
| 5,150 | 5,200 | 396 | 1,760 | 2,070 | 2,329 | 396 | 1,760 | 2,070 | 2,329 |
| 5,200 | 5,250 | 400 | 1,777 | 2,090 | 2,351 | 400 | 1,777 | 2,090 | 2,351 |
| 5,250 | 5,300 | 404 | 1,794 | 2,110 | 2,374 | 404 | 1,794 | 2,110 | 2,374 |
| 5,300 | 5,350 | 407 | 1,811 | 2,130 | 2,396 | 407 | 1,811 | 2,130 | 2,396 |
| 5,350 | 5,400 | 411 | 1,828 | 2,150 | 2,419 | 411 | 1,828 | 2,150 | 2,419 |
| 5,400 | 5,450 | 415 | 1,845 | 2,170 | 2,441 | 415 | 1,845 | 2,170 | 2,441 |
| 5,450 | 5,500 | 419 | 1,862 | 2,190 | 2,464 | 419 | 1,862 | 2,190 | 2,464 |
| 5,500 | 5,550 | 423 | 1,879 | 2,210 | 2,486 | 423 | 1,879 | 2,210 | 2,486 |
| 5,550 | 5,600 | 426 | 1,896 | 2,230 | 2,509 | 426 | 1,896 | 2,230 | 2,509 |

*(Continued)*

# 2015 Federal Tax Guide

**Earned Income Credit (EIC) Table** - *Continued*     (**Caution.** This is **not** a tax table.)

| If the amount you are looking up from the worksheet is— | | Single, head of household, or qualifying widow(er) and the number of children you have is— | | | | Married filing jointly and the number of children you have is— | | | |
|---|---|---|---|---|---|---|---|---|---|
| At least | But less than | 0 | 1 | 2 | 3 | 0 | 1 | 2 | 3 |
| | | Your credit is— | | | | Your credit is— | | | |
| 5,600 | 5,650 | 430 | 1,913 | 2,250 | 2,531 | 430 | 1,913 | 2,250 | 2,531 |
| 5,650 | 5,700 | 434 | 1,930 | 2,270 | 2,554 | 434 | 1,930 | 2,270 | 2,554 |
| 5,700 | 5,750 | 438 | 1,947 | 2,290 | 2,576 | 438 | 1,947 | 2,290 | 2,576 |
| 5,750 | 5,800 | 442 | 1,964 | 2,310 | 2,599 | 442 | 1,964 | 2,310 | 2,599 |
| 5,800 | 5,850 | 446 | 1,981 | 2,330 | 2,621 | 446 | 1,981 | 2,330 | 2,621 |
| 5,850 | 5,900 | 449 | 1,998 | 2,350 | 2,644 | 449 | 1,998 | 2,350 | 2,644 |
| 5,900 | 5,950 | 453 | 2,015 | 2,370 | 2,666 | 453 | 2,015 | 2,370 | 2,666 |
| 5,950 | 6,000 | 457 | 2,032 | 2,390 | 2,689 | 457 | 2,032 | 2,390 | 2,689 |
| 6,000 | 6,050 | 461 | 2,049 | 2,410 | 2,711 | 461 | 2,049 | 2,410 | 2,711 |
| 6,050 | 6,100 | 465 | 2,066 | 2,430 | 2,734 | 465 | 2,066 | 2,430 | 2,734 |
| 6,100 | 6,150 | 469 | 2,083 | 2,450 | 2,756 | 469 | 2,083 | 2,450 | 2,756 |
| 6,150 | 6,200 | 472 | 2,100 | 2,470 | 2,779 | 472 | 2,100 | 2,470 | 2,779 |
| 6,200 | 6,250 | 476 | 2,117 | 2,490 | 2,801 | 476 | 2,117 | 2,490 | 2,801 |
| 6,250 | 6,300 | 480 | 2,134 | 2,510 | 2,824 | 480 | 2,134 | 2,510 | 2,824 |
| 6,300 | 6,350 | 484 | 2,151 | 2,530 | 2,846 | 484 | 2,151 | 2,530 | 2,846 |
| 6,350 | 6,400 | 488 | 2,168 | 2,550 | 2,869 | 488 | 2,168 | 2,550 | 2,869 |
| 6,400 | 6,450 | 492 | 2,185 | 2,570 | 2,891 | 492 | 2,185 | 2,570 | 2,891 |
| 6,450 | 6,500 | 496 | 2,202 | 2,590 | 2,914 | 496 | 2,202 | 2,590 | 2,914 |
| 6,500 | 6,550 | 496 | 2,219 | 2,610 | 2,936 | 496 | 2,219 | 2,610 | 2,936 |
| 6,550 | 6,600 | 496 | 2,236 | 2,630 | 2,959 | 496 | 2,236 | 2,630 | 2,959 |
| 6,600 | 6,650 | 496 | 2,253 | 2,650 | 2,981 | 496 | 2,253 | 2,650 | 2,981 |
| 6,650 | 6,700 | 496 | 2,270 | 2,670 | 3,004 | 496 | 2,270 | 2,670 | 3,004 |
| 6,700 | 6,750 | 496 | 2,287 | 2,690 | 3,026 | 496 | 2,287 | 2,690 | 3,026 |
| 6,750 | 6,800 | 496 | 2,304 | 2,710 | 3,049 | 496 | 2,304 | 2,710 | 3,049 |
| 6,800 | 6,850 | 496 | 2,321 | 2,730 | 3,071 | 496 | 2,321 | 2,730 | 3,071 |
| 6,850 | 6,900 | 496 | 2,338 | 2,750 | 3,094 | 496 | 2,338 | 2,750 | 3,094 |
| 6,900 | 6,950 | 496 | 2,355 | 2,770 | 3,116 | 496 | 2,355 | 2,770 | 3,116 |
| 6,950 | 7,000 | 496 | 2,372 | 2,790 | 3,139 | 496 | 2,372 | 2,790 | 3,139 |
| 7,000 | 7,050 | 496 | 2,389 | 2,810 | 3,161 | 496 | 2,389 | 2,810 | 3,161 |
| 7,050 | 7,100 | 496 | 2,406 | 2,830 | 3,184 | 496 | 2,406 | 2,830 | 3,184 |
| 7,100 | 7,150 | 496 | 2,423 | 2,850 | 3,206 | 496 | 2,423 | 2,850 | 3,206 |
| 7,150 | 7,200 | 496 | 2,440 | 2,870 | 3,229 | 496 | 2,440 | 2,870 | 3,229 |
| 7,200 | 7,250 | 496 | 2,457 | 2,890 | 3,251 | 496 | 2,457 | 2,890 | 3,251 |
| 7,250 | 7,300 | 496 | 2,474 | 2,910 | 3,274 | 496 | 2,474 | 2,910 | 3,274 |
| 7,300 | 7,350 | 496 | 2,491 | 2,930 | 3,296 | 496 | 2,491 | 2,930 | 3,296 |
| 7,350 | 7,400 | 496 | 2,508 | 2,950 | 3,319 | 496 | 2,508 | 2,950 | 3,319 |
| 7,400 | 7,450 | 496 | 2,525 | 2,970 | 3,341 | 496 | 2,525 | 2,970 | 3,341 |
| 7,450 | 7,500 | 496 | 2,542 | 2,990 | 3,364 | 496 | 2,542 | 2,990 | 3,364 |
| 7,500 | 7,550 | 496 | 2,559 | 3,010 | 3,386 | 496 | 2,559 | 3,010 | 3,386 |
| 7,550 | 7,600 | 496 | 2,576 | 3,030 | 3,409 | 496 | 2,576 | 3,030 | 3,409 |
| 7,600 | 7,650 | 496 | 2,593 | 3,050 | 3,431 | 496 | 2,593 | 3,050 | 3,431 |
| 7,650 | 7,700 | 496 | 2,610 | 3,070 | 3,454 | 496 | 2,610 | 3,070 | 3,454 |
| 7,700 | 7,750 | 496 | 2,627 | 3,090 | 3,476 | 496 | 2,627 | 3,090 | 3,476 |
| 7,750 | 7,800 | 496 | 2,644 | 3,110 | 3,499 | 496 | 2,644 | 3,110 | 3,499 |
| 7,800 | 7,850 | 496 | 2,661 | 3,130 | 3,521 | 496 | 2,661 | 3,130 | 3,521 |
| 7,850 | 7,900 | 496 | 2,678 | 3,150 | 3,544 | 496 | 2,678 | 3,150 | 3,544 |
| 7,900 | 7,950 | 496 | 2,695 | 3,170 | 3,566 | 496 | 2,695 | 3,170 | 3,566 |
| 7,950 | 8,000 | 496 | 2,712 | 3,190 | 3,589 | 496 | 2,712 | 3,190 | 3,589 |
| 8,000 | 8,050 | 496 | 2,729 | 3,210 | 3,611 | 496 | 2,729 | 3,210 | 3,611 |
| 8,050 | 8,100 | 496 | 2,746 | 3,230 | 3,634 | 496 | 2,746 | 3,230 | 3,634 |
| 8,100 | 8,150 | 496 | 2,763 | 3,250 | 3,656 | 496 | 2,763 | 3,250 | 3,656 |
| 8,150 | 8,200 | 491 | 2,780 | 3,270 | 3,679 | 496 | 2,780 | 3,270 | 3,679 |
| 8,200 | 8,250 | 487 | 2,797 | 3,290 | 3,701 | 496 | 2,797 | 3,290 | 3,701 |
| 8,250 | 8,300 | 483 | 2,814 | 3,310 | 3,724 | 496 | 2,814 | 3,310 | 3,724 |
| 8,300 | 8,350 | 479 | 2,831 | 3,330 | 3,746 | 496 | 2,831 | 3,330 | 3,746 |
| 8,350 | 8,400 | 475 | 2,848 | 3,350 | 3,769 | 496 | 2,848 | 3,350 | 3,769 |
| 8,400 | 8,450 | 472 | 2,865 | 3,370 | 3,791 | 496 | 2,865 | 3,370 | 3,791 |
| 8,450 | 8,500 | 468 | 2,882 | 3,390 | 3,814 | 496 | 2,882 | 3,390 | 3,814 |
| 8,500 | 8,550 | 464 | 2,899 | 3,410 | 3,836 | 496 | 2,899 | 3,410 | 3,836 |
| 8,550 | 8,600 | 460 | 2,916 | 3,430 | 3,859 | 496 | 2,916 | 3,430 | 3,859 |
| 8,600 | 8,650 | 456 | 2,933 | 3,450 | 3,881 | 496 | 2,933 | 3,450 | 3,881 |
| 8,650 | 8,700 | 452 | 2,950 | 3,470 | 3,904 | 496 | 2,950 | 3,470 | 3,904 |
| 8,700 | 8,750 | 449 | 2,967 | 3,490 | 3,926 | 496 | 2,967 | 3,490 | 3,926 |
| 8,750 | 8,800 | 445 | 2,984 | 3,510 | 3,949 | 496 | 2,984 | 3,510 | 3,949 |
| 8,800 | 8,850 | 441 | 3,001 | 3,530 | 3,971 | 496 | 3,001 | 3,530 | 3,971 |
| 8,850 | 8,900 | 437 | 3,018 | 3,550 | 3,994 | 496 | 3,018 | 3,550 | 3,994 |
| 8,900 | 8,950 | 433 | 3,035 | 3,570 | 4,016 | 496 | 3,035 | 3,570 | 4,016 |
| 8,950 | 9,000 | 430 | 3,052 | 3,590 | 4,039 | 496 | 3,052 | 3,590 | 4,039 |
| 9,000 | 9,050 | 426 | 3,069 | 3,610 | 4,061 | 496 | 3,069 | 3,610 | 4,061 |
| 9,050 | 9,100 | 422 | 3,086 | 3,630 | 4,084 | 496 | 3,086 | 3,630 | 4,084 |
| 9,100 | 9,150 | 418 | 3,103 | 3,650 | 4,106 | 496 | 3,103 | 3,650 | 4,106 |
| 9,150 | 9,200 | 414 | 3,120 | 3,670 | 4,129 | 496 | 3,120 | 3,670 | 4,129 |
| 9,200 | 9,250 | 410 | 3,137 | 3,690 | 4,151 | 496 | 3,137 | 3,690 | 4,151 |
| 9,250 | 9,300 | 407 | 3,154 | 3,710 | 4,174 | 496 | 3,154 | 3,710 | 4,174 |
| 9,300 | 9,350 | 403 | 3,171 | 3,730 | 4,196 | 496 | 3,171 | 3,730 | 4,196 |
| 9,350 | 9,400 | 399 | 3,188 | 3,750 | 4,219 | 496 | 3,188 | 3,750 | 4,219 |
| 9,400 | 9,450 | 395 | 3,205 | 3,770 | 4,241 | 496 | 3,205 | 3,770 | 4,241 |
| 9,450 | 9,500 | 391 | 3,222 | 3,790 | 4,264 | 496 | 3,222 | 3,790 | 4,264 |
| 9,500 | 9,550 | 387 | 3,239 | 3,810 | 4,286 | 496 | 3,239 | 3,810 | 4,286 |
| 9,550 | 9,600 | 384 | 3,256 | 3,830 | 4,309 | 496 | 3,256 | 3,830 | 4,309 |
| 9,600 | 9,650 | 380 | 3,273 | 3,850 | 4,331 | 496 | 3,273 | 3,850 | 4,331 |
| 9,650 | 9,700 | 376 | 3,290 | 3,870 | 4,354 | 496 | 3,290 | 3,870 | 4,354 |
| 9,700 | 9,750 | 372 | 3,305 | 3,890 | 4,376 | 496 | 3,305 | 3,890 | 4,376 |
| 9,750 | 9,800 | 368 | 3,305 | 3,910 | 4,399 | 496 | 3,305 | 3,910 | 4,399 |
| 9,800 | 9,850 | 365 | 3,305 | 3,930 | 4,421 | 496 | 3,305 | 3,930 | 4,421 |
| 9,850 | 9,900 | 361 | 3,305 | 3,950 | 4,444 | 496 | 3,305 | 3,950 | 4,444 |
| 9,900 | 9,950 | 357 | 3,305 | 3,970 | 4,466 | 496 | 3,305 | 3,970 | 4,466 |
| 9,950 | 10,000 | 353 | 3,305 | 3,990 | 4,489 | 496 | 3,305 | 3,990 | 4,489 |
| 10,000 | 10,050 | 349 | 3,305 | 4,010 | 4,511 | 496 | 3,305 | 4,010 | 4,511 |
| 10,050 | 10,100 | 345 | 3,305 | 4,030 | 4,534 | 496 | 3,305 | 4,030 | 4,534 |
| 10,100 | 10,150 | 342 | 3,305 | 4,050 | 4,556 | 496 | 3,305 | 4,050 | 4,556 |
| 10,150 | 10,200 | 338 | 3,305 | 4,070 | 4,579 | 496 | 3,305 | 4,070 | 4,579 |
| 10,200 | 10,250 | 334 | 3,305 | 4,090 | 4,601 | 496 | 3,305 | 4,090 | 4,601 |
| 10,250 | 10,300 | 330 | 3,305 | 4,110 | 4,624 | 496 | 3,305 | 4,110 | 4,624 |
| 10,300 | 10,350 | 326 | 3,305 | 4,130 | 4,646 | 496 | 3,305 | 4,130 | 4,646 |
| 10,350 | 10,400 | 322 | 3,305 | 4,150 | 4,669 | 496 | 3,305 | 4,150 | 4,669 |
| 10,400 | 10,450 | 319 | 3,305 | 4,170 | 4,691 | 496 | 3,305 | 4,170 | 4,691 |
| 10,450 | 10,500 | 315 | 3,305 | 4,190 | 4,714 | 496 | 3,305 | 4,190 | 4,714 |
| 10,500 | 10,550 | 311 | 3,305 | 4,210 | 4,736 | 496 | 3,305 | 4,210 | 4,736 |
| 10,550 | 10,600 | 307 | 3,305 | 4,230 | 4,759 | 496 | 3,305 | 4,230 | 4,759 |
| 10,600 | 10,650 | 303 | 3,305 | 4,250 | 4,781 | 496 | 3,305 | 4,250 | 4,781 |
| 10,650 | 10,700 | 299 | 3,305 | 4,270 | 4,804 | 496 | 3,305 | 4,270 | 4,804 |
| 10,700 | 10,750 | 296 | 3,305 | 4,290 | 4,826 | 496 | 3,305 | 4,290 | 4,826 |
| 10,750 | 10,800 | 292 | 3,305 | 4,310 | 4,849 | 496 | 3,305 | 4,310 | 4,849 |
| 10,800 | 10,850 | 288 | 3,305 | 4,330 | 4,871 | 496 | 3,305 | 4,330 | 4,871 |
| 10,850 | 10,900 | 284 | 3,305 | 4,350 | 4,894 | 496 | 3,305 | 4,350 | 4,894 |
| 10,900 | 10,950 | 280 | 3,305 | 4,370 | 4,916 | 496 | 3,305 | 4,370 | 4,916 |
| 10,950 | 11,000 | 277 | 3,305 | 4,390 | 4,939 | 496 | 3,305 | 4,390 | 4,939 |
| 11,000 | 11,050 | 273 | 3,305 | 4,410 | 4,961 | 496 | 3,305 | 4,410 | 4,961 |
| 11,050 | 11,100 | 269 | 3,305 | 4,430 | 4,984 | 496 | 3,305 | 4,430 | 4,984 |
| 11,100 | 11,150 | 265 | 3,305 | 4,450 | 5,006 | 496 | 3,305 | 4,450 | 5,006 |
| 11,150 | 11,200 | 261 | 3,305 | 4,470 | 5,029 | 496 | 3,305 | 4,470 | 5,029 |
| 11,200 | 11,250 | 257 | 3,305 | 4,490 | 5,051 | 496 | 3,305 | 4,490 | 5,051 |
| 11,250 | 11,300 | 254 | 3,305 | 4,510 | 5,074 | 496 | 3,305 | 4,510 | 5,074 |
| 11,300 | 11,350 | 250 | 3,305 | 4,530 | 5,096 | 496 | 3,305 | 4,530 | 5,096 |
| 11,350 | 11,400 | 246 | 3,305 | 4,550 | 5,119 | 496 | 3,305 | 4,550 | 5,119 |
| 11,400 | 11,450 | 242 | 3,305 | 4,570 | 5,141 | 496 | 3,305 | 4,570 | 5,141 |
| 11,450 | 11,500 | 238 | 3,305 | 4,590 | 5,164 | 496 | 3,305 | 4,590 | 5,164 |
| 11,500 | 11,550 | 234 | 3,305 | 4,610 | 5,186 | 496 | 3,305 | 4,610 | 5,186 |
| 11,550 | 11,600 | 231 | 3,305 | 4,630 | 5,209 | 496 | 3,305 | 4,630 | 5,209 |
| 11,600 | 11,650 | 227 | 3,305 | 4,650 | 5,231 | 496 | 3,305 | 4,650 | 5,231 |
| 11,650 | 11,700 | 223 | 3,305 | 4,670 | 5,254 | 496 | 3,305 | 4,670 | 5,254 |
| 11,700 | 11,750 | 219 | 3,305 | 4,690 | 5,276 | 496 | 3,305 | 4,690 | 5,276 |
| 11,750 | 11,800 | 215 | 3,305 | 4,710 | 5,299 | 496 | 3,305 | 4,710 | 5,299 |
| 11,800 | 11,850 | 212 | 3,305 | 4,730 | 5,321 | 496 | 3,305 | 4,730 | 5,321 |
| 11,850 | 11,900 | 208 | 3,305 | 4,750 | 5,344 | 496 | 3,305 | 4,750 | 5,344 |
| 11,900 | 11,950 | 204 | 3,305 | 4,770 | 5,366 | 496 | 3,305 | 4,770 | 5,366 |
| 11,950 | 12,000 | 200 | 3,305 | 4,790 | 5,389 | 496 | 3,305 | 4,790 | 5,389 |
| 12,000 | 12,050 | 196 | 3,305 | 4,810 | 5,411 | 496 | 3,305 | 4,810 | 5,411 |
| 12,050 | 12,100 | 192 | 3,305 | 4,830 | 5,434 | 496 | 3,305 | 4,830 | 5,434 |
| 12,100 | 12,150 | 189 | 3,305 | 4,850 | 5,456 | 496 | 3,305 | 4,850 | 5,456 |
| 12,150 | 12,200 | 185 | 3,305 | 4,870 | 5,479 | 496 | 3,305 | 4,870 | 5,479 |
| 12,200 | 12,250 | 181 | 3,305 | 4,890 | 5,501 | 496 | 3,305 | 4,890 | 5,501 |
| 12,250 | 12,300 | 177 | 3,305 | 4,910 | 5,524 | 496 | 3,305 | 4,910 | 5,524 |
| 12,300 | 12,350 | 173 | 3,305 | 4,930 | 5,546 | 496 | 3,305 | 4,930 | 5,546 |
| 12,350 | 12,400 | 169 | 3,305 | 4,950 | 5,569 | 496 | 3,305 | 4,950 | 5,569 |
| 12,400 | 12,450 | 166 | 3,305 | 4,970 | 5,591 | 496 | 3,305 | 4,970 | 5,591 |
| 12,450 | 12,500 | 162 | 3,305 | 4,990 | 5,614 | 496 | 3,305 | 4,990 | 5,614 |
| 12,500 | 12,550 | 158 | 3,305 | 5,010 | 5,636 | 496 | 3,305 | 5,010 | 5,636 |
| 12,550 | 12,600 | 154 | 3,305 | 5,030 | 5,659 | 496 | 3,305 | 5,030 | 5,659 |
| 12,600 | 12,650 | 150 | 3,305 | 5,050 | 5,681 | 496 | 3,305 | 5,050 | 5,681 |
| 12,650 | 12,700 | 146 | 3,305 | 5,070 | 5,704 | 496 | 3,305 | 5,070 | 5,704 |
| 12,700 | 12,750 | 143 | 3,305 | 5,090 | 5,726 | 496 | 3,305 | 5,090 | 5,726 |
| 12,750 | 12,800 | 139 | 3,305 | 5,110 | 5,749 | 496 | 3,305 | 5,110 | 5,749 |

*(Continued)*

# 2014 Earned Income Credit Table

**Earned Income Credit (EIC) Table** - *Continued*  (**Caution.** This is **not** a tax table.)

| If the amount you are looking up from the worksheet is– | | Single, head of household, or qualifying widow(er) and the number of children you have is– | | | | Married filing jointly and the number of children you have is– | | | |
|---|---|---|---|---|---|---|---|---|---|
| At least | But less than | 0 | 1 | 2 | 3 | 0 | 1 | 2 | 3 |
| | | Your credit is– | | | | Your credit is– | | | |
| 12,800 | 12,850 | 135 | 3,305 | 5,130 | 5,771 | 496 | 3,305 | 5,130 | 5,771 |
| 12,850 | 12,900 | 131 | 3,305 | 5,150 | 5,794 | 496 | 3,305 | 5,150 | 5,794 |
| 12,900 | 12,950 | 127 | 3,305 | 5,170 | 5,816 | 496 | 3,305 | 5,170 | 5,816 |
| 12,950 | 13,000 | 124 | 3,305 | 5,190 | 5,839 | 496 | 3,305 | 5,190 | 5,839 |
| 13,000 | 13,050 | 120 | 3,305 | 5,210 | 5,861 | 496 | 3,305 | 5,210 | 5,861 |
| 13,050 | 13,100 | 116 | 3,305 | 5,230 | 5,884 | 496 | 3,305 | 5,230 | 5,884 |
| 13,100 | 13,150 | 112 | 3,305 | 5,250 | 5,906 | 496 | 3,305 | 5,250 | 5,906 |
| 13,150 | 13,200 | 108 | 3,305 | 5,270 | 5,929 | 496 | 3,305 | 5,270 | 5,929 |
| 13,200 | 13,250 | 104 | 3,305 | 5,290 | 5,951 | 496 | 3,305 | 5,290 | 5,951 |
| 13,250 | 13,300 | 101 | 3,305 | 5,310 | 5,974 | 496 | 3,305 | 5,310 | 5,974 |
| 13,300 | 13,350 | 97 | 3,305 | 5,330 | 5,996 | 496 | 3,305 | 5,330 | 5,996 |
| 13,350 | 13,400 | 93 | 3,305 | 5,350 | 6,019 | 496 | 3,305 | 5,350 | 6,019 |
| 13,400 | 13,450 | 89 | 3,305 | 5,370 | 6,041 | 496 | 3,305 | 5,370 | 6,041 |
| 13,450 | 13,500 | 85 | 3,305 | 5,390 | 6,064 | 496 | 3,305 | 5,390 | 6,064 |
| 13,500 | 13,550 | 81 | 3,305 | 5,410 | 6,086 | 496 | 3,305 | 5,410 | 6,086 |
| 13,550 | 13,600 | 78 | 3,305 | 5,430 | 6,109 | 493 | 3,305 | 5,430 | 6,109 |
| 13,600 | 13,650 | 74 | 3,305 | 5,450 | 6,131 | 489 | 3,305 | 5,450 | 6,131 |
| 13,650 | 13,700 | 70 | 3,305 | 5,460 | 6,143 | 485 | 3,305 | 5,460 | 6,143 |
| 13,700 | 13,750 | 66 | 3,305 | 5,460 | 6,143 | 482 | 3,305 | 5,460 | 6,143 |
| 13,750 | 13,800 | 62 | 3,305 | 5,460 | 6,143 | 478 | 3,305 | 5,460 | 6,143 |
| 13,800 | 13,850 | 59 | 3,305 | 5,460 | 6,143 | 474 | 3,305 | 5,460 | 6,143 |
| 13,850 | 13,900 | 55 | 3,305 | 5,460 | 6,143 | 470 | 3,305 | 5,460 | 6,143 |
| 13,900 | 13,950 | 51 | 3,305 | 5,460 | 6,143 | 466 | 3,305 | 5,460 | 6,143 |
| 13,950 | 14,000 | 47 | 3,305 | 5,460 | 6,143 | 462 | 3,305 | 5,460 | 6,143 |
| 14,000 | 14,050 | 43 | 3,305 | 5,460 | 6,143 | 459 | 3,305 | 5,460 | 6,143 |
| 14,050 | 14,100 | 39 | 3,305 | 5,460 | 6,143 | 455 | 3,305 | 5,460 | 6,143 |
| 14,100 | 14,150 | 36 | 3,305 | 5,460 | 6,143 | 451 | 3,305 | 5,460 | 6,143 |
| 14,150 | 14,200 | 32 | 3,305 | 5,460 | 6,143 | 447 | 3,305 | 5,460 | 6,143 |
| 14,200 | 14,250 | 28 | 3,305 | 5,460 | 6,143 | 443 | 3,305 | 5,460 | 6,143 |
| 14,250 | 14,300 | 24 | 3,305 | 5,460 | 6,143 | 439 | 3,305 | 5,460 | 6,143 |
| 14,300 | 14,350 | 20 | 3,305 | 5,460 | 6,143 | 436 | 3,305 | 5,460 | 6,143 |
| 14,350 | 14,400 | 16 | 3,305 | 5,460 | 6,143 | 432 | 3,305 | 5,460 | 6,143 |
| 14,400 | 14,450 | 13 | 3,305 | 5,460 | 6,143 | 428 | 3,305 | 5,460 | 6,143 |
| 14,450 | 14,500 | 9 | 3,305 | 5,460 | 6,143 | 424 | 3,305 | 5,460 | 6,143 |
| 14,500 | 14,550 | 5 | 3,305 | 5,460 | 6,143 | 420 | 3,305 | 5,460 | 6,143 |
| 14,550 | 14,600 | * | 3,305 | 5,460 | 6,143 | 417 | 3,305 | 5,460 | 6,143 |
| 14,600 | 14,650 | 0 | 3,305 | 5,460 | 6,143 | 413 | 3,305 | 5,460 | 6,143 |
| 14,650 | 14,700 | 0 | 3,305 | 5,460 | 6,143 | 409 | 3,305 | 5,460 | 6,143 |
| 14,700 | 14,750 | 0 | 3,305 | 5,460 | 6,143 | 405 | 3,305 | 5,460 | 6,143 |
| 14,750 | 14,800 | 0 | 3,305 | 5,460 | 6,143 | 401 | 3,305 | 5,460 | 6,143 |
| 14,800 | 14,850 | 0 | 3,305 | 5,460 | 6,143 | 397 | 3,305 | 5,460 | 6,143 |
| 14,850 | 14,900 | 0 | 3,305 | 5,460 | 6,143 | 394 | 3,305 | 5,460 | 6,143 |
| 14,900 | 14,950 | 0 | 3,305 | 5,460 | 6,143 | 390 | 3,305 | 5,460 | 6,143 |
| 14,950 | 15,000 | 0 | 3,305 | 5,460 | 6,143 | 386 | 3,305 | 5,460 | 6,143 |
| 15,000 | 15,050 | 0 | 3,305 | 5,460 | 6,143 | 382 | 3,305 | 5,460 | 6,143 |
| 15,050 | 15,100 | 0 | 3,305 | 5,460 | 6,143 | 378 | 3,305 | 5,460 | 6,143 |
| 15,100 | 15,150 | 0 | 3,305 | 5,460 | 6,143 | 374 | 3,305 | 5,460 | 6,143 |
| 15,150 | 15,200 | 0 | 3,305 | 5,460 | 6,143 | 371 | 3,305 | 5,460 | 6,143 |
| 15,200 | 15,250 | 0 | 3,305 | 5,460 | 6,143 | 367 | 3,305 | 5,460 | 6,143 |
| 15,250 | 15,300 | 0 | 3,305 | 5,460 | 6,143 | 363 | 3,305 | 5,460 | 6,143 |
| 15,300 | 15,350 | 0 | 3,305 | 5,460 | 6,143 | 359 | 3,305 | 5,460 | 6,143 |
| 15,350 | 15,400 | 0 | 3,305 | 5,460 | 6,143 | 355 | 3,305 | 5,460 | 6,143 |
| 15,400 | 15,450 | 0 | 3,305 | 5,460 | 6,143 | 352 | 3,305 | 5,460 | 6,143 |
| 15,450 | 15,500 | 0 | 3,305 | 5,460 | 6,143 | 348 | 3,305 | 5,460 | 6,143 |
| 15,500 | 15,550 | 0 | 3,305 | 5,460 | 6,143 | 344 | 3,305 | 5,460 | 6,143 |
| 15,550 | 15,600 | 0 | 3,305 | 5,460 | 6,143 | 340 | 3,305 | 5,460 | 6,143 |
| 15,600 | 15,650 | 0 | 3,305 | 5,460 | 6,143 | 336 | 3,305 | 5,460 | 6,143 |
| 15,650 | 15,700 | 0 | 3,305 | 5,460 | 6,143 | 332 | 3,305 | 5,460 | 6,143 |
| 15,700 | 15,750 | 0 | 3,305 | 5,460 | 6,143 | 329 | 3,305 | 5,460 | 6,143 |
| 15,750 | 15,800 | 0 | 3,305 | 5,460 | 6,143 | 325 | 3,305 | 5,460 | 6,143 |
| 15,800 | 15,850 | 0 | 3,305 | 5,460 | 6,143 | 321 | 3,305 | 5,460 | 6,143 |
| 15,850 | 15,900 | 0 | 3,305 | 5,460 | 6,143 | 317 | 3,305 | 5,460 | 6,143 |
| 15,900 | 15,950 | 0 | 3,305 | 5,460 | 6,143 | 313 | 3,305 | 5,460 | 6,143 |
| 15,950 | 16,000 | 0 | 3,305 | 5,460 | 6,143 | 309 | 3,305 | 5,460 | 6,143 |
| 16,000 | 16,050 | 0 | 3,305 | 5,460 | 6,143 | 306 | 3,305 | 5,460 | 6,143 |
| 16,050 | 16,100 | 0 | 3,305 | 5,460 | 6,143 | 302 | 3,305 | 5,460 | 6,143 |
| 16,100 | 16,150 | 0 | 3,305 | 5,460 | 6,143 | 298 | 3,305 | 5,460 | 6,143 |
| 16,150 | 16,200 | 0 | 3,305 | 5,460 | 6,143 | 294 | 3,305 | 5,460 | 6,143 |
| 16,200 | 16,250 | 0 | 3,305 | 5,460 | 6,143 | 290 | 3,305 | 5,460 | 6,143 |
| 16,250 | 16,300 | 0 | 3,305 | 5,460 | 6,143 | 286 | 3,305 | 5,460 | 6,143 |
| 16,300 | 16,350 | 0 | 3,305 | 5,460 | 6,143 | 283 | 3,305 | 5,460 | 6,143 |
| 16,350 | 16,400 | 0 | 3,305 | 5,460 | 6,143 | 279 | 3,305 | 5,460 | 6,143 |
| 16,400 | 16,450 | 0 | 3,305 | 5,460 | 6,143 | 275 | 3,305 | 5,460 | 6,143 |
| 16,450 | 16,500 | 0 | 3,305 | 5,460 | 6,143 | 271 | 3,305 | 5,460 | 6,143 |
| 16,500 | 16,550 | 0 | 3,305 | 5,460 | 6,143 | 267 | 3,305 | 5,460 | 6,143 |
| 16,550 | 16,600 | 0 | 3,305 | 5,460 | 6,143 | 264 | 3,305 | 5,460 | 6,143 |
| 16,600 | 16,650 | 0 | 3,305 | 5,460 | 6,143 | 260 | 3,305 | 5,460 | 6,143 |
| 16,650 | 16,700 | 0 | 3,305 | 5,460 | 6,143 | 256 | 3,305 | 5,460 | 6,143 |
| 16,700 | 16,750 | 0 | 3,305 | 5,460 | 6,143 | 252 | 3,305 | 5,460 | 6,143 |
| 16,750 | 16,800 | 0 | 3,305 | 5,460 | 6,143 | 248 | 3,305 | 5,460 | 6,143 |
| 16,800 | 16,850 | 0 | 3,305 | 5,460 | 6,143 | 244 | 3,305 | 5,460 | 6,143 |
| 16,850 | 16,900 | 0 | 3,305 | 5,460 | 6,143 | 241 | 3,305 | 5,460 | 6,143 |
| 16,900 | 16,950 | 0 | 3,305 | 5,460 | 6,143 | 237 | 3,305 | 5,460 | 6,143 |
| 16,950 | 17,000 | 0 | 3,305 | 5,460 | 6,143 | 233 | 3,305 | 5,460 | 6,143 |
| 17,000 | 17,050 | 0 | 3,305 | 5,460 | 6,143 | 229 | 3,305 | 5,460 | 6,143 |
| 17,050 | 17,100 | 0 | 3,305 | 5,460 | 6,143 | 225 | 3,305 | 5,460 | 6,143 |
| 17,100 | 17,150 | 0 | 3,305 | 5,460 | 6,143 | 221 | 3,305 | 5,460 | 6,143 |
| 17,150 | 17,200 | 0 | 3,305 | 5,460 | 6,143 | 218 | 3,305 | 5,460 | 6,143 |
| 17,200 | 17,250 | 0 | 3,305 | 5,460 | 6,143 | 214 | 3,305 | 5,460 | 6,143 |
| 17,250 | 17,300 | 0 | 3,305 | 5,460 | 6,143 | 210 | 3,305 | 5,460 | 6,143 |
| 17,300 | 17,350 | 0 | 3,305 | 5,460 | 6,143 | 206 | 3,305 | 5,460 | 6,143 |
| 17,350 | 17,400 | 0 | 3,305 | 5,460 | 6,143 | 202 | 3,305 | 5,460 | 6,143 |
| 17,400 | 17,450 | 0 | 3,305 | 5,460 | 6,143 | 199 | 3,305 | 5,460 | 6,143 |
| 17,450 | 17,500 | 0 | 3,305 | 5,460 | 6,143 | 195 | 3,305 | 5,460 | 6,143 |
| 17,500 | 17,550 | 0 | 3,305 | 5,460 | 6,143 | 191 | 3,305 | 5,460 | 6,143 |
| 17,550 | 17,600 | 0 | 3,305 | 5,460 | 6,143 | 187 | 3,305 | 5,460 | 6,143 |
| 17,600 | 17,650 | 0 | 3,305 | 5,460 | 6,143 | 183 | 3,305 | 5,460 | 6,143 |
| 17,650 | 17,700 | 0 | 3,305 | 5,460 | 6,143 | 179 | 3,305 | 5,460 | 6,143 |
| 17,700 | 17,750 | 0 | 3,305 | 5,460 | 6,143 | 176 | 3,305 | 5,460 | 6,143 |
| 17,750 | 17,800 | 0 | 3,305 | 5,460 | 6,143 | 172 | 3,305 | 5,460 | 6,143 |
| 17,800 | 17,850 | 0 | 3,305 | 5,460 | 6,143 | 168 | 3,305 | 5,460 | 6,143 |
| 17,850 | 17,900 | 0 | 3,298 | 5,451 | 6,133 | 164 | 3,305 | 5,460 | 6,143 |
| 17,900 | 17,950 | 0 | 3,290 | 5,440 | 6,122 | 160 | 3,305 | 5,460 | 6,143 |
| 17,950 | 18,000 | 0 | 3,282 | 5,429 | 6,112 | 156 | 3,305 | 5,460 | 6,143 |
| 18,000 | 18,050 | 0 | 3,274 | 5,419 | 6,101 | 153 | 3,305 | 5,460 | 6,143 |
| 18,050 | 18,100 | 0 | 3,266 | 5,408 | 6,091 | 149 | 3,305 | 5,460 | 6,143 |
| 18,100 | 18,150 | 0 | 3,258 | 5,398 | 6,080 | 145 | 3,305 | 5,460 | 6,143 |
| 18,150 | 18,200 | 0 | 3,250 | 5,387 | 6,070 | 141 | 3,305 | 5,460 | 6,143 |
| 18,200 | 18,250 | 0 | 3,242 | 5,377 | 6,059 | 137 | 3,305 | 5,460 | 6,143 |
| 18,250 | 18,300 | 0 | 3,234 | 5,366 | 6,049 | 133 | 3,305 | 5,460 | 6,143 |
| 18,300 | 18,350 | 0 | 3,226 | 5,356 | 6,038 | 130 | 3,305 | 5,460 | 6,143 |
| 18,350 | 18,400 | 0 | 3,218 | 5,345 | 6,028 | 126 | 3,305 | 5,460 | 6,143 |
| 18,400 | 18,450 | 0 | 3,210 | 5,335 | 6,017 | 122 | 3,305 | 5,460 | 6,143 |
| 18,450 | 18,500 | 0 | 3,202 | 5,324 | 6,007 | 118 | 3,305 | 5,460 | 6,143 |
| 18,500 | 18,550 | 0 | 3,194 | 5,314 | 5,996 | 114 | 3,305 | 5,460 | 6,143 |
| 18,550 | 18,600 | 0 | 3,186 | 5,303 | 5,986 | 111 | 3,305 | 5,460 | 6,143 |
| 18,600 | 18,650 | 0 | 3,178 | 5,293 | 5,975 | 107 | 3,305 | 5,460 | 6,143 |
| 18,650 | 18,700 | 0 | 3,170 | 5,282 | 5,965 | 103 | 3,305 | 5,460 | 6,143 |
| 18,700 | 18,750 | 0 | 3,162 | 5,272 | 5,954 | 99 | 3,305 | 5,460 | 6,143 |
| 18,750 | 18,800 | 0 | 3,154 | 5,261 | 5,943 | 95 | 3,305 | 5,460 | 6,143 |
| 18,800 | 18,850 | 0 | 3,146 | 5,250 | 5,933 | 91 | 3,305 | 5,460 | 6,143 |
| 18,850 | 18,900 | 0 | 3,138 | 5,240 | 5,922 | 88 | 3,305 | 5,460 | 6,143 |
| 18,900 | 18,950 | 0 | 3,130 | 5,229 | 5,912 | 84 | 3,305 | 5,460 | 6,143 |
| 18,950 | 19,000 | 0 | 3,122 | 5,219 | 5,901 | 80 | 3,305 | 5,460 | 6,143 |
| 19,000 | 19,050 | 0 | 3,114 | 5,208 | 5,891 | 76 | 3,305 | 5,460 | 6,143 |
| 19,050 | 19,100 | 0 | 3,106 | 5,198 | 5,880 | 72 | 3,305 | 5,460 | 6,143 |
| 19,100 | 19,150 | 0 | 3,098 | 5,187 | 5,870 | 68 | 3,305 | 5,460 | 6,143 |
| 19,150 | 19,200 | 0 | 3,090 | 5,177 | 5,859 | 65 | 3,305 | 5,460 | 6,143 |

*If the amount you are looking up from the worksheet is at least $14,550 but less than $14,590, and you have no qualifying children, your credit is $2
If the amount you are looking up from the worksheet is $14,590 or more, and you have no qualifying children, you cannot take the credit.

*(Continued)*

**Earned Income Credit (EIC) Table** - *Continued*  (**Caution.** This is **not** a tax table.)

| If the amount you are looking up from the worksheet is— | | Single, head of household, or qualifying widow(er) and the number of children you have is— | | | | Married filing jointly and the number of children you have is— | | | |
|---|---|---|---|---|---|---|---|---|---|
| At least | But less than | 0 | 1 | 2 | 3 | 0 | 1 | 2 | 3 |
| | | Your credit is— | | | | Your credit is— | | | |
| 19,200 | 19,250 | 0 | 3,082 | 5,166 | 5,849 | 61 | 3,305 | 5,460 | 6,143 |
| 19,250 | 19,300 | 0 | 3,074 | 5,156 | 5,838 | 57 | 3,305 | 5,460 | 6,143 |
| 19,300 | 19,350 | 0 | 3,066 | 5,145 | 5,828 | 53 | 3,305 | 5,460 | 6,143 |
| 19,350 | 19,400 | 0 | 3,058 | 5,135 | 5,817 | 49 | 3,305 | 5,460 | 6,143 |
| 19,400 | 19,450 | 0 | 3,050 | 5,124 | 5,807 | 46 | 3,305 | 5,460 | 6,143 |
| 19,450 | 19,500 | 0 | 3,042 | 5,114 | 5,796 | 42 | 3,305 | 5,460 | 6,143 |
| 19,500 | 19,550 | 0 | 3,034 | 5,103 | 5,786 | 38 | 3,305 | 5,460 | 6,143 |
| 19,550 | 19,600 | 0 | 3,026 | 5,093 | 5,775 | 34 | 3,305 | 5,460 | 6,143 |
| 19,600 | 19,650 | 0 | 3,018 | 5,082 | 5,764 | 30 | 3,305 | 5,460 | 6,143 |
| 19,650 | 19,700 | 0 | 3,010 | 5,071 | 5,754 | 26 | 3,305 | 5,460 | 6,143 |
| 19,700 | 19,750 | 0 | 3,002 | 5,061 | 5,743 | 23 | 3,305 | 5,460 | 6,143 |
| 19,750 | 19,800 | 0 | 2,994 | 5,050 | 5,733 | 19 | 3,305 | 5,460 | 6,143 |
| 19,800 | 19,850 | 0 | 2,986 | 5,040 | 5,722 | 15 | 3,305 | 5,460 | 6,143 |
| 19,850 | 19,900 | 0 | 2,978 | 5,029 | 5,712 | 11 | 3,305 | 5,460 | 6,143 |
| 19,900 | 19,950 | 0 | 2,970 | 5,019 | 5,701 | 7 | 3,305 | 5,460 | 6,143 |
| 19,950 | 20,000 | 0 | 2,962 | 5,008 | 5,691 | 3 | 3,305 | 5,460 | 6,143 |
| 20,000 | 20,050 | 0 | 2,954 | 4,998 | 5,680 | * | 3,305 | 5,460 | 6,143 |
| 20,050 | 20,100 | 0 | 2,946 | 4,987 | 5,670 | 0 | 3,305 | 5,460 | 6,143 |
| 20,100 | 20,150 | 0 | 2,938 | 4,977 | 5,659 | 0 | 3,305 | 5,460 | 6,143 |
| 20,150 | 20,200 | 0 | 2,930 | 4,966 | 5,649 | 0 | 3,305 | 5,460 | 6,143 |
| 20,200 | 20,250 | 0 | 2,922 | 4,956 | 5,638 | 0 | 3,305 | 5,460 | 6,143 |
| 20,250 | 20,300 | 0 | 2,914 | 4,945 | 5,628 | 0 | 3,305 | 5,460 | 6,143 |
| 20,300 | 20,350 | 0 | 2,906 | 4,935 | 5,617 | 0 | 3,305 | 5,460 | 6,143 |
| 20,350 | 20,400 | 0 | 2,898 | 4,924 | 5,607 | 0 | 3,305 | 5,460 | 6,143 |
| 20,400 | 20,450 | 0 | 2,890 | 4,913 | 5,596 | 0 | 3,305 | 5,460 | 6,143 |
| 20,450 | 20,500 | 0 | 2,882 | 4,903 | 5,585 | 0 | 3,305 | 5,460 | 6,143 |
| 20,500 | 20,550 | 0 | 2,874 | 4,892 | 5,575 | 0 | 3,305 | 5,460 | 6,143 |
| 20,550 | 20,600 | 0 | 2,866 | 4,882 | 5,564 | 0 | 3,305 | 5,460 | 6,143 |
| 20,600 | 20,650 | 0 | 2,858 | 4,871 | 5,554 | 0 | 3,305 | 5,460 | 6,143 |
| 20,650 | 20,700 | 0 | 2,850 | 4,861 | 5,543 | 0 | 3,305 | 5,460 | 6,143 |
| 20,700 | 20,750 | 0 | 2,842 | 4,850 | 5,533 | 0 | 3,305 | 5,460 | 6,143 |
| 20,750 | 20,800 | 0 | 2,834 | 4,840 | 5,522 | 0 | 3,305 | 5,460 | 6,143 |
| 20,800 | 20,850 | 0 | 2,826 | 4,829 | 5,512 | 0 | 3,305 | 5,460 | 6,143 |
| 20,850 | 20,900 | 0 | 2,818 | 4,819 | 5,501 | 0 | 3,305 | 5,460 | 6,143 |
| 20,900 | 20,950 | 0 | 2,810 | 4,808 | 5,491 | 0 | 3,305 | 5,460 | 6,143 |
| 20,950 | 21,000 | 0 | 2,802 | 4,798 | 5,480 | 0 | 3,305 | 5,460 | 6,143 |
| 21,000 | 21,050 | 0 | 2,794 | 4,787 | 5,470 | 0 | 3,305 | 5,460 | 6,143 |
| 21,050 | 21,100 | 0 | 2,786 | 4,777 | 5,459 | 0 | 3,305 | 5,460 | 6,143 |
| 21,100 | 21,150 | 0 | 2,778 | 4,766 | 5,449 | 0 | 3,305 | 5,460 | 6,143 |
| 21,150 | 21,200 | 0 | 2,770 | 4,756 | 5,438 | 0 | 3,305 | 5,460 | 6,143 |
| 21,200 | 21,250 | 0 | 2,762 | 4,745 | 5,428 | 0 | 3,305 | 5,460 | 6,143 |
| 21,250 | 21,300 | 0 | 2,754 | 4,734 | 5,417 | 0 | 3,305 | 5,460 | 6,143 |
| 21,300 | 21,350 | 0 | 2,746 | 4,724 | 5,406 | 0 | 3,305 | 5,460 | 6,143 |
| 21,350 | 21,400 | 0 | 2,738 | 4,713 | 5,396 | 0 | 3,305 | 5,460 | 6,143 |
| 21,400 | 21,450 | 0 | 2,730 | 4,703 | 5,385 | 0 | 3,305 | 5,460 | 6,143 |
| 21,450 | 21,500 | 0 | 2,722 | 4,692 | 5,375 | 0 | 3,305 | 5,460 | 6,143 |
| 21,500 | 21,550 | 0 | 2,714 | 4,682 | 5,364 | 0 | 3,305 | 5,460 | 6,143 |
| 21,550 | 21,600 | 0 | 2,706 | 4,671 | 5,354 | 0 | 3,305 | 5,460 | 6,143 |
| 21,600 | 21,650 | 0 | 2,698 | 4,661 | 5,343 | 0 | 3,305 | 5,460 | 6,143 |
| 21,650 | 21,700 | 0 | 2,690 | 4,650 | 5,333 | 0 | 3,305 | 5,460 | 6,143 |
| 21,700 | 21,750 | 0 | 2,682 | 4,640 | 5,322 | 0 | 3,305 | 5,460 | 6,143 |
| 21,750 | 21,800 | 0 | 2,674 | 4,629 | 5,312 | 0 | 3,305 | 5,460 | 6,143 |
| 21,800 | 21,850 | 0 | 2,666 | 4,619 | 5,301 | 0 | 3,305 | 5,460 | 6,143 |
| 21,850 | 21,900 | 0 | 2,658 | 4,608 | 5,291 | 0 | 3,305 | 5,460 | 6,143 |
| 21,900 | 21,950 | 0 | 2,650 | 4,598 | 5,280 | 0 | 3,305 | 5,460 | 6,143 |
| 21,950 | 22,000 | 0 | 2,642 | 4,587 | 5,270 | 0 | 3,305 | 5,460 | 6,143 |
| 22,000 | 22,050 | 0 | 2,634 | 4,577 | 5,259 | 0 | 3,305 | 5,460 | 6,143 |
| 22,050 | 22,100 | 0 | 2,626 | 4,566 | 5,249 | 0 | 3,305 | 5,460 | 6,143 |
| 22,100 | 22,150 | 0 | 2,618 | 4,555 | 5,238 | 0 | 3,305 | 5,460 | 6,143 |
| 22,150 | 22,200 | 0 | 2,610 | 4,545 | 5,227 | 0 | 3,305 | 5,460 | 6,143 |
| 22,200 | 22,250 | 0 | 2,602 | 4,534 | 5,217 | 0 | 3,305 | 5,460 | 6,143 |
| 22,250 | 22,300 | 0 | 2,594 | 4,524 | 5,206 | 0 | 3,305 | 5,460 | 6,143 |
| 22,300 | 22,350 | 0 | 2,586 | 4,513 | 5,196 | 0 | 3,305 | 5,460 | 6,143 |
| 22,350 | 22,400 | 0 | 2,579 | 4,503 | 5,185 | 0 | 3,305 | 5,460 | 6,143 |

| If the amount you are looking up from the worksheet is— | | Single, head of household, or qualifying widow(er) and the number of children you have is— | | | | Married filing jointly and the number of children you have is— | | | |
|---|---|---|---|---|---|---|---|---|---|
| At least | But less than | 0 | 1 | 2 | 3 | 0 | 1 | 2 | 3 |
| | | Your credit is— | | | | Your credit is— | | | |
| 22,400 | 22,450 | 0 | 2,571 | 4,492 | 5,175 | 0 | 3,305 | 5,460 | 6,143 |
| 22,450 | 22,500 | 0 | 2,563 | 4,482 | 5,164 | 0 | 3,305 | 5,460 | 6,143 |
| 22,500 | 22,550 | 0 | 2,555 | 4,471 | 5,154 | 0 | 3,305 | 5,460 | 6,143 |
| 22,550 | 22,600 | 0 | 2,547 | 4,461 | 5,143 | 0 | 3,305 | 5,460 | 6,143 |
| 22,600 | 22,650 | 0 | 2,539 | 4,450 | 5,133 | 0 | 3,305 | 5,460 | 6,143 |
| 22,650 | 22,700 | 0 | 2,531 | 4,440 | 5,122 | 0 | 3,305 | 5,460 | 6,143 |
| 22,700 | 22,750 | 0 | 2,523 | 4,429 | 5,112 | 0 | 3,305 | 5,460 | 6,143 |
| 22,750 | 22,800 | 0 | 2,515 | 4,419 | 5,101 | 0 | 3,305 | 5,460 | 6,143 |
| 22,800 | 22,850 | 0 | 2,507 | 4,408 | 5,091 | 0 | 3,305 | 5,460 | 6,143 |
| 22,850 | 22,900 | 0 | 2,499 | 4,398 | 5,080 | 0 | 3,305 | 5,460 | 6,143 |
| 22,900 | 22,950 | 0 | 2,491 | 4,387 | 5,069 | 0 | 3,305 | 5,460 | 6,143 |
| 22,950 | 23,000 | 0 | 2,483 | 4,376 | 5,059 | 0 | 3,305 | 5,460 | 6,143 |
| 23,000 | 23,050 | 0 | 2,475 | 4,366 | 5,048 | 0 | 3,305 | 5,460 | 6,143 |
| 23,050 | 23,100 | 0 | 2,467 | 4,355 | 5,038 | 0 | 3,305 | 5,460 | 6,143 |
| 23,100 | 23,150 | 0 | 2,459 | 4,345 | 5,027 | 0 | 3,305 | 5,460 | 6,143 |
| 23,150 | 23,200 | 0 | 2,451 | 4,334 | 5,017 | 0 | 3,305 | 5,460 | 6,143 |
| 23,200 | 23,250 | 0 | 2,443 | 4,324 | 5,006 | 0 | 3,305 | 5,460 | 6,143 |
| 23,250 | 23,300 | 0 | 2,435 | 4,313 | 4,996 | 0 | 3,305 | 5,460 | 6,143 |
| 23,300 | 23,350 | 0 | 2,427 | 4,303 | 4,985 | 0 | 3,294 | 5,446 | 6,129 |
| 23,350 | 23,400 | 0 | 2,419 | 4,292 | 4,975 | 0 | 3,286 | 5,436 | 6,118 |
| 23,400 | 23,450 | 0 | 2,411 | 4,282 | 4,964 | 0 | 3,278 | 5,425 | 6,108 |
| 23,450 | 23,500 | 0 | 2,403 | 4,271 | 4,954 | 0 | 3,270 | 5,415 | 6,097 |
| 23,500 | 23,550 | 0 | 2,395 | 4,261 | 4,943 | 0 | 3,262 | 5,404 | 6,087 |
| 23,550 | 23,600 | 0 | 2,387 | 4,250 | 4,933 | 0 | 3,254 | 5,394 | 6,076 |
| 23,600 | 23,650 | 0 | 2,379 | 4,240 | 4,922 | 0 | 3,246 | 5,383 | 6,066 |
| 23,650 | 23,700 | 0 | 2,371 | 4,229 | 4,912 | 0 | 3,238 | 5,373 | 6,055 |
| 23,700 | 23,750 | 0 | 2,363 | 4,219 | 4,901 | 0 | 3,230 | 5,362 | 6,045 |
| 23,750 | 23,800 | 0 | 2,355 | 4,208 | 4,890 | 0 | 3,223 | 5,352 | 6,034 |
| 23,800 | 23,850 | 0 | 2,347 | 4,197 | 4,880 | 0 | 3,215 | 5,341 | 6,024 |
| 23,850 | 23,900 | 0 | 2,339 | 4,187 | 4,869 | 0 | 3,207 | 5,330 | 6,013 |
| 23,900 | 23,950 | 0 | 2,331 | 4,176 | 4,859 | 0 | 3,199 | 5,320 | 6,002 |
| 23,950 | 24,000 | 0 | 2,323 | 4,166 | 4,848 | 0 | 3,191 | 5,309 | 5,992 |
| 24,000 | 24,050 | 0 | 2,315 | 4,155 | 4,838 | 0 | 3,183 | 5,299 | 5,981 |
| 24,050 | 24,100 | 0 | 2,307 | 4,145 | 4,827 | 0 | 3,175 | 5,288 | 5,971 |
| 24,100 | 24,150 | 0 | 2,299 | 4,134 | 4,817 | 0 | 3,167 | 5,278 | 5,960 |
| 24,150 | 24,200 | 0 | 2,291 | 4,124 | 4,806 | 0 | 3,159 | 5,267 | 5,950 |
| 24,200 | 24,250 | 0 | 2,283 | 4,113 | 4,796 | 0 | 3,151 | 5,257 | 5,939 |
| 24,250 | 24,300 | 0 | 2,275 | 4,103 | 4,785 | 0 | 3,143 | 5,246 | 5,929 |
| 24,300 | 24,350 | 0 | 2,267 | 4,092 | 4,775 | 0 | 3,135 | 5,236 | 5,918 |
| 24,350 | 24,400 | 0 | 2,259 | 4,082 | 4,764 | 0 | 3,127 | 5,225 | 5,908 |
| 24,400 | 24,450 | 0 | 2,251 | 4,071 | 4,754 | 0 | 3,119 | 5,215 | 5,897 |
| 24,450 | 24,500 | 0 | 2,243 | 4,061 | 4,743 | 0 | 3,111 | 5,204 | 5,887 |
| 24,500 | 24,550 | 0 | 2,235 | 4,050 | 4,733 | 0 | 3,103 | 5,194 | 5,876 |
| 24,550 | 24,600 | 0 | 2,227 | 4,040 | 4,722 | 0 | 3,095 | 5,183 | 5,866 |
| 24,600 | 24,650 | 0 | 2,219 | 4,029 | 4,711 | 0 | 3,087 | 5,173 | 5,855 |
| 24,650 | 24,700 | 0 | 2,211 | 4,018 | 4,701 | 0 | 3,079 | 5,162 | 5,845 |
| 24,700 | 24,750 | 0 | 2,203 | 4,008 | 4,690 | 0 | 3,071 | 5,151 | 5,834 |
| 24,750 | 24,800 | 0 | 2,195 | 3,997 | 4,680 | 0 | 3,063 | 5,141 | 5,823 |
| 24,800 | 24,850 | 0 | 2,187 | 3,987 | 4,669 | 0 | 3,055 | 5,130 | 5,813 |
| 24,850 | 24,900 | 0 | 2,179 | 3,976 | 4,659 | 0 | 3,047 | 5,120 | 5,802 |
| 24,900 | 24,950 | 0 | 2,171 | 3,966 | 4,648 | 0 | 3,039 | 5,109 | 5,792 |
| 24,950 | 25,000 | 0 | 2,163 | 3,955 | 4,638 | 0 | 3,031 | 5,099 | 5,781 |
| 25,000 | 25,050 | 0 | 2,155 | 3,945 | 4,627 | 0 | 3,023 | 5,088 | 5,771 |
| 25,050 | 25,100 | 0 | 2,147 | 3,934 | 4,617 | 0 | 3,015 | 5,078 | 5,760 |
| 25,100 | 25,150 | 0 | 2,139 | 3,924 | 4,606 | 0 | 3,007 | 5,067 | 5,750 |
| 25,150 | 25,200 | 0 | 2,131 | 3,913 | 4,596 | 0 | 2,999 | 5,057 | 5,739 |
| 25,200 | 25,250 | 0 | 2,123 | 3,903 | 4,585 | 0 | 2,991 | 5,046 | 5,729 |
| 25,250 | 25,300 | 0 | 2,115 | 3,892 | 4,575 | 0 | 2,983 | 5,036 | 5,718 |
| 25,300 | 25,350 | 0 | 2,107 | 3,882 | 4,564 | 0 | 2,975 | 5,025 | 5,708 |
| 25,350 | 25,400 | 0 | 2,099 | 3,871 | 4,554 | 0 | 2,967 | 5,015 | 5,697 |
| 25,400 | 25,450 | 0 | 2,091 | 3,860 | 4,543 | 0 | 2,959 | 5,004 | 5,687 |
| 25,450 | 25,500 | 0 | 2,083 | 3,850 | 4,532 | 0 | 2,951 | 4,994 | 5,676 |
| 25,500 | 25,550 | 0 | 2,075 | 3,839 | 4,522 | 0 | 2,943 | 4,983 | 5,665 |
| 25,550 | 25,600 | 0 | 2,067 | 3,829 | 4,511 | 0 | 2,935 | 4,972 | 5,655 |

\* If the amount you are looking up from the worksheet is at least $20,000 but less than $20,020, and you have no qualifying children, your credit is $1.
If the amount you are looking up from the worksheet is $20,020 or more, and you have no qualifying children, you cannot take the credit.

*(Continued)*

# 2014 Earned Income Credit Table

**Earned Income Credit (EIC) Table** - *Continued*  (**Caution.** This is **not** a tax table.)

| At least | But less than | Single, HoH or QW — 0 | 1 | 2 | 3 | MFJ — 0 | 1 | 2 | 3 |
|---|---|---|---|---|---|---|---|---|---|
| 25,600 | 25,650 | 0 | 2,059 | 3,818 | 4,501 | 0 | 2,927 | 4,962 | 5,644 |
| 25,650 | 25,700 | 0 | 2,051 | 3,808 | 4,490 | 0 | 2,919 | 4,951 | 5,634 |
| 25,700 | 25,750 | 0 | 2,043 | 3,797 | 4,480 | 0 | 2,911 | 4,941 | 5,623 |
| 25,750 | 25,800 | 0 | 2,035 | 3,787 | 4,469 | 0 | 2,903 | 4,930 | 5,613 |
| 25,800 | 25,850 | 0 | 2,027 | 3,776 | 4,459 | 0 | 2,895 | 4,920 | 5,602 |
| 25,850 | 25,900 | 0 | 2,019 | 3,766 | 4,448 | 0 | 2,887 | 4,909 | 5,592 |
| 25,900 | 25,950 | 0 | 2,011 | 3,755 | 4,438 | 0 | 2,879 | 4,899 | 5,581 |
| 25,950 | 26,000 | 0 | 2,003 | 3,745 | 4,427 | 0 | 2,871 | 4,888 | 5,571 |
| 26,000 | 26,050 | 0 | 1,995 | 3,734 | 4,417 | 0 | 2,863 | 4,878 | 5,560 |
| 26,050 | 26,100 | 0 | 1,987 | 3,724 | 4,406 | 0 | 2,855 | 4,867 | 5,550 |
| 26,100 | 26,150 | 0 | 1,979 | 3,713 | 4,396 | 0 | 2,847 | 4,857 | 5,539 |
| 26,150 | 26,200 | 0 | 1,971 | 3,703 | 4,385 | 0 | 2,839 | 4,846 | 5,529 |
| 26,200 | 26,250 | 0 | 1,963 | 3,692 | 4,375 | 0 | 2,831 | 4,836 | 5,518 |
| 26,250 | 26,300 | 0 | 1,955 | 3,681 | 4,364 | 0 | 2,823 | 4,825 | 5,508 |
| 26,300 | 26,350 | 0 | 1,947 | 3,671 | 4,353 | 0 | 2,815 | 4,815 | 5,497 |
| 26,350 | 26,400 | 0 | 1,939 | 3,660 | 4,343 | 0 | 2,807 | 4,804 | 5,486 |
| 26,400 | 26,450 | 0 | 1,931 | 3,650 | 4,332 | 0 | 2,799 | 4,793 | 5,476 |
| 26,450 | 26,500 | 0 | 1,923 | 3,639 | 4,322 | 0 | 2,791 | 4,783 | 5,465 |
| 26,500 | 26,550 | 0 | 1,915 | 3,629 | 4,311 | 0 | 2,783 | 4,772 | 5,455 |
| 26,550 | 26,600 | 0 | 1,907 | 3,618 | 4,301 | 0 | 2,775 | 4,762 | 5,444 |
| 26,600 | 26,650 | 0 | 1,899 | 3,608 | 4,290 | 0 | 2,767 | 4,751 | 5,434 |
| 26,650 | 26,700 | 0 | 1,891 | 3,597 | 4,280 | 0 | 2,759 | 4,741 | 5,423 |
| 26,700 | 26,750 | 0 | 1,883 | 3,587 | 4,269 | 0 | 2,751 | 4,730 | 5,413 |
| 26,750 | 26,800 | 0 | 1,875 | 3,576 | 4,259 | 0 | 2,743 | 4,720 | 5,402 |
| 26,800 | 26,850 | 0 | 1,867 | 3,566 | 4,248 | 0 | 2,735 | 4,709 | 5,392 |
| 26,850 | 26,900 | 0 | 1,859 | 3,555 | 4,238 | 0 | 2,727 | 4,699 | 5,381 |
| 26,900 | 26,950 | 0 | 1,851 | 3,545 | 4,227 | 0 | 2,719 | 4,688 | 5,371 |
| 26,950 | 27,000 | 0 | 1,843 | 3,534 | 4,217 | 0 | 2,711 | 4,678 | 5,360 |
| 27,000 | 27,050 | 0 | 1,835 | 3,524 | 4,206 | 0 | 2,703 | 4,667 | 5,350 |
| 27,050 | 27,100 | 0 | 1,827 | 3,513 | 4,196 | 0 | 2,695 | 4,657 | 5,339 |
| 27,100 | 27,150 | 0 | 1,819 | 3,502 | 4,185 | 0 | 2,687 | 4,646 | 5,329 |
| 27,150 | 27,200 | 0 | 1,811 | 3,492 | 4,174 | 0 | 2,679 | 4,635 | 5,318 |
| 27,200 | 27,250 | 0 | 1,803 | 3,481 | 4,164 | 0 | 2,671 | 4,625 | 5,307 |
| 27,250 | 27,300 | 0 | 1,795 | 3,471 | 4,153 | 0 | 2,663 | 4,614 | 5,297 |
| 27,300 | 27,350 | 0 | 1,787 | 3,460 | 4,143 | 0 | 2,655 | 4,604 | 5,286 |
| 27,350 | 27,400 | 0 | 1,780 | 3,450 | 4,132 | 0 | 2,647 | 4,593 | 5,276 |
| 27,400 | 27,450 | 0 | 1,772 | 3,439 | 4,122 | 0 | 2,639 | 4,583 | 5,265 |
| 27,450 | 27,500 | 0 | 1,764 | 3,429 | 4,111 | 0 | 2,631 | 4,572 | 5,255 |
| 27,500 | 27,550 | 0 | 1,756 | 3,418 | 4,101 | 0 | 2,623 | 4,562 | 5,244 |
| 27,550 | 27,600 | 0 | 1,748 | 3,408 | 4,090 | 0 | 2,615 | 4,551 | 5,234 |
| 27,600 | 27,650 | 0 | 1,740 | 3,397 | 4,080 | 0 | 2,607 | 4,541 | 5,223 |
| 27,650 | 27,700 | 0 | 1,732 | 3,387 | 4,069 | 0 | 2,599 | 4,530 | 5,213 |
| 27,700 | 27,750 | 0 | 1,724 | 3,376 | 4,059 | 0 | 2,591 | 4,520 | 5,202 |
| 27,750 | 27,800 | 0 | 1,716 | 3,366 | 4,048 | 0 | 2,583 | 4,509 | 5,192 |
| 27,800 | 27,850 | 0 | 1,708 | 3,355 | 4,038 | 0 | 2,575 | 4,499 | 5,181 |
| 27,850 | 27,900 | 0 | 1,700 | 3,345 | 4,027 | 0 | 2,567 | 4,488 | 5,171 |
| 27,900 | 27,950 | 0 | 1,692 | 3,334 | 4,016 | 0 | 2,559 | 4,478 | 5,160 |
| 27,950 | 28,000 | 0 | 1,684 | 3,323 | 4,006 | 0 | 2,551 | 4,467 | 5,150 |
| 28,000 | 28,050 | 0 | 1,676 | 3,313 | 3,995 | 0 | 2,543 | 4,456 | 5,139 |
| 28,050 | 28,100 | 0 | 1,668 | 3,302 | 3,985 | 0 | 2,535 | 4,446 | 5,128 |
| 28,100 | 28,150 | 0 | 1,660 | 3,292 | 3,974 | 0 | 2,527 | 4,435 | 5,118 |
| 28,150 | 28,200 | 0 | 1,652 | 3,281 | 3,964 | 0 | 2,519 | 4,425 | 5,107 |
| 28,200 | 28,250 | 0 | 1,644 | 3,271 | 3,953 | 0 | 2,511 | 4,414 | 5,097 |
| 28,250 | 28,300 | 0 | 1,636 | 3,260 | 3,943 | 0 | 2,503 | 4,404 | 5,086 |
| 28,300 | 28,350 | 0 | 1,628 | 3,250 | 3,932 | 0 | 2,495 | 4,393 | 5,076 |
| 28,350 | 28,400 | 0 | 1,620 | 3,239 | 3,922 | 0 | 2,487 | 4,383 | 5,065 |
| 28,400 | 28,450 | 0 | 1,612 | 3,229 | 3,911 | 0 | 2,479 | 4,372 | 5,055 |
| 28,450 | 28,500 | 0 | 1,604 | 3,218 | 3,901 | 0 | 2,471 | 4,362 | 5,044 |
| 28,500 | 28,550 | 0 | 1,596 | 3,208 | 3,890 | 0 | 2,463 | 4,351 | 5,034 |
| 28,550 | 28,600 | 0 | 1,588 | 3,197 | 3,880 | 0 | 2,455 | 4,341 | 5,023 |
| 28,600 | 28,650 | 0 | 1,580 | 3,187 | 3,869 | 0 | 2,447 | 4,330 | 5,013 |
| 28,650 | 28,700 | 0 | 1,572 | 3,176 | 3,859 | 0 | 2,439 | 4,320 | 5,002 |
| 28,700 | 28,750 | 0 | 1,564 | 3,166 | 3,848 | 0 | 2,431 | 4,309 | 4,992 |
| 28,750 | 28,800 | 0 | 1,556 | 3,155 | 3,837 | 0 | 2,424 | 4,299 | 4,981 |
| 28,800 | 28,850 | 0 | 1,548 | 3,144 | 3,827 | 0 | 2,416 | 4,288 | 4,971 |
| 28,850 | 28,900 | 0 | 1,540 | 3,134 | 3,816 | 0 | 2,408 | 4,277 | 4,960 |
| 28,900 | 28,950 | 0 | 1,532 | 3,123 | 3,806 | 0 | 2,400 | 4,267 | 4,949 |
| 28,950 | 29,000 | 0 | 1,524 | 3,113 | 3,795 | 0 | 2,392 | 4,256 | 4,939 |
| 29,000 | 29,050 | 0 | 1,516 | 3,102 | 3,785 | 0 | 2,384 | 4,246 | 4,928 |
| 29,050 | 29,100 | 0 | 1,508 | 3,092 | 3,774 | 0 | 2,376 | 4,235 | 4,918 |
| 29,100 | 29,150 | 0 | 1,500 | 3,081 | 3,764 | 0 | 2,368 | 4,225 | 4,907 |
| 29,150 | 29,200 | 0 | 1,492 | 3,071 | 3,753 | 0 | 2,360 | 4,214 | 4,897 |
| 29,200 | 29,250 | 0 | 1,484 | 3,060 | 3,743 | 0 | 2,352 | 4,204 | 4,886 |
| 29,250 | 29,300 | 0 | 1,476 | 3,050 | 3,732 | 0 | 2,344 | 4,193 | 4,876 |
| 29,300 | 29,350 | 0 | 1,468 | 3,039 | 3,722 | 0 | 2,336 | 4,183 | 4,865 |
| 29,350 | 29,400 | 0 | 1,460 | 3,029 | 3,711 | 0 | 2,328 | 4,172 | 4,855 |
| 29,400 | 29,450 | 0 | 1,452 | 3,018 | 3,701 | 0 | 2,320 | 4,162 | 4,844 |
| 29,450 | 29,500 | 0 | 1,444 | 3,008 | 3,690 | 0 | 2,312 | 4,151 | 4,834 |
| 29,500 | 29,550 | 0 | 1,436 | 2,997 | 3,680 | 0 | 2,304 | 4,141 | 4,823 |
| 29,550 | 29,600 | 0 | 1,428 | 2,987 | 3,669 | 0 | 2,296 | 4,130 | 4,813 |
| 29,600 | 29,650 | 0 | 1,420 | 2,976 | 3,658 | 0 | 2,288 | 4,120 | 4,802 |
| 29,650 | 29,700 | 0 | 1,412 | 2,965 | 3,648 | 0 | 2,280 | 4,109 | 4,792 |
| 29,700 | 29,750 | 0 | 1,404 | 2,955 | 3,637 | 0 | 2,272 | 4,098 | 4,781 |
| 29,750 | 29,800 | 0 | 1,396 | 2,944 | 3,627 | 0 | 2,264 | 4,088 | 4,770 |
| 29,800 | 29,850 | 0 | 1,388 | 2,934 | 3,616 | 0 | 2,256 | 4,077 | 4,760 |
| 29,850 | 29,900 | 0 | 1,380 | 2,923 | 3,606 | 0 | 2,248 | 4,067 | 4,749 |
| 29,900 | 29,950 | 0 | 1,372 | 2,913 | 3,595 | 0 | 2,240 | 4,056 | 4,739 |
| 29,950 | 30,000 | 0 | 1,364 | 2,902 | 3,585 | 0 | 2,232 | 4,046 | 4,728 |
| 30,000 | 30,050 | 0 | 1,356 | 2,892 | 3,574 | 0 | 2,224 | 4,035 | 4,718 |
| 30,050 | 30,100 | 0 | 1,348 | 2,881 | 3,564 | 0 | 2,216 | 4,025 | 4,707 |
| 30,100 | 30,150 | 0 | 1,340 | 2,871 | 3,553 | 0 | 2,208 | 4,014 | 4,697 |
| 30,150 | 30,200 | 0 | 1,332 | 2,860 | 3,543 | 0 | 2,200 | 4,004 | 4,686 |
| 30,200 | 30,250 | 0 | 1,324 | 2,850 | 3,532 | 0 | 2,192 | 3,993 | 4,676 |
| 30,250 | 30,300 | 0 | 1,316 | 2,839 | 3,522 | 0 | 2,184 | 3,983 | 4,665 |
| 30,300 | 30,350 | 0 | 1,308 | 2,829 | 3,511 | 0 | 2,176 | 3,972 | 4,655 |
| 30,350 | 30,400 | 0 | 1,300 | 2,818 | 3,501 | 0 | 2,168 | 3,962 | 4,644 |
| 30,400 | 30,450 | 0 | 1,292 | 2,807 | 3,490 | 0 | 2,160 | 3,951 | 4,634 |
| 30,450 | 30,500 | 0 | 1,284 | 2,797 | 3,479 | 0 | 2,152 | 3,941 | 4,623 |
| 30,500 | 30,550 | 0 | 1,276 | 2,786 | 3,469 | 0 | 2,144 | 3,930 | 4,612 |
| 30,550 | 30,600 | 0 | 1,268 | 2,776 | 3,458 | 0 | 2,136 | 3,919 | 4,602 |
| 30,600 | 30,650 | 0 | 1,260 | 2,765 | 3,448 | 0 | 2,128 | 3,909 | 4,591 |
| 30,650 | 30,700 | 0 | 1,252 | 2,755 | 3,437 | 0 | 2,120 | 3,898 | 4,581 |
| 30,700 | 30,750 | 0 | 1,244 | 2,744 | 3,427 | 0 | 2,112 | 3,888 | 4,570 |
| 30,750 | 30,800 | 0 | 1,236 | 2,734 | 3,416 | 0 | 2,104 | 3,877 | 4,560 |
| 30,800 | 30,850 | 0 | 1,228 | 2,723 | 3,406 | 0 | 2,096 | 3,867 | 4,549 |
| 30,850 | 30,900 | 0 | 1,220 | 2,713 | 3,395 | 0 | 2,088 | 3,856 | 4,539 |
| 30,900 | 30,950 | 0 | 1,212 | 2,702 | 3,385 | 0 | 2,080 | 3,846 | 4,528 |
| 30,950 | 31,000 | 0 | 1,204 | 2,692 | 3,374 | 0 | 2,072 | 3,835 | 4,518 |
| 31,000 | 31,050 | 0 | 1,196 | 2,681 | 3,364 | 0 | 2,064 | 3,825 | 4,507 |
| 31,050 | 31,100 | 0 | 1,188 | 2,671 | 3,353 | 0 | 2,056 | 3,814 | 4,497 |
| 31,100 | 31,150 | 0 | 1,180 | 2,660 | 3,343 | 0 | 2,048 | 3,804 | 4,486 |
| 31,150 | 31,200 | 0 | 1,172 | 2,650 | 3,332 | 0 | 2,040 | 3,793 | 4,476 |
| 31,200 | 31,250 | 0 | 1,164 | 2,639 | 3,322 | 0 | 2,032 | 3,783 | 4,465 |
| 31,250 | 31,300 | 0 | 1,156 | 2,628 | 3,311 | 0 | 2,024 | 3,772 | 4,455 |
| 31,300 | 31,350 | 0 | 1,148 | 2,618 | 3,300 | 0 | 2,016 | 3,762 | 4,444 |
| 31,350 | 31,400 | 0 | 1,140 | 2,607 | 3,290 | 0 | 2,008 | 3,751 | 4,433 |
| 31,400 | 31,450 | 0 | 1,132 | 2,597 | 3,279 | 0 | 2,000 | 3,740 | 4,423 |
| 31,450 | 31,500 | 0 | 1,124 | 2,586 | 3,269 | 0 | 1,992 | 3,730 | 4,412 |
| 31,500 | 31,550 | 0 | 1,116 | 2,576 | 3,258 | 0 | 1,984 | 3,719 | 4,402 |
| 31,550 | 31,600 | 0 | 1,108 | 2,565 | 3,248 | 0 | 1,976 | 3,709 | 4,391 |
| 31,600 | 31,650 | 0 | 1,100 | 2,555 | 3,237 | 0 | 1,968 | 3,698 | 4,381 |
| 31,650 | 31,700 | 0 | 1,092 | 2,544 | 3,227 | 0 | 1,960 | 3,688 | 4,370 |
| 31,700 | 31,750 | 0 | 1,084 | 2,534 | 3,216 | 0 | 1,952 | 3,677 | 4,360 |
| 31,750 | 31,800 | 0 | 1,076 | 2,523 | 3,206 | 0 | 1,944 | 3,667 | 4,349 |
| 31,800 | 31,850 | 0 | 1,068 | 2,513 | 3,195 | 0 | 1,936 | 3,656 | 4,339 |
| 31,850 | 31,900 | 0 | 1,060 | 2,502 | 3,185 | 0 | 1,928 | 3,646 | 4,328 |
| 31,900 | 31,950 | 0 | 1,052 | 2,492 | 3,174 | 0 | 1,920 | 3,635 | 4,318 |
| 31,950 | 32,000 | 0 | 1,044 | 2,481 | 3,164 | 0 | 1,912 | 3,625 | 4,307 |
| 32,000 | 32,050 | 0 | 1,036 | 2,471 | 3,153 | 0 | 1,904 | 3,614 | 4,297 |
| 32,050 | 32,100 | 0 | 1,028 | 2,460 | 3,143 | 0 | 1,896 | 3,604 | 4,286 |
| 32,100 | 32,150 | 0 | 1,020 | 2,449 | 3,132 | 0 | 1,888 | 3,593 | 4,276 |
| 32,150 | 32,200 | 0 | 1,012 | 2,439 | 3,121 | 0 | 1,880 | 3,583 | 4,265 |
| 32,200 | 32,250 | 0 | 1,004 | 2,428 | 3,111 | 0 | 1,872 | 3,572 | 4,254 |
| 32,250 | 32,300 | 0 | 996 | 2,418 | 3,100 | 0 | 1,864 | 3,561 | 4,244 |
| 32,300 | 32,350 | 0 | 988 | 2,407 | 3,090 | 0 | 1,856 | 3,551 | 4,233 |
| 32,350 | 32,400 | 0 | 981 | 2,397 | 3,079 | 0 | 1,848 | 3,540 | 4,223 |
| 32,400 | 32,450 | 0 | 973 | 2,386 | 3,069 | 0 | 1,840 | 3,530 | 4,212 |
| 32,450 | 32,500 | 0 | 965 | 2,376 | 3,058 | 0 | 1,832 | 3,519 | 4,202 |
| 32,500 | 32,550 | 0 | 957 | 2,365 | 3,048 | 0 | 1,824 | 3,509 | 4,191 |
| 32,550 | 32,600 | 0 | 949 | 2,355 | 3,037 | 0 | 1,816 | 3,498 | 4,181 |
| 32,600 | 32,650 | 0 | 941 | 2,344 | 3,027 | 0 | 1,808 | 3,488 | 4,170 |
| 32,650 | 32,700 | 0 | 933 | 2,334 | 3,016 | 0 | 1,800 | 3,477 | 4,160 |
| 32,700 | 32,750 | 0 | 925 | 2,323 | 3,006 | 0 | 1,792 | 3,467 | 4,149 |
| 32,750 | 32,800 | 0 | 917 | 2,313 | 2,995 | 0 | 1,784 | 3,456 | 4,139 |

*(Continued)*

**Earned Income Credit (EIC) Table** - *Continued*   (**Caution.** This is **not** a tax table.)

| If the amount you are looking up from the worksheet is— | | Single, head of household, or qualifying widow(er) and the number of children you have is— | | | | Married filing jointly and the number of children you have is— | | | |
|---|---|---|---|---|---|---|---|---|---|
| At least | But less than | 0 | 1 | 2 | 3 | 0 | 1 | 2 | 3 |
| | | Your credit is— | | | | Your credit is— | | | |
| 32,800 | 32,850 | 0 | 909 | 2,302 | 2,985 | 0 | 1,776 | 3,446 | 4,128 |
| 32,850 | 32,900 | 0 | 901 | 2,292 | 2,974 | 0 | 1,768 | 3,435 | 4,118 |
| 32,900 | 32,950 | 0 | 893 | 2,281 | 2,963 | 0 | 1,760 | 3,425 | 4,107 |
| 32,950 | 33,000 | 0 | 885 | 2,270 | 2,953 | 0 | 1,752 | 3,414 | 4,097 |
| 33,000 | 33,050 | 0 | 877 | 2,260 | 2,942 | 0 | 1,744 | 3,403 | 4,086 |
| 33,050 | 33,100 | 0 | 869 | 2,249 | 2,932 | 0 | 1,736 | 3,393 | 4,075 |
| 33,100 | 33,150 | 0 | 861 | 2,239 | 2,921 | 0 | 1,728 | 3,382 | 4,065 |
| 33,150 | 33,200 | 0 | 853 | 2,228 | 2,911 | 0 | 1,720 | 3,372 | 4,054 |
| 33,200 | 33,250 | 0 | 845 | 2,218 | 2,900 | 0 | 1,712 | 3,361 | 4,044 |
| 33,250 | 33,300 | 0 | 837 | 2,207 | 2,890 | 0 | 1,704 | 3,351 | 4,033 |
| 33,300 | 33,350 | 0 | 829 | 2,197 | 2,879 | 0 | 1,696 | 3,340 | 4,023 |
| 33,350 | 33,400 | 0 | 821 | 2,186 | 2,869 | 0 | 1,688 | 3,330 | 4,012 |
| 33,400 | 33,450 | 0 | 813 | 2,176 | 2,858 | 0 | 1,680 | 3,319 | 4,002 |
| 33,450 | 33,500 | 0 | 805 | 2,165 | 2,848 | 0 | 1,672 | 3,309 | 3,991 |
| 33,500 | 33,550 | 0 | 797 | 2,155 | 2,837 | 0 | 1,664 | 3,298 | 3,981 |
| 33,550 | 33,600 | 0 | 789 | 2,144 | 2,827 | 0 | 1,656 | 3,288 | 3,970 |
| 33,600 | 33,650 | 0 | 781 | 2,134 | 2,816 | 0 | 1,648 | 3,277 | 3,960 |
| 33,650 | 33,700 | 0 | 773 | 2,123 | 2,806 | 0 | 1,640 | 3,267 | 3,949 |
| 33,700 | 33,750 | 0 | 765 | 2,113 | 2,795 | 0 | 1,632 | 3,256 | 3,939 |
| 33,750 | 33,800 | 0 | 757 | 2,102 | 2,784 | 0 | 1,625 | 3,246 | 3,928 |
| 33,800 | 33,850 | 0 | 749 | 2,091 | 2,774 | 0 | 1,617 | 3,235 | 3,918 |
| 33,850 | 33,900 | 0 | 741 | 2,081 | 2,763 | 0 | 1,609 | 3,224 | 3,907 |
| 33,900 | 33,950 | 0 | 733 | 2,070 | 2,753 | 0 | 1,601 | 3,214 | 3,896 |
| 33,950 | 34,000 | 0 | 725 | 2,060 | 2,742 | 0 | 1,593 | 3,203 | 3,886 |
| 34,000 | 34,050 | 0 | 717 | 2,049 | 2,732 | 0 | 1,585 | 3,193 | 3,875 |
| 34,050 | 34,100 | 0 | 709 | 2,039 | 2,721 | 0 | 1,577 | 3,182 | 3,865 |
| 34,100 | 34,150 | 0 | 701 | 2,028 | 2,711 | 0 | 1,569 | 3,172 | 3,854 |
| 34,150 | 34,200 | 0 | 693 | 2,018 | 2,700 | 0 | 1,561 | 3,161 | 3,844 |
| 34,200 | 34,250 | 0 | 685 | 2,007 | 2,690 | 0 | 1,553 | 3,151 | 3,833 |
| 34,250 | 34,300 | 0 | 677 | 1,997 | 2,679 | 0 | 1,545 | 3,140 | 3,823 |
| 34,300 | 34,350 | 0 | 669 | 1,986 | 2,669 | 0 | 1,537 | 3,130 | 3,812 |
| 34,350 | 34,400 | 0 | 661 | 1,976 | 2,658 | 0 | 1,529 | 3,119 | 3,802 |
| 34,400 | 34,450 | 0 | 653 | 1,965 | 2,648 | 0 | 1,521 | 3,109 | 3,791 |
| 34,450 | 34,500 | 0 | 645 | 1,955 | 2,637 | 0 | 1,513 | 3,098 | 3,781 |
| 34,500 | 34,550 | 0 | 637 | 1,944 | 2,627 | 0 | 1,505 | 3,088 | 3,770 |
| 34,550 | 34,600 | 0 | 629 | 1,934 | 2,616 | 0 | 1,497 | 3,077 | 3,760 |
| 34,600 | 34,650 | 0 | 621 | 1,923 | 2,605 | 0 | 1,489 | 3,067 | 3,749 |
| 34,650 | 34,700 | 0 | 613 | 1,912 | 2,595 | 0 | 1,481 | 3,056 | 3,739 |
| 34,700 | 34,750 | 0 | 605 | 1,902 | 2,584 | 0 | 1,473 | 3,045 | 3,728 |
| 34,750 | 34,800 | 0 | 597 | 1,891 | 2,574 | 0 | 1,465 | 3,035 | 3,717 |
| 34,800 | 34,850 | 0 | 589 | 1,881 | 2,563 | 0 | 1,457 | 3,024 | 3,707 |
| 34,850 | 34,900 | 0 | 581 | 1,870 | 2,553 | 0 | 1,449 | 3,014 | 3,696 |
| 34,900 | 34,950 | 0 | 573 | 1,860 | 2,542 | 0 | 1,441 | 3,003 | 3,686 |
| 34,950 | 35,000 | 0 | 565 | 1,849 | 2,532 | 0 | 1,433 | 2,993 | 3,675 |
| 35,000 | 35,050 | 0 | 557 | 1,839 | 2,521 | 0 | 1,425 | 2,982 | 3,665 |
| 35,050 | 35,100 | 0 | 549 | 1,828 | 2,511 | 0 | 1,417 | 2,972 | 3,654 |
| 35,100 | 35,150 | 0 | 541 | 1,818 | 2,500 | 0 | 1,409 | 2,961 | 3,644 |
| 35,150 | 35,200 | 0 | 533 | 1,807 | 2,490 | 0 | 1,401 | 2,951 | 3,633 |
| 35,200 | 35,250 | 0 | 525 | 1,797 | 2,479 | 0 | 1,393 | 2,940 | 3,623 |
| 35,250 | 35,300 | 0 | 517 | 1,786 | 2,469 | 0 | 1,385 | 2,930 | 3,612 |
| 35,300 | 35,350 | 0 | 509 | 1,776 | 2,458 | 0 | 1,377 | 2,919 | 3,602 |
| 35,350 | 35,400 | 0 | 501 | 1,765 | 2,448 | 0 | 1,369 | 2,909 | 3,591 |
| 35,400 | 35,450 | 0 | 493 | 1,754 | 2,437 | 0 | 1,361 | 2,898 | 3,581 |
| 35,450 | 35,500 | 0 | 485 | 1,744 | 2,426 | 0 | 1,353 | 2,888 | 3,570 |
| 35,500 | 35,550 | 0 | 477 | 1,733 | 2,416 | 0 | 1,345 | 2,877 | 3,559 |
| 35,550 | 35,600 | 0 | 469 | 1,723 | 2,405 | 0 | 1,337 | 2,866 | 3,549 |
| 35,600 | 35,650 | 0 | 461 | 1,712 | 2,395 | 0 | 1,329 | 2,856 | 3,538 |
| 35,650 | 35,700 | 0 | 453 | 1,702 | 2,384 | 0 | 1,321 | 2,845 | 3,528 |
| 35,700 | 35,750 | 0 | 445 | 1,691 | 2,374 | 0 | 1,313 | 2,835 | 3,517 |
| 35,750 | 35,800 | 0 | 437 | 1,681 | 2,363 | 0 | 1,305 | 2,824 | 3,507 |
| 35,800 | 35,850 | 0 | 429 | 1,670 | 2,353 | 0 | 1,297 | 2,814 | 3,496 |
| 35,850 | 35,900 | 0 | 421 | 1,660 | 2,342 | 0 | 1,289 | 2,803 | 3,486 |
| 35,900 | 35,950 | 0 | 413 | 1,649 | 2,332 | 0 | 1,281 | 2,793 | 3,475 |
| 35,950 | 36,000 | 0 | 405 | 1,639 | 2,321 | 0 | 1,273 | 2,782 | 3,465 |

| If the amount you are looking up from the worksheet is— | | Single, head of household, or qualifying widow(er) and the number of children you have is— | | | | Married filing jointly and the number of children you have is— | | | |
|---|---|---|---|---|---|---|---|---|---|
| At least | But less than | 0 | 1 | 2 | 3 | 0 | 1 | 2 | 3 |
| | | Your credit is— | | | | Your credit is— | | | |
| 36,000 | 36,050 | 0 | 397 | 1,628 | 2,311 | 0 | 1,265 | 2,772 | 3,454 |
| 36,050 | 36,100 | 0 | 389 | 1,618 | 2,300 | 0 | 1,257 | 2,761 | 3,444 |
| 36,100 | 36,150 | 0 | 381 | 1,607 | 2,290 | 0 | 1,249 | 2,751 | 3,433 |
| 36,150 | 36,200 | 0 | 373 | 1,597 | 2,279 | 0 | 1,241 | 2,740 | 3,423 |
| 36,200 | 36,250 | 0 | 365 | 1,586 | 2,269 | 0 | 1,233 | 2,730 | 3,412 |
| 36,250 | 36,300 | 0 | 357 | 1,575 | 2,258 | 0 | 1,225 | 2,719 | 3,402 |
| 36,300 | 36,350 | 0 | 349 | 1,565 | 2,247 | 0 | 1,217 | 2,709 | 3,391 |
| 36,350 | 36,400 | 0 | 341 | 1,554 | 2,237 | 0 | 1,209 | 2,698 | 3,380 |
| 36,400 | 36,450 | 0 | 333 | 1,544 | 2,226 | 0 | 1,201 | 2,687 | 3,370 |
| 36,450 | 36,500 | 0 | 325 | 1,533 | 2,216 | 0 | 1,193 | 2,677 | 3,359 |
| 36,500 | 36,550 | 0 | 317 | 1,523 | 2,205 | 0 | 1,185 | 2,666 | 3,349 |
| 36,550 | 36,600 | 0 | 309 | 1,512 | 2,195 | 0 | 1,177 | 2,656 | 3,338 |
| 36,600 | 36,650 | 0 | 301 | 1,502 | 2,184 | 0 | 1,169 | 2,645 | 3,328 |
| 36,650 | 36,700 | 0 | 293 | 1,491 | 2,174 | 0 | 1,161 | 2,635 | 3,317 |
| 36,700 | 36,750 | 0 | 285 | 1,481 | 2,163 | 0 | 1,153 | 2,624 | 3,307 |
| 36,750 | 36,800 | 0 | 277 | 1,470 | 2,153 | 0 | 1,145 | 2,614 | 3,296 |
| 36,800 | 36,850 | 0 | 269 | 1,460 | 2,142 | 0 | 1,137 | 2,603 | 3,286 |
| 36,850 | 36,900 | 0 | 261 | 1,449 | 2,132 | 0 | 1,129 | 2,593 | 3,275 |
| 36,900 | 36,950 | 0 | 253 | 1,439 | 2,121 | 0 | 1,121 | 2,582 | 3,265 |
| 36,950 | 37,000 | 0 | 245 | 1,428 | 2,111 | 0 | 1,113 | 2,572 | 3,254 |
| 37,000 | 37,050 | 0 | 237 | 1,418 | 2,100 | 0 | 1,105 | 2,561 | 3,244 |
| 37,050 | 37,100 | 0 | 229 | 1,407 | 2,090 | 0 | 1,097 | 2,551 | 3,233 |
| 37,100 | 37,150 | 0 | 221 | 1,396 | 2,079 | 0 | 1,089 | 2,540 | 3,223 |
| 37,150 | 37,200 | 0 | 213 | 1,386 | 2,068 | 0 | 1,081 | 2,530 | 3,212 |
| 37,200 | 37,250 | 0 | 205 | 1,375 | 2,058 | 0 | 1,073 | 2,519 | 3,201 |
| 37,250 | 37,300 | 0 | 197 | 1,365 | 2,047 | 0 | 1,065 | 2,508 | 3,191 |
| 37,300 | 37,350 | 0 | 189 | 1,354 | 2,037 | 0 | 1,057 | 2,498 | 3,180 |
| 37,350 | 37,400 | 0 | 182 | 1,344 | 2,026 | 0 | 1,049 | 2,487 | 3,170 |
| 37,400 | 37,450 | 0 | 174 | 1,333 | 2,016 | 0 | 1,041 | 2,477 | 3,159 |
| 37,450 | 37,500 | 0 | 166 | 1,323 | 2,005 | 0 | 1,033 | 2,466 | 3,149 |
| 37,500 | 37,550 | 0 | 158 | 1,312 | 1,995 | 0 | 1,025 | 2,456 | 3,138 |
| 37,550 | 37,600 | 0 | 150 | 1,302 | 1,984 | 0 | 1,017 | 2,445 | 3,128 |
| 37,600 | 37,650 | 0 | 142 | 1,291 | 1,974 | 0 | 1,009 | 2,435 | 3,117 |
| 37,650 | 37,700 | 0 | 134 | 1,281 | 1,963 | 0 | 1,001 | 2,424 | 3,107 |
| 37,700 | 37,750 | 0 | 126 | 1,270 | 1,953 | 0 | 993 | 2,414 | 3,096 |
| 37,750 | 37,800 | 0 | 118 | 1,260 | 1,942 | 0 | 985 | 2,403 | 3,086 |
| 37,800 | 37,850 | 0 | 110 | 1,249 | 1,932 | 0 | 977 | 2,393 | 3,075 |
| 37,850 | 37,900 | 0 | 102 | 1,239 | 1,921 | 0 | 969 | 2,382 | 3,065 |
| 37,900 | 37,950 | 0 | 94 | 1,229 | 1,910 | 0 | 961 | 2,372 | 3,054 |
| 37,950 | 38,000 | 0 | 86 | 1,217 | 1,900 | 0 | 953 | 2,361 | 3,044 |
| 38,000 | 38,050 | 0 | 78 | 1,207 | 1,889 | 0 | 945 | 2,350 | 3,033 |
| 38,050 | 38,100 | 0 | 70 | 1,196 | 1,879 | 0 | 937 | 2,340 | 3,022 |
| 38,100 | 38,150 | 0 | 62 | 1,186 | 1,868 | 0 | 929 | 2,329 | 3,012 |
| 38,150 | 38,200 | 0 | 54 | 1,175 | 1,858 | 0 | 921 | 2,319 | 3,001 |
| 38,200 | 38,250 | 0 | 46 | 1,165 | 1,847 | 0 | 913 | 2,308 | 2,991 |
| 38,250 | 38,300 | 0 | 38 | 1,154 | 1,837 | 0 | 905 | 2,298 | 2,980 |
| 38,300 | 38,350 | 0 | 30 | 1,144 | 1,826 | 0 | 897 | 2,287 | 2,970 |
| 38,350 | 38,400 | 0 | 22 | 1,133 | 1,816 | 0 | 889 | 2,277 | 2,959 |
| 38,400 | 38,450 | 0 | 14 | 1,123 | 1,805 | 0 | 881 | 2,266 | 2,949 |
| 38,450 | 38,500 | 0 | 6 | 1,112 | 1,795 | 0 | 873 | 2,256 | 2,938 |
| 38,500 | 38,550 | 0 | * | 1,102 | 1,784 | 0 | 865 | 2,245 | 2,928 |
| 38,550 | 38,600 | 0 | 0 | 1,091 | 1,774 | 0 | 857 | 2,235 | 2,917 |
| 38,600 | 38,650 | 0 | 0 | 1,081 | 1,763 | 0 | 849 | 2,224 | 2,907 |
| 38,650 | 38,700 | 0 | 0 | 1,070 | 1,753 | 0 | 841 | 2,214 | 2,896 |
| 38,700 | 38,750 | 0 | 0 | 1,060 | 1,742 | 0 | 833 | 2,203 | 2,886 |
| 38,750 | 38,800 | 0 | 0 | 1,049 | 1,731 | 0 | 826 | 2,193 | 2,875 |
| 38,800 | 38,850 | 0 | 0 | 1,038 | 1,721 | 0 | 818 | 2,182 | 2,865 |
| 38,850 | 38,900 | 0 | 0 | 1,028 | 1,710 | 0 | 810 | 2,171 | 2,854 |
| 38,900 | 38,950 | 0 | 0 | 1,017 | 1,700 | 0 | 802 | 2,161 | 2,843 |
| 38,950 | 39,000 | 0 | 0 | 1,007 | 1,689 | 0 | 794 | 2,150 | 2,833 |
| 39,000 | 39,050 | 0 | 0 | 996 | 1,679 | 0 | 786 | 2,140 | 2,822 |
| 39,050 | 39,100 | 0 | 0 | 986 | 1,668 | 0 | 778 | 2,129 | 2,812 |
| 39,100 | 39,150 | 0 | 0 | 975 | 1,658 | 0 | 770 | 2,119 | 2,801 |
| 39,150 | 39,200 | 0 | 0 | 965 | 1,647 | 0 | 762 | 2,108 | 2,791 |

*If the amount you are looking up from the worksheet is at least $38,500 but less than $38,511, and you have one qualifying child, your credit is $1.
If the amount you are looking up from the worksheet is $38,511 or more, and you have one qualifying child, you  cannot take the credit.

*(Continued)*

# 2014 Earned Income Credit Table

**Earned Income Credit (EIC) Table** - *Continued*     (**Caution.** This is **not** a tax table.)

| If the amount you are looking up from the worksheet is– | | Single, head of household, or qualifying widow(er) and the number of children you have is– | | | | Married filing jointly and the number of children you have is– | | | |
|---|---|---|---|---|---|---|---|---|---|
| At least | But less than | 0 | 1 | 2 | 3 | 0 | 1 | 2 | 3 |
| | | Your credit is– | | | | Your credit is– | | | |
| 39,200 | 39,250 | 0 | 0 | 954 | 1,637 | 0 | 754 | 2,098 | 2,780 |
| 39,250 | 39,300 | 0 | 0 | 944 | 1,626 | 0 | 746 | 2,087 | 2,770 |
| 39,300 | 39,350 | 0 | 0 | 933 | 1,616 | 0 | 738 | 2,077 | 2,759 |
| 39,350 | 39,400 | 0 | 0 | 923 | 1,605 | 0 | 730 | 2,066 | 2,749 |
| 39,400 | 39,450 | 0 | 0 | 912 | 1,595 | 0 | 722 | 2,056 | 2,738 |
| 39,450 | 39,500 | 0 | 0 | 902 | 1,584 | 0 | 714 | 2,045 | 2,728 |
| 39,500 | 39,550 | 0 | 0 | 891 | 1,574 | 0 | 706 | 2,035 | 2,717 |
| 39,550 | 39,600 | 0 | 0 | 881 | 1,563 | 0 | 698 | 2,024 | 2,707 |
| 39,600 | 39,650 | 0 | 0 | 870 | 1,552 | 0 | 690 | 2,014 | 2,696 |
| 39,650 | 39,700 | 0 | 0 | 859 | 1,542 | 0 | 682 | 2,003 | 2,686 |
| 39,700 | 39,750 | 0 | 0 | 849 | 1,531 | 0 | 674 | 1,992 | 2,675 |
| 39,750 | 39,800 | 0 | 0 | 838 | 1,521 | 0 | 666 | 1,982 | 2,654 |
| 39,800 | 39,850 | 0 | 0 | 828 | 1,510 | 0 | 658 | 1,971 | 2,654 |
| 39,850 | 39,900 | 0 | 0 | 817 | 1,500 | 0 | 650 | 1,961 | 2,643 |
| 39,900 | 39,950 | 0 | 0 | 807 | 1,489 | 0 | 642 | 1,950 | 2,633 |
| 39,950 | 40,000 | 0 | 0 | 796 | 1,479 | 0 | 634 | 1,940 | 2,622 |
| 40,000 | 40,050 | 0 | 0 | 786 | 1,468 | 0 | 626 | 1,929 | 2,612 |
| 40,050 | 40,100 | 0 | 0 | 775 | 1,458 | 0 | 618 | 1,919 | 2,601 |
| 40,100 | 40,150 | 0 | 0 | 765 | 1,447 | 0 | 610 | 1,908 | 2,591 |
| 40,150 | 40,200 | 0 | 0 | 754 | 1,437 | 0 | 602 | 1,898 | 2,580 |
| 40,200 | 40,250 | 0 | 0 | 744 | 1,426 | 0 | 594 | 1,887 | 2,570 |
| 40,250 | 40,300 | 0 | 0 | 733 | 1,416 | 0 | 586 | 1,877 | 2,559 |
| 40,300 | 40,350 | 0 | 0 | 723 | 1,405 | 0 | 578 | 1,866 | 2,549 |
| 40,350 | 40,400 | 0 | 0 | 712 | 1,395 | 0 | 570 | 1,856 | 2,538 |
| 40,400 | 40,450 | 0 | 0 | 701 | 1,384 | 0 | 562 | 1,845 | 2,528 |
| 40,450 | 40,500 | 0 | 0 | 691 | 1,373 | 0 | 554 | 1,835 | 2,517 |
| 40,500 | 40,550 | 0 | 0 | 680 | 1,363 | 0 | 546 | 1,824 | 2,506 |
| 40,550 | 40,600 | 0 | 0 | 670 | 1,352 | 0 | 538 | 1,813 | 2,496 |
| 40,600 | 40,650 | 0 | 0 | 659 | 1,342 | 0 | 530 | 1,803 | 2,485 |
| 40,650 | 40,700 | 0 | 0 | 649 | 1,331 | 0 | 522 | 1,792 | 2,475 |
| 40,700 | 40,750 | 0 | 0 | 638 | 1,321 | 0 | 514 | 1,782 | 2,464 |
| 40,750 | 40,800 | 0 | 0 | 628 | 1,310 | 0 | 506 | 1,771 | 2,454 |
| 40,800 | 40,850 | 0 | 0 | 617 | 1,300 | 0 | 498 | 1,761 | 2,443 |
| 40,850 | 40,900 | 0 | 0 | 607 | 1,289 | 0 | 490 | 1,750 | 2,433 |
| 40,900 | 40,950 | 0 | 0 | 596 | 1,279 | 0 | 482 | 1,740 | 2,422 |
| 40,950 | 41,000 | 0 | 0 | 586 | 1,268 | 0 | 474 | 1,729 | 2,412 |
| 41,000 | 41,050 | 0 | 0 | 575 | 1,258 | 0 | 466 | 1,719 | 2,401 |
| 41,050 | 41,100 | 0 | 0 | 565 | 1,247 | 0 | 458 | 1,708 | 2,391 |
| 41,100 | 41,150 | 0 | 0 | 554 | 1,237 | 0 | 450 | 1,698 | 2,380 |
| 41,150 | 41,200 | 0 | 0 | 544 | 1,226 | 0 | 442 | 1,687 | 2,370 |
| 41,200 | 41,250 | 0 | 0 | 533 | 1,216 | 0 | 434 | 1,677 | 2,359 |
| 41,250 | 41,300 | 0 | 0 | 522 | 1,205 | 0 | 426 | 1,666 | 2,349 |
| 41,300 | 41,350 | 0 | 0 | 512 | 1,194 | 0 | 418 | 1,656 | 2,338 |
| 41,350 | 41,400 | 0 | 0 | 501 | 1,184 | 0 | 410 | 1,645 | 2,327 |
| 41,400 | 41,450 | 0 | 0 | 491 | 1,173 | 0 | 402 | 1,634 | 2,317 |
| 41,450 | 41,500 | 0 | 0 | 480 | 1,163 | 0 | 394 | 1,624 | 2,306 |
| 41,500 | 41,550 | 0 | 0 | 470 | 1,152 | 0 | 386 | 1,613 | 2,296 |
| 41,550 | 41,600 | 0 | 0 | 459 | 1,142 | 0 | 378 | 1,603 | 2,285 |
| 41,600 | 41,650 | 0 | 0 | 449 | 1,131 | 0 | 370 | 1,592 | 2,275 |
| 41,650 | 41,700 | 0 | 0 | 438 | 1,121 | 0 | 362 | 1,582 | 2,264 |
| 41,700 | 41,750 | 0 | 0 | 428 | 1,110 | 0 | 354 | 1,571 | 2,254 |
| 41,750 | 41,800 | 0 | 0 | 417 | 1,100 | 0 | 346 | 1,561 | 2,243 |
| 41,800 | 41,850 | 0 | 0 | 407 | 1,089 | 0 | 338 | 1,550 | 2,233 |
| 41,850 | 41,900 | 0 | 0 | 396 | 1,079 | 0 | 330 | 1,540 | 2,222 |
| 41,900 | 41,950 | 0 | 0 | 386 | 1,068 | 0 | 322 | 1,529 | 2,212 |
| 41,950 | 42,000 | 0 | 0 | 375 | 1,058 | 0 | 314 | 1,519 | 2,201 |
| 42,000 | 42,050 | 0 | 0 | 365 | 1,047 | 0 | 306 | 1,508 | 2,191 |
| 42,050 | 42,100 | 0 | 0 | 354 | 1,037 | 0 | 298 | 1,498 | 2,180 |
| 42,100 | 42,150 | 0 | 0 | 343 | 1,026 | 0 | 290 | 1,487 | 2,170 |
| 42,150 | 42,200 | 0 | 0 | 333 | 1,015 | 0 | 282 | 1,477 | 2,159 |
| 42,200 | 42,250 | 0 | 0 | 322 | 1,005 | 0 | 274 | 1,466 | 2,148 |
| 42,250 | 42,300 | 0 | 0 | 312 | 994 | 0 | 266 | 1,455 | 2,138 |
| 42,300 | 42,350 | 0 | 0 | 301 | 984 | 0 | 258 | 1,445 | 2,127 |
| 42,350 | 42,400 | 0 | 0 | 291 | 973 | 0 | 250 | 1,434 | 2,117 |
| 42,400 | 42,450 | 0 | 0 | 280 | 963 | 0 | 242 | 1,424 | 2,106 |
| 42,450 | 42,500 | 0 | 0 | 270 | 952 | 0 | 234 | 1,413 | 2,096 |
| 42,500 | 42,550 | 0 | 0 | 259 | 942 | 0 | 226 | 1,403 | 2,085 |
| 42,550 | 42,600 | 0 | 0 | 249 | 931 | 0 | 218 | 1,392 | 2,075 |
| 42,600 | 42,650 | 0 | 0 | 238 | 921 | 0 | 210 | 1,382 | 2,064 |
| 42,650 | 42,700 | 0 | 0 | 228 | 910 | 0 | 202 | 1,371 | 2,054 |
| 42,700 | 42,750 | 0 | 0 | 217 | 900 | 0 | 194 | 1,361 | 2,043 |
| 42,750 | 42,800 | 0 | 0 | 207 | 889 | 0 | 186 | 1,350 | 2,033 |
| 42,800 | 42,850 | 0 | 0 | 196 | 879 | 0 | 178 | 1,340 | 2,022 |
| 42,850 | 42,900 | 0 | 0 | 186 | 868 | 0 | 170 | 1,329 | 2,012 |
| 42,900 | 42,950 | 0 | 0 | 175 | 857 | 0 | 162 | 1,319 | 2,001 |
| 42,950 | 43,000 | 0 | 0 | 164 | 847 | 0 | 154 | 1,308 | 1,991 |
| 43,000 | 43,050 | 0 | 0 | 154 | 836 | 0 | 146 | 1,297 | 1,980 |
| 43,050 | 43,100 | 0 | 0 | 143 | 826 | 0 | 138 | 1,287 | 1,969 |
| 43,100 | 43,150 | 0 | 0 | 133 | 815 | 0 | 130 | 1,276 | 1,959 |
| 43,150 | 43,200 | 0 | 0 | 122 | 805 | 0 | 122 | 1,266 | 1,948 |
| 43,200 | 43,250 | 0 | 0 | 112 | 794 | 0 | 114 | 1,255 | 1,938 |
| 43,250 | 43,300 | 0 | 0 | 101 | 784 | 0 | 106 | 1,245 | 1,927 |
| 43,300 | 43,350 | 0 | 0 | 91 | 773 | 0 | 98 | 1,234 | 1,917 |
| 43,350 | 43,400 | 0 | 0 | 80 | 763 | 0 | 90 | 1,224 | 1,906 |
| 43,400 | 43,450 | 0 | 0 | 70 | 752 | 0 | 82 | 1,213 | 1,896 |
| 43,450 | 43,500 | 0 | 0 | 59 | 742 | 0 | 74 | 1,203 | 1,885 |
| 43,500 | 43,550 | 0 | 0 | 49 | 731 | 0 | 66 | 1,192 | 1,875 |
| 43,550 | 43,600 | 0 | 0 | 38 | 721 | 0 | 58 | 1,182 | 1,864 |
| 43,600 | 43,650 | 0 | 0 | 28 | 710 | 0 | 50 | 1,171 | 1,854 |
| 43,650 | 43,700 | 0 | 0 | 17 | 700 | 0 | 42 | 1,161 | 1,843 |
| 43,700 | 43,750 | 0 | 0 | 7 | 689 | 0 | 34 | 1,150 | 1,833 |
| 43,750 | 43,800 | 0 | 0 | * | 678 | 0 | 27 | 1,140 | 1,822 |
| 43,800 | 43,850 | 0 | 0 | 0 | 668 | 0 | 19 | 1,129 | 1,812 |
| 43,850 | 43,900 | 0 | 0 | 0 | 657 | 0 | 11 | 1,118 | 1,801 |
| 43,900 | 43,950 | 0 | 0 | 0 | 647 | 0 | ** | 1,108 | 1,790 |
| 43,950 | 44,000 | 0 | 0 | 0 | 636 | 0 | 0 | 1,097 | 1,780 |
| 44,000 | 44,050 | 0 | 0 | 0 | 626 | 0 | 0 | 1,087 | 1,769 |
| 44,050 | 44,100 | 0 | 0 | 0 | 615 | 0 | 0 | 1,076 | 1,759 |
| 44,100 | 44,150 | 0 | 0 | 0 | 605 | 0 | 0 | 1,066 | 1,748 |
| 44,150 | 44,200 | 0 | 0 | 0 | 594 | 0 | 0 | 1,055 | 1,738 |
| 44,200 | 44,250 | 0 | 0 | 0 | 584 | 0 | 0 | 1,045 | 1,727 |
| 44,250 | 44,300 | 0 | 0 | 0 | 573 | 0 | 0 | 1,034 | 1,717 |
| 44,300 | 44,350 | 0 | 0 | 0 | 563 | 0 | 0 | 1,024 | 1,706 |
| 44,350 | 44,400 | 0 | 0 | 0 | 552 | 0 | 0 | 1,013 | 1,696 |
| 44,400 | 44,450 | 0 | 0 | 0 | 542 | 0 | 0 | 1,003 | 1,685 |
| 44,450 | 44,500 | 0 | 0 | 0 | 531 | 0 | 0 | 992 | 1,675 |
| 44,500 | 44,550 | 0 | 0 | 0 | 521 | 0 | 0 | 982 | 1,664 |
| 44,550 | 44,600 | 0 | 0 | 0 | 510 | 0 | 0 | 971 | 1,654 |
| 44,600 | 44,650 | 0 | 0 | 0 | 499 | 0 | 0 | 961 | 1,643 |
| 44,650 | 44,700 | 0 | 0 | 0 | 489 | 0 | 0 | 950 | 1,633 |
| 44,700 | 44,750 | 0 | 0 | 0 | 478 | 0 | 0 | 939 | 1,622 |
| 44,750 | 44,800 | 0 | 0 | 0 | 468 | 0 | 0 | 929 | 1,611 |
| 44,800 | 44,850 | 0 | 0 | 0 | 457 | 0 | 0 | 918 | 1,601 |
| 44,850 | 44,900 | 0 | 0 | 0 | 447 | 0 | 0 | 908 | 1,590 |
| 44,900 | 44,950 | 0 | 0 | 0 | 436 | 0 | 0 | 897 | 1,580 |
| 44,950 | 45,000 | 0 | 0 | 0 | 426 | 0 | 0 | 887 | 1,569 |
| 45,000 | 45,050 | 0 | 0 | 0 | 415 | 0 | 0 | 876 | 1,559 |
| 45,050 | 45,100 | 0 | 0 | 0 | 405 | 0 | 0 | 866 | 1,548 |
| 45,100 | 45,150 | 0 | 0 | 0 | 394 | 0 | 0 | 855 | 1,538 |
| 45,150 | 45,200 | 0 | 0 | 0 | 384 | 0 | 0 | 845 | 1,527 |
| 45,200 | 45,250 | 0 | 0 | 0 | 373 | 0 | 0 | 834 | 1,517 |
| 45,250 | 45,300 | 0 | 0 | 0 | 363 | 0 | 0 | 824 | 1,506 |
| 45,300 | 45,350 | 0 | 0 | 0 | 352 | 0 | 0 | 813 | 1,496 |
| 45,350 | 45,400 | 0 | 0 | 0 | 342 | 0 | 0 | 803 | 1,485 |
| 45,400 | 45,450 | 0 | 0 | 0 | 331 | 0 | 0 | 792 | 1,475 |
| 45,450 | 45,500 | 0 | 0 | 0 | 320 | 0 | 0 | 782 | 1,464 |
| 45,500 | 45,550 | 0 | 0 | 0 | 310 | 0 | 0 | 771 | 1,453 |
| 45,550 | 45,600 | 0 | 0 | 0 | 299 | 0 | 0 | 760 | 1,443 |

*If the amount you are looking up from the worksheet is at least $43,750 but less than $43,756, and you have two qualifying children, your credit is $1.

If the amount you are looking up from the worksheet is $43,756 or more, and you have two qualifying children, you cannot take the credit.

**If the amount you are looking up from the worksheet is at least $43,900 but less than $43,941, and you have one qualifying child, your credit is $3.

If the amount you are looking up from the worksheet is $43,941 or more, and you have one qualifying child, you cannot take the credit.

*(Continued)*

**Earned Income Credit (EIC) Table** - *Continued*  (**Caution.** This is **not** a tax table.)

| At least | But less than | Single, HoH, QW — 0 | 1 | 2 | 3 | Married filing jointly — 0 | 1 | 2 | 3 |
|---|---|---|---|---|---|---|---|---|---|
| 45,600 | 45,650 | 0 | 0 | 0 | 289 | 0 | 0 | 750 | 1,432 |
| 45,650 | 45,700 | 0 | 0 | 0 | 278 | 0 | 0 | 739 | 1,422 |
| 45,700 | 45,750 | 0 | 0 | 0 | 268 | 0 | 0 | 729 | 1,411 |
| 45,750 | 45,800 | 0 | 0 | 0 | 257 | 0 | 0 | 718 | 1,401 |
| 45,800 | 45,850 | 0 | 0 | 0 | 247 | 0 | 0 | 708 | 1,390 |
| 45,850 | 45,900 | 0 | 0 | 0 | 236 | 0 | 0 | 697 | 1,380 |
| 45,900 | 45,950 | 0 | 0 | 0 | 226 | 0 | 0 | 687 | 1,369 |
| 45,950 | 46,000 | 0 | 0 | 0 | 215 | 0 | 0 | 676 | 1,359 |
| 46,000 | 46,050 | 0 | 0 | 0 | 205 | 0 | 0 | 666 | 1,348 |
| 46,050 | 46,100 | 0 | 0 | 0 | 194 | 0 | 0 | 655 | 1,338 |
| 46,100 | 46,150 | 0 | 0 | 0 | 184 | 0 | 0 | 645 | 1,327 |
| 46,150 | 46,200 | 0 | 0 | 0 | 173 | 0 | 0 | 634 | 1,317 |
| 46,200 | 46,250 | 0 | 0 | 0 | 163 | 0 | 0 | 624 | 1,306 |
| 46,250 | 46,300 | 0 | 0 | 0 | 152 | 0 | 0 | 613 | 1,296 |
| 46,300 | 46,350 | 0 | 0 | 0 | 141 | 0 | 0 | 603 | 1,285 |
| 46,350 | 46,400 | 0 | 0 | 0 | 131 | 0 | 0 | 582 | 1,274 |
| 46,400 | 46,450 | 0 | 0 | 0 | 120 | 0 | 0 | 581 | 1,264 |
| 46,450 | 46,500 | 0 | 0 | 0 | 110 | 0 | 0 | 571 | 1,253 |
| 46,500 | 46,550 | 0 | 0 | 0 | 99 | 0 | 0 | 560 | 1,243 |
| 46,550 | 46,600 | 0 | 0 | 0 | 89 | 0 | 0 | 550 | 1,232 |
| 46,600 | 46,650 | 0 | 0 | 0 | 78 | 0 | 0 | 539 | 1,222 |
| 46,650 | 46,700 | 0 | 0 | 0 | 68 | 0 | 0 | 529 | 1,211 |
| 46,700 | 46,750 | 0 | 0 | 0 | 57 | 0 | 0 | 518 | 1,201 |
| 46,750 | 46,800 | 0 | 0 | 0 | 47 | 0 | 0 | 508 | 1,190 |
| 46,800 | 46,850 | 0 | 0 | 0 | 36 | 0 | 0 | 497 | 1,180 |
| 46,850 | 46,900 | 0 | 0 | 0 | 26 | 0 | 0 | 487 | 1,169 |
| 46,900 | 46,950 | 0 | 0 | 0 | 15 | 0 | 0 | 476 | 1,159 |
| 46,950 | 47,000 | 0 | 0 | 0 | * | 0 | 0 | 466 | 1,148 |
| 47,000 | 47,050 | 0 | 0 | 0 | 0 | 0 | 0 | 455 | 1,138 |
| 47,050 | 47,100 | 0 | 0 | 0 | 0 | 0 | 0 | 445 | 1,127 |
| 47,100 | 47,150 | 0 | 0 | 0 | 0 | 0 | 0 | 434 | 1,117 |
| 47,150 | 47,200 | 0 | 0 | 0 | 0 | 0 | 0 | 424 | 1,106 |
| 47,200 | 47,250 | 0 | 0 | 0 | 0 | 0 | 0 | 413 | 1,095 |
| 47,250 | 47,300 | 0 | 0 | 0 | 0 | 0 | 0 | 402 | 1,085 |
| 47,300 | 47,350 | 0 | 0 | 0 | 0 | 0 | 0 | 392 | 1,074 |
| 47,350 | 47,400 | 0 | 0 | 0 | 0 | 0 | 0 | 381 | 1,064 |
| 47,400 | 47,450 | 0 | 0 | 0 | 0 | 0 | 0 | 371 | 1,053 |
| 47,450 | 47,500 | 0 | 0 | 0 | 0 | 0 | 0 | 360 | 1,043 |
| 47,500 | 47,550 | 0 | 0 | 0 | 0 | 0 | 0 | 350 | 1,032 |
| 47,550 | 47,600 | 0 | 0 | 0 | 0 | 0 | 0 | 339 | 1,022 |
| 47,600 | 47,650 | 0 | 0 | 0 | 0 | 0 | 0 | 329 | 1,011 |
| 47,650 | 47,700 | 0 | 0 | 0 | 0 | 0 | 0 | 318 | 1,001 |
| 47,700 | 47,750 | 0 | 0 | 0 | 0 | 0 | 0 | 308 | 990 |
| 47,750 | 47,800 | 0 | 0 | 0 | 0 | 0 | 0 | 297 | 980 |
| 47,800 | 47,850 | 0 | 0 | 0 | 0 | 0 | 0 | 287 | 969 |
| 47,850 | 47,900 | 0 | 0 | 0 | 0 | 0 | 0 | 276 | 959 |
| 47,900 | 47,950 | 0 | 0 | 0 | 0 | 0 | 0 | 266 | 948 |
| 47,950 | 48,000 | 0 | 0 | 0 | 0 | 0 | 0 | 255 | 938 |
| 48,000 | 48,050 | 0 | 0 | 0 | 0 | 0 | 0 | 244 | 927 |
| 48,050 | 48,100 | 0 | 0 | 0 | 0 | 0 | 0 | 234 | 916 |
| 48,100 | 48,150 | 0 | 0 | 0 | 0 | 0 | 0 | 223 | 906 |
| 48,150 | 48,200 | 0 | 0 | 0 | 0 | 0 | 0 | 213 | 895 |
| 48,200 | 48,250 | 0 | 0 | 0 | 0 | 0 | 0 | 202 | 885 |
| 48,250 | 48,300 | 0 | 0 | 0 | 0 | 0 | 0 | 192 | 874 |
| 48,300 | 48,350 | 0 | 0 | 0 | 0 | 0 | 0 | 181 | 864 |
| 48,350 | 48,400 | 0 | 0 | 0 | 0 | 0 | 0 | 171 | 853 |
| 48,400 | 48,450 | 0 | 0 | 0 | 0 | 0 | 0 | 160 | 843 |
| 48,450 | 48,500 | 0 | 0 | 0 | 0 | 0 | 0 | 150 | 832 |
| 48,500 | 48,550 | 0 | 0 | 0 | 0 | 0 | 0 | 139 | 822 |
| 48,550 | 48,600 | 0 | 0 | 0 | 0 | 0 | 0 | 129 | 811 |
| 48,600 | 48,650 | 0 | 0 | 0 | 0 | 0 | 0 | 118 | 801 |
| 48,650 | 48,700 | 0 | 0 | 0 | 0 | 0 | 0 | 108 | 790 |
| 48,700 | 48,750 | 0 | 0 | 0 | 0 | 0 | 0 | 97 | 780 |
| 48,750 | 48,800 | 0 | 0 | 0 | 0 | 0 | 0 | 87 | 769 |

| At least | But less than | Single, HoH, QW — 0 | 1 | 2 | 3 | Married filing jointly — 0 | 1 | 2 | 3 |
|---|---|---|---|---|---|---|---|---|---|
| 48,800 | 48,850 | 0 | 0 | 0 | 0 | 0 | 0 | 76 | 759 |
| 48,850 | 48,900 | 0 | 0 | 0 | 0 | 0 | 0 | 65 | 748 |
| 48,900 | 48,950 | 0 | 0 | 0 | 0 | 0 | 0 | 55 | 737 |
| 48,950 | 49,000 | 0 | 0 | 0 | 0 | 0 | 0 | 44 | 727 |
| 49,000 | 49,050 | 0 | 0 | 0 | 0 | 0 | 0 | 34 | 716 |
| 49,050 | 49,100 | 0 | 0 | 0 | 0 | 0 | 0 | 23 | 706 |
| 49,100 | 49,150 | 0 | 0 | 0 | 0 | 0 | 0 | 13 | 695 |
| 49,150 | 49,200 | 0 | 0 | 0 | 0 | 0 | 0 | ** | 685 |
| 49,200 | 49,250 | 0 | 0 | 0 | 0 | 0 | 0 | 0 | 674 |
| 49,250 | 49,300 | 0 | 0 | 0 | 0 | 0 | 0 | 0 | 664 |
| 49,300 | 49,350 | 0 | 0 | 0 | 0 | 0 | 0 | 0 | 653 |
| 49,350 | 49,400 | 0 | 0 | 0 | 0 | 0 | 0 | 0 | 643 |
| 49,400 | 49,450 | 0 | 0 | 0 | 0 | 0 | 0 | 0 | 632 |
| 49,450 | 49,500 | 0 | 0 | 0 | 0 | 0 | 0 | 0 | 622 |
| 49,500 | 49,550 | 0 | 0 | 0 | 0 | 0 | 0 | 0 | 611 |
| 49,550 | 49,600 | 0 | 0 | 0 | 0 | 0 | 0 | 0 | 601 |
| 49,600 | 49,650 | 0 | 0 | 0 | 0 | 0 | 0 | 0 | 590 |
| 49,650 | 49,700 | 0 | 0 | 0 | 0 | 0 | 0 | 0 | 580 |
| 49,700 | 49,750 | 0 | 0 | 0 | 0 | 0 | 0 | 0 | 569 |
| 49,750 | 49,800 | 0 | 0 | 0 | 0 | 0 | 0 | 0 | 558 |
| 49,800 | 49,850 | 0 | 0 | 0 | 0 | 0 | 0 | 0 | 548 |
| 49,850 | 49,900 | 0 | 0 | 0 | 0 | 0 | 0 | 0 | 537 |
| 49,900 | 49,950 | 0 | 0 | 0 | 0 | 0 | 0 | 0 | 527 |
| 49,950 | 50,000 | 0 | 0 | 0 | 0 | 0 | 0 | 0 | 516 |
| 50,000 | 50,050 | 0 | 0 | 0 | 0 | 0 | 0 | 0 | 506 |
| 50,050 | 50,100 | 0 | 0 | 0 | 0 | 0 | 0 | 0 | 495 |
| 50,100 | 50,150 | 0 | 0 | 0 | 0 | 0 | 0 | 0 | 485 |
| 50,150 | 50,200 | 0 | 0 | 0 | 0 | 0 | 0 | 0 | 474 |
| 50,200 | 50,250 | 0 | 0 | 0 | 0 | 0 | 0 | 0 | 464 |
| 50,250 | 50,300 | 0 | 0 | 0 | 0 | 0 | 0 | 0 | 453 |
| 50,300 | 50,350 | 0 | 0 | 0 | 0 | 0 | 0 | 0 | 443 |
| 50,350 | 50,400 | 0 | 0 | 0 | 0 | 0 | 0 | 0 | 432 |
| 50,400 | 50,450 | 0 | 0 | 0 | 0 | 0 | 0 | 0 | 422 |
| 50,450 | 50,500 | 0 | 0 | 0 | 0 | 0 | 0 | 0 | 411 |
| 50,500 | 50,550 | 0 | 0 | 0 | 0 | 0 | 0 | 0 | 400 |
| 50,550 | 50,600 | 0 | 0 | 0 | 0 | 0 | 0 | 0 | 390 |
| 50,600 | 50,650 | 0 | 0 | 0 | 0 | 0 | 0 | 0 | 379 |
| 50,650 | 50,700 | 0 | 0 | 0 | 0 | 0 | 0 | 0 | 369 |
| 50,700 | 50,750 | 0 | 0 | 0 | 0 | 0 | 0 | 0 | 358 |
| 50,750 | 50,800 | 0 | 0 | 0 | 0 | 0 | 0 | 0 | 348 |
| 50,800 | 50,850 | 0 | 0 | 0 | 0 | 0 | 0 | 0 | 337 |
| 50,850 | 50,900 | 0 | 0 | 0 | 0 | 0 | 0 | 0 | 327 |
| 50,900 | 50,950 | 0 | 0 | 0 | 0 | 0 | 0 | 0 | 316 |
| 50,950 | 51,000 | 0 | 0 | 0 | 0 | 0 | 0 | 0 | 306 |
| 51,000 | 51,050 | 0 | 0 | 0 | 0 | 0 | 0 | 0 | 295 |
| 51,050 | 51,100 | 0 | 0 | 0 | 0 | 0 | 0 | 0 | 285 |
| 51,100 | 51,150 | 0 | 0 | 0 | 0 | 0 | 0 | 0 | 274 |
| 51,150 | 51,200 | 0 | 0 | 0 | 0 | 0 | 0 | 0 | 264 |
| 51,200 | 51,250 | 0 | 0 | 0 | 0 | 0 | 0 | 0 | 253 |
| 51,250 | 51,300 | 0 | 0 | 0 | 0 | 0 | 0 | 0 | 243 |
| 51,300 | 51,350 | 0 | 0 | 0 | 0 | 0 | 0 | 0 | 232 |
| 51,350 | 51,400 | 0 | 0 | 0 | 0 | 0 | 0 | 0 | 221 |
| 51,400 | 51,450 | 0 | 0 | 0 | 0 | 0 | 0 | 0 | 211 |
| 51,450 | 51,500 | 0 | 0 | 0 | 0 | 0 | 0 | 0 | 200 |
| 51,500 | 51,550 | 0 | 0 | 0 | 0 | 0 | 0 | 0 | 190 |
| 51,550 | 51,600 | 0 | 0 | 0 | 0 | 0 | 0 | 0 | 179 |
| 51,600 | 51,650 | 0 | 0 | 0 | 0 | 0 | 0 | 0 | 169 |
| 51,650 | 51,700 | 0 | 0 | 0 | 0 | 0 | 0 | 0 | 158 |
| 51,700 | 51,750 | 0 | 0 | 0 | 0 | 0 | 0 | 0 | 148 |
| 51,750 | 51,800 | 0 | 0 | 0 | 0 | 0 | 0 | 0 | 137 |
| 51,800 | 51,850 | 0 | 0 | 0 | 0 | 0 | 0 | 0 | 127 |
| 51,850 | 51,900 | 0 | 0 | 0 | 0 | 0 | 0 | 0 | 116 |
| 51,900 | 51,950 | 0 | 0 | 0 | 0 | 0 | 0 | 0 | 106 |
| 51,950 | 52,000 | 0 | 0 | 0 | 0 | 0 | 0 | 0 | 95 |

*If the amount you are looking up from the worksheet is at least $46,950 but less than $46,997, and you have three qualifying children, your credit is $5.
If the amount you are looking up from the worksheet is $46,997 or more, and you have three qualifying children, you cannot take the credit.

**If the amount you are looking up from the worksheet is at least $49,150 but less than $49,186, and you have two qualifying children, your credit is $4.
If the amount you are looking up from the worksheet is $49,186 or more, and you have two qualifying children, you cannot take the credit.

*(Continued)*

# 2014 Earned Income Credit Table

**Earned Income Credit (EIC) Table** - *Continued*                                                                    (**Caution.** This is **not** a tax table.)

| If the amount you are looking up from the worksheet is– | | And your filing status is– | | | | | | | | If the amount you are looking up from the worksheet is– | | And your filing status is– | | | | | | | |
| | | Single, head of household, or **qualifying widow(er)** and the number of children you have is– | | | | **Married filing jointly** and the number of children you have is– | | | | | | Single, head of household, or **qualifying widow(er)** and the number of children you have is– | | | | **Married filing jointly** and the number of children you have is– | | | |
| | | 0 | 1 | 2 | 3 | 0 | 1 | 2 | 3 | | | 0 | 1 | 2 | 3 | 0 | 1 | 2 | 3 |
| At least | But less than | Your credit is– | | | | Your credit is– | | | | At least | But less than | Your credit is– | | | | Your credit is– | | | |
| 52,000 | 52,050 | 0 | 0 | 0 | 0 | 0 | 0 | 0 | 85 | 52,400 | 52,427 | 0 | 0 | 0 | 0 | 0 | 0 | 0 | 3 |
| 52,050 | 52,100 | 0 | 0 | 0 | 0 | 0 | 0 | 0 | 74 | | | | | | | | | | |
| 52,100 | 52,150 | 0 | 0 | 0 | 0 | 0 | 0 | 0 | 64 | | | | | | | | | | |
| 52,150 | 52,200 | 0 | 0 | 0 | 0 | 0 | 0 | 0 | 53 | | | | | | | | | | |
| 52,200 | 52,250 | 0 | 0 | 0 | 0 | 0 | 0 | 0 | 42 | | | | | | | | | | |
| 52,250 | 52,300 | 0 | 0 | 0 | 0 | 0 | 0 | 0 | 32 | | | | | | | | | | |
| 52,300 | 52,350 | 0 | 0 | 0 | 0 | 0 | 0 | 0 | 21 | | | | | | | | | | |
| 52,350 | 52,400 | 0 | 0 | 0 | 0 | 0 | 0 | 0 | 11 | | | | | | | | | | |

# 8. Corporate Tax Rate Schedule

**Corporate Tax Rate Schedule**
**For tax years beginning on or after Jan. 1, 1993**

| If taxable income is: | | Tax is: | Of the amount over— |
|---|---|---|---|
| Over— | But not over— | | |
| $ 0 | $ 50,000 | 15% | $ 0 |
| 50,000 | 75,000 | $ 7,500 + 25% | 50,000 |
| 75,000 | 100,000 | 13,750 + 34% | 75,000 |
| 100,000 | 335,000 | 22,250 + 39% | 100,000 |
| 335,000 | 10,000,000 | 113,900 + 34% | 335,000 |
| 10,000,000 | 15,000,000 | 3,400,000 + 35% | 10,000,000 |
| 15,000,000 | 18,333,333 | 5,150,000 + 38% | 15,000,000 |
| 18,333,333 | — | 35% | 0 |

## 9. Estate and Gift Tax Rates (2013 and Thereafter)

(Source: § 2001(c))

| Taxable Amount Over | Taxable Amount Not Over | Tax on Amount in 1st Column | Tax Rate on Excess Over Amount in 1st Column |
|---|---|---|---|
| $ 0 | $ 10,000 | $ 0 | 18% |
| $ 10,000 | $ 20,000 | $ 1,800 | 20% |
| $ 20,000 | $ 40,000 | $ 3,800 | 22% |
| $ 40,000 | $ 60,000 | $ 8,200 | 24% |
| $ 60,000 | $ 80,000 | $ 13,000 | 26% |
| $ 80,000 | $ 100,000 | $ 18,200 | 28% |
| $ 100,000 | $ 150,000 | $ 23,800 | 30% |
| $ 150,000 | $ 250,000 | $ 38,800 | 32% |
| $ 250,000 | $ 500,000 | $ 70,800 | 34% |
| $ 500,000 | $ 750,000 | $ 155,800 | 37% |
| $ 750,000 | $ 1,000,000 | $ 248,300 | 39% |
| $ 1,000,000 | | $ 345,800 | 40% |

Note that, for post-2005 decedents, estates are not taxed in the lower brackets because of the use of the "applicable exclusion amount," also known as the "unified credit." The same is true for post-2009 gifts. For spouses dying after 2010, the applicable exclusion amount may also include the deceased spousal unused exclusion amount.

# 10. Tables of Class Lives and Recovery Periods

## IRS Pub. 946, How to Depreciate Property (2013)

IRS Publication 946, *How to Depreciate Property*, Appendix B, consists of two parts. The first part, Table B-1, begins with the heading, SPECIFIC DEPRECIABLE ASSETS USED IN ALL BUSINESS ACTIVITIES, EXCEPT AS NOTED. The second part, Table B-2, begins with the heading, DEPRECIABLE ASSETS USED IN THE FOLLOWING ACTIVITIES. Both Table B-1 and Table B-2 must be consulted to determine the correct recovery period. First, look in Table B-1 for a description of the property. Second, look in Table B-2 for a description of the activity in which the property is being used.

If the property is described in Table B-1, use the recovery period shown in the appropriate column of Table B-1, *unless:* (1) the applicable activity is described in Table B-2; *and* the property is specifically included in the assets listed for that activity in Table B-2. If the latter two conditions apply, use the recovery period shown in the appropriate column of Table B-2.

If the property is not described in Table B-1, but the applicable activity is described in Table B-2, use the recovery period shown in the appropriate column of Table B-2 (regardless of whether the property is specifically included in the assets listed for that activity in Table B-2).

If the property is not described in Table B-1 and the applicable activity is not described in Table B-2, check the end of Table B-2 under *Certain Property for Which Recovery Periods Assigned*.

A complete version of IRS Pub. 946 is available online at www.irs.gov/pub/irs-pdf/p946.pdf and on Bloomberg BNA Tax and Accounting Center (taxandaccounting.bna.com).

# 11. MACRS Depreciation Tables

(Source: IRS Pub. 946, How to Depreciate Property (2013))

## 3-, 5-, 7-, 10-, 15-, and 20-Year Property (Half-Year Convention)

| Year | 3-year | 5-year | 7-year | 10-year | 15-year | 20-year |
|------|--------|--------|--------|---------|---------|---------|
| 1 | 33.33% | 20.00% | 14.29% | 10.00% | 5.00% | 3.750% |
| 2 | 44.45% | 32.00% | 24.49% | 18.00% | 9.50% | 7.219% |
| 3 | 14.81% | 19.20% | 17.49% | 14.40% | 8.55% | 6.677% |
| 4 | 7.41% | 11.52% | 12.49% | 11.52% | 7.70% | 6.177% |
| 5 | | 11.52% | 8.93% | 9.22% | 6.93% | 5.713% |
| 6 | | 5.76% | 8.92% | 7.37% | 6.23% | 5.285% |
| 7 | | | 8.93% | 6.55% | 5.90% | 4.888% |
| 8 | | | 4.46% | 6.55% | 5.90% | 4.522% |
| 9 | | | | 6.56% | 5.91% | 4.462% |
| 10 | | | | 6.55% | 5.90% | 4.461% |
| 11 | | | | 3.28% | 5.91% | 4.462% |
| 12 | | | | | 5.90% | 4.461% |
| 13 | | | | | 5.91% | 4.462% |
| 14 | | | | | 5.90% | 4.461% |
| 15 | | | | | 5.91% | 4.462% |
| 16 | | | | | 2.95% | 4.461% |
| 17 | | | | | | 4.462% |
| 18 | | | | | | 4.461% |
| 19 | | | | | | 4.462% |
| 20 | | | | | | 4.461% |
| 21 | | | | | | 2.231% |

## 3-, 5-, 7-, 10-, 15-, and 20-Year Property (Mid-Quarter Convention)

**Placed in Service in First Quarter**
**Depreciation rate for recovery period**

| Year | 3-year | 5-year | 7-year | 10-year | 15-year | 20-year |
|------|--------|--------|--------|---------|---------|---------|
| 1 | 58.33% | 35.00% | 25.00% | 17.50% | 8.75% | 6.563% |
| 2 | 27.78% | 26.00% | 21.43% | 16.50% | 9.13% | 7.000% |
| 3 | 12.35% | 15.60% | 15.31% | 13.20% | 8.21% | 6.482% |
| 4 | 1.54% | 11.01% | 10.93% | 10.56% | 7.39% | 5.996% |
| 5 | | 11.01% | 8.75% | 8.45% | 6.65% | 5.546% |
| 6 | | 1.38% | 8.74% | 6.76% | 5.99% | 5.130% |
| 7 | | | 8.75% | 6.55% | 5.90% | 4.746% |
| 8 | | | 1.09% | 6.55% | 5.91% | 4.459% |
| 9 | | | | 6.56% | 5.90% | 4.459% |
| 10 | | | | 6.55% | 5.91% | 4.459% |
| 11 | | | | 0.82% | 5.90% | 4.459% |
| 12 | | | | | 5.91% | 4.460% |

### Placed in Service in First Quarter
### Depreciation rate for recovery period

| Year | 3-year | 5-year | 7-year | 10-year | 15-year | 20-year |
|------|--------|--------|--------|---------|---------|---------|
| 13 | | | | | 5.90% | 4.459% |
| 14 | | | | | 5.91% | 4.460% |
| 15 | | | | | 5.90% | 4.459% |
| 16 | | | | | 0.74% | 4.460% |
| 17 | | | | | | 4.459% |
| 18 | | | | | | 4.460% |
| 19 | | | | | | 4.459% |
| 20 | | | | | | 4.460% |
| 21 | | | | | | 0.565% |

### Placed in Service in Second Quarter
### Depreciation rate for recovery period

| Year | 3-year | 5-year | 7-year | 10-year | 15-year | 20-year |
|------|--------|--------|--------|---------|---------|---------|
| 1 | 41.67% | 25.00% | 17.85% | 12.50% | 6.25% | 4.688% |
| 2 | 38.89% | 30.00% | 23.47% | 17.50% | 9.38% | 7.148% |
| 3 | 14.14% | 18.00% | 16.76% | 14.00% | 8.44% | 6.612% |
| 4 | 5.30% | 11.37% | 11.97% | 11.20% | 7.59% | 6.116% |
| 5 | | 11.37% | 8.87% | 8.96% | 6.83% | 5.658% |
| 6 | | 4.26% | 8.87% | 7.17% | 6.15% | 5.233% |
| 7 | | | 8.87% | 6.55% | 5.91% | 4.841% |
| 8 | | | 3.34% | 6.55% | 5.90% | 4.478% |
| 9 | | | | 6.56% | 5.91% | 4.463% |
| 10 | | | | 6.55% | 5.90% | 4.463% |
| 11 | | | | 2.46% | 5.91% | 4.463% |
| 12 | | | | | 5.90% | 4.463% |
| 13 | | | | | 5.91% | 4.463% |
| 14 | | | | | 5.90% | 4.463% |
| 15 | | | | | 5.91% | 4.462% |
| 16 | | | | | 2.21% | 4.463% |
| 17 | | | | | | 4.462% |
| 18 | | | | | | 4.463% |
| 19 | | | | | | 4.462% |
| 20 | | | | | | 4.463% |
| 21 | | | | | | 1.673% |

### Placed in Service in Third Quarter
### Depreciation rate for recovery period

| Year | 3-year | 5-year | 7-year | 10-year | 15-year | 20-year |
|------|--------|--------|--------|---------|---------|---------|
| 1 | 25.00% | 15.00% | 10.71% | 7.50% | 3.75% | 2.813% |
| 2 | 50.00% | 34.00% | 25.51% | 18.50% | 9.63% | 7.289% |
| 3 | 16.67% | 20.40% | 18.22% | 14.80% | 8.66% | 6.742% |
| 4 | 8.33% | 12.24% | 13.02% | 11.84% | 7.80% | 6.237% |
| 5 | | 11.30% | 9.30% | 9.47% | 7.02% | 5.769% |
| 6 | | 7.06% | 8.85% | 7.58% | 6.31% | 5.336% |

# MACRS Depreciation Tables

### Placed in Service in Third Quarter
### Depreciation rate for recovery period

| Year | 3-year | 5-year | 7-year | 10-year | 15-year | 20-year |
|------|--------|--------|--------|---------|---------|---------|
| 7    |        |        | 8.86%  | 6.55%   | 5.90%   | 4.936%  |
| 8    |        |        | 5.53%  | 6.55%   | 5.90%   | 4.566%  |
| 9    |        |        |        | 6.56%   | 5.91%   | 4.460%  |
| 10   |        |        |        | 6.55%   | 5.90%   | 4.460%  |
| 11   |        |        |        | 4.10%   | 5.91%   | 4.460%  |
| 12   |        |        |        |         | 5.90%   | 4.460%  |
| 13   |        |        |        |         | 5.91%   | 4.461%  |
| 14   |        |        |        |         | 5.90%   | 4.460%  |
| 15   |        |        |        |         | 5.91%   | 4.461%  |
| 16   |        |        |        |         | 3.69%   | 4.460%  |
| 17   |        |        |        |         |         | 4.461%  |
| 18   |        |        |        |         |         | 4.460%  |
| 19   |        |        |        |         |         | 4.461%  |
| 20   |        |        |        |         |         | 4.460%  |
| 21   |        |        |        |         |         | 2.788%  |

### Placed in Service in Fourth Quarter
### Depreciation rate for recovery period

| Year | 3-year | 5-year | 7-year | 10-year | 15-year | 20-year |
|------|--------|--------|--------|---------|---------|---------|
| 1    | 8.33%  | 5.00%  | 3.57%  | 2.50%   | 1.25%   | 0.938%  |
| 2    | 61.11% | 38.00% | 27.55% | 19.50%  | 9.88%   | 7.430%  |
| 3    | 20.37% | 22.80% | 19.68% | 15.60%  | 8.89%   | 6.872%  |
| 4    | 10.19% | 13.68% | 14.06% | 12.48%  | 8.00%   | 6.357%  |
| 5    |        | 10.94% | 10.04% | 9.98%   | 7.20%   | 5.880%  |
| 6    |        | 9.58%  | 8.73%  | 7.99%   | 6.48%   | 5.439%  |
| 7    |        |        | 8.73%  | 6.55%   | 5.90%   | 5.031%  |
| 8    |        |        | 7.64%  | 6.55%   | 5.90%   | 4.654%  |
| 9    |        |        |        | 6.56%   | 5.90%   | 4.458%  |
| 10   |        |        |        | 6.55%   | 5.91%   | 4.458%  |
| 11   |        |        |        | 5.74%   | 5.90%   | 4.458%  |
| 12   |        |        |        |         | 5.91%   | 4.458%  |
| 13   |        |        |        |         | 5.90%   | 4.458%  |
| 14   |        |        |        |         | 5.91%   | 4.458%  |
| 15   |        |        |        |         | 5.90%   | 4.458%  |
| 16   |        |        |        |         | 5.17%   | 4.458%  |
| 17   |        |        |        |         |         | 4.458%  |
| 18   |        |        |        |         |         | 4.459%  |
| 19   |        |        |        |         |         | 4.458%  |
| 20   |        |        |        |         |         | 4.459%  |
| 21   |        |        |        |         |         | 3.901%  |

<u>Residential Rental Property Mid-Month Convention Straight</u>
<u>Line — 27.5 Years</u>

### Month property placed in service

| Year | 1 | 2 | 3 | 4 | 5 | 6 |
|------|------|------|------|------|------|------|
| 1 | 3.485% | 3.182% | 2.879% | 2.576% | 2.273% | 1.970% |
| 2-9 | 3.636% | 3.636% | 3.636% | 3.636% | 3.636% | 3.636% |
| 10 | 3.637% | 3.637% | 3.637% | 3.637% | 3.637% | 3.637% |
| 11 | 3.636% | 3.636% | 3.636% | 3.636% | 3.636% | 3.636% |
| 12 | 3.637% | 3.637% | 3.637% | 3.637% | 3.637% | 3.637% |
| 13 | 3.636% | 3.636% | 3.636% | 3.636% | 3.636% | 3.636% |
| 14 | 3.637% | 3.637% | 3.637% | 3.637% | 3.637% | 3.637% |
| 15 | 3.636% | 3.636% | 3.636% | 3.636% | 3.636% | 3.636% |
| 16 | 3.637% | 3.637% | 3.637% | 3.637% | 3.637% | 3.637% |
| 17 | 3.636% | 3.636% | 3.636% | 3.636% | 3.636% | 3.636% |
| 18 | 3.637% | 3.637% | 3.637% | 3.637% | 3.637% | 3.637% |
| 19 | 3.636% | 3.636% | 3.636% | 3.636% | 3.636% | 3.636% |
| 20 | 3.637% | 3.637% | 3.637% | 3.637% | 3.637% | 3.637% |
| 21 | 3.636% | 3.636% | 3.636% | 3.636% | 3.636% | 3.636% |
| 22 | 3.637% | 3.637% | 3.637% | 3.637% | 3.637% | 3.637% |
| 23 | 3.636% | 3.636% | 3.636% | 3.636% | 3.636% | 3.636% |
| 24 | 3.637% | 3.637% | 3.637% | 3.637% | 3.637% | 3.637% |
| 25 | 3.636% | 3.636% | 3.636% | 3.636% | 3.636% | 3.636% |
| 26 | 3.637% | 3.637% | 3.637% | 3.637% | 3.637% | 3.637% |
| 27 | 3.636% | 3.636% | 3.636% | 3.636% | 3.636% | 3.636% |
| 28 | 1.97% | 2.273% | 2.576% | 2.879% | 3.182% | 3.485% |
| 29 | | | | | | |

### Month property placed in service

| Year | 7 | 8 | 9 | 10 | 11 | 12 |
|------|------|------|------|------|------|------|
| 1 | 1.667% | 1.364% | 1.061% | 0.758% | 0.455% | 0.152% |
| 2-9 | 3.636% | 3.636% | 3.636% | 3.636% | 3.636% | 3.636% |
| 10 | 3.636% | 3.636% | 3.636% | 3.636% | 3.636% | 3.636% |
| 11 | 3.637% | 3.637% | 3.637% | 3.637% | 3.637% | 3.637% |
| 12 | 3.636% | 3.636% | 3.636% | 3.636% | 3.636% | 3.636% |
| 13 | 3.637% | 3.637% | 3.637% | 3.637% | 3.637% | 3.637% |
| 14 | 3.636% | 3.636% | 3.636% | 3.636% | 3.636% | 3.636% |
| 15 | 3.637% | 3.637% | 3.637% | 3.637% | 3.637% | 3.637% |
| 16 | 3.636% | 3.636% | 3.636% | 3.636% | 3.636% | 3.636% |
| 17 | 3.637% | 3.637% | 3.637% | 3.637% | 3.637% | 3.637% |
| 18 | 3.636% | 3.636% | 3.636% | 3.636% | 3.636% | 3.636% |
| 19 | 3.637% | 3.637% | 3.637% | 3.637% | 3.637% | 3.637% |
| 20 | 3.636% | 3.636% | 3.636% | 3.636% | 3.636% | 3.636% |

## MACRS Depreciation Tables

### Month property placed in service

| Year | 7 | 8 | 9 | 10 | 11 | 12 |
|---|---|---|---|---|---|---|
| 21 | 3.637% | 3.637% | 3.637% | 3.637% | 3.637% | 3.637% |
| 22 | 3.636% | 3.636% | 3.636% | 3.636% | 3.636% | 3.636% |
| 23 | 3.637% | 3.637% | 3.637% | 3.637% | 3.637% | 3.637% |
| 24 | 3.636% | 3.636% | 3.636% | 3.636% | 3.636% | 3.636% |
| 25 | 3.637% | 3.637% | 3.637% | 3.637% | 3.637% | 3.637% |
| 26 | 3.636% | 3.636% | 3.636% | 3.636% | 3.636% | 3.636% |
| 27 | 3.637% | 3.637% | 3.637% | 3.637% | 3.637% | 3.637% |
| 28 | 3.636% | 3.636% | 3.636% | 3.636% | 3.636% | 3.636% |
| 29 | 0.152% | 0.455% | 0.758% | 1.061% | 1.364% | 1.667% |

## Nonresidential Real Property Mid-Month Convention Straight Line — 31.5 Years

### Month property placed in service

| Year | 1 | 2 | 3 | 4 | 5 | 6 |
|---|---|---|---|---|---|---|
| 1 | 3.042% | 2.778% | 2.513% | 2.249% | 1.984% | 1.720% |
| 2-7 | 3.175% | 3.175% | 3.175% | 3.175% | 3.175% | 3.175% |
| 8 | 3.175% | 3.174% | 3.175% | 3.174% | 3.175% | 3.174% |
| 9 | 3.174% | 3.175% | 3.174% | 3.175% | 3.174% | 3.175% |
| 10 | 3.175% | 3.174% | 3.175% | 3.174% | 3.175% | 3.174% |
| 11 | 3.174% | 3.175% | 3.174% | 3.175% | 3.174% | 3.175% |
| 12 | 3.175% | 3.174% | 3.175% | 3.174% | 3.175% | 3.174% |
| 13 | 3.174% | 3.175% | 3.174% | 3.175% | 3.174% | 3.175% |
| 14 | 3.175% | 3.174% | 3.175% | 3.174% | 3.175% | 3.174% |
| 15 | 3.174% | 3.175% | 3.174% | 3.175% | 3.174% | 3.175% |
| 16 | 3.175% | 3.174% | 3.175% | 3.174% | 3.175% | 3.174% |
| 17 | 3.174% | 3.175% | 3.174% | 3.175% | 3.174% | 3.175% |
| 18 | 3.175% | 3.174% | 3.175% | 3.174% | 3.175% | 3.174% |
| 19 | 3.174% | 3.175% | 3.174% | 3.175% | 3.174% | 3.175% |
| 20 | 3.175% | 3.174% | 3.175% | 3.174% | 3.175% | 3.174% |
| 21 | 3.174% | 3.175% | 3.174% | 3.175% | 3.174% | 3.175% |
| 22 | 3.175% | 3.174% | 3.175% | 3.174% | 3.175% | 3.174% |
| 23 | 3.174% | 3.175% | 3.174% | 3.175% | 3.174% | 3.175% |
| 24 | 3.175% | 3.174% | 3.175% | 3.174% | 3.175% | 3.174% |
| 25 | 3.174% | 3.175% | 3.174% | 3.175% | 3.174% | 3.175% |
| 26 | 3.175% | 3.174% | 3.175% | 3.174% | 3.175% | 3.174% |
| 27 | 3.174% | 3.175% | 3.174% | 3.175% | 3.174% | 3.175% |
| 28 | 3.175% | 3.174% | 3.175% | 3.174% | 3.175% | 3.174% |
| 29 | 3.174% | 3.175% | 3.174% | 3.175% | 3.174% | 3.175% |
| 30 | 3.175% | 3.174% | 3.175% | 3.174% | 3.175% | 3.174% |
| 31 | 3.174% | 3.175% | 3.174% | 3.175% | 3.174% | 3.175% |

### Month property placed in service

| Year | 1 | 2 | 3 | 4 | 5 | 6 |
|------|------|------|------|------|------|------|
| 32 | 1.720% | 1.984% | 2.249% | 2.513% | 2.778% | 3.042% |
| 33 | | | | | | |

### Month property placed in service

| Year | 7 | 8 | 9 | 10 | 11 | 12 |
|------|------|------|------|------|------|------|
| 1 | 1.455% | 1.190% | 0.926% | 0.661% | 0.397% | 0.132% |
| 2-7 | 3.175% | 3.175% | 3.175% | 3.175% | 3.175% | 3.175% |
| 8 | 3.175% | 3.175% | 3.175% | 3.175% | 3.175% | 3.175% |
| 9 | 3.174% | 3.175% | 3.174% | 3.175% | 3.174% | 3.175% |
| 10 | 3.175% | 3.174% | 3.175% | 3.174% | 3.175% | 3.174% |
| 11 | 3.174% | 3.175% | 3.174% | 3.175% | 3.174% | 3.175% |
| 12 | 3.175% | 3.174% | 3.175% | 3.174% | 3.175% | 3.174% |
| 13 | 3.174% | 3.175% | 3.174% | 3.175% | 3.174% | 3.175% |
| 14 | 3.175% | 3.174% | 3.175% | 3.174% | 3.175% | 3.174% |
| 15 | 3.174% | 3.175% | 3.174% | 3.175% | 3.174% | 3.175% |
| 16 | 3.175% | 3.174% | 3.175% | 3.174% | 3.175% | 3.174% |
| 17 | 3.174% | 3.175% | 3.174% | 3.175% | 3.174% | 3.175% |
| 18 | 3.175% | 3.174% | 3.175% | 3.174% | 3.175% | 3.174% |
| 19 | 3.174% | 3.175% | 3.174% | 3.175% | 3.174% | 3.175% |
| 20 | 3.175% | 3.174% | 3.175% | 3.174% | 3.175% | 3.174% |
| 21 | 3.174% | 3.175% | 3.174% | 3.175% | 3.174% | 3.175% |
| 22 | 3.175% | 3.174% | 3.175% | 3.174% | 3.175% | 3.174% |
| 23 | 3.174% | 3.175% | 3.174% | 3.175% | 3.174% | 3.175% |
| 24 | 3.175% | 3.174% | 3.175% | 3.174% | 3.175% | 3.174% |
| 25 | 3.174% | 3.175% | 3.174% | 3.175% | 3.174% | 3.175% |
| 26 | 3.175% | 3.174% | 3.175% | 3.174% | 3.175% | 3.174% |
| 27 | 3.174% | 3.175% | 3.174% | 3.175% | 3.174% | 3.175% |
| 28 | 3.175% | 3.174% | 3.175% | 3.174% | 3.175% | 3.174% |
| 29 | 3.174% | 3.175% | 3.174% | 3.175% | 3.174% | 3.175% |
| 30 | 3.175% | 3.174% | 3.175% | 3.174% | 3.175% | 3.174% |
| 31 | 3.174% | 3.175% | 3.174% | 3.175% | 3.174% | 3.175% |
| 32 | 3.175% | 3.174% | 3.175% | 3.174% | 3.175% | 3.174% |
| 33 | 0.132% | 0.397% | 0.661% | 0.926% | 1.190% | 1.455% |

## MACRS Depreciation Tables

### Nonresidential Real Property Mid-Month Convention Straight Line — 39 Years

#### Month property placed in service

| Year | 1 | 2 | 3 | 4 | 5 | 6 |
|---|---|---|---|---|---|---|
| 1 | 2.461% | 2.247% | 2.033% | 1.819% | 1.605% | 1.391% |
| 2-39 | 2.564% | 2.564% | 2.564% | 2.564% | 2.564% | 2.564% |
| 40 | 0.107% | 0.321% | 0.535% | 0.749% | 0.963% | 1.177% |

#### Month property placed in service

| Year | 7 | 8 | 9 | 10 | 11 | 12 |
|---|---|---|---|---|---|---|
| 1 | 1.177% | 0.963% | 0.749% | 0.535% | 0.321% | 0.107% |
| 2-39 | 2.564% | 2.564% | 2.564% | 2.564% | 2.564% | 2.564% |
| 40 | 1.391% | 1.605% | 1.819% | 2.033% | 2.247% | 2.461% |

### Straight Line Method (Half-Year Convention)

#### Recovery periods in years

| Year | 2.5 | 3 | 3.5 | 4 | 5 | 6 | 6.5 | 7 |
|---|---|---|---|---|---|---|---|---|
| 1 | 20.0% | 16.67% | 14.29% | 12.5% | 10% | 8.33% | 7.69% | 7.14% |
| 2 | 40.0% | 33.33% | 28.57% | 25.0% | 20% | 16.67% | 15.39% | 14.29% |
| 3 | 40.0% | 33.33% | 28.57% | 25.0% | 20% | 16.67% | 15.38% | 14.29% |
| 4 | | 16.67% | 28.57% | 25.0% | 20% | 16.67% | 15.39% | 14.28% |
| 5 | | | | 12.5% | 20% | 16.66% | 15.38% | 14.29% |
| 6 | | | | | 10% | 16.67% | 15.39% | 14.28% |
| 7 | | | | | | 8.33% | 15.38% | 14.29% |
| 8 | | | | | | | | 7.14% |

#### Recovery periods in years

| Year | 7.5 | 8 | 8.5 | 9 | 9.5 | 10 | 10.5 | 11 |
|---|---|---|---|---|---|---|---|---|
| 1 | 6.67% | 6.25% | 5.88% | 5.56% | 5.26% | 5.0% | 4.76% | 4.55% |
| 2 | 13.33% | 12.50% | 11.77% | 11.11% | 10.53% | 10.0% | 9.52% | 9.09% |
| 3 | 13.33% | 12.50% | 11.76% | 11.11% | 10.53% | 10.0% | 9.52% | 9.09% |
| 4 | 13.33% | 12.50% | 11.77% | 11.11% | 10.53% | 10.0% | 9.53% | 9.09% |
| 5 | 13.34% | 12.50% | 11.76% | 11.11% | 10.52% | 10.0% | 9.52% | 9.09% |
| 6 | 13.33% | 12.50% | 11.77% | 11.11% | 10.53% | 10.0% | 9.53% | 9.09% |
| 7 | 13.34% | 12.50% | 11.76% | 11.11% | 10.52% | 10.0% | 9.52% | 9.09% |
| 8 | 13.33% | 12.50% | 11.77% | 11.11% | 10.53% | 10.0% | 9.53% | 9.09% |
| 9 | | 6.25% | 11.76% | 11.11% | 10.52% | 10.0% | 9.52% | 9.09% |
| 10 | | | 5.56% | 10.53% | 10.0% | 9.53% | 9.09% |
| 11 | | | | | 5.0% | 9.52% | 9.09% |
| 12 | | | | | | | | 4.55% |

### Recovery periods in years

| Year | 11.5 | 12 | 12.5 | 13 | 13.5 | 14 | 15 | 16 |
|------|------|------|------|------|------|------|------|------|
| 1 | 4.35% | 4.17% | 4.0% | 3.85% | 3.70% | 3.57% | 3.33% | 3.13% |
| 2 | 8.70% | 8.33% | 8.0% | 7.69% | 7.41% | 7.14% | 6.67% | 6.25% |
| 3 | 8.70% | 8.33% | 8.0% | 7.69% | 7.41% | 7.14% | 6.67% | 6.25% |
| 4 | 8.69% | 8.33% | 8.0% | 7.69% | 7.41% | 7.14% | 6.67% | 6.25% |
| 5 | 8.70% | 8.33% | 8.0% | 7.69% | 7.41% | 7.14% | 6.67% | 6.25% |
| 6 | 8.69% | 8.33% | 8.0% | 7.69% | 7.41% | 7.14% | 6.67% | 6.25% |
| 7 | 8.70% | 8.34% | 8.0% | 7.69% | 7.41% | 7.14% | 6.67% | 6.25% |
| 8 | 8.69% | 8.33% | 8.0% | 7.69% | 7.41% | 7.15% | 6.66% | 6.25% |
| 9 | 8.70% | 8.34% | 8.0% | 7.69% | 7.41% | 7.14% | 6.67% | 6.25% |
| 10 | 8.69% | 8.33% | 8.0% | 7.70% | 7.40% | 7.15% | 6.66% | 6.25% |
| 11 | 8.70% | 8.34% | 8.0% | 7.69% | 7.41% | 7.14% | 6.67% | 6.25% |
| 12 | 8.69% | 8.33% | 8.0% | 7.70% | 7.40% | 7.15% | 6.66% | 6.25% |
| 13 | | 4.17% | 8.0% | 7.69% | 7.41% | 7.14% | 6.67% | 6.25% |
| 14 | | | | 3.85% | 7.40% | 7.15% | 6.66% | 6.25% |
| 15 | | | | | | 3.57% | 6.67% | 6.25% |
| 16 | | | | | | | 3.33% | 6.25% |
| 17 | | | | | | | | 3.12% |

### Recovery periods in years

| Year | 16.5 | 17 | 18 | 19 | 20 | 22 | 24 | 25 |
|------|------|------|------|------|------|------|------|------|
| 1 | 3.03% | 2.94% | 2.78% | 2.63% | 2.5% | 2.273% | 2.083% | 2.0% |
| 2 | 6.06% | 5.88% | 5.56% | 5.26% | 5.0% | 4.545% | 4.167% | 4.0% |
| 3 | 6.06% | 5.88% | 5.56% | 5.26% | 5.0% | 4.545% | 4.167% | 4.0% |
| 4 | 6.06% | 5.88% | 5.55% | 5.26% | 5.0% | 4.545% | 4.167% | 4.0% |
| 5 | 6.06% | 5.88% | 5.56% | 5.26% | 5.0% | 4.546% | 4.167% | 4.0% |
| 6 | 6.06% | 5.88% | 5.55% | 5.26% | 5.0% | 4.545% | 4.167% | 4.0% |
| 7 | 6.06% | 5.88% | 5.56% | 5.26% | 5.0% | 4.546% | 4.167% | 4.0% |
| 8 | 6.06% | 5.88% | 5.55% | 5.26% | 5.0% | 4.545% | 4.167% | 4.0% |
| 9 | 6.06% | 5.88% | 5.56% | 5.27% | 5.0% | 4.546% | 4.167% | 4.0% |
| 10 | 6.06% | 5.88% | 5.55% | 5.26% | 5.0% | 4.545% | 4.167% | 4.0% |
| 11 | 6.06% | 5.89% | 5.56% | 5.27% | 5.0% | 4.546% | 4.166% | 4.0% |
| 12 | 6.06% | 5.88% | 5.55% | 5.26% | 5.0% | 4.545% | 4.167% | 4.0% |
| 13 | 6.06% | 5.89% | 5.56% | 5.27% | 5.0% | 4.546% | 4.166% | 4.0% |
| 14 | 6.06% | 5.88% | 5.55% | 5.26% | 5.0% | 4.545% | 4.167% | 4.0% |
| 15 | 6.06% | 5.89% | 5.56% | 5.27% | 5.0% | 4.546% | 4.166% | 4.0% |
| 16 | 6.06% | 5.88% | 5.55% | 5.26% | 5.0% | 4.545% | 4.167% | 4.0% |
| 17 | 6.07% | 5.89% | 5.56% | 5.27% | 5.0% | 4.546% | 4.166% | 4.0% |
| 18 | | 2.94% | 5.55% | 5.26% | 5.0% | 4.545% | 4.167% | 4.0% |
| 19 | | | 2.78% | 5.27% | 5.0% | 4.546% | 4.166% | 4.0% |
| 20 | | | | 2.63% | 5.0% | 4.545% | 4.167% | 4.0% |
| 21 | | | | | 2.5% | 4.546% | 4.166% | 4.0% |

## MACRS Depreciation Tables

### Recovery periods in years

| Year | 16.5 | 17 | 18 | 19 | 20 | 22 | 24 | 25 |
|------|------|----|----|----|----|--------|--------|------|
| 22 | | | | | | 4.545% | 4.167% | 4.0% |
| 23 | | | | | | 2.273% | 4.166% | 4.0% |
| 24 | | | | | | | 4.167% | 4.0% |
| 25 | | | | | | | 2.083% | 4.0% |
| 26 | | | | | | | | 2.0% |

### Recovery periods in years

| Year | 26.5 | 28 | 30 | 35 | 40 | 45 | 50 |
|------|--------|--------|--------|--------|-------|--------|------|
| 1 | 1.887% | 1.786% | 1.667% | 1.429% | 1.25% | 1.111% | 1.0% |
| 2-6 | 3.774% | 3.571% | 3.333% | 2.857% | 2.50% | 2.222% | 2.0% |
| 7 | 3.773% | 3.572% | 3.333% | 2.857% | 2.50% | 2.222% | 2.0% |
| 8 | 3.774% | 3.571% | 3.333% | 2.857% | 2.50% | 2.222% | 2.0% |
| 9 | 3.773% | 3.572% | 3.333% | 2.857% | 2.50% | 2.222% | 2.0% |
| 10 | 3.774% | 3.571% | 3.333% | 2.857% | 2.50% | 2.222% | 2.0% |
| 11 | 3.773% | 3.572% | 3.333% | 2.857% | 2.50% | 2.222% | 2.0% |
| 12 | 3.774% | 3.571% | 3.333% | 2.857% | 2.50% | 2.222% | 2.0% |
| 13 | 3.773% | 3.572% | 3.334% | 2.857% | 2.50% | 2.222% | 2.0% |
| 14 | 3.773% | 3.571% | 3.333% | 2.857% | 2.50% | 2.222% | 2.0% |
| 15 | 3.774% | 3.572% | 3.334% | 2.857% | 2.50% | 2.222% | 2.0% |
| 16 | 3.773% | 3.571% | 3.333% | 2.857% | 2.50% | 2.222% | 2.0% |
| 17 | 3.774% | 3.572% | 3.334% | 2.857% | 2.50% | 2.222% | 2.0% |
| 18 | 3.773% | 3.571% | 3.333% | 2.857% | 2.50% | 2.222% | 2.0% |
| 19 | 3.774% | 3.572% | 3.334% | 2.857% | 2.50% | 2.222% | 2.0% |
| 20 | 3.773% | 3.571% | 3.333% | 2.857% | 2.50% | 2.222% | 2.0% |
| 21 | 3.774% | 3.572% | 3.334% | 2.857% | 2.50% | 2.222% | 2.0% |
| 22 | 3.773% | 3.571% | 3.333% | 2.857% | 2.50% | 2.222% | 2.0% |
| 23 | 3.774% | 3.572% | 3.334% | 2.857% | 2.50% | 2.222% | 2.0% |
| 24 | 3.773% | 3.571% | 3.333% | 2.857% | 2.50% | 2.222% | 2.0% |
| 25 | 3.774% | 3.572% | 3.334% | 2.857% | 2.50% | 2.222% | 2.0% |
| 26 | 3.773% | 3.571% | 3.333% | 2.857% | 2.50% | 2.222% | 2.0% |
| 27 | 3.774% | 3.572% | 3.334% | 2.857% | 2.50% | 2.223% | 2.0% |
| 28 | | 3.571% | 3.333% | 2.858% | 2.50% | 2.222% | 2.0% |
| 29 | | 1.786% | 3.334% | 2.857% | 2.50% | 2.223% | 2.0% |
| 30 | | | 3.333% | 2.858% | 2.50% | 2.222% | 2.0% |
| 31 | | | 1.667% | 2.857% | 2.50% | 2.223% | 2.0% |
| 32 | | | | 2.858% | 2.50% | 2.222% | 2.0% |
| 33 | | | | 2.857% | 2.50% | 2.223% | 2.0% |
| 34 | | | | 2.858% | 2.50% | 2.222% | 2.0% |
| 35 | | | | 2.857% | 2.50% | 2.223% | 2.0% |
| 36 | | | | 1.429% | 2.50% | 2.222% | 2.0% |
| 37 | | | | | 2.50% | 2.223% | 2.0% |

### Recovery periods in years

| Year | 26.5 | 28 | 30 | 35 | 40 | 45 | 50 |
|------|------|----|----|----|------|--------|------|
| 38 | | | | | 2.50% | 2.222% | 2.0% |
| 39 | | | | | 2.50% | 2.223% | 2.0% |
| 40 | | | | | 2.50% | 2.222% | 2.0% |
| 41 | | | | | 1.25% | 2.223% | 2.0% |
| 42 | | | | | | 2.222% | 2.0% |
| 43 | | | | | | 2.223% | 2.0% |
| 44 | | | | | | 2.222% | 2.0% |
| 45 | | | | | | 2.223% | 2.0% |
| 46 | | | | | | 1.111% | 2.0% |
| 47-50 | | | | | | | 2.0% |
| 51 | | | | | | | 1.0% |

## Straight Line Method (Mid-Quarter Convention)

### Placed in Service in First Quarter
### Recovery periods in years

| Year | 2.5 | 3 | 3.5 | 4 | 5 | 6 | 6.5 | 7 |
|------|-------|--------|--------|--------|--------|--------|--------|--------|
| 1 | 35.0% | 29.17% | 25.00% | 21.88% | 17.5% | 14.58% | 13.46% | 12.50% |
| 2 | 40.0% | 33.33% | 28.57% | 25.00% | 20.0% | 16.67% | 15.38% | 14.29% |
| 3 | 25.0% | 33.33% | 28.57% | 25.00% | 20.0% | 16.67% | 15.39% | 14.28% |
| 4 | | 4.17% | 17.86% | 25.00% | 20.0% | 16.67% | 15.38% | 14.29% |
| 5 | | | 3.12% | 20.0% | 16.66% | 15.39% | 14.28% |
| 6 | | | | | 2.5% | 16.67% | 15.38% | 14.29% |
| 7 | | | | | | 2.08% | 9.62% | 14.28% |
| 8 | | | | | | | | 1.79% |

### Recovery periods in years

| Year | 7.5 | 8 | 8.5 | 9 | 9.5 | 10 | 10.5 | 11 |
|------|--------|--------|--------|--------|--------|--------|-------|-------|
| 1 | 11.67% | 10.94% | 10.29% | 9.72% | 9.21% | 8.75% | 8.33% | 7.95% |
| 2 | 13.33% | 12.50% | 11.77% | 11.11% | 10.53% | 10.00% | 9.52% | 9.09% |
| 3 | 13.33% | 12.50% | 11.76% | 11.11% | 10.53% | 10.00% | 9.52% | 9.09% |
| 4 | 13.33% | 12.50% | 11.77% | 11.11% | 10.53% | 10.00% | 9.53% | 9.09% |
| 5 | 13.34% | 12.50% | 11.76% | 11.11% | 10.52% | 10.00% | 9.52% | 9.09% |
| 6 | 13.33% | 12.50% | 11.77% | 11.11% | 10.53% | 10.00% | 9.53% | 9.09% |
| 7 | 13.34% | 12.50% | 11.76% | 11.11% | 10.52% | 10.00% | 9.52% | 9.09% |
| 8 | 8.33% | 12.50% | 11.77% | 11.12% | 10.53% | 10.00% | 9.53% | 9.09% |
| 9 | | 1.56% | 7.35% | 11.11% | 10.52% | 10.00% | 9.52% | 9.09% |
| 10 | | | | 1.39% | 6.58% | 10.00% | 9.53% | 9.10% |
| 11 | | | | | | 1.25% | 5.95% | 9.09% |
| 12 | | | | | | | | 1.14% |

### Recovery periods in years

| Year | 11.5 | 12 | 12.5 | 13 | 13.5 | 14 | 15 | 16 |
|------|-------|-------|------|-------|-------|-------|-------|-------|
| 1 | 7.61% | 7.29% | 7.0% | 6.73% | 6.48% | 6.25% | 5.83% | 5.47% |
| 2 | 8.70% | 8.33% | 8.0% | 7.69% | 7.41% | 7.14% | 6.67% | 6.25% |

# MACRS Depreciation Tables

## Recovery periods in years

| Year | 11.5 | 12 | 12.5 | 13 | 13.5 | 14 | 15 | 16 |
|---|---|---|---|---|---|---|---|---|
| 3 | 8.70% | 8.33% | 8.0% | 7.69% | 7.41% | 7.14% | 6.67% | 6.25% |
| 4 | 8.69% | 8.33% | 8.0% | 7.69% | 7.41% | 7.14% | 6.67% | 6.25% |
| 5 | 8.70% | 8.33% | 8.0% | 7.69% | 7.41% | 7.14% | 6.67% | 6.25% |
| 6 | 8.69% | 8.34% | 8.0% | 7.69% | 7.41% | 7.14% | 6.67% | 6.25% |
| 7 | 8.70% | 8.33% | 8.0% | 7.69% | 7.41% | 7.14% | 6.67% | 6.25% |
| 8 | 8.69% | 8.34% | 8.0% | 7.69% | 7.41% | 7.15% | 6.66% | 6.25% |
| 9 | 8.70% | 8.33% | 8.0% | 7.70% | 7.40% | 7.14% | 6.67% | 6.25% |
| 10 | 8.69% | 8.34% | 8.0% | 7.69% | 7.41% | 7.15% | 6.66% | 6.25% |
| 11 | 8.70% | 8.33% | 8.0% | 7.70% | 7.40% | 7.14% | 6.67% | 6.25% |
| 12 | 5.43% | 8.34% | 8.0% | 7.69% | 7.41% | 7.15% | 6.66% | 6.25% |
| 13 | | 1.04% | 5.0% | 7.70% | 7.40% | 7.14% | 6.67% | 6.25% |
| 14 | | | | 0.96% | 4.63% | 7.15% | 6.66% | 6.25% |
| 15 | | | | | | 0.89% | 6.67% | 6.25% |
| 16 | | | | | | | 0.83% | 6.25% |
| 17 | | | | | | | | 0.78% |

## Recovery periods in years

| Year | 16.5 | 17 | 18 | 19 | 20 | 22 | 24 | 25 |
|---|---|---|---|---|---|---|---|---|
| 1 | 5.30% | 5.15% | 4.86% | 4.61% | 4.375% | 3.977% | 3.646% | 3.5% |
| 2 | 6.06% | 5.88% | 5.56% | 5.26% | 5.000% | 4.545% | 4.167% | 4.0% |
| 3 | 6.06% | 5.88% | 5.56% | 5.26% | 5.000% | 4.545% | 4.167% | 4.0% |
| 4 | 6.06% | 5.88% | 5.56% | 5.26% | 5.000% | 4.546% | 4.167% | 4.0% |
| 5 | 6.06% | 5.88% | 5.55% | 5.26% | 5.000% | 4.545% | 4.167% | 4.0% |
| 6 | 6.06% | 5.88% | 5.56% | 5.26% | 5.000% | 4.546% | 4.167% | 4.0% |
| 7 | 6.06% | 5.88% | 5.55% | 5.26% | 5.000% | 4.545% | 4.167% | 4.0% |
| 8 | 6.06% | 5.88% | 5.56% | 5.26% | 5.000% | 4.546% | 4.167% | 4.0% |
| 9 | 6.06% | 5.88% | 5.55% | 5.26% | 5.000% | 4.545% | 4.167% | 4.0% |
| 10 | 6.06% | 5.88% | 5.56% | 5.27% | 5.000% | 4.546% | 4.166% | 4.0% |
| 11 | 6.06% | 5.88% | 5.55% | 5.26% | 5.000% | 4.545% | 4.167% | 4.0% |
| 12 | 6.06% | 5.89% | 5.56% | 5.27% | 5.000% | 4.546% | 4.166% | 4.0% |
| 13 | 6.06% | 5.88% | 5.55% | 5.26% | 5.000% | 4.545% | 4.167% | 4.0% |
| 14 | 6.06% | 5.89% | 5.56% | 5.27% | 5.000% | 4.546% | 4.166% | 4.0% |
| 15 | 6.06% | 5.88% | 5.55% | 5.26% | 5.000% | 4.545% | 4.167% | 4.0% |
| 16 | 6.07% | 5.89% | 5.56% | 5.27% | 5.000% | 4.546% | 4.166% | 4.0% |
| 17 | 3.79% | 5.88% | 5.55% | 5.26% | 5.000% | 4.545% | 4.167% | 4.0% |
| 18 | | 0.74% | 5.56% | 5.27% | 5.000% | 4.546% | 4.166% | 4.0% |
| 19 | | | 0.69% | 5.26% | 5.000% | 4.545% | 4.167% | 4.0% |
| 20 | | | | 0.66% | 5.000% | 4.546% | 4.166% | 4.0% |
| 21 | | | | | 0.625% | 4.545% | 4.167% | 4.0% |
| 22 | | | | | | 4.546% | 4.166% | 4.0% |
| 23 | | | | | | 0.568% | 4.167% | 4.0% |
| 24 | | | | | | | 4.166% | 4.0% |
| 25 | | | | | | | 0.521% | 4.0% |
| 26 | | | | | | | | 0.5% |

## Recovery periods in years

| Year | 26.5 | 28 | 30 | 35 | 40 | 45 | 50 |
|------|--------|--------|--------|--------|--------|--------|-------|
| 1 | 3.302% | 3.125% | 2.917% | 2.500% | 2.188% | 1.944% | 1.75% |
| 2 | 3.774% | 3.571% | 3.333% | 2.857% | 2.500% | 2.222% | 2.00% |
| 3 | 3.774% | 3.571% | 3.333% | 2.857% | 2.500% | 2.222% | 2.00% |
| 4 | 3.774% | 3.571% | 3.333% | 2.857% | 2.500% | 2.222% | 2.00% |
| 5 | 3.774% | 3.571% | 3.333% | 2.857% | 2.500% | 2.222% | 2.00% |
| 6 | 3.774% | 3.572% | 3.333% | 2.857% | 2.500% | 2.222% | 2.00% |
| 7 | 3.773% | 3.571% | 3.333% | 2.857% | 2.500% | 2.222% | 2.00% |
| 8 | 3.774% | 3.572% | 3.333% | 2.857% | 2.500% | 2.222% | 2.00% |
| 9 | 3.773% | 3.571% | 3.333% | 2.857% | 2.500% | 2.222% | 2.00% |
| 10 | 3.774% | 3.572% | 3.333% | 2.857% | 2.500% | 2.222% | 2.00% |
| 11 | 3.773% | 3.571% | 3.333% | 2.857% | 2.500% | 2.222% | 2.00% |
| 12 | 3.774% | 3.572% | 3.333% | 2.857% | 2.500% | 2.222% | 2.00% |
| 13 | 3.773% | 3.571% | 3.334% | 2.857% | 2.500% | 2.222% | 2.00% |
| 14 | 3.774% | 3.572% | 3.333% | 2.857% | 2.500% | 2.222% | 2.00% |
| 15 | 3.773% | 3.571% | 3.334% | 2.857% | 2.500% | 2.222% | 2.00% |
| 16 | 3.774% | 3.572% | 3.333% | 2.857% | 2.500% | 2.222% | 2.00% |
| 17 | 3.773% | 3.571% | 3.334% | 2.857% | 2.500% | 2.222% | 2.00% |
| 18 | 3.774% | 3.572% | 3.333% | 2.857% | 2.500% | 2.222% | 2.00% |
| 19 | 3.773% | 3.571% | 3.334% | 2.857% | 2.500% | 2.222% | 2.00% |
| 20 | 3.774% | 3.572% | 3.333% | 2.857% | 2.500% | 2.222% | 2.00% |
| 21 | 3.773% | 3.571% | 3.334% | 2.857% | 2.500% | 2.222% | 2.00% |
| 22 | 3.774% | 3.572% | 3.333% | 2.857% | 2.500% | 2.222% | 2.00% |
| 23 | 3.773% | 3.571% | 3.334% | 2.857% | 2.500% | 2.222% | 2.00% |
| 24 | 3.774% | 3.572% | 3.333% | 2.857% | 2.500% | 2.222% | 2.00% |
| 25 | 3.773% | 3.571% | 3.334% | 2.857% | 2.500% | 2.222% | 2.00% |
| 26 | 3.774% | 3.572% | 3.333% | 2.857% | 2.500% | 2.223% | 2.00% |
| 27 | 2.358% | 3.571% | 3.334% | 2.858% | 2.500% | 2.222% | 2.00% |
| 28 | | 3.572% | 3.333% | 2.857% | 2.500% | 2.223% | 2.00% |
| 29 | | 0.446% | 3.334% | 2.858% | 2.500% | 2.222% | 2.00% |
| 30 | | | 3.333% | 2.857% | 2.500% | 2.223% | 2.00% |
| 31 | | | 0.417% | 2.858% | 2.500% | 2.222% | 2.00% |
| 32 | | | | 2.857% | 2.500% | 2.223% | 2.00% |
| 33 | | | | 2.858% | 2.500% | 2.222% | 2.00% |
| 34 | | | | 2.857% | 2.500% | 2.223% | 2.00% |
| 35 | | | | 2.858% | 2.500% | 2.222% | 2.00% |
| 36 | | | | 0.357% | 2.500% | 2.223% | 2.00% |
| 37 | | | | | 2.500% | 2.222% | 2.00% |
| 38 | | | | | 2.500% | 2.223% | 2.00% |
| 39 | | | | | 2.500% | 2.222% | 2.00% |
| 40 | | | | | 2.500% | 2.223% | 2.00% |
| 41 | | | | | 0.312% | 2.222% | 2.00% |
| 42 | | | | | | 2.223% | 2.00% |
| 43 | | | | | | 2.222% | 2.00% |
| 44 | | | | | | 2.223% | 2.00% |

# MACRS Depreciation Tables

### Recovery periods in years

| Year | 26.5 | 28 | 30 | 35 | 40 | 45 | 50 |
|------|------|----|----|----|----|-----|------|
| 45 | | | | | | 2.222% | 2.00% |
| 46 | | | | | | 0.278% | 2.00% |
| 47-50 | | | | | | | 2.00% |
| 51 | | | | | | | 0.25% |

## Placed in Service in Second Quarter
### Recovery periods in years

| Year | 2.5 | 3 | 3.5 | 4 | 5 | 6 | 6.5 | 7 |
|------|------|--------|--------|--------|-------|--------|--------|--------|
| 1 | 25.0% | 20.83% | 17.86% | 15.63% | 12.5% | 10.42% | 9.62% | 8.93% |
| 2 | 40.0% | 33.33% | 28.57% | 25.00% | 20.0% | 16.67% | 15.38% | 14.29% |
| 3 | 35.0% | 33.34% | 28.57% | 25.00% | 20.0% | 16.67% | 15.38% | 14.28% |
| 4 | | 12.50% | 25.00% | 25.00% | 20.0% | 16.66% | 15.39% | 14.29% |
| 5 | | | 9.37% | 9.37% | 20.0% | 16.67% | 15.38% | 14.28% |
| 6 | | | | 7.5% | 16.66% | 15.39% | 14.29% |
| 7 | | | | | 6.25% | 13.46% | 14.28% |
| 8 | | | | | | | 5.36% |

### Recovery periods in years

| Year | 7.5 | 8 | 8.5 | 9 | 9.5 | 10 | 10.5 | 11 |
|------|--------|--------|--------|--------|--------|--------|-------|-------|
| 1 | 8.33% | 7.81% | 7.35% | 6.94% | 6.58% | 6.25% | 5.95% | 5.68% |
| 2 | 13.33% | 12.50% | 11.77% | 11.11% | 10.53% | 10.00% | 9.52% | 9.09% |
| 3 | 13.33% | 12.50% | 11.76% | 11.11% | 10.53% | 10.00% | 9.52% | 9.09% |
| 4 | 13.34% | 12.50% | 11.77% | 11.11% | 10.53% | 10.00% | 9.53% | 9.09% |
| 5 | 13.33% | 12.50% | 11.76% | 11.11% | 10.52% | 10.00% | 9.52% | 9.09% |
| 6 | 13.34% | 12.50% | 11.77% | 11.11% | 10.53% | 10.00% | 9.53% | 9.09% |
| 7 | 13.33% | 12.50% | 11.76% | 11.11% | 10.52% | 10.00% | 9.52% | 9.09% |
| 8 | 11.67% | 12.50% | 11.77% | 11.12% | 10.53% | 10.00% | 9.53% | 9.09% |
| 9 | | 4.69% | 10.29% | 11.11% | 10.52% | 10.00% | 9.52% | 9.09% |
| 10 | | | 4.17% | 9.21% | 10.00% | 9.53% | 9.09% |
| 11 | | | | | 3.75% | 8.33% | 9.10% |
| 12 | | | | | | | 3.41% |

### Recovery periods in years

| Year | 11.5 | 12 | 12.5 | 13 | 13.5 | 14 | 15 | 16 |
|------|-------|-------|------|-------|-------|-------|-------|-------|
| 1 | 5.43% | 5.21% | 5.0% | 4.81% | 4.63% | 4.46% | 4.17% | 3.91% |
| 2 | 8.70% | 8.33% | 8.0% | 7.69% | 7.41% | 7.14% | 6.67% | 6.25% |
| 3 | 8.70% | 8.33% | 8.0% | 7.69% | 7.41% | 7.14% | 6.67% | 6.25% |
| 4 | 8.70% | 8.33% | 8.0% | 7.69% | 7.41% | 7.14% | 6.67% | 6.25% |
| 5 | 8.69% | 8.33% | 8.0% | 7.69% | 7.41% | 7.14% | 6.67% | 6.25% |
| 6 | 8.70% | 8.33% | 8.0% | 7.69% | 7.41% | 7.14% | 6.67% | 6.25% |
| 7 | 8.69% | 8.34% | 8.0% | 7.69% | 7.41% | 7.15% | 6.66% | 6.25% |
| 8 | 8.70% | 8.33% | 8.0% | 7.69% | 7.41% | 7.14% | 6.67% | 6.25% |
| 9 | 8.69% | 8.34% | 8.0% | 7.69% | 7.40% | 7.15% | 6.66% | 6.25% |
| 10 | 8.70% | 8.33% | 8.0% | 7.70% | 7.41% | 7.14% | 6.67% | 6.25% |
| 11 | 8.69% | 8.34% | 8.0% | 7.69% | 7.40% | 7.15% | 6.66% | 6.25% |

**Recovery periods in years**

| Year | 11.5 | 12 | 12.5 | 13 | 13.5 | 14 | 15 | 16 |
|------|------|-----|------|------|------|------|------|------|
| 12 | 7.61% | 8.33% | 8.0% | 7.70% | 7.41% | 7.14% | 6.67% | 6.25% |
| 13 | | 3.13% | 7.0% | 7.69% | 7.40% | 7.15% | 6.66% | 6.25% |
| 14 | | | | 2.89% | 6.48% | 7.14% | 6.67% | 6.25% |
| 15 | | | | | | 2.68% | 6.66% | 6.25% |
| 16 | | | | | | | 2.50% | 6.25% |
| 17 | | | | | | | | 2.34% |

**Recovery periods in years**

| Year | 16.5 | 17 | 18 | 19 | 20 | 22 | 24 | 25 |
|------|------|------|------|------|------|------|------|------|
| 1 | 3.79% | 3.68% | 3.47% | 3.29% | 3.125% | 2.841% | 2.604% | 2.5% |
| 2 | 6.06% | 5.88% | 5.56% | 5.26% | 5.000% | 4.545% | 4.167% | 4.0% |
| 3 | 6.06% | 5.88% | 5.56% | 5.26% | 5.000% | 4.545% | 4.167% | 4.0% |
| 4 | 6.06% | 5.88% | 5.56% | 5.26% | 5.000% | 4.545% | 4.167% | 4.0% |
| 5 | 6.06% | 5.88% | 5.55% | 5.26% | 5.000% | 4.546% | 4.167% | 4.0% |
| 6 | 6.06% | 5.88% | 5.56% | 5.26% | 5.000% | 4.545% | 4.167% | 4.0% |
| 7 | 6.06% | 5.88% | 5.55% | 5.26% | 5.000% | 4.546% | 4.167% | 4.0% |
| 8 | 6.06% | 5.88% | 5.56% | 5.26% | 5.000% | 4.545% | 4.167% | 4.0% |
| 9 | 6.06% | 5.88% | 5.55% | 5.27% | 5.000% | 4.546% | 4.167% | 4.0% |
| 10 | 6.06% | 5.88% | 5.56% | 5.26% | 5.000% | 4.545% | 4.167% | 4.0% |
| 11 | 6.06% | 5.88% | 5.55% | 5.27% | 5.000% | 4.546% | 4.166% | 4.0% |
| 12 | 6.06% | 5.89% | 5.56% | 5.26% | 5.000% | 4.545% | 4.167% | 4.0% |
| 13 | 6.06% | 5.88% | 5.55% | 5.27% | 5.000% | 4.546% | 4.166% | 4.0% |
| 14 | 6.06% | 5.89% | 5.56% | 5.26% | 5.000% | 4.545% | 4.167% | 4.0% |
| 15 | 6.06% | 5.88% | 5.55% | 5.27% | 5.000% | 4.546% | 4.166% | 4.0% |
| 16 | 6.06% | 5.89% | 5.56% | 5.26% | 5.000% | 4.545% | 4.167% | 4.0% |
| 17 | 5.31% | 5.88% | 5.55% | 5.27% | 5.000% | 4.546% | 4.166% | 4.0% |
| 18 | | 2.21% | 5.56% | 5.26% | 5.000% | 4.545% | 4.167% | 4.0% |
| 19 | | | 2.08% | 5.27% | 5.000% | 4.546% | 4.166% | 4.0% |
| 20 | | | | 1.97% | 5.000% | 4.545% | 4.167% | 4.0% |
| 21 | | | | | 1.875% | 4.546% | 4.166% | 4.0% |
| 22 | | | | | | 4.545% | 4.167% | 4.0% |
| 23 | | | | | | 1.705% | 4.166% | 4.0% |
| 24 | | | | | | | 4.167% | 4.0% |
| 25 | | | | | | | 1.562% | 4.0% |
| 26 | | | | | | | | 1.5% |

**Recovery periods in years**

| Year | 26.5 | 28 | 30 | 35 | 40 | 45 | 50 |
|------|------|------|------|------|------|------|------|
| 1 | 2.358% | 2.232% | 2.083% | 1.786% | 1.563% | 1.389% | 1.25% |
| 2 | 3.774% | 3.571% | 3.333% | 2.857% | 2.500% | 2.222% | 2.00% |
| 3 | 3.774% | 3.571% | 3.333% | 2.857% | 2.500% | 2.222% | 2.00% |
| 4 | 3.774% | 3.571% | 3.333% | 2.857% | 2.500% | 2.222% | 2.00% |
| 5 | 3.774% | 3.571% | 3.333% | 2.857% | 2.500% | 2.222% | 2.00% |
| 6 | 3.774% | 3.572% | 3.333% | 2.857% | 2.500% | 2.222% | 2.00% |
| 7 | 3.774% | 3.571% | 3.333% | 2.857% | 2.500% | 2.222% | 2.00% |

# MACRS Depreciation Tables

## Recovery periods in years

| Year | 26.5 | 28 | 30 | 35 | 40 | 45 | 50 |
|------|------|------|------|------|------|------|------|
| 8 | 3.773% | 3.572% | 3.333% | 2.857% | 2.500% | 2.222% | 2.00% |
| 9 | 3.774% | 3.571% | 3.333% | 2.857% | 2.500% | 2.222% | 2.00% |
| 10 | 3.773% | 3.572% | 3.333% | 2.857% | 2.500% | 2.222% | 2.00% |
| 11 | 3.774% | 3.571% | 3.333% | 2.857% | 2.500% | 2.222% | 2.00% |
| 12 | 3.773% | 3.572% | 3.334% | 2.857% | 2.500% | 2.222% | 2.00% |
| 13 | 3.774% | 3.571% | 3.333% | 2.857% | 2.500% | 2.222% | 2.00% |
| 14 | 3.773% | 3.572% | 3.334% | 2.857% | 2.500% | 2.222% | 2.00% |
| 15 | 3.774% | 3.571% | 3.333% | 2.857% | 2.500% | 2.222% | 2.00% |
| 16 | 3.773% | 3.572% | 3.334% | 2.857% | 2.500% | 2.222% | 2.00% |
| 17 | 3.774% | 3.571% | 3.333% | 2.857% | 2.500% | 2.222% | 2.00% |
| 18 | 3.773% | 3.572% | 3.334% | 2.857% | 2.500% | 2.222% | 2.00% |
| 19 | 3.774% | 3.571% | 3.333% | 2.857% | 2.500% | 2.222% | 2.00% |
| 20 | 3.773% | 3.572% | 3.334% | 2.857% | 2.500% | 2.222% | 2.00% |
| 21 | 3.774% | 3.571% | 3.333% | 2.857% | 2.500% | 2.222% | 2.00% |
| 22 | 3.773% | 3.572% | 3.334% | 2.857% | 2.500% | 2.222% | 2.00% |
| 23 | 3.774% | 3.571% | 3.333% | 2.857% | 2.500% | 2.222% | 2.00% |
| 24 | 3.773% | 3.572% | 3.334% | 2.857% | 2.500% | 2.222% | 2.00% |
| 25 | 3.774% | 3.571% | 3.333% | 2.857% | 2.500% | 2.222% | 2.00% |
| 26 | 3.773% | 3.572% | 3.334% | 2.857% | 2.500% | 2.222% | 2.00% |
| 27 | 3.302% | 3.571% | 3.333% | 2.857% | 2.500% | 2.223% | 2.00% |
| 28 |  | 3.572% | 3.334% | 2.858% | 2.500% | 2.222% | 2.00% |
| 29 |  | 1.339% | 3.333% | 2.857% | 2.500% | 2.223% | 2.00% |
| 30 |  |  | 3.334% | 2.858% | 2.500% | 2.222% | 2.00% |
| 31 |  |  | 1.250% | 2.857% | 2.500% | 2.223% | 2.00% |
| 32 |  |  |  | 2.858% | 2.500% | 2.222% | 2.00% |
| 33 |  |  |  | 2.857% | 2.500% | 2.223% | 2.00% |
| 34 |  |  |  | 2.858% | 2.500% | 2.222% | 2.00% |
| 35 |  |  |  | 2.857% | 2.500% | 2.223% | 2.00% |
| 36 |  |  |  | 1.072% | 2.500% | 2.222% | 2.00% |
| 37 |  |  |  |  | 2.500% | 2.223% | 2.00% |
| 38 |  |  |  |  | 2.500% | 2.222% | 2.00% |
| 39 |  |  |  |  | 2.500% | 2.223% | 2.00% |
| 40 |  |  |  |  | 2.500% | 2.222% | 2.00% |
| 41 |  |  |  |  | 0.937% | 2.223% | 2.00% |
| 42 |  |  |  |  |  | 2.222% | 2.00% |
| 43 |  |  |  |  |  | 2.223% | 2.00% |
| 44 |  |  |  |  |  | 2.222% | 2.00% |
| 45 |  |  |  |  |  | 2.223% | 2.00% |
| 46 |  |  |  |  |  | 0.833% | 2.00% |
| 47-50 |  |  |  |  |  |  | 2.00% |
| 51 |  |  |  |  |  |  | 0.75% |

### Placed in Service in Third Quarter
#### Recovery periods in years

| Year | 2.5 | 3 | 3.5 | 4 | 5 | 6 | 6.5 | 7 |
|------|------|------|------|------|------|------|------|------|
| 1 | 15.0% | 12.50% | 10.71% | 9.38% | 7.5% | 6.25% | 5.77% | 5.36% |
| 2 | 40.0% | 33.33% | 28.57% | 25.00% | 20.0% | 16.67% | 15.38% | 14.29% |
| 3 | 40.0% | 33.34% | 28.57% | 25.00% | 20.0% | 16.67% | 15.39% | 14.28% |
| 4 | 5.0% | 20.83% | 28.58% | 25.00% | 20.0% | 16.66% | 15.38% | 14.29% |
| 5 | | 3.57% | 15.62% | 20.0% | 16.67% | 15.39% | 14.28% |
| 6 | | | | 12.5% | 16.66% | 15.38% | 14.29% |
| 7 | | | | | 10.42% | 15.39% | 14.28% |
| 8 | | | | | | 1.92% | 8.93% |

#### Recovery periods in years

| Year | 7.5 | 8 | 8.5 | 9 | 9.5 | 10 | 10.5 | 11 |
|------|------|------|------|------|------|------|------|------|
| 1 | 5.00% | 4.69% | 4.41% | 4.17% | 3.95% | 3.75% | 3.57% | 3.41% |
| 2 | 13.33% | 12.50% | 11.76% | 11.11% | 10.53% | 10.00% | 9.52% | 9.09% |
| 3 | 13.33% | 12.50% | 11.77% | 11.11% | 10.53% | 10.00% | 9.52% | 9.09% |
| 4 | 13.33% | 12.50% | 11.76% | 11.11% | 10.52% | 10.00% | 9.52% | 9.09% |
| 5 | 13.34% | 12.50% | 11.77% | 11.11% | 10.53% | 10.00% | 9.53% | 9.09% |
| 6 | 13.33% | 12.50% | 11.76% | 11.11% | 10.52% | 10.00% | 9.52% | 9.09% |
| 7 | 13.34% | 12.50% | 11.77% | 11.11% | 10.53% | 10.00% | 9.53% | 9.09% |
| 8 | 13.33% | 12.50% | 11.76% | 11.11% | 10.52% | 10.00% | 9.52% | 9.09% |
| 9 | 1.67% | 7.81% | 11.77% | 11.11% | 10.53% | 10.00% | 9.53% | 9.09% |
| 10 | | 1.47% | 6.95% | 10.52% | 10.00% | 9.52% | 9.09% |
| 11 | | | | 1.32% | 6.25% | 9.53% | 9.10% |
| 12 | | | | | | 1.19% | 5.68% |

#### Recovery periods in years

| Year | 11.5 | 12 | 12.5 | 13 | 13.5 | 14 | 15 | 16 |
|------|------|------|------|------|------|------|------|------|
| 1 | 3.26% | 3.13% | 3.0% | 2.88% | 2.78% | 2.68% | 2.50% | 2.34% |
| 2 | 8.70% | 8.33% | 8.0% | 7.69% | 7.41% | 7.14% | 6.67% | 6.25% |
| 3 | 8.70% | 8.33% | 8.0% | 7.69% | 7.41% | 7.14% | 6.67% | 6.25% |
| 4 | 8.69% | 8.33% | 8.0% | 7.69% | 7.41% | 7.14% | 6.67% | 6.25% |
| 5 | 8.70% | 8.33% | 8.0% | 7.69% | 7.41% | 7.14% | 6.67% | 6.25% |
| 6 | 8.69% | 8.33% | 8.0% | 7.69% | 7.41% | 7.14% | 6.67% | 6.25% |
| 7 | 8.70% | 8.34% | 8.0% | 7.69% | 7.41% | 7.14% | 6.66% | 6.25% |
| 8 | 8.69% | 8.33% | 8.0% | 7.70% | 7.40% | 7.14% | 6.67% | 6.25% |
| 9 | 8.70% | 8.34% | 8.0% | 7.69% | 7.41% | 7.15% | 6.66% | 6.25% |
| 10 | 8.69% | 8.33% | 8.0% | 7.70% | 7.40% | 7.14% | 6.67% | 6.25% |
| 11 | 8.70% | 8.34% | 8.0% | 7.69% | 7.41% | 7.15% | 6.66% | 6.25% |
| 12 | 8.69% | 8.33% | 8.0% | 7.70% | 7.40% | 7.14% | 6.67% | 6.25% |
| 13 | 1.09% | 5.21% | 8.0% | 7.69% | 7.41% | 7.15% | 6.66% | 6.25% |
| 14 | | 1.0% | 4.81% | 7.40% | 7.14% | 6.67% | 6.25% |
| 15 | | | | 0.93% | 4.47% | 6.66% | 6.25% |
| 16 | | | | | | 4.17% | 6.25% |
| 17 | | | | | | | 3.91% |

# MACRS Depreciation Tables

## Recovery periods in years

| Year | 16.5 | 17 | 18 | 19 | 20 | 22 | 24 | 25 |
|------|------|------|------|------|------|------|------|------|
| 1 | 2.27% | 2.21% | 2.08% | 1.97% | 1.875% | 1.705% | 1.563% | 1.5% |
| 2 | 6.06% | 5.88% | 5.56% | 5.26% | 5.000% | 4.545% | 4.167% | 4.0% |
| 3 | 6.06% | 5.88% | 5.56% | 5.26% | 5.000% | 4.545% | 4.167% | 4.0% |
| 4 | 6.06% | 5.88% | 5.56% | 5.26% | 5.000% | 4.545% | 4.167% | 4.0% |
| 5 | 6.06% | 5.88% | 5.55% | 5.26% | 5.000% | 4.546% | 4.167% | 4.0% |
| 6 | 6.06% | 5.88% | 5.56% | 5.26% | 5.000% | 4.545% | 4.167% | 4.0% |
| 7 | 6.06% | 5.88% | 5.55% | 5.26% | 5.000% | 4.546% | 4.167% | 4.0% |
| 8 | 6.06% | 5.88% | 5.56% | 5.26% | 5.000% | 4.545% | 4.167% | 4.0% |
| 9 | 6.06% | 5.88% | 5.55% | 5.27% | 5.000% | 4.546% | 4.166% | 4.0% |
| 10 | 6.06% | 5.88% | 5.56% | 5.26% | 5.000% | 4.545% | 4.167% | 4.0% |
| 11 | 6.06% | 5.88% | 5.55% | 5.27% | 5.000% | 4.546% | 4.166% | 4.0% |
| 12 | 6.06% | 5.89% | 5.56% | 5.26% | 5.000% | 4.545% | 4.167% | 4.0% |
| 13 | 6.06% | 5.88% | 5.55% | 5.27% | 5.000% | 4.546% | 4.166% | 4.0% |
| 14 | 6.06% | 5.89% | 5.56% | 5.26% | 5.000% | 4.545% | 4.167% | 4.0% |
| 15 | 6.06% | 5.88% | 5.55% | 5.27% | 5.000% | 4.546% | 4.166% | 4.0% |
| 16 | 6.07% | 5.89% | 5.56% | 5.26% | 5.000% | 4.545% | 4.167% | 4.0% |
| 17 | 6.06% | 5.88% | 5.55% | 5.27% | 5.000% | 4.546% | 4.166% | 4.0% |
| 18 | 0.76% | 3.68% | 5.56% | 5.26% | 5.000% | 4.545% | 4.167% | 4.0% |
| 19 | | | 3.47% | 5.27% | 5.000% | 4.546% | 4.166% | 4.0% |
| 20 | | | | 3.29% | 5.000% | 4.545% | 4.167% | 4.0% |
| 21 | | | | | 3.125% | 4.546% | 4.166% | 4.0% |
| 22 | | | | | | 4.545% | 4.167% | 4.0% |
| 23 | | | | | | 2.841% | 4.166% | 4.0% |
| 24 | | | | | | | 4.167% | 4.0% |
| 25 | | | | | | | 2.604% | 4.0% |
| 26 | | | | | | | | 2.5% |

## Recovery periods in years

| Year | 26.5 | 28 | 30 | 35 | 40 | 45 | 50 |
|------|------|------|------|------|------|------|------|
| 1 | 1.415% | 1.339% | 1.250% | 1.071% | 0.938% | 0.833% | 0.75% |
| 2 | 3.774% | 3.571% | 3.333% | 2.857% | 2.500% | 2.222% | 2.00% |
| 3 | 3.774% | 3.571% | 3.333% | 2.857% | 2.500% | 2.222% | 2.00% |
| 4 | 3.774% | 3.571% | 3.333% | 2.857% | 2.500% | 2.222% | 2.00% |
| 5 | 3.774% | 3.571% | 3.333% | 2.857% | 2.500% | 2.222% | 2.00% |
| 6 | 3.774% | 3.572% | 3.333% | 2.857% | 2.500% | 2.222% | 2.00% |
| 7 | 3.773% | 3.571% | 3.333% | 2.857% | 2.500% | 2.222% | 2.00% |
| 8 | 3.774% | 3.572% | 3.333% | 2.857% | 2.500% | 2.222% | 2.00% |
| 9 | 3.773% | 3.571% | 3.333% | 2.857% | 2.500% | 2.222% | 2.00% |
| 10 | 3.774% | 3.572% | 3.333% | 2.857% | 2.500% | 2.222% | 2.00% |
| 11 | 3.773% | 3.571% | 3.333% | 2.857% | 2.500% | 2.222% | 2.00% |
| 12 | 3.774% | 3.572% | 3.334% | 2.857% | 2.500% | 2.222% | 2.00% |
| 13 | 3.773% | 3.571% | 3.333% | 2.857% | 2.500% | 2.222% | 2.00% |
| 14 | 3.774% | 3.572% | 3.334% | 2.857% | 2.500% | 2.222% | 2.00% |
| 15 | 3.773% | 3.571% | 3.333% | 2.857% | 2.500% | 2.222% | 2.00% |

### Recovery periods in years

| Year | 26.5 | 28 | 30 | 35 | 40 | 45 | 50 |
|------|------|------|------|------|------|------|------|
| 16 | 3.774% | 3.572% | 3.334% | 2.857% | 2.500% | 2.222% | 2.00% |
| 17 | 3.773% | 3.571% | 3.333% | 2.857% | 2.500% | 2.222% | 2.00% |
| 18 | 3.774% | 3.572% | 3.334% | 2.857% | 2.500% | 2.222% | 2.00% |
| 19 | 3.773% | 3.571% | 3.333% | 2.857% | 2.500% | 2.222% | 2.00% |
| 20 | 3.774% | 3.572% | 3.334% | 2.857% | 2.500% | 2.222% | 2.00% |
| 21 | 3.773% | 3.571% | 3.333% | 2.857% | 2.500% | 2.222% | 2.00% |
| 22 | 3.774% | 3.572% | 3.334% | 2.857% | 2.500% | 2.222% | 2.00% |
| 23 | 3.773% | 3.571% | 3.333% | 2.857% | 2.500% | 2.222% | 2.00% |
| 24 | 3.774% | 3.572% | 3.334% | 2.857% | 2.500% | 2.222% | 2.00% |
| 25 | 3.773% | 3.571% | 3.333% | 2.857% | 2.500% | 2.222% | 2.00% |
| 26 | 3.774% | 3.572% | 3.334% | 2.858% | 2.500% | 2.222% | 2.00% |
| 27 | 3.773% | 3.571% | 3.333% | 2.857% | 2.500% | 2.223% | 2.00% |
| 28 | 0.472% | 3.572% | 3.334% | 2.858% | 2.500% | 2.222% | 2.00% |
| 29 | | 2.232% | 3.333% | 2.857% | 2.500% | 2.223% | 2.00% |
| 30 | | | 3.334% | 2.858% | 2.500% | 2.222% | 2.00% |
| 31 | | | 2.083% | 2.857% | 2.500% | 2.223% | 2.00% |
| 32 | | | | 2.858% | 2.500% | 2.222% | 2.00% |
| 33 | | | | 2.857% | 2.500% | 2.223% | 2.00% |
| 34 | | | | 2.858% | 2.500% | 2.222% | 2.00% |
| 35 | | | | 2.857% | 2.500% | 2.223% | 2.00% |
| 36 | | | | 1.786% | 2.500% | 2.222% | 2.00% |
| 37 | | | | | 2.500% | 2.223% | 2.00% |
| 38 | | | | | 2.500% | 2.222% | 2.00% |
| 39 | | | | | 2.500% | 2.223% | 2.00% |
| 40 | | | | | 2.500% | 2.222% | 2.00% |
| 41 | | | | | 1.562% | 2.223% | 2.00% |
| 42 | | | | | | 2.222% | 2.00% |
| 43 | | | | | | 2.223% | 2.00% |
| 44 | | | | | | 2.222% | 2.00% |
| 45 | | | | | | 2.223% | 2.00% |
| 46 | | | | | | 1.389% | 2.00% |
| 47-50 | | | | | | | 2.00% |
| 51 | | | | | | | 1.25% |

# MACRS Depreciation Tables

### Placed in Service in Fourth Quarter
#### Recovery periods in years

| Year | 2.5 | 3 | 3.5 | 4 | 5 | 6 | 6.5 | 7 |
|---|---|---|---|---|---|---|---|---|
| 1 | 5.0% | 4.17% | 3.57% | 3.13% | 2.5% | 2.08% | 1.92% | 1.79% |
| 2 | 40.0% | 33.33% | 28.57% | 25.00% | 20.0% | 16.67% | 15.39% | 14.29% |
| 3 | 40.0% | 33.33% | 28.57% | 25.00% | 20.0% | 16.67% | 15.38% | 14.28% |
| 4 | 15.0% | 29.17% | 28.57% | 25.00% | 20.0% | 16.67% | 15.39% | 14.29% |
| 5 | | | 10.72% | 21.87% | 20.0% | 16.66% | 15.38% | 14.28% |
| 6 | | | | | 17.5% | 16.67% | 15.39% | 14.29% |
| 7 | | | | | | 14.58% | 15.38% | 14.28% |
| 8 | | | | | | | 5.77% | 12.50% |

#### Recovery periods in years

| Year | 7.5 | 8 | 8.5 | 9 | 9.5 | 10 | 10.5 | 11 |
|---|---|---|---|---|---|---|---|---|
| 1 | 1.67% | 1.56% | 1.47% | 1.39% | 1.32% | 1.25% | 1.19% | 1.14% |
| 2 | 13.33% | 12.50% | 11.76% | 11.11% | 10.53% | 10.00% | 9.52% | 9.09% |
| 3 | 13.33% | 12.50% | 11.77% | 11.11% | 10.53% | 10.00% | 9.52% | 9.09% |
| 4 | 13.33% | 12.50% | 11.76% | 11.11% | 10.52% | 10.00% | 9.52% | 9.09% |
| 5 | 13.33% | 12.50% | 11.77% | 11.11% | 10.53% | 10.00% | 9.53% | 9.09% |
| 6 | 13.34% | 12.50% | 11.76% | 11.11% | 10.52% | 10.00% | 9.52% | 9.09% |
| 7 | 13.33% | 12.50% | 11.77% | 11.11% | 10.53% | 10.00% | 9.53% | 9.09% |
| 8 | 13.34% | 12.50% | 11.76% | 11.11% | 10.52% | 10.00% | 9.52% | 9.09% |
| 9 | 5.00% | 10.94% | 11.77% | 11.11% | 10.53% | 10.00% | 9.53% | 9.09% |
| 10 | | | 4.41% | 9.73% | 10.52% | 10.00% | 9.52% | 9.09% |
| 11 | | | | | 3.95% | 8.75% | 9.53% | 9.09% |
| 12 | | | | | | | 3.57% | 7.96% |

#### Recovery periods in years

| Year | 11.5 | 12 | 12.5 | 13 | 13.5 | 14 | 15 | 16 |
|---|---|---|---|---|---|---|---|---|
| 1 | 1.09% | 1.04% | 1.0% | 0.96% | 0.93% | 0.89% | 0.83% | 0.78% |
| 2 | 8.70% | 8.33% | 8.0% | 7.69% | 7.41% | 7.14% | 6.67% | 6.25% |
| 3 | 8.69% | 8.33% | 8.0% | 7.69% | 7.41% | 7.14% | 6.67% | 6.25% |
| 4 | 8.70% | 8.33% | 8.0% | 7.69% | 7.41% | 7.14% | 6.67% | 6.25% |
| 5 | 8.69% | 8.33% | 8.0% | 7.69% | 7.41% | 7.14% | 6.67% | 6.25% |
| 6 | 8.70% | 8.34% | 8.0% | 7.69% | 7.41% | 7.14% | 6.67% | 6.25% |
| 7 | 8.69% | 8.33% | 8.0% | 7.69% | 7.41% | 7.14% | 6.67% | 6.25% |
| 8 | 8.70% | 8.34% | 8.0% | 7.69% | 7.40% | 7.15% | 6.66% | 6.25% |
| 9 | 8.69% | 8.33% | 8.0% | 7.70% | 7.41% | 7.14% | 6.67% | 6.25% |
| 10 | 8.70% | 8.34% | 8.0% | 7.69% | 7.40% | 7.15% | 6.66% | 6.25% |
| 11 | 8.69% | 8.33% | 8.0% | 7.70% | 7.41% | 7.14% | 6.67% | 6.25% |
| 12 | 8.70% | 8.34% | 8.0% | 7.69% | 7.40% | 7.15% | 6.66% | 6.25% |
| 13 | 3.26% | 7.29% | 8.0% | 7.70% | 7.41% | 7.14% | 6.67% | 6.25% |
| 14 | | | 3.0% | 6.73% | 7.40% | 7.15% | 6.66% | 6.25% |
| 15 | | | | | 2.78% | 6.25% | 6.67% | 6.25% |
| 16 | | | | | | | 5.83% | 6.25% |
| 17 | | | | | | | | 5.47% |

### Recovery periods in years

| Year | 16.5 | 17 | 18 | 19 | 20 | 22 | 24 | 25 |
|------|------|------|------|------|------|------|------|------|
| 1 | 0.76% | 0.74% | 0.69% | 0.66% | 0.625% | 0.568% | 0.521% | 0.5% |
| 2 | 6.06% | 5.88% | 5.56% | 5.26% | 5.000% | 4.545% | 4.167% | 4.0% |
| 3 | 6.06% | 5.88% | 5.56% | 5.26% | 5.000% | 4.545% | 4.167% | 4.0% |
| 4 | 6.06% | 5.88% | 5.56% | 5.26% | 5.000% | 4.546% | 4.167% | 4.0% |
| 5 | 6.06% | 5.88% | 5.55% | 5.26% | 5.000% | 4.545% | 4.167% | 4.0% |
| 6 | 6.06% | 5.88% | 5.56% | 5.26% | 5.000% | 4.546% | 4.167% | 4.0% |
| 7 | 6.06% | 5.88% | 5.55% | 5.26% | 5.000% | 4.545% | 4.167% | 4.0% |
| 8 | 6.06% | 5.88% | 5.56% | 5.26% | 5.000% | 4.546% | 4.167% | 4.0% |
| 9 | 6.06% | 5.88% | 5.55% | 5.26% | 5.000% | 4.545% | 4.167% | 4.0% |
| 10 | 6.06% | 5.88% | 5.56% | 5.27% | 5.000% | 4.546% | 4.166% | 4.0% |
| 11 | 6.06% | 5.88% | 5.55% | 5.26% | 5.000% | 4.545% | 4.167% | 4.0% |
| 12 | 6.06% | 5.89% | 5.56% | 5.27% | 5.000% | 4.546% | 4.166% | 4.0% |
| 13 | 6.06% | 5.88% | 5.55% | 5.26% | 5.000% | 4.545% | 4.167% | 4.0% |
| 14 | 6.06% | 5.89% | 5.56% | 5.27% | 5.000% | 4.546% | 4.166% | 4.0% |
| 15 | 6.06% | 5.88% | 5.55% | 5.26% | 5.000% | 4.545% | 4.167% | 4.0% |
| 16 | 6.06% | 5.89% | 5.56% | 5.27% | 5.000% | 4.546% | 4.166% | 4.0% |
| 17 | 6.07% | 5.88% | 5.55% | 5.26% | 5.000% | 4.545% | 4.167% | 4.0% |
| 18 | 2.27% | 5.15% | 5.56% | 5.27% | 5.000% | 4.546% | 4.166% | 4.0% |
| 19 | | | 4.86% | 5.26% | 5.000% | 4.545% | 4.167% | 4.0% |
| 20 | | | | 4.61% | 5.000% | 4.546% | 4.166% | 4.0% |
| 21 | | | | 4.375% | 4.545% | 4.167% | 4.0% |
| 22 | | | | | | 4.546% | 4.166% | 4.0% |
| 23 | | | | | | 3.977% | 4.167% | 4.0% |
| 24 | | | | | | | 4.166% | 4.0% |
| 25 | | | | | | | 3.646% | 4.0% |
| 26 | | | | | | | | 3.5% |

### Recovery periods in years

| Year | 26.5 | 28 | 30 | 35 | 40 | 45 | 50 |
|------|------|------|------|------|------|------|------|
| 1 | 0.472% | 0.446% | 0.417% | 0.357% | 0.313% | 0.278% | 0.25% |
| 2 | 3.774% | 3.571% | 3.333% | 2.857% | 2.500% | 2.222% | 2.00% |
| 3 | 3.774% | 3.571% | 3.333% | 2.857% | 2.500% | 2.222% | 2.00% |
| 4 | 3.774% | 3.571% | 3.333% | 2.857% | 2.500% | 2.222% | 2.00% |
| 5 | 3.774% | 3.571% | 3.333% | 2.857% | 2.500% | 2.222% | 2.00% |
| 6 | 3.773% | 3.572% | 3.333% | 2.857% | 2.500% | 2.222% | 2.00% |
| 7 | 3.774% | 3.571% | 3.333% | 2.857% | 2.500% | 2.222% | 2.00% |
| 8 | 3.773% | 3.572% | 3.333% | 2.857% | 2.500% | 2.222% | 2.00% |
| 9 | 3.774% | 3.571% | 3.333% | 2.857% | 2.500% | 2.222% | 2.00% |
| 10 | 3.773% | 3.572% | 3.333% | 2.857% | 2.500% | 2.222% | 2.00% |
| 11 | 3.774% | 3.571% | 3.333% | 2.857% | 2.500% | 2.222% | 2.00% |
| 12 | 3.773% | 3.572% | 3.333% | 2.857% | 2.500% | 2.222% | 2.00% |
| 13 | 3.774% | 3.571% | 3.334% | 2.857% | 2.500% | 2.222% | 2.00% |
| 14 | 3.773% | 3.572% | 3.333% | 2.857% | 2.500% | 2.222% | 2.00% |
| 15 | 3.774% | 3.571% | 3.334% | 2.857% | 2.500% | 2.222% | 2.00% |

# MACRS Depreciation Tables

### Recovery periods in years

| Year | 26.5 | 28 | 30 | 35 | 40 | 45 | 50 |
|------|------|------|------|------|------|------|------|
| 16 | 3.773% | 3.572% | 3.333% | 2.857% | 2.500% | 2.222% | 2.00% |
| 17 | 3.774% | 3.571% | 3.334% | 2.857% | 2.500% | 2.222% | 2.00% |
| 18 | 3.773% | 3.572% | 3.333% | 2.857% | 2.500% | 2.222% | 2.00% |
| 19 | 3.774% | 3.571% | 3.334% | 2.857% | 2.500% | 2.222% | 2.00% |
| 20 | 3.773% | 3.572% | 3.333% | 2.857% | 2.500% | 2.222% | 2.00% |
| 21 | 3.774% | 3.571% | 3.334% | 2.857% | 2.500% | 2.222% | 2.00% |
| 22 | 3.773% | 3.572% | 3.333% | 2.857% | 2.500% | 2.222% | 2.00% |
| 23 | 3.774% | 3.571% | 3.334% | 2.857% | 2.500% | 2.222% | 2.00% |
| 24 | 3.773% | 3.572% | 3.333% | 2.857% | 2.500% | 2.222% | 2.00% |
| 25 | 3.774% | 3.571% | 3.334% | 2.857% | 2.500% | 2.222% | 2.00% |
| 26 | 3.773% | 3.572% | 3.333% | 2.857% | 2.500% | 2.222% | 2.00% |
| 27 | 3.774% | 3.571% | 3.334% | 2.858% | 2.500% | 2.222% | 2.00% |
| 28 | 1.415% | 3.572% | 3.333% | 2.857% | 2.500% | 2.223% | 2.00% |
| 29 | | 3.125% | 3.334% | 2.858% | 2.500% | 2.222% | 2.00% |
| 30 | | | 3.333% | 2.857% | 2.500% | 2.223% | 2.00% |
| 31 | | | 2.917% | 2.858% | 2.500% | 2.222% | 2.00% |
| 32 | | | | 2.857% | 2.500% | 2.223% | 2.00% |
| 33 | | | | 2.858% | 2.500% | 2.222% | 2.00% |
| 34 | | | | 2.857% | 2.500% | 2.223% | 2.00% |
| 35 | | | | 2.858% | 2.500% | 2.222% | 2.00% |
| 36 | | | | 2.500% | 2.500% | 2.223% | 2.00% |
| 37 | | | | | 2.500% | 2.222% | 2.00% |
| 38 | | | | | 2.500% | 2.223% | 2.00% |
| 39 | | | | | 2.500% | 2.222% | 2.00% |
| 40 | | | | | 2.500% | 2.223% | 2.00% |
| 41 | | | | | 2.187% | 2.222% | 2.00% |
| 42 | | | | | | 2.223% | 2.00% |
| 43 | | | | | | 2.222% | 2.00% |
| 44 | | | | | | 2.223% | 2.00% |
| 45 | | | | | | 2.222% | 2.00% |
| 46 | | | | | | 1.945% | 2.00% |
| 47-50 | | | | | | | 2.00% |
| 51 | | | | | | | 1.75% |

## Straight Line Method (Mid-Month Convention)
### Month property placed in service

| Year | 1 | 2 | 3 | 4 | 5 | 6 |
|------|--------|--------|--------|--------|--------|--------|
| 1 | 2.396% | 2.188% | 1.979% | 1.771% | 1.563% | 1.354% |
| 2-40 | 2.500 | 2.500 | 2.500 | 2.500 | 2.500 | 2.500 |
| 41 | 0.104 | 0.312 | 0.521 | 0.729 | 0.937 | 1.146 |

| Year | 7 | 8 | 9 | 10 | 11 | 12 |
|------|--------|--------|--------|--------|--------|--------|
| 1 | 1.146% | 0.938% | 0.729% | 0.521% | 0.313% | 0.104% |
| 2-40 | 2.500 | 2.500 | 2.500 | 2.500 | 2.500 | 2.500 |
| 41 | 1.354 | 1.562 | 1.771 | 1.979 | 2.187 | 2.396 |

## 150% Declining Balance Method (Half-Year Convention)
### Recovery periods in years

| Year | 2.5 | 3 | 3.5 | 4 | 5 | 6 | 6.5 | 7 |
|------|-------|-------|--------|--------|--------|--------|--------|--------|
| 1 | 30.0% | 25.0% | 21.43% | 18.75% | 15.00% | 12.50% | 11.54% | 10.71% |
| 2 | 42.0% | 37.5% | 33.67% | 30.47% | 25.50% | 21.88% | 20.41% | 19.13% |
| 3 | 28.0% | 25.0% | 22.45% | 20.31% | 17.85% | 16.41% | 15.70% | 15.03% |
| 4 | | 12.5% | 22.45% | 20.31% | 16.66% | 14.06% | 13.09% | 12.25% |
| 5 | | | 10.16% | 16.66% | 14.06% | 13.09% | 12.25% |
| 6 | | | | 8.33% | 14.06% | 13.09% | 12.25% |
| 7 | | | | | 7.03% | 13.08% | 12.25% |
| 8 | | | | | | | | 6.13% |

### Recovery periods in years

| Year | 7.5 | 8 | 8.5 | 9 | 9.5 | 10 | 10.5 | 11 |
|------|--------|--------|--------|--------|--------|--------|--------|--------|
| 1 | 10.00% | 9.38% | 8.82% | 8.33% | 7.89% | 7.50% | 7.14% | 6.82% |
| 2 | 18.00% | 16.99% | 16.09% | 15.28% | 14.54% | 13.88% | 13.27% | 12.71% |
| 3 | 14.40% | 13.81% | 13.25% | 12.73% | 12.25% | 11.79% | 11.37% | 10.97% |
| 4 | 11.52% | 11.22% | 10.91% | 10.61% | 10.31% | 10.02% | 9.75% | 9.48% |
| 5 | 11.52% | 10.80% | 10.19% | 9.65% | 9.17% | 8.74% | 8.35% | 8.18% |
| 6 | 11.52% | 10.80% | 10.19% | 9.64% | 9.17% | 8.74% | 8.35% | 7.98% |
| 7 | 11.52% | 10.80% | 10.18% | 9.65% | 9.17% | 8.74% | 8.35% | 7.97% |
| 8 | 11.52% | 10.80% | 10.19% | 9.64% | 9.17% | 8.74% | 8.35% | 7.98% |
| 9 | | 5.40% | 10.18% | 9.65% | 9.17% | 8.74% | 8.36% | 7.97% |
| 10 | | | 4.82% | 9.16% | 8.74% | 8.35% | 7.98% |
| 11 | | | | | 4.37% | 8.36% | 7.97% |
| 12 | | | | | | | | 3.99% |

## MACRS Depreciation Tables

### Recovery periods in years

| Year | 11.5 | 12 | 12.5 | 13 | 13.5 | 14 | 15 | 16 |
|---|---|---|---|---|---|---|---|---|
| 1 | 6.52% | 6.25% | 6.00% | 5.77% | 5.56% | 5.36% | 5.00% | 4.69% |
| 2 | 12.19% | 11.72% | 11.28% | 10.87% | 10.49% | 10.14% | 9.50% | 8.94% |
| 3 | 10.60% | 10.25% | 9.93% | 9.62% | 9.33% | 9.05% | 8.55% | 8.10% |
| 4 | 9.22% | 8.97% | 8.73% | 8.51% | 8.29% | 8.08% | 7.70% | 7.34% |
| 5 | 8.02% | 7.85% | 7.69% | 7.53% | 7.37% | 7.22% | 6.93% | 6.65% |
| 6 | 7.64% | 7.33% | 7.05% | 6.79% | 6.55% | 6.44% | 6.23% | 6.03% |
| 7 | 7.64% | 7.33% | 7.05% | 6.79% | 6.55% | 6.32% | 5.90% | 5.55% |
| 8 | 7.63% | 7.33% | 7.05% | 6.79% | 6.55% | 6.32% | 5.90% | 5.55% |
| 9 | 7.64% | 7.33% | 7.04% | 6.79% | 6.55% | 6.32% | 5.91% | 5.55% |
| 10 | 7.63% | 7.33% | 7.05% | 6.79% | 6.55% | 6.32% | 5.90% | 5.55% |
| 11 | 7.64% | 7.32% | 7.04% | 6.79% | 6.55% | 6.32% | 5.91% | 5.55% |
| 12 | 7.63% | 7.33% | 7.05% | 6.78% | 6.55% | 6.32% | 5.90% | 5.55% |
| 13 | | 3.66% | 7.04% | 6.79% | 6.56% | 6.32% | 5.91% | 5.54% |
| 14 | | | | 3.39% | 6.55% | 6.31% | 5.90% | 5.55% |
| 15 | | | | | | 3.16% | 5.91% | 5.54% |
| 16 | | | | | | | 2.95% | 5.55% |
| 17 | | | | | | | | 2.77% |

### Recovery periods in years

| Year | 16.5 | 17 | 18 | 19 | 20 | 22 | 24 | 25 |
|---|---|---|---|---|---|---|---|---|
| 1 | 4.55% | 4.41% | 4.17% | 3.95% | 3.750% | 3.409% | 3.125% | 3.000% |
| 2 | 8.68% | 8.43% | 7.99% | 7.58% | 7.219% | 6.586% | 6.055% | 5.820% |
| 3 | 7.89% | 7.69% | 7.32% | 6.98% | 6.677% | 6.137% | 5.676% | 5.471% |
| 4 | 7.17% | 7.01% | 6.71% | 6.43% | 6.177% | 5.718% | 5.322% | 5.143% |
| 5 | 6.52% | 6.39% | 6.15% | 5.93% | 5.713% | 5.328% | 4.989% | 4.834% |
| 6 | 5.93% | 5.83% | 5.64% | 5.46% | 5.285% | 4.965% | 4.677% | 4.544% |
| 7 | 5.39% | 5.32% | 5.17% | 5.03% | 4.888% | 4.627% | 4.385% | 4.271% |
| 8 | 5.39% | 5.23% | 4.94% | 4.69% | 4.522% | 4.311% | 4.111% | 4.015% |
| 9 | 5.39% | 5.23% | 4.94% | 4.69% | 4.462% | 4.063% | 3.854% | 3.774% |
| 10 | 5.39% | 5.23% | 4.94% | 4.69% | 4.461% | 4.063% | 3.729% | 3.584% |
| 11 | 5.39% | 5.23% | 4.94% | 4.69% | 4.462% | 4.063% | 3.729% | 3.583% |
| 12 | 5.39% | 5.23% | 4.95% | 4.69% | 4.461% | 4.063% | 3.729% | 3.584% |
| 13 | 5.38% | 5.23% | 4.94% | 4.69% | 4.462% | 4.064% | 3.730% | 3.583% |
| 14 | 5.39% | 5.23% | 4.95% | 4.69% | 4.461% | 4.063% | 3.729% | 3.584% |
| 15 | 5.38% | 5.23% | 4.94% | 4.69% | 4.462% | 4.064% | 3.730% | 3.583% |
| 16 | 5.39% | 5.23% | 4.95% | 4.69% | 4.461% | 4.063% | 3.729% | 3.584% |
| 17 | 5.38% | 5.23% | 4.94% | 4.69% | 4.462% | 4.064% | 3.730% | 3.583% |
| 18 | | 2.62% | 4.95% | 4.7% | 4.461% | 4.063% | 3.729% | 3.584% |
| 19 | | | 2.47% | 4.69% | 4.462% | 4.064% | 3.730% | 3.583% |
| 20 | | | | 2.35% | 4.461% | 4.063% | 3.729% | 3.584% |
| 21 | | | | | 2.231% | 4.064% | 3.730% | 3.583% |

### Recovery periods in years

| Year | 16.5 | 17 | 18 | 19 | 20 | 22 | 24 | 25 |
|------|------|----|----|----|----|----|----|----|
| 22 | | | | | | 4.063% | 3.729% | 3.584% |
| 23 | | | | | | 2.032% | 3.730% | 3.583% |
| 24 | | | | | | | 3.729% | 3.584% |
| 25 | | | | | | | 1.865% | 3.583% |
| 26 | | | | | | | | 1.792% |

### Recovery periods in years

| Year | 26.5 | 28 | 30 | 35 | 40 | 45 | 50 |
|------|------|-----|-----|-----|-----|-----|-----|
| 1 | 2.830% | 2.679% | 2.500% | 2.143% | 1.875% | 1.667% | 1.500% |
| 2 | 5.500% | 5.214% | 4.875% | 4.194% | 3.680% | 3.278% | 2.955% |
| 3 | 5.189% | 4.934% | 4.631% | 4.014% | 3.542% | 3.169% | 2.866% |
| 4 | 4.895% | 4.670% | 4.400% | 3.842% | 3.409% | 3.063% | 2.780% |
| 5 | 4.618% | 4.420% | 4.180% | 3.677% | 3.281% | 2.961% | 2.697% |
| 6 | 4.357% | 4.183% | 3.971% | 3.520% | 3.158% | 2.862% | 2.616% |
| 7 | 4.110% | 3.959% | 3.772% | 3.369% | 3.040% | 2.767% | 2.538% |
| 8 | 3.877% | 3.747% | 3.584% | 3.225% | 2.926% | 2.674% | 2.461% |
| 9 | 3.658% | 3.546% | 3.404% | 3.086% | 2.816% | 2.585% | 2.388% |
| 10 | 3.451% | 3.356% | 3.234% | 2.954% | 2.710% | 2.499% | 2.316% |
| 11 | 3.383% | 3.205% | 3.072% | 2.828% | 2.609% | 2.416% | 2.246% |
| 12 | 3.383% | 3.205% | 2.994% | 2.706% | 2.511% | 2.335% | 2.179% |
| 13 | 3.383% | 3.205% | 2.994% | 2.590% | 2.417% | 2.257% | 2.114% |
| 14 | 3.383% | 3.205% | 2.994% | 2.571% | 2.326% | 2.182% | 2.050% |
| 15 | 3.383% | 3.205% | 2.994% | 2.571% | 2.253% | 2.110% | 1.989% |
| 16 | 3.383% | 3.205% | 2.994% | 2.571% | 2.253% | 2.039% | 1.929% |
| 17 | 3.383% | 3.205% | 2.994% | 2.571% | 2.253% | 2.005% | 1.871% |
| 18 | 3.383% | 3.205% | 2.994% | 2.571% | 2.253% | 2.005% | 1.815% |
| 19 | 3.383% | 3.205% | 2.994% | 2.571% | 2.253% | 2.005% | 1.806% |
| 20 | 3.384% | 3.205% | 2.993% | 2.571% | 2.253% | 2.005% | 1.806% |
| 21 | 3.383% | 3.205% | 2.994% | 2.571% | 2.253% | 2.005% | 1.806% |
| 22 | 3.384% | 3.205% | 2.993% | 2.571% | 2.253% | 2.005% | 1.806% |
| 23 | 3.383% | 3.205% | 2.994% | 2.571% | 2.253% | 2.005% | 1.806% |
| 24 | 3.384% | 3.205% | 2.993% | 2.571% | 2.253% | 2.004% | 1.806% |
| 25 | 3.383% | 3.205% | 2.994% | 2.571% | 2.253% | 2.005% | 1.806% |
| 26 | 3.384% | 3.205% | 2.993% | 2.571% | 2.253% | 2.004% | 1.806% |
| 27 | 3.383% | 3.205% | 2.994% | 2.571% | 2.253% | 2.005% | 1.806% |
| 28 | | 3.205% | 2.993% | 2.572% | 2.253% | 2.004% | 1.806% |
| 29 | | 1.602% | 2.994% | 2.571% | 2.253% | 2.005% | 1.806% |
| 30 | | | 2.993% | 2.572% | 2.253% | 2.004% | 1.806% |
| 31 | | | 1.497% | 2.571% | 2.253% | 2.005% | 1.806% |
| 32 | | | | 2.572% | 2.253% | 2.004% | 1.806% |
| 33 | | | | 2.571% | 2.252% | 2.005% | 1.806% |

# MACRS Depreciation Tables

### Recovery periods in years

| Year | 26.5 | 28 | 30 | 35 | 40 | 45 | 50 |
|------|------|----|----|-----|--------|--------|--------|
| 34 | | | | 2.572% | 2.253% | 2.004% | 1.806% |
| 35 | | | | 2.571% | 2.252% | 2.005% | 1.806% |
| 36 | | | | 1.286% | 2.253% | 2.004% | 1.806% |
| 37 | | | | | 2.252% | 2.005% | 1.806% |
| 38 | | | | | 2.253% | 2.004% | 1.806% |
| 39 | | | | | 2.252% | 2.005% | 1.806% |
| 40 | | | | | 2.253% | 2.004% | 1.806% |
| 41 | | | | | 1.126% | 2.005% | 1.806% |
| 42 | | | | | | 2.004% | 1.805% |
| 43 | | | | | | 2.005% | 1.806% |
| 44 | | | | | | 2.004% | 1.805% |
| 45 | | | | | | 2.005% | 1.806% |
| 46 | | | | | | 1.002% | 1.805% |
| 47 | | | | | | | 1.806% |
| 48 | | | | | | | 1.805% |
| 49 | | | | | | | 1.806% |
| 50 | | | | | | | 1.805% |
| 51 | | | | | | | 0.903% |

## 150% Declining Balance Method (Mid-Quarter Convention)

### Property Placed in Service in First Quarter
### Recovery periods in years

| Year | 2.5 | 3 | 3.5 | 4 | 5 | 6 | 6.5 | 7 |
|------|--------|--------|--------|--------|--------|--------|--------|--------|
| 1 | 52.50% | 43.75% | 37.50% | 32.81% | 26.25% | 21.88% | 20.19% | 18.75% |
| 2 | 29.23% | 28.13% | 26.79% | 25.20% | 22.13% | 19.53% | 18.42% | 17.41% |
| 3 | 18.27% | 25.00% | 21.98% | 19.76% | 16.52% | 14.65% | 14.17% | 13.68% |
| 4 | | 3.12% | 13.73% | 19.76% | 16.52% | 14.06% | 13.03% | 12.16% |
| 5 | | | 2.47% | 16.52% | 14.06% | 13.02% | 12.16% |
| 6 | | | | 2.06% | 14.06% | 13.03% | 12.16% |
| 7 | | | | | 1.76% | 8.14% | 12.16% |
| 8 | | | | | | | 1.52% |

### Recovery periods in years

| Year | 7.5 | 8 | 8.5 | 9 | 9.5 | 10 | 10.5 | 11 |
|------|--------|--------|--------|--------|--------|--------|--------|--------|
| 1 | 17.50% | 16.41% | 15.44% | 14.58% | 13.82% | 13.13% | 12.50% | 11.93% |
| 2 | 16.50% | 15.67% | 14.92% | 14.24% | 13.61% | 13.03% | 12.50% | 12.01% |
| 3 | 13.20% | 12.74% | 12.29% | 11.86% | 11.46% | 11.08% | 10.71% | 10.37% |
| 4 | 11.42% | 10.77% | 10.20% | 9.89% | 9.65% | 9.41% | 9.18% | 8.96% |
| 5 | 11.42% | 10.77% | 10.19% | 9.64% | 9.15% | 8.71% | 8.32% | 7.96% |
| 6 | 11.41% | 10.76% | 10.20% | 9.65% | 9.15% | 8.71% | 8.32% | 7.96% |
| 7 | 11.42% | 10.77% | 10.19% | 9.64% | 9.15% | 8.71% | 8.32% | 7.96% |
| 8 | 7.13% | 10.76% | 10.20% | 9.65% | 9.15% | 8.71% | 8.32% | 7.96% |
| 9 | | 1.35% | 6.37% | 9.64% | 9.14% | 8.71% | 8.32% | 7.96% |

# 2015 Federal Tax Guide

### Recovery periods in years

| Year | 7.5 | 8 | 8.5 | 9 | 9.5 | 10 | 10.5 | 11 |
|---|---|---|---|---|---|---|---|---|
| 10 | | | | 1.21% | 5.72% | 8.71% | 8.31% | 7.97% |
| 11 | | | | | | 1.09% | 5.20% | 7.96% |
| 12 | | | | | | | | 1.00% |

### Recovery periods in years

| Year | 11.5 | 12 | 12.5 | 13 | 13.5 | 14 | 15 | 16 |
|---|---|---|---|---|---|---|---|---|
| 1 | 11.41% | 10.94% | 10.50% | 10.10% | 9.72% | 9.38% | 8.75% | 8.20% |
| 2 | 11.56% | 11.13% | 10.74% | 10.37% | 10.03% | 9.71% | 9.13% | 8.61% |
| 3 | 10.05% | 9.74% | 9.45% | 9.18% | 8.92% | 8.67% | 8.21% | 7.80% |
| 4 | 8.74% | 8.52% | 8.32% | 8.12% | 7.93% | 7.74% | 7.39% | 7.07% |
| 5 | 7.64% | 7.46% | 7.32% | 7.18% | 7.04% | 6.91% | 6.65% | 6.41% |
| 6 | 7.64% | 7.33% | 7.04% | 6.78% | 6.53% | 6.31% | 5.99% | 5.80% |
| 7 | 7.64% | 7.33% | 7.04% | 6.77% | 6.54% | 6.31% | 5.90% | 5.54% |
| 8 | 7.64% | 7.33% | 7.04% | 6.78% | 6.53% | 6.31% | 5.91% | 5.54% |
| 9 | 7.64% | 7.33% | 7.04% | 6.77% | 6.54% | 6.31% | 5.90% | 5.54% |
| 10 | 7.63% | 7.32% | 7.04% | 6.78% | 6.53% | 6.31% | 5.91% | 5.54% |
| 11 | 7.64% | 7.33% | 7.04% | 6.77% | 6.54% | 6.31% | 5.90% | 5.54% |
| 12 | 4.77% | 7.32% | 7.03% | 6.78% | 6.53% | 6.31% | 5.91% | 5.54% |
| 13 | | 0.92% | 4.40% | 6.77% | 6.54% | 6.32% | 5.90% | 5.54% |
| 14 | | | 0.85% | 4.08% | 6.31% | 5.91% | 5.55% |
| 15 | | | | | | 0.79% | 5.90% | 5.54% |
| 16 | | | | | | | 0.74% | 5.55% |
| 17 | | | | | | | | 0.69% |

### Recovery periods in years

| Year | 16.5 | 17 | 18 | 19 | 20 | 22 | 24 | 25 |
|---|---|---|---|---|---|---|---|---|
| 1 | 7.95% | 7.72% | 7.29% | 6.91% | 6.563% | 5.966% | 5.469% | 5.250% |
| 2 | 8.37% | 8.14% | 7.73% | 7.35% | 7.008% | 6.411% | 5.908% | 5.685% |
| 3 | 7.61% | 7.42% | 7.08% | 6.77% | 6.482% | 5.974% | 5.539% | 5.344% |
| 4 | 6.92% | 6.77% | 6.49% | 6.23% | 5.996% | 5.567% | 5.193% | 5.023% |
| 5 | 6.29% | 6.17% | 5.95% | 5.74% | 5.546% | 5.187% | 4.868% | 4.722% |
| 6 | 5.71% | 5.63% | 5.45% | 5.29% | 5.130% | 4.834% | 4.564% | 4.439% |
| 7 | 5.38% | 5.23% | 5.00% | 4.87% | 4.746% | 4.504% | 4.279% | 4.172% |
| 8 | 5.38% | 5.23% | 4.94% | 4.69% | 4.459% | 4.197% | 4.011% | 3.922% |
| 9 | 5.38% | 5.23% | 4.95% | 4.69% | 4.459% | 4.061% | 3.761% | 3.687% |
| 10 | 5.38% | 5.23% | 4.94% | 4.69% | 4.459% | 4.061% | 3.729% | 3.582% |
| 11 | 5.38% | 5.23% | 4.95% | 4.69% | 4.459% | 4.061% | 3.729% | 3.582% |
| 12 | 5.38% | 5.22% | 4.94% | 4.69% | 4.460% | 4.061% | 3.730% | 3.582% |
| 13 | 5.38% | 5.23% | 4.95% | 4.69% | 4.459% | 4.061% | 3.729% | 3.582% |
| 14 | 5.38% | 5.22% | 4.94% | 4.69% | 4.460% | 4.061% | 3.730% | 3.582% |
| 15 | 5.38% | 5.23% | 4.95% | 4.68% | 4.459% | 4.061% | 3.729% | 3.582% |
| 16 | 5.37% | 5.22% | 4.94% | 4.69% | 4.460% | 4.061% | 3.730% | 3.582% |
| 17 | 3.36% | 5.23% | 4.95% | 4.68% | 4.459% | 4.061% | 3.729% | 3.582% |
| 18 | | 0.65% | 4.94% | 4.69% | 4.460% | 4.061% | 3.730% | 3.582% |
| 19 | | | 0.62% | 4.68% | 4.459% | 4.061% | 3.729% | 3.581% |

# MACRS Depreciation Tables

### Recovery periods in years

| Year | 16.5 | 17 | 18 | 19 | 20 | 22 | 24 | 25 |
|------|------|----|----|----|-----|-----|-----|-----|
| 20 | | | | 0.59% | 4.460% | 4.060% | 3.730% | 3.582% |
| 21 | | | | | 0.557% | 4.061% | 3.729% | 3.581% |
| 22 | | | | | | 4.060% | 3.730% | 3.582% |
| 23 | | | | | | 0.508% | 3.729% | 3.581% |
| 24 | | | | | | | 3.730% | 3.582% |
| 25 | | | | | | | 0.466% | 3.581% |
| 26 | | | | | | | | 0.448% |

### Recovery periods in years

| Year | 26.5 | 28 | 30 | 35 | 40 | 45 | 50 |
|------|------|------|------|------|------|------|------|
| 1 | 4.953% | 4.688% | 4.375% | 3.750% | 3.281% | 2.917% | 2.625% |
| 2 | 5.380% | 5.106% | 4.781% | 4.125% | 3.627% | 3.236% | 2.921% |
| 3 | 5.075% | 4.832% | 4.542% | 3.948% | 3.491% | 3.128% | 2.834% |
| 4 | 4.788% | 4.574% | 4.315% | 3.779% | 3.360% | 3.024% | 2.749% |
| 5 | 4.517% | 4.329% | 4.099% | 3.617% | 3.234% | 2.923% | 2.666% |
| 6 | 4.262% | 4.097% | 3.894% | 3.462% | 3.113% | 2.826% | 2.586% |
| 7 | 4.020% | 3.877% | 3.700% | 3.314% | 2.996% | 2.732% | 2.509% |
| 8 | 3.793% | 3.669% | 3.515% | 3.172% | 2.884% | 2.64% | 2.433% |
| 9 | 3.578% | 3.473% | 3.339% | 3.036% | 2.776% | 2.552% | 2.360% |
| 10 | 3.383% | 3.287% | 3.172% | 2.906% | 2.671% | 2.467% | 2.290% |
| 11 | 3.384% | 3.204% | 3.013% | 2.781% | 2.571% | 2.385% | 2.221% |
| 12 | 3.383% | 3.204% | 2.994% | 2.662% | 2.475% | 2.306% | 2.154% |
| 13 | 3.384% | 3.204% | 2.994% | 2.571% | 2.382% | 2.229% | 2.090% |
| 14 | 3.383% | 3.204% | 2.994% | 2.571% | 2.293% | 2.154% | 2.027% |
| 15 | 3.384% | 3.204% | 2.994% | 2.571% | 2.252% | 2.083% | 1.966% |
| 16 | 3.383% | 3.204% | 2.994% | 2.571% | 2.252% | 2.013% | 1.907% |
| 17 | 3.384% | 3.204% | 2.994% | 2.571% | 2.253% | 2.005% | 1.850% |
| 18 | 3.383% | 3.204% | 2.994% | 2.571% | 2.252% | 2.005% | 1.806% |
| 19 | 3.384% | 3.204% | 2.994% | 2.571% | 2.253% | 2.005% | 1.806% |
| 20 | 3.383% | 3.204% | 2.994% | 2.571% | 2.252% | 2.005% | 1.806% |
| 21 | 3.384% | 3.203% | 2.993% | 2.571% | 2.253% | 2.005% | 1.806% |
| 22 | 3.383% | 3.204% | 2.994% | 2.571% | 2.252% | 2.005% | 1.806% |
| 23 | 3.384% | 3.203% | 2.993% | 2.571% | 2.253% | 2.005% | 1.806% |
| 24 | 3.383% | 3.204% | 2.994% | 2.57% | 2.252% | 2.005% | 1.806% |
| 25 | 3.384% | 3.203% | 2.993% | 2.571% | 2.253% | 2.004% | 1.806% |
| 26 | 3.383% | 3.204% | 2.994% | 2.570% | 2.252% | 2.005% | 1.806% |
| 27 | 2.115% | 3.203% | 2.993% | 2.751% | 2.253% | 2.004% | 1.806% |
| 28 | | 3.204% | 2.994% | 2.570% | 2.252% | 2.005% | 1.805% |
| 29 | | 0.400% | 2.993% | 2.571% | 2.253% | 2.004% | 1.806% |
| 30 | | | 2.994% | 2.570% | 2.252% | 2.005% | 1.805% |
| 31 | | | 0.374% | 2.571% | 2.253% | 2.004% | 1.806% |
| 32 | | | | 2.570% | 2.252% | 2.005% | 1.805% |
| 33 | | | | 2.571% | 2.253% | 2.004% | 1.806% |
| 34 | | | | 2.570% | 2.252% | 2.005% | 1.805% |

### Recovery periods in years

| Year | 26.5 | 28 | 30 | 35 | 40 | 45 | 50 |
|------|------|-----|-----|--------|--------|--------|--------|
| 35 | | | | 2.571% | 2.253% | 2.004% | 1.806% |
| 36 | | | | 0.321% | 2.252% | 2.005% | 1.805% |
| 37 | | | | | 2.253% | 2.004% | 1.806% |
| 38 | | | | | 2.252% | 2.005% | 1.805% |
| 39 | | | | | 2.253% | 2.004% | 1.806% |
| 40 | | | | | 2.252% | 2.005% | 1.805% |
| 41 | | | | | 0.282% | 2.004% | 1.806% |
| 42 | | | | | | 2.005% | 1.805% |
| 43 | | | | | | 2.004% | 1.806% |
| 44 | | | | | | 2.005% | 1.805% |
| 45 | | | | | | 2.004% | 1.806% |
| 46 | | | | | | 0.251% | 1.805% |
| 47 | | | | | | | 1.806% |
| 48 | | | | | | | 1.805% |
| 49 | | | | | | | 1.806% |
| 50 | | | | | | | 1.805% |
| 51 | | | | | | | 0.226% |

### Property Placed in Service in Second Quarter
### Recovery periods in years

| Year | 2.5 | 3 | 3.5 | 4 | 5 | 6 | 6.5 | 7 |
|------|--------|--------|--------|--------|--------|--------|--------|--------|
| 1 | 37.50% | 31.25% | 26.79% | 23.44% | 18.75% | 15.63% | 14.42% | 13.39% |
| 2 | 37.50% | 34.38% | 31.38% | 28.71% | 24.38% | 21.09% | 19.75% | 18.56% |
| 3 | 25.0% | 25.00% | 22.31% | 20.15% | 17.06% | 15.82% | 15.19% | 14.58% |
| 4 | | 9.37% | 19.52% | 20.15% | 16.76% | 14.06% | 13.07% | 12.22% |
| 5 | | | 7.55% | 16.76% | 14.06% | 13.07% | 12.22% |
| 6 | | | | 6.29% | 14.07% | 13.07% | 12.22% |
| 7 | | | | | 5.27% | 11.43% | 12.23% |
| 8 | | | | | | | 4.58% |

### Recovery periods in years

| Year | 7.5 | 8 | 8.5 | 9 | 9.5 | 10 | 10.5 | 11 |
|------|--------|--------|--------|--------|--------|--------|--------|--------|
| 1 | 12.50% | 11.72% | 11.03% | 10.42% | 9.87% | 9.38% | 8.93% | 8.52% |
| 2 | 17.50% | 16.55% | 15.70% | 14.93% | 14.23% | 13.59% | 13.01% | 12.47% |
| 3 | 14.00% | 13.45% | 12.93% | 12.44% | 11.98% | 11.55% | 11.15% | 10.77% |
| 4 | 11.49% | 10.93% | 10.65% | 10.37% | 10.09% | 9.82% | 9.56% | 9.31% |
| 5 | 11.49% | 10.82% | 10.19% | 9.64% | 9.16% | 8.73% | 8.34% | 8.04% |
| 6 | 11.49% | 10.82% | 10.19% | 9.65% | 9.16% | 8.73% | 8.34% | 7.98% |
| 7 | 11.48% | 10.83% | 10.19% | 9.64% | 9.16% | 8.73% | 8.34% | 7.98% |
| 8 | 10.05% | 10.82% | 10.20% | 9.65% | 9.17% | 8.73% | 8.34% | 7.98% |
| 9 | | 4.06% | 8.92% | 9.64% | 9.16% | 8.73% | 8.34% | 7.99% |
| 10 | | | | 3.62% | 8.02% | 8.73% | 8.35% | 7.98% |
| 11 | | | | | | 3.28% | 7.30% | 7.99% |
| 12 | | | | | | | | 2.99% |

# MACRS Depreciation Tables

## Recovery periods in years

| Year | 11.5 | 12 | 12.5 | 13 | 13.5 | 14 | 15 | 16 |
|------|------|------|------|------|------|------|------|------|
| 1 | 8.15% | 7.81% | 7.50% | 7.21% | 6.94% | 6.70% | 6.25% | 5.86% |
| 2 | 11.98% | 11.52% | 11.10% | 10.71% | 10.34% | 10.00% | 9.38% | 8.83% |
| 3 | 10.42% | 10.08% | 9.77% | 9.47% | 9.19% | 8.92% | 8.44% | 8.00% |
| 4 | 9.06% | 8.82% | 8.60% | 8.38% | 8.17% | 7.97% | 7.59% | 7.25% |
| 5 | 7.88% | 7.72% | 7.56% | 7.41% | 7.26% | 7.12% | 6.83% | 6.57% |
| 6 | 7.64% | 7.33% | 7.04% | 6.78% | 6.55% | 6.35% | 6.15% | 5.95% |
| 7 | 7.64% | 7.33% | 7.04% | 6.79% | 6.55% | 6.32% | 5.91% | 5.55% |
| 8 | 7.64% | 7.33% | 7.05% | 6.78% | 6.55% | 6.32% | 5.90% | 5.55% |
| 9 | 7.64% | 7.33% | 7.04% | 6.79% | 6.54% | 6.32% | 5.91% | 5.55% |
| 10 | 7.63% | 7.33% | 7.05% | 6.78% | 6.55% | 6.32% | 5.90% | 5.54% |
| 11 | 7.64% | 7.33% | 7.04% | 6.79% | 6.54% | 6.32% | 5.91% | 5.55% |
| 12 | 6.68% | 7.32% | 7.05% | 6.78% | 6.55% | 6.32% | 5.90% | 5.54% |
| 13 | | 2.75% | 6.16% | 6.79% | 6.54% | 6.32% | 5.91% | 5.55% |
| 14 | | | | 2.54% | 5.73% | 6.33% | 5.90% | 5.54% |
| 15 | | | | | | 2.37% | 5.91% | 5.55% |
| 16 | | | | | | | 2.21% | 5.54% |
| 17 | | | | | | | | 2.08% |

## Recovery periods in years

| Year | 16.5 | 17 | 18 | 19 | 20 | 22 | 24 | 25 |
|------|------|------|------|------|------|------|------|------|
| 1 | 5.68% | 5.51% | 5.21% | 4.93% | 4.688% | 4.261% | 3.906% | 3.750% |
| 2 | 8.57% | 8.34% | 7.90% | 7.51% | 7.148% | 6.528% | 6.006% | 5.775% |
| 3 | 7.80% | 7.60% | 7.24% | 6.91% | 6.612% | 6.083% | 5.631% | 5.429% |
| 4 | 7.09% | 6.93% | 6.64% | 6.37% | 6.116% | 5.668% | 5.279% | 5.103% |
| 5 | 6.44% | 6.32% | 6.08% | 5.86% | 5.658% | 5.281% | 4.949% | 4.797% |
| 6 | 5.86% | 5.76% | 5.58% | 5.40% | 5.233% | 4.921% | 4.639% | 4.509% |
| 7 | 5.38% | 5.25% | 5.11% | 4.98% | 4.841% | 4.586% | 4.349% | 4.238% |
| 8 | 5.39% | 5.23% | 4.94% | 4.69% | 4.478% | 4.273% | 4.078% | 3.984% |
| 9 | 5.38% | 5.23% | 4.94% | 4.69% | 4.463% | 4.063% | 3.823% | 3.745% |
| 10 | 5.39% | 5.23% | 4.95% | 4.69% | 4.463% | 4.063% | 3.729% | 3.583% |
| 11 | 5.38% | 5.23% | 4.94% | 4.69% | 4.463% | 4.062% | 3.729% | 3.583% |
| 12 | 5.39% | 5.23% | 4.95% | 4.69% | 4.463% | 4.063% | 3.729% | 3.583% |
| 13 | 5.38% | 5.24% | 4.94% | 4.69% | 4.463% | 4.062% | 3.730% | 3.583% |
| 14 | 5.39% | 5.23% | 4.95% | 4.69% | 4.463% | 4.063% | 3.729% | 3.583% |
| 15 | 5.38% | 5.24% | 4.94% | 4.69% | 4.462% | 4.062% | 3.730% | 3.583% |
| 16 | 5.39% | 5.23% | 4.95% | 4.69% | 4.463% | 4.063% | 3.729% | 3.583% |
| 17 | 4.71% | 5.24% | 4.94% | 4.69% | 4.462% | 4.062% | 3.730% | 3.583% |
| 18 | | 1.96% | 4.95% | 4.69% | 4.463% | 4.063% | 3.729% | 3.583% |
| 19 | | | 1.85% | 4.69% | 4.462% | 4.062% | 3.730% | 3.583% |
| 20 | | | | 1.76% | 4.463% | 4.063% | 3.729% | 3.583% |
| 21 | | | | | 1.673% | 4.062% | 3.730% | 3.583% |
| 22 | | | | | | 4.063% | 3.729% | 3.583% |
| 23 | | | | | | 1.523% | 3.730% | 3.583% |
| 24 | | | | | | | 3.729% | 3.582% |

### Recovery periods in years

| Year | 16.5 | 17 | 18 | 19 | 20 | 22 | 24 | 25 |
|---|---|---|---|---|---|---|---|---|
| 25 | | | | | | | 1.399% | 3.583% |
| 26 | | | | | | | 1.343% | |

### Recovery periods in years

| Year | 26.5 | 28 | 30 | 35 | 40 | 45 | 50 |
|---|---|---|---|---|---|---|---|
| 1 | 3.538% | 3.348% | 3.125% | 2.679% | 2.344% | 2.083% | 1.875% |
| 2 | 5.460% | 5.178% | 4.844% | 4.171% | 3.662% | 3.264% | 2.944% |
| 3 | 5.151% | 4.900% | 4.602% | 3.992% | 3.525% | 3.155% | 2.855% |
| 4 | 4.859% | 4.638% | 4.371% | 3.821% | 3.393% | 3.050% | 2.770% |
| 5 | 4.584% | 4.389% | 4.153% | 3.657% | 3.265% | 2.948% | 2.687% |
| 6 | 4.325% | 4.154% | 3.945% | 3.501% | 3.143% | 2.850% | 2.606% |
| 7 | 4.080% | 3.932% | 3.748% | 3.351% | 3.025% | 2.755% | 2.528% |
| 8 | 3.849% | 3.721% | 3.561% | 3.207% | 2.912% | 2.663% | 2.452% |
| 9 | 3.631% | 3.522% | 3.383% | 3.069% | 2.802% | 2.574% | 2.378% |
| 10 | 3.426% | 3.333% | 3.213% | 2.938% | 2.697% | 2.489% | 2.307% |
| 11 | 3.384% | 3.205% | 3.053% | 2.812% | 2.596% | 2.406% | 2.238% |
| 12 | 3.383% | 3.205% | 2.994% | 2.692% | 2.499% | 2.325% | 2.171% |
| 13 | 3.384% | 3.205% | 2.994% | 2.576% | 2.405% | 2.248% | 2.106% |
| 14 | 3.383% | 3.205% | 2.994% | 2.571% | 2.315% | 2.173% | 2.042% |
| 15 | 3.384% | 3.205% | 2.994% | 2.571% | 2.253% | 2.101% | 1.981% |
| 16 | 3.383% | 3.204% | 2.994% | 2.571% | 2.253% | 2.031% | 1.922% |
| 17 | 3.384% | 3.205% | 2.994% | 2.571% | 2.253% | 2.005% | 1.864% |
| 18 | 3.383% | 3.204% | 2.993% | 2.571% | 2.253% | 2.005% | 1.808% |
| 19 | 3.384% | 3.205% | 2.994% | 2.571% | 2.253% | 2.005% | 1.806% |
| 20 | 3.383% | 3.204% | 2.993% | 2.571% | 2.253% | 2.005% | 1.806% |
| 21 | 3.384% | 3.205% | 2.994% | 2.572% | 2.253% | 2.005% | 1.806% |
| 22 | 3.383% | 3.204% | 2.993% | 2.571% | 2.253% | 2.005% | 1.806% |
| 23 | 3.384% | 3.205% | 2.994% | 2.572% | 2.253% | 2.004% | 1.806% |
| 24 | 3.383% | 3.204% | 2.993% | 2.571% | 2.253% | 2.005% | 1.806% |
| 25 | 3.384% | 3.205% | 2.994% | 2.572% | 2.253% | 2.004% | 1.806% |
| 26 | 3.383% | 3.204% | 2.993% | 2.571% | 2.253% | 2.005% | 1.806% |
| 27 | 2.961% | 3.205% | 2.994% | 2.572% | 2.253% | 2.004% | 1.806% |
| 28 | | 3.204% | 2.993% | 2.571% | 2.253% | 2.005% | 1.806% |
| 29 | | 1.202% | 2.994% | 2.572% | 2.253% | 2.004% | 1.806% |
| 30 | | | 2.993% | 2.571% | 2.252% | 2.005% | 1.806% |
| 31 | | | 1.123% | 2.572% | 2.253% | 2.004% | 1.806% |
| 32 | | | | 2.571% | 2.252% | 2.005% | 1.806% |
| 33 | | | | 2.572% | 2.253% | 2.004% | 1.806% |
| 34 | | | | 2.571% | 2.252% | 2.005% | 1.806% |
| 35 | | | | 2.572% | 2.253% | 2.004% | 1.806% |
| 36 | | | | 0.964% | 2.252% | 2.005% | 1.806% |
| 37 | | | | | 2.253% | 2.004% | 1.806% |
| 38 | | | | | 2.252% | 2.005% | 1.806% |
| 39 | | | | | 2.253% | 2.004% | 1.806% |

# MACRS Depreciation Tables

### Recovery periods in years

| Year | 26.5 | 28 | 30 | 35 | 40 | 45 | 50 |
|------|------|-----|-----|-----|--------|--------|--------|
| 40 | | | | | 2.252% | 2.005% | 1.806% |
| 41 | | | | | 0.845% | 2.004% | 1.806% |
| 42 | | | | | | 2.005% | 1.806% |
| 43 | | | | | | 2.004% | 1.806% |
| 44 | | | | | | 2.005% | 1.806% |
| 45 | | | | | | 2.004% | 1.805% |
| 46 | | | | | | 0.752% | 1.806% |
| 47 | | | | | | | 1.805% |
| 48 | | | | | | | 1.806% |
| 49 | | | | | | | 1.805% |
| 50 | | | | | | | 1.806% |
| 51 | | | | | | | 0.677% |

## Property Placed in Service in Third Quarter
### Recovery periods in years

| Year | 2.5 | 3 | 3.5 | 4 | 5 | 6 | 6.5 | 7 |
|------|--------|--------|--------|--------|--------|--------|--------|--------|
| 1 | 22.50% | 18.75% | 16.07% | 14.06% | 11.25% | 9.38% | 8.65% | 8.04% |
| 2 | 46.50% | 40.63% | 35.97% | 32.23% | 26.63% | 22.66% | 21.08% | 19.71% |
| 3 | 27.56% | 25.00% | 22.57% | 20.46% | 18.64% | 16.99% | 16.22% | 15.48% |
| 4 | 3.44% | 15.62% | 22.57% | 20.46% | 16.56% | 14.06% | 13.10% | 12.27% |
| 5 | | | 2.82% | 12.79% | 16.57% | 14.06% | 13.10% | 12.28% |
| 6 | | | | | 10.35% | 14.06% | 13.11% | 12.27% |
| 7 | | | | | | 8.79% | 13.10% | 12.28% |
| 8 | | | | | | | 1.64% | 7.67% |

### Recovery periods in years

| Year | 7.5 | 8 | 8.5 | 9 | 9.5 | 10 | 10.5 | 11 |
|------|--------|--------|--------|--------|--------|--------|--------|--------|
| 1 | 7.50% | 7.03% | 6.62% | 6.25% | 5.92% | 5.63% | 5.36% | 5.11% |
| 2 | 18.50% | 17.43% | 16.48% | 15.63% | 14.85% | 14.16% | 13.52% | 12.94% |
| 3 | 14.80% | 14.16% | 13.57% | 13.02% | 12.51% | 12.03% | 11.59% | 11.18% |
| 4 | 11.84% | 11.51% | 11.18% | 10.85% | 10.53% | 10.23% | 9.93% | 9.65% |
| 5 | 11.48% | 10.78% | 10.18% | 9.64% | 9.17% | 8.75% | 8.51% | 8.33% |
| 6 | 11.48% | 10.78% | 10.17% | 9.65% | 9.17% | 8.75% | 8.34% | 7.97% |
| 7 | 11.48% | 10.78% | 10.18% | 9.64% | 9.18% | 8.75% | 8.34% | 7.97% |
| 8 | 11.48% | 10.79% | 10.17% | 9.65% | 9.17% | 8.74% | 8.34% | 7.97% |
| 9 | 1.44% | 6.74% | 10.18% | 9.64% | 9.18% | 8.75% | 8.34% | 7.97% |
| 10 | | 1.27% | 6.03% | 9.17% | 8.74% | 8.34% | 7.97% |
| 11 | | | | 1.15% | 5.47% | 8.35% | 7.96% |
| 12 | | | | | | 1.04% | 4.98% |

### Recovery periods in years

| Year | 11.5 | 12 | 12.5 | 13 | 13.5 | 14 | 15 | 16 |
|------|--------|--------|--------|--------|--------|--------|--------|--------|
| 1 | 4.89% | 4.69% | 4.50% | 4.33% | 4.17% | 4.02% | 3.75% | 3.52% |
| 2 | 12.41% | 11.91% | 11.46% | 11.04% | 10.65% | 10.28% | 9.63% | 9.05% |
| 3 | 10.79% | 10.43% | 10.08% | 9.77% | 9.46% | 9.18% | 8.66% | 8.20% |

**Recovery periods in years**

| Year | 11.5 | 12 | 12.5 | 13 | 13.5 | 14 | 15 | 16 |
|---|---|---|---|---|---|---|---|---|
| 4 | 9.38% | 9.12% | 8.88% | 8.64% | 8.41% | 8.20% | 7.80% | 7.43% |
| 5 | 8.16% | 7.98% | 7.81% | 7.64% | 7.48% | 7.32% | 7.02% | 6.73% |
| 6 | 7.63% | 7.33% | 7.05% | 6.79% | 6.65% | 6.54% | 6.31% | 6.10% |
| 7 | 7.63% | 7.33% | 7.05% | 6.79% | 6.55% | 6.31% | 5.90% | 5.55% |
| 8 | 7.63% | 7.33% | 7.05% | 6.79% | 6.54% | 6.31% | 5.90% | 5.55% |
| 9 | 7.63% | 7.33% | 7.05% | 6.79% | 6.55% | 6.32% | 5.91% | 5.55% |
| 10 | 7.63% | 7.32% | 7.05% | 6.79% | 6.54% | 6.31% | 5.90% | 5.55% |
| 11 | 7.63% | 7.33% | 7.05% | 6.79% | 6.55% | 6.32% | 5.91% | 5.55% |
| 12 | 7.64% | 7.32% | 7.04% | 6.80% | 6.54% | 6.31% | 5.90% | 5.55% |
| 13 | 0.95% | 4.58% | 7.05% | 6.79% | 6.55% | 6.32% | 5.91% | 5.55% |
| 14 | | | 0.88% | 4.25% | 6.54% | 6.31% | 5.90% | 5.55% |
| 15 | | | | | 0.82% | 3.95% | 5.91% | 5.55% |
| 16 | | | | | | | 3.69% | 5.55% |
| 17 | | | | | | | | 3.47% |

**Recovery periods in years**

| Year | 16.5 | 17 | 18 | 19 | 20 | 22 | 24 | 25 |
|---|---|---|---|---|---|---|---|---|
| 1 | 3.41% | 3.31% | 3.13% | 2.96% | 2.813% | 2.557% | 2.344% | 2.250% |
| 2 | 8.78% | 8.53% | 8.07% | 7.66% | 7.289% | 6.644% | 6.104% | 5.865% |
| 3 | 7.98% | 7.78% | 7.40% | 7.06% | 6.742% | 6.191% | 5.722% | 5.513% |
| 4 | 7.26% | 7.09% | 6.78% | 6.50% | 6.237% | 5.769% | 5.364% | 5.182% |
| 5 | 6.60% | 6.47% | 6.22% | 5.99% | 5.769% | 5.375% | 5.029% | 4.871% |
| 6 | 6.00% | 5.90% | 5.70% | 5.51% | 5.336% | 5.009% | 4.715% | 4.579% |
| 7 | 5.45% | 5.38% | 5.23% | 5.08% | 4.936% | 4.667% | 4.420% | 4.304% |
| 8 | 5.38% | 5.23% | 4.94% | 4.69% | 4.566% | 4.349% | 4.144% | 4.046% |
| 9 | 5.39% | 5.23% | 4.94% | 4.69% | 4.460% | 4.064% | 3.885% | 3.803% |
| 10 | 5.38% | 5.23% | 4.94% | 4.69% | 4.460% | 4.064% | 3.729% | 3.584% |
| 11 | 5.39% | 5.23% | 4.94% | 4.69% | 4.460% | 4.064% | 3.730% | 3.584% |
| 12 | 5.38% | 5.23% | 4.95% | 4.69% | 4.460% | 4.064% | 3.729% | 3.584% |
| 13 | 5.39% | 5.22% | 4.94% | 4.69% | 4.461% | 4.064% | 3.730% | 3.584% |
| 14 | 5.38% | 5.23% | 4.95% | 4.69% | 4.460% | 4.064% | 3.729% | 3.584% |
| 15 | 5.39% | 5.22% | 4.94% | 4.70% | 4.461% | 4.064% | 3.730% | 3.584% |
| 16 | 5.38% | 5.23% | 4.95% | 4.69% | 4.460% | 4.064% | 3.729% | 3.584% |
| 17 | 5.39% | 5.22% | 4.94% | 4.70% | 4.461% | 4.064% | 3.730% | 3.584% |
| 18 | 0.67% | 3.27% | 4.95% | 4.69% | 4.460% | 4.065% | 3.729% | 3.584% |
| 19 | | | 3.09% | 4.70% | 4.461% | 4.064% | 3.730% | 3.584% |
| 20 | | | | 2.93% | 4.460% | 4.065% | 3.729% | 3.584% |
| 21 | | | | | 2.788% | 4.064% | 3.730% | 3.585% |
| 22 | | | | | | 4.065% | 3.729% | 3.584% |
| 23 | | | | | | 2.540% | 3.730% | 3.585% |
| 24 | | | | | | | 3.729% | 3.584% |
| 25 | | | | | | | 2.331% | 3.585% |
| 26 | | | | | | | | 2.240% |

## MACRS Depreciation Tables

### Recovery periods in years

| Year | 26.5 | 28 | 30 | 35 | 40 | 45 | 50 |
|------|--------|--------|--------|--------|--------|--------|--------|
| 1 | 2.123% | 2.009% | 1.875% | 1.607% | 1.406% | 1.250% | 1.125% |
| 2 | 5.540% | 5.250% | 4.906% | 4.217% | 3.697% | 3.292% | 2.966% |
| 3 | 5.227% | 4.968% | 4.661% | 4.036% | 3.559% | 3.182% | 2.877% |
| 4 | 4.931% | 4.702% | 4.428% | 3.863% | 3.425% | 3.076% | 2.791% |
| 5 | 4.652% | 4.450% | 4.207% | 3.698% | 3.297% | 2.973% | 2.707% |
| 6 | 4.388% | 4.212% | 3.996% | 3.539% | 3.173% | 2.874% | 2.626% |
| 7 | 4.140% | 3.986% | 3.796% | 3.387% | 3.054% | 2.778% | 2.547% |
| 8 | 3.906% | 3.773% | 3.607% | 3.242% | 2.94% | 2.686% | 2.471% |
| 9 | 3.685% | 3.571% | 3.426% | 3.103% | 2.829% | 2.596% | 2.397% |
| 10 | 3.476% | 3.379% | 3.255% | 2.970% | 2.723% | 2.510% | 2.325% |
| 11 | 3.383% | 3.205% | 3.092% | 2.843% | 2.621% | 2.426% | 2.255% |
| 12 | 3.383% | 3.205% | 2.994% | 2.721% | 2.523% | 2.345% | 2.187% |
| 13 | 3.383% | 3.205% | 2.994% | 2.605% | 2.428% | 2.267% | 2.122% |
| 14 | 3.383% | 3.205% | 2.994% | 2.571% | 2.337% | 2.192% | 2.058% |
| 15 | 3.383% | 3.205% | 2.994% | 2.571% | 2.253% | 2.118% | 1.996% |
| 16 | 3.383% | 3.206% | 2.994% | 2.571% | 2.253% | 2.048% | 1.937% |
| 17 | 3.383% | 3.205% | 2.994% | 2.571% | 2.253% | 2.005% | 1.878% |
| 18 | 3.383% | 3.206% | 2.994% | 2.571% | 2.253% | 2.005% | 1.822% |
| 19 | 3.383% | 3.205% | 2.994% | 2.571% | 2.253% | 2.005% | 1.806% |
| 20 | 3.383% | 3.206% | 2.993% | 2.571% | 2.253% | 2.005% | 1.806% |
| 21 | 3.383% | 3.205% | 2.994% | 2.571% | 2.253% | 2.005% | 1.806% |
| 22 | 3.383% | 3.206% | 2.993% | 2.571% | 2.253% | 2.005% | 1.806% |
| 23 | 3.383% | 3.205% | 2.994% | 2.571% | 2.253% | 2.005% | 1.806% |
| 24 | 3.383% | 3.206% | 2.993% | 2.571% | 2.253% | 2.005% | 1.806% |
| 25 | 3.382% | 3.205% | 2.994% | 2.571% | 2.253% | 2.004% | 1.806% |
| 26 | 3.383% | 3.206% | 2.993% | 2.571% | 2.253% | 2.005% | 1.806% |
| 27 | 3.382% | 3.205% | 2.994% | 2.571% | 2.253% | 2.004% | 1.806% |
| 28 | 0.423% | 3.206% | 2.993% | 2.571% | 2.253% | 2.005% | 1.806% |
| 29 | | 2.003% | 2.994% | 2.571% | 2.253% | 2.004% | 1.806% |
| 30 | | | 2.993% | 2.571% | 2.253% | 2.005% | 1.806% |
| 31 | | | 1.871% | 2.571% | 2.253% | 2.004% | 1.806% |
| 32 | | | | 2.571% | 2.253% | 2.005% | 1.806% |
| 33 | | | | 2.571% | 2.253% | 2.004% | 1.806% |
| 34 | | | | 2.571% | 2.253% | 2.005% | 1.806% |
| 35 | | | | 2.571% | 2.253% | 2.004% | 1.806% |
| 36 | | | | 1.607% | 2.253% | 2.005% | 1.806% |
| 37 | | | | | 2.253% | 2.004% | 1.805% |
| 38 | | | | | 2.254% | 2.005% | 1.806% |
| 39 | | | | | 2.253% | 2.004% | 1.805% |
| 40 | | | | | 2.254% | 2.005% | 1.806% |
| 41 | | | | | 1.408% | 2.004% | 1.805% |
| 42 | | | | | | 2.005% | 1.806% |
| 43 | | | | | | 2.004% | 1.805% |
| 44 | | | | | | 2.005% | 1.806% |

### Recovery periods in years

| Year | 26.5 | 28 | 30 | 35 | 40 | 45 | 50 |
|------|------|----|----|----|----|--------|--------|
| 45 | | | | | | 2.004% | 1.805% |
| 46 | | | | | | 1.253% | 1.806% |
| 47 | | | | | | | 1.805% |
| 48 | | | | | | | 1.806% |
| 49 | | | | | | | 1.805% |
| 50 | | | | | | | 1.806% |
| 51 | | | | | | | 1.128% |

## Property Placed in Service in Fourth Quarter
### Recovery periods in years

| Year | 2.5 | 3 | 3.5 | 4 | 5 | 6 | 6.5 | 7 |
|------|--------|--------|--------|--------|--------|--------|--------|--------|
| 1 | 7.50% | 6.25% | 5.36% | 4.69% | 3.75% | 3.13% | 2.88% | 2.68% |
| 2 | 55.50% | 46.88% | 40.56% | 35.74% | 28.88% | 24.22% | 22.41% | 20.85% |
| 3 | 26.91% | 25.00% | 23.18% | 22.34% | 20.21% | 18.16% | 17.24% | 16.39% |
| 4 | 10.09% | 21.87% | 22.47% | 19.86% | 16.40% | 14.06% | 13.26% | 12.87% |
| 5 | | 8.43% | 17.37% | 16.41% | 14.06% | 13.10% | 12.18% |
| 6 | | | | 14.35% | 14.06% | 13.10% | 12.18% |
| 7 | | | | | 12.31% | 13.10% | 12.19% |
| 8 | | | | | | 4.91% | 10.66% |

### Recovery periods in years

| Year | 7.5 | 8 | 8.5 | 9 | 9.5 | 10 | 10.5 | 11 |
|------|--------|--------|--------|--------|--------|--------|--------|--------|
| 1 | 2.50% | 2.34% | 2.21% | 2.08% | 1.97% | 1.88% | 1.79% | 1.70% |
| 2 | 19.50% | 18.31% | 17.26% | 16.32% | 15.48% | 14.72% | 14.03% | 13.40% |
| 3 | 15.60% | 14.88% | 14.21% | 13.60% | 13.03% | 12.51% | 12.03% | 11.58% |
| 4 | 12.48% | 12.09% | 11.70% | 11.33% | 10.98% | 10.63% | 10.31% | 10.00% |
| 5 | 11.41% | 10.74% | 10.16% | 9.65% | 9.24% | 9.04% | 8.83% | 8.63% |
| 6 | 11.41% | 10.75% | 10.16% | 9.65% | 9.17% | 8.72% | 8.32% | 7.95% |
| 7 | 11.41% | 10.74% | 10.16% | 9.64% | 9.17% | 8.72% | 8.31% | 7.96% |
| 8 | 11.41% | 10.75% | 10.16% | 9.65% | 9.17% | 8.72% | 8.32% | 7.95% |
| 9 | 4.28% | 9.40% | 10.17% | 9.64% | 9.17% | 8.72% | 8.31% | 7.96% |
| 10 | | 3.81% | 8.44% | 9.18% | 8.71% | 8.32% | 7.95% |
| 11 | | | | 3.44% | 7.63% | 8.31% | 7.96% |
| 12 | | | | | | 3.12% | 6.96% |

### Recovery periods in years

| Year | 11.5 | 12 | 12.5 | 13 | 13.5 | 14 | 15 | 16 |
|------|--------|--------|--------|--------|--------|--------|--------|--------|
| 1 | 1.63% | 1.56% | 1.50% | 1.44% | 1.39% | 1.34% | 1.25% | 1.17% |
| 2 | 12.83% | 12.31% | 11.82% | 11.37% | 10.96% | 10.57% | 9.88% | 9.27% |
| 3 | 11.16% | 10.77% | 10.40% | 10.06% | 9.74% | 9.44% | 8.89% | 8.40% |
| 4 | 9.70% | 9.42% | 9.15% | 8.90% | 8.66% | 8.43% | 8.00% | 7.61% |
| 5 | 8.44% | 8.24% | 8.06% | 7.87% | 7.69% | 7.52% | 7.20% | 6.90% |
| 6 | 7.63% | 7.33% | 7.09% | 6.96% | 6.84% | 6.72% | 6.48% | 6.25% |
| 7 | 7.63% | 7.33% | 7.05% | 6.78% | 6.53% | 6.31% | 5.90% | 5.66% |
| 8 | 7.62% | 7.33% | 7.05% | 6.78% | 6.53% | 6.31% | 5.90% | 5.54% |

# MACRS Depreciation Tables

### Recovery periods in years

| Year | 11.5 | 12 | 12.5 | 13 | 13.5 | 14 | 15 | 16 |
|---|---|---|---|---|---|---|---|---|
| 9 | 7.63% | 7.33% | 7.05% | 6.78% | 6.53% | 6.31% | 5.90% | 5.54% |
| 10 | 7.62% | 7.32% | 7.05% | 6.78% | 6.54% | 6.31% | 5.91% | 5.54% |
| 11 | 7.63% | 7.33% | 7.05% | 6.78% | 6.53% | 6.31% | 5.90% | 5.54% |
| 12 | 7.62% | 7.32% | 7.04% | 6.78% | 6.54% | 6.30% | 5.91% | 5.55% |
| 13 | 2.86% | 6.41% | 7.05% | 6.78% | 6.53% | 6.31% | 5.90% | 5.54% |
| 14 | | | 2.64% | 5.94% | 6.54% | 6.30% | 5.91% | 5.55% |
| 15 | | | | | 2.45% | 5.52% | 5.90% | 5.54% |
| 16 | | | | | | | 5.17% | 5.55% |
| 17 | | | | | | | | 4.85% |

### Recovery periods in years

| Year | 16.5 | 17 | 18 | 19 | 20 | 22 | 24 | 25 |
|---|---|---|---|---|---|---|---|---|
| 1 | 1.14% | 1.10% | 1.04% | 0.99% | 0.938% | 0.852% | 0.781% | 0.750% |
| 2 | 8.99% | 8.73% | 8.25% | 7.82% | 7.430% | 6.760% | 6.201% | 5.955% |
| 3 | 8.17% | 7.96% | 7.56% | 7.20% | 6.872% | 6.299% | 5.814% | 5.598% |
| 4 | 7.43% | 7.25% | 6.93% | 6.63% | 6.357% | 5.870% | 5.450% | 5.262% |
| 5 | 6.75% | 6.61% | 6.35% | 6.11% | 5.880% | 5.469% | 5.110% | 4.946% |
| 6 | 6.14% | 6.03% | 5.82% | 5.63% | 5.439% | 5.097% | 4.790% | 4.649% |
| 7 | 5.58% | 5.50% | 5.34% | 5.18% | 5.031% | 4.749% | 4.491% | 4.370% |
| 8 | 5.38% | 5.22% | 4.94% | 4.77% | 4.654% | 4.425% | 4.210% | 4.108% |
| 9 | 5.38% | 5.23% | 4.94% | 4.69% | 4.458% | 4.124% | 3.947% | 3.862% |
| 10 | 5.38% | 5.22% | 4.94% | 4.69% | 4.458% | 4.062% | 3.730% | 3.630% |
| 11 | 5.38% | 5.23% | 4.95% | 4.69% | 4.458% | 4.062% | 3.729% | 3.582% |
| 12 | 5.38% | 5.22% | 4.94% | 4.69% | 4.458% | 4.062% | 3.730% | 3.582% |
| 13 | 5.38% | 5.23% | 4.95% | 4.69% | 4.458% | 4.062% | 3.729% | 3.582% |
| 14 | 5.38% | 5.22% | 4.94% | 4.69% | 4.458% | 4.061% | 3.730% | 3.582% |
| 15 | 5.37% | 5.23% | 4.95% | 4.69% | 4.458% | 4.062% | 3.729% | 3.582% |
| 16 | 5.38% | 5.22% | 4.94% | 4.69% | 4.458% | 4.061% | 3.730% | 3.583% |
| 17 | 5.37% | 5.23% | 4.95% | 4.68% | 4.458% | 4.062% | 3.729% | 3.582% |
| 18 | 2.02% | 4.57% | 4.94% | 4.69% | 4.459% | 4.061% | 3.730% | 3.583% |
| 19 | | | 4.33% | 4.68% | 4.458% | 4.062% | 3.729% | 3.582% |
| 20 | | | | 4.10% | 4.459% | 4.061% | 3.730% | 3.583% |
| 21 | | | | | 3.901% | 4.062% | 3.729% | 3.582% |
| 22 | | | | | | 4.061% | 3.730% | 3.583% |
| 23 | | | | | | 3.554% | 3.729% | 3.582% |
| 24 | | | | | | | 3.730% | 3.583% |
| 25 | | | | | | | 3.263% | 3.582% |
| 26 | | | | | | | | 3.135% |

### Recovery periods in years

| Year | 26.5 | 28 | 30 | 35 | 40 | 45 | 50 |
|------|------|------|------|------|------|------|------|
| 1 | 0.708% | 0.670% | 0.625% | 0.536% | 0.469% | 0.417% | 0.375% |
| 2 | 5.620% | 5.321% | 4.969% | 4.263% | 3.732% | 3.319% | 2.989% |
| 3 | 5.302% | 5.036% | 4.720% | 4.080% | 3.592% | 3.209% | 2.899% |
| 4 | 5.002% | 4.766% | 4.484% | 3.905% | 3.458% | 3.102% | 2.812% |
| 5 | 4.719% | 4.511% | 4.260% | 3.738% | 3.328% | 2.998% | 2.728% |
| 6 | 4.452% | 4.269% | 4.047% | 3.578% | 3.203% | 2.898% | 2.646% |
| 7 | 4.200% | 4.041% | 3.845% | 3.424% | 3.083% | 2.802% | 2.567% |
| 8 | 3.962% | 3.824% | 3.653% | 3.278% | 2.968% | 2.708% | 2.490% |
| 9 | 3.738% | 3.619% | 3.470% | 3.137% | 2.856% | 2.618% | 2.415% |
| 10 | 3.526% | 3.426% | 3.296% | 3.003% | 2.749% | 2.531% | 2.342% |
| 11 | 3.383% | 3.242% | 3.132% | 2.874% | 2.646% | 2.447% | 2.272% |
| 12 | 3.382% | 3.204% | 2.994% | 2.751% | 2.547% | 2.365% | 2.204% |
| 13 | 3.383% | 3.204% | 2.994% | 2.633% | 2.451% | 2.286% | 2.138% |
| 14 | 3.382% | 3.204% | 2.994% | 2.570% | 2.359% | 2.210% | 2.074% |
| 15 | 3.383% | 3.204% | 2.994% | 2.571% | 2.271% | 2.136% | 2.011% |
| 16 | 3.382% | 3.204% | 2.994% | 2.570% | 2.253% | 2.065% | 1.951% |
| 17 | 3.383% | 3.204% | 2.994% | 2.571% | 2.253% | 2.005% | 1.893% |
| 18 | 3.382% | 3.204% | 2.994% | 2.570% | 2.253% | 2.005% | 1.836% |
| 19 | 3.383% | 3.204% | 2.993% | 2.571% | 2.253% | 2.005% | 1.806% |
| 20 | 3.382% | 3.204% | 2.994% | 2.570% | 2.253% | 2.005% | 1.806% |
| 21 | 3.383% | 3.204% | 2.993% | 2.571% | 2.253% | 2.005% | 1.806% |
| 22 | 3.382% | 3.204% | 2.994% | 2.570% | 2.253% | 2.005% | 1.806% |
| 23 | 3.383% | 3.205% | 2.993% | 2.571% | 2.253% | 2.005% | 1.806% |
| 24 | 3.382% | 3.204% | 2.994% | 2.570% | 2.253% | 2.005% | 1.805% |
| 25 | 3.383% | 3.205% | 2.993% | 2.571% | 2.253% | 2.005% | 1.806% |
| 26 | 3.382% | 3.204% | 2.994% | 2.570% | 2.252% | 2.005% | 1.805% |
| 27 | 3.383% | 3.205% | 2.993% | 2.571% | 2.253% | 2.004% | 1.806% |
| 28 | 1.268% | 3.204% | 2.994% | 2.570% | 2.252% | 2.005% | 1.805% |
| 29 | | 2.804% | 2.993% | 2.571% | 2.253% | 2.004% | 1.806% |
| 30 | | | 2.994% | 2.570% | 2.252% | 2.005% | 1.805% |
| 31 | | | 2.619% | 2.571% | 2.253% | 2.004% | 1.806% |
| 32 | | | | 2.570% | 2.252% | 2.005% | 1.805% |
| 33 | | | | 2.571% | 2.253% | 2.004% | 1.806% |
| 34 | | | | 2.570% | 2.252% | 2.005% | 1.805% |
| 35 | | | | 2.571% | 2.253% | 2.004% | 1.806% |
| 36 | | | | 2.249% | 2.252% | 2.005% | 1.805% |
| 37 | | | | | 2.253% | 2.004% | 1.806% |
| 38 | | | | | 2.252% | 2.005% | 1.805% |
| 39 | | | | | 2.253% | 2.004% | 1.806% |
| 40 | | | | | 2.252% | 2.005% | 1.805% |
| 41 | | | | | 1.971% | 2.004% | 1.806% |
| 42 | | | | | | 2.005% | 1.805% |
| 43 | | | | | | 2.004% | 1.806% |
| 44 | | | | | | 2.005% | 1.805% |

## MACRS Depreciation Tables

### Recovery periods in years

| Year | 26.5 | 28 | 30 | 35 | 40 | 45 | 50 |
|------|------|----|----|----|----|--------|--------|
| 45 | | | | | | 2.004% | 1.806% |
| 46 | | | | | | 1.754% | 1.805% |
| 47 | | | | | | | 1.806% |
| 48 | | | | | | | 1.805% |
| 49 | | | | | | | 1.806% |
| 50 | | | | | | | 1.805% |
| 51 | | | | | | | 1.580% |

## RATES TO FIGURE INCLUSION AMOUNTS FOR LEASED LISTED PROPERTY

### Table A-19. Amount A Percentages

| Recovery Period of Property Under ADS | First Tax Year During Lease in Which Business Use is 50% or Less | | | | | |
|---|---|---|---|---|---|---|
| | 1 | 2 | 3 | 4 | 5 | 6 |
| Less than 7 years | 2.1% | -7.2% | -19.8% | -20.1% | -12.4% | -12.4% |
| 7 to 10 years | 3.9% | -3.8% | -17.7% | -25.1% | -27.8% | -27.2% |
| More than 10 years | 6.6% | -1.6% | -16.9% | -25.6% | -29.9% | -31.1% |

| Recovery Period of Property Under ADS | First Tax Year During Lease in Which Business Use is 50% or Less | | | | | |
|---|---|---|---|---|---|---|
| | 7 | 8 | 9 | 10 | 11 | 12&Later |
| Less than 7 years | -12.4% | -12.4% | -12.4% | -12.4% | -12.4% | -12.4% |
| 7 to 10 years | -27.1% | -27.6% | -23.7% | -14.7% | -14.7% | -14.7% |
| More than 10 years | -32.8% | -35.1% | -33.3% | -26.7% | -19.7% | -12.2% |

### Table A-20. Amount B Percentages

| Recovery Period of Property Under ADS | First Tax Year During Lease in Which Business Use is 50% or Less | | | | | |
|---|---|---|---|---|---|---|
| | 1 | 2 | 3 | 4 | 5 | 6 |
| Less than 7 years | 0.0% | 10.0% | 22.0% | 21.2% | 12.7% | 12.7% |
| 7 to 10 years | 0.0% | 9.3% | 23.8% | 31.3% | 33.8% | 32.7% |
| More than 10 years | 0.0% | 10.1% | 26.3% | 35.4% | 39.6% | 40.2% |

| Recovery Period of Property Under ADS | First Tax Year During Lease in Which Business Use is 50% or Less | | | | | |
|---|---|---|---|---|---|---|
| | 7 | 8 | 9 | 10 | 11 | 12&Later |
| Less than 7 years | 12.7% | 12.7% | 12.7% | 12.7% | 12.7% | 12.7% |
| 7 to 10 years | 31.6% | 30.5% | 25.0% | 15.0% | 15.0% | 15.0% |
| More than 10 years | 40.8% | 41.4% | 37.5% | 29.2% | 20.8% | 12.5% |

## 12. ACRS Depreciation Tables
(Source: IRS Pub. 534, *Depreciating Property Placed in Service Before 1987*)

*Accelerated percentages for recovery property (other than recovery property used predominantly outside the United States)*

**Table 1.     3-Year Property, 5-Year Property, 10-Year Property, and 15-Year Public Utility Property.**

| If the recovery Year is: | And the class of property is | | | |
|---|---|---|---|---|
| | 3-Year | 5-Year | 10-Year | 15-Year Public Utility |
| | The applicable percentage is: | | | |
| 1 | 25 | 15 | 8 | 5 |
| 2 | 38 | 22 | 14 | 10 |
| 3 | 37 | 21 | 12 | 9 |
| 4 | | 21 | 10 | 8 |
| 5 | | 21 | 10 | 7 |
| 6 | | | 10 | 7 |
| 7 | | | 9 | 6 |
| 8 | | | 9 | 6 |
| 9 | | | 9 | 6 |
| 10 | | | 9 | 6 |
| 11 | | | | 6 |
| 12 | | | | 6 |
| 13 | | | | 6 |
| 14 | | | | 6 |
| 15 | | | | 6 |

**Table 2.     15-Year Real Property (other than low-income housing), assuming full-month convention, applicable to real property placed in service after 1980 and before March 16, 1984.**

| Year | Month Placed in Service | | | | | | | | | | | |
|---|---|---|---|---|---|---|---|---|---|---|---|---|
| | 1 | 2 | 3 | 4 | 5 | 6 | 7 | 8 | 9 | 10 | 11 | 12 |
| 1 | 12% | 11% | 10% | 9% | 8% | 7% | 6% | 5% | 4% | 3% | 2% | 1% |
| 2 | 10% | 10% | 11% | 11% | 11% | 11% | 11% | 11% | 11% | 11% | 11% | 12% |
| 3 | 9% | 9% | 9% | 9% | 10% | 10% | 10% | 10% | 10% | 10% | 10% | 10% |
| 4 | 8% | 8% | 8% | 8% | 8% | 8% | 9% | 9% | 9% | 9% | 9% | 9% |
| 5 | 7% | 7% | 7% | 7% | 7% | 7% | 8% | 8% | 8% | 8% | 8% | 8% |
| 6 | 6% | 6% | 6% | 6% | 7% | 7% | 7% | 7% | 7% | 7% | 7% | 7% |
| 7 | 6% | 6% | 6% | 6% | 6% | 6% | 6% | 6% | 6% | 6% | 6% | 6% |
| 8 | 6% | 6% | 6% | 6% | 6% | 6% | 5% | 6% | 6% | 6% | 6% | 6% |
| 9 | 6% | 6% | 6% | 6% | 5% | 6% | 5% | 5% | 5% | 6% | 6% | 6% |
| 10 | 5% | 6% | 5% | 6% | 5% | 5% | 5% | 5% | 5% | 5% | 6% | 5% |
| 11 | 5% | 5% | 5% | 5% | 5% | 5% | 5% | 5% | 5% | 5% | 5% | 5% |
| 12 | 5% | 5% | 5% | 5% | 5% | 5% | 5% | 5% | 5% | 5% | 5% | 5% |
| 13 | 5% | 5% | 5% | 5% | 5% | 5% | 5% | 5% | 5% | 5% | 5% | 5% |
| 14 | 5% | 5% | 5% | 5% | 5% | 5% | 5% | 5% | 5% | 5% | 5% | 5% |

| | | | | | | | | | | | |
|---|---|---|---|---|---|---|---|---|---|---|---|
| 15 | 5% | 5% | 5% | 5% | 5% | 5% | 5% | 5% | 5% | 5% | 5% | 5% |
| 16 | — | — | 1% | 1% | 2% | 2% | 3% | 3% | 4% | 4% | 4% | 5% |

**Table 3.** 18-Year Real Property, assuming full-month convention, applicable to real property (other than low-income housing) placed in service after March 15, 1984 and before June 23, 1984.

| Year | Month Placed in Service | | | | | | | | | | |
|---|---|---|---|---|---|---|---|---|---|---|---|
| | 1 | 2 | 3 | 4 | 5 | 6 | 7 | 8 | 9 | 10–11 | 12 |
| 1 | 10% | 9% | 8% | 7% | 6% | 6% | 5% | 4% | 3% | 2% | 1% |
| 2 | 9% | 9% | 9% | 9% | 9% | 9% | 9% | 9% | 9% | 10% | 10% |
| 3 | 8% | 8% | 8% | 8% | 8% | 8% | 8% | 8% | 9% | 9% | 9% |
| 4 | 7% | 7% | 7% | 7% | 7% | 7% | 8% | 8% | 8% | 8% | 8% |
| 5 | 6% | 7% | 7% | 7% | 7% | 7% | 7% | 7% | 7% | 7% | 7% |
| 6 | 6% | 6% | 6% | 6% | 6% | 6% | 6% | 6% | 6% | 6% | 6% |
| 7 | 5% | 5% | 5% | 5% | 6% | 6% | 6% | 6% | 6% | 6% | 6% |
| 8–12 | 5% | 5% | 5% | 5% | 5% | 5% | 5% | 5% | 5% | 5% | 5% |
| 13 | 4% | 4% | 4% | 5% | 5% | 4% | 4% | 5% | 4% | 4% | 4% |
| 14–18 | 4% | 4% | 4% | 4% | 4% | 4% | 4% | 4% | 4% | 4% | 4% |
| 19 | | | 1% | 1% | 1% | 2% | 2% | 2% | 3% | 3% | 4% |

**Table 4.** 18-Year Real Property, assuming mid-month convention, applicable to real property (other than low-income housing) placed in service after June 22, 1984 and before May 9, 1985.

| Year | Month Placed in Service | | | | | | | | | | | |
|---|---|---|---|---|---|---|---|---|---|---|---|---|
| | 1 | 2 | 3 | 4 | 5 | 6 | 7 | 8 | 9 | 10 | 11 | 12 |
| 1 | 9% | 9% | 8% | 7% | 6% | 5% | 4% | 4% | 3% | 2% | 1% | 0.4% |
| 2 | 9% | 9% | 9% | 9% | 9% | 9% | 9% | 9% | 9% | 10% | 10% | 10% |
| 3 | 8% | 8% | 8% | 8% | 8% | 8% | 8% | 8% | 9% | 9% | 9% | 9% |
| 4 | 7% | 7% | 7% | 7% | 7% | 8% | 8% | 8% | 8% | 8% | 8% | 8% |
| 5 | 7% | 7% | 7% | 7% | 7% | 7% | 7% | 7% | 7% | 7% | 7% | 7% |
| 6 | 6% | 6% | 6% | 6% | 6% | 6% | 6% | 6% | 6% | 6% | 6% | 6% |
| 7 | 5% | 5% | 5% | 5% | 6% | 6% | 6% | 6% | 6% | 6% | 6% | 6% |
| 8–12 | 5% | 5% | 5% | 5% | 5% | 5% | 5% | 5% | 5% | 5% | 5% | 5% |
| 13 | 4% | 4% | 4% | 5% | 4% | 4% | 5% | 4% | 4% | 4% | 5% | 5% |
| 14–17 | 4% | 4% | 4% | 4% | 4% | 4% | 4% | 4% | 4% | 4% | 4% | 4% |
| 18 | 4% | 3% | 4% | 4% | 4% | 4% | 4% | 4% | 4% | 4% | 4% | 4% |
| 19 | | 1% | 1% | 1% | 2% | 2% | 2% | 3% | 3% | 3% | 3% | 3.6% |

# ACRS Depreciation Tables

**Table 5.** 19-Year Real Property, assuming mid-month convention, applicable to real property (other than low-income housing) placed in service after May 8, 1985.

| Year | Month Placed in Service | | | | | | | | | | | |
|---|---|---|---|---|---|---|---|---|---|---|---|---|
| | 1 | 2 | 3 | 4 | 5 | 6 | 7 | 8 | 9 | 10 | 11 | 12 |
| 1 | 8.8 | 8.1 | 7.3 | 6.5 | 5.8 | 5.0 | 4.2 | 3.5 | 2.7 | 1.9 | 1.1 | 0.4 |
| 2 | 8.4 | 8.5 | 8.5 | 8.6 | 8.7 | 8.8 | 8.8 | 8.9 | 9.0 | 9.0 | 9.1 | 9.2 |
| 3 | 7.6 | 7.7 | 7.7 | 7.8 | 7.9 | 8.9 | 8.0 | 8.1 | 8.1 | 8.2 | 8.3 | 8.3 |
| 4 | 6.9 | 7.0 | 7.0 | 7.1 | 7.1 | 7.2 | 7.3 | 7.3 | 7.4 | 7.4 | 7.5 | 7.6 |
| 5 | 6.3 | 6.3 | 6.4 | 6.4 | 6.5 | 6.5 | 6.6 | 6.6 | 6.7 | 6.8 | 6.8 | 6.9 |
| 6 | 5.7 | 5.7 | 5.8 | 5.9 | 5.9 | 5.9 | 6.0 | 6.0 | 6.1 | 6.1 | 6.2 | 6.2 |
| 7 | 5.2 | 5.2 | 5.3 | 5.3 | 5.3 | 5.4 | 5.4 | 5.5 | 5.5 | 5.6 | 5.6 | 5.6 |
| 8 | 4.7 | 4.7 | 4.8 | 4.8 | 4.8 | 4.9 | 4.9 | 5.0 | 5.0 | 5.1 | 5.1 | 5.1 |
| 9 | 4.2 | 4.3 | 4.3 | 4.4 | 4.4 | 4.5 | 4.5 | 4.5 | 4.5 | 4.6 | 4.6 | 4.7 |
| 10–19 | 4.2 | 4.2 | 4.2 | 4.2 | 4.2 | 4.2 | 4.2 | 4.2 | 4.2 | 4.2 | 4.2 | 4.2 |
| 20 | 0.2 | 0.5 | 0.9 | 1.2 | 1.6 | 1.9 | 2.3 | 2.6 | 3.0 | 3.3 | 3.7 | 4.0 |

**Table 6.** Low-income housing, assuming full-month convention, applicable to low-income housing placed in service after 1980 and before May 9, 1985.

| Year | Month Placed in Service | | | | | | | | | | | |
|---|---|---|---|---|---|---|---|---|---|---|---|---|
| | 1 | 2 | 3 | 4 | 5 | 6 | 7 | 8 | 9 | 10 | 11 | 12 |
| 1 | 13% | 12% | 11% | 10% | 9% | 8% | 7% | 6% | 4% | 3% | 2% | 1% |
| 2 | 12% | 12% | 12% | 12% | 12% | 12% | 12% | 13% | 13% | 13% | 13% | 13% |
| 3 | 10% | 10% | 10% | 10% | 11% | 11% | 11% | 11% | 11% | 11% | 11% | 11% |
| 4 | 9% | 9% | 9% | 9% | 9% | 9% | 9% | 9% | 10% | 10% | 10% | 10% |
| 5 | 8% | 8% | 8% | 8% | 8% | 8% | 8% | 8% | 8% | 8% | 8% | 9% |
| 6 | 7% | 7% | 7% | 7% | 7% | 7% | 7% | 7% | 7% | 7% | 7% | 7% |
| 7 | 6% | 6% | 6% | 6% | 6% | 6% | 6% | 6% | 6% | 6% | 6% | 6% |
| 8 | 5% | 5% | 5% | 5% | 5% | 5% | 5% | 5% | 5% | 5% | 6% | 6% |
| 9 | 5% | 5% | 5% | 5% | 5% | 5% | 5% | 5% | 5% | 5% | 5% | 5% |
| 10 | 5% | 5% | 5% | 5% | 5% | 5% | 5% | 5% | 5% | 5% | 5% | 5% |
| 11 | 4% | 5% | 5% | 5% | 5% | 5% | 5% | 5% | 5% | 5% | 5% | 5% |
| 12 | 4% | 4% | 4% | 5% | 4% | 5% | 5% | 5% | 5% | 5% | 5% | 5% |
| 13 | 4% | 4% | 4% | 4% | 4% | 4% | 5% | 4% | 5% | 5% | 5% | 5% |
| 14 | 4% | 4% | 4% | 4% | 4% | 4% | 4% | 4% | 4% | 5% | 4% | 4% |
| 15 | 4% | 4% | 4% | 4% | 4% | 4% | 4% | 4% | 4% | 4% | 4% | 4% |
| 16 | — | — | 1% | 1% | 2% | 2% | 2% | 3% | 3% | 3% | 4% | 4% |

**Table 7.** Low-income housing, assuming full-month convention, applicable to low-income housing placed in service after May 8, 1985.

| If the Recovery Year is: | And the Month in the First Recovery Year the property is Placed in Service is: | | | | | | | | | | | |
|---|---|---|---|---|---|---|---|---|---|---|---|---|
| | 1 | 2 | 3 | 4 | 5 | 6 | 7 | 8 | 9 | 10 | 11 | 12 |
| | The applicable percentage is: | | | | | | | | | | | |
| 1 | 13.3 | 12.1 | 11.1 | 10.0 | 8.9 | 7.8 | 6.6 | 5.6 | 4.4 | 3.3 | 2.2 | 1.1 |
| 2 | 11.6 | 11.7 | 11.9 | 12.0 | 12.1 | 12.3 | 12.5 | 12.6 | 12.7 | 12.9 | 13.0 | 13.2 |
| 3 | 10.0 | 10.1 | 10.2 | 10.4 | 10.5 | 10.7 | 10.8 | 10.9 | 11.1 | 11.2 | 11.3 | 11.4 |
| 4 | 8.7 | 8.8 | 8.9 | 9.0 | 9.1 | 9.2 | 9.3 | 9.5 | 9.6 | 9.7 | 9.8 | 9.9 |
| 5 | 7.5 | 7.6 | 7.7 | 7.8 | 7.9 | 8.0 | 8.1 | 8.2 | 8.3 | 8.4 | 8.5 | 8.6 |
| 6 | 6.5 | 6.6 | 6.7 | 6.8 | 6.9 | 6.9 | 7.0 | 7.1 | 7.2 | 7.3 | 7.4 | 7.4 |
| 7 | 5.7 | 5.7 | 5.8 | 5.9 | 5.9 | 6.0 | 6.1 | 6.1 | 6.2 | 6.3 | 6.4 | 6.5 |
| 8 | 4.9 | 5.0 | 5.0 | 5.1 | 5.2 | 5.2 | 5.3 | 5.3 | 5.4 | 5.5 | 5.5 | 5.6 |
| 9 | 4.6 | 4.6 | 4.6 | 4.6 | 4.6 | 4.6 | 4.6 | 4.6 | 4.6 | 4.7 | 4.8 | 4.8 |
| 10 | 4.6 | 4.6 | 4.6 | 4.6 | 4.6 | 4.6 | 4.6 | 4.6 | 4.6 | 4.6 | 4.6 | 4.6 |
| 11 | 4.6 | 4.6 | 4.6 | 4.6 | 4.6 | 4.6 | 4.6 | 4.6 | 4.6 | 4.6 | 4.6 | 4.6 |
| 12 | 4.5 | 4.6 | 4.6 | 4.6 | 4.6 | 4.6 | 4.6 | 4.6 | 4.6 | 4.6 | 4.6 | 4.6 |
| 13 | 4.5 | 4.5 | 4.6 | 4.5 | 4.6 | 4.6 | 4.6 | 4.6 | 4.6 | 4.5 | 4.6 | 4.6 |
| 14 | 4.5 | 4.5 | 4.5 | 4.5 | 4.5 | 4.5 | 4.5 | 4.6 | 4.6 | 4.5 | 4.5 | 4.5 |
| 15 | 4.5 | 4.5 | 4.5 | 4.5 | 4.5 | 4.5 | 4.5 | 4.5 | 4.5 | 4.5 | 4.5 | 4.5 |
| 16 | 0.0 | 0.4 | 0.7 | 1.1 | 1.5 | 1.9 | 2.3 | 2.6 | 3.0 | 3.4 | 3.7 | 4.1 |

*Optional straight-line percentages for recovery property (other than recovery property used predominantly outside the United States)*

**Table 8.** 3-year property, 5-year property, 10-year property, and 15-year public utility property.

| If the recovery year is: | And the period elected is: | | | | | | | |
|---|---|---|---|---|---|---|---|---|
| | 3 | 5 | 10 | 12 | 15 | 25 | 35 | 45 |
| | The applicable percentage is: | | | | | | | |
| 1 | 17 | 10 | 5 | 4 | 3 | 2 | 1 | 1.1 |
| 2 | 33 | 20 | 10 | 9 | 7 | 4 | 3 | 2.3 |
| 3 | 33 | 20 | 10 | 9 | 7 | 4 | 3 | 2.3 |
| 4 | 17 | 20 | 10 | 9 | 7 | 4 | 3 | 2.3 |
| 5 | | 20 | 10 | 9 | 7 | 4 | 3 | 2.3 |
| 6 | | 10 | 10 | 8 | 7 | 4 | 3 | 2.3 |
| 7 | | | 10 | 8 | 7 | 4 | 3 | 2.3 |
| 8 | | | 10 | 8 | 7 | 4 | 3 | 2.3 |
| 9 | | | 10 | 8 | 7 | 4 | 3 | 2.3 |
| 10 | | | 10 | 8 | 7 | 4 | 3 | 2.3 |
| 11 | | | 5 | 8 | 7 | 4 | 3 | 2.3 |
| 12 | | | | 8 | 6 | 4 | 3 | 2.2 |
| 13 | | | | 4 | 6 | 4 | 3 | 2.2 |

| | | | | |
|---|---|---|---|---|
| 14 | 6 | 4 | 3 | 2.2 |
| 15 | 6 | 4 | 3 | 2.2 |
| 16 | 3 | 4 | 3 | 2.2 |
| 17 | | 4 | 3 | 2.2 |
| 18 | | 4 | 3 | 2.2 |
| 19 | | 4 | 3 | 2.2 |
| 20 | | 4 | 3 | 2.2 |
| 21 | | 4 | 3 | 2.2 |
| 22 | | 4 | 3 | 2.2 |
| 23 | | 4 | 3 | 2.2 |
| 24 | | 4 | 3 | 2.2 |
| 25 | | 4 | 3 | 2.2 |
| 26 | | 2 | 3 | 2.2 |
| 27 | | | 3 | 2.2 |
| 28 | | | 3 | 2.2 |
| 29 | | | 3 | 2.2 |
| 30 | | | 3 | 2.2 |
| 31 | | | 3 | 2.2 |
| 32 | | | 2 | 2.2 |
| 33 | | | 2 | 2.2 |
| 34 | | | 2 | 2.2 |
| 35 | | | 2 | 2.2 |
| 36 | | | 1 | 2.2 |
| 37 | | | | 2.2 |
| 38 | | | | 2.2 |
| 39 | | | | 2.2 |
| 40 | | | | 2.2 |
| 41 | | | | 2.2 |
| 42 | | | | 2.2 |
| 43 | | | | 2.2 |
| 44 | | | | 2.2 |
| 45 | | | | 2.2 |
| 46 | | | | 1.1 |

**Table 9.    15-year straight-line, assuming full-month convention, applicable to real property, including low-income housing, placed in service after 1980 and before March 16, 1984.**

| If the recovery year is | And the month in the 1st recovery year that the property is placed in service is: | | | | | | |
|---|---|---|---|---|---|---|---|
| | 1 | 2–3 | 4 | 5–6 | 7–8 | 9–10 | 11–12 |
| | The applicable percentage is: | | | | | | |
| 1 | 7 | 6 | 5 | 4 | 3 | 2 | 1 |
| 2 | 7 | 7 | 7 | 7 | 7 | 7 | 7 |
| 3 | 7 | 7 | 7 | 7 | 7 | 7 | 7 |
| 4 | 7 | 7 | 7 | 7 | 7 | 7 | 7 |
| 5 | 7 | 7 | 7 | 7 | 7 | 7 | 7 |
| 6 | 7 | 7 | 7 | 7 | 7 | 7 | 7 |

| | | | | | | | |
|---|---|---|---|---|---|---|---|
| 7 | 7 | 7 | 7 | 7 | 7 | 7 | 7 |
| 8 | 7 | 7 | 7 | 7 | 7 | 7 | 7 |
| 9 | 7 | 7 | 7 | 7 | 7 | 7 | 7 |
| 10 | 7 | 7 | 7 | 7 | 7 | 7 | 7 |
| 11 | 6 | 6 | 6 | 6 | 6 | 6 | 6 |
| 12 | 6 | 6 | 6 | 6 | 6 | 6 | 6 |
| 13 | 6 | 6 | 6 | 6 | 6 | 6 | 6 |
| 14 | 6 | 6 | 6 | 6 | 6 | 6 | 6 |
| 15 | 6 | 6 | 6 | 6 | 6 | 6 | 6 |
| 16 | | 1 | 2 | 3 | 4 | 6 | 6 |

**Table 10.**   18-year straight-line, assuming full-month convention, applicable to (1) real property (other than low-income housing) placed in service after March 15, 1984, and before June 23, 1984; and (2) low-income housing placed in service after March 15, 1984, and before May 9, 1985.

| | Month Placed in Service | | | | | | |
|---|---|---|---|---|---|---|---|
| Year | 1 | 2–3 | 4–5 | 6–7 | 8–9 | 10–11 | 12 |
| 1 | 6% | 5% | 4% | 3% | 2% | 1% | 0.5% |
| 2–10 | 6% | 6% | 6% | 6% | 6% | 6% | 6% |
| 11 | 5% | 5% | 5% | 5% | 5% | 5% | 5.5% |
| 12–18 | 5% | 5% | 5% | 5% | 5% | 5% | 5% |
| 19 | | 1% | 2% | 3% | 4% | 5% | 5% |

**Table 11.**   35-year straight-line, assuming full-month convention, applicable to (1) low-income housing placed in service after 1980 and before May 9, 1985; and (2) real property (other than low-income housing) placed in service after 1980 and before June 23, 1984 (i.e., 15-year real property and 18-year real property within the full-month convention effective date).

| | Month Placed in Service | | |
|---|---|---|---|
| Year | 1–2 | 3–6 | 7–12 |
| 1 | 3% | 2% | 1% |
| 2–30 | 3% | 3% | 3% |
| 31–35 | 2% | 2% | 2% |
| 36 | | 1% | 2% |

# ACRS Depreciation Tables

**Table 12.  35-year straight-line, assuming full-month convention, applicable to low-income housing placed in service after May 8, 1985.**

| If the Recovery Year is: | And the Month in the First Recovery Year the Property is Placed in Service is: | | | | | | | | | | | |
|---|---|---|---|---|---|---|---|---|---|---|---|---|
| | 1 | 2 | 3 | 4 | 5 | 6 | 7 | 8 | 9 | 10 | 11 | 12 |
| | The applicable percentage is: | | | | | | | | | | | |
| 1 | 2.9 | 2.6 | 2.4 | 2.1 | 1.9 | 1.7 | 1.4 | 1.2 | 1.0 | 0.7 | 0.5 | 0.2 |
| 2 | 2.9 | 2.9 | 2.9 | 2.9 | 2.9 | 2.9 | 2.9 | 2.9 | 2.9 | 2.9 | 2.9 | 2.9 |
| 3 | 2.9 | 2.9 | 2.9 | 2.9 | 2.9 | 2.9 | 2.9 | 2.9 | 2.9 | 2.9 | 2.9 | 2.9 |
| 4 | 2.9 | 2.9 | 2.9 | 2.9 | 2.9 | 2.9 | 2.9 | 2.9 | 2.9 | 2.9 | 2.9 | 2.9 |
| 5 | 2.9 | 2.9 | 2.9 | 2.9 | 2.9 | 2.9 | 2.9 | 2.9 | 2.9 | 2.9 | 2.9 | 2.9 |
| 6 | 2.9 | 2.9 | 2.9 | 2.9 | 2.9 | 2.9 | 2.9 | 2.9 | 2.9 | 2.9 | 2.9 | 2.9 |
| 7 | 2.9 | 2.9 | 2.9 | 2.9 | 2.9 | 2.9 | 2.9 | 2.9 | 2.9 | 2.9 | 2.9 | 2.9 |
| 8 | 2.9 | 2.9 | 2.9 | 2.9 | 2.9 | 2.9 | 2.9 | 2.9 | 2.9 | 2.9 | 2.9 | 2.9 |
| 9 | 2.9 | 2.9 | 2.9 | 2.9 | 2.9 | 2.9 | 2.9 | 2.9 | 2.9 | 2.9 | 2.9 | 2.9 |
| 10 | 2.9 | 2.9 | 2.9 | 2.9 | 2.9 | 2.9 | 2.9 | 2.9 | 2.9 | 2.9 | 2.9 | 2.9 |
| 11 | 2.9 | 2.9 | 2.9 | 2.9 | 2.9 | 2.9 | 2.9 | 2.9 | 2.9 | 2.9 | 2.9 | 2.9 |
| 12 | 2.9 | 2.9 | 2.9 | 2.9 | 2.9 | 2.9 | 2.9 | 2.9 | 2.9 | 2.9 | 2.9 | 2.9 |
| 13 | 2.9 | 2.9 | 2.9 | 2.9 | 2.9 | 2.9 | 2.9 | 2.9 | 2.9 | 2.9 | 2.9 | 2.9 |
| 14 | 2.9 | 2.9 | 2.9 | 2.9 | 2.9 | 2.9 | 2.9 | 2.9 | 2.9 | 2.9 | 2.9 | 2.9 |
| 15 | 2.9 | 2.9 | 2.9 | 2.9 | 2.9 | 2.9 | 2.9 | 2.9 | 2.9 | 2.9 | 2.9 | 2.9 |
| 16 | 2.9 | 2.9 | 2.9 | 2.9 | 2.9 | 2.9 | 2.9 | 2.9 | 2.9 | 2.9 | 2.9 | 2.9 |
| 17 | 2.9 | 2.9 | 2.9 | 2.9 | 2.9 | 2.9 | 2.9 | 2.9 | 2.9 | 2.9 | 2.9 | 2.9 |
| 18 | 2.9 | 2.9 | 2.9 | 2.9 | 2.9 | 2.9 | 2.9 | 2.9 | 2.9 | 2.9 | 2.9 | 2.9 |
| 19 | 2.9 | 2.9 | 2.9 | 2.9 | 2.9 | 2.9 | 2.9 | 2.9 | 2.9 | 2.9 | 2.9 | 2.9 |
| 20 | 2.9 | 2.9 | 2.9 | 2.9 | 2.9 | 2.9 | 2.9 | 2.9 | 2.9 | 2.9 | 2.9 | 2.9 |
| 21 | 2.8 | 2.8 | 2.8 | 2.8 | 2.8 | 2.8 | 2.8 | 2.8 | 2.8 | 2.8 | 2.8 | 2.8 |
| 22 | 2.8 | 2.8 | 2.8 | 2.8 | 2.8 | 2.8 | 2.8 | 2.8 | 2.8 | 2.8 | 2.8 | 2.8 |
| 23 | 2.8 | 2.8 | 2.8 | 2.8 | 2.8 | 2.8 | 2.8 | 2.8 | 2.8 | 2.8 | 2.8 | 2.8 |
| 24 | 2.8 | 2.8 | 2.8 | 2.8 | 2.8 | 2.8 | 2.8 | 2.8 | 2.8 | 2.8 | 2.8 | 2.8 |
| 25 | 2.8 | 2.8 | 2.8 | 2.8 | 2.8 | 2.8 | 2.8 | 2.8 | 2.8 | 2.8 | 2.8 | 2.8 |
| 26 | 2.8 | 2.8 | 2.8 | 2.8 | 2.8 | 2.8 | 2.8 | 2.8 | 2.8 | 2.8 | 2.8 | 2.8 |
| 27 | 2.8 | 2.8 | 2.8 | 2.8 | 2.8 | 2.8 | 2.8 | 2.8 | 2.8 | 2.8 | 2.8 | 2.8 |
| 28 | 2.8 | 2.8 | 2.8 | 2.8 | 2.8 | 2.8 | 2.8 | 2.8 | 2.8 | 2.8 | 2.8 | 2.8 |
| 29 | 2.8 | 2.8 | 2.8 | 2.8 | 2.8 | 2.8 | 2.8 | 2.8 | 2.8 | 2.8 | 2.8 | 2.8 |
| 30 | 2.8 | 2.8 | 2.8 | 2.8 | 2.8 | 2.8 | 2.8 | 2.8 | 2.8 | 2.8 | 2.8 | 2.8 |
| 31 | 2.8 | 2.8 | 2.8 | 2.8 | 2.8 | 2.8 | 2.8 | 2.8 | 2.8 | 2.8 | 2.8 | 2.8 |
| 32 | 2.8 | 2.8 | 2.8 | 2.8 | 2.8 | 2.8 | 2.8 | 2.8 | 2.8 | 2.8 | 2.8 | 2.8 |
| 33 | 2.8 | 2.8 | 2.8 | 2.8 | 2.8 | 2.8 | 2.8 | 2.8 | 2.8 | 2.8 | 2.8 | 2.8 |
| 34 | 2.8 | 2.8 | 2.8 | 2.8 | 2.8 | 2.8 | 2.8 | 2.8 | 2.8 | 2.8 | 2.8 | 2.8 |
| 35 | 2.8 | 2.8 | 2.8 | 2.8 | 2.8 | 2.8 | 2.8 | 2.8 | 2.8 | 2.8 | 2.8 | 2.8 |
| 36 | 0.0 | 0.3 | 0.5 | 0.8 | 1.0 | 1.2 | 1.5 | 1.7 | 1.9 | 2.2 | 2.4 | 2.7 |

**Table 13.** 45-year straight-line, assuming full-month convention, applicable to (1) low-income housing placed in service after 1980; and (2) real property (other than low-income housing) placed in service after 1980 and before June 23, 1983 (i.e., 15-year real property and 18-year real property within the full-month convention effective date).

| Year | Month Placed in Service | | | | | | | | | | | |
|------|------|------|------|------|------|------|------|------|------|------|------|------|
|      | 1 | 2 | 3 | 4 | 5 | 6 | 7 | 8 | 9 | 10 | 11 | 12 |
| 1 | 2.3% | 2.0% | 1.9% | 1.7% | 1.5% | 1.3% | 1.2% | 0.9% | 0.7% | 0.6% | 0.4% | 0.2% |
| 2–10 | 2.3% | 2.3% | 2.3% | 2.3% | 2.3% | 2.3% | 2.3% | 2.3% | 2.3% | 2.3% | 2.3% | 2.3% |
| 11–45 | 2.2% | 2.2% | 2.2% | 2.2% | 2.2% | 2.2% | 2.2% | 2.2% | 2.2% | 2.2% | 2.2% | 2.2% |
| 46 |  | 0.3% | 0.4% | 0.6% | 0.8% | 1.0% | 1.1% | 1.4% | 1.6% | 1.7% | 1.9% | 2.1% |

**Table 14.** 18-year straight-line, assuming mid-month convention, applicable to real property (other than low-income housing) placed in service after June 22, 1984, and before May 9, 1985.

| Year | Month Placed in Service | | | | | |
|------|------|------|------|------|------|------|
|      | 1–2 | 3–4 | 5–7 | 8–9 | 10–11 | 12 |
| 1 | 5% | 4% | 3% | 2% | 1% | 0.2% |
| 2–10 | 6% | 6% | 6% | 6% | 6% | 6.% |
| 11 | 5% | 5% | 5% | 5% | 5% | 5.8% |
| 12–18 | 5% | 5% | 5% | 5% | 5% | 5.% |
| 19 | 1% | 2% | 3% | 4% | 5% | 5.% |

**Table 15.** 19-year straight-line, assuming mid-month convention, applicable to real property (other than low-income housing) placed in service after May 8, 1985.

| Year | Month Placed in Service | | | | | | | | | | | |
|------|------|------|------|------|------|------|------|------|------|------|------|------|
|      | 1 | 2 | 3 | 4 | 5 | 6 | 7 | 8 | 9 | 10 | 11 | 12 |
| 1 | 5.0% | 4.6% | 4.2% | 3.7% | 3.3% | 2.9% | 2.4% | 2.0% | 1.5% | 1.1% | 0.7% | 0.2% |
| 2–13 | 5.3% | 5.3% | 5.3% | 5.3% | 5.3% | 5.3% | 5.3% | 5.3% | 5.3% | 5.3% | 5.3% | 5.3% |
| 14–19 | 5.2% | 5.2% | 5.2% | 5.2% | 5.2% | 5.2% | 5.2% | 5.2% | 5.2% | 5.2% | 5.2% | 5.2% |
| 20 | 0.2% | 0.6% | 1.0% | 1.5% | 1.9% | 2.3% | 2.8% | 3.2% | 3.7% | 4.1% | 4.5% | 5.0% |

**Table 16.** 35-year straight-line, assuming mid-month convention, applicable to real property (other than los-income housing) placed in service after June 22, 1984, and before May 9, 1985 (i.e., 18-year real property within the mid-month convention effective date).

| Year | Month Placed in Service | | | | |
|------|------|------|------|------|------|
|      | 1–2 | 3–6 | 7–10 | 11 | 12 |
| 1 | 3% | 2% | 1% | 0.4% | 0.1% |
| 2–30 | 3% | 3% | 3% | 3.0% | 3.0% |
| 31 | 2% | 2% | 2% | 2.6% | 2.9% |
| 32–35 | 2% | 2% | 2% | 2.0% | 2.0% |
| 36 |  | 1% | 2% | 2.0% | 2.0% |

# ACRS Depreciation Tables

**Table 17.** 35-year straight line, assuming mid-month convention, applicable to real property (other than low-income housing) placed in service after May 8, 1985 (i.e., 19-year property).

| If the Recovery Year is: | And the Month in the First Recovery Year the Property is Placed in Service is: | | | | | | | | | | | |
|---|---|---|---|---|---|---|---|---|---|---|---|---|
| | 1 | 2 | 3 | 4 | 5 | 6 | 7 | 8 | 9 | 10 | 11 | 12 |
| | The applicable percentage is: | | | | | | | | | | | |
| 1 | 2.7 | 2.5 | 2.3 | 2.0 | 1.8 | 1.5 | 1.3 | 1.1 | 0.8 | 0.6 | 0.4 | 0.1 |
| 2 | 2.9 | 2.9 | 2.9 | 2.9 | 2.9 | 2.9 | 2.9 | 2.9 | 2.9 | 2.9 | 2.9 | 2.9 |
| 3 | 2.9 | 2.9 | 2.9 | 2.9 | 2.9 | 2.9 | 2.9 | 2.9 | 2.9 | 2.9 | 2.9 | 2.9 |
| 4 | 2.9 | 2.9 | 2.9 | 2.9 | 2.9 | 2.9 | 2.9 | 2.9 | 2.9 | 2.9 | 2.9 | 2.9 |
| 5 | 2.9 | 2.9 | 2.9 | 2.9 | 2.9 | 2.9 | 2.9 | 2.9 | 2.9 | 2.9 | 2.9 | 2.9 |
| 6 | 2.9 | 2.9 | 2.9 | 2.9 | 2.9 | 2.9 | 2.9 | 2.9 | 2.9 | 2.9 | 2.9 | 2.9 |
| 7 | 2.9 | 2.9 | 2.9 | 2.9 | 2.9 | 2.9 | 2.9 | 2.9 | 2.9 | 2.9 | 2.9 | 2.9 |
| 8 | 2.9 | 2.9 | 2.9 | 2.9 | 2.9 | 2.9 | 2.9 | 2.9 | 2.9 | 2.9 | 2.9 | 2.9 |
| 9 | 2.9 | 2.9 | 2.9 | 2.9 | 2.9 | 2.9 | 2.9 | 2.9 | 2.9 | 2.9 | 2.9 | 2.9 |
| 10 | 2.9 | 2.9 | 2.9 | 2.9 | 2.9 | 2.9 | 2.9 | 2.9 | 2.9 | 2.9 | 2.9 | 2.9 |
| 11 | 2.9 | 2.9 | 2.9 | 2.9 | 2.9 | 2.9 | 2.9 | 2.9 | 2.9 | 2.9 | 2.9 | 2.9 |
| 12 | 2.9 | 2.9 | 2.9 | 2.9 | 2.9 | 2.9 | 2.9 | 2.9 | 2.9 | 2.9 | 2.9 | 2.9 |
| 13 | 2.9 | 2.9 | 2.9 | 2.9 | 2.9 | 2.9 | 2.9 | 2.9 | 2.9 | 2.9 | 2.9 | 2.9 |
| 14 | 2.9 | 2.9 | 2.9 | 2.9 | 2.9 | 2.9 | 2.9 | 2.9 | 2.9 | 2.9 | 2.9 | 2.9 |
| 15 | 2.9 | 2.9 | 2.9 | 2.9 | 2.9 | 2.9 | 2.9 | 2.9 | 2.9 | 2.9 | 2.9 | 2.9 |
| 16 | 2.9 | 2.9 | 2.9 | 2.9 | 2.9 | 2.9 | 2.9 | 2.9 | 2.9 | 2.9 | 2.9 | 2.9 |
| 17 | 2.9 | 2.9 | 2.9 | 2.9 | 2.9 | 2.9 | 2.9 | 2.9 | 2.9 | 2.9 | 2.9 | 2.9 |
| 18 | 2.9 | 2.9 | 2.9 | 2.9 | 2.9 | 2.9 | 2.9 | 2.9 | 2.9 | 2.9 | 2.9 | 2.9 |
| 19 | 2.9 | 2.9 | 2.9 | 2.9 | 2.9 | 2.9 | 2.9 | 2.9 | 2.9 | 2.9 | 2.9 | 2.9 |
| 20 | 2.9 | 2.9 | 2.9 | 2.9 | 2.9 | 2.9 | 2.9 | 2.9 | 2.9 | 2.9 | 2.9 | 2.9 |
| 21 | 2.8 | 2.8 | 2.8 | 2.8 | 2.8 | 2.8 | 2.8 | 2.8 | 2.8 | 2.8 | 2.8 | 2.8 |
| 22 | 2.8 | 2.8 | 2.8 | 2.8 | 2.8 | 2.8 | 2.8 | 2.8 | 2.8 | 2.8 | 2.8 | 2.8 |
| 23 | 2.8 | 2.8 | 2.8 | 2.8 | 2.8 | 2.8 | 2.8 | 2.8 | 2.8 | 2.8 | 2.8 | 2.8 |
| 24 | 2.8 | 2.8 | 2.8 | 2.8 | 2.8 | 2.8 | 2.8 | 2.8 | 2.8 | 2.8 | 2.8 | 2.8 |
| 25 | 2.8 | 2.8 | 2.8 | 2.8 | 2.8 | 2.8 | 2.8 | 2.8 | 2.8 | 2.8 | 2.8 | 2.8 |
| 26 | 2.8 | 2.8 | 2.8 | 2.8 | 2.8 | 2.8 | 2.8 | 2.8 | 2.8 | 2.8 | 2.8 | 2.8 |
| 27 | 2.8 | 2.8 | 2.8 | 2.8 | 2.8 | 2.8 | 2.8 | 2.8 | 2.8 | 2.8 | 2.8 | 2.8 |
| 28 | 2.8 | 2.8 | 2.8 | 2.8 | 2.8 | 2.8 | 2.8 | 2.8 | 2.8 | 2.8 | 2.8 | 2.8 |
| 29 | 2.8 | 2.8 | 2.8 | 2.8 | 2.8 | 2.8 | 2.8 | 2.8 | 2.8 | 2.8 | 2.8 | 2.8 |
| 30 | 2.8 | 2.8 | 2.8 | 2.8 | 2.8 | 2.8 | 2.8 | 2.8 | 2.8 | 2.8 | 2.8 | 2.8 |
| 31 | 2.8 | 2.8 | 2.8 | 2.8 | 2.8 | 2.8 | 2.8 | 2.8 | 2.8 | 2.8 | 2.8 | 2.8 |
| 32 | 2.8 | 2.8 | 2.8 | 2.8 | 2.8 | 2.8 | 2.8 | 2.8 | 2.8 | 2.8 | 2.8 | 2.8 |
| 33 | 2.8 | 2.8 | 2.8 | 2.8 | 2.8 | 2.8 | 2.8 | 2.8 | 2.8 | 2.8 | 2.8 | 2.8 |
| 34 | 2.8 | 2.8 | 2.8 | 2.8 | 2.8 | 2.8 | 2.8 | 2.8 | 2.8 | 2.8 | 2.8 | 2.8 |
| 35 | 2.8 | 2.8 | 2.8 | 2.8 | 2.8 | 2.8 | 2.8 | 2.8 | 2.8 | 2.8 | 2.8 | 2.8 |
| 36 | 0.2 | 0.4 | 0.6 | 0.9 | 1.1 | 1.4 | 1.6 | 1.8 | 2.1 | 2.3 | 2.5 | 2.8 |

**Table 18.**      45-year straight line, assuming mid-month convention, applicable to real property (other than low-income housing) placed in service after June 22, 1984 (i.e., 18-year property within the mid-month convention effective date and 19-year property).

| Year | Month Placed in Service | | | | | | | | | | | |
|---|---|---|---|---|---|---|---|---|---|---|---|---|
|  | 1 | 2 | 3 | 4 | 5 | 6 | 7 | 8 | 9 | 10 | 11 | 12 |
| 1 | 2.1% | 1.9% | 1.8% | 1.6% | 1.4% | 1.2% | 1.0% | 0.8% | 0.6% | 0.5% | 0.3% | 0.1% |
| 2–11 | 2.3% | 2.3% | 2.3% | 2.3% | 2.3% | 2.3% | 2.3% | 2.3% | 2.3% | 2.3% | 2.3% | 2.3% |
| 12–45 | 2.2% | 2.2% | 2.2% | 2.2% | 2.2% | 2.2% | 2.2% | 2.2% | 2.2% | 2.2% | 2.2% | 2.2% |
| 46 | 0.1% | 0.3% | 0.4% | 0.6% | 0.8% | 1.0% | 1.2% | 1.4% | 1.6% | 1.7% | 1.9% | 2.1% |

*Accelerated percentages for recovery property used predominantly outside the United States.*

**Table 19.**      3-year property, 5-year property, 10-year property, and 15-year public utility property.

*If the recovery year is:* — *And the recovery period is:*

| If the recovery year is: | 2.5 | 3 | 3.5 | 4 | 5 | 6 | 6.5 | 7 | 7.5 | 8 |
|---|---|---|---|---|---|---|---|---|---|---|
| | The applicable percentage is: | | | | | | | | | |
| 1 | 40 | 33 | 29 | 25 | 20 | 17 | 15 | 14 | 13 | 13 |
| 2 | 48 | 45 | 41 | 38 | 32 | 28 | 26 | 25 | 23 | 22 |
| 3 | 12 | 15 | 17 | 19 | 19 | 18 | 18 | 17 | 17 | 16 |
| 4 | | 7 | 13 | 12 | 12 | 12 | 13 | 13 | 13 | 12 |
| 5 | | | | 6 | 12 | 10 | 10 | 9 | 9 | 9 |
| 6 | | | | | 5 | 10 | 9 | 9 | 9 | 8 |
| 7 | | | | | | 5 | 9 | 9 | 8 | 8 |
| 8 | | | | | | | | 4 | 8 | 8 |
| 9 | | | | | | | | | | 4 |

*If the recovery year is:* — *And the recovery period is:*

| If the recovery year is: | 8.5 | 9 | 9.5 | 10 | 10.5 | 11 | 11.5 | 12 | 12.5 | 13 |
|---|---|---|---|---|---|---|---|---|---|---|
| | The applicable percentage is: | | | | | | | | | |
| 1 | 12 | 11 | 11 | 10 | 10 | 9 | 9 | 8 | 8 | 8 |
| 2 | 21 | 20 | 19 | 18 | 17 | 17 | 16 | 15 | 15 | 14 |
| 3 | 16 | 15 | 15 | 14 | 14 | 13 | 13 | 13 | 12 | 12 |
| 4 | 12 | 12 | 12 | 12 | 11 | 11 | 11 | 11 | 10 | 10 |
| 5 | 9 | 9 | 9 | 9 | 9 | 9 | 9 | 9 | 9 | 9 |
| 6 | 8 | 8 | 7 | 7 | 7 | 7 | 7 | 7 | 7 | 7 |
| 7 | 8 | 7 | 7 | 7 | 7 | 7 | 6 | 6 | 6 | 6 |
| 8 | 7 | 7 | 7 | 7 | 7 | 6 | 6 | 6 | 6 | 6 |
| 9 | 7 | 7 | 7 | 7 | 6 | 6 | 6 | 6 | 6 | 5 |
| 10 | | 4 | 6 | 6 | 6 | 6 | 6 | 6 | 6 | 5 |
| 11 | | | | 3 | 6 | 6 | 6 | 5 | 5 | 5 |
| 12 | | | | | | 3 | 5 | 5 | 5 | 5 |
| 13 | | | | | | | | 3 | 5 | 5 |
| 14 | | | | | | | | | | 3 |

# ACRS Depreciation Tables

If the recovery year is: — And the recovery period is:

The applicable percentage is:

| If the recovery year is: | 13.5 | 14 | 15 | 16 | 16.5 | 17 | 18 | 19 | 20 | 22 |
|---|---|---|---|---|---|---|---|---|---|---|
| 1 | 7 | 7 | 7 | 6 | 6 | 6 | 6 | 5 | 5 | 5 |
| 2 | 14 | 13 | 12 | 12 | 11 | 11 | 10 | 10 | 10 | 9 |
| 3 | 12 | 11 | 11 | 10 | 10 | 10 | 9 | 9 | 9 | 8 |
| 4 | 10 | 10 | 9 | 9 | 9 | 9 | 8 | 8 | 8 | 7 |
| 5 | 8 | 8 | 8 | 8 | 8 | 8 | 7 | 7 | 7 | 6 |
| 6 | 7 | 7 | 7 | 7 | 7 | 7 | 7 | 6 | 6 | 6 |
| 7 | 6 | 6 | 6 | 6 | 6 | 6 | 6 | 6 | 6 | 5 |
| 8 | 6 | 5 | 5 | 5 | 5 | 5 | 5 | 5 | 5 | 5 |
| 9 | 5 | 5 | 5 | 5 | 5 | 5 | 5 | 5 | 4 | 4 |
| 10 | 5 | 5 | 5 | 5 | 5 | 4 | 4 | 4 | 4 | 4 |
| 11 | 5 | 5 | 5 | 5 | 4 | 4 | 4 | 4 | 4 | 4 |
| 12 | 5 | 5 | 5 | 4 | 4 | 4 | 4 | 4 | 4 | 4 |
| 13 | 5 | 5 | 5 | 4 | 4 | 4 | 4 | 4 | 4 | 4 |
| 14 | 5 | 5 | 4 | 4 | 4 | 4 | 4 | 4 | 4 | 3 |
| 15 |  | 3 | 4 | 4 | 4 | 4 | 4 | 4 | 3 | 3 |
| 16 |  |  | 2 | 4 | 4 | 4 | 4 | 4 | 3 | 3 |
| 17 |  |  |  | 2 | 4 | 3 | 4 | 3 | 3 | 3 |
| 18 |  |  |  |  |  | 2 | 3 | 3 | 3 | 3 |
| 19 |  |  |  |  |  |  | 2 | 3 | 3 | 3 |
| 20 |  |  |  |  |  |  |  | 2 | 3 | 3 |
| 21 |  |  |  |  |  |  |  |  | 2 | 3 |
| 22 |  |  |  |  |  |  |  |  |  | 3 |
| 23 |  |  |  |  |  |  |  |  |  | 2 |

If the recovery year is: — And the recovery period is:

The applicable percentage is:

| If the recovery year is: | 25 | 26.5 | 28 | 30 | 35 | 45 | 50 |
|---|---|---|---|---|---|---|---|
| 1 | 4 | 4 | 4 | 3 | 3 | 2 | 2 |
| 2 | 8 | 7 | 7 | 6 | 6 | 4 | 4 |
| 3 | 7 | 7 | 6 | 6 | 5 | 4 | 4 |
| 4 | 6 | 6 | 6 | 6 | 5 | 4 | 4 |
| 5 | 6 | 6 | 6 | 5 | 5 | 4 | 3 |
| 6 | 6 | 5 | 5 | 5 | 4 | 4 | 3 |
| 7 | 5 | 5 | 5 | 5 | 4 | 3 | 3 |
| 8 | 5 | 5 | 4 | 4 | 4 | 3 | 3 |
| 9 | 4 | 4 | 4 | 4 | 4 | 3 | 3 |
| 10 | 4 | 4 | 4 | 4 | 3 | 3 | 3 |
| 11 | 4 | 4 | 4 | 3 | 3 | 3 | 3 |
| 12 | 3 | 3 | 3 | 3 | 3 | 3 | 3 |
| 13 | 3 | 3 | 3 | 3 | 3 | 3 | 2 |
| 14 | 3 | 3 | 3 | 3 | 3 | 3 | 2 |
| 15 | 3 | 3 | 3 | 3 | 3 | 2 | 2 |
| 16 | 3 | 3 | 3 | 3 | 3 | 2 | 2 |

| | | | | | | | |
|---|---|---|---|---|---|---|---|
| 17 | 3 | 3 | 3 | 3 | 2 | 2 | 2 |
| 18 | 3 | 3 | 3 | 3 | 2 | 2 | 2 |
| 19 | 3 | 3 | 3 | 3 | 2 | 2 | 2 |
| 20 | 3 | 3 | 3 | 3 | 2 | 2 | 2 |
| 21 | 3 | 3 | 3 | 3 | 2 | 2 | 2 |
| 22 | 3 | 3 | 2 | 2 | 2 | 2 | 2 |
| 23 | 3 | 3 | 2 | 2 | 2 | 2 | 2 |
| 24 | 2 | 2 | 2 | 2 | 2 | 2 | 2 |
| 25 | 2 | 2 | 2 | 2 | 2 | 2 | 2 |
| 26 | 1 | 2 | 2 | 2 | 2 | 2 | 2 |
| 27 | | 1 | 2 | 2 | 2 | 2 | 2 |
| 28 | | | 2 | 2 | 2 | 2 | 2 |
| 29 | | | 1 | 2 | 2 | 2 | 2 |
| 30 | | | | 2 | 2 | 2 | 2 |
| 31 | | | | 1 | 2 | 2 | 2 |
| 32 | | | | | 2 | 2 | 2 |
| 33 | | | | | 2 | 2 | 2 |
| 34 | | | | | 2 | 2 | 2 |
| 35 | | | | | 2 | 2 | 2 |
| 36 | | | | | 1 | 2 | 1 |
| 37 | | | | | | 1 | 1 |
| 38 | | | | | | 1 | 1 |
| 39 | | | | | | 1 | 1 |
| 40 | | | | | | 1 | 1 |
| 41 | | | | | | 1 | 1 |
| 42 | | | | | | 1 | 1 |
| 43 | | | | | | 1 | 1 |
| 44 | | | | | | 1 | 1 |
| 45 | | | | | | 1 | 1 |
| 46 | | | | | | 1 | 1 |
| 47 | | | | | | | 1 |
| 48 | | | | | | | 1 |
| 49 | | | | | | | 1 |
| 50 | | | | | | | 1 |
| 51 | | | | | | | 1 |

# ACRS Depreciation Tables

**Table 20.** 35-year accelerated, assuming full-month convention, applicable to (1) low-income housing placed in service after 1980 and before May 9, 1985; (2) real property (other than low-income housing) placed in service after 1980 and before June 23, 1984 (i.e., 18-year real property within the full-month convention effective date and 15-year real property).

| If the recovery year is: | And the month in the 1st recovery year in which the property is placed in service is: | | | | |
|---|---|---|---|---|---|
| | 1 | 2,3 | 4,5,6 | 7,8 | 9,10,11,12 |
| | The applicable percentage is: | | | | |
| 1 | 4 | 4 | 3 | 2 | 1 |
| 2 | 4 | 4 | 4 | 4 | 4 |
| 3 | 4 | 4 | 4 | 4 | 4 |
| 4 | 4 | 4 | 4 | 4 | 4 |
| 5 | 4 | 4 | 4 | 4 | 4 |
| 6 | 3 | 3 | 3 | 4 | 4 |
| 7 | 3 | 3 | 3 | 3 | 3 |
| 8 | 3 | 3 | 3 | 3 | 3 |
| 9 | 3 | 3 | 3 | 3 | 3 |
| 10 | 3 | 3 | 3 | 3 | 3 |
| 11 | 3 | 3 | 3 | 3 | 3 |
| 12 | 3 | 3 | 3 | 3 | 3 |
| 13 | 3 | 3 | 3 | 3 | 3 |
| 14 | 3 | 3 | 3 | 3 | 3 |
| 15 | 3 | 3 | 3 | 3 | 3 |
| 16 | 3 | 3 | 3 | 3 | 3 |
| 17 | 3 | 3 | 3 | 3 | 3 |
| 18 | 3 | 3 | 3 | 3 | 3 |
| 19 | 3 | 3 | 3 | 3 | 3 |
| 20 | 3 | 3 | 3 | 3 | 3 |
| 21 | 3 | 3 | 3 | 3 | 3 |
| 22 | 3 | 3 | 3 | 3 | 3 |
| 23 | 3 | 3 | 3 | 3 | 3 |
| 24 | 3 | 3 | 3 | 3 | 3 |
| 25 | 3 | 2 | 3 | 2 | 3 |
| 26 | 2 | 2 | 2 | 2 | 2 |
| 27 | 2 | 2 | 2 | 2 | 2 |
| 28 | 2 | 2 | 2 | 2 | 2 |
| 29 | 2 | 2 | 2 | 2 | 2 |
| 30 | 2 | 2 | 2 | 2 | 2 |
| 31 | 2 | 2 | 2 | 2 | 2 |
| 32 | 2 | 2 | 2 | 2 | 2 |
| 33 | 2 | 2 | 2 | 2 | 2 |
| 34 | 2 | 2 | 2 | 2 | 2 |
| 35 | 2 | 2 | 2 | 2 | 2 |
| 36 | | 1 | 1 | 2 | 2 |

# 2015 Federal Tax Guide

Table 21.    35-year accelerated, assuming mid-month convention, applicable to real property (other than low-income housing) placed in service after June 22, 1984, and before May 9, 1985 (i.e., 18-year real property within the mid-month effective date).

| If the recovery year is: | And the month in the 1st recovery year in which the property is placed in service is: | | | | | | |
|---|---|---|---|---|---|---|---|
| | 1 | 2 | 3 | 4–5 | 6–8 | 9–11 | 12 |
| | The applicable percentage is: | | | | | | |
| 1 | 4 | 4 | 3 | 3 | 2 | 1 | 0.2 |
| 2 | 4 | 4 | 4 | 4 | 4 | 4 | 4.0 |
| 3 | 4 | 4 | 4 | 4 | 4 | 4 | 4.0 |
| 4 | 4 | 4 | 4 | 4 | 4 | 4 | 4.0 |
| 5 | 4 | 4 | 4 | 4 | 4 | 4 | 4.0 |
| 6 | 3 | 3 | 3 | 3 | 4 | 4 | 4.0 |
| 7 | 3 | 3 | 3 | 3 | 3 | 3 | 3.8 |
| 8 | 3 | 3 | 3 | 3 | 3 | 3 | 3.0 |
| 9 | 3 | 3 | 3 | 3 | 3 | 3 | 3.0 |
| 10 | 3 | 3 | 3 | 3 | 3 | 3 | 3.0 |
| 11 | 3 | 3 | 3 | 3 | 3 | 3 | 3.0 |
| 12 | 3 | 3 | 3 | 3 | 3 | 3 | 3.0 |
| 13 | 3 | 3 | 3 | 3 | 3 | 3 | 3.0 |
| 14 | 3 | 3 | 3 | 3 | 3 | 3 | 3.0 |
| 15 | 3 | 3 | 3 | 3 | 3 | 3 | 3.0 |
| 16 | 3 | 3 | 3 | 3 | 3 | 3 | 3.0 |
| 17 | 3 | 3 | 3 | 3 | 3 | 3 | 3.0 |
| 18 | 3 | 3 | 3 | 3 | 3 | 3 | 3.0 |
| 19 | 3 | 3 | 3 | 3 | 3 | 3 | 3.0 |
| 20 | 3 | 3 | 3 | 3 | 3 | 3 | 3.0 |
| 21 | 3 | 3 | 3 | 3 | 3 | 3 | 3.0 |
| 22 | 3 | 3 | 3 | 3 | 3 | 3 | 3.0 |
| 23 | 3 | 3 | 3 | 3 | 3 | 3 | 3.0 |
| 24 | 3 | 3 | 3 | 3 | 3 | 3 | 3.0 |
| 25 | 3 | 2 | 3 | 2 | 2 | 3 | 3.0 |
| 26 | 2 | 2 | 2 | 2 | 2 | 2 | 2.0 |
| 27 | 2 | 2 | 2 | 2 | 2 | 2 | 2.0 |
| 28 | 2 | 2 | 2 | 2 | 2 | 2 | 2.0 |
| 29 | 2 | 2 | 2 | 2 | 2 | 2 | 2.0 |
| 30 | 2 | 2 | 2 | 2 | 2 | 2 | 2.0 |
| 31 | 2 | 2 | 2 | 2 | 2 | 2 | 2.0 |
| 32 | 2 | 2 | 2 | 2 | 2 | 2 | 2.0 |
| 33 | 2 | 2 | 2 | 2 | 2 | 2 | 2.0 |
| 34 | 2 | 2 | 2 | 2 | 2 | 2 | 2.0 |
| 35 | 2 | 2 | 2 | 2 | 2 | 2 | 2.0 |
| 36 | | 1 | 1 | 2 | 2 | 2 | 2.0 |

# ACRS Depreciation Tables

**Table 22.** 35-year accelerated, assuming mid-month convention, applicable to real property (other than low-income housing) placed in service after May 8, 1985 (i.e., 19-year real property).

| If the Recovery Year is: | And the Month in the First Recovery Year the Property is Placed in Service is: | | | | | | | | | | | |
|---|---|---|---|---|---|---|---|---|---|---|---|---|
| | 1 | 2 | 3 | 4 | 5 | 6 | 7 | 8 | 9 | 10 | 11 | 12 |
| | The applicable percentage is: | | | | | | | | | | | |
| 1 | 4.1 | 3.7 | 3.4 | 3.0 | 2.7 | 2.3 | 2.0 | 1.6 | 1.3 | 0.9 | 0.5 | 0.2 |
| 2 | 4.1 | 4.1 | 4.1 | 4.2 | 4.2 | 4.2 | 4.2 | 4.2 | 4.2 | 4.3 | 4.3 | 4.3 |
| 3 | 3.9 | 4.0 | 4.0 | 4.0 | 4.0 | 4.0 | 4.0 | 4.0 | 4.1 | 4.1 | 4.1 | 4.1 |
| 4 | 3.8 | 3.8 | 3.8 | 3.8 | 3.8 | 3.8 | 3.9 | 3.9 | 3.9 | 3.9 | 3.9 | 3.9 |
| 5 | 3.6 | 3.6 | 3.6 | 3.6 | 3.7 | 3.7 | 3.7 | 3.7 | 3.7 | 3.8 | 3.7 | 3.7 |
| 6 | 3.5 | 3.5 | 3.5 | 3.5 | 3.5 | 3.5 | 3.5 | 3.5 | 3.5 | 3.6 | 3.6 | 3.6 |
| 7 | 3.3 | 3.3 | 3.3 | 3.3 | 3.3 | 3.4 | 3.4 | 3.4 | 3.4 | 3.4 | 3.4 | 3.4 |
| 8 | 3.2 | 3.2 | 3.2 | 3.2 | 3.2 | 3.2 | 3.2 | 3.2 | 3.3 | 3.3 | 3.3 | 3.3 |
| 9 | 3.0 | 3.0 | 3.0 | 3.1 | 3.1 | 3.1 | 3.1 | 3.1 | 3.1 | 3.1 | 3.1 | 3.1 |
| 10 | 2.9 | 2.9 | 2.9 | 2.9 | 2.9 | 2.9 | 3.0 | 3.0 | 3.0 | 3.0 | 3.0 | 3.0 |
| 11 | 2.8 | 2.8 | 2.8 | 2.8 | 2.8 | 2.8 | 2.8 | 2.8 | 2.9 | 2.9 | 2.9 | 2.9 |
| 12 | 2.6 | 2.7 | 2.7 | 2.7 | 2.7 | 2.7 | 2.7 | 2.7 | 2.7 | 2.7 | 2.8 | 2.8 |
| 13 | 2.6 | 2.6 | 2.6 | 2.6 | 2.6 | 2.6 | 2.6 | 2.6 | 2.6 | 2.6 | 2.6 | 2.6 |
| 14 | 2.6 | 2.6 | 2.6 | 2.6 | 2.6 | 2.6 | 2.6 | 2.6 | 2.6 | 2.6 | 2.6 | 2.6 |
| 15 | 2.6 | 2.6 | 2.6 | 2.6 | 2.6 | 2.6 | 2.6 | 2.6 | 2.6 | 2.6 | 2.6 | 2.6 |
| 16 | 2.6 | 2.6 | 2.6 | 2.6 | 2.6 | 2.6 | 2.6 | 2.6 | 2.6 | 2.6 | 2.6 | 2.6 |
| 17 | 2.6 | 2.6 | 2.6 | 2.6 | 2.6 | 2.6 | 2.6 | 2.6 | 2.6 | 2.6 | 2.6 | 2.6 |
| 18 | 2.6 | 2.6 | 2.6 | 2.6 | 2.6 | 2.6 | 2.6 | 2.6 | 2.6 | 2.6 | 2.6 | 2.6 |
| 19 | 2.6 | 2.6 | 2.6 | 2.6 | 2.6 | 2.6 | 2.6 | 2.6 | 2.6 | 2.6 | 2.6 | 2.6 |
| 20 | 2.6 | 2.6 | 2.6 | 2.6 | 2.6 | 2.6 | 2.6 | 2.6 | 2.6 | 2.6 | 2.6 | 2.6 |
| 21 | 2.6 | 2.6 | 2.6 | 2.6 | 2.6 | 2.6 | 2.6 | 2.6 | 2.6 | 2.6 | 2.6 | 2.6 |
| 22 | 2.6 | 2.6 | 2.6 | 2.6 | 2.6 | 2.6 | 2.6 | 2.6 | 2.6 | 2.6 | 2.6 | 2.6 |
| 23 | 2.6 | 2.6 | 2.6 | 2.6 | 2.6 | 2.6 | 2.6 | 2.6 | 2.6 | 2.6 | 2.6 | 2.6 |
| 24 | 2.6 | 2.6 | 2.6 | 2.6 | 2.6 | 2.6 | 2.6 | 2.6 | 2.6 | 2.6 | 2.6 | 2.6 |
| 25 | 2.6 | 2.6 | 2.6 | 2.6 | 2.6 | 2.6 | 2.6 | 2.6 | 2.6 | 2.6 | 2.6 | 2.6 |
| 26 | 2.6 | 2.6 | 2.6 | 2.6 | 2.6 | 2.6 | 2.6 | 2.6 | 2.6 | 2.6 | 2.6 | 2.6 |
| 27 | 2.6 | 2.6 | 2.6 | 2.6 | 2.6 | 2.6 | 2.6 | 2.6 | 2.6 | 2.6 | 2.6 | 2.6 |
| 28 | 2.6 | 2.6 | 2.6 | 2.6 | 2.6 | 2.6 | 2.6 | 2.6 | 2.6 | 2.6 | 2.6 | 2.6 |
| 29 | 2.6 | 2.6 | 2.6 | 2.6 | 2.6 | 2.6 | 2.6 | 2.6 | 2.6 | 2.6 | 2.6 | 2.6 |
| 30 | 2.5 | 2.5 | 2.5 | 2.5 | 2.5 | 2.5 | 2.5 | 2.5 | 2.5 | 2.5 | 2.5 | 2.5 |
| 31 | 2.5 | 2.5 | 2.5 | 2.5 | 2.5 | 2.5 | 2.5 | 2.5 | 2.5 | 2.5 | 2.5 | 2.5 |
| 32 | 2.5 | 2.5 | 2.5 | 2.5 | 2.5 | 2.5 | 2.5 | 2.5 | 2.5 | 2.5 | 2.5 | 2.5 |
| 33 | 2.5 | 2.5 | 2.5 | 2.5 | 2.5 | 2.5 | 2.5 | 2.5 | 2.5 | 2.5 | 2.5 | 2.5 |
| 34 | 2.5 | 2.5 | 2.5 | 2.5 | 2.5 | 2.5 | 2.5 | 2.5 | 2.5 | 2.5 | 2.5 | 2.5 |
| 35 | 2.5 | 2.5 | 2.5 | 2.5 | 2.5 | 2.5 | 2.5 | 2.5 | 2.5 | 2.5 | 2.5 | 2.5 |
| 36 | 0.0 | 0.2 | 0.5 | 0.7 | 0.9 | 1.2 | 1.3 | 1.7 | 1.7 | 1.8 | 2.2 | 2.5 |

**Table 23.      35-year accelerated, assuming full-month convention, applicable to low-income housing placed in service after May 8, 1985.**

| If the Recovery Year is: | And the Month in the First Recovery Year the Property is Placed in Service is: | | | | | | | | | | | |
|---|---|---|---|---|---|---|---|---|---|---|---|---|
| | 1 | 2 | 3 | 4 | 5 | 6 | 7 | 8 | 9 | 10 | 11 | 12 |
| | The applicable percentage is: | | | | | | | | | | | |
| 1 | 4.2 | 3.9 | 3.6 | 3.2 | 2.8 | 2.5 | 2.1 | 1.8 | 1.4 | 1.1 | 0.7 | 0.4 |
| 2 | 4.1 | 4.1 | 4.1 | 4.2 | 4.2 | 4.2 | 4.2 | 4.2 | 4.2 | 4.2 | 4.3 | 4.3 |
| 3 | 3.9 | 3.9 | 4.0 | 4.0 | 4.0 | 4.0 | 4.0 | 4.0 | 4.0 | 4.1 | 4.1 | 4.1 |
| 4 | 3.8 | 3.8 | 3.8 | 3.8 | 3.8 | 3.8 | 3.8 | 3.8 | 3.9 | 3.9 | 3.9 | 3.9 |
| 5 | 3.6 | 3.6 | 3.6 | 3.6 | 3.7 | 3.7 | 3.7 | 3.7 | 3.7 | 3.7 | 3.7 | 3.7 |
| 6 | 3.4 | 3.5 | 3.5 | 3.5 | 3.5 | 3.5 | 3.5 | 3.5 | 3.5 | 3.6 | 3.6 | 3.6 |
| 7 | 3.3 | 3.3 | 3.3 | 3.3 | 3.3 | 3.4 | 3.4 | 3.4 | 3.4 | 3.4 | 3.4 | 3.4 |
| 8 | 3.2 | 3.2 | 3.2 | 3.2 | 3.2 | 3.2 | 3.2 | 3.2 | 3.3 | 3.3 | 3.3 | 3.3 |
| 9 | 3.0 | 3.0 | 3.0 | 3.1 | 3.1 | 3.1 | 3.1 | 3.1 | 3.1 | 3.1 | 3.1 | 3.1 |
| 10 | 2.9 | 2.9 | 2.9 | 2.9 | 2.9 | 2.9 | 3.0 | 3.0 | 3.0 | 3.0 | 3.0 | 3.0 |
| 11 | 2.8 | 2.8 | 2.8 | 2.8 | 2.8 | 2.8 | 2.8 | 2.8 | 2.8 | 2.8 | 2.9 | 2.9 |
| 12 | 2.6 | 2.7 | 2.7 | 2.7 | 2.7 | 2.7 | 2.7 | 2.7 | 2.7 | 2.7 | 2.7 | 2.8 |
| 13 | 2.6 | 2.6 | 2.6 | 2.6 | 2.6 | 2.6 | 2.6 | 2.6 | 2.6 | 2.6 | 2.6 | 2.6 |
| 14 | 2.6 | 2.6 | 2.6 | 2.6 | 2.6 | 2.6 | 2.6 | 2.6 | 2.6 | 2.6 | 2.6 | 2.6 |
| 15 | 2.6 | 2.6 | 2.6 | 2.6 | 2.6 | 2.6 | 2.6 | 2.6 | 2.6 | 2.6 | 2.6 | 2.6 |
| 16 | 2.6 | 2.6 | 2.6 | 2.6 | 2.6 | 2.6 | 2.6 | 2.6 | 2.6 | 2.6 | 2.6 | 2.6 |
| 17 | 2.6 | 2.6 | 2.6 | 2.6 | 2.6 | 2.6 | 2.6 | 2.6 | 2.6 | 2.6 | 2.6 | 2.6 |
| 18 | 2.6 | 2.6 | 2.6 | 2.6 | 2.6 | 2.6 | 2.6 | 2.6 | 2.6 | 2.6 | 2.6 | 2.6 |
| 19 | 2.6 | 2.6 | 2.6 | 2.6 | 2.6 | 2.6 | 2.6 | 2.6 | 2.6 | 2.6 | 2.6 | 2.6 |
| 20 | 2.6 | 2.6 | 2.6 | 2.6 | 2.6 | 2.6 | 2.6 | 2.6 | 2.6 | 2.6 | 2.6 | 2.6 |
| 21 | 2.6 | 2.6 | 2.6 | 2.6 | 2.6 | 2.6 | 2.6 | 2.6 | 2.6 | 2.6 | 2.6 | 2.6 |
| 22 | 2.6 | 2.6 | 2.6 | 2.6 | 2.6 | 2.6 | 2.6 | 2.6 | 2.6 | 2.6 | 2.6 | 2.6 |
| 23 | 2.6 | 2.6 | 2.6 | 2.6 | 2.6 | 2.6 | 2.6 | 2.6 | 2.6 | 2.6 | 2.6 | 2.6 |
| 24 | 2.6 | 2.6 | 2.6 | 2.6 | 2.6 | 2.6 | 2.6 | 2.6 | 2.6 | 2.6 | 2.6 | 2.6 |
| 25 | 2.6 | 2.6 | 2.6 | 2.6 | 2.6 | 2.6 | 2.6 | 2.6 | 2.6 | 2.6 | 2.6 | 2.6 |
| 26 | 2.6 | 2.6 | 2.6 | 2.6 | 2.6 | 2.6 | 2.6 | 2.6 | 2.6 | 2.6 | 2.6 | 2.6 |
| 27 | 2.6 | 2.6 | 2.6 | 2.6 | 2.6 | 2.6 | 2.6 | 2.6 | 2.6 | 2.6 | 2.6 | 2.6 |
| 28 | 2.6 | 2.6 | 2.6 | 2.6 | 2.6 | 2.6 | 2.6 | 2.6 | 2.6 | 2.6 | 2.6 | 2.6 |
| 29 | 2.6 | 2.5 | 2.5 | 2.5 | 2.6 | 2.6 | 2.6 | 2.6 | 2.6 | 2.6 | 2.6 | 2.6 |
| 30 | 2.5 | 2.5 | 2.5 | 2.5 | 2.5 | 2.5 | 2.5 | 2.5 | 2.5 | 2.5 | 2.5 | 2.5 |
| 31 | 2.5 | 2.5 | 2.5 | 2.5 | 2.5 | 2.5 | 2.5 | 2.5 | 2.5 | 2.5 | 2.5 | 2.5 |

*Optional straignt-line percentages for recovery property used predominantly outside the United States*

# ACRS Depreciation Tables

**Table 24.** 3-year property, 10-year property, and 15-year public utility property.

| If the recovery year is: | And the period elected is: | | | | | | | | |
|---|---|---|---|---|---|---|---|---|---|
| | 2.5 | 3 | 3.5 | 4 | 5 | 6 | 6.5 | 7 | 7.5 |
| | The applicable percentage is: | | | | | | | | |
| 1 | 20 | 17 | 14 | 13 | 10 | 8 | 8 | 8 | 7 |
| 2 | 40 | 33 | 29 | 25 | 20 | 17 | 16 | 14 | 14 |
| 3 | 40 | 33 | 29 | 25 | 20 | 17 | 16 | 14 | 14 |
| 4 | | 17 | 28 | 25 | 20 | 17 | 15 | 14 | 13 |
| 5 | | | | 12 | 20 | 17 | 15 | 14 | 13 |
| 6 | | | | | 10 | 17 | 15 | 14 | 13 |
| 7 | | | | | | 7 | 15 | 14 | 13 |
| 8 | | | | | | | | 8 | 13 |

| If the recovery year is: | And the period elected is: | | | | | | | | |
|---|---|---|---|---|---|---|---|---|---|
| | 8 | 8.5 | 9 | 9.5 | 10 | 10.5 | 11 | 11.5 | 12 |
| | The applicable percentage is: | | | | | | | | |
| 1 | 6 | 6 | 6 | 5 | 5 | 5 | 5 | 4 | 4 |
| 2 | 13 | 12 | 11 | 11 | 10 | 10 | 9 | 9 | 9 |
| 3 | 13 | 12 | 11 | 11 | 10 | 10 | 9 | 9 | 9 |
| 4 | 13 | 12 | 11 | 11 | 10 | 10 | 9 | 9 | 9 |
| 5 | 13 | 12 | 11 | 11 | 10 | 10 | 9 | 9 | 9 |
| 6 | 12 | 12 | 11 | 11 | 10 | 10 | 9 | 9 | 8 |
| 7 | 12 | 12 | 11 | 10 | 10 | 9 | 9 | 9 | 8 |
| 8 | 12 | 11 | 11 | 10 | 10 | 9 | 9 | 9 | 8 |
| 9 | 6 | 11 | 11 | 10 | 10 | 9 | 9 | 9 | 8 |
| 10 | | | 6 | 10 | 10 | 9 | 9 | 8 | 8 |
| 11 | | | | | 5 | 9 | 9 | 8 | 8 |
| 12 | | | | | | | 5 | 8 | 8 |
| 13 | | | | | | | | | 4 |

| If the recovery year is: | And the period elected is: | | | | | | | | |
|---|---|---|---|---|---|---|---|---|---|
| | 12.5 | 13 | 13.5 | 14 | 15 | 16 | 16.5 | 17 | 18 |
| | The applicable percentage is: | | | | | | | | |
| 1 | 4 | 4 | 4 | 4 | 3 | 3 | 3 | 3 | 3 |
| 2 | 8 | 8 | 8 | 8 | 7 | 7 | 7 | 6 | 6 |
| 3 | 8 | 8 | 8 | 7 | 7 | 7 | 6 | 6 | 6 |
| 4 | 8 | 8 | 8 | 7 | 7 | 7 | 6 | 6 | 6 |
| 5 | 8 | 8 | 8 | 7 | 7 | 7 | 6 | 6 | 6 |
| 6 | 8 | 8 | 8 | 7 | 7 | 6 | 6 | 6 | 6 |
| 7 | 8 | 8 | 7 | 7 | 7 | 6 | 6 | 6 | 6 |

| | | | | | | | | | |
|---|---|---|---|---|---|---|---|---|---|
| 8 | 8 | 8 | 7 | 7 | 7 | 6 | 6 | 6 | 6 |
| 9 | 8 | 8 | 7 | 7 | 7 | 6 | 6 | 6 | 6 |
| 10 | 8 | 8 | 7 | 7 | 7 | 6 | 6 | 6 | 6 |
| 11 | 8 | 7 | 7 | 7 | 7 | 6 | 6 | 6 | 6 |
| 12 | 8 | 7 | 7 | 7 | 6 | 6 | 6 | 6 | 5 |
| 13 | 8 | 7 | 7 | 7 | 6 | 6 | 6 | 6 | 5 |
| 14 | | 3 | 7 | 7 | 6 | 6 | 6 | 6 | 5 |
| 15 | | | 4 | 6 | 6 | 6 | 6 | 5 |
| 16 | | | | 3 | 6 | 6 | 6 | 5 |
| 17 | | | | | 3 | 6 | 5 | 5 |
| 18 | | | | | | | 2 | 5 |
| 19 | | | | | | | | 2 |

*If the recovery year is:*

*And the period elected is:*

| | 19 | 20 | 22 | 25 | 26.5 | 28 | 30 | 35 |
|---|---|---|---|---|---|---|---|---|
| | | | The applicable percentage is: | | | | | |
| 1 | 3 | 3 | 2 | 2 | 2 | 2 | 2 | 1 |
| 2 | 6 | 5 | 5 | 4 | 4 | 4 | 4 | 3 |
| 3 | 6 | 5 | 5 | 4 | 4 | 4 | 4 | 3 |
| 4 | 6 | 5 | 5 | 4 | 4 | 4 | 4 | 3 |
| 5 | 6 | 5 | 5 | 4 | 4 | 4 | 4 | 3 |
| 6 | 6 | 5 | 5 | 4 | 4 | 4 | 4 | 3 |
| 7 | 5 | 5 | 5 | 4 | 4 | 4 | 4 | 3 |
| 8 | 5 | 5 | 5 | 4 | 4 | 4 | 4 | 3 |
| 9 | 5 | 5 | 5 | 4 | 4 | 4 | 4 | 3 |
| 10 | 5 | 5 | 5 | 4 | 4 | 4 | 4 | 3 |
| 11 | 5 | 5 | 5 | 4 | 4 | 4 | 3 | 3 |
| 12 | 5 | 5 | 5 | 4 | 4 | 4 | 3 | 3 |
| 13 | 5 | 5 | 5 | 4 | 4 | 4 | 3 | 3 |
| 14 | 5 | 5 | 4 | 4 | 4 | 4 | 3 | 3 |
| 15 | 5 | 5 | 4 | 4 | 4 | 4 | 3 | 3 |
| 16 | 5 | 5 | 4 | 4 | 4 | 4 | 3 | 3 |
| 17 | 5 | 5 | 4 | 4 | 4 | 3 | 3 | 3 |
| 18 | 5 | 5 | 4 | 4 | 4 | 3 | 3 | 3 |
| 19 | 5 | 5 | 4 | 4 | 4 | 3 | 3 | 3 |
| 20 | 2 | 5 | 4 | 4 | 4 | 3 | 3 | 3 |
| 21 | | 2 | 4 | 4 | 4 | 3 | 3 | 3 |
| 22 | | | 4 | 4 | 3 | 3 | 3 | 3 |
| 23 | | | 2 | 4 | 3 | 3 | 3 | 3 |
| 24 | | | | 4 | 3 | 3 | 3 | 3 |
| 25 | | | | 4 | 3 | 3 | 3 | 3 |
| 26 | | | | 2 | 3 | 3 | 3 | 3 |
| 27 | | | | | 3 | 3 | 3 | 3 |
| 28 | | | | | | 3 | 3 | 3 |
| 29 | | | | | | 2 | 3 | 3 |
| 30 | | | | | | | 3 | 3 |
| 31 | | | | | | | 2 | 3 |

# ACRS Depreciation Tables

| | | |
|---|---|---|
| 32 | | 2 |
| 33 | | 2 |
| 34 | | 2 |
| 35 | | 2 |
| 36 | | 1 |

| *If the recovery year is:* | | *And the period elected is:* |
|---|---|---|
| | 45 | 50 |
| | | The applicable percentage is: |
| 1 | 1.1 | 1 |
| 2 | 2.3 | 2 |
| 3 | 2.3 | 2 |
| 4 | 2.3 | 2 |
| 5 | 2.3 | 2 |
| 6 | 2.3 | 2 |
| 7 | 2.3 | 2 |
| 8 | 2.3 | 2 |
| 9 | 2.3 | 2 |
| 10 | 2.3 | 2 |
| 11 | 2.3 | 2 |
| 12 | 2.2 | 2 |
| 13 | 2.2 | 2 |
| 14 | 2.2 | 2 |
| 15 | 2.2 | 2 |
| 16 | 2.2 | 2 |
| 17 | 2.2 | 2 |
| 18 | 2.2 | 2 |
| 19 | 2.2 | 2 |
| 20 | 2.2 | 2 |
| 21 | 2.2 | 2 |
| 22 | 2.2 | 2 |
| 23 | 2.2 | 2 |
| 24 | 2.2 | 2 |
| 25 | 2.2 | 2 |
| 26 | 2.2 | 2 |
| 27 | 2.2 | 2 |
| 28 | 2.2 | 2 |
| 29 | 2.2 | 2 |
| 30 | 2.2 | 2 |
| 31 | 2.2 | 2 |
| 32 | 2.2 | 2 |
| 33 | 2.2 | 2 |
| 34 | 2.2 | 2 |
| 35 | 2.2 | 2 |
| 36 | 2.2 | 2 |
| 37 | 2.2 | 2 |
| 38 | 2.2 | 2 |

| | | |
|---|---|---|
| 39 | 2.2 | 2 |
| 40 | 2.2 | 2 |
| 41 | 2.2 | 2 |
| 42 | 2.2 | 2 |
| 43 | 2.2 | 2 |
| 44 | 2.2 | 2 |
| 45 | 2.2 | 2 |
| 46 | 1.1 | 2 |
| 47 | | 2 |
| 48 | | 2 |
| 49 | | 2 |
| 50 | | 2 |
| 51 | | 1 |

# ACRS Depreciation Tables

Table 25.     35-year straight-line, assuming full-month convention, applicable to (1) low-income housing placed in service after 1980 and before May 9, 1985; (2) real property (other than low-income housing) placed in service after 1980 and before June 23, 1984 (i.e., 15-year real property and 18-year real property within the full-month convention effective date). Note: This table is identical to Table 11, and accordingly is not reproduced here.

Table 26.     35-year straight-line, assuming full-month convention, applicable to low-income housing placed in service after May 8, 1985. Note: This table is identical to Table 12, and accordingly is not reproduced here.

Table 27. 4     5-year straight-line, assuming full-month convention, applicable to (1) low-income housing placed in service after 1980; and (2) real property (other than low-income housing) placed in service after 1980 and before June 23, 1984 (i.e., 15-year real property and 18-year real property within the full-month convention effective date). Note: This table is identical to Table 13, and accordingly is not reproduced here.

Table 28.     35-year straight-line, assuming mid-month convention, applicable to real property (other than low-income housing) placed in service after June 22, 1984, and before May 9, 1985 (i.e., 18-year real property within the mid-month convention effective date). Note: This table is identical to Table 16, and accordingly is not reproduced here.

Table 30.     45-year straight-line, assuming mid-month convention, applicable to real property (other than low-income housing) placed in service after June 22, 1984 (i.e., 18-year real property within the mid-month convention effective date and 19-year property). Note: This table is identical to Table 18, and accordingly is not reproduced here.

Table 29.     35-year straight-line, assuming mid-month convention, applicable to real property (other than low-income housing) placed in service after May 8, 1985, (i.e., 19-year real property). Note: This table is identical to Table 17, and accordingly is not reproduced here.

# 13. Types of Payments and Information Forms to File

Below is an alphabetical list of some payments and the forms to file to report them. The list was developed to help you determine which form to file. However, it is not a complete list of all payments, and the absence of a payment from the list does not indicate that the payment is not reportable.

| Type of Payment | Report on Form |
| --- | --- |
| Abandonment | 1099-A |
| Accelerated Death Benefits | 1099-LTC |
| Advance earned income credit | W-2 |
| Agriculture payments | 1099-G |
| Allocated tips | W-2 |
| Annuities | 1099-R |
| Attorneys, fees and gross proceeds | 1099-MISC |
| Auto Reimbursements: | |
| Employee | W-2 |
| Nonemployee | 1099-MISC |
| Awards: | |
| Employee | W-2 |
| Nonemployee | 1099-MISC |
| Bank deposit interest paid to nonresident alien individual residing in Canada | 1042-S |
| Barter exchange income | 1099-B |
| Bonuses: | |
| Employee | W-2 |
| Nonemployee | 1099-MISC |
| Broker transactions | 1099-B |
| Cancellation of debt | 1099-C |
| Capital gain distributions | 1099-DIV |
| Car expenses: | |
| Employee | W-2 |
| Nonemployee | 1099-MISC |
| Cash of over $10,000 received in trade or business | 8300 |
| Charitable gift annuities | 1099-R |
| Christmas bonuses: | |
| Employee | W-2 |
| Nonemployee | 1099-MISC |
| Commissions: | |
| Employee | W-2 |
| Nonemployee | 1099-MISC |
| Commodities transactions | 1099-B |
| Compensation: | |
| Employee | W-2 |

| Type of Payment | Report on Form |
|---|---|
| Nonemployee/Independent contractor | 1099-MISC |
| Crop insurance proceeds | 1099-MISC |
| Damages | 1099-MISC |
| Death benefits: | 1099-R |
| Accelerated | 1099-LTC |
| Debt cancellation | 1099-C |
| Dependent care payments | W-2 |
| Direct rollovers | 1099-R, 5498 |
| Direct sales of consumer products for resale | 1099-MISC |
| Directors' fees | 1099-MISC |
| Discharge of indebtedness | 1099-C |
| Dividends | 1099-DIV |
| Education business expense reimbursement | W-2 |
| Education IRA contributions | 5498 |
| Education IRA distributions | 1099-R |
| Education loan interest | 1098-E |
| Employee business expense reimbursement | W-2 |
| Employee compensation | W-2 |
| Excess deferrals, excess contributions, distributions of | 1099-R |
| Farm rental income received as crops or livestock produced if you, the landlord, did not materially participate in farm's operation or management | 4835 |
| Fees: | |
| Employee | W-2 |
| Nonemployee | 1099-MISC |
| Fish purchases for cash | 1099-MISC |
| Fishing boat crew members proceeds | 1099-MISC |
| Fringe benefits to employees | W-2 |
| Foreclosures | 1099-A |
| Foreign persons income | 1042-S |
| 401(k) contributions | W-2 |
| 401(k) dividend | 1099-DIV |
| Gambling winnings | W-2G |
| Golden parachute: | |
| Employee | W-2 |
| Nonemployee | 1099-MISC |
| Grants, taxable | 1099-G |
| Health care services | 1099-MISC |
| Income tax refunds, state and local | 1099-G |
| Indian gaming profits paid to tribal members | 1099-MISC |

# Types of Payments and Information Forms to File

| Type of Payment | Report on Form |
|---|---|
| Interest Income | 1099-INT |
| Interest, mortgage | 1098 |
| IRA contributions | 5498 |
| IRA distributions | 1099-R |
| Life insurance contract distributions | 1099-R, 1099-LTC |
| Liquidation, distributions in | 1099-DIV |
| Loans, distribution from pension plan | 1099-R |
| Long-term Care Benefits | 1099-LTC |
| Medical Savings Accounts: | |
|   Contributions | 5498-MSA |
|   Distributions | 1099-MSA |
| Medical services | 1099-MISC |
| Medicare+Choice MSAs: | |
|   Contributions | 5498-MSA |
|   Distributions | 1099-MSA |
| Mileage: | |
|   Employee | W-2 |
|   Nonemployee | 1099-MISC |
| Military retirement | 1099-R |
| Mortgage interest | 1098 |
| Moving expense | W-2 |
| Nonemployee compensation | 1099-MISC |
| Nonqualified plan distribution | W-2 |
| Beneficiaries | 1099-R |
| Original issue discount (OID) | 1099-OID |
| Patronage dividends | 1099-PATR |
| Pension | 1099-R |
| Points | 1098 |
| Prizes: | |
|   Employee | W-2 |
|   Nonemployee | 1099-MISC |
| Profit-sharing plan | 1099-R |
| PS 58 costs | 1099-R |
| Punitive damages | 1099-MISC |
| Qualified plan distributions | 1099-R |
| Qualified state tuition program payments | 1099-G |
| Real estate transactions | 1099-S |
| Recharacterized IRA contributions | 1099-R, 5498 |
| Refunds, state and local tax | 1099-G |
| Rents | 1099-MISC |

| Type of Payment | Report on Form |
|---|---|
| Retirement | 1099-R |
| Roth conversion IRA: | |
|   Contributions | 5498 |
|   Distributions | 1099-R |
| Roth IRA contributions | 5498 |
| Roth IRA distributions | 1099-R |
| Royalties | 1099-MISC |
| Timber, pay-as-cut contract | 1099-S |
| Sales: | |
|   Real estate | 1099-S |
| Securities | 1099-B |
| Section 1035 exchange | 1099-R |
| SEP contributions | W-2, 5498 |
| SEP distributions | 1099-R |
| Severance pay | W-2 |
| Sick pay | W-2 |
| SIMPLE Contributions | W-2, 5498 |
| SIMPLE Distributions | 1099-R |
| Student loan interest | 1098-E |
| Substitute payments in lieu of dividends or tax-exempt interest | 1099-MISC |
| Supplemental unemployment | W-2 |
| Tax refunds, state and local | 1099-G |
| Tips | W-2 |
| Tuition (qualified) reimbursements or refunds | 1098-T |
| Unemployment benefits | 1099-G |
| Vacation allowance: | |
|   Employee | W-2 |
|   Nonemployee | 1099-MISC |
| Wages | W-2 |

## 14. Excise Tax List

| EXCISE TAX | RATE | DUE DATE AND FORM | X-REF TO FEDERAL EXCISE TAX NAVIGATOR |
|---|---|---|---|
| Alcohol Taxes: | | | |
| Distilled Spirits (per gallon) | $13.50 | 14th day after close of semimonthly period; TTB Form 5000.24 | Chapter 1.1 |
| Beer (per 31 gallon barrel) | $18.00 | 14th day after close of semimonthly period; TTB Form 5000.24 | Chapter 1.2 |
| First 60,000 barrels of produced by domestic brewer making 2,000,000 barrels or less | $7.00 | 14th day after close of semimonthly period; TTB Form 5000.24 | Chapter 1.2 |
| Wine up to 14% alcohol content (per gallon) | $1.07 | 14th day after close of semimonthly period; TTB Form 5000.24 | Chapter 1.3 |
| Wine more than 14% but less than 21% alcohol (per gallon) | $1.57 | 14th day after close of semimonthly period; TTB Form 5000.24 | Chapter 1.3 |
| Wine more than 21% but not more than 24% alcohol (per gallon) | $3.15 | 14th day after close of semimonthly period; TTB Form 5000.24 | Chapter 1.3 |
| Champagne and other sparkling wines (per gallon) | $3.40 | 14th day after close of semimonthly period; TTB Form 5000.24 | Chapter 1.3 |
| Artificially carbonated wines (per gallon) | $3.30 | 14th day after close of semimonthly period; TTB Form 5000.24 | Chapter 1.3 |
| Hard Cider (per gallon) | $0.226 | 14th day after close of semimonthly period; TTB Form 5000.24 | Chapter 1.3 |

| EXCISE TAX | RATE | DUE DATE AND FORM | X-REF TO FEDERAL EXCISE TAX NAVIGATOR |
|---|---|---|---|
| Tobacco Taxes: | | | |
| Small cigarettes (three pounds or less per 1,000) | $50.33 | 14<sup>th</sup> day after close of semimonthly period; TTB Form 5000.24 | Chapter 2.1 |
| Large cigarettes (more than three pounds per 1,000) | $105.69 | 14<sup>th</sup> day after close of semimonthly period; TTB Form 5000.24 | Chapter 2.1 |
| Cigarette papers (per 50 papers) | $0.0315 | 14<sup>th</sup> day after close of semimonthly period; TTB Form 5000.24 | Chapter 2.1 |
| Cigarette tubes (per 50 tubes) | $0.0630 | 14<sup>th</sup> day after close of semimonthly period; TTB Form 5000.24 | Chapter 2.1 |
| Small cigars (weighing three pounds or less per 1,000) | $50.33 | 14<sup>th</sup> day after close of semimonthly period; TTB Form 5000.24 | Chapter 2.2 |
| Large cigars (weighing more than three pounds per 1,000) | 52.75% of sales price, not exceeding $0.4026 per cigar | 14<sup>th</sup> day after close of semimonthly period; TTB Form 5000.24 | Chapter 2.2 |
| Pipe tobacco (per pound) | $2.8311 | 14<sup>th</sup> day after close of semimonthly period; TTB Form 5000.24 | Chapter 2.2 |
| Chewing tobacco (per pound) | $0.5033 | 14<sup>th</sup> day after close of semimonthly period; TTB Form 5000.24 | Chapter 2.2 |
| Snuff (per pound) | $1.51 | 14<sup>th</sup> day after close of semimonthly period; TTB Form 5000.24 | Chapter 2.2 |
| Roll-your-own-tobacco (per pound) | $24.78 | 14<sup>th</sup> day after close of semimonthly period; TTB Form 5000.24 | Chapter 2.2 |

# Excise Tax List

| EXCISE TAX | RATE | DUE DATE AND FORM | X-REF TO FEDERAL EXCISE TAX NAVIGATOR |
|---|---|---|---|
| Tobacco occupational taxes | $1,000 | July 1 each year; TTB Form 5630.5t | Chapter 2.2 |
| | $500 (small proprietors) | July 1 each year; TTB Form 5630.5t | Chapter 2.2 |
| Fuel Taxes:[1] | | | |
| *Aviation Fuel* (Including LUST Trust Fund Rate) | | | |
| Gasoline (per gallon) | $0.194 | Reported Quarterly; IRS Form 720 | Chapter 8.1 |
| Kerosene removed directly into aircraft fuel tank (per gallon) | | | |
|    Commercial Aviation | $0.044 | Reported Quarterly; IRS Form 720 | Chapter 8.1 |
|    Noncommercial Aviation | $0.219 | Reported Quarterly; IRS Form 720 | Chapter 8.1 |
| Kerosene removed directly from a terminal (per gallon) | | | |
|    Generally | $0.219 | Reported Quarterly; IRS Form 720 | Chapter 8.1 |
|    Terminal located in secure area of airport in commercial aviation | $0.044 | Reported Quarterly; IRS Form 720 | Chapter 8.1 |
| Surtax on fractional aircraft ownership program (per gallon) | $0.141 | Reported Quarterly; IRS Form 720 | Chapter 8.1 |

| EXCISE TAX | RATE | DUE DATE AND FORM | X-REF TO FEDERAL EXCISE TAX NAVIGATOR |
|---|---|---|---|
| *Motor Fuel* (Including LUST Trust Fund Rate) | | | |
| Gasoline (per gallon) | $0.184 | Reported Quarterly; IRS Form 720 | Chapter 8.1 |
| Diesel Fuel or Kerosene (per gallon) | $0.244 | Reported Quarterly; IRS Form 720 | Chapter 8.1 |
| Diesel-water Fuel Emulsion (per gallon) | | | |
| Generally | $0.244 | Reported Quarterly; IRS Form 720 | Chapter 8.1 |
| Reduced Rate (at least 14% water and registered emulsion additive) | $0.198 | Reported Quarterly; IRS Form 720 | Chapter 8.1 |
| Dyed diesel fuel (per gallon) | $.001 | Reported Quarterly; IRS Form 720 | Chapter 8.1 |
| Dyed diesel fuel or Kerosene used in certain intercity and local buses (per gallon) | $0.074 | Reported Quarterly; IRS Form 720 | Chapter 8.1 |
| *Special Fuels* | | | |
| "P Series" fuels (per gallon) | $0.184 | Reported Quarterly; IRS Form 720 | Chapter 8.2 |
| Liquefied petroleum gas (LPG) (per gallon) | $0.184 | Reported Quarterly; IRS Form 720 | Chapter 8.2 |
| Liquefied hydrogen (per gallon) | $0.184 | Reported Quarterly; IRS Form 720 | Chapter 8.2 |

# Excise Tax List

| EXCISE TAX | RATE | DUE DATE AND FORM | X-REF TO FEDERAL EXCISE TAX NAVIGATOR |
| --- | --- | --- | --- |
| Fischer-Tropsch process liquid fuel (except ethanol and methanol) derived from coal, including peat (per gallon) | $0.244 | Reported Quarterly; IRS Form 720 | Chapter 8.2 |
| Liquid hydrocarbons derived from biomass (per gallon) | $0.244 | Reported Quarterly; IRS Form 720 | Chapter 8.2 |
| Qualified ethanol produced from coal (per gallon) | $0.184 | Reported Quarterly; IRS Form 720 | Chapter 8.2 |
| Qualified methanol produced from coal (per gallon) | $0.184 | Reported Quarterly; IRS Form 720 | Chapter 8.2 |
| Partially exempt ethanol produced from natural gas (per gallon) | $0.114 | Reported Quarterly; IRS Form 720 | Chapter 8.2 |
| Partially exempt methanol produced from natural gas (per gallon) | $0.0925 | Reported Quarterly; IRS Form 720 | Chapter 8.2 |
| B-100 (100% biodiesel) (per gallon) | $0.244 | Reported Quarterly; IRS Form 720 | Chapter 8.2 |
| Compressed natural gas (CNG) (per energy equivalent of a gasoline gallon) | $0.183 | Reported Quarterly; IRS Form 720 | Chapter 8.2 |
| *Other Fuel* | | | |
| Crude oil (per barrel) | $0.08 | Reported Quarterly; IRS Form 720 | Chapter 12.3 |

| EXCISE TAX | RATE | DUE DATE AND FORM | X-REF TO FEDERAL EXCISE TAX NAVIGATOR |
|---|---|---|---|
| **Wagering Taxes:** | | | |
| State authorized wagering | 0.25% of wager amount | Monthly; IRS Form 11-C | Chapter 3.3 |
| Unauthorized wagers | 2% of wager amount | Monthly; IRS Form 11-C | Chapter 3.3 |
| *Wagering occupational tax* | | | |
| Authorized wagering | $50 per year | July 1 each year; IRS Form 11-C | Chapter 3.3 |
| Unauthorized wagering | $500 per year | July 1 each year; IRS Form 11-C | Chapter 3.3 |
| **Heavy Motor Vehicle Highway Use Tax:** | | | |
| Vehicles between 55,000 and 75,000 lbs. (per year) | $100 per year + $22 for each 1,000 pounds over 55,000 | Yearly; IRS Form 2290 | Chapter 9.1 |
| Vehicles over 75,000 pounds | $550 | Yearly; IRS Form 2290 | Chapter 9.1 |
| **Heavy Trucks and Trailer Retail Tax:** | | | |
| Truck chassis or body (suitable for use with a vehicle with gross weight in excess of 33,000 lbs.) | 12% of retail price | Reported Quarterly; IRS Form 720 | Chapter 9.2 |

# Excise Tax List

| EXCISE TAX | RATE | DUE DATE AND FORM | X-REF TO FEDERAL EXCISE TAX NAVIGATOR |
|---|---|---|---|
| Trailer and semi-trailer chassis or body (suitable for use with a trailer or semi-trailer exceeding 26,000 lbs) | 12% of retail price | Reported Quarterly; IRS Form 720 | Chapter 9.2 |
| Parts and accessories installed on a taxable vehicle installed within six months of the vehicle first being placed in service | 12% of retail price | Reported Quarterly; IRS Form 720 | Chapter 9.2 |
| Firearms Taxes: | | | |
| Transfer Tax (per firearm) | $5 (concealable weapon) | | |
| | $200 (all other firearms) | Per Transaction; ATF Form 5320.4 | Chapter 3.5 |
| *Firearms Sales Tax* | | | |
| Pistols and revolvers | 10% of sales price | Reported Quarterly; TTB Form 5300.26 | Chapter 3.5 |
| Firearms other than pistols and revolvers | 11% of sales price | Reported Quarterly; TTB Form 5300.26 | Chapter 3.5 |
| Ammunition (shells and cartridges) | 11% of sales price | Reported Quarterly; TTB Form 5300.26 | Chapter 3.5 |
| Making Tax | $200 per firearm made | Per Transaction; ATF Form 5320.4 | Chapter 3.5 |

| EXCISE TAX | RATE | DUE DATE AND FORM | X-REF TO FEDERAL EXCISE TAX NAVIGATOR |
|---|---|---|---|
| *Occupational Tax* | | | |
| Importers and manufacturers | $1,000 | Yearly; ATF Form 5630.7 | Chapter 3.5 |
| Dealers and small manufacturers and importers | $500 | Yearly; ATF Form 5630.7 | Chapter 3.5 |
| Highway Tire Tax: | | | |
| Tires with load capacity over 3,500 lbs | $0.0945 for each 10 lbs of load capacity over 3,500 lbs | Reported Quarterly; IRS Form 720 | Chapter 9.5 |
| Super single tires and Biasply tires | $0.04725 for each 10 lbs of load capacity over 3,500 lbs | Reported Quarterly; IRS Form 720 | Chapter 9.5 |
| Gas Guzzler Tax: | | | |
| Fuel economy standard ≥ 22.5mpg | $0 | Reported Quarterly; IRS Form 720 | Chapter 9.6 |
| Fuel economy standard ≥ 21.5mpg but < 22.5mpg | $1,000 | Reported Quarterly; IRS Form 720 | Chapter 9.6 |
| Fuel economy standard ≥ 20.5mpg but < 21.5mpg | $1,300 | Reported Quarterly; IRS Form 720 | Chapter 9.6 |
| Fuel economy standard ≥ 19.5mpg but < 20.5mpg | $1,700 | Reported Quarterly; IRS Form 720 | Chapter 9.6 |

## Excise Tax List

| EXCISE TAX | RATE | DUE DATE AND FORM | X-REF TO FEDERAL EXCISE TAX NAVIGATOR |
|---|---|---|---|
| Fuel economy standard ≥ 18.5mpg but < 19.5mpg | $2,100 | Reported Quarterly; IRS Form 720 | Chapter 9.6 |
| Fuel economy standard ≥ 17.5mpg but < 18.5mpg | $2,600 | Reported Quarterly; IRS Form 720 | Chapter 9.6 |
| Fuel economy standard ≥ 16.5mpg but < 17.5mpg | $3,000 | Reported Quarterly; IRS Form 720 | Chapter 9.6 |
| Fuel economy standard ≥ 15.5mpg but < 16.5mpg | $3,700 | Reported Quarterly; IRS Form 720 | Chapter 9.6 |
| Fuel economy standard ≥ 14.5mpg but < 15.5mpg | $4,500 | Reported Quarterly; IRS Form 720 | Chapter 9.6 |
| Fuel economy standard ≥ 13.5mpg but < 14.5mpg | $5,400 | Reported Quarterly; IRS Form 720 | Chapter 9.6 |
| Fuel economy standard ≥ 12.5mpg but < 13.5mpg | $6,400 | Reported Quarterly; IRS Form 720 | Chapter 9.6 |
| Fuel economy standard < 12.5mpg | $7,700 | Reported Quarterly; IRS Form 720 | Chapter 9.6 |
| Communications Tax on local telephone service, toll telephone service, and teletypewriter exchange service | 3% of amount paid | Reported Quarterly; IRS Form 720 | Chapter 11.2 |

| EXCISE TAX | RATE | DUE DATE AND FORM | X-REF TO FEDERAL EXCISE TAX NAVIGATOR |
|---|---|---|---|
| Transportation Taxes: | | | |
| *Air* (2015) | | | |
| Domestic passenger tickets for each flight segment except to or from rural airports | 7.5% of ticket amount | | |
| | plus $4.00 | Reported Quarterly; IRS Form 720 | Chapter 9.4 |
| Alaska and Hawaii passenger tickets (per departure) | $8.90 | Reported Quarterly; IRS Form 720 | Chapter 9.4 |
| International passenger tickets (arrivals and departures) | $17.70 | Reported Quarterly; IRS Form 720 | Chapter 9.4 |
| Air Cargo | $6.25% of amount paid | Reported Quarterly; IRS Form 720 | Chapter 9.4 |
| *Water Transportation* | | | |
| Passengers (per person; either embarkation or disembarkation) | $3 | Reported Quarterly; IRS Form 720 | Chapter 9.3 |
| Port use (Harbor Maintenance Tax) | 0.125% of cargo value | Reported Quarterly; CBP Form 349 | Chapter 11.3 |
| Recreational Equipment Tax: | | | |
| *Sport Fishing* | | | |
| Sport fishing equipment generally | 10% of sales price | Reported Quarterly; IRS Form 720 | Chapter 3.4 |

# Excise Tax List

| EXCISE TAX | RATE | DUE DATE AND FORM | X-REF TO FEDERAL EXCISE TAX NAVIGATOR |
|---|---|---|---|
| Fishing rods and poles | 10% of sales price; capped at $10 | Reported Quarterly; IRS Form 720 | Chapter 3.4 |
| Electric outboard motors | 3% of sales price | Reported Quarterly; IRS Form 720 | Chapter 3.4 |
| Tackle boxes | 3% of sales price | Reported Quarterly; IRS Form 720 | Chapter 3.4 |
| *Archery* | | | |
| Bows and other archery equipment | 11% of sales price | Reported Quarterly; IRS Form 720 | Chapter 3.4 |
| Arrows per shaft (for 2015) | $0.49 | Reported Quarterly; IRS Form 720 | Chapter 3.4 |
| Coal Severance Tax: | | | |
| Surface mines | lesser of $1.10 per ton or 4.4% of sales price | Reported Quarterly; IRS Form 720 | Chapter 12.1 |
| Underground mines | lesser of $0.55 per ton or 4.4% of sales price | Reported Quarterly; IRS Form 720 | Chapter 12.1 |
| Indoor Tanning Tax | 10% of amount paid | Reported Quarterly; IRS Form 720 | Chapter 3.6 |

| EXCISE TAX | RATE | DUE DATE AND FORM | X-REF TO FEDERAL EXCISE TAX NAVIGATOR |
|---|---|---|---|
| Foreign Insurance Tax (per dollar of premium paid): | | | |
| Casualty insurance and indemnity bonds | $0.04 | Reported Quarterly; IRS Form 720 | Chapter 4.1 |
| Life, sickness and accident insurance, and annuity contracts | $0.01 | Reported Quarterly; IRS Form 720 | Chapter 4.1 |
| Reinsurance of tax-able contracts | $0.01 | Reported Quarterly; IRS Form 720 | Chapter 4.1 |
| Healthcare Related Taxes:[2] | | | |
| Vaccines (per dose) | $0.75 | Reported Quarterly; IRS Form 720 | Chapter 5.4 |
| Medical Devices | 2.3% of sales price | Reported Quarterly; IRS Form 720 | Chapter 5.5 |

[1] Credits, refunds and payments use Forms 720, 4136 and 8849 depending on the fuel and payee. For a detailed discussion of credits, refunds, and payments of fuel excise taxes pertaining to specific situations and payees, see the Federal Excise Tax Navigator, chapter 14.

[2] For further discussion of healthcare related excise taxes including COBRA continuation requirements, Archer MSA and HSA contributions and the individual PPACA mandate, see Chapter 5 of the Federal Excise Tax Navigator.

## 15. Annual Lease Value Table for Employer-Provided Automobiles

| REV. PROC. 2014–21 TABLE 1 DEPRECIATION LIMITATIONS FOR PASSENGER AUTOMOBILES (THAT ARE NOT TRUCKS OR VANS) PLACED IN SERVICE IN CALENDAR YEAR 2014 ||
| --- | --- |
| *Tax Year* | *Amount* |
| 1st Tax Year | $ 3,160 |
| 2nd Tax Year | $ 5,100 |
| 3rd Tax Year | $ 3,050 |
| Each Succeeding Year | $ 1,875 |

| REV. PROC. 2014–21 TABLE 2 DEPRECIATION LIMITATIONS FOR TRUCKS AND VANS PLACED IN SERVICE IN CALENDAR YEAR 2014 ||
| --- | --- |
| *Tax Year* | *Amount* |
| 1st Tax Year | $ 3,460 |
| 2nd Tax Year | $ 5,500 |
| 3rd Tax Year | $ 3,350 |
| Each Succeeding Year | $ 1,975 |

| REV. PROC. 2014-21 TABLE 3 DOLLAR AMOUNTS FOR PASSENGER AUTOMOBILES (THAT ARE NOT TRUCKS OR VANS) WITH A LEASE TERM BEGINNING IN CALENDAR YEAR 2014 |||||||
| --- | --- | --- | --- | --- | --- | --- |
| Fair Market Value of Passenger Automobile || Tax Year During Lease |||||
| Over | Not Over | $1^{st}$ | $2^{nd}$ | $3^{rd}$ | $4^{th}$ | $5^{th}$ & later |
| $18,500 | $19,000 | 3 | 5 | 8 | 10 | 11 |
| 19,000 | 19,500 | 3 | 6 | 10 | 11 | 13 |
| 19,500 | 20,000 | 3 | 8 | 11 | 13 | 14 |
| 20,000 | 20,500 | 4 | 8 | 13 | 14 | 17 |
| 20,500 | 21,000 | 4 | 9 | 14 | 17 | 18 |
| 21,000 | 21,500 | 5 | 10 | 15 | 18 | 21 |
| 21,500 | 22,000 | 5 | 11 | 17 | 20 | 22 |
| 22,000 | 23,000 | 6 | 13 | 18 | 23 | 25 |
| 23,000 | 24,000 | 7 | 14 | 22 | 26 | 29 |
| 24,000 | 25,000 | 8 | 16 | 25 | 29 | 33 |
| 25,000 | 26,000 | 8 | 19 | 27 | 32 | 38 |
| 26,000 | 27,000 | 9 | 20 | 31 | 35 | 42 |
| 27,000 | 28,000 | 10 | 22 | 33 | 40 | 45 |
| 28,000 | 29,000 | 11 | 24 | 36 | 43 | 49 |
| 29,000 | 30,000 | 12 | 26 | 39 | 46 | 53 |
| 30,000 | 31,000 | 13 | 28 | 41 | 50 | 57 |
| 31,000 | 32,000 | 14 | 30 | 44 | 53 | 61 |
| 32,000 | 33,000 | 14 | 32 | 47 | 56 | 65 |
| 33,000 | 34,000 | 15 | 34 | 50 | 59 | 69 |
| 34,000 | 35,000 | 16 | 36 | 52 | 64 | 72 |

### REV. PROC. 2014-21
### TABLE 3 DOLLAR AMOUNTS FOR PASSENGER AUTOMOBILES (THAT ARE NOT TRUCKS OR VANS)
### WITH A LEASE TERM BEGINNING IN CALENDAR YEAR 2014

| Fair Market Value of Passenger Automobile | | Tax Year During Lease | | | | |
|---|---|---|---|---|---|---|
| 35,000 | 36,000 | 17 | 38 | 55 | 67 | 76 |
| 36,000 | 37,000 | 18 | 39 | 59 | 70 | 80 |
| 37,000 | 38,000 | 19 | 41 | 61 | 74 | 84 |
| 38,000 | 39,000 | 20 | 43 | 64 | 77 | 88 |
| 39,000 | 40,000 | 21 | 45 | 67 | 80 | 92 |
| 40,000 | 41,000 | 21 | 47 | 70 | 84 | 96 |
| 41,000 | 42,000 | 22 | 49 | 73 | 87 | 100 |
| 42,000 | 43,000 | 23 | 51 | 75 | 91 | 104 |
| 43,000 | 44,000 | 24 | 53 | 78 | 94 | 108 |
| 44,000 | 45,000 | 25 | 55 | 81 | 97 | 112 |
| 45,000 | 46,000 | 26 | 56 | 84 | 101 | 116 |
| 46,000 | 47,000 | 27 | 58 | 87 | 104 | 120 |
| 47,000 | 48,000 | 28 | 60 | 90 | 107 | 124 |
| 48,000 | 49,000 | 28 | 62 | 93 | 111 | 127 |
| 49,000 | 50,000 | 29 | 64 | 96 | 114 | 131 |
| 50,000 | 51,000 | 30 | 66 | 98 | 118 | 135 |
| 51,000 | 52,000 | 31 | 68 | 101 | 121 | 139 |
| 52,000 | 53,000 | 32 | 70 | 104 | 124 | 143 |
| 53,000 | 54,000 | 33 | 72 | 106 | 128 | 147 |
| 54,000 | 55,000 | 34 | 74 | 109 | 131 | 151 |
| 55,000 | 56,000 | 34 | 76 | 112 | 135 | 155 |
| 56,000 | 57,000 | 35 | 78 | 115 | 138 | 159 |
| 57,000 | 58,000 | 36 | 80 | 118 | 141 | 163 |
| 58,000 | 59,000 | 37 | 81 | 121 | 145 | 167 |
| 59,000 | 60,000 | 38 | 83 | 124 | 148 | 171 |
| 60,000 | 62,000 | 39 | 86 | 128 | 153 | 177 |
| 62,000 | 64,000 | 41 | 90 | 134 | 159 | 185 |
| 64,000 | 66,000 | 43 | 94 | 139 | 167 | 192 |
| 66,000 | 68,000 | 44 | 98 | 145 | 173 | 201 |
| 68,000 | 70,000 | 46 | 102 | 150 | 180 | 209 |
| 70,000 | 72,000 | 48 | 105 | 156 | 188 | 216 |
| 72,000 | 74,000 | 50 | 109 | 162 | 194 | 224 |
| 74,000 | 76,000 | 51 | 113 | 168 | 200 | 232 |
| 76,000 | 78,000 | 53 | 117 | 173 | 208 | 239 |
| 78,000 | 80,000 | 55 | 120 | 179 | 215 | 247 |
| 80,000 | 85,000 | 58 | 127 | 189 | 226 | 261 |
| 85,000 | 90,000 | 62 | 137 | 203 | 243 | 281 |
| 90,000 | 95,000 | 67 | 146 | 217 | 260 | 301 |
| 95,000 | 100,000 | 71 | 156 | 231 | 277 | 320 |
| 100,000 | 110,000 | 77 | 170 | 253 | 303 | 349 |
| 110,000 | 120,000 | 86 | 189 | 281 | 337 | 389 |
| 120,000 | 130,000 | 95 | 208 | 310 | 370 | 428 |
| 130,000 | 140,000 | 103 | 228 | 337 | 405 | 467 |

# Annual Lease Value Table for Employer-Provided Automobiles

| REV. PROC. 2014-21<br>TABLE 3 DOLLAR AMOUNTS FOR PASSENGER AUTOMOBILES (THAT ARE NOT TRUCKS OR VANS)<br>WITH A LEASE TERM BEGINNING IN CALENDAR YEAR 2014 | | | | | | |
|---|---|---|---|---|---|---|
| Fair Market Value<br>of<br>Passenger Automobile | | Tax Year During Lease | | | | |
| 140,000 | 150,000 | 112 | 247 | 366 | 438 | 507 |
| 150,000 | 160,000 | 121 | 266 | 394 | 473 | 545 |
| 160,000 | 170,000 | 130 | 284 | 423 | 507 | 585 |
| 170,000 | 180,000 | 138 | 304 | 451 | 541 | 624 |
| 180,000 | 190,000 | 147 | 323 | 479 | 575 | 663 |
| 190,000 | 200,000 | 156 | 342 | 507 | 609 | 703 |
| 200,000 | 210,000 | 164 | 361 | 536 | 643 | 742 |
| 210,000 | 220,000 | 173 | 380 | 565 | 676 | 781 |
| 220,000 | 230,000 | 182 | 399 | 593 | 710 | 821 |
| 230,000 | 240,000 | 190 | 418 | 622 | 744 | 860 |
| 240,000 | and over | 199 | 437 | 650 | 778 | 899 |

| REV. PROC. 2014-21<br>TABLE 4 DOLLAR AMOUNTS FOR TRUCKS AND VANS<br>WITH A LEASE TERM BEGINNING IN CALENDAR YEAR 2014 | | | | | | |
|---|---|---|---|---|---|---|
| Fair Market Value<br>of<br>Truck or Van | | Tax Year During Lease | | | | |
| Over | Not Over | 1st | 2nd | 3rd | 4th | 5th &<br>later |
| $19,000 | $19,500 | 2 | 4 | 5 | 7 | 8 |
| 19,500 | 20,000 | 2 | 5 | 7 | 8 | 10 |
| 20,000 | 20,500 | 3 | 6 | 8 | 10 | 12 |
| 20,500 | 21,000 | 3 | 7 | 10 | 11 | 14 |
| 21,000 | 21,500 | 3 | 8 | 11 | 14 | 15 |
| 21,500 | 22,000 | 4 | 9 | 12 | 15 | 18 |
| 22,000 | 23,000 | 5 | 10 | 15 | 17 | 21 |
| 23,000 | 24,000 | 5 | 12 | 18 | 21 | 24 |
| 24,000 | 25,000 | 6 | 14 | 20 | 25 | 28 |
| 25,000 | 26,000 | 7 | 16 | 23 | 28 | 32 |
| 26,000 | 27,000 | 8 | 18 | 26 | 31 | 36 |
| 27,000 | 28,000 | 9 | 20 | 28 | 35 | 40 |
| 28,000 | 29,000 | 10 | 21 | 32 | 38 | 44 |
| 29,000 | 30,000 | 11 | 23 | 35 | 41 | 48 |
| 30,000 | 31,000 | 11 | 26 | 37 | 45 | 52 |
| 31,000 | 32,000 | 12 | 27 | 41 | 48 | 56 |
| 32,000 | 33,000 | 13 | 29 | 43 | 52 | 60 |
| 33,000 | 34,000 | 14 | 31 | 46 | 55 | 64 |
| 34,000 | 35,000 | 15 | 33 | 49 | 58 | 68 |
| 35,000 | 36,000 | 16 | 35 | 51 | 62 | 72 |
| 36,000 | 37,000 | 17 | 37 | 54 | 65 | 76 |
| 37,000 | 38,000 | 18 | 38 | 58 | 69 | 79 |
| 38,000 | 39,000 | 18 | 41 | 60 | 72 | 83 |
| 39,000 | 40,000 | 19 | 43 | 63 | 75 | 87 |

| REV. PROC. 2014-21 TABLE 4 DOLLAR AMOUNTS FOR TRUCKS AND VANS WITH A LEASE TERM BEGINNING IN CALENDAR YEAR 2014 | | | | | | |
|---|---|---|---|---|---|---|
| Fair Market Value of Truck or Van | | Tax Year During Lease | | | | |
| 40,000 | 41,000 | 20 | 44 | 66 | 79 | 91 |
| 41,000 | 42,000 | 21 | 46 | 69 | 82 | 95 |
| 42,000 | 43,000 | 22 | 48 | 72 | 85 | 99 |
| 43,000 | 44,000 | 23 | 50 | 74 | 89 | 103 |
| 44,000 | 45,000 | 24 | 52 | 77 | 93 | 106 |
| 45,000 | 46,000 | 24 | 54 | 80 | 96 | 111 |
| 46,000 | 47,000 | 25 | 56 | 83 | 99 | 115 |
| 47,000 | 48,000 | 26 | 58 | 86 | 102 | 119 |
| 48,000 | 49,000 | 27 | 60 | 88 | 106 | 123 |
| 49,000 | 50,000 | 28 | 62 | 91 | 109 | 127 |
| 50,000 | 51,000 | 29 | 63 | 95 | 113 | 130 |
| 51,000 | 52,000 | 30 | 65 | 97 | 117 | 134 |
| 52,000 | 53,000 | 31 | 67 | 100 | 120 | 138 |
| 53,000 | 54,000 | 31 | 69 | 103 | 123 | 142 |
| 54,000 | 55,000 | 32 | 71 | 106 | 126 | 146 |
| 55,000 | 56,000 | 33 | 73 | 108 | 130 | 150 |
| 56,000 | 57,000 | 34 | 75 | 111 | 133 | 154 |
| 57,000 | 58,000 | 35 | 77 | 114 | 137 | 157 |
| 58,000 | 59,000 | 36 | 79 | 116 | 141 | 161 |
| 59,000 | 60,000 | 37 | 80 | 120 | 144 | 165 |
| 60,000 | 62,000 | 38 | 84 | 123 | 149 | 172 |
| 62,000 | 64,000 | 40 | 87 | 130 | 155 | 180 |
| 64,000 | 66,000 | 41 | 91 | 136 | 162 | 187 |
| 66,000 | 68,000 | 43 | 95 | 141 | 169 | 195 |
| 68,000 | 70,000 | 45 | 99 | 146 | 176 | 203 |
| 70,000 | 72,000 | 47 | 102 | 153 | 182 | 211 |
| 72,000 | 74,000 | 48 | 107 | 158 | 189 | 219 |
| 74,000 | 76,000 | 50 | 110 | 164 | 196 | 227 |
| 76,000 | 78,000 | 52 | 114 | 169 | 203 | 235 |
| 78,000 | 80,000 | 54 | 118 | 175 | 209 | 243 |
| 80,000 | 85,000 | 57 | 124 | 185 | 222 | 256 |
| 85,000 | 90,000 | 61 | 134 | 199 | 239 | 276 |
| 90,000 | 95,000 | 65 | 144 | 213 | 256 | 295 |
| 95,000 | 100,000 | 70 | 153 | 227 | 273 | 315 |
| 100,000 | 110,000 | 76 | 168 | 248 | 298 | 345 |
| 110,000 | 120,000 | 85 | 187 | 277 | 332 | 383 |
| 120,000 | 130,000 | 93 | 206 | 305 | 366 | 423 |
| 130,000 | 140,000 | 102 | 225 | 334 | 400 | 462 |
| 140,000 | 150,000 | 111 | 244 | 362 | 434 | 501 |
| 150,000 | 160,000 | 120 | 263 | 390 | 468 | 541 |
| 160,000 | 170,000 | 128 | 282 | 419 | 502 | 580 |
| 170,000 | 180,000 | 137 | 301 | 447 | 536 | 619 |
| 180,000 | 190,000 | 146 | 320 | 475 | 571 | 658 |
| 190,000 | 200,000 | 154 | 339 | 504 | 604 | 698 |

## Annual Lease Value Table for Employer-Provided Automobiles

| REV. PROC. 2014-21 TABLE 4 DOLLAR AMOUNTS FOR TRUCKS AND VANS WITH A LEASE TERM BEGINNING IN CALENDAR YEAR 2014 | | | | | | |
|---|---|---|---|---|---|---|
| Fair Market Value of Truck or Van | | Tax Year During Lease | | | | |
| 200,000 | 210,000 | 163 | 358 | 532 | 639 | 736 |
| 210,000 | 220,000 | 172 | 377 | 561 | 672 | 776 |
| 220,000 | 230,000 | 180 | 397 | 589 | 706 | 815 |
| 230,000 | 240,000 | 189 | 416 | 617 | 740 | 854 |
| 240,000 | and over | 198 | 435 | 645 | 774 | 894 |

# 16. AFR Tables

## 2014

### November 2014 AFR (Rev. Rul. 2014-28)

| | | Annual | Semiannual | Quarterly | Monthly |
|---|---|---|---|---|---|
| | | | Short-Term | | |
| | AFR | .39% | .39% | .39% | .39% |
| 110% | AFR | .43% | .43% | .43% | .43% |
| 120% | AFR | .47% | .47% | .47% | .47% |
| 130% | AFR | .51% | .51% | .51% | .51% |
| | | | Mid-Term | | |
| | AFR | 1.90% | 1.89% | 1.89% | 1.88% |
| 110% | AFR | 2.09% | 2.08% | 2.07% | 2.07% |
| 120% | AFR | 2.28% | 2.27% | 2.26% | 2.26% |
| 130% | AFR | 2.48% | 2.46% | 2.45% | 2.45% |
| 150% | AFR | 2.86% | 2.84% | 2.83% | 2.82% |
| 175% | AFR | 3.34% | 3.31% | 3.30% | 3.29% |
| | | | Long-Term | | |
| | AFR | 2.91% | 2.89% | 2.88% | 2.87% |
| 110% | AFR | 3.21% | 3.18% | 3.17% | 3.16% |
| 120% | AFR | 3.50% | 3.47% | 3.46% | 3.45% |
| 130% | AFR | 3.80% | 3.76% | 3.74% | 3.73% |

### October 2014 AFR (Rev. Rul. 2014-26)

| | | Annual | Semiannual | Quarterly | Monthly |
|---|---|---|---|---|---|
| | | | Short-Term | | |
| | AFR | .38% | .38% | .38% | .38% |
| 110% | AFR | .42% | .42% | .42% | .42% |
| 120% | AFR | .46% | .46% | .46% | .46% |
| 130% | AFR | .49% | .49% | .49% | .49% |
| | | | Mid-Term | | |
| | AFR | 1.85% | 1.84% | 1.84% | 1.83% |
| 110% | AFR | 2.03% | 2.02% | 2.01% | 2.01% |
| 120% | AFR | 2.22% | 2.21% | 2.20% | 2.20% |
| 130% | AFR | 2.40% | 2.39% | 2.38% | 2.38% |
| 150% | AFR | 2.78% | 2.76% | 2.75% | 2.74% |
| 175% | AFR | 3.25% | 3.22% | 3.21% | 3.20% |
| | | | Long-Term | | |
| | AFR | 2.89% | 2.87% | 2.86% | 2.85% |
| 110% | AFR | 3.18% | 3.16% | 3.15% | 3.14% |
| 120% | AFR | 3.47% | 3.44% | 3.43% | 3.42% |
| 130% | AFR | 3.76% | 3.73% | 3.71% | 3.70% |

## September 2014 AFR (Rev. Rul. 2014-22)

| | | Annual | Semiannual | Quarterly | Monthly |
|---|---|---|---|---|---|
| | | | **Short-Term** | | |
| | AFR | .36% | .36% | .36% | .36% |
| 110% | AFR | .40% | .40% | .40% | .40% |
| 120% | AFR | .43% | .43% | .43% | .43% |
| 130% | AFR | .47% | .47% | .47% | .47% |
| | | | **Mid-Term** | | |
| | AFR | 1.86% | 1.85% | 1.85% | 1.84% |
| 110% | AFR | 2.05% | 2.04% | 2.03% | 2.03% |
| 120% | AFR | 2.23% | 2.22% | 2.21% | 2.21% |
| 130% | AFR | 2.42% | 2.41% | 2.40% | 2.40% |
| 150% | AFR | 2.80% | 2.78% | 2.77% | 2.76% |
| 175% | AFR | 3.27% | 3.24% | 3.23% | 3.22% |
| | | | **Long-Term** | | |
| | AFR | 2.97% | 2.95% | 2.94% | 2.93% |
| 110% | AFR | 3.28% | 3.25% | 3.24% | 3.23% |
| 120% | AFR | 3.57% | 3.54% | 3.52% | 3.51% |
| 130% | AFR | 3.88% | 3.84% | 3.82% | 3.81% |

## August 2014 AFR (Rev. Rul. 2014-19)

| | | Annual | Semiannual | Quarterly | Monthly |
|---|---|---|---|---|---|
| | | | **Short-Term** | | |
| | AFR | .36% | .36% | .36% | .36% |
| 110% | AFR | .40% | .40% | .40% | .40% |
| 120% | AFR | .43% | .43% | .43% | .43% |
| 130% | AFR | .47% | .47% | .47% | .47% |
| | | | **Mid-Term** | | |
| | AFR | 1.89% | 1.88% | 1.88% | 1.87% |
| 110% | AFR | 2.08% | 2.07% | 2.06% | 2.06% |
| 120% | AFR | 2.27% | 2.26% | 2.25% | 2.25% |
| 130% | AFR | 2.45% | 2.44% | 2.43% | 2.43% |
| 150% | AFR | 2.84% | 2.82% | 2.81% | 2.80% |
| 175% | AFR | 3.32% | 3.29% | 3.28% | 3.27% |
| | | | **Long-Term** | | |
| | AFR | 3.09% | 3.07% | 3.06% | 3.05% |
| 110% | AFR | 3.41% | 3.38% | 3.37% | 3.36% |
| 120% | AFR | 3.71% | 3.68% | 3.66% | 3.65% |
| 130% | AFR | 4.03% | 3.99% | 3.97% | 3.96% |

# AFR Tables

## July 2014 AFR (Rev. Rul. 2014-20)

| | | Annual | Semiannual | Quarterly | Monthly |
|---|---|---|---|---|---|
| | | | Short-Term | | |
| | AFR | .31% | .31% | .31% | .31% |
| 110% | AFR | .34% | .34% | .34% | .34% |
| 120% | AFR | .37% | .37% | .37% | .37% |
| 130% | AFR | .40% | .40% | .40% | .40% |
| | | | Mid-Term | | |
| | AFR | 1.82% | 1.81% | 1.81% | 1.80% |
| 110% | AFR | 2.00% | 1.99% | 1.99% | 1.98% |
| 120% | AFR | 2.18% | 2.17% | 2.16% | 2.16% |
| 130% | AFR | 2.36% | 2.35% | 2.34% | 2.34% |
| 150% | AFR | 2.74% | 2.72% | 2.71% | 2.70% |
| 175% | AFR | 3.20% | 3.17% | 3.16% | 3.15% |
| | | | Long-Term | | |
| | AFR | 3.06% | 3.04% | 3.03% | 3.02% |
| 110% | AFR | 3.37% | 3.34% | 3.33% | 3.32% |
| 120% | AFR | 3.68% | 3.65% | 3.63% | 3.62% |
| 130% | AFR | 3.99% | 3.95% | 3.93% | 3.92% |

## June 2014 AFR (Rev. Rul. 2014-16)

| | | Annual | Semiannual | Quarterly | Monthly |
|---|---|---|---|---|---|
| | | | Short-Term | | |
| | AFR | .32% | .32% | .32% | .32% |
| 110% | AFR | .35% | .35% | .35% | .35% |
| 120% | AFR | .38% | .38% | .38% | .38% |
| 130% | AFR | .42% | .42% | .42% | .42% |
| | | | Mid-Term | | |
| | AFR | 1.91% | 1.90% | 1.90% | 1.89% |
| 110% | AFR | 2.10% | 2.09% | 2.08% | 2.08% |
| 120% | AFR | 2.29% | 2.28% | 2.27% | 2.27% |
| 130% | AFR | 2.49% | 2.47% | 2.46% | 2.46% |
| 150% | AFR | 2.87% | 2.85% | 2.84% | 2.83% |
| 175% | AFR | 3.36% | 3.33% | 3.32% | 3.31% |
| | | | Long-Term | | |
| | AFR | 3.14% | 3.12% | 3.11% | 3.10% |
| 110% | AFR | 3.46% | 3.43% | 3.42% | 3.41% |
| 120% | AFR | 3.77% | 3.74% | 3.72% | 3.71% |
| 130% | AFR | 4.10% | 4.06% | 4.04% | 4.03% |

# 2015 Federal Tax Guide

## May 2014 AFR (Rev. Rul. 2014-13)

| | | Annual | Semiannual | Quarterly | Monthly |
|---|---|---|---|---|---|
| | | | **Short-Term** | | |
| | AFR | .33% | .33% | .33% | .33% |
| 110% | AFR | .36% | .36% | .36% | .36% |
| 120% | AFR | .40% | .40% | .40% | .40% |
| 130% | AFR | .43% | .43% | .43% | .43% |
| | | | **Mid-Term** | | |
| | AFR | 1.93% | 1.92% | 1.92% | 1.91% |
| 110% | AFR | 2.12% | 2.11% | 2.10% | 2.10% |
| 120% | AFR | 2.31% | 2.30% | 2.29% | 2.29% |
| 130% | AFR | 2.52% | 2.50% | 2.49% | 2.49% |
| 150% | AFR | 2.90% | 2.88% | 2.87% | 2.86% |
| 175% | AFR | 3.39% | 3.36% | 3.35% | 3.34% |
| | | | **Long-Term** | | |
| | AFR | 3.27% | 3.24% | 3.23% | 3.22% |
| 110% | AFR | 3.59% | 3.56% | 3.54% | 3.53% |
| 120% | AFR | 3.93% | 3.89% | 3.87% | 3.86% |
| 130% | AFR | 4.25% | 4.21% | 4.19% | 4.17% |

## April 2014 AFR (Rev. Rul. 2014-12)

| | | Annual | Semiannual | Quarterly | Monthly |
|---|---|---|---|---|---|
| | | | **Short-Term** | | |
| | AFR | .28% | .28% | .28% | .28% |
| 110% | AFR | .31% | .31% | .31% | .31% |
| 120% | AFR | .34% | .34% | .34% | .34% |
| 130% | AFR | .36% | .36% | .36% | .36% |
| | | | **Mid-Term** | | |
| | AFR | 1.81% | 1.80% | 1.80% | 1.79% |
| 110% | AFR | 1.99% | 1.98% | 1.98% | 1.97% |
| 120% | AFR | 2.17% | 2.16% | 2.15% | 2.15% |
| 130% | AFR | 2.35% | 2.34% | 2.33% | 2.33% |
| 150% | AFR | 2.72% | 2.70% | 2.69% | 2.68% |
| 175% | AFR | 3.17% | 3.15% | 3.14% | 3.13% |
| | | | **Long-Term** | | |
| | AFR | 3.32% | 3.29% | 3.28% | 3.27% |
| 110% | AFR | 3.65% | 3.62% | 3.60% | 3.59% |
| 120% | AFR | 3.99% | 3.95% | 3.93% | 3.92% |
| 130% | AFR | 4.33% | 4.28% | 4.26% | 4.24% |

# AFR Tables

## March 2014 AFR (Rev. Rul. 2014-8)

|  |  | Annual | Semiannual | Quarterly | Monthly |
|---|---|---|---|---|---|
|  |  | **Short-Term** |  |  |  |
|  | AFR | .28% | .28% | .28% | .28% |
| 110% | AFR | .31% | .31% | .31% | .31% |
| 120% | AFR | .34% | .34% | .34% | .34% |
| 130% | AFR | .36% | .36% | .36% | .36% |
|  |  | **Mid-Term** |  |  |  |
|  | AFR | 1.84% | 1.83% | 1.83% | 1.82% |
| 110% | AFR | 2.02% | 2.01% | 2.00% | 2.00% |
| 120% | AFR | 2.21% | 2.20% | 2.19% | 2.19% |
| 130% | AFR | 2.39% | 2.38% | 2.37% | 2.37% |
| 150% | AFR | 2.77% | 2.75% | 2.74% | 2.73% |
| 175% | AFR | 3.23% | 3.20% | 3.19% | 3.18% |
|  |  | **Long-Term** |  |  |  |
|  | AFR | 3.36% | 3.33% | 3.32% | 3.31% |
| 110% | AFR | 3.69% | 3.66% | 3.64% | 3.63% |
| 120% | AFR | 4.04% | 4.00% | 3.98% | 3.97% |
| 130% | AFR | 4.38% | 4.33% | 4.31% | 4.29% |

## February 2014 AFR (Rev. Rul. 2014-6)

|  |  | Annual | Semiannual | Quarterly | Monthly |
|---|---|---|---|---|---|
|  |  | **Short-Term** |  |  |  |
|  | AFR | .30% | .30% | .30% | .30% |
| 110% | AFR | .33% | .33% | .33% | .33% |
| 120% | AFR | .36% | .36% | .36% | .36% |
| 130% | AFR | .39% | .39% | .39% | .39% |
|  |  | **Mid-Term** |  |  |  |
|  | AFR | 1.97% | 1.96% | 1.96% | 1.95% |
| 110% | AFR | 2.17% | 2.16% | 2.15% | 2.15% |
| 120% | AFR | 2.36% | 2.35% | 2.34% | 2.34% |
| 130% | AFR | 2.57% | 2.55% | 2.54% | 2.54% |
| 150% | AFR | 2.96% | 2.94% | 2.93% | 2.92% |
| 175% | AFR | 3.46% | 3.43% | 3.42% | 3.41% |
|  |  | **Long-Term** |  |  |  |
|  | AFR | 3.56% | 3.53% | 3.51% | 3.50% |
| 110% | AFR | 3.92% | 3.88% | 3.86% | 3.85% |
| 120% | AFR | 4.28% | 4.24% | 4.22% | 4.20% |
| 130% | AFR | 4.64% | 4.59% | 4.56% | 4.55% |

# 2015 Federal Tax Guide

## January 2014 AFR (Rev. Rul. 2014-1)

### Short-Term

| | | Annual | Semiannual | Quarterly | Monthly |
|---|---|---|---|---|---|
| | AFR | .25% | .25% | .25% | .25% |
| 110% | AFR | .28% | .28% | .28% | .28% |
| 120% | AFR | .30% | .30% | .30% | .30% |
| 130% | AFR | .33% | .33% | .33% | .33% |

### Mid-Term

| | | Annual | Semiannual | Quarterly | Monthly |
|---|---|---|---|---|---|
| | AFR | 1.75% | 1.74% | 1.74% | 1.73% |
| 110% | AFR | 1.92% | 1.91% | 1.91% | 1.90% |
| 120% | AFR | 2.10% | 2.09% | 2.08% | 2.08% |
| 130% | AFR | 2.27% | 2.26% | 2.25% | 2.25% |
| 150% | AFR | 2.63% | 2.61% | 2.60% | 2.60% |
| 175% | AFR | 3.07% | 3.05% | 3.04% | 3.03% |

### Long-Term

| | | Annual | Semiannual | Quarterly | Monthly |
|---|---|---|---|---|---|
| | AFR | 3.49% | 3.46% | 3.45% | 3.44% |
| 110% | AFR | 3.85% | 3.81% | 3.79% | 3.78% |
| 120% | AFR | 4.19% | 4.15% | 4.13% | 4.11% |
| 130% | AFR | 4.55% | 4.50% | 4.47% | 4.46% |

## 17. Actuarial Tables for Annuities (Table V)

(Source: IRS Pub. 939, *General Rule for Pensions and Annuities*)

**TABLE V—ORDINARY LIFE ANNUITIES**
**ONE LIFE—EXPECTED RETURN MULTIPLES**

| AGE | MULTIPLE | AGE | MULTIPLE | AGE | MULTIPLE |
|---|---|---|---|---|---|
| 5 | 76.6 | 42 | 40.6 | 79 | 10.0 |
| 6 | 75.6 | 43 | 39.6 | 80 | 9.5 |
| 7 | 74.7 | 44 | 38.7 | 81 | 8.9 |
| 8 | 73.7 | 45 | 37.7 | 82 | 8.4 |
| 9 | 72.7 | 46 | 36.8 | 83 | 7.9 |
| 10 | 71.7 | 47 | 35.9 | 84 | 7.4 |
| 11 | 70.7 | 48 | 34.9 | 85 | 6.9 |
| 12 | 69.7 | 49 | 34.0 | 86 | 6.5 |
| 13 | 68.8 | 50 | 33.1 | 87 | 6.1 |
| 14 | 67.8 | 51 | 32.2 | 88 | 5.7 |
| 15 | 66.8 | 52 | 31.3 | 89 | 5.3 |
| 16 | 65.8 | 53 | 30.4 | 90 | 5.0 |
| 17 | 64.8 | 54 | 29.5 | 91 | 4.7 |
| 18 | 63.9 | 55 | 28.6 | 92 | 4.4 |
| 19 | 62.9 | 56 | 27.7 | 93 | 4.1 |
| 20 | 61.9 | 57 | 26.8 | 94 | 3.9 |
| 21 | 60.9 | 58 | 25.9 | 95 | 3.7 |
| 22 | 59.9 | 59 | 25.0 | 96 | 3.4 |
| 23 | 59.0 | 60 | 24.2 | 97 | 3.2 |
| 24 | 58.0 | 61 | 23.3 | 98 | 3.0 |
| 25 | 57.0 | 62 | 22.5 | 99 | 2.8 |
| 26 | 56.0 | 63 | 21.6 | 100 | 2.7 |
| 27 | 55.1 | 64 | 20.8 | 101 | 2.5 |
| 28 | 54.1 | 65 | 20.0 | 102 | 2.3 |
| 29 | 53.1 | 66 | 19.2 | 103 | 2.1 |
| 30 | 52.2 | 67 | 18.4 | 104 | 1.9 |
| 31 | 51.2 | 68 | 17.6 | 105 | 1.8 |
| 32 | 50.2 | 69 | 16.8 | 106 | 1.6 |
| 33 | 49.3 | 70 | 16.0 | 107 | 1.4 |
| 34 | 48.3 | 71 | 15.3 | 108 | 1.3 |
| 35 | 47.3 | 72 | 14.6 | 109 | 1.1 |
| 36 | 46.4 | 73 | 13.9 | 110 | 1.0 |
| 37 | 45.4 | 74 | 13.2 | 111 | .9 |
| 38 | 44.4 | 75 | 12.5 | 112 | .8 |
| 39 | 43.5 | 76 | 11.9 | 113 | .7 |
| 40 | 42.5 | 77 | 11.2 | 114 | .6 |
| 41 | 41.5 | 78 | 10.6 | 115 | .5 |

# 18. Actuarial Tables

(Source: IRS Pub. 939, *General Rule for Pensions and Annuities*)

## Actuarial Tables

Table I (One Life) applies to all ages. Tables II–IV apply to males ages 35 to 90 and females ages 40 to 95.

Table I.—Ordinary Life Annuities—One Life—Expected Return Multiples

| Ages | | Multiples | Ages | | Multiples | Ages | | Multiples |
|---|---|---|---|---|---|---|---|---|
| Male | Female | | Male | Female | | Male | Female | |
| 6 | 11 | 65.0 | 41 | 46 | 33.0 | 76 | 81 | 9.1 |
| 7 | 12 | 64.1 | 42 | 47 | 32.1 | 77 | 82 | 8.7 |
| 8 | 13 | 63.2 | 43 | 48 | 31.2 | 78 | 83 | 8.3 |
| 9 | 14 | 62.3 | 44 | 49 | 30.4 | 79 | 84 | 7.8 |
| 10 | 15 | 61.4 | 45 | 50 | 29.6 | 80 | 85 | 7.5 |
| 11 | 16 | 60.4 | 46 | 51 | 28.7 | 81 | 86 | 7.1 |
| 12 | 17 | 59.5 | 47 | 52 | 27.9 | 82 | 87 | 6.7 |
| 13 | 18 | 58.6 | 48 | 53 | 27.1 | 83 | 88 | 6.3 |
| 14 | 19 | 57.7 | 49 | 54 | 26.3 | 84 | 89 | 6.0 |
| 15 | 20 | 56.7 | 50 | 55 | 25.5 | 85 | 90 | 5.7 |
| 16 | 21 | 55.8 | 51 | 56 | 24.7 | 86 | 91 | 5.4 |
| 17 | 22 | 54.9 | 52 | 57 | 24.0 | 87 | 92 | 5.1 |
| 18 | 23 | 53.9 | 53 | 58 | 23.2 | 88 | 93 | 4.8 |
| 19 | 24 | 53.0 | 54 | 59 | 22.4 | 89 | 94 | 4.5 |
| 20 | 25 | 52.1 | 55 | 60 | 21.7 | 90 | 95 | 4.2 |
| 21 | 26 | 51.1 | 56 | 61 | 21.0 | 91 | 96 | 4.0 |
| 22 | 27 | 50.2 | 57 | 62 | 20.3 | 92 | 97 | 3.7 |
| 23 | 28 | 49.3 | 58 | 63 | 19.6 | 93 | 98 | 3.5 |
| 24 | 29 | 48.3 | 59 | 64 | 18.9 | 94 | 99 | 3.3 |
| 25 | 30 | 47.4 | 60 | 65 | 18.2 | 95 | 100 | 3.1 |
| 26 | 31 | 46.5 | 61 | 66 | 17.5 | 96 | 101 | 2.9 |
| 27 | 32 | 45.6 | 62 | 67 | 16.9 | 97 | 102 | 2.7 |
| 28 | 33 | 44.6 | 63 | 68 | 16.2 | 98 | 103 | 2.5 |
| 29 | 34 | 43.7 | 64 | 69 | 15.6 | 99 | 104 | 2.3 |
| 30 | 35 | 42.8 | 65 | 70 | 15.0 | 100 | 105 | 2.1 |
| 31 | 36 | 41.9 | 66 | 71 | 14.4 | 101 | 106 | 1.9 |
| 32 | 37 | 41.0 | 67 | 72 | 13.8 | 102 | 107 | 1.7 |
| 33 | 38 | 40.0 | 68 | 73 | 13.2 | 103 | 108 | 1.5 |
| 34 | 39 | 39.1 | 69 | 74 | 12.6 | 104 | 109 | 1.3 |
| 35 | 40 | 38.2 | 70 | 75 | 12.1 | 105 | 110 | 1.2 |
| | | | | | | 106 | 111 | 1.0 |
| 36 | 41 | 37.3 | 71 | 76 | 11.6 | 107 | 112 | .8 |
| 37 | 42 | 36.5 | 72 | 77 | 11.0 | 108 | 113 | .7 |
| 38 | 43 | 35.6 | 73 | 78 | 10.5 | 109 | 114 | .6 |
| 39 | 44 | 34.7 | 74 | 79 | 10.1 | 110 | 115 | .5 |
| 40 | 45 | 33.8 | 75 | 80 | 9.6 | 111 | 116 | 0 |

### Adjustments to Tables I, II, V, VI and VIA. Payments Made Quarterly, Semiannually, or Annually

| | Number of whole months from annuity starting date to first payment date | | | | | | | | | | | |
|---|---|---|---|---|---|---|---|---|---|---|---|---|
| | 0–1 | 2 | 3 | 4 | 5 | 6 | 7 | 8 | 9 | 10 | 11 | 12 |
| Payments to be made: | | | | | | | | | | | | |
| Annually | +.5 | +.4 | +.3 | +.2 | +.1 | 0 | 0 | -.1 | -.2 | -.3 | -.4 | -.5 |
| Semiannually | +.2 | +.1 | 0 | 0 | -.1 | -.2 | | | | | | |
| Quarterly | +.1 | 0 | -.1 | | | | | | | | | |

Table II. — Ordinary Joint Life and Last Survivor Annuities — Two Lives — Expected Return Multiples

| Ages | | | | | | | | | | | | | | |
|---|---|---|---|---|---|---|---|---|---|---|---|---|---|---|
| | Male | 35 | 36 | 37 | 38 | 39 | 40 | 41 | 42 | 43 | 44 | 45 | 46 | 47 |
| Male | Female | 40 | 41 | 42 | 43 | 44 | 45 | 46 | 47 | 48 | 49 | 50 | 51 | 52 |
| 35 | 40 | 46.2 | 45.7 | 45.3 | 44.8 | 44.4 | 44.0 | 43.6 | 43.3 | 43.0 | 42.6 | 42.3 | 42.0 | 41.8 |
| 36 | 41 | 45.7 | 45.2 | 44.8 | 44.3 | 43.9 | 43.5 | 43.1 | 42.7 | 42.3 | 42.0 | 41.7 | 41.4 | 41.1 |
| 37 | 42 | 45.3 | 44.8 | 44.3 | 43.8 | 43.4 | 42.9 | 42.5 | 42.1 | 41.8 | 41.4 | 41.1 | 40.7 | 40.4 |
| 38 | 43 | 44.8 | 44.3 | 43.8 | 43.3 | 42.9 | 42.4 | 42.0 | 41.6 | 41.2 | 40.8 | 40.5 | 40.1 | 39.8 |
| 39 | 44 | 44.4 | 43.9 | 43.4 | 42.9 | 42.4 | 41.9 | 41.5 | 41.0 | 40.6 | 40.2 | 39.9 | 39.5 | 39.2 |
| 40 | 45 | 44.0 | 43.5 | 42.9 | 42.4 | 41.9 | 41.4 | 41.0 | 40.5 | 40.1 | 39.7 | 39.3 | 38.9 | 38.6 |
| 41 | 46 | 43.6 | 43.1 | 42.5 | 42.0 | 41.5 | 41.0 | 40.5 | 40.0 | 39.6 | 39.2 | 38.8 | 38.4 | 38.0 |
| 42 | 47 | 43.3 | 42.7 | 42.1 | 41.6 | 41.0 | 40.5 | 40.0 | 39.6 | 39.1 | 38.7 | 38.2 | 37.8 | 37.5 |
| 43 | 48 | 43.0 | 42.3 | 41.8 | 41.2 | 40.6 | 40.1 | 39.6 | 39.1 | 38.6 | 38.2 | 37.7 | 37.3 | 36.9 |
| 44 | 49 | 42.6 | 42.0 | 41.4 | 40.8 | 40.2 | 39.7 | 39.2 | 38.7 | 38.2 | 37.7 | 37.2 | 36.8 | 36.4 |
| 45 | 50 | 42.3 | 41.7 | 41.1 | 40.5 | 39.9 | 39.3 | 38.8 | 38.2 | 37.7 | 37.2 | 36.8 | 36.3 | 35.9 |
| 46 | 51 | 42.0 | 41.4 | 40.7 | 40.1 | 39.5 | 38.9 | 38.4 | 37.8 | 37.3 | 36.8 | 36.3 | 35.9 | 35.4 |
| 47 | 52 | 41.8 | 41.1 | 40.4 | 39.8 | 39.2 | 38.6 | 38.0 | 37.5 | 36.9 | 36.4 | 35.9 | 35.4 | 35.0 |

| Ages | | | | | | | | | | | | | | |
|---|---|---|---|---|---|---|---|---|---|---|---|---|---|---|
| | Male | 48 | 49 | 50 | 51 | 52 | 53 | 54 | 55 | 56 | 57 | 58 | 59 | 60 |
| Male | Female | 53 | 54 | 55 | 56 | 57 | 58 | 59 | 60 | 61 | 62 | 63 | 64 | 65 |
| 35 | 40 | 41.5 | 41.3 | 41.0 | 40.8 | 40.6 | 40.4 | 40.3 | 40.1 | 40.0 | 39.8 | 39.7 | 39.6 | 39.5 |
| 36 | 41 | 40.8 | 40.6 | 40.3 | 40.1 | 39.9 | 39.7 | 39.5 | 39.3 | 39.2 | 39.0 | 38.9 | 38.8 | 38.6 |
| 37 | 42 | 40.2 | 39.9 | 39.6 | 39.4 | 39.2 | 39.0 | 38.8 | 38.6 | 38.4 | 38.3 | 38.1 | 38.0 | 37.9 |
| 38 | 43 | 39.5 | 39.2 | 39.0 | 38.7 | 38.5 | 38.3 | 38.1 | 37.9 | 37.7 | 37.5 | 37.3 | 37.2 | 37.1 |
| 39 | 44 | 38.9 | 38.6 | 38.3 | 38.0 | 37.8 | 37.6 | 37.3 | 37.1 | 36.9 | 36.8 | 36.6 | 36.4 | 36.3 |
| 40 | 45 | 38.3 | 38.0 | 37.7 | 37.4 | 37.1 | 36.9 | 36.6 | 36.4 | 36.2 | 36.0 | 35.9 | 35.7 | 35.5 |
| 41 | 46 | 37.7 | 37.3 | 37.0 | 36.7 | 36.5 | 36.2 | 36.0 | 35.7 | 35.5 | 35.3 | 35.1 | 35.0 | 34.8 |
| 42 | 47 | 37.1 | 36.8 | 36.4 | 36.1 | 35.8 | 35.6 | 35.3 | 35.1 | 34.8 | 34.6 | 34.4 | 34.2 | 34.1 |
| 43 | 48 | 36.5 | 36.2 | 35.8 | 35.5 | 35.2 | 34.9 | 34.7 | 34.4 | 34.2 | 33.9 | 33.7 | 33.5 | 33.3 |
| 44 | 49 | 36.0 | 35.6 | 35.3 | 34.9 | 34.6 | 34.3 | 34.0 | 33.8 | 33.5 | 33.3 | 33.0 | 32.8 | 32.6 |
| 45 | 50 | 35.5 | 35.1 | 34.7 | 34.4 | 34.0 | 33.7 | 33.4 | 33.1 | 32.9 | 32.6 | 32.4 | 32.2 | 31.9 |
| 46 | 51 | 35.0 | 34.6 | 34.2 | 33.8 | 33.5 | 33.1 | 32.8 | 32.5 | 32.2 | 32.0 | 31.7 | 31.5 | 31.3 |
| 47 | 52 | 34.5 | 34.1 | 33.7 | 33.3 | 32.9 | 32.6 | 32.2 | 31.9 | 31.6 | 31.4 | 31.1 | 30.9 | 30.6 |
| 48 | 53 | 34.0 | 33.6 | 33.2 | 32.8 | 32.4 | 32.0 | 31.7 | 31.4 | 31.1 | 30.8 | 30.5 | 30.2 | 30.0 |
| 49 | 54 | 33.6 | 33.1 | 32.7 | 32.3 | 31.9 | 31.5 | 31.2 | 30.8 | 30.5 | 30.2 | 29.9 | 29.6 | 29.4 |
| 50 | 55 | 33.2 | 32.7 | 32.3 | 31.8 | 31.4 | 31.0 | 30.6 | 30.3 | 29.9 | 29.6 | 29.3 | 29.0 | 28.8 |
| 51 | 56 | 32.8 | 32.3 | 31.8 | 31.4 | 30.9 | 30.5 | 30.1 | 29.8 | 29.4 | 29.1 | 28.8 | 28.5 | 28.2 |
| 52 | 57 | 32.4 | 31.9 | 31.4 | 30.9 | 30.5 | 30.1 | 29.7 | 29.3 | 28.9 | 28.6 | 28.2 | 27.9 | 27.6 |
| 53 | 58 | 32.0 | 31.5 | 31.0 | 30.5 | 30.1 | 29.6 | 29.2 | 28.8 | 28.4 | 28.1 | 27.7 | 27.4 | 27.1 |
| 54 | 59 | 31.7 | 31.2 | 30.6 | 30.1 | 29.7 | 29.2 | 28.8 | 28.3 | 27.9 | 27.6 | 27.2 | 26.9 | 26.5 |
| 55 | 60 | 31.4 | 30.8 | 30.3 | 29.8 | 29.3 | 28.8 | 28.3 | 27.9 | 27.5 | 27.1 | 26.7 | 26.4 | 26.0 |
| 56 | 61 | 31.1 | 30.5 | 29.9 | 29.4 | 28.9 | 28.4 | 27.9 | 27.5 | 27.1 | 26.7 | 26.3 | 25.9 | 25.5 |
| 57 | 62 | 30.8 | 30.2 | 29.6 | 29.1 | 28.6 | 28.1 | 27.6 | 27.1 | 26.7 | 26.2 | 25.8 | 25.4 | 25.1 |
| 58 | 63 | 30.5 | 29.9 | 29.3 | 28.8 | 28.2 | 27.7 | 27.2 | 26.7 | 26.3 | 25.8 | 25.4 | 25.0 | 24.6 |
| 59 | 64 | 30.2 | 29.6 | 29.0 | 28.5 | 27.9 | 27.4 | 26.9 | 26.4 | 25.9 | 25.4 | 25.0 | 24.6 | 24.2 |
| 60 | 65 | 30.0 | 29.4 | 28.8 | 28.2 | 27.6 | 27.1 | 26.5 | 26.0 | 25.5 | 25.1 | 24.6 | 24.2 | 23.8 |

# Actuarial Tables

Table II.—Ordinary Joint Life and Last Survivor Annuities—Two Lives—Expected Return Multiples—Continued

| Ages | | | | | | | | | | | | | | |
|------|--------|------|------|------|------|------|------|------|------|------|------|------|------|------|
| | Male | 61 | 62 | 63 | 64 | 65 | 66 | 67 | 68 | 69 | 70 | 71 | 72 | 73 |
| Male | Female | 66 | 67 | 68 | 69 | 70 | 71 | 72 | 73 | 74 | 75 | 76 | 77 | 78 |
| 35 | 40 | 39.4 | 39.3 | 39.2 | 39.1 | 39.0 | 38.9 | 38.9 | 38.8 | 38.8 | 38.7 | 38.7 | 38.6 | 38.6 |
| 36 | 41 | 38.5 | 38.4 | 38.3 | 38.2 | 38.2 | 38.1 | 38.0 | 38.0 | 37.9 | 37.9 | 37.8 | 37.8 | 37.7 |
| 37 | 42 | 37.7 | 37.6 | 37.5 | 37.4 | 37.3 | 37.3 | 37.2 | 37.1 | 37.1 | 37.0 | 36.9 | 36.9 | 36.9 |
| 38 | 43 | 36.9 | 36.8 | 36.7 | 36.6 | 36.5 | 36.4 | 36.4 | 36.3 | 36.2 | 36.2 | 36.1 | 36.0 | 36.0 |
| 39 | 44 | 36.2 | 36.0 | 35.9 | 35.8 | 35.7 | 35.6 | 35.5 | 35.5 | 35.4 | 35.3 | 35.3 | 35.2 | 35.2 |
| 40 | 45 | 35.4 | 35.3 | 35.1 | 35.0 | 34.9 | 34.8 | 34.7 | 34.6 | 34.6 | 34.5 | 34.4 | 34.4 | 34.3 |
| 41 | 46 | 34.6 | 34.5 | 34.4 | 34.2 | 34.1 | 34.0 | 33.9 | 33.8 | 33.8 | 33.7 | 33.6 | 33.5 | 33.5 |
| 42 | 47 | 33.9 | 33.7 | 33.6 | 33.5 | 33.4 | 33.2 | 33.1 | 33.0 | 33.0 | 32.9 | 32.8 | 32.7 | 32.7 |
| 43 | 48 | 33.2 | 33.0 | 32.9 | 32.7 | 32.6 | 32.5 | 32.4 | 32.3 | 32.2 | 32.1 | 32.0 | 31.9 | 31.9 |
| 44 | 49 | 32.5 | 32.3 | 32.1 | 32.0 | 31.8 | 31.7 | 31.6 | 31.5 | 31.4 | 31.3 | 31.2 | 31.1 | 31.1 |
| 45 | 50 | 31.8 | 31.6 | 31.4 | 31.3 | 31.1 | 31.0 | 30.8 | 30.7 | 30.6 | 30.5 | 30.4 | 30.4 | 30.3 |
| 46 | 51 | 31.1 | 30.9 | 30.7 | 30.5 | 30.4 | 30.2 | 30.1 | 30.0 | 29.9 | 29.8 | 29.7 | 29.6 | 29.5 |
| 47 | 52 | 30.4 | 30.2 | 30.0 | 29.8 | 29.7 | 29.5 | 29.4 | 29.3 | 29.1 | 29.0 | 28.9 | 28.8 | 28.7 |
| 48 | 53 | 29.8 | 29.5 | 29.3 | 29.2 | 29.0 | 28.8 | 28.7 | 28.5 | 28.4 | 28.3 | 28.2 | 28.1 | 28.0 |
| 49 | 54 | 29.1 | 28.9 | 28.7 | 28.5 | 28.3 | 28.1 | 28.0 | 27.8 | 27.7 | 27.6 | 27.5 | 27.4 | 27.3 |
| 50 | 55 | 28.5 | 28.3 | 28.1 | 27.8 | 27.6 | 27.5 | 27.3 | 27.1 | 27.0 | 26.9 | 26.7 | 26.6 | 26.5 |
| 51 | 56 | 27.9 | 27.7 | 27.4 | 27.2 | 27.0 | 26.8 | 26.6 | 26.5 | 26.3 | 26.2 | 26.0 | 25.9 | 25.8 |
| 52 | 57 | 27.3 | 27.1 | 26.8 | 26.6 | 26.4 | 26.2 | 26.0 | 25.8 | 25.7 | 25.5 | 25.4 | 25.2 | 25.1 |
| 53 | 58 | 26.8 | 26.5 | 26.2 | 26.0 | 25.8 | 25.6 | 25.4 | 25.2 | 25.0 | 24.8 | 24.7 | 24.6 | 24.4 |
| 54 | 59 | 26.2 | 25.9 | 25.7 | 25.4 | 25.2 | 25.0 | 24.7 | 24.6 | 24.4 | 24.2 | 24.0 | 23.9 | 23.8 |
| 55 | 60 | 25.7 | 25.4 | 25.1 | 24.9 | 24.6 | 24.4 | 24.1 | 23.9 | 23.8 | 23.6 | 23.4 | 23.3 | 23.1 |
| 56 | 61 | 25.2 | 24.9 | 24.6 | 24.3 | 24.1 | 23.8 | 23.6 | 23.4 | 23.2 | 23.0 | 22.8 | 22.6 | 22.5 |
| 57 | 62 | 24.7 | 24.4 | 24.1 | 23.8 | 23.5 | 23.3 | 23.0 | 22.8 | 22.6 | 22.4 | 22.2 | 22.0 | 21.9 |
| 58 | 63 | 24.3 | 23.9 | 23.6 | 23.3 | 23.0 | 22.7 | 22.5 | 22.2 | 22.0 | 21.8 | 21.6 | 21.4 | 21.3 |
| 59 | 64 | 23.8 | 23.5 | 23.1 | 22.8 | 22.5 | 22.2 | 21.9 | 21.7 | 21.5 | 21.2 | 21.0 | 20.9 | 20.7 |
| 60 | 65 | 23.4 | 23.0 | 22.7 | 22.3 | 22.0 | 21.7 | 21.4 | 21.2 | 20.9 | 20.7 | 20.5 | 20.3 | 20.1 |
| 61 | 66 | 23.0 | 22.6 | 22.2 | 21.9 | 21.6 | 21.3 | 21.0 | 20.7 | 20.4 | 20.2 | 20.0 | 19.8 | 19.6 |
| 62 | 67 | 22.6 | 22.2 | 21.8 | 21.5 | 21.1 | 20.8 | 20.5 | 20.2 | 19.9 | 19.7 | 19.5 | 19.2 | 19.1 |
| 63 | 68 | 22.2 | 21.8 | 21.4 | 21.1 | 20.7 | 20.4 | 20.1 | 19.8 | 19.5 | 19.2 | 19.0 | 18.7 | 18.5 |
| 64 | 69 | 21.9 | 21.5 | 21.1 | 20.7 | 20.3 | 20.0 | 19.6 | 19.3 | 19.0 | 18.7 | 18.5 | 18.2 | 18.0 |
| 65 | 70 | 21.6 | 21.1 | 20.7 | 20.3 | 19.9 | 19.6 | 19.2 | 18.9 | 18.6 | 18.3 | 18.0 | 17.8 | 17.5 |
| 66 | 71 | 21.3 | 20.8 | 20.4 | 20.0 | 19.6 | 19.2 | 18.8 | 18.5 | 18.2 | 17.9 | 17.6 | 17.3 | 17.1 |
| 67 | 72 | 21.0 | 20.5 | 20.1 | 19.6 | 19.2 | 18.8 | 18.5 | 18.1 | 17.8 | 17.5 | 17.2 | 16.9 | 16.7 |
| 68 | 73 | 20.7 | 20.2 | 19.8 | 19.3 | 18.9 | 18.5 | 18.1 | 17.8 | 17.4 | 17.1 | 16.8 | 16.5 | 16.2 |
| 69 | 74 | 20.4 | 19.9 | 19.5 | 19.0 | 18.6 | 18.2 | 17.8 | 17.4 | 17.1 | 16.7 | 16.4 | 16.1 | 15.8 |
| 70 | 75 | 20.2 | 19.7 | 19.2 | 18.7 | 18.3 | 17.9 | 17.5 | 17.1 | 16.7 | 16.4 | 16.1 | 15.8 | 15.5 |
| 71 | 76 | 20.0 | 19.5 | 19.0 | 18.5 | 18.0 | 17.6 | 17.2 | 16.8 | 16.4 | 16.1 | 15.7 | 15.4 | 15.1 |
| 72 | 77 | 19.8 | 19.2 | 18.7 | 18.2 | 17.8 | 17.3 | 16.9 | 16.5 | 16.1 | 15.8 | 15.4 | 15.1 | 14.8 |
| 73 | 78 | 19.6 | 19.0 | 18.5 | 18.0 | 17.5 | 17.1 | 16.7 | 16.2 | 15.8 | 15.5 | 15.1 | 14.8 | 14.4 |

# 2015 Federal Tax Guide

Table II.—Ordinary Joint Life and Last Survivor Annuities—Two Lives—Expected Return Multiples—Continued

| Ages | | | | | | | | | | | | | |
| Male | | 74 | 75 | 76 | 77 | 78 | 79 | 80 | 81 | 82 | 83 | 84 | 85 |
| Male | Female | 79 | 80 | 81 | 82 | 83 | 84 | 85 | 86 | 87 | 88 | 89 | 90 |
| 35 | 40 | 38.6 | 38.5 | 38.5 | 38.5 | 38.4 | 38.4 | 38.4 | 38.4 | 38.4 | 38.4 | 38.3 | 38.3 |
| 36 | 41 | 37.7 | 37.6 | 37.6 | 37.6 | 37.6 | 37.5 | 37.5 | 37.5 | 37.5 | 37.5 | 37.5 | 37.4 |
| 37 | 42 | 36.8 | 36.8 | 36.7 | 36.7 | 36.7 | 36.7 | 36.6 | 36.6 | 36.6 | 36.6 | 36.6 | 36.6 |
| 38 | 43 | 36.0 | 35.9 | 35.9 | 35.9 | 35.8 | 35.8 | 35.8 | 35.8 | 35.7 | 35.7 | 35.7 | 35.7 |
| 39 | 44 | 35.1 | 35.1 | 35.0 | 35.0 | 35.0 | 34.9 | 34.9 | 34.9 | 34.9 | 34.8 | 34.8 | 34.8 |
| 40 | 45 | 34.3 | 34.2 | 34.2 | 34.1 | 34.1 | 34.1 | 34.1 | 34.0 | 34.0 | 34.0 | 34.0 | 34.0 |
| 41 | 46 | 33.4 | 33.4 | 33.3 | 33.3 | 33.3 | 33.2 | 33.2 | 33.2 | 33.2 | 33.1 | 33.1 | 33.1 |
| 42 | 47 | 32.6 | 32.6 | 32.5 | 32.5 | 32.4 | 32.4 | 32.4 | 32.3 | 32.3 | 32.3 | 32.3 | 32.3 |
| 43 | 48 | 31.8 | 31.8 | 31.7 | 31.7 | 31.6 | 31.6 | 31.5 | 31.5 | 31.5 | 31.5 | 31.4 | 31.4 |
| 44 | 49 | 31.0 | 30.9 | 30.9 | 30.8 | 30.8 | 30.8 | 30.7 | 30.7 | 30.7 | 30.6 | 30.6 | 30.6 |
| 45 | 50 | 30.2 | 30.1 | 30.1 | 30.0 | 30.0 | 29.9 | 29.9 | 29.9 | 29.8 | 29.8 | 29.8 | 29.8 |
| 46 | 51 | 29.4 | 29.4 | 29.3 | 29.2 | 29.2 | 29.2 | 29.1 | 29.1 | 29.0 | 29.0 | 29.0 | 28.9 |
| 47 | 52 | 28.7 | 28.6 | 28.5 | 28.5 | 28.4 | 28.4 | 28.4 | 28.3 | 28.3 | 28.2 | 28.2 | 28.1 |
| 48 | 53 | 27.9 | 27.8 | 27.8 | 27.7 | 27.6 | 27.6 | 27.5 | 27.5 | 27.5 | 27.4 | 27.4 | 27.4 |
| 49 | 54 | 27.2 | 27.1 | 27.0 | 26.9 | 26.9 | 26.8 | 26.8 | 26.7 | 26.7 | 26.6 | 26.6 | 26.6 |
| 50 | 55 | 26.4 | 26.3 | 26.3 | 26.2 | 26.1 | 26.1 | 26.0 | 26.0 | 25.9 | 25.9 | 25.8 | 25.8 |
| 51 | 56 | 25.7 | 25.6 | 25.5 | 25.5 | 25.4 | 25.3 | 25.3 | 25.2 | 25.2 | 25.1 | 25.1 | 25.0 |
| 52 | 57 | 25.0 | 24.9 | 24.8 | 24.7 | 24.7 | 24.6 | 24.5 | 24.5 | 24.4 | 24.4 | 24.3 | 24.3 |
| 53 | 58 | 24.3 | 24.2 | 24.1 | 24.0 | 23.9 | 23.9 | 23.8 | 23.7 | 23.7 | 23.6 | 23.6 | 23.5 |
| 54 | 59 | 23.6 | 23.5 | 23.4 | 23.3 | 23.2 | 23.2 | 23.1 | 23.0 | 23.0 | 22.9 | 22.9 | 22.8 |
| 55 | 60 | 23.0 | 22.9 | 22.8 | 22.7 | 22.6 | 22.5 | 22.4 | 22.3 | 22.3 | 22.2 | 22.2 | 22.1 |
| 56 | 61 | 22.3 | 22.2 | 22.1 | 22.0 | 21.9 | 21.8 | 21.7 | 21.6 | 21.6 | 21.5 | 21.5 | 21.4 |
| 57 | 62 | 21.7 | 21.6 | 21.5 | 21.3 | 21.2 | 21.1 | 21.1 | 21.0 | 20.9 | 20.8 | 20.8 | 20.7 |
| 58 | 63 | 21.1 | 21.0 | 20.8 | 20.7 | 20.6 | 20.5 | 20.4 | 20.3 | 20.2 | 20.2 | 20.1 | 20.0 |
| 59 | 64 | 20.5 | 20.4 | 20.2 | 20.1 | 20.0 | 19.9 | 19.8 | 19.7 | 19.6 | 19.5 | 19.4 | 19.4 |
| 60 | 65 | 19.9 | 19.8 | 19.6 | 19.5 | 19.4 | 19.3 | 19.1 | 19.0 | 19.0 | 18.9 | 18.8 | 18.7 |
| 61 | 66 | 19.4 | 19.2 | 19.1 | 18.9 | 18.8 | 18.7 | 18.5 | 18.4 | 18.3 | 18.3 | 18.2 | 18.1 |
| 62 | 67 | 18.8 | 18.7 | 18.5 | 18.3 | 18.2 | 18.1 | 18.0 | 17.8 | 17.7 | 17.7 | 17.6 | 17.5 |
| 63 | 68 | 18.3 | 18.1 | 18.0 | 17.8 | 17.6 | 17.5 | 17.4 | 17.3 | 17.2 | 17.1 | 17.0 | 16.9 |
| 64 | 69 | 17.8 | 17.6 | 17.4 | 17.3 | 17.1 | 17.0 | 16.8 | 16.7 | 16.6 | 16.5 | 16.4 | 16.3 |
| 65 | 70 | 17.3 | 17.1 | 16.9 | 16.7 | 16.6 | 16.4 | 16.3 | 16.2 | 16.0 | 15.9 | 15.8 | 15.8 |
| 66 | 71 | 16.9 | 16.6 | 16.4 | 16.3 | 16.1 | 15.9 | 15.8 | 15.6 | 15.5 | 15.4 | 15.3 | 15.2 |
| 67 | 72 | 16.4 | 16.2 | 16.0 | 15.8 | 15.6 | 15.4 | 15.3 | 15.1 | 15.0 | 14.9 | 14.8 | 14.7 |
| 68 | 73 | 16.0 | 15.7 | 15.5 | 15.3 | 15.1 | 15.0 | 14.8 | 14.6 | 14.5 | 14.4 | 14.3 | 14.2 |
| 69 | 74 | 15.6 | 15.3 | 15.1 | 14.9 | 14.7 | 14.5 | 14.3 | 14.2 | 14.0 | 13.9 | 13.8 | 13.7 |
| 70 | 75 | 15.2 | 14.9 | 14.7 | 14.5 | 14.3 | 14.1 | 13.9 | 13.7 | 13.6 | 13.4 | 13.3 | 13.2 |
| 71 | 76 | 14.8 | 14.5 | 14.3 | 14.1 | 13.8 | 13.6 | 13.5 | 13.3 | 13.1 | 13.0 | 12.8 | 12.7 |
| 72 | 77 | 14.5 | 14.2 | 13.9 | 13.7 | 13.5 | 13.2 | 13.0 | 12.9 | 12.7 | 12.5 | 12.4 | 12.3 |
| 73 | 78 | 14.1 | 13.8 | 13.6 | 13.3 | 13.1 | 12.9 | 12.7 | 12.5 | 12.3 | 12.1 | 12.0 | 11.8 |
| 74 | 79 | 13.8 | 13.5 | 13.2 | 13.0 | 12.7 | 12.5 | 12.3 | 12.1 | 11.9 | 11.7 | 11.6 | 11.4 |
| 75 | 80 | 13.5 | 13.2 | 12.9 | 12.6 | 12.4 | 12.2 | 11.9 | 11.7 | 11.5 | 11.4 | 11.2 | 11.0 |
| 76 | 81 | 13.2 | 12.9 | 12.6 | 12.3 | 12.1 | 11.8 | 11.6 | 11.4 | 11.2 | 11.0 | 10.8 | 10.7 |
| 77 | 82 | 13.0 | 12.6 | 12.3 | 12.1 | 11.8 | 11.5 | 11.3 | 11.1 | 10.8 | 10.7 | 10.5 | 10.3 |
| 78 | 83 | 12.7 | 12.4 | 12.1 | 11.8 | 11.5 | 11.2 | 11.0 | 10.7 | 10.5 | 10.3 | 10.1 | 10.0 |
| 79 | 84 | 12.5 | 12.2 | 11.8 | 11.5 | 11.2 | 11.0 | 10.7 | 10.5 | 10.2 | 10.0 | 9.8 | 9.6 |
| 80 | 85 | 12.3 | 11.9 | 11.6 | 11.3 | 11.0 | 10.7 | 10.4 | 10.2 | 10.0 | 9.7 | 9.5 | 9.3 |
| 81 | 86 | 12.1 | 11.7 | 11.4 | 11.1 | 10.7 | 10.5 | 10.2 | 9.9 | 9.7 | 9.5 | 9.3 | 9.1 |
| 82 | 87 | 11.9 | 11.5 | 11.2 | 10.8 | 10.5 | 10.2 | 10.0 | 9.7 | 9.4 | 9.2 | 9.0 | 8.8 |
| 83 | 88 | 11.7 | 11.4 | 11.0 | 10.7 | 10.3 | 10.0 | 9.7 | 9.5 | 9.2 | 9.0 | 8.7 | 8.5 |
| 84 | 89 | 11.6 | 11.2 | 10.8 | 10.5 | 10.0 | 9.8 | 9.5 | 9.3 | 9.0 | 8.7 | 8.5 | 8.3 |
| 85 | 90 | 11.4 | 11.0 | 10.7 | 10.3 | 10.0 | 9.6 | 9.3 | 9.1 | 8.8 | 8.5 | 8.3 | 8.1 |

# Actuarial Tables

Table II.—Ordinary Joint Life and Last Survivor Annuities—Two Lives—
Expected Return Multiples—Continued

| Ages | | | | | | |
|------|------|------|------|------|------|------|
| | **Male** | 86 | 87 | 88 | 89 | 90 |
| **Male** | **Female** | 91 | 92 | 93 | 94 | 95 |
| 35 | 40 | 38.3 | 38.3 | 38.3 | 38.3 | 38.3 |
| 36 | 41 | 37.4 | 37.4 | 37.4 | 37.4 | 37.4 |
| 37 | 42 | 36.5 | 36.5 | 36.5 | 36.5 | 36.5 |
| 38 | 43 | 35.7 | 35.7 | 35.6 | 35.6 | 35.6 |
| 39 | 44 | 34.8 | 34.8 | 34.8 | 34.8 | 34.8 |
| 40 | 45 | 33.9 | 33.9 | 33.9 | 33.9 | 33.9 |
| 41 | 46 | 33.1 | 33.1 | 33.1 | 33.0 | 33.0 |
| 42 | 47 | 32.2 | 32.2 | 32.2 | 32.2 | 32.2 |
| 43 | 48 | 31.4 | 31.4 | 31.4 | 31.4 | 31.3 |
| 44 | 49 | 30.6 | 30.5 | 30.5 | 30.5 | 30.5 |
| 45 | 50 | 29.7 | 29.7 | 29.7 | 29.7 | 29.7 |
| 46 | 51 | 28.9 | 28.9 | 28.9 | 28.9 | 28.9 |
| 47 | 52 | 28.1 | 28.1 | 28.1 | 28.1 | 28.0 |
| 48 | 53 | 27.3 | 27.3 | 27.3 | 27.3 | 27.2 |
| 49 | 54 | 26.5 | 26.5 | 26.5 | 26.5 | 26.5 |
| 50 | 55 | 25.8 | 25.7 | 25.7 | 25.7 | 25.7 |
| 51 | 56 | 25.0 | 25.0 | 24.9 | 24.9 | 24.9 |
| 52 | 57 | 24.3 | 24.2 | 24.2 | 24.2 | 24.1 |
| 53 | 58 | 23.5 | 23.5 | 23.4 | 23.4 | 23.4 |
| 54 | 59 | 22.8 | 22.7 | 22.7 | 22.7 | 22.7 |
| 55 | 60 | 22.1 | 22.0 | 22.0 | 22.0 | 21.9 |
| 56 | 61 | 21.4 | 21.3 | 21.3 | 21.3 | 21.2 |
| 57 | 62 | 20.7 | 20.6 | 20.6 | 20.6 | 20.5 |
| 58 | 63 | 20.0 | 19.9 | 19.9 | 19.9 | 19.8 |
| 59 | 64 | 19.3 | 19.3 | 19.2 | 19.2 | 19.2 |
| 60 | 65 | 18.7 | 18.6 | 18.6 | 18.5 | 18.5 |
| 61 | 66 | 18.1 | 18.0 | 17.9 | 17.9 | 17.9 |
| 62 | 67 | 17.4 | 17.4 | 17.3 | 17.3 | 17.2 |
| 63 | 68 | 16.8 | 16.8 | 16.7 | 16.7 | 16.6 |
| 64 | 69 | 16.2 | 16.2 | 16.1 | 16.1 | 16.0 |
| 65 | 70 | 15.7 | 15.6 | 15.5 | 15.5 | 15.4 |
| 66 | 71 | 15.1 | 15.0 | 15.0 | 14.9 | 14.8 |
| 67 | 72 | 14.6 | 14.5 | 14.4 | 14.4 | 14.3 |
| 68 | 73 | 14.1 | 14.0 | 13.9 | 13.8 | 13.8 |
| 69 | 74 | 13.6 | 13.5 | 13.4 | 13.3 | 13.2 |
| 70 | 75 | 13.1 | 13.0 | 12.9 | 12.8 | 12.7 |
| 71 | 76 | 12.6 | 12.5 | 12.4 | 12.3 | 12.2 |
| 72 | 77 | 12.1 | 12.0 | 11.9 | 11.8 | 11.8 |
| 73 | 78 | 11.7 | 11.6 | 11.5 | 11.4 | 11.3 |
| 74 | 79 | 11.3 | 11.2 | 11.1 | 11.0 | 10.9 |
| 75 | 80 | 10.9 | 10.8 | 10.7 | 10.5 | 10.5 |
| 76 | 81 | 10.5 | 10.4 | 10.3 | 10.2 | 10.1 |
| 77 | 82 | 10.2 | 10.0 | 9.9 | 9.8 | 9.7 |
| 78 | 83 | 9.8 | 9.7 | 9.5 | 9.4 | 9.3 |
| 79 | 84 | 9.5 | 9.3 | 9.2 | 9.1 | 8.9 |
| 80 | 85 | 9.2 | 9.0 | 8.9 | 8.7 | 8.6 |
| 81 | 86 | 8.9 | 8.7 | 8.6 | 8.4 | 8.3 |
| 82 | 87 | 8.6 | 8.4 | 8.3 | 8.1 | 8.0 |
| 83 | 88 | 8.3 | 8.2 | 8.0 | 7.9 | 7.7 |
| 84 | 89 | 8.1 | 7.9 | 7.8 | 7.6 | 7.5 |
| 86 | 91 | 7.7 | 7.5 | 7.3 | 7.1 | 7.0 |
| 87 | 92 | 7.5 | 7.3 | 7.1 | 6.9 | 6.8 |
| 88 | 93 | 7.3 | 7.1 | 6.9 | 6.7 | 6.6 |
| 89 | 94 | 7.1 | 6.9 | 6.7 | 6.5 | 6.4 |
| 90 | 95 | 7.0 | 6.8 | 6.6 | 6.4 | 6.2 |

# 19. Section 382 Long-Term Tax-Exempt Rates

**2014 Tax Year**

| Month | Source | Long-Term Rate | Ownership Change Rate |
|---|---|---|---|
| Jan. | Rev. Rul. 2014-1 | 3.49% | 3.26% |
| Feb. | Rev. Rul. 2014-6 | 3.56% | 3.56% |
| Mar. | Rev. Rul. 2014-8 | 3.36% | 3.56% |
| Apr. | Rev. Rul. 2014-12 | 3.32% | 3.56% |
| May | Rev. Rul. 2014-13 | 3.27% | 3.36% |
| June | Rev. Rul. 2014-16 | 3.14% | 3.32% |
| July | Rev. Rul. 2014-20 | 3.06% | 3.27% |
| Aug. | Rev. Rul. 2014-19 | 3.05% | 3.14% |
| Sept. | Rev. Rul. 2014-22 | 2.94% | 3.06% |
| Oct. | Rev. Rul. 2014-26 | 2.77% | 3.05% |
| Nov. | Rev. Rul. 2014-28 | 2.80% | 2.94% |

## 20. Guide to Common Returns/Forms

| FORM # | FORM TITLE | DUE DATE | AUTHORITY |
|---|---|---|---|
| 706 | U.S. Estate (and Generation-Skipping Transfer) Tax Return | 9 months after the date of death | § 6075(a); Reg. § 20-6075-1 |
| 706-NA | U.S. Estate (and Generation-Skipping Transfer) Tax Return [**Estate of nonresident not a citizen of the United States**] | 9 months after the date of death | § 6075(a); Reg. § 20-6075-1 |
| 709 | U.S. Gift (and Generation-Skipping Transfer) Tax Return | By April 15 of year following calendar year of gift | § 6075(b) |
| 940 | Employer's Annual Federal Unemployment (FUTA) Tax Return | One month after the tax year ends | Reg. § 31.6071(a)-1(c) |
| 941 | Employer's Quarterly Federal Income Tax Return | One month after the tax quarter ends | Reg. § 31.6071(a)-1(a)(1) |
| 945 | Annual Return of Withheld Federal Income Tax | One month after the tax year ends | Reg. § 31.6071(a)-1(a)(1) |
| 990 | Return of Organization Exempt from Income Tax | By the 15th day of the fifth month following the close of the tax-exempt organization's annual accounting period | Reg. § 1.6033-2(e) |
| 990-BL | Information and Initial Excise Tax Return for Black Lung Benefit Trusts and Certain Related Persons | By the 15th day of the fifth month following the close of the taxpayer's tax year | Reg. § 53.6071-1(d) |
| 990-PF | Return of Private Foundation or Section 4947(a)(1) Nonexempt Charitable Trust Treated as a Private Foundation | By the 15th day of the fifth month following the close of the organization's annual accounting period | Reg. § 1.6033-2(e) |
| 990-T | Exempt Organization Business Income Tax Return | By the 15th day of the fifth month following the close of the taxable year | § 6072(e) |
| 1040 | U.S. Individual Income Tax Return | By the 15th day of the fourth month after the close of the individual's taxable year | § 6072(a) |

| FORM # | FORM TITLE | DUE DATE | AUTHORITY |
|---|---|---|---|
| 1040-NR | U.S. Nonresident Alien Income Tax Return | If the nonresident alien has wages subject to withholding under §§ 3401–3406, by the 15th day of the fourth month following the close of the taxable year; for other nonresident aliens, by the 15th day of the sixth month after the close of the year | § 6072(c); Reg. § 301.6072-1(c) |
| 1040-ES | Estimated Tax for Individuals | By the 15th day of the fourth, sixth, and ninth months of the taxable year and the 15th day of the first month of the succeeding year | § 6654(e) |
| 1041 | U.S. Income Tax Return for Estates and Trusts | By the 15th day of the fourth month after the close of the taxable year | § 6072(a) |
| 1041-A | U.S. Information Return Trust Accumulation of Charitable Amounts | By the 15th day of the fourth month following the close of the trust's taxable year | Reg. § 1.6034-1(c) |
| 1041-ES | Estimated Income Tax for Estates and Trusts | By the 15th day of the fourth, sixth, and ninth months of the taxable year and the 15th day of the first month of the succeeding year | § 6654(e) |
| 1041-T | Allocation of Estimated Tax Payments to Beneficiaries (Under Code section 643(g)) | By the 65th day after the close of the tax year | § 643(g)(2) |
| 1042 | Annual Withholding Tax Return for U.S. Source Income of Foreign Persons | By March 15 of the succeeding year | Reg. § 1.1461-1(b)(1) |
| 1042-S | Foreign Person's U.S. Source Income Subject to Withholding | By March 15 of the year following the calendar year in which the amount subject to reporting was paid | Reg. § 1.1461-1(c)(1) |
| 1045 | Application for Tentative Refund | Or after the date of the filing of the return for the taxable year and within 12 months after the end of the year in which an NOL, unused credit, a net § 1256 contracts loss or claim of right adjustment rose | Reg. § 1.6411-1(c) |
| 1065 | U.S. Return of Partnership Income | By the 15th day of the fourth month after the end of the partnership's tax year | § 6072(a) |

# Guide to Common Returns/Forms

| FORM # | FORM TITLE | DUE DATE | AUTHORITY |
|---|---|---|---|
| 1065-B | U.S. Return of Income for Electing Large Partnerships | By the 15th day of the fourth month after the end of the partnership's tax year; furnish to partners by the first March 15th following the close of its taxable year | Instructions to Form 1065-B; § 6031(b) |
| 1066 | U.S. Real Estate Mortgage Investment Conduit (REMIC) Income Tax Return | By the 15th day of the fourth month after the end of the REMIC's tax year | Reg. § 1.860F-4 |
| 1120 | U.S. Corporation Income Tax Return | By the 15th day of the third month after the close of the year | § 6072(b) |
| 1120-C | U.S. Income Tax Return for Cooperative Associations | For cooperatives meeting the requirements of § 6072(d), by the 15th day of the ninth month after the end of the tax year; otherwise, by the 15th day of the third month after the end of its tax year | § 6072(d); § 6072(b) |
| 1120-F | U.S. Income Tax Return of a Foreign Corporation | If the corporation does not have an office or fixed place of business in the United States, by the 15th day of the sixth month after the close of the year; if the corporation does have an office or fixed place of business within the United States, by the 15th day of the third month following the close of the taxable year | § 6072(c); Reg. § 1.6072-2(a), (b) |
| 1120-FSC | U.S. Income Tax return of a Foreign Sales Corporation | By the 15th day of the third month after the close of the corporation's taxable year | § 6072(b) |
| 1120-H | U.S. Income Tax Return for Homeowners Associations | By the 15th day of the third month after the end of the association's tax year | § 6072(b); Instructions to Form 1120-H |
| 1120-IC-DISC | Interest Charge Domestic International Sales Corporation Return | By the 15th day of the ninth month after the end of the tax year | § 6072(b) |
| 1120-L | U.S. Life Insurance Company Income Tax Return | By the 15th day of the third month after the close of the corporation's taxable year | § 6072(b) |
| 1120-PC | U.S. Property and Casualty Insurance Company Income Tax Return | By the 15th day of the third month after the close of the corporation's taxable year | § 6072(b) |

| FORM # | FORM TITLE | DUE DATE | AUTHORITY |
|---|---|---|---|
| 1120-POL | U.S. Income Tax Return of Certain Political Organizations | By the 15th day of the third month after the close of the corporation's taxable year | § 6072(b) |
| 1120-REIT | U.S. Income Tax Return for Real Estate Investment Trusts | By the 15th day of the third month after the close of the corporation's taxable year | § 6072(b) |
| 1120-RIC | U.S. Income Tax Return for Regulated Investment Companies | By the 15th day of the third month after the close of the corporation's taxable year | § 6072(b) |
| 1120-S | U.S. Income Tax Return for an S Corporation | By the 15th day of the third month after the close of the corporation's taxable year | § 6072(b) |
| 1120-W | Estimated Tax for Corporations | By the 15th day of 4th, 6th, 9th and 12th months of the tax year | § 6655(c); Instructions to Form 1120-W |
| 1127 | Application for Extension of Time for Payment of Tax Due to Undue Hardship | By the date the tax is due | Reg. § 1.6161-1(c) |
| 1138 | Extension of Time for Payment of Taxes by a Corporation Expecting a Net Operating Loss Carryback | After the start of the tax year of the expected NOL but before the tax of the preceding tax year is required to be paid | Reg. § 1.6164-1(b)(1); Instructions to Form 1138 |
| 1139 | Corporation Application for Tentative Refund | Within 12 months of the end of the tax year in which an NOL, net capital loss, unused credit, or claim of right adjustment arose | Reg. § 1.6411-1(c) |
| 2438 | Undistributed Capital Gains Tax Return | By the 30th day after the end of the RIC's or REIT's tax year; also attach to 1120-RIC or 1120-REIT | Reg. § 1.857-6(f)(1); Instructions to Form 2438 |
| 2553 | Election by a Small Business Corporation | No more than 2 months and 15 days after the beginning of the tax year the election is to take effect; or any time during the tax year preceding the tax year it is to take effect | Reg. § 1.1362-6(a)(2)(ii) |

# Guide to Common Returns/Forms

| FORM # | FORM TITLE | DUE DATE | AUTHORITY |
|---|---|---|---|
| 3115 | Application for Change in Accounting Method | **Automatic change requests:** Original attached to timely filed federal tax return for the year of change, duplicate filed no earlier than the first day of the year of change and no later than when the original is filed with the tax return for the year of change. **Advance consent requests:** during the tax year for which the change is requested | Reg. § 1.446-1(e)(3)(i); Instructions to Form 3115 |
| 3520 | Annual Return to Report Transactions With Foreign Trusts and Receipt of Certain Foreign Gifts | By the due date that the tax return is due (including extensions) | Notice 97-34; Instructions to Form 3520 |
| 3520-A | Annual Information Return of Foreign Trust with a U.S. Owner | By the 15th day of the third month after the end of the trust's tax year | Notice 97-34; Instructions to Form 3520-A |
| 4361 | Application for Exemption from Self-Employment Tax for Use by Ministers, Members of Religious Orders and Christian Science Practitioners | By the due date, including extensions, of the taxpayer's tax return for the 2nd year in which the taxpayer had more than $400 of net earnings from self-employment, any of which came from services performed as a minister, member of a religious order or Christian Science practitioner | Reg. § 1.1402(e)-3A(a)(1) |
| 4466 | Corporation Application for Quick Refund of Overpayment of Estimated Tax | By the 15th day of the third month after the close of the taxable year, but before the corporation files its income tax return | § 6425(a)(1) |
| 4768 | Application for Extension of Time to File a Return and/or Pay U.S. Estate (and Generation-Skipping Transfer) Taxes | By the original due date of the applicable return for which the extension is sought | Reg. § 20.6081-1(b) |
| 4868 | Application for Automatic Extension of Time to File U.S. Individual Income Tax Return | By the regular due date of the return | Reg. § 1.6081-4T(b) |

| FORM # | FORM TITLE | DUE DATE | AUTHORITY |
|--------|-----------|----------|-----------|
| 4876-A | Election to be Treated as an Interest Charge DISC | For the corporation's first tax year, within 90 days after the start of the tax year. For a year not the corporation's first tax year, during the 90-day period immediately preceding the first day of that tax year | Reg. § 1.921-1T(b)(1); Instructions to Form 4876-A |
| 5213 | Election to Postpone Determination as to Whether the Presumption Applies That an Activity is Engaged in for Profit | Within 3 years after the due date of the tax return (determined without regard to extensions) for the first tax year the taxpayer engaged in the activity | Temp. Reg. § 12.9(c)(1); Instructions to Form 5213 |
| 5308 | Request for Change in Plan/Trust Year | By the last day of the end of the short period required to make the change | Rev. Proc. 87-27, 1987-1 C.B. 769 |
| 5471 | Information Return of U.S. Persons With Respect to Certain Foreign Corporations | Due when income tax return is due, including extensions | § 6046; Reg. § 1.6046-1(j)(1); Instructions to Form 5471 |
| 5472 | Information Return of a 25% Foreign-Owned U.S. Corporation or a Foreign Corporation Engaged in a U.S. Trade or Business | By the due date of the reporting corporation's income tax return (including extensions) | Reg. § 1.6038A-2(d) |
| 5500 | Annual Return/Report of Employee Benefit Plan | Generally, by the last day of the seventh month after the close of the plan year (DFEs have a special 9½ month rule) | § 6058(a); Reg. § 1.6058-1 |
| 5558 | Application for Extension of Time to File Certain Employee Plan Returns | By the return's normal due date (i.e., due date without extensions) | Reg. § 1.6081-11T(b) |
| 5578 | Annual Certification of Racial Nondiscrimination for a Private School Exempt from Federal Income Tax | By the 15th day of the fifth month following the end of the organization's calendar year or fiscal period | Instructions to Form 5578 |
| 5712 | Election to be Treated as a Possessions Corporation under Section 936 | By the due date (including extensions) of the first return to which the election will apply | § 936(e); Reg. § 1.936-1(a) |

# Guide to Common Returns/Forms

| FORM # | FORM TITLE | DUE DATE | AUTHORITY |
|---|---|---|---|
| 6069 | Return of Excise Tax on Excess Contributions to Black Lung Benefit Trust Under Section 4953 and Computation of Section 192 Deduction | By the 15th day of the fifth month following the close of the taxpayer's tax year | Reg. § 53.6071-1(d) |
| 7004 | Application for Automatic Extension of Time to File Certain Business Income Tax, Information, and Other Returns | By the due date of the applicable tax return | § 6081; Instructions to Form 7004 |
| 8038 | Information Return for Tax-Exempt Private Activity Bond Issues | By the 15th day of the 2nd calendar month after the close of the calendar quarter in which the bond is issued; may not be filed before the issue date | § 149(e)(2) |
| 8109 | Federal Tax Deposit Coupon Book (Corporation Estimated Tax) | On the 15th day of the fourth, sixth, ninth and last month of the year | § 6655(c) |
| 8264 | Application for Registration of a Tax Shelter | No later than the day on which an interest in the tax shelter is first offered for sale | Reg. § 301.6111-2; Instructions to Form 8264 |
| 8288 | U.S. Withholding Tax Return for Dispositions by Foreign Persons of U.S. Real Property Interests | By the 20th day after the date of the transfer | Reg. § 1.1445-1(c), -5(b)(5) |
| 8300 | Report of Cash Payments Over $10,000 Received in a Trade or Business | By the 15th day after the cash was received | Reg. § 1.6050I-1(e) |
| 8329 | Lender's Information Return for Mortgage Credit Certificates (MCCs) | By January 31 following the close of the calendar year in which the lender certified indebtedness loans | Reg. § 1.25-8T(a) |
| 8508 | Request for Waiver from Filing Information Returns Electronically (Forms W-2, W-2G, 1042-S, 1098 Series, 5498 Series, and 8027) | At least 45 days before the due date of the returns for which a waiver is requested | Instructions to Form 8508 |
| 8703 | Annual Certification of a Residential Rental Project | By March 31 after the close of the calendar year for which the certification is made | § 142(d)(7); Instructions to Form 8703 |

| FORM # | FORM TITLE | DUE DATE | AUTHORITY |
|---|---|---|---|
| 8716 | Election to Have a Tax Year Other Than a Required Tax Year | By the 15th day of the fifth month following the month that includes the first day of the taxable year for which the election will first be effective; or the due date (without regard to extensions) of the income tax return resulting from the § 444 election | Reg. § 1.444-3T(b) |
| 8804 | Annual Return for Partnership Withholding Tax (Section 1446) | By the 15th day of the fourth month following the close of the partnership's tax year (15th day of the 6 month for partnership's that keep their books and records outside of the United States or Puerto Rico | Reg. § 1.6031(a)-1(e) |
| 8805 | Foreign Partner's Information Statement of Section 1446 Withholding Tax | By the 15th day of the fourth month following the close of the partnership's tax year (15th day of the 6 month for partnership's that keep their books and records outside of the United States or Puerto Rico | Reg. § 1.6031(a)-1(e) |
| 8842 | Election to Different Annualization Periods for Corporate Estimated Tax | By the 15th day of the fourth month of the tax year for which the election is to apply | § 6655(e)(2)(C)(iii); Reg. § 1.6655(e)-1(b) |
| 8857 | Request for Innocent Spouse Relief | As soon as you become aware of a tax liability you believe only your spouse or former spouse should be held responsible; but in no case later than 2 years after the first IRS attempt to collect the tax from you that occurs after July 22, 1998; for taxpayers in a community property state, no later than 6 months before the expiration of the statute of limitations on assessment against your spouse or former spouse for the tax year for which relief is requested | § 6015(b), § 66(c); Reg. § 1.6015-5(b)(1); Reg. § 1.66-4(j)(2) |

## Guide to Common Returns/Forms

| FORM # | FORM TITLE | DUE DATE | AUTHORITY |
|---|---|---|---|
| 8870 | Information Return for Transfers Associated With Certain Personal Benefit Contracts | By the 15th day of the 5th month after the end of the charitable organization's tax year; for charitable remainder trusts, by April 15th of the year following the calendar year the premiums are paid | § 170(f)(10)(F)(iii); Reg. § 1.6033-2(e) |
| 8872 | Political Organization Report of Contributions and Expenditures | Vary depending on whether the form is due for a reporting period that occurs during an even-numbered year or an odd-numbered year | See Instructions to Form 8872 for details |
| 8892 | Application for Automatic Extension of Time To File Form 709 and/or Payment of Gift/Generation-Skipping Transfer Tax | If paying gift tax, by the due date of the Form 709, usually April 15 | Instructions to Form 8892 |

## 21. Guide to Information Returns

| Form | Title | What To Report | Amounts To Report | Due Date * | |
|---|---|---|---|---|---|
| | | | | To IRS | To Recipient (unless indicated otherwise) |
| 1042-S | Foreign Person's U.S. Source Income Subject to Withholding | Payments subject to withholding under Chapter 3 of the Code, including interest, dividends, royalties, pensions and annuities, gambling winnings, compensation for personal services, and distributions by publicly traded partnerships of income effectively connected with the conduct of a U.S. trade or business. | All amounts, except $10 or more for interest on U.S. deposits paid to Canadian nonresident aliens | March 15 | March 15 |
| 1097-BTC | Bond Tax Credit | Tax credit bond credits to shareholders. | All amounts | February 28, or, if filed electronically, March 31 | On or before the 15th day of the 2nd calendar month after the close of the calendar quarter (on or before May 15; August 15; November 15; February 15 of the following year) |

| Form | Title | What To Report | Amounts To Report | Due Date * | |
|------|-------|----------------|-------------------|------------|---|
| | | | | To IRS | To Recipient (unless indicated otherwise) |
| 1098 | Mortgage Interest Statement | Mortgage interest (including points) and certain mortgage insurance premiums you received in the course of your trade or business from individuals and reimbursements of overpaid interest. | $600 or more | February 28 or, if filed electronically, March 31 | (To Payer/ Borrower) January 31 |
| 1098-C | Contributions of Motor Vehicles, Boats, and Airplanes | Information regarding a donated motor vehicle, boat, or airplane. | Gross proceeds of more than $500 | February 28 or, if filed electronically, March 31 | |
| 1098-E | Student Loan Interest Statement | Student loan interest received in the course of your trade or business. | $600 or more | February 28 or, if filed electronically, March 31 | January 31 |
| 1098-T | Tuition Statement | Qualified tuition and related expenses, reimbursements or refunds, and scholarships or grants (optional). | See instructions | February 28 or, if filed electronically, March 31 | January 31 |
| 1099-A | Acquisition or Abandonment of Secured Property | Information about the acquisition or abandonment of property that is security for a debt for which you are the lender. | All amounts | February 28 or, if filed electronically, March 31 | (To Borrower) January 31 |
| 1099-B | Proceeds From Broker and Barter Exchange Transactions | Sales or redemptions of securities, futures transactions, commodities, and barter exchange transactions. | All amounts | February 28 or, if filed electronically, March 31 | January 31 or, March 15 for reporting by trustees and middlemen of WHFITs |

# Guide to Information Returns

| Form | Title | What To Report | Amounts To Report | Due Date * | |
|------|-------|----------------|-------------------|------------|--|
| | | | | To IRS | To Recipient (unless indicated otherwise) |
| 1099-C | Cancellation of Debt | Cancellation of a debt owed to a financial institution, the Federal Government, a credit union, RTC, FDIC, NCUA, a military department, the U.S. Postal Service, the Postal Rate Commission, or any organization having a significant trade or business of lending money. | $600 or more | February 28 or, if filed electronically, March 31 | January 31 |
| 1099-CAP | Changes in Corporate Control and Capital Structure | Information about cash, stock, or other property from an acquisition of control or the substantial change in capital structure of a corporation. | Amounts of stock or property valued at $100 million or more | February 28 or, if filed electronically, March 31 | (To Shareholders) January 31 |
| 1099-DIV | Dividends and Distributions | Distributions, such as dividends, capital gain distributions, or nontaxable distributions, that were paid on stock and liquidation distributions. | $10 or more, except $600 or more for liquidations | February 28 or, if filed electronically, March 31 | January 31 or March 15 for reporting by trustees and middlemen of WHFITs |
| 1099-G | Certain Government Payments | Unemployment compensation, state and local income tax refunds, agricultural payments, and taxable grants. | $10 or more for refunds and unemployment | February 28 or, if filed electronically, March 31 | January 31 |
| 1099-H | Health Coverage Tax Credit (HCTC) Advance Payments | Health insurance premiums paid on behalf of certain individuals. | All amounts | February 28 or, if filed electronically, March 31 | January 31 |

| Form | Title | What To Report | Amounts To Report | Due Date * | |
|------|-------|----------------|-------------------|------------|---|
| | | | | To IRS | To Recipient (unless indicated otherwise) |
| 1099-INT | Interest Income | Interest income. | $10 or more ($600 or more in some cases) | February 28 or, if filed electronically, March 31 | January 31 or March 15 for reporting by trustees and middlemen of WHFITs |
| 1099-K | Merchant Card and Third-Party Network Payments | Merchant card and third-party network payments. | All amounts (for merchant cards); $20,000 or more (and 200 or more transactions (for third-party network payments) | February 28 or, if filed electronically, March 31 | January 31 |
| 1099-LTC | Long-Term Care and Accelerated Death Benefits | Payments under a long-term care insurance contract and accelerated death benefits paid under a life insurance contract or by a viatical settlement provider. | All amounts | February 28 or, if filed electronically, March 31 | January 31 |
| 1099-MISC | Miscellaneous Income | • Rent or royalty payments; prizes and awards that are not for services, such as winnings on TV or radio shows. | $600 or more, except $10 or more for royalties | February 28 or, if filed electronically, March 31 | January 31 or, March 15 for reporting by trustees and middlemen of WHFITs |

# Guide to Information Returns

| Form | Title | What To Report | Amounts To Report | To IRS | To Recipient (unless indicated otherwise) |
|------|-------|----------------|-------------------|--------|--------------------------------------------|
| | | | | Due Date * | |
| | (Also use to report direct sales of $5,000 or more of consumer goods for resale) | • Payments to crew members by owners or operators of fishing boats including payments of proceeds from sale of catch. | All amounts | | |
| | | • Section 409A deferrals and income from nonqualified deferred compensation plans. | All amounts ($600 or more if deferrals) | | |
| | | • Payments to a physician, physicians' corporation, or other supplier or health and medical services. Issued mainly by medical assistance programs or health and accident insurance plans. | $600 or more | | |
| | | • Payments for services performed for a trade or business by people not treated as its employees. Examples: fees to subcontractors or directors and golden parachute payments. | $600 or more | | |
| | | • Fish purchases paid in cash for resale. | $600 or more | | |
| | | • Substitute dividends and tax-exempt interest payments reportable by brokers. | $10 or more | | |
| | | • Crop insurance proceeds. | $600 or more | | |
| | | • Gross proceeds paid to attorneys. | $600 or more | | |

| Form | Title | What To Report | Amounts To Report | Due Date * | |
|------|-------|----------------|-------------------|------------|---|
| | | | | To IRS | To Recipient (unless indicated otherwise) |
| 1099-OID | Original Issue Discount | Original issue discount. | $10 or more | February 28 or, if filed electronically, March 31 | January 31 or, March 15 for reporting by trustees and middlemen of WHFITs |
| 1099-PATR | Taxable Distributions Received From Cooperatives | Distributions from cooperatives to their patrons. | $10 or more | February 28 or, if filed electronically, March 31 | January 31 |
| 1099-Q | Payments from Qualified Education Programs (Under Sections 529 and 530) | Earnings from qualified tuition programs and Coverdell ESAs. | All amounts | February 28 or, if filed electronically, March 31 | January 31 |
| 1099-R | Distributions From Pensions, Annuities, Retirement or Profit-Sharing Plans, IRAs, Insurance Contracts, etc. | Distributions from retirement or profit-sharing plans, any IRA, insurance contracts, and IRA recharacterizations. | $10 or more | February 28 or, if filed electronically, March 31 | January 31 |
| 1099-S | Proceeds From Real Estate Transactions | Gross proceeds from the sale or exchange of real estate and certain royalty payments. | Generally, $600 or more | February 28 or, if filed electronically, March 31 | January 31 |
| 1099-SA | Distributions From an HSA, Archer MSA, or Medicare Advantage MSA | Distributions from an HSA, Archer MSA, or Medicare Advantage MSA. | All amounts | February 28 or, if filed electronically, March 31 | January 31 |

# Guide to Information Returns

| Form | Title | What To Report | Amounts To Report | Due Date * | |
| --- | --- | --- | --- | --- | --- |
| | | | | **To IRS** | **To Recipient** (unless indicated otherwise) |
| 3921 | Exercise of an Incentive Stock Option Under Section 422(b) | Transfer of an employer's stock to an employee pursuant to the exercise of an incentive stock option under section 422(b). | All amounts | February 28 or, if filed electronically, March 31 | January 31 |
| 3922 | Transfer of Stock Acquired Through an Employee Stock Purchase Plan Under Section 423(c) | Transfer(s) of stock acquired through an employee stock purchase plan under section 423(c). | All amounts | February 28 or, if filed electronically, March 31 | January 31 |
| 5471 | Information Return of U.S. Persons With Respect To Certain Foreign Corporations | U.S. persons who are officers, directors, or shareholders in certain foreign corporations report information as required by sections 6038 and 6046 and to report income from controlled foreign corporations under sections 951–965. | See form instructions | Due date of income tax return | None |
| 5472 | Information Return of a 25% Foreign-Owned U.S. Corporation or a Foreign Corporation Engaged in a U.S. Trade or Business | Reportable transactions that occur during the tax year of a reporting corporation with a foreign or domestic related party. | See form instructions | Due date of income tax return | None |

| Form | Title | What To Report | Amounts To Report | Due Date * | |
|------|-------|----------------|-------------------|------------|---|
| | | | | To IRS | To Recipient (unless indicated otherwise) |
| 5498 | IRA Contribution Information | Contributions (including rollover contributions) to any individual retirement arrangement (IRA) including a SEP, SIMPLE, and Roth IRA; Roth conversions; IRA recharacterizations; and the fair market value (FMV) of the account. | All amounts | May 31 | (To Participant) For FMV and required minimum distributions, January 31; for contributions, May 31 |
| 5498-ESA | Coverdell ESA Contribution Information | Contributions (including rollover contributions) to a Coverdell ESA. | All amounts | May 31 | April 30 |
| 5498-SA | HSA, Archer MSA, or Medicare Advantage MSA Information | Contributions to an HSA (including transfers and rollovers) or Archer medical savings account (MSA) and the fair market value of an HSA, Archer MSA, or Medicare Advantage MSA. | All amounts | May 31 | (To Participant) May 31 |
| 8027 | Employer's Annual Information Return of Tip Income and Allocated Tips | Receipts from large food or beverage operations, tips reported by employees, and allocated tips. | See separate instructions | Last day of February or, if filed electronically, March 31 | Allocated tips are shown on Form W-2, due January 31 |

# Guide to Information Returns

| Form | Title | What To Report | Amounts To Report | Due Date * To IRS | Due Date * To Recipient (unless indicated otherwise) |
|---|---|---|---|---|---|
| 8300 (IRS/FinCen form) | Report of Cash Payments Over $10,000 Received in a Trade or Business | Payments in cash (including certain monetary instruments) or foreign currency received in one transaction, or two or more related transactions, in the course of a trade or business. Does not apply to banks and financial institutions filing FinCen Form 104, and casinos that are required to report such transactions on FinCen Form 103, or, generally, to transactions outside the United States. | Over $10,000 | 15 days after date of transaction | (To Payer)<br><br>January 31 |
| 8308 | Report of a Sale or Exchange of Certain Partnership Interests | Sale or exchange of a partnership interest involving unrealized receivables or inventory items under section 751(a). | (Transaction only) | Generally, attach to Form 1065 or 1065-B | (To Transferor and Transferee) January 31 |
| 8935 | Airline Payment Report | Payments of any money or other property made by a commercial passenger airline carrier to a qualified airline employee. | Annual amount(s) paid | Within 90 days of the date of the airline payment(s) to the employee | Within 90 days of the date of the airline payment(s) to the employee |
| W-2G | Certain Gambling Winnings | Gambling winnings from horse racing, dog racing, jai alai, lotteries, keno, bingo, slot machines, sweepstakes, wagering pools, etc. | Generally, $600 or more; $1,200 or more from bingo or slot machines; $1,500 or more from keno | February 28 or, if filed electronically, March 31 | January 31 |

| Form | Title | What To Report | Amounts To Report | Due Date * | |
|---|---|---|---|---|---|
| | | | | To IRS | To Recipient (unless indicated otherwise) |
| 104 (FinCen form) | Currency Transaction Report | Each deposit, withdrawal, exchange of currency, or other payment or transfer by, through, or to financial institutions (other than casinos). | Over $10,000 | 15 days after date of transaction | Not required |
| 926 | Return by a U.S. Transferor of Property to a Foreign Corporation | Certain transfers of tangible and intangible property to a foreign corporation as required by section 6038B. | See form instructions | Attach to tax return | None |
| W-2 | Wage and Tax Statement | Wages, tips, other compensation, social security, Medicare, withheld income taxes; and advance earned income credit (EIC) payments. Include bonuses, vacation allowances, severance pay, certain moving expense payments, some kinds of travel allowances, and third-party payments of sick pay. | See separate instructions | (To SSA) Last day of February or, if filed electronically, March 31 | January 31 |
| TD F 90-22.1 | Report of Foreign Bank and Financial Accounts | Financial interest in or signature or other authority over a foreign bank account, securities account, or other financial account. | Over $10,000 | (To Treasury Dept.) June 30 | None |

* If any date shown falls on a Saturday, Sunday, or legal holiday, the due date is the next business day.

## 22. IRS Forms and Schedules for Claiming/Reporting Credits

| Code section | Credit | Individual (credit not from pass-through entity) | C Corp | Partnership/ S Corp | Trust/ Estate[1], [2] | Taxpayer with credit from pass-through entity[3] only | Cooperative[4] | Taxpayer with credit from cooperative only |
|---|---|---|---|---|---|---|---|---|
| | | IRS Form/ Schedule | IRS Form/ Schedule | IRS Form/ Schedule | IRS Form/ Schedule | IRS Form/ Schedule | IRS Form/ Schedule | IRS Form/ Schedule |
| 21 | Child and Dependent Care | 2441 | n/a | n/a | n/a | n/a | n/a | n/a |
| 22 | Elderly or Disabled | 1040 Sch. R | n/a | n/a | n/a | n/a | n/a | n/a |
| 23 | Adoption | 8839 | n/a | n/a | n/a | n/a | n/a | n/a |
| 24 | Child Tax | 1040 8812 | n/a | n/a | n/a | n/a | n/a | n/a |
| 25 | Mortgage Interest | 8396 | n/a | n/a | n/a | n/a | n/a | n/a |
| 25A | Education | 8863 | n/a | n/a | n/a | n/a | n/a | n/a |
| 25B | Retirement Savings | 8880 | n/a | n/a | n/a | n/a | n/a | n/a |
| 25C | Nonbusiness Energy | 5695 | n/a | n/a | n/a | n/a | n/a | n/a |
| 25D | Residential Energy Property | 5695 | n/a | n/a | n/a | n/a | n/a | n/a |
| 27/901 | Foreign Tax | 1116 | 1118 | Sch K/K-1 | 1116 Sch K-1 | 1116 1118 | 1118 | n/a |
| 27/936 | Possessions Tax | 1116 | 1118 | Sch K/K-1 | 1116 Sch K-1 | 1116 1118 | 1118 | n/a |

[1] Estate or trust whose only source of credit is from pass-through entities may not be required to complete source credit form unless the source credit can be allocated to the beneficiaries.

[2] An estate or non-grantor trust may, under appropriate authority, allocate some or all of a credit to a beneficiary on Sch. K-1. Grantor trusts, because they don't accumulate taxable income, would not claim a credit, but would pass it through, in toto, to the beneficiary.

[3] Partnerships, S Corporations, Estates, Trusts.

[4] Cooperatives with credit passed through from partnership or S corporation may not be required to complete source credit form unless source credit can or must be allocated to patrons. See the instructions for Form 1120-C.

| Code section | Credit | Individual (credit not from pass-through entity) | C Corp | Partnership/ S Corp | Trust/ Estate[1, 2] | Taxpayer with credit from pass-through entity[3] only | Cooperative[4] | Taxpayer with credit from cooperative only |
|---|---|---|---|---|---|---|---|---|
| | | IRS Form/ Schedule | IRS Form/ Schedule | IRS Form/ Schedule | IRS Form/ Schedule | IRS Form/ Schedule | IRS Form/ Schedule | IRS Form/ Schedule |
| 30 | Electric Vehicle | 8834 (non-business) 8834/ 3800 (business) | 8834/ 3800 | 8834 Sch K/K-1 | 8834/ 3800 | 8834/ 3800 | 8834/ 3800 | n/a |
| 30B | Alternative Motor Vehicle | 8910 (non-business) 8910/ 3800 (business) | 8910/ 3800 | 8910 Sch K/K-1 | 8910/ 3800 | 8910/ 3800 | 8910/ 3800 | n/a |
| 30C | Alternative Fuel/Vehicle Refueling | 8911 (non-business) 8911/ 3800 (business) | 8911/ 3800 | 8911 Sch K/K-1 | 8911/ 3800 | 8911/ 3800 | 8910/ 3800 | n/a |
| 30D | Plug-in Electric Vehicle | 8936 (non-business) 8936/ 3800 (business) | 8936/ 3800 | 8936 Sch K/K-1 | 8936/ 3800 | 8936/ 3800 | 8910/ 3800 | n/a |
| 32 | Earned Income | 1040 Sch EIC | n/a | n/a | n/a | n/a | n/a | n/a |
| 34 | Gasoline & Special Fuel | 4136 | 4136 | Sch K-1 | 4136 | 4136 | 4136 | n/a |
| 35 | Health Coverage | 8885 | n/a | n/a | n/a | n/a | n/a | n/a |
| 36 | First-time Homebuyer | 5405 | n/a | n/a | n/a | n/a | n/a | n/a |

# IRS Forms and Schedules for Claiming/Reporting Credits

| Code section | Credit | Individual (credit not from pass-through entity) | C Corp | Partnership/ S Corp | Trust/ Estate[1],[2] | Taxpayer with credit from pass-through entity[3] only | Cooperative[4] | Taxpayer with credit from cooperative only |
|---|---|---|---|---|---|---|---|---|
| | | IRS Form/ Schedule | IRS Form/ Schedule | IRS Form/ Schedule | IRS Form/ Schedule | IRS Form/ Schedule | IRS Form/ Schedule | IRS Form/ Schedule |
| 36A | Making Work Pay/ Government Retiree | 1040 Sch M | n/a | n/a | n/a | n/a | n/a | n/a |
| 36C | Adoption | 8839 | n/a | n/a | n/a | n/a | n/a | n/a |
| 40 | Alcohol/ Cellulosic Biofuel[5] | 6478/ 3800 | 6478/ 3800 | 6478 Sch K/K-1 | 6478/ 3800 Sch K-1 | 6478/ 3800 | 6478/ 3800 1099-PATR | 6478/ 3800 |
| 40A | Biodiesel/ Renewable Diesel[5a] | 8864/ 3800 | 8864/ 3800 | 8864 Sch K/K-1 | 8864/ 3800 Sch K-1 | 8864/ 3800 | 8864/ 3800 1099-PATR | 8864/ 3800 |
| 41 | Research | 6765/ 3800 | 6765/ 3800 | 6765 Sch K/K-1 | 6765/ 3800 Sch K-1 | 3800 only | 6765/ 3800 | n/a |
| 42 | Low-Income Housing | 8586/ 3800 | 8586/ 3800 | 8586 Sch K/K-1 | 8586/ 3800 Sch K-1 | 3800[6] 8586/ 3800[7] | 8586/ 3800 | n/a |
| 43 | Enhanced Oil Recovery | 8830[8] | | | | | | n/a |
| 44 | Disabled Access | 8826/ 3800 | 8826/ 3800 | 8826 Sch K/K-1 | 8826/ 3800 Sch K-1 | 3800 only | 8826/ 3800 | n/a |

[5] Before claiming a credit on Form 6478, the alcohol fuel mixture component of the credit must first be claimed as a § 4081 excise tax credit on Form 720. Any credit in excess of the § 4081 liability can be taken as a claim for payment on Form 8849 or as an income tax credit on Form 4136.

[5a] Before claiming a credit on Form 8864, the biodiesel mixture component of the credit must first be claimed as a § 4081 excise tax credit on Form 720. Any credit in excess of the § 4081 liability can be taken as a claim for payment on Form 8849 or as an income tax credit on Form 4136.

[6] For buildings placed in service before 2008.

[7] For buildings placed in service after 2007.

[8] Credit phased out. IRS has not issued updated forms or instructions.

| Code section | Credit | Individual (credit not from pass-through entity) | C Corp | Partnership/ S Corp | Trust/ Estate[1],[2] | Taxpayer with credit from pass-through entity[3] only | Cooperative[4] | Taxpayer with credit from cooperative only |
|---|---|---|---|---|---|---|---|---|
| | | IRS Form/ Schedule | IRS Form/ Schedule | IRS Form/ Schedule | IRS Form/ Schedule | IRS Form/ Schedule | IRS Form/ Schedule | IRS Form/ Schedule |
| 45 | Renewable Electricity/ Refined Coal/ Indian Coal | 8835/ 3800 | 8835/ 3800 | 8835 Sch K/K-1 | 8835/ 3800 Sch K-1 | 3800 only | 8835/ 3800 1099-PATR | 8835/ 3800 |
| 45A | Indian Employment | 8845/ 3800 | 8845/ 3800 | 8845 Sch K/K-1 | 8835/ 3800 Sch K-1 | 3800 only | 8845/ 3800 1099-PATR | 3800 only |
| 45B | Employer Tip Payments | 8846/ 3800 | 8846/ 3800 | 8846 Sch K/K-1 | 8846/ 3800 Sch K-1 | 3800 only | 8846/ 3800 | n/a |
| 45C | Orphan Drug | 8820/ 3800 | 8820/ 3800 | 8820 Sch K/K-1 | 8820/ 3800 Sch K-1 | 3800 only | 8820/ 3800 | n/a |
| 45D | New Markets | 8874/ 3800 | 8874/ 3800 | 8874 Sch K/K-1 | 8874/ 3800 Sch K-1 | 3800 only | 8874/ 3800 | n/a |
| 45E | Small Employer Pension | 8881/ 3800 | 8881/ 3800 | 8881 Sch K/K-1 | 8881/ 3800 Sch K-1 | 3800 only | 8881/ 3800 | n/a |
| 45F | Employer Child Care | 8882/ 3800 | 8882/ 3800 | 8882 Sch K/K-1 | 8882/ 3800 Sch K-1 | 3800 only | 8882/ 3800 | n/a |
| 45G | Railroad Track Maintenance | 8900/ 3800 | 8900/ 3800 | 8900 Sch K/K-1 | 8900/ 3800 Sch K-1 | 3800 only | 8900/ 3800 | n/a |
| 45H | Low-Sulfur Diesel Fuel | 8896/ 3800 | 8896/ 3800 | 8896 Sch K/K-1 | 8896/ 3800 Sch K-1 | 3800 only | 8896/ 3800 1099-PATR | 3800 only |

# IRS Forms and Schedules for Claiming/Reporting Credits

| Code section | Credit | Individual (credit not from pass-through entity) | C Corp | Partnership/ S Corp | Trust/ Estate[1], [2] | Taxpayer with credit from pass-through entity[3] only | Cooperative[4] | Taxpayer with credit from cooperative only |
|---|---|---|---|---|---|---|---|---|
| | | IRS Form/ Schedule | IRS Form/ Schedule | IRS Form/ Schedule | IRS Form/ Schedule | IRS Form/ Schedule | IRS Form/ Schedule | IRS Form/ Schedule |
| 45I | Marginal Well | [9] | | | | | | |
| 45J | Advanced Nuclear Facility | [10] | | | | | | |
| 45K | Nonconventional Fuels | 8907/ 3800 | 8907/ 3800 | 8907 Sch K/K-1 | 8907/ 3800 Sch K-1 | 3800 only | 8907/ 3800 | n/a |
| 45L | Energy Efficient Home | 8908/ 3800 | 8908/ 3800 | 8908 Sch K/K-1 | 8908/ 3800 Sch K-1 | 3800 only | 8908/ 3800 | n/a |
| 45M | Energy Efficient Appliance | 8909/ 3800 | 8909/ 3800 | 8909 Sch K/K-1 | 8909/ 3800 Sch K-1 | 3800 only | 8909/ 3800 1099-PATR | 3800 only |
| 45N | Mine Rescue Team | 8923/ 3800 | 8923/ 3800 | 8923 Sch K/K-1 | 8923/ 3800 Sch K-1 | 3800 only | 8923/ 3800 | n/a |
| 45O | Agricultural Chemical Security | 8931/ 3800 | 8931/ 3800 | 8931 Sch K/K-1 | 8931/ 3800 Sch K-1 | 3800 only | 8931/ 3800 1099-PATR | 8931/ 3800 |
| 45P | Employer Wage Differential Payment | 8932/ 3800 | 8932/ 3800 | 8932 Sch K/K-1 | 8932/ 3800 Sch K-1 | 3800 only | 8932/ 3800 1099-PATR | 8932/ 3800 |
| 45Q | Carbon Dioxide Sequestration | 8933/ 3800 | 8933/ 3800 | 8933 Sch K/K-1[11] | 8933/ 3800 Sch K-1 | 3800 only | 8933/ 3800 | n/a |

---

[9] Credit phased out. No form issued.

[10] Credit has never gone into effect. IRS has never issued forms or instructions.

[11] Special rules for partnerships with § 761 elections.

| Code section | Credit | Individual (credit not from pass-through entity) | C Corp | Partnership/ S Corp | Trust/ Estate[1], [2] | Taxpayer with credit from pass-through entity[3] only | Cooperative[4] | Taxpayer with credit from cooperative only |
|---|---|---|---|---|---|---|---|---|
| | | IRS Form/ Schedule | IRS Form/ Schedule | IRS Form/ Schedule | IRS Form/ Schedule | IRS Form/ Schedule | IRS Form/ Schedule | IRS Form/ Schedule |
| 45R | Small Employer Health Insurance | 8941/ 3800 | 8941/ 3800 | 8941 Sch K/K-1 | 8941/ 3800 Sch K-1 | 3800 only | 8941/ 3800 | n/a |
| 47 | Rehabilitation | 3468/ 3800 | 3468/ 3800 | 3468 Sch K/K-1 | 3468/ 3800 Sch K-1 | 3468/ 3800 | 3468/ 3800 1099-PATR | 3468/ 3800 |
| 48 | Energy | 3468/ 3800 | 3468/ 3800 | 3468 Sch K/K-1 | 3468/ 3800 Sch K-1 | 3468/ 3800 | 3468/ 3800 1099-PATR | 3468/ 3800 |
| 48A | Advanced Coal Project | 3468/ 3800 | 3468/ 3800 | 3468 Sch K/K-1 | 3468/ 3800 Sch K-1 | 3468/ 3800 | 3468/ 3800 1099-PATR | 3468/ 3800 |
| 48B | Qualified Gasification Project | 3468/ 3800 | 3468/ 3800 | 3468 Sch K/K-1 | 3468/ 3800 Sch K-1 | 3468/ 3800 | 3468/ 3800 1099-PATR | 3468/ 3800 |
| 48C | Advanced Energy Property Project | 3468/ 3800 | 3468/ 3800 | 3468 Sch K/K-1 | 3468/ 3800 Sch K-1 | 3468/ 3800 | 3468/ 3800 1099-PATR | 3468/ 3800 |
| 48D | Therapeutic Discovery Project | 3468/ 3800 | 3468/ 3800 | 3468 Sch K/K-1 | 3468/ 3800 Sch K-1 | 3468/ 3800 | 3468/ 3800 1099-PATR | 3468/ 3800 |
| 51 | Work Opportunity | 5884/ 3800 | 5884/ 3800 | 5884 Sch K/K-1 | 5884/ 3800 Sch K-1 | 5884/ 3800 | 5884/ 3800 1099-PATR | 5884/ 3800 |
| 53 | Prior Year Minimum Tax | 8801 | 8827 | 8827[13] | 8801 | n/a | 8827 | n/a |
| 54 | CREB Bond | 8912 | 8912 | 8912 Sch K/K-1 | 8912 Sch K-1 | 8912 | 8912 | n/a |

---

[13] Applicable for certain S corporations against built-in gain.

# IRS Forms and Schedules for Claiming/Reporting Credits

| Code section | Credit | Individual (credit not from pass-through entity) | C Corp | Partnership/ S Corp | Trust/ Estate[1, 2] | Taxpayer with credit from pass-through entity[3] only | Cooperative[4] | Taxpayer with credit from cooperative only |
|---|---|---|---|---|---|---|---|---|
| | | IRS Form/ Schedule | IRS Form/ Schedule | IRS Form/ Schedule | IRS Form/ Schedule | IRS Form/ Schedule | IRS Form/ Schedule | IRS Form/ Schedule |
| 54A | Tax Credit Bond | 8912 | 8912 | 8912 Sch K/K-1 | 8912 Sch K-1 | 8912 | 8912 | n/a |
| 54AA | Build America Bond | 8912 | 8912 | 8912 Sch K/K-1 | 8912 Sch K-1 | 8912 | 8912 | n/a |
| 1396 | Empowerment Zone | 8844/ 3800 | 8844/ 3800 | 8844 Sch K/K-1 | 8844/ 3800 Sch K-1 | 3800 only | 8844/ 3800 1099-PATR | 8844/ 3800 |
| 1397E | Qualified Zone Academy Bond | n/a | 8912 | 8912 Sch K/K-1 | n/a | 8912 | n/a | n/a |
| 1400C | D.C. First-Time Homebuyer | 8859 | n/a | n/a | n/a | n/a | n/a | n/a |
| 1400N(l) | Gulf/Midwestern Tax Credit Bond | 8912 | 8912 | 8912 | 8912 | 8912 | 8912 | n/a |
| 1400P | Disaster Housing | 5884-A / 3800 | 5884-A /3800 | 5884-A Sch K/K-1 | 5884-A /3800 | 5884-A / 3800 | 5884/ 3800 | 5884/ 3800 |
| 1400R | Disaster Employee Retention | 5884-A / 3800 | 5884-A /3800 | 5884-A Sch K/K-1 | 5884-A /3800 | 5884-A / 3800 | 5884-A /3800 1099-PATR | 5884-A /3800 |
| 5011 | Distilled Spirits | 8906/ 3800 | 8906/ 3800 | 8906 Sch K/K-1 | 8906/ 3800 | 3800 only | 8906/ 3800 | n/a |
| None | Community Development | 8847/ 3800 | 8847/ 3800 | 8847 Sch K/K-1 | 8847/ 3800 Sch K-1 | 3800 only | 8847/ 3800 | n/a |
| None | 2010 New Hire Retention | 5884-B/ 3800 | 5884-B/3800 | 5884-B Sch K/K-1 | 5884-B/3800 Sch K-1 | 5884-B/ 3800 | 5884-B/3800 | n/a |

## 23. Deductions Relevant to Real Estate Transactions

| Code Section | Title |
|---|---|
| § 162 | Trade Or Business Expenses |
| § 163 | Interest |
| § 164 | Taxes |
| § 165 | Losses |
| § 166 | Bad Debts |
| § 167 | Depreciation |
| § 168 | Accelerated Cost Recovery System |
| § 170 | Charitable, Etc., Contributions And Gifts |
| § 172 | Net Operating Loss Deduction |
| § 175 | Soil And Water Conservation Expenditures Endangered Species Recovery Expenditures |
| § 179 | Election To Expense Certain Depreciable Business Assets |
| § 179D | Energy Efficient Commercial Buildings Deduction |
| § 180 | Expenditures By Farmers For Fertilizer, Etc. |
| § 190 | Expenditures To Remove Architectural And Transportation Barriers To The Handicapped And Elderly |
| § 194 | Treatment Of Reforestation Expenditures |
| § 195 | Start-Up Expenditures |
| § 197 | Amortization Of Goodwill And Certain Other Intangibles |
| § 212 | Expenses For Production Of Income |
| § 263 | Capital Expenditures |
| § 263A | Capitalization And Inclusion In Inventory Costs Of Certain Expenses |
| § 1400I | Commercial Revitalization Deduction |
| § 1400L | Tax Benefits For New York Liberty Zone |
| § 1400N | Tax Benefits For Gulf Opportunity Zone |

# CHAPTER I. GROSS INCOME

# >>>>>>>>>>>>>>>>>>>>>>>>>>>>>>>

## I.A. Introduction to Gross Income

In broad terms, there are several steps required to determine the income tax liability of a taxpayer. The gross income of the taxpayer must be determined. Deductions allowable to the taxpayer must be identified. The taxable income of the taxpayer is computed by subtracting the allowable deductions from gross income. The income tax of the taxpayer is then computed by applying specified tax rates to the taxpayer's taxable income. After the taxpayer's income tax has been computed, it may be reduced by any tax credits available to the taxpayer.

Accordingly, the determination of a taxpayer's gross income is an important first step in determining income tax liability. The Internal Revenue Code provides that gross income generally includes income from whatever source derived [§ 61(a)]. The Supreme Court has interpreted this definition of gross income to include all items of income that are clearly realized accessions to wealth [*Commissioner v. Glenshaw Glass Co.*, 348 U.S. 426 (1955)]. Although judicial decisions have addressed the application of the accession-to-wealth concept to most of the more common transactions and many arcane transactions, the application of the concept is not always straightforward. Therefore, Congress has provided numerous statutory provisions under which certain items are included in gross income and others are excluded from gross income.

The Code provides that gross income includes, but is not limited to, the following items: (i) compensation for services (see I.C.), (ii) income derived from business (see I.H.), (iii) gains derived from property transactions (see I.I.), (iv) interest (see I.D.), (v) dividends (see I.E.), (vi) rents (see I.F.1.), (vii) royalties (see I.F.2.), (viii) alimony (see I.G.), (ix) pensions (see I.C.6.), (x) annuities (see I.M.3.), (xi) income from life insurance and endowment contracts (see I.M.2.), (xii) income from the discharge of indebtedness (see I.L.), (xiii) a distributive share of partnership income (see XIV.D.2.), (xiv) income from an interest in an estate or trust (see XVIII.F.), and (xiv) income in respect of a decedent (see Chapter XVIII.) [§ 61(a)].

This chapter discusses some of the more common items that are included in gross income. Chapter II discusses items that are excluded from gross income.

1

## I.B. Special Rules for Determining Gross Income

### I.B.1. Assignment of Income Doctrine

[502 T.M., IV.; ¶1020.]

The assignment of income doctrine was developed by the courts to address the issue of which taxpayer is required to include an income item in gross income. This issue often arises when a taxpayer attempts to minimize taxes by making a gratuitous transfer of income to a related person in a lower tax bracket or to a tax-exempt charitable organization. Under the assignment of income doctrine, income from personal services generally must be included in the gross income of the taxpayer who renders the services, and income from property transactions generally must be included in the gross income of the taxpayer who beneficially owns the property [*Lucas v. Earl*, 281 U.S. 111 (1930)].

---

**EXAMPLE:** Margaret owns stock in Corporation X. Margaret gave her son the right to receive dividends for the next two years. The corporation agreed to make dividend checks payable to her son. Margaret accomplished a legally effective transfer under state law. Because she failed to part with the stock as well as the dividends, Margaret must pay tax on the dividends received by her son from stock that she continues to own.

---

Special rules apply to the income of certain spouses who live in community property states (see I.B.2.) and the income of certain children (see I.B.3.).

### I.B.2. Income of Spouses Who Live in Community Property States

[515 T.M., XI.; TPS ¶3310.05.]

When spouses live in a community property state (Arizona, California, Idaho, Louisiana, Nevada, New Mexico, Texas, Washington, and Wisconsin) and file separate federal returns, special rules apply in determining which spouse is required to include an income item in gross income. Spouses (including same-sex spouses) residing in community property states are each liable for tax on one-half of the community income. Thus, each spouse must report one-half of the community income on his or her separate return [*United States. v. Mitchell*, 403 U.S. 190 (1971)]. These rules also generally apply to registered domestic partners residing in California, Nevada, and Washington.

The laws of the state in which the spouses live govern whether they have community property and community income or separate property and separate income for federal tax purposes. The following discussion summarizes the general rules.

Community income generally includes (i) income from community property, (ii) income from real estate that is treated as community property under the laws of the state where the property is located, and (iii) salaries, wages, net profits from a sole proprietorship, and other amounts received for services performed by either spouse while residing in a community property state. Community property generally includes (i) property acquired by the spouses while residing in a community property state, (ii) property the spouses agree to convert from separate property to community property, and (iii) property that cannot be identified as separate property.

Separate property generally includes (i) property that a spouse owned separately before the marriage, (ii) money earned while residing in a noncommunity property state, (iii) property a spouse receives separately as a gift or inheritance, (iv) property the spouses agree to convert from community property to separate property through an agreement valid under state law, and (v) any portion of a property bought with separate funds rather than community funds. Generally, income from separate property is treated as the separate income of the spouse who owns the property. However, in Idaho, Louisiana, Texas, and Wisconsin, income from most separate property is treated as community income.

Special rules apply for reporting community income when spouses live apart or when one spouse is a nonresident alien. The special rules apply to spouses who live apart if (i) they live apart at all times during the calendar year, (ii) they do not file a joint return for a tax year beginning or ending during the calendar year, (iii) they had earned income that is community income during the calendar year, and (iv) neither spouse transfers any of such earned income to the other before the end of the calendar year [§ 66(a)]. The special rules apply when one spouse is a nonresident alien as long as the other spouse does not elect to treat that nonresident alien spouse as a U.S. resident for federal income tax purposes. When these requirements are met, the following rules apply for reporting community income [§ 66(a), § 879(a)]:

1. income or loss from a trade or business carried on by a partnership is treated as the income or loss of the spouse who is the partner;

2. income or loss from any other trade or business is treated as the income or loss of the spouse carrying on the trade or business;

3. other earned income (including wages, salaries, professional fees, and pay for other personal services) is treated as the income of the spouse who performed the services and earned the income;

4. social security and equivalent railroad retirement benefits are treated as the income of the spouse who receives the benefits;

5. income from the separate property of one spouse is treated as the income of that spouse; and

6. all other community income is treated according to the normal community property rules.

A taxpayer is not responsible for the tax relating to an item of community income properly includible in his or her gross income if all of the following requirements are met [§ 66(c)]:

1. the taxpayer did not file a joint return for the tax year;

2. the taxpayer did not include the item of community income in gross income and that item would be treated as the income of the other spouse under the special rules discussed above;

3. the taxpayer establishes that he or she did not know of, and had no reason to know of, that item of community income; and

4. under all facts and circumstances, it would not be fair to include that item of community income in the taxpayer's gross income.

The IRS may disallow the benefits of the community property laws for an item of community income if a taxpayer treats the item as if only he or she is entitled to the income and the taxpayer does not notify his or her spouse of the nature and amount of the income by the due date (including extensions) for filing the return [§ 66(b)].

### I.B.3. Income of Children

[502 T.M., IV.C.7.; TPS ¶3310.03.F.5.]

Amounts received from the performance of services by a child are included in the gross income of the child, even if such amounts are received by the child's parents instead of the child [§ 73(a)]. However, a parent may elect to include his or her child's income on his or her return if all of the following requirements are met [§ 1(g)(7)]:

1. the child has income only from interest and dividends (including capital gain distributions and Alaska Permanent Fund dividends);
2. the child's gross income is more than $1,000 for 2014 ($1,050 for 2015) but less than $10,000 for 2014 ($10,500 for 2015) [Rev. Proc. 2013-35, 2013-47 I.R.B. 537, Rev. Proc. 2014-61, 2014-47 I.R.B. 860];
3. the child was under age 19 (under age 24 if a full-time student) at the end of the tax year;
4. the child is otherwise required to file a return;
5. the child does not file a joint return for the year;
6. no federal income tax was taken out of the child's income under the backup withholding rules;
7. no estimated tax payment was made (and no overpayment credit from a previous year was applied) under the child's name and social security number; and
8. the parent is eligible to make the election.

The following rules apply in determining whether a parent is eligible to make the election:

- If the child's parents are married to each other and file a joint return, the parents may make the election jointly.
- If the child's parents are married to each other and file separate returns, the eligible parent depends on whether or not the parents live together. If they live together, the parent with the greater taxable income is eligible to make the election. If they do not live together, the eligible parent depends on whether the custodial parent (the parent with whom the child lives for the greater part of the year) is considered married or unmarried for federal tax purposes. If the custodial parent is considered married, the custodial parent is eligible to make the election. If the custodial parent is considered unmarried, the parent with the greater taxable income is eligible to make the election.
- If the child's parents are divorced or legally separated, the eligible parent depends on whether or not the custodial parent has remarried. If the custodial parent has not remarried, the custodial parent is eligible to make the election. If the custodial parent has remarried, the stepparent (the new spouse of the custodial parent) is treated as the child's other parent and the rules discussed above are applied to the custodial parent and stepparent.
- If the child's parents were never married to each other, the eligible parent depends on whether the parents lived together all year. If they lived together all year, the parent with the greater taxable income is eligible to make the election. If they did not live together all year, the rules discussed above for divorced or separated parents apply.
- If one of the child's parents is deceased and the surviving parent remarries, the new spouse of the surviving parent is treated as the child's other parent for purposes of these rules.

The election is made by completing Form 8814, *Parent's Election To Report Child's Interest and Dividends,* and attaching it to the parent's timely filed return. A separate Form 8814 must be filed for each child whose income the parent elects to report on his or her return. If a parent makes the election to include a child's income on his or her return, the child is not required to file a return.

If a child has more than $2,000 for 2014 ($2,100 for 2015) in interest, dividends, and other unearned income, and the income is not or cannot be reported on a parent's return by filing Form 8814, part of that income may be taxed to the child at the parent's tax rate instead of the child's tax rate. See X.A.3. for a discussion of this so-called "kiddie tax."

### I.B.4. Income from Jointly Owned Property

[502 T.M., IV.B.2.c(2); TPS ¶1020.03.A.]

When two or more taxpayers jointly own property as joint tenants or tenants in common, the income from the property is allocated between the joint owners according to state law, as long as the joint ownership is not lacking in economic substance. Thus, for example, when two or more taxpayers acquire property through a proportionate contribution of capital, the income from the jointly owned property is generally allocated between the taxpayers in proportion to their ownership interests.

When spouses hold property as tenants by the entirety under state law, the income from the property is allocated between the spouses according to state law. If the spouses are entitled to equal shares of the income from the property under state law, then each spouse generally must include one-half of the income in his or her gross income for federal income tax purposes. On the other hand, if all the income from the property belongs to one spouse under state law, then that spouse generally must include all the income in his or her gross income for federal income tax purposes.

### I.B.5. Claim of Right Doctrine

[502 T.M., III.; TPS ¶1030.]

The claim of right doctrine was developed by the courts to address the issue of the proper tax year for reporting an item of income that a taxpayer received but may be required to repay. Under the claim of right doctrine, an item of income received under a bona fide claim of right without restrictions on its use must be included in gross income in the year of receipt, despite any potential repayment obligation [*N. Am. Oil Consol. v. Burnet*, 286 U.S. 417 (1932)]. If a taxpayer is required to repay such an item in a later year, the taxpayer may claim a deduction for the item in that year (see VII.K.). Because such a deduction is claimed in a year that is different from the year in which the item was included in gross income, the tax benefit produced by the deduction may potentially be smaller than the tax burden created by the income inclusion. A special provision applies to mitigate such an inequity if (i) the item was included in gross income in the prior tax year because it appeared the taxpayer had an unrestricted right to the item, (ii) a deduction is allowable for the current tax year because it has been established that the taxpayer did not have an unrestricted right to the item, and (iii) the amount of that deduction is more than $3,000. If the mitigation provision applies, the taxpayer's tax liability for the repayment year is treated as the lesser of (i) the tax liability for the repayment year as determined without the deduction, or (ii) the tax liability for the repayment year as determined without the deduction, minus the amount by which the tax liability for the income inclusion year would have been reduced if the income item had not been included in gross income in that year [§ 1341(a)].

### I.B.6. Tax Benefit Rule and Recoveries

[502 T.M., II.; TPS ¶1050.]

The tax benefit rule addresses the situation in which a taxpayer deducts an amount in one tax year and then recovers the amount in a later tax year. Under the tax benefit rule, the recovery of an amount deducted in a prior tax year is not included in gross income to the extent that the amount did not reduce the taxpayer's tax liability in the year it was deducted [§ 111(a)]. On the other hand, a recovery must be included in gross income to the extent the deduction resulted in a tax benefit in the year it was deducted. Similar rules apply to recoveries associated with tax credits (other than the investment tax credit and the foreign tax credit) [§ 111(b)].

*State or Local Income Tax Refunds.* The most common type of recovery is an income tax refund. A federal income tax refund is never included in gross income because federal income taxes are not deductible. A state or local income tax refund, on the other hand, generally must be included in gross income if the taxpayer deducted the associated tax in an earlier tax year. However, a state or local income tax refund is not included in gross income if, in the year the taxpayer paid the tax, the taxpayer did not itemize deductions or the taxpayer elected to deduct state or local general sales taxes instead of state or local income taxes. A taxpayer generally can use the State and Local Income Tax Refund Worksheet (Source: 2014 Form 1040 Draft Instructions) to determine the amount of a state or local tax refund that must be included in gross income.

2014 Form 1040—Lines 10 Through 13

**State and Local Income Tax Refund Worksheet—Line 10**     *Keep for Your Records*

| | |
|---|---|
| **Before you begin:** | ✓ Be sure you have read the **Exception** in the instructions for this line to see if you can use this worksheet instead of Pub. 525 to figure if any of your refund is taxable. |

1. Enter the income tax refund from **Form(s) 1099-G** (or similar statement). But **do not** enter more than the amount of your state and local income taxes shown on your 2013 Schedule A, line 5 ............ 1. _____

2. Enter your total itemized deductions from your 2013 Schedule A, line 29 ......... 2. _____

**Note.** If the filing status on your 2013 Form 1040 was married filing separately and your spouse itemized deductions in 2013, skip lines 3 through 5, enter the amount from line 2 on line 6, and go to line 7.

3. Enter the amount shown below for the filing status claimed on your **2013** Form 1040.

   • Single or married filing separately—$6,100
   • Married filing jointly or qualifying widow(er)—$12,200
   • Head of household—$8,950     } 3. _____

4. Did you fill in line 39a on your 2013 Form 1040?

   ☐ **No.**  Enter -0-.
   ☐ **Yes.**  Multiply the number in the box on line 39a of your 2013 Form 1040 by $1,200 ($1,500 if your 2013 filing status was single or head of household).     } 4. _____

5. Add lines 3 and 4 ....................................................... 5. _____

6. Is the amount on line 5 less than the amount on line 2?

   ☐ **No.** (STOP)  None of your refund is taxable.
   ☐ **Yes.**  Subtract line 5 from line 2 ........................................ 6. _____

7. **Taxable part of your refund.** Enter the **smaller** of line 1 or line 6 here and on Form 1040, line 10 ................................................................. 7. _____

**EXAMPLE:** In Year 1, Laura claimed the standard deduction on her return. In Year 2, Laura receives a refund of her Year 1 state income tax. Laura does not include any of the state income tax refund in her gross income for Year 2 because she did not itemize her deductions in Year 1.

**EXAMPLE:** In Year 1, Steve itemized his deductions and chose to deduct state general sales tax instead of state income tax. In Year 2, Steve receives a refund of his Year 1 state income tax. Steve does not include any of the state income tax refund in his gross income for Year 2 because he did not deduct his state income tax in Year 1.

If a taxpayer itemized his deductions and elected to deduct state or local income taxes instead of state or local general sales taxes before 2014, the amount of any state or local income tax refund included in gross income is limited to the amount by which the state or local income tax deduction he or she took exceeded the state or local general sales tax deduction he or she could have taken. The deduction for state or local general sales taxes expired December 31, 2013.

**EXAMPLE:** In Year 1, Alex itemized his deductions and elected to take an $11,000 state income tax deduction instead of a $10,000 state general sales tax deduction. In Year 2, Alex receives a $2,500 state income tax refund. The maximum amount of the refund Alex may have to include in gross income for Year 2 is $1,000 ($11,000 − $10,000).

*Itemized Deduction Recoveries.* Generally, if a taxpayer recovers an itemized deduction that he claimed in an earlier tax year, he must include the full amount of the recovery in gross income in the year received if all of the following conditions apply for the year of the deduction: (i) he or she had taxable income, (ii) his or her itemized deductions were not subject to the limitation on itemized deductions, (iii) his or her itemized deductions exceeded his or her standard deduction by at least the amount of the recovery, (iv) his or her deduction for the item recovered was greater than or equal to the amount of the recovery, (v) he or she had no unused tax credits, and (vi) he or she was not subject to alternative minimum tax (AMT). If one or more of these conditions does not apply, the taxpayer may be able to exclude at least part of the recovery from gross income.

*Non-Itemized Deduction Recoveries.* If a taxpayer recovers a non-itemized deduction (e.g., he or she receives a payment on a previously deducted bad debt), he or she generally must include the full amount of the recovery in gross income in the year received. However, if any part of the deduction did not reduce his or her tax, the recovery is included in gross income only to the extent that it reduced his or her tax in the year of the deduction.

### I.B.7. Bargain Purchase Rule

[501 T.M., VIII.B.1.h.; TPS ¶5410.04.]

Employees, independent contractors, and other service providers are sometimes offered the opportunity to purchase property from the service recipient (e.g., the employer) at less than fair market value. The difference between the property's fair market value and the bargain purchase price paid for the property is generally treated as compensation for services and included in gross income at the time of the transfer [§ 83(a); Reg. § 1.61-2(d)(2)(i)]. An employee can exclude a bargain purchase from gross income if it is a qualified employee discount. See XVII.D.2. for a discussion of qualified employee discounts.

### I.B.8. Bartering Transactions

[501 T.M., VIII.B.1.h(2); TPS ¶5410.05.D.1.]

When two taxpayers barter with each other and exchange property or services, they are generally required to include in gross income the fair market value of the property or services received in the bartering transaction. If a bartering transaction involves an exchange of services, the value that the taxpayers assign to the services will generally be accepted as the fair market value of those services, unless there is evidence to the contrary. Bartering income is generally reported on Schedule C of Form 1040.

---

**EXAMPLE:** Al, an accountant, agrees to provide accounting services to Bill, a housepainter, in exchange for the painting of his house by Bill. Al and Bill must each include in gross income the fair market value of the services provided by the other.

---

## I.C. Compensation

### I.C.1. General Rules on Compensation

[501 T.M.; TPS ¶1110.]

Compensation for services is generally included in the gross income of the recipient, whether paid in cash or property [§ 61(a)(1); Reg. § 1.61-2]. Special rules apply to compensation paid in the form of property (see I.C.2.). Compensation for services is reported by employers to employees on Form W-2, *Wage and Tax Statement*. Compensation for services is generally reported by service recipients to independent contractors and other service providers on Form 1099-MISC.

Compensation can take many forms including, but not limited to, wages, salaries, tips (see I.C.3.), commissions, bonuses (see I.C.7.), and severance pay [Reg. § 1.61-2(a)(1)]. The value of fringe benefits provided by an employer must be included in gross income, unless specifically excluded (see I.C.4.). The value of certain life insurance coverage provided by an employer also must be included in gross income (see I.C.5.). Deferred compensation and retirement pay are also generally includible in gross income (see I.C.6.).

Excessive payments for salaries and other compensation are included in the gross income of an employee even if the employer is denied a deduction for such payments because they are considered unreasonable compensation. If such excessive payments are made to a shareholder-employee, they may be taxable as dividends rather than compensation (see I.E.1.). If such excessive payments are determined to be payments for property rather than compensation, they are treated as part of the purchase price of the property and taxable to the extent of any gain [Reg. § 1.162-8].

### I.C.2. Noncash Compensation

[501 T.M., VIII.; TPS ¶1110.02.]

If a taxpayer receives property as compensation for services, the fair market value of the property (less any amount paid for the property) generally must be included in gross income in the year the property is received. However, if the property has restrictions that affect its value, no amount is included in gross income until the year in which the taxpayer's rights in the property become substantially vested [§ 83(a); Reg. § 1.83-1(a)(1)].

A taxpayer's rights in property become substantially vested when those rights are either (i) transferable, or (ii) not subject to a substantial risk of forfeiture [§ 83(a); Reg. § 1.83-3(b)]. A substantial risk of forfeiture exists if the taxpayer's rights in the property are conditioned upon the future performance of substantial services or upon the occurrence of a event related to a purpose for the transfer of the property and, if that condition is not satisfied, the possibility of forfeiture is substantial [§ 83(c)(1); Reg. § 1.83-3(c)]. A taxpayer's rights in property are transferable if they can be sold, assigned, or pledged to another person (other than the transferor of the property) and that person's rights in the property are not subject to a substantial risk of forfeiture (i.e., that person is not required to give up the property or its value if a forfeiture by the taxpayer occurs) [§ 83(c)(2); Reg. § 1.83-3(a)].

---

**EXAMPLE:** XYZ Corporation transfers 100 shares of stock to John as compensation for his services as an employee. The stock has a fair market value of $100 per share at the time of the transfer and John pays $10 per share for the stock. Under the terms of the transfer, John must resell the stock to XYZ for $10 per share if he leaves his job within three years of the date of the transfer. John's rights in the stock are subject to a substantial risk of forfeiture because he must perform substantial services for XYZ over a specified period of time and, if he does not, he must sell the stock back to XYZ at the price he paid for it (regardless of its value at that time). John's rights in the stock are not substantially vested in the year he buys it and, therefore, he does not include any amount in gross income for that year. John continues to work for XYZ for three years and the fair market value of the stock at the end of the three-year period is $200 per share. John must include $19,000 (100 shares × ($200 − $10)) in gross income after the three-year work condition is satisfied and his rights in the stock become substantially vested.

---

A taxpayer whose rights in property are not substantially vested at the time it is transferred to him or her may elect to include the fair market value of the property (less any amount paid for the property) in gross income for the year it is transferred to him or her by filing a written statement with the IRS within 30 days of the date of transfer. Once made, the election may be revoked only with IRS consent [§ 83(b)]. An advantage of making the election is that the taxpayer does not treat any subsequent appreciation of the property as compensation when the taxpayer's rights in the property become substantially vested. Instead, the taxpayer takes a basis in the property equal to the amount of compensation included in gross income in the year of the transfer (plus any amount paid for the property), and any gain from appreciation that occurs after the date of transfer is not recognized until the taxpayer disposes of the property [§ 83(b)(1)].

See XVII.B. for further discussion of the taxation of noncash compensation, including the taxation of stock options.

### I.C.3. Tips

[501 T.M., VIII.B.1.c.; TPS ¶1110.01.C.3.]

A taxpayer must include all tips received in gross income, including tips received directly, charged tips received from an employer, tips received under a tip-splitting or tip-pooling arrangement, and the value of noncash tips [Reg. § 1.61-2(a)(1)]. Taxpayers are required to keep a daily tip record, to report tips to their employers on a monthly basis, and to report tips on their federal income tax returns. The daily tip record can be kept by writing information in a tip diary (Form 4070A, *Employee's*

*Daily Record of Tips*, may be used for this purpose) or by retaining documents such as restaurant bills and charge slips. Tips may be reported to an employer on Form 4070, *Employee's Report of Tips to Employer*, or a statement containing similar information (note that there is a penalty for the failure to report tips to an employer). All tips received during the tax year must be reported with the taxpayer's wages on Form 1040. The tips reported to an employer during the year are included in the wages shown in box 1 of the Form W-2 received from the employer. Any tips not reported to an employer must also be reported as wages on Form 1040.

### I.C.4. Fringe Benefits

#### I.C.4.a. General Rule for Fringe Benefits

[501 T.M., VIII.C.; TPS ¶1110.05.B.]

Unless excluded under one of the many statutory exclusion provisions, the value of a fringe benefit received by an employee from an employer must be included in the employee's gross income [§ 61(a)(1); Reg. § 1.61-21]. A fringe benefit is a benefit other than salary, wages, and similar direct compensation that is provided in connection with the performance of services [Reg. § 1.61-21(a)(3)].

#### I.C.4.b. Excluded Fringe Benefits

[501 T.M., VIII.C.; TPS ¶1110.05.B.]

Many types of fringe benefits are statutorily excluded from gross income. The general categories of fringe benefits excluded from gross income are (i) no-additional-cost services, (ii) qualified employee discounts, (iii) working condition fringe benefits, (iv) de minimis fringe benefits, (v) qualified transportation fringe benefits, (vi) qualified moving expense reimbursements, and (vii) qualified retirement planning services [§ 132]. Specific types of fringe benefits statutorily excluded from gross income include (i) accident or health plan coverage provided to an employee [§ 106], (ii) qualified tuition reductions provided to an employee [§ 117(d)], (iii) meals or lodging furnished to an employee for the convenience of the employer [§ 119], (iv) benefits provided to an employee under a cafeteria plan [§ 125], (v) educational assistance provided to an employee [§ 127], (vi) dependent care assistance provided to an employee [§ 129], and (vii) adoption assistance provided to an employee [§ 137]. See XVII.D. and XVII.E. for a detailed discussion of the fringe benefits that are excluded from gross income.

#### I.C.4.c. Valuation of Fringe Benefits

[519 T.M., V.C.; TPS ¶5980.03.]

Generally, the amount of any fringe benefit included in gross income is equal to the amount by which the fair market value of the fringe benefit exceeds the sum of (i) the amount, if any, paid for the fringe benefit, and (ii) the amount, if any, of the fringe benefit that is specifically excluded from gross income [Reg. § 1.61-21(b)(1)]. However, there are special valuation rules that apply to certain types of fringe benefits, such as the personal use of employer-provided vehicles and personal flights on employer-provided aircraft. If one of the special valuation rules is used, it is determinative of the value of the benefit for both income and employment tax purposes.

An employer may choose to use any special valuation rule that applies. If an employer chooses to use a special valuation rule, its employees have the option of using either that special valuation rule or the general valuation rule. However, with one exception, an employee may not choose to use a special valuation rule that is not used by his employer. Under the exception, an employee may choose to use a special valuation rule not used by his employer if the employer failed to report the value of the benefit as wages on a timely filed return (including extensions) for the tax year in which the benefit was provided and any one of the following requirements is met [Reg. § 1.61-21(c)(3)(ii)]:

1. the employee includes the value of the benefit in gross income on a timely filed return for the tax year in which the benefit was provided;

2. the employee is not a control employee (generally, a 1% owner, a director, or an officer or employee whose compensation exceeds a specified inflation-adjusted amount); or

3. the employer demonstrates a good faith effort to treat the benefit correctly for reporting purposes.

### I.C.4.d. Valuation of Personal Use of Employer-Provided Vehicles

[519 T.M., V.C.2.; TPS ¶5980.03.A.]

An employee who uses an employer-provided vehicle must include the value of any personal use of that vehicle in gross income. The value of any business use of the vehicle generally can be excluded from the employee's gross income as a working condition fringe benefit. There are several different methods that may be used for valuing the personal use of an employer-provided vehicle. Under the general valuation method, the value equals the amount the employee would have to pay to lease the vehicle in an arm's-length transaction under comparable conditions [Reg. § 1.61-21(b)(4)]. Because this amount may be difficult to determine, several special valuation methods are available.

*Vehicle Cents-Per-Mile Valuation Method.* Under the vehicle cents-per-mile valuation method, the value of the personal use of an employer-provided vehicle is determined by multiplying the standard mileage rate (56 cents for 2014) by the number of miles the employee drives the vehicle for personal purposes during the year. This method generally may be used if the vehicle is reasonably expected to be used regularly in the employer's business, is used primarily by an employee, and is actually driven at least 10,000 miles during the calendar year. However, this method may not be used if the fair market value of the vehicle on the date it is made available to the employee exceeds an applicable dollar amount. For 2014, the applicable dollar amount is $16,000 if the vehicle is a passenger automobile and $17,300 if the vehicle is a truck or van [Reg. § 1.61-21(e); Notice 2014-11, 2014-13 I.R.B. 880; Notice 2013-80, 2013-52 I.R.B. 821].

*Automobile Lease Valuation Rule.* Under the automobile lease valuation rule, the value of the personal use of an employer-provided vehicle generally is determined by multiplying the Annual Lease Value of the vehicle by the percentage of the total mileage that the vehicle is used for personal purposes during the year. The Annual Lease Value of the vehicle is determined using the Annual Lease Value Table (see *Schedules & Tables 15.*) and is based on the fair market value of the vehicle as of the first date on which the vehicle is made available to any employee for personal use [Reg. § 1.61-21(d)(2)]. The following safe harbor rules apply in determining the fair market value of an employer-provided vehicle for this purpose [Reg. § 1.61-21(d)(5)]:

- If the vehicle is owned by the employer, the safe harbor value of the vehicle is the employer's cost of purchasing the vehicle (including sales tax, title, etc.) in an arm's-length transaction.

- If the vehicle is leased (or revalued) by the employer, the safe harbor value is the retail value of the vehicle as reported in a nationally recognized publication that regularly reports new or used vehicle retail values.

- In a case in which an employer has a fleet of 20 or more vehicles, the fleet-average value (the average of the fair market values of all vehicles in the fleet) may be used for purposes of determining the annual lease values for all vehicles in the fleet.

If an employer-provided vehicle is available for personal use for less than an entire calendar year but for continuous periods of at least 30 days, the value of the personal use is determined based on the pro-rated Annual Lease Value or a Daily Lease Value (an estimate of the daily cost of renting the vehicle based upon a day-to-day rental) [Reg. § 1.61-21(d)(4)].

*Commuting Valuation Rules.* Under the commuting valuation rule, the value of the personal use of an employer-provided vehicle used for commuting purposes is $1.50 per one-way commute (e.g., from home to work or from work to home). If more than one employee commutes in the same employer-provided vehicle, the amount includible in the gross income of each employee is $1.50 per one-way commute [Reg. § 1.61-21(f)(3)]. However, the commuting valuation rule may be used only if all of the following requirements are met [Reg. § 1.61-21(f)(1)]:

1. the vehicle is owned or leased by the employer, provided to one or more employees for use in connection with the employer's trade or business, and used in that trade or business;
2. the employer requires the employee to commute to and/or from work in the vehicle for bona fide noncompensatory reasons;
3. the employer has established a written policy under which the employee may not use the vehicle for personal purposes other than commuting or de minimis personal use;
4. the employee does not use the vehicle for any personal purpose other than commuting and de minimis personal use; and
5. the employee is not a control employee of the employer (generally, a 1% owner, a director, or an officer or employee whose compensation exceeds a specified inflation-adjusted amount).

There is a special commuting valuation rule for transportation that is provided by an employer to an employee due to the employee's unsafe commuting conditions. Under this rule, the value of the commuting use of the employer-provided transportation is $1.50 per one-way commute per employee if the following four requirements are met [Reg. § 1.61-21(k)(1)]:

1. the transportation is provided to an employee who would normally walk or use public transportation in commuting to and from work and is provided solely because of unsafe commuting conditions;
2. the employer has established a written policy under which the transportation is not provided for any personal purpose other than unsafe commuting conditions, and the employer's practice corresponds with that policy;
3. the employee does not use the transportation for any personal purpose other than unsafe commuting conditions; and
4. the employee is a qualified employee (generally, a non-exempt employee paid on an hourly basis and eligible for overtime pay).

### I.C.4.e. *Valuation of Personal Flights on Employer-Provided Aircraft*

[519 T.M., V.C.3.; TPS ¶5980.03.B.]

An employee who is provided a personal flight on an employer-provided aircraft must include the value of the flight in gross income. The value of a business flight on an employer-provided aircraft generally can be excluded from an employee's gross income as a working condition fringe benefit.

***Combined Flights.*** If an employee combines personal and business flights in one trip on an employer-provided aircraft, the determination of the amount that must be included in the employee's gross income depends on whether the employee's trip is primarily for personal purposes or primarily for business purposes. If the employee's trip is made primarily for personal purposes, the amount included in gross income is the value of the personal flights that would have been taken had there been no business flights. If the employee's trip is made primarily for business purposes, the amount included in gross income is the excess of (i) the value of all flights, over (ii) the value of the flights that would have been taken had there been no personal flights.

***Value of Employer-Provided Flights.*** The value of a flight on an employer-provided aircraft is determined based on the Standard Industry Fare Level (SIFL) formula. To compute that value, the appropriate aircraft multiple is multiplied by the product of the applicable SIFL cents-per-mile rate and the number of miles in the flight, and an applicable terminal charge is then added to that amount.

The aircraft multiple is based on the maximum certified takeoff weight of the aircraft and depends on whether or not the employee is a control employee (generally, a 5% owner, a director, an officer, or an employee among the top 1% most highly paid employees). The appropriate aircraft multiple is determined based on the following chart [Reg. § 1.61-21(g)(7)]:

| Maximum Certified Takeoff Weight | Aircraft Multiple (Control Employee) | Aircraft Multiple (Non-Control Employee) |
|---|---|---|
| 6,000 lbs. or less | 62.5% | 15.6% |
| 6,001–10,000 lbs. | 125% | 23.4% |
| 10,001–25,000 lbs. | 300% | 31.3% |
| 25,001 lbs. or more | 400% | 31.3% |

The SIFL cents-per-mile rate and terminal charge are revised semi-annually and issued by the Department of Transportation. The rates for 2014 are as follows [Rev. Rul. 2014-10, 2014-14 I.R.B. 906; Rev. Rul. 2014-25, 2014-40 I.R.B. 574]:

| Period of Flight | 1/1/14–6/30/14 | 7/1/14–12/31/14 |
|---|---|---|
| SIFL rate, up to 500 miles | $0.2515 | $0.2530 |
| SIFL rate, 501-1,500 miles | $0.1918 | $0.1929 |
| SIFL rate, over 1,500 miles | $0.1844 | $0.1855 |
| Terminal Charge | $45.98 | $46.25 |

The value of an employee's personal flight on an employer-provided aircraft is deemed to be zero if 50% or more of the regular seating capacity of the aircraft is occupied by individuals whose flights are primarily for the employer's business [Reg. § 1.61-21(g)(12)].

***Personal Flights by Commercial Airline Employees.*** A special rule applies for purposes of determining the value of a standby or space-available personal flight of an airline employee on the employer's commercial aircraft. Under this rule, the amount included in the employee's gross income is equal to 25% of the highest unrestricted coach fare in effect for that flight [Reg. § 1.61-21(h)].

*Frequent Flyer Miles.* Frequent flyer miles earned by an employee on an employer-provided business flight are not includible in gross income, even if used for personal purposes [Announcement 2002-18, 2002-10 I.R.B. 621].

### I.C.5. Life Insurance Coverage and Benefits

[501 T.M., VIII.C.16., 386 T.M., VII., 397 T.M., IV.E.; TPS ¶5930.01., .02.]

Generally, life insurance proceeds paid by reason of the death of the insured are excluded from the income of the beneficiary, whether paid under an individual, group-term life, split-dollar life, or other form of policy (see I.L.2.). However, when an employer pays premiums on a life insurance policy on the life of an employee under a group-term or split-dollar life insurance plan, there are often tax implications for the employee.

*Group-Term Life Insurance.* Subject to certain exceptions, an employee must include in gross income the cost of employer-provided group-term life insurance coverage in excess of $50,000, reduced by any amount the employee pays toward the coverage [§ 79(a)]. See XVII.B.4.a.

*Split-Dollar Life Insurance.* Split-dollar life insurance is a method of financing premium payments on a life insurance policy. Under such an arrangement, an employer and employee join in the purchasing of an insurance policy on the life of the employee (such a policy generally has a substantial investment element). Unless the arrangement is considered a loan between the employer and employee, under an arrangement in which the employer owns the policy, the employee must include in income (i) the cost of the current life insurance protection, (ii) the amount of policy cash value to which the employee has current access, and (iii) the value of other economic benefits provided to the employee. See XVII.B.4.b.

### I.C.6. Deferred Compensation and Retirement Pay

[320 T.M. through 388 T.M.; TPS ¶ 5510. through ¶5830.]

Deferred compensation generally must be included in the gross income of an employee when actually or constructively received. Retirement pay generally must be included in the gross income of an employee to the extent the employee did not contribute to the cost and did not pay taxes on the employer's contributions [Reg. § 1.61-11]. See XVII.A. and XVII.B. for discussions of deferred compensation and retirement pay.

### I.C.7. Bonuses and Awards

[501 T.M., VIII.C.10.; TPS ¶1320.]

Bonuses and awards received from an employer for outstanding work generally must be included in the employee's income as wages. Thus, for example, the value of a vacation trip received from an employer as a prize for meeting sales goals must be included in gross income. However, employee achievement awards generally can be excluded from gross income [§ 74(c)].

An employee achievement award is an item of tangible personal property that is awarded by an employer to an employee for length of service achievement or safety achievement as part of a meaningful presentation and under conditions and circumstances that do not create a significant likelihood of it being disguised compensation [§ 274(j)(3)].

The exclusion for employee achievement awards does not apply to a length of service award if it is received for less than five years of service or if the employee received another length of service award during the year or the previous four years.

The exclusion for employee achievement awards does not apply to a safety achievement award if the employee is a manager, administrator, clerical employee, or other professional employee or if more than 10% of the eligible employees previously received safety achievement awards during the year [§ 274(j)(4)].

The exclusion for employee achievement awards is limited to $1,600 for all employee achievement awards received during the year. There is also a $400 limitation for employee achievement awards that are not qualified plan awards (awards made as part of an established written plan or program that does not discriminate in favor of highly compensated employees) [§ 274(j)(2)].

### I.C.8. Employment Tax Withholding

[392 T.M.; TPS ¶5440.]

Generally, all compensation derived from employment, unless specifically excluded, is subject to employment tax withholding, including FICA (social security), FUTA (unemployment), and income tax withholding [§ 3121(a), § 3201, § 3306(b), § 3401(a)]. The only relevant consideration is that the payment is made in consideration for services performed by the employee. Thus, the medium and manner in which compensation is paid by an employer is generally immaterial in determining whether an amount is subject to employment tax withholding.

Salary advances and draws on accounts for future earnings are subject to employment taxes, whether paid directly to an employee or credited to an account from which he can draw. However, advances to cover legitimate expenses expected to be incurred in the course of doing business are not subject to employment tax withholding. Moreover, salary advances and drawing accounts may be exempt from employment tax withholding if the employer treats the amounts as a loan and gets a written statement from the employee regarding his indebtedness to the employer.

Fringe benefits are exempt from employment tax withholding if, at the time the benefits are provided, it is reasonable to believe that the employee will be able to exclude the benefit received from gross income [§ 3121(a)(20), § 3306(b)(16), § 3401(a)(19)]. Fringe benefits that do not qualify for exclusion from gross income are includible in compensation and subject to employment taxes on the excess of the benefit's fair market value over the amount, if any, paid by the employee for the benefit.

For further discussion of employment taxes, see Chapter XXII.

## I.D. Interest Income

### I.D.1. General Rules on Interest Income

[535 T.M.; TPS ¶1210.]

Generally, all interest received by or credited to a taxpayer must be included in gross income [§ 61(a)(4); Reg. § 1.61-7(a)]. However, interest on most state and local bonds (see I.D.6.) can be excluded from gross income and interest on certain U.S. savings bonds (see I.D.5.) can be excluded from gross income if the taxpayer pays higher education expenses in the tax year such bonds are redeemed. See II.B. and II.J. for detailed discussions of these exclusions.

Interest income can come from many sources, including bank accounts, money market funds, certificates of deposit, corporate obligations, and government obligations. The Supreme Court held that a mortgagee must recognize interest income upon purchasing a property in a foreclosure sale when the mortgagee's bid for the property includes unpaid accrued interest as well as principal [*Helvering v. Midland*

*Mut. Life Ins. Co.*, 300 U.S. 216 (1937)]. Lower courts have held that a mortgagee must recognize interest income even when the mortgagor voluntarily surrenders the property to the mortgagee in lieu of foreclosure. In that situation, the interest income is the amount by which the property's value exceeds the principal amount of the loan [*Mfr's Life Ins. Co. v. Commissioner*, 43 B.T.A. 867 (1941)].

Individual taxpayers who receive more than $10 of interest from a bank or other payer of interest should receive a Form 1099-INT, *Interest Income*, reporting that interest to them. Individual taxpayers with taxable interest income of more than $1,500 must report interest income on Schedule B of Form 1040, *U.S. Individual Income Tax Return*. Other taxpayers report interest income directly on the appropriate line on page 1 of Form 1040.

### I.D.2. Reporting Interest Income

#### I.D.2.a. Cash Method Taxpayers

[570 T.M., IV.B.; TPS ¶1210.01.D.]

A cash method taxpayer generally includes interest in gross income when it is actually or constructively received. Interest income is treated as constructively received in the tax year in which it is credited to the taxpayer's account, set apart for him, or otherwise made available so that he may draw on it at any time [Reg. § 1.451-1, § 1.451-2(a)]. See XI.B.1.c. for further discussion of the cash method of accounting.

---

**EXAMPLE:** Beth is a calendar year taxpayer. On Dec. 31, Year 1, Beth's bank credited $50 of interest to her savings account. Beth did not withdraw the interest or enter it into her books until Year 2. Beth must include the $50 of interest in gross income on her return for Year 1 because she constructively received it in Year 1.

---

#### I.D.2.b. Accrual Method Taxpayers

[570 T.M., IV.C.; TPS ¶1210.01.D.]

An accrual method taxpayer generally includes interest in gross income when it is earned, whether or not received. For this purpose, interest is earned when all events have occurred that fix the right to receive the interest and the amount of the interest can be determined with reasonable accuracy [Reg. § 1.451-1]. See XI.B.1.d. for further discussion of the accrual method of accounting.

#### I.D.2.c. Special Rule for Bonds Sold Between Interest Payment Dates

[535 T.M., VI.D.; TPS ¶1210.01.C.9. ]

If a taxpayer sells a bond between interest payment dates, part of the sales price is treated as representing interest that accrued before the date of the sale. The taxpayer must report that accrued interest as interest income for the year of the sale [Reg. § 1.61-7(d)].

#### I.D.2.d. Special Rule for Bonds Traded Flat

[535 T.M., VI.D.; TPS ¶1210.01.C.8.]

If a taxpayer buys a bond when interest has been defaulted or when interest has accrued but not yet been paid (e.g., when the bond is purchased between interest payment dates), the transaction is often described as trading a bond flat. The defaulted or unpaid interest is not treated as income to the taxpayer and, if it is later paid to the taxpayer, it is treated as a return of capital that reduces his basis in the bond. Any interest that accrues after the date the bond is purchased is treated as interest income to the taxpayer [Reg. § 1.61-7(c)].

### I.D.3. Interest on Debt Instruments

[535 T.M.; TPS ¶1840.]

Debt instruments are frequently issued at, and trade at, a discount. The discount on the debt instrument is treated as the equivalent of interest. Different tax rules apply for purposes of determining the discount on a debt instrument on the date it is originally issued (so-called original issue discount) and determining the discount on a debt instrument when it is traded on some date after the original issue date (so-called market discount). A special set of rules applies for determining the discount on short-term obligations. In some cases, debt instruments are issued with no interest or below-market interest. Interest may be imputed to those types of debt instruments.

### I.D.3.a. Original Issue Discount

[535 T.M., II.; TPS ¶1840.02.]

When a debt instrument is issued for a price that is less than its stated redemption price at maturity (i.e., it is issued at a discount), the difference between the issue price and the stated redemption price is known as original issue discount (OID). OID is treated as interest and generally must be included in gross income as it accrues over the term of the debt instrument [§ 1272, § 1273]. See III.F.2.a. for a detailed discussion of OID.

### I.D.3.b. Market Discount

[535 T.M., VI.A.; TPS ¶1840.03.B.]

When a debt instrument is purchased after the date on which it was originally issued, it is usually purchased for a price that is different from its issue price because the fair market value of the debt instrument at that time is usually different from its yield at the time it was issued. Market discount arises when the value of a debt instrument decreases after its issue date. Market discount is the amount by which the stated redemption price of a bond at maturity exceeds the taxpayer's basis in the bond immediately after he acquires it. Under the market discount rules, a taxpayer generally must treat any partial payment of principal on a market discount bond as interest income to the extent of the accrued market discount on the bond [§ 1276]. See III.F.2.b. for a detailed discussion of market discount.

### I.D.3.c. Discount on Short-Term Debt Instruments

[535 T.M., VI.E.; TPS ¶1840.09.A.]

The OID rules (see I.D.3.a.) and market discount rules (see I.D.3.b.) do not apply to certain types of short-term debt instruments (debt instruments with a fixed maturity date of not more than one year from the date of issue). Those types of short-term debt instruments are instead subject to special rules under which the discount or interest on a short-term debt instrument is included in gross income currently as it accrues [§ 1281]. See III.F.2.c. for a detailed discussion of short-term debt instruments.

### I.D.3.d. Imputed Interest

[535 T.M., III.; TPS ¶1840.04.]

Certain payments of principal on a debt instrument may be required to be recharacterized as payments of interest (i.e., interest is imputed on the debt instrument). Interest may be imputed on a debt instrument based on the provisions of

§ 1274 and § 483. Interest may also be imputed under the below-market loan rules (see I.D.3.e.).

Section 1274 applies to any debt instrument given in consideration for the sale or exchange of property if some of the payments due on the debt instrument are due more than six months after the sale or exchange, and the stated redemption price of the debt instrument at maturity exceeds either (i) its stated principal amount (if adequate stated interest is provided), or (ii) its imputed principal amount (if adequate stated interest is not provided). A debt instrument has adequate stated interest if its stated principal amount does not exceed its imputed principal amount. The imputed principal amount is the sum of the present values of all payments due under the debt instrument, using a discount rate equal to the Applicable Federal Rate (AFR) (see *Schedules & Tables 16.*). Section 1274 does not apply to (i) certain sales of farms for $1 million or less, (ii) sales of principal residences, (iii) sales involving payments of $250,000 or less, (iv) sales of certain patents, and (v) certain § 483(e) land transfers between related parties.

When § 1274 applies to a debt instrument, the issue price of the debt instrument is treated as its stated principal amount or its imputed principal amount (depending on whether or not adequate stated interest is provided), and imputed interest is taken into account as OID (see I.D.3.a.).

Section 483 applies to a payment on account of a sale or exchange of property that constitutes part of the sales price and that is due more than six months after the sale or exchange under a contract that provides for some payments due more than one year after the sale or exchange and that does not provide for adequate interest. Adequate interest is stated interest that is paid or compounded at least annually at a rate at least equal to the rate used in determining the issue price of a debt instrument under § 1274. Section 483 does not apply to a debt instrument whose issue price is determined under § 1274.

When § 483 applies to a debt instrument, the unstated interest under the debt instrument is taxable as interest. The unstated interest is equal to the amount by which the deferred payments due more than six months from the date of sale exceed the sum of the present value of all deferred payments and all payments of interest due under the debt instrument.

### I.D.3.e. Below-Market Loans

[535 T.M., VII.; TPS ¶1820.]

When the stated rate of interest on certain types of loans is below the Applicable Federal Rate (AFR) set by the IRS (see *Schedules & Tables 16.*), the forgone interest on such below-market loans must be included in the lender's gross income as imputed interest. The foregone interest for any period is equal to the interest that would have been payable for that period if interest was accrued at the AFR and payable annually on December 31, less any interest actually payable on the loan for that period [§ 7872(e)(2)].

The rules for below-market loans apply to (i) gift loans, (ii) compensation-related loans, (iii) corporation-shareholder loans, (iv) tax avoidance loans, (v) other below-market loans for which the interest arrangements have a significant effect on the federal tax liability of the lender or borrower, and (vi) certain loans made to qualified continuing care facilities under continuing care contracts. Compensation-related loans include both loans between employers and employees and loans between independent contractors and the persons for whom the contractors provide services. Tax avoidance loans are loans for which the avoidance of federal tax is one of the main purposes of the interest arrangements under the loans [§ 7872(c)(1)].

The tax treatment of a below-market loan depends on whether the loan is a demand loan, term loan, or gift loan. A demand loan is a loan payable at any time upon demand by the lender. A term loan is any loan that is not a demand loan. A gift loan, which may be either a demand loan or a term loan, is a loan for which the forgone interest is in the nature of a gift.

*Gift and Demand Loans.* A below-market demand or gift loan is treated as an arm's length transaction in which the following transfers are treated as occurring on December 31: (i) the lender makes a loan to the borrower in exchange for a note that requires payment of interest at the AFR and also makes an additional payment to the borrower in an amount equal to the forgone interest, and (ii) the borrower is treated as transferring the additional payment back to the lender as interest. The lender must report the amount of the additional payment (i.e., the foregone interest) as interest income [§ 7872(a)].

*Term Loans.* A below-market term loan other than a gift loan is generally treated as a transaction in which the lender makes a loan to the borrower and also makes an additional payment to the borrower in an amount equal to the excess of the amount loaned over the present value (based on the AFR) of all payments due under the loan. The additional payment is treated as original issue discount (OID) (see I.D.3.a.) and the lender must report the OID as interest income as it accrues over the term of the loan [§ 7872(b)].

*Exceptions to Below-Market Loan Rules.* In the case of a gift loan between individuals, the below-market loan rules do not apply to any day on which the total outstanding amount of loans between the individuals is $10,000 or less, unless the loan is directly used to buy or carry income-producing assets or the loan is a term loan that was previously subject to the below-market loan rules [§ 7872(c)(2), § 7872(f)(10)]. If the total outstanding amount of loans between such individuals is over $10,000 but $100,000 or less, then the foregone interest included in the gross income of the lender is limited to the amount of the borrower's net investment income for the year (net investment income is treated as zero if it is $1,000 or less). However, this limitation does not apply if the avoidance of federal tax is one of the main purposes of the interest arrangement under the loan [§ 7872(d)].

In the case of a compensation-related loan or corporation-shareholder loan, the below-market loan rules do not apply to any day on which the total outstanding amount of loans between the borrower and lender is $10,000 or less, unless the avoidance of federal tax is one of the main purposes of the loan interest arrangement or the loan is a term loan that was previously subject to the below-market loan rules [§ 7872(c)(3), § 7872(f)(10)].

In the case of a loan made to a qualified continuing care facility under a continuing care contract, the below-market loan rules do not apply if the lender or the lender's spouse is age 62 or older at the end of the calendar year [§ 7872(h)].

The below-market loan rules also do not apply to a below-market loan if the interest arrangement under the loan does not have a significant effect on the federal tax liability of the borrower or lender. Under this exception, the below-market loan rules do not apply to the following types of below-market loans [Reg. § 1.7872-5(b), § 1.7872-5T(b)]:

- loans made available by the lender to the general public on the same terms and conditions that are consistent with the lender's customary business practice;

- loans subsidized by a federal, state, or local government that are made available under a program of general application to the public;
- certain employee-relocation loans;
- gift loans made to a charitable organization (unless the total outstanding amount of loans by the lender to the organization is more than $250,000 at any time during the tax year);
- loans from a foreign lender to a U.S. borrower (unless the interest income imputed to the lender would be effectively connected with the conduct of a U.S. trade or business and not exempt from U.S. income tax under an income tax treaty); and
- other loans on which the interest arrangements can be shown to have no significant effect on the federal tax liability of the borrower or lender (determined based on all the facts and circumstances including whether items of income and deduction generated by the loan offset each other and the amount of those items, the cost of complying with the below-market loan rules, and non-tax reasons for structuring the transaction as a below-market loan).

### I.D.3.f. Election to Report All Interest as OID

[535 T.M., VI.C.; TPS ¶1840.03.]

A taxpayer may elect to treat all interest on a debt instrument acquired during the tax year as original issue discount (OID) (see I.D.3.a.). For purposes of this election, the interest covered includes stated interest, OID, de minimis OID, market discount, de minimis market discount, acquisition discount, and unstated interest. The election must be made for the tax year in which the taxpayer acquires the debt instrument and may not be revoked without IRS approval. The election is made by attaching a statement to the taxpayer's timely filed tax return that provides that the taxpayer is making the election under Reg. § 1.1272-3 and that identifies the debt instruments subject to the election [Reg. § 1.1272-3].

### I.D.4. Interest on U.S. Treasury Bills, Notes and Bonds

[501 T.M., X.A.1.c.(7); TPS ¶1210.01.C.10.]

Interest from U.S. Treasury bills, notes, and bonds is subject to federal income tax (such interest is generally exempt from state and local income taxes). Treasury notes and bonds have maturity periods of more than one year. They pay interest every six months. Treasury bills have maturity periods of less than one year. The difference between the discounted price paid for a Treasury bill and the face value received at maturity is treated as interest income. Treasury bills are subject to the rules on short-term debt instruments, discussed in I.D.3.c. and III.F.2.c. The U.S. Treasury also issues inflation-protected securities (TIPS), discussed in III.F.2.a.

### I.D.5. Interest on U.S. Savings Bonds

[501 T.M., X.A.1.c(7), 2.c.; TPS ¶1210.01.C.10.]

Interest from U.S. savings bonds is generally subject to federal income tax. U.S. savings bonds include series H, series HH, series E, series EE, and series I bonds. Series H and HH bonds were issued at face value and interest is payable twice a year. Series E and EE bonds were issued at a discount (i.e., interest on these bonds is equal to the difference between the purchase price and the redemption value) and interest is payable at maturity. Series I bonds were issued at face value and all accrued interest is payable at maturity.

Accrual method taxpayers report interest income from U.S. savings bonds in the year accrued. Cash method taxpayers report interest income from series H or HH bonds in the year received. Cash method taxpayers may choose to report interest income from series E, EE, and I bonds in one of two ways [§ 454(c); Reg. § 1.454-1]:

1. postpone reporting the interest income until the earlier of the year the bonds are redeemed or the year the bonds mature; or

2. report the increase in redemption value of the bonds as interest income in each year.

Interest received on the redemption of a qualified U.S. savings bond can be excluded from gross income if qualified higher education expenses were paid during the same year (see II.J.) [§ 135(a)].

### I.D.6. Interest on State and Local Bonds

[501 T.M., X.A.2.b.; TPS ¶1210.02.]

Interest on state and local bonds is generally exempt from federal income tax (see II.B.) [§ 103(a); Reg. § 1.103-1(a), § 1.61-7(b)]. However, interest on the following types of state and local bonds is not tax-exempt and must be included in gross income [§ 103(b)]:

- bonds not in registered form;
- private activity bonds that are not qualified bonds;
- arbitrage bonds;
- certain federally guaranteed bonds; and
- certain bonds issued for advance refunding.

State and local bonds include obligations issued by a state, the District of Columbia, a U.S. possession, or any political subdivision thereof [§ 103(c)]. Bonds issued after 1982 by Indian tribal governments are treated as issued by a state.

*Bonds Not in Registered Form.* Interest on a state or local bond is generally not tax-exempt unless the bond is in registered form. However, this rule does not apply to state or local bonds that are not of a type offered to the public and state or local bonds that have a maturity of one year or less. Interest on those types of bonds may be tax-exempt even if the bonds are not in registered form [§ 149(a)].

*Private Activity Bonds.* Interest on a private activity bond is not tax-exempt unless the bond is a qualified bond. Thus, interest on a private activity bond must be included in gross income if the private activity bond is not a qualified bond.

A private activity bond is a bond that is part of a state or local government bond issue and meets either a private loan financing test or a private business test [§ 141(a)]. A bond meets the private loan financing test if the amount of the proceeds to be used to make or finance loans to persons other than government units exceeds the lesser of 5% of the proceeds or $5 million [§ 141(c)]. A bond meets the private business test if it meets both of the following requirements [§ 141(b)]:

1. more than 10% of the proceeds is to be used for a private business use; and

2. more than 10% of the payment of principal and interest on the proceeds is either (i) secured by an interest in property to be used for a private business use (or payments for the property), or (ii) derived from payments for property (or borrowed money) used for a private business use.

A qualified bond is a private activity bond that is an exempt facility bond, a qualified mortgage bond, a qualified veterans' mortgage bond, a qualified small issue bond, a qualified student loan bond, a qualified redevelopment bond, or a qualified § 501(c)(3) bond [§ 141(e)].

In computing alternative minimum tax (AMT), an individual taxpayer must make an adjustment for interest from specified private activity bonds exempt from the regular tax. See X.A.2. for a discussion of AMT.

*Arbitrage Bonds.* Interest on an arbitrage bond issued by state or local governments is not tax-exempt. An arbitrage bond is a bond that is part of an issue any portion of the proceeds of which are reasonably expected to be used to buy (or to replace funds that were used to buy) higher yielding investments. A bond is treated as an arbitrage bond if the issuer intentionally uses any portion of the proceeds in this manner [§ 148(a)].

*Federally Guaranteed State and Local Bonds.* Interest on a federally guaranteed state or local bond is not tax-exempt unless the obligation is guaranteed by one of the following U.S. government agencies [§ 149(b)]:

- Federal Housing Administration;
- Department of Veterans Affairs;
- Federal National Mortgage Association;
- Federal Home Loan Mortgage Corporation;
- Government National Mortgage Association;
- Student Loan Marketing Association;
- Bonneville Power Authority (if guarantee made under Northwest Power Act as in effect on July 18, 1984);
- Federal home loan banks (if guarantee made after July 30, 2008, in connection with original bond issue during period beginning on that date and ending on December 31, 2010, and certain safety and soundness requirements met); or
- Resolution Funding Corporation.

A bond is federally guaranteed if (i) the payment of principal or interest on the bond is guaranteed by the United States, (ii) 5% or more of the proceeds of the issue of which the bond is a part is to be used in making loans on which the payment of principal or interest is guaranteed by the United States or is to be invested in federally insured deposits and accounts, or (iii) the payment of principal or interest on the bond is otherwise indirectly guaranteed by the United States [§ 149(b)(2)].

*Bonds Issued for Advanced Refundings.* Interest on a state or local bond is not tax-exempt if the bond is part of an issue that includes [§ 149(d)]:

- a bond issued to advance refund a private activity bond (other than a qualified § 501(c)(3) bond);
- a bond issued to advance refund a bond other than a private activity bond, when certain technical requirements are not satisfied; or
- a bond issued to advance refund any type of bond, when a device is employed in connection with the issuance to obtain a material financial advantage.

A bond is treated as issued to advance refund another bond if it is issued more than 90 days before the redemption of the refunded bond [§ 149(d)(5)].

## I.E. Dividends

### I.E.1. Definition of Dividends

[501 T.M., X.A.3.; TPS ¶1220.02., .06.]

Dividends are included in gross income [§ 61(a)(7)]. Dividends are distributions of money or other property received by a shareholder from a corporation with respect to its stock. Gross income also includes constructive dividends, which may occur when a corporation pays the expenses of or performs services for its shareholders, or permits a shareholder to make personal use of corporate property.

A distribution from a corporation is a dividend only to the extent that it is paid out of the current or accumulated earnings and profits of the corporation. If a distribution exceeds both the current and accumulated earnings and profits of the corporation, it is treated as a non-taxable return of capital that reduces the shareholder's basis in the corporation's stock and, to the extent it exceeds the shareholder's basis in the corporation's stock, it is treated as a capital gain [§ 301(c), § 316(a)].

---

**EXAMPLE:** All of the outstanding stock of X Corporation is owned by Bob, who has a $10,000 adjusted basis in his X stock, and Carol, who has a $5,000 adjusted basis in her X stock. During Year 1, X distributes $10,000 cash to each shareholder. X has current E&P of $5,000 and no accumulated E&P. Bob is taxed on his $10,000 distribution as follows: (i) $2,500 is a taxable dividend ($5,000 E&P × (Bob's $10,000 distribution/total $20,000 distribution)), and (ii) $7,500 is a nontaxable return of capital (Bob reduces his adjusted basis in his stock from $10,000 to $2,500). Carol is taxed on her $10,000 distribution as follows: (i) $2,500 is a taxable dividend ($5,000 E&P × (Carol's $10,000 distribution/total $20,000 distribution)), (ii) $5,000 is a nontaxable return of capital (Carol reduces her adjusted basis in her stock from $5,000 to $0), and (iii) $2,500 is taxed as capital gain.

---

See XIII.D. for further discussion of dividends paid by corporations to shareholders.

### I.E.2. Taxation of Dividends

[501 T.M., X.A.3.; TPS ¶1220.05.]

As a general rule, ordinary dividends are taxed as ordinary income. However, ordinary dividends that are qualified dividends are taxed at the same preferential tax rates as net capital gains [§ 1(h)(11), § 301(f)(4)]. Special rules apply to dividends paid in property, stock dividends, capital gain dividends, and liquidating dividends.

Taxpayers who receive $10 or more in dividends and other distributions from a corporation should receive a Form 1099-DIV, *Dividends and Distributions*, reporting those amounts to them. Individual taxpayers with ordinary dividends of more than $1,500 must report dividend income on Form 1040, Schedule B.

### I.E.2.a. Qualified Dividends

[501 T.M., X.A.3.; TPS ¶1220.05.]

Qualified dividends are dividends received from U.S. corporations and qualified foreign corporations on stock for which certain holding period requirements are met. Certain types of dividends are not eligible to be treated as qualified dividends [§ 1(h)(11)(B)].

*Qualified Foreign Corporations*. Dividends received from a foreign corporation are qualified dividends only if the foreign corporation is a qualified foreign corporation. A qualified foreign corporation is a foreign corporation that is either (i) incorporated in a U.S. possession, or (ii) eligible for the benefits of a comprehensive income tax treaty with the United States that includes an exchange of information program and that the Treasury Department has determined to be satisfactory for this purpose. A foreign corporation that does not meet either of those requirements will nevertheless be treated as a qualified foreign corporation with respect to any dividends paid on stock that is readily tradable on an established securities market in the United States. Under an exception to these rules, a foreign corporation is not treated as a qualified foreign corporation if it is a passive foreign investment company (PFIC) during its tax year in which the dividends are paid or during its previous tax year [§ 1(h)(11)(C)].

*Holding Period Requirements.* Dividends are qualified dividends only if they are paid on stock that meets certain holding period requirements. Generally, a shareholder must have held the stock for more than 60 days during the 121-day period that begins 60 days before the ex-dividend date. In the case of preferred stock on which the dividends are due to periods totaling more than 366 days, a shareholder must have held the stock for more than 90 days during the 181-day period that begins 90 days before the ex-dividend date. The holding period for stock includes the day the stock is sold but not the day it was acquired [§ 1(h)(11)(B)(iii)(I), § 246(c)].

---

**EXAMPLE:** Bob bought 1,000 shares of X Corporation stock on July 9. X, a U.S. corporation, declared a cash dividend of 10 cents per share with an ex-dividend date of July 16. Bob sold the 1,000 shares on Aug. 12. The 121-day period began on May 17 (60 days before the ex-dividend date) and ended on Sept. 14. Bob held the shares for only 34 days of the 121-day period (July 10 through Aug. 12). Thus, the dividends Bob receives from X are not qualified dividends.

**EXAMPLE:** Assume the same facts as in the previous example, except that Bob bought the 1,000 shares on July 15 and sold the stock on Sept. 16. Bob held the shares for a total of 63 days and for 61 days during the 121-day period (July 15 through Sept. 14). Thus, the dividends Bob receives from X are qualified dividends.

---

*Ineligible Dividends.* The following types of dividends are not qualified dividends [§ 1(h)(11)(B)(ii), § 1(h)(11)(B)(iii)(II)]:

- dividends paid on deposits with mutual savings banks, cooperative banks, credit unions, U.S. building and loan associations, U.S. savings and loan associations, federal savings and loan associations, and similar financial institutions (these amounts are treated as interest income);
- dividends from a corporation that is a tax-exempt organization or farmers' cooperative during the corporation's tax year in which the dividends were paid or during the corporation's previous tax year;
- dividends paid by a corporation on employer securities held on the date of record by an employee stock ownership plan (ESOP) maintained by that corporation; and
- dividends paid on any share of stock to the extent that the shareholder is obligated to make related payments for positions in substantially similar or related property (whether under a short sale or otherwise).

### I.E.2.b. Dividends Paid in Form of Property

[501 T.M., X.A.3.; TPS ¶1220.04.B.]

When a shareholder receives a dividend in the form of property (other than stock or stock rights), the amount of the dividend received is equal to the fair market value of the property received on the date of distribution, reduced (but not below zero) by the amount of any liability assumed or any liability to which the property is subject [§ 301(b)].

### I.E.2.c. Stock Dividends

[765 T.M., III.; TPS ¶4830.01.C.]

A corporation may distribute to shareholders its own stock or rights to acquire its stock (so-called stock rights). Generally, such stock dividends are not taxable to shareholders [§ 305(a)]. However, the fair market value of stock dividends must be included in a shareholder's gross income if any of the following conditions apply [§ 305(b)]:

- the distribution is payable in either stock or other property at the election of any shareholder;
- the distribution is disproportionate (i.e., the distribution results in the receipt of stock by some shareholders and the receipt of other property by other shareholders);
- the distribution results in the receipt of common stock by some shareholders and the receipt of preferred stock by other shareholders;
- the distribution is made with respect to preferred stock (unless the distribution merely results in an increase in the conversion ratio of convertible preferred stock to take into account a stock dividend or stock split); or
- the distribution consists of convertible preferred stock (unless the distribution will not result in a disproportionate distribution).

A shareholder's basis in stock or stock rights received as a nontaxable stock dividend generally is determined by allocating the adjusted basis of the stock on which the stock dividend was made between that stock (the old stock) and the new stock or stock rights in proportion to the fair market values of each on the date of distribution [§ 307(a); Reg. § 1.307-1]. However, a shareholder's basis in stock rights received in a nontaxable distribution is treated as zero if the fair market value of the stock rights on the date of distribution is less than 15% of the fair market value of the old stock (unless the shareholder makes an election to allocate part of the basis of the old stock to those stock rights) [Reg. § 1.307-2].

A shareholder's basis in stock or stock rights received as a taxable stock dividend is generally equal to the fair market value of the stock or stock rights on the date of distribution.

See XIII.D.2. for further discussion of stock dividends.

### I.E.2.d. Capital Gain Dividends

[740 T.M., IX.C., 742 T.M., IV.B.3.; TPS ¶1220.05.]

Capital gain distributions (also known as capital gain dividends) are amounts paid to shareholders by regulated investment companies (e.g., mutual funds) and real estate investment trusts with respect to capital gains of the RIC or REIT (see XIII.F. for a discussion of capital gain distributions paid by RICs and REITs). Capital gain dividends are reported as long-term capital gains, not dividends [§ 1(h)(11)(D)(iii)].

### I.E.2.e. Liquidating Dividends

[784 T.M., V.A.; TPS ¶5010.03.]

Liquidating distributions (also known as liquidating dividends) are distributions received by shareholders upon a partial or complete liquidation of a corporation (see XIII.E.3.b. for a discussion of liquidating distributions). Generally, liquidating distributions are treated as a nontaxable return of capital that reduce the shareholder's basis in the stock. However, to the extent that the distributions exceed the shareholder's basis, they are taxable as capital gain.

## I.F. Rents and Royalties

### I.F.1. Rents

[501 T.M., X.A.4.; TPS ¶1230.01.]

Rents are included in gross income [§ 61(a)(5)]. Rents are payments received for the use or occupation of property. A cash method taxpayer includes rent in gross income in the tax year it is actually or constructively received, regardless of when it was earned. Rent is constructively received when made available to the taxpayer (e.g., when credited to the taxpayer's bank account). An accrual method taxpayer generally includes rent in gross income in the tax year it is earned. If rent is received in the form of property or services instead of money, the amount of rent received is equal to the fair market value of the property or services received. Individual taxpayers report rental income and expenses on Form 1040, Schedule E.

Special rules apply to advance rent, lease cancellation payments, landlord expenses paid by the tenant, leasehold improvements made by a tenant, and security deposits.

*Advance Rent.* Rent received before the period it covers (so-called advance rent) is included in gross income in the year received, regardless of the period covered or the taxpayer's method of accounting [Reg. § 1.61-8(b)].

*Lease Cancellation Payments.* Payments received from a tenant for the cancellation of a lease are included in gross income in the year received, regardless of the taxpayer's method of accounting. Such payments are considered a substitute for rent [Reg. § 1.61-8(b)].

*Landlord Expenses Paid by Tenant.* If a tenant pays any of the taxpayer's expenses on the rental property (e.g., the tenant pays for property taxes or repairs and deducts the payment from rent), the taxpayer must treat the tenant's payment as rent and include it in gross income. The taxpayer may also deduct that amount if it qualifies as a deductible rental expense [Reg. § 1.61-8(c)].

*Leasehold Improvements.* If a tenant makes improvements to rental real estate as a substitute for rent, the taxpayer must treat the improvements as rent and include them in gross income. The intent of the parties, as determined by the facts and circumstances surrounding the lease, is controlling on the issue of whether improvements constitute rent [Reg. § 1.61-8(c)].

*Security Deposits.* A security deposit generally is not included in gross income if the taxpayer plans to return it to the tenant at the end of the lease. However, any portion of a security deposit retained by the taxpayer because the tenant did not live up to the terms of the lease must be included in gross income. When an amount called a security deposit is to be used as a final payment for rent, it is treated as advance rent and included in gross income when received.

### I.F.2. Royalties

[501 T.M., X.A.5.; TPS ¶1230.02.]

Royalties are included in gross income [§ 61(a)(6)]. Royalties include payments received from the leasing and licensing of tangible and intangible personal property, such as books, stories, plays, copyrights, trademarks, formulas, patents. Royalties may also be received from the exploitation of natural resources, such as oil, gas, coal, copper, and timber [Reg. § 1.61-8(a)]. Royalties are typically measured as a percentage of the income derived from the sale of a unit of the property. Individual taxpayers report royalties on Form 1040, Schedule E.

## I.G. Alimony

[515 T.M., II.; TPS ¶1310.]

Alimony and separate maintenance payments received from a spouse or ex-spouse are included in the gross income of the recipient spouse. Such payments are generally deductible by the payer spouse [§ 61(a)(8), § 71(a)]. See VII.B.11. for the deduction of alimony by the payer spouse. Child support payments are not includible in the gross income of the recipient spouse [§ 71(c)]. Special rules apply to transfers of property between spouses incident to divorce (see III.E.5.).

### I.G.1. Payments that Qualify as Alimony

[515 T.M., II.C.; TPS ¶1310.01.]

An alimony or separate maintenance payment is a payment to, or for the benefit of, a spouse or ex-spouse under a divorce or separation instrument for which the following requirements are met [§ 71(b), § 71(e)]:

1. the payment is in cash (i.e., not property);
2. the instrument does not designate the payment as not being alimony;
3. there is no liability to make any payment after the death of the recipient spouse;
4. in the case of spouses who are legally separated under a decree of divorce or separate maintenance, the spouses are not members of the same household; and
5. the spouses do not file a joint return with each other.

A divorce or separation instrument includes [§ 71(b)(2)]:

- a decree of divorce or separate maintenance or a written instrument incident to that decree;
- a written separation agreement; or
- a decree or any type of court order requiring a spouse to make payments for the support or separate maintenance of the other spouse.

Child support payments do not qualify as alimony [§ 71(c)]. Property settlement payments (i.e., transfers of property between spouses) also do not qualify as alimony because alimony includes only cash payments.

### I.G.2. Recapture of Alimony

[515 T.M., II.F.; TPS ¶1310.01.]

Because alimony payments are deductible but property settlement payments are not, there is a recapture rule that is designed to prevent spouses from disguising property settlement payments as alimony. If alimony payments end or decrease by a significant amount during the first three calendar years, then a portion of the alimony payments previously deducted by the payor spouse must be recaptured and included in his or her gross income. The recipient spouse is allowed a corresponding deduction since he or she previously included that amount in his or her gross income. The recapture rule presumes that the excess payments in the early years are at least partially property settlement payments instead of alimony [§ 71(f)(1)].

Under the recapture rule, the three calendar year period includes the first calendar year in which the spouse makes alimony payments and the following two calendar years. The alimony payments made in the third year are compared to the payments made in the first and second years. Generally, the payor spouse must recapture excess alimony payments in the third year if the alimony paid in the third year decreases by more than $15,000 from the second year or if the alimony paid in the second and third years decreases significantly from the alimony paid in the first year. More specifically, the excess alimony payments to be recaptured are the sum of the excess payments during the first year and excess payments for the second year. The excess alimony payments for the second year are equal to the excess, if any, of the amount of alimony paid during the second year over the sum of (i) $15,000, plus (ii) the amount of alimony paid during the third year. The excess alimony payments for the first year are equal to the excess, if any, the amount of alimony paid during the first year over the sum of (i) $15,000, plus (ii) the average of (a) the alimony paid in the third year and (b) the alimony paid in the second year reduced by any excess alimony payments for the second year [§ 71(f)(2)].

---

**EXAMPLE:** Under a divorce decree, Pete makes cash payments to his ex-wife, Pam, of $50,000 in Year 1, $30,000 in Year 2, and $5,000 in Year 3. The excess alimony payments for the second year are $10,000 ($30,000 − ($15,000 + $5,000)). The excess alimony payments for the first year are $22,500 ($50,000 − ($15,000 + (($5,000 + ($30,000 − $10,000))/2))). In Year 3, Pete may take a $5,000 deduction for the payments made in that year, but he must also recapture $32,500 ($10,000 + $22,500) in payments and include them in gross income. Pam can take a corresponding deduction for the $32,500 of alimony payments she previously included in her gross income.

---

The recapture rule does not apply in the following situations [§ 71(f)(5)]:

- either spouse dies during the first three years and the payments cease for that reason;
- the recipient spouse remarries during the first three years and the payments cease for that reason;
- the payments are temporary support payments made pursuant to a court order; or
- the payments vary in amount because they are determined by a pre-existing formula based on a fixed portion of income from a business, from property, or from compensation for employment or self-employment.

## I.H. Business Income

### I.H.1. Business Income in General

[501 T.M., IX.; TPS ¶1010.03.B.]

Gross income includes income derived from the operation of a business. Gross income from the operation of a manufacturing or merchandising business is generally equal to the total sales of the business less the cost of goods sold. The cost of goods sold is generally equal to inventory at the beginning of the year, plus purchases, minus inventory at the end of the year (in the case of a manufacturer, the costs of labor and overhead allocable to the manufactured goods are also added to cost of goods sold). For a manufacturing business, inventory generally includes raw materials, work in process, finished goods, and materials and supplies used in manufacturing the goods, and purchases generally include the costs of all raw materials or parts purchased for manufacture into finished goods. For a merchandising business, inventory generally includes the cost of merchandise on hand, and purchases generally include the cost of merchandise purchased for resale. The cost of goods sold generally does not include selling expenses, losses, and other items not ordinarily used in computing the costs of the goods that are sold. The cost of goods sold is determined based on the method of accounting consistently used by the taxpayer [§ 61(a)(2); Reg. § 1.61-3]. See XI.B. for a discussion of the accounting methods that may be used by a business.

A business that is primarily engaged in providing services generally will not have any cost of goods sold. Thus, the gross income of such a business is generally equal to its total sales.

Individual taxpayers report income and deductions from a business on Form 1040, Schedule C or C-EZ. See Chapter IV. for a discussion of deductions that can be claimed in determining the taxable income of a business.

### I.H.2. Farming Income

[608 T.M.; TPS ¶1010.03.B.5.]

A farming business is generally treated like any other business for purposes determining gross income. However, there are some special rules that apply specifically to farms and farmers. A farm is defined in the ordinarily accepted sense and encompasses livestock, dairy, poultry, fruit, and truck farms, as well as plantations, ranches, and all land used for farming operations. Farmers include all individuals, partnerships, or corporations that cultivate, operate, or manage farms for gain or profit, either as owners or tenants [Reg. § 1.61-4(d)]. Farmers report farming income and expenses on Form 1040, Schedule F. See IV.F.3. for a discussion of the deductions that can be claimed in determining the taxable income of a farming business.

The determination of gross income from a farming business depends on whether the farmer uses the cash method, accrual method, or crop method of accounting. See XI.H. for a discussion of the accounting methods that apply to farmers.

***Gross Income of Farmers Using Cash Method.*** A farmer using the cash method of accounting must include the following amounts in gross income: (i) cash and the value of any property received from the sale of livestock and produce raised by the farmer, (ii) profits from the sale of livestock and other items purchased by the farmer, (iii) incidental farm income, including breeding fees and fees from the rental of machinery and land, (iv) subsidy and conservation payments not otherwise excluded from gross income, and (v) gross income from all other sources [Reg. § 1.61-4(a)].

***Gross Income of Farmers Using Accrual Method.*** A farmer using the accrual method of accounting must use inventories. An accrual-method farmer must include the following amounts in gross income: (i) the sales price of all livestock and other products held for sale and sold during the year, (ii) the inventory value of all livestock and other products held for sale but not sold as of the end of the year (i.e., ending inventory), (iii) incidental farm income, including breeding fees and fees from the rental of machinery and land, (iv) subsidy and conservation payments not otherwise excluded from gross income, and (v) gross income from all other sources. An accrual-method farmer then subtracts the following amounts in determining gross income for the year: (i) the inventory value of all livestock and other products held for sale but not sold as of the beginning of the year (i.e., beginning inventory), and (ii) the cost of all livestock and other products purchased during the year (i.e., inventory purchases during the year) [Reg. § 1.61-4(b)].

Because of the difficulty of determining the actual cost of livestock and other farm products, accrual method farmers may value their inventories using the farm-price method or the unit-livestock-price method [Reg. § 1.471-6].

*Gross Income of Farmers Using Crop Method.* A farmer engaged in the production of crops may, with IRS consent, elect to use the crop method of accounting for his crop. Under the crop method, when a farmer does not harvest and dispose of his crop in the same tax year it was planted, he deducts the entire cost of producing the crop (including the cost of seed or young plants) in the year the income from the crop is realized [Reg. § 1.61-4(c)].

### I.H.3. Business Recoveries From Judgments and Settlements

[522 T.M., IV.A.; TPS ¶1340.04.A.]

When a taxpayer receives a payment from a judgment or settlement and the origin of the underlying claim is a nonpersonal business injury, there is no question that the amount of the recovery must be included in gross income. However, an issue often arises as to whether the recovery should be treated as ordinary income, capital gain, or a return of capital. If the nature of the underlying claim indicates that the recovery is compensation for lost profits, the recovery is treated as ordinary income. On the other hand, if the nature of the underlying claim is for loss of goodwill or harm to capital assets, the recovery is treated as a nontaxable return of capital to the extent of the taxpayer's basis. Any recovery in excess of basis is generally treated as capital gain. For a discussion of the underlying claim test, see II.F.2.

## I.I. Gains from Property Transactions

[501 T.M., X.C.; TPS ¶¶1410. through 1810.]

Gross income includes gains derived from dealings in property [§ 61(a)(3)]. Generally, the gain realized on a sale or exchange of property is equal to the amount realized by the taxpayer on the sale or exchange, less the taxpayer's adjusted basis in the property sold or exchanged. In certain cases, gain or loss realized on a sale or exchange of property is not recognized in the year of the sale or exchange and is instead deferred until some later year [Reg. § 1.61-6]. See Chapter III. for a discussion of the treatment of property transactions.

## I.J. Unemployment Compensation

[501 T.M., VIII.F.1.; TPS ¶1110.06.]

Gross income includes unemployment compensation received by an individual taxpayer [§ 85(a)]. Unemployment compensation generally includes any amount received under an unemployment compensation law of the United States or a state, including benefits paid by a state or the District of Columbia from the Federal Unemployment Trust Fund, state unemployment insurance benefits, railroad unemployment compensation benefits, and disability payments from a government program paid as a substitute for unemployment compensation. However, unemployment compensation does not include benefits received from an employer-financed fund and benefits received from as private fund to which the taxpayer voluntarily contributes (unless the taxpayer receives more than the amount contributed). Taxpayers who receive unemployment compensation should receive Form 1099-G, *Certain Government Payments*, reporting the total amount of unemployment compensation received during the year.

If a taxpayer repays any amount of unemployment compensation in the same year it was received, only the excess of the amount received over the amount repaid is included in gross income. If a taxpayer repays any amount of unemployment compensation that was included in his gross income in an earlier year, he can take a deduction for the amount repaid on his return for the year of repayment.

## I.K. Social Security Benefits

[501 T.M., VIII.F.4.; TPS ¶1170.02.A.]

A portion of social security benefits received by an individual taxpayer must be included in his gross income if certain requirements are met [§ 86(a)]. Social security benefits include (i) monthly retirement, survivor, and disability benefits received under Title II of the Social Security Act (reported to taxpayers on Form SSA-1099, *Social Security Benefit Statement*), and (ii) the social security equivalent benefit (SSEB) portion of tier 1 railroad retirement benefits received under the Railroad Retirement Act of 1974 (reported to taxpayers on Form RRB-1099, *Payments by the Railroad Retirement Board*). Social security benefits do not include supplemental security income (SSI) payments. Social security benefits are included in the gross income of the person who has the legal right to receive them.

A taxpayer must include a portion of social security benefits received in gross income if his provisional income exceeds a base amount. Provisional income is equal to the sum of (i) one-half of the social security benefits received, plus (ii) modified adjusted gross income [§ 86(b)(1)]. The base amount is $32,000 for married taxpayers filing jointly, $0 for married taxpayers who live with their spouses and file separately, and $25,000 for all other taxpayers [§ 86(c)(1)].

In determining provisional income, modified adjusted gross income is equal to: (i) adjusted gross income determined without regard to social security benefits, the § 135 exclusion of savings bonds interest, the § 137 exclusion of employer-paid adoption expenses, the § 199 domestic production activities deduction, the § 221 educational loan interest deduction, the § 222 qualified tuition deduction, the § 911 foreign income and housing costs exclusion, the § 931 exclusion of income from U.S. possessions, and the § 933 exclusion of income from Puerto Rico, plus (ii) tax-exempt interest received [§ 86(b)(2)].

---

**EXAMPLE:** Sarah is a retired single taxpayer who receives $10,000 of social security benefits during the year. Her adjusted gross income, not counting social security benefits, is $15,000 and she receives tax-exempt interest of $2,000. Sarah does not need to include any portion of her social security benefits in gross income because the sum of one-half of her social security benefits plus her modified adjusted gross income is $22,000 (($10,000 × 50%) + ($15,000 + $2,000)), and that amount is less than her base amount of $25,000.

---

If a portion of a taxpayer's social security benefits is includible in gross income, the determination of the amount includible depends on whether the taxpayer's provisional income is more or less than an adjusted base amount. The adjusted base amount is $44,000 for married taxpayers filing jointly, $0 for married taxpayers who live with their spouses and file separately, and $34,000 for all other taxpayers [§ 86(c)(2)].

If a taxpayer's provisional income does not exceed the adjusted base amount, the amount of his social security benefits included in gross income is the lesser of [§ 86(a)(1)]:

1. 50% of the social security benefits received; or
2. 50% of the excess of the provisional income over the base amount.

If a taxpayer's provisional income exceeds the adjusted base amount, the amount of his social security benefits included in gross income is the lesser of [§ 86(a)(2)]:

1. 85% of the social security benefits received; or

2. the sum of (i) 85% of the excess of the provisional income over the adjusted base amount, plus (ii) the lesser of (a) 50% of the difference between the base amount and the adjusted base amount, or (b) the amount that would be included in gross income if the taxpayer's provisional income was treated as not exceeding the adjusted base amount (as discussed above).

**EXAMPLE:** Bill and Beth, married taxpayers who file a joint return, receive $5,000 of social security benefits during the year. They have $31,000 of modified adjusted gross income for the year. Bill and Beth must include a portion of the social security benefits in gross income because their provisional income of $33,500 (($5,000 × 50%) + $31,000) exceeds their base amount of $32,000. Because their provisional income does not exceed their adjusted base amount of $44,000, the amount of social security benefits included in gross income is only $750, which is equal to the lesser of 50% of the social security benefits received ($5,000 × 50% = $2,500) or 50% of the excess of their provisional income over their base amount (($33,500 − $32,000) × 50% = $750).

**EXAMPLE:** Assume the same facts as in the previous example, except that Bill and Beth have $45,000 of modified adjusted gross income (instead of $31,000). Because provisional income of $47,500 (($5,000 × 50%) + $45,000) exceeds their adjusted base amount of $44,000, the amount of social security benefits includible in gross income is equal to the lesser of 85% of the social security benefits received or the following amount: the sum of (i) 85% of the excess of the provisional income over the adjusted base amount (($47,500 − $44,000) × 85% = $2,975), plus (ii) the lesser of (a) 50% of the difference between the base amount and the adjusted base amount (($44,000 − $32,000) × 50% = $6,000), or (b) the amount that would be included in gross income if the taxpayer's provisional income was treated as not exceeding the adjusted base amount, which is the lesser of 50% of the social security benefits received ($5,000 × 50% = $2,500) or 50% of the excess of the provisional income over the base amount (($47,500 − $32,000) × 50% = $7,750). Bill and Beth must include $4,250 of their social security benefits in gross income because 85% of the social security benefits received ($5,000 × 85% = $4,250) is less than $5,475 ($2,975 + $2,500).

# Gross Income

Taxpayers can generally use the Social Security Benefits Worksheet (Source: 2014 Form 1040 Draft Instructions) to determine if any of their benefits are taxable.

2014 Form 1040—Lines 20a and 20b

## Social Security Benefits Worksheet—Lines 20a and 20b

*Keep for Your Records*

**Before you begin:**
- ✓ Complete Form 1040, lines 21 and 23 through 32, if they apply to you.
- ✓ Figure any write-in adjustments to be entered on the dotted line next to line 36 (see the instructions for line 36).
- ✓ If you are married filing separately and you lived apart from your spouse for all of 2014, enter "D" to the right of the word "benefits" on line 20a. If you do not, you may get a math error notice from the IRS.
- ✓ Be sure you have read the **Exception** in the line 20a and 20b instructions to see if you can use this worksheet instead of a publication to find out if any of your benefits are taxable.

1. Enter the total amount from **box 5** of **all** your **Forms SSA-1099** and **Forms RRB-1099**. Also, enter this amount on Form 1040, line 20a .... 1. _____

2. Enter one-half of line 1 ................................................. 2. _____

3. Combine the amounts from Form 1040, lines 7, 8a, 9a, 10 through 14, 15b, 16b, 17 through 19, and 21 ........................................ 3. _____

4. Enter the amount, if any, from Form 1040, line 8b ..................................... 4. _____

5. Combine lines 2, 3, and 4 ................................................. 5. _____

6. Enter the total of the amounts from Form 1040, lines 23 through 32, plus any write-in adjustments you entered on the dotted line next to line 36 .............................. 6. _____

7. Is the amount on line 6 less than the amount on line 5?
   ☐ **No.** (STOP) None of your social security benefits are taxable. Enter -0- on Form 1040, line 20b.
   ☐ **Yes.** Subtract line 6 from line 5 ................................... 7. _____

8. If you are:
   - • Married filing jointly, enter $32,000
   - • Single, head of household, qualifying widow(er), or married filing separately and you **lived apart** from your spouse for all of 2014, enter $25,000
   - • Married filing separately and you lived with your spouse at any time in 2014, skip lines 8 through 15; multiply line 7 by 85% (.85) and enter the result on line 16. Then go to line 17
   } .............. 8. _____

9. Is the amount on line 8 less than the amount on line 7?
   ☐ **No.** (STOP) None of your social security benefits are taxable. Enter -0- on Form 1040, line 20b. If you are married filing separately and you **lived apart** from your spouse for all of 2014, be sure you entered "D" to the right of the word "benefits" on line 20a.
   ☐ **Yes.** Subtract line 8 from line 7 ................................... 9. _____

10. Enter: $12,000 if married filing jointly; $9,000 if single, head of household, qualifying widow(er), or married filing separately and you **lived apart** from your spouse for all of 2014 ........................................ 10. _____

11. Subtract line 10 from line 9. If zero or less, enter -0- ................................... 11. _____

12. Enter the **smaller** of line 9 or line 10 ................................... 12. _____

13. Enter one-half of line 12 ................................................. 13. _____

14. Enter the **smaller** of line 2 or line 13 ................................... 14. _____

15. Multiply line 11 by 85% (.85). If line 11 is zero, enter -0- .............................. 15. _____

16. Add lines 14 and 15 ................................................. 16. _____

17. Multiply line 1 by 85% (.85) ................................................. 17. _____

18. **Taxable social security benefits.** Enter the **smaller** of line 16 or line 17. Also enter this amount on Form 1040, line 20b ................................... 18. _____

(TIP) *If any of your benefits are taxable for 2014 and they include a lump-sum benefit payment that was for an earlier year, you may be able to reduce the taxable amount. See* Lump-Sum Election *in Pub. 915 for details.*

The following special rules apply in determining the amount of social security benefits received during a tax year:

1. The amount of social security benefits received by a taxpayer during a tax year is reduced by any social security benefits the taxpayer repaid during that year,

whether the repayment was for benefits received during that year or during a previous year [§ 86(d)(2)]. If the benefits repaid are more than the benefits received and a taxpayer's SSA-1099 or RRB-1099 shows net negative social security benefits received for the year, the benefits received in that year are not taxable and the taxpayer may claim an itemized deduction for the portion of the negative amount that represents benefits that were included in gross income in an earlier year.

2. A disabled taxpayer who receives workers' compensation generally receives a reduced amount of social security benefits that takes into account the amount of workers' compensation received. For federal tax purposes, the amount of social security benefits received must be increased by the workers' compensation received (i.e., the workers' compensation is treated as social security benefits for federal tax purposes) [§ 86(d)(3)].

3. A lump-sum payment of social security retirement benefits is generally included in gross income in the year received. However, if a lump-sum payment is attributable to earlier years, a taxpayer may elect to spread the payment back to the earlier years. When such an election is made, the amount included in gross income in the current year for the portion of the payment attributable to the earlier years is limited to the sum of the increases in gross income that would have occurred in the earlier years if the payment had actually been received in those years. This adjustment affects only the current year and no amended returns are filed for the earlier years [§ 86(e)].

## I.L. Discharge of Indebtedness Income

[540 T.M., II.; TPS ¶1040.]

Generally, income from the discharge of indebtedness (DOI) is included in gross income. For example, where a taxpayer and his or her bank modify a mortgage loan to reduce the principal balance of the loan, or where a credit card company settles a debt for less than the full amount the taxpayer owed, the taxpayer will typically realize income in an amount equal to the difference between the original amount owed and modified amount owed after the discharge. However, certain DOI amounts are excluded from gross income, including amounts from discharges occurring in a bankruptcy case under title 11, discharges occurring when the taxpayer is insolvent, discharges of qualified farm indebtedness, and, for certain taxpayers, discharges of qualified real property business indebtedness [§ 108(a)(1)]. Additionally, the discharge of certain student loans may also qualify for exclusion from income [§ 108(f)]. See II.A. for further discussion of DOI amounts that are excluded from gross income.

Sales of property, and in particular, real estate, frequently involve the cancellation or release of liabilities of the seller. In this situation, the nature of the liability is important. A disposition of property encumbered by a nonrecourse liability discharges the transferor from indebtedness, and the amount of the liability discharged is included in the transferor's amount realized, including instances where the amount of the nonrecourse debt exceeds the property's fair market value. The transferor realizes gain or loss from the disposition of the property depending on whether the indebtedness exceeds the transferor's basis in the property. No DOI income is realized, and therefore, none of the exclusions applicable to discharges of income, discussed below, are available [Reg. § 1.1001-2(a)].

A disposition of property subject to a recourse liability is treated differently. Like with nonrecourse debts, the amount of the recourse liability the transferee assumes is included in the transferor's amount realized. However, when the debt is discharged as part of the disposition, some of the income may be characterized as DOI income, rather than gain or loss from the sale or exchange of property. To the extent the fair market value of the property exceeds the transferor's basis, the transferor realizes gain. To the extent the recourse debt that is discharged exceeds the fair market value of the property, the transferor realizes DOI income, which may qualify for exclusion from income, as discussed below [Reg. § 1.1001-2(a)].

---

**EXAMPLE:** Andy owns property with a basis of $1,000 and a fair market value of $2,000. The property is subject to a nonrecourse mortgage in the amount of $3,000. Andy transfers the property to the lender and realizes $2,000 of gain ($3,000 amount realized − $1,000 basis). He does not realize any DOI income.

**EXAMPLE:** Olivia owns land with a basis of $1,000 and a fair market value of $2,000. The property is subject to a recourse liability of $3,000. Olivia transfers the property to the creditor, who agrees that Olivia will have no further liability to repay the debt. Olivia realizes $1,000 of gain on the disposition ($2,000 fair market value − $1,000 basis), and $1,000 of DOI income ($3,000 liability − $2,000 fair market value). If eligible, all or a portion of Olivia's DOI income may be excludible under one of the provisions described in II.A.

---

An individual taxpayer should receive a Form 1099-C, *Cancellation of Debt*, from a lender if the lender has discharged a debt the taxpayer owes to it, or if an identifiable event has occurred that is, or is deemed to be, a discharge of a debt of $600 or more. A taxpayer generally must report DOI income for the year to which Form 1099-C applies. However, if an identifiable event has occurred but the debt has not actually been discharged, the taxpayer is not required to report the DOI income until the year the debt is actually discharged.

The manner in which an individual taxpayer reports DOI income on his return depends on the nature of the debt. If the debt is a nonbusiness debt, the discharged amount is reported as "other income" on Form 1040. If the debt is a business debt, the discharged amount is reported on Schedule C or C-EZ of Form 1040. If the debt is a farming debt, the discharged amount is reported on Schedule F of Form 1040.

If a taxpayer includes DOI income in gross income in one tax year and repays the discharged amount in a later tax year, he may file Form 1040X, *Amended U.S. Individual Income Tax Return*, to claim a refund for the tax year in which the DOI income was included in gross income (subject to the three-year statute of limitations).

## I.M. Other Income

### I.M.1. Prizes and Awards

[501 T.M., XI.K.; TPS ¶1320.]

Prizes and awards generally must be included in gross income. Examples of prizes and awards include amounts received from raffles, drawings, sweepstakes, and television or radio giveaways. If a prize or award is received in the form of goods or services instead of cash, the fair market value of the goods or services must be included in gross income [§ 74(a); Reg. § 1.74-1(a)(2)].

Prizes and awards received in recognition of accomplishments in religious, charitable, scientific, educational, artistic, literary, or civic fields may be excluded from gross income if all of the following requirements are met [§ 74(b)]:

1. The taxpayer was selected without any action on his or her part to enter the contest or proceeding.

2. The taxpayer is not required to perform substantial future services as a condition of receiving the prize or award.

3. The prize or award is transferred by the payer directly to a government unit or tax-exempt charitable organization designated by the taxpayer.

See I.C.7. for a discussion of the tax treatment of employee achievement awards.

### I.M.2. Life Insurance

[529 T.M.; TPS ¶1170.01.]

Gross income generally includes income from life insurance contracts [§ 61(a)(10); Reg. § 1.61-10(a)]. However, gross income does not include amounts received under a life insurance contract by reason of the death of the insured [§ 101(a)(1)]. See II.E. for further discussion of the exclusion of life insurance proceeds. Note that the exclusion for life insurance proceeds does not apply to any interest income paid on life insurance proceeds held by an insurer under an agreement to pay interest [§ 101(c)].

### I.M.3. Annuities

#### I.M.3.a. Introduction to Annuities

[529 T.M.; TPS ¶1160.01.]

An annuity is a series of payments under a contract made at regular intervals over a period of more than one full year. The most common types of annuities include:

- fixed period annuities (definite amounts are paid at regular intervals for a definite length of time);

- single life annuities (definite amounts are paid at regular intervals for the life of one individual; the payments end when that individual dies);

- joint and survivor annuities (definite amounts are paid at regular intervals for the life of a first individual and, when that first individual dies, definite amounts are paid at regular intervals for the life of a second individual; the payments end when the second individual dies); and

- variable annuities (variable amounts are paid at regular intervals for a definite length of time or for life; the amounts paid often depend on variables such as cost-of-living indexes or profits earned by the annuity fund).

Annuities are usually sold by insurance companies, and are most commonly purchased by employers for employees as part of an employer retirement plan. However, commercial annuities can be purchased by individual taxpayers as an investment outside of the employment context, and private annuities can be sold by individuals and non-commercial organizations such as charities.

#### I.M.3.b. General Rules for Taxation of Annuities

[529 T.M., II.D.; TPS ¶1160.02.]

As a general rule, amounts received as an annuity under an annuity, endowment, or life insurance contract must be included in gross income [§ 61(a)(9), § 72(a)(1)]. However, a basic principle of annuity taxation is that the net cost of an annuity can be recovered tax free over the period during which the annuity payments are made. Thus, only amounts in excess of the net cost of the annuity are included in gross income.

Based on these principles, each monthly annuity payment received by a taxpayer must be segregated into two different amounts: (i) a tax free recovery of the net cost of the annuity, and (ii) the taxable balance. As a general rule, the tax-free portion of each annuity payment received by a taxpayer is determined based on an exclusion ratio equal to the taxpayer's investment in the contract over the taxpayer's total expected return under the contract [§ 72(b)(1)]. However, a special method applies in determining the tax-free portion of payments received as an annuity under a qualified retirement plan (such as a qualified stock bonus, pension, or profit sharing plan, a qualified employee annuity plan, or a § 403(b) tax-sheltered annuity contract) [§ 72(d)]. See XVII.A. for a discussion of this special method and the taxation of payments received as an annuity under a qualified retirement plan.

### I.M.3.c. Computing Taxable Part of Annuity Payments Received During Year

[529 T.M., II.D.; TPS ¶1160.02.A.]

*General Rule.* The taxable portion of the annuity payments a taxpayer received during the year is computed by subtracting the tax-free part of the annuity payments from the total amount of the annuity payments. The tax-free part of the annuity payments is equal to the tax-free part of each payment multiplied by the number of payments received during the year. Under the general rule, the tax-free part of each annuity payment is determined by multiplying the exclusion ratio by the first regular periodic annuity payment received. The exclusion ratio is equal to the ratio of the taxpayer's investment in the contract (see I.M.3.d.) to the taxpayer's total expected return under the contract (see I.M.3.e.).

---

**EXAMPLE:** Sam, age 65, paid $10,800 for an annuity that will pay him $100 a month for life. He received $1,200 ($100 × 12) of annuity payments during the year. Assuming Sam's expected return under the contract is $24,000, his exclusion ratio is 45% ($10,800 ÷ $24,000). The tax-free part of each annuity payment received by Sam is $45 ($100 × 45%). Thus, the tax-free part of the total annuity payments he received during the year is $540 ($45 × 12). Sam must include $660 ($1,200 − $540) of the annuity payments in gross income for the year.

---

The tax-free amount of each annuity payment generally does not change, even if the total amount of each annuity payment increases at a later date. As a result, any increase in the total amount of the annuity payments is fully taxable.

*Special Rule for Variable Annuity Payments.* The tax-free part of each variable annuity payment is determined by dividing the taxpayer's investment in the contract by the total number of periodic payments the taxpayer expects to receive under the contract. If the annuity is for a definite period, the total number of periodic payments is equal to the number of payments to be received each year multiplied by the number of years that payments will be received. If the annuity is for life, the total number of periodic payments is equal to the taxpayer's expected return multiple from the actuarial tables contained in Reg. § 1.72-9 [Reg. § 1.72-4(d)(3)(i)]. See I.M.3.e. for a discussion of expected return multiples.

---

**EXAMPLE:** Cathy, age 65, paid $12,000 for an annuity contract that will be paid in variable annual installments for her life. The annuity starting date was January 1 and the payments started on July 1. Cathy's expected return multiple from Table V of the actuarial tables is 20.0. The tax-free part of each variable annuity payment is $600 ($12,000 ÷ 20.0).

---

**EXAMPLE:** Assume the same facts as in the previous example, except that the annuity contract will be paid in variable annual installments for 15 years. The tax-free part of each variable annuity payment is $800 ($12,000 ÷ 15).

If this computation for variable annuity payments results in the tax-free part of the annuity payments for a year being more than the total annuity payments actually received for that year, the taxpayer may elect to re-compute the tax-free part of the annuity payments in the following year [Reg. § 1.72-4(d)(3)(ii)].

### I.M.3.d. Investment in the Contract

[529 T.M., II.D.5.; TPS ¶1160.02.A.3.]

A taxpayer's investment in the contract is the net amount paid for the annuity as of the annuity starting date [§ 72(c)]. The annuity starting date is the later of (i) the first day of the first period for which the taxpayer receives a payment under the contract, or (ii) the date on which the obligation under the contract becomes fixed [Reg. § 1.72-4(b)]. The net amount paid for the annuity is equal to the premiums and other amounts the taxpayer paid for the contract, minus the following amounts [Reg. § 1.72-6(a), § 1.72-7]:

1. any refunded premiums, rebates, dividends, or unrepaid loans the taxpayer received by the later of the annuity starting date or the date on which the taxpayer received his first payment;

2. any other tax-free amounts the taxpayer received under the contract by the later of the annuity starting date or the date on which the taxpayer received his first payment;

3. any additional premiums paid for double indemnity or disability benefits; and

4. the value of any refund feature contained in the contract.

**Refund Feature.** A contract contains a refund feature if (i) the expected return depends on the life of one or more individuals, (ii) the contract provides that payments will be made to a beneficiary or to the estate of the annuitant on or after the death of the annuitant if a stated amount or number of payments has not been paid to the annuitant before his death, and (iii) those payments are a refund of the amounts the taxpayer paid for the contract [Reg. § 1.72-7(a)].

The computation of the value of the refund feature requires reference to the actuarial tables to determine the likelihood that the annuitant will die before recovering the guaranteed minimum return on the contract. Different rules apply for purposes of determining the value of the refund feature for single life annuities, joint and survivor annuities, variable annuities, and contracts providing for more than one annuity element [Reg. § 1.72-7(b) through (e)]. For a single life annuity without survivor benefit, the value of the refund feature is treated as zero if (i) the payments are guaranteed for less than 2½ years, and (ii) the annuitant is under a specified age (depending on the actuarial table used). For a joint and survivor annuity, the value of the refund feature is treated as zero if (i) the payments are guaranteed for less than 2½ years, (ii) both annuitants are age 74 or younger, and (iii) the survivor's annuity is at least 50% of the first annuitant's annuity.

### I.M.3.e. Expected Return

[529 T.M., II.D.4.; TPS ¶1160.02.A.2.]

The taxpayer's expected return under the contract is the total amount he and any other eligible annuitants can expect to receive under the contract. The determination of the taxpayer's expected return depends on the type of annuity [§ 72(c)(3)].

*Fixed Period Annuity.* The expected return for a fixed period annuity is equal to the amount of payments to be received for each period multiplied by the fixed number of periods for which payments will be received [§ 72(c)(3)(B)].

---

**EXAMPLE:** Al paid $52,000 for an annuity that pays him $500 per month for 20 years. Al's expected return is $120,000 ($500 × (20 years × 12 months)).

---

*Single Life Annuity.* The expected return for a single life annuity is equal to the amount of payments to be received annually multiplied by the taxpayer's expected return multiple, as determined under the actuarial tables based on the taxpayer's age [Reg. § 1.72-5(a)]. For this purpose, a taxpayer's age is his age at his birthday nearest the annuity starting date. Generally, Tables V through VII are used for annuities purchased after June 30, 1986, and Tables I through IV are used for annuities purchased on or before June 30, 1986. See *Schedules and Tables 17 for Table V.*

---

**EXAMPLE:** Sue, age 66, paid $60,000 for an annuity that pays her $600 per month for life. Under Table V of the actuarial tables, Sue's expected return multiple is 19.2 years. Sue's expected return is $138,240 (($600 × 12) × 19.2).

---

*Joint and Survivor Annuity.* The expected return for a joint and survivor annuity depends on whether or not the payments will be the same for the two annuitants. If the payments will be the same, the expected return is equal to the amount of payments received annually multiplied by the annuitants' expected return multiple based on their joint life expectancies. However, if the payments will be different, the computation of the expected return must account for both the joint lives of the annuitants and the life of the survivor [Reg. § 1.72-5(b)].

---

**EXAMPLE:** Matt, age 70, bought a joint and survivor annuity providing payments of $500 a month for his life and, after his death, $500 a month for the remainder of the life of his 67-year-old wife, Sarah. Under Table VI of the actuarial tables, Matt and Sarah's joint expected return multiple is 22.0. Their expected return is $132,000 (($500 × 12) × 22.0).

**EXAMPLE:** Assume the same facts as in the previous example, except that Sarah will only receive payments of $350 a month after Matt's death. Because the payments are different, Matt's and Sarah's expected returns must be computed separately and then added together. Matt's expected return multiple is 16.0 under Table V, and his expected return is $96,000 (($500 × 12) × 16.0). Sarah's expected return multiple is determined by subtracting Matt's separate return multiple of 16.0 from their joint expected return multiple of 22.0, and her expected return is $25,200 (($350 × 12) × (22.0 – 16.0)). Thus, their total expected return under the contract is $121,200 ($96,000 + $25,200).

### I.M.3.f. Limitation on Exclusion

[529 T.M., II.D.3.; TPS ¶1160.02.]

The total amount of annuity payments that can be excluded from gross income is limited to the taxpayer's investment in the contract as of the annuity starting date (this limitation does not apply if the annuity starting date is before 1987). For this purpose, the investment in the contract is computed without any reduction for a refund feature [§ 72(b)(2)].

---

**EXAMPLE:** Sharon bought an annuity for $12,500. After certain adjustments (not including any reduction for a refund feature), her investment in the contract on the annuity starting date is $10,000. Sharon receives monthly annuity payments of $500 and she has an exclusion ratio of 20%. Thus, she can exclude $100 a month ($500 × 20%). Sharon will have excluded the full amount of her investment in the contract after 100 months of payments ($10,000 ÷ $100 per month). Thus, any annuity payments Sharon receives after 100 months will be fully taxable to her.

---

### I.M.3.g. Deduction of Unrecovered Investment in the Contract at Death

[529 T.M., II.D.7.; TPS ¶1160.02.B.2.]

If there is any unrecovered investment in the contract at the time of the taxpayer's death (in the case of a joint and survivor annuity, at the time of the last annuitant's death), that amount is allowed as a miscellaneous itemized deduction not subject to the 2% floor on the decedent's final income tax return [§ 72(b)(3)(A)].

### I.M.3.h. Tax Treatment of Amounts Not Received as an Annuity

[529 T.M., II.; TPS ¶1160.02.E.]

The annuity tax rules discussed above apply to periodic distributions received under an annuity, endowment, or life insurance contract. A taxpayer may also receive certain nonperiodic distributions under such a contract, such as cash withdrawals, dividends, and amounts received on a partial surrender of the contract. Nonperiodic distributions are treated as amounts not received as an annuity and are subject to a separate set of tax rules. The tax treatment of nonperiodic distributions depends on whether such distributions are received before the annuity starting date or on or after the annuity starting date.

***Nonperiodic Distributions Received On or After Annuity Starting Date.*** If a taxpayer receives a nonperiodic payment on or after the annuity starting date, the amount of the payment generally must be included in gross income [§ 72(e)(2)(A)].

***Nonperiodic Distributions Received Before Annuity Starting Date.*** If a taxpayer receives a nonperiodic payment before the annuity starting date from an annuity other than a qualified employer retirement plan annuity, the payment is first allocated to income on the contract and then to investment in the contract. The amount of the payment allocated to income on the contract must be included in gross income. The amount of the payment allocated to investment in the contract is not taxable [§ 72(e)(2)(B)].

The amount of the payment allocated to income on the contract is equal to the smaller of (i) the nonperiodic payment, or (ii) the amount by which the cash surrender value of the contract exceeds the taxpayer's investment in the contract immediately before the payment [§ 72(e)(3)].

**EXAMPLE:** Pete purchased an annuity contract from an insurance company. He received a $7,000 nonperiodic payment from the contract before the annuity starting date. Immediately before the payment, his investment in the contract was $10,000 and the contract had a cash surrender value of $16,000. Of the $7,000 payment, $6,000 ($16,000 − $10,000) must be allocated to income on the contract and included in Pete's gross income. The $1,000 ($7,000 − $6,000) balance of the payment is allocated to Pete's investment in the contract and is not taxable.

See XVII.A. for a discussion of the taxation of nonperiodic payments received from a qualified employer retirement plan annuity.

### I.M.4. Gambling Income

[527 T.M., VII.; TPS ¶1010.02.B.12.]

Gambling winnings must be included in gross income. Gambling winnings include, but are not limited to, winnings from lotteries, raffles, and slot machines. Gambling losses can be deducted up to the amount of the gambling winnings for the year if the taxpayer itemizes deductions [§ 165(d)]. See VII.J. for further discussion of the tax treatment of gambling winnings and losses.

### I.M.5. Illegal Income

[501 T.M., XI.F.; TPS ¶1010.02.B.9.]

Income received illegally and income received from illegal sources must be included in gross income [Reg. § 1.61-14(a)]. Illegal income includes income from illegal transactions such as embezzlement, extortion, theft, bribery, kickbacks, fraudulent schemes or devices, misappropriation, illegal diversion of funds, and illegal gambling.

### I.M.6. Miscellaneous Income

[501 T.M., XI., XII.; TPS ¶1010.02.B., .03.P.]

Numerous other items are also included in gross income. These other items include, but are not limited to, the following:

- income from an activity not engaged in for a profit, such as a hobby (however, see VIII.J. for a discussion of the treatment of hobby losses);
- fees for services (e.g., fees received as a corporate director, fiduciary of an estate, notary public, or election precinct official);
- jury duty fees;
- court awards and damages (other than compensatory damages for personal physical injuries or physical sickness);
- rewards for providing information;
- whistleblower's awards received from the IRS;
- strike and lockout benefits received from a union;
- benefits received under a credit card disability or unemployment insurance plan;
- Reemployment Trade Adjustment Assistance (RTAA) payments;
- business insurance proceeds received as reimbursement for loss of profits;
- the value of found money or property (so-called treasure trove);
- amortizable bond premium for certain municipal bonds held by dealers in tax-exempt securities [§ 75];

- loans from the Commodity Credit Corporation that the taxpayer elects to treat as income [§ 77];
- certain foreign taxes deemed to have been paid by domestic corporations electing the foreign tax credit [§ 78];
- the amount by which certain securities for which a bad debt deduction was claimed is restored in value [§ 80];
- moving expense reimbursements (for a discussion of moving expenses, see VII.B.6.) [§ 82];
- the amount of appreciation in property transferred to political organizations [§ 84];
- the amount of any alcohol and biodiesel fuels credit claimed by the taxpayer (see IX.A.7. and IX.A.21.) [§ 87];
- the amount of any qualified zone academy bond credit claimed by a bond holder (see IX.F.9.) [§ 1397E(j)];
- the amount of any clean renewable energy bond credit claimed by a bond holder (see IX.F.11.) [§ 54(g)];
- the amount of any Gulf tax credit bond credit claimed by a bond holder (see IX.F.) [§ 1400N(l)(6)];
- the amount of any qualified tax credit bond credit claimed by a bond holder (see IX.F.) [§ 54A(f)];
- the amount of any build America bond credit claimed by a bond holder (see IX.F.10.) [§ 54AA(f)];
- the amount of any interest paid on certain qualified tax credit bonds by a bond issuer (see IX.F.) [§ 6431(f)(1)(D)];
- the amount of any nuclear decommissioning costs required to be included in the cost of service for rate making purposes [§ 88]; and
- the amount of any illegal federal irrigation subsidy received [§ 90].

# CHAPTER II. EXCLUSIONS FROM GROSS INCOME

>>>>>>>>>>>>>>>>>>>>>>>>>>>>>>

## II.A. Discharge of Indebtedness

### II.A.1. Discharge of Indebtedness in General

[540 T.M., II.N.; TPS ¶1040.04.]

Generally, income from the discharge of indebtedness (DOI) is included in gross income (see I.L.). For example, where a taxpayer and his or her bank modify a mortgage loan to reduce the principal balance of the loan, or where a credit card company settles a debt for less than the full amount the taxpayer owed, the taxpayer will typically realize income in an amount equal to the difference between the original amount owed and modified amount owed after the discharge. However, certain DOI amounts are excluded from gross income, including discharges occurring in a bankruptcy case under title 11, discharges occurring when the taxpayer is insolvent, discharges of qualified farm indebtedness, and, for certain taxpayers, discharges of qualified real property business indebtedness [§ 108(a)(1)]. Additionally, the discharge of certain student loans may also qualify for exclusion from income [§ 108(f)].

While a taxpayer may realize gain on the disposition of property subject to nonrecourse indebtedness, no DOI income is realized, and therefore, none of the exclusions applicable to discharges of indebtedness, discussed below, are available. Conversely, when recourse debt is discharged as part of a disposition, some of the income may be characterized as DOI income, which may qualify for exclusion from income, as discussed below [Reg. § 1.1001-2(a)].

Excluded DOI income is reported on Form 982, *Reduction of Tax Attributes Due to Discharge of Indebtedness (and Section 1082 Basis Adjustment)*.

### II.A.2. Bankruptcy Exclusion

[540 T.M., II.N.2.a.; TPS ¶1040.04.B.]

Discharge of indebtedness occurring in a bankruptcy proceeding under title 11 of the U.S. Code is excluded from gross income if the taxpayer is under the jurisdiction of the bankruptcy court and the discharge is granted by the court, or pursuant to a court-approved plan [§ 108(d)(2)]. Taxpayers excluding DOI income under the bankruptcy exclusion must reduce certain tax attributes (see II.A.8.).

### II.A.3. Insolvency Exclusion

[540 T.M., II.N.2.a.; TPS ¶1040.04.C.]

Discharge of indebtedness occurring when a taxpayer is insolvent is excluded from gross income. "Insolvent" means the excess of liabilities over the fair market value of assets. A taxpayer's solvency is determined immediately before the discharge [§ 108(d)(3)]. The amount excluded is limited to the amount by which the taxpayer is insolvent [§ 108(a)(3)]. Taxpayers excluding DOI income under the insolvency exclusion must reduce certain tax attributes (see II.A.8.).

Liabilities include the entire amount of recourse debts, the amount of nonrecourse up to the fair market value of the property securing the debt, and the amount of nonrecourse debt in excess of the fair market value of the property securing the debt to the extent the excess nonrecourse debt is discharged [Rev. Rul. 92-53, 1992-2 C.B. 48].

---

**EXAMPLE:** Robert has assets with an aggregate fair market value of $70,000 and debts of $100,000. Robert is not in bankruptcy, but his creditors agree to reduce his indebtedness to $60,000. The amount of the indebtedness discharged is $40,000; however, Robert may exclude only $30,000 ($100,000 liabilities − $70,000 assets) under the insolvency exclusion. The remaining $10,000 (the amount of the discharge that exceeds the amount of his insolvency) is DOI income and is not excluded under the insolvency exclusion.

---

### II.A.4. Qualified Farm Indebtedness Exclusion

[540 T.M., II.N.2.b(2); TPS ¶1040.04.D.]

Discharged qualified farm indebtedness is excluded from gross income, regardless of the taxpayer's solvency. Indebtedness is qualified farm indebtedness if [§ 108(g)(2)]:

- the indebtedness was incurred directly in connection with the taxpayer's operation of the trade or business of farming; and
- 50% or more of the taxpayer's aggregate gross receipts for the three tax years preceding the tax year of the discharge is attributable to the trade or business of farming.

Additionally, the discharge must be made by a federal, state, or local government, a government agency or instrumentality, or any person actively and regularly engaged in the business of lending money, other than [§ 108(g)(1), § 49(a)(1)(D)(iv)]:

- a person related to the taxpayer (as defined in § 465(b)(3)(C));
- a person from whom the taxpayer acquired the property (or a person related to this person); or
- a person who receives a fee with respect to the taxpayer's investment in the property (or a person related to this person).

Taxpayers excluding DOI income under the qualified farm indebtedness exclusion must reduce certain tax attributes (see II.A.8.).

*Amount of Exclusion.* The amount of discharged qualified farm indebtedness that may be excluded from gross income is limited to the sum of [§ 108(g)(3)]:

1. the taxpayer's adjusted tax attributes; and

2. the aggregate adjusted bases of property used, or held for use, in a trade or business or for the production of income that the taxpayer held as of the beginning of the tax year following the tax year of the discharge.

For this purpose, a taxpayer's adjusted tax attributes are the sum of the following items [§ 108(g)(3)(B)]:

1. any net operating loss for the tax year of the discharge and any net operating loss carryover to that year;

2. any net capital loss for the tax year of the discharge and any capital loss carryover from that year;

3. any passive activity loss carryover from the tax year of the discharge; and

4. three times the sum of the following:
   - general business credit carryover to or from the tax year of the discharge;
   - minimum tax credit available as of the beginning of the tax year following the tax year of the discharge;
   - foreign tax credit carryover to or from the tax year of the discharge; and
   - passive activity credit carryover from the tax year of the discharge.

---

**EXAMPLE:** Tim operates a farming business and has qualified farm indebtedness of $5,000. Additionally, Tim owns property with an adjusted basis of $1,000 that is held for use in a trade or business, and he has a net operating loss carryover to Year 1 of $500. Tim is not insolvent and not in bankruptcy. His creditor, who is a qualified person, reduces Tim's debt to $2,500. Tim may exclude $1,500 ($1,000 basis of qualified property + $500 adjusted tax attributes) of the discharged qualified farm indebtedness from income. The remaining $1,000 is DOI income and is not excluded as qualified farm indebtedness.

---

### II.A.5. Qualified Real Property Business Indebtedness Exclusion

[540 T.M., II.N.2.b(3); TPS ¶1040.04.E.]

Taxpayers other than C corporations may exclude discharged qualified real property business indebtedness from gross income, regardless of the taxpayer's solvency. Qualified real property business indebtedness is debt (other than qualified farm indebtedness) [§ 108(c)(3)]:

- that the taxpayer incurred or assumed in connection with real property used in a trade or business;
- that is secured by that real property;
- that was either:
  - incurred or assumed before 1993; or
  - (i) incurred or assumed to acquire, construct, reconstruct, or substantially improve the property (qualified acquisition indebtedness), or (ii) incurred to refinance qualified pre-1993 real property business debt, up to the amount of debt refinanced; and
- for which the taxpayer makes an election on Form 982, *Reduction of Tax Attributes Due to Discharge of Indebtedness (and Section 1082 Basis Adjustment)*.

***Amount of Exclusion.*** The amount of discharged qualified real property business indebtedness that may be excluded is subject to two limitations [§ 108(c)(2); Reg. § 1.108-6]. First, the amount excluded is limited to the excess of:

1. the outstanding principal amount of the qualified real property business debt immediately before the discharge; over

2. the fair market value immediately before the discharge of the real property securing the debt, reduced by the outstanding principal amount of any other qualified real property business debt secured by that property.

Second, the amount excluded may not exceed the total adjusted bases of depreciable real property the taxpayer held immediately before the discharge of the debt, not including any depreciable real property acquired in contemplation of the discharge.

---

**EXAMPLE:** Sandy owns a building with a fair market value of $200,000 and a basis of $100,000, which is used in her trade or business. Sandy is neither insolvent nor in bankruptcy. The building is subject to two mortgages: the first mortgage is securing a $150,000 debt, and the second mortgage is securing a $90,000 debt. Sandy is personally liable for the debts. The second mortgage debt is reduced to $40,000, resulting in $50,000 of DOI income. Sandy may elect to exclude $40,000 ($90,000 principal amount of second mortgage – ($200,000 fair market property value – $150,000 principal amount of first mortgage)) of the discharged amount from gross income. The remaining $10,000 of DOI income may not be excluded as qualified real property business indebtedness.

---

### II.A.6. Qualified Principal Residence Indebtedness Exclusion [Expired]

[540 T.M., II.N.2.b(4); TPS ¶1040.04.F.]

The exclusion of discharged qualified principal residence indebtedness applies only to debt discharged before 2014 [§ 108(a)(1)(E)]. Therefore, discharged qualified principal residence indebtedness may no longer be excluded from gross income.

---

**EXAMPLE:** In 2008, Pam buys a main residence for $130,000 with a $30,000 down payment and a $110,000 recourse mortgage loan secured by the residence. In 2014, when the balance on the mortgage is $100,000, Pam loses her job and the value of her home has declined to $90,000. The lender agrees to allow a short sale of the home for $90,000 and to cancel the unpaid balance of Pam's debt. Pam has $10,000 ($100,000 debt – $90,000 paid in satisfaction of the debt) of DOI income that must be included in her gross income in 2014. In addition, Pam may not take a loss deduction for her home's decline in value because the loss was not incurred in a trade or business, in a transaction entered into for profit, or as a result of a casualty or theft. Had the debt been discharged after 2007 and before 2014, the $10,000 of DOI income would have been excluded as discharged qualified principal residence indebtedness.

---

### II.A.7. Coordination of Discharge of Indebtedness Exclusions

[540 T.M., II.N.2.; TPS ¶1040.04.C.2., .04.D.5., .04.E.]

The bankruptcy exclusion takes precedence over the insolvency exclusion, the qualified farm indebtedness exclusion, and the qualified real property business indebtedness exclusion, all of which are inapplicable to discharges occurring in title 11 cases. The insolvency exclusion takes precedence over the qualified farm indebtedness exclusion and the qualified real property business exclusion, which are inapplicable to a discharge to the extent a taxpayer is insolvent [§ 108(a)(2)]. Thus, the order of precedence of the exclusions is as follows:

1. bankruptcy exclusion
2. insolvency exclusion
3. qualified farm indebtedness exclusion and qualified real property business indebtedness exclusion.

**EXAMPLE:** Adam files for bankruptcy in June of Year 1. He has debts of $500,000 and assets of $300,000. In October of Year 1, $150,000 of indebtedness is discharged pursuant to a court-approved plan of bankruptcy. In November of Year 1, $100,000 of debt is discharged without regard to a court order or the court-approved plan of bankruptcy. The $150,000 discharged in October qualifies for the bankruptcy exclusion, while the $100,000 discharged in November qualifies for the insolvency exclusion. Following the October discharge, Adam has debts of $350,000 ($500,000 – $150,000) and assets of $300,000. Therefore, Adam may exclude only $50,000 of the November discharge, which reflects the amount by which he is insolvent immediately before the November discharge. The remaining $50,000 of DOI income is not excluded under either the bankruptcy or the insolvency exclusions.

### II.A.8. Reduction of Tax Attributes When Discharge of Indebtedness Excluded

#### II.A.8.a. Reduction of Tax Attributes for the Bankruptcy Exclusion and the Insolvency Exclusion

[540 T.M., II.N.2.a.(5); TPS ¶1040.04.G.]

A taxpayer excluding discharged debt from gross income must reduce certain tax attributes (not below zero) by the amount excluded. If all attributes are reduced to zero, any unaccounted for excluded amounts may still be excluded from income, despite the impossibility of further reducing attributes. For amounts excluded under the bankruptcy exclusion or the insolvency exclusion, the taxpayer's tax attributes generally are reduced in the following order [§ 108(b)(2); Reg. § 1.108-7(a)]:

1. net operating losses for the tax year of the discharge and net operating loss carryovers to that year;
2. general business credit carryovers to or from the tax year of the discharge;
3. minimum tax credits as of the beginning of the tax year immediately following the tax year of the discharge;
4. net capital losses for the tax year of the discharge and capital loss carryovers to that year;
5. basis of the taxpayer's property held at the beginning of the tax year immediately following the tax year of the discharge;
6. passive activity losses and credit carryovers from the tax year of the discharge; and
7. foreign tax credit carryovers to or from the tax year of the discharge.

Generally, the attributes are reduced on a dollar-for-dollar basis with the amount of excluded discharged debt. However, general business credit carryovers, minimum tax credits, foreign tax credit carryovers, and passive activity credit carryovers are reduced by 33 1/3 cents for each dollar of excluded discharged debt [§ 108(b)(3)]. The reductions are made after the determination of tax for the tax year of the discharge, and thus, tax attributes arising in, or carried to the tax year of discharge must be applied against income for that year before they are reduced [§ 108(b)(4); Reg. § 1.108-7(b)].

---

**EXAMPLE:** In a corporation's chapter 11 bankruptcy proceeding, the debtor receives a discharge in the amount of $100,000 in Year 1. The entire amount is excluded from the debtor's gross income under the bankruptcy exclusion. The debtor has a net operating loss of $75,000 from a previous year that may be carried over to Year 1 and $50,000 of income in Year 1. The net operating loss carryover is first applied to the debtor's Year 1 taxable income to reduce such income to zero, and leaving a remainder of $25,000 ($75,000 carryover − $50,000 of income) of the net operating loss carryover. The $100,000 of excluded income from the discharge must reduce the debtor's tax attributes. The amount first applies against the debtor's $25,000 remaining net operating loss carryover, reducing the carryover to zero. $75,000 of excluded income remains, which must be applied to reduce the debtor's tax attributes in the order outlined above.

---

*Reduction of Property's Basis.* Reductions of the taxpayer's basis in property must be made in the following order [§ 108(b)(2)(E), § 1017(a); Reg. § 1.1017-1(a)]:

1. real property held for investment or used in the taxpayer's trade or business (other than real property held for sale to customers in the ordinary course of business) if it secured the discharged debt;

2. personal property held for investment or used in the taxpayer's trade or business (other than inventory, accounts receivable, and notes receivable) if it secured the discharged debt;

3. other property held for investment or used in the taxpayer's trade or business (other than inventory, accounts receivable, notes receivable, and real property held for sale to customers in the ordinary course of business);

4. inventory, accounts receivable, notes receivable, and real property held primarily for sale to customers in the ordinary course of business; and

5. personal-use property not used in the taxpayer's trade or business and not held for investment.

Within each category, basis is reduced in proportion to adjusted basis. Basis cannot be reduced by more than (i) the excess of the total bases of the property and the amount of money the taxpayer held immediately after the discharge, over (ii) the taxpayer's total liabilities immediately after the discharge.

A taxpayer may elect on Form 982, *Reduction of Tax Attributes Due to Discharge of Indebtedness (and Section 1082 Basis Adjustment)*, to reduce the bases of depreciable property held at the beginning of the tax year immediately following the tax year of the discharge before reducing other tax attributes [§ 108(b)(5); Reg. § 1.108-4]. Under this election, basis of depreciable property is reduced in the following order [Reg. § 1.1017-1(c)]:

1. depreciable real property used in the taxpayer's trade or business or held for investment that secured the discharged debt;

2. depreciable personal property used in the taxpayer's trade or business or held for investment that secured the discharged debt;

3. other depreciable property used in the taxpayer's trade or business or held for investment; and

4. real property held primarily for sale to customers if the taxpayer elects to treat it as if it were depreciable property.

Basis reduction may not exceed the total adjusted bases of all the taxpayer's depreciable property. If the amount of excluded discharged debt exceeds the taxpayer's total bases in depreciable property, the excess must reduce the taxpayer's other tax attributes in the order listed above.

### II.A.8.b. Reduction for the Qualified Farm Indebtedness Exclusion

[540 T.M., II.N.2.b(2); TPS ¶1040.04.G.2.d.(7).]

After first reducing tax attributes by any amount excluded under the insolvency exclusion, remaining tax attributes are reduced (not below zero) by the amount of excluded discharged qualified farm indebtedness. The attributes are reduced in the same order described for the bankruptcy and insolvency exclusions (see II.A.8.a.), except that reductions to the taxpayer's basis in property are treated differently. For excluded qualified farm indebtedness, only the basis of qualified property is reduced. Qualified property is any property the taxpayer uses or holds for use in his trade or business or for the production of income. Further, the basis of qualified property is reduced in the following order [§ 1017(b)(4)]:

1. depreciable qualified property;

2. land that is qualified property and is used or held in the taxpayer's farming business; and

3. other qualified property.

The taxpayer may elect on Form 982, *Reduction of Tax Attributes Due to Discharge of Indebtedness (and Section 1082 Basis Adjustment)*, to treat real property held primarily for sale to customers as if it were depreciable qualified property [§ 1017(b)(3)(E)].

### II.A.8.c. Reduction for the Qualified Real Property Business Indebtedness Exclusion

[540 T.M., II.N.2.b(3); TPS ¶1040.04.G.]

A taxpayer electing to exclude discharged qualified real property business indebtedness from income must reduce the basis of depreciable real property (not below zero) by the amount excluded. Basis is reduced at the beginning of the tax year immediately following the tax year of the discharge. Taxpayers disposing of depreciable real property before this time must reduce the property's basis immediately before disposition [§ 108(c), § 1017(b)(3)(F)].

### II.A.9. Student Loans

[540 T.M., II.N.2.c.; TPS ¶1040.04.H.]

Certain student loans provide that all or a portion of the debt incurred to attend a qualified educational institution (as defined in § 170(b)(1)(A)(ii)) will be discharged if the recipient of the loan works for a certain period of time in certain professions for any of a broad class of employers. DOI income from the discharge of these student loans is excluded from gross income. The loan must have been made by one of the following entities [§ 108(f)(2); Reg. § 1.170A-9(c)(1)]:

- the federal government, a state or local government, or an instrumentality, agency, or subdivision thereof;

- a tax-exempt public benefit corporation that has assumed control of a state, county, or municipal hospital, and whose employees have been deemed public employees under state law; or

- an educational institution (a) receiving funds from an entity described in one of the previous two bullets for the purpose of making the loan, or (b) as part of an institutional program designed to encourage students to serve in occupations or areas with unmet needs and under which the services provided are for or under the direction of a governmental unit or a tax-exempt § 501(c)(3) organization.

A loan made to refinance a qualified student loan also qualifies if made by an educational institution or tax-exempt § 501(a) organization under a program designed as described in part (b) of the third bullet, above.

---

**EXAMPLE:** Stephanie attended law school and has student loan debt. The loans and the underlying loan documents did not address whether any of the debt would be forgiven if Stephanie worked in a particular profession for a specified period of time. Her law school offers a loan repayment assistance program (LRAP) to help reduce the student loan debt of graduates that engage in public service. The LRAP program is designed to encourage graduates to enter public service in occupations or areas with unmet needs. Under the LRAP program, the law school makes loans that refinance the graduates' original student loans. After the graduate works for a required period in a qualifying law-related public service position, the law school will forgive all or a part of the graduate's debt. After Stephanie graduates law school, she signs an LRAP promissory note and accepts the terms and conditions of the law school's LRAP loan. Stephanie's LRAP loan is a qualified student loan for purposes of the exclusion.

---

Taxpayers are not required to reduce any tax attributes as a result of the exclusion of discharged student loans from gross income.

### II.A.10. Deferral of Discharge of Indebtedness Income for Certain Reacquired Business Debt

[540 T.M., II.N.2.d.; TPS ¶1040.05.]

Taxpayers may defer DOI income arising from the reacquisition of an applicable debt instrument in 2009 or 2010. This deferred income is included ratably over a five-year period beginning with the fifth tax year following the tax year in which the repurchase occurs (for repurchase occurring in 2009) or with the fourth tax year following the tax year in which the repurchase occurs (for repurchase occurring in 2010). Applicable debt instruments are debt instruments issued by (i) a C corporation, or (ii) any other person in connection with the conduct of a trade or business by that person [§ 108(i)].

### II.A.11. Foregone Deductions

[501 T.M., X.B.2.d(4), 541 T.M., II.G.10.; TPS ¶1040.03.I.1.]

A taxpayer does not realize income from a discharge of indebtedness to the extent that the payment of the liability would have given rise to a deduction. Thus, if a cash method taxpayer has unpaid interest on a trade or business loan that is discharged, the amount is not included in the taxpayer's income because the interest, had it been paid, would have been deductible, even though the discharge of the principal might be taxable [§ 108(e)(2)].

### II.A.12. Purchase Price Reductions

[501 T.M., X.B.2.d(5), 541 T.M., II.G.8.; TPS ¶1040.03.H.1.]

Gross income does not include the amount by which a seller of property reduces the taxpayer's indebtedness incurred in purchasing the property, if the reduction does not occur in a bankruptcy proceeding or while the taxpayer is insolvent, and the reduction would otherwise be treated as income from the discharge of indebtedness. Instead, the reduction is treated as a purchase price adjustment, and the taxpayer must reduce his or her tax basis for the purchased property [§ 108(e)(5)].

### II.A.13. Application of Discharge of Indebtedness Exclusions to Partnerships, S Corporations, and Consolidated Groups

[541 T.M., II.G.4.f., II.G.4.g., VI.B.1.; TPS ¶1040.04.I., .04.J., .04.K.]

*Partnerships.* In computing taxable income, income resulting from the discharge of a partnership's indebtedness passes through to the partners pro rata (see Chapter XIV.). Exclusions and attribute reductions also generally occur at the partner level. The bankruptcy exclusion (see II.A.2.) and the insolvency exclusion (see II.A.3.) each apply at the partner level. Thus, if a partnership is insolvent, but a partner is not, the insolvency exclusion is not available for that partner. However, the determination of whether debt is qualified real property business indebtedness and the application of the limitations on the amount of qualified real property business indebtedness that may be excluded (see II.A.5.) occur at the partnership level. Therefore, it is the partnership's trade or business and the partnership's real property that is considered in determining whether the debt was incurred or assumed in connection with real property used in a trade or business. The election to exclude discharged qualified real property business indebtedness, though, is made at the partner level [§ 108(d)(6)].

*S Corporations.* While the items of income, gain, loss, deductions, and credits of an S corporation pass through to its shareholders (see Chapter XV.), exclusions and attribute reductions apply at the corporate level. Because shareholders are limited in the amount of S corporation losses they may deduct, a special attribute reduction rule applies. Losses disallowed because of a shareholder's insufficient basis are treated as a net operating loss of the S corporation for that year, which are subject to reduction under the bankruptcy, insolvency, and qualified farm indebtedness exclusions [§ 108(d)(7)].

*Consolidated Groups.* For members of a consolidated group, the insolvency exclusion is applied separately to each member that has excluded DOI income, and insolvency is determined based only on the assets (including stock and securities of other members) and liabilities (including liabilities to other members) of the member that realizes the excluded DOI income [Reg. § 1.1502-28(a)(1)].

## II.B. Municipal Bonds

[501 T.M., X.A.2.b.; TPS ¶1210.02.A.]

Interest on a state or local bond generally is not taxable. A state or local bond is an obligation of a state, territory, U.S. possession, the District of Columbia, or a political subdivision thereof. A political subdivision is any state or local governmental unit that is a municipal corporation or that has been delegated the right to exercise part of the sovereign power of the state or local governmental unit [§ 103; Reg. § 1.103-1]. Examples include port authorities, toll road commissions, and utility services authorities. Though such interest is excluded from gross income, tax-exempt interest is included in calculating modified adjusted gross income in some situations, including determining whether social security benefits are taxable [§ 86(b)(2)]. Payers must report tax-exempt interest on Form 1099-INT, *Interest Income*.

Some state and local obligations are taxable and must be included in income, including [§ 103(b), § 141, § 148, § 149]:

- private activity bonds that are not qualified private activity bonds (Note that tax-exempt interest on specified private activity bonds is a tax preference item for purposes of the alternative minimum tax [§ 57(a)(5)] (see X.A.2.c.));
- arbitrage bonds;
- bonds required to be registered that are not in registered form;
- certain federally guaranteed bonds; and
- bonds issued with respect to certain advance refunding.

For a discussion of taxable state and local obligations, see I.D.6.

## II.C. Gifts and Inheritances

[501 T.M., XI.B., XI.C.; TPS ¶1330.]

Gross income does not include the value of property received as gifts, bequests, devises, or inheritances. However, income produced by such property, or any gift, bequest, devise, or inheritance of the income generated from property, is included in gross income (e.g., interest or dividends). Further, any amount included in the income of a beneficiary under subchapter J (Estates, Trusts, Beneficiaries, and Decedents) is treated as a gift, bequest, devise, or inheritance of income from property, and is includible in the recipient's income [§ 102; Reg. § 1.102-1] (see Chapter XXI.).

The gift exclusion does not apply to any amount transferred by or for an employer to (or for the benefit of) an employee and such amounts are included in the recipient's gross income. However, the gift exclusion applies if the employer is related to the employee and the transfer is connected with a personal event or situation and is not an attempt to disguise compensation [Prop. Reg. § 1.102-1(f)]. Additionally, prizes and awards are not excluded from income as gifts (see I.M.1.).

For purposes of this rule, a gift is generally defined as a transfer or money or property primarily motivated by a "detached and disinterested generosity" and made out of "affection, respect, admiration, charity or like impulses," rather than out of moral or legal obligations, the anticipation of some economic benefit, or in return for services [*Commissioner v. Duberstein*, 363 U.S. 278 (1960)]. A bequest is a gift of personal property by will, while a devise is a gift of real property by will. An inheritance is real or personal property acquired by succession from a decedent's estate.

---

**EXAMPLE:** News Co. is a for-profit company that publishes a daily newspaper. News Co. has operated at a deficit for several years and publishes an advertisement seeking money from readers and the general public so that operations may continue. The advertisement states that failing to send money is sure to result in the paper's demise. News Co. subsequently receives $200,000 over the following months (from persons other than News Co. stockholders). The payments are taxable to News Co. because they were made in consideration of News Co. continuing to publish the newspaper, and thus were not 'voluntary' in that contributors expected something in return for their money.

---

## II.D. Sickness, Injury, and Death Benefits

### II.D.1. Accident, Health, and Disability Insurance

#### II.D.1.a. Contributions by an Employer to Accident and Health Plans

[389 T.M., IV.; TPS ¶5920.01., .02.]

Gross income does not include the value of employer-provided coverage under an accident or health plan [§ 106(a)]. An accident or health plan is an arrangement for the payment of amounts to employees in the event of personal injuries or sickness to the employee, the employee's spouse, the employee's dependents, or the employee's children under age 27 [Reg. § 1.105-5].

Excludible contributions include employer contributions to [Reg. § 1.106-1]:

- the cost of accident or health insurance, including qualified long-term care insurance (see XVII.C.1.a.);
- a separate trust or fund that provides accident or health benefits directly or through insurance (see XVII.C.1.a.);
- Archer Medical Savings Accounts (Archer MSAs) (see XVII.C.1.d.);
- Health savings accounts (HSAs), or health reimbursement accounts (HRAs) (see XVII.C.1.e.).

For a discussion of employer-provided accident and health coverage, see XVII.C.1.a.

#### II.D.1.b. Reimbursement for Medical Expenses

[389 T.M., III.B.; TPS ¶5920.01.B.2., .01.B.3.]

Amounts received through health insurance, whether provided by an employer or purchased directly by an individual, are excluded from gross income if they are payments or reimbursements of medical care expenses of the employee, the employee's spouse, the employee's dependent, or the employee's child under age 27 that would otherwise be deductible under § 213 [§ 105(b), § 105(c); Reg. § 1.105-2, § 1.105-3]. However, reimbursements for amounts deducted in a prior tax year are includible in gross income [§ 104(a)(3)].

---

**EXAMPLE:** Tony and Allison are married. Tony works for Conglomo Co., which pays $1,000 per month to an Insurance Co. to provide health insurance to Tony and Allison. Conglomo's health plan meets the qualification requirements. Allison files a claim and receives $2,000 from Insurance Co. as reimbursement for a medical bill she paid. Tony and Allison do not receive gross income as a result of Congolomo's payment of the health insurance premium or Insurance Co.'s reimbursement.

---

#### II.D.1.c. Disability Benefits and Other Accident and Health Benefits

[389 T.M., IV.; TPS ¶5920.01., .02., .03.]

Employees may generally exclude direct or indirect employer payments under an accident or health plan that are payments for permanent loss or use of a part or function of the body, or for permanent disfigurement if the benefit is determined without regard to any period the employee is absent from work [§ 105(b), § 105(c); Reg. § 1.105-2, § 1.105-3]. This benefit also applies to the employee's spouse or dependent. However, payments are not excluded if they are either (i) attributable to contributions of the employer that were not includible in the employee's gross income, or (ii) paid by the employer. To the extent an accident or health plan is funded by the employee, a ratable portion of the benefits generally may be excluded from an employee's income [§ 105; Reg. § 1.105-1(c)] (see XVII.C.1.c.).

Social security disability benefits are taxed on the same basis as other social security benefits [§ 86(d)(1)] (see I.K.).

If an individual purchases a disability insurance policy with his or her own funds, amounts received under the policy are excluded from gross income, except to the extent the individual deducts the premiums [§ 104(a)(3)].

### II.D.2. Employee Death Benefits Excludible from Gross Income

[529 T.M., II.C.3.; TPS ¶5930.03.]

Amounts paid as a survivor annuity on account of the death of a public safety officer may be excludible from gross income [§ 101(h)] (see XVII.C.2.).

Gross income does not include amounts an employer pays because of the death of an employee who is a specified terrorist victim or an astronaut who dies in the line of duty [§ 101(i)].

### II.D.3. Statutory Benefits Excludible from Income

#### II.D.3.a. Workers' Compensation Excludible from Income

[522 T.M., III.A.; TPS ¶1340.03.A.]

An amount received under a workers' compensation act (or under a statute in the nature of a workers' compensation act) as compensation for personal injuries or sickness incurred in the course of employment is excluded from gross income. This includes compensation paid under a workers' compensation act to the survivor(s) of a deceased employee. The amount may not be a retirement pension or annuity measured by the employee's age, length of service, or prior contributions, even if the employee's retirement is occasioned by a work injury or sickness [§ 104(a)(1); Reg. § 1.104-1(b)].

#### II.D.3.b. Pension, Annuity, or Similar Allowance for Personal Injury or Sickness Excluded from Income

[522 T.M., III.C.; TPS ¶1340.03.C.]

Taxpayers may exclude from income amounts received as a pension, annuity, or similar allowance for personal injuries or sickness as a result of active service in the armed forces of any country, the Coast and Geodetic Survey, or the Public Health Service, or as a disability annuity payable under section 808 of the Foreign Service Act of 1980. To qualify for the exclusion, the taxpayer must one meet the following requirements [§ 104(a)(4), § 104(b); Reg. § 1.104-1(e)]:

- The taxpayer must have been entitled to receive the amounts on or before September 24, 1975.
- On September 24, 1975, the taxpayer was a member of the armed forces, the Coast and Geodetic Survey, the Public Health Service, or the Foreign Service, or had a binding written commitment to become a member.
- The taxpayer receives the excludible amounts by reason of a combat-related injury.
- Upon application, the taxpayer would be entitled to receive disability compensation from the Department of Veterans' Affairs.

The amounts excludible may not be less than the maximum amount the taxpayer would be entitled to receive as disability compensation from the Department of Veterans' Affairs [§ 104(b)(4)].

### II.D.3.c. *Disability Income from Terroristic or Military Action Excluded from Income*

[522 T.M., III.D.; TPS ¶1340.03.D.]

Amounts received as disability income attributable to injuries suffered as a direct result of a terroristic or military action are excluded from a taxpayer's gross income. A terroristic or military action is any terroristic activity which a preponderance of evidence indicates was directed against the United States or its allies and any military action involving U.S. armed forces and resulting from actual or threatened violence or aggression against the United States or its allies [§ 104(a)(5), § 692(c)(2)].

## II.E. Life Insurance Excluded from Income

[529 T.M., I.; TPS ¶¶1170.01., 5930.01.D.]

Life insurance proceeds paid by reason of the death of the insured are generally excluded from the beneficiary's income. This is the case whether the payment is made to the insured's estate or to any beneficiary and whether the payment is made directly or to a trust. The exclusion does not apply to interest earned on any excludible benefit held by the insurer under an agreement to pay interest. Additionally, where a life insurance contract is transferred for valuable consideration, the death benefits are generally excludible only to the extent of the consideration paid to acquire the contract, plus any premiums or other consideration paid by the transferee [§ 101; Reg. § 1.101-1(a)(1)].

### II.E.1. *Employer-Owned Life Insurance*

[529 T.M., I.C.4., 386 T.M., III.A.; TPS ¶¶1170.01.A.2., 5930.01.D.]

For employer-owned life insurance contracts (also known as corporate-owned life insurance or COLI) issued after August 17, 2006, amounts received in excess of premiums and other amounts paid for the contract are taxed. An employer-owned life insurance contract is a life insurance contract owned by a person in a trade or business that is a beneficiary under the contract and that covers the life of an insured who is an employee. This rule does not apply if the proceeds are paid to the insured's heirs. However, proceeds may be payable tax-free to the employer if notice and consent requirements are met and the insured was an employee at any time during the 12-month period before his death or, at the time the contract was issued, was a director or a highly compensated person [§ 101(j)].

The notice and consent requirements are met if, before the issuance of the contract, the employee is notified in writing that his life is being insured and about the maximum face amount for which the employee could be insured. The employee must provide written consent to being insured under the contract and to coverage that may continue after the insured terminates employment. The employee must be informed in writing that an applicable policyholder will be a beneficiary of any proceeds payable upon the death of the employee [§ 101(j)(4)].

### II.E.2. *Accelerated Death Benefits and Viatical Settlements*

[529 T.M., I.C.2., 546 T.M., III.D.2.b.; TPS ¶1540.05.]

Accelerated death benefits, which are amounts received under a life insurance contract on the life of an insured who is terminally or chronically ill are treated as amounts paid by reason of the death of an insured, and thus, such amounts may be excluded from income [§ 101(a)(1), § 101(g)(1)]. This is the case whether the policy is surrendered to the insurance company or sold to a viatical settlement provider.

A terminally ill individual is a person who has been certified by a physician as having an illness or physical condition that can reasonably be expected to result in death within two years of the certification [§ 101(g)(4)(A)]. A chronically ill individual is a person who is not terminally ill, but has been certified by a licensed health care practitioner as meeting one of the following tests [§ 101(g)(4)(B), § 7702B(c)(2)]:

- the individual is unable to perform at least two activities of daily living (e.g., eating, bathing, and dressing) for a period of at least 90 days without substantial assistance; or
- the individual has a level of disability similar to the level of disability described in the first test; or
- the individual requires substantial supervision to be protected from threats to health and safety due to severe cognitive impairment.

The nontaxable portion of the amount paid to an chronically ill individual is limited to amounts incurred for qualified long-term care not covered by insurance [§ 101(g)(3)].

## II.F. Judgments and Settlements

### II.F.1. Damages for Personal Injury or Sickness Excluded from Income

[522 T.M., III.E.; TPS ¶1340.03.E.]

Damages (excluding punitive damages) for personal injuries or physical sickness received in a tort suit (or the settlement agreement) may be excluded from income [§ 104(a); Reg. § 1.104-1(c)(1)]. This exclusion may apply to that portion of the damages measured by the individual's lost income. Punitive damages generally are not excludible under this rule, and must be included in gross income. However, punitive damages are excludible where they are recovered pursuant to a wrongful death action for which the applicable state law permits only punitive damages to be awarded [§ 104(c)].

For purposes of this rule, damages means an amount received (other than workers' compensation) through prosecution of a legal suit or action, or through a settlement agreement in lieu of prosecution [§ 104(a)(2); Reg. § 1.104-1(c)(1)].

Emotional distress is not considered a physical injury or physical sickness. However, where emotional distress is attributable to a physical injury or physical sickness, damages for such distress may be excluded. Further, emotional distress damages may be excluded from income to the extent of amounts actually paid for medical care attributable to the emotional distress [§ 104(a); Reg. § 1.104-1(c)(1)].

---

**EXAMPLE:** Cory's leg is injured in an automobile accident. He requires surgery and several weeks of bed rest. Cory sues the person who hit him and a jury awards him damages for lost wages, unpaid medical bills, and pain and suffering. Because these damages are all directly linked to the personal physical injury, they are excludible from gross income.

---

### II.F.2. Application of Underlying Claims Test to Judgments and Settlements

[522 T.M., II.; TPS ¶1340.02.]

In determining whether an amount received as a judgment or a settlement must be included in gross income (as well as the character and deductibility of any amount that must be included), a taxpayer must consider the nature of the claim underlying judgment or settlement. Where the underlying claim involves income that would be excludible had the taxpayer received the amount without the operation of a judgment or settlement, the amount received by operation of the judgment or settlement is also excluded from the taxpayer's income. On the other hand, where the underlying claim involves income that would be includible had the taxpayer received the amount without the operation of a judgment or settlement, the amount received by operation of the judgment or settlement is also included in the taxpayer's income [*United States v. Gilmore*, 372 U.S. 39 (1963)].

### II.F.3. Taxability of Certain Personal Injury Liability Assignments

[522 T.M., VI.B.; TPS ¶2430.06.A.]

If a tortfeasor pays a qualified assignee to assume his or her liability to make periodic payments to an injured plaintiff as damages or as compensation under a workers' compensation act for personal physical injury or sickness, the assignee generally may exclude from gross income the amount he or she receives for assuming the liability. The exclusion is limited to amounts that do not exceed the aggregate cost of any qualified funding asset (as defined in § 130(d)) [§ 130].

Assignments of the liability must meet five requirements [§ 130(c)]:

1. The periodic payments must be excludible from the recipient's gross income under § 104(a)(1) or § 104(a)(2) as amounts received under a workers' compensation act as compensation for personal injuries (see II.D.3.a.) or sickness or as damages (other than punitive damages) received on account of personal physical injuries or physical sickness (see II.F.1.).

2. The periodic payments must be fixed and determinable as to the amount and time of payment.

3. The periodic payments cannot be accelerated, deferred, increased, or decreased by the recipient of the payments.

4. The assignee must assume the liability from a person that is party to the suit or agreement or the workers' compensation claim.

5. The assignee's obligation on account of the personal injuries or sickness must not be greater than the obligation of the person who assigned the liability.

The basis of a qualified funding asset must be reduced by the amount excluded from gross income as a result of the asset's purchase, and any gain recognized on the disposition of the asset is treated as ordinary income [§ 130(b)(1), § 130(b)(2)].

---

**EXAMPLE:** Lisa files a civil suit after being struck by a truck owned and operated by Moving Co. Lisa and Moving Co. enter into a settlement agreement under which Moving Co. agrees to make four annual payments of $100,000 to Lisa in settlement of all her claims. Moving Co. makes a qualified assignment of its liability to Settle Corp., a structured settlement company, for a lump-sum payment of $350,000. To fund the obligation, Settle Corp. purchases an annuity contract (which is a qualified funding asset) from an insurance company for $325,000. Lisa's four annual payments are excludible from her income as damages received on account of physical personal injuries. Settle Corp. must include $25,000 ($350,000 amount received − $325,000 cost of the annuity) in income. The remaining $325,000 received is excluded from Settle's income, and the annuity's basis is reduced by the amount excluded to zero.

---

## II.G. Exclusion of Employee Benefits

### II.G.1. Amounts Paid Under Cafeteria Plans

[397 T.M.; TPS ¶5940.]

A cafeteria plan is an employee benefit plan that allows a participating employee to choose between receiving cash, which is included in wages and is taxable, or qualified benefits, which are excluded from wages and are not taxable. An employee choosing to receive a qualified benefit under the plan does not include the value of the benefit in income solely because the employee could have received cash instead [§ 125(a); Prop. Reg. § 1.125-1(b)]. A common feature of a cafeteria plan is a flexible spending account where the employee forgoes cash, and the foregone amount is credited to a bookkeeping account maintained by the employer that the employer draws upon to reimburse the employee for certain expenses.

*Qualified Benefits.* Subject to certain exceptions, a qualified benefit is any benefit that is excludible from an employee's gross income under a specific Code provision, and that does not defer compensation. Qualified benefits may include [§ 125(f); Prop. Reg. § 1.125-1(a)(3)]:

- group-term life insurance up to $50,000 (see XVII.B.4.);
- accident and health benefits (other than Archer MSAs or long-term care insurance) (see XVII.C.1.a.);
- long-term or short-term disability coverage (see XVII.C.1.c.);
- adoption assistance (see XVII.E.1.);
- dependent care assistance (see XVII.E.2.);
- health savings accounts (HSAs) (see XVII.C.1.e.);
- flexible spending accounts (FSAs) (see XVII.C.4.); and
- a qualified cash or deferred arrangement that is part of a profit sharing plan or stock bonus plan (see XVII.A.3.).

### II.G.2. Incidental Fringe Benefits Excluded from Income

[394 T.M.; TPS ¶¶5960., 5980.]

Employees may exclude from gross income certain fringe benefits that fall into one of the following eight general categories [§ 132(a)]:

- no-additional-cost services (see XVII.D.1.);
- qualified employee discounts (see XVII.D.2.);
- working condition fringes (see XVII.D.3.);
- de minimis fringes (see XVII.D.4.);
- qualified transportation fringes (see XVII.D.5.);
- qualified moving expense reimbursements (see XVII.D.6.):
- qualified retirement planning expenses (see XVII.D.7.); and
- qualified military base realignment and closure fringes (see II.M.5.).

### II.G.3. Other Statutory Fringe Benefits Excluded from Income

[394 T.M.; TPS ¶¶5960., 5980.]

The following employee benefits, while not qualified benefits for purposes of a cafeteria plan [Prop. Reg. § 1.125-1(q)], may be excluded from income in whole or in part:

- scholarships (see II.H.);

- employer-provided meals and lodging (see XVII.E.4.);
- educational assistance programs (see XVII.E.3.) (for a discussion of scholarships, fellowships, and, tuition reduction, see II.H., and for education credits, see IX.B.5., and for education deductions, see IV.A.5.);
- certain statutory fringe benefits (see XVII.D.);
- long-term care insurance;
- long-term care services; and
- contributions to Archer MSAs (see XVII.C.1.d.).

## II.H. Scholarships, Fellowships, and Tuition Reductions

[518 T.M., II.; TPS ¶1350.]

*Qualified Scholarship.* A qualified scholarship is excluded from gross income if the taxpayer is a candidate for a degree at a qualified educational organization (as defined in § 170(b)(1)(A)(ii)). A qualified scholarship is any amount received by the taxpayer as a scholarship or fellowship grant to aid the taxpayer in the pursuit of study or research, and that is used for (i) tuition and fees required for enrollment or attendance, and for (ii) course-related expenses, such as fees, books, supplies, and equipment required of all students in the particular course of instruction. Incidental expenses, including room and board, travel, research, clerical help, or equipment and other expenses not required for enrollment or attendance, do not qualify [§ 117(b); Prop. Reg. § 1.117-6(c)].

---

**EXAMPLE:** Henry receives a scholarship from University for the current academic year and is enrolled in a creative writing class. Suggested supplies for the class include a thesaurus, however, students enrolled in the creative writing class are not required to obtain a thesaurus to take the class. If Henry buys the thesaurus using money received as a stipend from his scholarship, he may not include its cost in determining the amount of his qualified scholarship.

---

A candidate for a degree is defined as one the following [Prop. Reg. § 1.117-6(c)(4)]:

- a primary or secondary school student;
- an undergraduate or graduate student at a college or university pursuing an academic or professional degree; or
- a student at an educational organization that:
  — provides a program that is acceptable for full credit towards a bachelor's or higher degree, or offers a program of training to prepare students for gainful employment in a recognized occupation; and
  — is authorized under federal or state law to provide such a program and is accredited by a nationally recognized accreditation agency.

*Qualified Tuition Reduction.* Similarly, a qualified tuition reduction is excluded from a taxpayer's gross income. A qualified tuition reduction is the amount of any reduction in tuition provided to an employee of a qualified educational organization for the education (below the graduate level) at such organization or at another qualified educational organization of either the employee or any person treated as an employee (or whose use is treated as employee use) [§ 117(d)].

The following persons are treated as employees for the purpose of a qualified tuition reduction [§ 117(d)(2)(B), § 132(h)]:

- retired employees;
- disabled employees who separated from the employer's service because of the disability;
- widows and widowers of an employee who died while employed by the employer or while treated as an employee by reason of retirement or disability;
- spouses of employees; and
- dependent children of employees.

***Compensatory Amounts.*** Certain amounts that are compensatory in nature must be included in income. The exclusion for qualified scholarships and tuition reductions does not apply to the portion of any amount the taxpayer receives that represents payment for teaching, research, or other services that are required as a condition for receiving the scholarship or tuition reduction. This is the case even if all candidates for a degree are required to perform those services [§ 117(c); Prop. Reg. § 1.117-6(d)]. However, these rules do not apply to an amount received under the National Health Services Corps Scholarship Program or the Armed Forces Health Professions Scholarship and Financial Assistance Program [§ 117(c)(2)].

---

**EXAMPLE:** Laura receives a graduate school scholarship of $5,000. The scholarship was not received under either the National Health Services Corps Scholarship Program or the Armed Forces Health Professions Scholarship and Financial Assistance Program. A condition of the scholarship requires that Laura serve part-time as a teaching assistant. $2,000 of the scholarship represents compensation for the teaching assistant role. Laura's qualifying education expenses are at least $3,000. Assuming all other conditions are met, $3,000 of Laura's scholarship is excluded from income, while the $2,000 received for teaching must be included.

---

***Athletic Scholarship.*** An athletic scholarship that provides tuition and room and board may be excluded from income to the extent it is designated for qualifying tuition and course-related expenses, and to the extent that the taxpayer's athletic performance is not considered to be "other services" for which compensation is being paid. If playing for a school team is a condition for receiving the scholarship or tuition reduction, however, the amounts received under the scholarship or tuition reduction are included in gross income [Rev. Rul. 77-263, 1977-2 C.B. 47].

---

**EXAMPLE:** Diana, an ice hockey goalie, receives an ice hockey scholarship from College. The terms of the scholarship provide that she receive funds which may not exceed her expenses for tuition, fees, room and board, and required class supplies. Diana is expected to participate in ice hockey, but is not required to do so. If she fails to participate, the scholarship is not canceled, and she is not expected to participate in another activity in lieu of ice hockey. The expenses for room and board are not qualifying expenses and must be included in Diana's income, but the rest of the value of the scholarship may be excluded from her income.

---

Education credits and education deductions are discussed in IX.B.5. and IV.A.5., respectively.

## II.I. Capital Contributions

[501 T.M., IX.B.5.; TPS ¶1370.07.]

A contribution of money or property to the capital of a corporation is excluded from the corporation's income. The exclusion does not apply to money or property transferred to a corporation in consideration of goods or services rendered, or to any subsidy paid to induce the taxpayer to limit production. Similarly, contributions in aid of construction, or any other contributions as a customer or potential customer are not excluded from the corporation's income [§ 118(a), § 118(b); Reg. § 1.118-1].

Where a corporation requires additional funding to conduct its business and shareholders make contributions through voluntary pro rata payments credited to the corporation's surplus account or to a special account, the amounts received are excluded from the corporation's income even though there is no increase in the outstanding shares of the corporation's stock. The payments are in the nature of an assessment upon, and they represent an additional price paid for the shareholder's stock, and the amounts are treated as an addition to, and a part of, the corporation's operating capital.

---

**EXAMPLE:** A nonexempt condominium management corporation collects, and places in a separate bank account, a special assessment from its unit owner-stockholders for the replacement of outdoor furniture. The funds are contributions to capital and are not included in the corporation's gross income. The special assessment to replace the furniture enhanced the value of the unit owner-stockholders' property.

---

Nonshareholder contributions to the capital of a corporation are also excludible from the corporation's income. For example, where a governmental unit or civic group contributes land or other property to a corporation to induce it to locate in a particular community or to enable it to expand its operating facilities, the value of the contribution is excluded from the corporation's income [Reg. § 1.118-1]. Nonshareholder contributions generally must satisfy all the following requirements [*United States v. Chicago, Burlington & Quincy R.R.*, 412 U.S. 401 (1973)]:

- The contribution must become a permanent part of the corporation's working capital structure.
- The contribution must not be compensation.
- The contribution must be bargained for.
- The asset transferred must foreseeably benefit the corporation in an amount commensurate with its value.
- The asset must ordinarily be employed in, or contribute to, the production of additional income.

Contributions in aid of construction are not excludible from income. However, the term does not include an amount paid as a service charge for starting or stopping services. Certain regulated public utilities providing water or sewerage disposal services are excepted from the general rule on contributions in aid of construction. A contribution of money or property received by such a utility is an excludible capital contribution if all the following requirements are met [§ 118(c); Reg. § 1.118-2(a)]:

- The amount is a contribution in aid of construction.
- Where the contributed property is not a water or sewerage disposal facility, the amount satisfies certain expenditure rules.

- The amount, or any property acquired or constructed with the amount, is not included in taxpayer's rate base for ratemaking purposes.

For a discussion of capitalization of corporations, see XIII.B.

## II.J. Certain Savings Bond Income

[501 T.M., X.A.2.c., 518 T.M., II.E.3.; TPS ¶1370.09.]

Amounts realized from an individual's redemption of a qualified U.S. savings bond during a tax year in which the individual pays qualified higher education expenses are not included in that individual's gross income. The exclusion is not available for married individuals filing a separate return [§ 135(a)].

A qualified U.S. savings bond is any U.S. savings bond that is issued after 1989 to an individual at least 24 years old at the time of issuance, and that is issued at a discount under § 3105 of Title 31 of the U.S. Code. Qualified higher education expenses are tuition or fees required for the enrollment or attendance of the taxpayer, the taxpayer's spouse, or any dependent for whom the taxpayer is allowed a personal exemption deduction, at an accredited university, college, junior college, nursing school, or vocational school [§ 135(c)]. Qualified education expenses also include contributions to a qualified tuition program on behalf of a designated beneficiary, or to a Coverdell education savings account on behalf of an account beneficiary who is the taxpayer, the taxpayer's spouse, or any dependent for whom the taxpayer is allowed a personal exemption deduction (see II.L.). Qualified higher education expenses do not include expenses for any course involving sports, games, or hobbies that are not part of a degree program.

Additionally, qualified higher education expenses must be reduced by the sum of the following amounts:

- the tax-free portion of a qualified scholarship or fellowship (see II.H.);
- expenses used to figure the tax-free portion of distributions from a Coverdell education savings account or a qualified tuition program (529 plan) (see II.L.);
- any tax-free payments (other than gifts, bequests, devises, or inheritances) received as educational assistance; and
- any expenses used in figuring the American opportunity and lifetime learning credits (see IX.B.5.).

Where the aggregate proceeds (principal and interest) of all the taxpayer's redeemed U.S. savings bonds exceed the taxpayer's qualified education expenses for the tax year, the amount of interest that may be excluded is reduced pro rata by multiplying the amount that would otherwise be excluded by a fraction, the numerator of which is qualified educational expenses, and the denominator of which is the aggregate proceeds of qualified U.S. savings bonds redeemed.

---

**EXAMPLE:** Randy redeems his qualified U.S. savings bonds and receives $15,000, of which $10,000 is principal and $5,000 is interest. Randy's son has qualified educational expenses of $20,000. Randy may exclude the entire $5,000 of interest from his income.

**EXAMPLE:** Veronica redeems her qualified U.S. savings bonds and receives $20,000, of which $12,000 is principal and $8,000 is interest. Veronica's daughter has qualified educational expenses of $15,000. Veronica may exclude $6,000 (($15,000 expenses ÷ $20,000 proceeds), multiplied by $8,000 of otherwise excludible interest) of interest from her income.

---

*Phaseout of Exclusion.* The exclusion is subject to a phaseout of the excludible amount based on the taxpayer's modified adjusted gross income (MAGI). The phaseout begins for taxpayers with MAGI of $76,000 ($113,950 for joint returns) in 2014 ($77,200 and $115,750, respectively, for 2015). For taxpayers with MAGI above this threshold, the excludible amount is reduced by the same ratio to which the amount of MAGI exceeding the threshold bears to $15,000. Thus, the exclusion is completely phased out for taxpayers with MAGI of $91,000 ($143,950 for joint return) in 2014 ($92,200 and $145,750, respectively, for 2015) [Rev. Proc. 2013-35, 2013-47 I.R.B. 537, Rev. Proc. 2014-61, 2014-47 I.R.B. 860].

MAGI, for this purpose, is the taxpayer's adjusted gross income for the tax year after applying (i) the partial exclusion for social security and tier 1 railroad retirement benefits, (ii) the adjustments for limitations on passive activity losses and credits, and (iii) the deduction for certain retirement savings, and without regard to the following [§ 135(c)(4)]:

- excludible higher education savings bond interest;
- excludible adoption assistance payments;
- the domestic production activities deduction;
- the deduction for interest on certain qualifying education loans;
- the deduction for qualified tuition and related expenses;
- excludible foreign earned income or housing amounts;
- excludible income from U.S. possessions; and
- excludible income from Puerto Rican sources available to bona fide residents of Puerto Rico.

---

**EXAMPLE:** In 2014, Bobby redeems his qualified U.S. savings bonds and receives $10,000, of which $6,000 is principal and $4,000 is interest. Bobby is married and files a joint return. His 2014 MAGI is $115,450. The excess of Bobby's MAGI over the threshold is $1,500 ($115,450 − $113,950). Thus, Bobby's excludible interest is limited to $3,600 ($4,000 otherwise excludible interest − ($4,000 otherwise excludible interest, multiplied by ($1,500 ÷ $15,000))).

---

*Reporting:* Excluded interest from the redemption of qualified U.S. savings bonds for taxpayers with qualified education expenses is reported on Form 8815, *Exclusion of Interest from Series EE and I U.S. Savings Bonds Issued After 1989.*

## II.K. Certain Cost-Sharing Payments

[501 T.M., XII.B., 608 T.M., V.C.; TPS ¶1370.16.]

A taxpayer may exclude from income all or part of a government payment received under certain cost-sharing conservation, reclamation, and restoration programs. A payment, for this purpose, is any economic benefit conferred upon the taxpayer as a result of an improvement. The exclusion applies only to the portion of a payment that meets all of the following tests [§ 126(b); Temp. Reg. § 16A.126-1(a)]:

- The payment must be for a capital expense, as no payment that is properly associated with an amount allowable as a deduction for the tax year the amount is paid or incurred may be excluded.
- The payment must not increase the taxpayer's annual income from the property for which the payment is made by more than the greater of:

— 10% of the average annual income derived from the affected property before receiving the improvement; or

— $2.50, multiplied by the number of affected acres.

- The Secretary of Agriculture must certify that the payment was made primarily for the purpose of conserving soil and water resources, protecting or restoring the environment, improving forests, or providing a habitat for wildlife.

The excludible portion of a payment is the present fair market value of the right to receive annual income from the affected acreage of the greater of either [Reg. § 16A.126-1(b)(5)]:

- 10% of the prior average annual income from the affected acreage (i.e., the average of the gross receipts from the affected acreage for the last three tax years before the tax year in which the taxpayer begins to install the improvement); or

- $2.50, multiplied by the number of affected acres.

---

**EXAMPLE:** Walter owns a farm. 100 acres of his land were reclaimed under a rural abandoned mine program contract with the USDA. The total cost of the improvement is $500,000, of which the USDA paid $490,000 and Walter paid $10,000. The value of the cost-sharing improvement is $15,000. The present fair market value of the right to receive the annual income from the property of 10% of the prior average annual income of the affected acreage is $1,380. The present fair market value of the right to receive $250 ($2.50, multiplied by 100 acres) is $1,550. Walter may exclude $1,550 (the greater of $1,380 and $1,550) from income.

---

The amount of the exclusion is reported on Schedule F of Form 1040, *Profit or Loss From Farming*. A taxpayer may elect not to have these rules apply to all or part of any excludible portion [§ 126(c)].

## II.L. Coverdell Education Savings Accounts and Qualified Tuition Programs

### II.L.1. Coverdell Education Savings Accounts

[518 T.M., IV.; TPS ¶1370.18.]

Coverdell education savings accounts (Coverdell ESAs) are exempt from federal income tax (other than unrelated business income tax), and certain distributions from Coverdell ESAs for qualified education expenses are not included in a beneficiary's income. A Coverdell ESA is a trust or custodial account exclusively for the purpose of paying the qualified education expenses of an individual designated as the beneficiary. A taxpayer may contribute to both a Coverdell ESA and a qualified tuition program for the same beneficiary in the same year.

Where distributions from an account for the year do not exceed a designated beneficiary's qualified education expenses at an eligible educational institution, the beneficiary may exclude the value of the distributions from gross income. However, if the aggregate distributions exceed the beneficiary's qualified education expenses for that year, a portion of the distributions may be taxable to the beneficiary. In such a case, the beneficiary may exclude from income an amount bearing the same ratio to the amount that otherwise would be includible in gross income (without regard to the exclusion for qualified education expenses) as the qualified education expenses bear to the aggregate distributions. With some exceptions, a 10% penalty may be imposed to the extent a distribution is includible in income because it is not used for qualified educational expenses [§ 530(d)].

---

**EXAMPLE:** Joey receives an $850 distribution from his Coverdell ESA in Year 2. In Year 1, $1,500 had been contributed to the Coverdell ESA. Thus, at the end of Year 1, the account's basis was $1,500. There were no contributions in Year 2, and, after the distribution to Joey, the value (balance) of the account at the end of Year 2 was $950. The portion of the distribution to Joey that is basis is $708 ($850 distribution × ($1,500 basis plus contributions in Year 2 ÷ $1,800 value plus distributions in Year 2)). Therefore, the earnings included in the distribution equal $142 ($850 distribution − $708 basis in the distribution), which would be included in income but for the exclusion for education expenses. Joey's qualified educational expenses for Year 2 are $700. Of the distributed earnings, $117 ($142 distributed earnings × ($700 qualified education expenses ÷ $850 distribution)) is excluded from Joey's income, while $25 must be included ($142 − $117).

---

*Trust Instrument Requirements.* The written governing instrument creating the trust must meet the following requirements [§ 530(b)(1)]:

- the trustee or custodian may only accept contributions satisfying the following three conditions:
  - it is in cash;
  - it is made before the beneficiary is age 18 (unless the beneficiary is a special needs beneficiary); and
  - it would not result in total contributions for the year, excluding rollovers, being more than $2,000;
- the trustee or custodian is a bank or another person approved by the IRS;
- no part of the trust assets can be invested in life insurance contracts;
- the assets of the trust cannot be commingled with other property except in a common trust fund or common investment fund;
- except in the case of death or divorce, any balance to the credit of the designated beneficiary must be distributed within 30 days of the earlier of:
  - the beneficiary reaching age 30 (unless the beneficiary is a special needs beneficiary); or
  - the beneficiary's death.

*Qualified Education Expenses.* Qualified education expenses can be qualified higher education expenses and qualified elementary and secondary education expenses, as well as any contribution to a qualified tuition program on behalf of the designated beneficiary. Qualified higher education expenses include [§ 530(b)(2)(A)(i)]:

- expenses for tuition, fees, books, supplies, and equipment required for a designated beneficiary's enrollment or attendance at an eligible educational institution;
- in the case of a special needs beneficiary, expenses for special needs services incurred in connection with enrollment or attendance; and
- expenses for room and board incurred by a student who is enrolled at least half-time, to the extent the expenses are not more than the greater of either:

— the student's allowance for room and board that was included in the cost of attendance, as determined by the school, for a particular academic period and living arrangement; or

— the actual amount charged if the student is residing in housing owned or operated by the school.

An eligible educational institution generally includes accredited post-secondary educational institutions offering credit toward a bachelor's degree, associate's degree, graduate level or professional degree, or other recognized post-secondary credential. Additionally, certain proprietary and post-secondary vocational institutions are eligible educational institutions [§ 530(b)(2)(A)(i)].

Qualified elementary and secondary education expenses include the following [§ 530(b)(3)]:

- expenses for tuition, fees, academic tutoring, special needs services in the case of a special needs beneficiary, books, supplies, and other equipment incurred by a designated beneficiary in connection with enrollment or attendance at any public, private, or religious elementary or secondary school;

- expenses for room and board, uniforms, transportation, and supplementary items and services that are required or provided by a public, private, or religious elementary or secondary school in connection with enrollment or attendance; and

- expenses for the purchase of any computer technology or equipment, or internet access and related services, if it is to be used by the designated beneficiary and the beneficiary's family during any of the years the beneficiary is in elementary or secondary school (excluding expenses for software designed for sports, games, or hobbies, unless the software is predominantly educational in nature).

***Rollovers.*** Assets may generally be rolled over from one Coverdell ESA to another, or the designated beneficiary may be changed, without incurring tax. A change in the beneficiary of a Coverdell ESA is not a distribution includible in income where the new beneficiary is under age 30 and a family member of the old beneficiary. Similarly, an amount distributed from a Coverdell ESA is excluded from gross income to the extent the amount received is paid within 60 days into another Coverdell ESA for the same beneficiary, or a member of the beneficiary's family that is under age 30 (other than a special needs beneficiary). However, the rollover generally will not be excluded from income if the same provision excluding rollover distributions applied to any prior payment or distribution in the previous 12 months. A family member for purposes of these rules includes the following relatives of the beneficiary: spouse, children, siblings, parents, grandparents, stepparents, nieces, nephews, uncles, aunts, in-laws, and the spouse of any of those individuals, as well as first cousins (but not their spouses) [§ 530(d)(5), § 530(d)(6), § 529(e)(2)].

***Contribution Limits.*** The total maximum allowable contribution to all Coverdell ESAs established for the benefit of any one designated beneficiary is $2,000 per tax year. Similarly, each contributor to a Coverdell ESA is limited to a maximum contribution of $2,000 per tax year for any one designated beneficiary. The maximum amount an individual is allowed to contribute to a Coverdell ESA is phased out for taxpayers with modified adjusted gross income (MAGI) over $95,000 ($190,000 for joint returns). For taxpayers exceeding this MAGI threshold, the $2,000 maximum contribution amount is phased out ratably by an amount bearing the same ratio as the excess over the MAGI threshold bears to $15,000 ($30,000 for joint returns). Thus, the maximum contribution amount is phased out completely for taxpayers with MAGI of $110,000 ($220,000 for joint returns) [§ 530(c)].

MAGI, for this purpose, is a taxpayer's adjusted gross income for the tax year, increased by (i) excludible foreign earned income or housing amounts, (ii) excludible income from U.S. possessions, and (iii) excludible income from Puerto Rican sources available to bona fide residents of Puerto Rico [§ 530(c)(2)].

---

**EXAMPLE:** When Avery was born, two separate Coverdell ESAs were established for her. In Year 1, Avery's grandfather contributes $2,000 to one of her Coverdell ESAs. Because in any given tax year the total amount that may be contributed to Coverdell ESAs established for Avery's benefit may not exceed $2,000, no one else may contribute to any of Avery's accounts in Year 1. However, if Avery had a twin brother that also had a Coverdell ESA, Avery's grandfather would still be able to contribute $2,000 to his account in Year 1.

**EXAMPLE:** Doug is single and had a MAGI of $98,000 in Year 1. For each beneficiary in Year 1, Doug may contribute a maximum of $1,600 ($2,000 maximum contribution – ($2,000 maximum contribution, multiplied by ($3,000 excess MAGI ÷ $15,000))).

---

*Gift and GST Taxes.* For purposes of the federal gift tax and generation-skipping transfer (GST) tax, a contribution to a Coverdell ESA on behalf of a designated beneficiary is treated as a completed gift to the beneficiary that is not a future interest in property, and is not treated as a qualified transfer. Thus, contributions to a Coverdell ESA are eligible for the annual gift tax exclusion, but not for the educational expense exclusion. Donors contributing an aggregate amount exceeding the annual exclusion limitation for the year may elect to take the contributions into account ratably over the five-year period beginning with that calendar year. Distributions from a Coverdell ESA generally are not treated as a taxable gift. However, an exception applies to a transfer by reason of a change in the designated beneficiary (or rollover to a new beneficiary's account) if the new beneficiary is a generation below the generation of the old beneficiary and a member of the family of the old beneficiary. For purposes of the federal estate tax, an interest in a Coverdell ESA is generally not included in the gross estate of the donor or designated beneficiary. Amounts distributed on the death of a beneficiary, however, are included in the gross estate of the designated beneficiary [§ 530(d)(3)].

*Reporting.* The portion of any distribution from a Coverdell ESA that represents earnings is reported on Form 1099-Q, *Payments from Qualified Education Programs (Under Sections 529 and 530).*

### II.L.2. Qualified Tuition Programs (529 Plans)

[518 T.M., III.; TPS ¶1370.19.]

Qualified tuition programs (QTPs) are exempt from federal income tax (other than unrelated business income tax), and certain distributions for qualified higher education expenses are not included in a beneficiary's income. A QTP is a program established and maintained by either a state (or an agency or instrumentality thereof), or by one or more eligible educational institutions, under which a person may prepay, or contribute to an account established for paying, a student's qualified higher educational expenses at an eligible educational institution. An eligible taxpayer may contribute to both a QTP and a Coverdell ESA for the same beneficiary in the same year. For a discussion of Coverdell ESAs, see II.L.1.

A QTP must meet all the following requirements [§ 529(a), § 529(b)]:

- It must provide that purchases or contributions may only be made in cash.

- It must provide separate accounting for each designated beneficiary.

- It must provide that any contributor to, or designated beneficiary of, such program may not direct the investment of any contributions to the program, or any earnings thereon.

- It must prohibit any interest in the program to be used as security for a loan.

- It must provide adequate safeguards to prevent contributions on behalf of a designated beneficiary in excess of those necessary to provide for the beneficiary's qualified higher education expenses.

*Qualified Higher Education Expenses.* Qualified higher education expenses include [§ 529(e)(3)]:

- expenses for tuition, fees, books, supplies, and equipment required for a designated beneficiary's enrollment or attendance at an eligible educational institution;

- expenses for special needs services incurred in connection with enrollment or attendance of a special needs beneficiary; and

- expenses for room and board incurred by a student who is enrolled at least half-time, limited to the greater of either the student's allowance for room and board or the actual amount charged if the student is residing in housing owned or operated by the school.

An eligible educational institution generally includes accredited post-secondary educational institutions offering credit toward a bachelor's degree, associate's degree, graduate level or professional degree, or other recognized post-secondary credential. Additionally, certain proprietary and post-secondary vocational institutions are eligible educational institutions. Eligible educational institutions do not include elementary and secondary educational institutions or expenses [§ 529(e)(5)].

*Amounts Excludible.* The beneficiary of a QTP may exclude the amount of a distribution that provides a benefit to the beneficiary which, if paid for by the beneficiary directly, would be a payment of a qualified higher education expense. Additionally, the beneficiary may exclude cash distributions where the total distribution does not exceed the beneficiary's qualified educational expenses for the year. A portion of the cash distribution is generally included in the beneficiary's income if the aggregate distributions exceed the beneficiary's qualified education expenses for the year. In such a case, the beneficiary may exclude from income an amount bearing the same ratio to the amount that otherwise would be includible in gross income (without regard to the exclusion for qualified education expenses) as the qualified education expenses bear to the aggregate distributions. With some exceptions, a 10% penalty generally is imposed to the extent a distribution is includible in income because it is not used for qualified higher educational expenses [§ 529(c)(6)].

---

**EXAMPLE:** Joan receives a QTP distribution of $5,300. The earnings included in the distribution equal $950, which would be included in income but for the exclusion for education expenses. Joan's qualified educational expenses for the year are $5,200. Of the distributed earnings, $932 ($950 distributed earnings, multiplied by ($5,200 qualified education expenses ÷ $5,300 distribution)) is excluded from Joan's income, while $18 must be included ($950 − $932).

---

*Rollovers.* Assets may generally be rolled over from one QTP to another, or the designated beneficiary may be changed, without incurring tax. A change in the beneficiary of a QTP is not a distribution includible in income where the new beneficiary is a family member of the old beneficiary. Similarly, an amount distributed from a QTP is excluded from gross income to the extent the amount received is paid within 60 days into another QTP for the same beneficiary, or a member of the beneficiary's family. However, rollovers into another QTP for the same beneficiary generally will only be excluded from income if no similar rollover has occurred in the previous 12 months [§ 529(c)(3)(C)]. A family member for purposes of these rules includes a spouse, children, siblings, parents, grandparents, stepparents, nieces, nephews, uncles, aunts, in-laws, and the spouse of any of those individuals, as well as first cousins (but not their spouses) [§ 529(e)(2)].

*Gift and GST Taxes.* For purposes of the federal gift tax and generation-skipping transfer (GST) tax, a contribution to a QTP on behalf of a designated beneficiary is treated as a completed gift to the beneficiary that is not a future interest in property, and is not treated as a qualified transfer. Thus, contributions to a QTP are eligible for the annual gift tax exclusion, but not for the educational expense exclusion. Donors contributing an aggregate amount exceeding the annual exclusion limitation for the year may elect to take the contributions into account ratably over the five-year period beginning with that calendar year. Distributions from a QTP generally are not treated as a taxable gift. However, an exception applies to a transfer by reason of a change in the designated beneficiary (or rollover to a new beneficiary's account) if the new beneficiary is a generation below the generation of the old beneficiary and a member of the family of the old beneficiary. For purposes of the federal estate tax, an interest in a QTP is generally not included in the gross estate of the donor or designated beneficiary. Amounts distributed on the death of a beneficiary, however, are included in the gross estate of the designated beneficiary [§ 529(c)(2), § 529(c)(4), § 529(c)(5)].

*Reporting.* The portion of any distribution from a QTP that represents earnings is reported on Form 1099-Q, *Payments from Qualified Education Programs (Under Sections 529 and 530).*

## II.M. Exclusions Related to Military Service

### II.M.1. Combat Zone Pay

[501 T.M., VIII.G.3.c.; TPS ¶1110.08.A.2.c.(1).]

Enlisted members of the armed forces (including commissioned warrant officers) may exclude from gross income compensation (not including pensions or retirement pay) received for active service for any month during any part of which the member served in a combat zone or was hospitalized as a result of wounds, disease, or injury incurred while serving in a combat zone. The same rules apply to commissioned officers (excluding commissioned warrant officers), except that the exclusion may not exceed the maximum enlisted amount per month, which is the sum of (i) the highest rate of basic pay payable for that month to any enlisted member at the highest pay grade applicable to enlisted members, and (ii) the amount of any special pay for being subject to hostile fire or imminent danger an officer may be entitled to for that month. Compensation received during hospitalization is not eligible for exclusion for any month beginning more than two years after the date of combatant activities in the combat zone.

***Combat Zone.*** A combat zone is any area designated by the President as an area in which U.S. Armed Forces are or have engaged in combat. Members performing military service outside a combat zone are deemed to serve in the combat zone for purposes of the exclusion if their service is in direct support of military operations in the combat zone and qualifies them for special pay for being subject to hostile fire or imminent danger. Compensation may be excluded only for service performed on or after the date combatant activities are designated as having commenced [§ 112; Reg. § 1.112-1].

Areas currently eligible for the combat zone pay exclusion include the following:

- Afghanistan, beginning September 19, 2001 [Executive Order No. 13239; Notice 2002-17, 2002-9 I.R.B. 567].

- The following countries and areas in support of Operation Enduring Freedom in Afghanistan: Djibouti (July 1, 2002), Jordan (September 19, 2001), Kyrgyzstan (October 1, 2001), Pakistan (September 19, 2001), Somalia (January 1, 2004), Tajikistan (September 19, 2001), Uzbekistan (October 1, 2001), Yemen (April 10, 2002), and the Philippines (only for personnel deployed in the Philippines in conjunction with Operation Enduring Freedom) (January 9, 2002).

- Arabian Peninsula areas, beginning January 17, 1991, including the Persian Gulf, Red Sea, Gulf of Oman, a portion of the Arabian Sea, the Gulf of Aden, Bahrain, Iraq, Kuwait, Oman, Qatar, Saudi Arabia, and the United Arab Emirates [Executive Order No. 12744; Notice 2003-21, 2003-17 I.R.B. 817].

- The Kosovo area, beginning March 24, 1999, including the Federal Republic of Yugoslavia (Serbia and Montenegro), Albania, the Adriatic Sea, and a portion of the Ionian Sea [Executive Order No. 13119; Notice 99-30, 1999-22 I.R.B. 5].

- Bosnia and Herzegovina, Croatia, and Macedonia, beginning November 21, 1995 [Pub. L. No. 104-117; Notice 96-34, 1996-1 C.B. 379].

### II.M.2. Qualified Military Benefits

[501 T.M., VIII.G.3.b.; TPS ¶1110.08.A.2.b.]

Gross income does not include qualified military benefits. A qualified military benefit is any allowance or in-kind benefit (other than the personal use of a vehicle) a member or former member of the uniformed services, or that person's dependent, receives by reason of the member's status or service in the uniformed services, and that was excludible from gross income on September 9, 1986, under a law, regulation, or administrative practice then in effect. Additionally, the benefit must be excludible from gross income under the Code without regard to any provision of law not contained in the Code or a revenue act. Excludible benefits include [§ 134]:

- dependent care assistance programs (as in effect on November 11, 2003);
- travel benefits under Operation Hero Miles;
- state or local bonus payments by reason of service in a combat zone;
- medical benefits;
- professional education benefits;
- moving and storage benefits;
- group term life insurance benefits;
- housing allowances;
- family separation allowances;
- family counseling services;
- defense counsel services;

- burial and death services;
- educational assistance;
- dependent education;
- dental care for military dependents; and
- uniform allowances.

### II.M.3. Certain Reduced Uniform Services Retirement Pay

[501 T.M., VIII.G.4.f.; TPS ¶1110.08.C.1.b.]

If a member or former member of the uniformed services does not elect out of the Survivor Benefit Plan or the Retired Serviceman's Family Protection Plan, the amount of the reduction in retirement or retainer pay made to fund a survivor annuity for his or her spouse or children generally is excluded from gross income. In the case of amounts excludible as a reduced benefit under this provision, as well as under § 104(a)(4) as a disability payment (see II.D.1.c.), this reduced benefit exclusion applies. If a retired member waives part of his or her disability retired pay in favor of a nontaxable Department of Veterans' Affairs benefit, this reduced benefit exclusion is applied before other exclusions [§ 122; Reg. § 1.122-1].

### II.M.4. Pensions, Annuities, and Similar Allowances for Personal Injuries or Sickness

[522 T.M., III.C.; TPS ¶1340.03.C.]

Taxpayers may exclude from income amounts received as a pension, annuity, or similar allowance for personal injuries or sickness as a result of active service in the armed forces of any country [§ 104(a)(4)] (see II.D.3.b.).

### II.M.5. Qualified Military Base Realignment and Closure Fringe

[394 T.M., II.B.2.h.]

Certain housing payments made with respect to military base realignment and closures are excludible as qualified military realignment and closure fringe benefits [§ 132(a)(8), § 132(n)].

### II.M.6. Miscellaneous Military Benefits Excludible from Income

[501 T.M., VIII.G.4.b., VIII.G.4.d.; TPS ¶1110.08.C.2.]

Gross income does not include special pensions paid to persons on the Army and Navy medal of honor roll [§ 140(a)(6)]. Additionally, certain benefits received under laws administered by the Veterans' Administration are excluded from gross income [§ 140(a)(3)]. Such benefits include education, training, and subsistence allowances, disability compensation, disability pensions, grants for homes designed for wheelchair living, grants for motor homes for veterans who have lost their sight or use of their limbs, veteran's pensions paid to veterans or their families, and veteran's insurance proceeds and dividends paid either to veterans or their beneficiaries.

## II.N. Miscellaneous Items of Exclusion

### II.N.1. Disaster Mitigation Payments

[597 T.M., IV.E.; TPS ¶1370.20.]

Amounts an individual receives as qualified disaster relief payments are not includible in gross income. A qualified disaster relief payment is an amount paid to or for the benefit of an individual as a result of a qualified disaster [§ 139(b)]:

- to reimburse or pay reasonable and necessary personal, family, living, or funeral expenses;
- to reimburse or pay reasonable and necessary expenses incurred to repair or rehabilitate a personal residence (including a rented personal residence), or its contents;
- by a common carrier on account of death or personal physical injury; or
- by a federal, state, or local government to promote the general welfare.

However, to the extent any expense compensated by such a payment is otherwise compensated for by insurance or otherwise, the payment is not a qualified disaster relief payment.

A qualified disaster includes [§ 139(c)]:
- a disaster resulting from a terrorist or military action;
- a federally declared disaster;
- a disaster involving a common carrier accident, or any other event the IRS determines to be of a catastrophic nature; or
- for amounts paid by a federal, state, or local government to promote the general welfare, any disaster designated by federal, state, or local officials.

### II.N.2. Holocaust Reparation Payments

[501 T.M., XII.D.1.; TPS ¶1010.05.N.]

Qualified restitution payments to a person persecuted by Nazi Germany, or any of its allied or controlled regimes, on the basis of race, religion, physical or mental disability, or sexual orientation is excluded from gross income. The exclusion is available for persecuted persons, their estates, and their survivors, and it applies to interest earned by qualified escrow and settlement funds [Pub. L. No. 107-16, § 803; Pub. L. No. 107-358 § 2].

### II.N.3. Rental Value of Parsonages

[501 T.M., VIII.C.12.; TPS ¶1110.09.B.2.]

A "minister of the gospel" may exclude from gross income either (i) the rental value of a home (including utilities) furnished to him as part of his compensation, or (ii) a rental allowance paid as part of his compensation to the extent the allowance does not exceed the fair rental value of the home. The rental allowance must be provided as remuneration for services that are ordinarily the duties of a minister, and the exclusion is limited to amounts that would be considered reasonable compensation for the services performed [§ 107].

The term "minister of the gospel" extends to any duly ordained, commissioned, or licensed minister of a religious organization who performs sacerdotal functions, the conduct of religious worship, the administration and maintenance of religious organizations and their integral agencies, and the performance of teaching and administrative duties at theological seminaries [Reg. § 1.107-1].

Despite being excluded from gross income, the rental allowance amount is treated as compensation for purposes of determining benefits under qualified retirement plans [Rev. Rul. 73-258, 1973-1 C.B. 194] (see XVII.A.2.). Additionally, a taxpayer excluding the rental allowance from gross income may still deduct real estate taxes and qualified housing interest [§ 265(a)(6)(B); Rev. Rul. 87-32, 1987-1 C.B. 131].

### II.N.4. Lessee Improvements on Lessor's Property

[593 T.M., III.B.1.e.; TPS ¶1230.01.G.]

Gross income generally does not include the income (other than rent) a lessor of real property derives upon the termination of a lease that represents the value of such property attributable to buildings erected or other improvements made by the lessee. The following are exceptions to the general rule of exclusion [§ 109; Reg. § 1.109-1(a)]:

- The facts disclose that the buildings or improvements represent (in whole or in part) a liquidation in kind of lease rentals (i.e., the lessor receives the building in lieu of rental payments).

- Income in the form of rent is derived during the period of the lease and is attributable to buildings erected or improvements made by the lessee.

- The income is derived upon the termination of the lease, but is not attributable to the value of the buildings or improvements.

- After termination of the lease, the lessor derives the income incident to the ownership of such buildings or improvements.

---

**EXAMPLE:** Lease Corp. leases real property to Develop Corp. for a 50-year period beginning in Year 1. The lease states that Develop Corp. must erect a $5 million office building on the leased property, and must pay a lease rental of $100,000 per year beginning on the date the improvements are completed. The lease further states that all improvements will become Lease Corp.'s absolute property upon the lease's termination through forfeiture or otherwise, and that Lease Corp. is entitled to the remainder of any funds held in escrow upon termination of the lease. Develop Corp. puts $1 million in escrow for payment of the rental. The building is completed in Year 3. In Year 8, Develop Corp. encounters financial problems and forfeits the lease. As a result, Lease Corp. receives the $500,000 remaining in escrow. The erected building is worth only $2.7 million at the time of the termination because of its location is in an overbuilt section of the city. Lease Corp. does not include the $2.7 million in gross income. However, the $500,000 is in the nature of a substitute for rent, and therefore must be included in Lease Corp.'s income.

---

### II.N.5. Qualified Lessee Construction Allowances

[593 T.M., III.B.2.b(2); TPS ¶1230.01.I.]

A lessee may exclude from gross income amounts received in cash or as a rent reduction from a lessor under a short-term lease of retail space to reimburse the lessee for the cost of constructing or improving qualified long-term real property to be used in the lessee's trade or business at that retail space. The exclusion is limited to the amount expended by the lessee for the construction or improvement [§ 110; Reg. § 1.110-1(a), § 1.110-1(b)].

A short-term lease is a lease or other occupancy or use agreement of a retail space for no more than 15 years. Retail space is nonresidential real property that a lessee leases, occupies, or otherwise uses in its trade or business of selling tangible personal property or services to the general public. Qualified long-term real property is nonresidential real property that is part of, or otherwise present at, the retail space and that reverts to the lessor at the termination of the lease [§ 110(c); Reg. § 1.110-1(b)(2)].

***Required Statements.*** Both the lessor and the lessee must submit a statement attached to their federal income tax returns for the tax year in which the construction allowance was paid by the lessor or received by the lessee. The lessor's statement must contain the lessor's name (as well as the parent's name, in the case of a consolidated group), employer identification number, tax year, and the following information for each lease [Reg. § 1.110-1(c)(3)(i)]:

- the lessee's name (and the parent's name, in the case of a consolidated group);
- the lessee's address;
- the lessee's employer identification number;
- the location of the retail space;
- the amount of the construction allowance; and
- the amount of the construction allowance the lessor treats as nonresidential real property owned by the lessor.

The lessee's statement must contain the lessee's name (as well as the parent's name, in the case of a consolidated group), employer identification number, tax year, and the following information for each lease [Reg. § 1.110-1(c)(3)(ii)]:

- the lessor's name (and the parent's name, in the case of a consolidated group);
- the lessor's address;
- the lessor's employer identification number;
- the location of the retail space;
- the amount of the construction allowance; and
- the amount of the construction allowance that is a qualified lessee construction allowance.

### II.N.6. Gain from Sale of Principal Residence

[594 T.M., IV.B.; TPS ¶1530.01.]

Taxpayers may generally exclude from gross income gain realized from the sale or exchange of property if, during the five-year period ending on the date of the sale or exchange, the taxpayer owned and used the property as his or her principal residence for a period of at least two years, in the aggregate. The amount of the exclusion is generally limited to $250,000 ($500,000 for certain married taxpayers filing jointly, or certain sales by surviving spouses). The exclusion generally may be used only once in a two-year period; however, a reduced exclusion may apply to a sale occurring within the two-year period [§ 121; Reg. § 1.121-1]. Exclusion of the gain from the sale of a principal residence is discussed in detail in III.E.3.

### II.N.7. Amounts Received Under Insurance Contracts for Certain Living Expenses

[513 T.M., IV.B.; TPS ¶¶1520.10.F.1., 2350.03.C.4.b.(4).]

Gross income does not include amounts received under an insurance contract to indemnify a temporary increase in living expenses resulting from the loss of use or occupancy of a principal residence due to a casualty, or due to a governmental authority's denial of access to a principal residence because of a casualty (or threat of a casualty). To the extent the insurance payments exceed the taxpayer's temporary increase in living expenses, the taxpayer must include the amount in income.

A taxpayer's temporary increase in living expenses is the difference between the actual living expenses incurred during the period the taxpayer and his or her family could not use the home, over the normal living expenses (i.e., the same expenses the taxpayer would have incurred but for the casualty) for that period. Expenses include amounts paid to rent suitable housing, transportation, food, and utilities. Actual living expenses incurred as a result of the casualty must be reasonable and necessary and made in order to maintain the household's customary standard of living [§ 123; Reg. § 1.123-1].

The exclusion does not apply to insurance reimbursements for the following [Reg. § 1.123-1(a)(3)]:

- the loss of rental income;
- the loss of, or damage to, real or personal property; and
- living expenses incurred because of governmental condemnation of, or similar action with respect to, the principal residence that is not related to a casualty or the threat of a casualty.

---

**EXAMPLE:** After a fire, Julian vacates his apartment and moves into a motel for a month. Julian pays $800 per month in rent for the apartment, but none was charged for the month he was displaced. His motel rent for the month was $1,500. Julian typically paid $300 per month for food, but while he lived in the motel, his food expenses were $500. Julian receives $1,200 from his insurance company to cover his living expenses for the month. The difference between his actual expenses for the month ($2,000) and his normal living expenses ($1,100) is $900. The excess of the insurance payment over the temporary increase in Julian's living expenses is $300 ($1,200 − $900). Julian may exclude $900 of the insurance payment from income, but the $300 by which the insurance payment exceeds his increased living expenses must be included in income.

---

### II.N.8. Foster Care Payments

[513 T.M., IV.C.; TPS ¶1370.12.]

Payments received from a state, a political subdivision thereof, or a qualified foster care placement agency for either providing care for a qualified foster individual in the foster care provider's home or as a difficulty of care payment generally may be excluded from the foster care provider's income. Foster care payments (other than difficulty of care payments) are not excludible to the extent the payments are made for more than five qualified foster individuals over age 18. Difficulty of care payments are not excludible to the extent the payments are made for more than (i) 10 qualified foster individuals age 18 or under, and (ii) five qualified foster individuals over age 18 [§ 131(a), § 131(b)(4), § 131(c)(2)].

*Qualified Foster Individual.* A qualified foster individual is any person living in a foster family home and placed there by the state, a political subdivision thereof, or a qualified foster care placement agency. A qualified foster care placement agency is any placement agency licensed or certified by a state, a political subdivision thereof, or an entity designated by a state, or political subdivision thereof, for the foster care program of the state or political subdivision to make foster care payments to foster care providers [§ 131(b)(2), § 131(b)(3)].

*Difficulty of Care Payment.* Difficulty of care payments are additional compensation for providing the additional care required for physically, mentally, or emotionally handicapped qualified foster individuals in the foster care provider's home. The state must determine that there is a need for the additional compensation, and the payor must designate such amounts as compensation for this purpose [§ 131(c)(1)].

### *II.N.9. Energy Conservation Subsidies Provided by Public Utilities*

[512 T.M., IV.B.; TPS ¶1370.14.]

A taxpayer generally may exclude the value of a direct or indirect subsidy that a public utility provides to a customer for the purchase or installation of any energy conservation measure. An energy conservation measure is any installation or modification primarily designed to reduce the consumption of electricity or natural gas or to improve the management of energy demand for a dwelling unit. A dwelling unit includes a house, apartment, condominium, mobile home, boat, or similar property, and any appurtenant structures or property.

No deduction or credit is allowed for any expenditure to the extent an amount is excluded under this provision for a subsidy provided with respect to the expenditure. Additionally, a taxpayer must reduce the basis of any property funded with energy conservation subsidies by the amount excluded [§ 136].

### *II.N.10. Federal Subsidies for Prescription Drug Plans*

[395 T.M., III.D., 501 T.M., VIII.F.6.; TPS ¶1370.21.]

Amounts an employer receives from special federal subsidies for providing retiree prescription drugs under § 1860D-22 of the Social Security Act are excluded from gross income for purposes of both the regular tax and the alternative minimum tax. After 2012, the exclusion is no longer disregarded in determining whether a deduction is allowable with respect to retiree prescription drug expenses, and thus, the amount otherwise allowable as a deduction for retiree prescription drug expenses is reduced by the amount of the excludible subsidy payments received [§ 139A].

### *II.N.11. Indian Health Care Benefits*

[501 T.M., XII.A.3.g.; TPS ¶5920.01.B.2.]

An individual may exclude the value of qualified Indian health care benefits received. Qualified Indian health care benefits are [§ 139D]:

- any health service or benefit provided or purchased by the Indian Health Service through a grant to, or a contract or compact with, an Indian tribe or tribal organization or through Indian Health Service-funded programs of third parties;
- medical care (as defined in § 213) provided or purchased by, or amounts to reimburse for such medical care provided by, an Indian tribe or tribal organization for, or to, a member of an Indian tribe, including a spouse or dependent of the member;
- the value of coverage under an accident or health insurance plan (as defined in § 105) provided by an Indian tribe or tribal organization for medical care to a member or the member's spouse or dependent; and
- any other medical care provided by an Indian tribe or tribal organization that supplements, replaces, or substitutes for a federal program or service provided to Indian tribes or their members.

No exclusion is allowed to the extent the value of a qualified Indian health care benefit is otherwise excludible from gross income or deductible under another provision of chapter 1 of the Code.

### II.N.12. General Welfare Exclusion

[501 T.M., XII.C.; TPS ¶¶1010.02.C.8., 1370.12.]

Payments made under legislatively provided social benefit programs for the promotion of general welfare are excluded from the recipient's gross income [Rev. Rul. 76-373, 1976-2 C.B. 16]. To the extent payments reflect the value of services rendered, however, they are treated as compensation and are not within the general welfare exclusion. Some government benefits to which the IRS has applied the general welfare exclusion include:

- Pay-for-Performance Success payments under the Home Affordable Modification Program that reduce home mortgage principal residence balances;
- payments to financially distressed homeowners under the federal Housing Finance Agency Innovation Fund for the Hardest-Hit Housing Markets and the Department of Housing and Urban Development's Emergency Homeowners' Loan Program;
- affordable housing benefits provided to all qualified low-income individuals living or working in a country;
- Native American tribal government housing assistance grants;
- payments to assist low-income persons with utility costs;
- payments to assist adoptive parents with support and maintenance of adoptive children;
- payments to blind persons;
- reimbursements to qualified senior citizens or disabled persons of rehabilitation costs;
- one-time state payments to lower and middle income homeowners who buy and install energy efficient furnaces or boilers;
- relocation payments authorized under the Housing and Community Development Act of 1974; and
- reimbursements by a state agency for a disabled child's care.

However, the IRS has refused to apply the general welfare exclusion to:

- amounts received under federal flood mitigation programs not computed based on the recipient's financial situation or other needs;
- payments under a municipal government program to convert multifamily housing to single family homes because the program provides benefits to investment or business activities rather than addressing individual or family needs;
- state economic stimulus payments not based on individual need;
- payments made under the National Housing Act to mortgagees on behalf of limited-profit corporations formed to acquire and lease apartments in lower income housing projects;
- payments by a mortgage loan servicer to a mortgagee as part of a program that effectively reduces the interest rate on mortgage loans owned by members of the armed services;
- payments for a disabled child's care when child deemed to be employer.

### II.N.13. Other Statutory Exclusions

[501 T.M., XII.; TPS ¶1010.05.]

Statutes other than the Internal Revenue Code may exclude particular items from gross income, such as:

- federal relocation assistance payments made to persons displaced by federal or federally assisted programs [42 USC Ch. 61];
- compensation paid to individual volunteers under the National Older Americans Volunteer Program [Pub. L. No. 93-29];
- amounts received by individuals provided services under the Domestic Volunteer Service Act of 1973 for support services and as reimbursement for expenses [Pub. L. No. 93-113];
- compensation received by a hostage from the U.S. government while in captive status or while hospitalized because of the captivity [Pub. L. No. 96-449];
- financial assistance received under the Solar Energy and Energy Conservation Bank Act and subsidies under the National Energy Conservation Act of 1980 from a utility to a residential customer for energy conservation purposes [Pub. L. No. 96-294] (the § 136 exclusion for energy conservation subsidies provided by public utilities is discussed in II.N.9.); and
- a portion of the qualifying gain from a conservation sale of a qualifying mineral or geothermal interest [Pub. L. No. 109-432].

### II.N.14. Other Nonstatutory Exclusions

[501 T.M., XII.; TPS ¶1010.02.C.]

Certain non-statutory items are also excluded from gross income, including the following:

- unrealized appreciation (because no sale or disposition occurs);
- recoveries of the cost of goods sold (because it is a return of the taxpayer's originally invested capital);
- receipts that a taxpayer may have an obligation to repay (see claim of right doctrine discussed in I.B.5.);
- loan proceeds (because the taxpayer has an obligation to repay the loan);
- loan repayments (unless the lender has claimed a bad debt deduction);
- certain types of imputed income that reflect benefits derived from property owned and used by a taxpayer or from the personal services a taxpayer performs on his or her own behalf;
- rebates from utilities that represent a reduction in the purchase price of electricity;
- government granted transferrable rights, including air emission rights, oil and gas leases obtained in government-run lottery, and remediation credits;
- general welfare payments (see II.N.12.);
- rehabilitation cost reimbursements (if the property owners do not have complete dominion and control over the work and the government controls the project);
- car pool expense reimbursements from members of the car pool (unless the taxpayer is engaged in the trade or business of operating a car pool);
- certain waived fees or commissions of an executor or administrator;
- frequent flyer miles earned during business travel (see I.C.4.);
- leave contributed to an employer-sponsored leave bank for use by other employees if the plan treats payments made by the employer to the leave recipient as wages;
- medical loss ratio rebates (if recipient did not deduct premiums);

- purchase price rebates to nonbusiness retail customers representing a reduction in the purchase price;
- security deposits meant to guarantee performance of an obligation required to be repaid if the obligation is performed;
- Smart Grid Investment Grants made to corporations treated as a capital contribution by the Department of Energy that require that the taxpayer reduce the property's basis.

# CHAPTER III. PROPERTY TRANSACTIONS

>>>>>>>>>>>>>>>>>>>>>>>>>>>>

## III.A. Gain or Loss on a Property Transaction

[501 T.M.; TPS ¶1410.]

Generally, a taxpayer will have gain or loss when property is sold, exchanged, or otherwise disposed of. Gain realized is the excess of the amount realized (see III.A.2.) over the taxpayer's adjusted basis in the disposed of property (see III.A.3.). Loss realized is the excess of the taxpayer's adjusted basis in the disposed of property over the amount realized [§ 1001(a); Reg. § 1.1001-1(a)].

Not all property transactions require a taxpayer to include ("recognize") gain or loss in their income at the time of the transaction (see III.E.). A prerequisite to the inclusion of gain or loss in income is the occurrence of a realization event (see III.A.1.). If a realization event has occurred, several other issues must be addressed to determine the proper tax treatment, including:

- the amount realized in the transaction (see III.A.2.);
- the taxpayer's adjusted basis in the property sold, exchanged, or disposed of (see III.A.3.);
- the determination of whether gain or loss is recognized (see III.E.);
- the character of any gain or loss recognized (see III.B.);
- the applicability of any provisions excluding gain from income (see Chapter II.);
- the applicability of any provisions allowing a deduction for a loss (see Chapters IV. and VII.); and
- the timing of any gain or loss (see XI.B.).

### III.A.1. Realization Events for Property Transactions

[501 T.M., III.A.3., X.C.2.a., 562 T.M., I.A.; TPS ¶1420.01.]

A transaction involving property is treated as realization event if the taxpayer's relationship with the property is changed in a way that terminates or significantly reduces the taxpayer's interest in the property. Necessarily, a transaction with respect to the property must take place. The lack of a transaction typically precludes the occurrence realization event. With certain exceptions, including mark-to-market accounting for securities dealers (see III.F.1.), § 1256 contracts marked-to-market (see III.F.1.e.), and constructive sales treatment for appreciated financial positions (see III.F.1.h.), the mere increase or decrease in the value of property owned by a taxpayer generally is not a realization event [§ 1001; *Eisner v. Macomber*, 252 U.S. 189 (1920)]. Additionally, the disposition of property by gift generally is not, by itself, a realization event.

---

**EXAMPLE:** Shaun owns a valuable wine collection. From Year 1 to Year 2, the fair market value of the collection increases by $1,000. Shaun does not sell, exchange, or otherwise dispose of any portion of the collection. There has been no realization event, and, though Shaun's wealth has increased by $1,000, he is not currently taxed on the gain. If he had sold the wine collection in Year 2, a realization event would have occurred, and Shaun would include the $1,000 gain in income.

**EXAMPLE:** Rachel owns a home with a fair market value of $100,000. In Year 1, Rachel adds an addition to the home that increases the value of the home by $20,000. The construction of an addition to the home is not a realization event and Rachel is not taxed on the increased value of her home in Year 1.

**EXAMPLE:** Donald owns two parcels of land, each with a fair market value of $200,000. In Year 1, Donald transfers the title of one parcel to Tim for $200,000 in cash, and the other to Anna for stock with a fair market value of $200,000. A realization even has occurred with respect to both parcels of land.

---

Timing rules for taxpayers using the accrual method of accounting are discussed in Chapter XI.

### III.A.2. Computation of Amount Realized in Property Transactions

[501 T.M., X.C.3., 562 T.M., III.C.2., 774 T.M., X.B.; TPS ¶¶1410.02., 1440., 1630.07.a.]

The amount realized is the total value of the economic benefit the taxpayer receives upon the disposition of property. It includes the sum of any cash received, the fair market value of any non-cash property received, the amount of any liability from which the taxpayer is discharged or relieved, and any other economic benefit inuring to the benefit of the taxpayer as a result of the disposition [§ 1001(b); Reg. § 1.1001-1(a)]. A taxpayer subtracts the disposed of property's adjusted basis (see III.A.3.) from the amount realized on the disposition of an item of property to determine taxable gain or loss.

*Liabilities.* A taxpayer is treated as having been discharged from a liability if another person agrees to pay it, even where a creditor does not release the taxpayer from a recourse liability. Thus, when the buyer of property assumes the seller's mortgage, the amount of the mortgage is included in the seller's amount realized even if the seller continues to be liable to the mortgagee. Similarly, the disposition of property securing a nonrecourse liability of the taxpayer also discharges the taxpayer's liability for purposes of computing the amount realized. Even where the amount of the liability exceeds the fair market value of the property it secures, the full amount of the liability relieved is included in the amount realized [Reg. § 1.1001-2(a), § 1.1001-2(b)].

If a taxpayer makes a gift of property, and the donee assumes or takes such property subject to a liability, the amount of the relieved liability is included in the taxpayer's amount realized, even though gifts are not, in and of themselves, realization events. In addition, a donee's assumption of the donor's gift tax liability on a gift is a relieved liability [Reg. § 1.1001-2(a)].

**EXAMPLE:** Elisa owns property with a fair market value of $100,000 that is subject to a $40,000 mortgage. Elisa is personally liable on the mortgage. She sells the property to William for $60,000 in cash and William's assumption of the mortgage. Elisa's amount realized is $100,000 ($60,000 cash + $40,000 liability from which she was relieved). The result is the same even if the creditor does not release Elisa from the mortgage and the creditor can hold her liable if William fails to make the mortgage payments. Further, the result is the same if the Elisa was not personally liable on the mortgage and William takes title to the property subject to the nonrecourse mortgage.

**EXAMPLE:** Frank transfers to his nephew by gift property with a fair market value of $50,000 that is subject to a recourse mortgage of $10,000. Frank's nephew agrees to assume payments on the mortgage. Frank is treated as selling the property to his nephew to the extent he is relieved from liability. Therefore, Frank's amount realized on the transaction is $10,000.

The amount of a liability relieved is not treated as part of the taxpayer's amount realized in two instances. First, the amount realized on the disposition of property securing a recourse liability does not include amounts that are income from the discharge of indebtedness. Amounts that would be treated as income from the discharge of indebtedness if they were realized and recognized are similarly excluded from the amount realized (see I.L.). Second, the amount realized on the disposition of property does not include the amount of a liability from which the transferor is discharged if the transferor did not take the liability into account in determining the basis for the property when he acquired it [Reg. § 1.1001-2(a)(2), § 1.1001-2(a)(3)].

**EXAMPLE:** Heather borrows $10,000 from Sally to help purchase a $12,000 car. Heather secures the loan with the car's title. Later on, when the loan balance is $8,000 and the car is worth $7,000, Heather moves out of the country. She no longer has a need for the car, and Sally agrees to purchase it from Heather in exchange for cancelling the $8,000 debt. Heather's amount realized on the sale is $7,000 (the car's fair market value), and she has income from the discharge of indebtedness of $1,000 ($8,000 discharged debt − $7,000 amount realized).

**EXAMPLE:** Evan purchases a retail space from Tara under the following terms: Evan transfers $100,000 in cash, borrows $500,000 from a bank, and makes himself liable to Tara for 15% of the amount by which his gross sales from the retail space exceed $3 million over the next two years. Evan encounters financial problems months later and has to sell the retail space to a third party. The amount Evan realizes on the sale does not include any amount attributable to the contingent liability for the excess gross sales, because Evan did not take into account that liability in determining his adjusted basis when he purchased the shopping center.

*Costs that Reduce Amount Realized.* Certain costs and expenses a taxpayer incurs to facilitate the disposition of the property can reduce the amount realized, including [Reg. § 1.263(a)-1(e)(1), § 1.263(a)-1(e)(3)]:
- commissions paid to real estate agents and brokers;
- title insurance premiums;
- attorney fees for services related to the disposition;
- appraisal fees;

- real property transfer and stamp taxes; and
- deed and title preparation expenses.

The amount realized is reduced by the amount of any credit the seller allows to the purchaser to induce the purchase. Additionally, the amount realized is reduced by any amounts the taxpayer returns to the purchaser in the year of the disposition as a purchase price reduction.

---

**EXAMPLE:** Bradley puts his house on the market in Jan. In Apr., Sam offers Bradley $100,000 for the house, and Bradley accepts. Thereafter, Bradley learns that in Mar. the town in which the house is located enacted an ordinance that requires all homeowners to connect to the public sewer system. The town will not issue a use and occupancy permit until the house has been connected, or until Bradley has arranged a binding contract to connect the house. The cost of connecting the house is $7,000. Bradley and Sam amend the contract of sale so that Sam agrees to have the sewer work completed after closing, and Bradley agrees to credit Sam with $5,000 of the cost at closing. Bradley's amount realized is $95,000 ($100,000 − $5,000).

**EXAMPLE:** Jane sells a parcel of land to Sue for $70,000 in Year 1. Later in Year 1, Sue discovers Jane had operated a dump on the land, and she had concealed that fact from Sue. Still in Year 1, Jane agrees to return $15,000 of the purchase price, reflecting the fact that the land is only worth $55,000 ($70,000 − $15,000). Jane's amount realized is $55,000. Had the $15,000 been returned to Sue in Year 2, it would have been treated as a separate transaction, and not a year of sale price adjustment.

---

*Costs that Do Not Reduce Amount Realized.* Certain costs and expenses do not reduce the amount realized. An amount a taxpayer pays to make property more attractive and increase the chances of selling it does not reduce the taxpayer's amount realized. However, if the expenditure is a capital expenditure (see VIII.A.), the property's adjusted basis (see III.A.3.) is increased. In addition, expenditures a taxpayer incurs at the time the property is disposed of, even if those expenditures are incurred on account of the disposition, do not reduce the taxpayer's amount realized if such expenditures are otherwise deductible. This is the case even where the taxpayer does not claim the available deduction. Furthermore, personal expenditures, such as utility charges or repairs relating to property used for personal purposes, do not reduce the amount realized upon disposition of the property.

---

**EXAMPLE:** Lynne owns a dilapidated building, which she has been unable to sell. She pays a contractor $40,000 to make major repairs. Upon completion of the work, Lynne sells the building for $100,000. Lynne's amount realized is $100,000. The $40,000 expenditure is a capital expenditure that increases Lynne's adjusted basis in the building.

**EXAMPLE:** Cole sells his home on Aug. 20 for $80,000. At settlement, Cole must pay $150 in interest on the mortgage secured by the home, which represents interest for the first 20 days of Aug. He also must pay $50 water use charges, which represents his water use for the first 20 days of Aug. that will be billed to the purchaser. The $150 of interest is deductible as qualified residence indebtedness and, therefore, does not reduce the amount realized. Similarly, the $50 of water use charges is a personal expense, and it does not reduce the amount realized. Thus, Cole's amount realized is $80,000, regardless of whether he deducts the $150 interest expense.

---

*Open Transactions.* In some situations, the consideration to be received in a sale or exchange cannot immediately be valued, and thus, it is not possible to determine the amount of gain realized at the time of the transaction. Where this is the case, the taxpayer is not required to include in income any gain at the time of the transaction. Rather, the transaction remains open until payment is received, and at that time, the appropriate amount of gain is determined and taken into income. The character of the gain is determined by the nature of the earlier transaction. These "open transactions" typically arise in connection with sales of property in exchange for contingent payments based on the profits generated from the property [*Burnet v. Logan*, 283 U.S. 404 (1931)].

---

**EXAMPLE:** Nina is the operator and sole shareholder of the retail business Clothing Corporation. Her adjusted basis in the stock of Clothing Corporation is $500,000. In Year 1, Nina sells all the stock to Ray in exchange for 20% of the net profits of the business during Years 2 through 6. At the time of the sale, it is not possible to determine whether the business will be profitable. During Years 2 through 6, Nina's share of the profits of Clothing Corporation is $600,000, which Ray pays to Nina in Year 6. Nina is not required to include any gain in income in Year 1, the year of the sale. However, in Year 6, Nina includes $100,000 ($600,000 amount received − $500,000 adjusted basis in the stock) in income. This amount is treated as gain from the sale of the stock.

---

Taxpayers are rarely successful in invoking the open transaction doctrine to defer the inclusion of gain because most contract rights can be valued with reasonable accuracy. Rarely will property be considered not to have an ascertainable fair market value [Rev. Rul. 58-402, 1958-2 C.B. 15].

Contingent payment sales reported using the installment method are discussed in III.G.8.

*Receipt of Stock in an Insurance Company Demutualization.* Whether the open transaction doctrine applies to the sale of stock received in a demutualization is unsettled. A mutual insurance company is owned by its policyholders. When a mutual insurance company demutualizes and becomes a stock company, an eligible policyholder may receive stock in the new stock company. The IRS has argued that taxpayers have zero basis in the proprietary interest in the mutual insurance company and therefore zero basis in the stock received [Rev. Rul. 71-233, 1971-1 C.B. 113].

Courts are divided on the matter. At least one court has found that, where a taxpayer subsequently sold the stock of a demutualized company, the open transaction doctrine applied to the facts before them, and the IRS's assertion that the stock had zero basis was incorrect. In that instance, the taxpayer was not required to recognize gain because the amount received was less than the overall cost basis in the insurance policy. Another court has rejected the application of the open transaction doctrine and required the taxpayer to recognize the full amount realized as gain on the grounds that the taxpayer had no basis in the stock. Still another court rejected the application of the open transaction doctrine but found that the taxpayer had some ascertainable basis in the stock and, as a result, the taxpayer was required only to recognize some gain.

### III.A.3. Computation of Adjusted Basis in Property Transactions

[560 T.M., III., IV.; TPS ¶1430.]

Adjusted basis represents a taxpayer's investment in property for tax purposes. A taxpayer subtracts the adjusted basis of the disposed of property from the amount realized on the disposition of the property (see III.A.2.) to determine taxable gain or loss. The calculation of adjusted basis is generally a two-step process: (1) the taxpayer's basis in the property must be determined, and (2) that basis must be modified up or down by any applicable basis adjustments [§ 1011(a); Reg. § 1.1011-1].

### III.A.3.a. Basis

[560 T.M., III.; TPS ¶1430.02.]

Basis is a reflection of the taxpayer's investment in property for tax purposes at the time the taxpayer acquires the property. How property's basis is determined typically depends on how the property was acquired. The following rules to determine basis cover most situations [§ 1012(a), § 1014, § 1015]:

- Property acquired through purchase or construction has a basis equal to its cost (cost basis) (see III.A.3.a.(1)).
- Property acquired through gift has a basis equal to the donor's adjusted basis (substituted or carryover basis), however, for purposes of determining loss, the basis is the lower of the donor's adjusted basis or the property's fair market value at the time of the gift (see III.A.3.a.(2)).
- Property acquired by reason of the death of a decedent generally has a basis equal to the property's fair market value at the date of death (stepped-up basis) (see III.A.3.a.(3)).
- Property acquired in a tax-free transaction generally has a basis equal to the taxpayer's basis in the property transferred in exchange for the acquired property (substituted basis) (see III.A.3.a.(4)).

### III.A.3.a.(1) Property Acquired Through Purchase or Construction (Cost Basis)

[560 T.M., III.B.1.; TPS ¶1430.02.B.]

Property acquired through purchase has a basis equal to its cost, including the value of amounts the taxpayer pays in cash, property, debt instruments, or services. Similarly, property constructed by the taxpayer has a basis equal to the cost of construction. In either case, if the taxpayer pays all or a portion of the cost with borrowed funds, the calculation of cost basis is the same. Note, however, that if the amount of a nonrecourse note given as part of the purchase price of property unreasonably exceeds the value of the interests acquired, the taxpayer may not be allowed to include the nonrecourse amount in depreciable basis [*Franklin Est. v. Commissioner*, 544 F.2d 1045 (9th Cir. 1976)].

---

**EXAMPLE:** Randall acquires a parcel of land by paying $5,000 in cash and incurring a $50,000 mortgage. His cost basis in the land is $55,000.

**EXAMPLE:** Nancy pays a construction company $400,000 to build her a new home. She pays $50,000 in cash, borrows $250,000 from the bank, and borrows an additional $100,000 from the construction company. Nancy's basis in the new home is $400,000.

---

Where there is a fully taxable exchange of property, the taxpayer's cost basis in the property acquired is equal to its fair market value. The same principal applies where cash is given or received to account for differences in the fair market values of the properties exchanged. There is a strong presumption that the total values of the properties exchanged are equal. Where this is indeed the case, the rule may be restated to say that cash basis in the property acquired is equal to the fair market value of the property given up, increased by cash given up, and decreased by cash received.

---

**EXAMPLE:** Charlie owns land with a fair market value of $100,000. Lucy owns stock in a computer company worth $100,000. Charlie and Lucy make a taxable exchange of these properties. Charlie's cost basis in the stock is $100,000, and Lucy's cost basis in the land is $100,000. If, however, the fair market value of Charlie's land had been $90,000 and Charlie had included $10,000 in cash in the taxable exchange to account for the difference in value, Charlie's cost basis in the stock would have been $100,000, and Lucy's cost basis in the land would have been $90,000.

---

### III.A.3.a.(2) Property Acquired Through Gift (Carryover Basis)

[560 T.M., III.B.3.a.; TPS ¶1430.02.E.]

Property acquired through gift has a basis equal to the property's adjusted basis in the hands of the donor. Where the donor's adjusted basis in the property exceeds the property's fair market value at the time of the gift, however, the donee's basis in the property is its fair market value for purposes of determining loss [§ 1015(a); Reg. § 1.1015-1(a)(1)].

---

**EXAMPLE:** Arthur owns land with an adjusted basis of $80,000, and a fair market value of $100,000. Arthur gives the land as a gift to his nephew George. George's basis in the land is $80,000. Assume, alternatively, that Arthur's basis in the land was $120,000. For purposes of determining loss, George's basis in the land is $100,000 (the fair market value). For purposes of determining gain, George's basis in the land is $120,000. Thus, if George subsequently sells the land for $70,000, he has a loss of $30,000 ($70,000 − $100,000). If George sells the land for $150,000, he has a gain of $30,000 ($150,000 − $120,000). If George sells the land for a price between $100,000 and $120,000, he realizes neither gain nor loss.

---

*Part Gift and Part Sale.* In some cases, a transfer of property may be part gift and part sale. For such cases, the transferee's basis is the greater of either (i) the amount paid for the property, or (ii) the transferor's adjusted basis at the time of the transfer. For purposes of determining loss, however, the transferee's basis may not exceed the fair market value of the property at the time of the transfer [Reg. § 1.1015-4(a)].

---

**EXAMPLE:** Rita owns property with an adjusted basis of $20,000 and a fair market value of $50,000. She transfers the property to Julia in exchange for $12,000. Julia later sells the property for $55,000. Julia's basis in the property in determining her gain on the sale is $20,000, which is the greater of the adjusted basis of the property in Rita's hands or the amount Julia paid for the property. Thus, Julia realizes $35,000 of gain on the sale ($55,000 − $20,000). Had Julia paid $30,000 for the property, her basis in determining her gain on the sale would have been $30,000, and thus, she would have realized gain of $25,000 ($55,000 − $30,000).

**EXAMPLE:** Ryan owns property with an adjusted basis of $20,000 and a fair market value of $10,000. He transfers the property to Jason in exchange for $5,000. For purposes of determining gain, Jason's basis in the property is $20,000, which is the greater of the adjusted basis of the property in Ryan's hands or the amount Jason paid for the property. Thus, if Jason later sells the property for $30,000, he will realize $10,000 of gain ($30,000 − $20,000). For purposes of determining loss, Jason's basis in the property is $10,000, because a transferee's basis may not exceed fair market value in determining loss. Thus, if Jason later sells the property for $5,000, he will realize $5,000 of loss ($5,000 − $10,000).

*Gift Taxes.* Where gift taxes are paid on the gift, the donee's basis is increased by a portion of the gift tax. The portion to be added to basis is the pro rata portion of all of the gift tax paid by the donor for the year that is attributable to the gift in question. Thus, the portion is determined by multiplying the total amount a donor paid in gift taxes for the year by a fraction, the numerator of which is the amount of the gift in question, and the denominator of which is the total taxable gifts made by the donor for the year. It is immaterial whether the gift tax is paid by the donor or donee, however, where the done pays the tax, the transaction is treated as part gift, part sale [§ 1015(d)(6); Reg. § 1.1015-5(c)].

### III.A.3.a.(3) *Property Acquired from a Decedent (Stepped-Up Basis)*

[560 T.M., III.B.3.c.; TPS ¶1430.02.D.]

Property acquired from a decedent typically has a basis equal to its fair market value at the time of the decedent's death, regardless of the adjusted basis in the hands of the decedent. If an estate tax return is filed, fair market value is the value at which the property is included in the decedent's gross estate [§ 1014(a)(1); Reg. § 1.1014-1(a), § 1.1014-3(a)].

For decedents dying in 2010, an executor may elect to apply a special carryover basis rule. If elected, the estate does not pay an estate tax, and the basis of property acquired from the decedent is equal to the lesser of (i) the decedent's adjusted basis in the property, or (ii) the property's fair market value at the time of the decedent's death [Pub. L. No. 111-312, § 301(c)].

**EXAMPLE:** Matthew dies in a year that is not 2010. One of his assets is a parcel of land with an adjusted basis of $65,000. The land's fair market value, as reported on the estate tax return, is $100,000. Matthew's will devises the land to Ashley. Ashley's basis in the land is $100,000.

A taxpayer's receipt of appreciated property that the taxpayer gifted to the decedent within one year of the decedent's death is not eligible for a basis equal to fair market value. Instead, the taxpayer's basis in the property is equal to the adjusted basis in the decedent's hands at the time of death. Additionally, the general rule of basis equal to fair market value does not apply to property that constitutes a right to receive an item of income from a decedent [§ 1014(c), § 1014((e); Reg. § 1.1014-1(c)(1)].

**EXAMPLE:** Joey has a terminal illness. In Jan. of Year 1, Jesse gifts Joey property with a fair market value of $100,000 and an adjusted basis of $50,000. In Sept., Joey dies and devises the same property to Jesse. The fair market value of the property at the time of Joey's death has increased to $115,000. Jesse's basis in the property is $50,000.

### III.A.3.a.(4) Property Acquired in a Tax-Free Exchange (Exchanged or Substituted Basis)

[560 T.M., III.B.2.b.; TPS ¶1510.08.]

Subject to certain adjustments, the basis of property acquired in a tax-free exchange is generally determined in whole or in part by reference to basis of the property the taxpayer transferred [§ 1031(d); Reg. § 1.1031(d)-1]. Transactions resulting in an exchanged basis include the following:

- like-kind exchanges of property held for productive use or investment [§ 1031];
- certain exchanges of insurance policies [§ 1035];
- certain exchanges of stock for stock in the same corporation [§ 1036];
- certain exchanges of U.S. obligations [§ 1037];
- transfers of property to a controlled corporation solely in exchange for stock in that corporation [§ 351]; and
- transfers of stock or securities in a corporation solely in exchange for stock or securities in the same corporation or certain other corporations as part of a reorganization [§ 354].

**EXAMPLE:** Kevin exchanges land held as an investment for an apartment building held for investment in a tax-free like-kind exchange (see III.E.1.). Both the land and the apartment building have a fair market value of $400,000. Kevin's adjusted basis in the land is $150,000. Because Kevin acquires the apartment building in a tax-free exchange, his basis in the apartment building is determined by reference to his basis in the land. Thus, Kevin's basis in the apartment building is $150,000.

Basis adjustments required by § 1031(d) and § 358(a)(1) are discussed in III.E.1.e. and XIII.B.4., respectively.

### III.A.3.b. Adjustments to Basis

[560 T.M., IV.B.; TPS ¶1430.03.]

Adjustments to basis reflect changes in the taxpayer's investment in the property for tax purposes occurring while the taxpayer owns the property. An adjustment is made for expenditures, receipts, losses, or other items properly chargeable to a capital account. Common items requiring basis adjustments include the following [§ 1016; Reg. § 1.1016-2]:

- Basis is increased for the cost of capital improvements.
- Basis is increased for expenses incurred in protecting title and securing possession and use.
- Basis is decreased for depreciation, depletion, amortization, exhaustion, wear and tear, and obsolescence (depreciation and amortization are discussed in Chapter V.; depletion is discussed in VI.A.).
- Basis is decreased by any insurance or other reimbursement, and by any deductible loss not covered by insurance, in the case of a casualty or theft loss (see VIII.H.1.).
- Basis is decreased as a result of certain attribute reductions required following a discharge of indebtedness that is excluded from income (see II.A.8.).

**EXAMPLE:** Leslie purchases a building for $200,000. Before placing it into service, she spends $50,000 to improve the building. After the capital improvement, Leslie's adjusted basis in the building is $250,000. Several years later, Leslie spends $5,000 to repair the building to its original operating condition. The $5,000 expenditure does not increase Leslie's adjusted basis in the building because it is in the nature of a deductible repair, rather than a capital improvement.

### III.A.3.c. Bargain Sales to Charity, Certain Term Interests, and Certain Annuity Transfers

[560 T.M., IV.E.; TPS ¶1430.01.B.]

In certain circumstances, including bargain sales to charity, certain term interests, and certain annuity transfers, adjusted basis is determined without regard to the general rules discussed above.

*Bargain Sales to Charity.* When a taxpayer sells property to a charity for less than fair market value under circumstances that permit the taxpayer to claim a charitable contribution deduction, a special computation of adjusted basis is made. Generally, the adjusted basis for determining gain or loss from the sale is the adjusted basis multiplied by a fraction, the numerator of which is the amount realized from the bargain sale, and the denominator of which is the fair market value of the property [§ 1011(b); Reg. § 1.1011-2].

*Certain Term Interests.* If a taxpayer disposes of a term interest in property, such as a life estate, interest for a term of years, or an income interest in a trust, any adjusted basis that is determined under the rules for acquisition by gift, from a decedent, or in a marital transaction is disregarded. Only the portion of the adjusted basis that is so determined is disregarded. This rule also applies to dispositions by corporations of term interests acquired in transactions to which the nonrecognition rules for acquisition of corporate stock apply (see XIII.B.1.). The rule does not apply to dispositions of remainder interests, reversionary interests, or interests that ripen into full ownership of the entire property upon termination or failure of a preceding term interest. Further, the term interest adjusted basis rule does not apply if the term interest is disposed of by the taxpayer in a transaction in which the taxpayer's entire interest in the property is transferred to other persons, or if, in the same transaction in which the owner of the term interest disposes of it, the owners of the other interests in the property also dispose of their interests [§ 1001(e); Reg. § 1.1001-1(f)].

*Certain Annuity Transfers.* When an annuity is sold for value, the person who transfers the annuity must modify its adjusted basis by subtracting from it all amounts received under the annuity that were not included in his or her gross income. Amounts received under an annuity include amounts deemed to have been received under the annuity and amounts received by another person under the annuity but that were not included in that person's gross income. If amounts received by the taxpayer under the annuity exceed the adjusted basis, the adjusted basis is zero. In no event may the adjusted basis be less than zero [§ 1021; Reg. § 1.1021-1]. Dispositions of annuity contracts are discussed in III.C.6., and nontaxable exchanges of certain annuity contracts are discussed in III.E.4.

### III.A.3.d. Basis in Stocks and Bonds

[560 T.M., V.B.3.b.; TPS ¶1430.02.B.5.]

When a taxpayer disposes of stock in a corporation that was acquired at different times, special rules apply to determine the taxpayer's basis in the disposed of stock. Using the adequate identification method, a taxpayer may determine which shares of stock have been sold by physically selecting or earmarking the certificates representing that stock. The taxpayer is treated as disposing the stock represented by the certificates delivered to the transferee. The taxpayer makes an adequate identification of stock at the time of sale, transfer, delivery, or distribution if the taxpayer identifies the stock no later than the earlier of either (i) the settlement date, or (ii) the time for settlement required by SEC rules. The adequate identification method is treated as being satisfied even if the taxpayer intends or instructs his broker or agent to deliver other stock to the purchaser. A taxpayer must use the adequate identification method if the requirements of the method are met [Reg. § 1.1012-1(c)].

Unless the taxpayer uses the average basis method (discussed below), if the taxpayer does not adequately identify the lot from which the stock is sold or transferred, the taxpayer is treated as having first sold the stock that was first acquired [Reg. § 1.1012-1(c)(1)].

---

**EXAMPLE:** Jerry purchases 300 shares of Corporation stock for $300,000 in Year 1. He purchases an additional 200 shares of Corporation stock for $400,000 in Year 5. Jerry later uses the adequate identification method and transfers to a purchaser the certificates for the 200 shares of Corporation purchased in Year 5. The 200 shares of Corporation stock purchased in Year 5 are treated as having been sold, and Jerry's basis in the sold stock is $400,000. Had Jerry not met the requirements of the adequate identification method, the 200 shares of Corporation stock would have been treated as having first come from the shares purchased in Year 1. Accordingly, the basis of those 200 shares would have been $200,000 ($300,000 total basis in Year 1 shares × (200 Year 1 shares sold ÷ 300 total Year 1 shares)).

---

There are two exceptions to the adequate identification method. The confirmation document identification exception applies when the stock is left in the custody of a broker or agent. The taxpayer is treated as having sold stock designated by the taxpayer and confirmed by the broker, even if other certificates are delivered to the purchaser. The designation must be made to the broker or agent at the time of the disposition, and the confirmation must be made in writing within a reasonable time after the disposition. The fiduciary identification exception applies when stock is retained by a trustee or by the administrator or executor of an estate. The trust or estate is treated as transferring stock designated by the fiduciary and, in the case of a distribution, identified to the distribute. The exception applies even if certificates representing other stock are delivered to the purchaser [Reg. § 1.1012-1(c)(3), § 1.1012-1(c)(4)].

Taxpayers may also use the average basis method to determine the cost or other basis of identical shares of stock in a regulated investment company (mutual fund) or identical shares of stock acquired after 2010 in connection with a dividend reinvestment plan that were acquired at different prices and maintained by a custodian or agent in an account maintained for the acquisitions, redemption, sale, or other disposition of shares of the stock. Identical shares of stock, for this purpose, are stock with the same CUSIP number or other permitted security identifier number. Average basis is computed by averaging the bases of all identical stock in an account regardless of holding period. Shares sold or transferred are deemed to be the shares first acquired [Reg. § 1.1012-1(e)(7)].

---

**EXAMPLE:** Damon enters into an agreement with Custodian establishing an account for the periodic acquisition of shares of Company, a regulated investment company. Custodian acquires shares of Company for Damon's account in the following amounts and on the following dates:

- Jan. 1, Year 1: 35 shares for $200;
- Feb. 1, Year 1: 30 shares for $200;
- Mar. 1, Year 1: 20 shares for $200; and
- Apr. 1, Year 1: 15 shares for $200.

At Damon's direction, Custodian sells 40 shares of Company from the account on Jan. 15 of Year 2 for $10 per share. Damon elects to use the average basis method for the shares of Company. The average basis for the shares sold in Jan. of Year 2 is $8 ($800 total cost of purchased shares ÷ 100 total shares purchased). Thus, each share sold in Jan. of Year 2 results in $2 of income ($10 amount realized − $8 basis). Damon realizes $50 ($2 × 35 shares) of long-term capital gain for the 35 shares acquired in Jan. of Year 1, and $10 ($2 × 5 shares) short-term capital gain for the 5 shares acquired in Feb. of Year 1.

---

Taxpayers are required to apply the wash sale rules (see III.F.1.d.) in computing average basis regardless of whether the stock of security sold and the stock acquired are in the same account or different accounts [Reg. § 1.1012-1(e)(7)(iv)].

A taxpayer elects the average basis method by notifying the custodian or other agent for the taxpayer's account in writing by any reasonable means. The election may be made at any time and is effective for dispositions occurring after notification. A separate election must be made for each account for which the average basis method is permissible. A taxpayer may revoke the election by the earlier of either (i) one year from the date of making the election, or (ii) the first sale or other disposition of the stock following the election [Reg. § 1.1012-1(e)(9)].

Note that brokers required to file information returns reporting sales by customers must include on the return the customer's adjusted basis in the security [§ 6045(g); Reg. § 1.6045-1(d)(2)(i)].

### III.A.4. Purchase Price Allocation Rules

[560 T.M., V.B.; TPS ¶1450.]

Businesses generally have many assets, and as a result, the sale of a trade or business typically is a sale of multiple assets, rather than a sale of a single asset. Thus, a lump sum paid for a trade or business is the purchase price of multiple individual assets. Gain or loss on the sale of those assets must be figured separately because different assets may be treated differently under the tax laws. For example, the sale of a capital asset results in capital gain or loss (see III.B.), the sale of § 1231 property results in § 1231 gain or loss (see III.C.1.), and the sale of inventory results in ordinary gain or loss (see III.A.).

Taxpayers purchasing several assets for a lump sum must allocate the total purchase price among the acquired assets in order to determine each asset's basis. Just the same, a taxpayer selling several assets for a lump sum must allocate the total sales price among the sold assets in order to determine the amount realized for each asset. The purchase-price allocation rules apply to applicable asset acquisitions, which are direct or indirect transfers satisfying two criteria [§ 1060(a), § 1060(c); Reg. § 1.1060-1(a)(1), § 1.1060-1(b)]:

1. the transfer is of assets that constitute a trade or business; and

2. the transfer is one for which the transferee's basis in the assets is determined wholly by reference to the consideration paid for the assets (see III.A.3.a.(1)) (though a transfer is not excluded solely because nonrecognition rules apply to a portion of the assets transferred).

*Trade or Business.* A group of assets constitutes a trade or business where either [§ 355; Reg. § 1.1060-1(b)(2)]:

- the use of the assets would constitute an active trade or business in either the hands of the seller or the purchaser under the rules on distributions of stock and securities of controlled corporations; or

- the character of the assets is such that goodwill or going concern value could under any circumstances attach to the group.

A trade or business, for purposes of the controlled corporation distribution rules, is a group of activities carried on to earn income or profit in which the activities included in the group include every operation that forms a part of, or a step in, the process of earning income or such profit [Reg. § 1.355-3(b)(2)(ii)]. The determination of whether the character of the group of assets is such that goodwill or going concern value could under any circumstances attach to the group is made taking into account all of the facts and circumstances, including the following [Reg. § 1.1060-1(b)(2)(iii)]:

- the presence of intangible assets (whether or not they are amortizable intangibles);

- the existence of an excess of total consideration over the aggregate book value of the purchased tangible and intangible assets (other than goodwill and going concern value) in the purchaser's financial accounting books and records; and

- related transactions between the purchaser and seller in connection with the transfer, including lease agreements, licenses, and similar agreements.

---

**EXAMPLE:** Sara operates a car wash. She sells all of her car washing equipment and the building housing the car wash to Kristen. In Sara's hands, the building and the equipment constituted a trade or business. Because the transferred assets constitute a trade or business and Kristen's basis in the transferred assets is determined wholly by reference to the consideration she paid, Kristen's purchase of Sara's assets is an applicable asset acquisition.

---

*Nonrecognition Transactions.* A transaction will not fail to satisfy the "wholly by reference to" criterion solely because a portion of the group of assets exchanged is received in certain nonrecognition transactions, including like-kind exchanges (see III.E.1.), certain insurance policy exchanges, certain exchanges of stock in a corporation for stock in the same corporation, as well as any other provision that has the same effect as the like-kind nonrecognition provisions [§ 1060(c), § 1031, § 1035, § 1036; Reg. § 1.1060-1(b)(8)]. The fact that a purchaser determines basis in one or more of the transferred assets under the like-kind exchange basis determination rules is not taken into account in determining whether a transfer is an applicable asset acquisition. All assets transferred, including the nonrecognition assets, are taken into account in determining whether the group of assets constitutes a trade or business. However, if an applicable asset acquisition includes property, the basis of which is determined under an applicable nonrecognition provision, that property is excluded from the application of the purchase price allocation rules, and basis and amount realized for that property are determined under the applicable nonrecognition rules [Reg. § 1.1060-1(b)(8)].

---

**EXAMPLE:** Dora owns a travel agency business, which she sells to Bill. One of the business's assets is a building with a fair market value of $100,000. Bill transfers to Dora $400,000 in cash, plus appreciated land with a fair market value of $80,000. The like-kind nonrecognition rules allow Bill to defer the recognition of some gain on the transfer of the land. However, the transfer still qualifies as an applicable asset acquisition.

---

*Allocation of Consideration.* Where the buyer and seller have a written agreement on the allocation of any consideration or the fair market value of any asset, the agreement is binding unless the IRS determines the assigned allocations or fair market values are inappropriate. If the parties do not have a written agreement, or if the IRS deems their agreement inappropriate, the asset class allocation rules apply, under which assets acquired in an applicable asset acquisition are divided into seven classes among which the purchase price is allocated [§ 1060(a); Reg. § 1.1060-1(c)(2)].

The seven asset classes are as follows:
1. Class I: cash and general deposit accounts, including checking and savings accounts, but excluding certificates of deposit.
2. Class II: certificates of deposit, U.S. government securities, foreign currency, and actively traded personal property, including stock and securities.
3. Class III: accounts receivable, other debt instruments, and assets marked to market at least annually for federal income tax purposes, but excluding debt instruments issued by persons related to the target at the beginning of the day following the acquisition, certain contingent debt instruments, and debt instruments convertible into the stock of the issuer or other property.
4. Class IV: stock in trade of the taxpayer, or other inventory-type property.
5. Class V: all assets other than Class I, II, III, IV, VI, and VII assets.
6. Class VI: amortizable intangibles, except goodwill and going concern value.
7. Class VII: goodwill and going concern value, whether or not they are amortizable intangibles.

Consideration is allocated among asset classes sequentially, beginning with Class I. Within each class, consideration is allocated in proportion to an asset's fair market value on the purchase date. The amount allocated to an asset (other than those assets in Class VII) may not exceed its fair market value. For these purposes, the fair market value of an asset is determined without regard to mortgages, liens, pledges, and other liabilities [Reg. § 1.1060-1(c)(2), § 1.338-6].

---

**EXAMPLE:** Cindy sells all the assets of her business to Ivan for $300,000 in an applicable asset acquisition. The assets sold consist of $50,000 in cash, $40,000 of inventory, $60,000 of equipment, land worth $100,000, and a building worth $105,000. The cash is a Class I asset, and therefore, $50,000 of the total consideration is first allocated to the cash. There are no Class II or Class III assets. The inventory is a Class IV asset, and therefore, $40,000 is next allocated to the inventory. The remaining assets are all Class V assets, and $210,000 ($300,000 − $50,000 − $40,000) of the consideration is left to be allocated. Because the total value of the Class V assets is

$265,000, the remaining consideration must be allocated in proportion to each asset's fair market value. Thus, $47,547 is allocated to the equipment ($210,000 × ($60,000 ÷ $265,000)), $79,245 is allocated to the land ($210,000 × ($100,000 ÷ $265,000)), and $83,208 is allocated to the building ($210,000 × ($105,000 ÷ $265,000)).

Both the seller and the purchaser of a group of assets constituting a trade or business must attach Form 8594, *Asset Acquisition Statement*, to their income tax returns.

## III.B. Capital Gains and Losses

[507 T.M., II.A.3., III.A.2.; TPS ¶1610.]

The character of gain or loss realized must be classified as either ordinary or capital. This is because net capital gain is taxed differently than ordinary income, and deductions for net capital losses may be restricted in a way that deductions for ordinary losses are not. Generally, a taxpayer will have a capital gain or loss where he or she sells or exchanges a capital asset (see III.B.1.). Further, capital gain must be characterized as either short-term or long-term capital gain, depending on the holding period of the property (see III.B.3.). Ordinary income and loss, on the other hand, are gain or loss from the disposition of property that is not a capital asset. Dispositions of certain property held for longer than one year and used in a trade or business may also give rise to capital gain (see III.C.1.).

*Noncorporate Taxpayers.* In 2014, a noncorporate taxpayer's net capital gains are subject to tax rate groups with maximum rates of 0%, 15%, 20%, 25%, and 28%, depending on the type of asset, the holding period, and the taxpayer's income [§ 1(h)].

The 28% group consists of capital gain and loss from collectibles held for over a year and from the sale of certain small business stock, as well as long-term capital loss carryovers (see III.B.5.). Collectibles include items like art, rugs, antiques, precious metals, gems, stamps, coins, and alcoholic beverages. Gain from collectibles also includes gain on the sale or exchange of an interest in a partnership, S corporation, or trust that is attributable to the unrealized appreciation of such collectibles [§ 1(h)(4), § 1(h)(5)]. A portion of the gain from the sale of certain small business stock held for more than five years may be excluded from income under § 1202 (see III.C.5.). The amount of capital gain included in the 28% group is the amount of eligible gain, less the § 1202 exclusion [§ 1(h)(4), § 1(h)(7), § 1202].

The 25% group consists of unrecaptured § 1250 gain from property held for over a year (see III.D.3.). Unrecaptured § 1250 gain is the excess of [§ 1(h)(6)]:

1. the amount of long-term capital gain (not otherwise treated as ordinary income) that would be treated as ordinary income if § 1250 recapture applied to all depreciation on § 1250 property using 100% as the applicable percentage; over

2. any net loss from the 28% group.

Section 1250 treats gains attributable to certain depreciation (generally that amount of depreciation in excess of the amount allowable under the straight-line method) as ordinary income.

The remaining groups consist of long-term capital gains and losses that are not taxed under the 28% group or the 25% group, as well as qualified dividend income (see XIII.D. and I.E.). The 20% group applies to net capital gains that would otherwise be subject to the 39.6% regular income tax rate. The 15% group applies to net capital gains that would otherwise be subject to the 25%, 28%, 33%, or 35% regular income tax rates. The 0% group applies to net capital gains that would otherwise be subject to the 10% or 15% regular income tax rates.

An individual's capital gains and losses are reported on Form 8949, *Sales and Other Dispositions of Capital Assets*, and Schedule D of Form 1040, *Capital Gains and Losses*.

*Corporate Taxpayers.* Corporate taxpayers with net capital gains are subject to tax equal to the lesser of the following [§ 1201(a)]:

- the tax imposed under the corporate income tax (see X.B.), the unrelated business income tax (see XIX.D.), or the tax on insurance companies other than life insurance companies, whichever is applicable; or
- an alternative tax equal to the sum of the following amounts:
  - the tax imposed by the corporate income tax (see X.B.), the unrelated business income tax (see XIX.D.), or the tax on insurance companies other than life insurance companies, whichever is applicable, on the corporation's taxable income reduced by its net capital gain; and
  - 35% of the lesser of the corporation's net capital gain or taxable income.

Under this rule, a corporation's net capital gain is effectively taxed at a rate no higher than 35%. The alternative rate does not apply if the highest tax rate imposed by the applicable tax is less than 35%.

*Reporting.* Capital gains and losses are reported on Form 8949, *Sales and Other Dispositions of Capital Assets*. The capital gains and losses of an S corporation or partnership flow through to the respective shareholders and partners. An S corporation shareholder and a partnership partner report their proportionate shares of gain or loss on Schedule K-1, *Shareholder's/Partner's Share of Income, Deductions, Credits, etc.* Additionally, a beneficiary of a trust or estate also reports his or her share of the gain or loss on Schedule K-1.

### III.B.1. Capital Assets

[561 T.M.; TPS ¶1620.]

Capital gain or loss occurs on the sale or exchange of a capital asset. Generally speaking, a capital asset is an asset that is not easily sold in the regular course of business for cash, is owned for its role in contributing to profit generation, and the benefits of which will extend beyond a year. The determination of whether any individual item of property is a capital asset requires both a statutory analysis and an analysis of non-statutory doctrines.

A capital asset is property held by the taxpayer (whether or not connected with the taxpayer's trade or business), excluding the following [§ 1221(a)]:

- stock in trade, inventory, or other property held primarily for sale to customers in the ordinary course of the taxpayer's trade or business;
- depreciable or real property used in the taxpayer's trade or business;
- certain literary or artistic property;
- accounts or notes receivable arising from the taxpayer's trade or business;
- certain publications of the federal government;
- commodities derivative financial instruments held by commodities derivatives dealers;
- hedging transactions; and
- supplies of a type regularly consumed in the ordinary course of the taxpayer's trade or business.

These exclusions from capital asset status are construed narrowly [*Arkansas Best Corp. v. Commissioner*, 485 U.S. 212 (1988)].

Court decisions and other guidance have also clarified the definition of capital asset. Though contract rights are typically considered a property interest, only certain contract rights are capital assets. Licenses permitting the conduct of a business granted by governmental authorities are capital assets, as are proceeds from the transfer of a taxpayer's entire life interest in property. Additionally, oil, gas, and other mineral interests, as well as trade names, franchises, and trade secrets, are capital assets.

***Stock in Trade, Inventory, and Other Property Held for Sale to Customers.*** The broadest and, arguably, most significant exclusion from capital asset status applies to property held primarily for sale to customers in the ordinary course of a trade or business, including stock in trade and inventory [§ 1221(a)(1)]. Whether property is primarily held for sale to customers in the ordinary course of business is determined considering the surrounding facts and circumstances. The following are relevant factors in determining the taxpayer's purpose for holding an asset:

- the frequency and regularity of sales of the asset;
- the substantiality of sales from the asset as compared to the amount of net income the taxpayer derives from his regular business;
- the length of time the taxpayer held the asset;
- the nature and extent of the taxpayer's business, and the relationship of the asset to that business;
- the purpose for which the asset was acquired and held prior to sale;
- the extent of the taxpayer's advertising or other efforts to sell the asset; and
- the extent to which any improvements have been made to the asset.

For this purpose, property is primarily held for sale if that is the principal purpose, or the purpose of first importance. A substantial purpose of selling the property to customers is not sufficient if the taxpayer has an additional, simultaneous purpose for holding the property (e.g., for investment, or for use in a trade or business) [*Malat v. Riddell*, 383 U.S. 569 (1966)].

***Depreciable or Real Property Used in a Trade or Business.*** Trade or business property of a type that is eligible for depreciation under § 167 (see V.A.) and all real property used in a trade or business are excluded from capital asset status [§ 1221(a)(2)]. However, gain recognized from the sale, exchange, or involuntary conversion of such property may nevertheless be characterized as capital gain under § 1231 on property used in a trade or business and involuntary conversions (see III.C.1.).

***Certain Literary or Artistic Property.*** Copyrights, literary, musical, or artistic compositions, letters and memoranda, and other similar property (e.g., drafts of speeches, recordings, transcripts, drawings, etc.) are excluded from the definition of a capital asset if held by one of the following [§ 1221(a)(3)]:

- a taxpayer whose personal efforts created such property;
- a taxpayer for whom such property was prepared or produced (in the case of a letter, memorandum, or similar property); or
- a taxpayer whose basis in such property is determined by reference to the basis in the hands of a taxpayer described in one of the first two bullets.

"Other similar property" does not include a patent, invention, or design that may be protected under the patent laws, rather than the copyright laws [Reg. § 1.1221-1(c)(1)].

*Accounts and Notes Receivable.* Accounts and notes receivable that are acquired in the ordinary course of a trade or business for services rendered or from the sale of property described in the first category of excluded property (stock in trade, inventory, and other property held for sale to customers) are excluded from capital asset status [§ 1221(a)(4)]. Thus, cash basis taxpayers who sell merchandise or provide services are prevented from converting business income into capital gain by selling accounts receivable, and accrual basis taxpayers who acquire notes or accounts receivable on sales of merchandise or services may deduct ordinary losses if they sell the accounts or notes at less than full value.

*Publications of the Federal Government.* Publications of the U.S. government that are received by taxpayers from any U.S. governmental entity without charge or below the price at which they are sold to the general public are excluded from capital assets status. This rule applies to a publication in the hands of the person who receives it from the governmental entity, as well as any person whose basis in the publication, for purposes of computing gain, is determined by reference to the basis of the publication in the hands of such person who receives it from the governmental entity [§ 1221(a)(5)].

*Commodities Derivatives.* Commodities derivative financial instruments held by commodities derivative dealers are excluded from capital gain status. A commodities derivatives dealer is a person who, in the regular course of a trade or business, offers to enter into, assume, offset, assign, or terminate positions in commodities derivative financial instruments with customers. A commodities financial instrument is any contract or financial instrument with respect to commodities, the value or settlement price of which is calculated by, or determined by reference to, a specified index. Stock in a corporation, beneficial interests in a partnership or trust, notes, bonds, debentures, or other evidences of indebtedness, and § 1256 contracts are excluded from the definition of commodities financial instruments [§ 1221(a)(6), § 1221(b)(1)].

*Hedging Transactions.* Any hedging transaction that is clearly identified as such before the close of the day on which it was acquired, originated, or entered into is excluded from capital asset status [§ 1221(a)(7)]. Hedging transactions are discussed in III.F.1.g.

*Regularly Used Supplies.* Supplies of a type regularly used or consumed in the ordinary course of a taxpayer's trade or business are excluded from the definition of capital asset [§ 1221(a)(8)]. For example, the sale of excess jet fuel by an airline is treated as ordinary income.

### III.B.2. Sale or Exchange Requirement for Capital Assets

[562 T.M., I.; TPS ¶1630.]

Capital gain or loss treatment requires the sale or exchange of a capital asset. While a sale or exchange generally means a transfer of property in exchange for consideration, certain involuntary transactions, including foreclosures and condemnations of real property, are also treated as a sale or exchange.

### III.B.2.a. Debt

[562 T.M., I.B.1.; TPS ¶1630.02.]

In general, the collection or retirement of an outstanding obligation is not a sale or exchange. Where a taxpayer acquires debt at a discount and then, on maturity, receives the face value, the amount of the discount is treated as income from the collection of the obligation, and not as income from the sale or exchange of the obligation. However, if a debtor satisfies an obligation by transferring property to the creditor, it is typically treated as a sale or exchange [Rev. Rul. 67-74, 1967-1 C.B. 194].

---

**EXAMPLE:** The trustee of Trust is required to distribute $5,000 annually to Tommy, the beneficiary. The trustee distributes stock with a fair market value of $5,000 and an adjusted basis of $2,000. This transfer of property in satisfaction of the obligation is treated as a sale or exchange, and Trust realizes a $3,000 capital gain.

---

Additionally, in the case of debt instruments of an individual issued and purchased after June 9, 1997, or debt instruments of a partnership, estate, or trust issued after July 2, 1982, amounts the holder of a debt instrument receives on the retirement of the instrument are treated as amounts received in exchange for the instrument. Special rules, though, may treat a portion of such gain as ordinary income in the case of debt instruments issued at a discount with the intention to call the obligation before maturity, certain short-term government obligations issued at a discount, and certain short-term nongovernment obligations issued at a discount [§ 1271(a); Reg. § 1.1271-1].

In certain circumstances, the modification of the terms of a debt instrument will rise to the level of an exchange of properties. If the modification is significant, it will be treated as an exchange of the original debt instrument for a modified instrument that differs materially either in kind or in extent. A modification is an alteration of a legal right or obligation of either the holder or the issuer. This alteration generally may not occur by the operation of the original terms of the instrument, except for the substitution of a new obligor, the addition or deletion of a co-obligor, or a change in the recourse nature of the instrument. A modification is significant if, based on the facts and circumstances, the legal rights or obligations are altered in an economically significant way. Significant modifications may result from the following events [Reg. § 1.1001-3]:

- changes in yield;
- changes in timing of payments;
- substitutions of an obligor on a recourse debt;
- changes in security or credit enhancement;
- changes in priority;
- modifications resulting in an instrument that is not debt; and
- changes in status from recourse to nonrecourse.

### III.B.2.b. Contract Rights
[562 T.M., I.B.2.; TPS ¶1630.03.]

The cancellation, lapse, expiration, or other termination of the following items is treated as a sale or exchange of a capital asset [§ 1234A]:

- a right or obligation with respect to property that is, or on acquisition would be, a capital asset in the taxpayer's hands (other than a securities futures contract); or
- a § 1256 contract (see III.F.1.e.) not described in the first bullet that is a capital asset in the hands of the taxpayer.

Additionally, amounts received by a lessee for the cancellation of a lease, or by a distributor of goods for the cancellation of a distributor's agreement (where the distributor has a substantial capital investment in the distributorship) is treated as an amount received in exchange for such lease or agreement [§ 1241].

### III.B.2.c. Abandonment

[562 T.M., I.B.4.; TPS ¶1630.04.]

An abandonment of property generally is not treated as a sale or exchange, and therefore, typically results in ordinary loss. However, where the property is subject to indebtedness and the taxpayer voluntarily reconveys the property for no consideration in order to avoid an obligation, the conveyance may be treated as a sale or exchange, rather than an abandonment.

### III.B.2.d. Involuntary Dispositions

[562 T.M., I.B.3.; TPS ¶1630.05.]

Insurance proceeds from property destroyed by fire or other casualty generally results in ordinary gain or loss, rather than gain or loss from the sale or exchange of the property [*Helvering v. William Flaccus Oak Leather Co.*, 313 U.S. 247 (1941)] (see VIII.H.1.a.). A government entity's condemnation of real property, on the other hand, is treated as a sale or exchange. Any interest received to compensate for the delayed payment of the compensation award, however, is ordinary income. Additionally, real property sold pursuant to a foreclosure proceeding, as well as a voluntary reconveyance of real property to a mortgagee that terminates the mortgagor's obligation on the debt, is treated as a sale or exchange (see III.B.2.).

### III.B.2.e. Worthless Property

[562 T.M., I.B.5.; TPS ¶1630.06.]

Losses attributable to properties that become worthless generally are not treated as losses from the sale or exchange of the property. However, with the exception of losses from certain small business stock, losses from securities that are capital assets and that become worthless are treated as losses from the sale or exchange of a capital asset on the last day of the tax year it became worthless [§ 165(g)(1), § 1244; Reg. § 1.165-5(c)].

For noncorporate taxpayers, losses from the worthlessness of nonbusiness debts are typically treated as losses from the sale or exchange of a capital asset held for less than one year. A nonbusiness debt is a debt other than one [§ 166(d); Reg. § 1.166-5(a), § 1.166-5(b)]:

- created or acquired in connection with the taxpayer's trade or business; or
- the loss from the worthlessness of which is incurred in the taxpayer's trade or business.

### III.B.2.f. Adjustment of Prior Transactions

[562 T.M., III.C.1.; TPS ¶1630.07.B.]

In some instances, the character of a transaction depends on whether a related transaction that occurred in an earlier year was capital or noncapital in nature. In such a scenario, the later transaction may be viewed as an adjustment to the earlier transaction, rather than as an independent transaction. Thus, a capital gain or capital loss might occur despite there being no sale or exchange of a capital asset. The leading case in the area involved taxpayers that reported capital gain on the complete liquidation of their corporation. Five years after the liquidation, a judgment was rendered against the liquidated corporation. The former shareholders, who were transferees of the corporation's assets, paid the judgment for the corporation. These payments were held to be capital losses, rather than ordinary losses, because they were inextricably related to the earlier capital gain [*Arrowsmith v. Commissioner*, 344 U.S. 6 (1952)].

---

**EXAMPLE:** Erica is an executive of Standard Co. She purchases and sells Standard stock within a two-month period and realizes a capital gain of $50,000. A Standard shareholder later sues Erica alleging that her trading violated federal securities laws, and that under those laws Erica is required to repay Standard a portion of her profits from the transaction. Erica pays $35,000 to Standard to settle the suit. Erica must treat the payment as a capital loss because it relates to the earlier sale or stock, which produced capital gain.

---

### III.B.3. Holding Periods for Capital Assets

[562 T.M., V.D.; TPS ¶1640.]

The length of time a taxpayer held a capital asset that is sold or exchanged determines whether the gain or loss realized on the disposition is short-term or long-term gain or loss. In general, the holding period of property begins the day after the property is acquired and ends with the day the property is disposed of. Only whole days are taken into account. The sale or exchange of property held for one year or less produces short-term gain or loss, while the sale or exchange of property held for more than one year produces long-term gain or loss [§ 1222].

---

**EXAMPLE:** Jimmy purchases property at 8:00 a.m. on Jan. 1, Year 1. He sells the property at a gain at 11:00 p.m. on Jan. 1, Year 2. The holding period begins on Jan. 2, Year 1, the day after the acquisition, and it ends on Jan. 1, Year 2, the day of the disposition. Fractions of days are not counted. Therefore, Jimmy is treated as having held the property for exactly one year.

---

### III.B.3.a. Split Holding Periods

[562 T.M., V.D.; TPS ¶1640.02.B.]

If more than one asset is sold, the holding period is computed separately for each asset. Holding periods are split if a sale results in both long-term and short-term gain or loss.

---

**EXAMPLE:** Jan purchases an unimproved tract of land in Year 1. In July of Year 5, she builds a house on the land. Jan sells the land and the home in Dec. of Year 5. She must use a split holding period because the holding period for the land is long-term (more than one year), and the holding period for the house is short-term (less than one year). Gain or loss attributable to the land is long-term capital gain or loss, and gain or loss attributable to the house is short-term capital gain or loss.

**EXAMPLE:** Leo begins construction on an office building in Jan. of Year 1. As of May 30, Year 1, the portion of the building that is complete has a cost basis of $250,000. The building is completed on Apr. 30, Year 2, with a total cost of $1 million. Leo sells the building on June 1, Year 2. Because 25% ($250,000 ÷ $1 million) of the building was completed more than one year before the sale, Leo treats 25% of his gain from the sale as long-term capital gain. The remaining 75% is short-term capital gain because it was completed less than one year before the sale.

---

Where a taxpayer transfers assets to a controlled corporation in exchange for stock and securities of the corporation in a nontaxable § 351 transaction (see XIII.B.1.), the holding periods of the stock and securities are determined by reference to the aggregate proportion of short-term and long-term assets transferred. Each share of stock and each security has a split holding period. The fraction of each share of stock or security treated as a long-term asset is equal to the proportion of the total transferred assets that are long-term assets, and the fraction of each share of stock or security treated as a short-term asset is equal to the proportion of the total transferred assets that are short-term assets.

---

**EXAMPLE:** In exchange for $100,000 of stock in Controlled Corp., Sam contributes two assets to Controlled Corp. in a transaction qualifying under § 351. The first asset is real estate with a fair market value of $40,000 acquired more than one year before the § 351 transaction. The second asset is machinery with a fair market value of $60,000 acquired less than one year before the § 351 transaction. Each of Sam's shares of Controlled Corp. has a split holding period based on the proportion of long-term and short-term assets Sam transferred to Controlled Corp. Thus, if Sam were to sell one or more shares of the stock immediately following the § 351 transaction, for each share 40% of the gain or loss will be long-term and 60% of the gain or loss will be short term.

---

### III.B.3.b. Special Holding Period Situations

[562 T.M., V.D.; TPS ¶1640.02.C.]

In certain situations, it is difficult to determine when a taxpayer acquires or disposes of property. This determination requires an examination of the "bundle of rights" associated with the property at issue, and generally, a person is treated as the owner of property if he or she assumes the benefits and burdens of ownership, without regard to technicalities of title.

*Securities.* The holding period of securities purchased or sold through an organized exchange or over the counter generally begins on the day after the trade date (the date of the order to buy or sell, rather than the date of delivery and payment) of the purchase and ends on the trade date of the sale [Rev. Rul. 70-598, 1970-2 C.B. 168]. The execution of a contract to purchase securities in the future typically is not an acquisition, until the securities are actually purchased. Securities held in escrow until the satisfaction of a condition are considered sold at the closing of the transaction when the escrow is released.

*Real Estate.* In the case of real estate, it is possible that a taxpayer may acquire sufficient benefits and burdens of ownership to be regarded as the property's owner without a formal transfer of title. In general, a sale or exchange of real estate occurs at the earlier of either (i) the time a transfer of ownership by deed is executed and delivered, or (ii) the time the benefits and burdens of ownership are transferred to the buyer [Rev. Rul. 71-265, 1971-1 C.B. 223]. An unconditional contract to purchase land along with the assumption of substantial benefits and burdens of ownership is typically sufficient to begin or end a holding period. However, if a contract conditions title transfer on the performance of contractual obligations, the assumption of the benefits and burdens of ownership is insufficient to establish ownership. The holding period of property purchased at a federal tax sale begins at the time the owner's redemption period expires and the deed is executed to the purchaser. The holding period of property transferred in a condemnation proceeding terminates when title vests in the condemning authority, which is typically upon the filing of a declaration of taking or similar action.

*Options, Contract Rights, and Patents.* The holding period of property sold pursuant to an option contract begins for the purchaser and ends for the seller when the option is exercised, rather than when the option is granted [§ 1223(5)]. The holding period of a contract right (including the right to exercise an option) begins at the time a written contract is executed, and not at an earlier time when a down payment is made or a memorandum of understanding is prepared. A patent's holding period typically does not begin until the process or invention has been reduced to practice.

*Property Acquired from a Decedent.* Property acquired from a decedent, the basis of which is determined in whole or in part under the § 1014 step-up in basis to fair market value (see III.A.3.a.(3)) is generally treated as having a long-term holding period, regardless of the actual length of time the taxpayer has held the property [§ 1223(9)].

*Partnership Interests.* A partner's holding period in a partnership interest is determined separately from the partnership's holding period of partnership assets. A holding period in a partnership interest is divided if either (i) the partner acquired portions of an interest at different times, or (ii) the partner acquired portions of an interest in exchange for property in certain transactions giving rise to different holding periods. The holding period of a portion of a partnership interest is generally determined relative to the proportion the fair market value of the portion of the partnership interest bears to the fair market value of the entire partnership interest immediately after the acquisition. A partner selling all or a portion of his or her partnership interest recognizes long-term or short-term capital gain or loss in the same proportion as the holding period of the partnership interest is divided between long-term and short-term assets [Reg. § 1.1223-3]. Where a partnership terminates upon the sale of a partnership interest, partners may have to determine the holding periods of the partnership assets rather than the holding period of the partners' partnership interests (see sale of a partnership interest, discussed in XIV.H. and termination of a partnership, discussed in XIV.I.).

---

**EXAMPLE:** Jessica contributes $5,000 cash and a nondepreciable capital asset that she has held for two years to ABC Partnership in exchange for a 50% interest in ABC in a § 721 nonrecognition transaction. The fair market value of the capital asset is $10,000 and its basis is $5,000. Following the transaction, Jessica's basis in her interest in ABC is $10,000, and the fair market value of the interest is $15,000. Jessica's holding period in ⅓ of the ABC interest (attributable to her $5,000 cash contribution out of a total $15,000 contribution) begins the day after the contribution. Her remaining ⅔ interest in ABC (attributable to the $10,000 asset contributed out of a total $15,000 contribution) has a two-year holding period. Six months later, when Jessica's basis in ABC is $12,000 (as a result of a $2,000 allocation of partnership income to Jessica), she sells her entire interest in ABC for $17,000. Assuming ABC has no inventory or unrealized receivables and no collectibles or recapture property, Jessica will have $5,000 ($17,000 fair market value − $12,000 basis) of capital gain. Jessica has held ⅓ of her interest in ABC for less than one year, and therefore, ⅓ of the capital gain will be short-term capital gain. Jessica has held ⅔ of her interest in ABC for more than one year, and therefore, ⅔ of the capital gain will be long-term capital gain.

---

### III.B.3.c. Tacking Holding Periods

[562 T.M., VI.D.4.; TPS ¶1640.03.A.]

In some situations, a taxpayer may include, or "tack," the time another person held property, or the time the taxpayer held another asset, when computing his or her holding period for an asset. This applies to transactions where the taxpayer takes either a substituted basis (see III.A.3.a.(4)) or a carryover basis (see III.A.3.a.(2)) in acquired property [§ 1223(1), § 1223(2); Reg. § 1.1223-1(a), § 1.1223-1(b)].

The holding period of property received in a tax-free exchange includes the taxpayer's holding period in the property transferred. Transactions subject to this rule include the following:

- acquisitions of stock in tax-free corporate reorganizations (see XIII.E.1.);
- tax-free like-kind exchanges (see III.E.1.);
- involuntary conversions (see III.E.2.); and
- acquisitions of partnership interests in exchange for capital contributions (see XIV.C.).

The holding period of property received by gift generally includes the donor's holding period. This is the case even if the donee's basis is increased by the amount of gift tax the donee pays. Tacking may not be permitted, however, if the donee incurs a loss on the transaction that is determined by reference to the fair market value of the property.

---

**EXAMPLE:** Tanya purchases Small Corp. stock on Jan. 1 of Year 1. On Mar. 1 of Year 2, Small Corp. is acquired by Large Corp. in a tax-free reorganization. Pursuant to the reorganization, Tanya receives Large Corp. stock in exchange for her Small Corp. stock. One month later, on Apr. 1, Year 2, Tanya sells her Large Corp. stock at a gain. Tanya's gain is long-term capital gain because her holding period for the Small Corp. stock is included in computing the holding period of the Large Corp. stock. Therefore, Tanya is treated as having owned the Large Corp. stock since Jan. 1, year 1.

**EXAMPLE:** Maya purchases stock on June 1 of Year 1. On Feb. 1 of Year 2, Maya makes a gift of the stock to Maggie. Maggie sells the stock at a gain on July 1 of Year 2. Maggie includes the period of time Maya held the stock in computing her holding period. Maggie is treated as having owned the stock since June 1, Year 1, and therefore her gain is long-term capital gain.

---

A taxpayer who sells qualified small business (QSB) stock held for more than six months, and who subsequently purchases other QSB stock within 60 days of the sale, may elect to roll over the gain from the old stock into the new stock (see III.C.5.). In such a situation, the holding period of the new QSB stock includes the holding period of the old QSB stock [§ 1223(13)].

Tacking is also permitted in the following transactions:

- a partner's receipt of property distributed from a partnership [§ 1223(15), § 735(b)] (see XIV.F.);
- a corporation's receipt of property in a tax-free incorporation (see XIII.B.) or tax-free reorganization [§ 1223(2); Reg. § 1.1223-1(a)] (see XIII.E.);
- a partnership's receipt of property in a tax-free capital contribution to the partnership in exchange for an interest in profits or capital of the partnership [§ 1223(2), § 721; Reg. § 1.1223-1(b)] (see XIV.C.);

- stock or securities involving "wash sales" [§ 1223(3); Reg. § 1.1223-1(d)] (see III.F.1.d.);
- stock dividends [§ 1223(4); Reg. § 1.1223-1(e)] (see XIII.D.2.); and
- commodities delivered pursuant to certain futures contracts [§ 1223(7); Reg. § 1.1223-1(h)].

Tacking is not permitted for stock or securities acquired from a corporation by the exercise of rights to acquire such stock or securities. Instead, the holding period beings when the rights are exercised, rather than when the rights are acquired [§ 1223(5); Reg. § 1.1223-1(f)].

### III.B.4. Netting Rules and Calculating Net Capital Gain

[562 T.M., V.F.2.; TPS ¶1610.02.A.9.]

Long-term capital gains and losses are offset against each other to determine net long-term capital gain or loss. Similarly, short-term capital gains and losses are offset against each other to determine net short-term capital gain or loss. The excess of any net long-term capital gain over net short-term capital loss for a tax year is net capital gain, and a taxpayer with net capital gain for a tax year is liable for tax on such gain [§ 1222].

To determine whether a taxpayer has a tax liability on a net capital gain, the taxpayer first must separate his or her long-term capital gains and losses into three groups according to the tax rate group appropriate for the items of income and loss (see III.B.):

1. the 28% rate group (i.e., long-term capital gains and losses from collectibles, the sale of certain small business stock, and long-term capital loss carryovers);
2. the 25% rate group (i.e., unrecaptured § 1250 gain); and
3. the 0%/15%/20% rate group (i.e., other long-term capital gains and losses).

Within each rate group, long-term capital gains and losses are netted to determine net long-term gain for the rate group. Any net short-term capital loss first reduces net long-term gain from the 28% rate group, then from the 25% rate group, and finally from the 0%/15%/20% rate group. Any net loss from the 28% group first reduces net long-term gain from the 25% rate group, and then from the 0%/15%/20% rate group. Any net loss from the 0%/15%/20% rate group first reduces net long-term gain from the 28% group, and then from the 25% group. Any net capital gain remaining for each rate group is taxed at the rate group's marginal tax rate [§ 1(h)].

### III.B.5. Capital Loss Deduction Limitation & Carryover of Unused Losses

[562 T.M., V.E.; TPS ¶1610.02.B.1.b.]

Noncorporate taxpayers may offset capital losses to the full extent of capital gains. Where capital losses exceed capital gains for a tax year, the taxpayer may deduct up to $3,000 ($1,500 for married taxpayers filing separately) of capital losses against ordinary income [§ 1211].

---

**EXAMPLE:** In Year 1, Kelly has net long-term capital gain of $5,000, a net short-term capital loss of $9,000, and ordinary income of $55,000. Kelly may offset $5,000 of the capital losses against $5,000 of the capital gains. In addition, Kelly may deduct $3,000 of the remaining capital losses against her ordinary income. The remaining $1,000 of capital losses are not deductible in Year 1.

---

Net capital losses that are not deducted in the current tax year may be carried forward indefinitely to offset future capital gains or ordinary income. Such loss carryforwards retain their character as short-term or long-term capital loss, and are combined with losses arising in future years for purposes of computing net capital gain and loss. Where a taxpayer has both long-term and short-term capital losses that exceed the $3,000 limitation in the aggregate, the taxpayer's taxable income is first reduced by the short-term capital losses to the extent allowable, and then by the long-term losses [§ 1212(b); Reg. § 1.1212-1(b)(1)].

---

**EXAMPLE:** In Year 1, Art has a net short-term capital loss of $2,000, and net long-term capital loss of $2,000, and taxable ordinary income of $40,000. Art may deduct $3,000 of his $4,000 of capital loss in Year 1. The $1,000 loss carried forward from Year 1 is characterized as long-term capital loss. This is because Art's Year 1 income is first reduced by short-term capital losses ($2,000), and then by his long-term capital losses (limited to $1,000). The remaining $1,000 long-term capital loss retains its character going forward.

---

A taxpayer may not elect the year in which to take a carryover into account. Carryover losses generally must be used in the succeeding tax year, whether or not use in that year produces less tax benefit that if the loss were used in a later year. The amount allowed as a deduction in the year to which the loss is carried is the smaller of the following:

- the lesser of:
  - $3,000 ($1,500 for married taxpayers filing separately), or
  - the amount by which capital losses exceed capital gains; or
- the taxpayer's adjusted taxable income for the tax year.

A taxpayer's adjusted taxable income is taxable income, increased by (i) the amount of capital loss allowed as a deduction for the tax year, and (ii) the § 151 personal exemption deduction (see XII.E.1.). This provision is intended to prevent the reduction of capital loss carryovers in years where the taxpayer does not have sufficient income to take advantage of the deduction [§ 1212(b)(2)].

---

**EXAMPLE:** In 2013, Jason, an unmarried individual, has a short-term capital gain of $2,000, and long-term capital loss of $10,000, and thus a net long-term capital loss of $8,000. Jason has no income or itemized deductions, and he is allowed standard deduction of $5,950 and a personal exemption deduction of $3,900. Jason's taxable income for purposes of the carryover computation is ($12,850) ($0 income − $3,000 allowable capital loss deduction − $5,950 standard deduction − $3,900 personal exemption deduction). Jason's adjusted taxable income is ($5,950) (($12,850) taxable income + $3,000 capital loss allowed + $3,900 personal exemption deduction). Because Jason's adjusted taxable income is less than his allowable capital loss deduction, he is not required to reduce his net capital loss by the allowable capital loss deduction. Thus, Jason's full $8,000 net capital loss is carried over to 2014.

---

A special rule allows net capital losses from regulated futures contracts, foreign currency contracts, nonequity options, dealer equity options, and dealer securities futures contracts to be carried back to the three preceding tax years and used to offset gain from such contracts in those years. However, a carryback may not be used to the extent it would produce or increase a net operating loss in the carryback year [§ 1212(c)].

Generally, only the taxpayer who sustains the capital loss is entitled to take the deduction. It may not be carried to a different taxpayer's tax year. In the case of married taxpayers, though, a capital loss arising in a spouse's prior separate return year may be carried forward without restriction to a joint return year. Thus, a married couple who file separate returns in Year 1 may carry forward and combine any individually reported net capital loss carryover from Year 1 on a joint return filed in Year 2. However, capital losses incurred in a joint return year and carried forward to a separate return year must be allocated between the spouses based on their individual net capital losses that gave rise to the carryover. [Reg. § 1.1212-1(c)(1)].

Corporate taxpayers may also offset capital losses to the extent of their capital gains, but they may not deduct any amount of capital losses against ordinary income. A corporation's net capital losses may be carried back to the three preceding tax years or forward to the five succeeding tax years. All such losses are treated as short-term capital loss in the year to which they are carried. Generally, net capital loss must be carried back to the earliest allowable carryback year and used to offset capital gain net income. Any excess carried back loss is then carried forward to the succeeding tax year. Net capital loss may not be carried back to the extent it would produce or increase a net operating loss in the carryback year [§ 1212(a)(1)].

---

**EXAMPLE:** Enormous Co. has net capital gain in Year 1 of $7,000. In Year 2 and Year 3, Enormous has no net capital gain. In Year 4, Enormous Co. has a net capital loss of $10,000, and in Year 5 Enormous has $5,000 of net capital gain. Enormous's $10,000 loss in Year 4 must first be carried back to Year 1, in which it will offset all $7,000 of Year 1's net capital gain. The remaining $3,000 of net capital loss is carried forward to Year 5 because Enormous has no net capital gain in Year 2 or Year 3. The $3,000 balance is applied against Year 5's $5,000 of net capital gain, reducing Year 5's net capital gain to $2,000. Had Enormous had no net capital gain in Year 5 through Year 9, the $3,000 carryover would expire.

---

Capital losses attributable to foreign expropriation capital losses may not be carried back, but may be carried forward for 10 years. A foreign expropriation capital loss is a loss sustained by reason of the expropriation, intervention, seizure, or similar taking of property by a foreign country's government [§ 1212(a)(1)(C), § 1212(a)(2)(A); Reg. § 1.1212-1(a)(2)].

A corporation may not carry back a net capital loss to a tax year in which it was a regulated investment company (RIC) (see XIII.F.1.) or a real estate investment trust (REIT) (see XIII.F.2.). For capital losses incurred before December 23, 2010, RICs may carry forward the loss for eight years. For capital losses incurred after December 23, 2010, RICs may carry forward a net capital loss indefinitely [§ 1212(a)(3)].

If a corporation undergoes an ownership change, the amount of pre-change capital loss carryover available for use in the tax year of the ownership change and tax years thereafter may be limited. An ownership change is an increase in stock ownership of more than 50 percentage points for certain large shareholders over a three-year period [§ 382(g), § 383(b), Reg. § 1.383-1(b)] (see XIII.E.5.b.).

Similarly, consolidated groups may face limitations on the use of capital loss carryovers and carrybacks. Losses incurred by a group member in a tax year in which it was not part of the consolidated group that are carried forward or backward to consolidated return years are subject to separate return limitation year (SRLY) rules [Reg. § 1.1502-22(c)].

A C corporation's net capital loss may not be carried forward or backward to a tax year in which it has elected to be treated as an S corporation. An intervening S corporation year, though, is counted in determining the proper year to which a net capital loss carry forward or carryback may be taken into account for a C corporation. No carryovers arise at the entity level during the period an S corporation election is in effect because proportionate shares of net capital loss flow through to shareholders (see XV.B.) [§ 1371(b)].

## III.C. Application of Capital Gain Rules

### III.C.1. Property Used in a Trade or Business (§ 1231 Transactions)

[561 T.M., V.A.2.; TPS ¶1710.]

The definition of a capital asset specifically excludes property used in a trade or business that is either real property or property of a depreciable nature [§ 1221(a)(2)]. However, a net gain on the sale or exchange of such property (and certain other property used in a trade or business) may still be treated as a long-term capital gain. A net loss on the sale or exchange of such property, on the other hand, is treated as an ordinary loss. This provides taxpayers with the benefit of lower long-term capital rates on any gain and the ability to use any losses to reduce ordinary income that is subject to higher ordinary rates without the restrictions imposed on capital losses [§ 1231(a); Reg. § 1.1231-1(b)] (see III.B.5.).

Gains and losses on the sale or exchange of assets used in a trade or business and certain involuntary conversions are reported on Form 4797, *Sales of Business Property.*

### III.C.1.a. Section 1231 Transactions

[562 T.M., V.A.2.; TPS ¶1710.03.]

The terms of § 1231 limit the application of the rule treating gains as capital gains and losses as ordinary losses to a certain set of transactions, including the following transactions [§ 1231(a)(3), § 1231(b); Reg. § 1.1231-1(c)]:

- sales or exchanges of real property used in a trade or business and held for more than one year (excluding inventory property and property held primarily for sale to customers);
- sales or exchanges of depreciable property used in a trade or business and held for more than one year (excluding inventory property; property held primarily for sale to customers; copyrights; literary, musical, or artistic compositions; letters, memoranda, or similar property; and certain publications of the U.S. government);
- the cutting of timber when the taxpayer elects to treat the cutting as a sale or exchange under § 631(a);
- the disposal of timber, coal, and iron ore with a retained economic interest that is treated as a sale under § 631(b) or (c), and the disposal of timber by an outright sale of such timber;
- sales or exchanges of cattle and horses held for draft, breeding, dairy, or sporting purposes for at least two years, and other livestock (excluding poultry) held for draft, breeding, dairy, or sporting purposes for at least one year;

- unharvested crops sold, exchanged, or involuntarily converted with the land in one transaction to a single purchaser;
- involuntary conversions resulting from destruction, theft, seizure, requisition, or condemnation (or threat thereof) of property used in the trade or business; and
- involuntary conversions of capital assets held for more than one year in connection with the trade or business, or a transaction entered into for profit.

If aggregating the gains and losses from all the transactions listed above for a tax year results in a net loss, it is ordinary loss. If the result is a net gain, it is ordinary gain up to the amount of nonrecaptured § 1231 losses (see III.C.1.c.) from the previous five years, and any excess is long-term capital gain.

---

**EXAMPLE:** Immense Corp. manufactures and sells steel cable. The cable is delivered on reels that are depreciable property and that are returned to Immense. Purchasers of the steel cable make deposits on the reels that are refunded if the reels are returned to Immense within a year. If the reels are not returned, Immense keeps the deposit as the agreed-upon sales price. Most reels are returned within a year, and Immense keeps records showing depreciation and other charges to the capitalized cost of the reels. The reels are not property held for sale to customers in the ordinary course of business, and any gain or loss from their not being returned is eligible for capital gain or ordinary loss treatment depending on Immense's other § 1231 transactions.

---

### III.C.1.b. Involuntary Conversions

[562 T.M., I.B.3.b.; TPS ¶1710.03.C.]

The capital gain/ordinary loss rules generally apply to the compulsory or involuntary conversion of property used in a trade or business and capital assets held in connection with a trade or business or acquired in a transaction entered into for profit, if such assets are held for more than one year. However, conversions of property held for less than one year, conversions that are subject to the casualty loss rules of § 165(c)(3) (i.e., casualties to, and thefts of, personal use property), and conversions of property held for sale are not within § 1231.

Involuntary conversions that fall within § 1231 are netted in two steps [§ 1231(a); Reg. § 1.1231-1(e)(3)]:

1. Recognized losses from casualties and thefts of § 1231 assets are compared against gains from such occurrences. If the losses exceed the gains, the losses and gains are removed from the § 1231 computation and the net loss is deductible as an ordinary loss under the casualty loss rules. If the gains exceed the losses, the net gains are included in the second step computation.
2. All other § 1231 gains and losses are netted. A net gain produces capital gain, and a net loss produces ordinary loss.

---

**EXAMPLE:** In Year 1, a truck used in Marc's delivery business is destroyed by a fire. The truck had a basis of $900 and had been used in the business for two years. Insurance paid Marc $3,000, and thus $2,100 of gain is realized. He purchases a replacement truck for $2,500. Also in Year 1, Marc's uninsured stamp collection and personal use lawn furniture were stolen. The stamp collection had been maintained for several years as a profit making venture, and its theft produced a $2,000 loss. The lawn furniture had been held for two years and its theft produced a $500 loss. Marc also has a $100 loss from the sale of business furniture acquired several years earlier. Assume there are no losses to recapture and no deferral election is made. Upon netting the gains and losses from casualties and thefts of § 1231 assets, gains exceed the losses by $100 ($2,100 gain from fire − $2,000 loss from the stamp theft). All other § 1231 gains and losses (including the $100 gain from the Step 1 calculation) are then netted and they result in no gain or loss ($100 gain from Step 1 − $100 loss from the furniture sale). The $500 loss from the theft of the personal use lawn furniture is not considered in either step because § 1231 does not apply to personal casualty losses.

A taxpayer may elect to defer the recognition of any gain realized under § 1231 on the involuntary conversion of property in certain circumstances. If property is converted into money or other property through the receipt of insurance proceeds, a condemnation award, or upon a qualifying sale, the taxpayer may elect deferral if he or she timely purchases replacement property that is similar or related in service or use to the property converted. Deferral is available only to the extent the amount realized from the conversion is reinvested, and the replacement property's basis must be decreased by the amount of gain deferred [§ 1033].

### III.C.1.c. Section 1231 Loss Recapture

[561 T.M., V.A.2.; TPS ¶1710.03.F.]

If a taxpayer has a net § 1231 gain within the five years following a net § 1231 loss, the net § 1231 gain is treated as ordinary income (rather than long-term capital gain) to the extent of the net § 1231 losses for the five preceding tax years that have yet to be recaptured. Thus, a taxpayer with a net § 1231 gain in a given tax year must examine his or her previous five tax years for net § 1231 losses. If the taxpayer deducted net § 1231 losses against ordinary income in that five-year period, the taxpayer must recharacterize the present year's net § 1231 gain as ordinary income until all net § 1231 losses are recaptured. Losses are recaptured beginning with the earliest loss in the five-year period. Once the net § 1231 losses are recaptured, any remaining net § 1231 gain for the tax year are long-term capital gain [§ 1231(c)].

---

**EXAMPLE:** In Year 6, Jan has a $4,000 net § 1231 gain. In the previous five years, Jan had only a net § 1231 loss of $5,000 in Year 3 and a net § 1231 gain of $3,600 in Year 5. The Year 5 net § 1231 gain recaptured $3,600 of the Year 3 net § 1231 loss, leaving $1,400 ($5,000 − $3,600) of unrecaptured net § 1231 loss attributable to Year 3. Thus, in Year 6, $1,400 of Jan's net § 1231 gain is treated as ordinary income as a result of the recapture of the remaining portion of the Year 3 loss. The remaining $2,600 ($4,000 − $1,400) of Jan's Year 6 net § 1231 gain is long-term capital gain.

---

### III.C.2. Transfers of Certain Intangible Property

### III.C.2.a. Patent Transfers

[558 T.M., II.A.; TPS ¶1720.01.]

The transfer of a holder's patent or patent rights is treated as a sale or exchange of an asset held for more than one year, regardless of the actual length of time held, if the transfer satisfies certain requirements. The holder must transfer all substantial rights to the patent, or an undivided interest in all such rights. Transfers by gift, inheritance, or devise are not eligible. Special treatment as long-term capital gain is available regardless of whether the consideration for the transfer is payable periodically over a period that is generally coterminous with the transferee's use of the patent or contingent on the productivity, use, or disposition of the transferred property [§ 1235(a); Reg. § 1.1235-1(a)].

A holder is (i) an individual whose effort created the patent and who qualifies as the original and first inventor, or (ii) an individual who acquired an interest in the patent from the creator before the invention was tested and operated successfully under operating conditions (other that the creator's employer or a person related to the creator) [§ 1235(b); Reg. § 1.1235-2(d)].

A holder's transfer that otherwise qualifies for the special long-term capital gain treatment will not qualify if the transfer is made to a related person (as defined in § 1235(d)).

All substantial rights to a patent are transferred if the transferee acquires all rights that are of value at the time of the transfer (whether or not such rights are then held by the patent holder). The determination of whether all substantial rights have been transferred is a facts and circumstances analysis. Certain rights are deemed substantial, and therefore, the instrument of transfer does not transfer all substantial rights to a patent where it imposes (i) geographical limitations within the country of issuance, (ii) durational limitations, (iii) field of use limitations, or (iv) limitations on the claims or inventions covered by the patent. Certain rights are not considered substantial, including (i) the retention of legal title to secure the transferee's performance or payment in a transaction involving an exclusive license to manufacture, use, and sell for the life of the patent, and (ii) the retention of rights in the property that are not inconsistent with the passage of ownership (e.g., a security interest or a provision for forfeiture in the event of nonperformance) [Reg. § 1.1235-2(b)].

### III.C.2.b. Franchise, Trademark, and Trade Name Transfers

[559 T.M., II.; TPS ¶1720.04.]

In general, the transfer of a franchise, trademark, or trade name is not treated as a sale or exchange of a capital asset if the transferor retains any significant power, right, or continuing interest in the subject matter of the franchise, trademark, or trade name [§ 1253(a)]. A significant power, right, or continuing interest in a franchise, trademark, or trade name includes the following [§ 1253(b)(2)]:

- the right to disapprove of any assignments;
- the right to terminate the contract at will;
- the right to prescribe standards of quality of products used or sold, or of services furnished, and of the equipment and facilities used to promote such services;
- the right to limit products sold or advertised to those of the transferor;
- the right to require that the transferee purchase substantially all supplies and equipment from the transferor; and
- a right to payments contingent on the productivity, use, or disposition of the interest transferred.

Other rights may be deemed significant if the facts and circumstances indicate that the transferor has retained excessive control.

If a transferor does not retain any significant power, right, or continuing interest, a transferred franchise, trademark, or trade name may qualify for capital gain or loss treatment if it qualifies as a sale or exchange of a capital asset under the general rules (see III.B.).

### III.C.3. Real Property Subdivided for Sale

[561 T.M., IV.I.; TPS ¶1730.]

Capital assets do not include stock in trade, inventory, or other property held primarily for sale to customers in the ordinary course of the taxpayer's trade or business (see III.B.1.). However, a special safe harbor provision allows taxpayer-investors (excluding C corporations) to divide substantially unimproved land into parcels or lots and sell them without being deemed to hold the property primarily for sale to customers in the ordinary course of a trade or business. Thus, a taxpayer may still be eligible for capital gain or loss treatment on the sale of such land if the following requirements are satisfied [§ 1237(a)]:

1. the tract of property must not have been previously held primarily for sale to customers in the ordinary course of the taxpayer's trade or business (thereby excluding dealers in real estate);

2. the taxpayer must not hold any other real property primarily for sale to customers in the ordinary course of the taxpayer's trade or business during the year in which the sale of the lot or parcel occurs;

3. the taxpayer (or certain family members, controlled entities, lessees, or governmental entities) must not have substantially improved the lot or parcel in a way that substantially enhances the value of the property; and

4. the taxpayer must have held the property for at least five years (see III.B.3.), unless the property was acquired by inheritance or devise (a taxpayer acquiring property by gift may tack the donor's holding period onto his or her own holding period) [Reg. § 1.1237-1(d)].

The safe harbor is available for a single tract of land in a given tax year, and it applies to sales or exchange of lots or parcels of unimproved land severed from the larger tract. Two or more pieces of real property that were contiguous at any time held by the taxpayer (or that would have been contiguous but for the interposition of a road, street, railroad, stream or similar property) are considered a single tract [§ 1237(c); Reg. § 1.1237-1(g)]. There is no limit to the number of lots or parcels into which a tract of land may be divided. However, if a taxpayer holds a large number of lots for sale over a long period of time, or if other substantial evidence suggests the taxpayer holds the property for sale in the ordinary course of business, the IRS may deem the safe harbor inapplicable [Reg. § 1.1237-1(a)].

### III.C.3.a. Five Lot Rule for Subdivided Real Property

[561 T.M., IV.I.3., IV.I.7.; TPS ¶1730.04.]

If a taxpayer sells five or fewer lots from the same tract of real property, all the gain realized on the sales may qualify for capital gain treatment so long as the other requirements are met. However, the gain from any sale in or after the tax year in which the sixth lot is sold is gain from the sale or exchange of property held primarily for sale to customers in the ordinary course of business to the extent of 5% of the selling price [§ 1237(b)(1); Reg. § 1.1237-1(e)(2)(i)]. For purposes of computing gain, selling expenses are first used to offset the ordinary income portion of the gain, and any remaining expenses reduce the portion treated as capital gain [§ 1237(b)(2)]. If five years elapse after the sale of a lot from a tract without another sale from that tract, the remainder of the original tract is deemed a new tract for purposes of five lot rule, regardless of whether the pieces are contiguous [§ 1237(c); Reg. § 1.1237-1(g)].

The 5% rule applies to all lots sold from the tract in the year that the sixth lot is sold and for every year after that. Thus, if the taxpayer sells the first six lots from a tract in one year, 5% of the selling price of each lot sold (not just the sixth lot) is treated as ordinary income. On the other hand, if the taxpayer sells the first four lots in Year 1 and sells two more lots from the same tract in Year 2, only the gain realized from the lots sold in Year 2 is subject to the 5% rule [Reg. § 1.1237-1(e)(2)(ii)].

---

**EXAMPLE:** Wanda owns a tract of land and qualifies for the safe harbor. In Year 1, she sells two lots severed from the tract for $5,000 each. All of the gain is capital gain. In Year 2, she sells three more lots from the tract for $5,000 each. All of the gain is capital gain. In Year 3, Wanda sells a sixth lot from the tract for $5,000. Wanda's basis in the sixth lot was $2,500, and she had $200 of expenses in selling the lot. Wanda realizes $2,300 ($5,000 amount realized − $2,500 basis − $200 sales expenses) of gain on the sale. Five percent of the sales price is $250, which would generally be treated as ordinary income. However, Wanda's $200 of expenses are first used to offset the ordinary income portion of her gain. Therefore, only $50 ($250 − $200) of Wanda's income is treated as ordinary income. The remainder is treated as capital gain.

**EXAMPLE:** Roy owns a tract of land and qualifies for the safe harbor. In Year 1, he sells three lots, all the gain from which is capital gain. In Year 2, he sells three lots, 5% of the sales price of which is treated as ordinary income. Roy does not sell any lots in Year 3 through Year 7. In Year 8, Roy sells two lots. No portion of the gain is treated as ordinary income because the tract is treated as a new tract for purposes of the five lot rule.

---

### III.C.3.b. Improvements to Land Subdivided for Sale

[561 T.M., IV.I.6.; TPS ¶1730.07.]

The safe harbor does not apply if a taxpayer makes substantial improvements to the tract that enhances its value. Improvements made pursuant to a contract of sale are included for this purpose, regardless of whether the improvements are actually made by the taxpayer or the purchaser. Additionally, improvements to the tract made by certain family members, controlled entities, lessees, or governmental entities are attributed to the taxpayer. An improvement that does not increase the value of the lot by more than 10% is not considered substantial.

Improvements considered substantial include the following:

- the construction of shopping centers;
- the construction of commercial or residential buildings;
- the installation of hard surface roads; and
- the installation of utilities (e.g., sewers, water, gas, or electric lines).

Improvements considered insubstantial include the following:

- the construction of a temporary field office structure;
- surveying, clearing, filling, leveling, and draining operations; and
- the construction of minimum all-weather access roads.

Certain necessary improvements are not treated as substantial (even if they otherwise would be substantial improvements) if they meet the following requirements [§ 1237(b)(3); Reg. § 1.1237-1(c)(5)]:

1. the taxpayer held the property for 10 full years before the sale of a lot, even if the property was inherited;
2. the improvements are limited to water, sewer and drainage facilities, and roads;
3. the taxpayer demonstrates that, absent improvements, the lots sold would not have brought the prevailing local price for similar building sites; and

4. the taxpayer elects, in the manner described in Reg. § 1.1237-1(c)(5)(iii), the following:

— not to adjust the basis of the lot sold (or any other property held by the taxpayer) for any part of the cost of such improvements; and

— not to deduct any part of such cost as an expense.

Where a taxpayer sells both substantially improved lots and qualifying lots from the same tract, only the substantially improved lots are ineligible for the safe harbor [§ 1237(a)(2); Reg. § 1.1237-1(c)].

### III.C.4. Gain from Sale of Depreciable Property Between Related Taxpayers

[564 T.M., XII.A., 759 T.M., III.E.22.; TPS ¶1740.]

Gain resulting from the direct or indirect sale or exchange of depreciable property (including patent applications) between certain related persons is treated as ordinary income, rather than capital gain. For purposes of this rule, related persons are the following [§ 1239, § 267(b)]:

- a shareholder and a corporation if more than 50% of the stock of the corporations is owned directly or indirectly by or for that shareholder;

- a partner and a partnership if more than 50% of the capital interest or profits interest of the partnership is owned directly or indirectly by or for that partner;

- two corporations that are members of the same controlled group;

- a corporation and a partnership if the same persons own (i) more than 50% of the value of the outstanding stock of the corporation and (ii) more than 50% of the capital interest or profits interest in the partnership;

- an S corporation and another S corporation if the same persons own more than 50% of the value of the outstanding stock of each;

- an S corporation and a C corporation if the same persons own more than 50% of the value of the outstanding stock of each;

- a taxpayer and any trust in which the taxpayer or his spouse is a beneficiary (unless such beneficiary's interest is a remote contingent interest under § 318(a)(3)(B)(i));

- an employer and any person who is a related person with respect to the employer;

- a welfare benefit fund controlled directly or indirectly by an employer or any person who is a related person with respect to the employer; and

- an executor of an estate and a beneficiary of such estate, except in the case of a sale or exchange in satisfaction of a pecuniary bequest.

In determining ownership under the first six bullets, certain constructive ownership rules under § 267(c) apply [§ 1239(c)(2)].

Notably, sales of depreciable property between related individuals are not covered by the rule treating gain as ordinary income. The sale of depreciable property to an entity controlled by certain family members, however, may be subject to the rule, and thus any gain may be ordinary income.

---

**EXAMPLE:** Dean has owned a small shopping center for several years. It has an adjusted basis of $2 million and a fair market value of $4 million. His sister, Sylvia, obtains a mortgage from her bank and purchases the shopping center from Dean for cash. Dean's entire gain is capital gain (except for any amount subject to recapture) and the related party rules do not apply to him. Had Dean, instead, sold the shopping center to Family, Inc., a corporation wholly owned by Sylvia, the constructive ownership and related party rules would make Dean's entire gain ordinary income.

---

### III.C.5. Small Business Stock Transactions

### III.C.5.a. Ordinary Loss Treatment for Certain Small Business Stock

[560 T.M., II., III., IV., V., VI., VII.; TPS ¶1705.02., .03., .04., .05., .06., .07., .08.]

An individual incurring a loss on the sale, exchange, or worthlessness of certain small business stock ("§ 1244 stock") may treat any otherwise capital loss as an ordinary loss, up to a maximum annual limit of $50,000 of losses ($100,000 for married taxpayers filing joint returns). Section 1244 stock is stock meeting the following five requirements [§ 1244(c)(1); Reg. § 1.1244(c)-1]:

1. The stock must be common or preferred stock (stock issued on or before July 18, 1984, must be common stock; for stock issued on or before November 6, 1978, corporation must have adopted a § 1244 plan).
2. The issuer must be a domestic corporation.
3. The issuer must be a small business corporation.
4. The stock must be issued for money or other property, excluding stock or securities.
5. The issuing corporation must meet the gross receipts test during the five most recent tax years ending before the date the loss on the stock is sustained.

A corporation is a small business corporation if, at the time of the issuance of the stock in question (and including the stock issuance in question), the aggregate amount of money and other property the corporation has received for (i) the sale of its stock to shareholders, (ii) contributions to capital, and (iii) paid-in surplus, does not exceed $1 million. For this purpose, non-money property received in exchange for the corporation's stock is included in the calculation at its adjusted basis to the corporation, reduced by the amount of any liability to which the property is subject or that the corporation assumes. Once an amount has been paid to a corporation, that amount is fixed for purposes of the small business corporation calculation. Thus, a corporation reducing its capital account by redeeming stock, or through a partial liquidation, does not reduce the capital counted toward the $1 million limit [§ 1244(c)(3); Reg. § 1.1244(c)-2(b)(1)].

The gross receipts test requires that a corporation derive less than half of its gross receipts from passive investment income, that is, royalties, rents, dividends, interest, annuities, and sales or exchanges of stock or securities. The test is applied as of the time the loss on the sale of the stock is sustained [§ 1244(c)(1)(C); Reg. § 1.1244(c)-1(e)]. If a corporation was not in existence for five tax years before the date of the loss on the sale of the stock, the gross receipts test is applied using the number of tax years the corporation has existed. Where a corporation has not existed for a full tax year, the test is applied using the total period of the corporation's existence. The gross receipts test does not apply if, for the applicable testing period, the corporation's deductions (excluding net operating loss deductions and corporate dividends received deductions) exceed its gross income [§ 1244(c)(2); Reg. § 1.1244(c)-1(e)].

Section 1244 ordinary loss treatment is available only for individuals and individual partners of a partnership sustaining the loss. Losses sustained on stock held by a corporation (including an S corporation), a trust, or an estate will not qualify. Additionally, ordinary loss treatment is only available to an individual or partnership that acquires the stock upon its original issuance. Thus, the individual or partnership that sells the stock at a loss must also be the individual or partnership that acquired the stock from the issuing corporation. Acquisition of the stock from a shareholder by purchase, gift, devise, or otherwise will disqualify the acquiring individual from receiving ordinary loss treatment for the acquired stock [Reg. § 1.1244(a)-1(b)]. In the case of a partnership, the benefit of ordinary loss treatment is available only to individuals that were partners at the time of the original issuance, and the ordinary loss deduction is limited to the lesser of either (i) the partner's distributive share at the time of the stock's issuance, or (ii) the partner's distributive share at the time the loss is sustained [Reg. § 1.1244(a)-1(b)(2)].

The amount of capital loss that may be treated as ordinary loss under this rule is limited to $50,000 per taxpayer ($100,000 for married taxpayers filing a joint return) annually. Capital losses in excess of the annual limitation remain capital losses (see III.B.5.). If a taxpayer has insufficient ordinary income against which to deduct the now-ordinary loss, the excess loss is treated as a net operating loss that may be carried back or carried forward [§ 1244(d)(3)] (see VIII.G.).

Losses treated as ordinary losses under this provision are reported on Form 4797, *Sales of Business Property*. Capital losses are reported on Form 8949, *Sales and Other Dispositions of Capital Assets*.

### III.C.5.b. Exclusion of Certain Small Business Stock Gain

[760 T.M., IX., X.; TPS ¶1750.09.]

Subject to certain limits, a noncorporate taxpayer may generally exclude 50% of the gain from the sale or exchange of qualified small business (QSB) stock held for more than five years. The exclusion is increased to 75% for QSB stock acquired between February 18, 2009, and September 27, 2010, and to 100% for QSB stock acquired between September 28, 2010, and December 31, 2013. Additionally, gain on the sale of QSB stock acquired after December 21, 2000, in a qualified empowerment zone business is eligible for a 60% exclusion if the requirements for the general 50% exclusion are met.

For purposes of this rule, QSB stock is stock meeting all the following requirements [§ 1202(c)]:

1. It must be stock in a domestic C corporation.
2. It must originally have been issued after August, 10, 1993.
3. The corporation must have total gross assets not exceeding $50 million at all times beginning on or after August 10, 1993, and through the issuance of the stock (for this purpose, members of the same parent-subsidiary controlled group are treated as one corporation).
4. The taxpayer must have acquired the stock at its original issue (directly or through an underwriter) in exchange for money or other property (excluding stock), or as compensation for services provided to the corporation (excluding services as an underwriter of such stock).

5. During substantially all of the taxpayer's holding period of the stock, the corporation must be a C corporation and must meet the active business requirement.

6. The corporation must not have purchased, directly or indirectly, more than a de minimis amount of its stock from the taxpayer or a related party during the two years before, or two years after, the stock's issuance.

7. During the year before, or year after, the stock's issuance, the corporation must not redeem more than 5% of the aggregate value of all its stock as of the date one year before the stock's issuance.

The active business requirement is satisfied if both of the following conditions are met [§ 1202(e)]:

1. At least 80% of the value of the assets of the corporation must be used in the active conduct of one or more qualified trades or businesses, which is any trade or business other than one of the following [§ 1202(e)(3)]:

— any trade or business involving the performance of services in the fields of health, law, engineering, architecture, accounting, actuarial science, performing arts, consulting, athletics, financial services, brokerage services, or any trade or business where the principal asset is the reputation or skill of one or more employees;

— any banking, insurance, financing, leasing, investing, or similar business;

— any farming business (including the business of raising or harvesting trees);

— any business involving the production or extraction of products for which percentage depletion can be claimed (see VI.A.3.b.); or

— any business of operating a hotel, motel, restaurant, or similar business; and

2. The corporation must be an eligible corporation, which is any domestic corporation other than one of the following [§ 1202(e)(4)]:

— a DISC or former DISC;

— a corporation that has made, or whose subsidiary has made, a § 936 election;

— a regulated investment company (RIC), a real estate investment trust (REIT), or a real estate mortgage investment conduit (REMIC);

— a cooperative.

The five-year holding period required for the partial exclusion is measured slightly differently than the holding period generally required of capital assets (see III.B.3.). A taxpayer acquiring QSB stock in exchange for property (other than money or stock) is deemed to have acquired the stock on the date of the exchange, and the period during which the taxpayer held the other property may not be tacked. Tacking is available, however, where QSB stock is converted into other stock of the same corporation. In such a case, the newly acquired stock is also treated as QSB stock and the old stock's holding period may be tacked. Similarly, a taxpayer that receives QSB stock as a gift or by death may tack the transferor's holding period. In addition, a partner that receives qualifies small business stock from a partnership may tack the partnership's holding period. It is also possible to preserve QSB stock treatment and to tack holding periods when exchanging QSB stock for otherwise non-QSB stock in a reorganization under § 368 (see XIII.E.) or a contribution to a controlled corporation under § 351 (see XIII.B.1.) [§ 1202(i)(1)(A), § 1202(f), § 1202(h)].

A 60% exclusion is available if (i) the requirements for the 50% exclusion are met, (ii) the stock sold was acquired after December 21, 2000, and (iii) the stock is in a corporation that is a qualified empowerment zone business entity during substantially all of the taxpayer's holding period for the stock. A qualified empowerment zone business entity must satisfy the following requirements for the tax year [§ 1202(a)(2)(A), § 1397C(b)]:

1. every trade or business of the QSB is the active conduct of a qualified business within an empowerment zone;

2. at least 50% of the total gross income of the QSB is derived from the active conduct of such business;

3. a substantial portion of the use of the tangible property of the QSB (whether owned or leased) is within an empowerment zone;

4. a substantial portion of the intangible property of the QSB is used in the active conduct of any such business;

5. a substantial portion of the services performed for the QSB by its employees are performed in an empowerment zone;

6. at least 35% of the QSB's employees are residents of an empowerment zone;

7. less than 5% of the average of the aggregate unadjusted bases of the property of the QSB is attributable to collectibles (as defined in § 408(m)(2)) other than those held primarily for sale to customers in the ordinary course of such business; and

8. less than 5% of the average of the aggregate unadjusted bases of the property of the QSB is attributable to nonqualified financial property.

For each tax year, a taxpayer is limited in the amount of gain on a single issuing corporation's stock that may be used in computing the amount of the exclusion. The limitation is applied separately for each corporation. The limit is the greater of the following [§ 1202(b)]:

- $10 million ($5 million for married individuals filing separately), reduced by the aggregate amount of eligible gain taken into account by the taxpayer in prior tax years that was attributable to dispositions of stock issued by the corporation; or

- 10 times the aggregate adjusted bases of QSB stock issued by the corporation and disposed of by the taxpayer during the tax year.

---

**EXAMPLE:** Tiny Co. is a qualified small business. In 2000, Tiny Co. issues 1,000 shares of common stock. Mia purchases all 1,000 shares for $200,000. In Year 1 (a year in which the exclusion amount is 50%), Mia sells 500 shares for $7 million, realizing a $6.9 million gain ($7 million amount realized − $100,000 basis in the 500 shares). Mia may use the entire amount of the gain in computing her 50% exclusion, which amounts to $3.45 million. In Year 2 (a year in which the exclusion amount is 50%), Mia sells her remaining 500 shares of Tiny Co. stock for $10 million, realizing a $9.9 million gain ($10 million amount realized − $100,000 basis in the 500 shares). Mia previously used a $6.9 million gain from the sale of Tiny Co. stock in Year 1 in computing a 50% exclusion for that year. Thus, she is limited to the greater of (i) $3.1 million ($10 million − $6.9 million gain from disposition of Tiny Co. stock taken into account in Year 1), or (ii) $1 million (10 × $1,000 basis in the Tiny Co. stock sold in Year 2). Thus, Mia may use $3.1 million of gain in calculating her 50% exclusion, which amounts to $1.55 million.

---

For alternative minimum tax purposes, 7% of a taxpayer's excluded gain on the sale of QSB stock is treated as a tax preference item and, therefore, is added back to taxable income in computing alternative minimum taxable income [§ 57(a)(7)]. However, no amount is treated as a tax preference item for QSB stock subject to the 100% exclusion [§ 1202(a)(4)(C)].

The sale or exchange of QSB stock is reported on Form 8949, *Sales and Other Dispositions of Capital Assets.*

### III.C.5.c. Deferral of Certain Small Business Stock Gain

[760 T.M., VIII., X., XI.; TPS ¶¶1570.05., 1750.10.]

A taxpayer may defer gain on the sale of QSB stock if he or she rolls over the gain into a new investment in QSB stock within 60 days. Rollover treatment is available if all the following conditions are satisfied [§ 1045(a)]:

1. The taxpayer must not be a corporation.

2. The taxpayer must be the party selling the stock.

3. The taxpayer must have held the stock for more than six months.

4. The taxpayer must make a special election to claim rollover treatment.

For purposes of this rule, QSB stock has the same meaning as it does for the exclusion rule, discussed in III.C.5.b. [§ 1045(b)(1), § 1202(c)].

The six-month holding period required for deferral is measured slightly differently than the holding period generally required of capital assets (see III.B.3.). The six-month period does not include any holding period arising under the tacking rules of § 1223. Rules similar to those described for the five-year holding period required for exclusion apply in measuring whether the six-month holding period for deferral has been satisfied. In addition, only the first six months of the taxpayer's holding period for the new QSB are taken into account in determining whether the active business requirement has been satisfied [§ 1045(b)(4), § 1045(b)(5)]. For a discussion of the exclusion rules for small business stock gain, see III.C.5.b.

The amount of gain that may be deferred is limited. A taxpayer must recognize gain to the extent the amount realized on the sale of the QSB stock exceeds the cost of any QSB stock the taxpayer purchases during the 60 days after the sale date (reduced by any portion of that cost previously taken into account on an earlier sale of QSB stock) [§ 1045(a)].

---

**EXAMPLE:** Phil purchases 100 shares of QSB stock in Small Corp. on May 1 of Year 1 for $10,000. Phil sells all 100 shares on June 1 of Year 2 for $15,000, realizing a $5,000 capital gain. On June 15 of Year 2, Phil purchases QSB stock in Little, Inc. for $15,000, and he elects to claim rollover treatment. Phil may defer the recognition of all the gain realized on the Small Corp. stock. Had Phil purchased QSB stock in Little, Inc. for $12,000, he would recognize $3,000 ($15,000 − $12,000) of gain, and the remaining $2,000 of gain would be deferred.

**EXAMPLE:** Charlotte has held two blocks of QSB stock for more than six months each. On Aug. 10 of Year 1, Charlotte sells the first block, which has a basis of $50,000, for $80,000, realizing $30,000 of gain. On Aug. 20 of Year 1, she sells the second block, which has a basis of $30,000, for $60,000, realizing $30,000 of gain. On Aug. 30 of Year 1, Charlotte purchases a new block of QSB stock for $100,000. Charlotte elects to claim rollover treatment. She is not required to recognize gain on the sale of the first block because there is no excess of amount realized over the cost of the new QSB stock. On the sale of the second block, Charlotte must recognize gain to the extent the

$60,000 amount realized exceeds the cost of the new QSB stock, reduced by the amount of the cost taken into account for the sale of the first block ($100,000 − $80,000). Charlotte recognizes gain up to no more than $40,000 ($60,000 − $20,000). However, because she only realized $30,000 of gain on the sale of the second block, Charlotte recognizes only $30,000.

---

Taxpayers must reduce their basis in new QSB stock dollar for dollar to reflect the amount of gain deferred under this provision. If more than one purchase of QSB stock is made, the deferred gain reduces the basis of each subsequent purchase in the order in which the purchases were made [§ 1045(b)(3)].

An election to rollover gain must be made no later than the due date for filing the income tax return for the tax year in which the QSB stock is sold. A taxpayer must report the sale on Form 8949, *Sales and Other Dispositions of Capital Assets*, as if he or she was not making the election, and then the taxpayer must enter the amount of gain deferred as an adjustment, along with the appropriate code for the adjustment indicated in the instructions to Form 8949.

### III.C.6. Dispositions of Insurance, Endowment, and Annuity Contracts

[529 T.M., IV., 546 T.M., III.D., 562 T.M., I.B.12.; TPS ¶1540.]

The tax treatment of insurance policy transfers depends on the form of the transfer, which generally falls into one of the following categories:

- a policy surrender;
- a policy sale or taxable policy exchange;
- an accelerated death benefit; or
- a nontaxable policy exchange.

The treatment of gains from surrenders, sales, taxable exchanges, and death benefits are discussed in III.C.6.a., while nontaxable exchanges of insurance, endowment, and annuity contracts are discussed in III.E.4.

### III.C.6.a. Surrenders of Insurance, Endowment, and Annuity Contracts

[529 T.M., IV.A.2.a., 546 T.M., III.D.6., 562 T.M., I.B.12.b.; TPS ¶1540.02.]

A policy surrender is the transfer for cancellation of a life insurance, endowment, annuity, or qualified long-term care insurance policy to its issuer in exchange for the policy's cash surrender value. Upon surrender, the taxpayer may realize gain if the surrender proceeds exceed the basis of the policy surrendered, or loss if the opposite is true. Such gain is ordinary income because a surrender does not constitute a sale or exchange of a capital asset [Rev. Rul. 2009-13, 2009-21 I.R.B. 1029]. Losses on the surrender of a policy generally are not deductible.

### III.C.6.b. Sales or Taxable Exchanges of Insurance, Endowment, and Annuity Contracts

[529 T.M., IV.A.2.b., 546 T.M., III.D.3.b(4), 562 T.M., I.B.12.c.; TPS ¶1540.04.]

If a life insurance, endowment, annuity, or qualified long-term care insurance policy is sold or exchanged in a transaction other than a nontaxable exchange (see III.E.4.), then any gain realized on the transaction will be recognized. Despite the fact that insurance and annuity policies are typically capital assets (see III.B.1.), gain recognized on the sale or exchange is generally ordinary income. Where an insured sells a life insurance contract with a cash surrender value, gain recognized is ordinary to the extent of any inside build-up amount under the contract that would be taxed as ordinary income if the contract was surrendered (see III.C.6.a.). Amounts in excess of the inside build-up amount may be long-term capital gain. Additionally, where an unrelated U.S. person buys a term life insurance contract from an insured, the buyer may recognize long-term capital gain on the subsequent sale of the policy to another unrelated buyer [Rev. Rul. 2009-13, 2009-21 I.R.B. 1029].

Losses realized on the sale of a life insurance or endowment policy may not be recognized unless it was incurred in connection with the taxpayer's trade or business or in a transaction entered into for profit (see VIII.H.).

The adjusted basis of an annuity contract sold by the taxpayer may not be an amount less than zero [§ 1021].

### III.C.6.c. Accelerated Death Benefits Under Life Insurance Contracts

[546 T.M., III.D.2.b.; TPS ¶1540.05.]

Amounts received under a life insurance contract on the life of an insured who is terminally or chronically ill are treated as amounts paid by reason of the death of an insured that may be excluded from income [§ 101(a)(1), § 101(g)(1)]. Accelerated death benefits are discussed in II.E.

### III.C.7. Dealings in Real Property

[590 T.M., IV.C.; TPS ¶1550.]

Special rules frequently apply to dealings in real property, including the following:

- If land or depreciable property used in a trade or business and held for more than one year is sold, gains are treated as capital gains and losses are treated as ordinary losses [§ 1231] (see III.C.1.).
- Gains from the sale of depreciable property between related taxpayers are treated as ordinary income, rather than capital gain [§ 1239] (see III.C.4.).
- A special safe harbor allows certain taxpayers to divide substantially unim-proved land into parcels or lots and sell them without being deemed to hold the property primarily for sale to customers in the ordinary course of business, and thus the taxpayer remains eligible for capital gain or capital loss treatment [§ 1221, § 1237] (see III.C.3.).
- The cancellation of qualified real property business indebtedness may be ex-cluded from income [§ 108(a)(1)(D)] (see II.A.5.).
- No gain or loss is recognized on the exchange of property held for productive use in a trade or business or for investment if exchanged solely for property of a like kind held for productive use in a trade or business or for investment [§ 1031] (see III.E.1.).
- If property is compulsorily or involuntarily converted as a result of (or as a result of the threat or imminence of) destruction, theft, seizure, or requisition or condemnation into property similar or related in service or use, no gain or loss is recognized [§ 1033] (see III.E.2.).
- Certain amounts of gain upon the sale or exchange of a taxpayer's principal residence may be excluded, provided that certain ownership and use require-ments are met [§ 121] (see III.E.3.).
- A seller of real property who reacquires such real property from the buyer in full or partial satisfaction of indebtedness to the seller that arose from the sale and that is secured by the property generally recognizes only limited gain, may not recognize loss, and may not treat debt secured by the repossessed property as worthless or partially worthless as a result of the reacquisition [§ 1038] (see III.E.6.).

### III.C.8. Miscellaneous Capital Gain and Ordinary Income Issues

#### III.C.8.a. Cancellation of a Lease or Distributorship Agreement

[562 T.M., I.B.2.b., 593 T.M., IV.C.1.; TPS ¶1770.01.]

Payments a lessee receives for the cancellation of a lease are considered as received in exchange for the lease. This is the case whether the lease relates to real property or personal property. A good faith payment for a partial cancellation of a lease qualifies as an amount received for cancellation if the cancellation relates to a severable economic unit, such as a cancellation with respect to a portion of the premises under a lease or a reduction in the unexpired term of a lease. Payments made for other modifications of leases generally are not recognized as amounts received for cancellation and do not qualify for exchange treatment. This special provision does not apply to lessors [§ 1241; Reg. § 1.1241-1].

Similarly, payments a distributor of goods receives for cancellation of a distributorship agreement are considered as received in exchange for the agreement if the distributor has a substantial capital investment in the distributorship. An investment is not substantial unless it consists of a significant portion of the facilities for storing, transporting, processing, or otherwise dealing with the goods, or a substantial inventory of goods. This provision applies only to distributorship agreements for marketing, or marketing and servicing, of goods. It does not apply to agreements for selling intangible property or for rendering personal services (e.g., agreements establishing insurance agencies or securities brokerage agencies) [§ 1241; Reg. § 1.1241-1].

The character of income or loss from the transaction depends on whether the lease or distributorship agreement is a capital asset (see III.B.1.) or certain property used in a trade or business (see III.C.1.).

#### III.C.8.b. Small Business Investment Companies

[760 T.M., XII.B.; TPS ¶1770.02.]

Stock held as an investment is typically a capital asset that, in the event of a loss on its sale or exchange or worthlessness, produces capital loss. However, investors are entitled to an ordinary loss deduction for losses from the sale, exchange, or worthlessness of stock in a company that is licensed to operate as a small business investment company pursuant to Small Business Administration regulations [§ 1242; Reg. § 1.1242-1]. In computing losses on the sale of small business investment company stock, transactions for a tax year are not netted. Instead, each transaction is considered separately [Rev. Rul. 65-291, 1965-2 C.B. 290]. The limitation on the allowance of nonbusiness deductions in computing a net operating loss is inapplicable to any loss from the stock of a small business investment company [Reg. § 1.1242-1(b)].

A company licensed to operate as a small business investment company pursuant to Small Business Administration regulations is entitled to an ordinary loss deduction on losses from the sale, exchange, or worthlessness of stock received under the conversion privilege of certain convertible debentures [§ 1243; Reg. § 1.1243-1].

#### III.C.8.c. Recapture of Soil and Water Conservation Expenses

[607 T.M., V.C.6.; TPS ¶1770.03.]

Taxpayers engaged in the trade or business of farming have the option of electing to currently deduct certain expenditures for soil and water conservation for land used in farming (see IV.F.3.e.). These deductions are subject to recapture as ordinary income if the farm land to which they relate is disposed of at a gain within 10 years of its acquisition. This recapture provision takes precedence over any other income tax provision of the Code [Reg. § 1.1252-1(a)(2)].

The amount of gain that is recaptured and treated as ordinary income upon disposition is the lesser of (i) the applicable percentage of the total of the soil and water conservation expenditure deductions allowed during the holding period, or (ii) the amount of gain realized on the disposition. The applicable percentages are as follows [§ 1252; Reg. § 1.1252-1(a)]:

| When Farm Land Is Disposed Of | Applicable Percentage |
|---|---|
| Within five years of acquisition | 100% |
| Within the sixth year after acquisition | 80% |
| Within the seventh year after acquisition | 60% |
| Within the eighth year after acquisition | 40% |
| Within the ninth year after acquisition | 20% |
| Within the tenth year after acquisition and thereafter | 0% |

---

**EXAMPLE:** Tyler purchased farm land on Jan. 1 of Year 1. Also in Year 1, Tyler deducted $18,000 in soil and water conservation expenditures with respect to the land. He did not deduct any other soil and water conservation expenditures while he owned the property. Tyler sold the farm land on Apr. 10 of Year 6, realizing a gain of $22,500. Because Tyler sold the farm within the sixth year after its acquisition, 80% of the soil and water conservation expenditure deduction is subject to recapture. Thus, he is required to treat $14,400 as ordinary income ($18,000 × 80%). The remaining $8,100 of gain is treated as gain from the sale of property used in a trade or business under § 1231.

---

A taxpayer making a gift of farm land for which he or she has deducted expenditures for soil and water conservation does not recapture the deductions as ordinary gain, regardless of the length of time the taxpayer held the land. However, immediately after the transfer, the transferee will assume the transferor's aggregate amount of conservation expenditures and the transferor's holding period for the transferred land [Reg. § 1.1252-2(a)(1), § 1.1252-2(f)(1)]. There is also no recapture where farm land is transferred upon the death of a taxpayer who has deduced soil and water conservation expenditures. In this case, though, the transferor's soil and water conservation expenditures are not attributed to the transferee [Reg. § 1.1252-2(b)].

Gain on the disposition of farm land subject to recapture is reported on Form 4797, *Sales of Business Property.*

### III.C.8.d. Disposition of Certain Wetlands and Croplands

[501 T.M., IV.G.2.n.; TPS ¶1770.03.B.]

Gain on the disposition of converted wetland or highly erodible cropland first used for farming after March 1, 1986, is treated as ordinary income, while a loss on the disposition is treated as long-term capital loss. This provision applies notwithstanding any other income tax provision of the Code, unless the gain has been recognized as ordinary income under other provisions of Part IV of the Code [§ 1257(a)].

A converted wetland is land that has been drained or filled for the purpose of making the production of agricultural commodities possible, if the production would not have been possible but for such action, and if the lands are held by one of the following:

- the person who converted the wetland;
- any other person who uses the land for farming for any period of time after conversion; or
- a person whose adjusted basis in the property is determined by reference to the basis of the person in whose hands the property was converted wetland.

Highly erodible cropland is land used by the taxpayer for purposes other than the grazing of animals and that is either (i) classified as Class IV, VI, VII, or VIII land under the Department of Agriculture land capability classification system, or (ii) land that would have an excessive average annual rate of erosion compared to an established soil loss tolerance level. A taxpayer holding land, the adjusted basis of which is determined in part or in whole by reference to the basis of a person who held the property when it was a highly erodible cropland, is also treated as holding highly erodible cropland [§ 1257].

### III.C.8.e. Disposition of Certain Improved Conservation Property
[610 T.M., VII.D.5.; TPS ¶1770.04.]

All or a part of a government payment received under certain cost-sharing conservation, reclamation, and restoration programs may be excluded from income [§ 126] (see II.K.). If property acquired or improved by excludible payments is disposed of within 20 years after the taxpayer received the excludible funds, the taxpayer must treat as ordinary income the lesser of the following [§ 1255(a); Reg. § 16A.1255-1(a)]:

- the applicable percentage of the aggregate payments made with respect to such property that were excluded from gross income; or
- the excess of either the amount realized on (in the case of a sale, exchange or involuntary conversion), or fair market value of (in the case of any other disposition), such property over the adjusted basis of the property.

For purposes of this rule, the applicable percentage is 100% if the property acquired or improved by excludible payments is disposed of within 10 years after the date of the last excludible payment. If property acquired or improved by excludible payments is disposed of more than 10 years, but less than 20 years, after the date of the last excludible payment, the applicable percentage is 100%, reduced by 10% for each year or partial year in excess of 10 years. The applicable percentage is 0%, and no recapture is required, if the disposition occurs more than 20 years after the date of the last excludible payment [§ 1255(a)(3); Reg. § 16A.1255-1(a)(4)].

Special rules apply where improved property is disposed of by gift, at death, or in a tax-free transaction before the expiration of the 20-year period. A disposition of improved property by gift does not trigger recapture. Instead, the aggregate excluded payments, as well as the date of receipt of the last excludible payment, is the same in the hands of the transferee immediately after the disposition as it was in the hands of the transferor immediately before the disposition [Reg. § 16A.1255-2(a)(1), § 16A.1255-2(d)]. A transferee does not recognize gain on the receipt of improved property received at the death of the transferor. If the transferee's basis in the property is determined solely by reference to the fair market value of the property as of the transferor's date of death (or an alternate valuation date), the transferee's amount of aggregate excluded payments is zero [Reg. § 16A.1255-2(b)].

---

**EXAMPLE:** In Year 2, Betsy makes a gift to Cameron of a parcel of land with an adjusted basis of $40,000 and a fair market value of $65,000. At the time of the gift, the aggregate amount of tax-free payments was $24,000, all of which were received on

Jan. 15 of Year 1. Betsy realizes no gain on making the gift. The aggregate amount of the tax-free payments relating to the land in Cameron's hands is $24,000. If she later disposes of the land, the date of the last excludible payment on the land in Cameron's hands is Jan. 15 of Year 1.

---

If improved property is disposed of in certain tax-free transactions, the amount of gain recognized as ordinary income is limited to the excess (if any) of (i) the amount of gain recognized by the transferor (without regard to these recapture rules), over (ii) the amount of any gain recognized by the transferor as ordinary income under other provisions of § 1231-§ 1260 of the Code. In the event of a completely tax-free transfer that does not require recapture, the transferor's aggregate excluded payments and date of receipt of the last excludible payment carry over to the transferee [Reg. § 16A.1255-2(c)(1), § 16A.1255-2(d)].

---

**EXAMPLE:** Aaron holds a parcel of property with an adjusted basis of $15,000 and a fair market value of $40,000. On Jan. 4 of Year 6, he transfers the property to Develop Corp. in a § 351 transaction in exchange for $32,000 of Develop Corp. stock and $8,000 cash. On the date of the transfer, the aggregate amount of tax-free payments relating to the land is $18,000, all of which was received on Mar. 25 of Year 1. Aaron realizes $25,000 of gain on the transfer ($40,000 − $15,000). Without regard to these recapture rules, Aaron would recognize $8,000 of gain as a result of the cash boot received. Assume Aaron recognizes no other gain as ordinary income. Because Aaron sold the property within 10 years of the date of the last excludible payment, his applicable percentage is 100%. $18,000 ($18,000 × 100%) is less than the gain realized on the exchange ($25,000), and thus would typically be the amount recaptured. However, Aaron's recapture is limited to any excess of the $8,000 that would be gain absent these recapture rules, over any other gain treated as ordinary income under § 1231-§ 1260 of the Code ($0). Therefore, Aaron's recapture is limited to $8,000.

---

Gain on the disposition of conservation property that is subject to recapture is reported on Form 4797, *Sales of Business Property*.

### III.C.8.f. Disposition of Tobacco Quotas

[608 T.M., XI.K.; TPS ¶1770.05.]

In connection with the repeal of the tobacco marketing quota program, the U.S. Department of Agriculture offered to enter into a contract with each eligible tobacco quota holder to compensate them with annual payments from 2005 through 2014 for the lost value of the quota as a result of the repeal [Pub. L. No. 108-357, § 611, § 612]. The character of gain or loss on the quota payment depends on how the owner used the quota. If an owner used a quota in the trade or business of farming and, on the sale date, the owner's holding period for the quota was more than one year, the transaction is a § 1231 transaction (see III.C.1.). If an owner held a quota for either investment purposes or the production of income, but did not use the quota in a trade or business, any gain or loss is capital gain or loss.

In certain situations, some or all of the gain must be recharacterized as ordinary income. If an owner previously deducted (i) the cost of acquiring a quota, (ii) amounts for amortization, depletion, or depreciation, or (iii) amounts to reflect a reduction in the quota pounds, gain is treated as ordinary income up to the amount previously deducted.

Payments received are not subject to self-employment tax [Notice 2005-57, 2005-32 I.R.B. 267].

## III.D. Depreciation Recapture

[563 T.M.; TPS ¶1760.]

A taxpayer disposing of certain property on which he or she claimed depreciation or amortization deductions (see Chapter V.) may be required to treat some or all of the gain from the property as ordinary income. This recapture rule applies to both personal property (see III.D.2.) and real property (see III.D.3.), and it applies notwithstanding any other income tax provision of the Code [§ 1245(a)(1), § 1250(a)(1)].

Dispositions subject to the depreciation recapture rules are reported on Form 4797, *Sales of Business Property*, or Form 4684, *Casualties and Thefts*, as the case may be.

### III.D.1. Transactions Triggering Depreciation Recapture

[563 T.M., III.; TPS ¶1760.01.D.]

The depreciation recapture rules apply when there is gain upon a disposition of property that is subject to the rules (see III.D.2. and III.D.3.). For this purpose, a disposition includes sales, exchanges, involuntary conversions, the sale in a sale-leaseback transaction, and a transfer on foreclosure of a security interest. A disposition does not include a mere transfer or title to a creditor upon creation of a security interest, or to a debtor upon termination of a security interest [§ 1245(a)(1), § 1250(a)(1); Reg. § 1.1245-1(a), § 1.1250-1(a)].

Certain tax-free transactions in which the transferee takes the transferor's basis in the transferred property do not trigger recapture. Instead, the recapture is deferred until the transferee's later disposition of the property [§ 1245(b)(3), § 1250(d)(3)]. Similarly, recapture is not triggered in certain tax-free transfers of property in which the transferred property's basis becomes the basis for replacement property the transferor acquires. In that case, the recapture is deferred until the disposition of the replacement property [§ 1245(b)(4), § 1250(d)(4)].

The recapture rules do not apply to dispositions in which the taxpayer realizes a loss [Reg. § 1.1245-1(d), § 1.1250-1(a)(5)(i)].

### III.D.2. Section 1245

#### III.D.2.a. Section 1245 Property

[563 T.M., II.; TPS ¶1760.02.]

A gain on the disposition of "§ 1245 property" is treated as ordinary income to the extent of depreciation allowed or allowable on the property. Section 1245 property is property that (i) is or has been property of a character subject to an allowance for depreciation or amortization and (ii) is one of the following types of property [§ 1245(a)(3); Reg. § 1.1245-3(a)(1)]:

- personal property (both tangible and intangible);
- certain industrial facilities that satisfy all three of the following criteria:
  1. the property must not be a building or structural component of a building;
  2. the property must be tangible property; and
  3. the property's basis must reflect depreciation deductions for a period during which it was used in one of the following capacities:

— as an integral part of manufacturing, production, extraction, or furnishing of transportation, communications, electrical energy, gas, water, or sewage disposal;

— as a research facility in connection with any of the capacities described in the first bullet; or

— as a storage facility in connection with any of the capacities described in the first bullet for the bulk storage of fungible commodities, including commodities in a liquid or gaseous state;

• that portion of any real property (not included in the industrial facilities group of property, above) that has an adjusted basis that reflects adjustments for amortization deductions claimed under any one of the following twelve rules:

1. the amortization rules for pollution control facilities (see IV.F.5.g.);

2. the optional depreciable business asset expense deduction rules (see V.B.);

3. the clean fuel vehicle and clean fuel vehicle refueling property rules;

4. the deduction for capital costs incurred in complying with EPA sulfur regulations (see IV.F.5.j.);

5. the election to expense refineries (see IV.F.5.d.);

6. the energy efficient commercial buildings deduction (see IV.F.5.a.);

7. the advanced mine safety equipment expense deduction (see IV.F.5.b.);

8. the railroad grading and tunnel bores amortization rules;

9. the child care facilities amortization rules;

10. the architectural and transportation barrier removal expense deduction rules (see IV.F.5.i.);

11. the tertiary injectant expense deduction rules (see VI.E.2.); and

12. the reforestation expenditure rules (VI.B.5.a.);

• single purpose agricultural or horticultural structures;

• storage facilities, other than buildings or structural components of buildings, used in connection with the distribution of petroleum or any primary product of petroleum;

• any railroad grading or tunnel bore.

A leasehold of any § 1245 property is also § 1245 property, and thus, a disposition of the leasehold may result in recapture. A leasehold of land is not § 1245 property [Reg. § 1.1245-3(a)(2)].

### III.D.2.b. Computation of Depreciation Recapture for § 1245 Property

[563 T.M., IV.; TPS ¶1760.04.]

The depreciation recaptured and treated as ordinary income on the disposition of § 1245 property is the lesser of the following:

• the amount realized on the sale, exchange, or involuntary conversion of the property (or the fair market value of the property in the case of any other disposition) reduced by adjusted basis; or

• the recomputed basis reduced by adjusted basis.

Recomputed basis generally means the adjusted basis of any property increased by the depreciation deductions previously claimed on that property [§ 1245(a); Reg. § 1.1245-1(a)(1), § 1.1245-1(b)]. This includes any depreciation claimed by any other person with respect to whose basis in the property the taxpayer's basis is determined, except to the extent the other person recognized depreciation recapture income. It also includes depreciation deductions claimed on any property the basis of which is reflected in the taxpayer's basis in the property in question, except to the extent that depreciation recapture income was recognized on the predecessor property. Depreciation deductions that were allowable but not claimed are not taken into account [§ 1245(a)(2); Reg. § 1.1245-2(a)(4), § 1.1245-2(a)(7)].

---

**EXAMPLE:** Michelle purchased equipment for $40,000 and claimed depreciation deductions of $12,000. As a result, her adjusted basis in the equipment is $28,000. Michelle sells the equipment for $35,000. The amount realized reduced by the adjusted basis is $7,000 ($35,000 − $28,000). The recomputed basis is $40,000 ($28,000 adjusted basis + $12,000 depreciation deductions taken). Recomputed basis reduced by adjusted basis is $12,000 ($40,000 − $28,000). Michelle must report $7,000 (the lesser of $7,000 and $12,000) as ordinary income under the depreciation recapture rules.

**EXAMPLE:** Famous Corp. distributes § 1245 property to its shareholder as a dividend. The property has an adjusted basis of $2,000, a recomputed basis of $3,300, and a fair market value of $3,100. The fair market value of the property reduced by adjusted basis is $1,100. The recomputed basis of the property reduced by adjusted basis is $1,300. Famous Corp. must report $1,100 (the lesser of $1,100 and $1,300) as ordinary income under the depreciation recapture rules. This is the case despite the nonrecognition rule of § 311 because § 1245 applies notwithstanding any other income tax provision of the Code.

---

### III.D.3. Section 1250

#### III.D.3.a. Section 1250 Property

[563 T.M., II.; TPS ¶1760.03.]

A gain on the disposition of "§ 1250 property" is treated as ordinary income to the extent of depreciation allowed or allowable on the property. Section 1250 property is real property that is or has been property of a character subject to an allowance for depreciation under § 167 and that is not and has never been § 1245 property (see III.D.2.a.). Real property includes intangible real property (e.g., a leasehold of land or a building) and tangible real property (e.g., buildings, structural components of buildings, paved parking areas, and fences) [§ 1250(c); Reg. § 1.1250-1(a)(2)(i)].

Section 1250 property can become § 1245 property if there is a change in use before its disposition. Property that loses its character as § 1250 property can never again be § 1250 property in the taxpayer's hands, and the § 1245 property rules apply at disposition [Reg. § 1.1250-1(e)(4)].

#### III.D.3.b. Computation of Depreciation Recapture for § 1250 Property

[563 T.M., IV.; TPS ¶1760.05.]

The depreciation recaptured and treated as ordinary income on the disposition of § 1250 property is the applicable percentage of the lesser of the following amounts [§ 1250(a)(1)(A); Reg. § 1.1250-1(a)(1)]:

- additional depreciation; or
- the excess of amount realized on the sale, exchange, or involuntary conversion of the property (or the excess of the fair market value of the property in the case of any other disposition) over adjusted basis.

For § 1250 property held longer than one year, additional depreciation is the actual depreciation adjustments that are more than the depreciation figured using the straight-line method (see V.A.4.b(3)). For § 1250 property held for one year or less, all the depreciation is additional depreciation [§ 1250(b); Reg. § 1.1250-2(a)(1), § 1.1250-2(b)(1)]. Additional depreciation includes any depreciation claimed by any other person with respect to whose basis in the property the taxpayer's basis is determined, except to the extent the other person recognized depreciation recapture income. It also includes depreciation deductions claimed on any property the basis of which is reflected in the taxpayer's basis in the property in question, except to the extent that depreciation recapture income was recognized on the predecessor property. Depreciation deductions that were allowable but not claimed are not taken into account (except in computing straight-line depreciation that would have been claimed had the taxpayer used that method of depreciation). Straight-line depreciation that would have been claimed on the property includes the straight-line depreciation that would have been claimed by the predecessor taxpayer or on the predecessor property, as the case may be [Reg. § 1.1250-2(d)(3), § 1.1250-2(d)(4)].

The applicable percentage depends on the nature of the real property disposed of, its holding period, and the tax years in which the depreciation was claimed. A single item of § 1250 property may have more than one applicable percentage, depending on when depreciation deductions were taken. The applicable percentages are generally described in the following table [§ 1250(a)]:

| | **Years Depreciation Taken** | | |
|---|---|---|---|
| **Type of Property** | **1964-1969** | **1970-1975** | **1976-** |
| *Nonresidential Real Property* | 0%* | 100% | 100% |
| *Residential Rental Property* | 0%* | 0%* | 100% |
| *Low-Income Housing* | 0%* | 0%* | 100%, less 1% for each full month the property was held over 100 full months |
| * Certain property held longer than 120 months (or, in some cases, 200 months) has an applicable percentage of 0%. Property for which depreciation was taken in the designated years and that is disposed of currently will have been held in excess of that time period. | | | |

The holding period of § 1250 property for purposes of the applicable percentage rules is measured slightly differently than the holding period for other capital assets. The holding period generally begins with the day after the property's acquisition. For property that is constructed, reconstructed, or erected, the holding period begins on the first day of the month in which the property is placed in service. Where § 1250 property is acquired in a transaction in which the taxpayer's basis is determined by reference to the transferor's basis, the taxpayer may tack the transferor's holding period onto his or her own. If property is disposed of through foreclosure, the holding period ends on the date the foreclosure proceedings begin. A full month is the period beginning on a date in Month 1 and ending on the date before the corresponding date in Month 2 (or on the final date of Month 2, if Month 2 does not have a corresponding date) [§ 1250(d)(7), § 1250(e); Reg. § 1.1250-4].

**EXAMPLE:** Clark acquires low-income housing property on June 1, 2003. Foreclosure proceedings on the property begin on Apr. 3, 2014 (130 months after the property was acquired), and the property is ultimately disposed of as a result of the foreclosure proceedings. The applicable percentage is 70% (100% − (1% × 30 months in excess of 100 months)). Thus, 70% of the lesser of (i) additional depreciation, or (ii) the excess of amount realized (or fair market value) over adjusted basis, is subject to recapture.

The amount of depreciation recapture is determined separately for each item of § 1250 property. This includes situations where there is a single disposition of property that has two or more elements. The existence of separate elements is determined on a facts and circumstances basis. Such separate elements may include certain separate improvements made to the property or units of the property placed in service at different times [Reg. § 1.1250-1(a)(1), § 1.1250-1(a)(2)].

A taxpayer disposing of a group of assets that are part § 1250 property and part non-§ 1250 property must allocate the amount realized between the two types of property in proportion to their fair market values. When a taxpayer disposes of an item of § 1250 property that has more than one applicable percentage, the gain realized (or excess fair market value over adjusted basis) must be allocated to each portion of the item in the same proportion as the additional depreciation for each portion bears to the total additional depreciation [Reg. § 1.1250-1(a)(6)].

### III.D.4. Special Depreciation Recapture Rules

[563 T.M., III.B., IV.C.1.a(2), 565 T.M., III.C.; TPS ¶¶1760.04.C., 2950.02., 3550.08.]

*Installment Sales.* If property subject to depreciation recapture is sold in an installment sale, the taxpayer must recognize any recapture income as ordinary income in the year of the sale. Any gain in excess of the recapture income is then taken into account using the installment method [§ 453(i); Reg. § 1.1245-6(d)(1), § 1.1250-1(c)(6)]. For further discussion of installment sales, see III.G.

*Like-Kind Exchanges and Involuntary Conversions.* A like-kind exchange (see III.E.1.) or involuntary conversion (see III.E.2.) of § 1245 property or § 1250 property into similar or related property will not result in gain subject to recapture, except to the extent of gain recognized on the disposition and the fair market value of non-§ 1245 property or non-§ 1250 property acquired as replacement property [Reg. § 1.1245-4(d), § 1.1250-3(d)].

*Partnerships.* For purposes of the recapture rule, § 1245 property or § 1250 property distributed by a partnership to a partner is deemed to have the same basis to the partner as it does to the partnership. In the case of § 1245 property, in determining recomputed basis, the amount of adjustments added back for periods before the partnership's distribution is the excess of (i) the amount of recaptured gain that would have resulted had the partnership sold the property at its fair market value immediately before the distribution, over (ii) the amount of gain to which § 751(b) applied. In the case of § 1250 property, additional depreciation attributable to periods before the partnership's distribution is the excess of (i) the amount of recaptured gain that would have resulted had the partnership sold the property at its fair market value immediately before the distribution and had the applicable percentage been 100%, over (ii) the amount of gain to which § 751(b) would have applied (if any) if the applicable percentage had been 100% [§ 1245(b)(5), § 1250(d)(5)].

*Corporations.* A corporation that disposes of § 1250 property may be required to recapture additional amounts. Twenty percent of the excess of (i) the amount of gain that would be treated as ordinary income if the disposed of property was § 1245 property, over (ii) the amount treated as ordinary income under § 1250, must be recaptured as ordinary income [§ 291(a)(1)].

## III.E. Nonrecognition/Deferrals

Gain or loss is generally recognized on the sale or exchange of property [§ 1001(c)] (see III.A.). Certain transactions, though, do not require the current recognition of gain or loss, and, instead, defer the gain or loss until there is a subsequent taxable transaction. These transactions are described below.

### III.E.1. Like-Kind Exchanges

[567 T.M.; TPS ¶1510.]

No gain or loss is recognized if property held for productive use in a trade or business or for investment is exchanged solely for property of a like kind to be held for productive use in a trade or business or for investment [§ 1031(a)(1)]. Application of this rule is mandatory if a transaction qualifies as a like-kind exchange, regardless of whether a taxpayer desires nonrecognition treatment.

Qualification for nonrecognition treatment as a like-kind exchange requires the satisfaction of the following conditions:

- there must be a mutual, interdependent transfer of properties between two or more taxpayers (the exchange requirement) (see III.E.1.a.);
- the property that the taxpayer gives up must be of a like kind to that which the taxpayer receives (the like-kind property requirement) (see III.E.1.b.); and
- both the property that is given up and the property that is received must be business or investment property, and must not be excluded property (the qualifying property requirement) (see III.E.1.c.).

Unrecognized gain under the like-kind exchange rules is not a tax preference item for purposes of the alternative minimum tax. Therefore, like-kind exchanges are treated the same for alternative minimum tax purposes as for regular tax purposes.

Like-kind exchanges are reported on Form 8824, *Like-Kind Exchanges.* Any gain recognized as a result of receiving cash or unlike property is reported on Form 8949, *Sales and Other Dispositions of Capital Assets,* or Form 4797, *Sales of Business Property,* as applicable.

### III.E.1.a. The Exchange Requirement

[567 T.M., II.C.; TPS ¶1510.02.]

For nonrecognition treatment as a like-kind exchange, a transaction must constitute an exchange. Generally, this requires a reciprocal transfer of property, rather than a transfer of property solely for cash (i.e., a sale). Receipt of boot in addition to like-kind property, however, results only in the recognition of gain to the extent of the boot, rather than disqualifying the entire transaction as an exchange [§ 1031(a)(1), § 1031(b)] (see III.E.1.e.).

The transfer of the like-kind properties must be mutually dependent; the receipt of one must be conditioned upon the transfer of the other. There is no mutual dependence where one property is sold and the proceeds of the sale are used to reinvest in property of a like kind.

---

**EXAMPLE:** Jack sold a golf course to Arnold in exchange for a promissory note. Jack later agreed to buy a resort from Arnold. Arnold was unable to meet his payments to Jack under the promissory note, and Jack tried to characterize the resort as payment for the golf course. The two sales are not treated as an exchange because there was no intention to treat the transactions as an exchange at the time the original sales contracts were executed.

---

### III.E.1.b. Like-Kind Property

[567 T.M., II.F.; TPS ¶1510.03.]

Like-kind property is property of a similar nature or character, rather than a similar grade or quality [Reg. § 1.1031(a)-1(b)].

The exchange of personal property for similar personal property is an exchange of like-kind property. Depreciable tangible personal property is of a like kind to any property within the same General Asset Class or Product Class [Reg. § 1.1031(a)-2(b)(1)]. General asset classes are discussed in *Schedules & Tables 10.* Product classes are described in a six-digit product class within Sectors 31, 32, and 33 (pertaining to manufacturing industries) of the North American Industry Classification System (NAICS) [Reg. § 1.1031(a)-2(b)(3)]. Under certain circumstances, two properties can be in different General Asset Classes (and thus not be of a like class) and yet be of like kind. For example, cars, light general-purpose trucks, crossovers, sport-utility vehicles (SUVs), minivans, and cargo vans are all like-kind, even if in different asset classes.

Whether intangible personal properties (e.g., a patent or copyright) are of a like kind depends on the types of rights involved and the types of underlying properties to which the intangible personal properties relate. The goodwill or going concern value of one business is not of a like kind to the goodwill or going concern value of another business [Reg. § 1.1031(a)-2(c)]. Personal property used predominantly within the United States is not of a like kind to personal property used predominantly outside the United States (as determined based on the two-year period before the exchange, or, if the property was held for less than two years, based on the period of time the property was held) [§ 1031(h)(2)]. Livestock exchanged for livestock may be a like-kind exchange only if the animals are of the same sex [§ 1031(e)].

The exchange of real estate for real estate generally is an exchange of like-kind property. It is immaterial whether any real estate involved is improved or unimproved [Reg. § 1.1031(a)-1(b)]. Real property located in the United States is not of a like kind to real property located outside the United States [§ 1031(h)(1)]. The exchange of a fee interest in real estate for a lease of real estate with a remaining term of at least 30 years qualifies for like-kind treatment [Reg. § 1.1031(a)-1(c)].

### III.E.1.c. Qualifying Property

[567 T.M., II.D., III.; TPS ¶1510.04., .05., .06.]

To qualify for nonrecognition treatment as a like-kind exchange, both the property transferred and the property received must be held for the productive use in a trade or business or for investment purposes. Property held for productive use in a trade or business may be exchanged for like-kind property to be held for investment, and vice versa [§ 1031(a); Reg. § 1.1031(a)-1(a)].

The following kinds of property are excluded from eligibility for nonrecognition [§ 1031(a)(2); Reg. § 1.1031(a)-1(a)(1)]:

- stock in trade or other property held primarily for sale;
- stock, bonds, or notes;
- other securities or evidences of indebtedness or interest;
- interests in a partnership;
- certificates of trust or beneficial interests; and
- choses in action.

### III.E.1.d. Deferred Like-Kind Exchanges

[567 T.M., VI., VII.; TPS ¶1510.09.A., .11.]

*Starker Exchanges.* A non-simultaneous exchange may still qualify for nonrecognition treatment. Often referred to as a "Starker exchange" for the court decision that first directly considered delayed like-kind exchanges, a deferred exchange occurs when a taxpayer transfers property to another party in exchange for that party's promise to transfer like-kind property to the taxpayer on a future date [*Starker v. United States*, 602 F.2d 1341 (9th Cir. 1979)]. If the underlying properties would otherwise qualify for like-kind exchange treatment, the following two additional conditions must be satisfied [§ 1031(a)(3); Reg. § 1.1031(k)-1]:

- The replacement property must be identified on or before the 45th day after the taxpayer transferred his property; and
- The identified property must actually be received by the taxpayer by the earlier of (i) the 180th day after the taxpayer transferred his property, or (ii) the due date (including extensions) for filing the taxpayer's tax return for the year in which the taxpayer transferred his property.

Identification of replacement property requires designation in a written document signed by the taxpayer and delivered to the person obligated to transfer the property or any other person involved in the exchange, other than the taxpayer or a disqualified person (as defined in Reg. § 1.1031(k)-1(k)). The replacement property must be unambiguously described in the written document [Reg. § 1.1031(k)-1(c)].

A taxpayer may recognize gain or loss if he or she actually or constructively receives money or other property before actually receiving like-kind replacement property. If a taxpayer actually or constructively receives money or other property in the full amount of the consideration for the relinquished property before receiving the like-kind replacement property, the transaction is considered a sale and not a like-kind exchange, even though the taxpayer may ultimately receive like-kind property.

The IRS has established safe harbors under which a taxpayer is not considered to be in constructive receipt of the money or other property. These include [Reg. § 1.1031(k)-1(g)]:

- security or guarantee arrangements;
- qualified escrow accounts and qualified trusts;
- qualified intermediaries; and
- interest and growth factors.

*Reverse-Starker Exchanges.* A reverse-Starker exchange occurs where the taxpayer receives the replacement property *before* transferring the relinquished property to the other party. The regulations applicable to Starker exchanges are explicitly inapplicable to reverse-Starker exchanges. However, a safe harbor exists for so-called "parking arrangements," under which the IRS will not challenge (i) the qualification of property as either replacement property or relinquished property (as defined in Reg. § 1.1031(k)-1(a)), or (ii) the treatment of the exchange accommodation titleholder (EAT) as the beneficial owner of the property for tax purposes if the property is held in a qualified exchange accommodation arrangement (QEAA) [Rev. Proc. 2000-37, 2000-40 I.R.B. 308].

A parking arrangement is a device that may be used to avoid a direct reverse exchange of property. Under the parking arrangement safe harbor, an EAT can acquire the replacement property, hold it for up to 180 days until a buyer is found for the relinquishment property, and then transfer it to the taxpayer in a like-kind exchange. Alternatively, the taxpayer can currently acquire the replacement property in a like-kind exchange, and the EAT can hold the relinquished property up to 180 days until a buyer is found.

Several requirements must be satisfied for property to qualify under the safe harbor and be considered held in a QEAA. The EAT must not be a disqualified person (as defined in Reg. § 1.1031(k)-1(k)), and he or she must be a person who is subject to federal income tax (or if the EAT is a partnership or an S corporation, more than 90% of its interests or stock must be owned by such persons). The EAT need not hold legal title, but he or she must have indicia of ownership of the property that are treated as beneficial ownership under principles of commercial law (e.g., a contract for deed). Within five days after the transfer of qualified indicia of ownership of the replacement property to the EAT, the taxpayer and the EAT must enter into a QEAA that provides that the EAT is holding the property for the benefit of the taxpayer in order to facilitate a like-kind exchange. Within 45 days after the transfer of qualified indicia of ownership of the replacement property to the EAT, the relinquished property must be properly identified. Identification must be made in the same manner as the identification of replacement property in a Starker exchange, discussed above [Rev. Proc. 2000-37, 2000-40 I.R.B. 308].

The safe harbor does not apply to replacement property held in a QEAA if the property is owned by the taxpayer within the 180-day period ending on the date of transfer of qualified indicia of ownership of the property to an EAT. Thus, a taxpayer may not treat as a like-kind exchange a transaction in which the taxpayer transfers property to an EAT and receives the same property as replacement property in a purported exchange for other property of the taxpayer [Rev. Proc. 2000-37, 2000-40 I.R.B. 308; Rev. Proc. 2004-51, 2004-33 I.R.B. 294].

### III.E.1.e. *Boot and Basis in a Like-Kind Exchange*

[567 T.M., IX., X.; TPS ¶1510.07., .08.]

No gain or loss is recognized in a transaction that satisfies the requirements of a like-kind exchange [§ 1031(a)]. Gain or loss is deferred until there is a subsequent taxable transaction. However, nonrecognition treatment applies only to qualifying property exchanged solely for other qualifying property. An exchange that otherwise qualifies as a like-kind exchange but includes the transfer of cash or other boot is partially taxable.

A taxpayer that transfers non-cash boot along with like-kind property must recognize gain or loss on the difference between the boot's fair market value and its basis [§ 1001(a); Reg. § 1.1031(a)-1(a)(2)]. A taxpayer receiving cash or non-cash boot with like-kind property must recognize gain, but not in excess of the cash and fair market value of the non-cash boot received. Loss on such an exchange may not be recognized [§ 1031(b), § 1031(c); Reg. § 1.1031(b)-1(a), § 1.1031(c)-1]. Certain exchange expenses (e.g., brokerage commissions) may be used by the relinquishing party to reduce the amount realized in a like kind exchange [Rev. Rul. 72-456, 1972-2 C.B. 233].

---

**EXAMPLE:** Louis owns Blackacre, which has a fair market value of $11,000 and an adjusted basis of $8,000. He exchanges it for Whiteacre, which has a fair market value of $10,000, and $1,000 cash. Louis realizes $3,000 of gain ($11,000 amount realized − $8,000 basis in Blackacre), but only the $1,000 cash must be recognized and included in income. Had Louis's adjusted basis in Blackacre been $10,500, his gain realized would have been $500 ($11,000 − $10,500), and thus, only $500 of the cash received would have to be recognized and included in income.

---

The basis of property received in a like-kind exchange is the same as the basis of the property transferred. This amount is then decreased by the amount of (i) any cash received and (ii) any loss recognized in the exchange, and increased by the amount of (i) any gain recognized, (ii) any additional consideration paid in the exchange, and (iii) certain exchange expenses (e.g., brokerage fees) [§ 1031(d); Reg. § 1.1031(d)-1(a); Rev. Rul. 72-456, 1972-2 C.B. 233].

If the other party to the exchange assumes a liability of the taxpayer, the taxpayer is treated as having received cash. The taxpayer's assumption of a liability of the other party is treated as an additional cost incurred [§ 1031(d)].

---

**EXAMPLE:** Kristen uses Car 1, which has a fair market value of $10,000 and an adjusted basis of $5,000, in her trade or business. She exchanges Car 1 and $3,000 for Car 2, which has a fair market value of $13,000. Kristen realizes $5,000 of gain ($13,000 amount realized – ($5,000 basis in Car 1 + $3,000 cash)), but does not recognize any income. Kristen's adjusted basis in Car 2 going forward is $8,000 ($5,000 basis in Car 1 + $3,000 additional consideration paid in the exchange).

**EXAMPLE:** Gray exchanges investment property with an adjusted basis of $50,000 and a fair market value of $80,000 for other investment property with a fair market value of $60,000 and $20,000 cash. Gray's realized gain is $30,000 ($60,000 fair market value of property received + $20,000 cash received − $50,000 basis of property transferred). Of that amount, the $20,000 of cash must be recognized. Gray's basis in the new property is $50,000 ($50,000 basis of the old property − $20,000 cash received + $20,000 gain recognized).

---

If two or more like-kind properties are received in an exchange, the taxpayer's basis is allocated among the properties in proportion to their fair market values. If both like-kind property and boot are received in an exchange, the taxpayer's basis is first allocated to the boot in an amount equal to the boot's fair market value at the time of the exchange, and then to the like-kind property [Reg. § 1.1031(d)-1(c)].

### III.E.1.f. Like-Kind Exchanges Between Related Parties
[567 T.M., II.C.9., II.E.; TPS ¶1510.02.D.]

Because of the potential to shift income, special rules apply to exchanges between related parties. Exchanges between related taxpayers (as defined in § 1031(f)(3)) generally are ineligible for nonrecognition if the property is disposed of within two years of the exchange. However, this rule does not apply to dispositions (i) by reason of the death of either party, (ii) by reason of the compulsory or involuntary conversion of the exchanged property if the exchange occurred before the threat or imminence of the conversion, or (iii) where the IRS acknowledges that neither the exchange nor the disposition had a principal purpose of tax avoidance [§ 1031(f)]. Nonrecognition treatment is completely denied for any exchange that is part of a transaction (or series of transactions) structured to avoid the purposes of these related party rules. For any period where the property holder's risk of loss for the property is substantially diminished by (i) the holding of a put with respect to the property, (ii) another person's holding of a right to acquire the property, or (iii) a short sale or other transaction, the two-year period is tolled [§ 1031(g)].

---

**EXAMPLE:** Pursuant to a prearranged plan, Angie makes a gift of Whiteacre to her cousin, Barbara. Within a year, Barbara exchanges Whiteacre with Angie's mother, Catherine, for Blueacre. Barbara then makes a gift of Blueacre to Angie, who immediately sells Blueacre. The exchange between Barbara and Catherine is not entitled to nonrecognition treatment because of the anti-avoidance rule.

---

### III.E.2. Involuntary Conversions

[568 T.M.; TPS ¶1520.]

If property is compulsorily or involuntarily converted as a result of its destruction, theft, seizure, requisition, or condemnation (or threat or imminence of requisition or condemnation), recognition of the gain realized from the conversion may be deferred. The deferral is mandatory if the property is directly converted into property that is similar or related in service or use to the converted property. The deferral may be elected if the taxpayer receives insurance proceeds or a condemnation award as compensation for the conversion and uses the money to purchase qualified replacement property within a certain amount of time [§ 1033]. Losses from an involuntary conversion may be recognized if allowable under another provision of the Code, for example losses on property used in a trade or business or for the production of income (see III.C.1.), or losses on personal use property as a result of casualty or theft (see VIII.H.1.).

Deferred gain under the involuntary conversion rules is not a tax preference item for purposes of the alternative minimum tax. Therefore, involuntary conversions are treated the same for alternative minimum tax purposes as for regular tax purposes.

Gain or loss from casualty and theft is reported on Form 4684, *Casualties and Thefts*. Gain or loss on the involuntary conversion (other than by casualty or theft) of property used in a trade or business and capital assets held in connection with a trade or business or a transaction entered into for profit is reported on Form 4797, *Sales of Business Property*. Form 4797 is also used for gain from a casualty or theft on trade, business, or income-producing property held for more than one year for which the taxpayer must recapture gain as ordinary income. Gain on the involuntary conversion (other than by casualty or theft) of personal-use property is reported on Form 8949, *Sales and Other Dispositions of Capital Assets*.

### III.E.2.a. Conversion into Similar or Related Use Property

[568 T.M., III.; TPS ¶1520.08.A.]

Nonrecognition of gain is required where property is converted directly into property similar or related in use. Similar property is generally property that is functionally similar and has the same uses as the converted property. The treatment of a loss on a direct conversion depends on whether the replacement property qualifies as like-kind property under § 1031 (see III.E.1.b.). If so, § 1031 mandates nonrecognition of the loss. If the property is not like-kind property, recognition of the loss is mandatory and may potentially be used to offset gain.

If the like-kind exchange rules do not apply to the transaction, a taxpayer's basis in the replacement property is the same as his or her basis in the converted property, decreased by the amount of (i) any loss recognized on the conversion, and (ii) any money received on the conversion that was not expended in the acquisition of replacement property, and increased by the amount of (i) any gain recognized on the conversion, and (ii) any additional cash spent [§ 1033(a)(1), § 1033(b)(1); Reg. § 1.1033(b)-1(a)]. The holding period of the replacement property includes the holding period of the converted property [§ 1223(1)(A)].

---

**EXAMPLE:** Roger owns an asset with a fair market value of $500 and a basis of $100. The asset is destroyed in a fire and Roger's insurance company exercises its option under the policy to replace the asset with an asset of similar use and value and that is also of a like kind. The new asset has a fair market value of $500. Roger does not recognize any of the $400 gain ($500 amount realized − $100 basis in the converted property) realized on the conversion. The basis in the replacement property is $100, the same as the basis of the converted property. Alternatively, if (i) Roger's basis in the converted property had been $1,000, (ii) the replacement property had not been of a like-kind for purposes of § 1031, and (iii) the property had been used in Roger's trade or business, the $500 loss ($500 amount realized − $1,000 basis) would have been allowable as an ordinary loss deduction under § 1231. Roger's basis in the replacement property would have been $500 ($1,000 basis in the converted property − $500 loss recognized).

---

### III.E.2.b. Conversion into Money or Dissimilar Property

[568 T.M., IV.; TPS ¶1520.08.B.]

If a taxpayer's property is involuntarily converted into cash or unlike property, and if the taxpayer either (i) does not purchase, or does not satisfy the rules for purchasing, qualified replacement property, or (ii) does not properly elect nonrecognition treatment for qualified replacement property, gain is recognized [§ 1033(a)(2)].

Where a valid election is made and the taxpayer satisfies all of the necessary conditions, gain realized on the conversion is recognized only to the extent the amount realized exceeds the cost of the replacement property. The taxpayer's basis in the replacement property is its cost, decreased by the amount of any gain not recognized [§ 1033(a)(2)(A), § 1033(b)(2)].

The holding period of any replacement property begins on the date of acquisition.

---

**EXAMPLE:** Rudy owns an asset with a fair market value of $500 and a basis of $100. The asset is destroyed in a fire and Rudy receives $500 from her insurance company. She purchases qualified replacement property for $350. Rudy must realizes $400 of gain ($500 amount received − $100 basis) and must recognize $150 of it ($500 amount realized − $350 cost of replacement property). Rudy's basis in the new asset is $100 ($350 cost − $250 gain not recognized).

---

If a taxpayer receives unlike property, rather than cash, as conversion proceeds, the taxpayer recognizes gain or loss on the receipt of the unlike property and takes a cost basis in such property [§ 1012].

### III.E.2.c. Qualified Replacement Property

[568 T.M., VII.; TPS ¶1520.04.]

For the involuntary conversion nonrecognition rules to apply, a taxpayer must purchase qualifying replacement property that is similar or related in service or use to the converted property. In applying the similar or related in service test, consideration will be given to (i) whether the properties are of a similar service to the taxpayer, (ii) the nature of the business risks connected with the properties, and (iii) what the properties demand of the taxpayer in the way of management, services, and relations to tenants [Rev. Rul. 64-237, 1964-2 C.B. 319]. In general, the following categories of replacement property may qualify:

- similar use property [§ 1033(a)(1), § 1033(a)(2)];
- stock in the acquisition of control (80% of the total combined voting power of all voting classes of stock and 80% of the total shares of all other classes of stock) of a corporation owning similar use property [§ 1033(a)(2)];
- property that is like-kind, in the case of the condemnation of business or investment real property [§ 1033(g)]; and
- farm property, if drought, flood, or other weather-related conditions, or soil contamination, or other environmental contamination make it infeasible for a taxpayer to reinvest proceeds in involuntarily converted livestock [§ 1033(f)].

If a taxpayer's property that is held for productive use in a trade or business or for investment is compulsorily or involuntarily converted as a result of a federally declared disaster, tangible property of a type that is held for productive use in a trade or business will be treated as similar use property [§ 1033(h)(2)].

In most cases, the taxpayer must replace the converted property within two years after the close of the first tax year in which the taxpayer realizes any part of the gain upon the conversion. For condemned real property used in a trade or business or held for investment, the replacement period is extended to three years. If a taxpayer's principal residence or its contents are converted as a result of a federally declared disaster, the replacement period is extended to four years [§ 1033(a)(2)(B)(i), § 1033(g)(4), § 1033(h)(1)(B)]. Upon taxpayer request to an IRS Area Director, the IRS may extend the replacement period. A taxpayer should generally make such a request before the expiration of the replacement period, and the request should include all the details in connection with the involuntary conversion [§ 1033(a)(2)(B)(ii); Reg. § 1.1033(a)-2(c)(3)].

### III.E.2.d. Electing Nonrecognition for Replacement Property

[568 T.M., VI.; TPS ¶1520.09.]

A taxpayer that purchases qualified replacement property elects to defer gain on the involuntary conversion by excluding some or all of the gain on his or her tax return in the year realized. No affirmative statement of election is required, however, the taxpayer must provide on the tax return all details in connection with an involuntary conversion of property at a gain. This includes information on what replacement property was acquired, when it was acquired, and the cost to acquire it [Reg. § 1.1033(a)-2(c)(2)].

### III.E.2.e. Special Involuntary Conversion Rules

[568 T.M., II.D., VI.C., VII.C.3., VIII.G.; TPS ¶1520.03.E., .03.F., .04.E.3., .04.G., .04.H.]

***Principal Residences.*** An individual that realizes gain on the involuntary conversion of his or her principal residence may exclude up to $250,000 ($500,000 for married taxpayers filing jointly) of that gain from gross income [§ 121(d)(5)] (see

II.N.6.). If a taxpayer's residence or any of its contents is compulsorily or involuntarily converted as a result of a federally declared disaster, no gain is recognized on the receipt of insurance proceeds for unscheduled personal property that was part of the contents of the residence. Any other insurance proceeds received for the residence or its contents may be treated as received for the conversion of a single item of property (i.e., treated as a common pool of funds). If this pool of funds is used to purchase any property that is similar or related in service or use to the converted residence or its contents, the taxpayer may elect to limit gain recognition to the extent that the amount of the pool of funds exceeds the cost of the replacement property. The replacement period is four years [§ 1033(h)(1)]. For a discussion of nonrecognition transactions upon the sale of a principal residence, see III.E.3.

*Outdoor Advertising Displays.* Taxpayers may elect to treat outdoor advertising displays permanently affixed to the ground or permanently attached to a building or other structure as real property if the taxpayer has not elected to expense the cost of the display. Thus, an interest in real property purchased as replacement property for an involuntarily converted advertising display is considered to be of a like kind to the converted property. The taxpayer must attach a statement clearly indicating the election is being made to a timely filed return (including extensions) for the first tax year to which the election is to apply [§ 1033(g)(3); Reg. § 1.1033(g)-1(b)].

*Livestock.* If livestock are destroyed by or on account of disease, or are sold or exchanged because of disease, the disposition is treated as an involuntary conversion. Exposure to the disease, rather than actual contraction, is sufficient for this purpose [§ 1033(d); Reg. § 1.1033(d)-1(a)]. If a taxpayer sells or exchanges livestock (other than poultry) held for draft, breeding, or dairy purposes solely on account of drought, flood, or other weather-related conditions, the disposition is an involuntary conversion to the extent the sales or exchanges exceed the level of sales or exchanges that would have occurred in the normal course of the taxpayer's business. If the livestock dies before they can be sold, the involuntary conversion rules do not apply. Replacement livestock must be functionally the same as the converted livestock. Thus, dairy cows may replace dairy cows, but draft animals may not replace breeding or dairy animals [§ 1033(e); Reg. § 1.1033(e)-1]. If purchasing replacement livestock is infeasible because of drought, flood, or other weather conditions, or soil contamination or other environmental contamination, the converted livestock may be replaced with other farm property [§ 1033(f)].

*Replacement Property Acquired from Related Persons.* In the case of (i) a C corporation, (ii) a partnership in which one or more C corporations own (directly or indirectly) more than 50% of the capital interests or profits interests at the time of the involuntary conversion, or (iii) any other taxpayer if the aggregate amount of gain realized on involuntarily converted property for the tax year exceeds $100,000, nonrecognition treatment is disallowed if replacement property is acquired from a related person (as defined in § 1033(i)(3)) However, replacement property acquired from a related person qualifies for nonrecognition treatment if the related person acquired the property from an unrelated person during the replacement period for the involuntarily converted property [§ 1033(i)].

### III.E.3. Sale of Principal Residence

[594 T.M., IV., V.; TPS ¶1530.]

Taxpayers may generally exclude from gross income gain realized from the sale or exchange of property if, during the five-year period ending on the date of the sale or exchange, the taxpayer owned and used the property as his or her principal residence for a period of at least two years, in the aggregate. The amount of the exclusion is generally limited to $250,000 ($500,000 for certain married taxpayers filing jointly, or certain sales by surviving spouses) [§ 121(a); Reg. § 1.121-1(a)].

The exclusion is available each time a taxpayer meets the eligibility requirements, but no more frequently than once every two years. A taxpayer, however, may elect not to have the exclusion provision apply to a sale or exchange [§ 121(b)(3), § 121(f); Reg. § 1.121-2(b), § 1.121-4(g)].

The principal residence exclusion is neither an adjustment made to taxable income nor a tax preference item for purposes of the alternative minimum tax. Therefore, there are no alternative minimum tax consequences to the use of the exclusion.

A taxpayer that (i) has gain that he or she cannot exclude (or that he or she has elected not to exclude), (ii) received a Form 1099-S, or (iii) has a deductible loss, must report the sale on Form 8949, *Sales and Other Dispositions of Capital Assets.* The taxpayer must report the sale or exchange as if he or she was not taking the exclusion, and then must enter the amount of excluded gain as an adjustment, along with the appropriate code for the adjustment indicated in the instructions to Form 8949. A taxpayer that has a loss on the sale of his or her principal residence for which he or she receives a Form 1099-S must report the sale on Form 8949, even though the loss is not deductible because it is not incurred in a trade or business or in a transaction entered into for profit [§ 165(c)]. A taxpayer that used the home for business or to produce rental income must report the sale on Form 4797, *Sale of Business Property.*

### III.E.3.a. Definition of Principal Residence

[594 T.M., IV.D.; TPS ¶1530.01.B.]

Whether a taxpayer uses property as a residence is determined under a facts and circumstances test. A residence may include a houseboat, a house trailer, or the house or apartment a taxpayer is entitled to occupy as a tenant-shareholder in a cooperative housing corporation. It does not include personal property that is not a fixture under local law [Reg. § 1.121-1(b)(1)]. The determination of a taxpayer's principal residence is also a facts and circumstances test. Relevant factors include the following [Reg. § 1.121-1(b)(2)]:

- the taxpayer's place of employment;
- the principal place of abode of the taxpayer's family members;
- the address listed on the taxpayer's federal and state tax returns, driver's license, automobile registration, and voter registration;
- the taxpayer's mailing address for bills and correspondence;
- the location of the taxpayer's banks; and
- the location of the taxpayer's religious organization and recreational clubs.

Vacant land may qualify as a principal residence for purposes of the principal residence exclusion if all of the following conditions are met [Reg. § 1.121-1(b)(3)(i)]:

1. the vacant land is adjacent to the land containing the dwelling unit of the taxpayer's principal residence;
2. the taxpayer owned and used the vacant land as part of the taxpayer's principal residence;
3. the taxpayer sells or exchanges the dwelling unit in a sale or exchange within two years before or after the date of the sale or exchange of the vacant land; and
4. the taxpayer owned and used the land for two years within the five-year period ending on the date of the sale or exchange.

For purposes of the maximum exclusion amount (see III.E.3.c.), the sale or exchange of the dwelling unit and the vacant land are treated as one sale or exchange. In applying the rule prohibiting more than one excludible sale or exchange within two years (see III.E.3.c.), each transaction is disregarded with respect to the other transaction. Thus, separate sales of a dwelling unit and qualifying vacant land, alone, will not run afoul of the rule. However, the transactions are taken into account in applying the rule to the sale or exchange of any other principal residence. [Reg. § 1.121-1(b)(3)(ii)].

### III.E.3.b. Period of Ownership and Use of a Principal Residence

[594 T.M., IV.C.; TPS ¶1530.01.F.]

To qualify for the exclusion, a taxpayer must own and use a property as a principal residence for a period aggregating at least two years over the five year period ending with the sale or exchange. Occupancy of the residence is required for this purpose. Short temporary absences (e.g., vacations), though, will still count as periods of use [Reg. § 1.121-1(c)(2)(i)].

Periods during which the taxpayer resides in a facility (including a nursing home) licensed by a state or political subdivision to care for an individual in the taxpayer's condition may qualify as periods of use where the taxpayer [§ 121(d)(7); Reg. § 1.121-1(c)(2)(ii)]:

1. becomes physically or mentally incapable of self-care; and

2. owns property and uses such property as a principal residence for periods aggregating at least one year during the five-year testing period.

The ownership and use period of an unmarried taxpayer whose spouse is deceased includes the period for which the taxpayer's deceased spouse owned and used the property for purposes of the principal residence exclusion [§ 121(d)(2); Reg. § 1.121-4(a)(1)]. Additionally, a taxpayer's ownership and use period includes the holding period of a spouse or former spouse where such property is transferred incident to a divorce, as well as any period in which the taxpayer owns the property and the spouse or former spouse is granted use of the property under a divorce or separation instrument [§ 121(d)(3); Reg. § 1.121-4(b)]. Members of the uniformed services and the foreign service may elect to toll the five-year testing period for any period that individual or that individual's spouse is serving on qualified official extended duty [§ 121(d)(9)].

### III.E.3.c. Limitations on Exclusion of Gain from Sale of Principal Residence

[594 T.M., IV.B., IV.E.; TPS ¶1530.01.C.]

**Joint Returns.** Generally, the amount of gain that may be excluded from gross income is limited to $250,000 per qualifying transaction. The limitation is increased to $500,000 for married taxpayers filing jointly if (i) either spouse meets the ownership requirement, (ii) both spouses meet the aggregate use requirement, and (iii) neither spouse excluded gain from the sale of a former principal residence under the exclusion rule during the two years preceding the sale. If a couple fails to meet these requirements, the amount of the exclusion they may claim is the sum of each spouse's maximum exclusion determined separately and as if they were not married, with each spouse being treated as owning (but not necessarily using) the principal residence during the period that either spouse owned the property [§ 121(b); Reg. § 1.121-2(a)].

**EXAMPLE:** Bob and Lisa are married and file a joint return. They have both used a house Bob has owned for six years as their principal residence for the past three years. Bob purchased the home for $200,000. He and Lisa decide to sell the home for $650,000. They may exclude the $450,000 gain on the sale, even though Bob is the sole owner. Had Bob and Lisa not been married and had Lisa only used the home as her principal residence for one year, they would have been able to exclude $375,000 of the gain on the sale. Bob would have been entitled to the full $250,000 exclusion because he both owned and used the residence for two years over the last five years. Lisa would have been entitled to a prorated $125,000 exclusion because she is treated as owning the residence for the required two years (Bob's ownership period), but she only uses the residence for one year. Thus, because her use of the residence is half of the required amount, Lisa's exclusion is prorated by 50% to $125,000.

Where joint filers do not share a principal residence, an exclusion of $250,000 is available on a qualifying sale or exchange of the residence of one of the spouses. The rule limiting the exclusion to only one sale every two years does not prevent a married couple from filing a joint return with each spouse excluding up to $250,000 of gain from the sale or exchange of each spouse's principal residence, provided that each spouse would be permitted to exclude up to $250,000 of gain if they filed separate returns. If a single taxpayer who is otherwise eligible for the exclusion marries someone who previously used the exclusion within the prior two years, the first taxpayer remains eligible for a maximum exclusion of $250,000 [§ 121(d)(1)].

**EXAMPLE:** Dave and Sara are married and file a joint return. Dave has owned a house for six years and has used it as his principal residence for the entirety of that time. Sara has owned a house for 10 years and has used it as her principal residence for the entirety of that time. They decide to sell both residences and purchase one home together. Dave and Sara may exclude up to $250,000 of gain from the sale of their principal residences provided that each spouse would be permitted to exclude that amount if they filed separate returns.

***Dispositions Caused by Employment, Health, or Unforeseen Circumstances.***
A taxpayer that fails to qualify for the exclusion (either because they fail to meet the ownership and use requirements or have used the exclusion within two years of selling their current home) due to a change in place of employment, health, or other unforeseen circumstances may still exclude gain up to a fraction of the maximum exclusion limitation. In such a case, the exclusion limitation is equal to the full amount of the exclusion limitation ($250,000 or $500,000, as the case may be), multiplied by a fraction. The numerator of the fraction is the shortest of the following periods [§ 121(c); Reg. § 1.121-3(g)]:

- the time that the taxpayer owned the property during the five-year period ending with the sale or exchange;
- the time that the taxpayer used the property as a principal residence during the five-year period ending with the sale or exchange; or
- the time between the date of a prior sale or exchange for which the taxpayer used the principal residence exclusion and the date of the current sale or exchange.

142

The denominator of the fraction is two years, which may be expressed as either 730 days or 24 months, depending on the measure of time used in the numerator [§ 121(c); Reg. § 1.121-3(g)].

---

**EXAMPLE:** Dexter purchases a house that he uses as his principal residence. Twelve months after purchase, Dexter sells the house due to a change in the place of his employment. He has not excluded gain on the sale of a principal residence within the last two years. Dexter is eligible to exclude up to $125,000 ($250,000 full amount of the exclusion × (12 months of ownership and use ÷ 24 months)) of gain on the sale of the house.

---

The fractional exclusion is available only if the primary reason for the sale or exchange is a change in the place of employment, health, or unforeseen circumstances, or if a safe harbor is met. Whether the primary reason test is satisfied depends upon all the facts and circumstances. Relevant factors include the following [Reg. § 1.121-3(b)]:

- whether the sale or exchange and the circumstances giving rise to the sale or exchange are proximate in time;
- whether the suitability of the property as the taxpayer's principal residence materially changes;
- whether the taxpayer's financial ability to maintain the property materially changes;
- whether the taxpayer uses the property as a residence during the period of his or her ownership of the property;
- whether the circumstances giving rise to the sale or exchange are not reasonably foreseeable when the taxpayer begins using the property as a principal residence; and
- whether the circumstances giving rise to the sale or exchange occur during the period of the taxpayer's ownership and use of the property as a principal residence.

A sale or exchange is due to a change in the place of employment if the primary reason for the sale or exchange is a change in the location of employment for a qualified individual. A qualified individual includes the taxpayer, the taxpayer's spouse, a co-owner of the residence, or a person whose principal place of abode is in the same household as the taxpayer. A safe harbor provides that a sale or exchange is deemed due to a change in place of employment if the change occurs during the period of the taxpayer's ownership and use of the property as a principal residence, and the qualified individual's new place of employment is at least 50 miles farther from the residence sold or exchanged than was the former place of employment (or the residence sold or exchanged if there was no former place of employment) [Reg. § 1.121-3(c), § 1.121-3(f)].

A sale or exchange is due to health if the primary reason for the sale or exchange is to obtain, provide, or facilitate the diagnosis, cure, mitigation, or treatment of disease, illness, or injury for a qualified individual, or to obtain or provide medical or personal care for a qualified individual suffering from a disease, illness, or injury. A qualified individual includes the taxpayer, the taxpayer's spouse, a co-owner of the residence, a person whose principal place of abode is in the same household as the taxpayer, or certain family members of these individuals. A safe harbor provides that a sale or exchange is deemed due to health if a physician recommends the change of residence [Reg. § 1.121-3(d), § 1.121-3(f)].

A sale or exchange is due to unforeseen circumstances if the primary reason for the sale or exchange is the occurrence of an event that the taxpayer could not reasonably have anticipated before purchasing and occupying the residence. A safe harbor provides that a sale or exchange is deemed due to unforeseen circumstances if any of the following events occur during the taxpayer's ownership and use of the property as a principal residence [Reg. § 1.121-3(e), § 1.121-3(f)]:

- the involuntary conversion of the residence;
- a natural or man-made disaster or act of war or terrorism resulting in a casualty to the residence;
- in the case of a qualified individual (the taxpayer, the taxpayer's spouse, a co-owner of the residence, or a person whose principal place of abode is in the same household as the taxpayer), (i) death, (ii) cessation of employment as a result of which the qualified individual is eligible for unemployment compensation, (iii) a change in employment or self-employment status that results in the taxpayer's inability to pay housing costs and reasonable basis living expenses for the taxpayer's household, (iv) divorce or legal separation, or (v) multiple births resulting from the same pregnancy; or
- any other event or situation the IRS designates as an unforeseen circumstance.

*Gain Attributable to Nonqualified Use.* Gain from the sale or exchange of a principal residence allocated to periods of nonqualified use is not excluded from income. A period of nonqualified use is any period after 2008 during which the taxpayer, or the taxpayer's spouse or former spouse, does not use the property as a principal residence. Nonqualified use does not include the following [§ 121(b)(4)[5]]:

- any portion of the five-year testing period that is after the last date the property is used as the taxpayer's or taxpayer's spouse's principal residence;
- any period (not exceeding 10 years in the aggregate) during which the taxpayer serves on qualified official extended duty as a member of the uniformed services, the U.S. foreign service, or an employee of the intelligence community; or
- any period (not exceeding two years in the aggregate) that the taxpayer is temporarily absent because of a change in place of employment, health, or other unforeseen circumstances.

The amount of gain allocated to periods of nonqualified use is the amount of gain multiplied by a fraction, the numerator of which is the aggregate periods of nonqualified use during the period the taxpayer owned the property, and the denominator of which is the period the taxpayer owned the property.

Gain attributable to depreciation deductions allowed for periods after May 6, 1997, cannot be excluded from income, and such gain is not accounted for in determining the amount of gain allocated to nonqualified use [§ 121(b)(4)[5](D), § 121(d)(6); Reg. § 1.121-1(d)].

---

**EXAMPLE:** Jessie buys a property on Jan. 1 of Year 1 (a year after 2008) for $400,000. She uses it as a rental property for two years, claiming $20,000 of depreciation deductions and reducing the property's basis to $380,000. On Jan. 1 of Year 3, Jessie converts the property to her principal residence. She moves out on Jan. 1 of Year 5 and sells the property for $700,000 on Jan. 1 of Year 6. The total gain on the sale is $320,000 ($700,000 amount realized − $380,000 basis). The $20,000 attributable to the depreciation deductions is included in ordinary income pursuant to § 1250, and the remaining $300,000 is used to calculate gain attributable to nonqualified use. $120,000 ($300,000 gain × (2 years of nonqualified use ÷ 5 years of ownership)) is allocated to nonqualified use and is ineligible for the principal residence exclusion. The remaining $180,000 of gain is less than the exclusion limitation applicable to Jessie, and, assuming she otherwise qualifies, she may exclude that amount from gross income.

*Nonresidential Use and Depreciation.* The principal residence exclusion does not apply to gain allocable to any portion of sold or exchanged property that is separate from the dwelling unit and for the taxpayer does not satisfy the ownership and use requirement. Thus, if a portion of a property was used for residential purposes and another portion that is separate from the dwelling unit was used for nonresidential purposes, only the gain allocable to the residential portion is excludible. Allocations of basis and amount realized must be allocated between the residential and nonresidential portions using the same method of allocation the taxpayer used to determine depreciation adjustments, if applicable. Where the residential and nonresidential portions are within the same dwelling unit, no allocation is required and the entire amount of the gain is excludible, provided the taxpayer otherwise qualifies for the exclusion [Reg. § 1.121-1(e)]. Gain attributable to depreciation deductions allowed for periods after May 6, 1997, cannot be excluded from income [§ 121(d)(6)].

**EXAMPLE:** Terry, an attorney, buys a house in Year 1 (a year after 1997). The house is a single dwelling unit, but Terry uses a portion of the house as his law office. He claims depreciation deductions of $2,000 during the period he owns the house. In Year 5, Terry sells the house and realizes a gain of $13,000. He has no other § 1231 gains or losses or capital gains or losses for Year 5. Terry must recognize $2,000 of the gain as unrecaptured § 1250 gain. If Terry otherwise qualifies for the principal residence exclusion, he may exclude the remaining $11,000 of gain because gain does not have to be allocated to the business use portion of the property where the residential and nonresidential portions are within the same dwelling unit.

*Sale of Principal Residence Acquired in Like-Kind Exchange.* If a taxpayer acquires property in a like-kind exchange (see III.E.1.), the principal residence exclusion will not apply to a sale or exchange of the property that occurs within the five years following the acquisition [§ 121(d)(10)].

### III.E.3.d. Special Principal Residence Sale Rules

[594 T.M., IV.C., IV.G., IV.H.; TPS ¶1530.01.G., .01.H., .01.I., .01.J.]

*Cooperative Housing Corporation Stock.* A taxpayer who sells or exchanges stock in a cooperative housing corporation is eligible to exclude gain realized from such disposition if, for the five-year period ending with the sale or exchange, the taxpayer has owned the stock and has owned and used the property as his or her principal residence for a period aggregating at least two years. The amount of the exclusion is limited to the extent of gain realized on the unit that the taxpayer was entitled to occupy as a tenant-stockholder [§ 121(d)(4); Reg. § 1.121-4(c)].

*Involuntary Conversions.* If the basis of property acquired as a result of an involuntary conversion is determined under the involuntary conversion rules, then for purposes of the principal residence exclusion, the taxpayer is treated as owning and using the acquired property as his or her principal residence during any period of time that the taxpayer owned and used the converted property as his or her principal residence [§ 121(d)(5); Reg. § 1.121-4(d)]. For further discussion of involuntary conversions, see III.E.2.

*Sales of Remainders or Partial Interests.* A taxpayer may generally elect to exclude gain from the sale or exchange of a remainder interest in a principal residence, provided all other requirements for the exclusion are satisfied. If the election is made, the principal residence exclusion will not apply to any other interest in the principal residence that is sold or exchanged separately. Further, the election is not available for a sale or exchange of a remainder interest to a related party (as defined in § 121(d)(8)(B)). A taxpayer makes the election by excluding gain from the sale or exchange of the remainder interest on his or her tax return for the tax year of the sale or exchange [§ 121(d)(8); Reg. § 1.121-4(e)(2)].

A taxpayer may exclude gain from the sale or exchange of a partial interest (other than interests remaining after the sale or exchange of a remainder interest) in his or her principal residence if the interest sold or exchanged includes an interest in the dwelling unit, provided all other requirements for the exclusion are satisfied. Sales or exchanges of partial interests in the same principal residence are treated as a single sale or exchange. Only one maximum limitation amount of $250,000 ($500,000 for married taxpayers filing jointly) applies to the combined sales or exchanges of partial interests. In applying the rule prohibiting more than one excludible sale or exchange within two years (see III.E.3.c.), each partial interest transaction is disregarded with respect to the other partial interest transaction, but taken into account for sales or exchanges of any other principal residence [Reg. § 1.121-4(e)(1)].

*Expatriates.* The principal residence exclusion does not apply to sales or exchanges by certain nonresident alien individuals who have lost or surrendered their U.S. citizenship for tax avoidance purposes [§ 877A(a)(1), § 877A(a)(2)(A)].

*Trusts.* The principal residence exclusion generally is not available when a taxpayer's residence is owned by a trust, rather than by the taxpayer. However, if the taxpayer is treated as the owner of the trust under the grantor trust tax rules, the taxpayer will be considered the owner of the residence for purposes of exclusion [Reg. § 1.121-1(c)(3)].

### III.E.3.e. Reacquisition of Principal Residence in Satisfaction of Secured Debt

[594 T.M., V.C.; TPS ¶1530.02.]

A seller of real property, including a principal residence, who reacquires the property from the buyer in full or partial satisfaction of indebtedness to the seller that arose from the sale and that is secured by the property does not recognize loss on the reacquisition, and any gain recognized is limited to the lesser of the following amounts [§ 1038]:

- the sum of money and the fair market value of other property received before and upon the reacquisition, less the gain previously reported as income; or
- the gain on the original sale, less the sum of (i) the gain previously reported on the sale, and (ii) payments by the seller in connection with the reacquisition.

A taxpayer reacquiring a principal residence must also recognize gain on the sale of a principal residence that was previously excluded under § 121.

For further discussion of the reacquisition of real property, see III.E.6.a.

### III.E.4. Certain Insurance, Endowment, and Annuity Contracts

[529 T.M., IV.B.; TPS ¶1540.03.]

Exchanges of insurance, endowment, and annuity contracts qualify for nonrecognition treatment if they satisfy certain requirements. Only certain types of contracts are eligible to be exchanged tax-free, and only certain types of contracts may be received in the exchange. Additionally, the nonrecognition rule is inapplicable where the property is transferred to a foreign person [§ 1035].

For a discussion of gains on the surrender, sale, taxable exchange, or accelerated death benefits of insurance, endowment, and annuity contracts, see III.C.6.

### III.E.4.a. Eligible Insurance, Endowment, and Annuity Contract Policies and Exchanges

[529 T.M., IV.B.; TPS ¶1540.03.B.1.]

Nonrecognition treatment requires that an exchange fit one of the following forms [§ 1035(a)]:

- a life insurance contract is exchanged for either (i) another life insurance contract, (ii) an endowment contract, (iii) an annuity contract, or (iv) a qualified long-term care insurance contract;
- an endowment contract is exchanged for either (i) another endowment contract that provides for regular payments beginning no later than the date payments would have begun under the exchanged contract, (ii) an annuity contract, or (iii) a qualified long-term care insurance contract;
- an annuity contract is exchanged for either (i) another annuity contract, or (ii) a qualified long-term care insurance contract; or
- a qualified long-term care insurance contract is exchanged for another qualified long-term care insurance contract.

The insured or the annuitant under the policy exchanged must be the same as the insured or annuitant under the policy received [Reg. § 1.1035-1(c)]. Additionally, each policy involved in the exchange must be issued by an insurance company, though not necessarily a life insurance company [§ 1035(b)].

A life insurance contract is a contract that depends in part on the insured's life expectancy, but only if the contract is not ordinarily payable in full during the insured's life. An endowment contract is a contract that depends in part on the life expectancy of the insured, but which may be payable in full in a single payment during the insured's life. An annuity contract is a contract that depends in part on an annuitant's life expectancy, but which may be payable during the annuitant's life only in installments [§ 1035(b)].

A qualified long-term care insurance contract is a contract that does the following [§ 7702B(b)(1)]:

1. covers only qualified long-term care services;
2. generally does not pay or reimburse expenses reimbursable under Medicare;
3. is guaranteed renewable;
4. does not provide for a cash surrender value or other money that can be paid, assigned, pledged, or borrowed;
5. under which refunds and dividends may be used only to reduce future premiums or increase future benefits; and
6. contains certain consumer protection provisions.

A contract is also treated as a qualified long-term care insurance contract if an individual receives coverage for qualified long-term care services under a state long-term care plan, and the terms of the arrangement would satisfy the requirements for a long-term insurance contract if the arrangement were an insurance contract [§ 7702B(f)].

For purposes of the nonrecognition rule, a contract will not fail to be treated as a life insurance contract or an annuity contract solely because a qualified long-term care insurance contract is part of, or a rider on, such contract [§ 1035(b)]. If a long-term care insurance contract (whether or not qualified) is provided by a rider on, or as a part of, a life insurance contract or annuity contract, that portion of the contract providing long-term care insurance coverage is treated as a separate contract [§ 7702B(e)(1)].

### III.E.4.b. Boot and Basis for Insurance, Endowment, and Annuity Contracts

[529 T.M., IV.B.; TPS ¶1540.03.C.]

An eligible policy exchanged solely for another eligible policy in a qualifying exchange will not result in the recognition of gain, and the policyholder's basis in the replacement policy is the same as his or her basis in the exchanged policy [§ 1035(a), § 1035(d)(2)].

If cash or other boot is received in addition to the replacement policy, the exchange qualifies for partial nonrecognition. In such a scenario, the like-kind exchange rules (see III.E.1.e.) apply to determine the amount of gain (if any) that must be recognized and the basis of the replacement policy [§ 1035(d)(1)].

### III.E.5. Transfers of Property Between Spouses or Incident to Divorce

[515 T.M., IV.D.; TPS ¶1570.02.]

Generally, no gain or loss is recognized on the transfer of property from an individual to (or in trust for the benefit of) his or her spouse or to his or her former spouse if the transfer was incident to the divorce. Annulments and cessations of marriages that are void ab initio due to violations of state law constitute divorces for purposes of the nonrecognition rule [§ 1041(a); Reg. § 1.1041-1T(b), Q&A 8].

A transfer is considered incident to a divorce if (i) it occurs within a year after the marriage ceases (whether or not related to the cessation of the marriage), or (ii) it is related to the cessation of the marriage. A transfer is related to the cessation of the marriage if it is made pursuant to a divorce or separation instrument (as defined in § 71(b)(2)) and the transfer occurs within six years of the date on which the marriage ceases. Transfers not pursuant to a divorce or separation instrument, or occurring more than six years after the cessation of the marriage, create a presumption that the transfer is not related to the cessation of the marriage. The presumption may be rebutted only by showing that the transfer was made to effect the division of property owned by the former spouses at the time of the cessation of the marriage [§ 1041(c); Reg. § 1.1041-1T(b), Q&A 7].

The property acquired in a qualifying transfer is treated as having been acquired by gift, and the transferee's basis in the property is the same as the transferor's adjusted basis in the property. Unlike the basis rules for gifts (see III.A.3.a(2)), though, the transferor's adjusted basis is used to determine both gain and loss [§ 1041(b); Reg. § 1.1041-1T(d), Q&A 11].

Application of the nonrecognition rule is mandatory for qualifying transfers. Parties cannot elect to treat the transaction as a sale, even if it is, in reality, an arm's-length sale. Transferred property need not have been owned by the transferor during the marriage. The transfer of property acquired after the divorce may, nevertheless, be subject to the nonrecognition rule [§ 1041(a); Reg. § 1.1041-1T(a), Q&A 5].

The nonrecognition rule does not apply if the transferee spouse or former spouse is a nonresident alien [§ 1041(d)].

The nonrecognition rules does not apply if the property is transferred in trust, to the extent that the sum of the amount of liabilities assumed and the amount of liabilities to which the property is subject, exceeds the total of the adjusted basis of the property transferred. However, if gain is recognized as a result of such a transfer, that gain is added to the transferee's basis in the asset [§ 1041(e)].

A transfer of property to a third party on behalf of a spouse or former spouse will qualify for nonrecognition in the following circumstances [Reg. § 1.1041-1T(c), Q&A 9]:

- the transfer to the third party is required by a divorce or separation instrument;
- the transfer to the third party is pursuant to the written request of the spouse or former spouse; or
- the transferor receives written consent or ratification of the transfer to the third party from the spouse or former spouse.

In such a case, the property is treated as having been transferred first to the spouse or former spouse, and then immediately transferred by the spouse or former spouse to the third party. The nonrecognition rule will apply to the first deemed transaction, but not to the second [Reg. § 1.1041-1T(c), Q&A 9].

### III.E.6. Miscellaneous Nonrecognition Transactions

#### III.E.6.a. Reacquisition of Real Property in Satisfaction of Secured Debt

[590 T.M., IV.C.4.; TPS ¶1550.02.A.]

A seller of real property who reacquires the real property from the buyer in full or partial satisfaction of indebtedness to the seller that arose from the sale and that is secured by the property generally does not recognize gain or loss on the reacquisition. However, to the extent the seller receives money or other property (other than the purchaser's obligations) with respect to the sale before the reacquisition, he or she must recognize gain. This gain is limited to the amount of gain realized from the original sale, reduced by (i) amounts already reported in income and (ii) amounts the seller paid in connection with the reacquisition of property. Loss on the reacquisition may not be recognized, and no debt secured by the repossessed property may be treated as worthless or partially worthless as a result of the reacquisition [§ 1038; Reg. § 1.1038-1(a)(1)].

If, before the reacquisition, the seller claimed bad debt deductions (see VIII.I.) for indebtedness secured by the property, the seller is treated as receiving an amount of money equal to the previously claimed deductions when the property is reacquired. Additionally, the adjusted basis of the indebtedness is increased by the same amount on the date of reacquisition [§ 1038(c), § 1038(d); Reg. § 1.1038-1(f)(2)].

The partial recognition and previous bad debt deduction recapture rules do not apply if (i) the seller qualified for nonrecognition under the principal residence exclusion (see III.E.3.) when he or she sold the property that is reacquired, and (ii) the seller sells the reacquired residence within one year after the date it is reacquired

[§ 1038(e)]. The reacquisition of a principal residence in satisfaction of secured debt is discussed in III.E.3.e.

The basis of reacquired property is the adjusted basis of the buyer's debt, increased by (i) the gain resulting from the reacquisition, and (ii) the amount of money and the fair market value of other property paid by the seller in connection with the reacquisition of the property [§ 1038(c); Reg. § 1.1038-1(g)(1)]. The seller's holding period for the reacquired property includes the period for which he or she held the property before the original sale. It does not include the period of time the purchaser held the property [Reg. § 1.1038-1(g)(3)].

For a discussion of reacquisitions of real property sold in an installment sale and reported using the installment method, see III.G.10.

### III.E.6.b. Certain Exchanges of U.S. Obligations

[501 T.M., IV.F.4.p., 503 T.M., II.E.3.d(14); TPS ¶1570.01.]

No gain or loss is recognized on the surrender to the United States of U.S. obligations issued under Title 31, Chapter 31, in exchange solely for other obligations issued under that chapter, when so provided by regulations promulgated in connection with the issuance of such obligations. For this purpose, a Treasury Department circular offering to exchange U.S. obligations issued under the Second Liberty Bond Act for other obligations issued under that Act constitutes relevant regulations if the circular:

- contains a declaration that no gain or loss will be recognized for federal income tax purposes on the exchange; or
- grants the privilege of continuing to defer the reporting of the income of the bonds exchanged until such time as the bonds received in the exchange are redeemed or disposed of, or have reached final maturity, whichever is earlier.

Where the nonrecognition rule would apply but for the fact that nonqualifying property was received in the exchange, the exchange qualifies for partial nonrecognition. In such a scenario, the like-kind exchange rules (see III.E.1.e.) apply to determine the amount of gain (if any) that must be recognized and the basis of the obligation received. If there is an exchange of obligations issued at a discount, the original issue discount rules (see III.F.2.a.) may apply. Gain or loss that has been realized but not recognized on a qualifying exchange is recognized at the earlier of the time when the obligation received in the exchange (i) is disposed of or redeemed, or (ii) reaches final maturity. The holding period of an obligation received in a tax-free exchange includes the period during which the taxpayer held the obligation surrendered, but only if the surrendered obligation was a capital asset in the taxpayer's hands at the time of the exchange [§ 1037; Reg. § 1.1037-1].

### III.E.6.c. Sales of Qualified Stock to ESOPs and Eligible Worker-Owned Cooperatives

[354 T.M., III.A.; TPS ¶1570.03.]

A taxpayer (other than a C corporation) may generally elect nonrecognition of long-term capital gain in certain cases where qualified securities are sold to a qualifying employee stock ownership plan (ESOP) or eligible worker-owned cooperative (EWOC) and the taxpayer purchases qualified replacement property within the replacement period. If the amount realized on the sale of the qualified securities exceeds the cost of the replacement property, the taxpayer must recognize gain to the extent of the excess. The taxpayer's basis in the replacement property is the cost of the replacement property, reduced by the amount of gain not recognized by reason of the election [§ 1042].

### III.E.6.d. Rollover of Publicly Traded Securities Gain into Specialized Small Business Investment Companies

[760 T.M., XII.A.; TPS ¶1570.04.]

Individuals and C corporations may elect not to recognize capital gain on the sale of publicly traded securities if the sales proceeds are used to purchase common stock or a partnership interest in a specialized small business investment company (SSBIC) within 60 days after the sale. Where the taxpayer makes the election, gain on the sale of the publicly traded securities is recognized only to the extent the amount realized on the sale exceeds the following amount [§ 1044(a); Reg. § 1.1044(a)-1(a)]:

1. the cost of any common stock or partnership interest in an SSBIC purchased in the 60-day period, reduced by;

2. any portion of that cost previously taken into account under this nonrecognition rule.

An SSBIC is any partnership or corporation that is licensed by the Small Business Administration under § 301(d) of the Small Business Investment Act of 1958 (as in effect on May 14, 1993) [§ 1044(c)(3)].

There are certain limits on amounts that may be excluded under the nonrecognition provision. An individual may exclude up to $50,000 per tax year, and up to $500,000 cumulatively. Thus, for any given tax year, the individual's exclusion is limited to the lesser of (i) $50,000, or (ii) $500,000, reduced by the amount of gain excluded under the nonrecognition provision for all previous tax years. In the case of married taxpayers filing separate returns, the limits are $25,000 and $250,000, respectively. C corporations may exclude up to $250,000 per tax year, and up to $1 million cumulatively. Thus, for any given tax year, the C corporation's exclusion is limited to the lesser of (i) $250,000, or (ii) $1 million, reduced by the amount of gain excluded under the nonrecognition provision for all previous tax years. For purposes of the limitation, all corporations that are members of the same controlled group (as defined in § 52(a)) are treated as a single taxpayer, and any gain excluded by a predecessor to the C corporation is treated as having been excluded by the C corporation [§ 1044(b)].

A taxpayer must elect for nonrecognition treatment by the due date (including extensions) of the taxpayer's tax return for the year in which the publicly traded securities are sold. The election is made by reporting the entire gain from the sale of publicly traded securities on Form 8949, *Sales and Other Dispositions of Capital Assets*, as if not electing nonrecognition, and the taxpayer must then enter the amount of deferred gain as an adjustment, along with the appropriate code for the adjustment indicated in the instructions to Form 8949. The taxpayer must also attach a statement showing (i) how the unrecognized gain was calculated, (ii) the SSBIC in which the common stock or partnership interest was purchased, (iii) the date the SSBIC stock or partnership interest was purchased, and (iv) the basis of the SSBIC stock or partnership interest [Reg. § 1.1044(a)-1(b)].

For a discussion of other special rules relating to the stock of small business corporations, see III.C.5.

### III.E.6.e. Rollover of Gain from Qualified Small Business Stock to Another Qualified Small Business Stock

[760 T.M., VIII., X., XI.; TPS ¶¶1570.05., 1750.10.]

A taxpayer may defer gain on the sale of qualified small business (QSB) stock if he or she rolls over the gain into a new investment in QSB stock within 60 days. Rollover treatment is available if the following conditions are satisfied [§ 1045(a)]:

1. the taxpayer is not a corporation;

2. the taxpayer is the party selling the stock;

3. the taxpayer has held the stock for more than six months; and

4. the taxpayer makes a special election to claim rollover treatment.

For a discussion of rolling over gain from qualified small business stock, see III.C.5.

### III.E.6.f. Gain on Rollover of Empowerment Zone Investments [Expired]

[597 T.M., IV.J.; TPS ¶1570.06.]

Before 2014, a taxpayer could elect not to recognize capital gain on the sale of any qualified empowerment zone asset (QEZA) held for more than one year if the sales proceeds were used to purchase any QEZA (for the same zone as the asset sold) within 60 days after the sale. However, empowerment zone designations ended after 2013 [§ 1391(d)]. Where the taxpayer made the election, gain on the sale of QEZA was recognized only to the extent the amount realized on the sale exceeded the following amount [§ 1397B(a)]:

1. the cost of any replacement QEZA (for the same zone as the asset sold) the taxpayer purchased within the 60-day period, reduced by;

2. any portion of such cost previously taken into account under this nonrecognition rule.

There were three types of QEZA [§ 1397B(b)(1), § 1400F]:

1. any qualified empowerment zone stock (as defined under § 1397B(b)(1)(A) and § 1400F(b)(2));

2. any qualified empowerment zone partnership interest (as defined under § 1397B(b)(1)(A) and § 1400F(b)(3)); and

3. any qualified empowerment zone business property (as defined under § 1397B(b)(1)(A) and § 1400F(b)(4)).

For purposes of the nonrecognition rule, the District of Columbia Enterprise Zone was not treated as an empowerment zone. Additionally, the nonrecognition rule did not apply to gain attributable to real property, or an intangible asset, that was not an integral part of an enterprise zone business (as defined in § 1397C).

The taxpayer's basis in the replacement QEZA was the cost of the replacement QEZA, reduced by the amount of gain not recognized by reason of the election [§ 1397B(b)(4)].

### III.E.6.g. Stock Exchanged for Stock in the Same Corporation

[501 T.M., IV.F.4.i.; TPS ¶1510.06.B.]

A taxpayer does not recognize any gain realized from the exchange of common stock in a corporation solely for common stock in the same corporation, or from the exchange of preferred stock in a corporation solely for preferred stock in the same corporation. For this purpose, nonqualified preferred stock (as defined in § 351(g)(2)) is treated as property other than stock. Where the nonrecognition rule would apply but for the fact that nonqualifying property was received in the exchange, the exchange qualifies for partial nonrecognition. In such a scenario, the like-kind exchange rules (see III.E.1.e.) apply to determine the amount of gain (if any) that must be recognized and the basis of the stock received [§ 1036; Reg. § 1.1036-1].

## III.F. Financial Instruments

### III.F.1. Transaction in Stock, Securities, and Other Financial Instruments

[186 T.M.; TPS ¶1810.]

The tax consequences of a transaction in stock, securities, or other financial instruments may differ depending on whether the transaction is carried out by (i) an investor, (ii) a trader, or (iii) a dealer.

*Investors.* An investor is a taxpayer that buys and sells securities with the principal purpose of realizing income in the form of interest, dividends, and gain from appreciation in value of a period of one or more years. Most taxpayers are classified as investors unless his or her activities rise to the level of a trade or business. An investor's investment expenses are generally deductible as itemized deductions, and therefore are subject to the 2% floor on miscellaneous itemized deductions (see VII.I.) and are not deductible for alternative minimum tax purposes (see X.A.2.). An investor's securities are capital assets and his or her gain or loss is subject to the capital gain and loss rules (see III.B.).

*Traders.* A trader is a taxpayer engaged primarily in speculative activity from which he or she derives most of his or her income, typically seeking to profit from short-term market swings rather than interest, dividends, or appreciation in value. A trader's activities are substantial, regular, and continuous, and they amount to a trade or business. Expenses relating to the trade or business are deductible. Generally, a trader's securities are capital assets and his or her gain or loss is subject to the capital gain and loss rules (see III.B.). However, a trader may elect to apply the mark-to-market accounting rules applicable to securities dealers. If such an election is made, all gains and losses from trading are ordinary [§ 475(f)].

*Dealers.* A dealer is a taxpayer that acquires securities from sources not usually available to the general public and sells them at a markup to customers in the ordinary course of a trade or business. Expenses relating to the trade or business are deductible. Securities a dealer holds for sale to customers are treated as inventory, and therefore, are not capital assets. Special mark-to-market accounting rules, discussed below, apply to securities dealers [§ 475(a)].

*Mark-to-Market Accounting.* Securities dealers and electing securities traders (as well as electing dealers or traders in commodities) are subject to special mark-to-market accounting rules. Under the mark-to-market rules [§ 475(a)]:

- any security that is inventory in the dealer's hands must be included in inventory at its fair market value; and
- any security that is not inventory in the dealer's hands and that is held at the close of any tax year is treated as having been sold for its fair market value on the last business day of the tax year, and the dealer must take into account any gain or loss in determining gross income for the tax year.

Gain or loss recognized under the mark-to-market method is generally treated as ordinary income or loss [§ 475(d)(3)(A)]. However, these rules do not apply to any security held for investment, debt instruments originated in the ordinary course of business and not held for sale, and securities that are hedges of certain positions [§ 475(b)].

The election to use the mark-to-market method generally is made by filing a statement describing the election, the tax year for which the election is effective, and the trade or business for which the election is made. The statement must be filed no later than the due date (without regard to extensions) of the original tax return for the tax year immediately preceding the election year, or, if applicable, to a request for an extension of time to file that return. However, a new taxpayer that was not required to file a tax return for the tax year immediately preceding the election year makes the election by placing the statement on its books and records within two months and 15 days after the first day of the election year. A copy of the statement is then submitted with the new taxpayer's original tax return for the election year [Rev. Proc. 99-17, 1999-7 I.R.B. 52, § 5]. Once made, the election applies to all subsequent tax years and may be revoked only with IRS consent [§ 475(e)(3), § 475(f)(3)]. Automatic consent to the change in method of accounting may be obtained if (i) the taxpayer is a commodities dealer, securities trader, or commodities trader that has made a valid election, (ii) the method of accounting to which the taxpayer changes is in accordance with its election, and (iii) the year of change is the election year [Rev. Proc. 2011-14, 2011-4 I.R.B. 330, § 23]. Special mark-to-market rules apply for § 1256 contracts (see III.F.1.e.) and mixed straddles (see III.F.1.f.).

### III.F.1.a. Forward Contracts and Futures Contracts

[187 T.M., IV.; TPS ¶1810.01.E., .01.F.]

**Forward Contracts.** A forward contract is a contract negotiated in the present that gives the holder of the contract the right and the obligation to conduct a transaction involving a specific quantity and type of asset at a specific future time and for a specified price. They are often used to reduce uncertainty or to speculate on future price movements. Generally, a forward contract is treated as an open transaction that does not give rise to tax consequences until the forward contract is settled or closed out. A forward contract that is not entered into by a dealer, is not part of a properly identified hedging transaction, and is not a foreign currency forward contract will generally be a capital asset, and thus, gain or loss will generally be capital [§ 1221(a)]. Gain or loss attributable to the cancellation, lapse, expiration, or other termination of a forward contract for property that would be a capital asset in the taxpayer's hands is treated as gain or loss from the sale of a capital asset [§ 1234A].

**Futures Contracts.** A futures contract is a forward contract with highly standardized terms that trades on an organized futures exchange. It obligates one party to exchange some property at a future date for a cash payment, with the payment occurring at the time of delivery of the underlying property. A regulated futures contract is a contract requiring the establishment of a margin account that is adjusted daily to reflect changes in the futures prices and that is traded on, or subject to, the rules of a board or exchange subject to regulation by the Securities and Exchange Commission, the Commodity Futures Trading Commission, or any other exchange or board the IRS authorizes [§ 1256(g)]. A regulated futures contract is a type of § 1256 contract, and therefore, gain or loss generally is subject to the 60/40 rule (see III.F.1.e.). A securities futures contract is a contract for the sale or delivery of a single security or of a narrow-based security index [§ 1234B(c)]. It is not a § 1256 contract (see III.F.1.e.) unless it is a dealer securities futures contracts. Gain or loss from the sale, exchange, or termination of a securities futures contract (other than a dealer securities futures contract) will be treated as having the same character as the property underlying the contract would have in the taxpayer's hands [§ 1234B(a)(1)].

### III.F.1.b. Option Contracts

[188 T.M., II.A.; TPS ¶1810.01.C.2.]

An option is a contract sold for consideration (a "premium") by one party (the "writer" or "seller") to another party (the "holder" or "buyer") that offers the holder the right, but not the obligation, to buy or sell property at an agreed upon price (the "exercise price" or "striking price") before a certain time. If the holder does not exercise his or her right by the specified date (the "expiration date"), the writer's obligation lapses. Gain or loss attributable to the sale or exchange of an option is treated as gain or loss on the sale or exchange of the property underlying the option. The period for which the taxpayer has held the option determines whether any capital gain or loss is short-term or long-term [§ 1234; Reg. § 1.1234-1(a)].

*Put Options.* A "put" option is the right to sell to the writer, at any time before a specified date, a stated number of shares at a specified price. The purchase of a put option is a capital expenditure, and its cost may not be deducted. When a put option is exercised, the holder must reduce his or her amount realized on the sale of the underlying stock by the cost of the put, while the writer must reduce his or her basis in the stock purchased by the amount received for the put. When a put option expires without being exercised, the holder reports the cost of the put as a capital loss on the date it expires, while the writer reports the amount received for the put as a short-term capital gain. When a holder sells the put option, the holder reports the difference between the cost of the put and the amount received as a capital gain or loss. If the writer repurchases the put option, the difference between the amount paid and the amount received for the put is a short-term capital gain or loss [§ 1234; Reg. § 1.1234-1].

*Call Options.* A "call" option is the right to buy from the writer, at any time before a specified date, a stated number of shares at a specified price. The purchase of a call option is a capital expenditure, and its cost may not be deducted. When a call option is exercised, the holder adds the cost of the call to his or her basis in the stock purchased, while the writer increases the amount realized on the sale of the stock by the amount received for the call. When a call option expires without being exercised, the holder reports the cost of the call as a capital loss on the date it expires, while the writer reports the amount received for the call as a short-term capital gain. When a holder sells the call option, the holder reports the difference between the cost of the call and the amount received as a capital gain or loss. If the writer repurchases the call option, the difference between the amount paid and the amount received for the call is a short-term capital gain or loss [§ 1234; Reg. § 1.1234-1].

Gain or loss from the exercise or expiration of an option (other than a § 1256 contract) that is a capital asset is reported on Form 8949, *Sales and Other Dispositions of Capital Assets*.

For a discussion of stock options offered as compensation for the performance of services, see XVII.B.2.

### III.F.1.c. Short Sales

[188 T.M., II.D.; TPS ¶1810.02.B.]

A short sale is essentially a sale of property that the taxpayer does not possess. In a short sale of stock, a taxpayer generally will agree to deliver to a buyer a certain quantity of stock. The taxpayer borrows the necessary stock from a lender with an obligation (i) to return stock of the same class, from the same issuer, and in the same amount, and (ii) to pay the lender a fee and make substitute payments equal to the dividends the lender would otherwise have received from the stock. The taxpayer then sells the borrowed stock to the buyer, but remains liable to the lender. When the taxpayer repays the lender, he or she has "closed out" the short sale.

If the stock price decreases between the time of the short sale and the time the transaction is closed out, the taxpayer is able to purchase stock and fulfill his or her obligation to the lender while capturing the profit to the extent of the difference between the amount for which the stock was sold and the amount for which the replacement stock was purchased. On the other hand, if the stock price rises over that same time period, the taxpayer will have a loss.

---

**EXAMPLE:** Alex sells short 100 shares of Vast Corp. common stock. In exchange for a fee, Alex borrows from Barry 100 shares of Vast Corp. common stock at $2 per share to sell to Carl for $200. The price of Vast Corp. common stock subsequently falls to $1 per share. Alex closes out the short sale by buying 100 shares of Vast Corp. for $100 and delivering the shares to Barry. Alex realizes a gain of $100 (less fees).

---

Gain or loss is not realized until delivery of the property to close out the short sale. If the property used to close out the short sale is a capital asset, the gain or loss will be capital gain or loss. Generally, a taxpayer determines whether he or she has short-term or long-term capital gain or loss on a short sale by the amount of time he or she held the property eventually delivered to the lender to close the transaction [Reg. § 1.1233-1(a)(3)].

Special rules may override the general rule on the character of the gain or loss. If, on the date of the short sale, the taxpayer has held property substantially identical to the property sold short for one year or less, or if the taxpayer acquires substantially identical property after the short sale while it is still open, any gain from the closing of the short sale is a short-term gain. The holding period of the substantially identical property generally is treated as beginning on the date the short sale is closed, or, if earlier, the date such substantially identical property is disposed of. If the taxpayer has held substantially identical property for more than one year on the date of a short sale, any loss from the closing of the short sale is a long-term loss. If property sold short becomes substantially worthless, a taxpayer must recognize gain as if the short sale were closed out when the property became substantially worthless [§ 1233(b), § 1233(d), § 1233(h); Reg. § 1.1233-1(a), § 1.1233-1(c)].

Gain or loss from a short sale is reported on Form 8949, *Sales and Other Dispositions of Capital Assets*, in the year it closes.

### III.F.1.d. Wash Sales

[186 T.M., I.; TPS ¶1810.02.A.]

A wash sale is the sale or trade of stock or securities at a loss where, within 30 days before or after the date of the sale, the taxpayer (or the taxpayer's spouse or a corporation controlled by the taxpayer) does one of the following [§ 1091; Reg. § 1.1091-1]:

- buys substantially identical stock or securities;
- acquires substantially identical stock or securities in a fully taxable trade;
- acquires a contract or option to buy substantially identical stock or securities; or
- acquires substantially identical stock for his or her IRA or Roth IRA [Rev. Rul. 2008-5, 2008-3 I.R.B. 271].

The result of a wash sale is that the taxpayer's investment position is left substantially unaltered. The wash sale rule prevents the taxpayer from deducting the loss unless he or she is a dealer in stock or securities and the loss is sustained in a transaction made in the ordinary course of that business [§ 1091(a)]. The wash sale rule does not apply to gains.

Where the wash sale rule applies, the holding period of the stock or security disposed of is tacked onto the holding period of the replacement stock or security [§ 1223(3)]. The basis of the replacement property is the basis of the property sold, increased or decreased (as the case may be) by the difference between the price at which the replacement property was acquired and the price at which the original property was disposed of. Thus, in effect, if a loss is disallowed as a result of the wash sale rule, the amount of the disallowed loss is added to the cost of the replacement property to determine the replacement property's basis [§ 1091(d)].

---

**EXAMPLE:** David sells a bond with a basis of $100 for $80 and purchases a replacement bond for $90. The transaction qualifies as a wash sale. David's basis in the replacement bond is $110 ($100 basis in the original bond + ($90 cost of the replacement bond − $80 amount realized on sale of the original bond)). Had David purchased the replacement bond for $70, its basis would be $90 ($100 basis in the original bond + ($70 cost of the replacement bond − $80 amount realized on the sale of the original bond)).

---

The term "substantially identical stock or securities" is not defined. While older cases have held that to be identical, the stock or securities must be issued by the same issuer, it is not clear whether this holding applies to similar index funds issued by different mutual fund families.

If the number of replacement shares or securities differs from the number of shares or securities the taxpayer sold, the taxpayer must determine the particular shares to which the wash sale rule applies. Shares or securities purchased are matched in the order of purchase (beginning with the first share or security purchased) with an equal number of shares or securities sold. The property so matched is subject to the wash sale rule [§ 1091(b), § 1091(c); Reg. § 1.1091-1(c), § 1.1091-1(d)].

---

**EXAMPLE:** Sally sells five shares of stock, each having a basis of $1,000, for $950 each. Within 30 days after the sale, Sally purchases two substantially identical shares of stock. Though Sally realizes a $250 loss (5 shares × ($950 amount realized − $1,000 basis)) on the sale of the stock, the wash sale rule applies to two of the shares. Thus, $100 (2 shares × ($950 amount realized − $1,000 basis)) of the loss is disallowed. Had Sally purchased six substantially identical shares within 30 days after the sale, all of the loss would be disallowed, and the five replacement shares acquired first would receive the tacked holding period and basis adjustment.

---

### III.F.1.e. Section 1256 Contracts

[187 T.M., IV.C.; TPS ¶1810.03.B., .03.F.]

A § 1256 contract is one of the following [§ 1256(b)(1)]:

- a regulated futures contract;
- a foreign currency contract;
- a nonequity option;

- a dealer equity option; or
- a dealer securities futures contract.

Section 1256 contracts do not include (i) any securities futures contract or option on such a contract unless the contract or option is a dealer securities futures contract, or (ii) any interest rate swap, currency swap, basis swap, interest rate cap, interest rate floor, commodity swap, equity swap, equity index swap, credit default swap, or similar agreement [§ 1256(b)(2)].

Generally, § 1256 contracts are subject to mark-to-market rules, and such contracts that are held at the end of the tax year are treated as being sold for their fair market value on the last day of the tax year, with any resulting gain or loss taken into account for that year. Gain or loss for a § 1256 contract is treated as 60% long-term capital gain or loss and 40% short-term capital gain or loss [§ 1256(a)(1), § 1256(a)(3)].

Gain or loss on a § 1256 contract is reported on Form 6781, *Gains and Losses From Section 1256 Contracts and Straddles.*

### III.F.1.f. Straddles

[187 T.M., VII.; TPS ¶1810.03.]

A straddle is any set of offsetting positions on actively traded personal property, including stock options and contracts to buy stock. Stock, though, generally is not personal property subject to the straddle rules, except in the following situations [§ 1092(d)(3)]:

- the stock is of a type that is actively traded, and at least one of the offsetting positions is a position on that stock or substantially similar or related property; or
- the stock is in a corporation formed or availed of to take positions in property that offset positions taken by any shareholder.

Loss realized on the disposition of one leg of a straddle generally is deferred to the extent of any unrealized and unrecognized gain in any offsetting positions in the straddle. Such loss is deferred until the next tax year where the amount of unrealized and unrecognized gain in any offsetting positions is again calculated and compared to the amount of the deferred straddle loss. However, the loss deferral rules do not apply to hedging transactions [§ 1092, § 1092(e), § 1256]. Additionally, rules similar to the wash sale rule (see III.F.1.d.) apply to any disposition of a straddle position [Reg. § 1.1092(b)-1T].

---

**EXAMPLE:** In July of Year 1, Gilbert enters into a straddle. In Dec. of Year 1, Gilbert closes one position of the straddle at a loss of $15,000. At the end of the tax year, Gilbert has an unrecognized gain of $12,750 in the offsetting open position of the straddle. Gilbert's deductible loss in Year 1 is limited to $2,250 ($15,000 loss − $12,750 unrecognized gain in offsetting position). The unused $12,750 is deferred and carried forward to Year 2.

---

The holding period of a position in a straddle generally begins on the date the taxpayer no longer holds an offsetting position. However, this rule does not apply to any position the taxpayer held for more than one year before establishing the straddle [Reg. § 1.1092(b)-2T(a)].

Each position (whether or not it is part of a straddle) on which a taxpayer has unrecognized gain is reported on Form 6781, *Gains and Losses from Section 1256 Contracts and Straddles.*

*Mixed Straddles.* Special rules apply to loss positions that are part of a mixed straddle. A mixed straddle is a straddle [Reg. § 1.1092(b)-5T(e)]:

1. that is not part of a larger straddle;
2. in which all positions are held as capital assets;
3. in which at least one (but not all) of the positions is a § 1256 contract (see III.F.1.e.); and
4. for which a mixed straddle election has not been made.

Losses on a mixed straddle are treated as 60% long-term capital loss and 40% short-term capital loss if the following conditions apply [Reg. § 1.1092(b)-2T(b)(2)]:

1. gain or loss from the sale of one or more of the straddle positions that are § 1256 contracts would be considered gain or loss from the sale or exchange of a capital asset;
2. the sale of no position in the straddle, other than a § 1256 contract, would result in a long-term capital gain or loss; and
3. the taxpayer has not made a straddle-by-straddle identification election or mixed straddle account election to offset gains and losses from positions that are part of a mixed straddle [§ 1092(b)(2)(A)(i)(I), § 1092(b)(2)(A)(i)(II)].

---

**EXAMPLE:** In Mar. of Year 1, Tiffany enters into a long gold forward contract. In July of Year 1, she enters into an offsetting short gold regulated futures contract (a § 1256 contract). She does not make an election to offset gains and losses from positions in a mixed straddle. In Aug. of Year 1, Tiffany disposes of the long forward contract at a loss. Because the forward contract was part of a mixed straddle and the disposition of this non-§ 1256 position would not result in long-term capital loss, the loss recognized on the disposition of the forward contract is treated as 60% long-term and 40% short-term capital loss.

---

### III.F.1.g. Hedging Transactions

[187 T.M., VI.; TPS ¶1620.08.B.]

A hedging transaction is any transaction a taxpayer enters into in the normal course of a trade or business primarily to manage the risk of price changes, currency fluctuations, interest rates fluctuations, and other such risks. Property that is part of a clearly identified hedging transaction is not a capital asset (see III.B.1.). Similarly, where a short sale or option is part of a hedging transaction, any gain or loss on the short sale or option is ordinary [§ 1221(a)(7); Reg. § 1.1221-2(a)].

A taxpayer must identify a transaction as a hedging transaction by the close of the day on which the taxpayer enters the transaction. The taxpayer must also identify the item, items, or aggregate risk being hedged within 35 days after entering into the hedging transaction. Where identified as a hedging transaction, the identification is binding for gain on the transaction. Thus, the gain will be ordinary whether or not all of the requirements for treatment as a hedging transaction are satisfied. Losses from a transaction that has been improperly identified as a hedging transaction, though, are characterized under general tax principals and will generally be capital. However, a misidentified transaction will not be subject to this whipsaw regime if (i) the transaction is not a hedging transaction, (ii) the misidentification was due to inadvertent error, and (iii) all of the taxpayer's transaction in all open years are treated in a manner consistent with the hedging transaction principles [Reg. § 1.1221-2(f), § 1.1221-2(g)].

### III.F.1.h. Constructive Sales Treatment for Appreciated Financial Positions

[187 T.M., IV.B.1.b.; TPS ¶1810.06.B.]

Taxpayers must recognize gain (but not loss) on a constructive sale of any appreciated financial position in stock, a partnership interest, or certain debt instruments. Gain must be recognized as if the position were disposed of at its fair market value on the date of the constructive sale. This gives the taxpayer a new holding period for the position that begins on the date of the constructive sale [§ 1259(a)]. A constructive sale of an appreciated financial position occurs when the taxpayer enters into one of the following [§ 1259(c)]:

- a short sale of the same or substantially identical property;
- an offsetting notional principal contract relating to the same or substantially identical property;
- a futures or forward contract to deliver the same or substantially identical property; or
- an acquisition of the same or substantially identical property, if the appreciated financial position is a short sale, an offsetting notional principal contract, or a futures or forward contract.

A taxpayer is not treated as having made a constructive sale solely because he or she enters into a contract for sale of any stock, debt instrument, or partnership interest that is not a marketable security (as defined in § 453(f)) if the contract settles within a year after the date the contract is entered into [§ 1259(c)(2)].

These rules do not apply to any position with respect to debt if [§ 1259(b)(2)]:

1. the debt unconditionally entitles the holder to receive a specified principal amount;
2. the interest payments (or other similar amounts) on such debt are payable based on a fixed rate (or, to the extent provided in the regulations, at a variable rate); and
3. such debt is not directly or indirectly convertible into stock of the issuer or any related person.

### III.F.2. Taxation of Debt Instruments

### III.F.2.a. Original Issue Discount

[535 T.M.; TPS ¶1840.]

Original issue discount (OID) rules apply when a debt instrument's stated redemption price at maturity (SRPM) is greater than its issue price (or, in the case of a stripped bond or coupon, its acquisition price). A holder of a debt instrument (DI) having OID must include in gross income an amount equal to the sum of the daily portion of the OID for each day during the tax year the holder held the instrument, regardless of whether the holder uses the cash or accrual method of accounting [§ 1272(a)(1), § 1273(a)(1)]. The holder's basis in a DI is increased by the amount included in his or her gross income [§ 1272(d)(2)].

**Exceptions to OID Rule.** The OID rules generally do not apply to the following DIs [§ 1272(a)(2)]:

- tax-exempt obligations;
- U.S. savings bonds;
- instruments with a fixed maturity date not more than one year from the date of issue;

- obligations issued by individuals before March 2, 1984; and
- loans of $10,000 or less between individuals who are not in the business of lending money (unless the principal purpose of the loan is to avoid federal tax).

*De Minimis Rule.* If the total OID on a DI is less than .25% of SRPM multiplied by the number of full years from the date of the original issue to maturity, the DI is treated as having no OID [§ 1273(a)(3)].

---

**EXAMPLE:** Tara purchases at issuance a ten-year DI with an SRPM of $1,000, issued at $980 with OID of $20. The DI is treated as having no OID because $20 is less than $25 (.25% × ($1,000 SRPM × 10 full years from date of original issue to maturity)). If Tara holds the DI to maturity, she will recognize that $20 as capital gain.

---

*Stated Redemption Price at Maturity (SRPM).* SRPM is the sum of all payments due under a DI's terms, other than qualified stated interest. Qualified stated interest is stated interest that is unconditionally payable in cash or property (other than DIs of the issuer) at least annually at a single fixed rate [Reg. § 1.1273-1(b), § 1.1273-1(c)(1)].

*Issue Price.* The calculation of a DI's issue price depends on whether the DI was issued for (i) money, (ii) property where either the DI or the property is publicly traded, or (iii) property where neither the DI nor the property is publicly traded. Generally, the issue price of a DI will be one the following [§ 1273(b), § 1274; Reg. § 1.1273-2]:

- in the case of a DI issued for cash, the cash price;
- in the case of a publicly traded DI issued for non-publicly traded property, the fair market value of the DI;
- in the case of a non-publicly traded DI issued for publicly traded property, the fair market value of the property; or
- in the case of an untraded DI issued for untraded property:
  - if the DI bears adequate interest, the stated principal amount; or
  - if the DI does not bear adequate stated interest, the imputed principal amount.

*Adequate Stated Interest.* A DI has adequate stated interest if its stated principal amount is less than or equal to the imputed principal amount. The imputed principal amount is the sum of the present values of all payments due under the DI (including principal and stated interest) discounted at a rate equal to the applicable federal rate (AFR) appropriate to the DI as of the date of the sale or exchange that gave rise to the DI. Thus, if the DI has a yield to maturity that equals or exceeds the AFR as of the sale date, then it bears adequate stated interest [§ 1274(b), § 1274(c)(2)].

The IRS publishes the AFR monthly. The AFR for any DI is based on the yields of U.S. Treasury obligations with corresponding maturity terms, as follows [§ 1274(d)(1)]:

- for a DI with a term not over three years, the AFR is the federal short-term rate;
- for a DI with a term over three years, but not over nine years, the AFR is the federal mid-term rate; and
- for a DI with a term over nine years, the AFR is the federal long-term rate.

The test rate is the three-month rate, which is the lower of the following:

- the lowest AFR in effect during the three-month period ending with the first month in which there is a binding written contract for the sale; or

- the lowest AFR in effect during the three-month period ending with the month in which the sale or exchange occurs.

***Calculating OID.*** Regardless of whether the holder of a DI is on the cash or accrual method of accounting, the holder must recognize the DI's OID as interest income as it accrues on a daily basis under the constant yield method. The annual OID inclusion required under the constant yield method is determined under the following four steps [Reg. § 1.1272-1(b)(1)]:

1. Determine the DI's yield to maturity, which is the discount rate that, when used to compute the present value of all principal and interest payments (including qualified stated interest) due under the DI, produces an amount equal to its issue price.

2. Determine the accrual period over which OID accrual is measured, which may be of any length, provided that each accrual period is no longer than one year and each scheduled interest or principal payment occurs on either the final day or first day of an accrual period.

3. Determine the OID for each accrual period, which will equal the product of the DI's adjusted issue price (issue price, plus prior-period OID accruals, less prior-period payments) and the DI's yield, less the amount of any qualified stated interest allocable to the accrual period.

4. Determine the daily portions of OID by dividing the OID allocable to each accrual period by the number of days in each such period.

***Reporting.*** The holder of a DI with OID must include in income the daily portions of OID for each day during the tax year that the holder held the DI [§ 1272(a)(1)]. Interest income is reported on Form 1040, Form 1040A, or Form 1040EZ. However, Form 1040EZ may not be used if the taxpayer either (i) received a Form 1099-OID as a nominee for the actual owner, or (ii) had total interest and OID income for the tax year of more than $1,500. Forms 1040A and 1040EZ may not be used if the taxpayer is reporting more or less OID than the amount shown on Form 1099-OID, other than because the taxpayer is a nominee.

The issuer claims the OID as deductible interest (to the extent it is not disallowed by another provision of the Code) as it accrues on a daily basis under the same constant yield method that applies to the holder of the DI [§ 163(e)].

### III.F.2.a.(1) Stripped Bonds and Coupons

[535 T.M., II.H.; TPS ¶1840.03.D.]

If a taxpayer strips one or more coupons from a bond and sells the bond or the coupons, the bond and coupons are treated as separate debt instruments issued with OID. Stripped bonds and coupons include (i) zero coupon instruments available through the Treasury Department's Separate Trading of Registered Interest and Principal of Securities (STRIPS) program and through government-sponsored enterprises, such as the Resolution Funding and Financing Corporation, and (ii) instruments backed by U.S. Treasury securities that represent ownership interests in those securities. The holder of a stripped bond has the right to receive the principal payment (i.e., the redemption price) and the holder of a stripped coupon has a right to receive the interest on the bond.

The taxpayer who strips coupons from a bond and sells the bond or the coupons is required to include in gross income (to the extent not previously included in gross income) (i) the interest that accrued while the taxpayer held the bond, and (ii) the market discount that accrued before the date of sale. The amount included in income is added to the taxpayer's basis in the bond and coupons, and allocated between the items retained and the items sold based on their respective fair market values. Any items retained are treated as OID bonds originally issued on the date of the sale [§ 1286(b)].

The taxpayer who buys a stripped bond or a stripped coupon treats it as an OID bond originally issued on the date of purchase. If the taxpayer buys a stripped bond, the taxpayer has OID equal to the excess of the stated redemption price of the bond at maturity over the bond's ratable share of the purchase price. If the taxpayer buys a stripped coupon, the taxpayer has OID equal to the excess of the amount payable on the due date of the coupon over the coupon's ratable share of the purchase price [§ 1286(a)].

### III.F.2.a.(2) Variable Rate Debt Instruments

[535 T.M., IV.; TPS ¶1840.06.]

Special OID rules apply to certain debt instruments that provide for interest at varying rates, known as variable rate debt instruments (VRDI). A debt instrument is a VRDI if the following conditions are satisfied [Reg. § 1.1275-5(a)]:

1. its issue price does not exceed total noncontingent principal payments by more than a specified amount;

2. the debt instrument only provides for certain types of stated interest;

3. the debt instrument provides that any qualified floating rate or single objective rate in effect at any time is set at a current value of that rate; and

4. the debt instrument does not provide for any principal payments that are contingent.

In determining the OID on a VRDI, the debt instrument is first converted into a fixed rate debt instrument, and the general OID rules are then applied [Reg. § 1.1275-5].

**Inflation-Indexed Securities.** An inflation-indexed debt instrument is a debt instrument that is (i) issued for cash, (ii) indexed for inflation and deflation, and (iii) not otherwise a contingent payment debt instrument (see III.F.2.a(3)). Generally, holders of inflation-indexed securities must report as OID any increase in the inflation-adjusted principal amount of the debt instrument that occurs while he or she held the debt instrument during the tax year. The inflation-adjusted principal amount of an inflation-indexed debt instrument on any date is the debt instrument's outstanding principal amount, multiplied by the index ratio for that date. Basis in the debt instrument is increased by the OID included in income [Reg. § 1.1275-7].

Inflation-indexed securities include Treasury Inflation-Protected Securities (TIPS). TIPS are backed by the U.S. government and their principal amounts are adjusted for inflation or deflation that occurs over the term of the security, while their interest rates remain fixed. Anticipating that, as a result of financial conditions, TIPS may be issued at a premium that is more than de minimis, Treasury issued regulations providing that, if TIPS are issued with more than a de minimis amount of premium (as determined under the principles of Reg. § 1.1273-1(d)) on or after April 8, 2011, the coupon bond method, rather than the discount bond method, applies for taking interest into account [Reg. § 1.1275-7(g)(2), § 1.1275-7(h)(2)].

### III.F.2.a.(3) Contingent Payment Debt Instruments

[535 T.M., V; TPS ¶1840.07.]

Special OID rules also apply to debt instruments that provide for contingent payments. The rules that apply depend on whether the contingent payment debt instrument (CPDI) is issued for (i) money or publicly traded property, or (ii) nonpublicly traded property [Reg. § 1.1275-4(b)].

When a CPDI is issued for money or publicly traded property, the OID accruals are determined under the noncontingent bond method. Under this method, the amount of interest taken into account for each tax year is determined by constructing a projected payment schedule for the debt instrument and applying rules similar to those for accruing OID on a noncontingent debt instrument (i.e., the general OID rules). If the actual amount of a contingent payment is not equal to the projected amount, appropriate adjustments are made to reflect the difference [Reg. § 1.1275-4(b)].

When a CPDI is issued for nonpublicly traded property, the payments on the debt instrument are separated into noncontingent payments and contingent payments. The total amount of noncontingent payments is treated as a separate debt instrument. Each contingent payment is treated as a payment of principal in an amount equal to the present value of the payment, and the amount of the contingent payment in excess of the principal payment is treated as interest [Reg. § 1.1275-4(c)].

### III.F.2.b. Market Discount

[535 T.M., VI.A.; TPS ¶1840.03.B.]

Market discount arises when a DI purchased in the secondary market has decreased in value since its issue date, generally because of an increase in interest rates. A market discount bond is any DI that has been acquired subsequent to original issue at a discount. If the DI was not issued with OID, the amount of the market discount is the excess of the DI's SRPM measured on the acquisition date, over the purchaser's basis immediately after acquisition. If the DI was issued with OID, the market discount is the excess of the DI's adjusted issue price over the purchaser's basis immediately after acquisition. If the market discount on a DI is less than .25% of SRPM multiplied by the number of full years to maturity (after its acquisition by the taxpayer), the DI is treated as having no market discount [§ 1278(a)(2)].

The market discount provisions do not apply to the following DIs:

- instruments with a fixed maturity date not more than one year from the date of issue;
- U.S. savings bonds; and
- instruments issued as consideration in a sale if the recognition of gain by the seller has been deferred under the § 453B rules applicable to installment sales.

Generally, gain on the disposition of any market discount bond is treated as ordinary income to the extent it does not exceed the accrued market discount on the bond. The gain must be recognized notwithstanding any other Code provisions. If a market discount bond is disposed of in any transaction other than a sale, exchange, or involuntary conversion, the taxpayer is treated as having realized the bond's fair market value [§ 1276(a)(1), § 1276(a)(2)].

**Accruing Market Discount.** Market discount on any bond is generally accrued ratably on a daily basis. However, the holder may elect (on a bond-by-bond basis) to accrue market discount on a constant interest basis [§ 1276(b)]. A taxpayer makes the election to use the constant interest rate by attaching to his or her timely filed tax return a statement identifying the bond and stating that he or she is making a constant interest rate election for a given bond [Rev. Proc. 92-67, 1992-2 C.B. 429].

---

**EXAMPLE:** A DI with a stated principal amount of $100,000 payable at maturity is issued on Jan. 1 of Year 1. It matures on Jan. 1 of Year 11 and it bears a 7% coupon payable semiannually (i.e., $3,500 at six-month intervals, beginning with July 1 of Year 1). Its issue price is $100,000. Amber purchases the DI on Mar. 5 of Year 4 for $92,580. The $7,420 ($100,000 − $92,580) of market discount accrues on this DI while held by Amber at a rate of $2.9775 per day ($7,420 ÷ 2,492 days to maturity).

---

*Partial Payments of Principal.* If a market discount bond calls for partial payments of principal prior to maturity (e.g., an installment obligation), any such payment is included in gross income as ordinary income to the extent it does not exceed the accrued market discount. Where any portion of a partial payment of principal has been included in the holder's income under this rule, the amount of accrued discount is reduced by any amounts so included when the bond is subsequently disposed of [§ 1276(a)(3)].

*Election to Currently Include Accrued Discount in Income.* A taxpayer who acquires a market discount bond may elect to include market discount in gross income currently for the tax year to which it is attributable. Amounts included in income under this election are treated as interest. The election applies to all market discount bonds acquired by the taxpayer after the first day of the first tax year to which the election applies and to subsequent tax years. The holder's basis in the market discount bond is increased by any amounts included in income under this election [§ 1278(b)].

A taxpayer makes the election by attaching to his or her timely filed tax return a statement (i) that he or she has included market discount in gross income for the year under § 1278(b), and (ii) describing the method used to figure the accrued market discount for the year [Rev. Proc. 92-67, 1992-2 C.B. 429].

### III.F.2.c. Short-Term Debt Obligations

[535 T.M., VI.E.; TPS ¶1840.09.A.]

The OID rules (see III.F.2.a.) and market discount rules (see III.F.2.b.) do not apply to certain types of short-term debt instruments. A short-term debt instrument is a debt instrument (other than a tax-exempt debt instrument) with a fixed maturity date of not more than one year from the date of issue [§ 1283(a)(1)].

Under the short-term debt instrument rules, a taxpayer is required to include the discount and interest on a short-term debt instrument in gross income currently as it accrues [§ 1281(a)]. The short-term debt instruments that qualify under these rules include short-term debt instruments that are [§ 1281(b)]:

- held by a taxpayer using the accrual method of accounting;
- held primarily for sale to customers in the ordinary course of the taxpayer's trade or business;
- held by a bank, regulated investment company, or common trust fund;
- held by certain pass-through entities;
- identified as part of a hedging transaction; or
- a stripped bond or stripped coupon held by the person who stripped the bond or coupon.

In the case of qualifying short-term government debt instruments, a taxpayer includes the accrued acquisition discount in gross income [§ 1281(a)(1)]. Acquisition discount is the amount by which the stated redemption price of the short-term debt instrument at maturity exceeds the taxpayer's basis in the debt instrument [§ 1283(a)(2)]. The accrued acquisition discount on a short-term debt instrument may be determined by using either the ratable accrual method or the constant interest rate method [§ 1283(b)].

In the case of qualifying short-term nongovernment debt instruments, a taxpayer generally includes the accrued OID in gross income [§ 1283(c)(1)]. However, a taxpayer may instead elect to include accrued acquisition discount in gross income for such short-term debt instruments [§ 1283(c)(2)].

The OID and market discount rules generally apply to non-qualifying short-term debt instruments. However, if a taxpayer acquires a non-qualifying short-term debt instrument, the taxpayer also may elect to apply the short-term debt instrument current inclusion rules to that short-term debt instrument. If this election is made, it applies to all non-qualifying short-term debt instruments acquired in the tax year of the election and all later tax years. Such an election may not be revoked without IRS consent [§ 1282(b)].

### III.F.2.d. Imputed Interest

[535 T.M., III.; TPS ¶1840.04.]

Certain payments of principal on a debt instrument may be required to be recharacterized as payments of interest (i.e., interest is imputed on the debt instrument). Interest may be imputed on a debt instrument based on the provisions of § 1274 and § 483, or under the below-market loan rules. Imputed interest and below-market loans are discussed in I.D.3.d., and I.D.3.e., respectively.

### III.F.2.e. Bond Premium

[535 T.M., VI.B.; TPS ¶1840.03.C.]

A bond is acquired at a premium if its basis in the holder's hands immediately after acquisition exceeds the sum of all amounts payable on the bond after its acquisition, other than payments of qualified stated interest. Accordingly, a bond with a maturity value of $1,000 that is purchased for $1,050 has $50 of premium. If a taxpayer pays a premium to buy a bond, the premium is part of the taxpayer's basis in the bond.

**Election to Amortize Bond Premium.** If the bond yields taxable interest, the taxpayer may elect to amortize the premium. Thus, each year over the life of the bond, the taxpayer may use a part of the premium to reduce the amount of interest includible in income. If a taxpayer makes the election, he or she must reduce the basis of the bond by the amortization for the year. If a bond yields tax-exempt interest, the taxpayer must amortize the premium. The amortized amount is not deductible, but the taxpayer must reduce his or her basis in the bond by the amortization for the year. A dealer in taxable bonds, or anyone who holds taxable bonds for sale to customer in the ordinary course of business or would include them in inventory at the close of a tax year, cannot claim a deduction for amortizable bond premium [§ 171; Reg. § 1.171-1].

**Making the Election.** A taxpayer elects to amortize the premium on taxable bonds by reporting the amortization for the year on his or her tax return for the first tax year he or she wants the election to apply. A statement should be attached to the return specifying that the taxpayer is making this election under Reg. § 1.171-4. The election is binding for the tax year it is made and for subsequent tax years and applies to all taxable bonds held during or after the tax year in which the election is made. The election may be revoked only with IRS consent [Reg. § 1.171-4].

Bond premium amortization is subtracted from interest income from the bond. The bond's interest is reported on Schedule B, *Interest and Ordinary Dividends*, of Form 1040. Adjustments to the interest amount for bond premium amortization are reported as a negative number on the same form and should be identified as "ABP Adjustment."

*Calculating Amortizable Bond Premium.* For bonds issued after September 27, 1985, bond premium is amortized using the constant yield method on the basis of the bond's yield to maturity, determined using the bond's basis and compounding at the close of each accrual period. The bond premium allocable to an accrual period is determined under the following steps [Reg. § 1.171-2(a)(3)]:

1. Determine the holder's yield, which is the discount rate that, when used to compute the present value of all remaining payments to be made on the bond (including qualified stated interest), produces an amount equal to the holder's basis in the bond. Remaining payments include only the payments to be made after the date the holder acquires the bond, and yield is calculated as of the date the holder acquires the bond.
2. Determine the accrual period, which may be of any length, provided that each accrual period is no longer than one year and each scheduled interest or principal payment occurs on either the final day or first day of an accrual period.
3. Determine the bond premium allocable to the accrual period, which will equal the excess of the qualified stated interest allocable to the accrual period over the product of the holder's adjusted acquisition price (as defined in Reg. § 1.171-2(b)) at the beginning of the accrual period and the holder's yield.

---

**EXAMPLE:** On Feb. 1 of Year 1, Jeremy bought a taxable bond for $110,000. The bond's stated principal amount is $100,000, payable at maturity on Feb. 1 of Year 8. Thus, Jeremy's premium is $10,000 ($110,000 − $100,000). The bond pays qualified stated interest of $10,000 on Feb. 1 of each year. Jeremy's yield is 8.07439% compounded annually. He chooses to use annual accrual periods ending Feb. 1 of each year. To find his bond premium amortization for the accrual period ending on Feb. 1 of Year 2, Jeremy multiplies the adjusted acquisition price at the beginning of the period ($110,000) by his yield (8.07439%), which results in $8,881.83. That amount is subtracted from the qualified stated interest for the period ($10,000), which results in bond premium amortization for the period of $1,118.17.

---

## III.G. Installment Sales

[565 T.M.; TPS ¶3550.]

If a disposition of property qualifies as an installment sale, gain on the disposition generally must be reported using the installment method of accounting [§ 453(a)]. The installment method permits a taxpayer to defer the recognition of gain on the disposition.

An installment sale is a disposition of property where at least one payment is to be received after the end of the tax year in which the disposition occurs [§ 453(b)(1)]. A taxpayer that sells property in an installment sale generally receives an installment obligation from the buyer of the property. An installment obligation is the buyer's note, deed of trust, or other evidence that the buyer will make future payments to the taxpayer.

*Reporting Installment Sales.* Form 6252, *Installment Sale Income*, is used to report an installment sale in the year it takes place and to report payments received in later years. For an installment sale to a related person (see III.G.7.), Form 6252 may need to be filed each year until the installment obligation is paid off, whether or not a payment is received. Form 6252 must be attached to the taxpayer's tax return for each year it is required to be filed.

Form 6252 is not filed for an installment sale that results in a loss. When an installment sale results in a loss, the entire sale is reported on Schedule D, *Capital Gains and Losses*, Form 4797, *Sales of Business Property*, or Form 8949, *Sales and Other Dispositions of Capital Assets*, as applicable. Similarly, Form 6252 is not filed if the taxpayer elects not to report the sale using the installment method (see III.G.3.).

A taxpayer that files Form 6252 to report an installment sale is also required to file Schedule D or Form 4797 to report the installment sale income. Schedule D is used to report gain from an installment sale of personal use property. Form 4797 is used to report gain from an installment sale of business or investment property.

### III.G.1. Eligibility for the Installment Method

[565 T.M., II.; TPS ¶3550.03.]

The installment method generally cannot be used for dealer dispositions, dispositions of inventory, dispositions under a revolving credit plan, and dispositions of publicly traded property. All payments to be received in these types of dispositions must be treated as received in the year of the disposition.

*Dealer Dispositions.* The installment method generally cannot be used for dispositions by dealers [§ 453(b)(2)(A)]. For this purpose, a dealer disposition includes the following [§ 453(l)(1)]:

- sales of personal property by a taxpayer who regularly sells such property on an installment plan; and
- sales of real property held by a taxpayer for sale to customers in the ordinary course of the taxpayer's trade or business.

The dealer disposition restriction does not apply to sales of property used or produced in a farming trade or business [§ 453(l)(2)(A)]. The dealer disposition restriction also does not apply to the following types of sales, if such sales are made by the taxpayer to an individual and the taxpayer elects to pay interest on the deferred tax resulting from use of the installment method [§ 453(l)(2)(B)]:

- sales of timeshare rights of not more than six weeks per year in residential real property;
- sales of rights to use specified campgrounds for recreational purposes; and
- sales of residential lots on which the taxpayer (or any related person) is not to make any improvements.

If a dealer makes the election to pay interest on the deferred tax resulting from use of the installment method on one of the enumerated types of sales, the amount of interest owed each year is based on the tax owed on the payments received during the year from installment sales of timeshares and residential lots. The interest is computed at the applicable federal rate (AFR) under § 1274 (see III.F.2.a.) in effect on the date of the sale (compounded semiannually), and is added to the tax owed for that year. However, the AFR under § 1274 is determined without regard to the rule providing for the use of the lowest three-month rate. The period for which the interest is charged begins on the sale date and ends on the date the installment payment is received. No interest is charged for any payment received in the tax year of the sale in which the installment obligation arose [§ 453(l)(3)].

***Dispositions of Inventory.*** The installment method cannot be used for sales of personal property of a kind required to be included in inventory if on hand at the end of the tax year [§ 453(b)(2)(B)].

***Dispositions Under a Revolving Credit Plan.*** The installment method cannot be used for sales of personal property under a revolving credit plan [§ 453(k)(1)]. For this purpose, a revolving credit plan is an arrangement under which a customer agrees to pay a part of the outstanding balance of his account each billing month [Reg. § 1.453A-2(c)(1)].

***Dispositions of Publicly Traded Property.*** The installment method cannot be used for the following dispositions [§ 453(k)(2)]:

- sales of stock or securities that are traded on an established securities market; and
- sales of other property of a kind regularly traded on an established market (to the extent the regulations provide that such sales are ineligible).

### III.G.2. Computing Gain Using the Installment Method

[565 T.M., III.; TPS ¶3550.02.]

Under the installment method, gain on an installment sale of property is spread over the period during which installment payments are received, rather than being taxed entirely in the year of sale. Each payment a taxpayer receives on the installment sale will generally consist of three components: (i) gain on the sale of the property, (ii) a return of the taxpayer's adjusted basis in the property, and (iii) interest. Thus, only a portion of each installment payment is treated as gain. The interest portion of an installment payment is treated as ordinary income. The recovery of basis is not included in income.

The amount of gain recognized on an installment sale for any tax year is equal to the total installment payments received during the year multiplied by a gross profit percentage. The gross profit percentage is equal to the ratio of gross profit to total contract price [§ 453(c); Reg. § 15A.453-1(b)(2)(i)]. Special rules apply in determining the gross profit and total contract price on installment obligations received in a like-kind exchange (see III.G.9.c.).

***Gross Profit.*** The gross profit used in determining the gross profit percentage is equal to the selling price, less the taxpayer's adjusted basis in the property sold [Reg. § 15A.453-1(b)(2)(v)].

The selling price includes: (i) money received from the buyer, (ii) the fair market value of any property received from the buyer, (iii) the amount of debt paid, assumed, or taken by the buyer, and (iv) the amount of the taxpayer's selling expenses paid by the buyer. The selling price does not include any interest received from the buyer [Reg. § 15A.453-1(b)(2)(ii)].

The taxpayer's adjusted basis for installment sale purposes includes the taxpayer's adjusted basis for tax purposes, plus any selling expenses related to the sale of the property (e.g., commissions or attorney's fees) [Reg. § 15A.453-1(b)(2)(v)]. If the taxpayer sells depreciable property, any depreciation recapture income (see III.G.5.) must also be added to the taxpayer's adjusted basis.

*Total Contract Price.* The total contract price used in determining the gross profit percentage is equal to the selling price reduced by the amount of any qualifying indebtedness assumed, or taken subject to, by the buyer [Reg. § 15A.453-1(b)(2)(iii)]. The amount of qualifying indebtedness taken into account for this purpose is limited to the amount of the taxpayer's basis in the property.

Qualifying indebtedness includes (i) a mortgage or other debt secured by the property, and (ii) any unsecured debt assumed or incurred by the buyer incident to the purchase, holding, or operation of the property in the ordinary course of business. Qualifying indebtedness does not include (i) debt incurred by the taxpayer incident to the sale of the property, (ii) debt incurred by the taxpayer that is unrelated to the purchase, holding, or operation of the property in the ordinary course of business, or (iii) debt that is assumed or incurred by the taxpayer in contemplation of the sale of the property and that results in an accelerated recovery of the taxpayer's basis upon the installment sale [Reg. § 15A.453-1(b)(2)(iv)].

---

**EXAMPLE:** On July 1 of Year 1, Sam sells personal property for $50,000 in an installment sale. The installment sale is eligible for the installment method and Sam does not elect out of the installment method. The buyer pays the $50,000 selling price with a $10,000 cash down payment and a $40,000 installment note payable in eight quarterly installments of $5,000 (plus interest) beginning on Oct. 1 of Year 1. Sam has an adjusted basis of $29,000 in the property sold and he incurs $1,000 of selling expenses in the transaction. Sam's gross profit on the installment sale is $20,000 ($50,000 selling price − ($29,000 adjusted basis + $1,000 selling expenses)). The total contract price is $50,000. Thus, Sam's gross profit percentage is 40% ($20,000 gross profit ÷ $50,000 total contact price). For Year 1, Sam must report $6,000 of gain (($10,000 down payment + $5,000 installment payment) × 40%). For Year 2, Sam must report $8,000 gain ($20,000 installment payments × 40%). For Year 3, Sam must report $6,000 of gain ($15,000 installment payments × 40%).

**EXAMPLE:** Assume the same facts as in the previous example, except that the buyer pays the $50,000 selling price with a $10,000 down payment, a $10,000 assumption of qualifying indebtedness, and a $30,000 installment note payable in six quarterly installments of $5,000 (plus interest) beginning on Oct. 1 of Year 1. Sam's gross profit on the installment sale is $20,000, as in the previous example. However, the total contact price is $40,000 ($50,000 selling price − $10,000 qualifying indebtedness assumed). Thus, Sam's gross profit percentage is 50% ($20,000 gross profit ÷ $40,000 total contact price). For Year 1, Sam must report $7,500 of gain (($10,000 down payment + $5,000 installment payment) × 50%). For Year 2, Sam must report $10,000 gain ($20,000 installment payments × 50%). For Year 3, Sam must report $2,500 of gain ($5,000 installment payments × 50%).

---

A special rule applies to gain from the installment sale of depreciable property subject to depreciation recapture (see III.G.5.). Additionally, certain installment sales of property are subject to a special interest charge on the deferred tax resulting from the installment sale (see III.G.4.).

### III.G.3. Electing Out of Installment Sale Treatment

[565 T.M., IX.; TPS ¶3550.11.B.]

If a sale qualifies as an installment sale, any gain on the sale must be reported using the installment method unless the taxpayer elects out of the installment method [§ 453(d)(1)]. When a taxpayer elects out of the installment method, the taxpayer must report the entire gain in the year of the sale, even though all sales proceeds are not received in that year.

A taxpayer elects out of the installment method by reporting all gain from the sale on Form 4797, *Sales of Business Property*, and/or Form 8949, *Sales and Other Dispositions of Capital Assets*, for its tax return for the year of the sale. The election generally must be made by the due date (including extensions) for the filing of the return for the year of the sale [§ 453(d)(2)]. However, if a taxpayer files its return without making the election, it can still make the election by filing an amended return within six months of the return due date (including extensions) and writing "Filed pursuant to section 301.9100-2" at the top of the amended return [Reg. § 301.9100-2(d)]. In addition, the IRS may permit a late election in those rare circumstances when it concludes that the taxpayer had good cause for failing to make a timely election [Reg. § 15A.453-1(d)(3)].

An election out of the installment method may be revoked only with IRS consent. The IRS will not consent to revocation of the election if the tax year in which any payment was received has closed or if one of the purposes of the revocation is the avoidance of federal income tax. If the IRS consents to revocation of the election, the revocation is retroactive [§ 453(d)(3); Reg. § 15A.453-1(d)(4)].

### III.G.4. Interest Charge on Deferred Tax of an Installment Obligation

[565 T.M., V.B.; TPS ¶3550.05.A.]

A taxpayer using the installment method to report gain on a sale of property is required to pay interest to the IRS on the deferred tax related to the installment obligation if both of the following apply [§ 453A(b)]:

1. the property had a sales price over $150,000; and
2. the total balance of the taxpayer's nondealer installment obligations arising during, and outstanding at the end of, the tax year is more than $5 million.

Installment obligations arising from the disposition of farm property and personal use property are not subject to interest [§ 453A(b)(3)]. Installment obligations arising from the disposition of timeshares and residential lots are subject to the dealer interest rule (see III.G.1.) instead of this nondealer interest rule [§ 453A(b)(4)].

The interest on deferred tax is computed by multiplying the taxpayer's deferred tax by the underpayment rate in effect for the month with or within which the taxpayer's tax year ends. The deferred tax is equal to the amount of the taxpayer's unrecognized gain as of the end of the tax year multiplied by the taxpayer's maximum tax rate in effect for the tax year. The underpayment rate is published quarterly in the Internal Revenue Bulletin [§ 453(c)].

The interest on deferred tax is reported as additional tax on the taxpayer's tax return. Individuals report it on the "other taxes" line of Form 1040 or Form 1040A. Corporations report it on the "other taxes" line in Schedule J of Form 1120.

### III.G.5. Depreciation Recapture Income in an Installment Sale

[565 T.M., III.C.; TPS ¶3550.08.]

If a taxpayer sells property subject to the depreciation recapture rules (see III.D.) in an installment sale, the taxpayer must recognize any recapture income as ordinary income in the year of the sale. Any gain in excess of the recapture income is then taken into account using the installment method [§ 453(i)(1)].

Recapture income is the total amount of gain that would be treated as ordinary income under the depreciation recapture rules of § 1245 and § 1250 (including § 179 recapture (see V.B.)) if all payments to be received on the sale of property were to be received in the year of the sale [§ 453(i)(2)]. The recapture income is added to the taxpayer's adjusted basis in the property sold for purposes of applying the installment method to the gain in excess of depreciation recapture income.

---

**EXAMPLE:** Steve sells depreciable property to Bob for $100,000 payable in 10 annual installments of $10,000 (plus interest) beginning in the year after the year of the sale. The property has an adjusted basis of $20,000 and Steve has taken $30,000 of depreciation deductions on the property as of the time of the sale. Under the depreciation recapture rules, the entire $30,000 must be recaptured as ordinary income. Thus, Steve must recognize $30,000 of recapture income in the year of the sale, even though he does not receive any payments in that year. Steve's gross profit percentage for each $10,000 payment received after the year of sale is 50% (($20,000 adjusted basis + $30,000 recapture income added to basis) ÷ $100,000 total contact price).

---

If gain on an installment sale includes both unrecaptured § 1250 gain and adjusted net capital gain, the installment method may be used to report both types of gain. Unrecaptured § 1250 gain is taken into account before adjusted net capital gain [Reg. § 1.453-12(a)].

### III.G.6. Deemed Payments Received in an Installment Sale

[565 T.M., IV., V.C.; TPS ¶3550.04., .05.B.]

The gain recognized on an installment sale for any tax year is determined by multiplying the amount of payments received during the year under the installment obligation by a gross profit percentage. Payments received under the installment obligation include not only amounts the taxpayer actually receives from the buyer, but also certain amounts the taxpayer is deemed to receive from the buyer [Reg. § 15A.453-1(b)(3)(i)].

A taxpayer selling property in an installment sale is deemed to receive payments from the buyer on the installment obligation in the following situations [Reg. § 15A.453-1(b)(3)(i)]:

- the taxpayer receives cash or other property that is payable on demand or readily tradable (such as foreign currency, marketable securities, or certain evidences of indebtedness);
- the taxpayer receives an evidence of indebtedness secured by cash or a cash equivalent (such as a bank certificate of deposit or a treasury note);
- the taxpayer's qualifying indebtedness is assumed, or taken subject to, by the buyer (however, in this case, the amount of the payments received is limited to the amount of the taxpayer's adjusted basis in the property sold);
- the taxpayer sells encumbered property to a buyer that is the taxpayer's creditor, and the buyer cancels the taxpayer's debt;
- the taxpayer sells encumbered property to a buyer that is liable for the related debt; and
- the taxpayer receives an evidence of indebtedness from a person other than the buyer.

If a taxpayer secures a loan using an installment obligation arising from an installment sale of property over $150,000, then the net proceeds the taxpayer receives from the loan are treated as a payment received on the installment obligation. Under this pledge rule, the payment on the installment obligation is treated as received on the later of the date the loan becomes secured or the date the taxpayer receives the loan proceeds [§ 453A(d)].

### III.G.7. Related Party Installment Sales

[565 T.M., VI.; TPS ¶3550.07.]

Two special rules apply to installment sales between related persons. One rule applies when a taxpayer sells property to a related person in an installment sale, and the related person then resells the property before making all required installment payments. The other rule applies when a taxpayer sells depreciable property to a related person in an installment sale.

***Sale of Property to Related Person Followed by Resale.*** If a taxpayer sells property to a related person (as defined in § 453(f)(1)) in an installment sale (the first disposition) and the related person then resells the property in another transaction (the second disposition) within two years of the first disposition and before making all required installment payments on the first disposition, then the amount realized by the related person in the second disposition generally must be treated as a payment received by the taxpayer in the first disposition. The taxpayer treats this amount as a payment received on the date of the second disposition [§ 453(e)(1), § 453(e)(2)].

For any tax year, the amount the taxpayer treats as a payment received under this rule is limited to the excess of:

1. the lesser of (i) the total amount realized on the second disposition before the end of the tax year, or (ii) the total contract price for the first disposition; over

2. the sum of (i) the amount of payments received on the first disposition before the end of the tax year, and (ii) the amount of payments treated as received on the second disposition by reason of this rule for prior tax years [§ 453(e)(3)].

---

**EXAMPLE:** In Year 1, Sam sells farm land to his son, Bill, for $500,000, to be paid in five equal installments of $100,000 (plus interest) over five years. Sam's installment sale basis in the property is $250,000 and the property is not subject to any mortgages or liens. Sam's gross profit percentage is 50% (($500,000 selling price − $250,000 basis) ÷ $500,000 total contract price). Bill pays Sam $100,000 in Year 1 and Sam includes $50,000 ($100,000 × 50%) in income for that year. Bill pays Sam $100,000 in Year 2 before selling the farm land to a third party for $400,000. In Year 2, Sam treats $200,000 as payments received because of the second disposition, computed as $400,000 (the lesser of the amount realized on the second disposition ($400,000) or the total contact price for the first disposition ($500,000)), minus $200,000 (the sum of the payments received on the first disposition before the end of Year 2 ($200,000) and the payments treated as received on the second disposition before Year 2 ($0)). Thus, Sam has $300,000 of total payments received and treated as received in Year 2 ($100,000 received + $200,000 treated as received), and he reports installment sale income of $150,000 for Year 2 ($300,000 × 50%).

---

If the taxpayer can show to the satisfaction of the IRS that avoidance of federal income tax was not one of the principal purposes of the first or second disposition, then this rule does not apply to the second disposition [§ 453(e)(7)].

This rule also does not apply to the following transactions:

• a taxpayer's sale or exchange of stock to the issuing corporation is not treated as a first disposition;

- an involuntary conversion of property is not treated as a second disposition by the related person if the first disposition occurred before the threat of conversion; and

- a transfer of the property after the death of the taxpayer or the related person, whichever is earlier, is not treated as a second disposition [§ 453(e)(6)].

***Sale of Depreciable Property to Related Person.*** If a taxpayer sells depreciable property to a related person (as defined in § 453(g)(3)) in an installment sale, the installment method generally cannot be used to report the gain on the sale. Instead, the taxpayer must treat all payments from the buyer as received in the year of the sale [§ 453(g)(1)].

Under an exception to this rule, a taxpayer can use the installment method to report gain on the sale of depreciable property to a related person if it can show to the satisfaction of the IRS that avoidance of federal income tax was not one of the principal purposes of the sale [§ 453(g)(2)].

### III.G.8. Contingent Payment Sales

[565 T.M., III.D.; TPS ¶3550.02.B.]

Contingent payment sales are required to be reported using the installment method unless the taxpayer elects out of the installment method. Generally, a contingent payment sale is a sale of property for which the aggregate selling price cannot be determined by the end of the tax year in which the property is sold. However, a contingent payment sale does not include a transaction in which the installment obligation represents (i) a retained interest in the property that is the subject of the transaction, (ii) an interest in a joint venture or partnership, or (iii) an equity interest in a corporation [Reg. § 15A.453-1(c)(1)].

Although contingent payment sales must be reported using the installment method, special rules apply for allocating the taxpayer's basis to the payments to be received in a contingent payment sale. A different allocation rule applies for each of the following scenarios [Reg. § 15A.453-1(c)(1)]:

- the contingent payment sale has a stated maximum selling price;

- the contingent payment sale does not have a stated maximum selling price, but it has a fixed payment period; and

- the contingent payment sale does not have a stated maximum selling price or a fixed payment period.

### III.G.9. Transactions Involving Installment Obligations

#### III.G.9.a. Dispositions of Installment Obligations

[565 T.M., VIII.; TPS ¶3550.09.]

When a taxpayer makes a disposition of property in an installment sale, the taxpayer generally receives an installment obligation from the buyer. If a taxpayer uses the installment method to report the installment sale and disposes of the installment obligation before all payments are received from the buyer, the taxpayer is generally required to report a gain or loss on the disposition of the installment obligation [§ 453B(a)].

The computation of the gain or loss on the disposition of an installment obligation depends on whether the taxpayer sells or exchanges the installment obligation or disposes of it in some other manner. If the taxpayer sells or exchanges the installment obligation, gain or loss is equal to the difference between the amount realized on the sale or exchange and the taxpayer's basis in the obligation [§ 453B(a)(1)]. If the taxpayer disposes of the installment obligation in some other manner, gain or loss is equal to the difference between the fair market value of the obligation at the time of disposition and the taxpayer's basis in the obligation [§ 453B(a)(2)]. An installment obligation that is canceled or otherwise becomes unenforceable is treated as a disposition of the installment obligation in a manner other than by sale or exchange [§ 453B(f)].

Self-canceling installment notes (SCINs) between related parties are frequently used for estate planning purposes. A SCIN is a note in which the buyer's payment obligations terminate upon a certain event, typically the seller's death. In order for the installment method to apply to a SCIN, the term of the note must be less than the seller's normal life expectancy, and thus, it must be reasonably anticipated that the seller will survive the entire term of the note. Upon the death of a decedent, a SCIN is treated as having been automatically canceled and disposed of in a transaction other than a sale or exchange.

A taxpayer's basis in an installment obligation is equal to the unpaid balance on the obligation, less the product of that unpaid balance and the taxpayer's gross profit percentage [§ 453B(b)].

---

**EXAMPLE:** Several years ago, Steve sold property under the installment method for $100,000. Steve's adjusted basis in the property was $40,000 and, therefore, Steve's gross profit percentage is 60% (($100,000 − $40,000) ÷ $100,000). On a date when the unpaid balance on the installment note is $10,000, Steve sells the note for $8,000. Steve's basis in the installment note is $4,000 ($10,000 unpaid balance − ($10,000 unpaid balance × 60% gross profit percentage)). Therefore, Steve must recognize a gain on the sale of the installment note of $4,000 ($8,000 amount realized − $4,000 basis).

---

Any gain or loss that results from the disposition of an installment obligation is treated as resulting from the sale or exchange of the property for which the obligation was received [§ 453B(a)]. Thus, the character of the gain or loss on the sale of the installment obligation will be the same as the character of the gain on the original installment sale (e.g., ordinary gain or loss, capital gain or loss, or § 1231 gain or loss).

No recognition of gain or loss is required for the following transactions [§ 453B(c), § 453B(d), § 453B(g), § 453B(h)]:

- the transfer of an installment obligation between spouses (or former spouses) incident to a divorce;
- the transfer of an installment obligation as a result of the taxpayer's death;
- the distribution of an installment obligation to a parent corporation in complete liquidation of an 80% owned subsidiary; and
- the distribution of an installment obligation in complete liquidation of an S corporation.

### III.G.9.b. Installment Obligations Received in a Corporate Liquidation

[565 T.M., VIII.B.4.; TPS ¶3550.09.B.4.]

If a shareholder receives an installment obligation in exchange for its stock in a corporation as part of a complete liquidation of the corporation, then the payments the shareholder receives on the installment obligation (but not the receipt of the installment obligation itself) are generally treated as consideration received for the stock [§ 453(h)(1)(A)]. The shareholder reports the payments received on the installment obligation under the installment method, unless he or she elects out of the installment method [Reg. § 1.453-11(a)(1)].

The installment obligation received by the shareholder generally does not qualify for the installment method if the stock of the liquidating corporation is traded on an established securities market because sales of stock or securities traded on an established securities market do not generally qualify for the installment method [§ 453(k)(2); Reg. § 1.453-11(a)(2)(i)]. However, if the stock of the liquidating corporation is not traded on an established securities market, the installment method can be used for the installment obligation unless the corporation was formed, or availed of, for a principal purpose of avoiding limitations on the availability of installment method treatment through the use of a related party [Reg. § 1.453-11(c)(5)(i)].

An installment obligation received in a corporate liquidation is covered by these rules if the liquidating corporation acquired it in a sale or exchange of corporate assets during the 12-month period beginning on the date the plan of liquidation is adopted [Reg. § 1.453-11(c)(1)]. However, an installment obligation acquired in a sale or exchange of inventory, stock in trade, or property held for sale in the ordinary course of business is covered by these rules only if the installment obligation arises from a single sale to one person of substantially all of such property attributable to a trade or business of the corporation [§ 453(h)(1)(B); Reg. § 1.453-11(c)(4)].

### III.G.9.c. Installment Obligations Received in a Like-Kind Exchange

[565 T.M., VII.; TPS ¶3550.06.]

When a taxpayer exchanges property in a like-kind exchange (see III.E.1.) and receives not only like-kind property but also cash or non-cash boot, the taxpayer must report gain to the extent of the cash and the fair market value of the non-cash boot received [§ 1031(b)]. An installment obligation received in a like-kind exchange is treated as boot, and the following special rules apply for purposes of determining the installment sale income to be reported on the installment obligation each year:

- the total contract price must be reduced by the fair market value of the like-kind property received in the exchange;
- the gross profit must be reduced by any gain on the exchange that can be deferred; and
- any like-kind property the taxpayer receives in the exchange is not treated as a payment received on the installment obligation [§ 453(f)(6)].

---

**EXAMPLE:** Sarah exchanges property with a fair market value of $100,000 and adjusted basis of $40,000 for like-kind property with a fair market value of $20,000 and an $80,000 installment note. For purposes of determining the gross profit percentage to be used in computing gain on the installment note, the selling price is $100,000 ($80,000 installment note + $20,000 fair market value of the like-kind property received), the total contract price is $80,000 ($100,000 selling price − $20,000 fair market value of the like-kind property received), and the gross profit is $60,000 ($100,000 selling price − $40,000 adjusted basis). Thus, Sarah's gross profit percentage is 75% ($60,000 gross profit ÷ $80,000 total contract price). In the year of the exchange, Sarah does not report any gain on the installment note because the like-kind property received is not treated as a payment received on the installment note. In later years, Sarah must recognize as gain 75% of each payment received on the installment note.

---

### *III.G.10. Reacquisitions of Installment Sale Real Property*

[565 T.M., XI.D.; TPS ¶3550.13.C.]

Special rules apply if a taxpayer sells real property in an installment sale and later reacquires that property. The special reacquisition rules apply only if the buyer's installment obligation is secured by the property reacquired, and the taxpayer's reacquisition of the property discharges that installment obligation [§ 1038(a)]. In such a case, the taxpayer generally must report gain on the reacquisition equal to the difference between the total payments received on the sale (including any deemed payments received) and the total gain already reported as income. However, the amount of taxable gain is limited to the taxpayer's gross profit on the original sale, less the sum of the amount of gain already reported as income before reacquisition and the costs of reacquisition [§ 1038(b)].

The taxpayer takes a basis in the reacquired real property equal to the sum of the following amounts [§ 1038(c)]:

1. the taxpayer's adjusted basis in the installment obligation (i.e., the unpaid balance on the obligation, less the product of that unpaid balance and the taxpayer's gross profit percentage);

2. the taxpayer's reacquisitions costs; and

3. the taxpayer's taxable gain on the reacquisition.

For further discussion of reacquisitions of real property in satisfaction of secured debt, see III.E.6.a.

# CHAPTER IV. TRADE OR BUSINESS DEDUCTIONS

>>>>>>>>>>>>>>>>>>>>>>>>>>>>>>>>>

## IV.A. Common Trade or Business Deductions

[505 T.M.; TPS ¶¶2110, 2450.03.]

To be deductible, a business expense must be (i) related to a trade or business, (ii) ordinary and necessary, and (iii) paid or incurred in carrying on a trade or business [§ 162(a)].

*Trade or Business.* Whether or not a trade or business exists is a fact-specific inquiry. However, a primary purpose of generating income or profit is a prerequisite. Additionally, a taxpayer's involvement with the activity must be regular and continuous [*Commissioner v. Groetzinger*, 480 U.S. 23 (1987)]. Factors considered in the profit motive determination include the following [Reg. § 1.183-2(b)]:

- the manner in which the taxpayer conducts the activity;
- the expertise of the taxpayer or his or her advisors;
- the time and effort the taxpayer expends in conducting the activity;
- the expectation that assets used in the activity may appreciate in value;
- the success the taxpayer has had in conducting other similar or dissimilar activities;
- the taxpayer's history of income or losses with respect to the activity;
- the amount of occasional profits from the activity;
- the financial status of the taxpayer; and
- the taxpayer's personal pleasure, recreation, or other personal motives.

If a profit motive is present, an expense that is not a business expense nevertheless may be deductible as an expense for the production of income [§ 212] (see IV.B.). The factors considered in determining the existence of a profit motive are similar to the factors used to determine whether a profit motive exists for purposes of establishing the existence of a trade or business discussed above.

*Ordinary and Necessary.* Whether an expense is ordinary and necessary is also a fact-specific inquiry. An expense is ordinary if it is normal, usual, or customary in the type of business in which it is incurred [*Lilly v. Commissioner*, 343 U.S. 90 (1952)]. It need not be incurred often or habitually by the same taxpayer in order to be considered ordinary. An expense is necessary if it is appropriate or helpful to the business [*Welch v. Helvering*, 290 U.S. 111 (1933)]. A compulsory payment is not, by its nature, a necessary expense [*Commissioner v. Lincoln Savings & Loan Ass'n*, 403 U.S. 345 (1971)].

179

*Paid or Incurred in Carrying on a Trade or Business.* An individual is carrying on a trade or business if he or she is actively engaged in the trade or business. Merely seeking employment in, or looking for, a new trade or business does not qualify. However, certain expenditures related to new trades or businesses may be deductible as a start-up expense [§ 195]. Start-up expenses are discussed in IV.F.4.

Of the many expenses incurred in operating a business, some may be deducted while others must be capitalized. Generally, expenses that are a part of a taxpayer's investment in a business are capital expenses. Capital expenses are considered assets in the business, and their costs generally are recovered over a period of years through depreciation, amortization, or depletion. On the other hand, expenses that do not rise to that level of investment typically may be deducted currently as business expenses. Capital expenditures are discussed in VIII.A. Depreciation and amortization is discussed in Chapter V., and depletion is discussed in VI.A.

### IV.A.1. Advertising Expenses

[505 T.M., IV.F.; TPS ¶2120.]

A taxpayer generally may deduct reasonable advertising expenses that are directly related to business activities [Reg. § 1.162-1(a)]. This includes the cost of institutional or goodwill advertising made to keep the business's name before the public and that are related to patronage the business may expect in the future [Reg. § 1.162-20(a)(2)]. If advertising is directed towards obtaining future benefits significantly beyond those traditionally associated with ordinary product advertising or with institutional or goodwill advertising, the costs may require capitalization [Rev. Rul. 92-80, 1992-2 C.B. 57].

Expenditures for advertising that presents a taxpayer's views on economic, financial, social, or other subjects of a general nature may be deducted. Similarly, a taxpayer may deduct impartial advertising that (i) encourages the public to register and vote in elections or contribute to campaigns of a candidate or party, or (ii) involves sponsoring unbiased presentations of debates among candidates for political office [Rev. Rul. 62-156, 1962-2 C.B. 47]. However, a taxpayer may not deduct expenditures incurred in connection with (i) influencing legislation, (ii) the participation or intervention in any political campaign, or (iii) any attempt to influence the general public with respect to legislative matters, elections, or referendums [§ 162(e); Reg. § 1.162-20(c)(4)].

### IV.A.2. Compensation Paid

[394 T.M., III.C., 505 T.M., IV.A.; TPS ¶¶1320.05.B.2.b., 5420.01.]

An employer generally may deduct reasonable amounts paid to employees for the services they perform [§ 162(a)(1)]. Payments in the form of compensation that are not, in fact, for services rendered are not deductible. Whether a payment is compensation for services rendered or takes some other form (e.g., dividends, loans, interest) is a question of fact [Reg. § 1.162-7].

Deductible compensation payments may be in the form of cash, property, or services, and it includes wages, salaries, bonuses, commissions, or other non-cash compensation like vacation allowances and fringe benefits [Reg. § 1.162-7, § 1.162-9, § 1.162-10(a)]. A bonus is allowed as a deduction for compensation if it is made in good faith and as additional compensation for services actually rendered, and if, when added to other compensation, it does not exceed reasonable compensation for the services rendered [Reg. § 1.162-9]. Amounts paid or accrued by an employer on account of employees' injuries (even lump sum payments) are deductible to the extent the amounts paid are not compensated for by insurance or otherwise. Additionally, deductions are allowed for dismissal wages, unemployment benefits, guaranteed annual wages, amounts paid under sickness, accident, hospitalization, medical expense, recreational, welfare, or similar benefit plans if they are ordinary and necessary trade or business expenses [Reg. § 1.162-10].

The deduction is limited to reasonable compensation. Reasonable compensation is the amount that would ordinarily be paid for like services by like enterprises under like circumstances at the time the contract for services is made (not the time the reasonableness is questioned) [Reg. § 1.162-7(b)(3)]. Factors that may be relevant in determining if pay is reasonable include (i) the duties the employee performs, (ii) the volume of business handled, (iii) the complexities of the business, (iv) the amount of time required, (v) the cost of living in the area, and (vi) the ability and achievements of the employee performing the service.

Amounts disallowed as a deduction because they are unreasonable are recharacterized depending on the circumstances. For example, an excessive amount paid by a corporation, if it bears a relationship to stockholdings, might be recharacterized as a dividend [Reg. § 1.162-8].

*Certain Highly Compensated Employees.* Publicly held corporations may not deduct compensation paid to covered employees to the extent it exceeds $1 million for the tax year. Commissions and certain performance-based compensation are excluded for this purpose. Covered employees are (i) the chief executive officer, (ii) an individual acting in the chief executive officer's capacity, or (iii) an employee whose compensation is required to be reported to shareholders under the Securities Exchange Act of 1934 by virtue of being among the four highest compensated officers for the tax year (other than the chief executive officer). In the case of certain employers that participated in the Troubled Asset Relief Program and certain health insurance providers, a similar $500,000 limit applies [§ 162(m)].

*Excess Golden Parachute Payments.* Golden parachute restrictions in § 280G may limit the deduction for compensation paid under § 162. Golden parachutes and excess parachute payments are discussed in XVII.B.3.

*Awards.* While an employer's reasonable cash payments to an employee are deductible as compensation paid, an employer also may generally deduct amounts paid in tangible property to an employee as an award. However, the deduction for the cost of employee achievement awards given to any one employee during a tax year is limited to $400 for awards that are not qualified plan awards, and $1,600 for all awards, whether or not qualified plan awards. The receipt of an employee achievement award is excluded from an employee's income if the cost of the award does not exceed the amount allowed as a deduction to the employer [§ 74(c), § 274(j)].

An employee achievement award is an item of tangible personal property that is (i) given to an employee as either a length of service award (as defined in § 274(j)(4)(B)) or safety achievement award (as defined in § 274(j)(4)(C)), (ii) as part of a meaningful presentation, and (iii) under circumstances that do not create a significant likelihood the award is disguised compensation. A qualified plan award is an achievement award given as part of an established written plan or program that does not favor highly compensated employees (as defined in § 414(q)). An award is not a qualified plan award if the average cost of all the employee achievement awards given in a tax year that would otherwise be qualified plan awards is more than $400 (ignoring awards of nominal value) [§ 274(j)].

*Deferred Compensation.* Deferred compensation and retirement benefits are not deductible under § 162 as a trade or business expense, but they may be deductible under another provision [§ 404; Reg. § 1.162-10(a), § 1.162-10T] (see XVII.A. and XVII.B.).

### IV.A.3. Employee-Related Expenses

[505 T.M., II.B.6., IV; TPS ¶2130.]

An employee's performance of services is considered a trade or business for purposes of the trade or business expense deduction. However, an employee who performs services for which compensation is neither sought nor received lacks a profit motive, and the employee is not engaged in a trade or business.

An employee deducting ordinary and necessary expenses for his or her employment reports those expenses on Form 2106, *Employee Business Expenses.*

**Who Must File Form 2106**

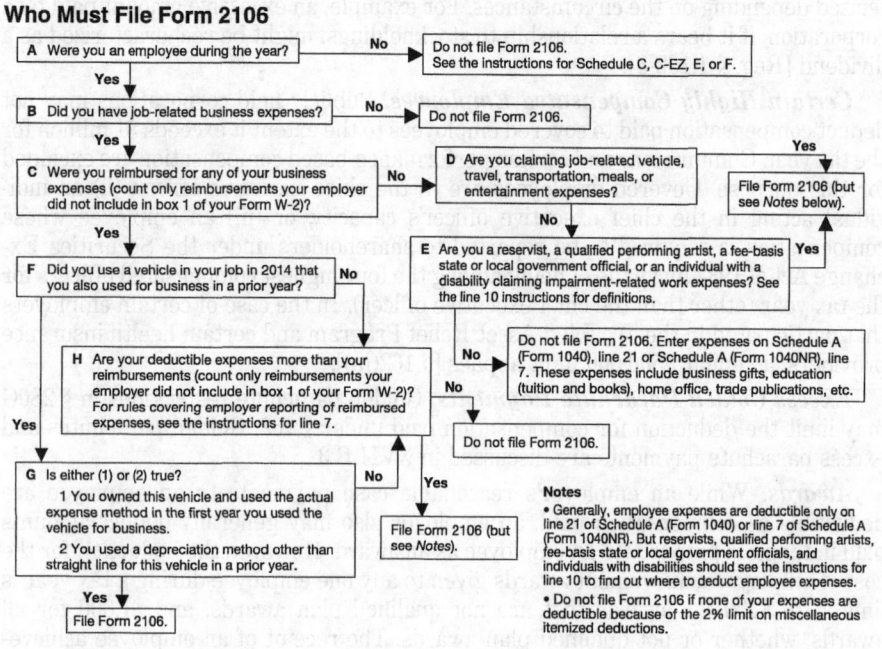

(Source: 2014 Draft Instructions for Form 2106)

### IV.A.3.a. Common Employee Expenses

[505 T.M., II.B.6., IV; TPS ¶2130.]

***Travel, Transportation, and Commuting Expenses***. The ordinary and necessary expenses of traveling away from home for business are deductible, including amounts spent for reasonable meals and lodging [§ 162(a)(2); Reg. § 1.162-2]. Expenses paid or incurred by an employee in getting from one work place to another (other than travel expenses while away from home) are deductible transportation expenses [Rev. Rul. 99-7, 1999-5 I.R.B. 4]. An employee's expenses in commuting from home to work, however, generally is not deductible [Reg. § 1.162-2(e)]. Travel, transportation, and commuting expenses are discussed in detail in IV.A.10.

*Meal and Entertainment Expenses.* Expenses of reasonable business meals and entertainment may be deductible if they are related to, or, in the case of an expense directly preceding or following a substantial and bona fide business discussion, associated with, the active conduct of the taxpayer's trade or business. The amount deductible is generally limited to 50% of the amount paid or incurred [§ 274(a)(1)(A), § 274(n)]. Meals and entertainment expenses are discussed in detail in IV.A.11.

*Uniforms and Work Clothing.* The cost of uniforms and other work clothing is generally deductible if the clothing is specifically required as a condition of employment and is not suitable for, or adaptable to, everyday wear [Rev. Rul. 70-474, 1970-2 C.B. 34]. An employer's cost in furnishing work clothing to employees is a deductible business expense of the employer [§ 162].

---

**EXAMPLE:** Ken is a cashier at Grocery Store. All of Grocery Store's employees are required to wear white shirts, black pants, and black shoes. Grocery Store does not reimburse employees for the expense. Ken purchases the required clothing and never wears the items for any activities other than his work at Grocery Store. Because his clothes are regular clothing items suitable for everyday wear, their cost is not a deductible ordinary and necessary business expense.

---

*Small Tools.* Employees required to furnish small tools for use in connection with their employment may be able to deduct or depreciate the cost of the tools. Similarly, the cost of small tools that an employer furnishes to an employee is a deductible business expense of the employer [§ 162].

*Union and Professional Dues.* Annual dues paid to labor unions and trade associations are generally deductible as ordinary and necessary business expenses [Reg. § 1.162-15(c)]. Similarly, dues paid to a professional association are deductible if membership in the association is intended to further a professional's business interests. Dues expenses are discussed in detail in IV.A.4.

*Educational Expenses.* Expenses for education may be deductible if the education (i) maintains or improves skills required by the employee's present occupation, or (ii) satisfies the express requirements of the employer, or the requirements of applicable law or regulations, imposed as a condition for retaining the employee's position, status, or level of compensation. However they are not deductible as a business expense if paid or incurred to meet minimum educational requirements for employment or to qualify the employee for a new trade or business [Reg. § 1.162-5(a), § 1.162-5(b)]. Educational expenses are discussed in detail in IV.A.5.

*Job Search Expenses.* Expenses paid or incurred in seeking new employment in the taxpayer's present occupation may be deductible. It is immaterial whether or not the search is successful. However, if there is a substantial lack of continuity between the taxpayer's previous employment and the search for a new job, the job search expenses are not deductible [Rev. Rul. 75-120, 1975-1 C.B. 55]. Further, no deduction is allowed for the expenses of seeking employment in a first job, or in a different occupation or profession.

---

**EXAMPLE:** From Year 1 through Year 6, Joan worked for a publisher as an editor. From Year 7 through Year 16, Joan had 4 children, was a full-time mother, and served as a volunteer in her community. She was not employed outside the home during that period. In Year 17, Joan decides to resume her career as an editor. She prints and mails resumes to several publishing companies to solicit employment. Because of the lapse of time between Joan's prior employment and her job search, the printing and mailing expenses are not deductible business expenses.

---

***Home Office Expenses.*** A deduction for a home office is available for any part of a taxpayer's home that is used regularly and exclusively for one the following uses [§ 280A(c)(1)]:

- the principal place of business for any trade or business in which the taxpayer engages;
- a place to meet or deal with patients, clients, or customers in the normal course of a trade or business; or
- a separate structure not attached the taxpayer's house or residence that is used in connection with a trade or business.

These expenses are distinguishable from lodging furnished to an employee for the employer's convenience, the value of which is excluded from the employee's income [§ 119]. Lodging furnished for an employer's convenience is discussed in XVII.E.4.

Home office expenses are discussed in detail in IV.D.7.

### IV.A.3.b. Reimbursement Arrangements

[503 T.M., II.B.4.b(2); TPS ¶2130.02.]

Employees may receive an advance, an allowance, or a reimbursement from their employer for business expenses they incur. How these amounts are reported depends on the type of plan under which the employee is reimbursed. Under an accountable plan, the employer does not report any reimbursements in the employee's income, and the employee may not deduct the expenses on his or her return. The employer, on the other hand, generally may deduct the reimbursed amounts, subject to any applicable limits. By contrast, under a nonaccountable plan, the employer includes the amount of any reimbursement or other expense allowance paid to the employee in the employee's wages. The employee, if he or she itemizes deductions, may deduct the business expenses on his or her return, subject to the 2% of adjusted gross income floor (see VII.C.).

***Accountable Plans.*** An accountable plan is an arrangement between an employer and employee that satisfies the following three basic requirements [Reg. § 1.62-2(c)]:

- the expenses must have a business connection;
- the expenses must be substantiated; and
- amounts received in excess of substantiated expenses must be returned to the employer.

The business connection requirement necessitates that the plan provide advances, allowances, or reimbursements for employee business expenses that (i) satisfy the requirements for deduction under § 161 through § 199, and (ii) are paid or incurred in connection with the employee's performance of services as an employee. Allowances under the plan may include per diems, meals and incidental expenses, and mileage allowances. Payments under the plan may be received from either the employer, the employer's agent, or a third party for whom the employee performs a service as an employee of the employer. If an amount is paid to an employee whether or not the employee incurs (or is reasonably expected to incur) a deductible employee business expense, the arrangement does not satisfy the business connection requirement, and all amounts paid under the arrangement are treated as paid under a nonaccountable plan [Reg. § 1.62-2(d)].

The substantiation requirement mandates that an employee furnish adequate substantiation of reimbursed expenses to the employer or other payor. The type of substantiation required depends on the nature of the reimbursed expense. Arrangements that reimburse travel, entertainment, the use of a passenger automobile or other listed property, or other business expenses governed by the § 274(d) substantiation requirements (see IV.C.1.) will meet the accountable plan substantiation requirement if they satisfy those § 274(d) substantiation requirements. If an expense is not governed by the § 274(d) substantiation requirements, the employee must provide the employer with information identifying the nature of the expense and showing that it was attributable to the employer's business activities [Reg. § 1.62-2(e)].

An accountable plan must require that an employee return to the employer any amount that exceeds the employee's properly substantiated expenses within a reasonable period of time. The plan may not give an employee the right to retain excess amounts. If a plan provides for the return of excess amounts, but the employee fails to return them, the excess amounts are treated as paid from a nonaccountable plan. Where money is advanced to an employee to defray expenses, (i) the amount must be reasonably calculated not to exceed anticipated expenditures, (ii) the advance must be made within a reasonable period of the day the anticipated expenditures are paid or incurred, and (iii) amounts exceeding the employee's substantiated expenses must be required to be returned to the employer within a reasonable time [§ 62(c)(2); Reg. § 1.62-2(c)(3)(ii), § 1.62-2(f)].

A reasonable period of time depends on the facts and circumstances. Generally, it is considered reasonable if employees receive advances within 30 days of the time they incur the expenses, adequately account for the expenses within 60 days after the expenses were paid or incurred, and return any amounts in excess of expenses within 120 days after the expenses were paid or incurred. Also, it is considered reasonable if an employer gives employees a periodic statement (at least quarterly) that asks them to either return or adequately account for outstanding amounts and they do so within 120 days [Reg. § 1.62-2(g)].

Typically, an employer is not required to withhold income tax on advances or reimbursements made under an accountable plan; however, such payments become subject to withholding and payment of employment taxes if the expenses are not substantiated within a reasonable period, or if amounts in excess of substantiated expenses are not returned within a reasonable period [Reg. § 1.62-2(h)] (see XXII.B.4.g.).

*Nonaccountable Plans.* An arrangement that does not satisfy all three criteria for an accountable plan is a nonaccountable plan. An employee cannot compel an employer providing a nonaccountable plan to treat payments as paid under an accountable plan by voluntarily substantiating expenses and returning any excess to the employer [Reg. § 1.62-2(c)(3)].

Expenses reimbursed under a nonaccountable plan are treated as wages, and the amounts are subject to income and employment tax withholding. However, if amounts for meal and entertainment expenses are deemed paid under a nonaccountable plan solely because of the percentage limit on deductible meal and entertainment expenses (see IV.D.5.), the nondeductible amounts are not treated as gross income and are not subject to income or employment tax withholding [Reg. § 1.62-2(c)(5)]. Expenses included in an employee's income may be deducted by the employee, subject to all applicable limitations and substantiation requirements [Reg. § 1.162-17(d)(1)(i)].

---

**EXAMPLE:** Little Corp. policy provides that employees who undertake business travel on Little's behalf are reimbursed for their business expenses. At the end of each quarter, employees report their total travel expenses for the quarter, but they are not required to provide supporting documentation or itemization to Little. The company this issues checks to each employee in the amount requested. Because Little Corp. does not require substantiation, the arrangement is a nonaccountable plan. In Year 1, Harrison, a Little Corp. employee, incurred $10,000 in deductible travel expenses and receives reimbursement from Little in the same amount. Harrison must report the $10,000 as wages, and the amount is subject to withholding and employment taxes. To deduct the expenses, Harrison must itemize his deductions and complete Form 2106, *Employee Business Expenses*.

---

**No Plan.** If an employer does not have an allowance or other reimbursement arrangement, employees paying or incurring business expenses may deduct the expenses as business expenses, subject to all applicable limitations and substantiation requirements.

### IV.A.3.c. Limitations on Business Expense Deductions

[503 T.M., II.B.4.; TPS ¶¶2130.03.B., 2150.03.]

The treatment of a deduction differs depending on whether the amount is deductible from gross income as an "above-the-line deduction" or from adjusted gross income as an itemized (or "below-the-line") deduction. Above-the-line deductions are deductible whether or not the taxpayer itemizes deductions and not subject to the 2% of adjusted gross income floor on miscellaneous itemized deductions. Itemized deductions are deductible only if the taxpayer itemizes deductions and, if they are miscellaneous itemized deductions, only to the extent that, in the aggregate, they exceed 2% of the taxpayer's adjusted gross income. Above-the-line deductions and itemized deductions are discussed in VII.B. and VII.C., respectively.

A taxpayer's status as an employee or a self-employed individual determines the limitations that apply to business expense deductions. For a self-employed individual, business expenses are an above-the-line deduction from gross income. Thus the self-employed individual may deduct his business expenses whether or not he or she itemizes deductions, and the expenses are subject only to the general limitations imposed on certain types of business expenses (e.g., the 50% limitation applicable to meal and entertainment expenses).

For employees, the following types of business expenses qualify as above-the-line deductions [§ 62(a)(2)]:

1. reimbursed business expenses of an employee paid under an accountable plan (see IV.A.3.b.);
2. certain business expenses of a qualified performing artist (see VII.B.2.);
3. certain expenses of public officials (see VII.B.3.);
4. certain educator expenses for years before 2014 (see VII.B.1.);
5. certain expenses of military reservists traveling more than 100 miles to attend meetings (see VII.B.4.);
6. certain unreimbursed employee moving expenses (see VII.B.6.); and
7. jury duty pay remitted to an employer [§ 62(a)(13)].

Unreimbursed business expenses and reimbursed business expenses paid to an employee pursuant to a nonaccountable plan are below-the-line deductions, and therefore, are only available if a taxpayer itemizes his or her deductions [Reg. § 1.62-1T(e)(3), § 1.62-2(c)(5)] (see VII.C.). In addition to the general limitations imposed on certain types of business expenses, these deductions are subject to the 2% floor on miscellaneous itemized deductions (see VII.I.).

The impairment-related work expenses of a handicapped taxpayer (see VII.J.) are below-the-line deductions. However, unlike other below-the-line deductions, they are not subject to the 2% of adjusted gross income floor [§ 67(b)(6); Reg. § 1.67-1T(b)(2)].

### IV.A.4. Dues Expenses

[505 T.M., IV.M.; TPS ¶2140.]

Generally, a taxpayer may not deduct amounts paid or incurred for membership in a club organized for business, pleasure, recreation, or any other social purpose, including country clubs, golf and athletic clubs, hotel clubs, sporting clubs, and airline clubs [§ 274(a)(3); Reg. § 1.274-2(a)(2)(iii)(a)]. However, unless one of their principal purposes is to conduct or provide access to entertainment activities for members or their guests, the following business organizations are exempted from the general disallowance rule [Reg. § 1.274-2(a)(2)(iii)(b)]:

- business leagues;
- trade associations;
- chambers of commerce;
- boards of trade;
- real estate boards;
- professional organizations (e.g., bar associations and medical associations); and
- civic or public service organizations (e.g., Kiwanis, Lions, Rotary, and similar organizations).

### IV.A.5. Educational and Professional Expenses

[505 T.M., IV.K., IV.L., 517 T.M., II.; TPS ¶2150.]

*Educational Expenses.* Expenses for education may be deductible if the education either (i) maintains or improves skills required by the employee's present occupation, or (ii) satisfies the express requirements of the employer, or the requirements of applicable law or regulations, imposed as a condition for retaining the employee's position, status, or level of compensation. However, educational expenses (even if otherwise deductible as business expenses) are not deductible as a business expense if paid or incurred either (i) to meet the minimum educational requirements for qualification in the employee's employment or other trade or business, or (ii) to qualify the employee for a new trade or business [Reg. § 1.162-5(a), § 1.162-5(b), § 1.162-5(c)].

**EXAMPLE:** Lisa is an attorney whose normal practice involves tax planning. She pays $150 to attend a course offered to practicing attorneys in the tax field to refresh their skills in connection with drafting tax opinion letters and structuring business transactions tax-effectively. Because the refresher course is related to Lisa's trade or business, she may deduct the $150 fee for the course as an educational expense.

**EXAMPLE:** Tammy is employed by an accounting firm, and her employer requires her to obtain a J.D. degree. She attends law school at night, completes her studies, and receives a J.D. degree. Tammy intends to continue practicing accounting after receiving the degree. Despite being required by her employer, Tammy's expenses for law school are not deductible because the course of study qualifies her for a new trade or business.

Travel, in and of itself, is not a deductible form of education [§ 274(m)(2)]. In certain situations, though, travel may be a deductible educational expense to the extent the expenses are attributable to a period of travel that is directly related to the duties of the individual in his or her employment or other trade or business. The travel is directly related to the individual's duties if the major portion of the activities during the period of travel directly maintains or improves skills required in the individual's employment or other trade or business [Reg. § 1.162-5(d)]. If an individual travels away from home primarily to obtain education, the expenses of which otherwise qualify as deductible educational expenses, expenses for travel, meals, and lodging while away may also be deductible. However, if the individual engages in personal activities (e.g., sightseeing, social visiting, or other recreation), the portion of the expenses attributable to those activities is nondeductible [Reg. § 1.162-5(e)].

For a discussion of excludible employer-provided educational expenses, see XVII.E.3.

*Professional Expenses.* Professionals (e.g., lawyers, accountants, physicians, and architects) generally may deduct certain expenses related to their professional practice. Typical deductible professional expenses include the cost of supplies, dues to professional societies, subscriptions to professional journals, rent paid for offices, the cost of utilities, the cost of an office assistant, and the cost of books, furniture, and professional instruments and equipment with a short useful life [§ 62(a)(1)].

For some expenses, it is important to distinguish between a professional individual working as an employee and a self-employed professional individual. A professional individual who is an employee is treated as an employee for purposes of deducting business expenses. Thus, the individual could not deduct the cost of utilities at his or her place of employment as an ordinary and necessary business expense. A self-employed professional, on the other hand, can deduct such costs as part of maintaining his or her office.

### IV.A.6. Insurance Premiums

[505 T.M., IV.E.; TPS ¶2170.]

Insurance premiums incurred in connection with the operation of a trade or business generally are deductible as business expenses. Premiums individuals pay for personal insurance for themselves and their families generally are personal expenses and generally are not deductible, except to the extent they qualify as deductible medical expenses (see VII.D.1.) or are allowed as a deduction for self-employed individuals [§ 262(a), § 213(d)(1), § 162(l)] (see VII.B.9.).

Exclusions from income for employer-provided accident, health, and disability insurance are discussed at II.D.1.

*Life Insurance.* Life insurance premiums are generally deductible only if the taxpayer is not directly or indirectly a beneficiary of the policy. Thus, a taxpayer who takes out a life insurance policy to protect him or herself from loss in the event of the death of the insured is a beneficiary and may not deduct the premiums. The deduction is not denied for premiums paid on certain annuity contracts [§ 264(a)(1), § 264(b); Reg. § 1.264-1(b)].

If the payment of life insurance premiums are part of an employee's compensation for the actual performance of services and the total amount of the employee's compensation (including the premiums) is reasonable, the employer may deduct the life insurance premium as a reasonable allowance for salaries and other compensation for services (see IV.A.2.) [§ 162(a)(1); Reg. § 1.162-7]. Employers may not deduct premiums paid on a life insurance policy insuring an individual solely in his or her capacity as a shareholder [Reg. § 1.162-7(b)(1)]. Similarly, if a taxpayer who is a partner in a partnership takes out an insurance policy on his or her own life and names the other partners as beneficiaries to induce them to retain their investments in the partnership, the taxpayer is considered an indirect beneficiary and the premiums are not deductible [Reg. § 1.264-1(b)].

*Health and Disability Insurance.* An employer may deduct health and disability insurance premiums for employees as a business expense if (the premiums are paid as part of compensation for the performance of services, (ii) the total amount of compensation paid (including the premiums) is reasonable, and (iii) the employer does not receive the insurance benefits [Rev. Rul. 58-90, 1958-1 C.B. 88]. Additionally, an employer may deduct payments for health and disability insurance made to an employee benefit plan, provided that such payments qualify as business expenses and do not constitute payments under a deferred compensation plan [Reg. § 1.162-10(a)] (see XVII.B.).

Self-employed individuals may deduct certain amounts paid for medical insurance coverage for themselves, their spouses, their dependents, and any of their children who are under age 27 at the end of the tax year [§ 162(l)(2)(B)] (see VII.B.9.).

*Property Insurance.* Taxpayers may deduct as a business expense premiums paid for insurance coverage that protects business property or income-producing property from fire, storm, theft, or similar losses [Reg. § 1.162-1(a), § 1.212-1(a)(1)]. However, no business expense deduction is allowed for insurance premiums that are capital expenditures (i.e., generally amounts paid for the acquisition, production, or improvement of a capital asset) [§ 263] (see VIII.A.).

*Liability and Malpractice Insurance.* A taxpayer may deduct premiums paid on liability insurance incurred in connection with the taxpayer's trade or business. Similarly, premiums paid on malpractice insurance that covers a taxpayer's personal liability for professional negligence resulting in injury or damage to patients or clients are deductible [Reg. § 1.162-1(a)].

*Other Insurance.* Premiums paid for the following kinds of insurance related to a trade or business also generally may be deducted:

- credit insurance that covers losses from business bad debts;
- workers' compensation insurance set by state law that covers any claims for bodily injuries or job-related diseases suffered by employees, regardless of fault;
- overhead insurance that pays for business overhead expenses during long periods of disability caused by a taxpayer's injury or sickness;
- car and other vehicle insurance that covers vehicles used in the taxpayer's business for liability, damages, and other losses (to the extent of the business use of any vehicle partly operated for personal use);
- business interruption insurance that pays for lost profits if a taxpayer's business is shut down due to a fire or other cause; and
- contributions to a state unemployment insurance fund are deductible as taxes if they are considered taxes under state law.

No deduction is available for premiums paid on (i) self-insurance reserve funds, (ii) insurance against loss of earnings due to sickness or disability, and (iii) insurance to secure a loan.

### IV.A.7. Expenses for the Repair of Tangible Property

[505 T.M., IV.D., 509 T.M., VI.B.7., VII.B.4.; TPS ¶2200.]

The cost of incidental repairs and routine maintenance to tangible property incurred in carrying on a trade or business generally are deductible as business expenses [Reg. § 1.162-1(a)]. However, expenditures that are for a betterment to the property, that restore the property, or that adapt the property to a new or different use are not deductible and must be capitalized or charged to the taxpayer's depreciation reserve [Reg. § 1.263(a)-3(d)]. Capital expenditures, including what constitutes a betterment, a restoration, and an adaptation to a new or different use, are discussed at VIII.A.

The line separating a deductible repair and a capital expenditure is indistinct and determinations depend heavily on the facts and circumstances of the expenditure. Deductible repairs are defined in the negative; that is, an amount is deductible as a repair only if it is not otherwise required to be capitalized [Reg. § 1.162-4(a)].

*Materials and Supplies.* Amounts paid to acquire or produce non-incidental materials and supplies are generally deductible in the tax year that the materials and supplies are first consumed in the taxpayer's operations. Amounts paid to acquire or produce incidental materials and supplies that the taxpayer carries on hand and for which the taxpayer neither keeps a record of consumption nor takes physical inventories at the beginning and end of the tax year are generally deductible in the year paid, provided taxable income is clearly reflected [Reg. § 1.162-3(a)]. Materials and supplies means tangible property used or consumed in the taxpayer's operations that is not inventory and that either [Reg. § 1.162-3(c)(1)]:

- is a component acquired to maintain, repair, or improve a unit of tangible property owned, leased, or serviced by the taxpayer and that is not acquired as part of any single unit of tangible property (including rotable, temporary, and standby emergency spare parts, as defined in Reg. § 1.162-3(c)(2) and § 1.162-3(c)(3));

- consists of fuel, lubricants, water, and similar items, reasonably expected to be consumed in 12 months or less;

- is a unit of property with an economic useful life of 12 months or less;

- is a unit of property with an acquisition or production cost of $200 or less; or

- is identified in published guidance as materials and supplies.

A taxpayer may elect to treat the cost of certain materials and supplies as a capital expenditure and as an asset subject to the allowance for depreciation [Reg. § 1.162-3(d)(1)].

*Routine Maintenance Safe Harbor.* Routine maintenance on a unit of property, including buildings, is deemed not to improve the property, and therefore is not required to be capitalized. Routine maintenance is the recurring activities a taxpayer expects to perform as a result of the taxpayer's use of the unit of property to keep the unit of property in its ordinarily efficient operating condition (e.g., inspection, cleaning, testing, and replacing damaged or worn parts with comparable replacement parts) [Reg. § 1.263(a)-3(i)].

*Safe Harbor for Small Taxpayers.* A taxpayer with average annual gross receipts for the three preceding tax years of $10 million or less may elect not to apply the rules requiring capitalization of improvement expenses to an eligible building property if the total amount paid during the tax year for repairs, maintenance, improvements, and similar activities performed on the building property does not exceed the lesser of either (i) 2% of the unadjusted basis of the building, or (ii)

$10,000. Eligible building property generally includes a building unit of property owned or leased by the taxpayer that has an unadjusted basis of $1 million or less [Reg. § 1.263(a)-3(h)].

*De Minimis Safe Harbor.* Electing taxpayers are not required to capitalize or treat as a material or supply certain amounts paid for the acquisition or production of a unit of property, and thus, such amounts may be deducted. A taxpayer with an applicable financial statement and certain accounting procedures in place may rely on the de minimis safe harbor to expense amounts paid for property that do not exceed $5,000 per invoice or item. A taxpayer without an applicable financial statement, but with certain accounting procedures in place, may rely on the safe harbor if the amount paid for the property does not exceed $500 per invoice or item. Amounts paid for land or property intended to be included in inventory are not eligible for the de minimis safe harbor. Additionally, if the taxpayer elects the application of the safe harbor, it must be applied to all eligible materials and supplies (other than certain rotable, temporary, and standby emergency spare parts) [Reg. § 1.263(a)-1(f)].

### IV.A.8. Rent and Royalty Expenses

[505 T.M., IV.C.; TPS ¶2210.]

Rent or royalty payments for the use of property are generally deductible in the year paid or accrued, if paid in connection with a taxpayer's trade or business [§ 162(a)(3); Reg. § 1.162-11].

*Taxes and Other Operating Expenses.* If the terms of a lease require the lessee to pay as additional rent a pro rata share of real estate taxes levied on the property and some or all of the property's operating expenses (e.g., insurance, maintenance, trash hauling, and security), the lessee may deduct these expenses as additional rent [Reg. § 1.162-11(a), § 1.61-8(c)].

*Advance Rents and Bonuses.* If a lessee pays for the use of property in advance of the year in which the property actually will be used, the lessee must capitalize the payment and amortize it proportionally over the base term of the lease (regardless of the lessee's method of accounting). Thus, for any tax year, the lessee may deduct only the amount that applies to his or her use of the rented property during that tax year. Bonus payments paid by a lessee to induce the lessor to enter into the lease are treated similarly. In each case, though, the lessor must include the payment in income in the year of receipt [Reg. § 1.162-11(a), § 1.61-8(b)].

*Cancellation or Termination of Lease.* Amounts a lessee pays to cancel a business lease generally may be deducted as a rent payment. However, a lessee must capitalize a lease termination payment if he or she incurs the payment in connection with the acquisition of another lease, because the payment permits the lessee to obtain a benefit (i.e., the acquisition of the second lease) that extends beyond the end of the year [Reg. § 1.263(a)-4(d)(6)].

*Unreasonable Rent Between Related Parties.* A lessee may not take a deduction for the payment of unreasonable rent. If rental payments between related parties are excessive in amount, the parties' relationship may create the presumption that the dealings were not arm's-length. Generally, rent paid to a related lessor is reasonable if it is the same amount the lessee would pay to an unrelated lessor for use of the same property.

*Improvements Made by Lessee.* Gross income generally does not include the income (other than rent) a lessor of real property derives upon the termination of a lease that represents the value of such property attributable to buildings erected or other improvements made by the lessee [§ 109] (see II.N.4.).

*Leases vs. Sales.* The characterization of a transaction as a lease or a sale may significantly impact a taxpayer. For instance, in a lease transaction, a lessee may generally deduct rental payments. However, if the property is purchased, the buyer may be able to deduct depreciation or interest if the purchase of the property is financed. A lessor who receives rental payments has ordinary income that may be offset by depreciation and interest deductions. However, a seller may realize capital gain upon the sale. Different taxpayers in different tax positions will find it advantageous to structure a transaction either as a sale or as a lease.

Whether a transaction is a sale or a lease is a question of the intent of the parties, as evidenced by the facts and circumstances surrounding the transaction and the agreement. Generally, the IRS considers a transaction to be a sale if any of the following conditions are present [Rev. Rul. 55-540, 1955-2 C.B. 39]:

- portions of the periodic payments are made specifically applicable to an equity to be acquired by the lessee;
- the lessee acquires title to the property upon payment of a stated amount of "rentals" that he or she is required to make under the terms of the contract;
- the total amount that the lessee is required to pay for a relatively short period of use constitutes an inordinately large proportion of the total sum required to be paid to secure the transfer of title;
- the agreed "rental" payments materially exceed the current fair rental value (this may indicate that the payments include an element other than compensation for the use of property);
- as determined at the time of entering into the original agreement, the property may be acquired under a purchase option at a price that is nominal in relation to the value of the property at the time when the option may be exercised, or that is a relatively small amount when compared with the total payments that are required to be made; or
- some portion of the periodic payments are specifically designated as interest or are otherwise readily recognizable as the equivalent of interest.

If the transfer involves real property, the essential question is whether the property will be used by another for a limited period of time and then returned to the owner (a lease), or whether the ultimate ownership passes to the other party and that party has full use of the property during the period before passage of title (a sale).

---

**EXAMPLE:** Carl enters into an agreement with Will to allow Will full occupancy of Carl's current residence for a 10-year period. The agreement provides that Will must pay $1,000 per month, plus 8% interest on the unpaid balance, for the full term of the agreement, and title to the property will pass to Will upon payment of the entire $120,000 ($1,000 × 12 months × 10 years). Will is required to pay all taxes and insurance, and he is entitled to prepay the entire remaining outstanding amount without penalty. If Will fails to make a payment, Carl is permitted to reoccupy the home. The agreement between Carl and Will is a sale, rather than a lease, because the only possibility of reversion to Carl is upon default in Will's payments, there is a prepayment privilege consistent with a sale, and title passes upon completion of the agreement if all of the terms are satisfied.

---

Certain leveraged lease transactions involving equipment may be considered sales, rather than leases.

*Royalties.* Royalties are compensation paid for the use of intangible personal property or in exchange for rights to exploit natural resources. In both cases, the amount of the royalty is typically measured as a percentage of the income derived from the sale of a unit of the property. Royalties are generally deductible as business expenses under much the same conditions that rent paid for business purposes is deductible.

### IV.A.9. Domestic Production Activities Deduction

[510 T.M., 599 T.M., XII.; TPS ¶2220.]

Eligible taxpayers are allowed a deduction equal to 9% of the lesser of (i) the taxpayer's qualified production activities income (QPAI) for the tax year, or (ii) taxable income (or in the case of an individual, adjusted gross income) for the tax year (determined without regard to the domestic production activities deduction). The amount of the deduction for any tax year is limited to 50% of the taxpayer's W-2 wages for that tax year [§ 199]. A special exception reduces the amount of the deduction for income attributable to domestic production of oil, gas, or primary products of oil or gas [§ 199(d)(9)].

The deduction for domestic production activities is reported on Form 8903, *Domestic Production Activities Deduction.*

### IV.A.9.a. Taxpayers Eligible for the Domestic Production Activities Deduction

[510 T.M., III.B., 599 T.M., XII.A.3.; TPS ¶2220.05.]

*Corporations and Expanded Affiliated Groups.* Corporations and expanded affiliated groups (EAGs) are eligible taxpayers for purposes of the domestic production activities deduction. An EAG is an affiliated group as defined under § 1504(a) (see XIII.C.8.a.), but using a 50% voting and value test, and including life insurance companies subject to tax under § 801 and corporations that have elected the possessions tax credit under § 936. Members of an EAG are considered a single corporation. Generally, the domestic production activities deduction must be allocated among the members of the EAG in proportion to each member's respective amount of qualified production activities income [§ 199(d)(4)].

*Individuals.* Individuals may be eligible taxpayers. The amount of an individual's domestic production activities deduction is determined using the individual's qualified production activities income or adjusted gross income (as defined in § 199(d)(2)) [§ 199(d)(2); Reg. § 1.199-8(b)].

*Pass-through Entities.* Partnerships, S corporations, estates and trusts, and other pass-through entities may be eligible taxpayers. In the case of a partnership or S corporation, the deduction is applied at the partner or shareholder level [§ 199(d)(1); Reg. § 1.199-5(b)(1)(i), 1.199-5(c)(1)(i)]. For estates and trusts, see XVIII.A.4.b(3).

If a taxpayer performs a qualifying activity pursuant to a contract, then only the taxpayer with the benefits and burdens of ownership is entitled to the deduction [Reg. § 1.199-3(f)(1)].

### IV.A.9.b. Calculating the Amount of the Domestic Production Activities Deduction

[510 T.M., III.A., 599 T.M., XII.C.; TPS ¶2220.02., .04.]

Taxpayers may deduct 9% of the lesser of (i) the taxpayer's qualified production activities income (QPAI) for the tax year, or (ii) taxable income (or in the case of an individual, adjusted gross income) for the tax year (determined without regard to the domestic production activities deduction). A special exception reduces the amount of the deduction for income attributable to domestic production of oil, gas, or primary products of oil or gas. Under the special rule, the deduction is reduced by 3% of the least of (i) the taxpayer's oil-related QPAI (as defined in § 199(d)(9)(B)) for the tax year, (ii) the taxpayer's QPAI for the tax year, or (iii) the taxpayer's taxable income determined without regard to the domestic production activities deduction [§ 199(a), § 199(d)(9)].

*Qualified Production Activities Income.* In general, QPAI for any tax year is the excess of a taxpayer's domestic production gross receipts, over the sum of (i) the cost of goods sold that are allocable to those receipts, and (ii) other expenses, losses, or deductions (other than the domestic production activities deduction) that are properly allocable to those receipts [§ 199(c)(1); Reg. § 1.199-1(c)].

*Domestic Production Gross Receipts.* Domestic production gross receipts (DPGR) are gross receipts derived from the following activities [§ 199(c)(4)(A); Reg. § 1.199-3(a)]:

- any lease, rental, license, sale, exchange, or other disposition of:
  - qualifying production property (i.e., tangible personal property, computer software, and sound recordings) manufactured, produced, grown, or extracted by the taxpayer in whole or in significant part within the United States [§ 199(c)(5); Reg. § 1.199-3(j)];
  - any qualified film produced by the taxpayer; or
  - electricity, natural gas, or potable water produced by the taxpayer in the United States;
- construction of real property performed in the United States by the taxpayer in the ordinary course of a construction trade or business; and
- engineering or architectural services performed in the United States by the taxpayer in the ordinary course of a trade or business with respect to the construction of real property in the United States.

DPGR does not include gross receipts derived from the following activities [§ 199(c)(4)(B); Reg. § 1.199-3(o), § 1.199-3(l), § 1.199-3(m)(6)(iii)]:

- the sale of food and beverages prepared by the taxpayer at a retail establishment;
- the transmission or distribution of electricity, natural gas, or potable water; or
- the lease, rental, license, sale, exchange, or other disposition of land.

Qualifying production property (QPP) is considered manufactured, produced, grown, or extracted (MPGE) by the taxpayer in whole or in significant part within the United States if either (i) the taxpayer's MPGE activities within the United States are substantial in nature, or (ii) the taxpayer satisfies the 20% safe harbor. Whether a taxpayer's MPGE activities in the United States are substantial in nature is a facts and circumstances analysis that considers, among other things, the relative value added by the taxpayer's activity, the relative cost of the taxpayer's activity, the nature of the QPP, and the nature of the activities the taxpayer performs within the United States. The taxpayer satisfies the safe harbor if the direct labor and overhead for MPGE the QPP within the United States accounts for 20% or more of the taxpayer's cost of goods sold of the QPP. In the case of a lease, rental, or license, the direct labor and overhead must account for 20% or more of the taxpayer's unadjusted depreciable basis in the qualified property [Reg. § 1.199-3(g)].

In determining DPGR, the United States includes the 50 states, the District of Columbia, the territorial waters of the United States, and the seabed and subsoil of submarine areas adjacent to the territorial waters of the United States over which the United States has exclusive rights. It does not include possessions and territories of the United States or the airspace or space over the United Space and these areas. For years before 2014, Puerto Rico was treated as part of the United States if all of the taxpayer's gross receipts from sources within Puerto Rico were taxable for United States federal income tax purposes [§ 199(d)(8)].

For purposes of determining DPGR, gross receipts are the taxpayer's receipts for the tax year that are recognized under the taxpayer's method of accounting for income tax purposes for the tax year (see XI.B.). Gross receipts are not reduced by the cost of goods sold or the cost of certain other non-capital asset property sold [Reg. § 1.199-3(c)]. A taxpayer is required to determine whether gross receipts qualify as DPGR on an item-by-item basis. A taxpayer must allocate its gross receipts between DPGR and non-DPGR using any reasonable method. If a taxpayer has the information readily available to specifically identify whether the gross receipts derived from an item are DPGR, then the taxpayer must use a specific identification method to determine DPGR [Reg. § 1.199-1(d)].

***Cost of Goods Sold Allocable to DPGR.*** The cost of goods sold (CGS) allocable to DPGR (as well as other expenses, losses, or deductions properly allocable to DPGR) must be subtracted from DPGR to determine QPAI. In the case of a sale, exchange, or other disposition of inventory, CGS is computed first by adding a taxpayer's beginning inventory to the purchases and production costs incurred by the taxpayer during the tax year and included in inventory costs. The taxpayer then reduces that amount by the taxpayer's ending inventory to arrive at CGS. CGS also includes the gross receipts from the sale or other disposition of non-inventory property. Thus, for non-inventory property, CGS includes the property's adjusted basis. A taxpayer must allocate CGS between DPGR and non-DPGR using any reasonable method. If a taxpayer has the information readily available to specifically identify CGS allocable to DPGR, then CGS allocable to DPGR is that amount, whether or not the taxpayer uses another allocation method to allocate gross receipts between DPGR and non-DPGR [Reg. § 1.199-4(b)].

***Other Expenses, Losses, or Deductions Properly Allocable to DPGR.*** Other expenses, losses, and deductions (other than the domestic production activities deduction) properly allocable to DPGR (as well as the cost of goods sold allocable to DPGR) must be subtracted from DPGR to determine QPAI [§ 199(c)(1)(B)(ii)]. Examples of costs that may not be treated as CGS include marketing, selling, advertising, and distribution costs, research and experimental expenditures, losses, charitable contributions, and interest. There are three methods a taxpayer may use to allocate and apportion deductions [Reg. § 1.199-4(d), § 1.199-4(e), § 1.199-4(f)]:

1. the § 861 method, which is available to all taxpayers, but required for those taxpayers with average annual gross receipts over $100 million or total assets over $10 million;

2. the simplified deduction method, available to any taxpayer with average annual gross receipts of $100 million or less or total assets of $10 million or less; and

3. the small business simplified overall method, which is available to qualifying small taxpayers.

A taxpayer using the simplified deduction method or the small business simplified overall method must use that method for all deductions. A taxpayer eligible to use the small business simplified overall method may choose at any time for any tax year to use the small business simplified overall method, the simplified deduction method, or the § 861 method for a tax year. A taxpayer eligible to use the simplified deduction method may choose at any time for any tax year to use the simplified deduction method or the § 861 method for a tax year. Regardless of the method chosen, net operating loss deductions are not allocated or apportioned to DPGR or gross income attributable to DPGR [Reg. § 1.199-4(c)].

### IV.A.9.c. W-2 Wage Limitation for the Domestic Production Activities Deduction

[510 T.M., III.A.2., 599 T.M., XIII.B.2.; TPS ¶2220.03.]

The domestic production activities deduction is limited to 50% of the taxpayer's W-2 wages. W-2 wages generally means the sum of the aggregate amounts the taxpayer is required to include on the Forms W-2 of the taxpayer's employees during the tax year, and it only includes amounts properly allocable to DPGR. It includes remuneration for services performed, the total amount of elective deferrals, compensation deferred under § 457, and the amount of designated Roth IRA contributions [§ 199(b)(2); Reg. § 1.199-2(e)].

The taxpayer must use one of three methods to compute W-2 wages [Rev. Proc. 2006-47, 2006-45 I.R.B. 869]:

1. the "Unmodified Box Method," which calculates W-2 wages by taking, without modification, the lesser of (i) the total entries in Box 1 (wages, tips, other compensation) of all Forms W-2 the taxpayer files for his or her employees, or (ii) the total entries in Box 5 (Medicare wages and tips) of all Forms W-2 the taxpayer files for his or her employees;

2. the "Modified Box 1 Method," which adjusts the total entries in Box 1 by subtracting amounts included in Box 1 that (i) are not wages for income tax withholding purposes, or (ii) are treated as wages under § 3402(o) for purposes of withholding, and by adding amounts reported in Box 12 of Forms W-2 that are properly coded D, E, F, G, or S; or

3. the "Tracking Wages Method," which requires the total amounts of wages paid to employees that are subject to income tax withholding and reported on Forms W-2 for the calendar year to be reduced by any included supplemental unemployment compensation benefits and increased by amounts reported in Box 12 of Forms W-2 that are properly coded D, E, F, G, or S.

A taxpayer may determine the amount of W-2 wages properly allocable to DPGR using any reasonable method that is satisfactory to the IRS based on all the facts and circumstances. Taxpayers may also avail themselves of certain safe harbor W-2 wage allocation methods dependent on the cost allocation method the taxpayer uses to determine expenses, losses, or deductions properly allocable to DPGR [Reg. § 1.199-2(e)(2)].

### IV.A.10. Travel and Transportation Expenses

### IV.A.10.a. Travel Away from Home

[505 T.M., IV.I.5., 519 T.M., II.; TPS ¶2310.01.]

The expenses of traveling away from home for business generally are deductible, including amounts spent for reasonable (i.e., non-lavish, non-extravagant) meals and lodging [§ 162(a)(2); Reg. § 1.162-2].

**Tax Home.** Business travel expenses are deductible only if incurred while a taxpayer is traveling away from his or her tax home. The taxpayer's travel must last overnight, or be long enough to require substantial sleep or rest [§ 162(a)(2); *Correll v. United States*, 389 U.S. 299 (1967)]. Thus, distance traveled, by itself, does not justify a deduction if the taxpayer returns home without stopping for sleep or rest.

A tax home is generally a taxpayer's regular or main place of business or post of duty, regardless of where he or she maintains a family home. It includes the city or general area in which the taxpayer's business or work is located. The tax home of a taxpayer who, due to the nature of his or her work, has no regular or main place of business may be the place he or she regularly lives. An itinerant who has neither a regular or main place of business nor a place he or she regularly lives cannot claim a travel expense deduction.

A member of Congress's tax home is his or her residence in his or her congressional district. However, a member of Congress may deduct not more than $3,000 per tax year for living expenses for travel away from home (including expenses while on official business in Washington, D.C.) [§ 162(a)]. A state legislator may elect to treat his or her residence within the represented legislative district as his or her tax home and may deduct limited business travel expenses. However, the election does not apply to any legislator whose residence within the represented district is within 50 miles of the state capitol building [§ 162(h); Reg. § 1.162-24].

A member of the U.S. armed services reserve is deemed to be away from home in pursuit of a trade or business for any period he or she is away from home in connection with such service. He or she must be more than 100 miles away from home for expenses to be deductible business expenses, limited to the per diem rate [§ 162(p), § 62(a)(2)(E)].

A taxpayer employed abroad is generally subject to the same rules for business travel costs as a domestic taxpayer, except for the foreign earned income and housing exclusion. A taxpayer employed abroad indefinitely generally cannot deduct foreign living costs because they are personal expenses. On the other hand, a taxpayer employed abroad temporarily can deduct living costs as business travel expenses [§ 911]. The foreign earned income and housing exclusion are discussed in XX.C.1.

***Combined Business and Personal Travel.*** A taxpayer engaging in some personal activities during a business trip can deduct travel expenses to and from the destination only if the trip primarily relates to business activities. However, expenses attributable to the taxpayer's personal activities are not deductible. A taxpayer may not deduct travel expenses to or from a destination where the trip is primarily for personal reasons, but expenses paid or incurred while at the destination that are properly allocable to the taxpayer's trade or business are deductible. Whether a taxpayer's trip is primarily for business or for personal activities depends on the facts and circumstances, though time spent on each type of activity is an important factor. A taxpayer traveling to a convention or seminar must show a sufficient relationship between his or her business and the meeting so that his or her business is advanced by attending [Reg. § 1.162-2(b), § 1.162-2(d)].

---

**EXAMPLE:** Melanie travels from her home in Atlanta to New Orleans. While in New Orleans, Melanie spends one week on business activities and three weeks on vacation. Her trip is primarily for personal reasons and neither her airfare nor her other expenses in traveling to and from New Orleans are deductible. However, Melanie's living expenses during the week she is engaged in business activities generally are deductible (subject to any applicable limitations).

---

Deductions for foreign business travel are subject to special allocation rules. Generally, taxpayers who engage in personal activities while traveling abroad (including possessions or territories of the United States) must allocate part of the cost of traveling to and from the foreign destination to his or her personal activities. The portion of the taxpayer's foreign transportation expenses attributable to personal activities is not deductible [§ 274(c), Reg. § 1.274-4]. The foreign travel expense allocation rules do not apply in the following situations [Reg. § 1.274-4(c), § 1.274-4(d), § 1.274-4(f)(5)]:

- the travel abroad does not exceed one week (excluding the day of departure and including the day of return);
- the taxpayer spends less than 25% of his or her time abroad on personal activities (including both the departure and return days);
- the taxpayer does not have substantial control over arranging the trip; or
- one of the taxpayer's major considerations in making the trip is not obtaining a vacation.

---

**EXAMPLE:** Mark flies from Portland to Tokyo for 10 days of business activities. He then flies to Singapore for a six-day vacation, returning home via Tokyo. Mark's travel expenses between Singapore and Tokyo are not deductible because they are personal expenses. He spends a total of 18 days abroad, including the two travel days between Portland and Tokyo, of which 12 days are business and six are personal. Thus, Mark can deduct 2/3 (12 business days ÷ 18 total days abroad) of his travel costs to Tokyo, while the remaining 1/3 of his travel costs are attributable to his vacation and are not deductible.

---

In addition to the foreign travel expense allocation rules, to deduct business travel expenses, a taxpayer traveling outside the North American area to attend a convention or seminar must show that (i) the meeting is directly related to the active conduct of his or her trade or business, and (ii) based on certain criteria, it is as reasonable for the meeting to be held outside of the North American area as it is for the meeting to be held within the North American area [§ 274(h)].

No deduction is permitted for travel expenses for the taxpayer's spouse, dependent, or other individual accompanying the taxpayer (or accompanying an officer or employee of the taxpayer), unless all of the following requirements are satisfied [§ 274(m)(3)]:

1. the accompanying person is an employee of the taxpayer;
2. the travel of the accompanying person is for a bona fide business purpose; and
3. the expenses would otherwise be deductible by the accompanying person.

### IV.A.10.b. Local Transportation and Commuting
[505 T.M., IV.I.4., 519 T.M., III.; TPS ¶2310.02.]

**Transportation Expenses.** Expenses paid or incurred by an employee in getting from one work place to another (other than travel expenses while away from home) are deductible transportation expenses [Reg. § 1.162-2(a); Rev. Rul. 99-7, 1999-5 I.R.B. 4]. Transportation expenses generally include the costs (e.g., air, train, bus, and taxi fares, vehicle operation and maintenance costs, tolls, and parking fees) of the following:

- getting from one workplace to another when traveling within the city or general area that is the taxpayer's tax home;

- visiting clients or customers;
- going to a business meeting away from the regular workplace; and
- getting from the taxpayer's home to a temporary workplace when there are one or more regular places of work.

*Commuting Expenses.* An employee's expenses in commuting from home to work generally are not deductible [Reg. § 1.162-2(e)]. The following are exceptions to the general rule [Rev. Rul. 99-7]:

- A taxpayer without a regular work location may deduct daily transportation expenses incurred in going between his or her residence and a temporary work location outside the taxpayer's metropolitan area.
- A taxpayer with one or more regular work locations away from his or her residence may deduct daily transportation expenses incurred in going between the taxpayer's residence and a temporary work location in the same trade or business, regardless of distance.
- If a taxpayer's residence is also his or her principal place of business, the taxpayer may deduct daily transportation expenses incurred in going between the residence and another work location in the same trade or business, regardless of whether the other work location is regular or temporary, and regardless of distance.

### IV.A.10.c. *Business and Personal Use of Automobiles*

[519 T.M., IV., V.; TPS ¶2310.05.]

A taxpayer who uses a personal automobile for business purposes generally can deduct certain car expenses using either (i) actual car expenses or (ii) the standard mileage rate. All of the costs associated with an automobile must be apportioned between deductible business use and nondeductible personal use [§ 262; Reg. § 1.262-1(a), § 1.262-1(b)(5)].

### IV.A.10.c.(1) *Actual Expense*

[519 T.M., IV.B.2.; TPS ¶2310.05.B.4.]

A taxpayer who does not elect to use the standard mileage rate may deduct actual car expenses. Actual car expenses include depreciation, licenses, gas, oil, tolls, lease payments, insurance, garage rent, parking fees, registration fees, repairs, and tires.

### IV.A.10.c.(2) *Standard Mileage Rate*

[519 T.M., VI.C.3.a(1); TPS ¶2310.05.B.2.]

Rather than keeping track of actual expenses, a taxpayer may use the standard mileage rate set by the IRS. In 2014, the standard mileage rate for all miles of business use is 56 cents per mile [Notice 2013-80, 2013-52 I.R.B. 821].

The deduction computed using the standard mileage rate for business miles is in lieu of deducting operating and fixed costs (e.g., depreciation, maintenance and repairs, tires, gas, oil, insurance, and registration fees) of the automobile. Not included in the standard mileage rate, and thus deductible as a separate item, are parking fees, tolls, interest relating to the purchase of the automobile, and state and local taxes to the extent they are allowable deductions [Rev. Proc. 2010-51, 2010-51 I.R.B. 883]. Because depreciation is considered a component of the standard mileage rate, the taxpayer's basis in the automobile must be reduced by the depreciation allowed. In 2014, the depreciation allowed is 22 cents per mile [Notice 2013-80].

To use the standard mileage rate, the taxpayer must choose to use it in the first year the automobile is placed in service in the taxpayer's business. For later years, the taxpayer may choose to use either the standard mileage rate or actual expenses. However, the standard mileage rate may not be used to compute deductible expenses if the taxpayer [Rev. Proc. 2010-51]:

- uses five or more cars at the same time (e.g., in fleet operations);
- claimed a depreciation deduction for the car using any method other than straight-line;
- claimed a deduction under § 179 for the election to expense certain depreciable business assets (see V.B.);
- claimed the additional first-year depreciation allowance (for example, under § 168(k) or § 168(n));
- used the Accelerated Cost Recovery System (ACRS) or the Modified Accelerated Cost Recovery System (MACRS);
- claimed actual car expenses after 1997 for a car the taxpayer leased; or
- is a rural mail carrier who received a qualified reimbursement [§ 162(o)].

### IV.A.10.c.(3) Mileage Allowances

[519 T.M., VI.C.3.a(2)(a); TPS ¶2310.05.B.3.]

In some circumstances, an employer may provide a mileage allowance to reimburse employees for automobile expenses. A mileage allowance is a payment under an accountable reimbursement arrangement (see IV.A.3.b.) that is [Rev. Proc. 2010-51, 2010-51 I.R.B. 883]:

- paid for ordinary and necessary business expenses incurred, or that the employer reasonably anticipates will be incurred, by an employee for transportation expenses in connection with the performance of services as an employee;
- reasonably calculated not to exceed the amount of expenses or anticipated expenses; and
- paid at the applicable standard mileage rate, a flat rate or stated schedule, or under any other IRS-specified rate or schedule.

A mileage allowance is paid at a flat rate or stated schedule if it is provided on a uniform and objective basis. The allowance may be paid periodically at a fixed rate, at a cents-per-mile rate, at a variable rate based on a stated schedule, at a rate that combines any of these rates, or on any other basis that is consistently applied and is in accordance with reasonable business practice [Rev. Proc. 2010-51].

### IV.A.10.c.(4) Fixed and Variable Rate (FAVR) Allowances

[519 T.M., VI.C.3.a(2)(b); TPS ¶2310.05.B.3.]

A fixed and variable rate allowance (FAVR allowance) is a mileage allowance that includes a combination of payments covering (i) periodic fixed payments of projected fixed costs of operating a standard automobile (e.g., depreciation, insurance, property taxes, and registration and license fees), and (ii) periodic variable payments of projected operating costs of using a standard automobile (e.g., gas, oil, tires, and routine maintenance and repairs) [Rev. Proc. 2010-51, 2010-51 I.R.B. 883].

**Limitations on Use of FAVR Allowances.** The allowance may be paid only for an automobile that meets all of the following requirements [Rev. Proc. 2010-51]:

1. It is owned or leased by the employee receiving the payment.
2. It costs (when new) at least 90% of the standard automobile cost taken into account for purposes of determining the FAVR allowance for the first calendar year the employee receives the allowance for the automobile.

3. Its model year not differ from the current calendar year by more than the number of years in the retention period.

A FAVR allowance may not be paid for any automobile for which the employee has claimed one of the following:

- depreciation using a method other than straight-line for its estimated useful life;
- additional first-year depreciation under § 179 (see V.B.);
- depreciation using the Accelerated Cost Recovery System (ACRS) (see V.A.5.) or the Modified Accelerated Cost Recovery System (MACRS) (see V.A.4.); or
- actual automobile expenses for an automobile the taxpayer leased.

The deduction computed using a FAVR allowance is in lieu of deducting operating and fixed costs (e.g., depreciation, maintenance and repairs, tires, gas, oil, insurance, and registration fees) of the automobile. Not included in the FAVR allowance, and thus deductible as a separate item, are parking fees, tolls, and interest payments relating to the purchase of the automobile to the extent otherwise deductible [Rev. Proc. 2010-51].

### IV.A.10.c.(5) Depreciation and § 179 Deductions

[519 T.M., IV.B.3., IV.B.4.; TPS ¶2310.05.B.5., .05.B.6.]

If a taxpayer uses actual expenses to figure the deduction for an automobile owned and used in the taxpayer's business, he or she may claim a depreciation deduction [§ 168] (see V.A.). In addition, a taxpayer may elect under § 179 to treat all or a portion of the cost of an automobile as a current expense (see V.B.).

### IV.A.11. Meal and Entertainment Expenses

[520 T.M.; TPS ¶2320.]

Generally, a taxpayer may deduct expenses to entertain a client, customer, or employee if the expenses have an adequate business connection by satisfying either the (i) directly-related test, or (ii) associated test. Entertainment includes any activity generally considered to constitute entertainment, amusement, or recreation (and for purposes of this provision, meals, unless otherwise specified) [§ 274(a)(1)(A); Reg. § 1.274-2(a)(1)].

The exclusion for meals furnished to an employee for the employer's convenience is discussed at XVII.E.4.

### IV.A.11.a. Directly-Related Test for Entertainment Expenses

[520 T.M., I.C.1.d(1); TPS ¶2320.01.D.1.]

An entertainment expense is directly related to a taxpayer's trade or business if the entertainment occurs either (i) during an active business discussion, or (ii) in a clear business setting directly in furtherance of the taxpayer's trade or business [Reg. § 1.274-2(c)].

*Active Business Discussion.* An active business discussion requires the satisfaction of the following four elements [Reg. § 1.274-2(c)(3)]:

1. The taxpayer must have more than a general expectation of deriving a business benefit, other than goodwill, at some future time. However, income or some other business benefit need not be shown to have actually resulted.

2. During the entertainment period, the taxpayer must actively engage in a business meeting or other bona fine business transaction. This requires that the taxpayer or the taxpayer's representative be present. An active business dis-

cussion is rebuttably presumed not to occur if the entertainment occurs under circumstances where there is little or no possibility of engaging in the active conduct of business due to substantial distractions (e.g., night clubs, theaters, sports events, essentially social gatherings, and group meetings that include nonbusiness associates at places like cocktail lounges, golf and country clubs, or vacation resorts) [Reg. § 1.274-2(c)(7)].

3. The principal character of a combined business and entertainment activity must be the active conduct of the taxpayer's business. This does not require the taxpayer to show he or she spent more time on business than entertainment. Rather, he or she must show that business was the principal feature of the activity. The principal character is rebuttably presumed not to be business if the activities occur on hunting or fishing trips, or on yachts or other pleasure boats.

4. The entertainment expense attributable to nonbusiness guests, even if they accompany business guests with whom the taxpayer has an active business discussion, may not be deducted. However, in some situations, this disallowance does not apply to a business guest's spouse and the taxpayer's own spouse [Reg. § 1.274-2(d)(4)].

**EXAMPLE:** Sally, a bank president, holds cocktail parties at her home for customers, potential customers, key bank employees, and their guests. She also hosts important customers at professional tennis matches. Sally does not initiate specific business discussions at either event. These entertainment costs contribute to the bank's growth, enhance its goodwill, and are genuine business expenses. However, none of the costs are deductible under the active business discussion alternative of the directly-related test for business connection. Though Sally generated substantial goodwill, she is presumed not to have engaged in the active conduct of business during such distracting events as a cocktail party and a tennis match.

**EXAMPLE:** Bret is a radiologist who hosts a holiday party for other doctors (who are his source of referrals), as well as his friends and neighbors. If 30% of the guests are referring doctors, and the other active business discussion requirements are met, then Bret has satisfied the directly-related test as to 30% of the cost of the party.

*Clear Business Setting.* A taxpayer alternatively may satisfy the directly-related test if the entertainment occurs in a clear business setting directly in furtherance of the taxpayer's trade or business. This test generally requires the taxpayer to show that any recipient of the entertainment should have known that the taxpayer's only significant motive in providing the entertainment was to further his or her business. The test is likely satisfied where there is no meaningful personal or social relationship between the taxpayer and the entertainment guests. Examples of clear business settings include (i) a hospitality room at a convention where goodwill is created through display or discussion of the taxpayer's products, (ii) entertaining business and civic leaders at the opening of a new hotel or theatrical production, where the clear purpose is to obtain business publicity, and (iii) entertainment where the principal effect is a price rebate (e.g., when a hotel owner occasionally provides free meals to a frequent guest). Entertainment occurring in distracting circumstances is unlikely to qualify as having been provided in a clear business setting [Reg. § 1.274-2(c)(4)].

### *IV.A.11.b. Associated Test for Entertainment Expenses*
[520 T.M., I.C.1.d(2); TPS ¶2320.01.D.2.]

An entertainment expense satisfies the associated test if it is both (i) associated with the active conduct of the taxpayer's trade of business, and (ii) directly before or after a substantial and bona fide business discussion. This allows a taxpayer to deduct entertainment costs where there is a clear business connection, but where no business actually is conducted during the entertainment. Thus, goodwill entertainment that cannot qualify under the directly-related test may be deductible under the associated test [§ 274(a)(1)(A); Reg. § 1.274-2(a)(1)(ii), § 1.274-2(d)].

*Associated with a Trade or Business.* An expense is associated with the taxpayer's trade of business where the taxpayer can show a clear business purpose for having the expense (e.g., getting new business, or encouraging the continuation of an existing business relationship) [Reg. § 1.274-2(d)(2)].

*Substantial and Bona Fide Discussion.* Whether a discussion is a substantial and bona fide business discussion is determined based on the facts and circumstances. The taxpayer must show that he or she actively engaged in a business meeting, negotiation, discussion, or other transaction to obtain income or some other specific business benefit. Additionally, the meeting, negotiation, discussion, or other transaction must be substantial in relation to the entertainment. The substantiality requirement is met if the principal character of the combined business and entertainment was the active conduct of business, however, the taxpayer need not spend more time on business than entertainment. A meeting officially scheduled at a convention, or sponsored by a business or professional organization, qualifies as a substantial and bona fide business discussion if (i) the expense was an ordinary and necessary trade or business expense, (ii) the organization sponsoring the convention or meeting scheduled a program of business activities, and (iii) the business program was the principal activity of the convention or meeting [Reg. § 1.274-2(d)(3)(i)].

*Directly Before or After.* Entertainment that occurs on the same day as the substantial business discussion is deemed to directly precede or follow the business discussion. If the entertainment occurs on a different day than the business discussion, the facts and circumstances determine whether the entertainment directly precedes or follows the business discussion. Factors considered in this analysis include (i) the place, date, and duration of the business discussion, (ii) whether the taxpayer or his or her business guests are from out of town, (iii) the dates of arrival and departure, and (iv) the reasons the entertainment occurred on a different day than the business discussion [Reg. § 1.274-2(d)(3)(ii)].

---

**EXAMPLE:** Madeline is a dental equipment supplier. She hosts several out-of-town dentists at dinner the night before they conduct substantial business discussions. The dinner qualifies as entertainment associated with the active conduct of Madeline's business.

---

### *IV.A.11.c. Entertainment Facilities*
[520 T.M., I.C.2.; TPS ¶2320.01.E.]

Expenses for the use of an entertainment facility generally are not deductible. This includes expenses for depreciation, as well as operating costs like rent, utilities, maintenance, and protection. The disallowance rule also applies to losses realized on the sale or other disposition of the facility, which are governed by the rules for nonbusiness property. However, costs that are deductible without regard to a business purpose (e.g., interest and taxes) are not affected by the disallowance rule. Similarly, out-of-pocket expenses like food, beverages, catering, and gas that the taxpayer provides during entertainment at a facility may be deducted, subject to the other applicable requirements or limitations for entertainment expenses [§ 274(a)(1)(B); Reg. § 1.274-2(a)(2)(i), § 1.274-2(e)(3)].

An entertainment facility is any property the taxpayer owns, rents, or uses for entertainment. Examples include yachts, hunting lodges, fishing camps, swimming pools, tennis courts, bowling alleys, cars, airplanes, apartments, hotel suites, and homes in vacation resorts. Facilities used only incidentally for entertainment (e.g., a car or airplane used primarily for business transportation) are not entertainment facilities [Reg. § 1.274-2(e)(2)].

***Club Dues.*** Dues or fees to any social, athletic, or sporting club or organization are treated as entertainment facility costs. Generally, a taxpayer may not deduct amounts paid or incurred for membership in a club organized for business, pleasure, recreation, or any other social purpose, including country clubs, golf and athletic clubs, hotel clubs, sporting clubs, and airline clubs [§ 274(a)(2), § 274(a)(3); Reg. § 1.274-2(a)(2)(iii)(a)]. Dues are discussed in IV.A.4.

### IV.A.11.d. Sports and Other Entertainment Tickets

[520 T.M., I.C.2.b(2); TPS ¶2320.01.E.5.]

Box seats and season tickets to theaters and sporting events are not treated as entertainment facilities. Instead, the cost of the seats or tickets is allocated to separate events, and the use of tickets to each event is analyzed to determine if it meets the business connection requirements for entertainment activities [Rev. Rul. 63-144, 1963-2 C.B. 129].

A taxpayer may not deduct any ticket cost in excess of the face value of the ticket unless the event qualifies as a charitable sports event. A charitable sports event is any sports event (i) that is organized for the primary purpose of benefitting a charitable organization that is exempt from tax, (ii) all of the net proceeds of which are contributed to such organization, and (iii) that utilizes volunteers for substantially all of the work performed in carrying out the event [§ 274(l)(1)].

The cost of renting a skybox or private luxury box for more than one event is not deductible to the extent its cost exceeds the cost of a regular seat. However, separately stated charges for food and beverages are deductible without regard to the skybox limit, subject to the other applicable requirements or limitations for entertainment expenses [§ 274(l)(2)].

### IV.A.11.e. Exceptions to the Entertainment Disallowance Rules

[520 T.M., I.C.3.; TPS ¶2320.01.F.]

***Food and Beverages for Employees.*** An employer's cost of running a company cafeteria or employee dining room on the employer's premises, including the cost of the meals served, is excepted from the entertainment disallowance rules. This exception applies even if guests are occasionally served in the cafeteria or dining room. Expenses deductible under this exception are subject to the 50% limit on meals [§ 274(e)(1), § 274(n); Reg. § 1.274-2(f)(2)(ii)] (see IV.D.5.).

***Entertainment Expenses Treated as Compensation.*** An employer who furnishes noncash benefits to an employee generally is not subject to the entertainment disallowance rules to the extent that the employer treats the cost of the benefit as compensation to the employee and withholds taxes accordingly. In the case of certain covered employees (described in § 274(e)(2)(B)(ii)), the exception applies only to the extent of the amount of expenses treated as compensation or includible in income. Expenses deductible under this exception are not subject to the 50% limit on business entertainment [§ 274(e)(2); Reg. § 1.274-2(f)(2)(iii)] (see IV.D.5.).

*Reimbursed Expenses.* An employee or independent contractor who incurs business entertainment costs for which he is reimbursed by his employer or client is not subject to the entertainment disallowance rules so long as the employer or client is subject to the entertainment disallowance rules. This rule is the corollary to the employer exception for entertainment expenses treated as compensation, and it insures that the entertainment disallowance rules apply at only one level. The exception applies to an employee if the employer does not treat the entertainment expense as compensation. Expenses deductible under this exception are not subject to the 50% limit on business entertainment cost [§ 274(e)(3); Reg. § 1.274-2(f)(2)(iv)] (see IV.D.5.).

*Recreational Activities for Employees.* The cost to an employer of recreational activities or facilities primarily for the benefit of his employees is excepted from the entertainment disallowance rules. The exception typically applies to the cost of holiday parties, annual picnics, and company swimming pools, baseball diamonds, bowling alleys, and golf courses. The exception does not apply if the recreational activities are provided in circumstances that discriminate in favor of highly-compensated employees (as defined in § 414(q)). The employer's cost of recreational activities, if excluded from the entertainment disallowance rules by this exception, is not subject to the 50% deduction limit on entertainment [§ 274(e)(4); Reg. § 1.274-2(f)(2)(v)] (see IV.D.5.).

*Business Meetings.* Entertainment costs incurred by a taxpayer that are directly related to business meetings of his or her employees, stockholders, agents, or directors are not subject to the entertainment disallowance rules (but are subject to the 50% deduction limitation (see IV.D.5.)). The exception does not apply if there are so many distractions that there is little possibility of engaging in the active conduct of business [§ 274(e)(5); Reg. § 1.274-2(f)(2)(vi)].

*Meetings of Business Leagues.* Expenses directly related to and necessary for attendance at a business meeting held by one of a variety of business leagues (e.g., chambers of commerce, real estate boards, boards of trade, certain professional associations, and trade associations) is excepted from the entertainment disallowance rules [§ 274(e)(6); Reg. § 1.274-2(f)(2)(vii)]. The taxpayer's cost of entertainment at these meetings is still subject to the 50% deduction limitation (see IV.D.5.).

*Items Available to the Public.* The cost to the taxpayer of goods, services, and facilities made available to the general public are not subject to the entertainment disallowance rules (nor to the 50% deduction limitation (see IV.D.5.)). The cost of sponsoring a television or radio entertainment program falls within this exception. Similarly, the cost of maintaining private recreational facilities (e.g., parks and golf courses) falls within this exception to the extent the facility is made available to the general public [§ 274(e)(7); Reg. § 1.274-2(f)(2)(viii)].

*Entertainment Sold to Customers.* The taxpayer's expenses for entertainment sold to customers for fair value are not subject to the entertainment disallowance rules (or the 50% deduction limitation (see IV.D.5.)). This exception ensures that a taxpayer in the business of selling entertainment can deduct the costs of producing that entertainment [§ 274(e)(8); Reg. § 1.274-2(f)(2)(ix)].

*Expenses Includible in the Income of Non-Employees.* Business entertainment costs for a non-employee that are included in the recipient's income as compensation or as a prize or award are not subject to the entertainment disallowance rules. The taxpayer must report the expense on an information return for the non-employee. While the taxpayer who qualifies for this exception is not subject to the 50% limit on deducting entertainment costs (see IV.D.5.), the non-employee is subject to both the entertainment disallowance rules and the 50% limit.

### IV.A.11.f. Business Gifts

[520 T.M., III.; TPS ¶2320.01.G.]

A taxpayer may deduct all or a portion of the cost of gifts given in the course of a trade or business. As with other deductible business expenses, the gift must be an ordinary and necessary expense, meaning the expenditure must be appropriate and helpful to the taxpayer's business, and it must be made with a reasonable expectation of a commensurate financial return. However, a taxpayer may not deduct more than $25 for business gifts given directly or indirectly to each person during the tax year. For this purpose, spouses are treated as a single taxpayer [§ 274(b); Reg. § 1.274-3].

The following items are exempt from the $25 limitation [§ 274(b)(1); Reg. § 1.274-3(b)(2)]:

- items clearly and permanently bearing the taxpayer's name that cost the taxpayer less than $4, and that are one of a number of identical items generally distributed by the taxpayer (e.g., specialty advertising items like pens and bags); and

- signs, display racks, or other promotional materials used on the business premises of the recipient.

### IV.A.12. Interest, Taxes, and Fees

[525 T.M., III., IV., 536 T.M., VIII.D., X.; TPS ¶¶2330.02.E., .03., 2340.03.B., .04.B.]

*Interest Expenses.* Trade or business interest is deductible in full by a noncorporate taxpayer, unless it is otherwise disallowed or limited by another provision. Trade or business interest is interest paid or accrued on debt properly allocable to a taxpayer's trade or business (other than the trade or business of performing services as an employee). Investment interest and passive activity interest are excluded from the definition of trade or business interest, and thus, trade or business interest is often referred to as "active" interest [§ 163(h)(2)(A), § 163(d), § 469]. Deductible investment interest is discussed at IV.B.2.a. and deductible passive activity interest is discussed at VIII.F. Deductible nonbusiness interest is discussed at VII.F.

For corporate taxpayers, interest expense is generally deductible with the following exceptions:

- Certain corporations have limited deductions for passive activity interest [§ 469(a)].

- Deductions for interest on debt used to acquire the stock or assets of another corporation are limited for all corporations [§ 279(a)].

- The deduction for certain interest paid by a corporation to related persons is limited [§ 163(j)].

*Taxes and Fees.* While some taxes are specifically deductible or nondeductible regardless of the existence of a trade or business, certain taxes, fees, and similar payments are deductible only if they are incurred in carrying on a trade or business or an investment activity [§ 162, § 164(a), § 164(c), § 212]. Such items include sales taxes, excise taxes, automobile inspection fees for vehicles used in the trade or business, tolls paid while on business travel, license fees paid in connection with the trade or business, and employer contributions to social security taxes. Deductible nonbusiness taxes are discussed at VII.E.

The following taxes are nondeductible, regardless of the existence of a trade or business or a for-profit activity [§ 275]:

- federal income taxes (except to the extent that a deduction is permitted for a portion of self-employment taxes [§ 164(f)] (see VII.B.7.));
- an employee's share of FICA taxes [§ 3101] (see XXII.B.1.a.);
- the wage taxes imposed on railroad employees and employee representatives [§ 3201, § 3211] (see XXII.B.1.e.);
- federal income taxes withheld at source on wages [§ 3402] (see XXII.A.);
- estate, inheritance, legacy, succession, and gift taxes;
- income taxes imposed by the authority of any foreign country or U.S. possession if the taxpayer elects to any extent the foreign tax credit [§ 901];
- taxes on real property to the extent they are treated as being imposed on another taxpayer under § 164(d);
- certain excise-type taxes imposed under the charitable, private foundation, pension, and corporate prohibited transactions provisions; and
- fees imposed on covered entities engaged in the business of manufacturing or importing branded prescription drugs [Pub. L. No. 111-148, § 9008(a), § 9008(f)].

### IV.A.13. Judgments and Settlements

[522 T.M., V.; TPS ¶1340.05.]

The underlying claims test applies to determine whether payments made under a judgment or settlement are deductible as a trade or business expense [*United States v. Gilmore*, 372 U.S. 39 (1963)]. Generally, amounts paid in judgment or settlement of a lawsuit (including punitive damages) are deductible if the acts giving rise to the litigation were performed in the ordinary conduct of the taxpayer's trade or business [§ 162(a); Rev. Rul. 80-211, 1980-2 C.B. 57]. Similarly, amounts paid for legal expenses in connection with litigation are allowed as deductible business expenses where such litigation is directly connected to, or proximately results from, the conduct of the taxpayer's business. However, if the litigation arises from a capital transaction, payments are required to be capitalized [*Woodward v. Commissioner*, 397 U.S. 572 (1970)].

Two-thirds of treble damages paid in connection with convictions for violations of the antitrust laws are not deductible [§ 162(g)] (see IV.D.4.). Additionally, fines and penalties paid to a government are not deductible [§ 162(f)] (see IV.D.2.).

The treatment of amounts received from a judgment or settlement, and the application of the underlying claims test to such amounts, is discussed in II.F.

### IV.A.14. Corporate Charitable Contributions

[794 T.M.; TPS ¶¶2390.07., 2395.]

Corporations are allowed a limited deduction for any charitable contribution made to, or for the use of, a qualified charitable organization [§ 170]. Charitable contributions are discussed in VII.G.

*Qualified Charitable Organizations.* The range of qualified charitable organizations for corporate donors is similar, though more limited, than for individual donors (see VII.G.1.). Specifically, domestic fraternal societies, orders, or associations, though they are qualified charitable organizations for individuals, are not qualified charitable organizations for corporations [§ 170(c)(4)]. Further, while both individuals and corporations may deduct contributions to a corporation, trust, or community chest, fund, or foundation organized and operated exclusively for charitable purposes, a corporation's contribution or gift to a trust, chest, fund, or foundation is only deductible if it is to be used within the United States or any U.S. possessions [§ 170(c)(2)(D)].

*Contributions as Constructive Dividends.* A contribution to charity is deductible only if it is a voluntary transfer of money or other property without expectation of economic consideration or other benefit to the transferor. If a closely-held corporation makes a contribution to a charity and the two entities are controlled by the same individuals, the test for donative intent focuses both on the anticipated benefit to the corporation and any expected benefit to the controlling shareholders. Depending on the circumstances, the transfer may be treated as a constructive dividend from the corporation to the shareholders followed by a constructive charitable contribution by the shareholders to the charity.

*Tax Year of Deduction.* Generally, charitable contributions are deductible in the tax year in which the contribution is made, whether the donor is a cash method or accrual method taxpayer. However, an accrual basis corporation may elect to treat a contribution made after the close of a tax year as made within the tax year if all of the following conditions are met [§ 170(a)(2)]:

1. the corporation's board of directors authorizes the contribution during the tax year;
2. payment of the contribution is made on or before the 15th day of the third month following the close of the tax year; and
3. the election is made at the time of the filing of the corporate income tax return for the tax year.

A corporation makes the election by reporting the contribution on its income tax return. Additionally the corporation must attach to the return a written declaration, verified by a corporate office under penalty of perjury, that the board resolution authorizing the contribution was adopted during the tax year and listing the date of the resolution [Reg. § 1.170A-11(b)(2)].

### IV.A.14.a. *Corporate Contributions of Appreciated Ordinary Income Property*

[794 T.M., IV; TPS ¶2390.07.B.]

Generally, the amount of a contribution of ordinary income property must be reduced by the amount of gain that would not have been long-term capital gain if the donor had sold the property for its fair market value [§ 170(e)(1)]. Contributions of appreciated ordinary income property are discussed in VII.G.2.a.

Two exceptions to the general rule offer corporations preferential treatment for gifts of certain ordinary income property: (i) contributions of inventory for the care of the ill, needy, or infants, and (ii) scientific property used for research. For these types of contributions, a corporation (other than an S corporation) may be able to claim a deduction equal to the lesser of either (i) the basis of the donated inventory or property plus half of the inventory or property's appreciation (i.e., gain if the donated inventory or property was sold at fair market value on the date of the donation), or (ii) two times the basis of the donated inventory or property [§ 170(e)(3)(B)].

*Contributions of Inventory for Care of Ill, Needy, or Infants.* A corporation that makes a qualified contribution of certain ordinary income property for use in caring for the ill, the needy, or infants may take advantage of the special reduction. A qualified contribution for this purpose is a charitable contribution of property described in § 1221(a)(1) or § 1221(a)(2) to a public charity or private operating foundation that meets all of the following requirements [§ 170(e)(3)(A)]:

1. the property contributed must be either (i) inventory property held primarily for sale to customers in the ordinary course of a trade or business, or (ii) property used in a trade or business of a character that is subject to a depreciation deduction, or real property used in a trade or business;

2. the donee's use of the property must be related to its exempt purpose or function, and the donee's use of the property must be solely to care for the ill, the needy, or infants;

3. the donee must not transfer the property in exchange for money, other property, or services;

4. the donor must receive a written statement from the donee representing that its use and disposition of the property will be in accordance with the requirements for a qualified contribution; and

5. any property subject to the Federal Food, Drug, and Cosmetic Act must satisfy the requirements of the Act on the date of transfer and for 180 days prior to the date of transfer.

Before 2014, certain charitable contributions of apparently wholesome food inventory by any taxpayer engaged in a trade or business qualified for the special reduction. Thus sole proprietorships, partnerships, and S corporations, among others, could take the special reduction. This provision expired for contributions made after 2013 [§ 170(e)(3)(C)].

***Scientific Property Used for Research.*** A corporation (other than S corporations, personal holding companies, and service organizations) that makes a qualified research contribution of certain ordinary income property for use in research may take advantage of the special reduction [§ 170(e)(4)(A)]. A qualified research contribution for this purpose is a contribution to a college, university, or certain scientific research organization that meets all of the following requirements [§ 170(e)(4)(B)]:

1. the contributed property must be tangible personal property that is inventory or property held primarily for sale to customers in the ordinary course of a trade or business;

2. the property must be constructed or assembled by the donor;

3. the contribution must be made not later than two years after the date the construction or assembly of the property is substantially completed;

4. the original use of the property must be by the donee;

5. the property must be scientific equipment or apparatus substantially all of the use of which by the donee is for research or experimentation, or for research training, in the United States in physical or biological sciences;

6. the donee must not transfer the property in exchange for money, property, or services; and

7. the donor must receive a written statement from the donee representing that its use and disposition of the property will be in accordance with the requirements for a qualified research contribution.

### IV.A.14.b. Percentage Limitations on Corporate Charitable Contributions

[794 T.M., V.; TPS ¶2390.07.C.]

A single percentage limitation applies to all gifts by corporations. The charitable contributions deduction for any tax year is limited to 10% of the corporation's taxable income [§ 170(b)(2)(A)]. For this purpose, taxable income is computed without regard to the following items [§ 170(b)(2)(C)]:

- the charitable contributions deduction;
- the dividends received deduction (see XIII.C.2.b.) and certain other deductions allowable only to corporations;
- any net operating loss carryback to the tax year (see VIII.G.3.);
- the deduction for income attributable to domestic production activities (see IV.A.9.); and
- any capital loss carryback to the tax year (see III.B.5.).

***Carryover of Excess Contributions.*** Charitable contributions that exceed the 10% limitation may be carried over to the succeeding five tax years (in order). Contributions actually made during any tax year are deductible before any carryovers to that year may be deducted, and carryovers from the earliest year are deducted first among carryover amounts [§ 170(d)(2)(A)].

An excess contribution is deductible in a carryover year to the extent of the lesser of [§ 170(d)(2)(A)]:

- the excess of the maximum amount deductible for the tax year under the 10% limitation over the sum of (i) contributions made during the year, and (ii) excess contributions made in tax years before the contribution year but that are deducible as carryovers for the year; or
- the portion of the excess not already deductible for a previous carryover year.

Carryovers of excess contributions may not be deducted to the extent it increases a net operating loss carryover [§ 170(d)(2)(B)].

### IV.A.15. Miscellaneous Business Expenses

#### IV.A.15.a. Social Security Payments for Employees of Foreign Subsidiaries

[514 T.M., III.C.; TPS ¶2270.02.]

Domestic corporations can deduct social security tax equivalents under § 3121(l) agreements for services performed by U.S. citizens employed by a foreign subsidiary. The U.S. employer must enter into a binding agreement with the IRS whereby the U.S. employer undertakes to pay the full FICA tax (employer and employee portions) on all U.S. citizens and residents employed by the foreign affiliate. The U.S. employer may deduct the payments made under such agreements. However, the deduction is not available for amounts for which the U.S. employer is compensated, and the deduction does not apply to payments that would not constitute wages under social security laws [§ 176, § 3121(l)].

#### IV.A.15.b. Contributions to Black Lung Benefit Trusts

[514 T.M., III.D.; TPS ¶2270.03.]

Taxpayers may deduct contributions to black lung benefits trusts that are tax-exempt under § 501(c)(21) (see XIX.B.1.) [§ 192(a)]. The amount deductible in any tax year is limited to the greater of the following amounts [§ 192(b)]:

- the amount necessary to fund (with level funding) the taxpayer's remaining unfunded liability for black lung claims filed, or expected to be filed, by, or with respect to, the taxpayer's past or present employees; or
- the aggregate amount necessary to increase each black lung liability trust to the amount required to pay all amounts payable from the trust for the tax year.

Payments must be in cash, U.S. public debt, securities, state or local government obligations that are not in default, or time deposits in U.S. banks or credit unions. To be deductible for a particular tax year, payments must be made by the taxpayer's income tax return due date, including extensions [§ 192(c)(3), § 192(c)(4)].

Amounts not deductible by reason of the limitation may be carried forward and treated as contributed to the trust in the succeeding tax year [§ 192(d)]. However, excess contributions that are not deducted or withdrawn are subject to a 5% excise tax payable each tax year by the person making the excess contribution [§ 4953(a)].

### IV.A.15.c. Employer Liability Trust Contributions

[505 T.M., IV.A.8.; TPS ¶2270.04.]

Contributions to an employer withdrawal liability payment fund trust that are properly allocable to the tax year are deductible. An employer withdrawal liability payment fund trust is a trust established to pay the withdrawal liability of an employer withdrawing from a multi-employer pension plan under § 4223 of ERISA [§ 194A].

### IV.A.15.d. Unused Business Credits

[505 T.M., IV.R.; TPS ¶2270.05.]

A taxpayer may deduct the part of certain unused business credits (as defined in § 196(c)) that had not been allowed because of the tax liability limitation on deduction of business credits and the expiration of the § 39 business credit carryover period. The unused credit may be allowed as a deduction for the first tax year following the last tax year the credit could have been allowed. The amount of the deduction for the investment tax credit (other than the § 47 rehabilitation credit) and the research credit is limited to 50% of the unused portion of the credit. The deduction may also be claimed for the tax year in which the taxpayer died or ceased to exist [§ 196].

Business credits are discussed in IX.A.

### IV.A.15.e. Payments for Professional Services

[505 T.M., IV.N.; TPS ¶2480.]

A taxpayer may deduct reasonable payments made for professional services in connection with the carrying on of a trade or business. Deductible expenses include accounting, business, and investment advice, maintenance of a corporate resident office, appraisals, and actuarial, legal, and management services [§ 162(a)].

## IV.B. Expenses for the Production of Income

[505 T.M., III.; TPS ¶2300.]

The existence of a trade or business is not a prerequisite for the deductibility of certain expenses. Individuals, trusts, and estates may deduct the ordinary and necessary expenses paid or incurred during a tax year (i) for the production or collection of income, (ii) for the management, conservation, or maintenance of property held for the production of income, or (iii) in connection with the determination, collection, or refund of any tax [§ 212, § 641(b); Reg. § 1.212-1]. While this deduction provision relaxes the trade or business requirement of the § 162 trade or business expenses deduction (see IV.A.), other restrictions on deductions, including the requirements that an expense be reasonable in amount and not a capital expenditure, continue to apply.

In contrast to trade or business expenses, which are above-the-line deductions used to compute adjusted gross income, expenses for the production of income for individuals are generally treated as below-the-line miscellaneous itemized deductions, which reduce adjusted gross income. One exception is deductions for expenses for the production of income attributable to property held for the production of rents or royalties, which is an above-the-line deduction [§ 62(a)(4)]. Miscellaneous itemized deductions are subject to a 2% floor (see VII.I.).

### IV.B.1. Basic Requirements

[505 T.M., III.; TPS ¶2300.01.]

To be deductible as an expense for the production of income, three things must be established:

1. the taxpayer's purpose in making the expenditure must be to earn a profit;
2. the taxpayer must show that the expense is ordinary and necessary; and
3. no other restrictions on the deductibility of the expenditure must apply.

*Activities Engaged in for a Profit.* Whether an activity involves the production of income and whether a taxpayer holds property for the production of income are questions of fact. The determination is similar to the determination of whether a profit motive exists for purposes of establishing the existence of a trade or business (see IV.A.).

*Ordinary and Necessary.* The ordinary and necessary requirement has generally been interpreted the same way it has for purposes of the trade or business expense deduction (see IV.A.). Generally speaking, an expenditure must be reasonable in amount, and it must bear a reasonable and proximate relation to the production or collection of taxable income, or to the management, conservation, or maintenance of property held for the production of income [Reg. § 1.212-1(d)].

*Production or Collection of Income.* Deductions are allowed for expenses paid or incurred for the production or collection of income [§ 212(1)]. An expense needs not be related to income of the current year in order to be deductible. The term "income" includes not merely income of the tax year, but also income that the taxpayer has realized in a prior tax year or may realize in subsequent tax years. The term is also not confined to recurring income; it applies as well to gains from the disposition of property. It is also immaterial whether the taxpayer actually realizes income. Further, expenses are deductible even if their purpose is merely to minimize an expected loss [Reg. § 1.212-1(b)].

---

**EXAMPLE:** Ethan owns a vacant lot that he hopes to sell at a gain in 5 or 6 years. He is concerned that he might be sued by someone who is injured on the property, so he buys liability insurance. Presuming the other requirements are satisfied, the cost of Ethan's insurance policy is deductible despite the fact that the lot does not currently produce any income.

---

*Management, Conservation, or Maintenance of Property Held for the Production of Income.* Deductions are allowed for expenses paid or incurred for the management, conservation, or maintenance of property held for the production of income [§ 212(2)]. No deduction is allowed for the expenses of maintaining property held for personal purposes, even if the taxpayer expects to sell that personal property at a gain. Thus, a taxpayer may not deduct the expenses of maintaining his or her residence, even though the residence has appreciated in value, because the taxpayer's use of the property as a dwelling makes it a personal expense. However, if the taxpayer's property is converted from personal use property to rental use property, the taxpayer's expenses become deductible [§ 262(a); § 280A(a); Reg. § 1.212-1(h)]. In the case of property that is used both for personal and investment purposes, the expenses of maintaining the property are allocated between the two uses and are deductible to the extent they relate to the investment use.

Expenses paid or incurred in defending or perfecting title to property and in recovering, developing, or improving property constitute a part of the cost of the property that must be capitalized and are not deductible expenses. Attorneys' fees paid in a suit to quiet title to lands are not deductible, however the expenses would be deductible if paid in connection with investment property and income that, if and when recovered, must be included in gross income [Reg. § 1.212-1(k)].

### IV.B.2. Certain Production of Income Expenses

### IV.B.2.a. Investment Interest and Other Investment Expenses

[523 T.M., III.C., 536 T.M., VIII.B.; TPS ¶2300.02.A.]

A taxpayer may deduct fees for services of investment counsel, custodial fees, clerical help, office rent, and similar expenses paid or incurred in connection with the taxpayer's investments [Reg. § 1.212-1(g)]. However, while fees paid for ongoing investment advice are deductible, one-time fees paid in connection with the acquisition of particular investments are akin to sales commissions or finder's fees, and they must be capitalized as part of the taxpayer's basis in the investments.

*Investment Interest.* A noncorporate taxpayer's deduction for investment interest is limited to the taxpayer's net investment income for the tax year. Investment interest disallowed by this limitation can be carried forward and deducted against net investment income is subsequent tax years. Property held for investment does not include an interest in a passive activity (as defined in § 469(c)) [§ 163(d)].

Where interest expense is passed through to the taxpayer from a partnership or S corporation, the determination whether it is investment interest is made at the entity level. Similarly, investment interest paid by a trust or estate is characterized as investment interest at the beneficiary level if the trust or estate income is actually distributed to the beneficiaries.

Investment interest is discussed in VII.F.4. Deductible trade or business interest and deductible passive activity interest are discussed at IV.A.12. and VIII.F., respectively. Deductible nonbusiness interest is discussed at VII.F.

### IV.B.2.b. Legal Expenses

[523 T.M., III.A.; TPS ¶2300.02.B.]

Attorneys' fees and other legal expenses paid or incurred for the production of income or for the management, conservation, or maintenance of property held for the production of income are typically deductible. However, legal expenses for defending or perfecting title to property and for recovering, developing, or improving property constitute a part of the cost of the property and are not deductible expenses. Attorneys' fees paid in a suit to quiet title to lands are also not deductible, however the expenses would be deductible if paid in connection with investment property and income that, if and when recovered, must be included in gross income. In addition, legal expenses incurred in connection with the determination, collection, or refund of taxes generally are deductible (see IV.B.3.). However, an expense that is not otherwise deductible in determining or contesting a liability does not become deductible merely because property the taxpayer holds for the production of income may be required to be used or sold to satisfy the liability [Reg. § 1.212-1(k), § 1.212-1(l), § 1.212-1(m)].

A corporation that pays the legal fees of an officer may be entitled to deduct the fees if the officer's crime arose from the entity's trade or business. However, no deduction is allowed if the officer's charged crime is personal in nature and could not have arisen in the course of the trade or business (e.g., murder).

### IV.B.3. Determination, Collection, or Refund of Any Tax

[505 T.M., III.G.; TPS ¶2480.02.J.]

A taxpayer may deduct the expenses paid or incurred in connection with the determination, collection, or refund of any tax, whether the taxing authority is the United States, a state, a municipality, or another taxing entity (including foreign governments). Further, the expenses may be incurred in connection with income, estate, gift, property, or any other tax. An expense paid or incurred in connection with a proceeding involved in determining or contesting a tax liability is deductible [Reg. § 1.212-1(l)]. However, expenses incurred in determining or contesting a liability asserted against the taxpayer are not deductible merely because property held for the production of income may be used or sold to satisfy the liability [Reg. § 1.212-1(m)].

Common expenses relating to the determination, collection, or refund of taxes include legal and professional fees paid for tax advice, for the preparation of an income tax return, for services rendered to pursue a claim for refund, for contesting a deficiency or a civil fraud penalty, and for defending criminal tax charges.

### IV.B.4. Expenses of Earning Tax-Exempt Income

[536 T.M., X.L.; TPS ¶2300.03.D.]

No deduction is allowed for expenses allocable to the production of tax-exempt income. This includes interest on debt incurred or continued to fund a taxpayer's investments in obligations or certificates that pay tax-exempt interest. If expenses relate to both taxable and tax-exempt income, the expenses must be allocated between the two classes, and the amount allocable to the tax-exempt income is not deductible [§ 265]. Expenses allocable to the production of tax-exempt income are discussed in VIII.D.

## IV.C. Substantiation of Expenses

In general, taxpayers should be able to prove that deducted expenses were legitimate and actually paid. Often this may be accomplished by maintaining a recordkeeping system and retaining supporting documents that are evidence of payments (e.g., receipts, invoices, and cancelled checks). Certain expenses, however, require special substantiation.

### IV.C.1. Special Substantiation Requirements for Certain Expenses

[519 T.M., VI.B.; TPS ¶2130.02.B.4.]

The following expenses are subject to specific substantiation requirements [§ 274(d)]:

- travel expenses (including meals and lodging while away from home) (see IV.A.10.a.);
- any item related to an activity that is of a type generally considered to constitute entertainment, amusement, or recreation, or with respect to a facility used in connection with such an activity (see IV.A.11.);
- gifts (see IV.A.11.f.); and

- expenses with respect to an item of the following "listed properties" [§ 280F(d)(4)]:

  — passenger automobiles, or any other property used for transportation (other than property, substantially all of which is used in a trade or business of providing transportation services);

  — property generally used for purposes of entertainment, recreation, or amusement;

  — any computer or peripheral equipment (except for equipment used exclusively at a regular business establishment and owned or leased by the person operating the establishment); and

  — any other property of a type specified by regulations.

For these categories of expenses, a deduction is allowed only if the taxpayer substantiates by adequate records, or by sufficient evidence corroborating the taxpayer's own statement, the following [§ 274(d)]:

- the amount of such expense or other item;
- the time and place of the travel, entertainment, amusement, recreation, or use of the facility or property, or the date and description of the gift;
- the business purpose of the expense or other item; and
- the business relationship to the taxpayer of persons entertained, using the facility or property, or receiving the gift.

***Adequate Records.*** Taxpayers must furnish either adequate records or sufficient evidence to corroborate the taxpayer's own statement. The maintenance of adequate records requires that the taxpayer keep (i) an account book, diary, log, statement of expense, trip sheets, or similar record, and (ii) documentary evidence like receipts and invoices. Taken together, these two items should establish each element of an expenditure or use. Further, the items should be prepared in such a manner than each recording of an element of an expense or use is made at or near the time of the expenditure or use. Documentary evidence should contain sufficient information to establish the amount, date, place, and essential character of the expenditure [Reg. § 1.274-5(c), § 1.274-5T(c)]. If employee expenses subject to these specific substantiation requirements are reimbursed under an accountable plan (see IV.A.3.b.), satisfaction of these specific substantiation requirements is also sufficient substantiation for purposes of the accountable plan [Reg. § 1.62-2(e)(2)].

Table 5-1. **How To Prove Certain Business Expenses**

| IF you have expenses for . . | THEN you must keep records that show details of the following elements . . . | | | |
|---|---|---|---|---|
| | Amount | Time | Place or Description | Business Purpose Business Relationship |
| Travel | Cost of each separate expense for travel, lodging, and meals. Incidental expenses may be totaled in reasonable categories such as taxis, fees and tips, etc. | Dates you left and returned for each trip and number of days spent on business. | Destination or area of your travel (name of city, town, or other designation). | Purpose: Business purpose for the expense or the business benefit gained or expected to be gained.<br><br>Relationship: N/A |
| Entertainment | Cost of each separate expense. Incidental expenses such as taxis, telephones, etc., may be totaled on a daily basis. | Date of entertainment. (Also see *Business Purpose*.) | Name and address or location of place of entertainment. Type of entertainment if not otherwise apparent. (Also see *Business Purpose*.) | Purpose: Business purpose for the expense or the business benefit gained or expected to be gained. For entertainment, the nature of the business discussion or activity. If the entertainment was directly before or after a business discussion: the date, place, nature, and duration of the business discussion, and the identities of the persons who took part in both the business discussion and the entertainment activity.<br><br>Relationship: Occupations or other information (such as names, titles, or other designations) about the recipients that shows their business relationship to you. For entertainment, you must also prove that you or your employee was present if the entertainment was a business meal. |
| Gifts | Cost of the gift. | Date of the gift. | Description of the gift. | |
| Transportation | Cost of each separate expense. For car expenses, the cost of the car and any improvements, the date you started using it for business, the mileage for each business use, and the total miles for the year. | Date of the expense. For car expenses, the date of the use of the car. | Your business destination. | Purpose: Business purpose for the expense.<br><br>Relationship: N/A |

(Source: IRS Pub. 463)

### IV.C.2. *Alternatives to Substantiation of Actual Expenses*

If an employer reimburses an employee for his or her expenses using a per diem or car allowance, the employee generally may use the allowance as proof for the amount of his or her expenses.

### IV.C.2.a. *Per Diem Allowances*

[519 T.M., VI.C.3.b.; TPS ¶2130.02.B.5.]

The amount of ordinary and necessary business expenses paid or incurred by an employee while traveling away from home will be deemed substantiated when an employer (or the employer's agent, or a third party) provides a per diem allowance to pay for such expenses. To satisfy the special substantiation rules for travel expenses (see IV.C.1.), an employee receiving a per diem allowance under an accountable plan (see IV.A.3.b.) need only substantiate the time, place, and business purposes of the travel expenses [Rev. Proc. 2011-47, 2011-42 I.R.B. 520].

A per diem allowance is a payment under an accountable plan that has the following characteristics [Rev. Proc. 2011-47]:

- it is paid with respect to an employee's lodging, meal, and incidental expenses (or for meal and incidental expenses, but not for lodging expenses alone) for business travel away from home;
- it is reasonably calculated not to exceed the amount of the expenses or anticipated expenses; and

- it is paid at or below the applicable federal per diem rate, a flat rate or stated schedule, or any other IRS-specified rate or schedule.

The federal per diem rate is the sum of the federal lodging expense rate and the federal meal and incidental expense rate for the date and place of travel. These rates for localities within the continental United States are established by the General Services Administration (www.gsa.gov/postal/content/104877), these rates for localities outside the continental United States are established by the Defense Department (www.defensetravel.dod.mil/site/perdiemcalc.cfm ), and these rates for foreign localities are established by the State Department (www.aoprals.state.gov/web920/per_diem.asp).

***Flat Rate or Stated Schedule.*** An allowance is considered to be paid according to a flat rate or stated schedule if it is provided on a uniform and objective basis. Such allowance may be paid with respect to the number of days away from home in connection with the performance of services as an employee or on any other basis that is consistently applied and in accordance with reasonable business practice [Rev. Proc. 2011-47].

***Incidental Expenses.*** Incidental expenses include the following [Rev. Proc. 2011-47]:

- fees and tips given to porters, baggage carriers, bellhops, hotel maids, stewards or stewardesses and others on ship, and hotel servants in foreign countries;

- transportation between places of lodging or business and places where meals are taken, if suitable meals cannot be obtained at the temporary duty site; and

- mailing costs associated with filing travel vouchers and payment of employer-sponsored charge card billings.

***Optional Per Diem Methods.*** Optional per diem methods are also available for (i) employees and self-employed individuals for computing the deductible costs of business meal and incidental expenses paid or incurred while traveling away from home, and (ii) computing the deductible costs of incidental expenses paid or incurred while traveling away from home by employees and self-employed individuals who do not pay or incur meal costs and are not reimbursed for the incidental expenses [Rev. Proc. 2011-47].

### IV.C.2.b. Standard Mileage Rate and Mileage Allowances

[519 T.M., VI.C.3.a.; TPS ¶2310.05.B.]

Rather than keeping track of actual automobile expenses, a taxpayer may use the standard mileage rate set by the IRS in lieu of deducting the automobile's operating and fixed costs. This amount generally may be used as proof for the amount of expenses. Similarly, if an employer provides a mileage allowance under an accountable plan to reimburse employees for automobile expenses, these amounts may also serve as proof for the amount of expenses (see IV.a.10.c.).

### IV.C.2.c. Cohan Rule

[519 T.M., 523 T.M., II.; TPS ¶2480.05.A.]

If a taxpayer provides sufficient evidence that he or she has incurred a deductible expense, but is unable to adequately substantiate the amount of the deduction, a court generally may estimate the amount of the expense, rather than disallow the deduction entirely [*Cohan v. Commissioner*, 39 F.2d 540 (2d Cir. 1930)]. However, because of perceived abuses and administrative difficulties, this rule does not apply to expenses subject to special substantiation requirements, for example, those discussed in IV.C.1. [§ 274(d); Reg. § 1.274-5T(a)].

## IV.D. Limitations on Trade or Business Deductions

### IV.D.1. Nondeductible Lobbying and Political Expenses

[613 T.M.; TPS ¶2180.]

***Lobbying Expenses.*** Generally, lobbying expenses are not deductible. Lobbying expenses, for this purpose, include amounts paid or incurred to (i) influence legislation, (ii) participate in, or intervene in, any political campaign on behalf of (or in opposition to) any candidate for public office, (iii) any attempt to influence the general public, or segments thereof, on elections, legislative matters, or referendums, and (iv) any direct communication with certain high-level executive branch officials in an attempt to influence the official actions or positions of that official [§ 162(e); Reg. § 1.162-29].

However, the following areas of lobbying expenses are exceptions to the general nondeductibility rule [§ 162(e)(2), § 162(e)(4), § 162(e)(5)]:

- legislative lobbying at the local level;
- certain in-house legislative lobbying expenditures that do not exceed $2,000 for the tax year;
- lobbying of administrative agencies and the executive branch of government on matters not relating to legislation; and
- professional lobbying that rises to the level of a trade or business.

***Political Expenses.*** No deduction is permitted for the expense of participating in, or intervening in, a political campaign on behalf of (or in opposition to) any candidate for public office. Thus, contributions or gifts paid to political parties or candidates are not deductible [§ 162(e)(1)(B)]. Further, the cost of an advertisement on a political issue that is expected to benefit one political group is considered an expenditure for political campaign purposes and is nondeductible [Rev. Rul. 62-156, 1962-2 C.B. 47].

In addition, indirect political contributions and costs of taking part in political activities are not deductible. Examples of such expenses include, advertising in a publication of a political party if the proceeds from the publication are for the use of a political party or candidate, admission to a dinner or program if any proceeds from the function are for the use of a political party or candidate, and admission to an inaugural ball, gala, parade, concert, or similar even if identified with a political party or candidate [§ 276(a)].

An individual's cost of obtaining or retaining an elective office is not deductible [*McDonald v. Commissioner*, 323 U.S. 57 (1944)].

### IV.D.2. Nondeductible Fines and Penalties

[524 T.M., V.; TPS ¶2230.]

Taxpayers may not deduct amounts paid as a fine or similar penalty to any government for violation of any law [§ 162(f)]. A fine or penalty for this purpose includes the following amounts [Reg. § 1.162-21(b)(1)]:

- amounts paid pursuant to conviction or a plea of guilty or nolo contendere for a crime (felony or misdemeanor) in a criminal proceeding;
- amounts paid as a civil penalty under federal, state, or local law;
- amounts paid in settlement of the taxpayer's actual or potential liability for a fine or penalty (civil or criminal); and
- amounts forfeited as collateral posted in connection with a proceeding that could result in imposition of a fine or penalty.

Compensatory damages paid to a government do not constitute a fine or penalty [Reg. § 1.162-21(b)(2)]. If it is unclear whether a statute imposes a punitive or compensatory penalty (or if the statute serves both purposes), then the facts and circumstances of the specific payment at issue, and the manner in which it is calculated, must be examined to determine the purpose for which the payment is intended. In the case of a settlement agreement (e.g., under the False Claims Act) that is silent or ambiguous on the matter, a similar investigation of the facts and circumstances surrounding the settlement must be made.

---

**EXAMPLE:** Large Co. is an interstate trucking company. The states in which Large Co. operates impose maximum weight limits on trucks operating on their highways. Failure to adhere to these limits results in fines payable to the appropriate state. Large Co. accumulates a number of overweight citations. In some instances, Large Co. contests the citation and is found liable by a court, and in other instances, Large Co. simply pays the fine without contest. None of the fines are deductible as a trade or business expense because each one is paid to a government for the violation of a law.

---

### IV.D.3. Nondeductible Illegal Bribes and Kickbacks

[524 T.M., I., II., III.; TPS ¶2240.]

Generally, no deduction is allowed for illegal bribes or kickbacks paid directly or indirectly to an official, employee, or agency or instrumentality of any government. If the payment would be illegal under federal or state law, the deduction is prohibited even if the payment occurs in a foreign jurisdiction where the payment is not illegal [§ 162(c); Reg. § 1.162-18(a)(1)]. Similarly, taxpayers are denied a deduction for payments made to any non-government officials or employees if the payment constitutes an illegal bribe, kickback, or any other illegal payment under federal or state law (where such state law is generally enforced) that subjects the payor to a criminal penalty or the loss of a license or privilege to engage in a trade or business [§ 162(c); Reg. § 1.162-18(b)(1)].

---

**EXAMPLE:** Assume there is a U.S. law that makes kickbacks on insurance sales illegal. If Karen, an insurance saleswoman, gives a kickback on a sale in country Z, Karen may not deduct the kickback as a business expense even if the payment is legal and routine in country Z.

---

Kickbacks, rebates, and bribes made by any provider of services, supplier, physician, or other person who provides items or services paid for under Medicare or Medicaid are specifically not deductible. Kickbacks include payments in consideration of the referral of a client, patient, or customer [§ 162(c)(3); Reg. § 1.162-18(c)].

### IV.D.4. Nondeductible Portion of Treble Damages

[522 T.M., IV.C.; TPS ¶2250.]

Generally, taxpayers may deduct the payment of legal judgments if the claim on which the judgment is based arose in the ordinary course of the taxpayer's trade or business. However, if a taxpayer is convicted of a criminal violation of the antitrust laws, or if the taxpayer pleads guilty or nolo contendere to such a charge, no deduction is allowed for 2/3 of any amount paid or incurred (i) on any treble damages award on account of the same violation or a related violation of the antitrust laws that occurred before the date of the final judgment of conviction, or (ii) in settlement of any suit based on the violation or a related violation. The remaining 1/3 amount paid or incurred is deductible. Further, attorneys' fees, court costs, and other costs incurred in connection with the proceedings are fully deductible if the alleged violation occurs in the ordinary course of the taxpayer's business [§ 162(g); Reg. § 1.162-22(a)].

The deductibility of judgment and settlement awards is discussed in IV.A.13.

### IV.D.5. Meal and Entertainment Expense Deduction Limitation

[520 T.M., II.E.2.a.; TPS ¶2320.02.B.]

Expenses of reasonable business meals and entertainment may be deductible if they are related to, or, in the case of an expense directly before or after a substantial and bona fide business discussion, associated with, the active conduct of the taxpayer's trade or business (see IV.A.11.). However, the amount deductible is generally limited to 50% of the amount paid or incurred [§ 274(a)(1)(A), § 274(n)].

The percentage reduction rule applies to business meals and entertainment expenses a taxpayer has while (i) traveling away from home (whether eating alone or with others) on business, (ii) entertaining customers at the taxpayer's place of business, a restaurant, or other location, or (iii) attending a business convention or reception, business meeting, or business luncheon at a club. Items subject to the percentage reduction rule include the following:

- taxes and tips relating to a business meal or entertainment activity;
- cover charges for admission to a nightclub;
- rent paid for a room in which the taxpayer holds a dinner or cocktail party; and
- amounts paid for parking at sports arenas.

Any amount otherwise allowable as a deduction without regard to its connection with the taxpayer's trade or business (e.g., interest, taxes (such as real property taxes), and casualty losses) is not subject to the disallowance rule, and thus is not subject to the percentage reduction rule [§ 274(f); Reg. § 1.274-6]. Additionally, there are several exceptions to the percentage reduction rule, including the following [§ 274(n)(2)]:

- expenses treated as compensation paid to an employee (and subject to withholding tax), or otherwise included in the recipient's gross income (see IV.A.11.e.);
- reimbursed expenses (but the percentage reduction rule applies instead to the person making the reimbursement) (see IV.A.11.e.);
- expenses for certain recreational activities for employees (e.g., holiday parties and summer picnics) (see IV.A.11.e.);
- expenses for services or facilities that are made available to the general public (e.g., promotional tickets or samples provided to customers) (see IV.A.11.e.);
- expenses for goods or services sold to customers in bona fide transaction for adequate consideration (see IV.A.11.e.);
- food or beverage costs excludible from the recipient's gross income as a de minimis employee fringe benefit [§ 132(e)] (see XVII.D.4.);
- the cost of tickets to sports events arranged for the primary purpose of benefiting certain charitable organizations [§ 274(l)(1)(B)] (see IV.A.11.d.);
- meal expenses of an employee reimbursed by an employer and otherwise deductible as moving expenses, if includible in the employee's income [§ 82]; and

- expenses for food or beverages provided (i) to crew members of certain commercial vessels, or (ii) on certain oil and gas platforms or drilling rigs (or integral and proximate support camps).

***Employees Subject to Federal Hours of Service Limitations.*** Certain employees subject to the Department of Transportation hours of service limitations are subject to an 80%, rather than 50%, limitation for expenses for food or beverages consumed while away from home during, or incident to, the period of duty subject to the limitation [§ 274(n)(3)].

### IV.D.6. Hobby Loss Limitations

[548 T.M.; TPS ¶2450.]

An individual, S corporation, partnership, or trust or estate that does not carry on a business or investment activity to make a profit cannot deduct expenses from the activity against other income. However, the expenses may offset gross income from the activity during the tax year [§ 183(a), § 183(b); Reg. § 1.183-1(a); Rev. Rul. 77-320, 1977-2 C.B. 78]. Hobby losses and the limitation on the deduction of expenses attributable to hobby losses are discussed in VIII.J.

### IV.D.7. Home Office and Vacation Home Limitations

#### IV.D.7.a. Home Offices

[547 T.M.; TPS ¶2460.02.]

Generally, no deduction is allowed for business expenses attributable to the business use of a dual-use residence (i.e., a dwelling that is used both as a residence and in connection with a trade or business) [§ 280A(a)]. However, a deduction for a home office is available for any part of a taxpayer's home that is used regularly and exclusively for one the following uses [§ 280A(c)(1)]:

- the principal place of business for any trade or business in which the taxpayer engages;
- a place to meet or deal with patients, clients, or customers in the normal course of a trade or business; or
- a separate structure not attached the taxpayer's house or residence that is used in connection with a trade or business.

A deduction is also available for the part of a taxpayer's home that is used regularly, but not necessarily exclusively, (i) as a storage unit for inventory or product samples, or (ii) for the provision of day care services for children or other specified individuals [§ 280A(c)(2), § 280A(c)(4)].

Additionally, where the taxpayer is an employee, the use of the home office must be for the convenience of the employer, and the taxpayer must not rent any part of his or her home to the employer and use the rented portion to perform services as an employee for that employer [§ 280A(c)(1), § 280A(c)(6)].

***Limitations.*** Allowable trade or business deductions are limited to amounts that are allocable to the business use portion of the dual-use residence. Further, in a given tax year, such amounts may not exceed the gross income derived for that tax year from the qualified business use of the dual-use residence, less (i) deductible personal expenses (e.g. real estate taxes and casualty losses) allocated to the qualifying business use of the residence, and (ii) expenses attributable to the business activity but not attributable to the residence (e.g. supplies and compensation paid). If deductions exceed gross income, the excess may be carried forward to the succeeding tax year [§ 280A(c)(5); Prop. Reg. § 1.280A-2(i)].

The limitations apply to individuals, trusts, estates, partnerships, and S corporations. The limitations do not apply to those expenses that are allowable as a deduction without regard to whether they qualify as a trade or business expense (e.g., state and local income taxes) [§ 280A(b); Prop. Reg. § 1.280A-1(a), § 1.280A-1(b)].

*Calculating the Deduction.* Direct expenses that are paid or incurred only for the business portion of the residence (e.g., painting or repairs only in the area used for business) generally are deductible in full. Unrelated expenses that are paid or incurred only for the non-business parts of the residence (e.g., lawn care or painting a room not used for business) are not deductible. Indirect expenses for keeping up and running the entire residence (e.g., insurance, utilities, and general repairs) are deductible based on the percentage of your home used for business. The business portion of indirect expenses may be determined using any reasonable method (e.g., allocation according to the percentage of total floor space used for business purposes) [Prop. Reg. § 1.280A-2(i)(3)]. A taxpayer who owns a home and qualifies to deduct expenses for its business use can claim a depreciation deduction for the business portion, as well. The recovery period for nonresidential real property is 39 years. The basis for depreciation is generally the prorated portion of the home's cost, increased for any permanent improvements the taxpayer has made to it and decreased for casualty losses or depreciation deducted in earlier years. Depreciation is discussed in Chapter V.

In the case of a residence used for day care services, expenses must be further allocated based on the length of time the portion of the residence used for day care services bears to the length of time that portion is available for all purposes [Prop. Reg. § 1.280A-2(i)(4)].

---

**EXAMPLE:** Isaac uses his basement to operate a day care business for children. The basement is 1,600 square feet and the residence is 3,200 square feet. The business percentage of the basement is 50% (1,600 ÷ 3,200). Isaac uses the basement for day care for 12 hours a day, 5 days a week, for a total of 3,120 hours a year. During the rest of the time, Isaac can use the basement. Because there are 8,760 hours in a year (24 × 365), Isaac can deduct 35.6% (3,120 ÷ 8,760) of any direct expenses for the basement. However, because his indirect expenses are for the entire house, Isaac can only deduct 17.8% (50% × 35.6%) of the indirect expenses.

---

*Safe Harbor Allocation Method.* As an alternative to the calculation, allocation, and substantiation of actual expenses, a taxpayer may elect to determine their allowable deduction for home office expenses by multiplying $5 by the area of the residence used for a qualified business use (not to exceed 300 square feet). The election is made by using the safe harbor method to compute the deduction on the taxpayer's timely filed income tax return for the tax year. A taxpayer who elects to use the safe harbor method cannot deduct any actual expenses for the business that relate to the use of the home, or any depreciation (including additional first-year depreciation) or § 179 expense for the portion of the home used for a qualified business use. The depreciation deduction allowable for that portion of the home is deemed to be zero for a year in which the taxpayer uses the safe harbor method and therefore is not subject to recapture [Rev. Proc. 2013-13, 2013-6 I.R.B. 478].

Figure A.  **Can You Deduct Business Use of the Home Expenses?** Do not use this chart if you use your home for the storage of inventory or product samples, or to operate a daycare facility. See *Exceptions to Exclusive Use*, earlier, and *Daycare Facility*, later.

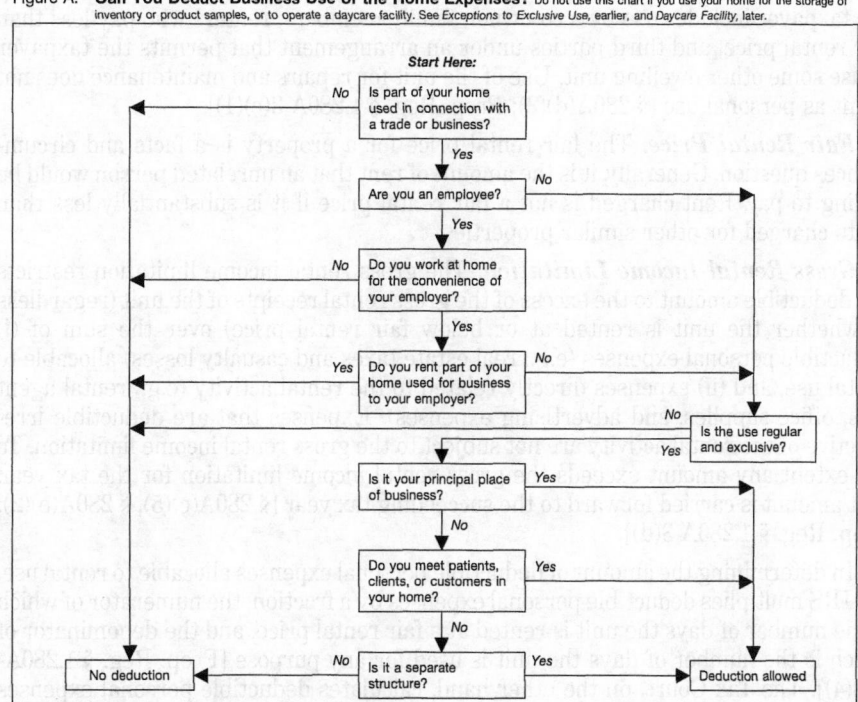

## IV.D.7.b. Vacation Home Rentals

[547 T.M., III.C.; TPS ¶2460.01.]

Expenses associated with renting a residence are generally deductible. However, if an individual, trust, estate, partnership, or S corporation makes personal use of a dwelling unit used as rental property, deductions otherwise allowable as trade or business expenses are disallowed to the extent allocable to the personal use. The portion of rental expenses allocable to the rental use of the property is determined by multiplying the expenses by a fraction, the numerator of which is the number of days the unit is rented at fair rental price during the tax year, and the denominator of which is the number of days the unit is used for any purpose during the tax year. The limitation does not apply to deductions that would be allowable for the tax year whether or not the dwelling unit was rented (e.g. certain taxes and casualty losses) [§ 280A(e); Prop Reg. § 1.280A-1(a), § 1.280A-1(b)]. If only a portion of the dwelling unit is rented, the allocation rule is applied to the expenses arising from the rented portion. Expenses attributable to the rented portion of the dwelling unit are determined using the same rules applicable to home offices (see IV.D.7.a.) [§ 280A(e)(1); Prop. Reg. § 1.280A-3(c)(2), § 1.280A-2(i)(3)].

Where the taxpayer's personal use of the dwelling unit exceeds the greater of (i) 14 days, or (ii) 10% of the days rented at a fair rental price, deductible expenses additionally are subject to a gross rental income limitation. However, if such a taxpayer rents the unit for fewer than 15 days during the tax year, no deduction for rental expenses is allowed and the rental income is excluded from gross income [§ 280A(d)(1), § 280A(g)].

*Personal Use.* A taxpayer is deemed to have used a dwelling unit for personal purposes if he or she uses any part of the unit for any part of the day. Personal use by the taxpayer includes use by a co-owner, family members, renters who pay less than fair rental price, and third parties under an arrangement that permits the taxpayer to use some other dwelling unit. Use of the unit for repairs and maintenance does not count as personal use [§ 280A(d)(2); Prop. Reg. § 1.280A-3(c)(1)].

*Fair Rental Price.* The fair rental price for a property is a facts and circumstances question. Generally, it is the amount of rent that an unrelated person would be willing to pay. Rent charged is not a fair rental price if it is substantially less than rents charged for other similar properties.

*Gross Rental Income Limitation.* The gross rental income limitation restricts the deductible amount to the excess of the gross rental receipts of the unit (regardless of whether the unit is rented at or below fair rental price) over the sum of (i) deductible personal expenses (e.g., real estate taxes and casualty losses) allocable to rental use, and (ii) expenses directly related to the rental activity (e.g., rental agent fees, office supplies, and advertising expenses). Expenses that are deductible irrespective of the rental activity are not subject to the gross rental income limitation. To the extent any amount exceeds the gross rental income limitation for the tax year, that amount is carried forward to the succeeding tax year [§ 280A(c)(5), § 280A(e)(2); Prop. Reg. § 1.280A-3(d)].

In determining the amount of deductible personal expenses allocable to rental use, the IRS multiplies deductible personal expenses by a fraction, the numerator of which is the number of days the unit is rented at a fair rental price, and the denominator of which is the number of days the unit is used for any purpose [Prop. Reg. § 1.280A-3(c)(4)]. The Tax Court, on the other hand, calculates deductible personal expenses allocable to rental use using the number of days in the tax year as the denominator [*Bolton v. Commissioner*, 77 T.C. 104 (1981)].

## IV.E. Losses and Bad Debts

[527 T.M., 538 T.M.; TPS ¶¶2350., 2360.]

Losses typically arise when there is either a total loss of value or a diminution in the value of an asset resulting from some transaction, event, or occurrence. Taxpayers generally may deduct any loss sustained during a tax year that is not compensated for by insurance or otherwise [§ 165(a)]. Common types of deductible losses under § 165 include casualty losses, theft losses, abandonment and obsolescence losses, losses on worthless securities, gambling or wagering losses, and farming losses.

Accounts receivable that will likely remain unpaid, uncollectible, and written off at tax time are considered bad debts. If the debt arises from a debtor-creditor relationship based on a valid and enforceable obligation to pay a determinable sum of money, and if the debt becomes worthless during the tax year, the taxpayer may deduct all or a part of the uncollectible amount. Business bad debts arise in connection with a taxpayer's trade or business and are fully deductible. Further, partially-worthless business bad debts may be deductible. Nonbusiness bad debts, however, are subject to the restrictions imposed on short-term capital losses and are deductible only when they become completely worthless [§ 166].

Section 165 losses and bad debts are discussed in VIII.H. and VIII.I., respectively.

## IV.F. Exceptions to Capitalization

With certain exceptions, taxpayers generally must capitalize expenditures for the acquisition of assets or rights with useful lives of more than one year. However, certain types of these expenditures have been statutorily carved out from the general rule and are deductible, either in the tax year the expenditures are made or over a period of years.

### IV.F.1. Circulation Expenses

[505 T.M., V.L.; TPS ¶2420.]

Publishers may elect to deduct the costs of establishing, maintaining, or increasing the circulation of a newspaper, magazine, or other periodical, including sales commissions for new and renewal subscriptions. Though they otherwise qualify as circulation expenditures, current deduction is not allowed for (i) expenditures for the purchase of land or depreciable property, or (ii) expenditures for the acquisition of circulation through the purchase of any part of the business of another publisher [§ 173(a); Reg. § 1.173-1(a)(1)].

The election to currently deduct circulation expenditures is made by attaching a statement to the tax return for the first tax year to which the election is applicable. Once made, the election is binding for all subsequent years, unless the IRS approves revocation [Reg. § 1.173-1(c)(2)].

A noncorporate taxpayer (including S corporations and personal holding companies) may elect to amortize over three years the circulation expenditures that would otherwise be deductible [§ 59(e)].

### IV.F.2. Research and Experimental Expenditures

[556 T.M.; TPS ¶2430.]

Taxpayers may elect to deduct the reasonable costs incurred in a trade or business for activities intended to provide information that would eliminate uncertainty about the development or improvement of a product. For this purpose, a product includes any pilot model, process, formula, invention, technique, patent, or similar property, and it includes products to be used by the taxpayer in his or her trade or business, as well as products to be held for sale, lease, or license. The costs of obtaining a patent (including attorneys' fees) are research and experimental expenditures [§ 174; Reg. § 1.174-2(a)].

The research and experimental expenditures deduction applies not only to costs paid or incurred for research or experimentation directly undertaken by the taxpayer, but also to expenditures for research or experimentation undertaken on the taxpayer's behalf by another person or organization. Thus, a taxpayer may qualify for the deduction by engaging a research institute, foundation, engineering company, or similar contractor to conduct its research [Reg. § 1.174-2(a)(10)]. In such a scenario, the taxpayer must still satisfy the trade or business requirement.

Research and experimental expenditures do not include expenditures for quality control testing, efficiency surveys, management studies, consumer surveys, advertising or promotions, the acquisition of another's patent, model, production, or process, or research in connection with literary, historical, or similar projects [Reg. § 1.174-2(a)(6)].

***Computer Software.*** The costs of developing computer software (whether or not the particular software is patented or copyrighted) so closely resembles research and experimental expenditures that taxpayers may treat the costs of developing software in the same manner as qualifying research expenditures. Accordingly, the costs attributable to the development of computer software (as defined in Rev. Proc. 2000-50, 2000-52 I.R.B. 601, § 2) may be treated as current expenses and deducted in full, or may be treated as capital expenditures recoverable through deductions for ratable amortization over a 60-month period beginning on the date of completion of development, or over a 36-month period beginning on the date the software is placed in service [§ 167(f)(1)].

***Accounting for Expenditures.*** Taxpayers may elect to deduct currently research or experimental expenditures that are paid or incurred during the tax year in connection with the taxpayer's trade or business. If adopted, this method applies to all research and experimental expenditures the taxpayer pays or incurs during the year the method is adopted, and to all subsequent tax years, unless the IRS authorizes a different method [§ 174(a)(1), § 174(a)(3); Reg. § 1.174-3(a)]. Expenditures that are otherwise allowable as a deduction under this method may, at the taxpayer's election, be amortized over a 10-year period beginning with the tax year in which the expenditures are made (rather than the month in which the taxpayer first realized benefits from the expenditures). Once made, this election is revocable only with IRS consent [§ 174(f)(2), § 59(e)].

A taxpayer that has not adopted the current expense method (or that has adopted the current expense method, but has received IRS permission) may elect to treat research or experimental expenditures as deferred expenses that may be amortized over a period of not less than 60 months (as selected by the taxpayer). Different amortization periods may be selected for separate projects. The deferred expense method applies only to expenditures that are chargeable to capital accounts, but that are not chargeable to property subject to an allowance for depreciation or depletion. Thus, this method may be utilized only if the property resulting from the research or experimental expenditures has no determinable useful life [§ 174(b); Reg. § 1.174-4(a)].

***Coordination with the Research Credit.*** No research and experimental expenditure deduction is allowed for that portion of a taxpayer's qualified research expenses (as defined in § 41(b)) or basic research expenses (as defined in § 41(e)(2)) that are otherwise allowable as a deduction for the tax year that is equal to the amount of the taxpayer's research credit determined for that year [§ 280C(c)(1)]. The § 41 research credit does not apply to amounts paid or incurred after 2013 [§ 41(h)] (see IX.A.8.).

***Alternative Minimum Tax Treatment.*** In determining the amount of the alternative minimum taxable income of noncorporate taxpayers, the amount of research and experimental expenditures allowable as a current deduction in computing the regular tax must be capitalized and amortized ratably over the 10-year period, beginning with the tax year in which the expenditures are made. There is no adjustment in the case of corporate taxpayers or the deferred expense method of deducting research or experimental expenditures. There is also no alternative minimum tax adjustment for individual taxpayers who materially participate (as defined in § 469(h)) in the activity giving rise to the current expense deduction [§ 56(b)(2)].

### IV.F.3. Farming Expenses

[607 T.M., II.; TPS ¶2440.]

In most respects, farming expenditures are governed by the rules generally applicable to trades or businesses and to production of income activities. However, some special provisions offer farmers tax advantages that are unavailable to other taxpayers. Farming losses are discussed in VIII.H.5.

### IV.F.3.a. Prepaid Farm Supplies and Poultry Costs

[607 T.M., II.D.12., IV.B.3.; TPS ¶2440.02.D.12., .04.B.3.]

The costs of incidental supplies and ordinary tools of short life or small cost that are used in a farming activity (e.g., hand tools, rakes, shovels) are allowable as business expenses [Reg. § 1.162-3(a)(2)]. The deduction of prepaid farm supplies and certain poultry costs by a cash method taxpayer (see XI.B.1.c.) in the year of payment, though, are generally subject to a special limitation. In this case, the deduction is limited to 50% of the taxpayer's other deductible farm expenses for the year [§ 464(f)].

***Expenses Subject to the Limitation.*** Prepaid farm supply expenses include the following items if paid for during the year [§ 464(f)(4)(B)]:

- the cost of feed, seed, fertilizer, and similar farm supplies not used or consumed during the year, but not including farm supplies that the farmer would have consumed during the year if not for a fire, storm, flood, other casualty, disease, or drought;
- the cost of poultry (including egg-laying hens and baby chicks) bought for use (or for both use and resale) in the farmer's farming business that, after being capitalized, would be deductible in the tax year after the year of purchase; and
- the cost of poultry purchased for resale and not resold or otherwise disposed of during the year.

Prepaid farm supplies do not include amounts paid for feed, seed, fertilizer, or similar supplies that are on hand at the close of the tax year due to fire, storm, or other casualty, or due to disease or drought [§ 464(d)].

***Taxpayers Subject to the Limitation.*** The limitation on prepaid farm supplies applies to a taxpayer for any tax year if the taxpayer meets all of the following conditions [§ 464(f)(2)]:

1. the taxpayer does not use the accrual method of accounting (see XI.B.1.d.);
2. the taxpayer has excess prepaid farm supplies (as defined in § 464(f)(4)(A)) for the tax year; and
3. the taxpayer is not a qualified farm-related taxpayer (as defined in § 464(f)(3)).

***Effect of the Limitation on Amounts Deductible.*** The limitation on prepaid farm supplies affects the timing of a deduction, rather than the overall amount deductible. Taxpayers subject to the limitation may not deduct the cost of excess prepaid farm supplies in the year paid [§ 464(f)(1)]. Instead, taxpayers may deduct the excess cost of farm supplies other than poultry in the year the supplies are used or consumed. The excess cost of poultry bought for use (or for both use and resale) in a farming business is capitalized and deducted ratably over the lesser of 12 months or their useful life in the trade or business. The excess cost of poultry bought for resale is deductible in the year that poultry is sold or otherwise disposed of [§ 464(a), § 464(b)]. To the extent the costs of prepaid farm supplies do not exceed 50% of the taxpayer's deductible farming expenses, their deduction is not affected by the special limitation.

---

**EXAMPLE:** Ernie is a cash basis taxpayer who owns and operates a farm. He is not a qualified farm-related taxpayer in Year 1. During Year 1, Ernie purchases $4,000 of fertilizer, $1,000 of feed, and $500 of seed for use on his farm in Year 2. He did not purchase any poultry. Ernie's prepaid farm supplies for Year 1 are $5,500 ($4,000 + $1,000 + $500). Assume Ernie's deductible farming expenses for Year 1 (including the prepaid farm supplies) total $15,500. His excess prepaid farm supplies for Year 1 are $500 ($5,500 prepaid farm supplies – ($10,000 deductible farm expenses other than prepaid farm supplies × 50%)). The excess prepaid farm supplies of $500 are deductible in Year 2, the year they will be actually used or consumed. The $5,000 of prepaid farm supplies that are not excess prepaid farm supplies are not subject to the special limitation, and thus this amount is deductible in Year 1, provided no other restriction applies. Alternatively, had Ernie been a qualified farm-related taxpayer in Year 1, the special limitation on prepaid farm supplies would not have applied and Ernie would have been able to deduct the entire $5,500 in Year 1, provided no other restrictions applied.

---

### IV.F.3.b. *Prepaid Feed Expenses*

[607 T.M., II.D.3., IV.B.2.; TPS ¶2440.02.D.3., .04.B.2.]

Subject to certain restrictions, the cost of feed purchased for livestock held for resale or otherwise used in farming is a deductible business expense. Feed purchased for livestock consumed by a farmer and the farmer's family, however, is considered a personal expenditure and is not deductible as a business expense. Additionally, the value of feed grown on the taxpayer's farm and of a taxpayer's labor is not a deductible expense [§ 262(a); Reg. § 1.162-12(a), § 1.262-1(a); Rev. Rul. 79-229, 1979-2 C.B. 210].

A farmer using the cash method of accounting (see XI.B.1.c.) may deduct in the year paid the cost of feed his or her livestock will consume in a later year if all of the following conditions are met [Rev. Rul. 79-229]:

1. the payment must be for the purchase of feed, rather than a deposit;

2. the prepayment must have a business purpose other than tax avoidance; and

3. deducting the prepayment must not result in a material distortion of the farmer's income.

In addition, any deduction for prepaid feed expenses is also subject to the general limitation on the deduction of prepaid farm supplies (see IV.F.3.a.).

*Non-Tax Business Purpose Requirement.* The degree of scrutiny applied to the taxpayer's motives may depend on whether the taxpayer is a farmer in the traditional sense or an investor in a farming tax shelter arrangement. In the case of a traditional farmer, a valid business purpose exists when the farmer acquires, or expects to receive, some business benefit as a consequence of the prepayment. Such benefits may include fixing maximum prices, assuring a feed supply, or securing preferential treatment in anticipation of a feed shortage. An investor's purposes likely will face closer scrutiny. For investors, a business practice of prepayment will not necessarily refute the existence of a primary tax avoidance motivation [Rev. Rul. 79-229].

### IV.F.3.c. Expenses for Fertilizer, Lime, and Other Soil Conditioners

[607 T.M., II.D.4., V.D.; TPS ¶2440.02.D.4., .05.D.]

Expenses to purchase fertilizer, lime, and other materials that enrich, neutralize, or condition farmland are generally deductible as business expenses in the year paid or incurred if the benefits of applying the materials do not last substantially longer than a year. Additionally, the expenses of applying such materials are also deductible [§ 162, § 263(a)(1)]. If the benefits last substantially longer than a year, the expenses may be classified as capital expenditures.

A farmer, however, may elect to deduct, rather than capitalize, the costs of fertilizer, lime, and other soil conditioners (including the costs of applying the materials to the land) that would otherwise be classified as a capital expenditure. This election is available only to taxpayers engaged in the business of farming and limited to expenditures with respect to land used in farming [§ 180(a)]. Expenditures for the initial preparation of land for farming that are classified as capital expenditures are not subject to the election [§ 180(b); Reg. § 1.180-1(b)].

The election is made by claiming a deduction on the taxpayer's timely filed tax return for the tax year (including extensions). The election is effective only for the tax year for which the deduction is claimed, and it may be revoked only with IRS consent [§ 180(c); Reg. § 1.180-2].

***Coordination with Soil and Water Conservation Expenditure Deduction.*** If a particular expenditure is both subject to the election to deduct costs of fertilizer and other soil conditioners and also subject to the election to deduct soil and water conservation or endangered species recovery expenditures, the expenditure is treated as a conservation expenditure [Reg. § 1.180-1(a)] (see IV.F.3.e.).

### IV.F.3.d. Costs of Raising Livestock and Breeding Fees

[607 T.M., II.D.1., V.A.2.; TPS ¶2440.02.D.1., .05.A.2.]

Cash basis taxpayers have the option to deduct or capitalize the costs of raising livestock, including breeding fees. Expenditures to purchase livestock, on the other hand, must be capitalized. Embryo transplants are considered analogous to breeding fees, and thus may be deducted in the year of payment if they represent the costs of raising (rather than acquiring) livestock [Reg. § 1.162-12(a)].

Corporations, partnerships, and tax shelters required to use the accrual method of accounting (see XI.B.1.d.) are required under the uniform capitalization rules (see XI.D.) to capitalize expenses incurred in raising and breeding livestock and add them to the basis of the calf, foal, or other livestock produced [§ 263A(a), § 263A(b)(1), § 263(d)].

---

**EXAMPLE:** Christina, a grain farmer using the cash method of accounting, maintains a small dairy herd. In Year 1, she purchases 10 dairy cows at auction for $2,500. During Year 1, she expends $5,000 for feed, medicine, veterinary fees, and other costs associated with the care and maintenance of the 10 cows. The $2,500 purchase price of the cattle is a capital expenditure that forms the initial cost basis of the animals, which are depreciable assets. Christina may deduct the other $5,000 in expenses for maintaining the cattle in Year 1.

---

### IV.F.3.e. Soil and Water Conservation, Erosion Prevention, and Endangered Species Recovery

[607 T.M., II.D.2., V.C.; TPS ¶2440.02.D.2., .05.C.]

Taxpayers engaged in the business of farming (as defined in Reg. § 1.175-3) may elect to deduct certain expenses that would otherwise be capitalized for soil and water conservation on land used in farming, prevention of erosion of land used in farming, or endangered species recovery. The amount of conservation or recovery expenditures that may be deducted in a tax year is limited to 25% of the taxpayer's gross income from farming. Any amounts exceeding this limitation are carried forward to succeeding tax years [§ 175].

*Making the Election.* A taxpayer elects to deduct soil and water conservation, erosion prevention, and endangered species recovery expenditures by claiming a deduction on the taxpayer's income tax return for the first tax year in which the expenditures are paid or incurred. A taxpayer that fails to make an election for the first year the expenditures are paid or incurred may make an election in a later year only with IRS consent. Consent is also required to revoke an election to deduct the expenditures. Once made, the election applies to all such expenditures by the taxpayer during and after the tax year of election [§ 175(d); Reg. § 1.175-6].

### IV.F.3.e.(1) Soil and Water Conservation, Erosion Prevention, and Endangered Species Recovery Expenditures Subject to Election

[607 T.M., V.C.2.; TPS ¶2440.05.C.2.]

*Land Used in Farming.* To be eligible for the election, expenditures for soil and water conservation and for erosion prevention must be paid or incurred in respect of land used in farming (as defined in Reg. § 1.175-4). However, expenditures for endangered species recovery need not be paid or incurred in respect of land used in farming [§ 175(a), § 175(c)(2)].

Expenditures that benefit both farmland and non-farmland are allocated on the basis of land areas, unless the taxpayer can establish another, more reasonable allocation method. Only the portion of the expenditure allocable to the land used for farming is subject to the election. The remainder must be capitalized under the general rules applicable to capital expenditures [Reg. § 1.175-7].

*Qualifying Expenditures.* To be eligible to make the election to deduct, an expenditure must be made for soil or water conservation on land used in farming, to prevent the erosion of land used in farming, or for endangered species recovery efforts. If made for such purposes, the following categories of expenditures qualify for elective treatment [Reg. § 1.175-2(a)(1)]:

- expenditures for the treatment or movement of earth, including leveling, conditioning, grading, terracing, contour furrowing, and restoration of soil fertility;
- expenditures for the construction, control, and protection of diversion channels, drainage ditches, earthen dams, watercourses, outlets, and ponds;
- expenditures for the eradication of brush;
- expenditures for the planting of windbreaks; and
- expenditures to achieve site-specific management actions recommended in recovery plans approved pursuant to the 1973 Endangered Species Act.

The following categories of expenditures are specifically excluded from the scope of the election to deduct [§ 175(c)(1), § 175(c)(3)]:

- expenditures in connection with depreciable property;

- expenditures that are classified as deductible farm expenses, rather than capital expenditures, without regard to the election; and

- expenditures in connection with the draining or filling of wetlands or land preparation for center pivot irrigation systems.

*Conservation or Recovery Plan Approval.* Regardless of any other provision, the election does not apply unless the expenditures are consistent with the plan approved by the Natural Resources Conservation Service of the Department of Agriculture or the recovery plan approved pursuant to the Endangered Species Act of 1973 for the area in which the land is located. If there is no federal plan, then the expenditures must be consistent with any plan of a comparable state agency [§ 175(c)(3)(A)].

### IV.F.3.e.(2) Limitations on the Amount of Deductible Soil and Water Conservation, Erosion Prevention, and Endangered Species Recovery Expenditures

[607 T.M., V.C.3.; TPS ¶2440.05.C.3.]

The maximum amount of soil and water conservation, erosion prevention, or endangered species recovery expenditures that may be deducted under the election in any tax year is limited to 25% of the gross income derived from farming (as defined in Reg. § 1.175-5(a)(2)) during that year. Gross income from farming does not include income from the sale of assets (e.g., farm machinery) and gains from the disposition of land [§ 175(b); Reg. § 1.175-5(a)].

*Net Operating Losses.* An amount deductible under the election is taken into account in determining a net operating loss for the year in which it is deducted. Once the deduction forms part of a net operating loss carryback or carryover, the deduction is no longer considered a soil or water conservation, erosion prevention, or endangered species recovery expenditure in the year to which it is carried, and, thus, it is not subject to the 25% limitation in that year [Reg. § 1.175-5(a)(3)]. Net operating losses are discussed in VIII.G.

*Carryover of Excess Amounts.* Amounts that exceed the 25% limitation for any tax year are carried forward and deducted in succeeding years, subject to the 25% limitation in the applicable carryover year. So long as the taxpayer remains engaged in the business of farming, amounts may be carried forward during the taxpayer's entire life or existence [Reg. § 1.175-5(b)].

---

**EXAMPLE:** In Year 1, Victor, a farmer using the cash method of accounting, has gross income derived from farming of $3,200. Victor had previously made an effective election to deduct soil and water conservation expenditures. In Year 1 he pays $900 in soil and water conservation expenditures. The maximum amount of soil and water conservation expenditures deductible in Year 1 is $800 ($3,200 gross income from farming × 25%). The excess $100 of soil and water conservation expenditures is carried over to Year 2. In Year 2, Victor has gross income derived from farming of $3,600. He pays $1,000 in soil and water conservation expenditures during Year 2, and he has $100 of carryover from Year 1. The maximum amount of soil and water conservation expenditures deductible in Year 2 is $900 ($3,600 gross income from farming × 25%). The excess $200 (($1,000 expended + $100 carryover) − $900 limitation) is carried over to Year 3.

---

### IV.F.3.e.(3) Recapture of Soil and Water Conservation, Erosion Prevention, and Endangered Species Recovery Deductions

[607 T.M., V.C.6.; TPS ¶2440.05.C.6.]

Deductions for soil and water conservation, erosion prevention, and endangered species recovery expenditures are subject to recapture as ordinary income if the farm land to which they relate is disposed of at a gain within 10 years of its acquisition. This recapture provision takes precedence over any other income tax provision of the Code [§ 1252; Reg. § 1.1252-1(a)(2)] (see III.C.8.c.).

### IV.F.3.f. Cost of Seeds and Plants

[607 T.M., II.D.11., V.A.3.b.; TPS ¶2440.02.D.11., .05.A.3.b.]

Generally, a cash basis farmer who purchases property for resale in a later tax year is required to account for the cost of the goods in the year of sale, rather than the year of purchase [Reg. § 1.61-4(a)]. However, expenditures for seeds and young plants purchased for further development and cultivation before sale in later years are deductible in the year of purchase, provided the farmer follows a consistent practice of deducting these costs from year to year [Reg. § 1.162-12(a)]. The exception only applies to a farmer who purchases the seeds or young plants for planting. Crops that are already planted do not qualify and the cost of growing them must be capitalized [Rev. Rul. 85-82, 1985-1 C.B. 57]. Further, the exception does not cover the purchase of plants for resale without any intervening development or cultivation. Farmers using the crop method of accounting are not eligible to deduct the cost of seedlings and young plants [Reg. § 1.162-12(a)].

The limitation on prepaid farm supplies applies to prepayments for seeds and is discussed in IV.F.3.a.

### IV.F.3.g. Miscellaneous Farming Deduction Rules

### IV.F.3.g.(1) Disallowance of Deductions for Production of Unharvested Crops Sold with Land

[607 T.M., IV.C.; TPS ¶1710.05.C.]

An unharvested crop is treated as property used in a trade or business if the following conditions are met [§ 1231(b)(4); Reg. § 1.1231-1(c)(5)]:

1. the unharvested crop is on land used in a trade or business;
2. the land is held for more than one year; and
3. the crop and the land are sold or exchanged at the same time and to the same person.

Gain from the simultaneous sale of the land and the unharvested crops are treated as capital gain. Deductions, including expenses and depreciation, that relate to the production of the unharvested crops are not allowed. Instead, the adjusted basis of the crops is increased by the amount of deductions disallowed under this rule [§ 268]. Property used in a trade or business (§ 1231 transactions) is discussed in III.C.1.

### IV.F.3.g.(2) Election to Capitalize Deductible Expenses of the Preproductive Period

[607 T.M., V.A.4.; TPS ¶2440.05.A.4.]

Farmers may elect to capitalize the deductible expenses incurred in the development of a farm, orchard, or ranch before the time a productive state is reached. The farmer may elect to deduct all such developmental expenses, capitalize all developmental expenses, or deduct part and capitalize the other part. The election, however, does not apply to expenses subject to the uniform capitalization rules (see XI.D.). The election to deduct or capitalize developmental expenses is irrevocable [Reg. § 1.162-12(a)].

### IV.F.4. Start-Up Expenditures

[534 T.M.; TPS ¶2470.]

Though business start-up and organization costs are generally capital expenditures, taxpayers may elect to deduct up to $5,000 of organizational expenditures. This amount is reduced (but not below zero) to the extent total start-up and organizational costs exceed $50,000. Thus, taxpayers with $55,000 or more of start-up and organizational costs are ineligible to deduct any amount. Any start-up expenditures that are not deducted may be treated as deferred expenses amortizable over a 180-month period beginning in the month the trade or business begins [§ 195(a), § 195(b); Reg. § 1.195-1(a)].

A taxpayer is deemed to have elected this provision for the tax year in which the related trade or business begins. However, taxpayers may forego the deduction by affirmatively electing to capitalize the expenditures on a timely-filed income tax return. Once made, the deemed election or the affirmative election is irrevocable and it applies to all start-up expenditures related to the relevant trade or business [Reg. § 1.195-1(b)].

Rules applying to the costs of organizing corporations and partnerships are discussed in XIII.C.2.d. and XIV.C.4.a., respectively.

*Start-Up Expenditures Defined.* Start-up expenditures fall within one of the following three categories [§ 195(c)(1)(A)]:

1. expenses paid or incurred in connection with investigating the creation or acquisition of an active trade or business;

2. expenses paid or incurred in connection with creating an active trade or business; and

3. expenses paid or incurred in connection with any activity engaged in for profit and for the production of income before the day the active trade or business begins, in anticipation of such activity becoming an active trade or business.

These include only amounts that, if paid or incurred in connection with the operation of an existing trade or business in the same field, would be deductible for the year in which paid or incurred. Expenses that qualify for deduction as interest or taxes (see IV.A.12.), or as research and development expenditures (IV.F.2.) are excluded [§ 195(c)(1)(B)].

*Investigatory Expenses.* Expenses paid or incurred in connection with investigating the creation or acquisition of an active trade or business include the cost of seeking and reviewing prospective businesses before reaching a decision to acquire or enter a business. However, it does not include expenses incurred after a taxpayer has reached the decision to acquire or establish a new business [Rev. Rul. 99-23, 1999-20 I.R.B. 3].

*When a Trade or Business Begins.* There are no regulations concerning when an active trade or business begins [§ 195(c)(2)]. Some courts have held that an entity is not carrying on a trade or business until the business begins to function as a going concern (i.e., when actual business or revenue producing operations begin) and perform the activities it was organized to perform, while other courts have held an entity is carrying on a trade or business as soon as there is a regular and continuous course of conduct [*Richmond Television Corp. v. Commissioner*, 345 F.2d 901 (4th Cir. 1965), *Blitzer v. United States*, 684 F.2d 874 (Ct. Cl. 1982)]. The IRS follows the first position – that an entity is not engaged in a trade or business for start-up expenditure purposes until the business begins to function as a going concern [TAM 9027002]. In the case of an acquisition of an active trade or business, the trade or business is treated as beginning when acquired by the taxpayer [§ 195(c)(2)(B)].

**Early Disposition of a Trade or Business.** If a taxpayer completely disposes of a trade or business at any time before the end of the amortization period, any deferred expenses attributable to the trade or business that have not been deducted may be deductible under the loss rules [§ 195(b)(2)] (see VIII.H.).

## IV.F.5. Other Exceptions to Capitalization

### IV.F.5.a. Energy Efficient Commercial Buildings [Expired]

[505 T.M., V.R.; TPS ¶2270.09.]

Before 2014, a taxpayer could deduct a portion of the cost of energy efficient building property (as defined in § 179D(c)(1)) placed in service during a tax year. The provision expired for property placed in service after 2013 [§ 179D(a), § 179D(h)].

### IV.F.5.b. Advanced Mine Safety Equipment [Expired]

[505 T.M., V.T.; TPS ¶2270.10.]

Before 2014, a taxpayer could elect to treat 50% of the cost of any qualified advanced mine safety equipment (as defined in § 179E(c) and § 179E(d)) as a deduction in the year placed in service. The provision expired for property placed in service after 2013 [§ 179E(a), § 179E(g)].

### IV.F.5.c. Railroad Rolling Stock Rehabilitation and Railroad Tie Expenses

[505 T.M., V.N., V.O.; TPS ¶2920.09., .10.]

A domestic common carrier by railroad can elect to deduct as repairs (see IV.A.7.) its expenditures to rehabilitate a unit of railroad rolling stock it uses if (i) the expense otherwise would be chargeable to a capital account, and (ii) during any 12-month period, the expenditures do not exceed an amount equal to 20% of the carrier's basis in such unit of rolling stock [§ 263(d); Reg. § 1.263(e)-1].

In addition, though the replacement of a wood railroad tie with one made of any other material is capital in nature, any domestic common carrier by rail (including a railroad switching or terminal company) that used the retirement-replacement method of accounting for depreciation of railroad track may deduct expenditures for replacement railroad ties and fastenings related to the ties to the same extent they would be deducted if they were made of wood [§ 263(f)].

### IV.F.5.d. Refinery Property [Expired]

[512 T.M., II.I.; TPS ¶2640.12.]

Before 2014, a taxpayer could elect to deduct 50% of the cost of qualified refinery property (as defined in § 179C(c) and § 179C(d)) placed in service during the tax year. The provision excludes property placed in service after 2013 [§ 179C(a), § 179C(c)(1)(B)].

### IV.F.5.e. Reforestation

[505 T.M., VI.C.7., 610 T.M., VII.C.; TPS ¶2640.03.]

Costs incurred for the reforestation of timber property normally are capital expenditures. However, taxpayers may elect on a property-by-property basis to deduct up to $5,000 ($10,000 for married taxpayers filing separately) of reforestation expenditures incurred per tract per year in connection with qualified timber property. To the extent the maximum limit is exceeded, the taxpayer can amortize the excess over 84 months. Reforestation expenditures are the direct costs incurred in connection with initial forestation or reforestation by means of planting or artificial or natural seeding, including expenditures for the preparation of the site, seeds or seedlings, and labor and tools (including depreciation of equipment like tractors and trucks). The deduction is not available for trusts [§ 194].

Timber transactions are discussed in VI.B.

### IV.F.5.f. Franchises, Trademarks, and Trade Names

[505 T.M., V.M.; TPS ¶1720.04.H.]

A transferee may deduct certain contingent serial payments made under an agreement to transfer, sell, or otherwise dispose of a franchise, trademark, or trade name. To be deductible, the payments must be (i) contingent on the productivity, use, or disposition of the franchise, trademark, or trade name, (ii) paid as part of a series of payments that are payable at least annually throughout the entire term of the transfer agreement, and (iii) substantially equal in amount or payable under a fixed formula [§ 1253(d)(1)].

### IV.F.5.g. Pollution Control Facility Amortization

[505 T.M., V.H., 530 T.M., XV.; TPS ¶2370.13.A.]

A taxpayer may elect to deduct the amortizable basis of any certified pollution control facility over a 60-month period (84-months for certain atmospheric pollution control facilities) [§ 169(a)]. A certified pollution control facility is a new identifiable treatment facility (defined in § 169(d)(4)) that meets the following conditions [§ 169(d)(1), § 169(d)(5)]:

1. the facility must be used in connection with a plant or other property in operation before January 1, 1976 (April 11, 2005, for certain atmospheric pollution control facilities);

2. the facility must be used to abate or control water or atmospheric pollution or contamination by removing, altering, disposing, storing, or preventing the creation or emission of pollutants, contaminants, wastes, or heat;

3. the state certifying authority having jurisdiction over the facility must certify to the federal certifying authority that the facility has been constructed, reconstructed, erected, or acquired in conformity with the state program or requirements for abatement or control of water or atmospheric pollution or contamination; and

4. the federal certifying authority must certify to the IRS that (i) the facility complies with the applicable regulations of federal agencies, and (ii) the facility is in furtherance of the general policy of the United States for cooperation with the states in prevention and abatement of water pollution and atmospheric pollution and contamination under the Federal Water Pollution Control Act and the Clean Air Act, respectively.

### IV.F.5.h. Certain Qualified Film and Television Productions [Expired]

[599 T.M., XI.; TPS ¶2270.08.]

Before 2014, a taxpayer could elect to deduct the cost of any qualified film or television production (as defined in § 181(d)), subject to certain limits. This provision expired for film and television productions commencing after 2013 [§ 181(a), § 181(f)].

### IV.F.5.i. Architectural and Transportation Barrier Removal

[505 T.M., V.K.; TPS ¶2270.01.]

Taxpayers may elect to deduct in the year paid or incurred expenditures for the removal of architectural and transportation barriers to the handicapped and elderly. Architectural and transportation barrier removal expenses are expenditures for the purpose of making any facility or public transportation vehicle owned or leased by the taxpayer for use in connection with a trade or business more accessible to, and usable by, handicapped and elderly individuals. Such expenses are qualified expenses if they meet certain standards established by the IRS with the concurrence of the Architectural and Transportation Barriers Compliance Board [§ 190(a), § 190(b); Reg. § 1.190-2(b)].

To make the election, a taxpayer must claim the deduction as a separate item on his or her timely filed income tax return for the tax year (including extensions) for which the election is to apply. Partnerships must claim the deduction on the partnership tax return for that tax year [Reg. § 1.190-3(a)].

**Limitation.** The deduction is limited to $15,000 per tax year. Amounts expended in excess of this limit are capital expenditures. In the case of a partnership, the limit applies to both the partnership and each partner. At the partner level, each partner applies the limitation to the aggregate of his or her shares of deductible architectural and transportation barrier removal expenses from each partnership in which he or she is a partner, as well as his or her own removal expenses [§ 190; Reg. § 1.190-1(b)].

**Depreciation Recapture.** All or a portion of a taxpayer's capital gains on the disposition of property may be treated as ordinary income if depreciation or amortization have been claimed on the property. Amounts a taxpayer elects to deduct for the removal of architectural and transportation barriers to the handicapped and elderly are treated as deductions allowable for amortization for purposes of the depreciation recapture rules [§ 1245(a)(2)(C), § 1245(a)(3)(C)] (see III.D.).

**Coordination with the Disabled Access Credit.** A taxpayer that takes the disabled access credit (see IX.A.11.) cannot receive a double benefit by taking an additional deduction or increasing basis for such amount [§ 44(d)(7)].

### IV.F.5.j. EPA Sulfur Regulation Compliance Costs

[505 T.M., VI.C.10.; TPS ¶2640.11.]

If a crude oil refiner is a small business refiner, the taxpayer may elect to deduct a portion of its qualified capital costs paid or incurred during the tax year to comply with Environmental Protection Agency regulations. A small business refiner is a refiner of crude oil that employs no more than 1,500 individuals in the refinery operations of the business on any day during the tax year, and has an average daily domestic refinery run or average retained production for all facilities for the one-year period ending December 31, 2002, not exceeding 205,000 barrels. The deduction is generally limited to 75% of applicable costs, phased out ratably as the average daily domestic refinery runs for the one-year period ending December 31, 2002, increases from 155,000 barrels to 205,000 barrels. For any property for which the taxpayer elects this deduction, the basis of the property must be reduced by the portion of the cost taken into account in determining the allowable deduction [§ 179B].

### IV.F.5.k. Mineral Exploration and Development Expenditures

[505 T.M., VI.C.5., VI.C.6.; TPS ¶2630.]

Development expenditures paid or incurred during a tax year are deductible if they are paid or incurred after the existence of ores or minerals in commercially marketable quantities has been disclosed. Development expenditures are those paid or incurred for the development of a mine or other natural deposit, other than an oil or gas well [§ 616].

A taxpayer may also elect to treat mining exploration expenditures paid or incurred during the tax year as a deduction. Mining exploration expenditures are those paid or incurred for the purpose of ascertaining the existence, location, extent, or quality of any deposit or ore or other mineral, if they are paid or incurred before the development stage of the mine. The deduction is subject to recapture when the mine reaches producing stages and when the property is sold [§ 617].

Mineral exploration and development costs are discussed in VI.D.

### IV.F.5.l. Capital Contributions to the Federal National Mortgage Association (Fannie Mae)

[505 T.M., IV.S.1.; TPS ¶2260.04.]

Any excess of the amount of capital contributions evidenced by a share of stock issued under § 303(c) of the Federal National Mortgage Association Charter Act over the fair market value of the stock as of its issue date is treated by the initial holder of the stock as trade or business expense [§ 162(d)].

### IV.F.5.m. Tertiary Injectants

[505 T.M., VI.C.8., 605 T.M., III.H.1.; TPS ¶2640.04.]

Taxpayers may deduct the cost of qualified tertiary injectants. The deduction is allowed for the later of either (i) the tax year in which the injectant is injected, or (ii) the tax year in which the expenses are paid or incurred. No deduction is allowed for expenditures for which the taxpayer has made an election under § 263(c) to deduct intangible drilling and development costs, or for which a deduction is allowed or allowable under any other income tax provision [§ 193].

Tertiary injectant expenses are discussed in VI.E.2.

# CHAPTER V. DEPRECIATION AND AMORTIZATION

>>>>>>>>>>>>>>>>>>>>>>>>>>>>>>>

## V.A. Depreciation of Realty and Tangible Property

[530 T.M., 531 T.M., 532 T.M.; TPS ¶2370]

Depreciation is an annual deduction that allows taxpayers to recover the basis of certain property over the property's useful life. It represents the decline in the value of property, and the erosion of investment in that property, that occurs over time. Depreciation may be caused by ordinary wear and tear or deterioration, and it may result from use, passage of time, or external factors like obsolescence, change in capacity, or other physical or environmental factors. Because taxpayers generally may not deduct the cost of an asset at the time of its acquisition, they are instead permitted depreciation deductions to recover their investment over a period of time extending beyond the year in which the outlay for the asset is made.

### V.A.1. Property that May Be Depreciated

[530 T.M., III.A.; TPS ¶2370.01.]

Most types of tangible property (except land) may be depreciated. To be depreciable, the property must meet all of the following requirements [§ 167; Reg. § 1.167(a)-1]:

1. it must be property the taxpayer owns;
2. it must be used in the taxpayer's trade or business or income-producing activity; and
3. it must have a determinable useful life, and that life must be longer than one year.

Certain intangible property, such as patents, copyrights, and computer software, is also depreciable. The amortization of intangible property is discussed in V.D.1.

***Property the Taxpayer Owns.*** A taxpayer is considered as owning property even if it is subject to a debt. A lessor may depreciate leased property only if the he or she retains the incidents of ownership in the property. Incidents of ownership in property include (i) the legal title to the property, (ii) the legal obligation to pay for the property, (iii) the responsibility to pay maintenance and operating expenses, (iv) the duty to pay any taxes on the property, and (v) the risk of loss if the property is destroyed, condemned, or diminished in value through obsolescence or exhaustion. The lessor depreciates his or her investment as it existed at the beginning of the lease and the cost of any subsequent improvements paid by the lessor. A lessee who makes improvements to the leased property may depreciate their cost [Reg. § 1.167(a)-4].

If property is held by one person for life with the remainder to another person, the life tenant takes depreciation as if he or she were the absolute owner. After the life tenant's death, the remainderman receives the income and is entitled to the remaining depreciation. Depreciation on property held by an estate is apportioned among the estate and the heirs, legatees, and devisees in proportion to the income of the estate allocable to each. Depreciation on property held in trust is apportioned between the income beneficiaries and the trustee in proportion to the trust income allocable to each. However, if the trust instrument or local law requires or permits the trustee to maintain a depreciation reserve, the depreciation deduction is allocated first to the trustee to the extent of the income set aside for the depreciation reserve. Any balance is apportioned between the income beneficiaries and the trustee in proportion to the income [§ 167(d); Reg. § 1.167(h)-1].

***Property Used in the Taxpayer's Trade or Business or Income-Producing Activity.*** Property is depreciable only if the taxpayer uses it in a trade or business or holds it for the production of income. Property held for sale (e.g., inventory) is not depreciable. With the exception of certain reusable containers used to ship products, containers for the products sold generally are considered part of inventory and also are not depreciable [§ 167(a); Reg. § 1.167(a)-2; Rev. Rul. 75-34, 1975-1 C.B. 271]. Supplies generally are currently deductible rather than subject to depreciation [Reg. § 1.162-3] (see IV.A.7.).

Taxpayers may not depreciate property used solely for personal activities. If property is used both for business or investment purposes and for personal purposes, the taxpayer may deduct depreciation based only on the business or investment use [Reg. § 1.167(a)-2].

***Property with a Determinable Useful Life Longer than One Year.*** Property has a determinable useful life if it wears out, decays, gets used up, becomes obsolete, or loses its value from natural causes. To be depreciable, the property must have a useful life extending substantially beyond the year it is placed in service. Non-inventory property with a useful life of one year or less that is used or consumed in the taxpayer's operations generally is considered a material or supply that may be deducted as a business expense [§ 167(a); Reg. § 1.162-3(c)(1)(iii), § 1.167(a)-2] (see IV.A.7.).

***Property that May Not Be Depreciated.*** Property that may not be depreciated includes:

- land;
- property placed in service and disposed of in the same year;
- equipment used to build capital improvements;
- § 197 intangibles (see V.D.1.); and
- certain term interests in property for any period during which the remainder interest is held directly or indirectly by a related person.

### V.A.2. Depreciation Period

[530 T.M., IX.C.; TPS ¶2370.04.]

A taxpayer may begin to depreciate property when he or she places it in service for use in a trade or business or for the production of income. Depreciation ends upon the earlier of either (i) the time the taxpayer has fully recovered the cost or other basis, or (ii) the time the taxpayer retires the property from service [Reg. § 1.167(a)-10(b)].

*Placed in Service.* Property is placed in service when it is ready and available for a specific use, whether in a business activity, an income-producing activity, a tax-exempt activity, or a personal activity. This is the case even if the taxpayer is not actually using the property.

---

**EXAMPLE:** Shipping Co. purchased a barge and outfitted it for use in Shipping's business. The outfitting was completed, and the barge was available for use in Dec. of Year 1. However, the barge was locked in ice, and was not actually used until May of Year 2. The barge was placed in service in Dec. of Year 1 because it was ready and available for its specified use, even though it was not actually used.

**EXAMPLE:** Power Co. built a power production facility. The machinery and equipment became operational and were available for use beginning in Year 1. However, further testing was necessary to eliminate defects that prevented the facility from attaining the planned production levels. The facility finally reached planned production levels in Year 2. The machinery and equipment were placed in service in Year 1 because they were ready and available for a specifically assigned function, even if they did not run as successfully as Power expected them to.

---

*Retired from Service.* Property is retired from service when the taxpayer permanently withdraws it from use in a trade or business or from use in the production of income because of any of the following events [Reg. § 1.167(a)-8(a)]:

- the taxpayer sells or exchanges the property;
- the taxpayer converts the property to personal use;
- the taxpayer abandons the property;
- the taxpayer transfers the property to a supplies or scrap account; or
- the property is destroyed.

### V.A.3. Amount to Be Depreciated

[530 T.M., V.; TPS ¶2370.03.]

The total amount of depreciation allowable for any asset is limited to its basis. Under ACRS (see V.A.5.) and MACRS (see V.A.4.), the annual depreciation deduction is computed by multiplying unadjusted basis by the recovery percentage for the tax year [§ 168(b)(1)]. Unadjusted basis is basis determined under the normal basis rules, except that depreciation adjustments are ignored and reductions are made for certain amortization, amounts deducted under the first-year expensing rules, amounts deducted under the special first-year additional allowance, certain portions of any applicable investment credit, and amounts reflecting personal use [Prop. Reg. § 1.168-2(d)(1)]. Basis rules are discussed in III.A.3.

### V.A.4. Modified Accelerated Cost Recovery System (MACRS)

[531 T.M.; TPS ¶2370.05.]

Nearly all tangible property placed in service after 1986 must be depreciated using the Modified Accelerated Cost Recovery System (MACRS). However, certain tangible property that falls into one of the following categories is excluded from MACRS [§ 168(f)]:

- the property is depreciated using a depreciation method not expressed in terms of years (e.g., the units-of-production method, machine hours or operating days method, income forecast method, mileage-based method, or standard automobile mileage rate) (see V.A.8.);

- the property is excluded public utility property;
- the property is a motion picture, television film, or a sound recording;
- the property is acquired in a churning transaction (as described in § 168(f)(5)); or
- special transition rules treat property that would otherwise be placed in service within the MACRS effective dates as being placed in service within the ACRS effective dates.

In order to determine an asset's MACRS deduction, the taxpayer must determine the property's recovery class and applicable recovery period (see V.A.4.a.), depreciation method (V.A.4.b.), and depreciation convention (V.A.4.c.).

Taxpayers must use either the General Depreciation System (GDS) or the Alternative Depreciation System (ADS) to depreciate property under MACRS. The depreciation system used will affect the taxpayer's depreciation method and recovery period. Generally, GDS must be used unless the taxpayer is specifically required by law to use ADS, or the taxpayer elects to use ADS. The discussion that follows in this section, V.A.4., will generally address GDS. ADS is discussed separately in V.A.4.g.

For property placed in service after 1980 and before 1987, the Accelerated Cost Recovery System (ACRS) applies (see V.A.5.).

### V.A.4.a. Recovery Classes of MACRS Property

[531 T.M., V.; TPS ¶2370.05.C.]

Under MACRS, there are 10 categories of property (discussed below) with a recovery period assigned to each category [§ 168(c)]. Property is either statutorily placed into one of these categories, or its category is determined based on its class life. Class lives and recovery periods of property are discussed in *Schedules & Tables 10.* [Rev. Proc. 87-56, 1987-2 C.B. 674; Rev. Proc. 88-22, 1988-1 C.B. 785].

Property with the following class lives receive the following MACRS classifications, each of which is discussed below [§ 168(e)(1)]:

| Class Life (in years) | MACRS Classification | Recovery Period |
|---|---|---|
| 4 or less | Three-Year Property | 3 Years |
| 5 – 9 | Five-Year Property | 5 Years |
| 10 – 15 | Seven-Year Property | 7 Years |
| 16 – 19 | 10-Year Property | 10 Years |
| 20 – 24 | 15-Year Property | 15 Years |
| 25 or more | 20-Year Property | 20 Years |

***Three-Year Property.*** The applicable recovery period for three-year property is three years. Three-year property consists of property with a class life of four years or less. Three-year property includes the following [§ 168(c), § 168(e)(3)(A); Rev. Proc. 87-56, 1987-2 C.B. 674]:

- tractor units for over-the-road use;
- any race horse over two years old when placed in service (all race horses placed in service after 2008 and before 2014 were deemed to be three-year property, regardless of age);
- any other horse (other than a race horse) over 12 years old when placed in service; and
- qualified rent-to-own property.

*Five-Year Property.* The applicable recovery period for five-year property is five years. Five-year property consists of property with a class life of between five and nine years. Five-year property includes the following [§ 168(c), § 168(e)(3)(B); Rev. Proc. 87-56]:

- automobiles, taxis, buses, and trucks;
- computers and peripheral equipment;
- office machinery (e.g., typewriters, calculators, copiers, etc.);
- any property used in research and experimentation;
- breeding cattle and dairy cattle;
- appliances, carpets, furniture, etc., used in a residential rental real estate activity; and
- certain geothermal, solar, and wind energy property.

*Seven-Year Property.* The applicable recovery period for seven-year property is seven years. Seven-year property consists of property with a class life of between 10 and 15 years. Seven-year property includes the following [§ 168(c), § 168(e)(3)(C); Rev. Proc. 87-56]:

- office furniture and fixtures (e.g., desks, files, safes, etc.);
- agricultural machinery and equipment;
- certain motorsports entertainment complex property placed in service before 2014;
- any natural gas gathering line placed in service after April 11, 2005; and
- any property that does not have a class life and has not been designated by law as being in any other class.

*10-Year Property.* The applicable recovery period for 10-year property is 10 years. Ten-year property consists of property with a class life of between 16 and 19 years. Ten-year property includes the following [§ 168(c), § 168(e)(3)(D); Rev. Proc. 87-56]:

- vessels, barges, tugs, and similar water transportation equipment;
- any single purpose agricultural or horticultural structure;
- any tree or vine bearing fruits or nuts; and
- qualified small electric meter and qualified smart grid systems placed in service on or after October 3, 2008.

*15-Year Property.* The applicable recovery period for 15-year property is 15 years. Fifteen-year property consists of property with a class life of between 20 and 24 years. Fifteen-year property includes the following [§ 168(c), § 168(e)(3)(E); Rev. Proc. 87-56]:

- certain improvements made directly to land or added to it (e.g., shrubbery, fences, roads, sidewalks, bridges, etc.);
- any retail motor fuels outlet (e.g., a convenience store);
- any municipal wastewater treatment plant;
- any qualified leasehold improvement property placed in service before 2014;
- any qualified restaurant property placed in service before 2014;
- initial clearing and grading land improvements for gas utility property;
- electric transmission property that is § 1245 property and that is used in the transmission at 69 or more kilovolts of electricity placed in service after April 11, 2005;

- any natural gas distribution line place in service after April 11, 2005, and before 2014; and
- any qualified retail improvement property placed in service before 2014.

*20-Year Property.* The applicable recovery period for 20-year property is 20 years. Twenty-year property consists of property with a class life of 25 years or more. Twenty-year property includes the following [§ 168(c), § 168(e)(3)(F); Rev. Proc. 87-56]:

- farm buildings (other than single purpose agricultural or horticultural structures);
- municipal sewers not classified as 25-year property; and
- initial clearing and grading land improvements for electric utility transmission and distribution plants.

*Water Utility Property.* The applicable recovery period for water utility property is 25 years. Water utility property is either (i) property that is an integral part of the gathering, treatment, or commercial distribution of water, and that, without regard to this provision would be 20-year property, or (ii) municipal sewers other than property placed in service under a binding contract in effect at all times since June 9, 1996 [§ 168(c), § 168(e)(5); Rev. Proc. 87-56].

*Residential Rental Property.* The applicable recovery period for residential rental property is 27½ years. Residential rental property includes any building or structure, including a mobile home, for which 80% or more of the gross rental income for the tax year is rental income from dwelling units. If any part of the building or structure is occupied by the taxpayer, the gross rental income includes the fair rental value of the part the taxpayer occupies. A dwelling unit is a house or an apartment used to provide living accommodations in a building or structure, but it does not include a unit in a hotel, motel, inn, or other establishment where more than half of the units are used on a transient basis (generally, for periods of less than 30 days) [§ 168(c), § 168(e)(2)(A); Rev. Proc. 87-56].

*Nonresidential Real Property.* The applicable recovery period for nonresidential real property is 39 years if placed in service after May 12, 1993. The applicable recovery period is 31½ years if placed in service before May 13, 1993, and after 1986. Nonresidential real property includes any building or structural component that is not residential real property and realty with a class life of 27½ years or more [§ 168(c), § 168(e)(2)(B); Rev. Proc. 87-56].

*Railroad Grading or Tunnel Bore Property.* The applicable recovery period for any railroad grading or tunnel bore is 50 years [§ 168(c), § 168(e)(4); Rev. Proc. 87-56].

*Special Rule for Qualified Indian Reservation Property.* MACRS property that is qualified Indian reservation property (as defined in § 168(j)(4)) placed in service before 2012 is assigned a shorter recovery period than the one to which it otherwise would be assigned [§ 168(j)].

### *V.A.4.b. Depreciation Methods Under MACRS*
[531 T.M., VI.B.; TPS ¶2370.05.D.]

Note: The declining balance method is abbreviated as DB and the straight line method is abbreviated as SL.

| Method | Type of Property | Benefit |
|---|---|---|
| GDS using 200% DB | • Nonfarm 3-, 5-, 7-, and 10-year property | • Provides a greater deduction during the earlier recovery years<br>• Changes to SL when that method provides an equal or greater deduction |
| GDS using 150% DB | • All farm property (except real property)<br>• All 15- and 20-year property (except qualified leasehold improvement property, qualified restaurant property, and qualified retail improvement property placed in service before January 1, 2014)<br>• Nonfarm 3-, 5-, 7-, and 10-year property | • Provides a greater deduction during the earlier recovery years<br>• Changes to SL when that method provides an equal or greater deduction |
| GDS using SL | • Nonresidential real property<br>• Qualified leasehold improvement property placed in service before January 1, 2014<br>• Qualified restaurant property placed in service before January 1, 2014<br>• Qualified retail improvement property placed in service before January 1, 2014<br>• Residential rental property<br>• Trees or vines bearing fruit or nuts<br>• Water utility property<br>• All 3-, 5-, 7-, 10-, 15-, and 20-year property (see § 168(b)(5))<br>• Property for which the taxpayer elected § 168(k)(4) | • Provides for equal yearly deductions (except for the first and last years) |
| ADS using SL | • Listed property used 50% or less for business<br>• Property used predominantly outside the United States<br>• Tax-exempt property<br>• Tax-exempt bond-financed property<br>• Farm property used when an election not to apply the uniform capitalization rules is in effect<br>• Imported property (see § 168(g)(6))<br>• Any property for which the taxpayer elects to use this method (see § 168(g)(7)) | • Provides for equal yearly deductions (except for the first and last years) |

(Source: IRS Pub. 946)

### V.A.4.b.(1) 200% Declining-Balance Method (Double Declining-Balance Method)

[531 T.M., VI.B.1.; TPS ¶2370.05.D.1.]

For any property in the three-, five-, seven-, or 10-year class, the taxpayer generally must use the 200% declining balance method over the applicable recovery period. The taxpayer must switch to the straight-line method (see V.A.4.b.(3)) for the first tax year in which the straight-line method, when applied to the adjusted basis at the beginning of the year, will yield a larger deduction [§ 168(b)(1)]. This switch to the straight-line method will occur in the following years for the following property classes:

| Property Class | Method | Year of Switch to Straight-Line |
|---|---|---|
| Three-Year Property | 200% DB | 3 |
| Five-Year Property | 200% DB | 4 |
| Seven-Year Property | 200% DB | 5 |
| 10-Year Property | 200% DB | 7 |

MACRS depreciation tables are available in *Schedules & Tables 11.* and provide percentages that reflect the preceding computations so that a taxpayer need only multiply unadjusted basis by the percentage found in the appropriate table.

---

**EXAMPLE:** Butch purchases an item of MACRS five-year property for $10,000. The 200% declining-balance method is the applicable depreciation method. The applicable depreciation rate is 40% (200% × 5 years). Using the half-year convention in the first tax year, the MACRS deduction is $2,000 ($10,000 × 40% × ½). The adjusted basis at the end of the first tax year is $8,000 ($10,000 basis − $2,000 deduction in year one). In the second tax year, the MACRS deduction is $3,200 ($8,000 × 40%). The adjusted basis at the end of the second tax year is $4,800 ($8,000 − $3,200). In the third tax year, 200% declining-balance depreciation is $1,920 ($4,800 × 40%), while straight-line depreciation is $1,371 ($4,800 ÷ 3½ remaining years). Thus, the MACRS deduction for the third tax year is $1,920, and the adjusted basis at the end of the third year is $2,880 ($4,800 − $1,920). In the fourth tax year, 200% declining-balance depreciation is $1,152 ($2,880 × 40%), while straight-line depreciation is $1,152 ($2,880 ÷ 2½ remaining years). Thus, the switch to the straight-line method occurs in the fourth tax year. The MACRS deduction for the fourth tax year is $1,152, and the adjusted basis at the end of the fourth year is $1,728 ($2,880 − $1,152). In the fifth tax year, the deduction is $1,152 ($1,728 ÷ 1½ remaining years), and the remaining adjusted basis is $576. In the sixth tax year, the deduction is $576, leaving basis at $0.

| Year | Basis to Start Year | 200% Declining-Balance | Straight-Line | Basis at End of Year |
|------|-----|------|------|------|
| 1 | $10,000 | $2,000 | $1,000 | $8,000 |
| 2 | $ 8,000 | $3,200 | $1,778 | $4,800 |
| 3 | $ 4,800 | $1,920 | $1,371 | $2,880 |
| 4 | $ 2,880 | $1,152 | $1,152 | $1,728 |
| 5 | $ 1,728 | $ 691 | $1,152 | $ 576 |
| 6 | $ 576 | $ 230 | $ 576 | $ 0 |

*Election to use 150% Declining-Balance Method.* In lieu of the 200% declining balance rate over the recovery period, a taxpayer may elect to use the 150% declining-balance method (see V.A.4.b.(2)). The election is irrevocable and may be made for one or more classes of property placed in service in a particular tax year. Once made for any class, the election applies to all property in that particular class placed in service during that year. The election is made by specifying the use of the 150% declining balance method on Form 4562, *Depreciation and Amortization* [§ 168(b)(2)(D), § 168(b)(5)].

### V.A.4.b.(2) 150% Declining-Balance Method
[531 T.M., VI.B.3.; TPS ¶2370.05.D.1.]

For any property in the 15- or 20-year class, and any property used in a farming business and placed in service after 1988, the taxpayer must use the 150% declining balance method over the applicable recovery period. The taxpayer must switch to the straight-line method (see V.A.4.b.(3)) for the first tax year in which the straight-line method, when applied to the adjusted basis at the beginning of the year, will yield a larger deduction. This switch to the straight-line method will occur in the following years for the following property classes:

| Property Class | Method | Year of Switch to Straight-Line |
|------|------|------|
| 15-Year Property | 150% DB | 7 |
| 20-Year Property | 150% DB | 9 |

*Calculation.* The 150% declining-balance rate of depreciation is calculated in the same manner as the 200% declining-balance rate of depreciation (see V.A.4.b.(1)), substituting 150% as the declining-balance percentage.

MACRS depreciation tables are presented in *Schedules & Tables 11.* and provide percentages that reflect the computations so that a taxpayer need only multiply unadjusted basis by the percentage found in the appropriate table.

### V.A.4.b.(3) Straight-Line Method
[531 T.M., VI.B.4.; TPS ¶2370.05.D.2.]

The straight-line method must be used for the following property [§ 168(b)(3)]:
- nonresidential real property;
- residential rental property;
- any railroad grading or tunnel bore;
- any tree or vine bearing fruit or nuts;
- any water utility property (described in § 168(e)(5));
- certain qualified leasehold improvement property (described in § 168(e)(6));
- qualified restaurant property (described in § 168(e)(7)); and

- qualified retail improvement property (described in § 168(e)(8)).

***Election in Lieu of Declining-Balance Method.*** In lieu of using the declining-balance method to depreciate property, a taxpayer may elect to use the straight-line method over the recovery period. The election is irrevocable and may be made for one or more classes of property placed in service in a particular tax year. Once made for any class, the election applies to all property in that particular class placed in service during that year. The election is made by specifying the use of the straight-line method on Form 4562, *Depreciation and Amortization* [§ 168(b)(3)(D), § 168(b)(5)].

***Calculation.*** The straight-line rate must be recalculated for each tax year in the recovery period. For any tax year, the straight-line rate is determined by dividing the number one by the years remaining in the recovery period at the beginning of the tax year. Thus, for five-year property, divide one by five, resulting in a 20% straight-line rate. The rate is applied to the adjusted basis of the property, reduced by prior depreciation deductions, but not reduced for salvage value. If the remaining recovery period at the beginning of the tax year is less than one year, the straight-line rate for that year is 100% [Rev. Proc. 87-57, 1987-2 C.B. 687].

MACRS depreciation tables are presented in *Schedules & Tables 11.* and provide percentages that reflect the computations so that a taxpayer need only multiply unadjusted basis by the percentage found in the appropriate table.

---

**EXAMPLE:** Whitney purchases an item of MACRS five-year property for $10,000. Whitney properly elects the straight-line method for the property. The straight-line rate is 20% (1 ÷ 5 year recovery period). Using the half-year convention, in the first tax year, the MACRS deduction is $1,000 ($10,000 basis × 20% × ½). The adjusted basis at the end of the first tax year is $9,000 ($10,000 − $1,000). In the second through fifth tax years, the MACRS deduction in each year is $2,000 ($10,000 × 20%). For the sixth tax year, the MACRS deduction is $1,000.

| Year | Basis to Start Year | Straight-Line | Basis at End of Year |
|---|---|---|---|
| 1 | $10,000 | $1,000 | $9,000 |
| 2 | $ 9,000 | $2,000 | $7,000 |
| 3 | $ 7,000 | $2,000 | $5,000 |
| 4 | $ 5,000 | $2,000 | $3,000 |
| 5 | $ 3,000 | $2,000 | $1,000 |
| 6 | $ 1,000 | $1,000 | $   0 |

---

## V.A.4.c. Depreciation Conventions Under MACRS

[531 T.M., VI.C.; TPS ¶2370.05.E.]

Under MACRS, averaging conventions establish when the recovery period begins and ends. The convention a taxpayer uses determines the number of months for which the taxpayer may claim depreciation in the year the property is placed in service and in the year the property is disposed of.

MACRS depreciation tables are presented in *Schedules & Tables 11.* and provide percentages that reflect the computation of the MACRS deduction, accounting for the various depreciation conventions, so that a taxpayer need only multiply unadjusted basis by the percentage found in the appropriate table.

### V.A.4.c.(1) Half-Year Convention

[531 T.M., VI.C.1.; TPS ¶2370.05.E.1.]

For property other than nonresidential real property, residential rental property, and railroad grading and tunnel bores, the half-year convention generally is used in calculating the MACRS deduction for the first year the property is placed in service. The half-year convention also generally applies in computing depreciation in the year property is disposed of, if disposed of before the end of the property's recovery period [§ 168(d)(1); Rev. Proc. 87-57, 1987-2 C.B. 687].

Under this convention, a taxpayer treats all property placed in service or disposed of during a tax year as placed in service or disposed of at the midpoint of the year. Thus, a ½ year of depreciation is allowed for the year the property is placed in service, and a ½ year of depreciation is allowed for the year the property is disposed of [§ 168(d)(4)].

### V.A.4.c.(2) Mid-Quarter Convention

[531 T.M., VI.C.4.; TPS ¶2370.05.E.2.]

The mid-quarter convention applies if, during any tax year, the total bases of depreciable property placed in service during the last three months of that tax year exceed 40% of the total bases of all depreciable personal property placed in service during that tax year. The basis of (i) any railroad grading or tunnel bore property, (ii) any property placed in service and disposed of during the same tax year, and (iii) any residential rental property or nonresidential real property is excluded for purposes of determining the total bases of depreciable property [§ 168(d)(3)].

In determining whether the mid-quarter convention applies, the depreciable basis of property the taxpayer placed in service during the tax year reflects the reduction in basis for amounts expensed under § 179 (see V.B.) and the part of the basis of property attributable to personal use. It does not, however, reflect any reduction in basis for any special depreciation allowance [Reg. § 1.168(d)-1(b)(4)].

---

**EXAMPLE:** Janet, a calendar-year taxpayer, purchases a truck costing $8,000, a desk costing $500, a safe costing $1,000, and a computer costing $3,000. Assume that Janet does not elect the special expensing deduction. The truck is placed in service in Jan., the desk and safe in Aug., and the computer in Nov. In Sept., Janet sells the truck and the desk. Because the truck and the desk were placed in service and disposed of in the same tax year, the depreciable basis of the truck and the desk are not taken into account in determining whether the mid-quarter convention applies. Because the computer was placed in service during the last three months of the tax year and its basis ($3,000) exceeds 40% of the aggregate basis of depreciable property placed in service during the tax year (safe and computer with an aggregate basis of $4,000), the mid-quarter convention applies to the truck, the desk, the safe, and the computer.

---

Under this convention, a taxpayer treats all property placed in service or disposed of during any quarter of the tax year as placed in service or disposed of at the midpoint of that quarter. Thus, 1½ months of depreciation is allowed for the quarter the property is placed in service, and 1½ months of depreciation is allowed for the quarter the property is disposed of. To calculate the depreciation deduction for the first tax year that property subject to the mid-quarter convention is placed in service, the taxpayer first must compute the depreciation deduction for the full tax year and then multiply the full year deduction by the following fraction for the quarter of the tax year the property is placed in service:

| Quarter of Tax Year | Fraction |
|---------------------|----------|
| First               | 7/8      |
| Second              | 5/8      |
| Third               | 3/8      |
| Fourth              | 1/8      |

### V.A.4.c.(3) Mid-Month Convention

[531 T.M., VI.C.2.; TPS ¶2370.05.E.3.]

The mid-month convention applies to nonresidential real property, residential rental property, and railroad grading and tunnel bores.

Under this convention, all property placed in service or disposed of during any month is treated as placed in service or disposed of on the midpoint of that month. Thus, ½ month of depreciation is allowed for the month the property is placed in service, and ½ month of depreciation is allowed for the month the property is disposed of [§ 168(d)(2), § 168(d)(4)(B)].

To calculate the depreciation deduction for the first tax year that property subject to the mid-month convention is placed in service, the taxpayer first must compute the depreciation deduction for the full tax year and then multiply the full year deduction by a fraction determined in accordance with the following formula: $[(N \times 2) - 1] \div 24$, where N is the number of months the property was in service during the first tax year. Therefore, if a calendar-year taxpayer places nonresidential real property in service in March of Year 1, the property will be in service for the 10 months of Year 1 (March through December). The fraction used in calculating the first-year depreciation deduction is 19/24.

### V.A.4.d. Determining MACRS Deduction for a Short Tax Year

[531 T.M., VII.C.; TPS ¶2370.05.E.6.]

Special rules apply to determine the depreciation deduction for property placed in service or disposed of in a short tax year (a tax year with less than 12 full months), or for taxpayers that have a short tax year during the recovery period (other than the year the property is placed in service or disposed of). The MACRS depreciation tables in *Schedules & Tables 11.* cannot be used to determine depreciation for a short tax year.

### V.A.4.d.(1) Depreciation Conventions for a Short Tax Year

[531 T.M., VII.C.2.b.; TPS ¶2370.05.E.6.a.]

*Mid-Month Convention for a Short Tax Year.* Under the mid-month convention (see V.A.4.c(3)), a taxpayer always treats property as placed in service or disposed of on the midpoint of the month it is placed in service or disposed of. This rule applies regardless of whether the tax year is a short tax year [Rev. Proc. 89-15, 1989-1 C.B. 816].

*Half-Year Convention for a Short Tax Year.* Under the half-year convention (see V.A.4.c(1)), a taxpayer treats property as placed in service or disposed of on the midpoint of the tax year it is placed in service or disposed of. If a short tax year begins on the first day of a month or ends on the last day of a month, the partial month is treated as a whole month in determining the midpoint. Thus, a short tax year beginning June 20 and ending December 31 consists of seven months, and the midpoint is in the middle of September (3½ months from the beginning of the tax year in June).

If a short tax year neither begins on the first day of a month nor ends on the last day of a month, the tax year consists of the number of days in the tax year, and the midpoint is determined by dividing that number by two. If the result of dividing the number of days in the tax year by two is not the first day or the midpoint of a month, the property is treated as placed in service or disposed of on the nearest preceding first day or midpoint of a month [Rev. Proc. 89-15].

*Mid-Quarter Convention for a Short Tax Year.* Under the mid-quarter convention (see V.A.4.c(2)), a taxpayer treats property as placed in service or disposed of on the midpoint of the quarter of the tax year in which it is placed in service or disposed of. For a short tax year of four full calendar months, the quarters consist of one month. For a short tax year of eight full calendar months, the quarters consist of two months. The midpoint of each quarter is either the first day or the midpoint of a month.

If the short tax year consists of an amount of time other than four full months or eight full months, the midpoint is determined by dividing the number of days in the short tax year by four (to establish quarters), and dividing the number of days in each quarter by two to establish the midpoint. If that midpoint is on a day other than the first day or midpoint of a month, the property is treated as placed in service or disposed of on the nearest preceding first day or midpoint of that month [Rev. Proc. 89-15].

### V.A.4.d.(2) Computing Depreciation For and After a Short Tax Year

[531 T.M., VII.C.2.c., VII.C.2.d.; TPS ¶2370.05.E.6.b., .05.E.6.c.]

*Property Placed in Service in a Short Tax Year.* To determine the amount of the MACRS depreciation deduction for property placed in service in a short tax year, a taxpayer must multiply the amount of depreciation for a full tax year by a fraction, the numerator of which is the number of months (including parts of a month) the property is treated as in service during the tax year (using the applicable convention), and the denominator of which is 12 [Rev. Proc. 89-15, 1989-1 C.B. 816].

*Depreciation After a Short Tax Year.* Two methods are allowed to compute depreciation deductions for subsequent tax years that fall within the recovery period: (i) the allocation method, or (ii) the simplified method. Whichever method is chosen must be used consistently.

Under the allocation method, the depreciation deduction for each subsequent tax year is calculated by allocating to that tax year the depreciation allowance for each full recovery year (or portion) that falls within the tax year. For each recovery year included in the tax year, multiply the depreciation attributable to that recovery year by a fraction, the numerator of which is the number of months (including parts of a month) included in both the tax year and the recovery year, and the denominator of which is 12. The allowable depreciation for the tax year is the sum of the depreciation figured for each recovery year [Rev. Proc. 89-15].

Under the simplified method, the depreciation deduction for a subsequent tax year is calculated by multiplying the unrecovered basis of the property at the beginning of the year by the applicable depreciation rate. If a later year in the recovery period is a short tax year, a taxpayer calculates depreciation for that year using the same formula, but multiplies the result by a fraction, the numerator of which is the number of months (including parts of a month) in the tax year, and the denominator of which is 12. Similarly, if the property is disposed of in a later tax year before the end of the recovery period, a taxpayer calculates depreciation for the year of disposition using the same formula, but multiplies the result by a fraction, the numerator of which is the number of months (including parts of a month) the property is treated as in service during the tax year (applying the applicable convention), and the denominator of which is 12 [Rev. Proc. 89-15].

### V.A.4.e. Accounting for MACRS Property

### V.A.4.e.(1) Single and Multiple Asset Accounts

[531 T.M., VII.D.4.; TPS ¶2370.05.H.]

**Single Asset Accounts.** MACRS property may be accounted for by treating each individual asset as an account (single asset account) or by combining two or more assets into one account (multiple asset account). However, a taxpayer is required to account for an asset in a single asset account if one of the following conditions apply [Reg. § 1.168(i)-7(b)]:

- the asset is used both in a trade or business (or for the production of income) and in a personal activity;
- the asset is both placed in service and disposed of during the same tax year;
- general asset account treatment for the asset terminates;
- the asset is accounted for in a multiple asset account and the asset is disposed of; or
- a portion of an asset is disposed of in a partial disposition to which the partial disposition rules of Reg. § 1.168(i)-8(d)(1) apply.

**Dispositions of Single Asset Account Property.** Depreciation ends for an asset upon the asset's disposition. Additionally, the single asset account terminates upon the asset's disposition. If a portion of an asset is disposed of in a partial disposition, that portion must be accounted for in a single asset account as of the first day of the tax year of the disposition [Reg. § 1.168(i)-8(h)(1), § 1.168(i)-8(h)(3)(i)]. Generally, for computing gain or loss, the adjusted basis of an asset disposed of is its adjusted depreciable basis (as defined in Reg. § 1.168(b)-1(a)(4)) at the time of disposition [Reg. § 1.168(i)-8(f)(1)].

**Multiple Asset Accounts.** Unless required to be accounted for in a single asset account or general asset account, MACRS property may be accounted for in a multiple asset account. Each multiple asset account must include only assets that [Reg. § 1.168(i)-7(a), § 1.168(i)-7(c)]:

- have the same applicable depreciation method;
- have the same applicable recovery period;
- have the same applicable convention; and
- are placed in service by the taxpayer in the same tax year.

The following special rules apply when establishing multiple asset accounts [Reg. § 1.168(i)-7(c)(2)(ii)]:

- assets subject to the mid-quarter convention may only be grouped into a multiple asset account with assets that are placed in service in the same quarter of the tax year;
- assets subject to the mid-month convention may only be grouped into a multiple asset account with assets that are placed in service in the same month of the tax year;
- passenger automobiles for which the depreciation allowance is limited under § 280F(a) must be grouped in a separate multiple asset account;

- assets not eligible for an additional first-year depreciation deduction (including assets for which the taxpayer elected not to deduct the additional first-year depreciation amount) must be grouped into a separate multiple asset account;
- assets eligible for an additional first-year depreciation deduction may only be grouped into a multiple asset account with assets for which the taxpayer claimed the same percentage of additional first-year depreciation (e.g., 30%, 50%, or 100%);
- listed property (see V.A.7.), except for passenger automobiles for which the depreciation allowance is limited (as described in the third bullet, above), must be grouped into separate multiple asset accounts;
- assets for which the depreciation allowance for the placed-in-service year is not determined by using an optional depreciation table must be grouped into separate multiple asset accounts; and
- mass assets (as defined in Reg. § 1.168(i)-8(b)(3)) that are, or will be, disposed of or converted and identified by a mortality dispersion table must be grouped into a separate multiple asset account.

***Dispositions of Multiple Asset Account Property.*** A taxpayer disposes of an asset from a multiple asset account when ownership of the asset is transferred or when the asset is permanently withdrawn from use in the taxpayer's trade or business or from use in the production of income. This includes a sale, exchange, retirement, physical abandonment, or destruction of an asset, as well as a transfer to a supplies, scrap, or similar account, and upon certain partial dispositions of assets [Reg. § 1.168(i)-8(b)(2)]. If an asset is disposed of by sale, exchange, or involuntary conversion, gain or loss must be recognized under the applicable Code provision. If the asset is disposed of by physical abandonment, loss must be recognized in the amount of the adjusted depreciable basis of the asset at the time of the abandonment. However, if the abandoned asset is subject to nonrecourse indebtedness, gain or loss is recognized under the applicable Code provision. If an asset is disposed of other than by sale, exchange, involuntary conversion, physical abandonment, or conversion to personal use (e.g., by transfer to a supplies or scrap account), gain is not recognized. Loss, though, must be recognized in the amount of the excess of the adjusted depreciable basis of the asset over its fair market value at the time of disposition [Reg. § 1.168(i)-8(e)].

Generally, the adjusted basis of an asset disposed of for computing gain or loss is its adjusted depreciable basis at the time of disposition. If the taxpayer accounts for the asset disposed of in a multiple asset account and it is impracticable from the taxpayer's records to determine the unadjusted depreciable basis of the asset disposed of, the taxpayer may use any reasonable method to make the determination. This method must be applied consistently to all the assets in the same account. To determine the adjusted depreciable basis of an asset disposed of in a multiple asset account, the depreciation allowed or allowable for the asset disposed of is computed by using the depreciation method, recovery period, and convention applicable to the multiple asset account in which the asset disposed of was included and by including the additional first-year depreciation deduction claimed for the asset [Reg. § 1.168(i)-8(f)].

If a taxpayer accounts for an asset disposed of in a multiple asset account, the following rules apply [Reg. § 1.168(i)-8(h)(2)]:

- as of the first day of the tax year in which the disposition occurs, the asset disposed of is removed from the multiple asset account and is placed into a single asset account;

- the unadjusted depreciable basis of the multiple asset account must be reduced by the unadjusted depreciable basis of the asset disposed of as of the first day of the tax year in which the disposition occurs;
- the depreciation reserve of the multiple asset account must be reduced by the depreciation allowed or allowable for the asset disposed of as of the end of the tax year immediately preceding the year of disposition, computed by using the depreciation method, recovery period, and convention applicable to the multiple asset account in which the asset disposed of was included and by including the additional first-year depreciation deduction claimed for the asset disposed of; and
- in determining the adjusted depreciable basis of the asset disposed of at the time of disposition, the depreciation allowed or allowable for the asset is computed by using the depreciation method, recovery period, and convention applicable to the multiple asset account in which the asset disposed of was included and by including the additional first-year depreciation deduction claimed for the asset disposed of.

### V.A.4.e.(2) General Asset Accounts

[531 T.M., VII.D.3.; TPS ¶2370.05.G.]

To simplify the computation of MACRS depreciation, taxpayers may group separate properties into one or more general asset accounts. The assets in any particular general asset account are then depreciated as a single asset using the applicable depreciation method, recovery period, and convention for the assets in the account.

MACRS property generally may be accounted for in one or more general asset accounts. However, an asset may not be accounted for in a general asset account if one of the following conditions applies [§ 168(g)(1); Reg. § 1.168(i)-1(c)(1)(i)]:

- the asset is used both in a trade or business (or for the production of income) and in a personal activity at any time during the tax year in which the taxpayer first places the asset in service; or
- the asset is both placed in service and disposed of in the same tax year.

Each general asset account must include only assets that [Reg. § 1.168(i)-1(c)(2)(i)]:

- have the same applicable depreciation method;
- have the same applicable recovery period;
- have the same applicable convention; and
- are placed in service by the taxpayer in the same tax year.

In addition, the following special rules apply when establishing general asset accounts [Reg. § 1.168(i)-1(c)(2)(ii)]:

- assets subject to the mid-quarter convention may only be grouped into a general asset account with assets that are placed in service in the same quarter of the tax year;
- assets subject to the mid-month convention may only be grouped into a general asset account with assets that are placed in service in the same month of the tax year;
- passenger automobiles for which the depreciation allowance is limited under § 280F(a) must be grouped in a separate general asset account;

- assets not eligible for an additional first-year depreciation deduction (including assets for which the taxpayer elected not to deduct the additional first-year depreciation amount) must be grouped into a separate general asset account;
- assets eligible for an additional first-year depreciation deduction may only be grouped into a general asset account with assets for which the taxpayer claimed the same percentage of additional first-year depreciation (e.g., 30%, 50%, or 100%);
- listed property (see V.A.7.), except for passenger automobiles for which the depreciation allowance is limited (as described in the third bullet, above), must be grouped into separate general asset accounts;
- assets for which the depreciation allowance for the placed-in-service year is not determined by using an optional depreciation table must be grouped into separate general asset accounts;
- mass assets (as defined in Reg. § 1.168(i)-8(b)(3)) that are, or will be, disposed of or converted and identified by a mortality dispersion table must be grouped into a separate general asset account; and
- assets whose change in use results in a shorter recovery period or a more accelerated depreciation method for which the depreciation allowance for the year of change is not determined by using an optional depreciation table must be grouped into a separate general asset account.

***Electing to Use a General Asset Account.*** An irrevocable election to establish a general asset account is made on a timely filed tax return (including extensions) for the year in which the property included in the general asset account is placed in service by filing a completed Form 4562, *Depreciation and Amortization*, with "General asset account election made under section 168(i)(4)" written at the top of the form [Reg. § 1.168(i)-1(l)(1), § 1.168(i)-1(l)(3)].

***Dispositions of General Asset Account Property.*** A taxpayer disposes of an asset from a general asset account when ownership of the asset is transferred or when the asset is permanently withdrawn from use in the taxpayer's trade or business or from use in the production of income (see V.A.2.) [Reg. § 1.168(i)-1(e)(1)].

Immediately before a disposition of any asset in a general asset account, the asset is treated as having an adjusted basis of zero, and thus, no loss is realized on the disposition. Similarly, if an asset is disposed of by transfer to a supplies or scrap account, the basis of the asset in that account is zero. Amounts realized on a disposition of an asset in a general asset account are recognized as ordinary income to the extent of the unadjusted depreciable basis (as defined in Reg. § 1.168(b)-1(a)(3)) of the general asset account and any expensed cost (as defined in Reg. § 1.168(i)-1(b)(5)) for assets in the account (except to the extent of amounts previously recognized as ordinary income upon the disposition of other assets in the account). The unadjusted depreciable basis of the account is the sum of the unadjusted depreciable bases of all assets in the account, disregarding any expensed cost for assets in the account. The recognition and character of any excess amount realized is determined under applicable Code provisions (other than the depreciation recapture rules (see III.D.)) [Reg. § 1.168(i)-1(b)(2), § 1.168(i)-1(e)(2)].

The general asset account's unadjusted depreciable basis and depreciation reserve are not reduced as a result of the disposition of an asset from the general asset account [Reg. § 1.168(i)-1(e)(2)(iii)].

***Dispositions of All General Asset Account Properties.*** If all assets (or the last asset) in a general asset account are disposed of, the taxpayer may choose to terminate the general asset account, and the general rules that otherwise apply to the disposition of an asset in a general asset account do not apply. Rather, the amount of gain or loss is determined by taking into account the adjusted depreciable basis of the general asset account (as defined in Reg. § 1.168(i)-1(b)(3)) at the time of the disposition. Gain subject to depreciation recapture is limited to the excess of the depreciation allowed or allowable for the general asset account over any amounts previously recognized as ordinary income under the general rule for dispositions [Reg. § 1.168(i)-1(e)(3)(ii)(A)].

*Qualifying Dispositions of General Asset Account Property.* A taxpayer that disposes of general asset account property in a qualifying disposition (as defined in Reg. § 1.168(i)-1(e)(3)(iii)(B)) he or she may elect, in lieu of applying the general rules for the disposition of general asset account property, to determine the amount of gain, loss, or deduction for the asset by taking into account the asset's adjusted basis. For this purpose, the adjusted depreciable basis of an asset at the time of the disposition is the asset's unadjusted basis, minus the depreciation allowed or allowable for the asset, computed using the depreciation method, recovery period, and convention applicable to the general asset account, and by including the additional first-year depreciation deduction claimed for the general asset account that is attributable to the asset disposed of [Reg. § 1.168(i)-1(e)(3)(iii)(A)].

The amount of gain subject to recapture is limited to the lesser of either (i) depreciation allowed or allowable for the asset, including any expensed cost, and (ii) the excess of the beginning cost over the previous gain. Beginning cost is the original unadjusted basis of the general asset account (plus any expensed cost in the case of personalty originally included in the general asset account). Previous gain is the cumulative amounts of gain previously recognized as ordinary income under the depreciation recapture rules or under the general rule for general asset account dispositions [Reg. § 1.168(i)-1(e)(3)(iii)(A)].

*Optional Method.* A taxpayer may elect to use the optional method to determine gain, loss, or deduction for a qualifying disposition of an asset. If elected, the following rules apply [Reg. § 1.168(i)-1(e)(3)(iii)(C)]:

* the asset is removed from the general asset account as of the first day of the tax year in which the qualifying disposition occurs, and it is placed into a single asset account;
* the unadjusted depreciable basis of the general asset account must be reduced by the unadjusted depreciable basis of the asset as of the first day of the tax year in which the disposition occurs;
* the depreciation reserve of the general asset account must be reduced by the depreciation allowed or allowable for the asset as of the end of the tax year immediately preceding the year of disposition; and
* for purposes of determining gain realized on subsequent dispositions that is subject to ordinary income treatment under the general rule and under the depreciation recapture rules, the amount of any expensed cost must be disregarded.

*Transfers of General Asset Account Property.* If an asset in a general asset account is transferred in a corporate or partnership nonrecognition transaction, special rules apply [Reg. § 1.168(i)-1(e)(3)(iv)(B), § 1.168(i)-1(e)(3)(iv)(C)]. Specifically, these special rules apply to the same nonrecognition transactions subject to the nontaxable transfer rules discussed in V.A.4.f. [§ 168(i)(7); Reg. § 1.168(i)-1(e)(3)(iv)(C)].

*Like-Kind Exchanges and Involuntary Conversions of General Asset Account Property.* If a taxpayer transfers all the assets (or the last asset) in a general asset account in a like-kind exchange (see III.E.1.) or an involuntary conversion (see III.E.2.), the general asset account terminates as of the first day of the year of disposition. Gain or loss for the general asset account is determined by taking into account the adjusted depreciable basis of the general asset account at the time of the disposition. The adjusted depreciable basis of the general asset account at the time of the disposition is treated as the adjusted depreciable basis of the relinquished MACRS property. The depreciation allowance for the general asset account in the year of disposition is determined in the same manner as the depreciation allowance for the relinquished MACRS property in the year of disposition [Reg. § 1.168(i)-1(e)(3)(v)(A), § 1.168(i)-6].

If a taxpayer transfers an asset (other than the last asset or all of the assets) in a general asset account in a like-kind exchange or an involuntary conversion, general asset account treatment for the asset terminates on the first day of the year of disposition. Gain or loss for the asset is determined by taking into account the asset's adjusted depreciable basis (i.e., the unadjusted depreciable basis of the asset less the depreciation allowed or allowable for the asset, computed using the depreciation method, recovery period, and convention applicable to the general asset account in which the asset was included). The depreciation allowance for the asset in the year of disposition is determined in the same manner as the depreciation allowance for the relinquished MACRS property in the year of disposition [Reg. § 1.168(i)-1(e)(3)(v)(B), § 1.168(i)-6].

*Abusive Transactions.* If an asset in a general asset account is disposed of in an abusive transaction, the general asset account treatment for the asset terminates on the first day of the tax year in which the disposition occurs. An abusive transaction is a transaction entered into or made with the principal purpose of achieving a tax benefit or result that would otherwise be unavailable [Reg. § 1.168(i)-1(e)(3)(vii)].

### V.A.4.f. Miscellaneous MACRS Rules

[531 T.M., VII.G.1., VII.I.2.a., .VII.J., VIII.; TPS ¶2370.05.I.]

*Improvements and Additions to MACRS Property.* The depreciation deduction for an improvement or addition to property must be computed in the same manner as the deduction would be computed if the property had been placed in service at the same time as the improvement or addition. Thus, the MACRS class for the improvement or addition is determined by the MACRS class of the property to which the improvement or addition is made. The recovery period for an improvement or addition begins on the later of (i) the date the improvement or addition is placed in service, or (ii) the date the property to which the improvement or addition is made is placed in service [§ 168(i)(6)].

*Nontaxable Transfers of MACRS Property.* If MACRS property is transferred in a corporate or partnership nontaxable transfer, the recipient of the property must determine the property's depreciation deduction in the same manner as would the transferor, to the extent the recipient's adjusted basis does not exceed the transferor's basis. Thus, the recipient effectively assumes the transferor's depreciation schedule as to the carryover basis amount. The following nonrecognition transactions are covered by these rules [§ 168(i)(7)]:

- a § 332 distribution in complete liquidation of a subsidiary (see XIII.E.3.);
- a § 351 transfer to a corporation controlled by a transferor (see XIII.B.1.);

- a § 361 transfer of property in exchange for stock or securities in a corporate reorganization (see XIII.E.1.);
- a § 721 transfer of property to a partnership in exchange for a partnership interest (see XIV.C.1.a.);
- a § 731 partnership distribution of property to a partner (see XIV.F.1.); and
- any transaction between members of the same affiliated group during any tax year for which the group makes a consolidated return (see XIII.C.8.d.).

Transfers of general asset account property in a corporate or partnership nonrecognition transaction is discussed in V.A.4.e.(2).

*Reacquisitions of MACRS Property.* If a taxpayer disposes of and then reacquires property, he or she must compute depreciation deductions as if the property had not been disposed of. It is unclear whether this rule applies only if the taxpayer anticipates the reacquisition of the property at the time of the disposition [§ 168(i)(7)(C)].

*Leasehold Improvements of MACRS Property.* If a building is erected, or if improvements are made, on leased property, and if the building or improvement is property to which MACRS applies, depreciation deductions must be determined under MACRS. A lessor that disposes of a leasehold improvement that was made by the lessor for the lessee of the property may take the adjusted basis of the improvement into account for purposes of determining gain or loss if the improvement is irrevocably disposed of or abandoned by the lessor at lease termination [§ 168(i)(8)].

### V.A.4.g. MACRS Alternative Depreciation System (ADS)

[531 T.M., V.A.1.c(1), V.R., VI.D.3.b.; TPS ¶2370.05.F.]

In certain situations, a taxpayer may be required (or may elect) to use the Alternative Depreciation System (ADS) to compute the depreciation deduction of MACRS property. The use of ADS is required for the following property [§ 168(g)]:

- listed property (see V.A.7.) used 50% or less in a qualified business use [§ 280F(b)(1)];
- any tangible property used predominantly outside the United States during the year (i.e., the property is physically located outside the United States for more than 50% of the tax year);
- any tax-exempt use property;
- any tax-exempt bond-financed property;
- all property used predominantly in a farming business and placed in service in any tax year during which an election not to apply the uniform capitalization rules (see XI.D.) to certain farming costs is in effect [§ 312(k)(3)]; and
- any property imported from a foreign country for which an Executive Order is in effect because the country maintains trade restrictions or engages in other discriminatory acts.

An election to use ADS generally must cover all property in the same property class that a taxpayer places in service during the year. However, the election for residential real property and nonresidential real property can be made on a property-by-property basis. Once the election is made, it is irrevocable [§ 168(g)(7)].

*Tax-Exempt Use Property.* For nonresidential real property and residential rental property, tax-exempt use property is that portion of the property leased to a tax-exempt entity in a disqualified lease. However, if the portion of this property leased to tax-exempt entities in disqualified leases is 35% of the property or less, the property is not treated as tax-exempt use property. Property is not treated as tax-exempt use property solely by reason of a short-term lease (i.e., a lease of less than three years). A disqualified lease is a lease of this type of property to a tax-exempt entity if any of the following criteria is met [§ 168(h)(1)]:

- tax-exempt financing was used to finance all or part of the property and the tax-exempt entity, or a related entity, participated in the financing;
- there is a fixed or determinable purchase price or sale option, or equivalent of such an option, involving the entity (or related entity);
- the lease term exceeds 20 years; or
- the property is the subject of a sale and leaseback, or a lease and leaseback, more than three months after the property was first used by the tax-exempt entity (or related entity).

For property other than nonresidential real property and residential rental property, tax-exempt use property is that portion of any tangible property leased to a tax-exempt entity. This property is not treated as tax-exempt use property solely by reason of a short-term lease [§ 168(h)(1)].

Tax-exempt use property does not include that portion of property leased to a tax-exempt entity that is predominantly used by the tax-exempt entity (either directly or through a partnership in which the entity is a partner) in an unrelated trade or business subject to the unrelated business tax (see XIX.D.). In addition, any portion of property used in this way is not counted in determining if the 35% threshold test for nonresidential real property and residential rental property has been exceeded [§ 168(h)(1)(D)].

***Tax-Exempt Bond-Financed Property.*** Tax-exempt bond-financed property is any property to the extent that it is directly or indirectly financed by an obligation, the interest on which is-tax exempt. If only a portion of a facility is financed with a tax-exempt bond, the bond proceeds are allocated to the property in the order in which the property is placed in service [§ 168(g)(5)].

***Computing Depreciation Deductions Using ADS.*** Under ADS, depreciation deductions are computed by using three components [§ 168(g)(2)]:

1. the straight-line method (see V.A.4.b(3)), disregarding salvage value;
2. the applicable convention (see V.A.4.c.) as determined for the particular type of property involved; and
3. the recovery period assigned for purposes of ADS.

Under ADS, recovery periods for most property generally are longer than under the General Depreciation System (GDS), and thus, cost recovery generally is slower. Like under GDS, the recovery period of property under ADS generally is based on the property's class life. For personal property with no class life, a 12-year recovery period applies. For nonresidential real property and residential rental property, the recovery period is 40 years. For railroad grading, tunnel bore, or water utility property, the recovery period is 50 years. Other property's recovery period generally is its class life [§ 168(g)(2)(C)]. ADS recovery periods are available in IRS Pub. 946, *How to Depreciate Property*.

### V.A.5. Accelerated Cost Recovery System (ACRS)

[531 T.M.; TPS ¶2370.06.]

Property depreciable under the Accelerated Cost Recovery System (ACRS) is called "recovery property." ACRS applies to most tangible depreciable property placed in service after 1980 and before 1987, and some property placed in service after 1986 that is subject to a transition rule. It continues to apply to depreciate property placed in service during this time until the property is either fully depreciated or disposed of. However, tangible property that falls into any of the following categories is excluded from ACRS [Pre-1987 § 168(e)]:

- the property is depreciated using a depreciation method not expressed in terms of years (e.g., the units-of-production method) (see V.A.8.);
- the property is excluded public utility property;
- the property is a motion picture, tape, or sound recording; or
- the property is acquired in a churning transaction.

For property placed in service after 1986, the Modified Accelerated Cost Recovery System (MACRS) generally applies (see V.A.4.).

### V.A.5.a. Recovery Classes of ACRS Property

[531 T.M., V.; TPS ¶2370.06.B.]

The period over which the unadjusted basis of an item of recovery property is depreciated and the rate applied depends on the class to which the item is assigned. Under ACRS, there are eight classes of property with a recovery period assigned to each category, as follows:

| ACRS Classification | Recovery Period |
|---|---|
| Three-Year Property | 3 Years |
| Five-Year Property | 5 Years |
| 10-Year Property | 10 Years |
| 15-Year Public Utility Property | 15 Years |
| 15-Year Real Property | 15 Years |
| Low-Income Housing Property | 15 Years |
| 18-Year Real Property | 18 Years |
| 19-Year Real Property | 19 Years |

Applicable depreciation percentages for each class of ACRS property are available in *Schedules & Tables 12*.

### V.A.5.b. Optional Straight-Line Percentages

[531 T.M., VI.E.3.b.; TPS ¶2370.06.D.]

Under ACRS, taxpayers may elect to recover the unadjusted basis of recovery property using percentages based on a straight-line method. The optional straight-line method incorporates the regular recovery period for the property or one of two longer periods [Pre-1987 § 168(b)(3); Prop. Reg. § 1.168-2(c)].

| ACRS Classification | Optional Recovery Period |
|---|---|
| Three-Year Property | 3, 5, or 12 Years |
| Five-Year Property | 5, 12, or 25 Years |
| 10-Year Property | 10, 25, or 35 Years |
| 15-Year Real Property | 15, 35, or 45 Years |
| 15-Year Public Utility Property | 15, 35, or 45 Years |
| Low-Income Housing Property | 15, 35, or 45 Years |
| 18-Year Real Property | 18, 35, or 45 Years |
| 19-Year Real Property | 19, 35, or 45 Years |

To compute the ACRS deduction using the straight-line percentages, a taxpayer multiplies the unadjusted basis of the recovery property by the appropriate percentage. Salvage value is disregarded for purposes of the computation. Straight-line percentages for each ACRS class and optional recovery period are available in *Schedules & Tables 12*.

**Special Rules for Three-, Five-, and 10-Year Property.** If a taxpayer elects a particular straight-line percentage for any item of three-, five-, or 10-year property, the same straight-line percentage must be used for all items of property in the same class placed in service during that same tax year. Additionally, once elected, use of a straight-line percentage is required throughout the recovery period. The half-year convention (see V.A.4.c.(1)) must be used for the year in which the property is placed in service, regardless of when during that year the property is actually placed in service. A taxpayer that holds the property for the entire recovery period is allowed a half-year of depreciation for the year following the end of the property's recovery period [Pre-1987 § 168(b)(3)(B)].

**Electing the Straight-Line Method.** The election to use the optional straight-line method must be made by the due date (including extensions) of the taxpayer's tax return for the tax year in which the property is placed in service for a depreciable use. Once made, the election may be revoked only with IRS consent, which is granted only in extraordinary circumstances [Pre-1987 § 168(f)(4); Prop. Reg. § 1.168-2(c)(1)].

### V.A.5.c. Transfers of ACRS Recovery Property

[531 T.M., II.D.; TPS ¶2370.06.E.]

**Corporate and Partnership Transfers.** If recovery property is transferred in a nonrecognition transaction involving a corporation or a partnership, the transferee is treated as the transferor to the extent of the carryover basis in the transferred recovery property. The transferee must use the same recovery period and method as the transferor to compute the ACRS deduction for the carried-over portion of the basis. If the transferee's basis exceeds the carryover basis, the transferee may use either the regular or optional straight-line percentages to the extent of the excess.

These carryover basis rules do not apply to any transfer of pre-1981 property described in the anti-churning rules (as described in pre-1987 § 168(e)(4)). The following nonrecognition transactions are covered by these rules [Pre-1987 § 168(f)(10); Prop. Reg. § 1.168-5(b)(2)]:

- a § 332 distribution in complete liquidation of a subsidiary (see XIII.E.3.);
- a § 351 transfer to a corporation controlled by a transferor (see XIII.B.1.);
- a § 361 transfer of property in exchange for stock or securities in a corporate reorganization (see XIII.E.1.);
- a former § 371 transfer of property as a result of receivership or bankruptcy proceedings;
- a § 721 transfer of property to a partnership in exchange for a partnership interest (see XIV.C.1.a.); and
- a § 731 partnership distribution of property to a partner (see XIV.F.1.).

**Related Party and Leaseback Transactions.** If ACRS recovery property is transferred to a related party (as defined in pre-1987 § 168(e)(4)(D)) in a transaction not involving the anti-churning rules (as described in pre-1987 § 168(e)(4)), the related party is required to use the same recovery period and method as used by the transferor, to the extent of the transferor's adjusted basis at the time of the transfer. Similarly, if a taxpayer acquires recovery property and leases it back to the person from whom it was acquired, the taxpayer is bound to use the same recovery period and method as used by the person from whom the property was acquired [Pre-1987 § 168(f)(10); Prop. Reg. § 1.168-5(b)(2)].

### V.A.5.d. ACRS Deduction in Short Tax Years

[531 T.M., VII.C.3.; TPS ¶2370.06.F.]

For a tax year that is less than 12 months, the ACRS deduction is prorated on a 12-month basis. Thus, the amount of the deduction for a short tax year is computed by multiplying the amount of a full tax year deduction by a fraction, the numerator of which is the number of months in the short tax year, and the denominator of which is 12. The full ACRS percentages are used during the remaining years of the recovery period, and the unrecovered basis is deductible in the first tax year after the recovery period. The short tax year rules, however, do not apply to any tax year in which 15-, 18-, or 19-year real property, or low-income housing property is placed in service or disposed of. Instead, the ACRS deduction is computed for the number of months (using either a full-month or mid-month convention) the property is in service during the tax year, regardless of the number of months in the tax year and the recovery period and method used [Pre-1987 § 168(f)(5); Prop. Reg. § 1.168-2(f)].

### V.A.6. Pre-ACRS Depreciation Methods

[530 T.M.; TPS ¶2370.08.]

Tangible depreciable property placed in service before 1981 and certain tangible depreciable property excluded from MACRS and ACRS is depreciated by first determining the property's basis, its estimated useful life, and its estimated salvage value as of the end of its useful life. Then, a depreciation method that yields a reasonable allowance is applied. Reasonable depreciation methods include the straight-line method, the declining-balance method, and the sum-of-the-years-digits method [Pre-1990 § 167]. However, a taxpayer may not depreciate an asset below a reasonable salvage value [Reg. § 1.167(a)-1(c)].

*Useful Life.* The useful life of an asset is an estimate of the period over which the asset may reasonably be expected to be useful to the taxpayer in his or her trade or business or income producing activity. Factors considered in estimating the useful life of an item include the frequency of use, age when acquired, the taxpayer's repair policy, and environmental conditions [Reg. § 1.167(a)-1(b)].

### V.A.7. Listed Property Limitations

[531 T.M., VII.B.; TPS ¶2370.10.]

For certain listed property, MACRS and ACRS deductions are limited, either in annual amount or in the method of depreciation. Generally, the limitations apply identically to MACRS and ACRS property [§ 280F]. Deductions for listed property are subject to the following special rules and limitations:

- If an individual taxpayer's use of listed property is not for his or her employer's convenience or is not required as a condition of employment, the taxpayer cannot deduct depreciation or rent expenses for the use of the property as an employee [§ 280F(d)(3); Reg. § 1.280F-6(a)] (see V.A.7.b.).

- If the listed property is not used predominantly (more than 50%) for qualified business use, the taxpayer cannot claim the § 179 deduction or a special depreciation allowance. Additionally, the taxpayer must figure any depreciation deduction under MACRS using the straight-line method over the Alternative Depreciation System (ADS) recovery period (see V.A.4.g.). For ACRS property, listed property that is not used predominantly in a qualified business use must be depreciated using the straight-line method over the earnings and profits life of the property (see V.A.7.c.). The taxpayer may also have to recapture any excess depreciation claimed in previous years [§ 280F(b), § 280F(d)(6); Reg. § 1.280F-3T(e), § 1.168(i)-6(d); pre-1987 Reg. § 1.280F-3T(c)(1)] (see V.A.7.e.).

- Annual limits apply to depreciation deductions (including § 179 deductions and special depreciation allowance) for certain passenger automobiles. The taxpayer may continue to deduct depreciation for the unrecovered basis resulting from these limits after the end of the recovery period [§ 280F(a)] (see V.A.7.d.).

### V.A.7.a. Listed Property Definition

[531 T.M., VII.B.2.; TPS ¶2370.10.B.2.]

Listed property is any of the following [§ 280F(d)(4)]:

- passenger automobiles;
- any other property used for transportation, unless it is an excepted vehicle;
- property generally used for entertainment, recreation, or amusement (including photographic, phonographic, communication, and video-recording equipment); and
- computers and related peripheral equipment, unless used at a regular business establishment (including a portion of a dwelling unit that is used regularly and exclusively for business) and owned or leased by the person operating the establishment.

***Passenger Automobiles.*** A passenger automobile is any four-wheeled vehicle made primarily for use on public streets, roads, and highways, with an unloaded gross vehicle weight of 6,000 pounds or less (gross vehicle weight of 6,000 pounds or less for trucks and vans). It includes parts, components, or other items physically attached to the automobile at the time of purchase, or usually included in the purchase price of an automobile. It does not include the following vehicles [§ 280F(d)(5); Reg. § 1.280F-6(c)]:

- ambulances, hearses, or combination ambulance-hearses used directly in a trade or business;
- vehicles used directly in the trade or business of transporting persons or property for pay or hire; and
- trucks or vans that are qualified nonpersonal use vehicles (i.e., vehicles that are not, by their nature, likely to be used more than a minimal amount for personal purposes).

Though certain vehicles may not be passenger automobiles, they still may be "other property used for transportation" (see below), and therefore still subject to the special rules for listed property. Annual depreciation limits for passenger automobiles is discussed in V.A.7.d.

***Other Property Used for Transportation.*** Other property used for transportation includes trucks, buses, boats, airplanes, motorcycles, and any other vehicle used to transport persons or goods. It does not include the following qualified nonpersonal use vehicles (i.e., vehicles that are not, by their nature, likely to be used more than a minimal amount for personal purposes) [Reg. § 1.280F-6(b)(2), § 1.274-5(k)]:

- clearly marked police and fire vehicles;
- unmarked vehicles used by law enforcement officers if the use if officially authorized;
- ambulances used as such, and hearses used as such;

- any vehicle with a loaded gross vehicle weight of over 14,000 pounds that is designed to carry cargo;
- bucket trucks (cherry pickers), cement mixers, dump trucks (including garbage trucks), flatbed trucks, and refrigerated trucks;
- combines, cranes and derricks, and forklifts;
- delivery trucks with seating only for the driver, or driver seating plus a folding jump seat;
- qualified moving vans;
- qualified specialized utility repair trucks;
- school buses used in transporting students and employees of schools;
- other buses with a capacity of at least 20 passengers that are used as passenger buses; and
- tractors and other special purpose farm vehicles.

***Computers and Related Peripheral Equipment.*** A computer is a programmable, electronically activated device capable of accepting information, applying prescribed processes to the information, and supplying the results of those processes with or without human intervention. It must consist of a central processing unit containing extensive storage, logic, arithmetic, and control capabilities. Related peripheral equipment is any auxiliary machine (whether on-line or off-line) that is designed to be placed under the control of the central processing unit. Computers and related peripheral equipment does not include the following [§ 168(i)(2)(B)]:

- any equipment that is an integral part of other property that is not a computer;
- typewriters, calculators, adding and accounting machines, copiers, duplicating equipment, and similar equipment; or
- equipment of a kind used primarily for the user's amusement or entertainment (e.g., video games).

### V.A.7.b. Employee Use of Listed Property

[531 T.M., VII.B.3.c.; TPS ¶2370.10.B.4.]

A taxpayer who is an employee can claim a depreciation deduction for the use of listed property (whether owned or rented) in performing services as an employee only if the taxpayer's use is a business use. If a taxpayer's use is not for the employer's convenience or is not required as a condition of employment, the taxpayer cannot deduct depreciation or rent expenses for the use of the property as an employee [§ 280F(d)(3); Reg. § 1.280F-6(a)].

***Employer's Convenience.*** Whether the use of listed property is for the convenience of the employer must be determined from all the facts. Generally, the use is for the employer's convenience if it is for a substantial business reason of the employer. Use of the property during the employee's regular working hours in carrying on the employer's business is generally considered to be use for the convenience of the employer [Reg. § 1.280F-6(a)(2)(i)].

***Condition of Employment.*** Whether the use of listed property is a condition of employment depends on all the facts and circumstances. The use of the property must be required for the employee to perform his or her duties properly. The employer need not explicitly require the employee to use the property. A mere statement by the employer that the use of the property is a condition of employment is not sufficient [Reg. § 1.280F-6(a)(2)(ii)].

**EXAMPLE:** Virginia is employed as a courier with Delivery Service Inc. She owns and uses a motorcycle to deliver packages to downtown offices for Delivery Service. Delivery Service explicitly requires all its couriers to own a small car or motorcycle for use in their employment with the company, and it reimburses couriers for their costs. Virginia's use of the motorcycle for delivery purposes is for the convenience of Delivery Service and is required as a condition of employment.

**EXAMPLE:** Drew is a pilot for Airline, a small charter airline. Airline requires its pilots to obtain 80 hours of annual flight time in addition to the number of hours of flight time spent with Airline. Pilots can usually obtain these hours by flying with the Air Force Reserve or by flying part-time for another airline. Drew owns his own small airplane. He uses the airplane to obtain the required flight hours. Drew's use of the airplane is not for the convenience of Airline and is not a required condition for employment.

### V.A.7.c. Listed Property Used Predominantly for Qualified Business Use

[531 T.M., VII.B.3.; TPS ¶2370.10.B.3., 10.B.5.]

A taxpayer may claim the § 179 deduction and/or a special depreciation allowance for listed property and may depreciate listed property using the MACRS General Depreciation System (GDS) and a declining-balance method if the property is used predominantly for a qualified business use [§ 280F(b)].

*Qualified Business Use.* A qualified business use is any use in the taxpayer's trade or business. It does not include the following [§ 280F(d)(6); Reg. § 1.280F-6(d)(2)]:

- use of property held merely for the production of income, or any similar investment use;
- leasing property to any 5% owner or related person (as defined in § 267(b)), to the extent that use of the property is by a 5% owner or related person of the owner or lessee of the property;
- use of property as compensation for the performance of services by a 5% owner or related person; or
- use of property as compensation for the performance of services by any person, other than a 5% owner or related person, unless an amount is included in that person's gross income for the use of the property, and, where required, there has been withholding of income tax on that amount.

A 5% owner of a corporation is any person who owns, or is considered to own, more than 5% of the outstanding stock of the corporation, or stock possessing more than 5% of the total combined voting power of all stock in the corporation. For noncorporate businesses, a 5% owner is any person who owns more than 5% of the capital or profits interest in the business [§ 280F(d)(6)(D)].

*Predominant Use.* Listed property is predominantly used in a qualified business use for any tax year if the business use percentage is more than 50%. If listed property is used for more than one purpose during the tax year, the taxpayer must allocate use among the various uses of that property. The percentage of investment use of listed property is not part of the percentage of qualified business use for purposes of the 50% test. However, the combined total business and investment use is taken into account in calculating the depreciation deductions for the property [Reg. § 1.280F-6(d)(3), § 1.280F-6(d)(4)].

For non-automobile listed property, the allocation of use of the property is made on the basis of the most appropriate unit of time [Reg. § 1.280F-6(e)(3)]. For passenger automobiles and other means of transportation, allocation of use of the property is made on the basis of mileage. The percentage of qualified business use is calculated by dividing the miles the vehicle is driven for purposes of the trade or business by the total number of miles driven during the year for any purpose [Reg. § 1.280F-6(e)(2)]. If someone else drives the taxpayer's automobile, that use is treated as business use only if one of the following conditions apply [Reg. § 1.280F-6(d)(3)(iv)]:

1. the use is directly connected with the taxpayer's business;

2. the taxpayer property reports the value of the use as income to the other person and withholds tax on the income where required; or

3. the taxpayer is paid fair market rent.

The predominant use test must be satisfied for each year of the listed property recovery period.

***Application of the Limitation.*** If any listed property depreciated under MACRS is not used predominantly in a qualified business during any tax year, the depreciation deduction must be computed using the Alternative Depreciation System (ADS) under MACRS (see V.A.4.g.). Additionally, no first-year expensing deduction is allowable for the property [§ 280F(b)(1)]. If any listed property depreciated under ACRS is not used predominantly in a qualified business use during any tax year, the property must be depreciated under ACRS using the straight-line method over the following earnings and profits life of the property [Reg. § 1.280F-3T(e)]:

| ACRS Classification | Earnings and Profits Life |
|---|---|
| Three-Year Property | 5 Years |
| Five-Year Property | 12 Years |
| 10-Year Property | 25 Years |
| 15-Year Public Utility Property | 35 Years |
| 18-Year Real Property | 40 Years |
| Low-Income Housing Property | 40 Years |

Tables with the recovery percentages for ACRS property depreciated using the straight-line method are available in *Schedules & Tables 12.*

Taxpayers may also have to recapture any excess depreciation claimed in previous years. Recapture of excess depreciation is discussed in V.A.7.e.

### V.A.7.d. Annual Depreciation Limits for Certain Passenger Automobiles

[519 T.M., IV.B.3.; TPS ¶2310.05.B.6.]

The yearly depreciation deduction (including the § 179 deduction and special depreciation allowance) that may be claimed for passenger automobiles (as defined in V.A.7.a.) is limited. The maximum deduction amounts for most passenger automobiles are as follows:

| Year | First | Second | Third | Succeeding Years |
|---|---|---|---|---|
| 2014 | $3,160 | $5,100 | $3,050 | $1,875 |
| 2013 | $3,160/$11,160* | $5,100 | $3,050 | $1,875 |
| 2012 | $3,160/$11,160* | $5,100 | $3,050 | $1,875 |
| 2011 | $3,160/$11,160* | $4,900 | $2,950 | $1,775 |

| 2010 | $3,160/$11,160* | $4,900 | $2,950 | $1,775 |
| 2009 | $2,960/$10,960* | $4,800 | $2,850 | $1,775 |
| 2008 | $2,960/$10,960* | $4,800 | $2,850 | $1,775 |

\* For passenger automobiles that are qualified property (i.e., acquired and placed in service during 2008 through 2013) the limitation on the amount of the additional first-year depreciation deduction is increased by $8,000 [§ 168(k)(2)(F)].

Vans and trucks, which are passenger automobiles built on a truck chassis (including minivans and sport utility vehicles built on a truck chassis), have higher limitation amounts that other passenger automobiles as a result of a higher inflation adjustment. The maximum deduction amounts for vans and trucks are as follows:

| Year | First | Second | Third | Succeeding Years |
| --- | --- | --- | --- | --- |
| 2014 | $3,460 | $5,500 | $3,350 | $1,975 |
| 2013 | $3,360/$11,360* | $5,400 | $3,250 | $1,975 |
| 2012 | $3,360/$11,360* | $5,300 | $3,150 | $1,875 |
| 2011 | $3,260/$11,260* | $5,200 | $3,150 | $1,875 |
| 2010 | $3,160/$11,160* | $5,100 | $3,050 | $1,875 |
| 2009 | $3,060/$11,060* | $4,900 | $2,950 | $1,775 |
| 2008 | $3,160/$11,160* | $5,100 | $3,050 | $1,875 |

\* For trucks and vans that are qualified property (i.e., acquired and placed in service during 2008 through 2013) the limitation on the amount of the additional first-year depreciation deduction is increased by $8,000 [§ 168(k)(2)(F)].

Unrecovered basis for a passenger automobile used exclusively for business or investment purposes is its adjusted basis, minus the deductions that were allowed for the prior tax years [§ 280F(d)(8)].

*Partial Personal Use.* If a taxpayer's automobile is not used exclusively for business or investment (but is used more than 50% for business or investment), the taxpayer must reduce the maximum deduction amount proportionately by multiplying the maximum amount by the percentage of business or investment use during the tax year [Reg. § 1.280F-2T(i)(1)]. For depreciation purposes, the unrecovered basis for the first tax year after the end of the recovery period for an automobile not used exclusively for business or investment purposes is its adjusted basis, minus the allowable deductions for the prior tax years as if the automobile had been used during the prior tax years exclusively for business or investment purposes [§ 280F(d)(8)]. An automobile not used predominantly (i.e., more than 50%) in a qualified business use for any tax year is subject to special rules, discussed in V.A.7.c.

*Short Tax Years.* If a taxpayer has a short tax year, the taxpayer must reduce the maximum deduction amount proportionately by multiplying the maximum amount by a fraction, the numerator of which is the number of months and partial months in the short tax year, and the denominator of which is 12 [Reg. § 1.280F-2T(i)(2)].

### V.A.7.e. Recapture of Excess Deduction

[531 T.M., VII.B.4.b.; TPS ¶2370.10.B.6.]

A taxpayer that used listed property more than 50% in a qualified business use (see V.A.7.c.) in the year it was placed in service must recapture (i.e., include in income) excess depreciation in the first year he or she uses it 50% or less in a qualified business use. The adjusted basis of the property must be increased by the same amount [§ 280F(b)(2); Reg. § 1.280F-3T(d)(1)]. Excess depreciation is the excess, if any, of [§ 280F(b)(2)(B); Reg. § 1.280F-3T(d)(2)]:

- the amount of the depreciation deductions allowable for the property (including any § 179 deduction and special depreciation allowance claimed) for tax years before the first tax year in which the property was not predominantly used in a qualified business use; over

- the amount of depreciation deductions that would have been allowable for those tax years if the taxpayer had not used the property predominantly for a qualified business use in the year it was placed in service (i.e., for MACRS property, without claiming a § 179 deduction or special depreciation allowance, and using the straight-line method and the ADS recovery period (see V.A.7.c.)).

Recapture of excess depreciation under § 280F(b)(2) is reported on Form 4797, *Sales of Business Property*.

---

**EXAMPLE:** In June of Year 1, Lance purchased and placed in service a pickup truck that cost $18,000. He used it only for qualified business use for Year 1 through Year 4. Lance claimed a § 179 deduction of $10,000 based on the purchase of the truck. He began depreciating it using the 200% declining-balance method over a five-year GDS recovery period. The truck's gross vehicle weight was over 6,000 pounds, so it was not subject to the passenger automobile limits. During Year 5, Lance used the truck 50% for business and 50% for personal purposes. Lance's total § 179 deduction in Year 1 is $10,000, and his depreciation claimed for Year 1 through Year 4 totals $6,618 (($8,000 × 20%) + ($8,000 × 32%) + ($8,000 × 19.2%) + ($8,000 × 11.52%)). Thus, Lance's total depreciation deductions claimed in Year 1 through Year 4 is $16,618 ($10,000 + $6,618). Had Lance not used the property predominantly for a qualified business use in Year 1, he could not have claimed the § 179 deduction, and he would have had to figure any depreciation deduction using the straight-line method over the ADS recovery period, which is five years. Thus, the amount of depreciation deductions that would have been allowed would have totaled $12,600 (($18,000 × 10%) + ($18,000 × 20%) + ($18,000 × 20%) + ($18,000 × 20%)). The excess depreciation that must be recaptured in Lance's gross income for Year 5 is $4,018 ($16,618 − $12,600).

---

### V.A.7.f. Inclusion of Listed Property in Income

[519 T.M., IV.C.8.b., 531 T.M., VII.B.4.b.; TPS ¶¶2310.05.C., 2370.10.B.6.]

*Leased Passenger Automobile Listed Property.* For automobiles leased for a term of 30 days or more, taxpayers must include in gross income an inclusion amount if the automobile is worth more than $18,500 ($19,000 for a van or truck) in 2014 [Reg. § 1.280F-7(a)(2); Rev. Proc. 2014-21, 2014-11 I.R.B. 641]. For each tax year that the automobile is leased, the inclusion amount is determined in three steps [Reg. § 1.280F-7(a)(2)]:

1. determine the dollar amount from the applicable table (available in *Schedules & Tables 15.*);

2. prorate the dollar amount for the number of days of the lease term included in the tax year; and

3. multiply the prorated dollar amount by the business or investment use for the tax year.

To determine the dollar amount from the applicable table, the fair market value of the automobile on the first day of the lease term is used to find the appropriate row of the table. The tax year in which the automobile is being used under the lease is used to find the appropriate column of the table. For the last tax year during any lease that does not begin and end in the same tax year, the preceding year's dollar amount is used.

---

**EXAMPLE:** On Jan. 17, 2014, Miriam leases a car for two years and places it in service in her business. The car has a fair market value of $31,250 on the first day of the lease term. She uses the car 75% for business and 25% for personal purposes during each year of the lease. For 2014 through 2016, Miriam must include the following amounts in gross income:

| Tax Year | Dollar Amount | Proration | Business Use | Inclusion Amount |
|---|---|---|---|---|
| 2014 | $14 | 349/365 | 75% | $10.04 |
| 2015 | $30 | 365/365 | 75% | $22.50 |
| 2016 | $44 | 16/365 | 75% | $ 1.44 |

---

*Leased Non-Passenger Automobile Listed Property.* A taxpayer that leases listed property (other than a passenger automobile) for business or investment use must include an amount in income in the first year his or her qualified business use percentage (see V.A.7.c.) is 50% or less. The inclusion amount is the sum of two numbers [Reg. § 1.280F-7(b)]:

1. the product of the following:
    - the fair market value of the property;
    - the business or investment use percentage for the recapture year; and
    - the first amount applicable percentage (see Reg. § 1.280F-7(b)(2)(i)); plus
2. the product of the following:
    - the fair market value of the property;
    - the average business or investment use for all tax years preceding the recapture year in which the lease was in effect; and
    - the second amount applicable percentage (see Reg. § 1.280F-7(b)(2)(ii)).

However, if (i) the lease term begins within nine months before the end of the taxpayer's tax year, (ii) the leased property is not predominantly used in a qualified business use during the first tax year, and (iii) the lease term continues into the next tax year, the inclusion amount is included in the lessee's gross income in the following tax year, rather than the tax year in which the lease begins. Additionally, the average business or investment use is computed using the percentage for both years, and the applicable percentage is the one applicable to the year in which the lease begins [Reg. § 1.280F-5T(g), § 1.280F-7(b)(1)].

### V.A.8. Depreciation Methods Not Expressed in a Term of Years

#### V.A.8.a. Unit-of-Production Method
[530 T.M., XI.E.1.; TPS ¶2370.05.B.2.]

The unit-of-production method is widely used in extraction industries (e.g., mining, oil and gas, timber) where the units of production are readily measurable. Each unit produced is intended to bear an equal proportion of the depreciation, but the annual depreciation allowance may vary because it depends on the number of units produced during the year. To calculate depreciation under the unit-of-production method, the cost of the asset (reduced by estimated salvage) is divided by total expected units of output during the asset's useful life. The resulting number is the depreciation factor per unit of output.

**EXAMPLE:** Drilling Co. purchases drilling equipment for $120,000. Drilling estimates that 100,000 tons of ore will be produced during the life of the equipment, and that the equipment's salvage value will be $20,000. The $100,000 ($120,000 − $20,000) basis of the equipment is divided by the 100,000 tons of anticipated production to ascertain a $1 depreciation factor per unit of output. If 40,000 tons are produced in the tax year, Drilling's depreciation deduction is $40,000 (40,000 tons × $1).

### V.A.8.b. Income Forecast Method

[530 T.M., XI.E.2., 599 T.M., VIII.G.; TPS ¶2380.01.F.3.]

Intangible property that is a § 197 intangible is amortized over 15 years, rather than depreciated (see V.D.). Intangible property that is not § 197 property may be depreciated, typically using a straight-line method, under which the basis of the property, less its salvage value, is deducted in equal annual increments over the asset's useful life [Reg. § 1.167(b)-1(a)]. The income forecast method generally cannot be used for any property that is a § 197 intangible. In lieu of the straight-line method, however, taxpayers may choose to depreciate the following intangible property using the income forecast method [§ 167(g)(6)]:

- motion picture films or video tapes;
- sound recordings;
- copyrights;
- books; and
- patents.

Under the income forecast method, any given tax year's depreciation deduction is equal to the product of the cost of the property and a fraction, the numerator of which is the net income from the property in the current tax year, and the denominator of which is the total income anticipated from the property through the end of the tenth tax year after the year the property is placed in service. The total anticipated income may be revised upwards or downwards at the end of any tax year based on new information, but the revision does not affect the amount of depreciation claimed in prior years [§ 167(g)(1)].

**EXAMPLE:** Michael, a film producer, leases films to a television network. Michael's cost of producing the films is $800,000, taking into account salvage value. It is estimated that the films will produce total revenue over their life in the amount of $1,200,000. Michael realizes income of $600,000 in Year 1, $150,000 in Year 2, and $300,000 in Year 3. Under the income forecast method, the depreciation deduction for Year 1 is $400,000 ($800,000 × ($600,000 ÷ $1,200,000)). The depreciation deduction for Year 2 is $100,000 ($800,000 × ($150,000 ÷ $1,200,000)). The depreciation deduction for Year 3 is $200,000 ($800,000 × ($300,000 ÷ $1,200,000)).

A look-back rule applies to ensure that the depreciation deductions taken under the income forecast method are consistent with the actual income earned from the property. In the third and tenth years after the property is placed in service, the taxpayer must compare depreciation deductions that were claimed to depreciation deductions that would have been claimed if the taxpayer had used actual, rather than estimated, income from the property. The taxpayer may owe or be owed interest on the hypothetical underpayment or overpayment of tax, which is reported on Form 8866, *Interest Computation Under the Look-Back Method for Property Depreciated Under the Income Forecast Method.*

The look-back rule does not apply to property with a cost basis of $100,000 or less. Additionally, no interest is owed or paid where the actual income from the property is within 10% of the estimated income in the third and tenth years [§ 167(g)(2), § 167(g)(3), § 167(g)(4)].

### V.A.8.c. Other Methods

[530 T.M., XI.E., TPS ¶2370.05.B.2.]

Other depreciation methods that are not expressed in a term of years include the following:

- the machine hours or operating days method;
- the mileage-based method;
- the standard automobile mileage rate;
- the retirement method; and
- the replacement method.

### V.A.9. Recapture of Depreciation Deductions Upon Disposition

[563 T.M., III.; TPS ¶1760.01.D.]

A taxpayer disposing of certain property on which he or she claimed depreciation or amortization deductions may be required to treat some or all of the gain from the property as ordinary income. Depreciation recapture is discussed in III.D.

## V.B. Section 179 First-Year Expensing

[532 T.M.; TPS ¶2370.11.]

A taxpayer (other than a trust or estate) may elect to treat up to a certain dollar amount of the aggregate cost of qualified first-year expensing property placed in service during the tax year as a deductible expense, rather than as a capital expenditure. The dollar limit in 2014 (and 2015) is $25,000. However, the limitation must be reduced (but not below zero) by the amount by which the cost of the property placed in service during the 2014 (or 2015) tax year exceeds $200,000.

### V.B.1. Property Qualifying for the § 179 Deduction

[532 T.M., II.C.1.; TPS ¶2370.11.B.]

Unless an exception applies, qualified first-year expensing property is any tangible property that satisfies the following conditions [§ 179(d)(1)]:

1. it is MACRS property (see V.A.4.);
2. it is § 1245 property (see III.D.2.a.); and
3. it is acquired by purchase for use in the active conduct of a trade or business.

Previously, certain depreciable computer software (as described in § 197(e)(3)(A)(i)) could qualify. Additionally, taxpayers could elect to include as qualified first-year expensing property certain qualified real property [§ 179(f)(1)]. However, these properties are not eligible to be qualified first-year expensing property in 2014.

*Partial Non-Business Use.* If qualified first-year expensing property is used for both business and non-business purposes, its cost must be allocated between the business and non-business portions, but no first-year expensing deduction is allowed if the non-business use is 50% or more [Reg. § 1.179-1(d)].

*Property that Does Not Qualify.* Qualified first-year expensing property generally does not include the following [§ 50(b), § 179(d)(1)]:

- property used outside the United States;
- property used for lodging;
- property used by certain tax-exempt organizations;
- property used by governmental units or foreign persons or entities; and
- air conditioning units and heating units.

*Property Acquired by Purchase.* Property is acquired by purchase for purposes of the first-year expensing deduction only if it is not one of the following [§ 179(d)(2); Reg. § 1.179-4(c)]:

- property acquired by one member of a controlled group from another component member of the same group;
- property the taxpayer acquires from another person and in which the taxpayer's basis is determined (in whole or in part) by reference to the adjusted basis of the property in the hands of the person from whom the taxpayer acquired the property, or under the stepped-up basis rules for property acquired from a decedent (see III.A.3.a(3)); or
- property acquired from a related person whose relationship to the person acquiring it would result in the disallowance of losses under § 267 (including only the taxpayer's spouse, ancestors, and lineal descendants as members of the individuals family under § 267(c)(4)) or § 707(b).

Section 179 expensing is not permitted for so much of the property's basis as is determined by reference to the basis of other property held at any time by the person acquiring the property in question. Thus, if the property is acquired in a like-kind exchange (see III.E.1.) or as replacement property for an involuntary conversion (see III.E.2.), only outlays in excess of the adjusted basis of the replaced property can qualify for § 179 expensing [§ 179(d)(3)].

*Partnership and S Corporation Property.* The determination whether partnership or S corporation property is § 179 property is made at the entity level. Thus, even if the partnership or S corporation interest is investment property for the partner or shareholder, if the entity uses the property in the active conduct of a trade or business, the partner or shareholder may elect to expense his or her share of the § 179 expense (assuming the partner or shareholder meaningfully participates in the management or operation of the entity).

### V.B.2. Limitations on § 179 Deduction

[532 T.M., II.B.; TPS ¶2370.11.C.]

Generally, the § 179 deduction is the cost of the qualifying property. However, the total amount that a taxpayer may elect to deduct under § 179 is subject to a dollar limit and an income limit [§ 179(b)].

### V.B.2.a. Dollar Limitation on § 179 Deduction

[532 T.M., II.A., II.B.; TPS ¶2370.11.C.1.]

A taxpayer may elect to treat up to $25,000 of the aggregate cost of § 179 property placed in service in 2014 (or 2015) as an expense, rather than a capital expenditure. However, this amount generally must be reduced (but not below zero) by the amount by which the cost of the § 179 property placed in service in the 2014 (or 2015) tax year exceeds $200,000 [§ 179(b)]. Thus, in most cases, no deduction is available to taxpayers that place $225,000 or more of § 179 property in service in 2014 (or 2015).

In previous years, an increased § 179 deduction was available for enterprise zone and renewal community businesses and for property in the New York Liberty Zone, Gulf Opportunity (GO) Zone, and Kansas Disaster Area, as well as for qualified disaster assistance property. These provisions have expired.

***Partnerships and S Corporations.*** The dollar limitation applies both to partnerships and S corporations, as well as to each partner and shareholder. First, the entity determines its § 179 deduction subject to the limits, then it allocates the deduction among its partners or shareholders. At the partner or shareholder level, the cost of the § 179 property that is allocated to the partner or shareholder is aggregated with the cost of any other § 179 property expended by the individual, including any amount allocated from other partnerships and S corporations. In computing the reduction of the limitation amount based on the cost of § 179 property placed in service during the tax year, the cost of § 179 property placed in service by a partnership or S corporation is not attributed to any partner or shareholder [§ 179(d)(8); Reg. § 1.179-2(b)(3), § 1.179-2(b)(4)].

If the tax years of a partner and a partnership, or a shareholder and an S corporation, do not coincide, then the amount of any § 179 deduction attributed to any partner or shareholder for a tax year is the amount attributable to the partnership year that ends within the partner or shareholder's tax year [Reg. § 1.179-2(b)(3)(iv), § 1.179-2(b)(4)].

***Controlled Groups.*** A controlled group of corporations (as defined in § 1563(a), but using "more than 50%" in place of "at least 80%") is treated as a single taxpayer for purposes of the dollar limitation. The expense deduction may be taken by any one component member or allocated among several members in any manner [§ 179(d)(7); Reg. § 1.179-2(b)(7)].

***Married Taxpayers.*** Married individuals filing a joint return are treated as a single taxpayer for purposes of the dollar limitation.

Married individuals who file separate returns are also treated as a single taxpayer for purposes of the dollar limitation, including the reduction of the limitation amount based on the cost of § 179 property placed in service during the tax year. The spouses either may allocate the dollar limit (after any reduction) equally between themselves or elect a different proportion by which to share the limitation, so long as they total 100% [§ 179(b)(4); Reg. § 1.179-2(b)(6)].

---

**EXAMPLE:** Gary and Patty are married and file separate calendar year tax returns for 2014. During 2014, they place in service $100,000 and $110,000, respectively, of § 179 property. If Gary and Patty had filed jointly, their dollar limitation would have been $15,000 ($25,000 − (($100,000 + $110,000) − $200,000)). Because they do not elect a sharing percentage, the dollar limitation for both Gary and Patty is determined by multiplying by 50% the dollar limitation that would have applied if they had filed jointly. Therefore, the 2014 dollar limitation for each of Gary and Patty is $7,500 ($15,000 × 50%). Gary and Patty could select other percentages so long as the total percentage elected totals 100%.

---

### V.B.2.b. Taxable Income Limitation

[532 T.M., II.B.2.; TPS ¶2370.11.C.2.]

The total cost that may be deducted each tax year is limited to the taxable income the taxpayer derives from the active conduct of any trade or business during that tax year. Taxable income is calculated without taking a deduction for the cost of any § 179 property into account.

***Carryover of Disallowed Amounts.*** If any amount of the cost of § 179 property is not deductible as a result of the taxable income limitation, that amount may be carried over to the next tax year and added to the cost of § 179 property placed in service during that tax year. If costs from more than one year are carried forward to a subsequent year in which only part of the total carryover can be deducted, the costs carried forward from the earliest year is used first. Unused amounts may be carried forward indefinitely. A taxpayer that placed more than one property in service in the tax year may select the properties for which all or a part of the costs will be carried forward. Absent a selection, the total carryover will be allocated equally among the properties the taxpayer elected to expense for the year [§ 179(b)(3); Reg. § 1.179-3].

Taxpayers who transfer (in a taxable or nontaxable transfer) § 179 property for which a carryover is outstanding must increase the basis of the property by the amount of any carryover for that property immediately before the transfer. This prevents taxpayers from having to recapture into ordinary income an amount that has not been deducted, and it prevents transferees from succeeding to the carryover because the property was not acquired by purchase [Reg. § 1.179-3(f)].

***Active Conduct of a Trade or Business.*** Taxpayers are generally considered to meet the active conduct of a trade or business requirement if they meaningfully participate in the management or operations of the business (see IV.A.). A mere passive investor does not actively conduct a trade or business. Employees are considered to be engaged in the active conduct of the trade or business of their employment. Therefore, wages, salaries, tips, and other compensation (not reduced by unreimbursed employee business expenses) derived by a taxpayer as an employee are included in the aggregate amount of taxable income for purposes of the limitation [Reg. § 1.179-2(c)(6)].

***Married Taxpayers.*** The taxable income limitation is applied to married individuals filing a joint return by aggregating each spouse's taxable income. If married individuals file separate returns, the taxable income limitation is determined by treating each spouse as a separate taxpayer [Reg. § 1.179-2(c)(7), § 1.179-2(c)(8)].

### V.B.2.c. Limitation for Certain Passenger Vehicles

[532 T.M., II.B.1.e.; TPS ¶2370.11.C.3.]

Taxpayers may not elect to expense more than $25,000 of the cost of any heavy sport utility vehicle (SUV) and certain other vehicles placed in service during the tax year. An SUV is a four-wheeled vehicle that satisfies all of the following conditions [§ 179(b)(5)]:

1. it must be primarily designed or can be used to carry passengers over public streets, roads, or highways, unless it is operated only on rails;
2. it must not be subject to the § 280F luxury automobile depreciation limits; and
3. it must be rated at 14,000 pounds or less of gross vehicle weight.

A vehicle is not considered an SUV for this purpose if it is a vehicle with any of the following qualities [§ 179(b)(5)(B)(ii)]:

- it is designed to seat more than nine passengers behind the driver's seat;

- it is equipped with a cargo area (open or enclosed by a cap) of at least six feet in interior length that is not readily accessible from the passenger compartment; or
- it has an integral enclosure fully enclosing the driver compartment and load carrying device, it does not have seating rearward of the driver's seat, and it has no body section protruding more than 30 inches ahead of the leading edge of the windshield.

### V.B.3. Recapture of § 179 Deduction

[532 T.M., II.D.; TPS ¶2370.11.F.]

Taxpayers may have to recapture a § 179 deduction if property is not used more than 50% in a trade or business for any tax year during the property's recovery period. The amount of recaptured income is the amount of the § 179 deduction claimed, less the total depreciation that would have been allowable had the § 179 deduction not been elected for prior tax years and the year of recapture. The recaptured amount is treated as ordinary income in the year of recapture. The basis of property for which § 179 recapture occurs is increased by the amount of the recapture immediately before the event that triggers the recapture. However, if § 1245 recapture applies (see III.D.2.), there is no § 179 recapture and no basis adjustment [§ 179(d)(10); Reg. § 1.179-1(e)].

If the recapture rule applies to an item of § 179 property under this provision, as well as under the provision limiting deductions for listed property (see V.A.7.e.), the amount of recapture is determined only under the listed property rules [Reg. § 1.179-1(e)(1)].

Recapture of the § 179 deduction is reported on Form 4797, *Sales of Business Property*.

### V.B.4. Exclusions from § 179 Eligibility

[532 T.M., II.E.; TPS ¶2370.11.G.]

***Estates and Trusts.*** Estates and trusts are not permitted to make the § 179 election. Further, an estate or trust that is a partner or S corporation shareholder cannot deduct its distributive share of the § 179 expenses allocated to it. The partnership or S corporation does not reduce its basis in the property by the amount allocated to the estate or trust [§ 179(d)(4); Reg § 1.179-1(f)(3)].

***Certain Lessors of Property.*** A lessor of property who is treated as the owner for tax purposes is the person who makes the § 179 election for property. However, lessors who merely hold the property for the production of income cannot make the election, even if the lessee uses the property in the active conduct of a trade or business. Noncorporate lessors may not make the election unless one of the following conditions is satisfied [§ 179(d)(5); Reg. § 1.179-1(i)]:

- the property was manufactured or produced by the lessor; or
- the lease term is less than 50% of the class life of the property, and for the first 12 months after the property is transferred to the lessee, the sum of the deductions for the property that are allowable to the lessor solely for trade or business purposes (aside from rents and reimbursed amounts) exceeds 15% of the rental income produced by the property.

### *V.B.5. Electing the § 179 Deduction*

[532 T.M., II.F.; TPS ¶2370.11.E.]

The election to take the § 179 first-year expensing deduction is made by filing Form 4562, *Depreciation and Amortization*, with the taxpayer's original tax return (whether or not filed timely) for the tax year to which the election applies, or with an amended return, filed by the due date (including extensions), for that tax year. If a taxpayer timely files his or her original return without making the election, he or she may still make the election by filing an amended return within six months of the due date of the return (excluding extensions), writing "Filed pursuant to section 301.9100-2" on the amended return.

The taxpayer must maintain records that permit specific identification of each piece of § 179 property and reflect how and from whom the property was acquired and when the property was placed in service.

In 2014, the election may be revoked only with IRS consent, which will be granted only in extraordinary circumstances. Previously, the election could be revoked without IRS consent [§ 179(c)(2)].

## V.C. Additional First-Year Depreciation (Bonus Depreciation) [Expired]

[532 T.M., III.; TPS ¶2370.12.]

Before 2014, under the additional first-year depreciation rules, a taxpayer could deduct (rather than capitalize and recover through MACRS) the specified percentage of the adjusted basis of qualified property. This bonus depreciation was allowable in the year in which the property was placed in service. The adjusted basis of the property was reduced by the amount of this bonus depreciation before the MACRS deduction for the year in which the property was placed in service and subsequent years was computed [§ 168(k)(1)(A)].

Bonus depreciation, however, expired at the end of 2013 and does not apply in 2014 [§ 168(k)(2)]. Nevertheless, the rules relating to the computation and the qualification of property for the deduction in prior years remain relevant for property placed in service during those years; for example, in determining the adjusted basis of the qualified property placed in service.

### *V.C.1. Qualified Bonus Depreciation Property*

[532 T.M., III.A.2.; TPS ¶2370.12.F.2.]

For purposes of the additional first-year depreciation allowance, there are three types of qualified property:

1. 30% qualified property (see V.C.1.a.);
2. 50% qualified property (see V.C.1.b.); and
3. 2008-2013 qualified property (see V.C.1.c.).

### *V.C.1.a. 30% Qualified Property*

[532 T.M., III.A.2.b.; TPS ¶2370.12.F.2.b.]

Thirty-percent qualified property is property that satisfies the following four conditions [Pre-2008 § 168(k)(2)(A)(i); Reg. § 1.168(k)-1(b)(4)]:

1. it must be MACRS property with a recovery period of 20 years or less (see V.A.4.a.), depreciable computer software (as defined in § 167(f)(1)(B)), water utility property (see V.A.4.a.), or qualified leasehold improvement property (as defined in Reg. § 1.168(k)-1(c));

2. its original use must begin with the taxpayer after September 10, 2001;
3. it must either:
- be acquired by the taxpayer after September 10, 2001, and before January 1, 2005, but only if no written binding contract for the acquisitions was in effect before September 11, 2001; or
- be acquired by the taxpayer pursuant to a written binding contract entered into after September 10, 2001, and before January 1, 2005; and
4. it must be placed in service by the taxpayer before January 1, 2005 (January 1, 2006, in the case of long production period property or specified aircraft).

*Qualified Leasehold Improvement Property.* Qualified leasehold improvement property is any improvement to the interior portion of a building that is nonresidential real property if the following three conditions are satisfied [Pre-2008 § 168(k)(3)(A); Reg. § 1.168(k)-1(c)(1)]:

1. it must be made under a lease by the lessee, sublessee, or lessor of that portion;
2. the portion must be set for occupancy by the lessee and sublessee; and
3. the improvement must be placed in service more than three years after the date the building was first placed in service.

Qualified leasehold improvement property does not include any improvement for which the expenditure is attributable to the enlargement of the building, any elevator or escalator, any structural component benefitting a common area, or the internal structural framework of the building. A commitment to enter into a lease is treated as a lease, and the parties to the commitment are treated as lessor and lessee. However, a lease between related persons is not considered a lease. For this purpose, related persons are members of an affiliated group (see XIII.C.8.a.) and persons related for purposes of § 267(b), but substituting "80% or more" for "more than 50%." [Pre-2008 § 168(k)(3)(B); Reg. § 1.168(k)-1(c)(2)].

*Long Production Period Property.* Long production period property is property that satisfies all of the following conditions [Pre-2008 § 168(k)(2)(B)]:

1. it must satisfy the first three conditions of the 30% qualified property definition, above;
2. it must have a recovery period of at least 10 years or be tangible personal property used in the trade or business of transporting persons or property;
3. it must be subject to the uniform capitalization rules (see XI.D.);
4. it must have an estimated production period exceeding two years or an estimated production period exceeding one year with a cost exceeding $1 million, determined as if those provisions apply to property that has a long useful life for purposes of the uniform capitalization rules; and
5. it must not be a specified aircraft (as defined in pre-2008 § 168(k)(2)(C)).

*Exceptions.* Thirty-percent qualified property does not include property subject to the MACRS Alternative Depreciation System (ADS) (see V.A.4.g.), other than by reason of the election to subject the property to that system, as determined after applying the listed property limitations (see V.A.7.). It also does not include qualified New York Liberty Zone leasehold improvement property (as defined in § 1400L(c)(2)) or any property for which the taxpayer elects to forego the additional first-year depreciation [Pre-2008 § 168(k)(2)(D); Reg. § 1.168(k)-1(b)(2)(ii)(A)].

*Special Rules.* In the case of self-constructed property, the third condition of the 30% qualified property definition is satisfied by a taxpayer who manufactures, constructs, or produces, property for the taxpayer's own use if he or she begins manufacturing, constructing, or producing the property after September 10, 2001, and before January 1, 2005 [Pre-2008 § 168(k)(2)(E)(i)].

*Sale-leaseback transactions are also subject to a special rule.* For purposes of the second and third conditions of the 30% qualified property definition, property that a person originally places in service after September 10, 2001, and that the person sells and leases back within three months after the date it is originally placed in service, is treated as originally placed in service not earlier than the date on which the property is used under the leaseback [Pre-2008 § 168(k)(2)(E)(ii); Reg. § 1.168(k)-1(b)(3)(iii)(A)].

For purposes of the second condition of the 30% qualified property definition, syndicated property is treated as placed in service no earlier than the date of the last syndicated sale. Property is syndicated property if the following three conditions are satisfied [Pre-2008 § 168(k)(2)(E)(iii); Reg. § 1.168(k)-1(b)(3)(iii)(B)]:

1. the property must be originally placed in service after September 10, 2001, by its lessor;

2. the property must be sold by the lessor or a subsequent purchaser within three months after the date the property was originally placed in service (or, if there are multiple units of property subject to the same lease, within three months after the date the final unit is placed in service, provided the period between the time the first unit is placed in service and the time the last unit is placed in service does not exceed 12 months);

3. the property's user after the last sale during the three-month period must remain the same as when the property was originally placed in service.

### V.C.1.b. 50% Qualified Property

[532 T.M., III.A.2.c.; TPS ¶2370.12.F.2.c.]

Fifty-percent qualified property is property that satisfies the following four conditions [Pre-2008 § 168(k)(4)(B); Reg. § 1.168(k)-1(b)(4)]:

1. it must be MACRS property with a recovery period of 20 years or less (see V.A.4.a.), depreciable computer software (as defined in § 167(f)(1)(B)), water utility property (see V.A.4.a.), or qualified leasehold improvement property (as defined in Reg. § 1.168(k)-1(c));

2. its original use must begin with the taxpayer after May 5, 2003;

3. it must either:

   • be acquired by the taxpayer after May 5, 2003, and before January 1, 2005, but only if no written binding contract for the acquisitions was in effect before May 6, 2003; or

   • be acquired by the taxpayer pursuant to a written binding contract entered into after May 5, 2003, and before January 1, 2005; and

4. it must be placed in service by the taxpayer before January 1, 2005 (January 1, 2006, in the case of long production period property or specified aircraft).

Qualified leasehold improvement property, long production period property, and specified aircraft have the same definitions as they have for purposes of identifying 30% qualified property (see V.C.1.a.).

*Exceptions.* The exceptions discussed for purposes of 30% qualified property (see V.C.1.a.) also apply for 50% qualified property. However, also excepted from 50% qualified property is property that the taxpayer elects to treat as 30% qualified property [Reg. § 1.168(k)-1(e)(1)(ii)(B)].

*Special Rules.* The special rules discussed for purposes of 30% qualified property (see V.C.1.a.) also apply for 50% qualified property. However, "May 5, 2003" replaces references to "September 10, 2001" [Pre-2008 § 168(k)(4)(C)].

### V.C.1.c. 2008-2013 Qualified Property

[532 T.M., III.A.2.d.; TPS ¶2370.12.F.2.d.]

In general, 2008-2013 qualified property is eligible for 50% bonus depreciation. In certain circumstances, though, the property may be eligible for 100% bonus depreciation (see V.C.1.c(1)). 2008-2013 qualified property is property that satisfies the following four conditions [§ 168(k)(2)(A); Reg. § 1.168(k)-1(b)]:

1. it must be MACRS property with a recovery period of 20 years or less (see V.A.4.a.), depreciable computer software (as defined in § 167(f)(1)(B)), water utility property (see V.A.4.a.), or qualified leasehold improvement property (as defined in Reg. § 1.168(k)-1(c));

2. its original use must begin with the taxpayer after December 31, 2007;

3. it must either:
   - be acquired by the taxpayer after December 31, 2007, and before January 1, 2014, but only if no written binding contract for the acquisitions was in effect before January 1, 2008; or
   - be acquired by the taxpayer pursuant to a written binding contract entered into after December 31, 2007, and before January 1, 2014; and

4. it must be placed in service by the taxpayer before January 1, 2014 (January 1, 2015, in the case of long production period property or specified aircraft).

*Qualified Leasehold Improvement Property.* Qualified leasehold improvement property, has the same definitions as it has for purposes of identifying 30% qualified property (see V.C.1.a.) [§ 168(k)(3)].

*Long Production Period Property.* Long production period property is defined slightly differently for purposes of 2008-2013 qualified property than for purposes of 30% qualified property or 50% qualified property. In this case, long production period property is property that satisfies all of the following conditions [§ 168(k)(2)(B)]:

1. it must satisfy all four conditions of the 2008-2013 qualified property definition, above;

2. it must have a recovery period of at least 10 years or be tangible personal property used in the trade or business of transporting persons or property;

3. it must be subject to the uniform capitalization rules (see XI.D.);

4. it must have an estimated production period exceeding one year with a cost exceeding $1 million, determined as if this provision also applies to property that has a long useful life for purposes of the uniform capitalization rules; and

5. it must not be a specified aircraft (as defined in § 168(k)(2)(C)).

*Exceptions.* The exceptions discussed for purposes of 30% qualified property (see V.C.1.a.) also apply for 2008-2013 qualified property [§ 168(k)(2)(D)].

*Special Rules.* The special rules discussed for purposes of 30% qualified property (see V.C.1.a.) also apply for 2008-2013 qualified property. However, "December 31, 2007" replaces references to "September 10, 2001," and "January 1, 2014" replaces references to "January 1, 2005" [§ 168(k)(2)(E)].

### V.C.1.c.(1) 2008-2013 Qualified Property Eligible for 100% Bonus Depreciation

[532 T.M., III.A.2.d(2); TPS ¶2370.12.F.2.d(2)]

The percentage allowance applicable to 2008-2013 qualified property is dictated by the dates on which the taxpayer acquires the qualified property and places it into service. 2008-2013 qualified property that is acquired after September 8, 2010, and before January 1, 2012, and that the taxpayer places in service before January 1, 2012 (January 1, 2013, in the case long production period property and specified aircraft), is eligible for a 100% first-year depreciation allowance, in lieu of the 50% allowance that is generally applicable to 2008-2013 qualified property [§ 168(k)(5)].

For 2008-2013 qualified property to be eligible for 100% bonus depreciation, the property's original use must begin with the taxpayer after September 8, 2010. Additionally, the property must either [§ 168(k)(2)(A), § 168(k)(5)]:

- be acquired by the taxpayer after September 8, 2010, and before January 1, 2012, but only if no written binding contract for the acquisitions was in effect before September 9, 2010; or
- be acquired by the taxpayer pursuant to a written binding contract entered into after September 8, 2010, and before January 1, 2012.

***Interaction with Listed Property Limitation on Passenger Automobiles.*** If an automobile is eligible for the 100% first-year allowance, but is also subject to the listed property depreciation limits (see V.A.7.d.), the listed property rules operate to limit the amount of the bonus depreciation deduction allowed. Thus, even if an automobile is eligible for a 100% first-year depreciation allowance, the listed property depreciation limitations may limit the amount of the bonus depreciation deduction to the lesser of either (i) the 100% first-year bonus depreciation, or (ii) the first-year limitation amount for passenger automobile listed property, plus $8,000 [§ 168(k)(2)(F); Rev. Proc. 2011-26, 2011-16 I.R.B. 664, § 3.03].

***Election Out of 100% Bonus Depreciation Allowance.*** Taxpayers may elect out of the additional first-year depreciation allowances provided for any qualified property placed in service during the tax year. Once made, the election applies to all property of the same class that the taxpayer placed in service in that year. As a result, that class of property is no longer eligible to be treated as qualified property for purposes of either the 100% allowance or the 50% allowance for 2008-2013 qualified property [§ 168(k)(2)(D)(iii); Reg. § 1.168(k)-1(e)(7)]. Procedures for electing to forego 2008-2013 bonus depreciation are discussed in V.C.1.c(2).

### V.C.1.c.(2) Election to Forego 2008-2013 Bonus Depreciation

[532 T.M., III.A.2.d(5); TPS ¶2370.12.F.2.d(5)]

A taxpayer may elect to forego bonus depreciation on any class of 2008-2013 qualified property. The election, if made, applies to all property of that class placed in service during that tax year. An election is made by attaching a statement to a timely-filed tax return (including extensions) for the year in which the property is placed in service. The statement should indicate the election being made and the class of property for which the election is being made. A taxpayer that timely filed its return without making the election could still make the election by filing the election statement with an amended return within six months of the due date of the original return (excluding extensions), writing "Filed pursuant to section 301.9100-2" on the amended return. The election generally may be revoked only with IRS consent [§ 168(k)(2)(D)(iii); Reg. § 1.168(k)-1(e)].

### V.C.1.c.(3) Election to Accelerate Minimum Tax and Research Credits in Lieu of 2008-2013 Bonus Depreciation

[532 T.M., III.A.2.d(5)(d); TPS ¶2370.12.F.2.d(5)(c)]

A corporate taxpayer may elect to forego bonus depreciation for certain 2008-2013 qualified property placed in service during and after its first tax year ending after March 31, 2008. If the election was made, the corporation must use the straight-line method (see V.A.4.b(3)) to depreciate the property, and could (i) increase its general business credit limitation (see IX.A.2.) for the amount of the research credit, or (ii) increase the limitation in § 53(c) by its bonus depreciation amount. As a result, the corporation could effectively utilize otherwise unusable credits from tax years beginning before 2006 that are allocable to research expenditures or alternative minimum tax liabilities. These increases in credits are refundable. The election is revocable only with IRS consent [§ 168(k)(4)].

The election was made by the due date (including extensions) of the federal income tax return for the taxpayer's first tax year ending after March 31, 2008. Even if a taxpayer does not place in service any eligible qualified property during its first tax year ending after that date, the taxpayer must make the election for that tax year in order to apply the election to eligible qualified property placed in service in subsequent tax years. The procedure for making the election depended on the ending date of the taxpayer's first tax year ending after March 31, 2008, and whether the taxpayer was a member of a controlled group [Rev. Proc. 2009-16, 2009-6 I.R.B. 449, § 3].

*Property Eligible for the Election.* Eligible qualified property is 2008-2013 qualified property, with the following exceptions:

- "March 31, 2008" is used in lieu of "December 31, 2007";
- the written binding contract limitation for specified aircraft is disregarded; and
- only adjusted basis attributable to manufacture, construction, or production after March 31, 2008, but before January 1, 2010, and after December 31, 2010, but before January 1, 2014, is taken into account under the longer production period rules.

*Bonus Depreciation Amount.* A corporation's bonus depreciation amount for a tax year is 20% of the excess (if any) of (i) the aggregate amount of depreciation that would be allowable under § 168 for eligible qualified property placed in service during that tax year if bonus depreciation applied to all qualified property (but disregarding the written binding contract exception for specified aircraft), over (ii) the aggregate amount of depreciation that would be allowed under § 168 for eligible qualified property placed in service during that tax year if bonus depreciation did not apply to the property. These aggregate amounts are determined without regard to certain elections [§ 168(k)(4)(C)].

*Allocation of the Bonus Depreciation Amount.* The bonus depreciation amount is allocated between an electing corporation's general business credit limitation and prior year § 53(c) minimum tax credit limitation as the taxpayer determines, within certain rules [§ 168(k)(4)(E)(i); Rev. Proc. 2009-16, 2009-6 I.R.B. 449]. However, the portion of the bonus depreciation amount that may be allocated to the general business credit limitation for any tax year is limited to the excess of the business credit increase amount (as defined in § 168(k)(4)(E)(iii)) over the bonus depreciation amount allocated to that limitation for all preceding tax years. Similarly, the portion of the bonus depreciation amount that may be allocated to the minimum tax credit limitation is limited to the excess of the minimum tax credit increase amount (as defined in § 168(k)(4)(E)(iv)) over the bonus depreciation amount allocated to that limitation for all preceding tax years [§ 168(k)(4)(E)(ii)].

### V.C.1.c.(4) Coordination of Elections

[532 T.M., III.A.2.d(5)(e); TPS ¶2370.12.F.2.d(5)(d)]

If a taxpayer makes both the election not to claim the 2008-2013 additional first-year depreciation for a class of property (see V.C.1.c(2)) and the election to accelerate the minimum tax and research credits in lieu of bonus depreciation (see V.C.1.c(3)), the taxpayer applies the election not to claim the 2008-2013 additional first-year depreciation first. Any class of property for which the election not to claim the 2008-2013 bonus depreciation has been made is not eligible qualified property for purposes of the election to accelerate the minimum tax and research credits in lieu of bonus depreciation [Rev. Proc. 2008-65, 2008-44 I.R.B. 1082, § 4.04].

### V.C.2. Biofuel Plant Property Bonus Depreciation [Expired]

[532 T.M., III.B.; TPS ¶2370.12.A.]

Before 2014, a taxpayer could deduct (rather than capitalize and recover through MACRS) 50% of the adjusted basis of qualified second generation biofuel plant property (as defined in § 168(l)(2) and § 168(l)(3)). The adjusted basis of the property was reduced by the amount of this additional first-year depreciation before the MACRS deduction for the year in which the property was placed in service and subsequent years was computed. If qualified second generation biofuel plant property ceased to be so qualified, the bonus depreciation deduction was recaptured in the same manner as the additional first-year expensing deduction when property ceases to be qualified first-year expensing property [§ 168(l)] (see V.B.3.).

### V.C.3. Reuse and Recycling Property Bonus Depreciation

[532 T.M., III.C.; TPS ¶2370.12.B.]

A taxpayer may deduct (rather than capitalize and recover through MACRS) 50% of the adjusted basis of qualified reuse and recycling property placed in service after August 31, 2008. The additional first-year depreciation is allowable in the tax year in which the property is placed in service. The adjusted basis of the property is reduced by the amount of this additional first-year depreciation before the MACRS deduction for the year in which the property is placed in service and subsequent years is computed [§ 168(m)].

*Reuse and Recycling Property.* Reuse and recycling property is any machinery and equipment used exclusively to collect, distribute, or recycle qualified reuse and recyclable materials. Qualified reuse and recyclable materials are scrap plastic, scrap glass, scrap textiles, scrap rubber, scrap packaging, recovered fiber, scrap ferrous and nonferrous metals, or certain electronic scrap generated by an individual or business [§ 168(m)(3)(A), § 168(m)(3)(B)].

*Qualified Reuse and Recycling Property.* Qualified reuse and recycling property is any reuse and recycling property that meets all of the following conditions [§ 168(m)(2)(A)]:

1. it must be MACRS property;

2. it must have a useful life of at least five years;

3. its original use must begin with the taxpayer after August 31, 2008; and

4. it must be acquired by the taxpayer either:

- by purchase after August 31, 2008, but only if no written binding contract for the acquisition was in effect before September 1, 2008; or

- pursuant to a written binding contract entered into after August 31, 2008.

It does not include any of the following [§ 168(m)(2)(B)]:

- 2008-2013 qualified property (see V.C.1.c.);
- property subject to the MACRS Alternative Depreciation System (ADS) (see V.A.4.g.), other than by reason of the taxpayer's election; or
- property for which the taxpayer elects to forego additional first-year depreciation.

## V.D. Amortization of Intangibles

[533 T.M.; TPS ¶2380.]

Generally, taxpayers may amortize ratably over a 15-year (180-month) period the capitalized costs of § 197 intangibles held in connection with a trade or business or in an activity engaged in for the production of income. The amortization period begins with the later of either (i) the month the § 197 intangible is acquired, or (ii) the month the trade or business or activity engaged in for the production of income begins. No amortization deduction is taken in the month a taxpayer disposes of the intangible.

If a taxpayer pays or incurs an amount that increases the basis of the § 197 intangible after the 15-year amortization period begins, the taxpayer amortizes that amount over the remainder of the 15-year period, beginning with the month the basis increase occurs.

### V.D.1. Section 197 Intangibles

#### V.D.1.a. Intangible Property Eligible for Amortization

[533 T.M., III.; TPS ¶2380.02.B.]

A § 197 intangible is one of the following twelve items [§ 197(d)]:

1. goodwill;
2. going concern value;
3. workforce in place;
4. business books and records, operating systems, or any other information base, including lists or other information concerning current or prospective customers;
5. a patent, copyright, formula, process, design, pattern, know-how, format, or similar item;
6. a customer-based intangible;
7. a supplier-based intangible;
8. any item similar to items 3 through 7;
9. a license, permit, or other right granted by a governmental unit or agency (including issuances and renewals);
10. a covenant not to compete entered into in connection with the acquisition of an interest in a trade or business;
11. any franchise, trademark, or trade name; and
12. a contract for the use of, or a term interest in, any item in this list.

*Goodwill:* The value of a trade or business that is attributable to the expectancy of continued customer patronage, whether due to the name of a trade or business, its reputation, or any other factor [Reg. § 1.197-2(b)(1)].

*Going Concern Value:* The additional element of value of a trade or business that attaches to property because it is an integral part of an ongoing business. It includes the value attributable to a trade or business's ability to continue to function and generate income without interruption notwithstanding a change in ownership. It also includes the value attributable to the use or availability of an acquired trade or business (e.g., the net earnings that otherwise would not be received during any period if the acquired trade or business was not available or operational). Going concern value does not include any other § 197 intangible [Reg. § 1.197-2(b)(2)].

*Workforce in Place:* The composition of a workforce (e.g., its experience, education, or training), the terms and conditions of employment, and any other value placed on employees or their attributes. Thus, the part of the purchase price of an acquired trade or business that is attributable to the existence of a highly-skilled workforce is amortized. Additionally, the cost of acquiring an existing employment contract or relationship with employees or consultants as part of the acquisition of a trade or business is also amortized as part of the workforce in place. However, a workforce in place does not include any covenant not to compete or other similar arrangement entered into in connection with a direct or indirect acquisition of an interest in a trade or business [Reg. § 1.197-2(b)(3)].

*Information Base:* The intangible value of technical manuals, training manuals or programs, data files, and accounting or inventory control systems. It also includes the cost of acquiring customer lists, subscription lists, insurance expirations, patient or client files, and lists of newspaper, magazine, radio, or television advertisers [Reg. § 1.197-2(b)(4)].

*Patents, Copyrights, Etc.:* Includes package designs, computer software, and any interest in a film, sound recording, video tape, book, or other similar property. However, certain property is excluded from this category if it is not acquired in a transaction involving the acquisition of assets constituting a trade or business (or a substantial portion of a trade or business). Additionally, certain computer software that is leased to a tax-exempt entity is subject to special rules [Reg. § 1.197-2(b)(5)].

*Customer-Based Intangibles:* The composition of market, market share, and any other value resulting from the future provision of goods or services pursuant to relationships with customers in the ordinary course of business. Thus, the portion of the purchase price of an acquired trade or business attributable to the existence of customer base, circulation base, undeveloped market or market growth, insurance in force, mortgage servicing contracts, investment management contracts, or other relationships with customers that involve the future provision of goods or services is amortized. Customer-based intangibles also include the deposit base and any similar asset of a financial institution. However, mortgage servicing rights that are acquired separately are excluded from this category and may be amortized over nine years [§ 167(f)(3); Reg. § 1.197-2(b)(6)].

The portion of the purchase price of an acquired trade or business attributable to accounts receivable or other similar rights to income for goods or services provided to customers before acquisition of the trade or business is not amortizable. Instead, it is allocated among the receivables and taken into account as payment is received or at the time a receivable becomes worthless [Reg. § 1.197-2(b)(6)].

*Supplier-Based Intangibles:* The value resulting from the future acquisition of goods or services pursuant to relationships (contractual or otherwise) in the ordinary course of business with suppliers of goods or services to be used or sold by the taxpayer. Thus, the portion of the purchase price of an acquired trade or business attributable to a favorable relationship with persons providing distribution services, or the existence of favorable supply contracts, is amortized. The amount paid for supplier-based intangibles does not include any amount required to be paid for the goods or services themselves, pursuant to the terms of the agreement or other relationship [Reg. § 1.197-2(b)(7)].

*Government-Granted License, Permit, Etc.:* Licenses, permits, and other rights granted by a government unit or agency, including those that have been granted for an indefinite period or are reasonably expected to be renewed for an indefinite period. Thus, the capitalized cost of acquiring a liquor license, a taxicab medallion or license, an airport landing or takeoff right, a regulated airline route, or a television of radio broadcasting license is amortized. The issuance or renewal of such a license, permit, or other right is treated as an acquisition of the license, permit, or other right. However, a right granted that constitutes an interest in land or an interest under a lease of tangible property is not a § 197 intangible. Further, rights to receive tangible property or services that are not acquired as part of a purchase of a trade or business, and certain rights of fixed duration or amount, are not § 197 intangibles [Reg. § 1.197-2(b)(8)].

*Covenants Not to Compete:* Covenants not to compete or similar arrangements entered into in connection with the direct or indirect acquisition of an interest in a trade or business (or a substantial portion thereof). An interest in a trade or business includes both the assets of a trade or business and stock in a corporation or an interest in a partnership that is engaged in a trade or business. An acquisition may be made in the form of an asset acquisition, a stock acquisition or redemption, or the acquisition or redemption of a partnership interest [Reg. § 1.197-2(b)(9)].

*Franchises, Trademarks, or Trade Names:* The term "franchise" includes any agreement that provides a party with the right to distribute, sell, or provide goods, services, or facilities, within a specified area. It includes distributorships or other similar contractual arrangements under which the transferee is permitted or licensed to operate or conduct a trade or business within a specified area. A license, permit, or other right granted by a governmental unit may constitute a franchise. The renewal of a franchise, trademark, or trade name is treated as an acquisition of that asset. Sports franchises acquired after October 22, 2004 (and any intangible asset acquired in connection with the acquisition of such a franchise, including player contracts), are also considered § 197 intangibles.

The term "trademark" includes any work, name, symbol, or device (or any combination thereof) adopted and used by a manufacturer or merchant to identify goods or services and distinguish them from those manufactured of sold by others. The term "trade name" includes any name used by a manufacturer or merchant to identify or designate a particular trade or business or the name or title used by a person or organization engaged in the business [Reg. § 1.197-2(b)(10)].

### V.D.1.b. Intangible Property Excluded from Amortization

[533 T.M., IV; TPS ¶2380.02.C.]

The following assets are not § 197 intangibles [§ 197(e)]:

- interests in corporations, partnerships, trusts, or estates;
- interests under financial contracts;
- interests in land;
- certain computer software;
- any of the following intangibles not acquired in a transaction involving the acquisition of a trade or business:

— any interest in a film, sound recording, video tape, book, or similar property;

— any right to receive tangible property or services under a contract or granted by a governmental unit or agency;

— any interest in a patent or copyright; and

— a contract right or license, permit, or other right granted by a governmental unit if the right (i) is acquired in the ordinary course of business and not as part of the purchase of a trade or business, and (ii) either has a fixed duration of less than 15 years or is fixed as to amount with an adjusted basis that is recoverable under a method similar to the unit-of-production method;

• any interest under an existing lease of tangible property or any existing indebtedness;

• any right to service indebtedness that is secured by residential real property unless acquired in a transaction involving the acquisition of a trade or business; and

• fees for professional services and transaction costs incurred in connection with a transaction in which any portion of the gain or loss is not recognized.

***Certain Computer Software.*** Section 197 intangibles do not include the following types of computer software [§ 197(e)(3)]:

• computer software that meets all of the following requirements:

— it is or has been readily available for purchase by the general public;

— it is subject to a nonexclusive license; and

— it has not been substantially modified (i.e., the cost of all modifications is not more than the greater of (i) 25% of the price of the publicly available unmodified software, or (ii) $2,000) [Reg. § 1.197-2(c)(4)(i)]; and

• computer software that is not acquired in a transaction (or series of related transactions) involving the acquisition of assets constituting a trade or business (or a substantial portion thereof).

Computer software includes all programs designed to cause a computer to perform a desired function, as well as any database or similar item that is in the public domain and is incidental to the operation of qualifying software [Reg. § 1.197-2(c)(4)(iv)].

***Certain Rights of Fixed Duration or Amount.*** Certain contract rights or licenses, permits, or other rights granted by a governmental unit are not § 197 intangibles if they are (i) acquired in the ordinary course of business and not as part of the purchase of a trade or business, and (ii) either have a fixed duration of less than 15 years or are fixed as to amount with an adjusted basis that is recoverable under a method similar to the unit-of-production method. However, the following rights are *not* subject to this exclusion [Reg. § 1.197-2(c)(13)(i)]:

• customer-related information bases, customer-based intangibles, or similar items;

• goodwill;

• going concern value;

• covenants not to compete; and

• franchises, trademarks, or trade names.

### V.D.1.c. Self-Created Intangibles

[533 T.M., III.B.1.c.; TPS ¶2380.02.D.]

Generally, § 197 does not apply to intangibles that are created (rather than acquired) by the taxpayer, unless they are created in connection with the acquisition of a trade or business. A § 197 intangible is created by the taxpayer to the extent that the taxpayer makes payments or otherwise incurs costs for its creation, production, development, or improvement, whether the actual work is performed by the taxpayer or by another person under a contract with the taxpayer entered into before the creation, production, development, or improvement occurs [§ 197(c)(2); Reg. § 1.197-2(d)(2)].

---

**EXAMPLE:** Auto Co., a car manufacturer, enters into a contract with Motor, Inc., under which Motor agrees to develop a design of an engine to be used in a new model of car. The design is developed solely for Auto's use, and the contract provides the Auto will retain all rights to the design. Auto pays Motor $200,000 for the creation of the design. The design is a self-created intangible and therefore Auto may not amortize the cost under § 197.

---

The self-created intangibles exception does not apply to the entering into (or renewal of) a contract for the use of an existing § 197 intangible. Thus, the exception does not apply to legal and other professional fees incurred by a licensee in connection with the entry into a contract for the use of know-how or similar property [Reg. § 1.197-2(d)(2)(ii)(B)].

***Exceptions to the Self-Created Intangibles Rule.*** The self-created intangibles rule does not apply to the following [§ 197(c)(2)(A); Reg. § 1.197-2(d)(2)(iii)(A)]:

- any license, permit, or other right that is granted by a governmental unit or an agency or instrumentality thereof;
- any covenant not to compete entered into in connection with the acquisition of a trade or business or a substantial portion thereof; or
- any franchise, trademark, or trade name.

***Reacquisitions of Self-Created Intangibles.*** If a taxpayer disposes of a self-created intangible and subsequently reacquires the intangible, the self-created intangibles rule does not apply to the reacquired intangible. However, this is the case only if the intangible is amortizable as a § 197 intangible by the initial acquirer and the transactions are not a series of related transactions [Reg. § 1.197-2(d)(2)(iii)(C)].

### V.D.2. Calculating the § 197 Amortization Deduction

[533 T.M., III.C.; TPS ¶2380.02.E., .02.K.]

***Amortization Period of § 197 Intangibles.*** The amount of the amortization deduction for a § 197 intangible generally is determined by amortizing the adjusted basis of the asset ratably over a 15-year period, beginning with the first day of the month in which the intangible was acquired. For property held in connection with the conduct of a trade or business, the amortization period begins with the first day of the month in which the active conduct of the trade or business begins, if that date is later than the first day of the month in which the intangible was acquired [§ 197(a); Reg. § 1.197-2(f)(1)(i)].

In the case of a short tax year, the amortization deduction is determined by reference to the number of months in the short year. No amortization deduction is claimed in the month of the intangible's disposition [Reg. § 1.197-2(f)(1)(iii), § 1.197-2(f)(1)(iv)]

---

> **EXAMPLE:** Corporation acquires a § 197 intangible on Sept. 15, Year 1, for $180,000. Beginning with the month beginning on Sept. 1, Year 1, Corporation amortizes the intangible at a rate of $1,000 per month ($180,000 adjusted basis ÷ 180 months). Had Corporation begun doing business on Oct. 10, Year 1, Corporation would amortize the intangible at a rate of $1,000 per month beginning on Oct. 1, Year 1.

---

***Basis of § 197 Intangibles.*** A taxpayer's basis in a § 197 intangible generally is the taxpayer's cost of acquiring the intangible. In determining an intangible's adjusted basis, salvage value is disregarded [Reg. § 1.197-2(f)(1)(ii)]. If additional consideration is required to be paid to the seller upon the occurrence of a contingency, any amount that is properly included in the basis of the intangible after the first month of the 15-year amortization period, but before the expiration of that period, is amortized ratably over the remainder of the 15-year period. An amount not properly included in the basis of the intangible until after the expiration of the 15-year period is amortized in full immediately upon inclusion in the basis of the asset [Reg. § 1.197-2(f)(2)].

***Intangibles Leased to Tax-Exempt Entities.*** For a § 197 intangible that would be tax-exempt use property (as defined in § 168(h)), the amortization period is not less than 125% of the lease term. For computer software that would be tax-exempt use property, the useful life of that leased computer software is not less than 125% of the lease term [§ 167(f)(1)(C), § 197(f)(10)].

### V.D.3. Disposition of § 197 Intangibles

[533 T.M., III.D.; TPS ¶2380.02.F.]

Section 197 intangibles are treated as depreciable property used in a trade or business. If the taxpayer held the intangible for more than one year, any gain on its disposition (up to the amount of allowable amortization) is § 1245 gain (see III.D.2.), which is treated as ordinary income. If multiple § 197 intangibles are disposed of in a single transaction (or in a series of related transactions) all of the intangibles are treated as if they were a single asset in determining the amount of gain that is ordinary income. Any remaining gain, or any loss, is a § 1231 gain or loss (see III.C.1.). If the taxpayer held the intangible for one year or less, any gain or loss on its disposition is an ordinary gain or loss [§ 197(f)(7); Reg. § 1.197-2(g)(8)].

***Loss Disallowance and Basis Adjustment.*** If a taxpayer disposes of a § 197 intangible and retains other amortizable intangibles acquired in the same transaction (or series of related transactions) in which the disposed of intangible was acquired, no loss is recognized. Instead, the adjusted basis of each remaining § 197 intangible is increased by a proportionate share of the nondeductible loss. Each retained intangible's proportionate share of the nondeductible loss is determined by multiplying the nondeductible loss amount by a fraction, the numerator of which is the retained intangible's adjusted basis on the date of the disposition, and the denominator of which is the total adjusted bases of all retained § 197 intangibles on the date of the disposition [§ 197(f)(1)(A); Reg. § 1.197-2(g)(1)(i)(A)].

An abandonment of a § 197 intangible, or any event rendering a § 197 intangible worthless, is treated as a disposition of the intangible for purposes of the loss disallowance and basis adjustment rules [Reg. § 1.197-2(g)(1)(i)(B)].

---

**EXAMPLE:** In Jan. of Year 1, Large Co. purchases Small Co. In the acquisition, Large acquires three patents. A portion of the purchase price of Small is allocated to the patents as follows: $180,000 to Patent 1; $360,000 to Patent 2; $540,000 to Patent 3. In Jan. of Year 3, after two years of amortization, the adjusted bases of the patents are as follows: $156,000 for Patent 1; $312,000 for Patent 2; and $468,000 for Patent 3. At that time, Large sells Patent 2 for $200,000. Large's loss of $112,000 ($200,000 − $312,000) is not recognized. The basis of Patent 1 is increased by $28,000 ($112,000 disallowed loss × ($156,000 Patent 1 basis ÷ $624,000 total basis of Patent 1 and Patent 3). The basis of Patent 3 is increased by $84,000 ($112,000 disallowed loss × ($468,000 Patent 1 basis ÷ $624,000 total basis of Patent 1 and Patent 3).

---

For taxpayers under common control, no loss is recognized on the disposition of a § 197 intangible by a member of a controlled group of corporations if, after the disposition, another member of that group retains other § 197 intangibles acquired in the same transaction as the disposed of intangible. If the group member that incurs the loss retains no § 197 intangibles, the bases of any intangibles retained by any other group member are not increased by the amount of the disallowed loss. Rather, the taxpayer that incurs the loss amortizes the disallowed loss over the period of time that the disposed of intangibles would have been amortized. However, the amount of any remaining disallowed loss is allowed in full when all other retained intangibles have been disposed of or become worthless [Reg. § 1.197-2(g)(1)(iv)].

The loss disallowance rule does not apply to a § 197 intangible that is not acquired in a transaction (or series of related transactions) in which the taxpayer acquires other § 197 intangibles. Thus, a loss may be recognized upon the disposition of a § 197 intangible that was separately acquired [Reg. § 1.197-2(g)(1)(ii)].

***Nonrecognition Transactions.*** If a taxpayer acquires a § 197 intangible in a nonrecognition transaction (see III.E.), the taxpayer is treated as the transferor for the portion of the adjusted basis of the intangible that does not exceed the transferor's adjusted basis. Thus, the taxpayer amortizes this part of the adjusted basis of the intangible's remaining amortization period in the hands of the transferor. In a like-kind exchange (see III.E.1.) or involuntary conversion (see III.E.2.) of a § 197 intangible, the taxpayer must continue to amortize the part of the adjusted basis of the acquired intangible that is not more than the adjusted basis in the exchanged or converted intangible over the remaining amortization period of the exchanged or converted intangible. The portion of the adjusted basis of the acquired intangible that is more than the adjusted basis of the exchanged or converted intangible is amortized over a new 15-year period [Reg. § 1.197-2(g)(2)(iii)].

***Covenants Not to Compete.*** If a taxpayer enters into a covenant not to compete (or any other arrangement having substantially the same effect) in connection with the direct or indirect acquisition of an interest in a trade or business, disposition or worthlessness of the covenant (or other arrangement) will not be considered to occur until the disposition or worthlessness of all interests in the trade or business. A covenant not to compete that is acquired in connection with a purchase of stock would continue to be amortized over its 15-year period, even after it expires or becomes worthless, unless all trades or businesses in which the interest was acquired by the purchase of stock or all of the purchaser's interests in those trades or businesses also are disposed of or become worthless [§ 197(f)(1)(B); Reg. § 1.197-2(g)(1)(iii)].

### V.D.4. Anti-Churning Rules

[533 T.M., III.F.4.; TPS ¶2380.02.J.]

Anti-churning rules prevent taxpayers from amortizing certain § 197 intangibles if the transaction in which the taxpayer acquired them did not result in a significant change in ownership or use. These rules apply to goodwill, going concern value, and any other § 197 intangible that is not otherwise depreciable or amortizable [Reg. § 1.197-2(h)(1)]. Under the anti-churning rules, these assets may not be amortized as § 197 intangibles if any of the following conditions apply [§ 197(f)(9)(A); Reg. § 1.197-2(h)(2)]:

- the taxpayer or a related person held or used the intangible at any time from July 25, 1991, through August 10, 1993;

- the taxpayer acquired the intangible from a person who held it at any time during the period described in the first bullet, and, as part of the transaction, the user did not change; or

- the taxpayer granted the right to use the intangible to a person (or a person related to that person) who held or used it at any time during the period described in the first bullet, and the transaction in which the taxpayer granted the right and the transaction in which the taxpayer acquired the intangible are part of a series of related transactions.

*Related Person.* For purposes of the anti-churning rules, a related person is defined by reference to § 267(b) and § 707(b)(1), but with a 20% threshold instead of a 50% threshold. Additionally, persons under common control (as determined under § 41(f)(1)(A) and (B)) are also considered related to each other. The determination of whether a relationship exists is made immediately before or immediately after the acquisition of the intangible. Thus, the rule cannot be avoided by acquiring the intangible simultaneously with entering into or leaving a related-person status. In a series of related transactions, the determination is made immediately before the earliest such transaction, or immediately after the last such transaction [§ 197(f)(9)(C); Reg. § 1.197-2(h)(6)].

A de minimis rule applies in certain circumstances. Two corporations are not treated as related if they are related only as a result of the substitution of "20%" for "50%" in § 267(f)(1)(A) and the beneficial ownership of each corporation in the other is less than 10% by vote and value [Reg. § 1.197-2(h)(6)(iv)].

*Exceptions to the Anti-Churning Rules.* The anti-churning rules do not apply in the following situations [§ 197(f)(9)(B); Reg. § 1.197-2(h)(5)]:

- The taxpayer acquires the intangible from a decedent and its basis is stepped up to fair market value.

- The intangible is amortizable as a § 197 intangible by the seller or transferor from whom the taxpayer acquired it. However, this rule does not apply if the transaction in which the taxpayer acquires the intangible and the transaction in which the seller or transferor acquires it are part of a series of related transactions.

- The gain-recognition exception applies.

*Gain Recognition Exception.* This exception to the anti-churning rules applies if the person from whom the taxpayer acquired the intangible (i) would not be related to the taxpayer if the 20% test for ownership of stock and partnership interests was replaced by a 50% test, and (ii) chose to recognize gain on the disposition of the intangible and pay income tax on the gain at the highest tax rate. If the exception applies, the anti-churning rules apply only to the extent the taxpayer's adjusted basis in the intangible exceeds the transferor's gain recognized [§ 197(f)(9)(B); Reg. § 1.197-2(h)(9)].

## V.E. Changes in Method of Accounting for Depreciation

[530 T.M., XIV.B.; TPS ¶2370.08.E.]

Changes in method of depreciation generally are treated as changes in method of accounting, which typically require IRS approval. Taxpayers must file Form 3115, *Application for Change in Accounting Method*, to request a change in method of accounting for depreciation. Examples of changes in method of accounting for depreciation include the following [Reg. § 1.446-1(e)(2)(ii)(d)(2)]:

- A change from an impermissible method of determining depreciation for depreciable property if the impermissible method was used in two or more consecutively filed tax returns.

- A change in the treatment of an asset from nondepreciable to depreciable, or vice versa.

- A change in the depreciation method, period of recovery, or convention of a depreciable asset.

- A change from not claiming to claiming the bonus depreciation allowance (see V.C.) if the taxpayer did not make the election to claim any bonus depreciation allowance.

- A change from claiming a 50% bonus depreciation allowance to claiming a 30% bonus depreciation allowance for qualified property.

Changes in depreciation that are not a change in method of accounting, and thus may only be made by filing an amended return, include the following [Reg. § 1.446-1(e)(2)(ii)(d)(3)]:

- an adjustment in the useful life of a depreciable asset for which depreciation is determined under § 167;

- a change in use of an asset in the hands of the same taxpayer;

- a late depreciation election or revocation of a timely valid depreciation election (including the election not to deduct the bonus depreciation allowance (see V.C.)); and

- any change in the placed in service date of a depreciable asset.

Note that if a taxpayer elected not to claim any bonus depreciation allowance, a change from not claiming to claiming the bonus depreciation allowance is a revocation of the election and is not an accounting method change. IRS approval is generally required to make a late depreciation election or revoke a depreciation election.

In certain situations, a taxpayer may obtain automatic consent to a change in accounting method. [Rev. Proc. 2007-16, 2007-4 I.R.B. 358, Rev. Proc. 2011-14, 2011-4 I.R.B. 330]. A taxpayer that does not qualify for automatic consent must use the advance approval request procedures [Rev. Proc. 97-27, 1997-1 C.B. 680] (see XI.B.3.).

# CHAPTER VI. NATURAL RESOURCES
## >>>>>>>>>>>>>>>>>>>>>>>>>>>>>

## VI.A. Depletion

[601 T.M., VI., 603 T.M., IV., 605 T.M., IV.; TPS ¶2610.]

Depletion is the using up of natural resources by mining, drilling, quarrying stone, or cutting timber. Just as owners of tangible personal property may claim depreciation to give tax effect to the deterioration or obsolescence of those assets in income-producing activities (see Chapter V.), owners of exhaustible natural resources are entitled to claim deductions for depletion as the resource is extracted and sold. The depletion deduction allows owners and operators to account for the reduction of a product's reserves [§ 611].

### VI.A.1. Taxpayers Eligible for the Depletion Deduction

[603 T.M., II., 605 T.M., I., II., IV.A.; TPS ¶2610.02.]

Taxpayers with an economic interest in timber, oil, gas, or minerals in place may take a deduction for depletion. An economic interest exists where the taxpayer (i) has acquired by investment an interest in such property, and (ii) secures, by any form of legal relationship, income derived from the extraction of that property as his or her sole source of income [Reg. § 1.611-1(b)(1)].

Each of the following property interests has been defined as an economic interest in certain contexts:

- mineral interests;
- royalty interests;
- working interests;
- overriding royalty interests;
- net profits interests;
- carved out or retained oil payments; and
- production payments pledged to the development of property or retained in a leasing transaction.

**Acquisitions by Investment.** A taxpayer has an investment in the property if he or she has a tax basis (even a $0 basis) in the natural resource in place. The basis can arise by any means, including purchase, gift, or inheritance.

**Legal Relationship.** A legal relationship to the property generally means the existence of some legal or equitable claim over the property that a court could recognize. ForExample, someone who drills an illegal slant well does not have a legal relationship to the field, while a lessee of the mineral estate does.

***Interest in the Timber, Oil, Gas, or Minerals in Place.*** An interest in minerals in place exists if the taxpayer has a right to share and participate in the proceeds derived from the production of the minerals. This is the case even if, under state law, the actual title to the minerals in place belongs to another person or entity [*Thomas v. Perkins*, 301 U.S. 655 (1937), *Anderson v. Helvering*, 310 U.S. 404 (1940)].

***Sole Source of Income.*** The taxpayer must rely on output in order to recover his or her investment in the property (e.g., a mineral leasing arrangement under which, as a lessee mine extracts ore, the royalty received by the landowner allows the landowner to recover his or her investment in the mineral estate leased out). The taxpayer must not have a source of financial protection other than the natural resource itself to recover capital. Thus, if a taxpayer can look to the sales proceeds from the disposition of the overlying surface land to help assure performance of a production payment, then the economic interest is lost. Minimal alternative sources may be ignored [*Anderson v. Helvering*, 310 U.S. 404 (1940), *Std. Oil of Indiana v. Commissioner*, 465 F.2d 246 (7th Cir. 1972)].

### VI.A.2. Identifying and Combining Non-Timber Property

[603 T.M., III., 605 T.M., II.F., II.G.; TPS ¶2610.04.]

Depletion is determined on a property-by-property basis. Therefore, a taxpayer with both a royalty interest and a net profits interest in a single mine has two properties and the depletion deductions for each must be computed separately. Once a property has been identified, though, it may, in certain circumstances, be combined with one or more other properties. Combination may yield important tax consequences, including the computation of cost depletion and percentage depletion (which is done property-by-property) and calculating gains and losses from dispositions.

***Identifying the Property.*** For mines, wells, and other natural deposits, the term "property" means each separate interest the taxpayer owns in each mineral deposit in each separate tract or parcel of land. Tracts and parcels generally are all contiguous areas described in a single conveyance or grant. Areas included in separate conveyances or grants from different owners are separate tracts or parcels. Thus, a taxpayer that simultaneously acquires three contiguous tracts from three different owners has three separate tracts, even if he or she operates them as a single unit. Dissimilar legal interests within the same tract or parcel of land are separate properties. Additionally, interests relating to more than one deposit within the same tract are also separate properties [§ 614(a); Reg. § 1.611-1(d)(1), § 1.614-1(a)].

---

**EXAMPLE:** Joe owns one tract of land under which lie three separate and distinct seams of coal. Joe owns three separate mineral interests, each of which is a separate property.

**EXAMPLE:** Hannah conducts mining operations on eight tracts of land as a single unit. She acquired her interests in each of the eight tracts from separate owners. Even if each tract of land contains part of the same mineral deposit, Hannah owns eight separate mineral interests, each of which is a separate property.

**EXAMPLE:** Samantha owns a tract of land under which lies one mineral deposit. She operates a well on part of the tract and leases the mineral rights in the remainder to another operator, retaining a royalty interest. Samantha owns two separate mineral interests, each of which is a separate property.

**EXAMPLE:** Martin acquires from a single owner, in a single deed, three noncontiguous tracts of mineral land for a single consideration. Even if each tract contains part of the same mineral deposit, Martin owns three separate mineral interests, each of which is a separate property.

*Identifying a Deposit.* Because each deposit is a separate property, taxpayers must be able to identify a deposit. The deposit refers to each separate resource. Thus, oil, gas, and distillates are separate properties because they are distinct natural resources. However, if a deposit underlies multiple tracts, the taxpayer has multiple interests, even though the deposit is not physically separated [Reg. § 1.614-1(a)(5)].

A waste bank or residue from prior mining, the extraction of ores or minerals from which is treated as mining, is not a separate mineral deposit. Rather, it is considered part of the mineral deposit from which it was extracted. However, if the owner of the waste bank or residue disposes of the deposit from which it came, then the waste bank or residue is a separate deposit. A waste bank or residue is also treated as a separate deposit if it cannot be attributed to a particular deposit of the owner [§ 613(c)(3), § 613(c)(4); Reg. § 1.614-1(c)].

### VI.A.2.a. Combining and Separating Operating Oil and Gas Interests
[605 T.M., II.F.2.; TPS ¶2610.05.]

An automatic aggregation rule provides that taxpayers must combine their operating interests in oil, gas, and geothermal properties that underlie one tract or parcel of land and treat them as one property, subject to a special election that allows taxpayers to treat one or more of such interests as separate properties. Taxpayers may not, however, combine operating interest in separate tracts or parcels [§ 614(b)].

---

**EXAMPLE:** Oil Co. owns two operating interests in Parcel A and three operating interests in Parcel B. Unless it elects otherwise, Oil Co.'s operating interests in Parcel A combine into a single property and its operating interests in Parcel B combine into a single property. Oil Co. may not, however, combine any interest in Parcel A with any interest in Parcel B, even if the same oil and gas reservoir underlies the two parcels.

---

*Operating Interest.* An operating interest is a mineral, oil, or gas interest in which the costs of production must be taken into account for purposes of computing the taxable income limitation in determining percentage depletion (see VI.A.3.b.), or in which such costs would be taken into account if the mine or well were in the production stage. Generally, if a taxpayer may claim trade or business expense deductions (see Chapter IV.) for exploiting the property, then he or she has an operating interest. Operating interests exclude royalty interest, production payments, and net profits interests [Reg. § 1.614-2(b), § 1.614-3(c)].

### VI.A.2.a.(1) Elective Separation of Oil, Gas, and Geothermal Properties
[605 T.M., II.F.2.; TPS ¶2610.05.B., .05.C., .05.E.]

Taxpayers may elect to treat one or more of its oil and gas interests as separate properties. However, a taxpayer may not have more than one combination of operating interest in one tract or parcel of land. Subsequently discovered or acquired operating interests in the same tract are added to the existing combination, unless the taxpayer elects to treat it as a separate property. If there is no existing combination, then the new interest is treated as a separate property, unless the taxpayer elects to combine it with another interest [§ 614(b)(2); Reg. § 1.614-8(a)(2)].

A taxpayer makes the election to treat operating interests as separate properties by filing a statement attached to his or her timely filed return (including extensions) for the first tax year in which the taxpayer makes any expenditure for development or operation of the operating mineral interest after the acquisition of the interest. The statement should identify by name, code number, or other means the operating mineral interests within the same tract that the taxpayer is electing to treat as either separate properties or in combination. The statement should also identify by name, code number or other means the tract of land, and it should set forth the facts upon which its treatment as a single tract is based. If a taxpayer is electing to treat all of its operating mineral interests in a tract as separate properties, the taxpayer may make a blanket election for all its interests in that tract at the time of the election, and he or she need only identify the tract [§ 614(b)(4); Reg. § 1.614-8(a)(3)].

For this purpose, expenditures for development include any intangible drilling or development costs, but it does not include delay rentals. Further, the acquisition of an option to acquire an economic interest in minerals in place does not constitution the acquisition of a mineral interest. Once made, the election to treat operating interests as separate properties is binding for all later years [§ 614(b)(4); Reg. § 1.614-8(a)(3)].

### VI.A.2.a.(2) *Unitizations and Pooling Arrangements*

[605 T.M., II.G.; TPS ¶2610.05.D.]

A unitization or pooling arrangement is an agreement under which two or more owners of operating mineral interests agree to (i) have the interest operating on a unified basis, and (ii) share in production on the basis of a stipulated percentage or fractional interest without regard to which owner's interest produced the mineral [Reg. § 1.614-8(b)(6)].

If the unitization or pooling arrangement is compulsory (e.g., under applicable state law) the taxpayer must combine the affected operating mineral interests. If the arrangement is voluntary, the affected operating mineral interests are aggregated only if they are (i) located in tracts or parcels that are continuous or in proximity, and (ii) either located in the same deposit, or, if located in two or more deposits, the joint development or production of the affected interests must be logical from the standpoint of geology, convenience, economy, or conservation [§ 614(b)(3); Reg. § 1.614-8(b)(2)].

***Interaction with the Combination and Separation Rules.*** The combination and separation rules do not apply for any of the taxpayer's operating interests that participate in unitization or pooling arrangements during the period in which they participate in that arrangement. Instead, all operating interests participating in the arrangement are treated as a single property [§ 614(b)(3)(A)].

**EXAMPLE:** Drilling Corp. owns operating Interests 1, 2, and 3 on Parcel. In Year 1, Drilling elected to treat Interest 1 as a separate property. Accordingly, Interests 2 and 3 were automatically combined. On July 14 of Year 2, Interests 1 and 2 became part of a compulsory pooling arrangement under state law. As of that date, Interests 1 and 2 are treated as a single property and will continue to be so treated until one or the other is no longer a part of that arrangement. Because the general combination and separation rules are simply suspended during a given interest's participation in a pooling arrangement, any preexisting combinations remain in force. If Drilling later acquires Interest 4 on Parcel, Interest 4 is automatically combined with Interest 3, absent Drilling's election otherwise. The combination occurs because Interest 3 is part of an existing combination (i.e., of Interest 2 and Interest 3), and the effect of that combination is deemed to continue despite the pooling of Interests 1 and 2, and the taxpayer cannot aggregate Interests 3 and 4.

---

### VI.A.2.b. Combining and Separating Mineral Interests

[603 T.M., III.F.; TPS ¶2610.06.]

The rules on combining and separating mineral interests (often called "aggregating" and "deaggregating" in this context) differ sharply from the rules for combining oil and gas interests (see VI.A.2.a.). Generally speaking, mineral interests are less prone to automatic combinations.

*Operating Interest.* Operating interest is defined in VI.A.2.a. Specifically for the purpose of determining whether a mineral interest is an operating mineral interest, "costs of production" exclude exploration or development expenditures, as well as taxes paid by holders of nonoperating interests [Reg. § 1.614-2(b), § 1.614-3(c)]

### VI.A.2.b.(1) Election to Aggregate Nonoperating Mineral Interests

[603 T.M., III.F.5.; TPS ¶2610.06.A.]

With IRS consent, a taxpayer that owns two or more separate nonoperating mineral interests in a single tract or parcel of land (or in two or more adjacent tracts or parcels) may elect to aggregate all such mineral interests and treat them as one property. A nonoperating mineral interest is an interest that is not an operating mineral interest. This includes royalties, production payments, and net profits interests [§ 614(e)].

*Making the Election.* A taxpayer must file an application for IRS permission to aggregate separate nonoperating mineral interests. The application must be filed by the later of (i) 90 days after the beginning of the first tax year for which aggregation is desired, or (ii) 90 days after the acquisition of one of the interests that is to be included in the aggregation. The taxpayer must establish that the principal purpose for the election is not tax avoidance. The application must include a description of the nonoperating mineral interests within the tract or tracts of land involved. If the IRS grants permission, a copy of the letter granting permission must be attached to the taxpayer return for the first tax year for which the permission applies. Once made, the election is binding unless the IRS consents to revocation [§ 614(e); Reg. § 1.614-5(e)(1), § 1.614-5(e)(4)].

### VI.A.2.b.(2) Election to Aggregate Operating Mineral Interests in an Operating Unit

[603 T.M., III.F.6.; TPS ¶2610.06.B.]

If a taxpayer owns two or more separate operating mineral interests that constitute part or all of an operating unit, the taxpayer may elect (i) to aggregate and treat as one property all such interests he or she owns that constitute one or more mines, and (ii) to treat as separate property each such interest not deemed to be included in the aggregation. A taxpayer may elect to form more than one aggregation of operating mineral interests within any one operating unit. However, no aggregation may include any operating mineral interest that is a part of a mine without including all of the operating mineral interests that are a part of such mine in the first tax year for which the election to aggregate is effective. Additionally, any operating mineral interest that thereafter becomes a part of that mine is included in the aggregation [§ 614(c)].

*Operating Unit.* An operating unit is mineral interests that are operated together for purpose of producing minerals. An operating unit of any particular taxpayer is determined on the basis of its own operations, recognizing that operating units may not be uniform in the particular extractive industry. Factors that indicate that mineral interests are operated together as a unit include the following [Reg. § 1.614-2(c)(1)]:

- common field or operating personnel;
- common supply and maintenance facilities;
- common processing or treatment plants; and
- common storage facilities.

*Making the Election.* An election must be made in a statement attached to the taxpayer's return for the tax year for which the election is made. It must be accompanied by a description of each separate interest within the operating unit that is to be treated as a separate property. Once made, the election is binding for all years unless the IRS consents to a change. An election to aggregate properties is effective on the first day of the tax year for which the election was made, except as to later-added properties [Reg. § 1.614-3(f)(5), § 1.614-3(f)(6)].

### VI.A.2.b.(3) *Elective Mineral Deaggregation Rule*

[603 T.M., III.F.7.; TPS ¶2610.06.C.]

The deaggregation rule allows taxpayers to elect to treat a single operating interest as several properties. If a single tract or parcel of land contains a mineral deposit that is being (or will be) extracted using several mines for which the taxpayer has made expenditures for development or operation, then the taxpayer can elect to allocate all of the tract or parcel of land and the mineral deposit contained therein to such mines. Additionally, the taxpayer may treat the part of the tract or parcel of land and the proportionate mineral deposits so allocated to each mine as a separate property [§ 614(c)(2); Reg. § 1.614-3(b)(1)].

Separate property resulting from a deaggregation election may later be combined with another property pursuant to an aggregation election. However, the taxpayer may not make a deaggregation election for any property that is already part of an elective aggregation [§ 614(c)(2); Reg. § 1.614-3(b)(1)].

The election requires the consent of the IRS. An application for consent must be accompanied by a statement explaining the reasons for the request to exercise the election for an aggregated property. The IRS will not grant consent where the principal purpose for the request to make the election is based on tax consequences [Reg. § 1.614-3(b)(1)].

### VI.A.2.b.(4) *Invalid Aggregations*

[603 T.M. III.F.12.; TPS ¶2610.06.D.]

If the taxpayer makes an invalid aggregation, the effect is the same as if the taxpayer had made no election at all, and the affected properties are treated separately. An invalid aggregation can occur either when the first or basic aggregation is made, or when additions to basic aggregations are made. In the case of an invalid basic aggregation, a taxpayer may seek IRS consent to make a correct aggregation.

An attempt to add another property to an operating mineral interest is ineffective when it is not aggregated with all the other interest in a single mine, or when it is actually not in the same operating unit as the aggregation to which it is purportedly added. These defective efforts do not destroy an existing valid aggregation, but the added property must be maintained separately. However, if an invalid addition is properly a part of a mine for which other interests previously have been validly aggregated, the invalid addition must be included in the aggregation of which it is properly a part [Reg. § 1.614-3(f)(8)].

### VI.A.3. Calculating Depletion for Non-Timber Property

[603 T.M., IV., 605 T.M., IV.; TPS ¶2610.07., .13.]

There are two ways of figuring depletion: (i) cost depletion (see VI.A.3.a.), and (ii) percentage depletion (see VI.A.3.b.). A taxpayer generally must use the method that provides the larger deduction. However, unless the taxpayer is an independent producer or royalty owner, he or she generally cannot use percentage depletion for oil and gas wells [§ 613(a), § 613A].

### VI.A.3.a. Cost Depletion

[603 T.M., III.C., IV.B., 605 T.M., IV.B.; TPS ¶2610.07.]

Taxpayers can claim cost depletion deduction for mines, oil and gas wells, other natural deposits, and timber. However, if percentage depletion (see VI.A.3.b.) results in a greater depletion for the year, the taxpayer must use that method. The calculation is performed annually and property-by-property [§ 611(a), § 613(a)]. To figure cost depletion a taxpayer must first determine the following:

- the property's basis for depletion;
- the total recoverable units of mineral in the property's natural deposits; and
- the number of units of mineral sold during the tax year.

Once those figures are determined, the cost depletion deduction is calculated in two steps. First, divide the property's basis for depletion by the total recoverable units to determine the rate per unit. Second, multiply the rate per unit by units sold during the tax year to determine the cost depletion deduction [Reg. § 1.611-2(a)(1)].

Certain unmetered gases are subject to a special depletion method [Reg. § 1.611-2(a)(4)].

### VI.A.3.a.(1) Basis for Depletion

[603 T.M., IV.B.1., 605 T.M., IV.B.1.; TPS ¶2610.08.A.]

To determine the basis for depletion, a property's adjusted basis is decreased by the following amounts [§ 612; Reg. § 1.612-1]:

- amounts recoverable through:
  - — depreciation deductions;
  - — deferred expenses (including deferred exploration and development costs); and
  - — deductions other than depletion;
- the residual value of land and improvements at the end of operations; and
- the cost or value of land acquired for purposes other than mineral production.

### VI.A.3.a.(2) Total Recoverable Units of Mineral and Units of Mineral Sold During the Tax Year

[603 T.M., IV.B.2., 605 T.M., IV.B.1.; TPS ¶2610.09.]

The total recoverable units of mineral is the sum of (i) the number of units of mineral remaining at the end of the year (including units recovered but not sold), and

(ii) the number of units of mineral sold during the tax year, as determined under the taxpayer's method of accounting. A taxpayer that uses the cash method of accounting (see XI.B.1.c.) treats units for which the taxpayer receives payment during the tax year (regardless of the year of sale) as units sold. A taxpayer that uses the accrual method of accounting (see XI.B.1.d.) computes units sold based on the taxpayer's inventories and method of accounting for inventory [Reg. § 1.611-2(a), § 1.611-2(c)].

---

**EXAMPLE:** Tripp, a mine operator, has an adjusted basis of $600 in a particular mining property. The number of units sold during the tax year totals 15 units, and the number of units remaining to be recovered from the property at the end of the tax year totals 85 units. Therefore, the recoverable units for the tax year total 100 (15 + 85). The rate per unit is $6 ($600 basis ÷ 100 total recoverable units). The depletion deduction for the tax year is $90 ($6 rate per unit × 15 units sold).

---

*Safe Harbor Method for Oil and Gas Property.* A taxpayer may elect to use a safe harbor method to determine an oil or gas property's total recoverable units. Under the safe harbor, the total recoverable units equals 105% of a property's proven reserves (both developed and undeveloped). To make the election, a taxpayer must attach a statement to a timely filed return (including extensions) for the first tax year for which the safe harbor is elected. The election is effective for the tax year in which it is made and for all later years. It may not be revoked in the year of election, but may be revoked in a later year. Once revoked, it may not be re-elected for the next five years [Rev. Proc. 2004-19, 2004-10 I.R.B. 563].

### VI.A.3.b. *Percentage Depletion*

[603 T.M., IV.C., 605 T.M., IV.C.; TPS ¶2610.13.]

To figure percentage depletion, a taxpayer multiplies a certain percentage (specified for each mineral) by his or her gross income from the property during the tax year. The percentage depletion deduction generally cannot be more than 50% (100% for oil and gas property) of a taxpayer's taxable income from the property, calculated without the depletion deduction and the domestic production activities deduction (see IV.A.9.) [§ 613(a)].

*Gross Income from the Property.* In figuring percentage depletion, the taxpayer subtracts from the gross income from the property (i) any rents or royalties the taxpayer paid or incurred for the property, and (ii) the part of any bonus the taxpayer paid for a lease on the property allocable to the product sold (or that otherwise gives rise to gross income) for the tax year [Reg. § 1.613-2(c)(5)].

*Taxable Income from the Property.* Taxable income from the property means gross income from the property, less all allowable deductions (except deductions for depletion or domestic production activities) attributable to mining processes, including mining transportation. These deductible items include operating expenses, certain selling expenses, administrative and financial overhead, depreciation, intangible drilling and development expenditures, exploration and development expenditures, deductible taxes (other than taxes capitalized or taken as a credit), and losses sustained [Reg. § 1.613-5(a)].

Additionally, the following rules apply in calculating taxable income from the property for purposes of the taxable income limit [Reg. § 1.613-5(b); Rev. Rul. 60-74, 1960-1 C.B. 253]:

- net operating loss deductions are not deducted from the gross income from the property;

- corporations may not deduct charitable contributions from the gross income from the property; and

- if, during the year, the taxpayer disposes of an item of § 1245 property (see III.D.2.) that was used in connection with mineral property, any allowable deduction for mining expenses must be reduced by the part of any gain the taxpayer must report as ordinary income that is allocable to the mineral property.

### VI.A.3.b.(1) Oil and Gas Property

[605 T.M., IV.C.; TPS ¶2610.13., .14.]

Taxpayers may not claim percentage depletion for an oil or gas well unless either (i) the taxpayer is an independent producer or a royalty owner, or (ii) the well produces natural gas that is sold under a fixed contract or is produced from geopressured brine [§ 613A(b), § 613A(c)]. Percentage depletion cannot be claimed on a lease bonus, advance royalty, or any other amount payable without regard to production from the property [§ 613A(d)(5); Reg. § 1.613A-3(j)].

*Independent Producers or Royalty Owners.* Independent producers and royalty owners (as described in § 613A(c)) are allowed a 15% depletion rate [§ 613A]:

- only as to their domestic production;

- of the first 1,000 barrels of oil per day, or 6 million cubic feet of natural gas per day; and

- for taxpayers who do not have significant refining or retailing operations.

The taxpayer's deduction for percentage depletion is limited to the smaller of (i) 100% of the taxpayer's taxable income from the property, calculated without the depletion deduction and the domestic production activities deduction, or (ii) 65% of the taxpayer's taxable income from all sources, calculated without the depletion deduction, the domestic production activities deduction, any net operating loss carryback, and any capital loss carryback. Any amount not deductible because of the 65% of taxable income limit can be carried over to the following tax year and added to the taxpayer's depletion allowance before applying any limits [§ 613(a), § 613A(d)].

*Natural Gas Wells.* Natural gas sold under a fixed contract (as defined in § 613(b)(3)(A)) qualifies for a percentage depletion rate of 22%. The natural gas must be sold under a contract effective from February 1, 1975, to the date of sale of the gas. Qualified natural gas from geopressured brine (as defined in § 613A(b)(3)(C)) is eligible for a percentage depletion rate of 10% [§ 613A(b)].

*Partnerships and S Corporations.* Depletion generally is computed separately by each partner, rather than by the partnership. The partnership allocates to each partner a proportionate share of the partnership's adjusted basis in each oil or gas property, and each partner makes his or her own determination of whether cost of percentage depletion is applicable. If a partner uses percentage depletion, the 65% of taxable income limit applies using that partner's taxable income from all sources. Similar rules apply for shareholders and S corporations [§ 613A(c)(7)(D), § 613A(c)(11)].

### VI.A.3.b.(2) Mines and Natural Deposits

[603 T.M., IX.; TPS ¶2610.15.]

Certain mines, wells, and other natural deposits (including geothermal deposits) qualify for percentage depletion. Geothermal deposits (as defined in § 613(e)(2)) qualify for a percentage depletion rate of 15%. However, for geothermal deposits, no percentage depletion is allowed on any lease bonus, advance royalty, or other amount payable without regard to production [§ 613(e)]. For mines and natural deposits, the applicable percentage depletion rates range from 22% to 5% and depend on the type of deposit [§ 613(b)]:

| Deposits | Rate |
|---|---|
| • sulphur and uranium; and<br>• if from deposits in the United States:<br> — anorthosite, clay, laterite, and nephelite syenite (to the extent that alumina and aluminum compounds are extracted therefrom), asbestos, bauxite, celestite, chromite, corundum, fluorspar, graphite, ilmenite, kyanite, mica, olivine, quartz crystals (radio grade), rutile, block steatite talc, and zircon, and ores of the following metals: antimony, beryllium, bismuth, cadmium, cobalt, columbium, lead, lithium, manganese, mercury, molybdenum, nickel, platinum and platinum group metals, tantalum, thorium, tin, titanium, tungsten, vanadium, and zinc. | 22% |
| • if from deposits in the United States:<br> — gold, silver, copper, and iron ore; and<br> — oil shale (except shale described in the 7½% category). | 15% |
| • metal mines (except metals from deposits in the United States described in the 22% and 15% categories), rock asphalt, and vermiculite; and<br>• if the 22%, 7½%, and 5% categories do not apply:<br> — ball clay, bentonite, china clay, sagger clay, and clay used or sold for use for purposes dependent on its refractory properties. | 14% |
| • asbestos (other than asbestos described in the 22% category), brucite, coal, lignite, perlite, sodium chloride, and wollastonite. | 10% |
| • clay and shale used or sold for use in the manufacture of sewer pipe or brick, and clay, shale, and slate used or sold for use as sintered or burned lightweight aggregates. | 7½% |
| • gravel, peat, pumice, sand, scoria, shale (except shale described in the 15% or 7½% categories), and stone (except stone described in the second 14% category, below);<br>• clay used, or sold for use, in the manufacture of drainage and roofing tile, flower pots, and kindred products; and<br>• if from brine wells:<br> — bromine, calcium chloride, and magnesium chloride. | 5% |
| • all other minerals not included in the above categories, excluding the following:<br> — soil, sod, dirt, turf, water, or mosses;<br> — minerals from sea water, the air, or similar inexhaustible sources (minerals, other than sodium chloride, extracted from brines pumped from a saline perennial lake in the United States is not considered to be from an inexhaustible source); and<br> — oil and gas wells. | 14% |

### VI.A.4. Timber Depletion

[610 T.M., VI.; TPS ¶2610.20.]

Timber depletion is similar to depletion for other natural resources, except that only cost depletion (see VI.A.3.a.) is used. Percentage depletion (see VI.A.3.b.) does not apply to timber property [Reg. § 1.611-1(a)(1)].

**Timber Accounts.** Taxpayers who claim depletion deductions for timber must maintain one or more timber accounts detailing the number and units of merchantable timber. Each account must generally include a block of timber. Each block may consist of further units dictated by the taxpayer's ordinary commercial practices (e.g., all the timber that will be directed to a particular mill). These lesser accounts are annually adjusted and form part of the overall timber account [Reg. § 1.611-3(c), § 1.611-3(d)].

**Timber Units.** For each timber account, a taxpayer must estimate the quantity of merchantable timber reasonably known, or on good evidence believed, to exist on the date of acquisition. Timber is measured using board feet, log scale, cords, or other units. If the taxpayer later determines that he or she has more or less units of timber, the original estimate must be adjusted [Reg. § 1.611-3(e)].

**Calculating Depletion for Timber Property.** To calculate cost depletion, a taxpayer takes the following steps [Reg. § 1.611-3(b)]:

1. Determine the cost or adjusted basis of the timber on hand at the beginning of the year.
2. Add the cost of any timber units acquired during the year and any additions to capital to the amount determined in 1.
3. Determine the number of timber units to take into account by adding the number of timber units acquired during the year to the number of timber units on hand in the account at the beginning of the year and then adding or subtracting any correction to the estimate of the number of timber units remaining in the account.
4. Divide the result of 2. by the result of 3. to find the depletion unit.
5. Multiply the depletion unit calculated in 4. by the number of timber units cut.

If timber products are unsold at the end of the year, the depletion allowable for that timber must be included as an item of cost in closing inventory. The inventory is the taxpayer's basis for determining gain or loss in the tax year he or she sells the timber products [Reg. § 1.611-3(b)(1)].

---

**EXAMPLE:** Paul bought a timber tract for $160,000 (the land and the timber were each worth $80,000). His basis for the timber is $80,000. Based on an estimated 1,000 units of standing timber, Paul's depletion unit is $80 per unit ($80,000 basis ÷ 1,000 units). Paul cuts 500 units of timber. His depletion allowance is $40,000 ($80 depletion unit × 500 units). Had Paul sold only 250 of the 500 units of cut timber, he would deduct $20,000 ($80 depletion unit × 250 units) of the allowable $40,000 of depletion that year. The remaining $20,000 depletion would be added to his closing inventory of timber products.

---

**Basis for Depletion.** Tax basis in timber starts with initial basis, however obtained, and increases with capital expenditures in connection with the planting of timber (e.g., the cost of seedlings or the expenses of preparing the site for planting or natural seeding) [Reg. § 1.611-3(a)].

*Election to Treat Cutting of Timber as Sale or Exchange.* Certain taxpayers that have held timber for more than one year may elect to treat the cutting of that timber as a sale or exchange (see VI.B.1.). The taxpayer also must reduce the timber account containing the timber by an amount equal to the adjusted depletion basis of the timber [§ 631(a); Reg. § 1.611-3(b)(3)].

## VI.B. Timber

[610. T.M.; TPS ¶2650.]

There are three principal forms of timber disposition that may have immediate tax consequences: (i) the cutting of timber by the taxpayer for sale or use in the taxpayer's trade or business, (ii) the transfer of timber with a retained economic interest, and (iii) an outright sale in which the taxpayer disposes of all of the economic interests in the timber.

### VI.B.1. Election to Treat Cutting of Timber as Sale or Exchange

[610 T.M., IV.; TPS ¶2650.02.]

An owner of timber (or a person having a contractual right to cut the timber) may elect to treat the cutting of timber used in his or her trade or business as a sale or exchange if the timber (or cutting right) has been held for at least one year as of the date of the cutting. Gain or loss on the cutting is recognized in an amount equal to the difference between the timber's fair market value on the first day of the tax year in which it is cut and its adjusted basis for depletion [§ 631(a); Reg. § 1.631-1].

Cut timber subject to the election automatically constitutes property used in the taxpayer's trade or business for purposes of § 1231 (see III.C.1.a.). Thus, gain is treated as long-term capital gain unless there is an overall net § 1231 loss, in which case the gain or loss will be ordinary gain or loss. The fair market value becomes the basis for figuring ordinary gain or loss on the sale or other disposition of the products cut from the timber. For purposes of depletion, the taxpayer must reduce the timber account containing the timber by an amount equal to the adjusted depletion basis of the timber [§ 631(a); Reg. § 1.631-1(d)].

*Making the Election.* The election must be made on Form T, *Forest Activities Schedule*, for the taxpayer's initial tax return for the tax year in which the election is first effective. Resulting gain or loss is reported on Form 4797, *Sales of Business Property*. The election is generally binding for the tax year in which it is made and all following tax years. It may be revoked only with IRS consent upon a showing of undue hardship [Reg. § 1.631-1(a)(3), § 1.631-1(c)].

---

**EXAMPLE:** Jack is the owner of woodlands that, at the beginning of Year 1, contained a volume of 1 million board feet (1,000 MBF) of timber with an adjusted basis of $100 per MBF. During Year 1, Jack cuts 700,000 board feet (700 MBF) of the timber, at which time the fair market value is $150 per MBF. A capital gain of $50 per MBF ($150 fair market value − $100 basis) is realized from the timber cut. A new adjusted basis of $150 per MBF now applies to the 700 MBF cut in Year 1. The adjusted basis of the remaining 300 MBF remains $100 per MBF. Jack makes an election under § 631(a) to treat the cutting of timber as a sale or exchange in Year 1. Jack will report capital gain income of $35,000 (700 MBF × $50 capital gain per MBF), even though no sale was consummated or cash dollars were received for the lumber manufactured from the cut timber. In Year 2, Jack processes 50 MBF of the cut timber for lumber. The additional cost of processing the cut timber is $20,000. Jack sells the manufactured lumber for $40,000. His Year 2 profit on the sale is $12,500

($40,000 amount received – ($20,000 processing expenses + ($150 per MBF basis in the cut timber × 50 MBF of cut timber))).

***Time Timber Is Cut.*** For purposes of the election, timber is considered to be cut at the time when, in the ordinary course of business, the quantity of timber felled is first definitely determined [Reg. § 1.631-1(a)(2)].

### VI.B.2. Dispositions of Timber

[610 T.M., II.; TPS ¶2650.03.]

Taxpayers may achieve § 1231 treatment (i.e., capital gains treatment for gains and ordinary loss treatment for losses) (see III.C.1.) on qualifying timber dispositions. This treatment is available whether the seller retains an economic interest in the timber, or if the disposition is outright. To qualify, a timber transaction must meet all of the following requirements [§ 631(b)]:

1. the taxpayer must be the owner of the timber;
2. the taxpayer must have held the timber for longer than one year before its disposal;
3. the taxpayer must make a disposal of the timber under a contract; and
4. by virtue of the contract of disposal, the taxpayer must have retained an economic interest in the timber or made an outright sale of the timber.

***Owner of Timber.*** The term "owner" means any person owning an interest in the timber, including sublessors and holders of a cutting contract. An owner must have a right to cut timber for sale on his or her own account, or for use in his or her trade or business [Reg. § 1.631-2(e)(2)].

***Contractual Disposal.*** A mutually binding and enforceable contract for the sale and purchase of standing timber, which may be either oral or written, must exist. An owner must surrender cutting rights in the timber to another, and must relinquish actual ownership or control over the standing timber. A disposal is not limited to a sale of standing timber. Rather, the term has been broadly stated to envision a lease, a cutting contract, or other timber disposition arrangement in which the timber is cut by someone other than the owner.

Disposal occurs on the date the timber is cut. Timber is deemed cut at the time when, in the ordinary course of business, the quantity of timber felled is first definitely determined. However, in the case of a disposition with a retained economic interest, if payment is made to the taxpayer under the contract before the timber is cut, the taxpayer may elect to treat the date of payment as the date of disposal. The election is made by attaching a statement to a timely filed return (including extensions) for the year in which the payment is received. The statement should specify the advance payments that are subject to the election and identify the contract under which the payments are made [§ 631(b); Reg. § 1.631-2(b), § 1.631-2(c)].

***Retention of Economic Interest.*** A taxpayer may retain an economic interest in timber by virtue of the contractual disposal. For this purpose, an economic interest generally is identified in the same way as for purposes of determining eligibility for the depletion deduction (see VI.A.1.). A retained economic interest in timber thus requires that the taxpayer be entitled to share in the proceeds to be derived from the timber, and the recovery of the taxpayer's capital investment in the timber must be contingent upon actual severance. Generally speaking, an economic interest is retained when the taxpayer is paid on a per unit basis, with payment being based on measurements or scaling performed after severance. A taxpayer that is assured of a fixed return independent of the severance of timber has not retained an economic interest.

*Outright Sale.* An outright sale of timber qualifies for § 1231 treatment in the same manner as a sale with a retained economic interest. However, the election to treat the date of payment (if before the date of cutting) as the date of disposal is not available in the case of an outright sale. Thus, the date of disposal in an outright sale is the date the timber is deemed cut [§ 631(b)].

### VI.B.3. Long-Term Timber Leases

[610 T.M., V.; TPS ¶2650.04.]

A long-term timber lease is an arrangement through which rights to timber are acquired for a sufficient period of time to allow planted or naturally regenerated seedling to grow into a crop of timber. Payments a landowner receives under a long-term timber contract are segmented into (i) proceeds realized from the sale of timber, and (ii) ordinary rental income. The transaction is treated as a sale of timber to the extent of the fair market value of the timber standing on the date the agreement is signed. Any amount paid in excess of the fair market value is treated as ordinary rental income from the land [Rev. Rul. 62-81, 1962-1 C.B. 153].

### VI.B.4. Timber Depletion

[610 T.M., VI.; TPS ¶2610.20.]

Taxpayers may deduct a reasonable allowance for the depletion of standing timber. Depletion is allowed to permit the tax-free recovery of a taxpayer's capital investment in timber as it is cut, based on the principle that depletion constitutes compensation for capital consumed in the production of income through the severance of timber [§ 611(a)]. Timber depletion is discussed in VI.A.4.

### VI.B.5. Miscellaneous Timber Issues

#### VI.B.5.a. Reforestation Expenditures

[610 T.M., VII.B., VII.C.; TPS ¶2650.07.B., .07.C.]

Direct costs incurred for the reforestation of timber property generally are capital expenditures and must be added to the adjusted basis of the timber and recovered either when the timber is sold or through the depletion allowance (see VI.A.4.) as the timber is harvested [Reg. § 1.611-3(a)]. These costs include the following [Rev. Rul. 75-467, 1975-2 C.B. 93]:

- preparation of the site (e.g. girdling, herbicide application, baiting of rodents, or brush removal to afford good growing conditions);
- costs of seed or seedlings; and
- labor and tool expenses (including depreciation of equipment like tractors, trucks, tree planters, and similar machines).

Reforestation expenses must be distinguished from silvicultural expenses. Silvicultural expenses are the costs of maintaining an established stand of timber (e.g., the cost of brush clearing and removal of unwanted trees after planting, fire, disease, and insect control, and fertilization). These ongoing expenses generally are currently deductible because they are in the nature of maintenance costs. However, a taxpayer may elect to capitalize silvicultural expenses as a carrying charge under § 266 [§ 162, § 266; Reg. § 1.263(a)-6(b)(19); Rev. Rul. 2004-62, 2004-25 I.R.B. 1072].

*Election to Deduct and Amortize Reforestation Expenses.* Though reforestation expenditures generally must be capitalized, taxpayers may elect on a property-by-property basis to deduct up to $10,000 ($5,000 for married taxpayers filing separately) of reforestation expenditures incurred per tract per year in connection with qualified timber property (as defined in § 194(c)(1)). To the extent the maximum limit is exceeded, the taxpayer may amortize the excess over 84 months. For individuals, the amortized reforestation costs are an above-the-line adjustment to gross income (see VII.B.16.). The deduction is not available for trusts [§ 62(a)(11), § 194].

The election is made by claiming the deduction on a timely filed return (including extensions) for the tax year in which the expense was paid or incurred. The taxpayer should attach a statement to the return for each qualified timber property for which an election is being made. The statement should contain the unique stand identification numbers, the total number of acres reforested during the tax year, the nature of the reforestation treatments, and the total amounts of qualified reforestation expenditures eligible to be amortized or deducted [Notice 2006-47, 2006-20 I.R.B. 892].

***Recapture of Amortized Amounts.*** Amounts amortized under § 194 are subject to recapture as ordinary income to the extent of gain recognized from the disposition of qualified timber property within 10 years after the tax year in which the qualifying reforestation expenditures were made [§ 1245(a)(3)]. Recapture on the disposition of § 1245 property is discussed in III.D.2.

### VI.B.5.b. Certain Timber Cost-Sharing Payments

[610 T.M., VII.D.; TPS ¶2650.07.D.]

Taxpayers may exclude from income all or part of a government payment received under certain cost-sharing conservation, reclamation, and restoration programs [§ 126] (see II.K.).

### VI.B.5.c. Timber Casualty Losses and Involuntary Conversions

[610 T.M., VII.K.; TPS ¶2650.07.H., .07.I.]

Subject to limitations, a taxpayer generally may deduct losses on business property, including timber, that arises from a disaster such as a storm, fire, or other casualty [§ 165(c)(3)] (see VIII.H.1.). Additionally, if property is compulsorily or involuntarily converted as a result of its destruction, theft, seizure, requisition, or condemnation (or threat or imminence of requisition or condemnation), then recognition of the gain realized from the conversion may be deferred [§ 1033] (see III.E.2.).

## VI.C. Intangible Development Costs

[605 T.M., III.C.; TPS ¶2620.]

The cost of developing oil, gas, or geothermal wells typically is a capital expenditure that may be recovered through depreciation (see V.A.) or depletion (see VI.A.). However, in certain cases, a taxpayer may elect to deduct intangible drilling and development costs (IDCs) for wells in the United States as a current business expense [§ 263(c)].

Foreign IDCs incurred for wells outside the United States do not qualify for the IDC election. In such a case, the taxpayer may either (i) elect to include these costs in the adjusted basis of the oil or gas property and recover them through any allowable depletion or depreciation deduction, or (ii) deduct the costs ratably over the 10-year period beginning with the tax year when the costs were paid or incurred. However, these rules do not apply to foreign nonproductive wells [§ 263(i)].

The election to deduct IDCs is often used in concert with the percentage depletion deduction (see VI.A.3.b.). If a taxpayer claims percentage depletion, he or she reduces the oil and gas property's basis by the depletion. If the well is a success, there is likely to be little benefit from extra basis from capitalized drilling expenses because it will be used up via percentage depletion. However, if the well is ultimately abandoned, the IDC deduction effectively accelerates the loss.

*Qualifying Taxpayers.* Only operators may claim the IDC deduction. An operator is a taxpayer who holds a working or operating interest in any tract or parcel of land either as a fee owner or under a lease or any other form of contract granting working or operating rights. The expenditures may by paid to another party to actually perform the work, so long as the payor is an operator [Reg. § 1.612-4(a)].

*Integrated Oil Companies.* An integrated oil company is required to reduce its IDC deductions by 30%. The portion that cannot be currently deducted is written off ratably over 60 months, beginning with the month in which the costs are paid or incurred [§ 291(b)(1)].

*Qualifying Expenditures.* Expenditures eligible for deduction are limited to the cost of items with no salvage value, including wages, fuel, repairs, hauling, and supplies related to drilling wells and preparing them for production. These amounts can be paid or incurred for [Reg. § 1.612-4(a)]:

- the drilling, shooting, and cleaning of wells;
- clearing of ground, draining, road making, surveying, and geological work as are necessary in preparation for the drilling of wells; and
- in the construction of derricks, tanks, pipelines, and other physical structures necessary for the drilling of wells and the preparation of wells for the production of oil or gas.

*Making the IDC Election.* A taxpayer makes the deduction election by claiming IDCs as a deduction on his or her return for the first tax year in which the taxpayer pays or incurs such costs. No formal statement is required. Once made, the election is binding on all properties the taxpayer owns and for all later years. A taxpayer that fails to deduct IDCs on that return is deemed to have elected to recover IDCs through depletion or depreciation, as the case may be [Reg. § 1.612-4(d), § 1.612-4(e)].

*Nonproductive Well "Dry Hole" Election.* If a taxpayer has elected to capitalize IDCs, he or she may elect to deduct as an ordinary loss the IDCs incurred in drilling a nonproductive well. The taxpayer must indicate and clearly state the election on his or her tax return for the year the well is completed. Once made, the election is binding for all later years [Reg. § 1.612-4(b)(4)].

*Recapture of IDC Deductions.* A taxpayer that recognizes gain on the disposition (as defined in Reg. § 1.1254-1(b)(3)) of an oil, gas, or geothermal property must treat that gain as ordinary income to the extent of the lesser of the following amounts [§ 1254; Reg. § 1.1254-1(a)]:

- the sum of (i) the IDC deductions that would otherwise have been included in the property's basis, and (ii) depletion deductions that reduced the property's basis; or
- the amount, if any, by which the amount realized on the sale, exchange, or involuntary conversion (or the fair market value of the property on any other disposition) exceeds the property's adjusted basis.

The following dispositions of natural resource property are not subject to IDC recapture [Reg. § 1.1254-2]:

- gifts [§ 1015(a)] (see III.A.3.a(2));
- transfers between spouses where no gain is recognized [§ 1041] (see III.E.5.);
- inheritances [§ 1014(a)] (see III.A.3.a(3));

- tax-deferred transfers between corporations and shareholders [§ 332, § 351, § 361] (see XIII.E.3., XIII.B.1., and XIII.E.1.);
- tax-deferred transfers between partners and partnerships [§ 721, § 731] (see XIV.C.1.a. and XIV.F.1.);
- like-kind exchanges [§ 1031] (see III.E.1.); and
- involuntary conversions [§ 1033] (see III.E.2.).

*Alternative Minimum Tax Treatment.* A portion of the IDCs that a taxpayer expenses is a tax preference item subject to the alternative minimum tax. This portion is the amount, if any, by which the excess intangible drilling costs (as defined in § 57(a)(2)(B)) arising in the tax year exceed 65% of the taxpayer's net income from such properties (as defined in § 57(a)(2)(C)) for the tax year. The tax preference IDC tests are applied separately to oil and geothermal properties (as one group) and to oil and gas properties (as a second group). The preference only applies in full to integrated oil companies. For independent producers, it applies only to the extent the preference exceeds 40% of the alternative minimum taxable income for the tax year [§ 57(a)(2)].

A taxpayer can elect to avoid the AMT on the IDCs by electing to deduct the IDCs ratably over 60 months, beginning with the month the IDCs are paid or incurred. Any portion of an IDC expense subject to this election is not treated as an item of tax preference [§ 59(e)].

## VI.D. Mineral Exploration and Development Costs

[601 T.M., III., 603 T.M., V.; TPS ¶2630.]

The cost of determining the existence, location, extent, or quality of any mineral deposit (other than oil and gas) typically is a capital expenditure that may be recovered through depletion (see VI.A.). Similarly, mining development expenditures to provide openings for transporting minerals are also generally capital expenditures. However, in certain circumstances, a taxpayer may elect to deduct certain exploration and development costs [§ 616, § 617].

### VI.D.1. Exploration Expenditures

[601 T.M., III., 603 T.M., V.A.; TPS ¶2630.01., ¶2630.02., ¶2630.03.]

Exploration expenditures are amounts paid or incurred for the purpose of ascertaining the existence, location, extent, or qualify of mineral deposits (other than oil or gas), and they are paid or incurred *before* the development stage of the mining operation. The development stage of the mine begins when, based on all the facts and circumstances, deposits of ore or other mineral are shown to exist in sufficient quantity and quality to reasonably justify commercial exploitation by the taxpayer [§ 617(a); Reg. § 1.617-1(a)].

### VI.D.1.a. Election to Deduct Exploration Expenditures

[601 T.M., III.E.3., 603 T.M., V.A.1.; TPS ¶2630.02.]

A taxpayer may elect to deduct domestic exploration expenditures paid or incurred during the tax year. The expenditures must be subjectively intended to result in the discovery of depletable minerals. They cannot be incurred in the search for oil and gas, even if it results in the discovery of minerals. Additionally the election is not available for exploration expenditures relating to any mineral for which percentage depletion (see VI.A.3.b.) is not allowed, though exploration expenditures for qualifying minerals are deductible even if only non-qualifying minerals are located [§ 617(a); Reg. § 1.617-1(b)(5)].

Subject to certain exceptions, the election generally is inapplicable to the following exploration expenditures [§ 617(a)(1); Reg. § 1.617-1(b)]:

- expenditures that would otherwise be allowable as deductions for the tax year;
- expenditures for depreciable property;
- expenditures attributable to the fractional share of a working or operating interest that the taxpayer does not own;
- expenditures reflected in the amount the taxpayer paid or incurred to acquire the mineral property;
- expenditures made in connection with nondepletable mineral property; and
- expenditures to develop new mining techniques (see IV.F.2.).

***Making the Election.*** A taxpayer makes the election to deduct exploration costs by taking the deduction on his or her timely filed tax return for the tax year in which the exploration expenditures were paid or incurred. The return must adequately describe and identify each property or mine, and it must clearly state how much is being deducted for each. Once made, the election applies to all later tax years. It may not be revoked without IRS consent [§ 617(a)(2)(B); Reg. § 1.617-1(c)].

### VI.D.1.b. Recapture of Exploration Expenditure Deductions

[601 T.M., III.E.7., III.E.8., VII.A., 603 T.M., V.A.2., V.A.3.; TPS ¶2630.03., .08.D.]

Exploration expenditures the taxpayer elected to deduct are recaptured as ordinary income on the occurrence of any of the following three events [§ 617(b), § 617(c), § 617(d)]:

1. when a mine for which exploration deductions have been claimed reaches the producing stage (as defined in Reg. § 1.616-2(b));
2. on receipt or accrual of a bonus or royalty for the property for which exploration deductions were claimed; or
3. upon disposition of a mining property (or portion thereof) for which exploration deductions have been claimed.

***Recapture Upon a Mine Reaching the Producing Stage.*** Where recapture is the result of a mine reaching the producing stage, the recapture may be accomplished in one of two ways, at the taxpayer's election:

1. through the disallowance of depletion deductions for the mineral properties until the disallowed depletion equals the amount of previously deducted exploration expenditures attributable to the mining operation; or
2. by electing to include in nondepletable gross income an amount equal to the previously deducted exploration expenditures attributable to the mining operation as of the date the mine reaches the producing stage.

---

**EXAMPLE:** In Year 1, Betty currently deducts $100,000 of exploration expenditures. In Year 2, the property enters the producing stage and the allowable deduction for depletion for that year would be $125,000. If Betty does not make an election to include $100,000 of exploration expenditures in income for Year 2, then she is restricted to a deduction of only $25,000 ($125,000 depletion − $100,000 previously deducted exploration expenditures) for depletion.

---

The election for any tax year may be made or changed until the time for filing the taxpayer's tax return (including extensions). It is an annual election, but, if made, the election applies to all the mines that reach the producing stage in that particular year and as to which the taxpayer has claimed current exploration deductions [Reg. § 1.617-3(a)(2)].

*Recapture Upon the Receipt or Accrual of a Bonus or Royalty.* Where recapture results from the receipt or accrual of a bonus or royalty from mine property before it reaches the producing stage, a taxpayer does not claim any depletion deduction for the tax year the bonus or royalty is received, or any later years, until the depletion the taxpayer would have deducted equals the exploration costs the taxpayer deducted [§ 617(c); Reg. § 1.617-3(a)(1)(ii)].

*Recapture Upon the Disposition of Property.* If a taxpayer realizes gain on the disposition of a property for which exploration expenditures were previously deducted, some or all of the gain must be recharacterized as ordinary income [§ 617(d), § 1254(a)]. The recapture of exploration expenditures is reported on Form 4797, *Sales of Business Property.*

### VI.D.2. Development Expenditures

[601 T.M., IV., 603 T.M., V.B.; TPS ¶2630.04., .05., .06., .07.]

Development is generally the process of providing openings for transporting minerals and obtaining further and more detailed information on the character and size of an ore body. The development stage of the mine begins when, based on all the facts and circumstances, deposits of ore or other mineral are shown to exist in sufficient quantity and quality to reasonably justify commercial exploitation by the taxpayer. The development stage ends when commercial production begins. The production stage begins when the major portion of the mineral production from the mine or natural deposit is obtained from workings other than those opened for the purpose of development, or when the principal activity of the mine or natural deposit is the production of developed ores or mineral, rather than the development of additional ores or mineral for mining [§ 616; Reg. § 1.616-1(a), § 1.616-2(b)].

### VI.D.2.a. Deduction of Development Expenditures

[601 T.M., IV.C.1., 603 T.M., V.B.; TPS ¶2630.05.]

A taxpayer may deduct costs paid or incurred during the tax year for the development of a domestic mine or other natural deposit (other than an oil or gas well), provided the expenditures are paid or incurred after the discovery of ores or minerals in commercially marketable quantities. These costs include depreciation on improvements used in the development of ores or minerals and costs incurred by a contractor for the taxpayer. They do not include the costs for the acquisition or improvement of depreciable property [§ 616; Reg. § 1.616-1].

Subject to certain exceptions, no deduction for development costs are available for the following development expenditures [Reg. § 1.616-1(b)]:

- expenditures that would otherwise be allowable as deductions for the tax year;
- expenditures for depreciable property;
- expenditures attributable to the fractional share of a working or operating interest that the taxpayer does not own; and
- expenditures reflected in the amount the taxpayer paid or incurred to acquire the mineral property.

If there are several mines or natural deposits within an aggregated property, the taxpayer may deduct the development expenditures for one mine or deposit and may defer the development expenditures made (see VI.D.2.b.) for another mine or deposit. A similar rule applies where there is more than one mine for a single underlying deposit. A taxpayer must treat all development expenditures for each mine or natural deposit consistently within a tax year [Reg. § 1.616-1(c)].

### VI.D.2.b. Election to Defer Development Expenditures

[601 T.M., IV.C.2., 603 T.M., V.B.; TPS ¶2630.06.]

Rather than deducting development costs in the year paid or incurred, taxpayers may elect to defer development costs for each individual mine or deposit. Deferred expenses are deducted ratably as the units of produced ores or minerals benefited by the expenses are sold. If the election is made during the development stage, the amount to which the election applies is the excess of the costs over the net proceeds from sales of minerals. If the election is made during the producing stage, the entire amount of the development costs is subject to the election. Deferred development expenditures are considered in computing the adjusted basis of the mine or deposit, except when computing the adjusted basis of the mine or deposit for purposes of cost depletion [§ 616(b), § 616(c); Reg. § 1.616-2].

*Amount of the Deduction.* The deduction for a tax year is calculated in a similar manner to the cost depletion deduction (see VI.A.3.a.). For any given tax year, the amount of the deduction is determined by multiplying the deferred expenses not previously deducted by a fraction, the numerator of which is the number of benefited units sold during the year, and the denominator of which is the sum of the following: (i) the number of benefited units sold during the year, (ii) the number of benefited units recovered during the year but unsold at the end of the year, and (iii) the number of benefited units that have not been recovered as of the end of the year [Reg. § 1.616-2(f)].

---

**EXAMPLE:** In Year 1, Isla paid $10,000 in development expenditures for a silver mine and was paid $1,000 from sales of silver in the same year. The mine's estimated silver reserve at the end of the exploratory period in the prior year was 100,000 pounds. Isla elected to defer the $9,000 excess of costs over its sales receipts. In Year 2, the silver mine entered the production stage and produced 10,000 pounds of silver, but Isla sold none of the output. She can deduct none of the deferred expenses in Year 2 because no silver was sold. If, in Year 3, Isla extracts 10,000 more pounds of silver and sells the 20,000 pounds, she can deduct $1,800 ($9,000 deferred expense × (20,000 pounds sold during the year ÷ (20,000 pounds of benefited units sold + 80,000 pounds of benefited units not yet recovered)).

---

*Making the Election.* The election to defer exploration expenditures is made year-by-year for each mine or natural deposit by a clear indication on the taxpayer's return or by a statement filed with the IRS office where the taxpayer files its return. The election must be made by the due date for the taxpayer's return (including extensions) for the tax year for which the election applies. Once made, the election is binding for expenditures for that tax year, and it may not be revoked for any reason [Reg. § 1.616-2(e)]. For partnerships, the election is made by the partnership, not the partner [§ 703(b)].

### VI.D.2.c. Recapture of Development Expenditure Deductions

[601 T.M., VII.A.; TPS ¶2630.07., .08.D.]

If a taxpayer realizes gain on the disposition of a property for which development expenditures were previously deducted, some or all of the gain must be recharacterized as ordinary income [§ 1254(a)]. The recapture of development expenditures is reported on Form 4797, *Sales of Business Property.*

### VI.D.3. Limitations on Both Exploration and Development Expenditures

[601 T.M., III.D.2.; TPS ¶2630.08.]

***Cut-Back of Deduction for Corporate Taxpayers.*** A corporation (other than an S corporation) may deduct only 70% of its exploration or development costs. It must capitalize the remaining 30% and amortize them over 60 months, beginning with the month the exploration costs are paid or incurred. A corporation also may elect to amortize mining exploration or development costs over 10 years.

The capitalized portion of a corporation's domestic exploration or development costs cannot be added to the property's basis to figure cost depletion. However, the amount amortized is treated as additional depreciation, and it is subject to recapture as ordinary income on a disposition of the property (see III.D.3.) [§ 291(b)].

***Foreign Exploration and Development Expenditures.*** If a taxpayer pays or incurs exploration or development costs for a mine or natural deposit located outside the United States, then the taxpayer may not deduct the costs in the current year. Rather, the taxpayer may elect to include the costs (other than costs for an oil, gas, or geothermal well) in the adjusted basis of the mineral property to figure cost depletion (see VI.A.3.a.). If this election is not made, the taxpayer must deduct the costs over the 10-year period beginning with the tax year in which he or she pays or incurs them [§ 616(d), § 617(h)].

### VI.D.4. Alternative Minimum Tax Treatment of Exploration and Development Costs

[601 T.M., III.E.10.b.; TPS ¶2630.08.B.]

Both exploration and development costs are taken into account in computing the alternative minimum tax. In figuring alternative minimum taxable income, these costs must be capitalized and amortized ratably over a 10-year period, beginning with the tax year in which the expenditures are made. Alternatively, taxpayers may make a 10-year write-off election under § 59(e) that conforms the regular tax deduction for exploration and development expenditures with the AMT. If elected, the deducted amounts are not counted for purposes of alternative minimum taxable income [§ 56(a)(2)(A), § 59(e)].

## VI.E. Miscellaneous Natural Resource Issues

### VI.E.1. Disposal of Coal or Domestic Iron Ore with a Retained Economic Interest

[601 T.M., VII.C.; TPS ¶2640.01.]

If a taxpayer disposes of coal (including lignite) or domestic iron ore, the disposition is treated as a disposition of a § 1231 asset (i.e., capital gains treatment for gains and ordinary loss treatment for losses) if the following conditions are satisfied [§ 631(c); Reg. § 1.631-3]:

- the taxpayer held the coal or domestic iron ore for more than one year before disposal;
- the disposing taxpayer is the owner of the coal or iron ore; and
- the disposal is under any form of contract by virtue of which the owner retains an economic interest in the coal or iron ore in place.

Section 1231 transactions are discussed in III.C.1.

### VI.E.2. Tertiary Injectant Expenses

[512 T.M., II.G., 605 T.M., III.H.1.; TPS ¶2640.04.]

Taxpayers may deduct the cost of qualified tertiary injectants. The deduction is allowed for the later of either (i) the tax year in which the injectant is injected, or (ii) the tax year in which the expenses are paid or incurred. No deduction is allowed for expenditures for which the taxpayer has made an election under § 263(c) to deduct intangible drilling and development costs (see VI.C.), or for which a deduction is otherwise allowed or allowable [§ 193].

A qualified tertiary injectant expense is any cost, whether or not capital in nature, that is paid or incurred for any tertiary injectant (other than certain hydrocarbons) used as part of a tertiary recovery method (as defined in § 193(b)(3)). Qualified tertiary injectant expenses can include the cost of production or acquisition of a tertiary injectant, as well as certain operating expenses related to the tertiary injectant's use [Rev. Rul. 2003-82, 2003-2 C.B. 125]. Drilling costs associated with the retrieval of tertiary injectants, however, generally are not allowable under § 193, but may be deductible as a development expenditure (see VI.D.2.).

### VI.E.3. Miscellaneous Natural Resource Deductions

[514 T.M., III.D., 603 T.M., IV.C.4.k., XIV.; TPS ¶2640.06.]

***Mine Equipment Expenditures Under Receding Face Doctrine.*** Under the receding face doctrine, certain otherwise-capital expenditures incurred in the mining business are currently deductible. Qualifying expenditures are those for additional equipment (including installation and housing), and the replacement of such equipment, needed to maintain production solely because of the recession of the working faces of the mine, provided the expenditures [Reg. § 1.612-2(a)]:

- do not increase the value of the mine;
- do not decrease the cost of production of mineral units; and
- do not restore property for which an allowance (e.g., depreciation) is or has been made.

***Mine Reclamation and Closing Costs.*** Accrual method taxpayers can elect to deduct currently on an annual basis additions to reserve accounts to cover the anticipated costs of certain mine reclamation and closure activity for surface mines and solid waste disposal sites during the tax years in which the taxpayer engages in the mining or waste disposal activity [§ 468].

***Black Lung Benefit Trust Contributions.*** Taxpayers may deduct a limited amount of contributions to black lung benefit trusts [§ 192(a)] (see IV.A.15.b.).

### VI.E.4. Delay Rentals, Royalties, and Bonuses

[603 T.M., VIII.; TPS ¶¶2630.01., 2640.08.]

***Delay Rentals.*** Many leases require that the lessee or operator mine remove the mineral within a certain time period. Delay rentals are amounts paid to a lessor to defer the commencement of mining operations. For the lessor, delay rental payments are taxed like rent, and are ordinary income and not subject to depletion. For the lessee, the uniform capitalization rules (see XI.E.) require that all pre-production, indirect costs be capitalized, rather than deducted. Proposed regulations, however, would provide that the lessee may elect to deduct or capitalize delay rental payments, except to the extent that the uniform capitalization rules apply [Reg. § 1.263A-2(a)(3)(ii); Prop. Reg. § 1.612-3(c)(2)].

*Royalties.* Advance royalties are royalties paid before extraction or drilling begins. They are recoupable out of later production via a credit against actual production royalty obligations due under the agreement as a result of the previously paid advance royalties. For the lessor, the advance royalties are ordinary income subject to depletion as received. The lessee generally may not deduct an advance royalty until the year the mineral or hydrocarbon product to which it relates is sold [Reg. § 1.612-3(b)].

Advance royalties paid or accrued in connection with mineral property as a result of a qualifying minimum royalty provision are deductible when paid or accrued, depending on the taxpayer's accounting method, at the taxpayer's election. A qualifying minimum royalty provision is a provision requiring a "substantially uniform amount of royalties be paid at least annually either over the life of the lease or for a period of at least 20 years, in the absence of mineral production requiring payment of aggregate royalties in a greater amount." The election is made by deducting the advance royalties in the year paid or accrued. Failure to deduct them is treated as an election to deduct royalties as the minerals are sold [Reg. § 1.612-3(b)(3); Rev. Rul. 77-489, 1977-2 C.B. 177].

*Bonuses.* A bonus is consideration unrelated to, and not recoupable from, production that is paid to acquire a lease or interest in a natural resource property. Thus, unlike a royalty payment, a bonus does not afford the payor a credit against future royalty payments once the resource is removed.

The payor must treat the bonus as a capital cost of the lease, which must be recovered through depletion. It must be restored to income and basis in the mineral property if the lessor abandons the lease before production. The lessor generally must treat the bonus payment as ordinary income. Bonuses in connection with coal or domestic iron ore may be afforded sale or exchange treatment in certain circumstances (see VI.E.1.). If the mineral or oil or gas is subject to depletion, the lessor is entitled to depletion on the bonus payment. The depletion deduction is prorated between it and the expected royalties on the basis of expected total production. Depletion on the bonus and on the royalties is deducted from the lessor's basis for depletion. If the economic interest for which a bonus was received expires, terminates, or is abandoned before there has been any income from the extraction of the mineral, the lessor must adjust his or her capital account by restoring the depletion deduction taken on the bonus, and a corresponding amount must be reported as income in the year of expiration, termination, or abandonment [Reg. § 1.612-3(a)].

### VI.E.5. Taxation of Production Payments

[601 T.M., XI.F.; TPS ¶2640.10.]

A mineral production payment is essentially a royalty limited in time or amount. It is a right to a specified share of the production from minerals in place, or the proceeds from such production. It must have an expected life at the time of its creation of a shorter duration than the economic life of the mineral property burdened by the production payment.

Generally, a production payment carved out of mineral property is treated as a mortgage loan on the property and does not qualify as an economic interest. Thus, the transferor reports the production used to pay the debt and claims associated depletion. A production payment retained on the sale of a mineral property is treated as if it was a purchase money mortgage and is also not an economic interest. This means that the seller of the underlying property (i) includes the production payment in determining the amount realized on the sale, (ii) may not deplete the production income received as the payment is made, and (iii) is obligated to report portions of the amounts received as interest. The buyer (i) includes the production payment in the basis of the property, (ii) reports the production income applied to pay off the production payment, and (iii) claims cost or percentage depletion on that production along with deductions for the interest portion of the amounts paid to the seller [§ 636; Reg. § 1.636-1(a)(1)].

### VI.E.6. Costs to Comply with EPA Sulfur Regulations

[512 T.M., II.H.; TPS ¶2640.11.]

If a crude oil refiner is a small business refiner, the taxpayer may elect to deduct a portion of its qualified capital costs paid or incurred during the tax year to comply with Environmental Protection Agency regulations [§ 179B] (see IV.F.5.j.).

### VI.E.7. Election to Expense Portion of Qualified Refinery Property [Expired]

[512 T.M., III.H.; TPS ¶2640.12.]

Before 2014, a taxpayer could elect to deduct 50% of the cost of qualified refinery property (as defined in § 179C(c) and § 179C(d)) placed in service during the tax year. The provision excludes property placed in service after 2013 [§ 179C(a), § 179C(c)(1)(B)].

### VI.E.8. Geological and Geophysical Expenditures

[605 T.M., III.B.3.; TPS ¶¶2620.02.B., 2640.06.C.]

Geological or geophysical expenses paid or incurred in connection with the domestic exploration for, or development of, oil and gas in the United States may be amortized over a 24-month period using the half-year convention (see V.A.4.c.(1)). If property to which these expenditures relate is retired or abandoned during the 24-month period, no deduction is permitted on account of the retirement or abandonment. The amortization deduction, though, would continue.

For major integrated oil companies (as defined in § 167(h)(5)(B)), the optional amortization period is extended to seven years [§ 167(h)].

### VI.E.9. Natural Resource Credits

[506 T.M., 512 T.M., 603 T.M., 605 T.M.; TPS ¶¶2640., 3140., 3170.]

Several credits related to natural resources may be available, including the following:

- the enhanced oil recovery credit (see IX.A.10.);
- the credit for producing fuel from nonconventional sources (see IX.A.26.);
- the mine rescue team training credit (see IX.A.31.);
- the renewable electricity production credit, including the refined coal production credit and the Indian coal production credit (see IX.A.12.);
- the low sulfur diesel fuel production credit (see IX.A.22.);
- the marginal oil and gas well production credit (see IX.A.23.);
- the carbon dioxide sequestration credit (see IX.A.32.);

- the qualifying advanced coal project credit (see IX.A.5.c.);
- the qualifying gasification project credit (see IX.A.5.d.);
- the alcohol fuels credit (see IX.A.7.);
- the biodiesel and renewable diesel fuels credit (see IX.A.21.); and
- the § 54B qualified forestry conservation bond credit (see IX.F.5.).

# CHAPTER VII. NONBUSINESS DEDUCTIONS

>>>>>>>>>>>>>>>>>>>>>>>>>>>>>>

## VII.A. Introduction to Nonbusiness Deductions

Deductions reduce the amount of a taxpayer's income subject to income tax. As a fundamental rule, taxpayers are only allowed to take those deductions that are specifically authorized by Congress in the Internal Revenue Code. Because deductions are a matter of legislative grace, taxpayers' claims for deductions may be closely scrutinized by the IRS to ensure that they clearly satisfy the letter of the law. Nonbusiness deductions that may be claimed by an individual taxpayer are discussed in this chapter. Deductions that may be claimed by a business, including a corporation, a partnership, or a sole proprietorship operated by an individual taxpayer, are discussed in Chapter IV.

The deductions that may be subtracted by an individual taxpayer in determining taxable income fall into several broad categories. First, an individual taxpayer may subtract specified types of statutory deductions from gross income in determining adjusted gross income (AGI) [§ 62]. These deductions used in determining AGI are generally referred to as "above-the-line deductions" (see VII.B.).

Second, an individual taxpayer may choose to subtract either one of the following from his or her AGI: (i) the remaining statutory deductions he is eligible to claim, or (ii) a standard deduction [§ 63]. The taxpayer's remaining statutory deductions are referred to as "below-the-line deductions" or, more commonly, "itemized deductions" (see VII.C.). The standard deduction is an annual inflation-adjusted amount that is based on the taxpayer's filing status. For a discussion of the standard deduction and the choice between the standard deduction and itemized deductions, see XII.E.

Finally, a taxpayer may subtract certain personal exemptions to determine the amount of his or her taxable income. Although personal exemptions are not generally referred to as deductions, they have the same effect as deductions because they reduce the amount of an individual taxpayer's income that is subject to income tax. For a discussion of personal exemptions, see XII.D.

Above-the-line deductions are reported directly on page one of an individual taxpayer's Form 1040, *U.S. Individual Income Tax Return*. Itemized deductions are reported on Schedule A and the total is carried to page two of Form 1040. Above-the-line deductions are generally more beneficial to a taxpayer than itemized deductions. Above-the-line deductions are deductible even if a taxpayer chooses to take the standard deduction instead of itemizing deductions. In addition, above-the-line deductions are not subject to the AGI limitations that apply to many itemized deductions. In fact, above-the-line deductions reduce the AGI limitations that may apply to a taxpayer's itemized deductions by reducing the amount of the taxpayer's AGI.

## VII.B. Above-the-Line Deductions

### VII.B.1. Classroom Expenses of Teachers [Expired]

[503 T.M., II.B.4.b(5); TPS ¶2130.03.B.6.]

Before 2014, certain teachers and educators could take an above-the-line deduction for up to $250 of expenses paid in connection with books, supplies, computer equipment, other equipment, and supplementary materials used in the classroom [§ 62(a)(2)(D)]. Taxpayers eligible for this deduction included individuals who were teachers, instructors, counselors, principals, or aides in a school providing elementary or secondary education (kindergarten through grade 12) and who worked at such a school for at least 900 hours during a school year [§ 62(d)(1)]. Above-the-line treatment (although not the ability to deduct the expenses as employee business expenses) expired December 31, 2013.

### VII.B.2. Business Expenses of Performing Artists

[503 T.M., II.B.4.b(3); TPS ¶2130.03.B.1.]

A qualified performing artist can take an above-the-line deduction for business expenses paid in connection with the performance of services in the performing arts as an employee [§ 62(a)(2)(B)]. The deduction is computed and reported on Form 2106, *Employee Business Expenses*, or Form 2106-EZ, *Unreimbursed Employee Business Expenses*. A qualified performing artist is an individual taxpayer who meets the following requirements for any tax year [§ 62(b)]:

1. the taxpayer performed services in the performing arts as an employee for at least two employers from whom he earned at least $200 each during the year;
2. the total amount of deductible business expenses paid by the taxpayer in connection with such services is more than 10% of the gross income he earned from such services; and
3. the taxpayer's adjusted gross income for the year (determined without regard to the deductible business expenses) does not exceed $16,000.

### VII.B.3. Business Expenses of Fee-Basis Government Officials

[503 T.M., II.B.4.b(4); TPS ¶2130.03.B.5.]

A state or local government official who is compensated in whole or in part on a fee basis can take an above-the-line deduction for business expenses paid in performing his or her duties as an employee [§ 62(a)(2)(C)]. The deduction is computed and reported on Form 2106, *Employee Business Expenses*, or Form 2106-EZ, *Unreimbursed Employee Business Expenses*.

### VII.B.4. Certain Business Expenses of Military Reservists

[503 T.M., II.B.4.b(6); TPS ¶2130.03.B.7.]

A member of the U.S. Armed Forces reserve (including the National Guard) can take an above-the-line deduction for business expenses paid in connection with the performance of his or her reserve duty for any period during which the taxpayer is more than 100 miles away from home [§ 62(a)(2)(E)]. Thus, a military reservist generally can deduct travel expenses such as transportation, meals, and lodging paid while traveling away from home for reserve duty; however, the deductible amount cannot exceed the general federal government per diem rate applicable to the relevant locality. The deduction is computed and reported on Form 2106, *Employee Business Expenses*, or Form 2106-EZ, *Unreimbursed Employee Business Expenses*.

### VII.B.5. Health Savings Account Contributions

[503 T.M., IV.H.; TPS ¶2010.01.A.2.]

A taxpayer generally can take an above-the-line deduction for contributions made to a health savings account (HSA) [§ 62(a)(19), § 223]. An HSA is an account set up exclusively for paying the qualified medical expenses of the taxpayer who established the HSA, or those of his spouse and dependents. The deduction for HSA contributions is computed and reported on Form 8889, *Health Savings Accounts (HSAs)*. For a detailed discussion of Health Savings Accounts, see XVII.C.1.e.

### VII.B.6. Moving Expenses

[503 T.M., IV.D.; TPS ¶2870.]

A taxpayer generally can take an above-the-line deduction for the expenses of moving from one home to another in connection with his or her job or business if the taxpayer meets both a distance requirement and a time requirement [§ 62(a)(15), § 217]. The deduction for moving expenses is computed and reported on Form 3903, *Moving Expenses*.

### VII.B.6.a. Deductible Moving Expenses

[503 T.M., IV.D.2.; TPS ¶2870.03.]

The following two types of moving expenses are deductible by a taxpayer who otherwise meets the requirements to deduct moving expenses [§ 217(b)]:

1. the reasonable expenses of moving household goods and personal effects from the old home to the new home; and

2. the reasonable expenses of traveling from the old home to the new home (including lodging costs, but not meals or sightseeing costs).

A taxpayer can deduct expenses attributable to a member of the taxpayer's household (e.g., spouse, children) if the taxpayer's old home and new home are both principal places of residence for that individual [Reg. § 1.217-2(b)(10)].

In the case of a foreign move, deductible moving expenses also include [§ 217(h)]:

1. the reasonable expenses of moving household goods and personal effects to and from storage; and

2. the reasonable expenses of storing household goods and personal effects during the period in which the new workplace continues to be the taxpayer's principal place of work.

### VII.B.6.b. Distance Requirement for Moving Expense Deduction

[503 T.M., IV.D.4.b.; TPS ¶2870.05.]

To qualify for the moving expense deduction, the distance between the taxpayer's new workplace and old home must be at least 50 miles more than the distance between the old workplace and the old home. If the taxpayer had no old workplace, then the new workplace must be at least 50 miles from his or her old home. In determining distance, a taxpayer must use the shortest of the more commonly traveled routes between the workplace and home [§ 217(a), § 217(c)(1)].

**EXAMPLE:** Beth works five miles away from her home. Beth accepts a new job that is 57 miles away from her home and she decides to move to a new home in the general area of her new job. Beth can take a deduction for the moving expenses paid in moving from her old home to her new home because the distance between her new workplace and her old home is 52 miles (57 – 5) more than the distance between her old workplace and her old home.

### VII.B.6.c. Time Requirement for Moving Expense Deduction
[503 T.M., IV.D.4.c.; TPS ¶2870.06.]

To qualify for the moving expense deduction, the taxpayer must meet one of the following two time requirements [§ 217(c)(2)]:

1. If the taxpayer is an employee, the taxpayer must work full time in the general area of his or her new workplace for at least 39 weeks during the 12 months immediately after the move.

2. If the taxpayer is self-employed, the taxpayer must work full time in the general area of his or her new workplace for at least 39 weeks during the first 12 months and for a total of 78 weeks during the first 24 months immediately after the move.

The time requirements do not apply if the taxpayer cannot satisfy them because one of the following applies: (i) the taxpayer dies, (ii) the taxpayer's job ends because he or she becomes disabled, (iii) the taxpayer is transferred for his or her employer's benefit, or (iv) the taxpayer is laid off or discharged for a reason other than willful misconduct [§ 217(d)(1)].

If a taxpayer has not met the time requirements before the due date (including extensions) for his or her tax return for the tax year in which the moving expenses are paid but it is possible that he or she may still meet those requirements, then he or she may elect to deduct the moving expenses for that year. However, if, in a later tax year, it becomes certain that the taxpayer will not meet the time requirements, then the taxpayer must include the moving expenses in gross income for that tax year [§ 217(d)(2), § 217(d)(3)].

### VII.B.6.d. Special Moving Expense Rules for Members of the Military
[503 T.M., IV.D.5.; TPS ¶2870.08.]

If an active duty member of the U.S. Armed Forces moves as a result of a permanent change of station, the distance and time requirements do not apply. If the taxpayer's spouse and/or dependents are moved to or from different locations than the taxpayer, those moves can be treated as part of the taxpayer's move [§ 217(g)].

### VII.B.6.e. Special Moving Expense Rules for Retirees or Survivors Working in Foreign Countries
[503 T.M., IV.D.7.; TPS ¶2870.09.D.]

An individual whose home and principal place of work are both outside the United States can deduct the expenses of moving to a new home in the United States if he or she permanently retires. The time requirements (see VII.B.6.c.) do not apply [§ 217(i)(1), § 217(i)(2)].

The spouse or dependent of an individual whose principal place of work was outside the United States at the time of his or her death can deduct the expenses of moving to a new home in the United States if (i) a spouse or dependent lived with the decedent outside the United States at the time of the decedent's death, and (ii) the move begins within six months of the date of the decedent's death. The time requirements (see VII.B.6.) do not apply [§ 217(i)(1), § 217(i)(3)].

### VII.B.7. Self-Employed Taxpayer's Payments of Self-Employment Tax

[525 T.M., II.J.; TPS ¶2340.02.I.]

A self-employed taxpayer is generally required to pay tax on his or her net earnings from self-employment; however, the taxpayer can take an above-the-line deduction for one-half of the self-employment tax paid [§ 164(f)]. The self-employment tax and the deduction for self-employment tax are both computed on Schedule SE of Form 1040. For a detailed discussion of the self-employment tax, see X.A.7.

### VII.B.8. Self-Employed Taxpayer's Contributions to SEPs, SIMPLEs, and Other Qualified Plans

[503 T.M., II.B.4.b(10); TPS ¶2010.01.A.2.]

A self-employed taxpayer can take an above-the-line deduction for contributions made to a pension, profit-sharing, annuity, or other qualified retirement plan [§ 62(a)(6)]. Qualified retirement plans include plans often used by small employers, such as simplified employee pensions (SEPs) (see XVII.A.) and savings incentive match plans for employees (SIMPLEs) (see XVII.A.9.).

### VII.B.9. Self-Employed Taxpayer's Payments for Health Insurance

[505 T.M., IV.E.4.; TPS ¶2170.03.B.1.]

A self-employed taxpayer generally can take an above-the-line deduction for amounts paid for health insurance coverage for the taxpayer, his or her spouse, and dependents (and children under the age of 27 at the end of the tax year). However, the amount of the deduction is limited to the taxpayer's net earnings from self-employment for the business under which the health insurance plan is established [§ 162(l)(1), § 162(l)(2)(A)].

### VII.B.9.a. Taxpayers Eligible for Self-Employed Health Insurance Deduction

[505 T.M., IV.E.4.; TPS ¶2170.03.B.1.]

The deduction is available to a self-employed taxpayer for amounts paid to a health insurance plan established under a business in which his or her services are a material income-producing factor. A general partner and a limited partner receiving guaranteed payments are both treated as self-employed taxpayers for this purpose. A more-than-2% shareholder is treated as a self-employed taxpayer if he received wages from the S corporation [§ 162(l)(5)].

In the case of a self-employed taxpayer filing Schedule C or C-EZ, or Schedule F, the insurance policy can be in the taxpayer's name or in the name of the taxpayer's business. In the case of a partner, the policy can be in the taxpayer's name or in the name of the partnership; however, if in the policy is in the taxpayer's name and the taxpayer pays the premiums, the partnership must reimburse the taxpayer and report the premium amounts as guaranteed payments on Schedule K-1. In the case of a more-than-2% S corporation shareholder, the policy can be in the taxpayer's name or the name of the corporation; however, if in the policy is in the taxpayer's name and the taxpayer pays the premiums the corporation must reimburse the taxpayer and report the premium amounts as wages on Form W-2.

The deduction is not available if the individual is eligible to participate in any subsidized health plan maintained by the taxpayer's employer or an employer of the individual's spouse, dependent, or child under age 27 at the end of the tax year. This rule applies whether or not the taxpayer actually participates in such a subsidized health plan [§ 162(l)(2)(B)].

A self-employed taxpayer cannot take the deduction for any amounts paid from retirement plan distributions that were nontaxable because he is a retired public safety officer.

### VII.B.9.b. Insurance Eligible for Self-Employed Health Insurance Deduction

[505 T.M., IV.E.4.; TPS ¶2170.03.B.1.]

The deduction can be taken for amounts paid by a self-employed taxpayer for medical, dental, and qualified long-term care insurance coverage. It can also be taken for Medicare premiums that a self-employed taxpayer voluntarily pays to obtain insurance in his or her name that is similar to qualifying private health insurance.

### VII.B.9.c. Computing the Self-Employed Health Insurance Deduction

[505 T.M., IV.E.4.; TPS ¶2170.03.B.1.]

Generally, a self-employed taxpayer can use the Self-Employed Health Insurance Deduction Worksheet (Source: 2014 Form 1040 Draft Instructions) to determine the amount of the deduction. However, a taxpayer may not use that Worksheet if any of the following apply:

- the taxpayer had more than one source of income subject to self-employment tax;
- the taxpayer files Form 2555, *Foreign Earned Income*, or Form 2555-EZ, *Foreign Earned Income Exclusion*; or
- the taxpayer uses amounts paid for qualified long-term care insurance in computing the deduction.

---

**Self-Employed Health Insurance Deduction Worksheet—Line 29**　　　*Keep for Your Records*

**Before you begin:** ✓ Be sure you have read the **Exception** in the instructions for this line to see if you can use this worksheet instead of Pub. 535 to figure your deduction.

1. Enter the total amount paid in 2014 for health insurance coverage established under your business (or the S corporation in which you were a more-than-2% shareholder) for 2014 for you, your spouse, and your dependents. Your insurance can also cover your child who was under age 27 at the end of 2014, even if the child was not your dependent. But do not include amounts for any month you were eligible to participate in an employer-sponsored health plan or amounts paid from retirement plan distributions that were nontaxable because you are a retired public safety officer .................. **1.** _____

2. Enter your net profit* and any other earned income** from the business under which the insurance plan is established, minus any deductions on Form 1040, lines 27 and 28. Do not include Conservation Reserve Program payments exempt from self-employment tax ................... **2.** _____

3. **Self-employed health insurance deduction.** Enter the **smaller** of line 1 or line 2 here and on Form 1040, line 29. **Do not** include this amount in figuring any medical expense deduction on Schedule A ................ **3.** _____

*If you used either optional method to figure your net earnings from self-employment, do not enter your net profit. Instead, enter the amount from Schedule SE, Section B, line 4b.

**Earned income includes net earnings and gains from the sale, transfer, or licensing of property you created. However, it does not include capital gain income. If you were a more-than-2% shareholder in the S corporation under which the insurance plan is established, earned income is your Medicare wages (box 5 of Form W-2) from that corporation.

### VII.B.9.d. Effect on Medical Expense Deduction and Self-Employment Tax

[505 T.M., IV.E.4.; TPS ¶2170.03.B.1.]

If a taxpayer claims the self-employed health insurance deduction and itemizes deductions, the taxpayer must subtract the amount of the self-employed health insurance deduction from any medical insurance used in computing his or her medical expense deduction (see VII.D.). However, a taxpayer may not subtract the self-employed health insurance deduction in computing net earnings from self employment for purposes of the self-employment tax (see X.A.7.) [§ 162(l)(3), § 162(l)(4)].

### VII.B.10. Penalties for Early Withdrawal from Savings

[503 T.M., II.B.4.b(12); TPS ¶2010.01.A.2.]

A taxpayer can take an above-the-line deduction for penalties paid to a bank or other financial institution for the premature withdrawal of funds from a savings account, certificate of deposit, or similar type of deposit [§ 62(a)(9)]. The bank or financial institution should report the amount of any penalties charged on a Form 1099-INT, *Original Issue Discount*, or Form 1099-OID, *Interest Income*, provided to the taxpayer.

### VII.B.11. Alimony Payments

[503 T.M., IV.B.; TPS ¶1310., ¶2010.01.A.2.]

A taxpayer can take an above-the-line deduction for the amount of alimony or separate maintenance payments made to a spouse or ex-spouse during the tax year [§ 62(a)(10), § 215(a)]. The spouse making the alimony payments is required to report the taxpayer identification number of the spouse receiving the payments on his or her tax return for the year of the deduction [§ 215(c)]. The recipient spouse generally must include the amount of the payments received in gross income (see I.G.).

### VII.B.12. IRA Contributions

[503 T.M., IV.E.; TPS ¶2010.01.A.2.]

An eligible taxpayer under age 70½ can generally take an above-the-line deduction for contributions made to a traditional individual retirement arrangement (IRA) [§ 62(a)(7), § 219]. A traditional IRA is any IRA other than a Roth IRA or a SIMPLE IRA. For a detailed discussion of IRAs, see XVII.A.5.

### VII.B.13. Student Loan Interest

[517 T.M., IV.; TPS ¶2150.01.E.3.]

A taxpayer generally can take an above-the-line deduction for interest paid on a qualified student loan [§ 62(a)(17), § 221(a)]. However, a taxpayer must meet certain eligibility requirements to take the deduction. Moreover, the amount of the deduction is subject to certain limitations.

### VII.B.13.a. Qualified Student Loan

[517 T.M., IV.B.; TPS ¶2150.01.E.3.a.]

A qualified student loan is a loan the taxpayer took out solely to pay qualified education expenses that were [§ 221(d)(1); Reg. § 1.221-1(e)(3)]:

1. for the taxpayer, the taxpayer's spouse, or any person who was a dependent of the taxpayer when the taxpayer took out the loan;
2. paid within a reasonable period of time before or after the taxpayer took out the loan; and

3. for education provided during an academic period in which the person is an eligible student.

However, loans from related persons and loans from qualified employer plans (or contracts purchased under a qualified employer plan) are not qualified student loans. For this purpose, related persons generally include a spouse, brothers and sisters, half brothers and half sisters, ancestors, lineal descendants, and certain entities [§ 221(d)(1); Reg. § 1.221-1(e)(3)(iii)].

*Qualified Education Expenses.* Qualified education expenses are the total costs of attending an eligible educational institution, including tuition and fees, room and board, books, supplies, equipment, transportation, and other necessary expenses. An eligible educational institution includes (i) any college, university, vocational school, or other postsecondary institution that is eligible to participate in a student aid program administered by the Department of Education, and (ii) an institution that conducts an internship or residency program leading to a degree or certificate awarded by a higher education institution, hospital, or health care facility that offers postgraduate training. Qualified education expenses must be reduced by the tax-free part of any scholarships and fellowships paid toward a student's costs of attending an eligible educational institution [§ 221(d)(2); Reg. § 1.221-1(e)(1), § 1.221-1(e)(2)].

*Dependent.* For purposes of the first requirement above, a taxpayer's dependent generally includes a qualifying child or qualifying relative, as defined in § 152 (see XII.D.2.). However, under certain exceptions to the § 152 definition, an individual can be a taxpayer's dependent even if the individual files a joint return or has gross income in excess of the exemption amount and even if the taxpayer is a dependent of another taxpayer [§ 221(d)(4)].

*Reasonable Period.* For purposes of the second requirement above, qualified education expenses are deemed to be paid within a reasonable period of time if either (i) they are paid with the proceeds of student loans that are part of a federal postsecondary education loan program, or (ii) they relate to a specific academic period and the loan proceeds used to pay them are disbursed within a period beginning 90 days before and ending 90 days after the end of that academic period. In any other case, the determination of whether the qualified education expenses are paid within a reasonable period of time is based on all the facts and circumstances [Reg. § 1.221-1(e)(3)(ii)].

*Eligible Student.* For purposes of the third requirement above, an eligible student is a student who is enrolled at least half-time in a program leading to a degree, certificate, or other recognized educational credential. A student is considered enrolled at least half-time if the student is taking at least half the normal full-time workload for his or her course of study (as determined by the eligible educational institution) [§ 221(d)(3), § 25A(b)(3)].

*Academic Period.* An academic period is a semester, trimester, quarter, or other period of study (e.g., summer school) as reasonably determined by an eligible educational institution. If the institution does not have academic periods but instead uses credit hours or clock hours, then each payment period may be treated as an academic period [Reg. § 1.25A-2(c)].

### VII.B.13.b. Taxpayer Eligibility for Deduction

[517 T.M., IV.A.2.; TPS ¶2150.01.E.3.a.]

A taxpayer can take the student loan interest deduction if he or she meets the following eligibility requirements [§ 221(c), § 221(e)(2); Reg. § 1.221-1(b)(1)]:

1. the taxpayer paid interest on a qualified student loan during the year;

2. the taxpayer is legally obligated to pay the interest on that qualified student loan;

3. the taxpayer's filing status is any status other than married filing separately; and

4. the taxpayer (and his or her spouse, if filing jointly) is not claimed as a dependent on another taxpayer's return for that year.

If a taxpayer is legally obligated to pay the interest on a qualified student loan but another person pays the interest on that loan, the taxpayer is treated as paying the interest that is paid by the other person [Reg. § 1.221-1(b)(4)].

A taxpayer cannot take a student loan interest deduction for any amount that is allowable as a deduction under another provision of the tax law (i.e., no double tax benefit is allowed) [§ 221(e)(1)]. Thus, for example, a taxpayer who pays qualified education expenses with a home equity loan and takes a mortgage interest deduction for the interest attributable to those expenses cannot also claim a student loan interest deduction for the interest.

### *VII.B.13.c. Determining Amount of Deduction*

[517 T.M., IV.C.; TPS ¶2150.01.E.3.b.]

The amount of the student loan interest deduction is subject to a maximum dollar limitation and a modified adjusted gross income limitation. The maximum deduction that can be taken for any tax year is $2,500 [§ 221(b)(1)]. Thus, a taxpayer's deduction is generally equal to the smaller of the amount of interest he or she paid on qualified student loans during the year or $2,500.

However, for both 2014 and 2015, a taxpayer's deduction is phased out if his or her modified adjusted gross income (MAGI) is between $65,000 and $80,000 ($130,000 and $160,000 if married filing jointly) [§ 221(b)(2); Rev. Proc. 2013-35, 2013-47 I.R.B. 537, § 3.26, Rev. Proc. 2014-61, 2014-47 I.R.B. 860]. Thus, for 2014, a taxpayer cannot take any deduction if his or her MAGI is $80,000 or more ($160,000 or more if married filing jointly).

For most taxpayers, MAGI is the taxpayer's adjusted gross income computed without taking into account the student loan interest deduction and the tuition and fees deduction (see VII.B.14.). Taxpayers also do not take the following into account in computing MAGI, if applicable: (i) the domestic production activities deduction (see IV.A.9.), (ii) the foreign earned income exclusion (see XX.C.1.a.), (iii) the foreign housing exclusion or deduction (see XX.C.1.c.), and (iv) the exclusions of income for bona fide residents of American Samoa or Puerto Rico [§ 221(b)(2)(C)].

Most taxpayers can compute their student loan interest deduction using the Student Loan Interest Deduction Worksheet (Source: 2014 Form 1040 Draft Instructions).

**Student Loan Interest Deduction Worksheet—Line 33**          *Keep for Your Records*

| | | |
|---|---|---|
| **Before you begin:** | ✓ | Figure any write-in adjustments to be entered on the dotted line next to line 36 (see the instructions for line 36). |
| | ✓ | Be sure you have read the **Exception** in the instructions for this line to see if you can use this worksheet instead of Pub. 970 to figure your deduction. |

| | | | |
|---|---|---|---|
| 1. | Enter the total interest you paid in 2014 on qualified student loans (see the instructions for line 33). **Do not** enter more than $2,500 ................................................................... | **1.** | |
| 2. | Enter the amount from Form 1040, line 22 ..................................... | **2.** | |
| 3. | Enter the total of the amounts from Form 1040, lines 23 through 32, plus any write-in adjustments you entered on the dotted line next to line 36 ......................... | **3.** | |
| 4. | Subtract line 3 from line 2 ...................................... | **4.** | |
| 5. | Enter the amount shown below for your filing status. | | |
| | • Single, head of household, or qualifying widow(er)—$65,000 | **5.** | |
| | • Married filing jointly—$130,000 | | |
| 6. | Is the amount on line 4 more than the amount on line 5? | | |
| | ☐ **No.**   Skip lines 6 and 7, enter -0- on line 8, and go to line 9. | | |
| | ☐ **Yes.**   Subtract line 5 from line 4 .................................... | **6.** | |
| 7. | Divide line 6 by $15,000 ($30,000 if married filing jointly). Enter the result as a decimal (rounded to at least three places). If the result is 1.000 or more, enter 1.000 ................................. | **7.** | . |
| 8. | Multiply line 1 by line 7 ................................................. | **8.** | |
| 9. | **Student loan interest deduction.** Subtract line 8 from line 1. Enter the result here and on Form 1040, line 33. **Do not** include this amount in figuring any other deduction on your return (such as on Schedule A, C, E, etc.) ..................................................... | **9.** | |

### VII.B.14. Tuition and Fees [Expired]

[503 T.M., IV.G.; TPS ¶2150.01.E.4.]

Before 2014, a taxpayer who met certain eligibility requirements could take an above-the-line deduction for qualified tuition and fees he or she paid during the year [§ 62(a)(18), § 222]. The deduction expired December 31, 2013.

The amount of the qualified tuition and fees deduction was subject to the following maximum dollar limitations, based on the amount of a taxpayer's modified adjusted gross income (MAGI) [§ 222(b)(2)(B)]:

• $4,000, for taxpayers with MAGI of $65,000 or less ($130,000 or less if married filing jointly);

• $2,000, for taxpayers with MAGI between $65,000 and $80,000 ($130,000 and $160,000 if married filing jointly); or

• $0, for taxpayer with MAGI of $80,000 or more ($160,000 or more if married filing jointly).

The deduction could not be claimed if the taxpayer claimed an education credit for the same student (see IX.B.5.) [§ 222(c)(2)].

***Qualified Tuition and Fees.*** Qualified tuition and fees are tuition and certain related expenses (as defined in Reg. § 1.25A-2(d)) that are [§ 222(d), § 25A(f)]:

1. required for enrollment or attendance at an eligible educational institution during the tax year;

2. paid in connection with an academic period beginning during the tax year or during the first three months of the following tax year; and

3. paid on behalf of the taxpayer, the taxpayer's spouse, or a dependent for whom the taxpayer can claim an exemption.

Qualified education expenses must be reduced by the tax-free part of any scholarships and fellowships [§ 222(d)(1)].

*Eligible educational institution.* An eligible educational institution is any college, university, vocational school, or other postsecondary institution that is eligible to participate in a student aid program administered by the Department of Education [§ 25A(f)(2); Reg. § 1.25A-2(b)].

*Taxpayer Eligibility for Deduction.* A taxpayer could take the qualified tuition and fees deduction if he or she met the following eligibility requirements [§ 222(c)(3), § 222(d)]:

1. he or she paid qualified tuition and fees for an eligible student for an academic period beginning during the year or the first three months of the following year;

2. the taxpayer's filing status was any status other than married filing separately;

3. the taxpayer (and his or her spouse, if filing jointly) was not claimed as a dependent on another taxpayer's return for that year; and

4. if the taxpayer was a nonresident alien for any part of the year, he or she made an election to be treated as a resident alien.

### VII.B.15. Domestic Production Activities Deduction

[510 T.M.; TPS ¶2220.]

A taxpayer can take the domestic production activities deduction for up to 9% of his or her qualified production activities income, which includes income from [§ 199(a), § 199(c)(4)(A)]:

- the lease, rental, license, sale, exchange, or other disposition of:

— tangible personal property, computer software, or sound recordings that the taxpayer manufactured, produced, grew, or extracted in whole or in significant part in the United States;

— a qualified film that the taxpayer produced; or

— electricity, natural gas, or potable water that the taxpayer produced in the United States;

- the construction of real property performed in the United States; and

- engineering or architectural services performed in the United States for the construction of real property in the United States.

The domestic production activities deduction is computed and reported on Form 8903, *Domestic Production Activities Deduction.* For a detailed discussion of the domestic production activities deduction, see IV.A.9.

### VII.B.16. Other Above-the-Line Deductions

[503 T.M., II.B.4.b.; TPS ¶2010.01.A.2.]

Other above-the-line deductions include:

- the deduction for reforestation amortization and expenses (see IV.F.5.e.) [§ 62(a)(11), § 194];

- the deduction for the repayment of supplemental unemployment compensation benefits required by the Trade Act of 1974 [§ 62(a)(12)];

- the deduction for jury duty pay remitted to an employer [§ 62(a)(13)];

- the Archer MSA deduction (see XVII.C.1.d.) [§ 62(a)(16), § 220];

- the deduction for attorney fees and court costs paid in connection with an action involving an unlawful discrimination claim (limited to amount includible in taxpayer's gross income from such action) [§ 62(a)(20)];

• the deduction for attorney fees and court costs paid in connection with a whistleblower award from the IRS (limited to amount includible in taxpayer's gross income from such award) [§ 62(a)(21)];

• the deduction for expenses related to income from the rental of personal property engaged in for profit;

• the deduction for contributions to a § 501(c)(18)(D) pension plan; and

• the deduction for contributions by certain chaplains to a § 403(b) plan.

Expenses or losses netted against income or gains from activities reported on Schedules C, D, E, and F of Form 1040 and Form 4797 are also above-the-line deductions. These expenses include:

• trade or business expenses reported on Schedule C, *Profit or Loss from Business (Sole Proprietorship)*, or Schedule C-EZ, *Net Profit from Business (Sole Proprietorship)*, and Schedule F, *Profit or Loss from Farming* (see Chapter IV.) [§ 62(a)(1)];

• expenses attributable to property held for the production of rents or royalties reported on Schedule E, *Supplemental Income and Loss* (see IV.A.8.) [§ 62(a)(4)]; and

• losses from the sale or exchange of property reported on Schedule D, *Capital Gains and Losses*, and Form 4797, *Sales of Business Property* (see III.B.) [§ 62(a)(3)].

On Schedule D, individual taxpayers can also deduct certain nonbusiness bad debts as an above-the-line deduction [§ 166(d)]. A nonbusiness bad debt is a debt other than (i) a debt created or acquired in connection with a trade or business of the taxpayer, or (ii) a debt the loss from the worthlessness of which is incurred in the taxpayer's trade or business. Nonbusiness bad debts are deductible only if they are totally worthless. They are reported as short-term capital losses on Form 8949, *Sales and Other Dispositions of Capital Assets*, and then on Schedule D. See VIII.I. for a detailed discussion of bad debts, including nonbusiness bad debts.

## VII.C. Itemized Deductions

[503 T.M., II.B.4.; TPS ¶2010.01.A.3.]

Itemized deductions include deductions for certain medical expenses (see VII.D.), taxes (see VII.E.), interest (see VII.F.), charitable contributions (see VII.G.), casualty and theft losses (see VII.H.), and miscellaneous itemized deductions (see VII.I. and VII.J.).

There are a number of limitations on itemized deductions that are based on the taxpayer's adjusted gross income (AGI) for the year. The deduction of medical expenses is generally allowed only to the extent that the taxpayer's deductible medical expenses exceed 10% of his or her AGI for the year (the 10% AGI floor) (see VII.D.). The deduction of certain types of miscellaneous itemized deductions is allowed only to the extent that such amounts exceed 2% of the taxpayer's AGI for the year (the 2% AGI floor) (see VII.I.). However, the deduction of other types of miscellaneous itemized deductions is not limited by the 2% AGI floor (see VII.J.).

In addition to the limitations on specific types of itemized deductions, there is also an overall limitation on itemized deductions for taxpayers whose AGI exceeds certain threshold amounts. See VII.L. for a discussion of this overall limitation.

## VII.D. Medical Expenses

[513 T.M., III.A.; TPS ¶2840.]

Taxpayers are allowed a deduction for unreimbursed medical expenses paid during the tax year to the extent that such expenses exceed 10% of their adjusted gross income (AGI) [§ 213(a)]. The AGI floor for taxpayers age 65 or older is 7.5%. The 7.5% floor applies to married couples if one spouse is 65 or older [§ 213(f)]. The deduction for medical expenses cannot be claimed unless a taxpayer itemizes deductions.

---

**EXAMPLE:** Dan, a 60-year-old single taxpayer, pays medical expenses of $4,750 for himself during the tax year. Dan's AGI for the year is $50,000 and he itemizes his deductions. Dan cannot deduct any of his medical expenses because they are less than 10% of his AGI ($50,000 × 10% = $5,000).

**EXAMPLE:** Assume the same facts as in the previous example, except that Dan is age 70 instead of age 60. Dan can deduct the amount by which his medical expenses exceed 7.5% of his AGI ($50,000 × 7.5% = $3,750). Thus, Dan can deduct $1,000 ($4,750 − $3,750) of his medical expenses for the year.

---

### VII.D.1. What Medical Expenses Are Deductible?

[513 T.M., III.A.4.; TPS ¶2840.03.]

Deductible medical expenses include [§ 213(d)(1)]:
- the costs of diagnosis, cure, mitigation, treatment, or prevention of disease (see VII.D.1.a.);

- the costs of treatments affecting any part or function of the body (see VII.D.1.a.);

- the costs of transportation primarily for, and essential to, medical care (see VII.D.1.b.);

- the costs of qualified long-term care services (see VII.D.1.c.);

- the costs of a qualified long-term care insurance contract (see VII.D.1.c.); and

- the costs of medical insurance (see VII.D.1.d.).

For a checklist of expenses that can and cannot be treated as deductible medical expenses, see the Medical and Dental Expenses Checklist (Source: IRS Pub. 17).

Table 21-1. **Medical and Dental Expenses Checklist.** See Publication 502 for more information about these and other expenses.

| You can include: | | You cannot include: | |
|---|---|---|---|
| • Bandages<br>• Birth control pills prescribed by your doctor<br>• Body scan<br>• Braille books<br>• Breast pump and supplies<br>• Capital expenses for equipment or improvements to your home needed for medical care (see the worksheet in Publication 502)<br>• Diagnostic devices<br>• Expenses of an organ donor<br>• Eye surgery—to promote the correct function of the eye<br>• Fertility enhancement, certain procedures<br>• Guide dogs or other animals aiding the blind, deaf, and disabled<br>• Hospital services fees (lab work, therapy, nursing services, surgery, etc.)<br>• Lead-based paint removal<br>• Legal abortion<br>• Legal operation to prevent having children such as a vasectomy or tubal ligation<br>• Long-term care contracts, qualified<br>• Meals and lodging provided by a hospital during medical treatment<br>• Medical services fees (from doctors, dentists, surgeons, specialists, and other medical practitioners)<br>• Medicare Part D premiums | • Medical and hospital insurance premiums<br>• Nursing services<br>• Oxygen equipment and oxygen<br>• Part of life-care fee paid to retirement home designated for medical care<br>• Physical examination<br>• Pregnancy test kit<br>• Prescription medicines (prescribed by a doctor) and insulin<br>• Psychiatric and psychological treatment<br>• Social security tax, Medicare tax, FUTA, and state employment tax for worker providing medical care (see *Wages for nursing services*, below)<br>• Special items (artificial limbs, false teeth, eye-glasses, contact lenses, hearing aids, crutches, wheelchair, etc.)<br>• Special education for mentally or physically disabled persons<br>• Stop-smoking programs<br>• Transportation for needed medical care<br>• Treatment at a drug or alcohol center (includes meals and lodging provided by the center)<br>• Wages for nursing services<br>• Weight-loss, certain expenses for obesity | • Baby sitting and childcare<br>• Bottled water<br>• Contributions to Archer MSAs (see Publication 969)<br>• Diaper service<br>• Expenses for your general health (even if following your doctor's advice) such as—<br>—Health club dues<br>—Household help (even if recommended by a doctor)<br>—Social activities, such as dancing or swimming lessons<br>—Trip for general health improvement<br>• Flexible spending account reimbursements for medical expenses (if contributions were on a pre-tax basis)<br>• Funeral, burial, or cremation expenses<br>• Health savings account payments for medical expenses<br>• Illegal operation, treatment, or medicine<br>• Life insurance or income protection policies, or policies providing payment for loss of life, limb, sight, etc.<br>• Maternity clothes | • Medical insurance included in a car insurance policy covering all persons injured in or by your car<br>• Medicine you buy without a prescription<br>• Nursing care for a healthy baby<br>• Prescription drugs you brought in (or ordered shipped) from another country, in most cases<br>• Nutritional supplements, vitamins, herbal supplements, "natural medicines," etc., unless recommended by a medical practitioner as a treatment for a specific medical condition diagnosed by a physician<br>• Surgery for purely cosmetic reasons<br>• Toothpaste, toiletries, cosmetics, etc.<br>• Teeth whitening<br>• Weight-loss expenses not for the treatment of obesity or other disease |

### VII.D.1.a. Medical Expenses Related to Disease and Treatments Affecting the Body

[513 T.M., III.A.4.; TPS ¶2840.03.B.]

Deductible medical expenses include the costs of diagnosis, cure, mitigation, treatment, or prevention of disease. Deductible medical expenses also include the costs of treatments affecting any part or function of the body [§ 213(d)(1)(A)]. More specifically, deductible medical expenses include, but are not limited to, the costs of [Reg. § 1.213-1(e)(1), § 1.213-1(e)(2)]:

- medical doctors, osteopathic doctors, eye doctors, dentists, acupuncturists, chiropractors, physical therapists, occupational therapists, psychiatrists, psychoanalysts, and psychologists;

- medical examinations;

- X-rays;

- laboratory services;

- diagnostic tests (e.g., a full-body scan, a pregnancy test, or a blood sugar test kit);

- clinic costs;

- nursing care (however, no deduction is allowed for nursing care for a healthy baby);

- hospital care, including meals and lodging;

- lodging expenses (limited to $50 per night) while away from home to receive outpatient medical care in a hospital or medical facility related to a hospital (however, no deduction is allowed if a significant element of the travel is personal pleasure, recreation, or vacation) [§ 213(d)(2)];

- prescription medicines and insulin (however, no deduction is allowed for non-prescription medicines and imported drugs not approved by the FDA) [§ 213(b)];
- medical aids such as eyeglasses, contact lenses, hearing aids, braces, crutches, wheelchairs, and guide dogs (including the cost of maintaining them);
- capital expenditures for special medical equipment or to accommodate a home for a disabled taxpayer;
- surgery to improve defective vision, such as laser surgery and radial keratotomy;
- a program to stop smoking and prescription medicines to alleviate nicotine withdrawal; and
- a weight loss program as treatment for a specific disease diagnosed by a doctor, including obesity.

These types of expenses are deductible only if they are paid primarily to alleviate or prevent a physical or mental defect or illness. Expenses that are merely beneficial to general health are not deductible. Thus, for example, the cost of a vacation recommended by a doctor is not deductible. Examples of other expenses that are not deductible as medical expenses include the costs of vitamins, diet food, illegal drugs, illegal operations, and cosmetic surgery (unless necessary to improve a deformity from a congenital abnormality, an injury, or a disfiguring disease) [§ 213(d)(9); Reg. § 1.213-1(e)(2)].

### VII.D.1.b. Medical Transportation Expenses

[513 T.M., III.A.4.i.; TPS ¶2840.03.C.]

Transportation costs are deductible as medical expenses if the transportation is primarily for, and essential to, medical care [§ 213(d)(1)(B); Reg. § 1.213-1(e)(1)(iv)]. Deductible medical expenses can include the costs of the following types of transportation if used primarily for medical reasons [Reg. § 1.213-1(e)(1)(iv)]:

- ambulance service;
- a personal vehicle; or
- bus, taxi, train, or airplane fare.

In the case of a personal vehicle used for medical reasons, the deduction can be based on either the taxpayer's actual out-of-pocket costs or the standard mileage rate. The deduction for actual costs can include oil and gas costs, but not depreciation, insurance, or repair and maintenance costs. The deduction using the standard mileage rate is 23.5 cents per mile for 2014 [Notice 2013-80, 2013-52 I.R.B. 821]. Parking fees and tolls can be deducted under either method [Rev. Proc. 2010-51, 2010-51 I.R.B. 883].

---

**EXAMPLE:** Sarah drove 1,000 miles for medical purposes during the year. She spent $175 for gas and $25 for oil. She also paid $50 for tolls and parking. Sarah's actual costs for medical travel are $250 ($175 + $25 + $50). However, if she uses the standard mileage rate, she can take a $285 deduction for medical travel ((1,000 miles × $0.235 per mile) + $50).

---

The transportation costs for regular visits to see a mentally ill dependent are deductible if the visits are recommended as part of the treatment for the dependent

[Rev. Rul. 58-533, 1958-2 C.B. 108]. The transportation costs for a nurse (or other person) to accompany a patient traveling for medical care are deductible if the patient is unable to travel alone and the nurse is needed to give the patient injections, medications, or other required treatment.

No deduction is allowed for travel undertaken merely for the general improvement of a taxpayer's health or for travel to another city for medical care for purely personal reasons [Reg. § 1.213-1(e)(1)(iv)].

### VII.D.1.c. Long-Term Care Expenses

[513 T.M., III.A.4.d(3); TPS ¶2840.03.D.]

Deductible long-term care expenses include the costs of qualified long-term care services and premiums paid under a long-term care insurance contract.

*Costs of Qualified Long-Term Care Services.* The costs of qualified long-term care services are deductible as medical expenses [§ 213(d)(1)(C)]. Qualified long-term care services include necessary diagnostic, preventive, therapeutic, curing, treating, mitigating, rehabilitative services, and maintenance and personal care services that are required by a chronically ill individual and provided pursuant to a plan of care prescribed by a licensed health care practitioner (generally, a physician, registered professional nurse, or licensed social worker) [§ 7702B(c)(1), § 7702B(c)(4)]. Maintenance and personal care services are services the primary purpose of which is to provide a chronically ill individual with needed assistance with his or her disabilities (including protection from self-harm due to severe cognitive impairment) [§ 7702B(c)(3)].

An individual is chronically ill if, within the previous 12 months, a licensed health care practitioner has certified that the individual meets any one of the following three requirements [§ 7702B(c)(2)]:

1. he or she is unable to perform at least two of six daily living activities (eating, toileting, transferring, bathing, dressing, and continence) without substantial assistance from another individual for at least 90 days due to a loss of functional capacity;
2. he or she has a level of disability similar to the disability discussed in 1.; or
3. he or she requires substantial supervision to be protected from threats to health and safety due to severe cognitive impairment.

*Premiums under Qualified Long-Term Care Insurance Contract.* Subject to certain limitations, premiums paid under a qualified long-term care insurance contract are deductible as medical expenses [§ 213(d)(1)(D)]. A qualified long-term care insurance contract is an insurance contract that provides coverage only for qualified long-term care services and that meets all of the following requirements [§ 7702B(b)]:

1. the contract is guaranteed renewable;
2. the contract provides that refunds and dividends under the contract (other than refunds on the death of the insured or on a complete surrender or cancellation of the contract) must be used only to reduce future premiums or increase future benefits;
3. the contract does not provide for a cash surrender value or other money that can be paid, assigned, pledged, or borrowed;
4. the contract does not pay or reimburse expenses incurred for services or items that would be reimbursed under Medicare (except where Medicare is a secondary payer or the contract makes per diem or other periodic payments without regard to expenses); and

5. the contract contains certain consumer protection provisions.

For 2014 and 2015, the amount of qualified long-term care insurance premiums that can be deducted for coverage of any individual is limited to the following amounts based on the age of the covered individual as of the end of each year [§ 213(d)(10); Rev. Proc. 2013-35, 2013-47 I.R.B. 537, Rev. Proc. 2014-61, 2014-47 I.R.B. 860]:

| Age | 2014 Dollar Limitation | 2015 Dollar Limitation |
|---|---|---|
| Age 40 or under | $ 370 | $ 380 |
| Age 41 to 50 | $ 700 | $ 710 |
| Age 51 to 60 | $1,400 | $1,430 |
| Age 61 to 70 | $3,720 | $3,800 |
| Age 71 or over | $4,660 | $4,750 |

### VII.D.1.d. Medical Insurance Premiums

[513 T.M., III.A.4.d(2); TPS ¶2840.03.E.]

Premiums paid for an insurance policy are deductible as a medical expense if the insurance covers deductible medical expenses such as hospitalization, surgical services, X-rays, prescription drugs, insulin, dental care, or the replacement of damaged or lost contact lenses [§ 213(d)(1)(D)].

If an insurance policy provides both medical coverage and another type of coverage, the portion of the premiums attributable to the medical coverage can be deducted only if those charges are separately stated in the insurance contract (or another statement) and are reasonable in relation to the total charges under the contract [§ 213(d)(6); Reg. § 1.213-1(e)(4)(i)(a)].

Insurance premiums and other medical and dental expenses paid on behalf of an employee under an employer-sponsored health insurance plan are not deductible by the employee as medical expenses unless the employer reports those amounts to the employee on Form W-2 as compensation. Expenses reimbursed to an employee under an employer's health reimbursement arrangement (HRA) are not deductible as medical expenses because an HRA is funded solely by the employer (see XVII.C.1.e.).

Premiums paid for coverage under Medicare Part B (medical insurance) and Medicare Part D (voluntary prescription drug insurance) are deductible as medical expenses [§ 213(d)(1)(D)]. Taxpayers covered under social security are automatically enrolled in Medicare Part A coverage (hospital insurance) and cannot deduct the payroll taxes paid for such coverage. However, taxpayers who are not covered under social security but voluntarily enroll in Medicare Part A coverage can deduct the premiums paid for such coverage.

When a taxpayer younger than age 65 pays premiums for medical insurance to cover the taxpayer, or the taxpayer's spouse or dependents after the taxpayer reaches age 65, the taxpayer can deduct the premiums as medical expenses in the year in which paid if the premiums are payable in equal installments (annually or more frequently) for a period of (i) 10 years or more, or (ii) until the year the taxpayer turns age 65 (but not for a period of less than 5 years) [§ 213(d)(7); Reg. § 1.213-1(e)(4)(i)(b)].

---

**EXAMPLE:** Paul, age 50, buys an insurance policy that will provide medical coverage for him and his wife after he reaches age 65. Under the terms of the policy, Paul will pay premiums of $2,000 per year for the next 15 years until he turns age 65. Paul can deduct those insurance premiums in the years paid.

**EXAMPLE:** Sandy, age 61, buys an insurance policy that will provide medical coverage for her and her husband after she reaches age 65. Under the terms of the policy, Sandy will pay premiums of $5,000 per year for the next four years until she turns age 65. Sandy cannot deduct those insurance premiums in the years paid.

### VII.D.2. Whose Medical Expenses Qualify for Deduction?

[513 T.M., III.A.2.b.; TPS ¶2840.02.]

A taxpayer generally can deduct medical expenses paid on behalf of the taxpayer, or the taxpayer's spouse or dependents [§ 213(a); Reg. § 1.213-1(a)(3)(i)]. A deduction can be taken for medical expenses paid for a person who was the taxpayer's spouse at the time the person received the medical services or at the time the taxpayer paid the medical expenses. For this purpose, a person is not considered a spouse of the taxpayer if they are legally separated under a decree of divorce or separate maintenance [Reg. § 1.213-1(e)(3)].

**EXAMPLE:** After Steve and Shirley got married, Steve paid the expenses for medical treatment that Shirley received before they were married. Steve can include those expenses in computing his medical expense deduction. This is true whether Steve and Shirley file a joint return or separate returns.

**EXAMPLE:** After Bill and Beth got married, Beth paid the expenses for medical treatment she received before they were married. If Bill and Beth file a joint return, those expenses can be included in computing the medical expense deduction. If Bill and Beth file separate returns, only Beth can include those expenses in computing the medical expense deduction.

A deduction can be taken for medical expenses paid for a person who was the taxpayer's dependent at the time the person received the medical services or at the time the taxpayer paid the medical expenses [Reg. § 1.213-1(e)(3)]. A person qualifies as a taxpayer's dependent if both of the following requirements are met [§ 213(a), § 152(a), § 152(b)(3)(A)]:

1. the person is a qualifying child (see VII.D.2.a.) or qualifying relative (see VII.D.2.b.) of the taxpayer; and

2. the person is a U.S. citizen, resident, or national, or a Canadian or Mexican resident.

### VII.D.2.a. Qualifying Child

[513 T.M., III.A.2.b(3); TPS ¶2840.02.]

A person is a qualifying child of the taxpayer if he or she meets all of the following requirements [§ 152(c)]:

1. the person is the taxpayer's son, daughter, stepchild, adopted child, foster child, brother, sister, stepbrother, stepsister, half brother, half sister, or a descendant of any of them (e.g., a grandchild, nephew, or niece);

2. the person was (i) under age 19 at the end of the year and younger than the taxpayer (or the taxpayer's spouse, if filing jointly), (ii) under age 23 at the end of the year, a full-time student, and younger than the taxpayer (or the taxpayer's spouse, if filing jointly), or (iii) permanently and totally disabled (no matter what age);

3. the person lived with the taxpayer for more than half of the year;

4. the person did not provide more than half of his or her own support during the year; and

5. the person did not file a joint return for the year (other than to claim a refund).

*Adopted Children.* Special rules apply for adopted children. A child is considered an adopted child of a taxpayer if he is legally adopted by the taxpayer or if he is lawfully placed with the taxpayer for legal adoption [§ 152(f)(1)(B)]. An adopted child can be a dependent of a taxpayer even if the child is not a U.S. citizen, resident, or national, or a Canadian or Mexican resident, as long as the child lives with the taxpayer as a member of his or her household during the year and the taxpayer is a U.S. citizen or national [§ 152(b)(3)(B)]. A taxpayer can deduct medical expenses paid for an adopted child before adoption if the child qualified as a dependent when the child received the medical services or when the taxpayer paid the medical expenses. A taxpayer can also deduct amounts paid to an adoption agency as repayment for medical expenses the agency paid for the child after adoption negotiations began.

*Children of Divorced or Separated Parents.* A child of divorced or separated parents can be treated as a dependent of both parents for purposes of the medical expense deduction. Each parent can take into account the medical expenses he or she paid for the child if the following requirements are met [§ 152(e)(1)]:

1. the child is in the custody of one or both parents for more than half the year;

2. the child receives over half his or her support from his or her parents during the year; and

3. the parents are (i) divorced or legally separated under a decree of divorce or separate maintenance, (ii) separated under a written separation agreement, or (iii) live apart at all times during the last six months of the year.

### VII.D.2.b. Qualifying Relative

[513 T.M., III.A.2.b(3); TPS ¶2840.02.]

A person is a qualifying relative of the taxpayer if all of the following requirements are met [§ 152(d)]:

1. the person is the taxpayer's (i) son, daughter, stepchild, adopted child, foster child, or a descendant of any of them, (ii) brother, sister, half brother, half sister, or a son or daughter of any of them, (iii) father or mother or an ancestor or sibling of either of them, (iv) stepfather, stepmother, stepbrother, stepsister, father-in-law, mother-in-law, brother-in-law, sister-in-law, son-in-law, daughter-in-law, or (v) any other person (except a spouse) who lived with the taxpayer all year as a member of his or her household;

2. the person was not a qualifying child of any taxpayer during the year (see VII.D.2.a.); and

3. the taxpayer provided over half the person's support during the year.

If a person is designated as a taxpayer's dependent in a multiple support agreement under which two or more individuals together provide over half the person's support, and no one individual alone provides over half the person's support, then the taxpayer can take a deduction for the medical expenses he or she pays for the person. The medical expenses paid by the other individuals cannot be deducted by anyone [§ 152(d)(3); Reg. § 1.213-1(a)(3)(i)].

### VII.D.3. When Are Medical Expenses Deductible?

[513 T.M., III.A.5.; TPS ¶2840.04.]

Medical expenses are deductible in the year they are paid, regardless of when the medical services are provided and regardless of the taxpayer's method of accounting [§ 213(a); Reg. § 1.213-1(a)(1)]. Medical expenses paid by check are treated as paid on the date the check is mailed or otherwise delivered. Medical expenses paid by credit card are treated as paid on the date they are charged to the credit card.

Generally, if a taxpayer and spouse file separate returns, each spouse can deduct only the medical expenses actually paid by that spouse. Medical expenses paid from a joint account are generally divided equally between the spouses. Similarly, if the spouses live in a community property state, the medical expenses paid out of community income are divided equally between the spouses.

If a taxpayer fails to deduct medical expenses on his or her return for the year they are paid, the taxpayer can file a Form 1040X, *Amended U.S. Individual Income Tax Return*, for that year. The taxpayer cannot claim the expenses as a deduction on a later year's return.

### VII.D.4. Reimbursements of Medical Expenses

[513 T.M., III.A.3.d.; TPS ¶2840.05.]

Medical expenses are deductible only to the extent that they are not reimbursed by insurance or otherwise [§ 213(a)]. Thus, a taxpayer must reduce his or her total medical expenses for the year by any medical expense reimbursements (including Medicare payments) received during the year.

If a taxpayer's medical expense reimbursements are more than his or her total medical expenses for the year, the excess reimbursements must be included in gross income to the extent they are attributable to medical insurance premium payments made by the taxpayer's employer. However, reimbursements are not includible in gross income if the taxpayer did not itemize deductions or if the taxpayer did not deduct the underlying medical expense because of the AGI floor on medical expense deductions.

## VII.E. Taxes

[525 T.M., I.; TPS ¶2340.01.]

Individual taxpayers can deduct certain taxes paid or accrued during the year. In determining the deductibility of taxes, the different types of taxes fall into three broad categories.

The first category of taxes includes those that the Code specifically enumerates as being deductible. These deductible taxes include [§ 164(a)]:

1. state and local income taxes (see VII.E.1.);
2. state and local general sales taxes (before 2014) (see VII.E.2.);
3. real estate taxes (see VII.E.3.);
4. personal property taxes (see VII.E.4.);
5. certain foreign taxes (see VII.E.5.); and
6. the generation-skipping transfer tax (see VII.E.6.).

Before 2014, the first two types of taxes in the list were alternatives — a taxpayer could elect to deduct one, but not both, of those types of state and local taxes.

The second category of taxes includes those that the Code specifically enumerates as not being deductible under any circumstances [§ 275] (see VII.E.7.).

The third category of taxes includes all taxes that are not specifically enumerated as being deductible or nondeductible. These types of taxes are deductible only if paid in connection with a trade or business activity or a for-profit activity (see IV.A.12.) [§ 164(a)].

### VII.E.1. State and Local Income Taxes

[525 T.M., II.D.; TPS ¶2340.02.D.]

Before 2014, an individual taxpayer who itemized could elect to deduct either (i) state and local income taxes, or (ii) state and local general sales taxes (see VII.E.2.). The election was made by checking the appropriate box on Form 1040, Schedule A, line 5. Although the deduction for state and local general sales taxes has expired, taxpayers can still deduct state and local income taxes.

State and local taxes are taxes imposed by a state, the District of Columbia, a U.S. possession, or a political subdivision thereof (such as a county or city) [§ 164(b)(2); Reg. § 1.164-1(a)]. State and local income taxes are income and profits taxes based on gross income, net income, taxable income, or a similar type of income. They do not include taxes based on value or taxes based on specific transactions [Reg. § 1.901-2(b)].

An individual taxpayer generally can claim a state and local income tax deduction for the following items:

- state and local income taxes withheld from wages and salary during the year;
- state and local income taxes paid during the year for a prior year (thus, for example, a taxpayer who files a 2013 state and local income tax return on April 15, 2014, can deduct any taxes paid with that return on his or her 2014 federal income tax return);
- state and local estimated tax payments made during the year (including any prior year state and local income tax refunds credited to the year); and
- mandatory contributions withheld from a taxpayer's salary during the year for the following benefit funds:
  - disability funds, including the California, New Jersey, and New York Non-occupational Disability Benefit Funds, the Rhode Island Temporary Disability Benefit Fund, and the Washington State Supplemental Compensation Fund;
  - unemployment compensation funds, including the Alaska, New Jersey, and Pennsylvania Unemployment Compensation Funds and the California Unemployment Insurance Trust Fund; and
  - state family leave programs, including the New Jersey Family Leave Insurance program and the California Paid Family Leave program.

The following special rules apply to the state and local income tax deduction for married taxpayers:

1. If the spouses file joint federal returns and joint state and local returns, the total state and local income taxes paid by both spouses can be deducted on the joint return.
2. If the spouses file separate federal returns and separate state and local returns, each spouse deducts the amount of state and local income taxes he or she actually paid on his or her separate federal return.
3. If the spouses file separate federal returns but file joint state and local returns, the spouses' deductions depend on whether or not they are jointly and individually liable for the state and local incomes taxes. If they are jointly and individu-

ally liable, then each spouse deducts the amount of state and local income taxes he or she actually paid on his or her separate federal return. However, if they are not jointly and individually liable, then each spouse's deduction is generally equal to his or her proportionate share of the total state and local income taxes paid by both spouses, with each spouse's share of the total taxes determined based on the ratio of his or her gross income to the total gross income of both spouses. Under this latter method, each spouse's deduction is limited to the amount of state and local income taxes he or she actually paid during the year.

### VII.E.2. State and Local General Sales Taxes [Expired]

[525 T.M., II.E.; TPS ¶2340.02.E.]

Before 2014, an individual taxpayer could elect to deduct either (i) state and local income taxes (see VII.E.1.), or (ii) state and local general sales taxes [§ 164(b)(5)(A)]. The election was made by checking the appropriate box on Form 1040, Schedule A, line 5. The deduction for sales taxes expired December 31, 2013. Unless that deduction is extended, a taxpayer may only deduct state and local income taxes.

State and local taxes are taxes imposed by a state, the District of Columbia, a U.S. possession, or a political subdivision thereof (such as a county or city) [§ 164(b)(2); Reg. § 1.164-1(a)]. Sales taxes are taxes imposed upon the sellers or buyers of tangible personal property. General sales taxes are sales taxes imposed at one rate on retail sales of a broad range of classes of items [§ 164(b)(5)(B); Reg. § 1.164-3(f)].

A taxpayer who elected to deduct state and local general sales taxes could deduct either the amount of the actual sales taxes paid or an amount based on the optional sales tax tables [§ 164(b)(5)(H)].

Actual sales taxes paid (including compensating use taxes paid) were deductible if the tax rate at which those taxes were imposed was the same as the general sales tax rate. Generally, no deduction was allowed for sales taxes imposed at a rate different than the general sales tax rate. However, sales taxes on food, clothing, medical supplies, and motor vehicles were deductible even if the tax rate was less than the general sales tax rate. In addition, when sales taxes on motor vehicles (sales taxes on cars, trucks, vans, sport utility vehicles, motorcycles, motor homes, and recreational vehicles that are bought or leased) were imposed at a rate higher than the general sales tax rate, a deduction could be taken for the amount of sales taxes that would have been paid on that vehicle at the general sales tax rate. No deduction was allowed for sales taxes paid for property used in a trade or business.

A taxpayer who chose to determine the state and local general sales tax deduction based on the optional sales tax tables could compute the deduction using the tables and worksheets in the instructions for Form 1040, Schedule A or the Sales Tax Deduction Calculator at www.irs.gov. The applicable amount from the tables was based on the state where the taxpayer lived, the taxpayer's income, and the number of exemptions the taxpayer claimed on his or her return. For this purpose, the taxpayer's income was equal to his or her adjusted gross income plus certain nontaxable items.

### VII.E.3. Real Estate Taxes

#### VII.E.3.a. Deductible Real Estate Taxes

[525 T.M., II.B.; TPS ¶2340.02.B.]

An individual taxpayer can deduct real estate taxes. Real estate taxes are taxes imposed on interests in real property and levied for the general public welfare. Real estate taxes are deductible only if they are based on the assessed value of real property and charged uniformly against all property under the jurisdiction of the taxing authority [Reg. § 1.164-3(b), § 1.164-4(a)].

A tenant-shareholder in a cooperative housing corporation can deduct the amount paid to the corporation that represents his or her share of the real estate taxes the corporation paid or incurred for the tenant shareholder's unit.

### VII.E.3.b. Amounts Not Deductible as Real Estate Taxes
[525 T.M., II.B.; TPS ¶2340.02.B.]

Certain payments related to real estate, such as taxes charged for local benefits, itemized charges for services, transfer taxes, and homeowners' association charges, are not deductible as real estate taxes.

*Taxes Charged for Local Benefits.* Taxes charged for local benefits or improvements of a kind that tend to increase the value of the taxpayer's property are not deductible as real estate taxes. Examples include assessments used to pay for new streets, sidewalks, public parking lots, water mains, sewer lines, and similar improvements. Under an exception, assessments used to pay for maintenance, repairs, or interest charges on such local benefits or improvements (e.g., assessments used to pay for repairs to streets or sidewalks) can be deducted as real estate taxes [Reg. § 1.164-2(g), § 1.164-4(a), § 1.164-4(b)].

*Itemized Charges for Services.* Itemized charges for services to specific property or persons are not deductible as real estate taxes, even when paid to the taxing authority. Thus, no deduction is allowed for a unit fee for delivery of service (e.g., $5 for every 1,000 gallons of water consumed), a periodic charge for residential service (e.g., $20 per month for trash removal), or a flat fee charged for a single service (e.g., $30 for mowing lawn that had grown higher than permitted under an ordinance). However, service charges used to maintain or improve services are deductible as real estate taxes if the charges are imposed at the same rate on all properties in the taxing jurisdiction, the funds collected are commingled with general revenue funds, and the amounts used to maintain or improve the services are not limited to the funds collected.

*Transfer Taxes.* Transfer taxes and similar charges on the sale of a personal residence are not deductible as real estate taxes. Seller-paid transfer taxes are treated as expenses of the sale. Buyer-paid transfer taxes are added to the buyer's basis in the property.

*Homeowners' Association Fees.* Homeowners' association fees are not deductible as real estate taxes because they are imposed by a homeowners' association, not a state or local government.

### VII.E.3.c. Apportionment of Real Estate Taxes between Buyer and Seller
[525 T.M., II.B.; TPS ¶2340.02.B.]

When real property is sold during the property tax year, the real estate taxes on that property must be divided between the buyer and the seller. Generally, the seller is treated as owning the property up to, but not including, the date of the sale, and the buyer is treated as owning the property beginning on the date of the sale. The buyer and seller generally split the real estate taxes according to the number of days in the real property tax year that each one owns the property [§ 164(d)(1); Reg. § 1.164-6(b)].

---

**EXAMPLE:** Sam sells his home to Patty on Sept. 1. The property tax year in the area is the calendar year. The real estate taxes for the property tax year are $730. The taxes are apportioned between Sam and Patty based on the number of days during the property tax year that each owned the home. Thus, $244 ($730 × (122/365)) is apportioned to Patty and $486 ($730 × (243/365)) is apportioned to Sam.

Generally, a cash method taxpayer can deduct real estate taxes in the year they are paid, and an accrual method taxpayer can deduct real estate taxes in the year they accrue under state law. However, an accrual method taxpayer may elect to accrue real estate taxes ratably over the period to which they relate and deduct them in his corresponding tax year(s) [§ 461(c)].

A number of special rules apply for purposes of determining the timing of a taxpayer's deduction for apportioned real estate taxes. These rules depend on the taxpayer's method of accounting and the date when the taxes become a lien or personal liability. Depending on the tax jurisdiction, real estate taxes may become a lien or personal liability before, during, or after the property tax year.

*Sales Before Property Tax Year But After Lien Date.* In some tax jurisdictions, real estate taxes become a lien or personal liability before the property tax year. If a property in such a jurisdiction is sold after the lien or personal liability date but before the beginning of the property tax year, then the seller has paid the taxes for the property tax year even though the buyer owns the property for the entire property tax year. In such a case, the buyer will typically reimburse the seller for the taxes at settlement and the taxes will be apportioned entirely to the buyer. The seller is not allowed a deduction for the taxes. The buyer may deduct the taxes according to his or her method of accounting. Thus, a cash method buyer can deduct the taxes in the year paid and an accrual method buyer can deduct the taxes in the year accrued [Reg. § 1.164-6(b)(1)(ii)].

---

**EXAMPLE:** The property tax year in Alpha County is the calendar year and real estate taxes become a lien on Nov. 1 of the preceding year. Steve owns a property in the county. On Nov. 1, Year 1, Steve pays $1,000 of real estate taxes on the property for Year 2. On Nov. 15, Year 1, Steve sells the property to Barbara, a cash method taxpayer. At settlement, Barbara reimburses Steve for the $1,000 of taxes. The taxes are apportioned entirely to Barbara. Barbara can deduct the $1,000 of real estate taxes in Year 1.

---

*Sales After Property Tax Year But Before Lien Date.* In some tax jurisdictions, real estate taxes become a lien or personal liability after the property tax year. If a property in such a jurisdiction is sold before the lien or personal liability date but after the beginning of the property tax year, then the buyer has paid the taxes for the property tax year even though the seller owns the property for the entire property tax year. In such a case, the seller will typically reimburse the buyer for the taxes at settlement and the taxes will be apportioned entirely to the seller. The buyer is not allowed a deduction for the taxes. The seller may deduct the taxes according to his or her method of accounting. Thus, a cash method seller can deduct the taxes in the year paid and an accrual method seller can deduct the taxes in the year accrued [Reg. § 1.164-6(b)(1)(iii)].

---

**EXAMPLE:** The property tax year in Beta County is the calendar year and real estate taxes become a lien on March 1 of the following year. Sharon, a cash method taxpayer, owned a property in the county throughout Year 1. On Jan. 31, Year 2,

Sharon sells the property to Ben. At settlement, Sharon reimburses Ben for $800 of Year 1 real estate taxes that Ben will be responsible for paying on the March 1 lien date. The taxes are apportioned entirely to Sharon. Sharon can deduct the $800 of real estate taxes in Year 2.

---

*Sales During Property Tax Year.* Generally, a cash method taxpayer can only deduct real estate taxes in the year they are paid. However, there are some special rules that apply to the timing of the deduction of real estate taxes when real property is sold during the property tax year.

A cash method seller may treat the real estate taxes apportioned to him as paid in the year of sale, even though the taxes are not actually paid in that year, if (i) the buyer is liable for the taxes under the laws of the tax jurisdiction, or (ii) the seller is liable for the taxes under the laws of the tax jurisdiction but the taxes are not payable until after the date of the sale [§ 164(d)(2)(A); Reg. § 1.164-6(d)(1)].

A cash method buyer may treat the real estate taxes apportioned to him as paid in the year of sale, even though the taxes are not actually paid in that year, if the seller is liable for the taxes under the laws of the tax jurisdiction [§ 164(d)(2)(A); Reg. § 1.164-6(d)(2)].

---

**EXAMPLE:** The property tax year in Kappa County is the calendar year and real estate taxes become a lien on Nov. 1 of the preceding year. Sally owned a property in the county. On July 1, Year 2, Sally sells the property to Bill, a cash method taxpayer. At settlement, $500 of the real estate taxes for Year 2 is apportioned to Bill. The taxes were paid by Sally on Nov. 1, Year 1, and Bill reimburses Sally for the taxes apportioned to him. Bill may deduct the $500 of real estate taxes in Year 2 even though Sally paid them in Year 1.

---

An accrual method seller or buyer may treat the real estate taxes apportioned to him as accruing on the date of the sale if those taxes would not otherwise be deductible in any year [§ 164(d)(2)(B); Reg. § 1.164-6(d)(6)].

---

**EXAMPLE:** The property tax year in Zeta County is the calendar year and real estate taxes become a lien on Nov. 1. Seth owned property in the county. Seth sells the property to Bob on May 1, Year 2. Assume the real estate taxes are apportioned $340 to Seth and $360 to Bob. Seth and Bob are both accrual method taxpayers and neither has elected to accrue real estate taxes ratably. Generally, Seth would not be allowed to deduct the $340 because he is an accrual method taxpayer and he sold the property before the Nov. 1 accrual date. Therefore, under the special rule, Seth can treat the $340 as accruing on the May 1 date of sale and deduct the taxes in his tax year that includes that date. Bob must deduct the $360 in his tax year that includes the Nov. 1 lien date because his deduction is not otherwise disallowed under the accrual method of accounting.

---

### VII.E.4. Personal Property Taxes

[525 T.M., II.C.; TPS ¶2340.02.C.]

An individual taxpayer can deduct personal property taxes. Personal property taxes are taxes that are charged on personal property on an annual basis (even if collected more or less frequently) and that are based on the value of the personal property [§ 164(b)(1); Reg. § 1.164-3(c)]. If a tax is based partly on the value of the personal property and partly on other criteria, the taxpayer can only deduct the part of the tax based on value.

---

**EXAMPLE:** Steve pays an annual motor vehicle registration fee for his car. The annual fee is equal to 1% of the value of the vehicle plus 50 cents for each 100 pounds of the vehicle's weight. Steve's car is valued at $2,000 and weighs 3,000 pounds. Steve's registration fee is $35 (($2,000 × 1%) + (3,000 pounds × $0.50)). Steve can deduct only $20 ($2,000 × 1%) of the fee as personal property tax.

---

### VII.E.5. Foreign Taxes

[525 T.M., II.I.; TPS ¶2340.02.H.]

Generally, an individual taxpayer can take either a deduction or a tax credit for foreign income taxes imposed on him by a foreign country or a U.S. possession [§ 164(a)(3)]. See XX.C.2. for a discussion of the foreign tax credit. An individual taxpayer can also take a deduction for foreign real estate taxes. See VII.E.3. for a general discussion of the deduction for real estate taxes.

### VII.E.6. Generation-Skipping Transfer Taxes

[525 T.M., II.F.; TPS ¶2340.02.F.]

An individual taxpayer can deduct any generation-skipping transfer tax paid [§ 164(b)(4)]. See XXI.D. for a discussion of the generation-skipping transfer tax.

### VII.E.7. Taxes Not Deductible

[525 T.M., III.; TPS ¶2340.03.]

The following types of taxes generally are not deductible [§ 275(a); Reg. § 1.164-2]:

- federal income taxes;
- the employee's share of employment taxes, such as social security, Medicare, and railroad retirement taxes (however, a taxpayer can take an above-the line deduction for one-half of self-employment tax paid — see VII.B.7.);
- estate, inheritance, legacy, and succession taxes (however, a deduction can be taken for federal estate tax attributable to income in respect of a decedent that is includible in the taxpayer's gross income — see VII.J.); and
- gift taxes.

In addition, fees such as per capita fees, license fees, and fines and penalties are generally not deductible.

### VII.F. Interest

[536 T.M.; TPS ¶2330.]

Individual taxpayers generally can deduct two types of interest: (i) mortgage interest (see VII.F.1.), including certain points (see VII.F.3.a.) and mortgage insurance premiums (before 2014) (see VII.F.2.), and (ii) investment interest (see VII.F.4.). Individual taxpayers can also deduct interest incurred in a trade or business (see IV.A.12.).

Personal interest is not deductible [§ 163(h)(1)]. Personal interest includes any interest that is not home mortgage interest, investment interest, business interest, or another special type of deductible interest (e.g., interest on qualified student loans)

[§ 163(h)(2)]. Thus, for example, the following types of interest are nondeductible personal interest:

- interest on car loans;
- interest on federal, state, or local income tax; and
- finance charges on credit cards, retail installment contracts, or revolving charge accounts incurred for personal expenses.

### VII.F.1. Mortgage Interest

[536 T.M., VIII.I.; TPS ¶2330.02.H.]

Individual taxpayers who itemize their deductions can take a mortgage interest deduction for qualified residence interest [§ 163(h)(2)(D)]. Qualified residence interest is interest paid or accrued on a secured debt (see VII.F.1.b.) on a qualified residence (see VII.F.1.a.) in which the taxpayer has an ownership interest. Qualified residence interest includes interest on home acquisition debt (see VII.F.1.c.), home equity debt (see VII.F.1.d.), and grandfathered debt (see VII.F.1.e.). There are certain dollar limitations on the deduction of interest on home acquisition debt and home equity debt.

### VII.F.1.a. Qualified Residence

[536 T.M., VIII.E.; TPS ¶2330.02.H.3.b.]

A qualified residence includes a taxpayer's main home and one second home [§ 163(h)(4)(A)]. A home includes a house, condominium, cooperative, mobile home, house trailer, boat, or similar property that has sleeping, cooking, and toilet facilities [Reg. § 1.163-10T(p)(1), § 1.163-10T(p)(3)(ii)].

*Main Home.* A taxpayer's main home is the home where he or she lives most of the time during the year (i.e., his or her principal residence). A taxpayer cannot have more than one main home at any time during the year [Reg. § 1.163-10T(p)(2)].

*Second Home.* A taxpayer's second home may be any home other than his main home. Generally, if a taxpayer has more than one second home, he or she can deduct qualified residence interest on only one second home. The taxpayer must make an election as to which home will be treated as a second home for interest deduction purposes.

Although a taxpayer generally can deduct qualified residence interest on only one second home during a tax year, there are exceptions under which a taxpayer can treat different homes as second homes for different parts of the year:

- If the taxpayer buys a new home during the tax year, he or she can choose to treat the new home as the second home as of the day of purchase.
- If the taxpayer's main home no longer qualifies as a main home, the taxpayer can choose to treat it as a second home as of the day the taxpayer stops using it as his or her main home.
- If the taxpayer's second home is sold during the year or becomes the taxpayer's main home, the taxpayer can choose a new second home as of the day the taxpayer sells the old one or begins using it as his or her main home.

If a taxpayer rents out a home during the year, the taxpayer cannot choose that home as a second home for interest deduction purposes unless he or she uses it as a home for more than 14 days or more than 10% of the number of days during the year that it was rented at fair market value, whichever is greater. If a taxpayer does not rent out a home during the year, the taxpayer can choose that home as a second home even if the taxpayer does not use it as a home during the year [§ 163(h)(4)(A)(i), § 163(h)(4)(A)(iii), § 280A(d)(1)].

---

**EXAMPLE:** In addition to her main home, Patty owns a beach house that she rents out for 180 days during the year. Patty must use the beach house as a home for more than 18 days (180 × 10%) during the year in order for it to qualify as her second home for purposes of the mortgage interest deduction.

---

### VII.F.1.b. Secured Debt

[536 T.M., VIII.I.3.; TPS ¶2330.02.H.3.c.]

A debt is a secured debt if the taxpayer signs an instrument (such as a mortgage, deed of trust, or land contract) that (i) makes the taxpayer's ownership in his or her home the security for payment of the debt, (ii) provides that the home could satisfy the debt in the event of default, and (iii) is recorded or otherwise perfected under any state or local law that applies [Reg. § 1.163-10T(o)(1)]. A debt is treated as secured on the date on which each of these three requirements is satisfied, regardless of when amounts are actually borrowed. The third requirement is treated as satisfied on the date the security interest was granted if the instrument is recorded within a commercially reasonable time after that date [Reg. § 1.163-10T(o)(3)].

---

**EXAMPLE:** Sam owns a home subject to a mortgage of $100,000. He sells the home for $500,000 to Karen, who pays $50,000 down and gives Sam a $450,000 note. Karen takes the home subject to the $100,000 mortgage and Sam continues to make payments on it. Sam does not record or otherwise perfect the $450,000 mortgage under the state law that applies. Thus, the $450,000 mortgage does not qualify as a secured debt and Karen cannot deduct any interest she pays on it as home mortgage interest.

---

Under these rules, a taxpayer's mortgage on his or her home is generally a secured debt if the home is put up as collateral for the debt and the lender can take the home to satisfy the debt in the event the taxpayer defaults. However, a wraparound mortgage is not a secured debt unless it is recorded or otherwise perfected under state law.

A debt is not a secured debt if it is secured solely by a security interest that attaches to the taxpayer's home without his or her consent, such as a mechanic's lien or a judgment lien. A debt is also not a secured debt if it is secured solely by a lien on the taxpayer's general assets [Reg. § 1.163-10T(o)(1)].

A taxpayer may elect to treat a debt secured by a qualified residence as not secured by a qualified residence. Such an election may be desirable because of the limitations on the deduction of acquisition debt (see VII.F.1.c.) and home equity debt (see VII.F.1.d.). If a taxpayer has interest that would be deductible as either home mortgage interest or under some other Code provision (e.g., as a business expense), he may wish to make this election so that he can take more of a deduction for interest on other debts that are deductible only as home mortgage interest. When a taxpayer makes this election, it is effective for the tax year in which it is made and all later tax years, and it may only be revoked with the consent of the IRS [Reg. § 1.163-10T(o)(5)].

*VII.F.1.c. Home Acquisition Debt*
[536 T.M., VIII.I.1.; TPS ¶2330.02.H.3.d.]

Home acquisition debt is any mortgage that is taken out after October 13, 1987, to buy, build, or substantially improve a qualified residence and that is secured by that qualified residence [§ 163(h)(3)(B)(i)]. An improvement is substantial if it adds value to the home, prolongs the useful life of the home, or adapts the home to a new use. Repairs that merely maintain a home in good condition are not substantial improvements.

The total amount of the mortgages on a taxpayer's qualified residences (i.e., his or her main home and second home) that can qualify as home acquisition debt is limited to $1 million, reduced (but not below zero) by the amount of the any grandfathered debt (see VII.F.1.e.). The $1 million limitation is reduced to $500,000 for married taxpayers who file separately. An amount in excess of the limitation may qualify as home equity debt (see VII.F.1.d.) [§ 163(h)(3)(B)(ii), § 163(h)(3)(D)(ii)].

---

**EXAMPLE:** Wendy owns two qualified residences: a main home with a $450,000 mortgage and a second home with a $250,000 mortgage. She incurs another $380,000 debt to substantially improve her main home. Wendy's total home acquisition debt is $1,080,000 ($450,000 + $250,000 + $380,000); however, only $1,000,000 of that debt qualifies as home acquisition debt for purposes of the mortgage interest deduction. The $80,000 balance ($1,080,000 − $1,000,000) may potentially qualify for the mortgage interest deduction on home equity debt.

---

*Refinanced Home Acquisition Debt.* A mortgage used to refinance home acquisition debt is also treated as home acquisition debt. However, the amount of such a mortgage that may be treated as home acquisition debt is limited to the balance of the original mortgage immediately before it is refinanced. An amount in excess of this limitation may instead qualify as home equity debt (see VII.F.1.d.) [§ 163(h)(3)(B)(i)].

*Later Qualification as Home Acquisition Debt.* A mortgage that does not qualify as home acquisition debt because it does not meet the requirements at the time it is taken out may qualify as home acquisition debt at a later date when it meets those requirements. Thus, for example, if a mortgage used to buy a home does not qualify as home acquisition debt at the time it is taken out because the home is not a qualified residence, it may qualify at the time the home later becomes a qualified residence (assuming it is secured by the qualified residence) [Notice 88-74, 1988-2 C.B. 385].

*Treatment as Home Acquisition Debt When Requirements Not Met.* In the following situations, a mortgage secured by a qualified residence can be treated as home acquisition debt even if the proceeds are not actually used to buy, build, or substantially improve the qualified residence [Notice 88-74]:

1. If a taxpayer buys a home and takes out a mortgage secured by the home within 90 days before or after the date he buys the home, the mortgage may be treated as home acquisition debt. However, the amount treated as home acquisition debt is limited to the cost of the home plus the cost of any substantial improvements to the home.

---

**EXAMPLE:** On June 3, Alan bought a home for $200,000 and paid with cash from the sale of his old home. On July 15, Alan took out a mortgage of $100,000 secured by the new home. Alan uses the $100,000 proceeds to invest in stock. Because Alan took out the mortgage within 90 days after he bought the new home, he can treat the mortgage as home acquisition debt. The entire amount of the mortgage can be treated as home acquisition debt because the $100,000 mortgage was less than the $200,000 cost of the home.

2. If a taxpayer builds or substantially improves a home and takes out a mortgage secured by the home before the work on the home is completed, the mortgage may be treated as home acquisition debt. However, the amount treated as home acquisition debt is limited to the amount of expenses incurred within 24 months before the date the mortgage is taken out.

3. If a taxpayer builds or substantially improves his or her home and takes out a mortgage secured by the home within 90 days after the work on the home is completed, the mortgage may be treated as home acquisition debt. However, the amount treated as home acquisition debt is limited to the amount of expenses incurred within the period beginning 24 months before the work is completed and ending on the date the mortgage is taken out.

---

**EXAMPLE:** On Jan. 31, Barbara began building a home on a lot she owned. She used $75,000 of her personal funds to build the home. On Oct. 31, she completed construction of the home. On Nov. 21, Barbara took out a $50,000 mortgage secured by the home. Because Barbara took out the mortgage within 90 days after she completed work on the home, she can treat the mortgage as home acquisition debt. The entire amount of the mortgage can be treated as home acquisition debt because the $50,000 mortgage was less than the $75,000 of expenses incurred within the period 24 months before the work was completed.

---

### VII.F.1.d. Home Equity Debt

[536 T.M., VIII.I.2.; TPS ¶2330.02.H.3.e.]

Home equity debt is any mortgage taken out after October 13, 1987, that is secured by a qualified residence but is not home acquisition debt [§ 163(h)(3)(C)(i)] (see VII.F.1.c.). Thus, home equity debt may include:

1. a mortgage taken out for reasons other than to buy, build, or substantially improve a qualified residence; and

2. a mortgage taken out to buy, build, or substantially improve a qualified residence to the extent it is more than the home acquisition debt limitation.

---

**EXAMPLE:** Tom originally bought his main home for cash, but last year he took out a $100,000 mortgage loan secured by his home for the purpose of paying his medical bills and college tuition for his children. The loan is home equity debt because it is secured by his qualified residence but it is not home acquisition debt.

---

There is a limit on the amount of debt that can be treated as home equity debt. The total home equity debt on a taxpayer's main home and second home is limited to the smaller of [§ 163(h)(3)(C)]:

- $100,000 ($50,000 if married filing separately); or

- the total of each home's fair market value, reduced (but not below zero) by the amount of the taxpayer's home acquisition debt and grandfathered debt.

---

**EXAMPLE:** Sue took out a mortgage to buy her main home ten years ago. The fair market value of her home is now $110,000 and the current balance of her original mortgage is now $95,000. A bank offers Sue a mortgage loan equal to 125% of the fair market value of the home, less any outstanding mortgages and liens. Sue takes out a mortgage loan of $42,500 (($110,000 × 125%) − $95,000) to consolidate her other debts. The amount of the $42,500 mortgage loan that Sue can treat as home equity debt is limited to $15,000, which is the smaller of the maximum home equity debt limit ($100,000) or her home's fair market value reduced by her home acquisition debt ($110,000 − $95,000 = $15,000).

---

### VII.F.1.e. Grandfathered Debt

[536 T.M., VIII.I.; TPS ¶2330.02.H.3.]

Grandfathered debt is any mortgage that was taken out on or before October 13, 1987, and that was secured by a qualified residence on October 13, 1987, and at all times thereafter. Unlike home acquisition debt and home equity debt, there is no dollar limitation on the amount of debt that can be treated as grandfathered debt. However, the amount of a taxpayer's grandfathered debt reduces the dollar limitations that apply to his or her home acquisition debt (see VII.F.1.c.) and home equity debt (see VII.F.1.d.) [§ 163(h)(3)(D)].

*Refinanced Grandfathered Debt.* A mortgage taken out after October 13, 1987, to refinance grandfathered debt is also treated as grandfathered debt to the extent it does not exceed the remaining principal on the original mortgage on the date of the refinancing (it is treated as home acquisition or home equity debt to the extent it exceeds the remaining principal). However, refinanced grandfathered debt can be treated as grandfathered debt only for the term remaining on the grandfathered debt when it was refinanced (after that, it is treated as home acquisition or home equity debt). Under an exception, if the debt before refinancing was like a balloon note (the principal was not amortized over the term of the debt), then the refinanced debt is treated as grandfathered debt for the term of the first refinancing (not to exceed 30 years) [§ 163(h)(3)(D)(iii), § 163(h)(3)(D)(iv)].

*Line-of-Credit.* A line-of-credit mortgage that existed on October 13, 1987, is grandfathered debt only to the extent of the amounts borrowed against the line-of-credit on or before October 13, 1987. Amounts borrowed against the line-of-credit after October 13, 1987, are either home acquisition debt or home equity debt, depending on how the proceeds are used.

### VII.F.2. Mortgage Insurance Premiums [Expired]

[594 T.M., II.D.2.g.; TPS ¶2330.02.H.3.h.]

Before 2014, taxpayers could deduct mortgage insurance premiums if [§ 163(h)(3)(E), § 163(h)(4)(E)]:

1. the premiums were paid or accrued in connection with home acquisition debt (see VII.F.1.c.);

2. the mortgage insurance was certain private mortgage insurance or mortgage insurance provided by the Department of Veterans Affairs, the Federal Housing Administration, or the Rural Housing Service; and

3. the insurance contract was issued after 2006.

The deduction for mortgage insurance premiums was phased out for taxpayers with adjusted gross income between $100,000 and $109,000 ($50,000 and $54,500 for married taxpayers filing separately) [§ 163(h)(3)(E)(ii)].

Special rules applied to prepaid mortgage insurance. When a taxpayer paid mortgage insurance premiums that were properly allocable to periods after the end of the tax year, the premiums were required to be treated as paid in the period to which they were properly allocated. For this purpose, premiums were required to be allocated ratably over the shorter of (i) the stated term of the mortgage, or (ii) 84 months. If a mortgage was satisfied before the end of its stated term, no deduction was allowed for mortgage insurance premiums properly allocable to periods after the mortgage was satisfied [§ 163(h)(4)(F); Reg. § 1.163-11(a)].

The deduction for mortgage insurance premiums expired December 31, 2013.

### VII.F.3. Points

[536 T.M., V.A.; TPS ¶2330.01.A.7.a.]

Lenders sometimes require or encourage borrowers to pay certain charges known as "points" in order to obtain a home mortgage (points are also often referred to as loan origination fees, maximum loan charges, loan discount, or discount points). Points are considered to be prepaid interest. Points are typically calculated as a percentage of the amount borrowed and are paid at the time of the loan closing.

### VII.F.3.a. Rules for Buyer-Paid Points

[536 T.M., V.A.; TPS ¶2330.01.A.7.a.]

Because points are prepaid interest, they generally must be capitalized and deducted ratably over the life of the mortgage [§ 461(g)(1)]. However, a cash method taxpayer can currently deduct the full amount of points paid if the points are paid on a mortgage incurred in connection with the purchase or improvement of, and secured by, his or her main home as long as the payment of points is an established business practice in the area where the mortgage is taken out and the amount of points does not exceed the amount of points generally charged in that area [§ 461(g)(2)].

***Safe Harbor for Current Deduction Exception.*** Under a safe harbor for the current deduction exception, a taxpayer can currently deduct the full amount of points paid in obtaining a mortgage if the following requirements are met [Rev. Proc. 94-27, 1994-1 C.B. 613]:

1. the taxpayer uses the cash method of accounting;
2. the taxpayer uses the mortgage to buy or build his or her main home;
3. the mortgage is secured by the taxpayer's main home;
4. the payment of points is an established business practice in the area where the mortgage is taken out;
5. the points were not more than the points generally charged in that area;
6. the points were not more than the sum of (i) the funds the taxpayer provided at or before closing, and (ii) any points paid by the seller;
7. the points were not paid in place of amounts that are ordinarily stated separately on the settlement statement, such as appraisal fees, inspection fees, title fees, attorney fees, and property taxes;
8. the amount of points is clearly shown on the settlement statement (such as Form HUD-1); and
9. the points were computed as a percentage of the principal amount of the mortgage.

***Mortgage Used for Home Improvement.*** Although the safe harbor for the current deduction exception applies only to points paid on a mortgage used to buy or build a taxpayer's main home, the IRS has taken the position that current deduction exception also applies to points paid on a mortgage used to substantially improve a taxpayer's main home if all of the safe harbor requirements except #2, #8, and #9 are satisfied [§ 461(g)(2)].

***Mortgage Refinancing.*** The IRS has taken the position that the current deduction exception generally does not apply to points paid to refinance an existing home mortgage because the mortgage proceeds are used to repay a debt, not to buy, build, or substantially improve a home. However, if a portion of the mortgage proceeds are used to substantially improve a taxpayer's main home, the points may be allocated between the improvements and the refinancing, with the points attributable to the improvements treated as currently deductible and the points attributable to repayment of the old mortgage treated as deductible ratably over the life of the new mortgage [Rev. Rul. 87-22, 1987-1 C.B. 146].

---

**EXAMPLE:** Martha, a cash method taxpayer, refinances the old mortgage on her main home with a new 15-year $100,000 mortgage that is secured by her home. She pays two points on the loan ($100,000 × 2% = $2,000) out of her private funds. The payment of points is an established practice in the area, the two points are not more than the amount generally charged there, and the points are not paid in place of amounts ordinarily stated separately on the settlement statement. Martha uses $75,000 of the loan proceeds to pay off the old mortgage and $25,000 of the loan proceeds to improve her home. She makes six monthly payments on the new mortgage during the year of the refinancing. Martha can currently deduct the $500 ($2,000 × ($25,000/$100,000)) of points allocated to the home improvements. She can also currently deduct $50 (6 monthly payments × ($1,500/180 months)) of the balance of points that must be ratably deducted over the life of the mortgage. Thus, she can currently deduct $550 of the points and she must deduct the remaining $1,450 balance ratably in later years.

---

The Eighth Circuit has held that where a taxpayer purchases his or her main home with short-term financing and later replaces that short-term loan with a permanent mortgage, the points paid on the permanent mortgage can be currently deducted because the permanent mortgage is sufficiently incurred in connection with the purchase of the home to fall within the current deduction exception [*Huntsman v. Commissioner*, 905 F.2d 1182 (8th Cir. 1990)]. However, the IRS has stated that it will not follow this holding in circuits other than the Eighth Circuit [AOD 1991-02].

***Mortgage on Second Home.*** The current deduction exception applies only to points paid to obtain a mortgage on a taxpayer's main home [§ 461(g)(2)]. Points paid to obtain a mortgage on the taxpayer's second home must be deducted ratably over the life of the mortgage.

### VII.F.3.b. Rules for Seller-Paid Points

[536 T.M., V.A.; TPS ¶2330.01.A.7.a.]

Loan placement fees paid by the seller to the lender to arrange for financing for the buyer are considered to be points. A buyer treats such seller-paid points as if he paid them and reduces the basis of the home by the amount of those points [Rev. Proc. 94-27, 1994-1 C.B. 613]. Thus, a buyer may be able to deduct seller-paid points. The buyer applies the rules discussed in VII.F.3.a. to determine whether he or she can currently deduct these points or whether the points must be deducted over the life of the mortgage. A seller cannot deduct such points, but can treat them as selling expenses that reduce the seller's amount realized from the sale of the home.

### VII.F.3.c. Deduction of Points Ratably Over Life of Mortgage

[536 T.M., V.A.; TPS ¶2330.01.A.7.a.]

If a taxpayer does not qualify to currently deduct points or chooses not to currently deduct points, then the points can be deducted ratably over the life of the mortgage if the following requirements are met [Rev. Proc. 87-15, 1987-1 C.B. 624]:

1. the taxpayer uses the cash method of accounting;
2. the mortgage is secured by a home (need not be main home);
3. the life of the mortgage is not more than 30 years;
4. if the life of the mortgage is more than 10 years, the terms of the mortgage are the same as the terms of other mortgages offered in the taxpayer's area for the same or a longer life; and
5. either (i) the mortgage amount is $250,000 or less, or (ii) the number of points paid on the mortgage is 6 or less (if mortgage life more than 15 years) or 4 or less (if mortgage life 15 years or less).

### VII.F.4. Investment Interest

[536 T.M., VIII.B.; TPS ¶2330.02.F.]

An individual taxpayer who itemizes deductions can deduct investment interest to the extent of his or her net investment income for the tax year [§ 163(d)(1)]. Investment interest generally includes any interest paid or accrued on money borrowed to buy investment property (however, it does not include home mortgage interest or passive activity interest) [§ 163(d)(3)]. Investment property includes [§ 163(d)(5), § 469(e)(1)]:

1. property that produces interest, dividends, annuities, or royalties not derived in the ordinary course of a trade or business;
2. property that produces gain or loss not derived in the ordinary course of a trade or business that is attributable to the disposition of the type of property discussed in 1. or property held for investment (other than an interest in a passive activity); and
3. an interest held in a trade or business activity (other than a passive activity) in which the taxpayer did not materially participate.

### VII.F.4.a. Computing Investment Interest Deduction

[536 T.M., VIII.B.; TPS ¶2330.02.F.2.c.]

A taxpayer's deduction for investment interest is limited to the amount of the taxpayer's net investment income for the tax year. Net investment income is equal to the taxpayer's investment income minus the taxpayer's investment expenses other than investment interest [§ 163(d)(4)(A)].

Investment income is generally the taxpayer's gross income from investment property (e.g., interest, dividends, annuities, and royalties). However, investment income does not include income used to compute income or loss from a passive activity. Investment income also does not include qualified dividends or net capital gains unless the taxpayer elects to treat them as investment income. A taxpayer may elect to include qualified dividends and/or net capital gains in investment income by entering the amount he elects to include on the appropriate line of Form 4952. However, if a taxpayer makes this election, the taxpayer must reduce his or her qualified dividends and/or net capital gains eligible for the lower capital gains tax rates by that same amount [§ 163(d)(4)(B), § 163(d)(4)(D)].

Investment expenses are the taxpayer's allowable deductions that are directly connected with the production of investment income. For purposes of computing net investment income, investment expenses do not include investment interest. Investment expenses also do not include expenses used to compute income or loss from a passive activity [§ 163(d)(4)(C), § 163(d)(4)(D)].

An individual taxpayer uses Form 4952, *Investment Interest Expense Deduction*, to compute and report his or her deduction for investment interest.

### VII.F.4.b. Carryover of Disallowed Investment Interest

[536 T.M., VIII.B.; TPS ¶2330.02.F.2.d.]

Any investment interest disallowed as a deduction due to the net investment income limitation can be carried over indefinitely and deducted as investment interest in later tax years (subject to the same limitation in those years) [§ 163(d)(2)].

The carryover of disallowed investment interest to later tax years is not limited by the taxpayer's taxable income for the tax year in which the investment interest is paid or accrued [Rev. Rul. 95-16, 1995-1 C.B. 9]. In other words, disallowed investment interest can be carried over to later tax years even if it is more than the taxpayer's taxable income in the year it was paid or accrued.

## VII.G. Charitable Contributions

[521 T.M.; TPS ¶2390.]

Individual taxpayers who itemize their deductions generally can take a deduction for charitable contributions made during the tax year. A charitable contribution is a donation or gift to, or for the use of, a qualified charitable organization [§ 170(c)]. A contribution is "for the use of" a qualified charitable organization when it is held for the organization in a legally enforceable trust or under a similar arrangement. For a discussion of the definition of a qualified charitable organization, see VII.G.1.

A charitable contribution generally may be made in the form of money or property. For special rules that apply to contributions of property, see VII.G.2. For other special charitable contribution rules, see VII.G.3. For limitations on the amount of the charitable contributions that can be deducted by a taxpayer, see VII.G.5. For the rules on when charitable contributions can be deducted, see VII.G.5. For the recordkeeping requirements that must be met by taxpayers making charitable contributions, see VII.G.6.

### VII.G.1. Qualified Charitable Organizations

[521 T.M., II.D.; TPS ¶2390.02.]

A qualified charitable organization includes any of the following five types of organizations [§ 170(c)]:

1. a corporation, trust, community chest, fund, or foundation organized and operated solely for religious, charitable, scientific, literary, or educational purposes, or for the prevention of cruelty to children and animals, or to foster national or international amateur sports competition (must be organized in the U.S., a U.S. possession, a state, or the District of Columbia);

2. a war veterans' organization, such as a post, auxiliary, trust or foundation (must be organized in the U.S. or a U.S. possession);

3. a domestic fraternal society, order, or association operating under a lodge system (contributions deductible only if used solely for religious, charitable, scientific, literary, or educational purposes, or for the prevention of cruelty to children and animals);

4. certain nonprofit cemetery companies; and

5. the United States, a U.S. possession, a state, the District of Columbia, an Indian tribal government, or a political subdivision thereof (contributions deductible only if used solely for public purposes).

Examples of organizations that are qualified charitable organizations include:

• churches, temples, synagogues, mosques, and other religious organizations;

• nonprofit charitable organizations (e.g., the United Way, the American Red Cross);

• nonprofit hospitals and medical research organizations;

• nonprofit educational organizations (e.g., colleges, museums, the Boy Scouts and Girl Scouts);

• nonprofit volunteer fire companies;

• nonprofit organizations that develop and maintain public parks and recreational facilities; and

• civil defense organizations.

Examples of organizations that are not qualified charitable organizations include:

• chambers of commerce and other business leagues or organizations;

• civic leagues and associations;

• country clubs and other social clubs;

• homeowners' associations;

• political organizations and candidates;

• labor unions; and

• foreign organizations (other than certain Canadian, Mexican, and Israeli charitable organizations).

Taxpayers can determine whether an organization is a qualified charitable organization by:

• contacting the organization itself;

• checking the IRS website (www.irs.gov) by clicking on "Tools" and "Exempt Organizations Select Check"; or

• calling the IRS at 1-877-829-5500.

### VII.G.2. Contributions of Property

[521 T.M., III.; TPS ¶2390.04.]

When a taxpayer makes a charitable contribution of property, the amount of the taxpayer's deduction is generally equal to the fair market value of the property at the time of the contribution. The fair market value of property is generally the price at which the property would change hands between a willing buyer and a willing seller if neither is under any compulsion to buy or sell and both have reasonable knowledge of the relevant facts [Reg. § 1.170A-1(c)(1)].

The contribution of a future interest in tangible personal property is treated as made only when all intervening interests in, and rights to the actual possession or enjoyment of, the property have either expired or have been transferred to a person other than the taxpayer or a related person [§ 170(a)(3); Reg. § 1.170A-5].

Special rules apply to contributions of appreciated property (see VII.G.2.a.). Special rules also apply to contributions of specific types of property, including (i) clothing and household items (see VII.G.2.b.), (ii) motor vehicles, boats, and airplanes (see VII.G.2.c.), (iii) intellectual property (see VII.G.2.d.), (iv) taxidermy property (see VII.G.2.e.), (v) property subject to a debt (see VII.G.2.f.), and (vi) partial interests in property, including qualified conservation contributions (see VII.G.2.g.).

### VII.G.2.a. Contributions of Appreciated Property

[521 T.M., III.C.; TPS ¶2390.04.B.]

Special rules apply to contributions of property that has appreciated in value (i.e., the fair market value of the property on the date of contribution is more than the taxpayer's adjusted basis in the property). The amount of the charitable deduction for such contributions may be required to be reduced by the amount of ordinary income or capital gain the taxpayer would recognize if he sold the property at its fair market value on the date of the contribution. The application of these rules depends on whether the appreciated property is ordinary income property or capital gain property. Note that a taxpayer is not required to reduce the amount of his or her charitable deduction if the taxpayer includes the ordinary income or capital gain in gross income in the same year as the contribution [§ 170(e)(1)(A); Reg. § 1.170A-4].

*Ordinary Income Property.* Ordinary income property is property on which the taxpayer would have recognized ordinary income or short-term capital gain if he had sold it at its fair market value on the date of contribution [Reg. § 1.170A-4(b)(1)]. Examples of ordinary income property are capital assets held for one year or less, inventory, and works of art and manuscripts created by the taxpayer. Property used in a trade or business is also considered ordinary income property to the extent of any depreciation recapture that would be treated as ordinary income if the taxpayer sold the property at its fair market value on the date of the contribution. For a detailed discussion of ordinary income property, see III.B.1.

The amount of a taxpayer's charitable deduction for a contribution of ordinary income property is equal to the fair market value of the property minus the amount that would be ordinary income or short-term capital gain if the taxpayer sold the property at its fair market value on the date of the contribution [Reg. § 1.170A-4(a)(1)]. Generally, this means that the taxpayer's charitable deduction for ordinary income property is limited to his or her basis in the property.

---

**EXAMPLE:** Laura contributes stock with a fair market value of $1,000 to a qualified charitable organization. She had held the stock for eight months as of the date of the contribution and her basis in the stock is $700. Laura's charitable deduction is limited to $700, which is equal to the $1,000 fair market value minus the $300 ($1,000 − $700) short-term capital gain she would have recognized if she had sold the stock at its fair market value on the date of the contribution.

---

*Capital Gain Property.* Capital gain property is property on which the taxpayer would have recognized long-term capital gain if he had sold it at its fair market value on the date of contribution [Reg. § 1.170A-4(b)(2)]. Capital gain property generally includes capital assets held for more than one year. For purposes of these charitable contribution rules, capital gain property also includes certain real property and depreciable property used in the taxpayer's trade or business and held for more than one year. For a detailed discussion of capital gain property, see III.B.1.

The amount of a taxpayer's charitable deduction for a contribution of capital gain property is generally equal to the fair market value of the property [Reg. § 1.170A-4(a)(1)]. However, there are certain exceptions under which the amount of a taxpayer's charitable deduction for a contribution of capital gain property is equal to the fair market value of the property minus the amount that would be long-term capital gain if the taxpayer sold the property at its fair market value on the date of the contribution. Under these exceptions, the taxpayer's charitable deduction for such capital gain property is generally limited to his or her basis in the property.

The following are the exceptions under which a taxpayer's charitable deduction for a contribution of capital gain property must be reduced by the amount that would be long-term capital gain [§ 170(e)(1)(B)]:

1. contributions of tangible personal property that the qualified charitable organization will put to a use that is unrelated to its exempt purpose or function;

2. contributions of tangible personal property that the qualified charitable organization will sell or exchange during the year the contribution is made and for which it has not made the required certification of exempt use;

3. contributions of property to certain private nonoperating foundations;

4. contributions of intellectual property (see VII.G.2.d.); and

5. contributions of certain taxidermy property (see VII.G.2.e.).

### VII.G.2.b. Contributions of Used Clothing and Household Items

[521 T.M., II.C.2.b(4); TPS ¶2390.06.G.]

Contributions of used clothing and household items are not deductible unless the clothing or household items (furniture, furnishings, electronics, appliances, linens, and similar items) are in good used condition or better. However, a taxpayer can deduct a contribution of a single clothing or household item that is not in good used condition if the deduction is for more than $500 and the taxpayer includes a qualified appraisal of the property with his or her return [§ 170(f)(16)].

There are no fixed formulas or methods for determining the fair market value of items of clothing and household items. Such items usually have a fair market value that is much lower than the price paid for them when they were new. For items of clothing, the valuation can be based on prices that buyers of such used items pay in used clothing stores. For household items, evidence such as photographs, receipts, and statements from the recipient should be retained in support of the valuation.

### VII.G.2.c. Contributions of Used Vehicles, Boats, and Airplanes

[521 T.M., VI.C.6.; TPS ¶2395.03.B.]

A taxpayer's deduction for the contribution of a qualified vehicle with a claimed value of more than $500 may be subject to limitation and must satisfy special substantiation requirements. A qualified vehicle includes (i) a motor vehicle manufactured mainly for use on public streets, roads, and highways (e.g., a car, truck, or SUV), (ii) a boat, and (iii) an airplane.

If the qualified charitable organization sells such a vehicle without making any significant intervening use of or material improvement to the vehicle before it is sold, the taxpayer's deduction cannot exceed the amount of the gross proceeds the organization received from the sale [§ 170(f)(12)(A)(ii)]. Thus, in such a case, the taxpayer's deduction is limited to the smaller of the fair market value of the vehicle on the date of contribution or the gross proceeds from the sale of the vehicle. However, this limitation does not apply and the taxpayer can deduct the fair market value of the vehicle if the qualified charitable organization [Notice 2005-44, 2005-25 I.R.B. 1287]:

1. made a significant intervening use of or a material improvement to the vehicle before it was sold; or

2. gave the vehicle to a needy individual (or sold it to a needy individual at a price well below fair market value) to further the organization's charitable purpose.

In determining the fair market value of a motor vehicle, a taxpayer can use the price listed for a private party sale of the vehicle in a used car pricing guide (a so-called blue book). The fair market value of boats and airplanes generally should be based on an appraisal.

A taxpayer who donates a qualified used vehicle should receive Copy B of Form 1098-C, *Contributions of Motor Vehicles, Boats, and Airplanes,* from the qualified charitable organization within 30 days of the sale of the vehicle (or, if one of the exceptions applies, within 30 days of the donation of the vehicle). Form 1098-C shows the gross proceeds from the sale of a qualified vehicle and Copy B must be attached to the taxpayer's return for the year of the donation. If the taxpayer e-files, the taxpayer must either (i) include Form 1098-C as a PDF attachment if the tax software program permits, or (ii) attach Copy B of Form 1098-C to Form 8453, *U.S. Individual Income Tax Transmittal for an IRS e-file Return,* and mail the forms to the IRS. If the taxpayer does not receive Copy B of Form 1098-C from the qualified charitable organization by the filing deadline, he or she can either (i) request an extension to file the return, or (ii) file the return without claiming the deduction and file an amended return after receiving Form 1098-C [§ 170(f)(12)(A)(i)].

### VII.G.2.d. Contributions of Intellectual Property

[521 T.M., VII.C.; TPS ¶2390.09.C.]

If a taxpayer contributes intellectual property to a qualified charitable organization, his or her initial charitable deduction is limited to the smaller of the taxpayer's basis in the contributed property or the fair market value of the property [§ 170(e)(1)(B)(iii)]. However, the taxpayer may be permitted an additional charitable deduction for the year of contribution and later years, based on a specified percentage of the income generated by the donated intellectual property in those years [§ 170(m)]. For purposes of these rules, intellectual property includes patents, copyrights, trademarks, trade names, trade secrets, know-how, certain software, and other similar property, or applications or registrations of such property [§ 170(m)(9)].

Additional charitable deductions can be claimed only if the taxpayer notifies the qualified charitable organization at the time of the contribution that he intends to claim additional charitable deductions for the income from the contributed intellectual property. The organization is required to file Form 8899, *Notice of Income From Donated Intellectual Property,* and to provide a copy to the taxpayer.

The amounts of additional charitable deductions that may be claimed by the taxpayer are computed based on the chart below as the specified percentage of the income generated by the donated intellectual property during each year of the 10-year period after the date of the contribution (but limited to the legal life of the property). However, additional charitable deductions are allowed only to the extent that the total amounts computed based on the chart exceed the initial charitable deduction claimed [§ 170(m)].

| Taxpayer's Tax Year Ending On or After Date of Contribution | Applicable Percentage |
|---|---|
| 1st | 100% |
| 2nd | 100% |
| 3rd | 90% |
| 4th | 80% |
| 5th | 70% |
| 6th | 60% |
| 7th | 50% |
| 8th | 40% |
| 9th | 30% |
| 10th | 20% |
| 11th | 10% |
| 12th | 10% |

### VII.G.2.e. Contributions of Taxidermy Property

[521 T.M., III.C.3.a(4); TPS ¶2390.04.B.2.d.]

If a taxpayer contributes taxidermy property to a qualified charitable organization, the charitable deduction is limited to the smaller of the taxpayer's basis in the contributed property or the fair market value of the property. This rule applies whether the taxpayer prepared, stuffed, or mounted the taxidermy property or the taxpayer paid someone else to prepare, stuff, or mount the taxidermy property [§ 170(e)(1)(B)(iv)]. Taxidermy property includes any work of art that (i) is the reproduction or preservation of an animal, (ii) is prepared, stuffed, or mounted for purposes of recreating one or more of the characteristics of the animal, and (iii) contains a part of the body of the dead animal. A taxpayer's basis in taxidermy property includes only the cost of preparing, stuffing, and mounting the property [§ 170(f)(15)].

### VII.G.2.f. Contributions of Property Subject to Debt

[521 T.M., II.E.2.e(2)(b); TPS ¶2390.01.C.5.b.]

If a taxpayer contributes property subject to a debt and the qualified charitable organization assumes the debt, the amount of the taxpayer's charitable deduction is determined by reducing the fair market value of the property by [§ 170(f)(5)(A); Reg. § 1.170A-3(b)]:

1. the amount of the outstanding debt assumed by the qualified charitable organization; and
2. the amount of any deductible interest the taxpayer pays on the debt that is attributable to the period after the date of the contribution.

If the contributed property is a bond, the fair market value must also be reduced by the amount of any interest (including bond discount) receivable on the bond that is attributable to any period before the date of the contribution to the extent that the interest is not includible in the taxpayer's income because of his or her accounting method [§ 170(f)(5)(B); Reg. § 1.170A-3(c)].

### VII.G.2.g. Contributions of Partial Interest in Property

[521 T.M., II.F.; TPS ¶2390.06.B.]

Generally, a taxpayer cannot take a charitable deduction for the contribution of a partial interest in property, such as a contribution of a right to use the taxpayer's property [§ 170(f)(3)(A)].

---

**EXAMPLE:** Paul owns an office building and he allows a qualified charitable organization to use the top floor of the building rent-free. Paul cannot take a charitable deduction because he has only contributed a partial interest in the property.

---

There are four exceptions under which a taxpayer can take a charitable deduction for the contribution of a partial interest in property. A taxpayer can take a charitable deduction for a contribution of [§ 170(f)(3), Reg. § 1.170A-7(b)]:

1. a remainder interest in the taxpayer's personal home or farm;
2. an undivided part of the taxpayer's entire interest in the property;
3. a partial interest that would be deductible if transferred to certain types of trusts; and
4. a qualified conservation contribution.

***Contribution of Remainder Interest in Personal Home or Farm.*** A taxpayer can take a charitable deduction for the contribution of an irrevocable remainder interest in a personal home or farm. A personal home includes any home that the taxpayer uses as a residence, including a vacation home. A farm includes any land the taxpayer uses for the production of crops, fruit, or other agricultural products, or for the sustenance of livestock [§ 170(f)(3)(B)(i); Reg. § 1.170A-7(b)(3), § 1.170A-7(b)(4)].

---

**EXAMPLE:** Alice gives her church a remainder interest in her home under which she will continue to live in her home during her lifetime but the home will pass to the church upon her death. Alice can take a charitable deduction for the value of the remainder interest.

---

***Contribution of Undivided Part of Entire Interest in Property.*** A taxpayer can take a charitable deduction for a contribution of an undivided portion of the taxpayer's entire interest in property. An undivided portion of a taxpayer's entire interest in property consists of a fraction or percentage of every substantial interest or right the taxpayer owns in the property that extends over the entire term of the taxpayer's interest in the property [§ 170(f)(3)(B)(ii); Reg. § 1.170A-7(b)(1)].

---

**EXAMPLE:** Dave contributes an undivided one-half interest in 100 acres of land to a qualified charitable organization. Dave and the organization share in the economic benefits of the land as tenants in common. Dave can take a charitable deduction for the value of the undivided one-half interest.

---

However, there are special rules that apply to a contribution of an undivided portion of a taxpayer's entire interest in tangible personal property. No deduction is allowed for such a contribution unless all interests in the tangible personal property immediately before the contribution are held by (i) the taxpayer, or (ii) the taxpayer and the qualified charitable organization receiving the contribution. If the taxpayer later makes an additional contribution of such tangible personal property, the fair market value of the later contribution is equal to the smaller of the fair market value at the time of the initial contribution or the fair market value at the time of the additional contribution. The taxpayer must recapture his or her charitable deduction for the contribution of such tangible personal property if, within a specified period, (i) the taxpayer does not contribute the rest of his or her interests in the property, or (ii) the qualified charitable organization does not take substantial physical possession of the property and use it for the organization's charitable purpose. For purposes of this recapture rule, the specified period is the earlier of (i) the date that is 10 years after the date of the initial contribution, or (ii) the date of the taxpayer's death [§ 170(o)(3)].

*Contribution of a Partial Interest to Certain Trusts.* Taxpayers can take charitable deductions for the contribution of certain partial interests (e.g., remainder interests, income interests) transferred in trust [§ 170(f)(2)]. If a taxpayer contributes a partial interest in property that is not transferred in trust, he can take a charitable deduction for the value of the partial interest if it would have been deductible had it been transferred in trust [§ 170(f)(3)(A); Reg. § 1.170A-7(b)(2)].

*Qualified Conservation Contribution.* Taxpayers can take charitable deductions for contributions of certain partial interests in real property known as qualified conservation contributions. A qualified conservation contribution is a contribution of a qualified real property interest to a qualified organization to be used exclusively for conservation purposes. A qualified real property interest is [§ 170(h)(2)]:

- the taxpayer's entire interest in the property (other than a mineral interest);
- a remainder interest in the property; or
- a restriction granted in perpetuity on the use of the property (e.g., an easement).

Qualified organizations include [§ 170(h)(3)]:

- governmental units;
- certain publicly supported charities; and
- organizations controlled by such governmental units or charities.

The contribution must be made for one of the following conservation purposes [§ 170(h)(4)]:

1. the preservation of land areas for outdoor recreation by, or for the education of, the general public;
2. the protection of a relatively natural habitat of fish, wildlife, or plants, or a similar ecosystem;
3. the preservation of open space (e.g., farmland, forest land) for the scenic enjoyment of the general public or under a clearly delineated government conservation policy (but only if such preservation yields a significant public benefit); or
4. the preservation of an historically important land area or certified historic structure (a building, structure, or land area listed in the National Register or a building located in a registered historic district and certified as being of historic significance to the district).

Such a conservation purpose must be protected in perpetuity.

In the case of a certified historic building in a registered historic district, a contribution of an easement or other restriction on the exterior of the building is deductible as a charitable contribution only if (i) the restriction preserves the entire exterior of the building and prohibits any change that is inconsistent with its historical character, (ii) the taxpayer and qualified organization enter into an agreement certifying that the organization is a qualified organization and has the resources and commitment to manage and enforce the restriction, and (iii) the taxpayer includes with the return a qualified appraisal, photographs of the building's entire exterior, and a description of all restrictions on development of the building [§ 170(h)(4)(B)]. A $500 filing fee applies if the taxpayer claims a deduction of more than $10,000 [§ 170(f)(13)]. If a rehabilitation credit was claimed for the building for any of the five years before the year of the contribution, the amount of the charitable deduction must be reduced [§ 170(f)(14)].

### *VII.G.2.h. Contributions of Food Inventory [Expired]*

[794 T.M., IV.B.; TPS ¶2390.04.B.1.b.]

Before 2014, a special enhanced deduction was available for contributions of food inventory by an individual taxpayer from his or her trade or business. In determining the amount of a taxpayer's charitable deduction for a contribution of food inventory, the fair market value was reduced by only one-half the amount that would be ordinary income or short-term capital gain if the taxpayer sold the food inventory at its fair market value on the date of the contribution. However, the charitable deduction computed under this rule was limited to twice the basis of the contributed food inventory. Thus, in effect, the charitable deduction for food inventory was equal to the lesser of (i) the basis plus one-half the appreciation, or (ii) two times the basis [§ 170(e)(3)(B)]. For individual taxpayers (but not C corporations), the charitable deduction for food inventory was limited to 10% of the taxpayer's total net income from all trades or businesses from which such contributions were made during the year [§ 170(e)(3)(C)(ii)].

The special deduction expired December 31, 2013.

### *VII.G.3. Special Charitable Contribution Rules*

### *VII.G.3.a. Out-of-Pocket Expenses Paid in Providing Services*

[521 T.M., II.C.1.c(1); TPS ¶2390.01.E.1.]

A taxpayer cannot take a charitable deduction for the value of services he or she performs for a qualified charitable organization. However, a taxpayer can take a charitable deduction for certain unreimbursed, out-of-pocket expenses incurred while performing such services if the expenses are directly connected with the services and the taxpayer incurred the expenses only because of the performance of such services [Reg. § 1.170A-1(g)]. For special substantiation requirements that apply to the charitable deduction for out-of-pocket expenses, see VII.G.6.c.

*Automobile Expenses.* A taxpayer can take a charitable deduction for any unreimbursed, out-of-pocket expenses directly related to the use of the taxpayer's automobile in performing services for a qualified charitable organization [Reg. § 1.170A-1(g)]. The taxpayer can either take a deduction for the actual automobile expenses paid or figure the deduction by using the standard mileage rate for charitable use of an automobile (14 cents per mile for 2014) [Notice 2013-80, 2013-52 I.R.B. 821]. A taxpayer who chooses to deduct actual automobile expenses can deduct gas and oil costs, but not costs such as repairs and maintenance, depreciation, registration fees, insurance, or tires. Under either method, the taxpayer can deduct the costs of parking fees and tolls. A taxpayer must keep reliable written records to substantiate the deduction.

*Travel.* A taxpayer can take a charitable deduction for reasonable travel expenses incurred while away from home in performing services for a qualified charitable organization [Reg. § 1.170A-1(g)]. However, such expenses are deductible only if there is no significant element of personal pleasure, recreation, or vacation involved in the travel and only if the taxpayer is on duty in a genuine and substantial sense throughout the trip. Deductible travel expenses include the costs of (i) air, rail or bus transportation, (ii) transportation between the taxpayer's hotel and the airport or station, (iii) lodging, and (iv) meals. If a taxpayer receives a per diem allowance to cover travel expenses, the charitable deduction for travel expenses must be reduced by the amount of the allowance received. If the amount of a per diem allowance received is more than the amount of the travel expenses, the taxpayer must include the excess amount in income.

---

**EXAMPLE:** Fred travels to Greece and works for several hours each morning on an archaeological dig sponsored by a qualified charitable organization. The rest of his day is free for recreation and sightseeing. Fred cannot take a charitable deduction for his travel expenses.

---

*Conventions.* If a taxpayer attends a convention as a representative of a qualified charitable organization, he can deduct his travel expenses (he cannot deduct personal expenses for sightseeing, theaters, nightclubs, etc.). If a taxpayer attends a church convention as a member of the church instead of its representative, he cannot deduct his travel expenses. However, he can deduct unreimbursed expenses incurred while performing services for his church.

*Uniforms.* A taxpayer can deduct the cost and upkeep of a uniform worn while performing service for a qualified charitable organization if the uniform is not suitable for everyday use [Reg. § 1.170A-1(g)].

*Church Deacons.* A church deacon (an individual in a permanent diaconate program established by a church) can take a charitable deduction for the unreimbursed expenses of vestments, books, and transportation necessary to serve the church as either a deacon candidate or an ordained deacon.

*Expenses of Foster Children.* A foster parent can take a charitable deduction for the unreimbursed expenses of feeding, clothing, and caring for a foster child if (i) the foster child was chosen for the taxpayer by a qualified charitable organization, (ii) the taxpayer does not have a profit motive (or any profit) in providing the foster care, and (iii) the expenses are incurred primarily to benefit the qualified charitable organization.

*Expenses of Underprivileged Youths.* A taxpayer can take a charitable deduction for unreimbursed out-of-pocket expenses paid to allow underprivileged youths to attend athletic events, movies, or dinners if the youths are selected by a qualified charitable organization whose goal is to reduce juvenile delinquency.

### VII.G.3.b. Benefits Received as a Result of Charitable Contributions

[521 T.M., II.E.2.d.; TPS ¶2390.01.C.4.a.]

If a taxpayer receives a benefit as a result of making a charitable contribution to a qualified charitable organization, the taxpayer can deduct the contribution only to the extent it exceeds the value of the benefit received [Reg. § 1.170A-1(h)(2)]. In other words, the taxpayer's charitable deduction is equal to the amount of the contribution reduced by the value of any benefit received. However, the amount of the contribution does not need to be reduced by the value of any token benefit (a small item or other benefit of token value) if the qualified charitable organization determines that the value of the benefit is not substantial and informs the taxpayer that he or she can deduct the contribution in full.

If a taxpayer pays more than $75 to a qualified charitable organization and the payment is partly a contribution and partly a payment for goods or services, the charitable organization must provide the taxpayer with a written statement that contains a good faith estimate of the value of the goods or services provided and that notifies the taxpayer that the taxpayer can only deduct the amount of the payment in excess of the value of the goods and services provided to him [Reg. § 1.170A-13(f)(7), § 1.170A-13(f)(8)].

***College Sports Tickets.*** If a taxpayer makes a charitable contribution to a college and, as a result, receives the right to buy tickets to athletic events at the college's stadium, the taxpayer can take a charitable deduction for only 80% of the contribution. The fair market value of the right to buy tickets is treated as being equal to 20% of the contribution. No charitable deduction is allowed for any portion of a contribution that is for the tickets themselves (instead of the right to buy tickets) [§ 170(l)].

---

**EXAMPLE:** Pam pays $800 a year to a university's athletic scholarship program and, as a result, she gets a right to buy one season ticket for the university's home basketball games. The payment includes $300 for one season ticket at the stated ticket price. Pam cannot take a charitable deduction for the $300 paid for the season ticket. Pam can take a $400 (($800 − $300) × 80%) charitable deduction for the balance of her annual payment to the athletic scholarship fund.

---

***Charity Benefit Tickets.*** If a taxpayer makes a contribution to a qualified charitable organization and receives tickets to a charity ball, banquet, show, sporting event, or other event, the taxpayer can take a charitable deduction only for the amount of the contribution in excess of the value of the tickets. The value of the tickets is the established charge for such tickets or, if there is no established charge, the reasonable value of the right to attend the event. Whether the taxpayer actually uses the tickets is irrelevant; however, the taxpayer can deduct the full amount of the contribution if he returns the tickets to the qualified charitable organization for resale.

***Membership Fees or Dues.*** If a taxpayer pays membership dues or fees to a qualified charitable organization, the taxpayer can take a charitable deduction only for the amount that is in excess of the value of the membership benefits he receives. If the membership dues or fees are $75 or less, the following membership benefits can be disregarded in determining the amount of the charitable deduction [Reg. § 1.170A-1(h)(3), § 1.170A-13(f)(8)(i)(B)]:

1. membership rights and privileges that can be used frequently, such as free or discounted admission, free or discounted parking, discounts on the purchase of goods and services, and preferred access to goods and services; and

2. admission to events open only to members if the organization reasonably projects that the cost per person will be $10.40 or less for 2014 ($10.50 for 2015) [§ 513(h)(2); Rev. Proc. 2013-35, 2013-47 I.R.B. 537, § 3.28, Rev. Proc. 2014-61, 2014-47 I.R.B. 860].

### VII.G.3.c. Expenses Related to Student Living with Taxpayer

[521 T.M., II.C.1.c(2); TPS ¶2390.01.E.2.]

A taxpayer can take a charitable contribution deduction of up to $50 per month for the qualifying expenses of an American or foreign student who lives with the taxpayer in his or her home under a written agreement with a qualified organization as part of a program to provide educational opportunities if the following requirements are met [Reg. § 1.170A-2]:

1. the student is not a relative or dependent of the taxpayer; and
2. the student is a full-time student in the 12th grade or lower at a school in the United States.

For this purpose, a qualified organization includes only the first three types of qualified charitable organizations listed in VII.G.1. Thus, for example, it does not include a U.S. or state government or a nonprofit cemetery company [Reg. § 1.170A-2(a)(1)].

Qualifying expenses generally include the cost of books, tuition, food, clothing, transportation, medical care, entertainment, and other amounts spent for the well-being of the student. They do not include general household expenses such as taxes, insurance, and repairs. They also do not include amounts not actually spent by the taxpayer such as the fair market value of the room used by the student or depreciation on the home [Reg. § 1.170A-2(a)(2)].

### VII.G.3.d. *Expenses of Whaling Captains*

[521 T.M., II.C.1.c(1); TPS ¶2390.01.E.3.]

A whaling captain recognized by the Alaska Eskimo Whaling Commission can take a charitable contribution deduction for up to $10,000 per year of reasonable and necessary whaling expenses paid to carry out sanctioned whaling activities [§ 170(n)].

### VII.G.4. Percentage Limitations on Charitable Deduction

[521 T.M., IV.; TPS ¶2390.05.]

Generally, a taxpayer's deduction for charitable contributions cannot be more than 50% of his or her adjusted gross income (AGI) (see VII.G.4.a.). However, in certain cases, a taxpayer's deduction may be further limited to 30% or 20% of his or her adjusted gross income (see VII.G.4.b. and VII.G.4.c.). Special limitations apply to capital gain property (see VII.G.4.d.). Before 2014, special limitations also applied to qualified conservation contributions (see VII.G.4.e.). For purposes of these limitations, adjusted gross income is computed without regard to any net operating loss carrybacks.

The various limitations on the deduction of charitable contributions must be applied in a specified order (see VII.G.4.f.). Charitable contributions that exceed the limits can be carried over and deducted in later years (see VII.G.4.g.).

### VII.G.4.a. *50% Limit*

[521 T.M., IV.B.1.; TPS ¶2390.05.B.1.]

A taxpayer's deduction for the total of all charitable contributions made during the year cannot be more than 50% of the taxpayer's AGI. Thus, the 50% limit is an overall limit on a taxpayer's deduction for all charitable contributions made during a year.

The 50% limit also applies to contributions a taxpayer makes to (and not merely for the use of) specified types of qualified charitable organizations known as 50% limit organizations (however, as discussed at VII.G.4.d., contributions of capital gain property to 50% limit organizations are subject to a special 30% limit). The following types of qualified charitable organizations are 50% limit organizations [§ 170(b)(1)(A); Reg. § 1.170A-9]:

1. churches and conventions or associations of churches;
2. educational organizations with a regular faculty and curriculum that normally have a regularly enrolled student body attending classes on site;

3. hospitals and certain medical research organizations associated with hospitals;

4. organizations operated for the benefit of publicly supported state colleges and universities;

5. governmental units;

6. publicly supported charities;

7. organizations that may not qualify as "publicly supported" but that meet other tests showing they respond to the needs of the general public and normally receive more than one-third of their support from the 50% limit organizations described above or from persons other than disqualified persons;

8. organizations controlled by, and operated for the benefit of, the 50% limit organizations described above;

9. private operating foundations;

10. private nonoperating foundations that make qualifying distributions of 100% of contributions within two-and-one-half months after the end of the year in which they receive the contributions; and

11. private foundations whose contributions are pooled into a common fund and that would qualify under #8 but for the right of substantial contributors to name the public charities that receive contributions from the fund.

### VII.G.4.b. 30% Limit

[521 T.M., IV.B.2.; TPS ¶2390.05.B.2.]

The 30% limit applies to the following contributions [§ 170(b)(1)(B)]:

1. contributions made to any qualified charitable organization other than a 50% limit organization (such as veterans' organizations, fraternal societies, nonprofit cemeteries, and certain private nonoperating foundations); and

2. contributions made for the use of any qualified charitable organization (including a 50% limit organization).

### VII.G.4.c. 20% Limit

[521 T.M., IV.B.3.; TPS ¶2390.05.B.3.]

The 20% limit applies to contributions of capital gain property to or for the use of any qualified charitable organization other than a 50% limit organization (see VII.G.4.d. for contributions of capital gain property to or for the use of a 50% limit organization) [§ 170(b)(1)(D)].

### VII.G.4.d. Special 30% Limit for Capital Gain Property

[521 T.M., IV.C.5.; TPS ¶2390.05.B.1.b.]

Contributions of capital gain property to or for the use of a 50% limit organization are subject to a special 30% limit instead of the 20% limit that applies to other qualified charitable organizations. However, the special 30% limit does not apply if the taxpayer determines the amount of its deduction for the capital gain property by reducing the fair market value by the amount of long-term gain he would have recognized had he sold the property at its fair market value on the date of the contribution. The special 30% limit also does not apply to qualified conservation contributions [§ 170(b)(1)(C)].

### VII.G.4.e. Special Limits for Qualified Conservation Contributions [Expired]

[521 T.M., IV.C.5.d.; TPS ¶2390.05.B.1.e.]

Before 2014, the deduction of qualified conservation contributions was subject to a special 50% limit (100% for qualified conservation contributions made by farmers and ranchers). The limit on the deduction for qualified conservation contributions was computed as 50% (100% for farmers and ranchers) of the taxpayer's adjusted gross income minus the taxpayer's deduction for all other charitable contributions. The special limit expired December 31, 2013 [§ 170(b)(1)(E)].

### VII.G.4.f. Application of the Limitations

[521 T.M., IV.D.; TPS ¶2390.05.]

The limits on the deduction of charitable contributions are applied in the following order [§ 170(b)(1)]:
1. the 50% limit;
2. the 30% limit;

3. the special 30% limit on contributions of capital gain property;
4. the 20% limit;

5. the 50% limit on qualified conservation contributions (before 2014); and
6. the 100% limit on qualified conservation contributions (before 2014).

The Applying the Deduction Limits Worksheet (Source: IRS Pub. 526) can be used to apply the deduction limits when more than one limit applies for the tax year.

Worksheet 2. **Applying the Deduction Limits**                           *Keep for your records*

If the result on any line is less than zero, enter zero. For other instructions, see *Instructions for Worksheet 2.*

**Step 1. Enter any qualified conservation contributions (QCCs).**

| | |
|---|---|
| 1. If you are a qualified farmer or rancher, enter any QCCs eligible for the 100% limit | 1 |
| 2. Enter any QCCs not entered on line 1. Do not include this amount on line 3, 4, 5, 6, or 8 | 2 |

**Step 2. List your other charitable contributions made during the year.**

| | |
|---|---|
| 3. Enter your contributions to 50% limit organizations. (Include contributions of capital gain property if you reduced the property's fair market value. Do not include contributions of capital gain property deducted at fair market value.) **Do not** include any contributions you entered on line 1 or 2 | 3 |
| 4. Enter your contributions to 50% limit organizations of capital gain property deducted at fair market value | 4 |
| 5. Enter your contributions (other than of capital gain property) to qualified organizations that are not 50% limit organizations | 5 |
| 6. Enter your contributions "for the use of" any qualified organization. (But do not enter here any amount that must be entered on line 8.) | 6 |
| 7. Add lines 5 and 6 | 7 |
| 8. Enter your contributions of capital gain property to or for the use of any qualified organization. (But do not enter here any amount entered on line 3 or 4.) | 8 |

**Step 3. Figure your deduction for the year and your carryover to the next year.**

| | |
|---|---|
| 9. Enter your adjusted gross income | 9 |
| 10. Multiply line 9 by 0.5. This is your 50% limit | 10 |

| | | Carryover |
|---|---|---|
| *Contributions to 50% limit organizations* | | |
| 11. Enter the smaller of line 3 or line 10 | 11 | |
| 12. Subtract line 11 from line 3 | 12 | |
| 13. Subtract line 11 from line 10 | 13 | |
| *Contributions not to 50% limit organizations* | | |
| 14. Add lines 3 and 4 | 14 | |
| 15. Multiply line 9 by 0.3. This is your 30% limit | 15 | |
| 16. Subtract line 14 from line 10 | 16 | |
| 17. Enter the smallest of line 7, 15, or 16 | 17 | |
| 18. Subtract line 17 from line 7 | 18 | |
| 19. Subtract line 17 from line 15 | 19 | |
| *Contributions of capital gain property to 50% limit organizations* | | |
| 20. Enter the smallest of line 4, 13, or 15 | 20 | |
| 21. Subtract line 20 from line 4 | 21 | |
| 22. Subtract line 17 from line 16 | 22 | |
| 23. Subtract line 20 from line 15 | 23 | |
| *Other contributions* | | |
| 24. Multiply line 9 by 0.2. This is your 20% limit | 24 | |
| 25. Enter the smallest of line 8, 19, 22, 23, or 24 | 25 | |
| 26. Subtract line 25 from line 8 | 26 | |
| 27. Add lines 11, 17, 20, and 25 | 27 | |
| 28. Subtract line 27 from line 10 | 28 | |
| 29. Enter the smaller of line 2 or line 28 | 29 | |
| 30. Subtract line 29 from line 2 | 30 | |
| 31. Subtract line 27 from line 9 | 31 | |
| 32. Enter the smaller of line 1 or line 31 | | 32 |
| 33. Add lines 27, 29, and 32. Enter the total here and on Schedule A (Form 1040), line 16 or line 17, whichever is appropriate | | 33 |
| 34. Subtract line 32 from line 1 | | 34 |
| 35. Add lines 12, 18, 21, 26, 30, and 34. Carry this amount forward to Schedule A (Form 1040) next year | | 35 |

## VII.G.4.g. Carryovers of Unused Charitable Contributions

[521 T.M., V; TPS ¶2390.05.C.]

Charitable contributions that exceed any applicable percentage limitation in the year of contribution may be carried over to the succeeding five tax years. Excess contributions carried over to succeeding tax years generally retain their character from the year of contribution (i.e., the excess amount of a contribution subject to the 50% limit is generally treated as a contribution subject to the 50% limit in each succeeding tax year). Contributions actually made during a tax year are deductible before contributions carried over to that year. Carryover contributions are deductible on a first-in, first-out basis (i.e., carryovers from earlier years are deductible before carryovers from later years) [§ 170(d)].

### *VII.G.5. Timing of Charitable Contribution Deduction*

[521 T.M., II.; TPS ¶2390.01.D.]

A charitable contribution is deductible only in the tax year it is actually paid. This rule applies to both cash method and accrual method taxpayers [Reg. § 1.170A-1(a)].

A charitable contribution is generally considered to be paid on the date of its unconditional delivery to a qualified charitable organization [Reg. § 1.170A-1(b)]. A contribution made by check is treated as delivered on the date the taxpayer mails it. A contribution charged to a credit card is treated as delivered on the date the charge is made. A contribution made through a pay-by-phone account is treated as delivered on the date the financial institution pays the amount. A contribution made by text message is treated as delivered on the date the text is sent

A contribution in the form of a stock certificate is generally treated as delivered on the date the properly endorsed certificate is mailed or otherwise delivered to the qualified charitable organization. However, if a stock certificate is delivered to the taxpayer's agent or the issuing corporation for transfer to the name of a qualified charitable organization, it is not considered to be delivered to the charitable organization until it is transferred on the books of the issuing corporation [Reg. § 1.170A-1(b)].

If a taxpayer's contribution to a qualified charitable organization is conditioned upon the occurrence of a future act or event to become effective, no deduction is allowed unless the possibility of the act or event occurring is so remote as to be negligible [Reg. § 1.170A-1(e)].

---

**EXAMPLE:** Nick transfers land to his hometown for as long as it is used as a public park. The city plans to use the land as a park and there is little chance that it will be used for a different purpose. Nick can take a deduction for the contribution of the land.

---

### *VII.G.6. Substantiation Requirements for Charitable Contributions*

[521 T.M., VI.; TPS ¶2395.]

Taxpayers must retain certain records to substantiate their charitable contribution deductions. The types of records required depend on (i) the type of contribution (cash or noncash), and (ii) the amount of the contribution.

### *VII.G.6.a. Substantiation of Cash Contributions*

[521 T.M., VI.B.; TPS ¶2395.01.]

Cash contributions include contributions paid by cash, check, debit card, credit card, electronic funds transfer, and payroll deduction. The substantiation requirements for cash contributions fall into two categories based on the amount of the contribution: (i) contributions of less than $250, and (ii) contributions of $250 or more. If the taxpayer receives any goods or services from the qualified charitable organization in connection with the contribution, the amount of the contribution is equal to the amount of payment to the organization minus the value of the goods and services received from the organization.

***Cash Contribution of Less than $250.*** A cash contribution of less than $250 must be substantiated by [§ 170(f)(17); Reg. § 1.170A-13(a)(1)]:

1. a bank record (e.g., canceled check, bank statement, or credit card statement);

2. a receipt, letter, or other written communication from the qualified charitable organization; or

3. payroll deduction records.

The documents must show the name of the qualified charitable organization, the date of the contribution, and the amount of the contribution. In the case of payroll deduction records, the taxpayer must retain (i) a pay stub, Form W-2, or other document furnished by his or her employer that shows the date and amount of the contribution and (ii) a pledge card or other document that shows the name of the qualified charitable organization.

*Cash Contribution of $250 or More.* A cash contribution of $250 or more must be substantiated by (i) an acknowledgement from the qualified charitable organization, or (ii) payroll deduction records. For this purpose, each payment or payroll deduction is treated as a separate contribution. If the taxpayer made more than one contribution of $250 or more, he may satisfy the requirements with a separate acknowledgement for each contribution or an acknowledgement that lists the dates and amounts of multiple contributions [§ 170(f)(8), § 170(f)(17); Reg. § 1.170A-13(a)(1), § 1.170A-13(f)].

If substantiated by an acknowledgement from the qualified charitable organization, the acknowledgement must be written, must be received by the taxpayer on or before the earlier of the date the return is filed or the due date of the return (including extensions), and must contain the following information [§ 170(f)(8); Reg. § 1.170A-13(f)]:

1. the name of the qualified charitable organization;

2. the date of the contribution (the date may be substantiated by a bank record or a receipt instead);

3. the amount of the contribution;

4. whether any goods or services were provided to the taxpayer as a result of the contribution (other than certain token items and membership benefits);

5. a description and good faith estimate of the value of any such goods or services provided (other than an intangible religious benefit such as admission to a religious ceremony); and

6. if intangible religious benefits were the only benefits provided, a statement to that effect.

If substantiated by payroll records, the taxpayer must retain (i) a pay stub, Form W-2, or other document furnished by his or her employer that shows the date and amount of the contribution (the date may be substantiated by a bank record or a receipt instead), and (ii) a pledge card or other document that shows the name of the qualified charitable organization and states that the organization does not provide the taxpayer with goods or service in return for the contributions. A single pledge card may be retained for all contributions made by payroll deduction.

### VII.G.6.b. Substantiation of Noncash Contributions

[521 T.M., VI.C.; TPS ¶2395.02.]

The substantiation requirements for a noncash contribution (e.g., a contribution of property) fall into the following four categories based on the amount of the deduction the taxpayer claims for the contribution: (i) deductions of less than $250, (ii) deductions of at least $250 but not more than $500, (iii) deductions more than $500 but not more than $5,000, or (iv) deductions over $5,000. If the taxpayer receives any goods or services from the qualified charitable organization in connection with the contribution, the taxpayer must reduce the amount of the contribution by the value of the goods and services received. If the taxpayer reduces his or her deduction for appreciated property under the rules discussed at VII.G.2.a., his contribution is the reduced amount.

***Deductions Less than $250.*** If a taxpayer claims a deduction of less than $250 for a noncash contribution, the contribution generally must be substantiated by a receipt, letter, or other written communication from the qualified charitable organization showing [Reg. § 1.170A-13(b)(1), § 1.170A-13(b)(2)]:

1. the name of the organization;
2. the date and location of the contribution; and
3. a reasonably detailed description of the property.

The receipt requirement is waived when the taxpayer leaves property at a qualified charitable organization's unattended drop site and in other similar situations where it is impractical for the taxpayer to get such a document from the organization.

For deductions of less than $250, a taxpayer must also keep reliable written records for each item of contributed property that include the following information [Reg. § 1.170A-13(b)(1)]:

1. the name and address of the qualified charitable organization;
2. the date and location of the contribution;
3. a reasonably detailed description of the property;
4. the fair market value of the property and how it was determined (including a copy of a signed appraisal, if any); and
5. the terms of any conditions attached to the property.

If the taxpayer must reduce the fair market value of the property by the amount of appreciation, the records must also show the amount of the reduction and how it was determined. If the taxpayer contributes only a partial interest in property, the records must also show (i) the amount claimed as a deduction for the current year, (ii) the amounts claimed as a deduction for any earlier years in which other partial interests in the property were contributed and the name and address of each organization to which such other interests were contributed, (iii) the place where any tangible property is located or kept, and (iv) the name of any person (other than the charitable organization) in possession of the property [Reg. § 1.170A-13(b)(2)].

***Deductions Between $250 and $500.*** If a taxpayer claims a deduction of at least $250 but not more than $500 for a noncash contribution, the contribution must be substantiated by an acknowledgement from the qualified charitable organization. The acknowledgement must be written, must be received by the taxpayer on or before the earlier of the date the return is filed or the due date of the return (including extensions), and must contain the following information [§ 170(f)(8); Reg.§ 1.170A-13(f)]:

1. the name of the qualified charitable organization;
2. the date and location of the contribution;
3. a reasonably detailed description of the property contributed (but not necessarily its value);
4. whether any goods or services were provided to the taxpayer as a result of the contribution (other than certain token items and membership benefits);
5. a description and good faith estimate of the value of any such goods or services provided (other than intangible religious benefits); and

6. if intangible religious benefits were the only benefits provided, a statement to that effect.

For deductions of between $250 and $500, a taxpayer must also keep reliable written records for each item of contributed property. The records must include the same information included in records for deductions of less than $250 (see discussion above).

***Deductions Between $500 and $5,000.*** If a taxpayer claims a deduction of more than $500 but not more than $5,000 for a noncash contribution, the contribution must be substantiated by the same type of acknowledgement that applies to deductions between $250 and $500 (see discussion above).

For deductions between $500 and $5,000, the taxpayer must also keep written records that include the same information as the written records required for deductions between $250 and $500 (see discussion above). However, the following additional information must also be included in the taxpayer's records for deductions between $500 and $5,000 [§ 170(f)(11)(B); Reg. § 1.170A-13(b)(3)]:

1. how the taxpayer acquired the contributed property (e.g., purchase, gift, bequest, inheritance, exchange);

2. the approximate date the taxpayer acquired the contributed property (if the property was created, produced, or manufactured by the taxpayer, the approximate date the property was substantially completed); and

3. the taxpayer's cost or other basis for the contributed property (including any adjustments to basis for property held less than one year).

Taxpayers should attach an explanatory statement to their return if they have reasonable cause for not providing information about the acquisition date or cost basis of the property. For contributions of publicly traded securities, information on the cost or other basis of the property is not required.

In determining whether a deduction for a noncash contribution is over $500, a taxpayer should combine his or her claimed deductions for all similar items of property contributed to the same qualified charitable organization during the year [§ 170(f)(11)(F)].

***Deductions over $5,000.*** If a taxpayer claims a deduction of more than $5,000 for a noncash contribution, the contribution must be substantiated by the same type of acknowledgement that applies to deductions between $500 and $5,000 (see discussion above) and the taxpayer must keep written records that include the same information as the written records required for deductions between $500 and $5,000 (see discussion above).

In addition to the required acknowledgement and written records, a taxpayer claiming a deduction of more than $5,000 for a noncash contribution must also obtain a qualified written appraisal of the contributed property from a qualified appraiser [§ 170(f)(11)(C); Reg. § 1.170A-13(c)].

In determining whether a deduction for a noncash contribution is over $5,000, a taxpayer must combine his or her claimed deductions for all similar items of property contributed to the same qualified charitable organization during the year [§ 170(f)(11)(F)].

***Special Substantiation Requirements for Qualified Conservation Contributions.*** In the case of a qualified conservation contribution, a taxpayer's written records must also include information on (i) the fair market value of the underlying property before and after the contribution, and (ii) the conservation purpose furthered by the contribution [Reg. § 1.170A-14(i)].

### VII.G.6.c. Substantiation of Out-of-Pocket Expenses Related to Services

[521 T.M., VI.; TPS ¶2395.]

If a taxpayer provides services to a qualified charitable organization and has unreimbursed out-of-pocket expenses related to those services, he must keep adequate records to prove the amount of the expenses. For any separate out-of-pocket expenses of $250 or more, the taxpayer must also obtain an acknowledgement from the qualified charitable organization that provides the following information [Reg. § 1.170A-13(f)(10)]:

1. a description of the services provided;

2. a statement of whether or not the organization provided the taxpayer with any goods or services to reimburse him for the expenses;

3. a description and good faith estimate of the value of any goods and services provided to reimburse the taxpayer; and

4. if the only benefit provided to the taxpayer was an intangible religious benefit, a statement to that effect.

## VII.H. Casualty and Theft Losses

[527 T.M., V.; TPS ¶2350.03.C., .03.D.]

Individual taxpayers are allowed a deduction for losses on personal-use property, but only if such losses result from a casualty or a theft [§ 165(c)(3)]. A casualty is the damage, destruction, or loss of property resulting from an identifiable event that is sudden, unexpected, or unusual. A theft is an illegal taking of property with the intent to deprive the owner of it. The deduction for casualty and theft losses on personal-use property is subject to certain limitations. The deduction is reported in Section A of Form 4684, *Casualties and Thefts*, and claimed as an itemized deduction in the Casualty and Theft Losses section on Schedule A of Form 1040.

Individual taxpayers are also allowed a deduction for losses incurred in a trade or business and losses incurred in a transaction entered into for profit, whether or not such losses result from a casualty or theft [§ 165(c)(1), § 165(c)(2)]. The deductions for casualty and theft losses on business and income-producing property are reported in Section B of Form 4684, *Casualties and Thefts*, and on Form 4797, *Sales of Business Property* (if required). An individual taxpayer claims the deduction for casualty and theft losses on business property as an above-the-line deduction on Schedule C of Form 1040. An individual taxpayer claims the deduction for casualty and theft losses on income-producing property as a miscellaneous itemized deduction not subject to the 2% floor on Schedule A of Form 1040.

See VIII.H. for a detailed discussion of the loss deductions allowable to individual taxpayers, including the deductions for casualty or theft losses, losses on business property, and losses on income-producing property.

## VII.I. Miscellaneous Itemized Deductions Subject to 2% AGI Floor

[504 T.M., II.A.1.; TPS ¶2910.]

In addition to the itemized deductions for medical expenses (see VII.D.), taxes (see VII.E.), interest (see VII.F.), charitable contributions (see VII.G.), and casualty and theft losses (see VII.H.), there are a number of miscellaneous itemized deductions. Certain types of miscellaneous itemized deductions are deductible only to the extent they exceed 2% of a taxpayer's adjusted gross income. Other types of miscellaneous itemized deductions are not subject to this 2% floor. Miscellaneous itemized deductions subject to the 2% floor include [§ 67; Reg. § 1.67-1T(a)(1)]:

1. unreimbursed employee expenses (see VII.I.1.);

2. expenses paid in connection with the determination, collection, or refund of any tax (see VII.I.2.); and

3. expenses paid for the production or collection of income or for the management, conservation, or maintenance of property held for the production of income (see VII.I.3.).

The total amount of these types of miscellaneous itemized deductions is deductible only to the extent it exceeds 2% of the taxpayer's adjusted gross income.

### VII.I.1. Unreimbursed Employee Expenses

[504 T.M., II.A.1.b(4)(b); TPS ¶2130.]

A taxpayer can deduct unreimbursed employee expenses as miscellaneous itemized deductions if they are ordinary and necessary expenses paid or incurred during the tax year in carrying on the taxpayer's trade or business of being an employee [§ 162(a)]. The deduction for unreimbursed employee expenses is computed and reported on Form 2106, *Employee Business Expenses*, or Form 2106-EZ, *Unreimbursed Employee Business Expenses*. Some of the more common types of unreimbursed employee expenses deductible as miscellaneous itemized deductions include (i) travel expenses, (ii) local transportation expenses, (iii) meal and entertainment expenses, (iv) the cost of uniforms and work clothing, (v) union and professional dues, (vi) work-related educational expenses, (vii) job search expenses, and (viii) home office expenses. For a detailed discussion of the deduction for unreimbursed employee expenses, see IV.A.3.

### VII.I.2. Expenses for the Determination, Collection, or Refund of Tax

[504 T.M., II.A.1.b(4)(d); TPS ¶2010.01.A.3.b(1)]

An individual taxpayer can deduct the ordinary and necessary expenses paid or incurred in connection with the determination, collection, or refund of any tax [§ 212(3); Reg. § 1.212-1(l)].

The most common example of this type of deduction is tax preparation fees. Deductible tax preparation fees include fees paid to an accountant or other tax return preparer to prepare tax returns, the cost of tax preparation software programs, the cost of tax publications, and fees paid for the electronic filing of tax returns. Tax preparation fees are generally deductible on the taxpayer's return for the year in which he pays the fees.

Credit card convenience fees charged by a card processor are deductible if they are incurred by a taxpayer when he uses a credit or debit card to pay federal taxes (including estimated taxes). Such fees are deductible for the tax year in which they are incurred [IR-2009-37 (4/7/2009)].

Legal fees paid in connection with the determination, collection, or refund of tax are also deductible. Thus, for example, a taxpayer can deduct legal fees paid in connection with the provision of tax advice in relation to a divorce.

### VII.I.3. Expenses for the Production of Income

[504 T.M., II.A.1.b(4)(c); TPS ¶2300.]

An individual taxpayer can deduct the ordinary and necessary expenses paid or incurred for the production or collection of income and for the management, conservation, or maintenance of property held for the production of income. To be deductible, such expenses must be reasonable and they must be closely related to one of those purposes [§ 212(1), § 212(2); Reg. § 1.212-1(d)]. Examples of these types of deductible expenses include (i) investment fees and expenses, (ii) fees to collect interest and dividends, (iii) service charges on dividend reinvestment plans, (iv) IRA administrative fees, (v) legal fees, (vi) appraisal fees, (vii) safe deposit box rental fees, (viii) expenses of an office used for investment purposes, (ix) computer depreciation, (x) indirect miscellaneous deductions from pass-through entities, (xi) losses on deposits with financial institutions, (xii) losses on IRAs, and (xiii) certain casualty and theft losses.

*Investment Fees and Expenses.* A taxpayer can deduct investment fees, custodial fees, trust administration fees, and other expenses paid for the management of investments that produce taxable income.

*Fees to Collect Interest and Dividends.* A taxpayer can deduct fees paid to a broker, bank, trustee or similar agent to collect interest on taxable bonds or dividends on shares of stock. Fees paid to brokers to buy or sell stocks and bonds are not deductible. The fees paid to buy such securities are included in the basis of the securities. The fees paid to sell such securities are taken into account in computing the gain or loss on the sale.

*Service Charges on Dividend Reinvestment Plans.* A taxpayer can deduct service charges paid as a subscriber in a dividend reinvestment plan, including charges for holding shares acquired through the plan, collecting and reinvesting cash dividends, keeping individual records, and providing detailed statements of account.

*IRA Administrative Fees.* A taxpayer can deduct fees that are billed separately by a trustee in connection with the administration of the taxpayer's IRA.

*Legal Fees.* A taxpayer can deduct legal fees paid in connection with the production or collection of taxable income. Thus, for example, a taxpayer can deduct legal fees paid in connection with the performance or retention of the taxpayer's job (e.g., legal fees to defend against criminal charges arising as a result of the taxpayer's job). As another example, a taxpayer can deduct legal fees paid in connection with the collection of taxable alimony.

*Appraisal Fees.* A taxpayer can deduct appraisal fees paid to determine the amount of a casualty loss or the fair market value of donated property.

*Safe Deposit Box Rental Fees.* A taxpayer can deduct safe deposit box rental fees if the safe deposit box is used to store taxable stocks and bonds or investment-related papers and documents. No deduction is allowed if the box is used only to store personal items or tax-exempt securities.

*Office Expenses.* A taxpayer can deduct the expenses of operating an office, such as rent expense and wages for clerical help, if the office is used for investment purposes.

*Computer Depreciation.* A taxpayer can deduct depreciation on a computer if it is used for investment purposes. Such a computer generally must be depreciated using the straight line method over the ADS recovery period. See V.A. for a detailed discussion of depreciation.

*Indirect Deductions from Pass-Through Entities.* A partner or shareholder in a partnership, an S corporation, or a nonpublicly offered mutual fund can deduct his or her share of the pass-through entity's deductions for investment expenses (note that publicly offered mutual funds do not pass through such deductions to shareholders). Partnerships and S corporations report such amounts on Schedule K-1. Nonpublicly offered mutual funds report such amounts on Form 1099-DIV.

*Losses on Deposits with Financial Institutions.* A taxpayer generally can deduct a loss for a deposit he had in an insolvent or bankrupt financial institution. The taxpayer may elect to deduct the loss in the year the financial institution becomes insolvent or bankrupt, even if the exact amount of loss has not been finally determined (if the actual loss turns out to be less than the estimated loss, the taxpayer must include the difference in income). If the deposit is federally insured, the loss must be deducted as a casualty loss. If the deposit is not federally insured, the loss can be deducted as (ii) an ordinary loss treated as a miscellaneous itemized deduction subject to the 2% AGI floor (limited to $20,000 per financial institution), (ii) a nonbusiness bad debt, or (iii) a casualty loss. If treated as a miscellaneous itemized deduction, the taxpayer should write "Insolvent Financial Institution" next to the amount on the appropriate line of Form 1040, Schedule A. If the taxpayer does not elect to deduct the loss in the year the financial institution becomes insolvent or bankrupt, the loss may be deducted as a nonbusiness bad debt in the year its amount is finally determined [§ 165(l); Notice 89-28, 1989-1 C.B. 667].

*Losses on IRAs.* If all of a taxpayer's traditional and Roth IRAs have been distributed and the taxpayer has a loss because the total distributions are less than the taxpayer's unrecovered basis in the IRAs, the taxpayer can deduct the loss as a miscellaneous itemized deduction subject to the 2% floor.

*Casualty and Theft Losses of Employees.* If a taxpayer has a casualty or theft loss from property he used in performing services as an employee, he can deduct the loss as a miscellaneous itemized deduction subject to the 2% AGI floor.

### VII.I.4. Other Miscellaneous Itemized Deductions Subject to the 2% Floor

[504 T.M., II.A.1.b(4)(c); TPS ¶2300.]

Certain other types of expenses are also deductible as miscellaneous itemized deductions subject to the 2% floor.

*Hobby Expenses.* A taxpayer can deduct hobby expenses (expenses on an activity not carried on to make a profit) as miscellaneous itemized deductions subject to the 2% floor. However, the amount of hobby expenses that can be deducted is limited to the amount of the income from the hobby (i.e., hobby losses are not deductible) (see VIII.J.) [§ 183].

*Excess Deductions on Termination of Estate.* The beneficiary of an estate can deduct the excess of estate's total deductions over its gross income in the year it terminates as a miscellaneous itemized deduction subject to the 2% floor [Reg. § 1.642(h)-2(a)].

*Repayments.* If a taxpayer repays an amount of $3,000 or less that he treated as ordinary income in an earlier year, he can deduct the amount of the repayment as a miscellaneous itemized deduction subject to the 2% floor (see VII.K.).

### VII.J. Miscellaneous Deductions Not Subject to 2% AGI Floor

[504 T.M., II.A.1.b(2) and (3); TPS ¶2910.01.B.2.]

In addition to the itemized deductions for medical expenses (see VII.D.), taxes (see VII.E.), interest (see VII.F.), charitable contributions (see VII.G.), and casualty and theft losses (see VII.H.), there are a number of miscellaneous itemized deductions. Certain miscellaneous itemized deductions are subject to a 2% floor and others are not.

The following miscellaneous itemized deductions are not subject to the 2% floor [§ 67(b)(6) through § 67(b)(12)]:

1. any deduction for impairment-related work expenses;

2. the § 691(c) deduction for federal estate tax attributable to income in respect of a decedent;

3. any deduction allowable in connection with personal property used in a short sale;

4. the § 1341 deduction for the repayment of more than $3,000 under a claim of right (see VII.K.);

5. the § 72(b)(3) deduction for any unrecovered investment in an annuity upon the death of a taxpayer;

6. the § 171 deduction for amortizable premium on taxable bonds;

7. the § 216 deduction for real estate taxes and mortgage interest passed through to and paid by a tenant-shareholder in a cooperative housing corporation;

8. deduction of gambling losses up to the amount of gambling winnings [§ 165(d)];

9. deduction of casualty and theft losses from income-producing property;

10. deduction of loss from other activities from Schedule K-1 (Form 1065-B), box 2; and

11. an ordinary loss attributable to a contingent payment debt instrument or inflation-indexed instrument.

***Impairment-Related Work Expenses.*** If a taxpayer has a physical or mental disability that limits the taxpayer being employed, or substantially limits one or more of the taxpayer's major life activities (such as performing manual tasks, walking, speaking, breathing, learning, and working), the taxpayer can deduct such impairment-related work expenses [§ 67(b)(6), § 190(b)(3)]. Impairment-related work expenses include the following types of expenses that qualify as ordinary and necessary business expenses [§ 67(d)]:

1. expenses for attendant care services at the taxpayer's place of work; and

2. other expenses in connection with the taxpayer's place of work that are necessary for him to be able to work.

***Gambling Losses.*** A taxpayer can deduct gambling losses to the extent of his or her gambling winnings for the year [§ 165(d)]. Gambling winnings are reported as income on the "other income" line of Form 1040, *U.S. Individual Income Tax Return* (see I.M.4.). Gambling losses, on the other hand, must be reported as "Other Miscellaneous Deductions" on Schedule A of Form 1040.

Taxpayers deducting gambling losses must be able to substantiate the losses. Generally, taxpayers should keep an accurate diary or similar record of their gambling winnings and losses that contains information about (i) the date and type of the specific wager or wagering activity, (ii) the name and address of the gambling establishment, (iii) the names of other persons present with the taxpayer, and (iv) the amount won or lost. A taxpayer should also retain other documentation to prove his or her winnings and losses, such as wagering tickets, canceled checks, credit records, bank withdrawals, and statements of winnings or payment slips provided by the gambling establishment.

## VII.K. Repayments of Income Received in Prior Year

[502 T.M., III.C.; TPS ¶1030.]

The treatment of repayments of amounts included in income in previous years under a claim of right (see I.B.5.) depends on the amount of the repayment and the type of income. As a general rule, a repayment can be deducted on the same form or schedule on which the income was previously reported. For example, repayments of amounts reported as self-employment income are deducted on Schedule C or Schedule F. Repayment of an amount reported as a capital gain is deducted as a capital loss on Schedule D. Repayments of wages, unemployment compensation, or other nonbusiness income of $3,000 or less may be claimed as a miscellaneous itemized deduction subject to the 2% floor (see VII.I.4.).

If the amount repaid is $3,000 or more, the taxpayer has the option to deduct the amount repaid as a miscellaneous itemized deduction not subject to the 2% floor (see VII.J.) or to recompute the tax for the tax year of the repayment without the deduction and subtract from that amount the reduction in tax that would have resulted from excluding the amount repaid from income for the year of the overpayment [§ 1341, § 67(b)(9)]. The resulting amount is effectively treated as a refundable credit.

*Repayment of social security benefits.* A special rule applies to repayments of social security benefits previously received. These amounts are generally reported to the taxpayer on Form SSA-1099 (or Form RRB-1099, for RRTA benefits). Instead of a deduction, the amount of social security benefits received during any tax year is reduced by any repayment, regardless of whether the amount repaid was received in that year or a prior year [§ 86(d)(2)] (see I.K.).

If the amounts repaid are more than the gross benefits received in the current tax year, the general rule will apply to the amount of the repayment in excess of the gross benefits received (amounts repaid in excess of current benefits up to $3,000 treated as a miscellaneous itemized deduction subject to 2% floor and amounts over $3,000 treated as miscellaneous itemized deduction not subject to 2% floor or claim of right tax recomputation, at the taxpayer's option).

## VII.L. Overall Limitation on Itemized Deductions

[504 T.M., II.A.2.; TPS ¶2905.]

An individual taxpayer whose adjusted gross income (AGI) exceeds a certain threshold amount must reduce his or her otherwise allowable itemized deductions by the lesser of [§ 68(a)]:

1. 3% of the excess of the taxpayer's AGI over the applicable threshold amount; or
2. 80% of the taxpayer's otherwise allowable itemized deductions.

The following are the applicable threshold amounts for 2014 [§ 68(b); Rev. Proc. 2013-35, 2013-47 I.R.B. 537, § 3.14]:

- $305,050 in the case of married taxpayers filing a joint return or a surviving spouse;
- $279,650 in the case of a head of household;
- $152,525 in the case of a married taxpayer filing a separate return; and
- $254,200 in the case of any other taxpayer.

The following are the applicable threshold amounts for 2015 [§ 68(b); Rev. Proc. 2014-61, 2014-47 I.R.B. 860]:

- $309,900 in the case of married taxpayers filing a joint return or a surviving spouse;
- $284,050 in the case of a head of household;
- $154,950 in the case of a married taxpayer filing a separate return; and
- $258,250 in the case of any other taxpayer.

For purposes of the 80% test, the following deductions are not treated as itemized deductions [§ 68(c)]:

- the medical expense deduction (see VII.D.);
- the investment interest deduction (see VII.F.4.);
- the deduction for casualty and theft losses (see VII.H.); and
- the deduction for gambling losses (see VII.J.).

The overall limitation is applied after any other applicable limitations on itemized deductions [§ 68(d)]. If a taxpayer's AGI exceeds the applicable threshold amount, the Itemized Deductions Worksheet (Source: 2014 Form 1040 (Schedule A) Draft Instructions) can be used to compute his or her allowable itemized deductions.

---

**EXAMPLE:** Bob is a single taxpayer. His adjusted gross income (AGI) for 2014 is $284,200. Bob's otherwise allowable itemized deductions for 2014 are $20,000, which includes a $5,000 medical expense deduction (after application of the 10% AGI limitation on medical expenses). In determining the overall limitation on his itemized deductions, Bob does not treat the $5,000 medical expense deduction as an itemized deduction. Thus, Bob's itemized deductions must be reduced by $900, which is the lesser of (i) 3% of the excess of his AGI over the applicable threshold amount (($284,200 − $254,200) × 3% = $900), or (ii) 80% of his otherwise allowable itemized deductions (($20,000 − $5,000) × 80% = $12,000). Bob can deduct $19,100 ($20,000 − $900) of his itemized deductions for 2014.

---

**Itemized Deductions Worksheet—Line 29**       *Keep for Your Records*

| | | |
|---|---|---|
| **1.** | Enter the total of the amounts from Schedule A, lines 4, 9, 15, 19, 20, 27, and 28 . . . . . . . . . . . . . . . . . . . . . . . . . . . . . . | **1.** |
| **2.** | Enter the total of the amount from Schedule A, lines 4, 14, and 20, plus any gambling and casualty or theft losses included on line 28 . . . . . . . . . . . . . . . . . . . . . . . . . . . . . . . . . . . . . . . . . . . . . . . . . . . . . . . . . . . . . . . . . | **2.** |

⚠ CAUTION    Be sure your total gambling and casualty or theft losses are clearly identified on the dotted lines next to line 28.

| | | |
|---|---|---|
| **3.** | Is the amount on line 2 less than the amount on line 1? | |
| | ☐ **No.** 🛑 Your deduction is not limited. Enter the amount from line 1 of this worksheet on Schedule A, line 29. **Do not** complete the rest of this worksheet. | |
| | ☐ **Yes.** Subtract line 2 from line 1 . . . . . . . . . . . . . . . . . . . . . . . . . . . . . . | **3.** |
| **4.** | Multiply line 3 by 80% (.80) . . . . . . . . . . . . . . . . . . . . . . . . . . . . . . . . . . | **4.** |
| **5.** | Enter the amount from Form 1040, line 38 . . . . . . . . . . . . . . . . . . . . . . . . . . | **5.** |
| **6.** | Enter $305,050 if married filing jointly or qualifying widow(er); $279,650 if head of household; $254,200 if single; or $152,525 if married filing separately . . . . . . . . . . . . . . . . . . . . . . | **6.** |
| **7.** | Is the amount on line 6 less than the amount on line 5? | |
| | ☐ **No.** 🛑 Your deduction is not limited. Enter the amount from line 1 of this worksheet on Schedule A, line 29. **Do not** complete the rest of this worksheet. | |
| | ☐ **Yes.** Subtract line 6 from line 5 . . . . . . . . . . . . . . . . . . . . . . . . . . . . . | **7.** |
| **8.** | Multiply line 7 by 3% (.03) . . . . . . . . . . . . . . . . . . . . . . . . . . . . . . . . . . | **8.** |
| **9.** | Enter the **smaller** of line 4 or line 8 . . . . . . . . . . . . . . . . . . . . . . . . . . . . . . . . . . . . | **9.** |
| **10.** | **Total itemized deductions.** Subtract line 9 from line 1. Enter the result here and on Schedule A, line 29 . . . . . . . . . . . . | **10.** |

# CHAPTER VIII. LOSSES AND LIMITATIONS ON LOSSES AND DEDUCTIONS

>>>>>>>>>>>>>>>>>>>>>>>>>>>>

## VIII.A. Capital Expenditures

[509 T.M.; TPS ¶2920.]

The characterization of a payment as either a capital expenditure or a business expense affects the timing of the taxpayer's cost recovery. Business expenses are currently deductible, while capital expenditures generally are amortized or depreciated over the asset's useful life. Typically, the difference between a deductible business expense and a capital expenditure is a matter of degree, rather than kind. The costs of incidental repairs and routine maintenance to tangible property incurred in carrying on a trade or business generally are business expenses [Reg. § 1.162-1(a)]. However, expenditures to acquire or produce a unit of real or personal property and expenditures to improve a unit of property the taxpayer owns generally are required to be capitalized [Reg. § 1.263(a)-2(d), § 1.263(a)-3(d)].

The line separating a deductible repair and a capital expenditure is indistinct and determinations depend heavily on the facts and circumstances of the expenditure. Section 263 lists expenditures that are required to be capitalized. Deductible repairs, on the other hand, are defined in the negative; that is, an amount is deductible as a repair only if it is not otherwise required to be capitalized [Reg. § 1.162-4(a)].

Deductible repairs and routine maintenance to property are discussed in IV.A.7.

### VIII.A.1. Tangible Property Costs Subject to Capitalization

[509 T.M., II.A.; TPS ¶2920.01.]

When compared to deductible repair expenses, capital expenditures generally may be thought of as more permanent increments in the value, utility, and longevity of a unit of property. Capital expenditures include (i) any amount paid for new buildings or for permanent improvements or betterments made to increase the value of any property or estate, or (ii) any amount paid in restoring property or in making good the exhaustion thereof for which an allowance is or has been made [§ 263(a); Reg. § 1.263(a)-1(a)].

### VIII.A.1.a. Expenditures for the Acquisition or Production of Tangible Property

[509 T.M., VI.; TPS ¶2920.01.B.2.c(3)]

Taxpayers generally must capitalize amounts paid to acquire or produce a unit of real or personal property, including leasehold improvements, land and land improvements, buildings, machinery and equipment, and furniture and fixtures. Such amounts include the invoice price, transaction costs, and costs for work performed prior to the date the property is placed in service. In addition, taxpayers must capitalize amounts paid to acquire real or personal property for resale, as well as amounts paid to defend or perfect title to property [Reg. § 1.263(a)-2(d)(1), § 1.263(a)-2(e)(1)]. An exception exists whereby a taxpayer may deduct amounts paid to acquire or produce materials and supplies in the tax year they are first used or consumed in the taxpayer's operations (see IV.A.7.). Taxpayers that elect application of the de minimis safe harbor (see IV.A.7.) may not capitalize amounts paid for the acquisition or production of a unit of property that otherwise qualifies for the de minimis safe harbor [Reg. § 1.263(a)-1(f)].

The uniform capitalization rules apply to property produced by the taxpayer or acquired by the taxpayer for resale [§ 263A] (see XI.D.).

***Facilitative Costs.*** Except as provided by the de minimis safe harbor, taxpayers must capitalize amounts paid to facilitate the acquisition of real or personal property. For this purpose, facilitative amounts include the following inherently facilitative amounts [Reg. § 1.263(a)-2(f)]:

- securing an appraisal or determining the value or price of property;
- negotiating the terms or structure of the acquisition and obtaining tax advice on the acquisition;
- application fees, bidding costs, or similar expenses;
- preparation and review of documents effectuating the property's acquisition;
- examining and evaluating property's title;
- conveying property between parties (including sales and transfer taxes, and title registration costs);
- finders' fees or brokers' commissions (including contingency fees);
- architectural, geological, survey, engineering, environmental, or inspection services pertaining to particular properties; and
- services provided by a qualified intermediary or other facilitator of a like-kind exchange (see III.E.1.).

Employee compensation and overhead are not treated as costs facilitating the acquisition of real or personal property. Taxpayers, though, may elect to treat such amounts as facilitative costs, and thus may capitalize such costs. Additionally, amounts paid in the process of investigating or otherwise pursuing the acquisition of real property is not a facilitative cost if it relates to activities performed in the process of determining whether to acquire real property and which real property to acquire [Reg. § 1.263(a)-2(f)(2)(iii), § 1.263(a)-2(f)(2)(iv)].

### VIII.A.1.b. Expenditures to Improve Tangible Property

[509 T.M., VII.; TPS ¶2200.01.C.1.d., .01.C.1.e., .01.C.1.f.]

Taxpayers must capitalize amounts paid to improve a unit of property. An expenditure is considered an improvement if the amount paid [Reg. § 1.263(a)-3(d)]:

- is for a betterment to the unit of property;

- restores the unit of property; or

- adapts property to a new or different use.

***Betterments.*** An amount is paid for a betterment to a unit of property only if it [Reg. § 1.263(a)-3(j)(1)]:

- ameliorates a material condition or defect that either existed before the taxpayer's acquisition of the unit of property or arose during the production of the unit of property, whether or not the taxpayer was aware of the condition or defect at the time of acquisition or production;

- is for a material addition, including a physical enlargement, expansion, extension, or addition of a major component to the unit of property or a material increase in the capacity, including additional cubic or linear space, of the unit of property; or

- is reasonably expected to materially increase the productivity, efficiency, strength, quality, or output of the unit of property.

An amount is paid to improve a building if it is paid for a betterment to a building structure or building system (as defined in Reg. § 1.263(a)-3(e)(2)(ii)), an individual condominium unit owned by the taxpayer and its structural components, and all or a portion of a building of which the taxpayer is a lessee [Reg. § 1.263(a)-3(j)(2)(ii)].

---

**EXAMPLE:** Mindy purchases a store located on a parcel of land that contains underground gasoline storage tanks left by a prior occupant. Assume that the parcel of land is the unit of property. The tanks leaked and caused soil contamination before Mindy's purchase. She is not aware of the contamination at the time of the purchase. The year after the purchase, Mindy discovers the contamination and incurs costs to remediate the soil. The remediation expenditures are for a betterment to the land because Mindy incurred the costs to ameliorate a material condition or defect that existed before she acquired the land. Thus, Mindy must capitalize the expenditure.

---

***Restorations.*** An amount is paid to restore a unit of property only if it [Reg. § 1.263(a)-3(k)(1)]:

- is for the replacement of a component of a unit of property for which the taxpayer has properly deducted a loss for that component (other than a casualty loss (see VIII.H.1.a.));

- is for the replacement of a component of a unit of property for which the taxpayer has properly taken into account the adjusted basis of the component in realizing gain or loss resulting from the sale or exchange of the component;

- is for the restoration of damage to a unit of property for which the taxpayer is required to take a basis adjustment as a result of a casualty loss (see VIII.H.1.a.), or relating to a casualty event, subject to certain limitations;

- returns the unit of property to its ordinarily efficient operating condition if the property has deteriorated to a state of disrepair and is no longer functional for its intended use;

- results in the rebuilding of the unit of property to a like-new condition after the end of its class life; or

- is for the replacement of a part or combination of parts that comprise a major component or a substantial structural part of a unit of property (as determined under Reg. § 1.263(a)-3(k)(6)).

An amount is paid to improve a building if it is paid to restore a building structure or building system (as defined in Reg. § 1.263(a)-3(e)(2)(ii)), an individual condominium unit owned by the taxpayer and its structural components, and all or a portion of a building of which the taxpayer is a lessee [Reg. § 1.263(a)-3(k)(2)].

---

**EXAMPLE:** Albert owns and operates a farm with several barns and outbuildings. He did not use or maintain one of the outbuildings on a regular basis, and it fell into a state of disrepair. The outbuilding previously was used for storage, but it can no longer be used for that purpose because the building is not structurally sound. Albert decides to restore the outbuilding and pays an amount to shore up the walls and replace the siding. The walls and siding are part of the building structure. Albert must treat the amounts paid to shore up the walls and replace the siding as a restoration of the building structure because the amounts return the building structure to its ordinarily efficient operating condition after it had deteriorated to a state of disrepair and was no longer functional for its intended use. Thus, Albert must capitalize the expenditure.

---

*Adaptations to a New or Different Use.* An amount is paid to adapt a unit of property to a new or different use if the adaptation is not consistent with the taxpayer's ordinary use of the unit of property at the time the taxpayer originally placed it in service. An amount is paid to improve a building if it is paid to adapt to a new or different use a building structure or building system (as defined in Reg. § 1.263(a)-3(e)(2)(ii)), an individual condominium unit owned by the taxpayer and its structural components, and all or a portion of a building of which the taxpayer is a lessee [Reg. § 1.263(a)-3(l)(2)].

---

**EXAMPLE:** Tim is a manufacturer and owns a manufacturing building that he has used for manufacturing since Year 1, when Tim placed it in service. In Year 30, Tim pays an amount to convert the manufacturing building into a showroom for his business. To convert the facility, Tim removes and replaces (with comparable, commercially available replacement material) various structural components to provide a better layout. He also repaints the building interiors as part of the conversion. The amount paid to convert the manufacturing building into a showroom adapts the building structure to a new or different use because the conversion is not consistent with Tim's ordinary use of the building structure at the time it was placed in service. Thus, Tim must capitalize the expenditure.

---

### VIII.A.1.c. Election to Capitalize Tangible Property Repair and Maintenance Costs

[509 T.M., VII.B.6.; TPS ¶2200.01.E.5.]

A taxpayer may elect to treat amounts paid for the repair and maintenance of tangible property as amounts paid to improve that property and as an asset subject to the allowance for depreciation if the taxpayer incurs these amounts in carrying on his or her trade or business and if the taxpayer treats these amounts as capital expenditures on its books and records. A taxpayer that makes this election in a tax year must capitalize all amounts paid for repairs and maintenance to tangible property that it treats as capital expenditures on its books and records in that tax year. Amounts for which the election is made are not treated as amounts paid for repair or maintenance, which would otherwise be deductible [Reg. § 1.263(a)-3(n)].

The election is made by attaching a statement titled "Section 1.263(a)-3(n) Election" to the taxpayer's timely filed tax return (including extensions) for the tax year in which the taxpayer pays amounts for repair and maintenance to tangible property. The statement must include the taxpayer's name, address, taxpayer identification number, and a statement that the taxpayer is making the election to capitalize repair and maintenance costs under Reg. § 1.263(a)-3(n). For consolidated groups, the election is made for each member of the group by the common parent. For partnerships and S corporations, the election is made by the partnership or S corporation, rather than by the shareholders or partners [Reg. § 1.263(a)-3(n)].

### VIII.A.2. Exceptions to Capitalization of Tangible Property

[509 T.M., IV, VII.B.4.d., VII.B.4.e.; TPS ¶2200.01.C.1.b., .03.A.]

***Materials and Supplies.*** Amounts paid to acquire or produce non-incidental materials and supplies are generally deductible in the tax year that the materials and supplies are first consumed in the taxpayer's operations. Amounts paid to acquire or produce incidental materials and supplies that the taxpayer carries on hand and for which the taxpayer neither keeps a record of consumption nor takes physical inventories at the beginning and end of the tax year are generally deductible in the year paid, provided taxable income is clearly reflected [Reg. § 1.162-3(a)] (see IV.A.7.).

***Safe Harbors for Deduction.*** Three safe harbors may allow taxpayers to avoid capitalization of certain expenditures that would otherwise be capital expenditures (see IV.A.7.):

- the routine maintenance safe harbor [Reg. § 1.263(a)-3(i)];
- the safe harbor for small taxpayers [Reg. § 1.263(a)-3(h)]; and
- the de minimis safe harbor [Reg. § 1.263(a)-1(f)].

Additional exceptions to the capitalization requirement for certain types of expenditures are discussed in IV.F.

### VIII.A.3. Optional Regulatory Accounting Method for Tangible Property

[509 T.M., VII.B.5.; TPS ¶2200.01.C.1.g.]

Certain regulated taxpayers may elect to use an optional simplified method to determine whether amounts paid to repair, maintain, or improve tangible property are treated as deductible expenses or capital expenditures. Taxpayers eligible to elect this regulatory accounting method are those taxpayers subject to the accounting rules of either: (i) the Federal Energy Regulatory Commissioner (FERC), (ii) the Federal Communications Commission (FCC), or (iii) the Surface Transportation Board (STB). Taxpayers that use FERC, FCC, or STB regulatory accounting rules, but that are not subject to FERC, FCC, or STB regulatory authority are not eligible to use the optional regulatory accounting method [Reg. § 1.263(a)-3(m)].

Under the optional regulatory accounting method, electing taxpayers must follow the applicable regulatory accounting rule in determining whether an amount paid improves property. If the amount paid is capitalized for regulatory accounting purposes, it must be capitalized for income tax purposes, as well. Amounts not capitalized for regulatory accounting purposes are not capitalized for tax purposes [Reg. § 1.263(a)-3(m)(3)].

A taxpayer that uses the optional regulatory accounting method must use it for all of the taxpayer's tangible property that is subject to regulatory accounting rules. The method does not apply to property that is not subject to regulatory accounting rules.

### VIII.A.4. Acquisition or Creation of Intangible Property

[509 T.M., VIII.; TPS ¶2920.01.B.2., .04.J.]

Generally, amounts paid or incurred for the following items must be capitalized [Reg. § 1.263(a)-4(b)(1)]:

- an amount paid to acquire an intangible;
- an amount paid to create certain intangibles (as described in Reg. § 1.263(a)-4(d));
- an amount paid to create or enhance a separate and distinct intangible asset;
- an amount paid to create or enhance a future benefit that is prospectively identified in published guidance as required to be capitalized; and
- an amount paid to facilitate an acquisition, creation, or enhancement of any of the intangibles described in the previous bullets (i.e., transaction costs).

Computer software development costs are discussed in IV.F.2. Amortization of intangible property is discussed in V.D.

## VIII.B. Transactions Between Related Taxpayers

### VIII.B.1. Disallowance of Losses Between Related Persons

[564 T.M., II.; TPS ¶2930.01.]

Generally, a deduction is disallowed for any loss from the direct or indirect sale or exchange of property between related persons. The related person loss disallowance rules do not affect gain recognition. Thus, if a taxpayer sells or exchanges several assets to a related person, some items may realize a loss and some items may realize a gain. In this scenario, the taxpayer would recognize all of the taxable gain (absent the application of another deferral or nonrecognition provision), but none of the losses. Netting of gains and losses is not allowed [§ 267(a)].

**Related Persons.** For purposes of the loss disallowance rule, the following are considered related persons [§ 267(b)]:

- the taxpayer and his or her siblings, half-siblings, spouses, ancestors (i.e., parents, grandparents, etc.), and lineal descendants (i.e., children, grandchildren, etc.);
- the taxpayer and a partnership in which the taxpayer directly or indirectly owns more than 50% of the capital interest or profits interest;
- the taxpayer and a corporation in which the taxpayer directly or indirectly owns more than 50% in value of the outstanding stock;
- the taxpayer and a tax-exempt charitable or educational organization directly or indirectly controlled (in any manner or method) by the taxpayer or by a member of the taxpayer's family, whether or not this control is legally enforceable;
- a grantor and fiduciary, or the fiduciary and beneficiary, of any trust;
- fiduciaries of two different trusts, or the fiduciary and beneficiary of two different trusts, if the same person is the grantor of both trusts;
- a trust fiduciary and a corporation of which more than 50% in value of the outstanding stock is directly or indirectly owned by or for the trust, or by or for the grantor of the trust;
- a corporation and a partnership if the same persons own more than 50% in value of the outstanding stock of the corporation and more than 50% of the capital interest, or the profits interest, in the partnership;

- two S corporations if the same persons own more than 50% in value of the outstanding stock of each corporation;

- two corporations, one of which is an S corporation, if the same persons own more than 50% in value of the outstanding stock of each corporation;

- an executor and a beneficiary of an estate (except in the case of a sale or trade to satisfy a pecuniary bequest);

- two corporations that are members of the same controlled group (however, under certain conditions, these losses are not disallowed but must be deferred); and

- two partnerships if the same persons own, directly or indirectly, more than 50% of the capital interests or the profit interests in both partnerships.

In determining whether a person directly or indirectly owns corporate stock, certain constructive ownership rules apply [§ 267(c); Reg. § 1.267(c)-1].

***Subsequent Sale Where Loss Previously Disallowed.*** If a taxpayer acquires property by purchase or exchange from a transferor who sustained a loss on the transaction that was disallowed as a result of the related party rules, any gain the taxpayer realizes on a sale or other disposition of the property is recognized only to the extent the gain exceeds the amount of the loss properly allocable to the property. This general rule also applies to a taxpayer's sale or other disposition of property if the basis of the property in the taxpayer's hands is determined directly or indirectly by reference to other property the taxpayer acquired from a transferor through a sale or exchange in which a loss sustained by the transferor was not allowable. The general rule is available only to the original transferee, but does not apply to an original transferee who acquired the property other than by purchase or exchange (e.g., a donee) [§ 267(d); Reg. § 1.267(d)-1(a)].

---

**EXAMPLE:** Don and Grace are married. Don sells Grace certain corporate stock with an adjusted basis of $800 for $500. The loss of $300 is not allowable to Don. Grace later sells the stock for $1,000. Although her realized gain is $500 ($1,000 amount realized − $500 basis), her recognized gain is only $200 ($500 realized gain − $300 loss not allowable to Don). In determining capital gain or loss, Grace's holding period begins on the date of the sale from Don to Grace.

---

***Corporate Liquidation Exception.*** The general loss disallowance rule for related party transactions does not apply to a complete corporate liquidation. A loss realized by a corporation in a distribution in complete liquidation is not subject to the disallowance rule. Additionally, any loss realized by the distributee-shareholder in a complete liquidation is not disallowed [§ 267(a)(1)].

However, the recognition of loss by a liquidating corporation on the distribution of property to a related person is disallowed if (i) the property is not distributed pro-rata among the shareholders, or (ii) the distributed property is property acquired by the liquidating corporation in a § 351 transaction (see XIII.B.1.), or as a contribution to capital, during the five years before the distribution (as well as any property, the adjusted basis of which is determined in whole or in part by reference to the adjusted basis of such property). For purposes of this rule, a related person has the same meaning as for the general loss disallowance rule (see VIII.B.1.) [§ 336(d)(1)]. Corporate liquidations are discussed in XIII.E.3.

*Exception for Transfers of Property Between Spouses or Incident to Divorce.*
The loss disallowance rule does not apply to any transfer of property between spouses
or incident to divorce that are covered by § 1041(a) (see III.E.5.).

*Exception for Controlled Groups.* Where a transaction involves members of a
controlled group (as defined in § 267(f)(1)), a loss realized by or a deduction ordinarily
allowed to a member of the controlled group is deferred (rather than denied) until the
property is transferred outside of the group [§ 267(f)(2)].

### VIII.B.2. Matching of Deductions and Income

[564 T.M., II.C.2.; TPS ¶2930.02.]

Under certain circumstances, a payer's deduction for a payment made may be
deferred until the tax year the recipient includes such payment in income. If, as a
result of a related payer and recipient using different accounting methods, a payer's
payment is not includible in the recipient's gross income but the payment would be
deductible to the payer at the end of his or her tax year, then no deduction is
permitted to the payer. Rather, the deduction is permitted when the payment is
includible in the recipient's gross income. For purposes of this matching rule, a
related person is the same as a related person for purposes of the loss disallowance
rule (see VIII.B.1.). Additionally, a personal service corporation and any owner-
employee (regardless of level of ownership) are treated as related persons
[§ 267(a)(2)].

---

**EXAMPLE:** Manufacturing Co. retains Accounting Firm, Inc. Because one individual owns 100% of the stock of both companies, the companies are related persons.
Manufacturing and Accounting use the calendar year as their tax years. In Nov. of
Year 1, Accounting completes accounting work for Manufacturing. Accounting bills
Manufacturing $10,000 for the work on Dec. 15 of Year 1. Manufacturing routinely
pays bills on a 45-day cycle. It pays the bill on Feb. 1 of Year 2. Manufacturing is an
accrual method taxpayer that would normally deduct the cost for the accounting work
when billed. Accounting uses the cash method and reports income in the year it is
received. Because the income is not includible by Accounting until Year 2, Manufacturing may not deduct the accounting cost until Year 2.

---

*Termination of Relationship.* Termination of related person status before entering into a transaction will preclude application of the matching rule. However, if
persons are related at the time of the transaction, termination of the relationship
before the amount is includible in the gross income of the recipient will not prevent
deferral of the deduction. Once a deduction is deferred under the related person
rules, it is not allowable until the amount is includible in the gross income of the
former related person [§ 267(a)(2)(B); Reg. § 1.267(a)-2T(b), Q&A-5].

*Payments to Related Foreign Persons.* A modified deduction matching principle applies to related foreign persons. Generally, a taxpayer must use the cash
method of accounting for deduction of amounts owed to a related foreign person. A
related foreign person is any non-U.S. person (within the meaning of § 7701(a)(30))
related to the taxpayer (within the meaning of the loss disallowance rule (see
VIII.B.1.)) by the close of the tax year in which the amount would otherwise be
deductible. This includes members of a controlled group without regard to the rule
excluding foreign corporations as members [Reg. § 1.267(a)-3].

Only certain income is covered by the modified matching principle, including
income other than capital gains, income of foreign corporations and nonresident alien

individuals that is not effectively connected with a U.S. business, and foreign-source interest. Neither the modified matching principle for related foreign persons nor the general deduction matching principle apply to items other than interest that are from sources outside the United States and that are not effectively connected income of a related foreign person [Reg. § 1.267(a)-3(b)(2)]. Income of a related foreign person that is effectively connected with the conduct of a U.S. business is allowable as a deduction on the day the amount is includible in the gross income of the related foreign person, so long as the amount is subject to full U.S. tax [Reg. § 1.267(a)-3(c)(1)].

### VIII.B.3. Special Loss and Deduction Limitation Rules Applicable to Related Parties

[564 T.M., III., VIII., XI.; TPS ¶¶1510.02.D., 2330.03.E.1., 4040.02.]

*Partners and Partnerships.* A transaction between a partnership and a partner is treated as a transaction between the partnership and a non-partner if the partner engages in the transaction in a capacity other than as a partner. Common examples include loans from a partner to the partnership, leases of property by a partner to the partnership, or sales of property between the partnership and its partners [§ 707].

No deduction is allowed for losses from the direct or indirect sale or exchange of property (other than the sale or exchange of an interest in the partnership) between (i) a partnership and a person directly or indirectly owning more than 50% of the capital interest or profits interest in the partnership, or (ii) two partnerships in which the same person directly or indirectly owns more than 50% of the capital interests or profits interests. If the property is later sold or exchanged, the rules applicable to the subsequent sale of property previously subject to the general loss disallowance rule apply (see VIII.B.1.) [§ 707(b)(1)]. Transactions between partnerships and partners are discussed XIV.D.3.

*Earnings Stripping.* No deduction is allowed for interest expense paid or accrued directly or indirectly [§ 163(j)]:

- by a taxpayer to a related person if no tax is imposed on the receipt of such interest;
- by a taxpayer to a person who is not a related person if there is a guarantee by a related person who is an exempt organization or a foreign person and no gross basis tax is imposed with respect to such interest; or
- by a taxable REIT subsidiary (as defined in § 856(l)) of a real estate investment trust to the trust.

However, the disallowance does not apply if the payer corporation is either an S corporation or a foreign corporation with no income effectively connected with a U.S. trade or business [Prop. Reg. § 1.163(j)-1(a)(1)].

For purposes of this rule, a related person is any person related to the taxpayer within the meaning of the general loss disallowance rule (see VIII.B.1.) or the § 707(b)(1) rule disallowing losses from the sale or exchange of property between partners and certain controlled partnerships. However, any interest paid or accrued to a partnership that is a related person is not treated as such to the extent less than 10% of the profits and capital interests in the partnership are held by persons not subject to income tax on such interest. Additionally, if a treaty reduces the rate of tax imposed on a partner's share of interest paid or accrued to a partnership, the partner's interests in the partnership are treated as held in part by a tax-exempt person and in party by a taxable person [§ 163(j)(4)].

Interest deductible as a business expense is discussed in IV.A.12. Investment interest deductible as an expense for the production of income is discussed in IV.B.2.a.

*Like-Kind Exchanges.* Like-kind exchanges between related parties still receive non-recognition treatment. However, if the taxpayer or the related party disposes of the property received in the exchange within two years of the last transfer, then both the taxpayer and the related party must recognize gain or loss on the exchanged property [§ 1031(f)(1)]. For purposes of this rule, a related person is any person related to the taxpayer within the meaning of the general loss disallowance rule (see VIII.B.1.) or the § 707(b)(1) rule disallowing losses from the sale or exchange of property between partners and certain controlled partnerships [§ 1031(f)(3)]. Like-kind exchanges are discussed in III.E.1.

## VIII.C. Acquisitions of Corporations to Avoid Tax

[780 T.M., VII.; TPS ¶2940.]

If a taxpayer directly or indirectly acquires control of a corporation and the principal purpose of the acquisition is the evasion or avoidance of income tax by securing a deduction, credit, or other allowance, the IRS may disallow all or part of the deduction, credit, or other allowance. "Other allowances" that may be disallowed, for this purpose, generally include anything in the Code that has the effect of diminishing tax liability (e.g., net operating losses, built-in losses, and credit carry-overs). The disallowance provision also applies where a corporation directly or indirectly acquires the property of another corporation (that was not controlled by the corporation or its shareholders) for which the corporation obtains a carryover basis (e.g., acquisition through a tax-free reorganization) [§ 269(a); Reg. § 1.269-1(a)].

*Acquisition of Control.* Control means beneficial ownership of at least 50% of the total combined voting power of all classes of stock of the corporation, or at least 50% of the total value of shares of all classes of stock of the corporation [§ 269(a)(2); Reg. § 1.269-5(a)]. However, constructive ownership rules do not apply for this purpose [Rev. Rul. 80-46, 1980-1 C.B. 62]. "Acquisition" is interpreted broadly. Acquisition of control can be accomplished through a single transaction or through a series of related transactions, and it includes the purchase of an existing corporation and the creation of a new corporation [Reg. § 1.269-3(b)].

*Application to Certain Liquidations.* The disallowance rule also may apply to certain liquidations occurring after a stock acquisition. If there is a stock purchase qualifying for a § 338 election (see XIII.E.4.), but no election is made, and the acquired corporation is liquidated under a plan adopted within two years after the acquisition date, the IRS can disallow any deduction, credit, or allowance that the acquiring corporation would not otherwise enjoy, if the principal purpose of the liquidation is the evasion or avoidance of tax [§ 269(b)].

*Principal Purpose of Evasion or Avoidance.* Tax evasion or avoidance is the principal purpose of a transaction if it exceeds any other purpose in importance. It does not have to be the sole purpose for the acquisition. All relevant facts and circumstances must be analyzed. In particular, the acquirer's motivation at the time of the acquisition should be considered [Reg. § 1.269-3(a)].

Examples of situations where a tax avoidance purpose may exist include the following [Reg. § 1.269-3(b), § 1.269-3(c), § 1.269-6]:

- a single business is divided into several corporations simply to take advantage of the progressive tax rates;

- a person with high earning assets transfers them to a newly formed corporation and retains assets producing net operating losses that are used in an attempt to secure refunds;
- a person acquires a corporation with net operating loss carryovers with the intent of changing the corporation's business to an entirely new and profitable business;
- a corporation acquires assets having in its hands a basis that is materially greater than its aggregate fair market value at the time of the acquisition and it uses the property to create tax-reducing losses or deductions; and
- a loss subsidiary acquires high earning assets from its parent corporation.

Additionally, a tax avoidance purpose is presumed when there is an ownership change of a "title 11 corporation," if the corporation does not carry on more than an insignificant amount of an active trade or business during and after its title 11 (bankruptcy) reorganization [§ 382; Reg. § 1.269-3(d)]. Ownership changes and limitations on the use of corporate tax attributes are discussed in XIII.E.5.b.

Examples of situations where the acquirer may be able to demonstrate the existence of a valid business purpose include the following:
- the seller insists on a stock sale instead of an asset sale;
- the acquirer believes the loss company can be made profitable;
- the acquirer believes the combined operations of several companies may present a stronger financial picture to prospective lenders of funds to be used in rehabilitating the loss business;
- the need for additional manufacturing space or a new manufacturing process;
- the creation of multiple corporations to limit tort liability; and
- the need to acquire a supplier or distributor to satisfy business needs.

***Coordination with Ownership Change Rules.*** The disallowance provision may apply notwithstanding the limitation or reduction of a deduction, credit, or other allowance under the ownership change rules of § 382 and § 383. The limitation or reduction of a tax attribute under those ownership change rules, though, is relevant to the determination of whether the acquisitions principal purpose is the evasion or avoidance of tax [Reg. § 1.269-7]. The ownership change rules are discussed in XIII.E.5.b.

## VIII.D. Expenses Related to Tax-Exempt Income

[504 T.M., III.A.2.a.; TPS ¶2960.]

Taxpayers generally may not deduct expenses allocable to tax-exempt income [§ 265]. Allowing such a deduction would afford taxpayers a double benefit: the deduction of expenses and tax-free income earned with those deductible expenses. The disallowance provision applies whether or not the taxpayer is currently receiving tax-exempt income and applies even if the income is less than the expenses incurred or if the taxpayer does not have a tax avoidance motive [§ 265(a)].

***Allocation Between Taxable and Tax-Exempt Income.*** Expenses directly allocable to either taxable or tax-exempt income are allocated to that income. If an expense relates to both taxable and tax-exempt income, the expenses must be apportioned between the two classes. The amount allocable to the tax-exempt income is not deductible. Expenses are allocated based on the facts and circumstances of each situation. One way allocation may be done is on the basis of the proportion of the taxpayer's exempt income and nonexempt income to his or her total income for the tax year. However, this method is not mandatory [Reg. § 1.265-1(c); Rev. Rul. 63-27, 1963-1 C.B. 57].

---

**EXAMPLE:** Lou receives $6,000 in interest, of which $4,800 was tax-exempt and $1,200 was taxable. In earning this income, Lou had $500 in expenses. He could not specifically identify the amount of each expense item attributable to each income item. As a result, Lou allocates the expenses in proportion to the exempt and nonexempt income. Thus, $400 ($500 expenses × ($4,800 tax-exempt interest ÷ $6,000 total interest)) is attributable to tax-exempt income and is not deductible. The remaining $100 ($500 expenses × ($1,200 tax-exempt interest ÷ $6,000 total interest)) is attributable to taxable income and is deductible.

---

Taxpayers must submit with their returns an itemized statement showing the amount of each type of tax-exempt income and the amount of expenses allocated to each type of such tax-exempt income. Amounts allocated to tax-exempt income by apportionment of expenses between taxable and tax-exempt income must be shown separately and the basis for apportionment must be provided. The itemized statement must state that each deduction claimed in the return is not attributable to exempt income [Reg. § 1.265-1(d)(1)].

*Certain Expenses of Ministers and Military Personnel.* Ministers of the gospel and military personnel are excepted from the disallowance rule for certain expenses. These taxpayers are allowed to deduct mortgage interest and real property taxes on their homes despite receiving tax-exempt housing allowances under the parsonage allowance (see II.N.3.) and the military housing allowance (see II.M.2.) [§ 265(a)(6)].

*Alternative Minimum Tax.* Tax-exempt interest on certain private activity bonds is an item of tax preference that must be added to the taxpayer income for purposes of calculating alternative minimum taxable income. Interest on such bonds is tax-exempt for purposes of the regular tax, but it is taxable for purposes of the alternative minimum tax. Any deductions allocable to this tax-exempt interest that were disallowed as expenses related to tax-exempt interest are deductible against this private activity bond interest for alternative minimum tax purposes [§ 57(a)(5)]. The alternative minimum tax for individuals and corporations is discussed in X.A.2. and X.B.2., respectively.

### VIII.D.1. Non-Interest Expenses Related to Tax-Exempt Income

[504 T.M., III.A.2.a(2); TPS ¶2960.02.]

Nearly all expenses allocable to the production of tax-exempt income (other than tax-exempt interest income) are nondeductible. Only certain expenses allocable to the production of tax-exempt interest income are nondeductible [§ 265(a)(1), § 265(a)(2)].

*Expenses Allocable to Tax-Exempt Income (Other than Tax-Exempt Interest).* Expenses that would otherwise be deductible are nondeductible if they are allocable to the production of tax-exempt income (excluding tax-exempt interest income). For example, legal fees and costs paid in connection with a lawsuit that results in the taxpayer receiving a tax-exempt award of damages are nondeductible. Similarly, insurance premiums paid to ensure receipt of tax-exempt insurance proceeds, expenses incurred in connection with a nontaxable gift, scholarship, or fellowship, and state and local income taxes paid or accrued on income that is exempt from federal income tax (except tax-exempt interest income) are nondeductible under the disallowance provision [§ 265(a)(1)].

*Expenses Allocable to Tax-Exempt Interest.* Only deductions for nonbusiness expenses and interest allocable to tax-exempt interest are disallowed. Nonbusiness expenses are expenses not incurred in a trade or business, but incurred (i) in the production or collection of income, (ii) for the management, conservation, or maintenance of property held for the production of income, or (iii) in connection with the determination, collection, or refund of any tax [§ 212, § 265(a)(1)]. For example, payments for investment advice, safe deposit and custodial facilities, clerical assistance, fiduciary services, and legal services made in connection with tax-exempt interest income are not deductible. On the other hand, deductions for depreciation, amortization, and tax expenses, which are deductible other than as an investment expense, are not disallowed.

---

**EXAMPLE:** Paula is a cash basis taxpayer. She invests in nontransferable, non-negotiable, nonrecourse participation certificates of Commercial Bank, participating in certain tax-exempt interest municipal bonds held by Commercial Bank. Paula's share of the tax-exempt interest received on these bonds for the tax year is $1,400. The interest is tax-exempt income to Paula. However, Commercial Bank only distributes $1,350 to Paula, retaining $50 as a service charge. Paula may not claim the $50 as a nonbusiness deduction. The service charge is directly related to her receipt of tax-exempt interest income.

**EXAMPLE:** Trust owns tax-exempt bonds and other taxable securities. The portion of the fiduciary fees for management, conservation, or maintenance of the trust that are allocable to the tax-exempt interest income of Trust are nondeductible.

---

### VIII.D.2. Interest Expenses Related to Tax-Exempt Income

[504 T.M., III.A.2.a(3); TPS ¶2960.03.]

To prevent double tax benefits to taxpayers who borrow money in order to purchase or carry property that produces tax-exempt income, no deduction is allowed for interest paid or accrued on such debt. Absent this disallowance, a taxpayer could receive the benefit of an interest deduction, as well as tax-free income from such a transaction [§ 265(a)(1), § 265(a)(2)].

*Interest Expenses Allocable to Tax-Exempt Income (Other than Tax-Exempt Interest).* Interest allocable to the production of tax-exempt income (other than tax-exempt interest income) is not deductible, regardless of any other provision that may allow the deduction of interest.

*Interest Expenses Allocable to Tax-Exempt Interest.* Interest on debt incurred or continued in order to fund a taxpayer's investments in obligations or certificates that pay tax-exempt interest is not deductible. Additionally, no deduction is allowed for interest on debt incurred or continued in order to purchase or carry shares of stock in a regulated investment company (see XIII.F.1.) that pays tax-exempt dividends [§ 265(a)(2), § 265(a)(4)].

The disallowance for tax-exempt securities only applies where the indebtedness is incurred or continued for the purpose of purchasing or carrying tax-exempt securities. All facts and circumstances are considered when examining the taxpayer's purpose in incurring or continuing each item of indebtedness. If the purpose of the debt is to fund the taxpayer's tax-exempt interest investments, interest on the debt is not deductible. Two factors indicate that debt was incurred or continued for tax-exempt investments: (i) the debt is secured by tax-exempt obligations, or (ii) a reasonable person would have sacrificed liquidity and security and sold his or her tax-exempt obligations, rather than incur the debt [§ 265(a)(2); Rev. Proc. 72-18, 1972-1 C.B. 740].

---

**EXAMPLE:** Lloyd borrows $5,000 and gives the proceeds to his wife, Cheryl. Cheryl uses the proceeds to buy tax-exempt securities. Interest paid by Lloyd on the debt is not deductible on their joint return.

**EXAMPLE:** Oscar borrows $100,000 against two brokerage accounts that consist mainly of tax-exempt securities. The debt is collateralized by the tax-exempt securities. Oscar uses the loan proceeds to buy stock in a small company and to buy a personal boat. The debt is in an amount approximately equal to the amounts in which Oscar regularly purchased tax-exempt bonds. In addition, a reasonable person would have sold some of the tax-exempt bonds in order to buy stock in a small company and a boat. The facts establish a direct relationship between the debt and Oscar's tax-exempt investment. Therefore, the debt is incurred to carry tax-exempt interest investments, and interest on the debt is nondeductible.

---

Absent direct evidence that a taxpayer's purpose for incurring or continuing debt was to purchase or carry tax-exempt securities, the interest deduction will not be disallowed if the taxpayer's investment in tax-exempt obligations is insubstantial. For a corporate taxpayer, insubstantial means that, during the tax year, the average amount of its tax-exempt obligations (valued at adjusted basis) does not exceed 2% of the average total assets (valued at adjusted basis) held in the active conduct of its trade or business. In the case of an individual taxpayer, insubstantial means that, during the tax year, the average amount of the taxpayer's tax-exempt obligations (valued at adjusted basis) does not exceed 2% of the average adjusted basis of the taxpayer's portfolio investments and any assets held for the active conduct of a trade or business. Portfolio investments, for this purpose, include transactions entered into for profit (including investment in real estate) that are not connected with the active conduct of a trade or business. This de minimis exception does not apply to dealers in tax-exempt obligations [Rev. Proc. 72-18].

### VIII.D.3. Special Rules for Financial Institutions

[504 T.M., III.A.2.a.(5); TPS ¶2960.04.]

Generally, no deduction is allowed for the portion of a financial institution's interest expense that is allocable to tax-exempt interest obligations, regardless of the taxpayer's purpose for the debt [§ 265(b)(1)]. However, tax-exempt obligations issued in 2009 or 2010 and held by a financial institution in an amount not exceeding 2% of the adjusted basis of the institution's assets are not taken into account for purposes of determining the portion of the institution's interest expense subject to the disallowance rule [§ 265(b)(7)].

A financial institution is any taxpayer that accepts deposits from the public in the ordinary course of business and is subject to federal or state supervision as a financial institution, or that is a corporation qualifying as a bank for federal income tax purposes [§ 265(b)(5), § 585(a)(2)]. The portion of the interest expense disallowed is calculated by multiplying the taxpayer's total interest expense by the average adjusted bases of its tax-exempt obligations acquired after August 7, 1986, divided by its average adjusted bases for all of its assets. The adjusted basis of the taxpayer's tax-exempt obligations must first be reduced (but not below zero) by the amount of debt on which interest is nondeductible because of the general provisions disallowing deductions for interest on debt related to tax-exempt income, including tax-exempt interest income (see VIII.D.2.) [§ 265(b)(2), § 265(b)(6)(A)(ii)].

---

**EXAMPLE:** National bank B incurs $360,000 in interest expense during the tax year. B's average adjusted basis in its tax-exempt obligations acquired after Aug. 7, 1986, is $1 million. The average adjusted basis of all B's assets is $6 million. Thus, $60,000 ($360,000 interest expense × ($1 million ÷ $6 million)) of B's interest expense is disallowed.

---

## VIII.E. At-Risk Rules

[550 T.M.; TPS ¶2970.]

The at-risk rules may limit the amount of a taxpayer's deductible losses generated by an activity to the amount the taxpayer is at risk in that activity. If losses are disallowed for a tax year under the at-risk rules, the loss is suspended and treated as a deduction allocable to the activity in question for the next tax year, where it again will be subject to the at-risk rules. Disallowed losses may be carried forward indefinitely [§ 465].

The at-risk rules are applied before the passive activity loss rules (see VIII.F.). Thus, unless the loss is allowed under the at-risk rules, the question of whether the loss is disallowed under the passive loss rule generally will not arise [Reg. § 1.469-2T(d)(6)(i)].

Because the rules for computing alternative minimum taxable income differ from the rules for computing regular taxable income, the at-risk limitation must be recalculated for alternative minimum tax purposes [§ 59(h)]. The limitation on losses under the at-risk rules is calculated on Form 6198, *At-Risk Limitations*.

### VIII.E.1. Taxpayers Subject to the At-Risk Rules

[550 T.M., III.; TPS ¶2970.01.]

The at-risk rules apply to individuals, estates, and trusts. S corporations and partnerships are not subject to the at-risk rules. However, shareholders and partners are subject to the rules at the individual level. In addition, closely held C corporations in which no more than five individuals own more than 50% of the value of the corporation's outstanding stock are also subject to the rules [§ 465(a)(1), § 542(a)(2)]. In determining percentage ownership of the closely held C corporation, the attribution rules of § 544 apply with one modification: stock owned by one partner is not considered to be owned by another partner merely because they are partners [§ 465(a)(3)(A)].

### VIII.E.2. Activities Subject to the At-Risk Rules

[550 T.M., IV.; TPS ¶2970.02.]

The at-risk rules apply to most activities engaged in to carry on a trade or business or produce income [§ 465(c)(1), § 465(c)(3)(A)]. They do not apply to personal activities, active businesses of C corporations, certain equipment leasing by C corporations, and certain real estate businesses.

*Exception for Personal Activities.* The at-risk rules do not apply to personal activities, which are those activities not engaged in to carry on a trade or business or produce income; accordingly, deductions generated by personal activities (e.g., taxes, casualty and theft losses, and charitable contributions) are not subject to the at-risk rules [§ 465(c)(1), § 465(c)(3)(A)].

**Exception for Active Business of C Corporations.** Losses of a qualified C corporation from a qualifying business are not subject to the at-risk rules. If a C corporation is sufficiently closely held to be subject to the at-risk rules (see VIII.E.1.), it will be a qualified C corporation if it is not (i) a personal holding company (see XIII.C.5.a.), or (ii) a personal services corporation (as defined in § 269A(b), but substituting "5%" for "10%") (see XIII.C.6.) [§ 465(c)(7)(B)].

A qualifying business is an active business that meets all of the following conditions [§ 465(c)(7)(C)]:

1. During the entire 12-month period ending on the last day of the tax year, the corporation had at least:

   — One full-time employee whose services were in the active management of the business; and

   — Three full-time non-owner employees (i.e., an employee that owns no more than 5% in value of the outstanding stock of the corporation at any time during the tax year) whose services were directly related to the business. A modified version of the § 318 constructive ownership rules apply: an owner of 5% or more (rather than 50% or more) of the value of the corporation's stock is considered to own a proportionate share of any stock owned by the corporation.

2. Deductions due to the business that are allowable to the corporation as business expenses and as contributions to certain employee benefit plans for the tax year exceed 15% of the gross income from the business.

3. The business must not involve the use, exploitation, sale, lease, or other disposition of master sound recordings, motion picture films, video tapes, or tangible or intangible assets associated with literary, artistic, musical, or similar properties.

4. The business must not involve (i) the leasing of equipment that is § 1245 property (see III.D.2.a.), or (ii) the purchasing, servicing, and selling of § 1245 property [§ 465(c)(6), § 465(c)(7)(E)(ii)].

In certain circumstances, a partnership's business may be attributed to a corporate partner in proportion with the corporation's profit interest and that portion of the partnership's business will be used in determining whether the corporation's business qualifies for the active business exception [§ 465(c)(7)(D)]. Additionally, for purposes of the active business exception, the component members of an affiliated group of corporations (as defined in § 1504(a)) (see XIII.C.8.a.) are treated as if they were a single corporation [§ 465(c)(7)(F)]. However, if a personal holding company (see XIII.C.5.a.) or a personal service corporation (see XIII.C.6.) is a member of an affiliated group, it cannot use the losses of other members of the group to offset its income, even if those losses come from businesses that qualify for the active business exception [§ 465(c)(7)(G)].

**Exception for Certain Equipment Leasing by C Corporations.** While a business generally does not satisfy the active business exception if the business involves equipment leasing, if several conditions are met, the equipment leasing activities may be considered in determining whether the active business requirement is satisfied. If a closely held C corporation is actively engaged in equipment leasing, the equipment leasing is treated as a separate activity not covered by the at-risk rules. A corporation is actively engaged in equipment leasing if 50% or more of its gross receipts for the tax year are from equipment leasing.

Equipment leasing, for this purpose, means the leasing, purchasing, servicing, and selling of equipment that is § 1245 property (see III.D.2.a.). It does not include assets associated with literary, artistic, or musical property, and therefore a corporation can neither exclude these leasing activities from the at-risk rules nor count them as equipment leasing for the gross receipts test. For purposes of the equipment leasing exception, the component members of a controlled group of corporations (see XIII.C.7.) generally are treated as if they were a single corporation. However, the at-risk rules will not apply to the equipment leasing losses of a component member of a controlled group if certain conditions are met [§ 465(c)(4), § 465(c)(5), § 465(c)(6)].

*De Facto Exception for Certain Real Estate Businesses.* As a practical matter, the at-risk rules do not apply to certain real estate businesses. If certain conditions are satisfied, a nonrecourse loan borrowed in connection with holding real property is included in the amount at risk, and thus it increases the amount of losses related to the activity that a taxpayer may deduct [§ 465(b)(6)]. Amounts at-risk are discussed in VIII.E.4.

### VIII.E.3. Determining Separate Activities Under the At-Risk Rules

[550 T.M., V.; TPS ¶2970.03.]

The at-risk rules prevent a taxpayer from using losses from one activity to offset income from other activities. The rules do not limit the ability to claim deductions from an activity against income from the same activity. Therefore, it is necessary to determine whether income and loss are from the same activity or separate activities. Generally, activities are not aggregated for purposes of the at-risk rules. However, several exceptions provide for the aggregation of activities that fall within certain categories.

*Active Participation Activities.* If a taxpayer actively participates in the management of a trade or business, then all activities comprising the trade or business are aggregated for purposes of the at-risk rules. If a trade or business is carried on by a partnership or an S corporation and at least 65% of any losses from the trade or business are allocable to individuals who actively participate in management, then all activities comprising the trade or business are aggregated [§ 465(c)(3)(B)].

*Certain Activities Conducted Through Partnerships and S Corporations.* Partners and S corporation shareholders may aggregate activities of their partnership or S corporation within each of the following categories [Reg. § 1.465-1T]:

- films and video tapes;
- § 1245 property (see III.D.2.a.) leased or held for lease [§ 465(c)(2)(A)(ii), § 465(c)(2)(B)];
- farms;
- oil and gas properties; and
- geothermal properties.

---

**EXAMPLE:** Partnership P produces two films during the tax year. P's partners may treat the production of both films as one activity for purposes of the at-risk rules.

---

*Real Property Activities.* For purposes of the qualified nonrecourse financing provisions (see VIII.E.4.), the activity of holding real property includes the holding of personal property and the provision of services that are incidental to that activity if real property is made available as living accommodations [§ 465(b)(6)(E)(i)].

### VIII.E.4. Determining the Amount At Risk

[550 T.M. VI.; TPS ¶2970.04., .07.]

A taxpayer is at risk in any activity for the sum of following [§ 465(b)]:

1. the money and adjusted basis of property the taxpayer contributed to the activity; and
2. amounts the taxpayer borrows for use in the activity if either:
   — the taxpayer is personally liable for repayment; or
   — the taxpayer pledges property (other than property used in the activity) as security for the loan.

*Amounts Borrowed.* Subject to certain exceptions, a taxpayer who borrows money to use in an activity is at risk to the extent he or she is personally liable for repayment or has pledged property (other than property used in the activity) as security for the borrowed amount (to the extent of the net fair market value of the taxpayer's interest in the property) [§ 465(b)(2)]. However, a taxpayer is not at risk for amounts borrowed from a person who has an interest (other than a creditor's interest) in the activity, or that is related to a person (other than the taxpayer) having an interest in the activity. Loans may be made by a person without an interest in the activity, but that is related to the taxpayer [§ 465(b)(3)(A)]. In addition, borrowed amounts are not excluded in the following situations [§ 465(b)(3)(B), § 465(b)(6)(A); Reg. § 1.465-8(a)(2)(ii)(B)]:

- amounts borrowed by a corporation from a person whose only interest in the activity is as a shareholder of the corporation;
- amounts borrowed from a person having an interest in the activity as a creditor; or
- amounts borrowed after May 3, 2004, secured by real property used in the activity of holding real property (other than mineral property) that, if nonrecourse, would be qualified nonrecourse financing.

A related person, for this purpose, is any person related to the taxpayer within the meaning of the § 267(b) general loss disallowance rule (see VIII.B.1.) or the § 707(b)(1) partnership disallowance rule (see VIII.B.3.), but, in each case, substituting 10% for 50%. Additionally, a lender and a person with an interest in the activity are considered related if they are engaged in businesses under common control (within the meaning of § 52(a) and § 52(b)) [§ 465(b)(3)(C)].

*Qualified Nonrecourse Financing.* A nonrecourse loan borrowed in connection with holding real property will be included in the amount at risk only if it is qualified nonrecourse financing. Qualified nonrecourse financing is a loan that meets all of the following conditions [§ 465(b)(6)]:

1. the taxpayer must borrow the money in connection with the activity of holding real property;
2. the loan must be secured by real property used in the activity;
3. the loan must not be convertible from a debt obligation to an ownership interest; and
4. the money must be loaned or guaranteed by any federal, state, or local government, or the taxpayer must borrow the money from a qualified person.

**EXAMPLE:** Charlie and Owen form a partnership that incurs a nonrecourse loan to purchase a residential building. The loan is secured by the building. Assuming the other requirements are met, the loan qualifies as qualified nonrecourse financing because the money was borrowed in connection with the activity of holding real property. Charlie and Owen are each at risk for their portion of the liability because the loan is secured by real property used in the activity of holding real property.

A qualified person is a person actively engaged in the business of lending money that meets the following criteria [§ 465(b)(6)(D), § 49(a)(1)(D)(iv)]:

1. the person must not be a related person to the taxpayer, or if the person is a related person, the financing must be commercially reasonable and on substantially the same terms as loans involving unrelated persons;

2. the taxpayer must not have acquired the property from the person, or from a person related to the person; and

3. the person must not receive a fee due to the taxpayer's investment in the real property, or be related to a person receiving such a fee.

In determining whether qualified nonrecourse financing is secured only by real property used in the activity of holding real property, property that is incidental to the activity of holding real property is disregarded. Also disregarded is other property if the total gross fair market value of that property is less than 10% of the total gross fair market value of all the property securing the financing [Reg. § 1.465-27(b)(2)(i)].

**EXAMPLE:** Veronica owns 11% of the stock of Bank. She also owns an office building that she leases to Company. Veronica sells the building to Company. Bank lends Company the money to finance the purchase. Company therefore acquired the building from a person related to the lender. As a result, the loan does not qualify as qualified nonrecourse financing. If the loan were guaranteed by a federal, state, or local government, it could qualify as qualified nonrecourse financing, notwithstanding the related-party aspect.

*Indemnification Agreements.* A taxpayer is not at risk if he or she has the benefit of an agreement that will indemnify or otherwise protect against the loss of his or her investment. Such an agreement may be express or it may arise by implication.

*Changes in Amount At Risk.* An activity may generate losses in multiple tax years. Therefore, the extent to which a taxpayer is at risk must be calculated anew each tax year, taking into account what has previously happened. Adjustments that may have to be made include the following [Prop. Reg. § 1.465-22, § 1.465-23]:

- to the extent the at-risk rules permit a loss to be deducted, the amount deducted reduces the amount at risk;
- an activity that generates taxable income that is not distributed increases the amount at risk;
- a taxpayer's contribution of additional money or property to the activity increases the amount at risk;
- a taxpayer's incurrence of additional debt may qualify for inclusion in the amount at risk; and
- a taxpayer's withdrawal of money or property from the activity decreases the amount at risk to the extent of the withdrawal.

## VIII.E.5. Recapture of Previously Allowed Losses

[550 T.M., II.A.4.; TPS ¶2970.07.B.]

A taxpayer's amount at risk cannot be negative. When the amount at risk reaches zero, losses are suspended. However, distributions of cash, reductions in liabilities, executions of indemnity agreements, and other events could nevertheless give rise to a negative at-risk amount. If the amount a taxpayer has at risk in any activity is less than zero at the end of a tax year, the taxpayer must recapture at least part of previously allowed losses. This is accomplished by including in gross income from the activity for the tax year an amount equal to the lesser of either (i) the absolute value of the negative at-risk amount, or (ii) the total amount of losses deducted in previous tax years beginning after 1978, less any amounts previously added to income from that activity under this recapture rule. The recapture of income automatically generates a suspended loss in the same amount that may be used in a succeeding tax year once the taxpayer has a sufficient amount at risk [§ 465(e)].

---

**EXAMPLE:** In Year 1, Matt invests $50,000 cash in an equipment leasing partnership and is also at risk for $150,000 of partnership indebtedness, giving him a total amount at risk of $200,000. His share of the partnership's Year 1 loss is $120,000, which he deducts in full on his Year 1 return, reducing his amount at risk to $80,000. In Year 2, Matt's share of partnership taxable income is $10,000, and the partnership distributes $150,000 cash to him. The contribution of income and distribution results in a negative at-risk amount of $60,000 ($80,000 + $10,000 share of partnership income − $150,000 cash distribution), so Matt is required to include $60,000 of recapture income from the activity during the year, and his amount at risk as of the beginning of Year 3 is $0. He also has a suspended loss of $60,000, available for possible use in Year 3.

---

## VIII.F. Passive Loss Rules

[549 T.M.; TPS ¶2980.]

The passive loss rules generally provide that deductions and credits from passive activities are allowed only to the extent of income from such activities. This rule is intended to prevent taxpayers from using losses and credits from tax shelters to offset income from other sources. The passive loss rules apply to individuals, estates, trusts (other than grantor trusts), personal service corporations, and closely held corporations. Though grantor trusts, partnerships, and S corporations are not directly subject to the rules, the passive loss rules apply to the owners of such entities. Deductions or credits that are disallowed may be carried forward indefinitely. Any unused passive activity loss (but not credits) may be used to offset nonpassive income upon a taxpayer's complete disposition of his interest in the passive activity in a fully taxable transaction [§ 469(a), § 469(b), § 469(g)(1)].

Passive activity losses generally are reported on Form 8582, *Passive Activity Loss Limitations*. Passive activity credits generally are reported on Form 8582-CR, *Passive Activity Credit Limitations*. Personal service corporations and closely held corporations report passive activity losses and credits on Form 8810, *Corporate Passive Activity Loss and Credit Limitations*. Partnerships and S corporations report income and expenses from rental real estate activities on Form 8825, *Rental Real Estate Income and Expenses of a Partnership or an S Corporation.*

### VIII.F.1. Passive Activities

[549 T.M., III.; TPS ¶2980.03., .04., .05.]

A taxpayer subject to the passive loss rules must identify which, if any, of his or her activities are passive activities. A passive activity is (i) any activity that involves the conduct of any trade or business in which the taxpayer does not materially participate for the tax year, or (ii) any rental activity (regardless of whether the taxpayer materially participates) to the extent the taxpayer is not engaged in the rental activities as a real estate professional [§ 469(c)(1), § 469(c)(2)]. The determination of whether the taxpayer is engaged in a passive activity first requires the identification of separate activities (see VIII.F.1.a.). Thereafter, those separate activities must be analyzed to determine whether any given activity involves the conduct of a trade or business (see VIII.F.1.b.) and whether the taxpayer materially participates in any trade or business (see VIII.F.1.c.).

### VIII.F.1.a. Grouping Activities Under the Passive Loss Rules

[549 T.M., III.A.; TPS ¶2980.03.]

***General Grouping Rules.*** Identifying a taxpayer's separate activities is a precondition to determining which of the taxpayer's activities are passive. A taxpayer may treat one or more trade or business activities, or rental activities, as a single activity if those activities form an appropriate economic unit for measuring gain or loss under the passive activity rules. Whether activities form an appropriate economic unit is a facts and circumstances question, and a taxpayer may use any reasonable method of applying the relevant facts and circumstances [Reg. § 1.469-4(c)]. Factors to be considered include the following [Reg. § 1.469-4(c)(2)]:

- the similarities and differences in the types of trades or businesses;
- the extent of common control;
- the extent of common ownership;
- the geographical location; and
- the interdependencies between or among activities, which may include the extent to which the activities:
  — buy or sell goods between or among themselves;
  — involve products or services that are generally provided together;
  — have the same customers;
  — have the same employees; or
  — use a single set of books and records to account for the activities.

Generally, when activities are grouped into appropriate economic units, a taxpayer may not regroup those activities in a later tax year. However, if the original grouping is clearly inappropriate or there is a material change in the facts and circumstances that makes the original grouping clearly inappropriate, a taxpayer must regroup the activities. Additionally, because the application of the net investment income tax (see X.A.4.) may cause taxpayers to reconsider their previous grouping determinations, a taxpayer may regroup activities in the first tax year beginning after 2013 in which the taxpayer is subject to the net investment income tax [Reg. § 1.469-4(e), § 1.469-11(b)(3)(iv)(A), § 1.469-11(b)(3)(iv)(B)].

Taxpayers must comply with disclosure requirements for their original groupings and the later addition and disposition of specific activities within those groupings. A statement must be filed in the tax year that a grouping is first made, when a new activity is added to an existing group, and when a clearly inappropriate grouping is regrouped. Special rules exist for groupings by partnerships and S corporations [Reg. § 1.469-4(e); Rev. Proc. 2010-13, 2010-4 I.R.B. 329].

The IRS may regroup a taxpayer's activities if the taxpayer's grouping fails to reflect one or more appropriate economic units and a principal purpose of the taxpayer's grouping is to circumvent the underlying purposes of the passive loss rules. Additionally, failure to comply with the disclosure requirements generally will result in each activity in a purported grouping being treated as separate activities, unless the taxpayer qualifies for relief for untimely disclosure [Reg. § 1.469-4(f); Rev. Proc. 2010-13].

*Rental Activity Grouping Rules.* Taxpayers generally may not group a rental activity with a trade or business activity. However, they may be grouped together if the activities form an appropriate economic unit and either [Reg. § 1.469-4(d)(1)]:
- the rental activity is insubstantial in relation to the trade or business activity;
- the trade or business activity is insubstantial in relation to the rental activity; or
- each owner of the trade or business activity has the same ownership interest in the rental activity, in which case the part of the rental activity that involves the rental of items of property for use in the trade or business activity may be grouped with the trade or business activity.

An activity involving the rental of real property and an activity involving the rental of personal property (other than personal property provided in connection with the real property) may not be treated as a single activity [Reg. § 1.469-4(d)(2)].

*Limitation on Grouping Certain Activities.* A taxpayer who owns an interest as a limited partner or limited entrepreneur in one of the following activities may not group that activity with any other activity in another type of business [Reg. § 1.469-4(d)(3)]:
- holding, producing, or distributing motion picture films or videotapes;
- farming;
- leasing any § 1245 property (see III.D.2.a.);
- exploring for, or exploiting, oil and gas resources; and
- exploring for, or exploiting, geothermal deposits as a trade or business or for the production of income.

However, a taxpayer who is a limited partner or limited entrepreneur in any of the above-described activities may group that activity with (i) another above-described activity that is the same type of business if the taxpayer is a limited partner or limited entrepreneur in the other activity, or (ii) another activity in the same type of business in which the taxpayer is not a limited partner or limited entrepreneur if the grouping is appropriate under the general facts and circumstances test [§ 465(c)(1); Reg. § 1.469-4(c), § 1.469-4(d)(3)(i)]. A limited entrepreneur is a person who has an interest in an enterprise other than as a limited partner and who does not actively participate in the management of the enterprise [§ 464(e)(2)].

*Activities Conducted Through Partnerships or S Corporations.* A partnership or S corporation must group its activities by following the general rules and by using the facts and circumstances analysis. Once the entity determines its activities, a partner or shareholder groups those activities with activities conducted directly by the partner or shareholder or with activities conducted through other partnerships or S corporations in accordance with the general rules [Reg. § 1.469-4(d)(5)].

### VIII.F.1.b. Trade or Business Activity for Purposes of the Passive Loss Rules
[549 T.M., III.B.1.; TPS ¶2980.03.C.]

Once a taxpayer has determined the scope of his or her separate activities, it is necessary to determine which of those activities are passive. Passive activities include any activity that involves the conduct of any trade or business in which the taxpayer does not materially participate for the tax year [§ 469(c)(1)].

A trade or business activity, for purposes of the passive loss rules, is any non-rental activity that meets one of the following conditions [Reg. § 1.469-4(b)(1)]:

1. it involves the conduct of a trade or business (see IV.A.);

2. it is conducted in anticipation of the commencement of a trade or business (see IV.F.4.); or

3. it involves deductible research or experimental expenditures (see IV.F.2.).

A trade or business activity is not a passive activity, however, if the taxpayer materially participates in the activity (see VIII.F.1.c.).

### VIII.F.1.c. Material Participation for Purposes of the Passive Loss Rules
[549 T.M., III.B.2.; TPS ¶2980.04.]

A trade or business activity is not a passive activity if a taxpayer materially participates in the activity. In making this determination, the participation of the taxpayer's spouse is taken into account. A taxpayer materially participates in a trade or business activity for a tax year if he or she meets any of the following seven tests [§ 469(h); Reg. § 1.469-5T(a)]:

1. The taxpayer participated in the activity for more than 500 hours during the tax year.

2. The taxpayer's participation was substantially all the participation in the activity of all individuals (including individuals who are not owners of interests in the activity) for the tax year.

3. The taxpayer participated in the activity for more than 100 hours during the tax year, and no one else (including individuals who are not owners of interests in the activity) participates more.

4. The activity is a significant participation activity and the taxpayer participated in all significant participation activities, in the aggregate, for more than 500 hours. A significant participation activity is a trade or business activity in which the taxpayer participated for more than 100 hours during the year and in which the taxpayer did not materially participate under any other material participation test.

5. The taxpayer materially participated in the activity for any five (whether or not consecutive) of the 10 immediately preceding tax years.

6. The activity is a personal service activity in which the taxpayer materially participated for any three (whether or not consecutive) preceding tax years. A personal service activity is an activity involving the performance of personal services in the fields of health (including veterinary services), law, engineering, architecture, accounting, actuarial science, performing arts, consulting, or any other trade or business in which capital is not a material income-producing factor.

7. Based on all the facts and circumstances, the taxpayer's participation in the activity was material because it was regular, continuous, and substantial. However, the taxpayer must have participated in the activity for more than 100

hours during the tax year. Participation in managing the activity does not count for the 100 hours requirement if any other person received compensation for managing the activity, or spent more hours managing the activity than the taxpayer did (regardless of whether he or she was compensated).

*Material Participation by Partners.* The passive loss rules apply at the partner level, rather than the partnership level. Thus, whether an individual general partner materially participates in a partnership activity is determined by the general partner's participation in the activity. The material participation tests are applied to the partnership's tax year that ends with or within the partner's tax year [Reg. § 1.469-2T(e)(1)]. Limited partners, however, generally are not treated as materially participating in activities conducted by the partnership. Only a limited partner who satisfies test 1, 5, or 6, above, will be treated as materially participating [Reg. § 1.469-5T(e)(2)].

*Material Participation by Corporate Entities.* The passive loss rules apply to two types of C corporations: closely held corporations (as defined in Reg. § 1.469-1T(g)(2)(ii)) and personal service corporations (as defined in Reg. § 1.469-1T(g)(2)(ii)). These corporations are treated as materially participating in an activity only if one or more shareholders together holding more than 50% in value of the outstanding stock of the corporation materially participate in the activity. The seven material participation tests apply to determine whether an individual is treated as materially participating in an activity of the corporation. For this purpose, all of the corporation's activities are treated as activities in which the individual holds an interest, and the individual's participation in all activities other than the corporation's activities is disregarded [§ 469(h)(4); Reg. § 1.469-1T(g)(3)]. Additionally, a closely held corporation also is treated as materially participating if it satisfies both of the following conditions [§ 465(c)(7)(C), § 469(h)(4)(B)]:

1. During the entire 12-month period ending on the last day of the tax year, the corporation had at least:

   — One full-time employee whose services were in the active management of the business; and

   — Three full-time non-owner employees (i.e., an employee that owns no more than 5% in value of the outstanding stock of the corporation at any time during the tax year) whose services were directly related to the business. A modified version of the constructive ownership rules of § 318 apply: an owner of 5% or more (rather than 50% or more) of the value of the corporation's stock is considered to own a proportionate share of any stock owned by the corporation.

2. Deductions due to the business that are allowable to the corporation as business expenses and as contributions to certain employee benefit plans for the tax year exceed 15% of the gross income from the business.

***Material Participation by Estates and Trusts.*** An estate or trust is treated as materially participating in an activity if the executor or the trustee is materially participating. For a grantor trust, however, the determination of material participation is made at the taxpayer level. It has been held that a trust may be treated as materially participating in an activity if the persons who conduct business on the trust's behalf, including, but not limited to, trustees, are materially participating [*Mattie K. Carter Trust v. United States*, 256 F. Supp. 2d 536 (N.D. Tex. 2003)]. However, the IRS has taken the position that, in order for a non-trustee to be considered as materially participating, the non-trustee must be a fiduciary. Further, to be considered a fiduciary, the non-trustee must be vested with some degree of discretionary power to act on behalf of the trust [TAM 200733023].

***Participation Definition.*** In general, any work done by an individual in any capacity in connection with an activity in which the individual owns an interest at the time the work is done is treated as participation of the individual in the activity. Additionally, an individual's participation in an activity includes the individual's spouse's participation [Reg. § 1.469-5(f)(1), § 1.469-5T(f)(3)]. There are two exceptions [Reg. § 1.469-5T(f)(2)]:

1. work done in connection with an activity is not treated as participation if:

   — the work is not of a type customarily done by an owner of such an activity; and

   — one of the principal purposes for the performance of the work is to avoid the disallowance of losses or credits under the passive loss rules; and

2. work done by an individual in the individual's capacity as an investor in an activity is not treated as participation in the activity unless the individual is directly involved in the day-to-day management of the activity.

A taxpayer may establish participation in an activity by any reasonable means, including the identification of services performed over a period of time and the number of hours spent performing such services based on appointment books, calendars, or narrative summaries. Maintenance of contemporaneous daily time reports, logs, or similar documents is not required if the taxpayer can otherwise substantiate the level of his or her participation in an activity [Reg. § 1.469-5T(f)(4)].

## Material Participation Flow Chart

(Note: For farming activities, retirees and surviving spouses may alternatively show material participation under Section 469(h)(3)).

1) During the taxable year, did the taxpayer participate in the activity for more than 500 hours?

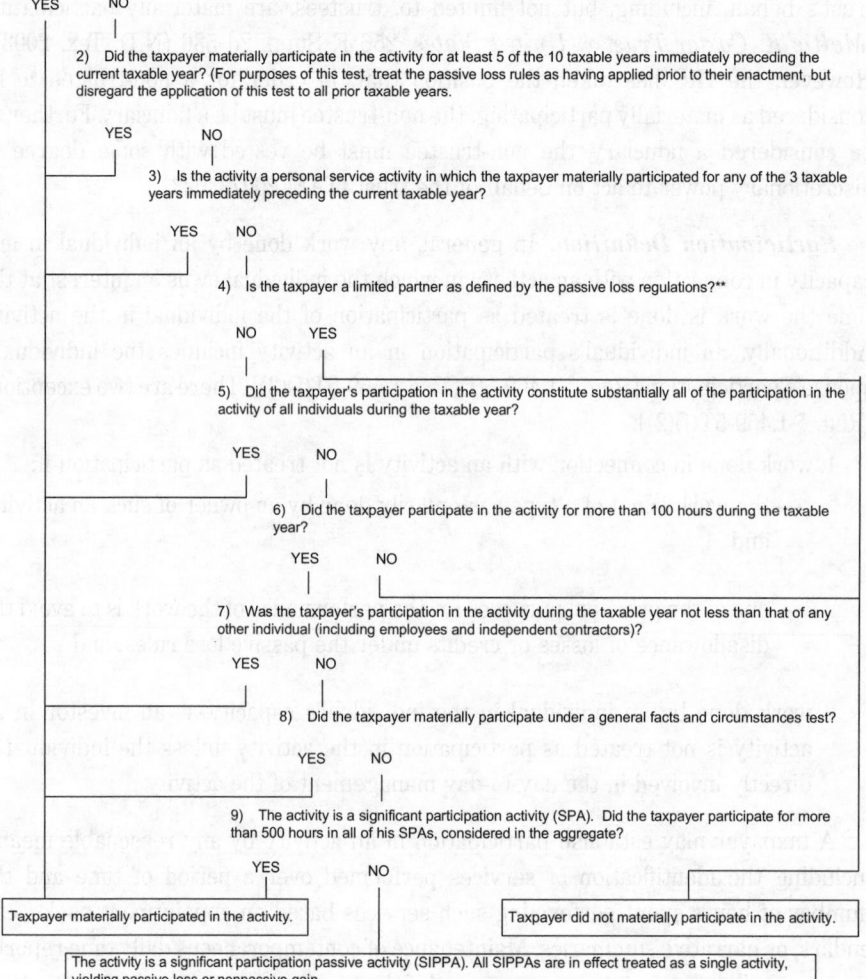

YES       NO

2) Did the taxpayer materially participate in the activity for at least 5 of the 10 taxable years immediately preceding the current taxable year? (For purposes of this test, treat the passive loss rules as having applied prior to their enactment, but disregard the application of this test to all prior taxable years.

YES       NO

3) Is the activity a personal service activity in which the taxpayer materially participated for any of the 3 taxable years immediately preceding the current taxable year?

YES       NO

4) Is the taxpayer a limited partner as defined by the passive loss regulations?**

NO       YES

5) Did the taxpayer's participation in the activity constitute substantially all of the participation in the activity of all individuals during the taxable year?

YES       NO

6) Did the taxpayer participate in the activity for more than 100 hours during the taxable year?

YES       NO

7) Was the taxpayer's participation in the activity during the taxable year not less than that of any other individual (including employees and independent contractors)?

YES       NO

8) Did the taxpayer materially participate under a general facts and circumstances test?

YES       NO

9) The activity is a significant participation activity (SPA). Did the taxpayer participate for more than 500 hours in all of his SPAs, considered in the aggregate?

YES       NO

| Taxpayer materially participated in the activity. | | Taxpayer did not materially participate in the activity. |

The activity is a significant participation passive activity (SIPPA). All SIPPAs are in effect treated as a single activity, yielding passive loss or nonpassive gain.

** For these purposes, the Tax Court and the Court of Federal Claims have ruled the members of LLCs and partners in LLPs are not considered limited partners under the regulations.

### VIII.F.1.d. Rental Activities

[549 T.M., III.B.3.; TPS ¶2980.05.]

Rental activities generally are passive activities even if a taxpayer materially participates. An activity is a rental activity if real or personal tangible property is used by customers, or held for use by customers, and the gross income (or expected gross income) from the activity represents amounts paid (or to be paid) mainly for the use of the property. It does not matter whether the use of the property by customers is pursuant to a lease, service contract, or other arrangement not called a lease [§ 469(j)(8); Reg. § 1.469-1T(e)(3)(i)].

There are several exceptions to the general passive rental activity rule. An activity is not treated as a passive rental activity if any of the following apply [Reg. § 1.469-1T(e)(3)(ii)]:

- The average period of customer use of the property is no more than seven days.

- The average period of customer use of the property is no more than 30 days, and the taxpayer provides significant personal services. Significant personal services include only services performed by individuals. Significant personal services do not include the following:

  — services needed to permit the lawful use of the property;

  — services to repair or improve property that would extend its useful life for a period substantially longer than the average rental; and

  — services that are similar to those commonly provided with long-term rentals of real estate (e.g., cleaning and maintenance of common areas or routine repairs).

- The taxpayer provides extraordinary personal services in making the rental property available for customer use (i.e., if the services are performed by individuals, and customers' use of the property is incidental to their receipt of the services).

- The rental is incidental to a nonrental activity. A rental activity is incidental to a nonrental activity if the taxpayer's principal purpose for holding the property during the tax year is to realize gain from its appreciation, and the gross rental income from the property is less than 2% of the lesser of the property's (i) unadjusted basis, or (ii) fair market value. The rental of property is incidental to a trade or business activity if all of the following apply:

  — the taxpayer owns an interest in the trade or business activity during the year;

  — the rental property was used mainly in that trade or business activity during the current year, or during at least two of the preceding five years; and

  — the taxpayer's gross rental income from the property is less than 2% of the lesser of the property's (i) unadjusted basis, or (ii) fair market value.

- The taxpayer customarily makes the rental property available during defined business hours for nonexclusive use by various customers.

- The taxpayer provides the property for use in a nonrental activity in his or her capacity as an owner of an interest in a partnership, S corporation, or joint venture.

- The rental is of the taxpayer's residence, and the § 280A limitations on the rental of a residence apply [§ 469(j)(10)] (see IV.D.7.).

- The taxpayer materially participates in the rental real estate activities as a real estate professional [§ 469(c)(7)] (see VIII.F.1.d(1)).

### VIII.F.1.d(1) Real Estate Professionals

[549 T.M., III.B.3.c.; TPS ¶2980.05.B.8.]

Rental real estate activities in which a taxpayer materially participates as a real estate professional are not treated as passive activities [§ 469(c)(7)]. A taxpayer qualifies as a real estate professional if he or she meets both of the following requirements [§ 469(c)(7)(B)]:

1. more than half of the personal services the taxpayer performs in trades or businesses during the tax year are performed in real property trades or businesses (i.e., real property development, redevelopment, construction, reconstruction, acquisition, conversion, rental, operation, management, leasing, or brokerage trades or businesses) in which the taxpayer materially participates; and

2. the taxpayer performed more than 750 hours of services during the tax year in real property trades or businesses in which he or she materially participates.

Personal services performed as an employee in real property trades or businesses do not count, unless the taxpayer is a 5% owner of the employer. While a spouse's participation is counted in determining material participation, taxpayers who file a joint return do not count a spouse's personal services in determining whether he or she meets the requirements for a real estate professional [§ 469(c)(7)(B)].

A closely held C corporation qualifies as a real estate professional if more than 50% of the gross receipts (not including portfolio income, as defined in Reg. § 1.469-2T(c)(3)) for its tax year came from real property trades or businesses in which it materially participated.

Each interest of a qualifying taxpayer in rental real estate is treated as a separate rental real estate activity unless the taxpayer elects to treat all interests in rental real estate as a single rental real estate activity. To make an election, the taxpayer must file with his or her original income tax return for the tax year a statement that the taxpayer (i) is a qualifying taxpayer for the tax year, and (ii) is making the election pursuant to § 469(c)(7)(A). In certain circumstances, taxpayers may make a late election on an amended return. An election is binding for the tax year in which it is made and all future tax years in which the taxpayer is a qualifying taxpayer. However, if there is a material change in the taxpayer's facts and circumstances, the taxpayer may revoke the election [Reg. § 1.469-9(e)(1); Rev. Proc. 2011-34, 2011-24 I.R.B. 875].

### VIII.F.1.d.(2) $25,000 Offset for Active Participation Rule

[549 T.M., V.C.; TPS ¶2980.05.C.]

Certain taxpayers that actively participate in rental real estate activities may offset nonpassive income with up to $25,000 ($12,500 for married taxpayers filing separately) of losses and credits from rental real estate activities [§ 469(i)]. However, if a taxpayer lives with his or her spouse at any time during the year and files a separate return, the taxpayer is ineligible to use the special allowance [§ 469(i)(5)(B)].

***Active Participation.*** Active participation is a less stringent standard than material participation and can be satisfied without regular, continuous, and substantial involvement in an activity. Active participation can be established through the significant and bona fide performance of purely management functions (e.g., approving new tenants, deciding on rental terms, approving capital and repair expenditures, etc.). Participation by the taxpayer's spouse is taken into account in determining whether a taxpayer actively participates.

Only individuals can actively participate in rental real estate activities. A decedent's estate, however, is treated as actively participating for its tax years ending within two years after the decedent's death, if the decedent would have satisfied the active participation requirement for the activity for the tax year he or she died [§ 469(i)(4)].

Limited partners are not treated as actively participating in a partnership's rental real estate activities. Additionally, a taxpayer is not treated as actively participating in a rental real estate activity unless his or her interest in the activity (including the taxpayer's spouse's interest) is at least 10% of the value of all interest in the activity throughout the year [§ 469(i)(6)].

---

**EXAMPLE:** Missy owns a rental apartment building. She makes all management decisions, periodically reviews building maintenance, arranges through brokers for advertising and showing of vacant apartments, and arranges through others for leasing, rent collection, and necessary repairs. Missy incurs a loss from the rental activity of $20,000. Although her rental activity is a passive activity, Missy can deduct the $20,000 loss under the $25,000 offset rule because she actively participates in the rental activity.

---

**Phaseout of Maximum Offset Amount.** The $25,000 ($12,500 for married taxpayers filing separately) offset amount is phased out ratably as the taxpayer's income increases. The amount is reduced by 50% of the amount by which the taxpayer's adjusted gross income (as defined in § 469(i)(3)(F)) exceeds $100,000 ($50,000 for married taxpayers filing separately), and is phased out completely where the taxpayer's adjusted gross income reaches $150,000 ($75,000 for married taxpayers filing separately) [§ 469(i)(3), § 469(i)(5)]. Special rules apply to rehabilitation investment credits from rental real estate activities, low-income housing credits, and commercial revitalization deductions [§ 469(i)(3)(B), § 469(i)(3)(C), § 469(i)(3)(D)].

### VIII.F.1.e. Passive Activity Credits

[549 T.M., IV.C.9.; TPS ¶2980.06.D.]

Passive activity credits for a tax year are allowed only against tax on income from passive activities. The credits are not allowed to the extent they exceed the taxpayer's regular tax liability allocable to all passive activities for the year. Passive activity credits are credits that are attributable to the tax year, arise in connection with the conduct of a passive activity, and arise under the following provisions [§ 469(d)(2)(A); Reg. § 1.469-3T(b)]:

- the general business credits [§ 38 through § 45R] (see IX.A.);

- the former Puerto Rico and possessions tax credit [§ 27(b)]; and

- carryover of the expired qualified electric vehicle credit [§ 30].

The amount of regular tax liability (as defined under § 26(b)) allocable to all passive activities for the tax year is the excess of (i) the taxpayer's regular tax liability for the tax year, over (ii) the amount of regular tax liability, determined by disregarding both passive activity gross income and passive activity deductions (see VIII.F.2.) for the year [Reg. § 1.469-3T(d)(1)].

### VIII.F.2. Computation of Passive Activity Loss and Carryovers

[549 T.M., II.F., IV.; TPS ¶2980.06.C., .06.E., .10.]

A taxpayer who owns an interest in a passive activity must compute the amount of the loss from the activity, which is then subject to the passive loss limitations. For taxpayers other than closely held C corporations, the passive activity loss for any tax year is the amount by which passive activity deductions exceed passive activity gross income. The taxpayer must aggregate all passive activity deductions and all passive activity gross income from his or her interests in all passive activities to determine whether he or she has an overall passive activity loss for the tax year. To the extent the taxpayer has net income from passive activities, passive activity credits can be used to offset the tax liability attributable to the net income [§ 469(d)].

*Passive Activity Gross Income.* Passive activity gross income includes all items of gross income from passive activities, including gains from dispositions of interests in passive activities. However, certain items of income from passive activities are excluded from passive activity gross income, including the following [Reg. § 1.469-2T(c)]:

- portfolio income and portfolio expenses (e.g., interest, dividends, annuities, and royalties not derived in the ordinary course of a trade or business, and gain or loss from the disposition of property that produces these types of income or the disposition of property held for investment);
- personal service income (e.g., salaries, wages, commissions, self-employment income from trade or business activities in which the taxpayer materially participates, deferred compensation, taxable social security and other retirement benefits, and payments from partnerships to partners for personal services);
- income from positive § 481 adjustments (see XI.B.3.) allocated to activities other than passive activities;
- income from oil and gas property, if any loss from a working interest in the property was treated as a nonpassive loss under a special rule concerning qualified working interests;
- any income from intangible property (e.g., patents, copyrights, or literary, musical, or artistic compositions) if the taxpayer's personal efforts significantly contributed to the creation of the property;
- income attributable to a state, local, or foreign income tax refund;
- income from a covenant not to compete; and
- income attributable to the reimbursement of a casualty or theft loss (see VIII.H.1.) included in gross income to recover all or part of a prior year loss deduction, if the loss deduction was not a passive activity deduction.

*Passive Activity Deductions.* A deduction is a passive activity deduction only if it (i) arises in connection with the conduct of an activity that is a passive activity for the tax year, or (ii) is a passive activity deduction that is carried over to the tax year from a prior year. The term generally includes losses from dispositions of property used in a passive activity at the time of the disposition and losses from a disposition of less than the taxpayer's entire interest in a passive activity. Passive activity deductions do not include the following [Reg. § 1.469-2T(d)]:

- deductions for expenses (other than interest expenses) that are clearly and directly allocable to portfolio income;
- deductions for losses from the disposition of property that produces portfolio income or that was held for investment;

- qualified home mortgage interest, capitalized interest expenses, and other interest expenses (other than self-charged interest) properly allocable to passive activities;

- miscellaneous itemized deductions that are subject to disallowance in whole or in part due to the 2% floor on miscellaneous itemized deductions (see VII.I.);

- deductions for charitable contributions (see VII.G.);

- deductions for any state, local, or foreign income tax (see VII.E.);

- items of loss or deduction that are carried to the tax year under the net operating loss rules (see VIII.G.), the percentage depletion limitation rules (see VI.A.), or the capital loss rules (see III.B.5.);

- deductions for casualty and theft losses (see VIII.H.1.), unless losses similar in cause and severity recur regularly in the activity; and

- net negative § 481 adjustments (see XI.B.3.) allocated to activities other than passive activities.

A deduction from a passive activity that is disallowed for a tax year under other sections of the Code is not a passive activity deduction for the tax year. The at-risk limitations (see VIII.E.) and the partnership and S corporation basis limitations (see XIV.D.2.f. and XV.B.2.a., respectively) are applied before a deduction is treated as a passive activity deduction for purposes of the passive loss rules [Reg. § 1.469-2T(d)(6)].

***Partnerships and S Corporations.*** Special rules for determining passive activity gross income and passive activity deductions apply to partnerships and S corporations. If participation is relevant, the character of each item of gross income and deduction allocated to a partner or shareholder is determined by reference to the participation of the partner or shareholder in the activity that generated the item [Reg. § 1.469-2T(e)(1)].

---

**EXAMPLE:** Howard is a calendar year taxpayer and a partner in Partnership, which has a natural business tax year that ends on Jan. 31. Partnership engages in a single trade or business activity during the tax year ending Jan. 31, Year 2. For the period from Feb. 1, Year 1, through Jan. 31, Year 2, Howard does not materially participate in this activity. On his Year 2 tax return, Howard's distributive share of Partnership's gross income and deductions from this activity must be treated as passive activity gross income and passive activity deductions, regardless of his participation in the activity for the period from Feb. 1, Year 2, through Dec. 31, Year 2.

---

If a transaction is treated under the partnership rules as a transaction between a partnership and a partner acting in a capacity other than a partner (see XIV.D.3.a.), the passive loss rules characterize income or deductions from the transaction in a manner consistent with the treatment under the partnership rules [Reg. § 1.469-2T(e)(2)(i)].

When a partner sells an interest in a partnership, and when a shareholder sells some or all of the stock in an S corporation, gain or loss must be allocated among activities. A portion of a taxpayer's gain or loss from disposing of such an interest is treated as gain or loss from disposing of an interest in each trade or business, rental, or investment activity in which the partnership or S corporation owns an interest on the applicable valuation date. If net gain is realized on a disposition, the gain is allocated (as described in Reg. § 1.469-2T(e)(3)(ii)(B)(1)) to those activities that would have produced net gain if the entity had sold its entire interest in its activities for fair market value on the applicable valuation date. Similarly, if net loss is realized on a disposition, the loss is allocated (as described in Reg. § 1.469-2T(e)(3)(ii)(B)(2)) only to those activities that would have produced a loss. An applicable valuation date is elected by the entity and is either (i) the beginning of the tax year of the entity in which the disposition occurs, or (ii) the date on which the disposition occurs. However, the beginning of the tax year cannot be used if certain significant events have occurred during the year that might make that date inappropriate [Reg. § 1.469-2T(e)(3)(ii)].

*Publicly Traded Partnerships.* The passive loss rules apply separately for each publicly traded partnership (PTP) (see XIV.D.4.b.) in which the taxpayer owns an interest. Because PTPs are treated separately, net income from one PTP cannot be offset by losses from any other PTP or by any other passive losses. Thus, a partner with net passive losses from a PTP cannot apply them against any other income. The partner must carry the losses forward and may either use them to offset income from that particular PTP in a later year, or use them when the partner disposes of his or her entire interest in the PTP [§ 469(k)].

*Carryover of Loss.* Where a taxpayer has a passive activity loss for a tax year, the passive activity deductions and passive activity credits that are disallowed because they exceed passive activity gross income may be carried over to subsequent tax years and allocated to the same passive activity. If the composition of a taxpayer's activities change, special rules apply to allocate suspended losses [§ 469(b); Reg. § 1.469-1(f)(4)].

### VIII.F.3. Disposition of Passive Activity Interests

[549 T.M., V.A.; TPS ¶2980.08.]

A taxpayer who disposes of his or her entire interest in a passive activity in a fully taxable transaction can use passive activity losses (but not credits) to offset nonpassive income in the year of disposition. In a transaction in which all gain or loss is recognized on the disposition of a passive activity, any loss from the activity for the tax year (including gain or loss recognized on the disposition) in excess of any net income or gain from other passive activities for the tax year is treated as a loss that is not from a passive activity. The person acquiring the interest cannot be related to the taxpayer [§ 469(g)].

---

**EXAMPLE:** Bianca purchases a rental activity interest for $100,000 in Year 1. During Year 1 and Year 2, Bianca incurs $20,000 of suspended passive activity losses as a result of $20,000 of depreciation claimed on rental property. At the end of Year 2, Bianca contracts to sell the rental activity for $100,000. She closes the sale in early Year 3. Her gain on the sale is $20,000 ($100,000 amount realized – ($100,000 basis – $20,000 depreciation)), which is included on her tax return for Year 3. The $20,000 gain is offset by the $20,000 of suspended passive activity losses. Had Bianca sold the rental activity for $95,000 and also had $9,000 of passive income and $5,000 of passive losses from other activities, her $15,000 gain ($95,000 amount realized – ($100,000 basis – $20,000 depreciation)) would have been offset by the $20,000 of suspended passive activity losses. The remaining $5,000 ($20,000 – $15,000) of suspended passive activity losses would have been offset against the net $4,000 of passive income ($9,000 passive income – $5,000 passive losses) from her other activities. The remaining $1,000 ($5,000 – $4,000) would have been a nonpassive loss that could be deducted against Bianca's other income.

---

***Dispositions by Installment Sale.*** Complete dispositions of a taxpayer's interest can be made by an installment sale (see III.G.). In such a case, the portion of the passive activity losses that are allowable for each tax year bears the same ratio to all the losses as the gain recognized on the sale during the tax year bears to the gross profit from the sale [§ 469(g)(3)].

***Dispositions by Gift.*** A taxpayer's gift of all or a part of an interest in a passive activity does not result in the allowance of suspended passive activity losses. Rather, the suspended passive activity losses are added to the basis of the property transferred immediately before the gift is made. As a result, the donor may not use the suspended losses in any year, and the losses are effectively recovered by the donee through the stepped-up basis [§ 469(j)(6)].

***Dispositions by Death.*** If an interest in an activity is transferred as a result of the death of the taxpayer, the suspended passive activity losses are generally allowed on the decedent's final tax return. However, the suspended losses are allowed only to the extent those losses exceed the step-up in the basis of the transferred interest that is available on the death of the decedent. If suspended losses are less than the step-up in basis or cannot be used in the decedent's final tax return, the suspended losses are never allowed [§ 469(g)(2)].

***Partial Dispositions.*** A taxpayer may treat a disposition of substantially all of an activity as a separate activity of which there was a complete disposition (thus allowing suspended losses) if the taxpayer can establish with reasonably certainty (i) the amount of deductions and credits allocable to that part of the activity for the tax year, and (ii) the amount of gross income and of any other deductions and credits allocable to that part of the activity for the tax year [Reg. § 1.469-4(g)].

## VIII.G. Net Operating Losses

[539. T.M.; TPS ¶2410.]

Taxpayers with deductions in excess of gross income for a tax year may, subject to limitations, deduct the excess from taxable income in previous or succeeding tax years. In any given tax year, a net operating loss (NOL) deduction is allowed in an amount equal to the sum of NOL carryovers or carrybacks to the tax year. The NOL deduction effectively averages a taxpayer's income and losses over a period of years, thus relieving some of the inequities caused by the determination of the income tax based on an annual accounting period. While losses from operating a business are the most common source of an NOL, deductions from a taxpayer's work as an employee, casualty and theft losses, moving expenses, or rental property, among other things, may also result in an NOL [§ 172].

### VIII.G.1. Taxpayers Eligible to Deduct Net Operating Losses

[539 T.M., II.; TPS ¶2410.02.]

Taxpayers eligible to take advantage of the NOL deduction include individuals, C corporations, estates and trusts, exempt organizations, insurance companies other than life insurance companies, and, in certain circumstances, personal holding companies. While partnerships and S corporations generally cannot use NOLs, partners and shareholders can use their separate shares of partnership or S corporation income and deductions to figure their individual NOLs [§ 172(a), § 641(a), § 512(b)(6), § 545(b)(4)].

Other entities ineligible to deduct NOLs include life insurance companies, regulated investment companies, corporations subject to the accumulated earnings tax, and cooperative organizations [§ 703(a)(2)(D), § 1363(b)(2), § 805(b)(4), § 535(b)(4), § 1382(c)].

### VIII.G.2. Calculating Net Operating Losses

[539 T.M., III.; TPS ¶2410.03.]

A taxpayer with deductions exceeding gross income may have an NOL. The amount of an NOL is equal to the taxpayer's gross income minus deductions, computed with certain modifications. The modifications that must be made in calculating an NOL depends on whether the taxpayer is a corporate or noncorporate taxpayer. If, after the required modifications, excess deductions remain, the NOL is equal to the excess as modified. If the modifications eliminate the excess of deductions over gross income, the taxpayer does not have an NOL [§ 172(c), § 172(d)]. Special rules for calculating NOLs apply to real estate investment trusts, public utilities, exempt organizations, and estates and trusts [§ 172(d)(5), § 172(d)(6), § 247(a), § 512(b)(6), § 642(d)].

NOLs for any tax year are determined under the laws applicable to that tax year. Thus, for purposes of determining the amount of an NOL deduction, the law of the loss year is controlling, rather than the law of the year in which the NOL is ultimately deducted [Reg. § 1.172-1(e)].

---

**EXAMPLE:** For Year 3, Tory's allowable deductions exceed her gross income. The law applicable in Year 3 applies for purposes of determining whether Tory incurred an NOL for Year 3, and, if so, the amount of the NOL. If Tory has an NOL for Year 3, the loss is an NOL carryback to each of the two tax years preceding the Year 3 loss year (i.e., Year 1 and Year 2). If the loss is not fully absorbed in the carryback period, the loss may be an NOL carryover to each of the 20 years following the Year 3 loss year (i.e., Year 4 through Year 23).

---

*Corporate Taxpayers.* A corporation's NOL is determined by subtracting its gross income from its deductions and applying the following modifications [§ 172(d); Reg. § 1.172-2]:

- the NOL deduction is disallowed (i.e., NOL carrybacks and carryovers from other tax years cannot be used to augment the NOL for the tax year);
- the dividends received deductions under § 243, § 244, and § 245 (see XIII.C.2.b.) are computed without regard to the aggregate limitations that normally limit these deductions;
- the dividends paid deduction (see XIII.C.2.c.) for dividends paid on public utility preferred stock is computed without regard to the § 247(a)(1)(B) limitation; and
- the domestic production activity deduction (see IV.A.9.) is disallowed.

*Noncorporate Taxpayers.* An individual or other noncorporate taxpayer's NOL is determined by subtracting gross income from deductions and applying the following modifications [§ 172(d); Reg. § 1.172-3]:

- the NOL deduction is disallowed (i.e., NOL carrybacks and carryovers from other tax years cannot be used to augment the NOL for the tax year);
- the deduction for personal exemption (see XII.D.1.), or any deduction in lieu of such deduction, is disallowed;
- the deduction of nonbusiness capital losses is limited to the amount of nonbusiness capital gains, and the deduction of business capital losses is limited to the

sum of (i) business capital gains, and (ii) any nonbusiness capital gains not required to offset either nonbusiness capital losses or ordinary nonbusiness deductions (as described in the following bullet);

- the deduction of ordinary nonbusiness deductions is limited to the amount of nonbusiness income;
- the exclusion for capital gains from small business stock under § 1202 (see III.C.5.b.) is not allowed; and
- the deduction for domestic production activities (see IV.A.9.) is disallowed.

### VIII.G.3. Carryback and Carryover of Net Operating Losses

[539 T.M., IV.; TPS ¶2410.04.]

In general, taxpayers may carry back NOLs two years and carry forward NOLs 20 years. An NOL must first be carried to the earliest of the tax years for which it is allowable as a carryback or carryover. If the NOL is not fully absorbed by the taxable income of that year, the remainder is carried to the next earliest tax year for which it is allowable as a carryback or carryover. If some portion of an NOL remains after the expiration of the carryover period, that amount is not deductible [§ 172(b)(2)].

### VIII.G.3.a. Election to Waive Carryback Period

[539 T.M., IV.C.; TPS ¶2410.04.D.]

A taxpayer may elect to relinquish the entire carryback period for an NOL. If a carryback period is waived, the NOL is carried forward for the allowable carryover period, which is not extended as a result of waiving the carryback period. The election is made by filing a statement showing that the taxpayer is making an election to waive the carryback period under § 172(b)(3). The statement should be attached to the taxpayer's return, which must be filed no later than the due date (including extensions) for the tax year in which the NOL arises. The election applies only to the NOL for which it is made; a separate election is required for each NOL. Once made, an election is irrevocable for that tax year [§ 172(b)(3)]. If an affiliated group of corporations files a consolidated return, the common parent may elect, on behalf of the group, to waive the carryback period [Reg. § 1.1502-21(b)(3)(i)].

### VIII.G.3.b. Exceptions to General Carryback and Carryover Periods

[539 T.M., IV.B.; TPS ¶2410.04.C.]

***Real Estate Investment Trusts (REITs).*** No carryback is allowed for NOLs incurred in a tax year in which an entity qualifies as a REIT. The carryover period remains 20 years. If an entity fails to qualify as a REIT in a tax year, the general carryback and carryover periods apply to NOLs incurred in that tax year. However, an NOL arising in a non-REIT year (i.e., a year in which the entity fails to qualify as a REIT) may not be carried back to a REIT year (i.e., a year in which the entity qualifies as a REIT) [§ 172(b)(1)(A), § 172(b)(1)(B); Reg. § 1.172-10].

***Specified Liability Losses.*** Specified liability losses are eligible for a 10-year carryback period [§ 172(b)(1)(C)]. A specified liability loss is the sum of the following amounts, to the extent they are taken into account in computing the NOL for the tax year [§ 172(f)(1)]:

- amounts allowable as a § 162 business expense deduction (see IV.A.) or a § 165 loss deduction (see VIII.H.) attributable to (i) product liability, or (ii) expenses incurred in the investigation or settlement of, or opposition to, claims against the taxpayer on account of product liability; and

- amounts allowable as a deduction for an amount paid in satisfaction of a liability under a federal or state law requiring the reclamation of land, the decommissioning of a nuclear power plant or any unit thereof, the dismantlement of a drilling system, the remediation of environmental contamination, or a worker's compensation payment, if the act (or failure to act) giving rise to the liability occurs at least three years before the beginning of the tax year, and the taxpayer used an accrual method of accounting throughout.

*Corporate Equity Reduction Interest Losses.* When certain corporations incur a corporate equity reduction interest loss (as defined in § 172(h)(1)) in connection with a corporate equity reduction transaction (as defined in § 172(h)(3)), the loss cannot be carried back to any tax year preceding the tax year of the corporate equity reduction transaction. The carryover period remains 20 years [§ 172(b)(1)(E)].

*Farming Losses.* Farming losses may be carried back five years. A taxpayer may elect to waive the special five-year carryback period in favor of the general two-year carryback period. The election is made by filing a statement showing that the taxpayer is making an election to waive the special five-year carryback period under § 172(i)(3). The statement should be attached to the taxpayer's return, which must be filed no later than the due date (including extensions) for the tax year in which the NOL arises. The general two-year carryback period may also be separately waived (see VIII.G.3.a.). The carryover period remains 20 years [§ 172(b)(1)(G), § 172(i)].

A farming loss is the amount that would be the NOL for a tax year if only income and deductions attributable to farming businesses are taken into account. However, farming losses cannot exceed the amount of the NOL for the tax year. A farming business is a trade or business involving the cultivation of land or the raising or harvesting of any agricultural or horticultural commodity, including the operation of a nursery or sod farm and the raising or harvesting of trees bearing fruit, nuts, or other crops or ornamental trees [§ 172(i), § 263A(e)(4)].

*Losses from Casualty, Theft, and Federally Declared Disasters.* A three-year carryback period applies for (i) individuals suffering losses of property arising from fire, storm, shipwreck, or other casualty, or from theft (see VIII.H.), and (ii) small businesses (as defined in § 172(b)(1)(F)(iii)) or taxpayers engaged in the trade or business of farming suffering NOLs attributable to federally declared disasters. The carryover period remains 20 years. Farming losses that qualify for five-year carryback periods are not treated as losses eligible for the three-year carryback period [§ 172(b)(1)(F)].

### VIII.G.3.c. Amount of Carrybacks and Carryovers

[539 T.M., V.C.; TPS ¶2410.05.B.]

The amount of the carryback to the earliest tax year in the carryback period (or, if the carryback period is waived or disallowed, the amount of the carryover to the earliest tax year in the carryover period) is the entire amount of the NOL. If an NOL is not fully absorbed by the taxable income of the first tax year to which it is carried, the amount available to be carried over to the other tax years in the carryback or carryover periods is equal to the excess of the NOL over the modified taxable income of the first tax year. If the remaining loss is not fully absorbed by the taxable income of that year, the amount available to be carried over to the next tax year is equal to the excess of the NOL over the sum of the modified taxable incomes of the intervening tax years. This process is repeated until the loss is completely absorbed or the carryover period ends. If the carryover period ends and a portion of the loss remains, no deduction is allowed for that portion [§ 172(b)(2); Reg. § 1.172-4(b)].

The following modifications to taxable income apply in determining a taxpayer's modified taxable income, which may not be less than zero [§ 172(b)(2)]:

- For all taxpayers, the amount of the NOL deduction is determined without regard to the NOL for the loss year or any tax year after the loss year.
- For all taxpayers, the deduction for domestic production activities (see IV.A.9.) is disallowed.
- For noncorporate taxpayers, the amount deductible on account of capital losses cannot exceed the amount includible on account of capital gains.
- For noncorporate taxpayers, the exclusion for capital gains from small business stock under § 1202 (see III.C.5.b.) is disallowed.
- For noncorporate taxpayers, the deduction for personal exemptions, or any deduction in lieu thereof, is disallowed.
- For all taxpayers, any deduction or limitation that is calculated with reference to a percentage of taxable income or adjusted gross income must be recomputed on the basis of the modified taxable income or modified adjusted gross income, determined after applying all the other modifications. For corporate taxpayers, the only item affected is the charitable contributions deduction. For individuals, several deductions and limitations may have to be recomputed, including the medical expense deduction, the casualty and theft loss deduction, the limit on miscellaneous itemized deductions, and the charitable contributions deduction.

### VIII.G.3.d. Recomputation of Tax for Carryback Year

[539 T.M., VI.B.; TPS ¶2410.06.B.]

A taxpayer determines his or her tax liability for any year without regard to any future NOLs that may ultimately be carried back to such year. When an NOL is carried back to a tax year before the loss year, the effect of the carryback is either (i) to create an NOL deduction if no NOL deduction was previously allowable for the prior tax year, or (ii) to increase the amount of any NOL deduction that was allowed for the prior tax year. Whether an NOL deduction is created or increased, it is necessary to recompute the taxpayer's income tax liability (as well as alternative minimum tax liability, but not self-employment tax liability) for the carryback year.

The NOL deduction is taken into account in arriving at the recomputed adjusted gross income. Any deductions or other items that are based on a percentage of adjusted gross income (except charitable contributions) must also be recomputed, including deductions for medical expenses and casualty and theft losses and the limitation on miscellaneous itemized deductions. Additionally, any credits based on or limited by the amount of tax must also be recomputed with reference to the recomputed tax liability. If the applicable statute of limitations has not expired for the carryback year, the taxpayer may claim a credit or refund of the overpayment, if any, resulting from the creation or increase of the NOL deduction.

### VIII.G.3.e. Limitation on Use of Carryovers in Certain Corporate Acquisitions

[539 T.M., II.B.9.; TPS ¶2410.02.C.9.]

In connection with a tax-free reorganization in which one corporation acquires the assets of another corporation, the acquiring corporation may succeed to the tax attributes of the transferor corporation, including NOLs. However, certain rules limit the acquiring corporation's use of the transferor corporation's NOL carryovers. A transferor corporation's NOL carryovers may be carried forward by the acquiring corporation, but they may not be carried back to offset income of the acquiring corporation for tax years preceding the acquisition [§ 381(c)(1)(A)]. Use of NOL carryovers is further restricted when there is a substantial change in the ownership of a loss corporation [§ 382] (see XIII.E.5.b.).

In addition, an acquiring corporation's use of a transferor corporation's NOL carryovers may be disallowed if the principal purpose of the acquisition was the evasion or avoidance of federal income tax [§ 269(a)] (see VIII.C.).

### VIII.G.4. Special Rules Relating to Net Operating Losses

### VIII.G.4.a. Carrybacks and Carryovers Used by Married Taxpayers

[539 T.M., VII.A.; TPS ¶2410.07.A.]

***All Joint Returns or All Separate Returns.*** If a married couple files a joint return for each of the tax years involved in the computation of an NOL carryback or carryover and for the year to which the loss is carried, the joint NOL carryover or carryback is computed in the same manner as the NOL carryover or carryback of an individual, using the joint NOLs and combined taxable income of both spouses. If a married couple files separate returns in each tax year involved in the computation of an NOL carryback or carryover and in the year to which the loss is carried, each spouse computes his or her individual NOL without regard to the income and deductions of the other spouse [Reg. § 1.172-7(c), § 1.172-7(f)].

***Change from Separate Returns to Joint Returns.*** If a married couple files a joint return in a tax year to which an NOL is carried forward or carried back, but they file separate returns for all the tax years involved in the computation of the carryover or carryback, the separate NOL carryover or carryback is a joint NOL carryover or carryback to the tax year in which the joint return is filed [Reg. § 1.172-7(b)].

***Change from Joint Returns to Separate Returns.*** If a married couple files separate returns in a tax year to which an NOL is carried over or carried back, but they file a joint return for one or more of the tax years involved in the computation of the carryover or carryback, the separate NOL carryover or carryback of each spouse must be computed under the general rules for determining the amount of carryovers or carrybacks, subject to the following two modifications [Reg. § 1.172-7(d)]:

- The NOL of any spouse for a year in which a joint return was filed is deemed to be the portion of the joint NOL attributable to the gross income and deductions of that spouse.

- If an NOL is carried forward or carried back to a tax year other than the first carryback or carryover year and taxable income for the intervening year was reported on a joint return, the taxable income of a particular spouse for the intervening year (which is subtracted from the NOL for the loss year to determine the amount of the loss that may be carried to the tax year in question) is deemed to be the sum of the following:

    — the portion of the combined taxable income of both spouses for the intervening year that is attributable to the gross income and deductions of the particular spouse; and

    — the portion of the combined taxable income of both spouses for the intervening year that is attributable to the other spouse, provided, however, that if the other spouse sustained an NOL in a tax year beginning on the same date as the loss year, then the portion must first be reduced by that NOL of the other spouse.

*Recurrent Use of Joint Returns.* If a married couple files a joint return in a tax year to which an NOL is carried forward or carried back, but they file separate returns for at least one (but not all) of the tax years involved in the computation of the carryover or carryback, the amount of the carryover or carryback is determined in accordance with the rules for changes from joint returns to separate returns, described immediately above. Because a joint return is filed for the tax year to which the loss is carried, the carryover or carryback is considered a joint NOL carryover or carryback [Reg. § 1.172-7(e)].

### VIII.G.4.b. Consolidated Returns

[539 T.M., VII.B.; TPS ¶¶2410.07.B., 5310.07.A.2.a.]

The consolidated NOL deduction for a tax year is the aggregate of the consolidated NOL carryovers and carrybacks to that year. The NOL carryovers and carrybacks to a tax year are comprised of the group's consolidated NOLs and any NOLs sustained by members of the group in separate return years that may be carried over or carried back to the year under consideration [Reg. § 1.1502-21(a), § 1.1502-21(b)]. The consolidated NOL is determined taking into account the following [Reg. § 1.1502-11(a), § 1.1502-21(e)]:

- the separate taxable income of each member of the group;
- any consolidated capital gain net income;
- any consolidated § 1231 net loss;
- any consolidated charitable contributions deductions;
- any consolidated dividends received deduction; and
- any dividends paid deduction on certain preferred stock of public utilities.

If a consolidated NOL can be carried forward or carried back to a separate return year (as defined in Reg. § 1.1502-1(e)) of a member of the group, the portion of the carryover or carryback that is attributable to that member must be apportioned to that corporation and carried forward or carried back to the separate return year, rather than to the group's corresponding consolidated return year [Reg. § 1.1502-21(b)(2)]. In addition, if losses are incurred by a group member in a tax year in which it did not join in the filing of a consolidated return (or joined the filing of a consolidated return with another group) and those losses are carried over or carried back to consolidated return years, the separate return limitation year (SRLY) rules limit the group's use of those losses [Reg. § 1.1502-21(c)].

Consolidated returns are discussed in XIII.C.8.c.

### VIII.G.4.c. Discharges of Indebtedness in Bankruptcy or While Insolvent

[539 T.M., VII.C.; TPS ¶2410.07.C.]

Discharges of indebtedness are generally included in a taxpayer's gross income (see I.L.). However, a taxpayer may exclude discharged debt from gross income in certain situations (see II.A.). If a taxpayer excludes discharge of indebtedness income under the insolvency exclusion or the bankruptcy exclusion, the taxpayer must reduce his or her tax attributes by the amount excluded. The first tax attribute that must be reduced is NOLs for the tax year of the discharge and NOL carryovers to that year [§ 108(b)(2)(A); Reg. § 1.108-7(a)(1)(i)] (see II.A.8.a.).

### VIII.G.5. Reporting Net Operating Loss Carryovers and Carrybacks

[539 T.M., VIII.A.; TPS ¶2410.09.A.]

*Reporting Carryovers.* If an individual's NOLs are carried over to a tax year after the loss year, the NOL deduction is reported as a negative "other income" amount on Form 1040. A corporation's NOLs carried over to a tax year after the loss year is reported as a deduction on Form 1120.

*Reporting Carrybacks and Requesting Refunds.* When an NOL is carried back to a tax year before the loss year, the taxpayer's return will have already been filed for the carryback year, and the taxpayer's income will have been computed without regard to the NOL deduction. The carried back NOL may reduce or eliminate the tax liability for the carryback year.

There are two methods to claim a refund or credit for the overpayment within the applicable limitations period: (i) the taxpayer may file an amended return for the carryback year, or (ii) the taxpayer may file an application for a tentative carryback adjustment. The deadline for filing an amended return is three years from the due date (including extensions) for filing the return for the loss year. A tentative carryback adjustment is requested on Form 1045, *Application for Tentative Refund*, or Form 1139, *Corporation Application for Tentative Refund*. The application must be filed on or after the due date for filing the return for the loss year and within 12 months after the loss year [§ 6411, § 6511(a), Reg. § 1.172-1(d)].

A corporation that expects to incur an NOL in its current tax year may extend the time to pay the tax for the immediately preceding tax year by filing Form 1138, *Extension of Time for Payment of Taxes by a Corporation Expecting a Net Operating Loss Carryback* [§ 6164(a)].

*Required Statement.* For NOL deductions attributable to both carrybacks and carryovers, a taxpayer must file with his or her return a statement setting forth the amount of the deduction and all material facts relating to the deduction. The statement must cover each carryback or carryover that forms part of the deduction and include a detailed schedule showing the computation of the deduction [Reg. § 1.172-1(c)].

### VIII.G.6. Alternative Minimum Tax Treatment

[539 T.M., IX.; TPS ¶2410.08.]

One of the adjustments to taxable income required of all taxpayers in computing alternative minimum taxable income (AMTI) is the substitution of the alternative tax net operating loss (ATNOL) deduction for the regular tax NOL deduction. Thus, a taxpayer must make two parallel NOL computations: the regular tax NOL deduction, which is used to offset the taxpayer's regular tax liability, and the ATNOL deduction, which applies in determining the taxpayer's minimum tax liability [§ 56(a)(4)].

The ATNOL deduction is equal to the regular tax NOL deduction modified in the following three ways [§ 56(d)(1)]:

1. The amount of the ATNOL deduction is limited to the sum of the following:
   — the lesser of:
      - the amount of the deduction attributable to NOLs (other than a deduction attributable to an applicable NOL for which an election is made under § 172(b)(1)(H)); or
      - 90% of the AMTI determined without regard to the NOL deduction and the deduction for domestic production activities (see IV.A.9.); plus
   — the lesser of:
      - the amount of the deduction attributable to an applicable NOL for which an election is made under § 172(b)(1)(H); or
      - AMTI determined without regard to the NOL deduction and the § 199 deduction, reduced by the first of these two numbers that are added to

calculate the ATNOL deduction limit (as determined under the first set of bullets).

2. In computing the NOL for purposes of the alternative minimum tax, all adjustments required in the computation of AMTI must be applied, and the NOL must be reduced by the items of tax preference (provided, however, that an item of tax preference is taken into account only to the extent that such item increased the amount of the NOL as determined for purposes of the regular tax).

3. In determining the ATNOL deduction, the amount of a carryback or carryover (see VIII.G.3.c.) must be calculated taking into account the limitation on the amount of ATNOL deduction, discussed in 1, above.

*Carrybacks and Carryovers.* The carryback and carryover periods for ATNOLs are the same as for regular tax NOLs (see VIII.G.3.). Additionally, an election to waive carryback of an NOL for regular tax purposes also applies for alternative minimum tax purposes. If a taxpayer does not elect to waive a carryback period for regular tax purposes, it may not waive it for AMT purposes [§ 172(b)(3)].

## VIII.H. Section 165 Losses

[527 T.M.; TPS ¶2350.]

Losses typically arise when there is either a total loss of value or a diminution in the value of an asset resulting from some transaction, event, or occurrence. Taxpayers generally may deduct any loss sustained during a tax year that is not compensated for by insurance or otherwise [§ 165(a)]. A transaction coming within the literal language of both the loss and bad debt provisions (see VIII.I.) must be treated as a bad debt [*Spring City Foundry Co. v. Commissioner*, 292 U.S. 182 (1934)].

*Elements of a Loss.* A loss may be deducted if the taxpayer establishes the following:

1. the loss is actually sustained and is evidenced by a closed and completed transaction (i.e., fixed by an identifiable event);

2. the loss is not compensated for by insurance or some other means;

3. the taxpayer is the person or entity who sustained the loss; and

4. if the taxpayer is an individual, the loss must have arisen from one of the following:

   — a trade or business;

   — a transaction entered into for profit; or

   — a casualty or theft.

A loss is sustained during a tax year in which the loss occurred, as evidenced by closed and completed transactions and as fixed by identifiable events that happened during the year. The loss may be sustained in a sale or exchange, or when property is abandoned, becomes worthless or obsolete, is taken by theft, or is damaged in a casualty [Reg. § 1.165-1(b), § 1.165-1(d)(1)]. The mere diminution in value of property, absent an event such as a sale or abandonment, is insufficient to support a loss deduction. Additionally, a loss is not evidenced by a closed and completed transaction if the taxpayer has a claim for reimbursement that provides a reasonable prospect of recovery, as determined by the facts and circumstances [Reg. § 1.165-1(d)(2)(i)].

No deduction is allowed where a loss is compensated for by insurance or otherwise. Thus, in calculating losses actually sustained, adjustments must be made for any insurance or other compensation received, as well as for any salvage value [§ 165(a);

Reg. § 1.165-1(a), § 1.165-1(c)(4)]. If a taxpayer suffers a casualty or theft loss that is covered by insurance but fails to file a claim, no deduction is permitted [§ 165(h)(5)(E)].

***Personal Losses Generally Not Deductible.*** Generally, an individual's nonbusiness losses are not deductible. Thus, a taxpayer may not claim a loss on the sale at a loss of a personal asset not used in a trade or business and not held in a transaction engaged in for profit [Reg. § 1.165-9]. However, personal casualty and theft losses (see VII.H.) are an exception to the general disallowance rule [§ 165(c)].

---

**EXAMPLE:** Daniel and Jane buy a house for $300,000 and exclusively use it as their personal residence. They make improvements of $40,000 and five years later sell it for $280,000. Their $60,000 loss ($280,000 – ($300,000 + $40,000)) is nondeductible.

---

***Unregistered Securities Generally Not Deductible.*** Subject to certain exceptions (as described in Reg. § 1.165-12(c)), a taxpayer may not deduct a loss on a bond or other obligation that is required to be in registered form, but which is not [§ 165(j)(1); Reg. § 1.165-12].

***Losses Deducted for Estate Tax Purposes Generally Not Deductible.*** If an estate sustains a loss and the loss is deducted for estate tax purposes, the estate cannot deduct the same loss for income tax purposes unless it elects to waive the estate tax deduction in favor of the income tax deduction [§ 2054, Reg. § 1.165-7(c), § 1.165-8(b), § 1.642(g)-1].

***Demolition Losses Generally Not Deductible.*** If a taxpayer demolishes a structure, generally no deduction is allowed for any amount expended for the demolition or any loss sustained on account of the demolition. Instead, the disallowed amounts are added to the basis of the land on which the demolished structure was located [§ 280B].

### VIII.H.1. Casualty and Theft Losses

### VIII.H.1.a. Casualty Losses

[527 T.M., V; TPS ¶2350.03.C.]

Taxpayers generally may deduct losses on business and nonbusiness property arising from a disaster such as a storm, fire, shipwreck, or other casualty. A casualty is the damage, destruction, or loss of property that results from an identifiable event that is sudden (i.e., swift, not gradual or progressive), unexpected (i.e., ordinarily unanticipated and unintended), or unusual (i.e., not a day-to-day occurrence and not typical of the activity engaged in). Deductible casualty losses can result from many different causes including [§ 165(c)(3); Reg. § 1.165-7]:

- car accidents;
- earthquakes;
- fires;
- floods;
- mine cave-ins;
- shipwrecks;
- sonic booms;
- storms (including hurricanes and tornadoes);
- terrorist attacks;
- vandalism; and

● volcanic eruptions.

The amount of the casualty loss is equal to the lesser of either (i) the adjusted basis of the property, or (ii) the loss of value by reason of the casualty (i.e., the fair market value of the property immediately before the casualty, less the fair market value immediately after the casualty), reduced by any compensation received from insurance or otherwise [§ 165(a); Reg. § 1.165-7(b)(1)].

### VIII.H.1.b. Theft Losses

[527 T.M., V.; TPS ¶2350.03.D.]

Subject to certain limitations, taxpayers generally may deduct losses attributable to the theft of his or her property, even if the property is not used in a trade or business or held in a transaction entered into for profit. A theft is the illegal taking and removing of money or other property with the intent to deprive the owner of it. Theft includes the taking of money or property by blackmail, burglary, embezzlement, extortion, kidnapping for ransom, larceny, and robbery [§ 165(c)(3); Reg. § 1.165-8].

The value of property lost by theft is treated as zero. Thus, the amount of the theft loss generally is the lesser of either (i) the adjusted basis of the property, or (ii) the fair market value of the property immediately before the theft, reduced by any compensation received from insurance or otherwise [§ 165(a); Reg. § 1.165-7(b)(1), § 1.165-8(c)].

### VIII.H.1.c. Limitations on Casualty and Theft Loss Deductions

[527 T.M., V.D.3.; TPS ¶2350.02.C.3.d.]

*De Minimis Limitation.* An individual taxpayer may not deduct the first $100 of each loss from casualty or theft. This limitation applies on a per casualty basis, rather than a per item of property or per year basis. Thus, if one casualty results in a loss sustained to more than one item of property, the $100 reduction is applied only once to the entire loss. Similarly, if a casualty results in a loss sustained in more than one year, the $100 reduction is applied only once, and if two separate casualties or thefts occur and result in losses within one year, the $100 reduction is applied twice – once to each casualty or theft loss. A casualty or theft that results in a loss of $100 or less will effectively be nondeductible [§ 165(h)(1); Reg. § 1.165-7(b)(4)(ii)].

If multiple taxpayers jointly own the property that sustains the loss, the $100 reduction applies to each taxpayer's loss. Married taxpayers filing a joint return for the first tax year in which the loss is allowable as a deduction are treated as a single taxpayer for this purpose. However, if married taxpayers file separately, each is subject to the $100 reduction [§ 165(h)(1), § 165(h)(5)(B); Reg. § 1.165-7(b)(4)(iii)].

If the loss is sustained on property used for both business and nonbusiness purposes, the $100 limitation applies only to that portion of the loss properly attributable to the nonbusiness use. Thus, if a car used 60% for business use and 40% for nonbusiness use sustains a $1,000 loss, the $100 limitation applies to the $400 nonbusiness portion of the loss [Reg. § 1.165-7(b)(4)(iv)].

*10% of Adjusted Gross Income Limitation.* After the application of the de minimis limitation, a further limitation applies to the amount an individual taxpayer may deduct as a result of a casualty or theft loss. The taxpayer may only deduct a net casualty loss to the extent it exceeds 10% of the individual's adjusted gross income for the tax year. A net casualty loss is the excess of personal casualty losses for the tax year over the personal casualty gains for that year. Adjusted gross income for this purpose is computed with a deduction for personal casualty losses to the extent of personal casualty gains. A personal casualty gain is the recognized gain from any involuntary conversion (see III.E.2.) of property not used in a trade or business or in a transaction entered into for profit that arises from fire, storm, shipwreck, or other casualty, or from theft (e.g., an insurance reimbursement that exceeds the adjusted basis of depreciated property subject to a casualty or theft) [§ 165(h)(2), § 165(h)(4), § 165(h)(5)].

---

**EXAMPLE:** Tommy's house is burglarized. After reimbursement by insurance, Tommy still has a $2,000 loss. His adjusted gross income in the tax year of the burglary is $29,500. Tommy first must apply the $100 reduction to reduce his loss to $1,900. He then applies the 10% of adjusted gross income limitation. Because $2,950 (10% × $29,500) exceeds $1,900, Tommy may not deduct the loss. Had Tommy's unreimbursed loss been $4,000, he would have been able to deduct $950 ($3,900 loss after $100 reduction − $2,950) of the loss.

---

The 10% of adjusted gross income limitation applies once to all losses in a tax year (after reducing each loss by $100). If multiple taxpayers jointly own the property that sustains the loss, the 10% rule applies separately to each taxpayer. Married taxpayers filing a joint return for the first tax year in which the loss is allowable as a deduction are treated as a single taxpayer for this purpose. However, if married taxpayers file separately, each is subject to 10% rule [§ 165(h)(2)(A), § 165(h)(5)(B)].

If the loss is sustained on property used for both business and nonbusiness purposes, the 10% limitation applies only to that portion of the loss properly attributable to the nonbusiness use [§ 165(h)(4)(B)].

If personal casualty gains exceed personal casualty losses in a tax year, the gains are treated as capital gains and the losses are treated as capital losses [§ 165(h)(2)(B)].

### VIII.H.1.d. Miscellaneous Casualty and Theft Loss Issues

[527 T.M., V.E.1.b., V.H.5., VI.; TPS ¶2350.03.C.3., .03.D.5., .05.C.]

*Loss of Bank Deposits.* Certain individuals who can estimate that there is a loss on his or her deposit (or part of it) in a bank or credit union because of the bankruptcy or insolvency of the institution, under certain circumstances, can elect to treat the estimated loss as a casualty loss. A taxpayer who does not exercise the election would still be entitled to a bad debt loss (see VIII.I.). The benefit of electing to treat the loss as a casualty or theft loss is that the loss may be claimed sooner and as an ordinary, rather than capital, loss. However, the 10% of adjusted gross income limitation, discussed above, may offset those advantages [§ 165(l)(1)].

To qualify, the taxpayer's deposit must be with a bank, a savings institution, a credit union in which the deposits are insured under federal law (or are insured, protected, or guaranteed under state law), or with a similar institution chartered and supervised under federal or state law. The taxpayer must be an individual who is none of the following [§ 165(l)(2)]:

1. an owner of at least 1% in value of the outstanding stock of the financial institution;

2. an officer of the financial institution;

3. a sibling, spouse, aunt, uncle, nephew, niece, ancestor (parent or grandparent), or lineal descendant (child or grandchild) of a person described in 1. or 2.; or

4. an otherwise related person (as defined in § 267(b)) for a person described in 1. or 2.

The election may be made if the loss can reasonably be estimated as of the close of the tax year. If the election is made, it will apply to all of the taxpayer's losses on deposits with that financial institution, and it may not be revoked without IRS consent. A taxpayer that elects treatment as a casualty or theft loss must forego any right to claim that loss as a deductible worthless debt under § 166, § 165(l)(1)(A), § 165(l)(6), or § 165(l)(7).

***Natural Disaster Losses.*** If a taxpayer suffers a loss as a result of a natural disaster, the taxpayer may elect to deduct the loss either in the tax year the loss occurred, or in the immediately preceding tax year. The loss must occur in the disaster area (as defined in § 165(h)(3)(C)(ii)) of a federally declared disaster (as defined in § 165(h)(3)(C)(i)). The election is also available if a taxpayer's home is located in a federally declared disaster area and the state or local government has ordered (within 120 days after the area is declared a disaster) the taxpayer to demolish or relocate the home because it has been rendered unsafe as a result of the disaster. If a taxpayer receives cash or property from an employer or an agency that dispenses disaster relief specifically for the purpose of restoring or rehabilitating property lost or damaged in the disaster, the amount received is considered compensation for property and reduces the amount of the deductible casualty loss. If the amount of the reimbursement exceeds the taxpayer's basis in the property before the casualty, the excess is treated as gain from an involuntary conversion [§ 165(i), § 165(k)] (see III.E.2.).

The election to treat the loss as occurring in the immediately preceding year is made on a return, amended return, or claim for refund clearly showing the election is being made. The election must be made by the later of (i) the unextended due date of the income tax return for the year of the disaster, or (ii) the date that any extension for filing the income tax return for the year immediately preceding the disaster expires. The election should note the city, town, county, and state in which the damaged or destroyed property was located [Reg. § 1.165-11(e)].

***Ponzi Scheme Losses.*** Losses from Ponzi schemes are theft losses and are not subject to the $100 and 10% of adjusted gross income limitations. Additionally, Ponzi scheme losses are not subject to the limitations on miscellaneous itemized deductions or the phaseout applicable to itemized deductions (see VII.C.) [Rev. Rul. 2009-9, 2009-14 I.R.B. 735].

### VIII.H.1.e. Casualty and Theft Loss Property Basis and Reporting Requirements

[527 T.M., V.F., V.G.; TPS ¶2350.05.]

***Basis.*** The basis of property damaged or destroyed by a casualty or theft must be reduced by the allowable loss deduction and any insurance or other reimbursement [Rev. Rul. 71-161, 1971-1 C.B. 76]. Amounts paid or incurred to replace or restore damaged or destroyed property that are not business expenses are capital expenditures and should be added to the remaining basis of the property [Reg. § 1.263(a)-3(k)(1)(iii)].

***Reporting.*** Gains or losses from a casualty or theft of business or nonbusiness property are reported on Form 4684, *Casualties and Thefts*. If a casualty or theft loss deduction is claimed for business or income-producing property, Form 4797, *Sales of Business Property*, may also be required.

### VIII.H.2. Abandonment and Obsolescence Losses

[527 T.M., III.B., III.C.; TPS ¶2350.03.A.]

*Abandonment.* Taxpayers may deduct losses by reason of abandonment, obsolescence, or worthlessness of business or investment property equal to the adjusted basis of the property immediately before the loss, reduced by any compensation for the loss [§ 165(b); Reg. § 1.165-2(a), § 1.168(i)-8(e)(2)].

Abandonment is a voluntary and permanent surrender of possession and use of property with the intention of immediately and permanently ending ownership, but without passing it on to anyone else. Generally, an abandonment is not treated as a sale or exchange of the property (see III.B.2.c.), and therefore gain or loss is typically ordinary gain or loss.

*Obsolescence.* If nondepreciable property that a taxpayer uses in a trade or business or in a transaction entered into for profit becomes obsolete and is permanently discarded from use, the obsolescence qualifies for the loss deduction. If cost recovery property is removed from service in a manner that does not constitute a sale, exchange, or abandonment, a deduction is allowed equal to the excess of the property's unrecovered tax basis over its scrap or salvage value. An obsolescence loss is allowed in the year it is sustained, though the tax year of the loss may not be the year the taxpayer actually abandons the use of the property [Reg. § 1.165-2(a); Prop. Reg. § 1.168-6(a)(3)]. If the property is depreciable property, the obsolescence should be reflected by a change in depreciation method, rather than by a loss deduction [Reg. § 1.165-2(b), § 1.167(a)-9].

Obsolescence is an event or cause that shortens the estimated useful life of an asset from what it was originally expected to be (e.g., a technological advance or a reasonably foreseeable economic change like developments in industry products, methods, markets, sources of supply, or legislative or regulatory changes). Obsolescence may also occur when property suddenly becomes useless in a business or profit transaction, or when the business or profit transaction itself is discontinued [Reg. § 1.167(a)-9, § 1.165-2(a)].

### VIII.H.3. Worthless Securities

[527 T.M., III.E.; TPS ¶2350.03.B.]

Securities that are capital assets (i.e., securities other than those held for sale by a securities dealer) that become completely worthless during the tax year are treated as having been sold on the last day of the tax year [§ 165(g)]. Thus, the worthlessness of the security satisfies the requirement that a loss be evidenced by a closed and completed transaction (see VIII.H.).

The rule applies to shares of stock in a corporation, the right to subscribe for or receive shares of stock in a corporation, as well as bonds, debentures, notes, and other evidences of indebtedness issued by a corporation or a government or political subdivision thereof, with interest coupons or in registered form [§ 165(g)(2)].

In order to take the loss deduction, a taxpayer must show the following [§ 165(g)]:

• the security had a basis;
• the security was not worthless in a prior year; and
• the security is worthless in the year claimed.

If a domestic corporation owns a security in an affiliated corporation (as defined in § 165(g)(3)), the domestic corporate owner is entitled to an ordinary loss (rather than capital loss) when the security becomes worthless [§ 165(g)(3)].

Worthless securities are reported on Form 8949, *Sales and Other Dispositions of Capital Assets.*

### VIII.H.4. Gambling or Wagering Losses

[527 T.M., VII.; TPS ¶2350.03.E.]

A taxpayer's gambling or wagering losses for a tax year are deductible only to the extent the taxpayer has gambling or wagering gains for that year. This limitation applies whether the taxpayer is a casual gambler or a professional gambler who pursues gambling as a trade or business [§ 165(d)].

### VIII.H.5. Farming Losses

[607 T.M., III.C.3., 608 T.M., XVII.; TPS ¶2350.03.H.]

Losses incurred from the operation of a farm as a trade or business are deductible. Such losses may result in a net operating loss (see VIII.G.), which may be used to offset other income for that tax year or may be carried back or forward to offset income in other tax years. However, farming losses arising from the operation of a farm for pleasure or recreation are not deductible [Reg. § 1.165-6(a)(1), § 1.165-6(a)(3)].

*Loss of Livestock or Crops.* If livestock used in the trade or business of farming die as a result of disease, exposure, or injury, the loss is deductible. Additionally, the loss is deductible if livestock purchased and used in a farming trade or business are destroyed by federal, state, or other governmental order. However, the death of livestock raised for sale does not qualify for the loss deduction [Reg. § 1.165-6(d), § 1.165-6(e)]. The cost of feed, pasture, and care of livestock is not considered part of the cost of the livestock in determining the amount of a loss; however these expenses may qualify for deduction as a trade or business expense [Reg. § 1.165-6(f)(1), § 1.162-12].

Generally, if a prospective crop being grown in a farming business is totally destroyed by frost, storm, flood, or fire, no loss deduction is allowed [Reg. § 1.165-6(c)].

*Limitation on Excess Farm Losses.* Taxpayers (other than C corporations) receiving an applicable subsidy (as defined in § 461(j)(3)) for any tax year may not deduct excess farm losses for that year. An excess farm loss generally is the excess of the taxpayer's aggregate deductions for the tax year that are attributable to the taxpayer's farming businesses (as defined in § 461(j)(4)(C)) over the sum of (i) the taxpayer's aggregate gross income or gain for that year attributable to the farming businesses, and (ii) the threshold amount for that year. The threshold amount is the greater of either (i) $300,000 ($150,000 for married taxpayers filing separately), or (ii) the net farm income the taxpayer has received over the previous five years [§ 461(j)(4)].

Losses due to fire, storm, or other casualty, disease, or drought are disregarded in the calculation of the excess farm limitation. Amounts disallowed by the limitation are treated as a deduction attributable to the farming business in the next tax year [§ 461(j)(4)(D), § 461(j)(2)].

For a partnership or S corporation, the excess farm losses limitation is applied at the partner or shareholder level. The excess farm loss limitation is applied before the passive loss rules [§ 461(j)(5), § 461(j)(7)].

Farming expenses are discussed in IV.F.3.

## VIII.I. Bad Debt Deductions

[538 T.M.; TPS ¶2360.]

Accounts receivable that will likely remain unpaid, uncollectible, and written off at tax time are considered bad debts. If the debt arises from a debtor-creditor relationship based on a valid and enforceable obligation to pay a determinable sum of money, and if the debt becomes worthless during the tax year, the taxpayer may deduct all or a part of the uncollectible amount.

A distinction is made between business bad debts and nonbusiness bad debts. Business bad debts arise in connection with a taxpayer's trade or business and are fully deductible. Further, partially-worthless business bad debts may be deductible. Nonbusiness bad debts are subject to the restrictions imposed on short-term capital losses and are deductible only when they become completely worthless [§ 166].

### VIII.I.1. Business Bad Debts

[538 T.M.; TPS ¶2630.]

Bona fide business bad debts are deductible as ordinary losses in the tax year the debt became partly or totally worthless. A business bad debt is a loss from the worthlessness of a debt that was either (i) created or acquired in the taxpayer's trade or business, or (ii) closely related to the taxpayer's trade or business when it became partly or totally worthless. Debts are closely related to a trade or business if the taxpayer's primary motive for incurring the debt is business related. All corporate loans are treated as business debts, regardless of the context [§ 166].

A taxpayer may claim a business bad debt only if he or she previously included the amount owed in gross income. Thus, a taxpayer using the accrual method of accounting (see XI.B.1.d.) can only claim a bad debt deduction for an uncollectible receivable if the taxpayer previously included the uncollectible amount in income. Cash method taxpayers, on the other hand, cannot claim a bad debt deduction for amounts owed because the taxpayer never included those amounts in income [Reg. § 1.166-1(c), § 1.166-1(e)].

Common types of business bad debts include loans to clients and suppliers, debts of an insolvent partner paid by the taxpayer, and certain business loans that the taxpayer guarantees. However, no deduction is allowed for the bad debts of political organizations, except by banks and certain suppliers of goods and services [§ 271(a), § 271(c)].

---

**EXAMPLE:** Tiffany owns a dress company. Motivated by the desire to retain one of her largest clients and keep a sales outlet, Tiffany guarantees the payment of a $20,000 note for her client, Dress Outlet. Dress Outlet later defaults on the loan and Tiffany pays the remaining $10,000 balance of the loan in full to the bank. Tiffany can claim a $10,000 business bad debt deduction because her guarantee was made in the course of her trade or business and for a good faith purpose.

---

Individuals claim the business bad debt deduction on Schedule C of Form 1040. Farmers claim the deduction on Schedule F of Form 1040. Corporations, S corporations, and partnerships report the deduction on their respective income tax return forms.

*Bona Fide Debt.* A debt is bona fide if all of the following conditions are satisfied [Reg. § 1.166-1(c)]:

1. the obligation arose from a true debtor-creditor relationship;

2. the debtor-creditor relationship is based on a valid and enforceable obligation to pay a fixed or determinable amount of money;

3. the lender has an intention to seek repayment; and

4. repayment is not contingent on an event that has not occurred.

Loans to family members and loans by shareholders to corporations are likely to receive extra scrutiny and may be considered gifts and capital contributions, respectively.

***Worthlessness.*** Whether a debt is worthless is determined based on the facts and circumstances. Generally, a debt becomes worthless when there is no longer any chance the amount owed will be paid. The taxpayer must show that he or she has taken reasonable steps to collect the debt, but was unable to do so. A judgment from a court is not necessary if the taxpayer can show a judgment would be uncollectible [Reg. § 1.166-2]. The following factors may be indicative of worthlessness:

- the insolvency or bankruptcy of the debtor;
- the debtor's lack of assets;
- the termination of the debtor's business;
- the death of a key employee of the debtor if no one else is capable of sustaining the business;
- the disappearance or incarceration of the debtor; and
- certain international political crises (e.g., where a debtor's assets are frozen by the U.S. government).

The expiration of the statute of limitations on enforcing payment on a debt does not establish that the debt is worthless. The debtor may waive or fail to assert the protection of the statute of limitations, in which case the debt remains enforceable. Additionally, voluntary cancellation of a debt does not establish worthlessness, and the cancellation of a debt established to be worthless does not preclude a deduction. A taxpayer who compromises a debt by accepting less than the full about because the debtor is unable to pay more is entitled to a worthless debt deduction for the unrecovered balance.

Securities that become worthless during a tax year are treated as having been sold on the last day of that tax year, resulting in a loss, rather than being treated as a bad debt. Worthless securities are discussed in VIII.H.3.

***Partial Worthlessness.*** Business debts may be deducted when partially worthless. If the taxpayer demonstrates that it can recover only part of a business debt, the taxpayer may deduct the worthless portion, provided that it is "charged off" [§ 166(a)(2); Reg. § 1.166-3(a)(2)]. A deduction for a partially worthless debt may be claimed either in the year that part of the debt becomes worthless, or in any subsequent year before the time the debt becomes wholly worthless. Thus, the taxpayer has the following options when a business debt becomes partially worthless:

- charge off and deduct the worthless portion in the current year;
- charge off and deduct the worthless portion in a subsequent year (but not later than the year the debt becomes wholly worthless);
- spread the charge-off and deduction of the worthless portion over more than one year; or
- deduct the entire amount in the year the debt becomes wholly worthless.

***Charge-Off Requirement.*** Most taxpayers are required to use the specific charge-off method. To satisfy the charge-off requirement, the taxpayer must take some action (normally a bookkeeping entry) that clearly establishes that a specific portion of the debt has become worthless and will no longer be treated as an asset [Reg. § 1.166-3(a)(2)]. When there has been a significant modification (within the meaning of Reg. § 1.1001-3) of a partially worthless debt instrument (see III.B.2.a.), the taxpayer may deduct an amount on account of the partially worthless debt even though no amount has been charged off within the tax year. This rule only applies if the modification would result in recognition of gain and if the debt was charged off and deducted in a previous tax year in accordance with the charge-off rules. If these conditions are satisfied, a modified debt is deemed charged off (in an amount limited to the difference between the tax basis of the debt and the greater of either the book basis or the fair market value of the debt) in the year in which gain is recognized [Reg. § 1.166-3(a)(3)].

*Nonaccrual Experience Method.* Certain accrual method taxpayers may use the nonaccrual experience method for bad debts instead of the specific charge-off method. To be eligible to use the nonaccrual experience method for accounts receivable for services performed, either (i) the services the taxpayer provides must be in the fields of accounting, actuarial science, architecture, consulting, engineering, health, law, or the performing arts, or (ii) the taxpayer's average annual gross receipts for any consecutive three-year period cannot exceed $5 million.

Under the nonaccrual experience method, a taxpayer does not accrue services-related income he or she expects to be uncollectible. Because the expected uncollectible amounts are not included in income, these amounts are not later deducted from income [§ 448(d)(5)].

*Recovery of a Bad Debt.* A taxpayer that claims a deduction for a bad debt on its tax return and later recovers all or a part of it must include the recovery in income. The amount included is limited to the amount that the deduction in the prior year reduced the amount of tax [§ 111(a); Reg. § 1.111-1]. The tax benefit rule and the recovery of amounts previously deducted are discussed in I.B.6.

*Coordination with Loss Rules.* A transaction coming within the literal language of both the loss provisions (see VIII.H.) and the bad debt provisions must be treated as a bad debt [*Spring City Foundry Co. v. Commissioner*, 292 U.S. 182 (1934)].

If mortgaged or pledged property is lawfully sold (whether to the creditor or another purchaser) for less than the amount of the debt, and the portion of the indebtedness remaining unsatisfied after the sale is wholly or partially uncollectible, the mortgagee or pledgee may claim a bad debt deduction for the tax year in which it becomes wholly worthless or is charged off as partially worthless [Reg. § 1.166-6].

### VIII.I.2. Nonbusiness Bad Debts

[538 T.M., IV.; TPS ¶2360.02.]

While related, there are several important differences in the treatment of business bad debts and nonbusiness bad debts. Business bad debts generally arise from the operation of a trade or business and are deductible as a business loss (see VIII.I.1.). Nonbusiness bad debts, on the other hand, are bad debts that are not business bad debts, and they are deductible as short-term capital losses (see III.B.3., III.B.4., and VII.B.16.). Further, nonbusiness bad debts must be completely worthless before they are deductible. Only noncorporate taxpayers and S corporations may claim nonbusiness bad debt deductions [§ 166(d); Reg. § 1.166-5].

## VIII.J. Hobby Losses

[548 T.M.; TPS ¶2450.]

Activities a taxpayer engages in as a hobby or for sport or recreation often are not entered into for profit. An individual, S corporation, partnership, trust, or estate that does not carry on a business or investment activity to make a profit cannot deduct expenses from the activity against other income. However, the expenses may offset gross income from the activity during the tax year [§ 183(a), § 183(b); Reg. § 1.183-1(a); Rev. Rul. 77-320, 1977-2 C.B. 78]. Allowable deductible expenses of an activity not engaged in for profit fall into the following categories, in the following order [§ 183(b); Reg. § 1.183-1(b)(1)]:

1. amounts that would be allowable as deductions without regard to whether the activity was engaged in for profit (e.g., certain taxes, casualty losses, etc.);

2. amounts that would be allowable as deductions if the activity was engaged in for profit, but only to the extent that the gross income exceeds the deductions described in 1.; and

3. amounts that would be allowable as deductions if the activity was engaged in for profit and would result in an adjustment to the basis of property, but only to the extent that the gross income exceeds the deductions described in 1. and 2.

---

**EXAMPLE:** Amber owns several horses as a hobby. Over the course of the year, she earns $1,000 offering horse rides at children's parties. She also incurs the following expenses and losses: $300 state and local real property taxes on a stable used to house the horses, $1,200 for feed, and $500 for a casualty loss attributable to one of the horses. First, the $300 state and local real property taxes and $400 of the casualty loss ($500, less the $100 casualty loss limitation under § 165(h)(1)) are deductible without regard to profit motive, and they are deducted from the $1,000 gain in full. Next, to the extent of the $300 of gross income remaining ($1,000 gross income − $300 real property taxes − $400 casualty loss), Amber may deduct those items that would be allowable as a deduction if the activity was engaged in for profit and that do not require basis adjustments. The $1,200 for feed falls into this category. However, only $300 is allowed as a deduction due to the gross income from the activity limitation. The remaining $900 may not be deducted.

---

The determination of whether a taxpayer is carrying on an activity for profit is a facts and circumstances analysis. Factors considered include the following [Reg. § 1.183-2(b)]:

- the manner in which the taxpayer conducts the activity;
- the expertise of the taxpayer or his or her advisors;
- the time and effort the taxpayer expends in conducting the activity;
- the expectation that assets used in the activity may appreciate in value;
- the success the taxpayer has had in conducting other similar or dissimilar activities;
- the taxpayer's history of income or losses with respect to the activity;
- the amount of occasional profits from the activity;
- the financial status of the taxpayer; and
- the taxpayer's personal pleasure, recreation, or other personal motives.

A profit motive is rebuttably presumed if the activity was profitable for three of the last five years (two of the last seven years in the case activities consisting in major part of breeding, training, showing, or racing horses), ending with the current tax year. A taxpayer may elect to delay the determination of whether the presumption applies until after the close of the fourth tax year following the first tax year in which the taxpayer engaged in the activity by filing Form 5213, *Election to Postpone Determination as to Whether the Presumption Applies That an Activity is Engaged in for Profit* [§ 183(d), § 183(e)].

Where the taxpayer is involved in several undertakings, those undertakings may constitute a single activity or separate activities for purposes of the hobby loss rules. The IRS generally will accept the taxpayer's characterization unless the characterization appears artificial and cannot reasonably be supported under the facts and circumstances. If the taxpayer engages in two or more separate activities, deductions and income from each separate activity are considered separately for purposes of applying the hobby loss rules [Reg. § 1.183-1(d)(1)].

To the extent they are allowable, hobby loss expenses are miscellaneous itemized deductions subject to the 2% floor (see VII.I.).

# CHAPTER IX. CREDITS

>>>>>>>>>>>>>>>>>>>>>>>>>>>>>>>>

## IX.A. Business Credits

### IX.A.1. List of Credits

[506 T.M., III.A.1.; TPS ¶3180.01.B.]

The general business credit for a tax year equals the sum of the business credit carryforwards carried to that tax year, the current year business credit, and the business credit carrybacks carried to that tax year [§ 38(a)]. The general business credit is composed of the following credits [§ 38(b)]:

- the § 46 investment credit (including the § 47(a) rehabilitation credit, § 48 energy credit, § 48A qualifying advanced coal project credit, § 48B qualifying gasification project credit, § 48C qualifying advanced energy project credit, and § 48D qualifying therapeutic discovery project credit) (see IX.A.5.);
- the § 51 work opportunity credit (including the § 1400L New York Liberty Zone business employee credit) (see IX.A.6.);
- the § 40 alcohol fuels credit (see discussion of second generation biofuel producer credit at IX.A.7.);
- the § 41 research credit (see IX.A.8.);
- the § 42 low-income housing credit (see IX.A.9.);
- the § 43 enhanced oil recovery credit (see IX.A.10.);
- the § 44 disabled access credit (see IX.A.11.);
- the § 45 renewable electricity production credit (see IX.A.12.);
- the § 1396 empowerment zone employment credit (including the § 1400H renewal community employment credit) (see IX.A.13.);
- the § 45A Indian employment credit (see IX.A.14.);
- the § 45B employer social security credit (see IX.A.15.);
- the § 45C orphan drug credit (see IX.A.16.);
- the § 45D new markets tax credit (see IX.A.17.);
- the § 45E small employer pension plan startup cost credit (see IX.A.18.);
- the § 45F employer-provided child care credit (see IX.A.19.);
- the § 45G railroad track maintenance credit (see IX.A.20.);
- the § 40A biodiesel fuels credit (see IX.A.21.);
- the § 45H low sulfur diesel fuel production credit (see IX.A.22.);
- the § 45I marginal oil and gas well production credit (see IX.A.23.);

431

- the § 5011 distilled spirits credit (see IX.A.24.);
- the § 45J advanced nuclear power facility production credit (see IX.A.25.);
- the § 45K nonconventional fuel source production credit (see IX.A.26.);
- the § 45L new energy efficient home credit (see IX.A.27.);
- the § 45M energy efficient appliance credit (see IX.A.28.);
- the business portion of the § 30B alternative motor vehicle credit (see IX.A.29.);
- the business portion of the § 30C alternative fuel vehicle refueling property credit (see IX.A.30.);
- the § 1400P(b) Hurricane Katrina housing credit;
- the § 1400R(a) Hurricane Katrina employee retention credit;
- the § 1400R(b) Hurricane Rita employee retention credit;
- the § 1400R(c) Hurricane Wilma employee retention credit;
- the § 45N mine rescue team training credit (see IX.A.31.);
- the § 45O agricultural chemicals security credit;
- the § 45P differential wage payment credit;
- the § 45Q carbon dioxide sequestration credit (see IX.A.32.);
- the business portion of the § 30D new qualified plug-in electric drive motor vehicle credit (see IX.A.33.);
- the § 45R small employer health insurance credit (see IX.A.34.); and
- the § 4612(e) trans-Alaska pipeline liability fund credit.

See *Schedules & Tables 22.* for a table of IRS forms and schedules for claiming and reporting credits.

### IX.A.2. Limitations on General Business Credit

[506 T.M., VI.B.1.b(3); TPS ¶3180.01.C.1.a.]

The aggregate amount of otherwise allowable general business credits that may be claimed for the tax year is limited to the excess, if any, of the taxpayer's net income tax for that year, over the greater of the taxpayer's tentative minimum tax for that year or the taxpayer's excess net regular tax liability [§ 38(c)(1)].

The net income tax equals the sum of the regular income tax and the alternative minimum tax (AMT), reduced by the sum of the following nonrefundable credits: the taxpayer's allowable household and dependent care credit, credit for the elderly and permanently disabled, adoption credit, child tax credit, home mortgage interest credit, education credits, elective deferrals and IRA contributions credit, nonbusiness energy property credit, residential energy efficient property credit, first-time D.C. homebuyer credit, foreign tax credit, plug-in electric vehicle credit, alternative motor vehicle credit, alternative fuel vehicle refueling property credit, and new qualified plug-in electric drive motor vehicle credit [§ 38(c)(1)].

The excess net regular tax liability equals 25% of the excess, if any, of the taxpayer's net regular tax liability over $25,000. The taxpayer's net regular tax liability equals the taxpayer's regular income tax reduced by the sum of the nonrefundable credits listed above [§ 38(c)(1)].

Note that if the taxpayer is subject to AMT, then the general business credits (other than specified credits and the § 1396 empowerment zone employment credit) are not allowable.

**EXAMPLE:** Taxpayer T has a regular tax liability for 2014 of $60,000, tentative minimum tax (TMT) of $50,000, a current year general business credit of $40,000, and nonrefundable credits of $2,000. T's AMT equals $0 because T's regular tax liability exceeds T's TMT. T is limited to $8,000 of general business credit for 2014, computed as follows:

| Step 1. | | |
|---|---|---|
| **Compute net income tax:** | | |
| | Regular tax liability plus AMT | $60,000 |
| | Less: Nonrefundable credits | ($2,000) |
| | Net income tax | $58,000 |
| **Step 2.** | | |
| **Compute net regular tax liability:** | | |
| | Regular tax liability | $60,000 |
| | Less: Nonrefundable credits | ($2,000) |
| | Net regular tax liability | $58,000 |
| **Step 3.** | | |
| **Compute excess net regular tax liability:** | | |
| | Net regular tax liability | $58,000 |
| | Less: | ($25,000) |
| | Excess net regular tax liability | $33,000 |
| **Step 4.** | | |
| **Compute 25% of excess from step 3:** | | |
| | Excess × 25% | $8,250 |
| **Step 5.** | | |
| **Compute greater of the two reductions:** | | |
| | TMT | $50,000 |
| | 25% of excess net regular tax liability | $8,250 |
| | Greater of the two | $50,000 |
| **Step 4.** | | |
| **Reduce net income tax:** | | |
| | Net income tax | $58,000 |
| | Minus greater of the two reductions ($50,000) | |
| | Credit Limitation | $8,000 |

*Specified Credits.* Special rules apply to the computation of the limitation for specified credits. First, the limitation is computed separately for each specified credit. Second, in computing the limitation, the taxpayer's tentative minimum tax is treated as being zero; accordingly, specified credits may be claimed against AMT. Third, in computing the limitation applicable to specified credits, the otherwise applicable limitation is reduced by the taxpayer's general business credits other than the specified credits [§ 38(c)(4)(A)]. The specified credits are as follows:

- the § 40 alcohol fuels credit;
- the § 42 low-income housing credit attributable to buildings placed in service after December 31, 2007;
- the § 45 renewable electricity production credit for electricity produced at a facility placed in service after October 22, 2004, during the four-year period beginning on the date the facility is placed in service;

- the § 45B employer social security credit;
- the § 45G railroad track maintenance credit;
- the § 48 energy credit;
- the § 47 rehabilitation credit attributable to qualified rehabilitation expenditures properly taken into account for periods after December 31, 2007;
- the § 51 work opportunity credit; and
- the § 45 renewable electricity production credit for electricity produced at an Indian coal production facility during the four-year period beginning on the later of January 1, 2006, or the date the facility is placed in service [§ 38(c)(4)(B)].

Special rules affect the application of the limitation to the § 1396 empowerment zone employment credit and the § 1400L(a) New York Liberty Zone business employee credit [§ 38(c)(2), § 38(c)(3)].

***Separate Returns.*** For married couples filing separate returns, the $25,000 amount applied in computing the limitation is $12,500 for each individual [§ 38(c)(6)(A)].

***Controlled Groups.*** For controlled groups of business entities, the $25,000 amount applied in computing the limitation is apportioned among the group's members [§ 38(c)(6)(B)].

***Estates and Trusts.*** For estates and trusts, the $25,000 amount applied in computing the limitation is reduced to an amount that bears the same ratio as the portion of the income of the estate or trust which is not allocated to beneficiaries [§ 38(c)(6)(D)].

### IX.A.3. Ordering Rules

[506 T.M., III.A.1.; TPS ¶3180.01.D.]

For purposes of compliance with the tax liability limitation on use of the general business credit, the components of the general business credit are treated as used on a first-in, first-out basis by offsetting the earliest-earned credits first, so that:

1. Carryforwards to the tax year are used before that year's current year general business credit and before carrybacks to that tax year are used;

2. Current year general business credits are used after carryforwards to the tax year are used, but before carrybacks to that tax year are used;

3. Carrybacks to a tax year are used only to the extent that carryforwards to that tax year and that year's current year general business credit have been fully used;

4. Carryforwards and carrybacks are used in first-in, first-out order; and

5. For credits arising in a single year, the credits are used in the order listed in IX.A.1., subject to the following:

- The components of the investment credit are used in the following order: rehabilitation credit, energy credit, qualifying advanced coal project credit, qualifying gasification project credit, qualifying advanced energy project credit and qualifying therapeutic discovery project credit.
- The renewal community employment credit is applied after the empowerment zone employment credit.
- The § 30 qualified plug-in electric vehicle credit for vehicles acquired before 2012 is applied after the § 30D new qualified plug-in electric drive motor vehicle credit.

- The new hire retention credit is applied after the small employer health insurance credit.
- General credits from an electing large partnership are applied after the new hire retention credit [§ 38(d)].

### IX.A.4. General Business Credit Carryover

[506 T.M., III.A.1.; TPS ¶3180.01.B.]

Any amount of the general business credit that is not allowed for the tax year because of the tax liability limitation in § 38(c) may be carried back to the first preceding tax year. Any remaining amount may be carried forward in succession to the next succeeding 20 tax years following the tax year in which the credit amount initially arose. However, the § 45I marginal well production credit has a five-year carryback period to make the total carryover period 25 years.

The carryback and carryforward periods are determined separately for the following credits:

- the § 1396 empowerment zone employment credit;
- the § 1400L New York Liberty Zone business employee credit;
- the § 40 alcohol fuels credit;
- the § 42 low-income housing credit attributable to buildings placed in service after December 31, 2007;
- the § 45 renewable electricity production credit for electricity produced at a facility placed in service after October 22, 2004, during the four-year period beginning on the date the facility is placed in service;
- the § 45B employer social security credit;
- the § 45G railroad track maintenance credit (no carryback or carryforward);
- the § 48 energy credit;
- the § 47 rehabilitation credit attributable to qualified rehabilitation expenditures properly taken into account for periods after December 31, 2007;
- the § 51 work opportunity credit; and
- the § 45 credit for coal produced at an Indian coal production facility during the four-year period beginning on the later of January 1, 2006, or the date the facility is placed in service.

No portion of the unused general business credit for any tax year attributable to a credit specified in § 38(b) or any portion thereof may be carried back to any tax year before the first tax year for which that specified credit or that portion is allowable without regard to any carryback [§ 196(a)].

Any portion of a qualified business credit determined for a tax year that has not been allowed or carried over to another tax year may be allowed as a deduction for the first tax year following the last tax year the credit could have been allowed. The deduction is not allowed for other credits. Qualified business credits are as follows [§ 196(c)]:

- the § 46 investment credit to the extent attributable to property the basis of which is reduced by § 50(c) (only 50% of this amount may be deducted [§ 196(d)(1)]);
- the § 51 work opportunity credit;
- the § 40 alcohol fuels credit;

- the § 41 research credit (other than such credit determined under § 280C(c)(3)) for tax years beginning after December 31, 1988 (only 50% of this amount may be deducted [§ 196(d)(2)]);
- the § 43 enhanced oil recovery credit;
- the § 1396 empowerment zone employment credit;
- the § 45A Indian employment credit;
- the § 45B employer social security credit; and
- the § 45D new markets tax credit.

If the taxpayer dies or ceases to exist before the first year following the last tax year the qualified business credits are allowed or carried over, the remaining amount may be allowed to the taxpayer as a deduction in the tax year the death or cessation occurs [§ 196(b)].

### IX.A.5. Investment Credit

[506 T.M., III.A.2., 512 T.M., 584 T.M., Part One, 603 T.M., XVIII.B.; TPS ¶3140.]

Taxpayers may claim a credit for investment in certain projects. The investment credit is the sum of the rehabilitation credit, the energy credit, the qualifying advanced coal project credit, the qualifying gasification project credit, the qualifying advanced energy project credit, and the qualifying therapeutic discovery project credit. The investment credit is a component of the general business credit.

No investment credit is permitted for property used predominantly outside the United States, for property used for lodging, for property used by tax-exempt organizations (other than farmers' cooperatives) except for property used predominantly in an unrelated trade or business subject to unrelated business income tax (see XIX.D.1.), or for property used by governmental entities or foreign persons [§ 50(b)].

### IX.A.5.a. Rehabilitation Credit

[584 T.M., Part One.; TPS ¶3140.02.]

Taxpayers may claim a credit based on a fixed percentage of their rehabilitation costs.

***Amount of Credit***. The rehabilitation credit is equal to the sum of [§ 47(a)]:

1. 20% of the taxpayer's qualified rehabilitation expenditures for any certified historic structure; and

2. 10% of the taxpayer's qualified rehabilitation expenditures for any other qualified rehabilitated building.

The rehabilitation credit generally is allowed in the tax year in which the property attributable to the qualified rehabilitation expenditures is placed in service. The amount of qualified rehabilitation expenditures must be reduced by the amount of qualified progress expenditures for which the § 47 rehabilitation credit was allowed for a tax year before the building was placed in service [§ 47(b)(2)].

***Qualified Rehabilitation Expenditures***. Qualified rehabilitation expenditures must be [§ 47(c)(2)(A)]:

1. properly chargeable to capital account;

2. for property for which depreciation deductions are allowable;

3. for property or for an addition or improvement to property that is nonresidential real property, is residential rental property, or is real property with a class life of more than 12.5 years; and

4. made in connection with the rehabilitation of a qualified rehabilitated building.

Qualified rehabilitation expenditures do not include expenditures for which the taxpayer does not use straight-line MACRS (unless the MACRS alternative depreciation system applies because the property is tax-exempt use or tax-exempt bond financing property), costs of acquiring a building or interest in a building, expenditures attributable to the enlargement of an existing building, expenditures attributable to the rehabilitation of a certified historic structure or building in a registered historic district unless the rehabilitation is a certified rehabilitation, expenditures for rehabilitation of a building that is allocable to the portion of such property that is or can reasonably be expected to be tax-exempt use property, or expenditures by a lessee of a building if the remaining term of the lease is less than the remaining MACRS recovery period [§ 47(c)(2)(B)].

*Qualified Rehabilitated Building.* A qualified rehabilitated building [§ 47(c)(1)]:

1. was first placed in service before 1936 (except for certified historic structures);

2. has been substantially rehabilitated;

3. was placed in service before the beginning of the rehabilitation;

4. retains in place at least 75% of its external walls (50% as external walls) and 75% of its internal structural framework; and

5. is depreciable or amortizable.

A building is substantially rehabilitated if the qualified rehabilitation expenditures during the 24-month (60-month for rehabilitation expected to be completed in phases set for in architectural plans before rehabilitation begins) period ending within the tax year exceed $5,000 or the adjusted basis if the building determined as of the beginning of the later of the holding period or the first day of the 24-month (or 60-month) period [§ 47(c)(1)(C)].

*Progress Expenditures.* A taxpayer may claim the credit for "qualified progress expenditures" before the building is placed in service if: (1) the building is rehabilitated by or for the taxpayer; (2) the normal rehabilitation period for the building is at least two years; and (3) it is reasonable to expect that the building will be a qualified rehabilitated building in the taxpayer's hands when it is placed in service [§ 47(d)(2)(A)]. If the building is not self-rehabilitated property, the amount of the qualified progress expenditure is limited to the portion of the overall cost of rehabilitation property attributable to the portion of the rehabilitation completed during the tax year. Any amounts paid that exceed the limitation are carried forward to the next tax year. Conversely, if the amount paid is less than the limitation, then the succeeding year's limitation is increased by the excess of the limitation over the amount paid [§ 47(d)(3)(C)].

If the qualified progress expenditure building is self-rehabilitated property, the expenditures are taken into account in the tax year for which the expenditure is chargeable to the capital account. If the building is not self-rehabilitated property, the expenditures are taken into account in the tax year in which they are paid [§ 47(d)(1)].

*Special Rules.* The basis of property for which the rehabilitation credit is claimed must be reduced by the amount of the credit. The basis is increased to the extent the credit is subsequently recaptured [§ 50(c)(2)].

No energy credit under § 48 is permitted on the portion of the basis of property that is attributable to qualified rehabilitation expenditures [§ 48(a)(2)(B)].

*IX.A.5.b. Energy Credit*

[512 T.M., III.A.2.; TPS ¶3140.03.]

Taxpayers are allowed a credit for a portion of the expenditures they make in placing energy property in service.

*Amount of Credit.* The energy credit for a tax year equals the product of the energy percentage and the basis of the energy property placed in service during that tax year. The energy percentage is 30% for [§ 48(a)(2)(A)(i), § 48(a)(5)]:

- qualified fuel cell property;
- qualified small wind energy property;
- qualified investment credit facility property;
- equipment that uses solar energy to generate electricity, to heat or cool a structure, or to provide solar process heat (other than for heating swimming pools); and
- equipment that uses solar energy to illuminate the inside of a structure using fiber-optic distributed sunlight.

The energy percentage is 10% for [§ 48(a)(2)(A)(ii)]:

- geothermal equipment;
- qualified microturbine property;
- combined heat and power system property; and
- qualified geothermal heat pump system property.

The energy credit for qualified fuel cell property is limited to $1,500 for each 0.5 kilowatts of capacity. The credit for microturbine property is limited to $200 for each kilowatt of capacity [§ 48(c)].

*Energy Property.* To be energy property, property must satisfy four conditions:

1. Either the construction, reconstruction, or erection of the property is completed by the taxpayer, or, the property is acquired by the taxpayer if the original use of the property commences with the taxpayer.

2. Depreciation or amortization must be allowable for the property.

3. The property must meet any performance and quality standards prescribed by the IRS after consultation with the Department of Energy that are in effect when the property is acquired.

4. The property must not be property that is part of a facility the production from which is allowed as part of the § 45 renewable electricity production credit, unless the property is part of a qualified investment credit facility.

*Investment Credit Facility Property.* For property placed in service after 2008, the construction of which began before January 1, 2014, taxpayers otherwise entitled to the § 45 renewable electricity production credit may irrevocably elect to take the energy credit in lieu of the production credit. The energy percentage is 30% for such property. If the taxpayer makes the election, no renewable electricity production credit for any year is allowed for any qualified investment credit facility. The election is made by attaching a statement to Form 3468, *Investment Credit* [§ 48(a)(5); Notice 2009-52, 2009-25 I.R.B. 1094].

A qualified investment facility is any of the following facilities [§ 48(a)(5)(C)]:

- qualified wind facility;
- qualified closed-loop biomass facility;
- qualified open-loop biomass facility;
- qualified geothermal facility;

- qualified landfill gas facility;
- qualified trash facility;
- qualified hydropower facility; and
- qualified marine and hydrokinetic renewable energy facility.

*Special Rules.* No credit is permitted for expenditures for property for which the taxpayer receives a grant under § 1603 of the 2009 American Recovery and Reinvestment Act for the tax year in which the grant is made or any subsequent tax year [§ 48(d)(1)].

No energy credit under § 48 is permitted on the portion of the basis of property attributable to qualified rehabilitation expenditures [§ 48(a)(2)(B)]. However, at the time the energy property is placed in service, the basis must be reduced, but not below zero, by the amount of qualified progress expenditures for the property for which the § 48(a) energy credit was allowed for a tax year before the property was placed in service.

### IX.A.5.c. Qualifying Advanced Coal Project Credit

[512 T.M., III.A.3., 603 T.M., XVIII.B.1.; TPS ¶3140.04.]

Taxpayers that have received certification from the IRS may claim a credit for a portion of the expenditures made in qualifying advanced coal projects [§ 48A(d)(2)]. The IRS was authorized to certify no more than $2.55 billion in advanced coal project credits [§ 48A(d)(3)], of which $1.3 billion was authorized in Phase I and $1.25 billion in Phase II. $658.5 million of the $1.3 billion was reallocated from Phase I and authorized for Phase III [Announcement 2013-43, 2013-46 I.R.B. 524].

*Amount of Credit.* The credit is the sum of: (1) 20% of the qualified investment for the tax year in integrated gasification combined cycle projects; (2) 15% of the qualified investment for the tax year in other advanced coal-based generation technologies for which application is made during the three-year period beginning on March 13, 2006; and (3) 30% of the qualified investment in advanced coal-based generation technologies for which application is made during the three-year period beginning on March 13, 2009. For the 30% credit, the advanced coal electricity project must capture and sequester at least 65% of the facility's carbon dioxide emissions (70% in the case of credits reallocated by the IRS) [§ 48A(a), § 48A(e)(1)(G)].

If the property is subsidized property, the basis of the property taken into account in determining credit is limited to the basis that would otherwise be taken into account, multiplied by (1 − (subsidized basis/property basis)) [§ 48A(b)(2)].

*Qualified Investment.* Qualified investment for a tax year equals the basis of eligible property placed in service by the taxpayer during the tax year that is part of a qualifying advanced coal project for which: (1) construction, reconstruction, or erection of the project is completed by the taxpayer, or the project is acquired by the taxpayer if the original use of the property commences with the taxpayer; and (2) depreciation or amortization is allowable for the property [§ 48A(b)(1)].

*Recapture.* In addition to the general recapture rules (see IX.A.5.k.), the credit is subject to recapture for any project that fails to capture and sequester at least 65% of the facility's carbon dioxide emissions (70% in the case of credits reallocated by the IRS) [§ 48A(i)].

### IX.A.5.d. Qualifying Gasification Project Credit

[512 T.M., III.A.4.; 603 T.M., XVIII.B.2.; TPS ¶3140.05.]

Taxpayers that have received certification from the IRS may claim a credit for a portion of the expenditures they make in qualifying gasification projects. The IRS was authorized to certify no more than $600 million in qualifying gasification project credits. All amounts have been allocated and no new allocation amounts have been authorized [§ 48B(d)(1); Announcement 2010-56, 2010-39 I.R.B. 398]. No qualifying gasification project credit is allowed for any qualified investment for which a qualifying advanced coal project credit is allowed under § 48A [§ 48B(e)].

*Amount of Credit.* The credit equals the sum of: (1) 30% of the qualified investment in qualifying gasification projects that include equipment that separates and sequesters at least 75% of the project's total carbon dioxide emissions; and (2) 20% of all other qualified investment in qualifying gasification projects for the tax year [§ 48B(a)].

If the property is subsidized property, the basis of the property taken into account in determining the credit is limited to the basis that would otherwise be taken into account, multiplied by (1 – (subsidized basis/property basis)) [§ 48B].

*Recapture.* In addition to the general recapture rules (see IX.A.5.k.), the 30% credit is subject to recapture for any project that fails to attain or maintain the separation and sequestration requirements [§ 48B(f)].

### IX.A.5.e. Qualifying Advanced Energy Project Credit

[512 T.M., III.A.5.; TPS ¶3140.09.]

Taxpayers that have received certification from the IRS may claim a credit for a portion of the expenditures made in qualifying advanced energy projects. $2.3 billion in credits were authorized and all amounts have been allocated [§ 48C(d)(1)(B); Notice 2013-12, 2013-10 I.R.B. 543]. No credit is allowable for an investment for which a § 48 energy credit, a § 48A qualifying advanced coal project credit, or a § 48B qualifying gasification project credit is allowed [§ 48C(e)].

*Amount of Credit.* The credit equals 30% of the qualified investment in qualifying advanced energy projects for the tax year [§ 48C(a)].

*Qualified Investment.* Qualified investment for a tax year equals the basis of eligible property placed in service by the taxpayer during the tax year that is part of a qualifying advanced energy project. The amount treated as qualified investment for all tax years for a qualifying advanced energy project is limited to the amount designated by the IRS as eligible for the credit [§ 48C(b)].

*Eligible Property.* Eligible property is property that: (1) is necessary for the production of advanced energy property; (2) is either tangible personal property, or other tangible property that not only is used as an integral part of the qualified investment credit facility but also is not a building or its structural components; and (3) is property for which depreciation or amortization is allowable [§ 48C(c)(2)].

### IX.A.5.f. The Qualifying Therapeutic Discovery Project Credit [Expired]

[506 T.M., III.A.2.g.; TPS ¶3140.10.]

Eligible taxpayers that made a qualified investment in a qualifying therapeutic discovery project were allowed a tax credit equal to 50% of those expenditures. The qualifying therapeutic discovery project credit applied only to qualified investments made in 2009 or 2010 allocable to depreciable property [§ 48D]. The qualifying therapeutic discovery project credit is a component of the investment credit.

One billion in credits were authorized and the entire amount has been allocated [§ 48D(d)(1)(B)].

### IX.A.5.g. *Progress Expenditures and the Investment Credit*

[506 T.M., III.A.2.; 512 T.M., III.A.6.; TPS ¶3140.01.B.]

For credits other than the rehabilitation credit (see IX.A.5.), the taxpayer may elect to increase its basis in eligible property by the qualified progress expenditures made for that year. If the eligible property is self-constructed property, the qualified progress expenditures equal the amount properly chargeable to capital account for the tax year. If the eligible property is not self-constructed property, the qualified progress expenditures for the property equal the lesser of: (1) the amount paid during the tax year to another person for construction, reconstruction, or erection of the property; or (2) the amount that represents that portion of the overall cost to the taxpayer of the construction by such other person that is properly attributable to that portion of such construction that is completed during the tax year [§ 48(b), § 48A(b)(3), § 48B(b)(3), § 48C(b)(2)].

***Eligible Property.*** Eligible property is progress expenditure property if: (1) the property is constructed by or for the taxpayer; (2) the normal construction period for the property is two years or more; and (3) it is reasonable to expect that the property will be energy property in the taxpayer's hands when it is placed in service [§ 48(b), § 48A(b)(3), § 48B(b)(3), § 48C(b)(2)].

### IX.A.5.h. *At-Risk Rules for Investment Credit*

[506 T.M., VI.B.2., 512 T.M., III.A.7.; TPS ¶3140.08.]

The investment credit is not allowed for any portion of the basis or cost of investment credit property for which the taxpayer is not "at risk." At-risk taxpayers include individuals, shareholders in S corporations and partners in partnerships (if the entity is engaged in an at-risk activity), and closely-held C corporations [§ 49(a)(1)].

The taxpayer is at risk to the extent of cash invested in an activity, plus the adjusted basis of any property contributed to the activity, plus the amount of any recourse debt incurred by the taxpayer for the activity. The credit base of otherwise qualified investment credit property must be reduced by the nonqualified nonrecourse financing incurred for the property as of the close of the tax year in which the property is placed in service [§ 49(a)(1)].

Qualified energy property is not subject to the at-risk rules if: (1) an energy tax credit is in effect for the property; (2) nonqualified nonrecourse financing does not exceed 75% of the basis of the property as of the close of the tax year the property is placed in service; and (3) the nonqualified nonrecourse financing for the property is a level payment loan, in which (a) each installment is substantially equal, (b) a portion of each installment is attributable to the repayment of principal, and (c) that portion is increased as the portion attributable to interest decreases [§ 49(a)(1)(F)].

A net decrease in nonqualified nonrecourse financing after the year the property is placed in service increases the amount at risk for the property. The increase is treated as if it occurred in the year the property is placed in service for investment credit purposes. The credit is taken on the tax return for the year in which the decrease in nonqualified nonrecourse financing occurs. A net increase in nonqualified nonrecourse financing after the year in which the property was placed in service decreases, and the resulting decrease in credits, applied as if reducing the credit base in the year the property was first placed in service, is recaptured [§ 49(a)(2), § 49(b)].

***Nonqualified Nonrecourse Financing.*** Nonqualified nonrecourse financing is nonrecourse financing other than qualified commercial financing (as defined in § 49(a)(1)(D)(ii)), including: (1) any amount for which the taxpayer is protected against loss through guarantees, stop-loss agreements, or other similar arrangements; and (2) any amount borrowed from a person that has a non-creditor interest in the activity in which the property is used, or any amount borrowed from a person that is related to a person, other than the taxpayer, that has such an interest [§ 49(a)(1)(D)].

### IX.A.5.i.  Investment Credit Claimed by Lessees

[506 T.M., III.A.2., 512 T.M., III.A.9.; TPS ¶3140.08.]

Upon an election by the lessor, a lessee of investment credit property will be treated as if the lessee acquired a portion or all of the property and may claim a portion or all of the investment credit if: (1) the lessee is the person that originally placed the property in service; (2) the property is sold and leased back by the lessee, or leased to the lessee, within three months after the date the property was originally placed in service; and (3) the lessee and lessor does not make an election to preclude application of the sale-leaseback rules. The election is not available to lessors that are mutual savings banks or other similar financial organizations, regulated investment companies (RICs), or real estate investment trusts (REITs) [§ 50(d)(4); Reg. § 1.48-4(a)(1)].

If the lessee is treated as acquiring the entire property, the lessee's investment amount is the property's fair market value, unless the lessor and lessee are members of a controlled group in which case the lessee is treated as having acquired the property for an amount equal to the lessor's basis. If the lessee is treated as acquiring a portion of the property, the lessee's investment amount equals the amount for which the lessee's investment would be if the lessee had acquired the entire property, multiplied by a fraction, the numerator of which is the term of the lease, and the denominator of which is the class life of the property [§ 50(d)(5)].

The election is made by filing a statement with the lessee, signed by the lessor and including the written consent of the lessee, on or before the due date (including any extensions of time) of the lessee's return for the lessee's tax year during which possession of the property is transferred to the lessee [Reg. § 1.48-4(f)].

### IX.A.5.j.  Claiming the Investment Credit

[506 T.M., III.A.2.; TPS ¶3140.01.B.]

The credit is claimed on Form 3468, *Investment Credit*. The credit amount is added to Form 3800, *General Business Credit*. Unlike other components of the general business credit, taxpayers whose only source of the credit is from partnerships or S corporations must attach Form 3468 to Form 3800.

### IX.A.5.k.  Recapture of Investment Credit

[506 T.M., II.E.3.g.; TPS ¶3140.07.]

Any required recapture is reported on Form 4255, *Recapture of Investment Credit*. All or a portion of the investment credit may have to be recaptured if the property to which the investment credit applies is disposed of or otherwise ceases to be investment credit property during the first five years the credit applies. Recapture of the investment credit does not apply to: (1) a transfer due to the death of the taxpayer; (2) a transfer between spouses or incident to divorce under § 1041 (however, a later disposition by the transferee is subject to recapture to the same extent as if the transferor had disposed of the property at the later date); (3) an acquisition transaction to which § 381(a) applies (see XIII.E.5.); and (4) a mere change in the form of conducting a trade or business if (a) the property is retained as investment credit property in that trade or business, and (b) the taxpayer retains a substantial interest in that trade or business [§ 50(a)].

For increases in the amount of nonqualified nonrecourse financing that has been excluded from the credit base, the recapture amount is equal to the aggregate decrease in credits for all prior tax years that would have resulted from reducing the credit base taking into account the amount of the net increase. The amount of nonqualified nonrecourse financing for the taxpayer shall not be treated as increased because of a transfer of evidence of indebtedness if the transfer occurs more than one year after the indebtedness was incurred [§ 49(b)].

### IX.A.6. Work Opportunity Credit [Expired]

[506 T.M., III.A.13., 514 T.M., IV.A.; TPS ¶3170.16.B.]

Employers may claim a credit for a portion of wages paid to certain new employees who are members of targeted groups. The work opportunity credit is a component of the general business credit. The employer must reduce the deduction for wages paid by the amount of the work opportunity credit, even if some or all of the credit is unused in the year it is generated [§ 280C(a)]. The work opportunity credit expired December 31, 2013 [§ 51(c)(4)].

*Amount of Credit.* The work opportunity tax credit equals 40% of the qualified first-year wages for that tax year [§ 51(a)]. The percentage is reduced to 25% for individuals who perform at least 120 hours but less than 400 hours of service for the employer during the one-year period beginning on the day the employee begins work for the employer. No credit applies to individuals performing less than 120 hours of service during the one-year period [§ 51(i)(3)]. The credit also includes 50% of qualified second-year wages that are paid to long-term family assistance recipients [§ 51(e)(1)(B)].

Qualified first-year wages are limited to $6,000 ($3,000 for a summer youth employee) for any one employee. For long-term family assistance recipients, the $6,000 limitation is increased to $10,000 [§ 51(e)(1)(B)].

The wage limitation is $6,000 for qualified veterans who are either a member of a family receiving food stamps for at three months during the one-year period before the date of hire, or who have been unemployed for at least four weeks but less than six months during the one-year period before the date of hire. For certain qualified veterans hired on or after November 22, 2011, the limitation is increased to $12,000 (for qualified veterans with a service-connected disability hired within one year of discharge from active duty), $14,000 (for those unemployed a total of six months or more during the one year period before the date of hire), or $24,000 (for those with a service-connected disability that have been unemployed a total of six months or more during the one year period before the date of hire) [§ 51(b)(3), § 51(d)(3)(A)].

*Targeted Group.* An individual is a member of a targeted group if the individual is:

- a qualified IV-A recipient (receiving assistance under certain state programs),
- a qualified veteran,
- a qualified ex-felon,
- a designated community resident,
- a vocational rehabilitation referral,
- a qualified summer youth employee,
- a qualified supplemental nutrition assistance program recipient,
- a qualified SSI (supplemental security income benefits) recipient, or

- a long-term family assistance recipient;

Additionally, on or before the day on which the individual begins work for the employer, the employer has received a certification from a designated local agency that the individual is a member of a targeted group. To meet this requirement, the employer may submit the a completed pre-screening notice and request (Form 8850, *Pre-Screening Notice and Certification Request for the Work Opportunity Credit*) to the designated local agency to request and obtain certification not later than the 28th day after the individual begins work for the employer [§ 51(d)(1)].

A disqualified individual is an individual that is a related individual, a nonqualifying rehire (an individual that was previously employed by the employer at any time), or a minimum employment individual (an individual that performs less than 120 hours of service for the employer) [§ 51(i)].

***Claiming the Credit.*** The credit is claimed on Form 5884, *Work Opportunity Credit*. The credit amount is added to Form 3800, *General Business Credit*, except for partnerships and S corporations, which must attach Form 5884 to their returns and report the amount on Schedule K. If the taxpayer's only source of this credit is from partnerships or S corporations, Form 5884 need not be completed and this credit is claimed directly on Form 3800.

A taxpayer may elect to forgo the work opportunity credit for a tax year by not claiming the credit on the return or amended return. The election may be made or revoked at any time before the expiration of the three-year period beginning on the due date for filing the income tax return for that tax year, without regard to extensions [§ 51(j)].

***Tax-Exempt Organizations.*** While the work opportunity credit is generally not available to tax-exempt organizations (except § 521 farmers' cooperatives), a qualified tax-exempt organization may claim the credit against the employer's share of FICA tax for hiring qualified [§ 3111(e)(3)]. Qualified tax-exempt organizations may claim the credit on Form 5884-C, *Work Opportunity Credit for Qualified Tax-Exempt Organizations Hiring Qualified Veterans*, which is filed after the employment tax return has been filed.

### IX.A.7. Second Generation Biofuel Producer Credit [Expired]

[506 T.M., III.A.7.b(5), 512 T.M., III.B.2.e.; TPS ¶3170.01.A.5.]

Taxpayers may claim a credit for qualified second generation biofuel production. The second generation biofuel producer credit (formerly named the cellulosic biofuel producer credit for fuel produced before January 3, 2013) is a component of the alcohol fuels credit [§ 40], which is a component of the general business credit.

The second generation biofuel production credit expired December 31, 2013 [§ 40(b)(6)(J)(i)]. The other components of the alcohol fuels income tax credit (alcohol mixture (gasohol), alcohol, and small ethanol producer credits) expired December 31, 2011 [§ 40(e)(1)].

***Eligibility.*** All producers of second generation biofuel must be registered with the IRS [§ 40(b)(6)(I)]. Form 637, *Application for Registration (For Certain Excise Tax Activities)*, is used to apply for registration.

***Amount of Credit.*** The second generation biofuel producer credit equals the second generation biofuel rate multiplied by the number of gallons of qualified second generation biofuel production [§ 40(b)(6)(A)]. The second generation biofuel rate is $1.01 per gallon [§ 40(b)(6)(B)].

*Claiming the Credit.* The credit is claimed on Form 6478, *Biofuel Producer Credit.* The credit amount is added to Form 3800, *General Business Credit,* except for partnerships and S corporations, which must attach Form 6478 to their returns and report the amount on Schedule K. If the taxpayer's only source of this credit is from partnerships or S corporations, Form 6478 need not be completed and this credit is claimed directly on Form 3800.

A taxpayer may elect to forgo the alcohol fuels credit for a tax year. The election may be made or revoked at any time before the expiration of the three-year period beginning on the due date, without regard to extensions, for filing the income tax return for that tax year [§ 40(f)].

*Recapture of Credit.* If the taxpayer uses the biofuel for which a credit has been taken for any purpose other than as qualified second generation biofuel, the credit amount applicable to the amount of biofuel is recaptured as a tax [§ 40(d)(3)(D)]. Recapture of the alcohol fuels credit is reported on Form 720, *Quarterly Federal Excise Tax Return.*

*Special Rules.* The second generation biofuel producer credit may not be claimed if the alternative fuel mixture excise tax credit is claimed for the same gallon of production [§ 40(c), § 6426(h)].

If the second generation biofuel producer credit ceases to apply because of the termination of the credit, any general business credit attributable to the second generation biofuel producer credit arising before the termination may not be carried to any tax year beginning after the three-tax-year period beginning with the tax year in which occurs the first day of the termination of the credit [§ 40(e)(2), § 40(b)(6)(J)(ii)]. If the credit expires, any unused second generation biofuel producer credit is deductible in the first tax year after the end of the three-year period for claiming the credit [§ 196(a), § 196(c)(3)].

### IX.A.8. Research Credit [Expired]

[506 T.M., III.A.3.; 556 T.M., VI.; 557 T.M., II.C.; TPS ¶3160.01.]

Taxpayers may claim a credit for certain research and experimental expenditures paid or incurred in carrying on a trade or business during the tax year. The research credit is a component of the general business credit.

The research credit expired December 31, 2013 [§ 41(h)].

### IX.A.8.a. Amount of Research Credit

[506 T.M., III.A.3.a., 556 T.M., VI.B., 557 T.M., II.C.; TPS ¶3160.04., .05.]

The research credit is an amount equal to the sum of the following separate credit computations [§ 41(a)]:

- 20% of the excess of qualified research expenses for the tax year over a base amount (incremental research credit); plus
- 20% of basic research payments (as defined in § 41(e)(1)(A)) made during the tax year (basic research credit); plus
- 20% of the taxpayer's expenditures for the tax year on qualified energy research undertaken by an energy research consortium (in § 41(f)(6)) for energy research (applicable to all such expenditures, not only those in excess of a base amount).

The base amount is computed by multiplying the fixed-base percentage by the taxpayer's average annual gross receipts for the four tax years preceding the tax year for which the credit is being determined (the credit year). The fixed-base percentage is the ratio that a taxpayer's total qualified research expenses for tax years beginning after 1983 and before 1989 bears to its total gross receipts for that period. A taxpayer's fixed-base percentage cannot exceed 16%. A taxpayer's base amount may not be less than 50% of the qualified research expenses for the credit year [§ 41(c)].

A start-up company rule applies if the first tax year in which the taxpayer had both gross receipts and qualified research expenses begins after December 31, 1983, or if there are fewer than three tax years in the 1984-1988 period in which the taxpayer both incurred qualified research expenses and had gross receipts. The taxpayer is assigned a fixed-base percentage of 3% for each of its first five tax years beginning after 1993 in which it incurs qualified research expenditures. The taxpayer's fixed-base percentages for its sixth through its 10th tax year beginning after 1993 is determined by multiplying an assigned fraction to certain previous years' ratios of qualified research expenditures to gross receipts. For tax years thereafter, the taxpayer's fixed-based percentage is its actual ratio of qualified research expenditures to gross receipts for any five tax years selected by the taxpayer from its fifth through 10th tax years after 1993 [§ 41(c)(3)].

*Alternative Simplified Credit.* Taxpayers may elect an alternative simplified credit calculation in place of the standard method of computing the incremental research credit. The alternative simplified research credit amount is equal to 14% of qualified research expenses that exceed 50% of the average qualified research expenses for the three preceding tax years. The rate is reduced to 6% if a taxpayer has no qualified research expenses in any one of the three preceding tax years [§ 41(c)(5)].

*Minimum Basic Research Amount.* The minimum basic research amount equals the greater of two fixed floors. The first floor equals 1% of the average of the sum of amounts paid or incurred during the base period for any in-house research expenses or contract research expenses. The second floor equals the amounts treated as contract research expenses during the base period by reason of the university basic research credit rules. For corporations not in existence for at least one full year of the three tax years in the base period, the minimum basic research amount for any base period is never less than 50% of the basic research payments for the tax year for which the university basic research credit amount is being determined. If the corporation was in existence for one or two full tax years in the base period, the fixed floor is computed for the year or years [§ 41(e)(4)].

### IX.A.8.b. Qualified Research

[506 T.M., III.A.3.c., III.A.3.d., III.A.3.g(2), III.A.3.h., 556 T.M., III.B., 557 T.M., II.C.; TPS ¶3160.03.]

*Qualified Research.* Qualified research is research: (1) for which expenditures may be treated as deductible expenses under § 174; (2) undertaken for the purpose of discovering information that is technological in nature and the application of which is intended to be useful in the development of a new or improved business component of the taxpayer; and (3) in which substantially all of the activities constitute elements of a process of experimentation for a functional purpose [§ 41(d)(1)]. Purposes that do not qualify as qualified research include: (1) research conducted for a business component after commercial production of the component has begun; (2) adaptation of existing business components to a particular customer's requirements; (3) duplication of existing business components; (4) market research, data canvassing, surveys, studies, etc.; (5) research conducted outside the United States, its possessions, or Puerto Rico; (6) research in the social sciences (including economics, business management and behavioral sciences), arts or humanities; (7) research funded by a grant, contract or otherwise by another person or a governmental entity; and (8) research on computer software to be used for internal use for the benefit of the taxpayer [§ 41(d)(4)].

*Qualified Research Expenses.* Qualified research expenses is the sum of in-house research expenses and contract research expenses paid or incurred during any tax year in any trade or business. Qualifying in-house research expenses include: (1) wages paid or incurred to an employee for qualified services; (2) amounts paid or incurred for supplies used in the conduct of qualified research; and (3) amounts paid or incurred to another person for the right to use computers in the conduct of qualified research. Contract research expenses are equal to 65% of any amount paid or incurred by the taxpayer to any person, other than an employee of the taxpayer, for qualified research. For amounts paid or incurred by the taxpayer to eligible small businesses, universities, and federal laboratories for qualified energy research, 100%, instead of 65%, of the amount constitutes contract research expenses [§ 41(b)].

### IX.A.8.c. Claiming the Research Credit

[506 T.M., III.A.3., 556 T.M., VI.B., 557 T.M., II.C.; TPS ¶3160.12.]

The credit is claimed on Form 6765, *Credit for Increasing Research Activities*. The credit amount is added to Form 3800, *General Business Credit,* except for partnerships and S corporations, which must attach Form 6765 to their returns and report the amount on Schedule K. If the taxpayer's only source of this credit is from partnerships or S corporations, Form 6765 need not be completed and this credit is claimed directly on Form 3800.

### IX.A.8.d. Special Rules for the Research Credit

[506 T.M., III.A.3.j.; 556 T.M., VI.B.6.; 557 T.M., II.C.5.a.; TPS ¶3160.02., .13.]

The deduction for research and experimental expenditures (see IV.F.2.) in the year the research credit is taken must be reduced by the amount of the research credit claimed on the tax return. If the research credit determined for the tax year exceeds the amount allowable as a deduction for qualified research expenses for the tax year because of the capitalization rules, the amount capitalized must be reduced by the excess. Alternatively, the taxpayer may elect to claim a reduced credit to avoid any reduction of the research expense deduction or the amount capitalized, which would be appropriate where the taxpayer is subject to the alternative minimum tax [§ 280(c)(1), § 280(c)(3)(A); Reg. § 1.280C-4]. An election to claim a reduced research credit in favor of a full deduction is made on Form 6765.

Clinical testing expenses taken into account for the orphan drug credit may not be taken into account for the research credit. However, those expenses are taken into account in determining base period research expenses in subsequent years [§ 45C(c)] (see IX.A.16.).

For a partner in a partnership, a shareholder in an S corporation, or a beneficiary of a trust or estate, the amount of credit that can be used in a particular tax year cannot exceed an amount equal to the amount of tax attributable to the income arising from that person's interest in the trade or business or entity [§ 41(g)].

### IX.A.8.e. Election to Accelerate Research Credit in Lieu of Bonus Depreciation

[532 T.M., III.A.2.d(5)(d), 556 T.M., VI.I.1.; TPS ¶¶2370.12.F.2.d.(3), 3201.07.]

Corporate taxpayers may elect to increase the part of the business credit limitation under § 38(c) attributable to the research credit in lieu of taking the § 168(k) additional first-year depreciation deduction (bonus depreciation) for qualified property placed in service after March 31, 2008, but before January 1, 2010. The election also applied to the minimum tax credit under § 53 (see IX.H.1.). The increases in credits are refundable [§ 168(k)(4)]. The election was extended through December 31, 2013, for the minimum tax credit but not for the research credit (see V.C.1.c.(3)).

For information about the election, see Rev. Proc. 2008-65, 2008-44 I.R.B. 1082, *amplified and supplemented by* Rev. Proc. 2009-16, 2009-6 I.R.B. 449, *modified by* Rev. Proc. 2009-33, 2009-29 I.R.B. 150]. The election is revocable only with consent of the IRS.

### IX.A.9. Low-Income Housing Credit

[506 T.M., III.A.9., 584 T.M., Part Two, I.; TPS ¶3150.]

Taxpayers may claim a credit for a portion of their investments in qualified low-income housing. The low-income housing credit is a component of the general business credit.

### IX.A.9.a. Eligibility for the Low-Income Housing Credit

[506 T.M., III.A.9., 584 T.M., Part Two, I., Part Two, II., Part Two, VI., Part Two, VII.; TPS ¶3150.03., .05., .06.]

The low-income housing credit is available for taxpayers that invest in projects providing low income housing for at least 15 years; however the credit is taken annually over a 10-year period, beginning with the tax year in which the building is placed in service, or, at the taxpayer's election, with the tax year after the year in which it is placed in service [§ 42(f)(1), § 42(i)(1)]. To be eligible, the taxpayer must enter an agreement with the appropriate state or local agency committing the building to extended use for low-income housing for a period that begins on the first day a building is part of a low-income housing project, and ends on a date not earlier than the date that is 15 years after the 15-year compliance period [§ 42(h)(6)].

For purposes of the credit, rehabilitation expenditures for any building are treated as a separate new building and are eligible for the credit if during any 24-month period the expenditures are at least equal to the greater of: (1) 20% of the adjusted basis of the building, or (2) $6,000 ($6,600 for 2015) per low-income housing unit [§ 42(e); Rev. Proc. 2014-61, 2014-47 I.R.B. 860].

*Qualified Low-Income Building.* A qualified low-income building is any building that: (1) is part of a qualified low-income housing project at all times during the testing period that begins on the first day in the compliance period on which the building is part of the project, and ends on the last day of the compliance period for the building; and (2) is subject to the amendments made by the 1986 Tax Reform Act, § 201. The compliance period for a building is the period of 15 tax years beginning with the first tax year of the credit period for the building [§ 42(c)(2)].

*Qualified Low-Income Housing Project.* A qualified low-income housing project is any project for residential rental property that satisfies one of the following conditions: (1) 20% or more of the residential units in the project are both rent-restricted and occupied by individuals whose income is 50% or less of area median gross income; or (2) 40% or more of the residential units in the project are both rent-restricted and occupied by individuals whose income is 60% or less of area median gross income [§ 42(g)].

### IX.A.9.b. Amount of Low-Income Housing Credit

[506 T.M., III.A.9.b., 584 T.M., Part Two, V., Part Two, VI.; TPS ¶3150.02., .04., .08.]

The low-income housing credit amount equals the applicable percentage multiplied by the qualified basis of each qualified low-income building and is computed for each tax year in the credit period and is prorated in the first year (any reduction is allowed in the eleventh year) [§ 42(a), § 42(f)(2)]. The credit amount is limited by the housing credit dollar amount allocated to the low-income building by the appropriate state or local agency [§ 42(h)(1)(A)]. The housing credit dollar amount limit does not apply to the extent the credit is attributable to eligible basis financed with certain tax-exempt obligations [§ 42(h)(4)]. To obtain a housing credit allocation, the taxpayer and the appropriate state or local agency must each complete portions of Form 8609, *Low-Income Housing Credit Allocation and Certification,* and the taxpayer must submit the form to the IRS.

If the building is a new building that is not federally subsidized, the percentage must be prescribed so that it yields, over a 10-year period, amounts of credit that have a present value equal to 70% of the qualified basis of the building. If the building is a new building that is federally subsidized or if it is an existing building, the percentage must be prescribed so that it yields, over a 10-year period, amounts of credit that have a present value equal to 30% of the qualified basis of the building [§ 42(b)(2)].

***Qualified Basis.*** Qualified basis in any qualified low-income building for any tax year equals the applicable fraction (proportion of low-income housing capacity in the building to total housing capacity in the building, determined by number of units or by floor space) multiplied by the eligible basis of the building [§ 42(c)(1)]. The eligible basis of a new building is its adjusted basis as of the close of the first tax year of the credit period. The eligible basis of a qualified existing building equals its adjusted basis as of the close of the first tax year of the credit period [§ 42(d)(1)].

The applicable percentage is reduced if the qualified basis increases after the close of the first tax year in the credit period. The applicable percentage that applies to that excess qualified basis equals two-thirds of the applicable percentage that would otherwise apply [§ 42(f)(3)].

Buildings located in qualified census tracts or difficult development areas are eligible for a 30% increase in the basis attributable to new construction or rehabilitation eligible for credits. In addition, for buildings placed in service after July 30, 2008, any building designated by a state housing agency as requiring the enhanced credit in order for such building to be financially feasible is also eligible for the 30% increase in basis [§ 42(d)(5)(B)].

***At-Risk Limitations.*** At-risk limitations apply, except that: (1) loans for low-income housing credit projects are not treated as nonqualified nonrecourse financing merely because the lender and taxpayer are related persons; (2) the general investment credit at-risk rule, limiting the amount of nonrecourse financing to 80% of the credit base of the property, does not apply; and (3) certain loans on low-income housing credit projects from certain nonprofit lenders are treated as qualified nonrecourse financing even if the lender is not a commercial lender and/or is the seller of the property (or is related to the seller) [§ 42(k)].

### IX.A.9.c. Claiming the Low-Income Housing Credit

[506 T.M., III.A.9., 584 T.M., Part Two, VI.E.; TPS ¶3150.13.]

The credit is claimed on Form 8586, *Low-Income Housing Credit.* The credit amount is added to Form 3800, *General Business Credit,* except for partnerships and S corporations, which must attach Form 8586 to their returns and report the amount on Schedule K. If the taxpayer's only source of this credit is from partnerships or S corporations, Form 8586 need not be completed and this credit is claimed directly on Form 3800.

Form 8609-A, *Annual Statement for Low-Income Housing Credit*, must be filed with the taxpayer's return for each year of the 15-year compliance period to report compliance with the requirements for taking the credit and to calculate the credit.

### IX.A.9.d. Recapture of Low-Income Housing Credit

[506 T.M., III.A.9.g., 584 T.M., Part Two, IX.B.; TPS ¶3150.09., .13.E.]

Failure to qualify for the credit during the compliance period or failure to maintain qualified basis throughout the compliance period will trigger recapture of the accelerated portion of the credit taken in previous years and disqualify the project for the credit in the current year. If the recapture event occurs in the second through eleventh years of the credit period, one-third of previously taken credits, plus interest, is recaptured. In year 12, the recapture fraction is reduced to 4/15; reduced to 3/15 in year 13; reduced to 2/15 in year 14; and reduced to 1/15 in year 15 [§ 42(j)].

The recapture amount is reported on Form 8611, *Recapture of Low-Income Housing Credit*, which is added as tax to the taxpayer's income tax return.

### IX.A.10. Enhanced Oil Recovery Credit

[506 T.M., III.A.5., 512 T.M., III.D., 605 T.M., V.A.; TPS ¶3170.03.A.]

Taxpayers are allowed a credit for a portion of their enhanced oil recovery costs. The enhanced oil recovery credit is a component of the general business credit. The credit equals 15% of the taxpayer's qualified enhanced oil recovery costs for the tax year [§ 43(a)], reduced by a phase-out amount, equal to the amount otherwise allowable multiplied by a fraction, the numerator of which is the excess of the reference price of oil per barrel over $28, and the denominator of which is $6 [§ 43(b)]. For 2013, the reference price for crude oil was $94.53 and the credit is entirely phased out.

### IX.A.11. Disabled Access Credit

[506 T.M., III.A.12.; 590 T.M., III.D.4.; TPS ¶3170.04.]

Eligible small business taxpayers may claim a credit for a portion of expenditures incurred to make facilities or programs accessible to disabled individuals. The disabled access credit is a component of the general business credit.

*Eligibility.* An eligible small business is any person or entity that had gross receipts for the preceding tax year that did not exceed $1 million, or employed 30 or fewer full-time employees during the preceding tax year [§ 44(b)].

*Amount of Credit.* The disabled access credit equals 50% of the eligible access expenditures that exceed $250 and do not exceed $10,250 [§ 44(a)].

*Eligible Access Expenditures.* Eligible access expenditures are amounts paid or incurred by an eligible small business for the purpose of enabling it to comply with the 1990 Americans with Disabilities Act (ADA). Eligible access expenditures also include amounts paid or incurred for qualified access purposes, provided they are reasonable and necessary to accomplish the purpose. Amounts paid or incurred in connection with facilities first placed in service after November 5, 1990, are not eligible [§ 44(c)].

*Qualified Access Purposes.* Qualified access purposes include [§ 44(c)(2)]:

- removing architectural, communication, physical, or transportation barriers that prevent a business from being accessible to, or usable by, individuals with disabilities;
- providing qualified interpreters or other effective methods of making aurally delivered materials available to individuals with hearing impairments;
- providing qualified readers, taped texts, and other effective methods of making visually delivered materials available to individuals with visual impairments;

- acquiring or modifying equipment or devices for individuals with disabilities; and

- providing other similar services, modifications, materials, or equipment.

***Claiming the Credit.*** The credit is claimed on Form 8826, *Disabled Access Credit*. The credit amount is added to Form 3800, *General Business Credit*, except for partnerships and S corporations, which must attach Form 8826 to their returns and report the amount on Schedule K. If the taxpayer's only source of this credit is from partnerships or S corporations, Form 8826 need not be completed and this credit is claimed directly on Form 3800.

***Special Rules.*** The disabled access credit reduces any deduction or other credit otherwise allowable with respect to the expenditures, and reduces the increase in basis that would otherwise occur on account of the expenditures [§ 44(d)(7)].

### IX.A.12. Renewable Electricity Production Credit

[506 T.M., III.A.6., 512 T.M., III.E.1., III.E.5.; 603 T.M., XVIII.C.3.; TPS ¶3170.05.]

Taxpayers may claim a credit for producing and selling renewable electricity (see IX.A.12.a. and b.), refined coal (see IX.A.12.c.), and Indian coal (see IX.A.12.d.). The renewable electricity production credit is a component of the general business credit. The renewable electricity credit expired for facilities placed in service after December 31, 2013, but may continue to apply to electricity produced at facilities placed in service before then. The refined coal credit expired for facilities placed in service after December 31, 2011, but may continue to apply to facilities placed in service before then. The Indian coal credit expired December 31, 2013.

### IX.A.12.a. Eligibility for the Renewable Electricity Production Credit

[506 T.M., III.A.6.a.; 512 T.M., III.E.1.; 603 T.M., XVIII.C.3.; TPS ¶3170.05.]

The renewable electricity production credit applies to electricity that is [§ 45(e)(1)]:

1. produced by the taxpayer from qualified energy resources;
2. produced by the taxpayer at a qualified facility during the credit period;
3. sold by the taxpayer to an unrelated person [§ 45(a)(2)]; and
4. produced in the United States or a U.S. possession.

***Qualified Energy Resources.*** Qualified energy resources consist of [§ 45(c)(1)]:

- wind;
- closed-loop biomass;
- open-loop biomass;
- geothermal energy;
- solar energy;
- small irrigation power;
- municipal solid waste;
- qualified hydropower production; and
- marine and hydrokinetic renewable energy.

***Qualified Facility.*** A qualified facility is any wind, closed-loop biomass, open-loop biomass, geothermal energy, solar energy, small irrigation power, marine and hydrokinetic renewable energy, landfill gas, trash, or qualified hydropower facility. A qualified facility does not include any facility that produces electricity from gas derived from the biodegradation of municipal solid waste if that biodegradation occurs in a facility the production from which a § 45K credit was allowed for the tax year or any prior tax year [§ 45(d)].

*Credit Period.* The renewable electricity production credit applies to facilities placed in service on or before December 31, 2013 (December 31, 2006, for solar energy facilities and December 31, 2008, for small irrigation facilities) [§ 45(d)]. Generally, the credit period is the 10-year period beginning on the date the facility was originally placed in service. However, for open-loop biomass , geothermal energy, solar energy, small irrigation power, landfill gas, and trash facilities placed in service before August 9, 2005, the credit period was a five-year period beginning on the placed-in-service date; consequently, electricity produced at such facilities is no longer eligible for the credit. For any qualified hydropower facility that produces incremental hydropower production, the credit period begins on the date the efficiency improvements or additions to capacity are placed in service [§ 45(a)(2), § 45(b)(4), § 45(d)(9)(B)].

### IX.A.12.b. Amount of Renewable Electricity Production Credit

[506 T.M., III.A.6.b., III.A.6.h., 512 T.M., III.E.2., III.E.8., 603 T.M., XVIII.C.3.b.; TPS ¶3170.05.A.1., .05.D.]

*Credit Rate.* For wind, closed-loop biomass, geothermal, and solar energy, the renewable electricity production credit amount generally equals 1.5 cents ($0.015) multiplied by the kilowatt hours of renewable electricity produced and sold by the taxpayer (increased by an inflation factor to 2.3 cents ($0.023) for 2014) [§ 45(a), § 45(b)(2); Notice 2014-36, 2014-22 I.R.B. 1058]. The renewable electricity production credit is reduced by one-half if it is produced and sold at any open-loop biomass facility, small irrigation power facility, landfill gas facility, trash facility, qualified hydropower facility, or marine and hydrokinetic renewable energy facility ($1.1 cents ($0.011) for 2014) [§ 45(b)(4); Notice 2014-36].

*Credit Reduction for Phaseout.* The credit is potentially reduced by a phaseout amount determined by a reference price relating to the price of electricity, adjusted for inflation. Due to the level of the reference prices, the renewable electricity production credit is not subject to phaseout for 2014 [§ 45(b)(1), § 45(b)(2)].

*Credit Reduction for Subsidies.* The credit allowable for any project is reduced by the subsidy reduction amount. The subsidy reduction amount equals the credit that would otherwise be allowable multiplied by the lesser of one-half or the reduction fraction, the numerator of which equals the sum, for the tax year and all prior tax years, of subsidy grants, subsidy bond proceeds, subsidized energy financing, and other project credits; and the denominator of which is the aggregate amount of additions to the capital account for the project for the tax year and all prior tax years. The subsidy reduction does not apply to certain closed-loop biomass facilities [§ 45(b)(3)].

### IX.A.12.c. Refined Coal Credit

[506 T.M., III.A.6.b.1(b), 512 T.M., III.E.2.a(2)(b), 603 T.M., XVIII.C.2.; TPS ¶3170.05.A.]

The credit for refined coal equals $4.375 (adjusted for inflation to $6.601 for 2014) per ton of qualified refined coal that: (1) is produced by the taxpayer at a refined coal production facility during the 10-year period beginning on the date the facility was originally placed in service; (2) is sold by the taxpayer to an unrelated person; and (3) is sold during that 10-year period and that tax year. Refined coal is a liquid, gaseous, or solid fuel produced from coal or high carbon fly ash meeting the requirements of § 45(c)(7).

*Credit Reduction for Phaseout.* The credit is potentially reduced by a phaseout amount determined by a reference price relating to the price of electricity, adjusted for inflation. Due to the level of the reference prices, the refined coal credit is not subject to phaseout for 2014 [§ 45(e)(8); Notice 2014-36, 2014-22 I.R.B. 1058].

The refined coal credit is also reduced by the subsidy reduction amount (see IX.A.12.c.).

The refined coal credit may not be claimed if production from the facility is eligible for the § 45K nonconventional fuel source credit [§ 45(e)(9)] (see IX.A.26.).

### IX.A.12.d. Indian Coal Credit [Expired]

[506 T.M., III.A.6.b(1)(c), 512 T.M., III.E.2.a(2)(b), 603 T.M., XVIII.C.3.; TPS ¶3170.05.B.9.]

The credit for producers of Indian coal equals the applicable dollar amount per ton of Indian coal that: (1) is produced by the taxpayer at an Indian coal production facility during the eight-year period beginning on January 1, 2006; (2) is sold by the taxpayer to an unrelated person; and (3) is sold during that eight-year period and that tax year [§ 45(e)(10)]. The applicable dollar amount is adjusted for inflation and was $2.308 per ton for 2013 [Notice 2013–33, 2013–22 I.R.B. 1140]. The Indian coal credit expired December 31, 2013 [§ 45(e)(10)(A)].

### IX.A.12.e. Claiming the Renewable Electricity Production Credit

[506 T.M., III.A.6., 512 T.M., III.E., 603 T.M., XVIII.C.3.a.; TPS ¶3170.05.J.]

The credit is claimed on Form 8835, *Renewable Electricity, Refined Coal, and Indian Coal Production Credit.* The credit amount is added to Form 3800, *General Business Credit,* except for partnerships and S corporations, which must attach Form 8835 to their returns and report the amount on Schedule K. If the taxpayer's only source of this credit is from partnerships or S corporations, Form 8835 need not be completed and this credit is claimed directly on Form 3800.

Beginning in 2009, taxpayers may elect to claim the § 48 energy credit for their investment in a qualified renewable electricity production facility in lieu of the renewable electricity production credit [§ 48(a)(5)] (see IX.A.5.b.). Taxpayers may also elect to receive a federal grant for their investments in renewable electricity production facilities in lieu of either credit under § 1603 of the 2009 American Recovery & Reinvestment Act [§ 48(d)(1)].

For allocation of the credit among cooperative patrons, see § 45(e)(11). For allocation of the credit to developers and investors in wind farms, see Rev. Proc. 2007-65, 2007-45 I.R.B. 970, *modified by* Announcement 2009-69, 2009-40, I.R.B. 475.

### IX.A.13. Empowerment Zone Employment Credit [Expired]

[506 T.M., III.A.14., 514 T.M., IV.G., 597 T.M., IV.AA.; TPS ¶3170.06.]

Employers may claim an empowerment zone employment credit for qualified zone wages paid to qualified zone employees. The empowerment zone employment credit is a component of the general business credit. The employer's deduction otherwise allowed for wages paid for a tax year is reduced by the amount of the empowerment zone employment credit claimed for that year [§ 280C(a)].

The empowerment zone credit expired December 31, 2013 [§ 1396(d)(1)(A)]. For renewal communities treated as empowerment zones, the credit (the renewal community employment credit under § 1400H) expired December 31, 2009 [§ 1400E(b)(1)].

*Amount of Credit.* The empowerment zone employment credit for any tax year equals the applicable percentage multiplied by the qualified zone wages paid or incurred during the calendar year ending with or within the tax year [§ 1396(a)]. For the originally designated empowerment zones, the applicable percentage is 20% [§ 1396(b)].

*Limitation.* Only the first $15,000 of qualified zone wages for each employee each year is taken into account in computing the credit (so that the maximum credit per employee is $3000). The $15,000 limitation is reduced by the amount of wages paid or incurred during that year which are taken into account in determining the work opportunity credit under § 51 [§ 1396(c)].

*Qualified Zone Wages.* Qualified zone wages are any wages paid or incurred by an employer for services performed by an employee while that employee is a qualified zone employee (as defined in § 1396(d)) [§ 1396(c)(1)].

*Empowerment Zone.* An empowerment zone is any one of the nominated areas designated by the appropriate government officials as empowerment zones, as determined by population, distress, size and poverty criteria [§ 1391, § 1392].

*Claiming the Credit.* The credit is claimed on Form 8844, *Empowerment Zone Employment Credit.* The credit amount is added to Form 3800, *General Business Credit,* except for partnerships and S corporations, which must attach Form 8844 to their returns and report the amount on Schedule K. If the taxpayer's only source of this credit is from partnerships or S corporations, Form 8844 need not be completed and this credit is claimed directly on Form 3800.

The instructions to Form 8844 contain a list of empowerment zone designations.

### IX.A.14. Indian Employment Credit [Expired]

[506 T.M., III.A.15., 514 T.M., IV.B.; TPS ¶3170.08.]

Employers of certain members of Indian tribes or their spouses may claim a credit for their qualified wages and employee health insurance costs. The Indian employment credit is a component of the general business credit. An employer's deduction otherwise allowed for wages paid for a tax year is reduced by the Indian employment credit claimed for that tax year [§ 280C(a)].

The credit does not apply to tax years beginning after December 31, 2013 [§ 45A(f)].

*Eligibility.* The employer must be engaged in a trade or business. The credit may not be claimed by tax-exempt organizations, except for § 521 farmers' cooperatives [§ 45A(c)(4), § 45A(e)(3)].

*Amount of Credit.* The amount of the Indian employment credit equals 20% of the net incremental Indian employment wages. Net incremental Indian employment wages equals the excess of qualified wages and qualified employee health insurance costs paid or incurred during a tax year, over the sum of qualified wages and qualified employee health insurance costs paid or incurred by the employer (or predecessor employer) during calendar year 1993 [§ 45A(a)]. The aggregate amount of qualified wages and qualified health insurance costs taken into account for any employee for any tax year is limited to $20,000 [§ 45A(b)].

*Qualified Employee.* A qualified employee: (1) must be an enrolled member of an Indian tribe or the spouse of an enrolled member of an Indian tribe; (2) must perform substantially all of the services for the employer during the period within an Indian reservation; (3) must maintain his or her principal place of abode while performing the services on or near the Indian reservation within which the services are performed; and (4) must not be an ineligible employee. An ineligible employee is an employee who is paid wages at an annual rate exceeding $45,000, a non-business employee, a related individual, a 5% owner of the employer, or a gaming employee [§ 45A(c)].

*Claiming the Credit.* The credit is claimed on Form 8845, *Indian Employment Credit.* The credit amount is added to Form 3800, *General Business Credit*, except for partnerships and S corporations, which attach Form 8845 to their returns and report the amount on Schedule K. If the taxpayer's only source of this credit is from partnerships or S corporations, Form 8845 need not be completed and this credit is claimed directly on Form 3800.

### IX.A.15. Employer Social Security Credit

[506 T.M., III.A.18., 514 T.M., IV.E.; TPS ¶3170.09.]

Employers in the food and beverage industry may claim a credit for excess social security and Medicare (FICA) tax paid or incurred during the tax year. The employer social security credit is a component of the general business credit. No deduction is allowed for any amount taken into account in determining the employer social security credit [§ 45B(c)].

*Amount of Credit.* The credit is equal to the excess employer social security tax paid on applicable tips received by an employee during any month, to the extent those tips: (1) are deemed to have been paid by the employer to the employee under § 3121(q), without regard to whether the tips are reported under § 6053; and (2) exceed the amount by which the wages, excluding tips, paid by the employer to the employee during that month are less than the total amount that would be payable at the 2007 federal minimum wage rate ($5.15) [§ 45B(b)(1)].

---

**EXAMPLE:** Employee B worked 100 hours and received $450 in tips for December 2014. B received $375 in wages (excluding tips) at the rate of $3.75/hr. If B had been paid $5.15/hr, B would have received $515 in wages. For purposes of the employer social security credit, the $450 in tips is reduced by $140 (the difference between $515 and $375) and only $310 of B's tips for December 2014 are taken into account.

---

*Claiming the Credit.* The credit is claimed on Form 8846, *Credit for Employer Social Security and Medicare Taxes Paid on Certain Employee Tips.* The credit amount is added to Form 3800, *General Business Credit*, except for partnerships and S corporations, which must attach Form 8846 to their returns and report the amount on Schedule K. If the taxpayer's only source of this credit is from partnerships or S corporations, Form 8846 need not be completed and this credit is claimed directly on Form 3800.

Taxpayers may claim or elect not to claim the credit at any time within three years from the due date of the return on either the original return or on an amended return [§ 45B(d)].

### IX.A.16. Orphan Drug Credit

[506 T.M., III.A.4.; TPS ¶3170.10.]

Taxpayers may claim a credit for a portion of their expenses incurred in developing drugs for treating rare diseases and conditions. The orphan drug credit, otherwise known as the clinical drug testing credit, is a component of the general business credit. The amount of the orphan drug credit reduces the otherwise allowable deduction for the expenses of clinical testing, or, if the expenses are capitalized, the orphan drug credit amount reduces the amount capitalized [§ 280C(b)].

***Amount of Credit.*** The orphan drug credit allowable for a tax year equals 50% of the taxpayer's qualified clinical testing expenses for that year. Qualified clinical testing expenses equal the sum of qualified in-house clinical testing expenses and qualified contract clinical testing expenses. Qualified clinical testing expenses do not include any amounts funded by any grant, contract, or otherwise by another person or by a governmental entity [§ 45C(a), § 45C(b)(1)].

***In-House Clinical Testing Expenses.*** In-house clinical testing expenses include [§ 45C(b)(1)]:

- wages paid or incurred to an employee for qualified services;
- amounts paid for incurred for supplies used in the conduct of clinical testing; and
- amounts paid or incurred to another person for the right to use computers in the conduct of qualified clinical testing, except to the extent that the taxpayer receives or accrues any amount from any other person for the right to use substantially identical personal property.

***Contract Clinical Testing Expenses.*** Contract clinical testing expenses are any amount paid or incurred by the taxpayer to any person, other than the taxpayer's employee, for qualified clinical testing [§ 45C(b)(1)].

***Qualified Clinical Testing.*** Qualified clinical testing is any human clinical testing that satisfies four conditions [§ 45C(b)(2)]:

1. it must be carried out under an exemption for a drug being tested for a rare disease or condition under § 505(i) of the Federal Food, Drug, and Cosmetic Act (FFDCA) or the regulations thereunder;

2. it must occur during the qualified period that begins when the drug is designated under the designation provision of the FFDCA and ends when an application for the drug is approved, or if the drug is a biological product, when a license for the drug is issued under the Public Health Service Act;

3. it must be conducted by or on behalf of the taxpayer designated under the FFDCA as the developer; and

4. it must be related to the use of the drug for the rare disease or condition for which it was designated under § 526 of the FFDCA.

***Claiming the Credit.*** The credit is claimed on Form 8820, *Orphan Drug Credit.* The credit amount is added to Form 3800, *General Business Credit,* except for partnerships and S corporations, which must attach Form 8820 to their returns and report the amount on Schedule K. If the taxpayer's only source of this credit is from partnerships or S corporations, Form 8820 need not be completed and this credit is claimed directly on Form 3800.

***Special Rules.*** Any qualified clinical testing expenses for which the taxpayer claims the orphan drug credit may not be taken into account for purposes of determining the § 41 research credit (see IX.A.8.). However, any qualified clinical testing expenses for any tax year that are qualified research expenses for purposes of the research credit are taken into account in determining base period research expenses for purposes of applying the research credit in subsequent tax years [§ 45C(c)].

### IX.A.17. New Markets Credit

[506 T.M., III.A.11., 585 T.M., 597 T.M., IV.EE.; TPS ¶3170.11.]

The new markets tax credit was created to increase investments in low income communities. The new markets credit is a component of the general business credit.

There is an annual national designated investment limitation on the total amount of new markets credits. The limitation was $3.5 billion for 2013 [§ 45D(f)(1)(G)]. There has been no credit allocation enacted for 2014.

*Eligibility.* The credit may be claimed by a taxpayer that holds a qualified equity investment (QEI) in a qualified Community Development Entity (CDE) on a credit allowance date of the investment that occurs during the tax year.

CDEs must provide notice to any taxpayer that acquires a QEI in the CDE at its original issue that the equity investment is a QEI entitling the taxpayer to claim the new markets credit. Notice is to be provided on Form 8874-A, *Notice of Qualified Equity Investment for New Markets Credit,* no later than 60 days after the date the taxpayer makes the investment in the CDE [Reg. § 1.45D-1(g)(2)(i)(A)].

*Amount of Credit.* The total credit is up to 39% of the investment to be applied over seven years beginning with the initial qualified investment and for each of the six anniversary dates of the initial investment date.

The amount of the credit is the applicable percentage of the amount paid to the CDE for the investment at its original issue. The applicable percentage is 5% of the investment for the first three credit allowance dates, and 6% for the other four credit allowance dates [§ 45D(a)].

*Qualified Community Development Entity (CDE).* A qualified community development entity is any domestic corporation or partnership that satisfies the following three requirements [§ 45D(c)]:

1. Its primary mission must be serving, or providing investment capital for, low-income communities or low-income persons.

2. It must maintain accountability to residents of low-income communities through their representation on any governing board of the entity or on any advisory board to the entity.

3. It must be certified by the Director of the Department of Treasury Community Development Financial Institutions Fund (CDFIF) as being a CDE. Certain entities qualify without certification but must register as CDEs with CDFIF.

The primary role of the CDE in the credit program is to receive and provide "Allocation" to projects. The CDE is awarded Allocation from Treasury and can receive capital from investors and provide the tax credit to such investors, up to the maximum amount of its Allocation. The Allocation must be used by the CDE within five years of receipt. CDEs must satisfy certain reporting requirements [Reg. § 1.45D-1(g)(2)]. A CDE may be only a corporation or partnership, or a single member LLC that has elected to be taxed as an association taxable as a corporation. An LLC that has not made such an election must therefore have at least two members at all times following its formation.

*Qualified Equity Investment.* A qualified equity investment is any equity investment for which the following three conditions are satisfied [§ 45D(b)]:

1. The investment must be in a CDE, the investment must be acquired by the taxpayer at its original issue, directly or through an underwriter, solely in exchange for cash (an investor may borrow funds from a lender to finance a portion of the investment).

2. At least 85% (75% for the seventh year of the credit period) of the cash must be used by the qualified community development entity to make qualified low-income community investments (determined based on credit periods, not tax year).

3. The investment must be designated for purposes of this section by the qualified community development entity.

*Claiming the Credit.* The credit is claimed on Form 8874, *New Markets Credit.* The credit amount is added to Form 3800, *General Business Credit,* except for partnerships and S corporations, which must attach Form 8874 to their returns and report the amount on Schedule K. If the taxpayer's only source of this credit is from partnerships or S corporations, Form 8874 need not be completed and this credit is claimed directly on Form 3800.

*Termination and Recapture of Credit.* The credit terminates at the end of the seven-year credit period, or upon any termination event that requires recapture of the credit amount claimed, unless the failure that triggers termination is corrected within six months of the date the CDE becomes aware or should have become aware of the failure [§ 45D(a), § 45D(g)].

Any termination event requires recapture of the credit amount claimed in its entirety, treated as an addition to tax in the termination year and is reported on the taxpayer's income tax return [§ 45D(g)(1)].

The credit is recaptured if the entity fails to continue to be a CDE, the proceeds of the investment cease to be used as required, or the interest is redeemed or otherwise cashed out within seven years, unless it corrects its failure within six months after the date it becomes aware or should have become aware of the failure. Only one correction is permitted for each QEI during the seven-year credit period [§ 45D(g)(3)]. The IRS may waive a requirement or extend a deadline if the waiver or extension does not materially frustrate the purposes of § 45D. A waiver or extension is requested by submitting a ruling request. The IRS may require appropriate adjustments of the CDE's requirements as a condition to a waiver or extension [Reg. § 1.45D-1(e)(5)].

The amount to be recaptured is the sum of the aggregate decrease in the general business credits allowed to the taxpayer for all prior tax years that would have resulted if no new markets credit had been allowed for the investment, plus interest at the statutory underpayment rate. No deduction is allowed for the interest [§ 45D(g)(2)].

*Special Rules.* Claiming the new markets tax credit requires an adjustment in the basis of the investment in the CDE by the amount of the credit on the date of the initial investment and on each of the six anniversary dates thereafter [§ 45D(h)]. The basis is reduced even if the credit is not currently useable and is carried forward. If a QEI is held by a partnership or S corporation, the basis in the partnership interest or S corporation stock must also be adjusted [Reg. § 1.45D-1(f)(1)]. The basis adjustment does not apply for purposes of § 1202 (partial exclusion of gain from certain small business stock), § 1400B (gain from DC Zone assets) or § 1400F (gain from certain qualified community assets) [§ 45D(h); Reg. § 1.45D-1(f)(1)].

### IX.A.18. Small Employer Pension Plan Startup Cost Credit

[506 T.M., III.A.16., 514 T.M., IV.F.; TPS ¶3170.12.]

Eligible employers may claim a credit for pension plan startup costs [§ 45E(a)]. The small employer pension plan startup cost credit is a component of the general business credit.

*Eligibility.* An eligible employer is an employer that had no more than 100 employees who received at least $5,000 of compensation from the employer for the preceding tax year. An eligible employer that becomes an ineligible employer for a subsequent year is treated as an eligible employer for the two years following the last year for which the employer was an eligible employer, unless the employer becomes ineligible because of an acquisition, disposition, or similar transaction involving an eligible employer [§ 45E(a), § 408(p)(2)(C)(i)].

An employer is not eligible if, during the three-year period immediately preceding the first tax year for which the small employer pension plan startup cost credit is otherwise allowable, the employer or any member of any controlled group including the employer, or any predecessor of either, established or maintained a qualified employer plan for which contributions were made, or benefits were accrued, for substantially the same employees as are in the qualified employer plan [§ 45E(c)].

All persons treated as a single employer under § 52(a) or § 52(b) or under § 414(m) or § 414(o) are treated as one person for purposes of the small employer pension plan startup cost credit. All eligible employer plans are treated as one eligible employer plan [§ 45E(e)(1)].

*Amount of Credit.* The credit equals 50% of the qualified startup costs paid or incurred by the taxpayer during the tax year [§ 45E(a)]. For the first credit year and each of the two following tax years, the credit is limited to $500 [§ 45E(b)]. No credit is allowed for any other tax year. The first credit year is the tax year that includes the date that the employer plan to which the startup costs relate becomes effective; however, the employer may elect to treat as the first credit year the tax year preceding the tax year that would otherwise be the first credit year [§ 45E(d)(3)].

No deduction is allowed for the portion of the qualified startup costs paid or incurred for the tax year that equals the credit claimed by the taxpayer [§ 45E(e)(2)].

*Qualified Startup Costs.* Qualified startup costs are any ordinary and necessary expenses of an eligible employer that either: (1) are paid or incurred in connection with the establishment or administration of an eligible employer plan, or (2) are paid or incurred in connection with the retirement-related education of employees with respect to an eligible employer plan. Qualified startup costs do not include any expenses in connection with a plan that does not have at least one employee eligible to participate that is not a highly compensated employee [§ 45E(d)(1)].

*Eligible Employer Plan.* An eligible employer plan is any plan meeting the requirements of § 401(a) that includes a trust exempt from tax under § 501(a), a qualified § 403(a) annuity plan, a § 408(k) SEP plan, and any § 408(p) SIMPLE retirement account. It does not include any plan maintained by an employer that has at all times been exempt from the income tax, or any government plan [§ 45E(d)(2)].

*Claiming the Credit.* The credit is claimed on Form 8881, *Credit for Small Employer Pension Plan Startup Costs*. The credit amount is added to Form 3800, *General Business Credit*, except for partnerships and S corporations, which must attach Form 8881 to their returns and report the amount on Schedule K. If the taxpayer's only source of this credit is from partnerships or S corporations, Form 8881 need not be completed and this credit is claimed directly on Form 3800.

An eligible employer may elect not to claim the credit for a tax year by not claiming it on the return for that year [§ 45E(e)(3)].

### IX.A.19. Employer-Provided Child Care Credit

[506 T.M., III.A.17.; 514 T.M., IV.C.; TPS ¶3170.13.]

Employers may claim a credit for qualified child care expenditures and for qualified child care resource and referral expenditures for the tax year. The employer-provided child care credit is a component of the general business credit. No deduction or credit is allowable under any other Code provision for the employer-provided child care credit [§ 45F(f)(2)].

*Amount of Credit.* The credit equals the sum of: (1) 25% of the taxpayer's qualified child care expenditures for the tax year; and (2) 10% of the taxpayer's qualified child care resource and referral expenditures for the tax year [§ 45F(a)]. Qualified child care resource and referral expenditures are any amounts paid or incurred under a contract to provide child care resource and referral services to an employee of the taxpayer [§ 45F(c)(3)].

The employer-provided child care credit for any tax year is limited to $150,000 per taxpayer [§ 45F(b)].

*Qualified Child Care Expenditure.* A qualified child care expenditure is an amount paid or incurred [§ 45F(c)(1)]:

- to acquire, construct, rehabilitate, or expand property that (a) is to be used as part of a qualified child care facility of the taxpayer, (b) is depreciable (or amortizable) property, and (c) is not part of the principal residence of the taxpayer or any employee of the taxpayer;

- for the operating costs of a qualified child care facility of the taxpayer, including costs related to the training of employees, to scholarship programs, and to the providing of increased compensation to employees with higher levels of child care training; or

- under a contract with a qualified child care facility to provide child care services to the taxpayer's employees.

*Qualified Child Care Facility.* A qualified child care facility must satisfy two conditions: (1) the principal use of the facility must be to provide child care assistance, and (2) it must meet the requirements of all applicable laws and regulations of the state or local government in which it is located, including the licensing of the facility as a child care facility. The first condition need not be satisfied if the facility is the principal residence of the facility's operator [§ 45F(c)(2)(A)].

A facility is not treated as a qualified child care facility unless: (1) enrollment in the facility is open to all of the taxpayer's employees during the tax year; (2) if the facility is the taxpayer's principal trade or business, at least 30% of the facility's enrollees are dependents of the taxpayer's employees; and (3) use of the facility, or eligibility to use the facility, must not discriminate in favor of highly compensated employees [§ 45F(c)(2)(B)].

*Claiming the Credit.* The credit is claimed on Form 8882, *Credit for Employer-Provided Childcare Facilities and Services*. The credit amount is added to Form 3800, *General Business Credit*, except for partnerships and S corporations, which must attach Form 8882 to their returns and report the amount on Schedule K. If the taxpayer's only source of this credit is from partnerships or S corporations, Form 8882 need not be completed and this credit is claimed directly on Form 3800.

*Recapture of Credit.* If, as of the close of any tax year, there is a recapture event for any qualified child care facility of the taxpayer, then the tax for that tax year is increased by a recapture amount equal to the applicable recapture percentage multiplied by the aggregate decrease in the credits allowed under § 38 for all prior tax years that would have resulted if the taxpayer's qualified child care expenditures by reason of acquiring, constructing, rehabilitating, or expanding property had been zero [§ 45F(d)(1)].

The applicable recapture percentage is as follows:

| Years 1-3 | 100% |
|---|---|
| Year 4 | 85% |
| Year 5 | 70% |
| Year 6 | 55% |
| Year 7 | 40% |
| Year 8 | 25% |
| Years 9-10 | 10% |
| After Year 10 | 0% |

Year 1 begins on the first day of the tax year in which the qualified child care facility is placed in service by the taxpayer [§ 45F(d)(2)].

A recapture event occurs if either: (1) the facility ceases to operate as a qualified child care facility (unless the cessation is caused by the casualty loss and the facility is restored within a reasonable period of time); or (2) there is a disposition of the taxpayer's interest in the facility (not including acquisition of the facility or an interest in it by a person that agrees in writing to assume the taxpayer's recapture liability in effect immediately before the disposition) [§ 45F(d)(3)].

The adjusted basis of any facility expenditures for which there are qualified child care expenditures by reason of acquiring, constructing, rehabilitating, or expanding property, for the facility must be reduced by the amount of the employer-provided child care credit arising from the expenditures. If there is a recapture amount determined for a facility the basis of which was so reduced, the basis of the facility as of immediately before the recapture event is increased by an amount equal to the recapture amount [§ 45F(f)(1)].

### IX.A.20. Railroad Track Maintenance Credit [Expired]

[506 T.M., III.A.20.; TPS ¶3170.17.]

Eligible taxpayers may claim a credit for qualified railroad track maintenance expenditures paid or incurred [§ 45G(a)]. The railroad track maintenance credit is a component of the general business credit. The credit expired December 31, 2013 [§ 45G(f)].

*Eligibility.* Eligible taxpayers include Class II (mid-size) and Class III (small) railroads, and any person that transports property using the rail facilities of a Class II or Class III railroad or that furnishes railroad-related property or services to a Class II or Class III railroad, but only with respect to miles of railroad track assigned to that person by that Class II or Class III railroad for purposes of the limitation on the credit [§ 45G(c)]. There are special rules for controlled groups [§ 45G(e)(2)].

*Amount of Credit.* The credit is equal to 50% of qualified maintenance expenditures made during the tax year, up to the maximum credit amount, which equals $3,500 multiplied by the sum of: (1) the number of miles of eligible railroad track owned or leased by the eligible taxpayer as of the close of the tax year, and (2) the number of miles of eligible railroad track assigned for purposes of the limitation to the eligible taxpayer by a Class II or Class III railroad that owns or leases that railroad track as of the close of the tax year. For eligible taxpayers other than Class II and Class III railroads, the maximum credit amount is $3,500 multiplied by the number of eligible railroad track assigned by a Class II or Class III railroad to the eligible taxpayer for the tax year [§ 45G(b)(1)]. Any amount of the otherwise computed credit that exceeds these amounts may not be carried to another tax year [Reg. § 1.45G-1(c)(2)(iii)].

*Claiming the Credit.* The credit is claimed by filing Form 8900, *Qualified Railroad Track Maintenance Credit.* The credit amount is added to Form 3800, *General Business Credit,* except for partnerships and S corporations, which must attach Form 8900 to their returns and report the amount on Schedule K [Reg. § 1.45G-1(a)]. Form 8900 must be filed if the taxpayer assigns any mile of railroad track, even if the taxpayer is not claiming the credit for that tax year [Reg. § 1.45G-1(d)(4)]. If the taxpayer's only source of this credit is from partnerships or S corporations, Form 8900 need not be completed and the credit is claimed directly on Form 3800.

*Special Rules.* The taxpayer's basis in the railroad track is reduced by the amount of the credit allowed, but not below zero [§ 45G(e)(3)]. The reduction is limited to the amount of qualified railroad track maintenance expenditures that are required to be capitalized [Reg. § 1.45G-1(e)(1)].

### IX.A.21. Biodiesel and Renewable Diesel Fuel Credit [Expired]

[506 T.M., III.A.19., 512 T.M., III.C.; TPS ¶3170.02.A.1.]

The biodiesel fuels credit is the sum of [§ 40A(a)]:

1. the biodiesel mixture credit;

2. the biodiesel credit; and

3. the small agri-biodiesel credit.

It is a component of the general business credit. The credit expired effective for fuel produced, and sold or used, after December 31, 2013 [§ 40A(g)].

*Eligibility.* Biodiesel may be taken into account for purposes of the biodiesel mixture credit or the biodiesel credit only if the taxpayer obtains a certification from the producer or importer of the biodiesel identifying the product and the percentage of biodiesel and agri-biodiesel in the product. Certification is not required for the small agri-biodiesel producer credit [§ 40A(b)(3)].

The biodiesel must be produced and used as fuel in the United States or its possessions [§ 40A(d)(5)].

*Biodiesel Mixture Credit.* The biodiesel mixture credit rate is $1 per gallon of biodiesel used by the taxpayer in the production of a qualified biodiesel mixture [§ 40A(b)(1)].

*Biodiesel Credit.* The biodiesel credit rate is $1 per gallon of biodiesel that is not in a mixture that is used by the taxpayer as a fuel in a trade or business or is sold by the taxpayer at retail and placed in the fuel tank of the buyer's vehicle [§ 40A(b)(2)].

*Small Agri-Biodiesel Producer Credit.* The small agri-biodiesel producer credit is available to eligible producers (generally agri-biodiesel producers whose capacity does not exceed 60 million gallons per year). The credit rate is 10 cents per gallon for no more than 15 million gallons per year of qualified agri-biodiesel production [§ 40A(b)(4)].

Renewable diesel is generally treated in the same manner as biodiesel for purposes of the biodiesel mixture credit and the biodiesel credit. However, there is no credit for small producers of renewable diesel [§ 40A(f)].

The biodiesel and renewable diesel fuel credit is reduced for any excise tax credit under § 6426 or payment under § 6427(e) [§ 40A(c)].

*Claiming the Credit.* The biodiesel mixture component of the credit must be claimed first as a credit on Schedule C of Form 720, *Quarterly Federal Excise Tax Return,* against the taxpayer's § 4081 excise tax liability reported on Form 720. Any credit in excess of the § 4081 liability may be taken on Form 8849, *Claim for Refund of Excise Tax Payments*; on Form 720, Schedule C; on Form 4136, *Credit for Federal Tax Paid on Fuels*; or on Form 8864, *Biodiesel and Renewable Diesel Fuels Credit.* The other two components of the credit (biodiesel and small agri-biodiesel producer credit) may be claimed only as an income tax credit on Form 8864.

*Special Rules.* The amount of the taxpayer's biodiesel and renewable diesel fuel credit must be included in the taxpayer's gross income [§ 87(2)].

An excise tax is imposed if a biodiesel and renewable diesel fuel credit is claimed for biodiesel that is subsequently used for a purpose for which the credit is not allowed or that is changed into a substance that does not qualify for the credit. The tax is reported on Form 720, *Quarterly Federal Excise Tax Return* [§ 40A(d)(3)].

### IX.A.22. Low-Sulfur Diesel Fuel Production Credit

[506 T.M., III.A.21., 512 T.M., III.F.; TPS ¶3170.18.]

Small business refiners may claim a credit for low sulfur diesel fuel produced during the tax year. The low sulfur diesel fuel production credit is a component of the general business credit. Deductions otherwise allowable to qualified refiners are reduced by the amount of credit determined for the tax year [§ 280C(d)].

*Eligibility.* A small business refiner is a refiner of crude oil that: (1) does not have more than 1,500 individuals engaged in the refinery operations of the business on any day during the tax year, and (2) has average daily domestic refinery run or average retained production for all of its facilities for the one-year period ending on December 31, 2002, of less than or equal to 205,000 barrels [§ 45H(c)(1)].

To claim the credit, the small business refiner must obtain certification from the IRS (in consultation with EPA) that the refiner's qualified costs for a facility will cause compliance with the applicable EPA regulations [§ 45H(e)].

*Amount of Credit.* The credit is equal to $0.05 multiplied by the number of gallons of low sulfur diesel fuel produced during the tax year by the small business refiner at that facility [§ 45H(a)]. The total credits allowed for all tax years cannot be more than the refiner's qualified costs limitation [§ 45H(b)(1)].

*Qualified Costs Limitation.* The total credits allowed to a refiner cannot exceed 25% of the qualified costs paid or incurred to comply with EPA highway diesel fuel regulations during the period beginning January 1, 2003, and ending on the earlier of the date one year after the date on which the refiner must comply with the EPA requirements with respect to the facility, or December 31, 2009. For refiners that had average daily refinery runs of more than 155,000 barrels in 2002, the 25% is reduced (but not below zero) by multiplying it by one minus the excess over 155,000 barrels divided by 50,000 barrels [§ 45H(b)(2)].

Qualified costs include expenditures for the construction of new process operation units or the dismantling and reconstruction of existing process units to be used in the production of low sulfur diesel fuel, associated adjacent or offsite equipment (including tankage, catalyst, and power supply), engineering, construction period interest, and site work [§ 45H(c)(2)].

*Claiming the Credit.* The credit is claimed on Form 8896, *Low Sulfur Diesel Fuel Production Credit.* The credit amount is added to Form 3800, *General Business Credit,* except for partnerships and S corporations, which must attach Form 8896 to their returns and report the amount on Schedule K. If the taxpayer's only source of this credit is from partnerships or S corporations, Form 8896 need not be completed and this credit is claimed directly on Form 3800.

A taxpayer may elect to forgo the low sulfur diesel fuel production credit for a tax year [§ 45H(g)].

### IX.A.23. Marginal Oil and Gas Well Production Credit

[506 T.M., III.A.22., 512 T.M., III.G., 605 T.M., V.B.; TPS ¶3170.19.]

A credit for producing oil and natural gas from marginal wells is available to taxpayers holding an operating interest in a marginal well. The marginal oil and gas well production credit is a component of the general business credit.

*Amount of Credit.* The marginal oil and gas well production credit for any tax year equals the credit amount ($3 per barrel of qualified crude oil production ($.50 per 1,000 cubic feet of qualified natural gas production) multiplied by an inflation adjustment factor) multiplied by the qualified crude oil production and the qualified natural gas production attributable to the taxpayer [§ 45I(b)(1)]. Qualified production is domestic crude oil or natural gas produced from a qualified marginal well (as defined in § 45I(c)(3)(A)).

The credit is reduced by a phase-out amount, but not below zero, calculated by using reference prices for oil and gas [§ 45I(b)(2)]. The credit is fully phased out if reference prices exceed $18 for crude oil and $2 for natural gas production. Because the prices of oil and natural gas have been high in recent years, the credit has been entirely phased out since enactment.

### IX.A.24. Distilled Spirits Excise Tax Carrying Credit

[506 T.M., III.A.23.; TPS ¶3170.20.]

Distillers and importers of distilled spirits and eligible wholesalers are eligible to claim the distilled spirits excise tax carrying credit, also known as the distilled spirits credit. The distilled spirits excise tax carrying credit is a component of the general business credit.

*Eligibility.* An eligible wholesaler is any person that: (1) holds a permit under the Federal Alcohol Administration Act as a wholesaler of distilled spirits; and (2) is not a state, a political subdivision of a state, a state agency, or a political subdivision agency [§ 5011(b)].

*Amount of Credit.* The distilled spirits credit for the tax year equals the number of qualified cases (stored cases for distillers and importers of distilled spirits that are not eligible wholesalers) of bottled distilled spirits multiplied by the average tax-financing cost per case (as defined in § 5011(c)) for the most recent calendar year ending before the beginning of the tax year [§ 5011(a)(1)].

*Claiming the Credit.* The credit is claimed by filing Form 8906, *Distilled Spirits Credit,* with the tax return for the year for which the credit is claimed. The credit amount is added to Form 3800, *General Business Credit,* except for partnerships and S corporations, which must attach Form 8906 to their returns and report the amount on Schedule K [Reg. § 1.45D-1(g)(2)]. Taxpayers that are not partnerships or S corporations, and for whom the only source of the credit is from passthrough entities, are not required to complete Form 8906 and can report the credit directly on Form 3800.

### IX.A.25. Advanced Nuclear Power Facilities Production Credit

[506 T.M., III.A.24., 512 T.M., VII.D.; TPS ¶3170.21.]

Taxpayers may claim a credit for producing electricity at a qualifying advanced nuclear power facility. The advanced nuclear power facilities production credit is a component of the general business credit.

*Eligibility.* The advanced nuclear power facility must be placed in service after August 8, 2005, and before January 1, 2021 [§ 45J(d)].

*Amount of Credit.* The credit is equal to 1.8 cents per kilowatt hour of electricity sold to an unrelated person during each tax year during the eight-year period starting with the date the facility was originally placed in service [§ 45J(a)].

The otherwise allowable advanced nuclear power production credit is reduced by the phase-out amount, which equals the credit that would otherwise be allowable multiplied by a fraction, the numerator of which is the reference price excess, and the denominator of which is three cents. The reference price excess equals the reference price for the calendar year in which the sale of the nuclear generated electricity occurs, less eight cents (adjusted for inflation) [§ 45J(c)(2)]. The credit is also subject to a limitation based on Treasury's allocation of the national megawatt capacity limitation, [§ 45J(c)(1)].

As of 2014, no facility has qualified for the credit and the IRS has not issued forms or instructions.

### IX.A.26. Nonconventional Source Fuels Credit [Expired]

[506 T.M., III.A.25., 512 T.M., III.H., 603 T.M., XVIII.A., 605 T.M., VII.B.; TPS ¶3170.22.]

Taxpayers may claim a credit for selling qualified nonconventional source fuels. The nonconventional source fuel credit is a component of the general business credit.

For all qualified fuels except coke and coke gas, the credit previously expired. For facilities producing coke and coke gas, the credit effectively expired December 31, 2013, because it is only available to facilities placed in service before January 1, 2010, and terminates four years after the date placed in service [§ 45K(g)(1)].

*Eligibility.* Producers of fuel from nonconventional sources are eligible for the credit, including those with royalty or net profits interests [§ 45K(d)(3)].

*Amount of Credit.* The credit is equal to $3 (inflation-adjusted to $3.59 for 2013) multiplied by the barrel-of-oil equivalent [§ 45K(a)] of qualified fuel produced within the United States or its possessions [§ 45K(d)(1)] by the taxpayer and sold to an unrelated person during the tax year [§ 45K(a)].

The amount of qualified fuel eligible for the credit during any tax year is limited to an average barrel-of-oil equivalent of 4,000 barrels per day, excluding any days before the facility is placed in service [§ 45K(g)(2)(A)].

The credit is reduced in proportion to any federal, state, and local grants, subsidized energy loans, and tax-exempt financing provided in connection with the project, determined as of the close of the tax year, and is further reduced for the energy credit and the enhanced oil recovery credit [§ 45K(b)].

*Claiming the Credit.* The credit is claimed on Form 8907, *Nonconventional Source Fuel Credit.* The credit amount is added to Form 3800, *General Business Credit,* except for partnerships and S corporations, which must attach Form 8907 to their returns and report the amount on Schedule K. If the taxpayer's only source of this credit is from partnerships or S corporations, Form 8907 need not be completed and this credit is claimed directly on Form 3800.

465

The credit is not allowed for any qualified nonconventional source fuel for which a credit is allowed under § 45 (electricity produced from certain renewable sources) [§ 45K(g)(2)(E)], or for any facility that received a credit under former § 29 [§ 45K(g)(2)(C)].

### IX.A.27. New Energy Efficient Home Credit [Expired]

[506 T.M., III.A.26., 512 T.M., VI.C., 590 T.M., III.D.5.; TPS ¶3170.23.]

Eligible contractors may claim a credit for building and selling eligible energy efficient homes. The new energy efficient home credit is a component of the general business credit. The credit does not apply to homes acquired after December 31, 2013 [§ 45L(g)]. If a new energy efficient home credit is allowed for an expenditure for any property, the increase in the basis of that property that would otherwise result from that expenditure must be reduced by the credit amount [§ 45L(e)].

*Eligibility.* An eligible contractor is the person that constructed the new energy efficient home, or, for a qualified new energy efficient home that is a manufactured home, the manufactured home producer [§ 45L(b)(1)]. The credit is not available to homebuyers.

Eligible homes must be: (1) certified qualified new energy efficient homes; (2) constructed by the eligible contractor; and (3) acquired by another person from the eligible contractor for use as a residence during the tax year [§ 45L(a)(1)]. Construction includes substantial reconstruction and rehabilitation [§ 45L(b)(3)]. Eligible homes may not be used by the contractor as a personal residence.

*Amount of Credit.* For certified new homes and certified manufactured homes, the credit amount is $2,000 per qualified home. For alternatively certified (under less stringent requirements) manufactured homes and Energy Star manufactured homes, the applicable amount is $1,000 [§ 45L(a)(2)].

*Claiming the Credit.* The credit is claimed on Form 8908, *Energy Efficient Home Credit.* The credit amount is added to Form 3800, *General Business Credit,* except for partnerships and S corporations, which must attach Form 8908 to their returns and report the amount on Schedule K. If the taxpayer's only source of this credit is from partnerships or S corporations, Form 8908 need not be completed and the credit is claimed directly on Form 3800.

Expenditures taken into account for the rehabilitation or energy credits may not be taken into account for purposes of the new energy efficient home credit [§ 45L(f)].

### IX.A.28. Energy Efficient Appliance Credit [Expired]

[506 T.M., III.A.27., 512 T.M., VI.D.; TPS ¶3170.24.]

Manufacturers may claim a credit for producing qualified energy efficient appliances, including dishwashers, clothes washers and refrigerators. The energy efficient appliance credit is a component of the general business credit. The energy efficient appliance credit does not apply to appliances acquired after December 31, 2013 [§ 45M(b)]. The energy efficient appliance credit is not available to tax-exempt organizations, except § 521 farmers' cooperatives [§ 45M(g)(1)].

*Amount of Credit.* The amount of the energy efficient appliance credit is the sum of credit amounts for each type of appliance. For each type of appliance, the eligible production is multiplied by the applicable amount per appliance for the credit amount for each appliance type [§ 45M(a)].

Eligible production is the number of the appliance produced by the taxpayer during the tax year less the average number of such appliance produced by the taxpayer during the preceding two-year period.

For 2013, the applicable amounts were:

- Dishwashers, $75

- Clothes washers, $225, and

- Refrigerators, $150 for those consuming at least 30% less energy than the 2001 energy conservation standards, and $200 for those consuming at least 35% less energy than the 2001 energy standards [§ 45M(b)].

The aggregate credit amount for a taxpayer for any tax year is $25 million, less the amount of the credit allowed for all prior years beginning after 2010, without taking into account clothes washers for which the $225 credit amount was claimed, or refrigerators for which the $200 credit amount was claimed. The credit amount allowed for the tax year may not exceed 4% of the taxpayer's average annual gross receipts for the three tax years preceding the tax year for which the credit is claimed [§ 45M(e)].

*Claiming the Credit.* The credit is claimed on Form 8909, *Energy Efficient Appliance Credit*. The credit amount is added to Form 3800, *General Business Credit*, except for partnerships and S corporations, which must attach Form 8909 to their returns and report the amount on Schedule K. If the taxpayer's only source of this credit is from partnerships or S corporations, Form 8909 need not be completed and the credit is claimed directly on Form 3800.

### IX.A.29. Alternative Motor Vehicle Credit

[506 T.M., III.A.28., 512 T.M., VI.F.; TPS ¶3130.06., ¶3170.25.]

Taxpayers may claim a credit for placing in service alternative motor vehicles. The business portion of the alternative motor vehicle credit is a component of the general business credit All components of the alternative motor vehicle credit, except the qualified fuel cell motor vehicle credit, expired before 2014. The qualified fuel cell motor vehicle credit expires for property purchased after December 31, 2014 [§ 30B(i)(4), § 30B(k)]. The credit is discussed in IX.D.1.

*Claiming the Credit.* The credit is claimed on Form 8910, *Alternative Motor Vehicle Credit*. The business portion is added to Form 3800, *General Business Credit*, except for partnerships and S corporations, which must attach Form 8910 to their returns and report the amount on Schedule K. If the taxpayer's only source of this credit is from partnerships or S corporations, Form 8910 need not be completed and this credit is claimed directly on Form 3800.

### IX.A.30. Alternative Fuel Vehicle Refueling Property Credit

[506 T.M., III.A.29., 512 T.M., VI.G.; TPS ¶3170.26.]

Taxpayers may claim a credit for placing in service qualified alternative-fuel vehicle refueling property. The business portion of the alternative fuel vehicle refueling property credit is a component of the general business credit. For property relating to hydrogen, the credit expires December 31, 2014. The credit expired for all other property December 31, 2013 [§ 30C(g)]. The credit is discussed in IX.D.2.

*Claiming the Credit.* The credit is claimed on Form 8911, *Alternative Fuel Vehicle Refueling Property Credit*. The business portion is added to Form 3800, *General Business Credit*, except for partnerships and S corporations, which must attach Form 8911 to their returns and report the amount on Schedule K. If the taxpayer's only source of this credit is from partnerships or S corporations, Form 8911 need not be completed and this credit is claimed directly on Form 3800.

### IX.A.31. Mine Rescue Team Training Credit [Expired]

[506 T.M., III.A.37., 603 T.M., XVIII.D.; TPS ¶3170.29.]

A credit is allowed for any taxpayer that employs individuals as miners in underground mines in the United States for the mine rescue team training expenses for each qualified mine rescue team employee [§ 45N]. The credit is a component of the general business credit. No deduction is allowed for those expenses for which the credit is claimed that would otherwise have been allowable as a deduction for the tax year in an amount equal to the claimed credit [§ 280C(e)].

The credit expired on December 31, 2013.

*Amount of Credit.* The credit is equal to the 20% of the expenditures the taxpayer paid or incurred during the tax year for mine rescue team training program costs of each employee, including the employee's wages while attending the program, but not over $10,000. The 20%/$10,000 limit applies per employee [§ 45N(a)].

*Claiming the Credit.* The credit is claimed on Form 8923, *Mine Rescue Team Training Credit.* The credit amount is added to Form 3800, *General Business Credit,* except for partnerships and S corporations, which must attach Form 8923 to their returns and report the amount on Schedule K. If the taxpayer's only source of this credit is from partnerships or S corporations, Form 8923 need not be completed and this credit is claimed directly on Form 3800.

### IX.A.32. Carbon Dioxide Sequestration Credit

[506 T.M., III.A.40., 512 T.M., VI.I.; TPS ¶3170.32.]

Taxpayers may claim a credit for sequestering qualified carbon dioxide ($CO_2$) that otherwise would have been released into the atmosphere. The carbon dioxide sequestration credit is a component of the general business credit.

*Eligibility.* To be eligible for the credit, the taxpayer must own a qualified industrial facility at which carbon capture equipment is placed in service and that captures not less than 500,000 metric tons of carbon dioxide during the tax year [§ 45Q(c)].

Qualified $CO_2$ is $CO_2$ from industrial sources that otherwise would have been released into the atmosphere as industrial emission of greenhouse gas and must be measured at the source of capture and verified at the point of disposal or injection [§ 45Q(b)]. It does not include $CO_2$ that is recaptured, recycled and re-injected as part of the enhanced oil and natural gas recovery process. The $CO_2$ must be captured and either disposed or used within the United States or its possessions [§ 45Q(d)(1)].

*Amount of Credit.* The credit is the sum of the secured carbon dioxide credit and the reused carbon dioxide credit.

The secured carbon dioxide credit is equal to $20 (adjusted for inflation to $21.51 for 2014) per metric ton of qualified $CO_2$ that the taxpayer captures at a qualified facility and disposes of in secure geological storage, and not used as a tertiary injectant in a qualified enhanced oil or natural gas recovery project [§ 45Q(a)(1)].

The reused carbon dioxide credit is equal to $10 (adjusted for inflation to $10.75 for 2014) per metric ton of qualified $CO_2$ that the taxpayer captures at a qualified facility and uses as a tertiary injectant in a qualified enhanced oil or natural gas recovery project, and disposes of in secure geological storage [§ 45Q(a)(2)].

*Claiming the Credit.* The credit is claimed on Form 8933, *Carbon Dioxide Sequestration Credit.* The credit amount is added to Form 3800, *General Business Credit,* except for partnerships and S corporations, which must attach Form 8933 to their returns and report the amount on Schedule K. If the taxpayer's only source of this credit is from partnerships or S corporations, Form 8933 need not be completed and this credit is claimed directly on Form 3800.

The credit is available until the end of the year in which the IRS certifies, in consultation with the EPA, that 75 million metric tons of qualified $CO_2$ have been taken into account for purposes of the credit [§ 45Q(e)].

*Recapture of Credit.* Taxpayers must recapture the benefit of any carbon dioxide sequestration credit allowable for any qualified $CO_2$ that ceases to be captured, disposed of, or used as a tertiary injectant in a manner consistent with the requirements to claim the credit [§ 45Q(d)(6)].

### IX.A.33. Qualified Plug-In Electric Drive Motor Vehicle Credit

[506 T.M., III.A.41., 512 T.M., VI.H.; TPS ¶3170.33.]

Taxpayers may claim a credit for placing in service new qualified plug-in motor vehicles for the tax year in which the vehicle is placed in service. The portion of the qualified plug-in electric drive motor vehicle credit attributable to depreciable property (i.e., business vehicles) is a component of the general business credit. The credit is discussed in IX.D.3.

*Claiming the Credit.* The credit is claimed on Form 8936, *Qualified Plug-in Electric Drive Motor Vehicle Credit.* The business portion is added to Form 3800, *General Business Credit,* except for partnerships and S corporations, which must attach Form 8936 to their returns and report the amount on Schedule K. If the taxpayer's only source of this credit is from partnerships or S corporations, Form 8936 need not be completed and this credit is claimed directly on Form 3800.

### IX.A.34. Small Employer Health Insurance Credit

[389 T.M., XVIII.B.2., 506 T.M., III.A.43., 514 T.M., IV.J.; TPS ¶3170.35.]

Eligible small employers may claim a credit for certain expenditures to provide health insurance coverage for their employees through a small business health options program (SHOP) exchange. For tax years 2010-2013, the credit applied to other forms of insurance coverage.

An employer's § 162 deduction for health insurance expenses must be reduced by the amount of any § 45R credit for that year [§ 280C(h); Reg. § 1.45R-5(c)].

### IX.A.34.a. Eligibility for Small Employer Health Insurance Credit

[389 T.M., XVIII.B., 506 T.M., III.A.43., 514 T.M., IV.J.; TPS ¶3170.35.C.]

Four requirements must be met for a taxpayer to be an eligible small employer: (1) it must offer health insurance coverage to its employees; (2) it must have no more than 25 full-time equivalent (FTE) employees for the tax year; (3) it must pay average annual wages (as defined in § 3121(a)) of no more than $50,000 adjusted for inflation ($50,800 for 2014; $51,600 for 2015); and (4) it must have a contribution arrangement through which it pays at least half of the insurance premiums for its employees at the employee-only coverage rate [§ 45R(d)(1); Rev. Proc. 2014-61, 2014-47 I.R.B. 860].

*Employee.* An employee is an individual who is an employee of the eligible small employer under the common law standard, but also includes leased employee (as defined in § 414(n)). Seasonal workers are not employees for purposes of the credit unless the seasonal worker provides services to the employer on more than 120 days during the tax year [Reg. § 1.45R-1(a)(5)].

For purposes of the credit, the following individuals are excluded from the definition of "employee":

- independent contractors;

- self-employed individuals;
- 2% shareholders of S corporations;
- 5% owners of other businesses; or
- Related individuals and dependents [§ 45R(e)(1)(A)].

FTEs are determined by dividing the total number of hours of service for which wages paid during the tax year by 2,080 [§ 45R(d)(2)].

*2014 Health Insurance Coverage.* For purposes of eligibility for the credit for tax years beginning in or after 2014, an employer must make a nonelective contribution on behalf of each employee who enrolls in a qualified health plan (QHP) offered to employees through a SHOP Exchange in an amount equal to a uniform percentage (not less than 50%) of the premium cost of the QHP [§ 45R(d); Reg. § 1.45R-1(a)(14), § 1.45R-2(a), § 1.45R-3(a)]. Transition relief is available for employers that are located in a county that does not having qualified health plans available for the calendar year 2014 SHOP Exchange. Those employers may provide health insurance coverage that qualifies under the pre-2014 rules [Notice 2014-6, 2014-2 I.R.B. 279].

*Pre-2014 Health Insurance Coverage.* For tax years beginning before 2014, see Notice 2010-44, 2010-22 I.R.B. 717, and Notice 2010-82, 2010-51 I.R.B. 857.

An employer located in a U.S. territory or foreign country that has income effectively connected with the conduct of a trade or business in the United States may claim the credit if the coverage for which it pays premiums is issued in and regulated by a state or the District of Columbia [Reg. § 1.45R-2(a)].

### IX.A.34.b. *Computing Small Employer Health Insurance Credit*

[389 T.M., XVIII.B., 506 T.M., III.A.43., 514 T.M., IV.J.; TPS ¶3170.35.B.]

The credit is calculated in three steps:

1. Calculate the maximum credit amount.

2. Reduce the maximum amount in accordance with the phaseout.

3. For employers receiving a state credit or subsidy for health insurance, determine the employer's actual premium payment.

*Maximum Credit Amount.* For tax years beginning in 2014, the maximum credit amount is 50% (35% for a tax-exempt eligible small employer) of the lesser of: (1) the aggregate amount of nonelective contributions the employer made for its employees under a contribution arrangement for qualified health plan premiums offered by the employer to its employees through an Exchange; or (2) the aggregate amount of nonelective contributions that the employer would have made to such an arrangement if each employee had enrolled in a qualified health plan that had a premium equal to the average premium for the small group market in the rating area in which the employee enrolls for coverage [§ 45R(b)].

The total premium cost per employee of a qualified health plan does not include employee contributions made pursuant to salary reduction arrangements [§ 45R(e)(3)].

*Phase-Out.* The credit phases out gradually for eligible small employers if the number of full time equivalent employees (FTEs) exceeds 10 or if the average annual wages exceed $25,000, adjusted for inflation ($25,400 for 2014; $25,800 for 2015), and is phased out completely for employers with 25 or more FTEs or an average annual per-employee wage of $50,000 or more, adjusted for inflation ($50,800 for 2014; $51,600 for 2015). The credit is reduced by the sum of:

- the maximum credit amount multiplied by a fraction, the numerator of which is the total number of the employer's FTEs in excess of 10 and the denominator of which is 15; and

- the maximum credit amount multiplied by a fraction, the numerator of which is the average annual wages paid by the employer in excess of $25,400 (or $25,800 for 2015) and the denominator of which is $25,400 ($25,800 for 2015) [§ 45R(c); Rev. Proc. 2014-61].

---

**EXAMPLE:** For the 2014 tax year, a taxable eligible small employer has 12 FTEs and average annual wages of $30,000. The employer pays $96,000 in health insurance premiums for its employees (which does not exceed the average premium for the small group market in the employer's state) and otherwise meets the requirements for the credit.

---

The credit is $32,907, calculated as follows:

1. Initial amount of credit determined before any reduction: (50% × $96,000) = $48,000

2. Credit reduction for FTEs in excess of 10: ($48,000 × 2/15) = $6,400

3. Credit reduction for average annual wages in excess of $25,000: ($48,000 × ($4,600 ÷ $25,400)) = $8,693

4. Total credit reduction: ($6,400 + $8,693) = $15,093

5. Total 2014 tax credit equals $32,907 ($48,000 − $15,093).

*State Credits and Subsidies.* Generally, the credit is not reduced if the employer receives a state tax credit for employee health insurance premiums or a state premium subsidy that is paid directly to the employer. If a state makes subsidy payments directly to an insurance company (or another entity licensed under state law to engage in the business of insurance), the state is treated as making the payments on behalf of the employer, and the premium payments are treated as an employer contribution.

However, the amount of the credit may not exceed the amount of the employer's net premium payments. Where a state tax credit or a subsidy is paid directly to an employer, the employer's net premium payments are calculated by subtracting the tax credit or subsidy from the employer's actual premium payments. Where a state subsidy payment is made directly to an insurance company, the employer's net premium payments are the employer's actual premium payments [Notice 2010-44].

If a state-administered program (such as Medicaid or another program that makes payments directly to a health care provider or insurance company on behalf of eligible individuals) makes payments that are not contingent on the maintenance of an employer-provided group health plan, those payments are not taken into account in calculating the credit [Notice 2010-44, 2010-22 I.R.B. 717, *amplified by* Notice 2010-82, 2010-51 I.R.B. 857].

### IX.A.34.c. *Claiming the Small Employer Health Insurance Credit*

[389 T.M., XVIII.B.2.g., 506 T.M., III.A.43., 514 T.M., IV.J.; TPS ¶3170.35.G.]

The credit is available for a maximum coverage period of two consecutive tax years beginning with the first tax year in which the employer (or any predecessor) offers one or more qualified health plans to its employees through an Exchange. The employer may claim the credit in any tax year of the credit period [§ 45R(a), § 45R(e)(2)].

The credit is claimed on Form 8941, *Credit for Small Employer Health Insurance Premiums.* For non-tax exempt employers, the credit amount is added to Form 3800, *General Business Credit,* except for partnerships, S corporations, cooperatives, estates and trusts, which must attach Form 8941 to their returns and report the amount on Schedule K. If the taxpayer's only source of this credit is from passthrough entities, Form 8941 need not be completed and this credit is claimed directly on Form 3800.

Tax exempt employers claim the credit on Form 8941 and then add the amount to Form 990-T, *Exempt Organization Business Income Tax Return,* as a refundable credit.

## IX.B. Nonrefundable Personal Credits

### IX.B.1. Household and Dependent Care Credit

[513 T.M., III.D.; TPS ¶3120.01.]

Eligible taxpayers may claim a nonrefundable credit for a portion of the qualifying child or dependent care expenses incurred while working out of the home or actively seeking employment.

*Eligibility.* To be eligible, the taxpayer must incur eligible employment-related expenses for the care of one or more "qualified persons," who include: (1) the taxpayer's dependent under age 13; (2) a dependent of the taxpayer who is physically or mentally incapable of self-care; or (3) a taxpayer's spouse who is physically or mentally incapable of self-care [§ 21(b)(1)].

CAN YOU CLAIM THE CREDIT?

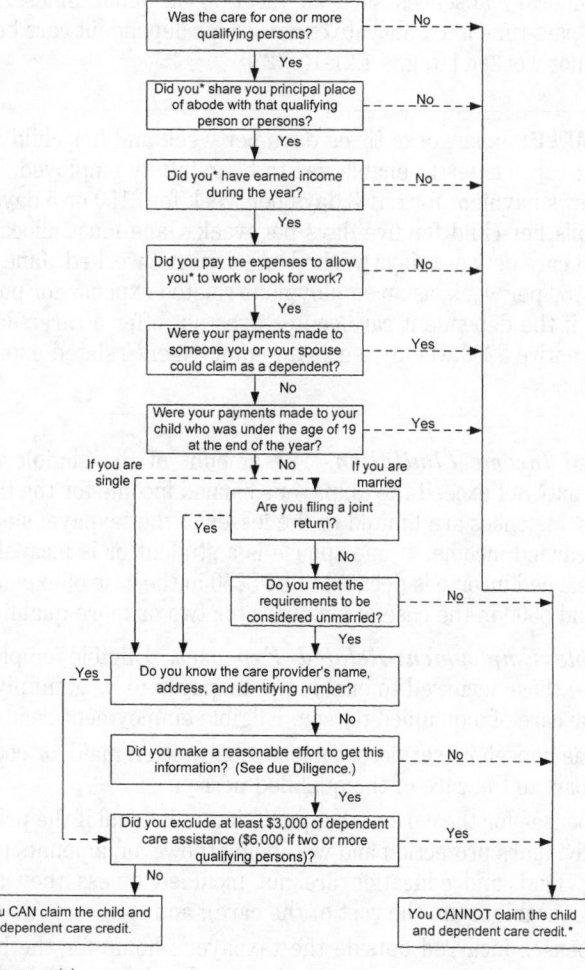

(Source: IRS Pub. 17)

*Amount of Credit.* The amount of the credit is equal to the applicable percentage multiplied by the eligible employment-related expenses. For taxpayers with adjusted gross income of $15,000 or less, the applicable percentage is 35%, reduced by one percentage point (but not below 20%) for each $2,000 or fraction thereof by which the taxpayer's AGI exceeds $15,000. The 20% figure is reached at an AGI of $43,000 [§ 21(a)(2)].

*Limitation on Expenses.* The maximum amount of eligible employment-related expenses that may be taken into account is $3,000 for expenses for one qualified person, and $6,000 for expenses for two or more qualified persons. The limitation amount is reduced by the amount excludable from the taxpayer's gross income for employer-provided dependent care assistance programs under § 129 [§ 21(c)] (see XVII.E.2.).

Expenses must be allocated in any year in which the taxpayer is gainfully employed or actively pursuing gainful employment for less than the full year, but not for short, temporary absences such as vacation or minor illness. A taxpayer who is employed part-time must allocate expenses for dependent care between days worked and days not worked [Reg. § 1.21-1(c)(2)].

---

**EXAMPLE:** Jane works three days per week and her child attends a qualifying dependent care center to enable her to be gainfully employed. The dependent care center allows payment for any 3 days per week for $150 or 5 days per week for $250. Jane enrolls her child for five days per week. Jane must allocate her expenses for dependent care between days worked and days not worked. Jane may claim 3/5 of the $250, or $150 per week, as an employment-related expense for purposes of the credit. However, if the dependent care center does not offer a three-day option, Jane may claim the entire $250 weekly fee as an employment-related expense for purposes of the credit.

---

*Earned Income Limitation.* The amount of the eligible employment-related expenses may not exceed the taxpayer's earned income for the tax year. For married taxpayers, expenses are limited to the lesser of the taxpayer's earned income or the spouse's earned income. If one spouse is a student or is incapable of self-care, that spouse's earned income is deemed to be $250 in the case of expenses for one qualified person, and $500 in the case of expenses for two or more qualified persons [§ 21(d)].

*Eligible Employment-Related Expenses.* Eligible employment related expenses are those incurred to enable the taxpayer to be gainfully employed and that are for the care of a qualified person. Eligible employment-related expenses include:

- some household services, such as a babysitter, maid, or cook, if related at least in part to the care of the qualified person;
- expenses for the care of the qualifying individual if the primary purpose is the individual's protection and well-being (however, amounts paid to provide clothing, food, and education are not included unless they are incident to, and inseparable from, the cost of the care); and
- expenses incurred outside the taxpayer's home for the benefit of a qualified person if that person regularly spends at least eight hours a day in the taxpayer's home.

A taxpayer may claim a credit for services provided outside the taxpayer's home by a dependent care center that (1) provides care for more than six individuals who do not reside at the facility; and (2) receives payment or grants for providing the services only if the center complies with all applicable state or local laws and regulations.

Eligible expenses can include amounts paid for items other than the care of a child (such as food and schooling) if the items are incidental to the care of the child and cannot be separated from the total cost. However, the cost of schooling for a child in kindergarten or above is not an eligible expense.

Eligible expenses can include the cost of a day camp, even if it specializes in a particular activity, such as computers or soccer. However, eligible expenses cannot include any expenses for sending a dependent to an overnight camp, summer school, or a tutoring program [§ 21(b)(2); Reg. § 1.21-1(d)].

**EXAMPLE:** To be gainfully employed, Natalie sends her nine-year-old child to a summer day camp that offers computer activities and recreational activities such as swimming and arts and crafts. The full cost of the summer day camp is eligible for the credit.

**EXAMPLE:** To be gainfully employed, Oliver sends his nine-year-old child to a math tutoring program for two hours per day during the summer. The cost of the tutoring program is eligible for the credit.

---

The credit is not permitted for payments to a dependent of the taxpayer or his spouse, a child of the taxpayer under age 19 at the end of the tax year, the taxpayer's spouse, or the parent of the taxpayer's child that is a qualified person [§ 21(e)(6); Reg. § 1.21-4(a)].

*Tax Liability Limitation.* The total amount of all nonrefundable personal credits, including the dependent care credit, is allowed to the full extent of the taxpayer's regular tax (as defined in § 26(b)) reduced by the foreign tax credit, plus any alternative minimum tax [§ 26(a)]. Unused credit may not be carried forward.

*Claiming the Credit.* The credit for child and dependent care expenses is claimed by completing Form 2441, *Child and Dependent Care Expenses,* and attaching it to Form 1040 or 1040A. The credit cannot be claimed on Form 1040EZ. The taxpayer identification number (TIN) must be provided for the qualifying individual, and the name, address and TIN of any service provider must be provided [§ 21(e)(9), § 21(e)(10)].

If the taxpayer is married at the close of the tax year, the taxpayer must file a joint return with his spouse in order to claim the credit [§ 21(e)(2)].

*Divorced or Separated Parents.* A child of divorced or legally separated taxpayers is considered the qualifying individual with respect to the custodial parent regardless of which parent may claim the dependency exemption for the child for that tax year [§ 21(e)(5), Reg. § 1.21-1(b)(5)(ii)].

### IX.B.2. Credit for the Elderly and Disabled

[513 T.M., III.E.; TPS ¶3120.02.]

Qualified individual taxpayers may claim a credit on account of being elderly or permanently and totally disabled.

*Eligibility.* A qualified individual is any individual who either has attained age 65 or retired on disability before the close of the tax year and who, at the time of retirement, was permanently and totally disabled [§ 22(b)]. A nonresident alien is not a qualified individual [§ 22(f)].

*Amount of Credit.* The credit is equal to 15% multiplied by the individual's "§ 22 amount" for the tax year. The § 22 amount is the initial amount, reduced by the benefits amount, and reduced by the excess adjusted gross income amount [§ 22(c)].

The initial amount is $5,000 for a single individual, or joint filers where only one spouse is a qualified individual; $7,500 in the case of a joint return where both spouses are qualified individuals; or $3,750 in the case of a married individual filing separately. If the taxpayer has not attained age 65, the initial amount is limited to the taxpayer's disability income for the tax year. For qualified individuals filing joint returns where one spouse has not attained age 65, the initial amount is limited to $5,000 plus the disability income for the spouse that has not attained age 65. For joint filers where neither spouse has attained age 65, the initial amount is limited to the sum of the spouses' disability income [§ 22(c)(2)].

An individual is permanently and totally disabled if he is unable to engage in any substantial gainful activity by reason of any medically determinable physical or mental impairment which can be expected to result in death or which has lasted or can be expected to last for a continuous period of not less than 12 months [§ 22(e)(3)].

The initial amount is reduced by the amounts received by the individual as a pension, annuity or disability benefit that is excludable from gross income. Amounts received as pensions, annuities, or other allowances for personal injuries or sickness resulting from active duty in the armed forces of any country, Public Health Service, Foreign Service, or U.S. Coast and Geodetic Survey do not reduce the initial amount [§ 22(c)(3)].

The initial amount is further reduced by one-half of the excess of the taxpayer's adjusted gross income over the adjusted gross income limitation amount. The adjusted gross income limitation amount is $7,500 for single taxpayers; $10,000 for married taxpayers filing joint returns; and $5,000 for married taxpayers filing separately [§ 22(d)].

---

**EXAMPLE:** A married couple, both over age 65, have AGI of $10,800 and combined nontaxable social security benefits of $6,600. Their credit for the elderly is computed as follows:

| Initial amount | $ 7,500 |
|---|---|
| Less: social security benefits | 6,600 |
| Reduced initial amount | 900 |
| Less: 1/2 AGI in excess of $10,000 | 400 |
| Creditable amount | 500 |
| Credit for the elderly: 500 X 15% | $    75 |

---

*Tax Liability Limitation.* The total amount of all nonrefundable personal credits, including the credit for the elderly and disabled, is allowed to the full extent of the taxpayer's regular tax (as defined in § 26(b)) reduced by the foreign tax credit, plus the alternative minimum tax [§ 26(a)]. Unused credit may not be carried forward.

*Claiming the Credit.* The credit for the elderly is claimed by completing Schedule R, *Credit for the Elderly or the Disabled,* and attaching it to Form 1040 or Form 1040A. The credit cannot be claimed on Form 1040EZ. If a taxpayer is claiming the credit as disabled, a physician's statement generally is required to support the condition.

Married taxpayer may claim the credit only on joint returns, unless the spouses live apart at all times during the tax year [§ 22(e)(1)].

### IX.B.3. Adoption Expense Credit

[513 T.M., III.F.; TPS ¶3120.03.]

Individual taxpayers may claim a credit for qualified expenses paid or incurred in adopting an eligible child. An individual taxpayer may claim both a credit and an exclusion from gross income in connection with the adoption of an eligible child, but the credit and exclusion may not be claimed for the same expenses [§ 23(b)(3)] (see XVII.E.1.).

*Eligibility.* An eligible child is an individual who either has not attained age 18 or is physically or mentally incapable of self-care [§ 23(d)(2)].

*Amount of Credit.* The maximum credit amount per child for 2014 is $13,190 ($13,400 for 2015) [Rev. Proc. 2013-35, 2013-47 I.R.B. 537; Rev. Proc. 2014-61, 2014-47 I.R.B. 860]. The unused portion of the credit may be carried forward up to five years after the tax year in which the credit arose [§ 23(c)].

For adoption of a child with special needs that becomes final during a tax year, even if the taxpayer has not paid the maximum credit amount in qualified adoption expenses, the taxpayer is treated as having paid qualified adoption expenses for the adoption in an amount equal to the excess (if any) of the credit amount for that year over the aggregate qualified adoption expenses actually paid or incurred for that adoption during that and all prior tax years [§ 23(a)(3)].

For 2014, the amount of the credit begins to phase out when the taxpayer's modified adjusted gross income (MAGI) exceeds $197,880 ($201,010 for 2015), and is completely eliminated when the MAGI reaches $237,880 ($241,010 for 2015) [§ 23(b)(2), § 23(h); Rev. Proc. 2013-35; Rev. Proc. 2014-61].

*Timing of Credit.* For any expense paid or incurred before the tax year in which the adoption becomes final, the credit is allowed for the tax year following the tax year during which the expense is paid or incurred. For any expense paid or incurred during or after the tax year in which the adoption becomes final, the credit is allowed for the tax year in which the expense is paid or incurred [§ 23(a)(2)].

If the adopted child is not a U.S. citizen or resident, the credit is allowed only if and when the adoption becomes final [§ 23(e); Rev. Proc. 2005-31, 2005-26 I.R.B. 1374; Rev. Proc. 2010-31, 2010-40 I.R.B. 413].

*Qualified Adoption Expenses.* Qualified adoption expenses are reasonable and necessary reasonable adoption fees, court costs, attorney fees, and other expenses that [§ 23(d)(1)]:

1. are directly related to the legal adoption of an eligible child by the taxpayer;

2. have as a principal purpose the legal adoption of an eligible child by the taxpayer;

3. are not incurred in violation of state or federal law or in carrying out any surrogate parenting arrangement;

4. are not expenses for the adoption by an individual of a child that is the child of that individual's spouse;

5. are not be reimbursed under an employer program (see XVII.E.1.) or otherwise; and

6. are not funded or reimbursed under any federal, state or local program [§ 23(b)(3)(B)].

*Special Needs Child.* A child with special needs is any child who: (1) the state has determined cannot or should not return to the home of his parents; (2) the state has determined has a special factor or condition (such as ethnic background, age, medical condition, etc.) for which it is reasonable to conclude that the child cannot be placed with adopting parents without providing adoption assistance; and (3) is a citizen or resident of the United States [§ 23(d)(3)].

*Tax Liability Limitation and Carryover.* The total amount of all nonrefundable personal credits, including the adoption credit, is allowed to the full extent of the taxpayer's regular tax (as defined in § 26(b)) reduced by the foreign tax credit, plus the alternative minimum tax [§ 26(a)]. Excess adoption credit may be carried forward five years, and are used on a first-in, first-out basis [§ 23(c)]. The credit was refundable (i.e., not limited to the taxpayer's tax liability) for tax years beginning in 2010 and 2011.

*Claiming the Credit.* The credit is claimed on Form 8839, *Qualified Adoption Expenses,* which is attached to the taxpayer's Form 1040. The credit cannot be claimed on Form 1040A or 1040EZ. A married taxpayer and spouse must file a joint return to claim the credit. Certain married individuals who file a separate return for the year, maintain a household for a qualified individual for more than one-half of the year, and do not share a household with the spouse at any time during the last six months of the year are considered unmarried for purposes of the credit [§ 23(f)(1)].

### IX.B.4. Child Tax Credit

[513 T.M., III.C.; TPS ¶3120.04.]

Taxpayers may claim a credit against tax for each qualifying child.

*Amount of Credit.* The credit is $1,000 for each qualifying child for whom the taxpayer is allowed a dependency exemption deduction under § 151 [§ 24(a)].

The total credit is reduced by $50 for each $1,000 or increment thereof that the taxpayer's modified adjusted gross income exceeds the threshold amount, which is $110,000 for joint filers, $75,000 for unmarried individuals, and $55,000 for married individuals filing separately [§ 24(b)].

*Qualifying Child.* A qualifying child is an individual who [§ 24(c)]:

1. is the child of the taxpayer or a descendant of such child, or is a brother, sister, stepbrother, or stepsister of the taxpayer or a descendant of any such relative;

2. lives with the taxpayer for more than one-half of such tax year;

3. has not provided over one-half of such individual's own support for the calendar year in which the tax year of the taxpayer begins;

4. has not attained the age of 17;

5. is younger than the taxpayer;

6. has not filed a joint return (other than only for a claim for refund) with their spouse for the tax year beginning in the calendar year in which the tax year of the taxpayer begins; and

7. is a citizen, national or resident alien of the United States.

For legally separated and divorced parents, if the custodial parent releases the dependency exemption to the noncustodial parent under § 152(e), the child is considered the qualifying child of the noncustodial parent, who is then entitled to claim the child tax credit [§ 24(c), § 152(c)].

*Refundable Portion of Credit.* Part of the child tax credit is nonrefundable and part is refundable. The total amount of all nonrefundable personal credits, including the nonrefundable portion of the child tax credit, is allowed to the full extent of the taxpayer's regular tax (as defined in § 26(b)) reduced by the foreign tax credit, plus any alternative minimum tax [§ 26(a)]. The refundable portion of the child tax credit is the "additional tax credit." The child tax credit is refundable to the extent of the lesser of: (1) the unclaimed portion of the nonrefundable credit amount, or (2) the greater of 15% of the taxpayer's earned income in excess of $3,000 (for 2014 and 2015), or, for taxpayers with three or more qualifying children, the excess of the taxpayer's social security taxes over his earned income credit for the tax year [§ 24(d); Rev. Proc. 2014-61, 2014-47 I.R.B. 860].

**EXAMPLE:** Sue had earned income of $22,000, but could only claim a $1,500 child tax credit for her two children, since that was the extent of her ordinary income tax liability. The unclaimed portion of the nonrefundable credit amount is $500 ($2,000 – $1,500). 15% of her earned income over $3,000 is $2,850 (($22,000 – $3,000) × .15). Sue may claim the lesser amount of $500 as the refundable portion of the credit.

*Claiming the Credit.* The child tax credit is claimed on Form 1040, 1040A, or 1040NR. The refundable portion or "additional child tax credit" is claimed on Form 8812, *Child Tax Credit,* and is attached to Form 1040, Form 1040A, or Form 1040NR. Taxpayers must include the name and taxpayer identification number of each qualifying child on the return in order to claim the child tax credit [§ 24(e)].

*Special Rules.* No credit is allowed for a short tax year, unless the tax year is less than 12 months because of the taxpayer's death [§ 24(f)].

### IX.B.5. Education Tax Credit

[517 T.M., V.; TPS ¶3120.05.]

Taxpayers may claim a credit for qualified tuition and related expenses paid for the taxpayers or their dependents. The education tax credit is the sum of the Hope Scholarship credit (or "the American Opportunity tax credit" for 2009 through 2017) and the Lifetime Learning credit.

### IX.B.5.a. The American Opportunity Tax Credit

[517 T.M., V.A.4.; TPS ¶3120.05.B.]

For tax years beginning after 2008 and before 2018, the Hope Scholarship credit is expanded and is known as the American Opportunity tax credit.

*Eligibility.* An eligible student for any academic period is a student who: (1) is enrolled in a program leading to a degree or other recognized education credential; (2) carries at least one-half of the normal full-time workload for the course of study the student is pursuing; and (3) has not been convicted of a federal or state felony offense for the possession or distribution of a controlled substance before the end of the tax year for which the credit is claimed [§ 25A(b)]. A nonresident alien for any portion of the tax year may not claim the credit unless the taxpayer elects to be treated as a U.S. resident under § 6013(g) or § 6013(h) [§ 25A(g)(7)].

If a child is claimed as a dependent by another taxpayer and incurs qualified tuition and related expenses, the taxpayer claiming the child as a dependent is deemed to have paid the expense and may claim the credit and the child may not claim the credit [§ 25A(g)(3)].

*Amount of Credit.* The credit is equal to 100% of the first $2,000 of all of the qualified tuition and related expenses paid by the taxpayer during the tax year (for education furnished to the eligible student during any academic period beginning in that year), plus 25% of the expenses that are more than $2,000 but not more than $4,000, for a total limit per student per year of $2,500. The credit applies only to the first four years of the qualified student's post-secondary education.

Allowable expenses includes tuition, fees, and course materials [§ 25A(i)].

**EXAMPLE:** Tom, an unmarried taxpayer, has two claimed dependents, Charmaine and Donna, who are each an eligible student attending an eligible educational institution. Tom pays $2,500 in allowable expenses for Charmaine and $5,000 in qualified tuition and related expenses for Donna. Tom can claim an American Opportunity Tax Credit of $2,125 for Charmaine (100% of the first $2,000, plus 25% of the expenses that are more than $2,000 but not more than $4,000) and a credit of $2,500 for Donna. The credit for Donna was the maximum allowed for any student because Tom paid at least $4,000. Tom's total American Opportunity Tax Credit is $4,625.

---

*Refundable Portion of Credit.* Up to 40% of the American Opportunity credit may be refundable, but not if the taxpayer is a child whose income is subject to the "kiddie" tax under § 1(g) (see X.A.3.), whether or not the child actually pays kiddie tax [§ 25A(i)(5)].

---

**EXAMPLE:** In 2014, 26-year-old Sarah paid $1,800 in qualified tuition and related expenses for herself. Her income is not subject to the "kiddie tax" under § 1(g)(2). Her adjusted gross income is $20,000 and her total tax liability is $1,024. The refundable portion of Sarah's American Opportunity credit is computed first and is $720 ($1,800 × 40%). The nonrefundable portion is $1,080 ($1,800 minus $720) but is limited to Sarah's $1,024 tax liability for a total allowable credit of $1,744.

---

### IX.B.5.b. The Lifetime Learning Credit

[517 T.M., V.A.4.; TPS ¶3120.05.C.]

*Eligibility.* An eligible student for any academic period is a student who is enrolled in one or more courses at an eligible educational institution and the course is either part of a postsecondary degree program leading to a degree, certificate or other educational credential or is taken to acquire or improve job skills. If the taxpayer is a nonresident alien individual for any portion of the tax year, the credit may not be claimed unless the taxpayer is treated as a resident alien for income tax purposes on account of an election to be treated as a U.S. resident under § 6013(g) or § 6013(h) [§ 25A(c)(2)(B), § 25A(g)(7)].

If a child is claimed as a dependent by another taxpayer and incurs qualified tuition and related expenses, the taxpayer claiming the child as a dependent is deemed to have paid the expense and may claim the credit and the child may not claim the credit [§ 25A(g)(3)].

*Amount of Credit.* The Lifetime Learning Credit for a taxpayer equals 20% of the year's total eligible expenditures up to $10,000, for himself and for dependents. The credit is available for all years of postsecondary education and for courses taken to acquire or improve job skills. The credit is available for an unlimited number of years and is available for one or more courses. Eligible expenditures equal the qualified tuition and related expenses paid by the taxpayer during that year for education furnished during any academic period beginning in that year. If the expenses are paid during a tax year for an academic period beginning during the first three months following that tax year, that academic period is treated as beginning during the tax year when the expenses are paid [§ 25A(c), § 25A(g)(4)].

### IX.B.5.c. Limitations on Education Tax Credit

[517 T.M., V.A.4.; TPS ¶3120.05.E.]

The otherwise allowable credit for a tax year is reduced, but not below zero, by the income limitation amount. The income limitation amount equals the otherwise allowable education credit for the tax year, multiplied by a fraction, the numerator of which is the excess of the taxpayer's modified adjusted gross income (MAGI) for that tax year over the threshold amount, and the denominator of which is the base amount.

The base amount is $20,000 joint filers and $10,000 for all other taxpayers. For the Lifetime Learning credit, the threshold amount is adjusted for inflation and for 2014 is $108,000 for joint filers and $53,000 for all other taxpayers ($110,000 for joint filers and $55,000 for other taxpayers for 2015) [§ 25A(d); Rev. Proc. 2013-35, 2013-47 I.R.B. 537; Rev. Proc. 2014-61, 2014-47 I.R.B. 860]. For the American Opportunity credit, the threshold amount is not adjusted for inflation and is $160,000 for joint filers and $80,000 for all other taxpayers [§ 25A(i)(4)].

---

**EXAMPLE:** Married taxpayers have calculated their Lifetime Learning credit to be $1,500 for 2014. Their MAGI is $120,000. The credit is reduced by $1,500 × (($120,000-$108,000) ÷ $20,000), or $900. Therefore, only $600 ($1,500-$900) is allowed for tax year 2014.

---

### IX.B.5.d. Qualified Tuition and Related Expenses
[517 T.M., V.A.4.; TPS ¶3120.05.B.]

Qualified tuition and related expenses means tuition and fees, including books, supplies, and equipment, required for the enrollment or attendance of a qualified person at an eligible educational institution for courses of instruction of the person at that institution. For taxpayers claiming the American Opportunity Credit, qualified tuition and related expenses also include course materials. For purposes of the Lifetime Learning Credit, qualified tuition and related expenses include expenses for any course of instruction at an eligible educational institution that is taken to acquire job skills or to improve job skills. Qualified tuition and related expenses do not include expenses for any course or other education involving sports, games, or hobbies, unless that course or other education is part of the qualified person's degree program. Qualified tuition and related expenses do not include student activity fees, athletic fees, insurance expenses, or other expenses unrelated to the qualified person's academic course of instruction. Qualified tuition and related expenses also do not include any expense for which an income tax deduction is allowed [§ 25A(f)(1), § 25A(g)(5), § 25A(i)(3)].

The amount of qualified tuition and related expenses otherwise taken into account for purposes of the credit for a qualified person for an academic period must be reduced by any amounts paid for the benefit of that person that are allocable to that academic period as:

- a qualified scholarship excludible from gross income;
- an educational assistance allowance;
- a payment for the person's educational expenses or attributable to the person's enrollment at an eligible educational institution that are excludible from gross income (other than gifts, bequests, devises, or inheritances).

This reduction is taken into account before applying the any of the fixed dollar limitations and before applying the income limitation [§ 25A(g)(2)].

### IX.B.5.e. Recapture of Education Tax Credit
[517 T.M., V.A.4.; ¶3120.05.G.]

The credit amount must be recaptured when there is in a subsequent year a refund of any amount taken into account in determining the amount of the credit. This is reported on Form 1040 or Form 1040A, and included on the "Tax" line. Taxpayers must write "ECR" to the left of the amount on the Tax line. This cannot be reported on Form 1040EZ. Refunds received in the same tax year in which the qualified tuition and related expenses are paid are subtracted from the gross payment [§ 25A(j); Reg. § 1.25A-5(f)(3)].

### IX.B.5.f. Claiming the Education Tax Credit

[517 T.M., V.A.4.; TPS ¶3120.05.F.]

The credit is claimed on Form 8863, *Education Credits (American Opportunity and Lifetime Learning Credits)*, which is attached to the taxpayer's Form 1040. An taxpayer who is married at the close of a tax year must file a joint return with his spouse in order to claim the education tax credit [§ 25A(g)(6)].

### IX.B.6. Retirement Savings Contributions Credit

[506 T.M., V.I.; TPS ¶3120.06.]

Taxpayers may claim a credit for elective deferrals and IRA contributions made during the tax year. The qualified retirement savings credit is also known as the "saver's credit."

*Eligibility.* To qualify for the retirement savings credit, an individual must be at least 18 years old at the end of the tax year, may not be claimed as a dependent on another taxpayer's return, and must not be a full-time student during five or more months of the calendar year. For 2014, only taxpayers filing joint returns with adjusted gross income (AGI) of $60,000 or less, head of household returns with AGI of $45,000 or less, and single returns (or separate returns filed by married taxpayers) with AGI of $30,000 or less, are eligible for the credit [§ 25B(b)].

*Amount of Credit.* The amount of the credit is equal to the applicable percentage of qualified retirement savings contributions of up to $2,000 [§ 25B(a)]. The credit rate depends on the taxpayer's modified AGI and the maximum is 50% [§ 25B(b), § 25B(e)]. Thus, the maximum annual credit amount is $1,000 (50% of $2,000). The following table sets forth the applicable percentages (i.e., credit rates) for 2014 [Notice 2013-73, 2013-49 I.R.B. 598]:

| Joint return | | Head of a Household | | All Other Cases | | Applicable Percentage |
|---|---|---|---|---|---|---|
| Over | Not over | Over | Not over | Over | Not over | |
| $0 | $36,000 | $0 | $27,000 | $0 | $18,000 | 50% |
| $36,000 | $39,000 | $27,000 | $29,250 | $18,000 | $19,500 | 20% |
| $39,000 | $60,000 | $29,250 | $45,000 | $19,500 | $30,000 | 10% |
| $60,000 | | $45,000 | | $30,000 | | 0% |

The applicable percentages for 2015 are [IRS News Release IR-2014-99 (Oct. 23, 2014)]:

| Joint return | | Head of a Household | | All Other Cases | | Applicable Percentage |
|---|---|---|---|---|---|---|
| Over | Not over | Over | Not over | Over | Not over | |
| $0 | $36,500 | $0 | $27,375 | $0 | $18,250 | 50% |
| $36,500 | $39,500 | $27,375 | $29,625 | $18,250 | $19,750 | 20% |
| $39,500 | $61,000 | $29,625 | $45,750 | $19,750 | $30,500 | 10% |
| $61,000 | | $45,750 | | $30,500 | | 0% |

The retirement savings credit does not reduce any deduction or exclusion that would otherwise apply for the savings contribution [Announcement 2001-106, 2001-44 I.R.B. 416].

*Qualified Retirement Savings.* The qualified retirement savings credit is available for contributions (or elective deferrals of compensation) to [§ 25B(d)(1)]:

- a § 401(k) plan;
- a tax-exempt organization or public school employee annuity under § 403(b);
- an eligible deferred compensation plan of a state or local government (§ 457 plan);
- a SIMPLE individual retirement account;
- a simplified employee pension (SEP);
- a traditional or Roth IRA; or
- a qualified retirement plan, in the case of voluntary after-tax employee contributions.

The amount of any contribution eligible for the credit is reduced by distributions received by the taxpayer and their spouse from any savings arrangement described above (including a Roth IRA, whether or not taxable) or any other retirement plan during the tax year for which the credit is claimed, the two preceding tax years, and the period after the end of the tax year for which the credit is claimed but before the due date (including extensions) for filing the taxpayer's return for that year. Distributions not includible in income as direct trustee-to-trustee transfers or other qualifying rollovers do not reduce contributions eligible for the credit [§ 25B(d)(2)].

*Tax Liability Limitation.* The total amount of all nonrefundable personal credits, including the retirement savings credit, is allowed to the full extent of the taxpayer's regular tax (as defined in § 26(b)) reduced by the foreign tax credit, plus any alternative minimum tax [§ 26(a)]. Unused credit may not be carried forward.

*Claiming the Credit.* The credit is claimed on Form 8880, *Credit for Qualified Retirement Savings Contributions*, which is attached to the taxpayer's Form 1040 or Form 1040A. Joint filers file one Form 8880.

## IX.C. Nonrefundable Personal Real Estate Credits

### IX.C.1. Credit for Interest on Certain Home Mortgages

[506 T.M., V.G.; TPS ¶3121.01.]

Individuals who hold qualified mortgage credit certificates may claim a credit for interest paid or accrued on qualified home mortgages.

*Eligibility.* To be eligible for the credit, the taxpayer's income must not exceed 115% of the area's median family income, which is established by the housing authorities and varies geographically. The indebtedness must be incurred by the taxpayer to acquire his principal residence, or as a qualified home improvement loan, or as a qualified rehabilitation loan for such residence. The residence must be a single-family residence that is the principal abode of the taxpayer and is located within the jurisdiction of the governmental authority issuing the mortgage credit certificate. The holder of the certificate must not have had an interest in a principal residence within three years of the date of execution of the certified mortgage except in the case of qualified home improvement and rehabilitation loans, or targeted area residences. The acquisition cost may not exceed 110% of the average area purchase price (varies geographically) for the typical single-family home. The mortgage to which the credit is applied must be obtained within a maximum of two years from the commencement date of the program [§ 25(e)].

A mortgage does not qualify if the residence is financed in any part by a qualified mortgage bond or a qualified veterans' mortgage bond [§ 25(c)(2)].

*Amount of Credit.* The credit amount is equal to the certificate credit rate multiplied by the interest paid or accrued during the tax year on the certified indebtedness amount. The certificate credit rate is the rate of credit specified by the issuer on the certificate and varies from not less than 10% to a maximum of 50% [§ 25(a)]. The amount of the deduction otherwise allowable for mortgage interest for the tax year must be reduced by the amount of the mortgage interest credit taken in such year [§ 163(g)].

*Limitation on Credit.* When the certificate credit rate is greater than 20%, the amount of the mortgage interest credit for any one tax year is limited to $2,000. If the residence is owned by more than one person, the $2,000 maximum is allocated to the taxpayers in accordance with their interest in the residence [§ 25(a)].

*Tax Liability Limitation and Carryover.* The total amount of all nonrefundable personal credits, including the retirement savings credit, is allowed to the full extent of the taxpayer's regular tax (as defined in § 26(b)) reduced by the foreign tax credit, plus any alternative minimum tax [§ 26(a)]. Excess retirement savings credit may be carried forward for up to three years [§ 25(e)(1)].

*Claiming the Credit.* The credit is claimed on Form 8396, *Mortgage Interest Credit*, which is attached to Form 1040.

*Recapture of Credit.* The credit is subject to recapture if the taxpayer disposes of the residence securing the mortgage within nine years of the date the taxpayer becomes liable in whole or in part of the federally-subsidized indebtedness [§ 25(i), § 143(m)]. The amount recaptured is reported on Form 8828, *Recapture of Federal Mortgage Subsidy.*

### IX.C.2. First-Time D.C. Homebuyer Credit [Expired]

[594 T.M., VI.C.; TPS ¶3121.02.]

A taxpayers who qualified as a first-time homebuyer of a principal residence in the District of Columbia could claim a credit for the acquisition. The first-time D.C. homebuyer credit expired December 31, 2011, and does not apply to property purchased after that date [§ 1400C(i)].

*Eligibility.* An individual is considered a first-time homebuyer if: (1) the individual and the individual's spouse have had no present ownership interest in a principal residence in the District of Columbia during the one-year period ending on the date of purchase of the principal residence for which the credit is being claimed; and (2) the individual has not been treated as a first-time homebuyer relating to any other principal residence [§ 1400C(c)].

*Amount of Credit.* The amount of the credit is equal to the purchase price up to $5,000 [§ 1400C(a)]. For a married taxpayer filing separately, the amount is limited to $2,500. If two or more unmarried taxpayers purchase a principal residence, the $5,000 amount is allocated among the taxpayers [§ 1400C(e)(1)]. The credit is phased out for taxpayers with modified adjusted gross income (MAGI) between $70,000 and $90,000 ($110,000 and $130,000 for joint returns).

*Carryover of Credit.* The first-time D.C. homebuyer credit is limited by an individual's tax liability, including alternative minimum tax, and certain other nonrefundable personal credits claimed. Any excess credit may be carried forward indefinitely to succeeding tax years [§ 1400C(d)].

*Claiming the Credit.* Because the credit has expired, only a credit carryforward may be claimed after 2011. The carryforward may be claimed on Form 8859, *Carry-*

*forward of the District of Columbia First-Time Homebuyer Credit,* which is attached to Form 1040.

***Special Rules.*** The taxpayer's basis in a property is reduced by the amount of any homebuyer credit claimed for such property [§ 1400C(h)].

No first-time D.C. homebuyer credit is allowed for the purchase of a residence for which the § 36 first-time homebuyer credit is allowable [§ 1400C(e)(4)].

### IX.C.3. Nonbusiness Energy Property Credit [Expired]

[506 T.M., V.K.; TPS ¶3121.03.]

Taxpayers may claim the nonbusiness energy property credit for expenditures for certain qualified energy efficient improvements and residential energy property expenditures placed in service or installed before 2014.

***Eligibility.*** The credit may be claimed for expenditures for qualified property placed in service or installed in 2006, 2007, or 2009 through 2013. If more than 20% of an item's use is for business purposes, then only the portion of the expenditures allocable to the nonbusiness use is eligible for the credit. Expenditures made from subsidized energy financing are not eligible for the credit [§ 25C(e)].

***Amount of Credit.*** For years after 2008, the allowable credit is equal to the sum of 10% of expenditures for qualified energy efficiency improvements plus the amount of residential property expenditures, subject to an overall cap of $500 for all property placed in service in all years [§ 25C(a)].

***Limitations on Credit.*** The credit amount allowed in a tax year for each item of energy-efficient building property is limited to $300. The maximum credit allowed for all exterior windows (including skylights) placed in service is $200 [§ 25C(b)].

***Tax Liability Limitation and Carryover.*** The total amount of all nonrefundable personal credits, including the nonbusiness energy property credit, is allowed to the full extent of the taxpayer's regular tax (as defined in § 26(b)) reduced by the foreign tax credit, plus any alternative minimum tax [§ 26(a)]. Unused credit may not be carried forward.

***Claiming the Credit.*** The credit is claimed on Form 5695, *Residential Energy Credits,* which is then attached to Form 1040.

***Special Rules.*** The increase in the taxpayer's basis that would otherwise result from credit-eligible expenditures is reduced by the amount of the nonbusiness energy property credit allowed for such expenditures [§ 25C(f)].

### IX.C.4. Residential Energy Efficient Property Credit

[512 T.M., VI.B.; TPS ¶3121.04.]

Taxpayers may claim a credit for a portion of expenditures associated with [§ 25D]:

- qualified solar electric property;
- qualified solar water heating property;
- qualified fuel cell power plants;
- qualified small wind energy property; or
- qualified geothermal heat pump property.

The residential energy efficient property credit does not apply to property placed in service after 2016 [§ 25D(g)].

***Eligibility.*** To be eligible for the residential energy efficient property credit, the property: (1) must be used to generate energy for a dwelling unit in the United States that the taxpayer uses as his residence; and (2) must not be used for a swimming pool, hot tub, or any other energy storage medium that has a function other than storage. Expenditures for onsite preparation, assembly, and original installation of qualified property, as well as expenditures for piping or wiring to interconnect such property to the dwelling unit, as well as labor costs allocable to such expenditures, are eligible for the credit [§ 25D(e)].

*Amount of Credit.* The credit is equal to 30% of the expenditures associated with qualified solar electric property, qualified solar water heating property, qualified fuel cell power plants, qualified small wind energy property, or qualified geothermal heat pump property [§ 25D(a)]. In the case of an expenditure for the construction (or reconstruction) of a structure, the expenditure is treated as made when the taxpayer's original use of the structure begins; otherwise, the expenditure is treated as made when the original installation is complete [§ 25D(e)(8)].

*Limitation on Credit.* There is no maximum credit for qualified solar electric property, qualified solar water heating property, qualified small wind energy property, and qualified geothermal heat pump property. For qualified fuel cell property, the maximum credit amount is $500 for each one-half kilowatt of capacity [§ 25D(b)]. For qualified fuel cell property, the maximum amount of expenditures that may be taken to account by all joint occupiers of the dwelling during the year is $1,667 for each half kilowatt of capacity. The amount allocated to each joint occupier is the lesser of (1) the expenses paid by the taxpayer, or (2) the taxpayer's proportionate share of the $1,667 limitation, based on amount paid. If a taxpayer is a tenant-stockholder in a cooperative housing corporation or a member of a condominium management association for a condominium that he/she owns, then the taxpayer is treated as having made his/her proportionate share of the cooperative corporation's or condominium association's qualifying expenditures [§ 25D(e)].

If more than 20% of an item's use is for business purposes, then only the portion of the expenditures allocable to the nonbusiness use is eligible for the credit [§ 25D(e)(7)]. See IX.A.5.b. for a discussion of the business credit for energy property.

*Qualified Solar Electric Property.* Qualified solar electric property is property that uses solar energy to generate electricity for use in the taxpayer's residence.

*Qualified Solar Water Heating Property.* Qualified solar water heating property is property used to heat water for use in the taxpayer's residence, if at least half of the energy that it uses to heat the water is derived from the sun.

*Qualified Fuel Cell Property.* Qualified fuel cell property is an integrated system (power plant) consisting of a fuel cell stack assembly and associated balance of plant components that: (1) converts a fuel into electricity using electrochemical means, (2) has an electricity-only generation efficiency of greater than 30%, and (3) generates at least 0.5 kilowatts of electricity. A qualified fuel cell power plant must be installed on or in connection with the taxpayer's principal residence.

*Qualified Geothermal Heat Pump Property.* Qualified geothermal heat pump property is equipment that uses the ground or ground water as a thermal energy source to heat the taxpayer's residence and meets the Energy Star program requirements in effect at the time the expenditure for the equipment is made [§ 25D(d)].

*Tax Liability Limitation and Carryover.* The total amount of all nonrefundable personal credits, including the nonbusiness energy property credit, is allowed to the full extent of the taxpayer's regular tax (as defined in § 26(b)) reduced by the foreign tax credit, plus any alternative minimum tax [§ 26(a)]. Excess nonbusiness energy property credit may be carried forward indefinitely to succeeding tax years [§ 25D(c)].

*Claiming the Credit.* The credit is claimed on Form 5695, *Residential Energy Credits,* which is then attached to Form 1040.

*Special Rules.* The basis increase that would otherwise result from the purchase of qualified property must be reduced by the amount of the residential energy efficient property credit allowed for such property [§ 25D(f)].

## IX.D. Automotive Credits

### IX.D.1. Alternative Motor Vehicle Credit

[506 T.M., III.A.28., 512 T.M., VI.F.; TPS ¶3131.02.]

Taxpayers may claim a credit for placing in service alternative motor vehicles. The business portion of the alternative motor vehicle credit is a component of the general business credit (see IX.A.29.). The alternative motor vehicle credit originally included credits for fuel cell, advanced lean burn technology, hybrid, and alternative fuel motor vehicles, as well as a plug-in conversion credit [§ 30B(a)]. However, all components of the alternative motor vehicle credit, except the qualified fuel cell motor vehicle credit, expired before 2014. The qualified fuel cell motor vehicle credit expires for property purchased after December 31, 2014 [§ 30B(k)(1)].

*Amount of Credit.* The new qualified fuel cell motor vehicle credit is [§ 30B(b)(1)]:

- $4,000 for a qualifying vehicle with a gross vehicle weight up to 8,500 pounds;
- $10,000 for a vehicle with a gross vehicle weight of more than 8,500 pounds but not more than 14,000 pounds;
- $20,000 for a vehicle with a gross vehicle weight of more than 14,000 pounds but not more than 26,000 pounds; and
- $40,000 for a vehicle with a gross vehicle weight of more than 26,000 pounds.

The credit may increase by amounts ranging from $1,000 to $4,000 if the vehicle achieves increases in fuel economy ranging from 150% to 300% of the 2002 model year city fuel economy [§ 30B(b)(2)(A)].

For purposes of the credit, a new qualified fuel cell motor vehicle is a motor vehicle that satisfies nine conditions [§ 30B(b)(3), § 30B(h)(7), § 30B(h)(10), § 30B(k)(1)]:

1. It must be propelled by power derived from one or more cells that convert chemical energy directly into electricity by combining oxygen with hydrogen fuel stored on board the vehicle in any form, whether or not it requires reformation before use.

2. If it is a passenger automobile or light truck, it must have received after August 7, 2005, a certificate that it meets or exceeds the Bin 5 Tier II emission level established in regulations prescribed by the EPA under § 202(i) of the Clean Air Act for that make and model year vehicle.

3. Its original use must begin with the taxpayer.

4. It must be acquired for use or lease by the taxpayer and not for resale.

5. It must be made by a manufacturer.

6. It must be purchased before January 1, 2015.

7. It must not be property used predominantly outside the United States, unless it is not subject to the MACRS alternative depreciation system.

8. It must be in compliance with the applicable provisions of the Clean Air Act (including waivers).

9. It must be in compliance with the motor vehicle safety provisions of 49 USC § 30101 through § 30169.

For procedures for manufacturers to follow to certify vehicles as new qualified fuel cell motor vehicles that taxpayers may rely on, see Notice 2008-33, 2008-12 I.R.B. 642.

***Claiming the Credit.*** The credit is claimed on Form 8910, *Alternative Motor Vehicle Credit.* The nonbusiness credit is nonrefundable, i.e., it may be claimed against the taxpayer's regular tax (as defined by § 26(a)) reduced by the foreign tax credit, plus any alternative minimum tax [§ 30B(g)(2)]. Unused credit may not be carried forward. For limitations applicable to the business credit, see IX.A.3.

A taxpayer may elect to forgo the credit for any vehicle [§ 30B(h)(9)].

***Recapture of Credit.*** Recapture applies if the property ceases to be eligible for the credit, including if there is a lease period of less than the vehicle's economic life, unless the cessation is by reason of conversion to a qualified plug-in electric drive motor vehicle [§ 30B(h)(8)].

***Special Rules.*** The amount of any deduction or other credit allowable for income tax purposes for a new qualified fuel cell motor vehicle must be reduced by the amount of the new qualified fuel cell motor vehicle credit allowed for that vehicle for the tax year and the basis of the vehicle must be reduced by the amount of such credit [§ 30B(h)(4), § 30B(h)(7)].

***Tax-Exempt Use Vehicles***. Under certain circumstances, the person who sells qualified alternative motor vehicles may claim the credit if the seller clearly discloses to the user the amount of any allowable credit. The property (1) must be used by a tax-exempt organization other than a § 521 cooperative, or by a government, foreign person, or foreign entity; (2) must not be used predominantly in an unrelated trade or business subject to the § 511 unrelated business income tax; and (3) must not be leased by the organization [§ 30B(h)(6)].

### IX.D.2. Alternative Fuel Vehicle Refueling Property Credit

[506 T.M., III.A.29., 512 T.M., VI.G.; TPS ¶3131.03.]

Taxpayers may claim a credit for placing in service qualified alternative-fuel vehicle refueling property. The business portion of the alternative fuel vehicle refueling property credit is a component of the general business credit (see IX.A.30.).

For property relating to hydrogen, the credit expires December 31, 2014. The credit expired for all other property December 31, 2013 [§ 30C(g)].

***Amount of Credit.*** The alternative-fuel vehicle refueling property credit equals 30% of the cost of the qualified alternative-fuel vehicle refueling property placed in service by the taxpayer during the tax year [§ 30C(a)]. The credit for all qualified property placed in service by the taxpayer during the tax year at a location is limited to $30,000 for depreciable (business) property, and $1,000 for non-depreciable (non-business) property [§ 30C(b)].

The cost of qualified alternative-fuel vehicle refueling property [Notice 2007-43, 2007-22 I.R.B. 1318]:

- includes all costs that must be capitalized as a cost of the property;
- does not include costs properly allocable to land, a building, or the structural components of a building; and
- does not include any amount expensed under § 179.

The cost of dual-use property used to store or dispense both alternative fuel and conventional fuel is included in the cost of qualified alternative-fuel vehicle refueling property only to the extent it exceeds the cost of equivalent conventional refueling property. Special rules apply to qualified alternative-fuel vehicle refueling property that is converted from previously non-qualified property [Notice 2007-43].

*Qualified Clean-Fuel Vehicle Refueling Property.* Qualified clean-fuel vehicle refueling property is any property that satisfies six conditions [§ 30C(c)]:

1. It must not be a building or its structural components.

2. It must be depreciable property unless it is installed on property used as the taxpayer's principal residence.

3. Original use must begin with the taxpayer.

4. It must be for the storage or dispensing of an alternative fuel into the fuel tank of a motor vehicle propelled by that fuel, but only if the storage or dispensing property is at the point where the fuel is delivered into the fuel tank of the motor vehicle, or for the recharging of motor vehicles propelled by electricity, but only if the recharging property is located at the point where the motor vehicles are recharged.

5. It must not be property used predominantly outside the United States, unless it is not subject to the MACRS alternative depreciation system.

6. It must be placed in service on or before the credit termination date.

*Claiming the Credit.* The credit is claimed on Form 8911, *Alternative Fuel Vehicle Refueling Property Credit.* The nonbusiness portion is nonrefundable, i.e., it is limited to the excess, if any, of the taxpayer's modified § 26(b) regular tax liability limitation over the taxpayer's tentative minimum tax [§ 30C(e)(2)]. Unused credit may not be carried forward. For limitations applicable to the business credit, see IX.A.3.

A taxpayer may elect to forgo the credit for any property [§ 30C(e)(4)].

*Recapture of Credit.* The alternative-fuel vehicle refueling property credit is subject to recapture rules when the property ceases to be alternative-fuel vehicle refueling property before the end of its recovery period [§ 30C(e)(5)].

*Special Rules.* The amount of any deduction or other credit allowable for income tax purposes for any property for which the alternative-fuel vehicle refueling property credit is allowed must be reduced by the amount of the credit allowed for that property for the tax year and the basis of the property must be reduced by the amount of the credit [§ 30C(e)(1), § 30C(e)(3)].

*Tax-Exempt Use Property.* Under certain circumstances, the person who sells qualified alternative fuel vehicle refueling property may claim the credit if the seller clearly discloses to the user the amount of any allowable credit. The property (1) must be used by a tax-exempt organization other than a § 521 cooperative, or by a government, foreign person, or foreign entity; (2) must not be used predominantly in an unrelated trade or business subject to the § 511 unrelated business income tax; and (3) must not be leased by the organization [§ 30C(e)(2)].

### IX.D.3. Qualified Plug-In Electric Drive Motor Vehicle Credit

[506 T.M., III.A.41., 512 T.M., VI.H.; TPS ¶3131.04.]

Taxpayers may claim a credit for placing in service new qualified plug-in motor vehicles for the tax year in which the vehicle is placed in service. The portion of the qualified plug-in electric drive motor vehicle credit attributable to depreciable property (i.e., business vehicles) is a component of the general business credit (see IX.A.33.).

The credit for two- and three-wheeled vehicles (but not for other vehicles) expired December 31, 2013.

*Amount of Credit.* The credit amount per vehicle equals the sum of [§ 30D(b)]:

1. the base amount ($2,500), plus

2. for a vehicle that draws its propulsion energy from a battery with not less than five kilowatt-hours (kwh) of capacity, $417 plus $417 for each kwh in excess of five kwh (not to exceed $5,000).

The total amount of the credit is limited to $7,500 per vehicle.

The full amount of the credit may be claimed for the first 200,000 new qualified plug-in electric-drive motor vehicles sold for use in the United States after December 31, 2009, after which taxpayers placing in service such a vehicle must claim a reduced credit amount [§ 30D(e)].

The credit amount for two- or three-wheeled plug-in vehicles acquired in 2012 and 2013 equals the lesser of (1) 10% of the cost of the qualified vehicle, or (2) $2,500 [§ 30D(g)(2)].

Per-vehicle credit amounts acknowledged by the IRS are available at *http://www.irs.gov/Businesses/Qualified-Vehicles-Acquired-after-12-31-2009*.

***Claiming the Credit.*** The credit is claimed on Form 8936, *Qualified Plug-in Electric Drive Motor Vehicle Credit*. The nonbusiness credit is nonrefundable, i.e., it may be claimed against the taxpayer's regular tax (as defined in § 26(b)) reduced by the foreign tax credit, plus any alternative minimum tax [§ 30D(c)(2)]. Unused credit may not be carried forward. For limitations applicable to the business credit, see IX.A.3.

A taxpayer may elect not to apply § 30D to a given qualifying vehicle [§ 30D(f)(6)].

Recapture applies for any vehicle that ceases to be eligible for the credit [§ 30D(f)(5)].

***Special Rules.*** The vehicle's cost basis must be reduced by the amount of the credit claimed against that vehicle [§ 30D(f)(1)]. In addition, any other deduction or credit allowed for such vehicle must be reduced by the qualified plug-in electric drive motor vehicle credit [§ 30D(f)(2)].

## IX.E. Foreign Tax Credit

[901 T.M.; TPS ¶3130.]

A credit is generally allowed against U.S. tax for foreign income taxes paid on income derived from operations or investments in a foreign country as a means of mitigating double taxation [§ 27, § 901]. In addition, the credit is allowed for foreign taxes paid by certain foreign subsidiaries [§ 902]. The foreign tax credit is claimed on Form 1116, *Foreign Tax Credit—Individual, Estate, Trust*, or Form 1118, *Foreign Tax Credit—Corporations*.

See XX.C.2. for a discussion of the foreign tax credit.

## IX.F. Bond Credits

Taxpayers that hold qualified tax credit bonds on any of the bonds' credit allowance dates during the tax year may claim an income tax credit [§ 54(a), § 54A(a), § 54AA(a), § 1397E(a)]. If the bond pays interest, the holder generally must include the interest in income notwithstanding the fact that the issuer may be a state or local government.

Tax credit bonds include forestry conservation bonds (see IX.F.5.), clean renewable energy bonds (CREBs) (see IX.F.6. and IX.F.11.), qualified school construction bonds (see IX.F.7.), qualified energy conservation bonds (see IX.F.8.), qualified zone academy bonds (QZABs) (see IX.F.9. and IX.F.12.), and Build America bonds (see IX.F.10.).

### IX.F.1. Amount of Credit

[506 T.M., 512 T.M., 597 T.M.; TPS ¶3132.]

For each credit allowance date during the tax year, the bond credit is equal to 25% of the "annual credit" amount for the particular bond. The annual credit amount is the product of (1) the applicable credit rate (as determined by Treasury), and (2) the outstanding face amount of the bond. The credit allowance dates are March 15, June 15, September 15, December 15, and the last day on which the bond is outstanding. For bonds issued during the three-month period ending on a credit allowance date, or redeemed or maturing during such period, the credit amount is prorated [§ 54A(b), § 54A(e)(1)].

The bond credit amount is multiplied by 70% for new clean renewable energy bond (new CREB) credits and for qualified energy conservation bond credits [§ 54C(b), § 54D(b)].

For Build America bonds (including recovery zone credit bonds), the credit allowable for each interest payment date is 35% (45% for recovery zone credit bonds) of the amount of interest payable by the bond issuer to the taxpayer on the interest payment date [§ 54AA(a), § 54AA(b), § 1400U-2(a)].

For certain qualified zone academy bonds (QZABs) issued after March 18, 2010, new CREBs, qualified school construction bonds, and qualified energy conservation bonds, issuers may irrevocably elect to receive a credit from the IRS instead of the credit being allowed to the bond's holder. The election to receive a payment in lieu of providing a tax credit to the bond holder is not available for QZABs issued with the 2011 national limitation [§ 6431(f)].

For qualified Build America bonds issued before 2011, the credit is disallowed to the holder, and is allowed to the state or local government issuing the bond in the form of a payment issued directly to the state or local government [§ 54AA(g)(1), § 6431(f)(1)(C)].

### IX.F.2. Limitation on Credit and Carryover

[506 T.M., 512 T.M., 597 T.M., TPS ¶3132.]

The bondholder may claim the credit against both regular income tax liability and the alternative minimum tax liability. The sum of the bond credits is generally limited to the taxpayer's total regular tax liability (as defined in § 26(b)), plus any alternative minimum tax, minus the sum of the taxpayer's nonrefundable credits [§ 54(c), § 54A(c)(1), § 54AA(c)(1)].

*Carryover of Credit.* Any unused credit may be carried forward to later tax years. For the QZAB credit, any excess over the limitation amount may be carried forward only to the first two years following the unused limitation year, determined on a first-in, first-out basis [§ 54A(c)(2), § 54E(c)(4), § 54AA(c)(2)].

### IX.F.3. Claiming the Credit

[506 T.M., 512 T.M., 597 T.M.; TPS ¶3132.]

Taxpayers will generally receive Form 1097-BTC from the issuer or payer, as well as Form 1099-INT if the bond pays interest. Taxpayers may claim bond credits on Form 8912, *Credit to Holders of Tax Credit Bonds*. The amount is then entered on Form 1040, Form 1041, or Form 1120. Partnerships and S corporations report the amount on Schedule K and issue Forms 1097-BTC to partners and shareholders. Amounts allocated to beneficiaries of estates and trusts must also be reported to the beneficiaries on Form 1097-BTC.

A regulated investment company (RIC) that meets the requirements of § 852(a) may elect to pass through the credits to its shareholders. The credits are not allowed to the RIC and the RIC must include in gross income as interest an amount equal to the amount that the RIC would have otherwise included in gross income for the credits. The dividends paid deduction is increased by the amount of such income. The shareholders include in income their proportionate share of interest income along with their share of the credits [§ 853A].

Issuers of bonds that elect to receive the credit payment from the IRS may request the payment by filing Form 8038-CP, *Return for Credit Payments to Issuers of Qualified Bonds,* no earlier than 90 days before and no later than 45 days before the interest payment date.

### IX.F.4. Inclusion in Income and Stripped Bonds

[506 T.M., 512 T.M., 597 T.M.; TPS ¶3132.]

The amount of any tax credit bond credit is generally includible in the gross income of the holder and is treated as interest income [§ 54(g), § 54A(f), § 54AA(f)(1)].

Ownership of the bond and entitlement to the bond credit may be separated [§ 54A(i)]. Taxation of stripped bonds and coupons is discussed at III.F.2.a.(1).

### IX.F.5. Qualified Forestry Conservation Bond Issuer Payments

[506 T.M., III.F., 512 T.M., VI.J.; TPS ¶¶3132.02.B., 3201.05.]

States (or their subdivisions) and § 501(c)(3) organizations may issue forestry conservation bonds (FCBs) allowing their holders to claim a tax credit in lieu of receiving interest [§ 54A(d)(1)(A)]. The total FCBs are subject to a national limitation of $500 million. Treasury makes allocations of the limitation among qualified forestry conservation purposes [§ 54B(c), § 54B(d)].

To qualify for the credit, the bond issuer: (1) must be a state, a political subdivision or instrumentality, or § 501(c) organization; (2) must use the bond issue 100% for qualified forestry conservation purposes (as defined in § 54B(e)); and (3) must designate the bond issue for purposes of the FCB provision [§ 54B(a)].

A qualified issuer of forestry conservation bonds may, in lieu of issuing bonds, elect to treat its allocation as a deemed payment of tax equal to 50% of the amount of its bond allocation. Qualified issuers are state and local governments and § 501(c)(3) organizations [§ 54B(h)].

### IX.F.6. New Clean Renewable Energy Bond

[512 T.M., III.J.; TPS ¶3132.02.C.]

A new CREB is an obligation (1) that is part of an issue 100% of the available project proceeds of which are to be used for capital expenditures incurred by governmental bodies, public power providers, or cooperative electric companies for qualified renewable energy facilities (as defined in § 54C(d)(9)), and (2) that is designated as a new CREB [§ 54C(a)]. The annual credit allowed is 70% of the annual credit amount determined under § 54(b).

The national limitation on the credit is $2.4 billion, which has been entirely allocated [§ 54C(c)].

### IX.F.7. Qualified School Construction Bond

[506 T.M., III.K.; TPS ¶3132.02.F.]

A qualified school construction bond (QSCB) is an obligation that is part of an issue 100% of the available project proceeds of which are to be used for the construction, rehabilitation, or repair of a public school facility or for the acquisition of land on which the facility is to be constructed with the proceeds [§ 54F(a)].

There is a national limitation on QSCBs of $11 billion for each of calendar years 2009 and 2010 and $0 thereafter. An additional $200 million of QSCBs for each of years 2009 and 2010 was allocated to purposes of the construction, rehabilitation, and repair of schools funded by the Bureau of Indian Affairs. For purposes of such allocations, Indian tribal governments are qualified issuers [§ 54F(c), § 54F(d)(4)].

*Eligible Issuer.* Eligible issuers of QSCBs include states, political subdivisions, large local educational agencies that are state or local governmental entities, and entities empowered to issue bonds on behalf of any such entity under rules similar to those for determining whether a bond issued on behalf of a state or political subdivision constitutes an obligation of that state or political subdivision. Eligible issuers also include otherwise eligible issuers in conduit financing issues [Notice 2009-35, 2009-17 I.R.B. 876].

### IX.F.8. Qualified Energy Conservation Bond

[512 T.M., VI.K.; TPS ¶3132.02.D.]

A qualified energy conservation bond (QECB) is an obligation that (1) is part of an issue 100% of the available project proceeds of which are to be used for one or more qualified conservation purposes (as defined in § 54D(f)), and (2) is so designated by the issuer [§ 54D(a)].

The national limitation on QECBs is $3.2 billion, which was entirely allocated in 2009 [§ 54D(d); Notice 2009-29, 2009-16 I.R.B. 849].

In the case of private activity bonds, only capital expenditures can be for qualified conservation purposes [§ 54D(f)].

### IX.F.9. Qualified Zone Academy Bond (Issued after October 3, 2008)

[597 T.M., IV.KK.; TPS ¶3132.02.E.]

A qualified zone academy bond (QZAB) is an obligation that is part of an issue 100% of the available project proceeds of which are to be used for a qualified purpose (as defined in § 54E(d)(3)) for a qualified zone academy established by an eligible local education agency [§ 54E(a), § 54E(b)]. No QZABs may be issued for the years 2014 and after [§ 54E(c)].

### IX.F.10. Build America Bond

[506 T.M., III.K.; TPS ¶3132.03.]

A Build America bond is an obligation that satisfies five conditions [§ 54AA(d)]:

1. it must not be a private activity bond;

2. it must generate interest that, except for the requirement under § 54AA(f)(1) that such income is includible in gross income for federal tax purposes, is otherwise excludible from gross income as interest on state and local bonds;

3. it must be issued before January 1, 2011;

4. its issuer must make an irrevocable election to have § 54AA apply; and

5. its issue price must not have a de minimis amount of premium over the stated principal amount of the bond.

Indian tribal government Tribal Economic Development bonds that otherwise satisfy the five conditions qualify as Build America bonds [§ 54AA(d)].

*Qualified Build America Bonds.* Qualified Build America bonds are Build America bonds that satisfy two conditions: (1) 100% of the excess of the issue's available project proceeds (as defined in § 54AA(g)(2)(A)) over the amounts in a reasonably required reserve for the issue must be used for capital expenditures; and (2) the issuer must make an irrevocable election to have this special rule apply. Tax credit bonds issued after March 28, 2010, that are new CREBs, QECBs, QZABs, or QSCBs for which the issuer has made an irrevocable election to be treated as a specified Build America bond are treated as qualified Build America bonds [§ 54AA(g)(2), § 6431(f)].

*Recovery Zone Economic Development Bonds.* Recovery zone economic development bonds (as defined in § 1400U-2) are otherwise treated as Build America bonds for purposes of the § 6431 credit. The national limitation for recovery zone economic development bonds is $10 billion, which was entirely allocated in 2009 [§ 1400U-1(a)(4); Notice 2009-50, 2009-26 I.R.B. 1118].

### IX.F.11. Clean Renewable Energy Bond Credits (Issued before October 4, 2008)

[506 T.M., III.G.1., 512 T.M., III.I.; TPS ¶3132.01.C.]

A clean renewable energy bond (CREB) is an obligation issued by a qualified issuer (as defined in § 54(j)] that is part of an issue 95% of the proceeds of which are used for capital expenditures incurred by qualified borrowers for one or more qualified projects.

The national limitation for clean renewable energy bond credits ("old CREBs") was $1.2 billion, which was entirely allocated before 2008.

Unlike the issuers of qualified zone academy bonds (QZABs), issuers of old CREBs must report issuance to the IRS in a manner similar to the information returns required for tax-exempt bonds [§ 54(j)(5)].

*Qualified Borrower.* A qualified borrower is a mutual or cooperative electric company or a governmental body [§ 54(j)(5)].

### IX.F.12. Qualified Zone Academy Bond Credit (Issued before October 4, 2008)

[597 T.M., IV.KK.; TPS ¶3132.04.]

A qualified zone academy bond (QZAB) issued before October 4, 2008, is an obligation that is part of an issue 95% or more of the proceeds of which are to be used for a qualified purpose for a qualified zone academy established by a state or local government. Old QZABs differ from other tax credit bonds. QZABs could be issued only to banks, insurance companies, or corporations actively engaged in the business of lending money [§ 1397E(d)(6)]. The credit allowance dates are the last day of the one-year period beginning on the date of issue, and each one-year anniversary date thereafter [§ 1397E(b), § 1397E(i)(1)].

The bond credit for old QZABs is equal to the product of (1) the applicable credit rate (as determined by Treasury), and (2) the face amount of the bond on the credit allowance date.

## IX.G. Refundable Credits

### IX.G.1. Taxes Withheld on Wages, Excess Social Security Withholding and Backup Withholding

#### IX.G.1.a. Credit for Withheld Income Tax

[506 T.M., IV.A.1.; TPS ¶3200.01.]

Taxpayers may claim a credit for income taxes withheld from their wages, including income taxes withheld from supplemental unemployment benefits, pensions and certain other deferred income, annuities, sick pay, certain tips, gambling winnings, certain payments from Indian casinos, and the value of certain vehicle fringe benefits [§ 31(a), § 3402] (see XXII.A.).

Taxpayers also are allowed a credit for taxes withheld under backup withholding, which applies to reportable payments for which the taxpayer is not in compliance with reporting or other requirements [§ 31(c), § 3406; Reg. § 1.31-1(a)] (see XXII.A.7.).

*Eligibility.* The credits are allowable to the taxpayer subject to income tax on the wages from which the income taxes were withheld and are allowable as a credit even if the employer has not remitted the tax to the federal government. If the payments for which there has been withholding are made to a trust, estate, partnership, or S corporation, on account of services performed by a beneficiary, partner, or shareholder, the latter individual is permitted to claim the credit. Spouses in community property states who file separate returns are each allowed to claim one-half of the income taxes withheld on each spouse's wages [§ 31(a)(1); Reg. § 1.31-1(a)].

For government employees, each head of a federal agency or instrumentality that files a withholding agent's return is treated as a separate employer. Each state, political subdivision of a state, and instrumentality of any state or political subdivision is a separate employer. A U.S. employer that has entered into an agreement to treat foreign affiliates as subject to withholding obligations is a separate employer from the foreign affiliate [§ 6413(c)(2)].

*Claiming the Credit.* The credit is claimed on the appropriate line of an income tax return (e.g., Form 1040) showing the tax liability against which the credit is claimed. The credit for income tax withheld from wages is allowable for the last tax year beginning in the calendar year of the withholding. Income taxes withheld under backup withholding are allowable as a credit for the tax year of the recipient in which the income is received [§ 31(a)(2), § 31(c)].

#### IX.G.1.b. Credit for Excess Employment Tax Withholding

[506 T.M., IV.C.; TPS ¶3200.01.B.2.]

Taxpayers may claim a credit for withholding on wages in excess of the maximum wage base for old-age, survivor and disability insurance (OASDI) under the Federal Insurance Contributions Act (FICA) or the Railroad Retirement Tax Act (RRTA). Excess FICA withholding exists if more than one employer withholds the employment taxes and the total amount withheld exceeds the amount that would have been withheld had the taxpayer earned all of the wages from one employer. The maximum wage base for OASDI for 2014 is $117,000 [§ 31(b); Notice 2013-72, 2013-48 I.R.B. 592]. For a discussion of FICA and RRTA withholding, see XX.B.

The credit for excess employment taxes withheld does not apply to a taxpayer with only one employer. If one employer withholds more than the maximum amount of employment taxes, the employer must make an adjustment for the excess withholding directly with the taxpayer, or, if that is not possible, the taxpayer must file a separate claim for refund [Rev. Rul. 54–221, 1954-1 C.B. 73].

For government employees, each head of a federal agency or instrumentality that files a withholding agent's return is treated as a separate employer. Each state, political subdivision of a state, and instrumentality of any state or political subdivision is a separate employer. A U.S. employer that has entered into an agreement to treat foreign affiliates as subject to withholding obligations is a separate employer from the foreign affiliate [§ 6413(c)(2)].

***Claiming the Credit.*** The credit for excess employment taxes withheld may be claimed on the appropriate line on Form 1040 or 1040A but not on Form 1040EZ. The credit is allowable for the last tax year beginning in the calendar year in which the wages were received [§ 31(b)(2)].

### IX.G.2. Tax Withheld on Nonresidents and Foreign Corporations

[506 T.M., IV.A.3.; TPS ¶3200.02.]

Certain nonresident individuals and foreign entities may claim a credit for income taxes withheld at the source on their U.S. source income [§ 33, § 1462]. Income taxes withheld at the source include:

- the § 1441 withholding tax on nonresident aliens' specified income items from U.S. sources;
- the § 1442 withholding tax on foreign corporations' specified income items from U.S. sources;
- the § 1443(a) withholding tax on foreign tax-exempt organizations;
- the § 1444 withholding tax on income from sources within the Virgin Islands;
- the § 1445 withholding tax on dispositions of U.S. real property interests by a foreign person; and
- the § 1446 withholding tax on foreign partners' shares of income effectively connected with the conduct of a U.S. trade or business.

***Amount of Credit.*** Credit against U.S. income tax liability is allowed for the amount of tax withheld at the source from amounts paid to nonresident aliens and foreign corporations [§ 33, § 1462].

***Claiming the Credit.*** Individuals claim the credit for tax withheld on nonresident aliens on Form 1040NR, *U.S. Nonresident Alien Income Tax Return.* Corporations file Form 1120-F, *U.S. Income Tax Return of a Foreign Corporation.* Payors of U.S. source income to nonresident aliens and foreign corporations must file Form 1042, *Annual Withholding Tax Return for U.S. Source Income of Foreign Persons,* and furnish to the recipient of such income Form 1042-S, *Foreign Person's U.S. Source Income Subject to Withholding,* by March 15 of the year following the year in which payment occurred [Reg. § 1.1461-1(c)].

For a detailed discussion of withholding on foreign persons, see XX.F.

### IX.G.3. Credit for Overpayment of Tax

[507 T.M., VIII.C.2.; TPS ¶3200.03.]

A taxpayer may claim a credit for an overpayment of tax. The taxpayer may elect to have all or part of an overpayment of income tax applied as a credit against his estimated income tax for the subsequent tax year or, because the credit is refundable, may file a claim for a refund of the overpayment. In addition, the IRS has the authority to credit such overpayment against any tax liability of the taxpayer [§ 37, § 6401].

***Eligibility.*** A credit for an overpayment is permitted only for the income tax liability of the same taxpayer. For married taxpayers, an overpayment from a separate return year may be applied as a credit against the taxpayer's portion of a joint liability for a year in which the taxpayer files a joint return; however, the overpayment may be credited against only so much of the joint liability that is attributable to the taxpayer. In addition, a taxpayer's share of an overpayment from a year in which a joint return was filed may be applied against the taxpayer's tax liability from a year in which the taxpayer filed a separate return. For married taxpayers filing separate tax returns, an overpayment on the taxpayer's return may not offset a deficiency on the spouse's return even if they file on a community property basis unless the tax liabilities are paid with community funds, in which case one spouse's overpayment may be available to offset the other's liability [Rev. Rul. 67-431, 1967-2 C.B. 411; Rev. Rul. 85-70, 1985-1 C.B. 361].

The sole shareholder of a corporation may not credit against his own tax an overpayment by the corporation. Similarly, overpayments made by a trust may not be credited against the liability of the beneficiary.

*Amount of Credit.* The overpayment is the amount payment of tax that exceeds the taxpayer's tax liability [§ 6401(c)].

The most common types of overpayments are [§ 6401]:

- excessive withholding or estimated tax payments;
- tax collected after expiration of the limitations period; and
- excess of refundable credits over tax liability.

In determining the amount of an overpayment, all adjustments must be taken into account, including those barred by the period of limitations. However, an overpayment will be credited or refunded only to the extent that adjustments decreasing the tax are the subject of a timely filed claim.

*Married Filers.* For married taxpayers filing jointly, each spouse has a separate interest in any overpayment that is determined by computing each spouse's tax liability as if they had filed separate returns. The liability from the joint return is then allocated based on a ratio of these separate liabilities. Each spouse's overpayment is computed by subtracting his share of the joint liability from his payment of the joint liability. The earned income credit is apportioned between them in determining their separate contributions to payment of the joint tax liability.

In community property states, each spouse is considered to receive one-half of the aggregate wages of both spouses, and each spouse receives credit for one-half of the aggregate taxes withheld from such wages so that each spouse is presumed to have a half interest in any overpayment, unless it is possible to determine the exact portion that a spouse contributes to the income and credit [Rev. Rul. 2004–71, 2004-30 I.R.B. 74 (Arizona, Wisconsin); Rev. Rul. 2004–72, 2004-30 I.R.B. 77 (California, Idaho, Louisiana); Rev. Rul. 2004–73, 2004-30 I.R.B. 80 (Nevada, New Mexico, Washington); Rev. Rul. 2004–74, 2004-30 I.R.B. 84 (Texas)].

For a discussion of application of overpayments against a taxpayer's non-tax debts, see XXIII.E.1.

*Claiming the Credit.* The election to have the overpayment applied as a credit against the following year's estimated tax liability is made on a timely filed original income tax return or amended return for the year of the overpayment. The election is irrevocable; conversely, a taxpayer that claims a refund may not later elect to have the overpayment applied as a credit.

If the election is made to apply the overpayment to a subsequent year, the amount is deemed paid on April 15 of the subsequent year. However, if a refund claim is not filed for a credited overpayment within three years of the deemed payment, the overpayment is forfeited [§ 6511(a), § 6513(b)(2)].

### IX.G.4. Earned Income Credit

Eligible low-income workers may claim a credit against tax for a portion of their earned income. The earned income credit (EIC) is refundable, i.e., the credit may be allowed even if in excess of the taxpayer's tax liability.

### IX.G.4.a. Eligibility for Earned Income Credit

[506 T.M., V.C.; TPS ¶3201.01.]

**Eligible Taxpayers.** Although originally enacted to provide a credit for taxpayers with children, currently both individuals with a "qualifying child," and individuals without a qualifying child may claim the credit. An individual who does not have a qualifying child for the tax year is eligible for the credit if: (1) the individual's principal place of abode is in the United States for more than half of the tax year; (2) the individual (or, if married, his or her spouse) has reached age 25, but not 65, by the end of the tax year; and (3) the individual may not be claimed as a dependent by another taxpayer for a tax year beginning in the same calendar year in which the individual's tax year begins [§ 32(c)(1)].

The following individuals are not eligible for the EIC: (1) the otherwise qualifying child of a taxpayer; (2) an individual that lives abroad and elects the foreign earned income and housing cost amount exclusion (see XX.C.1.); (3) a nonresident alien for any portion of the tax year, unless married to a U.S. citizen or resident and agreeing to subject his or her worldwide income to U.S. income tax [§ 32(c)(1)].

Only one taxpayer may actually treat a child as a qualifying child and taxpayers may not divide the various tax benefits between or among themselves, although different taxpayers may claim different children as their qualifying children [Notice 2006-86, 2006-41 I.R.B. 680].

Taxpayers who are married at the end of the tax year may not claim the credit unless they file a joint return. For this purpose, a taxpayer that is legally separated under a decree of divorce or separate maintenance is not considered to be married. In the case of a joint return, the credit is available if either spouse is an eligible individual and the earned income of the taxpayer for the preceding tax year is the sum of the earned income of each spouse for the preceding tax year [§ 32(d), § 7703(a)(2)].

**Qualifying Child.** A qualifying child must be a qualifying child under § 152(c) for purposes of the dependency exemption (see XII.D.2.a.), except that: (1) there is no requirement that the child does not provide over half of his own support; (2) the special rules for children of divorced or separated parents under § 152(e) are disregarded, i.e., a custodial parent waiving the dependency exemption is still entitled to any EIC; and (3) the requirement that the qualifying child have the same principal place of abode as the taxpayer for more than one-half of the tax year cannot be satisfied unless the abode is in the United States. Additionally, a qualifying child may not be married unless the taxpayer is entitled to a dependency exemption [§ 32(c)(3)].

**Earned Income.** Earned income consists generally of amounts includible in gross income that are wages, salaries, tips, and other employee compensation and net earnings from self-employment. Earned income does not include:

- any amount received as a pension or annuity;
- unemployment compensation or worker's compensation;

- income of a nonresident alien that is not effectively connected with the conduct of a trade or business within the United States;
- any amount received for services provided by an inmate at a penal institution;
- certain workfare payments earned by the taxpayer; or
- nontaxable employee compensation.

Taxpayers may elect to include in earned income amounts excluded from income as combat zone compensation for U.S. Armed Forces members [§ 32(c)(2)(A)].

Earned income includes the taxpayer's net earnings from self-employment, determined with regard to the deduction allowed for one-half of the self-employment taxes. Net earnings from self-employment includes the gross income derived from any trade or business, less any deductions allowed attributable to the trade or business, and the taxpayer's distributive share of income or loss from any trade or business carried on by a partnership. A taxpayer with minimal net earnings may elect to be treated as having received net earnings from self-employment equal to four times the amount of earnings needed to earn one quarter of coverage under § 213(d) of the Social Security Act [§ 32(c)(2)(A)(ii)].

*Disqualified Income.* For 2014, no EIC is allowed for the tax year for a taxpayer whose aggregate amount of disqualified income for the tax year exceeds $3,350 ($3,400 for 2015) [§ 32(j); Rev. Proc. 2013-35, 2013-47 I.R.B. 537; Rev. Proc. 2014-61, 2014-47 I.R.B. 860]. Disqualified income consists of interest and dividends, tax-exempt interest, net income (if greater than zero) from rents and royalties not derived in the ordinary course of business, capital gain net income, and net passive income (if greater than zero) that is not self-employment income. However, disqualified income does not include gain from selling business assets treated as long-term capital gain [§ 32(i)].

### IX.G.4.b. Amount of Earned Income Credit

[506 T.M., V.C.3.; TPS ¶3201.01.C.]

The amount of earned income credit is equal to the "credit percentage" multiplied by the portion of the taxpayer's earned income that does not exceed a specified "earned income amount" [§ 32(a)(1)]. Earned income credit amounts are available at *Schedules & Tables 7.* in the Earned Income Credit Table.

The earned income amounts, credit percentages and maximum credit amounts for 2014 are as follows [§ 32(b); Rev. Proc. 2013-35]:

| Number of Children | Earned Income Amount | Credit Percentage | Maximum Credit Amount |
|---|---|---|---|
| 0 | $6,480 | 7.65% | $496 |
| 1 | $9,720 | 34% | $3,305 |
| 2 | $13,650 | 40% | $5,460 |
| 3+ | $13,650 | 45% | $6,143 |

The earned income amounts, credit percentages and maximum credit amounts for 2015 are as follows [§ 32(b); Rev. Proc. 2014-61, 2014-47 I.R.B. 860]:

| Number of Children | Earned Income Amount | Credit Percentage | Maximum Credit Amount |
|---|---|---|---|
| 0 | $6,580 | 7.65% | $503 |
| 1 | $9,880 | 34% | $3,359 |
| 2 | $13,870 | 40% | $5,548 |
| 3+ | $13,870 | 45% | $6,242 |

*Credit Phaseout.* The credit begins to phase out if the taxpayer's adjusted gross income (or, if greater, the taxpayer's earned income) exceeds the phaseout amount. The earned income credit may not exceed the excess of: (1) the credit percentage multiplied by the earned income amount, over (2) the phaseout percentage multiplied by the portion of the taxpayer's adjusted gross income (or earned income amount, if greater) that exceeds the beginning phaseout amount [§ 32(a)(2)].

The 2014 earned income phaseout amounts for an unmarried taxpayer (including surviving spouses and heads of household) taxpayer are as follows [§ 32(b); Rev. Proc. 2013-35]:

| Number of Children | Beginning Phaseout Amount | End Phaseout Range | Phaseout Percentage |
|---|---|---|---|
| 0 | $8,110 | $14,590 | 7.65% |
| 1 | $17,830 | $38,511 | 15.98% |
| 2 | $17,830 | $43,756 | 21.06% |
| 3+ | $17,830 | $46,997 | 21.06% |

For married taxpayers filing a joint return, the beginning and ending phase-out amounts are each increased by $5,430.

The 2015 earned income phaseout amounts for an unmarried taxpayer (including surviving spouses and heads of household) taxpayer are as follows [Rev. Proc. 2014-61, 2014-47 I.R.B. 860]:

| Number of Children | Beginning Phaseout Amount | End Phaseout Range | Phaseout Percentage |
|---|---|---|---|
| 0 | $8,240 | $14,820 | 7.65% |
| 1 | $18,110 | $39,131 | 15.98% |
| 2 | $18,110 | $44,454 | 21.06% |
| 3+ | $18,110 | $47,747 | 21.06% |

For married taxpayers filing a joint return, the beginning and ending phase-out amounts are each increased by $5,520.

### IX.G.4.c. Claiming the Earned Income Credit

[506 T.M., V.C.; TPS ¶3201.01.E.]

The credit may be claimed on Forms 1040, 1040A, or 1040EZ. Taxpayers who claim the EIC for a qualifying child must attach Schedule EIC (Form 1040A/1040), *Earned Income Credit* to either Form 1040 or 1040A. Taxpayers must include on the tax return for the tax year his or her taxpayer identification number, and, if married, the spouse's taxpayer identification number [§ 32(c)(1)(E)]. Additionally, the taxpayer must include on the return the name, age, and taxpayer identification number of any qualifying child [§ 32(c)(1)(F)].

Individuals filing returns for less than a 12-month period are not permitted to claim the credit unless the short period is due to the individual's death [§ 32(e)].

***Improper EIC claims.*** Taxpayers who make improper EIC claims are barred from claiming the EIC for: (1) a period of 10 tax years if there is a final determination that the improper claim was due to fraud; (2) a period of two tax years if the improper claim was due to reckless or intentional disregard of rules and regulations other than through fraud; and (3) any subsequent year if the credit is denied as a result of assessment of a tax on account of the credit, other than on account of a mathematical or clerical error, unless the taxpayer provides evidence of eligibility for the credit [§ 32(k)].

### IX.G.5. Fuel Tax Credit

[607 T.M., VI.; TPS ¶3201.02.]

Taxpayers that purchase and use gasoline, diesel fuel, aviation fuel, or special motor fuels in farming, off-highway business purposes, and other qualified activities are entitled to recover overpaid excise taxes by claiming an income tax credit. The fuel tax credit is refundable.

***Eligibility.*** In order to claim the farming use credit: (1) the gasoline must be used in carrying on a trade or business; (2) the use must occur on a farm situated in the United States; and (3) the gasoline must be used for farming purposes [§ 6420(c)(1)].

The off-highway business use credit is available only for gasoline used by a person [§ 6421(a), § 6421(e)(2)]:

- in a trade or business or production-of-income activity of such person;
- other than as fuel in a highway vehicle that (at the time of the use) is registered or required to be registered for highway use by any state or foreign law;
- other than use in a motorboat; and
- in qualified mobile machinery.

The use of gasoline in vessels employed in the commercial fishing or whaling business is an off-highway business use.

For a detailed discussion of eligibility for other components of the fuel tax credit, see the Bloomberg BNA Federal Excise Tax Navigator, Chapter 12.3.

***Amount of Credit.*** The credit amount is equal to the federal excise taxes paid when the fuel was purchased. However, in some cases the credit may be less than the total excise tax paid. For gasoline, the credit is determined by multiplying the number of gallons of gasoline used during the tax year by $0.183 (the excise tax rate) [§ 34(a)(1), § 6420(a), § 6421(a)]. For diesel, kerosene, and special motor fuels, the credit is determined by multiplying the number of gallons used during the tax year by $0.243 (the excise tax rate)

***Claiming the Credit.*** Generally, the credit is claimed on Form 4136, *Credit for Federal Tax Paid on Fuels,* which is attached to the taxpayer's income tax return. Partnerships do not file Form 4136, but attach to Form 1065 a statement allocating gasoline or other fuel to each partner and describing the use of such gasoline or other fuel so that each partner may claim his proportionate share of the credit on his individual return. However, certain taxpayers must file claims against their excise taxes on Form 720, *Quarterly Federal Excise Tax Return,* or Form 8849, *Claim for Refund of Excise Taxes,* before filing Form 4136.

If a taxpayer entitled to a fuel tax credit deducted the tax paid as an expense, then the credit must be included in gross income. The year of inclusion depends on the taxpayer's accounting method. A cash basis taxpayer includes the credit in gross income for the tax year in which the relevant Form 4136 is filed. For accrual method taxpayers, the credit is included in income for the tax year in which the fuel was used [Rev. Rul. 67–2, 1967-1 C.B. 13].

### IX.G.6. Credit for Health Insurance Costs of Eligible Individuals [Expired]

[389 T.M., VII.D.6., 506 T.M., V.J.; TPS ¶3201.03.]

Individual taxpayers who suffered job displacements due to import competition and certain individuals receiving benefits from the Pension Benefit Guaranty Corporation (PBGC) may claim a credit for health insurance premiums paid. The credit for health insurance costs of eligible individuals is refundable [§ 35(a)].

The credit is available for coverage months that begin before January 1, 2014 [§ 35(b)(1)(B)].

*Eligibility.* An eligible individual is an individual that is: (1) receiving trade adjustment assistance (TAA) (including alternative TAA) due to job dislocation caused by import competition, or (2) at least 55 years of age and is receiving a benefit from PBGC for a termination of a pension plan under title IV of the Employee Retirement Income Security Act (ERISA). To be entitled to the credit, the insurance premiums must be paid for eligible coverage months (as defined in § 35(b)). No credit is allowed to an individual for whom a dependency deduction is allowed to another taxpayer for a tax year beginning in the calendar year in which such individual's tax year begins [§ 35(c), § 35(g)(4)].

*Amount of Credit.* The credit amount is equal to 72.5% of the amount paid for the coverage of the taxpayer and qualifying family members under qualified health insurance (as defined in § 35(e)) during eligible coverage months [§ 35(a)].

The amount of the credit is reduced by any payments made to the qualified health insurance provider on behalf of the eligible individual on an advance basis under § 7527 [§ 35(g)(1)].

*Qualifying Family Member.* A qualifying family member includes the taxpayer's spouse and any dependent for whom the taxpayer is entitled to a deduction. A family member that has other specified coverage is not a qualifying family member. In the case of divorced or legally separated parents, the custodial parent is deemed entitled to the dependency deduction unless the custodial parent signs a written declaration that he or she will not claim the child as a dependent and the noncustodial parent attaches the written declaration to the noncustodial parent's return for the tax year [§ 35(d)].

An eligible individual's family members may continue to be qualifying family members even upon the occurrence of certain events [§ 35(g)(9)]:

- The month in which the eligible individual is entitled to Medicare is treated as an eligible coverage month to determine the amount of credit for qualifying family members.
- Upon the eligible individual's final divorce, the ex-spouse is treated as an eligible individual for 24 months.
- Upon the eligible individual's death, the surviving spouse is treated as an eligible individual for 24 months.

*Qualifying Individual.* A qualifying individual is an individual who, as of the date he seeks to enroll in coverage, has an aggregate of creditable coverage of three months or longer, and who does not have other specified coverage and is not imprisoned. The term qualified health insurance does not include a flexible spending plan or similar arrangement, or insurance if substantially all of its coverage consists of "excepted benefits" [§ 35(e)(2)(B)].

*Other Specified Coverage.* "Other specified coverage" includes subsidized coverage (at least 50% of the cost is paid by an employer) and coverage under Medicare or Medicaid. Benefits from the Veterans Administration are not "other specified coverage" [§ 35(f)].

*Claiming the Credit.* The credit is claimed on Form 8885, *Health Coverage Tax Credit*, which is then attached to the taxpayer's Form 1040, Form 1040NR, Form 1040-SS, or Form 1040-PR.

For payments to be made on an advance basis to a qualified health insurance provider under § 7527, a qualified health insurance costs credit eligibility certificate issued by the Department of Labor or PBGC must be in effect for the taxpayer [§ 35(g)(1), § 7527].

*Special Rules.* Amounts taken into account in determining the credit may not be taken into account in determining the amount allowable under the § 213 itemized deduction for medical expenses or the § 162(l) deduction for health insurance expenses of self-employed individuals [§ 35(g)(2)].

Amounts distributed from a medical savings account are not eligible for the credit [§ 35(g)(3)].

### IX.G.7. Post-2013 Health Insurance Premium Credit (Affordability Credit)

[513 T.M., III.I.; TPS ¶3201.06.]

Beginning in 2014, some individuals who are responsible for maintaining health insurance (see XVII.C.5.a.) may be eligible for a refundable health insurance premium credit [§ 36B(a)]. The credit applies to tax years ending after December 31, 2013.

Generally, the taxpayer who enrolls in a plan offered through a health exchange reports his income to the health exchange. Based on information provided to the health exchange by the taxpayer and the IRS, the taxpayer receives a premium assistance credit during the year, which Treasury pays directly to the taxpayer's health care plan [2010 Patient Protection and Affordable Care Act (2010 PPACA), § 1411]. The taxpayer pays the balance remaining on the premium charged to the plan. Premium assistance credits may be used toward any level of plan purchased through a health exchange. Taxpayers are not limited to the benchmark plan on which the credit is based, but they must pay any difference between the premium assistance amount and the actual premium for their plan [§ 36B(f)(3)]. A taxpayer may choose not to claim the advance payments but claim the credit on his or her return (see IX.G.7.d.).

If an individual experiences a change in income during the benefit year that affects his or her eligibility for premium assistance, the individual must report this to the exchange, which will conduct an eligibility redetermination. Any resulting change in the amount of advance payments of the premium tax credit will require the exchange to recalculate the amount of advance payments to adjust for any advance payments already made. If the change impacts cost-sharing subsidies, the exchange must determine the individual eligible for the category of cost-sharing subsidies that corresponds to his or her expected annual household income for the benefit year.

### IX.G.7.a. Eligibility for Post-2013 Health Insurance Premium Credit
[513 T.M., III.I.2.; TPS ¶3201.06.B.]

The credit is available to a taxpayer who pays premiums for enrollment in a qualified health plan offered through a health exchange and whose household income for the tax year is at least 100% but not more than 400% of an amount equal to the federal poverty line (FPL) for a family the size of the taxpayer's family [§ 36B(c)(1)(A); Reg. § 1.36B-2(b)(1)]. An individual generally is not eligible for the premium credit if he or she can get other minimum essential coverage (not including coverage in the individual market). Other coverage includes Medicare, Medicaid, other government-sponsored coverage, or employer-sponsored coverage. An employee is deemed not able to obtain employer-sponsored coverage if the employer plan is unaffordable because the employer coverage requires a contribution of more than 9.5% of the employee's household income or if the plan does not provide minimum value because it pays less than 60% of the total allowed costs of benefits provided to the employee. The affordability test for individuals who are related to the employee and covered under the employer-sponsored plan because of that relationship is based on the employee's required contribution for self-only coverage, not for family coverage. This test applies both for the employee and for individuals who are related to the employee and are covered under the employer plan [§ 36B(c)(2)(B), § 36B(c)(2)(C); Reg. § 1.36B-2(c)(3)(v)(A)(1), § 1.36B-2(c)(3)(v)(A)(2)]. If the individual declines employer plan coverage because a health exchange determined that the coverage would be unaffordable, the employer plan is considered unaffordable for the full plan year [Reg. § 1.36B-2(c)(3)].

A taxpayer who can be claimed as a dependent on another person's return is not eligible for the credit, even if the taxpayer is not actually claimed as a dependent. Married taxpayers may not claim the credit unless they file jointly for the year [§ 36B(c)(1)(C)]. However, for 2014, a victim of domestic abuse satisfies the joint return filing requirement if the individual files the 2014 income tax return as married filing separately [Reg. § 1.36B-2T(b)(2)(ii)].

A lawful immigrant whose immigration status precludes eligibility for Medicaid and whose household income does not exceed 100% of FPL is treated as having a household income at FPL [§ 36B(c)(1)(B)]. Coverage is reduced if any person for whom the personal exemption is claimed on the taxpayer's income tax return is not lawfully present in the United States. An individual who is incarcerated or who is not lawfully present in the United States may not claim the credit unless the individual is an applicable taxpayer eligible for premium assistance by virtue of a family member who enrolls in a qualified health plan [§ 36B(e); Reg. § 1.36B-2(b)(4)].

### IX.G.7.b. Amount of Post-2013 Health Insurance Premium Credit
[513 T.M., III.I.3.; TPS ¶3201.06.C.]

The amount of the health care premium tax credit for the year is equal to the total of the premium assistance amounts for each coverage month that occurs during the tax year. The amount of the credit available to the taxpayer is reduced by the amount of any advance payment of the credit. Credit amounts are tied to the cost of the applicable benchmark plan.

### IX.G.7.c. Definitions Applicable to Post-2013 Health Insurance Premium Credit
[513 T.M., III.I.; TPS ¶3201.06.]

**Premium Assistance Amount.** The premium assistance amount for a coverage month is the lesser of: (1) the monthly premiums for that month for one or more

504

qualified health plans offered in the individual market that cover the taxpayer, the taxpayer's spouse, or the taxpayer's dependent who were enrolled through a state health exchange, or (2) any excess of the adjusted monthly premium for the month for the applicable second lowest cost silver plan for the taxpayer (often called the benchmark plan), over 1/12 of the taxpayer's contribution amount, which is the applicable percentage (listed below) multiplied by the taxpayer's household income for the year. The adjusted monthly premium is the amount an issuer would charge for the benchmark plan to cover the members of the coverage family, as adjusted for the age of each member but not for tobacco use [§ 36B(b)(2)].

The applicable percentages for 2014 are as follows [§ 36B(b)(3)(A)]:

| Household Income | Initial Premium Percentage | Final Premium Percentage |
|---|---|---|
| (as % of FPL) | | |
| 100% to 133% | 2.0% | 2.0% |
| 133% to 150% | 3.0% | 4.0% |
| 150% to 200% | 4.0% | 6.3% |
| 200% to 250% | 6.3% | 8.05% |
| 250% to 300% | 8.05% | 9.5% |
| 300% to 400% | 9.5% | 9.5% |

*Coverage Month.* A coverage month is any month in which, as of the first day of the month, the taxpayer, the taxpayer's spouse, or any dependent of the taxpayer is enrolled in a qualified health plan through a health exchange, as long as the premium for coverage is paid by the taxpayer by the unextended due date for filing the taxpayer's income tax return or through advance payment of the credit. It does not include any month for which the individual is eligible for minimum essential coverage (other than coverage in the individual market) [§ 36B(c)(2)].

*Household Income.* Household income is the taxpayer's modified adjusted gross income (MAGI) plus the aggregate MAGIs of all other individuals for whom the taxpayer properly claims a personal exemption deduction and who are required to file a tax return under § 1 [§ 36B(d)(2)].

For this purpose, MAGI includes: (1) any amount excluded from gross income for foreign earned income and housing by U.S. citizens and residents living abroad (see XX.C.1.); (2) tax-exempt interest received or accrued by the taxpayer during the tax year (see II.B.); and (3) social security benefits not included in the taxpayer's gross income (see I.K.).

*Benchmark Plan.* The applicable benchmark plan is the second lowest cost silver plan that applies to the taxpayer. A silver plan is a plan that covers at least 70% of the value of benefits provided and: (1) is in the rating area in which the individual resides; (2) is offered through an exchange in the area in which the individual resides; and (3) provides self-only coverage in the case of an individual who purchases self-only coverage, or family coverage in the case of any other individual. If family members live in different states and enroll in separate qualified health plans, the sum of the premiums for the applicable benchmark plans for each group of family members living in the same state is the premium for the applicable benchmark plan. Under a proposed rule that taxpayers may apply for 2014, if family members live in different states and enroll in separate qualified health plans, the sum of the premiums for the applicable benchmark plans for each group of family members living in the same state is the premium for the applicable benchmark plan [§ 36B(b)(3)(B); Prop. Reg. § 1.36B-3(f)(4)].

No benefits other than essential health benefits are considered, even if the individual's home state requires the additional benefits. If an individual enrolls in both a qualified health plan and a pediatric dental plan for a plan year, the portion of the premium for the plan that is properly allocable to pediatric dental benefits that are included in the essential health benefits required to be provided by a qualified health plan must be treated as a premium payable for a qualified health plan [§ 36B(b)(3)(D), § 36B(b)(3)(E)].

If a taxpayer files a joint return, but the credit is not allowed for one spouse because the spouse is not lawfully present in the United States, the taxpayer will be treated as having self-only coverage for this purpose unless a personal exemption deduction is allowed for another dependent who is lawfully present in the United States [§ 36B(b)(3)(B), § 36B(e); Reg. § 1.36B-3(f)(1), § 1.36B-3(l)].

A qualified health plan may cover more than one family under a single policy (for example, a parent and a 25-year-old child on the same policy), in which case each applicable taxpayer covered by the plan may claim a premium tax credit, using that taxpayer's applicable percentage, household income, and applicable benchmark plan, assuming he or she is eligible for the credit [Reg. § 1.36B-3(h)].

### IX.G.7.d. Claiming the Post-2013 Health Insurance Premium Credit

[513 T.M., III.I.4.; TPS ¶3201.06.D.]

A taxpayer who receives an advance credit payment must file an income tax return and reconcile the actual credit for the tax year computed on the taxpayer's tax return with the amount of advance payments. A taxpayer whose tax credit year exceeds the taxpayer's advance credit payments may receive the excess as an income tax refund. A taxpayer whose advance credit payments for the tax year exceed the taxpayer's premium tax credit owes the excess as an additional income tax liability [§ 36B(f); Reg. § 1.36B-4(a)(1)].

The maximum amount of the tax increase is based on a sliding scale starting at $600 for household income below 200% ($300 for an unmarried individual not filing as a surviving spouse or head of a household) of the FPL and topping out at $2,500 ($1,250 for an unmarried individual) for household income at 300% to less than 400% of the FPL. Married taxpayers who receive advance credit payments and file separate income tax returns are treated as receiving excess advance payments, and the advance credit payments are allocated equally to each taxpayer [§ 36B(a), § 36B(f)(1); Reg. § 1.36B-4(a)(3)].

No deduction is allowed for the portion of health plan premiums paid using the premium tax credit [§ 280C(g)].

### IX.G.8. Child Tax Credit

[513 T.M., III.C.; TPS ¶3120.04.]

Taxpayers may claim a credit against tax for each qualifying child (see IX.B.4.). A portion of the child tax credit may be refundable.

***Amount of Credit.*** The child tax credit amount is $1,000 for each qualifying child for whom the taxpayer is allowed a dependency exemption deduction under § 151 [§ 24(a)]. The total credit is reduced by $50 for each $1,000 or increment thereof that the taxpayer's modified adjusted gross income exceeds the threshold amount, which is $110,000 for joint filers, $75,000 for unmarried individuals, and $55,000 for married individuals filing separately [§ 24(b)].

*Refundable Portion of Credit.* The refundable portion of the child tax credit is the "additional child tax credit." The child tax credit is refundable to the extent of the lesser of: (1) the unclaimed portion of the nonrefundable credit amount, or (2) the greater of 15% of the taxpayer's earned income in excess of $3,000 for 2014, or, for taxpayers with three or more qualifying children, the excess of the taxpayer's social security taxes over his earned income credit for the tax year [§ 24(d)].

*Claiming the Credit.* The refundable additional child tax credit is claimed on Form 8812, *Child Tax Credit*, which is attached to Form 1040, or Form 1040A, or Form 1040NR.

### IX.G.9. First-Time Homebuyer Credit [Expired]

#### IX.G.9.a. First-Time Homebuyer Credit, Including Long-Time Residents

[506 T.M., V.M.; 594 T.M., VI.D.; TPS ¶3201.09.B.]

Eligible first-time homebuyers who purchased a principal residence in the United States (not including the U.S. territories) on or after April 9, 2008, and entered into a written binding contract before May 1, 2010, and closed before October 1, 2010, were eligible for the first-time homebuyer credit. The credit has expired [§ 36].

*Eligibility.* Taxpayers who claim the first-time homebuyer credit may not also claim the D.C. first-time homebuyer credit under § 1400C for the same purchase. For residences purchased before January 1, 2009, taxpayers may not claim the first-time homebuyer credit if the taxpayer's financing was from tax-exempt mortgage revenue bonds.

*Amount of Credit.* The credit amount is equal to 10% of the residence's purchase price, not to exceed $8,000 ($4,000 for married taxpayers filing separately). A taxpayer may elect to treat the purchase of a principal residence purchased after December 31, 2008, as having occurred on December 31 of the preceding year, depending on which tax year is most advantageous. Individuals serving on qualified official extended duty outside the United States for at least 90 days during the period from January 1, 2009, through April 30, 2010, that entered into a written binding contract before May 1, 2011, to close before July, 1, 2011, were required to complete the purchase before July 1, 2011 [§ 36(b)(1)]. The credit is subject to a phaseout based on the taxpayer's modified adjusted gross income [§ 36(b)(2)].

As of November 7, 2009, long-time residents of the same principal residence were eligible for a $6,500 credit ($3,250 for married filing separately). Further, for purchases after this date, an $800,000 purchase price limitation applied, such that no credit is available for residences for which the purchase price exceeded $800,000 [§ 36(b)(1)(D), § 36(b)(3)].

For purchases that were made after November 6, 2009, a homeowner that had owned and used a principal residence for five consecutive years during the prior eight years and subsequently bought another principal residence is also eligible for a $6,500 credit ($3,250 for married filing separately) [§ 36(c)(6)].

*Claiming the Credit.* The first-time homebuyer credit is claimed by attaching a Form 5405, *First-Time Homebuyer Credit and Repayment of the Credit*, to Form 1040.

#### IX.G.9.b. Recapture of First-Time Homebuyer Credit

[506 T.M., II.E.3.g(9); TPS ¶3201.09.B.]

For the first-time homebuyer credit, the term "recapture" refers to both:

- the repayment of what was, essentially, an interest-free loan over 15 years (the "repayment provision"); and
- upon any disposition of the residence that was not covered by an exception (e.g., death, involuntary conversion, transfers between spouses or transfers incident to divorce), the accelerated recapture of any remaining credit amount in the year of the sale (the "accelerated recapture provision") [§ 36(f)].

For principal residences purchased after December 31, 2008, taxpayers are not subject to a repayment requirement and are subject to the accelerated recapture provision only if they disposed of the residence in a manner not covered by one of the listed exceptions within three years of the purchase date [§ 36(f)(4)(D)].

For principal residences purchased before January 1, 2009, a taxpayer that received the credit is subject to the repayment requirement and obligated to repay 6 ⅔% of the credit amount (for purchases before January 1, 2009, that is $500 if the maximum $7,500 credit is allowed) for each tax year in the recapture period. The credit is recaptured ratably over 15 years, with no interest charge, beginning in the second tax year after the tax year in which the home was purchased. The taxpayer is required to file a return for the recapture years even if not otherwise required to file. If the taxpayer sells the home (or the home ceases to be used as the principal residence of the taxpayer or the taxpayer's spouse) before the credit is fully repaid, any remaining credit repayment amount is due on the tax return for the year in which the home is sold or ceases to be used as the principal residence. However, the credit repayment amount cannot exceed the amount of gain from the sale of the residence to an unrelated person [§ 36(f)].

Effective November 7, 2009, there is no recapture for members of the Armed Forces in the event of a disposition, or cessation of use, of such individual's principal residence after 2008 due to government orders received by the individual (or the individual's spouse) for qualified official extended duty service [§ 36(f)(4)(E)].

***Reporting Recapture.*** For years after the expiration of the credit, recapture of the first-time homebuyer credit is reported on Form 5405, *Repayment of the First-Time Homebuyer Credit*, which is attached to Form 1040.

### IX.G.10. Refundable Credit for Adoption Expenses [Expired]

[506 T.M., V.E.; 513 T.M., III.F.2.c.; TPS ¶3201.09.C.]

Taxpayers may claim a credit for the amount of qualified adoption expenses paid or incurred regarding an eligible child. The credit was refundable (i.e., allowed even if in excess of the taxpayer's tax liability) for tax years beginning in 2010 and 2011.

***Amount of Credit.*** The credit for qualified adoption expenses was limited to $12,170 of aggregate expenditures for each child for tax years beginning in 2010, and $13,360 for tax years beginning in 2011 [Rev. Proc. 2010-40, 2010-46 I.R.B. 663; Rev. Proc. 2009-50, 2009-45 I.R.B. 617]. The credit is subject to a phaseout based on the taxpayer's modified adjusted gross income (MAGI).

For a discussion of the nonrefundable credit for adoption expenses, including discussion of qualified expenses and eligible children, see IX.B.3.

### IX.G.11. American Opportunity Tax Credit

[506 T.M., V.F.2.b., 517 T.M., V.A.4.; TPS ¶¶3120.05.B. 3201.08.]

For tax years beginning after 2008 and before 2018, the Hope Scholarship credit under § 25A(b) is expanded and is known as the American Opportunity Tax Credit.

*Amount of Credit.* The credit is equal to 100% of the first $2,000 of all of the qualified tuition and related expenses paid by the taxpayer during the tax year for each eligible student, plus 25% of the expenses that are more than $2,000 but not more than $4,000, for a total credit per student of up to $2,500 [§ 25A(i)(1)].

Up to 40% of the American Opportunity credit is refundable (i.e., up to $1,000 per eligible student), unless the taxpayer is a child whose income is subject to the "kiddie" tax (see X.A.3.) [§ 25A(i)(5)].

See IX.B.5.a. for a full discussion of the American Opportunity Tax Credit.

## IX.H. Minimum Tax Credit

[506 T.M., IV.F., 532 T.M., III.A.2.d(5)(d), 556 T.M., VI.I.1., 587 T.M., V.D.; TPS ¶3190.]

### IX.H.1. Minimum Tax Credit

Taxpayers may be entitled to a credit against their regular tax for a portion of a prior year alternative minimum tax (AMT) liability. Despite its name, the credit is not taken directly against the taxpayer's AMT.

*Eligibility.* The credit is available to corporations, individuals, estates and trusts that: (1) have paid AMT for tax years beginning after 1986 and before the year in which the credit is claimed; and (2) have had AMT adjustments or preference items that were not exclusion items in the year the AMT was paid [§ 53(a)].

*Amount of Credit.* The credit amount equals any excess of the adjusted net minimum tax (ANMT) imposed for all prior tax years beginning after 1986, over the amount allowable as a minimum tax credit for the prior years. For corporate taxpayers, ANMT equals net minimum tax for the year. For noncorporate taxpayers, ANMT for a tax year equals AMT for that tax year reduced by the AMT the taxpayer would be required to pay if exclusion preferences were the only AMT adjustments for the tax year [§ 53(b), § 53(d)(1)].

In computing AMTI, adjustments can be either positive or negative; accordingly, ANMT may be negative in years when there are negative adjustments.

*Exclusion Preferences.* Exclusion preferences are AMT preferences and adjustments that reflect items permanently removed from taxable income, specifically:

- the adjustment for miscellaneous itemized deductions disallowed for AMT purposes;
- the adjustment for property and income tax deductions disallowed for AMT purposes;
- the adjustment for medical expense deductions disallowed for AMT purposes by raising the floor from 7.5% to 10%;
- the adjustment for interest deductions disallowed for AMT purposes;
- the adjustment for tax refunds not included in gross income for AMT purposes;
- the adjustment for standard deductions and personal exemptions disallowed for AMT purposes;
- the adjustment eliminating the phaseout of itemized deductions;
- the adjustment for excess depletion deductions disallowed for AMT purposes;

- the adjustment for certain tax-exempt interest exclusions disallowed for AMT purposes; and
- the adjustment for the small business stock sale gain exclusion disallowed for AMT purposes [§ 53(d)(1)(B)].

---

**EXAMPLE:** John is an unmarried individual. His taxable income for 2011 is $20,000. Thus, his regular tax liability is $2,575 (($8,500 × 10%) + ($11,500 × 15%)). John has one $50,750 AMT adjustment arising from circulation expenditure amortization, which is not an exclusion preference. His AMTI equals $70,750 ($20,000 + $50,750). Because the exemption amount is $48,450, John's taxable excess equals $22,300 ($70,750 minus $48,450). His TMT equals $5,798 ($22,300 × 26%). His AMT and ANMT both equal $3,223, the excess of the $5,798 TMT over the $2,575 regular tax liability. If John's AMT were computed with regard only to exclusion preferences, his AMTI would be $20,000, the same as his taxable income. His taxable excess would be zero ($20,000 minus $48,450). John's TMT would be zero, and his AMT would be zero. Thus, his ANMT equals $3,223 ($3,223 AMT minus zero AMT computed with regard only to exclusion preferences). Thus, John's ANMT equals his AMT, and this $3,223 amount is added to the minimum tax credits available for the first subsequent year in which he does not have AMT liability.

---

If the AMT adjustment were an exclusion preference (for example, for miscellaneous itemized deductions disallowed for AMT purposes), John's AMTI would be $70,750, his taxable excess would be $22,300 ($70,750 minus $48,450), his TMT would be $5,798, and his AMT would be $3,223 ($5,798 minus $2,575). Thus, John's ANMT would equal zero ($3,223 AMT minus $3,223 AMT computed with regard only to exclusion preferences) and there would be no minimum tax credit.

*Limitation on Credit and Carryover.* The minimum tax credit is limited to the excess of the taxpayer's regular tax liability for the tax year, reduced by nonrefundable credits, over the taxpayer's tentative minimum tax for the tax year [§ 53(c)]. Unused minimum tax credits are carried forward and may be used to offset regular tax liability indefinitely until exhausted. Excess credits may not be carried back.

*Claiming the Credit.* Individuals, estates, and trusts claim the credit by attaching Form 8801, *Credit for Prior Year Minimum Tax—Individuals, Estates, and Trusts,* to their income tax returns. Corporations claim the credit by attaching Form 8827, *Credit for Prior Year Minimum Tax—Corporations,* to their income tax returns.

### IX.H.2. Refundable Long-Term Unused Minimum Tax Credit [Expired]

[506 T.M., IV.F.3., 587 T.M., V.D.; TPS ¶3201.09.A.]

For tax years beginning after December 20, 2006, and before January 1, 2013, individual taxpayers may claim a refundable credit for long-term unused minimum tax credits from prior years [§ 53(e)(1), § 53(e)(4)]. The credit is claimed on Form 8801, *Credit for Prior Year Minimum Tax—Individuals, Estates, and Trusts.*

*Amount of Credit.* For tax years beginning after December 31, 2007, the AMT refundable credit amount (which may not exceed that year's long-term unused minimum tax credit) is equal to the greater of: (1) 50% of the long-term unused minimum tax credit for that tax year; or (2) the AMT refundable credit for the preceding tax year (not taking into account any increase in credit under § 53(f)(2)) [§ 53(e)(2)]. For the first two tax years beginning after 2007, the credit was increased by 50% of any interest and penalties attributable to the application of the minimum tax adjustment for incentive stock options (see XVII.B.2.) before October 3, 2008 [§ 53(f)(2)].

***Long-Term Unused Minimum Tax Credit.*** The long-term unused minimum tax credit for any tax year is the portion of the minimum tax credit attributable to the adjusted net minimum tax for tax years before the third tax year immediately preceding the tax year at issue, determined on a first-in, first-out basis [§ 53(e)(3)].

### IX.H.3. Election to Accelerate the Minimum Tax Credit in Lieu of Bonus Depreciation [Expired]

[532 T.M., III.A.2.d(5)(d); TPS ¶¶2370.12.F.2.d.(3)., 3201.07.]

Corporate taxpayers may elect to accelerate the minimum tax credit in lieu of taking the § 168(k) additional first-year depreciation deduction (bonus depreciation) for qualified property placed in service after March 31, 2008, but before January 1, 2014. The election also applied to the § 41 research credit for the period through January 1, 2010 (see IX.A.8.). The increases in credits are refundable [§ 168(k)(4)]. For a detailed discussion, see V.C.1.c.(2).

The minimum tax credit is accelerated by increasing the taxpayer's § 53(c) prior year alternative minimum tax limitation by its bonus depreciation amount. The minimum tax credit increase amount equals the portion of the § 53(b) minimum tax credit for the first tax year ending after March 31, 2008, determined by taking into account only the adjusted minimum tax for tax years beginning before January 1, 2006, determining credits on a first-in, first-out basis [§ 168(k)(4)(E)(iv)].

***Claiming the Credit.*** The refundable credit is claimed on Form 8827, *Credit for Prior Year Minimum Tax—Corporations.* Taxpayers generally must make the § 168(k)(4) election by the due date (including extensions) of the federal income tax return for the taxpayer's first tax year ending either after March 31, 2008, or after December 31, 2010, depending on whether the property in question was round 2 extension property or round 3 extension property [Rev. Proc. 2008-65, 2008-44 I.R.B. 1082, *amplified and supplemented by* Rev. Proc. 2009-16, 2009-6 I.R.B. 449, *modified by* Rev. Proc. 2009-33, 2009-29 I.R.B. 150].

The election is revocable only with consent of the IRS.

# CHAPTER X. COMPUTATION OF TAX

## >>>>>>>>>>>>>>>>>>>>>>>>>>>>>>>

Federal income tax liability is generally determined by multiplying taxable income by the appropriate tax rates. However, there are various income tax liability computations that are based on other amounts and to which other rates apply (e.g., the alternative minimum tax, the net investment income tax, the self-employment tax). In addition, credit recaptures are added to income tax liability even though their computation is not based on the application of tax rates.

Generally, federal income tax liability is computed only to the extent a statutory provision specifically so provides. The primary income tax rates and tax computation provisions are set forth in § 1 through § 15 of the Code, but there are other provisions scattered throughout the remainder of the Code.

Federal income tax liability is limited to taxes computed on taxable income or some other form of income. Other federal tax liabilities, such as gift, estate, generation-skipping, and excise taxes, are not income tax liabilities.

Most individuals and entities are subject to federal income tax. However, pass-through entities, such as partnerships and S corporations, are not subject to federal income tax. The income of such pass-through entities is passed through to their owners (e.g., their partners and shareholders) and taxed at the owner level. In addition, nonresident aliens and foreign corporations that do not receive income from U.S. sources are not subject to federal income tax.

The federal income tax liability of individuals is discussed at X.A. The federal income tax liability of C corporations is discussed at X.B. The federal income tax liability of estates and trusts is discussed in Chapter XVIII.

## X.A. Federal Income Tax Liability of Individuals

### X.A.1. Regular Income Tax

[507 T.M., II.; TPS ¶3310.]

Section 1 of the Code imposes an income tax on U.S. citizens, resident aliens, and in certain circumstances, nonresident aliens [§ 1, § 871(b), § 877(b)].

### X.A.1.a. Computation of the Regular Income Tax

[507 T.M., II.; TPS ¶3310.]

Generally, individual taxpayers are required to compute regular income tax liability by multiplying taxable income by specified rates. There are seven rates that apply to individuals: 10%, 15%, 25%, 28%, 33%, 35%, and 39.6%. To apply the rates, taxable income is divided into seven brackets that are based on the amount of taxable income. The lowest rate applies to the lowest bracket of taxable income, the next lowest rate to the next lowest bracket, and so on. The amount of taxable income within each bracket varies according to the filing status of the individual [§ 1]. For an additional discussion of the computation of the regular income tax for individual taxpayers, see XII.A.1.

*Tax Rate Schedules and Tax Computation.* The IRS provides four tax rate schedules for individual taxpayers that show the tax rates that apply to all levels of taxable income (see *Schedules & Tables 1.* for the 2014 tax rate schedules and *Schedules & Tables 2.* for the 2015 tax rate schedules). The tax rate schedules are based on the § 1 tax rate schedules, as adjusted for inflation by an annual revenue procedure (for 2014, see Rev. Proc. 2013-35, 2013-47 I.R.B. 537; for 2015, see Rev. Proc. 2014-61, 2014-47 I.R.B. 860). The applicable tax rate schedule depends on an individual taxpayer's filing status (see XII.C.). There is a separate tax rate schedule for each of the following four filing statuses: (i) married filing jointly (including surviving spouses), (ii) married filing separately, (iii) head of household, and (iv) single.

Each year in the Form 1040 instructions, the IRS provides a Tax Table (see *Schedules & Tables 4.* for the 2014 Tax Table) and a Tax Computation Worksheet (see *Schedules & Tables 3.* for the 2014 Tax Computation Worksheet) that taxpayers generally must use to compute their tax for the year. The Tax Table and Tax Computation Worksheet are based on the tax rate schedules for that year. Taxpayers with taxable income of less than $100,000 must use the Tax Table to compute their tax. Taxpayers with taxable income of $100,000 or more must use the Tax Computation Worksheet.

*Special Tax Rates for Net Capital Gain and Qualified Dividend Income.* Special tax rates apply to the net capital gain of individual taxpayers. An individual taxpayer's net capital gain is taxed at no more than the applicable maximum capital gains rate. There are five maximum capital gains rates: 0%, 15%, 20%, 25%, and 28% [§ 1(h)].

Net capital gain is the excess of net long-term capital gain over net short-term capital loss. Net long-term capital gain is the excess of net long-term capital gains over net long-term capital losses. Net short-term capital loss is the excess of short-term capital losses over short-term capital gains [§ 1222]. For purposes of the maximum capital gains rate computations, net capital gain is reduced (but not below zero) by the amount taken into account as investment income under § 163(d)(4)(B)(iii) for purposes of computing deductible investment interest expense [§ 1(h)(2)].

Qualified dividend income is treated as net capital gain. Thus, qualified dividend income is taxed at no more than the applicable maximum capital gains rate. Qualified dividend income is dividends received during the tax year from domestic corporations and qualified foreign corporations [§ 1(h)(11)]. See I.E.2.a. for further discussion of qualified dividend income.

The regular income tax liability of an individual taxpayer who has a net capital gain for the tax year is equal to the sum of six tax amounts [§ 1(h)(1)]:

1. The first tax amount is the tax that, in the absence of the maximum capital gains rates, would be imposed on the greater of the following two amounts: (i) taxable income reduced by the net capital gain, or (ii) the lesser of taxable income subject to tax at a rate below 25% or taxable income reduced by adjusted net capital gain.

2. The second tax amount is 0% of the lesser of: (i) the 5% gain, or (ii) the 5% gain limitation amount. The 5% gain is equal to the lesser of adjusted net capital gain or taxable income. The 5% gain limitation amount is equal to the excess of the

amount of taxable income that would otherwise be taxed at a rate below 25% over taxable income reduced by adjusted net capital gain.

3. The third tax amount is 15% of the lesser of (i) the amount by which the lesser of adjusted net capital gain or taxable income exceeds the amount on which the second tax amount is computed, or (ii) the amount by which taxable income that would otherwise be taxed at a rate below 39.6% exceeds the sum of the amounts on which the first and second tax amounts are computed.

4. The fourth tax amount is 20% of the amount by which the lesser of adjusted net capital gain or taxable income exceeds the sum of the amounts on which the second and third tax amounts are computed.

5. The fifth tax amount is 25% of the excess of limited unrecaptured § 1250 gain over any excess first tax amount. Limited unrecaptured § 1250 gain is the lesser of unrecaptured § 1250 gain or net capital gain determined without regard to any qualified dividend income. The excess first tax amount is any excess of the sum of the amount on which the first tax amount is computed plus net capital gain over taxable income.

6. The sixth tax amount is 28% of any excess of taxable income over the sum of the amounts subject to the first four tax amounts.

For purposes of these computations, adjusted net capital gain is the sum of (i) net capital gain (determined without regard to qualified dividend income) reduced (but not below zero) by unrecaptured § 1250 gain and 28% gain, and (ii) qualified dividend income [§ 1(h)(3)].

The 28% gain equals the excess, if any, of the 28% gross gain over the 28% gross loss. The 28% gross gain equals the sum of the collectibles gain and § 1202 gain. The 28% gross loss equals the sum of collectibles losses, net short-term capital loss, and the amount of long-term capital loss carried to the tax year. Collectibles gain or loss is the gain or loss from the sale or exchange of a collectible (works of art, antiques, gems, coins, stamps, etc.) that is a capital asset held for more than one year, but only to the extent taken into account in computing taxable income [§ 1(h)(4), [§ 1(h)(5)].

Unrecaptured § 1250 gain equals the excess, if any, of the § 1250 capital gain over the 28% loss. The § 1250 capital gain equals long-term capital gain not otherwise treated as ordinary income that would be treated as ordinary income if § 1250 depreciation recapture applied to all depreciation on § 1250 property using 100% as the applicable percentage. The 28% loss equals the excess of any 28% gross loss over 28% gross gain [§ 1(h)(6)].

For additional discussion of the taxation of net capital gain, see III.B.4.

***Reporting Regular Income Tax.*** An individual taxpayer generally reports the tax computed on the Tax Table or Tax Computation Worksheet directly on the "Tax" line of Form 1040. However, in the following situations, an individual taxpayer must use a special form or worksheet to compute his or her regular income tax:

- Individual taxpayers with net capital gain or qualified dividend income must compute their regular income tax using the Schedule D Tax Worksheet (Source: 2014 Form 1040 (Schedule D) Draft Instructions) or the Qualified Dividends and Capital Gain Tax Worksheet.

- Certain children who had more than $2,000 of unearned income during 2014 ($2,100 during 2015) are taxed on this income at their parents' tax rate instead of their own rate if their parents' rate is higher. Such children must compute their regular income tax on Form 8615, *Tax for Certain Children Who Have Unearned Income.* See X.A.3. for a discussion of this so-called kiddie tax.

- Individual taxpayers with income from farming or fishing may elect to compute their regular income tax using income averaging. Such taxpayers must compute their tax on Schedule J (Form 1040), *Income Averaging for Farmers and Fishermen.*

- Individual taxpayers who claimed the foreign income exclusion, housing exclusion, or housing deduction on Form 2555, *Foreign Earned Income,* or Form 2555-EZ, *Foreign Earned Income Exclusion,* must compute their regular income tax using the Foreign Earned Income Tax Worksheet (see Chapter XX.).

---

**Schedule D Tax Worksheet**  *Keep for Your Records*

Complete this worksheet only if line 18 or line 19 of Schedule D is more than zero. Otherwise, complete the Qualified Dividends and Capital Gain Tax Worksheet in the Instructions for Form 1040, line 44 (or in the Instructions for Form 1040NR, line 42) to figure your tax. Before completing this worksheet, complete Form 1040 through line 43 (or Form 1040NR through line 41).
Exception: Do not use the Qualified Dividends and Capital Gain Tax Worksheet or this worksheet to figure your tax if:
 • Line 15 or line 16 of Schedule D is zero or less and you have no qualified dividends on Form 1040, line 9b (or Form 1040NR, line 10b); or
 • Form 1040, line 43 (or Form 1040NR, line 41) is zero or less.
Instead, see the instructions for Form 1040, line 44 (or Form 1040NR, line 42).

1. Enter your taxable income from Form 1040, line 43 (or Form 1040NR, line 41). (However, if you are filing Form 2555 or 2555-EZ (relating to foreign earned income), enter instead the amount from line 3 of the Foreign Earned Income Tax Worksheet in the Instructions for Form 1040, line 44) .................... 1. ____
2. Enter your qualified dividends from Form 1040, line 9b (or Form 1040NR, line 10b) ............ 2. ____
3. Enter the amount from Form 4952 (used to figure investment interest expense deduction), line 4g ....... 3. ____
4. Enter the amount from Form 4952, line 4e* ......................... 4. ____
5. Subtract line 4 from line 3. If zero or less, enter -0- ..................... 5. ____
6. Subtract line 5 from line 2. If zero or less, enter -0-** .............. 6. ____
7. Enter the smaller of line 15 or line 16 of Schedule D ................................. 7. ____
8. Enter the smaller of line 3 or line 4 ............ 8. ____
9. Subtract line 8 from line 7. If zero or less, enter -0-** .............. 9. ____
10. Add lines 6 and 9 ............................................. 10. ____
11. Add lines 18 and 19 of Schedule D** ........................... 11. ____
12. Enter the smaller of line 9 or line 11 .......................... 12. ____
13. Subtract line 12 from line 10 ...................................... 13. ____
14. Subtract line 13 from line 1. If zero or less, enter -0- ........................................ 14. ____
15. Enter:
 • $36,900 if single or married filing separately;
 • $73,800 if married filing jointly or qualifying widow(er); or
 • $49,400 if head of household ............... 15. ____
16. Enter the smaller of line 1 or line 15 ........................ 16. ____
17. Enter the smaller of line 14 or line 16 ........... 17. ____
18. Subtract line 10 from line 1. If zero or less, enter -0- ................................. 18. ____
19. Enter the larger of line 17 or line 18 .......................... 19. ____
20. Subtract line 17 from line 16. This amount is taxed at 0%. ...................... 20. ____
If lines 1 and 16 are the same, skip lines 21 through 41 and go to line 42. Otherwise, go to line 21.
21. Enter the smaller of line 1 or line 13 ............................. 21. ____
22. Enter the amount from line 20 (if line 20 is blank, enter -0-) .......... 22. ____
23. Subtract line 22 from line 21. If zero or less, enter -0- .............. 23. ____
24. Enter:
 • $406,750 if single;
 • $228,800 if married filing separately;
 • $457,600 if married filing jointly or qualifying widow(er); or
 • $432,200 if head of household ............... 24. ____
25. Enter the smaller of line 1 or line 24 ....................... 25. ____
26. Add lines 19 and 20 ....................................... 26. ____
27. Subtract line 26 from line 25. If zero or less, enter -0- ............... 27. ____
28. Enter the smaller of line 23 or line 27 ............................ 28. ____
29. Multiply line 28 by 15% (.15) ................................................. 29. ____
30. Add lines 22 and 28 ............................................. 30. ____
If lines 1 and 30 are the same, skip lines 31 through 41 and go to line 42. Otherwise, go to line 31.

**Schedule D Tax Worksheet—*Continued***

| | | |
|---|---|---|
| 31. | Subtract line 30 from line 21 . . . . . . . . . . . . . . . . . . . . . . . . . . . . . . . . . . . . . . . . . . . . . . | 31. |
| 32. | Multiply line 31 by 20% (.20) . . . . . . . . . . . . . . . . . . . . . . . . . . . . . . . . . . . . . . . . . . . . . . | 32. |
| | **If Schedule D, line 19, is zero or blank, skip lines 33 through 38 and go to line 39. Otherwise, go to line 33.** | |
| 33. | Enter the **smaller** of line 9 above or Schedule D, line 19 . . . . . . . . . . | 33. |
| 34. | Add lines 10 and 19 . . . . . . . . . . . . . . . . . . . . . . | 34. |
| 35. | Enter the amount from line 1 above . . . . . . . . . . | 35. |
| 36. | Subtract line 35 from line 34. If zero or less, enter -0- . . . . . . . . . . . . . | 36. |
| 37. | Subtract line 36 from line 33. If zero or less, enter -0- | 37. |
| 38. | Multiply line 37 by 25% (.25) . . . . . . . . . . . . . . . . . . . . . . . . . . . . . . . . . . . . . . . . . . . . . . | 38. |
| | **If Schedule D, line 18, is zero or blank, skip lines 39 through 41 and go to line 42. Otherwise, go to line 39.** | |
| 39. | Add lines 19, 20, 28, 31, and 37 . . . . . . . . . . . . . . . . . . . . . . . . . . . . . . . . . . . . . . . . . . | 39. |
| 40. | Subtract line 39 from line 1 . . . . . . . . . . . . . . . . . . . . . . . . . . . . . . . . . . . . . . . . . . . . . . . | 40. |
| 41. | Multiply line 40 by 28% (.28) . . . . . . . . . . . . . . . . . . . . . . . . . . . . . . . . . . . . . . . . . . . . . . | 41. |
| 42. | Figure the tax on the amount on **line 19.** If the amount on line 19 is less than $100,000, use the Tax Table to figure the tax. If the amount on line 19 is $100,000 or more, use the Tax Computation Worksheet . . . . . . . . . | 42. |
| 43. | Add lines 29, 32, 38, 41, and 42 . . . . . . . . . . . . . . . . . . . . . . . . . . . . . . . . . . . . . . . . . . . | 43. |
| 44. | Figure the tax on the amount on **line 1.** If the amount on line 1 is less than $100,000, use the Tax Table to figure the tax. If the amount on line 1 is $100,000 or more, use the Tax Computation Worksheet . . . . . . . . . . | 44. |
| 45. | **Tax on all taxable income (including capital gains and qualified dividends).** Enter the **smaller** of line 43 or line 44. Also include this amount on Form 1040, line 44 (or Form 1040NR, line 42). (If you are filing Form 2555 or 2555-EZ, do not enter this amount on Form 1040, line 44. Instead, enter it on line 4 of the Foreign Earned Income Tax Worksheet in the Form 1040 instructions) . . . . . . . . . . . . . . . . . . . . . . . . . . . | 45. |

*If applicable, enter instead the smaller amount you entered on the dotted line next to line 4e of Form 4952.

**If you are filing Form 2555 or 2555-EZ, see the footnote in the Foreign Earned Income Tax Worksheet in the Instructions for Form 1040, line 44, before completing this line.

*IRS Computation of Income Tax.* An individual taxpayer may elect to have the IRS compute his or her regular income tax liability if he or she meets all of the following conditions [§ 6014; Reg. § 1.6014-2]:

1. the taxpayer elects to have the IRS compute his income tax liability by not showing any liability on his filed return;

2. the taxpayer files the return on or before the due date (not including extensions);

3. the taxpayer cannot be claimed as an exemption on another taxpayer's return and he has either (i) gross income exceeding his standard deduction, or (ii) unearned income exceeding twice his standard deduction;

4. the taxpayer does not itemize his deductions;

5. the taxpayer claims the full standard deduction or a standard deduction amount of zero;

6. the taxpayer's taxable income is less than $100,000;

7. all of the taxpayer's income for the year is from wages, salaries, tips, interest, dividends, taxable social security benefits, unemployment compensation, IRA distributions, pensions, or annuities;

8. the taxpayer does not request a direct deposit of any refund;

9. the taxpayer does not request the application of any portion of a refund to the following year's estimated taxes; and

10. the taxpayer does not file Form 2555, Form 2555-EZ, Form 4137, Form 4970, Form 4972, Form 6198, Form 6251, Form 8606, Form 8615, Form 8814, Form 8839, Form 8853, Form 8889, or Form 8919.

If the IRS computes an overpayment, the taxpayer will receive a refund from the IRS. If the IRS computes an underpayment, the taxpayer will receive a bill from the IRS. In the latter case, the tax is due by the later of (i) 30 days after the date of the bill, or (ii) the due date of the tax return. No interest or penalty accrues on the underpayment until after the tax is due [Reg. § 1.6014-2].

### X.A.1.b. Other Amounts Reported with the Regular Income Tax

[507 T.M.; TPS ¶3310.]

Individual taxpayers must report the following amounts on the "Tax" line of Form 1040 along with their regular income tax liability:

- If parents elect to report their child's interest and dividends on their own tax return, the tax on the first $2,000 for 2014 ($2,100 for 2015) of the child's interest and dividends is computed in Part II of Form 8814, *Parents' Election To Report Child's Interest and Dividends*, and reported on the "Tax" line of Form 1040. See I.B.3. for further discussion of this election.

- If an employee receives a lump-sum distribution or payment of his entire balance from all of his employer's qualified plans of one kind (e.g., pension, profit-sharing, or stock bonus plans) in which he has funds, and he elects to compute the tax on the distribution or payment using the 20% capital gain election and/or the 10-year tax option, the employee must compute the tax on Form 4972, *Tax on Lump-Sum Distributions*, and report the tax on the "Tax" line of Form 1040. See XVII.A.2.e. for further discussion of distributions from qualified plans.

- If an individual taxpayer claimed an education credit (see IX.B.5.) but then received tax-free educational assistance or a refund of qualified educational expenses after filing the return on which the credit was claimed, he must recapture any excess educational credit. To do this, the taxpayer must recompute his educational credit by reducing his qualified educational expenses by the amount of the refund or tax-free educational assistance. The taxpayer then reports on the "Tax" line of Form 1040 the amount by which his tax would have increased if it had been computed using the lower amount of the recomputed education credit.

- If an individual taxpayer is a shareholder in a controlled foreign corporation (CFC) (see XX.C.3.b.) and he makes a § 962 election to be taxed at the corporate tax rates on amounts included in his gross income under § 951(a), he must report this tax on the "Tax" line of Form 1040.

- If an individual taxpayer is a shareholder in a passive foreign investment company (PFIC) (see XX.C.3.c.) that is a § 1291 fund and he receives any excess distributions from the fund, he must compute the tax on the excess distributions in Part V of Form 8621, *Information Return by a Shareholder of a Passive Foreign Investment Company or Qualified Electing Fund*, and report the tax on the "Tax" line of Form 1040.

### X.A.2. Alternative Minimum Tax

[587 T.M.; TPS ¶3410.]

The alternative minimum tax (AMT) generally applies to taxpayers who have certain types of income that receive favorable treatment and/or certain types of deductions and credits. These tax benefits can significantly reduce the regular income tax liability of many taxpayers, especially high-income taxpayers. The AMT essentially sets a limit on the amount of these tax benefits that can be used to reduce the regular income tax liability of taxpayers. The AMT for individual taxpayers is computed and reported on Form 6251, *Alternative Minimum Tax — Individuals.*

The AMT system is separate and entirely distinct from, but parallel to, the regular tax system. Thus, the U.S. tax system is essentially a two-track tax system. A taxpayer must pay AMT to the extent that his tax under the AMT system exceeds his tax under the regular tax system. The AMT is an amount that is paid in addition to regular tax.

Most taxpayers can use the Worksheet To See if You Should Fill in Form 6251 (Source: 2014 Form 1040 Draft Instructions) to determine whether they are potentially subject to AMT. However, taxpayers that claimed or received any of the following items must complete Form 6251 to determine whether they owe AMT: (i) accelerated depreciation, (ii) tax-exempt interest from private activity bonds, (iii) intangible drilling, circulation, research, experimental, or mining costs, (iv) amortization of pollution-controlled facilities or depletion, (v) income or loss from tax-shelter farm activities, passive activities, partnerships, S corporations, or activities for which the taxpayer is not at risk, (vi) income from long-term contracts not computed using the percentage-of-completion method, (vii) interest paid on a home mortgage not used buy, build, or substantially improve the taxpayer's home, (viii) investment interest expense reported on Form 4952, (ix) net operating loss deduction, (x) AMT adjustments from an estate, trust, electing large partnership, or cooperative, (xi) § 1202 exclusion, (xii) stock from the exercise of an incentive stock option that was not disposed of in the same year, (xiii) a general business credit claimed on Form 3800 (if line 6 or line 25 of Form 3800 is more than zero), (xiv) qualified electric vehicle credit, (xv) alternative fuel vehicle refueling property tax, (xvi) credit for prior year minimum tax, or (xvii) foreign tax credit.

**Worksheet To See if You Should Fill in Form 6251—Line 45**          *Keep for Your Records*

| | |
|---|---|
| **Before you begin:** | ✓ Be sure you have read the **Exception** in the instructions for this line to see if you must fill in Form 6251 instead of using this worksheet. |
| | ✓ If you are claiming the foreign tax credit (see the instructions for line 48), enter that credit on line 48. |

1. Are you filing **Schedule A**?

   ☐ **No.** Skip lines 1 through 3; enter on line 4 the amount from Form 1040, line 38, and go to line 5

   ☐ **Yes.** Enter the amount from Form 1040, line 41 . . . . . . . . . . . . . . . . . . . . . . . . . . . . . . . . . . . . . **1.** _____

2. If you or your spouse was age 65 or older, enter the **smaller** of the amount on Schedule A, line 4, or 2.5% (0.25) of the amount on Form 1040, line 38. If zero or less, enter -0- . . . . . . . . . . . . . . . . . . . . . . . . . . . . . . . . . **2.** _____

3. Enter the total of the amounts from Schedule A, lines 9 and 27 . . . . . . . . . . . . . . . . . . . . . . . . . . . . **3.** _____

4. Add lines 1 through 3 . . . . . . . . . . . . . . . . . . . . . . . . . . . . . . . . . . . . . . . . . . . . . . . . . . . . . . . **4.** _____

5. Enter any tax refund from Form 1040, lines 10 and 21 . . . . . . . . . . . . . . . . . . . . . . . . . . . . . . . . . **5.** _____

6. If you completed the Itemized Deductions Worksheet in the Instructions for Schedule A, enter the amount from line 9 of that worksheet . . . . . . . . . . . . . . . . . . . . . . . . . . . . . . . . . . . . . . . . . . . . . . . . . . . . . . . . **6.** _____

7. Add lines 5 and 6 . . . . . . . . . . . . . . . . . . . . . . . . . . . . . . . . . . . . . . . . . . . . . . . . . . . . . . . . . . **7.** _____

8. Subtract line 7 from line 4 . . . . . . . . . . . . . . . . . . . . . . . . . . . . . . . . . . . . . . . . . . . . . . . . . . . . **8.** _____

9. Enter the amount shown below for your filing status

   • Single or head of household—$52,800
   • Married filing jointly or qualifying widow(er)—$82,100      } . . . . . . . . . .
   • Married filing separately—$41,050                                                              **9.** _____

10. Is the amount on line 8 more than the amount on line 9?

   ☐ **No.** (STOP) You do not need to fill in Form 6251. Do not complete the rest of this worksheet.

   ☐ **Yes.** Subtract line 9 from line 8 . . . . . . . . . . . . . . . . . . . . . . . . . . . . . . . . . . . . . . . . . . . **10.** _____

11. Enter the amount shown below for your filing status.

   • Single or head of household—$117,300
   • Married filing jointly or qualifying widow(er)—$156,500      } . . . . . . . . . .
   • Married filing separately—$78,250                                                              **11.** _____

12. Is the amount on line 8 more than the amount on line 11?

   ☐ **No.** Enter -0-. Skip line 13. Enter on line 14 the amount from line 10, and go to line 15.

   ☐ **Yes.** Subtract line 11 from line 8 . . . . . . . . . . . . . . . . . . . . . . . . . . . . . . . . . . . . . . . . . . . **12.** _____

13. Multiply line 12 by 25% (.25) and enter the **smaller** of the result or line 9 . . . . . . . . . . . . . . . . . . . . . . . . **13.** _____

14. Add lines 10 and 13 . . . . . . . . . . . . . . . . . . . . . . . . . . . . . . . . . . . . . . . . . . . . . . . . . . . . . . . **14.** _____

15. Is the amount on line 14 more than $182,500 ($91,250 if married filing separately)?

   ☐ **Yes.** (STOP) Fill in Form 6251 to see if you owe the alternative minimum tax.

   ☐ **No.** Multiply line 14 by 26% (.26) . . . . . . . . . . . . . . . . . . . . . . . . . . . . . . . . . . . . . . . . . . . **15.** _____

16. Add Form 1040, line 44 (minus any tax from Form 4972), and Form 1040, line 46. (If you used Schedule J to figure your tax on Form 1040, line 44, refigure that tax without using Schedule J before including it in this calculation) . . . . . . . . . . . . . . . . . . . . . . . . . . . . . . . . . . . . . . . . . . . . . . . . . . . . . . . . . . . . . . . **16.** _____

**Next.** Is the amount on line 15 more than the amount on line 16?

   ☐ **Yes.** Fill in Form 6251 to see if you owe the alternative minimum tax.

   ☐ **No.** You do not owe alternative minimum tax and do not need to fill out Form 6251. Leave line 45 blank.

## X.A.2.a. Computation of Alternative Minimum Tax

[587 T.M., I.D.; TPS ¶3410.01.C.]

Certain items of income and deduction are treated differently for AMT purposes than they are for regular tax purposes. Thus, the first step in computing AMT is to recompute these items of income and deduction for AMT purposes. The recomputed items result in certain adjustments (see X.A.2.b.) and tax preferences (see X.A.2.c.). A taxpayer must compute his or her alternative minimum taxable income (AMTI) by modifying regular taxable income by these adjustments and preferences (these modifications to regular taxable income apply only for AMT purposes, not regular tax purposes). Note that preferences always increase regular taxable income, while adjustments may either increase or decrease regular taxable income.

Once AMTI is computed, the following steps are taken to determine whether a taxpayer has an AMT liability:

1. Taxable AMTI is computed by subtracting an exemption amount from AMTI (see X.A.2.d.).

2. Pre-credit tentative minimum tax is computed by multiplying the taxable AMTI by the AMT tax rates (special rules apply when the taxpayer has capital gains) (see X.A.2.e.).

3. Tentative minimum tax is computed by subtracting the AMT foreign tax credit, if any, from pre-credit tentative minimum tax (see X.A.2.f.).

4. AMT liability is computed as the excess, if any, of tentative minimum tax over regular tax (see X.A.2.g.).

### X.A.2.b. Alternative Minimum Taxable Income: AMT Adjustments

[587 T.M., II.B.; TPS ¶3410.02.B.]

In computing AMTI, individual taxpayers make adjustments (increases or decreases) to regular taxable income for the following items:

- personal exemptions;
- standard deduction;
- medical expense deduction;
- deduction for taxes;
- home mortgage interest deduction;
- miscellaneous itemized deductions;
- overall limit on itemized deductions;
- tax refunds;
- investment interest deduction;
- net operating loss deduction;
- alternative tax net operating loss deduction;
- incentive stock options;
- pass-through from estates or trusts;
- pass-through from electing large partnerships;
- gain or loss on dispositions of property;
- post-1986 depreciation deduction;
- passive activity loss limitations;
- other loss limitations;
- circulation costs;
- long-term contracts;
- mining costs;
- research and experimental costs;
- income from certain pre-1987 installment sales;
- pollution control facilities;
- tax shelter farm activity loss limitations;
- biodiesel producer credit/biodiesel and renewable diesel fuel credit; and
- cooperative patron's adjustment.

### (1) Personal Exemptions

For regular tax purposes, an individual taxpayer can deduct personal exemptions for himself, his spouse, and his dependents (see XII.D.) [§ 151]. For AMT purposes, no personal exemptions are allowed [§ 56(b)(1)(E)]. Thus, in computing AMTI, personal exemptions must be added back to regular taxable income. For practical purposes, no adjustment needs to be made on Form 6251 because the income used as the starting point for computing AMTI on that form is the taxpayer's income before the personal exemptions are taken into account.

### (2) Standard Deduction

For regular tax purposes, an individual taxpayer who does not itemize his deductions can claim a standard deduction (see XII.E.) [§ 63(c)]. For AMT purposes, the standard deduction is not allowed [§ 56(b)(1)(E)]. Thus, in computing AMTI, the standard deduction must be added back to regular taxable income. For practical purposes, no adjustment needs to be made on Form 6251 because the income used as the starting point for computing AMTI on that form is the taxpayer's income before the standard deduction is taken into account.

### (3) Medical Expense Deduction

For regular tax purposes, individual taxpayers are generally allowed to deduct medical expenses only to the extent that they exceed 10% of adjusted gross income (AGI). However, if a taxpayer or his spouse is age 65 or older by the end of the tax year, the floor for the medical expense deduction is reduced to 7.5% of AGI (see VII.D.) [§ 213(a), § 213(f)]. For AMT purposes, the 10% floor on the medical expense deduction applies to all taxpayers [§ 56(b)(1)(B)]. Thus, in computing AMTI, taxpayers age 65 or older must add back to regular taxable income any portion of their medical expense deduction that exceeds the amount that would have been deductible if the 10% floor had been applied instead of the 7.5% floor.

### (4) Deduction for Taxes

For regular tax purposes, individual taxpayers are allowed to deduct a number of different types of taxes paid during the year (see VII.E.) [§ 164]. For AMT purposes, the following types of taxes (whether state and local or foreign taxes) are not deductible: (i) income taxes, (ii) real property taxes, (iii) personal property taxes, and (iv) general sales taxes (deductible for regular tax purposes before 2014) [§ 56(b)(1)(A)(ii)]. Thus, in computing AMTI, these taxes generally must be added back to regular taxable income. However, the disallowance of the deduction of taxes for AMT purposes does not apply when such taxes are taken as an above-the-line deduction [§ 56(b)(1)(A)]. Thus, in computing AMTI, no adjustment needs to be made to regular taxable income for taxes claimed as above-the-line deductions. See X.A.2.b.(8). for the AMT treatment of refunds of taxes claimed as above-the-line deductions.

### (5) Home Mortgage Interest Deduction

For regular tax purposes, individual taxpayers are allowed to deduct qualified residence interest, which includes interest on acquisition debt and home equity debt (see VII.F.1.). Acquisition debt is any debt that is incurred to buy, build, or substantially improve a qualified residence and that is secured by that qualified residence. Home equity debt is any debt other than acquisition debt that is secured by a qualified residence. A qualified residence includes the taxpayer's principal residence and a second residence designated by the taxpayer. For these purposes, a residence includes a house, condominium, cooperative, mobile home, house trailer, boat, or similar property that has sleeping, cooking, and toilet facilities [§ 163(h)(3); Reg. § 1.163-10T(p)].

For AMT purposes, individual taxpayers are allowed to deduct qualified housing interest, rather than qualified residence interest. The definition of qualified housing interest is narrower than the definition of qualified residence interest. Qualified housing interest is qualified residence interest on debt incurred to buy, build, or substantially improve a principal residence or a qualified dwelling that is a qualified residence. A qualified dwelling includes only a house, an apartment, a condominium, or a mobile home not used on a transient basis [§ 56(b)(1)(C)(i), § 56(e)].

Thus, for AMT purposes, individual taxpayers are not allowed to deduct interest on home equity debt because they can only deduct interest on a debt incurred to buy, build, or substantially improve a residence. Moreover, for AMT purposes, individual taxpayers cannot deduct interest on debt incurred on certain types of second residences, such as mobile homes used on a transient basis and boats. In computing AMTI, any qualified residence interest that does not meet the narrower definition of qualified housing interest must be added back to regular taxable income.

### (6) Miscellaneous Itemized Deductions

For regular tax purposes, individual taxpayers are allowed certain miscellaneous itemized deductions (e.g., unreimbursed employee expenses, tax preparation fees, and certain expenses related to investment income or property) to the extent that the total amount of such deductions exceed 2% of their adjusted gross income (see VII.I.) [§ 67]. For AMT purposes, such miscellaneous itemized deductions are not allowed [§ 56(b)(1)(A)(i)]. Thus, in computing AMTI, miscellaneous itemized deductions subject to the 2% floor must be added back to regular taxable income.

### (7) Overall Limit on Itemized Deductions

For regular tax purposes, an individual taxpayer's total itemized deductions are limited if his adjusted gross income exceeds a specified dollar amount (see VII.L.) [§ 68]. For AMT purposes, the overall limitation on itemized deductions does not apply [§ 56(b)(1)(F)]. Thus, in computing AMTI, a taxpayer must determine his total itemized deductions for regular tax purposes (after application of the overall limitation) and then subtract his total itemized deductions for AMT purposes (without application of the overall limitation). If the difference is positive, it is added to regular taxable income in computing AMTI. If the difference is negative, it is subtracted from regular taxable income in computing AMTI.

### (8) Tax Refunds

For regular tax purposes, individual taxpayers who take an itemized deduction for taxes must include any later refund (or other recovery) of those taxes in gross income in the year the refund is received (see I.B.6.). However, certain types of taxes that are deductible for regular tax purposes are not deductible for AMT purposes (see X.A.2.b.(4)). For AMT purposes, any later refund (or other recovery) of those taxes is excluded from gross income [§ 56(b)(1)(D)]. Thus, in computing AMTI, the amount of the refund must be subtracted from regular taxable income.

If a taxpayer takes an above-the-line deduction for such taxes, any later refund of those taxes is included in gross income for AMT purposes (as it is for regular tax purposes) [§ 111(a), § 56(b)(1)(A)]. Thus, in computing AMTI in this case, no adjustment needs to be made to regular taxable income.

If a taxpayer is subject to AMT in the year such taxes are deducted for regular tax purposes, but is subject to regular income tax in the year a refund of those taxes is received, then the refund is excluded from gross income for regular tax purposes (as it is for AMT purposes) because no tax benefit was received from the previous deduction of the taxes [§ 111(a)]. Thus, in computing AMTI in this case, no adjustment needs to be made to regular taxable income.

### (9) Investment Interest Deduction

For regular tax purposes, individual taxpayers can deduct investment interest to the extent of their net investment income (see VII.F.4.) [§ 163(d)(3)]. For AMT purposes, individual taxpayers can also deduct investment interest. However, there are two differences in the treatment of investment interest for regular tax and AMT purposes. First, interest on specified private activity bonds is generally tax-exempt for regular tax purposes but includible in gross income for AMT purposes. Second, all AMT adjustments and preferences under § 56, § 57 and § 58 must be taken into account in computing net investment income for AMT purposes [§ 56(b)(1)(C)(iii), § 56(b)(1)(C)(v)]. Thus, in computing AMTI, adjustments must be made to regular taxable income to take into account these differences.

### (10) Net Operating Loss Deduction and Alternative Tax Net Operating Loss Deduction

For regular tax purposes, a taxpayer can generally claim a net operating loss (NOL) deduction equal to the sum of its NOL carrybacks and carryforwards to a particular tax year (see VIII.G.). An NOL is generally carried back two years and then forward 20 years until the loss is fully utilized to offset income. However, a taxpayer may elect to forego the carryback period and just carryforward an NOL [§ 172].

For AMT purposes, a taxpayer must use the alternative tax net operating loss (ATNOL) deduction in lieu of the NOL deduction allowed for regular tax purposes. A taxpayer can generally claim an ATNOL deduction equal to the sum of its ATNOL carrybacks and carryforwards to a particular tax year. Once an ATNOL is calculated, it is carried back and carried forward in the same manner as NOLs under the regular tax system. If a taxpayer elected to forego the carryback period for regular tax purposes, that election also applies for AMT purposes. ATNOL carrybacks and carryforwards will absorb AMTI even though the taxpayer is not subject to AMT for that particular tax year. A taxpayer's ATNOL is computed in the same manner as the taxpayer's NOL, with two exceptions [§ 56(a)(4), § 56(d)]:

1. The amount of an ATNOL is computed by taking into account (i) all the § 56 and § 58 adjustments that applied in computing AMTI, and (ii) the § 57 tax preference items that applied in computing AMTI to the extent that such items increased the taxpayer's NOL for regular tax purposes.

2. The ATNOL deduction generally can be used to offset only 90% of AMTI, determined without regard to the ATNOL deduction (in comparison, the NOL deduction can be used to completely offset regular taxable income).

Thus, in computing AMTI, the NOL deduction must be added back to, and the ATNOL deduction must be subtracted from, regular taxable income.

### (11) Incentive Stock Options

For regular tax purposes, no income is recognized by an employee at the time an incentive stock option (ISO) is granted to him or at the time he exercises the ISO. Instead, taxation is deferred until the employee sells the underlying stock (see XVII.B.2.) [§ 421(a)(1)]. For AMT purposes, an employee is required to recognize income at the time he exercises an ISO in which he is substantially vested. The amount of income recognized is equal to the excess of the fair market value of stock on the exercise date over the amount the employee pays for the stock. Thus, in computing AMTI for the year in which such an ISO is exercised, that income amount must be added to regular taxable income. The taxpayer is also required to increase his adjusted basis in the underlying stock by the amount of this adjustment for AMT purposes (see X.A.2.b.(14)) [§ 56(b)(3)].

If an employee exercises an ISO and sells the underlying stock in the same tax year, no AMT adjustments are necessary because the tax treatment is the same for regular tax and AMT purposes.

### (12) Pass-Through from Estates and Trusts

If the taxpayer is the beneficiary of an estate or trust, an AMT adjustment may be passed through to the taxpayer from the estate or trust on Schedule K-1 (Form 1041). The adjustment is reported by the taxpayer on the specified line of Form 6251. See Chapter XVIII. for a detailed discussion of the income taxation of estates and trusts.

### (13) Pass-Through from Partnerships and S Corporations

If the taxpayer is a partner in a partnership or a shareholder in an S corporation, AMT adjustments may be passed through to the taxpayer on Schedule K-1 (Form 1065) or Schedule K-1 (Form 1120S), respectively. The adjustments are reported by the taxpayer on the appropriate lines of Form 6251. See Chapter XIV. for a detailed discussion of partnerships. See Chapter XV. for a detailed discussion of S corporations.

In the case of a taxpayer who is a partner in an electing large partnership, a "net passive AMT adjustment" (for limited partners) and a "net other AMT adjustment" (for general partners and limited partners) may be passed through to the taxpayer on Schedule K-1 (Form 1065-B). The net passive AMT adjustment is reported by the taxpayer on Form 6251 with his AMT adjustments from other passive activities. The net other AMT adjustment is reported by the taxpayer on the specified line of Form 6251.

### (14) Gain or Loss on Dispositions of Property

The amount of gain or loss recognized on the disposition of property is different for regular tax purposes (see III.A.) and AMT purposes if the adjusted basis of such property is different for such purposes. The adjusted basis of property may be different for regular tax and AMT purposes when the deductions related to such property are different for such purposes and those deductions reduce the taxpayer's adjusted basis in the property. Examples of deductions that reduce the taxpayer's adjusted basis in the related property include the deductions for depreciation, mining costs, circulation costs, research and experimental costs, and pollution control amortization [§ 56(a)(6)]. Thus, in computing AMTI, an adjustment must be made to regular taxable income to account for any difference in the amount of gain or loss on the disposition of these types of property.

### (15) Post-1986 Depreciation

For regular tax purposes, depreciation on property placed in service after 1986 generally must be computed using the Modified Accelerated Cost Recovery System (MACRS) (see V.A.4.) [§ 168]. For AMT purposes, depreciation on most real and personal property placed in service after 1986 and before 1999 must be computed using the Alternative Depreciation System (ADS) (see V.A.4.g.) [§ 56(a)(1)]. Thus, in computing AMTI, an adjustment to regular taxable income must be made for the difference between regular tax depreciation and AMT depreciation on most types of property placed in service after 1986 and before 1999. No adjustment is needed for certain types of property (as discussed below).

***Property Placed in Service After 1986 and Before 1999.*** For AMT purposes, depreciation is computed using ADS class lives instead of MACRS recovery periods, but the same conventions are generally used for both regular tax and AMT purposes. The following depreciation methods are used for AMT purposes [§ 56(a)(1)(A)]:

- For § 1250 property, AMT depreciation is computed using the straight line method over 40 years.
- For tangible property (other than § 1250 property) depreciated using the straight line method for regular tax purposes, AMT depreciation is computed using the straight line method over the period of the property's ADS class life.
- For any other tangible property, AMT depreciation is computed using the 150% declining balance method switching to the straight line method over the period of the property's ADS class life.

***Property Placed in Service After 1998.*** Generally, no AMT adjustment is necessary for property placed in service after 1998. However, an AMT adjustment is required for the following property placed in service after 1998 [§ 56(a)(1)(A)]:

- tangible property depreciated for regular tax purposes using the 200% declining balance method; and
- Section 1250 property not depreciated for regular tax purposes using the straight line method.

***Property for Which No Adjustment Required.*** No AMT adjustment is required for the following types of depreciable personal property placed in service after 1986 [§ 56(a)(1)(B) and § 56(a)(1)(C)]:

- property expensed under § 179 (see V.B.);
- property the taxpayer elects to depreciate under the ADS for regular tax purposes;
- property depreciated under a depreciation method not expressed in terms of years (e.g., the unit-of-production method);
- certain public utility property if the taxpayer does not use a normalization method of accounting;
- film and videotapes that are generally depreciated under the income forecast method;
- sound recordings;
- natural gas gathering lines (if placed in service after April 11, 2005); and
- certain property placed in service after 1986 that is eligible for transitional relief.

**(16) Passive Activity Loss Limitations**

For regular tax purposes, individual taxpayers can deduct losses from passive activities only to the extent of their income from other passive activities (see VIII.F.). Under a special rule, a passive activity loss of a taxpayer is computed without regard to qualified residence interest [§ 469]. For AMT purposes, the tax preferences and adjustments of § 56 and § 57 must be taken into account in computing passive activity income and losses. In addition, for AMT purposes, the passive activity loss of a taxpayer is computed without regard to qualified housing interest, instead of qualified residence interest (see X.A.2.b.(5)) [§ 58(b)]. Thus, in computing AMTI, adjustments must be made to regular taxable income to account for these differences.

**(17) Other Loss Limitations**

For regular tax purposes, individual taxpayers can deduct losses from certain types of activities only to the extent of the amount they have at risk with respect to those activities (see VIII.E.) [§ 465]. Moreover, partners and S corporation share-holders generally can deduct their share of losses passed through from the partner-ship or S corporation only to the extent of their basis in the pass-through entity (see Chapter XIV. and Chapter XV.) [§ 704(d), § 1366(d)]. For AMT purposes, the tax preferences and adjustments of § 56, § 57, and § 58 must be taken into account in computing these loss limitations [§ 59(h)]. Thus, in computing AMTI, adjustments must be made to regular taxable income to account for these differences.

### (18) Circulation Costs

For regular tax purposes, taxpayers can take a current deduction for circulation expenditures (expenditures paid or incurred to establish, maintain, or increase the circulation of newspapers, magazines, or other periodicals) that would otherwise be required to be capitalized for regular tax purposes (see IV.F.1.) [§ 173]. For AMT purposes, such circulation expenditures must be capitalized and amortized over a three-year period beginning with the tax year in which the expenditures are paid or incurred [§ 56(b)(2)(A)(i)]. Thus, in computing AMTI, the amount by which the current-year deduction for regular tax purposes exceeds the current-year amortiza-tion for AMT purposes must be added back to regular taxable income.

If a taxpayer sustains a loss on a disposition of property for which circulation expenditures have not been fully amortized for AMT purposes, the taxpayer can deduct the unamortized portion of the expenditures in the year of the disposition for AMT purposes. In computing AMTI in the year of the disposition, a subtraction is made from regular taxable income for the lesser of (i) the unamortized circulation expenditures, or (ii) the amount that would be allowed as a loss deduction under § 165(a) if the circulation expenditures had remained capitalized [§ 56(b)(2)(B)].

For regular tax purposes, a taxpayer may elect to amortize circulation expendi-tures over a three-year period (instead of taking a current deduction) [§ 59(e)]. If a taxpayer makes such an election, no AMT adjustments are required.

### (19) Long-Term Contracts

For regular tax purposes, taxpayers are required to use the percentage-of-completion method to account for long-term contracts, except for home construction contracts, small contractor construction contracts, and residential construction con-tracts (see XI.E.) [§ 460]. For AMT purposes, taxpayers are required to use the percentage-of-completion method to account for long-term contracts, except home construction contracts [§ 56(a)(3)]. Thus, in computing AMTI, an adjustment to regular taxable income must be made to account for the difference between the percentage-of-completion method used for AMT purposes and another method used for regular tax purposes. Generally, this adjustment will only apply in the case of small contractor construction contracts and residential construction contracts. In determining the percentage of completion of such contracts for AMT purposes, the § 460(b)(3) simplified methods of cost allocation must be used [§ 56(a)(3)].

### (20) Mining Costs

For regular tax purposes, mining exploration and development costs generally must be capitalized and amortized over the life of the mine. However, a taxpayer may elect to currently deduct such costs in the year they are paid or incurred (see VI.D.) [§ 616, § 617]. For AMT purposes, mining exploration and development costs must be capitalized and amortized over a 10-year period beginning with the tax year in which the expenditures are paid or incurred [§ 56(a)(2)(A)]. Thus, in computing AMTI, an adjustment must be made to regular taxable income for the difference between the mining exploration and development costs deducted in the current year for regular tax and AMT purposes.

527

If a taxpayer sustains a loss on a disposition of property for which mining exploration and development costs have not been fully amortized for AMT purposes, the taxpayer can deduct the unamortized portion of the expenditures in the year of the disposition for AMT purposes. In computing AMTI in the year of the disposition, a subtraction is made from regular taxable income for the lesser of (i) the unamortized mining exploration and development costs, or (ii) the amount that would be allowed as a loss deduction under § 165(a) if the mining exploration and development costs had remained capitalized [§ 56(b)(2)(B)].

For regular tax purposes, a taxpayer may elect to amortize mining costs over a 10-year period (instead of amortizing them over the life of the mine or taking a current deduction) [§ 59(e)]. If a taxpayer makes such an election, no AMT adjustments are required.

### (21) Research and Experimental Costs

For regular tax purposes, individual taxpayers may take a current deduction for research and experimental expenditures (expenditures paid or incurred in connection with a trade or business that represent research or development costs in the experimental or laboratory sense) that would otherwise be required to be capitalized for regular tax purposes (see IV.F.2.) [§ 174; Reg. § 1.174-2(a)(1)]. For AMT purposes, such research and experimental expenditures must be capitalized and amortized over a 10-year period beginning with the tax year in which the expenditures are paid or incurred [§ 56(b)(2)(A)(ii)]. Thus, in computing AMTI, the amount by which the current-year deduction for regular tax purposes exceeds the current-year amortization for AMT purposes must be added back to regular taxable income.

If a taxpayer sustains a loss on a disposition of property for which research and experimental expenditures have not been fully amortized for AMT purposes, the taxpayer can deduct the unamortized portion of the expenditures in the year of the disposition for AMT purposes. In computing AMTI in the year of the disposition, a subtraction is made from regular taxable income for the lesser of (i) the unamortized research and experimental expenditures, or (ii) the amount that would be allowed as a loss deduction under § 165(a) if the research and experimental expenditures had remained capitalized [§ 56(b)(2)(B)].

For regular tax purposes, a taxpayer may elect to amortize research and experimental expenditures over a 10-year period (instead of taking a current deduction) [§ 59(e)]. For AMT purposes, a taxpayer who materially participates in an activity may elect to take a current deduction for research and experimental expenditures (instead of amortizing them over 10 years) [§ 56(b)(2)(D)]. If a taxpayer makes either of these elections, no AMT adjustments are required.

### (22) Pre-1987 Installment Sales

For regular tax purposes, the installment method can generally be used to report gains from nondealer dispositions of property (see III.G.) [§ 453]. For AMT purposes, the installment method does not apply to any nondealer disposition of property after August 16, 1986, but before January 1, 1987, if an installment obligation to which the proportionate disallowance rule applied arose from the disposition. Thus, in computing AMTI, an adjustment must be made to regular taxable income to account for this difference.

### (23) Pollution Control Facilities

For regular tax purposes, a taxpayer may elect to amortize the basis of a certified pollution control facility over a 60-month period (see IV.F.5.g.) [§ 169]. For AMT purposes, the treatment of a pollution control facility depends on when the facility was placed in service. A certified pollution control facility placed in service after 1986 and before 1999 is depreciated under § 168(g) of the alternative depreciation system (ADS) using the straight line method with a 24-year class life. A certified pollution control facility placed in service after 1998 is depreciated under the Modified Accelerated Cost Recovery System (MACRS) using the straight line method and the same recovery periods and convention used for regular tax purposes. Thus, in computing AMTI, an adjustment must be made to regular taxable income to account for these differences.

### (24) Tax Shelter Farm Activity Loss Limitations

For AMT purposes, an adjustment must be made for tax shelter farm activity losses. A loss from a tax shelter farm activity is not allowed as a deduction for AMT purposes (an exception applies if the taxpayer is insolvent). A tax shelter farming activity includes (i) any farming syndicate (as defined in § 464(c)), or (ii) any other activity consisting of farming that is a passive activity (within the meaning of § 469(c)). The rules on tax shelter farm activity losses are applied before the rules on passive activity losses (see X.A.2.b.(16)).

In computing whether the taxpayer has a loss from a tax shelter farming activity, AMT adjustments and preference items must be taken into account (to the extent an adjustment or preference item is taken into account for this purpose, it should not again be separately taken into account in computing the taxpayer's AMTI). A tax shelter farm activity loss must be computed on an activity-by-activity basis. Thus, losses from one farming activity may not offset gains from another farming activity. Any disallowed tax shelter farm activity loss may be carried forward to the next tax year and treated as a deduction allocable to the same farm activity in that year.

### (25) Second Generation Biofuel Producer Credit/Biodiesel and Renewable Diesel Fuels Credit

For regular tax purposes, taxpayers can claim the second generation biofuel producer credit (see IX.A.7.) and the biofuel and renewable diesel fuels credit (see IX.A.21.) [§ 40, § 40A]. The credits are nonrefundable credits that can be offset against a taxpayer's regular tax liability. If a taxpayer claims either of these credits, it must include the amount of the credit claimed in gross income [§ 87].

The biofuel producer credit and the biofuel and renewable diesel fuels credit cannot be claimed against a taxpayer's AMT liability. Thus, any amount of these credits included in gross income for regular tax purposes is not includible in gross income for AMT purposes and must be subtracted from regular taxable income in computing AMTI [§ 56(a)(7)].

These credits expired December 31, 2013.

### (26) Cooperative Patron's Adjustment

For regular tax purposes, taxpayers that are patrons of a cooperative may be required to include distributions received from the cooperative in gross income (see XIII.F.4.). For AMT purposes, certain adjustments must be made to the amounts included in income for regular tax purposes. The amount of a patron's AMT adjustment is reported to the patron on Form 1099-PATR, *Taxable Distributions Received From Cooperatives*, in box 9.

### X.A.2.c. Alternative Minimum Taxable Income: AMT Tax Preferences

[587 T.M., II.C.; TPS ¶3410.02.C.]

In computing AMTI, taxpayers increase their regular taxable income for the following tax preference items:

- depletion;
- tax-exempt interest income from specified private activity bonds;
- gains on qualified small business stock;
- intangible drilling and development costs; and
- accelerated depreciation on certain pre-1986 property.

### (1) Depletion

For regular tax purposes, taxpayers are allowed a depletion deduction for mines, oil and gas wells, other natural deposits, and timber (see VI.A.) [§ 611]. In computing AMTI, a tax preference for depletion must be added back to regular taxable income. The tax preference for depletion is based on the amount by which the taxpayer's depletion deduction for a property exceeds his adjusted basis in that property as of the end of the tax year. For this purpose, a property's adjusted basis is determined by taking into account any AMT adjustments made in the current year or previous years (other than the current year depletion deduction). The excess depletion computation is made on a property-by-property basis. Thus, the excess depletion of one property cannot be reduced by the adjusted basis of another property. The tax preference does not apply to certain independent oil and gas producers and royalty owners that claim percentage depletion for oil and gas wells [§ 57(a)(1); Reg. § 1.57-1(h)].

### (2) Tax-Exempt Interest Income from Specified Private Activity Bonds

For regular tax purposes, interest received on a state or local bond that is a qualified private activity bond is excluded from taxable income (see II.B.) [§ 103]. In computing AMTI, a tax preference for interest received on a specified private activity bond must be added back to regular taxable income. In determining the amount of the tax preference, the specified private activity bond interest is reduced by any related deduction that would be allowable if such interest were included in regular taxable income. A specified private activity bond is generally a private activity bond issued after August 7, 1986, the interest on which is excluded from taxable income for regular tax purposes. However, the following private activity bonds are not considered specified private activity bonds: (i) qualified § 501(c)(3) bonds, (ii) certain housing bonds, (iii) refunding bonds, (iv) bonds issued in 2009 and 2010, and (v) certain bonds issued before September 1, 1986. Exempt-interest dividends paid by a regulated investment company (RIC), such as a mutual fund, are treated as interest on specified private activity bonds to the extent that the dividends are attributable to interest on such bonds received by the RIC, minus an allocable share of the expenses paid or incurred by the RIC in earning the interest [§ 57(a)(5)].

### (3) Gain on Qualified Small Business Stock

For regular tax purposes, an exclusion from taxable income is allowed for 50% of any gain on the sale or exchange of qualified small business stock held for more than five years (see III.C.5.) [§ 1202(a)]. In computing AMTI, a tax preference for 7% of the excluded gain must be added back to regular taxable income. The tax preference does not apply to any qualified small business stock acquired after September 27, 2010, and before January 1, 2014 [§ 57(a)(7), § 1202(a)(4)(C)].

### (4) Intangible Drilling and Development Costs

For regular tax purposes, an operator in the development of oil and gas properties and geothermal wells may elect to currently deduct intangible drilling and development costs (IDCs) instead of capitalizing such costs (see VI.C.) [§ 263(c); Reg. § 1.612-4(a)]. In computing AMTI, a tax preference for IDCs must be added back to regular taxable income. The tax preference is equal to the excess IDCs for the tax year over 65% of the net income from oil, gas, and geothermal properties for the tax year. Excess IDCs are the excess of the amount of the IDCs the taxpayer currently deducted for the tax year over the amount of the amortization deduction the taxpayer would have had for the tax year if those IDCs had instead been capitalized and amortized using straight-line recovery of intangibles. The net income from oil, gas, and geothermal properties is the gross income from such properties, less any deductions allocable to those properties (reduced by the excess IDCs). The tax preference is computed separately for oil and gas properties and geothermal wells. The tax preference is limited or eliminated for certain independent producers [§ 57(a)(2)].

### (5) Depreciation on Certain Pre-1986 Property

The amounts of accelerated depreciation that would have been treated as tax preference items under the provisions in effect immediately before the Tax Reform Act of 1986 continue to be treated as tax preference items. Under those provisions, there is a depreciation tax preference for real property and leased personal property placed in service before 1981 in an amount equal to the excess of any accelerated depreciation deductions allowable on the property for the tax year over the amount that would have been allowable as a deduction for the tax year if the property had been depreciated using a straight line method for each tax year of its useful life.

There is also a depreciation tax preference for certain property placed in service after 1980 but before 1987 and depreciated under the Accelerated Cost Recovery System (ACRS). For leased personal property, the tax preference is equal to the excess of the ACRS depreciation deduction over the depreciation deduction that would have been allowable if the straight line depreciation method had been used over the applicable recovery period (5 years for 3-year property, 8 years for 5-year property, 15 years for 10-year property, and 22 years for 15-year public utility property). For 19-year real property and low-income housing, the tax preference is equal to the excess of the ACRS depreciation deduction over the depreciation deduction that would have been allowable if the straight line depreciation method (disregarding salvage value) had been used over the applicable recovery period (19 years for 19-year property and 15 years for low-income housing) [§ 57(a)(6)]. For further discussion of ACRS depreciation, see V.A.5.

### X.A.2.d. Exemption Amount

[587 T.M., III.B.; TPS ¶3410.03.B.]

After a taxpayer's AMTI is determined (see X.A.2.b. and X.A.2.c.), the next step in computing AMT is to subtract an exemption amount from AMTI. The amount, if any, by which the taxpayer's AMTI exceeds the taxpayer's applicable exemption amount is the taxable AMTI on which the taxpayer's AMT is computed. If a taxpayer's AMTI is less than his or her exemption amount (i.e., he has no taxable AMTI), then he or she is not subject to AMT.

***Exemption Amounts.*** The applicable exemption amounts are based on filing status and adjusted annually for inflation. The following exemption amounts apply to noncorporate taxpayers for 2014 and 2015 [Rev. Proc. 2013-35, 2013-47 I.R.B. 537, Rev. Proc. 2014-61, 2014-47 I.R.B. 860]:

| Filing Status | 2014 Exemption Amount | 2015 Exemption Amount |
|---|---|---|
| Married filing jointly | $82,100 | $83,400 |
| Married filing separately | $41,050 | $41,700 |
| Single | $52,800 | $53,600 |
| Head of Household | $52,800 | $53,600 |
| Surviving Spouse | $82,100 | $83,400 |
| Estate or Trust | $23,500 | $23,800 |

*Phase-Out of Exemption Amounts.* For higher-income taxpayers, the exemption amounts are phased out at a rate of 25 cents per dollar for each dollar of AMTI in excess of a phase-out amount. The phase-out ranges for the exemption amounts for 2014 and 2015, based on dollar amounts of AMTI, are as follows [Rev. Proc. 2013-35, Rev. Proc. 2014-61]:

| Filing Status | Begin Phase-out (2014) | Complete Phase-out (2014) | Begin Phase-out (2015) | Complete Phase-out (2015) |
|---|---|---|---|---|
| Married filing jointly | $156,500 | $484,900 | $158,900 | $492,500 |
| Married filing separately | $ 78,250 | $242,450 | $ 79,450 | $246,250 |
| Single | $117,300 | $328,500 | $119,200 | $333,600 |
| Head of Household | $117,300 | $328,500 | $119,200 | $333,600 |
| Surviving Spouse | $156,500 | $484,900 | $158,900 | $492,500 |
| Estate or Trust | $ 78,250 | $172,250 | $ 79,450 | $174,650 |

*Special Rule for Married Taxpayers Filing Separately.* If a taxpayer is married filing separately and his AMTI is greater than the AMTI amount at which the exemption is completely phased out ($242,450 for 2014 and $246,250 for 2015), then the taxpayer is required to increase his or her AMTI for purposes of computing the AMT. The purpose of this rule is to prevent married individuals from filing separately in order to obtain a more favorable AMT exemption. The amount by which a taxpayer's AMTI is increased under this rule is equal to the lesser of:

1. 25% of the excess of the taxpayer's AMTI (before this adjustment) over the AMTI amount at which the exemption is completely phased out; or

2. the exemption amount.

---

**EXAMPLE:** Steve and Sarah are married individuals who file separate returns for 2014. Steve has AMTI of $150,000 and, thus, his exemption is partially phased out. Steve's exemption amount is $23,113 ($41,050 – (($150,000 - $78,250) × 25%)). Sarah has AMTI of $245,000 and, thus, her exemption is completely phased out (her AMTI exceeds the $242,450 AMTI amount at which the exemption is completely phased out). In addition to having a $0 exemption, Sarah must increase her AMTI by $638, which is the lesser of (i) $638 (($245,000 - $242,450) × 25%), or (ii) $41,050. When combined, Steve and Sarah's total AMTI minus exemptions is equal to $372,525 (($150,000 + $245,638) – ($23,113 + $0)). Note that, if Steve and Sarah had filed jointly, their AMTI would have been $395,000 ($150,000 + $245,000) and their exemptions would have been $22,475 ($82,100 − (($395,000 - $156,500) × 25%)). Thus, their total AMTI minus exemptions would have also been equal to $372,525 ($395,000 - $22,475).

***Special Rule for Children Subject to Kiddie Tax.*** A special rule applies to the AMT exemption for children subject to the so-called kiddie tax. Under the kiddie tax rule, a child's net unearned income is taxed at his parent's tax rate if that rate is higher than the child's tax rate (see X.A.3.). The AMT exemption for a child subject to the kiddie tax is limited to the sum of the child's earned income plus an amount that is adjusted annually for inflation [§ 59(j)]. The inflation-adjusted amount is $7,250 for 2014 ($7,400 for 2015) [Rev. Proc. 2013-35, Rev. Proc. 2014-61].

**EXAMPLE:** For 2014, Timmy is subject to the kiddie tax on his net unearned income. He has $3,000 of earned income for the year. Timmy's AMT exemption for the year is limited to $10,250 ($3,000 + $7,250).

### X.A.2.e. Pre-Credit Tentative Minimum Tax

[587 T.M., III.C.; TPS ¶3410.03.C.]

The pre-credit tentative minimum tax is generally determined by multiplying the taxpayer's taxable AMTI (also known as the "taxable excess") (see X.A.2.b., c., and d.) by the AMT tax rates. For 2014, the AMT tax rates are [§ 55(b)(1)(A); Rev. Proc. 2013-35, 2013-47 I.R.B. 537.]:

- 26% on the first $182,500 ($91,250 if married filing separately) of taxable AMTI; and

- 28% on taxable AMTI over $182,500 ($91,250 if married filing separately).

For 2015, the taxable AMTI above which the 28% rate applies is $185,400 ($92,700 if married filing separately) [Rev. Proc. 2014-61, 2014-47 I.R.B. 860].

**EXAMPLE:** Jim is a single taxpayer with AMTI of $102,800 for 2014. Thus, Jim's taxable AMTI is $50,000, which is equal to his $102,800 AMTI minus his $52,800 exemption. Jim's pre-credit tentative minimum tax is $13,000 ($50,000 × 26%).

However, the computation of the pre-credit tentative minimum tax is more complicated if the taxpayer has capital gains for the tax year. The rules are designed to take into consideration the capital gains rates of § 1(h) in such a case. A taxpayer with capital gains computes pre-credit tentative minimum tax based on the following steps [§ 55(b)(3)]:

| COMPUTE: | "Taxable Excess" (TE) by subtracting the exemption amount, if any, from AMTI |
|---|---|
| MULTIPLY: | The first $182,500 of the taxable excess by 26% and any amount over $182,500 by 28% |
| ADD: | These two amounts |
| EQUALS: | FIGURE 1 |
| COMPUTE: | Net Capital Gain (which is equal to the excess, if any, of net long-term capital gain over net short-term capital loss) = NCG |

| | |
|---|---|
| COMPUTE: | Adjusted Net Capital Gain (which is equal to NCG reduced, but not below zero, by the sum of unrecaptured § 1250 gain plus 28% rate gain plus qualified dividend income) = ANCG |
| COMPUTE: | The sum of ANCG plus any unrecaptured § 1250 gain |
| COMPUTE: | The lesser of NCG or the sum of ANCG plus unrecaptured § 1250 gain |
| COMPUTE: | The excess, if any, of TE over the amount computed immediately above |
| EQUALS: | The § 55(b)(3)(A) amount |
| MULTIPLY: | The first $182,500 of the § 55(b)(3)(A) amount by 26% and any amount over $182,500 by 28% |
| ADD: | These two amounts |
| EQUALS: | The § 55(b)(3)(A) tentative minimum tax (TMT) |
| COMPUTE: | The amount of taxable income that, if not for § 1(h)(1)(B), would be taxed at a rate under 25% minus the excess, if any, of taxable income over ANCG |
| EQUALS: | The § 1(h)(1)(B) excess amount |
| COMPUTE: | The lesser of ANCG (as computed for AMTI purposes) or TE |
| COMPUTE: | The lesser of the amount computed immediately above or the § 1(h)(1)(B) excess amount |
| EQUALS: | The § 55(b)(3)(B) amount |
| MULTIPLY: | The § 55(b)(3)(B) amount by 0% |
| EQUALS: | The § 55(b)(3)(B) TMT |
| COMPUTE: | The lesser of ANCG (as computed for AMTI purposes) or TE |
| SUBTRACT: | The§ 55(b)(3)(B) amount from the amount computed immediately above. |
| EQUALS: | The § 55(b)(3)(C)(i) amount |
| COMPUTE: | Taxable income reduced by net capital gain (as computed for regular tax purposes) |
| COMPUTE: | The lesser of the amount of taxable income taxed at a rate below 25% or taxable income reduced by the adjusted net capital gain (as computed for regular tax purposes) |
| COMPUTE: | The greater of the two amounts computed immediately above |
| EQUALS: | The § 1(h)(1)(A) amount |
| ADD: | The § 1(h)(1)(A) amount and the § 1(h)(1)(B) excess amount |
| SUBTRACT: | The amount computed immediately above from the amount of taxable income that would be taxed at a rate below 39.6% |
| EQUALS: | The § 55(b)(3)(C)(ii) amount |
| COMPUTE: | The lesser of the § 55(b)(3)(C)(i) or the § 55(b)(3)(C)(ii) amounts |
| EQUALS: | The § 55(b)(3)(C) amount |
| MULTIPLY: | The § 55(b)(3)(C) amount by 15% |
| EQUALS: | The § 55(b)(3)(C) TMT |
| COMPUTE: | The lesser of ANCG (as computed for AMTI purposes) or TE |
| SUBTRACT: | The sum of the §§ 55(b)(3)(B) and (C) amounts from the amount computed immediately above. |
| EQUALS: | The § 55(b)(3)(D) amount |
| MULTIPLY: | The § 55(b)(3)(D) amount by 20% |

| EQUALS: | The § 55(b)(3)(D) TMT |
|---|---|
| COMPUTE: | The sum of the § 55(b)(3)(A), (B), (C), and (D) amounts |
| SUBTRACT: | The sum computed immediately above from TE |
| EQUALS: | The § 55(b)(3)(E) amount |
| MULTIPLY: | The § 55(b)(3)(E) amount by 25% |
| EQUALS: | The § 55(b)(3)(E) TMT |
| ADD: | The TMT amounts for § 55(b)(3)(A), (B), (C), (D), and (E) |
| EQUALS: | FIGURE 2 |
| COMPUTE: | The lesser of FIGURE 1 or FIGURE 2 |
| EQUALS: | The taxpayer's Pre-Credit Tentative Minimum Tax |

### X.A.2.f. Tentative Minimum Tax and the AMT Foreign Tax Credit

[587 T.M., III.D.; TPS ¶3410.03.D.]

A taxpayer's tentative minimum tax is determined by subtracting the AMT foreign tax credit, if any, from the pre-credit tentative minimum tax (see X.A.2.e.). The AMT foreign tax credit is generally computed in the same manner as the regular foreign tax credit. However, the computation of the overall limit on the foreign tax credit is modified for AMT purposes.

For regular tax purposes, the amount of a taxpayer's foreign tax credit that can be claimed is limited to his tentative U.S. tax multiplied by a fraction, the numerator of which is his foreign source taxable income and the denominator of which is his worldwide taxable income (see XX.C.2.) [§ 904]. For AMT purposes, this overall limit is generally computed in the same manner, with the following exceptions [§ 59(a)(1)]:

- the pre-credit tentative minimum tax is used instead of the tentative U.S. tax;
- foreign source AMTI is used instead of foreign source taxable income (i.e., AMT adjustments and preference items are taken into account); and
- worldwide AMTI is used instead of worldwide taxable income (i.e., AMT adjustments and preference items are taken into account).

A taxpayer may also elect to use a simplified method under which foreign source taxable income is treated as the numerator for AMT purposes [§ 59(a)(3)]. If this election is made, the taxpayer will not need to recompute the numerator used for regular tax purposes in order to take into account AMT adjustments and preference items.

Any AMT foreign tax credit that is disallowed due to the limitation may be carried back one year and carried forward 10 years. However, the amount of the credit allowable in the carryover years will again be subject to the limitation in those years [§ 904(c)]. Note that the AMT foreign tax credit will expire without generating any benefits if the taxpayer is subject to the regular tax during the entire carryover period.

A taxpayer's AMT foreign tax credit may be different than his regular foreign tax credit because of the differences in the computation of the overall limit. It may also be different because the AMT foreign tax credit must be computed and offset against tentative minimum tax each year, even if no AMT is due for the year. Thus, the AMT foreign tax credit is effectively applied against a different tax base than the regular foreign tax credit.

No regular or AMT foreign tax credit is allowed if a taxpayer chooses to deduct his accrued foreign taxes in lieu of claiming the credit. The choice that is made for regular tax purposes also applies for AMT purposes.

### *X.A.2.g. Computation of AMT Liability*

[587 T.M., III.E.; TPS ¶3410.03.E., .03.F.]

The amount of a taxpayer's AMT liability is equal to the excess of tentative minimum tax (see X.A.2.f.) over regular tax. For purposes of this comparison, regular tax is the taxpayer's regular tax liability for the year, except that the following two types of adjustments are made [§ 55(c), § 26(b)]:

- certain taxes are disregarded (e.g., the AMT and most of the taxes discussed in X.A.8.); and
- the only nonrefundable credit allowed is the foreign tax credit.

If tentative minimum tax is more than the regular tax amount, the taxpayer has an AMT liability equal to the excess amount and he must pay the AMT liability in addition to his regular tax liability. If tentative minimum tax is less than the regular tax amount, the taxpayer does not have any AMT liability and he only pays his regular tax liability.

---

**EXAMPLE:** Patty has tentative minimum tax of $250,000 and regular tax of $175,000. Thus, her AMT liability is $75,000 ($250,000 - $175,000). Patty must pay the $75,000 AMT liability in addition to her regular tax liability.

---

As a general rule, nonrefundable personal credits are allowed to offset both the regular tax liability (reduced by the regular foreign tax credit) and the AMT liability [§ 26(a)]. However, nonrefundable personal credits in excess of the regular tax and AMT liabilities cannot be used to create a refund. Some, but not all, of these unused credits may be carried forward to other tax years under the credit carryover rules. See IX.B. for a discussion of nonrefundable personal credits.

Credits based on the taxpayer's prepayments of income tax (e.g., the credits for taxes withheld and estimated taxes paid) are also allowed to offset both the regular tax liability and AMT liability when computing the amount of taxes due [§ 31 through § 34, § 6315, § 6413].

### *X.A.3. Kiddie Tax on Unearned Income of Certain Children*

[507 T.M., II.A.2.; TPS ¶3310.03.F.]

A special tax may apply to a child's unearned income. When this so-called kiddie tax applies, a portion of the child's net unearned income is taxed at his parent's tax rate if that rate is higher than his own rate. See X.A.3.a. for a discussion of children subject to the kiddie tax. See X.A.3.b. for the determination of a child's net unearned income and the computation of the kiddie tax. The kiddie tax is computed and reported on Form 8615, *Tax for Certain Children Who Have Unearned Income.*

### *X.A.3.a. Children Subject to Kiddie Tax*

[507 T.M., II.A.2.b.; TPS ¶3310.03.F.1.]

The kiddie tax applies to any child who meets all of the following conditions [§ 1(g)(2)]:

1. the child has more than $2,000 of net unearned income for 2014 ($2,100 for 2015) (see X.A.3.b.);
2. the child meets an age requirement;
3. at least one of the child's parents is alive at the end of the tax year; and
4. the child is required to file a return for the year and does not file a joint return.

*Age Requirement.* A child meets the age requirement if, as of the end of the tax year, he meets any of the following tests [§ 1(g)(2)(A)]:

1. he was under age 18;

2. he was age 18 and did not have earned income that was more than half his support; or

3. he was a full-time student over age 18 but under age 24 and did not have earned income that was more than half his support.

A child's earned income generally includes salaries, wages, tips, and other payments received for personal services performed [see § 911(d)(2)]. A child's support generally includes all amounts spent by the child, a parent, or another person to provide the child with food, lodging, clothing, education, medical and dental care, recreation, transportation, and similar necessities. However, a scholarship received by a child who is a full-time student is not considered support [§ 152(c)(1)(D), § 152(f)(5)].

### X.A.3.b. Computing the Kiddie Tax

[507 T.M., II.A.2.d.; TPS ¶3310.03.F.2., .03.F.3., .03.F.4.]

When the kiddie tax rules apply to a child, the child's income tax for the tax year is computed as the greater of [§ 1(g)(1)]:

1. the tax that would be imposed on the child's taxable income for the year if the kiddie tax rules were not applied; or

2. the sum of (i) the tax that would be imposed on the child's taxable income for the year if it were reduced by his net unearned income, plus (ii) the child's share of the allocable parental tax.

The kiddie tax is the additional amount of tax imposed on a child when his net unearned income is taxed at his parent's tax rate instead of his own tax rate.

*Net Unearned Income.* The net unearned income of a child is the child's unearned income reduced by the sum of [§ 1(g)(4), § 63(c)(5)(A); Rev. Proc. 2013-35, 2013-47 I.R.B. 537, Rev. Proc. 2014-61, 2014-47 I.R.B. 860]:

1. the limited standard deduction that applies to dependents whose personal exemption is allowable to another taxpayer ($1,000 for 2014 and $1,050 for 2015); plus

2. the greater of (i) the limited standard deduction, or (ii) the child's allowable itemized deductions directly connected with the production of the unearned income.

Thus, for 2014, the kiddie tax will not apply when a child's net unearned income is less than $2,000 ($2,100 for 2015).

Unearned income is all taxable income other than earned income (see X.A.3.a.), including taxable interest, dividends (including capital gain distributions), capital gains, rents, royalties, taxable social security benefits, pension and annuity income, taxable scholarship and fellowship grants, unemployment compensation, alimony, and taxable distributions received as the beneficiary of a trust other than a qualified disability trust (as defined in § 642(b)(2)(C)(ii)). A child's unearned income includes all income produced by property transferred to the child, including property given to the child as a gift.

Itemized deductions are directly connected with the production of unearned income if they are for expenses paid for the production or collection of such income or for the management, conservation, or maintenance of property held for the production of such income. They include expenses such as custodian fees and service charges, service fees to collect unearned income, and certain investment counsel fees. These types of expenses are miscellaneous itemized deductions that are deductible only to the extent that, when added together with other similar expenses, they exceed 2% of the child's adjusted gross income (see VII.I.).

*Child's Share of Allocable Parental Tax.* The allocable parental tax is the hypothetical additional tax that would be imposed on the child's parent if the parent's taxable income included the net unearned income of all the parent's children (including stepchildren and adopted children) subject to the kiddie tax. More specifically, the allocable parental tax is equal to the excess of (i) the tax that would be imposed on the sum of the parent's taxable income plus the net unearned income of all the parent's children subject to the kiddie tax, over (ii) the tax that would be imposed on the parent's taxable income if the kiddie tax rules were not applied [§ 1(g)(3)(A)].

A child's share of the allocable parental tax of a parent is determined by multiplying the allocable parental tax by a fraction, the numerator of which is the child's net unearned income and the denominator of which is the net unearned income of all the parent's children subject to the kiddie tax [§ 1(g)(3)(B)].

In computing the allocable parental tax, the parent whose taxable income is taken into account is determined as follows [§ 1(g)(5); Reg. § 1.1(i)-1T]:

- If the child's parents are married and file a joint return, their joint taxable income is used.
- If the child's parents are married and file separate returns, the taxable income of the parent with the higher taxable income is used.
- If the child's parents are unmarried, divorced, legally separated, or otherwise treated as unmarried for federal tax purposes, the taxable income of the custodial parent is used (if such custodial parent files a joint return with a non-parent spouse, the joint taxable income from that return is used).
- If the child's parents are unmarried but living together with the child, the taxable income of the parent with the higher taxable income is used.

The name and social security number of the parent whose taxable income is used in the computation is required to be reported by the child on Form 8615 [§ 1(g)(6)].

### X.A.3.c. Election Out of Kiddie Tax

[507 T.M., II.A.2.e.; TPS ¶3310.03.F.5.]

If certain requirements are met, a parent whose taxable income is used in computing the kiddie tax may elect to report the child's interest and dividend income on the parent's return by filing Form 8814, *Parent's Election To Report Child's Interest and Dividends* (see I.B.3.). If this election is made, the child will not be required to file a federal return or Form 8615.

### X.A.4. Net Investment Income Tax

[507 T.M., II.E.; TPS ¶3310.03.H.]

Individual taxpayers may be subject to the net investment income tax if they have unearned income and their adjusted gross income exceeds certain threshold amounts. The net investment income tax is imposed on U.S. citizens and resident aliens, but not nonresident aliens. It is also imposed on estates and most trusts [§ 1411(a), § 1411(e)]. The net investment income tax is computed on Form 8960, *Net Investment Income Tax – Individuals, Estates, and Trusts*, and reported on the appropriate line of the "Other Taxes" section of Form 1040.

### X.A.4.a. Computation of Net Investment Income Tax

[507 T.M., II.E.1., II.E.5.; TPS ¶3310.03.H.1., .03.H.4.]

The net investment income tax is equal to 3.8% of the lesser of [§ 1411(a)(1), § 1411(b)]:

1. the taxpayer's net investment income (see X.A.4.b.); or
2. the excess of the taxpayer's modified adjusted gross income (see X.A.4.c.) over the following applicable threshold amount:
   - $250,000 if married filing jointly or surviving spouse;
   - $125,000 if married filing separately; or
   - $200,000 if single or head of household.

---

**EXAMPLE:** Brad is an unmarried U.S. citizen. In Year 1, Brad has modified adjusted gross income (MAGI) of $190,000, including $50,000 of net investment income. Brad is not liable for the net investment income tax for Year 1 because his $190,000 MAGI is less than his $200,000 threshold amount. In Year 2, Brad has MAGI of $220,000, including $50,000 of net investment income. Brad's liability for the net investment income tax for Year 2 is $760, which is equal to 3.8% of the lesser of (i) his $50,000 of net investment income, or (ii) the $20,000 amount by which his MAGI ($220,000) exceeds his threshold amount ($200,000).

---

***Applicable Threshold for Short Tax Years.*** The applicable threshold amount is generally not prorated for a taxpayer with a short tax year. However, it is prorated when the short tax year results from a change in tax year. In that case, the applicable threshold amount is computed by multiplying the regular threshold amount by a fraction, the numerator of which is the number of months in the short period and the denominator of which is 12 months [Reg. § 1.1411-2(d)(2)].

### X.A.4.b. Net Investment Income

[507 T.M., II.E.3.; TPS ¶3310.03.H.2.]

Net investment income is the excess of a taxpayer's gross investment income over his investment deductions. More specifically, net investment income is equal to [§ 1411(c)(1)]:

1. the sum of:
   - gross income from interest, dividends, annuities, royalties, and rents (not including such income derived in the ordinary course of a trade or business that is not a § 1411(c)(2) trade or business) (see X.A.4.b.(2));
   - other gross income derived from a § 1411(c)(2) trade or business (see X.A.4.b.(3)); and
   - net gain attributable to the disposition of property (not including property held in a trade or business that is not a § 1411(c)(2) trade or business) (see X.A.4.b.(4)); minus
2. the deductions properly allocable to such gross income or net gain (see X.A.4.b.(5)).

#### (1) Section 1411(c)(2) Trade or Business

The net investment income tax generally does not apply to income derived in the ordinary course of a trade or business or to net gain attributable to the disposition of property held by a trade or business. However, it does apply to the income and net gain of a § 1411(c)(2) trade or business. A § 1411(c)(2) trade or business includes (i) a trade or business that is a passive activity with respect to the taxpayer, and (ii) a trade or business engaged in trading financial instruments or commodities [§ 1411(c)(2)].

A passive activity is (i) any activity that involves the conduct of any trade or business in which the taxpayer does not materially participate for the tax year, or (ii) any rental activity (regardless of whether the taxpayer materially participates) to the extent the taxpayer is not engaged in the rental activities as a real estate professional (see VIII.F.) [§ 469(c)(1), § 469(c)(2)]. A taxpayer may treat one or more trade or business activities or rental activities as a single activity if the activities form an appropriate economic unit for measuring gain or loss under the passive activity rules. Generally, activities that have been grouped cannot be regrouped in later years. However, a taxpayer may regroup activities in the first tax year beginning after 2013 in which the taxpayer is subject to the net investment income tax [Reg. § 1.469-11(b)(3)(iv)(A)].

### (2) Gross Income from Interest, Dividends, Etc.

Net investment income generally includes gross income from interest, dividends, annuities, royalties, and rents.

*Interest and Dividends.* Gross income from interest and dividends generally includes any items treated as interest and dividends for regular income tax purposes. It also includes substitute interest, substitute dividends, distributions from previously taxed earnings and profits, and certain excess distributions [Reg. § 1.1411-1(d)(3), § 1.1411-1(d)(6)].

*Annuities.* Gross income from annuities includes the amount received as an annuity under an annuity, endowment, or life insurance contract that is includible in gross income under § 72(a) and § 72(b), and amounts not received as an annuity under an annuity contract that are includible in gross income under § 72(e). Gross income from annuities also includes gain recognized on the sale of an annuity to the extent the sales price does not exceed the surrender value. If the sales price exceeds the surrender value, the portion of the gain attributable to the excess of the surrender value over the annuity basis is treated as gross income from annuities, and the portion attributable to the excess of the sales price over the surrender value is treated as net gain attributable to the disposition of property [Reg. § 1.1411-1(d)(1)].

*Royalties.* Gross income from royalties includes amounts received from mineral, oil, and gas royalties, and amounts received for the privilege of using patents, copyrights, secret processes and formulas, goodwill, trademarks, trade brands, franchises, and other similar property. Gross income from rents includes amounts received (or to be received) principally for the use of, or right to use, tangible property [Reg. § 1.1411-1(d)(10), § 1.1411-1(d)(11)].

*Interest, Dividends, Etc., of § 1411(c)(2) Trade or Business.* Net investment income includes gross income from interest, dividends, annuities, royalties, and rents that are derived in the ordinary course of a § 1411(c)(2) trade or business. In the case of an individual who operates a sole proprietorship, the determination of whether an item of gross income is derived from a § 1411(c)(2) trade or business is made at the individual level. In the case of an individual who owns an interest in a trade or business through one or more pass-through entities (e.g., partnerships, S corporations), the determination of whether an item of gross income is derived from a trade or business that is a passive activity with respect to the taxpayer is made at the individual level and the determination of whether an item of gross income is derived from a trade or business of trading in financial instruments or commodities is made at the pass-through entity level [Reg. § 1.1411-4(b)].

### (3) Other Gross Income of § 1411(c)(2) Trade or Business

Net investment income generally includes all gross income of a § 1411(c)(2) trade or business that is not otherwise discussed in X.A.4.b.(2). and X.A.4.b.(4).

### (4) Net Gain Attributable to Disposition of Property

Net gain from a disposition of property is taken into account for purposes of computing the net investment income tax only to the extent that it is taken into account for purposes of computing regular taxable income. In determining whether a disposition of property has occurred and the amount of net gain from that disposition, the rules that apply for regular income tax purposes also generally apply for net investment income tax purposes [Reg. § 1.1411-4(d)(1), § 1.1411-4(d)(3)].

The amount of net gain included in net investment income may not be less than zero. However, up to $3,000 of losses from the disposition of capital assets may be used to offset gain from the disposition of assets other than capital assets that are subject to § 1411 [§ 1211(b); Reg. § 1.1411-4(d)(2)]. See III.B.5. for further discussion of the allowance of such losses.

***Disposition of Property Held by § 1411(c)(2) Trade or Business.*** Net gain from the disposition of property that is held by a § 1411(c)(2) trade or business is taken into account in determining net investment income [Reg. § 1.1411-4(d)(4)].

***Disposition of Interest in Partnership or S Corporation.*** Gains and losses from the disposition of an interest in a partnership or S corporation are taken into account in determining net investment income only to the extent that such gains and losses would be taken into account if all of the partnership's or S corporation's property were sold for fair market value immediately before the disposition of that interest [§ 1411(c)(4)].

### (5) Properly Allocable Deductions

In determining net investment income, the items of gross income and net gain discussed above are reduced by properly allocable deductions. Only amounts paid or incurred to produce such gross income or net gain may be deducted for this purpose and those amounts may be deducted only to the extent of such gross income and net gain. Excess amounts may be carried over to other tax years for net investment income tax purposes only to the extent allowed under the carryover rules that apply for regular tax purposes [Reg. § 1.1411-4(f)(1)].

***Deductions Allowed.*** The types of deductions that can be taken into account in computing net investment income include [Reg. § 1.1411-4(f)(2) and § 1.411-4(f)(3)]:

- certain deductions allocable to gross income from rents and royalties;
- trade or business deductions allocable to a § 1411 trade or business;
- penalties on early withdrawal of savings;
- a portion of the net operating loss deduction (see below);
- investment expense;
- investment interest expense;
- state and local income taxes; and
- foreign income taxes.

***Net Operating Loss Deduction.*** Only a portion of the regular tax net operating loss (NOL) deduction (see VIII.G.) can be deducted for net investment income tax purposes. The portion of the regular tax NOL deduction that can be deducted for net investment income tax purposes is computed based on the following steps [Reg. § 1.1411-4(h)]:

1. The applicable portion of the NOL for each loss year is determined. The applicable portion of the NOL is equal to the lesser of (i) the amount of the NOL for the loss year that the taxpayer would have incurred if only items of gross income that are used to determine net investment income and only properly allocable deductions were taken into account in determining the NOL in accordance with § 172(c) and § 172(d), or (ii) the amount of the NOL for the loss year.

2. The amount of the NOL carried from each loss year and deducted in the current tax year is multiplied by a fraction, the numerator of which is the applicable portion of the NOL from step 1 and the denominator of which is the total NOL for the loss year. The result is the § 1411 NOL amount for that loss year.

3. The amount of the NOL deduction for the tax year that is properly allocable to net investment income is equal to the sum of the § 1411 NOL amounts for each NOL carried to and deducted in the current tax year.

***Other Loss Deductions.*** Losses that exceed gains from dealings in property can be deducted in determining net investment income if such losses are not taken into account in determining net gain attributable to the disposition of property (as discussed above, the amount of such net gain included in net investment income may not be less than zero). Thus, for example, the $3,000 capital loss deduction under § 1211(b) may be allowed as a deduction in determining net investment income [Reg. § 1.1411-4(f)(4)].

***Application of Regular Tax Deduction Limitations.*** Properly allocable itemized deductions that are subject to the 2% AGI limitation (see VII.I.) or the overall itemized deductions limitation (see VII.L.) for regular income tax purposes are deductible for net investment income purposes only to the same extent they would be deductible for regular income tax purposes [Reg. § 1.1411-4(f)(7)].

### (6) Amounts Not Included in Net Investment Income

Net investment income generally does not include distributions from qualified plans or items taken into account in computing self-employment income [§ 1411(c)(5) and § 1411(c)(6)]. Under a special rule that applies to a taxpayer engaged in a trade or business of trading financial instruments or commodities, properly allocable deductions that do not reduce the taxpayer's net earnings from self-employment are not considered to be taken into account in computing self-employment income and may therefore be considered in determining the taxpayer's net investment income [Reg. § 1.1411-9(b)].

### X.A.4.c. Modified Adjusted Gross Income

[507 T.M., II.E.4.; TPS ¶3310.03.H.3.]

Modified adjusted gross income (MAGI) is the taxpayer's adjusted gross income for income tax purposes, modified by certain amounts related to the foreign income exclusion. More specifically, MAGI is equal to adjusted gross income, increased by the excess of (i) the amount of the foreign earned income exclusion under § 911(a)(1), over (ii) the amount of any deductions or exclusions disallowed under § 911(d)(6) with respect to the foreign earned income exclusion. For this purpose, adjusted gross income includes all of the taxpayer's items of income, whether or not they are subject to the net investment income tax [§ 1411(d)].

### X.A.5. Additional Medicare Tax

[392 T.M., II.A.1.a.; TPS ¶5440.03.A.2.]

An additional Medicare tax of 0.9% applies to an individual taxpayer's Medicare wages, Railroad Retirement Tax Act (RRTA) compensation, and self-employment income over a specified threshold amount. The threshold amounts are $250,000 if married filing jointly, $125,000 if married filing separately, and $200,000 if using any other filing status (e.g., single, head of household, or surviving spouse) [§ 3101(b)(2)]. Medicare wages and self-employment income are combined in applying the applicable threshold. RRTA compensation is compared separately to the applicable threshold.

For employees, the Medicare tax rate is 1.45% for wages up to the threshold and 2.35% (1.45% plus 0.9%) for wages over the threshold (the employer portion of the Medicare tax remains at 1.45%) [§ 3101(b)(1)]. For self-employed taxpayers, the Medicare tax rate is 2.9% for self-employment income up to the threshold and 3.8% (2.9% plus 0.9%) for self-employment income over the threshold. Employers are responsible for withholding the 0.9% additional Medicare tax on an employee's Medicare wages or RRTA compensation in excess of $200,000 for a calendar year, regardless of the employee's filing status. For a detailed discussion of the Medicare tax, see XXII.B.

An individual taxpayer must file Form 8959, *Additional Medicare Tax*, to compute the amount of any additional Medicare tax owed if any of the following apply:

- Medicare wages and tips on any single Form W-2 (box 5) are greater than $200,000;
- RRTA compensation on any single Form W-2 (box 14) is greater than $200,000;
- Medicare wages and tips plus self-employment income are greater than the threshold amount for the taxpayer's filing status; or
- RRTA compensation and tips are greater than the threshold amount for the taxpayer's filing status.

The taxpayer's additional Medicare tax from Form 8959 is reported on the appropriate line in the "Other Taxes" section of Form 1040. Any additional Medicare tax withheld by the taxpayer's employer is reported on Form 1040 with other federal income tax withheld.

### X.A.6. Tax for Failure to Maintain Minimum Health Insurance Coverage

[389 T.M., XVII.A.; TPS ¶3310.03.G.]

For tax years beginning after 2013, individual taxpayers must maintain minimum essential health insurance coverage for each month and they are subject to a penalty tax for the failure to maintain such coverage for themselves or their dependents [§ 5000A(a), § 5000A(b)].

*Exemptions.* An individual is not required to maintain minimum essential coverage for any month that he or she [§ 5000A(d)(2) through § 5000A(d)(4); Reg. § 1.5000A-3]:

- is not a U.S. citizen or national or an alien lawfully present in the United States;
- has obtained a religious exemption as described in § 1402(g);
- is a member of a tax-exempt health care sharing ministry; or
- is in jail.

In addition, the IRS does not impose the penalty if [Reg. § 1.5000A-3]:

- the individual has a short gap in coverage;
- the individual would suffer a hardship if he or she were to obtain coverage through a qualified health plan;
- the individual cannot afford coverage;
- the individual has household income that is below the filing threshold; or
- the individual is a member of an Indian tribe.

*Penalty Tax.* An individual taxpayer who does not maintain minimum essential health insurance coverage for himself or his dependents during a tax year must pay a penalty tax that is equal to the lesser of [§ 5000A(c)]:

1. the sum of the monthly penalty amounts for the months in the tax year during which one or more such failures occurred; or

2. an amount equal to the national average premium for qualified health plans that have a bronze level of health coverage, provide coverage for the family size involved, and are offered through health insurance exchanges for the relevant plan year.

For purposes of the tax computation, a monthly penalty amount is equal to one-twelfth of the greater of (i) the flat dollar amount, or (ii) a specified percentage of the taxpayer's household income. For 2014, the flat dollar amount is $95 ($325 for 2015) and the specified percentage is 1.0% (2.0% for 2015) [§ 5000A(c)(2), § 5000A(c)(3)].

For a detailed discussion of the tax for failure to maintain minimum health coverage, see XVII.C.5.a.

### X.A.7. Self-Employment Tax

[392 T.M., II.; TPS ¶3340.]

The Self-Employment Contributions Act (SECA) imposes a tax on the self-employment income of each individual [§ 1401]. Every self-employed U.S. citizen and resident alien with net earnings from self-employment of $400 or more is liable for self-employment taxes, even if there is otherwise no liability to file an income tax return [§ 6017].

### X.A.7.a. Rate, Computation, and Collection of Self-Employment Tax

[392 T.M., II.B.1.; TPS ¶3340.01., .02., .03.]

*Rate of Tax.* SECA has two components: old, age, survivor and disability insurance (OASDI) and hospital insurance (HI or Medicare). The OASDI tax rate is 12.4%. The HI tax rate is generally 2.9%, but is increased by an additional 0.9% (3.8% total) for self-employment income in excess of $200,000 ($250,000 for a joint return) [§ 1401].

*Maximum and Minimum Earnings Subject to Self-Employment Tax.* Self-employment income subject to SECA tax is determined by an individual's net earnings from self-employment. However, no amount of an individual's net earnings from self-employment is subject to the OASDI portion of SECA tax to the extent that net earnings exceed the OASDI taxable wage base in effect for the calendar year in which the individual's tax year begins, minus the amount of any wages paid to the individual during the tax year. This base amount is adjusted annually by the Social Security Administration. The OASDI contribution and benefit taxable wage base is $118,500 for 2015 ($117,000 for 2014). All net earnings from self-employment are subject to the HI portion of SECA taxes without regard to the taxable wage base limit applicable to OASDI [§ 1402(b)(1); 79 Fed. Reg. 64,455 (Oct. 29, 2014)].

Self-employment income that is exempt from SECA also includes net earnings that are less than $400 in any tax year. However, if net earnings from self-employment are not less than $400, all self-employment income, including the portion under $400, is nonetheless subject to tax. This occurs when the individual's wages from employment and net earnings from self-employment exceed the taxable wage base for a particular year [§ 1402(b)(2)].

Self-employed individuals may deduct one-half of the individual's SECA tax liability to allow for the fact that employees do not pay tax on the value of the employer's FICA contributions. The deduction may be treated as a trade or business expense in determining the individual's taxable income or as a reduction in computing the individual's self-employment earnings subject to SECA tax. In the latter case, in computing net self-employment earnings subject to SECA tax, the deduction is equal to one-half of the product of the individual's net earnings from self-employment before the deduction and the combined OASDI and HI rates in effect for the tax year. This deduction is reflected by multiplying earnings by 92.35% (100% - 7.65%). No deduction is allowed for the additional 0.9% HI tax increase [§ 164(f), § 1402(a)(12)].

### X.A.7.b. Income Subject to Self-Employment Tax

### X.A.7.b.(1) Included Net Earnings from Self-Employment

[392 T.M., II.B.2.a(1); TPS ¶3340.04.A.]

Self-employment income subject to tax is determined by an individual's net earnings from a trade or business carried on as a sole proprietor or by a partnership of which he or she is a member. If an individual is engaged in more than one trade or business, net earnings from self-employment consist of the aggregate of the net earnings from all such trades or businesses [§ 1402(a); Reg. § 1.1402(a)-2(c)]. The trade or business must, however, be carried on by an individual, either personally or through agents or employees.

*Partnerships*. A member of a partnership includes as self-employment income his distributive share of the net income or loss from all partnerships of which he is a member. The term "partnership" generally includes, for these purposes, an organization recognized as a partnership under § 761 (see XIV.B.). Thus, a partnership that is not valid under state law but that is recognized as a partnership for federal income tax purposes is a partnership for self-employment tax purposes [§ 1402(a); Reg. § 1.1402(a)-2(f)].

A partner's distributive share of the income or loss of a partnership is determined under § 704 (see XIV.D.2.). Consequently, only the ordinary net income or loss derived by the partnership in carrying on the partnership's trade or business is subject to SECA tax. Any ordinary net income or loss of the partnership derived from sources that are unrelated to the trade or business carried on by it is excluded in determining net earnings from self-employment. In addition, a partner's distributive share is determined without regard to the nature of his partnership interest. Thus, a limited or inactive partner normally must include his distributive share of the partnership's ordinary net income or loss in determining net earnings from self-employment. However, the distributive share of the income or loss of a limited partner may be excluded in determining net earnings from self-employment to the extent that such amounts are not received as guaranteed payments for services actually performed by the limited partner for the partnership [§ 1402(a)(13); Reg. § 1.1402(a)-2(g)].

The tax year for purposes of computing SECA tax is the same as the tax year for income tax purposes. If the tax year of a partner does not correspond to that of the partnership, the partner is required to compute SECA tax on his distributive share of the ordinary income or loss of the partnership for the partnership tax year ending within his tax year [Reg. § 1.1401-1(a), § 1.1402(a)-2(e)].

### X.A.7.b.(2) *Excluded Net Earnings from Self-Employment*

[392 T.M., II.B.2.a(2); TPS ¶3340.04.B.]

***Rental Income.*** Rental income and deductions attributable to leased real estate and from personal property leased with the real estate are excluded when determining self-employment income subject to SECA, unless the rentals are received by an individual in the course of a trade or business as a real-estate dealer. An individual who is engaged in the business of selling real estate to customers with a view to the gains and profits that may be derived from such sales is a real-estate dealer. On the other hand, an individual who holds real estate for investment or speculation and receives rentals from the property is not considered a dealer [§ 1402(a)(1); Reg. § 1.1402(a)-4].

Payments for the use or occupancy of entire private residences or living quarters in duplex or multiple-housing units generally are rentals from real estate. Except in the case of real-estate dealers, such payments may be excluded in determining net earnings from self-employment even though such payments are in part attributable to personal property furnished under the lease. If payments for the use or occupancy of rooms or space include substantial and significant services for the convenience of the occupant, and that are other than those customarily rendered in connection with renting real estate, the rental payments are included in determining net earnings from self-employment. Such payments typically include rent paid for rooms in hotels, boarding homes, tourist homes, or for space in parking lots, warehouses, or storage garages. Services that are customarily rendered in connection with leased property and that do not constitute a material portion of the rental payments, such as heat, light, water, trash collection, maintenance of common areas, etc., are not considered to be rendered to the occupant and are, therefore, excluded from self-employment earnings [Reg. § 1.1402(a)-4(c)(1), § 1.1402(a)-4(c)(2)].

---

**EXAMPLE:** C owns a building containing four apartments. During the tax year, C receives $1,400 from apartments 1 and 2, which are rented without services rendered to the occupants, and $3,600 from apartments 3 and 4, which are rented with services rendered to the occupants. C's fixed expenses for the four apartments aggregate $1,200 during the tax year. In addition, C has $500 of expenses attributable to the services rendered to the occupants of apartments 3 and 4. In determining C's net earnings from self-employment, C includes the $3,600 received from apartments 3 and 4, and the expenses of $1,100 ($500 plus one-half of $1,200) attributable thereto. The rentals and expenses attributable to apartments 1 and 2 are excluded. Therefore, C has $2,500 of net earnings from self-employment for the tax year from the building.

---

***Farm Income.*** Income attributable to rent paid in "crop shares" is excluded from self-employment earnings. Income attributable to rent paid through the U.S. Department of Agriculture's conservation reserve program (CRP) to individuals who are receiving Social Security retirement or disability payments also is excluded from self-employment earnings [§ 1402(a)(1)].

The exclusion does not apply if the owner or lessee materially participates in the production or management of the agricultural or horticultural commodity. Such income is referred to as "includible farm rental income." An owner or lessee materially participates in the "production" of a commodity if the individual provides physical labor or pays incurred expenses in producing a particular commodity, including activities such as planting, cultivating or harvesting crops, and the furnishing of machinery, implements, seed, or livestock. An owner or lessee materially participates in the "management of production" by making managerial decisions regarding production, such as when to plant, cultivate, dust, spray, or harvest the crop, and includes advising and consulting, making inspections, and making decisions as to matters such as rotation of crops, the type of crops to be grown, the type of livestock to be raised, and the type of machinery and implements to be furnished [§ 1402(a)(1); Reg. § 1.1402(a)-4(b)].

*Dividend and Interest Income.* Dividends and interest are excluded from self-employment earnings unless such income is received in the course of a trade or business as a dealer in stocks or securities. A dealer in stocks and securities may exclude dividends and interest on stocks and securities that are held for speculation or investment from self-employment earnings. A dealer in stocks and securities is a person with an established place of business who is regularly engaged in the business of purchasing stocks and securities for the purpose of reselling them to customers [§ 1402(a)(2); Reg. § 1.1402(a)-5(c), § 1.1402(a)-5(d)].

*Income from the Sale of Capital Assets.* Net earnings from self-employment that are subject to SECA taxes do not include any gain or loss that is considered gain or loss from the sale or exchange of a capital asset [§ 1402(a)(3)(A); Reg. § 1.1402(a)-6(a)].

*Other Dispositions of Property.* Gains and losses attributable to the sale, exchange, involuntary conversion, or other disposition of property are excluded in determining net earnings from self-employment if such property is neither [§ 1402(a)(3)(C)]:

1. stock in trade or other property of a kind that would properly be includible in inventory if on hand at the close of the tax year, nor

2. property held primarily for sale to customers in the ordinary course of the trade or business.

*Ministers and Members or Religious Orders.* An individual who is a duly ordained, commissioned, or licensed minister of a church or a member of a religious order computes his or her net earnings from self-employment derived from the performance of service without regard to [§ 1402(a)(8), § 1402(c)(4)]:

1. the exclusion for the rental value of a parsonage;

2. the exclusion relating to meals and lodging furnished for the employer's convenience; or

3. the foreign earned income exclusion and housing cost exclusion and deduction.

Consequently, a minister's net earnings from self-employment includes the rental value of any parsonage or any parsonage allowance provided after the minister retires, as well as any other retirement benefit received from a church plan after the minister retires [§ 1402(a)(8)].

*Retirement Payments to Partners.* Periodic payments made by a partnership to a retired partner are generally excluded from self-employment income provided such payments are made pursuant to a written plan that provides bona fide retirement benefits for partners generally, or to a class of partners. The payment of benefits that are not customarily included in a pension or retirement plan, such as layoff benefits, do not qualify as excludible retirement benefits. A partner's eligibility for retirement benefits must also be based on age, physical condition, or years of service, and must continue at least until death [§ 1402(a)(10); Reg. § 1.1402(a)-17(b)].

*Alternative Methods for Computing Net Earnings.* Optional methods of computing net earnings from self-employment are available to individuals engaged in farming and nonfarming self-employment, or both, provided certain requirements are satisfied. By using the optional methods, individuals can continue to maintain Social Security coverage in tax years in which net earnings are negligible or a loss occurs [§ 1402(a); Reg. § 1.1402(a)-15].

***Statutory Exclusions from Trade or Business Liability.*** The only statutory exceptions to the general rule that all trades and businesses are subject to self-employment taxes include those for:

- public officials, such as the President, members of Congress, a judge, and a notary public [§ 1402(c)(1); Reg. § 1.1402(c)-2(b)];

- service performed by an individual as an employee, other than certain services performed by newspaper distributors, sharecroppers; employees of foreign governments instrumentalities and international organizations; fishing crews; real estate agents and direct sellers; and employees of churches and church-controlled organizations [§ 1402(c)(2), § 1402(d)]; and

- ministers who have obtained an exemption, members of religious orders who have taken a vow of poverty, members of religious orders who have not taken a vow of poverty but who have obtained an exemption, and Christian Science practitioners who have obtained an exemption. An exemption is filed on Form 4361, *Application for Exemption From Self-Employment Tax for Use by Ministers, Members of Religious Orders and Christian Science Practitioners* [§ 1402(c)(4), § 1402(c)(5), § 1402(e)(1)].

### X.A.7.c. SECA Filing Requirements

[392 T.M., II.B.1.c.; TPS ¶3340.06.]

An individual computes his or her SECA tax liability on Schedule SE to Form 1040, *Self-Employment Tax*. Schedule SE has two sections: Section A — Short Schedule SE; and Section B — Long Schedule SE. An individual uses Short Schedule SE if the individual:

1. did not receive wages or tips during the tax year;
2. is not a minister, member of a religious order, or Christian Science practitioner who received IRS approval not to be taxed on earnings from these sources but owes SECA tax on other earnings;
3. is not using one of the optional methods to compute his net self-employment earnings; and
4. did not receive church employee income reported on Form W-2 of $108.28 or more.

Section B has two Parts - Part I, Self-Employment Tax, and Part II, Optional Methods to Figure Net Earnings. An individual claims the business expense deduction equal to one-half of his SECA tax liability. If an individual's only self-employment income is from earnings as a minister, member of a religious order, or Christian Science practitioner who filed Form 4361 and received IRS approval not to be taxed on those earnings, he is not required to file Schedule SE; instead, he is directed to write "Exempt—Form 4361" on Form 1040, Line 56.

### X.A.8. Other Taxes

[507 T.M., II.A.; TPS ¶3310.]

There are numerous other taxes that individual taxpayers may be required to report in the "Other Taxes" section of Form 1040. This section provides a brief description of these various other types of taxes.

### X.A.8.a. Unreported Social Security and Medicare Tax

[507 T.M., II.A., 392 T.M., IV.B.1.; TPS ¶¶5440.01.B.11., 5440.03.B.1.]

Individual taxpayers must pay any social security and Medicare taxes that have not been reported or collected in the following situations:

- If an employee received $20 or more in cash tips for any month and did not report the full amount to his employer, he is required to pay the social security and Medicare tax on the unreported tips. This tax is computed and reported on Form 4137, *Social Security and Medicare Tax on Unreported Tip Income*.

- If an employee received wages and his employer did not withhold social security and Medicare tax from those wages, he is required to pay the employee share of that tax on the wages. This tax is computed and reported on Form 8919, *Uncollected Social Security and Medicare Taxes on Wages*.

- If an employee's employer did not withhold social security or Medicare tax on his tips or on the taxable cost of his group-term life insurance over $50,000, he is required to pay the employee share of that tax. The amount of the employee's share of the tax should be reported to him by his employer on Form W-2 in box 12 with codes A and N or M and N.

For a detailed discussion of the social security and Medicare tax, see XXII.B.

### X.A.8.b. Additional Taxes on IRAs, Other Qualified Retirement Plans, Etc.

[507 T.M., II.A., 370 T.M., X.D.; TPS ¶5610.10.A.3.]

Individual taxpayers are required to pay additional taxes on the following:

- early distributions from a qualified retirement plan (including an IRA) or modified endowment contract that was not rolled over in a qualified rollover contribution;

- taxable distributions received from a Coverdell education savings account (ESA) or a qualified tuition program (QTP);

- excess contributions made to an IRA, Roth IRA, Coverdell education savings account (ESA), Archer MSA, or health savings account (HSA); and

- excess accumulations in a qualified retirement plan (including an IRA).

These taxes are computed and reported on Form 5329, *Additional Taxes on Qualified Plans (including IRAs) and Other Tax-Favored Accounts*.

For a detailed discussion of IRAs, other qualified retirement plans, annuities, modified endowment contracts, HSAs, and Archer MSAs, see Chapter XVII. For a detailed discussion of Coverdell ESAs and qualified tuition programs, see II.L.

### X.A.8.c. Household Employment Taxes

[392 T.M., II.A.2.f(4)(b), 391 T.M., III.B.; TPS ¶5440.02.C.1.]

An individual taxpayer who has a household employee may be required to pay household employment taxes. A person is a household employee if the taxpayer hires the person to do household work and the taxpayer has the right to control what work the person will do and how the person will do it. Household work includes work done in and about the taxpayer's home by workers such as babysitters, nannies, housekeepers, cooks, cleaning people, health aides, private nurses, drivers, caretakers, yard workers, and similar domestic workers. Self-employed workers are not household employees. Workers hired through an agency are not household employees if the agency is responsible for who does the work and how it is done [Reg. § 31.3121(a)(7)-1(a)(2)].

For 2014, a taxpayer must file Schedule H (Form 1040), *Household Employment Taxes*, with his return to determine his total household employment taxes if any of the following apply [§ 3121(a)(7)(B), § 3121(x), § 3306(b)(6); Notice 2013-72, 2013-48 I.R.B. 592]:

1. the taxpayer paid any one household employee cash wages of $1,900 or more during 2014;

2. the taxpayer withheld federal income tax at the request of any household employee during 2014; or

3. the taxpayer paid total cash wages of $1,000 or more to all household employees during any calendar quarter in 2013 or 2014.

If the first rule applies, the taxpayer and employee must pay equal shares of social security and Medicare taxes on the employee's wages. If the third rule applies, the taxpayer must pay federal unemployment (FUTA) tax on his employees' wages.

The taxpayer must also file a Form W-2 for each household employee to whom the first or second rule applies.

### X.A.8.d. Repayment of First-Time Homebuyer Credit

[507 T.M., II.A.20., 506 T.M., V.M.; TPS ¶3201.09.B.]

Individual taxpayers who purchased a home as their primary residence in 2008, 2009, or 2010 may have been eligible to claim a first-time homebuyer credit (certain taxpayers serving on qualified official extended duty outside the United States were also eligible to claim the credit for homes purchased in 2011). Under some circumstances, taxpayers who claimed the first-time homebuyer credit are required to repay the credit. A taxpayer who is required to repay the credit does so by including it as an increase in tax on his return.

Taxpayers who claimed the first-time homebuyer credit for a home purchased in 2008 are required to repay the entire amount of the credit over a 15-year period [§ 36(f)]. If such a taxpayer owned and used the home as his or her principal residence during all of 2014, the taxpayer must continue repaying the credit on the 2014 return. In this case, the repayment amount is entered directly on the appropriate line on Form 1040. However, if such a taxpayer disposed of the home during 2014 or if it ceased to be his or her main home during 2014, the taxpayer generally must repay the balance of the unpaid credit on the 2014 return. In this case, the taxpayer must complete Form 5405, *Repayment of the First-Time Homebuyer Credit*, and then enter the repayment amount from that form on the appropriate line of Form 1040.

Taxpayers who claimed the first-time homebuyer credit for a home purchased in 2009 or 2010 were not required to repay the credit as long as they owned and used the home as their principal residence for at least 36 months beginning on the purchase date. However, if a taxpayer's home was destroyed or condemned (or sold under threat of condemnation) during that 36-month period, the taxpayer was not required to repay the credit as long as he acquired a new home within two years of the event. If such an event occurred during 2012 and the taxpayer did not acquire a new home by the end of the two-year period in 2014, he must repay part of the credit during 2014. In this case, the taxpayer determines the repayment amount by completing Part III of Form 5405 and enters that amount on the appropriate line of Form 1040.

See IX.G.9.b. for an additional discussion of this issue.

### X.A.8.e. Additional Tax on Retirement Benefits and Deferred Compensation

[507 T.M., II.A., 370 T.M., 385 T.M., 396 T.M.; TPS ¶¶5550., 5715., 5720.]

The following additional taxes on retirement benefits and deferred compensation must be reported on the "total tax" line of Form 1040:

- Tax on excess qualified plan benefits received by 5% owners. The 5% owners of a business maintaining a qualified pension or annuity plan are subject to a 10% tax on the amount of any benefits received in excess of the benefits provided for them under the plan formula [§ 72(m)(5)].

- Tax on compensation received from a nonqualified deferred compensation plan that fails to meet the requirements of § 409A (see XVII.B.1.e.). This tax is equal to 20% of the amount required to be included in income, plus an interest amount. The income subject to the tax is generally reported to the taxpayer in box 12 of Form W-2 with code Z or in box 15b of Form 1099-MISC [§ 409A(a)(1)(B)].

- Tax on compensation received from a nonqualified deferred compensation plan described in § 457A if the compensation would have been includible in the taxpayer's income in an earlier tax year but for the fact that the amount was not determinable until the current tax year. This tax is equal to 20% of the amount required to be included in income, plus an interest amount [§ 457A].

- Tax on golden parachute payments (see XVII.B.3.). This tax is equal to 20% of any excess parachute payments received by the taxpayer. The tax amount is generally reported to taxpayers in box 12 of Form W-2 with code K [§ 280G].

- Tax on insider stock compensation from an expatriated corporation. This tax is equal to 15% of the value of non-statutory stock options and certain other stock-based compensation held by the taxpayer or a family member from an expatriated corporation or its expanded affiliated group in which the taxpayer was an officer, director, or more-than-10% owner [§ 4985].

### X.A.8.f. Additional Tax on HSAs and MSAs

[507 T.M., II.A., 389 T.M., XI., XII.; TPS ¶5920.08.]

The following additional taxes on health savings accounts (HSAs) (see XVII.C.1.e.) and medical savings accounts (MSAs) (see XVII.C.1.d.) must be reported on the "total tax" line of Form 1040:

- Tax on distributions from HSAs, Archer MSAs, and Medicare Advantage MSAs. A 20% tax generally applies to HSA and Archer MSA distributions that are not rolled over to a similar account or used to pay qualified medical expenses [§ 223(f)(4)]. A 50% tax generally applies to Medicare Advantage MSA distributions that are not used to pay qualified medical expenses [§ 138(c)(2)].

- Tax for failure to remain an eligible individual during the HSA testing period. A 10% tax applies to HSA contributions that must be included in the taxpayer's income because he fails to remain an eligible individual during the testing period. A taxpayer is an eligible individual only if he is covered under a high deductible health plan and he has no other coverage except certain permitted coverage. The testing period is the 12-month period beginning on the first day of the month in which the qualified HSA distribution is contributed to the HSA [§ 106(e)(3), § § 106(e)(4)(A)].

The taxes related to HSAs are computed on Form 8889, *Health Savings Accounts (HSAs).* The taxes related to MSAs are computed on Form 8853, *Archer MSAs and Long-Term Care Insurance Contracts.*

See X.A.8.b. for a discussion of additional taxes on excess contributions to HSAs and Archer MSAs.

### X.A.8.g. Additional Taxes

[507 T.M., II.A.; TPS ¶3310.]

The following are some additional taxes that must be reported on the "total tax" line of Form 1040:

- Tax on accumulation distribution of trusts. Taxpayers that are beneficiaries of certain domestic trusts created before March 1, 1984, must pay a tax on any accumulation distribution received from the trust during the year. A distribution may be an accumulation distribution if the trust accumulated income rather than distributing it each year. The tax is computed and reported on Form 4970, *Tax on Accumulation Distribution of Trusts.* For further discussion of the tax on accumulation distributions, see XVIII.C.8.

- Tax on recapture of a charitable contribution deduction relating to a fractional interest in tangible personal property. Such a charitable contribution deduction must be recaptured if, within a specified period, the taxpayer does not contribute his remaining interest in the property or the charitable organization does not use the property for its charitable purpose. For further discussion of this recapture of a charitable contribution deduction, see VII.G.2.g.

- Tax on nonresident alien for income that is not effectively connected with U.S. trade or business. Nonresident aliens are generally subject to a 30% tax on income that is not effectively connected with a U.S. trade or business, unless a lower treaty tax rate applies (see XX.D.1.b.). This tax is generally reported on Form 1040NR, *U.S. Nonresident Income Tax Return.* However, a taxpayer who was a nonresident alien for only part of the year may be required to report this tax on noneffectively connected income on the "total tax" line of Form 1040.

### X.A.8.h. Recapture Amounts

[507 T.M., II.A.; TPS ¶3110.]

Individual taxpayers must report the following tax credit recapture amounts on the "total tax" line of Form 1040:

- the investment credit (see IX.A.5.);
- the low-income housing credit (see IX.A.9.);
- the Indian employment credit (see IX.A.14.);
- the new markets credit (see IX.A.17.);
- the credit for employer-provided child care facilities (see IX.A.19.);
- the alternative motor vehicle credit (see IX.D.1.);
- the alternative fuel vehicle refueling property credit (see IX.D.2.); and
- the qualified plug-in electric drive motor vehicle credit (see IX.D.3.).

***Recapture of Federal Mortgage Subsidy.*** If a taxpayer sells or otherwise disposes of his home during the first nine years after receiving a federally subsidized loan, he must recapture the federal mortgage subsidy and report it on the "total tax" line of Form 1040 for the year of disposition. A taxpayer has a federal mortgage subsidy if he received either of the following two types of mortgage loans: (i) a mortgage loan financed from the proceeds of any tax-exempt qualified mortgage bond, or (ii) a mortgage loan with a mortgage credit certificate for which the mortgage interest credit can be claimed. The recapture of a federal mortgage subsidy is computed and reported on Form 8828, *Recapture of Federal Mortgage Subsidy.*

### X.A.8.i. Interest Amounts

[507 T.M., II.A.; TPS ¶3310.]

Individual taxpayers must report the following interest amounts on the "total tax" line of Form 1040:

- interest on the tax due on installment income from the sale of certain residential lots and timeshares (see III.G.1.) [§ 453(l)(3)];

- interest on the deferred tax on gain from certain installment sales with a sales price over $150,000 (see III.G.4.) [§ 453A(c)];

- interest computed under the look-back method for completed long-term contracts (see Form 8697, *Interest Computation Under the Look-Back Method for Completed Long-Term Contracts*) (see XI.E.2.e.) [§ 460(b)];

- interest computed under the look-back method for property depreciated under the income forecast method (see Form 8866, *Interest Computation Under the Look-Back Method for Property Depreciated Under the Income Forecast Method*) (see V.A.8.b.) [§ 167(g)]; and

- interest related to distributions from, and dispositions of, stock of a § 1291 fund (see Part V of Form 8621, *Information Return by a Shareholder of a Passive Foreign Investment Company or Qualified Electing Fund*) [§ 1291(c)].

## X.B. Federal Income Tax Liability of C Corporations

### X.B.1. Regular Income Tax

[507 T.M., III.A.; TPS ¶3320.02.]

Corporations generally compute their federal income tax liability on taxable income at the regular corporate tax rates. The four corporate tax rates of 15%, 25%, 34%, and 35% are applied at various taxable income thresholds. However, the corporate tax rate structure is made more complex by the phase out of the lower rates for corporations with taxable income in excess of certain specified amounts. For corporations with taxable income in excess of $100,000, the lower rates are phased out by an additional 5% surtax on taxable income between $100,000 and $335,000. For corporations with taxable income in excess of $15,000,000, the lower rates are phased out by an additional 3% surtax on taxable income between $15,000,000 and $18,333,333 [§ 11(b)].

When the corporate tax rate phaseouts are taken into account, the corporate tax rate structure is as follows:

| If taxable income is: | | Then tax is: | | |
|---|---|---|---|---|
| Over- | But not over- | This amount: | Plus this percent: | Of the amount over: |
| $          0 | $       50,000 | — | 15% | $          0 |
| $     50,000 | $       75,000 | $       7,500 | 25% | $     50,000 |
| $     75,000 | $     100,000 | $     13,750 | 34% | $     75,000 |
| $   100,000 | $     335,000 | $     22,250 | 39% | $   100,000 |
| $   335,000 | $ 10,000,000 | $   113,900 | 34% | $   335,000 |
| $ 10,000,000 | $ 15,000,000 | $ 3,400,000 | 35% | $ 10,000,000 |
| $ 15,000,000 | $ 18,333,333 | $ 5,150,000 | 38% | $ 15,000,000 |
| $ 18,333,333 | — | — | 35% | $          0 |

See XIII.C.2. for a detailed discussion of application of the regular income tax to C corporations.

### X.B.2. Alternative Minimum Tax (AMT)

[752 T.M.; TPS ¶3420.]

The alternative minimum tax (AMT) for corporations is similar to the AMT for individuals (see X.A.2.). However, there are some differences that are noted in the following discussion. The AMT for corporations is computed and reported on Form 4626, *Alternative Minimum Tax – Corporations*.

### X.B.2.a. Corporations Subject to AMT

[752 T.M., I.; TPS ¶3420.01.B.]

All corporations subject to the regular income tax are also subject to the AMT, with two exceptions. Under the first exception, all corporations are exempt from AMT in their first year of existence. Under the second exception, certain small corporations are exempt from AMT [§ 55(e)].

Note that S corporations are not subject to AMT because they are not subject to the regular income tax. However, an S corporation must compute AMT adjustments and preferences as if it were an individual and pass those items through to its shareholders. For further discussion of S corporations, see Chapter XV.

***Small Corporation Exception.*** A corporation is automatically exempt from AMT for the first tax year of its existence (regardless of the amount of its gross receipts) [§ 55(e)(1)(C)]. However, after a corporation's first tax year, it is exempt from AMT only if it meets certain gross receipts tests under the small corporation exception.

For the first relevant three-tax-year period (or portion thereof) that the corporation is in existence, it qualifies as a small corporation if its annual gross receipts do not exceed $5,000,000. The relevant three-tax-year period is the three-tax-year period ending before the tax year in question. If the corporation is not in existence for an entire three-tax-year period, the test is applied on the basis of the period during which the corporation is in existence [§ 55(e)(1)(B)].

---

**EXAMPLE:** X Corp. is formed on Jan. 1, Year 1. In Year 1, X has gross receipts of $6 million. X is exempt from AMT in Year 1 because Year 1 is its first year in existence. In Year 2, X has gross receipts of $3 million. For Year 2, the relevant three-tax-year period is the three-tax-year period ending before Year 2. X was only in existence for one previous tax year ending before Year 2 and this period (Year 1) is considered X's first relevant three-tax-year period. X does not qualify as a small corporation exempt from AMT for Year 2 because its average annual gross receipts for its first relevant three-tax-year period ($6 million) exceeded $5 million.

For relevant three-tax-year periods after the first three-tax-year period, a corporation qualifies as a small corporation if its average annual gross receipts for all three-tax-year periods ending before the relevant tax year (other than the first three-tax-year period) do not exceed $7,500,000 [§ 55(e)(1)(A)].

**EXAMPLE:** Y Corp. is formed on Jan. 1, Year 1. In Year 1, Y has gross receipts of $4 million. Y is exempt from AMT in Year 1 because Year 1 is its first year in existence. In Year 2, Y has gross receipts of $8 million. For Year 2, the relevant three-tax-year period is the three-tax-year period ending before Year 2. Y was only in existence for one previous tax year ending before Year 2 and this period (Year 1) is considered Y's first relevant three-tax-year period. Y qualifies as a small corporation exempt from AMT for Year 2 because its average annual gross receipts for its first relevant three-tax-year period ($4 million) do not exceed $5 million. In Year 3, Y has gross receipts of $10 million. For Year 3, the relevant three-tax-year period is the three-tax-year period ending before Year 3. Y was only in existence for the two previous years ending before Year 3 and this period (Years 1 and 2) is considered Y's second relevant three-tax-year period. Y qualifies as a small corporation exempt from AMT for Year 3 because its average annual gross receipts for its second relevant three-tax-year period (($4 million + $8 million)/2 = $6 million) do not exceed $7.5 million.

Special rules apply for purposes of these gross receipts tests [§ 55(e)(1)(D), § 448(c)(2) and § 448(c)(3)]:

- Only tax years beginning after December 31, 1993, are taken into account for purposes of the tests.
- All persons treated as a single employer under § 52(a), § 52(b), § 414(m), or § 414(o) are treated as one person for purposes of the tests.
- The existence of any predecessor of the corporation is taken into account for purposes of the tests.
- Gross receipts for any tax year are reduced by returns and allowances made during the year.
- Gross receipts for any tax year of less than 12 months are annualized by multiplying the gross receipts for the short period by 12 and dividing the result by the number of months in the short period.

If a corporation qualifies as a small corporation for any tax year, its credit for prior year minimum tax liability (see IX.H.) is limited to the amount by which the corporation's regular tax liability (reduced by other credits) exceeds 25% of any excess of the corporation's regular tax liability (reduced by other credits) over $25,000 [§ 55(e)(5)].

A corporation that initially qualifies as a small corporation but later ceases to be a small corporation is subject to AMT prospectively. In this case, the AMT is applied only for AMT adjustments and preferences that relate to transactions and expenditures that occur after the first day of the first tax year for which the corporation no longer qualifies as a small corporation (the so-called change date). The AMT computation is modified as follows (except for items that were acquired by the corporation in a carryover or transferred basis transaction and that were subject to AMT in the hands of the transferor) [§ 55(e)(2) through § 55(e)(4)]:

- the depreciation adjustments and pollution control facility adjustments do not apply to property placed in service before the change date;

- the mining exploration and development cost adjustment does not apply to costs paid or incurred before the change date;

- the adjustment for long-term contracts does not apply to contracts entered into before the change date;

- the adjustment for the alternative tax net operating loss deduction applies beginning on the change date;

- the adjustment of depreciation to adjusted current earnings (ACE) does not apply;

- the limitation on the allowance of negative ACE adjustments applies only to prior tax years that begin on or after the change date; and

- certain other ACE adjustments apply beginning on the change date.

### X.B.2.b. Computation of Corporate AMT

[752 T.M., I.C.; TPS ¶3420.01.C.]

Although the computation of AMT by corporations is similar to the computation of AMT by individuals, there are some differences. For both individual and corporate taxpayers, certain items of income and deduction are treated differently for AMT purposes than they are for regular tax purposes. Thus, the first step in computing AMT is to recompute these items of income and deduction for AMT purposes. The recomputed items result in certain adjustments (see X.B.2.c.(1)) and tax preferences (see X.B.2.c.(2)). In determining alternative minimum taxable income (AMTI), regular taxable income is modified by these adjustments and preferences.

Although many of the AMT adjustments apply to both corporations and individual taxpayers, there are some adjustments that apply only to corporations and other adjustments that apply only to individuals. One important adjustment that applies only to corporations is the adjusted current earnings (ACE) adjustment (see X.B.2.c.(3)). In computing AMTI, corporations apply the ACE adjustment and the adjustment for the alternative tax net operating loss (ATNOL) deduction (see X.B.2.c.(4)) after all other adjustments and preferences have been applied.

Once AMTI is determined, the basic steps taken by a corporation to determine whether it has an AMT liability are the same steps taken by individual taxpayers:

1. Taxable AMTI is computed by subtracting an exemption amount from AMTI (see X.B.2.d.).

2. Pre-credit tentative minimum tax is computed by multiplying the taxable AMTI by the AMT tax rate (see X.B.2.e.).

3. Tentative minimum tax is computed by subtracting the AMT foreign tax credit, if any, from pre-credit tentative minimum tax (see X.B.2.f.).

4. AMT liability is computed as the excess, if any, of tentative minimum tax over regular tax (see X.B.2.g.).

### X.B.2.c. Alternative Minimum Taxable Income (AMTI)

### X.B.2.c.(1) AMT Adjustments

[752 T.M., II.B.; TPS ¶3420.02.B.]

In determining AMTI, corporations must make many of the same adjustments that are made by individual taxpayers. There are also specific adjustments that are made only by corporations.

In computing AMTI, both corporations and individual taxpayers make adjustments (increases or decreases) to regular taxable income for the following items:

- post-1986 depreciation deduction (see X.A.2.b.(15));
- pollution control facilities (see X.A.2.b.(23));
- mining costs (see X.A.2.b.(20));
- circulation costs (see X.A.2.b.(18). (applies only to personal holding companies);
- gain or loss on dispositions of property (see X.A.2.b.(14));
- long-term contracts (see X.A.2.b.(19));
- tax shelter farm activity loss limitations (see X.A.2.b.(24).; applies only to personal service corporations);
- passive activity loss limitations (see X.A.2.b.(16). (applies only to closely held corporations and personal service corporations);
- other loss limitations (see X.A.2.b.(17));
- biodiesel producer credit/biodiesel and renewable diesel fuels credit (see X.A.2.b.(25));
- pass-through from estates and trusts (see X.A.2.b.(12));
- pass-through from electing large partnerships (see X.A.2.b.(13));
- cooperative patron's adjustment (see X.A.2.b.(26)); and
- pre-1987 installment sales (see X.A.2.b.(22).).

In addition to those adjustments, corporations must also make adjustments for the following:

- merchant marine capital construction funds;
- special deduction for certain insurance organizations;
- special deduction for cooperatives; and
- the domestic production activities deduction.

***Merchant Marine Capital Construction Funds.*** For regular tax purposes, corporations can take a deduction for a deposit to a merchant marine capital construction fund for the replacement, construction, or reconstruction of certain shipping vessels built in the United States. In addition, earnings on the deposits in such a fund are not taxable for regular tax purposes. For AMT purposes, the regular tax benefits associated with such merchant marine capital construction funds are not available. Thus, the following two adjustments must be made to regular taxable income in computing AMTI: (i) the deduction for the deposits to a capital construction fund must be added back, and (ii) the earnings on those deposits must be added [§ 56(c)(2)].

***Special Deduction for Certain Insurance Organizations.*** For regular tax purposes, Blue Cross/Blue Shield and certain other health insurance organizations can take a deduction for the excess of (i) 25% of the sum of the insurance claims and liabilities incurred under cost-plus contracts, and the expenses incurred in connection with the administration of such cost-plus contracts and the adjustment and settlement of such claims, over (ii) the organization's adjusted surplus as of the beginning of the year [§ 833(b)]. For AMT purposes, this deduction is not allowed and a corporation must add back the deduction to regular taxable income in computing AMTI [§ 56(c)(3)].

*Cooperative's Adjustment.* A cooperative can take a deduction for certain distributions from patronage-sourced and nonpatronage-sourced income for both regular tax and AMT purposes (see XIII.F.4.b.) [§ 1382(b), § 1382(c)]. However, the income from which such distributions are computed may differ for regular tax and AMT purposes because of the adjustments and preferences that apply in determining AMTI. Thus, the amount of the deduction may differ for regular tax and AMT purposes and an adjustment must be made for the difference in computing AMTI.

*Domestic Production Activities Deduction.* For regular tax purposes, a corporation can take a domestic production activities deduction equal to 9% of the smaller of (i) its qualified production activities income, or (ii) its taxable income (see IV.A.9.) [§ 199(a)(1)]. For AMT purposes, a corporation's AMTI is substituted for taxable income in computing the domestic production activities deduction [§ 199(d)(6)]. Thus, an adjustment for the difference between the regular tax deduction and the AMT deduction must be made to regular taxable income in computing AMTI.

### X.B.2.c.(2) AMT Tax Preferences

[752 T.M., II.C.; TPS ¶3420.02.C.]

In determining AMTI, corporations add the same tax preference items that are added by individual taxpayers, except for the preference for the § 1202 exclusion for gains on the sale of qualified small business stock. The preference items that must be added to taxable income include the preferences for [§ 57]:

- depletion (see X.A.2.c.(1));
- tax-exempt interest from specified private activity bonds (see X.A.2.c.(2));
- intangible drilling and development costs (see X.A.2.c.(4)); and
- accelerated depreciation on certain pre-1986 property (see X.A.2.c.(5)).

### X.B.2.c.(3) Adjusted Current Earnings (ACE) Adjustment

[752 T.M., III.; TPS ¶3420.03.]

In computing AMTI, a corporation must make an adjustment to taxable income if the amount of its adjusted current earnings (ACE) is different from the amount of its AMTI [§ 56(c)(1)]. The starting point for computing ACE is pre-ACE AMTI, which is AMTI determined without regard to the ACE adjustment and the adjustment for the alternative tax net operating loss deduction. Once pre-ACE AMTI is computed, adjustments are made to certain tax items for ACE purposes [§ 56(g)]. As a result of these adjustments, certain tax items are treated differently for ACE purposes than they are for regular tax or AMT purposes. Thus, ACE essentially represents a third tax regime that is separate from the regular tax regime and the AMT regime.

*Adjustments to Pre-ACE AMTI.* The adjustments made to pre-ACE AMTI in determining ACE include the following [§ 56(g)(4)]:

- Depreciation for property placed in service before 1994 is computed using special ACE depreciation rules (no depreciation adjustment is made for property placed in service after 1993). The following ACE depreciation rules generally apply: (i) depreciation for property placed in service after 1989 but before 1994 is computed using the alternative depreciation system, (ii) depreciation for MACRS property placed in service before 1990 is computed by applying straight line depreciation to the property's AMT basis over the remainder of the property's recovery period under the alternative depreciation system, (iii) depreciation for ACRS property is computed by applying straight line depreciation to the property's regular tax basis over the remainder of the property's recovery period under the alternative depreciation system, and (iv) the depreciation for most other property is computed using the depreciation method used for regular tax purposes. For further discussion of depreciation, see V.A.

- Income items that are excluded for AMT purposes but taken into account in determining earnings and profits (see XIII.D.1.a.) (other than income from discharge of indebtedness) are included in income for ACE purposes.

- Expense items that are deductible for regular tax or AMT purposes but not taken into account in determining earnings and profits (see XIII.D.1.a.) are not allowed as deductions for ACE purposes.

- Certain adjustments made to more accurately reflect earnings and profits (see XIII.D.1.a.) must also be made for ACE purposes. These adjustments relate to intangible drilling costs, circulation costs, organizational expenditures, LIFO inventory, and installment sales.

- For ACE purposes, any loss on the exchange of a pool of debt obligations for another pool with substantially the same effective interest rates and maturities is disallowed.

- For ACE purposes, the small life insurance company deduction is disallowed and the election by small property and casualty companies to be taxed on only investment income does not apply.

- For ACE purposes, the depletion allowance for property placed in service after 1989 must be determined under the cost depletion method (see VI.A.3.a.).

- For ACE purposes, a corporation's adjusted basis in assets in which there is net unrealized built-in loss after an ownership change is determined based on the proportionate share of the fair market value of the corporation's assets immediately before the ownership change. For further discussion of ownership changes, see XIII.E.5.b.

- For ACE purposes, the basis of property subject to an ACE adjustment is determined according to the ACE rules.

*Computation of ACE Adjustment.* If a corporation's ACE exceeds its AMTI, it must make a positive ACE adjustment that increases its AMTI by 75% of the excess amount. If a corporation's AMTI exceeds its ACE, it must make a negative ACE adjustment that reduces its AMTI by 75% of the excess amount. However, the negative ACE adjustment for any tax year is limited to the excess, if any, of the total positive ACE adjustments for all previous tax years over the total negative ACE adjustments for all previous tax years [§ 56(g)(1) through § 56(g)(3)].

---

**EXAMPLE:** V Corp. has ACE of $200 and pre-ACE AMTI of $100 for the year. V must make a positive ACE adjustment that increases its AMTI by $75 (($200 - $100) × 75%).

**EXAMPLE:** W Corp. has ACE of $200 and pre-ACE AMTI of $400 for the year. In previous tax years, W had total positive ACE adjustments of $500 and total negative ACE adjustments of $300. W must make a negative ACE adjustment that reduces its AMTI by $150 (($400 - $200) × 75%). Note that the negative ACE adjustment was not limited because W's total positive ACE adjustments from previous tax years exceeded its total negative ACE adjustments from previous tax years by more than $150.

---

The ACE adjustment does not apply to S corporations, regulated investment companies (RICs), real estate investment trusts (REITs), or real estate mortgage investment conduits (REMICs) [§ 56(g)(6)].

The Adjusted Current Earnings (ACE) Worksheet (Source: 2014 Form 4626 Draft Instructions) can be used to compute the ACE adjustment.

**Adjusted Current Earnings (ACE) Worksheet**

*Keep for Your Records*

▶ See ACE Worksheet Instructions.

| | | | | | |
|---|---|---|---|---|---|
| 1 | Pre-adjustment AMTI . Enter the amount from line 3 of Form 4626 . . . . . . . . . . . . . . . . . . . . . . . . . . . . . . . . . . | | | **1** | |
| 2 | ACE depreciation adjustment: | | | | |
| a | AMT depreciation . . . . . . . . . . . . . . . . . . . . . . . . . . . . . . . . . . . . . . . . . . . . . | | **2a** | | |
| b | ACE depreciation: | | | | |
| | (1) Post-1993 property . . . . . . . . . . . . . . . . . . . | **2b(1)** | | | |
| | (2) Post-1989, pre-1994 property . . . . . . . . . . . . . | **2b(2)** | | | |
| | (3) Pre-1990 MACRS property . . . . . . . . . . . . . . | **2b(3)** | | | |
| | (4) Pre-1990 original ACRS property . . . . . . . . . . | **2b(4)** | | | |
| | (5) Property described in sections 168(f)(1) through (4) . . . . . . . . . . . . . . . . . . . . . . . . . . . . . . . . | **2b(5)** | | | |
| | (6) Other property . . . . . . . . . . . . . . . . . . . . . . | **2b(6)** | | | |
| | (7) Total ACE depreciation. Add lines 2b(1) through 2b(6) . . . . . . . . . . . . . . | **2b(7)** | | | |
| c | ACE depreciation adjustment. Subtract line 2b(7) from line 2a . . . . . . . . . . . . . . . . . . . . . . . . . . | | | **2c** | |
| 3 | Inclusion in ACE of items included in earnings and profits (E&P): | | | | |
| a | Tax-exempt interest income . . . . . . . . . . . . . . . . . . . . . . . . . . . . . . . . . . . | | **3a** | | |
| b | Death benefits from life insurance contracts . . . . . . . . . . . . . . . . . . . . . . . . . | | **3b** | | |
| c | All other distributions from life insurance contracts (including surrenders) . . . . . . . . . . | | **3c** | | |
| d | Inside buildup of undistributed income in life insurance contracts . . . . . . . . . . . . . . . | | **3d** | | |
| e | Other items (see Regulations sections 1.56(g)-1(c)(6)(iii) through (ix) for a partial list) . . . . . . . . . . . . . . . . . . . . . . . . . . . . . . . . . . . . . . . . . . . . . . . . . . . . | | **3e** | | |
| f | Total increase to ACE from inclusion in ACE of items included in E&P. Add lines 3a through 3e | | | **3f** | |
| 4 | Disallowance of items not deductible from E&P: | | | | |
| a | Certain dividends received . . . . . . . . . . . . . . . . . . . . . . . . . . . . . . . . . . . . . | | **4a** | | |
| b | Dividends paid on certain preferred stock of public utilities that are deductible under section 247 . . . . . . . . . . . . . . . . . . . . . . . . . . . . . . . . . . . . . . . . . . . . . . . . | | **4b** | | |
| c | Dividends paid to an ESOP that are deductible under section 404(k) . . . . . . . . . . . . . . | | **4c** | | |
| d | Nonpatronage dividends that are paid and deductible under section 1382(c) . . . . . . . . | | **4d** | | |
| e | Other items (see Regulations sections 1.56(g)-1(d)(3)(i) and (ii) for a partial list) . . . . . . . | | **4e** | | |
| f | Total increase to ACE because of disallowance of items not deductible from E&P. Add lines 4a through 4e . . . . . . . . . | | | **4f** | |
| 5 | Other adjustments based on rules for figuring E&P: | | | | |
| a | Intangible drilling costs . . . . . . . . . . . . . . . . . . . . . . . . . . . . . . . . . . . . . . . | | **5a** | | |
| b | Circulation expenditures . . . . . . . . . . . . . . . . . . . . . . . . . . . . . . . . . . . . . . | | **5b** | | |
| c | Organizational expenditures . . . . . . . . . . . . . . . . . . . . . . . . . . . . . . . . . . . . | | **5c** | | |
| d | LIFO inventory adjustments . . . . . . . . . . . . . . . . . . . . . . . . . . . . . . . . . . . . | | **5d** | | |
| e | Installment sales . . . . . . . . . . . . . . . . . . . . . . . . . . . . . . . . . . . . . . . . . . . | | **5e** | | |
| f | Total other E&P adjustments. Combine lines 5a through 5e . . . . . . . . . . . . . . . . . . . . | | | **5f** | |
| 6 | Disallowance of loss on exchange of debt pools . . . . . . . . . . . . . . . . . . . . . . . . . . . . . | | | **6** | |
| 7 | Acquisition expenses of life insurance companies for qualified foreign contracts . . . . . . . . . . . . . . . . . . . . . . . | | | **7** | |
| 8 | Depletion . . . . . . . . . . . . . . . . . . . . . . . . . . . . . . . . . . . . . . . . . . . . . . . . . . . . | | | **8** | |
| 9 | Basis adjustments in determining gain or loss from sale or exchange of pre-1994 property . . . . . . . . . . . . . . | | | **9** | |
| 10 | **Adjusted current earnings.** Combine lines 1, 2c, 3f, 4f, and 5f through 9. Enter the result here and on line 4a of Form 4626 . . . . . . . . . . . . . . . . . . . . . . . . . . . . . . . . . . . . . . . . . . . . . . . . . . . . . . . . . . . . . . . . . . . . . . . | | | **10** | |

(Source: Based on August 15, 2014 IRS Draft)

### X.B.2.c.(4) Alternative Tax Net Operating Loss

[752 T.M., IV.A.; TPS ¶3420.04.]

For regular tax purposes, a corporation can generally claim a net operating loss (NOL) deduction equal to the sum of its NOL carrybacks and carryforwards to a particular tax year. An NOL is generally carried back two years and then forward 20 years until the loss is fully utilized to offset income. A corporation may elect to forego the carryback period and just carryforward an NOL [§ 172]. See VIII.G. for a discussion of the NOL deduction and NOL carryovers.

For AMT purposes, a corporation must use the alternative tax net operating loss (ATNOL) deduction in lieu of the NOL deduction allowed for regular tax purposes. A corporation can generally claim an ATNOL deduction equal to the sum of its ATNOL carrybacks and carryforwards to a particular tax year. Once an ATNOL is calculated, it is carried back and carried forward in the same manner as NOLs under the regular tax system. If a corporation elected to forego the carryback period for regular tax purposes, that election also applies for AMT purposes. ATNOL carrybacks and carryforwards will absorb AMTI even though the corporation is not subject to AMT for that particular tax year. A corporations's ATNOL is computed in the same manner as its NOL, with two exceptions [§ 56(a)(4), § 56(d)]:

1. The amount of an ATNOL is computed by taking into account all the § 56 and § 58 adjustments and the § 57 tax preference items that applied in computing AMTI to the extent that such items increased the corporation's NOL for regular tax purposes.

2. The ATNOL deduction generally can be used to offset only 90% of AMTI, determined without regard to the ATNOL deduction (in comparison, the NOL deduction can be used to completely offset regular taxable income).

For corporations, the starting point in computing AMTI is taxable income before the NOL deduction. Therefore, a corporation need not add back its regular tax NOL in computing AMTI. A corporation subtracts its ATNOL deduction in computing AMTI.

### X.B.2.d. Exemption

[752 T.M., V.B.; TPS ¶3420.05.B.]

After a corporation's AMTI is determined (see X.B.2.c.), the next step in computing AMT is to subtract an exemption amount from AMTI. The amount, if any, by which the corporation's AMTI exceeds its exemption amount is the taxable AMTI on which its AMT is computed. If a corporation's AMTI is less than its exemption amount (i.e., it has no taxable AMTI), then it is not subject to AMT.

The exemption amount for corporations is generally $40,000. This exemption amount is not adjusted annually for inflation. However, the $40,000 exemption amount is phased out for corporations with AMTI over $150,000. Under this phase out rule, the $40,000 exemption amount is reduced (but not below zero) by 25% of the amount by which the corporation's AMTI exceeds $150,000. Thus, the exemption is fully phased out for a corporation with AMTI over $310,000 [§ 55(d)(2) and § 55(d)(3)(D)].

---

**EXAMPLE:** Z Corp. has AMTI of $200,000. Z's exemption amount is equal to $27,500 ($40,000 − (($200,000 - $150,000) x 25%)).

---

*Exemption for Controlled Groups.* Only one $40,000 AMT exemption is available to a controlled group of corporations. The exemption is allocated among the group members equally, unless they have elected to allocate it in a different manner. The phase-out of the exemption is applied by taking into account the AMTI for the entire controlled group [§ 1561(a)].

### X.B.2.e. Pre-Credit Tentative Minimum Tax

[752 T.M., V.C.; TPS ¶3420.05.C.]

The pre-credit tentative minimum tax is generally determined by multiplying the corporation's taxable AMTI (i.e., the excess of the corporation's AMTI over its exemption amount) (see X.B.2.c. and d.) by the corporate AMT tax rate of 20% [§ 55(b)(1)(B)(i)].

---

**EXAMPLE:** Assume the same facts as in the previous example. Z's taxable AMTI is $172,500 ($200,000 AMTI - $27,500 exemption). Z's pre-credit tentative minimum tax is $34,500 ($172,500 x 20%).

---

### X.B.2.f. Tentative Minimum Tax and the AMT Foreign Tax Credit

[752 T.M., V.D.; TPS ¶3420.05.D.]

A corporation's tentative minimum tax is determined by subtracting its AMT foreign tax credit, if any, from its pre-credit tentative minimum tax (see X.B.2.e.). The AMT foreign tax credit is generally computed in the same manner as the regular foreign tax credit. However, the computation of the overall limit on the foreign tax credit is modified for AMT purposes.

For regular tax purposes, the amount of a corporation's foreign tax credit that can be claimed is limited to its pre-credit U.S. tax multiplied by a fraction, the numerator of which is its foreign source taxable income and the denominator of which is its worldwide taxable income (see XX.C.2.) [§ 904]. For AMT purposes, this overall limit is generally computed in the same manner, with the following exceptions [§ 59(a)(1)]:

- the pre-credit tentative minimum tax is used instead of the pre-credit U.S. tax;
- foreign source AMTI is used instead of foreign source taxable income (i.e., AMT adjustments and preference items are taken into account); and
- worldwide AMTI is used instead of worldwide taxable income (i.e., AMT adjustments and preference items are taken into account).

A corporation may also elect to use a simplified method under which foreign source taxable income is treated as the numerator for AMT purposes (note that worldwide AMTI remains the denominator for AMT purposes). This election may be made only for the first tax year after 1997 for which the taxpayer claims the AMT foreign tax credit [§ 59(a)(3)]. If this election is made, the corporation will not need to recompute the numerator to take into account AMT adjustments and preference items.

A corporation's AMT foreign tax credit may be different than its regular foreign tax credit because of the differences in the computation of the overall limit. It may also be different because the AMT foreign tax credit must be computed and offset against tentative minimum tax each year, even if no AMT is due for the year. Thus, the AMT foreign tax credit is effectively applied against a different tax base than the regular foreign tax credit.

No regular or AMT foreign tax credit is allowed if a corporation chooses to deduct its accrued foreign taxes in lieu of claiming the credit. The choice that is made for regular tax purposes also applies for AMT purposes.

### X.B.2.g. Computation of AMT Liability

[752 T.M., V.E.; TPS ¶3420.05.E.]

The amount of a corporation's AMT liability is equal to the excess of tentative minimum tax (see X.B.2.f.) over regular tax. For this purpose, regular tax is the corporation's regular tax liability for the year, except that the following two types of adjustments are made [§ 55(c), § 26(b)]:

- certain taxes are disregarded (e.g., the AMT, accumulated earnings tax, personal holding company tax); and
- the only nonrefundable credit allowed is the foreign tax credit.

If tentative minimum tax is more than the regular tax amount, the corporation has an AMT liability equal to the excess amount and it must pay the AMT liability in addition to its regular tax liability. If tentative minimum tax is less than the regular tax amount, the corporation does not have any AMT liability and it only pays its regular tax liability.

---

**EXAMPLE:** P Corp. has tentative minimum tax of $250,000 and regular tax of $175,000. Thus, P's AMT liability is $75,000 ($250,000 - $175,000). P must pay the $75,000 AMT liability in addition to its regular tax liability.

---

As a general rule, no nonrefundable credits other than the regular foreign tax credit are allowed to offset the regular tax and AMT liability of a corporation. However, a corporation can use any investment tax credit attributable to the regular percentage investment income tax credit for property placed in service before 1991 to offset up to 25% of its tentative minimum tax.

Credits based on the taxpayer's prepayments of income tax (e.g., the credits for taxes withheld and estimated taxes paid) are allowed to offset both the regular tax liability and AMT liability when computing the amount of taxes due [§ 31 through § 34, § 6315, § 6413].

### X.B.3. Other Taxes

[796 T.M., 797 T.M.; TPS ¶¶5140., 5150.]

In addition to the regular income tax and the alternative minimum tax, C corporations may also be subject to other income taxes, including the accumulated earnings tax and the personal holding company tax. The accumulated earnings tax is a tax imposed on earnings that a corporation accumulates beyond the reasonable needs of its business (see XIII.C.4.). The personal holding company tax is a tax imposed on a corporation's undistributed personal holding company income (see XIII.C.5.).

# CHAPTER XI. ACCOUNTING PERIODS AND METHODS

>>>>>>>>>>>>>>>>>>>>>>>>>>>>>>>

All taxpayers must compute their taxable income and file their federal income tax returns on the basis of an annual accounting period known as a tax year. Generally, taxpayers can use either the calendar year or a fiscal year as their tax year. However, special types of tax years may be used in some situations. Moreover, there are a number of rules that limit the tax year that may be used by certain taxpayers. See XI.A. for a discussion of tax years.

All taxpayers must use permissible methods of accounting in computing their taxable income. A method of accounting includes not only a taxpayer's overall method of accounting for income and deductions, but also the accounting treatment used for any material item. The most common types of permissible accounting methods are the cash method and the accrual method (see XI.B.). However, there are a number of special accounting methods that must be used in certain situations. Some of the more common types of special accounting methods include the methods used to account for inventory (see XI.C.), the uniform capitalization of certain costs (see XI.D.), long-term contracts (see XI.E.), installment sales (see XI.F.), and property rentals (see XI.G.). Special accounting method rules also apply to farmers (see XI.H.). The IRS has the authority to require a taxpayer to change its method of accounting if that method does not clearly reflect income (see XI.I.).

## XI.A. Accounting Periods

### XI.A.1. Tax Year

[574 T.M., II.; TPS ¶3520.01.]

Taxable income is computed on the basis of a tax year [§ 441(a)]. Generally, a tax year can be either the calendar year or a fiscal year [§ 7701(a)(23)]. The calendar year is a period of 12 months ending on December 31 [§ 441(d)]. A fiscal year is a period of 12 months ending on the last day of a month other than December [§ 441(e)]. Although taxable income generally must be computed for a tax year of exactly 12 full months, there are two exceptions: (i) short tax years (see XI.A.1.b.), and (ii) 52-53-week tax years (see XI.A.1.c.).

### XI.A.1.a. Determination of a Taxpayer's Tax Year

[574 T.M., II.; TPS ¶3520.01.]

Generally, if a taxpayer keeps books and records using an annual accounting period that is either the calendar year or a fiscal year, the taxpayer must use that annual accounting period as its tax year. However, a taxpayer must use the calendar year as its tax year under each of the following circumstances [§ 441(b), § 441(c); Reg. § 1.441-1(b)(1)]:

- The taxpayer does not keep books and records.
- The taxpayer keeps books and records but does not use an annual accounting period for that purpose.
- The taxpayer keeps books and records using an annual accounting period but its annual accounting period is not a fiscal year.

Notwithstanding these general rules, there are substantial limitations that restrict the ability of many individuals and entities to adopt a fiscal year as their tax year (see XI.A.2.).

### XI.A.1.b. Short Tax Years

[574 T.M., VII.; TPS ¶3520.01.C., .13.]

If a taxpayer is required to file a short-period return for a period of less than 12 months, the taxpayer generally must compute its taxable income for a fractional part of a year, known as a short tax year [§ 443, § 7701(a)(23)]. A short-period return generally must be filed under the following circumstances:

- If a taxpayer changes its annual accounting period, it generally must file a short-period return. However, a short-period return is not required if the short period results from a change to or from a 52-53-week tax year (see XI.A.1.c.) and the short period is (i) six days or less (the short period is treated as part of following tax year), or (ii) 359 days or more (the short period is treated as a full tax year). If required to file a short-period return in this situation, the taxpayer's short tax year is the period beginning on the day after the end of its old tax year and ending on the day before the first day of its new tax year [§ 443(a)(1); Reg. § 1.443-1(a)(1)].
- If a taxpayer is in existence for only part of what would otherwise be its tax year, it must file a short-period return. Thus, a short-period return generally must be filed for a taxpayer's initial tax year and its final tax year. If required to file a short-period return in this situation, the taxpayer's short tax year is the period during which the taxpayer was in existence [§ 443(a)(2)].
- If a taxpayer's partnership tax year automatically terminates, the taxpayer must file a short-period return [§ 708(b)(1), § 706(c)].
- If a taxpayer's S corporation status terminates, the taxpayer must file a short-period return [§ 1362(e)].
- If a corporate taxpayer enters or exits an affiliated group filing consolidated returns, the taxpayer must file a short-period return [Reg. § 1.1502-76(b)].
- If a corporate taxpayer is acquired in a certain tax-free reorganization, liquidation transaction, or stock purchase treated as an asset sale under § 338, the taxpayer must file a short-period return [§ 338(a), § 381(b)(1)].

**Annualizing Income.** In computing its taxable income for a short tax year, a taxpayer is sometimes required to annualize income. For example, income must be annualized if a short tax year results from a change in a taxpayer's annual accounting method [§ 443(b); Reg. § 1.443-1(b)]. However, income is not annualized if a short tax year results because a taxpayer was not in existence for a full year [Reg. § 1.443-1(a)(2)].

Income is annualized by placing the short-period taxable income on an annual basis. First, annualized income must be computed by multiplying the short-period taxable income by 12 and then dividing the result by the number of months in the short period. Next, annualized tax is computed in the ordinary way on that annualized income. Finally, the actual tax is computed by multiplying the annualized tax by the number of months in the short period and dividing the result by 12 [§ 443(b)(1)].

**EXAMPLE:** At the end of Year 1, X Corp. changes its tax year from a calendar year to a fiscal year ending June 30. X has a short tax year for the period beginning Jan. 1, Year 2, and ending June 30, Year 2. X's taxable income for that short period is $50,000. X must annualize its income for purposes of its short-period return. Its annualized income is $100,000 ($50,000 × (12/6)).

A taxpayer may apply to the IRS for permission to use an alternative method of annualizing income if the short period includes the peak period of a cyclical business or a substantial amount of nonrecurring income, or if the short-period taxable income is abnormally high for any other reason. Under this alternative method, the tax is the greater of: (i) the tax on the taxable income for the short period, or (ii) an amount determined by multiplying the tax on the actual taxable income for the 12-month period beginning on the first day of the short period by a fraction, the numerator of which is the short-period taxable income and the denominator of which is the 12-month taxable income [§ 443(b)(2); Reg. § 1.443-1(b)(2)].

### XI.A.1.c. 52-53-Week Tax Years

[574 T.M., IV.; TPS ¶3520.10.]

A taxpayer may elect a 52-53-week tax year in certain circumstances. A 52-53-week tax year is a fiscal year that always ends on the same day of the week and for which the year-end may be either (i) the date on which the selected day of the week last occurs in a specified calendar month, or (ii) the date on which the selected day of the week falls that is nearest to the last day of a specified calendar month. In the first situation, the tax year always ends within the selected month and may end on the last day of the month or as many as six days before the end of the month. In the second situation, the tax year may end on the last day of the selected month or as many as three days before or three days after the end of the month. The length of the tax year is usually 52 weeks (364 days), but occasionally 53 weeks (371 days) to make up the shortfall of days when compared to the calendar year. Thus, out of every 28 years, there generally are 23 52-week years and five 53-week years [§ 441(f); Reg. § 1.441-2].

**EXAMPLE:** If a taxpayer elects a 52-53-week tax year that always ends on the last Wednesday in November, then its 2014 tax year ends on Nov. 26, 2014.

**EXAMPLE:** If a taxpayer elects a 52-53-week tax year that always ends on the Wednesday nearest to the end of November, then its 2014 tax year ends on Dec. 3, 2014.

Note that a 52-53-week tax year is always considered a fiscal year, even if the last day of the calendar month of reference is December 31. On the other hand, a 52-53-week tax year is never considered a short tax year, even when it consists of only 364 days.

*Advantages of 52-52-Week Tax Year.* A 52-53-week tax year can often be advantageous from a business perspective because it can provide consistency in the comparison of operating results without the necessity of making any complicated adjustments. For example, it allows the easy comparison of four-week periods without the adjustments for extra days that may be necessary for calendar-month comparisons. In addition, it enables simplification or elimination of adjustments for accruals such as weekly wages or other expenses normally accrued on a weekly basis.

*Eligibility to Elect 52-53-Week Tax Year.* A taxpayer is eligible to elect a 52-53-week tax year if it is otherwise eligible to use a fiscal year as its tax year (i.e., the taxpayer keeps books and records using an annual accounting period that is a fiscal year) (see XI.A.1.a.) [Reg. § 1.441-2(a)(3)].

*Procedures for Electing 52-53-Week Tax Year.* Most taxpayers can adopt a 52-53-week tax year for their initial tax year without obtaining the prior approval of the IRS. However, the election of a 52-53-week tax year by an existing taxpayer with an established tax year is treated as a change in accounting period that requires IRS approval (see XI.A.4.). A taxpayer that adopts or changes to a 52-53-week tax year must file a statement with its return for the year of adoption or change that contains the following information [Reg. § 1.441-2(b)]:

1. the calendar month with reference to which the new 52-53-week tax year ends;

2. the day of the week on which the 52-53-week tax year will always end; and

3. whether the 52-53-week tax year will always end on (i) the date on which that day of the week last occurs in the calendar month, or (ii) the date on which that day of the week falls that is nearest to the last day of that calendar month.

*Computation of Taxable Income for 52-53-Week Tax Year.* In computing taxable income for a 52-53-week tax year, all items of income and deduction generally must be determined on the basis of the 52-53-week tax year. However, particular tax items (e.g., depreciation or amortization) may be determined as though the 52-53-week tax year were a tax year consisting of 12 calendar months, provided that the practice is consistently followed and clearly reflects income. If a pass-through entity (e.g., partnership, S corporation) or one of its owners, or both, use a 52-53-week tax year and their tax years end with reference to the same calendar month, then for purposes of determining the tax year in which tax items from the pass-through entity are taken into account by the owner of the pass-through entity, the owner's tax year is deemed to end on the last day of the pass-through entity's tax year [Reg. § 1.441-2(d), § 1.441-2(e)].

### XI.A.2. Restrictions on Tax Year

[574 T.M., III.; TPS ¶3520.02.]

Substantial limitations restrict the ability of many individuals and entities to adopt a fiscal year as their tax year. The limitations are generally intended to prevent taxpayers from creating tax deferral benefits. Tax deferral benefits are created by manipulating tax years to create a disparity between the tax year of an entity and the tax years of its owners to which it passes through its tax items. Because the potential for manipulation is the greatest with pass-through entities, the limitations generally apply to entities such as partnerships, S corporations, and PSCs. The primary method used to restrict a pass-through entity's manipulation of tax years is the imposition of a "required tax year."

### XI.A.2.a. Required Tax Year of Partnerships

[574 T.M., III.B.; TPS ¶3520.03.]

A partnership generally must use a required tax year as its tax year. The required tax year of a partnership is [§ 706(b)]:

- the tax year of a majority of its partners ("the majority interest tax year");

- if there is no majority interest tax year, the tax year common to all of its principal partners (i.e., partners with a 5% or more interest in partnership capital or profits); or
- if there is neither a majority interest tax year nor a tax year common to all principal partners, the tax year that results in the least aggregate deferral of income.

However, if certain requirements are met, a partnership may instead choose to use one of the following tax years [§ 706(b)]:

- a tax year for which a business purpose is established;
- a tax year elected under § 444; or
- a 52-53-week tax year ending with reference to its required tax year or a tax year elected under § 444.

For a discussion of these special tax years, see XI.A.3.d. For further discussion of the tax year of a partnership, see XIV.D.4.d.

### XI.A.2.b. Required Tax Year of S Corporations

[574 T.M., III.C.; TPS ¶3520.04.]

An S corporation generally must use a required tax year as its tax year. The required tax year of an S corporation is the calendar year. However, if certain requirements are met, an S corporation may instead choose to use one of the following tax years [§ 1378; Reg. § 1.1378-1(a)]:

- a tax year for which a business purpose is established;
- a tax year elected under § 444; or
- a 52-53-week tax year ending with reference to its required tax year or a tax year elected under § 444.

For a discussion of these special tax years, see XI.A.3.d. For further discussion of the tax year of an S corporation, see XV.C.4.d.

### XI.A.2.c. Required Tax Year of Personal Service Corporation

[574 T.M., III.D.; TPS ¶3520.05.]

A personal service corporation (PSC) generally must use a required tax year as its tax year. The required tax year of a PSC is the calendar year. However, if certain requirements are met, a PSC may instead choose to use one of the following tax years [§ 441(i)]:

- a tax year for which a business purpose is established;
- a tax year elected under § 444; or
- a 52-53-week tax year ending with reference to its required tax year or a tax year elected under § 444.

For a discussion of these special tax years, see XI.A.3.d. For further discussion of the tax year of a PSC, see XIII.C.6.b.

### XI.A.2.d. Tax Year of Individual Taxpayers

[574 T.M., III.I.; TPS ¶3520.09.]

Because individual taxpayers do not normally keep books and records, they are generally required to use the calendar year as their tax year. However, a new taxpayer (i.e., a taxpayer subject to U.S. taxation for the first time) may adopt a fiscal year as his tax year by filing his first federal return using that fiscal year. Once a fiscal year is adopted, it cannot be changed without IRS approval [Reg. § 1.441-1(c)(1)].

### XI.A.3. Initial Tax Year

#### XI.A.3.a. General Requirements for Adopting Initial Tax Year

[574 T.M., V.; TPS ¶3520.11.A.]

A taxpayer adopts its initial tax year by filing its first federal income tax return using that tax year. The return must be filed by the original due date, not including any extensions. Generally, no IRS approval is required to adopt an initial tax year. However, under certain circumstances, a taxpayer with a required tax year may be required to obtain IRS approval to adopt its initial tax year (see XI.A.3.d.) [Reg. § 1.441-1(c)(1)].

A corporation is generally required to file its first federal income tax return for the year of its incorporation. A partnership is generally required to file its first federal income tax return for the first year in which it receives income or incurs deductible expenses. An individual, estate, or trust is required to file its first return when its income first meets certain filing thresholds.

Newly organized C corporations and individual taxpayers are not generally limited in their adoption of an initial tax year, although most individual taxpayers adopt the calendar year because they would be required to maintain books and records to adopt a fiscal year. Most other taxpayers are subject to substantial limitations that restrict the initial tax year that may be adopted (see XI.A.2.).

#### XI.A.3.b. Requirements for Adopting Fiscal Year

[574 T.M., V.A.; TPS ¶3520.11.A.]

Taxpayers that adopt a fiscal year as their initial tax year must establish and maintain adequate books and records no later than the end of the first fiscal year. If adequate books and records do not exist by the end of the first fiscal year, the calendar year must be used as the tax year.

#### XI.A.3.c. Requirements for Adopting 52-53-Week Tax Year

[574 T.M., V.B.; TPS ¶3520.11.A.]

Taxpayers may generally adopt a 52-53-week tax year as their initial tax year without IRS approval. However, partnerships, S corporations, and personal service corporations may only adopt a 52-53-week tax year without IRS approval if the 52-53-week year ends with reference to either the taxpayer's required tax year or a tax year elected under § 444 (see XI.A.3.d.).

#### XI.A.3.d. Special Requirements for Partnerships, S Corporations, and PSCs

[574 T.M., V.C.; TPS ¶3520.11.A.]

Partnerships, S corporations, and personal service corporations (PSCs) may adopt one of the following tax years as their initial tax year without IRS approval: (i) the required tax year, (ii) a tax year elected under § 444, or (iii) a 52-53-week tax year that ends with reference to its required tax year or a tax year elected under § 444. If such an entity wishes to adopt any other tax year as its initial tax year it must establish a business purpose and obtain IRS approval [Reg. § 1.441-1(c)(2)]. See XI.A.2. for a discussion of the required tax years of such entities.

*Section 444 Election.* A partnership, S corporation, or PSC is eligible to elect a tax year that generates up to three months of deferral relative to its required tax year, as long as it has not terminated a § 444 election previously in effect and it is not a member of a tiered structure [§ 444(a), § 444(b), § 444(d)]. Such an entity terminates a § 444 election when it (i) changes to its required tax year, (ii) liquidates, (iii) willfully fails to comply with § 7519, or (iv) becomes a member of a tiered structure [Reg.

§ 1.444-1T(a)(5)]. Such an entity is a member of a tiered structure if the entity directly owns any portion of a deferral entity or if a deferral entity directly owns any portion of it. A deferral entity is a partnership, S corporation, PSC, or trust [Reg. § 1.444-2T].

A § 444 election is made by filing Form 8716, *Election to Have a Tax Year Other Than a Required Tax Year*, by the earlier of (i) the 15th day of the fifth month following the month that includes the first day of the tax year for which the election will first be effective, or (ii) the due date (not including extensions) of the return resulting from the election [Reg. § 1.444-3T(b)].

If a partnership or S corporation makes a § 444 election to use a tax year other than its required tax year, it must make required payments under § 7519 for each year the election is in effect (note that a PSC is not required to make these payments). Section 7519 effectively requires such an entity to pay approximately the same amount in required payments as the entity's partners or shareholders would have paid in actual tax payments for the deferral period had the entity changed to its required tax year. These payments are made with Form 8752, *Required Payment or Refund Under Section 7519*, and are due on or before May 15 of the calendar year following the calendar year in which the applicable election year begins. However, the required payment under § 7519 need not be made if the entity establishes a business purpose for its tax year [§ 444(c)(1); Reg. § 1.7519-1T, § 1.7519-2T].

*Business Purpose.* A partnership, S corporation, or PSC may use a tax year other than its required tax year if it satisfies the IRS that it has a business purpose for doing so. See XI.A.4.a. for a discussion of establishing a business purpose.

### XI.A.3.e. Consequences of Adopting Improper Tax Year

[574 T.M., V.A., VI.E.; TPS ¶3520.11.A., .12.E.]

If a taxpayer adopts an improper tax year, it must either (i) adopt a proper tax year according to the procedures set forth in Rev. Proc. 85-15, 1985-1 C.B. 516, or (ii) request IRS approval to change its tax year (see XI.A.4.) [Rev. Rul. 85-22, 1985-1 C.B. 154]. Under Rev. Proc. 85-15, a taxpayer adopts a proper tax year by filing an amended return and attaching Form 1128, *Application to Adopt, Change, or Retain a Tax Year*. The taxpayer should type or write "FILED UNDER REV. PROC. 85-15" at the top of page 1 of Form 1128.

### XI.A.4. Change or Retention of Tax Year

[574 T.M., VI.; TPS ¶3520.12.]

Once a taxpayer has adopted a tax year, it must use that tax year in all later years, unless it obtains IRS approval to change its tax year [§ 442; Reg. § 1.441-1(e), § 1.442-1(a)]. Under certain circumstances, a partnership, S corporation, or personal service corporation (PSC) is required to change its tax year, unless it obtains IRS approval to retain its tax year [Reg. § 1.441-1(e)]. Thus, IRS approval generally must be obtained to either change or retain a tax year. There is, however, an exception for partnerships, S corporations, and personal service corporations that make an election under § 444 to change to a new tax year or to retain an existing tax year [§ 444] (see XI.A.3.d.).

Generally, the change or retention of a tax year will be approved by the IRS if, based on all facts and circumstances, the taxpayer establishes a business purpose for the requested tax year and agrees to any terms, conditions, and adjustments prescribed by the IRS. Such terms, conditions, and adjustments may include adjustments necessary to neutralize the tax effects of a substantial distortion of income that would otherwise result from the requested tax year. Generally, the requirement of a

571

business purpose will be satisfied, and adjustments to neutralize any tax conse-quences will not be required, if the requested tax year coincides with the taxpayer's required tax year (see XI.A.2.), ownership tax year (see XI.A.4.a), or natural business year (see XI.A.4.a.). For a partnership, S corporation, or PSC, deferral of income to partners, shareholders, or employee-owners will not be considered an acceptable business purpose [Reg. § 1.442-1(b)].

In certain cases, a taxpayer may obtain automatic IRS approval to change or retain its tax year (see XI.A.4.b.). However, the standard procedure for obtaining IRS approval to change or retain a tax year is the IRS's non-automatic approval procedure provided in Rev. Proc. 2002-39, 2002-22 I.R.B. 1046 (see XI.A.4.a.).

### XI.A.4.a. Non-Automatic Approval Procedure

[574 T.M., VI.B.; TPS ¶3520.12.C.]

Under the IRS's non-automatic approval procedure, a taxpayer's request to change or retain its tax year will normally be approved if the taxpayer (i) establishes a business purpose for the requested tax year, and (ii) agrees to the IRS's prescribed terms and conditions [Rev. Proc. 2002-39, 2002-22, I.R.B. 1046, § 5.01].

*Business Purpose*. A taxpayer can establish a business purpose to change or retain its tax year by showing that the requested tax year is its natural business year. A taxpayer can show that the requested tax year is its natural business year by meeting one of the following tests:

1. the 25% gross receipts test;
2. the annual business cycle test;
3. the seasonal business test; or
4. the facts and circumstances test.

Under the 25% gross receipts test, the requested tax year may be the taxpayer's natural business year if, for each of the previous three years, at least 25% of the taxpayer's gross receipts were generated in the last two months of that year. If there is more than one tax year that meets this test, the taxpayer's natural business year is the year that produces a highest three-year average [Rev. Proc. 2006-46, 2006-45 I.R.B. 859, § 5.07(1)].

Under the annual business cycle test, a taxpayer has a natural business year if the taxpayer's gross receipts for the short period created by the change and the previous three tax years indicate that the taxpayer has peak and non-peak periods of business. The taxpayer's natural business year is deemed to end at, or soon after, the highest peak period of business. A safe harbor provides that one month after the close of the highest peak period is deemed to be soon after the close of the highest peak [Rev. Proc. 2002-39, § 5.03(1)].

Under the seasonal business test, a taxpayer has a natural business year if the taxpayer's gross receipts for the short period created by the change and the previous three tax years indicate that the taxpayer's business is operational for only part of the year and, as a result, the taxpayer has insignificant gross receipts during the period the business is not operational. The taxpayer's natural business year is deemed to end at, or soon after, the operations end for the season. A safe harbor provides that an amount less than 10% of total gross receipts for the year is deemed to be insignificant, and one month is deemed to be soon after the end of operations [Rev. Proc. 2002-39, § 5.03(2)].

Under the facts and circumstances test, a taxpayer that cannot establish a busi-ness purpose under any of the three other business purpose tests may attempt to do so based on the facts and circumstances. The IRS rarely grants permission to change or retain a tax year under this test [Rev. Proc. 2002-39, § 5.02(1)(b)].

For S corporations, the IRS also regards the existence of an ownership tax year as a valid business purpose. An ownership tax year is a tax year that, as of the first day of the first effective year, constitutes the tax year of one or more shareholders holding more than 50% of the corporation's issued and outstanding shares of stock [Rev. Proc. 2006-46, § 6.06(1)].

*Terms and Conditions.* The IRS has provided a number of standard terms and conditions to which a taxpayer must agree. In certain cases, the IRS may determine that, based on the unique facts of a particular case and in the interest of sound tax administration, adjustments may be made to the standard terms and conditions or additional terms and conditions may be imposed.

*Procedural Requirements.* A taxpayer generally must complete, sign, and file Form 1128, *Application to Adopt, Change, or Retain a Tax Year*, to request IRS approval to change or retain its tax year (an electing S corporation must instead complete, sign, and file Form 2553, *Election by a Small Business Corporation*). Form 1128 must be filed no earlier than the day following the end of the first effective year and no later than the due date (excluding extensions) of the return for the first effective year. The following additional information must be provided if the taxpayer establishes a business purpose by showing that the requested tax year is a natural business year:

- If the 25% gross receipts test is used, the taxpayer must provide its gross receipts for the most recent 47 months.
- If the annual business cycle test or seasonal business test is used, the taxpayer must provide its gross receipts and approximate inventory costs for each month in the requested short period and each month of the three previous tax years.

### XI.A.4.b. Automatic Approval Procedure

[574 T.M., VI.B.; TPS ¶3520.12.B.]

The IRS provides different automatic approval procedures for pass-through entities (Rev. Proc. 2006-46, 2006-45 I.R.B. 859), C corporations (Rev. Proc. 2006-45, 2006-45 I.R.B. 851), tax-exempt organizations (Rev. Proc. 85-58, 1985-2 C.B. 740), and individual taxpayers (Rev. Proc. 2003-63, 2003-32 I.R.B. 304). Approval to change or retain a tax year is automatic if the appropriate procedures are followed and certain terms and conditions are met.

*Pass-Through Entities.* Partnerships, S corporations, electing S corporations, and personal service corporations that comply with the applicable provisions of Rev. Proc. 2006-46 are deemed to have automatic approval to change or retain their tax year. Automatic approval is available to such pass-through entities in the following circumstances [Rev. Proc. 2006-46, § 4.01]:

- the taxpayer wants to change to its required tax year or a 52-53-week tax year ending with reference to its required tax year;
- the taxpayer wants to change to or retain a natural business year that satisfies the 25% gross receipts test or a 52-53-week tax year ending with reference to such a year;
- the taxpayer is an S corporation or electing S corporation that wants to change to or retain its ownership tax year or a 52-53-week tax year ending with reference to its ownership year;

- the taxpayer wants to change from a 52-53-week tax year that references a particular calendar month to a non-52-53-week tax year that ends on the last day of the same calendar month, or vice versa; or
- the taxpayer is required to change its tax year as a term or condition of the approval of a related taxpayer's change of its tax year.

However, this automatic approval procedure is not available if [Rev. Proc. 2006-46, § 4.02]:

- the taxpayer is under IRS examination (unless it obtains the consent of the appropriate district director);
- the taxpayer is before an IRS area office with respect to an income tax issue and its tax year is an issue under consideration;
- the taxpayer is before a federal court with respect to an income tax issue and its tax year is an issue under consideration; or
- the taxpayer is a partnership or S corporation and, on the date it would otherwise file its application with the IRS Service Center, its tax year is an issue under consideration by an IRS area office or federal court with respect to a partner's or shareholder's federal income tax return.

This automatic approval procedure is also not available if the taxpayer changed its tax year at any time within the most recent 48-month period ending with the last month of the requested tax year. For this purpose, the following changes are not considered prior changes in the taxpayer's tax year [Rev. Proc. 2006-46, § 4.02(5)]:

- a prior change to a required tax year or ownership tax year;
- a prior change from a 52-53-week tax year to a non-52-53-week tax year that ends with reference to the same calendar month, or vice versa; or
- a prior change in tax year by an S corporation, electing S corporation, or personal service corporation to comply with the common tax year requirements applicable to affiliated groups of corporations filing consolidated returns.

A partnership or PSC applies for automatic approval to change or retain its tax year by filing Form 1128, *Application to Adopt, Change, or Retain a Tax Year,* no earlier than the day following the end of the first effective year and no later than the due date (including extensions) for filing the return for the first effective year. An S corporation or electing S corporation applies for automatic approval to change or retain its tax year by filing Form 2553, *Election by a Small Business Corporation,* any time during the tax year immediately before the tax year for which the election is to be effective, or before the 16th day of the 3rd month of the tax year for which the election is to be effective [Rev. Proc. 2006-46, § 7].

*Corporations.* Corporations that comply with the provisions of Rev. Proc. 2006-45 are deemed to have automatic approval to change or retain their tax year. This procedure applies to all corporations that are not excluded under a long list of exceptions. The excluded corporations include [Rev. Proc. 2006-45, § 4.02]:

- a corporation that has changed its tax year at any time within the most recent 48-month period ending with the last month of the requested tax year (subject to special rules under which certain changes in tax year are not considered prior changes);
- a corporation that has an interest in a pass-through entity or a controlled foreign corporation (CFC) as of the end of the first effective year (subject to special rules under which such an interest is disregarded if certain conditions are met);

- a corporation that is a shareholder of an interest charge domestic international sales corporation (IC-DISC) as of the end of the short period (subject to special rules under which such an interest is disregarded if certain conditions are met);
- a corporation that is an IC-DISC;
- a corporation that is an S corporation or a corporation that is requesting a change in tax year that is within an S termination year;
- a corporation that attempts to make an S corporation election for the tax year immediately following the short period (unless the change is to a permitted tax year, or from a 52-53-week tax year or to a non-52-53-week tax year that ends with reference to the same month, and vice versa);
- a corporation that is a personal service corporation (PSC);
- a corporation that is a CFC (with certain exceptions);
- a corporation that is a tax-exempt organization (with certain exceptions);
- a corporation that has a § 936 election in effect;
- a corporation that is a cooperative association with a loss in the short period and that is required to effect a change in tax year (with certain exceptions);
- a corporation that has a required tax year, unless the corporation is changing to its required tax year;
- a corporation that ceases to be a member of a consolidated group and that requests to change its tax year during the group's tax year in which it leaves the group; and
- a corporation that is a member of a consolidated group and that requests to change to or from a 52-53-week tax year, unless the requested tax year is identical to the tax year of the consolidated group.

A corporation applies for automatic approval to change or retain its tax year by filing Form 1128, *Application to Adopt, Change, or Retain a Tax Year*, on or before the due date (including extensions) for filing its return for the first effective year [Rev. Proc. 2006-45, § 7]. A subsidiary corporation that is required to change its tax year to conform to the tax year of its affiliated group does not need to file Form 1128 or obtain IRS approval [Reg. § 1.442-1(c)].

*Tax-Exempt Organizations*. Tax-exempt organizations (see Chapter XIX.) that comply with the provisions of Rev. Proc. 85-58 are deemed to have automatic approval to change or retain their tax year. An organization may not use this procedure if it has changed its tax year within calendar years ending with the calendar year that includes the short period resulting from the change in tax year.

A tax-exempt organization applies for automatic approval to change its tax year by timely filing the appropriate information return for the short period required to effect the change of tax year (e.g., Form 990, Form 990-PF, Form 990-BL, or Form 1065). The form should indicate that a change in tax year is being made.

*Individual Taxpayers*. Most individual taxpayers use the calendar year as their tax year because they do not qualify to use a fiscal year. However, an individual taxpayer who uses a fiscal year is deemed to have automatic approval to change to the calendar year if he or she complies with the provisions of Rev. Proc. 2003-62. An individual taxpayer applies for automatic approval to change to a calendar year by filing Form 1128, *Application to Adopt, Change, or Retain a Tax Year*, on or before the due date (including extensions) for filing its return for the short period required to effect the change.

The automatic approval procedure of Rev. Proc. 2003-62 does not apply to newly married taxpayers requesting to change to their spouse's tax year. Such taxpayers are instead subject to the automatic approval procedure of Reg. § 1.442-1(d). Under that procedure, a newly married taxpayer may obtain automatic approval to change his or her tax year to conform to the tax year of his or her spouse so that a joint return may be filed for the first or second tax year of that spouse ending after the date of the marriage. To obtain automatic approval, the taxpayer adopting the tax year of his or her spouse must file a return for the short period required by the change on or before the 15th day of the fourth month following the end of the short period. The short-period return must contain a statement at the top of page one indicating the return is filed in accordance with Reg. § 1.442-1(d). Form 1128 does not need to be filed. If the due date for the short-period return falls before the date of the marriage, the tax year of the other spouse cannot be adopted until the other spouse's second tax year after the date of the marriage.

## XI.B. Accounting Methods

[570 T.M., II.; TPS ¶3530.01.]

The computation of income for federal tax purposes depends upon the taxpayer's method of accounting. Although not defined in the Code or regulations, a method of accounting implies a set of rules under which a taxpayer determines when and how it records items of income and expense in its books, how it prepares its financial statements, and how it computes its taxable income. For income tax purposes, a method of accounting is essentially concerned with the timing of income and deductions.

A method of accounting includes not only a taxpayer's overall method of accounting for income and deductions, but also the accounting treatment used for any material item [Reg. § 1.446-1(a)(1)]. An item is generally any recurring incidence of income or expense. A material item is any item that concerns the timing of income or deductions [Reg. § 1.446-1(e)(2)(ii)(a)].

### XI.B.1. Permissible Methods of Accounting

[570 T.M., III.; TPS ¶3530.02.]

The method of accounting chosen by a taxpayer generally must conform to the taxpayer's books (see XI.B.1.a.) and it must clearly reflect income (see XI.B.1.b.) [§ 446(a), § 446(b)]. Subject to those two rules, a taxpayer may compute its taxable income using any of the following methods of accounting [§ 446(c)]:

1. the cash method (see XI.B.1.c.);
2. the accrual method (see XI.B.1.d.);
3. any other method permitted by the Code (see XI.B.1.e.); or
4. any combination of methods permitted under the regulations for particular material items (see XI.B.1.f.).

A taxpayer engaged in more than one trade or business may use different methods of accounting for each trade or business [§ 446(d)].

### XI.B.1.a. Conformity Requirement

[570 T.M., III.C.; TPS ¶3530.02.A.1.]

A taxpayer is generally required to compute taxable income using the same method of accounting that it regularly uses in keeping its books [§ 446(a)]. However, this does not necessarily mean that a taxpayer is required to use the same method of accounting it uses to prepare its financial statements. The books of a taxpayer constitute contemporaneous records of original entry from which an income statement and balance sheet can be prepared and any entries to reconcile those records with the amounts shown in the tax return.

### XI.B.1.b. Clear Reflection of Income Requirement

[570 T.M., III.E.; TPS ¶3530.02.A.2.]

No method of accounting is acceptable unless, in the opinion of the IRS, it clearly reflects income. A method of accounting that reflects the consistent application of generally accepted accounting principles (GAAP) in accordance with the accounting practices of the taxpayer's trade or business will normally be regarded as clearly reflecting income, as long as all items of income and expense are treated consistently from year to year [Reg. § 1.446-1(a)(2), § 1.446-1(c)(2)(ii)].

### XI.B.1.c. Cash Method of Accounting

[570 T.M., III.A.1.; TPS ¶3530.02.B.1.]

The cash method of accounting is used by most individual taxpayers and many small businesses. The cash method is often advantageous to taxpayers because of its simplicity and the control it provides over the timing of the recognition of income and expenses. Because of this control element, Congress prohibits certain types of taxpayers from using the cash method.

### XI.B.1.c.(1) Treatment of Income Under Cash Method

[570 T.M., III.A.1.; TPS ¶3530.02.B.1.]

Under the cash method, a taxpayer must recognize income in the year it is actually or constructively received. Income is constructively received by a taxpayer in the year in which it is credited to the taxpayer's account, set apart for the taxpayer, or otherwise made available so that he may draw upon it at any time. A taxpayer does not need to have possession of income for there to be constructive receipt. However, if a taxpayer's control of its receipt is subject to substantial limitations or restrictions, there is no constructive receipt [Reg. § 1.451-1(a), § 1.451-2(a)].

Examples of income that is constructively received include (i) interest, dividends, or other earnings on deposits or accounts with financial institutions, (ii) interest coupons that have matured and are payable, and (iii) dividends on corporate stock that are subject to the demand of the shareholder [Reg. § 1.451-2(b)].

Example: Steve is a calendar year taxpayer who uses the cash method of accounting. His bank credited interest to his bank account in Dec. of Year 1. Steve did not withdraw it or enter it in his books until Jan. of Year 2. Steve must include the interest in his gross income for Year 1 because he constructively received it in that year.

Interest, dividends, or other earnings payable on a deposit or account with a financial institution are not constructively received to the extent that they are not subject to withdrawal at the time credited. However, the following are not considered substantial limitations or restrictions on the taxpayer's control of the receipt of such earnings [Reg. § 1.451-2(a), § 1.451-2(b)]:

- a requirement that the deposit or account, and the earnings thereon, must be withdrawn in multiples of even amounts;
- a requirement that the earnings may be withdrawn only upon a withdrawal of all or a part of the deposit or account; or
- a requirement that notice of intention to withdraw must be given in advance of the withdrawal.

If dividends on corporate stock are declared payable on December 31 but the corporation follows its usual practice of paying the dividends by checks mailed so that the shareholders will not receive them until January of the following year, the dividends are not considered to be constructively received in December.

### XI.B.1.c.(2) Treatment of Expenses Under Cash Method

[570 T.M., III.A.1.; TPS ¶3530.02.B.1.]

Under the cash method, a taxpayer generally can deduct expenses in the year they are paid. However, an expenditure that results in the creation of an asset having a useful life that extends substantially beyond the end of the tax year must be capitalized and deducted over the period to which it relates [Reg. § 1.461-1(a)(1)].

Under a special 12-month rule, a taxpayer is not required to capitalize amounts paid to create certain rights or benefits for the taxpayer if the rights or benefits do not extend beyond the earlier of [Reg. § 1.263(a)-4(f)]:

1. 12 months after the right or benefit begins; or

2. the end of the tax year after the tax year in which the payment is made.

---

**EXAMPLE:** Laura is a calendar year, cash method taxpayer. She pays $3,000 in Year 1 for a business insurance policy that is effective for 36 months, beginning on July 1 of Year 1. Because this expense does not qualify for the 12-month rule, it must be capitalized and deducted over the period to which it relates. Laura can only deduct $500 ($3,000 × (6 mos./36 mos.)) of the expense in Year 1.

**EXAMPLE:** Assume the same facts as in the previous example, except that the business insurance policy is only effective for 12 months beginning on July 1 of Year 1. Under the 12-month rule, the full $3,000 expense can be deducted in Year 1.

---

### XI.B.1.c.(3) Taxpayers Prohibited From Using Cash Method

[570 T.M., III.A.1.; TPS ¶3530.02.B.1.]

*General Rule.* The following types of taxpayers are generally prohibited from using the cash method of accounting [§ 448(a)]:

1. a C corporation;

2. a partnership with a C corporation as a partner; and

3. a tax shelter.

A tax shelter includes (i) an enterprise (other than a C corporation) in which interests have been offered for sale in an offering required to be registered with any federal or state agency authorized to regulate securities offerings, (ii) an enterprise (other than a C corporation) for which more than 35% of losses are allocated to limited partners or limited entrepreneurs (a so-called syndicate), or (iii) any entity, plan, or arrangement that has as its principal purpose the avoidance or evasion of federal income tax [§ 448(d)(3), § 461(i)(3)].

A trust is treated as a C corporation with respect to its activities that constitute an unrelated trade or business (see Chapter XVIII.) [§ 448(d)(6)].

*Exceptions.* There are three exceptions under which a C corporation or a partnership with a C corporation as a partner may use the cash method of accounting [§ 448(b)]:

1. A corporation or partnership with a C Corporation as a partner may use the cash method if, for each prior tax year beginning after 1985, its average annual gross receipts are $5 million or less.

2. A farming business may generally use the cash method. However, see XI.H. for a discussion of farming businesses that must use the accrual method.

3. A qualified personal service corporation (PSC) may use the cash method (see XIII.C.6.c.).

### *XI.B.1.d. Accrual Method of Accounting*

[570 T.M., III.A.2.; TPS ¶3530.02.B.2.]

Under the accrual method of accounting, the timing of the recognition of an item of income or expense generally coincides with the economic activity that gives rise to it, rather than the related cash transfer. Thus, the accrual method normally results in a matching of related income and expense items in the proper year.

### *XI.B.1.d.(1) Treatment of Income Under Accrual Method*

[570 T.M., III.A.2.; TPS ¶3530.02.B.2.]

Under the accrual method, a taxpayer generally must recognize income when (i) all events have occurred that fix the taxpayer's right to receive the income, and (ii) the amount of the income can be determined with reasonable accuracy (referred to as "the all events test") [Reg. § 1.446-1(c)(1)(ii), § 1.451-1(a)]. Under the first part of the all events test, a taxpayer's right to income is fixed when either the amount is unconditionally due or the taxpayer has performed. Thus, accrual method taxpayers generally must recognize income when it is paid, due, or earned, whichever occurs first. Under the second part of the all events test, the amount of income can be determined with reasonable accuracy if a reasonable basis for calculation exists. The exact amount need not be known.

*Advance Payments.* Special rules apply to advance payments. An accrual method taxpayer receives advance payments for goods or services to be provided in future years generally must include those advance payments in income in the year they are received. However, as discussed below, there are certain exceptions under which the deferral of advance payments is permitted.

*Advance Payments for Goods.* Advance payments for goods include (i) amounts received under an agreement for the sale in a future tax year of goods held for sale in the ordinary course of the taxpayer's trade or business, and (ii) amounts received under an agreement for the building, installing, constructing, or manufacturing of items for which the agreement is not completed during the current tax year [Reg. § 1.451-5(a)].

Generally, advance payments for goods held for sale in the ordinary course of the taxpayer's trade or business must be included in gross income in the tax year the payments are received. However, under an alternative method, a taxpayer may instead include such advance payments in gross income in the earlier of [Reg. § 1.451-5(b)]:

1. the tax year in which the income is properly accrued under the method of accounting the taxpayer uses for tax purposes; or

2. the tax year in which the income is included in gross receipts under the method of accounting the taxpayer uses for financial reporting purposes.

Under an exception for inventory goods, a taxpayer can defer the advance payment income until the end of the second tax year following the year in which the advance payment is received if it meets all of the following requirements on the last day of the tax year [Reg. § 1.451-5(c)(1)]:

1. it accounts for the advance payments under the alternative method discussed above;

2. it has received a substantial advance payment on the agreement; and

3. it has enough substantially similar goods on hand (or available through its normal supply source) to satisfy the agreement.

A taxpayer has received a substantial advance payment under an agreement for future sale if, by the end of the tax year, the total advanced payments received during that tax year and the preceding tax years are more than the total costs reasonably estimated to be includible in inventory because of the agreement [Reg. § 1.451-5(c)(3)].

*Advance Payments for Services.* The following exceptions apply to advance payments for services:

1. An accrual method taxpayer that receives an advance payment for services he agrees to provide by the end of the immediately succeeding tax year may elect to defer the advance payment income until that succeeding year [Rev. Proc. 2004-34, 2004-22 I.R.B. 991].

2. An accrual method taxpayer that receives prepaid subscription payments may elect to defer the prepaid subscription income over the period of the subscription liability [§ 455].

3. An accrual method taxpayer that receives prepaid dues payments as a qualified membership organization may elect to defer the prepaid dues income over the period of the services or privileges liability (but not to exceed 36 months) [§ 456].

*Uncollectible Amounts.* Certain accrual method taxpayers may adopt a nonaccrual experience method under which they can defer recognition on the portion of their receivables from the performance of services that they determine, based on past experience, will not be collected. The nonaccrual experience method may be adopted by the following taxpayers [§ 448(d)(5); Reg. § 1.448-2(a)]:

1. taxpayers that provide services in the fields of health, law, engineering, architecture, accounting, actuarial science, performing arts, or consulting; and

2. taxpayers that provide services in other fields and that meet the $5 million gross receipts test for all prior tax years (the $5 million gross receipts test is met for a prior tax year if the taxpayer's average annual gross receipts for the three-tax-year period ending with that prior tax year is $5 million or less).

### XI.B.1.d.(2) Treatment of Expenses Under Accrual Method

[570 T.M., III.A.2.; TPS ¶3530.02.B.2.]

Under the accrual method, a taxpayer generally can deduct or capitalize business expenses when (i) all events have occurred that fix the fact of the taxpayer's liability and the amount of the liability can be determined with reasonable accuracy (i.e., the all-events test is met), and (ii) economic performance has occurred [§ 461(h); Reg. § 1.446-1(c)(1)(ii), § 1.461-1(a)(2)]. Thus, in determining the timing of deductions under the accrual method, the all-events test is not treated as met until economic performance has occurred.

*Economic Performance.* The following principles apply in determining when economic performance occurs [§ 461(h)(2); Reg. § 1.461-4]:

- If the taxpayer's expense is for property or services provided to the taxpayer by another person, economic performance occurs as the property or services are provided.

- If the taxpayer expense is for the taxpayer's use of another person's property, economic performance occurs as the taxpayer uses the property.

- If the taxpayer's expense is for property or services the taxpayer provides to another person, economic performance occurs as the taxpayer provides the property or services.
- If the taxpayer is required to make payments under workers' compensation laws or in satisfaction of a tort liability, economic performance occurs as the taxpayer makes the payments.
- For a deduction for compensation paid, economic performance generally occurs as the employee renders services to the taxpayer; however, deductions for compensation or other benefits paid to an employee in a year after economic performance occurs are subject to the rules governing deferred compensation, etc. (see XVII.B.).
- For a deduction for taxes paid, economic performance generally occurs as the taxes are paid.
- Other liabilities for which economic performance is considered to occur as the taxpayer makes payments include: (i) liabilities arising out of tort, breach of contract, violation of law, or a workers' compensation act (ii) rebates, refunds, and similar payments, (iii) awards, prizes, and jackpots, and (iv) liabilities arising out of insurance, warranty, or service contracts.
- For a deduction for interest, economic performance occurs with the passage of time, not as payments are made.

***Recurring Item Exception.*** Under an exception to the economic performance rule, certain recurring items may be treated as incurred during a tax year even though economic performance has not yet occurred. This recurring item exception applies if the following requirements are met [§ 461(h)(3); Reg. § 1.461-5(b)(1)]:

1. the all-events test is met;
2. economic performance occurs by the earlier of (i) 8½ months after the end of the tax year, or (ii) the date the taxpayer files a timely return (including extensions) for the tax year;
3. the expense item is recurring in nature and the taxpayer consistently treats similar items as incurred in the tax year in which the all-events test is met;
4. either (i) accruing the expense item in the year in which the all-events test is met results in a better match with the income to which it relates than accruing the item in the year of economic performance, or (ii) the expense item is not material.

An expense item is generally considered recurring in nature if it is incurred from one tax year to the next. Factors to be considered in this determination are the frequency with which the item and similar items are incurred, and how the taxpayer reports those items for tax purposes. A new expense or an expense not incurred every year can be treated as recurring if it is reasonable to expect that it will be incurred regularly in the future [Reg. § 1.461-5(b)(3)].

In determining whether the accrual of an expense item in a particular tax year results in a better match with the income to which it relates, generally accepted accounting principles are an important factor (but not necessarily dispositive). Under those principles, expenses directly associated with the income of a period are properly allocable to that period. Expenses that cannot be associated with the income of a particular period should be assigned to the period in which they are incurred. However, the matching requirement is deemed to be met for taxes, rebates, refunds, awards, prizes, jackpots, and payments under insurance, warranty, and services contracts [Reg. § 1.461-5(b)(5)].

In determining whether an expense item is material, important factors include the size of the expense item (both in absolute terms and in relation to the taxpayer's income and other expenses) and how the item is treated for financial reporting purposes. If an expense item is material for financial reporting purposes, it is also considered material for tax purposes. In some cases, an expense item that is immaterial for financial reporting purposes may be material for tax purposes [Reg. § 1.461-5(b)(4)].

---

**EXAMPLE:** Barry, a calendar year taxpayer, buys office supplies in Dec. of Year 1 and receives the supplies and bill during that month. Barry pays the bill in Jan. of Year 2. Barry can take a deduction for the office supplies expense in Year 1 because all events have occurred to fix the liability, the amount of the liability can be determined, and economic performance has occurred.

**EXAMPLE:** Assume the same facts as in the previous example, except that the supplies are not delivered to Barry until Jan. of Year 2. If Barry buys supplies on a recurring basis and otherwise meets the requirements of the recurring item exception, he can take a deduction for the office supplies expense in Year 1 even though economic performance did not occur until Year 2.

---

The recurring item exception applies to a liability reported on an amended return if economic performance for the liability occurs after the date the taxpayer files a timely return but within 8½ months after the end of the tax year [Reg. § 1.461-5(b)(2)]. The recurring item exception does not apply to liabilities arising out of tort, breach of contract, violation of law, or a workers' compensation act. It also does not apply to an interest expense [Reg. § 1.461-5(c)].

*Exception for Reserves for Estimated Expenses.* For financial accounting purposes, taxpayers often set up reserves for contingent liabilities and other estimated expenses. These amounts generally cannot be currently deducted for tax purposes because all events that fix the fact of the taxpayer's liability have not yet occurred (i.e., the all-events test is not met). However, under an exception to this rule, certain reserves for estimated expenses are deductible if the Code specifically provides for such deduction [§ 461(h)(5)].

*Exception for Contested Liabilities.* A contested liability is contingent and generally cannot be deducted. However, a current deduction is allowed if all of the following requirements are met: (i) the taxpayer contests an asserted liability, (ii) the taxpayer transfers money or other property to provide for satisfaction of the asserted liability, (iii) the contest as to the asserted liability continues to exist after the transfer, and (iv) a current deduction would be allowed but for the fact that the asserted liability is contested [§ 461(f)].

*Exception for Items Owed to Related Cash-Method Taxpayer.* An accrual method taxpayer cannot deduct expense items and interest owed to a related cash method taxpayer until the tax year those amounts are paid. This rule creates a matching of the timing of the accrual method taxpayer's deduction and the cash method taxpayer's income inclusion. For purposes of this rule, the provisions of § 267(b) apply in determining whether two taxpayers are related [§ 267(a)(2)].

### XI.B.1.e. Special Methods of Accounting

[570 T.M., III.A.3.; TPS ¶3530.02.B.5.]

Although the cash method and the accrual method are the two primary methods of accounting, a taxpayer may use any other method of accounting permitted under the Code [§ 446(c)(3); Reg. § 1.446-1(c)(1)(iii)]. The Code provides a wide variety of accounting methods for the treatment of particular items, including rules for inventory accounting (see XI.C.), uniform capitalization rules (see XI.D.), depreciation rules (see V.A.), § 179 expensing rules (see V.B.), and rules for the amortization or start-up and organizational expenditures (see IV.F.4.). Other important accounting methods are provided for long-term contracts (see XI.E.) and installment sales (see XI.F.). In addition, a special set of accounting methods applies to farmers (see XI.H.).

### XI.B.1.f. Hybrid Method of Accounting

[570 T.M., III.A.4.; TPS ¶3530.02.B.6.]

Taxpayers are not required to use a particular method of accounting for all items. Two or more accounting methods may be combined as long as the combination clearly reflects income and is used consistently. If the combination includes any special methods, the requirements for such methods must be met [§ 446(c)(4); Reg. § 1.446-1(c)(1)(iv)].

There are certain limitations on the combinations that may be used by a taxpayer. If a taxpayer uses the cash method for determining income, it must also use the cash method to determine expenses. If a taxpayer uses the accrual method to determine expenses, it must also use the accrual method to determine income. However, a taxpayer required to use the accrual method to account for inventory (see XI.C.) may use the cash method for other items of income or expense [Reg. § 1.446-1(c)(1)(iv)].

### XI.B.2. Adoption of Method of Accounting

[572 T.M., III.; TPS ¶3530.03.]

A taxpayer filing its first federal income tax return generally may, without IRS approval, choose any appropriate method of accounting. Similarly, a taxpayer filing a return on which an item is reported for the first time may, without IRS approval, choose any appropriate method of accounting to reflect that item in its return. Generally, no other requirements need be satisfied to adopt a method of accounting (however, for certain special methods of accounting, a form or election statement may need to be attached to the return) [Reg. § 1.446-1(e)(1)].

A taxpayer that conducts more than one distinct trade or business can normally adopt different methods of accounting for each trade or business. However, the accounting method used for each trade or business must clearly reflect the income of that trade or business [§ 446(d); Reg. § 1.446-1(d)].

Once a method of accounting has been adopted, IRS approval is required to change that method of accounting [Reg. § 1.446-1(e)(2)]. This is true even if the adopted accounting method is improper. For a discussion of changes in accounting method, see XI.B.3.

### XI.B.3. Changes in Method of Accounting

[572 T.M., I.C.; TPS ¶3530.04.]

Under certain circumstances, a taxpayer may wish to voluntarily change its method of accounting (see XI.B.4.a.). In other cases, a taxpayer may be required to change its method of accounting, either because a change is statutorily mandated (see XI.B.3.b.) or because the IRS determines that the taxpayer's method of accounting does not clearly reflect income (see XI.B.3.c.).

A change in method of accounting includes not only a change in the overall plan of accounting for gross income or deductions, but also a change in the treatment of any material item. A material item is one that affects the proper time for inclusion of income or allowance of a deduction. The correction of mathematical errors, posting errors, or errors in the computation of tax liability is not considered a change in a method of accounting [Reg. § 1.446-1(e)(2)(ii)].

Examples of some common changes in accounting method include:

- a change from the cash method to the accrual method, or vice versa;
- a change from the cash or accrual method to the long-term contract method, and vice versa;
- a change in the method used to value inventory;
- certain changes in computing depreciation or amortization; and
- a change involving the adoption, use, or discontinuation of a specialized method of computing taxable income (e.g., the crop method).

When a taxpayer's method of accounting is changed, the change is generally deemed to occur retroactively on the first day of the tax year of the change. This results in the possibility that certain tax items will be accounted for twice, or not at all. Thus, there are certain mechanisms that are used to transition from the old accounting method to the new accounting method. The most common transition mechanism is the § 481(a) adjustment. A § 481(a) adjustment is made in conjunction with a change in method of accounting in order to prevent amounts from being duplicated or omitted. Another common transition mechanism is the cut-off method. Under the cut-off method, only transactions initiated after a certain date are accounted for under the new method of accounting.

### XI.B.3.a. Voluntary Changes in Method of Accounting

[572 T.M., IV.; TPS ¶3530.06.]

A taxpayer may wish to voluntarily change its method of accounting if (i) it concludes that its current accounting method is proper but it desires to use another more favorable accounting method, or (ii) it concludes that its current accounting method is improper.

Generally, voluntary changes in a method of accounting are subject to the rules of § 446, although there are certain types of accounting method changes that are instead subject to the rules of other Code sections. Under the rules of § 446, a voluntary accounting method change may be either an automatic change (see XI.B.3.a.(1)) or a non-automatic change (see XI.B.3.a.(2)). Additional factors that may need to be considered by a taxpayer when making a voluntary accounting method change include [Rev. Proc. 97-27, 1997-1 C.B. 680; Rev. Proc. 2011-14, 2011-4 I.R.B. 330]:

- restrictions that apply when the taxpayer is under IRS examination, before an IRS appeals office, or before a federal court;
- the terms and conditions associated with the change; and
- special considerations for changes involving the LIFO method.

Voluntary changes in method of accounting generally are made by filing Form 3115, *Application for Change in Accounting Method.*

*Restrictions.* A taxpayer under examination generally may not file Form 3115 to request an accounting method change, unless (i) the taxpayer is in the 90-day or 120-day window period, (ii) permission is received from the revenue agent, or (iii) the issue is pending. Under the 90-day rule, a taxpayer under examination generally may file Form 3115 during the first 90 days of any tax year if it has been under examination for at least 12 consecutive months as of the first day of the tax year. Under the 120-day rule, a taxpayer may file Form 3115 during the 120-day period following the date an examination ends, regardless of whether a subsequent examination has begun [Rev. Proc. 97-27, § 6.01(3); Rev. Proc. 2011-14, § 7.03(3)].

A taxpayer before an appeals office or a federal court may file Form 3115 to request an accounting method change; however, the taxpayer will not receive audit protection (see below) if the method of accounting to be changed is an issue under consideration. A copy of Form 3115 must be provided to the appeals officer or counsel for the government, as appropriate [Rev. Proc. 97-27, § 6.01; Rev. Proc. 2011-14, § 6.02(3)].

*Terms and Conditions.* The IRS has authority to impose certain terms and conditions when it grants a requested change in accounting method. One significant term and condition concerns the manner in which the taxpayer converts from the old accounting method to the new accounting method. For this purpose, the IRS may grant the change on a cut-off basis or make the change subject to a § 481(a) adjustment [Rev. Proc. 97-27, § 2.03; Rev. Proc. 2011-14, § 2.06].

Another important term or condition involves audit protection. Generally, a taxpayer that voluntarily requests a change in accounting method receives audit protection for all tax years before the year of the change for the item being changed. Audit protection is especially important to taxpayers changing from an impermissible method of accounting to a permissible method of accounting because it precludes the IRS from including a § 481(a) adjustment in income for an earlier year, charging interest on a deficiency, or imposing an accuracy-related penalty. However, audit protection is not normally available if the purported accounting method change is made improperly, the change relates to an involuntary accounting method change made by the IRS in an earlier tax year, the change relates to an issue that is under consideration by IRS appeals or a federal court, or there is a pending criminal investigation relating to the taxpayer's federal tax liability for a tax year before the year of the change [Rev. Proc. 97-27, § 9.02(4); Rev. Proc. 2011-14, § 7.02(4)].

*Special Considerations for LIFO Inventory Changes.* Special rules apply for accounting method changes involving the LIFO inventory method (see XI.C.4.c.). While voluntary LIFO method changes are generally made using the cut-off method, involuntary LIFO changes generally must be made with a § 481(a) adjustment. Once a taxpayer using an erroneous LIFO method is contacted by the IRS for examination, it cannot voluntarily change to a proper method without IRS consent. Thus, taxpayers using an erroneous LIFO method have an incentive to voluntarily change to a proper LIFO method before being contacted by the IRS. By making a voluntary change, taxpayers can ensure that the cut-off method will apply and that no § 481(a) adjustment will need to be made to the years under examination for an understatement of income from use of the erroneous method in those years [Rev. Proc. 97-27, § 2.06; Rev. Proc. 2011-14, § 22.01(3)].

### XI.B.3.a.(1) Automatic Changes in Method of Accounting

[572 T.M., VI.; TPS ¶3530.06.]

Over the years, the IRS has created automatic change procedures for certain common accounting method changes. The IRS provides the qualification criteria, terms and conditions, and procedural rules for automatic accounting method changes in Rev. Proc. 2011-14, 2011-4 I.R.B. 330. The specific accounting method changes covered by the revenue procedure are listed in the appendix to Rev. Proc. 2011-14 and certain other relevant IRS pronouncements. If a taxpayer complies with all the applicable provisions of the revenue procedure, it is deemed to have obtained IRS approval to change its accounting method. Such approval is granted only for the changes of accounting method and affected items that are clearly and expressly identified in the taxpayer's application, and only to the extent that the taxpayer complies with all the applicable provisions of the revenue procedure and implements the change in accounting method on its federal income tax return for the requested year of change.

An automatic accounting method change is made by filing Form 3115, *Application for Change in Accounting Method*, with the taxpayer's timely filed return for the year of the change and filing a copy of Form 3115 with the IRS National Office. Form 3115 should reference the automatic change number provided in Rev. Proc. 2011-14 for the particular method change requested. Unlike a non-automatic accounting method change (see XI.B.3.a.(2)), no user fee is required and no ruling letter is issued by the IRS.

### XI.B.3.a.(2) Non-Automatic Changes in Method of Accounting

[572 T.M., V.; TPS ¶3530.]

If a taxpayer wishes to voluntarily change a method of accounting that does not qualify under the automatic change procedures (see XI.B.3.a.(1)), the taxpayer must formally request advance approval from the IRS National Office to make the change [Rev. Proc. 97-27, 1997-1 C.B. 680]. The IRS has the authority to grant or deny requested method changes [§ 446(e)]. Based on this authority, the IRS National Office has developed ruling policies on various types of accounting method change requests.

The procedure for requesting advance approval from the IRS National Office is similar to the procedure for requesting a letter ruling. A taxpayer requests approval by filing Form 3115, *Application for Change in Accounting Method*, with the National Office by the last day of the tax year of change [Reg. § 1.446-1(e)(3)(i)]. A request for a non-automatic change in accounting method must be accompanied by a user fee, the amount of which is set forth in the first annual revenue procedure each year.

After receiving the request and screening for the appropriate user fee, the IRS National Office studies the request and asks for any necessary additional information. If it decides to grant the request, it issues its ruling letter. If the IRS is leaning toward a denial of the request, it offers the taxpayer or its representative the option to hold a conference to discuss the issue.

### XI.B.3.b. Statutorily Mandated Changes in Method of Accounting

[572 T.M., VII.; TPS ¶3530.]

A statutorily mandated change in accounting method is a change required by law. Such a change often results from a Code provision that either disallows or requires the use of a particular method of accounting by certain taxpayers. Thus, for example, § 448 provides that the cash method of accounting generally cannot be used by a corporation, a partnership with a C corporation as a partner, or a tax shelter. In a situation in which an entity no longer qualifies to use the cash method under this rule, it must make a statutorily mandated change to the accrual method.

The terms and conditions of a statutorily mandated change in accounting method are often unique to that specific change and are generally included in the Code provision or its legislative history, although sometimes further clarified by the regulations. Where clear guidance on the terms and conditions of a statutorily mandated change is not provided, the terms and conditions must generally be determined through analogy.

Generally, a taxpayer does not need to file Form 3115 or pay a user fee when making a statutorily mandated change in accounting method. However, in some cases, a particular statement may be required to be attached to the tax return for the year of change.

### XI.B.3.c. IRS-Initiated Changes in Method of Accounting

[572 T.M., IX.; TPS ¶3530.05.]

When the IRS determines that a taxpayer is using an erroneous method of accounting, it may change the taxpayer's method of accounting to a method that, in the opinion of the IRS, clearly reflects income [§ 446(b)]. The IRS generally has broad discretion in selecting the new method of accounting to be used by a taxpayer. When the IRS requires a taxpayer to change to a new method of accounting, it may also require the taxpayer to file amended returns to reflect the change in method of accounting for any affected tax years. If the IRS is already examining the intervening years, it might simply make a consistent adjustment for each affected tax year. Once a taxpayer has been required to change to a new method of accounting, the taxpayer must continue to use that method unless it obtains IRS approval to change to another method.

For an IRS accounting method change to be effective, the examining agent, appeals officer, or counsel for the government must notify the taxpayer in writing that it is treating the change as a change in method of accounting. The notice must (i) state that the timing issue is being treated as an accounting method change or clearly label the adjustment as a § 481(a) adjustment, and (ii) describe the new method of accounting [Rev. Proc. 2002-18, 2002-13 I.R.B. 678, § 7.01(4)].

If the IRS discovers the taxpayer's erroneous method of accounting understates income, it normally makes the accounting method change in the earliest year under audit, and requires that the taxpayer take a § 481(a) adjustment into account entirely in the year of change [Rev. Proc. 2002-18, § 5.04]. However, the IRS sometimes uses a cut-off method instead of computing a § 481(a) adjustment. Under the cut-off method, the new accounting method is used starting on the first day of the change.

In the interest of settling a case, the IRS may agree to a resolution of the case that does not mandate the typical involuntary change treatment. This is most likely to occur when the taxpayer is before the Appeals Division, and in cases in which it is not clear that the taxpayer's current method of accounting is erroneous. The Appeals Division can agree to reduce the amount of the § 481(a) adjustment, spread the adjustment over multiple years, or provide for a year of change that is later than the earliest year under audit.

When the IRS chooses to resolve an issue without changing a taxpayer's method of accounting, a closing agreement is required and the accounting method issues can be resolved on the basis of alternative timing or time value of money [Rev. Proc. 2002-18, § 8.01].

For issues resolved on an alternative-timing basis, the IRS adjusts the taxpayer's taxable income to reflect the adjustment, as well as any collateral adjustments that must be made to taxable income to reflect resolution of the issue. The IRS may require the taxpayer to file amended returns to correct any affected succeeding tax year for which a tax return has been filed as of the date of the closing agreement. The taxpayer must reflect the resolution on the returns for any affected succeeding tax year for which a tax return has not been filed. Because the resolution does not constitute a change in method of accounting, the taxpayer must continue to file its returns using its current method of accounting for all items not covered by the closing agreement [Rev. Proc. 2002-18, § 8.03(1)].

For issues resolved on a time-value-of-money basis, the taxpayer must pay the specified amount required by the resolution. The IRS will not change or otherwise propose adjustments to taxable income with respect to the taxpayer's method of accounting for the tax years covered by the closing agreement. Because the resolution does not constitute a change in method of accounting, the taxpayer must continue to file its returns using its current method of accounting for all items not covered by the closing agreement [Rev. Proc. 2002-18, § 8.03(2)].

## XI.C. Inventory

[578 T.M.; TPS ¶3590.]

Inventory is essential to measuring the income of a business that sells goods because inventory enables a business to properly match the cost of goods sold with the revenues from the sales of those goods in determining its gross income for a particular period. Thus, businesses that engage in manufacturing or production and in wholesale and retail merchandising usually are required to maintain inventory. On the other hand, service-oriented businesses generally do not have to maintain inventory. See XI.C.1. for a discussion of taxpayers required to maintain inventory.

Inventory includes any goods acquired or produced by a business for sale to its customers. The ending inventory of a business is equal to its beginning inventory, plus the value of inventory items purchased or produced during the year, minus the value of inventory items sold during the year. See XI.C.2. for a discussion of the types of items included in inventory.

When inventory is used, a dollar amount must be placed on it that represents its value for financial accounting and tax purposes. There are two basic decisions that must be made by a taxpayer for any inventory:

1. the method of valuation (see XI.C.3.); and

2. assumptions concerning the flow of costs (see XI.C.4.).

### XI.C.1. Inventory Accounting Requirements

[578 T.M., III.; TPS ¶3590.01.B.]

A taxpayer is required to maintain an inventory to clearly reflect income if the production, purchase, or sale of merchandise is an income-producing factor in the taxpayer's business [§ 471(a); Reg. § 1.471-1]. When a taxpayer is required to maintain an inventory, it generally must use an accrual method to account for purchases and sales of inventory items [Reg. § 1.446-1(c)(2)(i)].

There is, however, an exception to the accrual method requirement for two types of small taxpayers: (i) qualifying taxpayers, and (ii) qualifying small business taxpayers. These small taxpayers can either (i) account for purchases and sales of inventory items using the cash method, or (ii) account for items that would otherwise be inventory as materials or supplies that are not incidental.

*Qualifying Taxpayers.* A qualifying taxpayer is a taxpayer (i) that has average annual gross receipts of less than $1 million for each three-year period ending on or after December 17, 1998, and (ii) that is not a tax shelter as defined under § 443(d)(3) [Rev. Proc. 2001-10, 2001-2 I.R.B. 272].

*Qualifying Small Business Taxpayers.* A qualifying small business taxpayer is a taxpayer (i) that has average annual gross receipts of less than $10 million for each three-year period ending on or after December 31, 2000, (ii) whose principal business activity is an eligible business, (iii) that is not prohibited from using the cash method under § 448, and (iv) that has not changed from the cash method because it became ineligible to use the cash method under Rev. Proc. 2002-28, 2002-18 I.R.B. 815. A taxpayer's principal business activity is an eligible business if it meets any of the following requirements [Rev. Proc. 2002-28,§ 4.01(1)(a)]:

- its principal business activity is described in a North American Industry Classification System (NAICS) code other than codes 211 and 212 (mining activities), codes 31 through 33 (manufacturing), code 42 (wholesale trade), codes 44 through 45 (retail trade), or codes 5111 and 5122 (information industries) (see return instructions for information about NAICS codes);
- its principal business activity is the provision of services (including the provision of property incident to those services); or
- its principal business activity is the fabrication or modification of tangible personal property upon demand in accordance with customer design or specifications.

*Accounting for Non-Incidental Materials and Supplies.* A qualifying taxpayer or qualifying small business taxpayer can account for items that would otherwise be inventory as materials and supplies that are not incidental. If a taxpayer chooses to do this, it can deduct the cost of those items that would otherwise be included in inventory in the tax year in which the materials and supplies are first used in the taxpayer's operations or are consumed in the taxpayer's operations [Reg. § 1.162-3(a)(1)]. A qualifying taxpayer that is a producer can use any reasonable method to determine the amount of its deduction for non-incidental materials and supplies consumed and used in its business. A qualifying small business taxpayer must use the specific identification (see XI.C.4.a.), FIFO (see XI.C.4.b.), or average cost method (see XI.C.4.d.) to determine the amount of its deduction for non-incidental materials and supplies consumed and used in its business [Rev. Proc. 2001-10].

### XI.C.2. Types of Items Included in Inventory

[578 T.M., V, VI.A.; TPS ¶3590.01.C.]

Inventory should include all finished and partly finished goods and any other goods that are intended to become a physical part of the merchandise [Reg. § 1.471-1]. Thus, inventory should generally include:

- merchandise or stock in trade;
- raw materials;
- work in process;
- finished products; and
- supplies that become a physical part of an item intended for sale.

The following types of merchandise should be included in inventory:

- goods the taxpayer has purchased (when title passes to the taxpayer);
- goods under contract for sale that have not yet been segregated and applied to the contract;
- goods out on consignment; and
- goods held for sale in display rooms or booths located away from taxpayer's place of business.

On the other hand, the following types of merchandise should not be included in inventory:

- goods the taxpayer has sold (when title passes to the buyer);

- goods consigned to the taxpayer; and
- goods ordered for future delivery (when taxpayer does not yet have title).

### XI.C.3. Methods for Valuation of Inventory

[578 T.M., IV.A.; TPS ¶3590.04.]

The valuation of inventory is considered a method of accounting for federal income tax purposes [Reg. § 1.446-1(e)(2)(ii)(a)]. Inventory must be valued using a method that conforms to the best accounting practices for the taxpayer's trade or business and that clearly reflects income [§ 471(a); Reg. § 1.471-2(a)]. The rules on inventory valuation methods are not uniform, but must instead give effect to the trade customs that come within the scope of the best accounting practice in the taxpayer's particular trade or business. Among the factors taken into consideration in determining whether an inventory method clearly reflects income are its conformity with generally accepted accounting principles (GAAP) and its consistent use from year to year. Greater weight is placed on consistent use of a particular method than on the actual method itself, so long as the method is a permissible one [Reg. § 1.471-2(a)].

The following methods generally may be used for the valuation of inventory:

1. cost (see XI.C.3.a.);
2. lower of cost or market (see XI.C.3.b.);
3. retail (see XI.C.3.c.).

A special inventory valuation method known as the mark-to-market method applies to dealers in securities (see XI.C.3.d.).

### XI.C.3.a. Cost Method

[578 T.M., IV.A.1.; TPS ¶3590.05.A.]

The cost method is the primary method of inventory valuation. Under this method, the value of inventory generally includes all direct and indirect costs associated with it. The following rules apply for purposes of the cost method [Reg. § 1.471-3]:

1. For goods on hand at the beginning of the tax year, cost means the ending inventory price of the goods for the previous tax year.
2. For goods purchased during the year, cost generally means the invoice price, minus trade and other discounts, plus transportation and other charges incurred in acquiring the goods. Cost may also include other amounts required to be capitalized under the uniform capitalization rules (see XI.D.).
3. For goods produced during the year, cost means all direct and indirect costs required to be capitalized under the uniform capitalization rules (see XI.D.).

### XI.C.3.b. Lower of Cost or Market Method

[578 T.M., IV.A.2.; TPS ¶3590.05.B.]

Under the lower of cost or market method, the market value of each inventory item on the inventory date is compared with the item's cost, and the lower of the two amounts is used as the inventory value [Reg. § 1.471-4(c)].

For normal goods, market value is the usual bid price on the inventory date. It is based on the volume of inventory the taxpayer usually buys. If no market exists, or if quotations are nominal because of an inactive market, market value must be determined using the best available evidence of fair market price on the dates nearest the taxpayer's inventory date. Such evidence may include (i) specific purchases or sales made at a reasonable volume and in good faith, and (ii) compensation amounts paid for cancellation of contracts for purchase commitments [Reg. § 1.471-4(a), § 1.471-4(b)].

The lower of cost or market method may be used for (i) goods purchased and on hand, and (ii) direct materials, direct labor, and certain indirect costs for goods being manufactured and finished goods on hand. However, this method may not be used for (i) goods being manufactured or on hand for delivery at a fixed price on a firm sales contract, or (ii) goods accounted for under the LIFO method.

### XI.C.3.c. Retail Method

[578 T.M., VI.A.; TPS ¶3590.10.C.5.]

Retail merchants may use the retail method of inventory valuation if they designate that they are using that method on their return, they keep accurate records, and they consistently use that method (unless the IRS authorizes a method change). Under the retail method, the total retail selling price of goods on hand at the end of the tax year in each department (or of each class of goods) is reduced to approximate cost by using an average markup expressed as a percentage of the total retail selling price [Reg. § 1.471-8].

### XI.C.3.d. Mark-to-Market Method for Dealers in Securities

[578 T.M., VI.B.; TPS ¶3590.06.A.]

Dealers in securities must use the mark-to-market method to value their inventory of securities. Under this method, each security held for sale must be valued at its fair market value. The carrying value of each security must be adjusted up or down to its fair market value at the end of each year. When a dealer's securities are marked to market at the end of the year, it must recognize a corresponding gain or loss as if the security had been sold for its fair market value. The character of such gain or loss is ordinary [§ 475].

### XI.C.4. Cost Flow Assumptions

[578 T.M., IV.B.; TPS ¶3590.02.]

Many inventory items are identical or interchangeable even though manufactured or purchased at different times for different costs. It is often impractical to keep track of which specific items are sold and which ones remain on hand. Therefore, certain assumptions must be made as to which costs should be used in determining the value of inventory items on hand at year end. The following inventory cost flow assumptions generally can be used for this purpose:

1. the specific identification method (see XI.C.4.a.);
2. the FIFO method (see XI.C.4.b.);
3. the LIFO method(see XI.C.4.c.); and
4. the average cost method (see XI.C.4.d.).

### XI.C.4.a. Specific Identification Method

[578 T.M., IV.B.1.; TPS ¶3590.02.B.]

Under the specific identification method, each unit in ending inventory is valued at its actual production or purchase price. The costs of specific goods are traced to particular invoices to determine which goods remain on hand at year end and what the costs of those goods were when they were produced or purchased. Thus, no cost flow assumption is needed with the specific identification method [Reg. § 1.471-2(d)].

The specific identification method is normally used when inventory is composed of large, relatively expensive items produced or purchased as individual units that are not interchangeable. This method is impractical in most other situations.

### XI.C.4.b. FIFO Method

[578 T.M., IV.B.2.; TPS ¶3590.02.C.]

Under the first-in, first-out (FIFO) method, the first goods produced or purchased are assumed to be the first goods sold. Ending inventory is assumed to consist of the last goods produced or purchased, and the value of ending inventory is determined based on the costs of the goods that were most recently produced or purchased [Reg. § 1.471-2(d)].

The FIFO method is the method most often used for intermingled goods when specific identification is not feasible. However, taxpayers may elect to use the LIFO method (see XI.C.4.c.) instead of the FIFO method.

**EXAMPLE:** A taxpayer began the year with 50 units of inventory and bought 250 more units during the year. Thus, it had 300 units available for sale at one time or another during the year. It sold 230 units during the year and it still had 70 unsold units in ending inventory. The costs for the beginning inventory and purchases are as follows:

|  | Units | Unit Cost | Total Cost |
|---|---|---|---|
| Beginning inventory | 50 | $ 10.00 | $   500 |
| Purchases: | | | |
| Feb. | 40 | $ 10.50 | $   420 |
| May | 50 | $ 11.00 | $   550 |
| Aug. | 60 | $ 11.50 | $   690 |
| Nov. | 100 | $ 12.00 | $ 1,200 |
| Totals | 300 | | $ 3,360 |
| Units sold | 230 | | |
| Ending inventory | 70 | | |

The taxpayer uses the FIFO method to determine the value of its ending inventory and cost of goods sold. Under the FIFO method those amounts are determined as follows:

| | Units of Inventory | | | Dollars of Cost | |
|---|---|---|---|---|---|
| | Sold | Not Sold | Unit Cost | Goods Sold | Ending Inv. |
| Beginning inventory | 50 | | $ 10.00 | $   500 | |
| Purchases: | | | | | |
| Feb. | 40 | | $ 10.50 | $   420 | |
| May | 50 | | $ 11.00 | $   550 | |
| Aug. | 60 | | $ 11.50 | $   690 | |
| Nov. | 30 | 70 | $ 12.00 | $   360 | $ 840 |
| Totals | 230 | 70 | | $ 2,520 | $ 840 |

### XI.C.4.c. LIFO Method

[578 T.M., IV.B.3., VII.; TPS ¶3590.02.D.]

Under the last-in, first-out (LIFO) method, the last goods produced or purchased are assumed to be the first goods sold. Ending inventory is assumed to consist of the first goods produced or purchased, and the value of ending inventory is determined based on the costs of those goods. Thus, in determining the value of ending inventory, the costs of the goods in beginning inventory are taken into account first, followed by the costs of the goods produced or purchased during the year (in chronological order) [§ 472; Reg. § 1.472-1].

The LIFO method and FIFO method (see XI.C.4.b.) produce different income results, depending on the trend of price levels at the time. In times of rising prices, LIFO produces lower ending inventory, higher costs of goods sold, and lower income than does FIFO. In times of falling prices, the opposite is true.

---

**EXAMPLE:** Assume the same facts as in the example in XI.C.4.b., except that the taxpayer uses the LIFO method to determine the value of its ending inventory and cost of goods sold. Under the LIFO method, those amounts are determined as follows:

| | Units of Inventory | | | Dollars of Cost | |
|---|---|---|---|---|---|
| | Sold | Not Sold | Unit Cost | Goods Sold | Ending Inv. |
| Beginning inventory | | 50 | $ 10.00 | | $ 500 |
| Purchases: | | | | | |
| Feb. | 20 | 20 | $ 10.50 | $ 210 | $ 210 |
| May | 50 | | $ 11.00 | $ 550 | |
| Aug. | 60 | | $ 11.50 | $ 690 | |
| Nov. | 100 | | $ 12.00 | $ 1,200 | |
| Totals | 230 | 70 | | $ 2,650 | $ 710 |

---

To elect the LIFO method, a taxpayer must file Form 970, *Application To Use LIFO Inventory Method,* (or a similar statement) with its timely filed return for the tax year it first uses the LIFO method [Reg. § 1.472-3].

The rules for the LIFO method are very complex. There are two basic methods that may be used to compute inventory under LIFO: the specific goods method and the dollar-value method.

*Specific Goods Method.* Under the specific goods method, specific inventory items are traced from their purchase into cost of goods sold, in reverse order of acquisition [Reg. § 1.472-1].

*Dollar-Value Method.* Under the more popular dollar-value method, similar inventory items are grouped into pools and each pool is essentially accounted for as if it were a single inventory item. Increases and decreases in the size of each pool are measured by its dollar value, with beginning and ending inventory expressed in constant dollars using the price of inventory items in the year LIFO was adopted (the base year). If the dollar value of inventory increases during the current year (as measured in base year dollars), the amount of that increase is multiplied by a price index for the current year in order to obtain an estimate of the price of the additional goods produced or purchased during that year. This estimate is treated as the cost of the pool's new layer of inventory. The applicable price index can be computed using one of several different methods, including (i) the double-extension method, (ii) the index method, (iii) the link-chain method, or (iv) the retail method. For a description of the first three methods, see Reg. § 1.472-8. For a description of the retail method, see Reg. § 1.471-8.

*Simplified Dollar-Value Method.* The simplified dollar-value method is a variation of the dollar-value method and was created to provide the tax benefits of LIFO to small businesses that might not otherwise use LIFO. To be eligible to elect this simplified method, a taxpayer must have average annual gross receipts of $5 million or less for its three preceding tax years. Under the simplified dollar-value method, a taxpayer's inventory pools are determined based on the major categories included in certain government price indexes. The change in the government price index during the year for each appropriate category is used to estimate the cost of each pool's new layer of inventory [§ 474].

### XI.C.4.d. Average Cost Method

[578 T.M., IV.B.4.; TPS ¶3590.02.E.]

Under the average cost method, both the goods sold and those remaining in ending inventory are assumed to have a unit cost equal to the average cost of all goods available for sale by the taxpayer during the year. This average is computed by dividing the total cost of goods that were available for sale by the total number of units available for sale. The average cost of the items is then multiplied by the number of units on hand at the end of the year to determine the value of the taxpayer's ending inventory. The IRS has provided two safe harbors under which the average cost method for inventories will be deemed to clearly reflect income [Rev. Proc. 2008-43, 2008-30 I.R.B. 186].

## XI.D. Uniform Capitalization Rules

[576 T.M.; TPS ¶3570.]

The uniform capitalization rules require taxpayers to capitalize the direct costs and an allocable portion of the indirect costs associated with certain property produced or acquired for resale. Such costs are included in the basis of the property. Thus, they are not currently deductible but must instead be capitalized and recovered through depreciation and amortization or, for inventory property, included in inventory costs [§ 263A(a)].

### XI.D.1. Property Subject to Uniform Capitalization Rules

[576 T.M., II., III.; TPS ¶3570.01.B.]

The uniform capitalization rules apply to [§ 263A(b); Reg. § 1.263A-1(a)(3)]:

- real property and tangible personal property produced by a taxpayer; and
- real property and personal property acquired by a taxpayer for resale.

*Property Produced by Taxpayer.* The uniform capitalization rules generally apply to real property and tangible personal property produced by a taxpayer (a so-called producer). A taxpayer is treated as producing such property if it constructs, builds, installs, manufactures, develops, improves, creates, raises, or grows the property. A taxpayer is not considered to be producing property unless, under federal tax principles, it is considered an owner of the property produced. Property produced for a taxpayer under a contract with another party is treated as property produced by the taxpayer to the extent the taxpayer makes payments or otherwise incurs costs in connection with the property. The uniform capitalization rules apply only to property produced by a taxpayer for use in its trade or business or for sale to customers. They do not apply to property produced for personal purposes [§ 263A(g); Reg. § 1.263A-2(a)].

***Property Acquired by Taxpayer for Resale.*** The uniform capitalization rules generally apply to real property and personal property acquired for resale by a retailer, wholesaler, or other taxpayer (a so-called reseller). However, certain small resellers are exempt (see XI.D.2.). Personal property includes both tangible and intangible property. Property acquired for resale includes stock in trade and other property includible in inventory if on hand at the end of the tax year. It also includes property held by the taxpayer primarily for sale to customers in the ordinary course of the taxpayer's trade or business [Reg. § 1.263A-3(a)].

***Additional Rules on the Application of the Uniform Capitalization Rules.*** Additional rules on the application of the uniform capitalization rules include the following [Reg. § 1.263A-1(a)(3)]:

- The uniform capitalization rules generally apply to foreign persons.
- Taxpayers engaged in a farming business are required to capitalize certain costs under the uniform capitalization rules.
- Taxpayers engaged in the production/resale of creative property are required to capitalize certain costs under the uniform capitalization rules.
- The uniform capitalization rules generally apply to inventories valued at cost, lower of cost or market, or market. However, the rules do not apply to inventories valued at market if the market valuation used by the taxpayer generally equals the property's fair market value.

### XI.D.2. Property Exempt from Uniform Capitalization Rules

[576 T.M., II., III.; TPS ¶3570.02.]

The uniform capitalization rules do not apply to the following:

- resellers of personal property with average annual gross receipts of $10 million or less [§ 263A(b)(2)(B); Reg. § 1.263A-1(b)(1)];
- certain producers that use a simplified production method and have total indirect costs of $200,000 or less [Reg. § 1.263A-1(b)(12)];
- property produced for personal use (i.e., property produced for uses not connected with a trade or business or an activity conducted for profit) [§ 263A(c)(1)];
- property produced under long-term contracts, other than certain home construction contracts under § 460(e)(1) [§ 263A(c)(4); Reg. § 1.263A-1(b)(2)];
- property provided to customers in connection with services (must be de minimis in amount and not included in inventory) [Reg. § 1.263A-1(b)(11)];
- property produced for which substantial construction occurred before March 1, 1986 [Reg. § 1.263A-1(b)(10)];
- timber and certain ornamental trees raised, harvested, or grown, including the underlying land [§ 263A(c)(5); Reg. § 1.263A-1(b)(4)];
- research and experimental expenditures deductible under § 174 [§ 263A(c)(2); Reg. § 1.263A-1(b)(9)];
- intangible drilling and development costs of oil and gas or geothermal wells, or any amortization deduction allowable under § 59(e) [§ 263A(c)(3); Reg. § 1.263A-1(b)(7)];

- costs allocable to natural gas acquired for resale (to the extent such costs would otherwise be allocable to cushion gas stored underground) [Reg. § 1.263A-1(b)(8)]; and

- qualified creative expenses paid or incurred as a freelance writer, photographer, or artist that are otherwise deductible [§ 263A(h); Reg. § 1.263A-1(b)(5)].

### XI.D.3. Costs Required to Be Capitalized

[576 T.M., II., III.; TPS ¶3570.04.]

Taxpayers subject to the uniform capitalization rules must capitalize all direct costs and certain indirect costs properly allocable to property produced or acquired for resale. However, a taxpayer does not take into account any cost that would not otherwise be taken into account in computing taxable income for the year [§ 263A(a)(2); Reg. § 1.263A-1(e)(1)].

**Direct Costs.** A producer must capitalize direct material costs and direct labor costs. A reseller must capitalize the acquisition costs of property acquired for resale.

Direct material costs include the costs of those materials that either (i) become an integral part of the property produced, or (ii) are consumed in the ordinary course of production and can be identified or associated with particular units (or groups of units) of property produced. Direct labor costs include the costs of labor that can be identified or associated with particular units (or groups of units) of property produced [Reg. § 1.263A-1(e)(2)].

**Indirect Costs.** Taxpayers subject to the uniform capitalization rules must capitalize all indirect costs properly allocable to property produced or acquired for resale. Indirect costs are all costs other than the direct costs discussed above. Indirect costs are properly allocable to property produced or acquired for resale when the costs directly benefit or are incurred by reason of the performance of production or resale activities. Indirect costs may be allocable to both production and resale activities, as well as other activities that are not subject to the uniform capitalization rules. Taxpayers must make a reasonable allocation of indirect costs between production, resale, and other activities [Reg. § 1.263A-1(e)(3)(i)].

Indirect costs that must be capitalized include indirect labor, officers' compensation, pension costs, employee benefit expenses, indirect materials, purchasing costs, handling costs, storage costs, depreciation, amortization, depletion, rent, taxes, insurance, utilities, repairs and maintenance, engineering and design costs, spoilage, tools and equipment, quality control, bidding costs, licensing and franchise costs, interest, and capitalizable service costs [Reg. § 1.263A-1(e)(3)(ii)].

There are certain indirect costs that are not required to be capitalized, including selling and distribution costs, research and experimental expenditures, § 179 costs, § 165 losses, cost recovery allowances on temporarily idle equipment and facilities, taxes assessed on the basis of income, strike expenses, warranty and product liability costs, on-site storage costs, unsuccessful bidding expenses, and deductible service costs [Reg. § 1.263A-1(e)(3)(iii)]. In addition, package design costs are not required to be capitalized, unless the package design is purchased from another person [Reg. § 1.263(a)-4(l), *Ex.* 9].

**Service Costs.** Service costs are a type of indirect cost that can be identified specifically with a service department or function or that directly benefit or are incurred by reason of a service department or function. The treatment of service costs depends on the type of service costs involved. There are three types of service costs [Reg. § 1.263A-1(e)(4)]:

1. Capitalizable service costs (service costs that directly benefit or are incurred by reason of the performance of production or resale activities) are required to be capitalized.

2. Deductible service costs (service costs that do not directly benefit or are not incurred by reason of the performance of production or resale activities) are not required to be capitalized.

3. Mixed service costs (service costs that partly benefit or are incurred by reason of production and resale activities and partly benefit or are incurred by reason of) other activities must be allocated between capitalizable service costs and deductible service costs.

*Interest Costs.* Generally, interest must be capitalized to the extent it is paid or incurred during the production period of certain designated property, which includes (i) real property, (ii) tangible personal property with a class life of 20 years or more that is primarily for the taxpayer's own use, (iii) tangible personal property with an estimated production period of more than one year and estimated production costs of more than $1 million, and (iv) tangible personal property with an estimated production period of more than two years. The amount of interest required to be capitalized is determined using the avoided cost method under which interest on any debt directly attributable to production expenditures for a designated property is capitalized and interest on any other debt is assigned to that property and capitalized to the extent that the taxpayer's interest costs could have been reduced if production expenditures had not been incurred. The total amount of capitalized interest is added to the basis of the designated property, not to the basis of the assets used to produce the property [§ 263A(f); Reg. § 1.263A-8, § 1.263A-9].

### XI.D.4. Cost Allocation Methods

[576 T.M., II., III.; TPS ¶3570.05., .07.C., .08.C.]

In allocating direct and indirect costs to property produced or acquired for resale, a taxpayer may use a general cost allocation method or a simplified cost allocation method. The general methods include:

- the specific identification method [Reg. § 1.263A-1(f)(2)];
- the burden rate method [Reg. § 1.263A-1(f)(3)(i)];
- the standard cost method [Reg. § 1.263A-1(f)(3)(ii)]; and
- any other reasonable allocation method [Reg. § 1.263A-1(f)(4)].

The simplified methods include:

- the simplified service cost method [Reg. § 1.263A-1(h)];
- the simplified production method [Reg. § 1.263A-2(b)]; and
- the simplified resale method [Reg. § 1.263A-3(d)].

## XI.E. Accounting for Long-Term Contracts

[575 T.M.; TPS ¶3610.]

Taxable income from a long-term contract (see XI.E.1.) generally must be determined under the percentage-of-completion method (see XI.E.2.) [§ 460(a)]. However, the percentage-of-completion method is not required to be used for certain home construction contracts and small contractor construction contracts. Certain other methods are used to determine taxable income under those types of exempt long-term contracts (see XI.E.3.).

### *XI.E.1. Long-Term Contract*

[575 T.M., II.; TPS ¶3610.01.]

A long-term contract is a contract for the manufacture, building, installation, or construction of property that is not completed within the same tax year it is entered into [§ 460(f)(1); Reg. § 1.460-1(b)(1)]. Thus, contracts for services generally do not qualify as long-term contracts.

***Special Rule for Manufacturing Contracts.*** A manufacturing contract qualifies as a long-term contract only if it is for the manufacture of [§ 460(f)(2); Reg. § 1.460-2(a)]:

1. a unique item of personal property that is not normally carried in the taxpayer's finished goods inventory; or

2. an item of personal property that normally requires more than 12 calendar months to complete.

***Completion of Long-Term Contract.*** A long-term contract is completed upon the earlier of (i) final completion and acceptance of the subject matter of the contract, or (ii) the use of the subject matter of the contract by the customer for its intended purpose when the taxpayer has incurred at least 95% of the total allocable contract costs attributable to the subject matter [Reg. § 1.460-1(c)(3)(i)]. Final completion of the contract is generally determined based on all the relevant facts and circumstances. However, final completion is determined without regard to (i) whether any contractual term provides for additional compensation that is contingent on successful performance, (ii) whether the taxpayer has an obligation to assist or supervise assembly or installation, or (iii) whether a dispute exists at the time the taxpayer tenders the subject matter to the customer. A taxpayer may not delay completion of a contract for the principal purpose of deferring tax [Reg. § 1.460-1(c)(3)(iv)].

### *XI.E.2. Percentage-of-Completion Method*

[575 T.M., V.B.; TPS ¶3610.03.A.1.]

The percentage-of-completion method generally must be used to account for long-term contracts entered into after January 10, 2001. Under the percentage-of-completion method, a taxpayer must include in income the portion of the total contract price that corresponds to the percentage of the contract that the taxpayer completed during the tax year. The percentage of the contract that the taxpayer completed during the tax year is determined by comparing the contract costs actually incurred with the estimated total contract costs. Thus, the contract price is included in the taxpayer's gross income in the periods that the related contract costs are incurred [Reg. § 1.460-4(b)(1)].

The total contract price is the amount that the taxpayer reasonably expects to receive under the contract. Total contract price includes [Reg. § 1.460-4(b)(4)]:

- holdbacks, retainages, and cost reimbursements;

- contingent compensation (as soon as the taxpayer can reasonably predict the amount that will be earned, even if the all-events test discussed at XI.B.1.d(1) has not yet been met); and

- an allocable share of the gross receipts attributable to non-long-term contract activity (if such activity is incident to or necessary for the manufacture, building, installation, or construction of the contract's subject matter).

### XI.E.2.a. Computation of Income from Long-Term Contract

[575 T.M., V.B.; TPS ¶3610.03.A.1.]

Under the percentage-of-completion method, the income from a long-term contract that is reported for a tax year is computed based on the following steps [Reg. § 1.460-4(b)(2)]:

1. A completion factor is computed for the contract (the completion factor is equal to the ratio of the cumulative allocable contract costs incurred through the end of the tax year to the estimated total allocable contract costs).
2. Cumulative gross receipts for the current tax year are computed by multiplying the total contract price by the completion factor from step 1.
3. Current-year gross receipts are computed by subtracting cumulative gross receipts for the immediately preceding tax year from the cumulative gross receipts for the current tax year from step 2.
4. Current-year income from the contract is computed by subtracting allocable contract costs incurred during the current tax year from current-year gross receipts from step 3.

### XI.E.2.b. Special Rules for Certain Contract Costs

[575 T.M., V.B.; TPS ¶3610.03.A.1.]

Special rules apply to contract costs incurred before the tax year in which the contract is entered and contract costs incurred after the tax year in which the contract is completed. If a taxpayer reasonably expects to enter into a long-term contract in a future tax year, he must capitalize any allocable contract costs that are incurred in a tax year before the year in which the contract is entered [Reg. § 1.460-4(b)(5)(iv)]. If a taxpayer incurs any allocable contract costs in a tax year after the year in which the contract is completed, he must account for those costs using a permissible method of accounting [Reg. § 1.460-4(b)(5)(v)].

### XI.E.2.c. Allocation Between Long-Term Contract Activities and Other Activities

[575 T.M., V.B.; TPS ¶3610.01.C.]

When a taxpayer provides additional items or services (e.g., spare parts, training) in addition to the property that is the subject matter of the contract, income and costs must be allocated between the long-term contract activities and the other activities. Generally, the income and costs attributable to the long-term contact activities are accounted for under the percentage-of-completion method, and the income and costs attributable to other activities are accounted for under another permissible method of accounting [Reg. § 1.460-1(d)].

### XI.E.2.d. Election of 10% Method

[575 T.M., V.B.; TPS ¶3610.02.E.]

Taxpayers otherwise required to use the percentage-of-completion method may elect to apply the 10% method. The 10% method is identical to the percentage-of-completion method, except that contract income and costs are not taken into account for any tax year in which less than 10% of the estimated total contract costs have been incurred by the end of the year. Such deferred contract income and costs are taken into account in the first year in which the 10% threshold is met. The 10% method is taken into account in applying the look-back method (see XI.E.2.e.) and in determining alternative minimum taxable income. In all other respects, the 10% method is identical to the percentage-of-completion method [§ 460(b)(5)].

### *XI.E.2.e. The Look-Back Method*

[575 T.M., V.B.; TPS ¶3610.02.A.3.]

When the percentage-of-completion method is used, a taxpayer is either required to pay, or entitled to receive, interest on the amount of the tax liability that is deferred or accelerated as a result of underestimating or overestimating the amount of the total contract price or the contract costs. Upon completion of a long-term contract, a look-back method must be used to determine the amount of such interest. Under the look-back method, a taxpayer must compute the income that would have been reported in each year of the contract if the actual total contract price and contract costs had been used (instead of the estimated total contract price and contract costs). If the taxpayer underestimated income in any year of the contract, it owes the government interest on the imputed underpayment of tax from that tax year through the year the contract is completed. Conversely, if the taxpayer overestimated income in any year of the contract, it is due a refund of interest on the overpayment of tax from that tax year through the year the contract is completed [§ 460(b)(2); Reg. § 1.460-6].

***Computation of Interest under Look-Back Method.*** A three-step procedure is used to compute the interest charged or credited under the look-back method [§ 460(b)(2); Reg. § 1.460-6(c)]:

1. The income from the contract is reallocated by applying the percentage-of-completion method to the long-term contract using actual total contract price and costs (instead of estimated total contract price and costs).

2. The underpayment or overpayment of tax is determined by comparing the tax based on the reallocated income with the tax based on the reported income.

3. The interest rate applicable for overpayments is applied to the underpayment or overpayment and the resulting amount is paid by, or credited to, the taxpayer.

The amount of any interest due from, or payable to, a taxpayer as a result of applying the look-back method is computed on Form 8697, *Interest Computation Under the Look-Back Method for Completed Long-Term Contracts.*

***Contracts Exempt from Look-Back Method.*** The look-back method does not apply to a contract if [§ 460(b)(3)(B); Reg. § 1.460-6(b)(3)]:

1. the contract has a total contract price that does not exceed the lesser of (i) $1 million, or (ii) 1% of the taxpayer's average annual gross receipts for the three tax years immediately preceding the tax year in which the contract is completed; and

2. the contract must be completed within two years of the contract commencement date.

***De Minimis Exception to Look-Back Method.*** Taxpayers may elect not to apply the look-back method to a tax year beginning after the tax year in which the contract is completed if [§ 460(b)(6)]:

1. the cumulative taxable income or loss under the contract as of the end of such tax year is within 10% of the cumulative look-back taxable income or loss as of the end of the most recent year in which the look-back method was applied; or

2. the cumulative taxable income or loss under the contract as of the end of each prior contract year is within 10% of the cumulative look-back taxable income or loss as of the end of that prior contract year.

***Simplified Look-Back Method for Certain Entities.*** For a partnership, S corporation, or trust (other than certain closely held entities), a simplified look-back method applies at the entity level. Under the simplified method, the amount of taxes deemed overpaid or underpaid in any year is determined by multiplying the amount of contract income overreported or underreported for the year by the highest corporate tax rate (the highest individual tax rate is used if more than 50% of the interests in the entity are held by individuals directly or through one or more pass-through entities at all times during the year) [§ 460(b)(4)].

### XI.E.3. Exempt Long-Term Contracts

[575 T.M., V.D.; TPS ¶3610.03.A.2.]

The percentage-of-completion method is not required to be used for the following types of long-term contracts [§ 460(e); Reg. § 1.460-3(b), § 1.460-3(c)]:

- home construction contracts; and
- small contractor construction contracts.

These types of long-term contracts may be accounted for using the percentage-of-completion method (PCM), the exempt-contract percentage-of-completion method (EPCM) (see XI.E.3.a.), or the completed-contract method (CCM) (see XI.E.3.b.) [Reg. § 1.460-4(c)]. A special rule applies to residential construction contracts that are not home construction contracts (see XI.E.3.c.).

***Home Construction Contracts.*** A home construction contract is a construction contract for which 80% of the total estimated contract costs are reasonably expected to be attributable to (i) dwelling units in buildings containing four or less dwelling units, and (ii) improvements to real property directly related to, and located at the site of, those dwelling units [§ 460(e)(6)(A); Reg. § 1.460-3(b)(2)].

***Small Contractor Construction Contracts.*** A small contractor construction contract is a construction contract of a taxpayer whose has average annual gross receipts of $10 million or less for the three tax years immediately before the tax year the contract is entered into and who estimates that construction under the contract will be completed within two years [§ 460(e)(1)(B); Reg. § 1.460-3(b)(1)(ii)].

### XI.E.3.a. Exempt-Contract Percentage-of-Completion Method

[575 T.M., V.D.; TPS ¶3610.03.B.]

The exempt-contract percentage-of-completion method (EPCM) is similar to the percentage-of-completion method (PCM) (see XI.E.2.). However, under the EPCM, the percentage of completion may be determined by comparing costs other than contract costs (e.g., direct labor costs) or by comparing the work actually performed with the estimated total work to be performed, as long as such method is consistently applied and clearly reflects income. In addition, the following rules do not apply to the EPCM: (i) the look-back method (see XI.E.2.e.), (ii) the treatment of contract costs incurred after the year the contract is completed (see XI.E.2.b.), and (iii) the 10% method (see XI.F.2.d.) [Reg. § 1.460-4(c)(2)].

### XI.E.3.b. Completed-Contract Method

[575 T.M., V.D.; TPS ¶3610.03.B.2.]

Under the completed-contract method (CCM), a taxpayer includes the entire gross contract price in income and takes a deduction for all contract costs in the year the contract is completed (the completion year). However, the following special rules apply when a disputed claim exists after the subject matter of the contract has been tendered to the customer [Reg. § 1.460-4(d)(4)]:

- If a disputed claim involves a customer request for a reduction in gross contract price or the performance of additional work, and the taxpayer is assured of either a profit or a loss regardless of the outcome of the dispute, the gross contract price is reduced by any amount in dispute before being taken into account in the completion year.

- If a disputed claim involves the taxpayer's request for an increase in the gross contract price, and the taxpayer is assured of either a profit or a loss regardless of the outcome of the dispute, the gross contract price is taken into account in the completion year.

- If the taxpayer is assured a profit on the contract, all contract costs incurred by the end of the completion year are taken into account in the completion year.

- If the taxpayer is assured a loss on the contract, the contract costs incurred by the end of the completion year are reduced by any amount in dispute before being taken into account in the completion year.

- If, as a result of the disputed claim, the taxpayer cannot determine whether a profit or loss will ultimately be realized, the taxpayer may not take any of the gross contract price or contract costs into account in the completion year.

- Any part of the gross contract price and contract costs not taken into account in the completion year as a result of the disputed claim must be taken into account in the year the dispute is resolved.

### XI.E.3.c. Special Rule for Residential Construction Contracts

[575 T.M., V.D.; TPS ¶3610.02.C.3.]

A residential construction contract is a construction contract that would otherwise qualify as a home construction contract except that the building constructed contains more than four dwelling units. A taxpayer may account for a residential construction contract using either the percentage-of-completion method (PCM) or the percentage-of-completion, capitalized-cost method (PCCM). Under PCCM, a taxpayer must determine the income from the contract using PCM for 70% of the contract and its selected exempt method for 30% of the contract [Reg. § 1.460-3(c), § 1.460-4(e)].

### XI.E.4. Cost Allocation Rules

[575 T.M., VII.; TPS ¶3610.03.B.]

Specific cost allocation methods must be used when accounting for long-term contracts under the percentage-of-completion method (PCM), the completed-contract method (CCM), and the percentage-of-completion/capitalized-cost method (PCCM). These cost allocation rules do not apply to exempt construction contracts that are accounted for under a method other than PCM or CCM [Reg. § 1.460-5(a)].

Under the cost allocation method for long-term contracts subject to PCM, direct and indirect costs generally must be allocated in the same manner as direct and indirect costs are capitalized to taxpayer-produced property under Reg. § 1.263A-1(e) through § 1.263A-1(h). However, a taxpayer may elect to use a simplified cost-to-cost method described in Reg. § 1.460-5(c) to allocate such costs [Reg. § 1.460-5(b), § 1.460-5(c)].

Under the cost allocation method for long-term contracts subject to CCM, direct costs must be allocated in the same manner as direct costs are capitalized to taxpayer-produced property under Reg. § 1.263A-1(e) through (h). However, indirect costs may be allocated as provided under the provisions of either Reg. § 1.263A-1(e)(3) or Reg. § 1.460-5(d)(2) [Reg. § 1.460-5(d)].

Under the cost allocation method for long-term contracts subject to PCCM, costs allocable to a residential construction contract (or a qualified ship contract) must be determined under the PCM cost allocation rules. However, the simplified cost-to-cost method may not be elected in this case [Reg. § 1.460-5(e)].

## XI.F. Installment Sales

[565 T.M.; TPS ¶3550.]

An installment sale is a sale or other disposition of property in which the seller receives at least one payment after the end of the tax year in which the sale occurs. If a sale qualifies as an installment sale, the seller must report gain from the sale using the installment method (see III.G.), unless it makes an election not to use the installment method [§ 453].

## XI.G. Section 467 Rental Agreements

[593 T.M., II.F.; TPS ¶3580.]

Generally, rent for the use of property is treated differently by cash method taxpayers and accrual method taxpayers. A cash method taxpayer accounts for such rent in the year the rent is paid, while an accrual method taxpayer accounts for such rent in the year the rental obligation is incurred. However, when a rental agreement for the use of property is a § 467 rental agreement, both cash method and accrual method taxpayers must use the accrual method to account for income and deductions under the agreement [§ 467(a); Reg. § 1.467-1(a)].

### XI.G.1. Definition of § 467 Rental Agreement

[593 T.M., II.F.; TPS ¶3580.01.A.]

A § 467 rental agreement is a rental agreement for the use of tangible property that involves total payments of more than $250,000 and that has either (i) increasing or decreasing rent, or (ii) deferred or prepaid rent. A rental agreement has increasing or decreasing rent if the annualized fixed rent allocated to one period of the lease term exceeds the annualized fixed rent allocated to any other period (disregarding any rent holidays of three months or less). A rental agreement has deferred or prepaid rent if the cumulative amount of rent allocated or payable as of the end of the calendar year exceeds the cumulative amount of rent payable or allocated as of the end of the succeeding calendar year [§ 467(d); Reg. § 1.467-1(c)].

### XI.G.2. General Rule: Accrual Method

[593 T.M., II.F.; TPS ¶3580.01.A.]

Generally, the income taken into account under a § 467 rental agreement for any tax year is equal to the sum of [§ 467(a), § 467(b)(1)]:

1. the rent that accrues for the year (determined by allocating rent to the lease periods in accordance with the agreement, and taking into account the present value of any amounts that are allocated to that year but not paid until a later year); and

2. interest on any amounts taken into account for prior tax years that remain unpaid.

### XI.G.3. Special Rule: Constant Rental Accrual

[593 T.M., II.F.6.c.; TPS ¶3580.01.B.]

Income under a § 467 rental agreement must be taken into account on a constant rental basis (referred to as "rent leveling") if [§ 467(b)(2), § 467(b)(3)]:

- the rental agreement fails to allocate rent to the lease periods; or
- the rental agreement is a disqualified leaseback or long-term agreement, as defined in § 467(b)(4).

The constant rental amount allocable to a tax year is the amount that, if paid at the end of each lease period, would result in a total present value equal to the present value of the total payments required under the agreement [§ 467(e)(1)].

### XI.G.4. Recapture of Prior Understated Inclusions

[593 T.M., II.F.6.e.; TPS ¶3580.02.]

If a taxpayer leases property under a leaseback or long-term agreement to which the constant rental accrual method (see XI.G.3.) did not apply, and the taxpayer disposes of the property during the term of the agreement, then a portion of the gain on the disposition must be recaptured as ordinary income. The portion of the gain treated as ordinary income is equal to the excess of the amounts that would have been included in income under the constant rental accrual method over the amounts that were actually included in income under the rental agreement [§ 467(c)(3)].

## XI.H. Accounting Methods for Farmers

### XI.H.1. General Methods of Accounting for Farmers

[608 T.M., XX., 578 T.M., II.B.3.b(4); TPS ¶3530.02.B.5., .07.].

Farmers generally have the choice of using either the cash method or accrual method of accounting, even though the accrual method is normally required for most taxpayers for whom inventories are a material income producing factor [Reg. § 1.61-4]. There are certain types of farming businesses that are required to use the accrual method (see below). Certain farmers may elect to use a special crop method of accounting (see below). For discussion of special rules that apply in determining the gross income of a farmer, see I.H.2. For discussion of special rules that apply in determining deductions and losses of a farmer, see IV.F.3. and VIII.H.5., respectively.

*Accrual Method Requirement for Certain Farming Businesses.* The following types of farming businesses are required to use the accrual method [§ 447, § 448(b)(1)]:

- a corporation (other than a family corporation) that had gross receipts of more than $1 million for any tax year beginning after 1975;
- a family corporation that had gross receipts of more than $25 million for any tax year beginning after 1985;
- a partnership with one of the above types of corporations as a partner; or
- a tax shelter.

A family corporation is a corporation that meets one of the following ownership requirements [§ 447(d)(2)(C), § 447(h)]:

- members of the same family own at least 50% of the shares of the voting stock and at least 50% of the shares of all other classes of stock;
- members of the two families have owned, directly or indirectly, since October 4, 1976, at least 65% of the shares of the voting stock and at least 65% of the shares of all other classes of stock; or
- members of the three families have owned, directly or indirectly, since October 4, 1976, at least 50% of the shares of the voting stock and at least 50% of the shares of all other classes of stock.

The accrual method requirement does not apply to an S corporation, a farming business operating a nursery or sod farm, or a farming business raising or harvesting trees other than fruit and nut trees (unless they are tax shelters) [§ 447(a), § 447(c)].

*Crop Method.* A farmer who does not harvest and dispose of its crop in the same tax year the crop is planted may, with IRS approval, use a special method of accounting known as the crop method. Under the crop method, a farmer deducts the entire cost of producing such a crop in the year he or she realizes the income from the crop, and not earlier [Reg. § 1.162-12(a)].

### XI.H.2. Inventory Valuation Methods for Farmers

[608 T.M., XX.D.3.; TPS ¶3590.06.D.]

Farmers generally may use any one of the following four methods of valuing inventory:

1. cost;

2. lower of cost or market;

3. the farm-price method; and

4. the unit-livestock-price method.

The first two methods may be used by most taxpayers and are discussed at XI.C.3. The farm-price method and the unit-livestock-price method are special methods available only to farmers.

*Farm-Price Method.* Under the farm-price method, each inventory item (whether raised or purchased) is valued at its market price less the direct costs of disposition. The costs of disposition include broker's fees and commissions, freight and handling charges, and marketing costs. If this method is used, it must be applied to all property produced by the taxpayer in the trade or business of farming, except livestock that is valued under the unit-livestock-price method [Reg. § 1.471-6(d)].

*Unit-Livestock-Price Method.* Under the unit-livestock-price method, livestock is grouped or classified by kind and age with a standard unit price used for each animal within a group or class. The standard unit prices should reasonably approximate the normal costs of producing animals in each classification or group. Classifications and standard unit prices are subject to IRS approval [Reg. § 1.471-6(e)].

If the unit-livestock-price method is used, it must be applied to all livestock raised, regardless of whether they are held for sale or for draft, breeding, or dairy purposes. The standard unit prices must be reevaluated annually and adjusted upward or downward to reflect increases or decreases in the costs of raising livestock [Reg. § 1.471-6(f)].

If this method is used, all livestock purchased generally must be included in inventory at cost, except that livestock purchased for draft, breeding, or dairy purposes can either be included in inventory or capitalized and depreciated after maturity. If purchased livestock is not mature at the time of purchase, the cost should be increased at the end of each tax year in accordance with the established unit prices (however, no increase is made at the end of the year for livestock purchased during the last six months of the year) [Reg. § 1.471-6(g)].

## XI.I. Section 482 Allocations of Income and Deductions Between Related Taxpayers

[551 T.M.; TPS ¶3600.]

Under § 482, the IRS has authority to make allocations between and among commonly controlled business entities if they do not report their true taxable income (i.e., the taxable income that would have resulted for such entities if they had dealt with each other at arm's length). The IRS may allocate income, deductions, credits, allowances, basis, or any other item or element affecting taxable income. The purpose of § 482 is to ensure that taxpayers clearly reflect income attributable to controlled transactions and to prevent tax avoidance with respect to such transactions. Under § 482, a controlled taxpayer is placed on tax parity with an uncontrolled taxpayer by determining the true taxable income of the controlled taxpayer [§ 482; Reg. § 1.482-1(a), § 1.482-1(b)]. For a detailed discussion of § 482, see XX.C.5.

# CHAPTER XII. INDIVIDUALS
>>>>>>>>>>>>>>>>>>>>>>>>>>>>>>>>

## XII.A. Return Filing Requirements

### XII.A.1. Who Must File a Return?

[507 T.M., I.A.4., II.B.2.b(3)(a); TPS ¶¶3820.02.A.1., 3310.04.F.]

Generally, every individual who is a citizen or resident of the United States is liable for federal income tax. U.S. citizens and residents are subject to tax on their worldwide income (i.e., all income received from sources within or without the United States) [Reg. § 1.1-1(a), § 1.1-1(b)].

*Resident and Nonresident Aliens.* Any individual who is not a U.S. citizen is classified as either a resident or nonresident alien. A resident alien generally is any individual who meets a green card test or substantial presence test (see XX.A.). A nonresident alien is any alien who is not a resident alien [§ 7701(b)(1)]. As discussed above, a resident alien is taxed on worldwide income in the same manner as a U.S. citizen. A nonresident alien generally is subject to tax only on U.S.-source income.

*Election of Nonresident Alien to Be Treated as Resident Alien.* A nonresident alien who is married to a U.S. citizen or resident alien may be treated as a resident alien and file a joint return with his or her spouse if both spouses so elect. The election is made by attaching a statement to the spouses' joint income tax return for the first year for which the election is to be effective. The statement must contain the name, address, and taxpayer identification number of each spouse, along with a statement that they are making the election for the nonresident spouse to be treated as a resident. The election is effective until it is revoked, suspended, or terminated [§ 6013(g); Reg. § 1.6013-6].

### XII.A.1.a. General Filing Requirement

[507 T.M., I.; TPS ¶3820.02.A.1.]

An individual liable for federal income tax generally must file a federal income tax return for any tax year in which his or her gross income exceeds a specified threshold amount. The specified threshold amount is based on a taxpayer's filing status (see XII.C.) and age, and is generally equal to the taxpayer's exemption amount (see XII.D.) plus the taxpayer's basic standard deduction amount (XII.E.1.) and any additional standard deduction for age (see XII.E.2.) [§ 6012(a)(1)(A), § 6012(a)(1)(B)].

The filing threshold amounts for 2014 and 2015 are as follows [Rev. Proc. 2013-35, 2013-47 I.R.B. 537; Rev. Proc. 2014-61, 2014-47 I.R.B. 860]:

| Filing Status and Age | 2014 Threshold | 2015 Threshold |
|---|---|---|
| Single, under 65 | $ 10,150 | $ 10,300 |
| Single, 65 or older | $ 11,700 | $ 11,850 |
| Married filing jointly, both spouses under 65* | $ 20,300 | $ 20,600 |
| Married filing jointly, one spouse 65 or older* | $ 21,500 | $ 21,850 |
| Married filing jointly, both spouses 65 or older* | $ 22,700 | $ 23,100 |
| Married filing separately (any age) | $  3,950 | $  4,000 |
| Head of household, under 65 | $ 13,050 | $ 13,250 |
| Head of household, 65 or older | $ 14,600 | $ 14,800 |
| Surviving spouse, under 65 | $ 16,350 | $ 16,600 |
| Surviving spouse, 65 or older | $ 17,550 | $ 17,850 |

*If a taxpayer's filing status is married filing jointly but the taxpayer does not live with his or her spouse at the end of the tax year, the filing threshold amount is $3,950 for 2014 ($4,000 for 2015), regardless of the taxpayer's age [Reg. § 1.6012-1(a)(2)(iii)(b)].

For this purpose, gross income generally includes all income received in the form of money, goods, property, and services that is not exempt from tax. It generally includes gains, but not losses, reported on Schedules C, D, and F. It also includes income from sources outside the United States and income from the sale of a main home, even if otherwise excludible from income. With certain exceptions, it does not include social security benefits [§ 61, § 6012(c)]. For an additional discussion of the filing requirements for individual taxpayers, see XXIII.A.1.a(1).

### XII.A.1.b. Dependent Filing Requirement

[507 T.M., I.A.; TPS ¶3820.02.A.1.]

An individual who can be claimed as a dependent by another taxpayer generally must file a federal income tax return if [§ 6012(a)(1)(C)]:

1. unearned income exceeds the minimum standard deduction for dependents (see XII.E.3.) plus any additional standard deductions for age or blindness (see XII.E.2.);

2. total gross income (earned income and unearned income) exceeds the basic standard deduction (see XII.E.1.); or

3. the standard deduction would be zero (see XII.E.).

Based on these rules, an individual who can be claimed as a dependent by another taxpayer must file a return if any one of three specified threshold amounts is exceeded: (i) the unearned income threshold, (ii) the earned income threshold, or (iii) the gross income threshold. The dependent filing threshold amounts for 2014 are as follows [Rev. Proc. 2013-35, 2013-47 I.R.B. 537]:

- A single dependent who is under 65 and not blind must file a return if: (i) unearned income exceeds $1,000 (ii) earned income exceeds $6,200, or (iii) gross income is more than the greater of $1,000 or earned income (up to $5,850) plus $350.

- A single dependent who is either 65 or older or blind must file a return if: (i) unearned income exceeds $2,550, (ii) earned income exceeds $7,750, or (iii) gross income is more than the greater of $2,550 or earned income (up to $5,850) plus $1,900.

- A single dependent who is both 65 or older and blind must file a return if: (i) unearned income exceeds $4,100, (ii) earned income exceeds $9,300, or (iii) gross income is more than the greater of $4,100 or earned income (up to $5,850) plus $3,450.

- A married dependent who is under 65 and not blind must file a return if: (i) unearned income exceeds $1,000, (ii) earned income exceeds $6,200, (iii) gross income is at least $5 and spouse files separately and itemizes, or (iv) gross income is more than the greater of $1,000 or earned income (up to $5,850) plus $350.

- A married dependent who is either 65 or older or blind must file a return if: (i) unearned income exceeds $2,200, (ii) earned income exceeds $7,400, (iii) gross income is at least $5 and spouse files separately and itemizes, or (iv) gross income is more than the greater of $2,200 or earned income (up to $5,850) plus $1,550.

- A married dependent who is both 65 or older and blind must file a return if: (i) unearned income exceeds $3,400, (ii) earned income exceeds $8,600, (iii) gross income is at least $5 and spouse files separately and itemizes, or (iv) gross income is more than the greater of $3,400 or earned income (up to $5,850) plus $2,750.

The dependent filing threshold amounts for 2015 are as follows [Rev. Proc. 2014-61, 2014-47 I.R.B. 860]:

- A single dependent who is under 65 and not blind must file a return if: (i) unearned income exceeds $1,050, (ii) earned income exceeds $6,300, or (iii) gross income is more than the greater of $1,050 or earned income (up to $5,950) plus $350.

- A single dependent who is either 65 or older or blind must file a return if: (i) unearned income exceeds $2,600, (ii) earned income exceeds $7,850, or (iii) gross income is more than the greater of $2,600, or earned income (up to $5,950) plus $1,900.

- A single dependent who is both 65 or older and blind must file a return if: (i) unearned income exceeds $4,150, (ii) earned income exceeds $9,400, or (iii) gross income is more than the greater of $4,150 or earned income (up to $5,850) plus $3,450.

- A married dependent who is under 65 and not blind must file a return if: (i) unearned income exceeds $1,050, (ii) earned income exceeds $6,300, (iii) gross income is at least $5 and spouse files separately and itemizes, or (iv) gross income is more than the greater of $1,050 or earned income (up to $5,950) plus $350.

- A married dependent who is either 65 or older or blind must file a return if: (i) unearned income exceeds $2,300, (ii) earned income exceeds $7,550, (iii) gross income is at least $5 and spouse files separately and itemizes, or (iv) gross income is more than the greater of $2,300 or earned income (up to $5,950) plus $1,600.

- A married dependent who is both 65 or older and blind must file a return if: (i) unearned income exceeds $3,550, (ii) earned income exceeds $8,800, (iii) gross income is at least $5 and spouse files separately and itemizes, or (iv) gross income is more than the greater of $3,550 or earned income (up to $5,950) plus $2,850.

Unearned income includes taxable interest, ordinary dividends, capital gains distributions, unemployment compensation, taxable social security benefits, pensions, annuities, and distributions of unearned income from a trust. Earned income includes salaries, wages, tips, professional fees, and taxable scholarship and fellowship grants. Gross income is the total of unearned income and earned income.

### XII.A.1.c. Other Filing Requirements

[507 T.M., I.A.; TPS ¶3820.02.A.1.]

A taxpayer not otherwise required to file a federal income tax return under the general or dependent filing requirements (see XII.A.1.a. and XII.A.1.b.) is nevertheless required to file a return if any of the following apply:

1. the taxpayer owes alternative minimum tax or any of the special taxes reported in the "Other Taxes" section of Form 1040 (see X.A.);

2. the taxpayer (or spouse, if filing jointly) received distributions from an HSA, Archer MSA, or Medicare Advantage MSA;

3. the taxpayer had at least $400 of net earnings from self-employment [§ 1402(b)(2)];

4. the taxpayer had at least $108.28 of wages from a church or qualified church-controlled organization that are exempt from employer social security and Medicare taxes [§ 1402(j)(2)(B)]; or

5. advance payments of the premium tax credit (see IX.G.7.) were made for the taxpayer, the taxpayer's spouse, or a dependent who enrolled in coverage through the Health Insurance Marketplace.

### XII.A.1.d. Exception to Filing Requirements for Certain Children

[507 T.M., I.A.; TPS ¶3820.02.A.1.]

The return filing requirements do not apply to a taxpayer who is under age 19 or a full-time student under age 24 if his or her parents make an election to report his or her income on their return [§ 1(g)(7)]. Parents may make this election by completing and attaching Form 8814, *Parent's Election To Report Child's Interest and Dividends*, to their timely filed return (see I.B.3.).

### XII.A.1.e. Filing Return When Not Required

[507 T.M., I.A.; TPS ¶3820.02.A.1.]

A taxpayer who is not otherwise required to file a federal income tax return should nevertheless file a return if he or she:

1. is eligible for a refund of federal income tax withheld (see XXII.A.); or

2. is eligible for a refundable tax credit (see IX.G.).

### XII.A.2. What Form Must Be Used to File Return?

[507 T.M., II.; TPS ¶3820.01.]

Taxpayers generally must use one of three forms in the Form 1040 series to file their federal income tax return. Forms 1040EZ and 1040A are the shortest and simplest forms but can be used only if certain requirements are satisfied. Taxpayers who do not qualify to file Form 1040EZ, *Income Tax Return for Single and Joint Filers with No Dependents*, or Form 1040A, *U.S. Individual Income Tax Return*, must file Form 1040, *U.S. Individual Income Tax Return* [Reg. § 1.6012-1(a)(6), § 1.6012-1(a)(7), § 1.6012-1(a)(8)].

### XII.A.2.a. Form 1040EZ

[507 T.M., II.; TPS ¶3820.01.]

A taxpayer can file Form 1040EZ only if all 11 of the following apply:

1. The taxpayer's filing status is single or married filing jointly.
2. The taxpayer (and spouse, if married filing jointly) is under age 65 and not blind at the end of the tax year.
3. The taxpayer does not claim any dependents.
4. The taxpayer's taxable income is less than $100,000.
5. The taxpayer has income only from wages, salaries, tips, taxable interest ($1,500 or less), Alaska Permanent Fund dividends, unemployment compensation, and taxable scholarship and fellowship grants.
6. The taxpayer's tips (if any) are included in boxes 5 and 7 of Form W-2.
7. The taxpayer does not claim any adjustments to income.
8. The taxpayer does not choose to itemize deductions.
9. The taxpayer does not claim any tax credits other than the earned income credit.
10. The taxpayer does not owe any household employment taxes on wages paid to household employees.
11. The taxpayer is not a debtor in a Chapter 11 bankruptcy case filed after October 16, 2005.

### XII.A.2.b. Form 1040A

[507 T.M., II.; TPS ¶3820.01.]

A taxpayer can file Form 1040A only if all six of the following apply:

1. The taxpayer's taxable income is less than $100,000.
2. The taxpayer's income is only from wages, salaries, tips, interest, ordinary dividends (including Alaska Permanent Fund dividends), unemployment compensation, taxable scholarship and fellowship grants, capital gain distributions (other than distributions including unrecaptured § 1250 gain, § 1202 gain, or collectibles gain), IRA distributions, pensions and annuities, and taxable social security and railroad retirement benefits.
3. The taxpayer's only adjustments to income are for educator expenses, tuition and fees, the student loan interest deduction, and the IRA deduction.
4. The taxpayer does not itemize deductions.
5. The taxpayer does not claim any tax credits other than the earned income credit, the credit for child and dependent care expenses, the credit for the elderly and disabled, the education credits, the retirement savings contribution credit, the child tax credit, and the additional child tax credit.
6. The taxpayer does not have an alternative minimum tax (AMT) adjustment on stock he acquired from the exercise of an incentive stock option.

### XII.A.2.c. Form 1040

[507 T.M., II.; TPS ¶3820.01.]

A taxpayer can use Form 1040 to report all types of income, deductions, and credits. If any one of the following applies, a taxpayer is required to file Form 1040 instead of Form 1040EZ or Form 1040A:

1. The taxpayer has taxable income of $100,000 or more.

2. The taxpayer has adjusted gross income of more than $150,000 and must reduce the dollar amount of his exemptions.

3. The taxpayer has itemized deductions.

4. The taxpayer has income, adjustments to income, or tax credits that cannot be reported on Form 1040EZ or Form 1040A.

5. The taxpayer has self-employment income.

6. The taxpayer has income as a partner in a partnership, shareholder in an S corporation, or beneficiary of an estate or trust.

7. The taxpayer is an employee and his or her employer did not withhold social security and Medicare tax.

8. The taxpayer received $20 or more in tips during a month and did not report them all to his or her employer.

9. The taxpayer's Form W-2 shows uncollected employee tax on tips or group-term life insurance.

10. The taxpayer's Form W-2 shows an amount in box 12 with code Z (income under § 409A on a nonqualified deferred compensation plan).

11. The taxpayer received a qualified health savings account (HSA) funding distribution from his or her IRA.

12. The taxpayer received a distribution from a foreign trust.

13. The taxpayer can exclude foreign earned income received as a U.S. citizen or resident.

14. The taxpayer is a bona fide resident of Puerto Rico or American Samoa and can exclude income from sources in Puerto Rico or American Samoa.

15. The taxpayer is required to repay the first-time homebuyer credit.

16. The taxpayer owes household employment taxes.

17. The taxpayer owes additional Medicare tax (or has such tax withheld) and must file Form 8959.

18. The taxpayer owes net investment income tax and must file Form 8960.

19. The taxpayer is eligible for the health coverage tax credit.

20. The taxpayer is claiming the adoption credit or received employer-provided adoption benefits.

21. The taxpayer has an AMT adjustment on stock he or she acquired from the exercise of an incentive stock option.

22. The taxpayer owes excise tax on insider stock compensation from an expatriated corporation.

23. The taxpayer had foreign financial assets and must file Form 8938.

24. The taxpayer is a debtor in a bankruptcy case filed after October 16, 2005.

25. The taxpayer must file other forms with his or her return to report certain exclusions, taxes, or transactions.

### XII.A.2.d. Form 1040NR/1040NR-EZ

[507 T.M., II.; TPS ¶3820.01.]

A nonresident alien is generally required to file Form 1040NR, *U.S. Nonresident Alien Income Tax Return*, or Form 1040NR-EZ, *U.S. Income Tax Return for Certain Nonresident Aliens with No Dependents*, if he or she engaged in a trade or business in the United States or had income from sources within the United States during the year. However, a nonresident alien who is married to a U.S. citizen or resident and elects to be treated as a U.S. resident for the year (see XII.A.1.) files a joint return with his or her spouse on Form 1040, 1040A, or 1040EZ [Reg. § 1.6012-1(b)].

### XII.A.3. When and Where Must Return Be Filed?

#### XII.A.3.a. Return Due Date

[507 T.M., II.; TPS ¶3820.02.E.1.]

An individual taxpayer generally must file his or her federal income tax return by April 15 of the year following the year for which the return is being filed. However, an individual taxpayer who uses a fiscal year instead of a calendar year must file his or her return by the 15th day of the fourth month after the end of his fiscal year. If the due date of a return is on a Saturday, Sunday, or legal holiday, the due date is extended to the next business day [§ 6072(a), § 7503].

A nonresident alien who files a federal income tax return is generally subject to the same rules. However, the due date for the return of a nonresident alien who did not earn wages subject to U.S. income tax withholding is June 15 of the year following the year for which the return is being filed (if using a fiscal year, the 15th day of the sixth month after the end of the fiscal year) [§ 6072(c)]. For an additional discussion of return due dates, see XXIII.A.1.c.

#### XII.A.3.b. Extensions of Time to File Return

[507 T.M., II.; TPS ¶3820.02.F.1.]

An individual taxpayer may obtain an automatic six-month extension of time to file his or her federal income tax return. The request for automatic extension must be filed by the regular due date for the taxpayer's return. Any tax due with the return must also be paid by the regular due date in order to avoid penalties and interest [Reg. § 1.6081-4].

An automatic six-month extension can be obtained in one of three ways [Reg. § 1.6081-4]:

1. by filing a paper Form 4868, *Application for Automatic Extension of Time to File U.S. Individual Income Tax Return*, by mail;

2. by filing Form 4868 electronically using a tax software package or a tax professional; or

3. by paying all or part of the tax due with the return on the internet or by phone (Form 4868 is not required to be filed under this option).

For an additional discussion of extensions of time to file, see XXIII.A.1.d.(1).

***Extensions for Citizens and Residents Outside the United States.*** U.S. citizens and residents who live outside of the United States and Puerto Rico are allowed an automatic two-month extension to file their federal income tax return and to pay the tax due if their main place of business or military post of duty is outside the United States. However, interest is charged on any tax paid after the regular due date. The two-month extension is obtained by attaching an explanation to the taxpayer's return when it is filed.

Taxpayers using the automatic two-month extension can also obtain an additional four-month extension to file their return (but not to pay tax) by filing Form 4868 and checking the "out of the country" box [Reg. § 1.6081-5(a)(5), § 1.6081-4(a)].

***Combat Zone Extensions.*** Individual taxpayers serving in an area designated by the President as a combat zone are allowed an automatic extension of at least 180 days to file their federal income tax return and to pay any tax due or file a claim for refund.

Eligible taxpayers include members of the military, Red Cross personnel, accredited correspondents, and civilians and merchant marines under the direction or control of the military. The extension period is generally 180 days from the later of the last day the taxpayer is in the combat zone or the last day the taxpayer is hospitalized for injury from service in the combat zone. In addition to the 180 days, the due date is also extended by the number of days the taxpayer had left to take action with the IRS at the time he entered the combat zone. These combat zone extension rules also apply to taxpayers deployed outside the United States and away from their permanent duty station while participating in a designated contingency operation [§ 7508(a); Reg. § 301.7508-1].

### XII.A.3.c. Methods of Filing

[507 T.M., II.; TPS ¶3820.01.E., .02.G.2.]

A federal income tax return can be filed electronically, by mail, or by private delivery service. The determination of whether a return is filed on time and where it is filed depends on the method used for filing the return.

*Filing electronically.* An electronic return is considered to be filed on time if the authorized electronic return transmitter (a participant in the IRS e-file program) electronically postmarks the transmission of the return to the IRS by the due date. The authorized electronic return transmitter electronically postmarks a return when it receives the transmission of the return on its host system. The date and time in the taxpayer's time zone is the date and time used for purposes of the electronic postmark. For an additional discussion of electronic filing, see XXIII.A.1.f.

*Filing by mail.* A paper return filed by mail is considered filed on time if it is postmarked by the due date and mailed in an envelope that is properly addressed and has enough postage. If filed by registered mail, the postmark date is the date of the registration. If filed by certified mail, the postmark date is the date of the certified mail receipt. A return filed by mail must be sent to the appropriate IRS mailing address (see *Schedules & Tables 6.*).

*Filing by private delivery service.* A paper return filed by an IRS-designated private delivery service is considered to be filed on time if it is postmarked by the due date. The postmark date is the date the private delivery service records in its database or marks on the mailing label. Private delivery services designated by the IRS include certain DHL, FedEx, and UPS delivery services. Lists of IRS designated private delivery services and the mailing addresses to which returns filed by private delivery service must be sent are provided at IRS.gov.

### XII.A.4. Special Filing Rules for Final Income Tax Return of Decedent

[804 T.M., XV.C.; TPS ¶6170.]

When a taxpayer dies, a final income tax return must be filed for the deceased taxpayer (the decedent) for the year of death. If the taxpayer dies before filing an income tax return for a previous year, that return must also be filed on his or her behalf. The personal representative of the decedent's estate is generally responsible for filing the final return and any previous returns not filed. The personal representative is the executor named in the decedent's will or, when no will exists, the administrator appointed by the court [§ 6012(b)(1); Reg. § 1.6012-3(b)(1)].

Generally, the final income tax return of the decedent is filed based on the same rules that apply to all individual taxpayers. However, special rules that apply are discussed below.

### *XII.A.4.a. Filing Requirement for Final Return*

[804 T.M., XV.C.; TPS ¶6170.]

The gross income, age, and filing status of the decedent determine whether a return is required to be filed for the decedent for the year of death. If a return is required to be filed for the year of death, it must be prepared on Form 1040, Form 1040A or Form 1040EZ for the year of death, regardless of when during the year the death occurred. If the decedent was a nonresident alien who would have been required to file Form 1040NR, that form must be filed instead [Reg. § 1.6012-3(b)(1), § 1.6012-1(a)].

### *XII.A.4.b. Filing Status for Final Return*

[804 T.M., XV.C.; TPS ¶6170.02.C.]

The decedent's filing status on the final income tax return generally depends on whether he or she was married or unmarried on the date of death. If the decedent was married on the date of death, the personal representative and the surviving spouse can file a joint return for the decedent and surviving spouse. If no personal representative has been appointed by the due date for filing the decedent's final return, the surviving spouse may make an election to file a joint return with the decedent. However, when the personal representative is later appointed, he or she may revoke the surviving spouse's election by filing a separate return for the decedent within one year from the due date (including extensions). In such a case, the joint return of the surviving spouse will be treated as a separate return by excluding the decedent's tax items and recalculating the tax liability [§ 6013(a)(3); Reg. § 1.6013-1(d)(5)].

### *XII.A.4.c. Who Files and Signs Final Return*

[804 T.M., XV.C.; TPS ¶6170.01.C., .02.C.]

If a personal representative has been appointed for the decedent, that person must sign and file the decedent's final income tax return. If the decedent was married and a joint return is being filed with the surviving spouse, the surviving spouse must also sign the return.

If no personal representative has been appointed by the time the decedent's final income tax return is due, the person responsible for filing and signing the final return depends on the decedent's marital status on the date he or she died. If the decedent was married on the date of death, the surviving spouse must file the decedent's final return, sign the return, and write "Filing as surviving spouse" in the signature area. If the decedent was unmarried on the date of death, the person in charge of the decedent's property must file the decedent's final return, sign the return, and write "personal representative" in the signature area.

### *XII.A.4.d. When and Where Final Return Is Filed*

[804 T.M., XV.C.; TPS ¶6170.01.B.]

The final income tax return of the decedent is due on the same date the return would have been due had he or she not died. Thus, for example, if the decedent was a calendar year taxpayer, the return is due on April 15, regardless of when during the year the death occurred [Reg. § 1.6072-1(b)]. The personal representative (or surviving spouse in the case of a joint return) can obtain an extension on behalf of the decedent. The final income tax return of the decedent can be filed electronically or filed with the Internal Revenue Service Center for the place where the personal representative (or other person filing the decedent's final return) lives.

### XII.A.4.e. Special Information Included on Final Return

[804 T.M., XV.C.; TPS ¶6170.]

On the final income tax return filed for a decedent, the word "DECEASED," the decedent's name, and the date of death must be written across the top of the return. If the final return is a separate return, the decedent's name is written in the name field on the return and the personal representative's name and address is written in the address field on the return. If the final return is a joint return, the names and address of the decedent and the surviving spouse are written in the name and address fields on the return.

### XII.A.4.f. Treatment of Items of Income, Deduction, and Credit on Final Return

[804 T.M., XV.C.; TPS ¶6170.04.]

**Income Items.** The decedent's income items includible on the final income tax return are generally determined in the same manner as if he or she were still alive, except that the taxable period ends on the date of death. Thus, the accounting method the decedent used before death will determine what items of income are included in the final return. If the decedent used the cash method, only those items actually or constructively received before death are included. If the decedent used the accrual method, only those items normally accrued before death are included. See XI.B. for a discussion of accounting methods.

**Deductions.** Generally, the decedent's deductions allowed on the final income tax return are determined in the same manner. Thus, if the decedent used the cash method, only those deductible items he paid before death are allowed and if the decedent used the accrual method, only those deductible items accrued before death are allowed. However, there are special rules that apply to the deductions for medical expenses and losses.

**Deduction for Medical Expenses.** If the decedent incurred medical expenses before death that had not been paid as of the date of death and the decedent used the cash method of accounting, the personal representative (or other person filing the decedent's final return) may elect to treat such medical expenses paid out of the estate during the one-year period after the date of death as paid by the decedent at the time they were incurred. As a result, such medical expenses are deductible on the decedent's final return [§ 213(c)]. For a general discussion of the medical expense deduction, see VII.D.

**Deduction for Loss Carryovers.** If the decedent had net operating loss carryovers or capital loss carryovers from prior years, they are lost if they are not deducted on the decedent's final return because they cannot be deducted on the estate's income tax return. For a general discussion of losses, see Chapter VIII.

**Standard Deduction, Exemptions, and Credits.** If the decedent's deductions are not itemized on the final income tax return, the full amount of the standard deduction can be taken on the final return, regardless of the decedent's date of death. Similarly, the full amount of the decedent's exemptions can be taken on the final return, regardless of the decedent's date of death. Any tax credits that applied to the decedent before death can be claimed on the final return.

### XII.A.4.g. Tax Forgiveness for Certain Decedents

[804 T.M., XV.C.; TPS ¶6170.]

Income tax liability may be forgiven for a decedent who dies due to service in a combat zone, due to military actions, as a result of a terrorist attack, or while serving in the line of duty as an astronaut.

### XII.A.4.h. Claiming Refund Due to Decedent

[804 T.M., XV.C.; TPS ¶6170.]

If the decedent is due a refund because of income tax withholding, estimated tax payments, or refundable credits, Form 1310, *Statement of Person Claiming Refund Due a Deceased Taxpayer*, generally must be filed to claim the refund. However, Form 1310 is not required to be filed to claim the refund if either of the following apply:

- the refund is claimed by the decedent's surviving spouse on an original or amended joint return filed with the decedent; or
- the refund is claimed by the decedent's personal representative on an original return filed for the decedent and a copy of the court certificate showing the personal representative's appointment is attached to the return.

If the personal representative files a claim for refund on a Form 1040X, *Amended U.S. Individual Income Tax Return*, or on Form 843, *Claim for Refund and Request for Abatement*, and the court certificate has already been filed with the IRS, the personal representative can attach Form 1310 to that form and write "Certificate Previously Filed" at the bottom.

## XII.B. Computing Income Tax Liability

[507 T.M., II.A.; TPS ¶3310.]

In the most basic terms, an individual taxpayer's regular income tax is computed by multiplying his or her taxable income by the appropriate tax rates. Once regular income tax is computed, the taxpayer's total income tax liability is determined by subtracting certain tax credits (see Chapter IX.) and adding any other income taxes that apply (see Chapter X.). Any estimated taxes paid by the taxpayer (see XXII.F.) and any taxes withheld by the taxpayer's employer (see XXII.A.) are credited against the taxpayer's total income tax liability in determining the amount due from or to be refunded to the taxpayer.

### XII.B.1. Taxable Income

[507 T.M., II.A.; TPS ¶3310.]

Taxable income is equal to gross income less allowable deductions and exemptions. An individual taxpayer filing Form 1040 takes the following steps to determine taxable income for the year:

1. The taxpayer computes adjusted gross income (AGI) by subtracting certain adjustments to income (so-called above-the-line deductions) from gross income. For a discussion of gross income, see Chapter I. For a discussion of above-the-line deductions, see VII.B.

2. The taxpayer subtracts itemized deductions or the standard deduction from the amount determined in step 1. For a discussion of itemized deductions, see VII.C. For a discussion of the standard deduction and the choice between taking itemized deductions or the standard deduction, see XII.E.

3. The taxpayer subtracts his or her exemptions from the amount determined in step 2 to determine taxable income. For a discussion of exemptions, see XII.D.

### XII.B.2. Regular Income Tax

[507 T.M., II.A.; TPS ¶3310.]

Once an individual taxpayer has computed taxable income for the year (see XII.B.1.), the taxpayer determines the amount of regular income tax by applying the applicable tax rates to his or her taxable income. For 2014, the following seven tax rates apply to individual taxpayers: 10%, 15%, 25%, 28%, 33%, 35%, and 39.6%. The application of these tax rates depends on the taxpayer's filing status (see XII.C.) and the amount of taxable income. Five tax rate schedules based on filing status are provided in § 1 and updated each year by an annual revenue procedure (for 2014, see Rev. Proc. 2013-35, 2013-47 I.R.B. 537; for 2015, see Rev. Proc. 2014-61, 2014-47 I.R.B. 860). Each year, the IRS provides a Tax Table (see *Schedules & Tables 4.*) and a Tax Computation Worksheet (see *Schedules & Tables 3.*) in the Form 1040 instructions. They are based on the § 1 tax rate schedules and generally must be used by taxpayers to compute their tax. A taxpayer with taxable income of less than $100,000 must use the Tax Table to compute the tax. A taxpayer with taxable income of $100,000 or more must use the Tax Computation Worksheet. For a detailed discussion of the determination of an individual taxpayer's regular income tax, see X.A.1.

### XII.B.3. Total Income Tax Liability

[507 T.M., II.A.; TPS ¶3310.]

Once an individual taxpayer has computed regular income tax for the year, he or she subtracts any applicable tax credits and adds any other applicable income taxes to determine his total tax liability for the year. For a discussion of tax credits, see Chapter IX. For a discussion of the other income taxes (e.g., the alternative minimum tax, the net investment income tax), see X.A.

## XII.C. Filing Status

[507 T.M., II.B.; TPS ¶3310.04.]

A taxpayer must determine his or her filing status before determining filing requirements and the amount of income tax. There are five filing statuses that can be used by individual taxpayers [§ 1]:

1. married filing jointly;
2. married filing separately;
3. single;
4. head of household; and
5. surviving spouse.

A taxpayer's marital status is a key factor in determining proper filing status (see XII.C.1.). A married taxpayer generally may choose either to file a return with his or her spouse or to file a return separately (see XII.C.2.). Thus, the taxpayer may choose married filing jointly status (see XII.C.3.) or married filing separately status (see XII.C.4.). An unmarried taxpayer generally files using single status (see XII.C.7.). However, certain taxpayers who are unmarried (or considered unmarried) and meet certain other requirements may choose to file using head of household status (see XII.C.5.). Finally, a taxpayer whose spouse has died may choose surviving spouse status under certain circumstances (see XII.C.6.).

### XII.C.1. Determining Marital Status

[507 T.M., II.B.2.b(7); TPS ¶3310.04.G.]

Generally, a taxpayer's filing status depends on whether he or she is considered married or unmarried. Marital status is generally determined as of the last day of the taxpayer's tax year [§ 7703(a)(1)]. Thus, a calendar year taxpayer who is married as of December 31 is treated as married for the tax year, regardless of the number of days during the tax year he or she was actually married. Similarly, a calendar year taxpayer who is divorced as of December 31 is treated as unmarried for the tax year.

### XII.C.1.a. Definition of Marriage

[507 T.M., II.B.2.b(7); TPS ¶3310.04.G.]

The definition of marriage has recently been expanded for federal tax purposes. Section 3 of the Defense of Marriage Act (DOMA) defined the word "marriage" as meaning only a legal union between one man and one woman as husband and wife, and defined the word "spouse" as referring only to a person of the opposite sex who is a husband or wife. The U.S. Supreme Court, however, has held that Section 3 of DOMA is unconstitutional [*United States v. Windsor*, 133 S. Ct. 2675 (2013)]. Based on this decision, the IRS has adopted a general rule recognizing a marriage of same-sex individuals that is validly entered into in a state whose laws authorize the marriage of two individuals of the same sex. The IRS has indicated that this rule applies even if the married couple is domiciled in a state that does not recognize the validity of same-sex marriages. The rule, however, does not apply to individuals who have entered into a registered domestic partnership, civil union, or other similar formal relationship that is not denominated as a marriage under state law. The IRS began applying these rules on September 16, 2013; however, taxpayers wishing to rely on the rules for earlier periods may choose to do so as long as the § 6511 limitations period has not expired [Rev. Rul. 2013-17, 2013-38 I.R.B. 201].

### XII.C.1.b. Married Status

[507 T.M., II.B.2.b(7); TPS ¶3310.04.G.]

Two taxpayers are considered married for the entire tax year if they meet any one of the following tests on the last day of the year [§ 7703; Rev. Rul. 58-66, 1958-1 C.B. 60, *amplified and clarified by* Rev. Rul. 2013-17, 2013-38 I.R.B. 201]:

1. they are married and living together;
2. they are living together in a common law marriage in a state that recognizes common law marriage;
3. they are married and living apart but are not legally separated under a decree of divorce or separate maintenance; or
4. they are separated under an interlocutory (not final) decree of divorce.

Taxpayers who are considered married for the entire tax year generally can use either married filing jointly status (see XII.C.3.) or married filing separately status (see XII.C.4.). See XII.C.2. for a discussion of the factors involved in choosing between these two filing statuses.

A taxpayer who lives apart from his or her spouse at the end of the year may be able to use head of household status (see XII.C.5.), even if not divorced or legally separated from the spouse [§ 7703(b)].

A taxpayer whose spouse died during the tax year is considered married for the entire year. The filing status of the taxpayer and deceased spouse depends on whether the taxpayer remarried before the end of the year. If the taxpayer remarried before the end of the year, the taxpayer can use married filing jointly status with the new spouse and the deceased spouse uses married filing separately status. If the taxpayer did not remarry before the end of the year, the taxpayer can use married filing jointly status with the deceased spouse [§ 6013(a)(2)]. In the latter situation, the taxpayer may be able to use surviving spouse status for the following two years (see XII.C.6.).

### XII.C.1.c. Unmarried Status

[507 T.M., II.B.2.b(7); TPS ¶3310.04.G.]

A taxpayer is considered unmarried for the entire tax year if any one of the following tests is met on the last day of the year [§ 7703]:

1. the taxpayer is unmarried;
2. the taxpayer is legally separated from his or her spouse under a decree of divorce or separate maintenance;
3. the taxpayer is divorced from his or her spouse under a final decree of divorce; or
4. the taxpayer has obtained a court decree of annulment holding that no valid marriage ever existed.

A taxpayer who is considered unmarried for the entire tax year generally uses single filing status (see XII.C.7.). However, an unmarried taxpayer who has a qualifying person living with him or her may be able to use head of household status (see XII.C.5.) or surviving spouse status (see XII.C.6.) in certain circumstances.

If two taxpayers obtain a divorce for the sole purpose of filing tax returns as unmarried individuals, and at the time of the divorce they intend to, and do in fact, remarry in the next tax year, the taxpayers must file as married individuals for both tax years [Rev. Rul. 76-255, 1976-2 C.B. 40].

### XII.C.2. Choice of Filing Status for Married Taxpayers

[507 T.M., II.B.2., II.B.5.; TPS ¶3310.04.A., .04.D.]

Taxpayers who are considered married at the end of the year (see XII.C.1.) may generally choose to use either married filing jointly status or married filing separately status. Married filing jointly status is usually more advantageous for married taxpayers because the tax on a joint return is generally lower than the combined tax on two separate returns. However, in certain situations, it may be preferable to file separate returns. In some cases, the combined tax on separate returns will be lower than the tax on a joint return. Moreover, a taxpayer may prefer to file a separate return because both spouses have joint responsibility for the tax on a joint return. Thus, for example, if one spouse believes the other spouse is not reporting all income, he or she may prefer to file a separate return.

### XII.C.2.a. Filing Joint Return After Separate Returns

[507 T.M., II.B.2.b.(7); TPS ¶3310.04.A.1.]

Married taxpayers who file separate returns generally can amend and file a joint return any time within three years from the due date (excluding extensions) of the separate returns [§ 6013(b); Reg. § 1.6013-2]. However, such an amended return cannot be filed after any of the following events:

- either spouse files a petition with the Tax Court regarding a notice of deficiency for the tax year;
- either spouse institutes a suit for refund for the tax year in a district court or the Court of Federal Claims; or
- either spouse has entered into a § 7121 closing agreement or a § 7122 compromise for the tax year.

An amended return using joint filing status is filed on Form 1040X, *Amended U.S. Individual Income Tax Return.*

### XII.C.2.b. Filing Separate Returns After Joint Return

[507 T.M., II.B.2.b.(7); TPS ¶3310.04.A.1.]

Married taxpayers who file a joint return are generally not permitted to amend and file separate returns any time after the due date of the joint return [Reg. § 1.6013-1]. However, an exception applies when one of the spouses dies during the year, the surviving spouse elects to file a joint return with the deceased spouse, and a personal representative is later appointed for the deceased spouse. The personal representative can disaffirm the surviving spouse's election to file a joint return and instead file a separate return for the deceased spouse. The personal representative must disaffirm the surviving spouse's election within one year from the due date (including extensions) of the joint return [§ 6013(a)(3); Reg. § 1.6013-1(d)(5)]. For a discussion of the filing of the final return of a deceased spouse, see XII.A.4.

### XII.C.3. Married Filing Jointly

[507 T.M., II.B.2.; TPS ¶3310.04.A.]

Taxpayers may choose married filing jointly status if they are considered married and both spouses agree to file a joint return for the year. A joint return can be filed even if one spouse has no income or deductions. If both spouses have income, they should compare the amount of their tax on a joint return with the amount of their combined tax on two separate returns to determine which filing status results in the lower combined tax.

For the year in which one spouse dies, the surviving spouse may elect married filing jointly status with the deceased spouse. For a discussion of the filing of the final income tax return of a deceased spouse, see XII.A.4.

If a U.S. citizen or resident is married to a nonresident alien at the end of the year, the spouses may elect to file a joint return. When such an election is made, the nonresident alien is treated as a resident alien (see XII.A.1.) [§ 6013(g)].

When a joint return is filed, both spouses include all their income, exemptions, deductions, and credits on the joint return. Generally, each spouse must sign the joint return (see XII.C.3.a.) and they can each be held responsible, jointly and individually, for the tax and any penalties and interest due on the joint return (see XII.C.3.b.). However, in some cases, an innocent spouse may be relieved of liability for the tax, penalties, and interest on a joint return (see XII.C.3.c.). In addition, when the IRS uses a refund on a joint return to offset the debts of one spouse, the other spouse (the injured spouse) can request his or her portion of the refund (see XII.C.3.d.).

### XII.C.3.a. Signing Joint Return

[507 T.M., II.B.2.; TPS ¶3310.04.A.]

Generally, both spouses must sign a return for it to be considered a joint return [Reg. § 1.6013-1(a)(2)]. If one spouse will be away from home at the time the return is to be filed, the return should be prepared early and sent to that spouse for his or her signature so that it can be filed on time. However, the following are exceptions in which a joint return can be signed on behalf of a spouse who cannot sign [Reg. § 1.6013-1(a)(2), § 1.6012-1(a)(5)]:

1. If Spouse 1 dies before signing the return, the executor or administrator of the estate must sign for Spouse 1. However, if no executor or administrator has been appointed, Spouse 2 can sign for Spouse 1 and write "Filing as surviving spouse" next to the signature.

2. Spouse 1 can authorize Spouse 2 to sign the return if Spouse 1 cannot sign it because of injury or disease. In such a case, Spouse 2 signs for Spouse 1 and writes the words "By (Spouse 2's name), Husband (or Wife)" next to the signature. A signed, dated statement should be attached to the return that includes the return form number, the tax year, an explanation of why Spouse 1 cannot sign, and a statement that Spouse 1 has authorized Spouse 2 to sign the return for Spouse 1.

3. Spouse 1 can sign a joint return for Spouse 2 when Spouse 2 is mentally incompetent and Spouse 1 is the guardian of the Spouse 2.

4. Spouse 1 can sign a joint return for Spouse 2 when Spouse 2 is serving in a combat zone, even if Spouse 1 does not have a power of attorney or other similar statement. A signed statement should be attached to the return explaining that Spouse 2 is serving in a combat zone.

5. Spouse 1 can sign a joint return for Spouse 2 for any other reason if given a valid power of attorney by Spouse 2. Form 2848, *Power of Attorney and Declaration of Representative*, can be used for this purpose. A copy of the power of attorney must be attached to the joint return.

### XII.C.3.b. Joint Liability of Spouses
[507 T.M., II.B.2.; TPS ¶3310.04.A.]

Generally, both spouses may be held responsible, jointly and individually, for any tax, interest, or penalties due on a joint return [§ 6013(d)(3)]. Thus, if one spouse does not report the correct tax on the return or does not pay the tax due, the other spouse may be held responsible.

If spouses get divorced after filing one or more joint returns, the spouses are jointly and individually responsible for any tax, interest, and penalties due on the returns, even if the divorce decree states that one spouse will be responsible for all amounts due on previously filed joint returns.

### XII.C.3.c. Innocent Spouse Relief from Joint Liability
[645 T.M.; TPS ¶3825.]

Although spouses generally have joint liability for the tax on a joint return, there are three types of relief available under which one spouse may be relieved of joint responsibility for the other spouse's tax items that were incorrectly reported on a joint return [§ 6015]:

- innocent spouse relief;
- separation of liability; and
- equitable relief.

To request one of these types of relief, a taxpayer must submit Form 8857, *Request for Innocent Spouse Relief*, or a written statement containing the same information. If a taxpayer requests relief from joint and several liability, the IRS is required to notify the other spouse of the request and allow the other spouse to provide information for consideration. A taxpayer who files using married filing separately status in a community property state may also be able to qualify for such relief.

***Innocent Spouse Relief.*** Innocent spouse relief provides a taxpayer with relief from additional tax he or she owes if his or her spouse or former spouse failed to report income, reported income improperly, or claimed improper deductions or credits. A taxpayer qualifies for innocent spouse relief only if he or she establishes that all three of the following apply [§ 6015(b)]:

1. The taxpayer filed a joint return that has an understatement of tax that is solely attributable to the other spouse's erroneous item.

2. The taxpayer did not know, and had no reason to know, that there was an understatement of tax at the time he or she signed the return.

3. It would be unfair to hold the taxpayer liable for the understatement of tax (taking into account all the facts and circumstances).

***Separation of Liability Relief.*** Separation of liability relief provides for an allocation between the taxpayer and a spouse or former spouse of any additional tax owed due to an erroneous item. A taxpayer qualifies for separation of liability relief if, at the time he or she signed the return, the taxpayer did not have actual knowledge of the erroneous item and, at the time relief is requested, the taxpayer meets any one of the following requirements for the spouse with whom the joint return was filed [§ 6015(c)]:

1. the taxpayer is divorced or legally separated from the spouse;

2. the taxpayer is widowed; or

3. the taxpayer has not been a member of the same household as the spouse at any time during the previous 12 months.

***Equitable Relief.*** Equitable relief may be available to a taxpayer who does not qualify for innocent spouse relief or separation of liability relief. Equitable relief may apply if an item attributable to the taxpayer's spouse was not reported properly on their joint return or if the correct amount of tax was reported on their joint return but it remains unpaid. A taxpayer qualifies for equitable relief if the taxpayer establishes that, based on all the facts and circumstances, it would unfair to hold the taxpayer liable for the understatement or underpayment of tax [§ 6015(f)].

### XII.C.3.d. Injured Spouse Refund Allocations

[645 T.M. XII.; TPS ¶3825.13.]

The IRS is authorized to offset federal tax refunds due to taxpayers in order to pay past-due child support, federal non-tax debts, state income tax obligations, and certain unemployment compensation debts owed to a state. When a taxpayer files a joint return with a spouse who is responsible for such a debt and the taxpayer is entitled to part of the refund from the return, the taxpayer can request his or her portion of the refund by filing Form 8379, *Injured Spouse Allocation*. Form 8379 may be filed with the original joint return, an amended joint return, or by itself. If Form 8379 is filed with an original joint return, "INJURED SPOUSE" should be written on the top left corner of the first page of the return and the form will be processed before the offset occurs. If Form 8379 is filed by itself, both spouses' social security numbers should be reported in the same order they were reported on the original joint return and the injured spouse should sign the form.

### XII.C.4. Married Filing Separately

[507 T.M., II.B.5.; TPS ¶3310.04.D.]

Taxpayers may choose married filing separately status if they are considered married (see XII.C.1.) and they do not agree to file a joint return for the year. However, a taxpayer who qualifies to use head of household filing status cannot use married filing separately status. A taxpayer may qualify to use head of household status if considered unmarried because he or she lives apart from his or her spouse and meets certain other requirements (see XII.C.5.) [§ 7703(b)].

A married taxpayer who files a separate return reports only his or her (not the spouse's) income, exemptions, deductions, and credits on the return. The taxpayer can claim an exemption for the spouse only if the spouse had no gross income, is not filing a return, and is not the dependent of another person.

Married filing separately status generally is not as beneficial as married filing jointly status because:

1. the tax rate is higher for a separate return than it is for a joint return;

2. the standard deduction cannot be claimed if the other spouse itemizes deductions on his or her separate return;

3. the alternative minimum tax (AMT) exemption allowed on a separate return is half the AMT exemption allowed on a joint return;

4. the capital loss deduction limit that applies for a separate return is half the limit that applies for a joint return; and

5. certain types of tax credits that can be claimed on a joint return cannot be claimed on a separate return.

### XII.C.5. Head of Household

[507 T.M., II.B.3.; TPS ¶3310.04.B.]

A taxpayer generally can use head of household filing status if all the following requirements are met [§ 2(b)(1); Reg. § 1.2-2(b)(1)]:

1. the taxpayer is unmarried or considered to be unmarried on the last day of the tax year (see XII.C.5.a.);

2. the taxpayer pays more than half the cost of maintaining a home for the year (see XII.C.5.b.); and

3. a qualifying person lives with the taxpayer in that home for more than half the year (see XII.C.5.c.).

However, a taxpayer cannot use head of household status if he or she is eligible for surviving spouse filing status or is a nonresident alien (see XII.C.6.) [§ 2(b)(1), § 2(b)(3)(A)].

The tax rates that apply for head of household filing status are generally lower than the rates that apply for married filing separately or single filing status.

### XII.C.5.a. Considered Unmarried

[507 T.M., II.B.3.b.; TPS ¶3310.04.B.2.]

A taxpayer may qualify for head of household filing status if he or she is unmarried or considered to be unmarried. A taxpayer is considered to be unmarried on the last day of the tax year if:

1. the taxpayer is legally separated from his or her spouse under a decree of divorce or separate maintenance on the last day of the year [§ 2(b)(2)(A)];

2. the taxpayer's spouse did not live in the taxpayer's home during the last six months of the year, the taxpayer's home was the main home of a dependent child for more than half the year, and the taxpayer pays more than half the cost of maintaining the home during the year [§ 2(c), § 7703(b)]; or

3. the taxpayer's spouse was a nonresident alien at any time during the year and the taxpayer does not elect to treat the spouse as a U.S. resident [§ 2(b)(2)(B)].

However, a taxpayer is not considered to be unmarried for the year if his or her spouse died during the year [§ 2(b)(2)(C)].

### XII.C.5.b. Maintaining a Home

[507 T.M., II.B.3.d., II.B.3.e.; TPS ¶3310.04.B.3.]

A taxpayer may qualify for head of household filing status only if he or she pays more than half the cost of maintaining a home during the year. The cost of maintaining a home is the cost incurred for the mutual benefit of the individuals who live in it as their main home. It includes expenses such as rent, mortgage interest, real estate taxes, insurance, repairs, utilities, and food. It does not include the costs of clothing, education, medical treatment, life insurance, transportation, or vacations [Reg. § 1.2-2(d)].

The taxpayer and the qualifying person (see XII.C.5.c.) must actually live in the home he or she pays more than half the cost of maintaining. However, a physical change in the location of the home will not disqualify the taxpayer from head of household status [Reg. § 1.2-2(c)].

### XII.C.5.c. Qualifying Person

[507 T.M., II.B.3.d.; TPS ¶3310.04.B.3.]

Generally, a taxpayer can qualify for head of household filing status only if a qualifying person lives with him or her for more than half the year [§ 2(b)(1)(A)]. However, a taxpayer can qualify for head of household status for a qualifying person who is his father or mother even if the parent does not live with him or her during the year [§ 2(b)(1)(B); Reg. § 1.2-2(b)(1), § 1.2-2(b)(4)]. Thus, for example, the taxpayer may qualify to file as head of household when a parent lives in a rest home or a home for the elderly, as long as the taxpayer pays more than half the cost of maintaining that home for the parent.

A qualifying person is a person who is a qualifying child or a qualifying relative for purposes of the dependent exemption (see XII.D.2.). Generally, a qualifying child is the taxpayer's son, daughter, adopted child, foster child, stepchild, or descendant of any of them (such as a grandchild), and a qualifying relative is the taxpayer's father, mother, grandparent, other direct ancestor, stepfather, stepmother, brother, sister, half brother, half sister, stepbrother, stepsister, aunt, uncle, niece, nephew, or in-law. See XII.D.2.a. for a full discussion of the definition of a qualifying child and XII.D.2.b. for a full discussion of the definition of a qualifying relative.

A taxpayer qualifies for head of household status for a qualifying child if [§ 2(b)(1)(A)(i); Reg. § 1.2-2(b)(3)(i)]:

1. the qualifying child is single (whether or not the taxpayer can claim an exemption for the child);

2. the qualifying child is married and the taxpayer can claim an exemption for the child; or

3. the qualifying child is married and the only reason the taxpayer cannot claim an exemption for the child is that the child can be claimed as an exemption on another taxpayer's return.

A taxpayer qualifies for head of household status for a qualifying relative only if the taxpayer can claim an exemption for the relative [§ 2(b)(1)(A)(ii); Reg. § 1.2-2(b)(3)(ii)].

However, a taxpayer does not qualify for head of household status for the following persons even if the taxpayer can claim an exemption for them [§ 2(b)(3)(B)]:

1. a child who the taxpayer can claim as an exemption as noncustodial parent based on a written declaration that the custodial parent will not claim an exemption for the child (see XII.D.2.a.(6). and XII.D.2.b.(4));

2. a person who the taxpayer can claim as an exemption under a multiple support agreement (see XII.D.2.b.(3)); and

3. a person who the taxpayer can claim as an exemption only because the person lived with the taxpayer for the entire year.

Under no circumstances can the same person be claimed as a qualifying person by more than one taxpayer for the same tax year [Reg. § 1.2-2(b)(2)].

---

**EXAMPLE:** Mike is a single taxpayer who pays the entire cost of maintaining his home. Mike's 18-year-old unmarried son, Kyle, lived with him for the entire year. Kyle did not provide more than half his own support and he is not the qualifying child of any other taxpayer. Kyle is a qualifying child of Mike and, because Kyle is single, he is also a qualifying person of Mike for head of household purposes. Mike can file as head of household even if he cannot claim an exemption for Kyle.

---

### XII.C.6. Surviving Spouse

[507 T.M., II.B.2.c.; TPS ¶3310.04.A.2.]

A taxpayer can use surviving spouse filing status for the two years following the year in which his spouse died if [§ 2(a); Reg. § 1.2-2(a)]:

1. he was entitled to file a joint return with his spouse in the year the spouse died;

2. he has not remarried as of the last day of the year for which he is claiming surviving spouse filing status; and

3. he pays over half the cost of maintaining a home for a child or stepchild who lived in his home the entire year and for whom he can claim an exemption (see XII.D.2.).

A taxpayer may use surviving spouse filing status only for the two years following the year of his spouse's death. He may elect to use married filing jointly status (see XII.C.3.) for the year of the spouse's death.

---

**EXAMPLE:** Tiffany's husband died in Year 1. During Year 2 and Year 3, Tiffany does not remarry and she continues maintain a home for her daughter, who lives with her and for whom she can claim an exemption. For Year 1, Tiffany can elect to file a joint return for herself and her deceased husband. For Year 2 and Year 3, Tiffany can file using surviving spouse filing status. After Year 3, Tiffany can file as single or head of household (if eligible), unless she remarries.

---

The tax rates that apply for surviving spouse status are the same tax rates that apply for married filing jointly status [§ 1(a)].

### XII.C.7. Single

[507 T.M., II.B.4.; TPS ¶3310.04.C.]

A taxpayer generally must use single filing status if he was unmarried or considered unmarried (see XII.C.1.) on the last day of the year and he is not eligible to use any other filing status. Thus, a taxpayer must use single filing status if:

1. he had never been married as of the end of the year;

2. he was legally separated under a decree of divorce or separate maintenance as of the end of the year; or

3. he was widowed before the beginning of the year, did not remarry before the end of the year, and does not have a dependent child.

## XII.D. Exemptions

[513 T.M., III.B.; TPS ¶2830.]

Individual taxpayers are allowed certain exemptions from tax. Exemptions are treated like deductions because they reduce the amount of a taxpayer's taxable income for the year [§ 151(a)]. There are two types of exemptions for which taxpayers may qualify: (i) personal exemptions (see XII.D.1.), and (ii) dependent exemptions (see XII.D.2.).

The exemption amount is the same for each type of exemption and it is adjusted annually for inflation [§ 151(d)]. The exemption amount is $3,950 for 2014 ($4,000 for 2015) [Rev. Proc. 2013-35, 2013-47 I.R.B. 537; Rev. Proc. 2014-61, 2014-47 I.R.B. 860]. The benefit of the personal and dependent exemptions is phased out and reduced for high income taxpayers (see XII.D.3.).

Exemptions are claimed in the "Exemptions" section on page 1 of Form 1040. The taxpayer must provide the name, relationship, and social security number of each dependent for whom an exemption is claimed. No exemption will be allowed for any individual for whom a social security number is not provided [§ 152(e)].

### XII.D.1. Personal Exemptions

[513 T.M., III.B.2.; TPS ¶2830.02.]

A taxpayer generally can claim one personal exemption for himself or herself. If the taxpayer is married, he or she may also be allowed to claim a second personal exemption for his or her spouse. The exemption amount is $3,950 for 2014 ($4,000 for 2015) [Rev. Proc. 2013-35, 2013-47 I.R.B. 537; Rev. Proc. 2014-61, 2014-47 I.R.B. 860].

### XII.D.1.a. Taxpayer's Own Exemption

[513 T.M., III.B.2.a.; TPS ¶2830.02.A.]

Taxpayers can always claim a personal exemption for themselves, with one exception [§ 151(b)]. If a taxpayer can be claimed as a dependent by another taxpayer, he or she is not allowed to claim a personal exemption for himself or herself [§ 151(d)(2)]. This is true even if the other taxpayer does not actually claim the taxpayer as a dependent.

### XII.D.1.b. Taxpayer's Exemption for Spouse

[513 T.M., III.B.2.b.; TPS ¶2830.02.B., .02.C.]

A married taxpayer may be allowed to take a personal exemption for a spouse. Note that a taxpayer can never take a dependent exemption (see XII.D.2.) for a spouse because one spouse can never be a dependent of the other spouse.

The determination whether a taxpayer can take a personal exemption for a spouse depends on whether the taxpayer and spouse file a joint return or separate returns and, in the latter case, on the spouse's personal circumstances [§ 151(b)]. Special rules apply for the tax year in which the taxpayer's spouse dies. No personal exemption can be taken for an ex-spouse.

*Joint Return.* If a taxpayer and spouse file a joint return, the taxpayer can take a personal exemption for the spouse [Reg. § 1.151-1(b)].

*Separate Returns.* If a taxpayer and spouse file separate returns, the taxpayer generally cannot take a personal exemption for the spouse. Instead, the taxpayer's spouse takes a personal exemption on his or her own return. However, a taxpayer can take a personal exemption for a spouse (including a nonresident alien spouse) on a separate return if the spouse has no gross income, is not filing a return, and is not a dependent of another taxpayer [§ 151(b); Reg. § 1.151-1(b)]. These rules apply whether the taxpayer is using married filing separately status or head of household status.

*Year of Spouse's Death.* A taxpayer whose spouse dies during the year may be able to claim a personal exemption for the deceased spouse depending on whether the taxpayer remarries during the year, the taxpayer's filing status, and the deceased spouse's personal circumstances. A taxpayer who remarries during the year cannot take a personal exemption for the deceased spouse. However, a taxpayer who does not remarry during the year may elect to file a joint return with the deceased spouse and, if such an election is made, can take a personal exemption for the deceased spouse on the joint return. If such a taxpayer does not elect to file a joint return with the deceased spouse, the taxpayer can take a personal exemption for the deceased spouse on his or her separate return only if the deceased spouse had no gross income, no return is filed for the deceased spouse, and the deceased spouse was not a dependent of another taxpayer [Rev. Rul. 71-158, 1971-1 C.B. 50; Rev. Rul. 71-159, 1971-1 C.B. 50].

If a taxpayer has no gross income and does not file a return for the year his or her spouse dies, and the taxpayer remarries during that year, the taxpayer's new spouse may claim a personal exemption for the taxpayer on a joint or separate return. If the new spouse claims a personal exemption for the taxpayer on a separate return, a personal exemption can also be claimed for the taxpayer on the deceased spouse's final separate return.

*Ex-Spouse.* A taxpayer cannot take a personal exemption for an ex-spouse. For this purpose, marital status is determined as of the last day of the tax year. Thus, if the taxpayer and spouse obtain a final decree of divorce or separate maintenance during the year, the taxpayer cannot take a personal exemption for the spouse, even though they were married for part of the year.

### XII.D.2. Dependent Exemptions

[513 T.M., III.B.3.; TPS ¶2830.03.]

A taxpayer generally can take an exemption for each person that he or she can claim as a dependent (even if the dependent files his or her own return) [§ 151(c)]. The exemption amount is $3,950 for 2014 ($4,000 for 2015) [Rev. Proc. 2013-35, 2013-47 I.R.B. 537; Rev. Proc. 2014-61, 2014-47 I.R.B. 860].

A taxpayer cannot take a dependent exemption for any person for a tax year in which the taxpayer (or his or her spouse, if filing jointly) is a dependent of another taxpayer [§ 152(b)(1)].

There are two types of persons that generally can be claimed as dependents [§ 152(a)]:

1. a qualifying child (see XII.D.2.a.); and

2. a qualifying relative (see XII.D.2.b.).

However, a person who is a qualifying child or qualifying relative cannot be claimed as a dependent if:

- the person is married and files a joint return with his or her spouse (unless the person and spouse file the joint return only for the purpose of claiming a refund of income tax withheld or estimated tax paid) [§ 152(b)(2)]; or

- the person is not a U.S. citizen/resident/national, Canadian resident, or Mexican resident (unless the person is an adopted child who lives with the taxpayer for the entire year and the taxpayer is a U.S. citizen or national) [§ 152(b)(3)].

### XII.D.2.a. Qualifying Child

[513 T.M., III.B.3.c.; TPS ¶2830.03.A.1.]

A qualifying child is a child who meets all of the following five tests [§ 152(c)(1)]:

1. a relationship test (see XII.D.2.a.(1));
2. an age test (see XII.D.2.a.(2));
3. a residency test (see XII.D.2.a.(3));
4. a support test (see XII.D.2.a.(4)); and
5. a filing test (see XII.D.2.a.(5)).

Only one taxpayer can claim a child as a dependent during the year. Thus, there are special rules that apply to determine who can claim a child as a dependent when the child meets the five tests with respect to two or more taxpayers. One special rule applies when a child's parents are divorced, separated, or living apart (see XII.D.2.a.(6)). Another special rule provides a set of tie-breakers that apply to other situations in which a child meets the five tests with respect to two or more taxpayers (see XII.D.2.a.(7)).

### XII.D.2.a.(1) Relationship Test

[513 T.M., III.B.3.c.(2); TPS ¶2830.03.A.4.]

To be the qualifying child of a taxpayer, a child must be the taxpayer's son, daughter, adopted child, stepchild, foster child, brother, sister, half brother, half sister, stepbrother, stepsister, or a descendant of any of them (for example, a grandchild or a niece or nephew) [§ 152(c)(1)(A), § 152(c)(2), § 152(f); Reg. § 1.151-3(a)].

### XII.D.2.a.(2) Age Test

[513 T.M., III.B.3.c.(3); TPS ¶2830.03.A.1.]

To be the qualifying child of a taxpayer, a child must meet any one of the following three tests [§ 152(c)(1)(C), § 152(c)(3)]:

1. the child is under age 19 at the end of the taxpayer's tax year;
2. the child is a student under age 24 at the end of the taxpayer's tax year; or
3. the child is permanently and totally disabled at any time during the taxpayer's tax year, regardless of his or her age.

For purposes of the first and second tests, the child must be younger than the taxpayer [§ 152(c)(3)]. If the taxpayer is married and files a joint return, the child must be younger than either the taxpayer or his spouse, but is not required to be younger than both.

---

**EXAMPLE:** Jack and Jill, both age 21, are married and file a joint return. Jack's 22-year-old brother, Jim, is an unmarried student who lives with them the entire year. Jim cannot be a qualifying child of Jack because he is not younger than either Jack or Jack's wife.

**EXAMPLE:** Assume the same facts as in the previous example, except that Jill is instead 23. Jim can be Jack's qualifying child even though he is not younger than Jack because he is younger than Jack's wife, Jill.

---

*Student.* A child qualifies as a student if, for some part of any five calendar months during the year (not necessarily consecutive calendar months), the child is either: (i) a full-time student at a school that has a regular teaching staff and course of study and a regularly enrolled student body, or (ii) a student taking a full-time, on-farm training course given by a school or government agency. A school includes an elementary school, junior or senior high school, college or university, and technical, trade, or mechanical school. Full-time students are students enrolled for the number of hours or courses the school considers to be full-time attendance and include students who work on co-op jobs in private industry as a part of a school's regular course of classroom and practical training [§ 152(f)(2); Reg. § 1.151-3(b), § 1.151-3(c)].

*Permanently and Totally Disabled.* A child is permanently and totally disabled if the child cannot engage in any substantial gainful activity because of a physical or mental condition, and a doctor has determined either that the condition has lasted (or can be expected to last) continuously for at least a year or that the condition can lead to death [§ 152(c)(3)(B), § 22(e)(3)].

### XII.D.2.a.(3) Residency Test

[513 T.M., III.B.3.c(4); TPS ¶2830.03.A.1.]

To be the qualifying child of a taxpayer, a child must have lived with the taxpayer for more than half the year [§ 152(c)(1)(B)]. However, there are exceptions that apply for (i) temporary absences, (ii) children who were born or died during the year, and (iii) kidnapped children.

*Temporary Absences.* Temporary absences of the taxpayer or the child from the taxpayer's home do not count in determining whether a child lived with the taxpayer for more than half the year. A child is considered to have lived with the taxpayer during periods of time when the child or the taxpayer is temporarily absent due to special circumstances such as illness, education, business, military service, or vacation.

*Child Born or Died During Year.* A child who was born or died during the year is considered to have lived with the taxpayer for more than half the year if the taxpayer's home was the child's home for more than half the time the child was alive during the year. For this purpose, any hospital stay following the birth of the child is not counted. A dependent exemption can be claimed for a child who was born alive and lived only briefly; however, an exemption cannot be claimed for a stillborn child.

*Kidnapped Child.* A child who has been kidnapped is considered to have lived with the taxpayer for more than half the year if [§ 152(f)(6)(A)]:

1. the child is presumed by law enforcement authorities to have been kidnapped by someone who is not a member of the taxpayer's family or the child's family; and

2. in the year of the kidnapping, the child lived with the taxpayer for more than half the portion of the year before the date of the kidnapping.

If these requirements are met, the child is considered to live with the taxpayer for more than half of each year during the period the child is treated as kidnapped. However, treatment of the child as kidnapped ends during the first tax year that begins after the calendar year in which the child is determined to be dead or the calendar year in which the child would have turned age 18, whichever is earlier [§ 152(f)(6)(D)].

### XII.D.2.a.(4) Support Test

[513 T.M., III.B.3.e.; TPS ¶2830.03.A.1.]

To be the qualifying child of a taxpayer, a child cannot provide more than half his or her own support during the year [§ 152(c)(1)(D)]. The total amount of a child's support during a year generally includes amounts spent to provide the child with food, lodging, clothing, education, medical/dental care, recreation, transportation, and similar necessities [Reg. § 1.152-1(a)(2)(i)]. Scholarships received by the child are not taken into account in determining whether the child provided more than half his or her own support [§ 152(f)(5)]. Foster care payments provided by a government agency in support of a child are considered support provided by the government, not the child.

**EXAMPLE:** Alan had a 16-year-old son, Jake, who worked a part-time job. Alan provided $5,000 of his son's support for the year and Jake provided $7,500 of his own support. Jake is not a qualifying child of Alan for the year because Jake provided more than half his own support for the year.

### XII.D.2.a.(5) Filing Test

[513 T.M., III.B.3.c.(1); TPS ¶2830.03.A.1.]

To be the qualifying child of a taxpayer, a child cannot file a joint return with the child's spouse for that year. There is, however, an exception to this rule if the child and the child's spouse file the joint return only for the purpose of claiming a refund of income tax withheld or estimated tax paid [§ 152(c)(1)(E)].

**EXAMPLE:** Harry and Sally are married and file a joint return. They supported their 18-year-old daughter, Sarah, and she lived with them for the entire year while her husband was overseas on military duty. Sarah filed a joint return with her husband for the year. Sarah is not a qualifying child of Harry and Sally since she filed a joint return with her husband.

**EXAMPLE:** Ted and Alice had 17-year-old son, Steve, who was married. Steve and his wife had $800 of wages from part-time jobs and no other income. Although neither Steve nor his wife is required to file a tax return, they file a joint return for the year to claim a refund for taxes that were withheld from their wages. Steve may be a qualifying child of Ted and Alice despite the fact that he is married and filed a joint return with his wife.

### XII.D.2.a.(6) Special Rule When Parents Divorced, Separated, or Living Apart

[513 T.M., III.B.3.h.; TPS ¶2830.03.A.1.]

A child can be the qualifying child of only one taxpayer during any tax year. In most cases in which the parents of a child are divorced, separated, or otherwise living apart during the year, the child will be the qualifying child of the custodial parent as a result of the residency test (see XII.D.2.a.(3)). However, a child may instead be treated as the qualifying child of a noncustodial parent if the custodial parent signs a written declaration that he or she will not claim the child as a dependent for that year. This rule applies only if all of the following requirements are met [§ 152(e)(1); Reg. § 1.152-4(b)]:

1. the parents must either: (i) be divorced or separated under a decree of divorce or separate maintenance, (ii) be separated under a written separation agreement, or (ii) have lived apart at all times during the last six months of the year (this last rule may apply to parents who never married);

2. the child must have received more than half his or her support for the year from the parents; and

3. the child must be in custody of one or both of the parents for more than half the year.

The requirements of this rule are also considered to be met if: (i) a pre-1985 decree of divorce or separate maintenance or written separation agreement provided that the noncustodial parent can claim the child as a dependent, (ii) the provision was not changed after 1984, and (iii) the noncustodial parent provided at least $600 of support for the child during the year [§ 152(e)(3)].

***Custodial Parent.*** The custodial parent is the parent with whom the child lived for the greater number of nights during the calendar year. The other parent is the noncustodial parent [§ 152(e)(4); Reg. § 1.152-4(d)].

***Written Declaration.*** The written declaration of the custodial parent must unconditionally release the custodial parent's claim to the child as a dependent, must specify the years for which it is effective, and must name the noncustodial parent to whom the exemption is released. The custodial parent may use Form 8332, *Release/Revocation of Release of Claim to Exemption for Child by Custodial Parent,* or a similar statement to make the written declaration to release the exemption to the noncustodial parent. The noncustodial parent must attach a copy of that form or statement to his or her return. If a divorce decree or separation agreement went into effect after 1984 and before 2009, the noncustodial parent may be able to attach certain pages from that decree or agreement to the return in lieu of Form 8332 [§ 152(e)(2); Reg. § 1.152-4(e)(1), § 1.152-4(e)(2)].

***Revocation of Written Declaration.*** The custodial parent can revoke a written declaration releasing his or her claim to the child as a dependent by providing written notice of the revocation to the noncustodial parent on Form 8332 or a similar statement. The revocation may not take effect until the calendar year after the calendar year in which the written notice is provided to the noncustodial parent. The custodial parent must attach a copy of the written notice to the return for each tax year for which the custodial parent claims the child as a dependent as a result of the revocation [Reg. § 1.152-4(e)(3)].

***Application of Rule for Other Tax Purposes.*** If a child is treated as a qualifying child of the noncustodial parent under this rule, only the noncustodial parent can claim the dependent exemption and the child tax credit for that child. However, the custodial parent (or other eligible taxpayer) can claim the child as a qualifying child for purposes of head of household filing status (see XII.C.5.), the credit for child and dependent care expenses (see IX.B.1.), the exclusion for dependent care assistance (see XVII.E.2.), and the earned income credit (IX.G.4.) [Reg. § 1.152-4(f)].

### XII.D.2.a.(7) Special Rule When Child Is Qualifying Child of Two or More Taxpayers

[513 T.M., III.B.3.c.(5); TPS ¶2830.03.A.1.]

Only one taxpayer can claim a child as a dependent for a tax year (i.e., the exemption for a child cannot be divided between two or more taxpayers). Thus, if a child is the qualifying child of two or more taxpayers, the following tie-breaker rules apply to determine which taxpayer can claim the child as a dependent [§ 152(c)(4)]:

1. if the taxpayers who can claim the child are parents of the child, the parent with whom the child lived for the longer portion of the year is entitled to the exemption;

2. if the taxpayers who can claim the child are parents of the child and the child lived with each one for an equal amount of time during the year, the parent with the highest adjusted gross income (AGI) for the year is entitled to the exemption;

3. if only one of the taxpayers who can claim the child is a parent of the child, that parent is entitled to the exemption;

4. if one or more of the taxpayers who can claim the child are parents of the child but no parent actually claims the child, the non-parent taxpayer with the highest AGI for the year is entitled to the exemption if his or her AGI is higher than the highest AGI of any parent who can claim the child; or

5. if no parent can claim the child but two or more non-parent taxpayers can claim the child, the taxpayer with the highest AGI is entitled to the exemption.

These tie-breaker rules do not apply to parents who are divorced, separated, or living apart for the last six months of the tax year when the custodial parent of a child has signed a written declaration releasing the child's exemption to the noncustodial parent (see XII.D.2.a.(6)).

---

**EXAMPLE:** Joan and her 5-year-old daughter, Rose, lived with Joan's mother, Lisa, for the entire year. Joan is unmarried and her AGI for the year is $10,000. Lisa's AGI for the year is $15,000. Rose's father did not live with Joan or Rose during the year and Joan has not signed a written declaration releasing Rose's exemption to him. Rose is the qualifying child of both Joan and Lisa (but no one else) during the year. Both Joan and Lisa claim an exemption for Rose for the year. Joan is entitled to the exemption as Rose's parent and Lisa's exemption will be disallowed. Note that if Joan did not claim an exemption for Rose, Lisa would be allowed an exemption for Rose because her AGI is higher than Joan's AGI.

---

### XII.D.2.b. Qualifying Relative

[513 T.M., III.B.3.d.; TPS ¶2830.03.A.2.]

A qualifying relative is a person who meets all three of the following tests [§ 152(d)(1)]:

1. a relationship or household member test (see XII.D.2.b.(1));

2. a gross income test (see XII.D.2.b.(2)); and

3. a support test (see XII.D.2.b.(3)).

A child cannot be a qualifying relative of a taxpayer if the child is a qualifying child of that taxpayer or any other taxpayer (see XII.D.2.a.) [§ 152(d)(1)(D)]. A child is not the qualifying child of another taxpayer who (i) does not file an income tax return because not required to file, or (ii) files an income tax return only for the purpose of claiming an income tax refund of income tax withheld or estimated tax paid.

---

**EXAMPLE:** Henry's 18-year-old daughter, Jane, lives with him and meets all the tests to be his qualifying child. Jane is not Henry's qualifying relative because she is a qualifying child of Henry.

**EXAMPLE:** Assume the same facts as in the previous example, except that Jane instead lives with Henry's parents and meets all the tests to be their qualifying child.

Jane is not Henry's qualifying relative because she is the qualifying child of another taxpayer.

---

If a child's parents are divorced, separated, or living apart and the child is not a qualifying child of either parent, the child may be a qualifying relative of one of the parents (see XII.D.2.b.(4)).

### XII.D.2.b.(1) Relationship or Household Member Test

[513 T.M., III.B.3.d.(2); TPS ¶2830.03.A.2.]

To be a qualifying relative of a taxpayer, a person must either (i) bear a specified relationship to the taxpayer, or (ii) live with the taxpayer for the entire year as a member of the taxpayer's household [§ 152(d)(1)(A), § 152(d)(2)].

*Relationship.* A person can be a qualifying relative of the taxpayer if the person is the taxpayer's: (i) son, daughter, adopted child, stepchild, foster child, or a descendant of any of them, (ii) father, mother, grandparent, or a direct ancestor of any of them, or (iii) brother, sister, aunt, uncle, half brother, half sister, child of half brother or half sister, stepfather, stepmother, stepbrother, stepsister, or a specified in-law (son, daughter, father, mother, brother, or sister) [§ 152(d)(2)]. A qualifying relative also includes a person who bears any of these relationships to the taxpayer's spouse if the taxpayer and spouse file a joint return. Any of these relationships that are established by marriage are not considered to end upon death or divorce. A person who bears one of these relationships to the taxpayer (or his spouse, if filing jointly) need not live with the taxpayer to be a qualifying relative of the taxpayer.

---

**EXAMPLE:** Adam and his wife, Amy, began supporting her elderly father several years ago. Amy's father did not live with them. Amy's father was a qualifying relative of Adam and Amy since the time they began supporting him. Amy died last year, but Adam continues to support her father. Despite Amy's death, Adam's father-in-law continues to be his qualifying relative.

---

*Member of Household.* A person who does not bear one of the above relationships to the taxpayer (or his spouse, if filing jointly) can be a qualifying relative of the taxpayer if the person lives with the taxpayer for the entire year as a member of the taxpayer's household [§ 152(d)(2)(H)]. Thus, a person may be a qualifying relative of a taxpayer without being related to the taxpayer. In determining whether a person lives with the taxpayer for the entire year, temporary absences due to special circumstances (e.g., illness, education, business, military service, or vacation) are not taken into account. A person who lives with the taxpayer from the beginning of the year until his death and a person who lives with the taxpayer from birth through the end of the year (excluding any hospital stay following birth) can be a qualifying relative. However, a person who was the taxpayer's spouse at any time during the year cannot be a qualifying relative of the taxpayer by living with the taxpayer for the entire year. A person who lives with the taxpayer in violation of local law cannot be a qualifying relative [§ 152(f)(3); Reg. § 1.152-1(b)].

### XII.D.2.b.(2) Gross Income Test

[513 T.M., III.B.3.d.(3); TPS ¶2830.03.A.2.]

For a person to be a qualifying relative of the taxpayer, the person's gross income for the calendar year in which the taxpayer's tax year begins must be less than the exemption amount for that year. The exemption amount is $3,950 for 2014 ($4,000 for 2015) [§ 152(d)(1)(B); Rev. Proc. 2014-61, 2014-47 I.R.B. 860].

For purposes of the gross income test, gross income generally includes all income in the form of money, property, and services that is not exempt from tax [§ 61]. However, the gross income of an individual who is permanently and totally disabled at any time during the year does not include income for services the individual performs at a sheltered workshop (as defined in § 152(d)(4)(B)) if: (i) the availability of medical care at the workshop is the main reason for the individual's presence there, and (ii) the income comes solely from activities at the workshop that are incident to such medical care [§ 152(d)(4)].

### XII.D.2.b.(3) Support Test

[513 T.M., III.B.3.e.; TPS ¶2830.03.A.2.]

For a person to be a qualifying relative of the taxpayer, the taxpayer must provide more than half that person's total support during the calendar year in which the taxpayer's tax year begins [§ 152(d)(1)(C)]. If no one provides more than half a person's total support, a taxpayer may be deemed to provide more than half the person's total support under a multiple support agreement [§ 152(d)(3)].

***Total Support.*** To determine if the taxpayer has provided more than half of a person's total support, the amount the taxpayer contributed to that person's support must be compared with the amount of total support the person received from all sources. The total support a person receives from all sources includes amounts spent to provide the person with food, lodging, clothing, education, medical/dental care, recreation, transportation, and similar necessities [Reg. § 1.152-1(a)(2)(i)]. Total support includes the person's own funds used for his or her support. Total support also includes tax-exempt income the person received and used for his or her own support, such as certain social security benefits, welfare benefits, nontaxable life insurance proceeds, Armed Forces allotments, nontaxable pensions, and tax-exempt interest. However, total support does not include scholarships or Survivors' and Dependents' Educational Assistance payments received by the person, even if used for his or her own support [§ 152(f)(5)].

Generally, the amount of an item of support is the amount of the expense incurred in providing that item. In the case of lodging provided as support, the amount of support is the fair rental value of the lodging. In the case of property provided as support, the amount of support is the fair market value of the property [Reg. § 1.152-1(a)(2)(i)].

For purposes of determining a person's total support, expenses not directly related to any one member of the household (e.g., the cost of food) must be divided among the members of the household.

---

**EXAMPLE:** Ralph's parents, Tim and Sue, live with him, his wife, and their only child in a house he owns. Tim receives a tax-exempt pension of $4,200, which he spends equally between Sue and himself on clothing and transportation ($2,100 share for each of Ralph's parents). The fair rental value of the house is $5,000 per year ($1,000 share for each of Ralph's parents) and the food expense of the household is also $5,000 per year ($1,000 share for each of Ralph's parents). Ralph pays $600 of medical expenses for his mother during the year. Ralph provides over half of his mother's total support for the year (($1,000 food + $1,000 lodging + $600 medical expenses) ÷ ($1,000 food + $1,000 lodging + $2,100 clothing and transportation + $600 medical expenses)). Thus, his mother can be a qualifying relative. However,

Ralph provides less than half of his father's total support for the year (($1,000 food + $1,000 lodging) ÷ ($1,000 food + $1,000 lodging + $2,100 clothing and transportation)). Thus, his father cannot be a qualifying relative.

---

*Multiple Support Agreement.* When two or more taxpayers would each be able to take an exemption for a person as a qualifying relative but for the support test (i.e., none of the taxpayers provide more than half the person's support) and the taxpayers together provide more than half the person's support, they may sign a multiple support agreement allowing one, but only one, of the taxpayers to claim a dependent exemption for that person as a qualifying relative. The taxpayer who claims the exemption under the multiple support agreement must have provided more than 10% of the person's support for the year. The other taxpayers must sign a statement agreeing not to claim the exemption for the year. The taxpayer claiming the exemption must attach Form 2120, *Multiple Support Declaration,* or a similar multiple support declaration to his or her return identifying each of the other taxpayers and must keep as records the signed statements of the other taxpayers [§ 152(d)(3)].

---

**EXAMPLE:** Tom, Dick, and Harry are brothers who provide the total support for their mother during the year. Tom and Dick each provide 45% of the support, while Harry provides the remaining 10% of the support. Tom and Dick can agree that one of them will take an exemption for their mother as a qualifying relative by having the other one sign a statement agreeing not to take an exemption. Harry is not eligible to take an exemption for the mother because he does not provide over 10% of her support. Harry does not need to sign any statement.

---

### XII.D.2.b.(4) Special Rule When Parents Divorced, Separated, or Living Apart

[513 T.M., III.B.3.h.; TPS ¶2830.03.A.2.]

In most cases, a child of parents who are divorced, separated, or living apart for the last six months of the year will be a qualifying child of one of the parents (see XII.D.2.a.). However, a child who is not a qualifying child of either parent may instead be a qualifying relative of one of the parents. The child will be a qualifying relative of the custodial parent if the gross income and support tests are both met. However, the child may instead be treated as a qualifying relative of the noncustodial parent if both those tests are met and the custodial parent signs a written declaration that he or she will not claim the child as a dependent for the year [§ 152(e)]. The same rule that applies to a custodial parent's release of a claim to a child as a qualifying child also applies to the release of the claim to a child as a qualifying relative (XII.D.2.a.(6)). However, that rule does not apply when the parents have a multiple support agreement in effect (see XII.D.2.b.(3)) [§ 152(e)(5)].

### XII.D.3. Phaseout of Personal and Dependent Exemptions

[513 T.M., III.B.4.b.; TPS ¶2830.01.C.]

The benefit of the personal and dependent exemptions is reduced for taxpayers with adjusted gross income (AGI) above a beginning phaseout threshold [§ 151(d)(3)]. A taxpayer's exemption amount is reduced by 2% for each $2,500 ($1,250 if married filing separately), or fraction thereof, by which the taxpayer's AGI exceeds the applicable beginning phaseout threshold. The exemption is totally phased out if the taxpayer's AGI exceeds a completed phaseout amount.

The beginning phaseout thresholds and complete phaseout amounts for 2014 are as follows [Rev. Proc. 2013-35, 2013-47 I.R.B. 537]:

| Filing Status | Beginning Phaseout | Completed Phaseout |
|---|---|---|
| Married filing jointly/Surviving spouse | $ 305,050 | $ 427,550 |
| Married filing separately | $ 152,525 | $ 213,775 |
| Single | $ 254,200 | $ 376,700 |
| Head of household | $ 279,650 | $ 402,150 |

The beginning phaseout thresholds and complete phaseout amounts for 2015 are as follows [Rev. Proc. 2014-61, 2014-47 I.R.B. 860]:

| Filing Status | Beginning Phaseout | Completed Phaseout |
|---|---|---|
| Married filing jointly/Surviving spouse | $ 309,900 | $ 432,400 |
| Married filing separately | $ 154,950 | $ 216,200 |
| Single | $ 258,250 | $ 380,750 |
| Head of household | $ 284,050 | $ 406,550 |

**EXAMPLE:** Jim and Jan are married taxpayers filing a joint return for 2014. For the year they have AGI of $330,050 and they claim two personal exemptions totaling $7,900 ($3,950 × 2). Because their AGI exceeds the $305,050 beginning phaseout threshold for taxpayers who are married filing jointly, their exemptions are subject to phaseout. Their exemptions are reduced by 20% ((($330,050 - $305,050)/$2,500)) × 2%). Thus, their exemption amount is $6,320 ($7,900 – ($7,900 × 20%)).

## XII.E. Standard Deduction

[503 T.M., II.B.5.; TPS ¶2820.]

Most individual taxpayers who do not elect to itemize deductions for the tax year may claim a standard deduction. The standard deduction is a fixed amount that may be subtracted from adjusted gross income. The amount of a taxpayer's standard deduction is based on his filing status (see XII.C.). The standard deduction is unlike any other deduction because it does not require a taxpayer to prove that expenditures have been made.

*Choice Between Itemized Deductions and Standard Deduction.* Most individual taxpayers have a choice of itemizing their deductions or taking the standard deduction. Because deductions reduce taxable income, a taxpayer will benefit by choosing to use the method that results in the greatest amount of deductions.

The amount of a taxpayer's itemized deductions is determined by completing Schedule A (Form 1040). Itemized deductions are allowed for expenses such as mortgage interest, taxes, charitable contributions, medical expenses, employee expenses, and similar items (see VII.C.).

The amount of a taxpayer's basic standard deduction is a fixed dollar amount based on a taxpayer's filing status and is adjusted annually for inflation (see XII.E.1.). Taxpayers who are age 65 or older and/or blind generally qualify for an additional standard deduction (see XII.E.2.). The standard deduction for a taxpayer who can be claimed as a dependent on another taxpayer's return is generally limited (see XII.E.3.) [§ 63(c)].

Although the choice to use the standard deduction generally eliminates the need for a taxpayer to track expenses and apply the sometimes complex rules for the various types of itemized deductions, it is generally beneficial for a taxpayer to at least make an estimate as to whether his or her itemized deductions would be greater than the standard deduction.

*Taxpayers Ineligible for Standard Deduction.* The following types of taxpayers are not eligible for the standard deduction (i.e., their standard deduction is zero) and they should itemize their deductions [§ 63(c)(6)]:

- a married taxpayer who uses married filing separately filing status and whose spouse itemizes deductions on his or her return;

- a taxpayer who files a return for a short tax year due to a change in his or her annual accounting period; and

- a taxpayer who is a nonresident alien, unless he or she is married to a U.S. citizen or resident and elects to be treated as a resident alien (see XII.A.1.).

### XII.E.1. Basic Standard Deduction

[503 T.M., II.B.5.c.(1); TPS ¶2820.01.]

The basic standard deduction amount depends on a taxpayer's filing status (see XII.C.) and is adjusted annually for inflation [§ 63(c)(2)]. The basic standard deduction amounts for 2014 and 2015 are as follows [Rev. Proc. 2013-35, 2013-47 I.R.B. 537, Rev. Proc. 2014-61, 2014-47 I.R.B. 860]:

| Filing Status | 2014 Amount | 2015 Amount |
|---|---|---|
| Single or Married Filing Separately | $ 6,200 | $ 6,300 |
| Married Filing Jointly or Surviving Spouse | $ 12,400 | $ 12,600 |
| Head of Household | $ 9,100 | $ 9,250 |

### XII.E.2. Additional Standard Deduction for Elderly and Blind

[503 T.M., II.B.5.c.(3); TPS ¶2820.02.]

Taxpayers who are age 65 or older and/or blind may qualify for additional standard deductions on top of the basic standard deduction [§ 63(c)(3), § 63(f)]. The additional standard deduction amount is $1,200 for 2014 ($1,250 for 2015) if the taxpayer's filing status is married filing separately, married filing jointly, or surviving spouse, and $1,550 for 2014 ($1,550 for 2015) if the taxpayer's filing status is single or head of household [Rev. Proc. 2013-35, 2013-47 I.R.B. 537, Rev. Proc. 2014-61, 2014-47 I.R.B. 860].

*Additional Standard Deduction for Age.* A taxpayer must be age 65 on the last day of the year to qualify for the additional standard deduction for age. A taxpayer is considered to turn age 65 on the day before his 65th birthday.

---

**EXAMPLE:** Jill is a single taxpayer filing a tax return for 2014. She was born on Jan. 1, 1950. Jill can take a $1,550 additional standard deduction for age on her 2014 return because she is considered to have turned age 65 on Dec. 31, 2014.

---

*Additional Standard Deduction for Blindness.* A taxpayer must be blind on the last day of the year to qualify for the additional standard deduction for blindness. If a taxpayer is not totally blind, he must obtain a certified statement from an ophthalmologist or optometrist stating that (i) he cannot see better than 20/200 in the better eye with glasses or contact lenses, (ii) his field of vision is 20 degrees or less, or (iii) his vision can be corrected beyond these limits by contact lenses but he can only wear them for brief periods due to pain, infection, or ulcers. The taxpayer should keep the statement for his records [§ 63(f)(4)].

*Determining Amount of Additional Standard Deductions.* Age and blindness are two separate categories for purposes of the additional standard deduction. A taxpayer is allowed an additional standard deduction amount for each category into which he or she falls and, if he or she is married filing jointly or he or she is married filing separately and can claim an exemption for his or her spouse, each category into which the spouse falls. For example, a taxpayer and spouse who file a joint return may take four additional standard deductions if they are both age 65 or older and they are both blind. Thus, for 2014 and 2015, the following standard deductions apply for taxpayers who are age 65 or older and/or blind [Rev. Proc. 2013-35, 2013-47 I.R.B. 537, Rev. Proc. 2014-61, 2014-47 I.R.B. 860]:

| Filing Status | Categories | 2014 Amount | 2015 Amount |
|---|---|---|---|
| Single | 1 | $ 7,750 | $ 7,850 |
| Single | 2 | $ 9,300 | $ 9,400 |
| Head of Household | 1 | $ 10,650 | $ 10,800 |
| Head of Household | 2 | $ 12,200 | $ 12,350 |
| Married Filing Jointly or Surviving Spouse | 1 | $ 13,600 | $ 13,850 |
| Married Filing Jointly or Surviving Spouse | 2 | $ 14,800 | $ 15,100 |
| Married Filing Jointly or Surviving Spouse | 3 | $ 16,000 | $ 16,350 |
| Married Filing Jointly or Surviving Spouse | 4 | $ 17,200 | $ 17,600 |
| Married Filing Separately | 1 | $ 7,400 | $ 7,550 |
| Married Filing Separately | 2 | $ 8,600 | $ 8,800 |
| Married Filing Separately | 3 | $ 9,800 | $ 10,050 |
| Married Filing Separately | 4 | $ 11,000 | $ 11,300 |

**EXAMPLE:** Matt, 66, and Sarah, 58, are married and file a joint return for 2014. Neither is blind and neither can be claimed as a dependent of another taxpayer. They decide not to itemize their deductions for the year. Their standard deduction is $13,600 (basic standard deduction of $12,400 plus additional standard deduction of $1,200 because Matt is 65 or older).

**EXAMPLE:** Assume the same facts as in the previous example, except that Matt and Sarah are both blind. Their standard deduction is $16,000 (basic standard deduction of $12,400 plus three additional standard deductions of $1,200).

### XII.E.3. Standard Deduction for Dependents

[503 T.M., II.B.5.c.(2); TPS ¶2820.01.B.]

*Basic Standard Deduction for Dependents.* The basic standard deduction of an individual who may be claimed as a dependent on another taxpayer's return (whether or not actually claimed) may be limited. The basic standard deduction for such an individual for 2014 (and 2015) is generally limited to the greater of [§ 63(c)(5); Rev. Proc. 2013-35, 2013-47 I.R.B. 537, Rev. Proc. 2014-61, 2014-47 I.R.B. 860]:

- $1,000 ($1,050 for 2015); or
- the individual's earned income plus $350 ($350 for 2015).

For this purpose, earned income includes salaries, wages, tips, professional fees, and other amounts received by the individual for works he actually performs. It also includes any part of a scholarship or fellowship grant that must be included in the individual's gross income.

**EXAMPLE:** Tim is a 23-year-old single taxpayer who can be claimed as a dependent on his parents' tax return. For 2014, he has wages of $500, interest income of $800, and no itemized deductions. His standard deduction for 2014 is $1,000 because that amount is greater than his earned income of $500 plus $350.

**EXAMPLE:** Assume the same facts as in the previous example, except that Tim's wages for 2014 are $4,000 (instead of $500). His standard deduction for 2014 is $4,350 (his $4,000 earned income plus $350) because that amount is greater than $1,000.

*Additional Standard Deductions for Dependents.* If an individual who can be claimed as a dependent on another taxpayer's return is 65 or older and/or blind, his standard deduction is increased by the applicable additional standard deduction amount (see XII.E.2.).

**EXAMPLE:** Assume the same facts as in the previous example, except that Tim is also blind. His standard deduction for the year is $5,900 (the $4,350 basic standard deduction plus the $1,550 additional standard deduction amount for blindness).

**Standard Deduction Worksheet for Dependents—Line 40**       *Keep for Your Records*

Use this worksheet **only** if someone can claim you, or your spouse if filing jointly, as a dependent.

| | |
|---|---|
| 1. | Is your **earned income*** more than $650? |
| | ☐ **Yes.** Add $350 to your earned income. Enter the total |
| | ☐ **No.** Enter $1,000         } ........................... 1. _____ |
| 2. | Enter the amount shown below for your filing status. |
| | • Single or married filing separately—$6,200 |
| | • Married filing jointly or qualifying widow(er)—$12,400    } ........................... 2. _____ |
| | • Head of household—$9,100 |
| 3. | **Standard deduction.** |
| | a. Enter the **smaller** of line 1 or line 2. If born after January 1, 1950, and not blind, **stop here** and enter this amount on Form 1040, line 40. Otherwise, go to line 3b ........................... 3a. _____ |
| | b. If born before January 2, 1950, or blind, multiply the number on Form 1040, line 39a, by $1,200 ($1,550 if single or head of household) ........................... 3b. _____ |
| | c. Add lines 3a and 3b. Enter the total here and on Form 1040, line 40 ........................... 3c. _____ |

\* *Earned income includes wages, salaries, tips, professional fees, and other compensation received for personal services you performed. It also includes any taxable scholarship or fellowship grant. Generally, your earned income is the total of the amount(s) you reported on Form 1040, lines 7, 12, and 18, minus the amount, if any, on line 27.*

(Source: 2014 Form 1040 Draft Instructions)

## XII.F. Estimated Taxes for Individuals

### XII.F.1. Liability for Estimated Tax

[581 T.M., II.A.; TPS ¶3330.01.A.1.]

Estimated tax is the method used to pay tax on income that is not subject to withholding. Estimated tax is used to pay income tax and self-employment tax, the additional Medicare tax, as well as other taxes and amounts reported on a taxpayer's tax return. This includes income from interest, dividends, alimony, rent, gains from sales of assets, and prizes and awards. Taxpayers may have to pay estimated tax if the amount of income tax withheld from their salary, pension, or other income is not enough.

The Code does not specifically define the term "estimated tax" as it relates to individuals, but rather it imposes an addition to tax (i.e., a penalty) if an individual fails to prepay sufficient amounts of his or her income tax liability for the current tax year. Accordingly, estimated tax may be defined as the minimum amount of payment required to be made to avoid the imposition of that penalty. Any individual who would otherwise be subject to the penalty must make installment payments of estimated tax. Accordingly, estimated tax payments are not required where the amount of income tax withheld at the source by an employer or other payer equals or exceeds the minimum amount of payments otherwise required. For example, if an individual's income consists entirely or predominantly of wages, the employer usually withholds sufficient tax so that estimated tax payments are not required [§ 6654(a)].

No penalty is imposed for underpayment of estimated tax if the tax shown on the return (or if no return is filed, the tax) for the tax year, reduced by the credit for income taxes withheld, is less than $1,000 [§ 6654(e)(1)]. The penalty for underpayment of estimated tax also is not imposed for any tax year if all the following conditions are met [§ 6654(e)(2)]:

1. the preceding tax year is a 12-month period;

2. the individual does not have any liability for tax for the preceding tax year; and

3. the individual is a U.S. citizen or resident throughout the entire preceding tax year.

In addition, the IRS may waive the underpayment of estimated tax penalty [§ 6654(e)(3)]:

- if by reason of casualty, disaster, or other unusual circumstances it would be against equity and good conscience to impose the penalty; or

- when the individual retires or becomes disabled and the underpayment was due to reasonable cause.

### XII.F.2. Due Dates for Estimated Tax Payments

[581 T.M., II.A.4.; TPS ¶3330.01.A.3.]

Most individuals who are required to pay estimated tax must do so in four installments. Subject to certain exceptions and special rules described below, for calendar year taxpayers the payments are due on April 15, June 15, and September 15 of the tax year, and January 15 of the succeeding tax year. For fiscal year taxpayers, the due dates are the 15th day of each of the fourth, sixth, and ninth months of the fiscal year, and the first month of the succeeding fiscal year [§ 6654(c), § 6654(k)]. In lieu of paying the January 15 installment, an individual may avoid an estimated tax penalty by filing his or her income tax return for the tax year and paying in full the amount of tax shown on the return as payable on or before January 31 [§ 6654(h)].

When an estimated tax payment is due on a Saturday, Sunday, or legal holiday, the payment may be made on the next succeeding business day [§ 7503; Reg. § 301.7503-1(b)].

Special provisions apply to the payment of estimated tax by individuals who qualify as farmers or fishermen. Instead of paying estimated tax in installments, a farmer or fisherman may pay the entire amount required to be paid as estimated tax in a single installment on January 15 of the succeeding tax year. Alternatively, a farmer or fisherman can skip the payment of any estimated tax and file the return and pay the entire tax due on March 1 of the succeeding tax year [§ 6654(h), § 6654(i)(1)].

Nonresident alien individuals (other than those whose wages are subject to U.S. income tax withholding) are not required to make their first installment payment of estimated tax until June 15, and must pay their estimated tax in three, rather than four, installments. The remaining two installments are due on September 15 and January 15 [§ 6654(j)].

For an individual serving in the U.S. Armed Forces (or in support of the Armed Forces) or in qualifying deployment in a contingency operation, the time period for the payment of estimated tax may be postponed [§ 7508(a)]. The IRS also may grant a postponement of the time for paying estimated tax by up to one year for individuals affected by a federally declared disaster or a terroristic or military action [§ 7508A(a)].

Upon application to the IRS showing undue hardship, an individual may be granted a reasonable extension of time to pay his estimated tax. Such extension cannot exceed six months unless the individual is abroad. The extension is of limited use, however, because it does not relieve the individual from the penalty imposed for underpayment of estimated tax. The application for extension is made on Form 1127, *Application for Extension of Time for Payment of Tax* [§ 6161(a)(1); Reg. § 1.6161-1].

### XII.F.3. *Calculating Estimated Tax Payments*

[581 T.M., II.A.5.; TPS ¶3330.01.A.4.a.]

To determine the amount of the estimated tax payments an individual is required to make, the individual's tax liability must be computed. For this purpose, an individual's "tax" is the sum of income tax and self-employment tax, reduced by the credits allowed against income tax (other than the credit for taxes withheld from wages) [§ 6654(f)].

The amount of any installment of estimated tax required to be paid is the lowest of the amounts computed under one of three alternatives discussed below. Different alternatives may be used to compute the amount of different installments for the same tax year. An even lower amount may be payable if an exception to the underpayment penalty applies. Generally, the amount of any required installment is 25% of the required annual payment [§ 6654(d), § 6654(e)]. The term "required annual payment" means the lesser of [§ 6654(d)(1)(B)]:

- 90% of the tax shown on the individual's return for the tax year (or, if no return is filed, 90% of the tax for such year) (Alternative 1); or
- 100% of the tax shown on the return of the individual for the preceding tax year (Alternative 2).

### XII.F.3.a. *Alternative 1 — Tax Shown on Current Year's Return*

[581 T.M., II.A.5.b.; TPS ¶3330.01.A.4.b.]

Under Alternative 1, the amount of each quarterly installment required to be paid is 22.5% (25% x 90%) of the tax shown on the individual's income tax return for the tax year, or 22.5% of the actual tax due for the year if no return is filed. Nonresident alien individuals who are allowed to pay their estimated tax in three installments must pay 45% (50% x 90%) of the current year tax for the first installment and 22.5% for each of the next two installments. The "tax shown on the return" means the tax shown on a timely filed original return for the year, and not the tax ultimately determined to be due on an amended return or as a result of an audit [§ 6654(d)(1)(A), § 6654(d)(1)(B)(i), § 6654(j)(3)(A)].

### XII.F.3.b. Alternative 2 — Tax Shown on Prior Year's Return

[581 T.M., II.A.5.c.; TPS ¶3330.01.A.4.c.]

Alternative 2 requires quarterly installment payments generally equal to 25% (25% x 100%) of the tax shown on the individual's return for the preceding tax year. However, if the individual's adjusted gross income as shown on the tax return for the preceding tax year exceeds $150,000 ($75,000 for a married individual who files a separate tax return for the current year), the amount of the required installment is increased to 27.5% (25% x 110%) of the tax shown on the prior year's return. The amount of the first installment is doubled for nonresident aliens who pay tax in three installments. Alternative 2 can be used only if the preceding tax year was a 12-month period, and a return was filed for that year [§ 6654(d)(1)(B), § 6654(d)(1)(C), § 6654(j)(3)(A)].

### XII.F.3.c. Alternative 3 — Tax on Annualized Income

[581 T.M., II.A.5.d.; TPS ¶3330.01.A.4.d.]

Under Alternative 3, the amount of each required installment is equal to the excess, if any, of [§ 6654(d)(2)(B)]:

1. the "applicable percentage" of the tax for the tax year, computed by placing on an annualized basis the individual's taxable income, alternative minimum taxable income, and "adjusted self-employment income" for the months in the tax year ending before the due date of the installment; over

2. the aggregate amount of any prior required installments for the tax year.

The "applicable percentage" of the tax is 22.5%, 45%, 67.5%, and 90% for the first, second, third, and fourth installment payments, respectively. For a nonresident alien individuals who pay estimated tax in three installments, the applicable percentage is 45%, 67.5%, and 90%, respectively [§ 6654(d)(2)(C)(ii), § 6654(j)(3)(B)].

An individual's taxable income for a period is placed on an annual basis by annualizing the individual's adjusted gross income and subtracting his annualized itemized deductions or standard deduction, whichever is greater, and his personal exemptions, determined as of the due date of the installment payment. Adjusted gross income and itemized deductions are annualized by dividing such amounts for the months in the tax year that end before the due date of the installment by the number of such calendar months and multiplying the result by 12. Similarly, alternative minimum taxable income (AMTI) is computed by annualizing the AMTI (computed without regard to the exemption amount) for such period and then subtracting the applicable exemption amount. The annualized adjusted self-employment income required to be taken into account is the annualized net income from self-employment for the months in the individual's tax year that end before the installment's due date; provided, however, that for purposes of computing the old age, survivors, and disability (OASDI) portion of the tax, self-employment income is limited to the excess of the computation base for the tax year over the annualized amount of wages paid to the taxpayer during the installment period [§ 6654(d)(2)(B), § 6654(d)(2)(C); Reg. § 1.6654-2(a)(2)].

### XII.F.3.d. Estimated Tax Treatment of Married Couples

[581 T.M., II.A.5.e.; TPS ¶3330.01.A.4.e.]

Spouses may compute their estimated tax requirements individually or jointly. Joint payments are based on the spouses' joint income and deductions, and the sum of their separate self-employment taxes. Joint payments, however, cannot be made if one of the following applies:

- either spouse is a nonresident alien (including a nonresident alien who is a bona fide resident of Puerto Rico or a possession to which § 931 applies during the entire tax year), unless such person elects under § 6013(g) or § 6013(h) to be treated as a U.S. resident for the entire tax year;
- the spouses are separated under a decree of divorce or separate maintenance; or
- the spouses have different tax years.

The manner of paying estimated tax does not affect the taxpayers' choice whether to file a joint return or separate returns [§ 6013(a), § 7703(a)(2)].

### XII.F.4. How to Pay Estimated Tax

[581 T.M., II.C.; TPS ¶3330.01.C.]

Payments of estimated tax may be made by any commercially acceptable means. These include payments by check or money order. An individual also may remit estimated tax payments by electronic funds transfer (EFT) or by credit or debit card [§ 6311(a), § 6311(e)(3); Reg. § 301.6311-1(a)(1)(i), § 301.6311-2].

**Payment by Check or Money Order.** Checks and money orders should be accompanied by a payment voucher from Form 1040-ES. Once a taxpayer files his first estimated tax payment-voucher, the IRS generally furnishes pre-printed vouchers with the taxpayer's name, address, and social security number imprinted. Payments of estimated tax, together with the appropriate payment-voucher, must be mailed to the IRS at the post office box for the location in which the taxpayer legally resides. Because only the U.S. Postal Service can deliver to a post office box; private delivery services cannot be used. Payments should not be sent to the same address to which the individual sends his tax return.

An estimated tax payment by check or money order is considered made when received by the IRS at the proper address. The payment of an estimated tax installment is also considered timely made if the envelope containing the payment bears a timely postmark, even though it is received by the IRS after the due date prescribed for payment, provided the payment is actually received and accounted for. If the payment is sent by U.S. registered or certified mail, the registration date or the date of the postmark on the taxpayer's certified mail receipt is treated as the postmark date on the envelope [§ 7502(a), § 7502(c)(1)(B), § 7502(d)(2); Reg. § 301.7502-1(c)(2)].

**Payment by EFT or Credit or Debit Card.** EFT payments are considered deposited when the funds are withdrawn from the taxpayer's account, provided the amount is not returned or reversed. Payments by credit card or debit card are deemed made when the issuer of the card properly authorizes the transaction, provided the payment is actually received by the IRS in the ordinary course of business and is not returned pursuant to error resolution procedures [Reg. § 1.6302-4, § 31.6302-1(h)(8), § 301.6311-2(b)].

# CHAPTER XIII. C CORPORATIONS

>>>>>>>>>>>>>>>>>>>>>>>>>>>>>>

## XIII.A. Introduction

A C corporation is treated as an entity that is separate from its owners for legal purposes. As a result, the shareholders of a C corporation are at risk only for the amounts they have invested in the corporation, i.e., they have limited liability. However, this treatment of a C corporation as a separate entity results in a double tax on its earnings for federal income tax purposes. The earnings are first taxed at the corporate level and then, after the earnings are distributed to the shareholders as dividends, they are taxed again at the shareholder level. Thus, the choice to use a C corporation as the entity for operating a business has both advantages and disadvantages (see Chapter XVI. for further discussion of the advantages and disadvantages of operating a business as a C corporation).

A C corporation should be distinguished from an S corporation, which is treated as a pass-through entity that is not separate from its owners (see Chapter XV. for a detailed discussion of S corporations). However, to simplify the discussion of C corporations, a C corporation will simply be referred to as a "corporation" throughout the remainder of this chapter.

## XIII.B. Formation of Corporation

[758 T.M.; TPS ¶4710.]

A corporation is generally formed when one or more persons transfer money and/or property to the corporation in exchange for stock in the corporation.

### XIII.B.1. Nonrecognition Rule for Property Transfers to Corporations

[758 T.M.; TPS ¶¶4610.03.A., 4710.01.]

When persons transfer property to a corporation solely in exchange for stock in the corporation and those persons are in control of the corporation immediately after the exchange, no gain or loss is recognized on the transfer [§ 351(a)]. This § 351 nonrecognition treatment applies whether the corporation is being formed or is already operating.

---

**EXAMPLE:** Steve transfers property worth $20,000 to a corporation in exchange for $20,000 of stock in the corporation. He is in control of the corporation immediately after the exchange. Steve does not recognize any gain or loss on the transfer of property to the corporation.

---

Section 351 nonrecognition treatment applies to transfers of property to a corporation by individuals, trusts, estates, partnerships, associations, companies, and other corporations [Reg. § 1.351-1(a)]. However, it does not apply to: (i) a transfer of property to a corporation that is an investment company, or (ii) a transfer of property in a bankruptcy or similar proceeding where the stock received in the exchange is used to pay the transferor's creditors [§ 351(e); Reg. § 1.351-1(c)].

When two or more persons transfer property to a corporation in exchange for stock, the exchange may qualify for § 351 nonrecognition treatment even if each transferor does not receive stock in proportion to his interest in the property transferred. However, such a disproportionate transfer will be treated according to its true nature for tax purposes. Thus, for example, the transfer may be treated as if the stock were first received in proportion and then some of it was used to make gifts, pay compensation for services, or satisfy the transferor's obligations [Reg. § 1.351-1(b)].

### XIII.B.1.a. Property

[758 T.M., III.B.; TPS ¶4710.01.B.2.]

Section 351 nonrecognition treatment generally applies to a transfer of any type of property in exchange for stock. Thus, it applies to a transfer of real property, personal property, or intangible property. However, nonrecognition treatment does not apply when stock is issued in exchange for: (i) services, (ii) debt of the corporation that is not evidenced by a security, or (iii) accrued interest on debt of the corporation. These items are not considered to be property for purposes of the nonrecognition rule [§ 351(d); Reg. § 1.351-1(a)(1)(i)].

---

**EXAMPLE:** Donna transfers property worth $20,000 and renders services valued at $5,000 to a corporation in exchange for $25,000 of stock in the corporation. She is in control of the corporation immediately after the exchange. Donna does not recognize any gain or loss on the transfer of property to the corporation but she must include $5,000 in income as an amount received for services rendered to the corporation.

---

Nonrecognition treatment also does not apply when the property transferred by a person is of a relatively small value in comparison to the value of the stock or securities already owned by the person and the primary purpose of the transfer is to qualify the property transfers of other persons for nonrecognition treatment [Reg. § 1.351-1(a)(1)(ii)]. Under a safe harbor rule, the property transferred will not be considered to be of a relatively small value if its fair market value is at least 10% of the fair market value of the stock or securities already owned.

### XIII.B.1.b. Stock

[758 T.M., III.H.; TPS ¶4710.01.B.6.]

Section 351 nonrecognition treatment applies when property is transferred solely in exchange for stock. For this purpose, stock generally includes common stock (whether voting or nonvoting) and qualified preferred stock. It does not include nonqualified preferred stock, stock rights, stock warrants, or securities [§ 351(g)(1); Reg. § 1.351-1(a)(1)].

Nonqualified preferred stock is preferred stock that has any of the following features: (i) the holder has a right to require the issuer or a related person to redeem or buy the stock; (ii) the issuer or a related person is required to redeem or buy the stock; (iii) the issuer or a related person has the right to redeem or buy the stock and, on the issue date, it is more likely than not that the right will be exercised; or (iv) the dividend rate on the stock varies with reference to interest rates, commodity prices, or similar indices [§ 351(g)(2)].

### XIII.B.1.c. Control

[758 T.M., III.E.; TPS ¶4710.01.B.8.]

Section 351 nonrecognition treatment applies only when the persons who transfer property to a corporation in exchange for its stock are in control of the corporation immediately after the exchange. Persons are considered in control of the corporation if they own at least 80% of the total combined voting power and at least 80% of the outstanding shares of each class of nonvoting stock [§ 368(c); Reg. § 1.351-1(a)(1)].

---

**EXAMPLE:** Fred and Mary organize a new corporation and transfer property they own to the corporation in exchange for all of its stock. At the time of the exchange, the property has a fair market value of $400,000 with a basis of $200,000 and the stock has a par value of $400,000. No gain is recognized by Fred or Mary.

**EXAMPLE:** Assume the same facts as in the previous example, except that the corporation is already operating and already owned by a current owner, and Fred and Mary transfer the same property in exchange for 75% of each class of the corporation's stock (i.e., the current owner's stock interest is reduced to 25%). The stock received by Fred and Mary has a total fair market value of $400,000. Fred and Mary must recognize a $200,000 gain on the exchange ($400,000 value of stock received − $200,000 basis in property transferred) because they are not in control of the corporation immediately after the exchange.

---

### XIII.B.2. Receipt of Boot in Transfer of Property to Corporation

[758 T.M., IV.; TPS ¶4710.01.D.1.b.]

If persons transferring property to a corporation receive money or other property ("boot") in addition to stock in an exchange that would otherwise qualify for § 351 nonrecognition treatment, they must recognize gain to the extent of the value of the boot received (i.e., the amount of money received plus the fair market value of other property received). No loss is recognized on the receipt of boot [§ 351(b); Reg. § 1.351-2].

---

**EXAMPLE:** Pam transfers property with a fair market value of $40,000 and an adjusted basis of $25,000 to a corporation in exchange for stock worth $30,000, property worth $6,000, and $4,000 of cash. Pam is in control of the corporation immediately after the exchange. Pam realizes a gain of $15,000 ($40,000 FMV − $25,000 adjusted basis) on the exchange, but she only recognizes gain to the extent of the boot she receives in the exchange. Thus, Pam recognizes a gain of $10,000 on the exchange ($6,000 FMV of property received $4,000 of money received).

---

The receipt of nonqualified preferred stock, stock warrants, stock rights, or securities is treated as the receipt of boot, not stock. For a discussion of what qualifies as the receipt of stock for purposes of the § 351 nonrecognition rule, see XIII.B.1.b.

### XIII.B.3. Assumption of Liabilities in Transfer of Property to Corporation

[758 T.M., IV.; TPS ¶4710.01.D.1.c.]

If a corporation assumes the liabilities of a person transferring property in exchange for its stock, the assumption of the liabilities by the corporation generally is not treated as boot received by the transferor [§ 357(a)]. There are, however, two exceptions to this rule:

- If the principal purpose of the assumption of liabilities is to avoid federal income tax on the exchange or is not a bona fide business purpose, the assumption of the liabilities is treated as boot [§ 357(b)].

- If the amount of the liabilities assumed by the corporation exceeds the transferor's adjusted basis in the property transferred, then the transferor must recognize gain for the excess amount (unless the liabilities assumed would give rise to a deduction when paid) [§ 357(c)].

---

**EXAMPLE:** Donald transfers property with a fair market value of $31,000, an adjusted basis of $20,000 and a mortgage of $5,000 to a corporation in exchange for stock worth $20,000 and $6,000 cash. Donald is personally liable on the mortgage and, as part of the exchange, the corporation assumes the mortgage. Immediately after the exchange, Donald is in control of the corporation. Donald realizes a gain of $11,000 on the exchange (($20,000 FMV of stock received $6,000 cash received $5,000 liability assumed) − $20,000 adjusted basis in property). Although the $6,000 cash is treated as boot, the $5,000 liability is not (note that the liability does not exceed Donald's adjusted basis in the property). Thus, Donald recognizes a gain of only $6,000 on the exchange.

---

### XIII.B.4. Tax Treatment of Transferors

[758 T.M., VII.B.; TPS ¶4710.01.D.]

As discussed in XIII.B.1., no gain or loss is recognized by persons that transfer property to a corporation solely in exchange for its stock if they are in control of the corporation immediately after the exchange. A person's basis in stock received in a § 351 transaction is equal to its adjusted basis in the property transferred to the corporation, decreased by the amount of any money and the fair market value of any other property received from the corporation, and increased by the amount of any gain recognized [§ 358(a)(1)]. A person's basis in any boot received from the corporation in a § 351 transaction is equal to the fair market value of the boot on the date of the exchange [§ 358(a)(2)].

### XIII.B.5. Tax Treatment of Corporation

[758 T.M., VII.C.; TPS ¶4710.01.E.]

No gain or loss is recognized by a corporation upon the receipt of money or property in exchange for its stock [§ 1032(a)]. Generally, a corporation that receives property in a § 351 nonrecognition transaction takes a basis in the property equal to the basis of the property in the hands of the person who transferred the property to the corporation, increased by the amount of any gain recognized by that person [§ 362(a)]. However, this increase for the gain recognized by the transferor is limited to the fair market value of the property if the gain is attributable to the assumption of a liability [§ 362(d)].

### *XIII.B.6. Reporting Requirements in Transfer of Property to Corporation*

[759 T.M., VIII.; TPS ¶4710.01.G.]

If § 351 nonrecognition treatment applies to a transfer of property in exchange for stock, the corporation and certain persons transferring property to the corporation (transferors) are required to file a statement with their tax return for the tax year of the transaction that includes the following information [Reg. § 1.351-3(a), § 1.351-3(b)]:

- the name and taxpayer identification number of the corporation (reported by the transferors) or each transferor (reported by the corporation);
- the date of the transfer of assets;
- the aggregate fair market value and basis of the property transferred as of the date of the exchange; and
- the date and control number of any private letter ruling issued by the IRS in connection with the exchange.

Transferors subject to these reporting requirements are persons that transferred property in exchange for stock and, immediately after the exchange, owned at least 1% of the outstanding stock of the corporation by vote and value (5% if the stock of the corporation is publicly traded) [Reg. § 1.351-3(d)(1)].

## XIII.C. Taxation of a Corporation

### *XIII.C.1. Corporation Filing Requirements*

#### *XIII.C.1.a. Who Must File Corporation Return*

[750 T.M., II.; TPS ¶3820.02.B.1.]

All domestic corporations other than tax-exempt corporations are required to file an income tax return for a tax year, whether or not they have taxable income for the year [§ 6012; Reg. § 1.6012-2].

#### *XIII.C.1.b. Form to File Corporation Return*

[750 T.M., II.A.; TPS ¶¶3820.02.B.1., 4610.04.A.]

A corporation generally must file Form 1120, *U.S. Corporation Income Tax Return*, to report income, gains, losses, deductions, and credits, and to calculate income tax liability. However, certain corporations are required to file special returns. For example, S corporations file Form 1120S, insurance companies file Form 1120-L or Form 1120-PC, and foreign corporations file Form 1120-F.

Certain entities may elect to be classified as an association taxable as a corporation. For example, although an LLC generally is treated as a partnership if it has more than one owner and is disregarded as an entity separate from its owner if it has only one owner, an LLC may elect to be classified as an association taxable as a corporation. An LLC or any other entity that makes an election to be classified as an association taxable as a corporation must file Form 1120 and attach Form 8832, *Entity Classification Election*, for the year of the election.

Form 1120 must be signed and dated by the president, vice president, treasurer, assistant treasurer, chief accounting officer, or any other corporate officer authorized to sign the return. It may be signed by a receiver or bankruptcy trustee if such fiduciary has possession of or holds title to substantially all the property or business of a corporation [§ 6062, § 6012(b)(3)].

Corporations generally have the option of filing either a paper Form 1120 or an electronic Form 1120. However, a corporation is required to file all returns (including Form 1120) electronically if it has assets of $10 million or more and it is required to file at least 250 federal returns of all types during the calendar year that ends with or within its tax year [Reg. § 301.6011-5, § 301.6037-2].

An affiliated group of corporations may elect to file a consolidated Form 1120 for all group members instead of separate Form 1120 for each group member. See XIII.C.8. for a discussion of consolidated returns.

### XIII.C.1.c. When to File Corporation Return

[750 T.M., II.A.; TPS ¶4610.04.A.]

*Due Date of Return.* A corporation is required to file its return by the 15th day of the 3rd month after the end of its tax year. However, if the due date falls on a Saturday, Sunday, or legal holiday, the due date is extended to the next business day [§ 6072(b), § 7503].

---

**EXAMPLE:** Alpha Corporation is a calendar year taxpayer. It generally must file its return by March 15th. However, if March 15th falls on a Saturday, it must file its return by March 17th.

**EXAMPLE:** Beta Corporation is a fiscal year taxpayer with a tax year ending June 30. It generally must file its return by September 15th. However, if September 15th falls on a Sunday, it must file its return by September 16th.

---

A new corporation filing a short-period return generally must file by the 15th day of the 3rd month after the date the short period ends. A corporation that dissolved during the year generally must file by the 15th day of the 3rd month after the date it dissolved.

*Extension of Time to File Return.* A corporation can receive a 6-month automatic extension of time to file its return by filing Form 7004, *Application for Automatic Extension of Time To File Certain Business Income Tax, Information and Other Returns.* However, an extension of time to file the return does not extend the time to pay the tax due on the return [§ 6081(a); Reg. § 1.6081-3].

*Penalty for Late Filing of Return.* A corporation that does not file its return by the due date (including extensions) is subject to a penalty equal to 5% of the unpaid tax for each month or part of a month the return is late, up to a maximum of 25%. If a return is over 60 days late, the minimum penalty is the smaller of the tax due or $135. The late filing penalty is reduced by the amount of any penalty for late payment of tax (see XIII.C.1.d. for a discussion of the late payment penalty). The late filing penalty is not imposed if the corporation can prove that the failure to file in time was due to a reasonable cause [§ 6651(a)(1); Reg. § 301.6651-1(a)(1)].

### XIII.C.1.d. Payment of Corporation Income Tax

[750 T.M., II.; TPS ¶3820.02.H.]

*Date and Method of Payment.* A corporation is required to pay the tax due on its return in full no later than the original due date of its return (i.e., by the 15th day of the 3rd month after the end of its tax year). Corporations must use electronic funds transfer to deposit all federal taxes, including income taxes. Deposits are generally made using the Electronic Federal Tax Payment System (EFTPS), a free service provided by the Department of Treasury. However, deposits may also be made through a third party, such as a tax professional, financial institution, or payroll service [Reg. § 1.6302-1, § 31.6302-1(h)].

***Penalty for Late Payment of Tax.*** A corporation that does not pay its tax when due is subject to a penalty equal to 0.5% of the unpaid tax for each month or part of a month the tax is not paid, up to a maximum of 25%. The late payment penalty is not imposed if the corporation can prove that the failure to pay in time was due to a reasonable cause [§ 6651(a)(2); Reg. § 301.6651-1(a)(2)].

### XIII.C.1.e. Corporate Estimated Tax Payments

[750 T.M., II.B.; TPS ¶4610.04.C.]

***Due Dates for Installments.*** A corporation generally must make estimated tax payments if it expects its total tax for the year to be $500 or more. Estimated tax payments are made in installments that are due by the 15th day of the 4th, 6th, 9th, and 12th months of corporation's tax year [Reg. § 1.6655-1(f)(2)(ii)]. However, if the due date of an installment payment falls on a Saturday, Sunday, or legal holiday, the due date is extended to the next business day [§ 6655(c), § 7503].

---

**EXAMPLE:** Alpha Corporation is a calendar year taxpayer. It generally must make installment payments of estimated tax by April 15th, June 15th, September 15th, and December 15th.

**EXAMPLE:** Beta Corporation is a fiscal year taxpayer with a tax year ending June 30. It generally must make installment payments of estimated tax by October 15th, December 15th, March 15th, and June 15th.

---

***Computing Installment Amounts.*** The amount of each installment of estimated tax is computed using Form 1120-W, *Estimated Tax for Corporations*. There are several methods that can be used to compute the installment payments and a corporation can generally choose the method that results in the smallest installment payments. Under the general method, each installment is equal to 25% of the income tax expected for the current tax year. If the corporation filed a return with a positive tax liability for the previous year and that return was not a short-period return, it can compute each installment as 25% of its income tax for the previous year (however, a corporation that had taxable income of $1 million or more for any of the three preceding tax years may use this method only for the first required installment). If a corporation's income is expected to vary during the year because, for example, it operates a business on a seasonal basis, it may be able to lower the amount of one or more installments by using the annualized income installment method and/or the adjusted seasonal installment method [§ 6655(d)].

***Paying Estimated Tax.*** Corporations must use electronic funds transfer to deposit all federal taxes, including estimated taxes. Deposits are generally made using the Electronic Federal Tax Payment System (EFTPS), a free service provided by the Department of Treasury. However, deposits may also be made through a third party, such as a tax professional, financial institution, or payroll service.

***Penalty for Underpayment of Estimated Tax.*** A corporation that does not pay a required installment of estimated tax by its due date may be subject to a penalty that is computed on Form 2220, *Underpayment of Estimated Tax by Corporations*, and depends on the amount of the underpayment, the period during which the underpayment was due and unpaid, and the IRS interest rate for underpayments. The penalty is figured separately for each installment due date [§ 6655(a) and § 6655(b), § 6621].

*Refund for Overpayment of Estimated Tax.* A corporation that has overpaid its estimated tax may apply for a quick refund if the overpayment is at least 10% of its estimated tax liability and at least $500. Form 4466, *Corporation Application for Quick Refund of Overpayment of Estimated Tax*, is used to compute the expected tax liability and the amount of the overpayment. Form 4466 must be filed after the end of the tax year and before the corporation files its return, but no later than the 16th day of the 3rd month after the end of the tax year.

### XIII.C.1.f. Corporate Accounting Methods and Periods

[570 T.M., 574 T.M.; TPS ¶4610.02.B.2.]

*Accounting Method.* A corporation is generally required to use the accrual method of accounting instead of the cash method if: (i) its average annual gross receipts for the three preceding tax years are more than $5 million, or (ii) it is engaged in the business of farming (regardless of its average annual gross receipts) [§ 447, § 448]. However, a personal service corporation is required to use the cash method (see XIII.C.6.) [§ 448(b)(2)].

*Accounting Period.* A corporation may generally choose to use either the calendar year or a fiscal year as its tax year [§ 441]. However, a personal service corporation is normally required to use a calendar year for its tax year (see XIII.C.6.) [§ 441(i)].

### XIII.C.2. Computation of Corporate Income Tax

[750 T.M., II.A.; TPS ¶4610.02.B.]

A corporation's income tax is computed by applying the graduated corporate income tax rates (see XIII.C.2.a) to its taxable income for the year. The taxable income of a corporation is generally computed using the same basic principles that apply to individual taxpayers (see XII.B.). It must report most of the same income items (see Chapter I.) in gross income and it is allowed many of the same deductions (see Chapters IV. and VII.) and credits (see Chapter IX.). However, corporate deductions differ from individual deductions in the following ways:

- a corporation is not allowed any personal or dependency exemptions;
- the standard deduction is not available to a corporation;
- there is no distinction between above-the-line and below-the-line deductions for a corporation;
- there is no 2% floor on miscellaneous itemized deductions for a corporation;
- a corporation cannot take deductions that, by their terms, apply only to individuals (e.g., the medical expense deduction, the alimony deduction);
- a corporation's charitable contribution deduction is limited to a percentage of its taxable income; and
- a corporation can take a net operating loss deduction for losses from prior and subsequent years.

In addition, there are a number of special deductions that are allowed only to corporations, including the dividends received deduction (see XIII.C.2.b.), the dividends paid deduction (see XIII.C.2.c.), and the deduction for organizational expenses (see XIII.C.2.d.).

### XIII.C.2.a. Corporate Income Tax Rates

[750 T.M., II.A.; TPS ¶4610.02.B.3.]

Income tax is imposed on a corporation based on the following set of graduated income tax rates [§ 11(b)(1)]:

| If taxable income is: | | Then tax is: | | |
|---|---|---|---|---|
| Over- | But not over- | This amount: | Plus this percent: | Of the amount over: |
| $ 0 | $ 50,000 | — | 15% | $ 0 |
| $ 50,000 | $ 75,000 | $ 7,500 | 25% | $ 50,000 |
| $ 75,000 | $ 100,000 | $ 13,750 | 34% | $ 75,000 |
| $ 100,000 | $ 335,000 | $ 22,250 | 39% | $ 100,000 |
| $ 335,000 | $ 10,000,000 | $ 113,900 | 34% | $ 335,000 |
| $ 10,000,000 | $ 15,000,000 | $ 3,400,000 | 35% | $ 10,000,000 |
| $ 15,000,000 | $ 18,333,333 | $ 5,150,000 | 38% | $ 15,000,000 |
| $ 18,333,333 | — | — | 35% | $ 0 |

Note that the maximum corporate tax rate is 35%. However, corporations that have significant amounts of taxable income lose the benefit of the lower graduated rates through the imposition of a surtax. Thus, for corporations with taxable income in excess of $100,000, the benefit of the lower rates is phased out through a 5% surtax on taxable income between $100,000 and $335,000. Similarly, for corporations with taxable income in excess of $15 million, the benefit of the lower rates is phased out through a 3% surtax on taxable income between $15,000,000 and $18,333,333.

A personal service corporation is taxed at a flat rate of 35% [§ 11(b)(2)]. See XII.C.6. for a discussion of personal service corporations.

### XIII.C.2.b. Corporate Dividends Received Deduction

[764 T.M., VI., 503 T.M., V.A.1.; TPS ¶4810.02.]

In order to reduce the number of times that corporate earnings are taxed, C corporations are allowed a deduction for dividends they receive from another corporation. The dividends received deduction allows a corporation to partially or fully offset the gross income it must recognize from such dividends with a deduction for the dividends. The amount of the dividends received deduction varies based on factors such as the nature of the corporation paying the dividends, the level of ownership in the corporation paying the dividends, and the type of stock on which the dividends are paid. Limitations apply to the dividends received deduction in certain circumstances.

The dividends received deduction does not apply to certain dividends received from:
- mutual savings banks, cooperative banks, domestic building and loan associations, and certain other savings institutions [§ 243(d)(1)];
- regulated investment companies [§ 243(d)(2)];
- real estate investment trusts [§ 243(d)(3)];
- tax-exempt corporations [§ 246(a)(1)];
- exempt farmers' cooperative associations [§ 246(a)(1)];
- Federal Home Loan Banks [§ 246(a)(2)];
- DISCs or former DISCs [§ 246(d)]; or
- corporations deriving most of their income from U.S. possessions [§ 246(e)].

### XIII.C.2.b.(1) Dividends Received from Domestic Corporations

[764 T.M., VI.B., 503 T.M., V.A.1.a.; TPS ¶4810.02.A., .02.C.]

A corporation is generally allowed a deduction for dividends received from another domestic corporation in an amount equal to [§ 243]:

- 70% of the amount of dividends received from a corporation in which it owns less than 20% of the voting power or value of the stock;
- 80% of the amount of dividends received from a corporation in which it owns 20% or more (but less than 80%) of the voting power and value of the stock; or
- 100% of the amount of dividends received from a corporation that is a member of the same affiliated group if certain requirements are met (as discussed at XIII.C.8.a., an affiliated group is a group of corporations in which there is common ownership of 80% or more of the voting power and value of the stock of each corporation).

If the corporation receiving the dividends is a small business investment company, it is allowed a dividends received deduction of 100% of the amount of any dividends received from another domestic corporation, regardless of its level of stock ownership in that corporation [§ 243(a)(2)]. A small business investment company is a company licensed by the Small Business Administration to provide financing to small businesses.

### XIII.C.2.b.(2) Dividends Received from Foreign Corporations

[764 T.M., VI.D., 503 T.M., V.A.1.c.; TPS ¶4810.02.D.]

A corporation is allowed a deduction for a percentage of the U.S.-source portion of dividends received from a foreign corporation if it owns 10% or more of the voting power and value of the foreign corporation. The U.S.-source portion of the dividends received from such a foreign corporation is equal to the total dividends received from the corporation multiplied by the ratio of its undistributed U.S. earnings to its total undistributed earnings. The dividends received deduction is equal to the following percentage of the U.S.-source portion of the dividends received [§ 245]:

- 70% if the ownership interest in the foreign corporation is between 10 and 20%;
- 80% if the ownership interest in the foreign corporation is 20% or more; or
- 100% if the foreign corporation is wholly owned and all of its gross income is effectively connected with the conduct of a trade or business within the U.S.

### XIII.C.2.b.(3) Limitations on Dividends Received Deduction

[764 T.M., VI.C., 503 T.M., V.A.1.a.; TPS ¶4810.02.E.]

There are a number of limitations that reduce the dividends received deduction. These limitations include a taxable income limitation, a holding period limitation, a limitation for debt-financed portfolio stock, and a limitation for public utility preferred stock.

**Taxable Income Limitation.** The aggregate amount of the dividends received deduction a corporation is allowed for a tax year is limited to 80% of its taxable income for dividends received from 20%-or-more-owned corporations and 70% of its taxable income for dividends received from less-than-20%-owned corporations. If a corporation received dividends from both types of corporations, the 80% limitation is applied first and then the 70% limitation is applied after reducing taxable income by the dividends received from 20%-or-more-owned corporations. For purposes of the limitation, taxable income is computed without taking into account the net operating loss deduction, the domestic production activities deduction, the dividends received deduction itself, the dividends paid deduction for public utilities, the adjustment for the nontaxable portion of an extraordinary dividend, and any capital loss carryback to the tax year. The limitation does not apply if the corporation had a net operating loss for the year. It also does not apply to dividends received by a small business investment company [§ 246(b)].

*Holding Period Limitation.* The dividends received deduction is not allowed for dividends received on stock unless the stock has been held for more than 45 days during the 91-day period that begins on the date 45 days before the ex-dividend date [§ 246(c)(1)(A)]. In the case of dividends received on preferred stock that are attributable to a period of more than 366 days, the dividends received deduction is not allowed unless the preferred stock has been held for more than 90 days during the 181-day period that begins on the date 90 days before the ex-dividend date [§ 246(c)(2)]. These holding periods are reduced by any periods during which the corporation receiving the dividends: (i) has an option to sell, or has made a short sale of, substantially identical stock or securities; (ii) is the grantor of an option to buy substantially identical stock or securities; or (iii) has diminished its risk of loss by holding one or more other positions in substantially similar or related property [§ 246(c)(4)].

The dividends received deduction is disallowed to the extent the corporation receiving the dividend is under an obligation to make related payments with respect to positions in substantially similar or related property [§ 246(c)(1)(B)].

*Limitation for Debt-Financed Portfolio Stock.* The deduction for dividends received on portfolio stock is reduced when the corporation uses debt to acquire or carry that portfolio stock. Stock held by a corporation is generally portfolio stock unless, on the ex-dividend date, (i) the corporation owned 50% or more of the voting power and value of the stock in the other corporation, or (ii) the corporation owned 20% or more of the voting power and value of the stock in the other corporation and 5 or fewer corporate shareholders owned 50% or more of the voting power and value of the stock in the other corporation [§ 246A(c)(2)].

The deduction for dividends received on debt-financed portfolio stock is allowed only to the extent that the portfolio stock on which the dividend is received is not financed by debt. Thus, the percentage used to compute the deduction for dividends received on debt-financed portfolio stock must be reduced to account for the debt used to acquire or carry the portfolio stock. The reduced deduction percentage is computed by multiplying the normal deduction percentage of 70% or 80% by a percentage equal to the difference between 100% and the average indebtedness percentage (the ratio of the average amount of debt used on the stock to the average adjusted basis of the stock during a specified base period). However, the amount of any reduction in the dividends received deduction cannot exceed the amount of the interest deduction allocable to the dividend [§ 246A(a), § 246A(d)].

The reduction in the dividends received deduction for debt-financed portfolio stock does not apply to the 100% deduction for dividends received from members of the same affiliated group and dividends received by small business investment companies [§ 246A(b)].

*Limitation for Public Utility Preferred Stock.* A corporation that receives preferred stock dividends from a public utility is generally allowed a dividends received deduction for those dividends; however, the amount of its dividends received deduction must be reduced by the amount of the dividends paid deduction allowed to the public utility [§ 244]. See XIII.C.2.c. for a discussion of the dividends paid deduction.

### XIII.C.2.c. Corporate Dividends Paid Deduction

[503 T.M., V.A.2.d.; TPS ¶2730.01.A.]

A public utility is generally allowed a deduction for 40% of the dividends it pays on its preferred stock (the deduction percentage is computed by dividing 14% by the maximum corporate tax rate, which is 35% for 2014). However, this dividends paid deduction is limited to 40% of the public utility's taxable income for the year, before the dividends paid deduction [§ 247].

### XIII.C.2.d. Corporate Organizational Expense Deduction

[ 750 T.M., I.E.; TPS ¶4610.02.B.1.c.]

A corporation is generally required to capitalize any organizational expenses it pays or incurs before it begins operations. However, a corporation may instead elect to deduct up to $5,000 of organizational expenses and to amortize the balance of its organizational expenses over a period of 180 months beginning in the month that operations begin. The deduction must be reduced on a dollar-for-dollar basis by any amount by which its organizational expenses exceed $50,000 [§ 248(a); Reg. § 1.248-1(a)].

A corporation is deemed to make the election to deduct organizational expenses for the year in which it begins operations; however, it may forego that deemed election by affirmatively electing to capitalize all its organizational expenses for that year [Reg. § 1.248-1(c)].

Organizational expenses are expenses that are directly incident to the creation of the corporation, chargeable to the corporation's capital account, and of such a character that they would be amortizable over the life of the corporation if it had a limited life. Examples of organizational expenses include: (i) legal expenses for the drafting of the corporate charter, bylaws, and minutes, (ii) necessary accounting expenses, (iii) expenses for the organizational meetings of directors, and (iv) incorporation fees [§ 248(b); Reg. § 1.248-1(b)].

### XIII.C.3. Corporate Alternative Minimum Tax (AMT)

[752 T.M.; TPS ¶3420.]

In addition to the regular income tax, most corporations are also subject to the alternative minimum tax (AMT), which is designed to prevent taxpayers with substantial economic income from avoiding all income tax liability through the use of exclusions, deductions, and credits. However, small corporations with average annual gross receipts of $7.5 million or less for the previous three-year period are exempt from AMT ($5 million or less for the corporation's first three-year period). First-year corporations are also exempt from AMT [§ 55(e)].

A corporation's AMT is the amount by which its tentative minimum tax exceeds its regular income tax [§ 55(a)]. A corporation's tentative minimum tax is determined by computing 20% of the amount by which its alternative minimum taxable income (AMTI) exceeds a $40,000 exemption amount, and then subtracting any alternative minimum foreign tax credit [§ 55(b)(1)(B), § 55(d)(2)]. A corporation's AMTI is its taxable income modified by certain adjustments and tax preferences described in § 56, § 57, and § 58 [§ 55(b)(2)]. See X.B.2. for further discussion of the alternative minimum tax.

### XIII.C.4. Accumulated Earnings Tax

[796 T.M.; TPS ¶5140.]

Because of the double tax on corporations, corporations may have an incentive to accumulate their earnings at the corporate level in order to avoid the tax at the shareholder level. However, a 20% penalty tax known as the accumulated earnings tax is generally imposed on any corporation that accumulates earnings for the purpose of avoiding income tax on shareholders [§ 532(a)]. The accumulated earnings tax is imposed in addition to the corporate-level income tax and other corporate-level taxes.

The accumulated earnings tax does not apply to: (i) personal holding companies, (ii) tax-exempt corporations, (iii) passive foreign investment companies, and (iv) S corporations [§ 532(b)].

### XIII.C.4.a. Tax Avoidance Purpose

[796 T.M., V; TPS ¶5140.01.B.]

A corporation is generally considered to accumulate earnings for the purpose of avoiding income tax on shareholders if it accumulates earnings beyond the reasonable needs of the business [§ 533(a)]. A holding company or investment company that accumulates earnings is presumed to do so for the purpose of avoiding income tax on shareholders [§ 533(b)].

***Reasonable Needs of the Business.*** An accumulation of earnings is generally beyond the reasonable needs of the business if it exceeds the amount a reasonable businessman would consider appropriate for current and reasonably anticipated future business needs. The need to accumulate earnings must be directly connected with the needs of the corporation itself and must be for bona fide business purposes [Reg. § 1.537-1(a)].

Earnings are accumulated for the reasonable needs of the business if the corporation reasonably anticipates that the accumulated amount is required for the future needs of the business and it has specific, definite, and feasible plans for the use of that amount [§ 537(a)(1); Reg. § 1.537-1(b)]. The determination of whether earnings are accumulated for the reasonable needs of the business is based on the facts and circumstances. For example, earnings are considered accumulated for reasonable needs when they are accumulated to: (i) provide for an expansion of the business, (ii) acquire another business in a stock or asset purchase, (iii) retire corporate debt, (iv) provide necessary working capital for the business, (v) provide investments in or loans to suppliers or customers, or (vi) provide for the payment of reasonably anticipated product liability losses [Reg. § 1.537-2(b)]. On the other hand, earnings are not considered accumulated for reasonable needs when they are accumulated to: (i) make personal loans to shareholders, (ii) make loans to persons that have no connection to the business, (iii) make loans to another commonly controlled corporation, (iv) make investments unrelated to the business, or (v) provide against unrealistic hazards [Reg. § 1.537-2(c)].

Earnings are also accumulated for the reasonable needs of the business if they are accumulated to redeem the corporation's stock included in a deceased shareholder's gross estate. However, the amount accumulated for this purpose cannot exceed the reasonably anticipated estate/inheritance taxes, funeral expenses, and administration expenses incurred by the shareholder's estate [§ 537(b)(1), § 303; Reg. § 1.537-1(c)].

***Burden of Proof.*** Generally, the corporation bears the burden of proving that its earnings are not accumulated beyond the reasonable needs of the business [§ 533(a)]. However, in a Tax Court proceeding involving a notice of deficiency, the IRS bears the burden of proving that the corporation's earnings are accumulated beyond the reasonable needs of the business if: (i) the IRS has not provided the proper notification to the corporation, or (ii) the corporation has submitted a statement to the IRS providing the grounds (and related facts) for its position that its earnings have not been accumulated beyond the reasonable needs of the business [§ 534].

### XIII.C.4.b. Computing Accumulated Earnings Tax

[796 T.M., II.A.; TPS ¶5140.03.]

The amount of accumulated earnings tax imposed on a corporation is equal to 20% of accumulated taxable income [§ 531].

*Accumulated Taxable Income.* Accumulated taxable income is calculated by making the following adjustments to the corporation's taxable income [§ 535]:

- a deduction is allowed for federal income taxes and excess profits taxes (other than the accumulated earnings tax and the personal holding company tax) accrued or deemed to be paid during the year;
- a deduction is allowed for income, war profits, and excess profits taxes of foreign countries or U.S. possessions accrued or deemed to be paid during the year (to the extent a foreign tax credit was taken and no deduction was allowed in calculating taxable income);
- a deduction is allowed for the amount of charitable contributions disallowed in calculating taxable income due to the 10% taxable income limitation;
- the dividends received deduction is disallowed;
- the dividends paid deduction on the preferred stock of a public utility is disallowed;
- the net operating loss deduction is disallowed;
- a deduction is allowed for net capital losses for the year, reduced by the lesser of the nonrecaptured capital gains deductions from prior years or the accumulated earnings and profits as of the end of the previous year;
- a deduction is allowed for net capital gains for the year, reduced by the taxes attributable to those gains;
- capital loss carrybacks or carryforwards are not taken into account;
- a special dividends paid deduction is subtracted; and
- the accumulated earnings credit is subtracted.

*Special Dividends Paid Deduction.* In calculating accumulated taxable income, a special dividends paid deduction can be subtracted from taxable income [§ 535(a)]. The dividends paid deduction is equal to the sum of the dividends paid during the tax year and the consent dividends for the tax year [§ 561(a)].

Dividends paid during the year are amounts distributed by a corporation to its shareholders out of its current and accumulated earnings and profits [§ 562(a), § 316]. A dividend paid on or before the 15th day of the third month following the end of a tax year is treated as paid during that tax year [§ 563(a)].

A consent dividend is a hypothetical dividend that is not actually paid by the corporation. Under the consent dividend procedures, a shareholder can consent to have certain amounts treated as a dividend paid by the corporation to the shareholder and simultaneously contributed back to the corporation by the shareholder as a contribution of capital. The shareholder reports the dividend as income and increases its basis in its stock. The corporation takes a deduction for the dividend and decreases its earnings and profits account. A consent dividend can only be paid on common stock or preferred stock with unlimited participation [§ 565].

*Accumulated Earnings Credit.* In calculating accumulated taxable income, an accumulated earnings credit can be subtracted from taxable income [§ 535(a)]. The accumulated earnings credit is generally equal to the amount of earnings accumulated for the reasonable needs of the business minus the amount of the net capital gains deduction taken in calculating accumulated taxable income [§ 535(c)(1)]. However, a safe harbor provides for a minimum accumulated earnings credit. The minimum credit is equal to the amount by which $250,000 exceeds the accumulated earnings and profits at the end of the previous year (reduced by the amount of any dividends paid after the end of the year but treated as paid during the year). For personal service corporations, the minimum credit is calculated using $150,000 instead of $250,000 [§ 535(c)(2), § 535(c)(4)]. See XIII.C.6. for a discussion of personal service corporations.

*Special Rules for Foreign Corporations.* In determining the amount of the net capital gains deduction for purposes of the accumulated taxable income calculation, a foreign corporation only takes into account gains or losses that are effectively connected with the conduct of a trade or business within the United States and that are not exempt from tax under a treaty [§ 535(b)(9)].

In calculating accumulated taxable income, a controlled foreign corporation is allowed a special deduction for the amount of the subpart F income that is included in the gross income of a U.S. shareholder [§ 535(b)(10)].

*Holding and Investment Companies.* In calculating accumulated taxable income, a mere investment or holding company is not allowed a deduction for net capital losses and its deduction for net capital gains is limited [§ 535(b)(8)].

### XIII.C.5. Personal Holding Company Tax

[797 T.M.; TPS ¶5150.]

Because corporate tax rates have historically been significantly lower than individual tax rates, individual taxpayers had an incentive in the past to incorporate their investment portfolios so that their investment income could be taxed at the lower corporate rates. A 20% penalty tax known as the personal holding company tax is imposed on personal holding companies to eliminate the incentive to do this. The personal holding company tax is imposed in addition to the corporate-level income tax and other corporate-level taxes. However, corporations that are subject to the personal holding company tax are not subject to the accumulated earnings tax [§ 532(b)(1)]. See XIII.C.4. for a discussion of the accumulated earnings tax.

### XIII.C.5.a. Definition of Personal Holding Company

[797 T.M., II.A.; TPS ¶5150.01.]

A corporation is a personal holding company subject to the personal holding company tax if both of the following tests apply to it [§ 542(a)]:

- at least 60% of its adjusted ordinary gross income for the year is personal holding company income (the "income test"); and
- more than 50% of the value of its outstanding stock is owned, directly or indirectly, by five or fewer individuals at any time during the last half of its tax year (the "stock ownership test").

*Income Test.* A corporation meets the income test if at least 60% of its adjusted ordinary gross income for the year is personal holding company income [§ 542(a)(1)]. Personal holding company income generally includes dividends, interest, rents, royalties, annuities, amounts received from shareholders for the use of corporate property, amounts received under personal service contracts, and income from estates and trusts [§ 542(a)]. Adjusted ordinary gross income is gross income after: (i) the exclusion of gains from the sale of capital assets and business property, and (ii) certain adjustments for interest, rents, and royalties [§ 543(b)].

In the case of an affiliated group of corporations filing a consolidated return (see XIII.C.8.), the income test is generally applied using the affiliated group's consolidated adjusted ordinary gross income and consolidated personal holding company income, and no member of the affiliated group is considered to meet the income test unless the affiliated group meets the test [§ 542(b)(1)]. However, the income test is instead applied to each separate member of the affiliated group if:

- any member derived 10% or more of its adjusted ordinary gross income from sources outside the group and 80% or more of that amount is personal holding company income [§ 542(b)(2)]; or
- any member of the group does not fall within the definition of a personal holding company [§ 542(b)(3)].

**Stock Ownership Test.** A corporation meets the stock ownership test if more than 50% of the value of its outstanding stock is owned, directly or indirectly, by five or fewer individuals at any time during the last half of its tax year [§ 542(a)(2)]. Certain constructive ownership rules apply in determining stock ownership [§ 544]. The following entities are treated as individuals for purposes of the stock ownership test [§ 542(a)(2)]:

- a qualified trust that is part of a stock bonus, pension, or profit-sharing plan of an employer;
- a trust that is part of a plan that pays supplemental unemployment compensation; and
- a private foundation.

**Ineligible Corporations.** The following types of corporations are not treated as personal holding companies subject to the personal holding company tax even if they meet both the income and stock ownership tests [§ 542(c)]:

- tax-exempt corporations;
- banks and domestic building and loan associations;
- life insurance companies;
- surety companies;
- foreign corporations;
- certain lending or finance companies;
- small business investment companies; and
- corporations undergoing bankruptcy proceedings.

### XIII.C.5.b. Computing Personal Holding Company Tax

[797 T.M., IX., X.; TPS ¶5150.04.]

The amount of personal holding company tax imposed on a corporation that is a personal holding company is equal to 20% of its undistributed personal holding company income [§ 541].

**Undistributed Personal Holding Company Income.** Undistributed personal holding company income is calculated by making the following adjustments to the corporation's taxable income [§ 545(a), § 545(b)]:

- a deduction is allowed for federal income taxes and excess profits taxes (other than the personal holding company tax and the accumulated earnings tax) accrued or deemed to be paid during the year;
- a deduction is allowed for income, war profits, and excess profits taxes of foreign countries or U.S. possessions accrued or deemed to be paid during the year (to the extent a foreign tax credit was taken and no deduction was allowed in calculating taxable income);
- a deduction is allowed for the amount of charitable contributions disallowed in calculating taxable income due to the 10% taxable income limitation;
- the dividends received deduction is disallowed;
- the dividends paid deduction on the preferred stock of a public utility is disallowed;
- the general net operating loss deduction is disallowed (however, a deduction is allowed for the net operating loss for the preceding tax year, computed without regard to certain special deductions);
- a deduction is allowed for net capital gains for the year, reduced by the taxes attributable to those gains;
- the deductions allowed for trade or business expenses and depreciation allocable to property are limited to the rent received for the use of the property (unless it is established that the rent received was the highest rent obtainable, the property was held by a business carried on for profit, and there was a reasonable expectation that the rental would result in a profit or that the property was necessary to the business); and
- a special dividends paid deduction is subtracted.

***Special Dividends Paid Deduction.*** In calculating undistributed personal holding company income, a special dividends paid deduction can be subtracted from taxable income [§ 545(a)]. The dividends paid deduction is equal to the sum of the dividends paid during the tax year and the consent dividends for the tax year [§ 561(a)].

Dividends paid during the year are amounts distributed by a corporation to its shareholders out of its current and accumulated earnings and profits [§ 562(a), § 316]. A dividend paid on or before the 15th day of the third month following the end of a tax year is treated as paid during that tax year [§ 563(a)].

A consent dividend is a hypothetical dividend that is not actually paid by the corporation. Under the consent dividend procedures, a shareholder can consent to have certain amounts treated as a dividend paid by the corporation to the shareholder and simultaneously contributed back to the corporation by the shareholder as a contribution of capital. The shareholder reports the dividend as income and increases its basis in its stock. The corporation takes a deduction for the dividend and decreases its earnings and profits account. A consent dividend can only be paid on common stock or preferred stock with unlimited participation [§ 565].

***Foreign Corporations.*** In determining the amount of the net capital gains deduction for purposes of the undistributed personal holding company income calculation, a foreign corporation only takes into account gains or losses that are effectively connected with the conduct of a trade or business within the United States and that are not exempt from tax under a treaty [§ 545(b)(7)].

***Deficiency Dividend Procedure.*** If a determination establishes that a corporation is liable for the personal holding company tax for a tax year, the corporation can pay a deficiency dividend and deduct it from personal holding company income in order to reduce or eliminate its personal holding company tax liability. The corporation, however, remains liable for any interest or penalties associated with the personal holding company tax. For this purpose, a determination includes: (i) a court decision, judgment, decree, or other order; (ii) a closing agreement with the IRS under § 7121; or (iii) any other agreement with the IRS relating to the corporation's liability for the personal holding company tax [§ 547].

### XIII.C.6. Personal Service Corporations

[551 T.M., IV.E.3.; TPS ¶5110.]

Personal service corporations are subject to a number of special rules. Generally speaking, a personal service corporation is a corporation in the business of providing personal services to clients or customers. However, there are different definitions of a personal service corporation that apply for different purposes. For example, there are different definitions for purposes of the rules that address income reallocation, accounting periods, accounting methods, income tax computations, the passive activity loss limitations, and the at risk limitations.

### XIII.C.6.a. Personal Service Corporation Income Reallocation Rules

[551 T.M., IV.E.3.; TPS ¶5110.02.]

The IRS has the authority to reallocate income and deductions between personal service corporations and their employee-owners if substantially all of the services of the personal service corporation are performed for one other entity and the principal purpose for forming or using the personal service corporation was tax avoidance [§ 269A(a)].

For this purpose, a personal service corporation is a corporation whose principal activity is the performance of services by employee-owners [§ 269A(b)(1)]. An employee-owner is an employee who, during any day of the tax year, owns more than 10% of the outstanding stock of the corporation [§ 269A(b)(2)].

### XIII.C.6.b. Personal Service Corporation Accounting Periods

[574 T.M., III.D.; TPS ¶5110.04.C.]

Most corporations can use either a calendar year or a fiscal year as their tax year. However, a personal service corporation is generally required to use a calendar year as its tax year. A personal service corporation can use a fiscal year only if it (i) establishes a business purpose for a fiscal year and obtains approval from the IRS, (ii) makes a § 444 election to use a tax year other than a calendar year by filing Form 8716, *Election To Have a Tax Year Other Than a Required Tax Year* (note that the deferral period of the elected tax year may not be longer than three months), or (iii) uses a 52-53-week tax year that ends with reference to the calendar year [§ 441(i), § 444].

A personal service corporation has the same general definition as it does under the income reallocation rules — a corporation whose principal activity is the performance of services by employee-owners (see XIII.C.6.a.). However, for this purpose, an employee-owner is an employee who, during any day of the tax year, owns *any* of outstanding stock of the corporation [§ 441(i)(2), § 444(f), § 269A(b)].

### XIII.C.6.c. Personal Service Corporation Accounting Methods and Income Tax Computations

[570 T.M., III.D.1.b(2); TPS ¶5110.04.A., .04.B.]

Most corporations are required to use the accrual method of accounting and are subject to a graduated income tax rate structure in computing their income tax.

However, a qualified personal service corporation can elect to use the cash method of accounting [§ 448(b)(2)]. Moreover, a qualified personal service corporation pays tax at a flat rate of 35% [§ 11(b)(2)].

For these purposes, a qualified personal service corporation is a corporation (i) whose principal activity involves the performance of services in the fields of health, law, engineering, architecture, accounting, actuarial science, the performing arts, or consulting, and (ii) substantially all of whose stock (95% or more by value) is held by employees performing services for the corporation in those fields, retired employees who had performed such services, and persons who acquired the stock by reason of the death of such employees or retired employees [§ 448(d)(2); Reg. § 1.448-1T(e)(5)].

### XIII.C.6.d. Personal Service Corporation Passive Loss Limitations

[549 T.M., III.B.2.j.; TPS ¶5110.04.D.]

Most corporations can deduct losses attributable to passive activities. However, a personal service corporation cannot deduct passive activity losses unless it materially participates in the activity [§ 469(a)(2)(C)]. A personal service corporation is treated as materially participating in an activity only if one or more shareholders that own more than 50% of the value of its stock materially participate in the activity [§ 469(h)(4)]. See VIII.F. for further discussion of the passive loss limitations.

For purposes of this rule, a personal service corporation is corporation whose principal activity is the performance of services by employee-owners and more than 10% of whose stock (by value) is owned by employee-owners. An employee-owner is an employee who, during any day of the tax year, owns any of the outstanding stock of the corporation [§ 469(j)(2), § 269A(b)].

### XIII.C.6.e. Personal Service Corporation At-Risk Limitations

[550 T.M., IV.C.2.; TPS ¶5110.04.E.]

A closely held corporation is subject to the at-risk limitations on losses unless it is a "qualified C corporation." Personal service corporations are specifically excluded from the definition of a qualified C corporation and, therefore, personal service corporations are subject to the at-risk limitations on losses [§ 465(c)(7)]. See VIII.E. for further discussion of the at-risk limitations.

A personal service corporation has the same general definition as it has under the income reallocation rules for this purpose — a corporation whose principal activity is the performance of services by employee-owners (see XIII.C.6.a.). However, for this purpose, an employee-owner is an employee who, during any day of the tax year, owns more than 5% of the outstanding stock of the corporation [§ 465(c)(7)(B)(ii), § 269A(b)].

### XIII.C.7. Controlled Groups of Corporations

[750 T.M., III., 554 T.M., VIII.; TPS ¶5160.]

Controlled groups of corporations generally may file consolidated returns (see XIII.C.8.). However, controlled groups are subject to limitations on tax benefits such as the graduated income tax brackets, the accumulated earnings credit, and the alternative minimum tax exemption amount. Controlled groups include parent-lsubsidiary groups, brother-sister groups, and combined groups.

*Parent-Subsidiary Controlled Group.* A parent-subsidiary controlled group is one or more chains of corporations connected through stock ownership with a common parent corporation for which both of the following tests are met [§ 1563(a)(1)]:

- the common parent owns at least 80% of the voting power or value of at least one of the other corporations; and
- at least 80% of the voting power or value of each corporation (other than the common parent) is owned by one or more of the other corporations.

---

**EXAMPLE:** X Corporation owns 80% of the vote and value of stock of Y Corporation. Y Corporation owns 80% of the vote and value of stock of Z Corporation. X, Y, and Z are a parent-subsidiary controlled group.

---

*Brother-Sister Controlled Group.* A brother-sister controlled group is a group of two or more corporations in which five or fewer persons (individuals, estates, or trusts only) own more than 50% of the voting power or value. The stock ownership of each person is taken into account only to the extent that it is identical for each corporation [§ 1563(a)(2)].

---

**EXAMPLE:** Al owns 55% of X Corporation, 51% of Y Corporation, and 55% of Z Corporation. Bill owns 45% of X Corporation and 25% of Y Corporation. Chris owns 24% of Y Corporation and 45% of Z Corporation. All ownership percentages are by both vote and value. X, Y, and Z are a brother-sister controlled group because Al has identical stock ownership of 51% with respect to each corporation.

---

*Combined Group.* A combined group is a group of three or more corporations, each of which is a member of a parent-subsidiary controlled group or a brother-sister controlled group and one of which is both a common parent of a parent-subsidiary controlled group and a member of a brother-sister controlled group [§ 1563(a)(3)].

*Limitations on Tax Benefits.* The following limitations apply to the tax benefits of a controlled group of corporations [§ 1561]:

- the income tax of the group must be computed using only one set of graduated corporate income tax brackets (see XIII.C.2.a.);
- the accumulated earnings tax of the group must be computed using only one $250,000 (or $150,000) accumulated earnings credit (see XIII.C.4.); and
- the alternative minimum tax of the group must be computed using only one $40,000 exemption amount (see XIII.C.3.).

These tax benefits generally must be divided equally among the members of the controlled group unless all members consent to an apportionment plan providing for an unequal allocation of such amounts [§ 1561].

### XIII.C.8. Consolidated Returns

[754 T.M.; TPS ¶5310.]

An affiliated group of corporations may elect to file a consolidated return in lieu of filing a separate return for each member of the affiliated group [§ 1501].

### XIII.C.8.a. Affiliated Group

[754 T.M., III.A.; TPS ¶5310.01.]

An affiliated group of corporations is one or more chains of includible corporations connected through stock ownership with a common parent corporation for which both of the following tests are met [§ 1504(a)]:

- the common parent directly owns at least 80% of the voting power and value of at least one of the other includible corporations; and

- at least 80% of the voting power and value of each includible corporation (other than the common parent) is directly owned by one or more of the other corporations.

An includible corporation is any corporation except [§ 1504(b)]:

- a tax-exempt corporation;
- a life insurance company;
- a foreign corporation;
- a corporation electing the possessions tax credit;
- a regulated investment company (RIC);
- a real estate investment company (REIT);
- a domestic international sales corporation (DISC); or
- an S corporation.

### XIII.C.8.b. Election to File Consolidated Return

[754 T.M., VII.A.; TPS ¶5310.02.]

The election to file a consolidated return is made when the common parent files Form 1120 for the affiliated group and attaches Form 851, *Affiliation Schedule*, to provide information about the members of the group [Reg. § 1.1502-75(h)(1)]. Once an election to file a consolidated return is made, a consolidated return must be filed for all subsequent years unless the group makes an election to discontinue filing consolidated returns [Reg. § 1.1502-75(a)(2)].

All corporations that were members of the affiliated group at any time during the tax year must consent to the filing of the consolidated return [§ 1501; Reg. § 1.1502-75(a)(1)]. Each member of the affiliated group must file Form 1122, *Authorization and Consent of Subsidiary Corporation to be Included in a Consolidated Tax Return*, for the first year in which the consolidated return is filed. Corporations becoming members of the group in subsequent years are not required to file Form 1122 [Reg. § 1.1502-75(h)(2)].

In order to discontinue filing a consolidated return, the common parent must obtain the permission of the IRS by making an application to discontinue the filing of a consolidated return and by establishing that the group has good cause to discontinue filing a consolidated return. Sufficient good cause can ordinarily be established if there has been a substantial adverse change in the law affecting the group's tax liability [Reg. § 1.1502-75(c)].

### XIII.C.8.c. Consolidated Returns

[754 T.M., 756 T.M.; TPS ¶5310.]

The consolidated return of an affiliated group must be filed on the basis of the common parent's tax year. Thus, each member of the affiliated group generally must adopt the tax year of the common parent [Reg. § 1.1502-76(a)]. However, each member is generally free to choose its own accounting method [Reg. § 1.1502-17(a)].

The common parent is the sole agent of the affiliated group for all purposes related to the group's federal income tax liability [Reg. § 1.1502-77]. However, the common parent and each subsidiary that was a member of the affiliated group during any part of the consolidated return year are severally liable for the group's consolidated tax liability for that year [Reg. § 1.1502-6(a)].

### *XIII.C.8.c.(1) Consolidated Taxable Income*

[756 T.M., II.; TPS ¶5310.07.]

The consolidated taxable income of an affiliated group filing a consolidated return is determined by taking into account the separate taxable income of each member of the group and certain items of income and deduction that are required to be determined on a consolidated basis. The items of income and deduction required to be determined on a consolidated basis include [Reg. § 1.1502-11(a)]:

- the net operating loss deduction (see Reg. § 1.1502-21);
- capital gain and loss (see Reg. § 1.1502-22);
- § 1231 net gain and loss (see Reg. § 1.1502-23);
- the charitable contributions deduction (see Reg. § 1.1502-24);
- the dividends-received deduction (see Reg. § 1.1502-26); and
- the deduction for dividends paid on certain public utility stock (see Reg. § 1.1502-27).

The separate taxable income of a group member is determined as if the member filed a separate return, with the following modifications made for amounts taken into account based on the consolidated return regulations [Reg. § 1.1502-12]:

- no amounts determined on a consolidated basis (see above) are taken into account;
- transactions between members of the group are taken into account based on the intercompany transaction rules under Reg. § 1.1502-13 (see XIII.C.8.d.);
- excess loss amounts are included in income based on the rules under Reg. § 1.1502-19 (see XIII.C.8.e);
- built-in losses are taken into account based on the rules under Reg. § 1.1502-15;
- in computing depreciation deductions, property does not lose its character as new property upon transfer from one group member to another if: (i) the transfer is an intercompany transaction under Reg. § 1.1502-13, or (ii) the transferee gets a carryover basis in the property;
- the limitations on deductions for mine exploration expenditures and percentage depletion are taken into account under Reg. § 1.1502-16 and Reg. § 1.1502-44, respectively;
- the deduction for additions to reserves for bad debts of certain thrift institutions is taken into account under Reg. § 1.1502-42;
- basis is determined under Reg. § 1.1502-31 and § 1.1502-32; and
- earnings and profits are determined under Reg. § 1.1502-33.

There are a number of limitations on the use of a corporation's losses in determining the consolidated taxable income of an affiliated group:

- The separate return limitation year (SRLY) rules limit the use of the built-in losses of a group member that were incurred in tax years in which it did not join in the filing of the group's consolidated return [Reg. § 1.1502-15].
- The § 382 limitation (see XIII.E.5.b.) has been coordinated with the consolidated return regulations and, following an ownership change for a loss group (or subgroup), the amount of consolidated taxable income of the group for any post-change year that may be offset by pre-change consolidated group attributes may not exceed the § 382 limitation for that year [Reg. § 1.1502-90 through § 1.1502-99].

- The at-risk rules (see VIII.E.) apply to limit the use of losses from business and income-producing activities of the common parent and group members;
- Losses on transactions involving the stock of the common parent are disallowed [Reg. § 1.1502-13(f)(6)(i)(A)].
- The unified loss rule of Reg. § 1.1502-36 and the loss disallowance rule of Reg. § 1.1502-35 disallow the deduction of losses incurred upon the transfer of subsidiary stock in certain situations;
- If a group member disposes of subsidiary stock, losses of the subsidiary cannot be used to offset the gain on the disposition of the stock [Reg. § 1.1502-11(b)].
- If a group member pays preferred dividends to persons that are not group members, the losses and credits of the group may not be used to offset the group member's "disqualified separately computed income" [§ 1503(f)].
- Dual consolidated losses (i.e., the net operating losses of a U.S. corporation that is subject to the income tax of a foreign country) may not be used to reduce the taxable income of any other member of a U.S. consolidated group [§ 1503(d)(1)].

### XIII.C.8.c.(2) Consolidated Personal Holding Company Tax, Accumulated Earnings Tax, and AMT

[756 T.M., III., V.; TPS ¶5310.09., .10.]

In addition to income tax, an affiliated group of corporations filing a consolidated return is also generally subject to the personal holding company tax, the accumulated earnings tax, and the alternative minimum tax (AMT). The AMT of the group is determined on a consolidated basis. Depending on the circumstances, the accumulated earning tax and personal holding company tax of the group may be determined on either a consolidated basis or a separate company basis.

The personal holding company tax of a group is generally determined on a consolidated basis. However, if the group is an ineligible affiliated group or if one of its members is excluded from the definition of personal holding company, the personal holding company tax must be determined on a separate company basis, with each member separately determining whether it is subject to the personal holding company tax [Reg. § 1.1502-2(b), § 1.1502-2(c)].

The accumulated earnings tax is not applicable to personal holding companies. Thus, if the group determines its personal holding company status on a consolidated basis, the accumulated earnings tax will apply only if the group is not a personal holding company. If the group determines its personal holding company status on a separate company basis, the accumulated earnings tax will apply only to members that are not personal holding companies [Reg. § 1.1502-2(d), § 1.1502-43].

### XIII.C.8.c.(3) Consolidated Tax Liability and Consolidated Tax Credits

[756 T.M., II., V.; TPS ¶5310.08.]

The consolidated tax liability of an affiliated group filing a consolidated return is determined by adding together the various federal taxes that are imposed on the group (the income tax, the personal holding company tax, the accumulated earnings tax, and the alternative minimum tax) and then reducing this amount by any allowable credits [Reg. § 1.1502-2]. Allowable credits are determined on a consolidated basis and are subject to the SRLY rules (see XIII.C.8.c.(1)) [Reg. § 1.1502-3].

*XIII.C.8.c.(4) Allocation of Consolidated Tax Liability*

[755 T.M., VIII.; TPS ¶5310.11.]

Although each group member is severally liable for the group's consolidated tax liability, it is necessary to allocate the group's tax liability among the various members, primarily for the purpose of determining each member's earnings and profits. The amount of the tax liability allocated to a member as its share of the group tax liability results in a decrease in its earnings and profits [§ 1552; Reg. § 1.1552-1(a)].

*XIII.C.8.c.(5) Estimated Tax Payments by Consolidated Group*

[754 T.M., IX.; TPS ¶5310.02.E.]

In the first two years in which an affiliated group of corporations files a consolidated return, it may make estimated tax payments on either a consolidated or separate basis. If made on a separate basis, the amount of any estimated tax payments made by a member is credited against the group's tax liability. Once consolidated returns have been filed for two consecutive years, estimated tax payments must be made on a consolidated basis [Reg. § 1.1502-5(a)].

*XIII.C.8.d. Consolidated Returns — Intercompany Transactions*

[756 T.M., II.A.2.; TPS ¶5310.04.]

The consolidated return regulations contain a set of rules for taking into account items of income, gain, loss, and deduction arising from transactions between two group members. The purpose of these intercompany transaction rules is to clearly reflect the taxable income of members of the group as a whole by preventing intercompany transactions between two members from creating, accelerating, deferring, or avoiding consolidated taxable income. The intercompany transaction rules replace the general timing rules of the Code with two special rules: a matching rule and an acceleration rule. The matching rule requires that the separate-entity attributes of the two members' items must be re-determined to the extent necessary to produce the same effect on consolidated taxable income as if the two members were divisions of a single corporation and the intercompany transaction were a transaction between divisions. The acceleration rule takes the two members' items into account immediately if they cannot be taken into account under the matching rule to produce the effect of treating the members as divisions of the same corporation. Special rules apply to intercompany obligations [Reg. § 1.1502-13].

*XIII.C.8.e. Consolidated Returns — Investment Adjustments and Excess Loss Accounts*

[755 T.M., II., III.; TPS ¶5310.05.]

A group member's basis in the stock of a subsidiary is adjusted under the consolidated return regulations to take into account the subsidiary's items of income, gain, loss, and deduction, including its: (i) taxable income or loss, (ii) tax-exempt income, (iii) noncapital, nondeductible expenses, and (iv) distributions with respect to its stock. The purpose of these adjustments is to treat the member and subsidiary as a single entity, avoiding distortions in consolidated taxable income that would result in the absence of the adjustments. The basis adjustments are tiered upward within the affiliated group, starting with the lowest tier subsidiaries and working up to the common parent [Reg. § 1.1502-32].

If a subsidiary's items of loss and deduction exceed its items of gain and income, the member must make a negative basis adjustment to the subsidiary stock. If the negative basis adjustment exceeds the member's basis in the subsidiary stock, the member must treat the difference as an excess loss account in the subsidiary stock.

The excess loss account is treated as negative basis for all federal tax purposes. When the member disposes of the subsidiary stock to which the excess loss account relates, it must treat the amount of the excess loss account as income or gain from the disposition [Reg. § 1.1502-19].

### XIII.C.8.f. Advantages and Disadvantages of Filing Consolidated Return

[754 T.M., IV., V.; TPS ¶5310.]

There are a number of potential tax advantages for an affiliated group of corporations filing a consolidated return:

- the losses of one group member generally can be used to offset the income or gains of other group members [Reg. § 1.1502-21, § 1.1502-22, § 1.1502-23];

- dividends received by one group member from other group members generally are not taxable (i.e., they are not included in the gross income of the recipient member) [Reg. § 1.1502-13(f)(2)(ii)];

- gains on transactions between group members may be deferred [Reg. § 1.1502-13(c), § 1.1502-13(d)];

- a group member's tax basis in stock it owns in another group member (i.e., a subsidiary) may be increased when it is adjusted to reflect the other member's items of taxable income or loss, tax-exempt income, nondeductible expenses, and distributions [Reg. § 1.1502-32];

- deductions or credits that are subject to the income limitation and that would otherwise not be allowed in a separate return of a group member may be allowed in a consolidated return when the limitation is applied based on the aggregate income of all members of the group;

- foreign taxes paid by a group member that would otherwise not be allowed as a credit in a separate return as a result of the § 904 limitations may be allowed as a credit in a consolidated return when those limitations are applied on an aggregate basis to the foreign taxes paid by all members of the group [Reg. § 1.1502-4(c), § 1.1502-4(d)];

- a group member that is a personal holding company will not be subject to the personal holding company tax if the group meets various consolidated personal holding company tests [§ 542(b)];

- depreciable property can be transferred from one group member to another without losing the benefit of rapid depreciation methods [Reg. § 1.1502-12(g)];

- group members may make contributions to the group's profit-sharing plan on behalf of a group member that is prevented from making contributions due to a lack of earnings and profits;

- to the extent the filing of a consolidated return reduces the aggregate tax payable by all members of the group, the group's estimated tax payments will be lower [Reg. § 1.1502-5(a)];

- the amount of gain recognized by a consolidated group upon a complete liquidation or a stock redemption is limited [Reg. § 1.1502-13(f)(4), § 1.1502-13(f)(5)];

- the aggregate stock owned by all members of the group is used for purposes of applying § 332(b)(1), § 351(a), § 732(f), and § 904(d) [Reg. § 1.1502-34]; and

- the consolidated return regulations allow the group to take current advantage of the favorable tax attributes of a group member (such as losses), while at the same time preserving the business and legal advantages of a separate corporation (such as limited liability).

There are also a number of potential disadvantages to filing a consolidated return:

- the unified loss rule disallows the deduction of losses in certain situations in which one group member transfers shares of the stock it owns in another group member [Reg. § 1.1502-35, § 1.1502-36];

- compliance with the consolidated return regulations and the associated record-keeping requirements can be costly and an administrative burden;

- once the election to file a consolidated return is made, it is difficult to undo;

- a group member that has a tax year different from its parent is required to change to the parent's tax year [Reg. § 1.1502-76(a)];

- if a group member is required to file a short period return when it changes to the parent's tax year, its carryover period for net operating loss carryovers and capital loss carryovers may be shortened by as much as 11 months [Reg. § 1.1502-76(b)];

- a group member's excess loss account in the stock of a subsidiary must be included in income upon a disposition of the stock [Reg. § 1.1502-19];

- deductions or credits that are subject to the income limitation and that would otherwise be allowed in a separate return of a group member may not be allowed in a consolidated return when the income limitation is applied based on the aggregate income of all members of the group;

- a bad debt deduction is not allowed for a debt owed by one group member to another [Reg. § 1.1502-13(g)(7)(ii), *Ex. 3*];

- losses on transactions between group members may be deferred [Reg. § 1.1502-13(c), § 1.1502-13(d)];

- because the § 1231 gains and losses of all group members are set off against each other in a consolidated return, one member's § 1231 loss that would have been treated as an ordinary loss in a separate return may be required to offset another member's § 1231 gain that would have been treated as a capital gain in a separate return [Reg. § 1.1502-23]; and

- a group member's tax basis in stock it owns in another group member (i.e., a subsidiary) may be decreased when it is adjusted to reflect the other member's items of taxable income or loss, tax-exempt income, nondeductible expenses, and distributions [Reg. § 1.1502-32].

## XIII.D. Distributions by a Corporation

[764 T.M.; TPS ¶4810.]

When a corporation distributes money or property to its shareholders, the distribution often has tax consequences for both the corporation and the shareholders. The tax consequences are different for distributions made when the corporation is in the process of shutting down its operations (so-called liquidating distributions) and distributions made while the corporation is continuing its operations (so-called nonliquidating distributions). This section discusses the tax consequences of nonliquidating distributions. See XIII.E.3. for a discussion of the tax consequences of liquidating distributions.

The most basic type of nonliquidating distribution involves a corporation's distribution of money or property (other than its own stock) to a shareholder (see XIII.D.1.). However, there are two types of nonliquidating distributions that have special tax consequences:

1. a nonliquidating distribution in which a corporation distributes its own stock to a shareholder (see XIII.D.2. for a discussion of these so-called stock dividends); and

2. a nonliquidating distribution in which a corporation distributes money or property to a shareholder in exchange for the shareholder's stock in the corporation (see XIII.D.3. for a discussion of these so-called stock redemptions).

### XIII.D.1. Nonliquidating Corporate Distributions

[764 T.M.; TPS ¶4810.01.]

A nonliquidating distribution is a distribution of money or property by a corporation to a shareholder with respect to its stock. Thus, a nonliquidating distribution must be made to a shareholder in its capacity as a shareholder. A distribution made to a shareholder in its capacity as an employee or creditor of the corporation is not treated as a nonliquidating distribution [§ 301(a); Reg. § 1.301-1(c)].

### XIII.D.1.a. Tax Consequences of Nonliquidating Corporate Distribution to Shareholder

[764 T.M., V.; TPS ¶4810.01.C., .01.D.]

Generally, a shareholder is subject to the following tax treatment when it receives a nonliquidating distribution of money or property from a corporation with respect to its stock [§ 301(c), § 316(a)]:

1. first, the distribution is treated as a taxable dividend to the extent of the corporation's current and accumulated earnings and profits;

2. next, any portion of the distribution that does not qualify as a taxable dividend is treated as a nontaxable return of capital to the extent of the shareholder's adjusted basis in the stock of the corporation (this portion of the distribution is applied against and reduces the shareholder's adjusted basis in the stock);

3. finally, any portion of the distribution that exceeds the shareholder's adjusted basis in the stock of the corporation is taxable as capital gain.

The amount of a distribution received by a shareholder is equal to the amount of any money received, plus the fair market value of any property received, reduced (but not below zero) by the amount of any liability that is assumed or that the property is taken subject to [§ 301(b)].

The determination of the portion of a distribution treated as a dividend is determined based on the corporation's earnings and profits (E&P). E&P is a unique tax measure that is not the same as taxable income or retained earnings. E&P is essentially an economic concept of a corporation's ability to pay dividends without distributing any of the capital contributed to the corporation by shareholders or creditors. Although E&P is not clearly defined in the Code, § 312 and the related regulations address certain aspects of its computation.

---

**EXAMPLE:** All of the outstanding stock of X Corporation is owned by Bob, who has a $10,000 adjusted basis in his X stock, and Carol, who has a $5,000 adjusted basis in her X stock. During Year 1, X distributes $10,000 cash to each shareholder. X has current E&P of $5,000 and no accumulated E&P. Bob is taxed on his $10,000 distribution as follows: (i) $2,500 is a taxable dividend ($5,000 E&P x (Bob's $10,000 distribution/total $20,000 distribution)), and (ii) $7,500 is a nontaxable return of capital (Bob reduces his adjusted basis in his stock from $10,000 to $2,500). Carol is taxed on her $10,000 distribution as follows: (i) $2,500 is a taxable dividend ($5,000 E&P x (Carol's $10,000 distribution/total $20,000 distribution)), (ii) $5,000 is a nontaxable return of capital (Carol reduces her adjusted basis in her stock from $5,000 to $0), and (iii) $2,500 is taxed as capital gain.

---

A shareholder's adjusted basis for any property received in a distribution is equal to the fair market value of the property on the date of distribution [§ 301(d)].

### XIII.D.1.b. Tax Consequences of Nonliquidating Distribution to Corporation

[764 T.M., VIII.; TPS ¶4810.01.C., .01.D.]

Generally, a corporation does not recognize gain or loss when it makes a nonliquidating distribution of money or property to a shareholder with respect to its stock [§ 311(a)(1)]. However, if a corporation distributes appreciated property, it must recognize gain as if the property were sold to the shareholder at fair market value. For this purpose, the fair market value of the property cannot be treated as less than the amount of any liability assumed by the shareholder or any liability to which the property is subject [§ 311(b), § 336(b)].

---

**EXAMPLE:** X Corporation distributes property with a fair market value of $100,000 and an adjusted basis of $120,000 to its shareholder. X does not recognize any loss on the distribution.

**EXAMPLE:** Assume the same facts as in the previous example, except that X's adjusted basis in the property is $60,000 instead of $120,000. X must recognize gain of $40,000 ($100,000 − $60,000) on the distribution.

**EXAMPLE:** Assume the same facts as in the immediately above example, except that the property is subject to a liability of $150,000, which the shareholder assumes. X must recognize a gain of $90,000 ($150,000 − $60,000) on the distribution.

---

### XIII.D.2. Distributions of Stock and Stock Rights (Stock Dividends)

[765 T.M.; TPS ¶4830.01.]

A corporation may make a nonliquidating distribution to a shareholder of its own stock or rights to acquire its stock (so-called stock rights). Such a distribution of stock or stock rights is generally referred to as a stock dividend. The rules that apply to stock dividends are different from the general rules that apply to nonliquidating distributions (see XIII.D.1. for a discussion of those rules).

### XIII.D.2.a. Tax Consequences of Stock Dividends to Shareholder

[765 T.M., III.; TPS ¶4830.01.C.]

If a corporation makes a distribution of stock or stock rights to a shareholder with respect to its stock (i.e., a stock dividend), the shareholder generally does not recognize income from the distribution [§ 305(a), § 305(d)]. The shareholder's adjusted basis in the stock for which the stock dividend was made must be allocated between that stock (the "old stock") and the stock received in the distribution (the "new stock"). This allocation generally is made based on the relative fair market values of the old stock and the new stock on the date of distribution [§ 307(a)]. However, in the case of a distribution of stock rights with a fair market value of less than 15% of the fair market value of the stock with respect to which the distribution was made, the shareholder's adjusted basis in the stock rights is treated as zero unless the shareholder makes an election to allocate the adjusted basis based on the above rule [§ 307(b)].

---

**EXAMPLE:** X Corporation distributes to its shareholders of one additional share of its stock for each four shares of its stock that are held by the shareholders. X has five shareholders who each own 400 shares of stock. On the date of the distribution, the fair market value of the stock is $100 per share and each shareholder has an adjusted basis of $50 per share in the stock already owned. Each shareholder receives a distribution of 100 additional shares of stock. The shareholders do not recognize income on the distribution of the additional shares. Each shareholder must allocate its $20,000 adjusted basis in the old stock (400 shares x $50 per share) between that old stock and the new stock received in the distribution based on the relative fair market values of the old stock (400 shares x $100 per share = $40,000) and the new stock (100 shares x $100 per share = $10,000). Thus, each shareholder allocates $16,000 of adjusted basis ($20,000 x ($40,000/$50,000)) to the old stock and $4,000 of adjusted basis ($20,000 x ($10,000/$50,000) to the new stock.

---

There are several exceptions under which a shareholder must recognize income upon a distribution of stock or stock rights. A distribution of stock or stock rights is treated as a taxable distribution of property under the general rules that apply to nonliquidating distributions (see XIII.D.1.) if [§ 305(b)]:

1. the distribution is payable in either stock or other property at the election of any shareholder;
2. the distribution is disproportionate (i.e., the distribution results in the receipt of stock by some shareholders and the receipt of other property by other shareholders);
3. the distribution results in the receipt of common stock by some shareholders and the receipt of preferred stock by other shareholders;
4. the distribution is made with respect to preferred stock (unless the distribution merely results in an increase in the conversion ratio of convertible preferred stock to take into account a stock dividend or stock split); or
5. the distribution consists of convertible preferred stock (unless the distribution will not result in a disproportionate distribution).

### XIII.D.2.b. Tax Consequences of Stock Dividends to Corporation

[765 T.M., III.I.3.; TPS ¶4830.01.D.]

A corporation does not recognize gain or loss when it makes a nonliquidating distribution of stock or stock rights to a shareholder with respect to its stock [§ 311(a)(2)].

### XIII.D.3. Distributions in Redemption of Stock (Stock Redemption)

[767 T.M.; TPS ¶4820.01.]

A stock redemption is a transaction in which a corporation acquires its own stock from a shareholder in exchange for money or property [§ 317(b)]. When a corporation redeems a small portion of the stock of a large shareholder, the redemption resembles a nonliquidating distribution (the shareholder receives money or property from the corporation and there is no significant change in the shareholder's percentage ownership interest in the corporation). In contrast, when a corporation redeems the stock of a small shareholder, the transaction more closely resembles a sale or exchange of the stock to a third party. Thus, a stock redemption is treated as a nonliquidating distribution in some situations and a sale or exchange in other situations.

### XIII.D.3.a. Tax Consequences of Stock Redemption to Shareholders

[767 T.M., IV.A.1., IV.B.1.; TPS ¶4820.01.A.]

Generally, a shareholder treats a stock redemption like a nonliquidating distribution. However, a shareholder must treat a stock redemption like a sale or exchange of the stock if the redemption falls into one of the following categories [§ 302(b), § 303]:

- the redemption completely terminates the shareholder's ownership interest in the corporation;
- the redemption is substantially disproportionate with respect to the shareholder;
- the redemption is not essentially equivalent to a dividend for the shareholder;
- the redemption involves stock of a noncorporate shareholder and is in partial liquidation of the corporation;
- the redemption is made by a regulated investment company (RIC) that issues only stock redeemable at the demand of a shareholder and it is made at the demand of the shareholder; or
- the redemption is made to pay estate, inheritance, or other death taxes.

When a stock redemption is treated like a nonliquidating distribution, the shareholder must recognize dividend income to the extent of the corporation's E&P (see XIII.D.1. for further discussion of the tax consequences of a nonliquidating distribution). On the other hand, when a stock redemption is treated like a sale or exchange of stock, the shareholder generally recognizes capital gain or loss in an amount equal to the amount realized (i.e., the amount of money and fair market value of property received from the corporation) minus the shareholder's adjusted basis in the redeemed stock.

**Stock Redemption in Complete Termination of Shareholder's Ownership Interest.** If a stock redemption completely terminates a shareholder's ownership interest in the corporation, it is treated as a sale or exchange of the stock instead of a nonliquidating distribution. The constructive ownership rules of § 318(a) generally must be taken into account in determining whether a stock redemption completely terminates a shareholder's ownership interest. However, an individual shareholder may waive the application of the § 318(a)(1) family attribution rules if (i) the shareholder has no interest in the corporation immediately after the redemption (other than an interest as a creditor), (ii) the shareholder does not acquire an interest in the corporation within 10 years of the date of the redemption (other than an interest acquired by bequest or inheritance), and (iii) the shareholder agrees to retain certain records and to notify the IRS if it acquires an interest in the corporation within 10 years. A shareholder that is a corporation, partnership, estate, or trust (i.e., an entity shareholder) may waive the application of the § 318(a)(1) family attribution rules if (i) the entity shareholder and each related person meet the three requirements discussed above for individual shareholders, and (ii) each related person agrees to joint and several liability for any deficiency resulting from a prohibited acquisition of an ownership interest in the corporation [§ 302(b)(3), § 302(c); Reg. § 1.302-4].

**Stock Redemption that Is Substantially Disproportionate.** If a stock redemption is substantially disproportionate with respect to a shareholder, it is treated as a sale or exchange of the stock instead of a nonliquidating distribution. A stock redemption is substantially disproportionate with respect to a shareholder only if all of the following requirements are met [§ 302(b)(2); Reg. § 1.302-3]:

1. the shareholder owns less than 50% of the corporation's voting stock immediately after the redemption;

2. the shareholder's percentage of ownership of the corporation's voting stock after the redemption is less than 80% of its percentage of ownership of that stock before the redemption;

3. the shareholder's percentage of ownership of the corporation's common stock (whether voting or nonvoting) after the redemption is less than 80% of its percentage of ownership of that stock before the redemption; and

4. the redemption is not made pursuant to a plan for a series of redemptions that, in the aggregate, fails to meet the first three requirements.

***Stock Redemption that Is Not Essentially Equivalent to a Dividend.*** If a stock redemption is essentially equivalent to a dividend for the shareholder, then the liquidating distribution rules apply and the shareholder recognizes dividend income to the extent of the corporation's E&P. On the other hand, if a stock redemption is not essentially equivalent to a dividend for the shareholder, then the sale or exchange rules apply and the shareholder recognizes capital gain or loss. The determination of whether or not a stock redemption is essentially equivalent to a dividend is based on all the facts and circumstances. Generally, a redemption must result in a meaningful reduction of the shareholder's proportionate interest in the corporation in order to be considered not essentially equivalent to a dividend [§ 302(b)(1); Reg. § 1.302-2; *United States v. Davis*, 397 U.S. 301 (1970)].

***Stock Redemption of Noncorporate Shareholder in Partial Liquidation of Corporation.*** A redemption of the stock of a noncorporate shareholder that results in a partial liquidation of the corporation is treated as a sale or exchange of the stock instead of a nonliquidating distribution. A redemption is in partial liquidation of a corporation if (i) it is not essentially equivalent to a dividend (as determined at the corporate level rather than the shareholder level), (ii) it is made pursuant to a plan, and (iii) it occurs no later than the end of the tax year after the tax year in which the plan was adopted. A redemption is not essentially equivalent to a dividend at the corporate level if the redemption is attributable to the corporation ceasing to conduct an active business that had been carried on for at least five years and, immediately after the redemption, the corporation is still conducting another active business that has been carried on for at least five years [§ 302(b)(4), § 302(e)].

### XIII.D.3.b. Tax Consequences of Stock Redemption to Corporation

[767 T.M., IV.A.2., IV.B.2.; TPS ¶4820.01.D.]

A corporation treats a stock redemption like a nonliquidating distribution. Generally, it recognizes no gain or loss when it redeems its own stock for money or property [§ 311(a)]. However, if it distributes appreciated property in redemption of its stock, it must recognize gain on the distribution as if the property had been sold to the shareholder at its fair market value [§ 311(b)]. See XIII.D.1. for further discussion of the tax consequences to a corporation for a nonliquidating distribution.

## XIII.E. Corporate Reorganizations, Divisions, Liquidations, and Acquisitions

### XIII.E.1. Corporate Reorganizations

[771 T.M., 772 T.M., 774 T.M.; TPS ¶4910.]

Generally, when a taxpayer exchanges one type of property for another type of property, the taxpayer must recognize a gain or loss on the exchange [§ 1001]. However, a corporation does not recognize gain or loss upon an exchange of property solely for stock or securities in another corporation if the exchange is part of a plan of reorganization and the other corporation is a party to the reorganization [§ 361].

In the most basic sense, a corporate reorganization is transaction designed to effect the readjustment of a continuing interest in a corporation under a modified corporate form [§ 1.368-1(b), § 1.368-2(g)]. In order to qualify as a tax-free corporate reorganization, a transaction must meet a number of statutory and judicial requirements. The transaction must fall within one of seven types of statutory reorganization. See XIII.E.1.a. for a discussion of the types of corporate reorganization. The exchange must be made pursuant to a plan of reorganization. See XIII.E.1.b. for the definition of a plan of reorganization. The other corporation must be a party to the reorganization. See XIII.E.1.c. for the definition of a party to a reorganization. In addition, a number of judicially developed requirements must be met. See XIII.E.1.d. for a discussion of these additional requirements.

When a transaction qualifies as a reorganization, the parties to the reorganization are generally entitled to nonrecognition treatment for tax purposes. See XIII.E.1.e. for a discussion of the tax consequences for corporations and shareholders involved in acquisitive reorganizations.

### XIII.E.1.a. Types of Statutory Reorganizations

[770 T.M., VII.B.; TPS ¶4910.01.A.1.]

Seven types of corporate reorganizations qualify for nonrecognition treatment. Each qualifying type of reorganization is defined in § 368 and is typically referred to by the § 368 subparagraph in which it is defined.

### XIII.E.1.a.(1) "A" Reorganizations

[771 T.M, III.A.; TPS ¶4910.01.B.]

An "A" Reorganization is a statutory merger or consolidation that is effected pursuant to the operation of a state or foreign law [§ 368(a)(1)(A); Reg. § 1.368-2(b)(1)(ii)]. In a merger, one corporation is absorbed by another corporation. In a consolidation, two or more corporations are combined into a newly created corporation. In each type of transaction, the shareholders of the corporations that cease to exist become shareholders of the surviving corporation.

**Triangular Mergers.** In a typical "A" merger, the stock of the acquiring corporation is exchanged for the assets of the target corporation and the target corporation assets are combined with the acquiring corporation assets in the same corporation. However, a triangular merger can also qualify as an "A" reorganization. In a triangular merger, the stock of one corporation (the controlling corporation) that controls another corporation (the controlled subsidiary) is exchanged for the assets of the target corporation, but the target corporation is merged with the controlled subsidiary of the controlling corporation instead of the controlling corporation itself. In a forward triangular merger, the target corporation is merged into the controlled subsidiary [§ 368(a)(2)(D)]. In a reverse triangular merger, the controlled subsidiary is merged into the target corporation, with the target effectively becoming a subsidiary of the controlling corporation [§ 368(a)(2)(E)].

### XIII.E.1.a.(2) "B" Reorganizations

[771 T.M., IV.A.; TPS ¶4910.01.C.]

A "B" reorganization is a transaction in which: (i) one corporation (the acquiring corporation) acquires the stock of another corporation (the target corporation) in exchange solely for all or part of its voting stock, and (ii) the acquiring corporation has control of the target corporation immediately after the acquisition [§ 368(a)(1)(B); Reg. § 1.368-2(c)].

*Solely for voting stock.* To qualify as a "B" reorganization, voting stock must be the only consideration used by the acquiring corporation in the transaction. The voting stock can be common or preferred stock. Moreover, the voting stock can be either the voting stock of the acquiring corporation or the voting stock of a corporation that is in control of the acquiring corporation (but not both) [§ 368(a)(1)(B); Reg. § 1.368-2(c)].

The solely-for-voting-stock requirement has been strictly construed by the IRS and the courts. The use of any non-voting-stock consideration, no matter how small, will disqualify the transaction as a "B" reorganization.

*Control.* To qualify as a "B" reorganization, the acquiring corporation must have control of the target corporation immediately after the acquisition. Control means the ownership of stock possessing at least 80% of the combined voting power of all classes of voting stock and at least 80% of the number of shares of all other classes of stock [§ 368(c)]. A transaction may qualify as a "B" reorganization even if the acquiring corporation already had control of the target corporation immediately before the acquisition [§ 368(a)(1)(B); Reg. § 1.368-2(c)].

*Triangular "B" Reorganizations.* When the voting stock of a corporation that is in control of the acquiring corporation is used as the consideration in a "B" reorganization, the transaction is referred to as a triangular "B" reorganization because three parties are involved. Such a transaction will qualify as a "B" reorganization only if the voting stock of the controlling corporation is the sole consideration used in the transaction. Thus, the voting stock of the acquiring corporation may not be used as consideration in a triangular "B" reorganization [Reg. § 1.368-2(c)].

### XIII.E.1.a.(3) "C" Reorganizations

[771 T.M., III.C.; TPS ¶4910.01.D.]

A "C" reorganization is a transaction in which: (i) one corporation (the acquiring corporation) acquires substantially all the assets of another corporation (the target corporation) in exchange solely for all or part of its voting stock, and (ii) the target corporation liquidates by distributing the stock and other property it receives in the exchange, as well as any assets it retained, to its shareholders pursuant to the plan of reorganization [§ 368(a)(1)(C), § 368(a)(2)(G); Reg. § 1.368-2(d)(1)].

*Substantially All the Assets.* To qualify as a "C" reorganization, the acquiring corporation must acquire substantially all the assets of the target corporation. There is no precise definition of "substantially all." In determining whether substantially all the assets of the target corporation have been acquired, the nature of the assets transferred by the target is significant, with more importance assigned to those assets that were essential to the target's business.

For advance ruling purposes, the IRS has ruled that the acquiring corporation will be considered to acquire substantially all the assets of the target corporation if it acquires 70% of the target's gross assets and 90% of the target's net assets [Rev. Proc. 77-37, 1977-1 C.B. 568].

*Solely for Voting Stock.* A "C" reorganization is subject to a solely-for-voting-stock requirement similar to the requirement for a "B" reorganization (see XIII.E.1.a.(2)). However, there are two exceptions that make the solely-for-voting-stock requirement more flexible for "C" reorganizations.

Under the first exception, if the acquiring corporation otherwise uses only voting stock as consideration in a "C" reorganization, liabilities assumed by the acquiring corporation are disregarded (i.e., not treated as non-voting-stock consideration) [§ 368(a)(1)(C); Reg. § 1.368-2(d)(1)].

Under the second exception, if the acquiring corporation acquires 80% of the fair market value of all target corporation assets solely for voting stock, the transaction may qualify as a "C" reorganization despite the use of non-voting-stock consideration to acquire an additional portion of the target assets. In other words, the acquiring corporation may acquire up to 20% of the fair market value of the target corporation assets using non-voting-stock consideration without disqualifying the transaction as a "C" reorganization. Liabilities assumed by the acquiring corporation are treated as non-voting-stock consideration for purposes of this exception [§ 368(a)(2)(B); Reg. § 1.368-2(d)(2), § 1.368-2(d)(3), § 1.368-2(d)(4)].

***Triangular "C" Reorganizations.*** When the voting stock of a corporation that is in control of the acquiring corporation is used as the consideration in a "C" reorganization, the transaction is referred to as a triangular "C" reorganization because three parties are involved. Such a transaction will qualify as a "C" reorganization only if the voting stock of the controlling corporation is the sole consideration used in the transaction. Thus, the voting stock of the acquiring corporation may not be used as consideration in a triangular "C" reorganization.

### *XIII.E.1.a.(4) "D" Reorganizations*

[772 T.M.; TPS ¶4910.01.E.]

A "D" reorganization is a transaction in which: (i) a corporation transfers all or part of its assets to another corporation, (ii) the transferor corporation and/or its shareholders are in control of the transferee corporation immediately after the transfer, and (iii) pursuant to the plan of reorganization, the transferee corporation distributes its stock or securities to its shareholders in a fully or partially tax-free reorganization or division [§ 368(a)(1)(D)]. Thus, a "D" reorganization is essentially a reshuffling of assets among corporations under common control. There are two types of "D" reorganizations: (i) a reorganization involving the division of a corporation into two or more separate corporations (a divisive "D" reorganization), and (ii) a reorganization that does not involve the division of a corporation (a non-divisive "D" reorganization).

***Non-divisive "D" Reorganizations.*** To qualify as a non-divisive "D" reorganization, the transferor corporation must transfer substantially all of its assets to the transferee corporation and it must then liquidate by distributing the stock and other property received in the exchange, as well as any retained assets, to its shareholders [§ 368(a)(1)(D), § 354(b)(1)]. The transferor corporation and/or its shareholders must have control of the transferee corporation immediately after the transfer. For non-divisive "D" reorganizations, control means the ownership of stock possessing at least 50% of the combined voting power of all classes of voting stock or at least 50% of the value of shares of all classes of stock [§ 368(a)(2)(H)(i), § 304(c)(1)].

***Divisive "D" Reorganizations.*** If the corporation does not transfer substantially all its assets to the transferee corporation, then the transaction is tested as a divisive "D" reorganization and the transferor corporation must distribute the transferee corporation's stock in a transaction that satisfies the requirements for a corporate division (see XIII.E.2. for a discussion of corporate divisions) [§ 368(A)(1)(D), § 355]. The transferor corporation and/or its shareholders must have control of the transferee corporation immediately after the transfer. For divisive "D" reorganizations, control means the ownership of stock possessing at least 80% of the combined voting power of all classes of voting stock and at least 80% of the number of shares of all other classes of stock [§ 368(c)].

### XIII.E.1.a.(5) "E" Reorganizations

[774 T.M., III.; TPS ¶4910.01.F.]

An "E" reorganization is a recapitalization, which is a reshuffling of a capital structure within the framework of an existing corporation [§ 368(a)(1)(E); *Helvering v. Southwest Consolidated Corp.*, 315 U.S. 194 (1942)]. In other words, an "E" reorganization involves a change in the capital structure of a single corporation through an exchange of stock or securities for other stock or securities.

Examples of "E" reorganizations include exchanges of equity for equity (such as when a corporation exchanges common stock for preferred stock or preferred stock for common stock) and equity for debt (such as when a corporation discharges its bonds by issuing preferred stock to bondholders) [Reg. § 1.368-2(e)].

### XIII.E.1.a.(6) "F" Reorganizations

[774 T.M., II.; TPS ¶4910.01.G.]

An "F" reorganization is a mere change in identity, form, or place of organization of a single corporation [§ 368(a)(1)(F)]. An "F" reorganizations includes transactions such as a reincorporation in another state and a change in the form of organization [Rev. Ruls. 57-276, 67-376; PLRs 8551017, 8448080].

### XIII.E.1.a.(7) "G" Reorganizations

[790 T.M., XIII.B.3., 791 T.M., VI.B.2.; TPS ¶4910.01.H.]

A "G" reorganization is a transaction in which a corporation transfers all or part of its assets to another corporation in bankruptcy and, pursuant to the plan of reorganization, the transferee corporation distributes its stock or securities to its shareholders in a fully or partially tax-free reorganization or division [§ 368(a)(1)(G)]. Thus, like a "D" reorganization, a "G" reorganization may be either a divisive or a non-divisive reorganization.

### XIII.E.1.b. Plan of Reorganization

[750 T.M., III.A.; TPS ¶4910.01.A.9.]

A plan of reorganization must provide for the execution of one of the seven types of statutory reorganizations and for the satisfaction of each of the related requirements for nonrecognition treatment. The actions contemplated in the plan of reorganization must be ordinary and necessary to the conduct of the corporation's business and must result in the continuation of that business by a corporation that is a party to the reorganization [Reg. § 1.368-1(c), § 1.368-2(g)].

### XIII.E.1.c. Party to Reorganization

[770 T.M., VIII.A.1.; TPS ¶4910.01.A.3.]

A party to a reorganization includes: (i) a corporation that results from a reorganization, (ii) both corporations involved in a reorganization in which one corporation acquires stock or assets of the other corporation, and (iii) a corporation that controls an acquiring corporation that is a party to reorganization [§ 368(b); Reg. § 1.368-2(f)].

### XIII.E.1.d. Other Reorganization Requirements

[770 T.M., VII.A.; TPS ¶4910.01.A.]

In addition to the statutory requirements, there are several judicially developed requirements that generally must be satisfied for a transaction to qualify as a tax-free reorganization. These requirements include the business purpose requirement, the continuity of interest requirement, and the continuity of business enterprise requirement.

***Business Purpose.*** The reorganization provisions provide nonrecognition treatment for "certain specifically described exchanges incident to... readjustments of corporate structures... as are required by business exigencies..." [Reg. § 1.368-1(b)]. Thus, a transaction must have a valid business purpose to qualify for tax-free reorganization treatment. The business purpose requirement grew out of a well-known Supreme Court case, the crux of which is that a transaction should not be respected for tax purposes if it has no motive other than the accomplishment of a tax purpose [*Gregory v. Helvering*, 293 U.S. 465 (1935)].

The business purpose required is presumably a valid non-tax purpose for undertaking the transaction in the first place. Provided that a transaction is entered into for a valid business purpose (which is ordinarily the case if the transaction is between unrelated parties negotiating at arm's length), the board of directors is evidently free to choose the most favorable structure based upon after-tax value to shareholders, without fear that the putative reorganization will be disqualified on the ground that the choice of that particular structure (as distinct from the reason for the transaction itself) was to secure a tax advantage.

It is not clear whether the required business purpose must be the business purpose of the corporation or the business purpose of the shareholders. The regulations seem to emphasize corporate business purpose [Reg. § 1.368-1(b), § 1.368-1(c)]; however, some cases have indicated that shareholder business purpose will be sufficient to meet the requirement [*Lewis v. Commissioner*, 176 F.2d 646 (1st Cir. 1949); *Parshelsky v. Commissioner*, 303 F.2d 14 (2d Cir. 1962)].

***Continuity of Interest.*** The purpose of the continuity of interest requirement is to prevent transactions that resemble sales from qualifying for tax-free reorganization treatment. To satisfy this requirement, a substantial part of the value of the proprietary interests in the target corporation must be preserved in the reorganization [Reg. § 1.368-1(e)(1)(i)]. Thus, the target corporation shareholders must receive a definite and substantial interest in the acquiring corporation in exchange for their target stock in order to preserve their proprietary interests in the target corporation. The continuity of interest requirement does not apply to single entity reorganizations, such as "E" and "F" reorganizations.

In determining whether the target shareholders receive a definite and substantial interest in the acquiring corporation, only the stock of the acquiring corporation is taken into account. Consideration such as cash and debt is not taken into account [Reg. § 1.368-1(e)(1)(i)]. There is no bright line rule on the quantity of equity consideration that the target shareholders must receive. However, the IRS has ruled that a 50% equity continuity of interest, by value, is adequate [Rev. Rul. 66-224, 1966-2 C.B. 114]. The target shareholders must hold their equity interest in the acquiring corporation for a sufficiently long period of time. All facts and circumstances are taken into consideration in determining whether, in substance, the proprietary interests in the target corporation are preserved [Reg. § 1.368-1(e)(1)(i)].

***Continuity of Business Enterprise.*** The purpose of the continuity of business enterprise requirement is to ensure that the reorganization transaction is not merely a step in winding up the business activity of the target corporation. Thus, for example, where one corporation acquired the assets of another corporation and then sold them pursuant to a preconceived plan, the transaction did not qualify as a tax-free reorganization because the business of that corporation was not continued [*Std. Realization Co. v. Commissioner*, 10 T.C. 708 (1948)].

Under the continuity of business enterprise requirement, the acquiring corporation must either continue the target corporation's business (business continuity) or use a significant portion of the target corporation's assets in a business (asset continuity). The determination of whether there is business or asset continuity is based on all the facts and circumstances [Reg. § 1.368-1(d)].

### XIII.E.1.e. Tax Consequences of Reorganizations

[770 T.M., VIII.; TPS ¶4910.02.]

In acquisitive reorganizations ("A", "B", "C", non-divisive "D", and non-divisive "G" reorganizations), the acquiring corporation generally acquires the stock or assets of the target corporation in exchange for its stock. In some cases, the acquiring corporation also transfers property other than its stock in the exchange. The following is a discussion of the tax consequences to the acquiring corporation, the target corporation, and the target shareholders in an acquisitive reorganization.

### XIII.E.1.e.(1) Tax Consequences to Acquiring Corporation in Reorganization

[770 T.M., VIII.D.; TPS ¶4910.02.B.]

**Nonrecognition of Gain or Loss.** The acquiring corporation does not recognize gain or loss when it exchanges its stock for the stock or assets of the target corporation [§ 1032]. However, if the acquiring corporation transfers property other than its stock as part of the transaction, it must generally recognize gain or loss on the exchange of that property under the general rules that apply to sales and exchanges of property [§ 1001]. See Chapter III. for a discussion of the general rules that apply to sales or exchanges of property.

---

**EXAMPLE:** X Corporation acquires substantially all the assets of Y Corporation solely in exchange for its voting stock in a "C" reorganization. X recognizes no gain or loss on the transfer of its stock to Y.

---

**Basis.** The acquiring corporation generally takes a basis in the stock or assets of the target corporation equal to the basis of that property in the hands of the transferor (i.e., a carryover basis), increased by the amount of any gain recognized by the transferor [§ 362(b)]. Thus, in the case of a stock acquisition, the acquiring corporation takes a basis in the target stock equal to the basis of the target shareholders in that stock, increased by the amount of any gain recognized by the target shareholders. Similarly, in the case of an asset acquisition, the acquiring corporation takes a basis in the assets equal to the target corporation's basis in the assets, increased by the amount of any gain recognized by the target corporation.

---

**EXAMPLE:** Assume the same facts as in the previous example and that Y's basis in the assets immediately before the transaction is $250,000. X takes a $250,000 basis in the assets.

---

**Nonrecognition of Gain or Loss on Subsequent Liquidation of Target.** If the acquiring corporation acquires the stock of the target corporation and subsequently liquidates the target, no gain or loss is recognized if the transaction qualifies as the complete liquidation of a subsidiary. See XIII.E.3. for a discussion of the tax treatment of the complete liquidation of a subsidiary.

### *XIII.E.1.e.(2) Tax Consequences to Target Corporation in Reorganization*

[770 T.M., VIII.C.; TPS ¶4910.02.C.]

*Nonrecognition of Gain or Loss on Exchange.* In a reorganization in which the acquiring corporation acquires the assets of the target corporation solely in exchange for its stock, the target corporation does not recognize gain or loss on the exchange [§ 361(a)]. However, if the target corporation receives money or other property ("boot") in addition to the stock of the acquiring corporation, the tax treatment of the target corporation depends on whether or not the target distributes the boot to its shareholders. If the target distributes the boot to its shareholders, it does not recognize any gain or loss on the exchange. If the target does not distribute the boot to its shareholders, it must recognize gain (but not loss) on the exchange. The amount of gain recognized is limited to the value of the boot not distributed to shareholders [§ 361(b)].

---

**EXAMPLE:** Y Corporation transfers substantially all of its assets to X Corporation solely in exchange for stock and securities of X in a "D" reorganization. Y recognizes no gain or loss on the transfer of its assets to X.

**EXAMPLE:** Assume the same facts as in the previous example, except that Y Corporation also receives money and other property from X (in addition to the stock and securities) and that, after the reorganization transaction, Y distributes all the stock, securities, money, and other property to its shareholders in complete liquidation. Y recognizes no gain or loss on the transfer of its assets to X.

---

*Treatment of Liabilities.* When a liability of the target corporation is assumed by the acquiring corporation in a reorganization transaction, the acquiring corporation's assumption of the liability is not treated as boot received by the target corporation unless it appears that the principal purpose of the assumption of the liability was the avoidance of federal income tax or the assumption of the liability was not otherwise done for a bona fide business purpose [§ 357(a), § 357(b)]. If the reorganization involved is a divisive "D" reorganization and the sum of the total liabilities assumed is greater than the adjusted basis of the property transferred, then the excess amount must be recognized as gain from the sale or exchange of the property [§ 357(c)].

*Nonrecognition of Gain or Loss on Distribution.* Generally, the target corporation does not recognize any gain or loss on the distribution of property to its shareholders pursuant to a plan of reorganization [§ 361(c)(1)]. However, if any of the property distributed is property other than stock or debt of the target corporation or stock or debt of another party to the reorganization that the target corporation received in the reorganization, then the target corporation must recognize gain as if that property were sold to its shareholders at its fair market value [§ 361(c)(2)].

### *XIII.E.1.e.(3) Tax Consequences to Target Shareholders in Reorganization*

[770 T.M., VIII.B.; TPS ¶4910.02.A.]

*Nonrecognition of Gain or Loss.* In a reorganization in which the acquiring corporation acquires the stock or securities of the target corporation from the target shareholders solely in exchange for its stock or securities, the target shareholders generally do not recognize gain or loss on the exchange [§ 354(a)(1)]. However, the nonrecognition rule does not apply to the extent that the principal amount of any securities received exceeds the principal amount of any securities surrendered

[§ 354(a)(2)(A)]. Nonqualified preferred stock (as defined in § 351(g)(2)) is not treated as stock or securities for purposes of the nonrecognition rule [§ 354(a)(2)(C)].

---

**EXAMPLE:** X Corporation acquires all of the stock of Y Corporation solely in exchange for X voting stock in a "B" reorganization. As part of the plan of reorganization, D, a shareholder in Y, exchanges all of his shares of Y stock for X stock. D recognizes no gain or loss on the transfer of his shares to X.

---

If the target shareholders receive boot in addition to the stock or securities of the acquiring corporation, they generally must recognize gain (but not loss) on the exchange. The amount of gain recognized is limited to the value of the boot (i.e., the amount of money plus the fair market value of other property) [§ 356(a)(1)]. If the exchange has the effect of a distribution of a dividend, then any gain is taxed as a dividend to the extent of undistributed earnings and profits, and the balance of any gain is taxed as gain from the sale or exchange of property [§ 356(a)(2)]. In determining whether the receipt of boot has the effect of a dividend distribution, the factors used to distinguish redemptions that are treated like sales and exchanges from redemptions that are treated like distributions apply (see XIII.D.3.a.). In the context of a reorganization, a boot payment does not have the effect of a dividend distribution if, by viewing the reorganization "exchange" as a whole, the exchange does not have the effect of a dividend distribution.

---

**EXAMPLE:** X Corporation acquires all the assets of Y Corporation in a statutory merger that qualifies as an "A" reorganization. As part of the plan of reorganization, B, a shareholder in Y, exchanges all of his shares of Y stock for X stock and $50 cash. B's shares of Y stock had a fair market value of $200 and an adjusted basis of $75. B realizes a gain of $125 ($200 − $75) on the transfer of his Y stock to X. However, assuming the exchange does not have the effect of a dividend distribution, the amount of gain recognized by B is limited to $50, the amount of the boot received in the exchange.

---

***Basis.*** The target shareholders generally take a basis in the stock or securities of the acquiring corporation received that is the same as their basis in the target corporation stock or securities surrendered (i.e., a substituted basis). However, if the target shareholders also receive boot from the acquiring corporation, their basis in the acquiring corporation stock or securities must be decreased by the amount of money and fair market value of other property received, and must be increased by the amount of gain recognized on the exchange [§ 358(a)].

---

**EXAMPLE:** Assume the same facts as in the previous example. B takes a $75 basis in the X Corporation stock, which is equal to his basis in the Y Corporation stock ($75), decreased by the amount of money and other property he received ($50), and increased by the amount of gain he recognized on the exchange ($50).

---

The target shareholders' basis in the acquiring corporation stock or securities received in the reorganization must be allocated among the classes of stock or securities received [§ 358(b)].

### XIII.E.2. Corporate Divisions

[776 T.M.; TPS ¶4920.]

In certain situations, it may be desirable to divide a corporation into two or more entities. In such a corporate division, the parent (the distributing corporation) generally distributes the stock of the subsidiary (the controlled corporation) to its shareholders. Under general tax principles, this type of transaction would normally be taxable to the distributing corporation and its shareholders; however, nonrecognition treatment can be achieved for such a transaction if certain requirements are satisfied. See XIII.E.2.a. for the requirements that must be satisfied for a corporate division to qualify for nonrecognition treatment. See XIII.E.2.b. for a discussion of the tax consequences to the distributing corporation and its shareholders.

Three types of corporate division may qualify for nonrecognition treatment:

1. In a spin-off, the distributing corporation makes a distribution of stock of a controlled corporation to its shareholders, and the shareholders do not surrender any of their stock in the distributing corporation. The distribution is usually pro rata.

2. In a split-off, the distributing corporation makes a distribution of stock of a controlled corporation to its shareholders, and the shareholders surrender a portion of their stock in the distributing corporation for stock in the controlled corporation. The distribution is usually not pro rata.

3. In a split-up, the distributing corporation makes a distribution of stock of two or more controlled corporations to its shareholders in exchange for all of their stock in distributing corporation, resulting in a complete liquidation of distributing corporation.

### XIII.E.2.a. Corporate Divisions — Requirements for Nonrecognition Treatment

[776 T.M., II.; TPS ¶4920.01.B.]

A corporate division qualifies for nonrecognition treatment if it meets all of the following requirements:

1. The distributing corporation must make a distribution to its shareholders of all of its stock in the controlled corporation or enough of its stock in the controlled corporation to constitute control of controlled corporation [§ 355(a)(1)(A), § 355(a)(1)(D)]. Control means the ownership of stock possessing at least 80% of the combined voting power of all classes of voting stock and at least 80% of the total number of shares of all other classes of stock [§ 368(c)].

2. Both the distributing corporation and the controlled corporation must be engaged in the active conduct of a trade or business immediately after the distribution or, if the distributing corporation had no assets other than the stock of the controlled corporation immediately before the distribution, the controlled corporation must be engaged in the active conduct of a trade or business immediately after the distribution. Such trade or business must have been actively conducted throughout the five-year period before the distribution [§ 355(a)(1)(C), § 355(b); Reg. § 1.355-3].

3. The transaction must not be used principally as a device for the distribution of the earnings and profits of the distributing corporation and/or the controlled corporation [§ 355(a)(1)(B); Reg. § 1.355-2(d)].

4. The transaction must be carried out for a valid business purpose other than the avoidance of federal income tax (this is the business purpose requirement discussed at XIII.E.1.d.) [Reg. § 1.355-2(b)].

5. The persons who owned the business before the distribution must own a sufficient amount of stock in each of the corporations in which the business is conducted after the distribution in order to establish a continuity of interest in the business (this is the continuity of interest requirement discussed at XIII.E.1.d.) [Reg. § 1.355-2(c)].

### XIII.E.2.b. Tax Consequences of Corporate Divisions

[776 T.M., IX., X., XI.; TPS ¶4920.05.]

***Nonrecognition of Gain and Loss.*** If a corporate division satisfies all of the requirements discussed in XIII.E.2.a., then the distributing corporation and its shareholders recognize no gain or loss on the distributing corporation's distribution of stock in the controlled corporation to its shareholders [§ 355(a)(1), § 355(c)(1)]. However, if the distributing corporation also distributes appreciated property to the shareholders, the distributing corporation must recognize gain on that property as if it sold it to the shareholders at fair market value [§ 355(c)(2)].

***Basis.*** The shareholders generally take a basis in the stock of the controlled corporation that is the same as their basis in any distributing corporation stock they exchanged in the transaction. However, if the distributing corporation also distributed other property in the transaction, the shareholders must: (i) decrease their basis by the amount of money or fair market value of any other property received and the amount of any loss recognized, and (ii) increase their basis by any amount treated as a dividend and the amount of any gain recognized [§ 358(a)(1)]. The shareholders take a basis in any other property received equal to the fair market value of that property on the date of the distribution [§ 358(a)(2)].

***Exception for Distributions in Connection with Acquisitions.*** Nonrecognition treatment does not apply to a corporate division that is part of a plan or series of related transactions in which one or more new shareholders will acquire a 50% or greater interest in the distributing corporation or the controlled corporation [§ 355(e)(2)(A)]. Any 50% or greater acquisition that takes place within the four-year period beginning two years before the date of the distribution is deemed to be part of such a plan [§ 355(e)(2)(B)].

### XIII.E.3. Corporate Liquidations

[784 T.M.; TPS ¶5010.]

Generally, distributions made by a corporation to its shareholders with respect to its stock are treated as dividends taxable to the shareholders as ordinary income [§ 301]. However, special rules apply to distributions made by a corporation to shareholders in complete liquidation of the corporation.

### XIII.E.3.a. Complete Liquidation of Corporation

[784 T.M.; TPS ¶5010.01.]

A distribution is considered to be in complete liquidation of a corporation if it is a single distribution or one of a series of distributions made in complete cancellation or redemption of all the corporation's stock pursuant to a plan of liquidation [§ 346(a); Reg. § 1.332-2(c)].

The Code does not explicitly define what entails a plan of liquidation. It implies that the adoption of a resolution by the shareholders of the liquidating corporation authorizing the distribution of all the corporation's assets in complete cancellation or redemption of its stock is considered to be the adoption of a plan of liquidation in the case of a liquidation that occurs within one tax year [§ 332(b)(2)]. However, it also implies that a more formal plan of liquidation is required in the case of a liquidation involving a series of distributions over a period of more than one tax year [§ 332(b)(3)]. The IRS requires only that the liquidating corporation must file Form 966, *Corporate Dissolution or Liquidation*, with its final return, and that a corporation receiving a liquidating distribution must file a statement with its return specifying certain information about the distribution and making a representation as to the date on which the plan of liquidation was adopted [Reg. § 1.332-6].

When a series of distributions is made, it is essential that liquidation status exists at the time of the first distribution and continues until the liquidation is completed. The liquidation is considered to be completed when the liquidating corporation ceases to be a going concern and its activities are merely for the purpose of winding up its affairs, paying its debts, and distributing any remaining balance to its shareholders. A complete liquidation can occur even if the corporation is not legally dissolved and it retains a nominal amount of assets to preserve its legal existence [Reg. § 1.332-2(c)].

A distribution to a noncorporate shareholder in partial liquidation of a corporation is treated as a distribution in redemption of stock (see XIII.D.3.), not a complete liquidation [§ 302(a), § 302(b)(4)]. A distribution is considered to be in partial liquidation of a corporation if: (i) the distribution is not essentially equivalent to a dividend, and (ii) the distribution is made pursuant to a plan and occurs within the tax year the plan is adopted or the succeeding tax year. A distribution is not essentially equivalent to a dividend if: (i) the distribution is attributable to the distributing corporation's ceasing to conduct a trade or business that was actively conducted during the preceding five-year period (or it consists of assets of such a trade or business), and (ii) immediately after the distribution, the distributing corporation is actively engaged in another such trade or business [§ 302(e)].

For a discussion of the general tax consequences of a complete liquidation to the liquidating corporation and its shareholders, see XIII.E.3.b. and c. For a discussion of the special rules that apply to the complete liquidation of a subsidiary, see XIII.E.3.d. and e.

### XIII.E.3.b. Tax Consequences to Shareholders in Corporate Liquidation
[784 T.M., VIII.A.3.; TPS ¶5010.03.]

***Recognition of Gain or Loss.*** A shareholder that receives a distribution in complete liquidation of a corporation must treat the distribution as full payment in exchange for the stock it holds in the corporation [§ 331(a)]. Thus, the shareholder must recognize gain or loss on the stock equal to the amount of the liquidating distribution received less its adjusted basis in the stock [§ 331(c), § 1001].

---

**EXAMPLE:** X Corporation has 100 shares of stock outstanding. A owns 70 shares of X stock with a basis of $90,000 and B owns 30 shares of X stock with a basis of $20,000. X's only asset is $100,000 of cash. Upon complete liquidation of X, $70,000 in cash is distributed to A and $30,000 of cash is distributed to B. A recognizes a loss of $20,000 ($70,000 − $90,000) and B recognizes a gain of $10,000 ($30,000 − $20,000).

---

***Basis.*** If property is distributed to a shareholder as part of a complete liquidation and the shareholder recognizes gain or loss on the distribution of the property, the shareholder takes a basis in the property equal to the fair market value of the property on the date of distribution [§ 334(a)].

---

**EXAMPLE:** D owns 1,000 shares of Z Corporation stock with a basis of $400,000. Upon the complete liquidation of Z, a building with a fair market value of $1 million and a mortgage of $500,000 is distributed to D. D recognizes a gain of $100,000 (($1 million − $500,000) − $400,000) on the liquidation of Z. D takes a basis of $1 million in the building.

---

### XIII.E.3.c. Tax Consequences to Liquidating Corporation
[784 T.M., VIII.A.1.; TPS ¶5010.02.]

A liquidating corporation generally must recognize gain or loss on the distribution of property to its shareholders in complete liquidation as if it sold the distributed property to the shareholders at fair market value [§ 336(a)]. Thus, a liquidating corporation recognizes a gain or loss on such a distribution equal to the fair market value (FMV) of the distributed property less its basis in that property [§ 1001]. However, if the property distributed in a complete liquidation is subject to a liability, or a shareholder assumes a liability in connection with the liquidating distribution of the property, then the fair market value used in computing the corporation's gain or loss may not be less than the amount of that liability [§ 336(b)].

---

**EXAMPLE:** X Corporation makes a liquidating distribution to shareholder B of property with a fair market value of $10,000 and an adjusted basis of $5,000. The property is subject to a liability of $8,000. X Corporation recognizes gain of $5,000 ($10,000 FMV − $5,000 basis) on the distribution.

**EXAMPLE:** Assume the same facts as in the previous example, except that the property is instead subject to a liability of $12,000. X Corporation recognizes gain of $7,000 ($12,000 deemed FMV − $5,000 basis) on the distribution.

---

There are two exceptions under which a corporation does not recognize any gain or loss when it makes a liquidating distribution:

1. A corporation that makes a liquidating distribution as part of a corporate reorganization recognizes no gain or loss on the distribution [§ 336(c), § 361(c)(4)]. See XIII.E.1. for a discussion of corporate reorganizations.

2. A controlled subsidiary that makes a liquidating distribution to its parent recognizes no gain or loss on the distribution [§ 337(a)]. A controlled subsidiary is a subsidiary in which the parent owns at least 80% of the voting power and value [§ 337(c), § 332(b), § 1504(a)(2)]. See XIII.E.3.d. for a discussion of complete liquidations of subsidiary corporations.

There are also a two exceptions under which a liquidating corporation's recognition of loss may be limited when it makes a liquidating distribution of property:

1. A corporation does not recognize any loss on a liquidating distribution to a related person (as defined in § 267(b)) unless the distribution is a pro rata distribution to all shareholders and the distribution does not include any property acquired by the corporation as a capital contribution or as part of a § 351 transaction during the five-year period before the distribution [§ 336(d)(1)].

2. A corporation may recognize only a limited amount of loss on a liquidating distribution of property acquired as a capital contribution or as part of a § 351 transaction if the property was acquired for the principal purpose of recognizing loss through a liquidating distribution. Property acquired during the two-

year period before the distribution is deemed to be acquired for such purpose. The amount of loss that may be recognized is limited to the portion of the loss that is attributable to the period after the property was acquired. The limitation is applied by reducing the corporation's adjusted basis in the property by the amount of built-in loss in the property on the date it was acquired [§ 336(d)(2)].

---

**EXAMPLE:** Shareholder D makes a contribution to the capital of Corporation Z of loss property for the purpose of having Z recognize the loss in connection with its complete liquidation. On the date of contribution, the property has a fair market value of $100 and an adjusted basis of $1,000. After adopting a plan of liquidation, Z sells the property to an unrelated party for $60. On the sale of the property, Z realizes a loss of $940 ($60 amount realized – $1,000 adjusted basis). However, the amount of the loss that Z can recognize is limited since the property was acquired for the purpose of recognizing loss through a liquidating distribution. Z can only recognize a loss of $40 ($60 amount realized – ($1,000 adjusted basis – $900 built-in loss on date of contribution).

---

### XIII.E.3.d. Complete Liquidation of Subsidiary

[784 T.M., II.; TPS ¶5010.05.]

As discussed in XIII.E.3.b. and c., a liquidating corporation and its shareholders generally must recognize gain or loss on distributions of property in complete liquidation of the corporation. However, special rules apply to the complete liquidation of a controlled subsidiary. A controlled subsidiary is a subsidiary in which the parent owns at least 80% of the total voting power and at least 80% of the total stock value [§ 337(c), § 332(b), § 1504(a)(2)].

***Nonrecognition of Gain or Loss.*** When a controlled subsidiary makes a distribution of property to its parent in complete liquidation, neither the parent nor the subsidiary recognizes gain or loss on the distribution [§ 332(a), § 337(a)]. For this purpose, any transfer of property by the subsidiary to the parent in satisfaction of debt is treated as a distribution of property to its parent in complete liquidation [§ 337(b)(1)].

When a controlled subsidiary makes liquidating distributions of property to minority shareholders in addition to the parent, the nonrecognition rules do not apply to the liquidating distributions to the minority shareholders. Instead, the general rules discussed in XIII.E.3.b. and c. apply to liquidating distributions to minority shareholders. Thus, a minority shareholder must recognize gain or loss on a liquidating distribution as if it had sold its stock [§ 331(a), § 1001]. A controlled subsidiary recognizes gain on a liquidating distribution to a minority shareholder as if it had sold the property [§ 336(a)]. A controlled subsidiary cannot recognize loss on a liquidating distribution to a minority shareholder [§ 336(d)(3)].

There are two other exceptions to the subsidiary liquidation rules. First, when a controlled subsidiary makes a liquidating distribution to a parent that is a tax-exempt organization, the nonrecognition rules do not apply unless the parent will use the distributed property in an unrelated business [§ 337(b)(2)]. Second, when the controlled subsidiary is a U.S. holding company and its parent is a foreign corporation, the nonrecognition rules do not apply and any liquidating distribution is generally taxed as a dividend under § 301 [§ 332(d)]. See XIII.D.1. for a discussion of the taxation of dividends.

***Basis.*** The parent generally takes a basis in property received in a liquidating distribution that is the same as its basis in the hands of the controlled subsidiary (i.e., carryover basis). However, the parent takes a basis equal to the fair market value of the property on the date of distribution if: (i) the controlled subsidiary recognizes gain or loss on the liquidating distribution, or (ii) the parent's total adjusted basis in the property would exceed its fair market value immediately after the liquidation [§ 334(b)].

Minority shareholders take a basis in property received in a liquidating distribution that is equal to its fair market value on the date of distribution [§ 334(a)].

### XIII.E.3.e. Section 336(e) Election

[784 T.M., XI.D.; TPS ¶5010.07.C.]

A corporation that owns 80%, by voting power and value, of the stock in a subsidiary may elect to treat a sale, exchange, or distribution of all such stock (a "qualified stock disposition") as a sale, exchange, or distribution by the subsidiary of all its assets. If such an election is made, the subsidiary recognizes gain or loss on the deemed sale of the assets, but the parent recognizes no gain or loss on the sale, exchange, or distribution of its stock in the subsidiary [§ 336(e)]. The § 336(e) election is similar to the § 338(h)(10) election. If both elections are available for a particular transaction, the rules of § 338(h)(10) must be applied. See XIII.E.4.b. for a discussion of the § 338(h)(10) election.

### XIII.E.4. Taxable Acquisitions and the § 338 Election

[770 T.M.; TPS ¶5010.07.]

A corporate business can be acquired through a purchase of the stock of the corporation or through a purchase of the assets of the corporation. Although the two types of acquisitions achieve the same overall economic result (the acquisition of a corporate business), they have different business and tax consequences. For business purposes, the purchaser of a corporate business normally prefers to acquire the corporation's stock because a stock acquisition is easier to accomplish and it avoids interruptions in the corporation's contractual and other relationships. For tax purposes, on the other hand, the purchaser of a corporate business often has an incentive to acquire the corporation's assets instead. In an asset acquisition, the purchaser gets a "step-up" in the basis of the acquired assets to its cost for those assets (in a stock acquisition, the purchaser gets a basis in the stock equal to its cost for the stock, but it would just take the seller's basis in the acquired assets). The step-up in the basis of the assets is beneficial to the purchaser because it will potentially result in depreciation or amortization benefits and less gain recognition on any subsequent disposition of those assets.

As a result of this disparity in the tax treatment of two transactions that essentially have the same economic result, § 338 affords a corporate purchaser the convenience of a stock purchase with the tax benefits of an asset purchase by allowing the purchaser to elect to treat a stock purchase as an asset purchase (primarily through its most common form, a § 338(h)(10) election). See XIII.E.4.a. for a discussion of the general § 338 election and XIII.E.4.b. for a discussion of the § 338(h)(10) election.

### XIII.E.4.a. Section 338 Election

[788 T.M.; TPS ¶5010.07.B.]

A corporation that purchases 80%, by vote and value, of the stock of a target corporation (excluding certain nonvoting preferred stock) within a 12-month period (i.e., a "qualified stock purchase") may elect to treat the stock purchase as an asset acquisition. If the election is made, the target corporation ("old target") is treated as if it sold all of its assets at the close of the first day on which the purchaser had acquired 80% of the target's stock (i.e., the "acquisition date"). The target corporation is then treated as a new corporation ("new target"), unrelated to old target, that purchases, on the day after the acquisition date, old target's assets at a price that reflects the price paid for the target's stock, adjusted for the target's liabilities and other items. New target is required to allocate the deemed purchase price among its assets according to a prescribed residual method. Old target's tax attributes are extinguished, and new target starts with a clean slate [§ 338(a), § 338(c), § 338(d)].

A § 338 election must be made no later than the 15th day of the 9th month after the month in which the acquisition occurs. Once made, the election is irrevocable [§ 338(g)].

The principal effect of a § 338 election on the target corporation is that the target's aggregate basis in its assets is "stepped up" under § 1012 to the price that the purchaser paid for target's stock (adjusted for assumed liabilities and other items). Unless a § 338(h)(10) election is made (see XIII.E.4.b.), the price for new target's basis step-up is a double tax: one level of tax incurred by the seller on the sale of the target stock and another level of tax on old target's deemed sale of its assets. The seller is responsible for any tax liability arising from the stock sale. The deemed asset sale occurs on the acquisition date, and any tax liability resulting from the deemed asset sale is the responsibility of old target. Absent contractual provisions to the contrary, the tax liability resulting from the deemed asset sale is borne economically by the purchaser since it is the owner of new target. This is a costly transaction for the purchaser and is used only in very limited circumstances.

Federal income tax rules apply to treat the parties as if they had engaged in the actual transactions that are deemed to occur as a result of a § 338 election, except to the extent provided in § 338 and the related regulations. Those rules may characterize the transaction as something other than, or in addition to, a sale and purchase of assets, but in all cases it must be a taxable transaction.

Certain consistency rules require the consistent treatment of acquisitions during a consistency period beginning one year before the acquisition of the target corporation and ending one year after it. Under the asset consistency rules, if a purchaser does not make a § 338 election for an acquisition of target stock and the purchaser (or a member of its affiliated group) purchases assets from the target (or members of the target's affiliated group) within a year before or after the acquisition date of the target stock, the purchaser must, under limited circumstances, take a carryover basis in the acquired assets. The stock consistency rules are a backstop to the asset consistency rules [§ 338(e), § 338(f)].

### XIII.E.4.b. Section 338(h)(10) Election

[788 T.M., V.; TPS ¶5010.07.B.2.d(2)]

The double tax from a § 338 election may be avoided or mitigated if the seller and purchaser are eligible to make a joint § 338(h)(10) election. If that election is made, the qualified stock purchase of old target is treated as a sale of the assets of old target followed by a liquidation of old target, and the sale of old target stock is ignored. The treatment of new target is generally the same as in a § 338 election, except that the parties typically agree that the seller will bear the economic burden of any tax due on the deemed sale of the assets. A § 338(h)(10) election is generally the only way to achieve a basis step-up for new target but avoid a double tax [§ 338(h)(10); Reg. § 1.338(h)(10)-1(d)].

A § 338(h)(10) election can be made only if the target is (i) a domestic corporation that is a subsidiary member of a consolidated group, (ii) a domestic corporation that is a subsidiary member of an affiliated group not filing a consolidated return, or (iii) an S corporation [Reg. § 1.338(h)(10)-1(c)].

### XIII.E.5. Tax Attributes

### XIII.E.5.a. Carryover of Corporate Tax Attributes

[780 T.M., II.; TPS ¶4930.01.]

When one corporation acquires the assets of another corporation in a specified type of tax-free transaction and the latter corporation ceases to exist, the tax attributes of the disappearing corporation generally carry over to the acquiring corporation [§ 381(a)]. The carryover of tax attributes applies in the case of "A" reorganizations, "C" reorganizations, non-divisive "D" reorganizations, "F" reorganizations, non-divisive "G" reorganizations, and complete liquidations of subsidiaries [§ 381(a)]. The carryover of tax attributes does not apply to "B" reorganizations, "E" reorganizations, or corporate divisions because such transactions do not involve the acquisition of assets by another corporation. See XIII.E.1. for a discussion of the various types of reorganizations and XIII.E.3. for a discussion of complete liquidations of subsidiaries.

A non-exclusive list of the tax attributes to which the carryover rules apply is provided § 381(c) and includes, among other things, net operating loss carryforwards, capital loss carryforwards, tax credit carryovers, the earnings and profits (E&P) account, methods of accounting, inventory methods, and depreciation methods. However, the acquiring corporation generally does not succeed to the net operating loss carrybacks or capital loss carrybacks of the disappearing corporation [§ 381(b)].

### XIII.E.5.b. Limitations on Use of Corporate Tax Attributes

[780 T.M., III., IV., V.; TPS ¶4930.02., .03., .04.]

*Limitation on Use of NOL Carryovers.* When an "ownership change" occurs for a corporation with net operating losses (NOLs), a limitation applies to the amount of the corporation's post-change taxable income that can be offset by its pre-change net operating losses (NOLs) [§ 382(a)]. An ownership change occurs if the percentage of stock owned by one or more 5% shareholders has increased by more than 50% over the lowest percentage of stock owned by such shareholders during the three-year period before the testing date [§ 382(g)(1), § 382(i)(1)]. A 5% shareholder is any person holding 5% or more of the corporation's stock at any time during the testing period [§ 382(k)(7)].

Two types of ownership change trigger the limitation:

- a change in the percentage ownership of a 5% shareholder [§ 382(g)(2)]; or
- a tax-free reorganization other than a divisive "D" reorganization, an "F" reorganization, or a divisive "G" reorganization [§ 382(g)(3)].

When the limitation is triggered, the amount of the corporation's post-change taxable income that can be offset by its pre-change NOLs is generally limited to an amount equal to the value of the corporation's stock immediately before the ownership change multiplied by the long-term tax-exempt rate (see *Schedules & Tables 19*) [§ 382(b)(1)]. Recognized built-in gains increase the amount of the limitation [§ 382(h)(1)(A)]. Recognized built-in losses are subject to the limitation as if they were pre-change NOLs [§ 382(h)(1)(B)]. The limitation is generally treated as zero if the corporation does not continue to operate the pre-change business enterprise at all times during the two-year period after the ownership change [§ 382(c)(1)]. Any unused portion of the limitation can be carried over and used in the following year [§ 382(b)(2)].

For the year of the ownership change, the corporation's taxable income generally must be prorated between the pre-change and post-change portions of the year based on number of days. Pre-change NOLs can be used to offset the taxable income for the pre-change portion of the year but are subject to the limitation for the post-change portion of the year [§ 382(b)(3)].

*Limitation on Use of Capital Loss and Tax Credit Carryovers.* Based on rules similar to the rules that apply to NOL carryovers (see above), when an ownership change occurs for a corporation with pre-change capital losses or pre-change credits, the amount of the corporation's post-change taxable income that can be offset by its pre-change capital losses and credits is limited [§ 383, § 382; Reg. § 1.383-1(b)]. Pre-change capital losses include capital loss carryovers and recognized built-in losses that are capital losses [Reg. § 1.383-1(c)(2)]. Pre-change credits include unused general business credit carryovers, unused minimum tax credit carryovers, and excess foreign tax credit carryovers [Reg. § 1.383-1(c)(3)]. The limitation that applies for purposes of capital loss carryovers and credit carryovers is essentially the same limitation that applies for purposes of NOL carryovers.

*Ordering Rules for Absorption of Limitation.* The limitation on pre-change losses and credits is absorbed in the following order [Reg. § 1.383-1(d)]:

- recognized built-in losses that are capital losses;
- capital loss carryovers;
- recognized built-in losses that are ordinary losses;
- NOL carryovers;
- excess foreign tax credit carryovers;
- unused general business credit carryovers; and
- unused minimum tax credit carryovers.

### XIII.E.5.c. Limitation on Use of Corporate Preacquisition Losses

[780 T.M., V; TPS ¶4930.04.]

When one corporation acquires another corporation in a certain type of stock or asset acquisition and one of the corporations has net unrealized built-in gains, the other corporation cannot offset pre-acquisition losses against the built-in gains of that corporation during the five-year period following the date of acquisition [§ 384(a)]. Pre-acquisition losses include NOL carryovers and recognized built-in losses [§ 384(c)(3)]. The limitation generally applies when the acquiring corporation acquires the target corporation through an acquisition of 80%, by vote and value, of the target corporation stock or through an acquisition of the target corporation assets in an "A", "C", or "D" reorganization [§ 384(a)(1), § 384(c)(5)]. However, the limitation does not apply if both corporations are members of the same controlled group at all times during the five-year period [§ 384(b)].

## XIII.F. Special Corporations

Certain types of corporations are subject to special tax rules that are a variation of the rules that apply to regular C corporations. This section covers the basic rules that apply to some of the more common types of special corporations, including the regulated investment company (RIC), the real estate investment trust (REIT), the real estate mortgage investment conduit (REMIC), and the cooperative organization. The rules that apply to S corporations are covered in Chapter XV. The rules that apply to other highly specialized types of corporations, such as insurance companies, are beyond the scope of this product.

### XIII.F.1. Regulated Investment Companies (RICs)

[740 T.M.; TPS ¶5170.]

Regulated investment companies (RICs) are companies registered with the Securities and Exchange Commission (SEC) to issue their shares to the public and to invest the funds they receive for those shares in the securities of other issuers. RICs act as financial intermediaries, allowing investors to pool funds for investment purposes and to thereby obtain the benefits of investment diversification, professional management, and economies of scale. The most common and well-known form of RIC, the mutual fund, continuously offers its shares to the public and stands by to redeem those shares at their current net asset value at any time.

An investment company must meet a number of requirements to qualify as a RIC (see XIII.F.1.a. for the RIC qualification requirements). Unlike a regular corporation, a RIC is allowed to deduct the dividends it distributes to its shareholders and, thus, it is generally subject to corporate tax only on its undistributed income (see XIII.F.1.b. for the taxation of RICs). The shareholders of a RIC generally treat distributions from a RIC in the same manner as distributions from a regular corporation (see XIII.F.1.c. for the taxation of RIC shareholders).

### XIII.F.1.a. Qualification as a RIC

[740 T.M., I. through VII.; TPS ¶5170.01.]

A domestic corporation is generally eligible for RIC tax status if it is registered with the SEC as a management company or a unit investment trust at all times during the tax year. Certain common trust funds are also eligible [§ 851(a); Reg. § 1.851-1]. However, a corporation with undistributed earnings and profits that were accumulated during a tax year in which it was not a RIC must distribute those earnings and profits before it can elect RIC status [§ 852(a)(2)].

To qualify for RIC tax status, an eligible corporation must meet several requirements, including a source of income test, two diversification tests, and a distribution requirement. If a corporation is eligible and meets the qualification requirements, it must make an election to be treated as a RIC for the first tax year for which such status is desired.

*Source of Income Test.* A RIC must derive a substantial portion of its gross income from passive investments. A corporation qualifies for RIC status for a tax year only if at least 90% of its gross income for the year is derived from (i) dividends, (ii) interest (including tax-exempt interest), (iii) payments with respect to securities loans, (iv) gains from the sale or other disposition of stock, securities, or foreign currencies, (v) other income derived from a business of investing in stock, securities, or foreign currencies, and (vi) net income derived from interests in certain publicly traded partnerships [§ 851(b)(2)].

*Investment Diversification Tests.* A RIC must invest primarily in passive investment assets and its investments must be diversified. A corporation qualifies for RIC tax status only if it meets both of the following two tests at the end of each quarter of the tax year [§ 851(b)(3)]:

1. at least 50% of the value of its total assets consists of (i) cash, (ii) cash items (including receivables), (iii) government securities, (iv) securities of other RICs, and (v) securities of any other issuer to the extent that the value of such securities is not greater than 5% of the value of the RICs total assets and that

such securities do not constitute more than 10% of the issuer's outstanding voting securities; and

2. not more than 25% of the value of its total assets is invested in (i) the securities of any one issuer (other than government securities or securities of another RIC), (ii) the securities of two or more issuers controlled by the RIC (other than securities of another RIC) and engaged in the same, similar, or related trades or businesses, or (iii) the securities of one or more publicly traded partnerships.

*Distribution Requirement*. A RIC must be used primarily as a conduit to pass through income to its shareholders. A corporation qualifies for RIC status only if the amount of deductible dividends it distributes to its shareholders for the tax year is greater than or equal to the sum of [§ 852(a)]:

- 90% of its taxable income other than net capital gain; and
- 90% of its net tax-exempt income.

*Election of RIC Tax Status*. If an eligible corporation meets all the qualification requirements, it may elect RIC tax status by computing its taxable income as a RIC on Form 1120-RIC, *U.S. Income Tax Return for Regulated Investment Companies*, for the first tax year for which such status is desired. Once made the election is irrevocable [§ 851(b)(1); Reg. § 1.851-2(a)]. However, note that RIC tax status can effectively be revoked by intentionally failing one of the qualification requirements.

### XIII.F.1.b. Taxation of RICs

[740 T.M., VIII.; TPS ¶5170.02.]

A RIC is essentially a conduit for passing through earnings to its shareholders. It does this by distributing its earnings to shareholders in the form of dividends. Unlike a regular corporation, a RIC is allowed a deduction for the dividends it pays to shareholders. As a result, a RIC is taxable only on the portion of its taxable income not distributed to shareholders. Because a RIC is required to distribute at least 90% of its taxable income to its shareholders, only a small portion of its taxable income is subject to tax at the corporate level. The amounts distributed to shareholders are taxable only at the shareholder level. Thus, most of the earnings of a RIC are not subject to the double taxation that applies to the earnings of regular corporations.

For purposes of determining its corporate level tax, a RIC is subject to income tax on (i) its investment company taxable income, and (ii) the undistributed portion of its net capital gain.

*Investment Company Taxable Income*. Investment company taxable income is equal to regular taxable income (computed as if the RIC were a regular corporation) with the following adjustments [§ 852(b)(2)]:

- a deduction for dividends paid to shareholders is allowed (computed without regard to capital gain dividends and exempt-interest dividends)
- net capital gain is excluded;
- the net operating loss deduction and the dividends received deduction are not allowed; and
- an election may be made to accrue original issue discount (OID) on short-term government obligations.

Generally, investment company taxable income is taxed at ordinary corporate income tax rates. However, investment company taxable income is taxed at the highest corporate tax rate if the RIC is a personal holding company or if it fails to comply with regulations prescribing the records to be kept for purposes of determining the actual ownership of its stock [§ 852(b)(1)].

*Undistributed Net Capital Gain.* Net capital gain is excluded from the computation of investment company taxable income. However, a RIC is taxable on the undistributed portion of its net capital gain. Specifically, a RIC is taxable on the excess of its net capital gain over a deduction for dividends paid to shareholders determined by reference to capital gains dividends only [§ 852(b)(3)(A)]. A capital gain dividend qualifies for deduction only if the RIC designates it as a capital gain dividend in a written notice mailed to shareholders no later than 60 days after the end of the tax year. If the total amount designated as capital gain dividends is more than the amount of net capital gain for the year, only a pro rata portion of each dividend is treated as a capital gain dividend [§ 852(b)(3)(C)].

A RIC may elect to avoid the double tax on a designated amount of undistributed net capital gain by paying the tax on that gain and treating the gain as if it had been distributed to its shareholders. In such a case, the tax paid by the RIC is treated as if it were paid by the shareholders and the shareholders get a credit or refund for the tax they have been deemed to pay. The ultimate effect of this special constructive distribution treatment is that the designated amount of undistributed net capital gain is taxed only at the shareholder level, with the RIC paying the shareholder-level tax on behalf of the shareholders. To elect this special treatment, a RIC must designate the amount of undistributed net capital gain subject to the treatment in a written statement mailed to shareholders within 60 days after the end of its tax year [§ 852(b)(3)(D)].

### XIII.F.1.c. Taxation of RIC Shareholders

[740 T.M., VIII.; TPS ¶5170.03.]

Shareholders of a RIC generally treat distributions from the RIC in the same manner as distributions from a regular corporation [Reg. § 1.852-4(a)]. Thus, such distributions are generally taxable as dividends to the extent of the RIC's earnings and profits. If the distribution is not covered by earnings and profits, it is treated as a return of capital to the shareholder that reduces the adjusted basis of the shareholder's stock. If the nondividend portion of a distribution exceeds the adjusted basis of the stock, the excess is treated as a gain from the sale of the stock [§ 301(c)].

Special treatment applies to RIC distributions that are designated as capital gain dividends or tax-exempt interest dividends. RIC shareholders treat capital gain dividends distributed by the RIC as long-term capital gain, regardless of their holding period for their RIC shares [§ 852(b)(3)(B); Reg. § 1.852-4(b)]. This treatment also applies to undistributed net capital gain that the RIC elects to pass through to shareholders as constructive dividends (see XIII.F.1.b.). RIC shareholders treat tax-exempt interest dividends distributed by the RIC as tax-exempt interest for all tax purposes [§ 852(b)(5)(B)].

Generally, RIC shareholders are taxable on dividends distributed by the RIC (other than tax-exempt interest dividends) in the year they are received. However, a special rule applies to dividends distributed by a RIC after the end of its tax year. If a RIC declares a dividend in October, November, or December of one tax year, but doesn't actually pay the dividend until January of the following year, the dividend is deemed to be received by the shareholders on December 31 [§ 852(b)(7)].

A shareholder's gain or loss on the sale of RIC stock is generally subject to the same rules that apply to normal sales of stock, with gain or loss characterized as either long-term or short-term depending on the shareholder's holding period for the stock. However, if a shareholder sells RIC stock that was held for less than six months, and the shareholder was allowed long-term capital gain treatment for capital gain dividends paid on that stock, the shareholder must treat any loss on the sale of the stock as long-term capital loss to the extent of the amount of capital gain dividends that were allowed to be treated as long-term capital gain [§ 852(b)(4)].

### XIII.F.2. Real Estate Investment Trusts (REITs)

[742 T.M.; TPS ¶5180.]

Real estate investment trusts (REITs) are investment vehicles that obtain funds from investors, invest those funds in real estate and real estate assets (including mortgages), and pass through the investment earnings to their investors. The use of a REIT as an investment vehicle allows numerous investors to pool their funds and invest in large portfolios of real estate assets, thereby obtaining the benefits of investment diversification and professional asset management.

An entity must meet a number of requirements to qualify for REIT tax status (see XIII.F.2.a. for the REIT qualification requirements). A REIT is subject to tax only on its undistributed income and certain specially defined income (see XIII.F.2.b. for the taxation of REITs). The shareholders of a REIT generally treat distributions from a REIT in the same manner as distributions from a regular corporation (see XIII.F.2.c. for the taxation of REIT shareholders).

### XIII.F.2.a. Qualification as a REIT

[742 T.M., III.; TPS ¶5180.01.]

A corporation, trust, or association is eligible for REIT tax status if [§ 856(a)]:

1. it is managed by one or more directors or trustees;
2. its beneficial ownership is held by 100 or more persons for at least 355 days during the tax year and is evidenced by transferable shares or certificates;
3. it is not closely held at any time during the last half of the tax year;
4. it is not an insurance company, bank, or other financial institution; and
5. it would be taxable as a domestic corporation but for the REIT tax provisions.

To qualify for REIT tax status, an eligible entity must meet several requirements, including source of income tests, investment asset tests, and a distribution requirement. If an entity is eligible and meets the qualification requirements, it must make an election to be treated as a REIT for the first tax year for which such status is desired.

*Source of Income Tests.* A REIT must derive a substantial portion of its gross income from passive real estate investments. An entity qualifies for REIT tax status only if it satisfies both of the following two tests on an annual basis [§ 856(c)]:

1. at least 75% of its gross income must be derived from the following real estate sources: (i) rents from real property, (ii) interest on obligations secured by mortgages on real property, (iii) interest on interests in real property, (iv) gain from the disposition of non-inventory real property, (v) dividends on, and gain from the sales of, shares of other REITs, (vi) real property tax refunds and abatements, (vii) income and gains derived from foreclosure property, (viii) certain mortgage, purchase, and lease commitment fees, (ix) gains from the dispositions of real estate assets (other than prohibited transactions), and (x) income from qualified temporary investments; and
2. at least 95% of its gross income must be derived from the real estate sources listed in (1) and the following other sources: (i) other interest, (ii) other dividends, (iii) gain from dispositions of stock and securities, and (iv) in the case of

a timber REIT, mineral royalty income from real property owned and held in connection with the trade or business of producing timber.

An entity that fails to meet the requirements of one or both of these tests for a tax year may nevertheless be considered to have met the requirements of both tests for that year if (i) the failure to meet the requirements is due to reasonable cause and not willful neglect, and (ii) the entity attaches a schedule to its timely filed return for that year the provides a description of each item of the entity's gross income described in the two tests [§ 856(c)(6)].

*Investment Asset Tests*. A REIT must invest primarily in passive real estate investment assets and its non-real estate investment assets must be diversified. An entity qualifies for REIT tax status only if [§ 856(c)(4)]:

1. at least 75% of the value of its assets is represented by real estate assets, cash, cash items (including receivables), and government securities;
2. not more than 25% of the value of its assets is represented by securities (other than government securities);
3. not more than 25% of the value of its assets is represented by securities of one or more taxable REIT subsidiaries;
4. not more than 5% of the value of its assets is represented by the securities of any one issuer (other than a government or a taxable REIT subsidiary); and
5. it does not hold the securities of any one issuer (other than a government or a taxable REIT subsidiary) that constitute more 10% of the total voting power or total value of that issuer's outstanding securities.

*Distribution Requirements*. A REIT must be used primarily as a conduit to pass through income to its shareholders. An entity qualifies for REIT tax status only if the amount of dividends (other than capital gain dividends) it distributes to its shareholders for the tax year is at least [§ 857(a)(1)]:

1. the sum of 90% of its REIT taxable income and 90% of the excess of its net income from foreclosure property over the tax imposed on such property; minus
2. any excess noncash income (as defined in § 857(e)).

*Election of REIT Status*. If an eligible entity meets all the qualification requirements, it may elect REIT tax status by computing its taxable income as a REIT on Form 1120-REIT, *U.S. Income Tax Return for Real Estate Investment Trusts*, for the first tax year for which such status is desired [§ 856(c)(1); Reg. § 1.856-2(b)]. The election may be revoked in a later year if the revocation is made within the first 90 days of the tax year for which the revocation is desired to be effective [§ 856(g)(2)].

### XIII.F.2.b. Taxation of REITs

[742 T.M., IV.B.; TPS ¶5180.02.]

A REIT is essentially a conduit for passing through earnings to its shareholders. It does this by distributing its earnings to shareholders in the form of dividends. Unlike a regular corporation, a REIT is allowed a deduction for the dividends it pays to shareholders. As a result, a REIT is taxable only on that portion of its taxable income not distributed to shareholders. Because a REIT is required to distribute at least 90% of its taxable income to its shareholders, only a small portion of its taxable income is subject to tax at the corporate level. The amounts distributed to shareholders are taxable only at the shareholder level. Thus, most of the earnings of a REIT are not subject to the double taxation that applies to the earnings of regular corporations.

For purposes of determining its corporate level tax, a REIT is subject to tax on the following categories of income:

1. real estate investment trust taxable income;

2. undistributed net capital gain;

3. net income from foreclosure property;

4. net income from prohibited transactions;

5. shortfall amount from failure to meet the source of income tests; and

6. income from redetermined rents, redetermined deductions, and excess interest.

***Real Estate Investment Trust Taxable Income.*** A REIT is taxable on real estate investment trust taxable income at the regular corporate income tax rates [§ 857(b)(1)]. Real estate investment trust taxable income is equal to regular taxable income (computed as if the REIT were a regular corporation) with the following adjustments [§ 857(b)(2), § 857(b)(3)(A)(i)]:

- a deduction for dividends paid to shareholders is allowed (computed without regard to dividends attributable to net income from foreclosure property and capital gain dividends);

- the dividends received deduction is not allowed;

- net capital gain is excluded

- net income from foreclosure property is excluded;

- net income from prohibited transactions is excluded;

- a deduction is allowed for certain special taxes paid; and

- any adjustments attributable to a change in accounting period are disregarded.

***Undistributed Net Capital Gain.*** A REIT is taxable on undistributed net capital gain at the rates provided in § 1201(a). Undistributed net capital gain is equal to the excess of net capital gain over the deduction for dividends paid to shareholders determined with reference to capital gain dividends only [§ 857(b)(3)(A)(ii)]. A capital gain dividend qualifies for deduction only if the REIT designates it as a capital gain dividend in a written notice mailed to shareholders no later than 30 days after the end of the tax year. However, if the total amount designated as capital gain dividends is more than the amount of net capital gain for the year, only a pro rata portion of each dividend is treated as a capital gain dividend [§ 857(b)(3)(C)].

A REIT may elect to avoid the double tax on a designated amount of undistributed net capital gain by paying the tax on that gain and treating the gain as if it had been distributed to its shareholders. In such a case, the tax paid by the REIT is treated as if it were paid by the shareholders and the shareholders get a credit or refund for the tax they have been deemed to pay. The ultimate effect of this special constructive distribution treatment is that the designated amount of undistributed net capital gain is taxed only at the shareholder level, with the REIT paying the shareholder-level tax on behalf of the shareholders. To elect this special treatment, a REIT must designate the amount of undistributed net capital gain subject to the treatment in a written statement mailed to shareholders within 60 days after the end of its tax year [§ 852(b)(3)(D)].

***Net Income from Foreclosure Property.*** A REIT is taxable on net income from foreclosure property at the highest corporate income tax rate. Foreclosure property is real property acquired by the REIT as a result of a default or imminent default on a lease of such property or on a debt secured by such property. Net income from foreclosure property is equal to the sum of gain from the sale or disposition of foreclosure property and gross income derived from foreclosure property, reduced by any allowable deductions directly connected with the production of such gain or income [§ 857(b)(4), § 856(e)].

***Net Income from Prohibited Transactions***. A REIT is subject to a 100% tax on the amount of net income from prohibited transactions. A prohibited transaction is a sale or disposition of property (other than foreclosure property) held primarily for sale to customers in the ordinary course of a trade or business. Net income from a prohibited transaction is equal to gain from the prohibited transaction, reduced by any allowable deductions directly connected with such transaction [§ 857(b)(6), § 1221(a)(1)].

***Shortfall Amount from Source of Income Tests***. A REIT that fails one or both of the source of income tests may nevertheless be deemed to meet those tests under certain circumstances (see XIII.F.2.a.). However, in this situation, the REIT is taxable on a "shortfall" amount. A shortfall amount, if any, must be determined for purposes of each source of income test. The shortfall amount is the excess of the amount of qualifying income required to meet the source of income test (i.e., 75% or 95% of gross income) over the actual amount of qualifying income. If there is a shortfall amount for both tests, the greater of the two shortfall amounts is used to compute the tax. The tax is equal to the applicable shortfall amount multiplied by a ratio, the numerator of which is the REIT's real estate investment trust taxable income for the year and the denominator of which is the REIT's gross income for the year [§ 857(b)(5)].

***Income from Redetermined Rents, Redetermined Deductions, and Excess Interest***. A REIT is subject to a 100% tax on income from redetermined rents, redetermined deductions, and excess interest. Redetermined rents are rents from real property to the extent that the amount of the rents would be reduced under § 482 to clearly reflect income as a result of services rendered by a taxable REIT subsidiary to a tenant of the REIT. Redetermined deductions are deductions of the taxable REIT subsidiary to the extent that the amount of the deductions would be decreased under § 482 to clearly reflect income between the taxable REIT subsidiary and the REIT. Excess interest is deductions for interest payments by the taxable REIT subsidiary to the REIT to the extent that the interest payments are in excess of a commercially reasonable interest rate [§ 857(b)(7)].

### XIII.F.2.c. Taxation of REIT Shareholders

[742 T.M., IV.B.; TPS ¶5180.03.]

Shareholders of a REIT generally treat distributions from the REIT in the same manner as distributions from a regular corporation [Reg. § 1.857-6(a)]. Thus, such distributions are generally taxable as dividends to the extent of the REIT's earnings and profits. If the distribution is not covered by earnings and profits, it is treated as a return of capital to the shareholder that reduces the adjusted basis of the shareholder's stock. If the nondividend portion of a distribution exceeds the adjusted basis of the stock, the excess is treated as a gain from the sale of the stock [§ 301(c)].

Special treatment applies to REIT distributions that are designated as capital gain dividends. REIT shareholders treat capital gain dividends distributed by the REIT as long-term capital gain, regardless of their holding period for their RIC shares [§ 857(b)(3)(B); Reg. § 1.857-6(b)]. This treatment also applies to undistributed net capital gain that the REIT elects to pass through to shareholders as constructive dividends (see XIII.F.2.b.).

Generally, REIT shareholders are taxable on dividends distributed by the REIT in the year they are received. However, a special rule applies to dividends distributed by a REIT after the end of its tax year. If a REIT declares a dividend in October, November, or December of one tax year, but doesn't actually pay the dividend until January of the following year, the dividend is deemed to be received by the shareholders on December 31 [§ 857(b)(9)].

A shareholder's gain or loss on the sale of REIT stock is generally subject to the same rules that apply to normal sales of stock, with gain or loss characterized as either long-term or short-term, depending on the shareholder's holding period for the stock. However, if a shareholder sells REIT stock that was held for less than six months, and the shareholder was allowed long-term capital gain treatment for capital gain dividends paid on that stock, the shareholder must treat any loss on the sale of the stock as long-term capital loss to the extent of the amount of capital gain dividends that were allowed to be treated as long-term capital gain [§ 857(b)(8)].

### XIII.F.3. Real Estate Mortgage Investment Conduits (REMICs)

[741 T.M., V.; TPS ¶5190.]

Real estate mortgage investment conduits (REMICs) are entities organized to hold a fixed pool of real estate mortgages and to issue multiple-class interests backed by those mortgages. An entity must meet a number of requirements to qualify for REMIC tax status (see XIII.F.3.a.). A REMIC is subject to tax only on certain specially defined income (see XIII.F.3.b.). The taxation of the holders of interests in a REMIC depends on whether they hold a regular interest or a residual interest in the REMIC (see XIII.F.3.c.). Special rules apply to the transfer of property to a REMIC upon its formation (see XIII.F.3.d.).

### XIII.F.3.a. Qualification as a REMIC

[741 T.M., V.; TPS ¶5190.01.]

Any type of entity can qualify for REMIC tax status if it meets several requirements, including an asset test, investment interest tests, and arrangements tests. If an entity is eligible and meets the qualification requirements, it must make an election to be treated as a REMIC for the first tax year for which such status is desired. A REMIC must use the calendar year as its tax year [§ 860D(a)(5)].

*Asset Test.* An entity qualifies as a REMIC only if substantially all of its assets consist of qualified mortgages and other permitted investments. The entity must meet this test by the end of the third month beginning after the startup day (generally, the day on which it issues all of its regular and residual interests), and at all times thereafter [§ 860D(a)(4), § 860G(a)(9)].

Substantially all of an entity's assets consist of qualified mortgages and other permitted investments if the entity owns no more than a de minimis amount of other assets. Under a safe harbor, the amount of other assets owned is de minimis if the total of the adjusted bases of those assets is less than 1% of the total of the adjusted bases of all assets owned by the REMIC [Reg. § 1.860D-1(b)(3)].

Qualified mortgages include (i) obligations principally secured by interests in real property, (ii) qualified replacement mortgages, and (iii) regular interests in other REMICs. Permitted investments include (i) cash flow investments, (ii) qualified reserve assets, and (iii) foreclosure property [§ 860G(a)(3) through § 860G(a)(7)].

*Investment Interest Tests.* An entity qualifies as a REMIC only if (i) all of the interests in the entity are regular or residual interests, and (ii) the entity has one, and only one, class of residual interests [§ 860D(a)(2) and § 860D(a)(3)].

A regular interest is an interest in a REMIC that (i) is designated as a regular interest, (ii) is issued on the startup day, (iii) has fixed terms, (iv) unconditionally entitles the holder to receive a specified principal amount, and (v) on which interest, if any, is payable based on a fixed rate or consists of a specified, invariable portion of the interest on qualified mortgages [§ 860G(a)(1)]. A residual interest is an interest in a REMIC that (i) is not a regular interest, (ii) is designated as a residual interest, and (iii) is issued on the startup day [§ 860G(a)(2)].

***Arrangements Tests.*** An entity qualifies as a REMIC only if [§ 860D(a)(6), § 860E(e)(5)]:

1. it has made reasonable arrangements to ensure that residual interests are not held by disqualified organizations (governmental organizations, tax-exempt organizations, and certain cooperatives); and

2. it has made reasonable arrangements to ensure that if a residual interest is acquired by a disqualified organization, the information necessary for the computation of the tax on transfers of residual interests to disqualified organizations will be provided to the disqualified organization and the IRS.

***Election of REMIC Tax Status.*** If an entity desires REMIC tax status and meets all of the REMIC qualification requirements, it must elect REMIC tax status during the first tax year of its existence. REMIC tax status is elected by timely filing Form 1066, *U.S. Real Estate Mortgage Investment Conduit Income Tax Returns*. Generally, the election applies to the entity's first tax year and all of its later years [§ 860D(b)(1); Reg. § 1.860D-1(d)]. However, if an entity ceases to meet the REMIC qualifications at any time during a tax year, its REMIC tax status is terminated for that year and all later years, unless the IRS determines that the termination was inadvertent and the entity takes steps to correct the inadvertent termination [§ 860D(b)(2)].

### XIII.F.3.b. Taxation of REMICs

[741 T.M., VI.; TPS ¶5190.03.]

A REMIC is generally not subject to federal income tax. Rather, the income of a REMIC is passed through to the holders of interests in the REMIC and taxed to them [§ 860A]. Although a REMIC is generally not subject to federal income tax, it is subject to the following taxes:

1. a 100% tax on the amount of net income from prohibited transactions [§ 860F(a)];

2. a 100% tax on the amount of contributions made to the REMIC after the startup day [§ 860G(d)]; and

3. a tax on net income from foreclosure property at the highest corporate income tax rate [§ 860G(c)].

A REMIC must compute and report its taxable income or loss each year because the taxation of the residual interest holders of a REMIC is based on the REMIC's taxable income or loss. The taxable income or loss of a REMIC is computed using the accrual method of accounting and determined in the same manner as an individual taxpayer, except that the following modifications must be made [§ 860C(b)]:

1. the regular interests in the REMIC are treated as debt of the REMIC;

2. any market discount on bonds is included in gross income for the tax years to which it is attributable under the rules of § 1276(b)(2);

3. no item of income, gain, loss, or deduction allocable to a prohibited transaction is taken into account;

4. the deductions not allowed to partnerships under § 703(a)(2) are not allowed (other than the § 212 deduction for expenses incurred in the production of income); and

5. the amount of any net income from foreclosure property is reduced by the § 860G(c) penalty tax imposed on such net income.

### XIII.F.3.c. Taxation of REMIC Interest Holders

[741 T.M., VII., VIII.; TPS ¶5190.04.]

The taxation of the holders of interests in a REMIC depends on whether they hold regular interests or residual interests in the REMIC.

*Taxation of Regular Interest Holders in REMICs.* A regular interest in a REMIC is treated as debt instruments for all federal tax purposes. Thus, it may be subject to the original issue discount, market discount bond, and amortizable bond premium rules, and other Code provisions that apply to debt instruments. The holder of a regular interest in a REMIC must use the accrual method of accounting to determine the amounts includible in gross income with respect to its interest in the REMIC. If a regular interest holder disposes of its interest in the REMIC, it must treat the gain on the disposition as ordinary income to the extent it does not exceed the excess, if any, of (i) the amount that would have been includible in gross income if the yield on the regular interest were 110% of the applicable federal rate as of the beginning of the holding period, over (ii) the amount actually includible in gross income [§ 860B].

*Taxation of Residual Interest Holders in REMICs.* The holder of a residual interest in a REMIC is taxable on its daily portion of the REMIC's taxable income or loss for each day during the tax year on which it held its residual interest. A residual interest holder's daily portion of the REMIC's taxable income or loss is determined by allocating the REMIC's quarterly taxable income or loss on a pro rata basis to each day in the quarter, and then allocating the daily amount of the REMIC's taxable income or loss among the residual interest holders in proportion to their respective holdings on each day [§ 860C(a)].

A residual interest holder must treat the amount of REMIC taxable income or loss allocated to it as ordinary income or loss. However, the amount of ordinary loss that may be taken into account by a residual interest holder for any quarter is limited to the amount of its adjusted basis in its residual interest as of the end of that quarter. Any loss disallowed under this rule can be carried forward indefinitely and used in later quarters [§ 860C(e)].

A residual interest holder is required to take into account a minimum amount of the REMIC's taxable income for each tax year. The amount of taxable income taken into account for any tax year may not be less than the excess inclusion for that year. The excess inclusion is determined on a quarterly basis. It is equal to the excess, if any, of (i) the amount of the REMIC's taxable income taken into account by the residual interest holder for the quarter, over (ii) the sum of the daily accruals allocated to the residual interest holder during the quarter. The daily accrual allocated to the residual interest holder for a day is determined by allocating to each day in the quarter the residual interest holder's pro rata portion of (i) its adjusted issue price in its residual interest at the beginning of the quarter, multiplied by (ii) 120% of the long-term federal rate [§ 860E].

### XIII.F.3.d. Taxation of Transfers to REMIC Upon Formation

[741 T.M., VI.; TPS ¶5190.02.]

Special rules apply to the transfer of property to a REMIC upon its formation. The tax consequences are tailored to the situation in which mortgages are contributed to the REMIC by the sponsor in exchange for regular and residual interests (note that, in many cases, the regular and residual interests are subsequently sold to investors). A taxpayer that transfers property to a REMIC in exchange for regular or residual interests in the REMIC does not recognize gain or loss on the transfer. The taxpayer's adjusted bases in the interests received from the REMIC are generally equal to the adjusted bases of the property it transferred to the REMIC. The REMIC's adjusted bases in the property received from the taxpayer is equal to the fair market value of that property immediately after the transfer [§ 860F(b)].

### XIII.F.4. Cooperative Organizations

[744 T.M.; TPS ¶5200.]

A cooperative is an organization established for the purpose of purchasing and marketing the products of its members and/or procuring supplies for resale to its members. The profits of a cooperative are distributed to its members in proportion to their patronage (i.e., business transacted with the cooperative). Although cooperatives are generally taxable like regular corporations, there are some special tax rules that apply only to cooperatives and their members. Members of a cooperative are known as patrons.

### XIII.F.4.a. Eligiblity for Cooperative Tax Rules

[744 T.M., II.; TPS ¶5200.01.]

A corporation operating on a cooperative basis is generally eligible for the special tax rules that apply to cooperatives. However, the following corporations are not eligible even if operating on a cooperative basis: (i) tax-exempt corporations, (ii) mutual savings banks, (iii) insurance companies, and (iii) corporations engaged in furnishing electricity or telephone service to persons in rural areas. An organization that qualifies as an exempt farmers' cooperative under § 521 is also eligible for the special tax rules that apply to cooperatives [§ 1381(a)].

### XIII.F.4.b. Taxation of Cooperatives

[744 T.M., IV.; TPS ¶5200.03.]

Cooperatives are generally taxable like regular corporations. Generally, a cooperative determines gross income in the same manner as a regular corporation and can take the same deductions as a regular corporation. However, there are some additional deductions that may be claimed by cooperatives [§ 1382]:

- All eligible cooperatives are allowed to deduct certain distributions from patronage sourced income.
- Exempt farmers' cooperatives are allowed to deduct certain distributions from nonpatronage sourced income.

If a cooperative claims a deduction for amounts paid in redemption of nonqualified written notices of allocation or nonqualified per-unit retain certificates (see below), the cooperative's tax for the tax year is equal to the lesser of [§ 1383]:

- the tax computed with such deductions; or
- the tax computed without such deductions, minus the decrease in tax for any prior tax years that would result from treating such nonqualified notices or certificates as qualified notices or certicates.

*Cooperative Deduction for Distributions from Patronage Sourced Income*. All eligible cooperatives can deduct the following types of distributions from patronage sourced income that are paid during the payment period (the period beginning on the first day of the cooperative's tax year and ending on the 15th day of the 9th month after the end of that year) [§ 1382(b), § 1388]:

- patronage dividends (a patronage dividend is an amount that is paid by a cooperative to a patron under an obligation to pay the patron based on the quantity or value of business done with the cooperative and that is determined by reference to the net earnings of the cooperative from business done with its patrons);

- payments in redemption of nonqualified written notices of allocation (a written notice of allocation is a written notice that discloses to the recipient the stated dollar amount allocated to him by the cooperative and the portion of that amount that constitutes a patronage dividend; it is nonqualified if it is not issued with a notice of right of redemption, it cannot be redeemed at its stated dollar amount within 90 days of receipt, or the patron has not agreed to include it in his gross income at its stated dollar amount);

- per-unit retain allocations (a per-unit retain allocation is an allocation by a cooperative to a patron that is made with respect to products marketed for him and that is fixed without reference to the net earnings of the cooperative); and

- payments in redemption of nonqualified per-unit retain certificates (a per-unit retain certificate is a written notice that discloses to the recipient the stated dollar amount of a per-unit retain allocation made to him by the cooperative; it is nonqualified if the patron has not agreed to include it in his gross income at the stated dollar amount).

*Exempt Farmer's Cooperative Deduction for Distributions from Nonpatronage Sourced Income*. An exempt farmers' cooperative can take additional deductions for the following amounts [§ 1382(c)]:

- amounts paid during the year as dividends on capital stock;

- amounts paid during the payment period in money, qualified written notices of allocation, or other property to patrons with respect to earnings derived from nonpatronage sources or from business done for the United Sates or any of its agencies; and

- amounts paid during the payment period in money or other property in redemption of a nonqualified written notice of allocation that was paid to a patron with respect to earnings derived from nonpatronage sources or from business done for the United States or any of its agencies.

### XIII.F.4.c. Taxation of Cooperative Patrons

[744 T.M., V.; TPS ¶5200.04.]

Patrons of a cooperative must include in gross income the following payments that are allowable as special deductions to the cooperative (see XIII.F.4.b.) [§ 1385(a)]:

- the amount of patronage dividends paid in money, a qualified written notice of allocation, or other property (except a nonqualified written notice of allocation) and received during the tax year;

- the amount of per-unit retain allocations paid in qualified per-unit retain certificates and received during the tax year; and

- the amount of nonpatronage distributions paid by an exempt farmers' cooperative in money, a qualified written notice of allocation, or other property (except a nonqualified written notice of allocation) and received during the tax year.

Patrons of a cooperative must also treat as ordinary income any gain recognized on the redemption, sale, or other disposition of a nonqualified written notice of allocation or a nonqualified per-unit retain certificate to the extent the stated dollar value of such notice or certificate exceeds its basis. The basis of such notice or certificate in the hands of the patron to whom it was paid generally is zero. However, if the notice or certificate was acquired from a decedent, its basis in the hands of the patron is the same as it was in the hands of the decedent [§ 1385(c)].

# CHAPTER XIV. PARTNERSHIPS

>>>>>>>>>>>>>>>>>>>>>>>>>>>>>>>

## XIV.A. Introduction to Partnerships

In general, a partnership is a joint undertaking (other than a corporation or a trust) by two or more taxpayers to conduct a business or investment activity for profit. The rules governing the taxation of partnerships combine both an aggregate approach and an entity approach. Generally, the use of the partnership form allows for a great deal of flexibility in structuring and reporting transactions. However, there are limitations on that flexibility, including a set of anti-abuse rules.

*Aggregate Approach.* The aggregate approach treats a partnership as a group of taxpayers, each of whom is viewed as owning an interest in all partnership assets and an interest in all partnership income, gains, losses, deductions, and credits (the so-called partnership tax items). Under this approach, a partnership is viewed as an aggregate of co-owners of property who use those assets for a common purpose. In implementing this concept of aggregate co-ownership, the partnership is treated as a mere conduit that passes through its tax items to the partners who then report their shares of those items on their own tax returns. The partnership itself is not subject to tax.

*Entity Approach.* The entity approach treats the partnership business as being separate and distinct from the taxpayers who own the business (i.e., the partners). Under this approach, the partnership entity is viewed as owning the property and conducting the operations. In implementing this concept of entity ownership, the amount, character, and timing of the partnership's tax items are determined at the partnership level (the partnership's tax items are then passed through to the partners under the aggregate approach, as discussed above).

*Partnership Flexibility.* Partners are granted a significant degree of flexibility in structuring partnership transactions, and in determining when and how the results of a particular partnership transaction are reported and allocated among the partners. The partnership agreement is generally used by partners to set forth the rules for the treatment of the partnership's transactions. Partners have a variety of choices available in determining how partnership transactions will be treated for tax purposes. For example, partners can use the partnership agreement to provide for special allocations of partnership items among the partners. This flexibility is a key advantage to operating a business in partnership form.

*Anti-Abuse Rules.* There are limitations on the flexibility of the partnership form of doing business. Under a broadly applicable set of anti-abuse rules, the IRS has the authority to recast a partnership transaction to more accurately reflect the underlying economic arrangements of the partners if it concludes that the transaction attempts to use the partnership in a manner inconsistent with the intent of the partnership provisions of subchapter K of the Code. The anti-abuse rules are intended to eliminate improper tax avoidance by partnerships [Reg. § 1.701-2].

## XIV.B. Classification as Partnership

### XIV.B.1. Partnership Characteristics

[710 T.M., II.; TPS ¶¶4010.01., 4020.]

For federal tax purposes, a partnership is defined to include a syndicate, group, pool, joint venture, or other unincorporated organization through or by means of which any business, financial operation, or venture is carried on. An organization cannot be a partnership if it falls within the federal tax definition of a corporation or a trust or estate [§ 761(a)].

A partnership must be a separate business entity. Certain relationships that resemble partnerships but that do not constitute separate business entities cannot be partnerships for federal tax purposes. Examples include relationships involving the co-ownership of property, the sharing of expenses, or a simple joint undertaking without the sharing of profits.

Although the requirement is not expressly stated in the Code, a partnership must have at least two owners. A business entity with one owner cannot be a partnership.

The federal tax definition of partnership is broader in scope than the common law meaning of partnership. Moreover, an organization may be a partnership under federal tax law even if it is not considered a separate entity under state law. Thus, the federal tax definition of partnerships may include arrangements generally not considered partnerships under the common law or state statutes. Conversely, an arrangement that constitutes a state law partnership may not be considered a federal tax law partnership in some cases.

### XIV.B.2. Check-the-Box Entity Classification Regulations

[700 T.M., III.; TPS ¶¶4010.01.B., 4020.03.]

The check-the-box entity classification regulations have simplified the classification of business entities [Reg. § 301.7701-1 through § 301.7701-3]. Under the check-the-box rules, certain listed business entities must always be classified as corporations. All other business entities (eligible entities) may elect their classification or simply use their default classification. An eligible entity with two or more members may elect to be either a partnership or an association taxable as a corporation. The election is made on Form 8832, *Entity Classification Election*. If a domestic eligible entity with two or more members does not make the election, it defaults to partnership status. If a foreign eligible entity with two or more members does not make the election, it defaults to either: (i) an association taxable as a corporation, if all owners have limited liability, or (ii) a partnership, if at least one owner does not have limited liability. See XVI.C. for further discussion of the check-the-box rules.

### XIV.B.3. Election to Be Excluded from Partnership Provisions

[710 T.M., II.B.4.; TPS ¶4020.05.]

In certain circumstances, the owners of an unincorporated organization that would otherwise be classified as a partnership for federal tax purposes may elect out of the application of the partnership provisions of Subchapter K of the Code. Such an election may be desirable for a variety of reasons including the following:

- Owners may wish to make inconsistent elections for purposes of depreciation, the installment method, intangible drilling costs, etc.

- Owners may wish to enter into like-kind exchanges of ownership interests, which are not available for exchanges of partnership interests.

- A purchaser of the partnership assets may desire a step-up in basis for the assets and the § 754 basis adjustment election may not be practicable.

The election to be excluded from the partnership provisions applies only to the provisions of Subchapter K of the Code. Thus, the election does not affect the partnership status of the organization under provisions contained in other subchapters of the Code.

### XIV.B.3.a. Eligibility for Election to Be Excluded from Partnership Provisions

[710 T.M., II.B.4.a.; TPS ¶4020.05.A.]

The election out of the partnership provisions may only be made by one of the following types of unincorporated organizations [§ 761(a)]:

- an organization used for investment purposes only;

- an organization used for the joint production, extraction, or use of property; or

- an organization used by dealers in securities for a short period for the purpose of underwriting, selling, or distributing a particular issue of securities.

The election out of the partnership provisions may be made by such an organization only if the income of its owners can be adequately determined without the computation of partnership taxable income [§ 761(a); Reg. § 1.761-2(a)(1)]. The election is not available for a syndicate, group, pool, or joint venture that is classified as an association, or any group operating under an agreement that creates an organization classified as an association [Reg. § 1.761-2(a)(1)].

*Investing Partnerships.* An unincorporated organization may be eligible to elect out of the application of the partnership provisions if it is owned by a group of participants who jointly purchase, retain, sell, or exchange investment property and it meets the following three requirements [Reg. § 1.761-2(a)(2)]:

1. the participants own the property as co-owners;

2. the participants reserve the right separately to take or dispose of their shares of any property acquired or retained; and

3. the participants do not actively conduct a trade or business or irrevocably authorize some representative to purchase, sell, or exchange the investment property (although each separate participant may delegate authority to purchase, sell, or exchange his share of investment property for a period of time no longer than one year).

*Partnerships Used for Joint Production, Extraction, or Use of Property.* An unincorporated organization may be eligible to elect out of the application of the partnership provisions if it is owned by a group of participants who jointly produce, extract, or use property, and it meets the following three requirements [Reg. § 1.761-2(a)(3)]:

1. the participants own the property as co-owners (either in fee or under a lease or other form of contract granting exclusive operating rights);

2. the participants reserve the right separately to take in kind or dispose of their shares of any property produced, extracted, or used; and

3. the participants do not jointly sell services or the property produced or extracted (although each separate participant may delegate authority to sell his share of the property produced or extracted for a period of time no longer than the minimum needs of the industry or one year).

However, an organization may not elect out of the partnership provisions if one of its principal purposes is cycling, manufacturing, or processing for persons who are not members of the organization.

### XIV.B.3.b. *Procedures for Election to Be Excluded from Partnership Provisions*

[710 T.M., II.B.4.c.; TPS ¶4020.05.B.]

The election out of the partnership provisions is made by attaching a statement to a Form 1065, *U.S. Return of Partnership Income*, filed with the appropriate IRS service center by the due date (including extensions) for the first tax year to which the election is to apply [Reg. § 1.761-2(b)]. The Form 1065 filed for the election year need only include the following information (in lieu of the information customarily required on Form 1065) [Reg. § 1.761-2(b)(2)(i)]:

- the name and address of the organization;
- the names, addresses, and identification numbers of all members (i.e., owners) of the organization;
- a statement that the organization qualifies for the election under § 761(a) and Reg. § 1.761-2(a);
- a statement that all of the members of the organization elect that it be excluded from the partnership provisions; and
- a statement indicating where a copy of the organizational agreement is available (or from whom it is available, if an oral agreement).

If an organization qualifies for the election but does not meet these filing requirements, the organization may be deemed to have made the election if all the surrounding facts and circumstances show that the members of the organization intended to secure exclusion from the partnership provisions beginning with the organization's first tax year [Reg. § 1.761-2(b)(2)(ii)]. The following are examples of factors that may indicate such requisite intent:

- There was an agreement among the members of the organization at the time it was formed that the organization would be excluded from the partnership provisions beginning with its first tax year.
- Members owning substantially all the capital interests in the organization report their respective shares of the organization's items of income, deduction, and credit on their personal tax returns as if the election to exclude the organization from the partnership provisions had been made.

An organization that qualifies for the exclusion from the partnership provisions of Subchapter K may request a partial exclusion — an exclusion from only certain provisions of Subchapter K — instead of a full exclusion. A request for a partial exclusion must be filed with the IRS within 90 days after the beginning of the first tax year for which the partial exclusion is desired. The request must include the sections of Subchapter K from which exclusion is requested, along with certain other required information [Reg. § 1.761-2(c)].

### XIV.B.4. Qualified Joint Venture (Married Couple)

[710 T.M., II.B.2.i.; TPS ¶4020.02.H.]

If a married couple who file jointly conduct a trade or business through a qualified joint venture, the joint venture is not treated as a partnership for federal tax purposes. A joint venture is a qualified joint venture if (i) the only members of the joint venture are the spouses, (ii) both spouses materially participate in the trade or business, and (iii) both spouses elect to have the joint venture treated as a qualified joint venture. When a qualified joint venture election is made, all items of income, gain, loss, deduction, and credit are divided between the spouses in accordance with their respective interests in the joint venture, and each spouse takes those items into account as if they were attributable to a trade or business conducted by the spouse as a sole proprietor [§ 761(f)]. Form 1065 would not be required and each spouse would account for his or her respective share on the appropriate form, such as Schedule C or Schedule E.

## XIV.C. Formation of Partnership

[711 T.M.; TPS ¶4030.]

Generally, taxpayers acquire an interest in a partnership by contributing money, property, or services to the partnership. See XIV.C.1. for a discussion of the tax consequences related to contributions of money and other property. See XIV.C.2. for a discussion of the tax consequences related to contributions of services.

Partnerships generally create capital accounts to track the equity of the partners in the partnership. Capital accounts must be established and maintained in order for special allocations made by the partnership to be respected. See XIV.C.3. for a discussion of the partner's capital accounts.

### XIV.C.1. Contributions of Property to Partnership

### XIV.C.1.a. Nonrecognition Rule for Contributions of Property to Partnership

[711 T.M., II.A.; TPS ¶¶4010.02.A.1., 4030.01.B.]

Taxpayers often acquire an interest in a partnership by contributing property (including money) to the partnership. Generally, neither the partner nor a partnership recognizes gain or loss when the partner contributes property to the partnership in exchange for a partnership interest. This nonrecognition rule applies whether the partnership is being formed or is already operating [§ 721(a); Reg. § 1.721-1(a)].

There are, however, some exceptions to the application of the nonrecognition rule to contributions of property. A contribution of property to a partnership in exchange for a partnership interest may result in the recognition of gain or loss if:

- the partnership is an investment company;
- the contribution of property is recharacterized as a disguised sale of the property;
- the contributed property is subject to liabilities; or
- the partner receives boot in addition to the partnership interest.

***Contributions to Investment Company Partnerships.*** A partner recognizes gain (but not loss) when the partner transfers property to a partnership that would be treated as an investment company if it were incorporated, and the transfer results in diversification of the partner's investment portfolio. A partnership is generally treated as an investment company if, immediately after the receipt of the transferred

711

property, over 80% of its assets (by value) are held for investment and consist of readily marketable stocks and securities. A transfer generally results in diversification of a partner's investment portfolio if one or more other partners transfer non-identical property to the partnership [§ 721(b); Reg. § 1.351-1(c)].

***Contributions Treated as Disguised Sales.*** A contribution of property by a partner to a partnership followed by a distribution of money or other property from the partnership to the partner is treated as a sale of property by the partner to the partnership if (i) the distribution would not have been made but for the contribution, and (ii) the partner's right to the distribution does not depend on the success of partnership operations. The determination of whether a contribution and distribution constitute a disguised sale is based on all the facts and circumstances. If a contribution and distribution occur within two years of each other, they are presumed to be a disguised sale unless the facts clearly indicate otherwise. Such transfers must be reported on Form 8275, *Disclosure Statement*, and attached to the partner's return if the partner treats them as a contribution and distribution (rather than a sale) and the distribution from the partnership to the partner is not considered a guaranteed payment, reasonable preferred return, or an operating cash flow distribution [Reg. § 1.707-3, § 1.707-8].

***Contributions of Property Subject to Liability.*** When a partner contributes property subject to a liability to a partnership, the partnership generally assumes the liability and the partner is relieved of the liability. Any decrease in a partner's individual liabilities due to the assumption of those liabilities by the partnership is treated as a constructive distribution of money by the partnership to the partner [§ 752(b); Reg. § 1.752-1(c)]. A partner generally must recognize gain to the extent that any money distributed exceeds the partner's adjusted basis in its partnership interest immediately before the distribution [§ 731(a)(1)].

***Contributions for Which Boot Received.*** If a partner contributes property to a partnership in exchange for a partnership interest and also receives other money or property ("boot") in the transaction, the partner is generally required to recognize gain in the amount of the boot received because the receipt of boot is treated as a partial sale or distribution [§ 707, § 731].

### XIV.C.1.b. Basis Issues upon Contribution of Property to Partnership
[714 T.M., II.; TPS ¶4030.01.E.1.]

When a taxpayer acquires an interest in a partnership by contributing money or other property to the partnership, the taxpayer must determine its initial basis in its partnership interest and the partnership must determine its initial basis in any contributed property.

***Partnership Basis in Contributed Property.*** The partnership's initial basis in the contributed property generally is equal to the contributing partner's adjusted basis in the property immediately before the contribution (i.e., a carryover basis). However, if the partnership qualifies as an investment company, the contributing partner must recognize any built-in gain (i.e., the excess of the fair market value over adjusted basis) in the property at the time of contribution, and the partnership must increase its basis in the property by the amount of that gain [§ 723]. The partnership's holding period in the property includes the period of time the contributing partner held the property [§ 1223(2)].

***Partner Basis in Partnership Interest.*** The contributing partner's initial basis in the partnership interest is equal to the partner's basis in the contributed property (i.e., a substituted basis), increased by the amount of any gain recognized by the partner at the time of the contribution [§ 722]. For further discussion of a partner's initial basis in a partnership interest acquired by contribution of property, see XIV.E.1.a.

### XIV.C.1.c. Mandatory Special Allocations for Property Contributed to Partnership

[711 T.M., I.B.; TPS ¶4010.04.C.]

The partnership must allocate among its partners any income, gain, loss, or deduction related to contributed property in a manner that will account for any difference between the fair market value of the property and the contributing partner's adjusted basis in the property at the time it is contributed (i.e., the built-in gain or loss) [§ 704(c)(1)(A)]. For purposes of determining the amount of such items allocated to partners other than the contributing partner, the basis of the contributed property in the hands of the partnership is treated as being equal to the property's fair market value at the time of the contribution [§ 704(c)(1)(C)]. Thus, if the partnership sells the contributed property, any built-in gain or loss is allocated to the contributing partner.

If the partnership distributes the contributed property to a partner other than the contributing partner within seven years of the date it was contributed, the contributing partner must recognize the built-in gain or loss on the date of distribution [§ 704(c)(1)(B)]. In addition, if a partner contributes appreciated property to the partnership and the contributing partner receives a distribution of other property from the partnership within seven years of the contribution, the partner must recognize gain on the distribution in an amount equal to the lesser of [§ 737(a), § 737(b)]:

- the excess of (i) the fair market value of the distributed property, over (ii) the partner's adjusted basis in its partnership interest immediately before the distribution (reduced by the amount of any money received in the distribution); or
- the net precontribution gain of the partner.

For further discussion of the special distribution rules that apply to partners that contribute property to a partnership, see XIV.F.5.

### XIV.C.1.d. Character of Partnership Gain or Loss on Sale of Contributed Property

[711 T.M., II.A.1.e(2); TPS ¶4030.01.E.5.]

To prevent a taxpayer from changing the character of a potential gain or loss inherent in an asset by contributing the asset to a partnership, the character of any gain or loss recognized by a partnership upon the sale or other disposition of certain contributed assets is determined by reference to the character of the asset in the hands of the contributing partner immediately before its contribution to the partnership. This rule applies only to unrealized receivables, inventory items, and capital loss property (property that was a capital asset with an adjusted basis in excess of its fair market value immediately before the partner contributed it to the partnership). The rule applies to such property in the following manner:

- A partnership must realize ordinary income or loss upon the disposition of unrealized receivables contributed to the partnership [§ 724(a)].
- A partnership must realize ordinary income or loss upon the disposition of inventory items contributed to the partnership if the disposition of inventory items occurs within five years of their contribution [§ 724(b)].

- A partnership must realize capital loss upon the disposition of capital loss property contributed to the partnership if the disposition of the property occurs within five years of its contribution [§ 724(c)].

If a partnership disposes of any of these types of assets in a nonrecognition transaction, the characterization rules also generally apply to any substituted basis property received by the partnership in the transaction. However, they do not apply to C corporation stock received in a § 351 nonrecognition transaction [§ 724(d)(3)]. See XIII.B.1. for further discussion of § 351 nonrecognition transactions.

### XIV.C.2. Contributions of Services to Partnership

[711 T.M., III.; TPS ¶¶4010.04.G., 4030.02.]

A partner can acquire an interest in a partnership in exchange for services performed or to be performed for the partnership. The partnership interest received by the partner is treated as compensation to the partner for the services performed or to be performed. The tax treatment of this type of transaction generally depends on whether the partnership interest received by the partner is a capital interest (see XIV.C.2.a.) or a profits interest (see XIV.C.2.b.). That determination is generally made at the time the partnership interest is received [Rev. Proc. 93-27, 1993-2 C.B. 343; Rev. Proc. 2001-43, 2001-34 I.R.B. 191].

### XIV.C.2.a. Treatment of Partnership Capital Interest

[711 T.M., III.D.; TPS ¶4030.02.C.]

A capital interest in a partnership is defined as the right to be repaid the amount of any contributions made to the partnership upon a complete liquidation of the partnership [Reg. § 1.721-1(b)(1)]. If a partner receives a capital interest in a partnership in exchange for services performed or to be performed for the partnership, the partner must include the fair market value of the partnership interest in gross income as compensation for services in the first tax year in which the partner is vested in the interest (i.e., the first year in which the partner can transfer the interest or the interest is not subject to a substantial risk of forfeiture) [§ 83(a); Reg. § 1.721-1(b)(1)]. In such a case, the partnership treats the fair market value of the partnership interest as a guaranteed payment to the partner (to the extent that the partner treats it as compensation for services). The partnership can capitalize or deduct the payment, depending on the nature of the services involved [Reg. § 1.721-1(b)(2), § 1.83-6].

### XIV.C.2.b. Treatment of Partnership Profits Interest

[711 T.M., III.C.; TPS ¶4030.02.D.]

A profits interest in a partnership is defined as any partnership interest other than a capital interest. If a partner receives a profits interest in a partnership in exchange for services performed or to be performed for the partnership, the transaction generally is not a taxable event for the partner or the partnership [Rev. Proc. 93-27, 1993-2 C.B. 343]. Although the receipt of a profits interest is generally not a taxable event, a partner receiving a profits interest is required to report its distributive share of the partnership profits as the profits are earned by the partnership.

There are three exceptions under which the receipt of a profits interest may be a taxable event to a partner receiving the profits interest. Under each exception, the determination must be made based on an application of case law and IRS guidance to the specific facts involved. A partner may be taxable on the receipt of a profits interest if [Rev. Proc. 93-27]:

- the profits interest relates to a substantially certain and predictable stream of income from partnership assets (e.g., income from high-quality debt securities or a high-quality lease);
- the partner disposes of the profits interest within two years; or
- the profits interest is a limited partnership interest in a publicly traded partnership.

### XIV.C.3. Partnership Capital Accounts

[711 T.M., I.B.; TPS ¶¶4010.04.B., 4030.01.H.]

The partners' capital accounts play a fundamental role in determining the economic and tax relations between the partners. A partnership is required to establish and maintain capital accounts in order for special allocations made by the partnership to be respected [Reg. § 1.704-1(b)(2)(iv)]. For further discussion of partnership allocations, see XIV.D.2.

A partner's capital account represents the partner's equity in the partnership. Initially, a partner's capital account reflects the amount of cash and the net fair market value of property the partner invested in the partnership. A partner's capital account is adjusted for the allocable share of partnership income or loss, partnership distributions, and additional capital contributions, all measured by fair market values [Reg. § 1.704-1(b)(2)(iv)(b), § 1.704-1(d)(1), and § 1.704-1(e)(1)].

The partners' capital accounts may be, but are not required to be, adjusted periodically for changes in the fair market value of partnership assets. Generally, such adjustments are made to the capital accounts in connection with contributions or distributions of money or other property, the admission of a new partner (including the admission of a service partner receiving a profits interest), and the issuance of noncompensatory stock options [Reg. § 1.704-1(b)(2)(iv)(f)].

A partner's capital account is separate and distinct from the partner's adjusted tax basis in its partnership interest since the capital accounts are established using fair market values instead of tax basis. Thus, there is an inevitable disparity between the records maintained by the partnership to comply with the special allocation regulations and the records needed to reflect tax basis [Reg. § 1.704-1(b)(2)(iv)(g), § 1.704-1(b)(4)(i), § 1.704-1(b)(5), Ex. (18)(ix)].

### XIV.C.4. Treatment of Partnership Formation Expenditures

[711 T.M., II.C.4.a., II.C.4.c.; TPS ¶4010.04.I.]

Many of the formation expenditures of a new business cannot be deducted currently as trade or business expenses because they will benefit the business for as long as it remains in operation. Such expenditures generally must be capitalized. However, taxpayers may elect to deduct certain types of formation expenditures instead of capitalizing them. A partnership may make an election to deduct (i) organizational expenses, and (ii) start-up expenses. There is a separate election for each of these types of formation expenses and a partnership may make both elections, if applicable.

### XIV.C.4.a. Partnership Organizational and Syndication Expenses

[711 T.M., II.C.4.b., II.C.4.c.; TPS ¶4010.04.I.]

A partnership may elect to deduct up to $5,000 of its organizational expenses in the tax year in which it begins business. The $5,000 deduction limitation is reduced (but not below zero) by the excess of the partnership's organizational expenses over $50,000. Any organizational expenses not deductible in the year in which the partnership begins business may be amortized and deducted ratably over a 180-month

715

period beginning with the month in which it begins business. A partnership is deemed to make the election unless it affirmatively chooses to forgo the deemed election by capitalizing its organizational expenses on its tax return for the year in which it begins business [§ 709; Reg. § 1.709-1].

Organizational expenses are expenses that are (i) incident to the creation of the partnership, (ii) chargeable to capital account, and (iii) of a character that, if expended incident to the creation of a partnership having an ascertainable life, would be amortized over such life. Examples of organizational expenses include legal, accounting, and other professional fees incident to the organization of the partnership, and filing fees for certificates and permits [§ 709(b)(3); Reg. § 1.709-2(a)].

Syndication expenses (expenses connected with the selling and marketing of interests in the partnership) are not eligible for the election and must be capitalized [§ 709(a)]. Examples of syndication fees include brokerage fees, registration fees, underwriting fees, the costs of promotional materials used to solicit potential investors, and other selling or promotional costs [Reg. § 1.709-2(b)].

### XIV.C.4.b. Partnership Start-up Expenses

[711 T.M., II.C.4.d.; TPS ¶4010.04.I.]

A partnership may elect to deduct up to $5,000 of its start-up expenses in the tax year in which it begins business. The $5,000 deduction limitation is reduced (but not below zero) by the excess of the partnership's start-up expenses over $50,000. Any start-up expenses not deductible in the year in which the partnership begins business may be amortized and deducted ratably over a 180-month period beginning with the month in which it begins business [§ 195].

Start-up expenses generally include expenses connected with (i) investigating the creation of the partnership or an active trade or business of the partnership, (ii) creating an active trade or business of the partnership, and (iii) any activity engaged in for profit before the day on which the active trade or business of the partnership begins, in anticipation of such activity becoming an active trade or business [§ 195(c)].

## XIV.D. Taxation of Partnership Operations

### XIV.D.1. Taxable Income of Partnership

[712 T.M., I.; TPS ¶4040.01.]

A partnership is not taxable as an entity [§ 701]. However, a partnership is required to separately determine its taxable income as an entity because it must report its income or loss to the IRS and the partners. The partnership's income or loss, including certain separately stated items of income, gain, loss, deduction, and credit, is allocated to the partners. Each partner reports its distributive share of partnership income or loss on its separate tax return. For further discussion of the determination of the partners' distributive shares of partnership income or loss, see XIV.D.2.

### XIV.D.1.a. Computation of Partnership Taxable Income

[712 T.M., II.A.; TPS ¶4040.01.A.]

A partnership computes its taxable income in the same manner as an individual, except that some items must be separately stated and some deductions are not allowed [§ 703(a)]. Certain items of income, gain, loss, deduction, and credit must be segregated and separately stated to the partners because the tax character of the items at the partnership level is required to be preserved and passed through to the partners [§ 702(b)]. The items required to be separately stated are items that potentially have varying tax consequences to the different partners depending on the partners' circumstances. Separately stated items include (but are not limited to) [§ 703(a)(1), § 702(a); Reg. § 1.703-1(a)(1), § 1.702-1(a), § 1.199-5(b)(1)]:

- net rental real estate income or loss;
- other net rental income or loss;
- guaranteed payments;
- interest income;
- ordinary and qualified dividends;
- royalties;
- net short-term capital gain or loss;
- net long-term capital gain or loss;
- collectibles gain or loss;
- unrecaptured § 1250 gain;
- net § 1231 gain or loss;
- gambling income and losses;
- recoveries of tax benefit items;
- the § 179 expensing deduction;
- the charitable contributions deduction;
- dividends taxed as net capital gain;
- dividends eligible for certain dividends received deductions;
- certain taxes paid or accrued to foreign countries or U.S. possessions;
- deductible soil and water conservation expenditures;
- deductible expenses for the production of income under § 212;
- deductible medical, dental and similar expenses under § 213;
- deductible alimony and similar payments under § 215;
- deductible amounts representing taxes and interest paid to cooperative housing corporations under § 216;
- deductible intangible drilling and development costs;
- deductible mining exploration expenditures;
- gain or loss realized by the partnership on a distribution to a partner in exchange for the partner's interest in unrealized receivables or substantially appreciated inventory;
- any item subject to a special allocation under the partnership agreement;
- information used in computing the net investment income tax; and
- information used in computing the domestic production activities deduction.

Although a partnership generally computes its taxable income in the same manner as an individual, it is not allowed to take the following deductions allowed to individuals [§ 703(a)(2); Reg. § 1.703-1(a)(2)]:

- the standard deduction;
- the deduction for personal exemptions;
- the additional itemized deductions for individuals under § 212, § 213, § 215 and § 216;
- the deduction for taxes paid or accrued to foreign countries or U.S. possessions;
- the deduction for charitable contributions;

- the net operating loss deduction; and
- the depletion deduction for oil and gas wells.

### XIV.D.1.b. Elections

[712 T.M., II.C.; TPS ¶4040.01.A.]

In computing the taxable income of a partnership, elections affecting the computation of partnership items of income, gain, loss, deduction, and credit are generally made by the partnership. For example, elections relating to tax year, accounting methods, inventory methods, depreciation, and § 179 expensing are made by the partnership instead of the partners. However, the following elections are made separately by the partners [§ 703(b); Reg. § 1.703-1(b)]:

- the § 108(b)(5) or § 108(c)(3) election relating to discharge of indebtedness income;
- the § 617 election relating to the deduction and recapture of certain mining exploration expenditures;
- the § 901 election to take a credit instead of a deduction for foreign taxes paid or incurred; and
- the § 871(d)(1) and § 882(d)(1) elections afforded to nonresident alien individuals and foreign corporations to be taxed on a net basis with respect to income from U.S. real property that is not effectively connected with a U.S. trade or business.

### XIV.D.2. Partners' Distributive Shares of Partnership Taxable Income

### XIV.D.2.a. Distributive Shares and Partnership Allocations

[712 T.M., III.D.; TPS ¶¶4040.01.B., 4090.01.]

Each partner must include its distributive share of the partnership's items of income, gain, loss, deduction, and credit in its tax return for any partnership tax year ending with or within the partner's tax year [§ 702(a), § 706(a)].

---

**EXAMPLE:** Ken, a calendar year taxpayer, is a partner in a partnership with a tax year ending Nov. 30. Ken will include his distributive share of the partnership items of income, gain, loss, deduction, or credit from the partnership's tax year beginning Dec. 1, Year 1, and ending Nov. 30, Year 2, in his individual tax return for his tax year ending Dec. 31, Year 2.

---

A partner's distributive share of partnership items is the amount of those items for which the partner is responsible for federal tax purposes. It is not the amount actually distributed to the partner. A partner is taxable on its distributive share of partnership items, whether or not the partnership ever actually distributes those amounts to it.

A partner is also generally subject to self-employment tax on its distributive share of any income or loss from a trade or business carried on by the partnership; however, there is an exception for certain limited partners. See X.A.7. for further discussion of the self-employment tax.

Generally, each partner's distributive share of partnership items of income, gain, loss, deduction, and credit is determined by the partnership agreement [§ 704(a)]. However, the allocations made to the partners under the partnership agreement are respected only if they have substantial economic effect (see XIV.D.2.b.) [§ 704(b)(2)]. If an allocation fails the substantial economic effect standard or the partnership agreement does not provide for the allocation of a partnership item, the allocation is made in accordance with the partners' respective interests in the partnership (see XIV.D.2.c.) [§ 704(b)]. Special allocation rules apply for certain items allocated in accordance with the partners' interests in the partnership (see XIV.D.2.d.).

If an allocation of a partnership item does not have substantial economic effect, is not made in accordance with partner's interest in the partnership, and is not made in accordance with one of the special allocation rules, then the item must be reallocated in accordance with the partner's interest in the partnership.

### XIV.D.2.b. Allocations Based on Partnership Agreement: Substantial Economic Effect

[712 T.M., IV.; TPS ¶¶4040.01.B., 4090.01.A.]

Each partner's distributive share of partnership items is generally determined by the partnership agreement. The partnership agreement is not required to provide for all partnership items to be allocated among partners in an identical manner. Thus, partnership items need not be allocated among partners in the same proportion as the partnership distributions made to the partners. Different allocation ratios may be used for different partnership items. However, allocations made according to the partnership agreement will not be respected unless they have substantial economic effect.

The substantial economic effect standard is designed to ensure that the allocations made to the partners for tax purposes also reflect the underlying economic arrangement of the partners. An allocation must meet two different tests to have substantial economic effect: (i) the allocation must have economic effect, and (ii) the economic effect of the allocation must be substantial. These tests are applied as of the end of the partnership tax year to which the allocation relates [Reg. § 1.704-1(b)(2)]. The economic effect test is a relatively objective test that provides clear safe harbors within which recognition of the economic effect is assured. In contrast, the substantiality test is a more open-ended test, designed to police for formally correct allocations that nevertheless lack an economically substantial effect on the underlying economics of the partners' relations.

***Economic Effect Test.*** Under the economic effect test, an allocation will have economic effect only if it is consistent with the underlying economic arrangement of the partners. Thus, if the allocation involves a corresponding economic benefit or burden, the partner to whom the allocation is made must receive the corresponding economic benefit or bear the corresponding economic burden [Reg. § 1.704-1(b)(2)(ii)(a)]. The economic effect of an allocation can be established by meeting any one of three different tests: (i) a general test, (ii) an alternate test, or (iii) an economic effect equivalence test.

Under the general test, an allocation will have economic effect if the partnership agreement provides that [Reg. § 1.704-1(b)(2)(ii)(b)]:

- the partnership must track partnership interests using capital accounts determined and maintained in accordance the rules specified in Reg. § 1.704-1(b)(2)(iv);
- any liquidating distributions made upon the liquidation of the partnership or a partner's interest in the partnership must be made in accordance with the positive balances of the partners' capital accounts; and
- any partner with a deficit balance in its capital account following the liquidation of the partnership or the partner's interest in the partnership must be uncon-

ditionally required to restore that deficit balance by contributing cash or other property to the partnership.

Under the alternate test, an allocation will be treated as having economic effect even if the third requirement of the general test is not met. If the first two requirements of the general test are met and the partnership agreement contains a qualified income offset provision, an allocation will be treated as having economic effect to the extent that the allocation does not cause or increase a deficit balance in the partner's capital account as of the end of the partnership tax year to which the allocation relates [Reg. § 1.704-1(b)(2)(ii)(d)]. A qualified income offset provision provides that a partner who unexpectedly receives a specified type of adjustment, allocation, or distribution will be allocated items of income or gain in an amount and manner sufficient to eliminate any resulting deficit balance as quickly as possible. In determining whether an allocation causes or increases a deficit balance in a partner's capital account, a partner's capital account must be reduced by the following types of adjustments, allocations, and distributions:

- reasonably expected depletion adjustments with respect to oil and gas properties of the partnership that are deducted by the partner without regard to the limitations of the partner allocation rules;

- reasonably expected allocations of loss and deduction resulting from certain partnership Code provisions that override the § 704(b) allocation provisions; and

- reasonably expected distributions from the partnership in excess of increases in the partner's capital account expected to occur by the end of the tax year in which the distributions are expected to be made.

Allocations that do not meet the general test or the alternate test may nevertheless be deemed to have economic effect if, as of the end of each partnership tax year, an immediate or subsequent liquidation of the partnership would produce the same economic results to the partners as would occur if the general test was met (regardless of the economic performance of the partnership in subsequent years) [Reg. § 1.704-1(b)(2)(ii)(i)].

***Substantiality Test.*** Even if an allocation satisfies the mechanical requirements of the economic effect test, it will not be respected as having substantial economic effect unless the economic effect of the allocation is substantial. The economic effect of an allocation is generally considered to be substantial if there is a reasonable possibility that the allocation will substantially affect the dollar amounts to be received by the partners from the partnership, independent of the tax consequences.

The economic effect of an allocation is not considered to be substantial if, at the time the allocation becomes part of the partnership agreement, (i) the after-tax consequences of at least one partner may be enhanced compared to such consequences if the allocation were not contained in the partnership agreement, and (ii) there is a strong likelihood that the after-tax consequences of no partner will be substantially diminished compared to such consequences if the allocation were not contained in the partnership agreement. This rule is intended to protect against allocation arrangements that attempt to improve the tax position of some partners without adversely affecting the tax position of the other partners. In determining whether the after-tax consequences of a partner are enhanced or diminished by an allocation, the comparison is made in present value terms, and the partner's own tax attributes, apart from those related to its participation in the partnership, are taken into account [Reg. § 1.704-1(b)(2)(iii)(a)].

In addition to the general rule that applies in determining when the economic effect of an allocation is not substantial, there are two specific types of allocation arrangements under which the economic effect of allocations will not be considered substantial. A "shifting allocations" arrangement involves potentially offsetting allocations that occur in the same tax year as the allocation at issue, and a "transitory allocations" arrangement involves potentially offsetting allocations that occur over more than one tax year.

Under a shifting allocations arrangement, an allocation is not considered substantial if the allocation provides a net tax benefit to the partners but, when all other allocations for the tax year are taken into account, the non-tax economic effect of the entire arrangement on the partners is not materially altered. Thus, there is a rebuttable presumption that the economic effect of an allocation in a particular partnership tax year is not substantial if, at the time the allocation becomes part of the partnership agreement, there is a strong likelihood that (i) the total tax liability of the partners will be less than it would be if the allocation was not contained in the partnership agreement, and (ii) the net increases and decreases that will be recorded to the partners' capital accounts for that year will not differ substantially from the net increases and decreases that would be recorded if the allocation was not contained in the partnership agreement [Reg. § 1.704-1(b)(2)(iii)(b)].

Under the transitory allocations arrangement, an allocation is not considered substantial if the allocation provides a net tax benefit to the partners but, when all other allocations covering multiple tax years are taken into account, the non-tax economic effect of the entire arrangement on the partners is not materially altered. Thus, there is a rebuttable presumption that the economic effect of one or more allocations in a particular partnership tax year is not substantial if the partnership agreement provides for the possibility that the allocations will be largely offset by other allocations and, at the time the allocations become part of the partnership agreement, there is a strong likelihood that (i) the total tax liability of the partners will be less than it would be if the allocations were not contained in the partnership agreement, and (ii) the net increases and decreases that will be recorded to the partners' capital accounts for that year will not differ substantially from the net increases and decreases that would be recorded if the original and offsetting allocations were not contained in the partnership agreement. However, this presumption does not apply if there is a strong likelihood that the offsetting allocations will not, in large part, be made within five years after the original allocations are made [Reg. § 1.704-1(b)(2)(iii)(c)].

For purposes of applying these rules in determining when the economic effect of an allocation is not substantial, the fair market value of each partnership asset is presumed to be equal to its adjusted tax basis at the time of the determination. Therefore, it is not possible to use the likelihood of appreciation to assert a substantial likelihood of a future allocation of income to offset a current allocation of depreciation or cost recovery deductions [Reg. § 1.704-1(b)(2)(iii)(c)].

### XIV.D.2.c. *Allocations of Partnership Items Based on Partner's Interest in Partnership*

[712 T.M., IV.D.; TPS ¶4090.01.C.]

If an allocation of a partnership item does not meet the substantial economic effect test, or if the partnership agreement does not expressly provide for the allocation of partnership items, the allocation may nevertheless be respected if it is in accordance with the partner's interest in the partnership [§ 704(b)]. The partner's interest in the partnership signifies the manner in which the partners' have agreed to share the economic benefit or burden associated with the partnership item [Reg. § 1.704-1(b)(1)(i)]. There are two tests that may be used to analyze whether an allocation is made in accordance with the partner's interest in the partnership: an objective test and a subjective test.

The objective test may be applied if the allocation meets the first two tests of the general economic effect test, but not the third (see XIV.D.2.b. for discussion of the general economic effect test). In other words, the objective test may be applied if the allocation does not have economic effect despite the fact that the partnership agreement provides that the partnership must track partnership interests using capital accounts and that any liquidating distributions must be made in accordance with the partners' positive balances in their capital accounts. Under the objective test, the partners' interests in the partnership with respect to an allocation are determined by comparing (i) the manner in which distributions would be made if all partnership property were sold at its book value and the partnership was liquidated immediately after the end of the tax year to which the allocation relates, and (ii) the manner in which distributions would be made if all partnership property were sold at book value and the partnership was liquidated immediately after the end of the prior tax year. In each case, the result is adjusted to reflect any reasonably expected adjustment, allocation, or distribution in connection with the alternate economic effect test [Reg. § 1.704-1(b)(3)(iii)].

If an allocation does not meet the objective test for determining whether it is in accordance with the partners' interests in the partnership, it may still be respected if it meets a subjective test that takes into account all facts and circumstances relating to the economic arrangement of the partners. Under the subjective test, the following facts and circumstances are among those that will be considered in determining a partner's interest in the partnership [Reg. § 1.704-1(b)(3)]:

- the partners' relative contributions to the partnership;
- the interests of the partners in economic profits and losses (if different than their interests in taxable income and loss);
- the interests of the partners in cash flow and other non-liquidating distributions; and
- the rights of the partners in liquidating distributions.

### XIV.D.2.d. Special Allocation Rules for Certain Partnership Items that Do Not Have Economic Effect

[712 T.M., IV.F.; TPS ¶4090.01.D.]

An allocation may be respected if it is in accordance with the partner's interest in the partnership (see XIV.D.2.c.). Generally, this determination requires an analysis based on certain objective and subjective tests. However, special rules apply in determining whether certain types of allocations are made in accordance with the partner's interest in the partnership.

***Allocations to Reflect Book-Tax Disparities.*** An asset of a partnership may be reflected in the partners' capital accounts at a value different from the partnership's adjusted tax basis in that asset if the contributing partner's tax basis in the asset was different from its fair market value at the time of contribution. Although depreciation, amortization, depletion, and gain or loss on such an asset are determined based on its tax basis, the partners' capital accounts are adjusted to reflect only the book amounts of those items. Thus, the allocation of any book-tax difference cannot have economic effect [Reg. § 1.704-1(b)(4)(i)]. Such tax items must be allocated among the partners in a manner that takes into account the variation between the partnership's adjusted basis in the property and the fair market value of the property at the time of contribution. The purpose of this rule is to require built-in gain or loss with respect to contributed property to be allocated to the contributing partner in order to prevent the shifting of tax consequences among partners [§ 704(c)(1)(A)]. The regulations provide three methods deemed reasonable for taking this difference into account: (i) the traditional method, (ii) the traditional method with curative allocations, and (iii) the remedial allocation method. Other allocation methods may be considered reasonable in appropriate circumstances [Reg. § 1.704-3(a)].

Under the traditional method, when a partnership disposes of contributed property, it allocates the gain or loss on the property attributable to the period prior to the contribution (i.e., the built-in gain or loss) to the contributing partner. It also allocates cost recovery deductions (e.g., depreciation, amortization, depletion) attributable to the property to reduce the built-in gain or loss. Generally, this is done by determining the amount of the cost recovery deductions to which the partners are economically entitled, and then first allocating those deductions to the noncontributing partners up to the amount of their share of the economic deductions (i.e., the deductions for book purposes) and next allocating the remaining amount to the contributing partner. Thus, the tax deductions generally follow the book deductions for the contributing partners. However, under a ceiling rule, the total depreciation, amortization, depletion, and gain or loss allocated to the partners cannot exceed the amount of the partnership's depreciation, amortization, depletion, and gain or loss. This rule applies if there are insufficient partnership tax items to allow noncontributing partners to be allocated tax items equal to their share of book items [Reg. § 1.704-3(b)].

The traditional method with curative allocations may be used to correct distortions caused by the traditional method ceiling rule. Under this method, the partnership eliminates the distortions by making reasonable curative allocations of other partnership tax items so that equal allocations of book and tax items may be made to noncontributing partners. A curative allocation is an allocation of an item for tax purposes that differs from the allocation of the item as reflected in the books. A curative allocation is reasonable only to the extent it does not exceed the amount necessary to offset the effect of the ceiling rule for the current tax year or, in the case of a curative allocation upon a disposition of the property, for prior tax years [Reg. § 1.704-3(c)].

The remedial allocation method may also be used to correct distortions caused by the traditional method ceiling rule. Under this method, the partnership eliminates the distortions by creating remedial items and allocating those items to the partners as follows: (i) the partnership first determines the amount of its book items and the partners' distributive shares of those items, (ii) it then allocates the corresponding tax items using the traditional method, and (iii) if the ceiling rule causes the book allocation of an item to a noncontributing partner to differ from the tax allocation of that item to the partner, it creates a remedial item of income, gain, loss, or deduction equal to the full amount of the difference and allocates that item to the noncontributing partner. A remedial allocation to a noncontributing partner must have the same tax attributes as the tax item limited by the ceiling rule. The created remedial tax items do not exist independently and have no effect on the capital accounts [Reg. § 1.704-3(d)].

***Allocations of Tax Credits.*** Allocations of tax credits and the recapture of tax credits are not reflected in adjustments to the partners' capital accounts. Thus, such allocations cannot have economic effect and must be made in accordance with the partners' interests in the partnership. Allocations of investment tax credits are deemed to be made in accordance with the partners' interests in the partnership. Allocations of other tax credits must be made in the same proportion as any corresponding book loss or deduction is allocated to the partners' capital accounts, without regard to whether such amounts are deductible for tax purposes [Reg. § 1.704-1(b)(4)(ii)].

***Allocations of Excess Percentage Depletion.*** Depletion of natural resources owned by the partnership (other than oil and gas produced and sold by the partnership) must be computed at the partnership level. Although the deduction for percentage depletion is not limited by the partnership's tax basis in the related property, no capital account adjustments are made for any percentage depletion deduction in excess of basis. Therefore, excess percentage depletion deductions cannot have economic effect and must be allocated in accordance with the partners' interests in the partnership. In such a case, the excess percentage depletion deductions are allocated based on the relative proportions of the partners' distributive shares of gross income from the related mineral property [Reg. § 1.704-1(b)(4)(iii)].

***Allocations Attributable to Oil and Gas Properties.*** Depletion and gain or loss on oil and gas properties owned by the partnership are computed at the partner level, not the partnership level. Thus, the partnership must allocate to each partner its proportionate share of adjusted tax basis in, and amounts realized from, such properties. These items are generally allocated in accordance with the partners' interests in partnership capital. However, they may be allocated in accordance with the partners' interests in partnership profits if (i) the partnership agreement so provides, (ii) no written provision has been made for the profits interest of any partner to be reduced for any purpose other than to reflect admission of a new partner, and (iii) no partner expects its profits interest to be reduced under an agreement with another partner or partners [§ 613A(c)(7)(D); Reg. § 1.704-1(b)(4)(v), § 1.613A-3(e)(2)].

### XIV.D.2.e. *Allocations of Partnership Items Attributable to Nonrecourse Liabilities*

[712 T.M., IV.E.; TPS ¶4090.01.D.5.]

When a partnership borrows money and no partner bears the risk of economic loss with respect to the related liability, the liability is a nonrecourse liability (e.g., when a lender makes a loan to a limited liability company with regard to the LLC's property, the members generally are not at risk, and the liability is characterized as a nonrecourse liability). The lender's sole recourse on a nonrecourse liability is against the assets of the partnership. Therefore, the allocation of deductions attributable to a nonrecourse liability cannot have economic effect because the lender bears the economic risk of loss if the partnership defaults on the loan. Thus, deductions attributable to a nonrecourse liability (so-called nonrecourse deductions) must be allocated in accordance with the partners' interests in the partnership [Reg. § 1.704-2(b)(1)]. Under a safe harbor, nonrecourse deductions are deemed to be allocated in accordance with the partners' interests in the partnership if they meet certain conditions [Reg. § 1.704-2(e)]. If the safe harbor does not apply, an allocation of nonrecourse deductions will be respected if it satisfies the objective test or subjective test discussed in XIV.D.2.c.

The rules on the allocation of deductions attributable to nonrecourse liabilities are interrelated with the rules on the allocation of liabilities for purposes of determining the partners' adjusted bases in their partnership interests. Under the latter set of rules (see XIV.E.3.), a partnership may include in an asset's adjusted basis the amount borrowed to acquire or construct an asset and it may then recover that amount (e.g., through depreciation) over the period the asset is owned. If the adjusted basis of such an asset is reduced below the outstanding balance of the liability, the amount by which the outstanding balance exceeds the adjusted basis is the minimum amount of gain the partnership would be required to recognize if it sold the asset (so-called minimum gain). Each year, minimum gain may increase or decrease as changes occur in the amount by which the outstanding liability balance exceeds the adjusted basis of the asset. Allocations attributable to a decrease in minimum gain during the year (so-called minimum gain chargeback) cannot have economic effect because they merely offset nonrecourse deductions previously claimed by the partnership. Thus, in order to prevent distortions of the economic arrangement of the partners, the minimum gain must be allocated to the same partners to whom the nonrecourse deductions attributable to the asset were allocated [Reg. § 1.704-2(b)(2)].

*Nonrecourse Deductions.* The amount of nonrecourse deductions for each tax year is equal to the net increase in minimum gain, reduced (but not below zero) by the total distribution of the proceeds of a nonrecourse liability that are allocable to the increase in minimum gain. However, increases in minimum gain from conversions, refinancing, or other changes to a debt instrument do not generate nonrecourse deductions. Ordering rules provide that nonrecourse deductions consist first of depreciation and cost recovery deductions on partnership assets subject to nonrecourse liabilities (but only to the extent of the minimum gain increase for each property). To the extent that the nonrecourse deductions exceed the amount of such depreciation and cost recovery deductions, a pro rata portion of the other partnership losses, deductions, and nondeductible expenses for the tax year are treated as nonrecourse deductions [Reg. § 1.704-2(c)].

*Minimum Gain.* The amount of minimum gain is determined by first computing, for each nonrecourse liability, the amount of gain the partnership would realize if it sold the encumbered property for no consideration other than full satisfaction of the liability. For each tax year, the net increase or decrease in minimum gain is determined by comparing the minimum gain on the last day of the immediately preceding tax year with the minimum gain on the last day of the current tax year [Reg. § 1.704-2(d)(1)].

*Partner's Share of Minimum Gain.* Each partner's share of minimum gain is significant for purposes of the operation of the minimum gain chargeback provision required by the safe harbor (see below) and for purposes of the alternate test for economic effect (see XIV.D.2.b.), under which each partner must be obligated to contribute its share of the minimum gain in satisfaction of a deficit in its capital account. A partner's share of minimum gain as of the end of a partnership tax year equals (i) the sum of that nonrecourse deductions allocated to that partner and the distributions made to that partner of proceeds of a nonrecourse liability allocable to an increase in minimum gain, minus (ii) the sum of the partner's aggregate share of decreases in minimum gain and decreases in minimum gain resulting from revaluations of partnership property subject to nonrecourse liabilities [Reg. § 1.704-2(g)(1)].

*Safe Harbor.* Under the safe harbor, nonrecourse deductions are deemed to be allocated in accordance with the partners' interests in the partnership if [Reg. § 1.704-2(e)]:

- capital accounts are strictly maintained in accordance with the regulations, liquidation proceeds are distributed in accordance with the positive balances in the partners' capital accounts, and either (i) partners with deficit balances in their capital accounts have an unconditional deficit restoration obligation, or (ii) the partnership agreement contains a qualified income offset provision;

- nonrecourse deductions are allocated among the partners in a manner that is reasonably consistent with allocations of some other significant partnership item (i.e., a partnership item with substantial economic effect) relating to the asset securing the nonrecourse liability other than minimum gain;

- the partnership agreement contains a minimum gain chargeback provision; and

- all other material allocations under the partnership agreement are valid.

The minimum gain chargeback provision requirement provides that if there is a net decrease in the minimum gain for the tax year, each partner must be allocated items of partnership income and gain equal to that partner's share of the net decrease in minimum gain. A partner's share of the net decrease in minimum gain is equal to the amount of the total net decrease multiplied by the partner's percentage share of the minimum gain at the end of the immediately preceding tax year [Reg. § 1.704-2(f)].

### XIV.D.2.f. Limitations on Deduction of Partnership Losses

[712 T.M., III.C.; TPS ¶4040.01.D.]

A partner's deduction of its distributive share of partnership losses may be subject to several limitations including: (i) a basis limitation, (ii) the at-risk limitations, and (iii) the passive activity loss limitations.

*Basis Limitation.* A partner's distributive share of partnership loss for a tax year is deductible only to the extent of the partner's adjusted basis in its partnership interest at the end of the partnership tax year in which the loss occurred. Any excess loss may be carried forward and deducted in later years, subject to the same limitation in those years [§ 704(d); Reg. § 1.704-1(d)(1)].

Before applying the basis limitation, the partner's basis must first be adjusted to take into account all partnership items for the partnership tax year (other than the losses), capital contributions, and distributions. If a partner's distributive share of the partnership loss items exceeds its basis in its partnership interest after such adjustments, then the partner is allowed a deduction for only a portion of each loss item (based on the proportion that each loss item bears to the total of all loss items) [Reg. § 1.704-1(d)(2)].

*At-Risk and Passive Activity Loss Limitations.* The at-risk and passive activity loss rules are generally applied at the partner level and serve as another set of overall limitations on a partner's ability to deduct losses passed through from the partnership [§ 465, § 469]. Thus, any loss available to a partner after application of the basis limitation is allowed as a deduction only to the extent of the partner's amount at risk in the activity at the end of the tax year [Reg. § 1.469-2T(d)(6)(iv)]. A partner generally is at risk to the extent of its basis in the partnership interest plus its share of partnership recourse liabilities (i.e., partnership liabilities guaranteed by the partners). Any loss allowed to the partner after application of both the basis limitation and the at-risk rules may be limited under the passive activity loss rules [Reg. § 1.469-2T(d)(6)(i)]. See Chapter VIII. for a discussion of the at-risk rules and passive activity loss rules.

### XIV.D.2.g. Rules Affecting Special Types of Partners

[6580 T.M., IV.G., 478 T.M., II.D.; TPS ¶¶6710.03.D.4., 7170.01.E.1.]

Special rules apply to certain types of partners. One special set of rules applies to tax-exempt organizations, charitable organizations, and qualified plans (collectively, "exempt organizations") that are partners in a partnership. Another special set of rules applies to foreign persons that are partners in a partnership.

*Exempt Organization Partners*. Although exempt organizations generally are not subject to income tax, they are taxable on their unrelated business taxable income (UBTI). Thus, when an exempt organization is a partner in a partnership, a determination must be made as to whether the exempt organization's distributive share of the partnership's income is UBTI. This depends on whether the trade or business carried on by the partnership is an unrelated trade or business with respect to the exempt organization. If a trade or business regularly carried on by the partnership is an unrelated trade or business with respect to the exempt organization, then the exempt organization must include in its UBTI an amount equal to its distributive share of the partnership's income from that trade or business, less its distributive share of deductions directly connected with that income [§ 512].

*Foreign Partners*. A foreign partner of a partnership that has income effectively connected with the conduct of a trade or business in the United States is subject to U.S. tax on its distributive share of that income [§ 875(1), § 871(b), § 882(a)]. A partnership is required to pay withholding tax on any portion of its effectively connected income that is allocable to such foreign partners [§ 1446].

### XIV.D.3. Transactions Between Partnerships and Partners

[712 T.M., VI.; TPS ¶4040.02.A.]

Transactions between a partnership and its partners involving transfers of property or the performance of services are not uncommon. A partner may or may not be acting in its capacity as a partner when it is involved in such a transaction with the partnership. The determination of whether or not a partner is acting in its capacity as a partner is made on a case-by-case basis taking into account all relevant facts and circumstances. If a partner is not acting in its capacity as a partner, the transaction generally is treated in the same manner as a transaction between two unrelated parties. If the partner is acting in its capacity as a partner, the payment by the partnership to the partner is treated as either a distributive share of partnership income or a guaranteed payment. For a discussion of transactions in which a partner is not acting in its capacity as a partner, see XIV.D.3.a. For a discussion of guaranteed payments, see XIV.D.3.b. For a discussion of distributive shares of partnership income, see XIV.D.2.

### XIV.D.3.a. Transactions in Non-Partner Capacity

[710 T.M., II.A.1.c(4); TPS ¶4040.02.B.]

Generally, a transaction between a partnership and a partner who is not acting in its capacity as a partner is treated as a transaction between the partnership and a person who is not a partner [§ 707(a); Reg. § 1.707-1(a)]. In other words, such a transaction is treated as a transaction between unrelated parties. Examples of transactions between a partner and partnership in which the partner may not be acting in its capacity as a partner include loans, sales of property, leases of property, and the rendering of services [Reg. § 1.707-1(a)].

Transactions in which a partner is not acting in its capacity as a partner generally are taxed according to general tax principles instead of the partnership tax rules [Reg. § 1.707-1(a)]. Thus, items of income, gain, loss, deduction, and credit from such transactions generally are required to be reported by the partner and the partnership based on their respective tax years and tax accounting methods. However, under a loss deferral rule, the deduction of the party making the payment (whether the partner or the partnership) is generally deferred until the time at which the party receiving the payment is required to recognize income [§ 267(a)(2), § 267(e)]. Special rules apply if the transaction constitutes a sale or exchange of property between a partnership and a partner who owns more than a 50% interest in the capital and profits of the partnership (or between two partnerships in which the same persons own more than a 50% interest in the capital and profits). Under those rules, any gain on the transaction may be required to be recognized as ordinary income instead of capital gain and any loss on the transaction may be disallowed [§ 707(b)].

The partnership rules also contain the following provisions aimed at preventing disguised allocations and disguised sales:

- If a partner performs services for a partnership (or transfers property to a partnership) and there is a related allocation and distribution by the partnership to the partner, the two must be viewed together as part of a single transaction that is properly characterized as a transaction between the partnership and a partner not acting in its capacity as a partner [§ 707(a)(2)(A)]. This provision is designed to prevent payments made for services (or property) from being disguised as partnership allocations and distributions.

- If a partner transfers money or other property to a partnership as a purported contribution and there is a related transfer of money or other property by the partnership to the partner as a purported distribution, the two must be viewed together as part of a single transaction that is properly characterized as a sale or exchange of property [§ 707(a)(2)(B)]. This provision is designed to prevent sales or exchanges of property from being disguised as contributions and distributions.

### XIV.D.3.b. Transactions in Partner Capacity: Guaranteed Payments

[712 T.M., VI.; TPS ¶4040.02.C.]

A payment made by a partnership to a partner acting in its capacity as a partner is treated as a guaranteed payment if the payment is for services rendered or for the use of capital and the payment is determined without regard to partnership income [§ 707(c); Reg. § 1.707-1(c)]. In other words, a guaranteed payment is a payment that is fixed and payable irrespective of partnership income. All other payments by a partnership to a partner acting in its capacity as a partner are treated as distributive shares of partnership income. If a partner is to receive a minimum payment from the partnership, the guaranteed payment is the amount by which the minimum payment is more than the partner's distributive share of the partnership income before taking into account the guaranteed payment.

---

**EXAMPLE:** C is a partner in ABC Partnership. The partnership agreement provides that C is entitled to a fixed annual payment of $100,000, determined without regard to the income of the partnership. C's distributive share of partnership income is 10%. The partnership has $500,000 of income, after deducting C's guaranteed payment. C has a guaranteed payment of $100,000 and a distributive share of $50,000 ($500,000 × 10%).

**EXAMPLE:** X is a partner in XY Partnership. The partnership agreement provides that X is entitled to receive the greater of 30% of the partnership income (as determined before taking into account any guaranteed payments), or $100,000. The partnership has $600,000 of income. X is entitled to $180,000 ($600,000 × 30%) as a distributive share. No part of this amount is a guaranteed payment.

**EXAMPLE:** Assume the same facts as in the previous example, except that the partnership has only $200,000 of income. X has a distributive share of $60,000 ($200,000 × 30%) and a guaranteed payment of $40,000 ($100,000 − $60,000).

---

Guaranteed payments are treated as payments made by the partnership to a person who is not a partner for purposes of the application of the § 61(a) rules on gross income inclusions and the § 162(a) rules on trade or business expense deductions [§ 707(c); Reg. § 1.707-1(c)]. For all other purposes, guaranteed payments are treated as payments made by the partnership to a person who is a partner (i.e., they are treated as a distributive share of partnership income).

A partnership is entitled to deduct a guaranteed payment to the same extent that a payment made to an unrelated party under the same circumstances would be deductible. Thus, a guaranteed payment is deductible to the extent it is properly classifiable as a trade or business expense, but it must be capitalized to the extent it is properly classifiable as a capital expenditure [§ 162(a), § 263]. A partnership may claim a deduction for a guaranteed payment at the time permitted under its method of tax accounting [Reg. § 1.703-1(b)(1)].

A partner receiving a guaranteed payment must report the payment as ordinary income for his tax year with or within which ends the partnership's tax year in which the partnership paid or accrued the payment under its method of tax accounting [§ 61(a), § 706(a)]. Thus, the timing of the partner's inclusion in income is matched with the timing of the corresponding partnership deduction (or capitalization). This required matching can result in an acceleration or deferral of the partner's inclusion of the guaranteed payment in income.

---

**EXAMPLE:** P, a calendar year taxpayer, is a partner in PQ Partnership, a fiscal year taxpayer with a tax year ending June 30. P receives a total of $100,000 of guaranteed payments from PQ during PQ's tax year ending June 30 of Year 2. Of this amount, $60,000 is received between July 1 and Dec. 31 of Year 1 and $40,000 is received between Jan. 1 and June 30 of Year 2. P must include the entire $100,000 of guaranteed payments in income for his tax year ending Dec. 31 of Year 2 because that is P's tax year within which PQ's tax year of payment ends. This results in a deferral of P's inclusion of the $60,000 received in Year 1 until Year 2.

---

Guaranteed payments for services are subject to self-employment tax. Guaranteed payments for the use of capital are subject to self-employment tax to the extent that the partnership is engaged in a trade or business. See Chapter X.A.7. for further discussion of the self-employment tax.

### XIV.D.4. Partnership Filing Requirements

### XIV.D.4.a. Who Must File a Partnership Return

[710 T.M., II., 910 T.M., V.A.3.; TPS ¶4010.05.G.]

Every domestic partnership (including an LLC classified as a partnership for federal tax purposes) must file an income tax return for each tax year unless it has no income, deductions, or credits for the year [§ 6031(a); Reg. § 1.6031(a)-1(a)(1), § 1.6031(a)-1(a)(3)].

A foreign partnership generally must file a U.S. income tax return if it has income effectively connected with the conduct of a trade or business in the United States (ECI) or gross income derived from sources in the United States (U.S. source income) [§ 6031(e); Reg. § 1.6031(a)-1(b)(1)]. This is true even if the foreign partnership's principal place of business is outside the United States and even if all the foreign partnership's partners are foreign persons. However, a foreign partnership with U.S.

source income is not required to file a U.S. income tax return if it qualifies under either of the following two exceptions [Reg. § 1.6031(a)-1(b)(2), § 1.6031(a)-1(b)(3)]:

1. A foreign partnership that had U.S. partners during the tax year is not required to file a U.S. return if it meets all of the following requirements for the year: (i) it had no effectively connected income, (ii) it had U.S. source income of $20,000 or less, (iii) less than 1% of each partnership tax item was allocable in the aggregate to direct U.S. partners, and (iv) it is not a withholding foreign partnership (as defined in Reg. § 1.1441-5(c)(2)(i)).

2. A foreign partnership that had no U.S. partners at any time during the tax year is not required to file a U.S. return if it meets all of the following requirements for the year: (i) it had no effectively connected income, (ii) all required Forms 1042 and 1042-S have been filed by the partnership or a withholding agent, and (iii) it is not a withholding foreign partnership.

### XIV.D.4.b. Forms Filed by Partnership

[710 T.M., II., 634 T.M., II.D.; TPS ¶4010.05.G.]

A partnership generally must file Form 1065, *U.S. Return of Partnership Income*. A Schedule K-1 must be attached to Form 1065 for each person who was a partner at any time during the tax year, and a copy of Schedule K-1 must be furnished to the relevant partner [§ 6031(b)].

Form 1065 generally must be signed by a general partner (or an LLC member manager) [§ 6063]. However, when a return is made for a partnership by a receiver, trustee, or assignee, the fiduciary must sign the return instead. Returns and forms signed by a receiver or bankruptcy trustee on behalf of a partnership must be accompanied by a copy of the order or instructions of the court authorizing signing of the return or form.

A partnership generally has the option of filing either a paper Form 1065 or an electronic Form 1065. However, a partnership is required to file Form 1065, Schedules K-1, and related forms and schedules electronically if it has more than 100 partners [§ 6011(e)(2); Reg. § 301.6011-3].

An unincorporated organization that elects to be excluded from the application of the partnership provisions of Subchapter K (see XIV.B.3.) must file Form 1065 for the year of the election; however, it does not file Form 1065 in later years [Reg. § 1.6031(a)-1(c)].

Certain special types of partnerships are required to file returns other than Form 1065. An electing large partnership must file Form 1065-B, *U.S. Return of Income for Electing Large Partnerships*. A publicly traded partnership treated as a corporation under § 7704 must file Form 1120, *U.S. Corporation Income Tax Return*.

*Electing Large Partnerships*. Certain partnerships with 100 or more partners may elect to apply simplified reporting provisions. However, this election may not be made by a partnership if substantially all of its partners perform services or if its principal activity is the buying and selling of commodities. Accordingly, the electing large partnership provisions are most commonly elected by investing partnerships. Once the election is made, it applies to all subsequent tax years and may be revoked only with IRS consent [§ 771, § 775].

Under the simplified reporting provisions that apply to electing large partnerships, the number of partnership items that must be separately reported to the partners is greatly reduced. Most partnership deductions and credits are combined at the partnership level, and capital gains and losses are netted at the partnership level.

In addition, most elections are made at, and most limitations are applied at, the partnership level [§ 772, § 773].

***Publicly Traded Partnerships.*** A partnership is classified as a publicly traded partnership if the interests in the partnership are traded on an established securities market or are readily tradable on a secondary market. A publicly traded partnership is taxed as a corporation unless more than 90% of its gross income for the tax year consists of interest, dividends, rents from real property, gains from the sale of real property, and income and gains derived from the exploitation of natural resources [§ 7704].

### XIV.D.4.c. When to File Partnership Return

[712 T.M., II.; TPS ¶4010.05.G.]

A domestic partnership is generally required to file Form 1065 by the 15th day of the 4th month after the end of its tax year (e.g., by April 15th for a calendar year taxpayer) [§ 6072(a)]. However, if the due date falls on a Saturday, Sunday, or legal holiday, the due date is extended to the next business day [§ 7503]. A partnership must furnish Schedule K-1 (information on a partner's share of partnership items) to each partner on or before the day on which Form 1065 is filed [§ 6031(b)].

A partnership generally can receive a five-month extension of time to file Form 1065 by filing Form 7004, *Application for Automatic Extension of Time To File Certain Business Income Tax, Information and Other Returns.* However, an extension of time to file the return does not extend the time to pay the § 7519 payment for partnerships electing not to have a required tax year (generally, partnerships with a September, October, or November year-end) [§ 6081(a); Reg. § 1.6081-2].

A partnership that keeps its books and records outside the United States and Puerto Rico can receive a 2-month extension to file and pay (i.e., an extension to the 15th day of the 6th month after the end of its tax year) without filing Form 7004 by attaching a statement to its return stating that it qualifies for this special extension of time to file and pay. If the partnership needs additional time, it can file Form 7004 to request an additional extension of three months (i.e., if needed, it can obtain a total extension of five months like domestic partnerships) [Reg. § 1.6081-5].

A partnership is subject to a penalty if it fails to timely file Form 1065 or to show required information on Form 1065. The penalty is imposed for each month (or fraction thereof) during which the failure continues (not to exceed 12 months). The amount of the monthly penalty is equal to $195 multiplied by the number of persons who were partners in the partnership during any part of the tax year [§ 6698].

A partnership is also subject to a penalty for the failure to furnish an accurate Schedule K-1 to a partner on a timely basis or to include all required information on a Schedule K-1. The amount of the penalty is generally $100 for each Schedule K-1 for which such a failure occurs (up to a maximum of $1.5 million). However, the penalty amount is reduced to $30 ($250,000 maximum) if the failure is corrected within 30 days or to $60 ($500,000 maximum) if the failure is corrected after more than 30 days but on or before August 1 of the calendar year in which the due date occurs. The penalty does not apply if the failure occurs on a de minimis number of Schedules K-1 [§ 6722].

### *XIV.D.4.d. Partnership Accounting Methods and Periods*

[712 T.M., II.D., II.E.; TPS ¶4010.04.K., .04.J.]

A partnership determines its method of accounting separately from its partners. Generally, a partnership can use any permissible method of accounting. However, a partnership cannot use the cash method of accounting if [§ 448]:

- it has at least one corporate partner, average annual gross receipts of more than $5 million, and it is not a farming business; or
- it is a tax shelter (as defined in § 448(d)(3)).

A partnership generally must use a "required" tax year as its tax year. A partnership's required tax year is [§ 706(b)]:

- the tax year of a majority of its partners (the majority interest tax year);
- if there is no majority interest tax year, the tax year common to all of its principal partners (i.e., partners with a 5% or more interest in partnership capital or profits); or
- if there is neither a majority interest tax year nor a tax year common to all principal partners, the tax year that results in the least aggregate deferral of income.

However, if certain requirements are met, a partnership may instead choose to use one of the following tax years:

- a tax year for which a business purpose is established;
- a tax year elected under § 444; or
- a 52-53-week tax year ending with reference to its required tax year or a tax year elected under § 444.

A partnership will be deemed to have established a business purpose for a tax year if it complies with the applicable provisions of Rev. Proc. 2006-46, which provide that the business purpose requirement is deemed to be satisfied if the partnership's tax year coincides with its required tax year or a natural business year. A partnership's natural business year may be established using a 25% gross receipts test, an annual business cycle test, or a seasonal business test. In rare circumstances, a partnership may also be able to establish a business purpose for a tax year using a facts-and-circumstances test [Rev. Proc. 2006-46, 2006-45 I.R.B. 859; Rev. Proc. 2002-39, 2002-22 I.R.B. 1046].

A partnership may make a § 444 election to use a tax year other than the required tax year or a year for which a business purpose is established if the selected tax year produces three months or less of tax deferral for the partners. Generally, this means that a partnership may make a § 444 election to use a fiscal tax year with a September, October, or November year-end. The § 444 election is made by filing Form 8716, *Election to Have a Tax Year Other Than a Required Tax Year*. If a partnership makes a § 444 election, it must make required payments to the IRS that reflect the tax deferral received by the partners due to the partnership's use of the fiscal year [§ 444].

### *XIV.D.4.e. Partnership Audits*

[710 T.M., III.A.10.; TPS ¶4010.05.H.]

The TEFRA audit procedures allow for the unified audit of most partnerships, permitting the IRS to treat a partnership as a separate entity for purposes of audits, administrative and judicial appeals, and refund claims for partnership items. However, electing large partnerships and certain small partnerships are not subject to the TEFRA audit procedures. See XXIII.C.2. for further discussion of this issue.

### XIV.D.5. Family Partnerships

[722 T.M.; TPS ¶4095.]

Family partnerships have often been used in an attempt to shift income from family members in higher tax brackets to family members in lower tax brackets or to transfer wealth from older family members to younger family members. In the past, the courts attempted to limit potential abuse from the use of family partnerships by limiting who may be a partner in a family partnership. In response, Congress enacted § 704(e). Under that provision, a person will be recognized as a partner for federal income tax purposes if that person owns a capital interest in a partnership in which capital is a material income-producing factor, whether or not such interest is derived by purchase or gift from any other person [§ 704(e)(1)]. Thus, a person that acquires a partnership capital interest by purchase or gift from a family member is generally recognized as a partner if capital is a material income-producing factor for the partnership. A partnership interest purchased from a family member is treated as created by gift from the selling family member [§ 701(e)(3)]. When a person's interest in a partnership is created by gift, the person's distributive share of partnership income is includible in gross income, except to the extent that (i) the distributive share is determined without allowance of reasonable compensation for services rendered to the partnership by the donor, or (ii) the portion of the distributive share attributable to donated capital is greater than the proportion attributable to the donor's capital [§ 701(e)(2)].

## XIV.E. Partner Basis in Partnership Interest

[714 T.M.; TPS ¶4055.]

There are two distinct concepts of basis that apply in the context of a partnership. First, a partnership has an adjusted basis in its assets (often referred to as "inside basis"). Second, each partner has an adjusted basis in its partnership interest (often referred to as "outside basis"). Although these two concepts of basis are separate and distinct, there is a relationship between the two under which the total amount of the partners' adjusted bases in their partnership interests should theoretically be equal to the total adjusted basis of the partnership in its assets (i.e., outside basis should be equal to inside basis). However, events that occur during the operation of the partnership may upset this equality between outside and inside basis in certain circumstances.

Note that a partner's adjusted basis in its partnership interest is separate and distinct from the partner's capital account (see XIV.C.3.) for the following reasons:

- A partner's basis in its partnership interest reflects its share of partnership liabilities, while the partner's capital account does not.
- In the case of transactions between the partner and partnership involving property, a partner's basis in its partnership interest is adjusted by the tax basis of the property, while the partner's capital account is adjusted by the fair market value of the property.

### XIV.E.1. Partner's Initial Basis in Partnership Interest

### XIV.E.1.a. Basis in Partnership Interest Acquired by Contribution of Money or Property

[714 T.M., II.A.1.; TPS ¶4055.02.A.]

If a partner acquires its partnership interest in return for a contribution of money and/or property to the partnership, the partner's initial basis in its partnership interest generally is equal to the amount of money contributed plus its adjusted basis in the property contributed. However, if the partnership would be treated as an investment company if it were incorporated, the amount of any gain the partner recognizes on the transfer of property to the partnership must also be added to the partner's initial basis in its partnership interest [§ 722, § 721(b)].

***Contribution of Property Encumbered by Recourse Liabilities.*** If a partner contributes property encumbered by recourse liabilities to a partnership, the partnership is treated as having assumed the liabilities to the extent that the amount of the liabilities does not exceed the fair market value of the property at the time of contribution [§ 752(c); Reg. § 1.751-1(e)]. The partnership's assumption of the liabilities is treated as a deemed cash distribution from the partnership to the contributing partner [§ 752(b)]. Any increase in the contributing partner's share of partnership liabilities upon the contribution of the encumbered property is treated as a deemed cash contribution by the partner to the partnership [§ 752(a)]. Thus, upon the contribution of encumbered property, the partner's basis in its partnership interest must be decreased by the deemed distribution and increased by the deemed contribution [§ 722, § 733]. These two basis adjustments are netted against each other and only the net decrease or increase is treated as a deemed distribution or contribution [Reg. § 1.752-1(f)].

Any net decrease treated as a deemed distribution cannot reduce the contributing partner's basis in the partnership interest below zero and the contributing partner must recognize gain to the extent the deemed distribution exceeds its basis in the partnership interest [§ 733, § 731(a), § 741]. The contributing partner does not increase its basis in its partnership interest by the amount of that gain.

The other partners' bases in their partnership interests also must be increased by any increase in their shares of partnership liabilities upon the contribution of encumbered property to the partnership [§ 752(a)].

---

**EXAMPLE:** Ashley acquired a 20% interest in a partnership by contributing property in which she had an adjusted basis of $8,000 and a $4,000 mortgage. The partnership assumed payment of the mortgage. Ashley's initial basis in her partnership interest is $4,800, which is equal to her $8,000 adjusted basis in the contributed property, minus the $4,000 deemed distribution for the partnership's assumption of the liability, plus the $800 ($4,000 × 20%) deemed contribution for her share of the partnership liability. The other partners must increase their bases in their partnership interests by their $3,200 ($4,000 × 80%) share of that partnership liability.

**EXAMPLE:** Assume the same facts as in the previous example, except that the contributed property had a mortgage of $12,000 instead. Ashley's initial basis in her partnership is zero because the $9,600 net decrease in basis adjustments related to the liability — the $12,000 decrease plus the $2,400 ($12,000 × 20%) increase — cannot reduce her $8,000 basis from the contributed property below zero. Ashley must recognize a gain of $1,600 ($9,600 − $8,000). This gain does not increase Ashley's basis in her partnership interest.

---

For additional discussion of the inclusion of recourse partnership liabilities in a partner's basis in its partnership interest, see XIV.E.2.b.

***Contribution of Property Encumbered by Nonrecourse Liabilities.*** Although the general rules that apply to contributions of property encumbered by recourse liabilities (see XIV.C.1.a.) also generally apply to contributions of property encumbered by nonrecourse liabilities, the rules governing the allocation of nonrecourse liabilities are different. The contributing partner is generally allocated its share of nonrecourse liabilities equal to the sum of (i) the partner's share of partnership minimum gain determined in accordance with the rules of § 704(b) and the related regulations, and (ii) the amount of any taxable gain that would be allocated to the partner under § 704(c) if the partnership disposed of all partnership property subject to one or more nonrecourse liabilities of the partnership in full satisfaction of the liabilities [Reg. § 1.752-3(a)(1), § 1.752-3(a)(2)]. The remaining balance of the nonrecourse liability may be allocated to the other partners in accordance with their shares of partnership profits or in accordance with one of the two alternative methods set forth in the regulations [Reg. § 1.752-3(a)(3)].

For additional discussion of the inclusion of nonrecourse partnership liabilities in a partner's basis in its partnership interest, see XIV.E.2.b.

### XIV.E.1.b. Basis in Partnership Interest Acquired by Other than Contribution of Money or Property

[714 T.M., II.B.; TPS ¶4055.02.A.6.]

If a partner acquires its partnership interest other than by a contribution of money and/or property to the partnership, the general income tax principles for tax basis apply (see III.A.3. for a discussion of these principles). Thus, the following rules apply in determining the partner's initial basis in a partnership interest acquired other than by contribution:

- The initial basis of a partnership interest acquired by purchase is equal to its cost [§ 1012; Reg. § 1.742-1].

- The initial basis of a partnership interest acquired from a decedent is the fair market value of the partnership interest on the date of death or the alternate valuation date, increased by the estate's (or other successor's) allocable share of partnership liabilities on that date and decreased to the extent that the fair market value of the partnership interest is attributable to items constituting income in respect of a decedent [§ 1014; Reg. § 1.742-1].

- The initial basis of a partnership interest acquired by gift generally is equal to the donor's adjusted basis in the partnership interest immediately before the gift. However, for purposes of determining loss realized upon a disposition of the partnership interest by the donee, the donee's basis is limited to the fair market value of the partnership interest at the time of the gift [§ 1015].

### XIV.E.2. Inclusion of Partnership Liabilities in Basis

[714 T.M., III.; TPS ¶4055.02.B.]

Although a partnership's income and losses are allocated to its partners, a partner may deduct its share of the partnership's losses only to the extent of the partner's adjusted basis in its partnership interest as of the end of the partnership tax year in which the losses occur [§ 704(d)]. For this purpose, a partner's adjusted basis in its partnership interest includes the partner's share of the partnership's liabilities [§ 752, § 722, § 733(1)]. A principal purpose for permitting partners to include their shares of the partnership liabilities in their adjusted bases in their partnership interests is to support deductions claimed by the partners for partnership items attributable to those liabilities (e.g., depreciation deductions). Thus, the determination of a partner's share of partnership liabilities is an important factor in determining whether the partner has enough basis to absorb the losses allocated to the partner.

### XIV.E.2.a. Partnership Liability

[714 T.M., III.D.2.a.; TPS ¶4055.02.B.2.b.]

A partner's basis in its partnership interest includes the partner's share of a partnership liability only if, and to the extent that, the liability [Reg. § 1.752-1(a)(4)(i)]:

- creates or increases the partnership's basis in any of its assets (including capitalized items allocable to future periods, such as organizational expenses);
- gives rise to a current deduction to the partnership; or
- is a nondeductible, noncapital expense of the partnership.

A partner's share of accrued but unpaid expenses or accounts payable of a cash basis partnership are not treated as a partnership liability for this purpose.

### XIV.E.2.b. Partner's Share of Partnership Liability

[714 T.M., III.D.; TPS ¶4055.02.B.2.]

The determination of a partner's share of a partnership liability depends on whether the liability is a recourse liability or a nonrecourse liability. A partnership liability is a recourse liability if any partner or related person bears the economic risk of loss for the liability [Reg. § 1.752-1(a)(1)]. A partnership liability is a nonrecourse liability if no partner or related person bears the economic risk of loss for the liability [Reg. § 1.752-1(a)(2)]. For this purpose, a person generally is considered related to a partner if the person and the partner bear a relationship to each other that is specified in § 267(b) or § 707(b)(1), with certain modifications [Reg. § 1.752-4(b)].

**Partner's Share of Recourse Liability.** A partner's share of a recourse liability is equal to the portion of that liability, if any, for which the partner or a related person bears the economic risk of loss [Reg. § 1.752-2(a), § 1.752-4(b)]. A partner or related person bears the economic risk of loss for a partnership liability to the extent that it would be obligated to make a payment to the creditor or a contribution to the partnership for the liability if the partnership were constructively liquidated (the obligation of the partner or related person is reduced to the extent it is entitled to reimbursement from another partner or person related to that other partner) [Reg. § 1.752-2(b)(1), § 1.752-2(b)(5)]. However, this general rule does not apply in de minimis situations in which the partner or related person guarantees a partnership loan that would constitute qualified nonrecourse financing (within the meaning of § 465(b)(6)) if the guarantor had made the loan to the partnership, and the partner has a 10% or less interest in each partnership item for every tax year it is a partner [Reg. § 1.752-2(d)(2)].

The following events are deemed to occur simultaneously in a constructive liquidation of a partnership [Reg. § 1.752-2(b)(1)]:

- all partnership liabilities become payable in full;
- all partnership assets other than assets securing a liability have a value of zero;
- all partnership assets are disposed of in a fully taxable transaction for no consideration except relief from liabilities for which the creditor's right to reimbursement is limited solely to one or more partnership assets;
- all items of partnership income, gain, loss, and deduction are allocated to the partners; and
- the partnership liquidates.

---

**EXAMPLE:** XY partnership is a cash basis partnership formed by X and Y, who each contribute $20,000 in cash and share equally in the partnership profits and losses. The partnership borrows $60,000 to purchase depreciable business equipment. The debt is a partnership liability and it creates a $60,000 basis in the partnership assets. Partner X is required to pay the creditor if the partnership defaults on the liability and, thus, X bears the economic risk of loss for the entire $60,000 liability. X's basis in his partnership interest is $80,000 ($20,000 + $60,000). Partner Y does not bear any economic risk of loss for the liability. Y's basis in his partnership interest is only $20,000.

---

A partner or related person also bears the economic risk of loss for a partnership liability to the extent that it makes a nonrecourse loan to the partnership and the economic risk of loss for that liability is not borne by another partner [Reg. § 1.752-2(c)]. This rule does not apply in the de minimis situation in which the loan constitutes qualified nonrecourse financing and the partner has a 10% or less interest in each partnership item for every tax year it is a partner [Reg. § 1.752-2(d)(1)].

***Partner's Share of Nonrecourse Liability.*** A partner's share of a nonrecourse liability is equal to the sum of [Reg. § 1.752-3(a)]:

- the partner's share of minimum gain (so-called first tier allocations);
- the amount of any gain that would be allocated to the partner if the partnership disposed of all partnership assets subject to nonrecourse liabilities in a taxable transaction in full satisfaction of the liabilities and for no other consideration (so-called second tier or § 704(c) minimum gain allocations); and
- the partner's share of excess nonrecourse liabilities not allocated under (1) or (2), as determined in accordance with the partner's share of partnership profits (so-called third tier allocations).

See XIV.D.2.e. for a discussion of the determination of a partner's share of minimum gain.

### XIV.E.2.c. Effect of Change in Partner's Share of Partnership Liabilities on Basis

[714 T.M., III.D.2.; TPS ¶4055.02.B.1.b.]

A change in a partner's share of the partnership liabilities has the following effect on the partner's adjusted basis in its partnership interest:

- An increase in a partner's share of the partnership liabilities, or an increase in a partner's individual liabilities because of its assumption of the partnership's liabilities, is treated as a deemed cash contribution by the partner to the partnership and increases the partner's adjusted basis in the partnership interest [§ 752(a), § 722; Reg. § 1.752-1(b)].
- A decrease in a partner's share of the partnership liabilities, or a decrease in a partner's individual liabilities because of an assumption of those liabilities by the partnership, is treated as a deemed cash distribution from the partnership to the partner and decreases the partner's adjusted basis in the partnership interest. [§ 752(b), § 733(1); Reg. § 1.752-1(c)]. However, a partner's adjusted basis in its partnership interest cannot be reduced below zero and the partner must recognize gain to the extent that the amount of a deemed distribution exceeds the partner's adjusted basis in its partnership interest [§ 731(a)(1)].

A partner is treated as assuming a partnership liability only if (i) the partner is personally obligated to pay the liability, (ii) the creditor knows that the liability was assumed by the partner, (iii) the creditor can demand payment from the partner, and

(iv) no other partner will bear the economic risk of loss on that liability immediately after the assumption [Reg. § 1.752-1(d)].

If property contributed to a partnership by a partner or property distributed by a partnership to a partner is subject to a liability, the transferee is treated as having assumed the liability to the extent it does not exceed the fair market value of the property at the time of contribution or distribution [Reg. § 1.752-1(e)].

If a partner's share of partnership liabilities both increases and decreases as a result of the same transaction (e.g., a contribution of encumbered property to the partnership), the increases and decreases are netted. A net increase is treated as a deemed contribution that increases adjusted basis. A net decrease is treated as a deemed distribution that decreases adjusted basis [Reg. § 1.752-1(f)].

### XIV.E.3. Adjustments to Partner's Basis in Partnership Interest

[714 T.M., IV.; TPS ¶4055.02.C.]

A partner's adjusted basis in its partnership interest is increased or decreased by certain items. A partner's adjusted basis is increased by [§ 705(a)(1)]:

- the partner's additional contributions to the partnership (including an increased share of partnership liabilities or an assumption of the partnership liabilities by the partner);
- the partner's distributive share of taxable and nontaxable partnership income; and
- the partner's distributive share of the excess of deductions for depletion over the basis of the property subject to depletion.

A partner's adjusted basis is decreased by [§ 705(a)(2), § 705(a)(3)]:

- the money and adjusted basis of property distributed to the partner by the partnership (including a decreased share of partnership liabilities or an assumption of the partner's individual liabilities by the partnership);
- the partner's distributive share of partnership losses;
- the partner's distributive share of nondeductible, noncapital partnership expenses; and
- the partner's deduction for depletion for any partnership oil and gas wells, to the extent the deduction does not exceed the proportionate share of the adjusted basis allocated to the partner.

Under an alternate rule, a partner's adjusted basis in its partnership interest can be determined by using the partner's share of the adjusted basis of the partnership property that would be distributed if the partnership terminated [§ 705(b); Reg. § 1.705-1(b)]. This alternate rule may be used if:

- the circumstances are such that the partner cannot practicably apply the general rules; or
- in the opinion of the IRS, it is reasonable to conclude that the result produced under the alternate rule will not vary substantially from the result under the general rules.

## Worksheet for Adjusting the Basis of a Partner's Interest in the Partnership

*Keep for Your Records*

1. Your adjusted basis at the end of the prior year. Do not enter less than zero. Enter -0- if this is your first tax year . . . . . . . . . . . . . . . . . . . . . . . . . . . **1.** _____

   Increases:

2. Money and your adjusted basis in property contributed to the partnership less the associated liabilities (but not less than zero) . . . . . . . . . . . . . . . . . . . **2.** _____

3. Your increased share of or assumption of partnership liabilities. (Subtract your share of liabilities shown in item K of your 2013 Schedule K-1 from your share of liabilities shown in item K of your 2014 Schedule K-1 and add the amount of any partnership liabilities you assumed during the tax year (but not less than zero)) . . . . . . . . . . . . . . . . . . . . . . . . . . . . . . . . . . . . . . . . . . . **3.** _____

4. Your share of the partnership's income or gain (including tax-exempt income) reduced by any amount included in interest income with respect to the credit to holders of clean renewable energy bonds . . . . . . . . . . . . . . . . . . . . . . **4.** _____

5. Any gain recognized this year on contributions of property. Do not include gain from transfer of liabilities . . . . . . . . . . . . . . . . . . . . . . . . . . . . . . . **5.** _____

6. Your share of the excess of the deductions for depletion (other than oil and gas depletion) over the basis of the property subject to depletion . . . . . . . . . . . **6.** _____

   Decreases:

7. Withdrawals and distributions of money and the adjusted basis of property distributed to you from the partnership. Do not include the amount of property distributions included in the partner's income (taxable income) . . . . . . . . . **7.** _____

   **Caution:** A distribution may be taxable if the amount exceeds your adjusted basis of your partnership interest immediately before the distribution.

8. Your decreased share of partnership liabilities and any decrease in your individual liabilities because they were assumed by the partnership. (Subtract your share of liabilities shown in item K of your 2014 Schedule K-1 from your share of liabilities shown in item K of your 2013 Schedule K-1 and add the amount of your individual liabilities that the partnership assumed during the tax year (but not less than zero)) . . . . . . . . . . . . . . . . . . . . . . . . . . . . . . **8.** _____

9. Your share of the partnership's nondeductible expenses that are not capital expenditures . . . . . . . . . . . . . . . . . . . . . . . . . . . . . . . . . . . . . . . **9.** _____

10. Your share of the partnership's losses and deductions (including capital losses). However, include your share of the partnership's section 179 expense deduction for this year even if you cannot deduct all of it because of limitations . . . . . . **10.** _____

11. The amount of your deduction for depletion of any partnership oil and gas property, not to exceed your allocable share of the adjusted basis of that property . . . . . . . . . . . . . . . . . . . . . . . . . . . . . . . . . . . . . . . . . . **11.** _____

12. Your adjusted basis in the partnership at the end of this tax year. (Add lines 1 through 6 and subtract lines 7 through 11 from the total. If zero or less, enter -0-.) . . . . . . . . . . . . . . . . . . . . . . . . . . . . . . . . . . . . . . . . . **12.** _____

   **Caution:** The deduction for your share of the partnership's losses and deductions is limited to your adjusted basis in your partnership interest. If you entered zero on line 12 and the amount figured for line 12 was less than zero, a portion of your share of the partnership losses and deductions may not be deductible. (See *Basis Rules*, earlier, for more information.)

(Source: 2014 Form 1065 (Schedule K-1) Draft Instructions)

## XIV.F. Partnership Distributions to Partners

[716 T.M.; TPS ¶4050.]

Partnerships often make distributions of money or property to their partners. Partnership distributions may be liquidating or nonliquidating distributions. Liquidating distributions are distributions that result in the termination of a partner's entire interest in the partnership [Reg. § 1.761-1(d)]. Non-liquidating distributions include distributions of a partner's share of the partnership's income and other distributions that do not result in the termination of a partner's interest in the partnership. Generally, liquidating and nonliquidating distributions are treated in the same manner; however, there are a few important differences that are discussed in this section. Special rules apply to liquidating distributions made to retiring partners (see XIV.G.) and distributions made upon the termination of a partnership (see XIV.I.).

### XIV.F.1. Gain or Loss Recognition on Partnership Distribution

[716 T.M., II.A., III.A., IV.A.; TPS ¶4050.01.B.1., .02.A.]

A partnership generally does not recognize any gain or loss on the distribution of money or property to a partner [§ 731(b)]. A partner recognizes gain on a distribution only to the extent that the amount of cash or marketable securities received by the partner exceeds the partner's adjusted basis in the partnership interest [§ 731(a)(1), § 731(c)(1)(a)]. Thus, no gain is recognized by a partner on a distribution of property other than marketable securities. Any gain recognized by a partner under these rules is treated as capital gain from a sale of the partnership interest on the date of the distribution [§ 731(a), § 741].

---

**EXAMPLE:** Partnership X makes a $30,000 cash distribution to partner Bob. Bob's has an adjusted basis of $50,000 in his partnership interest. Bob does not recognize any gain on the distribution.

**EXAMPLE:** Assume the same facts as in the previous example, except that Partnership X instead makes a $60,000 cash distribution to Bob. Bob recognizes a capital gain of $10,000 ($60,000 − $50,000) on the distribution.

---

A partner may also be required to recognize gain on a distribution if the partner made a contribution of appreciated property to the partnership (see XIV.F.5.) or if the distribution is disproportionate (see XIV.F.6.).

A partner generally does not recognize loss on a distribution. However, a partner that receives a liquidating distribution consisting solely of money, unrealized receivables, and inventory may recognize loss on the distribution to the extent that the partner's adjusted basis in the partnership interest exceeds the sum of the money and the adjusted basis of the assets received by the partner [§ 731(a)(2)]. Any loss recognized by a partner on a liquidating distribution is treated as capital loss from a sale of the partnership interest on the date of the distribution [§ 731(a), § 741].

---

**EXAMPLE:** Partnership Z distributes cash of $2,000 and inventory with fair market value of $9,000 and an adjusted basis of $7,000 to partner Mary in complete liquidation of her partnership interest. Mary's basis in her partnership interest before the liquidating distribution was $10,000. Mary may recognize a capital loss of $1,000 (($2,000 $7,000) − $10,000) on the liquidating distribution.

---

### XIV.F.2. Partner's Basis in Distributed Partnership Assets

[716 T.M., II.B., III.B., IV.B.; TPS ¶4050.01.B.2., .02.A.1.]

If a partner receives assets other than cash in a distribution, the basis the partner takes in those assets depends on whether the distribution is a liquidating distribution or a nonliquidating distribution. As a general rule, a partner takes a carryover basis in assets received in a nonliquidating distribution and a substituted basis in assets received in a liquidating distribution.

### XIV.F.2.a. Partner's Basis in Distributed Partnership Assets upon Nonliquidating Distribution

[716 T.M., III.B.; TPS ¶4050.01.B.2.]

When a partner receives assets other than cash in a nonliquidating distribution, the partner generally takes a basis in the distributed assets equal to the partnership's basis in those assets immediately before the distribution (i.e., a carryover basis) [§ 732(a)(1)]. However, the basis taken in the distributed assets is limited to the partner's basis in its partnership interest reduced by any cash received in the distribution [§ 732(a)(2)].

**EXAMPLE:** Carol has an adjusted basis of $20,000 in her partnership interest in Partnership X. Partnership X makes a nonliquidating distribution to Carol of cash of $2,000 and property in which the partnership has an adjusted basis of $16,000. Carol takes a $16,000 basis in the distributed property.

**EXAMPLE:** Assume the same facts as in the previous example, except that Carol has an adjusted basis of only $15,000 in her partnership interest in Partnership X. Carol's basis in the distributed property is limited to $13,000 ($15,000 − $2,000).

### XIV.F.2.b. Partner's Basis in Distributed Partnership Assets upon Liquidating Distribution

[716 T.M., IV.B.; TPS ¶4050.02.A.1.]

When a partner receives assets other than cash in a liquidating distribution, the partner generally takes a basis in the distributed assets equal to the partner's basis in its partnership interest (i.e., a substituted basis) reduced by any cash received in the distribution [§ 732(b)].

**EXAMPLE:** Assume the same facts as in Example 1, except that the distribution results in the termination of Carol's entire interest in Partnership X. Carol takes an $18,000 basis ($20,000 − $2,000) in the distributed property.

### XIV.F.2.c. Allocation of Partner's Basis Among Distributed Partnership Assets

[716 T.M., III.B., IV.B.; TPS ¶4050.01.B.2., .02.A.1.]

When a partner's basis in assets received in a distribution is measured by the partner's basis in its partnership interest reduced by any cash received in the distribution and the partner receives more than one asset in the distribution, the basis amount must be allocated among the distributed assets. The basis amount is allocated under the following rules [§ 732(c)(1)]:

- The allocable basis amount is first allocated to any unrealized receivables and inventory items received in the distribution by assigning a basis to each item equal to the partnership's adjusted basis in the item immediately before the distribution. If the total of these assigned bases is more than the allocable basis amount, the assigned bases must be decreased by the difference.

- Any remaining allocable basis amount is allocated to the other distributed assets by assigning a basis to each asset equal to the partnership's adjusted basis in the asset immediately before the distribution. If the total of these assigned bases is more than the remaining allocable basis amount, the assigned bases must be decreased by the difference. If the total of these assigned bases is less than the remaining allocable basis amount, the assigned bases must be increased by the difference.

A basis decrease for any excess amount is allocated under the following rules [§ 732(c)(3)]:

- The basis decrease amount is first allocated to assets with unrealized depreciation to the extent of that unrealized depreciation. If the basis decrease is less than the total unrealized depreciation, then it must be allocated to those assets in proportion to their respective amounts of unrealized depreciation.

- Any remaining basis decrease amount is allocated among all the distributed assets in proportion to their respective assigned bases amounts (after the application of step 1).

A basis increase for any deficit amount is allocated under the following rules [§ 732(c)(2)]:

- The basis increase amount is first allocated to assets with unrealized appreciation to the extent of that unrealized appreciation. If the basis increase amount is less than the total unrealized appreciation, then it must be allocated to those assets in proportion to their respective amounts of unrealized appreciation.

- Any remaining basis increase amount is allocated among all the distributed assets in proportion to their respective fair market values.

---

**EXAMPLE:** Lisa has a $55,000 adjusted basis in her partnership interest in Partnership Z. Lisa receives a liquidating distribution of Assets A and B, neither of which is unrealized receivables or inventory. Asset A has a fair market value of $40,000 and an adjusted basis of $5,000 in the hands of the partnership. Asset B has a fair market value of $10,000 and an adjusted basis of $10,000 in the hands of the partnership. In determining her basis in Assets A and B, Lisa first assigns a basis of $5,000 to Asset A and $10,000 to Asset B (their adjusted bases in the hands of the partnership). Since the total of these assigned bases ($15,000) is less than the allocable basis amount ($55,000), the assigned bases must be increased by the $40,000 difference. Lisa first allocates the basis increase amount to Asset A to the extent of its unrealized appreciation of $35,000 ($40,000 FMV − $5,000 basis). Since Asset B does not have any unrealized appreciation, the remaining $5,000 ($40,000 − $35,000) of the basis increase amount must be allocated among the assets in proportion to their fair market values, with $4,000 ($5,000 × ($40,000/$50,000)) allocated to Asset A and $1,000 ($5,000 × ($10,000/$50,000)) allocated to Asset B. As a result, Lisa takes a basis of $44,000 ($5,000 $35,000 $4,000) in Asset A and a basis of $11,000 ($10,000 $1,000) in Asset B.

---

### XIV.F.2.d. Special Basis Adjustment for Distributed Partnership Assets

[716 T.M., III.C.2.b., IV.C.3.; TPS ¶4050.03.]

A partner that acquired all or part of its partnership interest in a sale or exchange or upon the death of another partner may elect under § 732(d) to apply a special basis adjustment in determining its basis in any distributed assets if [§ 732(d); Reg. § 1.732-1(d)(1)(iii)]:

- the partnership distribution is made to the partner within two years after it acquired the partnership interest; and

- the partnership did not elect to make the optional basis adjustment under § 754 (based on § 743) for partnership property when the partner acquired its partnership interest (see XIV.H.3. for a discussion of this optional basis adjustment for partnership property).

If a partner elects to apply this special § 732(d) basis adjustment, the partner's basis in the distributed assets is the same as it would have been if the partnership had elected the optional § 754 basis adjustment with respect to the distributed assets [§ 732(d); Reg. § 1.732-1(d)(1)(iii)]. However, the assigned basis is not reduced by any depreciation or depletion that would have been allowed or allowable if the partnership had elected the optional § 754 basis adjustment [Reg. § 1.732-1(d)(1)(iv)].

---

**EXAMPLE:** Stan purchased a 25% interest in Partnership X for $17,000 in cash. At the time of the purchase, the partnership owned inventory with a fair market value of $16,000 and an adjusted basis of $14,000. Thus, Stan's share of the inventory was $4,000 ($16,000 × 25%) and had a basis of $3,500 ($14,000 × 25%). Partnership X did not elect to make the optional basis adjustment for partnership property at the time of Stan's purchase. Within two years of acquiring the partnership interest, Stan withdraws from the partnership and receives a liquidating distribution of cash of $1,500, inventory with a basis of $3,500, and other property with a basis of $6,000. Stan elects to make the special § 732(d) basis adjustment for purposes of determining his basis in the inventory received. As a result of the election, his basis in the inventory received is increased by $500 (25% of the $2,000 difference between the $16,000 FMV of the inventory and the partnership's $14,000 basis in the inventory at the time Stan acquired his partnership interest). Stan must allocate $15,500 of basis ($17,000 basis in partnership interest − $1,500 cash received) among the assets received in the liquidating distribution. He allocates $4,000 ($3,500 $500) to the inventory received and the $11,500 balance to the other asset received.

---

A partner must make the § 732(d) election for the tax year of the distribution if the distribution includes any property subject to depreciation, amortization, or depletion. Otherwise, the election must be made by the first tax year in which the basis of the distributed assets is relevant in determining the partner's income tax [Reg. § 1.732-1(d)(2)]. The partner must attach a statement to its tax return for the year the election is made stating that the partner is electing to adjust the basis of the distributed assets under § 732(d), showing a computation of the special basis adjustment, and listing the assets to which the adjustment has been allocated [Reg. § 1.732-1(d)(3)].

The special § 732(d) basis adjustment is required to be made if all of the following conditions existed when the partner acquired its partnership interest [§ 732(d); Reg. § 1.732-1(d)(4)]:

1. the fair market value of all partnership property (other than money) was more than 110% of its adjusted basis to the partnership;

2. if there had been a liquidation of the partner's interest in the partnership immediately after it was acquired, an allocation of the partner's basis in the partnership interest under the general rules would have increased the partner's basis in the assets that could be depreciated, amortized or depleted, and would have decreased the partner's basis in the other assets; and

3. if the partnership had elected the optional basis adjustment for partnership property, the election would have changed the partner's basis in the assets actually distributed.

If a partner elects to make the special § 732(d) basis adjustment and notifies the partnership, or if the special § 732(d) basis adjustment is required, the partnership must provide a statement to the partner that provides it with the information necessary to compute the special § 732(d) basis adjustment [Reg. § 1.732-1(d)(5)].

### XIV.F.3. Partner's Character and Holding Period for Distributed Partnership Assets

[716 T.M., III.B.2.; TPS ¶4050.05.]

When a partner receives a distribution of property from a partnership, the character of the distributed property in the hands of the partner is generally determined by the partner's purpose for holding the property. However, a special rule applies to unrealized receivables and inventory items. A partner who receives a distribution of unrealized receivables and/or inventory items (so-called ordinary income assets) generally must treat the character of the gain or loss on any later sale of those assets as ordinary income or loss [§ 735(a)]. This rule prevents a partner who receives a distribution of ordinary income assets from converting the ordinary income assets into capital assets by changing the purpose for which it holds those assets. If the partner subsequently sells the ordinary income assets, it generally must recognize ordinary income or loss rather than capital gain or loss (i.e., there is an ordinary income taint associated with such assets).

In the case of inventory items, the ordinary income taint applies only if the partner sells the inventory items within five years from the date of distribution [§ 735(a)(2)]. In other words, if the partner sells the inventory items more than five years after the date of distribution, the gain or loss on the sale may be capital gain or loss as long as the assets are capital assets in the hands of the partner [Reg. § 1.735-1(a)(2)]. In the case of unrealized receivables, the ordinary income taint applies regardless of how long the unrealized receivables are held by the partner [§ 735(a)(1)].

If the partner subsequently contributes an asset having ordinary income taint to another partnership in exchange for a partnership interest in that partnership, the ordinary income taint stays with the asset in the hands of the acquiring partnership and also attaches to the partner's interest in that partnership [§ 735(c)(2)(A)]. However, if the partner subsequently contributes an asset having ordinary income taint to a C corporation in a nonrecognition transaction, the ordinary income taint stays with the asset in the hands of the C corporation but does not attach to the stock received by the partner [§ 735(c)(2)(B)].

A partner is permitted to add the partnership's holding period to its own holding period in property distributed to the partner by the partnership. This rule applies for both liquidating and nonliquidating distributions. However, this rule does not apply for purposes of determining the five-year period used to determine whether there is ordinary income taint on the distribution of inventory items [§ 735(b)].

### XIV.F.4. Partnership's Basis in Undistributed Assets

[716 T.M., III.C., IV.C.; TPS ¶4050.07.]

When a partnership distributes property to a partner, the partnership's adjusted basis in its undistributed assets is not adjusted unless the partnership has elected to make an optional basis adjustment under § 754 (based on § 734) or unless the partnership is required to make a basis adjustment because there is a substantial basis reduction with respect to the distribution (i.e., a mandatory basis adjustment) [§ 734(a)].

The optional and mandatory basis adjustment rules are designed to resolve the discrepancy that may arise between the partnership's adjusted basis in its assets (the inside basis) and the partners' adjusted bases in their partnership interests (the outside basis). This discrepancy may result in the double taxation of gains or the duplication of losses. For example, if a partner's partnership interest is liquidated for cash, the partner must recognize gain equal to the excess of the cash received over the partner's adjusted basis in the partnership interest. This gain represents the partner's share of appreciation in the partnership assets. However, if the partnership's adjusted basis in its assets is not adjusted for this gain, the remaining partners will be subject to tax on the same gain when the partnership later sells its assets. The optional basis adjustment is designed to prevent such a double taxation of gains. The mandatory basis adjustment is designed to prevent a duplication of losses when there is a substantial basis reduction with respect to a distribution.

There is a substantial basis reduction with respect to a distribution if there would be a reduction of more than $250,000 in the basis of the undistributed assets if the partnership made the optional basis adjustment [§ 734(d)]. However, a securitization partnership (a partnership the sole business of which is to issue securities that provide for a fixed principal amount and that are primarily serviced by cash flows of a discrete pool of receivables or other assets that by their terms convert into cash on a finite period) is not treated as having a substantial basis reduction with respect to a distribution [§ 734(e), § 743(f)(2)].

When there is a distribution of assets to a partner by a partnership for which the optional basis adjustment election is in effect or for which there is a substantial basis reduction, the partnership makes the following basis adjustments:

- The basis of the undistributed assets is increased by the amount of any gain recognized by a partner as a result of the distribution (this adjustment applies only in the case of the optional basis adjustment) [§ 734(b)(1)(A)].

- The basis of the undistributed assets is decreased by the amount of any loss recognized by a partner as a result of the distribution [§ 734(b)(2)(A)].

- The basis of the undistributed assets is increased by any amount by which the partner's basis in the assets received is less than the partnership's basis in those assets (this adjustment applies only in the case of the optional basis adjustment) [§ 734(b)(1)(B)].

- The basis of the undistributed assets is decreased by any amount by which the partner's basis in the assets received is greater than the partnership's basis in those assets [§ 734(b)(1)(B)].

These special basis adjustments are generally allocated to undistributed assets that are similar in character to the distributed assets giving rise to the adjustments [§ 734(c), § 755(a), § 755(b)].

If the application of the special basis adjustment results in an increase in the basis of assets that the partnership is depreciating under MACRS or ACRS, the amount of the adjustment is treated as newly purchased property placed in service on the date of the distribution. If it results in a decrease in the basis of assets that the partnership is depreciating, the amount of the adjustment must be accounted for over the remaining recovery period of those assets, beginning with the recovery period in which the basis is decreased [Reg. § 1.734-1(e)].

A partnership that adjusts the basis of its undistributed assets under these rules must attach a statement to the partnership return for the year of the distribution providing information on the computation of the adjustment and the assets to which the adjustment is allocated [Reg. § 1.734-1(d)].

### XIV.F.5. Special Distribution Rules for Contributing Partners

[716 T.M., III.E.; TPS ¶4050.04.]

In the past, some taxpayers tried to use partnerships as a device for making tax-free exchanges of property that did not qualify for § 1031 like-kind exchange nonrecognition treatment by taking advantage of the fact that property contributions to a partnership and property distributions from a partnership are both nonrecognition transactions (for a discussion of like-kind exchanges, see III.E.1.). In order to limit the ability of taxpayers to use partnerships for this purpose, two special provisions now provide exceptions to the general nonrecognition rule for partnership distributions.

### XIV.F.5.a. Contributed Property Distributed to Other Partner

[716 T.M., III.E.1.; TPS ¶4050.04.B.]

If a partner contributes property to a partnership and the partnership distributes that property to another partner within seven years of the date it was contributed, the contributing partner must recognize the built-in gain or loss in the contributed property on the date of distribution [§ 704(c)(1)(B)(i); Reg. § 1.704-4(a)]. The character of the contributing partner's gain or loss is the same as the character of the gain or loss that would have been recognized if the partnership had instead sold the property to the other partner [§ 704(c)(1)(B)(ii); Reg. § 1.704-4(b)]. The contributing partner's basis in its partnership interest is increased by the amount of the gain recognized or decreased by the amount of loss recognized [§ 704(c)(1)(B)(iii); Reg. § 1.704-4(e)].

This rule does not apply to (i) property contributed on or before October 3, 1989, (ii) distributions in certain partnership liquidations, (iii) deemed distributions resulting from a partnership termination due to a sale or exchange of a 50% or more interest in the partnership. (iv) certain complete transfers of all assets and liabilities to another partnership, (v) an incorporation of a partnership in which the partnership is liquidated, or (vi) a distribution of an undivided interest in property to the extent that the undivided interest does not exceed the undivided interest contributed by the other partner in the same property [Reg. § 1.704-4(c)].

### XIV.F.5.b. Other Property Distributed to Contributing Partner

[716 T.M., III.E.2.; TPS ¶4050.04.C.]

If a partner contributes appreciated property to the partnership and the contributing partner receives a distribution of other property from the partnership within seven years of the contribution of the appreciated property, the partner must recognize gain on the distribution in an amount equal to the lesser of [§ 737(a), § 737(b)]:

- the excess of (i) the fair market value of the distributed property, over (ii) the partner's adjusted basis in its partnership interest immediately before the distribution (reduced by the amount of any money received in the distribution); or
- the net precontribution gain of the partner.

The following apply for purposes of this rule:

- The fair market value of the distributed property is not reduced by the amount of any liability assumed (or taken subject to) by the partner [Reg. § 1.737-1(e), Ex. 2].

- The partner's adjusted basis in its partnership interest must first be adjusted for all basis adjustments resulting from the distribution and for any other distribution or transaction that is part of the same distribution, except for (i) increases for the amount of any precontribution gain recognized, and (ii) decreases for the partner's adjusted basis in the distributed property [Reg. § 1.737-1(b)(3)].

- Net precontribution gain is equal to the net gain, if any, the partner would recognize if all the property contributed by the partner within seven years of the distribution, and held by the partnership immediately before the distribution, were distributed to another partner (other than a partner that owns more than 50% of the partnership) [§ 737(b); Reg. § 1.737-1(c)(1)].

The gain recognized under this rule is in addition to any gain recognized under the general distribution rules (i.e., the gain recognized if the money distributed to the partner is greater than the partner's basis in its partnership interest). The character of this gain is determined by reference to the character of the net precontribution gain [§ 737(a); Reg. § 1.737-1(d)].

When this rule applies, the partner's adjusted basis in its partnership interest and the partner's adjusted basis in any property contributed during the seven-year period is increased by the amount of any gain recognized [§ 737(c); Reg. § 1.737-3(a)].

This rule does not apply to (i) deemed distributions resulting from a partnership termination due to a sale or exchange of a 50% or more interest in the partnership, (ii) certain complete transfers of all assets and liabilities to another partnership, or (iii) an incorporation of a partnership in which the partnership is liquidated. In addition, any part of a distribution that consists of property the partner previously contributed to the partnership is not taken into account in making the computations [§ 737(d)(1); Reg. § 1.737-2].

### XIV.F.6. Special Rules for Disproportionate Distributions

[716 T.M., III.E.; TPS ¶4050.06.]

Special disproportionate distribution rules may apply when a distribution has the potential to shift the reporting of the partners' respective shares of the partnership's ordinary income and capital gain. These rules are intended to prevent a partnership from manipulating its distributions so that partners in high marginal tax brackets report the partnership's capital gain while partners in low brackets report the partnership's ordinary income.

The disproportionate distribution rules apply only if the partnership has unrealized receivables or substantially appreciated inventory items (so-called § 751 property). In addition, the disproportionate distribution rules apply only if a distribution to a partner is disproportionate. A distribution to a partner is considered disproportionate only if the partner receives a distribution of § 751 property that is greater than its allocable share of the partnership's § 751 property or if a partner receives a distribution of other property that has the effect of decreasing its allocable share of the partnership's § 751 property [Reg. § 1.751-1(b)(1)(i)]. Thus, the disproportionate distribution rules do not apply to a distribution to the extent that the distribution consists of the partner's allocable share of the partnership's § 751 property or its allocable share of the partnership's other property [Reg. § 1.751-1(b)(1)(ii)].

The disproportionate distribution rules also do not apply to [§ 751(b)(2)]:

- a distribution of property to a partner that contributed the property to the partnership; or

- a distribution of property to a retiring partner or the successor-in-interest of a deceased partner to the extent that the distribution is treated as a distributive share of partnership income or a guaranteed payment.

Under the disproportionate distribution rules, a distribution of property is generally treated as a sale or exchange of that property to the extent that it consists of [§ 751(b)(1)]:

- a distribution of a partner's interest in § 751 property (unrealized receivables and substantially appreciated inventory items) in exchange for that partner's interest in partnership property that is not § 751 property; or

- a distribution of a partner's interest in partnership property that is not § 751 property in exchange for that partner's interest in § 751 property.

For this purpose, inventory items of the partnership are considered to have substantially appreciated only if, at the time they are distributed, the total fair market value of the items is more than 120% of the partnership's adjusted basis in the items [§ 751(b)(3)].

When the disproportionate distribution rules apply to a distribution, part of the distribution is treated as a deemed sale or exchange of property between the partnership and the partner and part of the distribution is treated as a distribution of property under the general distribution rules (see XIV.F.1. for the general distribution rules) [Reg. § 1.751-1(b)(1)(iii)]. The disproportionate distribution rules operate by creating two fictions, a deemed distribution and a deemed exchange.

When a partner receives a distribution of § 751 property that is greater than its allocable share of the partnership's § 751 property, the partner is first deemed to receive a distribution of its allocable share of the partnership's other property. This deemed distribution is generally subject to nonrecognition treatment under the general distribution rules. The partner is then deemed to transfer that other property back to the partnership in exchange for the excess portion of the § 751 property it actually received in the distribution. This deemed exchange is treated as a taxable sale or exchange. As a result, the partnership must recognize ordinary income on the excess portion of § 751 property it transfers to the partner and the partner must recognize capital gain or loss on the other property it transfers to the partnership [Reg. § 1.751-1(b)(2)].

When a partner receives a distribution of other property that is greater than its allocable share of the partnership's other property (and the partner's share of the partnership's § 751 property is therefore reduced or eliminated), the partner is first deemed to receive a distribution of its allocable share of the partnership's § 751 property. This deemed distribution is generally subject to nonrecognition treatment under the general distribution rules. The partner is then deemed to transfer that § 751 property back to the partnership in exchange for the excess portion of the other property it actually received in the distribution. This deemed exchange is treated as a taxable sale or exchange. As a result, the partnership must recognize capital gain or loss on the excess portion of other property it transfers to the partner and the partner must recognize ordinary income on the § 751 property it transfers to the partnership [Reg. § 1.751-1(b)(3)].

## XIV.G. Partnership Payments to Retiring and Deceased Partners

[716 T.M.; TPS ¶4080.]

Special rules apply to payments made by a partnership to a retiring partner or a deceased partner's successor-in-interest in termination of the partner's entire interest in the partnership.

In determining the application of these special rules, a partner is treated as a retiring partner if he ceases to be a partner in the partnership under local law. For federal income tax purposes, a retiring partner and a deceased partner's successor-in-interest are treated as partners until their interests in the partnership have been completely liquidated [Reg. § 1.736-1(a)(1)(ii)].

To determine the tax consequences of partnership payments to a retiring partner or the successor-in-interest of a deceased partner, the payments must first be classified into various categories. First, the amount of the payments made in consideration for the partner's interest in the partnership property (so-called § 736(b) payments) must be determined. After that, the amount of the other payments (so-called § 736(a) payments) can be determined. The § 736(a) payments must be further categorized as either payments of the partner's distributive share of partnership income or guaranteed payments [§ 736; Reg. § 1.736-1(a)(2), § 1.736-1(a)(3)].

### XIV.G.1. Payments to Retiring or Deceased Partner in Respect of Partnership Property (§ 736(b) Payments)

[716 T.M., V.A.; TPS ¶4080.02.A.]

Payments to a retiring partner or the successor-in-interest of a deceased partner that are made in consideration for the partner's interest in the partnership property are treated as distributions (see XIV.F. for a detailed discussion of the tax treatment of distributions) [§ 736(b)(1); Reg. § 1.736-1(b)(1)]. Thus, the following tax consequences generally apply to the recipient of such payments:

- gain is recognized only to the extent that the amount of any cash and marketable securities distributed is more than the partner's adjusted basis in its partnership interest; and
- loss is recognized only if the distribution consists solely of money, unrealized receivables, and inventory items.

However, the following special rules apply to payments made in consideration for the partner's interest in the partnership's unrealized receivables and goodwill [§ 736(b)(2), § 736(b)(3); Reg. § 1.736-1(b)(2), § 1.736-1(b)(3)]:

- Payments made for a partner's share of the partnership's unrealized receivables are not treated as made in exchange for partnership property if the partner was a general partner and capital is not a material income-producing factor for the partnership. Such payments are instead treated as § 736(a) payments.
- Payments made for a partner's share of the partnership's goodwill are not treated as made in exchange for partnership property if the partner was a general partner, capital is not a material income-producing factor for the partnership, and the partnership agreement does not provide for goodwill payments to such partners. Such payments are instead treated as § 736(a) payments.

For purposes of these rules, the partners' valuation of a partner's interest in partnership property under an arm's-length agreement generally will be treated as correct. However, if the valuation reflects only the partner's net interest in the property (total assets less liabilities), then it must be adjusted so that the value of, and basis for, the partner's interest in partnership property includes the partner's share of partnership liabilities [Reg. § 1.736-1(b)(1)].

### XIV.G.2. Other Payments (§ 736(a) Payments)

[716 T.M., V.B.; TPS ¶4080.02.B.]

Payments to a retired partner or the successor-in-interest of a deceased partner that are not made in exchange for the partner's interest in partnership property are treated as either distributive shares of partnership income or guaranteed payments [§ 736(a)]. This rule also applies to any payments made for the partner's share of unrealized receivables and goodwill that are not treated as made in exchange for partnership property (see XIV.G.1.).

To the extent that such payments are determined with regard to the partnership's income, they are treated as a distributive share of partnership income and they retain the same character they had in the hands of the partnership. These types of payments are included in income in the recipient's tax year that includes the end of the partnership tax year for which the payments are a distributive share [§ 736(a)(1); Reg. § 1.736-1(a)].

To the extent such payments are determined without regard to the partnership's income, they are treated as guaranteed payments and reported as ordinary income. These types of payments are included in income in the recipient's tax year that includes the end of the partnership tax year in which the partnership is entitled to deduct them as guaranteed payments [§ 736(a)(2); Reg. § 1.736-1(a)].

## XIV.H. Partner Disposition of Partnership Interest

### XIV.H.1. Tax Consequences to Selling Partner on Sale of Partnership Interest

#### XIV.H.1.a. Recognition of Gain or Loss on Sale of Partnership Interest

[718 T.M., II.A.2.c.; TPS ¶4070.01.A.1.]

Generally, a partner who sells its interest in a partnership recognizes a gain or loss equal to the amount realized on the sale minus the partner's adjusted basis in the partnership interest [§ 741(a), § 1001(a)]. The amount realized on the sale is generally equal to the sum of any money received plus the fair market value of any property received by the partner for his partnership interest [§ 1001(b)]. The amount realized also includes the partner's share of any partnership liabilities to the extent the partner is relieved of those liabilities [§ 752(d); Reg. § 1.752-1(h)]. For a discussion of the determination of a partner's adjusted basis in the partnership interest, see XIV.E.

The like-kind exchange nonrecognition provisions do not apply to exchanges of partnership interests [§ 1031(a)(2)(D)]. Therefore, a partner who exchanges a partnership interest for another partnership interest generally must recognize gain or loss on the exchange.

#### XIV.H.1.b. Character of Gain or Loss on Sale of Partnership Interest

[718 T.M., II.A.2.c.; TPS ¶4070.01.A.2., .01.A.3.]

A partnership interest is considered to be a capital asset. Therefore, a partner's gain or loss on the sale or exchange of a partnership interest is generally treated as capital gain or loss. However, any portion of the gain or loss on the sale or exchange of a partnership interest that is attributable to the partner's share of the partnership's unrealized receivables or inventory items is treated as ordinary income or loss because it is considered to be gain or loss from the sale or exchange of property that is not a capital asset [§ 741(a), § 51(a)].

Unrealized receivables generally include rights to payment for services rendered and rights to payment for goods delivered to the extent the payment would be treated as received for property other than a capital asset. Such rights to payment are treated as unrealized receivables for this purpose only if they were received under a contact or agreement that existed at the time of the sale of the partnership interest and they have not already been included in income. Unrealized receivables also include potential gain that would be ordinary income if certain types of partnership property were sold at their market value on the date of the payment [§ 751(c)].

Inventory items generally include (i) stock in trade or other property that would properly be included in the partnership's inventory if on hand at the end of the tax year, (ii) property that is held primarily for sale to customers in the normal course of business, (iii) property that, if sold or exchanged by the partnership, would not be a capital asset or § 1231 property (real or depreciable business property held more than one year), and (iv) property held by the partnership that would be considered inventory if held by the partner selling the partnership interest [§ 751(d)].

The gain or loss attributable to the partner's share of the partnership's unrealized receivables and inventory items is the amount that would have been allocated to the partner if the partnership had sold all of its property for cash at fair market value immediately before the partner's sale or exchange of the partnership interest. This portion of the gain or loss is treated as ordinary income or loss. The remainder of the gain or loss is treated as capital gain or loss [Reg. § 1.741-1(a), § 1.751-1(a)(2)].

---

**EXAMPLE:** Sue is a partner in ABC partnership. At the end of the year, her adjusted basis in her partnership interest is zero. Her share of the partnership's unrealized receivables and inventory items is $4,000. Sue sells her partnership interest for $10,000 cash and reports a $10,000 gain on the sale ($10,000 amount realized − $0 adjusted basis). She must treat $4,000 of the gain as ordinary income and the $6,000 balance as capital gain.

---

A loss incurred from the abandonment or worthlessness of a partnership interest is generally treated as an ordinary loss if the transaction is not a sale or exchange and the partner does not receive an actual or deemed distribution from the partnership [Rev. Rul. 93-80, 1993-2 C.B. 239]. Otherwise, the entire loss is treated as a capital loss.

### XIV.H.1.c. Reporting Requirements for Sale of Partnership Interest
[720 T.M., II.F.1.; TPS ¶4070.01.A.4.]

A partner who sells or exchanges any part of its interest in a partnership that has unrealized receivables or inventory items must file with its income tax return for the year of the sale or exchange a statement containing the following information: (i) the date of the sale or exchange, (ii) the amount of any gain or loss attributable to the unrealized receivables and inventory items, and (iii) the amount of any gain or loss attributable to capital gain or loss on the sale of the partnership interest [Reg. § 1.751-1(a)(3)].

The partner must also provide the partnership with written notification of the sale or exchange within 30 days of the transaction (or by January 15 of the following calendar year, if sooner). When a partnership is notified of such a sale or exchange of a partnership interest, it must file Form 8308, *Report of a Sale or Exchange of*

*Certain Partnership Interests*, with its return for its tax year that includes the last day of the calendar year in which the sale or exchange took place.

A partner who sells or exchanges a partnership interest at a gain generally may report the sale on the installment method under § 453 (see III.G.). However, any portion of the gain allocable to unrealized receivables or inventory items may not be reported on the installment sale. That amount must be treated as ordinary income in the year of the sale or exchange.

### XIV.H.1.d. Application of Net Investment Income Tax to Sale of Partnership Interest

[718 T.M., II.A.6.; TPS ¶4070.01.A.5.]

The sale or exchange of a partnership interest may trigger the net investment income tax. The net investment income tax is generally equal to 3.8% of a partner's net investment income [§ 1411(a)(1)]. For a discussion of the net investment income tax, see X.A.4.

The net investment income generally includes net gain attributable to partnership interests that are (i) not held in a trade or business, (ii) held in a trade or business that is a passive activity, or (iii) held in a trade or business of trading financial interests or commodities. However, the amount of such net gain that is treated as net investment income is limited to the amount of the net gain that would be taken into account by the partner selling or exchanging the partnership interest if all of the partnership's property were sold for its fair market value immediately before the sale or exchange of the partnership interest [§ 1411(c)(4)].

### XIV.H.2. Tax Consequences to Purchasing Partner on Sale of Partnership Interest

[718 T.M., II.A.; TPS ¶4070.02.]

A taxpayer who purchases an interest in a partnership generally takes a basis in the partnership interest equal to its cost [§ 742, § 1012; Reg. § 1.742-1]. The purchasing partner steps into the shoes of the selling partner and acquires all its rights in the partnership, including its undivided interest in the partnership assets. However, the basis of the partnership assets generally is not adjusted upon a sale or exchange of a partnership interest. This could potentially result in a situation in which the purchasing partner will be taxed on gain attributable to appreciation in the value of the partnership assets that occurred before he purchased the partnership interest (even though this prior appreciation is normally reflected in his purchase price for the partnership interest). The partnership may elect to make an optional basis adjustment to the partnership assets in order to prevent such a result (see XIV.H.3.).

### XIV.H.3. Tax Consequences to Partnership on Sale of Partnership Interest

[718 T.M., II.A.2.; TPS ¶4070.02.]

The partnership's adjusted basis in its assets is not adjusted as a result of the sale or exchange of a partnership interest unless the partnership elects to make an optional basis adjustment under § 754 (based on § 743) or unless the partnership is required to make a basis adjustment because there is a substantial built-in loss immediately after the sale or exchange (i.e. a mandatory basis adjustment) [§ 743(a)].

The optional and mandatory basis adjustment rules are designed to resolve the discrepancy that may arise between the partnership's adjusted basis in its assets (the inside basis) and the partners' adjusted bases in their partnership interests (the outside basis). Generally, the price a purchasing partner pays for a partnership interest will reflect increases or decreases in the value of the partnership's assets that are not reflected in the partnership's adjusted bases in those assets. Thus, a purchasing partner may potentially have to report a gain attributable to appreciation in the partnership assets that occurred before its purchase of the partnership interest. However, a partnership may elect to make an optional basis adjustment to the partnership assets to provide the purchasing partner with a share of the partnership's basis in the partnership assets (inside basis) that is equal to the purchasing partner's basis in its partnership interest (outside basis). The optional basis adjustment essentially eliminates the purchasing partner's distributive share of partnership income or loss attributable to the appreciation or depreciation that occurred in the partnership assets before the partner purchased the partnership interest. The mandatory basis adjustment is required when there is a substantial built-in loss in the partnership assets in order to prevent the purchasing partner from claiming losses for depreciation that occurred in the partnership assets before the partner purchased the partnership interest.

For purposes of the mandatory basis adjustment, there is a substantial built-in loss in the partnership assets if the partnership's adjusted basis in the partnership property exceeds the fair market value of those assets by more than $250,000 [§ 743(d)(1)]. However, an electing investment partnership (a partnership that meets the requirements of § 743(e)(6) and elects to be treated as an investment partnership) and a securitization partnership (a partnership the sole business of which is to issue securities that provide for a fixed principal amount and which are primarily serviced by cash flows of a discrete pool of receivables or other assets that by their terms convert into cash on a finite period) are not treated as having substantial built-in losses [§ 743(e), § 743(f)].

When there is a sale or exchange of a partnership interest, and there is an optional basis adjustment in effect or there is a substantial built-in loss requiring a mandatory basis adjustment, one of the following adjustments must be made to the partnership's adjusted basis in its partnership assets [§ 743(b); Reg. § 1.743-1(b)]:

- If the purchasing partner's basis in its partnership interest is more than the purchasing partner's share of the partnership's adjusted basis in the partnership assets, the partnership's adjusted basis in the partnership assets is increased by the amount of the difference.
- If the purchasing partner's share of the partnership's adjusted basis in the partnership assets is more than purchasing partner's basis in its partnership interest, the partnership's adjusted basis in the partnership assets is decreased by the amount of the difference.

For purposes of these adjustments, the purchasing partner's share of the partnership's adjusted basis in the partnership assets is equal to the sum of the purchasing partner's share of the partnership's previously taxed capital, plus the purchasing partner's share of the partnership liabilities. The purchasing partner's share of the partnership's previously taxed capital is equal to (i) the amount of cash the purchasing partner would receive upon a liquidation of the partnership immediately after its purchase of the partnership interest, plus (ii) the amount of tax loss that would be allocated to the purchasing partner from this hypothetical transaction, minus (iii) the amount of tax gain that would be allocated to the purchasing partner from this hypothetical transaction [Reg. § 1.743-1(d)].

These special basis adjustments are allocated among the partnership's assets in accordance with the rules of § 755. Under those rules, the special basis adjustments are generally allocated to partnership property of a like character [§ 743(c), § 755(a) and § 755(b)].

If a partnership makes a nonliquidating distribution of property subject to a special basis adjustment to the partner to whom the adjustment applies (i.e., the purchasing partner), the special basis adjustment is taken into account in determining the partnership's adjusted basis in the property for purposes of computing that partner's basis in the property; however, if the partnership makes such a nonliquidating distribution of such property to another partner, the special basis adjustment is not taken into account. If the partnership makes a liquidating distribution of property to the purchasing partner in complete liquidation of its partnership interest, the partnership's adjusted basis in the distributed property immediately before the distribution includes any special basis adjustment related to partnership property in which the purchasing partner relinquishes an interest as a result of the liquidation of its partnership interest [Reg. § 1.743-1(g)].

If a partner to whom a special basis adjustment applies transfers its partnership interest, the new purchasing partner's special basis adjustment, if any, is determined without reference to the prior purchasing partner's special basis adjustment [Reg. § 1.743-1(f)].

A partnership that adjusts the basis of its undistributed assets under these rules must attach a statement to the partnership return for the year of the distribution providing information on the name and taxpayer identification number of the purchasing partner, the computation of the adjustment, and the assets to which the adjustment is allocated [Reg. § 1.743-1(k)].

## XIV.I. Termination of Partnership

[718 T.M.; TPS ¶4060.]

A partnership continues to exist for tax purposes unless a terminating event occurs [§ 708(a)]. There are five types of events that may cause the termination of a partnership:

1. The operations of the partnership are discontinued.

2. The operations of the partnership are no longer carried on in partnership form.

3. A sale or exchange of 50% or more of the total interest in the capital and profits of the partnership occurs during any 12-month period.

4. A merger or consolidation of the partnership with another partnership occurs.

5. A division of the partnership occurs.

Upon the termination of a partnership, the partnership's tax year closes. The tax consequences of the termination depend on the type of termination involved.

### XIV.I.1. Discontinuation of Operations

[718 T.M., II.B.2.; TPS ¶4060.01.B., .02.]

A partnership terminates when the operations of the partnership are discontinued and no part of any business, financial operation, or venture of the partnership continues to be carried on by any of its partners. There must be a complete cessation of partnership activity to cause such a termination. Thus, if partners agree to dissolve a partnership but continue to carry on business through a winding up period, the partnership is not terminated until the winding up period is complete [§ 708(b)(1)(A); Reg. § 1.708-1(b)(1)].

When a termination occurs under this rule, the partnership's tax year closes on the date the winding up of the partnership's affairs is completed. All partnership assets are treated as distributed to the partners on the date of termination and the rules on liquidating distributions apply (see XIV.F.) [Reg. § 1.708-1(b)(3)].

### XIV.I.2. Operations No Longer Carried on in Partnership Form

[718 T.M., II.B.2.; TPS ¶4060.01.C., .02.]

A partnership terminates if it is converted into a sole proprietorship or a corporation, but not if it is converted into a limited liability company (LLC).

*Conversion into Sole Proprietorship.* A partnership generally terminates if only one person remains as the owner of a business that was previously owned by two or more persons in the form of a partnership. However, there are two exceptions under which a partnership does not terminate in this situation:

1. If only one partner remains due to the death of one or more partners, the partnership does not terminate if the successors-in-interest of the deceased partners continue to share in the profits and losses of the partnership [Reg. § 1.708-1(b)(1)(i)].

2. If only one partner remains due to the retirement or death of one or more partners, and a series of payments is to be made in liquidation of the partnership interests of those partners, the partnership does not terminate until the final payment is made [Reg. § 1.708-1(b)(1)(ii)].

When a termination occurs for this reason, the partnership's tax year closes on the first date that only one partner remains. On that date, the partnership becomes a disregarded entity (i.e., a sole proprietorship) unless it elects to be classified as a corporation.

*Conversion into Corporation.* A partnership terminates if the partners convert the partnership into a corporation under a local law conversion statute, or by electing status as an association taxable as a corporation under the check-the-box regulations. [§ 301.7701-3(a), § 301.7701-3(c)]. In addition, a partnership can be converted into a corporation by making actual transfers in one of the following ways:

- The partners contribute their partnership interests to a corporation in exchange for stock in the corporation and the partnership is then liquidated.

- The partnership liquidates and distributes its assets to the partners and the partners then contribute the partnership assets to a corporation in exchange for stock.

- The partnership contributes all of its assets to a corporation in exchange for stock and the partnership then distributes the stock to the partners in liquidation of the partnership.

When a termination occurs for this reason, the closing of the partnership's tax year depends on which incorporation method was used.

*Conversion into LLC.* A partnership does not terminate if converted into an LLC [Rev. Rul. 95-37, 1995-1 C.B. 130]. In such case, the partnership's tax year does not close and the LLC can continue to use the partnership's taxpayer identification number. Although such a conversion does not result in a sale, exchange, or liquidation of any partnership interest, it may result in a change to partners' bases in their partnership interests if the partnership has recourse liabilities that become nonrecourse liabilities.

### XIV.I.3. Sale or Exchange of 50% Interest in Capital and Profits

[718 T.M., II.B.2.; TPS ¶4060.01.D., .02.]

A partnership terminates if there is a sale or exchange of 50% or more of the total interest in partnership profits and capital within a 12-month period (known as a technical termination). A partnership does not terminate unless there is both a sale or exchange of a 50% or more interest in the partnership profits and a sale or exchange of a 50% or more interest in the partnership capital during that period. In determining whether there has been a sale or exchange of a 50% or more interest within a 12-month period, the sales or exchanges made by all partners during that period are aggregated. However, more than one sale or exchange of the same partnership interest during a 12-month period is counted only once. For purposes of the rule, a sale or exchange includes a sale or exchange to a third party and a sale or exchange to another partner. However, a sale or exchange does not include a disposition of a partnership interest by gift, bequest, or inheritance. It also does not include the liquidation of a partnership interest or a contribution of capital by a partner to the partnership [§ 708(b)(1)(B); Reg. § 1.708-1(b)(2)].

When a termination occurs for this reason, the partnership's tax year closes on the date of the sale or exchange causing the termination [Reg. § 1.708-1(b)(3)]. For tax purposes, the partnership is deemed to contribute all of its assets and liabilities to a new partnership in exchange for an interest in the new partnership and, immediately thereafter, the partnership is deemed to liquidate by distributing interests in the new partnership to the purchaser and other remaining partners, followed by either a continuation of the business by the new partnership or its dissolution and winding up [Reg. § 1.708-1(b)(4)].

### XIV.I.4. Merger or Consolidation of Partnerships

[718 T.M., III.B.1.; TPS ¶4060.01.E., .02.]

Under certain circumstances, two or more partnerships may merge into one of the existing partnerships or two or more partnerships may consolidate into a new partnership. In these situations, a partnership whose partners own more than 50% of the capital and profits of the resulting partnership is considered to be a continuing partnership. If more than one partnership could be considered a continuing partnership under this rule, then the partnership credited with contributing the greatest value of assets will be the only partnership considered a continuing partnership. Any merging or consolidating partnership that is not considered a continuing partnership is terminated for federal income tax purposes. If none of the merging or consolidating partnerships is considered a continuing partnership, then all the partnerships are terminated and a new partnership results [§ 708(b)(2)(A); Reg. § 1.708-1(c)].

The resulting merged or consolidated partnership uses the tax year of the partnership that is considered the continuing partnership. On its return, the resulting partnership should state that it is a continuation of the continuing partnership, should use the employer identification number (EIN) of the continuing partnership, and should provide the names and EINs of the other merging or consolidating partnerships. The tax year of any merging or consolidating partnership that is terminated is treated as closing on the date of the merger or consolidation [Reg. § 1.708-1(c)(2)].

### XIV.I.5. Division of Partnership

[718 T.M., III.B.3.; TPS ¶4060.01.F., .02.]

In certain circumstances, an existing partnership can divide into two or more partnerships. A partnership resulting from the division is considered to be a continuation of the prior partnership if its partners had an interest of 50% or more in the capital and profits of the prior partnership. Any other resulting partnership is not a continuation of the prior partnership but is instead considered a new partnership. If the partners of none of the resulting partnerships had a 50% or more capital and profits interest in the prior partnership, then the prior partnership is treated as terminated for federal income tax purposes [§ 708(b)(2)(B); Reg. § 1.708-1(d)].

The partnership that is treated as a continuation of the prior partnership uses the tax year and employer identification number (EIN) of the prior partnership. On its return, it should state that it is a continuation of the prior partnership, should set forth the respective distributive shares of the partners for the periods before and after the date of the division, and should provide the names and EINs of all new partnerships resulting from the division. All new partnerships resulting from the division file separate returns for the tax year beginning on the day after the date of division. They should provide the name and EIN of the prior partnership on those returns. If the prior partnership is treated as terminated, its tax year closes on the date of division [Reg. § 1.708-1(d)(2)].

# CHAPTER XV. S CORPORATIONS
>>>>>>>>>>>>>>>>>>>>>>>>>>>>>>>

## XV.A. Election of S Corporation Status

### XV.A.1. Introduction to S Corporations

Subchapter S of the Internal Revenue Code permits certain corporations with relatively few shareholders to elect to be taxed as pass-through entities similar to partnerships. Corporations that make this election are known as S corporations. A key advantage to electing S corporation status is the avoidance of the double tax that is imposed on C corporations. The earnings of a C corporation are first taxed at the corporate level and then, when the earnings are distributed to the shareholders as dividends, they are taxed again at shareholder level. In contrast, the earnings of an S corporation are not taxed at the corporate level. Instead, an S corporation passes through its items of income, gain, loss, deduction, and credit to its shareholders and the shareholders report those items on their personal income tax returns. The shareholders are taxed on the S corporation's earnings at their individual income tax rates. Because S corporation earnings are subject to only one layer of tax, distributions to shareholders generally are tax-free.

#### XV.A.1.a. Advantages of S Corporation Status

[731 T.M., I.A.; TPS ¶4210.02.]

In addition to avoidance of the double tax imposed on C corporation earnings, there are other advantages in electing to be treated as an S corporation instead of a C corporation. S corporations are exempt from the alternative minimum tax (AMT), the accumulated earnings tax, and the personal holding company tax [§ 1363(a)]. S corporations can use the cash method of accounting [§ 448(a)]. In addition, S corporation shareholders can deduct their share of a net operating loss of an S corporation in the year the loss occurs, subject to certain limitations [§ 1366(a)].

#### XV.A.1.b. Disadvantages of S Corporation Status

[731 T.M., II.A., V.A.; TPS ¶4210.02.]

There are also certain disadvantages in electing to be treated as an S corporation instead of a C corporation. Compared to a C corporation, an S corporation is inflexible due to its eligibility requirements (e.g., the requirements limiting the number of shareholders and capital structure) [§ 1361(b)(1)]. Shareholders of an S corporation do not qualify for the favorable passive activity loss treatment available to the shareholders of a closely held C corporation [§ 469(e)(2)]. Two-percent shareholders of an S corporation generally do not qualify for the exclusion of fringe benefits paid to them in their capacity as employees of the S corporation [§ 1372]. In addition, the

§ 1202 exclusion of gain on the sale of qualified small business stock does not apply to the sale of S corporation stock [§ 1202(c)].

For further discussion of the advantages and disadvantages of electing S corporation status, see Chapter XVI.

### XV.A.2. Eligibility to Elect S Corporation Status

[730 T.M., II.; TPS ¶4230.]

A corporation is eligible to elect S corporation status only if it meets all of the following requirements [§ 1361(b), § 1378]:

1. it has no more than 100 shareholders;

2. all of its shareholders are individuals, estates, certain trusts, or certain exempt organizations;

3. none of its shareholders is a nonresident alien;

4. it is a U.S. corporation;

5. it is not an ineligible corporation;

6. it has only one class of stock; and

7. it uses a permissible tax year (see XV.C.4.d.).

### XV.A.2.a. Shareholder Limitation on S Corporation Election

[730 T.M., II.D.; TPS ¶4230.01.C.]

A corporation may not elect S corporation status if it has more than 100 shareholders [§ 1361(b)(1)(A)]. For purposes of the 100-shareholder limitation, members of the same family are treated as a single shareholder. Members of the same family are defined as a common ancestor, any lineal descendant of the common ancestor, and any spouse or former spouse of the common ancestor or a lineal descendant. An individual cannot be treated as a common ancestor if he or she is more than six generations removed from the youngest generation of lineal descendants that are shareholders. In determining lineal descendants, adopted children and foster children are treated as children by blood. Spouses are treated as members of the same family. The estate of a deceased individual is treated as a member of the same family of which the deceased individual was a member [§ 1361(c)(1)].

### XV.A.2.b. Eligible and Ineligible Shareholders for S Corporation Election

[730 T.M., II.E.; TPS ¶4230.01.D.]

An S corporation election may be made by a corporation only if all of its shareholders are eligible shareholders. Shareholders must all be individuals, estates, certain trusts, or certain exempt organizations [§ 1361(b)(1)(B)]. Thus, corporations and partnerships are not eligible shareholders. Individual shareholders must all be U.S. citizens or residents. Thus, nonresident aliens are not eligible shareholders [§ 1361(b)(1)(C)].

*Eligible Trusts.* Trusts permitted to be S corporation shareholders include [§ 1361(c)(2), § 1361(d); Reg. § 1.1361-1(h)]:

- a grantor trust (a trust treated as owned by a U.S. citizen or resident under § 671–§ 679);

- a trust that was a grantor trust immediately before the death of the deemed owner;

- a testamentary trust (a trust to which stock has been transferred by a will);

- a voting trust (a trust created primarily to exercise the voting power of the stock transferred to it);

- an electing small business trust (ESBT); and
- a qualified subchapter S trust (QSST).

A trust that was a grantor trust immediately before the death of a deemed owner is permitted to be an S corporation shareholder only for the two-year period beginning on the date of the deemed owner's death [§ 1361(c)(2)(A)(ii)]. A testamentary trust is permitted to be an S corporation shareholder only for the two-year period beginning on the date the stock is transferred to it [§ 1361(c)(2)(A)(iii)].

An electing small business trust (ESBT) can be an S corporation shareholder [§ 1361(c)(2)(A)(v)]. A trust generally can elect to be treated as an electing small business trust (ESBT) if it has no beneficiaries other than individuals, estates, or certain charitable organizations, and no interest in the trust was acquired by purchase. However, an ESBT election cannot be made by a qualified subchapter S trust (QSST), tax-exempt trust, charitable remainder annuity trust, or charitable remainder unitrust [§ 1361(e)]. Special rules apply to the taxation of an ESBT. The portion of the ESBT that consists of S corporation stock is treated as a separate trust and its tax liability is determined with the following modifications: (i) the highest tax rate for estates and trusts applies, (ii) the AMT exemption is zero, and (iii) the only items taken into account are pass-through items from S corporations, gain or loss from the disposition of S corporation stock, interest expense on debt incurred to acquire S corporation stock, and state or local income taxes or administrative expenses allocable to the first two items [§ 641(c)].

A qualified subchapter S trust (QSST) can be an S corporation shareholder if the income beneficiary of the trust so elects [§ 1361(d)(1)]. A trust qualifies as a QSST only if all of the income of the trust is distributed, or required to be distributed, currently to one individual who is a U.S. citizen or resident and the terms of the trust require that: (i) during the current income beneficiary's life, there can only be one income beneficiary, (ii) any corpus distributed during the current income beneficiary's life may only be distributed to that income beneficiary, (iii) the current income beneficiary's income interest in the trust will terminate on the earlier of the income beneficiary's death or the termination of the trust, and (iv) upon termination of the trust during the life of the current income beneficiary, the trust will distribute all its assets to that income beneficiary [§ 1361(d)(3)]. If an income beneficiary makes the election to have a QSST treated as an S corporation shareholder, the portion of the trust that consists of S corporation stock is treated like a grantor trust and the income beneficiary is treated as the deemed owner. Thus, all of the S corporation's income or loss allocated to the stock held by the deemed grantor trust is reportable for income tax purposes by the income beneficiary [§ 1361(d)(1)(B)].

A foreign trust is not permitted to be an S corporation shareholder [§ 1361(c)(2)(A); Reg. § 1.1361-1(h)(2)].

***Eligible Exempt Organizations.*** Exempt organizations permitted to be S corporation shareholders include [§ 1361(c)(6)]:
- a stock bonus, pension, or profit-sharing plan that qualifies under § 401(a) (including an employee stock ownership plan (ESOP));
- an organization exempt from tax under § 501(a); and
- a § 501(c)(3) charitable organization.

### *XV.A.2.c. Eligible and Ineligible Corporations for S Corporation Election*

[730 T.M., II.B., II.C.; TPS ¶4230.01.A., .01.B.]

An S corporation election generally may be made by a U.S. corporation; however, certain types of U.S. corporations are ineligible to make an S corporation election. An S corporation election may not be made by a foreign corporation.

A subsidiary of an S corporation may not make an S corporation election. However, a wholly owned domestic subsidiary of an S corporation may make a QSub election to be treated as part of its parent S corporation for federal income tax purposes.

***Ineligible Corporations.*** The following types of U.S. corporations are ineligible corporations and may not make an S corporation election [§ 1361(b)(2)]:

- financial institutions that use the reserve method of accounting for bad debts;
- insurance companies subject to taxation under Subchapter L of the Code;
- corporations that have elected to claim the Puerto Rico and possessions tax credit under § 936; and
- DISCs or former DISCs.

***Qualified Subchapter S Subsidiaries (QSubs).*** A subsidiary of an S corporation may not make an S corporation election because it has a corporation as a shareholder. However, a subsidiary of an S corporation that meets certain requirements can be treated as a qualified subchapter S subsidiary (QSub) if the parent S corporation makes an election to do so on Form 8869, *Qualified Subchapter S Subsidiary Election*. A Qsub is not considered to be a separate corporation for federal tax purposes and all its tax items are treated as tax items of the parent S corporation [§ 1361(b)(3)(A); Reg. § 1.1361-4(a)].

A subsidiary of an S corporation is eligible to be treated as a QSub if it meets all of the following requirements [§ 1361(b)(3)(B); Reg. § 1.1361-2(a)]:

1. it is a U.S. corporation;
2. it is not an ineligible corporation; and
3. it is 100% owned by the parent S corporation.

### *XV.A.2.d. Single Class of Stock Requirement for S Corporation Election*

[730 T.M., II.F.; TPS ¶4230.01.E.]

A corporation may not make an S corporation election if it has more than one class of stock [§ 1361(b)(1)(D)]. For purposes of this requirement, a corporation is treated as having only one class of stock if all its outstanding shares of stock confer identical rights to distribution and liquidation proceeds [Reg. § 1.1361-1(l)(1)]. The determination of whether all outstanding shares of stock of the corporation confer identical rights is made based on the corporate charter, articles of incorporation, bylaws, applicable state law, and binding agreements relating to distribution and liquidation proceeds. In making this determination, the following are generally disregarded and do not create a second class of stock [Reg. § 1.1361-1(l)(2)]:

- state laws that require a corporation to pay or withhold income taxes on behalf of shareholders (resulting in constructive distributions to those shareholders);
- buy-sell agreements among shareholders;
- agreements restricting the transferability of stock;
- redemption agreements; and
- governing provisions that provide that, as a result of a change in stock ownership, distributions are to be made on the basis of the shareholders' varying

interests in the corporation's income in the current or immediately preceding tax year.

In determining whether a corporation has more than one class of stock, differences in voting rights among shares of stock are disregarded. Thus, for example, common stock with both voting and nonvoting rights may be considered one class of stock [§ 1361(c)(4); Reg. § 1.1361-1(l)(1)].

Stock that is issued in connection with the performance of services and that is substantially nonvested (i.e., restricted stock) is not treated as a second class of stock [Reg. § 1.1361-1(b)(4)]. A deferred compensation plan that has a current payment feature (e.g., payment of dividend equivalent amounts that are taxed currently as compensation) is not treated as a second class of stock [Reg. § 1.1361-1(b)(4)].

Instruments, obligations, and arrangements other than stock may be treated as a second class of stock in certain circumstances. An instrument, obligation, or arrangement issued by a corporation is generally treated as a second class of stock if it constitutes equity (or otherwise results in the holder being treated as an owner of stock) and the principal purpose it is issued is to circumvent the rights to distribution or liquidation proceeds conferred by the corporation's stock [Reg. § 1.1361-1(l)(4)(ii)]. A call option, warrant, or similar instrument issued by a corporation is generally treated as a second class of stock if it is substantially certain to be exercised and it has a strike price substantially below the fair market value of the underlying stock on the date it is issued [Reg. § 1.1361-1(l)(4)(iii)].

There are, however, a number of safe harbors under which instruments, obligations, or arrangements other than stock are not treated as a second class of stock. The safe harbors apply to the following:

- straight debt;
- certain short-term unwritten advances;
- certain proportionately held obligations; and
- certain options (for example, call options with a strike price that is at least 90% of the fair market value of the underlying stock).

The straight debt safe harbor applies to debt if: (i) it is a written unconditional promise to pay a specified amount of money on demand or on a specified date, (ii) it does not provide for an interest rate or payment dates that are contingent on profits, the borrower's discretion, or similar factors, (iii) it is not convertible into stock or any other equity interest, and (iv) the creditor is an individual (other than a nonresident alien), an estate, a trust that would be an eligible shareholder, or a person actively and regularly engaged in the business of lending money [§ 1361(c)(5); Reg. § 1.1361-1(l)(5)].

### XV.A.3. Making the S Corporation Election

[730 T.M., III.; TPS ¶4240.]

An S corporation election is made by filing Form 2553, *Election by a Small Business Corporation* [Reg. § 1.1362-6(a)(2)]. An S corporation election is valid only if all persons who are shareholders on the date of the election consent to the election [§ 1362(a)(2)]. The IRS will generally notify a corporation whether or not its S corporation election is accepted within 60 days of the date Form 2553 is filed.

An entity that elects to be treated as an association taxable as a corporation (e.g., an LLC) and that also elects to be an S corporation on Form 2553 is not required to file Form 8832, *Entity Classification Election*. It will be treated as an S corporation as of the effective date of the S corporation election made on Form 2553.

An S corporation election is effective for the tax year for which it is made and all succeeding tax years until it is terminated [§ 1362(c)]. For a discussion of the termination of an S corporation election, see XV.A.4.a.

### XV.A.3.a. Shareholder Consent for S Corporation Election

[730 T.M., III.D.; TPS ¶4240.02.B.]

A shareholder consents to an S corporation election by signing and dating the consent statement section of Form 2553 or a separate statement that provides the same information. A shareholder's consent is binding and may not be withdrawn after a valid election is made by the corporation [Reg. § 1.1362-6(b)(3)].

Generally, consent must be provided by all persons who are shareholders on the date of the election. When the election is made during the first two months and 15 days of the year during which the election is to take effect, consent must also be provided by all persons who were shareholders during a portion of the year before the election date but who are not shareholders on the election date (see XV.A.3.b.) [§ 1362(b)(2)].

### XV.A.3.b. S Corporation Election Due Date

[730 T.M., III.B.; TPS ¶4240.01.]

An S corporation election generally may be made at any time during the tax year preceding the tax year the election is to take effect or during the first two months and 15 days of the tax year the election is to take effect [§ 1362(b)(1)]. However, an S corporation election made during the first two months and 15 days of the tax year will be treated as not taking effect until the following tax year if [§ 1362(b)(2); Reg. § 1.1362-6(a)(2)(ii)(B)]:

1. the corporation does not meet all of the S corporation eligibility requirements on one or more days during the portion of the year before the election date; or

2. consent is not provided by all persons who were shareholders during the portion of the year before the election date.

An S corporation election made after the first two months and 15 days of the tax year is generally treated as taking effect for the following tax year [§ 1362(b)(3)]. However, if the corporation can show that the failure to make the S corporation election on time was due to a reasonable cause, the IRS has authority to treat the election as taking effect for the current tax year [§ 1362(b)(5)]. The following requirements must be satisfied for a grant of relief for a late S corporation election [Rev. Proc. 2013-30, 2013-36 I.R.B. 173]:

1. the corporation intended to be classified as an S corporation on the date the election was intended to be effective;

2. the corporation requests relief within three years and 75 days after the date the election was intended to be effective;

3. the failure to qualify as an S corporation was solely because Form 2553 was not timely filed by the due date;

4. the corporation has reasonable cause for its failure to make a timely election and has acted diligently to correct the mistake upon its discovery; and

5. the corporation files a completed Form 2553 with any required statements, and Form 2553 is signed by a corporate officer and by all persons who were shareholders at any time during the period that began on the first day of the tax year for which the election is to be effective and ends on the day the completed Form 2553 is filed.

A corporation that does not meet those requirements generally must request a private letter ruling and pay a user fee to request relief for a late election.

## XV.A.4. Termination of S Corporation Elections

### XV.A.4.a. Termination of S Corporation Election

[730 T.M., IV.; TPS ¶4250.01.]

An S corporation election is terminated if: (i) it is revoked by the shareholders, (ii) the corporation ceases to meet the S corporation election eligibility requirements, or (iii) the corporation has excess passive investment income for three consecutive years. If an S corporation election is terminated, the corporation generally may not make a new S corporation election for five years (see XV.A.4.e.).

*Revocation.* An S corporation election is terminated if it is revoked by shareholders who hold more than 50% of the stock in the corporation on the date the revocation is made. An S corporation election may be revoked for any tax year for which the election is effective, including the first tax year. The election is revoked by filing a revocation statement with the same IRS service center with which Form 2553 was filed. Shareholders consent to the revocation by signing written statements of consent that are attached to the revocation statement filed with the IRS [§ 1362(d)(1)(B); Reg. § 1.1362-2(a)(1), § 1.1362-2(b)(1)].

The effective date of the revocation generally depends on the date the revocation is made. If the revocation is made during the first two months and 15 days of the tax year, it is effective as of the beginning of that tax year. If the revocation is made later during the tax year, it is not effective until the following tax year. However, if the shareholders specify an effective date for the revocation that is on or after the date the revocation is made, the revocation is effective on that specified date [§ 1362(d)(1)(C), § 1362(d)(1)(D); Reg. § 1.1362-2(a)(2)].

The revocation of an S corporation election may be rescinded at any time before it becomes effective. The rescission may be made only if consent is obtained from each shareholder who consented to the revocation and each person who became a shareholder between the dates of the revocation and the rescission. The revocation is rescinded by filing a statement with the same IRS service center with which the revocation was filed [Reg. § 1.1362-2(a)(4), § 1.1362-6(a)(4)].

*Ceasing to Meet Eligibility Requirements.* An S corporation election is automatically terminated if the corporation ceases to meet any of the eligibility requirements for making an S corporation election. For example, if the number of shareholders increases to more than 100, an ineligible person becomes a shareholder, or the corporation issues a second class of stock, the election is automatically terminated. The election is treated as terminated on the date the corporation first ceases to meet one of the eligibility requirements [§ 1362(d)(2); Reg. § 1.1362-2(b)]. See XV.A.2. for a detailed discussion of the S corporation election eligibility requirements.

*Excess Passive Investment Income.* An S corporation election is automatically terminated if the corporation has accumulated earnings and profits at the end of three consecutive tax years and, for each of those years, its passive investment income is more than 25% of its gross receipts. If both of these requirements are met for three consecutive years, the termination becomes effective on the first day of the fourth tax year [§ 1362(d)(3)(A); Reg. § 1.1362-2(c)(1), § 1.1362-2(c)(2)].

Accumulated earnings and profits include [Reg. § 1.1362-2(c)(3)]:

- the accumulated earnings and profits of the corporation from any period during which it was a C corporation (i.e., any period before the S corporation election was made); and
- the accumulated earnings and profits of certain acquired or predecessor corporations.

Passive investment income generally includes gross receipts from royalties, rents, dividends, interest, and annuities. However, it does not include dividends from stock held in an 80%-or-more-owned C corporation to the extent the dividends are attributable to the C corporation's earnings and profits derived from the active conduct of a trade or business [§ 1362(d)(3)(C); Reg. § 1.1362-2(c)(5)].

### XV.A.4.b. *Termination of QSub Election*

[730 T.M., II.C.1.b.; TPS ¶4250.01.E.]

A qualified subchapter S subsidiary (QSub) election (see XV.A.2.c.) is terminated if: (i) it is revoked by the parent S corporation, (ii) the S election of the parent S corporation is terminated, or (iii) an event occurs that renders the subsidiary ineligible for QSub status (i.e., it is no longer wholly owned by its S corporation parent) [§ 1361(b)(3)(C); Reg. § 1.1361-5(a)]. If a corporation's QSub election is terminated, the corporation generally may not make a new QSub election or an S corporation election for five years (see XV.A.4.e.).

### XV.A.4.c. *Mid-Year Terminations of S Corporation Elections*

[730 T.M., IV.D.; TPS ¶4250.03.]

If an S corporation election is terminated on a day other than the first day of the corporation's tax year, then the corporation's tax year is split into two shorts years: one short year for the portion of the year during which the corporation was an S corporation (the S short year) and another short year for the portion of the year during which the corporation was a C corporation (the C short year). The S short year ends on the day before the effective date of the termination and the C short year begins on the effective date of the termination. Generally, S corporation items must be allocated between the S short year and the C short year on a daily, pro rata basis. However, if consent is obtained from all persons who were shareholders at any time during the S short year and all persons who were shareholders on the first day of the C short year, a corporation may instead elect to report taxable income or loss for each short year based on the income or loss shown on the corporation's books under normal accounting rules (the so-called "closing-of-the-books" election) [§ 1362(e); Reg. § 1.1362-3].

### XV.A.4.d. *Inadvertent Terminations of S Corporation Elections*

[730 T.M., IV.C.3.; TPS ¶4250.02.]

The IRS has the authority to waive certain inadvertent terminations in order to mitigate the harsh effects of a termination resulting from an accidental cause [§ 1362(f)]. The IRS may waive an inadvertent termination that results from [§ 1362(f)(1)]:

- the corporation ceasing to meet the S corporation eligibility requirements (or, in the case of a QSub, the QSub eligibility requirements);
- the corporation having excess passive investment income for three consecutive years;
- the corporation failing to timely file the S corporation election; or
- the corporation failing to obtain all the necessary shareholder consents.

The IRS may not waive a termination resulting from a revocation of the S corporation election by the shareholders.

The IRS may grant relief for an inadvertent termination if: (i) the terminating event was inadvertent in the eyes of the IRS, (ii) the corporation corrects the event in a timely manner, and (iii) the corporation and its shareholders agree to make such adjustments as required by the IRS. The corporation has the burden of establishing that the termination was inadvertent. To obtain a finding of inadvertence, a corporation must submit a ruling request to the IRS containing a detailed explanation of the event causing termination, when and how the event was discovered, the steps taken to return the corporation to S corporation status, and the date of the corporation's S election [Reg. § 1.1362-4].

If the IRS grants relief for an inadvertent termination, it will waive the termination and treat the corporation as if it never lost S corporation status.

### XV.A.4.e. New Election After S Corporation Election Termination

[730 T.M., III.F.; TPS ¶4250.08.D.]

Generally, a corporation may not re-elect S corporation status (or QSub status) for five years after its S corporation election (or QSub election) is terminated. This rule also applies to a successor corporation of a corporation whose election was terminated. However, in some cases, a corporation or successor corporation may obtain IRS consent for a new election before the expiration of the five-year waiting period [§ 1362(g); Reg. § 1.1362-5(a)].

The five-year waiting period for a new election includes the tax year of the termination plus the next four tax years [§ 1362(g)]. A successor corporation is a corporation that meets the following two requirements [Reg. § 1.1362-5(b)]:

1. 50% or more of its stock is owned, directly or indirectly, by the same persons who owned 50% or more of the stock in the corporation whose election was terminated on the date the election was terminated; and

2. a substantial portion of its assets were assets of the corporation whose election was terminated, or it acquires a substantial portion of the assets of that corporation.

A corporation must submit a private letter ruling request to obtain IRS consent for a new election before the expiration of the five-year waiting period. The corporation has the burden of establishing that the IRS should consent to the election. Consent is ordinarily denied unless [Reg. § 1.1362-5(a)]:

- more than 50% of the corporation's stock is owned by persons who did not own any stock in the corporation on the date of the termination; or

- the corporation shows that the event that caused the termination was not reasonably within the control of the corporation or shareholders having a substantial interest in the corporation, and that the event was not part of a plan to terminate the election.

A corporation may make a new election within the five-year waiting period without IRS consent if the termination occurred for one of the following reasons [Reg. § 1.1362-5(c)]:

- the corporation revoked its election effective on the first day of the first tax year for which the election was to be effective; or

- the corporation failed to meet the S corporation eligibility requirements on the first day of the first tax year for which the election was to be effective.

## XV.B. Taxation of S Corporation Shareholders

### XV.B.1. Passthrough of S Corporation Items

[731 T.M., II.A.; TPS ¶4270.01.]

An S corporation is not liable for income tax (see XV.C. for a detailed discussion of the taxation of S corporations). Instead, an S corporation passes through its items of income, gain, loss, deduction, and credit (so-called "S corporation items") to its shareholders to be taken into account on their individual income tax returns. S corporation items passed through to shareholders generally retain their tax character as determined at the corporate level. The tax character of any S corporation item is determined as if such item were realized directly from the source from which realized by the S corporation, or incurred in the same manner as incurred by the S corporation. Thus, an S corporation must separately report to shareholders any S corporation items whose unique tax character could affect the computation of any shareholder's individual tax liability (so-called "separately stated items"). All S corporation items not required to be separately stated are aggregated and reported to shareholders as a single amount of ordinary income or loss (so-called "nonseparately computed income or loss"). An S corporation reports the separately stated items and nonseparately computed income or loss to shareholders on Schedule K-1 [§ 1366(a), § 1366(b)].

### XV.B.1.a. Separately Stated S Corporation Items

[731 T.M., II.A.1.; TPS ¶4270.01.B.]

Separately stated items include, but are not limited to [Reg. § 1.1366-1(a)(2), § 1.199-5(c)(1)]:

- net rental real estate income or loss;
- other net rental income or loss;
- interest income;
- ordinary and qualified dividends;
- royalties;
- net short-term capital gain or loss;
- net long-term capital gain or loss;
- collectibles gain or loss;
- unrecaptured § 1251 gain;
- net § 1231 gain or loss;
- gambling income and losses;
- recoveries of tax benefit items;
- the § 179 expense deduction;
- the charitable contribution deduction;
- investment interest expense;
- itemized deductions;
- expenses related to portfolio income;
- tax-exempt income;
- tax credits;
- foreign taxes paid or accrued;
- alternative minimum tax (AMT) adjustment and preference items;
- information used in computing the net investment income tax (see X.A.4.); and
- information used in computing the domestic production activities deduction (see IV.A.9.).

### XV.B.1.b. Allocation of S Corporation Items

[731 T.M., II.A.1.; TPS ¶4270.02.]

S corporation items (separately stated items and nonseparately computed income or loss) pass through to shareholders on a daily, pro rata basis. A shareholder's pro rata share of each S corporation item for a year is determined by assigning an equal portion of the item to each day in the tax year and then dividing that portion of the item among all shares outstanding on that day on a pro rata basis [§ 1377(a)(1); Reg. § 1.1377-1(a)(1)]. For purposes of the allocation rules, a shareholder who disposes of stock in the S corporation during the year is treated as a shareholder on the day of the disposition and a shareholder who dies during the year is treated as a shareholder on the day of death [Reg. § 1.1377-1(a)(2)(ii)].

---

**EXAMPLE:** X corporation is a calendar-year S corporation. At the beginning of the year, X had one shareholder, Beth. However, at the end of the day on Oct. 31, Beth sold 25% of her stock to David. X had non-separately computed income of $10,000 for the year. The $10,000 of income is allocated between Beth and David on a daily, pro rata basis. The $8,329 ($10,000 × (304/365)) of income attributable to the period from Jan. 1 through Oct. 31 is allocated 100% to Beth. Of the $1,671 ($10,000 × (61/365)) of income attributable to the period from Nov. 1 through Dec. 31, $1,253 ($1,671 × 75%) is allocated to Beth and $418 ($1,671 × 25%) is allocated to David.

---

If a shareholder terminates its entire interest in an S corporation during the year, the S corporation may elect to close its books on the termination date and apply the pro rata allocation rules as if the tax year consisted of two tax years, with the first tax year ending on the termination date. Consent must be provided by the shareholder whose interest terminated and by all shareholders to whom shares were transferred. In the case of a redemption of shares by the S corporation, consent must be provided by all persons who were shareholders during the tax year [§ 1377(a)(2)].

If a corporation's S election terminates during the year, the pro rata allocation rules apply for purposes of allocating S corporation items between the resulting S short year and C short year (see XV.A.4.c.).

### XV.B.1.c. Shareholder Reporting of S Corporation Items

[731 T.M., II.A.3.; TPS ¶4270.05.]

An S corporation shareholder must report its pro rata share of S corporation items (separately stated items and nonseparately computed income or loss) on its tax return for its tax year within which the S corporation's tax year ends [§ 1366(a), § 1366(c)]. Thus, if the shareholder uses a different tax year than the S corporation, the shareholder effectively defers the reporting of its share of S corporation items.

---

**EXAMPLE:** Mary, a calendar year taxpayer, owns all of the stock of X Corporation, an S corporation with a fiscal tax year ending Sept. 30. For its tax year ending Sept. 30, Year 2, X earns $10,000 of income and passes that income through to Mary. Mary reports the $10,000 of income on her return for her tax year ending Dec. 31, Year 2. There is a deferral of the reporting of three months of income because the income earned by X from Oct. 1, Year 1, through Dec. 31, Year 1, is not reported by Mary until Dec. 31, Year 2.

---

A shareholder's reporting of S corporation items is accelerated if the shareholder is an individual who dies during the year or an estate or trust that terminates during the year. In that case, the S corporation items must be reported on the final return of the shareholder. Death or termination generally results in accelerated reporting of S corporation items because the shareholder's final tax year will usually end before the S corporation's tax year ends [§ 1366(a)(1)].

In filing an individual return, each shareholder generally must treat S corporation items consistently with the S corporation's treatment of those items on its return. If an S corporation shareholder treats an item inconsistently, it must file a statement with the IRS identifying the inconsistency [§ 6037(c)].

### XV.B.2. Limitations on S Corporation Losses and Deductions

[731 T.M., II., III.; TPS ¶4270.06.]

A shareholder's deduction of its share of S corporation losses and deductions may be subject to several limitations including: (i) a basis limitation (see XV.B.2.a.), (ii) the at-risk and passive activity loss limitations (see XV.B.2.b.), and (iii) limitations that apply to specific types of S corporation items (see XV.B.2.c.).

### XV.B.2.a. Basis Limitation on S Corporation Losses and Deductions

[731 T.M., III.B.1.; TPS ¶¶4270.06.A., 4280.04.]

The amount of a shareholder's pro rata share of S corporation losses and deductions that can be deducted on its return is limited to the sum of: (i) the shareholder's adjusted basis in its stock in the S corporation, and (ii) the shareholder's adjusted basis in debt the S corporation owes to it [§ 1366(d)(1)]. However, the amount of any losses or deductions disallowed by this basis limitation generally can be suspended (i.e., carried forward) and deducted by the shareholder in succeeding tax years, subject to the same limitation in those years [§ 1366(d)(2)(A)]. See XV.B.3. for a discussion of the determination of an S shareholder's adjusted basis in S corporation stock and debt.

If a shareholder transfers his or her S corporation stock to a spouse or ex-spouse in a § 1041 nonrecognition transaction incident to divorce, the amount of any losses or deductions disallowed by the basis limitation in the year the stock is transferred can be suspended and deducted by the spouse or ex-spouse in succeeding tax years [§ 1366(d)(2)(B)]. See III.E.5. for a discussion of transfers of property by spouses incident to divorce.

The amount of any losses or deductions disallowed by the basis limitation in the last year the corporation is an S corporation are treated as incurred by the shareholder on the last day of the so-called post-termination transition period; however, the shareholder's deduction of those amounts is limited to its adjusted basis in the stock of the corporation on the last day of the post-termination transition period [§ 1366(d)(3)]. The post-transition termination period is generally the one-year period beginning on the day after the last day of the corporation's last tax year as an S corporation [§ 1377(b)].

The basis limitation does not apply to an S corporation shareholder's deduction of its pro rata share of a charitable contribution of appreciated property to the extent that the shareholder's pro rata share of the contribution exceeds its pro rata share of the basis in the contributed property [§ 1366(d)(4)].

### XV.B.2.b. At-Risk and Passive Activity Loss Limitations on S Corporation Losses and Deductions

[731 T.M., II.G., III.D.; TPS ¶4270.06.B., .06.C.]

The at-risk and passive activity loss rules are generally applied at the shareholder level and serve as another set of overall limitations on an S corporation shareholder's ability to deduct losses and deductions passed through from the S corporation [§ 465, § 469]. Thus, any loss or deduction available to a shareholder after application of the basis limitation is allowed as a deduction only to the extent of the shareholder's amount at risk in the activity at the end of the tax year [Reg. § 1.469-2T(d)(6)(iv)]. A shareholder generally is at risk to the extent of its basis in the S corporation stock plus its basis in any loans made to the S corporation. Any loss or deduction allowed to the shareholder after application of both the basis limitation and the at-risk rules may be limited under the passive activity loss rules [Reg. § 1.469-2T(d)(6)(i)]. See VIII.E. and VIII.F. for a discussion of the at-risk rules and passive activity loss rules, respectively.

### XV.B.2.c. Shareholder Level Limitations for Specific S Corporation Items

[731 T.M., III.B.; TPS ¶4270.06.D., .06.E.]

After the basis, at-risk, and passive activity loss limitations are applied, certain shareholder level limitations on specific types of pass-through loss and deduction items must also be considered. For example, the deductions for interest, charitable contributions, section 179 expenses, domestic production activities, and miscellaneous itemized deductions are all subject to certain limitations. See Chapter IV. and VII. for a discussion of the limitations on the deduction of these types of items.

### XV.B.3. Shareholder Basis in S Corporation Stock and Debt

[731 T.M., III.; TPS ¶4280.]

A shareholder's basis in the stock he owns in an S corporation is important for determining whether distributions made by the S corporation are taxable to him and for determining the amount of any gain or loss he must recognize upon a sale of the stock. A shareholder's basis in a loan he makes to an S corporation is important for determining whether he has any gain or loss when the S corporation repays the loan. Both types of basis are also important for determining whether there are any limitations on the deduction of losses or other amounts passed through to the shareholder by the S corporation (see XV.B.2.).

### XV.B.3.a. Shareholder Basis in S Corporation Stock

[731 T.M., III.A.1.; TPS ¶4280.02.]

A shareholder's initial basis in S corporation stock depends on how he acquired the stock. Certain adjustments must be made to the shareholder's basis in the stock at the end of each year during which he owns the stock.

***Initial Basis.*** The rules that apply in determining an S shareholder's initial basis in the stock of an S corporation are generally the same rules that apply in determining a shareholder's initial basis in the stock of a C corporation (see III.A.3.d.). The following rules apply:

- If a shareholder acquires S corporation stock from an existing shareholder, his initial basis in the stock is equal to his cost for the shares [§ 1012(a)].
- If a shareholder acquires stock as part of a § 351 transaction upon the organization of an S corporation, his initial basis in the stock is equal to the amount of

any money and the basis of any other property transferred to the S corporation in exchange for the stock [§ 358(a)].

- If a shareholder receives stock in a tax-free reorganization, his initial basis in the stock is equal to his basis in the stock exchanged, minus the amount of any boot received (i.e., the amount of money and fair market value of property received), plus or minus the amount of any gain or loss recognized on the exchange [§ 358(a)].

- If a shareholder receives stock in exchange for services provided to an S corporation, the value of the stock he receives upon becoming vested (less any amount he pays for the stock) is treated as compensation and his basis in the stock is equal to the amount included in his income as compensation (plus any amount he pays for the stock) [Reg. § 1.83-4(b)].

- A shareholder who receives stock as a gift generally gets a carryover basis in the stock equal to the donor shareholder's basis in the stock [§ 1015(a)].

- A shareholder who receives stock by inheritance generally gets a stepped-up basis in the stock equal to its fair market value on the date of the deceased shareholder's death (or on the alternate valuation date, if elected) [§ 1014(a)].

***Adjustments to Basis.*** Once an S corporation shareholder's initial basis in his S corporation stock has been determined, certain adjustments must be made to his stock basis each year [§ 1367; Reg. § 1.1367-1(a)]. Each shareholder's stock basis is increased by his share of the following items passed through by the S corporation [§ 1367(a)(1); Reg. § 1.1367-1(b)]:

- separately stated items of income (including tax-exempt income);

- nonseparately computed income; and

- the amount by which any depletion deductions exceed the basis of the related property subject to depletion.

Each shareholder's stock basis is decreased (but not below zero) by his share of the following items passed through by the S corporation [§ 1367(a)(2); Reg. § 1.1367-1(c)]:

- distributions not includible in income;

- separately stated items of loss and deduction;

- nonseparately computed loss;

- any expense that is not deductible and not properly chargeable to a capital account; and

- the amount by which the basis of oil and gas property subject to depletion exceeds the depletion deductions related to that property.

To the extent that a shareholder's stock basis is decreased to zero by the amount of such items, any additional amounts decrease the shareholder's basis in debt owed to him by the S corporation (see XV.B.3.b.).

The adjustments to basis are computed on a share-by-share basis. The basis of a share of stock is increased or decreased by an amount equal to the shareholder's pro rata portion of the above items that is attributable to that share. The pro rata portion of an item is determined on a per share, per day basis in accordance with the allocation rules (see XV.B.1.b.) [Reg. § 1.1367-1(b)(2), § 1.1367-1(c)(3)].

The adjustments to basis are determined as of the end of the S corporation's tax year and are generally effective on that date. However, when a shareholder disposes of stock during the S corporation's tax year, the adjustments with respect to that stock are effective immediately before the disposition. An adjustment for a nontaxable item is determined for the tax year in which the item would have been includible or deductible under the S corporation's method of accounting if it was subject to tax [Reg. § 1.1367-1(d)].

**Worksheet for Figuring a Shareholder's Stock Basis**

*Keep for Your Records*

1. Your stock basis at the beginning of the year . . . . . . . . . . . . . . . .     1. _____

**Increases:**

2. Money and your adjusted basis in property contributed to the corporation . . . . . . . . . . . . . . . . . . . . . . . . . . . . . . . . . . . . . .     2. _____

3. Your share of the corporation's income (including tax-exempt income) reduced by any amount included in income with respect to clean renewable energy or (for bonds issued before October 4, 2008) qualified zone academy bonds . . . . . . . . . . . . . . . . . . . . .     3. _____

4. Other increases to basis, including your share of the excess of the deductions for depletion (other than oil and gas depletion) over the basis of the property subject to depletion . . . . . . . . . . . . . . . . . .     4. _____

**Decreases:**

5. Distributions of money and the fair market value of property (excluding dividend distributions reportable on Form 1099-DIV and distributions in excess of basis (the sum of lines 1 through 4)) . . . . . . . . . . . . . . . . . . . . . . . . . . . . . . . . . . . . . . . . . . . . .     5. ( _____ )

6. Enter **(a)** your share of the corporation's nondeductible expenses and the depletion deduction for any oil and gas property held by the corporation (but only to the extent your share of the property's adjusted basis exceeds the depletion deduction); **or (b)** if the election under Regulations section 1.1367-1(g) applies, your share of the corporation's deductions and losses (include your entire share of the section 179 expense deduction even if your allowable section 179 expense deduction is smaller) adjusted, if the corporation made a charitable contribution of property as described in (4) under *Basis Rules* . . . . . . . . . . . . . . . . . . . . . . . . . . . . . .     6. ( _____ )

7. If the election under Regulations section 1.1367-1(g) applies, enter the amount from 6(a) above. Otherwise, enter the amount from 6(b) . . . . . . . . . . . . . . . . . . . . . . . . . . . . . . . . . . . . . . . . . . . . .     7. ( _____ )

8. Enter the smaller of **(a)** the excess, as of the beginning of the tax year, of the amount you are owed for loans you made to the corporation over your basis in those loans; **or (b)** the sum of lines 1 through 7. This amount increases your loan basis . . . . . . . . . . . .     8. ( _____ )

9. Your stock basis in the corporation at the end of the year. Combine lines 1 through 8 . . . . . . . . . . . . . . . . . . . . . . . . . . . . . . . . . . .     9. _____

(Source: 2014 Form 1120S (Schedule K-1) Draft Instructions)

### XV.B.3.b. Shareholder Basis in S Corporation Debt

[731 T.M., III.A.2.; TPS ¶4280.03.]

A shareholder is considered to have basis in debt owed to him by the S corporation only if there is a bona fide debt of the S corporation that runs directly to the shareholder. Whether debt is bona fide debt to a shareholder is determined under general federal tax principles and depends on all the facts and circumstances [Prop. Reg. § 1.1366-2(a)(2)(i)].

A shareholder's initial basis in debt owed to him by the S corporation is the face amount of the loan made to the S corporation. His basis in S corporation debt is increased by the face amount of any additional loans he makes to the S corporation and decreased by any principal payments made by the S corporation to him [§ 1366(d)(1)(B), § 1012]. Generally, all adjustments for pass-through items are made to the shareholder's basis in his stock rather than his basis in debt. However, there are two exceptions under which a shareholder's basis in S corporation debt is adjusted by pass-through items:

1. A shareholder's basis in S corporation debt is decreased by the types of items that decrease his basis in the S corporation stock (other than distributions) to the extent that the amount of those items for the year exceeds his stock basis. In other words, the amount of such items is first applied to decrease the shareholder's basis in his stock and, if his stock basis is reduced to zero, then any additional amounts are applied to decrease his basis in debt [§ 1367(b)(2)(A)]. See XV.B.3.a. for a discussion of the types of items that decrease a shareholder's basis in his stock.

2. If a shareholder's basis in debt was decreased under the rule discussed in 1., then the basis in debt is increased in each subsequent year to the extent that the types of items that increase stock basis for that year exceed the types of items that decrease stock basis for that year. However, the total amount of basis in debt that is restored under this rule cannot exceed the amount by which the basis in debt was decreased under the rule discussed in 1. [§ 1367(b)(2)(B)]. See XV.B.3.a. for a discussion of the types of items that increase a shareholder's basis in his stock.

---

**EXAMPLE:** Tom is a 100% shareholder in X Corporation, a calendar-year S corporation. Tom's stock basis is $5,000 at the beginning of the year. Tom previously made a $10,000 loan to X and X has not made any payments on the loan. During the year, X passes through an operating loss of $12,000 to Tom. Tom may deduct the entire amount of the loss. His stock basis is decreased to zero for the first $5,000 of the loss. His basis in debt is reduced from $10,000 to $3,000 to reflect the $7,000 balance of the loss. Tom's basis in debt will be increased in each subsequent year to the extent that pass-through items of income exceed pass-through items of loss and deduction for that year; however, the total increase to Tom's basis in debt during those years may not be more than $7,000.

---

### XV.B.4. Treatment of S Corporation Distributions

[731 T.M., IV.; TPS ¶4290.]

The tax treatment of nonliquidating distributions of property (including money) by an S corporation to its shareholders depends on whether or not the S corporation has accumulated earnings and profits. Earnings and profits is essentially an economic concept of a corporation's ability to pay dividends without distributing any capital contributed by shareholders or creditors. It is computed by making certain adjustments to taxable income.

An S corporation generally will not have accumulated earnings and profits unless it was a C corporation before it was an S corporation or it succeeded to the accumulated earnings and profits of a C corporation that it acquired.

While subchapter S contains special rules on the tax treatment of nonliquidating distributions by S corporations, it does not contain any rules on distributions in complete liquidation of the corporation, distributions in redemption of shareholder stock, or tax-free distributions of stock. S corporations making those types of distributions are subject to the same rules that apply to C corporations. See Chapter XIII. for a discussion of those rules.

### XV.B.4.a. Distribution from S Corporation with No Accumulated Earnings and Profits

[731 T.M., IV.A.; TPS ¶4290.03.]

A shareholder who receives a distribution of property from an S corporation that does not have any accumulated earnings and profits treats the distribution as a nontaxable return of capital to the extent of his adjusted basis in the S corporation stock and as a gain from the sale or exchange of property to the extent the distribution exceeds his adjusted basis in the stock [§ 1368(b)].

---

**EXAMPLE:** X Corporation has been an S corporation since it was first formed and it has no accumulated earnings and profits. Al is the sole shareholder of X and his adjusted basis in the X stock at the end of the year is $3,500. During the year, X distributed $5,000 of property to Al. The first $3,500 of the distribution is tax-free to Al. The $1,500 balance of the distribution is taxed to Al as a gain from the sale or exchange of property. Note that Al's basis in his X stock is reduced to zero as a result of the distribution.

---

### XV.B.4.b. Distribution from S Corporation with Accumulated Earnings and Profits

[731 T.M., IV.B.; TPS ¶4290.04.]

A shareholder who receives a distribution of property from an S corporation that has accumulated earnings and profits treats the distribution as follows [§ 1368(c)]:

1. nontaxable return of capital to the extent it does not exceed his adjusted basis in the stock and does not exceed the corporation's accumulated adjustments account (AAA);

2. gain from the sale or exchange of property to the extent it exceeds his adjusted basis in the stock but does not exceed the corporation's AAA;

3. a dividend to the extent it exceeds the corporation's AAA but does not exceed the corporation's accumulated earnings and profits;

4. a nontaxable return of capital to the extent it exceeds the corporation's accumulated earnings and profits but does not exceed his adjusted basis in the stock; and

5. a gain from the sale or exchange of property to the extent it exceeds both the corporation's accumulated earnings and profits and his adjusted basis in the stock.

An S corporation's accumulated adjustments account (AAA) represents an accumulation of the corporation's earnings that were previously taxed but not distributed (see XV.B.4.c.).

---

**EXAMPLE:** X Corporation is an S corporation that was formerly a C corporation and, at the end of the year, it has accumulated earnings and profits of $1,000 and an AAA balance of $10,000. Bob is the sole shareholder of X and, at the end of the year, he has an adjusted basis of $8,000 in his X stock. During the year, X distributed $18,000 of property to Bob. The first $8,000 of the distribution is treated as a nontaxable return of capital. The next $2,000 of the distribution is treated as a gain from the sale of property. The next $1,000 of the distribution is treated as a dividend. The $7,000 balance of the distribution in is treated as a gain from the sale of property.

---

If multiple distributions are made by the S corporation during the year and the total amount of distributions is greater than the balance in the AAA account at the end of the year, the balance in the AAA account must be allocated among the distributions in proportion to their respective sizes [§ 1368(c)].

An S corporation with accumulated earnings and profits may elect to distribute earnings and profits first. If such an election is made, the first two tiers of tax treatment discussed above are not applied. Thus, the distribution is first treated as a taxable dividend to the shareholder to the extent it does not exceed the S corporation's accumulated earnings and profits. An S corporation may make this election only if it obtains the consent of all shareholders to whom distributions are made during the tax year [§ 1368(e)(3)].

### XV.B.4.c. Accumulated Adjustments Account

[731 T.M., IV.C.; TPS ¶4290.04.E.]

The accumulated adjustments account (AAA) tracks the S corporation's ability to make tax-free distributions to shareholders. The AAA represents an accumulation of previously taxed, but undistributed, earnings of the S corporation. Therefore, to the extent the corporation has a positive balance in the AAA, tax-free distributions can generally be made to shareholders.

On the first day of the first year for which the corporation is an S corporation, the balance of the AAA is zero [Reg. § 1.1368-2(a)(1)]. The AAA is then increased and decreased in a manner similar to the adjustments that are made to stock basis (see XV.B.3.a.) except that: (i) AAA can be adjusted below zero, (ii) AAA is not adjusted for tax-exempt income and related expenses, and (iii) AAA is not adjusted for federal taxes attributable to tax years in which the corporation was a C corporation [§ 1368(e)(1)(A)].

AAA is increased by the sum of the following items [Reg. § 1.1368-2(a)(2)]:

- separately stated items of income and gain (other than tax-exempt income);
- nonseparately computed income; and
- excess depletion deductions.

AAA is decreased by the sum of the following items [Reg. § 1.1368-2(a)(3)]:

- separately stated items of loss and deduction;
- nonseparately computed loss;
- nondeductible, noncapitalized expenses (other than expenses attributable to tax-exempt income and federal taxes attributable to C corporation status); and
- shareholders' excess depletion deductions for oil and gas property.

Although the AAA account may become negative, any net negative adjustment for the year is not taken into account for purposes of determining the tax treatment of distributions made during the year. A net negative adjustment is the amount by which the decreases to AAA for the year exceed the increases to AAA for the year. When there is a net negative adjustment for the year, the AAA balance from the beginning of the year is used to determine the tax treatment of the distributions made during the year [§ 1368(e)(1)(C)].

---

**EXAMPLE:** X Corporation is a calendar-year S corporation with $100,000 of accumulated earnings and profits. At the beginning of the year, X has a $20,000 AAA balance and its shareholders have an aggregate stock basis of $20,000. During the year, X does not have any items that increase AAA and it has a $30,000 net loss that decreases AAA. X distributes $20,000 to its shareholders. Since there is a net negative adjustment of $30,000, the tax treatment of the distribution is determined based on the AAA balance at the beginning of the year. The distribution is not taxable to the shareholders because it does not exceed the $20,000 AAA balance or the shareholders' $20,000 basis in their stock. The AAA and the shareholders' stock basis are both reduced to zero by the $20,000 distribution. X's AAA balance at the beginning of the following year is negative $30,000.

### XV.B.4.c.(1) AAA Adjustments for Redemptions, Reorganizations, and Divisions

[731 T.M., IV.C.; TPS ¶4290.04.E.5.]

When an S corporation makes a redemption distribution treated as a distribution in exchange for stock under § 302(a) or § 303(a), the AAA is adjusted in an amount equal to the pro rata share of the corporation's AAA attributable to the redeemed stock as of the date of the redemption (whether positive or negative). When an S corporation makes both redemption distributions and ordinary distributions during the year, the AAA is first adjusted for the ordinary distributions and then for the redemption distributions [§ 1368(e)(1)(B); Reg. § 1.1368-2(d)(1)].

When an S corporation acquires the assets of another S corporation in a tax-free liquidation or reorganization to which § 381(a) applies, the AAA of the acquiring corporation after the transaction is equal to the sum of the AAA of both corporations before the transaction (whether positive or negative) [Reg. § 1.1368-2(d)(2)].

When an S corporation (distributing corporation) with accumulated earnings and profits transfers part of its assets constituting an active trade or business to another corporation (controlled corporation) in a § 368(a)(1)(D) reorganization and, immediately after the transfer, the stock and securities of the controlled corporation are distributed in a § 355 nonrecognition transaction, the AAA of the distributing corporation is allocated between distributing corporation and controlled corporation based on the fair market value of the assets [Reg. § 1.1368-2(d)(3)].

### XV.B.4.c.(2) Order of AAA Adjustments

[731 T.M., IV.C.1.; TPS ¶4290.04.E.7.]

Adjustments to the AAA must be computed in the following order [Reg. § 1.1368-2(a)(5)]:

1. adjustments are made for the items that increase the AAA;

2. adjustments are made for the items that decrease the AAA;

3. the AAA is decreased (but not below zero) for ordinary distributions;

4. the AAA is decreased by any net negative adjustment; and

5. the AAA is adjusted for redemption distributions (whether positive or negative).

### XV.B.4.c.(3) Allocation of AAA Among Multiple Distributions

[731 T.M., IV.C.6.; TPS ¶4290.04.C.]

If an S corporation makes more than one distribution during the tax year, the AAA must be allocated among distributions if the AAA has a positive balance at the end of the year and the sum of distributions made during the year is greater than the AAA balance at the end of the year. The amount allocated to each distribution is computed by multiplying the AAA balance at the end of the year by a fraction, the numerator of which is the amount of the distribution and the denominator of which is the total of all distributions made during the year [Reg. § 1.1368-2(b)].

### XV.B.4.d. S Corporation Distributions of Appreciated Property

[731 T.M., IV.E.; TPS ¶4290.05.]

If an S corporation distributes appreciated property (i.e., property with a fair market value greater than its adjusted basis) with respect to its stock, the S corporation must recognize gain on the distribution as if the property were sold to the distributee shareholder at fair market value [§ 311(b)(1)]. The gain passes through to all shareholders under the pro rata allocation rules (see XV.B.1.b.). The gain also increases the corporation's AAA.

---

**EXAMPLE:** X Corporation is an S corporation with two shareholders, Carol and Diane, who each own 50% of its stock. At the beginning of the year, X has an AAA of $40,000 and each shareholder has a $25,000 adjusted basis in her stock. During the year, X makes a distribution to Carol of $10,000 cash and a distribution to Diane of property with a fair market value of $10,000 and an adjusted basis of $2,000. X recognizes gain of $8,000 ($10,000 − $2,000) on the distribution of property to Diane. The gain increases the AAA to $48,000, and $4,000 ($8,000 × 50%) of the gain passes through to each of the shareholders. The distributions reduce the AAA to $28,000 ($48,000 − $10,000 − $10,000). Each shareholder's basis in her stock is $19,000 at the end of the year because the $25,000 basis at the beginning of the year is increased by the $4,000 gain passed through and decreased by the $10,000 distribution. Note that Carol is taxable on half the gain from the property even though the property was distributed to Diane.

---

### XV.B.4.e. Distributions Following Termination of S Corporation Status

[731 T.M., IV.G.; TPS ¶4290.09.]

A special rule allows a corporation that has terminated its S election to make tax-free distributions of income that was previously passed through and taxed to shareholders but never distributed to them. Any cash distribution with respect to the corporation's stock that is made during a specified period after the termination is applied against and reduces the adjusted basis of a shareholder's stock to the extent of the balance in the AAA as of the last day of the last S year [§ 1371(e)(1)]. The rule applies only to cash distributions, not property distributions. The distributions are tax-free only to the extent of the shareholder's adjusted basis in its stock. To qualify for this tax-free treatment, the distributions must be made during the post-termination transition period. The post-termination transition period is [§ 1377(b)(1)]:

- The period beginning on the last day of the last S year and ending one year later (or the due date for filing the return for the last S year, if later);

- The 120-day period beginning on the date of any audit determination that adjusts an S corporation item that arose during the most recent continuous period during which the corporation was an S corporation; or

- The 120-day period beginning on the date of a determination that the corporation's S election had terminated for a previous tax year.

### XV.B.5. Treatment of S Corporation Fringe Benefits and Qualified Retirement Plans

[731 T.M., V; TPS ¶4300.]

Often, shareholders of an S corporation are also its employees. Such shareholder-employees may receive compensation for providing services to the S corporation. The compensation received from the S corporation may take many forms, including salaries, bonuses, fringe benefits, and coverage in qualified retirement plans.

### XV.B.5.a. S Corporation Fringe Benefits

[731 T.M., V.; TPS ¶4300.04.]

Corporations generally can provide certain fringe benefits to their employees on a tax-free basis, with the employee excluding the value of the fringe benefit from income. The rules for fringe benefits provided by S corporations are similar to the rules that apply to C corporations (see XVII.D. for a detailed discussion of fringe benefits). However, two special rules apply to fringe benefits provided by S corporations. Shareholder-employees of an S corporation who own more than 2% of the voting power or value of the outstanding stock of the S corporation on any day during the tax year cannot exclude the value of certain fringe benefits provided by the S corporation, including group term life insurance, coverage under an accident and health plan, meals and lodging furnished for the convenience of the employer, and benefits provided under a cafeteria plan [§ 1372]. However, such shareholder-employees can generally take an above-the-line deduction for the amount of any health insurance premiums the S corporation pays on their behalf [§ 162(l)(1), § 162(l)(5)].

### XV.B.5.b. S Corporation Qualified Retirement Plans

[731 T.M., V.B.; TPS ¶4300.02.]

The rules for qualified retirement plans established by S corporations are generally similar to the rules that apply to C corporations in terms of the qualification requirements, the taxation of employees, and the treatment of employers (see XVII.A.2. for a detailed discussion of qualified retirement plans). However, there are some special rules that apply to S corporations in the context of qualified retirement plans:

- An S corporation cannot deduct contributions to an employee stock ownership plan (ESOP) that are used by the ESOP to repay principal or interest on a loan used to acquire stock of the S corporation [§ 404(a)(9)(C)].
- An S corporation cannot deduct dividends paid in cash on S corporation stock held by an ESOP [§ 404(k)(1)].
- S corporation shareholders do not qualify for the tax-free rollover of gain on the sale of S corporation stock to an ESOP [§ 1042(c)(1)].
- A distribution with respect to S corporation stock that constitutes qualifying employer securities is generally not treated as a prohibited transaction when it is used to repay a loan that was used to acquire the securities. However, this relief from the prohibited transaction penalties does not apply in the case of a distribution with respect to S corporation stock that is allocated to a participant unless the plan provides that stock with a fair market value of not less than the amount of the distribution will be allocated to the participant for the year in which the distribution would have been allocated to the participant [§ 4975(f)(7)].

## XV.C. Taxation of S Corporation

### XV.C.1. Applicable S Corporation Tax Rules

[731 T.M., I.A.; TPS ¶4260.]

The tax treatment of S corporations has traditionally been compared to the tax treatment of partnerships because of the pass-through of income, gain, loss, deduction, and credit items to the shareholders. And, in fact, many of the rules that apply to S corporations are similar to the rules that apply to partnerships. However, S corporations and partnerships are governed by different subchapters of the Internal Revenue Code and important differences exist. For some tax purposes, S corporations are subject to the same rules that apply to C corporations, such as the rules that apply to the formation of the corporation, distributions of property, redemptions of stock, complete liquidations, and tax-free reorganizations and divisions. See Chapter XIII. for a discussion of these rules.

### XV.C.2. S Corporation Taxes

[731 T.M., I.A.1.; TPS ¶4260.01.]

S corporations are exempt from all taxes imposed on C corporations, including the regular income tax, the alternative minimum tax, the accumulated earnings tax, and the personal holding company tax [§ 1363(a)]. However, the following special taxes may be imposed on S corporations in certain situations:

- the tax on built-in gains (see XV.C.5.);
- the tax on excess net passive income (see XV.C.6.); and
- the LIFO recapture tax (see XV.C.7.).

### XV.C.3. Computation of S Corporation Taxable Income

[731 T.M., I.A.3.; TPS ¶4260.02.A.]

Although an S corporation is not itself subject to income tax, the taxable income of an S corporation must be computed in order to determine the amount and character of the S corporation items to be passed through to shareholders. See XV.B.1. for a discussion of the pass-through of S corporation items to shareholders.

The taxable income of an S corporation is computed in the same manner as the taxable income of an individual, with four exceptions [§ 1363(b)]:

1. Items of income, gain, loss, deduction, and credit must be separately stated if their separate treatment could affect any shareholder's income tax liability (see XV.B.1.a.).

2. Certain deductions are not allowed, including the personal exemptions deduction, the charitable contributions deduction, the net operating loss deduction, the deduction for foreign taxes paid or incurred, the depletion deduction for oil and gas wells, and deductions that, by their terms, apply only to individuals (e.g., the medical expense deduction, the alimony deduction).

3. The § 248 rules for organizational expenditures apply (see XIII.C.2.d.).

4. The § 291 rules for corporate preference items apply if the S corporation was a C corporation for any of the three preceding tax years.

### XV.C.3.a. Elections Affecting S Corporation Items

[731 T.M., I.A.7.; TPS ¶4260.02.B.]

In computing the taxable income of an S corporation, elections affecting the computation of S corporation items are generally made at the corporate level [§ 1363(c)(1)]. For example, elections relating to tax year, accounting methods, inventory methods, depreciation, and § 179 expensing are made by the S corporation instead of the shareholders. However, the following elections are made at the shareholder level instead of the corporate level:

- the § 617 election relating to the deduction and recapture of certain mining exploration expenditures [§ 1363(c)(2)(A)];

- the § 901 election to take a credit instead of a deduction for foreign taxes paid or incurred [§ 1363(c)(2)(B)];
- the § 59(e) election to amortize certain expenditures that would otherwise be deducted and treated as tax preferences for alternative minimum tax purposes [§ 59(e)(4)(C)]; and
- the election not to apply the § 263A uniform capitalization rules to plants produced in a farming business [Reg. § 1.263A-4(d)(3)(i)].

### XV.C.3.b. S Corporation Carryovers

[731 T.M., I.A.5.; TPS ¶4260.09.]

No carryforwards or carrybacks arise in tax years in which a corporation is an S corporation. S corporation items that would potentially be subject to carryover treatment, such as net operating losses, are passed through to the shareholders in those years [§ 1371(b)(2), § 1366(a)].

Carryforwards or carrybacks that arise in tax years in which a corporation is a C corporation cannot be carried to tax years in which the corporation is an S corporation (with an exception for purposes of the built-in gains tax (see XV.C.5.)). However, the tax years in which the corporation is an S corporation are treated as tax years for purposes of counting the number of years to which a corporate-level item can be carried back or carried forward [§ 1371(b)(1), § 1371(b)(3)].

### XV.C.4. S Corporation Filing Requirements

### XV.C.4.a. Who Must File S Corporation Return

[731 T.M., I.; TPS ¶4410.01.A.1.]

Every corporation is required to file an income tax return for each tax year in which it is in existence, whether or not it has taxable income for the year [§ 6012(a)(2), Reg. § 1.6012-2(a)]. Thus, an S corporation must file an income tax return for each tax year in which it is in existence [§ 6037]. Termination of S status does not relieve an S corporation of its obligation to file a return. If an S election is terminated and the corporation reverts to a C corporation during a tax year, the corporation generally must file two returns for the tax year, one for the short year during which it was an S corporation (the S short year) and one for the short year during which it was a C corporation (the C short year) [§ 1362(e)].

### XV.C.4.b. Form to File S Corporation Return

[731 T.M., I.; TPS ¶4410.01.A.2.]

An S corporation must file Form 1120S, *U.S. Income Tax Return for an S Corporation,* for each tax year in which its S election is in effect [Reg. § 1.6012-2(h)]. A Schedule K-1 must be attached to Form 1120S for each person who was a shareholder at any time during the tax year and a copy of the Schedule K-1 must be furnished to the relevant shareholder [§ 6037(b)].

Form 1120S must be signed and dated by the president, vice president, treasurer, assistant treasurer, chief accounting officer, or any other corporate officer authorized to sign the return. It may be signed by a receiver or bankruptcy trustee if such fiduciary has possession of, or holds title to, substantially all the property or business of the corporation [§ 6062, § 6012(b)(3)].

An S corporation generally has the option of filing either a paper Form 1120S or an electronic Form 1120S. However, an S corporation is required to file all returns (including Form 1120S) electronically if: (i) it has assets of $10 million or more, and (ii) it is required to file at least 250 federal returns of all types during the calendar year that ends with or within its tax year [Reg. § 301.6011-5, § 301.6037-2].

### XV.C.4.c. When to File S Corporation Return

[731 T.M., I.; TPS ¶4410.01.A.3., .01.A.4., .01.B.]

An S corporation is generally required to file Form 1120S by the 15th day of the 3rd month after the end of its tax year (i.e., by March 15th for a calendar year taxpayer) [§ 6072(b)]. However, if the due date falls on a Saturday, Sunday, or legal holiday, the due date is extended to the next business day [§ 7503]. An S corporation must furnish Schedule K-1 (information on a shareholder's share of S corporation items) to each shareholder on or before the day on which Form 1120S is filed [§ 6037(b)].

If an S corporation dissolved during the year, it generally must file Form 1120S by the 15th day of the 3rd month after the date it dissolved. If an S election is terminated and the corporation reverts to a C corporation during the year, the return for the S short year is due on the due date for the return for the C short year, generally the 15th day of the 3rd month after the end of the C short year [§ 1362(e)(6)(B)].

---

**EXAMPLE:** X Corporation is a calendar-year S corporation that revokes its S election effective on May 31 of the tax year. The revocation creates an S short year covering Jan. 1 through May 30 and a C short year covering May 31 through Dec. 31. The due date for both the Form 1120S for the S short year and the Form 1120 for the C short year is March 15th of the following year.

---

An S corporation can receive a 6-month extension of time to file Form 1120S by filing Form 7004, *Application for Automatic Extension of Time To File Certain Business Income Tax, Information and Other Returns*. However, an extension of time to file the return does not extend the time to pay any tax due on the return (e.g., the built-in gains tax) [§ 6081(a); Reg. § 1.6081-3].

An S corporation is subject to a penalty if it fails to file a timely Form 1120S or to show required information on Form 1120S. The penalty is imposed for each month (or fraction thereof) during which the failure continues (not to exceed 12 months). The amount of the monthly penalty is equal to $195 multiplied by the number of persons who were shareholders in the S corporation during any part of the tax year [§ 6699].

An S corporation is also subject to a penalty for the failure to furnish an accurate Schedule K-1 to a shareholder on a timely basis or to include all required information on a Schedule K-1. The amount of the penalty is generally $100 for each Schedule K-1 for which such a failure occurs (up to a maximum of $1.5 million). However, the penalty amount is reduced to $30 ($250,000 maximum) if the failure is corrected within 30 days or to $60 ($500,000 maximum) if the failure is corrected after more than 30 days but on or before August 1 of the calendar year in which the due date occurs. The penalty does not apply if the failure occurs on a de minimis number of Schedules K-1 [§ 6722].

### XV.C.4.d. S Corporation Accounting Methods and Periods

[731 T.M., IX.D., IX.E.; TPS ¶¶4230.02., 4260.05.]

An S corporation determines its method of accounting independently from its shareholders. An S corporation may generally use any permissible accounting method (see XI.B.).

An S corporation is required to use one of the following tax years (see XI.A.) [§ 1378; Reg. § 1.1378-1(a)]:

- a tax year ending on December 31 (i.e., the calendar year);
- a tax year for which a business purpose is established (i.e., an ownership year or a natural business year);
- a tax year elected under § 444; or
- a 52-53-week tax year ending with reference to the calendar year or a tax year elected under § 444.

An S corporation will be deemed to have established a business purpose for a tax year if it complies with the applicable provisions of Rev. Proc. 2006-46. Under Rev. Proc. 2006-46, the business purpose requirement is satisfied if the S corporation's tax year coincides with an ownership year or a natural business year. A tax year coincides with an ownership year if it is the same tax year as the tax year of a majority of the S corporation's shareholders. A tax year coincides with a natural business year if 25% or more of the S corporation's gross receipts were earned during the last two months of that tax year for each of the three most recent years [Rev. Proc. 2006-46, 2006-45 I.R.B. 859].

An S corporation may make a § 444 election to use a tax year other than the calendar year or a year for which a business purpose is established if the selected tax year produces three months or less in tax deferral for the shareholders. Generally, this means that an S corporation may make a § 444 election to use a fiscal tax year with a September, October, or November year-end. The § 444 election is made by filing Form 8716, *Election to Have a Tax Year Other Than a Required Tax Year*. If an S corporation makes a § 444 election, it must make required payments to the IRS that reflect the tax deferral received by the shareholders due to the S corporation's use of the fiscal year [§ 444].

### XV.C.5. Tax on S Corporation Built-In Gains

[731 T.M., I.C.; TPS ¶4260.07.]

If a corporation converts from a C corporation to an S corporation and, during a specified period after the conversion (the recognition period) (see XV.C.5.a.), it disposes of assets that had appreciated during the years it was a C corporation, then it is subject to a corporate-level tax on the unrealized appreciation (the built-in gain) in those assets on the date of the conversion. The amount of the built-in gains tax is equal to the S corporation's net recognized built-in gain (see XV.C.5.b.) multiplied by the maximum corporate income tax rate (see XV.C.5.c.) [§ 1374(a), § 1374(b)(1)].

The built-in gains tax does not apply to a corporation that has been an S corporation for all tax years since it was formed [§ 1374(c)(1)]. Moreover, the tax does not apply to a corporation that converted from C corporation status to S corporation status before 1987 [Pub. L. No. 99-514].

### XV.C.5.a. Recognition Period for S Corporation Built-In Gains

[731 T.M., I.C.5.a.; TPS ¶4260.07.B.2.]

The recognition period is generally the 10-year period beginning on the first day of the first tax year in which the corporation was an S corporation. However, the recognition period was reduced to 7 years for assets disposed of in tax years beginning in 2009 and 2010 and to 5 years for assets disposed of in tax years beginning in 2011, 2012, and 2013 [§ 1374(d)(7)].

### *XV.C.5.b. Net Recognized Built-In Gain*

[731 T.M., I.C.5.a.; TPS ¶4260.07.B.7.]

The amount of net recognized built-in gain is generally equal to the amount of taxable income the S corporation would have had for the year if only the built-in gains and losses recognized on the disposition of assets during the recognition period are taken into account.

However, the amount of net recognized built-in gain is subject to two limitations:

1. Net recognized built-in gain may not be greater than the S corporation's taxable income for the year (computed with certain modifications) [§ 1374(d)(2)(A)].

2. Net recognized built-in gain may not be greater than the excess of the S corporation's net unrealized built-in gain over its net recognized built-in gains for all prior tax years during the recognition period [§ 1374(c)(2)]. For this purpose, net unrealized built-in gain is the amount by which the fair market value of the corporation's assets as of the beginning of its first S corporation year exceeds the adjusted bases of the assets at that time [§ 1374(d)(1)].

---

**EXAMPLE:** X Corporation is a calendar-year C corporation that elects to become an S corporation on Jan. 1. X has a net unrealized built-in gain of $50,000 on Jan. 1. X's taxable income for the year is $9,600. X would have had $20,000 of taxable income for the year if it only took into account built-in gains and losses recognized on the disposition of assets. X's net recognized built-in gain for the year is $9,600.

---

### *XV.C.5.c. Computation of Built-in Gains Tax*

[731 T.M., I.C.6.; TPS ¶4260.07.C.]

The following steps must be taken in computing the built-in gains tax:

1. determine the amount of the net recognized built-in gain (see XV.C.5.b.);

2. reduce the net recognized built-in gain from step 1 by a deduction for any net operating loss carryforwards and capital loss carryforwards that arose in tax years during which the corporation was a C corporation [§ 1374(b)(2)];

3. compute the tentative built-in gains tax by multiplying the amount computed in step 2 by the maximum corporate income tax rate in § 11(b) (35% in 2014) [§ 1374(b)(1)]; and

4. compute the built-in gains tax by reducing the tentative built-in gains tax computed in step 3 by any business credits that carry forward from tax years during which the corporation was a C corporation [§ 1374(b)(3)].

### *XV.C.6. Tax on S Corporation Excess Net Passive Income*

[731 T.M., I.B.; TPS ¶4260.08.]

If an S corporation has accumulated earnings and profits from a period when it was a C corporation and its passive investment income for the year is more than 25% of its gross receipts, then it is subject to a corporate-level tax on the excess passive investment income. The tax is equal to the S corporation's excess net passive income (see XV.C.6.b.) multiplied by the maximum corporate income tax rate in § 11(b) (35% in 2014) [§ 1375(a)]. No credits are allowed against the tax, except the credit for certain uses of gasoline and special fuels [§ 1375(c), § 34].

If an S corporation has both accumulated earnings and profits and passive investment income in excess of 25% of gross receipts for three consecutive years, its S corporation election is terminated (see XV.A.4.a.).

### XV.C.6.a. Definition of Passive Investment Income

[731 T.M., I.B.2.c.; TPS ¶4260.08.B.5.]

Passive investment income generally includes gross receipts from royalties, rents, dividends, interest, and annuities. However, it does not include dividends from stock held in an 80%-or-more-owned C corporation to the extent the dividends are attributable to the C corporation's earnings and profits derived from the active conduct of a trade or business [§ 1375(b)(3), § 1362(d)(3)(C); Reg. § 1.1362-2(c)(5)].

### XV.C.6.b. Definition of Excess Net Passive Income

[731 T.M., I.B.3.a.; TPS ¶4260.08.B.2.]

Excess net passive income is equal to net passive investment income multiplied by the ratio of the amount of passive investment income in excess of 25% of gross receipts over the total amount of passive investment income. Net passive investment income is passive investment income (see XV.C.6.a.) reduced by deductions directly connected with the production of that income. The amount of excess net passive income for the year is limited to the S corporation's taxable income (computed with certain modifications) [§ 1375(b)(1), § 1375(b)(2)].

---

**EXAMPLE:** X Corporation is an S corporation that was previously a C corporation and has substantial accumulated earnings and profits. During the year, X has gross receipts of $105,000, passive investment income of $50,000, and $1,000 of deductions directly connected with the production of that income. Its taxable income for the year is $26,000. X's net passive investment income is $49,000 ($50,000 − $1,000). Its excess net passive income is computed by multiplying that amount by the ratio of its passive investment income in excess of 25% of its gross receipts (($50,000 − ($105,000 × 25%)) = $23,750) over its total amount of passive investment income ($50,000), but is subject to the taxable income limitation ($26,000). Thus, X has excess net passive income of $23,275 ($49,000 × ($23,750/$50,000)). Its tax on excess net passive income is $8,146 ($23,275 × 35%).

---

### XV.C.6.c. Waiver of S Corporation Excess Net Passive Income Tax

[731 T.M., I.B.3.b.; TPS ¶4260.08.E.]

If an S corporation initially determines that it had no accumulated earnings and profits (AE&P) at the end of a tax year and it is later determined that the S corporation did have accumulated earnings and profits at the end of the year, the IRS has the authority to waive the tax on excess net passive income if the S corporation can establish that [§ 1375(d)]:

1. its initial determination that it had no AE&P was made in good faith; and

2. it distributed the AE&P within a reasonable period after it was determined that it had AE&P.

### XV.C.7. S Corporation LIFO Recapture Tax

[731 T.M., I.F.; TPS ¶4260.06.]

If a C corporation using the LIFO inventory method (see XI.C.4.c.) makes an S corporation election, it must include a LIFO recapture amount in gross income for its last tax year as a C corporation [§ 1363(d)(1)]. The LIFO recapture amount is equal to the excess of the corporation's inventory amount computed using the FIFO (first-in-first-out) method over its inventory amount computed using the LIFO (last-in-first-out) method [§ 1363(d)(3)]. Any increase in tax that results from including the

LIFO recapture amount in gross income must be paid in four equal installments. The first installment must be paid on or before the due date (excluding extensions) for the last C corporation return and the remaining three installments must be paid on or before the due dates (excluding extensions) of the corporation's returns for the three succeeding tax years. No interest is payable if the installments are paid by the due dates [§ 1363(d)(2)].

The LIFO recapture tax also applies if a C corporation transfers LIFO inventory assets to an S corporation in a tax-free reorganization or other nonrecognition transaction in which the transferred assets constitute transferred basis property [Reg. § 1.1363-2(a)].

# CHAPTER XVI. CHOICE OF ENTITY
>>>>>>>>>>>>>>>>>>>>>>>>>>>>>>>

## XVI.A. Introduction

The organizers of a new business have a wide variety of legal forms to choose from in implementing that new venture. These choices might also be examined when an expanding business needs to change its legal structure. The check-the-box regulations, which took effect in 1997, permit great flexibility in the choice of business entity.

The owners and managers of a business must carefully analyze the available options and determine which form of business entity is the most appropriate for the new (or restructured) enterprise. A variety of tax and non-tax considerations may dictate or influence this choice.

## XVI.B. Types of Business Organizations

[700 T.M., II.A.; TPS ¶4220.01.]

Taxpayers may choose among a myriad of different business forms for operating a business. The most common types of business form are the sole proprietorship, the partnership, the C corporation, the S corporation, and the limited liability company (LLC).

### XVI.B.1. Sole Proprietorship

[700 T.M., II.B.; TPS ¶4220.01.]

A sole proprietorship is a business conducted in one owner's individual capacity and without the organization of a separate legal entity for holding and conducting that business. The business owner merely utilizes a certain portion of his or her directly owned assets for business purposes.

Because no separate entity exists for federal income tax purposes, no separate income tax return is required for this business. Rather, the owner of a sole proprietorship separately reports the income from that business activity directly on the owner's federal income tax return. Income or loss is reported on the Schedule C of the sole proprietor's Form 1040, *U.S. Individual Income Tax Return.* If several sole proprietorships are conducted by one individual, multiple Schedule Cs will be required to be included in that individual's income tax return. If the sole proprietorship is a farming operation, the income or loss will be reported on a Schedule F to be included as part of the individual's Form 1040.

In contrast, if the taxpayer is actively engaged in the management of his or her investment assets, no separate reporting of that activity on an IRS form is required (or permitted); rather, the various items (e.g., interest, dividends, and capital gains) will be reported similarly to all investors who are passive.

Although no separate identity exists for federal income tax purposes, the proprietor may adopt a separate name under which the business is conducted. That business name may be required to be registered with state or local authorities under an "assumed name" or similar state law statute.

For federal income tax purposes, a disposition of a sole proprietorship is not the disposition of a separate "business entity." Rather, the transfer of a sole proprietorship interest is considered the transfer of the various individual assets of the sole proprietorship and will be treated as separate property disposition transactions. Accordingly, the amount of any gain or loss, and the character of the gain or loss, will be measured by reference to each of the various specific assets being transferred, rather than by reference to the sole proprietorship business as an "entity."

### XVI.B.2. Partnership

[700 T.M., II.D.; TPS ¶4020.]

A partnership is an association of two or more persons who organize as co-owners to carry on a business for profit. The business carried on by a partnership can be any trade, occupation, or profession. Any individual or entity, including domestic and foreign persons, trusts, estates, corporations, and other partnerships, may be a partner in a partnership. There are no limitations on the number of partners.

For federal income tax purposes, a partnership includes a syndicate, group, pool, joint venture, or unincorporated organization through, or by means of which, any business, financial operation, or venture is carried on, and that is not, for federal income tax purposes, a corporation, trust, or estate [§ 761(a)]. However, an organization may be excluded from the application of the partnership provisions at the election of all the members of the organization if the organization is availed of [§ 761(a); Reg. § 1.761-2(a)(1)]:

- for investment purposes only and not for the active conduct of a business;
- for the joint production, extraction, or use of property, but not for the purposes of selling services or property produced or extracted; or
- by dealers in securities for a short period for the purpose of underwriting, selling, or distributing a particular issue of securities, if the income of the members of the organization may be adequately determined without the computation of partnership taxable income.

For state law purposes, a partnership is recognized as an entity that is separate from its members. For example, the assets of the firm are treated as belonging to a business unit and are considered to be separate and distinct from the individual assets of its members. Title to property, particularly real estate, may be acquired by a partnership in the name of the partnership. However, whether an entity is an entity separate from its owners for federal income tax purposes is a matter of federal law and does not depend on whether the entity is recognized as an entity under local law [Reg. § 301.7701-1(a)(1)].

A partnership is managed by its partners and the partners may appoint one or more managing partners who have the primary management responsibility. Ostensibly, however, all partners can act on behalf of the partnership.

### XVI.B.2.a. Limited Partnership

[700 T.M., II.E.; TPS ¶4010.02.]

A limited partnership is a partnership formed by two or more persons under the limited partnership laws of a state. The partnership must have one or more general partners and one or more limited partners. Because the limited partnership statute does require that at least one partner be a general partner, an alternative business format may be the organization of a limited liability partnership (see XVI.B.2.b.) or a limited liability limited partnership (see XVI.B.2.c.) that limits the liability of every owner of the entity.

To enable the formation of a limited partnership, an authorizing state statute must be in effect and must provide for the formation of limited partnerships. When organized to achieve limited partnership status, the partnership must substantially comply with the requirements of the applicable state limited partnership statute. If the partnership so complies, the liability of a limited partner for the partnership debts or obligations is limited to the extent of the capital which that partner has contributed or agreed to contribute. The general partner remains personally liable, however, for the debts of this partnership. A corporation may function as the general partner. If the corporation is insubstantial, the question arises whether the partnership itself has been transformed (for U.S. tax purposes) into a corporation.

Most states have enacted the Revised Uniform Limited Partnership Act (RULPA) to enable the formation of limited partnerships in their respective jurisdictions. This Act provides that two or more persons desiring to form a limited partnership shall file in the office of the Secretary of State of the state in which the limited partnership has its principal office a signed certificate of limited partnership.

### XVI.B.2.b. Limited Liability Partnership

[700 T.M., II.F.; TPS ¶4020.02.]

The search for possible relief from liability by professional practice entities has encouraged states to enact limited liability partnership (LLP) provisions to facilitate an alternative form of doing business. The LLP follows the basic structure of a general partnership but has unique features that allow partners to benefit from partial limited liability. This form of business may be appropriate for any partnership that cannot operate as a limited partnership (thus attaining limited liability for the limited partners) because of the active conduct of the partners in the business.

In an LLP, partners often remain personally liable for their own wrongful acts and the acts of those whom they directly supervise, but their personal assets are protected from claims involving the wrongful acts of another partner. Creditors and others, however, still have recourse against partnership assets, including individual partners' investments. State statutes vary on the types of businesses that may be conducted by an LLP.

Whether a partner in an LLP is treated as a general partner or a limited partner can have ancillary effects, such as impacting the deductibility of certain expenses. For example, for purposes of deducting passive activity losses, a limited partner is presumed not to materially participate in the partnership and, therefore, generally is limited as to deductions that may be taken [§ 469(c), § 469(h)(2)]. In contrast, in a general partnership, all partners are considered general partners and therefore should not be affected by this limited partner rule.

### XVI.B.2.c. Limited Liability Limited Partnership

[700 T.M., II.G.; TPS ¶4020.02.]

A limited liability limited partnership (LLLP) is a limited partnership providing traditional limited liability to the limited partners. This form of entity also provides, however, limited liability to the general partners to the same extent permitted to a partner in an limited liability partnership. The LLLP format is not authorized by all states. Therefore, before the LLLP format is chosen in a state that authorizes organization as an LLLP, it is important to ascertain whether the limited liability of the general partners of the LLLP will be respected in a foreign state (a state other than the state of organization) where activity is being conducted.

### XVI.B.2.d. Publicly Traded Partnership

[700 T.M., II.H.; TPS ¶4020.04.]

A publicly traded partnership (also often referred to as a "master limited partnership") is a vehicle for holding assets in a limited partnership form while permitting liquidity to the holder of the interest through a listing of the partnership ownership units on a stock exchange or other comparable market. A publicly traded partnership (PTP) is often used to hold oil and gas assets, equipment leasing assets, minerals, and real estate.

One of two methods of creating a PTP usually is utilized: (i) a "roll-up" of existing partnership interests that already hold such assets, in exchange for interests (such as partnership units or depositary rights) in the PTP, or (ii) the "roll-out," which involves a corporate reorganization or liquidation followed by the transfer of assets to the PTP in exchange for partnership interests. The beneficial interest in the underlying partnership interest in the PTP is then assigned to a unit or depositary right, registered and listed, and sold to the public.

Although organized as a partnership under state law, a PTP is treated as a corporation for federal tax purposes, except in the case of PTPs where 90% or more of the gross income is "qualifying income" (i.e., passive-type income or natural resource-type income) [§ 7704]. The exception for the PTP having passive-type income is to enable federal tax treatment equivalent to regulated investment company status.

### XVI.B.3. C Corporation

[700 T.M., II.J.; TPS ¶4610.01.]

A regular corporation (also known as a C corporation) is an entity created by state law that is separate and distinct from its owners. A corporation may be formed only through compliance with a state incorporation statute. Although the requirements vary from state to state, annual board meetings and corporate resolutions can be critical to maintaining corporate status and protecting the shareholders with limited liability. Of all the available business entity choices, the limited liability of the regular corporation is most widely understood.

A corporation can be closely held (i.e., have only one or a small number of shareholders) or can be publicly held (i.e., have a large number of owners with the shares sold on a public market). Some states also have separate business law code provisions for the organization of closely held corporations, sometimes identified as "statutory close corporation" provisions.

A corporation is managed by its directors and officers. These directors and officers do not need to be owners of any shares of the corporation. The directors are elected by the shareholders. The shareholders (in their capacity as shareholders) have no power to commit the corporation to obligations made to others.

A corporation is subject to federal income tax separately from its owners. The profits accumulated after payment of this corporate level tax are subject to further federal income tax when those profits are distributed to the shareholder/owners as dividends (i.e., there is a second level of tax at the shareholder level on distributed corporate earnings).

There are a number of special rules that apply to corporations that are personal service corporations. In the broadest sense, a personal service corporation is a corporation that performs personal services as part of its business. However, there is no single definition of a personal service corporation and a corporation may be a personal service corporation under some provisions of the Code, but not under others.

The IRS is authorized to reallocate income and deductions between a personal service corporation and its employee-owners if: (i) the personal service corporation performs substantially all of its services for one other corporation, partnership, or other entity, and (ii) the principal purpose the employee-owners formed the personal service corporation was to avoid tax by obtaining tax benefits that wouldn't have been available to them if they were not operating as a corporation [§ 269A(a)]. For this purpose, a corporation is a personal service corporation if its principal activity is the performance of personal services and those services are substantially performed by its employee-owners (employees who own more than 10% of the outstanding stock of the corporation) [§ 269A(b)].

Personal service corporations are subject to special rules in areas other than income reallocation, including income tax computation, accounting methods, and accounting periods. In addition, personal service corporations may be subject to the passive-loss limitations and the at-risk rules in situations in which other corporations are not. Finally, the personal service income of a personal service corporation may trigger the personal holding company tax and the accumulated earnings tax.

### XVI.B.4. S Corporation

[700 T.M., II.K.; TPS ¶4220.]

An S corporation is a special type of corporation for federal income tax purposes that satisfies the qualification requirements of Subchapter S of the Internal Revenue Code. When an S corporation is organized under state law incorporation statutes, it is generally not specially designated as an "S corporation" for local law purposes.

By making an S corporation election, a corporation achieves special "pass-through" status for federal income tax purposes (and for state income tax purposes, in certain states). All shareholders of the corporation must consent to this election. To be eligible for S corporation status, the corporation must: (i) be a domestic corporation, (ii) not be an ineligible corporation, (iii) not have more than 100 shareholders, (iv) not have a shareholder who is not an individual, estate, a certain type of trust, a qualified plan or a tax-exempt charitable organization, (v) not have any nonresident alien shareholders, and (vi) not have more than one class of stock [§ 1361].

The effect of the S corporation election is that the corporation ordinarily will bear no federal income tax consequences at the entity level. All corporate level income will be treated as currently received directly by the shareholders without regard to whether that income actually is distributed by the corporation on a current basis to the shareholders.

In determining the shareholder's income tax liability, the shareholder is treated as in receipt of:

1. those items of income (including tax-exempt income), gain, loss, deduction, or credit the separate treatment of which could affect the liability for income tax of any shareholder; and

2. nonseparately computed income or loss (the remaining portion of the total income of the corporation after allocation of the income and other items where required as "separately stated").

An S corporation can own the stock of a domestic subsidiary. That corporation, if owned 100% and if electing status as a "qualified subchapter S subsidiary," is not treated as a separate entity for federal tax purposes. Rather, all assets, liabilities, and items of income, deduction, and credit of that subsidiary are to be treated as assets, liabilities, and such items of the parent S corporation itself.

### XVI.B.5. Limited Liability Company

[700 T.M., II.I., TPS ¶4100.]

A limited liability company (LLC), formed and operated pursuant to a state statute, is a hybrid entity that provides insulation from liabilities to the same extent as a corporation. Traditionally, an LLC is treated as a partnership for federal tax purposes. This combination of the protection for all owners from personal liability for the obligations of the entity, coupled with favorable pass-through federal income tax treatment, has spurred the enactment of LLC legislation in all states.

Under the check-the-box entity classification regulations, depending on circumstances and an election, an LLC may be classified as a partnership, an association taxed as a corporation, or a disregarded entity.

Ordinarily the members of an LLC have the option of participating directly in the management of the business or designating certain members or nonmembers as managers.

Delaware permits a LLC to register separate series of ownership interests (together, a "series LLC"). This innovative concept allows LLCs to establish separate series of members, managers, or interests, with separate rights, powers, or duties, including rights to profits and losses, with respect to specific property or obligations. For purposes of Delaware law, each of the series established in an LLC functions as a distinct state law entity. For example, separate series in a single LLC can, but are not required to, have a separate business purpose or business objective. The most discussed characteristic of the series LLC is the ability of each series to shield property from liabilities incurred in or against other series in the LLC. Thus, an LLC that operates two businesses might place each business into a separate series so that liabilities of one do not jeopardize the assets of the other. While this effect is available under other states' LLC laws through the use of subsidiary single-member LLCs, these lower-tier LLCs would carry with them additional fees and state tax filing requirements. The simplicity of a single fee and state tax return in Delaware offers relief from this multiple entity treatment.

## XVI.C. Check-the-Box Entity Classification Regulations

[700 T.M., III.D.; TPS ¶4020.03.]

Under the check-the-box entity classification regulations, most unincorporated business entities may elect their entity classification for federal income tax purposes. An organization qualifies to make the election if it is an eligible business entity (see XVI.C.1.). The choice of entity classification generally depends on how many owners an eligible entity has (see XVI.C.2.). If an eligible entity does not make a classification election, it is classified based on a set of default classification rules (see XVI.C.3.). The check-the-box regulations contain a set of rules for making an entity classification election (see XVI.C.4.).

### XVI.C.1. Qualification for Entity Classification Election

[700 T.M., III.D.; TPS ¶4020.03.]

To qualify for the entity classification election, an organization must be separate from its owners for federal tax purposes, it must be a business entity, and it must be an eligible entity.

Whether an organization is an entity separate from its owners for federal tax purposes is a matter of federal tax law. An entity formed under local law is not always recognized as a separate entity for federal tax purposes. A joint venture or other contractual arrangement may create a separate entity for federal tax purposes if the participants carry on a trade, business, financial operation, or venture and they divide the profits. However, a joint undertaking to merely share expenses does not create a separate entity. Similarly, mere co-ownership of property does not create a separate entity [Reg. § 301.7701-1(a)].

A business entity is any entity separate from its owners that is not properly classified as a trust or otherwise subject to special treatment under the Code (e.g., REMICs, qualified settlement funds). A business entity includes an entity with a single owner that may be disregarded as an entity separate from its owner [Reg. § 301.7701-2(a)].

An eligible entity is any business entity that is not classified as a corporation under one of the following eight categories of per se corporations [Reg. § 301.7701-3(a), § 301.7701-2(b)]:

1. a business entity organized under a federal or state statute, or under a statute of a federally recognized Indian tribe, if the statute describes or refers to the entity as incorporated or as a corporation, body corporate, or body politic;

2. a business entity organized under a state statute, if the statute describes or refers to the entity as a joint-stock company or joint-stock association;

3. an insurance company;

4. a state-chartered business entity conducting banking activities, if any of its deposits are insured under the Federal Deposit Insurance Act or a similar federal statute;

5. a business entity wholly owned by a state or any political subdivision thereof;

6. a business entity that is taxable as a corporation under a provision of the Code other than § 7701(a)(3);

7. a foreign business entity designated by the IRS as a per se corporation (see Reg. § 301.7701-2(b)(8) for a list of such foreign business entities); and

8. an entity created or organized under the laws of more than one jurisdiction (i.e., a business entity with multiple charters) if the entity is treated as a corporation in one or more of those jurisdictions.

An association is also treated as an eligible entity. An association includes a business entity that elects to be treated as a corporation under Reg. § 301.7701-3 (see XVI.C.2.) and a foreign entity that becomes an association taxable as a corporation under the foreign default rule (see XVI.C.3.).

### *XVI.C.2. Entity Classification Election*

[700 T.M., III.D.6.; TPS ¶4020.03.D.]

The entity classification that may be elected by an eligible entity depends on the number of owners it has. An eligible entity with two or more owners may elect to be classified as either an association taxable as a corporation or a partnership. An eligible entity with a single owner may elect to be classified as either an association taxable as a corporation or a disregarded entity [Reg. § 301.7701-3(a)]. For federal tax purposes, a disregarded entity is treated as if it is not separate from its owner. If it is owned by an individual, it is treated as a sole proprietorship. If it is owned by a corporation, it is treated in the same manner as a branch or division of the corporation [Reg. § 301.7701-2(a)].

### XVI.C.3. Default Entity Classification Rules

[700 T.M., III.D.7.; TPS ¶4020.03.E.]

If an eligible entity does not make an entity classification election, its tax status is determined under the default classification rules. An eligible entity's default classification depends on (i) the number of owners it has, (ii) whether it is a domestic or foreign entity, and (iii) if it is a foreign entity, whether any owner has unlimited liability.

A domestic eligible entity that does not make the election defaults to one of the following two entity classifications [Reg. § 301.7701-3(b)(1)]:

1. a partnership, if it has two or more owners; or

2. a disregarded entity, if it has one owner.

A foreign eligible entity that does not make the election defaults to one of the following three entity classifications [Reg. § 301.7701-3(b)(2)]:

1. a partnership, if it has two or more owners and at least one owner does not have limited liability;

2. an association taxable as a corporation, if all owners have limited liability; or

3. a disregarded entity, if it has a single owner that does not have limited liability.

The default rules apply only to eligible entities formed after 1996. Eligible entities in existence before January 1, 1997, retain their existing entity classification (unless they have elected to change their classification) [Reg. § 301.7701-3(b)(3)(i)].

### XVI.C.4. Procedures for Making Entity Classification Election

#### XVI.C.4.a. Who Should Make the Entity Classification Election?

[700 T.M., III.D.8.a.; TPS ¶4020.03.G.1.]

An eligible entity needs to make an entity classification election only if:

- it desires to use an initial classification that is different from the classification it would be assigned under the default classification rules; or

- it desires to change its classification.

Although an eligible entity desiring to use its default classification need not make the election, protective elections are permitted by the IRS.

The following types of eligible entities are deemed to have made the election to be an association taxable as a corporation [Reg. § 301.7701-3(c)(1)(v)]:

- an eligible entity that is tax-exempt under § 501(a);

- a real estate investment trust (REIT); and

- an eligible entity that timely files Form 2553 to elect classification as an S corporation (if it meets all other requirements to qualify as an S corporation).

#### XVI.C.4.b. How Is the Entity Classification Election Made?

[700 T.M., III.D.8.b., III.D.8.c.; TPS ¶4020.03.G.2., .03.G.4., and .03.G.5.]

An eligible entity makes the election by filing Form 8832, *Entity Classification Election*, with the IRS service center designated on the form. The IRS will not accept the election unless all information required by the form and instructions (including the taxpayer identification number of the electing entity) is provided on Form 8832 [Reg. § 301.7701-3(c)(1)(i)]. The election must be signed by (i) each member of the electing entity who is an owner at the time the election is filed, and (ii) any officer, manager, or member of the electing entity who is authorized to make the election and who represents to have such authorization under penalties of perjury [Reg. § 301.7701-3(c)(2)(i)].

An election is effective on the date specified on Form 8832 or, if no date is specified, on the date the election is filed. However, an effective date specified on Form 8832 will be respected only if it is not more than 75 days before and not more than 12 months after the date on which the election is filed. If the specified effective date is too early or too late, the election will be treated as effective 75 days before (if too early) or 12 months after (if too late) the date on which the election is filed [Reg. § 301.7701-3(c)(1)(iii)].

### *XVI.C.4.c. Additional Notifications*

[700 T.M., III.D.8.b.; ¶4020.03.G.3.]

If an eligible entity is required to file a federal tax or information return for the tax year for which the election is made, a copy of Form 8832 must be attached to that return. If not, a copy of Form 8832 must be attached to the federal tax or information return of every direct or indirect owner of the entity for the owner's tax year that includes the date on which the election was effective. The election will not be invalidated by the failure to meet such requirements, but penalties may be imposed [Reg. § 301.7701-3(c)(1)(ii)].

### *XVI.C.4.d. Election to Change Entity Classification*

[700 T.M., III.D.8.d.; ¶4020.03.G.2.]

An eligible entity may elect to change its existing entity classification (based on the same rules discussed in XVI.C.4.b.). However, an eligible entity generally cannot make an election to change its existing entity classification during the 60-month period after the effective date of its previous election. An entity classification election made on the date of formation of an eligible entity is not considered to be a change and, therefore, another election to change classification within 60 months of formation does not trigger this rule. In addition, the IRS may permit an election within 60 months if more than 50% of the ownership interests in the entity are owned by persons who did not own an interest in the entity on the filing date or effective date of the previous election [Reg. § 301.7701-3(c)(1)(iv)].

### *XVI.C.4.e. Relief for Late Entity Classification Elections*

[700 T.M., III.D.8.b(5); ¶4020.03.G.5.]

Eligible entities seeking to make a late entity classification election (for an initial classification or for a change in classification) may request relief under Rev. Proc. 2009-41, 2009-39 I.R.B. 439. This relief is available for an eligible entity that has not filed a federal tax return or information return for the first year in which the election was intended because the due date has not passed for that year's return, or for an eligible entity that has filed all required federal tax returns or information returns consistent with the requested classification. In addition, the eligible entity must have reasonable cause for its failure to make a timely election.

An eligible entity may request relief within three years and 75 days from the requested effective date by filing with the applicable IRS service center a completed and appropriately signed Form 8832. The IRS service center will determine whether the requirements for granting the late entity classification election have been satisfied and will notify the entity of its determination. Eligible entities not meeting these requirements may request a letter ruling for late entity classification relief.

## XVI.D. Comparison of Different Types of Business Organization

[700 T.M.; ¶4220.]

The form of an entity generally does not determine its ultimate success or failure as a business venture. However, the tax and non-tax attributes of each form can significantly affect the business's ability to raise capital as well as to generate and retain earnings. For example, a C corporation is subject to entity-level taxation, unlike the other forms of entities, but is generally a more viable entity for raising capital. Thus, the specific advantages and disadvantages of each form should be carefully weighed before the form is selected. This discussion will focus on the tax considerations of selecting the form of an entity; however, it is important to recognize that there are also many non-tax considerations that will come into play in making this choice. This discussion does not contain any separate analysis of LLCs because LLCs are generally treated as partnerships or disregarded entities for federal tax purposes.

In weighing the tax advantages and disadvantages of a particular form of entity, the ramifications of the choice should be considered for the entire life of the enterprise — beginning with its formation, during its operating stage, and upon its liquidation or disposition. At the formation stage, the major tax considerations include the limitations that may be placed on the types of persons who may own an interest in the entity, the tax consequences of forming the entity, and the accounting period and methods available to the entity. At the operating stage, the important tax considerations include the extent to which the entity itself is subject to taxation, the methods of allocating profits and losses among the entity's owners, the ability of the owners to utilize tax losses generated by the entity, the taxation of distributions to the owners by the entity, and the availability of tax-free fringe benefits to the entity's owners. At the liquidation/disposition stage, the major considerations in selecting a form of business entity are the tax consequences of a sale of an interest in a business entity, the sale of all or a portion of the assets of the entity, or the liquidation of an owner's interest in the entity.

Obviously, one particular type of entity may not be the optimal choice for all the phases in the life of a business. Thus, the ease of later converting from one form of entity to another is also an important consideration.

### XVI.D.1. Formation Stage

### XVI.D.1.a. Limitations on Ownership

[700 T.M., V.C.; ¶4220.02.C.]

**Sole Proprietorship.** A sole proprietorship is, by definition, limited to a single owner. As a practical matter, the owner must be an individual (although a decedent's estate could conceivably be the owner of a sole proprietorship).

**Partnership.** For federal tax purposes, there are no limitations on the number of partners a partnership can have or who can be a member of the partnership, provided the partnership has at least two members and at least one member is a general partner. Thus, individuals, estates, trusts, corporations, foreign persons, and tax-exempt entities can all be partners of a partnership for federal tax purposes. However, in certain cases, state law may impose some limitations on who can be a member of a partnership. For example, state law may only recognize individuals who are licensed physicians as members of a partnership providing medical services.

A partnership can have different classes of partners, each having different economic rights in the partnership.

*C Corporation.* As in the case of a partnership, no limitations are imposed on the number or type of persons who can hold stock in a C corporation for federal income tax purposes. However, as in the case of a partnership, state law may prohibit an unlicensed individual from being a shareholder in a professional corporation.

A C corporation can have different classes of stock carrying different economic and voting rights.

*S Corporation.* Unlike a C corporation or partnership, substantial restrictions are placed on the number and types of taxpayers who can be shareholders in an S corporation. An S corporation may not have more than 100 shareholders. All members of a family (and their estates), up to seven generations, are treated as one shareholder for purposes of this limit. Only individuals (other than nonresident aliens), estates, certain trusts, and certain tax-exempt organizations can be S corporation shareholders. Furthermore, an S corporation is limited to a single class of stock, although differences in voting rights are permitted. Thus, an S corporation cannot issue stock that is preferred as to dividends or rights in liquidation [§ 1361(b)(1), § 1361(c)].

### XVI.D.1.b. Tax Consequences on Formation

[700 T.M., V.A.; TPS ¶4220.02.B.]

*Sole Proprietorship.* No gain or loss is recognized upon the formation of a sole proprietorship. The assets of the business should, however, be clearly separated from the owner's personal assets to facilitate the maintenance of adequate books and records for the business.

*Partnership.* A partnership (including an LLC) can be formed tax-free. Generally, no gain is recognized by either the partnership or the contributing partners on the contribution of property to a partnership in exchange for an interest in the partnership [§ 721]. Unlike a transfer of property to a corporation in exchange for stock, nonrecognition treatment applies to the transferor on a contribution of property to a partnership regardless of whether the transferor has 80% control of the partnership.

However, gain is recognized to a contributing partner if the partner is relieved of liabilities in excess of the basis of the property he or she contributes to the partnership [§ 752(b), § 731]. The amount of liabilities that a partner is relieved of is determined by reducing the amount of the personal liabilities of the partner that are assumed by the partnership by the partner's share of partnership liabilities immediately following the transfer [Reg. § 1.722-1, *Ex. 2*]. Because netting of liabilities is allowed in this manner, it is less likely that gain will be recognized on the transfer of encumbered property to a partnership than if such property is transferred to a corporation [§ 357(c)(1)].

A partner also has taxable income to the extent an interest in the partnership is received in exchange for services performed (or to be performed) for the partnership [§ 83; Reg. § 1.83-3(f)].

A partnership's basis in assets it receives as a contribution to capital is equal to the basis of the property in the hands of the contributing partner increased by the amount of gain recognized to the partner on the contribution [§ 723]. A partner's initial basis in his or her partnership interest is generally equal to the sum of the amount of money plus the basis to the partner of other property contributed to the partnership and is increased by the amount of gain recognized by the partner on the contribution [§ 722].

*C Corporation.* A corporation can be formed tax-free; however, the requirements for nonrecognition treatment at the shareholder level are stricter than those for a partnership. A corporation recognizes no gain or loss on the receipt of money or property in exchange for its stock [§ 1032].

Nonrecognition treatment applies to the transferor shareholders only if: (i) the property is exchanged solely for stock in the corporation, and (ii) immediately after the transfer, the transferor shareholders control the corporation [§ 351]. For this purpose, control is defined as ownership of stock possessing at least 80% of the total combined voting power of all classes of voting stock and at least 80% of the total number of shares of all nonvoting classes of the corporation's stock [§ 351(a), § 368(c)]. Gain is recognized by a transferor shareholder who receives property other than stock in the corporation [§ 351(b)]. The assumption by the corporation of transferor-shareholder liabilities may be treated as the receipt of nonqualifying property. If encumbered property is transferred to a corporation in exchange for its stock, or if the corporation otherwise assumes liabilities of the transferor, gain is recognized by the transferor shareholder to the extent the liabilities effectively transferred to the corporation exceed the total adjusted basis of the property contributed by the transferor shareholder [§ 357(c)(1)]. However, certain liabilities, including those that would be deductible by the transferor if paid, are ignored [§ 357(c)(3)(A)].

As with the formation of a partnership, nonrecognition treatment does not apply if the stock is received in exchange for services performed (or to be performed) for the corporation [§ 83; Reg. § 1.83-3(f)].

The corporation takes a basis in the property received equal to the basis of the property in the hands of the transferor shareholder increased by any gain recognized by the shareholder on the transfer [§ 362(a)]. The shareholder's basis in any stock received is equal to the shareholder's basis in the property transferred, increased by any gain recognized by the shareholder and decreased by any money and the fair market value of any other nonqualifying property received by the shareholder [§ 358(a)(1)].

*S Corporation.* An S corporation is subject to the same rules that govern the formation of a C corporation.

### XVI.D.1.c. Selection of Accounting Period and Method

[700 T.M., VI.B.5., VI.B.6.; TPS ¶4220.02.D., .02.E.]

*Sole Proprietorship.* Because a sole proprietorship is not an entity separate from its owner, the tax year of the sole proprietorship's owner is the tax year on which the sole proprietorship reports its income or loss. Virtually all individuals use the calendar year for tax reporting purposes, although an individual is allowed to change to a fiscal year with the IRS's permission.

A sole proprietor is generally eligible to use the cash method of accounting unless the sole proprietorship is a tax shelter. However, a sole proprietorship generally will not fall within the definition of a tax shelter as long as its owner is active in the business.

*Partnership.* If one or more partners with the same tax year own a majority interest in partnership capital and profits, the partnership must use the tax year of those partners. If a majority of its partners are not using the same tax year, the partnership must use the same tax year as that of all of its principal partners. If all of the partnership's principal partners are not using the same tax year, the partnership must use the tax year end that provides the least aggregate deferral to its partners, unless it can establish a business purpose for another tax year

[§ 706(b)(1)(B)]. In certain cases, a partnership may elect to use a tax year not satisfying the above requirements, provided the partnership agrees to make non-interest bearing tax deposits that are designed to compensate the IRS for the loss of revenue resulting from the partners' deferral of income tax [§ 444(c)(1), § 7519]. Generally, only tax years providing a deferral of income for three months or less can be adopted under this option [§ 444(b)(1)]. Thus, for example, a newly formed partnership otherwise required to use a calendar year can elect to adopt a year ending with the month of September, October, or November.

A partnership generally is entitled to use either the cash method or the accrual method of accounting. However, a partnership cannot use the cash method if: (i) it is a tax shelter, or (ii) it has a C corporation (other than a personal service corporation) as a partner and the partnership's average annual gross receipts exceed $5 million as computed under a three-year test [§ 448(a)(2), § 448(a)(3), § 448(b)(3)]. For these purposes, a tax shelter includes, among other things: (i) a partnership whose interests have been offered for sale in any offering required to be registered with any federal or state agency regulating the offering of securities for sale, and (ii) a partnership more than 35% of whose losses are allocated to limited partners during a year [§ 448(d)(3), § 461(i)(3)]. Once a partnership uses the accrual method, it cannot change to the cash method without the consent of the IRS.

*C Corporation.* Generally, a corporation is free to adopt any tax year it wishes. However, a corporation that is a personal service corporation (PSC) generally must use the calendar year as its tax year unless it establishes a business purpose for another year end to the satisfaction of the IRS. For this purpose, a PSC is a corporation whose principal activity is the performance of personal services that are substantially performed by shareholder-employees. Certain PSCs otherwise required to adopt a calendar tax year may elect to adopt a deferral fiscal year ending with the month of September, October, or November. However, if a PSC elects to use a deferral fiscal year, it may be subject to a limitation on the amount it can deduct in a year for compensation and other payments it makes to its shareholder-employees.

A C corporation is required to use the accrual method of accounting unless: (i) it is a qualified PSC, or (ii) its average annual gross receipts are $5 million or less as computed under a three-year test. A qualified PSC for these purposes is a corporation substantially all of the activities of which involve performing services in the fields of health, law, engineering, architecture, accounting, actuarial science, performing arts, or consulting, and substantially all of the stock of which is held (directly or indirectly) by employees who perform the services, retired employees who formerly performed the services, the estates of such an employee, or certain persons who acquired the stock of such an employee upon his or her death. Once a C corporation has used the accrual method, it cannot change to the cash method, even if it satisfies one of these tests, without the consent of the IRS.

*S Corporation.* Generally, an S corporation must use a calendar tax year, unless it establishes a business purpose for a fiscal year to the satisfaction of the IRS. However, certain S corporations otherwise required to adopt a calendar tax year may elect to adopt a deferral tax year that ends with the month of September, October, or November. An S corporation electing to use a deferral tax year must make tax deposits designed to offset the loss of revenue to the IRS caused by the deferral of income to the shareholders through the corporation's use of a fiscal year.

An S corporation generally is eligible to use either the cash method or the accrual method of accounting. However, an S corporation cannot use the cash method if it is a tax shelter [§ 448(a)(3)]. For this purpose, a tax shelter includes, among other things: (i) an S corporation if its stock has been offered for sale in any offering required to be registered with any federal or state agency regulating sales of securities, and (ii) an S corporation if more than 35% of its losses for a year are allocated to persons who do not actively participate in the business [§ 448(d)(3), § 461(i)(3)].

### XVI.D.2. Operating Stage

#### XVI.D.2.a. Federal Taxation of Business Entities

[700 T.M., VI.B.1.; TPS ¶4220.03.A.1.]

*Sole Proprietorship.* A sole proprietorship is not treated as an entity separate from its owner for federal income tax purposes. Thus, the income generated by the sole proprietorship is simply included on its owner's individual income tax return along with his or her other items of income and deduction.

Because a sole proprietorship is not an entity separate from its owner, a sole proprietor generally is not taxed on cash or property withdrawn from the business. Thus, the double tax problem associated with a distribution of cash from a C corporation is irrelevant to a sole proprietor.

A sole proprietor is subject to self-employment taxes on the earnings from his or her business [§ 1402(a)].

*Partnership.* While a partnership is treated as an entity separate from its owners for some tax purposes, it is not a separate tax-paying entity [§ 701]. The partnership's items of income, gain, loss, deduction, and credit are passed through to its owners (i.e., the partners) and included in their income tax returns for the year that includes or ends with the end of the partnership's tax year [§ 706].

Although partners are taxed on the pass-through of the partnership's earnings, they generally are not taxed on cash or property withdrawn from the business. Thus, partnerships are not subject to a double tax like C corporations, whose earnings are taxed first at the corporate level and then again at the shareholder level when distributed to them as dividends.

General partners and limited partners providing services are subject to self-employment taxes on the earnings from their business [§ 1402(a)].

*C Corporation.* Unlike a sole proprietorship or a partnership, a C corporation is subject to an entity-level federal income tax on its taxable income. A separate set of corporate tax brackets applies to C corporations (see XIII.C.2.a. for the corporate tax brackets). The federal tax rates imposed on the first $75,000 of taxable income of a C corporation may be lower than the individual income tax rate at that income level, depending on the individual's filing status, etc. Thus, income tax savings may be achieved by operating a business as a C corporation if its taxable income is not expected to greatly exceed $75,000 for the long term and its earnings are retained, rather than distributed to its shareholders. However, note that a qualified personal service corporation — a corporation substantially all of whose activities involve performing services in the fields of health, law, engineering, architecture, accounting, actuarial science, performing arts, or consulting — is taxed at a flat 35% tax rate and does not benefit from the lower tax brackets that generally apply to C corporations.

A C corporation does not, however, have complete flexibility to accumulate its income to avoid the second level of tax at the shareholder level. A corporation that accumulates (rather than distributes) its income may be subject to one of two penalty taxes, which are in addition to the regular income tax:

1. A corporation that accumulates its earnings beyond its reasonable business needs may be subject to the accumulated earnings tax (AET). The AET is a penalty

tax assessed at a rate equal to 20% of the corporation's "accumulated taxable income" in excess of its business needs. A corporation is allowed to accumulate at least $250,000 of earnings ($150,000 in the case of certain PSCs), however, regardless of its business needs, before the tax is assessed. The AET is not imposed if the corporation is subject to the personal holding company tax [§ 531 through § 537].

2. If the corporation is closely held and has significant amounts of passive income (such as interest, dividends, rents, and certain royalties), it may be subject to the personal holding company penalty tax if it fails to distribute its earnings to its shareholders as dividends. The personal holding company tax is assessed at a rate equal to 20% of the corporation's "undistributed personal holding company income" [§ 541 through § 547].

Even if the penalty taxes do not apply to the corporation, any current income tax savings that can be generated by operating as a C corporation must be weighed against the fact that a shareholder-level tax is imposed when the earnings are distributed to the shareholders as dividends, or when the corporation liquidates.

The dividends-received deduction is another advantage of operating as a C corporation. Unlike other types of taxpayers, a C corporation can exclude from its income a portion of the dividend income it receives from other corporations. The amount of the exclusion, which takes the form of a deduction, ranges from 100% for dividends from a member of the recipient corporation's affiliated group, to 80% for dividends from other corporations that are at least 20% owned by the recipient, to 70% for dividends received from corporations in which the recipient owns less than 20% [§ 243].

**S Corporation.** A corporation that has been an S corporation since its inception is generally not subject to any corporate-level taxes. Like a partnership, its items of income, gain, loss, deduction, and credit pass through to its shareholders and are reported by them on their individual income tax returns. An S corporation may, however, be subject to corporate-level taxes if it was originally formed as a C corporation and converted to S status after its initial tax year. If an S corporation has accumulated earnings and profits from its years as a C corporation, and it has passive income including interest, rents, royalties, and dividends exceeding 25% of its gross receipts, it could be subject to a 35% passive income tax. Also, an S corporation that was formerly a C corporation can be subject to a 35% built-in gains tax on the C corporation appreciation in its assets that are disposed of during its first 10 years as an S corporation.

S corporation shareholders are not subject to the self-employment tax on their earnings from an S corporation. On the other hand, the S corporation and its shareholder-employees with wages are subject to FICA taxes on those wages.

### XVI.D.2.b. Allocation of Items of Income, Gain, Loss, Deduction, and Credit
[700 T.M., VI.B.2.; TPS ¶4220.03.]

**Sole Proprietorship.** Allocation of items of income, gain, loss, deduction, and credit of a sole proprietorship to its owner is not an issue because a sole proprietorship is, by definition, limited to a single owner.

**Partnership.** The ability to make special allocations of partnership items of income, gain, loss, deduction, and credit is one of the primary advantages that the partnership form of organization has over an S corporation. Partners generally have much more flexibility in allocating these items among themselves than do S corporation shareholders. Partners, through the partnership agreement, generally can provide for the allocation of the partnership's items of income or loss among themselves in any manner, provided that the allocation has "substantial economic effect" or otherwise reflects the partners' economic interests in the partnership [§ 704(b); Reg. § 1.704-1(b)]. The partnership agreement can provide for special allocations of specific items of partnership income or expense (e.g., depreciation) or of the partnership's "bottom line" profit or loss. An allocation typically satisfies the substantial economic effect, or the economic interests, standard if the partner who receives the allocation of income or loss for tax purposes also receives the corresponding economic benefit or burden [Reg. § 1.704-1(b)(2)(ii)(a)].

*C Corporation.* The allocation issue does not arise for a C corporation because its items of income, gain, loss, deduction, and credit do not pass through to its share-holders. However, "special" allocations can effectively be achieved through additional preferred classes of stock with varying dividends paid to the holders of those shares.

*S Corporation.* S corporations are subject to a rigid one-class-of-stock require-ment. As a result, an S corporation's items of income, gain, loss, deduction, and credit are allocated among its shareholders on a daily pro rata basis (sometimes called the per-share per-day basis) [§ 1377]. No special allocations of S corporation income or loss are permitted. This is a clear disadvantage to using an S corporation instead of a partnership. There are, however, some limited techniques that can be used to indirectly achieve the effect of special allocations. For example, debt instruments and compensation to shareholder/employees can sometimes be used as a means to achieve the same result as a special allocation by a partnership.

### XVI.D.2.c. Limitations on Use of Losses

[700 T.M., VI.B.7.; TPS ¶4220.03.C.]

*Sole Proprietorship,* The losses generated by a sole proprietorship are reported directly on its owner's individual income tax return. However, three limitations may apply to the deductibility of losses by the sole proprietor. First, a net loss from an activity not engaged in for profit may be totally nondeductible under the hobby-loss rules (see VIII.J.) [§ 183]. Second, the deductibility of a loss generated by a sole proprietorship may be limited under the at-risk rules (see VIII.E.). Finally, if the business enterprise constitutes a passive activity with respect to the owner, any losses from the activity may be disallowed under the passive activity loss rules (see VIII.F.).

*Partnership.* The losses of a partnership are passed through to its partners. Losses passed through to a partner from a partnership are potentially subject to three limitations on their deductibility: (i) the general basis limitation, (ii) the at-risk limitation, and (iii) the passive activity loss rules. All three limitations are applied at the partner level. Note that, for purposes of the general basis limitation, a partner's outside basis is increased by the amount of partnership level debt allocated to it. Partnership losses are nondeductible if the partnership is not engaged in an activity undertaken to make a profit.

*C Corporation.* A C corporation is not a pass-through entity. If a C corporation generates a net operating loss for a year, that loss generates a tax benefit to the corporation only to the extent the loss can be carried back or forward to a year in which the corporation has taxable income. Generally, a net operating loss can be carried back two years and forward 20 years [§ 172(b)(1)(A)]. The inability of share-holders of a C corporation to offset their own income with losses of the corporation is an important consideration in selecting a form of business entity, particularly if the business is expected to generate losses in its early stages. If the corporation is operated as a C corporation, no tax benefit is obtained from the losses until the corporation generates a taxable income.

In addition to the overall limitation on the use of losses by a C corporation, two special limitations apply on an activity basis to limit the deductibility of losses incurred by a C corporation:

1. Closely held C corporations are subject to both the at-risk rules and the passive activity loss rules (although in a modified form) [§ 465(a)(1)(B), § 469(a)(2)(B)].

2. Personal service corporations (PSCs) are fully subject to the passive activity loss rules, whether closely held or not [§ 469(a)(2)(C)].

*S Corporation.* Losses of an S corporation are passed through to its shareholders. Like losses passed through from a partnership, losses passed through to a shareholder from an S corporation are subject to three limitations on their deductibility: (i) the general basis limitation, (ii) the at-risk limitation, and (iii) the passive activity loss rules. All three limitations are applied at the shareholder level. Unlike partnerships and partners, the outside basis of S corporation shareholders is not increased by their share of S corporation level debt for purposes of the general basis limitation.

### XVI.D.2.d. Treatment of Distributions

[700 T.M., VII.; TPS ¶4220.03.D.]

*Sole Proprietorship.* Because a sole proprietorship is not an entity separate from its owner, a sole proprietor is not taxed on cash withdrawn from the business. Thus, the double tax problem associated with a distribution of cash from a C corporation is irrelevant to a sole proprietor.

There are also generally no tax consequences on the withdrawal of property by a sole proprietor from his or her business. However, if the investment tax credit was claimed on the property when it was originally placed in service, any unearned investment tax credit must be recaptured if the property is taken out of business use [§ 50(a)(1)].

*Partnership.* Generally, a partner is taxed on a distribution of cash from a partnership only to the extent the amount of money received exceeds his or her basis in his or her partnership interest [§ 731(a)(1)]. Distributions of money not in excess of the partner's basis are treated as a non-taxable return of capital. Distributions that do not exceed a partner's basis are generally taxed as capital gain [§ 731(a)]. However, a portion of the gain could be characterized as ordinary income if the partnership holds certain ordinary income assets [§ 751(b)]. Because a partner's basis includes the partner's share of partnership level debt to third parties, distributions from a partnership generally have a larger basis to reduce than do distributions from an S corporation.

Generally, no gain or loss is recognized by a partnership on the distribution of property, including money, to one of its partners [§ 731(b)]. Gain is generally recognized by a distributee partner if, as part of the transaction, the partner receives a distribution of money (whether actual or constructive) that exceeds the partner's basis in his or her partnership interest [§ 731(a)(1)]. The partner takes a basis in the distributed property equal to the partnership's basis in the property [§ 732(a)(1)]. However, the distributee partner's basis in the property received cannot exceed the basis of such partner's partnership interest reduced by any money received in the distribution [§ 732(a)(2)]. In certain cases, gain may also be recognized by a distributee partner who contributed appreciated assets to the partnership [§ 737(a)]. A partner never recognizes a loss on a distribution unless it is in liquidation of his or her partnership interest [§ 731(a)(2)].

*C Corporation.* Distributions from a C corporation with respect to its stock (i.e., dividends) are taxable to its shareholders at capital gains rates provided the distributions do not exceed the corporation's current or accumulated earnings and profits [§ 301]. Because a corporate-level tax is imposed on the corporation's earnings when they are generated, and a shareholder-level tax is imposed on the earnings when they are distributed, two levels of tax are imposed on the earnings of a C corporation that are distributed to its shareholders. The corporation receives no deduction for amounts paid to its shareholders as dividends.

Several planning techniques are available to reduce the incidence of the double tax. One straightforward method is to distribute funds from the corporation to its owners in the form of compensation rather than dividends. Provided the compensation paid to the shareholders is reasonable for the services they perform for the corporation, the corporation is entitled to a deduction for the compensation, and the corporate-level tax on the amount paid to the shareholders as compensation is avoided. However, note that FICA taxes would apply to the compensation paid to the shareholder-employee.

If a shareholder that is a C corporation qualifies for the dividends received deduction, the second level of tax is, at least in part, deferred until the earnings are subsequently distributed by the distributee corporation to its noncorporate shareholders.

A C corporation generally recognizes gain on the distribution of appreciated property. For tax purposes, the corporation is treated as if it had sold the property to the distributee shareholder(s) at fair market value [§ 311(b)]. Thus, a corporate level tax may be imposed on the distribution. No loss, however, is recognized on a nonliquidating distribution of depreciated property [§ 311(a)].

The corporation's shareholders report the receipt of the property as a taxable dividend (i.e., ordinary income), except to the extent the amount of the distribution exceeds the corporation's current and accumulated earnings and profits. Any excess distribution is treated as a non-taxable return of capital to the extent of a shareholder's adjusted basis in its stock, and as capital gain to the extent it exceeds the shareholder's adjusted basis in its stock [§ 301(c)]. The amount of the dividend is generally equal to the fair market value of the property distributed [§ 301(b)]. The distributee shareholder's basis in the property equals its fair market value [§ 301(d)].

*S Corporation.* Cash distributions received by a shareholder with respect to his or her stock in an S corporation that does not have accumulated earnings and profits (AE&P) are tax-free to the extent the distributions do not exceed the shareholder's stock basis. To the extent a distribution exceeds the shareholder's basis, the shareholder reports a capital gain.

The taxation of distributions from an S corporation with AE&P is more complex. Such distributions are considered a tax-free return of basis to the extent they do not exceed the lesser of the corporation's accumulated adjustments account (AAA) or the shareholder's stock basis. A distribution that exceeds the corporation's AAA is taxed as a dividend to the corporation's shareholders to the extent of the corporation's AE&P. Any distributions in excess of both AAA and AE&P are taxed as a tax-free return of the shareholder's remaining basis (if any); any excess is taxed as capital gain.

Like a C corporation, an S corporation recognizes gain on the distribution of appreciated property to a shareholder [§ 311(b)]. However, unless the S corporation is subject to one of the special S corporation level taxes, the entire gain passes through to the S corporation's shareholders, and no corporate level tax is imposed. Because S shareholders are required to report the gain recognized by the corporation on the distribution, the partnership form of doing business has an advantage over the

S corporation form with respect to distributions of appreciated property. As with a C corporation, no loss is recognized by an S corporation upon a nonliquidating distribution of depreciated property [§ 311(a)].

The S corporation's shareholders report the fair market value of the property received as a distribution subject to the same rules that apply to a distribution of money. However, the corporation's AAA and the shareholder's basis in the corporation will have been increased by the amount of gain recognized by the corporation on the distribution. A shareholder's basis in the property received in the distribution equals its fair market value.

### XVI.D.2.e. Compensation-Related Issues

[700 T.M., XII.; TPS ¶4220.03.E.]

***Fringe Benefits.*** The C corporation form of entity has a significant advantage over the other forms of entity because it may provide certain fringe benefits to its owners on a tax-free basis. These tax-free fringe benefits include accident and health plans, cafeteria plans, group-term life insurance, dependent care assistance programs, and certain miscellaneous statutory fringe benefits covered under § 132.

Generally, a C corporation can deduct the cost of these tax-free fringe benefits provided to its shareholder-employees, while its shareholder-employees do not include the value of the benefits in income. However, part or all of the benefits provided to highly compensated employees under certain benefit plans may be taxable if the plans do not satisfy certain nondiscrimination requirements.

Because fringe benefits can only be excluded by "employees," they generally cannot be provided on a tax-free basis to sole proprietors, partners, or shareholders owning (directly or indirectly) more than 2% of the stock in an S corporation. However, partners and more-than-2% S corporation shareholders are eligible for the miscellaneous fringe benefits provided under § 132 (e.g., working condition fringe benefits, de minimis fringe benefits) [Reg. § 1.132-1T(b)].

***Qualified Retirement Plans.*** Before 2002, special rules imposed penalty taxes on qualified plan loans to sole proprietors, partners owning a 10% or more capital or profits interest in the partnership, and S corporation shareholders owning more than 5% of the outstanding stock in the S corporation. However, those rules were repealed and qualified plan loans to such owner-employees are now generally permitted under the regular statutory exemptions. Thus, a qualified plan's ability to make such loans is no longer an advantage of C corporation status.

***Unreasonable Compensation.*** By paying compensation rather than dividends to its employee-shareholders, a C corporation can reduce the amount of its income subject to the corporate-level tax and avoid the double tax on the payment of dividends to shareholders. However, the IRS may reclassify compensation paid to a shareholder-employee as a dividend if it is excessive [Reg. § 1.162-8]. If the compensation is reclassified as a dividend, the C corporation loses its deduction for the excessive amount of compensation, and the recipient is required to include the payment in income as a dividend. Thus, two levels of tax are imposed. Certain otherwise deductible compensation is automatically disallowed as a deduction to the extent that the amounts exceed $1 million [§ 162(m)].

As a general rule, unreasonable compensation is not an issue for pass-through entities, because there is no double tax to be avoided by paying out the entity's earnings as compensation rather than dividends. A reasonable compensation issue could arise, however, with respect to an S corporation. An S corporation shareholder's distributive share of S corporation income is not subject to self-employment taxes.

Thus, an S corporation shareholder may have an incentive to forgo salary payments in order to increase its distributive share of S corporation income. This would allow for more tax-free distributions not subject to self-employment taxes (see below). This tax-avoidance approach is closely monitored by the IRS.

*Self-Employment Tax.* A sole proprietor is subject to self-employment taxes on the earnings from his or her business [§ 1402(a)].

A general partner is subject to self-employment taxes on his or her distributive share of the income attributable to a trade or business carried on by the partnership [§ 1402(a)]. A limited partner is not subject to self-employment taxes on his or her distributive share of partnership income; however, a limited partner is subject to self-employment taxes on guaranteed payments to the extent such payments are made for services rendered to the partnership [§ 1402(a)(13)].

Because members of an LLC classified as a partnership are neither general partners nor limited partners, the application of self-employment taxes to LLC members is not clear. The IRS issued two sets of proposed regulations in the 1990s, but never finalized either set. Accordingly, it remains unclear in what circumstances an LLC member should be treated as a general partner for self-employment tax purposes and in what circumstances a member should be treated as a limited partner. Case law suggests that LLC members providing services may indeed be subject to the self-employment taxes on their earnings. For example, in one case, self-employment taxes were imposed on the earnings of partners in a law firm organized as a limited liability partnership [*Renkemeyer v. Commissioner*, 136 T.C. 137 (2011)].

An S corporation shareholder is not subject to self-employment taxes on his or her share of undistributed S corporation income. However, like compensation paid to a shareholder-employee of a C corporation, wages paid to a shareholder-employee of an S corporation are subject to FICA and other payroll taxes.

### XVI.D.3. Disposition/Liquidation Stage

#### *XVI.D.3.a. Sale of Equity Interest*

[700 T.M., IX.; TPS ¶4220.04.A.]

*Sole Proprietorship.* A sole proprietor cannot simply sell an equity interest in his or her business. Instead, each asset is considered to have been sold separately, even if the business is sold pursuant to a single contract to a single buyer. The amount paid for the assets of a sole proprietorship must be allocated to all of the assets sold, including goodwill.

A sole proprietor recognizes gain or loss separately on each asset sold. The character of the gain or loss depends on whether the asset was a capital asset, ordinary income asset, or asset used in the trade or business. Because a sole proprietorship is not an entity separate from its owner, only one tax is imposed on the sale of the assets of the business.

*Partnership.* A partnership is a legal entity separate from its owners. Thus, a partner can sell all or a portion of his or her equity interest in a partnership without causing a sale of the underlying assets of the partnership [§ 741]. The amount of gain (or loss) to be reported by a partner on the sale of a partnership interest equals the excess of the sum of the amount of money plus the fair market value of other consideration received over the partner's basis in the portion of his or her partnership interest that is sold [§ 752(d)]. The gain or loss recognized on the sale is normally a capital gain or loss unless the partnership holds certain ordinary income assets (e.g., unrealized receivables, depreciation recapture potential, or substantially appreciated inventory), in which case the partner recognizes ordinary income on at least a portion of the sale [§ 741, § 751(a)].

The purchaser takes a cost basis in the partnership interest that is acquired. The purchaser's basis includes his or her share of the partnership's liabilities [§ 1012, § 752(a)]. The partnership's basis in its assets is generally unaffected by the sale of a partner's interest [§ 743(a)]. Thus, the purchasing partner generally is taxed on his or her share of the built-in gain in the partnership's assets when the partnership sells the assets, even though the purchasing partner has paid the selling partner for the full value of the partnership's assets as of the date of the sale. However, under § 754, a partnership may elect to adjust the basis of its assets to reflect the difference between the purchasing partner's basis in his or her partnership interest and the purchasing partner's share of the partnership's basis in its assets [§ 754, § 743(b)]. Any basis increase constitutes a basis adjustment to partnership property with respect to the purchasing partner only and allows the purchasing partner to claim increased depreciation deductions or report a lesser amount of income from the disposition of partnership assets [§ 743(b)]. The § 754 election to adjust partnership assets is optional for basis increases, but mandatory for substantial basis reductions or built-in losses exceeding $250,000 [§ 734, § 743].

The special § 754 basis adjustment election is available only to partnerships. Because an S corporation cannot adjust the basis of its assets when shareholders sell their stock, the partnership form of entity offers an advantage over an S corporation to a prospective purchaser.

*C Corporation.* A shareholder who sells his stock in a C corporation generally recognizes capital gain or loss on the sale. However, a shareholder that is an individual or partnership may qualify for ordinary loss treatment on a sale of C corporation stock if the stock is § 1244 stock. The amount of the loss that can qualify for ordinary loss treatment in any year is limited to $50,000 ($100,000 if a joint return is filed) [§ 1244].

The purchaser of the stock takes a cost basis in the stock acquired [§ 1012]. The basis of the corporation's assets is generally not affected by the sale or exchange of its stock. However, if the stock purchase constitutes a qualified stock purchase by a corporate buyer, an election can be made to treat the stock sale as an asset sale and step up the basis of the corporation's assets, albeit at the cost of a corporate-level tax [§ 338]. Similarly, if a corporation owns at least 80% of the stock of another corporation (the target) and it sells all of its stock in the target, it can elect to treat the stock sale as an asset sale in order to give a non-corporate purchaser a step-up in basis in the assets of the target [§ 336]. In stock sales treated as asset sales, the character of income at the corporate level will reflect that of the underlying assets.

*S Corporation.* The tax consequences on the sale of stock in an S corporation do not differ significantly from the consequences of a sale of C corporation stock. The seller generally reports capital gain (or loss) to the extent the sales proceeds exceed (or are less than) the seller's basis in the stock sold, and the purchaser takes a cost basis in the stock acquired [§ 1012]. Like stock of a C corporation, a loss on the sale of stock of an S corporation can qualify for ordinary loss treatment if the stock is § 1244 stock [§ 1244]. However, the amount of gain or loss to be reported by the S shareholder may be significantly more or less than the gain or loss that would be reported if the corporation were a C corporation, because the shareholder's basis will have been adjusted for corporate items of income or loss passed through to the shareholder during the current and prior years.

An S corporation can be the target in a qualified stock purchase deemed to be an asset sale in order to give a corporate buyer a step-up in the basis of the S corporation's assets [§ 338(h)(10)]. An S corporation can also be the target in a qualified stock purchase deemed to be an asset sale in order to give a non-corporate buyer a step-up in the basis of the S corporation's assets [§ 336(e)]. The character of income recognized on such deemed asset sales will reflect the character of the underlying assets.

### XVI.D.3.b. Sale of Assets of Entity

[700 T.M., IX.; TPS ¶4220.04.B.]

**Sole Proprietorship.** A sole proprietor recognizes gain or loss separately on each asset sold. The character of the gain or loss depends on whether the asset was a capital asset, ordinary income asset, or asset used in the trade or business. Because a sole proprietorship is not an entity separate from its owner, only one tax is imposed on the sale of the assets of the business.

**Partnership.** A single level of tax is imposed on the gain or loss recognized by a partnership on the sale of its assets, because the gains or losses are not taxed at the partnership level but are passed through directly to the partners [§ 701, § 702]. The character of the gains or losses is determined at the partnership level [§ 702(b)]. Partners do not recognize gain on the distribution of the sales proceeds, because the basis in their partnership interests will have been increased by their shares of the partnership's gain passed through to them [§ 705].

**C Corporation.** A corporate-level 35% tax is imposed on any net gain recognized by a C corporation on the sale of its assets. For a C corporation, ordinary income and capital gains are taxed at the same rate. In addition, a shareholder-level tax is generally imposed when the sales proceeds are distributed to the shareholders [§ 331]. Thus, unlike other types of entities, a double tax is generally imposed on the sale of a C corporation's assets if the proceeds from the sale are distributed to the shareholders. This potential double taxation on the sale of assets is generally viewed as the most significant disadvantage of a C corporation.

**S Corporation.** As with a partnership, gains and losses recognized by an S corporation on the sale of its assets pass through to its owners [§ 1366]. Generally, no corporate-level tax is imposed unless the corporation was formerly a C corporation (see XVI.D.2.a. for the tax consequences when an S corporation was formerly a C corporation). The shareholders do not recognize gain on the distribution of the sales proceeds, except to the extent the amount of the distribution exceeds the shareholders' basis in their stock.

### XVI.D.3.c. Liquidation of Entity

[700 T.M., IX.; TPS ¶4220.04.D.]

**Sole Proprietorship.** The liquidation concept does not apply to a sole proprietorship. The business of a sole proprietorship ends when its owner ceases to conduct the trade or business. If the assets of a sole proprietorship are sold, the owner recognizes gain or loss separately on each asset (see XVI.D.3.b.). If the assets are not sold but are simply withdrawn from business use, there are generally no tax consequences except for potential investment tax credit recapture or certain depreciation or expensing deduction recapture on the property when it ceases to be employed in a qualifying business use.

**Partnership.** If a partnership makes an in-kind liquidating distribution of its assets to its partners, the partnership recognizes no gain or loss on the distribution [§ 731(b)]. This nonrecognition rule applies to distributions of installment obligations received on the sale of the partnership's assets, as well as other types of property [Reg. § 1.453-9(c)(2)].

The partners generally recognize no gain or loss on the receipt of the liquidating distributions [§ 731(a)]. However, gain is recognized by a partner to the extent the amount of money the partner receives (either directly or constructively by reason of a relief of partnership liabilities) exceeds the partner's basis in his or her partnership interest [§ 731(a)(1)]. In certain cases gain may also be recognized when a partner who contributed appreciated assets to the partnership, directly or indirectly, receives a property distribution [§ 737(a)]. In such cases, the partner's interest in the partnership is increased by the gain recognized [§ 737(c)]. A partner recognizes loss on a liquidating distribution only if the partner's interest is completely liquidated, the partner receives no property other than cash and certain ordinary income assets, and the sum of the amount of money received and the basis of the ordinary income assets received is less than the partner's basis in his or her partnership interest [§ 731(a)(2)].

The distributee partners take a substituted basis in the property received (i.e., their basis in any property received equals the basis of their partnership interests reduced by any money received) [§ 732(b)]. However, a partner's basis in certain ordinary income assets is limited to the partnership's basis in those assets [§ 732(c)].

*C Corporation.* A C corporation generally recognizes gain or loss on the distribution of its assets in complete liquidation just as if the corporation has sold its assets at their fair market value [§ 336(a)].

A shareholder recognizes gain (usually capital gain) to the extent the value of the assets received in complete liquidation exceeds his or her stock basis [§ 331]. No gain or loss is recognized, however, by a parent corporation on the liquidation of a controlled subsidiary [§ 332]. If qualifying installment notes are received as part of the liquidation, the shareholders are entitled to report some or all of their gain on the installment method [§ 453(h)]. A shareholder recognizes a capital loss if the value of the assets received in liquidation is less than the shareholder's stock basis, although some or all of the loss may qualify as an ordinary loss if the stock is § 1244 stock [§ 331, § 1244].

The shareholder's basis in any property received is generally the fair market value of the property [§ 334(a)]. In the case of the liquidation of a controlled subsidiary into its parent corporation, the parent corporation takes a carryover basis in the subsidiary's assets [§ 334(b)].

Because the corporation recognizes gain or loss on the distribution of its assets in liquidation, and its shareholders recognize gain or loss on the receipt of the liquidating distributions, two levels of tax are imposed on the liquidation of a C corporation.

*S Corporation.* The rules governing the recognition of gain or loss applicable to a C corporation generally apply to the liquidation of an S corporation. However, unless the S corporation was previously a C corporation and is subject to the built-in gains tax, only a single level of tax at the shareholder level is imposed on the liquidation of an S corporation. Upon distribution of corporate property, the corporate-level gain on the deemed sale of the property passes through the shareholders, retaining its character at the shareholder level. Further, a shareholder recognizes gain (generally capital gain) to the extent the value of property received in the liquidation exceeds his or her stock basis [§ 331]. As with a shareholder in a C corporation, an S corporation shareholder may report his or her gain on the liquidation on the installment sale method if qualifying installment notes are received in the liquidation [§ 453(h)]. A shareholder recognizes a loss on the liquidation of the corporation in the same manner as a C corporation shareholder.

### *XVI.D.3.d. Tax-Free Reorganizations*

[700 T.M., X.; TPS ¶4220.04.E.]

The ability to engage in tax-free reorganizations is another factor to consider in selecting a form of business entity. Tax-free reorganizations are available only to corporations, including S corporations [§ 368]. However, S corporations are more limited than C corporations in the types of reorganizations in which they can engage in that the S corporation eligibility requirements restrict an S corporation's ability to engage in certain reorganizations if its S status is to be retained. While partnerships cannot engage in corporate reorganizations, the ease with which they can be formed and liquidated may allow transactions similar to corporate reorganizations to be structured between two partnerships.

## COMPARISON OF BUSINESS ENTITIES

| Applicable Factor | C Corporation | S Corporation | Sole Proprietor | Partnership | Limited Liability Company |
|---|---|---|---|---|---|
| **I. Formation** | | | | | |
| A. Method | Articles of Incorporation | Articles of Incorporation | None | Partnership agreement | Articles of Organization |
| B. Owner Eligibility | | | | | |
| 1. Number of Owners | No limit | 100; 75 for tax years beginning before 2005 | One | Two or more for general partnership; one or more general and one or more limited for limited partnership | No limit |
| 2. Type of Owners | No limitation | Only individuals and certain trusts and estates for tax years beginning before 1998; certain tax-exempt organizations also for tax years beginning after 1997 | Individual | No limitation | No limitation |

## COMPARISON OF BUSINESS ENTITIES (Continued)

| Applicable Factor | C Corporation | S Corporation | Sole Proprietor | Partnership | Limited Liability Company |
|---|---|---|---|---|---|
| 3. Affiliate limits | No limitation | May own 80% or more of C Corporation stock and 100% of qualified sub-chapter S subsidiary; No subsidiaries (except name holding) for tax years beginning before 1997 | No limitation | No limitation | No limitation |
| C. Capital Structure | | | | | |
| 1. Equity | No limitations (multiple classes permitted) | Only one class of stock | No stock | No limitations (multiple classes permitted) | No limitations (multiple classes permitted) |
| 2. Debt | No specific limits on debt/equity ratio | Safe-harbor for debt | No specific limits | No specific limits | No specific limits |
| D. Status Determination | | | | | |
| 1. Election by Entity | No election requirement | Required election | No election requirements | No election requirement but state law filing | No election requirement but state law filing |
| 2. Owner Consents | None required | Consent required | None required | None required | None required |
| E. Liability | Limited to shareholder's capital contributions | Limited to shareholder's capital contributions | Unlimited | General partners jointly and severally liable. Limited partners generally limited to capital contributions | Limited to member's capital contributions |

## COMPARISON OF BUSINESS ENTITIES (Continued)

| Applicable Factor | C Corporation | S Corporation | Sole Proprietor | Partnership | Limited Liability Company |
|---|---|---|---|---|---|
| **II. Operational Phase** | | | | | |
| A. Tax Year | Any year permitted (limit for personal service corporation) | Generally calendar year | Calendar year | Generally calendar year | Generally calendar year |
| B. Tax on Income | Corporate level | Owner level | Individual level | Owner level | Member level |
| C. Elections | Corporate level | Corporate level | Individual level | Partnership level | Entity level |
| D. Allocation of Income/Deductions | Not permitted (except through multiple equity structure) | Not permitted (except through debt/equity structure) | N/A | Permitted if substantial economic effect | Permitted if substantial economic effect |
| E. Character of Income/Deductions | No flow-through to shareholders | Flow-through to shareholders | Flow-through to individual | Flow-through to partners | Flow-through to members |
| F. Net Operating Losses | No flow-through | Flow-through to shareholders (limited to tax basis) | Flow-through to individual | Flow-through to partners (limited to tax basis) | Flow-through to members (limited to tax basis) |
| G. Net Capital Losses | No flow-through, but three-year carryback and five-year carryforward | Flow-through to shareholders | Flow-through to individual | Flow-through to partners | Flow-through to members |
| H. Effect of Statutory Limitations | Imposed at corporate level | Imposed at shareholder level | Imposed at individual level | Imposed at partner level | Imposed at member level |

## COMPARISON OF BUSINESS ENTITIES (Continued)

| Applicable Factor | C Corporation | S Corporation | Sole Proprietor | Partnership | Limited Liability Company |
|---|---|---|---|---|---|
| **III. Compensation Arrangements** | | | | | |
| A. Fringe Benefits | Shareholder-officers qualify for benefits | Certain benefits includible in 2% + shareholder's income | Generally subject to limits applicable to individuals | Limited participation for partners | Limited participation for members |
| B. Retirement Benefits | Shareholder-officers included in qualified plans | Certain limits on shareholder-employees; ESOPs available for tax years beginning after 1997 (although certain special tax breaks available to C corporations will not be available) | Generally subject to limits applicable to individuals | Certain limits applicable to partners | Certain limits applicable to members |
| C. Reasonable Compensation Limits | Applicable to shareholder-employees | Applicable to shareholder-employees | N/A | May be applicable in a family partnership context where capital is a material factor | May be applicable in a family LLC context where capital is a material factor |
| | | | | | |

## COMPARISON OF BUSINESS ENTITIES (Continued)

| Applicable Factor | C Corporation | S Corporation | Sole Proprietor | Partnership | Limited Liability Company |
|---|---|---|---|---|---|
| **IV. Transactions with Owners** | | | | | |
| A. Distribution of Cash | Dividends to extent of earnings and profits | No effect until previously taxed income fully recovered | No effect | No effect except in calculation of basis | No effect except in calculation of basis |
| B. Distribution of Property | Dividend treatment; gain recognition to distributing entity | Gain recognition to distributing entity | No effect | No gain or loss to entity but partners may recognize gain on certain appreciated property distributions | No gain or loss to entity but members may recognize gain on certain depreciated property distributions |
| C. Purchase of Owner's Interest | | | | | |
| 1. Partial Interest | Probable dividend treatment | Tax-free; but gain for proceeds in excess of tax basis | N/A | N/A | N/A |
| 2. Entire Interest | Capital gain treatment, with exceptions | Capital gain treatment after basis recovered | Cannot sell entity interest; sale of business is viewed as a sale of each asset | Capital gain treatment except ordinary income for ordinary income assets and certain § 736 payments | Capital gain treatment except ordinary income for ordinary income assets and certain § 736 payments |
| D. Property Sales to Entity by Owner | Possible dividend treatment or contribution to capital | Any excess value treated as distribution or contribution | N/A | Any excess value treated as distribution or contribution | Any excess value treated as distribution or contribution |

## COMPARISON OF BUSINESS ENTITIES (Continued)

| Applicable Factor | C Corporation | S Corporation | Sole Proprietor | Partnership | Limited Liability Company |
|---|---|---|---|---|---|
| E. Property Sales to Owner by Entity | Possible dividend treatment or contribution to capital | Any excess value treated as distribution or contribution | N/A | Any excess value treated as distribution or contribution | Any excess value treated as distribution or contribution |
| **V. Termination of Entity or Owner Interest** | | | | | |
| A. Sale of Interest by Owner to Third Person | Capital gain; no effect on basis of corporation's assets | Capital gain; no effect on basis of corporation's assets | Cannot sell entity interest; sale of business is viewed as a sale of each asset | Capital gain, subject to § 751 ordinary income categorization | Capital gain, subject to § 751 ordinary income categorization |
| B. Death of Owner | Estate continues as shareholder: FMV at date of death (or alternate valuation date) is basis for shares; no effect on basis of corporation's affects | Estate continues as shareholder: FMV at date of death (or alternate valuation date) is basis for shares; no effect on basis of corporation's assets | Estate takes over business | Estate as partner subject to agreement, FMV at date of death is basis for interest | Estate as member subject to agreement, FMV at date of death is basis for interest |
| C. Liquidation Distributions | | | | | |
| 1. Effect to Distributor | Gain recognition if appreciated property distributed; no increase in shareholder basis for gain | Gain recognition if appreciated property distributed; increase in shareholder basis for gain | N/A | No gain recognition on asset distributions | No gain recognition on asset distributions |

815

## COMPARISON OF BUSINESS ENTITIES (Continued)

| Applicable Factor | C Corporation | S Corporation | Sole Proprietor | Partnership | Limited Liability Company |
|---|---|---|---|---|---|
| 2. Effect to Recipient | Capital gain on excess value received over basis | Capital gain on excess value received over basis | N/A | Substituted basis in assets equal to basis in partnership interest; gain may be recognized depending on assets distributed | Substituted basis in assets equal to basis in LLC interest; gain may be recognized depending on assets distributed |
| D. Entity Reorganizations | Tax-free to shareholders if qualifying under reorganization provisions (§ 354 & § 368) | Tax-free to shareholders if qualifying under reorganization provisions (§ 354 & § 368) | N/A | No taxability on merger of partnership | No taxability on merger of LLC |
| E. Carryover of Tax Attributes | Carryover of tax attributes to successor entity if tax-free reorganization | Carryover of tax attributes to successor entity if tax-free reorganization | N/A | N/A | N/A |

# CHAPTER XVII. EMPLOYEE BENEFITS AND OTHER COMPENSATION ARRANGEMENTS

>>>>>>>>>>>>>>>>>>>>>>>>>>>>>>

## XVII.A. Retirement Plans

### XVII.A.1. Introduction

An employer offers retirement plans for several reasons: to attract good workers, to keep them happy while working and making the business profitable, to reward them for their past efforts, and to help provide them with income when they retire. Employers also benefit from certain income tax advantages from sponsoring retirement programs that are described in detail below.

### XVII.A.2. Qualified Retirement Plans

#### XVII.A.2.a. Tax Benefits

[351 T.M., I.C., 353 T.M., II.A.1.a.; TPS ¶5510.02.]

Both the employer adopting a retirement plan and the employees who participate receive substantial tax benefits if a plan is qualified. First, the employer receives an immediate tax deduction for certain contributions it makes to a qualified plan. Second, participants are not taxed on their benefits until such benefits are distributed. Third, the plan's income and gains on the investment of its assets are generally tax-exempt while such amounts remain in the plan.

#### XVII.A.2.b. Plan Document and Operational Requirements

[351 T.M., II.C.; TPS ¶5520.01.]

For a retirement plan to qualify as a "qualified plan" under § 401(a), both its written terms and its operation must comply with numerous requirements in the Internal Revenue Code (I.R.C.), Treasury regulations, and other administrative guidance. These rules are generally intended to prevent employers from providing discriminatory benefits or limiting coverage to highly-compensated employees. Applicable rules include minimum coverage requirements, age and service requirements, benefit accrual requirements, nondiscrimination in benefits or contributions, limits on contributions and benefits, vesting requirements, limitations on distribution of benefits, top-heavy rules and limitations on the alienation of benefits. Qualified plans also generally are subject to the Employee Retirement Income Security Act of 1974 (ERISA), although compliance or noncompliance with ERISA does not affect a plan's qualified tax status. ERISA also imposes exclusive benefit and fiduciary rules as well as reporting and disclosure, participation, vesting, funding, and enforcement requirements.

### XVII.A.2.c. Types of Qualified Plans

[350 T.M., III.C.; TPS ¶5510.03.]

Qualified plans are generally broken down into two types of plans: defined contribution and defined benefit plans.

***Defined Contribution Plans.*** A defined contribution plan is a retirement plan that provides for an individual account for each participant to which employer and employee contributions can be made, and that consists of income, expenses, gains, and losses, and any forfeitures of accounts of other participants that are allocated to such participant's account [§ 414(i)]. Thus, under a defined contribution plan, the participant bears the risk of gain or loss on plan investments. Defined contribution plans include profit-sharing plans, stock bonus plans, money purchase pension plans, thrift plans, § 401(k) plans and other cash and deferred arrangements, and employee stock ownership plans.

***Defined Benefit Plans.*** A defined benefit plan specifies the level of benefits to which participants will be entitled upon retirement. The employer's contributions are determined actuarially on the basis of the benefits payable, mortality, work force turnover, earnings on plan investments, and other factors. Participants do not share in any actuarial or investment gains, nor do they bear the risk of actuarial or investment losses.

Defined benefit plans involve different economic considerations than defined contribution plans. First, because benefits are predetermined under a defined benefit plan, these plans necessarily involve more fixed costs for the employer than defined contribution plans. Second, contributions generally must be made in amounts at least equal to those required under minimum funding standards set by the I.R.C. and ERISA.

Some defined benefit plans are termed "hybrid" plans because their design provides features common to both defined contribution and defined benefit plans. The most common hybrid plan is a cash balance plan. In such a plan, the benefit formula is commonly stated in terms of a notional or hypothetical account balance to which the sponsor provides annual "pay credits" based on each year's compensation and "interest credits" on the balance of the account [§ 412, § 430].

### XVII.A.2.d. Contribution and Benefit Limitations

[350 T.M., III.C.3., 351 T.M., VI., 358 T.M., III.A.7.c.,VIII.A.; TPS ¶¶5520.08.A., 5560.01.C.]

The I.R.C. limits the extent to which a qualified plan may provide tax-favored contributions or benefits on behalf of any participant.

***Defined Contribution Plans.*** Under all defined contribution plans, the maximum contribution that can be made to a participant's account cannot exceed the lesser of: (i) $40,000, as adjusted for inflation ($53,000 for 2015, and $52,000 for 2014); or (ii) 100% of the employee's compensation [§ 415(c)(1), IRS News Release IR-2014-99 (Oct. 23, 2014); Notice 2013–73, 2013–49 I.R.B. 598].

In applying this limit, compensation means the participant's annual compensation from the sponsoring employer. Generally, all compensation for personal services rendered in the course of employment with the sponsoring employer is included, whether in the form of wages, salaries, commissions, tips or bonuses [§ 415(c)(3)(A), § 415(c)(3)(B); Reg. § 1.415(c)-2].

*Defined Benefit Plans.* The I.R.C. limits the maximum benefit that a participant can accrue under a qualified defined benefit plan in the form of an annual life annuity. That benefit cannot exceed the lesser of: $160,000, as adjusted for inflation (for 2014 and 2015, this amount is $210,000); or 100% of the participant's average compensation for his or her three consecutive most highly compensated years of service with the employer [§ 415(b)(1); Reg. § 1.415(b)-1(a)(1); IRS News Release IR-2014-99 (Oct. 23, 2014); Notice 2013–73].

A participant's three consecutive most highly compensated years are the period of consecutive calendar years during which the participant had the greatest aggregate compensation from the employer. For shorter periods of service, a participant's high three years of service is computed by averaging the participant's compensation during the participant's longest consecutive period of employment over the actual period of service (including fractions of years, but not less than one year) [§ 415(b)(3); Reg. § 1.415(b)-1(a)(5)(ii)].

Adjustments are made to the dollar limit for benefits starting before age 62 and after age 65. If benefits begin before age 62, the dollar limit is reduced to an annual benefit that is the actuarial equivalent of an annual benefit equal to the regular dollar limit beginning at age 62. If benefits begin after age 65, the dollar limit is increased to an annual benefit (beginning when benefit payments begin) that is the actuarial equivalent to the regular dollar limit beginning at age 65 [§ 415(b)(2)(C), § 415(b)(2)(D); Reg. § 1.415(b)-1(d)(1), § 1.415(b)-1(e)(1)].

The defined benefit plan dollar limit also is subject to a special reduction in the case of an employee with less than 10 years of participation in the plan. For such employees, the dollar limit is multiplied by a fraction, the numerator of which is the number of years of participation in the plan, and the denominator of which is 10. The result is the employee's dollar limitation [§ 415(b)(5); Reg. § 1.415(b)-1(g)(1)].

*Compensation Limits.* For purposes of determining contributions and benefits, a qualified plan may not take into account compensation in excess of a specified dollar amount. The limit is $200,000, as adjusted for inflation in $5,000 increments ($265,000 for 2015, $260,000 for 2014) [§ 401(a)(17); IRS News Release IR-2014-99 (Oct. 23, 2014); Notice 2013–73].

*Deferral Limits.* Certain defined contribution plans that permit employee elective deferrals are subject to a deferral limitation, as adjusted for inflation. For example, a participant in a § 401(k) plan may only defer up to $18,000 in 2015 ($17,500 in 2014). This limit applies to all elective deferrals made by an individual to all plans that permit such contributions [§ 401(a)(30), § 402(g)(1)(B), § 402(g)4); IRS News Release IR-2014-99 (Oct. 23, 2014); Notice 2013–73].

| Qualified Retirement Plan/Benefit | Code Section | Annual Limitation |
|---|---|---|
| Maximum deferral limit — Sec. 401(k) plan | Sec. 402(g)* | $ 18,000 |
| Defined benefit plan — maximum annual benefit | Sec. 415(b), (d) | $ 210,000* |
| Defined contribution plan — maximum annual addition | Sec. 415(c) | $ 53,000 |
| "Highly-compensated employee" threshold | Sec. 414(q) | $ 120,000 |
| Qualified plans — annual compensation limit | Sec(s). 401(a)(17), 404(l), 408(k)(3)(C), 408(k)(6)(D)(ii), 505(b)(7) | $ 265,000 |

| Qualified Retirement Plan/Benefit | Code Section | Annual Limitation |
|---|---|---|
| Governmental plans that as of 7/1/93, allowed COLAs to Sec. 401(a)(17) limit to be taken into account | Sec. 401(a)(17) | $ 395,000 |
| Amount to determine the maximum ESOP account balance subject to 5-yr. distribution period; amount to determine lengthening of 5-yr. distribution period | Sec. 409(o) | $ 1,070,000 |
|  |  | $ 210,000 |
| Compensation threshold for SEP participation | Sec. 408(k)(2)(C)** | $ 600 |
| Deferral limit for SIMPLE plan | Sec. 408(p)(2)(E)* | $ 12,500 |
| Deferral limit for Sec. 457 plans | Sec. 457(e)(15)* | $ 18,000 |
| Definition of "control employee" for fringe benefit valuation purposes | Reg. Sec. 1.61-21(f)(5)(i) | $ 105,000 |
|  | Reg. Sec. 1.61-21(f)(5)(iii) | $ 215,000 |
| Definition of "key employee" in top-heavy plan | Sec. 416(i)(1)(A)(i) | $ 170,000 |
| Catch-up contributions for participants age 50 or older — Secs. 401(k), 403(b), eligible Sec. 457 plans | Sec. 414(v)(2)(B)(i) | $ 6,000 |
| Catch-up contributions for participants age 50 or older — SIMPLE plans | Sec. 414(v)(2)(B)(ii) | $ 3,000 |

*For participants who separated from service before January 1, 2015, the limitation for defined benefit plans under § 415(b)(1)(B) is computed by multiplying the participant's compensation limitation, as adjusted through 2014, by 1.0178.

**As amended by Pub. L. No. 107-147, § 411(j)(1)(A).

### XVII.A.2.e. Distributions

### XVII.A.2.e.(1) Timing

[353 T.M., III.A.; TPS ¶5520.16.B.]

A profit-sharing plan must provide for distribution of funds accumulated under the plan after a fixed number of years, the attainment of a stated age, or upon the prior occurrence of some event such as layoff, illness, disability, retirement, death or termination of employment. Unlike a pension plan, profit-sharing plans may make in-service distributions (for example, after the participant has participated for a fixed number of years). A "fixed number of years" for this purpose means at least two years. A profit-sharing CODA is subject to additional restrictions (see XVII.A.3.). After-tax contributions (also referred to as voluntary contributions) made to a qualified plan by an employee are permitted to be withdrawn before retirement or termination of service, and the employee may also withdraw the earnings attributed to the after-tax contributions [Reg. § 1.401-1(b)(1)(iii); Rev. Rul. 71-295, 1971-2 C.B. 184, Rev. Rul. 69-277, 1969-1 C.B. 116].

Unlike profit-sharing or stock bonus plans, pension plans generally cannot make in-service distributions, such as hardship withdrawals or distributions upon the passage of a fixed period of years. Some exceptions apply to this rule: (i) working retirement distributions can be made to employees who have reached age 62 and who have not separated from employment at the time of the distribution; and (ii) distributions can be made to participants who have attained normal retirement age under the plan even if the participant has not severed employment [§ 401(a)(36); Reg. § 1.401(a)-1(b)(1)(i)].

### XVII.A.2.e.(2) Distributions Other than In-Service Distributions

[370 T.M., I.B., IV., VIII., & IX.; TPS ¶5520.10.]

*Form of Distributions.* Generally, the form in which a qualified retirement plan benefit may be distributed is determined by the overall plan design. For example, a qualified plan may provide that a benefit distribution may be made in the form of annuity payments, installment payments, or a single lump-sum payment. In general, a plan cannot be amended to remove a meaningful distribution option for benefits that have already accrued. However, distribution options may be removed prospectively for benefits accrued after the date of the option removal. Certain benefit forms are required in qualified plans, however, and are discussed below [§ 411(d)(6)].

*Survivor Annuities.* In general, distributions from a qualified retirement plan must be made in the form of either a qualified joint and survivor annuity (QJSA) or a qualified preretirement survivor annuity (QPSA), unless: (i) the participant waives his or her right to receive benefits in such form in writing and the waiver is accompanied by a written consent signed by the participant's spouse, or (ii) the benefit is valued at $5,000 or less. For federal tax purposes, including all retirement plan purposes, the term "spouse" includes an individual lawfully married lawfully to a person of the same sex. The IRS has adopted a general rule recognizing marriages of same-sex spouses that were validly entered into in a domestic or foreign jurisdiction the laws of which authorize the marriage of two individuals of the same sex, even if the married couple resides in a domestic or foreign jurisdiction that does not recognize the validity of same-sex marriages [§ 401(a)(11)(B), § 411(a)(11); *United States v. Windsor*, 133 S. Ct. 2675 (2013); Rev. Rul. 2013-17, 2013-38 I.R.B. 201; Rev. Rul. 58-66, 1958-1 C.B. 60].

The survivor annuity rules apply to the following types of qualified plans:

- any defined benefit plan;
- any defined contribution plan that is subject to minimum funding standards (i.e., a money purchase pension plan or target benefit plan, but not a profit-sharing or stock bonus plan);
- any other defined contribution plan unless (i) the plan provides that the participant's benefit is payable in full to the participant's surviving spouse, (ii) the participant does not elect to receive benefits in the form of a life annuity, and (iii) with respect to the participant, the plan was not a direct or indirect transferee in a plan to plan transfer of benefits from a defined benefit plan or defined contribution plan that is subject to the minimum funding standards.

The joint and survivor annuity rules generally require that a married participant who retires receive his or her benefit in the form of a QJSA absent a written election to receive a different form of benefit payment accompanied by a written spousal consent. The terms and conditions of the QJSA, and the right to make this election, must be set out in a written explanation that the plan must provide to each participant within a reasonable period of time before the annuity starting date [§ 401(a)(11)(A)(i), § 417(a)(1)(B), § 417(a)(3)].

Plans subject to the survivor annuity rules must also provide benefits in the form of a QPSA to a participant's surviving spouse if the participant dies with a vested benefit before the participant's annuity starting date. Under a QPSA, the surviving spouse will receive periodic payments over the spouse's lifetime. A qualified plan that is subject to the survivor annuity rules must provide an annuity that is the actuarial equivalent in value of at least 50%, and no more than 100%, of the participant's vested account balance as of the participant's date of death [§ 401(a)(11)(A)(ii), § 417(c)(2)].

***Restrictions on Certain Cash-Out Distributions.*** A qualified plan's ability to distribute any portion of a participant's benefit without the participant's consent may be restricted. A qualified plan must provide that a participant's nonforfeitable benefit worth more than $5,000 cannot be distributed in a single sum without the participant's consent. If the benefit is $5,000 or less, however, the plan need not obtain consent before distributing it in a single sum unless the distribution takes place after the participant's annuity starting date. However, if the benefit is more than $1,000 but less than $5,000, the plan sponsor may roll over the distribution involuntarily without the consent of the participant to an IRA, but must provide notice to the participant that the rollover is taking place [§ 402(f)(1)(A), § 411(a)(11)(A), § 417(e)(1); Reg. § 1.411(a)-11(c)(3)].

***Minimum Required Distributions.*** A qualified plan must make minimum required distributions (MRDs). The MRD rules determine the latest date by which benefit payments under a qualified plan must begin and establish the maximum time period over which such payments may be made. These rules assure that qualified plans are used to provide retirement benefits rather than to defer the receipt of income indefinitely, i.e., as estate planning tools. Failure to make required distributions results in an excise tax on the payee (unless waived by the IRS) equal to 50% of the amount by which the MRD exceeds the amount actually distributed during the year [§ 401(a)(9), § 4974].

In general, distributions to a participant in a qualified plan must begin by the participant's required beginning date (RBD) and must be paid over:

- the participant's lifetime;
- the lifetimes of the participant and a designated beneficiary; or
- a period, which may be a term certain, not extending beyond (i) the participant's life expectancy or (ii) the joint life expectancies of the participant and his or her designated beneficiary.

A participant's RBD is April 1 of the calendar year following the later of (i) the calendar year in which the participant turns age 70½; or (ii) the calendar year in which the participant retires. For a 5% or more owner of the employer, however, distributions must begin no later than April 1 of the calendar year following the year in which the 5% owner turns age 70½. A plan may require, by its terms, however, that the participant begin receiving distributions by April 1 of the year after the participant reaches age 70½, even if the participant has not retired or is not a 5% owner [§ 401(a)(9)(A), § 401(a)(9)(C)].

**Example.** Jessica is employed by ABC Corporation and is a participant in the ABC Corporation § 401(k) and defined benefit plans. Both plans include language that a participant's RBD does not begin until April 1 of the calendar year following the later of the year in which a participant turns 70½ or the year in which the participant retires. On March 15, 2014, Jessica turned 70. Assuming she is not a 5% owner, if Jessica is still employed by ABC Corporation on January 1, 2015, she will not be required to take a minimum distribution from either plan on April 1, 2015, even though she turned 70½ in 2014. Jessica's minimum distributions will begin on April 1 of the calendar year following the calendar year in which she eventually retires.

***Rollovers.*** A qualified retirement plan must allow participants to have any distribution that is eligible for rollover treatment transferred directly to an eligible retirement plan specified by the participant in a direct rollover. This rule applies to any part of the otherwise taxable portion of a distribution from a qualified plan that can be rolled over tax free (termed an "eligible rollover distribution"), except for [§ 402(c)(4)]:

- a distribution that is one of a series of payments based on life expectancy or paid over a period of 10 years or more;
- a required minimum distribution;
- a corrective distribution;
- a hardship distribution; or
- dividends on employer securities.

A qualified plan may implement a direct rollover by any reasonable means of delivery to the recipient retirement plan, such as a wire transfer or mailing a check to the trustee or custodian. The plan also may allow the employee to deliver a check to the recipient plan, so long as the payee line of the check is made out in a manner that will ensure that the check is negotiable solely by the recipient plan [Reg. § 1.401(a)(31)-1, Q&As-3 & -4].

In order for an eligible rollover distribution that is distributed to the participant (i.e., not through a direct rollover) to receive tax-free rollover treatment, it must be contributed to another qualified plan, tax-sheltered annuity, or individual retirement arrangement no later than the 60th day following the day it is received. The IRS may waive the 60-day requirement upon the filing of a private letter ruling request with the IRS by the taxpayer if failing to waive it would be against equity or good conscience, including cases of casualty, disaster, or other events beyond the reasonable control of the individual subject to the 60-day requirement. Automatic approval (requiring no application for a waiver) may be granted if a delay is due to a financial institution's error [Rev. Proc. 2003-16, 2003-4 I.R.B. 357]. Any taxable amount that is not rolled over is included in income in the year it is received. Any taxable distribution paid to a participant is also subject to mandatory withholding of 20%, even if the participant intends to roll the distribution over later [§ 402(c)(3), § 408(d)(3)(I)].

The plan administrator must give participants a written explanation of the rollover and withholding rules within a reasonable time before making an eligible rollover distribution. The notice must be designed to be easily understood and must explain [§ 402(f)]:

- the availability of the direct rollover option;
- the rules that require income tax withholding on eligible rollover distributions;
- the rules under which the participant may roll over the distribution within 60 days of receipt; and
- any other special tax rules that may apply to the distribution.

If a distributee is under age 59 ½ at the time of a distribution, any taxable portion not rolled over may be subject to a 10% additional tax on early distributions under § 72(t) (see XVII.A.2.e.(6)).

### XVII.A.2.e.(3)  In-Service Distributions

[370 T.M., III.; TPS ¶5550.06., .08.]

In-service distributions or withdrawals are distributions made to a plan participant during the course of his or her employment with the employer. In-service distributions can take many different forms, including payments at a stated age, loans and hardship withdrawals. The availability of in-service distributions is often a desirable feature in a plan to encourage employee participation.

*Attainment of a Stated Age.* A common form of permissible in-service distribution provided for under qualified plans is a distribution that is available upon the participant's attainment of a stated age, even though the participant remains in the employ of the employer. Many qualified profit-sharing or stock bonus plans provide that distributions may take place at the attainment of age 59 ½ because the 10% additional income tax imposed on early distributions from qualified plans under § 72(t) (see XVII.A.2.e.(6)) does not apply [§ 72(t)(2)(A)(i); Reg. § 1.401-1(b)(1)(ii)].

A defined benefit plan may allow participants who have attained age 62 or who have reached normal retirement age under the plan to take distributions while still employed. For this purpose, a plan's normal retirement age must be an age that is not earlier than the earliest age that is reasonably representative of the typical retirement age for the industry in which the covered workforce is employed. Generally, a good faith determination by the employer that an age between 55 and 62 is a normal retirement age will be given deference, assuming that the determination is reasonable under the facts and circumstances [§ 401(a)(36); Reg. § 1.401(a)-1(b)(1)(i), § 1.401(a)-1(b)(2)(iii)].

*Loans.* Subject to special limits discussed below, both pension and profit-sharing plans may provide for loans to participants. To retain the qualified status of a plan, the loans must be offered on a uniform and nondiscriminatory basis. Although benefits provided under a qualified plan generally may not be anticipated, assigned, or alienated, a loan made to a participant or beneficiary that is secured by the participant's vested accrued benefit will not be treated as an assignment or alienation of the plan assets if: (i) the plan's loan provisions only permit plan assets to be used as security for loans from the plan; and (ii) the plan loan is exempt from the excise tax on prohibited transactions. A plan loan is exempt from the excise tax on prohibited transactions if loans [§ 401(a)(4), § 401(a)(13), § 4975(d)(1); Reg. § 1.401(a)-13(b)(1), § 1.401(a)-13(d)(2)]:

- are available to all participants and beneficiaries on a reasonably equivalent basis;
- are not made available to highly-compensated employees in an amount greater than the amount available to other employees;
- are made in accordance with specific provisions set forth in the plan;
- bear a reasonable rate of interest; and
- are adequately secured.

Generally, the amount of a plan loan, plus the amount of all other outstanding loans to the participant, cannot exceed the lesser of (i) $50,000 or (ii) the greater of: (a) one-half of the participant's vested accrued benefit, or (b) $10,000. The loan must be evidenced by an enforceable agreement either in writing or in another form approved by the IRS. The agreement must specify the loan amount, the term of the loan, and the repayment schedule. If a loan does not satisfy the repayment or enforceable agreement requirements, the balance due under the loan is treated as a deemed distribution from the plan at the time the loan is made. If the loan meets those requirements but, at the time the loan is made, the loan amount exceeds the statutory amount limit, only the excess amount is a deemed distribution [Reg. § 1.72(p)-1, Q&As-3(b), -4A, -17].

*Hardship Distributions.* Hardship distributions to participants in a § 401(k) plan are permitted on account of an immediate and heavy financial need, as determined by the plan administrator or a duly-appointed delegate. Hardship distributions from a § 401(k) plan are limited to the amount of a participant's elective deferrals and generally do not include any income earned on the deferred amounts. If the plan permits, certain employer matching contributions and employer discretionary contributions may also be included in the hardship distributions [Reg. § 1.401(k)-1(d)(3)(i)].

A distribution must be made both on account of an immediate and heavy financial need of the participant and as is necessary to satisfy that financial need. The determination of the existence of an immediate and heavy financial need and of the amount necessary to meet the need must be made in accordance with nondiscriminatory and objective standards set forth in the plan. A distribution on account of hardship must be limited to the distributable amount. The distributable amount is equal to a participant's total elective deferrals as of the date of distribution, reduced by the amount of previous distributions of elective contributions [Reg. § 1.401(k)-1(d)(3)(ii), § 1.401(k)-1(d)(3)(iii)].

Whether a participant has an immediate and heavy financial need is determined based on all relevant facts and circumstances. For example, the need to pay funeral expenses would generally be an immediate and heavy financial need, while the purchase of a boat or television would not. A financial need may be immediate and heavy even if it was reasonably foreseeable or voluntarily incurred by the participant [Reg. § 1.401(k)-1(d)(3)(iii)(A)].

A distribution is deemed to be on account of an immediate and heavy financial need of the participant (i.e., meets a safe-harbor classification) if the distribution is for [Reg. § 1.401(k)-1(d)(3)(iii)(B)]:

- expenses for medical care previously incurred by the participant and the participant's family;
- costs directly related to the purchase of a principal residence (excluding mortgage payments);
- payment of tuition, related educational fees, and room and board expenses, for the next 12 months of postsecondary education for the participant, or the participant's spouse, children, or dependents;
- payments necessary to prevent the eviction of the participant from the participant's principal residence or foreclosure on the mortgage on that residence;
- funeral expenses; or
- certain expenses relating to the repair of damage to the participant's principal residence.

A distribution may not be treated as necessary to satisfy an immediate and heavy financial need of a participant to the extent the amount of the distribution is in excess of the amount required to relieve the financial need or to the extent the need may be satisfied from other resources that are reasonably available to the participant (e.g., a loan). The amount of an immediate and heavy financial need may include any amounts necessary to pay any federal, state, or local income taxes or penalties reasonably anticipated to result from the distribution [Reg. § 1.401(k)-1(d)(3)(iv)(A)].

This determination of what is necessary to satisfy an immediate and heavy financial need is made on the basis of all relevant facts and circumstances. The participant's resources are deemed to include those assets of the participant's spouse and minor children that are reasonably available to the participant.

---

**EXAMPLE:** A vacation home owned jointly by John, a participant in a § 401(k) plan, and his spouse, generally will be deemed a resource of John's.

---

Under a safe harbor, a distribution is deemed necessary to satisfy an immediate and heavy financial need of an employee if the amount distributed is not in excess of the amount of the need and all of the following requirements are satisfied [Reg. § 1.401(k)-1(d)(3)(iv)(E)]:

1. the employee has obtained all distributions, other than hardship distributions, and all nontaxable loans currently available under all plans maintained by the employer; and

2. the employee is prohibited under the terms of the plan or an otherwise legally enforceable agreement from making elective contributions or employee contributions to the plan and all other plans maintained by the employer for at least six months after the receipt of the hardship distribution.

### XVII.A.2.e.(4) Taxation of Distributions

[370 T.M., II.A. & II.B.; TPS ¶5550.06.B., .06.C.]

The form of the benefit distribution determines the manner in which the distribution is taxed [§ 72, § 402].

*Lump Sums.* A lump-sum distribution is a distribution of the balance to the credit of a participant (i.e., his or her entire interest) from a qualified plan during a single tax year of the recipient, which is paid [§ 402(e)(4)(D)]:

- on account of the participant's death;
- after the participant reaches age 59 ½;
- for self-employed individuals, on account of the participant's becoming disabled; or
- for all other individuals, on account of the participant's separation from the employer's service.

Generally, a lump sum distribution is subject to tax to the extent of the participant's basis in his or her total benefits. In most cases, participants will have a zero basis in the benefits and there is no special tax advantage to taking a lump sum distribution [§ 72(e)(2)(A)]. Before 2000, however, recipients of lump-sum distributions could use an income averaging treatment known as "forward averaging," which taxed the lump-sum distribution at a lower rate than other income received by the participant [Former § 402(d)].

*In-Service Distributions.* For an in-service distribution, the amount of the distribution allocable to after-tax contributions is excluded from the participant's gross income and the remainder of the distribution is taxable to the participant. The nontaxable portion of the distribution is the ratio of the amount of after-tax contributions to the total amount in the participant's account. This ratio is deemed the exclusion ratio [§ 72(e)(1)(A), § 72(e)(2)].

---

**EXAMPLE:** Charlie, age 40, has made total after-tax contributions of $10,000 to a § 401(a) qualified plan. He requests an in-service distribution. As of the date of distribution, his account is valued at $50,000. The exclusion ratio is equal to $10,000 (total amount of after-tax contributions) / $50,000 (value of the employee's account on the date of valuation) = 0.2 (20%).

---

*Non-Annuity Distributions Before Annuity Starting Date.* If a distribution is made before the annuity starting date, it is taxed in a manner similar to post-retirement distributions in that the entire payment is taxed as ordinary income to the participant if the participant has no basis. If the participant has some basis in the benefit, a portion of the payment will be a nontaxable recovery basis and the remainder will be ordinary income. To determine the taxation of a preretirement payment from a defined contribution plan, the recipient's investment in the plan is divided by the value of the vested portion of the total account balance. The result is the nontaxable amount of the distribution and the remainder is ordinary income [§ 72(e)(2)(B), § 72(e)(8)].

*Annuities.* In general, payments to a participant from a qualified plan as an annuity are includible as ordinary income as received. The amount that is includible as ordinary income depends on a participant's basis in his or her interest in the plan or "investment in the contract." Investment in the contract generally is the premium or other consideration paid by the employee, i.e., nondeductible contributions that have not been recovered on a tax-free basis. Generally, if the participant has basis or an investment in the contract, part of the distribution is nontaxable and the rest is ordinary income [§ 72(c)(2), § 402(a), § 403(a); Reg. § 1.61-11(a), § 1.72-4(d)(1)].

An amount is considered to be received as an annuity if it is payable at regular intervals over more than one year measured from the annuity starting date. The annuity starting date is the first day of the first period for which an amount is payable as an annuity. Each payment received as an annuity consists of: (i) a recovery of cost and (ii) amounts to be included in gross income. The nontaxable and taxable portions are determined by applying the exclusion ratio which is the ratio of the investment in the contract, or cost basis under the plan, as of the annuity starting date, to the expected return under the contract. The expected return represents the total amount receivable. In a life annuity, the expected return equals the anticipated annual annuity payment multiplied by the appropriate life expectancy factor set forth in a table published under applicable regulations. The table used to determine the expected number of payments depends on whether the payments are based on the life of one or more than one individual. In the case of an annuity payable based on the life of more than one individual, the total number of monthly annuity payments expected to be received is based on the combined ages of the annuitants at the annuity starting date [§ 72(b), § 72(c)(4), § 72(d)(1)(B); Reg. § 1.72-1(b), § 1.72-1(c), § 1.72-2(b)(2), § 1.72-2(b)(3), § 1.72-9].

---

**EXAMPLE:** Mary, who contributed $10,000 to her employer's qualified retirement plan, retires at age 65 and is paid an annuity of $200 per month over both her life and that of her spouse. Mary's spouse is age 70. Because the combined age of the annuitants when annuity payments commence is 135, the number of annuity payments is considered to be 260 under the applicable table. The exclusion ratio therefore is: ($10,000/260 = $38.46). The amount of each monthly annuity payment to Mary of $200 that may be recovered tax-free therefore is $38.46 per month. The remaining $161.54 per month is taxable.

---

Where payments are made less frequently than monthly, i.e., quarterly, semiannually or annually, an adjustment to the annuitant's life expectancy may be required. A second adjustment may be required where the interval between the annuity starting date and the first annuity payment is less than the interval between subsequent annuity payments. The amount of the adjustments is determined pursuant to regulations. The adjustment to the annuitant's life expectancy may result in up to a 0.5% variance. In a term-certain annuity, the expected return equals each payment times the number of such payments.

If the annuity is payable to a primary annuitant and more than one survivor annuitant, the combined ages of the annuitants is the sum of the age of the primary annuitant and the youngest survivor annuitant. If the annuity is payable to more than one survivor annuitant but there is no primary annuitant, the combined ages of the annuitants is the sum of the age of the oldest survivor annuitant and the youngest survivor annuitant. In addition, any survivor annuitant whose entitlement to payments is contingent on an event other than the death of the primary annuitant is disregarded [Notice 98-2, 1998-2 I.R.B. 22].

If the excludible amount is greater than the amount of the annuity payment, then each annuity payment will be completely excluded from gross income until the entire investment is recovered. Annuity payments received after the investment is recovered are fully includible in gross income. If annuity payments cease by reason of death, a deduction for the unrecovered investment in the contract, if any, is allowed on the distributee's last income tax return [Notice 98-2].

If, in connection with the commencement of annuity payments, the taxpayer receives a lump-sum payment, the payment will be taxable as if received before the annuity starting date, and the investment in the contract is determined as if such payment had been so received [§ 72(d)(1)(D), § 72(e)].

---

**EXAMPLE:** Frank, age 57, retires and begins receiving retirement benefits in the form of a joint and 50% survivor annuity to be paid for the joint lives of Frank and his spouse, age 57. Frank contributed $31,000 to the plan. Frank's annuity starting date is July 1, 1998. On Frank's annuity starting date, in connection with receiving the first annuity payment, Frank receives a single sum payment of $10,000. Had the single sum payment of $10,000 been received before Frank's annuity starting date, then $2,000 would have been considered as a recovery of Frank's investment in the contract. Frank will receive a monthly retirement benefit of $1,500 per month, and his spouse will receive a monthly survivor benefit of $750 upon Frank's death.

Because the $10,000 is treated as if received before the annuity starting date, Frank will include $8,000 in income as a result of the single sum payment ($10,000 minus $2,000) and for purposes of determining the tax-free portion of each annuity payment, Frank's investment in the contract is $29,000 (the after-tax contributions to the plan minus the $2,000 portion of the single sum payment representing the recovery of Frank's investment in the contract). The expected number of monthly payments for two annuitants whose combined ages are 114 is 360. The tax-free portion of each $1,500 monthly annuity payment is $80.56, determined by dividing Frank's remaining investment ($29,000) by the expected number of payments (360).

Upon Frank's death, if Frank has not recovered the full $29,000 investment, his spouse will also exclude $80.56 from each $750 monthly annuity payment. Any annuity payments received after the 360 monthly payments have been made will be fully includible in gross income. If Frank and his spouse both die before 360 monthly payments have been made, a deduction is allowed for the last income tax return in the amount of the unrecovered investment.

---

*Losses.* Assuming a participant itemizes deductions, a deductible ordinary loss occurs in the tax year in which a cash distribution from a plan, representing the balance to the employee's credit, is less than unrecovered employee contributions [Rev. Rul. 72-305, 1972-1 C.B. 116].

### XVII.A.2.e.(5) Distributions in Kind – Property Distributions

[370 T.M., II.C.; TPS ¶5550.06.E.]

Special tax rules apply if the distribution from a qualified plan consists totally or partially of securities of the employer corporation. If a taxpayer receives securities of the participant's employer as a distribution in-kind from a qualified plan, part or all of the net unrealized appreciation (NUA) on the securities is shielded from current tax. NUA is the difference between the fair market value of the securities at the time of distribution and their cost or other basis to the distributing trust. If the distribution consists in part of securities that have appreciated and part that have depreciated, the "net" unrealized appreciation is the net increase in value of all of the securities included in the distribution. The amount of NUA shielded from current tax depends upon whether the distribution qualifies as a lump-sum distribution (see XVII.A.2.e.(4)). If the distribution qualifies as a lump-sum distribution, all of the NUA is excludible at the time of distribution. If it does not, only that portion of the NUA that is attributable to nondeductible employee contributions is excludible [§ 402(e)(4)].

NUA is not taxed until the recipient sells or disposes of the securities. The recipient pays some tax on the employer securities at the time of distribution, however. The amount subject to tax generally is the cost basis of the distributing trust in the securities, because the recipient pays tax on the value of the securities at the time of distribution. If only part of the NUA is excluded (because the distribution is not a lump-sum distribution but some of the appreciation is attributable to nondeductible employee contributions), some of the appreciation is taxed. Such taxable amounts are added to the recipient's basis in the securities [Reg. § 1.402(a)-1(b)(3)(vi); Rev. Rul. 80-258, 1980-2 C.B. 137].

---

**EXAMPLE:** Sally receives a lump-sum distribution, including employer securities on which there is NUA. The cost basis in the securities is $1,200. Upon distribution, their value is $1,700. Sally pays tax on $1,200 at the time of distribution; $500 is NUA. Three years later, Sally sells the securities for $2,000. Of the $800 gain ($2,000 - $1,200), $500 is NUA, taxable as long-term capital gain. The additional $300 is taxed as a long-term capital gain.

---

### XVII.A.2.e.(6) Additional 10% Tax on Early Distributions

[370 T.M., X.D.1.; TPS ¶5550.08.B.]

Generally, the taxable portion of distributions made before the date on which a participant attains age 59½ is subject to the imposition of a 10% additional income tax. To the extent a distribution is a nontaxable return of nondeductible contributions or is rolled over into another plan or an IRA, the 10% additional tax does not apply. There is no general financial hardship exception to the 10% additional tax, but distributions made under certain circumstances, such as the following, are not subject to the tax [§ 72(t)]:

- death;
- disability;
- distributions under a qualified domestic relations order (QDRO) (except for IRA distributions);
- substantially equal periodic payments over the life expectancy of the participant (or joint life expectancies where there is a beneficiary);

- amounts distributed to pay for qualified educational and first-time homebuyer expenses;
- amounts distributed to pay for certain deductible medical expenses;
- distributions to unemployed individuals for health insurance premiums; and
- distributions after separation from service where the participant has attained age 55.

The plan administrator is not required to withhold the amount of the § 72(t) additional income tax from an early distribution from a qualified plan. The recipient of an early distribution generally reports the § 72(t) additional income tax on Form 5329, *Additional Taxes on Qualified Plans (Including IRAs) and Other Tax-Favored Accounts.*

### XVII.A.2.f. Employer Deductions

[371 T.M., III., IV.; TPS ¶5550.08.B.]

In order to be deductible, contributions to a qualified plan must be "ordinary and necessary" business expenses. Contributions made to a qualified plan on an employee's behalf, when considered together with other compensation paid to that employee, must constitute a reasonable allowance for compensation for the services actually rendered. An employer may deduct the administrative expenses associated with operation of a qualified plan that it pays, such as legal, actuarial, accounting, and trustee fees, so long as they are ordinary and necessary business expenses [§ 162, § 212; Reg. § 1.404(a)-1(b)].

***Deductions for Defined Contribution Plans.*** The limit on the deductibility of contributions to a qualified profit-sharing or stock bonus plan is 25% of the compensation paid or accrued to participants [§ 404(a)(3)(A); Reg. § 1.404(a)-9].

---

**EXAMPLE:** Corporation B sponsors a qualified profit-sharing plan. During the corporation's 2015 tax year, a total of $150,000 in compensation is paid to participants. The corporation can contribute and deduct up to $37,500, provided such a contribution can be made under the plan's terms.

---

"Compensation" for deduction purposes is all of the compensation paid or accrued, including certain salary reduction amounts, except compensation that is deductible as a contribution to a qualified plan. Hence, except for an employee's pre-tax contributions to certain plans, an employer's contributions under a profit-sharing or stock bonus plan and under any other qualified plan on behalf of the employees covered by the profit-sharing or stock bonus plan are not counted [§ 404(a)(12); Reg. § 1.404(a)-9(b)(2)].

Generally, contributions in excess of the deduction limit generally may be carried over and deducted in a later year (the "carryforward year") in the order of time, to the extent that, when added to any contributions for the carryforward year, the resulting amount does not exceed the percentage limit of compensation paid or accrued during the succeeding year. Excess contributions are subject to a 10% excise tax, however [§ 404(a)(3)(A)(ii), § 4972].

The employer's contribution deduction also depends upon the plan's compliance with the Code's limit on maximum annual additions under defined contribution plans (see XVII.A.2.d.). To the extent that the annual additions to a participant's account in a qualified defined contribution plan exceed the maximum annual addition limit, the employer's otherwise allowable deduction will be denied. Contributions that are not deductible because they cause an employee's account to receive contributions in excess of the maximum annual addition limit may not be carried over and deducted [§ 404(j)].

*Deductions for Defined Benefit Plans.* Because defined benefit plans promise a specific level of benefits rather than a particular level of annual contributions, an employer usually must employ an actuary to determine the contribution necessary to fund promised benefits. Thus, rather than limiting the employer's deduction to a percentage of participants' compensation, as is the case with defined contribution plans, the deduction limits for defined benefit pension plans are based upon the amount needed to satisfy the I.R.C.'s minimum funding standard for the year.

Generally, the deductible limit for single-employer defined benefit plans is the greater of: (i) any excess of the sum of the year's target normal cost (generally the cost of benefits accrued in the year) plus the amount necessary to fully fund the funding target, plus a cushion amount, which is 50% of the funding target plus additional amounts reflecting projections of the participants' compensation and statutory compensation limits, minus the value of plan assets; or (ii) the minimum required contributions [§ 404(o), § 430].

### XVII.A.2.g. Employment Taxes, Withholding and Reporting

[392 T.M., III.A.3.b(2)(a); TPS ¶5550.01.]

Contributions (including employer contributions) to a qualified pension, annuity, profit-sharing or stock bonus plan whose trust is exempt from tax are exempt from income tax withholding and FICA [§ 3121(a)(5), § 3306(b)(5), § 3401(a)(12)]. However, salary reduction contributions made by an employee to a cash or deferred arrangement, such as a § 401(k) plan, are included in the definition of wages for purposes of FICA and FUTA taxes (but not income tax withholding) [§ 3121(v)(1), § 3306(r)(1)]. For a detailed discussion of the employment taxes, withholding and reporting requirements for distributions from a qualified plan, see XXII.A.6.a.

### XVII.A.3. Cash or Deferred Arrangements, Including § 401(k) Plans

[358 T.M., III.; TPS ¶5560.01.C.]

A cash or deferred arrangement (CODA), such as a § 401(k) plan, is an arrangement, generally forming part of a qualified profit-sharing or stock bonus plan, under which an eligible employee may elect to have certain payments made to a trust under the plan for the employee's benefit, or to the employee directly in cash. Because a CODA is part of a qualified profit-sharing or stock bonus plan, other employer contributions may be permitted in addition to the elective deferrals by employees. Many CODAs have been established in the form of savings plans. Under such arrangements, typically the employee may contribute a percentage of pay as a basic contribution by directing that this amount be the subject of an elective deferral. To effectuate elective deferrals, participants enter into binding salary reduction agreements whereby they agree to reduce their salary by the amount they elect to be contributed to the CODA. Subject to statutory limits and nondiscrimination requirements, employers can make deductible matching contributions to the plan equal to part or all of the employee's elective deferral [§ 401(k)(2)(A)].

### XVII.A.3.a. Automatic Contribution Arrangements

[358 T.M., II.B.2.; TPS ¶5560.01.C.2.]

A qualified CODA may include an arrangement under which the employer automatically reduces the compensation of eligible employees by a percentage specified in the plan. Such amounts will be treated as CODA contributions, unless an employee affirmatively elects not to have any contribution made or elects a different contribution percentage. Many § 401(k) plan sponsors use automatic contribution arrangements as a technique for increasing participation in their § 401(k) plans. The underlying theory is that more employees will participate in a § 401(k) plan or will participate at a higher level if they do not have to take affirmative steps to initiate participation or to designate a specific salary reduction percentage [Reg. § 1.401(k)-1(a)(3)(ii); Rev. Rul. 2000-8, 2000-8 I.R.B. 617].

### XVII.A.3.b. Designation of Elective Contributions as Roth Contributions

[358 T.M., VI.; TPS ¶5560.01.C.3.g.]

A CODA may allow an employee to designate some or all elective contributions as designated Roth contributions. Designated Roth contributions are elective contributions under a CODA that, unlike pre-tax elective contributions, are subject to federal income tax at the time they are deducted from employee compensation. The investment gain attributable to designated Roth contributions, like gain on pre-tax contributions, accumulates on a tax-free basis. However, in contrast to pre-tax elective contributions, a qualified distribution of an amount attributable to designated Roth contributions is not subject to federal income tax. This is comparable to the tax treatment of a Roth IRA. Like regular § 401(k) contributions, designated Roth contributions are subject to FICA taxation at the time they are made. For a discussion of Roth IRAs, see XVII.A.6. [§ 402A(d)(1), § 3121(v)(1)(A)].

### XVII.A.3.c. Annual Deferral Limitation

[358 T.M., VIII.; TPS ¶5560.01.C.3.a.]

Elective deferrals under qualified cash and deferred arrangements (including designated Roth contributions) (see XVII.A.3.b.) are subject to a special annual limitation. This limitation is $15,000 per year, as adjusted for inflation ($18,000 for 2015, $17,500 for 2014). This limit applies to all elective deferrals made by an individual to plans that permit such contributions [§ 401(a)(30), § 402(g)(1)(B), § 402(g)(4); IRS News Release IR-2014-99 (Oct. 23, 2014); Notice 2013–73, 2013-49 I.R.B. 598].

A plan may allow an individual age 50 or over to make additional elective deferrals each year, up to a dollar limit, if certain requirements provided under that section are satisfied. These additional elective deferrals are typically referred to as "catch-up contributions." Catch-up contributions are not subject to any otherwise applicable limitations on elective deferrals, including the § 402(g) elective deferral limit, the § 415 defined contribution limit (discussed below), or a plan-imposed limit. Catch-up contributions must be available to all catch-up eligible individuals who participate under any plan maintained by the employer that provides for elective deferrals. The applicable catch-up contribution amount is $5,000 as adjusted for inflation. For 2015, the applicable amount is $6,000 ($5,500 for 2014) [§ 414(v); IRS News Release IR-2014-99 (Oct. 23, 2014); Notice 2013–73].

### XVII.A.3.d. Restrictions on Distribution

[358 T.M., III.D.; TPS ¶5560.01.C.3.a.]

Amounts held by a plan that are attributable to elective contributions under a qualified CODA may not, in general, be distributed before the employee's death, disability, severance from employment, hardship, or attainment of age 59½ , except upon plan termination [§ 401(k)(2)(B)]. After-tax employee contributions, and rollovers to a CODA, are not subject to these restrictions [§ 402(c), § 408(d)(3)(A)]. A "severance from employment" occurs when an employee ceases to be an employee of the employer maintaining the plan, e.g., when an employee terminates employment with his or her employer and goes to work for an unrelated employer. An employee who is transferred to an employer that is a member of the employer's controlled group of employers does not have a severance from employment [Reg. § 1.401(k)-1(d)(2)]. An employee does not have a severance from employment if he or she transfers employment to another employer maintaining the § 401(k) plan, even if the employer is unrelated to the employee's former employer [Notice 2002-4, 2002-1 C.B. 298]. Distributions may not be made upon termination of the plan if, at the time the plan is terminated or within the period ending 12 months after distribution of all its assets, the employer maintains any other defined contribution plan, other than an ESOP, a SEP, a SIMPLE IRA plan, a § 403(b) plan, a § 457(b), or a § 457(f) plan.

Hardship is the only circumstance in which a distribution may be made before age 59½ to an active employee. The regulations provide that hardship distributions are permitted only if: (i) the distribution is made on account of an immediate and heavy financial need of the employee; and (ii) the distribution is necessary to satisfy the financial need. Hardship distributions from a CODA are limited to elective contributions net of allocable income. Even though a hardship distribution may be permitted, it may be subject to the additional 10% tax on premature distributions (see XVII.A.2.e.(b)). [Reg. § 1.401(k)-1(d)(3)(ii)(A)]. Hardship distributions are discussed in more detail in XVII.A.2.e.(3).

Once an event occurs that permits distribution of benefits under a CODA, those distributions are subject to the general requirements for qualified pension, profit-sharing and stock bonus plans relating to the form and time in which distributions may be made or must be made. See XVII.A.2.e. for a general discussion of distributions from qualified plans.

### XVII.A.3.e. Employment Taxes and Income Tax Withholding

[358 T.M., I.C.; TPS ¶5440.01.]

Amounts contributed to a CODA are subject to FICA and FUTA withholding but are exempt from income tax withholding [§ 3121(v)(1)(A), § 3306(r)(1)(A), § 3401(a)(12)(A)] (see XXII.A.5.b.).

### XVII.A.4. Tax-Sheltered Annuities (§ 403(b) Plans)

[373 T.M., III.; TPS ¶5630.]

Tax-sheltered annuities (TSAs), sometimes called § 403(b) plans because of the I.R.C. section under which they are regulated, often are the basic funding vehicle for retirement plans maintained by colleges, universities, hospitals and other tax-exempt employers. Individual employees of such employers also may use TSAs as a means of saving on a pre-tax basis, through salary reduction agreements. The motivating factor behind the adoption of most TSAs, whether on a salary reduction basis or as the funding vehicle for an employer-sponsored plan, is the favorable federal tax treatment afforded such arrangements for the recipients. Contributions may be made without causing current income recognition to participants, and earnings may accumulate free of current income tax.

A TSA is purchased on behalf of an individual by his employer. The employer must be either: (i) a public school; or (ii) a religious, charitable, educational, scientific or similar organization that the IRS has recognized as qualifying for tax-deductible contributions [§ 403(b)(1)(A)].

To be eligible for a TSA, an individual must be a common law employee of the organization rather than self-employed as a sole proprietor, independent contractor or partner [Reg. § 1.403(b)-2(b)(9)].

### XVII.A.4.a. Funding

[373 T.M., III.E.; TPS ¶5630.02.]

TSAs are funded by one of four kinds of investments:

1. annuity contracts;
2. custodial accounts;
3. retirement income accounts; or
4. face amount certificates.

*Annuity Contracts.* An annuity contract may take the form of an individual annuity contract in the employee's name or a group annuity contract taken out by an employer that provides separate accounts for eligible employees [Reg. § 1.403(b)-2(b)(2), § 1.403(b)-8(c)(1)].

Annuity contracts are attractive for their portability. An employee leaving one employer to go to work for another may have the new employer make TSA contributions to the existing contract (assuming the new employer is eligible to make TSA contributions) [Reg. § 1.403(b)-10(b); Rev. Rul. 68-33, 1968-1 C.B. 175].

To qualify as a TSA, an annuity contract must preclude distributions to the employee of funds that are attributable to salary reduction contributions until the employee reaches age 59½, except in the case of death, disability, separation from employment, or financial hardship. The annuity contract must be nontransferable [§ 403(b)(11); Reg. § 1.403(b)-6(d)(1)(ii)].

*Custodial Accounts.* Use of a custodial account avoids the need to invest through an annuity contract issued by an insurance company. A TSA must be invested in stock of a regulated investment company (a mutual fund). The entity holding a custodial account's investments must be a bank or other similar firm approved by the IRS. Custodial accounts qualify as TSAs only if the employee may not receive distributions before age 59½, except in the case of death, disability, separation from employment, or financial hardship [§ 403(b)(7), § 851].

*Retirement Income Accounts.* Churches and certain related organizations may offer TSAs in the form of retirement income accounts. These organizations are [§ 403(b)(9)(B), § 414(e)(3)(A); Reg. § 1.403(b)-9(a)(1)]:

- churches;
- conventions or associations of churches; and
- organizations (whether or not incorporated) controlled by or associated with a church or convention or association of churches if their principal purpose is administering or funding a program of benefits for employees of a church or convention or association of churches.

A retirement income account generally is a defined contribution program of contributions on behalf of an eligible employee. It is not subject to the requirement that its custodian be a bank or other firm approved by the IRS. More significant, the retirement income account may be commingled in a common investment fund with other church funds. The portion of the fund held by retirement income accounts must be used for the exclusive purpose of providing benefits for eligible employees and their beneficiaries [Reg. § 1.403(b)-2(b)(15), § 1.403(b)-9(a)(2), § 1.403(b)-9(a)(6)].

*Face-Amount Certificates.* A face-amount certificate, as defined in the Investment Company Act of 1940, is treated as an eligible TSA if it is nontransferable.

These certificates are contracts issued by mutual fund companies [§ 401(g); § 2(a)(15) of the Investment Company Act of 1940 (15 U.S.C., sec. 80a-2)].

***TSAs Funded Through Salary Reduction Agreements.*** The simplest and least costly form of a TSA from the employer's perspective is a TSA funded through a salary reduction agreement with the employee. Such arrangements offer substantial tax advantages and flexibility to the employees at little cost to the employer [Reg. § 31.3121(a)(5)-2].

### XVII.A.4.b. Nondiscrimination Requirements

[373 T.M., III.I.; TPS ¶5630.03.A., .04.B.]

Certain restrictions apply to an employer, other than a church, wishing to offer salary reduction TSAs. The restrictions prevent employers from discriminating in favor of highly-compensated employees. Unless the nondiscrimination requirements are met, employees may be taxable on their contributions. In addition, the employer must accept any salary reduction amount of more than $200 per year [§ 403(b)(12)(A)(ii); Reg. § 1.403(b)-5(b)(3)(i)].

In addition, many of the nondiscrimination rules that apply to qualified retirement plans also apply to contributions to TSAs that are not made pursuant to a salary reduction agreement. These include the requirements relating to minimum age and length of service, employer contributions, coverage, and vesting. However, these rules do not apply to church or government plans [§ 403(b)(12)(A); Reg. § 1.403(b)-5(d)].

### XVII.A.4.c. Contributions

[373 T.M., III.L.; TPS ¶5630.05.A.]

The principal tax advantage of a TSA is its ability to receive contributions without requiring the employee to pay current federal income tax on those amounts until they are distributed. Earnings on these amounts also are not taxable until distribution.

***Salary Reduction Contributions.*** An employee makes salary reduction contributions to a TSA by directing the employer to reduce his or her salary and divert the amount of the reduction to the TSA. The employee does not have to pay current federal income tax on the amount of the reduction.

Contributions funded through salary reduction elections often are called "elective deferrals" because they are made at the employee's election and they defer payment of federal income taxes on the amount contributed until it is distributed from the TSA. Generally, an employee cannot make more than a statutory amount of salary reductions per year. This limit is $18,000 for 2015 ($17,500 for 2014). The dollar limit includes any salary reduction contributions the employee makes under a § 401(k) plan (see XVII.A.3.), a salary reduction simplified employee pension (SARSEP (see XVII.A.8.d.)), or a SIMPLE plan (see XVII.A.9.). TSA salary reduction contributions also count towards the annual limits on salary reduction deferrals to certain other types of deferred compensation arrangements. However, two catch-up elections allow employees to contribute deferrals in excess of the statutory amount. The age 50 catch-up election permits employees who are at least 50 before the end of the tax year to make additional contributions of up to $6,000 for 2015 ($5,500 for 2014) [§ 402(g)(1), § 414(v)(2)(B), § 415(c)(1); IRS News Release IR-2014-99 (Oct. 23, 2014); Notice 2013–73, 2013–49 I.R.B. 598.] Further, certain employees who have 15 years of service with an eligible employer may contribute amounts in excess of the annual limit (usually $3,000 a year, up to $15,000 total, but more in the case of employees with many years of service who did not make maximum contributions in prior years) [§ 402(g)(7)(A)(ii); Reg. § 1.403(b)-4(c)(3)(i) through § 1.403(b)-4(c)(3)(iii)].

Church employees may elect to make additional contributions of up to $10,000 in a year. Annual additions under this rule for all years may not exceed a lifetime maximum of $40,000 [§ 415(c)(7)(A)].

When an employee makes more than the annual dollar amount limit in salary reduction contributions for a year, the employee must pay income tax on the amount of such contributions in excess of the limit [§ 402(g)(1), § 403(b)(1)(E); Reg. § 1.403(b)-4(a), § 1.403(b)-4(f)(1)].

The employee will be taxed a second time on the same amount when it is actually distributed from the TSA unless [§ 402(g)(2)(A)(ii); Reg. § 1.403(b)-4(f)(4)]:

1. it is withdrawn before April 15 of the year after the year in which it was contributed; and

2. the withdrawal includes any earnings on the excess amount.

By making a withdrawal by April 15, not only does the employee avoid being taxed a second time; the employee also avoids the 10% additional tax on early distributions from qualified plans under § 72(t), which also applies to TSAs [§ 402(g)(2)(C)].

***Overall Contributions.*** Subject to the various exceptions outlined above for church employees, the maximum contribution that can be made to a participant's account (including salary deferrals) cannot exceed the lesser of: (i) $40,000, as adjusted for inflation ($53,000 for 2015, $52,000 for 2014); or (ii) 100% of the employee's compensation. This is the same "annual addition" limit that applies to qualified plans as well as other defined contribution plans [§ 415(c)(1); IRS News Release IR-2014-99 (Oct. 23, 2014); Notice 2013–73.]

### XVII.A.4.d. Minimum Distributions

[373 T.M., III.K.1.; TPS ¶5630.05.C.]

Like qualified plans and IRAs, TSA distributions generally are limited in their ability to postpone distributions after age 70 1/2 and after death. For benefits earned after 1986, an employee generally must begin receiving distributions from his or her TSA no later than April 1 of the year after the year in which the employee turns age 70 1/2. Once distributions have commenced, the payments must continue over [§ 403(b)(10); Reg. § 1.403(b)-6(e)]:

- the employee's lifetime or the joint lifetimes of the employee and a designated beneficiary; or

- a period of years in installment payments, but the period cannot exceed the life expectancy of the employee or the joint life expectancy of the employee and a designated beneficiary.

### XVII.A.4.e. Loans and Hardship Withdrawals

[373 T.M., III.K.2.; TPS ¶5630.05.C.1., .05.D.]

Loans to employees may be made from a TSA annuity contract within certain limits. Failure to comply with these limits causes the loan to be considered a taxable distribution. The rules applicable to TSA loans are the same as those that apply to loans from qualified plans (see XVII.A.2.e.(3)). Distributions of salary reduction contributions from custodial accounts and annuity contracts may also be made before age 59½ on account of "financial hardship." The rules for a hardship withdrawal are the same as those that apply to hardship withdrawals from § 401(k) plans (see XVII.A.2.e.(3)) [§ 403(b)(7)(A)(ii), § 403(b)(11); Reg. § 1.403(b)-6(d)(1)(i)].

### XVII.A.4.f. Taxation of Distributions

[373 T.M., III.N.1. & III.N.7.; TPS ¶5630.06.D.]

Distributions from TSAs are treated much like distributions from qualified plans and IRAs. TSA distributions generally are taxable to the employee, but they are eligible for tax-free rollovers, i.e., a distribution from a TSA is not taxable to the employee to the extent it is rolled over into another eligible retirement plan within 60 days. The requirements for a rollover basically are the same as those that apply to qualified plan distributions (see XVII.A.2.e.(2)) [§ 402(c)(8)(B), § 403(b)(8), § 403(b)(10)].

Distributions to employees generally are subject to federal income tax (i.e., an employee will rarely have a tax "basis" in a TSA distribution). The taxable part of a distribution also may be subject to a 10% tax penalty if the employee is not yet age 59½ (even if the distribution is made on account of financial hardship (see XVII.A.2.e.(4)) [§ 72(t); Reg. § 1.403(b)-7(a)].

### XVII.A.4.g. Employment Taxes and Withholding

[373 T.M., III.O.; TPS ¶5630.06.]

Amounts contributed to the TSA of an employee are not "wages" for federal income tax withholding purposes, even if the contributions are made through salary reductions [Rev. Rul. 65-208, 1965-2 C.B. 414].

If a contribution to the employee's TSA is made through salary reduction, it will be subject to employment taxes. On the other hand, if the employer's contribution is not made through salary reduction, it will not be subject to employment taxes. There is no federal income tax withholding on any salary reductions [§ 3121(a)(5)(D), § 3121(a)(5)(E), § 3306(b)(5)(E)]. For a discussion of the employment taxes and income tax withholding requirements on distributions from TSAs, see XXII.A.6.a.

### XVII.A.5. Individual Retirement Arrangements (IRAs)

[367 T.M., I.B.; TPS ¶5610.01.]

The term IRA or traditional IRA refers to any one of three vehicles accorded the same special tax treatment by the I.R.C.:

- an individual retirement account;
- an individual retirement annuity; and
- a group individual retirement account sponsored by an employer or labor union.

An "individual retirement account" is a trust or custodial account established by an individual with a bank or similarly qualified firm acting as trustee or custodian. An "individual retirement annuity" is an annuity contract issued by an insurance company into which the individual pays premiums instead of contributions. A "group individual retirement account established by an employer or labor union" is essentially an individual retirement account, but a single account is established with a bank or custodian by the employer or employee association. The tax advantages of an IRA are that (i) contributions made to an IRA can be fully or partially deductible, and (ii) generally, amounts in a traditional IRA are not taxed until distributed.

### XVII.A.5.a. Eligibility Requirements

[367 T.M., I.; TPS ¶5610.02.]

Subject to limitations, individuals can open and make contributions to an IRA to the extent they (or, in the case of individuals filing a joint return, their spouse) received taxable compensation during the year, and they were not age 70 ½ by the end of the year. Except for rollover contributions, all IRA contributions must be made in cash [§ 219].

### XVII.A.5.b. Contributions

[367 T.M., III.A.; TPS ¶5610.02.B.2.].

A contribution is considered made for a tax year if [§ 219(f)(3)]:

- it is contributed during that tax year; or
- it is contributed after the tax year has ended but before the due date for filing the IRA owner's federal income tax return for that year.

Contributions to an IRA are subject to annual limits. Although IRA contributions generally are deductible, the deductible amount may be reduced or eliminated if the IRA owner is an active participant in one of certain types of retirement plans. The contribution limit applies not only to contributions made by the owner to his IRA but also to contributions made to the IRA by others on behalf of the owner, such as a relative or employer [§ 219(b)(1), § 408(a)(1)].

The maximum annual contribution is adjusted annually for inflation and is $5,500 for both 2014 and 2015 [Rev. Proc. 2013-35, 2013-47 I.R.B. 537, IRS News Release IR-2014-99 (Oct. 23, 2014)]. Individuals who have, or will have, attained age 50 by the end of a year may make additional catch-up IRA contributions of up to $1,000 (not indexed for inflation) [§ 219(b)(5)].

### XVII.A.5.c. Deductible Amounts

[367 T.M., III.A.4.; TPS ¶5610.03.A.4.b.]

The maximum deductible amount generally is the lesser of the maximum annual contribution amount (discussed in XVII.A.5.b.) or the amount of taxable compensation the individual has for the year.

---

**EXAMPLE:** Martha, who is 34 years old and single, earns $24,000 in 2015. Her IRA contributions for 2015 are limited to $5,500.

**EXAMPLE:** Alejandro, an unmarried college student working part time, earns $3,500 in 2015. His IRA contributions for 2015 are limited to $3,500, the amount of his compensation.

---

If both spouses have enough taxable compensation, each may contribute to his or her own IRA and deduct up to his or her own limit [§ 219(b)(1)].

*Active Participant Limitations.* An individual who is an "active participant" in an employer-maintained retirement plan may not make a *deductible* contribution to an IRA unless the individual's adjusted gross income (AGI) for the tax year falls below certain prescribed amounts, as adjusted for inflation. If it does fall below the prescribed amounts, a full or partial deduction will be available, depending on the individual's income level.

For tax years beginning in 2015, the applicable dollar amount for single individuals who are active participants that begins the phase-out is modified AGI of $61,000 for 2015 ($60,000 for 2014). A complete phase-out is attained when AGI reaches $71,000 ($70,000 for 2014) [§ 219(g)(3)(B)(ii), § 219(g)(8); IRS News Release IR-2014-99 (Oct. 23, 2014); Rev. Proc. 2013-35, 2013-47 I.R.B. 537].

For married individuals filing jointly who are active participants, the phase-out range for 2015 is AGI of $98,000 through $118,000 ($96,000 through $116,000 for 2014). For a married active participant who files separately, the phase-out range is

AGI of $1 through $10,000. The $10,000 dollar limit is not subject to inflationary increases [§ 219(g)(3)(B), § 219(g)(4); IRS News Release IR-2014-99 (Oct. 23, 2014); Notice 2013–73; Rev. Proc. 2013-35].

An individual is not considered an active participant in an employer-sponsored retirement plan merely because the individual's spouse is an active participant. However, the maximum deductible IRA contribution for an individual who is not an active participant but whose spouse is an active participant is phased out. For 2014, the phase-out begins when AGI for the tax year exceeds $183,000 ($181,000 for 2014), and the deduction is fully phased out when AGI reaches $193,000 ($191,000 for 2014) [§ 219(g)(7); Rev. Proc. 2013-35; IRS News Release IR-2014-99 (Oct. 23, 2014)].

*Nondeductible Contributions.* Any nondeductible contributions may be withdrawn as excess contributions or may be left in the IRA as designated nondeductible contributions. Once in an IRA, nondeductible contributions generate tax-free earnings just as deductible contributions do.

An IRA owner must report all nondeductible contributions on Form 8606, *Nondeductible IRAs*. The form is filed along with Form 1040 or 1040A. An IRA owner who fails to file Form 8606 is subject to a penalty of $50 per failure, unless the failure is shown to be due to reasonable cause [§ 6693(b)(2)].

---

**EXAMPLE:** Richard is 29 years old and single. In 2015, he was covered by a retirement plan at work. His salary is $62,000. His modified AGI is $75,000. Richard makes a $5,500 IRA contribution for 2015. Because he was covered by a retirement plan and his modified AGI is above $71,000, he cannot deduct his $5,500 IRA contribution. If he decides to leave his contribution in his IRA, he must designate it as a nondeductible contribution by reporting it on Form 8606.

---

### XVII.A.5.d. Compensation for IRA Purposes

[367 T.M., III.A.4.b.; TPS ¶5610.03.A.4.b.]

For IRA purposes, "compensation" includes wages, salaries, professional fees for providing personal services (e.g., commissions), severance payments under an unfunded welfare plan, net earnings by sole proprietors, taxable alimony, and differential wage payments to individuals on active duty in the military for more than 30 days. Compensation does not include interest and dividends, any deferred compensation (including any pension or annuity payment), foreign earned income or any unemployment compensation [§ 85(b), § 219(f)(1); Prop. Reg. § 1.219(a)-1(b)(3)].

### XVII.A.5.e. Excise Tax

[367 T.M., III.A.5.d.; TPS ¶5610.03.A.4.b.]

An excise tax of 6% is imposed per year on the amount of an excess contribution for the tax year in which it is made and for each subsequent year at the end of which the excess contribution remains in the IRA. An excess contribution is an IRA contribution that is not deductible, not a rollover contribution, and not designated as a nondeductible contribution. If an excise tax is due, the taxpayer must file Form 5329, *Additional Taxes on Qualified Plans (Including IRAs) and Other Tax-Favored Accounts*, together with the individual's Form 1040 [§ 4973, § 6693(b)(2); Prop. Reg. § 54.4973-1].

### XVII.A.5.f. Distributions

[367 T.M., III.D.2.; TPS ¶5610.03.D.2.]

*Minimum Distributions.* An IRA owner generally must begin to receive distributions from a traditional IRA by April 1 of the year that follows the year in which he or she attains age 70 ½. An excise tax is imposed on the IRA owner for failure to receive required minimum distributions in an amount equal to 50% of the shortfall between the actual amount distributed and the required minimum distribution [§ 408(a)(6), § 4974(a)].

*Early Distributions.* The I.R.C. generally imposes an additional tax on a distribution to an IRA owner before age 59½, unless the distribution complies with an exception to the premature distribution rules under § 72(t) (XVII.A.2.e.(6)). The additional tax is 10% of the taxable amount of the distribution. The 10% additional tax does not apply to the extent a distribution is a nontaxable return of nondeductible contributions or is rolled over into another IRA or a qualified plan within 60 days of distribution [§ 72(t)(1)].

An individual may withdraw up to $10,000 (during the individual's lifetime) from his or her IRA for expenses of purchasing a home for the first time without incurring the 10% early withdrawal penalty. The withdrawal must be used within 120 days to pay costs (such as any reasonable settlement, financing or other closing costs) of acquiring, constructing, or reconstructing a principal residence of a first-time homebuyer. The 10% additional income tax on early withdrawals applies to any amount not so used. If the 120-day rule cannot be satisfied due to a delay or cancellation of the acquisition or construction of the residence, the taxpayer may recontribute the amount withdrawn to an IRA before the end of the 120-day period without incurring adverse tax consequences [§ 72(t)(2)(F), § 72(t)(8)].

The first-time homebuyer must not have had an ownership interest in a principal residence during the 2-year period ending on the date of acquisition of the principal residence. The acquisition date is the date on which the individual enters a binding contract to acquire the principal residence or begins construction or reconstruction of that principal residence. The individual's spouse also must satisfy the ownership interest requirement as of the date the contract is entered into or construction begins [§ 72(t)(8)].

### XVII.A.5.g. Employment Taxes and Withholding

[367 T.M., VIII.A.; TPS ¶5610.12.]

Amounts paid by an employer to an employee that are contributed by the employee to an IRA or that are paid directly into the employee's IRA by the employer are considered taxable income and are subject to FICA and FUTA taxes. Employer contributions to an IRA that is part of a SEP arrangement (see XVII.A.8.), are not taxable and are not included in wages for FICA or FUTA purposes unless the contributions are made pursuant to a salary reduction election [§ 3121(a)(5)(C), § 3306(b)(5)(C); Reg. § 1.219-1(c)(4)].

Contributions to an IRA by a self-employed individual are neither excludible nor deductible in figuring compensation subject to self-employment taxes [Rev. Rul. 78-6, 1978-1 C.B. 273].

IRA distributions are subject to federal income tax withholding (see XXII.A.6.a.). Federal income tax withholding is mandatory on the payer for all distributions from an IRA, but the recipient may elect out of withholding for any reason [§ 3405(a)].

### XVII.A.5.h. Model Forms to Establish an IRA

[367 T.M., II.B.1.; TPS ¶5610.400.]

The IRS has released several model forms to establish an IRA. Form 5305, *Traditional Individual Retirement Trust Account*, establishes a trust under which an individual deposits funds or assets as a settlor with a trustee. Form 5305-A, *Traditional Individual Retirement Custodial Account*, establishes a custodial agreement under which an individual deposits funds or assets with a custodian. The terms of the form are identical to those of the Form 5305 other than the designation of a "custodian" rather than a "trustee." The only difference in their legal effect arises under trust or custodianship statutory or common law of the state in which the IRA is situated.

### XVII.A.5.i. Spousal and Inherited IRAs

[367 T.M., I.B.; TPS ¶5610.03.A.4.a., .13.A.]

**Spousal IRA.** A "spousal IRA" is a type of IRA into which a contribution is made in whole or in part from the compensation of the other spouse. Deductible IRA contributions may be made for each spouse (including, for example, a homemaker who does not work outside the home) if the combined compensation of both spouses is at least equal to the contributed amount. To be eligible to make a spousal contribution, the individual and the spouse must file a joint federal income tax return for the tax year, and the amount of compensation (if any) includible in the individual's gross income for that year must be less than the compensation includible in the gross income of the spouse for the tax year [§ 219(c)(2)].

---

**EXAMPLE:** H and W are married and file joint tax returns. H will receive $50,000 in salary in 2015. W does not work outside the home and will have no income in 2015. H and W will each contribute $5,500 to an IRA in 2015. H may deduct $5,500 for the contribution to his IRA. W also may deduct, on H and W's joint return for 2015, the entire $5,500 for the contribution to her IRA, because the spousal IRA will be computed based on the compensation of both spouses.

---

**Inherited IRA.** "An inherited IRA" describes an IRA after the death of its owner. The beneficiary is said to have inherited his or her ownership of the IRA. Because these IRAs are subject to certain minimum distribution rules after the original IRA owner's death, inherited IRAs may not be commingled with the beneficiary's personal IRA funds. Deductions for any amount contributed to an "inherited IRA" are prohibited and designated nondeductible contributions cannot be made to an inherited IRA. Therefore, a beneficiary cannot make contributions to an IRA that was established by a decedent.

Funds held in inherited IRAs are not exempt from the bankruptcy estate. Funds held in an inherited IRA are not set aside for the purpose of retirement and thus are not retirement funds for purposes of the Bankruptcy Code [*Clark v. Rameker*, 134 S. Ct. 2242 (2014)].

### XVII.A.5.j. IRAs and Divorce

[367 T.M., III.D.3.; TPS ¶5610.03.D.]

Upon divorce, a decree or property settlement may require an IRA owner to split his IRA with his or her ex-spouse or convey the entire interest in the IRA to the ex-spouse. Special rules shield both spouses from current federal income tax on such transfers. To be tax free, the transfer of the interest in an IRA must be pursuant to a divorce decree or a written instrument incident to the divorce (a property settle-ment), which is valid under state law. If the assets are held in a single IRA, the IRA owner can withdraw those assets that are to go to the ex-spouse and roll them over to a second IRA and assign ownership to the ex-spouse. Alternatively, an IRA owner can arrange for a direct transfer of assets from the trustee, custodian, or insurance company sponsoring his IRA to the sponsor of an IRA already established and owned by the ex-spouse. Any amount so transferred in connection with the divorce is not considered a distribution to either the IRA owner or the ex-spouse [§ 408(d)(6); Reg. § 1.408-4(g)(1)].

Once the transfer is made, the ex-spouse's interest in the transferee IRA is his or her own for all tax purposes. For example, if the ex-spouse is age 70½, minimum required distributions must begin.

### XVII.A.6. Roth IRAs

[367 T.M., X.A.; TPS ¶5610.07.]

There are several significant differences between traditional IRAs and Roth IRAs. For example, contributions to a Roth IRA are never deductible; contributions to a Roth IRA can be made after the owner has attained age 70 ½; and qualified distributions from a Roth IRA are not includible in gross income or subject to any minimum distribution rules. Similar to traditional IRAs, the assets of a Roth IRA grow tax free while held in the trust.

### XVII.A.6.a. Contributions

[367 T.M., X.C.; TPS ¶5610.07.A.]

Two types of contributions can be made to a Roth IRA: (i) regular contributions; and (ii) qualified rollover contributions. The maximum annual regular contributions an individual can make to all Roth IRAs maintained for his or her benefit is subject to dollar and adjusted gross income limitations. Under the annual IRS "dollar limitation," the maximum annual contributions cannot exceed the maximum amount allowed as a deduction for a traditional IRA — the lesser of the deductible amount or 100% of the individual's compensation — minus the contributions for the tax year to all other individual retirement plans maintained for the individual's benefit. For tax years beginning in 2014 and 2015, the maximum amount is $5,500. The maximum amount for a tax year is increased by a $1,000 "catch-up amount" for individuals who reach age 50 before the close of the tax year. Thus, the total amount that can be contributed by individuals aged 50 and over is $6,500 for 2014 and 2015 [§ 219(b)(5), § 408A(c)(2)(A); Rev. Proc. 2013-35, 2013-47 I.R.B. 537; IRS News Release IR-2014-99 (Oct. 23, 2014)].

The amount of an individual's Roth IRA contributions for a tax year determined above is phased out between certain levels of adjusted gross income (the "AGI limitation"). The AGI limitation is based on the participant's modified adjusted gross income. Under the AGI limitation, a participant's Roth IRA contribution is multiplied by a fraction determined by dividing the participant's modified adjusted gross income for the tax year over the applicable dollar amount by $15,000 ($10,000 for a joint return or a married individual filing a separate return). For 2015, the applicable amount is $183,000 for a joint return ($181,000 for 2014), $116,000 for any other taxpayer (other than a married taxpayer filing separately) ($114,000 for 2014), and $0 for a married individual filing a separate return [§ 408A(c)(3)(B)(ii); IRS News Release IR-2014-99 (Oct. 23, 2014); Notice 2013-73]. The effect of the AGI limitation is that the maximum contribution to a Roth IRA for 2015 is phased out for unmarried taxpayers with modified AGI between $116,000 to $131,000 (for 2014, $114,000 to

$129,000), for married individuals filing jointly with modified AGI between $183,000 to $193,000 (for 2014, $181,000 to $191,000), and for married individuals filing separately with AGI between $0 and $10,000 [§ 408A(c)(3); Reg. § 1.408A-3, Q&A-3(b); IRS News Release IR-2014-99 (Oct. 23, 2014); Notice 2013–73, 2013-49 I.R.B. 598].

A "qualified rollover contribution" is a rollover to a Roth IRA from another such account, or from another type of individual retirement plan.

### XVII.A.6.b. Conversions, Reconversions and Recharacterizations

[367 T.M., X.D.; TPS ¶5610.07.B.]

A taxpayer can withdraw all or part of the assets from a traditional IRA and reinvest them within 60 days in a Roth IRA. The amount that is withdrawn and timely contributed to a Roth IRA is called a conversion contribution. If amounts are properly and timely rolled over, the 10% additional tax on early distributions under § 72(t) will not apply. However, a part or all of the distribution from the traditional IRA may be included in gross income and subjected to ordinary income tax (except for the part that is a return of nondeductible contributions). Generally, a taxpayer can also convert a SEP-IRA and SIMPLE IRA (after two years from date of participation) to a Roth IRA [Reg. § 1.408A-4, Q&A-4].

A rollover or conversion to a Roth IRA may be reversed by transferring funds to a traditional IRA by the due date (including extensions) of the tax year in which the conversion was made. A taxpayer who makes a Roth conversion followed by a recharacterization may not make another Roth conversion until the later of the tax year following the tax year of the initial conversion or, if later, 30 days after the recharacterization [§ 408A(d)(6); Reg. § 1.408A-5, Q&As-1(b), -9(a)(1)].

A regular contribution plus earnings to a Roth IRA may be later recharacterized as an IRA contribution and earnings if the taxpayer was ineligible to make the contribution (e.g., exceeded the AGI limitation) or simply wishes to change his/her mind. A recharacterization is accomplished only by means of a direct trustee-to-trustee transfer, as opposed to a distribution and subsequent rollover, but a direct trustee-to-trustee transfer is permitted even if the IRAs are maintained by the same trustee. In order to effect a recharacterization, the individual must make an election and notify the trustees of both IRAs of the election. An individual makes the election to recharacterize a contribution to an IRA for a tax year by notifying, on or before the date of the transfer, both the trustee of the first IRA and the trustee of the second IRA that the individual has elected to treat the contribution as having been made to the second IRA, instead of the first IRA, for federal tax purposes [Reg. § 1.408A-5, Q&As-1, -6(a)].

---

**EXAMPLE:** In 2015, Debbie makes a $5,000 regular contribution for 2015 to her traditional IRA (first IRA). Before the due date (plus extensions) for filing her federal income tax return for 2015, Debbie decides that she would prefer to contribute to a Roth IRA instead. Debbie instructs the trustee of the first IRA to transfer in a trustee-to-trustee transfer the amount of the contribution, plus attributable net income, to the trustee of a Roth IRA (second IRA). Debbie notifies the trustee of the first IRA and the trustee of the second IRA that she is recharacterizing her $5,000 contribution for 2015. On her federal income tax return for 2015, Debbie treats the $5,000 as having been contributed to the Roth IRA for 2015 and not to the traditional IRA. As a result, for federal tax purposes, the contribution is treated as having been made to the Roth IRA for 2015 and not to the traditional IRA. The result would be the same if the conversion amount had been transferred in a tax-free transfer to another traditional IRA before the recharacterization.

### XVII.A.6.c. *Distributions*

[367 T.M., X.E.; TPS ¶5610.07.C.]

A distribution from a Roth IRA is not includible in the owner's gross income if it is a qualified distribution. A qualified distribution is one that is both [§ 408A(d)(2)(A); Reg. § 1.408A-6, Q&A-1(b)]:

1. made after a 5-tax-year period; and
2. made on or after the date on which the owner attains age 59½, made to a beneficiary or the estate of the owner on or after the date of the owner's death, attributable to the owner's being disabled within the meaning of § 72(m)(7), or to which § 72(t)(2)(F) applies (exception for first-time home purchase).

The 5-tax-year period begins on the first day of the individual's tax year for which the individual or the individual's spouse first made a Roth IRA contribution, or if earlier, the first day of the individual's tax year in which the first conversion contribution is made to any Roth IRA of the individual. The 5-tax-year period ends on the last day of the individual's fifth consecutive tax year beginning with the tax year described in the preceding sentence [§ 408A(d)(2)(B)].

Nonqualifying Roth IRA distributions are included in gross income to the extent that the amount of the distribution, when added to all other prior Roth IRA distributions that were not included in income, exceeds the owner's contributions [Reg. § 1.408A-6, Q&A-4].

No minimum distributions are required to be made from a Roth IRA while the owner is alive.

### XVII.A.6.d. *Model Forms to Establish a Roth IRA*

[367 T.M., X.H.; TPS ¶5610.07.E.]

The IRS has issued three model Roth IRA forms for use by trustees and custodians. The first two forms issued were Form 5305-R, *Roth Individual Retirement Trust Account*, and Form 5305-RA, *Roth Individual Retirement Custodial Account*, which serve as IRS-approved model forms for use by financial institutions to establish Roth IRAs for their customers.

The IRS also has issued Form 5305-RB, *Roth Individual Retirement Annuity Endorsement* agreement. Form 5305-RB is a model annuity endorsement that meets the requirements of § 408A and has been approved by the IRS. The form is used as an endorsement to an insurance company's annuity contract and is not filed with the IRS, but kept for recordkeeping purposes.

### XVII.A.7. Deemed IRAs

[368 T.M., III.; TPS ¶5610.08.]

Employers sponsoring qualified plans, or a § 403(a) or § 403(b) annuity plan, can allow employees to make voluntary contributions to a separate account or annuity established under the plan and have the contributions treated as traditional IRA or Roth IRA contributions. A separate account or annuity in a qualified employer plan is a "deemed IRA" that is treated as an IRA, not like a qualified employer plan, if the deemed IRA is established under the plan and meets the requirements applicable to either traditional IRAs or Roth IRAs or is an individual retirement annuity. Because a deemed IRA is not considered a qualified employer plan, it is not subject to rules governing employer plans [§ 408(q)(1)].

A qualified plan and a deemed IRA generally are treated as separate entities, and each entity is subject to the rules applicable to that entity. Therefore, issues regarding eligibility, participation, disclosure, nondiscrimination, contributions, distributions, investments, and plan administration generally must be resolved under the separate rules applicable to each entity. Thus, for example, deemed IRAs do not have to be made available in the nondiscriminatory manner required of qualified plans. The deemed IRA and contributions to it are subject to the exclusive benefit and fiduciary rules of ERISA to the extent otherwise applicable to the plan; however, they are not subject to the ERISA reporting and disclosure, participation, vesting, funding, and enforcement requirements applicable to the underlying plan [Reg. § 1.408(q)-1(c); ERISA § 4(c)].

The reporting and withholding rules on plan and IRA distributions apply separately depending on whether the distributions are made from a deemed IRA or a qualified plan. Thus, for example, the reporting rules for required minimum distributions apply separately for the two portions of the plan. Similarly, a total distribution of amounts held in the qualified employer plan and the deemed IRA is reported on two Forms 1099-R, *Distributions From Pensions, Annuities, Retirement or Profit-Sharing Plans, IRAs, Insurance Contracts, etc.* Also, the 20% withholding rules do not apply to a distribution from the deemed IRA but do apply to a distribution from the plan, and the tax on early distributions applies separately to the two entities [Reg. § 1.408(q)-1(e)].

### *XVII.A.8. Simplified Employee Pensions (SEP)*

[368 T.M., II.A.; TPS ¶5620.01.]

A SEP arrangement is a written program calling for contributions by the employer to the participating IRAs of its employees. SEPs provide a simplified, cost-effective means for employers to provide retirement benefits for their employees (and for employees to save for their own retirement) where the employer does not wish to incur the costs and administrative burdens associated with maintaining a traditional tax-qualified retirement plan [§ 408(k)].

Under a SEP arrangement, the employer contributes to individual traditional IRAs for covered employees. Employees may also make contributions as they normally would to an IRA if they participate in a grandfathered SARSEP (see XVII.A.8.d.). Self-employed individuals are treated as employees for this purpose. SEPs may be set up with banks, insurance companies or other qualified financial institutions. Employees are responsible for making investment decisions about their SEP accounts. The employer generally has no filing requirements for the SEP itself.

### *XVII.A.8.a. Requirements*

[368 T.M., II.E.; TPS ¶5620.02.A., .02.B.]

SEP IRAs must meet the following basic requirements [§ 408(k)(1) through § 408(k)(5); IRS News Release IR-2014-99 (Oct. 23, 2014); Notice 2013-73, 2013-49 I.R.B. 598]:

1. The SEP must be an individual retirement account or an individual retirement annuity.

2. The employer must make contributions to the SEPs of all employees (with certain exceptions) who (i) have reached age 21, (ii) have worked at least three of the preceding five years for the employer, and (iii) have received at least $450

in compensation, as adjusted for inflation ($600 for 2015 and $550 for 2014) from the employer for the year. An employer may adopt a requirement that is less stringent than the one imposed by the I.R.C. – for example, the employer can adopt a 2-years-out-of-5 service requirement, or may choose to impose no such requirement at all.

3. The contributions must not discriminate in favor of highly-compensated employees.

4. Employees must be able to withdraw the employer's contributions without any penalty.

5. The employer's contribution must be allocated among the SEPs of the employees pursuant to a written formula that specifies how the contribution is divided and how much of the contribution each employee can expect to receive.

6. All SEP contributions must be fully vested when made.

### XVII.A.8.b. Contributions and Deductions

[368 T.M., II.G., II.H.; TPS ¶5620.02.D., .02.E.]

The primary tax advantage of a SEP is that it enables the employer to make contributions to the IRAs of eligible employees with no current federal income tax liability to the employees as long as contributions do not exceed the lesser of 25% of the employee's compensation from the employer or $40,000 (as adjusted for inflation) ($53,000 for 2015 and $52,000 for 2014). A SEP contribution also lowers the maximum amount that an employer can deduct for contributions to any profit-sharing or stock bonus plan it also maintains [§ 402(h)(2), § 404(h)(3), § 415(a)(2); Reg. § 1.415(c)-1(a)(2)(i)(C); IRS News Release IR-2014-99 (Oct. 23, 2014); Notice 2013–73, 2013–49 I.R.B. 598].

---

**EXAMPLE:** Corporation Q establishes a SEP for the benefit of its eligible employees. Employee B earns $100,000 in compensation from Q in 2015. For 2015 the most Q can contribute to the IRA of B (without causing B to recognize taxable income) is $25,000 (25% of $100,000). This is because 25% of B's compensation is less than $53,000 (the applicable limit for 2015).

---

An employee may make deductible contributions to the IRA that is used to receive the employer's SEP contribution, just as he could to any other IRA. Conversely, a SEP can cover an employee who already has an IRA or who wishes to continue funding an IRA; an existing IRA of the employee even can be used to receive his employer's SEP contribution [§ 408(j)].

SEPs are treated similarly to qualified defined contribution plans for purposes of the deduction limits. In general, an employer may deduct up to 25% of the compensation paid to employees covered by a SEP arrangement [§ 404(h)(1)].

### XVII.A.8.c. Distributions

[368 T.M., II.F.; TPS ¶5620.02.C.]

A SEP must permit employees to withdraw previous employer contributions at any time. A SEP generally is subject to the same tax rules as IRAs. Distributions from a SEP are taxed as distributions from an IRA for federal income tax purposes. Thus, they are subject to the same minimum required distribution rules that apply after the IRA owner reaches age 70 ½ and after death as any other IRA. A distribution from a SEP is eligible for tax-free rollover into an IRA, qualified plan or certain other plans in the same manner as any IRA distribution. SEPs also can receive rollover contributions in the same manner as any IRA (see XVII.A.5.). Participant loans are not permitted from SEPs. No SEP assets can be used as collateral [§ 408(k)(4), § 402(h)(3)].

### XVII.A.8.d. SARSEPs

[368 T.M., II.A. & II.G.9.; TPS ¶5620.02.D.7.]

Certain employers provide for SEPs that are funded through salary reductions. These arrangements are called "SARSEPs." Due to the introduction of SIMPLE plans (see XVII.A.9.), SARSEPs cannot be established after December 31, 1996. SARSEPs established before January 1, 1997, however, can continue to receive contributions. An employer cannot continue to sponsor a SARSEP if it has more than 25 employees at any time during the preceding plan year. Further, at least 50% of the employer's eligible employees must make, or have in effect, a salary reduction election for their SEPs in order for an existing SARSEP to remain available [§ 408(k)(6), § 408(k)(7)(C)].

*Deferral Limit.* If an employee makes salary reduction contributions to his IRA under a SEP arrangement by directing the employer to reduce his salary and divert the amount of the reduction to his IRA, the employee can avoid current federal income tax on the amount of the reduction, so long as contributions comply with the § 402(g) limit on elective deferrals ($18,000 in 2015, $17,500 in 2014). This limit is in addition to the limit described in XVII.A.8.b. [§ 402(g)(1); IRS News Release IR-2014-99 (Oct. 23, 2014); Notice 2013–73, 2013–49 I.R.B. 598].

### XVII.A.8.e. Model Form to Establish a SEP

[368 T.M., II.C.2.; TPS ¶5620.02.A.3.]

A SEP can be established by adopting Form 5305-SEP, *Simplified Employee Pension—Individual Retirement Accounts Contribution Agreement.*

### XVII.A.8.f. Withholding and Employment Taxes

[368 T.M., II.I.; TPS ¶5620.02.G.]

SEP contributions other than SARSEP contributions by an employer are exempt from FICA and FUTA taxes (see XXII.A.6.a.). Any allocations that exceed the general defined contribution plan limit of 25% of compensation or $40,000 (as adjusted for inflation) ($53,000 for 2015), are not exempted [§ 415(c), § 3121(a)(5)(C), § 3306(b)(5)(C); Prop. Reg. § 1.408-7(f)(2); IRS News Release IR-2014-99 (Oct. 23, 2014); Notice 2013-73].

Amounts deferred under a SARSEP are subject to FICA and FUTA taxes when deferred [§ 3121(a)(5)(C), § 3306(b)(5)(C)].

|  | SEP-IRA | SARSEP | SIMPLE IRA and SIMPLE § 401(k) | Qualified Plan |
|---|---|---|---|---|
| **Contribution Deadline** | Due date of employer's tax return (including extensions). | Due date of employer's tax return (including extensions). Salary deferrals must be deposited as soon as they can be segregated from the employer's assets, but no later than the 15th day of the month following the month received. | Salary deferral contributions to SIMPLE IRAs must be made within 30 days after the end of the month for which the contributions are to be made. Matching or non-elective contributions are due on the due date of the employer's tax return (including extensions). Salary deferral contributions to SIMPLE § 401(k)s follow the qualified plan rule. | Salary deferrals must be deposited as soon as they can be segregated from the employer's assets, but no later than the 15th day of the month following the month received. Employer contributions are due on the due date of the employer's tax return (including extensions). <br><br>**Note:** For a defined benefit plan subject to minimum funding requirements, contributions are due in quarterly installments (April 15, July 15, October 15, and January 15 of the following year). |

|  | SEP-IRA | SARSEP | SIMPLE IRA and SIMPLE § 401(k) | Qualified Plan |
|---|---|---|---|---|
| **Contribution Limit** | Lesser of $53,000 for 2015 ($52,000 for 2014, $51,000 for 2013) or 25%[1] of participant's compensation.[2]<br><br>Participants age 50 and older can make catch-up contributions of $6,000 for 2015 ($5,500 for 2014 and 2013). | Lesser of 25%[1] of participant's compensation[2] or $18,000 for 2015 ($17,500 for 2013, $17,000 for 2012).<br><br>Participants age 50 and older can make catch-up contributions of $6,000 for 2015 ($5,500 for 2014 and 2013). | **Employee:** Salary reduction contributions up to $12,500 for 2015 ($12,000 for 2014 and 2013).<br><br>Participants age 50 and older can make catch-up contributions of $3,000 for 2015 ($2,500 for 2014 and 2013).<br><br>**Employer contributions:** *Either* dollar-for-dollar matching contributions, up to 3% of employee's compensation,[3] *or* fixed nonelective contributions of 2% of compensation.[2] | **Defined Contribution Plans:**<br>*Money Purchase:* Lesser of $53,000 for 2015 ($52,000 for 2014, $51,000 for 2013) or 100%[1] of participant's compensation.[2]<br><br>*Profit Sharing:* Lesser of $53,000 for 2015 ($52,000 for 2014, $51,000 for 2013) or 100%[1] of participant's compensation.[2]<br><br>*401(k):* Employee elective deferrals of $18,000 for 2015 ($17,500 for 2014 and 2013). Participants age 50 and older can make catch-up contributions of $6,000 for 2015 ($5,500 for 2014 and 2013).<br><br>**Defined Benefit Plans:** Limit on annual benefit is no greater than the lesser of $215,000 for 2015 ($210,000 for 2014, $205,000 for 2013) or 100% of the participant's average compensation for his or her highest 3 consecutive calendar years. |

|  | SEP-IRA | SARSEP | SIMPLE IRA and SIMPLE § 401(k) | Qualified Plan |
|---|---|---|---|---|
| **Deduction Limit** | 25%[1] of all participants' compensation. | 25%[1] of all participants' compensation.[2] | Same as maximum contribution. | **Defined Contribution Plans:** *Money Purchase:* 25%[1] of all participants' compensation.[2]<br><br>*Profit-Sharing:* 25%[1] of all participants' compensation.[2]<br><br>**Defined Benefit Plans:** Based on actuarial assumptions and computations.<br><br>Combined deduction limit for defined benefit and defined contribution plan is greater of 25% of all participants' compensation or amount necessary to meet minimum funding standards of defined benefit plans. |
| **Deadline to Set Up Plan** | Due date of employer's tax return (including extensions).<br><br>May use Form 5305-SEP. | Cannot be set up after 1996. | Any date from January 1 through October 1 of the calendar year.<br><br>For a new employer that comes into existence after October 1, as soon as administratively feasible.<br><br>May use Forms 5304-SIMPLE or 5305-SIMPLE. | By the end of the tax year.<br><br>Must adopt written plan document: IRS-approved master or prototype plan or individually designed plan. |

|  | SEP-IRA | SARSEP | SIMPLE IRA and SIMPLE § 401(k) | Qualified Plan |
|---|---|---|---|---|
| **Salary Deferrals** | Not permitted. | Allowed up to contribution limit, above. | Allowed up to contribution limit, above. | **Defined Contribution Plans:** Allowed up to contribution limit, above.<br>**Defined Benefit Plan:** Not permitted. |
| **Nondis-crimination Testing** | Not applicable. | Salary reduction elections may be limited for the group of highly- compensated employees based on the averages for the non-highly- compensated employees (see § 408(k)(6)(A)(iii)). | Not applicable to SIMPLE IRAs. SIMPLE § 401(k)s are deemed to satisfy non-discrimination requirements. | **Defined Contribution Plans:** Employee elective deferrals or contributions, and employer matches or nonelective contributions, must be limited for the group of highly- compensated employees based on the averages for the non-highly- compensated employees, unless the plan is designed as a safe harbor plan or has a compliant automatic enrollment feature.<br>**Defined Benefit Plan:** Must demonstrate that it does not discriminate in favor of highly- compensated employees by satisfying general test (i.e., each rate group under the plan satisfies § 410(b) as though it were a separate plan) or adopting a design-based safe harbor. |

|  | **SEP-IRA** | **SARSEP** | **SIMPLE IRA and SIMPLE § 401(k)** | **Qualified Plan** |
|---|---|---|---|---|
| **Form 5500 Filing** | Not required if employer furnishes employee with a copy of the completed and unmodified Form 5305-SEP used to create the SEP, and notifies each SEP participant in writing of any employer contributions made under the contribution agreement to the participant's IRA each year. DOL Reg. § 2520.104-48. | Not required if employer complies with employee notice requirements under DOL Reg. § 2520.104-49. | Not required for SIMPLE IRAs. Required for SIMPLE § 401(k)s. | Required. |
| **Employer Eligibility** | Any employer. | Any employer. | Employers that had no more than 100 employees who earned at least $5,000 in the previous year. | Any employer. |

|  | SEP-IRA | SARSEP | SIMPLE IRA and SIMPLE § 401(k) | Qualified Plan |
|---|---|---|---|---|
| **Employee Eligibility** | Must include all employees who (1) are at least 21 years old, (2) who have been employed for 3 of the 5 preceding years, and (3) who earn at least $600 in 2015 ($550 in 2014 and 2013). This amount is subject to adjustment for inflation. | Must include all employees who (1) are at least 21 years old, (2) who have been employed for 3 of the 5 preceding years, and (3) who earn at least $600 in 2015 ($550 in 2014 and 2013). This amount is subject to adjustment for inflation. | SIMPLE IRAs must include employees who earned at least $5,000 in any 2 preceding calendar years and who are reasonably expected to earn $5,000 in the current year. SIMPLE § 401(k)s follow the rule for qualified plans. | Must include employees who are at least 21 years old and who have performed at least 1 year of service. |

[1] Net earnings from self-employment must take the contribution into account.

[2] Compensation generally is limited to $265,000 for 2015 ($260,000 for 2014, $255,000 for 2013).

[3] Under a SIMPLE § 401(k) plan, compensation generally is limited to $265,000 for 2015 ($260,000 for 2014, $255,000 for 2013).

[4] A § 401(k) plan must be included in a money purchase or profit-sharing plan and the combined employer contributions and elective deferrals are limited to the lesser of $53,000 for 2015 ($52,000 for 2014, $51,000 for 2013) or 100% of participant's compensation.

### XVII.A.9. SIMPLE Plans

[368 T.M., I.A.; TPS ¶5560.11.A.]

A SIMPLE plan refers to a simplified retirement plan for small businesses known as a savings incentive match plan for employees. SIMPLE plans provide an alternative retirement plan for small employers that do not wish to assume the top-heavy or nondiscrimination rules or other administrative burdens applicable to other types of tax-exempt retirement plans (e.g., qualified plans or SEPs). SIMPLE plans may be established in IRA or § 401(k) form. By establishing a SIMPLE plan, the employer must provide eligible employees with a salary reduction option in which they may choose between cash or contributions to the plan. Participation in a SIMPLE plan must be voluntary.

### *XVII.A.9.a. Requirements*

[368 T.M., I.C.; TPS ¶5560.11.A.]

To be eligible to maintain a SIMPLE plan, an employer generally must have had 100 or fewer employees who received at least $5,000 each in compensation from it for the preceding year. In addition, an employer generally cannot make contributions under a SIMPLE plan for a given calendar year if the employer, or a predecessor employer, maintains a qualified plan under which its employees benefit [§ 408(p)(2)(C)(i)(I)].

A SIMPLE IRA is an individual retirement account described in § 408(a) or an individual retirement annuity described in § 408(b), the terms of which permit only employer contributions under a SIMPLE plan or rollovers or transfers from a SIMPLE IRA.

Generally, a SIMPLE § 401(k) cash or deferred arrangement is deemed to satisfy the special nondiscrimination tests applicable to employee elective deferrals and employer matching contributions if the plan satisfies the contribution requirements applicable to SIMPLE plans.

### *XVII.A.9.b. Contributions*

[368 T.M., I.E.; TPS ¶5560.11.B.3., .11.C.]

Under a SIMPLE plan, an employer must make either a 100% matching employer contribution for the employee's salary reduction contribution (subject to a maximum of 3% of compensation) or a 2% nonelective employer contribution. No other contributions are permitted under a SIMPLE plan [§ 408(p)(2)(A), § 408(p)(2)(B)].

---

**EXAMPLE:** Samantha works for the ABC Company, a small business with 50 employees. ABC Company has a SIMPLE IRA plan for its employees and will make a 2% nonelective contribution for each of them. Under this option, even if Samantha does not contribute to her SIMPLE IRA, she would still receive an employer contribution to her SIMPLE IRA equal to 2% of compensation. If Samantha's annual compensation is $50,000, ABC Company must still make a contribution of $1,000 (2% of $50,000) to her SIMPLE IRA account.

---

The annual dollar limit on salary reduction contributions under SIMPLE plans is $10,000, as indexed in $500 increments for inflation. For 2015, the indexed dollar limit is $12,500 ($12,000 in 2014). Participants who are age 50 or older before the end of the plan year may make additional catch-up contributions of up to $3,000 for 2015 ($2,500 for 2014). [§ 408(p)(2)(E)(i), § 414(v)(2)(B), § 414(v)(2)(C); IRS News Release IR-2014-99 (Oct. 23, 2014); Notice 2013-73, 2013-49 I.R.B. 598.]

The qualification rules of § 401(a) do not apply to SIMPLE plans. For example, § 415(c) does not apply to limit the amount of contributions that can be made each year under a SIMPLE plan. [Notice 98-4, 1998-2 C.B. 25, Q&A-I-6].

### *XVII.A.9.c. Model Forms to Establish a SIMPLE Plan*

[368 T.M., I.B.3.; TPS ¶5560.11.B.7.]

The IRS has released various forms to establish a SIMPLE IRA. Form 5305-S, *SIMPLE Individual Retirement Trust Account*, establishes a trust to be used to receive employer contributions under a SIMPLE arrangement, which are deposited with a trustee. Form 5305-SA, *SIMPLE Individual Retirement Custodial Account*, establishes a custodial account to be used to receive employer contributions under a SIMPLE arrangement, which are deposited with a custodian.

The IRS has also provided a model amendment in that may be used to assist employers in adopting a plan that contains SIMPLE § 401(k) provisions. The amendment gives plan sponsors a way to incorporate SIMPLE § 401(k) provisions in plans containing cash or deferred arrangements and matching contributions [Rev. Proc. 97-9, 1997-1 C.B. 624].

### XVII.A.9.d. Withholding and Employment Taxes

[368 T.M., I.E.8.; TPS ¶5440.01.B.2.]

Contributions to a SIMPLE IRA are excludible from federal income tax by the employee and are not subject to federal income tax withholding. However, salary reduction contributions to a SIMPLE IRA are subject to FICA and FUTA taxes and must be reported on Form W-2. Matching and nonelective employer contributions to a SIMPLE IRA are not subject to FICA or FUTA taxes, and are not required to be reported on Form W-2 [Notice 98-4, 1998-2 C.B. 25, Q&A-I-1].

Employment taxes and income tax withholding are discussed in greater detail below at XXII.A.6.

### XVII.A.10. ESOPs

[354 T.M., I.B.; TPS ¶5560.03.A.]

An ESOP is a defined contribution plan under which contributions are required to be primarily invested in employer securities. ESOPs are permitted to acquire employer securities in debt-financed transactions under a statutory prohibited transaction exemption. Thus, an ESOP has a combined strategic advantage of tying participant benefits to the stock performance of the corporate employer while, at the same time, providing capital to the employer by providing a market for its stock. Like a stock bonus plan, distributions under an ESOP are typically made in employer stock; however, under certain circumstances, distributions may be made in cash, subject to the participant's right to demand stock [§ 4975(d)(3), § 4975(e)(7)].

An ESOP is entitled to certain tax advantages. A loan to an ESOP is exempt from the Code's prohibited transaction rules, and an employer can guarantee the plan's payment to the lender without causing a prohibited transaction. Employers sponsoring ESOPs that use loans to acquire employer securities also may make greater deductible contributions than may be made to ordinary stock bonus plans. Under some circumstances, ESOP participants may receive greater annual allocations to their accounts than participants in ordinary defined contribution plans. ESOPs also may engage in certain tax-favored transactions. For example, a corporate shareholder may sell stock to an ESOP and defer payment of federal income tax on any gain from the sale if certain conditions are satisfied. Further, the sponsoring employer may deduct the amount of dividends paid on its stock held by an ESOP.

### XVII.A.10.a. ESOP Plan Requirements

[354 T.M., II.; TPS ¶5560.03.B.]

An ESOP must be a defined contribution plan that is a qualified stock bonus plan or a combination stock bonus/money purchase plan. An ESOP must include a written provision that it is designed to invest primarily in "qualifying employer securities." [§ 4975(e)(7); Reg. § 54.4975-11(b)].

### XVII.A.10.b. ESOP Contribution Limits

[354 T.M., II.D.5.; TPS ¶5560.03.E.2.]

Because an ESOP is a defined contribution plan, it is subject to the general contribution limit on annual additions to defined contribution plans. Therefore, contributions to participants cannot exceed the lesser of: (i) $40,000, as adjusted for inflation (for 2015, this amount is $53,000 and for 2014, this amount is $52,000); or (ii) 100% of the employee's compensation [§ 415(c)(1); IRS News Release IR-2014-99 (Oct. 23, 2014); Notice 2013-73, 2013-49 I.R.B. 598].

### *XVII.A.10.c. ESOP Deductions*

[354 T.M., II.D.6., III.B.; TPS ¶5560.03.E.1., .03.E.3.]

***Employer Contributions.*** An employer that sponsors an ESOP can deduct up to 25% of covered compensation of ESOP participants for contributions that are used by the ESOP to repay the principal amount of an exempt loan to the ESOP and can deduct an unlimited amount for contributions used to repay the interest on such a loan [§ 404(a)(9)].

***Dividends.*** An employer may deduct the amount of any applicable dividends paid in cash for applicable employer securities held by an ESOP if, pursuant to the plan, the dividends are paid in cash to participants within certain timeframes or, at the election of participants, are reinvested in qualifying employer securities. The deduction does not apply to S corporations. The 10% additional tax under § 72(t) on distributions before age 59 ½ does not apply to distributions of dividends on stock held by an ESOP [§ 72(t)(2)(A)(vi), § 404(k); Announcement 2008-56, 2008-26 I.R.B. 1192].

### *XVII.A.10.d. Withholding and Employment Taxes*

[370 T.M., X.A.1.; TPS ¶5550.11.]

Employees' elective compensation deferrals paid into an ESOP are wages for FICA and FUTA purposes, but not for federal income tax withholding purposes. Any employer contributions are not subject to FICA and FUTA and are not subject to withholding [§ 3401(a)(12)(A)].

### *XVII.A.11. Portability and Rollovers Among Retirement Arrangements*

[367 T.M., III.E., 370 T.M., VIII.; TPS ¶5520.10.D.]

Tax-free rollovers of retirement benefits are permitted to be made to eligible retirement plans under limited circumstances. An "eligible retirement plan" (i.e., a plan that is permitted to accept the transfer of an eligible rollover distribution) includes an IRA, a qualified plan, an annuity plan, a § 457(b) state or local government (but not tax-exempt organization) plan and a § 403(b) tax-sheltered annuity. Although qualified plans and other eligible retirement plans are required to make available rollovers to other plans, nothing in the I.R.C. requires plans to accept rollovers [§ 402(c)(8)]. The definition of an eligible rollover distribution is discussed in detail in XVII.A.2.e.(2).

If a distribution from a retirement plan or IRA is paid directly to a participant, the participant can also deposit all or a portion of it into an IRA or a retirement plan within 60 days. Unlike a direct transfer of benefits from one plan to another, any amount that is paid directly to a participant may be subject to mandatory 20% income tax withholding [§ 3405(a)].

In addition to rollovers between eligible retirement plans and contributions of distributed amounts within 60 days, amounts can be moved between plans through a trustee to trustee transfer. In such a case, a transfer takes place between the trustees of two eligible retirement plans without any type of distribution to the participant. Such amounts are not subject to income tax withholding. Unlike a rollover, a transfer may involve assets with a value equal to the participant's total accumulated benefits or account balance, including any after-tax employee contributions. Further, a transfer of assets may be preferable to a rollover where the IRS permits the years of participation in the transferor plan to be added to those in the transferee plan. However, benefits that are considered "protected benefits," such as the form of certain benefits generally cannot be eliminated through a transfer or pursuant to any plan amendment or action having the effect of amending a plan to transfer such benefits [Reg. § 1.411(d)-4, Q&A-3(a)(1)].

Rollovers between IRAs present a special problem. Generally, an IRA distribution can be rolled over to another IRA only if the IRA owner has not rolled over an earlier distribution during the 1-year period ending on the day of the distribution [§ 408(d)(3)(B); Reg. § 1.408-4(b)(4)(i)].

---

**EXAMPLE:** B withdraws $1,000 from his IRA on Oct. 1, 2015, and uses the money to open a second IRA within 60 days. Three months later, B makes another withdrawal from the first IRA. The withdrawal is not eligible for rollover treatment and must be taxed as ordinary income (except to the extent it is a return of any nondeductible contributions).

---

The IRS now follows the Tax Court's decision in *Bobrow v. Commissioner*, T.C. Memo 2014-21, and strictly interprets the 1-year IRA restriction to prevent a taxpayer from making more than one nontaxable rollover in a single year, even from separate IRAs. Before the Tax Court's ruling, the IRS's position was that the 1-year IRA restriction applied independently to each IRA. The IRS will not apply the Tax Court's interpretation to any rollover that involves an IRA distribution occurring before January 1, 2015 [Announcement 2014-15, 2014-16 I.R.B. 973].

The following chart shows what types of rollovers are permitted between different plans and any restrictions that may apply:

## ROLLOVER CHART

9/16/2014

| | | Roll To | | | | | | | |
|---|---|---|---|---|---|---|---|---|---|
| | | Roth IRA | Traditional IRA | SIMPLE IRA | SEP-IRA | Governmental 457(b) | Qualified Plan[1] (pre-tax) | 403(b) (pre-tax) | Designated Roth Account (401(k), 403(b) or 457(b)) |
| **Roll From** | Roth IRA | YES[2] | NO | NO | NO | NO | NO | NO | NO |
| | Traditional IRA | YES[3] | YES[2] | NO | YES[2] | YES[4] | YES | YES | NO |
| | SIMPLE IRA | YES,[3] after two years | YES,[2] after two years | YES[2] | YES,[2] after two years | YES,[4] after two years | YES, after two years | YES, after two years | NO |
| | SEP-IRA | YES[3] | YES[2] | NO | YES[2] | YES[4] | YES | YES | NO |
| | Governmental 457(b) | YES[3] | YES | NO | YES | YES | YES | YES | YES[3,5] |
| | Qualified Plan[1] (pre-tax) | YES[3] | YES | NO | YES | YES[4] | YES | YES | YES[3,5] |
| | 403(b) (pre-tax) | YES[3] | YES | NO | YES | YES[4] | YES | YES | YES[3,5] |
| | Designated Roth Account (401(k), 403(b) or 457(b)) | YES | NO | NO | NO | NO | NO | NO | YES[6] |

[1] Qualified plans include, for example, profit-sharing, 401(k), money purchase and defined benefit plans
[2] Only one rollover in any 12-month period
[3] Must include in income
[4] Must have separate accounts
[5] Must be an in-plan rollover
[6] Any amounts distributed must be rolled over via direct (trustee-to-trustee) transfer to be excludable from income
For more information regarding retirement plans and rollovers, visit Tax Information for Retirement Plans.

### XVII.A.12. Creditors' Rights to Retirement Assets

[351 T.M., XI., 367 T.M., IX.A.; TPS ¶¶5590.05.A., 5610.13.A.]

*Qualified Plans, IRAs and TSAs.* For a retirement plan to be qualified under the I.R.C. it must prohibit the assignment or alienation of a participant's interest in the plan subject to certain limited exceptions, such as for qualified domestic relations orders or for the enforcement or collection on a judgment resulting from an unpaid federal tax assessment. Section 541(c)(2) of the Bankruptcy Code allows a debtor to exclude from the bankruptcy estate any property that is subject to a restriction on transfer that is enforceable under "applicable nonbankruptcy law." The anti-alienation rules of the I.R.C. are considered such restrictions. Thus, if a participant files for bankruptcy, the participant's interest in a qualified plan may be excluded from the bankruptcy estate under this provision [§ 401(a)(13); ERISA § 206(d)(1); Reg. § 1.401(a)-13(b)(2)].

A debtor may exempt retirement funds held in a qualified pension or profit-sharing plan (including a governmental or church plan), annuity plan, traditional or Roth IRA, hybrid plan, eligible governmental or tax-exempt organization deferred compensation plan, or employee-contribution-only plan that is exempt from taxation. This includes plans exempt from taxation under § 401, § 403, § 408, § 408A, § 414, § 457 or § 501(a) [Bankruptcy Code § 522(b)(3)(C), § 522 (d)(12)]. The exemption for traditional and Roth IRAs (other than a SEP or a SIMPLE IRA) is subject to a $1 million cap (subject to certain exceptions), as such dollar amount is adjusted to reflect changes in the Consumer Price Index [Bankruptcy Code § 522(n)].

*IRAs.* IRAs are not protected by the federal law prohibiting the assignment or alienation of plan benefits. Accordingly, judgment creditors may attach assets of IRAs. However, assets held in traditional or Roth IRAs are protected from creditors when the IRA owner files for bankruptcy. A debtor in a federal bankruptcy proceeding is entitled to exempt from his or her bankruptcy estate up to $1 million held in a traditional or Roth IRA that has received a favorable determination in effect as of the date of the commencement of the bankruptcy case [11 U.S.C. § 522(b) and § 522(n)]. For a discussion of creditors' rights to inherited IRAs, see XVII.A.5.i.

## XVII.B. Nonqualified Deferred Compensation

### XVII.B.1. Nonqualified Plans

#### XVII.B.1.a. Uses for Nonqualified Plans

[385 T.M., I.B.; TPS ¶5710.01.]

Plans that fail to meet the qualified plan requirements or that were never intended to be qualified plans are generally referred to as nonqualified plans. These plans are not subject to the qualified plan requirements under § 401(a) and are not subject to exacting rules relating to funding, nondiscrimination, employee coverage, distribution, and other requirements. Because nonqualified plans do not meet the requirements under § 401(a), an employer may not take an immediate deduction for any contribution it makes. Instead, an employer's deduction is matched with the employee or service provider's recognition of income [§ 404(a)(5)].

Non-tax qualified deferred compensation arrangements generally involve an agreement by an employer to make payments to an individual for his or her future services. These arrangements are often used as a device to defer the timing of taxation on compensation, either: (i) as a means of forced savings; or (ii) to reduce the overall tax burden on such compensation by (a) postponing receipt until a year in which the individual is in a lower tax bracket, (b) spreading income that would otherwise have to be entirely recognized in a single tax year over a number of years, to minimize the impact of progressive tax rates, or (c) postponing tax on the appreciation of property or build-up of amounts credited to an employee's deferred compensation account.

The flexibility of nonqualified arrangements makes them suitable to a wide variety of specific business purposes. The most common use of such arrangements is to compensate and retain key personnel.

#### XVII.B.1.b. Advantages and Disadvantages

[385 T.M., I.B.; TPS ¶5710.01.]

The major advantages of a nonqualified plan over a qualified plan include:

- They are relatively simple to adopt and maintain.
- Unlike qualified plans, they allow selective participant coverage and individual tailoring.
- They permit greater latitude than qualified plans in structuring vesting and/or forfeitability.
- They can be exempt from certain exacting and time-consuming provisions of ERISA.
- Various other statutory requirements may not apply.
- They can be used to alleviate cash-flow problems of the employer.

The major negative factor is the employer's inability to deduct any amounts which may be set aside to pay the benefits until the amounts are includible in the employee's income. Other disadvantages include:

- A lack of security exists in nonqualified plan benefits for an employee until the benefits become substantially vested and taxable.

- Because nonqualified plan benefits are subject to the claims of general creditors of the employer, there is greater potential for benefit forfeiture by the employee.
- Distributions from nonqualified plans are generally subject to FICA and FUTA taxes and income tax withholding, whereas distributions from qualified plans may not be, or will be only at the employee's election.

### XVII.B.1.c. Structuring Arrangements to Defer Compensation

### XVII.B.1.c.(1) General Tax Principles

[385 T.M., IV.A.; TPS ¶5710.02.A.]

When drafting nonqualified deferred compensation arrangements, in addition to the numerous rules and restrictions applicable to most such arrangements under § 409A, (see XVII.B.1.e.), tax practitioners must be aware of the application of the constructive receipt and economic benefit doctrines. If either doctrine applies to the arrangement, some, if not all, of its objectives, including the deferral of income, will be negated. If either doctrine applies, the employee will be taxed on the deferred amounts even though he or she has yet to receive the benefits involved [§ 451; Reg. § 1.451-2(a)].

### XVII.B.1.c.(2) Constructive Receipt Doctrine

[385 T.M., VI.; TPS ¶5710.03.]

Under the constructive receipt doctrine, a taxpayer may not simply turn his or her back on current income and choose to receive it, and pay tax on it, at a later date. Instead, a cash method taxpayer must include compensation in income in the year it is actually or "constructively" received.

Income is "constructively received" by a taxpayer when it is credited to his or her account, set apart for him/her, or otherwise made available so that he/she may draw upon it at any time, or so that he/she could have drawn upon it during the tax year if notice of intention to withdraw had been given. However, income is not constructively received if the taxpayer's control of its receipt is subject to substantial limitations or restrictions [§ 451; Reg. § 1.451-2(a)].

### XVII.B.1.c.(3) Economic Benefit Doctrine

[385 T.M., VII.; TPS ¶5710.04.A.]

The economic benefit doctrine provides that an individual may be taxed on the value of any economic or financial benefit conferred as compensation, whatever the form or mode by which it is effected. Income taxation occurs whether or not the individual ever had the option to receive cash.

Where a plan is funded (i.e., assets are set aside to pay for benefits), the IRS requires the value of an employee's right to deferred compensation to be included in income in the year that the right "vests," i.e., the year in which it can no longer be forfeited because of some significant condition on its receipt, such as continued service for the employer. The principal issue that arises under the economic benefit doctrine is whether the employer has in fact funded its promise to pay deferred compensation by setting aside money or other property for that purpose and/or granting the employee significant rights to the property directly such that the employee receives more than a mere promise to pay money in the future.

***Annuities and Insurance Contracts.*** Where an employer purchases an annuity or other insurance contract to fund its obligation under a deferred compensation agreement, the employee will not be taxed under the economic benefit doctrine if the employer is the applicant, owner and beneficiary of the contract and retains all incidents of ownership.

***Trusts.*** Where an employer uses a trust to provide for benefits, the employee-beneficiary is not taxed under the economic benefit doctrine as long as the funds remain subject to the claims of the employer's general creditors (i.e., the employee has no rights to the funds other than by virtue of his status as a general creditor). Generally, a fund will remain subject to the claims of an employer's general creditors unless it is irrevocably given to a trustee, escrow agent, or some other independent party to be paid to the employee under the plan's terms.

### XVII.B.1.c.(4) Compensatory Transfers of Restricted Property

[384 T.M., III.; TPS ¶5710.04.E.1.]

Rules under § 83 primarily supplement the economic benefit doctrine in the area of compensatory transfers of employer stock and similar property subject to complex restrictions and forfeiture conditions. Section 83 is largely associated with nonqualified compensatory stock plans and similar bonus arrangements in which such restrictions and forfeiture provisions play a major role [§ 83, § 402(b)]. The basic rule under § 83 is that, if property is transferred to an individual as compensation for the performance of services, the individual will be taxed on the excess of the property's fair market value over the amount, if any, the employee paid for the property, as soon as the property [Reg. § 1.83-1(a)(1)]:

- is no longer subject to a "substantial risk of forfeiture"; or
- becomes freely transferable, whichever occurs first.

The excess is taxed as ordinary income and otherwise treated the same as additional salary (e.g., it is subject to withholding and employment taxes). Any gain realized when the property is sold, however, will be taxed as capital gain. "Property" for § 83 purposes includes virtually any item of value except cash or an unfunded and unsecured promise to pay deferred compensation, even though § 83 focuses primarily on stock, nonstatutory stock options, and similar property. Fair market value must be determined without regard to any restrictions on transfer, "other than a restriction which by its terms will never lapse" (a "non-lapse restriction") [§ 83(a)(1); Reg. § 1.83-5(a)].

Recognizing that most non-competition agreements are not enforced, the IRS takes the position that property that will be forfeited if an individual violates a non-competition and consulting agreement will not be considered subject to a substantial risk of forfeiture unless evidence is provided relating to the individual's age, skills, and health and the employer's history of enforcing such agreements, indicating that the agreement may actually be enforced [Reg. § 1.83-3(c)(2)].

### XVII.B.1.c.(5) Section 83(b) Elections to Accelerate Taxation

[384 T.M., III.D.; TPS ¶5710.04.E.4.]

Recipients of restricted property may elect to include in income for the tax year in which the property is transferred to them the excess of the property's fair market value at the time of transfer over the amount, if any, they paid for the property. This is true even if the property is non-transferable and is subject to a substantial risk of forfeiture and, thus, would ordinarily not be taxable until a later time. If a recipient makes this election, the recipient will not be taxed again when the property finally vests. This election, known as the "§ 83(b) election," provides a means of assuring that appreciation of the property that occurs after the election will be taxed as capital gains rather than compensation income when the property is disposed of. The election of current taxation is most beneficial where substantial appreciation is anticipated before vesting will occur [§ 83(b); Reg. § 1.83-2].

---

**EXAMPLE:** Corporation X transfers 1,000 shares of its stock to employee Y in 2012 for $80 per share at the time when the stock has a value of $100 per share. The stock is non-transferable and is subject to a substantial risk of forfeiture that expires in 2014, at which time it is worth $200 per share, or $200,000 total. The stock is ultimately sold in 2015 for $210 per share. If no § 83(b) election is made and the stock becomes substantially vested in 2014, Y has $120,000 (($200 - $80) × 1,000) of compensation income in 2014 and an additional $10,000 (($210 - $200) × 1,000) of capital gains in 2015. If, however, Y elected in 2012 to be currently taxed on the receipt of the stock, he will have $20,000 in compensation income in 2012, no additional income in 2014, and capital gains of $110,000 (($210 - $100) × 1,000) in 2015.

---

In addition to being taxed at generally lower rates than those applicable to ordinary income, capital gains, unlike ordinary compensation income, are not subject to employment taxes. Further, if the election is made and the property is held until the recipient dies, the property's basis will be stepped up to its date-of-death value, allowing it to be sold free of tax. Finally, the fact that the employee can defer tax on any appreciation until he or she sells or disposes of the property can confer a substantial benefit. These advantages must be weighed against the fact that, if the election is made, (i) the recipient initially will be taxed at an earlier date, and (ii) if the property is later forfeited, the resulting loss will be a capital loss that may not be fully deductible [§ 1211; Reg. § 1.83-2(a)].

An election made under § 83(b) must be made in accordance with IRS regulations and must be filed with the IRS no later than 30 days after the date that the property is transferred to the service provider. The IRS has released sample language that can be used to make a § 83(b) election [§ 83(b)(2); Reg. § 1.83-2(c), § 1.83-2(e); Rev. Proc. 2012-29, 2012-28 I.R.B. 49].

### XVII.B.1.d. *Taxation of Deferred Compensation*

### XVII.B.1.d.(1) *Nonqualified Trusts*

[384 T.M., V.A., 385 T.M., VIII.D.; TPS ¶5710.05.B.1.]

From the employee's perspective, the safest way to secure the payment of non-qualified benefits is for the employer to transfer funds to an irrevocable, nongrantor trust outside of the reach of its creditors. Generally, if an employer contributes to a nonqualified, nongrantor trust, and the employee's interest is substantially vested, the contribution is includible in the employee's income as compensation. An employee's interest in such a trust is vested if it is "transferable." Property is transferable if the transferee's rights in and to the property are not subject to a substantial risk of forfeiture. The company may deduct payments (assuming the maintenance of separate accounts for each employee) in the year in which the employee's rights in the trust's assets are no longer subject to a substantial risk of forfeiture, i.e., when the contributions are made, or when the employee vests, if later [§ 402(b); Reg. § 1.402(b)-1(a)(1)].

Generally, amounts distributed or made available from a nonqualified, nongrantor trust will be taxable to the employee under rules applicable to the taxation of annuities. Under those rules, the employee may recover a portion of each payment tax free. The total amount the employee can recover tax free is his or her "investment in the contract," which is the total of his or her own contributions to the trust, plus any amounts previously included in his gross income [§ 72, § 402(b)(1); Reg. § 1.402(b)-1(c)(1)]. Taxation of annuities is discussed in detail in XVII.A.2.e.(4).

An employer may deduct contributions it makes to a nonqualified, nongrantor trust at the time the employee recognizes income. Therefore, an employer will not lose a deduction for its contribution to a nonqualified nongrantor trust merely because its employees are not taxed currently on such contributions. Instead, the employer's deduction will be deferred until the employee recognizes income [§ 83(h), § 404(a)(5); Reg. § 1.404(a)-12(b)(1)].

If employee contributions to a nonqualified, nongrantor trust are incidental, any income earned by the trust will not be currently taxed to the employee under the grantor trust rules. Employee contributions are incidental if they do not exceed the employer's contributions. In most cases, the trust itself will pay tax on its accumulated income. If employee contributions are not incidental, the trust will be treated as a grantor trust with respect to the employees who benefit from it, and each employee will be taxable on the trust earnings allocable to his or her account [§ 402(b)(1), § 671 through § 679; Reg. § 1.402(b)-1(b)(6)].

### XVII.B.1.d.(2) Rabbi Trusts

[385 T.M., VIII.B.; TPS ¶5710.05.B.2.]

A "rabbi trust" is an irrevocable trust established by an employer to provide nonqualified deferred compensation to certain employees, which, because the grantor retains administrative powers, is treated as a grantor trust. The trustee of a rabbi trust is a fiduciary who receives assets contributed by the employer to support its deferred compensation obligations. The assets can be used only to pay the promised benefits, usually upon retirement, death, or termination of employment without cause, but must also be held available to pay the claims of creditors in the event of insolvency or bankruptcy. The IRS has determined that the participants whose benefits are funded in this manner are not currently taxed on contributions to the trust under the economic benefit doctrine, the constructive receipt doctrine, or the statutory rules on restricted property [§ 83, § 402(b); Reg. § 1.83-3(e)]. See Rev. Proc. 92-64, 1992-33 I.R.B. 11 (model rabbi trust and guidance for requesting rulings on nonqualified deferred compensation plans that use such trusts).

### XVII.B.1.d.(3) Reporting, Withholding and Employment Taxes

[384 T.M., V.B.; TPS ¶5710.13.]

Compensation deferred under an unfunded nonqualified deferred compensation plan is generally subject to federal income tax withholding in the same year that it is taxable to the employee. Thus, it is generally subject to withholding in the year that it is finally paid, although it may be subject to withholding earlier if for some reason the constructive receipt and/or economic benefit doctrines apply and require it to be taxed earlier [Reg. § 31.3401(a)-1(a), § 31.3402(a)-1(b)]. Compensation deferred under nonqualified deferred compensation plans is subject to FICA and FUTA taxes upon performance of the services for which such compensation is received, or, if later, when there is no substantial risk of forfeiture of the right to receive these amounts. However, an amount deferred may be taken into account at an even later date if all or a portion of the amount deferred is not "reasonably ascertainable" until such later date [§ 3121(v)(2)(A), § 3306(r)(2)(A); Reg. § 31.3121(v)(2)-1(e)(1)].

*XVII.B.1.e. Application of § 409A*

*XVII.B.1.e.(1) Coverage*

[385 T.M., IV.; TPS ¶5715.01.]

Section 409A makes significant changes to the law applicable to nonqualified deferred compensation plans. Arrangements that are subject to § 409A generally must satisfy requirements that fall into one of four categories:

1. written plan requirements;

2. election rules;

3. distribution rules; and

4. acceleration restrictions.

*Covered Plans.* The application of § 409A is very broad. It applies to every nonqualified deferred compensation plan, i.e., any plan that provides for the deferral of compensation other than the following types of plans [§ 409A(d)(1), § 409A(d)(3); Reg. § 1.409A-1(a)(2), § 1.409A-1(a)(5)]:

- tax-qualified retirement plans;

- tax-deferred annuity plans and contracts;

- simplified employee pensions (SEPs);

- SIMPLE plans;

- § 501(c)(18) trusts (generally, pension funds created before June 25, 1959);

- qualified governmental excess benefit arrangements; or

- any bona fide vacation leave, sick leave, compensatory time, disability pay or death benefit plan.

*Short-Term Deferrals.* A deferral of compensation does not occur if, absent an election by the service provider to otherwise defer the payment of the compensation to a later period, an amount of compensation is actually or constructively received by the service provider by the later of: (i) the 15th day of the third month following the service provider's first tax year in which the amount is no longer subject to a substantial risk of forfeiture; or (ii) the 15th day of the third month following the end of the service recipient's first tax year in which the amount is no longer subject to a substantial risk of forfeiture [Reg. § 1.409A-1(b)(4)(i)].

---

**EXAMPLE:** On Nov. 1, 2014, Employer W awards a bonus to its employee, David, such that David has a legally binding right to the payment as of Nov. 1, 2014. Under the bonus plan, the bonus will be determined based on services performed during the period from Jan. 1, 2015, through Dec. 31, 2016. The bonus is scheduled to be paid as a lump sum payment on Feb. 15, 2017. Under the bonus plan, David will forfeit the bonus unless he continues performing services through the scheduled payment date (Feb. 15, 2017). Provided that at all times before the scheduled payment date David is required to continue to perform services to retain the right to the bonus, and the bonus is paid on or before Mar. 15, 2018, the bonus plan will not be considered to have provided for a deferral of compensation because the amount paid will be considered a short-term deferral.

---

*Certain Stock Options Grants Not Subject to § 409A.* The grant of either an incentive stock option or an option under an employee stock purchase plan is not a deferral of compensation under § 409A. An option to purchase stock of the service recipient other than an incentive stock option or an option granted under an employee stock purchase plan does not provide for a deferral of compensation subject to § 409A if the purchase price may never be less than the fair market value of the underlying stock on the date of grant [Reg. § 1.409A-1(b)(5)(ii)].

***Separation Pay Arrangements.*** A separation pay plan that provides for separation pay upon an actual involuntary separation from service or pursuant to a window program does not provide for a deferral of compensation and, therefore, is not subject to § 409A, to the extent that the plan provides that [Reg. § 1.409A-1(b)(9)(iii); Notice 2013–73, 2013-49 I.R.B. 598]:

1. the separation pay (other than reimbursements and certain other separation payments) may not exceed two times the lesser of:

    a. the sum of the service provider's annualized items of compensation; or

    b. the maximum amount that may be taken into account for compensation purposes under a qualified plan under § 401(a)(17) ($265,000 in 2015, and $260,000 in 2014); and

2. the separation pay must be paid no later than the end of the second year following the year in which the separation from service occurs.

***Common Law Doctrines Still Apply.*** Although § 409A made many fundamental changes, it does not alter or affect the application of any other provision of the I.R.C. or common law tax doctrine (see XVII.B.1.c.). Deferred compensation that is not required to be included in income under § 409A still may be includible in income under § 451, the constructive receipt doctrine, the economic benefit doctrine, or any other applicable provision [Notice 2005-1, 2005-2 I.R.B. 274, § I].

***Correcting Mistakes.*** The IRS permits limited corrections of certain operational failures under § 409A(a) for inadvertent and unintentional errors. The IRS also provides methods for voluntary correction of many types of failures of plan documents to comply with § 409A. Generally, the service recipient must take commercially reasonable steps to identify and correct all other nonqualified deferred compensation plans that have substantially similar document failures [Notice 2008-113, 2008-51 I.R.B. 1305, § III, Notice 2010-6, 2010-3 I.R.B. 275].

### XVII.B.1.e.(2) Tax Consequences of Noncompliance

[385 T.M., IV.H.; TPS ¶5715.01.A.]

The potential consequences of violating § 409A are severe, even for minor or inadvertent violations. All tax consequences are imposed on the service provider and not the service recipient, although the latter may be subject to reporting requirements. The adverse consequences may include: (i) deferred compensation is currently includible in income; (ii) an additional "interest" tax is imposed during the period of deferral; and (iii) an additional 20% penalty tax is imposed on the deferred compensation. These adverse consequences are further compounded by application of the plan aggregation rules, which provide that all plans of the same type are aggregated and treated as having violated § 409A with respect to the participant [§ 409A(a)(1), § 409A(d)(6)].

If at any time during a tax year, a plan fails to meet or is not operated in accordance with the requirements of § 409A, all amounts deferred under the plan for the tax year and all preceding tax years by any participant with respect to whom the failure relates are includible in gross income for the tax year to the extent not subject to a substantial risk of forfeiture and not previously included in gross income. Inclusion in current income and the interest and additional tax apply only with respect to the participants for whom the requirements of the statute are not met, not to the entire plan [§ 409A(a)(1)(A); Prop. Reg. § 1.409A-4(a)(1)(ii)].

The rights of a person to compensation are subject to a substantial risk of forfeiture if the person's rights to the compensation are conditioned upon the future performance of substantial services by any individual. An amount is not subject to a substantial risk of forfeiture merely because the right to the amount is conditioned, directly or indirectly, upon refraining from performing services [§ 409A(d)(4); Reg. § 1.409A-1(d)(1)].

### XVII.B.1.e.(3) Written Plan Requirement

[385 T.M., IV.D.2.d(2); TPS ¶5715.01.C.]

The material terms of a nonqualified deferred compensation plan must be in writing. A plan must specify the following items in order to satisfy the written plan requirement [Reg. § 1.409A-1(c)(3)]:

1. the amount that the service provider has a right to be paid (or, in the case of an amount determinable under an objective, nondiscretionary formula, the terms of such formula);

2. the schedule or triggering events that will result in a payment of the amount;

3. the 6-month delay requirement for payments to specified employees of publicly-traded companies upon separation from service (no later than the time such provision may be applicable); and

4. the conditions under which a deferral or subsequent deferral election may be made.

### XVII.B.1.e.(4) Election Rules

[385 T.M., IV.E.; TPS ¶5715.01.G.]

In general, to avoid potential current inclusion in income, a nonqualified deferred compensation plan must provide that compensation for services performed during a tax year may be deferred at the participant's election only if the election to defer is made by the close of the preceding tax year. For performance-based compensation based on services performed over a period of at least 12 months, the election may be made no later than six months before the end of the service period. In the first year that an employee becomes eligible for participation in a nonqualified deferred compensation plan, the election may be made within 30 days after the date that the employee initially is eligible [§ 409A(a)(4)(B)].

***Subsequent Changes in Elections.*** Section 409A allows for changes that further delay or change the already-elected form of payment if [§ 409A(a)(4)(C); Reg. § 1.409A-2(b)(1)]:

1. the change does not take effect until at least 12 months after the date on which the change is made;

2. in the case of payments made on account of separation from service, a specified time (or pursuant to a fixed schedule), or following a change in control, the first payment must be deferred for at least five years from the date the payment otherwise would have been made; and

3. in the case of any change related to a payment made on account of a specified time (or pursuant to a fixed schedule), the change cannot be made less than 12 months before the date of the first scheduled payment.

### XVII.B.1.e.(5) Distribution Rules

[385 T.M., IV.F.; TPS ¶5715.01.H.]

Under § 409A, compensation deferred under a nonqualified deferred compensation plan may be made only at a fixed date or under a fixed schedule or for the following reasons [§ 409A(a)(2); Reg. § 1.409A-3(a)]:

1. separation from service;
2. a participant's disability (as defined under § 409A(a)(2)(C));
3. death;
4. a change in the ownership or effective control of the corporation or in the ownership of a substantial portion of the assets of the corporation; or
5. the occurrence of an unforeseeable emergency (as defined under § 409A(a)(2)(B)(ii)).

**Specified Employees.** Specified employees of publicly traded corporations who separate from service may not take distributions earlier than six months after the date of the separation from service or upon death. An employee of a service recipient with publicly traded stock is a "specified employee" if he or she: (i) owns more than 5% of the stock of the service recipient or of any member of its controlled group; (ii) owns more than 1% of the stock and has compensation from the service recipient in excess of $150,000 per year (not indexed); or (iii) is an officer of the service recipient with compensation in excess of $170,000 per year (as indexed for 2014 and 2015). Officer status is based on the nature of one's duties, not on title, and is limited to the 50 highest-paid officers [§ 409A(a)(2)(B)(i), § 416(i); IRS News Release IR-2014-99 (Oct. 23, 2014); Notice 2013-73, 2013-49 I.R.B. 598].

### XVII.B.1.e.(6) Prohibition on Acceleration

[385 T.M., IV.F.3.e.; TPS ¶5715.01.H.5.]

Generally, a nonqualified deferred compensation plan may not permit the acceleration of the time or schedule of any payment under the plan. However, if the requirements of § 409A otherwise are satisfied for deferring compensation, a service recipient may waive or accelerate the satisfaction of a condition constituting a substantial risk of forfeiture applicable to such deferral [§ 409A(a)(3)].

---

**EXAMPLE:** If a plan provides for a lump sum payment of a vested benefit upon separation from service, and the benefit vests under the plan only after 10 years of service, the service recipient may reduce the vesting requirement to five years of service, even if a service provider becomes vested as a result and qualifies for a payment in connection with a separation from service.

---

### XVII.B.1.e.(7) Reporting, Withholding and Employment Taxes

[385 T.M., IV.H.; TPS ¶5715.01.J.]

**Deferrals.** All deferrals for the year under a nonqualified deferred compensation plan must be separately reported on a Form 1099 or a Form W-2, regardless of whether the compensation is includible in gross income. However, until further guidance is issued, the IRS has placed a moratorium on this reporting requirement [Notice 2010-6, 2010-3 I.R.B. 275, § III.A].

**Amounts Included in Income.** An employer is required to include in total wages any amounts includible in an employee's gross income as a result of the application of § 409A. Such amounts are reported as wages paid on line 2 of Form 941 and in box 1 of Form W-2 and in box 12 of Form W-2 using code Z. Amounts includible in gross income in the applicable calendar year that are neither actually nor constructively received by an employee during that calendar year are treated as wages on December 31 of that year. Until the IRS provides further guidance, a payer is required to report in box 7 of Form 1099-MISC and in box 15b of Form 1099-MISC amounts includible in the gross income of a nonemployee that were not treated as wages as nonemployee compensation [Notice 2010-6, § III.B].

The amount includible in gross income and required to be reported by an employer or payer for each of these calendar years equals the portion of the total amount deferred under the nonqualified deferred compensation plan that, as of December 31 of that year, was not subject to a substantial risk of forfeiture and had not been included in income in a previous year, plus any amounts of deferred compensation paid or made available to the employee or nonemployee under the plan during that calendar year [Notice 2010-6, § III.B.1].

*Income Tax Withholding.* Employers are required to withhold tax on income arising from violations of § 409A as if these amounts were wages received in the year of the violation. Amounts included in income are treated as supplemental wages for purposes of determining the amount of tax to be withheld regardless of whether the employer paid other wages to the employee during the calendar year. This withholding obligation does not extend to the additional 20% tax or interest penalties imposed by § 409A – the service provider is responsible for reporting and paying those amounts and may have to make estimated tax payments in order to avoid liability for tax underpayments [Notice 2008-115, § III.B].

*FICA Taxes.* The tax treatment of deferred compensation for FICA purposes is not affected by § 409A. Thus, remuneration for employment constituting wages within the meaning of § 3121(a) is taken into account for FICA tax purposes in accordance with the rules for wage inclusion under § 3121(a) or § 3121(v)(2), as appropriate. (See XXII.) For SECA tax purposes, deferred compensation that complies with or is exempt from § 409A is not included in SECA income until actually or constructively received [§ 1401, § 1402(a), § 3121(a), § 3121(v)(2); Notice 2005-1, 2005-2 I.R.B. 274, Q&As-36-37].

### XVII.B.2. Compensatory Stock Arrangements

[383 T.M., I.C.; TPS ¶5810.01.]

Generally, for federal tax purposes, there are two types of stock options granted to employees — statutory stock options and nonstatutory stock options. A statutory stock option includes incentive stock options (ISOs) and options granted under an employee stock purchase plan. All other options are nonstatutory stock options (NSOs).

There are three points at which significant tax consequences occur for compensatory stock options:

1. the grant of the option;

2. the exercise of the option (when the employee acquires stock by paying the option's exercise price); and

3. the ultimate sale or other disposition of the stock acquired.

### XVII.B.2.a. Incentive Stock Options

[381 T.M., II.B.; TPS ¶5820.02.]

An ISO is an option to purchase stock in a corporation, issued to an employee of the corporation, which meets certain statutory requirements. By satisfying the relevant I.R.C. qualification requirements for such an option, the employee obtains preferential tax treatment. Without such treatment, the employee would pay federal income tax when the option was exercised, on the amount of the spread between the stock's value and the exercise price paid by the employee — which would be the case with an NSO. With preferential tax treatment, the employee does not recognize income until the stock is sold or otherwise disposed of, which may be several years after the option is exercised.

*Plan Terms.* An ISO must be granted pursuant to a written plan. The plan must specifically set forth the following two items [§ 422(b)(1)]:

1. the total number of shares that may be purchased pursuant to the exercise of options granted under the plan; and

2. the employees or class of employees who are eligible to participate in the plan.

All other terms of the plan can be set forth in the terms of the option issued to the employee.

*Shareholder Approval.* The shareholders of the granting corporation must approve the plan within 12 months before or after the date the plan is adopted [§ 422(b)(1); Reg. § 1.422-2(b)(2), § 1.422-2(b)(3)].

*Duration of Plan and ISO.* To be an ISO, an option must be granted to the employee within 10 years from the earlier of the date the plan is adopted, or the date the shareholders approve the plan [§ 422(b)(2); Reg. § 1.422-2(a)(2)(ii), § 1.422-2(c)]. To be an ISO, an option may not, by its terms, be exercised more than 10 years (five years in the case of a 10% or more stock owner) after the date on which it is granted [§ 422(b)(3); Reg. § 1.422-2(a)(2)(iii), § 1.422-2(d)].

---

**EXAMPLE:** ABC Corp adopts an ISO plan on Feb. 1, 2005, and its shareholders approve the plan on Apr. 1, 2005. ABC Corp can grant ISOs under this plan until Jan. 31, 2015. An ISO granted on Jan. 31, 2015, would have to be exercised no later than Jan. 31, 2025.

---

*Exercise Price.* An ISO's exercise price must be not less than 100% (110% in the case of a 10% or more stock owner) of the stock's fair market value at the time the option is granted. The exercise price is the amount of money or other consideration which, pursuant to the terms of an option, must be paid to purchase a share of stock subject to the option. Any reasonable valuation method may be used to determine whether, at the time an option is granted, the exercise price satisfies the exercise price requirement. This includes valuation methods used for estate tax purposes [§ 422(b)(4), § 422(6), § 422(c)(5); Reg. § 1.421-1(e), § 1.421-2(a)(2)(iv), § 1.421-2(e), § 1.422-2(f)].

*Restrictions on Transferability.* By its terms, an ISO must be nontransferable by the employee. The only exceptions are for transfers by will or by state laws of descent and distribution. During the employee's lifetime, the option may be exercisable only by him [§ 422(b)(5); Reg. § 1.422-2(a)(2)(v), § 1.421-1(b)(2)].

*Aggregate Value of Stock.* The aggregate fair market value of the stock with respect to which an ISO is exercisable for the first time by an employee during any particular calendar year under all plans of the individual's employer corporation and its parent and subsidiary corporations cannot exceed $100,000 [§ 422(d)(1)].

**EXAMPLE:** An employer with an ISO plan hires a new employee who becomes eligible to participate in the plan. The employer grants the employee five options, each of which entitles the employee to purchase $100,000 of the employer's stock. The vesting schedule for the options is such that options for no more than $100,000 worth of stock become exercisable in any one future calendar year. This series of options does not violate the limit on the amount of stock subject to options, because the limit is a per annum limit.

*Employee's Tax Treatment.* The employee has no tax consequences from the grant of an ISO, regardless of whether any portion of the ISO is vested upon grant. The employee similarly has no income tax consequences from the exercise of an ISO [§ 421(a)(1), § 422(a); Reg.§ 1.83-3(a)(2)].

Because an employee does not recognize taxable income on account of the grant of an ISO and because the employee generally does not pay the exercise price or any other consideration for the ISO until the time of exercise, the employee's basis in an ISO at the *date of grant* will generally be $0. Upon *exercise* of the ISO, the employee's basis in ISO stock will be the amount the employee paid upon exercise of the ISO [§ 422(a), § 1011].

The tax treatment of the *disposition* of ISO stock depends upon whether the stock is disposed of within the statutorily required holding period for such stock. The qualifying disposition period begins on the date of exercise and ends on the date that is the later of [§ 422(a)(1)]:

- two years from the date of the ISO grant; or
- one year from the date on which the ISO stock was transferred to the employee upon exercise.

For purposes of computing these periods, the date of grant or exercise, as appropriate, is excluded, and the last day of the period is included.

If an employee disposes of ISO stock after completion of the statutory holding period, the employee will recognize the difference between the amount received in such disposition over the employee's basis in the ISO stock as capital gain [§ 1001(a)].

An employee loses favorable tax treatment if he or she disposes of the shares acquired by exercise of an ISO before the end of the statutory holding period [Reg. § 1.421-1(c)(2)]. The income that an optionee would have recognized when the option was exercised, but for the special ISO rules, is recognized as ordinary compensation income in the tax year of a disqualifying disposition. The amount of compensation income equals the stock's fair market value on the date it was transferred to the optionee, less the optionee's basis in the shares (the exercise price plus any amount paid for the ISO) [§ 83(a), § 421(b); Reg. § 1.421-2(b)(1)]. Capital gain income also is recognized if the shares have appreciated since the exercise of the ISO. The gain is long-term capital gain if the shares have been held for more than the long-term capital gains holding period [§ 1221].

**EXAMPLE:** Employee N is granted an ISO on January 20, 2014, at an exercise price of $100 per share. The shares of the grantor corporation have a value of $100 per share on that date (i.e., the exercise price equaled the fair market value). N exercises the ISO on October 1, 2014, when the fair market value of the shares is $120 per share. N sells the stock on the market on April 1, 2015 for $125 per share. Because N sells the shares before the end of the statutory holding period (two years after the date of grant of the ISO and one year after the date the stock is transferred to the employee), the sale is a disqualifying disposition. N will recognize a gain of $25 per share, of which $20 will be ordinary income and $5 will be short-term capital gain. (The gain will be short-term because the shares were not held for more than one year.)

An individual who leaves employment has three months within which to exercise the ISO or the preferential tax treatment is lost and a disposition will be considered a disqualifying disposition. An individual who is disabled has up to one year [§ 422(a)(2), § 422(c)(6); Reg. § 1.421-1(h), § 1.422-1(a)(1)(i)(B)].

The statutory holding period is waived if an ISO is exercised after an optionee's death by his estate or by a person who acquired the right to exercise the option by bequest or inheritance or by reason of the optionee's death [§ 421(c)(1)(A)].

---

**EXAMPLE:** Daughter is given the right to exercise Employee's ISO under the provisions of Employee's will. After Employee's death, Daughter exercises the ISO and acquires stock. She sells all of the shares a few months after acquiring them; i.e., she does not wait until one year after the stock was transferred to her. She is entitled to the preferential tax treatment afforded ISOs even though she disposes of the stock before the end of the statutory holding period.

---

*Alternative Minimum Tax Treatment.* For alternative minimum tax (AMT) purposes, an ISO essentially is treated as an NSO. An employee must recognize income for AMT purposes when the employee exercises an ISO to the extent that the fair market value of the stock transferred to the employee exceeds the option price at the time the employee exercises the option. If the ISO does not have a readily ascertainable fair market value on the date of grant, then no regular tax or AMT consequences are triggered until the option is exercised or otherwise disposed of, even if the option's fair market value becomes ascertainable before such time. Upon exercise, the employee generally must include in alternative minimum taxable income (AMTI) the difference between the fair market value of the stock received and the amount paid for the stock (and for the option (if any)) as compensation income [§ 56(b)(3)].

---

**EXAMPLE:** During Year 1, Jesse receives an ISO to acquire 100 shares of stock for $10 per share. Jesse does not exercise the option until Year 2. The ISO has a readily ascertainable fair market value on the date of grant of $50. For AMT purposes, Jesse must include $50 compensation income in AMTI in Year 1. For regular tax purposes, the granting of an ISO is not a taxable event.

**EXAMPLE:** In the example above, assume instead that the ISO does not have a readily ascertainable fair market value on the date of grant. No income is recognized on the grant date. Upon exercise, Jesse recognizes $30 of ordinary income for AMT purposes ($40 (fair market value) less $10 (option price)), and $0 for regular tax purposes.

---

If a taxpayer recognizes AMT in the year an ISO is exercised but later sells the stock at a loss, it creates inequitable results because the loss generally is a capital loss deductible only to the extent of AMT capital gain plus $3,000. For tax years beginning after December 20, 2006, but before January 1, 2013, a minimum tax credit ameliorated this to a degree by allowing a credit against regular tax for subsequent years if the taxpayer's regular tax was greater than the taxpayer's "adjusted net minimum tax" imposed for all prior tax years beginning after 1986. In certain cases, this credit was refundable [§ 53(e)] (see IX.H.).

**Employer's Deduction.** An employer may not take a compensation deduction on the grant or exercise of an ISO. If an optionee makes a disqualifying disposition, however, the employer may deduct the amount of the optionee's resulting compensation income. The employer's deduction is taken in the tax year in which the disposition occurs [§ 83, § 421(a)(2), § 421(b); Reg. § 1.421-2(b)(1)].

**Employment Taxes, Withholding and Reporting.** ISOs are not taxed for FICA or FUTA purposes. There is no withholding on ISOs, even where one is sold in a disqualifying disposition [§ 421(b), § 3121(a)(22), § 3306(b)(19)].

A corporation that transfers stock pursuant to an individual's exercise of an ISO is required to file a Form 3921, *Exercise of an Incentive Stock Option Under Section 422(b)*, with the IRS for that calendar year on or before February 28 of the year following the year in which the ISO exercise occurs (or March 31 if filing electronically). A corporation that is required to file a Form 3921 must also file an information statement with each employee named in that return. Employers can meet this requirement by sending Copy B of the Form 3921 to the employee [§ 6039; Reg. § 1.6039-1(a)(2), § 1.6039-1(c)].

---

**EXAMPLE:** On January 1, 2014, Astro Corp. grants an ISO to Yolanda, an employee of Astro Corp., to purchase 50 shares of Astro Corp. stock. Yolanda exercises the ISO on July 1, 2014, receives her shares immediately, and eventually sells the shares on January 2, 2016. Because Astro Corp. issues stock on exercise of its ISOs, it must file Form 3921 with the IRS and furnish Yolanda with Copy B of the form.

---

### XVII.B.2.b. Nonstatutory Stock Options

[383 T.M., II.A.1.; TPS ¶5810.01., .02.A.]

Nonstatutory stock options (NSOs) are stock options that do not meet the requirement of an incentive stock option (ISO). An NSO must be in writing (in paper or electronic form), and the writing must be adequate to establish an option right or privilege that is enforceable under applicable law.

No particular combination of words is necessary, but the writing should express:
- the selling price;
- the number of shares subject to the option; and
- the period of time during which the option will remain open.

**Income Tax Treatment.** The timing of an employee's recognition of compensation income, if any, caused by the grant of an NSO depends upon whether that option has a "readily ascertainable fair market value" at the time it is granted. If it does, the employee will be taxed immediately. If it does not, the employee generally will not be taxed until the employee exercises the option. At either date, the income that is taxable to the employee will be taxed as ordinary compensation income.

Most NSOs will not have a readily ascertainable fair market value due to the restrictive way in which the regulations define the term. As a result, most NSOs do not cause taxation to the employee when they are granted and are not taxable until the employee exercises the option, even if the fair market value becomes readily ascertainable after the grant [Reg. § 1.83-7(b)].

In determining whether an option has a readily ascertainable fair market value, options are divided into two categories:

1. those that are actively traded on an established market; and
2. those that are not.

*Options Actively Traded on an Established Market.* An option that is actively traded on an *established market* is deemed to have a readily ascertainable fair market value. If an option has a "readily ascertainable fair market value" at the date of grant, the employee will recognize ordinary compensation income. The employee includes in income the fair market value of the option, less any amount paid for the option, for the tax year of the receipt of the option [Reg. § 1.83-7(b)(1)].

An employee holds an option taxed at grant with a basis that includes both the amount of income taxed at grant and any amount paid for the option by the employee. If the employee pays nothing for the option, the option's basis in the hands of the employee is the amount included in income at grant [Reg. § 1.83-7(b)(1)].

---

**EXAMPLE:** On July 1, 2014, Price, Inc. grants to Brady, a key employee of the corporation, in consideration for services rendered or to be rendered to Price, Inc., an option to buy 2,000 shares of Price, Inc. common stock. The exercise price is $10 per share. The option has a readily ascertainable fair market value because this option is actively traded. The option may be exercised, in whole or in part, at any time over the 5-year period following the date of its grant year.

On July 1, 2017, when the fair market value of the Price Inc. stock is $40 per share, Brady exercises the option in full, acquiring 2,000 shares for $10 per share. On July 1, 2019, Brady sells the 2,000 shares for $50 per share.

If this option is taxable at grant, Brady includes the value of the option (less any amount paid) in income for the tax year of receipt of the option. Assuming the fair market value of the option is $20 per share, Brady includes $40,000 in income for his 2014 tax return.

---

Property acquired upon the exercise of a compensatory option taxed at grant has a basis equal to the amount paid upon the exercise of the option plus any basis that the employee had in the option itself [§ 83(a), § 83(f)].

---

**EXAMPLE:** Under the facts of the above example, Brady would hold Price, Inc. stock with a basis of $30 per share ($10 per share exercise price plus $20 per share basis in the option, which is the amount of the readily ascertainable fair market value of the option that was included in income at grant).

---

The remaining bargain inherent in the property as a result of the appreciation of the underlying stock in excess of the sum of the exercise price, plus the amount included in income at grant, is not taxed until the employee disposes of the stock acquired with the option. The holding period of the stock acquired pursuant to the exercise of a compensatory option taxed at grant begins only with the day after the exercise. The holding period of the option is not tacked to the holding period of the underlying stock.

Before the employee may sell the stock and receive long-term capital gain treatment, the employee must hold the property for the requisite long-term holding period (e.g., more than one year for long-term capital gain treatment) [§ 1001(a)].

*Options Not Actively Traded on an Established Market.* An option that is not actively traded on an established market will not have a readily ascertainable fair market value unless the fair market value "can otherwise be measured with reasonable accuracy." There is a presumption that an untraded option does not have a readily ascertainable fair market value unless certain conditions are met, such as transferability and the absence of restrictions that impair the option's value. The effect of the presumption is that untraded options almost never have a readily ascertainable fair market value at the date of grant. As a result, untraded options usually will be taxed when they are exercised rather than when they are granted [Reg. § 1.83-7(b)(2)].

For options that do not have a readily ascertainable fair market value at grant, there will be a tax-significant event upon the *exercise* of the option, and not at the date of the *grant* of the option. Generally, in the tax year an employee exercises the option, the employee must include in gross income the difference between the value of the stock acquired and the exercise price. The amount is considered ordinary compensation income [§ 83(e)(3), § 83(e)(4)].

When such an option is not taxed at grant, however, the difference between the share value of the common stock on the exercise date and the per share exercise price is taxed to the employee as the compensation income arising under § 83(a) from the option transaction. The transaction's compensatory aspect is considered closed upon option exercise [§ 83(a); Reg. § 1.61-2(d)(2)(i)].

The property acquired pursuant to the exercise of an option that is not taxed at grant takes a basis equal to the sum of the property's cost (the exercise price) and the option's basis in the hands of the option holder [Reg. § 1.83-1(b)(2)].

---

**EXAMPLE:** On July 1, 2014, when Price, Inc. stock had a fair market value of $30 per share, Price Inc. granted to Brady, in consideration of services rendered to Price, Inc., an option to buy 2,000 shares of P common stock. The option price was $30 per share. On July 1, 2017, when the fair market value of the Price, Inc. stock is $45 per share, Brady exercises the option in full, acquiring 2,000 shares for $30 per share. The basis in the stock acquired is $45 per share (the sum of the exercise price of $30 per share and the amount included in income of $15 per share).

---

The employee's holding period in the underlying stock begins the day on which the property is acquired pursuant to the exercise of the option. There is no tacking of holding periods. Property acquired pursuant to the exercise of a compensatory option taxed at exercise is normally investment property and is taxable only when that property is disposed of [§ 83(f); Reg. § 1.83-4(a)].

---

**EXAMPLE:** In the above example, if Brady sells the property for $50 per share on July 1, 2019, a gain of $5 per share will be recognized ($50 per share amount realized less $45 share adjusted basis in the stock). This gain is long-term capital gain.

---

*Employer Deduction.* Generally, employers may take a trade or business expense deduction for nonstatutory stock options. The deduction may be taken for the amount included in income by the employee. The deduction is available if the amounts meet the "ordinary and necessary" requirement test applicable to deducting business expenses, and the amount reasonably compensates personal services actually rendered [§ 83, § 162(a)(1)].

A publicly held corporation's deduction for compensation paid or accrued with respect to a "covered employee" is limited to $1 million per year [§ 162(m)(1)]. A covered employee is [§ 162(m)(3)]:

- the principal executive officer of the corporation (or an individual acting in such capacity) as of the close of the tax year; or
- any employee whose total compensation for the employee's tax year is required to be reported to the company's shareholders because the employee is one of the three highest paid officers for the tax year (other than the principal executive officer or principal financial officer).

The $1 million compensation deduction limit applies to all remuneration for services. The limit applies to the year in which the deduction would otherwise be taken. Thus, for NSOs, the deduction normally is taken in the year the option is exercised. Among the types of compensation that are not subject to the limit and are not counted in determining whether other compensation exceeds $1 million is compensation paid solely because the executive has attained one or more performance goals [§ 162(m)(4)].

***Employer Gain or Loss***. The employer's use of property to compensate an employee is considered a disposition of that property. In most cases, the employer does not recognize gain (or is denied the benefit of recognizing loss) in an NSO transaction because the property used to compensate employees is the employer's own stock. The employer's disposition of its own stock is protected from gain recognition (and denied loss recognition) under § 1032. This section extends to transfers of employer stock as compensation for services [§ 1032; Reg. § 1.1032-1(a)].

***Employment Taxes and Withholding.*** When an employee recognizes ordinary compensation income upon exercise of an NSO, the employer must report the amount on Form W-2, withhold for purposes of federal income taxes as well as for FICA and must include such compensation in wages for purposes of FUTA [§ 3101, § 3301, § 3401].

The duty to pay employment taxes and to withhold belongs to the employer in most situations. The employer is potentially subject to penalties for failure to discharge these duties. The obligation to pay employment taxes and to withhold occurs at the same time that income is recognized under § 83. In the case of NSOs as compensation, stocks are eligible for the flat withholding rate that applies to "supplemental wage payments" if the employer has withheld taxes from the employee's regular wages [§ 3102(a), § 3111(a), § 3301, § 3402(a), § 3403, § 6672; Reg. § 31.3402(g)-1].

### XVII.B.2.c. Employee Stock Purchase Plans
[381 T.M., III.; TPS ¶5830.02., .07.]

An "employee stock purchase plan" (ESPP) is a program that gives employees preferential treatment on the exercise of stock options. The exercise price for the options may be as low as 85% of the stock's value, such that an employee could exercise his option immediately upon its grant and acquire stock in the employer at a 15% discount. Stock under an ISO plan, by contrast, must be purchased at a price that is at least 100% of fair market value on the date of grant of the option.

By meeting the I.R.C.'s requirements for an ESPP, employees obtain preferential tax treatment on the exercise of their options. Without such treatment, they would pay tax when the options were exercised, on the amount of the "spread" between the stock's value and its exercise price. With preferential tax treatment, the employee is not taxed until the stock is sold or otherwise disposed of, which may be several years after the tax year in which the option is exercised.

*Corporate Stock.* The stock subject to option must be stock in the employee's employer, its parent or its subsidiary.

---

**EXAMPLE:** S Corp. is 100% owned by P Corp. An employee of S may be granted options to purchase the stock of P Corp. under an ESPP.

---

*Eligible Participants.* An ESPP must provide that options are to be granted only to individuals who are employees of the employer corporation or its parent or its subsidiary. An option may not be issued to an independent contractor. Options, pursuant to a qualified ESPP, generally must be granted to all employees of the corporation, subject to certain limited exceptions for recently-hired, part-time, or highly-compensated employees, as well as 5% owners [§ 423(b)(1), § 423(b)(3), § 423(b)(4); Reg. § 1.423-2(b), § 1.423-2(d)(1), § 1.423-2(e)(1)].

---

**EXAMPLE:** Employee B owns 6,000 shares of the common stock of X Corp, the only class of X Corp. stock outstanding. X Corp. has 100,000 shares of its common stock outstanding. Because B owns 6% of the combined voting power or value of all classes of X Corp. stock, X Corp. cannot grant an option to B under its ESPP.

---

*Maximum Shares.* An ESPP must set forth the total number of shares that may be purchased pursuant to the exercise of options granted under the plan. By its terms, an ESPP also must provide that no employee may purchase stock under the plan (including any other such plan or plans of his employer corporation or its related corporations) at a rate that exceeds $25,000 in fair market value of such stock for each calendar year in which any such option granted to such individual is outstanding at any time [§ 423(b)(8); Reg. § 1.423-2(c)(3), § 1.423-2(i)(1)].

*Exercise Price.* The exercise price for an option granted under an employee stock purchase plan may not be less than the lesser of [§ 423(b)(6); Reg. § 1.423-2(g)(1)]:

1. 85% of the fair market value of a share of stock at the time of the option's grant; or

2. 85% of the fair market value of a share of stock at the time of the option's exercise.

The exercise price may be stated either as a percentage or as a dollar amount. If the price is a dollar amount, the price must be fixed at the date of grant as being no less than 85% of the fair market value of a share of stock at the date of grant.

*Option Duration.* The plan terms must provide that options cannot be exercised more than 27 months after the date of grant. If the exercise price is determined solely as a percentage of the stock's fair market value at the date of exercise, however, the plan terms can permit options to be exercised up to five years from the date of grant [§ 423(b)(7); Reg. § 1.423-2(h)(1)].

*Restrictions on Transfer.* Under the terms of the ESPP, an option must be nontransferable by the employee. The only exceptions are for transfers by will or by the state laws of descent and distribution. During the employee's lifetime, the option may be exercisable only by him [§ 423(b)(9); Reg. § 1.423-2(j)].

*Shareholder Approval.* The shareholders of the corporation granting the stock subject to options must approve the employee stock purchase plan within 12 months before or after the date the plan is adopted. [Reg. § 1.423-2(c)].

*Taxation to Employee.* An employee exercising an option granted under an employee stock purchase plan is afforded preferential tax treatment. An employee does not recognize any income upon the grant of an option under an employee stock purchase plan. An employee does not realize any income as a result of the transfer of stock to him upon the exercise of an option granted under an employee stock purchase plan [§ 421(a)(1); Reg. § 1.421-2(a)(1)(i)].

When an employee sells shares acquired through exercise of an option granted under an ESPP, the employee's gain (if any) generally is taxed as a capital gain. This gain is the difference between the sale proceeds and the employee's basis in the stock (which is the exercise price plus any amount paid by the employee to acquire the option) [§ 1221].

Notwithstanding the general rule that provides capital gain treatment, some gain will be taxed as ordinary compensation income at the time of the stock's sale or other disposition if, when the option was granted, the exercise price was less than 100% of the stock's fair market value. Most employee stock purchase plans contain such a "bargain" element at the date of grant, to encourage employee participation in the program [§ 423(c); Reg. § 1.423-2(k)(1)(i)].

---

**EXAMPLE:** In 2014, Employee C receives an option under an ESPP to purchase 100 shares of Employer Corp stock. At the date of grant, the stock has a value of $100 per share. In 2015, when the stock has appreciated to $120 per share, C exercises all 100 options. Under the plan's terms, C pays an exercise price equal to 85% of the stock's fair market value at the date of grant, for a total of $8,500. In 2017 (after the statutory holding period has expired), C sells the stock. The stock still has a value of $120 per share. The amount of compensation (ordinary) income C must recognize in 2017 is the amount by which the fair market value of the disposed stock at the time the option was granted ($10,000) exceeds the price paid for the stock ($8,500), or $1,500.

---

An employee loses preferential tax treatment if he disposes of the acquired stock before the end of the 2-year period beginning on the day of the grant of the option or before the end of the 1-year period beginning on the day of the transfer of the shares by the corporation. The statutory holding period is waived if an option granted under an ESPP is exercised after an employee's death by the employee's estate or by a person who acquired the right to exercise the option by bequest or inheritance or by reason of the employee's death [§ 421(c)(1)(A), § 423(a)(1); Reg. § 1.421-2(b)(1), § 1.423-1(a)(1)]. If the employee does not qualify for preferential tax treatment, the employee generally realizes ordinary income in the year of exercise, in the amount of the "spread" (the difference between the fair market value of the stock received and the exercise price paid) [§ 83(a), § 421(b); Reg. § 1.421-2(b)(1)].

Unlike with the exercise of an ISO, an employee will not recognize alternative minimum taxable income on the exercise of a purchase right under a § 423 plan. There is nothing in § 56 that subjects the exercise of purchase rights under a § 423 plan to AMT.

*Employer Deduction.* An employer granting an option under an ESPP does not receive a deduction for the grant of the option or for a transfer of stock to the employee upon exercise of the option [§ 421(a)(2); Reg. § 1.421-2(a)(1)(ii)]. However, if an option is not treated at the date of exercise as having been issued under an ESPP (for example, because the employee does not then meet the employment requirement), the employer's tax consequences are the same as those for an employer issuing a nonstatutory stock option. The employer may deduct an amount equal to the amount that the employee must recognize as compensation income. The deduction is taken in the employer's tax year coincident with or within which the employee's year of income recognition ends [§ 83, § 421(a)(2), § 421(b); Reg. § 1.421-2(b)(1)]. The rules applicable to the $1 million compensation deduction limit (see XVII.B.2.b.) also apply [§ 162(m)].

*Withholding, Employment Taxes and Reporting.* With respect to options granted under an ESPP, the remuneration from the disposition of stock acquired by an employee pursuant to exercise of the option or upon the exercise of the option is excluded from wages for FICA, FUTA or federal income tax withholding purposes. Also, federal income tax withholding is not required on disqualifying dispositions or when compensation is recognized in connection with an employee stock purchase plan discount [§ 421(b), § 423(c), § 3121(a)(22), § 3306(b)(19)].

A corporation that transfers stock pursuant to an individual's exercise of an option under an employee stock purchase plan (i.e., where the option price is between 85% and 100% of the stock's value) is required to file a return with the IRS. The return is required only with respect to the first transfer of such shares by the employee who exercised the purchase right, including the first transfer of legal title to a recognized broker or financial institution. The returns and information statements for employee stock purchase plans must be made on Form 3922, *Transfer of Stock Acquired Through an Employee Stock Purchase Plan Under Section 423(c),* or its designated successor, as provided in the instructions thereto [§ 6039(a)(2), § 6039(c)(2); Reg. § 1.6039-1(b), § 1.6039-2(b)].

### XVII.B.3. Golden Parachutes

[396 T.M.; TPS ¶5720.]

A "golden parachute" is an arrangement designed to provide payments and/or continued benefits to management or key employees in the event of a change in ownership or control of the employer. Typically, a golden parachute is part of a compensation package in which a key employee is given benefits, consisting of cash payments and continued noncash benefits, if the executive is terminated as a result of a change in the ownership or control of the company. In this way, golden parachutes are used to provide the executive with financial protection from the possibility that the acquiring corporation will terminate the executive in order to make room for its own management team.

The golden parachute statutes employ two sets of consequences or "penalties" to encourage compliance with congressional intent. Corporations undergoing a change in control are denied deductions for any and all excess parachute payments. In addition, the recipient-individual (disqualified individual) of these payments must pay an extra 20% excise tax in addition to regular taxes. The employer must withhold the excise tax if the payment constitutes "wages" within the meaning of § 3401 [§ 280G, § 4999(a)].

*Affected Individuals.* Only officers, certain shareholders and the highest paid group of individuals providing services (either as employees or independent contractors) to a corporation (including subsidiaries) undergoing a change in control transaction may be subject to the excise tax under these rules [§ 280G(c)].

*Parachute Payment.* The term "parachute payment" means any payment in the nature of compensation to (or for the benefit of) a disqualified individual if [§ 280G(b)(2)(A)]:

1. the payment is contingent on a change in the ownership or effective control of the corporation, or a substantial portion of the assets of the corporation, and

2. the aggregate present value of the compensation payments that are contingent on such change equals or exceeds an amount equal to 3 times the base amount.

There is a presumption that payments made pursuant to an agreement entered into within one year before a change in control are contingent on the change [§ 280G(b)(2)(C); Reg. § 1.280G-1, Q&A-25].

*Base Amount.* Calculating the base amount is fundamental to the determination of whether an executive will be subject to the excise tax, and whether a corporation will lose deductions for payments made on account of the change in control. Generally, the base amount is the simple average of includible compensation over the base period. The base period consists of the five tax years of the individual ending before the year of the change in control. For most individuals, the base period will be the five calendar years preceding the calendar year of the change in control. If the disqualified individual did not work for the corporation (or a predecessor or related entity as defined below) for the entire 5-year period, only those years of employment (or service) are counted in the base period [§ 280G(b)(3)(A); Reg. § 1.280G-1, Q&A-35(a)].

The base amount equals the sum of the includible compensation for the years of the base period, divided by the number of years in the base period.

---

**EXAMPLE:** If a disqualified individual has worked for a company for 10 years, and the individual received includible compensation of $150,000, $200,000, $225,000, $225,000, and $250,000 for the five years preceding the year of the change in control, then the individual's base amount equals:

($150,000 + $200,000 + $225,000 + $225,000 + $250,000) ÷ 5

= $1,050,000 ÷ 5

= $210,000.

---

*Excess Parachute Payment.* The amount of excess parachute payments with respect to any disqualified individual is equal to the total parachute payments to him, reduced by the greater of [§ 280G(b); Reg. § 1.280G-1, Q&As-38, -39]:

1. except in the case of securities violation parachute payments, the portion of each such payment that constitutes reasonable compensation for services previously rendered; and

2. the applicable portion of the base amount allocable to such payment.

*Exceptions.* Payments to or from the following plans are specifically exempted from the excess parachute payments restrictions [§ 280G(b)(6); Reg. § 1.280G-1, Q&A-8]:

1. a qualified plan;

2. a § 403(a) annuity;

3. a SEP under § 408(k); and

4. a SIMPLE plan under § 408(p).

### XVII.B.4. Employer-Provided Insurance Benefits

[TPS ¶5930.]

Nonqualified employer-provided insurance benefits can take a variety of forms. When benefits are provided through group-term life insurance, the employee generally may exclude the cost of up to $50,000 of coverage from gross income, if the plan meets certain nondiscrimination rules, and the employer generally can deduct the cost of such insurance as an ordinary and necessary business expense.

A split-dollar life insurance arrangement is a method of financing premiums on a whole life insurance policy that most commonly is used as an executive compensation technique. It is, according to the IRS definition, an "arrangement whereby the party with the need and the party with the ability to pay premiums join in purchasing an insurance contract in which there is a substantial investment element." It, therefore, is not a type of insurance coverage but a way to finance insurance.

### XVII.B.4.a. Group-Term Life Insurance

[501 T.M. VIII.C.16.c.; TPS ¶¶1170.01.K., 5930.01.B.]

In general, employees may receive, tax-free, up to $50,000 of group-term life insurance coverage each year. Group-term life insurance is term life insurance coverage (i.e., coverage for a fixed period of time) under a policy carried by an employer that provides a general death benefit to a group of employees, with the amount of coverage provided to each employee based on a formula that prevents individual selection. The value of any coverage in excess of $50,000 over any amount paid by the employee toward the purchase of the insurance during the year, however, is taxable to the employee and must be included on the employee's Form W-2 [§ 79(a)].

The value of group-term life insurance coverage included in an employee's income is determined under an IRS Uniform Premiums Table that provides the amount included in income for each $1,000 of coverage based on the employee's age [§ 79(c); Reg. § 1.79-3(d)].

---

**EXAMPLE:** Heather, age 38, is provided with $100,000 of group-term life insurance coverage by her employer. The employer pays a premium of $5.00 a month for that coverage. Heather must include in gross income the cost of the coverage in excess of $50,000. Under the Uniform Premium Table, the cost of coverage for a 38-year-old employee is equal to $0.09 per $1,000 of coverage. Thus, the amount includible in Heather's gross income is $4.50 per month (($100,000 - $50,000) × ($0.09/$1,000)). Note that the $5.00 of monthly premiums actually paid by the employer for the coverage is irrelevant for purposes of determining the amount includible in gross income.

---

Group-term life insurance must satisfy certain nondiscrimination requirements. If a group-term life insurance plan discriminates in favor of highly-compensated employees, those employees lose the benefit of the $50,000 exclusion and must recognize income equal to the greater of the employer's actual premium paid on their behalf or the amount determined under regulations [§ 79(d); Reg. § 1.79-3].

*Exceptions to Inclusion in Gross Income.* There are three exceptions under which an employee is not required to include the cost of group-term life insurance coverage in gross income [§ 79(b)]:

1. A former employee does not include the cost of group-term life insurance provided by his former employer if his employment has terminated and he is disabled.

2. An employee does not include the cost of group-term life insurance for any period during which the employer or a tax-exempt organization is the sole beneficiary under the policy.

3. An employee does not include the cost of group-term life insurance provided under the trust of a qualified pension, profit-sharing, or stock bonus plan if the proceeds are payable to a participant in the trust or an annuity program, or to a beneficiary of such participant.

### XVII.B.4.b. Split-Dollar Life Insurance Arrangements

[386 T.M., VI.; TPS ¶5930.02.C.]

A split-dollar life insurance arrangement involves the use of a whole life insurance policy. Because split-dollar normally requires a "split" in the ownership of a life insurance policy having an "investment element," term policies are not usable in a split-dollar situation. In a split-dollar arrangement, at least some parts of the policy must be split. For example, the rights to cash values available during the insured's lifetime and the death proceeds may be split between the employer and the employee (or the employee's beneficiary). The premiums need not be split; employer pay-all split-dollar is treated as split-dollar insurance for income tax purposes.

The standard "split" of the cash value element of whole life insurance under a split-dollar arrangement generally is one of the following types:

- The employer is entitled to recover from the cash value the total premiums that it paid, regardless of the cash value in the policy at any given time.

- Under classic split-dollar, known as "equity" split-dollar, the employer has an interest in the policy equal to the lesser of the policy's cash value or the total premiums it paid. The employee gets the benefit of any increase in the cash surrender value that exceeds these premium contributions. This gives the employee an interest in the cash surrender value by limiting the employer's interest to its premium contributions (even if less than the cash surrender value).

Typically, under a split-dollar arrangement either: (i) the employer is entitled to the entire cash surrender value, regardless of the amount of premiums it pays; or (ii) the employer is entitled to the greater of the premiums it pays or the policy's cash surrender value of the policy at any given time. The balance of the death proceeds or the amount at risk "owned" by the employee, or a third-party owner, such as a spouse or an irrevocable trust, is the total of the death proceeds provided under the policy that exceeds the amount returnable to the employer. If the policy is terminated during the employee's lifetime, the employer would be entitled to receive the amounts due it from the cash surrender value and the owner of the amount at risk would be entitled to the balance of the policy if any. If the insured dies, however, the policy's beneficiary would be entitled to the death proceeds, less the employer's interest in the policy at that time, which would be repaid to the employer.

***Taxation.*** Split-dollar arrangements are taxable under one of two mutually exclusive regimes: the economic benefit or the loan regime. Under the economic benefit, the employee is taxed on the value of the current life insurance protection, the amount of policy cash value to which the employee has current access and the value of any other economic benefits provided, minus any amounts contributed by the employee. Generally, in a split-dollar arrangement between an employer and employee, the employee must include the economic benefits in gross income for the year the benefits are provided [Reg. § 1.61-22(b)(3), § 1.61-22(d)(2)(i) through § 1.61-22(d)(2)(iii)].

Under the loan regime, the premiums paid by the employer are treated as a series of loans to the employee so long as the employee is obligated to repay the employer. If the payments are not below market-rate loans, they are subject to original issue discount rules (see III.F.2.a.), and if they are below market, they are subject to market discount interest rate rules (see III.F.2.b.). The premiums are considered taxable compensation to the employee if the employee is not expected to repay the premiums but owns the policy [Reg. § 1.61-22, § 1.7872-15(a)].

Where the employer owns the policy, the employee is taxed on the value of the current life insurance protection, the amount of policy cash value to which the employee has current access and the value of any other economic benefits provided, minus any amounts contributed by the employee. Generally, in a split-dollar arrangement between an employer and employee, the employee must include the economic benefits in gross income for the year the benefits are provided [Reg. § 1.61-22].

## XVII.C. Sickness, Injury and Death Benefits

### XVII.C.1. Accident, Health and Disability Insurance

### XVII.C.1.a. Contributions by an Employer to Accident and Health Plans

[389 T.M., IV.; TPS ¶5920.01., .02.]

Gross income does not include the value of employer-provided coverage under an accident or health plan [§ 106(a)]. An accident or health plan is an arrangement for the payment of amounts to employees in the event of personal injuries or sickness to the employee, the employee's spouse, the employee's dependents, or the employee's children under age 27. The plan may be either insured or noninsured, and it is not required to be in writing [Reg. § 1.105-5].

Excludible contributions include employer contributions to [Reg. § 1.106-1]:
- the cost of accident or health insurance, including qualified long-term care insurance;
- a separate trust or fund that provides accident or health benefits directly or through insurance; and
- Archer Medical Savings Accounts (Archer MSAs), or health savings accounts (HSAs).

Employees for purposes of this exclusion include:
- current employees;
- full-time life insurance agents who are current statutory employees;
- retired employees;
- former employees for whom coverage is maintained based on the employment relationship;
- a widow or widower of an individual who died while an employee; and
- a widow or widower of a retired employee.

If a self-insured health plan discriminates in favor of highly-compensated individuals, the amount of any benefits deemed to be discriminatory is taxable to those individuals. For purposes of the nondiscrimination rule, a highly-compensated individual is [§ 105(h)(5)]:
- one of the five highest paid officers;
- a shareholder owning more than 10% of the value of the employer's stock; or

- an employee among the highest paid 25% of all employees (other than those employees who are nonparticipants and those who may be excluded for purposes of the eligibility test).

### XVII.C.1.b. Reimbursement for Medical Expenses

[389 T.M., III.B.; TPS ¶5920.01.B.2., .01.B.3.]

Amounts received through employer-provided health insurance are excludible from gross income if they are payments or reimbursements of medical care expenses of the employee, the employee's spouse, the employee's dependent, or the employee's child under age 27 that would otherwise be deductible under § 213 (see VII.D.1.) [§ 105(a), § 105(b); Reg. § 1.105-2]. However, reimbursements for amounts deducted in a prior tax year are includible in gross income (see II.D.1.b.) [§ 104(a)(3)].

### XVII.C.1.c. Disability Benefits and Other Accident and Health Benefits

[389 T.M., IV.; TPS ¶5920.01., .02., .03.]

Employees may generally exclude direct or indirect employer payments under an accident or health plan that are payments for permanent loss or use of a part or function of the body, or for permanent disfigurement if the benefit is determined without regard to any period the employee is absent from work [§ 105(a), § 105(c); Reg. § 1.105-3]. This benefit also applies to the employee's spouse or dependent.

Amounts (other than reimbursements for medical care) that an employee receives through accident or health insurance for personal injuries or sickness that are determined with regard to the period the employee is absent for work (disability insurance) generally must be included in gross income if the amounts are either (i) attributable to contributions of the employer which were not includible in the employee's gross income, or (ii) paid by the employer. However, to the extent an accident or health plan is funded by the employee, a ratable portion of the benefits generally may be excluded from an employee's income [§ 105; Reg. § 1.105-1(c)].

If an employee is covered by an accident or health insurance plan through a cafeteria plan and the amount of the insurance premiums was not included in the employee's income, the employee is not considered to have paid the premiums and must include any benefits received in income. However, if the amount of the premium was included in income, the employee is considered to have paid the premiums and the benefits received are not taxable [§ 105(a); Reg. § 1.105-1(a)].

---

**EXAMPLE:** Susan is an employee of the Springfield Co., which provides long-term disability insurance for its employees as part of a cafeteria plan. Employees have the option of paying for the insurance as a deduction from their paychecks on a pre-tax or post-tax basis. Paying for the insurance pre-tax reduces the employee's taxable income by the amount of the premium and the amount subject to FICA tax. Paying for the insurance post-tax results in the premium amount being included in income and being subject to FICA. Susan elects to pay for the insurance post-tax and later becomes totally disabled and receives monthly disability benefits equal to 60% of her salary. Because Susan paid the premiums herself, the benefits are nontaxable. If Susan had paid the premiums on a pre-tax basis, her income would have been less in the years she was working, but the disability benefits would be taxable because the amount of the premiums was not included in her income. If Springfield Co. provided the disability insurance as a benefit without charge to its employees, the value of the insurance would be nontaxable to the employee, but any disability benefits paid would be taxable.

---

If an employee is required by terms of the disability insurance policy to repay all or part of the employer-provided benefits if the employee receives a social security disability award, the repayment would be deductible if the disability benefit was taxable but would be nondeductible if the disability benefit was not taxable. Note that social security disability benefits are taxed on the same basis as other social security benefits (see I.K.) [§ 86(d)(1)].

If an individual purchases a disability insurance policy with his or her own funds, amounts received under the policy are excludible from gross income, except to the extent the individual deducted the premiums [§ 104(a)(3)].

### XVII.C.1.d. Archer Medical Savings Accounts (Archer MSAs)

[389 T.M., XII.; TPS ¶5920.08.A.]

Distributions from an Archer MSA are excluded from the employee's income where the amounts are used exclusively for the qualified medical expenses of the employee, the employee's spouse, or the employee's dependents, including transportation for medical care, qualified long-term care service, and medical insurance (including Medicare Part B). For a discussion of deductible medical expenses, see VII.D.1. Distributions not used to pay qualified medical expenses are included in income and, unless the account holder is 65 or older or the distributions are made on account of death or disability, subject to an additional 20% tax [§ 220(f)].

Additionally, certain contributions to an Archer MSA by eligible individuals are deductible, and contributions by an eligible individual's employer may be excluded from his or her income. Earnings on amounts in an account are exempt from federal income tax (other than unrelated business income tax) [§ 220(a), § 220(b)(5), § 220(e)(1), § 220(f)(1)].

After 2007, no new Archer MSAs may be established; however, new contributions may still be made by or on behalf of account holders who previously had Archer MSA contributions and employees covered by a high deductible health plan maintained by an Archer MSA-participating employer [§ 220].

An Archer MSA is a trust or custodial account created exclusively for paying the qualified medical expenses of the account holder. They are generally available to employees covered under a high deductible health plan of a small employer (on average, no more than 50 employees either of the two preceding years), and similarly situated individuals that are self-employed, provided that those individuals are not covered under any other health plan, other than one providing certain permitted coverage. Permitted other coverage includes [§ 220(c)]:

- Medicare supplemental insurance;

- workers' compensation, tort liability, or auto insurance;

- insurance for a specific illness or specified disease; and

- insurance that provides fixed payments for hospitalization.

A high deductible health plan for these purposes is a health plan with an annual deductible between $2,200 and $3,250 for individual coverage in 2014 ($2,200 and $3,300 in 2015), and between $4,350 and $6,550 for family coverage in 2014 ($4,450 and $6,650 in 2015). Maximum out-of-pocket expenses with respect to allowed costs, including the deductible, must not exceed $4,350 for individual coverage in 2014 ($4,450 in 2015), and $8,000 for family coverage in 2014 ($8,150 in 2015) [Rev. Proc. 2013-35, 2013-47 I.R.B. 537, Rev. Proc. 2014-61, 2014-47 I.R.B. 860, § 3.26].

Out-of-pocket expenses do not include premiums. Plans prevented by state law from having a deductible for preventive care do not fail to qualify as a high deductible health plan merely for that fact [§ 220(c)(2)].

The annual contribution is limited to 65% of the annual deductible under the high deductible health plan for individual coverage, and 75% of the annual deductible for family coverage. The employee and the employer may not each make contributions to the Archer MSA in the same year. An employee may not contribute more than he or she earned for the year from the employer providing the high deductible health plan. Contributions for a year can be made through the due date for the individual's tax return for the year, not including extensions. An excise tax of 6% for each tax year is imposed on an account holder for excess individual and employer contributions, unless timely remitted to the account holder [§ 4973].

Assets may generally be rolled over from one Archer MSA to another, or to a health savings account (HSA), without incurring tax if the rollover is completed within 60 days of the distribution. However, the rollover generally will not be excluded from income if the same provision excluding rollover distributions applied to any prior payment or distribution in the previous 12 months [§ 220(f)(5)].

Medicare Advantage MSAs are a type of Archer MSA available to Medicare enrollees. Contributions from Medicare trust funds may be transferred to the MSA tax-free, income earned on the account is tax-exempt, and the account holder may use the funds to pay for qualifying medical expenses with no tax imposed on withdrawals made for such purposes. Amounts withdrawn and used for other purposes are treated as taxable income to the account holder, and a 50% penalty tax may apply [§ 138(c)(2)].

Contributions to an employee's Archer MSA are reported on Form 8853, *Archer MSAs and Long-Term Care Insurance Contracts*, and Form 5498-SA, *Archer MSA, or Medicare Advantage MSA Information*, with distributions reported on Form 8853 only.

### XVII.C.1.e. Health Savings Accounts (HSAs) and Health Reimbursement Accounts (HRAs)

### XVII.C.1.e.(1) HSAs

[389 T.M., XI.; TPS ¶5920.08.C.]

Distributions from an HSA used to pay qualified medical expenses are excluded from the account holder's income. An HSA is a trust or custodial account created exclusively for paying the qualified medical expenses of the account holder. Contributions to an HSA by eligible individuals are generally deductible, and contributions by an eligible individual's employer may be excluded from his or her income. Earnings on amounts in an HSA account are exempt from federal income tax (other than unrelated business income tax) [§ 223]. An employee may contribute pre-tax dollars to an HSA as part of a cafeteria plan (see XVII.C.3.).

An individual eligible for an HSA for any month [§ 223(b)(6), § 223(b)(7), § 223(c)(1)]:

- must be covered under a high deductible health plan on the first day of that month;
- must not be covered under any other plan (other than certain permitted insurance) that is not a high deductible health plan;
- must not be enrolled in Medicare; and
- cannot be claimed as a dependent on another person's tax return.

A high deductible health plan for purposes of an HSA [Rev. Proc. 2013-25, 2013-21 I.R.B. 1110, Rev. Proc. 2014-30, 2014-20 I.R.B. 1009]:

- has an annual deductible of at least $1,250 for individual coverage and $2,500 for family coverage in 2014 ($1,300 and $2,600 in 2015), with no maximum deductible; and

- provides that maximum out-of-pocket expense for allowed costs, including the deductible, must not exceed $6,350 for individual coverage and $12,700 for family coverage in 2014 ($6,450 and $12,900 in 2015).

The amount that may be contributed annually to an HSA is subject to a dollar limitation. The limit is $3,300 for individual coverage and $6,550 for family coverage in 2014 ($3,350 and $6,650 in 2015). These limits are increased by $1,000 in the case of individuals age 55 and older at the end of the tax year. The limits are decreased by the amount of any contributions to an Archer MSA in the same tax year.

Distributions from an HSA to pay the qualified medical expenses of the individual and his or her spouse or dependents are excludible from income. Distributions that are not for qualified medical expenses are includible in income and subject to an additional 20% tax on distributions, unless the distribution was made on account of death, disability, or after the individual became eligible for Medicare. If, upon death, the HSA designates a surviving spouse as beneficiary, then the HSA becomes the HSA of the surviving spouse and is excluded from income. If the HSA passes to a named beneficiary other than the surviving spouse, the HSA ceases to be an HSA and the beneficiary is required to include the HSA in gross income for the tax year that includes the date of death. The amount includible in income is reduced by the amount in the HSA that is used, within one year of the death, to pay qualified medical expenses incurred before death [§ 223(f)].

***Rollovers.*** Rollover contributions may be made to an HSA from an Archer MSA or other HSA [§ 223(d)(1)(A)]. If the individual does not remain an eligible individual for a full year after the contribution, the rollover contribution amount is includible in gross income and is subject to a 10% additional tax unless the individual dies or becomes disabled [§ 106(e)(3), § 106(e)(4)(A)].

In addition, a one-time rollover may be made from an IRA to an HSA. The rollover must be made by a direct trustee-to-trustee transfer. Rollovers from SEPs or SIMPLE retirement accounts are not allowed. The amount that can be rolled over from an IRA to an HSA is generally the maximum deductible HSA contribution amount. If the individual does not remain an eligible individual for a full year after the contribution, the rollover contribution amount is includible in the individual's gross income and is subject to a 10% additional tax unless the individual dies or becomes disabled [§ 408(d)(9)].

Contributions to and distributions from an employee's HSA are reported on Form 8889, *Health Savings Accounts (HSAs)*.

### XVII.C.1.e.(2) HRAs

[389 T.M., III.B.2.d.; TPS ¶5920.09.A.]

HRAs are popular because they allow employees to carry forward unused amounts in their accounts for use in future years. This feature allows HRAs to be used as a vehicle for providing post-retirement medical care on a "defined contribution" basis (i.e., the employer's liability is limited to the amounts in an employee's HRA account). However, an HRA may or may not provide for an increase in the amount available for reimbursement of medical care expenses after the employee retires or otherwise terminates employment. The "carryforward" feature, which can be used whether or not the HRA is designed to provide retiree healthcare benefits, contrasts with the "use it or lose it" rule applicable to health flexible spending accounts (FSAs) (see XVII.C.4.) under which amounts in an employee's account must be forfeited, unless special limited exceptions exist, if not used to pay for medical expenses of the employee, the employee's spouse, and dependents by the end of the tax year.

An HRA is an arrangement [Notice 2002-45, 2002-28 I.R.B. 93, § I]:

- that is paid for solely by the employer and is not provided pursuant to an employee's salary reduction election or otherwise under a cafeteria plan;

- that reimburses the employee for qualified medical expenses (i.e., those that qualify under § 213(d)) incurred by the employee and the employee's spouse and dependents;

- that provides reimbursements up to a maximum dollar amount for a coverage period (note: there is no statutory limit on the amount of money an employer can contribute to an HRA; therefore, the limit is the plan-provided limit); and

- under which any unused portion of the maximum dollar amount at the end of a coverage period is carried forward to increase the maximum reimbursement amount in later coverage periods.

To the extent that an HRA is an employer-provided accident or health plan, coverage and reimbursements of medical expenses of the employee, the employee's spouse, dependents and adult children who are under the age of 27 at the end of the tax year, generally are excludible from the employee's gross income. Self-employed persons are not eligible for an HRA [§ 105, § 106].

To qualify for the exclusion from the employee's gross income, an HRA can only provide benefits that reimburse expenses for medical care as defined in § 213(d). Only drugs and medicines obtained by prescription (even if a prescription is not required for the drug or medicine) or insulin may be reimbursed with excludible income through an HRA [§ 106(f); Notice 2010-59, 2010-39 I.R.B. 396].

Employer HRA contributions cannot come from employee salary reduction contributions or otherwise be provided under a § 125 cafeteria plan. An accident or health plan funded with salary reduction contributions is a cafeteria plan and is not an HRA.

Starting in 2014, non-retiree stand-alone HRAs (i.e., HRAs that are not integrated with another health plan) and HRAs that are used to reimburse individual market coverage are not permitted under the Affordable Care Act (ACA). Stand-alone HRAs for retirees are permitted, however. The market reforms under the ACA generally do not apply to a retiree-only HRA and therefore would not impact an employer's choice to offer such a vehicle [Notice 2013-54, 2013-40 I.R.B. 287].

There are no reporting requirements for HRAs on an individual's income tax return. In addition, there are no federal income taxes or employment taxes on amounts the employer contributes to the HRA if the amounts are used for qualified medical expenses. A participant cannot deduct qualified medical expenses as an itemized deduction on Schedule A for any distributions from their HRA. However, if an unused contribution is paid to a participant in cash at the end of the year, or upon termination of employment, any distribution from the HRA would no longer be qualified and would be included in income and subject to employment taxes.

### XVII.C.2. Death Benefits

[529 T.M., I.C.3.a., I.C.3.b.; TPS ¶5930.03.]

An amount paid as a survivor annuity on account of the death of a public safety officer (i.e., law enforcement officers, firefighters, rescue squads, and ambulance crews) killed in the line of duty is excluded from the beneficiary's income to the extent the annuity is attributable to the officer's service as a public safety officer. The survivor annuity must be provided under a governmental plan to the officer's surviving spouse (or former spouse) or to a child of the officer. The exclusion does not apply if (i) the death was caused by the officer's intentional misconduct or the officer's intent to bring about his or her own death, (ii) the officer was voluntarily intoxicated at the time of death, (iii) the officer was performing his or her duties in a grossly negligent manner at the time of death, or (iv) the action of the individual to whom payment is to be made substantially contributed to the officer's death [§ 101(h)].

### XVII.C.3. Exclusion of Amounts Paid under Cafeteria Plans

[397 T.M.; TPS ¶5940.]

A cafeteria plan is an employee benefit plan that allows a participating employee to choose between receiving cash, which is included in wages and is taxable, or qualified benefits, which are excluded from wages and are not taxable. An employer's contributions toward, or direct payment of, most qualified benefits under a cafeteria plan are not subject to income tax withholding [§ 3401(a)(18); Notice 97-9, 1997-1 C.B. 365] and, with the exception of adoption assistance, not subject to FICA and FUTA [§ 3121(a)(18), § 3306(b)(13)]. An employee choosing to receive a qualified benefit under the plan does not include the value of the benefit in income solely because the employee could have received cash instead [§ 125(a); Prop. Reg. § 1.125-1(b)]. A common feature of a cafeteria plan is a flexible spending account where the employee forgoes cash, and the foregone amount is credited to a bookkeeping account maintained by the employer that the employer draws upon to reimburse the employee for certain health expenses. An employee contribution to a flexible spending account cannot exceed $2,550 in 2015 [§ 125(i); Prop. Reg. § 1.125-5; Rev. Proc. 2014-61, 2014-47 I.R.B. 860, § 3.16].

While former employees may be included in a cafeteria plan, the plan may not be established predominantly for the benefit of former employees. Spouses and beneficiaries of participants may receive benefits from a cafeteria plan (e.g., family medical coverage or dependent care assistance), but may not participate in the plan unless they are also employees [Prop. Reg. § 1.125-1(g)(3), § 1.125-1(g)(4)(i)]. Self-employed individuals and 2% shareholders (as defined in § 1372(b)) of S corporations are not considered employees for this purpose [Prop. Reg. § 1.125-1(g)(2)].

Subject to certain exceptions, a qualified benefit is any benefit that is excludible from an employee's gross income under a specific I.R.C. provision, and that does not defer compensation. The term also includes certain group term life insurance coverage. Qualified benefits may include [§ 125(f); Prop. Reg. § 1.125-1(a)(3)]:

- accident and health benefits (other than Archer MSAs or long-term care insurance) (see XVII.C.1.a.);
- disability coverage (see XVII.C.1.c.);
- adoption assistance (see XVII.E.1.);
- dependent care assistance (see XVII.E.2.);
- health savings accounts (HSAs) (see XVII.C.1.e.);
- flexible spending accounts (see XVII.C.4.); and

- a qualified cash or deferred arrangement that is part of a profit sharing plan or stock bonus plan (see XVII.A.3.).

The following benefits, while possibly excludible from gross income, are not qualified benefits for purposes of a cafeteria plan [Prop. Reg. § 1.125-1(q)]:

- scholarships (see II.H.);
- employer-provided meals and lodging (see XVII.E.4.);
- educational assistance programs (see XVII.E.3.);
- certain fringe benefits (see XVII.D.);
- long-term care insurance;
- long-term care services; and
- contributions to Archer MSAs (see XVII.C.1.d.).

A cafeteria plan may not discriminate in favor of highly-compensated employees. For plans that discriminate as to eligibility to participate, contributions, or benefits, highly-compensated employees must include in income the value of taxable benefits they could have elected to receive [§ 125(b); Prop. Reg. § 1.125-7(m)]. A highly-compensated employee is an employee who is one of the following [§ 125(e)(1); Prop. Reg. § 1.125-7(a)(3), § 1.125-7(a)(9)]:

- an officer;
- a shareholder owning more than 5% of the voting power or value of all classes of the employer's stock;
- received more than $120,000 (2015 amount — for 2014, the amount is $115,000) in pay for the preceding year (however, an employer may elect to disregard this test if the employee was not also in the top 20% of the highest paid employees for the preceding year); or
- a spouse or dependent of a person described above.

Additionally, qualified benefits provided to key employees under a cafeteria plan cannot exceed 25% of the aggregate qualified benefits provided for all employees under the plan. To the extent a cafeteria plan favors key employees, they must include in income the value of taxable benefits they could have elected to receive. A key employee is an employee that is one of the following [§ 416(i)(1); Prop. Reg. § 1.125-7(a)(10)]:

- an officer with annual pay exceeding $170,000 (2014 and 2015 number);
- an employee that is a 5% owner of the employer's business; or
- an employee that is a 1% owner of the employer's business, and whose annual pay exceeds $150,000.

A plan maintained under a collective bargaining agreement is treated as nondiscriminatory and does not favor highly-compensated or key employees [§ 125(g)(1)].

Certain simple cafeteria plans are treated as meeting the nondiscrimination requirements. A simple cafeteria plan is a plan established and maintained by an eligible employer that meets contribution and participation requirements. An eligible employer is an employer that employed an average of 100 or fewer employees during either of the two preceding years. An employer that did not exist throughout the prior year is eligible if it reasonably expects to employ an average of 100 or fewer employees in the current year. An employer that establishes a simple cafeteria plan during a year it is an eligible employer continues to be an eligible employer in subsequent years where it does not employ an average of 200 or more employees [§ 125(j)(5)].

All employees who had at least 1,000 hours of service in the preceding year must be eligible to participate in the simple cafeteria plan, and each employee eligible to participate must be able to elect any benefit available under the plan. The following employees may be excluded from the plan [§ 125(j)(4)]:

- employees under age 21 at the close of the plan year;
- employees with less than one year of service with the employer as of any day during the plan year;
- employees covered under a collective bargaining agreement where there is evidence that the benefits covered under the plan were the subject of good faith bargaining; or
- nonresident alien employees with no U.S.-source income.

A simple cafeteria plan must require an employer to provide minimum contributions for each employee eligible to participate in the plan in an amount equal to either [§ 125(j)(3)]:

- a uniform percentage (not less than 2%) of the employee's compensation for the plan year (without regard to any employee salary reduction contribution); or
- the lesser of either:
  — 6% of the employee's compensation for the plan year; or
  — twice the amount of the salary reduction contributions of each qualified employee (unless the rate of contribution to any salary reduction contribution of a highly-compensated or key employee is greater than the rate of contribution to any other employee).

### XVII.C.4. Flexible Spending Accounts (FSAs)

[397 T.M., IV.K.2.; TPS ¶5940.03.B.4.]

A flexible spending account (FSA) is a salary reduction program that provides employees with coverage that reimburses specified, incurred expenses (subject to reimbursement maximums and any other reasonable conditions). An expense for qualified benefits must not be reimbursed from the FSA unless it is incurred during a period of coverage [Prop. Reg. § 1.125-5(a)(1)]. An employer may establish health FSAs and dependent care FSAs. Employees covered by an FSA can reduce their pay and have the amounts deposited in their FSA. Generally, no contribution or benefit from a FSA may be carried over to any subsequent plan year or period of coverage. Unused benefits or contributions remaining at the end of the plan year (or at the end of a grace period, if applicable) are forfeited [Prop. Reg. § 1.125-5(c)(1)].

*Health FSAs.* A health FSA may reimburse medical expenses (as defined in § 213(d) (see VII.D.1.)) and is permitted to limit payment or reimbursement to only certain medical expenses. However, qualified medical expenses do not include amounts paid for medicine or drugs, except for prescribed drugs (whether or not available over the counter) or insulin [§ 106(f)]. A health FSA may not reimburse employees for premium payments for other health coverage, including premiums for COBRA coverage, accidental death and dismemberment insurance, long-term disability or short-term disability insurance or for health coverage under a plan maintained by the employer of the employee or the employer of the employee's spouse or dependent. Also, a health FSA may not reimburse expenses for long-term care insurance premiums or for long-term care services for the employee or employee's spouse or dependent [Prop. Reg. § 1.125-5(k)(4)].

Salary reduction contributions to a health FSA are limited to $2,500 in 2014 ($2,550 in 2015) [§ 125(i); Rev. Proc. 2013-35, 2013-47 I.R.B. 537, Rev. Proc. 2014-61,

2014-47 I.R.B. 860, § 3.16], and unused benefits remaining at the end of the play year (or grace period, if applicable) are forfeited. The grace period must apply to all participants and may not extend beyond 2 ½ months after the end of the plan year (March 15 for calendar year plans).

Reimbursing advance payments for orthodontia services does not violate the prohibition against deferring compensation in a cafeteria plan [Prop. Reg. § 1.125-5(k)(3)(i)].

---

**EXAMPLE:** Employer D sponsors a calendar year cafeteria plan that offers a health FSA. Employee K elects to a salary reduction of $2,500 for a health FSA for the 2014 plan year. K's dependent requires orthodontic treatment, but K's accident and health insurance does not cover orthodontia. Following normal practice, the orthodontist charges $3,000, all due in 2014, for treatment to begin in 2014 and end in 2015. K pays the $3,000 in 2014. In 2014, D's cafeteria plan may reimburse $2,500 to K without violating the prohibition against deferring compensation in a cafeteria plan [Prop. Reg. § 1.125-5(k)(3)(ii)].

---

*Dependent Care FSAs.* A dependent care FSA may reimburse employees for dependent care costs subject to the limitations that apply to dependent care assistance programs (see XVII.E.1.). Accordingly, the maximum reimbursement is limited to $5,000 per employee ($2,500 for married filing separately).

### XVII.C.5. Minimum Health Care

### XVII.C.5.a. Individual Responsibilities

[389 T.M., XVII.A.; TPS ¶5920.16.B.; ¶HCRA 110.2., ¶HCRA 120., ¶HCRA 130.]

For each month beginning in 2014 and thereafter, individuals are personally responsible for obtaining for themselves and their dependents health care coverage that meets the requirements for minimum essential coverage. A tax penalty applies unless the individual purchases health insurance or is exempt from the penalty [§ 5000A(a); Reg. § 1.5000A-1 through § 1.5000A-5].

Plans that may provide minimum essential coverage include [§ 5000A(f)(1); Reg. § 1.5000A-2]:

- an eligible employer-sponsored plan;
- grandfathered health plans (generally, group health plans or health insurance coverage in existence on March 23, 2010);
- certain government coverage;
- health plans offered in the individual market in the state in which the individual resides; and
- other coverage recognized by the Secretary of HHS, in coordination with the Treasury Secretary, such as a health benefits risk pool.

An individual is treated as having minimum essential coverage for a calendar month if, for at least one day during the month, the individual is enrolled in and entitled to receive benefits under a program or plan that is minimum essential coverage [Reg. § 1.5000A-1(b)(1)].

*Penalty.* For each month that an individual does not have minimum essential coverage for himself or herself or dependents, the individual must pay a penalty equal to the lesser of (i) the sum of the "monthly penalty amounts" for months in the tax year during which one or more failures occurred, or (ii) an amount equal to the national average premium for qualified health plans that have a bronze level of coverage, cover the family size involved, and are offered through health exchanges for the relevant plan years (i.e., the plan years beginning in the calendar year with or within which the tax year ends).

The monthly penalty amount for any month is equal to 1/12th of the greater of: (i) a calculated flat dollar amount; or (ii) a specified percentage of the excess of household income (defined with respect to "modified adjusted gross income") over the gross income filing threshold under § 6012(a)(1). The specified percentage of household income is 1% for the 2014 tax year, 2% for 2015, and 2.5% for 2016 and later [§ 5000A(c)(2)(B)].

In determining the flat dollar amount, the penalty amount for each person who did not have minimum essential coverage is: (i) $95 for 2014; (ii) $325 for 2015; (iii) $695 for 2016; and (iv) $695, as indexed for inflation in $50 increments, after 2016 [§ 5000A(c)].

The penalty amount for individuals younger than age 18 is reduced by 50%. The flat dollar amount for a family is limited to 300% of the penalty amount for the calendar year with or within which the tax year ends, as determined without regard to the reduction for individuals under age 18 [§ 5000A(c)(2), [§ 5000A(c)(3); Reg. § 1.5000A-4(b)(2)].

---

**EXAMPLE:** *Unmarried taxpayer, no coverage for the year.* Taxpayer G, a calendar year taxpayer, is unmarried and has no dependents. G does not have minimum essential coverage for any month in 2016. G's household income is $120,000. G's applicable filing threshold is $12,000. The annual national average bronze plan premium for G is $5,000.

Flat Dollar Amount: $695 (the lesser of $695 and $2,085 ($695 × 3)).

Percentage of Household Income Amount: $2,700 (($120,000 − $12,000) × 0.025).

Monthly Penalty Amount: $225 (the greater of $58 ($695/12) or $225 ($2,700/12)).

National Average Premium: The penalty amount for the year is $2,700 ($225 × 12); and the sum of the monthly national average bronze plan premiums is $5,000.

Therefore, the payment imposed on G for 2016 is $2,700 (the lesser of $2,700 or $5,000).

**EXAMPLE:** *Married taxpayers, no coverage for the year.* In 2016, Taxpayers H and J, calendar year taxpayers, are married and file a joint return. H and J have three children: K, age 21, L, age 15, and M, age 10. No member of the family has minimum essential coverage for any month in 2016. H and J's household income is $250,000. H and J's applicable filing threshold is $24,000. The annual national average bronze plan premium for a family of 5 (2 adults, 3 children) is $15,000.

Flat Dollar Amount: The applicable dollar amount is $2,780 (($695 × 3 adults) + (($695/2) × 2 children)). The flat dollar amount is $2,085 (the lesser of $2,780 and $2,085 ($695 × 3)).

Percentage of Household Income: $5,650 (($250,000 − $24,000) × 0.025).

Monthly Penalty Amount: $470.83 (the greater of $173.75 ($2,085/12) or $470.83 ($5,650/12)).

National Average Premium: The sum of the monthly penalty amounts is $5,650 ($470.83 × 12); and the annual national average bronze plan premium is $15,000.

Therefore, the payment imposed on H and J for 2016 is $5,650 (the lesser of $5,650 or $15,000).

---

*Exemptions.* An individual is not required to maintain minimum essential coverage for any month that he or she [§ 5000A(d)(2) through § 5000A(d)(4); Reg. § 1.5000A-3]:

- is not a U.S. citizen or national or an alien lawfully present in the United States;

- has obtained an exemption certifying that he or she is a member of a recognized religious sect or division, as described in § 1402(g), and an adherent of its established tenets or teachings;

- is a member of a tax-exempt health care sharing ministry; or

- is in jail.

In addition, the IRS does not impose the penalty in several other circumstances. Reasons for exemption include the following: (i) the individual has a short gap in coverage; (ii) the individual would suffer a hardship if he or she were to obtain coverage through a qualified health plan; (iii) the individual cannot afford coverage; (iv) the individual has household income that is below the filing threshold; or (v) the individual is a member of an Indian tribe [Reg. § 1.5000A-3].

*Penalty Assessment.* The penalty is assessed in the same manner as an assessable penalty and must be paid upon notice and demand by the IRS. However, an individual who fails to pay the penalty does not face criminal penalties and is not subject to a lien or levy for the failure. Refunds and credits can be offset to collect the penalty [§ 5000A(g)(1), § 5000A(g)(2); Reg. § 1.5000A-5(b)].

*Premium Tax Credits and Cost-Sharing Reductions.* Some individuals who must pay health care premiums may be eligible for a premium assistance credit [§ 36B]. Cost-sharing subsidies also may be available. Generally, the taxpayer who enrolls in a plan offered through the health exchange reports his income to the health exchange. The taxpayer applying for the credit must provide the health exchange with information related to income for the tax year ending two years before the enrollment period. The IRS is permitted to disclose income information from individuals' tax returns to the Department of Health and Human Services and to state health exchanges that request the information to verify whether the individuals are eligible for the credit [§ 6103(l)(21); Reg. § 301.6103(l)(21)-1]. Based on the information provided, the taxpayer receives a premium assistance credit that the Treasury pays to the taxpayer's insurance plan. The taxpayer pays the remainder of the total premium charged to the plan. If an individual experiences a change in income during the benefit year that affects his or her eligibility for premium assistance, the individual must report this to the exchange, which will conduct an eligibility redetermination. Any resulting change in the amount of advance payments of the premium tax credit will require the exchange to recalculate the amount of advance payments to adjust for any advance payments already made. If the change impacts cost-sharing subsidies, the exchange must determine the individual eligible for the category of cost-sharing subsidies that corresponds to his or her expected annual household income for the benefit year [§ 36B].

For a detailed discussion of the premium tax credit, see IX.G.7.

### *XVII.C.5.b. Employer Responsibilities*

[389 T.M., XVIII.; TPS ¶5920.16.C.; ¶HCRA 140.]

No law requires employers to provide health plan coverage to employees. However, numerous rules and penalties apply to employers and group health plans that do not provide coverage or provide limited or unaffordable coverage.

Employer shared responsibility provisions are scheduled to take effect in 2015 (delayed from 2014), with an additional delay to 2016 for employers averaging fewer than 100 employees. Employers with fewer than 50 full-time or full-time equivalent employees are not subject to employer shared responsibility provisions. Under these provisions, a penalty is imposed on employers that do not sponsor health coverage or sponsor coverage that is not affordable for some employees or does not provide sufficient value, if at least one full-time employee is eligible to receive a premium tax credit or cost-sharing reduction from the government [§ 4980H].

*Amount of Excise Tax.* The excise tax payment is determined monthly, but for a year generally is [§ 4980H(a), § 4980H(b), and § 4980H(c)(1); Reg. § 54.4980H-1(a)(41), § 54.4980H-1(a)(42)]:

- $2,000 multiplied by the number of full-time employees minus 30 under the no-coverage prong of the law, or
- $3,000 multiplied by the number of full-time employees who are allowed a premium tax credit or cost-sharing reduction due to the plan's unaffordability or failure to provide minimum value or, if less, the no-coverage amount.

These dollar amounts are subject to adjustment for inflation. Any amount paid as an excise tax is not deductible [§ 275(a)(6), § 4980H(c)(5), § 4980H(c)(7)].

*Small Business Health Care Tax Credit.* Small business health care tax credits are available to employers of 25 or fewer full-time employees who pay average annual wages of no more than $50,000 per full-time employee, as adjusted for inflation, and who have a contribution arrangement through which they pay at least half of the insurance premiums for employees at the employee-only coverage rate [§ 45R] (see IX.A.34.).

*Reporting Obligation.* Health insurance providers, including issuers of qualified health plans and sponsors of self-insured group health plans, must report coverage information regarding covered individuals to the IRS. Every person (including self-insured plans) that provides minimum essential coverage to an individual must make a return, at a time to be prescribed by the IRS, and furnish information statements to individuals by January 31 of the year following the calendar year for which the return was required to be made. The IRS delayed the effective date for the reporting requirements by one year from 2014 to 2015. The IRS will not impose penalties for failure to report for coverage in 2014, but employers may report voluntarily for 2014 [§ 6055; Notice 2013-45, 2013-31 I.R.B. 116].

The return and the information statement must include the name, address, and taxpayer identification number of each individual covered under the policy, the dates the individual was covered, and certain details about the health insurance coverage. A return relating to employer-provided coverage also must include identifying information about the employer, details about the premium and other information about the coverage [§ 6055(b)]. The penalties for failure to comply with information reporting requirements apply [§ 6724(d)(1)(B)(xxiv), § 6724(d)(2)(GG)].

Employers that may be subject to the excise tax also must report on the health insurance they offer beginning in 2015 [§ 6056].

## XVII.D. Fringe Benefits Excludible from Income

[394 T.M.; TPS ¶¶5960., 5980.]

Employees may exclude from gross income certain fringe benefits that fall into one of the following eight general categories [§ 132(a)]:

- no-additional-cost services (see XVII.D.1.);
- qualified employee discounts [see XVII.D.2.);
- working condition fringes (see XVII.D.3.);
- de minimis fringes (see XVII.D.4.);
- qualified transportation fringes (see XVII.D.5.);
- qualified moving expense reimbursements (see XVII.D.6.);
- qualified retirement planning services (see XVII.D.7.); and
- qualified military base realignment and closure fringes (see II.M.5.).

The value of a fringe benefit excluded from gross income is not considered wages for purposes of income tax withholding, FICA, or FUTA [§ 3401(a)(19), § 3121(a)(20), § 3306(b)(16)].

### XVII.D.1. No-Additional-Cost Services

[394 T.M., II.B.2.b.; TPS ¶5960.02.A.]

A no-additional-cost service fringe is a service an employer provides to an employee that does not cause the employer to incur any substantial additional costs, and its value is generally excludible from the employee's income. The service must be offered to customers in the ordinary course of the line of business in which the employee performs substantial services. Often these services are excess capacity services; for example, airline, bus, or train tickets, and hotel rooms provided to employees in those lines of business for free or at reduced rates.

An employer incurs substantial additional costs if the employer or its employees spend a substantial amount of time providing the service to employees, even if the time spent would otherwise be idle or if the services are provided outside normal business hours. For this purpose, any lost revenue must be counted as a cost, and costs are not reduced by any amount an employee pays for the service. There is generally no substantial additional cost for services provided that are merely incidental to the primary service being provided to the employee, for example, an in-flight meal provided to an airline employee flying on a space-available basis, or a maid service provided to a hotel employee renting a hotel room on a space-available basis [§ 132(b); Reg. § 1.132-2(a)].

For purposes of the no-additional-cost services exclusion, the following individuals are generally treated as employees [§ 132(h); Reg. § 1.132-1(b)]:

- current employees;
- former employees who retired or left on disability;
- widows or widowers of individuals who died while an employee;
- widows or widowers of a former employee who retired or left on disability;
- partners who perform services for a partnership; and
- spouses and dependent (or orphaned) children of employees.

Employers may make reciprocal agreements whereby one employer may provide a no-additional-cost service to the employee of an unrelated employer, and it may still qualify as a no-additional-cost service excludible from the employee's gross income. The following three requirements must be met [Reg. § 1.132-2(b)]:

895

- The service provided by the unrelated employer must be the same type of service generally provided to customers in both the line of business in which the employee works and in the line of business in which the service is provided.

- The employers have a written reciprocal agreement under which a group of employees from each employer (all of whom perform substantial services in the same line of business) may receive no-additional-cost services from the other employer.

- Neither employer incurs any substantial additional cost in providing the service to the unrelated employees or because of the written agreement.

---

**EXAMPLE:** National Airline and Country Airline have a written reciprocal agreement whereby employees of one airline may fly on the other airline on a space-available basis at a reduced rate. Amelia is an employee of National Airline and flies on a Country Airline flight where space was available. The value of the flight is excluded from Amelia's income.

---

The exclusion for no-additional-cost services is available to highly-compensated employees (as defined in § 414(q)) only if the service is provided on a nondiscriminatory basis, and thus is available on substantially the same terms (i) to all employees, or (ii) to each member of a group of employees that is defined under a reasonable classification the employer set up that does not favor of highly-compensated employees [§ 132(j)(1); Reg. § 1.132-2(a)(4), § 1.132-8].

### XVII.D.2. Qualified Employee Discounts

[394 T.M., II.B.2.c.; TPS ¶5960.02.B.]

Qualified employee discounts are excluded from an employee's gross income. A qualified employee discount is a price reduction an employer gives an employee on property or services offered to customers in the ordinary course of the line of business in which the employee performs substantial services. The employee may generally exclude the value of the discount from his wage, up to the following limits [§ 132(c)(1); Reg. § 1.132-3(a)]:

- for services, 20% of the price charged to nonemployee customers; and

- for merchandise or other property, the gross profit percentage (as defined in Reg. § 1.132-3(c)) multiplied by the price charged to nonemployee customers.

For purposes of the qualified employee discount exclusion, the following individuals are generally treated as employees [§ 132(h); Reg. § 1.132-1(b)]:

- current employees;

- former employees who retired or left on disability;

- widows or widowers of individuals who died while an employee;

- widows or widowers of a former employee who retired or left on disability;

- partners who perform services for a partnership; and

- spouses and dependent (or orphaned) children of employees.

---

**EXAMPLE:** Carl works at a clothing retail store. He purchases for $60 an item of clothing from his employer that is sold to customers for $100. The employer's gross profit percentage is 40%. Carl may exclude all $40 (40% gross profit percentage, multiplied by $100 price for nonemployees) of the $40 discount ($100 price for nonemployee customers - $60 discounted price) from his income.

---

The exclusion does not apply to discounts on real property or on personal property of a kind commonly held for investment (e.g., stock and bonds) [§ 132(c)(4); Reg. § 1.132-3(a)(2)].

The exclusion for qualified employee discounts is available to highly-compensated employees (as defined in § 414(q)) only if the service is provided on a nondiscriminatory basis, and thus is available on substantially the same terms (i) to all employees, or (ii) to each member of a group of employees that is defined under a reasonable classification the employer set up that does not favor of highly-compensated employees [§ 132(j)(1); Reg. § 1.132-3(a)(6), § 1.132-8].

### XVII.D.3. Working Condition Fringes

[394 T.M., II.B.2.a.; TPS ¶5960.02.C.]

The value of a working condition fringe is excluded from an employee's income. A working condition fringe is property or services provided to an employee to the extent that the employee could deduct the cost of the property or services as a business expense (see IV.A.3.) or depreciation expense (see V.A.) if he or she had paid for it personally [§ 132(d)]. These benefits are not subject to nondiscrimination rules, and they may not be provided to employees' spouses or children. Certain benefits do not qualify as working condition fringes and are not eligible for the exclusion, including [Reg. § 1.132-5(a)]:

- a service or property provided in connection with a flexible spending account in which the employer agrees to provide the employee with a certain level of unspecified non-cash benefits with a pre-determined cash value over a period of time;

- an employer-provided physical examination program, even if mandatory;

- a cash payment to the employee, unless the employee is required to (i) use the payment for expenses in connection with a specific prearranged activity or undertaking for which a trade or business deduction or a depreciation deduction is allowable, (ii) verify the payment is actually so used, and (iii) return any unused funds;

- any item to the extent the employee could deduct its cost as an expense for a trade or business other than the trade or business of being an employee of the employer.

For purposes of the exclusion for working condition fringes, the following individuals are generally treated as employees [Reg. § 1.132-1(b)(2)]:

- current employees;

- partners who perform services for a partnership;

- directors of the employer; and

- independent contractors who perform services for the employer.

**EXAMPLE:** Tina works for Huge Co. and, at Huge's request, is moving to another job site in another state. Huge pays Tina's real estate broker's commission on the sale of her house to assist her relocation. Tina may not exclude the value of the commission as a working condition fringe because, had she paid the commission directly, the expense would not have been deductible as a business expense.

**EXAMPLE:** Paul is an employee of Company, Inc. Unrelated to either Company's trade or business or Paul's trade or business of being an employee of Company, Paul is a member of the board of directors of Business Co. Company provides Paul with air transportation to Business's board of directors meeting. Paul may not exclude the value of the air transportation as a working condition fringe. However, if Business had regularly purchased significant goods and services from Company, Paul's membership on Business's board of directors would be related to Paul's trade or business of being an employee of Company, and Paul would be able to exclude the value of the air transportation as a working condition fringe.

Subject to certain requirements, the value of goods manufactured for sale to customers that are provided to employees for product testing are excludible as a working condition fringe [Reg. § 1.132-5(n)]. An auto salesperson's use of a demonstrator car may be a working condition fringe where the use is primarily to facilitate the salesperson's performance of services and there are substantial restrictions on personal use [§ 132(j)(3); Reg. § 1.132-5(o)]. Additionally, the fact that an employer's payment of an employee's dues and fees for a social, athletic, or sporting club membership is not deductible (see IV.A.11.c.) does not preclude the benefit from being a working condition fringe to the employee. Such amounts may qualify for exclusion where (i) the employer has not treated the amount as compensation, (ii) the amount would be deductible as an ordinary and necessary business expense, and (iii) the employee substantiates the expenses [Reg. § 1.132-5(s)(1)].

**EXAMPLE:** Eric is an employee of Organization. Organization provides Eric a country club membership worth $10,000 so that Eric can develop client relationships and make business contacts. Organization does not treat this amount as compensation, and Eric substantiates that he used the country club 40% for business purposes. The business use of the membership is considered a working condition fringe. Eric may exclude $4,000 ($10,000 membership value multiplied by 40% business use) from his gross income. The remaining $6,000 does not qualify as a working condition fringe.

*Cell Phones.* Where an employer provides an employee with a cell phone primarily for noncompensatory business reasons, the employee's use of the cell phone for reasons related to the employer's trade or business is treated as a working condition fringe, and, for purposes of the working condition fringe, the substantiation requirements the employee would otherwise have to meet for a trade or business deduction are deemed satisfied (see IV.C.). Further, the value of any personal use of the cell phone is treated as a de minimis fringe (see XVII.D.4.) [Notice 2011-72, 2011-38 I.R.B. 407].

### XVII.D.4. De Minimis Fringes

[394 T.M., II.B.2.d.; TPS ¶5960.02.D.]

The value of any property or service an employer provides to an employee that is so small as to make accounting for it unreasonable or administratively impractical may be excluded from an employee's gross income as a de minimis fringe. The frequency such benefits are provided is taken into account in determining whether an item is a de minimis fringe. Thus, the aggregate value of a frequently provided small benefit may not qualify as de minimis. Where a benefit is not de minimis as a result of its value or frequency, no amount of the benefit is a de minimis fringe. Examples of de minimis fringes include occasional personal use of a company copying machine, non-cash holiday gifts with a low fair market value, occasional tickets to theater or sporting events, and certain meals. The benefits are not subject to nondiscrimination rules [§ 132(e); Reg. § 1.132-6].

Occasional meals, money for meals, or local transportation fare is excludible from an employee's income as a de minimis fringe if the benefit is reasonable and is provided because overtime work requires extension of the employee's normal work schedule. However, meal money or local transportation fare calculated based on the number of hours the employee worked is not a de minimis fringe [Reg. § 1.132-6(d)(2)(i)].

---

**EXAMPLE:** Big, Inc. offers employees meal money of $10 per hour for each hour over eight hours the employee works. The amount is not a de minimis fringe benefit.

---

*Eating Facilities.* An eating facility operated by an employer is a de minimis fringe if (i) the facility is located on or near the employer's business premises, and (ii) the revenue derived therefrom normally equals or exceeds the facility's direct operating costs (i.e., the cost of food and beverages and the labor costs of the persons whose services are performed primarily at the eating facility) [§ 132(e)(2); Reg. § 1.132-7].

The exclusion for employer-provided cafeterias and dining rooms is available to highly-compensated employees (as defined in § 414(q)) only if the service is provided on a nondiscriminatory basis, and thus is available on substantially the same terms (i) to all employees, or (ii) to each member of a group of employees that is defined under a reasonable classification the employer set up that does not favor of highly-compensated employees [§ 132(e)(2); Reg. § 1.132-7(a)(1)(ii), § 1.132-8]. In addition, each cafeteria or dining room is treated as a separate facility (regardless of whether food is or is not prepared in a separate kitchen or other area) for purposes of the nondiscrimination rule [§ 132(e)(2); Reg. § 1.132-8(b)(2)].

---

**EXAMPLE:** Elite Co. has multiple dining rooms for employees, as well as a separate room reserved for top executives. The food available and prices charged in each dining room are identical. Elite's dining facilities are not an excludible de minimis fringe benefit for the highly-compensated employees.

---

*Local Transportation.* If an employer provides local transportation (such as a taxi fare) to employees commuting to or from work under unusual circumstances and because it is unsafe to use other means of transportation, the employee may exclude the amount by which the value of the benefit exceeds $1.50 per one-way commute. Unusual circumstances include the employee working outside normal hours or a temporary change in the employee's work schedule [Reg. § 1.132-6(d)(2)(ii), § 1.132-6(d)(2)(iii)].

Where an employer provides an employee with a cell phone primarily for non-compensatory business reasons, the employee's use of the cell phone for reasons related to the employer's trade or business is treated as a working condition fringe, and, for purposes of the working condition fringe, the substantiation requirements the employee would otherwise have to meet for a trade or business deduction are deemed satisfied (see IV.C.). The value of any personal use of the cell phone is treated as a de minimis fringe [Notice 2011-72, 2011-38 I.R.B. 407].

### XVII.D.5. Qualified Transportation Fringes

[394 T.M., II.B.2.e.; TPS ¶5960.02.G.]

An employee may exclude the following qualified transportation fringe benefits [§ 132(f)(1); Reg. § 1.132-9(b), Q&A -1]:

- transportation in a commuter highway vehicle between the employee's home and workplace;
- a transit pass;
- qualified parking; and
- qualified bicycle commuting reimbursement.

The maximum amounts that may be excluded in 2014 and 2015 are [§ 132(f)(2), § 132(f)(5)(F); Reg. § 1.132-9(b), Q&A -7; Rev. Proc. 2014-61, 2014-47 I.R.B. 860]:

- $130 per month for combined commuter highway vehicle transportation and transit passes;
- $250 per month for qualified parking; and
- $20 per month for qualified bicycle commuting reimbursement if the employee (i) regularly uses a bicycle for a substantial portion of travel between home and work, and (ii) does not receive any other qualified transportation fringe.

---

**EXAMPLE:** Tom's employer provides him qualified parking for each month of 2015. The value of the parking is $265 per month, and Tom does not pay any amount for it. Because the fair market value of the parking exceeds the maximum exclusion amount by $15 ($265 - $250), $180 ($15, multiplied by 12 months) must be included in Tom's income in 2015. The $15 is subject to income tax withholding, FICA, and FUTA.

---

*Commuter Highway Vehicles.* A commuter highway vehicle is any highway vehicle (i) seating at least six adults (other than the driver), and (ii) at least 80% of the mileage of which is reasonably expected to be for transporting employees between their home and work with employees occupying at least half of the passenger seats. A transit pass is any pass, token, farecard, voucher, or similar item that entitles a person to ride for free or at a reduced rate (i) on mass transit or (ii) in a vehicle operated by a person in the business of transporting people for pay or hire, and which seats at least six adults (other than the driver).

*Qualified Parking.* Qualified parking is employer-provided parking on or near the employer's business premises, and includes parking at or near a location (other than another employee's home) from which employees commute to work using mass transit, commuter highway vehicles, or carpools.

*Qualified Bicycle Commuting.* A qualified bicycle commuting reimbursement is an employer's reimbursement for reasonable expenses (e.g., the purchase, improvement, repair, or storage of a bicycle) incurred for a bicycle regularly used to travel between an employee's home and work [§ 132(f)(5)].

Qualified transportation fringes (other than a qualified bicycle commuting reimbursement) are generally excludible from income even where, at the employee's election, they are provided in lieu of otherwise includible compensation [§ 132(f)(4); Reg. § 1.132-9(b), Q&A -11].

An employer may provide the benefits directly or through a bona fide reimbursement arrangement. In the case of a reimbursement arrangement, the employer must implement reasonable procedures to ensure an amount equal to the reimbursement was actually incurred for transportation in a commuter highway vehicle, a transit pass, or qualified parking [Reg. § 1.132-9(b), Q&A -16(c)].

---

**EXAMPLE:** Mary submits a used monthly transit pass to her employer and certifies that she purchased it. The employer has no reason to doubt Mary's certification and reimburses her within a reasonable time. The reimbursement is excluded from Mary's income to the extent it does not exceed the monthly maximum excludible amount.

---

Cash reimbursements for transit passes qualify for exclusion only if a voucher or similar item the employee can exchange only for a transit pass is not readily available for direct distribution to employees. A voucher is readily available for direct distribution to employees only if an employee can obtain it from a voucher provider that does not impose fare media charges or other restrictions that cause the vouchers not to be readily available. A voucher is not readily available where the average annual fare media charges the employer reasonably expects to incur for vouchers purchased from a voucher provider exceed 1% (disregarding reasonable delivery charges) of the average annual value of the vouchers [§ 132(f)(3); Reg. § 1.132-9(b), Q&A -16(b)].

For the purpose of qualified transportation fringes, a self-employed individual is not treated as an employee. Additionally, an individual who is both a 2% shareholder of an S corporation and an officer or common law employee of that S corporation is not treated as an employee [§ 132(f)(5)(E), § 401(c)(1); Reg. § 1.132-9(b), Q&A -24].

### XVII.D.6. Qualified Moving Expense Reimbursement

[394 T.M., II.B.2.f.; TPS ¶¶5960.02.H., 1370.10.]

Amounts received directly or indirectly from an employer that are payment for, or reimbursement of, moving expenses that could be deducted if the employee paid them directly (see VII.B.6.) are excluded from an employee's gross income as a qualified moving reimbursement fringe. The exclusion does not apply to expenses the employee deducted in a previous year [§ 132(g)].

### XVII.D.7. Qualified Retirement Planning Services

[394 T.M., II.B.2.g.; TPS ¶5960.02.K.]

The value of qualified retirement planning advice or information to an employee and his or her spouse that is provided by an employer maintaining a qualified employer retirement plan is excluded from the employee's income. The exclusion applies to information and advice regarding the qualified plan, as well as regarding retirement planning generally. It does not apply to services related to retirement planning, such as tax preparation, accounting, legal, or brokerage services.

The exclusion does not apply to highly-compensated employees unless the services are available on substantially the same terms to each member of the group of employees normally provided education and information regarding the employer's qualified retirement plan [§ 132(m)].

## XVII.E. Other Benefit Arrangements

### XVII.E.1. Employer-Provided Adoption Assistance

[397 T.M., IV.G.; TPS ¶¶5960.02.J., 1370.15.]

An employee may exclude from income amounts an employer pays or incurs pursuant to a qualified employer adoption assistance program for the employee's expenses in connection with the adoption of a child. The maximum exclusion amount for 2014 is $13,190 ($13,400 for 2015). Where an employee adopts a special needs child, the qualified adoption expenses are increased to the extent necessary to equal the maximum exclusion amount. Thus, an employee who receives adoption assistance in adopting a special needs child may exclude the maximum amount, regardless of actual adoption expenses. The maximum exclusion amount phases out for taxpayers with modified adjusted gross incomes in 2014 in excess of $197,880 ($201,010 for 2015), and is completely phased out for taxpayers with modified adjusted gross incomes in 2014 of $237,880 or more ($241,010 for 2015). The phaseout applies to the adoption of both special needs children and non-special needs children [§ 137(a), § 137(b); Rev. Proc. 2014-61, 2014-47 I.R.B. 860, § 3.19].

A qualified adoption assistance program is not required to be funded (i.e., assets set aside by the employer to pay benefits as they become due), but there must be a separate written plan for the benefit of its employees that meets the following requirements [§ 137(b), § 137(c)(2)]:

1. It must benefit employees who qualify under rules set up by the employer that do not favor highly-compensated employees (as defined in § 414(q)) or their dependents (not considering employees excluded from the plan who are covered by a collective bargaining agreement where there is evidence that adoption assistance was the subject of good faith bargaining).

2. Not more than 5% of the amount of adoption assistance expenses or reimbursements paid or incurred during the year may be provided to shareholders or owners (or their spouses or dependents) who own more than 5% of the stock or the capital or profits interest in the employer at any point in the year.

3. The employer must give reasonable notice of the plan to eligible employees.

4. Employees receiving assistance must provide reasonable substantiation that payments or reimbursements are qualified adoption expenses.

Employer-provided adoption assistance benefits are reported on Form 8839, *Qualified Adoption Expenses.*

An employer-provided adoption assistance program that meets the enumerated requirements may be offered through a cafeteria plan (see XVII.C.3.). For a discussion of the adoption credit, see IX.B.3.

Government payments to assist adoptive parents with the support and maintenance of adoptive children are generally excludible from gross income (see II.N.12.).

### XVII.E.2. Employer-Provided Child and Dependent Care

[394 T.M., III.B.; TPS ¶5980.02.]

Eligible expenses an employer pays or incurs for dependent care assistance provided to an employee under a qualified dependent care assistance program may be excluded from the employee's income. The maximum exclusion is $5,000 per taxpayer ($2,500 for married filing separately) [§ 129(a)]. Expenses are excludible only to the extent they do not exceed the lesser of the employee's or the employee's spouse's earned income [§ 129(b)(1)].

However, if an employee's spouse is a full-time student or is incapable of caring for him or herself, for purposes of the income limitation, the spouse is deemed to have earned income for each month of full-time matriculation or incapacitation in the following amounts [§ 129(b)(2), § 21(d)(2)]:

- $250 per month if the employee cares for one qualifying individual; or
- $500 per month if the employee cares for more than one qualifying individual.

---

**EXAMPLE:** David is a full-time employee and has three children. His spouse is a full-time student for nine months of the year. David's maximum employer-provided dependent care exclusion for the year is $4,500, which is the lesser of (i) his earned income for the year, or (ii) his spouse's deemed earned income for the year ($500, multiplied by 9 months).

---

A dependent care assistance program need not be funded (i.e., assets set aside to pay for dependent care benefits). There must be a separate written plan for the benefit of employees that meets the following requirements [§ 129(d)]:

1. The program must not discriminate with respect to contributions or benefits in favor of highly-compensated employees (as defined in § 414(q) or their dependents.

2. It must benefit employees who qualify under rules set up by the employer that do not favor highly-compensated employees or their dependents (not considering (i) employees under age 21 or who have not completed one year of service, and (ii) employees excluded from the plan who are covered by a collective bargaining agreement).

3. Not more than 25% of the amount of dependent care assistance expenses or reimbursements paid or incurred during the year are provided to shareholders or owners (or their spouses or dependents) that own more than 5% of the stock or the capital or profits interest in the employer at any point in the year.

4. Employees must be notified about the availability and terms of the program.

5. The plan must provide employees with written statements by January 31 outlining the amounts paid or expenses incurred in providing dependent care assistance to the employee during the previous calendar year.

6. The average benefits provided to non-highly-compensated employees must be at least 55% of the average benefits provided to highly-compensated employees (not considering (i) employees earning less than $25,000 where benefits are provided through a salary reduction agreement, (ii) employees under age 21 or who have not completed one year of service, and (iii) employees excluded from the plan who are covered by a collective bargaining agreement where there is evidence that dependent care benefits were the subject of good faith bargaining).

Expenses eligible for exclusion must be for dependent care assistance services that would be considered employment-related expenses if paid by the employee directly (see IX.B.1.). Employment-related expenses must be both (i) incurred to enable the employee or his or her spouse to remain gainfully employed while there is at least one qualifying individual with respect to the employee, and (ii) for the care of a qualifying individual or for household services that are attributable in part to the care of the qualifying individual [§ 129(e)(1), § 21(b)(2); Reg. § 1.21-1(d)(1)]. A qualifying individual must be one of the following [§ 21(b)(1)]:

- a dependent of the employee under age 13;

- a dependent of the employee of any age who is physically or mentally incapable of self-care; or

- the spouse of an employee that is physically or mentally incapable of self-care.

Employment-related expenses may be incurred for services provided inside or outside the employee's home. However, services provided outside the employee's home must be provided to either (i) a dependent of the employee under age 13, or (ii) a spouse or dependent of an employee who is physically or mentally incapable of caring for him or herself and who spends at least eight hours a day in the employee's household [§ 129(e)(1)]. Day care centers that provide care for more than six individuals must comply with all applicable state and local laws and regulations [§ 129(e)(1), § 21(b)(2)].

---

**EXAMPLE:** Megan is a participant in her employer's dependent care assistance program. She places her invalid parent in a residential nursing home. The employer's reimbursement of any of Megan's expenses of caring for her parent is not excludible from income. Had Megan, instead, hired a nurse whose job was to provide care for Megan's parent and who lived in Megan's home, any reimbursement for the cost of hiring the nurse would be excludible from income. Additionally, assuming the parent spent at least eight hours a day in Megan's household, reimbursement for any care provided outside the household would also be excludible.

---

Payments an employer makes directly to the dependent of an employee, and that are otherwise included in the employee's income, are not eligible for exclusion if the payments are made to either (i) an individual for whom the employee or employee's spouse may take a dependent personal exemption deduction, or (ii) the employee's child who is under age 19 at the end of the tax year [§ 129(c)].

For the purposes of employer-provided dependent care assistance programs, a self-employed individual is treated as an employee [§ 129(e)(3)].

Dependent care assistance benefits are reported on Form 2441, *Child and Dependent Care Expenses*.

An employer-provided dependent care assistance program may be offered on a stand-alone basis or through a cafeteria plan (see XVII.C.3.). For a discussion of the child and dependent care credit, see IX.B.1.

### XVII.E.3. Employer-Provided Educational Expenses

[394 T.M., III.A.; TPS ¶5980.05.]

Amounts paid or expenses incurred by an employer for the benefit of an employee under a qualified education assistance program may be excluded from the employee's income. The maximum exclusion is limited to $5,250 per year [§ 127(a)].

An educational assistance plan need not be funded (i.e., assets set aside to pay for educational assistance benefits). However, such a plan must be a separate written plan that meets the following requirements [§ 127(b)]:

- It must benefit employees who qualify under rules set up by the employer that do not favor highly-compensated employees (as defined in § 414(q)) or their dependents (not considering employees excluded from the plan who are covered by a collective bargaining agreement where there is evidence that educational assistance was the subject of good faith bargaining).

- Not more than 5% of the amount of educational assistance expenses or reimbursements paid or incurred during the year are provided for shareholders or owners (or their spouses or dependents) that own more than 5% of the stock or the capital or profits interest in the employer at any point in the year;

- The program may not allow eligible employees to choose between educational assistance and other remuneration includible in gross income.
- The employer must give reasonable notice of the plan to eligible employees.

Educational assistance is (i) an employer's payment of expenses incurred by or on behalf of an employee for education (including expenses for tuition, books, supplies, and equipment), and (ii) an employer's provision of courses of instruction for an employee (including books, supplies, and equipment). It does not include payment for, or provision of, meals, lodging, transportation, or tools and supplies that an employee may retain after completing the course of instruction, and it generally does not include any payment for, or provision of, courses or other education relating to sports, games, or hobbies, unless it has a reasonable relationship to the employer's business or is a required part of a degree program [§ 127(c)(1), Reg. § 1.127-2(c)(3)].

For purposes of the educational assistance exclusion, an employee is one of the following individuals [Reg. § 1.127-2(d), § 1.127-2(h)(1)]:

- a current employee;
- a retired, disabled, or laid-off employee;
- a present employee on leave (e.g., as part of the U.S. Armed Forces); and
- a self-employed individual.

A program that provides benefits to spouses or dependents of employees is not a qualified educational assistance program.

For a discussion of scholarships, fellowships, and, tuition reduction, see II.H., for education credits, see IX.B.5., and for education deductions, see IV.A.3.a.

### XVII.E.4. Meals or Lodging Furnished for Employer's Convenience

[520 T.M., IV.A.; TPS ¶1130.]

The value of meals and lodging an employer provides to an employee, an employee's spouse, or an employee's dependents may be excluded from the employee's gross income if they are both furnished on the employer's business premises and for the employer's convenience.

Meals are furnished for the convenience of the employer if they are provided for a substantial noncompensatory business reason [§ 119; Reg. § 1.119-1(a), § 1.119-1(b)]. Examples of noncompensatory business reasons include meals furnished [Reg. § 1.119-1(f)]:

- to employees that need to be on call for emergencies during meals if the emergencies requiring a job call during a meal either actually have occurred or reasonably can be expected to occur in the employee's business (e.g., a civil service physician employed at a state medical institution and required to be available for duty at all times);
- to employees restricted to a short meal period for business reasons, and who cannot be expected to eat elsewhere in such a short period (e.g., a bank teller whose peak workload occurs during meal time); and
- because security reasons prevent the employee from leaving the employer's premises for meal breaks (e.g., casino employees that are forbidden from leaving the casino during their shift because of the risk they could walk out with cash or tokens).

An employee may exclude all meals furnished on an employer's business premises if that employee is entitled to exclude employer-provided lodging on the business premises [Reg. § 1.119-1(a)(2)(i)].

Lodging is furnished for the convenience of the employer if there is a primary noncompensatory business necessity for providing the lodging, and if the employee could not properly perform his or her duties without being furnished the lodging. The employee must be required to accept the lodging as a condition of employment [§ 119(a)(2); Reg. § 1.119-1(b)]. Examples of noncompensatory reasons include lodging furnished:

- on remote work sites that are inaccessible by normal transportation or so remote that lodging facilities are unavailable (e.g., a construction supervisor on a project in a remote area in Alaska 40 miles from the nearest city on a route that is occasionally impassible due to weather, and who is subject to call during off-hours);

- as an essential part of the performance of the employee's duties (e.g., a governor's official residence); or

- as a necessity to enable the employee to be available for duty at all times or for longer than normal working hours (e.g., a portion of the non-medical staff of a state psychiatric institution required to be on call 24 hours a day to respond to emergencies).

A business premises, for purposes of the exclusion, means either (i) a place where the employee performs a significant portion of his or her duties, or (ii) a place where the employer conducts a significant portion of his or her business.

Cash allowances or reimbursements for meals and lodging are not eligible for exclusion. Only meals and lodging furnished in kind may be excluded from the employee's gross income. Additionally, if the employee has the option to receive additional compensation in lieu of meals or lodging in kind, the value of the meals or lodging is not excludible [Reg. § 1.119-1(e)].

# CHAPTER XVIII. INCOME TAXATION OF ESTATES AND TRUSTS

>>>>>>>>>>>>>>>>>>>>>>>>>>>>>>>

## XVIII.A. Taxation of Estates, Non-Grantor Trusts, and Beneficiaries

### XVIII.A.1. Overview

[852 T.M., I., II., III.; TPS ¶6120.01.]

Subchapter J of the Internal Revenue Code governs the treatment of fiduciary income tax (i.e., the income taxation of trusts and estates) and income in respect of decedents. Generally, the income tax rules applicable to individuals apply to both estates and trusts.

For purposes of Subchapter J, only decedents' estates qualify as "estates." This includes both testate estates subject to administration and intestate estates. A decedent's estate consists only of assets subject to probate administration. Thus, property that is not subject to administration, such as property that passes by right of survivorship or by contract directly upon an owner's death, is not included in the definition of an estate, notwithstanding that such property or interests is included in the decedent's gross estate for federal estate tax purposes. Generally, only one-half of community property and its income are included in the estate for federal income tax purposes, even if the entire community is subject to administration. The other one-half of the income is directly attributable to the surviving spouse.

*Guardianship Estates.* Guardianship estates are not subject to the rules of Subchapter J, notwithstanding the fact that the guardian is considered a fiduciary [§ 7701(a)(6)]. Instead, the guardian is responsible for filing an individual federal income tax return on behalf of the ward [§ 6012(b)(2); Reg. § 1.6012-3(b)(3)]. This applies to the guardian of a minor as well as the guardian of an incompetent adult.

In general, the term "trust" as used for federal income tax purposes refers to an arrangement created either by a will or by an inter vivos declaration whereby trustees take title to property for the purpose of protecting or conserving it for the beneficiaries under the ordinary rules applied in chancery or probate courts. Usually the beneficiaries of such a trust do no more than accept the benefits thereof and are not the voluntary planners or creators of the trust arrangement. The key element of a trust is the purpose of protecting or conserving property for the beneficiaries. Trusts exist for various reasons under state law, but not all trusts are taxable as trusts under Subchapter J. Although most are taxed as trusts under the general provisions of Subchapter J, some are taxed as corporations while others are treated as grantor trusts [Reg. § 301.7701-4(a)].

***Business Trusts.*** If a trust is engaged in a business, it may be treated as a business entity or a trust for federal income tax purposes, depending upon the activities of the trust and the creation and transfer of the beneficial interests. The mere fact that the trust is engaged in a business does not automatically result in its being taxed as a business entity. The regulations provide that business trusts created by the beneficiaries simply as a device to carry on a profit-making business that normally would have been carried on through business organizations that are classified as corporations or partnerships under the Code do not qualify as trusts under Subchapter J [Reg. § 301.7701-4(b)].

***Investment Trusts.*** An investment trust is a trust that facilitate(s) direct investment in the assets held by the trust or a trust with trust interests that are substantially equivalent to undivided interests in the trust corpus. An investment trust with a single class of ownership interests, representing undivided beneficial interests in the assets of the trust is classified as a trust if there is no power under the trust agreement to vary the investment of the certificate holders. An investment trust with multiple classes of ownership interests ordinarily is classified as a business entity; however, an investment trust with multiple classes of ownership interests, in which there is no power under the trust agreement to vary the investment of the certificate holders, will be classified as a trust if the trust is formed to facilitate direct investment in the assets of the trust and the existence of multiple classes of ownership interests is incidental to that purpose [Reg. § 301.7701-4(c)].

***Liquidating Trusts.*** A liquidating trust organized for the primary purpose of liquidating and distributing the assets transferred to it will be treated as a trust for federal income tax purposes if its activities are all reasonably necessary to, and consistent with, the accomplishment of that purpose. This assumes that the trust was established to liquidate and distribute assets and not to carry on a profit-making business that normally would be conducted through business organizations classified as corporations or partnerships. Bondholders' protective committees, voting trusts, and other agencies formed to protect the interests of security holders during insolvency, bankruptcy, or corporate reorganization proceedings are analogous to liquidating trusts but if subsequently utilized to further the control or profitable operation of a going business on a permanent continuing basis, they will lose their classification as trusts for tax purposes [Reg. § 301.7701-4(d)].

***Environmental Remediation Trusts.*** An organization is treated as an environmental remediation trust if: (i) it is organized as a trust under state law; (ii) its primary purpose is collecting and disbursing amounts for environmental remediation of an existing waste site to resolve, satisfy, mitigate, address, or prevent the liability or potential liability of persons imposed by federal, state, or local environmental laws; (iii) all contributors to it have actual or potential liability or a reasonable expectation of liability under federal, state, or local environmental laws for environmental remediation of the waste site; and (iv) it is not a qualified settlement fund under Reg. § 1.468B-1(a). Environmental remediation trusts include trusts formed pursuant to an order of a governmental authority, as well as trusts formed by taxpayers to avoid future liability or potential liability under federal, state, or local environmental laws [Reg. § 301.7701-4(e)].

***Gifts to Minors.*** Where the donee is a minor or under age 21 (or such other age as provided by applicable state law), the gift may be made to an adult as custodian for that minor pursuant to a state statute. Many states have adopted the Uniform Gifts to Minors Act, the Uniform Transfers to Minors Act, or a variation of those statutes. The donee of a gift in a custodial account is vested with both legal and equitable title.

For federal income tax purposes, the custodianship does not create a taxable entity separate from the minor. The minor is the owner and taxpayer; however, the custodian may qualify as a fiduciary required to file a return on behalf of the minor.

Estates and non-grantor trusts are recognized as separate taxpayers and generally compute taxable income and tax liability in the same manner as individuals [§ 641(b)]. Various special rules apply in the calculation of taxable income of the trust or estate, including:

- The foreign tax credit is denied to the extent allocable to the beneficiaries [§ 642(a)].
- The personal exemption is limited to $600 for estates, $300 for trusts required to distribute all income currently, and $100 for all other trusts [§ 642(b)].
- Depreciation, depletion, and amortization are allocable between the trust or estate and the beneficiaries in accordance with the terms of the governing instrument or on the basis of the income actually retained and distributed [§ 642(e), § 642(f), § 167(d), § 611(b)].
- No standard deduction is allowed [§ 63(c)(6)(D)].
- The § 170 charitable deduction is generally denied, but § 642(c) permits a deduction to estates and certain trusts for amounts of gross income paid for a charitable purpose.

The most significant special rule is the distribution deduction (see XVIII.A.5.), which is permitted for certain amounts distributed to beneficiaries [§ 651, § 661]. The effect of the distribution deduction is to allocate the liability for federal income tax between the trust or estate and the beneficiaries as follows: (i) to the extent that a trust or estate accumulates income, the tax is imposed on the trust or estate, and (ii) to the extent that a trust or estate distributes income, the tax is imposed on the beneficiary or beneficiaries [§ 652, § 662]. The distribution deduction essentially acts as a conduit, shifting federal income tax liability for the trust's or estate's income from the trust or estate to the beneficiary.

### XVIII.A.2. Federal Income Taxes Applicable to Trusts and Estates

#### XVIII.A.2.a. Regular Income Tax

[852 T.M., IV.C.1.; TPS ¶6110.01.]

Trusts and estates have their own income tax rates [§ 1(e)]. The tax brackets for trusts and estates are compressed vis-à-vis individual income tax brackets, meaning that it takes less income for a trust or estate to get taxed at the highest marginal rate. The tax rate schedules for 2014 and 2015 are as follows [Rev. Proc. 2013-35, 2013-47 I.R.B. 537, § 3.01, Rev. Proc. 2014-61, 2014-47 I.R.B. 860, § 3.01]:

| If 2014 taxable income is: | The tax is: |
| --- | --- |
| Not over $2,500 | 15% of taxable income |
| Over $2,500 but not over $5,800 | $375 plus 25% of the excess over $2,500 |
| Over $5,800 but not over $8,900 | $1,200 plus 28% of the excess over $5,800 |
| Over $8,900 but not over $12,150 | $2,068 plus 33% of the excess over $8,900 |
| Over $12,150 | $3,140.50 plus 39.6% of the excess over $12,150 |

| If 2015 taxable income is: | The tax is: |
|---|---|
| Not over $2,500 | 15% of taxable income |
| Over $2,500 but not over $5,900 | $375 plus 25% of the excess over $2,500 |
| Over $5,900 but not over $9,050 | $1,225 plus 28% of the excess over $5,900 |
| Over $9,050 but not over $12,300 | $2,107 plus 33% of the excess over $9,050 |
| Over $12,300 | $3,179.50 plus 39.6% of the excess over $12,300 |

Net capital gains are taxed at preferential rates of 0%, 15%, or 20%, depending on the taxpayer's ordinary income tax rate [§ 1(h)].

### XVIII.A.2.b. Alternative Minimum Tax

[852 T.M., IV.C.2.; TPS ¶6120.07.]

Estates and trusts are also subject to the alternative minimum tax (AMT), in a similar manner as individuals, to the extent the tentative minimum tax exceeds the regular tax for the year [§ 55, § 59(c)]. Tentative minimum tax is imposed on a portion of the estate's or trust's taxable income, after being adjusted for certain deductions, increased for preference items, and decreased by the available exemption. For tax years beginning in 2014, the tentative minimum tax is the sum of: (1) 26% of the amount up to $182,500 ($185,400 for 2015), plus (2) 28% of the amount exceeding $182,500 ($185,400 for 2015) [§ 55(b)(1)(A); Rev. Proc. 2013-35, § 3.10, Rev. Proc. 2014-61, 2014-47 I.R.B. 860, § 3.10]. A trust or estate is entitled to an exemption amount of $23,500 for tax years beginning in 2014 ($23,800 for 2015), which is phased out if the trust's or estate's alternative minimum taxable income (AMTI) exceeds the threshold amount of $78,250 ($79,450 for 2015) [§ 55(d)(1)(D), 55(d)(3)(C), 55(d)(4)(B)(ii); Rev. Proc. 2013-35, Rev. Proc. 2014-61]. The exemption amount is reduced by 25% of the excess over the threshold amount [§ 55(d)(1)(D), 55(d)(3)(C)]. Thus, for tax years beginning in 2014, if the estate's or trust's AMTI exceeds $172,250 ($174,650 for 2015), there is no available exemption amount.

AMTI is computed without the benefit of certain deductions and exclusions, and certain other deductions are recomputed for purposes of computing AMTI [§ 56-§ 58]. For a discussion of AMT, see Chapter X.

**Interaction with Distributable Net Income.** DNI (see XVIII.A.5.a.), by definition, begins with taxable income, subject to certain statutory modifications. AMTI also begins with taxable income, adjusted for certain items and increased by certain preferences. As adjustments are made to taxable income for alternative minimum tax purposes, those adjustments are also made to the computation of DNI. The distribution deduction is then adjusted according to § 59(c). The result of this is that many of the adjustments to taxable income will increase DNI and thus increase the distribution deduction so that the adjustments to taxable income will be offset by the corresponding adjustment to the distribution deduction. But this will not always be true, because the distribution deduction is limited by the amount of actual or required distributions. If the distribution deduction is increased at the estate's or trust's level, this will affect the computation of one or more of the beneficiary's alternative minimum tax. The increased distribution deduction will result in some or all of the beneficiaries being treated as having more income for purposes of computing the respective beneficiary's alternative minimum tax.

### XVIII.A.2.c. Net Investment Income Tax

[852 T.M., IV.C.6.; TPS ¶6110.01.]

The net investment income tax (NIIT), which is effective for tax years beginning after 2012, imposes an additional 3.8% tax on an estate's or trust's unearned income [§ 1411]. This additional tax effectively raises the highest tax rate on ordinary income and capital gains to 43.6% and 23.8%, respectively (see XVIII.E.).

### XVIII.A.3. Dual Track System: "Simple" Trusts vs. Estates and "Complex" Trusts

[852 T.M., V.D.; TPS ¶6130.]

Subchapter J adopts a dual system for the income taxation of trusts, estates, and their beneficiaries. One set of rules applies to "simple" trusts (see XVIII.A.7.), and the other set of rules applies to all estates and to "complex" trusts (see XVIII.A.8.).

Simple trusts and their beneficiaries are taxed under § 651 and § 652. A simple trust is a trust (i) all the fiduciary accounting income (FAI) of which is required to be distributed currently, (ii) that does not provide for any charitable transfers within § 642(c), and (iii) that does not make a distribution during the current year of an amount other than current income. The determination of whether a trust is a simple or complex trust is made each year.

Complex trusts and all estates are taxed under § 661 and § 662. A complex trust is any trust other than a simple trust. An estate of a decedent includes property of all kinds held by any legal representative who has the responsibility to collect assets, pay debts, and distribute the remainder [§ 641(a)].

### XVIII.A.4. Determining Taxable Income – Exemptions, Deductions, and Credits

### XVIII.A.4.a. Gross Income and Exclusions

[852 T.M., IV.B.1.; TPS ¶6120.02.A.]

The general definition of gross income applies to an estate or trust [§ 641(b)]. Gross income represents "undeniable accessions to wealth, clearly realized, and over which the taxpayer has complete dominion" [*Commissioner v. Glenshaw Glass Co.*, 348 U.S. 426 (1955)]. Some common items of gross income for estates and trusts are interest, dividends, rents, royalties, gross income derived from business, the distributive share of a partnership's gross income, income from life insurance contracts, gains derived from dealings in property, and income in respect of a decedent [§ 61] (see I.A.).

*Gains Derived from Dealings in Property.* An estate or trust will have gross income when it sells, exchanges, or otherwise disposes of an asset for an amount in excess of its adjusted basis in the property [§ 61(a)(3), § 1001, § 1014] (see III.A.).

*Income in Respect of a Decedent.* An estate or trust will have gross income if it collects an item of income in respect of a decedent (IRD) or transfers an item of IRD in a taxable disposition [§ 61(a)(14), § 691(a)] (see XVIII.F.).

*Exclusions.* Exclusions from gross income applicable to individuals are also available to trusts and estates. Some examples include tax exempt interest (see II.B.), or gains realized in a like-kind exchange (see III.E.1.) or a sale of a principal residence (see III.E.3.) [§ 103, § 121, § 1031].

### XVIII.A.4.b. Deductions

[852 T.M., IV.B.2.; TPS ¶6120.02.B.]

An estate or trust is entitled to the deductions allowed to individuals, with certain exceptions, modifications, and additions.

### XVIII.A.4.b.(1) Trade or Business Expenses

[852 T.M., IV.B.2.b.; TPS ¶6120.02.]

If an estate or trust is engaged in a trade or business, it is entitled to deduct "all the ordinary and necessary expenses paid or incurred during the tax year in carrying on [such] trade or business" [§ 162(a)] (see IV.A.). This deduction is limited by other statutory provisions, such as the limitation on meals and entertainment expenses [§ 274] (see IV.D.5.).

### XVIII.A.4.b.(2) Net Operating Losses

[852 T.M., IV.B.2.c.; TPS ¶6120.02.F.]

If an estate or trust is engaged in a trade or business it may have a net operating loss (NOL). In general, an NOL is the amount by which the deductions exceed gross income, with certain modifications [§ 172(c)]. An NOL can be carried back two tax years preceding the year of loss and may be carried forward 20 tax years after the year of loss [§ 172(b)] (see VIII.G.).

A trust's or estate's NOL is computed under the general rules, with two exceptions: (i) the NOL is computed without taking into account the charitable contribution deduction under § 642(c) or the distribution deduction under § 651 or § 661, and (ii) in computing gross income and deductions for purposes of § 172, a trust will exclude that portion of the income and deductions attributable to the grantor or another person under the grantor trust rules [Reg. § 1.642(d)-1(a), (b)].

To the extent an NOL is carried back to a prior year of an estate or trust, it will reduce DNI (see XVIII.A.5.a.) for that year. This in turn may reduce the income that a beneficiary was required to report with respect to a distribution in that carryback year, thereby permitting the estate beneficiary to recompute his tax liability for such prior year based upon the revised DNI of the estate after allowance of the net operating loss deduction. Any resulting overpayment of taxes may be refunded to the beneficiary provided the refund is allowed or a claim for refund or credit is timely filed by the beneficiary within the period prescribed by § 6511(d)(2) (special period of limitations for NOLs) [Rev. Rul. 61-20, 1961-1 C.B. 248].

Special provisions also allow an unused NOL carryover in the year of termination to be deducted by the beneficiaries who succeed to the property of the estate or trust upon termination [§ 642(h)]. Further, an NOL incurred by the decedent (rather than by his or her estate) does not carry over to the estate. Instead, it must be used on the decedent's final income tax return or carried back to prior income tax returns of the decedent [Rev. Rul. 74-175, 1974-1 C.B. 52].

### XVIII.A.4.b.(3) Deduction for Domestic Production Activities

[510 T.M., III., 852 T.M, IV.B.2.d.; TPS ¶2220.01.]

Generally, the deduction attributable to domestic production activities is the lesser of [§ 199]:

1. 9% of qualified production activities income (QPAI) for the tax year;
2. 9% of taxable income (determined without regard to § 199) for the tax year; or
3. 50% of the W-2 wages for the tax year.

The domestic production activities deduction is discussed at IV.A.9.

*Estates and Non-grantor Trust.* An estate or non-grantor trust calculates each beneficiary's share (and its own share, if any) of the QPAI from the estate or trust at the estate or trust level. The beneficiary is not permitted to use another cost allocation method to recompute its share of QPAI from the estate or trust or to reallocate costs of the estate or trust. The QPAI of an estate or non-grantor trust (which can be less than zero) is allocated to each beneficiary and to the estate or trust based on the relative proportion of the estate's or trusts DNI for the tax year that is distributed or required to be distributed to the beneficiary or is retained by the estate or trust. For a tax year during which the estate or trust has no DNI, QPAI and W-2 wages are all allocated to the estate or trust [Reg. § 1.199-5(e)].

*Grantor Trusts.* An owner of a grantor trust computes its QPAI for the portion of the trust the grantor owns as if that QPAI had been generated by activities performed directly by the owner, and the owner takes into account the owner's share of W-2 wages of the trust that are attributable to the owned portion of the trust [§ 199(d)(1)(B); Reg. § 1.199-5(d)].

### XVIII.A.4.b.(4) Expenses for Production of Income

[523 T.M., I.C., III., 505 T.M., III., IV., 852 T.M., IV.B.2.e.; TPS ¶¶2300.01., 2480.01.]

An estate or trust is entitled to a deduction for the ordinary and necessary expenses it pays or incurs [§ 212]: (i) for the production of income; (ii) for the management, conservation, or maintenance of property held for the production of income; or (iii) in connection with the determination, collection, or refund of any tax (see IV.B.). If property is held for the production of income, expenses paid or incurred to maintain that property qualify for the deduction, even if the property does not produce income as anticipated [*Bingham Trust v. Commissioner*, 325 U.S. 365 (1945)].

Reasonable amounts paid or incurred by the fiduciary of an estate or trust on account of administration expenses, including fiduciaries' fees and expenses of litigation, which are ordinary and necessary in connection with the performance of the duties of administration, are deductible [Reg. § 1.212-1(i)]. Most estate administration expenses qualify under § 212 because estate or trust property is usually held for the production of income. Expenses of administering estates are deductible, notwithstanding that all of the estate assets are not held for the production of income. For example, many estates include personal assets, such as jewelry and residences, which may not be held for the production of income. Nevertheless, an estate or trust may deduct certain expenses under § 212 that an individual would not be able to deduct. Some of these expenses are deductible in full in determining adjusted gross income, such as trustees' fees [§ 67(e)]. Other expenses are subject to the limitations on miscellaneous itemized deductions [§ 67(c)(3)(B)].

If the administrative expenses exceed the income for the year in question, they will not be deductible to the beneficiary unless they are incurred in the final year of the estate or trust, in which case they would be an excess deduction, allowable under § 642(h). Excess deductions in a non-final year do not create an NOL as defined in § 172 and, therefore, are wasted.

### XVIII.A.4.b.(5) Depreciation, Depletion, and Amortization

[852 T.M., IV.B.2.f.; TPS ¶6120.02.G.]

An estate or trust may be entitled to a depreciation deduction equal to a reasonable allowance for exhaustion, wear, tear, and obsolescence of certain property used in a trade or business or held for the production of income [§ 167, § 168] (see Chapter V.).

*Estates.* To the extent an heir, legatee, or devisee is entitled to an allocation of an estate's fiduciary accounting income (FAI), he or she is also allocated a proportionate share of the depreciation, depletion, or amortization deduction [§ 167(d), § 611(b)(4); Reg. § 1.167(h)-1(c)].

*Trusts.* In the case of a trust, the beneficiary's share of the depreciation, depletion, or amortization deduction is determined in accordance with the provisions of the trust instrument In the absence of such provisions, the deduction is determined on the basis of trust income allocable to each. If the trustee is required to maintain a reserve for depreciation or depletion, or has the discretion to do so, the deduction is first allocated to the trustee to the extent such reserve is set aside]. Any depreciation in excess of the reserve amount is allocated among the income beneficiaries and the trustee in proportion to the trust income allocated to each [§ 167(d), § 611(b)(4); Reg. § 1.167(h)-1(b)].

### XVIII.A.4.b.(6) Casualty and Theft Losses

[852 T.M., IV.B.2.g.; TPS ¶2350.02.]

An estate or trust may deduct losses not compensated for by insurance (i) incurred in a trade or business, (ii) incurred in a transaction entered into for profit, or (iii) arising from fire, storm, shipwreck, other casualty, or from theft [§ 165(c)]. The deduction for losses arising from fire, storm, shipwreck, other casualty, or from theft is subject to a $100 disallowance and is only allowable to the extent that the loss exceeds 10% of AGI (determined at the entity level) [§ 165(h)] (see IV.E.1.).

*Related Party Transactions.* Losses that arise in a transaction between related parties are disallowed [§ 267] (see VIII.B.1.). In the context of trusts and estates, related parties include [§ 267(b)]:

- a grantor and a fiduciary of the same trust;
- a fiduciary of a trust and a fiduciary of another trust, if the same person is a grantor of both trusts;
- a fiduciary of a trust and a beneficiary of such trust;
- a fiduciary of a trust and a beneficiary of another trust, if the same person is a grantor of both trusts;
- a fiduciary of a trust and a corporation more than 50% in value of the outstanding stock of which is owned, directly or indirectly, (i) by or for the trust or (ii) by or for a person who is a grantor of the trust; and
- an executor of an estate and a beneficiary of such estate, except in the case of a sale or exchange in satisfaction of a pecuniary bequest.

### XVIII.A.4.b.(7) Capital Losses

[852 T.M., IV.B.2.h.; TPS ¶1610.01.]

An estate or trust is entitled to deduct losses from the sale or exchange of capital assets up to the amount of capital gains plus $3,000 in excess of such gains [§ 1211(b)]. To the extent these losses are not fully deductible in the tax year incurred, they are permitted to be carried forward for an unlimited number of years until the loss is used [§ 1212(b)] (see III.B.5.). These losses also carry over to the beneficiaries succeeding to the property on the termination of an estate or trust. Similarly to § 165 losses, § 267 will disallow capital losses if the transaction occurs between related parties.

### *XVIII.A.4.b.(8)  Bad Debts*

[852 T.M., IV.B.2.i.; TPS ¶2360.01.]

If an estate or trust loans money and the debt becomes worthless, the bad debt may be deductible [§ 166]. If the estate or trust is engaged in a trade or business and the debt was created or acquired in that trade or business, the estate or trust may deduct the debt when and to the extent it becomes wholly or partially worthless [§ 166(a), § 166(d)(2)(A)]. The adjusted basis of the debt (or its worthless portion) is used to compute the bad debt deduction. The same rules apply even if the debt was not created or acquired in a trade or business, as long as the loss that occurs when the debt becomes wholly or partially worthless is proximately related to the conduct of a trade or business [§ 166(a), § 166(d)(2)(B); Reg. § 1.166-5(b)] (see IV.F.2.).

*Nonbusiness Bad Debts.* If a nonbusiness bad debt becomes totally worthless, it is treated as the sale or exchange of a short-term capital asset, resulting in a short-term capital loss [§ 166(d)(1)] (see VIII.F.).

### *XVIII.A.4.b.(9)  Interest Paid or Accrued*

[852 T.M., IV.B.2.j., 536 T.M., VIII.; TPS ¶¶6120.02.H., 2330.02.]

If an estate or trust paid or accrued interest on an indebtedness, it may deduct the interest expense subject to the limitations on investment and personal interest [§ 163(a), § 163(d), § 163(h)] (see VII.E.).

### *XVIII.A.4.b.(10)  State, Local, and Foreign Taxes*

[852 T.M., IV.B.2.k., 525 T.M., II.; TPS ¶2340.02.]

An estate or trust may deduct certain paid or accrued taxes, such as a state or local tax on real or personal property or a state income tax [§ 164] (see VII.E.). An estate or trust also may deduct state, local, or foreign taxes paid or accrued in carrying on a trade or business or an income-producing activity [§ 164(a)] (see IV.A.12.).

### *XVIII.A.4.b.(11)  Charitable Deduction*

[852 T.M., IV.B.2.l.; TPS ¶6120.02.E.]

Trusts and estates are allowed a charitable deduction for income tax purposes under § 642(c) in lieu of the § 170 charitable contribution deduction allowed to individuals. The deduction is available for charitable contributions paid from income (not principal) pursuant to the terms of the governing instrument [§ 642(c)(1)]. Trusts and estates can deduct any amount of the gross income that is paid to qualified charitable donees, including any undistributed income from prior tax years. Accordingly, if it qualifies as a charitable gift, no percentage limitation applies to the available deduction attributable to the contribution. This is in contrast to the rule applicable to individual taxpayers, who cannot deduct charitable contributions in excess of specified percentages of their AGI [§ 170(b)].

Estates are also allowed a deduction for any amount that is, pursuant to the terms of the governing instrument, "permanently set aside" during the tax year for a designated charitable purpose. Designated charitable purposes include purposes specified in § 170 and amounts used exclusively for (i) religious, charitable, scientific, literary, or educational purposes; (ii) the prevention of cruelty to children or animals; or (iii) the establishment, acquisition, maintenance, or operation of a nonprofit public cemetery. In contrast, individuals and most trusts (other than certain trusts established on or before October 9, 1969) may deduct charitable contributions only when those contributions are actually paid, and not merely when charitable pledges are made [§ 642(c)(2)].

*Contributions to Foreign Charities*. Unlike individuals, trusts and estates may receive a charitable deduction for contributions to foreign charities [Reg. § 1.642(c)-1(a)(2)].

### XVIII.A.4.b.(12) Deduction for Estate Taxes Paid

[862 T.M., VI., 852 T.M. IV.B.2.m.; TPS ¶6150.05.]

If an estate or trust collects an item of IRD (see XVIII.F.), the estate or trust may be allowed a deduction for the estate tax attributable to such item [§ 691(c)]. The estate or trust deduction is computed based only on the portion of the income that was not paid, credited, or supposed to be distributed to the beneficiaries during the year, determined by ignoring the potential § 691(c) deduction [§ 691(c)(1)(B); Reg. § 1.691(c)-2(a)(2)]. The portion paid, credited, or distributed to the beneficiaries is based on the allocation of DNI to such beneficiary under § 652 or § 662.

### XVIII.A.4.b.(13) Personal Exemption

[852 T.M., IV.B.2.n.; TPS ¶6120.02.C.]

Estates and trusts are entitled to a personal exemption in 2014 and 2015 as follows [§ 642(b), § 151(d); Rev. Proc. 2013-35, 2013-47 I.R.B. 537, § 3.23(1), Rev. Proc. 2014-61, 2014-47 I.R.B. 860, § 3.23(1).]:

| | |
|---|---|
| Estates | $600 |
| Trusts Required to Distribute All Income Currently | $300 |
| Qualified Disability Trusts | $3,950 ($4,000 for 2015) |
| All Other Trusts | $100 |

### XVIII.A.4.b.(14) Adjusted Gross Income Limitation

[852 T.M., IV.B.2.o.; TPS ¶6120.02.A.]

Some of the deductions available to an estate or trust are limited by the AGI of the estate or trust. For example, personal casualty losses (see XVIII.A.4.b.(6)) are deductible only to the extent they exceed 10% of AGI and some miscellaneous itemized deductions (see XVIII.A.4.b.(15)) are allowed only to the extent they exceed 2% of AGI (note that estates and trusts are exempt from the overall limit on itemized deductions) [§ 165(h)(2), § 67(a), § 67(e)].

AGI is computed in the same way as for an individual, with statutory exceptions depending upon the deduction being claimed. Generally, the AGI of an estate or trust means gross income, reduced by the following allowable deductions:

1. deductions attributable to carrying on a trade or business [§ 62(a)(1)];

2. losses from the sale or exchange of property [§ 62(a)(3)];

3. deductions attributable to property held for the production of rents or royalties, or maintenance of such property, including deductions for (i) depreciation, (ii) depletion, (iii) interest, (iv) taxes, and (v) ordinary and necessary expenses [§ 62(a)(4)]; and

4. penalties arising from premature withdrawal of funds from a certificate of deposit, time savings account, or similar class of deposit if the transaction was entered into for profit [§ 62(a)(9)].

For the limitation on personal casualty losses, the deductions for costs paid or incurred in connection with the administration of the estate or trust are deducted from gross income to compute AGI [§ 165(h)(5)(C)]. For the limitation on miscellaneous itemized deduction, (i) only those costs of administration that would not have been incurred if the property were not held in such trust or estate are deducted from gross income to compute AGI [§ 67(e)(1)], and (ii) the personal exemption and distribution deductions under § 651 or § 661 are deducted from gross income to compute AGI for purposes of imposing the limitation on miscellaneous itemized deductions.

### XVIII.A.4.b.(15) Miscellaneous Itemized Deductions

[852 T.M., IV.B.2.p.; TPS ¶6120.02.A.]

Generally, an estate or trust is entitled to claim miscellaneous itemized deductions only to the extent they exceed 2% of AGI [§ 67(a)]. In this context, an estate or trust computes its AGI in the same manner as an individual (see VII.I.), but with three unique deductions [§ 67(e)]:

1. the distribution deduction under § 651 or § 661;

2. the special personal exemption for estates and trusts; and

3. the deduction for costs that are paid or incurred in connection with the administration of the estate or trust that would not have been incurred if the property were not held in such estate or trust.

Thus, costs of administration that are incurred only because the property is held in an estate or trust, and that would not have been incurred otherwise, are above-the-line deductions for purposes of § 67 and are not miscellaneous itemized deductions subject to the 2% floor.

The following costs are subject to the 2% floor [Reg. § 1.67-4(b)]:

- Ownership costs that are chargeable to or incurred by an owner of property simply by reason of being the owner of the property, such as (i) condo fees, (ii) insurance premiums, (iii) maintenance and lawn services, (iv) automobile registration and insurance costs, and (v) certain partnership costs deemed to be passed through to and reportable by a partner.

- The costs of preparing all tax returns (e.g., gift tax returns), except for estate and GST tax returns, fiduciary income tax returns, and the decedent's final individual income tax return.

- Investment advisory fees, including fees for related services that would not be provided to an individual investor as part of an investment advisory fee (but excluding certain incremental costs of investment advice beyond the amount normally charged to an individual investor).

- Appraisal fees, other than for determining the value of assets (i) as of a decedent's date of death (or the alternate valuation date), (ii) for making distributions, and (iii) as required to prepare the estate's or trust's tax returns or a GST tax return.

Examples of fiduciary expenses that are not subject to the 2% floor include [Reg. § 1.67-4(b)(6)]:

- probate court fees and costs;

- fiduciary bond premiums;

- legal publication costs of notices to creditors or heirs;

- the cost of certified copies of the decedent's death certificate; and

- costs related to fiduciary accounts.

For tax years beginning before 2015, an estate or trust may deduct all investment and advisory costs and other costs that are bundled as part of one commission or fee paid to a trustee or executor, disregarding the 2% floor on miscellaneous itemized deductions [Notice 2011-37, 2011-20 I.R.B. 785]. However, for tax years beginning in

2015 and thereafter, bundled fees must be allocated (using any reasonable method) between costs that are subject to the 2% floor and those that are not [Reg. § 1.67-4(c)].

### XVIII.A.4.b.(16) Losses from Pass-Through Entities and Passive Activity Losses

[852 T.M., IV.B.2.q.; TPS ¶2980.01.]

Generally, the passive loss rules that apply to individuals (see VIII.F.) also apply to estates and trusts [§ 469]. Thus, an estate or trust must materially or actively participate in a trade or business in order to deduct losses attributable thereto. However, to date, the IRS has not issued guidance under § 469 defining material or active participation for an estate or trust.

A district court has held that the material participation of a trust in ranch operations (i.e., business activities) should be determined by reference to the persons and agents who conducted the ranch's business on the trust's behalf, including the trustee [*Mattie K. Carter Trust v. United States*, 256 F. Supp. 2d 536 (N.D. Tex. 2003)]. However, the IRS has rejected the conclusion in *Mattie K. Carter Trust* and has continued to hold the position that only the activities of trustees can be considered in determining whether a trust materially participates in an activity [TAM 200733023, TAM 201317010].

Generally, any rental activity is considered a passive activity, even if the taxpayer materially participates therein [§ 469(c)(2)]. Thus, losses incurred are not allowable as deductions. However, there is an exception for rental real estate activities. A taxpayer's rental real estate activities are not considered passive and, thus, losses incurred as a result of those activities are deductible, if (i) more than one-half of the personal services performed in trades or businesses by the taxpayer during the tax year is performed in real property trades or businesses in which the taxpayer materially participates, and (ii) the taxpayer performs more than 750 hours of services during the year in real property trades or businesses in which the taxpayer materially participates [§ 469(c)(7)]. In this context, the Tax Court has held that a trust is capable of performing personal services and therefore can satisfy the rental real estate activity exception [*Frank Aragona Trust v. Commissioner*, 142 T.C. No. 9 (3/27/14)]. The IRS has not acquiesced in the Tax Court's holding in *Aragona Trust*.

### XVIII.A.4.b.(17) Deductions Allowed to Individuals but Not to Trusts and Estates

[852 T.M., IV.B.2.r.; TPS ¶6120.02.]

There are deductions allowed to individuals but not to estates or trusts. For example, an estate or trust is not entitled to a standard deduction [§ 63(c)(6)(D)]. In addition, an estate or trust cannot elect to expense the cost of certain depreciable assets [§ 179(d)(4)].

Further, certain deductions are taken on the decedent's final return rather than by the estate on its income tax return. For example, medical expenses of the decedent paid by the estate during the first year after the decedent's death are deducted either in the decedent's final income tax return or on the estate's estate tax return [§ 213(c)]. In addition, if an annuitant dies before recovering his or her investment in an annuity contract, the deduction for the unrecovered investment is allowed on the decedent's final income tax return [§ 72(b)(3)].

### XVIII.A.4.b.(18) Distribution Deduction Available to Estates or Trusts

[852 T.M., IV.B.2.s.; TPS ¶6120.03.]

Generally, trusts and estates receive an income tax deduction for distributions of taxable DNI to their beneficiaries [§ 651, § 661]. DNI that is deemed to consist of tax-exempt income is not deductible. The distribution deduction is discussed in detail at XVIII.A.5.

### XVIII.A.4.b.(19) Disallowance of Double Deductions for Administration Expenses

[852 T.M., IV.B.2.t.; TPS ¶6120.02.I.]

Estate administration expenses are allowable as deductions in determining either estate tax liability or income tax liability, but not both [§ 642]. A fiduciary may only deduct certain administration expenses once, either on the estate tax return or the income tax return [§ 642(g); Reg. § 1.642(g)-2]. These expenses include legal and accounting fees, court fees, fiduciary's commissions, and expenses incurred in selling assets. The deduction for administration expenses is allowed only if the executor files the appropriate statement attached to Form 1041, *U.S. Income Tax Return for Estates and Trusts*, that the deductible amount has not been allowed as an estate tax deduction [§ 642(g)]. Further, if administration expenses are deducted by an estate for income tax purposes, the executor must waive the right to such an allowance as an estate tax deduction in the future.

### XVIII.A.4.b.(20) Nondeductibility of Expenses Allocated to Tax-Exempt Interest

[852 T.M., IV.B.2.u.; TPS ¶2960.01.]

An estate or trust cannot deduct expenses allocated to tax-exempt income [§ 265]. For example, if an indebtedness is incurred or continued in order to purchase or carry an obligation that produces tax-exempt income, the interest on the debt is not deductible [§ 265(a)(2)] (see VIII.D.). Further, expenses otherwise deductible under § 212 that are incurred to produce tax-exempt income are not deductible for income tax purposes [§ 265(a)(1)].

### XVIII.A.4.b.(21) Carryovers and Excess Deductions

[852 T.M., IV.B.2.v.; TPS ¶6120.04.G.]

Generally, if an estate or trust has deductions in excess of income, the deductions are lost. However, there are several exceptions. For example:

- Net operating losses may be carried back two years and carried forward up to 20 years [§ 172] (see VIII.G.3.).
- Capital losses can be carried forward by an estate or trust during the administration of the estate or trust [§ 1212(b)] (see III.B.5.).
- In the year of termination, certain carryovers and excess deductions pass through to the beneficiaries [§ 642(h)] (see XVIII.C.5.).

Excess deductions may be passed to a trust that is a residuary beneficiary of an estate [Rev. Rul. 57-31, 1957-1 C.B. 201].

### XVIII.A.4.b.(22) Distributions by Cemetery Perpetual Care Funds

[852 T.M., IV.B.2.w.; TPS ¶6120.02.]

A distribution by a cemetery perpetual care trust for the care and maintenance of gravesites is deductible [§ 642(i), § 651, § 661]. The amount of the deduction is limited to $5 per gravesite [§ 642(i)(2)].

### XVIII.A.5. Distribution Deduction

[852 T.M., V.E.1., V.F.2.; TPS ¶6130.01., .02.C.]

Because of the ability to get an income tax deduction for distributions that carry out DNI, one may view the taxability of trust and estate income as "he who gets the income, pays the tax." If the trust or estate keeps any income, the trust or estate will pay tax on such retained income. In this way, the trust or estate is a separate taxpayer, like an individual or a C corporation. If the trust or estate distributes income to a beneficiary, the beneficiary will pay tax on such distributed income. In this way, the trust or estate is a conduit, similar to a partnership or S corporation.

### XVIII.A.5.a. Distributable Net Income

[852 T.M., V.B.; TPS ¶6120.03.B.]

Distributable Net Income (DNI) is a mechanism that (i) quantifies the trust's or estate's distribution deduction, (ii) quantifies the amount of income attributed to beneficiaries, and (iii) characterizes the amounts distributed [§ 651(b), § 642(i), § 661(c), § 652(b), § 662(b)]. DNI serves as a ceiling on the amount of the distribution deduction to the trust or estate and on the amount of income to the beneficiaries [§ 651(b), § 661(c)]. DNI is neither fiduciary accounting income nor federal taxable income; it consists of the trust's or estate's taxable income, with certain modifications.

***Tax Exempt Interest.*** Tax-exempt interest (including exempt-interest dividends) is included in DNI but is reduced by (i) expenses not allowed in computing the estate's or trust's taxable income because they were attributable to tax-exempt interest, and (ii) the portion of tax-exempt interest deemed to have been used to make a charitable contribution [§ 643(a)(5)].

***Personal Exemption.*** The estate's or trust's personal exemption is not included in the calculation of DNI [§ 643(a)(2)].

***Distribution Deduction.*** DNI is computed without taking into account the distribution deduction [§ 643(a)(1)].

***Capital Gains.*** Capital gains are not automatically included in DNI. However, they can be included if (i) the gain is allocated to income in the accounts of the estate or trust or by notice to the beneficiaries under the governing instrument or local law, (ii) the gain is allocated to principal and is actually distributed to the beneficiaries during the tax year, (iii) the gain is used to determine the amount that is distributed or required to be distributed, or (iv) charitable contributions are made out of the gain. Generally, in determining the amount of capital gain included in DNI, the exclusion for gain from the sale or exchange of qualified small business stock is not taken into account [§ 643(a)(3)].

***Capital Losses.*** Capital losses are excluded in figuring DNI unless they enter into the computation of any capital gain that is distributed or required to be distributed during the year [§ 643(a)(3)].

***Extraordinary Dividends.*** In the case of a simple trust, extraordinary dividends (whether in cash or in property) and taxable stock dividends are excluded from DNI if the fiduciary makes a good faith determination that they are allocable to principal under the governing instrument and local law [§ 643(a)(4)].

***Example of DNI Computation.***

Under the terms of the trust instrument, the income of a trust is required to be currently distributed to B during B's life. Capital gains are allocated to principal and all expenses are charged against principal. During the tax year, the trust has the following items of income and expenses:

| Dividends from domestic corporations | $ 30,000 |
|---|---|
| Extraordinary dividends allocated to principal by the trustee in good faith | $ 20,000 |
| Taxable interest | $ 10,000 |
| Tax-Exempt Interest | $ 10,000 |
| Long-term capital gains | $ 10,000 |
| Trustee's commissions and miscellaneous expenses allocated to principal | $  5,000 |

The "income" of the trust determined under § 643(b) (i.e., FAI) that is currently distributable to B is $50,000, consisting of (i) $30,000 of dividends, (ii) $10,000 of taxable interest, and (iii) $10,000 of tax-exempt interest. The trustee's commission and miscellaneous expenses allocated to tax-exempt interest is $1,000 (($10,000/ $50,000) × $5,000).

The trust's DNI is $45,000, computed as follows:

| Dividends from domestic corporations | | $ 30,000 |
|---|---|---|
| Taxable interest | | $ 10,000 |
| Nontaxable interest | $  10,000 | |
| Expenses allocated to tax-exempt interest | ($   1,000) | |
| | | $   9,000 |
| Total | | $ 49,000 |
| Expenses | ($5,000 − $1000 allocated to tax-exempt interest) | $   4,000 |
| DNI | | $ 45,000 |

### XVIII.A.6. Credits

[852 T.M., IV.C.5.; TPS ¶6120.]

In computing income tax liability, an estate or trust is generally entitled to the credits otherwise allowed to an individual [Reg. § 1.641(b)-1]. Generally, the credits are allocated between the trust or estate and the beneficiaries, in accordance with allocation of income.

*Foreign Tax Credit.* The foreign tax credit is allocated to beneficiaries based on their "proportionate share" of foreign taxes paid by the estate or trust [§ 901(b)(5)].

Some of the credits that an estate or trust may claim include:

- a credit for federal income tax withheld on wages and backup withholding [§ 31] (see IX.G.1.);
- the general business credit [§ 38(a)] (see IX.A.);
- the low-income housing credit [§ 42] (see IX.A.9.); and
- the foreign tax credit [§ 901] (see Chapter XX.).

Some of the credits that an estate or trust may not claim include:

- the credit for the elderly and the permanently and totally disabled [§ 22] (see IX.B.2.);
- the child tax credit [§ 24] (see IX.B.4.); and
- the earned income tax credit [§ 32] (see IX.G.4.).

### XVIII.A.7. Taxation of Simple Trusts

[852 T.M., V.E.; TPS ¶6110.02.D.]

The gross income of a simple trust is technically subject to income tax. However, because of the distribution deduction and the fact that a simple trust is required to distribute all of its income currently, simple trusts typically do not incur any income tax liability [§ 651, § 652]. Accordingly, the beneficiaries generally report the trust's ordinary income, net of deductions.

A simple trust is taxed on (i) ordinary income in excess of FAI, (ii) capital gains that are not a part of DNI, (iii) "phantom income," and (iv) receipts from other trusts and estates that are principal for accounting purposes, but income for tax purposes (often referred to as "trapping" distributions because income is trapped inside the trust). Phantom income is taxable income allocated, but not actually distributed, to the trust by another entity (e.g., a trust's share of S corporation or partnership income that is not actually distributed to the trust during the tax year); thus, the income is included in the trust's taxable income, but not in its accounting income.

A simple trust will have taxable income when its fiduciary accounting income (FAI) is less than its DNI, because the distribution deduction is limited to the lower of FAI or DNI [§ 651]. Thus, in such a situation, the distribution deduction will not carry out all of the DNI, leaving some DNI to be taxed to the simple trust. FAI will be less than DNI when charges against income for accounting purposes are greater than deductions allowed for income tax purposes.

### XVIII.A.7.a. Distribution Deduction

[852 T.M., V.E.1.; TPS ¶6110.02.D.]

Generally, a simple trust is entitled to a deduction for the amount of FAI it is required to distribute [§ 651]. If the trust's FAI exceeds its DNI for the tax year, the distribution deduction is limited to DNI. For this purpose, DNI does not include any net tax-exempt income [§ 651(b); Reg. § 1.651(b)-1].

---

**EXAMPLE:** A simple trust has $40,000 of dividend income and $2,000 of trustee's fees. The fees are charged one-half against income and one-half against principal. The fees are deductible for income tax purposes under § 212. The trust's distribution deduction is equal to $38,000, computed as follows:

| (1) FAI: | |
|---|---|
| Dividends | $ 40,000 |
| ½ of Trustee's Fee | ($ 1,000) |
| Total | $ 39,000 |
| (2) DNI: | |
| Dividends | $ 40,000 |
| Trustee's Fee | ($ 2,000) |
| Total | $ 38,000 |
| (3) § 651(b) DNI = | $ 38,000 |
| (4) § 651 Distribution Deduction = | $ 38,000 |

Because DNI ($38,000) is less than FAI ($39,000), the distribution deduction is limited to DNI.

---

### XVIII.A.7.b. Taxation of Beneficiary of Simple Trust

[852 T.M., V.E.2.; TPS ¶6130.01.]

In a simple trust, there is one tier of beneficiaries: those entitled to receive currently the trust's FAI for the year. The amount of trust income taxable to beneficiaries is the lesser of FAI or DNI (reduced by net tax-exempt income), whether or not the income is actually distributed by the trust [§ 652(a); Reg. § 1.652(a)-1]. If there is more than one income beneficiary, the income is apportioned between them in proportion to the FAI each is required to receive. Further, the character of the income (e.g., tax-exempt or capital gain) in the hands of the beneficiary is the same as the character in the hands of the trust. Finally, the income is included in the beneficiary's tax year that ends with or includes the end of the trust's year for the distribution.

### XVIII.A.7.b.(1) Allocation of Income

[852 T.M., V.E.3.; TPS ¶6130.01.B.4.]

Generally, income is allocated to beneficiaries in accordance with the terms of the trust or local law. Otherwise, classes of income are allocated to the beneficiaries in proportion to their inclusion in DNI. If an allocation has economic effect independent of its tax consequences, or if local law or the terms of the trust requires that different classes of trust income be allocated to different beneficiaries, then the allocation will be effective for determining the character of the income in the hands of the beneficiary [Reg. § 1.652(b)-2].

### XVIII.A.7.b.(2) Allocation of Deductions

[852 T.M., V.E.4.; TPS ¶6130.01.B.5.]

Generally, all of a simple trust's deductions, other than the capital loss deduction, indirectly accrue to the benefit of the beneficiary because the deductions reduce DNI. This is true even if the deductions are allocated to principal under state law.

*Direct Expenses*. Deductible items directly attributable to one class of income (e.g., rental income, royalties, etc) are allocated thereto [Reg. § 1.652(b)-3(a)]. If a direct expense exceeds the class of income to which it is attributable, the excess expense is treated as an indirect expense, subject to the limitations on passive activity losses if applicable. But, if the excess deduction is directly attributable to tax-exempt interest it cannot reduce any other income item [Reg. § 1.652(b)-3(d)].

*Indirect Expenses*. Indirect expenses are expenses that are not directly attributable to a specific class of income but are allocated to the trust as a whole. Examples include the trustee's compensation, fees for renting a safe-deposit box, and state income and personal property taxes [Reg. § 1.652(b)-3(c)]. Indirect expenses may be allocated by the trustee to any class or classes of income [Reg. § 1.652(b)-3(b)]. However, a portion must be allocated to any tax-exempt income.

### XVIII.A.7.c. When Distribution Is Taxable to Income Beneficiary

[852 T.M., V.E.6.; TPS ¶6130.01.B.]

The tax year for simple trusts is the calendar year [§ 644(a)]. The amount of income for the tax year required to be distributed currently by a simple trust is included in the gross income of the beneficiaries to whom the income is required to be distributed, whether it is distributed or not [§ 652(a)]. In most cases, the income beneficiary also is on the calendar year, so that he or she will have gross income in the calendar year in which the income is required to be distributed. If the tax year of a beneficiary is different from that of the trust (e.g., if the beneficiary uses a fiscal year), the amount that the beneficiary is required to include in gross income is based upon the amount of income of the trust for any tax year or years of the trust ending within or with the beneficiary's tax year [§ 652(c)].

### XVIII.A.7.d. Death of Income Beneficiary

[852 T.M., V.E.7.; TPS ¶6130.02.B.]

When a beneficiary of a simple trust dies during a trust year, problems may arise in determining whether the trust income should be reported on the beneficiary's final return or on the estate's income tax return. In some cases, the beneficiary will have received an actual income distribution before death. In other cases, the beneficiary's estate may have the right to receive a distribution of the trust's income for the year, including the income accrued for that year before the beneficiary's death.

The final income tax return of a cash method beneficiary includes gross income resulting from trust income actually distributed to the beneficiary for the trust's tax year, even though the trust year will not end with or within the beneficiary's final tax year. The balance of the income required to be distributed by the trust, but not actually distributed to a cash-basis beneficiary, will be income in respect of a decedent (IRD), to be reported when it is paid to the estate or its successor. The estate will report the IRD when it is distributed to the estate, which may be later than when it is required to be distributed [Reg. § 1.652(c)-2].

### XVIII.A.7.e. Simple Trust Case Study

A trust has two beneficiaries, J and B, to which it must distribute all income currently. J is entitled to 1/4 of the income, and B is entitled to 3/4. Aside from any trust distributions, the only other items of income that J and B have are wages from employment, totaling $75,000 and $90,000, respectively. The trust has the following items:

- $20,000 of taxable interest;
- $500,000 from the sale of a commercial property used in an active trade/business and purchased 7 years ago for $400,000;
- $70,000 of rents;
- $6,000 of property maintenance expenses;
- $10,000 of interest from municipal bonds; and
- $10,000 of trustee fees (allocable ½ to income and ½ to principal).

| Item | FAI | Gross Income | Tentative Taxable Income | § 643(a) DNI | § 651(b) DNI |
|------|-----|--------------|--------------------------|--------------|--------------|
| Taxable Interest | $ 20,000 | $ 20,000 | $ 20,000 | $ 20,000 | $ 20,000 |
| Rent | $ 70,000 | $ 70,000 | $ 70,000 | $ 70,000 | $ 70,000 |
| Municipal Bonds | $ 10,000 | X | X | $ 9,000** | X |
| Long-term Capital Gains | X | $100,000 | $100,000 | X | X |
| Trustee Fee | ($ 5,000) | X | ($ 9,000)* | ($ 9,000) | ($ 9,000) |
| Property Maintenance Expense | ($ 6,000) | X | ($ 6,000) | ($ 6,000) | ($ 6,000) |
| Personal Exemption | X | X | ($300) | X | X |
| Total | $ 89,000 | $190,000 | $174,700 | $ 84,000 | $ 75,000 |

> \*Part of the trustee fee is allocable to tax-exempt interest and, thus, is not available for purposes of calculating tentative taxable income ((\$10,000 tax-exempt interest/\$100,000 total income) × \$10,000 trustee fee).
> \*\*\$10,000 tax-exempt interest − \$1,000 trustee fee allocated thereto.

*Note:* The \$100,000 of capital gain is excluded from DNI because it was allocated to principal and not distributed.

The distribution deduction for this trust is \$75,000, because FAI > § 651(b) DNI.

*Computation of the Trust's Taxable Income.*

| Tentative Taxable Income | \$ 174,700 |
|---|---|
| Distribution Deduction | (\$ 75,000) |
| Taxable Income | \$ 99,700* |

*This represents the \$100,000 of capital gains taxable to the trust less the trust's \$300 personal exemption.

*Computation of the Beneficiaries' Taxable Income.*

| | J | B |
|---|---|---|
| Taxable Interest | \$5,000 (1/4 × \$20,000) | \$15,000 (3/4 × \$20,000) |
| Rent | \$16,000 [(1/4 × \$70,000) − (1/4 × \$6,000)] | \$48,000 [(3/4 × \$70,000) − (3/4 × \$6,000)] |
| Municipal Bonds (tax-exempt) | \$1,250 [(1/4 × \$10,000) − (1/4 × \$5,000)] | \$3,750 [(3/4 × \$10,000) − (3/4 × \$5,000)] |
| Total Allocation of FAI | \$22,250 (1/4 × \$89,000) | \$66,750 (3/4 × \$89,000) |
| Total Taxable Income | \$21,000 | \$63,000 |

### Net Investment Income Tax Consequences.

A trust is subject to an additional 3.8% tax on the lesser of (i) its undistributed net investment income, or (ii) the amount by which its AGI exceeds the § 1411 threshold amount (\$12,150 for 2014, \$12,300 for 2015) [Rev. Proc. 2013-35, 2013-47 I.R.B. 537, § 3.01, Rev. Proc. 2014-61, 2014-47 I.R.B. 860, § 3.01] (see XVIII.E.). Because the trust does not have any undistributed net investment income, it will not incur any net investment income tax liability.

An individual is subject to an additional 3.8% tax on the lesser of (i) net investment income, or (ii) the amount by which the individual's modified AGI exceeds the § 1411 threshold amount (\$250,000 for married individuals filing jointly or surviving spouses, \$125,000 for married individuals filing separately, and \$200,000 for single individuals and heads of household) (see Chapter X.). Although rent and taxable interest are both items of net investment income, because neither J nor B has modified AGI over \$200,000, neither will incur net investment income tax liability.

### XVIII.A.8. Taxation of Complex Trusts and Estates

### XVIII.A.8.a. Introduction

[852 T.M., V.F.; TPS ¶6130.02.A.]

A complex trust is any trust that is not a simple trust. Thus, a complex trust is a trust (i) that is not required to distribute all its income currently, (ii) where amounts other than income are paid, credited, or required to be distributed, or (iii) where amounts are paid, permanently set aside, or used for charitable purposes. All estates are taxed as complex trusts [Reg. § 1.661(a)-1].

For a complex trust and any estate, a tier system is used to distinguish between (i) mandatory distributions of current FAI ("first tier"), and (ii) all other distributions, including distributions of principal, accumulated income, and discretionary distributions of current income ("second tier") [§ 661(a), § 662(a)]. The effect of the statutory definition of a second tier distribution is that any distribution from an estate or trust can carry out income to the beneficiary even though, for fiduciary accounting purposes, the distribution is of corpus.

First-tier distributions include any FAI that must be distributed currently. Income is required to be distributed currently if the will or trust requires income to be distributed at least annually, regardless of whether it is actually distributed. In the case of an intestate estate, income must be distributed currently if state law so provides.

There are a number of special rules that apply to complex trusts and estates, including the tier classification for distributions, the rules for distributions of specific sums or property, the timing rules for distributions, the separate share rule, and the rules for distributions in kind and charitable trusts.

### XVIII.A.8.b. Distribution Deduction

[852 T.M., V.F.2.; TPS ¶6130.02.C.]

Generally, a complex trust or estate is allowed a distribution deduction for all amounts paid, credited, or required to be distributed, with two limitations [§ 661]. First, the distribution deduction cannot exceed the trust's DNI. Second, no deduction is allowed for a distribution of net tax-exempt income. In essence, the computation of the distribution deduction for simple trusts and complex trusts is similar. However, the specific computations are different.

There are three basic categories of distributions:

1. Gifts or bequests of specific sums of money or property payable in no more than three installments, which are excluded from income because they qualify as gifts or devises [§ 663, § 102]. These do not carry out DNI of an estate or trust and do not factor into the calculation of a complex trust's or estate's distribution deduction [Reg. § 1.663(a)-1].

2. Distributions of FAI required to be distributed currently (i.e., first-tier distributions), which carry out DNI first, dollar-for-dollar.

3. All other distributions (i.e., second-tier distributions), such as (i) mandatory distributions of principal or accumulated income, (ii) discretionary distributions of income or principal, and (iii) mandatory annuity distributions paid out of principal or required to be paid out of principal [Reg. § 1.662(a)-3(b)]. These carry out any DNI remaining after the first-tier distributions.

### XVIII.A.8.c. Satisfaction of Legal Obligations of Grantor, Trustee, or Beneficiary

[852 T.M., V.F.3.; TPS ¶6130.02.]

When the trustee or another person has the discretion to make a distribution to a beneficiary to satisfy the grantor's obligation to support or maintain the beneficiary, the distribution may be taxable to the grantor (or another person) under the grantor trust rules (see XVIII.B.). A distribution is taxable to the grantor under the grantor trust rules if (i) the grantor has the discretion to satisfy his/her legal obligations without the consent of an adverse party, (ii) the trustee is required to satisfy the grantor's legal obligation to support or maintain another, or (iii) the trustee has discretion to satisfy the grantor's obligation to support his/her spouse [§ 677(a)].

If the trustee has the discretion to make a distribution for the support or maintenance of a nonspousal beneficiary whom the grantor is legally obligated to support, the grantor will not be taxed on trust income unless the trustee exercises the discretion and actually makes a distribution. Then, how and when the grantor is taxed will depend on whether the distribution is made from current FAI, from principal, or from accumulated FAI. If the distribution is made from current FAI, the grantor trust rules apply and the grantor is treated as owning that portion of the trust [§ 677(b)].

If the distribution to satisfy the grantor's nonspousal support obligation is made from principal or accumulated FAI, the grantor is taxed as a second-tier beneficiary under § 662 [§ 677(b)]. In this case, DNI will only reflect items of gross income and deductions not attributable to the grantor under the grantor trust rules.

Similar rules apply if a trustee, other than the grantor, has the discretion to make distributions that satisfy the trustee's obligation to support or maintain a beneficiary. If the trustee exercises his or her discretion, the trustee is treated as the owner of the income of the trust to the extent the distribution is paid out of FAI [§ 678(a), § 678(c)]. To the extent the distribution is paid out of principal or accumulated FAI, the trustee is treated as a second-tier beneficiary [§ 678(a), § 678(b); Reg. § 1.662(a)-3(b)].

### XVIII.A.8.d. Allowances for Support of Surviving Spouse or Dependents; Elective Share

[852 T.M., V.F.4.; TPS ¶6130.02.]

An allowance payable from an estate to a surviving spouse or family member for support can qualify as a first-tier distribution if required to be paid out of income. Additionally, if the allowance is required to be paid either out of income or principal, it will be treated as a first-tier distribution to the extent the estate's FAI was not paid, credited, or required to be distributed to other beneficiaries [Reg. § 1.662(a)-2(c)]. In all other cases, the allowance qualifies as another amount properly paid, credited, or required to be distributed (i.e., a second-tier distribution) [Reg. § 1.662(a)-3(b)].

For purposes of determining the amount of DNI and applying § 661(a) and § 662(a), the elective share is treated as a separate share (see XVIII.A.8.g.) of the estate [§ 663(c)]. Each share will calculate its DNI based on its portion of the estate's gross income that is included in the estate's DNI, plus its portion of any applicable deductions. The allocation of gross income is made in accordance with the amount of income to which the separate share is entitled under the governing instrument and local law. Thus, only income that is allocable to a surviving spouse's elective share for a tax year and distributed to the spouse in satisfaction of the elective share is treated as a distribution subject to § 661 and § 662. Therefore, a surviving spouse is taxed on the estate's income earned during administration only to the extent of the spouse's right to share in that income under state law.

### XVIII.A.8.e. 65-Day Rule — § 663(b) Election for Trusts and Estates

[852 T.M., V.F.5.; TPS ¶6130.03.B.]

For discretionary distributions, whether of income or principal, the year of payment by the estate or trust will generally be the year of deduction and will set the year for determining inclusion of the payment. But if, within the first 65 days of the tax year of a trust or estate, an amount is properly paid or credited, and if the fiduciary makes a proper election, the distribution is treated as having been made on the last day of the preceding tax year [§ 663(b)]. The election must be made no later than the deadline for filing Form 1041 for the tax year in which the distribution is treated as having been made, plus extensions [Reg. § 1.663(b)-2(a)(1), (2)].

If the estate or trust is required to file Form 1041, the election must be made on the return under "Other Information." If a return is not required, the election is made by filing a statement with the IRS where the return would otherwise be filed [Reg. § 1.663(b)-2(a)(2)].

### XVIII.A.8.f. Taxation of Distributions to Beneficiaries

[852 T.M., V.F.6.; TPS ¶.6130.02.B.]

Beneficiaries are taxed on distributions from complex trusts and estates. However, the amount of income taxable to beneficiaries is limited to the trust's or estate's DNI [§ 662(b)]. There is a tier system that acts to prioritize the allocation of DNI to beneficiaries. DNI is initially allocated to first-tier beneficiaries based on their share of FAI. Any residual DNI is allocated to second-tier beneficiaries up to their proportionate share of distributions.

### XVIII.A.8.f.(1) First-Tier Distributions

[852 T.M., V.F.6.a.; TPS ¶6130.02.B.2.]

The amount of FAI required to be distributed currently to a beneficiary is included in the beneficiary's gross income, whether distributed or not [§ 662(a)(1)]. If the amount of FAI that must be distributed currently exceeds DNI (computed without the charitable deduction) for the year, then each beneficiary includes only his/her pro rata share of DNI in gross income ((Amount of FAI Required to be Distributed to Beneficiary/Total FAI) × DNI) [Reg. § 1.662(a)-2(b)].

---

**EXAMPLE:** A trust has $30,000 of FAI and $12,000 of DNI. One-third of FAI is to be distributed to J and two-thirds to B. If the trust is required to distribute all of its income, then J will have gross income of $4,000 (1/3 × $12,000) and B will have gross income of $8,000 (2/3 × $12,000). If the trust is required to distribute one-fourth of its FAI currently ($7,500), then each beneficiary would have gross income in the amount of income required to be distributed to him or her, subject to the characterization rules. J would have $2,500 of gross income (1/3 × $7,500) and B would have $5,000 of gross income (2/3 × $7,500). There would be $4,500 of DNI ($12,000 − $7,500) left to be allocated to any second-tier beneficiaries.

---

### XVIII.A.8.f.(2) Second-Tier Distributions

[852 T.M., V.F.2.d.; TPS ¶6130.02.B.3.]

All other amounts properly paid, credited, or required to be distributed currently are included in the beneficiary's gross income [§ 662(a)(2)]. To the extent first-tier distributions equal or exceed DNI, second-tier distributions are not included in the beneficiary's gross income and are treated as nontaxable gifts or bequests [§ 102]. If first-tier distributions are less than DNI, then the residual DNI is allocated to the second-tier beneficiaries (up to the applicable value of their distributions). The second-tier beneficiaries will have gross income to the extent of their proportionate share of the DNI that was not allocated to the first-tier beneficiaries. If there are no first-tier distributions, second-tier distributions are included in a beneficiary's gross income to the extent of his or her proportionate share of DNI, based on the percentage of second-tier distributions that the beneficiary received.

If second-tier distributions exceed the remaining DNI, the DNI is allocated pro rata among the second-tier beneficiaries based on the respective amounts they received. This allocation is made among all second-tier beneficiaries, even to a beneficiary who is not entitled to share in the earnings of the estate or trust, and even if the DNI allocated to a beneficiary exceeds that beneficiary's share of the estate's or trust's income.

---

**EXAMPLE:** A trust is required to distribute all income ($30,000) currently, one-third to J and two-thirds to B. The trust has DNI of $12,000. In addition, the trustee has discretion to distribute principal to J and B. The trustee exercises its discretion to distribute $15,000 of principal to J and $15,000 of principal to B. The trust has no tax-exempt interest. In this case, J and B would have $4,000 and $8,000 of income, respectively, based on their share of FAI. Because the first-tier distributions carried out all of the trust's DNI, the $15,000 distribution of principal to both J and B will be treated as a non-taxable gift.

---

### XVIII.A.8.f.(3) When Are Distributions Taxable to Beneficiaries?

[851 T.M., V.F.6.; TPS ¶6130.02.B.]

If a beneficiary and an estate or trust have the same tax year, the gross income resulting from distributions to the beneficiary for that year will be included in the beneficiary's gross income for that year. If their tax years differ, the beneficiary will have gross income for its tax year that includes the last day of the tax year of the estate or trust [§ 662(c)].

### XVIII.A.8.f.(4) Final Return of Deceased Beneficiary

[852 T.M., V.F.6.d(2); TPS ¶6130.03.D.]

When the income beneficiary of a trust dies, his or her final income tax return includes his or her share of the trust income before his or her death. The gross income for the last tax year of a beneficiary on the cash basis method of accounting includes only the income actually distributed to the beneficiary before his or her death. Income required to be distributed by the trust, but actually distributed to the deceased beneficiary's estate, is included in the estate's gross income as an item of IRD (see XVIII.F.).

### XVIII.A.8.g. Separate Share Rule

[852 T.M., V.I.; TPS ¶6130.03.C.]

For the sole purpose of determining DNI, where a single trust or estate has more than one beneficiary, substantially separate and independent shares of different beneficiaries are treated as separate trusts or estates [§ 663(c)]. The separate share rule may apply in situations where separate and independent accounts are not maintained for each share and where no physical segregation of assets is made or required. Separate share treatment is not elective [Reg. § 1.663(c)-1].

A surviving spouse's statutory elective share of a decedent's estate is typically treated as a separate share. A revocable trust that elects to be treated as part of a decedent's estate is a separate share and may itself contain other separate shares. Although a specific bequest is not a separate share, income on bequeathed property if the specific bequest recipient is entitled to the income is considered a separate share. Further, a pecuniary formula bequest is a separate share (i) if it is entitled to income and to share in appreciation and depreciation, or (ii) if it must be paid or credited in no more than three installments [Reg. § 1.663(c)-4(a), § 1.663(c)-4(b)].

A share with multiple beneficiaries may be a separate share and the same person may be a beneficiary of more than one separate share [Reg. § 1.663(c)-3(c), § 1.663(c)-4(c)].

***Separate Shares and DNI***. If separate shares are created, DNI is subdivided per share, so that the amount of gross income resulting from distributions to a beneficiary of a share is determined by the DNI allocated to such shares. In addition, the trust or estate distribution deduction is allocated per share, based on the respective distributions and DNI per share [Reg. § 1.663(c)-2(b)].

### XVIII.A.8.h. Complex Trust Case Study

J and B are beneficiaries of a trust that requires that one-half of the income be paid annually to J and permits the trustee to make discretionary distributions of principal to J or B. Aside from any trust distributions, the only other items of income that J and B have are wages from employment, totaling $75,000 and $90,000, respectively. Both are single. The trust has the following items:

- $20,000 of taxable interest;
- $500,000 from the sale of a commercial property used in an active trade/business and purchased 7 years ago for $400,000;
- $70,000 of rents;
- $6,000 of property maintenance expenses; and
- $10,000 of trustee fees (allocable ½ to income and ½ to principal).

During 2014, the trustee pays one-half of the income to J and exercised its discretion to pay $50,000 of principal to both J and B.

| Item | FAI | Gross Income | Tentative Taxable Income | DNI |
|---|---|---|---|---|
| Taxable Interest | $ 20,000 | $ 20,000 | $ 20,000 | $ 20,000 |
| Rent | $ 70,000 | $ 70,000 | $ 70,000 | $ 70,000 |
| Long-term Capital Gains | X | $ 100,000 | $ 100,000 | X |
| Trustee Fee | ($ 5,000) | X | ($ 10,000) | ($ 10,000) |
| Property Maintenance Expense | ($ 6,000) | X | ($ 6,000) | ($ 6,000) |
| Personal Exemption | X | X | ($ 100) | X |
| Total | $ 79,000 | $ 190,000 | $ 173,900 | $ 74,000 |

*Note:* The $100,000 of capital gain is excluded from DNI because it was allocated to principal and not distributed.

For a complex trust (or estate), the distribution deduction is the sum of the first-tier and second-tier distributions, limited by DNI. The distribution deduction for this trust is $75,000, because DNI ($74,000) < actual amount distributed to J and B, i.e., the sum of the first-tier and second-tier distributions ($39,500 + $50,000 + $50,000 = $139,500).

*Computation of the Trust's Taxable Income.*

| Tentative Taxable Income | $ 173,900 |
|---|---|
| Distribution Deduction | ($ 74,000) |
| Taxable Income | $ 99,900* |

*This represents the $100,000 of capital gains taxable to the trust less the trust's $100 personal exemption.

*Computation of the Beneficiaries' Taxable Income.*

|  | J | B |
|---|---|---|
| **First-Tier*** | | |
| Rent** | $70,000 − $6,000 − $5,000 = $59,000 <br> $39,500 × 59/74 =$31,493 | N/A |
| Taxable Interest*** | $20,000 − $5,000 = $15,000 <br> $39,500 × 15/74 = $8,007 | N/A |
| **Second-Tier**** | | |
| Rent | $17,250 × 59/74 = $13,753 | $17,250 × 59/74 = $13,753 |
| Taxable Interest | $17,250 × 15/74 = $3,497 | $17,250 × 15/74 = $3,497 |
| Nontaxable Gift***** | $50,000 − $17,250 = $32,750 | $50,000 − $17,250 = $32,750 |

*First-tier distributions carry out DNI to the extent of the lesser of the distribution amount or total DNI.

**The required distribution of FAI to J ($79,000 × ½ = $39,500) includes both taxable interest and rent. To determine how much of each class of income makes up J's first-tier distribution, first determine the percentage of DNI represented by each. In 2014, the trust had $70,000 of rent. There are two deductions that can be taken against rent: property maintenance fees ($6,000) and part of the trustee fee (in this case, assume that the trustee allocates ½ of the trustee fee ($5,000) to each rent and taxable interest). In situations where items of income included in DNI are taxed at different rates, it is beneficial to exhaust allowable deductions on the income items that are taxed at the highest rate first, the next highest rate second, and so on. Because rent makes up 59/74 of DNI, we multiply $39,500 by that fraction to arrive at the amount of rent that is included in J's first-tier distribution.

***In 2014, the trust had $20,000 of taxable interest. There is one deduction that can be taken against rent: part of the trustee fee. Because taxable interest makes up 15/74 of DNI, we multiply $39,500 by that fraction to arrive at the amount of taxable interest that is included in J's first-tier distribution.

****Second-tier distributions also carry out DNI, but only if there is some left over after taking into account the first-tier distributions. In this case, there is $34,500 of DNI remaining ($74,000 − $39,500). Because J and B each received $50,000 distributions of principal, ½ of the residual DNI is allocated to each. To determine the character of the second tier distributions, multiply each beneficiary's DNI allocation ($34,500/2 = $17,250) by the proportion that represents the percentage of DNI made up by each class of income (59/74 for rent, 15/74 for taxable income).

*****Because second tier distributions exceeded DNI, the excess is treated as a nontaxable gift. To determine the amount that is distributed to J and B as a nontaxable gift, subtract from the total amount of the second-tier distributions ($50,000 each) the amount of residual DNI allocated thereto ($17,250 each).

*Net Investment Income Tax Consequence.* A trust is subject to an additional 3.8% tax on the lesser of (i) its undistributed net investment income, or (ii) the amount by which its AGI exceeds the § 1411 threshold amount ($12,150 for 2014, $12,300 for 2015) [Rev. Proc. 2013-35, 2013-47 I.R.B. 537, § 3.01, Rev. Proc. 2014-61, 2014-47 I.R.B. 860, § 3.01]. Because the trust does not have any undistributed net investment income, it will not incur any net investment income tax liability.

Single individuals are potentially subject to the net investment income tax if their modified AGI exceeds $200,000 (see Chapter X.). Although rent and taxable interest are both items of net investment income, because neither J nor B has modified AGI over $200,000, neither will incur net investment income tax liability.

### XVIII.A.9. Distributions of Non-Cash Assets

[852 T.M., V.G.; TPS ¶6120.04.C.]

An estate or complex trust may make distributions in cash or in kind (i.e., with non-cash assets). Distributions in kind can arise in various contexts, including:

- A beneficiary may be entitled to receive a distribution of income, but instead may consent to a distribution of other property.
- A beneficiary may be entitled to receive a distribution of specific property and may receive a distribution of that specific property.
- A beneficiary may be entitled to receive a distribution of specific property and may receive different property instead.
- A beneficiary may be entitled to receive a certain amount of cash or assets, payable out of income or principal, and may receive a distribution in kind.
- A trustee may exercise a discretionary power to distribute principal, and make a distribution in kind.

*Valuation of Asset for Computing Distribution Deduction and Distribution Amounts.* If a distribution is made in kind and gain or loss is recognized by reason of the distribution, by election or otherwise, the fair market value of the asset will be used for computing the distribution deduction. On the other hand, if gain or loss is not recognized, the adjusted basis of the asset immediately before the distribution will be used [§ 643(e)(2)].

*Basis to Beneficiary.* The beneficiary's basis in the property distributed in kind by an estate or trust is the adjusted basis of the property in the hands of the estate or trust immediately before the distribution, adjusted for any gain or loss recognized to the estate or trust on the distribution [§ 643(e)(1)].

### XVIII.A.9.a. Gain or Loss on Distributions in Kind

[852 T.M., V.G.1.; TPS ¶6120.04.C.]

An estate or complex trust recognizes gain or loss on a distribution of property in kind to a beneficiary only in the following situations:

1. The distribution satisfies the beneficiary's right to receive either (i) a specific dollar amount (whether payable in cash, in unspecified property, or both), or (ii) a specific property other than the property distributed [Reg. § 1.661(a)-2(f); *Kenan v. Commissioner*, 114 F.2d 217 (2d Cir. 1940)]; or
2. An election is made to recognize the gain or loss on the estate's income tax return [§ 643(e)(3)].

Generally, the gain or loss is the difference between the fair market value of the property at the time of distribution and the estate's basis in the property [§ 1001].

### XVIII.A.9.a.(1) "Kenan" Gain/Loss

[852 T.M., V.G.1.; TPS ¶6120.04.C.]

The fiduciary of an estate or trust may have the discretion to satisfy a pecuniary obligation by distributing non-cash assets. The distribution of appreciated (or depreciated) non-cash assets by an estate or trust in satisfaction of a pecuniary obligation creates a realization event for the estate or trust [Reg. § 1.661(a)-2(f)); *Kenan v. Commissioner*]. That is, the difference between the trust's basis in the property and its fair market value is included in determining the trust's taxable income. No part of the distribution carries out DNI; thus, no part of the distribution is taxable to the beneficiary. The beneficiary's basis in the distributed property is the property's fair market value at the date of distribution.

### XVIII.A.9.a.(2) Specific Gifts/Bequests

[852 T.M., V.C.; TPS ¶6130.03.A.]

A specific gift/bequest is a gift/bequest of (i) a specific sum of money, or (ii) specifically-identified property. For income tax purposes, an amount that can be paid or credited only from the income of the estate or trust is not considered a specific gift/bequest. A specific gift/bequest of money or property paid or credited in not more than three installments is not considered an amount properly paid to a beneficiary for purposes of determining either the estate's or trust's distribution deduction or the beneficiary's gross income [§ 663(a)]. As such, the amount of a specific gift/bequest is neither (i) deductible by trust, nor (ii) taxable to the beneficiary.

### XVIII.A.9.a.(3) Election to Recognize Gain or Loss on Distributions to Beneficiaries

[852 T.M., V.G.2.; TPS ¶6120.04.C.3.]

Generally, a trust or estate may elect to recognize gain or loss on distributions of non-cash assets to beneficiaries as if the property had been sold to the beneficiary at its fair market value [§ 643(e)(3)]. Although § 643(e)(3) states that a fiduciary may elect to recognize loss from a distribution to a beneficiary, the loss will be disallowed under the related-party rules [§ 267]. However, the related party rules do not disallow the recognition of loss when a distribution is in discharge of a pecuniary bequest (see XVIII.A.9.a.(1)).

If the election is made, the trust or estate recognizes gain and adjusts its basis in the asset accordingly. Because any gain recognized by reason of the estate's or trust's § 643(e)(3) election is taxable to the estate or trust, the gain is not taken into account for purposes of computing DNI. Receipt of property with built-in gain or loss is not a realization event for the beneficiary; that is, the beneficiary realizes no gain or loss with respect to the property distributed in kind.

If the fiduciary elects to recognize gain or loss, the election applies to all noncash distributions during the tax year, except charitable distributions and specific bequests [§ 643(e)(3)(B)]. Once made, the election may be revoked only with the consent of the IRS [§ 643(e)(3)]. To make the election, the fiduciary must report the transaction on Form 8949, *Sales and Other Dispositions of Capital Assets*, and/or Form 1041, Schedule D, as applicable, and check the box on line 7 in the "Other Information" section of Form 1041.

### XVIII.A.9.b. Inclusion of Gain or Loss in DNI

[852 T.M., V.G.3.; TPS ¶6120.03.B.]

A gain or loss recognized by a trust or estate on a distribution is reflected in DNI where:

- the gain or loss is ordinary (i.e., not from the sale of a capital asset); or
- the gain or loss is from the sale of exchange of a capital asset in the year of the estate's or trust's termination (in this situation, capital losses are taken into account to the extent of capital gains).

Capital gains realized in a year other than the year of the estate's or trust's termination are a part of DNI if the capital gains are allocated to income, or if the capital gains are allocated to principal and actually paid, credited, or required to be distributed. Losses from the sale or exchange of capital assets are excluded from the calculation of DNI, except to the extent such losses are taken into account in determining capital gains during the tax year [§ 643(a)(3); Reg. § 1.643(a)-3].

## XVIII.B. Taxation of Grantor Trusts

### XVIII.B.1. Grantor Trust Rules

[819 T.M., I., III.A.1.; TPS ¶6120.05.A., .05.B.]

To the extent that a trust is treated as a grantor trust, it is ignored as a taxpayer and the person who is deemed to be the "owner" of the trust is required to report the income, deductions, and credits of the trust on his or her own federal income tax return [§ 671-§ 678]. The grantor trust rules apply if the rights or powers of a person are sufficient to deem the person the owner of the trust. Generally, the grantor trust rules apply to the person who creates (or "settles") the trust (i.e., the grantor). However, under § 678, a person other than the grantor may be treated as the owner of a trust. The various grantor trust rules are discussed below.

***Spousal Attribution.*** The grantor is treated as holding any power or interest held by his or her spouse [§ 672(e)].

***Trusts Established by Foreign Grantors.*** A trust (foreign or domestic) is treated as a grantor trust only if the person deemed to own the trust is a U.S. citizen or resident or a domestic corporation [§ 672(f)(1)].

***Assignment of Income Doctrine.*** Income is taxed to the person who earns it (see I.B.1.). An individual taxpayer cannot assign income previously earned to a trust in an attempt to shift the income tax responsibility to the trust (or to the trust beneficiaries). Thus, for example, a grantor will be taxed on future income that the grantor assigns to an irrevocable trust to which the grantor trust rules do not apply [Reg. § 1.671-1(c)].

### XVIII.B.2. Reversionary Interests

[819 T.M., V.; TPS ¶6120.05.D.]

The grantor of a trust is treated as the owner of the portion of a trust in which the grantor (or, in certain cases, the grantor's spouse) has a reversionary interest in the trust's principal or income, the value of which (at the time of the transfer to trust) exceeds 5% of the value of the portion of the trust that the grantor owns [§ 673(a)]. Whether the reversionary interest is beyond the 5% threshold is determined by reference to IRS actuarial tables [§ 7520].

***Lineal Descendant Exception.*** Where a lineal descendant of the grantor holds all the present interests in any portion of a trust, the 5% limitation rule does not apply if the grantor's reversionary interest in that trust is to take effect only by reason of the death of the beneficiary before reaching age 21 [§ 673(b)].

### XVIII.B.3.  Powers that Do Not Trigger Grantor Trust Status

#### XVIII.B.3.a. Power to Control Beneficial Enjoyment

[819 T.M., VI.; TPS ¶6120.05.E.]

A grantor is taxable as the owner of a trust or portion of a trust over which the grantor or a nonadverse person (or both) has the power to dispose of the beneficial enjoyment of either the trust's income or principal, exercisable without an adverse party's approval or consent [§ 674(a); Reg. § 1.674(a)-1(a)]. However, several delineated powers can be exercised without causing the grantor to be taxable as the owner of the trust [§ 674(b)]:

- the power to apply income in support of a dependent;
- a power affecting beneficial enjoyment after the occurrence of an event;
- certain testamentary powers;
- the power to determine beneficial enjoyment of charitable beneficiaries;
- the power to distribute principal;
- the power to withhold income temporarily or during a disability; or
- the power to allocate between principal and income.

#### XVIII.B.3.b. Powers Exercisable by Independent Trustee

[819 T.M., VI.D.; TPS ¶.6120.05.G.]

Certain powers that are solely exercisable by an independent trustee do not cause the grantor to be treated as the owner of the trust. An independent trustee can exercise the power to:

- distribute, apportion, or accumulate income to or for a beneficiary; and
- pay out principal to or for a beneficiary.

The power must be solely exercisable by a trustee or trustees, none of whom is the grantor and no more than half of whom are related or subordinate parties. This permits an independent trustee to allocate income without restriction.

This exception is not available where the grantor (or certain other individuals) has a power to add one or more beneficiaries to the class of beneficiaries designated to receive the trust income or principal, unless the power is to provide for after-born or after-adopted children [§ 674(c)].

#### XVIII.B.3.c. Power to Allocate Income Limited by a Standard

[819 T.M., VI.E.; TPS ¶6120.05.F.]

A grantor is not taxable as the trust's owner merely because a nonadverse trustee or group of co-trustees holds a power to distribute, apportion, or accumulate income to or for a beneficiary or beneficiaries, if the power is limited by a reasonably definite external standard set forth in the trust instrument [§ 674(d)]. The exception to grantor trust treatment for this permissible trustee power is not available if the grantor or the grantor's spouse (if living with the grantor) is a trustee; however, unlike the § 674(c) exception (see XVIII.B.3.b.), any of the trustees may be related or subordinate to the grantor. A clearly measurable standard under which the holder of a power is legally accountable is deemed a reasonably definite standard for this purpose. [Reg. § 1.674(d)-1].

This exception does not apply if any person has a power to add a beneficiary to receive the trust's income or principal, unless the power is to provide for after-born or after-adopted children [§ 674(d); Reg. § 1.674(d)-2(b)].

### XVIII.B.4. Powers that May Cause Trust to Not Meet Grantor Trust Exceptions in § 674

#### XVIII.B.4.a. Power to Remove Trustee

[819 T.M., VI.F.; TPS ¶6120.05.H.]

If the grantor holds an unrestricted power to remove, substitute, or add trustees and to designate any person (including the grantor) as the replacement trustee, then the trustees' powers are deemed to be exercisable by the grantor for purposes of determining grantor trust status. This can cause the trust to not fall within one of the exceptions listed in XVIII.B.3., and for the grantor to be treated as the owner of the trust income. However, a power in the grantor to remove or discharge an independent trustee on the condition that he or she substitute another independent trustee will not cause the grantor to be treated as the income owner. Further, a power in the grantor to appoint a new independent trustee should not cause grantor trust treatment [Reg. § 1.674(d)-2].

#### XVIII.B.4.b. Power to Add Beneficiaries

[819 T.M., VI.D., VI.C.5.c.; TPS ¶6120.05.I.]

The exceptions to the grantor trust rules listed in XVIII.B.3. are not available where the grantor has a power to add to the beneficiaries designated to receive the trust's income or principal (unless the power is to provide for after-born or after-adopted children) [Reg. § 1.674(d)-2(b)]. This limitation does not apply to (i) a power held by a beneficiary to substitute other beneficiaries to succeed to his/her interest in the trust, or (ii) a power to control the beneficial enjoyment that is exercisable only by will.

### XVIII.B.5. Administrative Powers

[819 T.M., VII.; TPS ¶6120.05.J.]

The grantor is treated as the owner of any portion of a trust if, under the terms of the trust instrument or circumstances attendant to its operation, administrative control is exercisable primarily for the benefit of the grantor rather than for the beneficiaries. There are four categories of administrative controls that, if not prohibited, can trigger grantor trust status [§ 675]:

1. power exercisable by the grantor or a nonadverse party that enables the grantor to purchase, exchange, or otherwise deal with or dispose of the trust's income or principal for less than adequate consideration;

2. power exercisable by the grantor or a nonadverse party that enables the grantor to borrow (directly or indirectly) trust income or principal without adequate interest or security;

3. actual borrowing of trust assets without full repayment during the tax year (this rule will not apply if the terms of the loan provide for adequate interest and security, and the loan is made by a trustee other than (i) the grantor, or (ii) a related or subordinate trustee subservient to the grantor); and

4. certain administrative powers exercisable in a nonfiduciary capacity.

*Note:* A power exercisable by a trustee is presumed to be a power exercisable in a fiduciary capacity, i.e., for the interest of the beneficiary [Reg. § 1.675-1(b)(4)].

### *XVIII.B.6. Power to Revoke*

[819 T.M., VIII.; TPS ¶6120.05.K.]

If a power to revest in the grantor title to any portion of a trust is exercisable by the grantor or a nonadverse party without the approval or consent of an adverse party, the grantor is treated as the owner of that portion of the trust. The power to revest title to the trust assets includes any power to revoke, terminate, alter or amend, or to appoint. The grantor will not be treated as the trust's owner based on a deferred power to revest or revoke 5% or less of the trust funds [§ 676].

### *XVIII.B.7. Income for the Benefit of the Grantor*

[819 T.M., IX.; TPS ¶6120.05.L.]

The grantor is treated as the owner of any portion of a trust, the income of which is or may be (without the approval or consent of an adverse party) [§ 677; Reg. § 1.677(a)-1, § 1.677(b)-1]:

- distributed to the grantor or the grantor's spouse;
- held or accumulated for future distribution to the grantor or the grantor's spouse;
- applied to the payment of premiums on policies of insurance on the life of the grantor or the grantor's spouse; or
- actually applied or distributed to discharge the grantor's (or the grantor's spouse's) legal obligation of support.

### *XVIII.B.8. Persons Other than Grantor Treated as Substantial Owners*

[819 T.M., X.; TPS ¶6120.05.]

There are situations where someone other than the grantor may be treated as the owner of a portion of a trust. A third person is treated as the owner of any portion of a trust as to which the third person has (i) a power exercisable alone to vest the trust principal or income in himself or herself (i.e., a *Mallinckrodt* power); or (ii) a power derived from a *Mallinckrodt* power that has been partially released or modified and now constitutes a power that, had it been retained by the grantor, would have caused the grantor to be treated as the trust's owner under § 671-§ 677 [§ 678(a); *Mallinckrodt v. Nunan*, 146 F.2d 1 (8th Cir. 1945), *cert. denied*, 324 U.S. 871 (1945)].

### *XVIII.B.9. Foreign Trusts Established by U.S. Grantor with U.S. Beneficiaries*

[819 T.M., XI.; TPS ¶6120.05.M.]

A U.S. person who directly or indirectly transfers property to a foreign trust is treated as the owner for his/her tax year of that portion of the trust attributable to the transferred property if, for that year, the trust has a U.S. beneficiary [§ 679(a)(1)]. A trust is treated as having a U.S. beneficiary for the tax year unless (i) under the terms of the trust no part of the income or principal of the trust may be paid or accumulated during the tax year to or for the benefit of a U.S. person, or (ii) if the trust were terminated at any time during the tax year, no part of the income or principal of the trust could be paid to or for the benefit of a U.S. person [679(c)(1)]. Special attribution of ownership rules apply so that any amount paid to a controlled foreign corporation, a foreign partnership having a U.S. partner, or a foreign trust having a U.S. beneficiary is treated as an amount paid or accumulated for the benefit of a U.S. person [§ 679(c)(2)].

Additionally, the grantor is treated as the owner of the trust when:

- a trust subsequently acquires a U.S. beneficiary [§ 679(b)];
- a nonresident alien becomes a U.S. resident within five years after directly or indirectly transferring property to a foreign trust [§ 679(a)(4)]; or
- a domestic trust is transformed into a foreign trust (i.e., an outbound trust migration) [§ 679(a)(5)].

However, a grantor is not treated as the owner of the trust under § 679 if (i) the transfer of property to a foreign trust occurs because of the transferor's death (e.g., upon the creation of a testamentary trust), or (ii) the transfer of property to a foreign trust is in exchange for consideration of at least the fair market value of the transferred property [§ 679(a)(2)].

### XVIII.B.10. Foreign Trusts Indirectly Funded by U.S. Persons

[819 T.M., IV.D.8.; TPS ¶6120.05.O.]

Under certain circumstances, a U.S. beneficiary of a foreign trust will be treated as the owner of a trust established by a foreign person. If, under the grantor trust rules (before applying § 672(f)(5)), a foreign person would be treated as the owner of a portion of a trust, a U.S. beneficiary who transferred property to that foreign person will instead be treated as the grantor, unless the transfer was: (i) a sale for full and adequate consideration, (ii) a gift that qualifies for the annual exclusion, or (iii) a transfer that the U.S. beneficiary can demonstrate was wholly unrelated to any transaction involving the trust [§ 672(f)(5); Reg. § 1.672(f)-5(a)].

### XVIII.B.11. Grantor Trust Return Requirements

[819 T.M., III.G.; TPS ¶6120.08.]

Items of income, deduction, and credit attributable to any portion of a grantor trust are not reported by the trust on Form 1041, *U.S. Income Tax Return for Estates and Trusts*, but are shown on a separate statement to be attached to Form 1041 and reported by the grantor on his/her own income tax return [Reg. § 1.671-4]. There are multiple optional reporting methods available to certain types of grantor trusts and special rules for widely held fixed investment trusts [Reg. § 1.671-4, § 1.671-5].

A foreign trust with a U.S. owner must file Form 3520-A, *Annual Information Return of Foreign Trust with a U.S. Owner*, in order for the U.S. owner to satisfy its annual information reporting requirements under § 6048(b). A U.S. person who, during the tax year, is treated as the owner of any part of the assets of a foreign trust under the grantor trust rules must file Form 3520, *Annual Return to Report Transactions with Foreign Trusts and Receipt of Certain Foreign Gifts*. Form 3520 is generally due on the date that the U.S. person's income tax return is due, including extensions. A penalty applies if Form 3520 is not timely filed or if the information is incomplete or incorrect. The initial penalty is equal to the greater of $10,000 or (i) 35% of the gross value of any property transferred to a foreign trust for failure by a U.S. transferor to report the creation of or transfer to a foreign trust, or (ii) 35% of the gross value of the distributions received from a foreign trust for failure by a U.S. person to report receipt of the distribution, or (iii) 5% of the gross value of the portion of the trust's assets treated as owned by a U.S. person for failure by the U.S. person to report the U.S. owner information.

## XVIII.C. Other Fiduciary Income Tax Rules and Issues

### XVIII.C.1. Tax Years of Trusts and Estates

[852 T.M., IV.A.; TPS ¶6120.04.E.]

A trust must use the calendar year as its tax year [§ 644(a)]. By contrast, an estate has the option of choosing either the calendar year or the fiscal year as its tax year [§ 441(b)(1), § 644]. A fiscal year is a 12-month period ending on the last day of any month other than December [§ 441(e)]. Thus, an estate could select a year beginning February 1 and ending January 31 or a year beginning December 1 and ending November 30 (although its first year may begin on a day other than the first of a month and its last year may end on a date other than the last day of a month).

### XVIII.C.2. Multiple Trust Rule

[852 T.M., III.F.; TPS ¶6120.04.D.]

Two or more trusts will be treated as one trust if (i) the trusts have substantially the same grantor and beneficiaries, and (ii) a principal purpose of the trusts is the avoidance of federal income tax. Thus, where a substantial independent purpose exists and tax avoidance is not a principal purpose for the existence of separate trusts, the trusts will not be aggregated for federal income tax purposes. For purposes of applying the multiple trust rule, spouses are treated as one person [§ 643(f)].

### XVIII.C.3. Pre-Need Funeral Trusts

[852 T.M., V.K.; TPS ¶6120.06.]

Under a pre-need funeral arrangement, an individual enters into a contract with a business providing funeral or burial services or property, to purchase and pay for services or merchandise for the benefit of a specified person in advance of that person's death and the seller deposits all or a portion of the amount paid into an income-producing trust. The amounts remain in trust during the beneficiary's lifetime and are paid to the seller upon the beneficiary's death. To the extent a pre-need funeral trust would otherwise be treated as a grantor trust, the trustee may elect to have the trust taxed generally as a nongrantor trust if the trust meets certain qualifications (i.e., if the trust satisfies the requirements of a qualified funeral trust (QFT)) [§ 685]. Thus, the income tax rates generally applicable to trusts and estates apply, with each beneficiary's interest in the trust treated as a separate trust. A QFT, however, is not entitled to a deduction in lieu of a personal exemption [§ 685(a)(2)]. The tax on the annual earnings is payable by the trustee; the usual trust conduit rules are not applicable [§ 685(a)(1)].

No gain or loss is recognized on any amount refunded to the purchaser on the cancellation of the contract and the purchaser takes a carryover basis in any assets received upon cancellation [§ 685(d)]. Amounts received from the trust by the seller are treated as payments for services and merchandise and are includible currently in the seller's gross income [Rev. Rul. 87-127, 1987-2 C.B. 156].

The trustee elects QFT status by filing Form 1041-QFT, *U.S. Income Tax Return for Qualified Funeral Trusts.*

### XVIII.C.4. Commencement and Termination of Trusts and Estates

[852 T.M., III.C., III.E.; TPS ¶6120.04.B.]

The estate commences as a taxable entity for federal income tax purposes at the time of an individual's death. The trust's existence as a taxpaying person begins as of the time of the first funding of the trust (assuming a true trust and not a grantor trust). After an estate or trust is considered terminated, the gross income, deductions, and credits are considered to be the gross income, deductions, and credits of the beneficiaries succeeding to the property of the estate or trust [Reg. § 1.641(b)-3(d)].

***Termination of the Estate.*** The estate is deemed to exist for federal income tax purposes only during the period of administration or settlement. The period of administration or settlement is the period actually required by the administrator or executor to perform the ordinary duties of administration, such as the collection of assets and the payment of debts, taxes, legacies, and bequests, regardless of whether the period required is equivalent to the period specified under applicable local law for the settlement of estates. If the administration period is unreasonably prolonged, the estate is considered terminated for federal income tax purposes after the expiration of a reasonable period for the performance by the executor of all the administration duties. Further, an estate is considered terminated when all the assets have been distributed, except for a reasonable amount set aside in good faith for the payment of unascertained or contingent liabilities and expenses. Thus, no bright-line rule can be applied in this context, as estate or income tax controversies and extended periods for the payment or final determination of estate taxes sometimes will cause an estate to exist for a significant period of time. However, if the estate has joined in making a valid election under § 645 to treat a qualified revocable trust as part of the estate, the estate will not be considered terminated before the end of the § 645 election period [Reg. § 1.641(b)-3(a)].

***Termination of the Trust:*** The determination whether a trust has terminated depends upon whether the property held in trust has been distributed to the persons entitled to succeed to the property upon termination of the trust. The termination of the trust does not depend upon the technicality of whether the trustee has rendered the final accounting. A trust does not automatically terminate upon the happening of the event by which the duration of the trust is measured. A reasonable time is permitted after such event for the trustee to perform the duties necessary to complete the administration of the trust. However, the winding up of a trust cannot be unduly postponed and if the distribution of the trust corpus is unreasonably delayed, the trust is considered terminated for federal income tax purposes after the expiration of a reasonable period for the trustee to complete the administration of the trust. Further, a trust will be considered as terminated when all the assets have been distributed except for a reasonable amount set aside in good faith for the payment of unascertained or contingent liabilities and expenses (not including a claim by a beneficiary in that capacity) [Reg. § 1.641(b)-3(b)].

### XVIII.C.5. Unused Losses and Deductions on Trust or Estate Termination

[852 T.M., IV.B.2.v(2); TPS ¶6120.04.G.]

Deductions do not pass directly to beneficiaries because they are part of the DNI computational process. Consequently, excess tax deductions are not normally available to estate and trust beneficiaries, except for the tax year in which a trust or estate terminates [§ 642(h)]. During the year of termination, the following items are allowed as deductions to the beneficiaries succeeding to the property of the estate or trust:

- a net operating loss carryover [§ 642(h)(1), § 172];
- a capital loss carryover [§ 642(h)(1), § 1212]; or
- deductions in excess of the trust's or estate's gross income for the year of termination [§ 642(h)(2)].

***Excess Deductions.*** The personal exemption of the estate or trust and the charitable deduction, if any, are not taken into account for purposes of computing the excess deductions [§ 642(h)]. In addition, deductions that result in an NOL (and any gross income offset by such deductions) are not taken into account for purposes of computing the excess deductions [Reg. § 1.642(h)-2(b)]. The NOL passes through to the succeeding beneficiaries separately and is subject to the carryover rules (see XVIII.A.3.b.(4)). Thus, the NOL cannot be taken into account a second time for the purposes of computing the excess deductions. The excess deductions only can be used in the beneficiary's tax year in which or with which the truest or estate terminates. Further, these deductions can only be used as itemized deductions and not in computing the beneficiary's adjusted gross income, and are subject to the 2% threshold and other limitations applicable to an individual's deductions (see VIII.E.) [Reg. § 1.642(h)-2(a)].

If two or more beneficiaries succeed to the property of the terminating estate or trust, the passed-through items are allocated proportionately among them [Reg. § 1.642(h)-4].

### XVIII.C.6. Income Taxation of Charitable Remainder Trusts and Beneficiaries

[865 T.M.; TPS ¶6280.03.B.5.]

When an individual makes a transfer of a remainder interest in trust to a charity, the charitable deduction is only allowed if the form of the gift is a charitable remainder annuity trust (CRAT), a charitable remainder unitrust (CRUT), or a pooled income fund.

*CRAT*. A CRAT is a trust from which a fixed sum (not less than 5% or more than 50% of the initial net fair market value of its assets when placed in trust) is to be distributed at least annually, with at least one of the recipients being a noncharitable beneficiary. That is, the annuity beneficiary receives a specified amount each year without regard to the actual income of the trust for that year. The income interest may be either a life estate or for a term of years (not in excess of 20 years) [§ 664(d)(1)(A)]. The remainder, which must have an actuarial value that is at least 10% of the initial value of the property transferred into the trust, must be transferred to, or for the use of, a qualified charity. Generally, no amount other than the annuity amount may be paid from the trust to a noncharitable beneficiary [§ 664(a)(1)].

*CRUT*. A CRUT is a trust under which a fixed percentage (not less than 5% or more than 50% of the fair market value of its assets (valued annually)) must be distributed at least annually and at least one of the recipients must be a noncharitable beneficiary. The income interest may be either a life estate or for a term of years (not in excess of 20 years) [§ 664(d)(2)(A)]. The remainder, which must have an actuarial value that is at least 10% of the value of the property when transferred to the trust, is distributable to, or for the use of, a qualified charity [§ 664(d)(2)(C), § 664(d)(2)(D)]. Generally, no amount other than the unitrust amount may be paid from the trust to a noncharitable beneficiary [§ 664(d)(2)(B)].

A charitable remainder trust (CRT) is exempt from income tax [§ 664(c)]. In any tax year in which a CRT has unrelated business income the income is subject to a 100% excise tax that is reported on Form 4720, *Return of Certain Excise Taxes Under Chapters 41 and 42 of the Internal Revenue Code* [§ 512]. Additionally, a CRT may be liable for taxes on:

- self-dealing [§ 4941];
- excess business holdings [§ 4943];
- jeopardizing investments [§ 4944]; and

- taxable expenditures [§ 4945].

Distributions made to the noncharitable beneficiary of the trust are taxable to the beneficiary to the extent of the income received by the trust in the current year and undistributed income from prior years. The character of that income is determined by ordering rules, which have the effect of ensuring that the highest-taxed income is distributed first from the trust [§ 664(b)].

The determination of the character of amounts distributed or deemed distributed at any time during the tax year of the trust is made as of the end of that tax year. The tax rate(s) to be used in computing the recipient's tax on the distribution is the tax rate applicable, in the year in which the distribution is required to be made, to the classes of income deemed to make up that distribution, and not the tax rate applicable to those classes of income in the year the income is received by the trust [Reg. § 1.664-1(d)(1)(ii)(a)].

A CRT must file an annual information return, Form 5227, *Split-Interest Trust Information Return,* on or before the 15th day of the fourth month following the close of its tax year.

### XVIII.C.7. Pooled Income Funds

[865 T.M., XVII.; TPS ¶6280.03.C.]

A pooled income fund is an arrangement by which the donor contributes an irrevocable remainder interest to a charity, retaining for himself or herself (or others) an income interest for life [§ 642(c)(5)(A)]. Each income beneficiary receives annually an amount of income determined by the rate of return earned by the fund for that year. The donor may claim an income (or estate or gift) tax charitable deduction for the value of the remainder interest transferred to a pooled income fund [§ 642(c)(3)].

The property transferred to the fund must be commingled with property transferred by other individual donors to the fund [§ 642(c)(5)(B)]. Generally, the fund must be maintained by the organization to which the remainder interest is contributed or, under certain circumstances, by a supporting organization [Reg. § 1.642(c)-5(b)(5)].

A pooled income fund is taxed as a trust for federal income tax purposes, regardless of whether the fund qualifies as a trust under local law, and the grantor trust rules do not apply. Thus, a pooled income fund must file Form 1041. Additionally, a pooled income fund must file an annual information return, Form 5227, *Split-Interest Trust Information Return.*

### XVIII.C.8. Throwback Rules

[856 T.M., II.; TPS ¶6130.04.]

All income of a simple trust is treated as distributed during the current year. However, the beneficiary of a complex trust is taxed on the income distributed (or required to be distributed) but the trust is taxed on the retained income. This creates the possibility of immediate income tax savings, because the income can be split among several taxable entities (with income directed to the beneficiary subject to the lowest marginal rate to produce an overall tax savings). If, in a later year, the income previously taxed to the trust could be distributed to a high bracket taxpayer without further tax, the income tax savings in the earlier accumulation year could be permanently achieved. To preclude this, "throwback rules" require, in general, that the recipient of a distribution of accumulated trust income be taxed as if that income had been received when it was earned [§ 665-§ 667].

The throwback rules apply only to foreign trusts, domestic trusts that were at any time foreign trusts, and pre-March 1, 1984 multiple trusts [§ 665(c)].

*Compliance.* The amount, year, and character of any distributions subject to the throwback rules is determined on Form 1041, Schedule J. A beneficiary of a domestic trust who receives a distribution subject to the throwback rules computes his/her additional income tax liability on Form 4970, *Tax on Accumulation Distribution of Trusts.* Beneficiaries of foreign trusts must use Form 3520, *Annual Return to Report Transactions with Foreign Trusts and Receipt of Certain Foreign Gifts.*

## XVIII.D. Compliance for Estates and Non-Grantor Trusts

### XVIII.D.1. Filing and Due Date of Return

[852 T.M.; TPS ¶6120.08.]

An estate must file a return if it has gross income of $600 or more, or if any beneficiary is a nonresident alien [§ 6012(a)(3), (5)]. A trust must file a return if it has any taxable income, if it has gross income of $600 or more (regardless of the amount of taxable income), or if it has a beneficiary who is a nonresident alien [§ 6012(a)(4), § 6012(a)(4)(5)]. The estate or trust fiduciary must file Form 1041, *U.S. Income Tax Return for Estates and Trusts,* and pay the tax on the taxable income of the estate or trust. The due date of the return is the 15th day of the 4th month following the close of the estate's or trust's tax year [§ 6072(a)]. Generally, foreign estates or trusts must file Form 1040-NR, *U.S. Nonresident Alien Income Tax Return.* A trust can obtain an automatic five month extension of time to file its income tax return by filing Form 7004, *Application for Automatic Extension of Time to File Certain Business Income Tax, Information, and Other Returns,* on or before the due date for filing Form 1041 [Reg. § 1.6081-6].

If an estate or trust is required to file Form 1041, it must also provide Schedule K-1 to each beneficiary (i) who receives a distribution from the estate or trust during the tax year, or (ii) to whom any item is allocated during the tax year [§ 6034A(a)]. The Schedule K-1 must show the information required to be shown on the estate's or trust's own Form 1041 [§ 6034A(a)].

For a discussion of penalties for late filing and failure to provide information, see Chapter XXIII.

### XVIII.D.2. Payment of Estimated Tax

[852 T.M., IV.C.3.; TPS ¶6120.04.F.]

Generally, trusts must pay estimated tax on a quarterly basis [§ 6654(l)(1)]. However, the following entities do not have to pay estimated tax for any tax year ending before the date two years after the date of the decedent's death: (i) the decedent's estate, and (ii) any trust that was treated in its entirety as a grantor trust, and to which the residue of the decedent's estate will pass under his will [§ 6654(l)(2)]. Estimated tax rules are discussed in Chapter XXII.

---

**EXAMPLE:** Decedent (D) died on Jan. 1, 2014. The decedent's estate will not have to pay estimated tax for the 2013 tax year, which ended Apr. 15, 2014, or the 2014 tax year, which will end on Apr. 15, 2015. However, the estate would have to pay estimated tax for the 2015 tax year, because that year will end on Apr. 15, 2016, which is more than 2 years after the date of D's death (i.e., Jan. 1, 2016).

---

If a trust makes estimated tax payments, the trustee has 65 days from the end of its tax year to elect to treat all or any portion of the payment as made by a beneficiary [§ 643(g)]. The election is made on Form 1041-T and reported on Schedule K-1.

### XVIII.D.3. Payment of Income Tax Liability

[852 T.M.; TPS ¶6120.08.]

The fiduciary must pay any income tax liability on the due date of Form 1041 and is subject to late payment penalties and interest (see Chapter XXIII.).

*Personal Liability of Fiduciary.* The fiduciary is required to make and file the return and pay the estate's or trust's tax. The fiduciary is personally liable for the payment of the estate's or trust's income tax liability up to and after his or her discharge from fiduciary duties if, before distribution and discharge, he or she had notice of the tax obligations or failed to exercise due diligence in ascertaining whether or not the obligations existed. Liability for the tax also follows the assets of the estate distributed to heirs, devisees, legatees, and distributees, who may be required to discharge the amount of the tax due and unpaid to the extent of the distributive shares received by them [Reg. § 1.641(b)-2(a)]. A fiduciary may be discharged from personal liability at the discretion of the IRS [§ 2204]. To request such a discharge, the fiduciary must file Form 5495, *Request for Discharge from Personal Liability Under Internal Revenue Code Section 2204 or 6905.*

### XVIII.D.4. Withholding on Distributions to Covered Expatriates

[837 T.M., V.D.10.; TPS ¶7150.08.B.2.c.]

In the case of a distribution (whether direct or indirect) of any property from a nongrantor trust to a covered expatriate who was a beneficiary of the trust on the day before his or her expatriation date, the trustee must deduct and withhold from such distribution 30% of the taxable portion thereof [§ 877A(f)(1)(A), (f)(5)]. The covered expatriate is treated as waiving any reduction in withholding on the trust distributions under a U.S. treaty unless the covered expatriate agrees to such other treatment as the IRS may require [§ 877A(f)(4)(B)]. The taxable portion of the distribution means the portion that would be includible in the covered expatriate's gross income if he/she continued to be subject to tax as a citizen or resident of the United States [§ 877A(f)(2)]. If the distribution takes the form of appreciated property, the trust will recognize gain as if the distributed property had been sold to the expatriate at fair market value [§ 877A(f)(1)(B)].

The covered expatriate must file Form W-8CE, *Notice of Expatriation and Waiver of Treaty Benefits*, with the trustee annually to notify the trustee of the covered expatriate's status and that he or she has waived any applicable tax treaty benefits. The covered expatriate must also file Form 8854, *Initial and Annual Expatriation Statement*, each year to report either the receipt or absence of distributions from the trust. It will remain to be seen how all the foregoing will be enforced in cases where the trust is a foreign trust.

## XVIII.E. Net Investment Income Tax

### XVIII.E.1. Application of Net Investment Income Tax to Trusts and Estates

[852 T.M., IV.C.6.; TPS ¶6110.01.]

Section 1411 imposes a 3.8% tax on the net investment income of certain individuals, trusts, and decedents' estates. However, the following are not subject to the net investment income tax:

- a trust/estate all of the unexpired interests in which are devoted to one or more charitable purposes as described in § 170(c)(2)(B) [Reg. § 1.1411-3(b)(1)(i)];

- a trust exempt from tax under § 501 [Reg. § 1.411-3(b)(1)(ii)];

- a charitable remainder trust (but special rules apply for distributions from a charitable remainder trust to persons subject to § 1411) [Reg. § 1.1411-3(b)(1)(iii)];

- trusts that are statutorily exempt from income taxes [Reg. § 1.1411-3(b)(1)(iv)];

- a trust, or any portion of a trust, that is treated as a grantor trust [Reg. § 1.1411-3(b)(1)(v)];

- electing Alaska Native Settlement Trusts subject to taxation under § 646 [Reg. § 1.1411-3(b)(1)(vi)];

- Cemetery Perpetual Care Funds to which § 642(i) applies [Reg. § 1.1411-3(b)(1)(vii)]; and

- foreign trusts and estates [Reg. § 1.1411-3(b)(1)(viii), (ix)].

Taxpayers determine and report the net investment income tax on Form 8960, *Net Investment Income Tax — Individuals, Estates, and Trusts*, and attach it to Form 1041. Because the net investment income tax is subject to the estimated tax provisions, trusts and estates that anticipate liability must adjust their estimated tax payments to account for the 3.8% increase.

For trusts and estates subject to § 1411, an additional tax of 3.8% is imposed on the lesser of: (i) undistributed net investment income for the tax year, or (ii) the amount by which the trust's or estate's AGI exceeds the threshold amount ($12,150 for 2014 and 12,300 for 2015). Therefore, for 2014, an estate or trust is only subject to the tax if it has undistributed net investment income and also has an AGI over $12,150 [§ 1411(a)(2); Rev. Proc. 2013-35, 2013-47 I.R.B. 537, § 3.01, Rev. Proc. 2014-61, 2014-47 I.R.B. 860, § 3.01].

*Adjusted Gross Income.* The AGI for an estate or trust is determined in the same way as an individual except that an estate or trust also can deduct (i) the deduction for personal exemption under § 642(b), (ii) the distribution deduction allowed under § 651 or § 661, and (iii) costs that are paid or incurred in connection with the administration that would not have been incurred if the property were not held in an estate or trust (i.e., expenses that are not subject to the 2% floor) [§ 1411(a)(2)(B)(i), § 67(e)].

*Investment Income.* For purposes of the net investment income tax, investment income is defined as: (i) the gross income from interest, dividends, annuities, royalties, and rents derived from a trade or business that is a passive activity with respect to the taxpayer or that is a trade or business of trading in financial instruments or commodities; (ii) other gross income derived from a trade or business that is a passive activity with respect to the taxpayer or that is a trade or business of trading in financial instruments or commodities; and (iii) the net gain attributable to the disposition of property (other than the disposition of property in an active business that is not trading in financial instruments or commodities) [§ 1411(c)(1)(A)(i)-(iii)]. For a detailed discussion of net investment income, see Chapter X.

### XVIII.E.2. Undistributed Net Investment Income

[852 T.M., IV.C.6.c.; TPS ¶6110.01.]

An estate's or trust's undistributed net investment income is the estate's or trust's net investment income reduced by distributions of net investment income to beneficiaries and by deductions under § 642(c) [Reg. § 1.1411-3(e)]. For a trust or estate, distributions generally carry out items of income that comprise DNI. When one is calculating the items of net investment income that comprise DNI, direct expenses are allocated against the income to which they directly relate, while indirect expenses may be allocated against any item of income comprising DNI chosen by the fiduciary. However, if the trust or estate has tax-exempt income, then a portion of indirect expenses must be allocated to such income based on a fraction, the numerator of which is the amount of tax-exempt income and the denominator of which is the total gross amount of all items of income that comprises DNI. The other special allocation rule is where a trust or estate is entitled to a charitable deduction under § 642(c), the charity is considered to have received a proportionate amount of the gross income items that comprise DNI. Distributions made to beneficiaries that qualify for the distribution deduction then carry out to the recipient beneficiaries a proportionate share of all items of net income comprising DNI.

An estate's or trust's net investment income is reduced by distributions of net investment income to beneficiaries, limited to the lower of (i) the deduction allowed under § 651 or § 661, or (ii) the net investment income of the estate or trust [Reg. § 1.1411-3(e)(3)(i)]. All distributions to beneficiaries that qualify for the distribution deduction are deemed to consist of the same proportion of each class of income as the total of each class of income bears to DNI [Reg. § 1.1411-3(e)(3)].

### XVIII.E.3. Beneficiary's Share of Net Investment Income from Trusts and Estates

[852 T.M., IV.C.6.d.; TPS ¶6110.01.]

For purposes of the net investment income tax, the general rule regarding distributions from estates and trust to beneficiaries applies; that is, a beneficiary is deemed to receive a proportionate amount of each item of DNI based on the ratio of the amount of the distribution to the amount of the DNI [§ 652, § 662].

---

**EXAMPLE:** A trust earns during the tax year $10,000 of interest and $15,000 of dividends, and also has $25,000 of capital gains that are a part of DNI. The trust paid trustee commissions of $6,000 and distributed $47,000 to its beneficiary. The DNI of the trust is $44,000 (($10,000 interest + $15,000 dividends + $25,000 capital gains) − $6,000 trustee commissions). Because the trustee commissions are an indirect expense, the trustee may charge such commissions against any item of income comprising DNI. So, the trustee charges the entire commission against the interest income. The trust is entitled to a distribution deduction of $44,000 (the total amount of its DNI) and the beneficiary is deemed to have received $4,000 of interest, $15,000 of dividends, and $25,000 of capital gains.

---

### XVIII.E.4. Application of § 1411 to Electing Small Business Trusts (ESBTs)

[852 T.M., IV.C.6.g.; TPS ¶6110.01.]

Generally, the portion of any ESBT that consists of stock in one or more S corporations is treated as a separate trust and the amount of income tax imposed on such separate trust is determined with certain modifications detailed in § 641(c). However, § 1411 consolidates the ESBT into a single trust solely for purposes of determining the AGI threshold (i.e., solely for purposes of determining the amount subject to tax under § 1411). The ESBT first separately calculates the undistributed net investment income of the S portion and non-S portion as separate trusts and then totals the two results. Then the ESBT determines its adjusted gross income solely for purposes of § 1411 by adding the net income or net loss of the S portion to the non-S portion as a single item of income or loss. Lastly, the ESBT pays tax on the lesser of the combined undistributed net income or the excess of its adjusted gross income over the threshold amount [Reg. § 1.1411-3(c)(1)].

### XVIII.E.5. Application of § 1411 to Charitable Remainder Trusts

[852 T.M., IV.C.6.h.; TPS ¶6110.01.]

Although § 1411 does not apply to charitable remainder trusts, because annuity and unitrust distributions to the recipient beneficiaries may consist of net investment income, special rules apply to maintain the character and distribution ordering rules for CRTs. If items of net investment income comprise all or part of a distribution from a CRT, such items will retain their character as net investment income in the hands of the recipient and, if there are two or more recipients, it is apportioned among them based on their respective shares of the total distribution [Reg. § 1.1411-3(d)].

## XVIII.F. Income in Respect of a Decedent

[862 T.M.; TPS ¶6150.]

Generally, items of gross income that accrued before the death of the decedent but were not reported as gross income before death are to be included in gross income, in the year received, by the eventual recipients [§ 691]. Certain income of persons who die while serving in the U.S. Armed Forces or as a result of specified terrorist attacks is exempt from tax [§ 692].

Items of a decedent's gross income that are not properly includible in his/her gross income in the tax year in which he/she died (or in a prior tax year) are referred to as income in respect of a decedent (IRD) [§ 691(a)(1)]. Generally, IRD refers to items of income to which a taxpayer was entitled before death, but that were not reported before death because of the taxpayer's method of accounting. IRD includes [Reg. § 1.691(a)-1(b)]:

- all accrued income of a decedent who used the cash method of accounting;
- income that accrued solely by reason of the decedent's death in the case of a decedent who used the accrual method of accounting; and
- income to which the decedent had a contingent claim at the time of death.

Typical items that constitute IRD include:

- alimony, compensation, salary, commissions, bonus payments, or similar items that the decedent economically earned, but did not receive, before death;
- dividends, interest, rents, and similar items accrued at the time of the decedent's death;
- income from a capital asset that was sold before the decedent's death, where the proceeds were not received before death;
- payments received after the decedent's death on an installment obligation owing to the decedent and created before his/her death;
- business profits of a sole proprietorship that have been realized, but not received, at the time of the decedent's death;
- certain items that had been deducted by the decedent for income tax purposes before death that are restored after death by reason of a refund or a reimbursement claim;
- distributions of a decedent's retirement plan or IRA, to the extent not made from previously taxed contributions; and

- the account balance of an Archer MSA or Health Savings Account, unless the account holder's spouse is the designated beneficiary of the account.

IRD is included in gross income for the tax year received by [§ 691(a)(1)]:

- the estate of the decedent, if the right to receive the amount is acquired by the estate;
- the person who, by reason of the decedent's death, acquires the right to receive the amount (if the estate doesn't acquire the amount); or
- the person who acquires from the decedent (by bequest, devise, or inheritance), the right to receive the amount, if the amount is received after distribution by the decedent's estate of the right.

*Character of IRD Items.* The character of an item of IRD is determined by reference to the decedent. The item is treated as if the estate or other recipient had acquired it in the transaction in which the right to receive the income was originally derived, and the amount includible in gross income has the same character in the hands of the estate or other recipient that it would have had in the hands of the decedent had the decedent lived and received the amount [§ 691(a)(3)].

*Deductions in Respect of a Decedent.* The Code also provides special treatment for expenditures referred to as deductions in respect of a decedent (DRD). DRD includes the following items of a decedent that were not properly allowable to the decedent for the tax year of his or her death or a prior period:

1. trade or business expenses [§ 162];
2. interest expenses [§ 163];
3. certain taxes paid/accrued [§ 164];
4. expenses for the production of income [§ 212];
5. the allowance for deduction for the depletion of mines, oil and gas wells, other natural deposits, and timber [§ 611]; and
6. the foreign tax credit [§ 27].

A DRD item generally is allowed to the estate of the decedent, but, if the estate is not liable for the obligation giving rise to the deduction or credit, the DRD item is allowable to the person who receives an interest in the decedent's property subject to the obligation [§ 691(b)].

*Estate Tax Deduction.* There is a special income tax deduction for the portion of any estate tax paid by the decedent's estate that is attributable to the value of the IRD items [§ 691(c)].

*Compliance.* If received by the decedent's estate, IRD items are reported on Form 1041. If received by an individual, IRD items are included for gross income tax purposes at the appropriate place on that individual's Form 1040.

# CHAPTER XIX. TAX-EXEMPT ORGANIZATIONS
>>>>>>>>>>>>>>>>>>>>>>>>>>>>>>

## XIX.A. Section 501(c)(3) Charitable Organizations

[450 T.M., VII.; TPS ¶6510.01.]

Section 501(c)(3) exempts from tax certain charitable organizations, including organizations that are organized and operated exclusively for:

- charitable purposes;
- educational purposes;
- religious purposes;
- scientific purposes;
- testing for public safety;
- literary purposes;
- educational purposes;
- the fostering of national or international sports competition; or
- the prevention of cruelty to children or animals.

To receive and maintain the exemption, no part of the organization's net earnings may inure to the benefit of any private shareholder or individual. Further, no substantial part of the organization's activities can be the influencing of legislation. Finally, the organization may not participate or intervene in any political campaign on behalf of (or in opposition to) any candidate for public office.

The significance of an organization being a charitable organization is that (1) contributions to the organization qualify for the income tax, gift tax, and estate tax charitable contribution deductions, (2) the organization can qualify for tax-exempt financing, and (3) the organization may qualify for exemption from state and local taxes, favorable postal rates, etc. Section 501(c)(3) organizations are characterized as private foundations (see XIX.C.1.) or public charities, and a variety of tax consequences depend on this characterization.

*Cooperative Hospital Service Organizations* [§ 501(e)]. Organizations that qualify as cooperative hospital service organizations are considered charitable organizations under § 501(c)(3) if the organization is organized and operated solely to perform, on a centralized basis, one or more of the following services, which, if performed by a § 501(e) hospital on its own behalf, would constitute the exercise or performance of its exempt purposes:

- data processing;

- purchasing (including group insurance);
- warehousing;
- billing and collection; and
- food, clinical, industrial engineering, laboratory, printing, communications, record center, and personnel services (including selection, testing, training and education of personnel).

*Cooperative Educational Investment Organizations* [§ 501(f)]. Organizations that qualify as cooperative educational investment organizations are considered § 501(c)(3) charitable organizations. A cooperative educational investment organization must be comprised solely of members that are organizations described in § 170(b)(1)(A)(ii) or § 170(b)(1)(A)(iv) (i.e., schools, colleges, and organizations administering property for the benefit of certain government-supported colleges and universities), and must be organized and operated solely to hold and commingle the money contributed by members, to invest and reinvest such money in stock and securities, and to remit the net income to the members. Section 501(f) provides that certain cooperative service organizations that are organized and controlled by schools or universities, or organizations operated for the benefit of certain state and municipal colleges and universities for the collective investment of the members' funds in stocks or securities, are treated as organizations organized and operated exclusively for charitable purposes. Section 501(f) does not apply to private organizations that furnish services to the members even though only educational organizations may receive such services.

*Charitable Risk Pools* [§ 501(n)]. Qualified charitable risk pools are treated as § 501(c)(3) charitable organizations. A qualified charitable risk pool is an organization organized and operated solely to pool insurable risks of its members, other than medical malpractice risks, and to provide information to its members with respect to loss control and risk management. Because the qualified charitable risk pool must be organized and operated solely to pool insurable risks of its members, no profit or other benefit may be provided to any member of the organization other than through providing members with insurance coverage below the cost of comparable commercial coverage. Only charitable tax-exempt organizations described in § 501(c)(3) may be members of a qualified charitable risk pool.

*Provider-Sponsored Organizations* [§ 501(o)]. An organization will not fail to be treated as organized and operated exclusively for charitable purposes under § 501(c)(3) solely because a hospital that is owned and operated by the organization participates in a provider-sponsored organization (as defined in § 1855(d) of the Social Security Act), regardless of whether the provider-sponsored organization is exempt from tax. Persons with a material financial interest in the provider-sponsored organization are, however, treated as a private shareholder or individual with respect to the hospital. This provision means that the inurement and intermediate sanctions provisions of the Code would apply to doctors who own an interest in a provider-sponsored organization and thus are treated as insiders of the hospital itself, even though the physicians may not own a facility or department of the hospital.

### XIX.A.1. Organizational Requirements

[450 T.M., IV.A.; TPS ¶6510.02.B.]

To qualify as a § 501(c)(3) tax-exempt organization, an organization must be organized exclusively for one or more exempt purposes. To meet the organizational test, the articles of organization must (1) limit the organization's purposes to one or more exempt purposes, (2) not expressly empower the organization to engage, other than as an insubstantial part of its activities, in activities that do not further its exempt purpose(s), and (3) contain an express or implied provision dedicating its assets to an exempt purpose upon dissolution [Reg. § 1.501(c)(3)-1(b)]. The organizational test is satisfied if the purposes stated in the articles of organization (not the bylaws or other rules/regulations) are limited in some way by reference to § 501(c)(3). The organizational test is not satisfied by the fact that actual operations are for exempt purposes.

## XIX.A.2. Operational Requirements

[451 T.M., II.B.; TPS ¶6510.02.C.]

To qualify as a § 501(c)(3) tax-exempt organization, an organization must operate primarily in pursuance of one or more tax-exempt purposes constituting the basis of its tax exemption [Reg. § 1.501(c)(3)-1(c)(1)]. To meet the operational requirements:

1. the organization may not be operated primarily to conduct an unrelated trade or business [Reg. § 1.501(c)(3)-1(e)(1)];

2. the net earnings of the organization may not inure to the benefit of any person in a position to influence the activities of the organization [Reg. § 1.501(c)(3)-1(c)(2)];

3. the organization must operate to provide a public benefit, not a private benefit [Reg. § 1.501(c)(3)-1(d)(1)(ii)];

4. the organization may not engage in substantial legislative lobbying [Reg. § 1.501(c)(3)-1(c)(3)]; and

5. the organization may not participate or intervene in any political campaign [Reg. § 1.501(c)(3)-1(c)(3)].

A single nonexempt purpose, if substantial in nature, will result in denial or loss of exemption. Note, however, that an organization may engage in activities that do not further any exempt purpose if those activities are "insubstantial" [Reg. § 1.501(c)(3)-1(c)(1)].

Failure to meet the operational requirements may result in loss of tax exemption or imposition of excise taxes, depending on the type and severity of the violation (see XIX.A.6., XIX.A.7., and XIX.D.1.).

## XIX.A.3. Churches and Religious Organizations

[484 T.M., V.; TPS ¶6510.02.A.2.]

Organizations that are organized and operated exclusively for the advancement of religion or for religious purposes, including churches, are eligible for tax exemption as charitable organizations [§ 501(c)(3); Reg. § 1.501(c)(3)-1(d)(2)].

Because the terms "religion" and "religious" are not defined in either the Code or regulations, judicial construction of the terms has been required. Although courts have considered whether a particular organization is a religious organization, the scope of the term "religious" has been left imprecise deliberately due to constitutional considerations. Due to the constitutional implications concerning the scope of the term "religious," organizations claiming exemption as religious organizations are frequently denied exemption on the ground that they operate for a substantial nonexempt purpose, or on the ground that they operate for a private benefit, rather than on the ground that their claimed religious purposes are not religious purposes within the meaning of the exemption provisions.

A church is a type of religious organization. As in the case of the term "religious," a precise definition of the term "church" has not been formulated. At minimum, however, the concept of a church seems to require a body of believers or communicants that assembles regularly in order to worship. Churches are distinguished from other religious organizations because churches enjoy special advantages. For example, churches automatically qualify as public charities, whereas other religious organizations must satisfy the requirements of a publicly supported organization or a supporting organization to escape classification as private foundations [§ 170(b)(1)(A)(i), § 509(a)(1)]. Also, unlike most other charitable organizations, churches are not required to file an annual information return [§ 6033(a)(3)(A)(i)].

Certain communal religious and apostolic associations are granted exemption from income taxation in their own right, but not as charitable organizations [§ 501(d)]. Exemption is available even if the association engages in business for the common benefit of its members, provided that (1) the organization has a common or community treasury; and (2) the members of the organization include in their gross income their entire pro rata share, whether distributed or not, of the organization's taxable income for the year [Reg. § 1.501(d)-1]. Communal religious or apostolic associations must file an annual information return on Form 1065 [Reg. § 1.6033-2(e)].

### XIX.A.4. Supporting Organizations

[459 T.M., II.B.; TPS ¶6810.04.]

A supporting organization is an organization that performs its exempt purpose by giving support to other tax-exempt organizations. Supporting organizations are considered public charities and must satisfy the requirements of § 501(c)(3), as well as three additional requirements, to be tax exempt. The additional requirements that an organization must satisfy are that [§ 509(a)(3)]:

- it must be organized and operated exclusively for the benefit of, to perform the functions of, or to carry out the purposes of a public charity;
- it must be operated, supervised, or controlled by or in connection with a public charity;
- it cannot be controlled directly or indirectly by a disqualified person, other than foundation managers and public charities.

There are three types of supporting organizations. In order to be considered a Type I supporting organization, the organization must be subject to a substantial degree of direction from the supported organization [Reg. § 1.509(a)-4(g)]. The required relationship is comparable to that of a parent and subsidiary. In order to be considered a Type II supporting organization, there must be common supervision or control by the persons supervising or controlling both the supporting organization and the supported organization to ensure that the supporting organization will be responsive to the needs and requirements of the supported organization [Reg. § 1.509(a)-4(h)]. In order to be considered a Type III supporting organization, the supporting organization must meet: (1) the notification requirement, (2) the responsiveness test, and (3) the integral part test [Reg. § 1.509(a)-4(i)]. If a Type I or Type III supporting organization supports an organization that is controlled by a donor, then the supporting organization is treated as a private foundation, not a public charity [§ 509(f)(2)].

### XIX.A.5. Donor Advised Funds

[450 T.M., VIII.B.5.; TPS ¶6510.03.D.]

A donor advised fund (DAF) is an account established by a charitable organization to which donors may contribute and thereafter provide nonbinding advice or recommendations with regard to distributions from the fund or the investment of assets in the fund [§ 4966(d)(2)]. Donors who make contributions to charities for maintenance in a DAF generally claim a charitable contribution deduction at the time of the contribution. Although sponsoring charities frequently permit donors (or other persons appointed by donors) to provide nonbinding recommendations concerning the distribution or investment of assets in a DAF, sponsoring charities must have legal ownership and control of such assets following the contribution. If the sponsoring charity does not have such control (or permits a donor to exercise control over amounts contributed), the donor's contributions may not qualify for a charitable deduction, and, in the case of a community foundation, the contribution may be treated as being subject to a material restriction or condition by the donor.

DAFs are hybrid creatures. Although categorized as part of a "public" charity, like a foundation, a DAF is funded from a single source and is subject to certain of the private foundation rules (see XIX.C.2.), which prohibit self-dealing, excess business holdings and jeopardizing investments; mandate qualifying distributions equal to the organization's minimum investment return; impose a set of requirements concerning program expenditures, termed taxable expenditures; and levy a tax on net investment income. Like a public charity, the contributions to a DAF are, subject to the support fraction computation rules, deemed to be public support to the charitable recipients.

Certain distributions from a DAF are subject to tax. A "taxable distribution" is any distribution from a DAF to (1) any natural person; or (2) to any other person for any purpose other than one that, generally, is charitable or, if for a charitable purpose, the sponsoring organization does not exercise expenditure responsibility with respect to the distribution. In the event of a taxable distribution, an excise tax equal to 20% of the amount of the distribution is imposed against the sponsoring organization. In addition, an excise tax equal to 5% of the amount of the distribution is imposed against any manager of the sponsoring organization who knowingly approved the distribution, not to exceed $10,000 on any one taxable distribution.

If a donor, a donor advisor, or a person related to a donor or donor advisor of a DAF provides advice as to a distribution that results in any such person receiving, directly or indirectly, a more than incidental benefit, an excise tax equal to 125% of the amount of such benefit is imposed on the person who advised as to the distribution, and on the recipient of the benefit [§ 4967(a)]. In addition, if a manager of the sponsoring organization agreed to the making of the distribution, knowing that the distribution would confer a more than incidental benefit on a donor, a donor advisor, or a person related to a donor or donor advisor, the manager is subject to an excise tax equal to 10% of the amount of such benefit, not to exceed $10,000. Persons subject to the tax are jointly and severally liable for the tax [§ 4967(c)(1)].

### XIX.A.6. Lobbying and Political Activities

[451 T.M., IX.; TPS ¶6510.04.]

A charitable organization may not, as a substantial part of its activities, carry on propaganda or otherwise attempt to influence legislation. Further, a charitable organization cannot directly or indirectly participate or intervene in any political campaign on behalf of or in opposition to any candidate for public office. If the organization engages in substantial legislative activities or any political campaign activities, the organization is an "action" organization and exemption will be denied [Reg. § 1.501(c)(3)-1(c)(3)].

An organization may elect, on Form 5768, *Election/Revocation of Election by an Eligible Section 501(c)(3) Organization To Make Expenditures To Influence Leg-*

*islation*, to utilize an expenditure test to determine whether or not its legislative activities are substantial. The expenditure test establishes the lobbying nontaxable amount [§ 501(h), § 4911]. The permitted annual level of expenditures for legislative efforts (i.e., the lobbying nontaxable amount) is 20% of the first $500,000 of an organization's expenditures for an exempt purpose, including legislative but not including fundraising activities, plus 15% of the next $500,000, 10% of the next $500,000, and 5% of any exempt purpose expenditures over $1,500,000, up to a maximum of exceed $1,000,000. A specific limitation amounting to 25% of the lobbying nontaxable amount is imposed by § 4911(c)(4) on attempts to influence the general public on legislative matters, or "grass roots lobbying."

Expenditures in excess of the lobbying nontaxable amount (i.e., "excess lobbying expenditures") are subject to a 25% excise tax [§ 4911(a)]. An organization will lose its exemption if it normally spends more than 150% of the permissible amounts [§ 501(h)(1), § 501(h)(2)(B), § 501(h)(2)(D)].

Further, excise taxes are imposed on the political expenditures of charitable organizations [§ 4955]. The term "political expenditure" generally refers to any amount paid or incurred in any participation or intervention in any political campaign either on behalf of or in opposition to any candidate for public office. The initial tax on the charitable organization is equal to 10% of the political expenditure. Under certain circumstances, an organization manager who agreed to the making of a political expenditure is subject to an excise tax equal to 2.5% of the political expenditure (up to $5,000). An additional tax of 100% of the amount of the political expenditure is imposed on a charitable organization if the expenditure is not corrected within the taxable period. If an additional tax is imposed on the charitable organization, an additional tax equal to 50% of the amount of the political expenditure (up to $10,000) is also imposed on any organization manager who refused to agree to all or part of the correction. A charitable organization or manager liable for the excise tax on political expenditures must report the tax on Form 4720, *Return of Certain Excise Taxes on Charities and Other Persons Under Chapters 41 and 42 of the Internal Revenue Code.*

### XIX.A.7. Excess Benefit Transactions

[476 T.M., VI.; TPS ¶6510.03.B.]

Excise taxes are imposed when a public charity (other than a private foundation), a social welfare organization, or a qualified nonprofit health insurance issuer engages in an excess benefit transaction with certain disqualified persons [§ 4958(a)]. The term "excess benefit transaction" refers to any transaction in which an economic benefit is provided by an applicable tax-exempt organization directly or indirectly to or for the use of any disqualified person if the value of the economic benefit exceeds the value of the consideration received by the organization for providing the benefit [§ 4958(c)]. However, in excess benefit transactions with supporting organizations and donor advised funds, the entire amount of the transaction is the excess benefit.

The initial tax on disqualified persons is 25% of the excess benefit. Organization managers (i.e., a director, officer, trustee, or similar) who willingly and in the absence of reasonable cause participated in the transaction knowing it was an excess benefit transaction are jointly and severally liable for an initial tax equal to 10% of the excess benefit (up to $20,000 per act). When an initial tax is imposed on a disqualified person, an additional tax equal to 200% of the excess benefit may be imposed on the person if the transaction is not corrected within the taxable period. Organization managers are not subject to an additional tax. The IRS has authority to abate both the initial and additional tax if the excess benefit transaction is corrected within a specified time period [§ 4961(a), § 4962(a), § 4963].

*Disqualified Persons.* For purposes of the excise tax on excess benefit transactions, a "disqualified person" is [§ 4958(f)]:

- any person who, at any time during the five-year period ending on the date of the transaction, was in a position to exercise substantial influence over the organization's affairs (i.e., an "insider");
- a member of the family of an insider;
- an entity controlled by an insider or insider's family member;
- in the case of a supporting organization, a substantial contributor, a substantial contributor's family member, or an entity controlled by either;
- in the case of a DAF, a donor or donor advisor; or
- in the case of an organization that sponsors a DAF, an investment advisor.

### XIX.A.8. Participation in Tax Shelter Transactions

[451 T.M., XII.; TPS ¶7010.02.G.]

Tax-exempt organizations are subject to excise taxes when the entity acts as an accommodation party to a prohibited tax shelter transaction [§ 4965(a)]. The tax rate depends on whether the entity knew or had reason to know that the transaction was a prohibited tax shelter transaction. Managers of tax-exempt organizations may also be subject to the tax if they approve or cause the organization to participate in a prohibited tax shelter transaction, knowing or having reason to know that the transaction was a prohibited tax shelter transaction. For purposes of the manager-level tax, "tax-exempt entities" include: (1) entities described in § 501(c), § 501(d), and § 170(c); (2) Native American tribal governments; (3) tax-qualified pension plans, IRAs, and similar tax-favored savings arrangements [Reg. § 53.4965-2(a)]. A tax-exempt organization that participates in a prohibited tax shelter transaction must report it to the IRS on Form 8886-T, *Disclosure by Tax-Exempt Entity Regarding Prohibited Tax Shelter Transaction.*

### XIX.A.9. Compliance for § 501(c)(3) Organizations: Applying for and Maintaining Exempt Status

[450 T.M., 451 T.M.; TPS ¶7010.01., .02.]

#### XIX.A.9.a. Applying for Exempt Status

[450 T.M., IX.A.; TPS ¶7010.01.]

An organization that wishes to be tax exempt as a charitable organization must file either Form 1023, *Application for Recognition of Exemption Under § 501(c)(3) of the Internal Revenue Code*, or Form 1023-EZ, *Streamlined Application for Recognition of Exemption Under § 501(c)(3) of the Internal Revenue Code* [Reg. § 1.501(a)-1T(a)(2)]. An organization can use Form 1023-EZ if it has gross receipts of $50,000 or less and assets of $250,000 or less, unless it is specifically designated ineligible [Rev. Proc. 2014-40, 2014-30 I.R.B. 229, § 2.01].

The organization must file Form 1023 or Form 1023-EZ within 15 months (or 27 months if filed pursuant to the automatic 12-month extension) from the end of the month of its organization. Form 1023-EZ must be filed electronically. If the organization does not file or files late, it will not be treated as exempt under § 501(c)(3) for any period before the filing of the notice, unless it submits, and the IRS approves, Form 1023, Schedule E.

Churches, conventions or associations of churches, and integrated auxiliaries of churches are not required to file Form 1023 (and are ineligible to file Form 1023-EZ). Also, any organization other than a private foundation with gross receipts that are normally not more than $5,000 does not need to file either Form 1023 or Form 1023-EZ. Further, any subordinate organization other than a private foundation covered by a group exemption or a parent and certain nonexempt charitable trusts does not need to file an application for exempt status.

There is an $850 user fee for initial applications for exempt status using Form 1023 for organizations seeking exemption under § 501(c) whose actual or anticipated average annual gross receipts exceed $10,000 [Rev. Proc. 2014-8, 2014-1 I.R.B. 242, § 6.09]. There is a $400 user fee for applications for exemption under § 501 or § 521 from organizations other than pension, profit-sharing, and stock bonus plans that have had annual gross receipts averaging not more than $10,000 during the preceding four years, or new organizations anticipating gross receipts averaging not more than $10,000 during their first four years. An additional user fee of $3,000 must be paid for a group exemption letter. The user fee for Form 1023-EZ is $400 [Rev. Proc. 2014-40, § 4.04]. Unlike Form 1024 (discussed at XIX.B.2.), organizations applying for exemption under § 501(c)(3) need not file Form 8718 when paying the user fee.

### XIX.A.9.b. Annual Information Return

[452 T.M., II.B.; TPS ¶7010.02.A.]

Most exempt organizations are required to file an annual return, even if it did not file an application for exemption, on or before the 15th day of the fifth calendar month following the close of the organization's tax year [§ 6033(a)(1)]. The annual return must be filed even if the organization has not yet been recognized as being exempt [Reg. § 1.6033-2(c)].

The annual return for public charities is Form 990, *Return of Organization Exempt From Income Tax*. Public charities must also file Schedule A to Form 990. If a charity received a contribution of $5,000 or more, it must file Schedule B to Form 990. Private foundations file their annual returns on Form 990-PF, *Return of Private Foundation or Section 4947(a)(1) Nonexempt Charitable Trust Treated As a Private Foundation* [§ 6033(c)].

Exempt organizations other than private foundations with gross receipts of more than $50,000 and less than $200,000 and total assets of less than $500,000 may use Form 990-EZ, *Short Form Return of Organization Exempt From Income Tax*, to meet the annual filing requirements. An organization other than a § 509(a)(3) supporting organization whose gross receipts are normally not more than $50,000 must electronically file Form 990-N (e-Postcard) unless they choose to file a complete Form 990 or Form 990-EZ instead [§ 6033(i)]. Form 990-N is filed at http://epostcard.form990.org.

If an exempt organization fails to file a timely annual return, or files an incomplete or incorrect return, the organization is subject to a penalty of $20 per day for each day the failure to file continues [§ 6652(c)(1)(A)]. The maximum penalty that can be imposed for any one return is limited to the lesser of $10,000 or 5% of the organization's gross receipts for the tax year. These monetary penalties do not apply to organizations with annual gross receipts that normally do not exceed $50,000 (i.e., organizations required to file Form 990-N). In any year in which an organization has gross receipts of more than $1 million, the penalty for failure to file the return or to file a complete return is $100 per day, with a maximum penalty of $50,000. If an organization fails to provide the required electronic notice for three consecutive years, the organization's exempt status will be revoked [§ 6033(j)].

A penalty may also be imposed on the managers of an exempt organization. If an organization fails to file a return or files an incomplete return, the IRS may demand in writing that the organization file the return or supply the missing information within a reasonable period after the demand is mailed [§ 6652(b)(1)(B)]. If the organization does not comply with the demand, a $10 per day penalty is imposed on the person or persons responsible for the failure to comply, for each day the failure to comply continues. The penalty imposed on all such persons for any one return is limited to $5,000.

***Public Disclosure Requirements***. A tax exempt organization must make available for public inspection and copying its three most recent annual information returns and its application for exemption [§ 6104]. Any person who fails to comply with the public inspection and copying requirements is subject to a penalty of $20 per day until the requirement is satisfied [§ 6652(c)(1)(C)]. The maximum penalty that can be imposed on all persons for failing to disclose annual returns is $10,000. There is no limit on the penalty for failure to disclose the exemption application.

### XIX.A.9.c. Revocation or Modification of Determination Letter

[450 T.M., IX.A.1.d.; TPS ¶6510.07.B.]

A ruling or determination letter may be revoked or modified by: (1) notice to the organization, presumably after audit; (2) enactment of legislation or ratification of a tax treaty; (3) a U.S. Supreme Court decision; (4) issuance of temporary or final regulations; (5) publication of a revenue ruling, revenue procedure, or other statement in the Internal Revenue Bulletin; or (6) automatically, pursuant to § 6033(j), for failure to file a required annual return or notice for three consecutive years [Rev. Proc. 2014-9, 2014-2 I.R.B. 281, § 12]. The revocation or modification may be retroactive if the organization omitted or misstated a material fact or operated in a manner materially different from that originally represented. A court may overturn a retroactive revocation if it finds that the organization did not omit or misstate a material fact or operate in a manner materially different from that originally represented.

### XIX.A.9.d. Other Reporting Requirements

[452 T.M., II.; TPS ¶7010.]

***Disclosure of Nondeductibility of Contributions***. Each fundraising solicitation by or on behalf of an organization that is not a permissible donee for purposes of the charitable deduction (e.g., lobbying groups, social clubs, political organizations, political action committees, trade associations, and labor unions) must contain an express statement that contributions or gifts to the organization are not deductible as charitable contributions for federal income tax purposes [§ 6113]. The statement of nondeductibility of contributions must appear in a conspicuous and easily recognizable format. An organization is subject to a penalty of $1,000 for each day on which the failure to comply with the requirement for disclosing the nondeductibility of contributions occurred, up to a maximum of $10,000 for all failures to comply during a calendar year [§ 6710]. The penalty is not imposed, however, if the failure to comply was due to reasonable cause.

***Disclosure Relating to Quid Pro Quo Contributions***. Organizations that are qualified recipients of charitable contributions must inform donors that quid pro quo contributions in excess of $75 are only deductible to the extent that the contributions exceed the value of goods or services provided by the organization [§ 6115]. The notice must be in writing and provide the donor with a good-faith estimate of the value of goods or services furnished to the donor by the organization. A quid pro quo contribution is defined as a payment made partly as a contribution and partly in consideration for goods or services furnished to the donor by the charitable organization. Organizations that fail to comply with the disclosure requirements are subject to a penalty of $10 for each contribution for which the organization fails to make the required disclosure, subject to a maximum of $5,000 for each fundraising event or mailing [§ 6714]. If reasonable cause can be shown for failure to comply with the disclosure requirements, then no penalty is imposed.

*Contributions of Motor Vehicles, Boats, and Airplanes.* If a donor contributes a motor vehicle, boat, or airplane with a claimed value of more than $500, the donee organization must file Form 1098-C, *Contributions of Motor Vehicles, Boats, and Airplanes*, and furnish a contemporaneous written acknowledgement of the contribution to the donor. The organization is subject to penalties under § 6720 if it knowingly furnishes a false or fraudulent acknowledgement, or fails to furnish an acknowledgement in the manner, at the time, and showing the information required by § 170(f)(12).

*Contributions of Intellectual Property.* A donee organization that received a charitable gift of qualified intellectual property must file Form 8899, *Notice of Income From Donated Intellectual Property*, if the property produces net income for the year. The organization may be subject to a penalty if it fails to file Form 8899 by the due date, fails to include all of the required information, or fails to include correct information [§ 6721, § 6722, § 6723, § 6724].

*Disposition of Donated Property.* An organization must file Form 8282, *Donee Information Return (Sale, Exchange or Other Disposition of Donated Property)*, if it sells, exchanges, consumes, or otherwise disposes of (with or without consideration) any portion of charitable deduction property within three years after the date the organization received the property [§ 6050L(a)]. An organization does not need to file Form 8282 if the property disposed of had a value of $500 or less or if the property was consumed or distributed for a charitable purpose. The organization may be subject to a penalty (generally $50 per form) if it fails to file Form 8282 by the due date, fails to include all of the information required to be shown, or includes incorrect information on the filed form [§ 6721, § 6722, § 6723, § 6724].

## XIX.B. Other Exempt Organizations

### XIX.B.1. Types of Tax-Exempt Noncharitable Organizations

[450 T.M., V.; TPS ¶6520.]

In addition to § 501(c)(3) organizations, certain noncharitable organizations qualify for exemption from federal income taxation if they satisfy certain specific requirements:

*Instrumentalities of the United States* [§ 501(c)(1)]: Corporate instrumentalities of the United States specifically exempted from tax by Congress (e.g., FDIC, Federal Reserve Banks, etc.).

*Title and Real Property Holding Companies* [§ 501(c)(2)]: Corporations (but not trusts) organized for the exclusive purpose of holding title to property, collecting the income from the property, and remitting the net income to another organization that itself is exempt from tax under § 501(a).

*Social Welfare Organizations* [§ 501(c)(4)]: Nonprofit civic organizations that operate exclusively for the promotion of social welfare (i.e., primarily engaged in promoting the common good and general welfare of the people of a community) or local associations of employees, the membership of which is limited to the employees of a designated person(s) in a particular municipality and the net earnings of which are devoted exclusively to charitable, educational, or recreational purposes.

*Labor, Agricultural, or Horticultural Organizations* [§ 501(c)(5)]: Labor, agricultural, and horticultural organizations are tax exempt. Labor organizations are associations of workers who have combined to protect or promote their interests by bargaining collectively with their employers to secure better working conditions, wages, and similar benefits. Agricultural and horticultural organizations are organizations involved in the art or science of cultivating land, including preparing the soil, the planting of seeds, the raising and harvesting of crops or aquatic resources, and the rearing, feeding, and management of livestock.

*Trade Associations/Business Leagues* [§ 501(c)(6)]: Nonprofit business leagues, chambers of commerce, real estate boards, boards of trade, and professional football leagues, if no part of the organization's net earnings inure to the benefit of any private or individual shareholder.

*Social Clubs* [§ 501(c)(7)]: Clubs that are organized and operated for pleasure, recreation, and other nonprofit purposes, are exempt from tax if substantially all of the club's activities are for such purposes, and no part of the club's net earnings inures to the benefit of any private shareholder. This generally encompasses social and recreation clubs that are supported solely by membership fees, dues and assessments, as well as fees charged to members for the use of facilities. Exemption as a social club is less desirable than other categories of exemption, because the club's income other than its "exempt function" income (generally, income originating from members and amounts set aside for charitable and similar purposes) is subject to the UBIT (see XIX.D.5.).

*Fraternal Benefit Societies* [§ 501(c)(8)]: Fraternal benefit societies, orders, or associations that (1) operate under the lodge system (or operate for the exclusive benefit of the members of a fraternity that operates under the lodge system), and (2) provide for the payment of life, sick, accident, or other benefits to members or their dependents.

*Voluntary Employees' Beneficiary Associations* [§ 501(c)(9)]: Organizations consisting of employees whose eligibility is defined by reference to objective standards that constitute an employment-related common bond that provide for the payment of life, sick, accident, or other benefits to the members, their dependents or designated beneficiaries, no part of whose net earnings inures to the benefit of any private shareholder or individual.

*Domestic Fraternal Organizations* [§ 501(c)(10)]: Domestic fraternal societies, orders, or associations operating under the lodge system that (1) devote their net earnings exclusively to fraternal, religious, charitable, scientific, literary, or educational purposes, and (2) do not provide for the payment of life, sick, accident, or other benefits.

*Teachers' Retirement Fund Associations* [§ 501(c)(11)]: Local teachers' retirement fund associations are exempt from tax if (1) no part of the organization's net earnings (other than the payment of retirement benefits) inures to the benefit of any private shareholder or individual, or (2) the organization derives its income solely from public taxes, assessment from the teaching salaries of members, and investments.

*Life Insurance, Irrigation, Telephone and Similar Organizations* [§ 501(c)(12)]: Benevolent life insurance companies, mutual ditch or irrigation companies, mutual or cooperative telephone companies, or similar organizations are exempt from tax if 85% or more of the organization's income consists of amounts collected for the sole purpose of satisfying losses and expenses.

*Cemetery Companies* [§ 501(c)(13)]: Mutual cemetery companies that are owned and operated exclusively for the benefit of their members, nonprofit cemetery companies, and corporations chartered solely for burial or cremation purposes, that are not permitted by their charters to engage in any business not necessarily incident to those purposes, and no part of the net earnings of which inures to the benefit of a private shareholder or individual.

*Nonprofit Credit Unions and Mutual Insurance Funds* [§ 501(c)(14)]: Nonprofit mutual credit unions without capital stock that are formed and operated under a state credit union law and certain nonprofit mutual corporations or associations organized before September 1, 1957, are exempt from tax. However, federal credit unions are instrumentalities of the United States exempt under § 501(c)(1) rather than under § 501(c)(14).

*Small Insurance Companies* [§ 501(c)(15)]: An insurance company (as defined in § 816(a)), other than life (including interinsurers and reciprocal underwriters), is exempt from tax if its gross receipts for the tax year do not exceed $600,000, and more than 50% of those receipts consist of premiums. A mutual insurance company may qualify as tax-exempt under an alternative test requiring that gross receipts do not exceed $150,000 and premiums make up more than 35% of those receipts.

*Crop-Financing Corporations* [§ 501(c)(16)]: Corporations organized by § 521 farmers' cooperative marketing associations or purchasing associations, or the members thereof, that are operated in conjunction with the § 521 organization and are formed to finance the ordinary crop operations of the members or other producers.

*Supplemental Unemployment Compensation Trusts* [§ 501(c)(17)]: Certain trusts forming part of a plan providing for the payment of supplemental unemployment compensation benefits are exempt from tax. Supplemental unemployment compensation benefits are benefits paid to an employee because of the employee's involuntary separation from employment as a result of a reduction in labor force, a discontinuance of a plant or operation, or other similar conditions.

*Employee-Funded Pension Trusts* [§ 501(c)(18)]: Trusts created before June 25, 1959, that form part of a pension plan and that are funded only by employee contributions, are exempt as long as there are no fundamental changes in the character of the trust or its beneficiaries.

*Organizations of Past or Present Members of the Armed Forces* [§ 501(c)(19)]: Domestic posts or organizations of past or present members of the United States armed forces (including an auxiliary unit or society of such individuals, and a trust or foundation for such a post or organization) are exempt from tax if at least 75% of the organization's members are past or present members of the armed forces and substantially all other members are cadets, or spouses, widows, widowers, ancestors, or lineal descendents of past or present members or veterans of the armed forces or of cadets. No part of the net earnings of the organization may inure to the benefit of any private shareholder or individual.

*Group Legal Services Organizations* [§ 501(c)(20)]: Group legal services organizations are no longer exempt from tax [§ 120(e)].

*Black Lung Benefit Trusts* [§ 501(c)(21)]: Irrevocable domestic trusts created to satisfy, in whole or in part, a coal mine operator's liability for black lung benefits under the Black Lung Benefits Revenue Act of 1977.

*Multi-Employer Plan Trusts* [§ 501(c)(22)]: Trusts established by sponsors of multi-employee benefit plans are exempt from tax if the purpose of the trust is exclusively to pay an amount described in ERISA § 4223(c) or (h) and to pay reasonable and necessary administrative expenses in connection with the establishment and operation of the trust.

*Armed Forces Insurance Associations* [§ 501(c)(23)]: Any association organized before 1880 more than 75% of the members of which are present or past members of the United States armed forces and a principal purpose of which is to provide insurance and other benefits to veterans or their dependents.

*Employee Benefit Trusts* [§ 501(c)(24)]: A trust described in ERISA § 4049, as in effect on the date of enactment of the Single Employer Pension Plan Amendments Act of 1986, is qualified to be exempt from tax.

*Title-Holding Corporations or Trusts* [§ 501(c)(25)]: A corporation or trust, having no more than 35 shareholders of beneficiaries (who have certain rights) and only one class of stock or beneficial interest, organized for the exclusive purposes of acquiring real property, holding title to and collecting the income from such property, and remitting the income to one or more qualifying shareholders or beneficiaries.

*State-Sponsored High-Risk Health Insurance Pools* [§ 501(c)(26)]: Membership organizations that have been established by a state to provide medical care on a not-for-profit basis to certain delineated individuals.

*State-Sponsored Workers' Compensation Organizations* [§ 501(c)(27)]: An organization is exempt if it is organized and operated under state law exclusively to provide workmen's compensation insurance that is either required by state law or for which state law provides significant disincentives if an employer fails to purchase the insurance. There are special rules for organizations created before June 1, 1996.

*National Railroad Retirement Investment Trust* [§ 501(c)(28)]: The National Railroad Retirement Investment Trust (NRRIT), established under § 15(j) of the Railroad Retirement Act of 1974.

*CO-OP Health Insurance Issuers* [§ 501(c)(29)]: Qualified nonprofit health insurance issuers that received a loan or grant under the consumer operated and oriented plan program established under the Patient Protection and Affordable Care Act.

*Religious and Apostolic Organizations* [§ 501(d)]: Religious or apostolic associations or corporations are exempt from tax, if the organization has a common or community treasury. The organization may engage in business for the common benefit of the members, provided, however, that the members include in their gross income as a dividend their pro rata share, whether actually distributed or not, of the taxable income of the organization for the tax year of the organization ending with or during the individual's tax year.

*Credit Counseling Organizations* [§ 501(q)]: Organizations that provide credit counseling services are entitled to tax exemption only if they are § 501(c)(3) charitable organizations or § 501(c)(4) social welfare organizations and satisfy numerous requirements set forth in § 501(q). The organization must tailor its services to the specific needs and circumstances of consumers and must provide services to consumers who are unable to pay its fees. Additionally, an organization cannot refuse to serve a consumer on the ground that the customer is not eligible for debt management plan enrollment or the unwillingness of the consumer to enroll in a debt management plan.

*Farmers' Cooperatives* [§ 521]: Farmers', fruit growers', or similar associations organized and operated on a cooperative basis to (1) market the products of members or other producers and remit the proceeds (less expenses) based upon quantity or the value of products furnished, or (2) purchase supplies and equipment for the use of members or other persons at cost, plus necessary expenses are exempt from tax. A farmers' cooperative may issue capital stock, provided that any dividend is based on the value of the consideration for the stock and is fixed at a rate that does not exceed the legal rate of interest in the state of incorporation or 8% per annum, whichever is greater. Further, at least 85% of such stock (other than nonvoting preferred stock, the owners of which may not participate beyond the fixed dividends), must be owned by the producers who market their products and purchase their supplies or equipment through the association. Exemption will not be denied if the organization accumulates and maintains a reserve required by state law or a reasonable reserve for necessary purposes (e.g., the erection of facilities, the purchase of machinery and equipment, or the retirement of indebtedness incurred for such purposes). A farmers' association may (1) market products of nonmembers, provided the value of such products does not exceed the value of the products marketed for members, and (2) purchase supplies and equipment for nonmembers, provided that the value of the purchases for nonmembers does not (a) exceed the value of the purchases for members, and (b) exceed 15% of the value of all purchases. Note, however, that exempt farmers' cooperatives are subject to the corporate income tax [§ 1381] (see XIII.F.4.).

*Political Organizations* [§ 527]: A party, committee, association, fund, or other organization that is organized and operated primarily to accept contributions and/or make expenditures to influence the selection, nomination, election, or appointment of any individual to any federal, state, or local public office, or office in a political organization, or the election of Presidential or Vice-Presidential electors, is exempt from tax. An organization will be treated as meeting the operational test if, between elections, it is not supporting any specific candidate, but is engaged in activities that are related to and support the process of election of candidates. A political organization is subject to the highest rate of corporate income tax imposed by § 11 on its "political organization taxable income." "Political organization taxable income" is defined as the organization's gross income other than "exempt function income," less the deductions directly connected with the production of such includible gross income. "Exempt function income" includes amounts received as: (1) a contribution of money or other property; (2) membership dues; (3) proceeds from the conduct of bingo games as described in § 513(f)(2); and (4) proceeds from a political fundraising or entertainment event or from the sale of political campaign materials other than amounts received in the ordinary course of a trade or business. However, such amounts must be segregated in a separate account or accounts for the "exempt function" of the organization. A specific deduction of $100 is allowed, but no § 172 net operating loss deduction nor any dividends received deduction is allowed. If a § 527 organization has capital gains and if a lesser tax would result, the organization may, under § 527(b)(2), use the § 1201(a) alternative tax, computed with reference to its political organization taxable income.

*Qualified Tuition Programs* [§ 529]: A program established and maintained by a state or an agency/instrumentality thereof, or by one or more eligible educational institutions (including private institutions) under which persons may purchase tuition credits or certificates on behalf of a designated beneficiary that entitle the beneficiary to a waiver or payment of his/her qualified higher education expenses is exempt from tax. In the case of a QTP maintained by a state or a state agency or instrumentality, a person may also make contributions to an account that is established for the purpose of meeting qualified higher education expenses of the designated beneficiary of the account (see II.L.2.).

### XIX.B.2. Compliance for Noncharitable Tax-Exempt Organizations

[452 T.M., II.A.; TPS ¶7010.01., .02.]

Other than § 501(c)(3), § 501(c)(4), § 501(c)(9), § 501(c)(17), and § 501(c)(20) organizations and § 527 political organizations seeking exempt status pursuant to § 527(i), the Code does not require the organization to apply for recognition of exemption. However, most organizations do apply for recognition of exemption to confirm, and avoid litigation over, their qualification for exemption.

Generally, a noncharitable organization applies for exemption under § 501(a) by using Form 1024, *Application for Recognition of Exemption Under Section 501(a)*. Form 8718, *User Fee for Exempt Organization Determination Letter Request*, must be filed with Form 1024 and requires that a $850 user fee be included with the initial exemption application under § 501(a) [Rev. Proc. 2014-8, 2014-1 I.R.B. 242, § 6.09]. For organizations with annual gross receipts normally not more than $10,000 for the preceding four years or new organizations that anticipate gross receipts normally not more than $10,000 during the first four years, the user fee is $400. The user fee is $3,000 for group exemption letters.

*Farmers Cooperatives*. Farmers cooperatives must use Form 1028, *Application for Recognition of Exemption Under Section 521 of the Internal Revenue Code*, and pay an $850 user fee [Rev. Proc. 2014-8, § 6.09]. The user fee is $400 for organizations with annual gross receipts averaging not more than $10,000 during the preceding four years, or new organizations that anticipate gross receipts averaging not more than $10,000 during the first four years. An organization that is recognized as exempt under § 521 must file an annual return on Form 1120-C, *U.S. Income Tax Return for Cooperative Associations* (see XIII.F.4.).

*Political Organizations*. Political organizations must electronically file Form 8871, *Political Organization Notice of Section 527 Status*, to apply for exemption. There are five types of organizations that do not need to file Form 8871:

1. persons required to report under the Federal Election Campaign Act of 1971 as a political committee;
2. organizations that reasonably anticipate that their annual gross receipts will always be less than $25,000;
3. organizations described in § 501(c) that are subject to § 527(f)(1) because they have made an "exempt function" expenditure;
4. political committees of a state or local candidate; and
5. state or local committees of a political party.

A political organization that transfers $500 or more per calendar year to a single recipient, or that receives aggregate contributions of at least $200 from a single contributor during a calendar year must file, either monthly or quarterly, Form 8872, *Political Organization Report of Contributions and Expenditures*. Section 527(j) excludes some organizations from this filing requirement. Tax-exempt political organizations with gross receipts of $25,000 or more are required to file Form 990. Political organizations that receive contributions of $5,000 or more from any one contributor must include Form 990, Schedule B. A tax-exempt political organization is not required to file Form 990 if it is (1) not required to file Form 8871 (including an organization required to file as a political committee with the FEC), or (2) a caucus or association of state or local officials. Organizations with taxable political expenditures under § 527(f) must file Form 1120-POL, *U.S. Income Tax Return for Certain Political Organizations*.

*Annual Information Return.* Generally, organizations exempt from tax under § 501(a) must file Form 990 (see XIX.A.9.b.).

## XIX.C. Private Foundations

### XIX.C.1. Definition of Private Foundation

[450 T.M., VIII.B.; TPS ¶6810.01.]

A private foundation is any § 501(c)(3) organization other than a public charity [§ 509(a)]. There are four types of organizations excepted from private foundation status:

- public organizations;
- publicly supported organizations;
- qualified supporting organizations; or
- organizations organized and operated exclusively for testing for public safety.

*Public Organizations.* The first group of organizations excepted from private foundation status consists of those organizations engaging in certain legislatively favored activities. Churches, educational organizations, hospitals and medical research organizations, supporting organizations of state colleges and universities, and governmental units are deemed per se to be public charities without regard to their actual control or sources of support because they serve a public function [§ 509(a)(1)].

*Publicly Supported Organizations.* Publicly supported organizations are considered public charities. An organization qualifies as a publicly supported organization if more than 1/3 of its support is normally received from the public, including gifts, grants, contributions, membership fees, and exempt function income, and not more than 1/3 of its support is from investment income and unrelated business taxable income (UBTI), (less unrelated business income tax (UBIT) imposed thereon) [§ 509(a)(2)].

*Qualified Supporting Organizations.* Qualified supporting organizations are considered public charities. A qualified supporting organization is organized and operated exclusively for the benefit of, to perform the functions of, or to carry out the purposes of one or more public charities or publicly supported organizations [§ 509(a)(3)(A)]. The organization must be operated supervised or controlled by a public charity or publicly supported organization, or supervised, controlled, or operated in connection therewith [§ 509(a)(3)(B)]. Finally, a supporting organization must not be controlled by certain disqualified persons [§ 509(a)(3)(C)].

### XIX.C.2. Restrictions and Taxes Applicable to Private Foundations

[450 T.M., VIII.C.; TPS ¶¶6860, 6870, 6880, 6890, 6900, 6910.]

There are significant operating restrictions on private foundations, including excise taxes on:

- the net investment income of a private foundation (other than an exempt operating foundation) for the tax year [§ 4940(a)];
- various acts of self-dealing [§ 4941];
- the failure to meet minimum requirements for distribution of a private foundation's income [§ 4942];
- retention of excess business holdings [§ 4943];
- jeopardizing investments [§ 4944];
- taxable expenditures [§ 4945]; and

- the termination of an organization's status as a private foundation [§ 507].

Further, donations to private foundations are subject to more stringent limitations for purposes of the income tax charitable deduction than apply to gifts to public charities.

The IRS has discretionary authority to abate a qualified first tier tax (see XIX.C.2.), including interest, if the private foundation establishes that the occurrence of a taxable event was both due to reasonable cause and not due to willful neglect, and the taxable event was corrected within the correction period [§ 4962(a)]. A "qualified first tier tax" is defined as any excise tax imposed on a private foundation, except for the initial tax on self-dealing [§ 4962(b)].

A private foundation and the foundation managers are eligible for abatement of any second tier tax (including interest, additions to the tax, and additional amounts) if the taxable event is corrected within the correction period [§ 4961(a)]. Unlike the abatement of the initial tax, the abatement of the additional tax is not dependent on the discretion of the IRS. If the investment is removed from jeopardy within the correction period, then the additional tax will not be assessed. If the additional tax was already assessed, the assessment will be abated. If the additional tax was collected, it will be credited or refunded as an overpayment.

### XIX.C.2.a. Taxation of Net Investment Income

[468 T.M., I.B.; TPS ¶6860.01.]

Most private foundations, except exempt operating foundations, are subject to a 2% excise tax on their net investment income for the tax year [§ 4940(a)]. Private foundations that satisfy certain charitable distribution requirements and that were not liable for the tax on undistributed income in any of the previous five tax years are eligible for a reduced rate of 1% [§ 4940(e)].

A private foundation's net investment income is equal to its gross investment income (to the extent excluded from computation of UBIT), plus its capital gain net income, reduced by allowable deductions [§ 4940(c)]. To the extent they are excluded from the computation of UBIT, the following items are included in a private foundation's gross investment income: interest, dividends, rents, payments with respect to securities loans, royalties, and income from sources substantially similar to the preceding sources (e.g., notional principal contracts, annuities, and other ordinary and routine investments) [§ 4940(c)(2)]. In computing net investment income, a private foundation may deduct all the ordinary and necessary expenses paid or incurred for the production or collection of gross investment income or for the management, conservation, or maintenance of property held for the production of gross investment income.

**Exempt Operating Foundation.** For purposes of the private foundation rules, an exempt operating foundation is a foundation that satisfies the following requirements [§ 4940(d)(2)]:

1. the foundation makes sufficient distributions in directly accomplishing its exempt purpose and satisfies either an assets test, an endowment test, or a support test (i.e., the foundation is an operating foundation);
2. the foundation has been publicly supported for at least 10 tax years;
3. the foundation's governing body consists of individuals at least 75% of whom are not disqualified individuals and is broadly representative of the general public; and
4. a disqualified individual is not an officer of the foundation at any time during the tax year.

The excise tax on net investment income is reported on Form 990-PF, *Return of Private Foundation or Section 4947(a)(1) Nonexempt Charitable Trust Treated as a Private Foundation*, and estimated payments of the foundation's liability are calculated on Form 990-W, *Estimated Tax on Unrelated Business Taxable Income for Tax-Exempt Organizations* [§ 6655(g)(3)].

### XIX.C.2.b. Taxes on Self-Dealing

[470 T.M., IV.; TPS ¶6870.01.]

An initial tax is imposed on each act of self-dealing between a disqualified person and a private foundation. The initial tax on disqualified persons is equal to 10% of the amount involved in the act of self-dealing for each year (or portion of a year) in the taxable period [§ 4941(a)]. The initial tax on foundation managers is equal to 5% of the amount involved in the act of self-dealing, if the manager knowingly and willfully participated in the transaction in the absence of reasonable cause. The maximum aggregate amount of tax collectible as an initial tax from all foundation managers for any act of self-dealing is $20,000 [§ 4941(c)(2)]. If the self-dealing transaction is not corrected during the taxable period, an additional tax may be imposed on the disqualified person (200%) and foundation managers (50%). The private foundation, itself, is not liable for the tax on self-dealing transactions.

*Taxable Period*. For any act of self-dealing, "taxable period" means the period beginning with the date on which the act of self-dealing occurs and ending on the earliest of (1) the date of mailing of the notice of deficiency for the initial tax, (2) the date the initial tax is assessed, or (3) the date on which correction of the act of self-dealing is completed [§ 4941(e)(1)].

Disqualified persons include:

- substantial contributors;
- foundation managers;
- owners of more than 20% of the total combined voting power of a corporation, the profits interest of a partnership, or the beneficial interest in a trust or unincorporated enterprise, if the corporation, partnership, trust, or unincorporated enterprise is a substantial contributor;
- family members of disqualified persons described above (including spouses, ancestors, descendants, and spouses of descendants);
- corporations, partnerships, trusts, or estates of which persons described above own more than 35% of the combined voting power, profits interest, or beneficial interest; or
- government officials.

Acts of self-dealing include any direct or indirect engagement in one of the following activities by a private foundation and a disqualified person [§ 4941(d)(1)]:

- sales or exchanges;
- leases;
- lending money;
- furnishing goods, services, or facilities;
- payment of compensation to a disqualified person;
- transfer to or use of a private foundation's income or assets by or for the benefit of a disqualified person; or
- agreement to pay money or other property to a government official.

The tax on self-dealing is reported on Form 4720, *Return of Certain Excise Taxes Under Chapters 41 and 42 of the Internal Revenue Code.*

### XIX.C.2.c. Failure to Distribute Income

[880 T.M., I.B.; TPS ¶6880.01.A.]

There is an initial excise tax of 30% on a private foundation's undistributed income that has not been distributed before the first day of the second (or any succeeding) tax year following the tax year for which the income was required to be distributed [§ 4942(a)]. Thus, if a calendar year private foundation has a required distributable amount for 2014 equal to $50,000 and it distributes only $20,000 of its 2014 undistributed income by December 31, 2015, it is subject to a 30% excise tax, effective January 1, 2016, on the $30,000 of undistributed income for 2014. The failure to distribute is reported on Form 990-PF, and the initial excise tax is reported on Form 4720.

A second-tier tax, equal to 100% of the undistributed income, is imposed on a foundation that fails to distribute the required amount within the "taxable period" [§ 4942(b)]. The taxable period begins on the first day of the tax year and ends on the earlier of (1) the date the notice of deficiency for the initial tax is mailed, or (2) the date on which the initial tax is assessed [§ 4942(j)(1)]. For example, assume a calendar-year private foundation has $10,000 in undistributed income for 2014 that remains undistributed on December 31, 2015. If the IRS mails a notice of deficiency to the foundation on August 1, 2016, then the foundation's taxable period begins on January 1, 2014 and ends on August 1, 2016.

### XIX.C.2.d. Excess Business Holdings

[473 T.M., I.B.; TPS ¶6890.03.]

Generally, a private foundation and all of its disqualified persons may not hold more than 20% of the voting stock, profits interest, or beneficial interest of a business enterprise that is not related to the private foundation's exempt purpose [§ 4943(c)(2)]. The limit is increased to 35% where a third person has effective control of the business enterprise. There is an initial tax imposed at a rate of 10% on the value of a private foundation's excess business holdings during any tax year that ends during the taxable period [§ 4943(a)(1)]. The taxable period begins on the first day on which the private foundation has excess business holdings and ends on the earliest of (1) the date of mailing of the notice of deficiency, (2) the date on which the excess is eliminated, or (3) the date on which the initial tax is assessed [§ 4943(d)(2)]. Excess business holdings are reported on Form 990-PF and any tax due is reported on Form 4720.

The initial tax is payable by the foundation. Foundation managers are not liable. Although the tax is imposed on the last day of the tax year, the amount of the tax and the value of the excess business holdings is determined as of the date during the tax year on which the private foundation's excess business holdings were the greatest [§ 4943(a)(2)].

An additional tax equal to 200% of the value of the private foundation's excess business holdings is imposed if the private foundation still has excess business holdings at the close of the taxable period [§ 4943(b)].

***Application to Donor Advised Funds and Supporting Organizations***. The excise tax on excess business holdings also applies to donor advised funds, Type III supporting organizations, and § 501(c)(3) organizations that meet the organizational and operational tests of qualified supporting organizations and that are not controlled by a disqualified person [§ 4943(e), § 4943(f)].

### XIX.C.2.e. Taxes on Jeopardizing Investments

[468 T.M., II.C.; TPS ¶6900.02.]

A private foundation is liable for a 10% excise tax on any amount of income or principal invested in a way that jeopardizes its exempt purpose(s) [§ 4944(a)(1)]. An initial 10% excise tax (up to $10,000 per investment) also is imposed on a foundation manager who willfully and knowingly participated in the making of a jeopardizing investment (unless the participation was due to reasonable cause). An investment is considered to jeopardize the carrying out of a private foundation's exempt purpose(s) if it is determined that, in making the investment, the foundation managers failed to exercise ordinary business care and prudence in providing for the long-term and short-term financial needs of the foundation to carry out its exempt purposes.

When an initial tax has been imposed on a private foundation for making a jeopardizing investment, an additional 25% tax may be imposed if the investment is not removed from jeopardy within the taxable period [§ 4944(b)]. If an additional tax is imposed on the private foundation, then an additional 5% tax (up to $20,000) is imposed on any foundation manager who refused to agree to all or part of the removal of the investment from jeopardy.

No types of investments are treated as per se jeopardizing investments [Reg. § 53.4944-1(a)(2)(i)]. However, certain categories of investments are closely scrutinized to ascertain whether the foundation managers have satisfied the requisite standard of care, including:

- trading in securities on margin;
- trading in commodity futures;
- investments in working interests in oil and gas wells;
- the purchase of puts, calls, and straddles;
- the purchase of warrants; and
- short sales.

### XIX.C.2.f. Taxes on Taxable Expenditures

[474 T.M., III.B.; TPS ¶6910.02.]

There is an initial tax on private foundations of 20% of the amount of each taxable expenditure [§ 4945(a)(1)]. The initial tax on foundation managers is equal to 5% (up to $10,000) of the amount of the taxable expenditure, provided an initial tax is imposed on the private foundation, and the manager willfully agreed to the making of the expenditure knowing that it was a taxable expenditure and did not have reasonable cause to do so [§ 4945(a)(2)].

The categories of taxable expenditures are [§ 4945(d)]:

- expenditures to influence legislation;
- expenditures to influence public elections or carry on voter registration drives;
- grants to individuals for travel, study, or similar purposes;
- grants to other private foundations; and
- expenditures for noncharitable purposes.

When an initial tax has been imposed on a private foundation for making a taxable expenditure, an additional tax equal to 100% of the amount of the expenditure may be imposed if the expenditure is not corrected within the taxable period [§ 4945(b)]. If an additional tax is imposed on the private foundation, an additional tax equal to 50% of the expenditure (up to $20,000) is also imposed on any foundation manager who refused to agree to all or part of the correction. The taxable period within which a taxable expenditure must be corrected to avoid imposition of the additional tax begins on the date on which the expenditure is made, and ends on the earlier of the mailing of a notice of deficiency for the initial tax or the date on which the initial tax is assessed [§ 4945(i)(2)].

If multiple foundation managers are liable for the initial or additional tax for the making of a taxable expenditure, then they are jointly and severally liable [§ 4945(c)(1)].

### XIX.C.2.g. Penalty for Repeated Violations

[452 T.M., V.E.; TPS ¶6870.05.C.]

Private foundations and/or foundation managers can also be subject to a penalty for repeated violations of IRC Chapter 42. If the foundation or manager was previously liable for any of the excise taxes on private foundations or their managers, or the act or failure that gave rise to the imposition of the excise tax was willful and flagrant, then the foundation or manager is liable for a penalty equal to the amount of the tax [§ 6684]. The foundation or manager is not liable for the penalty if the act or failure to act was due to reasonable cause.

### XIX.C.3. Termination of Private Foundation Status

[877 T.M., XIV.; TPS ¶6850.01.]

There are four authorized methods for termination of private foundation status [§ 507(a), § 507(b)]:

1. Voluntary termination by the private foundation after notifying the IRS.
2. Involuntary termination by the IRS if there have been either willful repeated acts (or failures to act) or a willful and flagrant act (or failure to act) giving rise to tax liability under one of the excise taxes described in XIX.C.2.
3. Transfer of all of the private foundation's assets to one or more eligible public charities followed by a voluntary termination.
4. Conversion to a public charity.

The private foundation is subject to a termination tax equal to the lesser of the aggregate tax benefit resulting from tax-exempt status of the organization or the value of its net assets [§ 507(c)]. If a private foundation voluntarily terminates its status by either transferring its net assets to a public charity or by converting to a public charity, no termination tax is imposed. In all other cases, the IRS has discretionary authority to abate the unpaid portion of the tax if it determines that action is being taken to assure that the foundation's assets are preserved for charitable purposes [§ 507(g)]. A terminating foundation that has paid a part of the tax cannot use the abatement procedures as its remedy, but instead must file a claim for a refund.

An organization must use Form 8940, *Request for Miscellaneous Determination*, to obtain a determination about termination of private foundation status.

## XIX.D. Taxation of § 501 Organizations — Unrelated Business Income Tax

[450 T.M., I.; TPS ¶6510.01.]

An exempt organization is not subject to tax on its income (including dues and contributions) from an activity that is substantially related to the charitable, educational, or other purpose that is the basis for the organization's exemption, even if the activity is a trade or business.

### *XIX.D.1. Imposition of Unrelated Business Income Tax*

[462 T.M.; TPS ¶6710.]

The unrelated business income tax (UBIT) is imposed on an exempt organization's "unrelated business taxable income." Unrelated business taxable income (UBTI) is equal to the gross income subject to the tax, reduced by the allowable deductions and computed with certain specified modifications [§ 512(a)(1)]. An organization must include in UBTI the gross income (as defined in § 61) (see Chapter I.) derived from any regularly conducted trade or business that is not substantially related to its exempt purpose [§ 512(a)(1), § 513(a)]. The exclusions from gross income that are generally applicable for income tax purposes apply to the UBIT (see Chapter II.). In computing UBTI, an organization can take into account deductions that are directly connected with the carrying on of the unrelated trade or business (see Chapter IV.). Further, numerous items are excluded from UBTI as modifications under § 512(b), including dividends, interest, royalties, and certain rents.

*"Trade or Business" Requirement.* For purposes of the UBIT, a trade or business includes any activity carried on for the primary purpose of producing income or generating profit from the sale of goods or the performance of services [§ 513(c); Reg. § 1.513-1(b)]. The IRS may fragment a particular business activity into component parts, some of which may be treated as related activities and others of which may be taxed as unrelated businesses. Thus, for purposes of the UBIT, the term "trade or business" does not necessarily refer to an aggregate of assets, activities, and goodwill that would comprise a single business under a common understanding of the term.

*"Regularly Carried On" Requirement.* In determining whether a trade or business is regularly carried on, the most important considerations are (1) whether the business activity is carried on with a frequency and continuity similar to comparable commercial activities of nonexempt organizations, and (2) whether the activity is pursued in a manner generally similar to such commercial activities [§ 512(a)(1); Reg. § 1.513-1(c)(1)]. The activities of an exempt organization's agent are attributed to the organization for purposes of determining whether a business activity is regularly conducted.

*"Not Substantially Related" Requirement.* A trade or business is a substantially related business if the conduct of the business activity has a causal relationship that contributes importantly to the achievement of an organization's exempt purpose(s) [Reg. § 1.513-1(d)(2)]. In determining whether a trade or business contributes importantly to the achievement of an organization's exempt purposes, one factor is to consider is the size and extent of the business activity in relation to the nature and extent of the exempt function that the activity purports to serve [Reg. § 1.513-1(d)(3)].

Certain activities are not considered unrelated trades or businesses, including:

- a business in which substantially all of the work is performed without compensation (i.e., the "volunteer exception") [§ 513(a)(1); Reg. § 1.513-1(e)];
- a trade or business that is carried on by a charitable organization, or by a state college or university, primarily for the convenience of its members, students, patients, officers, or employees (i.e., the "convenience exception") [§ 513(a)(2)];
- the selling of merchandise, substantially all of which was received by the organization as gifts or contributions (i.e., the "donations exception") [§ 513(a)(3)];
- entertainment or recreational activities traditionally conducted at agricultural fairs and expositions [§ 513(d)(1), § 513(d)(2)];

- trade shows and similar activities designed to promote the products or services of an industry [§ 513(d)(1), § 513(d)(3)];
- income derived by a hospital from the performance of various services (specifically listed in § 501(e)(1)(A)) at cost for specified small hospitals [§ 513(e)];
- certain bingo games [§ 513(f)];
- income derived by mutual or cooperative telephone and electric companies from the rental of their poles [§ 513(g)];
- income derived by charitable organizations and war veterans organizations from the distribution of low-cost articles (for 2014, an article costing $10.40 or less; for 2015, an article costing $10.50 or less) incidental to the solicitation of charitable contributions [§ 513(h); Rev. Proc. 2013-35, 2013-47 I.R.B. 537, § 3.28(1), Rev. Proc. 2014-61, 2014-47 I.R.B. 860, § 3.29(i)];
- amounts received from the exchange or rental of mailing lists among charitable organizations and war veterans organizations [§ 513(h)]; and
- the solicitation and receipt of qualified sponsorship payments [§ 513(i)].

The following exempt organizations are not subject to the UBIT:

- instrumentalities of the United States [§ 501(c)(1)];
- farmers' cooperatives [§ 521] (see XIII.F.4.);
- shipowners' protection and indemnity associations [§ 526];
- political organizations [§ 527]; and
- homeowners associations [§ 528].

### *XIX.D.2. Calculation of UBTI — Exclusions*

[462 T.M., IV.C.; TPS ¶6710.04.C.]

Various items of income and the related deductions are expressly excluded from the computation of UBTI [§ 512(b)].

Items of investment income that are not derived from debt-financed property and related deductions are excluded from the computation of UBTI. Such items include dividends, interest, annuities, payments with respect to securities loans, loan commitment fees, and royalties [§ 512(b)(1), § 512(b)(2)]. In the context of UBTI, royalties generally consist of payments for the use of a right, such as a trademark, trade name, or copyright. Royalties do not include payments for services rendered.

All rents from real property and all rents from personal property leased therewith, provided that the rents attributable to the personal property do not exceed 10% of the total rents from all property leased, are excluded from UBTI [§ 512(b)(3)(A)]. Payments for the use or occupancy of rooms or other space where services are also rendered do not constitute rent from real property. There are two exceptions to the rental exclusion rule [§ 512(b)(3)(B)]. First, the exclusion does not apply if more than 50% of the total rent received or accrued under the lease is attributable to personal property. Second, the exclusion is not available if the determination of the amount of rent depends in whole or in part on the income or profits derived by any person from the leased property, other than an amount based on a fixed percentage of receipts or sales.

Gains or losses from the sale, exchange, or other disposition of property other than stock in trade or other property of a kind that would properly be includible in inventory if on hand at the close of the tax year or property held primarily for sale to customers in the ordinary course of a trade or business are excluded from UBTI [§ 512(b)(5)]. The exclusion also applies to gains or losses recognized in connection with the organization's investment activities from the lapse or termination of options to buy or sell securities or real property and all gains or losses from the forfeiture of good-faith deposits for the purchase, sale, or lease of real property in connection with the organization's investment activities.

The following items of research income, and all deductions directly connected with such research income, are excluded in computing UBTI [§ 512(b)(7), § 512(b)(8), § 512(b)(9)]:

- income derived from research for the United States, or any of its agencies or instrumentalities, or for any state or political subdivision thereof;

- in the case of a college, university, or hospital, income derived from research performed for any person; and

- in the case of an organization operated primarily for the purpose of carrying on fundamental research, the results of which are freely available to the general public, income from research performed for any person.

Any item of unrelated income from debt-financed property is included in UBTI, regardless if it is of a class that is otherwise excluded under § 512(b)(1), § 512(b)(2), § 512(b)(3), or § 512(b)(5) [512(b)(4)].

### XIX.D.3. Unrelated Debt-Financed Income

[465 T.M.; TPS ¶6720.]

### XIX.D.3.a. Inclusion of Debt-Financed Income in UBTI

[465 T.M., I.B.; TPS ¶6720.01.]

Income and deductions from debt-financed property is taken into account in computing UBTI. Debt-financed property is property having the following two basic characteristics: (1) the property is held to produce income, and (2) there was acquisition indebtedness on the property at any time during the tax year or, if the property was disposed of during the tax year, at any time during the 12 month period ending with the date of disposition [§ 514(b)]. Property held to produce income includes property held to produce recurring payments (e.g., dividends, interest, royalties, and rents), recurring income (e.g., securities, mineral production payments, leased equipment, and rental real estate), and gain upon disposition.

Debt-financed property does not include [§ 514(b)(1)]:

- certain property with a use substantially related to the organization's exempt purpose;

- property used to derive research income;

- property used in businesses excepted from the unrelated business tax by the volunteer, convenience, and donations exceptions;

- brownfield property;

- property acquired for prospective exempt use; and

- life income contracts.

The debt/basis percentage is used to determine the amount of income and deductions related to debt-financed property that is taken into account in computing UBTI. The debt/basis percentage is a fraction, the numerator of which is the average acquisition indebtedness and the denominator of which is the average adjusted basis [§ 514(a)(1)]. The debt/basis percentage cannot exceed 100%.

### XIX.D.3.b. Definition of Acquisition Indebtedness

[465 T.M., III.B.; TPS ¶6720.02.]

Acquisition indebtedness is the unpaid amount of [§ 514(c)(1)]:

1. indebtedness incurred by an organization in acquiring or improving property;
2. indebtedness incurred before the acquisition or improvement of the property, if the indebtedness would not have been incurred but for the acquisition or improvement; and
3. indebtedness incurred after the acquisition or improvement of the property, if the indebtedness would not have been incurred but for the acquisition or improvement and the incurrence of the indebtedness was reasonably foreseeable at the time of the acquisition or improvement.

An extension, renewal, or refinancing of a pre-existing obligation is not treated as the creation of new indebtedness [§ 514(c)(3)]. Further, acquisition indebtedness does not include indebtedness the incurrence of which is inherent in the performance or exercise of an organization's exempt purpose or function [§ 514(c)(4)].

Generally, if property is acquired subject to a mortgage, the amount of indebtedness secured by the mortgage is considered an indebtedness of the organization incurred in acquiring the property regardless of whether the organization assumed or agreed to pay the indebtedness [§ 514(c)(2)(A)]. However, when property subject to a mortgage that is acquired by bequest or devise, the mortgage is not treated as acquisition indebtedness for a 10-year period following the date of acquisition [§ 514(c)(2)(B)]. If an organization acquires property by gift subject to a mortgage that was placed on the property more than five years before the gift, and the property was held by the donor more than five years before the gift, the indebtedness secured by such mortgage is not treated as acquisition indebtedness during a period of 10 years following the date of the gift.

When property is acquired subject to a lien similar to a mortgage, the amount of indebtedness secured by the lean is treated as indebtedness incurred in acquiring the property. A lien is similar to a mortgage if title to property is encumbered by the lien for the benefit of a creditor [Reg. § 1.514(c)-1(b)(2)]. Where state law provides that a lien for taxes or assessments made by a state or political subdivision thereof attaches to property before the time when the taxes or assessments become due and payable, the lien is treated as similar to a mortgage only after: (1) the taxes or assessments become due and payable; and (2) the organization has had an opportunity to pay the taxes or assessments in accordance with state law.

Acquisition indebtedness does not include the obligation of an exempt organization to pay an annuity, provided [§ 514(c)(5)]:

- the value of the annuity is less than 90% of the value of the property received in the exchange;
- the annuity is payable over the lives of one or two individuals in being at the time the annuity is issued; and
- the annuity is payable under a contract that (1) does not guarantee a minimum number of payments or specify a maximum number of payments, and (2) does not provide for any adjustment of the amount of the annuity payments by reference to the income received from the transferred property or any other property.

Finally, acquisition indebtedness does not include an obligation to finance the purchase, rehabilitation, or constructing of housing for low and moderate income persons, to the extent the debt is insured by the Federal Housing Administration [§ 514(c)(6)].

### XIX.D.4. Calculation of UBTI — Deductions

[462 T.M., IV.B.; TPS ¶6710.04.B.]

In computing UBTI, an organization may utilize deductions allowed for income tax purposes that are directly connected with the carrying on of the unrelated trade or business [§ 512(a)(1)]. A deduction is directly connected with the conduct of an unrelated trade or business if it has a proximate and primary relationship to the conduct of the business [Reg. § 1.512(a)-1(a)]. If an exempt organization's assets or personnel are employed both in an unrelated trade or business and in exempt activities, then deductions attributable to such assets or personnel must be allocated between the two uses on a reasonable basis [Reg. § 1.512(a)-1(c)].

Deductions for charitable contributions and net operating losses are also available [§ 512(b)(6), § 512(b)(10), § 512(b)(11)]. For all non-trust exempt organizations subject to the UBIT, and for state colleges and universities, the charitable contributions deduction is limited to 10% of the organization's UBTI, computed without regard to the charitable contributions deduction [§ 512(b)(10)]. The deduction is allowed regardless of whether the charitable gift is directly connected with the conduct of an unrelated trade or business. To qualify for the deduction, the contribution must be made to another organization; i.e., use of funds by an organization in administering its own exempt programs does not qualify for the charitable contributions deduction [Reg. § 1.512(b)-1(g)(3)].

Except for purposes of computing the net operating loss deduction, an exempt organization is allowed a specific deduction of $1,000 in computing its UBTI [§ 512(b)(12)]. Only one specific deduction is allowed for each tax year, regardless of the number of unrelated trades or businesses carried on by the organization.

### XIX.D.5. Special Rules for Certain Exempt Organizations

[462 T.M., IV.D.; TPS ¶6710.04.D.]

The determination of the UBTI of social clubs, voluntary employees' beneficiary associations (VEBAs), and supplemental unemployment compensation benefit trusts (SUBs) is different than it is for other exempt organizations [§ 512(a)(3)]. Generally, exempt organizations are taxed only on income from regularly conducted trades or businesses. Most of their investment income is not taxed by virtue of modifications authorizing exclusion of dividends, interest, and other passive income. In contrast, social clubs, VEBAs, and SUBs are taxed on virtually all of their income, including investment income, except receipts from members. The different treatment for social clubs, VEBAs, and SUBs is accomplished by a special definition of unrelated business taxable income for such organizations and a special rule for nonrecognition of gain on the disposition of exempt function property.

### XIX.D.6. Computing UBIT

[462 T.M., V.; TPS ¶6710.05., .06.]

The UBIT on exempt trusts is computed using the income tax rates applicable to estates and trusts [§ 511(b)(1), § 1(e)] (see XVII.A.2.). For all other organizations, the UBIT is computed using the corporate rates [§ 511(a)(1), § 11] (see XIII.C.2.). An exempt organization computes its UBTI using the method of accounting regularly used in keeping its books and records [§ 446(a)]. However, if gross receipts from unrelated business activities exceed $5 million, the organization is required to use the accrual method of accounting [§ 448(a)(1), § 448(b)(3), § 448(d)(6)].

*Alternative Minimum Tax*. Organizations subject to the unrelated business income tax are also subject to the alternative minimum tax with respect to the adjustments and items of tax preference that enter into the computation of UBTI [§ 55(b)]. Exempt organizations that meet the definition of a small corporation are exempt from the alternative minimum tax [§ 55(e)(1)(A), § 55(e)(1)(C)].

*Compliance*. An exempt organization with gross income of $1,000 or more from an unrelated trade or business must file Form 990-T, *Exempt Organization Business Income Tax Return*, to report UBIT [Reg. § 1.6012-2(e), § 1.6012-3(a)(5)]. Exempt organizations required to make quarterly estimated payments of UBIT use Form 990-W, Estimated Tax on Unrelated Business Taxable Income for Tax-Exempt Organizations [§ 6655(g)(3)].

# CHAPTER XX. U.S. INTERNATIONAL TAXATION
>>>>>>>>>>>>>>>>>>>>>>>>>>>>>>>

## XX.A. Classification of Taxable Persons

[900 T.M., I., 905 T.M., I.; TPS ¶7110.03.]

There are four classes of "person" for U.S. income tax purposes: individuals, corporations, partnerships, and trusts and estates. Individuals and most corporations are treated as separate taxable entities [§ 7701(a)(1)] (see Chapter XIII.). Partnerships are not separately taxable; their income and other tax attributes are recognized in the hands of their owners (see Chapter XIV.). Estates and trusts are normally taxed in the same manner as individuals on income that they retain, but distributed income becomes taxed to the beneficiary (see Chapter XXI.).

Under U.S. international tax rules, as under most countries' tax systems, taxpayers are further classified into "resident" and "nonresident" [§ 7701(b)(1)]. The difference, normally, is that resident taxpayers — no matter what kind of persons — are subject to income taxation on their worldwide income, while nonresidents are subject to income tax only on income from sources within the taxing country [§ 61(a), § 2(d), § 11(d)]. Worldwide income tax liability is often called "residence-based" taxation; even if a country does not impose tax on worldwide income, residents are subject to the full scope of whatever tax it does impose.

The U.S. system treats both U.S. citizens (wherever they reside) and resident alien individuals as income tax residents under this distinction. Citizens are defined by law as any person born or naturalized in the United States [8 USC §§ 1401-1459, §§ 1481-1489]. "Resident" alien individuals are defined positively by a pair of tests. First, "lawful permanent residents" under immigration law ("green card" holders) are residents as long as they hold that status [§ 7701(b)(1)(A)]. Second, other aliens are considered resident for tax purposes if they are in the United States under a day-count test, which requires presence of at least 31 days in the year under consideration [§ 7701(b)(3)]. In applying the day-count test, if the number of days an alien is present in the current year, plus one-third of the days present in the prior year, plus one-sixth of the days present in the second prior year equals 183 or more, the person is a resident alien. The law makes exceptions for days present for certain special purposes, for example, as a diplomat, as a student or teacher, or as a medical patient [§ 7701(b)(5)]. Some income tax treaties can negate the statutory determination of residence for some purposes.

Corporations are not formally classified as resident or nonresident; domestic corporations (formed under U.S. federal or state laws) are taxed on worldwide income analogously to resident individuals; foreign corporations (any corporation that is not resident) is subject to source taxation [§ 7701(a)(4), § 7701(a)(5), § 7701(a)(30)(C); Reg. § 301.7701-5].

Partnerships are not themselves subject to income tax, and their status as resident or nonresident has been made fairly irrelevant. For instance, compare § 861(a)(1)(B) with Reg. § 1.861-2(a)(2), addressing the sourcing of interest payments of a foreign partnership. There is no general rule for their residence, thus, their status as "domestic" (formed under U.S. or state law) or "foreign" is more important [§ 7701(a)(4), § 7701(a)(5), § 7701(a)(30)(C); Reg. § 301.7701-5].

Similarly, trusts are classified as "domestic" or "foreign" according to whether they have a U.S. trustee and are subject to primary U.S. legal jurisdiction, and then are subject to tax as "U.S. persons" or nonresident aliens according to their domestic or foreign status [§ 7701(a)(30)(E), § 7701(a)(31); Reg. § 301.7701-7]. Although estates do not have a formal classification, they tend to be categorized along principles similar to those used for trusts.

With legal entities, in order to classify a taxpayer as domestic, foreign, resident or nonresident, it is also necessary to categorize it as one of the types of legal entities that the U.S. system recognizes [Reg. §§ 301.7701-1 through -7] (see Chapter XVI.). If an entity is a "business entity," that is, it exists for some income-earning purpose other than mere conservation of property for beneficial owners, specific rules are applied, although slightly differently for domestic entities than for foreign entities [Reg. § 301.7701-2(a)].

Foreign legal entities that are business entities are mandatorily considered to be corporations if they operate as insurance companies or banking institutions, or are owned by governments, or are legal entities of a kind listed in the regulations (and referred to as "per se" corporations) [Reg. § 301.7701-2(b)]. If a foreign entity does not fall into these categories, a second-level test is applied [Reg. § 301.7701-2(c)]. Although not frequently encountered, it is possible for some joint arrangements to be considered business entities for U.S. tax purposes and be subject to the entity classification process [Reg. § 301.7701-1(a)(2)]. If the entity has at least one owner that has unlimited legal liability for the debts or liabilities of the entity, it will default to partnership status. Contrarily, if it has no owners with unlimited liability, it will default to corporate status. Foreign entities that are not foreign "per se" corporations — referred to as foreign eligible entities in the regulations — may elect to be treated as either corporate or partnership, as the case may be, under the same procedure as is used for domestic entities making status elections [Reg. § 301.7701-2(b)(2), § 301.7701-3(b), § 301.7701-3(c).]

Finally, an important special rule applies to both domestic and foreign eligible entities that have pass-through status, either because they default to it, have elected it, or have a single owner. In this case, they disappear for most U.S. tax purposes; these are referred to as "disregarded entities" [Reg. § 301.7701-2(a)]. The most common exception to disregarded status is with respect to employment taxes (subtitle C and § 1402 dealing with self-employment tax). Both the disregarded entity and its owner retain all liabilities for withholding, payment, and filing as separate entities.

## XX.B. Source Rules for Income, Deductions, and Losses

[900 T.M., I.H., 905 T.M.; TPS ¶7110.04.]

The geographic source of income, deduction, and loss is pertinent to the U.S. taxation of income in four main contexts. First, U.S. persons are taxed on their worldwide income, and a foreign tax credit is available to offset foreign taxes paid on income from foreign sources [§ 901]. Second, nonresidents, who are taxed only on U.S. source gross income must determine which income items have a U.S. source; foreign persons who are taxed on a net basis must determine which income items are included (one element of which is the source of the income), and they must determine which deductions are attributable to that income to arrive at U.S. taxable income. Third, people who are "withholding agents" (responsible for withholding U.S. tax on U.S. source payments to foreign persons) may be liable in their own right for failure to withhold [§§ 1441-1446]. Thus, they must be aware of the source of income that they are paying to a foreign person to administer this responsibility. Fourth, U.S. individuals who qualify for preferential treatment arising from residence or substantial presence in a foreign country may exclude from gross income only foreign-source earned income [§ 911].

The principal U.S. source rules for income are statutory [§ 861-§ 862]. For many years, the Code has set out specific and fairly detailed rules by which the source of traditional income items may be determined. More recently enacted rules address more complex types of income.

| Income Type | General Source Rule |
|---|---|
| Interest | U.S. if paid by a U.S. or state government; a U.S. corporation; a U.S. citizen or noncorporate resident; if paid by or allocable to a U.S. business of a foreign person; or paid by a foreign partnership predominantly in U.S. business, even if not allocable to its U.S. business. Otherwise foreign. |
| Dividends | U.S. if paid by a U.S. corporation (that is not a "possession" corporation under § 936), including a DISC (a tax-benefitted corporation making foreign sales); a foreign corporation with material income from U.S. business or if dividend is eligible for exclusion as a U.S. dividend. Otherwise foreign. |
| Personal Services | U.S. if the services are performed in the U.S.; otherwise foreign (apportioned by time spent at locations or other methods). |
| Rent or Royalties | U.S. to the extent the property is used in the United States; foreign to the extent it is not. |
| Gains from Sales of U.S. Property | U.S. |
| Gains from Sale of Inventory | For property purchased and sold, the place of sale (where the right, title and interest pass to the buyer). Passage of title and the risk of loss are the most significant elements. |
| Social Security Benefits | U.S. if paid by the U.S. |
| Guarantee Fees | U.S. if paid by a U.S. corporation or U.S. resident, or by a foreign corporation if the expense is deductible. |
| Railroad Rolling Stock Usage Fees | U.S. if received by a non-railroad owner, and the property is used in North America, unless used in Canada or Mexico for more than 90 days in a year. If received by a railroad, the normal rule for rents applies. |

### XX.B.1. Inventory Sales

[905 T.M. VII.B.; TPS ¶7110.04.B.6.]

The sourcing rule for gain from selling inventory in the above table applies only to sales of purchased property. Manufacturers or producers must take additional steps to determine the source of income from selling property that they make [§ 863(b), § 865(b)]. First, they divide their gross income into an amount attributed to manufacturing and an amount attributed to sale of the product. The default, and commonly most favorable, method simply attributes 50% of the gross income to each activity. A taxpayer that regularly sells property to independent buyers, at prices reasonably reflecting income from production activity, can use that "independent factory price" to divide the income from other sales of that product. Alternatively, with advance permission from IRS, a taxpayer could report production income recorded on its books as the appropriate amount, attributing the remainder to sales [Reg. § 1.863-3].

Once the gross income attributable to production is determined, it is sourced as U.S. or foreign income, according to the adjusted tax basis of the taxpayer's production assets within and outside the U.S. Then, the amount that had been attributed to sales is sourced using the sales rule described in the table.

### XX.B.2. Other Personal Property Sales

[905 T.M. VII.A.; TPS ¶7110.04.B.6.]

Gain from selling property other than inventory is treated as having a source in the United States if sold by a U.S. person, or outside the United States if sold by a foreign person. Before that rule is applied, the amount of gain equal to depreciation taken in the United States on depreciable property is first resourced as U.S. gain. A second special rule sources gain from selling an intangible property as if it were a royalty (i.e., where the property is used) if the payments are contingent on use, productivity, or disposition of the property. The depreciation recapture rule just noted applies to sales of intangibles as well [§ 865(a)].

Sourcing gain under the general residence rule can be avoided by a U.S. resident (including a U.S. corporation) selling property through a foreign office that it maintains in a foreign country, if that country imposes an income tax of at least 10% on the gain. In addition, sourcing under the general rule can be avoided by a corporation selling stock of an 80% affiliate in a country in which the affiliate conducts an active business, if it earns at least 50% of its gross income over a three-year test period from the active business in that country.

Gain from selling property by a foreign person becomes U.S. source, however, notwithstanding all of the rules just described, if the foreign person maintains a U.S. office, and that office materially participates in the solicitation, negotiation or completion of the sale (so that under U.S. principles, that gain is attributable to that office). To promote exports, however, this rule is waived in the case of inventory property sold for use, consumption or disposition outside the United States, and a foreign office of the taxpayer also materially participates in making the sale.

### XX.B.3. New or Mixed Source Income

[905 T.M., IX., X., XI.; TPS ¶7110.04.C.]

Over the years, economic development, new technologies, and tax policy developments have led to new source rules for new kinds of income, or mixed source income. The principal statutory additions are:

*Transportation Income.* Trips that begin and end in the United States are deemed to generate 100% U.S. income. Trips that have one endpoint in the United States generate 50% U.S. source income [§ 863(c)(1)].

*International Communications Income.* Income from transmissions between the United States and a foreign country is 50% U.S. source if earned by a U.S. person. If earned by a foreign person (other than a controlled foreign corporation) that is not engaged in a U.S. trade or business, the income is deemed to be foreign unless it is earned by a U.S. office of that person, in which case it is all U.S. source. If earned by a foreign person engaged in a U.S. trade or business but not attributed to an office, the income is apportioned based on the percentage of U.S. assets, activities, and risks [§ 863(e); Reg. § 1.863-9].

*Space or Ocean Activity Income.* Income earned in space or on the ocean outside the jurisdiction of any country, and not sourced by one of the rules above, is U.S. source if earned by a U.S. person or foreign source if earned by a foreign person (other than a controlled foreign corporation) that is not engaged in a U.S. trade or business. If earned by a foreign person engaged in a U.S. trade or business but not attributed to an office, the income is apportioned based on the percentage of U.S. assets, activities, and risks [§ 863(d); Reg. § 1.863-8]. For purposes of U.S. source oil, gas and mineral exploration on the continental shelf, income earned in those activities is not ocean activity income [§ 638].

### XX.B.4. Filling Voids in the Source Rules

[905 T.M., XV.; TPS ¶7110.04.B.10., .04.B.11., 04.B.12.]

Although the Code and regulations cover an increasing number of income types, they do not identify all activities for which an income-source rule is needed. When there is no specific rule, courts and the IRS have stepped in to fill the void, applying various analyses to reach a result. Among these techniques are substitution and analogy. Under the first technique, payments that actually or in effect substitute for a payment with an established source have been given the source of the payment for which they substitute. For example, interest paid by a foreign guarantor of a U.S. company's debt was treated as U.S. source under a substitution theory, because it substituted for interest that otherwise would be paid by a U.S. person [Rev. Rul. 70-377, 1970-2 C.B. 175].

The second technique analyzes a payment to see what activity with an established source rule is most closely analogous to the payment under examination, and assigns that source to it. So, for example, courts have sourced guarantee fees by analogy to services income, because the act of guaranteeing a loan seemed more like a service than a loan; and letter of credit commissions have been sourced under interest sourcing rules, because the transactions seemed like an extension of credit.

### XX.B.5. Deductions and Losses

[900 T.M., I.J.; TPS ¶7110.04.D.]

Part of the mechanism for determining taxable income from a specific source is sometimes spoken of as identifying the "source" of deductions. More precisely, deductions are not "sourced;" they are attributed. That is, the deductions are identified with items of gross income that have been sourced, and in that way follow the income to a source. As a result, one does not search for the situs of a deduction, but for the relationship between that deduction and a class or item of gross income.

The Code does not direct which items of deduction are allocated to income from a particular source. Instead, it establishes a general two-step process, which the regulations term "allocation" and "apportionment" [§ 861(b), § 862(b); Reg. § 1.861-8; § 1.861-8T]. First, a deductible item is associated with a class of gross income to which it is directly related, in the sense that it was incurred as a result of, or in connection with, an activity that would earn income of that class. This is known as "allocation." A "class" of gross income is any kind of income listed in the Code (§ 61) (see Chapter I.), or an identifiable subdivision of that kind of income. Items of expense or deduction that relate to multiple classes of gross income (or that are related to all or no classes of income) are distributed among the classes under an apportionment formula.

Once a deduction has been allocated to one or more classes of gross income, it is "apportioned" between foreign source income and U.S. source income by use of a ratio. The specific ratio may be relative amounts of gross income, gross receipts or sales, units produced, time spent, assets used to produce the income, or any other reasonable ratio that reflects a factual connection between the deduction and the income [Reg. § 1.861-8T].

The regulations contain a number of special rules for particular kinds of expenses:

- Interest expense must almost always be apportioned by reference to the value of assets used in activities that generate income, not simply by gross income [Reg. §§ 1.861-9 through -12]. There are some limited situations, such as in the case of nonrecourse loans, in which a gross income apportionment is permitted [Reg. § 1.861-10].

- Research and experimentation expense must be allocated and apportioned over activities in broad product categories (normally 3-digit product codes under the Standard Industrial Classification (SIC) system or its replacements), notwithstanding that a narrow product may have been the objective of the research [Reg. § 1.861-17].

- Interest and various other expenses incurred by corporations that are in an affiliated group must be allocated and apportioned on an affiliated group basis (whether or not a consolidated return is filed) [Reg. § 1.861-14, § 1.861-14T].

- State income tax deductions are apportioned under specific rules that account for the fact that states' determinations of taxable income may differ from the federal amount [Reg. § 1.861-8(e)(6), § 1.861-8(g)].

- Losses from the sale of property are generally allocated to the class of gross income that would have been earned if the sale had produced a gain. (A class need not have income in it to support an allocation or an apportionment of deductions to it.) In the case of losses from selling shares of stock, the regulations track the rules for gain in general, but first require an allocation to recapture any dividend or other inclusion of earnings that had been received within two years of the loss [Reg. § 1.865-1, § 1.861-2.]

This discussion of allocating and apportioning deductions and losses considers the subject in the context of apportioning deductions between foreign source income and U.S. source income. This methodology is also used, however, to determine taxable income in special categories in most situations under which that special category receives special income tax treatment. For this reason the special category generating the need to make the computation is referred to as a "statutory grouping" of income (e.g., foreign source income is the statutory grouping), and the remainder is referred to as the "residual grouping" (e.g., in the case of foreign source income, the residual grouping is U.S. source income).

## XX.C. Foreign Activities of U.S. Taxpayers

### XX.C.1. Foreign Earned Income and Housing Cost Exclusions

[918 T.M., I.; TPS ¶7150.03.]

A qualified individual may exclude all or a portion of foreign earned income and exclude or deduct certain amounts related to foreign housing costs [§ 911]. However, any amount so excluded or deducted is taken into account for determining liability for the net investment income tax [§ 1441(d)]. If foreign earned income is not excluded, a taxpayer can instead claim a credit or deduction for foreign taxes paid on the income [§ 901].

#### XX.C.1.a. Basic Qualifications for § 911 Exclusion

[918 T.M., I.B., I.J.; TPS ¶7150.03.B.]

To claim the exclusion, an individual must have a tax home in a foreign country and be:

- a U.S. citizen who can establish an uninterrupted period of residency in a foreign country (or countries) over the entire tax year, or
- a U.S. citizen or resident alien who was physically present in a foreign country (or countries) for 330 full days (in the aggregate) over any consecutive 12-month period [§ 911(d)(1), § 911(d)(3)].

The 330 days need not be consecutive. A full day is a continuous period of 24 hours from midnight to midnight [Reg. § 1.911-2(d)(2)].

Also, a resident alien who is a citizen of a country that has an income tax treaty with the United States may usually qualify by applying the nondiscrimination clause found in most bilateral U.S. tax treaties [§ 7701(b)(1)(A); Rev. Rul. 91-58, 1991-2 C.B. 340].

#### XX.C.1.b. Foreign Earned Income for Purposes of § 911 Exclusion

[918 T.M., I.C.1.; TPS ¶7150.03.D.]

A limited amount of compensation for personal services performed in a foreign country is excludable from gross income. The annual limit is adjusted for inflation and is $99,200 for 2014 ($100,800 for 2015) [§ 911(b); Rev. Proc. 2013-35, 2013-47 I.R.B. 537, Rev. Proc. 2014-61, 2014-47 I.R.B. 860]. To determine an individual's maximum exclusion amount, the annual exclusion amount is multiplied by the fraction of qualifying days over the total days in the tax year.

---

**EXAMPLE:** In 2014, Sandy returned to the United States after having spent 185 qualifying days in Country A, during which she earned $32,000 in foreign income. Sandy's maximum exclusion for 2014 would be $50,279 ($99,200 × 185/365), however, because her actual foreign earned income was $32,000, she may exclude only $32,000 from gross income.

---

Amounts received as a pension or annuity or from a qualified retirement plan or as a U.S. government salary are not included in foreign earned income and may not be excluded from gross income [§ 911(b)(1)(B)].

#### XX.C.1.c. Foreign Housing Costs

[918 T.M., I.C.2.; TPS ¶7150.03.E.]

Foreign housing expenses are also excludable from gross income to the extent the costs are provided by an employer and exceed an annual base amount, subject to a limitation amount [§ 911(c)(2); Rev. Proc. 2013-35, 2013-47 I.R.B. 537]. These amounts are 16% and 30%, respectively, of the maximum foreign earned income exclusion amount for the year multiplied by the number of qualifying days and are computed on a daily basis [§ 911(c)(1), § 911(c)(2)].

---

**EXAMPLE:** The base amount for 2014 is $15,872 ($99,200 × 16%), resulting in a daily rate of $43.48 ($15,872/365), and the limitation amount is $29,760 ($99,200 × 30%), resulting in a daily rate of $81.53 ($29,760/365). Thus, the maximum annual exclusion for foreign housing costs in 2014 is $13,888 ($29,760 − $15,872), or a daily rate of $38.05 ($81.53 − $43.48). In the above example, since Sandy had 185 qualifying days and a maximum foreign earned income exclusion of $50,279 ($15,084 − $8,045), she can exclude $7,039 in housing costs.

---

Eligible housing costs are those that are reasonable expenses (i.e., not extravagant), and are paid or incurred by (or on behalf of) an individual (and any immediate family members) while in a foreign country. This includes rent and associated expenses (e.g., utilities and home insurance), but not amounts that qualify as deductible interest or taxes [§ 911(c)(3)]. A partial exclusion of foreign housing costs is not permitted [Reg. § 1.911-4(d)(1)].

Qualified individuals who are self-employed or do not have an employer-provided housing allowance can instead claim a deduction for housing costs, but only to the extent of the excess of one's foreign earned income exclusion over the housing cost amount exclusion for the tax year [§ 911(c)(4); Reg. § 1.911-4(e)]. Any portion of the housing cost amount that is disallowed due to the limitation can be carried over only once to the next tax year [§ 911(c)(4)(C); Reg. § 1.911-4(e)(2)]. In cases where an individual has self-employment income and employee wages, a portion of the housing cost amount is attributed to each income amount.

### XX.C.1.d. Making, Revoking, and Reelecting the Election

[918 T.M., I.G.; TPS ¶7150.03.F.]

The § 911 exclusions and deductions are elective and are made separately on Form 2555, *Foreign Earned Income*, which also must contain adequate information to determine a taxpayer's status as a qualified individual, and be filed with an income tax return [Reg. § 1.911-7(a)(1)-(2)]. Unless revoked, the election applies to all subsequent tax years [§ 911(e)(1)].

To revoke an election, a statement to that effect must be filed with the income tax return for the first tax year for which the revocation is to be effective and will remain effective for all later years [§ 911(e)(2); Reg. § 1.911-7(b)(1)]. Separate statements are required when revoking elections for both the foreign earned income exclusion and housing cost exclusion.

Once revoked, another election cannot be made without IRS consent until five tax years have passed [§ 911(e)(2); Reg. § 1.911-7(b)(1)]. Furthermore, if an individual claims a foreign tax credit on income excluded under § 911, the IRS will revoke one or both of the elections [Rev. Rul. 90-77, 1990-2 C.B. 183].

### XX.C.2. Foreign Tax Credit or Deduction

[901 T.M., I.B., 902 T.M., 904 T.M., 6380 T.M.; TPS ¶7150.02.]

The foreign tax credit is intended to reduce or avoid double taxation that would otherwise arise when foreign source income of a U.S. taxpayer is subject to taxation in the United States and a foreign country. There are two kinds of credits designed to mitigate this outcome. First, a direct credit is available to a U.S. person who pays or accrues creditable foreign income taxes which can be applied against U.S. tax liability [§ 901, § 903; Reg. § 1.901-1, § 1.903-1]. Typically, foreign taxes in this context will arise from income generated by the operations of foreign branches or disregarded entities, as well as withholding levied on payments of passive income from foreign persons. Second, an indirect credit is available for foreign taxes that are deemed to have been paid by the U.S. shareholder of a foreign subsidiary upon the distribution of a dividend [§ 902; Reg. § 1.902-1]. If a credit is not taken, a deduction may be taken instead [§ 901(n), § 164(a)(3); Reg. § 1.901-1(h)(2)].

### XX.C.2.a. Eligible Taxpayers

[901 T.M., III.; TPS ¶7150.02.B.]

The foreign tax credit is available to U.S. citizens and resident aliens and domestic corporations [§ 901(b); Reg. § 1.901-1(a)]. Likewise, partners in partnerships [§ 901(b)(5), § 704(b); Reg. § 1.704-1(b)(4)(ii)], shareholders of S corporations [§ 1363(c)(2)(B)], and estate and trust beneficiaries are all entitled to claim a proportionate credit [§ 901(b)(5)]. A nonresident alien and a foreign corporation engaged in a U.S. trade or business may also claim the credit in connection with creditable foreign tax on effectively connected foreign source income [§ 901(b)(4), § 906(a)].

### XX.C.2.b. Creditable Foreign Taxes

[901 T.M., II.; TPS ¶7150.02.E.]

To claim the foreign tax credit, a foreign levy must be creditable, meaning it has to be:

- a compulsory tax (or a tax imposed in lieu of an income tax);
- a tax on realized net income; and
- a tax that is imposed on or accrued and paid by the taxpayer-claimant [Reg. § 1.901-2(a)].

In evaluating a foreign levy, the predominant character must be that of an income tax, with reference made to U.S. law. Thus, a creditable foreign tax is one that is triggered by a taxable realization event and is based on the gross receipts and reaches the net income of the taxpayer; i.e., a certification by a foreign country that a levy is a tax is not enough [Reg. § 1.901-2(a)(2)(i), § 1.901-2(b)]. Provided it meets the requirements of an eligible tax, a tax in lieu of an income tax (e.g., a withholding tax on interest payments) may be creditable if it is imposed as a substitute for an otherwise applicable income tax and does not confer a special economic benefit [§ 903; Reg. § 1.903-1(a)].

Certain kinds of foreign taxes do not qualify for the credit. For instance, the denial of double benefits rule prevents one from claiming a foreign tax credit or itemized deduction for foreign taxes paid on income that is excluded from U.S. gross income or for which only an itemized deduction is permitted. Similarly, foreign taxes that arise in connection with operations in countries under an international boycott are not creditable [§ 908]. Moreover, customs duties, penalties and fines, interest, and similar obligations are not considered a tax [Reg. § 1.901-2(a)(2)(i)]. A tax payment that results in a "subsidy" for a taxpayer (or related person), such as through the use of rebates, credits, and refunds also does not qualify for the credit [§ 901(i); Reg. § 1.901-2(e)(2), § 1.901-2(e)(3)]. Certain "dual-capacity" taxpayers who receive a special economic benefit linked to a foreign levy have the burden of demonstrating what portion is the true tax [Reg. § 1.902-1(a)(2), § 1.902-1(b)(1)]. Likewise, a so-called "soak-up" tax, the liability for which depends on its creditability in a second country, is disqualified [Reg. § 1.901-2(c)]. More recently, rules were adopted that suspend the foreign tax credit in certain splitter transactions, which often arise in the parent-subsidiary context, by disallowing the splitting of foreign taxes for crediting until the year the related income is taken into account [§ 909; Reg. § 1.909-2T].

### XX.C.2.c. Indirect Credit

[902 T.M., II.; TPS ¶7150.02.F.2., .02.G.]

In contrast to the direct tax, an indirect credit is available to a domestic corporation for creditable foreign tax paid on a dividend received from a foreign subsidiary (or a deemed dividend with respect to a subpart F inclusion under § 951) [§ 78, § 902, § 960; Reg. § 1.902-1]. The parent corporation is treated as having paid the foreign tax directly by either including the dividend amount and foreign tax in its gross income, if the dividend represents all of the earnings and profits of the foreign subsidiary, or determining a credit proportional to the amount of distributed earnings and profits. To be eligible, however, the corporation must own at least 10% of the voting stock of the foreign company. Where multiple tiers of foreign subsidiaries are involved, the tax moves up the chain of ownership from the tax pool of the subsidiary that issued the dividend. Although an individual U.S. shareholder is not entitled to the indirect credit, special relief is provided elsewhere in the Code that allows one to elect to be taxed at corporate rates on the deemed dividend [§ 962].

As with the direct credit, the indirect credit is also available in limited circumstances to a foreign corporation in relation to foreign source income that is effectively connected with a U.S. trade or business [§ 901(b)(4), § 9061(a)].

### XX.C.2.d. Limitations

[904 T.M.; TPS ¶7150.02.H.]

The foreign tax credit is limited to the lesser of a taxpayer's foreign income taxes paid or accrued (or deemed paid) or the pre-credit U.S. tax on foreign source income [§ 904(a)]. In other words, the credit cannot exceed a taxpayer's U.S. tax liability attributed to foreign income so as to offset U.S. tax on U.S. source income. Although the rules on figuring the amount of the credit can be complicated, the basic formula is based on a ratio of foreign-to-worldwide taxable income multiplied by the total pre-credit U.S. tax, which provides a general (or overall) credit limit for the tax year. What can complicate the calculation is the interplay of the income sourcing rules [§ 861, § 862; Reg. § 1.861-1, § 1.862-1] with the rules for allocating and apportioning deductions [§ 861(b), § 862(b), § 863(a), 861(b); Reg. § 1.861-8, § 1.861-8T], particularly so when a taxpayer has multiple streams and different types of foreign and U.S. source income.

In addition to the general limitation on the foreign tax credit, separate limitations must be calculated for each type of foreign source income, most of which will fall into one of two categories (or baskets), general income and passive income [§ 904(d); Reg. § 1.904-1]. The separate limit treats all of a taxpayer's foreign source income and corresponding expenses in each category as a single unit. The credit amount is thus limited to the U.S. tax on the taxable income in each category and the usable credit is the sum of the limitations. Taxpayers cannot cross-credit foreign taxes paid on income in one category to another category.

Any excess foreign tax credits that go unused in a tax year may be carried back one year or forward until depleted for up to 10 years [§ 904(c); Reg. § 1.904-2]. Typically, excess credits will arise when the tax rate in a foreign jurisdiction is higher than the U.S. rate, and may also be caused by U.S. rules that allocate deductions to foreign income that are not allowed as deductions by a foreign country.

A limited exemption from the foreign tax credit limit is available if [§ 904(j)]:

1. a claim is based entirely on passive income;

2. all of one's foreign income and associated taxes are reported on a qualified payee statement (e.g., Form 1099-INT or a Schedule K-1); and

3. the creditable foreign taxes for the tax year do not exceed $300 ($600 for joint returns).

In this case, however, carryback and carryover of unused foreign tax credits is not permitted.

### XX.C.2.e. Election

[901 T.M., IV.G., VI.; TPS ¶7150.02.C.]

The foreign tax credit requires an affirmative election, made annually, and is computed and claimed on Form 1116, *Foreign Tax Credit (Individual, Estate, or Trust)*, or Form 1118, *Foreign Tax Credit — Corporations*, and filed with one's tax return [Reg. § 1.905-2(a)(2)]. However, separate forms must be used for each applicable category of foreign source income. Proof of foreign taxes paid, such as receipts or tax returns, need not be attached to the form, but taxpayers must produce authentic documentation to substantiate a claim if requested by the IRS; if unavailable, certain forms of secondary evidence will suffice [Reg. § 1.905-2(a)(2), § 1.905-2(b)]. Generally, the election applies to all creditable foreign income taxes for the tax year, meaning one cannot simply choose to credit some foreign taxes and/or deduct others in the same year [Reg. § 1.901-1(c)].

### XX.C.2.f. Deduction for Foreign Taxes

[902 T.M., III.E.5.; TPS ¶7150.02.C.2.]

A deduction for foreign taxes paid may be taken instead of the credit [§ 901(n), § 164, § 275]. In some circumstances, a deduction may even be available for otherwise uncreditable foreign taxes, provided the general tests for deductibility can otherwise be met [§ 901(j)(3), § 901(k)(7)]. Individuals claim the deduction claimed on Schedule A (Form 1040) and corporations on Form 1120, Line 17. Generally, a credit is preferred to a deduction, because a credit is a dollar-for-dollar offset against U.S. tax due, though there are circumstances in which this is not the case.

### XX.C.3. Foreign Corporations Owned By U.S. Persons

[919 T.M., 920 T.M., 6380 T.M.; TPS ¶7150.07.A.]

Although U.S. taxpayers are subject to tax on worldwide income, the taxation of the earnings of foreign corporations to their U.S. shareholders (individuals and corporations) is usually deferred until repatriated as dividends, because the law respects the separate tax status of the corporation as a distinct legal person. The primary advantage of deferral is that it allows foreign income to be taxed at a lower effective rate than U.S. source income, assuming the foreign tax rate is less than the U.S. rate. However, the deferral principle is subject to several exceptions that were placed in the Code over time in order to address the tax avoidance potential engendered by deferral through the use of various entities and structures often situated in tax havens.

### XX.C.3.a. Transfers, Mergers, and Liquidations Involving Foreign Corporations

[919 T.M., II., III.; TPS ¶7150.07.A.]

The Code is replete with nonrecognition provisions providing for the tax-free transfer of appreciated assets among domestic corporations of the same corporate group, based on the premise that gain is preserved and will be taxed at a later date, when an asset is eventually disposed of or upon the distribution of dividends. However, because the United States has limited taxing jurisdiction over a foreign corporation, transfers of appreciated assets involving foreign corporations can result in gain going untaxed. To address this limitation, § 367 deems away the corporate status of a foreign corporation. It thereby cancels out the benefit of nonrecognition, in some instances altogether, and imposes current tax on the gain. In other instances, § 367 imposes stringent conditions on the availability of nonrecognition. Stated differently, § 367 modifies the general corporation nonrecognition rules (see Chapter XIII.) in most instances involving a foreign corporation to reflect the reality of the international corporate environment. The vast majority of these rules are contained in corresponding regulations.

Broadly speaking, there are three basic contexts in which this issue arises:

1. outbound transfers whereby appreciated assets held in the United States by a U.S. person are transferred to a foreign corporation [§ 367(a)];

2. inbound transfers whereby the liquidation of a foreign subsidiary or reorganization of a foreign corporation can result in the repatriation of the foreign corporation's earnings and profits to the United States [§ 367(b)]; and

3. wholly foreign transactions involving transfers and other reorganizations whereby appreciated assets are transferred from one foreign person to another who is ultimately controlled by a U.S. person [§ 367(b)].

Series of transactions come within the range of outbound transfers under § 367(a) and require current gain recognition, including subsidiary liquidations [§ 332]; transfers to controlled corporations [§ 352]; stock and property transfers occurring in reorganizations entitled to nonrecognition treatment [under § 354 and § 361]; various other forms of these transactions [under § 356]; and transactions not involving an actual transfer of property but where assets move into the beneficial ownership of a foreign corporation.

An important exception is available for property transferred to a foreign corporation for use in an active trade or business of the corporation outside the United States, but it is restricted considerably [§ 367(a)(3)(A); Reg. § 1.367(a)-2T(b)]. For example, the exception is not available in a transfer of inventory and certain intellectual property nor upon the transfer of accounts receivable and similar financial assets, many of which are easily disposed of and typically have gain built in [§ 367(a)(3)(B)(i)]. Also, in a transfer of stock or securities to a foreign corporation, a U.S. shareholder who holds less than 5% of the total vote and value of the foreign corporation is not subject to gain recognition. Other exceptions are available, but are generally subject to substantive and procedural conditions. Furthermore, § 367 establishes various recaptures to claw back tax benefits such as deductions for branch losses and property depreciation despite that property may be used in an actual active trade or business [§ 367(a)(3)(C); Reg. § 1.367(a)-4T(b)].

An outbound transfer of intangibles by a U.S. person to a foreign corporation under § 351 or § 361 receives special treatment [§ 367(d)]. Rather than impose one-time current gain recognition upon the transfer, the transaction is recast as a sale in consideration for deemed royalty payments over the course of the useful life of the intangible, which is based on the actual income stream attributable to the intangible and taxed to the transferor, beginning in the year of transfer [§ 367(d)(2)(A)(ii)(I); Reg. § 1.367(d)-1T(c)(1), § 1.367(d)-1T(c)(3)]. The provision covers a wide swath of intellectual property and any similar items [§ 367(d)(1)]. A subsequent sale of the intangible by the transferee is a taxable event.

As for inbound and wholly foreign transfers, the scope of transactions covered by the § 367(b) regime extends the gamut from incorporations and reorganizations to divisions and liquidations. The basic premise underlying the corresponding regulations is that all earnings of a controlled foreign corporation (CFC) should be subject to U.S. tax as ordinary income, irrespective of the form of a transaction, if they are repatriated or move in a structure in which they would no longer be subject to U.S. tax as earnings in the future. Thus, in various inbound transfers that move assets from a CFC to a domestic corporation, such as a liquidation or reorganization of a foreign subsidiary, a "toll charge" is levied on the CFC's foreign earnings in the form of a constructive dividend [Reg. §§ 1.367(b)-3 through -5]. In wholly foreign transactions, which have no current impact on any U.S. person, current taxation generally is not imposed if the assets remain in a CFC, but instead by adjusting the earning and profits of the affected foreign entities, certain tax attributes are preserved to protect against future erosion of the tax base and allow for future recognition [§ 367(b); Reg. § 1.367(b)-1]. However, if the assets move to a foreign corporation that is not a CFC in transactions involving § 351 or § 367(b), then current tax is imposed on the net accumulated earnings pursuant to § 1248 to prevent certain U.S. shareholders from changing their tax position vis-à-vis the foreign corporation. Section 1248, which serves as a backstop for subpart F and is closely bound to the § 367(b) regulations, governs the taxation of U.S. shareholders who own 10% of the foreign corporation that was a CFC during the five-year period ending on the date of the sale or exchange of the stock [Reg. § 1.1248-2(b)]. The effect of this is that it prevents the further deferral of the foreign corporation's earnings.

Finally, the recognition of gain under § 367 can often be deferred if a taxpayer enters into a gain recognition agreement (GRA) with the IRS [Reg. § 1.367(a)-8]. Under a GRA, a taxpayer agrees to recognize gain upon the occurrence of a triggering event, such as the sale of the asset transferred to the foreign corporation, while the agreement is effective, which is typically a five-year period.

### XX.C.3.b. Controlled Foreign Corporations

[926 T.M., III., IV., V.; TPS ¶7150.04.A.]

The most prevalent anti-deferral regime targets the controlled foreign corporation (CFC), the pertinent Code provisions for which are contained in subpart F of chapter 1 [§§ 951-965]. The CFC provisions are intended to prevent a U.S. shareholder from utilizing a foreign corporation in a low tax jurisdiction to shelter specific kinds of income by subjecting the income to current taxation. Although the CFC regime is primarily focused on passive investment income, it also captures certain kinds of active business income.

For a foreign corporation to qualify as a CFC, U.S. shareholders must own more than 50% of the voting power or value of the entity at any time during the tax year [§ 957(a)]. A "U.S. shareholder," for this test, is one that owns at least 10% of the voting power of all of the voting stock of the foreign corporation [§ 951(b)]. Importantly, the stock ownership test can also be met indirectly or constructively, based on the facts and circumstances [§ 958(a)(2), § 958(b)]. If a foreign corporation is a CFC for an uninterrupted period of at least 30 days in a tax year, qualifying U.S. shareholders must currently include certain kinds of earnings of the CFC in their gross income on a pro rata basis, reflecting direct and indirect ownership and the number of days the foreign corporation was controlled during the year [§ 951(a)]. For this purpose, however, the attribution rules in § 958(b) used to determine stock ownership do not apply.

There are two basic components of CFC earnings subject to current inclusion: subpart F income and CFC earnings invested in U.S. property. Subpart F income consists of two components that target the channeling of income outside the CFC's home country: foreign base company income and insurance income [§ 951(a)(1), § 951(a)(2)]. The catchall foreign base company income is the primary target of the CFC regime, as it covers passive investment income (e.g., dividends, rents, royalties, and interest) and sales and services income [§ 954(a)]. A fourth category captures insurance income, that is, any income derived in connection with an insurance or annuity contract that would be subject to the same Code provisions that are applicable to domestic insurers, whereas as a fifth category concerns oil and gas related income. There are various exceptions and some special rules, such as for highly-taxed income and certain active businesses in banking or finance [§ 954(b)(4), § 954(h)]. An exclusion is also available under certain circumstances for subpart F income of a de minimis amount and for that of a bona fide foreign insurance business [§ 954(e)(2)(B)].

As for the earnings of a CFC that are invested in U.S. property, because a CFC has avenues for investing as such for the benefit of its U.S. shareholders, the possibility exists that a taxable dividend distribution can be avoided. To prevent this outcome, subpart F requires U.S. shareholders to currently include their pro rata shares of the undistributed earnings of a CFC so invested [§ 951(a)(1)(B), § 956(a)]. "U.S. property" in this context refers to tangible property situated in the United States, stock of a U.S. corporation, obligations of a related person, and the right of use within the United States as to various types of intellectual property, but it does not include U.S. government debt, bank deposits, export property, among other property [§ 956(c)]. Several exceptions also apply for purposes of investment or financing activities of bona fide businesses engaged in the insurance, securities, or commodities.

U.S. corporate shareholders of CFCs are entitled to a foreign tax credit for their pro rata share of foreign taxes paid by a CFC in relation to includible amounts of subpart F income [§ 960].

### XX.C.3.c. *Passive Investment Foreign Corporations*

[6300 T.M., II., III.; TPS ¶7150.04.B.]

A foreign corporation is a passive investment foreign corporation (PFIC) if it meets one of two tests during the tax year: (i) at least 75% of its gross income is passive, or (ii) at least 50% of its average assets (on an adjusted or fair market value basis) are assets that produce or could produce passive income [§ 1297(a)]. These tests are applied on a look-through basis in certain circumstances, such as in the case of 25%-owned subsidiaries and passive income from a related person [§ 1297(c)]. The significance for U.S. shareholders of a PFIC is that in targeting the sheltering of passive investment income from U.S. taxation, the PFIC rules subject distributions to a tax-and-interest regime. Tax is levied at the maximum ordinary income tax rate upon receipt of an "excess distribution" or upon disposition of PFIC stock and is accompanied by an interest charge [§ 1291(a), § 1291(c)]. The regime applies in both instances to any distribution or gain that exceeds 125% of the average distributions of the PFIC for the prior three years, with the tax-and-interest charge levied on amounts allocated equally over each year on a daily pro rata basis reflecting one's holding period and class of stock. The interest charge is treated as interest on an underpayment of tax when due, thus, it is characterized as a nondeductible personal interest expense for individuals [§ 1291(c)(1); Reg. § 1.163-9T(b)(2)].

Narrow exceptions to PFIC status obtained under these tests are available under certain conditions, such as for 10% shareholders of a CFC that is a PFIC (who are instead subject to subpart F), start-up companies and other corporations if they can show that they were not (nor any predecessors) previously PFICs and will not be in the succeeding two years, and tax-exempt organizations that are shareholders of a PFIC [§ 1297(d), § 1298(b)(2), § 1298(b)(3); Reg. § 1.1291-1(e)].

The taint of PFIC stock remains indefinitely, except that once a corporation loses its PFIC status, the taint of prior earnings can be purged voluntarily with a mark-to-market election to be taxed as though the stock was sold for fair market value [§ 1298(b)(1)].

There are also some other avenues available to mitigate the often harsh results of the PFIC regime. For example, provided a PFIC furnishes the information necessary to determine a U.S. shareholder's annual inclusions, one can elect out of the PFIC regime by making a qualified electing fund (QEF) election, the tradeoff for which is current taxation of one's pro rata share of the PFIC's earnings [§ 1291(d)(1)]. If a QEF election is made, the shareholder can also elect to defer payment of the tax until the earlier of an excess distribution or disposition of the PFIC stock, but this is subject to an interest charge [§ 1294]. Furthermore, a shareholder who makes a QEF election is also allowed to make a one-time mark-to-market election, which results in the current taxation of prior year PFIC earnings [§ 1291(d)(2)]. A mark-to-market election can also be made by a U.S. shareholder holding marketable PFIC stock [§ 1296].

Shareholders of a PFIC are eligible for the foreign tax credit, to the extent an excess distribution is allocated to the current year. To the extent an excess distribution is allocable to prior years, foreign taxes may reduce the special tax computed under the PFIC rules, but may not otherwise be claimed as a credit. Those who make a QEF election are not subject to this limitation.

### XX.C.3.d. Accumulated Earnings Tax

[926 T.M., II.D.3.; TPS ¶7150.04.C.]

As with domestic corporations, any foreign corporation (other than a PFIC) with U.S. shareholders that accumulates earnings beyond its reasonable operational needs becomes vulnerable to an annual penalty tax levied at a flat rate of 20% on its accumulated U.S.-source taxable income [§ 532] (see XIII.C.4.).

### XX.C.4. Interest Charge Domestic International Sales Corporations

[934 T.M., II.; TPS ¶7170.02.B.5.]

The interest charge domestic international sales corporation (DISC) regime is the only remaining export incentive under the Code. A DISC is a tax-exempt domestic corporation, essentially a "paper" entity, formed to reap specific tax benefits on income generated by qualified U.S. exports, including income from related sales, leasing, and managerial activities as well as certain professional services associated with foreign construction projects [§§ 991-995; Reg. § 1.927(a)-1T]. The current DISC regime can be used both to reduce a domestic corporation's taxable income and to defer tax on up to $10 million in qualified export income annually on a cumulative basis. Since a DISC is not subject to U.S. tax at the entity level, taxation is imposed on the shareholders, typically on a combination of actual and deemed dividends, who are also subject to an interest charge on undistributed DISC income.

For instance, in a traditional DISC structure, a U.S. producer forms a commission-based DISC and pays into it deductible commissions from qualified exports, up to the greater of 4% of gross receipts or 50% of net income, thereby reducing its taxable income and resulting in a tax-free net profit to the DISC. As the export-related income accumulates within the DISC, tax is deferred until the income is distributed (or deemed distributed) to the shareholders. And since DISC distributions are treated as dividends, individual shareholders can take advantage of the reduced tax rate on qualified dividends. However, some types of income are deemed distributed and, therefore, taxed currently in the hands of shareholders, such as taxable income in excess of the $10 million annual threshold [§ 995(b); Reg. § 1.995-2].

An interest charge will apply in the event DISC income remains undistributed at the end of the year. A shareholder's interest payment to the IRS is based on the amount of tax deferred by the shareholder after the end of the year, as if the income had been distributed and taxed to the shareholder as ordinary income [§ 995(f)] and computed at a T-bill rate. The interest payment is reported on IRS Form 8404, *Interest Charge on DISC-Related Deferred Tax Liability*, which is due by March 30 after the full year for which tax deferral was obtained. In recent years, these payments have been modest, given the low rates that Treasury bills have been yielding. Nonetheless, if all of a DISC's accumulated income is distributed at the end of the year, shareholders should not be subject to an interest charge since there is no deferred tax liability.

To qualify for DISC status, a U.S. corporation must meet the following requirements:

- file an election to be treated as an interest charge DISC;
- have a single class of stock;
- maintain a minimum capitalization of $2,500 on each day of the tax year; and
- hold at least 95% of its gross receipts and assets in the form of qualified export receipts and qualified export assets [§ 992(a)(1)].

To elect DISC treatment, IRS Form 4876-A, *Election To Be Treated as an Interest Charge DISC*, which requires shareholder consent, is generally filed within the first 90 days of the corporation's first tax year.

### XX.C.5. Transfer Pricing

#### XX.C.5.a. General Concepts

[886 T.M., II., III.; TPS ¶¶3600.01., 02., 7150.06.A.]

Transfer pricing concerns the amount charged for goods, services, transfers of royalties, rents, and loans in transactions between commonly controlled entities. Because the price charged by one entity and paid by another ultimately determines the amount of income received in any given transaction, the amount of tax liability can vary greatly. Commonly controlled taxpayers can easily shift income through intercompany transactions to reduce their overall tax liability. Transfer pricing has now become a major means by which tax authorities assess income.

Although § 482, the sole provision on transfer pricing in the Code, makes no explicit mention of the phrase "transfer pricing," it delegates authority to the IRS to distribute or allocate gross income between or among controlled businesses in order to "prevent evasion of taxes or to clearly reflect income." The law only applies in situations where there are two or more businesses (which need not be entities) that are controlled directly or indirectly by the same interests. Although "control" is defined in the regulations, the definition is broad, and fact-based, as it does not specify a certain level of shareholding or voting interest [Reg. § 1.482-1(i)(4)].

Extensive regulations under § 482 provide for and implement the guiding principle for allocation of income among entities: the arm's length standard [Reg. § 1.482-1]. Both the United States and the Organisation for Economic Co-Operation and Development (OECD) use this standard when negotiating treaties and in transfer pricing practice. The objective of the arm's length standard is to place "a controlled taxpayer on tax parity with an uncontrolled taxpayer by determining the true taxable income of the controlled taxpayer." To do this, practitioners look to a "comparable transaction" that would have happened between uncontrolled taxpayers in order to find the price with which the income should be calculated, which is also called the arm's length result. Controlled taxpayers are referred as the "tested party" or "tested parties," while an uncontrolled taxpayer is referred to as the "comparable."

A comparable transaction must be sufficiently similar to a tested one that it provides a reliable measure of an arm's length result [Reg. § 1.482-1(d)(2)]. This is called the standard of comparability, since the higher degree of comparability means a more reliable result. In many situations, closely similar comparables may not exist. The regulations provide a list of factors that must be evaluated when decided whether a transaction is comparable: functions performed, contractual terms, risks, economic conditions, and the nature of property or services [Reg. § 1.482-1(d)(1)]. The regulations recognize that one factor may be more important than another, depending on the circumstances of the transaction or the taxpayer.

Evaluation of the functions performed among the tested parties and comparables is often called functional analysis and is one of the most important aspects of a transfer pricing outcome. The functional analysis tells the story about how the company makes its profit, including all economically significant activities. Functions that may be included in a functional analysis include [Reg. § 1.482-1(d)(3)(i)]:

- research and development;
- product design and engineering;
- manufacturing, production and process engineering;
- product fabrication, extraction, and assembly;
- purchasing and materials management;
- marketing and distribution functions, including inventory management, warranty administration, and advertising activities;
- transportation and warehousing; and
- managerial, legal, accounting and finance, credit and collection, training, and personnel management services

### XX.C.5.b. Methods

[890 T.M., 7:IV., 7:VII.; TPS ¶¶3600.03., 7150.06.A.]

In order to determine the arm's length price that should apply between controlled entities, the regulations provide approved methods and stipulate that the "best method" must be used [Reg. § 1.482-3(a)]. This means that, under the facts and circumstances, the method used must provide the most reliable measure of the arm's length result [Reg. § 1.482-1(c)]. There are four factors that are taken into consideration when determining which method is the best:

1. the degree of comparability between the controlled transaction and uncontrolled transactions;
2. the quality of the data;
3. the reliability of the assumptions underlying the method; and
4. the sensitivity of results to deficiencies in the data or assumptions used.

The regulations identify five basic transfer pricing methods, which are divided into transaction-based methods and profit-based methods. The transaction-based methods are:

- a comparable uncontrolled transaction method,
- a resale price method (used in conjunction with tangible property or services), and
- a cost-plus method (used in conjunction with tangible property or services) [Reg. § 1.482-3(b)-(d)].

The profit-based methods are the profit split method and a comparable profits method [Reg. § 1.482-5, § 1.482-6]. The comparable profits methods is also known as the transactional net margin method. There are also special methods for cost sharing arrangements and services [Reg. § 1.482-7, § 1.482-9]. Unspecified methods are also allowable, but have been disfavored.

### XX.C.5.c. Advance Pricing Agreements

[890 T.M., 8:II.; TPS ¶¶3600.05.D., 7150.06.C.2.]

An Advance Pricing Agreement (APA) is an agreement between the taxpayer and the IRS that binds the taxpayer to a defined transfer pricing methodology (TPM). In return, if the agreement is satisfied, the IRS will not challenge on audit whether the transactions included in the agreement were conducted at arm's length. The agreement may be unilateral (i.e., with the IRS only), bilateral (i.e., involving the taxpayer, the taxpayer's affiliate, the IRS and a foreign tax authority), or multilateral (i.e., involving the taxpayer, the taxpayer's affiliate, the IRS and more than one foreign tax authority). The APA program is administered by the IRS Advance Pricing and Mutual Agreement (APMA) program and is designed to promote certainty between the taxpayer and the IRS.

There are a variety of issues when considering whether or not to pursue an APA. One of the obvious reasons for a taxpayer to pursue an APA is that it would produce a certain result so that the taxpayer can rely on a particular methodology and avoid being challenged upon exam. The greatest hurdle that taxpayers have reported is the level of information disclosure that is required in the APA process, which has been said to require more information than a request for a private letter ruling but less than the information required during examination. In addition, the selection of a TPM may interfere with business operations and accounting systems that have been pre-set with another particular TPM in mind. Finally, the cost of requesting an APA may be great, considering the user fee paid to the IRS (up to $50,000) and the costs involved to complete an APA request, including fees paid to economists or analysts and consultants. In some cases, the costs may be outweighed by the benefit of having certainty with respect to TPM and examination periods.

To request an APA, a taxpayer initiates the process by requesting a prefiling conference with the APMA program office. This conference allows the taxpayer and an officer from APMA to determine the suitability of an APA and provides the taxpayer an opportunity to ask questions about what information, documentation, and analyses would be appropriate for the transactions that it would like to cover in the APA. The taxpayer should then file a complete APA request, which includes a package of information regarding the taxpayer, controlled entities, description of the organizational structure, and detailed analyses of the transactions to be covered. Once the application is processed, a team leader is designated and forms an APA team consisting of economists and examiners within the IRS. The APA team and the taxpayer then conduct meetings and agree on a case plan. Once finished, the APA Director and the taxpayer both sign the agreement, which has the legal effect of a binding agreement between the taxpayer and the IRS [Rev. Proc. 2006-9, 2006-2

I.R.B. 278, *amplified by* Rev. Proc. 2006-54, 2006-49 I.R.B. 1035, *modified by* Rev. Proc. 2008-31. 2008-23 I.R.B. 1133].

For each tax year covered by the APA, the taxpayer must file an annual report with the IRS to demonstrate compliance with the agreement's terms and conditions. The taxpayer may seek a renewal of the APA by requesting another profiling conference. An APA may be revoked due to fraud or malfeasance or canceled due to misrepresentation, mistake as to a material fact, failure to state a material fact, failure to file a timely annual report, or lack of good faith compliance with the terms and conditions of the APA.

### XX.C.6. Foreign Currency Transactions and Translation

[921 T.M., II.; TPS ¶7150.09.]

Because U.S. tax liability is determined and reported in U.S. dollars, a transaction conducted in foreign currency raises the matter of the accompanying treatment of the currency for U.S. tax purposes. Generally, there are three contexts in which questions pertaining to foreign currency translation will arise for taxpayers:

1. when a single transaction is closed in a foreign currency, e.g., the purchase or sale of a forward currency contract or an asset denominated in a foreign currency;

2. when a foreign branch of a domestic company conducts business using foreign currency; and

3. when tax items derived from interests in foreign equity emerge, such as a claim for foreign tax credits or upon a dividend distribution to a shareholder.

The U.S. tax treatment of foreign currency is based on the general rule that equates foreign currency with property, not money, meaning gain or loss realized and recognized in a transaction is measured by comparing value or sale price to cost basis [§ 1001(a), § 1001(c), § 1012] (see III.A.). This of course raises issues related to the timing, amount, source, and character (ordinary or capital) of the gain or loss. To address the tax-significant events in which foreign currency features, specific concepts apply to U.S. and foreign persons, as appropriate, including individuals, which become the beginning point in evaluating a foreign currency transaction.

### XX.C.6.a. Functional and Nonfunctional Currency

[921 T.M., II.D., III.C.; TPS ¶7150.09.A.]

Each taxpayer is considered to have a single "functional currency," based upon which gain or loss is measured [§ 985]. There is a statutory presumption that a taxpayer's functional currency is the U.S. dollar [§ 985(b)(1)(A)]. Likewise, each "qualified business unit" (QBU) of a taxpayer is considered to have a single functional currency, which may be different than the U.S. dollar [§ 989(a)]. This determination is made by identifying the primary currency of the locale in which the unit or entity conducts its operations and keeps its book and records [§ 985(b)(1)(B)]. In contrast, a nonfunctional currency is any currency other than the functional currency of a taxpayer or QBU and includes legal tender as well as assets and financial instruments denominated in such currency. An election is available to a QBU to have the U.S. dollar as its functional currency, provided it keeps books and records in dollars and conducts its accounting based on a separate transaction basis [§ 985(b)(3)]. A change in the functional currency of a qualified business unit is permitted, but the unit must then recognize gain or loss on the conversion and make corresponding adjustments to earnings and profits and assets bases [Reg. § 1.985-5].

### *XX.C.6.b. Qualified Business Unit*

[921 T.M., II.C.; TPS ¶7150.09.A.]

A "qualified business unit" (QBU) is a unit that is clearly identifiable as a separate trade or business of the taxpayer and one that maintain separate books and records [§ 989(a)]. Hence, a corporation is a QBU, as is a partnership, trust, or estate of its partner or beneficiary, and multiple QBUs may exist in any such entity, even in the case where a unit operates a trade or business that is not entirely different than that of its owner. An individual cannot be a QBU, but a trade or business managed by an individual, such as a sole proprietorship, may qualify as one.

### *XX.C.6.c. Transactions in Nonfunctional Currency*

[921 T.M., III.C.; TPS ¶7150.09.B.]

For taxpayers with the U.S. dollar as their functional currency, gain or loss from foreign currency transactions is measured in dollars as to each individual transaction, but when a foreign currency is the functional currency of a QBU, the measurement is done using that currency and the resulting amount is translated into dollars at the spot rate [§ 988(c)(1)(A)]. Recognition of gain or loss occurs only when a transaction has closed, i.e., the date when a payment is remitted or an asset is otherwise disposed of. In this case, any resulting gain or loss attributed to exchange rate fluctuations between the functional and nonfunctional currencies of a taxpayer and its QBU is characterized separately from the underlying transaction as ordinary (not capital) gain or loss, with source determined generally by the residence of the taxpayer or the QBU, as the case may be.

Certain transactions with nonfunctional currency are specifically addressed in the Code, including transactions involving dispositions of nonfunctional currency, debt instruments, accounts payable and receivable, and various financial instruments, such as forward, futures and options contracts [§ 988(c)(1)]. Some of these transactions can be undertaken as hedging transactions to manage currency fluctuation and, provided certain conditions are met, allows a taxpayer to treat the hedging component as an integrated part of the underlying transaction [§ 988(d)].

The same rules apply to the business and investment transactions engaged in by individuals, other than "personal transactions" (i.e., those for which no deductible expenses is allowed) resulting in gain of less than $200 [§ 988(a), (e)].

### *XX.C.6.d. Translation of Foreign Income and Taxes Paid*

[921 T.M., VIII.; TPS ¶7150.09.C.]

Certain circumstances require the translation of a foreign functional currency into U.S. dollars for a taxpayer to determine its U.S. tax liability. For example, for a U.S. business with one or more foreign branch QBUs operating with a functional currency other than the U.S. dollar, the following steps are necessary to arrive at the amount of taxable income to include on its return [§ 987]:

1. The profit or loss of each QBU is computed in its functional currency.
2. The resulting sum is converted into U.S. dollars using the average exchange for the tax year.
3. If the QBUs use different functional currencies, adjustments must be made for inter-branch transfers of property, including remittances, which are calculated on the date of remittance as made on a pro-rata basis out of each QBU's accumulated earnings and profits, as well as for gain or loss, which is treated as ordinary income or loss.

Likewise, when a foreign corporation has distributed a dividend to its U.S. shareholders, the translation of its earnings and profits may be required. Earnings and profits are determined first in a QBU's functional currency, and the resulting distributed amount is translated at the current exchange rate on the distribution date [§ 986(b), § 989(b)]. In the case of a deemed dividend distribution requiring current inclusion in a taxpayer's taxable income under Subpart F of the Code, generally the amount is translated using the average exchange rate for the tax year, though various methods for determining the appropriate exchange rate exist.

In addition, for purposes claiming the foreign tax credit, the foreign income taxes paid must be translated into U.S. dollars. Generally, taxpayers on the accrual method of accounting translate foreign income tax payments using the average exchange rate for the tax year [§ 986(a)]. However, there are a number of circumstances in which the appropriate exchange rate is the rate in effect on the date that the foreign tax is paid.

## XX.D. U.S. Activities of Foreign Persons

### XX.D.1. Income from a U.S. Trade or Business

[907 T.M., VI.B., 908 T.M., III.; TPS ¶7130.03.]

For purposes of this discussion, a foreign person includes: nonresident aliens, foreign corporations, foreign partnerships and partners, and foreign trusts and estates and their beneficiaries. The United States imposes tax on foreign persons based on the following [§ 864(c), § 871(b)(1)] :

1. whether they are engaged in a trade or business within the United States;
2. whether that individual or corporation has income effectively connected with the conduct of a trade or business within the United States; and
3. whether the source of that income is U.S.-source or foreign-source.

The phrase "trade or business" is a creature of judicial and administrative conclusions based on factual situations. To be a "trade or business," activities conducted by a foreign person must be "considerable, continuous, regular, and substantial" as opposed to "sporadic, irregular, and minimal" [Rev. Rul. 73-522, 1973-2 C.B. 226]. Also, the activities must be conducted "within" the United States and the fact that some activities amount to a foreign trade or business has no bearing on whether the activities constitute a U.S. trade or business.

The relevant conduct needs usually to be "active," and contribute to income-generating activities, though not necessarily result in profit. Thus, while as a general rule the performance of personal services in the United States will by statute give rise to a trade or business, provided one stays more than 90 days and earns over $3,000, there are several exceptions and exemptions, depending on the circumstances [§ 864(b)]. Ministerial, clerical, or collection-related activities usually do not rise to the level of constituting a trade or business. The same applies for promotional activities and direct sales, but add in concluding transactions and they could qualify as a trade or business. The activities of foreign persons involved in the trading of U.S. securities or commodities will not give rise to a U.S. trade or business [§ 864(b)(2)]. Furthermore, the income of nonresident alien employees of foreign governments or international organizations is specifically exempted from taxation [§ 893].

A common situation in determining whether a person's activities constitute a trade or business arises when a third person, an agent, acts on behalf of the foreign person. Under common law principles of agency, actions of the agent are imputed to the independent principal. But the actions of independent contractors, commission agents, and brokers require a more extensive analysis. Some courts have looked at whether the relationship between the agent and the foreign person occurred with "regularity." Case law indicates that actions of agents who act exclusively or almost exclusively for a foreign person may be imputed to the foreign person.

Due to the highly factual nature of this inquiry, the IRS does not ordinarily issue rulings on whether a foreign person is engaged in a U.S. trade or business; however, certain corporate taxpayers under the jurisdiction of the IRS Large Business & International group may discuss this as a "likely suitable" issue with a pre-filing agreement with the IRS [Rev. Proc. 2009-14, § 3.06, 2009-3 I.R.B. 324].

### XX.D.1.a. Effectively Connected Income

[907 T.M., VI.B., 908 T.M., III.B.; TPS ¶7130.04.]

If a foreign person is found to engage in a U.S. trade or business during a tax year, the person is subject to U.S. tax at graduated rates on a net-basis on the portion of taxable income that is effectively connected with that trade or business [§ 871(b), § 882(a)]. Other income that is classified as fixed or determinable annual or periodical ("FDAP") income is taxed separately on a gross basis at a flat 30% rate [§ 871(a), § 881(a))].

U.S. source income that is not FDAP income or capital gain is effectively connected income [§ 864(c)(3)]. Chiefly, this refers to inventory sales taking place in the United States.

To determine whether U.S.-source FDAP income or capital gain is effectively connected to a U.S. trade or business, the Code provides two tests, and with each prescribes that "due regard" is to be given to whether or not the asset or income was accounted for through the trade or business [§ 864(c)(2)]. The first test is the "asset-use" test, which provides that income derived from assets used in or held for use in the trade or business is effectively connected income. Assets "used in or held for use in" refers to three categories of assets: assets held for the principal purpose of promoting the present conduct of the trade or business in the US; assets acquired and held in the ordinary course of the trade or business; and assets otherwise held in a "direct relationship" to trade or business. This test is most likely to apply to a passive item of income in relation to a business that does not ordinarily generate that type of income. For example, interest earned by a sales business which may be from accounts receivable or from passive investment. The second test is the "business-activities" test, which looks to whether the activities of the trade or business were a material factor in the realization of the income. Unlike the asset-use test, which is relevant primarily when the foreign corporation's trade or business-activities as such do not give rise directly to the investment income at issue, this test ordinarily applies to investment income that arises directly from the active conduct of the taxpayer's U.S. trade or business (e.g., banking).

In addition, the regulations provide a third test, the "active and material participation" test, for determining whether certain U.S.-source investment income earned by a foreign person engaged in the active conduct of a "banking, financing, or similar business" in the United States is effectively connected income [Reg. § 1.864-4(c)(5)]. This test applies in place of the asset-use or business-activities test in determining whether U.S.-source dividend or interest income or gain or loss from the sale or exchange of stocks or securities is effectively connected income.

As a general rule, a foreign person's foreign source income cannot be effectively connected income. However, some types of foreign source income are treated as effectively connected if they are attributable to a U.S. office maintained by the taxpayer [§ 864(c)(4)]. These items are:

1. rents, royalties, or gains from the sale of intangible property;

2. dividends, interest, or gains or loss from the sale of stocks or securities;

3. income, gain or loss from the sale of goods or merchandise through a U.S. office; and

4. income or gain that is equivalent to items 1. through 3.

Under special rules, income attributable to a U.S. life insurance business is effectively connected [§ 864(c)(4)(C)].

Computation of taxable income for a foreign person is calculated by taking the gross income that is effectively connected income and deducting amounts for: (i) expenses that are allocable or apportionable to the US trade or business; (ii) charitable contributions; (iii) casualty and theft losses; or (iv) in the case of an individual, a single personal exemption.

### XX.D.1.b. Income Not Effectively Connected

[907 T.M., VI.C., 908 T.M., IV; TPS ¶7120.03.]

Certain categories of non-effectively connected U.S.-source income of a foreign person are subject to tax on a gross basis at a flat rate of 30% [§ 871(a), § 881]. Unlike net-basis taxation for effectively connected income, there are no graduated rates and no deductions permitted. Income subject to this tax includes fixed or determinable annual or periodical income (FDAP) and other FDAP-like income. The 30% tax applies, for example, to interest (including original issue discount), dividends, rent, royalties, and compensation. Payment of the 30% tax is enforced by the withholding of tax at source by the payor under § 1441 and § 1442.

There are some exceptions to gross-basis taxation. Among the most important of these is the exemption for "portfolio interest" paid on certain portfolio debt [§ 871(h), § 881(c)]. In broad terms, "portfolio interest" is interest from debt instruments held for investment purposes. To qualify, obligations must be issued in registered form and the beneficial owner should provide the withholding agent with an owner's statement. However, this exemption is narrowly tailored and there are several categories of interest that do not qualify as such, including interest received by a 10% shareholder, interest received by a controlled foreign corporation from a related person, and certain contingent interest [§§ 871(h)(3)-(4), §§ 881(c)(3)-881(c)(5)]. There are also exceptions for certain bank deposit interest and interest-like payments under notional principal contracts [§ 871(i), § 881(d); Reg. § 1.863-7(a)(1)].

If a foreign person is unable to take advantage of an exception to the 30% rate, a reduced rate or an exemption might be provided by a relevant income tax treaty between the United States and the person's country of residence. Many U.S. income tax treaties provide for a reduced rate or an exemption for tax withheld at source for certain types of FDAP income, including investment income. Foreign persons claiming a treaty rate should file IRS Form 8833, *Treaty-Based Return Position Disclosure Under § 6114 or § 7701(b)*.

### XX.D.2. Branch Profits Tax

[6480 T.M., II., 908 T.M., III.D.; TPS ¶7120.04.C.]

The imposition of corporate income tax on effectively connected income is the equivalent of tax that would be imposed if a U.S. trade or business were incorporated as a U.S. subsidiary of a foreign corporation, rather than an unincorporated operation. A U.S. subsidiary of a foreign corporation would normally pay a 30% tax on dividends distributed to the foreign corporation (without an applicable tax treaty). To achieve a similar tax result, the foreign corporation is made liable for a 30% tax computed on its "dividend equivalent amount" (DEA) [§ 884]. This is referred to as a "branch profits tax," although it is imposed on most income that is effectively connected to a trade or business, even if formally there is no established branch. Thus, the branch profits tax substitutes for the taxation of the foreign corporation's shareholders while ensuring that U.S. income is taxed twice, in accord with the U.S. two-tier system for taxing corporate profits. The branch profits tax is not premised on the foreign corporation maintaining a fixed place of business or having other common indicia of a branch or substantial presence in this country. The only trigger for the tax is that the foreign corporation has income that is effectively connected with a U.S. trade or business.

To determine the DEA, the corporation first calculates its "effectively connected earnings and profits" (ECEP) [§ 884(d); Reg. § 1.884-1(f)]. This figure represents the earnings and profits that are attributable to actual or deemed effectively connected income (without regard to actual distributions during the year). Next, the corporation determines whether its U.S. net equity increased or decreased during the tax year. If there was an increase in U.S. net equity, the corporation is deemed to have reinvested in U.S. assets a portion of its current-year ECEP equal to the increase. The remaining ECEP, if any, is the DEA, which is treated as "distributed" to the head office. Consequently, if all the ECEP for the year is reinvested, the increase in U.S. net equity will be equal to the amount of ECEP, and the DEA (i.e., ECEP minus the increase in U.S. net equity) will be zero. If there was a decrease in U.S. net equity, the corporation is deemed to have distributed all its current-year ECEP to the head office rather than reinvesting it in U.S. assets. In addition, the corporation is treated as having disinvested from U.S. assets (i.e., distributed to the head office) the ECEP from years before the current year in an amount equal to the decrease in U.S. net equity. Thus, the DEA is equal to the current year's ECEP plus the decrease in U.S. net equity. The final tax would be 30% of the DEA.

The branch profits tax may be reduced or eliminated by an applicable income tax treaty, but such treaty provisions are subject to certain requirements designed to preclude foreign corporations from treaty shopping.

### XX.D.3. Dispositions of a U.S. Real Property Interest

[912 T.M., III., IV.; TPS ¶7140.02., 03.]

Section 897 imposes a tax on capital gains derived by foreign persons from the disposition of U.S. real property interests (USRPIs). Absent this, U.S. tax on gains so derived could be avoided by ensuring, through appropriate planning measures, that the gains did not qualify as effectively connected income. Section 897 provides a strict rule: gain (or loss) derived by a foreign person from the disposition of a USRPI is treated as income effectively connected with the conduct of a U.S. trade or business irrespective of whether the person's U.S. real estate activities in fact amount to the conduct of a U.S. trade or business. By characterizing the USRPI gains as such, U.S. income tax is imposed via § 871(b) and § 882(a).

A USRPI is defined as [Reg. § 1.897-1(c)(1)]:

- a direct "interest in real property" located in the United States or Virgin Islands;
- an interest in a partnership meeting certain USRPI ownership tests; or
- an interest in a domestic corporation, unless it is demonstrated that the corporation has not been a real property holding company (i.e., a corporation

whose assets consist predominantly of USRPIs) during the shorter of the time the foreign person held the interest in the corporation or at any time within the five-year period ending on the date the interest was disposed of.

The term "disposition" is defined as any transfer that would constitute a disposition by the transferor for any purpose of the Code and regulations [Reg. § 1.897-1(g)]. Thus, in addition to an outright sale, the term "disposition" may also include a capital contribution, redemption, distribution, or gift of a USRPI. The severance of crops or timber and the extraction of minerals do not alone constitute the disposition of a USRPI. However, for § 897 to operate, the disposition must generate gain or loss under § 1001 (see III.A.1.) [Reg. § 1.897-1(h)].

Two special operational rules apply for FIRPTA purposes. First, an anti-abuse rule provides that if a foreign person owns a pure USRPI and also owns an USRPI solely as a creditor, the interests are aggregated and treated as interests other than pure creditor's interests [Reg. § 1.897-1(d)(4)]. Second, the nonrecognition provisions of the Code generally do not apply to defer recognition of gain or loss unless the transferor of the USRPI receives in return an interest the sale of which would be subject to U.S. tax [§ 897(e)(1)].

The denial of nonrecognition treatment to a foreign corporation may violate the nondiscrimination provisions of an applicable income tax treaty. To preempt potential discrimination claims by foreign corporations, foreign corporations may elect to be treated as U.S. corporations for purposes of FIRPTA, provided they satisfy certain requirements [§ 897(i)]. This election thus enables a foreign corporation to avail itself of the nonrecognition provisions.

The collection of the tax imposed by FIRPTA is implemented by withholding [§ 1445; Reg. § 1.1445-2(a)]. Generally, the purchaser of a USRPI is obligated to withhold 10% of the amount realized by the foreign person and pay over to the IRS, as a portion of the purchase price instead of making a full payment to the foreign seller. This withholding represents a prepayment of the foreign seller's U.S. tax obligation with respect to the gain derived from the disposition of a USRPI. The withholding, which may be more or less than the foreign person's final U.S. tax obligation, is credited on the U.S. income tax return.

There are several exceptions and limitations. For example, FIRPTA withholding does not apply to foreign persons who purchase property for use principally as a residence, so long as its cost is not more than $300,000. Other exemptions include cases where the transferor furnishes a certification of non-foreign status, where the property transferred is U.S. stock that is regularly traded on an established securities market (or the company issues a certification of non-USRPI status). Importantly, if the tax that will be due on the gain would be less than the 10% tax required to be withheld, a "withholding certificate" may be obtained from the IRS that reduces or excuses withholding [Reg. § 1.1445-3]. Form 8288-B, *Application for Withholding Certificate for Dispositions by Foreign Persons of U.S. Real Property Interests*, is used to apply for withholding certificates.

### XX.D.4. Exempt Income of Foreign Persons

[907 T.M., VI.C., X.D., 908 T.M., III.B.; TPS ¶7120.02.]

If an item is excluded from gross income by a substantive provision of the Code, it is not included in the gross income of a foreign person, regardless of whether or not that person is engaged in a U.S. trade or business. The general income exemption provisions apply equally to domestic and foreign taxpayers. In addition, the Code provides some specific exclusions from gross income that are available only to foreign persons.

Exemptions specific to foreign individuals include: certain annuities received under qualified plans, certain gambling winnings from table games of chance that are not effectively connected to a U.S. trade or business, compensation received by participants in training or exchange programs, and certain U.S. savings bond income [§ 871(f), § 871(j), § 872(b)(3), § 872(b)(4)].

Exemptions specific to foreign entities include income from railroad rolling stock and income from communications satellites [§ 883(a)(3), § 883(b)].

Both individuals and foreign entities may receive exemptions on income from international operations and exemptions provided under a relevant tax treaty.

Some, but not all, types of U.S.-source income of a foreign government or international organization is exempt from U.S. tax [§ 892]. On the other hand, U.S.-source income of a foreign government received directly or indirectly from the conduct of a commercial activity in the United States is not exempt. Instead, as to that income, the foreign government is treated as a corporate resident of its country. U.S.-source income derived by a foreign central bank of issue from U.S. obligations (or the obligations of any U.S. agency or instrumentality), or from interest on deposits with persons carrying on the banking business, is also not included in its gross income. The exclusion does not apply to obligations that are held for, or used in connection with, the conduct of commercial banking functions or other commercial activities.

Finally, a non-resident employee of a foreign government or an international organization does not include wages from that entity in gross income [§ 893]. However, in the former case, the services rendered must be similar to those performed abroad by U.S. government employees, and the foreign government must grant an equivalent exemption. The exemption does not apply to aliens who are employees of a controlled commercial entity of the foreign government, or whose services are primarily in connection with a commercial activity (within or without this country) carried on by the foreign government.

## XX.E. U.S. Income Tax Treaties

### XX.E.1. Overview

[938 T.M., 943 T.M., 945 T.M., 6896 T.M.; TPS ¶7160.]

Persons engaged in cross-border investment or economic activities are subject to overlapping tax jurisdiction and, as such, are vulnerable to double taxation. To mitigate this burden, income tax treaties generally provide either for taxation in the source country where the item of income is earned or for taxation in the country where the income recipient is a resident. Income tax treaties, thus, supplement the operation of treaty countries' internal income tax laws by resolving conflicts when two countries tax the same item of income.

In addition to income tax treaties, there are various other types of tax treaties and executive-level agreements.

***Estate and Gift Tax Treaties.*** Also called "transfer tax" treaties, these treaties serve an equivalent role to income tax treaties in coordinating two taxing jurisdictions' exercise of rights over gifts and transfers at death.

***Social Security Totalization Agreements.*** These executive agreements coordinate the social security taxation of individuals from one country who work temporarily in another country and "totalize" (i.e., coordinate) the provision of ultimate social security benefits for individuals who have worked in and paid social security tax to, both countries, but may or may not have accumulated enough coverage to qualify for benefits in one or both.

*Shipping and Aircraft Agreements.* Also known as "transportation tax" agreements, these executive agreements cover the taxation of international transportation by these two modes and ancillary services provided in support of that activity.

*Tax Information Exchange Agreements (TIEAs).* TIEAs are limited international executive level agreements that aid both in administering and coordinating two countries' tax systems and in preventing undue tax avoidance, by authorizing various country-to-country discussions and exchanges of information.

### XX.E.2. Qualification for Treaty Benefits

[936 T.M., II., 938 T.M., II.; TPS ¶7160.03.A.]

Tax treaties provide benefits for people who are "residents" in either of the two countries that are parties to the treaty. For example, in the U.S. Model Income Tax Convention (Model Treaty), Article 4 defines residency as all persons whose status exposes them to worldwide taxation by the United States are U.S. residents. These include U.S. citizens, foreign individuals who are U.S. residents (i.e., individuals who either have the requisite immigration status or meet the "substantial presence" test) [§ 7701(b)] and all corporations incorporated in the U.S.

Another core requirement to qualify for tax treaty benefits is that the person claiming the benefit of a reduced rate under the provisions of a treaty must be the beneficial owner of the income for which the benefit is sought. Under U.S. tax principles, beneficial ownership is a multifaceted concept that first considers legal rights, including title, but puts great emphasis on economic substance. In this regard, beneficial ownership of income flowing through a fiscally transparent entity or paid with respect to certain financial instruments, whether hybrid or not, poses special challenges. In the U.S. Model Treaty, Article 22 (Limitations on Benefits) denies treaty benefits to certain persons or corporations. Accordingly, to qualify for U.S. treaty benefits, a person must be both a resident under Article 4 and not be disqualified under Article 22 of the U.S. Model Treaty.

### XX.E.3. Treatment of Common Types of Income

[938 T.M., IV. through IX.; TPS ¶7160.01.A.]

Most treaties reduce or eliminate tax imposed by the source country on common types of income received by residents of the other country. For example, the U.S. Model treaty provides a 15% rate for dividends, and a 5% rate to recipients that are corporations owning at least 10% of the voting stock of the corporation paying the dividends. Articles in treaties that cover interest and royalties may provide differing rates for certain types of payments.

### XX.E.4. Exchange of Information

[940 T.M., V.; TPS ¶7160.04.]

Income tax treaties can provide three ways for information to be exchanged between treaty partners: (i) upon request; (ii) automatically; and (iii) spontaneously. Requested information must relate to a specific case; fishing expeditions are generally not permitted. Automatic exchange of information entails the systematic transmission of information on certain categories of income (or with respect to certain industries) that have their source in one contracting state and that are received in the other contracting state. Spontaneous information exchange occurs when one country comes across information that may be of use to its treaty partner, and it then shares that information.

TIEAs often mirror the exchange of information provisions that already exist in income tax treaties. Some treaty partners may not agree to a treaty, but will agree to a TIEA. In other cases, TIEAs may provide more circumstances in which various kinds of tax or financial information may be provided by one country to the other. The agreements normally include information that might otherwise be subject to nondisclosure laws (e.g., bank secrecy).

### XX.E.5. FATCA Intergovernmental Agreements

[6565 T.M., IX.; TPS ¶7170.07.D.]

Intergovernmental agreements (IGAs) are bilateral executive agreements between the United States and many countries entered into for the purpose of implementing the Foreign Account Tax Compliance Act (FATCA). The IGA, of which there are two standard models, was developed by the Treasury Department and is essentially a form of TIEA intended to address foreign law restrictions on account holder information that might conflict with the reporting obligations under FATCA. Under an IGA, foreign financial institutions resident in or organized in the FATCA partner country are able to comply with the reporting obligations without violating local law in that country. IGAs have the status of executive agreements, not treaties, under U.S. law. However, IGAs may be viewed differently by FATCA partners, who may accord IGAs the status of treaties, making them subject to ratification processes. Thus, under some circumstances, IGAs exist as a supplement to an existing TIEA or an existing income tax treaty, and in others, they independently authorize information to be provided to the IRS.

### XX.E.6. Treaty Competent Authority Procedures

[940 T.M.; TPS ¶¶3600.05.E.; 7160.03.I.]

Income tax treaties establish a procedure for persons denied treaty benefits by a treaty country to appeal to the tax authorities of their own country of residence or citizenship to intervene with the authorities of the other treaty country in support of treaty protection. The process is known as a "mutual agreement procedure" ("MAP") or an appeal to the "competent authority." The U.S. Model Treaty contains a typical provision establishing the framework for the mutual agreement procedure to be conducted between the competent authorities of the contracting states. However, national tax authorities must supply specific procedures for taxpayers. In the U.S. tax system, the administration of competent authority is delegated to the IRS Deputy Commissioner (International). For procedures for requesting assistance with double taxation, denial of treaty benefits, discrimination, and questions of allocation of income and deductions, see Rev. Proc. 2006-54, 2006-49 I.R.B. 1035.

## XX.F. Select Withholding Obligations

[915 T.M., 6820 T.M.; TPS ¶7170.]

The U.S. tax liability of many foreign persons is satisfied by withholding at the source of the income. The Code requires U.S. payors to withhold tax from certain U.S. source payments to foreign persons and pay it over to the government. The general withholding rate is 30% of the gross amount of the payment. However, a different rate may apply to some kinds of income; certain types of income are exempt from withholding; and treaties may lower the rate or excuse withholding altogether. Generally, a foreign person's income is subject to withholding in five situations:

1. A foreign person receives (and beneficially owns) U.S. source fixed or determinable annual or periodical (FDAP) income that is not effectively connected to
   a U.S. trade or business [§ 881(a)].

2. A foreign individual receives payment for personal services, which though it is
   statutorily effectively connected income may still be subject to withholding if an
   exception does not apply [§ 1441(c)(1); Reg. § 1.1441-4(b)(1)].

3. A foreign person has effectively connected income attributed from a U.S.
   partnership [§ 1446].

4. A foreign person has gain from a transaction involving a U.S. real property
   interest, and certain other transactions covered by the Foreign Investment in
   Real Property Tax Act (FIRPTA) [§ 897, § 1445].

5. A foreign person is not properly documented under Foreign Account Tax
   Compliance Act (FATCA) provisions, and is therefore subject to withholding
   [§§ 1471-1474].

Under FATCA, special rules apply separately to payments made to foreign
financial institutions or other entities which may have U.S. account holders or U.S.
owners, but withholding in this case is being used as a "stick" to force disclosure of
information.

### XX.F.1. Income Subject to Withholding

[915 T.M.; TPS ¶7170.01.D.]

Withholding is required only for FDAP income and for items of income treated as
such for withholding purposes [§ 1441, § 1442]. Generally, provided the foreign payee
properly establishes its claim, withholding is not required for income that is effectively connected to a U.S. trade or business, because is taxed at graduated rates on a
net basis. However, there are three exceptions: (i) compensation for personal services; (ii) a foreign partner's share of effectively connected income; and (iii) income
from disposition of a U.S. real property interest [§ 1441(c)(1), § 1445, § 1446]. Withholding is also not required for income that is tax-exempt under the Code (although
it might be subject to reporting), nor of course is it applied to income from foreign
sources [Reg. § 1.6049-4(b)(5), § 1.6049-8].

### XX.F.1.a. Fixed or Determinable Annual or Periodical Income

[915 T.M.; TPS ¶7170.01.D.2.]

FDAP income is defined only in the regulations under § 1441 and encompasses all
income covered by § 61, except as specifically excluded in regulations or administrative pronouncements [Reg. § 1.1441-2(b)(1)(i)]. Because gain from selling property
and insurance premiums are the only specifically excepted items, characterization as
FDAP income and the prima facie obligation to withhold tax applies to a wide variety
of income items. Exclusion from the obligation to withhold depends, then, on an
exemption from the underlying tax, or a specific exemption from withholding for the
particular income item, and not on general arguments about the character of the
income.

### XX.F.1.a.(1) Exceptions and Special Rules

[915 T.M., XVIII.; TPS ¶ 7170.01.D.3.]

***Personal Services Income.*** Compensation for personal services is always effectively connected income, but when paid to a nonresident alien individual it is nonetheless subject to withholding, unless the income is compensation that is:

- subject to wage withholding or otherwise exempt under the rules relating to
  this form of withholding;

- earned by commuters from Mexico or Canada; or

- exempt by treaty [§ 1441(c)(1); Reg. § 1.1441-4(b)].

***Certain Corporate Distributions.*** While U.S source dividends are generally
subject to withholding, several kinds of corporate distributions are not [Reg. § 1.1441-
3(c)]. No withholding is required from a distribution of stock or stock rights, or on a
distribution treated as in full or part payment for stock (unless it is with respect to
stock that is a U.S. real property interest under FIRPTA) [Reg. § 1.1441-3(c)(1)]. Nor
is withholding required on a dividend paid by a grandfathered 80-20 corporation, to
the extent that the dividend is exempted from tax in the hands of a foreign person by
reason of the rules governing dividends from grandfathered 80-20 corporations that
have substantial foreign business income [§ 871(i), § 1441(c)(1), § 1442(a)]. Capital
gain dividends so designated by a regulated investment company are also not subject
to withholding (again with modifications made to accommodate FIRPTA).

A dividend is subject to withholding on the date considered paid, that is, if that
date and the record date differ. Furthermore, a dividend that is paid as part of an
exchange is considered paid when the exchange is made [Reg. § 1.1441-2(b)(3),
§ 1.1441-2(e)(4)].

Although only the dividend portion of a corporate distribution is taxable, a withholding agent is required to withhold 30% of an entire distribution, except as otherwise excused. The regulations are reasonably liberal in granting exceptions, however;
they permit a distributing corporation to elect not to withhold (by reducing the
amount withheld) on amounts in excess of current or accumulated earnings and
profits, stock or rights distributions, or capital gain distributions, and to coordinate
withholding on amounts that are also covered by FIRPTA withholding [Reg. § 1.1441-
3(c)(2)]. If a corporation does not know precisely what its earnings and profits
situation is at the time of a distribution, it may base withholding on a reasonable
estimate. If it later determines that it underwithheld, it will be liable for the shortfall,
as it would be for any underwithholding, but the regulations waive penalties for the
failure to withhold and deposit the tax if the payment is made quickly after the year
of the distribution, and in any event, they do not treat the corporation's payment of its
withholding agent's liability as an additional distribution subject to more withholding
[Reg. § 1.1441-3(c)(2)(ii)].

***Certain Interest Payments.*** In general, taxable U.S. source interest payments,
including some original issue discount (OID), must have tax withheld from them
[§ 1441(b), § 1441(c)(8); Reg. § 1.1441-2(b)(3), § 1.1441-3(b)]. Withholding is also required under the branch interest provisions [§ 884(f)]. There are several exceptions to
the interest withholding rules. Perhaps the broadest is the exception for qualifying
portfolio interest [§ 871(h), § 1441(c)(9)]. In addition, interest paid by banks and other
financial institutions on deposits and by grandfathered 80-20 corporations may be
partially or wholly exempt from withholding [§ 1441(c)(10); Reg. § 1.1441-2(a)(2)].

OID is subject to withholding on redemption of an original issue discount obligation or on interim sales if the withholding agent knows or has reason to know that the

sale was part of a plan to avoid tax [Reg. § 1.1441-2(a)(6), § 1.1441-2(b)(3)]. This may differ from the amount that is taxable to the holder, and the time that it is taxable, so that the holder of an OID obligation may owe tax or need to claim a refund of withholding, depending on circumstances. Because short-term obligations are not included in the definition of original issue discount obligation, no withholding is required on redemption of them, just as there is no tax on the OID in them [§ 871(g)(1)(B)(i); Reg. § 1.1441-2(a)(3)]. Furthermore, OID obligations issued as portfolio interest obligations are exempted from withholding [Reg. § 1.1441-2(a)(1)].

Interest on debt obligations that accrues between interest payment dates, like OID, may create a mismatch between withholding and tax liability. Liability for tax on interest between payment dates is normally the seller's obligation; a buyer customarily pays separately for it, acquires a basis in it, and does not incur taxable income until that basis is repaid. On the other hand, the buyer of bonds sold between interest dates is not required to withhold on the accrued but unpaid interest, and the issuer of the obligation must withhold on the full interest payment, without regard to the fact that the obligation was sold between interest payment dates [Reg. § 1.1441-2(a)(5)].

***Qualified Plans and Annuities.*** Pensions and annuities are subject to withholding if any part of the services for which they are paid were performed in the United States or, in the case of annuities, the contract is written in the United States. Some services are divided between the United States and foreign countries. Since the general withholding rule is that only U.S. source FDAP income is subject to withholding, withholding would be required for the portion of pension payments attributable to U.S. employment and to plan earnings.

Withholding is not required, however, on lump sum distributions from a qualified benefit plan and on annuities paid under a qualified benefit plan, if the amounts are exempt from tax because:

- they are attributable to foreign employment; and
- at least 90% of the persons covered by the plan are U.S. citizens or residents [§ 871(f), § 1441(c)(7)].

### XX.F.1.b. Partnerships

[915 T.M., XXI.; TPS ¶7170.01.E.]

The pass-through nature of partnerships presents some special withholding situations. A foreign partnership is a foreign "person" and, therefore, subject to withholding in principle when it is paid U.S. source FDAP income. However, if a partnership is a pass-through in its home country, it is not viewed as the "beneficial owner" of income in its own right, and withholding issues should be handled between the withholding agent and the partners directly [Reg. § 1.1441-5(c)(1)]. At the same time, a domestic partnership is not subject to withholding under § 1441 or § 1442, and without special withholding rules for U.S. partnerships receiving U.S. source FDAP income, the partnership could serve as a mechanism for foreign partners to escape U.S. withholding on this class of income. Thus, U.S. partnerships are required to withhold on FDAP income allocable to foreign partners [Reg. § 1.1441-5(b)(2)].

Similarly, if a partnership (domestic or foreign) earns items of effectively connected income, the U.S. tax effects of this fall on the partners, and if they are foreign, some means of managing withholding on this income is necessary to prevent the use of the partnership to avoid withholding altogether.

### XX.F.1.b.(1) Withholding on FDAP Income Paid to a Foreign Partnership

[915 T.M., XXI.C.; TPS ¶7170.01.E.]

If a foreign partnership is "undocumented," that is, it has not provided a Form W-8IMY, *Certificate of Foreign Intermediary, Foreign Flow-Through Entity, or Certain U.S. Branches for United States Tax Withholding and Reporting,* to a withholding agent, presumption rules must be used to determine what form of entity it is, and whether it is U.S. or foreign. If the conclusion is reached that it is a partnership, and foreign, it is not the beneficial owner of its income, and the status of the partners must be considered to see how withholding will be applied. A lack of documentation of the partnership will normally mean that the partners are presumed to be foreign [Reg. § 1.1441-1(b)(3), § 1.1441-5T(d)(2), § 1.1441-5T(d)(3)]. (This would be true, even if some of the partners are in fact U.S. persons.) This will mean withholding from any U.S. source FDAP income paid to the partnership.

### XX.F.1.b.(2) Withholding on FDAP Income by a U.S. Partnership

[915 T.M., XXI.A.; TPS ¶7170.01.E.]

A U.S. partnership is a U.S. person, and as such is not subject to withholding from FDAP income paid to it, either after having documented itself as a U.S. person or after being presumed to be a U.S. person under applicable presumption rules. (Backup withholding might be required if improper documentation or a tax identification number mismatch has occurred.) However, as a pass-through entity, the partnership may receive FDAP income that will be allocable to a foreign partner. In that case, the U.S. partnership is itself required to withhold from the foreign partner's allocable share of the FDAP income received by the partnership [Reg. § 1.1441-5(b)(2)(i)].

### XX.F.1.b.(3) Withholding on Foreign Partner's Share of Partnership Effectively Connected Income

[915 T.M., XXI.B.; TPS ¶7170.01.E.]

A partnership (domestic or foreign) with income, gain, or loss effectively connected with a U.S. trade or business must withhold at a special rate from any effectively connected income that is allocable to a foreign partner [§ 1446(a)]. The withholding is based on the percentage of partnership ECI that is allocable to foreign partners, and is determined at the highest tax rate attributable to that foreign partner [§ 1446(b)].

### XX.F.1.c. Estates and Trusts

### XX.F.1.c.(1) Domestic Trusts and Estates

[915 T.M., XXII.A.; TPS ¶7170.01.F.]

Domestic trusts and estates are, like domestic partnerships, not themselves subject to withholding. However, they must withhold on income attributable to a foreign beneficiary, to the extent that it constitutes an item subject to withholding [Reg. § 1.1441-5T(b)(2)(iii)]. Simple trusts, complex trusts, and estates all are required to withhold from income items that are subject to withholding, are included in their distributable net income, and are distributed to a foreign beneficiary. For a discussion of simple trusts and complex trusts and estates, see XVIII.A.7. and 8. If an item is required to be distributed currently but is not actually distributed at the end of the tax year, they must withhold on it by the time the annual report of payments must be sent to the beneficiaries and the IRS.

The difference between simple and complex trusts (or estates) under this rule is that income received by a complex trust that is not required to be distributed currently is not later included in distributable net income, and the trust has paid tax on it. Thus, while the withholding rule is stated in the same way for both kinds of trust regarding when they must withhold, trust rules distinguish between them in the amount included in the distributable net income base on which that withholding is calculated. The IRS position is that if the U.S. fiduciary of a complex trust with foreign beneficiaries receives U.S. source FDAP income but retains the income, pays tax at the trust level on it in the tax year of receipt, and then distributes that income to a foreign beneficiary in a subsequent year, the later distribution is not subject to withholding [Rev. Rul. 86-76, 1986-1 C.B. 284].

The source and character of income of a simple trust follow a current distribution into the hands of the beneficiary, and are the controlling factors in determining the withholding obligation of the U.S. fiduciary. Basically, the conduit rule of § 652 applies [Rev. Rul. 68-605, 1968-2 C.B. 390; Rev. Rul. 80-15, 1980-1 C.B. 365].

---

**EXAMPLE:** U.S. Estate has only foreign beneficiaries. In Year 1, Estate receives $1,000 in U.S. source interest that would be FDAP income in the hands of the foreign beneficiary if the obligor had paid him directly. Estate's executor makes no distribution to the foreign beneficiaries in that year, and the $1,000 is taxable to Estate [§ 641]. In Year 2, Estate receives an additional U.S. source interest payment of $500 from the same obligor. In Year 2, the executor distributes $1,000 to the foreign beneficiaries. Estate includes the $500 Year 2 interest in gross income in that year, but receives a deduction in the amount of the distribution limited, however, to the amount of its Year 2 distributable net income of $500 [§ 661]. Hence, Estate pays no tax in Year 2. The foreign beneficiaries are required to include the amount of the Year 2 distribution in their gross income limited, however, to the extent of the $500 of Estate's distributable net income [§ 662]. Since the $500 excess they receive in Year 2 was taxed to Estate in year 1, it is not subject to withholding, but the $500 required to be included in their gross income is [Rev. Rul. 86-76, 1986-1 C.B. 284].

---

### XX.F.1.c.(2) Foreign Trusts and Estates

[915 T.M., XXII.D.; TPS ¶7170.01.F.]

Foreign complex trusts and foreign estates are normally considered to be beneficial owners of income paid to them. A withholding agent may rely on Form W-8BEN-E, *Certificate of Status of Beneficial Owner for United States Tax Withholding and Reporting (Entities)*, or may use certain other documentation to determine the trust's status as a beneficial owner. In the absence of documentation, a trust presumed to be foreign is presumed to be complex [Reg. § 1.1441-5(e)(4), § 1.1441-5(e)(6)]. As a beneficial owner, a foreign complex trust (with a proper certification) may be able to claim income tax treaty benefits where applicable.

A foreign simple trust is not a beneficial owner of income paid to it. In procedures similar to those used for partnerships, a foreign simple trust must certify its own U.S. or foreign status, and then provide certifications of the beneficiaries, to secure any reductions of withholding or to avoid the application of the presumption rules [Reg. § 1.1441-5(e)(3)]. Foreign simple trusts may become withholding trusts, under principles similar to those applied to withholding foreign partnerships [Reg. § 1.1441-5(e)(5)(v)].

### XX.F.1.c.(3) Foreign Grantor Trusts

[915 T.M., XXII.D.; TPS ¶7170.01.F.2.]

Foreign grantor trusts are not considered to be the beneficial owners of their income and are treated similarly to simple trusts for purposes of documentation and withholding and may become withholding trusts, under principles similar to those applied to withholding foreign partnerships [Reg. § 1.1441-5(e)(3)(i), § 1.1441-5(e)(5)(v)].

### XX.F.1.d. Dispositions of a U.S. Real Property Interest

[912 T.M., III., IV.; TPS ¶7170.01.G.]

The transferee (normally the purchaser) who receives an interest in U.S. real property from a foreign person is required to withhold tax on the proceeds [§ 1445]. The tax is an amount equal to 10% of the amount realized by the foreign transferor (or a lesser amount established under an agreement with the IRS, discussed below). The amount of cash that changes hands in the transaction, if any, affects neither the duty to withhold nor the amount required to be withheld [§ 1445(a); Reg. § 1.1445-1(b)(1)].

In enacting a withholding regime for gain on U.S. real property dispositions, Congress departed from the theory of the Code that underpins withholding in general: withholding works best only where there is a high proportion of net income in the proceeds from the transaction. Where real property is concerned only the gain component of the proceeds is gross income subject to tax [§ 61(a)(3), § 1001(a)]. That is, in order to determine gain, the taxpayer's basis must be taken into account. From the standpoint of the buyer-withholding agent, no easy mechanism exists for him to make a determination of the gain element in order to withhold only in reference to it.

In addition, particularly where real estate is concerned, noncash consideration such as assumed mortgages may form a significant part of the price. From what does the buyer withhold if no cash changes hands? And, because the withholding obligation arises only as to foreign persons, in what way can the buyer determine that his seller is a foreign person subject to the tax regime for gain from the disposition of a U.S. real property interest? Or, more pragmatically, in what way can the buyer determine that his seller is not a foreign person and thus properly ignore the withholding rule?

The regulations address each of those issues in an attempt to arrive at a workable system that turns in part on certifications to be made to the transferee or to the IRS. However, because the buyer is ultimately liable for the duty to withhold, and the penalties attenuate for failing to do so in an appropriate case, the withholding rules in this area bring a new richness to the concept of caveat emptor.

Note, too, that because of the relatively low rate of withholding, the tax withheld may not entirely satisfy a foreign seller's underlying tax liability. This leads to two reasons why the foreign seller will be required to file a tax return and pay any additional tax that is due. First, because the gain is treated as effectively connected income, the seller is required to file a return even if withholding covers the tax and there is no remaining liability. Second, when the withholding is insufficient to cover the liability, a return is due so that the difference can be reported and paid. The seller remains entirely liable for the total amount of the underlying tax, notwithstanding the fact that the buyer has fulfilled the withholding obligation completely [Reg. § 1.1445-1(f)].

While, in general, the mechanism for withholding and paying over the amount of tax, and penalties potentially applicable to the buyer for failure properly to do so, parallel those for other kinds of income subject to withholding, there are some wrinkles that are peculiar to dispositions of U.S. real property interests.

First, the regulations provide that a transfer means any kind of transaction that amounts to a disposition for any purpose of the Code. Transfers for that purpose thus include distributions to shareholders of corporations, partners of a partnership, and beneficiaries of a trust or estate, and through the regulations' identification of a transferor, further include sales, exchanges, gifts, or any other kind of transfer [Reg. § 1.1445-1(g)(3), § 1.1445-1(g)(4)]. However, the obligation to withhold is imposed only when a transfer results in an amount realized under U.S. tax concepts, so that such transfers as gifts or amounts passing in an estate are not subject to withholding [Reg. § 1.1445-1(b)(1)].

Second, for purposes of these provisions, the amount realized to which the 10% gross tax applies includes:

- cash paid or to be paid (not including stated or unstated interest of original issue discount);
- the fair market value of the property; and
- the outstanding amount of any liability to which the U.S. real property is subject both immediately before and after the transfer [Reg. § 1.1445-1(g)(5)].

Finally, the seller must be a foreign person. In general, the foreign person identification system for withholding purposes dovetails with the kind of foreign person who is subject to tax on gain treated as effectively connected income upon the disposition of a U.S. real property interest [§ 897]. However, the regulations provide a mechanism under which transfers by some foreign persons otherwise subject to that tax do not require withholding.

### XX.F.2. FATCA Withholding

[6565 T.M.; TPS ¶7170.07.]

The Foreign Account Tax Compliance Act (FATCA) generally requires foreign financial institutions (FFIs) to identify U.S. account holders and report them to the IRS [§ 1471(b)(1)]. It also requires foreign entities that are not FFIs, i.e. nonfinancial foreign entities (NFFEs), to provide information regarding their ownership to withholding agents, including identifying any U.S. owners that hold an interest of more than 10% in the NFFE [§ 1472(a)]. FFIs and NFFEs that do not comply with the FATCA rules suffer a 30% withholding tax on withholdable payments to them.

A withholdable payment generally includes any payment of U.S. source fixed or determinable annual or periodical (FDAP) income, and starting in 2017, any gross proceeds from the sale or other disposition of any property that can produce U.S. source income in the form of interest or dividends [Reg. § 1.1473-1(a)]. It does not include the following, however:

- short-term obligations;
- U.S. trade or business income;
- certain excluded nonfinancial payments;
- gross proceeds from sales of fractional shares;
- offshore payments of U.S. source FDAP income before 2017; and
- certain payments made under collateral arrangements before 2017 [Reg. § 1.1473-1(a)(4)].

FFIs are financial institutions that are not U.S. financial institutions, including not only banks and custodial institutions, but also investment entities such as mutual funds, private equity funds, and hedge funds (the debt and equity interests in which are their "accounts"); as well as entities managing money or financial assets on behalf of others; certain insurance companies that issue cash value insurance or annuity contracts; and holding companies and treasury centers of affiliated groups that include one or more FFIs as a member [§ 1471(d)(5); Reg. § 1.1471-5(d), § 1.1471-5(e)]. FFIs generally are required to enter into an agreement with the IRS (an FFI agreement) under which they agree to do the following:

- perform due diligence with respect to their account holders;
- report their U.S. accounts to the IRS annually;
- comply with IRS requests for additional information;
- obtain a waiver of foreign law restrictions on reporting this information to the IRS for each U.S. account, or close the account if no waiver is obtained; and
- withhold a 30% tax on any "passthru payments" made to recalcitrant account holders who do not comply with the FFI's requests or provide a waiver and nonparticipating FFIs (NPFFIs) [§ 1471(b)(1)].

FFIs that enter into such agreements are known as participating FFIs (PFFIs). FFIs that do not comply with an FFI agreement or that are not otherwise exempted from the requirement to do so are referred to as NPFFIs.

Certain entities are exempted from the FATCA requirements to varying degrees, including foreign governments and their controlled entities, international organizations, foreign central banks, governments of U.S. territories, and certain retirement fund [§ 1471(f); Reg. § 1.1471-6]. FFIs that are deemed to be FATCA compliant (deemed-compliant FFIs) may either be registered-deemed compliant FFIs or certified deemed-compliant FFIs. Deemed-compliant FFIs do not need to enter into FFI agreements, but must still comply with the due diligence and withholding requirements applicable to their particular categories [Reg. § 1.1471-5(f)]. NFFEs that are exempted from FATCA withholding are referred to as excepted NFFEs [Reg. § 1.1472-1(c)].

PFFIs and registered deemed-compliant FFIs must register with the IRS, either electronically via the IRS website (www.irs.gov/fatca-registration) or on Form 8957, *Foreign Account Tax Compliance Act (FATCA) Registration* [Reg. § 1.1471-4(a), § 1.1471-5(f)(1)]. Upon registration, the FFI is assigned a global intermediary identification number (GIIN) [Reg. § 1.1471-1(b)(57)]. The date that the IRS issues a GIIN to a PFFI is the effective date of its FFI agreement [Reg. § 1.1471-1T(b)(35)]. The IRS has a standard FFI agreement [Rev. Proc. 2014-38, 2014-29 I.R.B. 131].

As enacted, FATCA's effective date was January 1, 2013. However, the IRS and Treasury have been implementing the law gradually: FATCA withholding on U.S. source FDAP payments became effective July 1, 2014, whereas withholding on gross proceeds does not until January 1, 2017 [Reg. § 1.1471-2(a)(1), § 1.1472-1T(b)(1), § 1.1473-1(a)(1)(ii)]. Also phased in are the dates by which FFIs have to enter into FFI agreements, complete account due diligence, implement passthru payment withholding, and report to the IRS. In addition, grandfathering rules exempt from FATCA withholding payments on certain obligations outstanding on July 1, 2014 [Reg. § 1.1471-2T(b)(2)(i)(A)(1)]. The IRS has also designated calendar years 2014 and 2015 as a transition period during which its enforcement and administration of the FATCA provisions, as well as certain related provisions, will be limited [Notice 2014-33, 2014-21 I.R.B. 1033].

FATCA due diligence requires PFFIs to identify and document their account holders to determine which accounts are U.S. accounts, which are foreign accounts, and which are held by recalcitrant account holders or NPFFIs [Reg. § 1.1471-4(c)(1)]. PFFIs will generally divide their accounts into four categories: preexisting individual accounts, preexisting entity accounts, new individual accounts, and new entity accounts. Preexisting accounts are accounts that are outstanding on the effective date of the FFI agreement, and new accounts are ones opened after that date [Reg. § 1.1471-1(b)(101), § 1.1471-1(b)(104)]. Each type of account has a different set of thresholds and implementation dates.

Similar payee identification procedures apply to withholding agents other than PFFIs. Withholding agents must report (both to the payee and the IRS), withhold, and deposit any withheld tax as required [Reg. § 1.1474–1(a)]. Reporting requires identifying the payee and the character and source of payments. The information collected to identify the payee will allow the withholding agent to determine if withholding is required.

Once a withholding agent identifies a payee, it must reliably associate the with-holdable payment with documentation supporting the payee's claimed "chapter 4 status" [Reg. § 1.1471-3(b)]. As with chapter 3 withholding, the withholding agent generally uses withholding certificates — Forms W-8 or W-9 — to do this, but depending on the chapter 4 status claimed, additional documentary evidence may be required [Reg. § 1.1471-3(d)]. The withholding agent must apply the same rules for reliably associating a payment with a withholding statement or documentary evidence and the same standards of knowledge that apply to all payee documentation. For certain payments made before July 1, 2017, a withholding agent may rely on a version of a withholding certificate issued before 2013 to establish the payee's chapter 4 status [Reg. § 1.1471-3T(d)(1)].

## XX.G. Select Reporting Obligations

### XX.G.1. Foreign Bank and Financial Accounts

[947 T.M., XIII.; TPS ¶7170.02.B.1.c.]

Any U.S. person having an interest in or signature authority over one or more foreign financial accounts with an aggregate value over $10,000 during a tax year must file a Financial Crimes Enforcement Network (FinCEN) Form 114, *Report of Foreign Bank and Financial Accounts* (FBAR), by June 30 following the calendar year for which the report is made, In addition to a foreign bank or securities account, a "financial account" includes commodities futures and options accounts, mutual funds, and life insurance and annuity policies with a cash value. Although it resembles a tax filing, FBARs are not tax reports and the requirement for them is not in the Internal Revenue Code. They are required by title 31 of the U.S. Code and regulations under that title. The FBAR is required to be filed via the Treasury Department's FinCEN electronic-filing system and no extension of time to file is permitted. However, a filing deferral is available until June 30, 2015, for certain employees and officers of a financial institution with signature authority only.

### XX.G.2. Foreign Financial Assets

[947 T.M., XIV.; TPS ¶7170.02.B.1.b.]

Any individual, including a resident alien and a nonresident alien who is taxed as a U.S. resident or is a resident of Puerto Rico or U.S. Possession, must file Form 8938, *Statement of Specified Foreign Financial Assets*, if the individual has interests in foreign financial assets, such as a foreign bank or securities account, the value of which exceeds a specific threshold, generally $50,000 on the last day of the tax year or $75,000 at any time during the tax year. The thresholds vary depending on the filing status of an individual. For joint filers, the respective amounts are $100,000 and $150,000, and $400,000 and $600,000 if either spouse is a qualified individual under the foreign earned income and housing cost exclusion [§ 911(d)(1)]. Similarly, the reporting threshold for an individual residing abroad is $200,000 and $300,000 [§ 911(d)(1)]. There are a number of reporting exceptions to address instances of duplicative reporting with other IRS Forms. If triggered, Form 8938 must be filed with an individual's U.S. income tax return, irrespective of whether tax liability is affected by one's foreign financial asset profile. The failure to file the form is subject to an initial penalty of $10,000, up to a maximum of $50,000 in a single tax period.

Although Form 8938 is similar to the FBAR, the two reporting requirements are intended for different purposes and, therefore, a taxpayer must file both forms, if applicable.

As of this writing, Form 8938 has been proposed to, but does not yet, apply to domestic entities, which would include corporations, partnerships, and certain trusts.

### XX.G.3. FATCA Reporting Obligations

[6565 T.M., II.D., II.E.; TPS ¶7170.07.B.]

Withholding agents and certain intermediaries must report withholdable payments under FATCA by filing an income tax return on Form 1042, *Annual Withholding Tax Return for U.S. Source Income of Foreign Persons*, which is the same form used to report U.S. source FDAP payments under § 1441 and § 1442 [Reg. § 1.1474-1(c)(1)]. The return must report the aggregate number of withholdable payments and the tax that withheld for the preceding calendar year. Although withholding agents must obtain withholding certificates and other documentation to determine whether FATCA withholding is appropriate, they need not be attached to the return. Form 1042 itself, however, must be filed even if no FATCA withholding was required. Participating and registered deemed-compliant FFIs generally must file a Form 1042 in the same manner as other withholding agents [Reg. § 1.1474-1(c)(2)]. Form 1042 is filed with the IRS by March 15 of the year following the calendar year in which the payment is made.

Withholding agents must also file with the IRS an information return on Form 1042-S, *Foreign Person's U.S. Source Income Subject to Withholding*, for each separate type of payment made to a single recipient [Reg. § 1.1474-1T(d)(1)(i), § 1.1474-1(d)(4)]. A copy must also be provided to the recipient of the income and any intermediary or flow-through entity [Reg. § 1.1474-1T(d)(1)(i)]. As with Form 1042, reporting on Form 1042-S is required whether or not any FATCA withholding tax was applied to the payment [Reg. § 1.1474-1T(d)(1)(i)]. Financial institutions filing Form 1042-S must use magnetic media, which includes electronic filing [Reg. § 301.1474-1(a)]. Withholding agents other than financial institutions file Forms 1042-S using magnetic media only if they are filing 250 or more Forms 1042-S [Reg. § 1.1474-1(e)].

Form 8966, *FATCA Report*, is used to report account holder information to the IRS. Participating FFIs and other entities use this form to provide aggregate information regarding accounts held by recalcitrant account holders and nonparticipating FFIs, as well as other account holders. Form 8966 is required is filed by March 31 for the preceding calendar year, but for 2014 reporting, the IRS proactively granted an automatic 90-day extension for all filers [Reg. § 1.1471-4(d)(3)(vi)]. Financial institutions must file electronically with the IRS [Reg. § 301.1474-1(a)]. Other withholding agents follow the 250-threshhold noted above.

Coordination of FATCA with other reporting obligations under chapters 3 and 61 and § 3406 is necessary because reporting and withholding under those regimes could also apply. FATCA withholding may be credited against withholding required under § 1441 through § 1443 and payments that are subject to withholding under § 1445 and

§ 1446 are not subject to FATCA withholding [Reg. § 1.1474-6T(b)(1), § 1.1474-6(c)(1), § 1.1474-6(d)(1)]. The same forms (Forms 1042 and 1042-S) are used for reporting under chapters 3 and 4. Also, if FATCA withholding is applied to a withholdable payment that is also a reportable payment under chapter 61, then no backup withholding under § 3406 is required [Reg. § 1.1474-6T(f)]. Similarly, reporting under FATCA will satisfy chapter 61 reporting obligations in certain circumstances [Reg. § 1.6049-4T(c)(4)(i)].

### XX.G.4. Currency Transactions of Over $10,000

[644 T.M., XII.; TPS ¶7170.02.B.6.]

A financial institution, including a bank, securities brokerage, and a currency exchange, must file FinCEN Form 104, *Currency Transaction Report*, in connection with a U.S. or foreign currency transaction totaling over $10,000. Multiple transactions by the same person in a single day that, taken together, exceed this amount must also be reported if the financial institution has knowledge of the circumstances. The form must be filed with the IRS center in Detroit, MI, within 15 days after the transaction date and a copy must be kept for five years from the date filed.

### XX.G.5. Cash Payments of Over $10,000

[644 T.M., XII., 915 T.M., VII.; TPS ¶3820.05.G.2.]

Any person who is engaged in a U.S. trade or business and receives a cash payment (including a check or money order) of more than $10,000 from a customer in a single transaction or series of related transactions must file Form 8300, *Report of Cash Payments Over $10,000 in a Trade or Business*, with the IRS within 15 days after the date of payment. The IRS, in turn, files the form with FinCEN. Form 8300 can be filed electronically through the FinCEN e-filing system or mailed to the IRS center in Detroit, MI. In addition, by January 31 of the following calendar year, the business must notify the customer, in writing, that a Form 8300 was filed with respect to the transaction. A copy of the filed form must be kept for five years from the date it was filed.

## XX.H. Select Compliance Issues

### XX.H.1. International Boycotts

[926 T.M.,VII.B.4.; TPS ¶7150.10.A.]

Generally, cooperation with an international boycott means agreeing, as a condition of doing business in a country or with its government or people, to refrain from doing business with or in another country or its people, which the Code discourages and, consequently, imposes the filing of a detailed report upon persons who participate in a transaction (direct or indirect) with or in a boycotting country [§ 999].

The Code provisions that apply to international boycotts require reporting certain operations, which, in turn, could cause the loss of certain tax benefits, such as foreign tax credits and tax deferral of foreign earnings [§ 999]. In general, persons who have operations in, or related to, boycotting countries must file Form 5713, *International Boycott Report*, to report those operations, the receipt of boycott requests, and boycott agreements. Specifically, Form 5713 must be filed by persons who:

- have such operations;
- are members of a controlled group, one member of which has such operations;
- are U.S. shareholders (within the meaning of subpart F) of a foreign corporation that has such operations;

- are partners in a partnership that has such operations; or
- are treated as owners of a trust that has such operations.

A non-U.S. person need not file Form 5713 unless the person claims a foreign tax credit or owns stock in an interest charge domestic international sales corporation. Form 5713 is due, in duplicate, by the due date of the taxpayer's U.S. income tax return, including extensions. Normally, the form does not have to be filed in connection with an international boycott that is approved of by the U.S. government.

The Treasury Department publishes a list, updated quarterly, of foreign countries that may require participation in, or cooperation with, an international boycott. Currently, Iraq, Kuwait, Lebanon, Libya, Qatar, Saudi Arabia, Syria, United Arab Emirates, and Yemen are on this list.

IRS agents with examinations involving taxpayer's with activities in, or in connection with, those countries, attempt to ensure that the taxpayer has complied with the reporting requirements and the substantive taxable income aspects of the boycott provisions of the Code.

The willful failure to file a required boycott report is a felony punishable by fine and imprisonment. Participation in or cooperation with an international boycott may result in a denial of the foreign tax credit for foreign taxes paid on boycott income, the benefits of treatment as a domestic international sales corporation may be diminished, and the Subpart F income of a controlled foreign corporation may be increased [§ 908, § 995(b)(1)(F)(ii), § 952(a)(3)]

### XX.H.2. Illegal Payments

[926 T.M., VII.B.5.; TPS ¶7150.10.B.]

Bribes, kickbacks or other similar payments made by a U.S. person to foreign government officials to influence official action in order to obtain or retain business violate the Foreign Corrupt Practices Act and are, therefore, considered illegal by the Code [§ 162(c)]. However, payments made to those officials to facilitate or expedite routine administrative action or that are made to nongovernmental persons are not within this prohibition. If proscribed payments are made:

- the amounts are not deductible as a business expense [§ 162(c)(1)] (see IV.D.3.);
- they limit the benefits available under the domestic international sales corporation provisions [§ 995(b)(1)(F)(iii)];
- they increase a controlled foreign corporation's Subpart F income [§ 954(a)(2)]; and
- they cannot be used to decrease its earnings and profits [§ 964(a)].

### XX.H.3. Foreign Books and Records

[623 T.M., I.D., II.D.17., 932 T.M., II.H.]

All persons who are liable for U.S. tax are required to keep books and records sufficient to determine their correct tax liability [§ 6001; Reg. § 1.6001-1]. A taxpayer who maintains some or all books and records outside the United States is subject to the same requirements for verification and substantiation, as if they were located in the United States and must be retained for as long as they may become material to the administration of any of the revenue laws [Reg. § 31.6001-1(e)(2)].

When an international examiner determines during the course of an audit that books and records located outside of the United States are necessary to verify income or substantiate deductions, the examiner asks the taxpayer to make the material available for examination in the United States. The agent's request is in writing, normally on Form 4564, *Information Document Request.* The taxpayer initially must respond within 60 days, but, in practice, this is subject to reasonable extensions upon consultation with the agent. If the taxpayer is unable or unwilling to produce the records in the United States but is willing to have them inspected at their foreign location, the agent may arrange for a foreign site inspection. If not, then formal document request is given to the taxpayer, who then has 90 days to comply [§ 982(c)]. Failure to comply at this point risks an unfavorable adjustment and may lead to a negligence penalty [§ 6662].

### XX.H.4. Departing Aliens

[907 T.M., XI.; TPS ¶7170.06.]

Before leaving the United States, an alien generally must file a certificate verifying compliance with U.S. income tax laws, including payment of any taxes due. Alternatively, the alien can present evidence that no certificate is required [§ 6851(d)]. In the absence of one or the other, the departing alien may be subject to examination by the IRS at the point of departure [Reg. § 1.6851-2(a)]. However, exceptions to this rule are provided for the following persons:

- diplomatic representatives, their families and certain servants;
- certain employees of foreign governments or international organizations and members of their households whose compensation is exempt from U.S. income tax and who have received no U.S. source gross income; and
- certain alien students, trainees, exchange visitors, and their spouses and children who have received no U.S. source income other than that allowed by regulation.

If the IRS believes that the collection of tax may be jeopardized by an alien's departure, it is authorized to terminate the alien's tax year and immediately demand payment of tax for that tax year and the preceding tax year [§ 6851(a)]. The compliance certificate requirements may apply to avoid the operation of that process or to complement it.

### XX.H.5. Expatriation

[907 T.M., XII., 918 T.M., IV., 919 T.M., VII.; TPS ¶7150.08.B.]

An important concern from a tax policy perspective is the expatriation of entities and individuals, which is the termination of U.S. status motivated by a desire to avoid U.S. worldwide taxation. More specifically, as concerns domestic entities, the benefit perceived by some taxpayers of being a U.S.-based corporation or partnership while avoiding the tax disadvantages of operating in the United States is accomplished by interposing a surrogate foreign corporation to hold the assets or business (directly or indirectly) of the former domestic entity. The Code targets an inversion generally by nullifying the associated tax benefits associated with the inversion or taxing the gain accrued to the U.S. entity up to the inversion date but without taking into account of offsets for net operating losses or foreign tax credits [§ 7874].

For individuals, because the United States asserts worldwide taxing jurisdiction over only U.S. taxpayers, U.S. citizens and resident aliens may expatriate (i.e., relinquish citizenship or terminate residency status) to avoid U.S. tax on foreign source income, which becomes particularly relevant in the case of high net-worth individuals who hold considerable portfolios of appreciated financial assets. As of June 17, 2008, an expatriating individual is subject to tax that is computed as if all of his or her assets held at that time were sold at fair market value on the day before expatriation [§ 877A]. A covered expatriate is subjected to the deemed sale treatment if one of the following tests is met:

- if the individual's average annual net federal income tax for the five years before the expatriation date exceeds a specific amount, which is adjusted annually ($157,000 for 2014 and $160,000 for 2015) [Rev. Proc. 2013-35, 2013-47 I.R.B. 537, Rev. Proc. 2014-61, 2014-47 I.R.B. 860];

- if the individual's net worth is $2 million or more as of the expatriation date; or

- if in the case where an individual's income and net worth fall below the above thresholds, the individual has failed to certify, or submit evidence of, compliance with requirements of U.S. tax laws for the previous five tax years.

Other than some items of deferred income, which are subject to a special withholding tax, there is no continuing taxation once this deemed sale has occurred [§ 877A(b)(1), § 877A(b)(7)].

# CHAPTER XXI. ESTATE, GIFT, AND GENERATION-SKIPPING TRANSFER TAX

>>>>>>>>>>>>>>>>>>>>>>>>>>>>>>

## XXI.A. Federal Transfer Tax System

Federal transfer taxes are imposed on the shifting of wealth. There are three different transfer taxes: (1) the estate tax, (2) the gift tax, and (3) the generation-skipping transfer (GST) tax. The estate tax applies to transfers of wealth that occur upon the donor's death. The gift tax applies to transfers that occur during the donor's lifetime. The GST tax can apply to both lifetime and post mortem transfers, but only when the donee is two or more generations younger than the donor (37.5 years for non-family members).

## XXI.B. Estate Tax

### XXI.B.1. Introduction

[800 T.M., IV.A.2.; TPS ¶6180.02.]

The federal estate tax is imposed on the transfer of property at death [§ 2001(a)]. The amount of tax depends on the value of the property transferred. The tax is not limited to property transfers controlled by a will or by the operation of the local laws of descent and distribution (i.e., property transferred for local "probate" purposes). Rather, the federal estate tax extends to other transfers that are essentially equivalent to testamentary transfers of property and that occur outside the scope of the probate system. Therefore, various types of transferred property, even though not "owned" (in the property sense) at death, are includible in the gross estate for federal estate tax purposes.

### XXI.B.2. The Gross Estate

#### XXI.B.2.a. Property Owned at Death

[817 T.M., II.; TPS ¶6190.01.]

The gross estate of a U.S. citizen or resident decedent includes all of the decedent's property, real or personal, tangible or intangible, wherever situated [§ 2031, § 2033]. If the decedent is a co-owner of property, the decedent's interest generally is included in the decedent's gross estate. Accordingly, if the decedent owned a fractional interest in property, the value of that fractional interest is included in the decedent's gross estate.

Property owned at death is reported on Form 706, Schedules A (real estate), B (stocks and bonds), and C (mortgages, notes, and cash). Other property interests not reported on a specific schedule are reported on Form 706, Schedule F.

### XXI.B.2.b. Marital Property Interests

[802 T.M.; TPS ¶6190.01.K.]

If a person is married at the time of death, the surviving spouse may have an interest in property titled in the decedent's name. In states that have adopted a community property system, each spouse is a one-half owner of each community asset, regardless of how the asset is titled. The gross estate of the deceased spouse includes, in effect, the decedent's one-half interest in each community asset (however titled) [§ 2033].

In states that have not adopted a community property regime, the property titled solely in the decedent's name may be burdened by inchoate marital property claims of the surviving spouse. These inchoate claims include property subject to statutory elective rights. Even though the property titled in the decedent's name is burdened by such a marital property claim, the amount of the decedent's gross estate is not reduced by those claims. Property passing to a spouse as a result of such a claim would qualify for the marital deduction (see XXI.B.4.d.).

Jointly-owned property is reported on Form 706, Schedule E.

### XXI.B.2.c. Transfers Within Three Years of Death

[818 T.M., II.; TPS ¶6200.01.]

Generally, transfers (other than transfers for adequate consideration) by the decedent within three years of the date of death are included in the decedent's gross estate if the interest transferred would have been included in the decedent's gross estate under § 2036, § 2037, § 2038, or § 2042 (each described below) if the transferred interest had been retained by the decedent on the decedent's date of death [§ 2035]. These transfers are reported on Form 706, Schedule G.

### XXI.B.2.d. Transfers with Retained Interests and Powers

[50 T.M., II., III.; 52 T.M., II., III.; TPS ¶6200.]

**Transfers with Retained Life Estate.** Incomplete transfers are included in the transferor's gross estate [§ 2036(a)]. The transferor's gross estate includes all property interests of which the transferor (at any time) made a transfer (other than a transfer for adequate consideration), by trust or otherwise, under which the transferor retained for life (or for any period not ascertainable without reference to his or her death or that does not end before his or her death) either [Reg. § 20.2036-1(a)]:

1. the possession, enjoyment, or the right to the income of the property; or
2. the right to designate the person(s) who will possess or enjoy the property or the income it generates.

**Transfers Taking Effect at Death.** The decedent's gross estate includes the value of property that the decedent transferred (other than for adequate consideration) if [§ 2037(a)]:

1. the decedent retained a reversionary interest in the property the value of which (immediately before the death of the decedent) exceeds 5% of the value of the property; and
2. ownership of the interest by the donee can be obtained only by surviving the decedent.

*Revocable Transfers.* The decedent's gross estate includes the value of any interest of which the decedent at any time made a transfer (other than a transfer for adequate consideration) if enjoyment of the interest was subject at the date of the transferor's death to any change through the exercise of a power by the transferor (alone or with any other person) to alter, amend, revoke, or terminate (or if any such power is relinquished during the three-year period ending on the date of the transferor's death) [§ 2038(a); Reg. § 20.2038-1(a)].

Transfers with retained interests and powers are reported on Form 706, Schedule G.

### XXI.B.2.e. Annuities

[821 T.M., II.; TPS ¶6210.02.]

The decedent's gross estate includes the value of (1) an annuity under a contract or agreement payable to the decedent (or the decedent possessed the right to an annuity) for life (or for any period not ascertainable without reference to the decedent's death or for any period that does not end before the decedent's death), and (2) an annuity or other payment (other than life insurance) under such contract or agreement receivable by any beneficiary by reason of surviving the decedent [§ 2039(a); Reg. § 20.2039-1(b)(1)].

The decedent's gross estate includes the value of the annuity receivable by any beneficiary by reason of surviving the decedent to the extent that the value of the annuity or other payment is attributable to contributions made by the decedent (or the decedent's employer) [§ 2039(b); Reg. § 20.2039-1(a)]. In other words, § 2039 includes in the decedent's gross estate the value of the survivor's annuity, not the value of the decedent's annuity immediately before death.

Annuities are reported on Form 706, Schedule I.

### XXI.B.2.f. Joint Survivorship Interests

[823 T.M.; TPS ¶6220.]

The joint tenancy with right of survivorship form of ownership provides that, upon the death of an owner, the surviving owner or surviving owners succeed to the interest of the deceased owner. Accordingly, if property is owned by two persons as joint tenants with right of survivorship, the death of one of the two joint tenants causes the surviving joint tenant to become the sole and outright owner of the property.

The decedent's gross estate includes the entire value of any joint tenancy property, except to the extent that the surviving joint tenant provided consideration for the acquisition of the property [§ 2040(a); Reg. § 20.2040-1(a)(2)]. To the extent that the property was acquired by the decedent and the other joint owner or owners by gift, devise, bequest, or inheritance, the decedent's fractional share of the property is included in his or her gross estate [§ 2040(a); Reg. § 20.2040-1(a)(1)].

A special rule is provided for certain survivorship property owned by spouses, which causes inclusion in the gross estate of the deceased spouse of one-half of the value of the survivorship property, regardless of which spouse provided consideration for the property [§ 2040(b)].

Jointly held property is reported on Form 706, Schedule E.

### XXI.B.2.g. Powers of Appointment

[825 T.M., IV.A.; TPS ¶6230.04.]

The decedent's gross estate includes certain property not owned by the decedent, but over which the decedent possessed at death a power of appointment [§ 2041(a); Reg. § 20.2041-1(a)]. This rule applies only to a "general" power of appointment, not to a "special" or "limited" power of appointment. A general power of appointment is a power that may be exercised in favor of:

- the decedent;
- the estate of the decedent;
- the creditors of the decedent; or
- the creditors of the estate of the decedent [Reg. § 20.2041-1(c)].

Generally, any other power of appointment is a special power of appointment [§ 2041(a)(3); Reg. § 20.2041-3(a)(3)].

Although § 2041 applies to a general power of appointment possessed at the moment of the decedent's death, it also applies to a general power of appointment exercised or released during the decedent's lifetime in a disposition that, if it had been a transfer of property owned by the decedent, would have caused the property to be includible in the decedent's gross estate under § 2035 to § 2038.

*5-or-5 Powers.* Generally, a lapse (due to inaction) of a power is treated as a release, causing the value of the power to be included in the decedent's gross estate. However, the lapsed power is not includible if its value did not exceed the greater of (1) $5,000, or (2) 5% of the value, at the time of the lapse, of the property from which the exercise of the lapsed power could have been satisfied [§ 2041(b)(2)].

Powers of appointment are reported on Form 706, Schedule H.

### XXI.B.2.h. Proceeds of Life Insurance

[826 T.M., I.; TPS ¶6240.01.]

The decedent's gross estate includes the proceeds of life insurance on the life of the decedent that are payable to (1) the decedent's estate, or (2) other beneficiaries (if the decedent possessed at the time of death any incident of ownership) [§ 2042].

*Incidents of Ownership.* The meaning of "incidents of ownership" is not limited to ownership in a technical sense, and it includes the right of the insured (or the estate of the insured) to the economic benefits of the policy, such as the power to change the beneficiary, to surrender or cancel the policy, to assign the policy, to revoke an assignment, to pledge the policy for a loan, or to obtain from the insurer a loan against the surrender value of the policy. "Incident of ownership" also includes a reversionary interest if the value of the reversionary interest exceeds 5% of the value of the policy immediately before the death of the decedent [Reg. § 20.2042-1(c)(2)–(6)].

Life insurance proceeds are reported on Form 706, Schedule D.

### XXI.B.2.i. Transfers for Insufficient Consideration

[50 T.M., V.B.; TPS ¶6250.02.]

Various transfers, interests, or powers may be subject to the federal estate tax. If the transfer, interest, or power were to be disposed of for adequate consideration, the consideration received would be subject to inclusion in the gross estate, and there would be no need for a special inclusion rule for the previously owned transfer, interest, or power. Section 2043(a) seeks to require full consideration for such transfers, interests, or powers by providing that trusts, interests, rights, or powers enumerated and described in § 2035 to § 2038 and § 2041 are not subject to inclusion in the gross estate if made, created, exercised, or relinquished for adequate consideration. If adequate consideration is not received, the gross estate includes only the excess of the fair market value of the property at the time of death over the value of the consideration received by the decedent.

### XXI.B.2.j. Property for Which Marital Deduction Previously Allowed

[843 T.M., VI.F.; TPS ¶6270.05.D.]

The estate and gift tax marital deductions (see XXI.B.4.d. and XXI.C.4.f.) for transfers to the decedent's spouse may take several forms. One widely used form of marital deduction transfer is the "qualified terminable interest property" (QTIP) transfer. The surviving spouse's gross estate includes the value of the QTIP interest for which an estate or gift tax marital deduction previously was allowed to the first spouse to die [§ 2044].

Property for which the marital deduction was previously allowed is reported on Form 706, Schedule F.

### XXI.B.2.k. Disclaimed Property

[848 T.M., III.; TPS ¶6320.08.]

Even though a person becomes the owner of property because of a gift, devise, or bequest, the person may disclaim certain property interests. If the person makes a qualifying disclaimer, the person is treated as if he or she never owned the property, and the disclaimed property is not included in the disclaimant's gross estate [§ 2046, § 2518(a)].

### XXI.B.3. Estate Tax Valuation Rules

[830 T.M., II., 833 T.M., I.A.; TPS ¶6290.]

Generally, property included in the decedent's gross estate is valued as of the decedent's date of death [§ 2031(a)]. However, the executor may elect an alternate valuation date, if doing so would reduce both the value of the gross estate and the sum of the estate and generation-skipping transfer taxes due [§ 2032(a), § 2032(c)]. The alternate valuation date is six months after the decedent's date of death, and if it is elected, each property included in the decedent's gross estate must be valued as of the alternative valuation date [§ 2032(a); Reg. § 20.2032-1(a)].

*Fair Market Value Standard.* Typically, an item includible in the decedent's gross estate is valued at its fair market value at the time of the decedent's death [Reg. § 20.2031-1(b)]. The fair market value is the price at which the property would change hands between a willing buyer and a willing seller, neither being under any compulsion to buy or to sell and both having reasonable knowledge of relevant facts. There is a penalty of 20% of the estate tax underpayment attributable to a substantial valuation understatement (or 40% for a gross valuation misstatement) [§ 6662(a), § 6662(g), § 6662(h)].

*Special Use Valuation.* An executor may elect to value certain real property used in a closely held farming or other business at its "special use value" (rather than its fair market value, which is based on the property's "highest and best use") by completing the notice of election on Form 706, Schedule A-1, and submitting a recapture agreement [§ 2032A]. For estates of decedents dying in 2014, the aggregate decrease in the value of qualified real property resulting from special use valuation cannot exceed $1,090,000 ($1,100,000 for 2015). [Rev. Proc. 2013-35, 2013-47 I.R.B. 537, § 3.33, Rev. Proc. 2014-61, 2014-47 I.R.B. 860, § 3.34].

### *XXI.B.4. Estate Tax Deductions*

To calculate the decedent's taxable estate, allowable deductions are subtracted from the gross estate [§ 2051]. These deductions are discussed below.

### *XXI.B.4.a. Deduction for Estate Expenses, Indebtedness, and Taxes*

[840 T.M., II.A.; ¶6260.01.A.]

In calculating the taxable estate, a deduction from the decedent's gross estate is allowed for certain expenses, indebtedness, and taxes [§ 2053]. The deductions can be separated into two categories of expenses and claims. The first category includes amounts that are payable out of property subject to claims and that are allowable for purposes of the probate proceeding for the decedent. The items within this first category are [§ 2053(a)]:

- funeral expenses;
- administration expenses of the estate;
- claims against the estate; and
- unpaid mortgage indebtedness on property if the gross value of the decedent's interest in the property, undiminished by any mortgage indebtedness, is included in the gross estate.

The items in the second category are expenses [§ 2053(b)]:

1. incurred in administering property included in the gross estate but not subject to claims; and
2. that would be allowed if (a) the property were subject to claims, and (b) the expense is paid before the expiration of the period of limitation for assessment.

*Note:* Certain administration expenses may be claimed as a deduction in calculating either (1) the amount of the taxable estate subject to the estate tax, or (2) the amount of the estate's taxable income subject to the income tax. Double deduction (on both the estate tax return and an income tax return) is disallowed [§ 642(g)]; however, deductible amounts may be split between the estate tax return and the income tax return. To claim an income tax deduction, the executor must file a statement in duplicate that the amounts have not been claimed as an estate tax deduction and waiving the right to the estate tax deduction [Reg. § 1.642(g)-1].

Funeral and administrative expenses are reported on Form 706, Schedule J. Mortgages, liens, and debts of the decedent are reported on Form 706, Schedule K.

### *XXI.B.4.b. Losses*

[840 T.M., III.; TPS ¶6260.04.]

In calculating the taxable estate, a deduction from the decedent's gross estate is allowed for losses incurred during estate administration arising from fires, storms, shipwrecks, or other casualties, or from theft, when such losses are not compensated for by insurance or otherwise [§ 2054].

*Note:* Certain losses may be claimed as a deduction in calculating either (1) the amount of the taxable estate subject to the estate tax, or (2) the amount of the estate's taxable income subject to the income tax. Double deduction (on both the estate tax return and an income tax return) is disallowed [§ 642(g)]; however, deductible losses may be split between the estate tax return and the income tax return. To claim an income tax loss, the executor must file a statement in duplicate that the amounts have not been claimed as an estate tax deduction and waiving the right to the estate tax deduction [Reg. § 1.642(g)-1].

Losses are reported on Form 706, Schedule L.

### XXI.B.4.c. Charitable Deduction

[839 T.M., II.; TPS ¶6280.]

An estate may deduct the value of qualifying contributions to, or for the benefit of, certain charitable organizations (including federal, state, and local governments) for public, charitable, religious, and other similar purposes [§ 2055(a)]. To qualify for the deduction, the transferred property must be included in the decedent's gross estate [§ 2055(d)].

**Split-Interest Transfers.** A transfer may qualify for the estate tax charitable deduction even if one of the beneficiaries is a noncharitable entity. These transfers must be in the form of one of the following:

- a charitable lead trust, with an annuity or unitrust payment made to a charitable income beneficiary, and a payment of the remainder to a noncharitable beneficiary [§ 2055(e)(2)(A)];
- a charitable remainder trust, with an annuity or unitrust payment made to a noncharitable income beneficiary, and a payment of the remainder to a charity [§ 170(f)(2), § 2055(e)(2)(B)];
- a remainder interest in a farm or personal residence, or an undivided portion of a decedent's entire interest [§ 2055(e)(3)(I); Reg. § 20.2055-2(e)(2)];
- a copyrighted work of art separate from its copyright [§ 2055(e)(4)]; or
- a qualified conservation easement [§ 170(f)(3)(B), § 2055(f)].

Charitable, public, and similar gifts and bequests are reported on Form 706, Schedule O.

### XXI.B.4.d. Marital Deduction

### XXI.B.4.d.(1) General Rules

[843 T.M., II.A.; TPS ¶6270.01.A.]

An unlimited estate tax marital deduction is available for transfers from a decedent to the decedent's surviving spouse. To be eligible for the deduction, the following requirements must be met:

1. The decedent must be survived by a spouse [§ 2056(a)].
2. The surviving spouse must be a U.S. citizen (unless the "qualified domestic trust" (QDOT) is used) [§ 2056(d); Reg. § 20.2056A-1(a)(1)(i)].
3. The property passing to the surviving spouse must be included in the decedent's gross estate [§ 2056(a); Reg. § 20.2056(a)-2(b)(1)].
4. The property passing to the surviving spouse must be subject to inclusion in the gross estate of the surviving spouse (to the extent the property is not consumed or transferred by the surviving spouse before death) [§ 2056(b); Reg. § 20.2056(b)-1(b)].

The following types of transfers to the surviving spouse qualify for the marital deduction:

- an outright transfer to the surviving spouse;
- a life estate to the surviving spouse with a testamentary general power of appointment in the surviving spouse;
- a QTIP bequest;
- an estate trust, which distributes all principal and accumulated income to the estate of the surviving spouse; and
- a QDOT for transfers for the benefit of a non-citizen surviving spouse.

***Same-Sex Married Couples.*** A couple legally married in a state that recognizes same-sex marriage is considered married for federal tax purposes [*United States v. Windsor*, 133 S. Ct. 2675 (2013)]. This includes couples legally married in a state that recognizes same-sex marriages but residing in a state that does not recognize same-sex marriages [Rev. Rul. 2013-17, 2013-38 I.R.B. 201]. Although many I.R.C. sections are couched in "husband" and "wife" terminology, legally married same-sex couples fall within their purview.

The marital deduction is claimed on Form 706, Schedule M.

### XXI.B.4.d.(2) QTIP Marital Deduction

[843 T.M., VI.F.; TPS ¶6270.05.D.]

The QTIP marital deduction applies to property: (1) that passes from the decedent, (2) in which the surviving spouse has a qualifying income interest for life (typically as the beneficiary of QTIP held in trust), and (3) to which an election is made by the estate of the first spouse to die.

For property to qualify for the marital deduction as QTIP, the surviving spouse must have, during his or her lifetime, either an entitlement to all of the income of the property, payable at least annually, or the right to use the property. In addition, no person can have the power to appoint any of the property to anyone other than the surviving spouse.

### XXI.B.4.d.(3) Marital Deduction for Transfers to Non-Citizen Surviving Spouse

[842 T.M., III.; TPS ¶6270.05.G.]

Generally, transfers to a non-citizen surviving spouse do not qualify for the marital deduction [§ 2056(d)]. However, property transferred to a QDOT for the benefit of a non-citizen surviving spouse qualifies for the estate tax marital deduction [§ 2056(d)(2), § 2056A]. There is a special mechanism that imposes estate tax on (1) any non-hardship distribution of principal (but not of income) from the QDOT to the surviving spouse, and (2) the value of the property remaining in the QDOT on the date of death of the non-citizen surviving spouse [§ 2056A(b)(1), § 2056A(b)(3)].

### XXI.B.4.e. Deduction for State Death Taxes

[840 T.M., IV.; TPS ¶6260.03.B.]

For purposes of calculating the taxable estate, a deduction from the decedent's gross estate is allowed for any estate, inheritance, legacy, or succession taxes paid to any state attributable to any property included in the decedent's gross estate [§ 2058(a)]. To be deductible, the state death tax must be claimed before the later of [§ 2058(b)]:

- four years after the filing of the estate tax return;
- if a Tax Court petition has been filed, 60 days after the Tax Court's decision becomes final;
- if an extension of the period of limitation for the payment of the tax has been granted, the date of the expiration of the period of the extension; or
- if a claim for refund or credit of an overpayment of estate tax has been timely filed, the latest of the expiration of: (1) 60 days from the date of mailing by the IRS to the taxpayer of a notice of the disallowance of any part of the claim; (2) 60 days after a decision by a court becomes final in a timely refund suit; or (3) two years after a notice of the waiver of disallowance is filed.

### XXI.B.5. Calculation of Estate Tax

#### XXI.B.5.a. Estate Tax Rates

[800 T.M., IV.A.4.; TPS ¶6180.02.D.8.]

A single unified rate schedule applies for determining estate and gift taxes [§ 2001, § 2502]. The top rate for estates and gifts is 40% [§ 2001(c)]. The estate tax is determined by applying the unified rate schedule to the aggregate of cumulative lifetime transfers and transfers at death [§ 2001(b)].

If elected, reduced federal estate tax rates are available for estates of certain qualified decedents, i.e., U.S. citizens and residents: (1) who are killed in action while serving in a combat zone, (2) who die from injuries suffered in the line of duty while serving in a combat zone, (3) who are specified terrorist victims, or (4) who are astronauts who die in the line of duty [§ 2201(b)].

#### XXI.B.5.b. Calculation of Tentative Estate Tax

[800 T.M., IV.A.4.; TPS ¶6180.02.D.]

Calculation of the tentative estate tax involves a multi-step process to account for the integration of the gift and estate taxes [Reg. § 20.0-2(b)]:

Step 1: Determine the amount of the taxable estate [§ 2051].

Step 2: Determine the amount of adjusted taxable gifts [§ 2001(b)]. "Adjusted taxable gifts" are the taxable gifts made by the decedent during his/her life, but excluding any gifts that are includible in the decedent's gross estate (because the lifetime transfer was deemed incomplete under § 2035–§ 2043).

Step 3: Calculate the tentative estate tax on the sum of the taxable estate and the amount of adjusted taxable gifts [§ 2001(b)(1)].

Step 4: Calculate the aggregate amount of gift tax that would have been payable on lifetime gifts made by the decedent using the § 2001(c) rates at the time of the decedent's death (rather than the rates at the time of the gifts) [§ 2001(b)(2)].

Step 5: The tentative estate tax is the excess of the tax in step 3 over the tax in step 4.

#### XXI.B.5.c. Estate Tax Credits

#### XXI.B.5.c.(1) The Unified Credit

[844 T.M., II.B.; TPS ¶6300.01.]

There is a unified credit against the tentative estate tax that is equivalent to the amount of estate tax that would be due on the applicable exclusion amount [§ 2010(a), § 2010(c)]. The applicable exclusion amount is the basic exclusion amount plus, in some cases, the deceased spousal unused exclusion (DSUE) amount [§ 2010(c)]. As adjusted for inflation, the basic exclusion amount is $5,340,000 for estates of decedents dying in 2014 ($5,430,000 for 2015), resulting in a credit of $2,081,800 ($2,117,800 for 2015) [Rev. Proc. 2013-35, 2013-47 I.R.B. 537, § 3.32, Rev. Proc. 2014-61, 2014-47 I.R.B. 860, § 3.33].

*Portability.* Married couples can effectively combine their unified credit amounts if the predeceased spouse's estate elects portability on a timely filed Form 706, *United States Estate (and Generation-Skipping Transfer) Tax Return*. This election gives the surviving spouse access to the DSUE amount (i.e., the predeceased spouse's basic exclusion amount that was not used for either estate or gift tax purposes), which is added to the surviving spouse's own basic exclusion amount [§ 2010(c)].

### XXI.B.5.c.(2) Other Credits

[844 T.M., IV.–VII.; TPS ¶6300.03., .04.]

***Credit for Gift Tax on Pre-1977 Gifts.*** There is a credit for any gift tax paid that is attributable to lifetime transfers made before 1977, if any amount of the gifted property is included in the value of the decedent's gross estate (because the lifetime transfer was deemed incomplete under § 2035–§ 2043) [§ 2012(a)]. The credit cannot exceed the lesser of (1) the gift tax paid, or (2) the estate tax attributable to the inclusion of the gift in the gross estate.

***Credit for Prior Federal Estate Tax Paid.*** There is a credit for certain estate taxes previously paid by the estate of another person who died within 10 years before, or within two years after, the decedent's death [§ 2013(a)]. The credit phases out over a 10-year period, in two-year intervals, from the date of death of the decedent [§ 2013(a)(1)–§ 2013(a)(4)]. This credit is claimed on Form 706, Schedule Q.

***Credit for Death Tax Paid to Foreign Government.*** There is a credit for amounts of inheritance, legacy, or succession taxes paid to any foreign country attributable to property (1) situated within the foreign country, and (2) included in the decedent's U.S. gross estate [§ 2014(a)]. The amount of the credit is limited to the amount of U.S. estate tax attributable to the property that generates the foreign tax [§ 2014(b)]. To claim this credit, the estate must utilize Form 706, Schedule Q, and Form 706-CE.

***Credit for Death Taxes on Remainders.*** If the payment of the federal estate tax allocable to reversionary and remainder interests in property that are included in a decedent's gross estate is postponed under § 6163(a), and if any foreign death taxes are incurred, the credit for death taxes on remainders provides for the use of the foreign death tax credit based upon when the respective taxes are paid [§ 2015].

***Recovery of Taxes Claimed as Credit.*** An estate must notify the IRS if any foreign death tax that was paid, for which a credit under § 2014 was claimed, is subsequently recovered from or refunded by the foreign country that initially collected the tax [§ 2016]. The IRS will then recalculate the federal estate tax to determine whether any additional tax is due.

### XXI.B.6. Returns and Payment of Estate Tax

### XXI.B.6.a. Duty to File Estate Tax Return

[822 T.M., I.C.; TPS ¶¶3820.03.A., 6300.06.]

An estate must file Form 706 only if (1) the gross estate exceeds the basic exclusion amount for the calendar year of the decedent's date of death, or (2) the executor elects portability [§ 6018(a)(1)].

The liability for payment of estate tax is imposed on the executor [§ 2002]. The executor is generally the personal representative acting under a decedent's will or, if none, the person in possession of the decedent's property [§ 2203].

### XXI.B.6.b. Due Date of Estate Tax Return

[822 T.M., IV.B.; TPS ¶3820.03.A.]

Form 706 is due within nine months of the decedent's date of death [§ 6075(a)]. The estate may get an automatic six-month extension by filing Form 4768, *Application for Extension of Time To File a Return and/or Pay U.S. Estate (and Generation-Skipping Transfer) Taxes*, on or before the due date for filing Form 706.

### XXI.B.6.c. Due Date for Payment of Estate Tax

[822 T.M., IV.F., G.; TPS ¶6300.05.A.]

Any estate tax payable is due as of the due date of the estate tax return, and any extension of the due date for filing Form 706 does not necessarily extend the due date for payment of the tax [Reg. § 20.6075-1, § 20.6081-1(e)]. Accordingly, payment of the estate tax generally is required on the date nine months after the decedent's death. The tax must be paid in cash (or by check); other property is not permitted as payment [§ 6311; Reg. § 301.6311-1, § 301.6311-2].

*Deferral of Payment.* The IRS may extend, at its discretion, the due date for payment of estate tax for a period not to exceed one year [§ 6161(a)(1)]. If the estate demonstrates reasonable cause, the IRS may extend the due date for a period not to exceed 10 years [§ 6161(a)(2)]. Further, an executor generally may elect to pay the estate tax attributable to a qualifying interest in a closely held business in installments over a period not longer than 14 years from the date the tax would otherwise be due [§ 6166(a)]. Another extension exists for certain reversionary or remainder interests [§ 6163].

### XXI.B.7. Special Estate Tax Provisions for Nonresident Aliens

[837 T.M., VI.; TPS ¶6310.01.]

The estate of a decedent, who was not a citizen or resident of the United States but who owned property situated therein, may be subject to the U.S. estate tax and required to file Form 706 [§ 2101–§ 2108, § 6018(a)(2)]. Generally, the estate of a nonresident non-citizen must file Form 706-NA, *United States Estate (and Generation- Skipping Transfer) Tax Return — Estate of nonresident not a citizen of the United States*, if the part of the gross estate that is situated in the United States exceeds $60,000, reduced (but not below zero) by the amount of adjusted taxable gifts made by the decedent after 1976 [§ 6018(a)(1), § 6018(a)(2)].

Although the nonresident non-citizen's estate is subject to tax at the same rates as estates of U.S. citizens, the unified credit is only $13,000 [§ 2102(a), § 2102(b)]. The nonresident alien's estate may avail itself of [§ 2106(a)(1)–§ 2106(a)(4)]:

- a deduction for a pro rata share of expenses, debts, and losses;
- a charitable deduction;
- a marital deduction (if the surviving spouse is a U.S. citizen); and
- a deduction for state death taxes.

*Note:* A bilateral tax treaty between the decedent's country of domicile and the United States may prescribe other estate tax treatment, and such a treaty overrides the otherwise-applicable statutory provisions.

## XXI.C. Gift Tax

### XXI.C.1. In General

[845 T.M., I.; TPS ¶6320.]

The federal gift tax is imposed on the (direct or indirect) gratuitous inter vivos transfer of property by an individual to a donee in exchange for less than full and adequate consideration [§ 2501(a)(1)]. The property transferred may be real, personal, tangible, or intangible, and can include forgiveness of a debt, assignment of a judgment, designation of an individual as the beneficiary of a life insurance policy, creation of a joint tenancy or tenancy in common. Donative intent is not required for the transfer to be considered a gift for gift tax purposes. The tax applies when any individual who is a U.S. citizen or resident transfers property with a value in excess of the amount of allowable exclusions and deductions. The gift tax is an excise tax imposed upon the donor's transfer, and the donor is primarily and personally liable for the tax [§ 2502(c)].

### XXI.C.2. Transfers Subject to Gift Tax

#### XXI.C.2.a. General Rules Applicable to Gift Tax

[845 T.M., III.; TPS ¶6320.01.]

Although the gift tax is imposed on "the transfer of property by gift," donative intent is not required for a transfer to be taxable [*Commissioner v. Wemyss*, 324 U.S. 303 (1945)]. If property is transferred for less than full and adequate consideration, the excess of the value of the transferred property over the value of consideration received is a "gift" for gift tax purposes [§ 2512(b)]. Further, the gift tax applies to both direct and indirect transfers. Indirect transfers subject to the gift tax may include:

- transfers in trust;
- certain assignments of benefits;
- cancellation of indebtedness;
- the ability to withdraw funds deposited by another from a joint account; and
- below-market interest rate loans.

#### XXI.C.2.b. Completion of Gift

[845 T.M., IV.; TPS ¶6320.06.]

The fundamental requirement for imposition of the gift tax is that there be a completed, irrevocable transfer of property by gift [*Burnet v. Guggenheim*, 288 U.S. 280 (1933)]. A gift is made when the donor completes the gift rather than when the donee receives the benefit of the gift [Reg. § 25.2511-2(b)]. A gift is complete to the extent that the donor relinquishes all dominion and control over the transferred property. As a general rule, to the extent that the transferor retains any power to revoke the gift or to change the disposition of the property, the gift is incomplete [Reg. § 25.2511-2(b), § 25.2511-2(c)].

#### XXI.C.2.c. Specific Transfers

[845 T.M., V.A., VI.C., VII.E.2.; TPS ¶6320.03., .07.]

**Gifts By Husband or Wife to Third Party.** Married persons may treat a gift made by one spouse to a third party as made one-half by each spouse [§ 2513]. This concept, known as "gift splitting," is discussed at XXI.C.4.b.

**Exercise or Release of Powers of Appointment.** Generally, the exercise, release, or lapse of a *special* power of appointment does not constitute a transfer of property for gift tax purposes [§ 2514(a)–§ 2514(c)]. However, the exercise or release of a *general* power of appointment is considered a transfer of property for gift tax purposes [§ 2514(a), § 2514(b)]. Generally, a lapse of a general power of appointment is considered a release of the power, unless the amount subject to the power does not exceed the greater of $5,000 or 5% of the aggregate value out of which the power could have been exercised [§ 2514(e)].

**Treatment of Generation-Skipping Transfer (GST) Tax.** For any taxable gift that is a direct skip, the amount of the gift is increased by the amount of any GST tax imposed on the transferor attributable to the gift [§ 2515].

*Transfers Incident to Divorce.* Transfers made pursuant to a written agreement between spouses (1) with regard to their marital and property rights, or (2) to provide a reasonable allowance for the support of minor children are deemed to be made for full and adequate consideration [§ 2516]. The agreement must be entered into within a three-year period that includes the two years prior to, and one year after, the divorce occurs.

*Dispositions of Certain Life Estates.* If an individual terminates his/her interest in qualified terminable interest property (QTIP) during the individual's lifetime, the disposition is treated as a transfer of all interests in the property other than the qualifying income interest [§ 2519(a)]. The transfer of the income interest is subject to tax under the general gift tax rules [§ 2511].

*Below-Market Interest Rate Loans.* Where a donor loans money, with the loan made on a below-interest or no-interest (i.e., below market rate) basis, the value of the interest-free use of such funds is a gift for gift tax purposes [§ 7872].

### XXI.C.3. Gift Tax Valuation Rules

[845 T.M., VII.; TPS¶6320.09.]

The determination of the value of a gift is based on the fair market value of the property on the date the transfer is complete [§ 2512(a); Reg. § 25.2512-1]. There is a penalty of 20% of the gift tax underpayment attributable to a substantial valuation understatement (or 40% for a gross valuation misstatement) [§ 6662(a), § 6662(g), § 6662(h)].

*Special Rules for Intra-Family Transfers of Nonpublicly Traded Property.* To combat estate freezing transactions, special valuation rules apply to certain gifts within families [§ 2701–§ 2704].

### XXI.C.4. Gift Tax Exclusions and Deductions

### XXI.C.4.a. Gift Tax Annual Exclusion

[845 T.M., IX.A.; TPS ¶6330.01.A.]

In determining the amount of taxable gifts made during the calendar year, an individual donor may exclude the first $14,000 (per donee) of gifts made in 2014 (and 2015) [§ 2503(b); Rev. Proc. 2013-35, 2013-47 I.R.B. 537, § 3.34, Rev. Proc. 2014-61, 2014-47 I.R.B. 860, § 3.35]. The exclusion is available only for gifts of present interests in property, not future interests [Reg. § 25.2503-3(a), (b)].

*Gifts to Minors.* Certain gifts in trust for the benefit of a minor (i.e., a person below the age of 21) are not considered gifts of future interests and, thus, the gift tax annual exclusion applies [§ 2503(c)].

*Crummey Powers.* Typically, gifts in trust have restrictions on the beneficiary's right to use, possess, or enjoy the transferred property. Those types of restrictions mean that the gift does not qualify as a present interest and, thus, the donor cannot access the per-donee annual exclusion. However, if a trust beneficiary has a right to withdraw funds from the trust, even though that right is not exercised, the donor will be able to claim the annual exclusion for a transfer to trust [*Crummey v. Commissioner*, 397 F.2d 82 (9th Cir. 1968)]. The right to withdraw is known as a "*Crummey* power". The beneficiary must be notified of, and have a reasonable opportunity to exercise, the right [Rev. Rul. 83-108, 1983-2 C.B. 167; Rev. Rul. 81-7, 1981-1 C.B. 474].

### *XXI.C.4.b. Gift Splitting*

[845 T.M., XIII.A.2.d.; TPS ¶6330.03.]

Married persons may elect to treat a gift made by one spouse as if it was made one-half by each spouse [§ 2513]. Gift splitting allows the spouses to combine their annual exclusions to make up to $28,000 of tax-free gifts per donee during 2014 (and 2015) [§ 2503(b); Rev. Proc. 2013-35, 2013-47 I.R.B. 537, § 3.34, Rev. Proc. 2014-61, 2014-47 I.R.B. 860, § 3.35]. Both spouses must consent for a gift to be split [§ 2513(a)(2)].

### *XXI.C.4.c. Gifts to Non-Citizen Spouse*

[842 T.M., IX.; TPS ¶6310.07.A.]

Although the gift tax marital deduction (see XXI.C.4.f.) generally is disallowed for transfers to a non-citizen spouse, the first $145,000 of present interest gifts made in 2014 ($147,000 for 2015) from a donor to his/her non-citizen spouse are not subject to the gift tax [§ 2523(i); Rev. Proc. 2013-35, 2013-47 I.R.B. 537, § 3.34, Rev. Proc. 2014-61, 2014-47 I.R.B. 860, § 3.35].

### *XXI.C.4.d. Gift Tax Exclusion for Educational and Medical Expenses*

[845 T.M., IX.B.; TPS ¶6330.04.]

There is an unlimited gift tax exclusion for qualified transfers to pay a donee's educational or medical expenses [§ 2503(e)]. This exclusion is in addition to the per donee annual exclusion [Reg. § 25.2503-6(a)] (see XXI.C.4.a.). To be excluded, the payment must be made on behalf of the donee either (1) directly to a qualifying educational institution for the donee's tuition, or (2) directly to a health care provider for the donee's medical expenses [§ 2503(e)(2); Reg. § 25.2503-6(b)].

### *XXI.C.4.e. Gift Tax Charitable Deduction*

[839 T.M., XI.; TPS ¶6330.06.]

There is an unlimited gift tax deduction for gratuitous transfers of property to, or for the use of, certain charitable recipients [§ 2522]. The deduction is permitted for qualifying transfers to four prescribed categories of donees: (1) governments, (2) any corporation, trust, community chest, fund, or foundation that is organized and operated exclusively for religious scientific, literary, or educational purposes, (3) certain fraternal societies (if the property is used for a charitable purpose), or (4) certain war veterans organizations [§ 2522(a)(1)–§ 2522(a)(4)]. Further, certain split-interest gifts are eligible for the deduction [§ 2522(c)(2)] (see XXI.B.4.c.).

### *XXI.C.4.f. Gift Tax Marital Deduction*

[845 T.M., X.A.; TPS ¶6330.05.]

Qualifying lifetime gifts to, or for the benefit of, the donor's spouse are deductible (without limitation as to amount) from the calculation of taxable gifts if the following requirements are met [§ 2523(a), § 2523(b), § 2523(i)]:

1. the spouses are married to each other at the time of the gift;
2. the interest transferred to the donee spouse is not a nondeductible terminable interest; and
3. the donee spouse is a U.S. citizen.

Gifts from the donor to his/her non-citizen spouse do not qualify for the unlimited gift tax marital deduction, but are eligible for an annual exclusion of up to $145,000 for gifts made in 2014 ($147,000 for 2015) [§ 2523(i)(2); Rev. Proc. 2013-35, 2013-47 I.R.B. 537, § 3.34, Rev. Proc. 2014-61, 2014-47 I.R.B. 860, § 3.35].

Generally, gifts of terminable interest property (e.g., life estates, interests in property for a term of years, most annuity interests, etc.) do not qualify for the marital deduction. However, the following terminable interests do qualify for the deduction:

- life estate with power of appointment in the donee spouse [§ 2523(e)];
- QTIP [§ 2523(f)]; or
- certain gifts of an income interest in a charitable remainder trust [§ 2523(g)].

### XXI.C.5. Disclaimers

[848 T.M., III.; TPS ¶6320.08.]

If a qualified disclaimer is made for any interest in property, the disclaimed interest is treated as if it had never been transferred to the person making the disclaimer [§ 2518(a)]. The transaction is treated as though ownership in the disclaimed property never vests in the person disclaiming. The disclaimed property passes directly from the original transferor to the transferee who receives the property as a result of the disclaimer, and there is no taxable gift by the disclaimant [Reg. § 25.2518-1(b)].

### XXI.C.6. Calculation of Gift Tax

### XXI.C.6.a. Gift Tax Imposed on Cumulative Transfers

[845 T.M., XII.; TPS ¶6330.07.]

The gift tax rate applicable to gifts during a year is based on the donor's aggregate lifetime taxable gifts, which is the sum of (1) taxable gifts made in prior periods, plus (2) taxable gifts made in the current period [§ 2502(a)]. Although the gift tax rates are no longer progressive for gifts made after 2009 (because of the interaction of the rate and credit amounts, the 40% rate essentially operates as a flat rate), this aggregation historically permitted the progressive gift tax rate schedule to apply to cumulative lifetime gifts. In effect, the progressive gift tax rate schedule for current year gifts started where the progressive rate schedule stopped for gifts made in prior periods. More specifically, the gift tax payable for current year gifts is the excess of (1) the tentative gift tax payable on the total of (a) all taxable gifts made by the donor during the current year plus (b) all taxable gifts made by the donor in prior periods, over (2) the tentative gift tax payable on taxable gifts in all previous periods [§ 2502(a)].

### XXI.C.6.b. Unified Credit Exemption Equivalent

[845 T.M., XII.E.; TPS ¶6330.07.]

For gifts made in 2014, the applicable credit amount (determined by reference to the basic exclusion amount for estate tax purposes) is $2,081,800 ($2,117,800 for 2015), which effectively excludes from gift tax the donor's first $5,340,000 ($5,430,000 for 2015) of lifetime gifts [§ 2505(a)(1), § 2010(c); Rev. Proc. 2013-35, 2013-47 I.R.B. 537, § 3.32, Rev. Proc. 2014-61, 2014-47 I.R.B. 860, § 3.33]. The basic exclusion amount is indexed for inflation. Thus, if a taxpayer uses the entire applicable credit amount and the basic exclusion amount increases in a later year, the taxpayer may claim the additional amount in the later year. The amount of the available credit is reduced by the sum of amounts allowable as a credit for all preceding calendar years [§ 2502(a)(2)]. In the case of a surviving spouse whose deceased spouse's estate made the portability election on its estate tax return, the amount of available credit is increased by the deceased spousal unused exclusion amount [§ 2505(a), § 2010(c)(2)(B)].

### XXI.C.7. Returns and Payment of Gift Tax

[822 T.M., IX.; TPS ¶3820.03.B.]

Generally, a donor must file a gift tax return, Form 709, *United States Gift (and Generation-Skipping Transfer) Tax Return*, for any calendar year that he/she gives gifts to a donee totaling more than the annual exclusion amount ($14,000 for gifts given in 2014 and 2015) [Rev. Proc. 2013-35, 2013-47 I.R.B. 537, § 3.34, Rev. Proc. 2014-61, 2014-47 I.R.B. 860, § 3.35]. The gift tax return for a calendar year is due on April 15 of the following calendar year [§ 6075(b)(1)]. Similarly, any gift tax due for a calendar year is due and payable on April 15 of the following calendar year [§ 6161(a)].

### XXI.C.8. Gifts Received from Foreign Sources

[845 T.M., VII.E.; TPS ¶6320.10.]

A U.S. person who receives more than $15,358 in 2014 ($15,601 in 2015) in gifts from foreign corporations or partnerships or more than $100,000 in gifts from nonresident aliens or foreign estates must report the gifts to the IRS on Form 3520, *Annual Return to Report Transactions With Foreign Trusts and Receipt of Certain Foreign Gifts* [§ 6039F; Notice 97-34, 1997-1 C.B. 422; Rev. Proc. 2013-35, 2013-47 I.R.B. 537, § 3.38, Rev. Proc. 2014-61, 2014-47 I.R.B. 860, § 3.39].

## XXI.D. Generation-Skipping Transfer Tax

### XXI.D.1. Taxable Generation-Skipping Transfers

[850 T.M., IV.; TPS ¶6340.02.]

A generation-skipping transfer (GST) tax is imposed at a 40% rate on certain transfers made to a beneficiary who is at least two generations below the transferor's generation [§ 2601, § 2602, § 2613, § 2641, § 2651]. For non-family members, this tax may apply when the donor is at least 37.5 years older than the recipient [§ 2651(d)]. Family members are assigned to generations based on their relationships rather than on their ages [§ 2651].

There are three types of generation-skipping transfers: (1) a direct skip, (2) a taxable termination, and (3) a taxable distribution to a skip person [§ 2611(a)]. A direct skip is a transfer to a skip person (i.e., a person two or more generations younger than the transferor, or a trust for the benefit of a skip person) [§ 2613(a)]. Generally, a taxable termination is the termination (by death, lapse of time, release of power, or otherwise) of an interest in property held in a trust for the benefit of a skip person [§ 2612(a)]. A taxable distribution is any distribution from a trust to a skip person that is not a taxable termination or a direct skip [§ 2612(b)]. If the parent of the skip person predeceases the transferor, a gift to the skip person is not a generation-skipping transfer [§ 2613(a)].

The following transfers are not subject to GST tax [§ 2611(b), § 2642(c)]:

- transfers not subject to gift tax because of the unlimited exclusion for direct payment of medical and tuition expenses;
- certain transfers to the extent that the property transferred was previously subject to GST tax; and
- direct skips and certain transfers to trust that qualify for the gift tax annual exclusion or the medical and tuition expense payment exclusion.

### XXI.D.2. GST Exemption

[850 T.M., V.; TPS ¶6340.03.]

Every individual is allowed a lifetime exemption for generation-skipping transfers adjusted for inflation annually [§ 2631, § 2010(c)]. The exemption for transfers made in 2014 is $5,340,000 ($5,430,000 for 2015) [Rev. Proc. 2013-35, 2013-47 I.R.B. 537, § 3.32, Rev. Proc. 2014-61, 2014-47 I.R.B. 860, § 3.33]. If a taxpayer uses the entire exemption and the exemption amount increases in a later year, the taxpayer may claim the additional amount in the later year. Although any unused GST exemption is automatically allocated to lifetime transfers that are treated as direct skips, the transferor may opt out of the automatic allocation on a timely filed Form 709, *United States Gift (and Generation-Skipping Transfer) Tax Return* [§ 2631, § 2632(b)(1), § 2632(b)(3); Reg. § 26.2632-1(b)(1)(i)].

### XXI.D.3. Computation of GST Tax Rate

[850 T.M., VII.; TPS ¶6340.04.]

The amount of GST tax imposed on a generation-skipping transfer is determined by multiplying the taxable amount by the applicable rate [§ 2602]. The applicable rate is determined by multiplying the maximum estate tax rate (40%) and the inclusion ratio for the transfer [§ 2641(a)].

The inclusion ratio is a mechanism that accounts for the portion of the generation-skipping transfer that is not exempt from the GST tax after application of the transferor's exemption amount. The inclusion ration for any property transferred in a generation-skipping transfer is the excess of 1 over either the applicable fraction determined for the trust from which the transfer is made, or in the case of a direct skip, the applicable fraction determined for the skip [§ 2642(a)(1)].

In contrast to the inclusion ration, the applicable fraction is the mechanism that accounts for the portion of the generation-skipping transfer that is exempt from the GST tax due to allocation of the transferor's exemption amount. The numerator of the applicable fraction is the amount of GST exemption allocated to the trust (or in the case of a direct skip, allocated to the property transferred in the skip) [§ 2642(a)(2)(A)]. The denominator is the value of the property transferred to the trust (or involved in the direct skip), reduced by the sum of (1) any federal estate tax or state death tax actually recovered from the trust attributable to the transferred property, and (2) any estate or gift tax charitable deduction attributable to the property [§ 2642(a)(2)(B)].

### XXI.D.4. Returns and Payment of GST Tax

[850 T.M., VIII.; TPS ¶6340.05.]

In the case of a taxable termination, the trustee is responsible for filing Form 706-GS(T), *Generation-Skipping Transfer Tax Return For Terminations*, and paying the GST tax [Reg. § 26.2662-1(b)(2), § 26.2662-1(c)(1)(ii)]. In the case of a taxable distribution, the transferee is responsible for filing Form 706-GS(D), *Generation-Skipping Transfer Tax Return For Distributions*, and paying the GST tax. A trust involved in a taxable distribution must file Form 706-GS(D-1), *Notification of Distribution From a Generation-Skipping Trust* [Reg. § 26.2662-1(b)(1), § 26-2662-1(c)(1)(i)]. Transferors must file Form 709 and pay the GST tax for direct skips made during his/her lifetime [Reg. § 26.2662-1(b)(3)(i), § 26.2662-1(c)(1)(iii)]. If a direct skip occurs upon the transferor's death, the executor is responsible for filing Form 706, *United States Estate (and Generation-Skipping Transfer) Tax Return*, Schedules R and R-1, and paying the GST tax [Reg. § 26.2662-1(b)(3)(ii), § 26.2662-1(c)(1)(v)].

If the tax is triggered by a decedent's death, it is due within nine months after the date of the decedent's death. In other cases, the appropriate return must be filed on or before the 15th day of the 4th month after the close of the calendar year in which the transfer occurred [Reg. § 26.2662-1(d)(1)].

## XXI.E. Gifts and Bequests from Expatriates

[837 T.M., VI.D., 845 T.M., XIV.B.; TPS ¶6310.04.C.]

There is a tax imposed at a rate of 40% on covered gifts and bequests received by U.S. persons from certain expatriates [§ 2801]. Section 2801 is a pseudo inheritance/income tax, as the tax is paid by the U.S. person *receiving* the gift or bequest [§ 2801(b)]. The tax applies to gifts and bequests acquired directly or indirectly from an individual who, at the time of the acquisition, is a "covered expatriate" [§ 2801(e)(1), § 2801(f), § 877A(g)(1)]. There are exceptions for otherwise taxable transfers (e.g., gifts of U.S.-situs tangible personal property) and for otherwise deductible transfers to spouses and charities [§ 2801(e)(2), § 2801(e)(3)]. Status as a covered expatriate is determined by reference to the objective standards relating to net income and net worth, and other compliance tests in § 877(a)(2)(A), § 877(a)(2)(B) and § 877(a)(2)(C), with certain exceptions.

The tax applies only to the extent that the value of covered gifts and bequests received by any U.S. person during the year exceeds the gift tax annual exclusion, which is $14,000 for gifts made in 2014 (and 2015) [§ 2801(c), § 2503(b); Rev. Proc. 2013-35, 2013-47 I.R.B. 537, § 3.34, Rev. Proc. 2014-61, 2014-47 I.R.B. 860, § 3.35]. The IRS has not yet provided a form for reporting the tax on covered gifts or bequests, but has indicated that it is developing a Form 708. It said that taxpayers will be given a reasonable time in which to report and pay the tax after the new form is published [Announcement 2009-57, 2009-29 I.R.B. 158].

# CHAPTER XXII. WITHHOLDING AND EMPLOYMENT TAXES

>>>>>>>>>>>>>>>>>>>>>>>>>>>>>>>

## XXII.A. Income Tax Withholding

### XXII.A.1. Liability for Withholding Taxes

#### XXII.A.1.a. Employer Liability for Withholding Taxes

[392 T.M., III.A.1.a.; TPS ¶5440.01.]

Employers must deduct and withhold income tax on the amount of wages that are actually or constructively paid to any employee. The tax applies irrespective of the irregular performance of the employee's services, the frequency of the payments, or the amount of wages that are paid at any one time. It is also immaterial that an employer-employee relationship no longer exists when payment is made [§ 3402(a)(1), § 3403; Reg. § 31.3401(d)-1(b), § 31.3402(a)-1(b), § 31.3403-1].

#### XXII.A.1.b. Deemed Employers Liable for Withholding Taxes

[392 T.M., III.A.1.b.; TPS ¶5430.01.A.4.]

In certain instances, the burden of collecting withholding taxes shifts to persons other than the actual employer. If the person for whom the employee's services are performed does not possess legal control of the payment of wages for the services, the person having control is deemed to be the employer. A deemed employer also includes any person who pays wages on behalf of a nonresident alien individual, foreign partnership, or foreign corporation not engaged in a trade or business in the United States or Puerto Rico [§ 3401(d); Reg. § 31.3401(d)-1(e)].

#### XXII.A.1.c. Authorized Agent Liable for Withholding Taxes

[392 T.M., III.A.1.c.; TPS ¶5440.03.B.1.e.]

Any person, in addition to the actual employer, who pays or controls the payment of wages may obtain authorization to act as the agent of the employer for purposes of withholding income taxes. An application to act as the agent of an employer that is properly executed by the employer is filed by the agent with the district director with whom the agent will file returns and pay taxes using Form 2678, *Employer/payor Appointment of Agent*. To the extent that an agent is authorized to act on behalf of the employer, all provisions of law, including penalties, which apply to an employer, also apply to the agent. However, each employer for whom the agent acts still remains subject to such laws as well [§ 3504; Reg. § 31.3504-1(a)].

### XXII.A.1.d. Third-Party Payors Liable for Withholding Taxes

[392 T.M., III.A.1.d.; TPS ¶3875.06.C.]

A lender, surety, or other person who pays wages directly to employees of an employer is treated as an employer for purposes of withholding and is liable for the payment of taxes otherwise required to be deducted and withheld by the employer. A lender, surety, or other person who advances funds to an employer also is liable for the payment of withholding taxes if [§ 3505]:

1. the third party knows that the advance will be used to pay wages of the employer's employees; and

2. the third party has actual notice or knowledge that the employer does not intend to or is unable to pay the amount required to be deducted and withheld by the employer.

### XXII.A.2. Computation of Withholding Taxes

### XXII.A.2.a. Payroll Periods

[392 T.M., III.A.2.a.; TPS ¶5440.03.A.]

The computation of the amount of tax that is withheld from the wages of each employee is determined based on an employee's payroll period. A "payroll period" is the period of service for which the employer ordinarily pays wages to an employee. It is immaterial in determining the amount withheld that wages are not consistently paid at regular intervals [§ 3401(b); Reg. § 31.3401(b)-1(a)].

---

**EXAMPLE:** If an employee is ordinarily paid on Friday of each week, but in a particular week is paid a portion of his accrued wages on another day and the balance on Friday, the payroll period is still weekly. Similarly, if the employee is away on business for a period that exceeds the normal payroll period, the wages he receives upon his return are taxed as if they had been paid at the time the employer ordinarily makes payment.

---

Withholding taxes normally are computed based on daily, weekly, biweekly, semi-monthly, monthly, quarterly, semiannual, or annual payroll periods. An employee may have only one payroll period. When an employee has no payroll period, the tax withheld is determined as if the employee were paid on a daily or miscellaneous period based on the number of days (including Sundays and holidays) in the period covered by the wage payment. If wages are paid to an employee for a payroll period of more than one year, the payroll period is deemed to be an annual payroll period [§ 3402(b)(1); Reg. § 31.3401(b)-1(b), Reg. § 31.3402(g)-2].

### XXII.A.2.b. Withholding Exemptions, Allowances and Withholding Certificates

[392 T.M., III.A.2.b.; TPS ¶5440.03.A.]

**Exemptions.** The amount of tax that is withheld from an employee's wages is determined in part by the number of withholding exemptions and allowances claimed by the employee. Withholding exemptions correspond to the exemptions that an employee is entitled to claim in computing his annual income tax. An employee who has filed a valid withholding exemption certificate with his employer is entitled to claim one exemption for himself unless the employee is claimed as a dependent on another tax return. An employee also may be entitled to additional exemptions as described below. However, additional exemptions typically are not permitted if the employee is a nonresident alien [§ 3402(f)(1), § 3402(f)(6)].

In addition to the exemptions to which an employee is personally entitled, an employee (other than a nonresident alien) may claim an exemption for each individual who may reasonably be expected to be claimed as the employee's dependent for the tax year, provided such individual is living at the time such individual is claimed. If the employee is married and the employee's spouse is not employed, the employee may also claim any withholding exemptions that the spouse could claim if the spouse were employed. If the spouse is in fact employed, an employee may still claim any exemption that the employed spouse is entitled to claim, provided the spouse has not claimed such exemption [§ 3402(f)(1)(B), § 3402(f)(1)(C); Reg. § 31.3402(f)(1)-1(d)(1)].

*Allowances*. An unmarried employee with only one employer and a married employee with only one employer and whose spouse is not an employee receiving wages subject to withholding may claim a standard deduction allowance equal to one withholding exemption. This allowance may not be claimed, however, if the employee has withholding exemption certificates in effect with respect to more than one employer. In addition to the standard deduction allowance, employees may claim additional withholding allowances for various estimated deductions and credits based on the amount of wages the employee "reasonably" expects to receive during the tax year [§ 3402(f)(1)(E), § 3402(m)].

*Withholding Certificates*. On or before the employee's employment commencement date, an employee must furnish the employer with a signed withholding exemption certificate, Form W-4, indicating the number of withholding exemptions that he or she intends to claim. If no certificate is filed, the number of withholding exemptions is considered to be zero. The number of withholding exemptions is also considered to be zero if the employee files an invalid certificate or indicates that the information in the certificate is false, and the employee fails to provide an amended certificate when requested by the employer. Employers are required to submit copies of withholding certificates to the IRS when requested by written notice or as directed in published guidance [§ 3401(e), § 3402(f)(2)(A); Reg. § 31.3402(f)(2)-1(e), § 31.3402(f)(2)-1(g), § 31.3402(f)(5)-1(c)].

### XXII.A.2.c. Withholding Methods

[392 T.M., III.A.2.c.; TPS ¶5440.03.A.4.]

The amount of tax that an employer is required to withhold from an employee's wages may be determined through use of alternative methods, the most common of which are the percentage method and the wage bracket method. Different methods may be used by the employer with respect to different groups of employees [§ 3402(a)(1); Reg. § 31.3402(a)-1(a)].

### XXII.A.2.c.(1) Percentage Method

[392 T.M., III.A.2.c(1); TPS ¶5440.03.A.4.]

The percentage method of withholding computes the amount of the tax required to be withheld as follows [§ 3402(b)]:

1. Multiply the dollar amount of one withholding allowance for the appropriate payroll period by the number of withholding allowances claimed on Form W-4 by the employee.
2. Subtract the product of step 1 from the amount of wages paid to the employee during the payroll period.

3. Compute the amount to be withheld on the resulting amount in step 2 according to the appropriate tables contained in IRS Pub. 15, *Circular E, Employer's Tax Guide,* for the employee's wage level and marital status.

In determining the amount to be deducted and withheld under the percentage method, the employer may compute the employee's wages to the nearest whole dollar. Therefore, any fractional part of any dollar may be disregarded unless it amounts to one half dollar or more, in which case it is increased to one dollar. If the employer chooses not to round the employee's wages to the nearest dollar, it may still reduce the last digit of such wages to zero [§ 3402(b)(4)].

### XXII.A.2.c.(2) Wage Bracket Withholding Method

[392 T.M., III.A.2.c(2); TPS ¶5440.03.A.4.]

In lieu of the percentage method, an employer may choose to withhold taxes using the wage bracket tables in IRS Pub. 15, *Circular E, Employer's Tax Guide* [§ 3402(c)]. To use the wage bracket tables, the employer merely identifies the tax that must be withheld from the table that corresponds to the employee's payroll period, wage payment, withholding allowances claimed, and marital status. In determining the amount required to be withheld, the employer may elect to compute the tax to the nearest whole dollar if the employee's wages exceed the highest wage bracket provided in the applicable table [§ 3402(c)(5)].

### XXII.A.2.c.(3) Annualized Wage Withholding Method

[392 T.M., III.A.2.c(3); TPS ¶5440.03.A.4.]

In lieu of the percentage and wage bracket methods, employers may compute the amount of tax that is withheld from an employee's wages on the basis of the employee's annual wages. Under this method, the employer determines the employee's withholding tax as if the employee were paid on a yearly basis and then withholds a prorated portion of the annual tax that corresponds to the employee's payroll period. To determine the amount of tax that is required to be withheld, the following procedures apply [§ 3402(h)(2); Reg. § 31.3402(h)(2)-1]:

1. Multiply the amount of the employee's wages for the payroll period by the number of periods in the calendar year.

2. Determine the amount of tax that would be required to be withheld using the percentage withholding method on the amount determined in step 1 as if that amount were the actual wages for the calendar year and the payroll period were an annual payroll period.

3. Divide the amount determined in step 2 by the number of payroll periods in the calendar year and withhold that amount.

### XXII.A.2.c.(4) Supplemental Wage Withholding Method

[392 T.M., III.A.2.c(6); TPS ¶5440.03.A.5.]

Supplemental wages are all wages paid by an employer that are not regular wages. Examples of supplemental wages include bonuses, overtime pay, back pay, reported tips, commissions, wages paid under reimbursement or other expense allowances, nonqualified deferred compensation includible in wages, wages paid as noncash fringe benefits, sick pay paid by a third party as an agent of the employer, amounts includible in gross income under § 409A, income recognized on the exercise of a nonqualified stock option, wages from imputed income for health coverage for a nondependent, and wage income recognized on the lapse of a restriction on restricted property transferred from an employer to an employee. Amounts defined as supplemental wages are considered supplemental wages regardless of whether the employer has paid the employee any regular wages during either the calendar year of the payment or any prior calendar year [§ 3402(o); Reg. § 31.3402(g)-1(a)(1)(i)].

Employers may treat overtime pay as regular wages rather than supplemental wages. In addition, employers may treat tips, defined as including all tips that are reported to the employer pursuant to § 6053, as regular wages rather than supplemental wages. Any such treatment is not required to be applied uniformly to all employees of the employer. An employer, however, cannot treat commissions, third-party sick pay paid by agents of the employer, or taxable fringe benefits as anything other than supplemental wages [Reg. § 31.3402(g)-1(a)(1)(iv), § 31.3402(g)-1(a)(1)(v)].

The optional flat rate of withholding on supplemental wages is allowed only if:

1. all supplemental wage payments previously made by any one employer during the calendar year do not exceed $1 million;

2. the supplemental wages are either not paid concurrently with regular wages or are separately stated on the employer's payroll records; and

3. income tax has been withheld from the employee's regular wages during the calendar year of the payment or the preceding calendar year.

If these conditions are met, the employer may determine the tax to be withheld from supplemental wages by using a flat percentage rate of 28% or the corresponding rate in effect under § 1(i)(2) for tax years beginning in the calendar year in which the payment is made. The optional flat rate on supplemental wage is currently 25% based on the corresponding rate in effect under § 1(i)(2) [Reg. § 31.3402(g)-1(a)(7)].

If a supplemental wage payment, together with all other supplemental wage payments paid by an employer to an employee during the calendar year, exceeds $1 million, a mandatory withholding rate on the supplemental wages in excess of that amount applies, equal to the maximum rate of tax in effect under § 1 for tax years beginning in that calendar year. The maximum rate under § 1 is currently 39.6% for annual supplemental wages in excess of $1 million [§ 1; Reg. § 31.3402(g)-1(a)(2)].

### XXII.A.2.c.(5) Other Withholding Methods

[392 T.M., III.A.2.c(8); TPS ¶5440.03.A.4.]

An employer may use any method of withholding that produces substantially the same amount required to be withheld using the percentage and wage bracket methods described above [§ 3402(h)(4)].

### XXII.A.2.c.(6) Wage Withholding Amounts and W-4 Filing Procedures for Nonresident Alien Employees

[392 T.M., III.A.2.d.; TPS ¶5440.03.A.4.]

A nonresident alien employee completing Form W-4 for withholding on wages must [Notice 2005-76, 2005-46 I.R.B. 947]:

1. not claim exemption from withholding;

2. request withholding as if single, without regard to marital status;

3. claim only one allowance, unless a resident of Canada, Mexico or South Korea; and

4. write "Nonresident Alien" or "NRA" above the dotted line on line 6.

An employer must calculate income tax withholding on wages of a nonresident alien employee by adding an amount, determined based on the payroll period, to the wages of the employee. The employer determines the income tax to be withheld by applying the tables to the sum of the wages paid for the payroll period plus the additional amount. The added amount is used solely to calculate the amount of income tax withholding; it is not income or wages to the employee; does not affect income, FICA or FUTA tax liability for the employer or the employee; and is not included in any box on Form W-2. [The amount that must be added to the nonresident alien employee's wages is the highest wage amount to which a zero withholding rate applies as shown in the Table for the Percentage Method of Withholding for a single person for each payroll period, as published periodically in IRS Pub. 15, *Circular E, Employer's Guide*. If the employer uses the percentage method, the employer should next subtract an amount for withholding allowances for the payroll period and then apply the percentage method withholding tables to the remainder. If the employer uses the wage bracket method, the employer should not subtract an amount for withholding allowance(s) but should apply the wage bracket tables to the sum of the gross wages and the additional amount added.]

These rules do not affect [Notice 2005-76]:

- the determination of withholding on supplemental wages that are subject to mandatory flat rate withholding or to which the employer is applying an optional flat rate of income tax withholding; or

- nonresident aliens who have no wages subject to federal income tax withholding under § 3402 (e.g., because of eligibility for a tax treaty withholding exemption).

### XXII.A.2.d. Voluntary Income Tax Withholding

[392 T.M., III.B.5.a.; TPS ¶5440.01.C.3.]

An employee may enter into an agreement with an employer that provides for withholding on amounts that are otherwise exempt from income tax withholding. An agreement to withhold on exempt payments may be entered into only for amounts that are otherwise includible in the gross income of the employee and must be applicable to all such amounts paid by the employer to the employee. A voluntary withholding agreement is effective for the period agreed to by the employer and the employee, and either party may terminate the agreement before the end of such period by furnishing a signed written notice to the other [§ 3402(p)(3); Reg. § 31.3402(p)-1(a), § 31.3402(p)-1(b)(2)].

### XXII.A.3. Compensation Subject to Income Tax Withholding

[392 T.M., III.A.3.a.; TPS ¶5440.01.A.]

As a general rule, all compensation derived from employment, unless specifically excluded, is subject to income tax withholding. The employer's designation of a payment of compensation as salary, fees, bonuses, or commissions is immaterial. The only relevant consideration is that the payment be made in consideration for services performed by an employee. Typically, the factors for eligibility for the payment provide the most accurate test to determine whether a payment is in consideration for services. The factors considered include the value of services performed by the employee, the length of employment, and the employee's prior wages [§ 3401(a); Reg. § 31.3401(a)-1(a)(2)].

---

**EXAMPLE:** A participant (P) in a voluntary downsizing program receives a lump sum payment from the company (C). The payment amount is calculated based upon P's employment with C, using a formula taking into account P's years of service and salary. The payment is considered compensation within the employment relationship, although not for work actually done and, thus, is subject to employment taxation.

---

*Cancellation of Employment Contracts/Dismissal Payments.* Remuneration for services, unless specifically excepted, constitutes wages even though at the time it is paid the relationship of employer and employee no longer exists between the parties. Payments received in consideration for the cancellation of an employment contract are treated as wages subject to income tax withholding. Similarly, payments by an employer on account of an employee's dismissal or involuntary separation are subject to tax withholding regardless of whether the employer is legally bound by contract or statute to make such payments [Reg. § 31.3401(a)-1(a)(5); Rev. Rul. 2004-110U, 2004-2 C.B. 960, Rev. Rul. 73-166, 1973-1 C.B. 411, Rev. Rul. 72-572, 1972-2 C.B. 535].

*Signing Bonuses.* Bonuses paid by an employer for signing or ratifying an employment contract are wages subject to income tax withholding [Rev. Rul. 2004-109, 2004-50 I.R.B. 958].

*Recovered Wages or Back Pay.* Amounts received in a judgment or as an award in a suit to recover wages that are expressly designated as something other than wages, such as attorney's fees or liquidated damages, are exempt from wage withholding [Rev. Rul. 80-364, 1980-2 C.B. 294]. Nonetheless, to the extent that an award or judgment is designated as "back pay," it is subject to tax withholding even if an employment relationship never existed [Rev. Rul 78-176, 1978-1 C.B. 303].

*Employer Payment of Employee's Employment Taxes.* If an employer pays the employee portion of the FICA tax or an amount required under a state unemployment compensation law without deducting the required tax from the employee's wages, the employer's payments are treated as additional compensation subject to income tax withholding [Reg. § 31.3401(a)-1(b)(6)].

### XXII.A.4. Employees Subject to Withholding

### XXII.A.4.a. Employer-Employee Relationship

[392 T.M., III.A.4.a.; TPS ¶5440.02.A.]

Unless otherwise excluded, employers are required to withhold income taxes on the wages paid to all employees. The term "employee" includes any officer, employee or elected official of the United States, a state, the District of Columbia, or any political subdivision thereof. It also includes most corporate officers. A director of a corporation, however, is not an employee of the corporation with regard to services performed as a director for federal income tax withholding purposes [§ 3401(c); Reg. § 31.3401(c)-1(f)].

The existence of an employer-employee relationship for purposes of income tax withholding is determined under common law rules. Although no single factor is determinative, an employer-employee relationship normally exists when the person for whom services are performed has the right to control and direct the individual who performs the services as to the result and the means by which that result is accomplished [Reg. § 31.3401(c)-1(a), § 31.3401(c)-1(b)].

The IRS has established the Voluntary Classification Settlement Program (VCSP), an optional program that allows taxpayers to voluntarily reclassify workers as employees in future tax periods for federal employment tax purposes and obtain relief with limited federal employment tax liability for the past non-employee treatment. The VCSP allows for voluntary reclassification of workers as employees outside of the examination context and without the need to go through normal administrative correction procedures applicable to employment taxes [Announcement 2012-45, 2012-51 I.R.B. 724].

### XXII.A.4.b. Statutory Exceptions to Wage Withholding Requirements

[392 T.M., III.A.4.b.; TPS ¶¶5440.02.C. 5710.13.A.3.]

*Public Officials.* Authorized fees paid to public officials such as notaries public, clerks of courts, sheriffs, etc., for services rendered in the performance of their official duties are excepted from wages and hence are not subject to withholding. On the other hand, salaries paid to such officials by the government, or by a government agency or instrumentality, are subject to withholding [Reg. § 31.3401(a)-2(b)(1)].

*Agricultural Workers.* Remuneration paid by an employer for agricultural labor is exempt from withholding if paid in a medium other than cash. In addition, cash wages paid by an employer in any calendar year for agricultural labor are exempt from withholding if the employee's wages for the year are less than $150 and the employer's total expenditures for such labor for the year are less than $2,500 [§ 3401(a)(2)].

*Domestic Workers.* Domestic service performed in the private home of the employer is not subject to withholding provided that the home is not used primarily for the purpose of supplying board or lodging to the general public as a business enterprise. A "private home" generally is defined as a fixed place of abode for an individual or family. Service performed in a nursing home, convalescent home, or hospital may qualify as domestic service in a private home if the facts and circumstances indicate that the room or suite is the residence of the patient [§ 3401(a)(3); Reg. § 31.3401(a)(3)-1(a)(1)]. Domestic service performed for a local college club or local chapter of a college fraternity or sorority is also exempt from withholding, provided the club or fraternity or sorority is not used primarily for the purpose of providing board or lodging to students or the general public as a business enterprise [Reg. § 31.3401(a)(3)-1(b)(1)].

Domestic service that is exempt from withholding generally is limited to services of a household nature performed in or about the home, college club, or fraternal organization. Services of a household nature include services performed by cooks, waiters, butlers, housekeepers, maids, caretakers, gardeners, and handymen. The term does not include services of a private secretary, tutor, or librarian, even though performed in a private home or local club or fraternal organization [Reg. § 31.3401(a)(3)-1(a)(2), § 31.3401(a)(3)-1(b)(2), § 31.3401(a)(3)-1(c)].

*Employees of Foreign Governments.* Services performed by a citizen or resident of the United States in the employ of a foreign government are not subject to withholding. This exception applies to services performed by ambassadors, ministers, and other diplomatic officers and employees, as well as to services performed as a consular or other officer or employee of a foreign government or nondiplomatic representative of a foreign government [§ 3401(a)(5); Reg. § 31.3401(a)(5)-1(a)(1)].

*Employees of International Organizations.* Services performed by a citizen or resident of the United States in the employ of an international organization are not subject to withholding. Examples of organizations that qualify as international organizations include the United Nations, the World Health Organization, the International Monetary Fund, and the World Bank [§ 3401(a)(5); Reg. § 31.3401(a)(5)-1(b)(1)].

*Ministers and Members of Religious Orders.* Services performed by a duly ordained, commissioned, or licensed minister in the exercise of his ministry, or by a member of a religious body in performing duties required by such order are exempt from withholding. An individual is not considered duly ordained, commissioned, or licensed for these purposes unless he or she is qualified to exercise all ecclesiastical duties of the particular religious organization [§ 3401(a)(9); Rev. Rul. 65-124, 1965-1 C.B. 60, Rev. Rul. 78-301, 1978-2 C.B. 103].

*Newspaper Distributors*. Delivering or distributing newspapers or shopping news to the ultimate consumer is exempt from withholding if such services are performed by an employee who is under the age of 18. The sale of newspapers or magazines also is exempt from withholding, without regard to the seller's age, if made at a fixed price under an arrangement in which the seller's compensation is based on the retention of the excess of such price over the amount at which the newspapers or magazines are charged to the seller [§ 3401(a)(10)].

*Fishing Crews*. Services performed by an individual on a boat engaged in catching fish (or other forms of aquatic life) are exempt from withholding if [§ 3401(a)(17); Reg. § 31.3401(a)(17)-1(a)]:

1. the individual's remuneration for such services is entirely based on, and derived from, the amount of the fish caught (or the proceeds from the sale of the catch); and

2. the operating crew of such boat (or each boat from which the individual receives a share of the catch in the case of a fishing operation involving more than one boat) is normally made up of fewer than 10 individuals.

*Nonresident Aliens*. A 30% income tax withholding rate is imposed on the income of nonresidential aliens derived from sources within the United States (see XX.D.1.). This rate does not apply, however, to wages, salaries, or other compensation paid to a nonresident alien for personal services if such income is effectively connected with the conduct of a trade or business in the United States. Instead, such wages are subject to the regular graduated withholding rates applicable to U.S. citizens and residents unless otherwise excepted by regulations [§ 1441(c)(4), § 3401(a)(6); Reg. § 1.1441-4(b)(1)].

*Citizens Performing Services Outside United States*. Wages paid to U.S. citizens performing services in a foreign country for an employer other than the United States (or any agency thereof) are exempt from withholding if at the time of payment [§ 3401(a)(8)(A)]:

- it is reasonable to believe the employee's wages will be excluded from gross income under § 911; or

- the employer is required by the laws of the foreign country to withhold income tax upon such wages.

A reasonable belief that an employee will be able to exclude any amounts paid as compensation for services performed in a foreign country under § 911 (see XX.C.1.) may be based upon any evidence reasonably sufficient to induce such belief. In the absence of a reasonable belief to the contrary, an employer may presume that wages paid to an employee for the performance of services in a foreign country are excluded from gross income under § 911 if the employee properly executes and furnishes to the employer a statement to the effect that the employee will be entitled to the exclusion [Reg. § 31.3401(a)(8)(A)-1(a)(1)(i), § 31.3401(a)(8)(A)-1(a)(2)(i)].

*United States Possessions*. Withholding is not required on wages paid to a U.S. citizen for the performance of services in a U.S. possession for an employer other than the United States (or an agency thereof) if at the time of payment [§ 3401(a)(8)(A)(ii), § 3401(a)(8)(B)]:

- it is reasonable to believe that at least 80% of the wages that will be paid to the employee during the calendar year will be attributable to the performance of services in such possession (other than Puerto Rico); or

- the employer is required by the laws of the possession to withhold income tax upon such wages.

*Puerto Rico.* Wages paid for services performed in Puerto Rico by a U.S. citizen for an employer other than the United States (or an agency thereof) are exempt from withholding if it is reasonable to believe that the employee will be a bona fide resident of Puerto Rico for the entire calendar year. The employer's belief that an employee will be a bona fide resident of Puerto Rico for the entire calendar year may be based upon any evidence reasonably sufficient to induce such belief. In the absence of reasonable belief to the contrary, an employer may presume that an employee will be a bona fide resident of Puerto Rico for the entire calendar year if: (1) the employer does not know that the employee has maintained a place of residence outside Puerto Rico during the current or preceding calendar year; or (2) the employee files a statement with the employer under penalties of perjury indicating that the employee has at all times been and intends to remain a resident of Puerto Rico for the current calendar year [§ 3401(a)(6), § 3401(a)(8)(C); Reg. § 31.3401(a)(8)(C)-1(b)].

*Real Estate Agents and Direct Sellers.* Services performed by certain qualified real estate agents and direct sellers are exempt from withholding. A "qualified" real estate agent is a licensed real estate agent whose remuneration for services is substantially related to sales or other output (including appraisal activities) rather than to the number of hours worked. The services of the agent must be performed pursuant to a written contract between the agent and the person for whom the services are performed that provides that the agent is not to be treated as an employee with respect to such services for federal employment tax purposes [§ 3508(a), § 3508(b)].

A "direct seller" includes any person engaged in the trade or business of [§ 3508(b)(2); Prop. Reg. § 31.3508-1]:

- selling (or soliciting the sale of) consumer products to the ultimate consumer or for resale to a buyer on a buy-sell basis, a deposit commission basis, or any similar basis, provided the sale or resale of the product occurs in a place other than a permanent retail establishment; or

- delivering or distributing newspapers or shopping news. The services of the seller must be performed pursuant to a written contract between the seller and the person for whom the services are performed that provides that the seller will not be treated as an employee with respect to such services for federal employment tax purposes.

### XXII.A.5. Withholding on Wages Excluded from Income

#### XXII.A.5.a. Military Pay

[392 T.M., III.A.3.b(1); TPS ¶5440.01.A.]

While wages paid to members of the U.S. armed forces generally are subject to withholding, including additional compensation received for sea duty, foreign duty, hazardous duty and diving duty, withholding on wages received by a member of the armed forces does not apply in any month in which the member receives wages that are exempt from gross income under § 112 (see II.M.1.) due to service in an area designated as a combat zone, or in which the member has been hospitalized as a result of wounds, disease or injury incurred while serving in a combat zone [§ 3401(a)(1), § 3401(h)].

#### XXII.A.5.b. Qualified Plans

[392 T.M., III.A.3.b(2)(a); TPS ¶5440.01.B.2.a.]

Employer contributions to a qualified pension, annuity, profit-sharing or stock bonus plan described in § 401(a) or § 403(a) (see XVII.B.) are not subject to income tax withholding. Deferred amounts made on behalf of an employee to a trust that is part of a § 401(k) qualified cash or deferred arrangement are also exempted. Distributions, however, may be subject to income tax withholding. Withholding on distributions from qualified plans is discussed in XXII.A.6.a., below [§ 3401(a)(12)].

### XXII.A.5.c. Nonqualified Plans

[392 T.M., III.A.3.b(2)(b); TPS ¶5440.01.B.2.b.]

Payments to a former employee pursuant to an unfunded deferred compensation agreement normally are subject to withholding at the time of actual or constructive receipt. However, no withholding is required with respect to amounts paid to an employee upon retirement that are taxable as annuities under § 72 unless withholding is elected by the employee. In addition, if the employee's wages are exempt from withholding at the time of employment, any deferred compensation payments paid with respect to such wages also would qualify for exemption [§ 3402(o)(1)(B), § 3405; Reg. § 31.3401(a)-1(b)(1)(i), § 31.3402(o)-2].

Unless certain statutory requirements are met at all times during a tax year, § 409A requires that all amounts deferred under a nonqualified deferred compensation plan (within the meaning of § 409A) for the tax year and all preceding tax years are includible in gross income to the extent not subject to a substantial risk of forfeiture and not previously included in gross income (see XVII.B.1.e.). Amounts required to be included in income under § 409A are treated as wages for income tax withholding purposes [§ 409A, § 3401(a)].

### XXII.A.5.d. Stock Options

[392 T.M., III.A.3.b(2)(c); TPS ¶5440.01.B.2.c.]

When an employer transfers stock to an employee or former employee in connection with the exercise of a nonqualified stock option or nonqualified stock purchase plan (see XVII.B.2.), the excess of the fair market value of the property over the price paid constitutes wages that are subject to income tax withholding. The amount received by an employee in cancellation of a nonstatutory option also is subject to income tax withholding. With respect to statutory stock options, no income tax withholding is required on a disqualifying disposition or in connection with a discount from an employee stock purchase plan [§ 83, § 421(b), § 423(c); Rev. Rul. 79-305, 1979-2 C.B. 350].

### XXII.A.5.e. Moving Expenses

[392 T.M., III.A.3.b(3); TPS ¶5440.01.B.4.]

Wages subject to withholding do not include remuneration paid to, or on behalf of, an employee for moving expenses incurred or expected to be incurred by the employee to the extent that the employer has reason to believe that, at the time of payment, the employee will be entitled to deduct the payment under § 217 (see VII.B.6.). Reasonable belief may be based upon any evidence sufficient to induce such belief, even though the deduction subsequently may be disallowed [§ 3401(a)(15); Reg. § 31.3401(a)(15)-1(a)].

### XXII.A.5.f. Dependent Care Assistance

[392 T.M., III.A.3.b(4); TPS ¶5440.01.B.7.]

Any payment made, or benefit furnished, to or for the benefit of an employee, is exempt from income tax withholding if, at the time of such payment or such furnishing, it is reasonable to believe that the employee will be able to exclude the payment or benefit from gross income under a dependent care assistance program that satisfies the requirements of § 129 (see XVII.E.2.) [§ 3401(a)(18)].

### XXII.A.5.g. Accident and Health Plan Payments

[392 T.M., III.A.3.b(5); TPS ¶5440.01.B.3.]

Payments to employees of amounts that are attributable to employer contributions and includible in gross income under § 105(a) by an employee under an uninsured accident or health plan for a period of absence from work due to injury or sickness (see XVII.C.1.c.) are treated as wages subject to withholding. However, an exclusion from gross income is provided with respect to amounts paid to reimburse the employee for expenses incurred for medical care (as defined in § 213) of the employee, his spouse, or his dependents. Payments made under a self-insured medical reimbursement plan also are exempt from withholding [§ 105(b), § 105(h)(6), § 3401(a)(20); Reg. § 31.3401(a)-1(b)(8)].

Employer payments for the permanent loss of use of a member or function of the body, or permanent disfigurement, of the employee, his or her spouse or dependent also are exempt from tax under § 105(a) (see II.D.1.c.), and thus withholding, if the payments are based on the nature of the injury and without regard to the employee's absence from work [§ 105(c)].

### XXII.A.5.h. Tips

[392 T.M., III.A.3.c(2); TPS ¶5440.01.B.11.b.]

Tips paid to an employee are exempt from withholding if [§ 3401(a)(16)]:

- paid in a medium other than cash; or
- the cash tips received by the employee in the course of his or her employment are less than $20 in any calendar month.

Payments to employees from service charges imposed by the establishment are not considered in applying the $20 calendar month threshold. Such amounts are treated as wages paid by the employer and are subject to withholding regardless of the amount of any tips received by the employee during the month.

### XXII.A.5.i. Sales Commissions

[392 T.M., III.A.3.c(3); TPS ¶5440.01.B.11.e.]

Withholding is not required on noncash remuneration paid for services rendered by a retail commission salesman if the salesman ordinarily is compensated solely on the basis of cash commissions. The exception does not apply if the salesman is paid a salary in addition to commissions or the salesman ordinarily is compensated with noncash remuneration [§ 3402(j); Reg. § 31.3402(j)-1(a)(2)].

### XXII.A.5.j. Meals and Lodging

[392 T.M., III.A.3.c(4); TPS ¶5440.01.B.11.c.]

The value of meals and lodging furnished by an employer for the benefit of employees is exempt from withholding if such value is excludible from the gross income of the employee under § 119 (see XVII.E.4.) [Reg. § 31.3401(a)-1(b)(9)].

## XXII.A.6. Nonwage Payments Subject to Income Tax Withholding

### XXII.A.6.a. Withholding on Deferred Compensation Distributions

[392 T.M., III.B.3.; TPS ¶5440.01.C.1.]

Income tax withholding generally is required on any distribution or payment from certain employer deferred compensation plans, individual retirement plans, and commercial annuities. For these purposes, an "employer deferred compensation plan" includes any qualified pension, annuity, profit-sharing, or stock bonus plan (see XVII.B.). Also included in this definition are employer-sponsored individual retirement plans (i.e., IRAs) and tax-sheltered annuity programs sponsored by government employers and certain tax-exempt entities [§ 3405; Reg. § 35.3405-1T, Q&As-17, -20, -22, -23].

Certain plan distributions are exempt from these withholding requirements. For example, plan distributions are exempt from the pension withholding rules if it is reasonable to believe that the distribution will be excluded from the employee's gross income. Thus, any portion of a distribution that represents the employee's nondeductible contributions to the plan is not subject to withholding [§ 3405(e)(1)(B)(ii)]. Additional amounts not subject to withholding include [§ 3405(e)(1)(B)(ii)]:

- distributions of dividends that are paid in cash from an employee stock ownership plan;
- any net unrealized appreciation attributable to employer securities received in a lump sum distribution; and
- the first $5,000 of any lump sum distribution that is payable on account of death.

The amount that is withheld from any deferred compensation payment depends on whether the distribution is a periodic payment, non-periodic payment, or an eligible rollover distribution. In the case of a periodic payment, the payor is required to withhold from such payment the amount that would be required if the payment were a payment of wages paid to an employee. Thus, the amount to withhold varies according to the withholding certificate filed by the recipient with the payor. If no certificate is filed, the amount to withhold is the same as if the recipient were married and claiming three withholding exemptions [§ 3405(a)(1), § 3405(a)(4)]. In the case of a non-periodic payment, the amount to withhold generally is equal to 10% of the amount distributed [§ 3405(b)(1)].

Except for eligible rollover distributions, withholding is not required on any periodic or non-periodic payment if the recipient elects not to have withholding apply. An election not to have withholding apply is not honored, however, if the recipient fails to disclose his Social Security number to the payor, or if the IRS notifies the payor that the Social Security number that is disclosed is incorrect. An election not to have withholding apply remains in effect until it is revoked [§ 3405(a)(2), § 3405(b)(2), § 3405(e)(12); Reg. § 35.3405-1T, Q&A-1, § d].

The payor of any distribution subject to withholding must notify each recipient of the right to elect not to have withholding apply and of the right to revoke any prior election. For periodic payments, notice of the election must be provided no earlier than six months before the first payment and no later than when making the first payment. Notice before the first payment does not relieve the payor of his obligation to notify the recipient of his rights at the time of the first payment, however. Thereafter, notice must be provided to the recipient at least once each calendar year. In addition, if the recipient's benefits are suspended due to his reemployment, the first payment upon recommencement of benefits is treated as a first payment for purposes of the notice requirements. For nonperiodic distributions, notice must be provided by the payor to the recipient at the time of the distribution. Because notice provided at the time of payment may result in delaying the payment of benefits, the regulations require that notice also be provided not earlier than six months before each distribution and not later than at a time that will provide the recipient with reasonable time to elect not to have withholding apply. What qualifies as a "reasonable time" generally depends on the facts and circumstances of each distribution [§ 3405(e)(10)(B); Reg. § 35.3405-1T, Q&As-4, -9, 15].

For eligible rollover distributions (see XVII.A.2.e.(2)), withholding is required at a rate of 20% on amounts that are not transferred directly to an eligible transferee plan. No election to forego withholding on eligible rollover distributions is permitted. The plan administrator/payor does not have to withhold tax from an eligible rollover distribution that is less than $200. All eligible distributions made from the same plan within the same tax year are aggregated in determining if the $200 floor has been reached. If a distributee elects to have a portion of an eligible rollover distribution paid to an eligible retirement plan in a direct rollover and wants to receive the balance, the 20% withholding requirement applies only to the portion of the eligible rollover distribution that the distributee receives and not to the portion that is paid in the direct rollover [§ 3405(c); Reg. § 31.3405(c)-1, Q&As-6, -14].

The plan administrator of a qualified plan and the payor of an annuity have the responsibility for complying with the 20% tax withholding requirement on eligible rollover distributions. The distributee and the plan administrator or payor may enter into an agreement to withhold more than 20% [§ 3402(p); Reg. § 31.3402(p)-1, § 31.3405(c)-1, Q&As-3, -4].

A plan administrator who fails to withhold 20% from an eligible distribution is not liable for taxes, interest or penalties if he or she reasonably relies on "adequate information" provided by a distributee. Although the plan administrator is obligated to maintain the records and make the returns and reports required under these regulations, the employer maintaining the plan is ultimately responsible [Reg. § 31.3405(c)-1, Q&As-7, -15].

### XXII.A.6.b. Withholding on Supplemental Unemployment Compensation

[392 T.M., III.B.2.; TPS ¶5440.01.C.2.]

A payor of supplemental unemployment compensation (SUB) benefits that are includible in the recipient's income must withhold income taxes. SUB benefits are defined as amounts paid to an employee, pursuant to a plan to which an employer is a party, because of the employee's involuntary separation from employment (whether or not such separation is temporary), resulting from a reduction in the employer's work force, the discontinuance of a plant or operation, or other similar circumstance, but only to the extent that such benefits are includible in the employee's gross income. A "separation from employment" occurs when the employee is no longer performing any service for the employer [§ 3402(o)(1), § 3402(o)(2)(A); Reg. § 31.3402(o)-1].

Whether SUB payments also are subject to FICA and FUTA tax depends on whether such benefits are characterized as wages or as SUB payments. SUBs, which include severance payments made to involuntarily terminated workers, are wages subject to FICA [*United States v. Quality Stores, Inc.*, 134 S. Ct. 1395 (2014)].

### XXII.A.6.c. Gambling Winnings

[392 T.M., III.B.1.; TPS ¶3820.04.E.]

The proceeds from certain gambling wagers are subject to income tax withholding by the payor in an amount equal to the product of the third lowest rate of tax under § 1(c) and the payment amount (see X.) [§ 3402(q)(1)]. Withholding taxes apply to the following situations [§ 3402(q)(3)]:

- For a state-conducted lottery, if the proceeds exceed $5,000.
- For a sweepstakes, wagering pool, or lottery (other than a state lottery), if the proceeds exceed $5,000.
- For any other wagering transaction (including wagers placed in a parimutuel pool on horse races, dog races or jai alai), if the proceeds exceed $5,000 and are at least 300 times as large as the amount wagered.

The "proceeds" from any wager are determined by reducing the amount received by the amount of the wager. Any amounts not received in cash must be taken in account according to the fair market value of the property received. When the proceeds from any wager are paid periodically, the payments are aggregated for purposes of determining whether or not such payments are subject to withholding [§ 3402(q)(4); Reg. § 31.3402(q)-1(c)(1)(iv)].

Gambling winnings subject to withholding do not include any payments from a slot machine or a bingo or keno game. "Windfall" winnings from no-cost lotteries or drawings are also exempt from withholding taxes. Withholding under § 3402(q) is not required on any payment of winnings to a nonresident alien individual or a foreign corporation if such payment is subject to withholding under either § 1441(a) or § 1442(a) (relating to withholding on nonresident aliens and foreign corporations, respectively) (see XX.D.1.) [§ 3402(q)(2), § 3402(q)(5); Reg. § 31.3402(q)-1(d) *Ex.* 10].

When a payor of monetary or nonmonetary proceeds pays the federal tax required to be withheld on those proceeds under § 3402(q) without deducting the tax from the proceeds, the proceeds paid to the winner are deemed to include the amount of the federal tax paid by the payor. When gambling amounts are subject to withholding, the payor must file Form 945, *Annual Return of Withheld Federal Income Tax*, and supply Form W-2G to the recipient [Notice 93-7, 1993-1 C.B. 297].

### XXII.A.6.d. Withholding on Golden Parachute Payments

[392 T.M., III.B.6.; TPS ¶5440.01.C.4.]

The recipient of an "excess parachute payment" is subject to a 20% tax that is withheld by the employer along with any amount of such payment that is subject to the general rules that apply to withholding on wages.

### XXII.A.7. Backup Withholding

[392 T.M., III.B.4.; TPS ¶3820.04.G.]

In certain circumstances, payors are required to deduct and withhold income tax from payments that exceed $10 that are "reportable payments" in an amount equal to the product of the payments and the fourth lowest tax rate imposed on unmarried individuals other than surviving spouses and heads of households (currently 28%). Backup withholding is required if [§ 3406(a)(1)]:

- the payee fails to provide his taxpayer identification number (TIN) to the payor in the manner required;
- the IRS notifies the payor that the TIN furnished by the payee is incorrect;
- the IRS notifies the payor that the payee has failed to report properly interest, dividends, or patronage dividends; or
- the payee fails to certify under the penalties of perjury when required to do so that he is not subject to backup withholding.

Backup withholding is not required where [§ 3406(g)(1), § 3406(g)(2)]:

- the payee is exempt from withholding;
- the payee has satisfied the requirements preventing the application of the backup withholding rules; or
- the amount received by the payee is subject to withholding under some other provision of the Code.

Payees exempt from withholding include tax-exempt organizations, individual retirement accounts, governmental entities, and international organizations. Qualified nominees acting as custodians or middlemen are also exempt from backup withholding. In the case of a payee waiting for a taxpayer identification number, a limited exception from withholding applies for a period of 60 days if the payee certifies to the payor that he is awaiting the receipt of a TIN [§ 3406(g)(1), § 3406(g)(3); Reg. § 31.3406(g)-1(a), § 1.6049-4(c)(1)(ii)(O)].

Reportable payments subject to backup withholding include payments of dividends, patronage dividends, interest, rents, salaries, wages, premiums, compensation for services, and amounts received by brokers and barter exchanges [§ 3406(b)].

For interest and dividends on new accounts and instruments, the payee must certify under penalties of perjury that the IRS has not notified the payee that he is subject to backup withholding due to underreporting of dividends or interest. The payee on these accounts or instruments must also certify that the TIN provided to the payor is the payee's correct number. If the payee fails to make either of these certifications, or if after making such certifications the payor is notified by the IRS that the payee's TIN is incorrect or that backup withholding is required due to underreporting, the payor must implement backup withholding [§ 3406(d), § 3406(e); Reg. § 31.3406(d)-1, § 31.3406(e)-1].

Where one of the situations described above exists for required backup withholding, the payor must withhold and deposit backup withholding amounts in a manner similar to that used for withholding and deposit of employment taxes (see XXII.C.1.b.). Payors must treat amounts withheld as backup withholding as "non-payroll" taxes. Payors must report backup withholding annually on Form 945, *Annual Return of Withheld Federal Income Tax* [Reg. § 31.6011(a)-4(b)].

## XXII.B. Federal Insurance Contributions Act (FICA) and Federal Unemployment Tax (FUTA) Taxes

### XXII.B.1. Rate of Tax

### XXII.B.1.a. FICA Taxes

[392 T.M., II.A.1.a(1); TPS ¶5440.03.A.2.]

FICA taxes, or social security taxes, are imposed on both employees and employers. FICA tax is comprised of two elements: old-age, survivor and disability insurance (OASDI) and hospital insurance (HI or Medicare). OASDI taxes are used to fund retirement and disability benefits, while HI taxes are used to provide health and medical benefits for the aged and disabled. The OASDI portion of FICA tax only applies to wages that are not in excess of the taxable wage base. This base amount is adjusted annually by the Commissioner of Social Security. The OASDI contribution and benefit taxable wage base is $118,500 for 2015 ($117,000 for 2014). Any wages paid in excess of this amount are exempt from the OASDI portion of FICA taxation. The HI portion of FICA tax, however, applies to all wages paid during the year, i.e., there is no annual Medicare wage base limitation [§ 3101, § 3111, § 3121(a)(1), § 3306(b)(1); 79 Fed. Reg. 64,455 (Oct. 29, 2014)].

The OASDI portion of wages is 6.2% for both the employer and employee portion. The Medicare portion of wages is 1.45% for both the employer and employee portion, except that an employee's Medicare tax on wages in excess of $200,000 ($250,000 for a joint return) is subject to an additional 0.9% rate (for a total of 2.35%) [§ 3101(a), § 3101(b)(1), § 3111(a); Reg. § 31.3101-2(b)(2)].

Certain individuals also must pay a 3.8% unearned income Medicare contribution tax (the net investment income tax) [§ 1411] (see X.). The employer is not required to withhold for this tax.

### XXII.B.1.b. FUTA Taxes

[392 T.M., II.A.1.b(1).; TPS ¶5440.03.A.3.]

Taxes under the Federal Unemployment Tax Act (FUTA) are imposed on employers. The wage base limitation applicable to FUTA contributions is a statutory amount that periodically has been adjusted legislatively. The 2014 FUTA tax rate of 6% is imposed on the first $7,000 of taxable wages paid during a calendar year. Amounts received in excess of that limit are not subject to FUTA taxation [§ 3301(2)].

Most employers never actually pay FUTA taxes at the rate of 6% due to credits they receive for the payment of state unemployment taxes. Total credits are limited, however, to 90% of the deemed federal tax rate of 6%. The net federal rate after applying the maximum credit is therefore 0.6%. Generally, there are two types of credits that an employer may use to reduce the federal unemployment tax: the "normal" credit and the "additional" credit. Under limited circumstances, a third type of credit, a "successor" credit, also is available to employers that acquire the business of another employer [§ 3302(a), § 3302(c)(1), § 3302(d)(1)].

### XXII.B.1.c. Application of Wage Bases Where There Is More than One Employer

[392 T.M., II.A.2.f(1); TPS ¶5440.01.B.1.]

The FICA and FUTA wage base limitations relate to the amount of wages received during the calendar year rather than the amount of wages accrued during such year. Thus, if an employee receives wages from more than one employer during any calendar year, the annual wage base limitations apply separately to each employer. The employee may, however, be eligible for a credit or a refund of the excess employee portion of the FICA tax that applies to wages above the FICA wage base [Reg. § 31.3121(a)(1)-1(a)(2), § 31.3306(b)(1)-1(a)(2); 79 Fed. Reg. 64,455 (Oct. 29, 2014)].

---

**EXAMPLE:** Employee (E) is employed by X for the first 5 calendar months of 2015 and is paid $80,000. For the remainder of the year, E is employed by Y and is paid $80,000. The entire $160,000 is subject to FICA tax, even though the taxable wage base for 2015 is $118,500, because the wage base applies separately to each employer (i.e., X and Y each must withhold FICA tax on the first $118,500 of wages paid to E). In addition, X and Y each must pay unemployment taxes on the first $7,000 paid to E in 2015. However, E may obtain a credit or refund on his 2015 individual tax return for the excess of the employee portion of the total OASDI tax withheld from the wages paid in 2015 above $118,500 (see IX.G.1.).

---

### XXII.B.1.d. Concurrent Employment/Common Paymaster

[392 T.M., II.A.2.f(1)(b); TPS ¶5440.01.B.1.]

When two or more related corporations concurrently employ the same individual during a calendar quarter and compensate that individual through a common paymaster that is one of the employing corporations, each corporation is considered to have paid only the remuneration actually paid by it to the employee, but the total amount of the employee and employer tax is determined as though the individual had only one employer. Thus, FICA and FUTA taxes are paid only on the aggregate wages of all related employers up to the taxable wage base. If the related corporations do not compensate their common employees through a common paymaster, the employee is treated as being employed by separate employers. A common paymaster is defined for these purposes as any member of a related group of corporations that disburses remuneration to employees of related corporations and is responsible for keeping books and payroll records with respect to such employees [§ 3121(s), § 3306(p); Reg. § 31.3121(s)-1(a), § 31.3121(s)-1(b)(2), § 31.3306(p)-1(a)].

### XXII.B.1.e. Railroad Retirement Tax Act (RRTA)

[392 T.M., II.A.3.d(9); TPS ¶5440.01.A.]

Railroad employers are subject to employment taxes that are separate from the FICA and FUTA systems covering most other employers. As such, payments subject to railroad retirement taxes are exempt from FICA, FUTA, and the Self-Employment Contributions Act (SECA). Instead, railroad employers are subject to the RRTA in determining railroad worker retirement benefits and the Railroad Unemployment Insurance Act in determining unemployment and sickness insurance benefits. "Compensation" for computation of RRTA taxes has the same meaning as the term "wages" under § 3121(a), except as specifically limited by the RRTA or regulations [The rules appear in § 3201–§ 3233; Reg. § 31.3231(e)-1(a)(1)].

A railroad employer files an annual Form CT-1, *Employer's Annual Railroad Retirement Tax Return*, to report RRTA taxes. All Form CT-1 returns must be filed by the last day of the second month following the end of the calendar year (e.g., February 28th in a non-leap year).

Although railroad employers are not subject to FICA, they are still required to withhold income tax from their railroad employees and must file Form 941 or Form 944 for this purpose. Railroad employers use Form W-2 to report wage payments to employees and to the Social Security Administration (SSA). RRTA taxes are shown in Box 14, and Boxes 3, 4, 5, 6 and 7, relating to OASDI and Medicare, should be left blank. Railroad employers use Form W-3 to transmit Forms W-2 to SSA. Form W-3 provides a box to indicate that the employer is a railroad, alerting SSA to the fact that the information reported reflects RRTA rather than FICA and Medicare.

If an employer has employees covered under FICA and Medicare as well as RRTA, the Forms W-2 must be segregated by type, and separate Forms W-3 prepared for each batch. For liability for withholding on income taxes, see XXII.A.1.

### XXII.B.2. Liability and Collection

### XXII.B.2.a. FICA Taxes

[392 T.M., II.A.1.a(3); TPS ¶3200.01.B.2.a.]

An employer collects the employee portion of the FICA tax by deducting the tax from the wages of each of its employees at the time of payment. The employer must collect and pay the tax in cash, even if the employee receives remuneration for services in a form other than cash [§ 3102(a); Reg. § 31.3102-1(a)].

The employer is liable for the employee portion of the tax (in addition to the employer portion of the tax) whether or not the tax is collected from the employee. If the employer withholds less than the correct amount or fails to withhold any part of the tax, the employer is nevertheless liable for the correct amount [§ 3102(b)].

When an employer fails to remit withheld income and employment taxes to the government, the IRS may assert the Trust Fund Recovery Penalty, which is equal to the total amount of tax not paid to the government, against persons who are responsible for collecting, accounting for, and paying over the trust fund taxes but willfully fail to do so [§ 6672].

### XXII.B.2.b. FUTA Taxes

[392 T.M., II.A.1.b(3); TPS ¶5430.01.A.3.]

Unlike FICA taxes, which are imposed on both employers and employees, only employers are liable for federal unemployment taxes. An employer is liable for unemployment taxes with respect to wages actually or constructively paid during the calendar year to employees who are not agricultural or domestic workers if, during the current or preceding calendar year, the employer [§ 3306(a); Reg. § 31.3301-1]:

- paid wages of $1,500 or more in any calendar quarter; or
- employed one or more individuals for some portion of a day in each of 20 or more calendar weeks.

### XXII.B.3. Compensation Subject to Tax

[392 T.M., II.A.1.b(3); TPS ¶5440.01.A.]

For purposes of FICA and FUTA, all wages derived from employment (including benefits), unless specifically excepted, are subject to tax. It is immaterial that wages are designated as salaries, fees, bonuses or commissions, as long as the payment is made in consideration for services performed. The medium and manner in which wages are paid also is immaterial in determining whether the payment of wages is subject to FICA or FUTA. Thus, it makes no difference that wages are paid on an hourly, weekly, monthly, or annual basis, or in a form other than cash [§ 3121(a), § 3306(b); Reg. § 31.3121(a)-1(c), § 31.3121(a)-1(d), § 31.3121(a)-1(e), § 31.3306(b)-1(c), § 31.3306(b)-1(d), § 31.3306(b)-1(e)].

### XXII.B.4. Statutory Exceptions and Inclusions

### XXII.B.4.a. Deferred Compensation Benefits

[392 T.M., II.A.2.f(2); TPS ¶5440.01.B.2.]

***Contributions to Tax-Qualified Arrangements.*** Contributions to many forms of deferred compensation benefits are excluded from the definition of wages for purposes of FICA and FUTA, including [§ 3121(a)(5), § 3306(b)(5)]:

- contributions to a qualified pension, annuity, profit-sharing or stock bonus plan whose trust is exempt from tax (e.g., plans qualified under § 401(a)) (see XVII.A.2.);
- contributions to a SEP (see XVII.A.8.); and
- contributions to a tax sheltered annuity plan (e.g., a § 403(b) plan) (see XVII.A.4.).

However, salary reduction contributions made by an employee to a cash or deferred arrangement (see XVIII.A.3.), a tax-sheltered annuity, a SIMPLE retirement account (see XVII.A.8.), or a simplified employee pension plan (SEP) (see XVIII.A.9.) are included in the definition of wages for purposes of FICA and FUTA taxes [§ 3121(v)(1), § 3306(r)(1)].

***Nonqualified Arrangements.*** Amounts required to be included in income under § 409A are treated as wages for FICA and FUTA tax purposes. To the extent that the requirements of § 409A are met, an amount deferred is only taken into income as wages for FICA and FUTA purposes as of the later of when:

- the services are performed; or
- the right to the amount deferred no longer is subject to a substantial risk of forfeiture.

However, a deferred amount under a nonaccount balance-type plan may be taken into account at a later date if all or a portion of the amount deferred is not "reasonably ascertainable" until that later date [§ 409A, § 3121(v)(2), § 3306(r)(2); Reg. § 31.3121(v)(2)-1, § 31.3121(v)(2)-2, § 31.3306(r)(2)-1].

**Statutory Stock Options.** Effective for stock acquired pursuant to options exercised after October 22, 2004, the transfer of stock pursuant to the exercise of an ISO or any disposition of such stock is excluded from the definition of wages subject to FICA and FUTA taxes [§ 421(b), § 3121(a)(22), § 3306(b)(19)] (see XVII.B.2.a.).

### XXII.B.4.b. Accident and Disability Payments

[392 T.M., II.A.2.f(3)(b); TPS ¶5440.01.B.3.]

Generally, payments to employees of amounts that are includible in income under an accident or health plan for a period of absence from work due to injury or sickness are treated as wages (see XVII.C.). However, for purposes of FICA and FUTA taxes, any payment or series of payments by an employer to an employee or any of the employee's dependents after the termination of the employee's employment relationship as a result of disability are exempt if paid under a plan established by the employer, unless the payment or payments would have been paid if the employee's employment had not been terminated. Disability payments by an employer to an employee also are exempt from FICA and FUTA taxes if paid by the employer after the expiration of six calendar months following the last calendar month in which the employee worked for the employer [§ 3121(a)(4), § 3121(a)(13), § 3306(b)(4), § 3306(b)(10)].

### XXII.B.4.c. Fringe Benefits

[392 T.M., II.A.2.f(5)(e); TPS ¶5440.01.B.5.]

Fringe benefits provided by an employer to its employees (see XVII.D.) are exempt from FICA and FUTA taxation if at the time such benefits are provided it is reasonable to believe that the employee will be able to exclude the benefit from income. Fringe benefits that do not qualify for exclusion from income are subject to FICA and FUTA taxation on the excess of the benefit's fair value over the amount, if any, paid by the employee for the benefit [§ 3121(a)(20), § 3306(b)(16)].

### XXII.B.4.d. Moving Expenses

[392 T.M., II.A.2.f(5)(a); TPS ¶5440.01.B.4.]

Compensation paid to an employee for moving expenses incurred or expected to be incurred by the employee are not considered wages subject to FICA or FUTA if, at the time of payment, the employer reasonably believes that the employee will be entitled to deduct such payment for federal income tax purposes. Reasonable belief may be based upon any evidence sufficient to induce the belief, even though the deduction later may be disallowed (see VII.B.6.) [§ 3121(a)(11), § 3306(b)(9)].

### XXII.B.4.e. Dependent Care Assistance

[392 T.M., II.A.2.f(5)(b); TPS ¶5440.01.B.7.]

Any payment or benefit furnished to, or for the benefit of, an employee under a qualified dependent care assistance program is exempt from FICA and FUTA taxation if at the time of payment or furnishing such benefit it is reasonable to believe the employee will be able to exclude the payment or benefit from gross income [§ 3121(a)(18), § 3306(b)(13)] (see XVII.E.2.).

### XXII.B.4.f. Domestic Workers

[392 T.M., II.A.2.f(4)(b); TPS ¶5440.01.B.11.a.]

Remuneration for domestic service in the private home of the employer is exempt from FICA if payment is in a medium other than cash, payment is made to an individual under age 18 for domestic service that is not the principal occupation of such individual, or the cash remuneration paid to the employee (including domestic service performed on a farm operated for profit) by the employer in any calendar year is less than $1,000 (adjusted for inflation). For 2015, the threshold amount is $1,900. [§ 3121(a)(7), § 3121(b)(21); 79 Fed. Reg. 64,455 (Oct. 29, 2014)].

For FUTA purposes, remuneration for domestic service in the private home is exempt from tax if the payments are less than $1,000 for each calendar quarter and the individual performing such service is not regularly employed by the employer to perform such service [§ 3306(a)(3), § 3306(b)(6)].

### XXII.B.4.g. Employer Reimbursements

[392 T.M., II.A.2.f(5)(f); TPS ¶5440.01.B.9.]

Amounts paid by an employer to an employee, either as an advance or reimbursement, for ordinary and necessary expenses reasonably expected to be incurred in the business of the employer are exempt from FICA and FUTA. To qualify for the exclusion, reimbursements must be made under an accountable plan. An accountable plan is an arrangement between an employer and employee that satisfies the following three basic requirements [Reg. § 1.62-2(c)]:

- the expenses must have a business connection;
- the expenses must be substantiated; and
- amounts received in excess of substantiated expenses must be returned to the employer.

For a detailed discussion of accountable plans, see IV.A.3.b.

The expense must be identified by the employer, either by making a separate payment to the employee or by specifically indicating the separate amounts if both wages and reimbursed expenses are combined in a single payment to the employee. The expense must be identified at the time of payment to be excluded from FICA tax. In determining whether a payment to an employee is attributable to an ordinary and necessary expense incurred in the business of the employer, the general rules relating to deductible employer expenses apply (see IV.A.). Thus, excludible reimbursements do not include nondeductible personal, living, or family expenses [§ 162; Reg. § 31.3121(a)-1(h), § 31.3121(a)-3, § 31.3306(b)-1(h), § 31.3306(b)-2].

### XXII.B.4.h. Tips

[392 T.M., II.A.2.f(4)(e); TPS ¶5440.01.B.11.b.]

Tips paid in cash and received by an employee in the course of employment are exempt from FICA and FUTA if the aggregate amount of tips received during any calendar month is less than $20. Tips in a medium other than cash also are exempt from employment taxes and are not reported to the employer [§ 3121(a)(12), § 3306(s)].

Cash tips include amounts received by check or other monetary exchange medium, including amounts designated by customers who pay their bills with a credit card and designate a portion of the bill as a tip. Tips are considered to be received by an employee in the course of employment whether the tips are received from a person other than an employer or are paid to the employee by the employer. However, only those tips that are received by an employee on his own behalf are treated as remuneration paid to the employee. Thus, when employees practice tip splitting (e.g., waiters paying a portion of their tips to busboys), each employee who receives a portion of the tip left by a customer of the employer is considered to have received tips in the course of employment. Service charges imposed by an establishment and paid to employees are not considered to be tips. Such amounts are treated as wages paid by the employer and are subject to employment taxes regardless of the tips received by the employee during the month [Reg. § 31.3121(a)(12)-1, § 31.3121(q)-1(c)].

An employee is required to report tips to his or her employer by the 10th day of the month following the month in which they were received. An employer may adopt a system under which some or all of an employer's tipped employees furnish their tip statements electronically. An employer that chooses to establish an electronic tip reporting system may select the type(s) of electronic systems (e.g., telephone or computer) to be used by its employees, but the system must ensure that the information received is the information transmitted by the employee and must document all occasions of access that result in the transmission of a tip statement. The electronic tip statement must contain exactly the same information that must be reported on a paper tip statement and must contain the employee's electronic signature [§ 6053(a); Reg. § 31.6053-1(b), § 31.6053-1(c)(2), § 31.6053-1(d)].

FICA taxes on tips are reported quarterly on Form 941 in the same general manner as nontip wages (see XXII.C.1.). However, an employer must report and withhold FICA only on tips that are reported to the employer. An employer is not liable for its portion of the FICA taxes on tips an employee fails to report to the employer until the IRS makes notice and demand for the taxes to the employer. The employer is not liable to withhold and pay the employee share of FICA taxes on the unreported tips [§ 3102(c)].

If an employee fails to report tips to his employer, the employee must pay his portion of the FICA tax owed by completing Form 4137, *Social Security and Medicare Tax on Unreported Tip Income*, and file it with Form 1040 for the year in which the employee actually receives the tips. An employee who fails to report tips that must be reported to an employer is subject to a penalty equal to 50% of the employee portion of the FICA taxes on those tips, unless the employee attaches a satisfactory explanation showing that the failure was due to reasonable cause and not due to willful neglect [§ 6652(b); Rev. Rul. 2012-18, 2012-26 I.R.B. 1032, Q&A-5].

### XXII.B.4.i. Meals and Lodging

[392 T.M., II.A.2.f(5)(d); TPS ¶5440.01.B.11.c.]

The value of meals and lodging furnished by or on behalf of an employer to employees, their spouses or dependents is exempt from employment taxes if it is reasonable for the employer to believe that the employee will be able to exclude these items from income at the time that they are furnished [§ 3121(a)(19), § 3306(b)(14)] (see XVII.E.4.).

### XXII.B.4.j. Noncash Sales Commissions

[392 T.M., III.A.3.c(3); TPS ¶5440.01.B.11.e.]

Income tax withholding is not required on noncash compensation paid for services rendered by a retail salesman if the salesman ordinarily is compensated solely on the basis of cash commissions. The employer must, however, include the fair market value of the noncash wages in the employee's total wages reported on Form W-2. The exception for noncash wages does not apply to the extent that the salesman is compensated for services performed in a capacity other than as a retail salesman, or if the salesman is paid a salary in addition to commissions or where the salesman ordinarily is compensated with non-cash compensation [§ 3402(j); Reg. § 31.3402(j)-1(a)(2)].

### XXII.B.4.k. Transfers of Nonqualified Compensation Interests Pursuant to Divorce

[392 T.M., II.A.2.f(2)(c); TPS ¶5440.01.B.2.b.(1).]

IRS guidance addresses how FICA, FUTA and income tax withholding apply to an employee's transfer of interests in nonqualified deferred compensation plans and nonstatutory stock options (NSOs) to a former spouse pursuant to divorce and how such transactions must be reported by employers. The transfer of interests in NSOs and in nonqualified deferred compensation from the employee spouse to the nonemployee former spouse incident to a divorce does not result in a payment of wages for FICA and FUTA tax purposes. The NSOs are subject to FICA and FUTA taxes at the time of exercise by the nonemployee spouse to the same extent as if the options had been retained by the employee spouse and exercised by the employee spouse. The nonqualified deferred compensation also remains subject to FICA and FUTA taxes to the same extent as if the rights to the compensation had been retained by the employee spouse. To the extent FICA and FUTA taxation apply, the wages are the wages of the employee spouse. The employee portion of the FICA taxes is deducted from the wages as and when the wages are taken into account for FICA tax purposes. The employee portion of the FICA taxes is deducted from the payment to the nonemployee spouse [Rev. Rul. 2004-60, 2004-1 C.B. 1051].

The income recognized by the nonemployee spouse on the exercise of the NSOs is subject to withholding, as are the amounts distributed to the nonemployee spouse from nonqualified deferred compensation plans. The amounts to be withheld for income tax withholding are deducted from the payments to the nonemployee spouse. The supplemental wage flat rate may be used to determine the amount of income tax withholding [Rev. Rul. 2004-60].

### XXII.B.4.l. Combat Zone Compensation

[501 T.M., VIII.G.3.c.; TPS ¶5440.01.B.12.]

Income tax withholding generally is not required on remuneration paid for active service as a member below the grade of commissioned officer in the U.S. Armed Forces for any month during any part of which the member served in a combat zone, or was hospitalized as a result of wounds, disease, or injury incurred while serving in a combat zone [§ 112(c)(2), § 3401(a)(1); Reg. § 1.112-1(b)] (see II.M.1.).

### XXII.B.4.m. Damages and Settlements

[392 T.M., II.A.2.d., II.A.2.e.; TPS ¶5440.01.E.]

The amount of any damages (other than punitive damages) received as the result of a suit or settlement agreement (whether as a lump-sum or as periodic payments) on account of personal physical injuries or physical sickness are excluded from gross income (see II.F.1.). Accordingly, FICA and FUTA are not withheld on such damages. Emotional distress generally is not treated as a physical injury or physical sickness. However, the amount of damages for emotional distress that does not exceed the amount paid for medical care attributable to emotional distress are considered damages attributable to physical injury or physical sickness and thus are excludible from gross income (and not subject to FICA and FUTA) if such amounts were not previously deducted as a medical expense [§ 104(a)].

In the context of a settlement agreement, determining whether the payment is excludible from gross income (and therefore exempt from FICA and FUTA) depends on the nature of the claim that was the actual basis of the settlement (i.e., the origin of the claim) and the types of income permitted to be recovered under the statute (see II.F.2.). For example, if the statute allows for the recovery of back pay, front pay, or severance pay, the IRS has taken the position that payments to settle a claim arising from such a statute are amounts paid in lieu of the recoverable types of income. Therefore, the payments constitute wages subject to employment taxes. This applies even if the employment relationship no longer exists at the time the payment is made.

### XXII.B.5. Employees Subject to FICA and FUTA Tax

[392 T.M., II.A.3.c., II.A.4.; TPS ¶5440.02.A.]

Unless otherwise excluded, FICA and FUTA is based on the amount of wages paid to common law employees and corporate officers [§ 3121(d), § 3306(i)]. The rules set forth in XXII.A.4. for determining an employer-employee relationship for income tax withholding purposes apply equally in determining such a relationship for FICA and FUTA tax purposes. The following additional occupational categories are deemed to be employees for purposes of FICA and FUTA, regardless of their treatment under common law [§ 3121(d)(3), § 3306(c)(14), § 3306(i)]:

- agent and commission drivers who distribute meat, vegetables, fruit, bakery goods, beverages (other than milk) or laundry and dry cleaning for a principal and not as part of their own business;
- insurance salesmen;
- home workers who perform services according to the specifications provided by the person for whom the services are performed with materials that are furnished by such person and are later returned to such person; and
- traveling salesmen engaged on a full-time basis to solicit orders from wholesalers, retailers, contractors or operators of hotels, restaurants or other similar establishments for merchandise for resale or use in the business operations of the principal.

Certain employers may enter into an agreement with the IRS to extend social security coverage (but not unemployment insurance coverage) to otherwise exempt service [§ 3121(l), § 3121(r)].

### XXII.B.6. Statutory Nonemployees Excluded From FICA and FUTA

[392 T.M., II.A.3.d.; TPS ¶5440.02.C.]

Notwithstanding the broad parameters of employee service subject to FICA and FUTA, generally, certain categories of individuals or service listed below are statutorily excluded from coverage. For the most part, the requirements for these exclusions mirror those set forth under the exclusions for federal income tax withholding set forth in XXII.A.4.b. [§ 3121(b), § 3306(c)]:

- certain agricultural employees;
- certain student employees;
- employees of foreign governments;
- employees of international organizations;
- services performed by a nonresident alien temporarily present in the United States as a nonimmigrant under § 101(a)(15)(F), § 101(a)(15)(J), § 101(a)(15)(M) or § 101(a)(15)(Q) of the Immigration and Nationality Act, if the

services are performed to carry out the purpose for which the individual was admitted;

- certain service performed by a child less than 18 years of age in the employ of a parent;

- duly ordained, commissioned, or licensed ministers (FICA exemption only);

- newspaper distributors under 18 years of age;

- certain fishing crews; and

- services performed by certain qualified real estate agents and direct sellers.

Special rules may apply to employers in U.S. possessions.

### XXII.B.7. Government Employees

[392 T.M., II.A.3.d(3); TPS ¶5440.02.C.8.]

***Federal Employees.*** Wages paid to federal government employees are not subject to FUTA [§ 3306(c)(6)]. Wages paid to all federal employees are subject to the Medicare portion of FICA, regardless of the hiring date [§ 3121(u)]. Wages paid to federal employees hired after 1983 generally are subject to the old-age, survivor and disability insurance portion of FICA (OASDI). However, wages paid to federal employees hired before 1984 and who participate in the Civil Service Retirement System (CSRS) or other similar pre-1984 retirement systems are exempt from the OASDI portion of FICA [§ 3121(b)(5)].

***State and Local Government Employees.*** Wages paid to employees of state and local governments and their political subdivisions are not subject to FUTA [§ 3306(c)(7)]. Wages paid to state and local governments employees generally are taxable under FICA for services performed by employees who are either [§ 3121(b)(7)]:

- covered under an agreement entered into pursuant to § 218 of the Social Security Act; or

- not covered under a § 218 agreement and not a member of a public retirement system.

For the Medicare portion of FICA only, wages paid for services performed by employees hired or rehired after March 31, 1986, and who are not covered under a § 218 agreement are taxable. However, wages paid to certain employees hired before April 1, 1986, may be exempt [§ 3121(u)].

Additionally, wages of less than $1,600 (2015 and 2014 amount) paid to election workers are exempt from FICA. Wages paid to emergency workers hired on a temporary basis are exempt [§ 3121(b)(7); 79 Fed. Reg. 64,455 (Oct. 29, 2014)].

Special rules may apply to government employers in U.S. possessions.

## XXII.C. Reporting and Paying Employment Taxes

### XXII.C.1. FICA and Withheld Income Taxes

#### XXII.C.1.a. Reporting Requirements

[392 T.M., IV.A.1.a.; TPS ¶5440.03.B.1.a.]

FICA taxes and withheld income taxes are reported together by employers on the same form. Generally, employers that withhold income and FICA taxes file Form 941, *Employer's Quarterly Federal Tax Return.* A different version of Form 941 must be used by employers who report wages paid to employees in American territories. Form 941-SS is used by employers to report wages paid to employees in American

Samoa, Guam, the Commonwealth of the Northern Mariana Islands, and the U.S. Virgin Islands. Form 941-PR is used to report wages paid to employees in Puerto Rico [Reg. § 31.6011(a)-1(a)(1), § 31.6011(a)-3(a), § 31.6011(a)-4(a)(1), § 31.6011(a)-5(a)].

Form 944, *Employer's Annual Federal Tax Return*, is used instead of Form 941 by employers that have been notified by the IRS of their eligibility to use Form 944. Form 944 is limited to employers with estimated annual employment tax liability of $1,000 or less. Employers that do not receive IRS notification may contact the IRS to request to use Form 944 if they anticipate that their annual employment tax liability will meet the eligibility threshold [Reg. § 31.6011(a)-1(a)(5), § 31.6011(a)-4(a)(4)].

Employers of agricultural workers must report withheld Social Security and federal income taxes on Form 943, *Employer's Annual Tax Return for Agricultural Employees* [Reg. § 31.6011(a)-4(a)(3)].

Employers must report on an annual basis any Social Security or federal unemployment tax obligations for wages paid to domestic workers on Schedule H of their individual income tax return (Form 1040) (see X.). Employers who file Schedule H must pay FICA and FUTA taxes and any withheld income taxes by the due date for their individual income tax returns, not including any extensions, for the applicable year [§ 3510; Reg. § 31.6011(a)-4(a)(2)].

Form 943 is an annual return for agricultural employees that is due one month after the calendar year ends.

The remaining employment tax returns are quarterly returns that are due one month after the end of each calendar quarter. However, if a tax must be deposited and the full amount of the tax is timely paid, the return is due by the tenth day of the second month following the calendar quarter (or year, if Form 943 is filed) [Reg. § 31.6071(a)-1(a)(1)].

**Applicable due dates are as follows:**

| Return and Period | General Due Date | Due Date if Timely Paid |
|---|---|---|
| **Form 943:** | | |
| Calendar year | January 31 | February 10 |
| **Forms 941, 941-SS, 941-PR:** | | |
| 1st Quarter | April 30 | May 10 |
| 2nd Quarter | July 31 | August 10 |
| 3rd Quarter | October 31 | November 10 |
| 4th Quarter | January 31 | February 10 |
| | | |
| **Form 944:** | | |
| Calendar year | January 31 | February 10 |

The IRS may extend the deadline for filing employment tax returns (including those for withheld income taxes) and the payment of employment and withheld income taxes for up to one year for taxpayers affected by a federally declared disaster or terroristic or military action [§ 7508A(a)]. The IRS must extend these deadlines for taxpayers serving in, or in support of, the Armed Forces in an area designated as a combat zone, in deployment or in a qualifying contingency operation, or hospitalized as a result of injury received during service in such an area [§ 7508(a)].

### XXII.C.1.b. Deposits

[392 T.M., IV.A.1.b.; TPS ¶5440.03.B.1.b.]

Social Security and withheld income taxes generally are deposited before the time that the appropriate return is due with a financial institution qualified as a depositary for federal taxes. All taxpayers that make federal tax deposits must use electronic funds transfers (EFT). Deposits are not required for taxes reported on Schedule H and are paid when the employer's Form 1040 is due (without regard to extensions) [§ 3510(a)(3), § 6302(h)].

An employer is classified as either a "monthly depositor" or a "semi-weekly depositor." This status is determined for each calendar year and is based on the amount of employment taxes which the employer reported for the one-year lookback period ending on June 30 of the preceding year. Employers that file Form 944 for the calendar year may remit employment taxes with their timely filed return for that tax year and are not required to deposit under the monthly or semi-weekly rules during that tax year, except that an employer that files Form 944 whose actual employment tax liability exceeds the $1,000 eligibility threshold does not qualify for this exception [Reg. § 31.6302-1(b), § 31.6302-1T(b)(4), § 31.6302-1T(c)(5)].

A monthly depositor is any employer that reported aggregate employment taxes of $50,000 or less during the lookback period. Monthly depositors must deposit each month's accumulated employment taxes by EFT on or before the 15th day of the following month [Reg. § 31.6302-1(b)(2), § 31.6302-1(c)(1)].

An employer that reported more than $50,000 in aggregate employment taxes for the lookback period is considered a semi-weekly depositor. For semi-weekly depositors, taxes accumulated for payments made on Wednesday, Thursday, and/or Friday must be deposited by EFT on or before the following Wednesday; and taxes accumulated for payments made on Saturday, Sunday, Monday, and/or Tuesday must be deposited by EFT on or before the following Friday. Semi-weekly depositors have a minimum of three business days after the end of the semi-weekly period to deposit taxes. Business days include every calendar day other than Saturdays, Sundays, or legal holidays in the District of Columbia. If any of the three weekdays following the close of a semi-weekly period is a legal holiday, the employer has an additional day for each day that is a legal holiday by which to make the required deposit [§ 7503; Reg. § 31.6302-1(b)(3), § 31.6302-1(c)(2)].

Monthly and semi-weekly depositors that accumulate employment taxes of $100,000 or more during any deposit period must make a deposit on the first business day after that threshold is satisfied (i.e., the "one-day" rule), and an employer that reaches this threshold immediately becomes a semi-weekly depositor for the remainder of the calendar year and for the following calendar year [Reg. § 31.6302-1(b)(2)(ii), § 31.6302-1(c)(3)].

The IRS will notify employers before the beginning of each calendar year whether they are monthly or semi-weekly depositors. A new employer is treated as a monthly depositor until it reports more than $50,000 of employment taxes for the prior July 1 through June 30 lookback period or until it accumulates $100,000 or more of employment taxes on any day during the month [Reg. § 31.6302-1(b)].

An employer with less than $2,500 of accumulated employment taxes for a calendar quarter may remit its taxes with its quarterly return. Penalties are abated if an employer shows that a failure to deposit the full amount of taxes is due to reasonable cause [§ 6656; Reg. § 31.6302-1(f)(4)] (see XXIII.).

A deposit of taxes by EFT is deemed made when the amount is withdrawn from the taxpayer's account, provided the U.S. Government is the payee and the amount is not returned or reversed. For taxpayers making EFTs, reasonable cause for abatement of the penalty can be established by relying on the records of the bank instructed to make the EFT and/or relying on the taxpayer's records [Reg. § 31.6302-1(h)(8)].

### XXII.C.1.c. Information Returns

[392 T.M., IV.A.1.c.; TPS ¶5440.03.B.1.c.]

Form W-2, *Wage and Tax Statement*, must be furnished to each employee from whom Social Security and income taxes have been withheld. Form W-2 also must be furnished to employees from whom income tax would have been withheld if the employee had claimed no more than one withholding exemption on Form W-4. Form W-2 must show the total wages and other compensation paid, the total wages subject to Social Security tax, the amounts deducted for income tax and Social Security tax purposes, and (though not taxable) the cost of employer-sponsored health coverage [§ 6051(a); Reg. § 31.6051-1(a)(1)(i)].

Form W-2 must be furnished to employees not later than January 31 following the calendar year in which the employee was subject to withholding. However, if the employee separates from service before the close of the calendar year, the employer may furnish Form W-2 at any time after termination and before January 31 of the following calendar year. Form W-2 may be furnished to an employee electronically with the recipient's consent [Reg. § 31.6051-1(d)(1), § 31.6051-1(j)].

Form W-3, *Transmittal of Income and Tax Statements*, must be filed with the Social Security Administration along with Copy A of all Form W-2s provided to the employer's employees. Form W-3 must be filed on or before the last day of February or, if filed electronically, March 31 following the calendar year for which the form applies; however, if a final return for a period ending before December 31 has been filed, Form W-3 must be filed on or before the last day of the second calendar month following the period for which the final return is filed [§ 6071(b); Reg. § 31.6051-2(a); § 31.6071(a)-1(a)(3)].

### XXII.C.2. FUTA

### XXII.C.2.a. Annual FUTA Return

[392 T.M., IV.A.2.a.; TPS ¶5440.03.B.2.a.]

FUTA taxes are reported on Form 940, *Employer's Annual Federal Unemployment Tax Return*. FUTA tax returns must be filed on or before the last day of the first calendar month following the period for which it is made. However, a return may be filed on or before the 10th day of February if timely deposits were made in full payment of FICA taxes due for the period. Upon written application, an employer may be granted an extension of up to 90 days for filing the Form 940. Employers who employ domestic workers must report FUTA taxes on an annual basis on Schedule H of Form 1040. A taxpayer required to deposit FUTA taxes must use EFT to make all deposits of those taxes [Reg. § 31.6011(a)-3(a), § 31.6071(a)-1(c), § 31.6081(a)-1(b), § 31.6302-1(h)(2)(iii)].

### XXII.C.2.b. Deposits of FUTA Taxes

[392 T.M., IV.A.2.b.; TPS ¶5440.03.B.2.b.]

FUTA taxes must be deposited with an authorized financial institution by the last day of the month following the end of any calendar quarter, other than the final quarter, in which the employer's undeposited tax liability exceeds $500. If the undeposited FUTA tax in any calendar quarter other than the final quarter of the year is $500 or less, a deposit is not required. The undeposited amount is added to the amount of the employer's tax liability in the succeeding quarter in determining whether the $500 threshold is reached [Reg. § 31.6302(c)-3(a)(1), § 31.6302(c)-3(a)(2)].

### XXII.C.3. Employment Tax Record Retention

[392 T.M., IV.A.3.; TPS ¶3820.05.E.1.]

Employers must keep accurate records of employment taxes for a minimum of four years after the later of the due date of the return or the date the tax is paid. Although the employer is not required to adopt any particular method of accounting or form of recordkeeping system, it must adopt a method or system that will enable the IRS to ascertain the amount of the employer's tax liability, if any. An employer claiming an exemption from any employment tax must maintain adequate records to establish the exemption [Reg. § 31.6001-1].

# CHAPTER XXIII. PROCEDURE AND ADMINISTRATION

>>>>>>>>>>>>>>>>>>>>>>>>>>>>>>>>

## XXIII.A. Tax Returns

### XXIII.A.1. Income Tax Returns

[623 T.M., I.D.1.; TPS ¶3820.01.]

The United States relies on a "self-assessment" system under which persons subject to income tax must file returns and report the tax due to the IRS.

Every person who is liable for income tax is required to file a return and furnish information pursuant to forms and regulations published by the IRS [§ 6011]. If any person fails to make a return required under the law, or makes a fraudulent return, the IRS is authorized to file a return for the taxpayer based on its knowledge or from information obtained from testimony or otherwise [§ 6020(b)].

A document is an income tax return for purposes of the filing requirement if it purports to be a return, contains sufficient data to calculate the tax liability, is an honest and reasonable attempt to satisfy tax law requirements, and is signed under penalties of perjury. A "frivolous return" is not considered a return and may be subject to a $5,000 penalty [§ 6702] (see XXIII.D.1.f.).

### XXIII.A.1.a. Filing Requirements

### XXIII.A.1.a.(1) Individuals

[507 T.M., II.A.; TPS ¶3820.01.A.]

***Citizens and Residents.*** Every U.S. citizen or resident whose gross income for the tax year exceeds a filing threshold must file an income tax return using one of three forms in the Form 1040 series (see XII.A.2.). The threshold is generally the taxpayer's exemption amount plus the basic standard deduction. For a detailed discussion of individual filing requirements, including filing status, see XII.A.

***Nonresident Aliens.*** Nonresident aliens must file returns on Form 1040NR, *U.S. Nonresident Alien Income Tax Return*, if they engaged in a trade or business in the United States (regardless of whether they have income from the trade or business, U.S. source income, or the income is exempt from taxation), and in certain other circumstances (see XX.D.).

### *XXIII.A.1.a.(2) Corporations*

[750 T.M., II.A.; 648 T.M., XIX.C.; TPS ¶3820.02.]

Every domestic corporation not expressly exempt from tax must file an income tax return, regardless of whether it has taxable income and regardless of the amount of its gross income [§ 6012(a)(2); Reg. § 1.6012-2(a)(1)]. Every foreign corporation engaged in a trade or business in the United States at any time during the tax year must file an income tax return, even if it has no income from U.S. sources or its income is exempt from tax under a treaty.

Returns are generally filed on Form 1120. However, certain corporate taxpayers must file specialized returns. These include:

- cooperatives (Form 1120-C);
- foreign corporations (Form 1120-F);
- foreign sales corporations (Form 1120-FSC);
- homeowner associations (Form 1120-H);
- interest charge domestic sales corporations (Form 1120-IC-DISC);
- life insurance companies (Form 1120-L);
- property and casualty insurance companies (Form 1120-PC);
- political organizations (Form 1120-POL);
- real estate investment companies (Form 1120-REIT);
- regulated investment companies (Form 1120-RIC); and
- electing small business corporations ("S Corporations") (Form 1120S).

For 2014 tax years, corporations with assets that equal or exceed $10 million and that issued audited financial statements reporting all or a portion of the corporation's operations for all or a portion of the corporation's tax year may be required to file Schedule UTP, *Uncertain Tax Position Statement*, with Form 1120. A Schedule UTP is required if the corporation (or a related party) has recorded a reserve with respect to a tax position in audited financial statements, or the corporation or related party did not record a reserve for that tax position because the corporation expects to litigate the position [Reg. § 1.6012-2(a)(4)].

### *XXIII.A.1.a.(3) Partnerships*

[710 T.M., II.A., 634 T.M., II.D.1.; TPS ¶3820.05.A.]

Although partnerships are not subject to federal income tax, they are required to file information returns on Form 1065, *U.S. Return of Partnership Income*, for each tax year in which they are engaged in a U.S. trade or business or have income from U.S. sources. They must report the names, identifying numbers, and addresses of all partners and each partner's distributive share of the items of income, gain, loss, deductions, and credits. The Form 1065 must be signed by a partner, and must cover the partnership's tax year, irrespective of the tax years of its partners [§ 6031].

Every partnership required to file a return must furnish its partners with a copy of Schedule K-1, *Partner's Share of Income, Deductions, Credits, etc.* The copy must be furnished to each person who was a partner (or who held an interest as nominee for another person) at any time during the tax year. These copies must be furnished not later than the due date for filing the partnership return (the 15th day of the fourth month following the close of the tax year of the partnership unless an extension is obtained).

In the case of an electing large partnership, the copies must be provided to the partners on or before March 15 of the year following the close of the tax year.

An "electing investment partnership" must attach a notice to each annual statement that it sends to a partner, alerting the partner to the fact that the partnership has elected to be treated as an electing investment partnership and instructing transferor and transferee partners as to procedures they must follow if an interest in the partnership is transferred.

Nominees who hold partnership interests for others must furnish the partnership with the names and addresses of the actual owners of the interests.

A partnership that has no income from sources within the United States need not file a return [Reg. § 1.6031(a)-1(a)(3)]. Foreign partnerships, in general, are not required to file partnership returns. A foreign partnership is required to file a partnership return for any tax year if for that year the partnership has either (i) gross income derived from sources within the United States, or (ii) gross income that is effectively connected with the conduct of a trade or business within the United States [§ 6031(a); Reg. § 1.6031-1].

### XXIII.A.1.a.(4) S Corporations

[700 T.M., VI.E.4.; TPS ¶4410.01.A.1.]

Each S corporation must file a tax return for the tax year on Form 1120S, *U.S. Income Tax Return for an S Corporation*. The return must be filed without regard to the amount of the S corporation's gross income for the tax year. Form 1120S shows specifically the items of gross income and the allowable deductions and each shareholder's pro rata share of those items [§ 6012(a)(2), § 6037; Reg. § 1.6012-2(a)(2)].

### XXIII.A.1.a.(5) Estates and Trusts

[852 T.M., 804 T.M., XV.C.; TPS ¶3820.02.C.]

An estate must file Form 1041, *U.S. Income Tax Return for Estates and Trusts*, if it has gross income of $600 or more, or if any beneficiary is a nonresident alien [§ 6012(a)(3), § 6012(a)(5)]. A trust must file Form 1041 if it has any taxable income, if it has gross income of $600 or more (regardless of the amount of taxable income), or if it has a beneficiary who is a nonresident alien [§ 6012(a)(4), § 6012(a)(5)] (see XVIII.D.1.).

### XXIII.A.1.a.(6) Other Entities

[741 T.M., IX.N.3., 540 T.M., III.F.5., 738 T.M., VIII.A.; TPS ¶5190.09.]

***REMICs.*** Real Estate Mortgage Investment Conduits (REMICs) are treated like partnerships and REMIC residual interest holders are treated like partners. REMICs must file an annual income tax return on Form 1066, *U.S. Real Estate Mortgage Investment Conduit Income Tax Return*. For the first tax year of the REMIC's existence, the REMIC election is made by timely filing Form 1066 and by providing certain information either on that return or in a separate statement attached to the return [§ 860F(e)].

***Bankruptcy Estates.*** The trustee of an individual's bankruptcy estate under chapter 7 or 11 of the Bankruptcy Code must file an income tax return on Form 1041 and attach Form 1040 showing the tax computation. An individual's bankruptcy estate computes tax in the same manner as an individual [§ 1398]. No separate return is required for the estates of individuals under other chapters of the Bankruptcy Code or from bankruptcy estates arising from corporation or partnership bankruptcies, although the trustee might be responsible for filing the corporate or partnership returns [§ 1398, § 1399].

*Settlement Funds.* All designated and qualified settlement funds under § 468B must file income tax returns on Form 1120-SF, *U.S. Income Tax Return for Settlement Funds.*

### XXIII.A.1.b. Taxpayer Identifying Numbers

[623 T.M., I.D.1.a.; TPS ¶3820.01.D.].

Taxpayer identifying numbers (TINs) are required on all tax and information returns and other documents filed with the IRS [§ 6109; Reg. § 301.6109-1]. TINs include:

- social security numbers (SSNs);
- employer identification numbers (EINs), used on all business returns, not just on employment tax returns;
- IRS individual taxpayer identification numbers (ITINs); and
- adoption taxpayer information numbers (ATINs).

A SSN is obtained by filing Form SS-5, *Application for a Social Security Card,* with the Social Security Administration.

An EIN is obtained by filing Form SS-4, *Application for Employer Identification Number,* with the IRS. Taxpayers may also obtain it online at www.irs.gov.

Any individual who is not eligible to obtain an SSN (i.e., nonresident aliens) and is required to furnish a taxpayer identification number must apply for an IRS ITIN on Form W-7, *Application for IRS Individual Taxpayer Identification Number.* An applicant must submit documentary evidence required by the IRS to establish alien status and identity. Examples of acceptable documentary evidence for this purpose include an original or certified copy of a passport, driver's license, birth certificate, identity card, or immigration documentation. Subject to exceptions specified in the instructions (e.g., information reporting by holders of income generating financial accounts), Form W-7 requires attachment of the return or other filing that generated the need for the ITIN.

Individuals who have SSNs but later become nonresident aliens must continue to use the SSN. Individuals that have ITINs who later become U.S. citizens or resident aliens must obtain an SSN [Reg. § 301.6109-1(d)(4)(i)].

*Adoptions.* An adoptive child may not have an SSN, or, if the child does have an SSN, the taxpayer adopting the child (the prospective adoptive parent) may be unable to obtain the SSN because of confidentiality laws. To alleviate this problem, the IRS will issue an ATIN to a child who is in the process of being adopted (a prospective adoptive child).

An ATIN automatically expires two years after the date of issuance, unless extended by the IRS. A prospective adoptive parent may apply for an ATIN on Form W-7A, *Application for Taxpayer Identification Number for Pending Adoptions,* for a child if (i) the prospective adoptive parent is eligible to claim a personal exemption for the child; (ii) the child is placed with the prospective adoptive parent for legal adoption by an authorized placement agency; (iii) the Social Security Administration will not assign the prospective adoptive parent an SSN for the child (for example, because the adoption is not final); and (iv) the prospective adoptive parent has used all reasonable means to obtain the child's assigned SSN, but has been unsuccessful in obtaining this number.

Once the adoption becomes final, the adoptive parent must apply for an SSN for the child.

The ATIN procedures do not apply to adoptions involving alien children, a child who is a foster child or is otherwise in the custody of a government agency or court, or a child for whom the adoptive parent has been able to obtain the SSN from the birth parent [Reg. § 301.6109-3].

***Identity Theft.*** The IRS has special procedures for processing tax returns for identity theft victims or taxpayers who believe their information has been compromised. See the IRS website at www.irs.gov or call 1-800-908-4490.

### XXIII.A.1.c.  When to File

### XXIII.A.1.c.(1)  Due Dates

[623 T.M., I.C.1., 907 T.M., VIII.J., 750 T.M., II.A., 634 T.M., II.D.; TPS ¶3820.02.E.]

***Individuals, Estates, and Trusts.*** Individuals, estates, and trusts must file income tax returns on or before the 15th day of the fourth month following the close of their fiscal year (i.e., on or before April 15 for calendar year taxpayers) [§ 6072(a)].

---

**EXAMPLE:** Individual T, a sole proprietor, operates on a fiscal year ending June 30. T's tax return for the fiscal year ended June 30, 2014, must be filed on or before Oct. 15, 2014.

---

A U.S. citizen or resident who has a tax home outside the United States or in Puerto Rico automatically receives a two-month extension of time to file (i.e., the return is not due until the 15th day of the sixth month following the close of the tax year). The automatic extension also applies to U.S. citizens or residents on military or naval service outside the United States and Puerto Rico [§ 6081].

***Nonresident Aliens.*** Nonresident alien individuals whose wages are not subject to withholding and foreign corporations not having an office in the United States must file their returns on or before the 15th day of the sixth month following the close of the fiscal year (i.e., on or before June 15 for calendar year taxpayers). Nonresident aliens whose wages are subject to withholding must file their returns on or before the 15th day of the fourth month following the close of their tax year (i.e., April 15 for calendar year taxpayers) [§ 6072(c)].

---

**EXAMPLE:** T is a nonresident alien with wages subject to withholding. T uses a fiscal year ending June 30. T is required to file his return for the year ending June 30, 2014, on or before Oct. 15, 2014.

---

***Decedents.*** The final income tax return of a decedent (covering the portion of the last year he was alive) must be filed by the executor, administrator, or other person responsible for the estate by the 15th day of the fourth month following the close of what would have been the decedent's tax year (i.e., April 15 for calendar year decedents) [Reg. § 1.6072-1(b)].

---

**EXAMPLE:** Individual X, a calendar year taxpayer, died on June 9, 2014. The last income return for X is due on or before Apr. 15, 2015.

---

***Corporations.*** Domestic corporations and foreign corporations having an office or place of business in the United States must file their income tax returns on or before the 15th day of the third month following the close of their fiscal year (March 15 for calendar year taxpayers) [§ 6072(b)].

**EXAMPLE:** Corporation X operates on a fiscal year ending Oct. 31. Its tax return for fiscal year ending Oct. 31, 2014, must be filed on or before Jan. 15, 2015.

*Partnerships.* Partnerships having an office or place of business in the United States must file their income tax returns on or before the 15th day of the fourth month following the close of their fiscal year (i.e., April 15 for calendar year taxpayers).

### XXIII.A.1.c.(2) Timely Mailing Rule

[627 T.M., I.C.1.; TPS ¶3860.01.A.2.]

A tax return's date of filing is generally the date it is physically delivered to the IRS. The "timely mailing/timely filing" rule provides a different rule for the convenience of taxpayers. If a tax return is mailed to the IRS on or before the last day for filing and is thereafter delivered to the IRS, the U.S. postmark stamped on the cover in which the return is mailed will be the date of delivery and consequently the date of filing [Reg. § 301.7502-1(a)]. If a return is sent by registered or certified mail, or by private delivery service, the date stamped on the receipt is the date of filing [Reg. § 301.7502-1(a)]. To qualify for this rule, the return must be deposited in the U.S. mail in an envelope or other appropriate wrapper, with postage prepaid and proper IRS address [§ 7502].

If a timely mailed return is lost in the mail, the return is treated as not filed. The taxpayer assumes the risk of nondelivery, and cannot presume the timely filing of a return unless the return is sent by registered or certified mail. If the return is mailed after the due date, it is not considered filed until actually received by the IRS. The mailbox rule also applies to returns mailed to the IRS from a foreign country. A return mailed in a foreign country to the IRS will be accepted as timely filed if mailed from and officially postmarked by the country on or before midnight of the last date prescribed for filing, including any extension.

Income tax returns may be filed by hand-carrying the return to a person assigned the responsibility to receive hand-carried returns in the local IRS office [Reg. § 1.6091-2(d)].

Taxpayers can also use commercial or private delivery services designated by the IRS and take advantage of the timely mailing/timely filing rule. The IRS has currently designated the following commercial or private delivery services [Notice 2004-83, 2004-52 I.R.B. 1030]:

- DHL Express (DHL) — DHL Same Day Service, DHL Next Day 10:30 am, DHL Next Day 12:00 pm, DHL Next Day 3:00 pm, and DHL 2nd Day Service.
- Federal Express — Priority Overnight, Standard Overnight, 2 Day Service, International Priority, and International First.
- United Parcel Service — Next Day Air, Next Day Air Saver, 2nd Day Air, 2nd Day Air A.M., Worldwide Express Plus, and Worldwide Express.

Note that, because these services provide delivery services to the United States from foreign countries, they are options for taxpayers filing returns from countries with unreliable mail services.

A return that is filed electronically with an electronic return transmitter is deemed to be filed on the date of the electronic postmark given by the authorized electronic return transmitter. The IRS may enter into an agreement with an electronic return transmitter or prescribe in forms, instructions, or other appropriate guidance the procedures under which the electronic return transmitter is authorized to provide taxpayers with an electronic postmark to acknowledge the date and time that the electronic return transmitter received the electronically filed document. An electronic postmark is defined to mean a record of the date and time (in a particular time zone) that an authorized electronic return transmitter receives the transmission of a taxpayer's electronically filed document on its host system. If the taxpayer and a transmitter are in different time zones, the time in the taxpayer's time zone controls the timeliness of the filed document [Reg. § 301.7502-1(d)].

### XXIII.A.1.c.(3) Weekend and Holiday Rule

[627 T.M., I.C.1.; TPS ¶3820.02.E.]

When the last day for filing a return falls on a Saturday, Sunday, or legal holiday, the time for filing is extended to the next day that is not a Saturday, Sunday, or legal holiday. Legal holidays include those recognized as legal holidays in the District of Columbia and any statewide legal holiday of the state where the return must be filed [§ 7503]. Legal holidays in the District of Columbia for 2015 are [Reg. § 301.7503-1(b); D.C. Code Ann. § 28-2706]:

- January 1—New Year's Day
- January 19—Birthday of Martin Luther King, Jr.
- February 16—Washington's Birthday
- April 16—District of Columbia Emancipation Day
- May 25—Memorial Day
- July 4—Independence Day
- September 7—Labor Day
- October 12—Columbus Day
- November 11—Veterans Day
- November 26—Thanksgiving Day
- December 25—Christmas Day

### XXIII.A.1.d. Extensions of Time to File

### XXIII.A.1.d.(1) Individual Returns

[634 T.M., II.; TPS ¶3820.02.F.]

An individual taxpayer can obtain an automatic six-month extension of time to file by filing an application on Form 4868, *Application for Automatic Extension of Time to File U.S. Individual Income Tax Return*, on or before the due date of the return (i.e., April 15 for calendar year taxpayers). Form 4868 need not be signed, but must be filed with the appropriate IRS office for where the taxpayer lives, as indicated on Form 4868. Accordingly, a third party such as a relative or return preparer may submit the automatic extension. Form 4868 may also be filed electronically using IRS e-file by either the taxpayer or a return preparer. Form 4868 must include a proper estimate of the tax for the tax year, but full payment is not required to obtain the extension. An automatic extension, however, does not extend the time for payment of the tax. The IRS can terminate an automatic extension by mailing to the taxpayer a notice of termination at least 10 days before the termination date [§ 6081; Reg. § 1.6081-4].

*Taxpayer out of the Country.* U.S. citizens or residents whose tax homes and abodes are outside the United States (including Puerto Rico) and U.S. citizens or residents who are in the armed forces on duty outside the United States and Puerto Rico are granted an automatic extension of time to file (and to pay) until the 15th day of the sixth month following the close of the tax year without requesting an extension.

If a U.S. citizen or resident whose tax home and abode are within the United States but is "out of the country" on the regular due date of the return, the taxpayer is allowed two extra months to file and pay any amount due without requesting an extension. If additional time beyond the two months is needed, the taxpayer must file Form 4868 (and check the box on line 8) and will be allowed an additional four months to file the return [Reg. § 1.6081-4(a), § 1.6081-5]. If an extension beyond six months is desired, the taxpayer must submit a letter to the IRS explaining the need for the extension. Where the taxpayer first obtains an extension under these provisions, and then seeks an additional four-month extension on Form 4868, the automatic six-month extension runs concurrently [Reg. § 1.6081-5(a)].

---

**EXAMPLE:** T is a U.S. citizen whose tax home is in France. T is a calendar year taxpayer and therefore has until June 15, 2015, to file his 2014 return without requesting an extension. If T should file Form 4868 to obtain an automatic six-month extension, the time by which he must file the return is extended to Oct. 15, 2015 (i.e., an additional four months).

---

### XXIII.A.1.d.(2) Partnerships

[634 T.M., II.; TPS ¶3820.02.F.]

Partnerships required to file Form 1065 are allowed an automatic five-month extension of time to file the return by submitting an application on Form 7004, *Application for Automatic Extension of Time to File Certain Business Income Tax, Information, and Other Returns.* Electing large partnerships required to file Form 1065-B, *U.S. Return of Income for Electing Large Partnerships,* will be allowed an automatic six-month extension of time to file the return by submitting an application on Form 7004. No further extension is allowed [Reg. § 1.6081-2].

A six-month extension is granted to partnerships that keep their records and books of account outside the United States and Puerto Rico. No application is required. Such partnerships may receive an additional extension by submitting Form 7004 [Reg. § 1.6081-5].

### XXIII.A.1.d.(3) Corporations

[634 T.M., II.; TPS ¶3820.02.F.]

A corporation (including an S corporation) or an affiliated group of corporations may obtain an automatic six-month extension of time for filing its income tax return by filing Form 7004, *Application for Automatic Extension of Time To File Certain Business Income Tax, Information, and Other Returns,* provided that the application is timely filed, properly signed, and a remittance is made of the amount of the tax properly estimated to be due [§ 6081(b); Reg. § 1.6081-3(a)]. For consolidated groups, the application must include a statement listing the name and address of each member of the affiliated group if the group will file a consolidated return [Reg. § 1.6081-3(a)(4)].

A six-month extension is granted to (i) domestic corporations that transact their business and keep their records and books of account outside the United States and Puerto Rico; (ii) foreign corporations that maintain an office or place of business within the United States; and (iii) domestic corporations whose principal income is from sources within the possessions of the United States.

### XXIII.A.1.d.(4) Estates and Trusts

[634 T.M., II.; TPS ¶3820.02.F.]

Estates and trusts that are required to file Form 1041, *U.S. Income Tax Return for Estates and Trusts*, are allowed an automatic five-month extension of time to file the return by submitting Form 7004, *Application for Automatic Extension of Time to File Certain Business Income Tax, Information, and Other Returns* [Reg. § 1.6081-6] (see XVIII.D.1.).

### XXIII.A.1.d.(5) Federally Declared Disasters

[627 T.M., I.E.18.; TPS ¶3820.02.F.5.]

In the case of a federally declared disaster, the IRS has the authority to postpone tax-related deadlines for affected taxpayers, including filing and paying tax, for a period of up to one year. The IRS also has the authority to suspend interest, penalties, additional amounts, and additions to tax that normally would accrue during the time the tax-related act is postponed [§ 7508A(a); Rev. Proc. 2007-56, 2007-34 I.R.B. 388].

When the original due date precedes the first day of the postponement period, and the extended due date falls within the postponement period, the following rules apply [Reg. § 301.7508A-1(b)(3)(ii)]:

- If an affected taxpayer received an extension of time to file, filing will be timely on or before the last day of the postponement period, and the taxpayer is eligible for relief from penalties and additions to tax related to the failure to file during the postponement period.

- If an affected taxpayer received an extension of time to pay, payment will be timely on or before the last day of the postponement period, and the taxpayer is eligible for relief from interest, penalties, and additions to tax and additional amounts related to the failure to pay during the postponement period.

An affected taxpayer is [Reg. § 301.7508A-1(d)(1)]:

- any individual whose principal residence is located in a covered disaster area;

- any individual who is a relief worker affiliated with a recognized government or philanthropic organization and who is assisting in a covered disaster area;

- any individual whose principal residence is not located in a covered disaster area, but whose records necessary to meet a deadline for a tax-related act are maintained in a covered disaster area;

- the spouse of an affected taxpayer, solely with regard to a joint return;

- any business entity or sole proprietor whose principal place of business is located in a covered disaster area;

- any individual, business entity, or sole proprietor not located in a covered disaster area, but whose records necessary to meet a deadline for a tax-related act are maintained in a covered disaster area;

- an estate or trust that has tax records necessary to meet a deadline for a tax-related act and that are maintained in a covered disaster area;

- any individual visiting the covered disaster area who was killed or injured as a result of the disaster; or

- any other person determined by the IRS to be affected by a federally declared disaster.

### *XXIII.A.1.d.(6) Terroristic and Military Actions*

[627 T.M., I.E.18.; TPS ¶3820.02.F.6.]

In the case of a terroristic or military action, the IRS has the authority to postpone tax-related deadlines for a period of up to one year, regardless of whether the federal government has declared a disaster area in connection with the action [§ 7508A(a); Rev. Proc. 2007-56, 2007-34 I.R.B. 388].

### *XXIII.A.1.d.(7) Service in a Combat Zone*

[627 T.M., I.E.19.; TPS ¶3820.02.F.7.]

Tax-related deadlines, including filing deadlines, are automatically extended for individual taxpayers serving in the Armed Forces, or in support of the Armed Services, in an area designated by the President as a combat zone (see II.M.1.), or who are deployed outside the United States away from his or her permanent duty station while participating in an operation designated as a contingency operation (or that became a contingency operation by operation of law), or hospitalized outside of the United States as a result of injury received in service in such area or operation [§ 7508(a); Rev. Proc. 2007-56, 2007-34 I.R.B. 388].

### *XXIII.A.1.e. Where to File*

[623 T.M., I.C.; TPS ¶3820.02.G.]

In general, returns must be filed with the designated IRS service center or hand-carried to the local IRS office. For a list of mailing addresses for filing individual returns, see *Schedules & Tables 6*. [§ 6091; Reg. § 1.6091-2]. However, if a return is required to be filed with a particular IRS service center, a return is not considered filed if it is mailed to the wrong center.

A taxpayer with no legal residence or principal place of business in an area covered by an IRS office may also file with a tax attache at a U.S. embassy.

Amended returns are generally filed in the same manner as the original returns to which they relate [Reg. § 1.6091-2(e)].

***Return Lost in Mail.*** If a return is mailed by the taxpayer by ordinary mail but is lost by the U.S. Postal Service before delivery to the IRS, the return is not deemed filed. The taxpayer bears the risk of nondelivery (see XXIII.A.1.c.(2)).

### *XXIII.A.1.f. Electronic Filing*

[620 T.M., 1:III.B.; TPS ¶3820.01.E.]

Individuals may file either paper income tax returns or file Forms 1040, 1040A, 1040-EZ, and 1040-NR electronically. However, neither amended returns nor late-filed returns can be filed electronically. The IRS provides four methods through which individuals can file over the internet using its e-file system:

- *Free File.* Individuals with income below a certain level (adjusted gross income of $60,000 for 2014 returns) can use a variety of free commercial tax preparation software online to prepare and file returns electronically. Some of the software also supports state returns. Free File is available at http://www.irs-.gov/uac/Free-File:-Do-Your-Federal-Taxes-for-Free.

- *IRS Free File Fillable Forms.* All taxpayers can use online fillable forms, also available at http://www.irs.gov/uac/Free-File:-Do-Your-Federal-Taxes-for-Free. Free File Fillable Forms uses a fill-in-the-blank format that performs some basic math calculations and provides for electronic filing. There are no income restrictions for using Free File Fillable Forms. It does not support any state tax returns.

- *Commercial Tax Software.* Most commercial tax preparation software also provides for electronic filing.
- *Paid Tax Preparer.* While the use of e-filing is optional for preparers who prepare a small number of returns each year, returns prepared by preparers who reasonably expect to file 11 or more returns for taxpayers must be filed electronically, unless the preparer obtains a hand-signed and dated statement containing the taxpayer's choice to have the return filed in paper format [§ 6011(e)(3); Reg. § 301.6011-7].

---

**EXAMPLE:** Tax return preparer X is an accountant who recently graduated from college with an accounting degree and has opened his own practice. X has not prepared individual income tax returns for compensation in the past and does not plan to focus his practice on individual income tax return preparation. X has no plans to, and does not, employ or engage any other tax return preparers. X estimates that he may be asked by some clients to prepare and file their individual income tax returns for compensation, but X expects that the number of people who do ask him to provide this service will be no more than seven in 2014. In fact, X actually prepares and files six paper Form 1040 (U.S. Individual Income Tax Return) returns in 2014. Due to a growing client base, and based upon his experience in 2014, X expects that the number of individual income tax returns he will prepare and file in 2015 will at least double. X is not required to electronically file the individual income tax returns he prepares and files in 2014. However, X must electronically file all individual income tax returns that he prepares and files in 2015 that are not otherwise excluded from the electronic filing requirement [Reg. § 301.6011-7(e), *Ex.* 1].

---

Rev. Proc. 2007-40, 2007-26 I.R.B. 1488, and Pub. 1345, *Handbook for Authorized IRS e-file Providers of Individual Income Tax Returns*, outline the requirements and procedures for participating in the IRS e-file program. Rev. Proc. 2000-24, 2000-22 I.R.B. 1133, provides guidance for electronic filing of Form 1040-NR.

*E-file Providers.* Individuals, businesses, and organizations that want to become "Authorized IRS e-file Providers" must apply for acceptance into the program by creating an IRS e-services account and submitting an e-file application on www.irs-.gov/Tax-Professionals/e-services---Online-Tools-for-Tax-Professionals, and must pass a suitability check.

Applicants may be rejected from the program for a variety of reasons, including [IRS Pub. 3112, *IRS e-file Application and Participation*]:

- conviction of a criminal tax offense;
- failure to file timely and accurate federal, state, or local tax returns due;
- failure to timely pay any federal, state, or local tax liabilities;
- assessment of penalties;
- suspension or disbarment from practice before the IRS or a state or local tax agency;
- disreputable conduct or other facts that may adversely impact the IRS e-file Program;
- misrepresentation on an application;
- unethical practices in return preparation;
- assessment against the applicant of a penalty for failing to be diligent in determining eligibility for the earned income credit;

- stockpiling returns before official acceptance into the program;
- knowingly and directly or indirectly employing or accepting assistance from any firm, organization, or individual that is denied participation in, or is suspended or expelled from, the program; and
- knowingly and directly or indirectly accepting employment as an associate, correspondent, or as a subagent from, or sharing fees with, any firm, organization, or individual that is denied participation in, or is suspended or expelled from, the program.

***Electronic Return Signatures.*** Taxpayers and the preparer/transmitter generally use Form 8879, *IRS e-file Signature Authorization,* to "sign" the return. Taxpayers either provide their own Personal Identification Number (PIN) or authorize the preparer/transmitter to generate a PIN on their behalf. The preparer/transmitter also must provide his Electronic Filing Identification Number (EFIN) and PIN before transmitting the completed return. Form 8879 is not mailed to the IRS but must be retained by the preparer for three years.

***Transmitting Paper Attachments and Other Documents.*** Form 8453, *U.S. Individual Income Tax Transmittal for an IRS e-file Return,* is used to send any required paper forms or supporting documentation that cannot be transmitted electronically. Electronic return preparers must mail Form 8453 to the IRS within three business days after receiving acknowledgement that the IRS has accepted the electronically filed return. Taxpayers that must mail in any documentation not listed on Form 8453 cannot file the return electronically.

***Payment.*** A taxpayer who electronically files a balance due return must pay any tax that is due. Failure to make full payment of any tax that is due on or before the due date of the return (without regard to extensions) will result in the imposition of interest and may result in the imposition of penalties. Taxpayers who e-file balance due returns may pay by electronic funds withdrawal, credit card, check (using Form 1040-V, *Payment Voucher*), or through the Electronic Federal Tax Payment System (EFTPS). Taxpayers may also request an installment agreement [IRS Pub. 1345].

***Refunds.*** An e-file preparer should advise the taxpayer of the option to receive a refund by paper check or direct deposit, and must accept any direct deposit election to any eligible financial institution designated by the taxpayer. A separate fee may not be charged for a direct deposit. The IRS has stated that neither it nor Treasury's Financial Management Service is responsible for the misapplication of a direct deposit that is caused by error, negligence, or malfeasance on the part of the taxpayer, electronic filer, financial institution, or any of their agents.

***Refund Anticipation Loans.*** A Refund Anticipation Loan (RAL) is money borrowed by a taxpayer based on the taxpayer's anticipated income tax refund. The IRS is not involved with RALs; rather, a RAL is a contract between the taxpayer and a lender. An entity that is involved in the IRS e-file program has an obligation to every taxpayer who applies for an RAL to advise the taxpayer as to the various aspects of RALs. Specifically, an e-file provider must advise the taxpayer that if a direct deposit is not timely, the taxpayer may be liable to the lender for additional interest on the RAL. In addition, electronic filers may assist taxpayers in applying for a RAL, and may charge a flat fee for doing so. The fee must be identical for all clients and must not be related to the amount of the refund or RAL. Electronic filers may not accept a fee from a financial institution for any service connected with an RAL that is contingent upon the amount of the refund or RAL. IRS e-file providers that assist taxpayers in applying for a RAL must obtain the taxpayer's written consent to disclose tax information to the lending financial institution in connection with an application for an RAL [Reg. § 301.7216-3(b)].

Corporations may file either paper income tax returns or file electronically. However, corporations (including S corporations) with assets of $10 million or more that are required to file at least 250 returns (including information returns such as Forms W-2 and 1099) must file using magnetic media [Reg. § 301.6011-5].

### XXIII.A.1.g. Signature Requirement

[634 T.M., II.B.3.b.; TPS ¶3820.01.B.2.]

To be valid, a return must contain the signature of the taxpayer or an authorized person attesting that the return is made under the penalties of perjury [§ 6065]. A return not supported by an oath is not a valid return. A signature on a tax return is prima facie (but not conclusive) evidence that the signer has knowledge of the contents of the return.

A return can be signed by an agent of an individual taxpayer. For example, an authorized representative may sign for the taxpayer when the taxpayer is ill or will be absent from the country for at least 60 days before the return is due [Reg. § 1.6012-1(a)(5)]. The agent must have a power of attorney except that, with oral consent, a spouse may sign the incapacitated taxpayer's name followed by the words: "By [Name], Husband (or Wife)." A dated statement must be attached to the return signed by the spouse who is signing the return and must contain the name of the return being filed, the tax year, the reason for the inability of the spouse who is incapacitated to sign the return, and that the spouse who is incapacitated consented to the signing of the return.

If a decedent taxpayer dies intestate, the transferee of the decedent's property may sign the decedent's unfiled returns without proof of authority if there is a balance due; however, proof of authority may be needed for a return claiming an overpayment [CCA 201334040].

In the case of a timely but unsigned return, IRS policy generally is not to consider such returns delinquent if the taxpayer files a signed return after the IRS's request for signature [IRS Policy Statement P-3-5 (7-26-11)].

### XXIII.A.1.h. Payment of Tax

[539 T.M., VIII.A.1.c.; TPS ¶3820.02.H.]

Income taxes are generally due and payable at the time and place fixed for filing returns. The granting of an extension of time for filing of the return generally does not postpone the date for payment [§ 6151(a)]. However, for individuals who elect to have their tax computed by the IRS, payment is not required until 30 days after the IRS mails a notice to the taxpayer of the amount due and demands payment [§ 6151(b)].

The IRS will accept payment by any commercially acceptable means, i.e., check, draft, money order, or other means of payment guaranteed by a U.S. financial institutions and collectible in U.S. currency [§ 6311]. This includes payment of taxes by credit card or debit card as prescribed by the IRS. If the taxpayer pays the tax by credit card or debit card, payment is deemed made when the issuer of the credit card or debit card properly authorizes the transaction, provided the payment is actually received by the United States in the ordinary course of business and is not returned [Reg. § 301.6311-2].

Special rules regarding creditor status, billing error resolution, and privacy protections apply to the use of a credit or debit card transaction to pay taxes. The IRS is not considered a creditor under the Truth in Lending Act (TILA). If there is a billing error or dispute, the payment is not subject to TILA, the Electronic Fund Transfer Act (EFTA), or any similar state law provisions, if the error alleged relates to the underlying tax liability instead of either an account-related error, such as improper computation or numerical transposition, or a payment authorization issue [§ 6311(d)(3)].

***Corporate NOL Carrybacks***. Corporations expecting a net operating loss carryback may obtain an extension of time for payment of tax. If a corporation in any tax year files a statement with the IRS on Form 1138, *Extension of Time for Payment of Taxes By a Corporation Expecting a Net Operating Loss Carryback*, the corporation can obtain an extension of time for payment of any tax due for the immediately preceding tax year equal to the reduction of tax attributable to the expected carryback. The statement must include the following information [§ 6164(a); Reg. § 1.6164-1(b)(1)]:

- the estimated amount of the expected net operating loss;
- the facts and circumstances that caused the loss;
- the amount of the reduction in tax that is attributable to the expected loss carryback; and
- the portion of the tax on which payment is to be extended.

### XXIII.A.1.i. Recordkeeping Requirement

[626 T.M., III.G.3.; TPS ¶3850.]

Every person liable for any federal tax or its collection is required to keep records, render statements, file returns and comply with such rules and regulations as prescribed by the IRS [§ 6001]. For example, taxpayers must maintain adequate books and records to substantiate claimed deductions (see IV.C.). Records must be retained as long as they may be considered material in the administration of the tax law [Reg. § 1.6001-1(e)]. At a minimum, taxpayers should retain records that support items shown on a return until the period of limitations for that return expires (see XXIII.C.3.). Records that support continuing items, such as tax basis, should be kept for longer periods.

### XXIII.A.2. Frequently Filed Information Returns

[643 T.M.; TPS ¶3820.05.]

The Code requires payers of income and certain other persons to report a wide range of transactions. This section discusses some of the more common information return requirements. Information returns relating to foreign transactions are discussed in Chapter XX. Employment tax information returns are discussed in XXII.C.1.c. A guide to information returns is in *Schedules & Tables 21*.

### XXIII.A.2.a. Dividends and Other Reportable Payments

[643 T.M., III.A., III.B., III.C.; TPS ¶3820.05.C.1.]

***Dividends and Other Corporate Distributions***. Corporations must report dividend distributions of $10 or more during a calendar year on Form 1099-DIV, *Dividends and Distributions*. Distributions that must be reported include all distributions (in cash or stock) to shareholders that are made out of current or accumulated earnings and profits, and received from either a domestic corporation or qualified foreign corporation [§ 6042(a)]. Distributions that constitute a return of capital are not reportable [Reg. § 1.6042-3(a)]. However, if the payer cannot determine with certainty the portion of the payment that is attributable to capital at the time the information return is filed, the entire payment must be treated as a dividend [§ 6042(b)(3); Reg. § 1.6042-3(c)]. Payments made by a stock broker to any person as a substitute for a dividend (including dividends received on stock borrowed to cover short sales) must also be reported [§ 6042(b)(1)].

***Dividends Not Subject to Reporting.*** Distributions or payments by a foreign corporation need not be reported if the corporation is not engaged in business within the United States, and does not have an office or place of business or a paying agent in the United States [Reg. § 1.6042-3(b)(1)]. Payments or distributions to (i) a state or local government (including any agencies thereof), (ii) a corporation, (iii) an exempt organization, (iv) a real estate investment trust or a regulated investment company, or (v) a dealer in securities registered under federal or state securities laws are not required to be reported [§ 6042(b)(2)(B), § 6049(b)(4)].

***Dividends-in-Kind.*** Dividends paid in property, such as the shares of stock of a corporation, are reportable on information returns. The reportable amount is the fair market value of the property as of the date of the distribution if the shareholder recipient is an individual, partnership, trust or estate, or corporation [§ 6042(b)(1)(A)].

***Corporate Liquidating Distributions and Redemptions.*** Distributions, in partial or complete liquidation or redemption of a corporation, of $600 or more during the calendar year to any shareholder must be reported on Form 1099-DIV [§ 6043].

***Patronage Dividends.*** Farm cooperatives and other cooperative corporations that make payments of $10 or more to any person during a calendar year must file Form 1099-PATR, *Taxable Distributions Received from Cooperatives* [§ 6044].

### XXIII.A.2.b. Information Reporting for Interest

[643 T.M., III.A., III.B., III.C.; TPS ¶3820.05.C.2.]

Every person who makes payments of interest aggregating $10 or more to any other person during a calendar year, or who receives payments of interest as a nominee and makes payments aggregating $10 or more to any other person during a calendar year, is required to file an annual information return on Form 1099-INT, *Interest Income* [§ 6049(a)]. For this purpose, interest includes [§ 6049(b)]:

- interest on any obligation (evidence of indebtedness) issued by a corporation in registered form or of a type offered to the public;
- interest on bank deposits;
- amounts paid by mutual savings banks, savings and loan associations, building and loan companies, credit unions, or similar organizations on deposits, shares, or investment certificates (whether or not such payments are designated as interest);
- interest on amounts held by insurance companies;
- interest on deposits with stockbrokers;
- interest paid on amounts held by investment companies and securities dealers;
- amounts includible in gross income for regular interests in REMICs;
- the amount of credit allowed on a clean renewable energy bond; and
- amounts includible in gross income for holders of qualified tax credit bonds.

***Interest Exempt from Reporting.*** For purposes of information reporting, the term "interest" does not include (i) interest on any note or other obligation issued by an individual not engaged in a trade or business, or (ii) any amount paid to one of the following [§ 6049(b)(2)]:

- a corporation;
- an exempt organization;
- the United States or any wholly owned agency thereof;
- a state or its political subdivision;
- a foreign government or political subdivision thereof;
- a registered securities or commodities dealer; or
- a real estate investment trust.

*Original Issue Discount.* The issuer of any bond or other evidence of indebtedness in registered or bearer form issued with original issue discount is required to file Form 1099-OID, *Original Issue Discount*, for each holder of this debt required to include in gross income at least $10 in OID [Reg. § 1.6049-4].

### XXIII.A.2.c. Information Reporting for Miscellaneous Income

[643 T.M., III.E.; TPS ¶3820.05.D.]

Every person engaged in a trade or business must file an information return Form 1099-MISC, *Miscellaneous Income*, if, in the course of the trade or business, payments are made to another person for "rents, salaries, wages, premiums, annuities, compensation, emoluments, or other fixed or determinable gains, profits or income" of $600 or more in any tax year. This includes payments for services performed for a trade or business by individuals who are not treated as employees, as well as prizes and awards. The return must show (i) the amount of the gains or income, and (ii) the name and address of the recipient of the payment [§ 6041(a)]. The payer also must furnish a written statement to each payee whose name is reported in an information return filed with the IRS [§ 6041(d)]. The statement, which is to be provided by January 31 of the year following the calendar year in which the payments are made, must contain the name, address, and telephone number of the person filing the return and the aggregate amount of payments shown thereon.

Any person who must furnish statements to recipients may do so electronically, provided the recipient has consented to receive the statement electronically. The statement may be furnished in a manner similar to the one permitted for Form W-2 or in another manner provided by IRS.

The following payments are exempt from reporting requirements [Reg. § 1.6041-3]:

- payments to corporations (other than payments of attorneys' fees and payments for medical and health care services);
- income earned outside the United States and excludible under the law;
- salaries and profits distributed by partnerships to their partners;
- reimbursed travel or business expenses, if the employee accounts to the employer;
- payments of wages and other income required to be reported on Form W-2, *Wage and Tax Statement*, or other forms;
- payments by a broker to a customer;
- payments made to corporations (except for attorneys' fees, medical and health insurance payments, and patronage dividends);
- payments for merchandise, freight, storage and similar charges;
- payments of rent made to real estate agents;

- payments representing earned income for services rendered outside of the United States and made to a U.S. citizen, if such amounts are excludible from gross income under the foreign earned income exclusion;
- payment of salaries and profits by a partnership to its individual partners;
- payments of interest on corporate bonds;
- payments of commissions to general agents by fire insurance companies or other companies insuring property, except when specifically directed by the IRS to be filed;
- payments made under reimbursement or other expense allowance arrangements;
- payments for medical care under a flexible spending arrangement or a health reimbursement arrangement that is treated as employer-provided coverage under an accident or health plan;
- payments of interest on obligations of the United States, or a state, territory, or political subdivision, or the District of Columbia;
- payments made to employees for services performed in Puerto Rico;
- payments made as an allowance or reimbursement for traveling or other bona fide ordinary and necessary expenses;
- payments to an informant as an award, fee, or reward for information relating to criminal activity;
- payments by a person carrying on the banking business of interest on a deposit evidenced by a negotiable time certificate of deposit;
- payments made to principals by persons carrying on the banking business, and by persons which are mutual savings banks, cooperative banks, building and loan associations, homestead associations, credit unions, or similar organizations chartered and supervised by law, of funds collected when acting in the capacity of collection agents;
- payments made under legislatively provided social benefit programs for the promotion of general welfare that are not includible in gross income; and
- payments made under structured settlement arrangements to personal injury claimants.

*Payments to Attorneys*. Payers making payments in the course of their trade or business to attorneys in connection with legal services generally must file Form 1099-MISC if the payments total $600 or more during a calendar year (whether or not such services are performed for the payer) [§ 6045(f)].

### XXIII.A.2.d. Information Reporting by Brokers

[643 T.M., III.D.; TPS ¶3820.05.F.]

Every person doing business as a broker is required to file Form 1099-B, *Proceeds from Broker and Barter Exchange Transactions*, for each sale by a customer of the broker in the ordinary course of its brokerage business. The broker must file a Form 1099-B showing the name, address, and TIN of the customer for whom the sale was effected, the property sold, the CUSIP number (if known), the gross proceeds, and the date of the sale [§ 6045].

The term "broker" includes a dealer, a barter exchange, and any other person who (for consideration) regularly acts as a middleman for property or services. The term can include real estate brokers [§ 6045(c)(1)].

For purposes of the broker reporting requirements, the term "sale" means any disposition for cash of securities, commodities, regulated futures contracts, or forward contracts, and includes redemptions of stock, retirements of indebtedness, and short sales when conducted for cash. However, grants or purchases of options, exercises of call options, or enterings into contracts that require delivery of personal property or an interest in personal property are not treated as sales and are not required to be reported [Reg. § 1.6045-1(a)(9)].

Real estate transactions must be reported on Form 1099-S, *Proceeds from Real Estate Transactions*, and a written statement furnished to the seller. The reporting requirement falls upon one of the following persons involved in the real estate transaction, in the following order [§ 6045(c)(1)]:

1. the person (including any attorney or title company) responsible for closing the transaction;

2. the mortgage lender;

3. the seller's broker;

4. the buyer's broker; or

5. the buyer.

### XXIII.A.2.e. Other Information Returns

[644 T.M.; TPS ¶3820.05.G.]

***Mortgage Interest and Mortgage Insurance Premiums***. Any person who, in the course of a trade or business, receives mortgage interest aggregating $600 or more for any calendar year on any one mortgage from any individual must file Form 1098, *Mortgage Interest Statement*, and furnish a statement to the payer [§ 6050H(a); Reg. § 1.6050H-1(a), § 1.6050H-2(a)]. The reporting requirement also applies to persons who receive premiums (including prepaid premiums) for mortgage insurance from any individual aggregating $600 or more for any calendar year [§ 6050H(h)].

***Receipt of Cash of More than $10,000***. Any person engaged in a trade or business who, in the course of such trade or business, receives more than $10,000 in cash in one transaction (or two or more related transactions) must file Form 8300, *Report of Cash Payments Over $10,000 Received in a Trade or Business*, and furnish a written statement to the payer [§ 6050I].

***Cancellation of Indebtedness by Financial Institutions***. Certain financial institutions (including finance companies and credit card companies), government agencies, and organizations that discharge the indebtedness of any person during any calendar year in the amount of $600 or more must file Form 1099-C, *Cancellation of Debt*, showing the name, address, and taxpayer identification number of each person whose indebtedness was discharged during the calendar year, the date of the discharge, and the amount of the indebtedness discharged. Organizations must have a significant money-lending business to be required to file Form 1099-C [§ 6050P].

***Long-Term Care Benefits***. Any person who pays long-term care benefits must file Form 1099-LTC, *Long Term Care and Accelerated Death Benefits*, and provide a payee statement to the recipient of the benefits [§ 6050Q].

***Higher Education and Tuition Related Expenses***. The following must file Form 1098-T, *Tuition Statement*, annually and provide each student with a statement [§ 6050S]:

- an eligible educational institution that: (i) receives payments of qualified tuition and related expenses, (ii) makes reimbursements or refunds of qualified tuition and related expenses, or (iii) enrolls any individual for any academic period;

- any person engaged in a trade or business of making payments to any individual under an insurance arrangement as reimbursements or refunds of qualified tuition and related expenses; and

- any person engaged in a trade or business that, in the course of such trade or business, receives from any individual interest aggregating $600 or more for any calendar year on one or more educational loans.

### XXIII.A.2.f. False Information Returns

[637 T.M., VI.C.; TPS ¶3820.05.H.]

If any person willfully files a fraudulent information return reporting payments purportedly made to a taxpayer, the taxpayer can bring a civil action for damages against the person filing the information return [§ 7434(a)]. A taxpayer can recover the greater of [§ 7434(b)]:

- $5,000; or

- the sum of any actual damages sustained as a proximate result of the filing of the fraudulent information return (including costs incurred in resolving with the IRS any deficiency asserted as a result of the filing), the costs of the action, and reasonable attorney's fees.

This type of action must be brought within the later of six years from the date of the filing of the fraudulent information return or one year after the false return would have been discovered by exercise of reasonable care [§ 7434(c)].

### XXIII.A.3. Confidentiality and Disclosure of Returns and Return Information

[625 T.M., 626 T.M.; TPS ¶3823.]

As a general rule, returns and return information are confidential, and except as specifically excepted, no officer or employee of the United States may disclose any return or return information [§ 6103(a)].

For purposes of the disclosure rules, a return means any tax or information return, declaration of estimated tax or claim for refund, and any amendment or supplement thereto, including supporting schedules, attachments, or lists that are part of the return [§ 6103(b)(1)]. Return information includes [§ 6103(b)(2)]:

- the taxpayer's identity, including name, address, and taxpayer identification number;

- the nature, source, or amount of the taxpayer's income, payments, receipts, deductions, exemptions, credits, assets, liabilities, net worth, tax liability, tax withheld, deficiencies, overassessments, or tax payments;

- whether the taxpayer's return is being audited or otherwise investigated;

- any other data received, recorded, prepared, furnished, or collected by the IRS with respect to a return or the determination of a tax liability;

- any information the IRS obtains from any source or develops through any means that relates to a taxpayer's return or to the liability or potential liability of any person under the internal revenue laws for any tax, penalty, interest, fine, forfeiture or other imposition or offense;

- any part of any written determination (e.g., a private letter ruling, determination letter, or technical advice memorandum) or background file document relating to such written determination that is not open to public inspection;

- any advance pricing agreement (APA) that a taxpayer enters into with the IRS, any background information related to the APA, or any application for an APA; and

- any closing agreement or similar agreement, and any background information related to such an agreement or request for such an agreement.

***Exceptions to Disclosure Prohibition.*** The IRS can disclose returns and return information to certain entities and persons for specific purposes. These include [§ 6103]:

- disclosures to other governmental agencies (such as state tax officials) for tax administration purposes and other specified uses, including the investigation of and response to terrorist activities;

- disclosures to members of the public when required for tax administration purposes (such as investigations or tax collection activities);

- disclosures of tax returns and tax information to the taxpayer, the taxpayer's designee, and to certain other persons having a material interest (as defined in § 6103(e)).

***Liability for Disclosure of Return/Return Information.*** A taxpayer may bring a federal district court action for damages against the United States if any officer or employee of the United States knowingly or negligently discloses any return or return information of the taxpayer in violation of § 6103. A cause of action also may be brought against any person who is not an officer or employee of the United States who knowingly or negligently discloses any return or return information of a taxpayer [§ 7431].

The amount of damages recoverable is the sum of (i) the greater of $1,000 for each act of unauthorized disclosure, or the sum of the actual damages plus punitive damages in the case of a willful or grossly negligent disclosure, (ii) the costs of the action, and (iii) in some cases, reasonable attorney's fees [§ 7431(c)].

A wrongful disclosure of confidential information by the IRS may also constitute a crime. Current or former IRS employees are subject to a fine not exceeding $5,000 or imprisonment of up to five years, or both [§ 7213].

### XXIII.A.4. Return Preparers and Preparer Penalties

### XXIII.A.4.a. Definition of Return Preparer for Purposes of Return Preparer Rules

[634 T.M., VII.A.; TPS ¶3830.10.A.]

A tax return preparer is any person who prepares for compensation (or who employs one or more persons who prepare for compensation) a tax return or a claim for refund. A person is deemed to be a tax return preparer if he or she prepares a "substantial portion" of a return or refund claim [§ 7701(a)(36)(A); Reg. § 301.7701-15(a)]. Preparers outside the United States are included, regardless of the person's nationality, residence, or business location if the person otherwise meets the definition [Reg. § 301.7701-15(e)]. The term also includes persons engaged in other businesses who prepare returns as part of a "package deal" in lieu of payment for their goods or services, or who prepare returns and purchase refunds at a discount [Rev. Rul. 86-55, 1986-1 C.B. 373]. Certain persons are excluded from the definition of income tax return preparer, including Volunteer Income Tax Assistance programs and their volunteers, and low-income taxpayer clinics and their employees or volunteers [Reg. § 301.7701-15(f)].

A person is not a tax return preparer merely because he or she (i) furnishes typing, or other mechanical assistance, (ii) prepares a return or claim for refund for an employer (or employees of an employer) by whom the taxpayer is regularly and continuously employed, (iii) prepares as a fiduciary of a trust or estate any return or claim for refund, or (iv) prepares a claim for refund for a taxpayer in response to a notice of deficiency issued to the taxpayer or in response to any waiver of restriction after the commencement of an audit of the taxpayer [§ 7701(a)(36)(B)].

***Signing v. Non-Signing Tax Return Preparer.*** A "signing tax return preparer" is any tax return preparer who signs, or who is required to sign, a return or claim for refund as a tax return preparer. The signing tax return preparer is the individual preparer who has the primary responsibility for the overall substantive accuracy of the preparation of the return or refund claim [Reg. § 301.7701-15(b)(1)]. A "non-signing tax return preparer" is any tax return preparer who is not a signing tax return preparer but who prepares all or a substantial portion of a return or claim for refund with respect to events that have occurred at the time the advice is rendered [Reg. § 301.7701-15(b)(2)]. For purposes of the penalty, only one individual associated with a firm can be a preparer. For example, if the preparer who signs the return is associated with a firm, that individual — and no other individual associated with the firm — is deemed to be the preparer. A person can be a return preparer even if he or she does not sign the return. If two or more individuals can be treated as the tax return preparer but neither has signed the return or refund claim, only one can be the preparer. In such cases, the individual with overall supervisory responsibility for the position giving rise to the understatement generally will be considered to be the preparer [Reg. § 1.6694-1(b)].

### XXIII.A.4.b. Understatement of Taxpayer's Liability by Return Preparer

### XXIII.A.4.b.(1) Imposition of Penalty for Understatement of Taxpayer's Liability by Return Preparer

[634 T.M., VII.C.; TPS ¶3830.10.A.]

The IRS may impose a penalty against a return preparer if any part of an understatement on a tax return or refund claim was due to an "unreasonable" position and the return preparer knew or should have known of the position. A position that was "adequately disclosed" is considered to be unreasonable unless there was a "reasonable basis" for the position. A position that is not disclosed on the return is considered to be unreasonable unless there was "substantial authority" for the position. In the case of tax shelters and reportable transactions, a position is considered to be unreasonable unless there was a "reasonable belief" that the position would "more likely than not" be sustained on its merits. The penalty is equal to the greater of (i) $1,000, or (ii) 50% of the income derived (or to be derived) by the preparer with respect to the return or claim. No penalty will be imposed if the preparer can establish reasonable cause for the understatement and that the preparer acted in good faith [§ 6694(a)]. The penalty increases to the greater of (i) $5,000 or (ii) 50% of the income derived (or to be derived) by the preparer with respect to the return or claim if the understatement was due to willful conduct or a reckless or intentional disregard of rules or regulations [§ 6694(b)].

***Reliance on Taxpayer's Information/Duty to Verify.*** A return preparer generally may rely in good faith upon information furnished by the taxpayer. A preparer also may rely in good faith and without verification on information and advice provided by another advisor, another return preparer, or other party (including another advisor or return preparer at the preparer's firm). The preparer is not required to verify independently the taxpayer's information; therefore, the preparer is not required to audit, examine, or review books and records, other documents, or the taxpayer's business operations. However, the preparer cannot ignore the implications of information furnished either by the taxpayer or others. If such information appears to be incorrect or incomplete, the preparer must make reasonable inquiries. If a Code section requires that the taxpayer have specific documents before claiming deductions, the return preparer must make appropriate inquiries to determine whether such documents exist as a condition to claiming the deduction [Reg. § 1.6694-1(e)(1)].

*Reasonable Belief/More Likely than Not Standards*. The preparer penalty applies if the tax return preparer knew (or reasonably should have known) of the position and either (i) the position is with respect to a tax shelter or a reportable transaction to which § 6662A applies, and it was not reasonable to believe that the position would "more likely than not" be sustained on its merits, (ii) for an undisclosed position, there was not "substantial authority," or (iii) for a disclosed position, there was no "reasonable basis" for the position.

The "reasonable belief that the position would more likely than not be sustained on its merits" standard will be satisfied if the tax return preparer analyzes the pertinent facts and authorities and, in reliance upon that analysis, reasonably concludes in good faith that the position has a greater than 50% likelihood of being sustained on its merits, based on all the facts and circumstances. A preparer's diligence, in turn, will be determined taking into account the preparer's experience with the area of tax law and familiarity with the taxpayer's affairs, as well as the complexity of the issues and facts in the case. A tax return preparer may meet the reasonable belief standard if a position is supported by a well-reasoned construction of the applicable statutory provision despite the absence of other types of authority, or if the return preparer relies on information or advice furnished by a taxpayer, advisor, another tax return preparer, or other party (even when the advisor or tax return preparer is within the tax return preparer's same firm [Reg. § 1.6694-2(b)(1)].

### XXIII.A.4.b.(2) Adequate Disclosure to Avoid Preparer Penalty

[634 T.M., VII.C.3.e.; TPS ¶3830.10.A.5.b.]

For a signing preparer, a position may be disclosed in one of three ways [Reg. § 1.6694-2(d)(3)(i)]:

1. The position may be disclosed on a properly completed and filed Form 8275, *Disclosure Statement*, or Form 8275-R, *Regulation Disclosure Statement*, as appropriate, or on the tax return in accordance with an annual revenue procedure [Rev. Proc. 2014-15, 2014-5 I.R.B. 456].

2. If the position does not meet the "substantial authority" threshold, disclosure of the position is adequate if the tax return preparer provides the taxpayer with a prepared tax return that includes the appropriate disclosure.

3. For tax returns or claims for refund that are subject to penalties other than the accuracy-related penalty for substantial understatements under § 6662(b)(2) and § 6662(d), the tax return preparer advises the taxpayer of the penalty standards applicable to the taxpayer under § 6662.

For a non-signing preparer, the position may be disclosed in one of three ways [Reg. § 1.6694-2(c)(3)(ii)]:

1. The position may be disclosed on a properly completed and filed Form 8275 or Form 8275-R, or in accordance with the annual revenue procedure (e.g., Rev. Proc. 2014-15).

2. A non-signing tax return preparer may meet the disclosure standards if he/she advises the taxpayer of all opportunities to avoid penalties under § 6662 that could apply to the position and advises the taxpayer of the standards for disclosure to the extent applicable.

3. Disclosure of a position is adequate if a non-signing tax return preparer advises another tax return preparer that disclosure under § 6694(a) may be required.

### XXIII.A.4.b.(3) Reasonable Cause to Avoid Penalty

[634 T.M., VII.C.3.e.; TPS ¶3830.10.A.7.]

The IRS may decline to impose the return preparer penalty if, after considering the facts and circumstances, the understatement was due to reasonable cause, and the preparer acted in good faith, using the following factors [Reg. § 1.6694-2(d)]:

- the nature of the error that caused the understatement;
- the frequency of errors;
- the materiality of errors;
- the preparer's normal office practice;
- reliance on the advice of another preparer; and
- the preparer's reliance on a generally accepted administrative or industry practice.

### XXIII.A.4.b.(4) Preparer Penalty Due to Willful, Reckless, or Intentional Conduct

[634 T.M., VII.C.4.; TPS ¶3830.10.A.8.]

The preparer understatement penalty increases to the greater of (i) $5,000, or (ii) 50% of the income derived (or to be derived) by the preparer for the return or claim if the understatement was due to willful conduct or a reckless or intentional disregard of rules or regulations. A preparer willfully attempts to understate tax liability if he or she disregards information furnished by the taxpayer or by other persons, so as to reduce the taxpayer's tax liability. A reckless or intentional disregard of a rule or regulation occurs if the preparer takes a position on a return or refund claim that is contrary to provisions of the Code, temporary or final Treasury regulations, or revenue rulings or other IRS published guidance. Ignorance of the rule or regulation is no excuse if the preparer makes little or no effort to determine whether such a rule or regulation exists [§ 6694(b)].

### XXIII.A.4.b.(5) Assessment, Collection, and Refund of Penalty

[634 T.M., VII.C.10.; TPS ¶3830.10.A.9.]

The preparer penalties may be assessed without regard to the notice of deficiency procedures. The general preparer understatement penalty must be assessed within three years after the related return is filed. The increased preparer understatement penalty for a willful understatement can be assessed at any time [§ 6696(b)].

### XXIII.A.4.c. Other Assessable Penalties Against Return Preparers

### XXIII.A.4.c.(1) Penalty for Failure to Furnish Copy of Return to Taxpayer

[634 T.M., VII.E.3.; TPS ¶3830.10.B.1.]

An income tax return preparer must furnish the taxpayer with a completed copy of the income tax return or claim for refund no later than the time the original return or claim for refund is presented to the taxpayer for signature [§ 6107(a)]. The preparer must provide a complete copy of the return or refund claim filed with the IRS to the taxpayer in any media (including electronic) that is acceptable to both the preparer and the taxpayer. For an electronically filed return, a complete copy consists of the electronic portion of the return or refund claim, including all schedules, forms, .pdf attachments, and jurats, that was filed with the IRS. The copy provided to the taxpayer must include all of the information submitted to the IRS to enable the taxpayer to determine what schedules, forms, electronic files, and other supporting materials have been filed with the return [Reg. § 1.6107-1(a)].

A preparer who fails to provide a copy of the return or claim at the appropriate time is subject to a penalty of $50 for each such failure, up to a maximum of $25,000 per calendar year, unless the failure is due to reasonable cause [§ 6695(a)].

### XXIII.A.4.c.(2)  Failure to Sign Return

[634 T.M., VII.E.1.; TPS ¶3830.10.B.2.]

Return preparers are required to sign returns that they prepare [Reg. § 1.6695-1(b)(1)]. For electronically filed returns, tax return preparers may use signature methods other than traditional pen-to-paper signature or facsimile signature stamps (e.g., electronic or digital methods). For example, the return preparer may sign original returns, amended returns, and requests for filing extensions using a rubber stamp, mechanical device, or computer software program, provided that either a facsimile of the individual preparer's signature or the printed name is included [Reg. § 1.6695-1(b)(2)]. The information may be provided on a replica of an official form. If more than one preparer is involved, the preparer who must sign the return is the preparer who has the primary responsibility for the overall substantive accuracy of the preparation of the return [Reg. § 1.6695-1(b)(4), *Ex.* 1].

Failure to sign a return subjects the preparer to a penalty of $50 for each such failure, up to a maximum of $25,000 per calendar year, unless the failure is due to reasonable cause [§ 6695(b)].

### XXIII.A.4.c.(3)  Failure to Furnish Identification Number

[634 T.M., VII.E.2.; TPS ¶3830.10.B.3.]

A preparer must provide his or her tax identification number and that of his or her employer (if applicable) on the return or refund claim that is filed with the IRS [§ 6109(a)(4)]. This number is generally a preparer tax identification number (PTIN). The preparer may request a PTIN on Form W-7P or electronically from the IRS. [Reg. § 1.6109-2(a)].

Failure to furnish the identifying number subjects the preparer to a penalty of $50 for each such failure, up to a maximum of $25,000 per calendar year, unless the failure is due to reasonable cause [§ 6695(c)].

### XXIII.A.4.c.(4)  Failure to Retain Copy or List

[634 T.M., VII.E.4.; TPS ¶3830.10.B.4.]

An income tax return preparer must (i) retain a completed copy of each return or refund claim or retain a record or list of the name, TIN number, the tax year and type of return for each taxpayer for whom a return or claim was prepared, (ii) retain a record, for each return or refund claim presented to the taxpayer, of the name of the individual preparer required to sign the return or refund claim, and (iii) upon request by the IRS, make available the copy or record of returns and refund claims or the record of the individuals required to sign [§ 6107(b)]. The copy of each return or claim for refund or list of names must be maintained for at least three years after the close of the return period. The preparer may retain a photocopy of the return or claim or may use an electronic (paperless) storage system that meets IRS requirements [Reg. § 1.6107-2].

A penalty of $50 is imposed for each failure, up to $25,000 for any return period, unless the failure is due to reasonable cause and not willful neglect [§ 6695(d)].

### XXIII.A.4.c.(5) Failure to File Correct Information Returns

[634 T.M., VII.E.5.; TPS ¶3830.10.B.5.]

Employers of income tax return preparers are required to retain (and make available to the IRS on request) a record of the preparers employed or engaged during a return period [§ 6060]. A penalty of $50, up to a maximum of $25,000, is imposed on each failure to file a return as required or to include required information in a return unless the failure is due to reasonable cause [§ 6695(e)].

### XXIII.A.4.c.(6) Penalty for Negotiating Check Issued to Taxpayer

[634 T.M., VII.E.7.; TPS ¶3830.10.B.6.]

If a return preparer endorses or otherwise negotiates a check issued to the taxpayer with respect to a return or refund claim prepared by him, a $500 penalty is imposed for each such check [§ 6695(f)]. However, the penalty does not apply solely as a result of the preparer having affixed the taxpayer's name to a refund check for the purpose of depositing the check into the taxpayer's account if authorized by the taxpayer or the taxpayer's representative [Reg. § 1.6695-1(f)(1)].

### XXIII.A.4.c.(7) Penalty for Disclosing Return Information

[634 T.M., VII.G.2.; TPS ¶3830.10.B.7.]

A return preparer who discloses any information furnished to him or her for, or in connection with, the preparation of a return, or who uses any information provided for any purpose other than to prepare or assist in preparing the return, is subject to a penalty of $250 for each such disclosure or use, but the total penalty imposed in any calendar year shall not exceed $10,000 [§ 6713].

### XXIII.A.4.c.(8) Failing to Exercise Due Diligence in Determining Eligibility for Earned Income Credit

[634 T.M., VII.E.6.; TPS ¶3830.10.B.8.]

A paid tax return preparer who fails to comply with the due diligence requirements for determining a taxpayer's eligibility for, or amount of, the earned income credit is subject to a $100 penalty for each such failure [§ 6695(g)]. To avoid the penalty, the return preparer must complete Form 8867, *Paid Preparer's Earned Income Credit Checklist*, and (i) in the case of a signing tax return preparer filing the return or refund claim electronically, electronically file the completed Form 8867 with the tax return or refund claim, (ii) in the case of a signing tax return preparer not electronically filing a return or refund claim, provide the taxpayer with the completed paper Form 8867 for inclusion with the filed return or refund claim, or (iii) in the case of a non-signing tax return preparer, provide the signing tax return preparer with the completed Form 8867 in either electronic or paper format for inclusion with the filed tax return or refund claim [Reg. § 1.6695-2(b)(1)].

## XXIII.B. Excise Taxes

[623 T.M., I.C.4.; TPS ¶3820.03.E.]

Taxpayers subject to environmental, fuel, manufacturer, and retail excise taxes, communications and air transportation excise taxes, and a variety of miscellaneous excise taxes must file Form 720, *Quarterly Federal Excise Tax Return*. Additionally, various excise taxes are imposed on taxpayers who engage in prohibited transactions between a disqualified person and a qualified plan; who fail to meet minimum funding standards; or who make excess contributions for tax-sheltered annuity plan investments in mutual funds. Form 5330, *Return of Excise Taxes Related to Employee Benefit Plans*, must be filed to report these excise taxes. Form 5329, *Additional Taxes on Qualified Plans (including IRAs) and Other Tax Favored Accounts*, is used to report excise taxes imposed on taxpayers who make excess payments to IRAs (see XVII.A.5.e.). An annual return on Form 4720, *Return of Certain Excise Taxes Under Chapters 41 and 42 of the Internal Revenue Code*, must be filed by every foundation manager or other person who is subject to the tax on self-dealing, the tax on failure to distribute income, the tax on excess business holdings, the tax on investments which jeopardize charitable purposes, or the tax on taxable expenditures.

For a complete list of excise taxes and their filing and payment requirements, see *Schedules & Tables 14*.

## XXIII.C. Assessment and Collection of Tax

### XXIII.C.1. Examination: Audits, Assessments, Appeals

[623 T.M.; TPS ¶3850.]

Under the self-assessment system of federal income, taxpayers are required to fill out tax returns, determine their own tax liabilities, file the returns, and pay the tax shown on the returns. The vast majority of income tax returns and tax liabilities reported are accepted by the IRS after preliminary screening without being subjected to audit. Examinations of those returns that are selected for audit are conducted by the examination or compliance functions of the submission processing centers and the area offices.

### XXIII.C.1.a. Submission Processing Center Audits

[623 T.M., II.C.1.; TPS ¶3850.01.B.]

The IRS submission processing centers (or "campuses") handle, entirely by direct correspondence with the taxpayer, routine errors or omissions such as a failure to sign the return, attach a schedule, or submit the correct amount of tax shown to be due on the return. In submission processing center examinations, the taxpayer is contacted by correspondence. Computer-generated programs and manual inspection techniques are used to select returns for audit by an area office. Three of the most important of these audit programs are:

- mathematical and clerical error program;
- information return program; and
- earned income tax credit/revenue strategy program.

*Mathematical and Clerical Error Program.* The IRS can summarily assess additional tax arising from mathematical or clerical errors and the correction is not subject to the notice of deficiency procedures [§ 6213(b)]. Instead, the taxpayer has 60 days after a correction notice is sent to file a request for abatement. A mathematical or clerical error is defined as [§ 6213(g)(2)]:

- mathematical errors in addition, subtraction, multiplication or division shown on any return;
- incorrect use of IRS tables if such incorrect use is apparent from other information on the return;

- entries on a return that are inconsistent with another entry on the return;
- an omission of information that is required to be supplied on the return to substantiate an entry on the return;
- an entry on a return of a deduction or credit in an amount that exceeds a statutory limit (expressed as a dollar amount or as a percentage, ratio or fraction), if the items determining the limit appear on the return, such as where the taxpayer claims a standard deduction greater than the dollar or percentage limits applicable to that taxpayer;
- an entry on a return claiming the credit with respect to earnings from self-employment to the extent the self-employment tax on such earnings has not been paid;
- an omission of a correct taxpayer identification number in connection with the claiming of certain types of tax credits (e.g., the earned income credit, dependent care credit, or the child tax credit);
- an omission of certain information in connection with the claiming of certain types of tax credits, etc.;
- the inclusion on a return of a tax identification number required if such number is of an individual whose age affects the amount of certain types of credits and the computation of the credit on the return reflects the treatment of such individual as being of an age different from the individual's age based on such taxpayer identification number;
- an entry on the return claiming the child tax credit if the taxpayer is a noncustodial parent of such child;
- an omission of the required reduction in the making work pay credit or the correct social security number; and
- an omission of amounts required to be recaptured with respect to the first-time homebuyer credit or information that must be provided to claim the credit.

*Information Returns Program.* An automated document matching program (identifies returns where the amounts reported such as wages, interest or dividends do not correspond with the amounts reported on information returns such as Form W-2 or Form 1099 filed with the IRS by employers and payers.

*Earned Income Tax Credit/Revenue Strategy Program.* This program covers a broad range of items that appear on their face to be unallowable under the law. The main audit issues are earned income credit, dependent exemptions, filing status, Schedule C gross receipts, child tax credit, child care credit, education credit, adoption credit, false inflated income, and false inflated withholding.

### XXIII.C.1.b. Office and Field Audit Procedures

### XXIII.C.1.b.(1) Audit Procedures

[623 T.M., II.C.; TPS ¶3850.01.C.]

Routine audits involving simple issues are assigned to tax auditors for office interview. All corporate and more complicated individual returns are assigned to a revenue agent for field audit, which may involve an examination of the taxpayer's books and records.

*Time and Place of Examination.* IRS employees select the time and place of an examination on a case-by-case basis, but the regulations indicate that it generally is considered reasonable to schedule an examination on a normally scheduled workday and to hold office examinations at the office within the area that is closest to the taxpayer's residence [Reg. § 301.7605-1(b)(1)]. A taxpayer has no right to set conditions on the time and place of the audit; a taxpayer is limited to objecting to the IRS's designation of time and place as being unfair or improper.

*Witnesses.* Taxpayers have the right to use the services of any person they may select as a witness for the purposes of explaining their books, records or returns to the examiner, provided that person is the most knowledgeable of the taxpayer's accounting system [§ 7521(c); Rev. Proc. 68-29, 1968-2 C.B. 913].

*Recognition of Taxpayer's Representative.* A taxpayer's representative has the right to be present whenever the taxpayer is interviewed or interrogated in connection with the audit. The IRS cannot require the taxpayer to attend an interview, except by issuing an administrative summons [§ 7521(c)].

*Repetitive Examinations.* The IRS has a policy against repetitive examinations of particular return issues. If an issue was examined in either of the two preceding years and resulted in no change or a small tax change, the issue is eliminated from the audit plan for the current year unless some information indicates that the issue is worth examining. In a case where this policy is not followed, the taxpayer should request that examination of the issue be discontinued. The examiner will review the files or seek information from the taxpayer to determine whether this policy is applicable.

*Third Party Contact.* In the course of an examination, the IRS may seek to obtain information from parties other than the taxpayer being examined. During an examination, however, no IRS officer or employee may contact any person other than the taxpayer concerning the determination or collection of the tax liability of the taxpayer without providing advance notice to the taxpayer. Further, the IRS periodically must provide the taxpayer with a record of persons it contacted concerning the determination or collection of the taxpayer's tax liability. The notice and record requirements do not apply (i) to pending criminal tax matters; (ii) if the collection of the tax liability is in jeopardy; (iii) if the IRS determines for good cause shown that disclosure may involve reprisal against any person; or (iv) if the taxpayer authorized the contact [§ 7602(c)].

### XXIII.C.1.b.(2) Examination Outcomes

[623 T.M., II.C.; TPS ¶3850.01.C.]

There are four possible outcomes of an audit:

1. No Change: The examiner proposes no change in the taxpayer's tax liability.
2. Agreed: The examiner proposes adjustments to the taxpayer's tax liability, and the taxpayer is willing to agree to the changes and to sign a waiver of restrictions on assessment as to all adjustments.
3. Unagreed: The examiner proposes adjustments to tax liability, and the taxpayer disagrees with all adjustments and refuses to sign a waiver of restrictions on assessment as to any of the adjustments.
4. Partially Agreed: The examiner proposes adjustments, and the taxpayer is willing to agree with some of the changes and to sign a waiver with respect to some of the adjustments, but not as to all adjustments.

If the examiner proposes no change, the liability shown on the return is accepted as filed, and the taxpayer is so notified. If the examiner proposes adjustments and the taxpayer does not wish to contest them, the taxpayer is asked to sign a waiver form, which permits immediate assessment of the deficiency, and to pay the deficiency, with interest. By signing the waiver, taxpayers waive their rights to a 90-day notice of deficiency and authorize the IRS to assess the deficiency immediately [§ 6213(d)]. The signing of the waiver effectively precludes the taxpayer from filing a petition for review in the Tax Court, since the 90-day notice is required before the taxpayer can file a petition for review by the Tax Court.

If the taxpayer wishes to contest one or more of the examining agent's adjustments, the taxpayer must decide which appeal procedure to use. The taxpayer can first request an informal conference with the auditor's supervisor (group manager) to try and resolve the matter. If that conference does not resolve the matter, the taxpayer can (i) appeal to the IRS Appeals office, (ii) wait for the IRS to issue a 90-day letter and file a petition with the Tax Court, or (iii) sign a waiver, pay the deficiency, and file a claim for refund.

If the taxpayer wishes to appeal to the Appeals office or the Tax Court, the taxpayer should not sign the waiver. Refusal to sign usually forces the IRS to issue a 30-day letter to the taxpayer after which the taxpayer can file a protest with Appeals. If the taxpayer is not successful in Appeals or does not make an appeal, a 90-day letter (notice of deficiency) is issued by the IRS. The taxpayer can then proceed to file a petition with the Tax Court.

At the conclusion of an office audit or field audit, the examiner explains the proposed adjustments to the taxpayer and gives the taxpayer a copy of the report. If the taxpayer disagrees with some or all of the proposed tax changes and refuses to sign a waiver of restrictions on assessment, the area office usually sends the taxpayer a 30-day letter. The 30-day letter, however, is not statutory and may not be sent if insufficient time remains on the statute of limitations for assessment. In such cases, the examiner may proceed directly to issuance of a 90-day notice of deficiency.

Possible taxpayer responses to a 30-day letter are as follows:

- Agreement. The taxpayer can agree to all adjustments. Under this approach, the taxpayer signs and returns the waiver agreement, thereby consenting to the immediate assessment and collection of the additional tax. When the area office receives the waiver, it closes the case. The taxpayer is then sent notice and demand for the amount of the deficiency, plus accrued interest.

- Protest. The taxpayer can protest the findings and request a hearing with the area Appeals office. The written request can be made using small case procedures if the proposed deficiency or refund is $25,000 or less. Otherwise, the protest must be a formal written protest.

- Tax Court. The taxpayer can choose to forego the administrative appeal option and file a petition with the Tax Court. The taxpayer should allow the 30-day period to expire, and upon receipt of the statutory notice of deficiency (90-day letter), file a petition for review. Under this option the taxpayer is not required to pay the proposed deficiency until the Tax Court decision becomes final. After filing the petition the taxpayer, if he chooses, may voluntarily make an advance payment of the proposed deficiency to stop the running of interest.

- Refund Litigation. The taxpayer can choose to pay the deficiency and file a refund suit in federal district court or the U.S. Court of Federal Claims. The taxpayer should execute the waiver of restrictions on assessment which is enclosed with the 30-day letter, pay the deficiency, and file a claim for refund. Upon denial of the claim by the IRS or after the expiration of six months, the taxpayer can file a suit for refund in federal district court or the Court of Federal Claims.

- Request More Time. The taxpayer can request a short extension of time within which to respond to the 30-day letter. The IRS usually grants an extension of time to reply if the taxpayer shows reasonable circumstances.

- Ignore. If the taxpayer ignores the 30-day letter (preliminary determination of a deficiency), the IRS issues a statutory notice of deficiency (90-day letter). If the taxpayer then ignores the 90-day letter, the IRS will assess the tax and send the taxpayer a notice and demand for payment. If the taxpayer ignores this notice, the IRS commences collection actions.

### XXIII.C.1.c. Consents Extending Period of Limitations for Assessment of Tax

[623 T.M., III.E.; TPS ¶3850.02.D.]

The general period of limitations within which the IRS must assess taxes is three years from the date the return was filed or the due date of the return, whichever is later [§ 6501]. There are numerous exceptions to this three-year rule (see XXIII.C.3.b.).

*Types of Consent Forms.* Form 872, *Consent to Extend the Time to Assess Tax*, is used by the IRS to extend the period of limitations for a fixed time and Form 872-A, *Special Consent to Extend the Time to Assess Tax*, is used to extend the statutory period indefinitely. Form 872 sets a specific expiration date for the extension; however, Form 872 can be renewed and extended by subsequent agreements executed before the expiration date. Form 872-A is open-ended in that it provides for extending the period of limitations on assessment to a date 90 days after (1) the IRS issues a 90-day letter; (2) the case is completed and the final tax liability is assessed; or (3) the taxpayer or the IRS gives written notice of an election to terminate the consent on Form 872-T, *Notice of Termination of Special Consent to Extend the Time to Assess Tax*.

The IRS generally requests the taxpayer to sign a consent agreement in the following situations:

- the limitations period for the tax year under examination expires within 180 days and there is insufficient time to complete the audit and administrative processing of the case;

- the limitations period for the tax year expires within 365 days (formerly 180) days and the taxpayer has requested or intends to request that the case be sent to the Appeals office for consideration;

- the limitations period for a year before the year under examination expires within 180 days and it appears that substantial additional tax is due for the prior year;

- the limitations period will expire within 210 days for a case that will be (or has been) placed in suspense;

- the limitations period for the tax year under examination expires within 180 days and the case is included in the Coordinated Industry Case (CIC) Program (formerly the CEP program) or involves a case in which the Form 6658, *Notice of Special Investor Action*, procedure is applicable.

When requested to consent to an extension agreement, the taxpayer has three options:

1. the taxpayer can refuse to sign the waiver;

2. the taxpayer can sign an unconditional waiver extending the period of limitations for a fixed period or indefinite period; or

3. the taxpayer can agree to enter into a restricted waiver, under which the period of limitations is waived only with respect to specific tax issues.

*Consequences of Taxpayer Refusal to Extend Period of Limitations.* If the taxpayer refuses to sign a waiver, the IRS usually terminates the audit and proceeds to issue a statutory notice of deficiency (90-day letter). In lieu of issuing the 90-day letter, the IRS can (i) accelerate the audit, examination, and appeals procedures, (ii) make a jeopardy assessment, or (iii) forgo the audit.

In some cases, a restricted waiver limiting the consent to one or two issues can be used. The IRS may agree to a restricted waiver in limited circumstances, such as cases being held in suspense or abeyance by the IRS pending appeals or audit action in a related case, other cases involving the same issue, or cases where the delay in completing the examination is entirely within the IRS's control.

*Effect of Waiver of the Period of Limitations on Assessment on Claims for Refund.* There is a statutory period of limitations for the filing of refund claims. Generally, a claim for credit or refund of an overpayment of tax must be filed within three years from the time the return is filed or within two years from the time the tax is paid, whichever period expires later. Form 872 extending the period for assessment of a tax also provides that the taxpayer has the right to file a claim for credit or refund during the time covered by the extension and for six months thereafter [§ 6511(a)].

*Deposit to Stop Running of Interest on an Underpayment.* During the period of time that a taxpayer's return is undergoing audit and/or appeal procedures, interest accrues on any underpayment that is ultimately determined (see XXIII.D.2.). A taxpayer can stop the running of interest by making either a payment or a deposit against the anticipated tax liability. Any payment that is made is subject to the claim-for-refund procedures and limitations as well as review by the Joint Committee if the applicable threshold is met. The procedures governing a deposit are very different [§ 6603; Rev. Proc. 2005-18, 2005-13 I.R.B. 798].

### XXIII.C.1.d. Deficiency Assessments

[623 T.M., II.E.; TPS ¶3850.03.B.]

*Deficiency Defined.* A deficiency assessment results from a finding that a tax return understates the taxpayer's liability or that the taxpayer failed to file a return. A deficiency assessment cannot occur until the IRS takes a number of steps required by statute. For example, the IRS must send the taxpayer a notice of deficiency and then refrain from further action for the 90-day period during which time the taxpayer is authorized to file a petition for a redetermination in the Tax Court [§ 6211(a), § 6212(a), § 6213(a)].

A deficiency is defined as the excess of the correct tax over the sum of the tax shown on the taxpayer's return plus any prior deficiency assessments. The sum, however, is first reduced by the amount of any rebates made. A "rebate" is the amount of an abatement, credit, refund, or other repayment made on the ground that the tax imposed under the income, estate and gift, or excise tax provisions was less than the excess of (i) the sum of the tax shown on the taxpayer's return plus any prior deficiency assessments over (ii) the rebates previously made. A rebate includes a refund of taxes resulting from a tentative NOL carryback, as well as a credit against unpaid taxes allowed as a result of a tentative NOL carryback [§ 6211].

The income tax imposed and the tax shown on the return both are determined without regard to (i) payments on account of estimated tax; (ii) the credit for taxes withheld on wages; (iii) the credit for tax withheld at the source for nonresident aliens and foreign corporations; (iv) and any credits resulting from the collection of amounts assessed through termination assessments. In addition, if an individual with gross income of less than $10,000 elects to have the IRS compute his or her income tax, the IRS's computation is treated as having been made by the taxpayer and shown by the taxpayer on his or her return [§ 6211(b), § 6211(c)].

---

**EXAMPLE:** Taxpayer C files an individual return for calendar year 2009 on Apr. 15, 2010, showing total tax liability of $3,000, a tax payment of $3,500 (from withholding on wages), and an overpayment of $500. The refund of $500 is paid to C. A subsequent audit determines C's 2009 tax liability to be $3,400. A deficiency of $400 is determined as follows: the correct tax liability of $3,400 exceeds the tax liability shown on the return of $3,000 by $400.

---

*Notice of Deficiency.* A deficiency in tax, unlike tax liabilities reported on a return, cannot be summarily assessed. By law, before a deficiency can be assessed, the IRS must (i) determine the amount of the deficiency and (ii) give notice to the taxpayer of the proposed deficiency and an opportunity for judicial review before making payment. No assessment of a deficiency of income, estate or gift tax may be made and no levy or collection proceeding in court may be commenced until 90 days (150 days for taxpayers outside the United States) after a 90-day letter (notice of deficiency) has been mailed to the taxpayer's "last known address" [§ 6213(a)]. Moreover, if a petition for redetermination is filed with the Tax Court during the 90-day (or 150-day) period, the assessment cannot be made until the decision of the Tax Court becomes final [§ 6513(a)].

If, in response to the notice, the taxpayer files a timely petition for review with the Tax Court, the assessment cannot be made until the decision of the Tax Court becomes final [§ 6213(a)]. Still, the IRS is allowed to make a supplemental assessment when the original assessment is incomplete or imperfect [§ 6204(a)]. The IRS generally is prohibited from issuing any additional deficiency notice to the taxpayer for the same taxable year and for the same type of tax [§ 6212(a)].

If the taxpayer petitions the Tax Court and has not previously had its dispute considered by the Appeals office, a taxpayer may take the matter to the Appeals office, provided that the IRS Counsel who is defending the case consents and provided that the review does not interfere with deadlines established by the Tax Court. If, on the other hand, the taxpayer pays the tax and files an administrative claim for refund, and if the taxpayer receives a notice of proposed disallowance of the claim, the taxpayer may request that the claim be considered by the IRS Appeals Office.

If a timely petition is not filed with the Tax Court, the IRS may make the assessment at any time after the expiration of the 90-day (or 150-day) period without further notice. The period commences on the mailing date (postmark) of the notice, but the last day cannot end on a Saturday, Sunday or legal holiday in the District of Columbia [§ 6213].

*Exceptions to Restrictions on Assessment of Deficiencies.* There are six situations in which the IRS can make summary assessments of deficiencies and ignore the notice of deficiency requirement [§ 6213(b), § 6851]:

1. mathematical or clerical errors;
2. tentative carryback adjustments;
3. amounts that are paid as taxes;
4. jeopardy and termination assessments;

5. orders of criminal restitution; and

6. computational adjustments.

### XXIII.C.2. TEFRA Partnership Audit Procedures

[624 T.M.; TPS ¶3855.]

Before enactment of the Tax Equity and Fiscal Responsibility Act of 1982 (TE-FRA), the IRS audited partnership return items at the partner level. Due to the administrative burden associated with applying those audit procedures to partnerships with large numbers of partners, Congress enacted the TEFRA audit procedures to effectively move the audit of partnership return items to the partnership level.

The TEFRA audit procedures require all partners in a partnership subject to the procedures to report their "partnership items" consistently with the partnership's tax reporting. The partnership's tax reporting is then subject to audit at the partnership level (with varying participation rights for the partners), and the tax effect of the partnership adjustments on the partners' taxable income is accomplished by a mathematical computation and bill. The goals of the TEFRA audit procedures are (i) the attainment of consistency in tax reporting and audit results for the partnership and the partners, and (ii) the creation of efficiencies by applying unified audit procedures at the partnership level.

The application of the TEFRA audit procedures depends on:

1. whether the partnership is subject to the procedures (see XXIII.C.2.a.);

2. the partnership items to which the procedures apply (see XXIII.C.2.b.); and

3. the partner category within which a partner falls (see XXIII.C.2.c.).

### XXIII.C.2.a. Partnerships Subject to TEFRA Audit Procedures

[624 T.M., II.; TPS ¶3855.02.]

The TEFRA audit procedures generally apply to all entities that are required to file a partnership return because they meet the § 761(a) definition of a partnership [§ 6231(a)(1)(A), § 6031(a)] (see XIV.B.1.). They also apply to other entities that actually file a partnership return [§ 6233]. However, partnerships that qualify under the small partnership exception generally are not subject to the TEFRA audit procedures.

**Small Partnership Exception.** Under the small partnership exception, the TE-FRA audit procedures do not apply to a partnership if (i) it has ten or fewer partners (spouses count as one partner), (ii) it has a partner that is a partnership, S corporation, or trust, or (iii) it has a partner that is a nonresident alien [§ 6231(a)(1)(B)(i)].

A partnership that qualifies under the small partnership exception may elect to have the TEFRA audit procedures apply. The election is made by attaching to the partnership return a statement signed by all persons who were partners at any time during the partnership tax year. Once made, the election is effective for the year of the election and all later years. It may not be revoked without IRS consent [§ 6231(a)(1)(B)(ii); Reg. § 301.6231(a)(1)-1(b)].

**Foreign Partnerships.** Because the TEFRA audit procedures apply only to partnerships that are required to file a partnership return, they do not apply to a foreign partnership unless the foreign partnership has (i) gross income derived from sources within the United States, or (ii) gross income that is effectively connected with the conduct of a trade or business within the United States [§ 6231(a)(1), § 6031(e)].

A special disallowance rule applies if a foreign partnership is required to file a partnership return but does not do so. In such a case, the U.S. partners may not claim any deductions, losses, or credits from the foreign partnership if, at any time after the end of the partnership's tax year, either (i) the tax matters partner resides outside the United States, or (ii) the partnership books and records are maintained outside the United States [§ 6231(f)].

### XXIII.C.2.b. Types of Items Subject to TEFRA Audit Procedures

[624 T.M., III.B.; TPS ¶3855.03.]

The TEFRA audit procedures apply only to "partnership items." Partnership items are items that are more appropriately determined at the partnership level than at the partner level. The following items are partnership items [§ 6231(a)(3); Reg. § 301.6231(a)(3)-1(a)]:

- partnership income, gain, loss, deduction, or credit;
- nondeductible partnership expenditures (e.g., charitable contributions);
- items that may be § 57(a) tax preference items for any partner;
- tax-exempt partnership income;
- the amount, character, and changes in partnership liabilities;
- the partnership aspects of the investment tax credit and investment tax credit recapture;
- the partnership aspects of the at-risk determination;
- the partnership aspects of the oil and gas wells depletion allowance;
- the partnership aspects of the determination of the § 751 treatment of unrealized receivables and inventory items;
- guaranteed payments;
- optional § 754 basis adjustments; and
- items relating to partnership contributions, distributions, and transactions between partners and the partnership.

The TEFRA audit procedures do not apply to items that are not partnership items (so-called non-partnership items). However, certain items known as affected items receive special treatment. Affected items are items that are affected by partnership items when those partnership items flow through to the partners' returns. An extended statute of limitations generally is provided for such affected items [§ 6231(a)(4), § 6231(a)(5); Reg. § 301.6231(a)(5)-1].

In certain situations, items that were once considered partnership items may be converted to non-partnership items. The audit procedures that apply to such converted items depend on the nature of the events that caused the conversion [§ 6231(b)].

### XXIII.C.2.c. Application of TEFRA Audit Procedures to Different Categories of Partners

[624 T.M., III.A.; TPS ¶3855.04.]

The application of the TEFRA audit procedures to a partner depends on the partner category within which the partner falls. Different audit procedures apply to different categories of partners, including (i) the tax matters partner, (ii) notice and non-notice partners, (iii) pass-through partners, and (iv) indirect partners.

**Tax Matters Partner.** One of the principal purposes of the TEFRA audit procedures is to allow a unified audit proceeding at the partnership level. One partner, the tax matters partner (TMP), has principal responsibility for acting on behalf of the partnership in the partnership audit and any related litigation. Some of the TMP's most important rights and responsibilities include:

- the right to extend the statute of limitations for the audit of the partnership items;
- the right to enter into administrative settlement of partnership items on behalf of non-notice partners that have not joined a 5% notice group (see below);
- the right to settle with the IRS or settle any Tax Court litigation;
- the responsibility to provide notice to partners of all significant procedural stages and filings associated with the TEFRA partnership audit and litigation.

The TMP is determined in the following order of priority [§ 6231(a)(7)]:

1. If the partnership designates a specific partner as the TMP on the partnership return or in a filing with the IRS Service Center where the partnership return is filed, that partner is the TMP.

2. If the partnership does not designate a TMP, the general partner with the largest profits interest is the TMP.

3. If no TMP can be clearly determined under 1. or 2., the IRS may designate the TMP for the partnership.

***Notice and Non-Notice Partners.*** For most partnerships subject to the TEFRA audit procedures, every partner other than the TMP is a notice partner. However, for partnerships with more than 100 partners, only partners that have at least a 1% profits interest are notice partners. All other partners generally are non-notice partners. However, non-notice partners can band together with other non-notice partners to form a 5% notice group or 5% litigation group that essentially gives the members of the group the same status and rights as a notice partner [§ 6231(a)(8), § 6223].

A notice partner is entitled to receive the Notice of Beginning of Administrative Proceeding (NBAP) and the Notice of Final Partnership Administrative Adjustment (FPAA) directly from the IRS. A notice partner may file a petition contesting the adjustments contained in the FPAA if the TMP fails to do so.

***Pass-Through Partners.*** A pass-through partner is an individual or entity through which other persons (so-called indirect partners) hold an interest in the partnership. Until the pass-through partner files an identification statement with the IRS identifying the indirect partners who are the ultimate beneficiaries of the partnership flow-through items, the pass-through partner is obligated to furnish to indirect partners all notices and information received from the IRS, the TMP, or other pass-through partners within 30 days of receipt [§ 6231(a)(9), § 6223(h)].

***Indirect Partners.*** An indirect partner is a partner that claims an interest in the partnership flow-through items through a pass-through partner. Until the pass-through partner files an identification statement with the IRS identifying the indirect partner, the indirect partner (i) has no right to receive notices or information directly from the IRS, the TMP, or other pass-through- partners, and (ii) has an unlimited statute of limitations for partnership item adjustments [§ 6231(a)(10), § 6229(e)].

***Statute of Limitations.*** Under the TEFRA audit procedures, § 6229 sets forth a statute of limitations for partnership items and affected items that is based on the filing date of the partnership return. The courts have held that the § 6229 limitations period for assessments is not a separate limitations period from the § 6501 limitations period that applies under the non-TEFRA audit procedures (see XXIII.C.3.). Instead, § 6229 merely provides a minimum amount of time for assessing tax attributable to partnership items and it complements § 6501, which normally sets forth the maximum period for the assessment of any tax [*Rhone-Poulenc Surfactants & Specialties LP v. Commissioner*, 114 T.C. 533 (2000)].

### XXIII.C.3. Statute of Limitations for Assessment

[627 T.M.; TPS ¶3860.]

### XXIII.C.3.a. General Rule for Assessments

[627 T.M.; TPS ¶3860.]

In general, the amount of any income, employment, or estate or gift tax must be assessed within three years after the return was filed (whether or not the return was filed on or after the date prescribed). No proceeding in court, without assessment for the collection of the tax, can begin after the expiration of this three-year period. For these purposes, the term "return" means the return required to be filed by the taxpayer [§ 6501(a)]. If a taxpayer fails to file a return, there is no statute of limitations, and the IRS may assess the tax or commence collection proceedings without assessment at any time [§ 6501(c)(3)]. The filing of a return of a pass-through entity (such as an estate, trust, partnership, or S corporation) does not start the running of the period of limitations for assessment of tax against an individual who must report the items shown on the entity return. Instead, the individual's income tax return is treated as separate and distinct from the entity return, and the statute of limitations must be computed separately for each return [§ 6501(a)].

Income tax returns, including filing requirements and filing dates, are discussed in XXIII.A.1.

### XXIII.C.3.b. Exceptions to General Rule for Assessments

[627 T.M.; TPS ¶3860.01.B., .01.F.].

There are a number of exceptions to the three-year rule.

*False or Fraudulent Return*. If a taxpayer files a false or fraudulent return with the intent to evade tax or in the case of a willful attempt in any manner to defeat or evade tax, there is no time limit for the IRS to assess tax for that tax year or period [§ 6501(c)(1), § 6501(c)(2)].

*Extended Limitations Period for Listed Transactions*. The assessment period of limitations is extended for a "listed transaction" if a taxpayer fails to include on any return or statement for a tax year any information concerning a listed transaction that is required to be included with the return or statement. The period of limitations for assessing tax on such a transaction does not expire before the date that is one year after the earlier of (i) the date on which the IRS is furnished the required information, or (ii) the date that a material advisor (as defined in § 6111) satisfies the list maintenance requirements for a request by the IRS [§ 6501(c)(10)].

*Omission of More than 25% from Gross Income*. If a taxpayer omits from gross income an amount properly includible therein that is in excess of 25% of the amount of gross income stated in the return, the tax may be assessed, or a proceeding in court for the collection of that tax may be begun without assessment, at any time within six years after the return was filed.

*Prompt Assessment of Estate or Corporate Tax*. In certain situations involving a tax return required to be filed by a decedent or the decedent's estate during administration (other than an estate tax return) or by a corporation contemplating or in the process of dissolution, the IRS must assess the tax within 18 months after the fiduciary or corporation files a written request for prompt assessment [§ 6501(d)].

*Statutory Extensions of Statute of Limitations on Assessment.* The period of limitations for assessment is extended by Code provisions in a number of situations. These include:

- Net Operating Loss or Capital Loss Carryback — A deficiency attributable to a NOL or capital loss carryback may be assessed at any time before the expiration of the period within which a deficiency for the tax year of the NOL that results in such carryback may be assessed [§ 6501(h)].

- Foreign Tax Credit Carryback — A deficiency attributable to the carryback of excess foreign taxes under the foreign tax credit provisions can be assessed at any time before the end of one year following the expiration of the period within which a deficiency for the tax year in which the excess foreign taxes arose can be assessed [§ 6501(i)].

- Business Credit Carrybacks — A deficiency attributable to a reduced carryback of a general business credit can be assessed at any time before the expiration of the period within which a deficiency for the tax year in which the unused credit arose may be assessed [§ 6501(j)].

- Tentative Carryback Adjustments — If an amount has been tentatively refunded or credited by reason of a NOL, capital loss, or credit carryback from a later tax year, a deficiency may be assessed at any time before the expiration of the period within which a deficiency for the later year in which the carryback arose may be assessed. The deficiency is not limited to items attributable to the tentative carryback; however, the amount of the assessment for the carryback year cannot exceed the amount of tax refunded or credited as a result of the carryback, reduced by any deficiency attributable to the carryback that may be assessed [§ 6501(k)].

- Adjustment in Barred Year — The IRS can reduce a claimed NOL or credit carryover or carryback in an open tax year by making adjustments to a barred year that effectively increase the amount of the NOL or credit used in the barred year and thereby reduce the amount available for use in the open year [Rev. Rul. 69-543, 1969-2 C.B. 1].

- Election to File Joint Return After Separate Return — In certain circumstances, if an individual taxpayer files a separate return for a year in which the taxpayer could have filed a joint return with his or her spouse, and then files a joint return after the due date of the original return, the joint return replaces the separate return. If a substitute joint return is filed under this provision, a deficiency may be assessed at any time within one year after the date the joint return is filed, regardless of when the return is deemed filed [§ 6013(b)].

- Involuntary Conversions — If a taxpayer defers gain resulting from an involuntary conversion, the statute of limitations on the gain year(s) stays open until the taxpayer notifies the IRS in writing either (i) that a timely replacement has been made, or (ii) that no timely replacement has been made [§ 1033(a)(2)(C)(i)].

- Installment Sale — If a taxpayer uses the installment method to report gain from the sale of property to a related person and the related person disposes of the property within the next two years and before all payments are received by the taxpayer, the period for assessing a deficiency on the first disposition expires not less than two years after the date on which the person making the first disposition notifies the IRS that there was a second disposition of the property [§ 453(e)(1)].

- Transfers to Foreign Persons — For any information that must be reported to the IRS pursuant to an election under § 1295(b), § 1298(f), § 6038, § 6038A, § 6038B, § 6038D, § 6046, § 6046A, or § 6048, the time for assessment of any tax for any tax period to which such information relates does not expire before the date that is three years after the date on which the IRS is provided with the required information [§ 6501(c)(8)].

### XXIII.C.3.c. Tolling of Statute of Limitations for Assessment

[627 T.M.; TPS ¶3860.01.F.]

In certain circumstances, an event suspends the running of the period of limitations for assessment. These include:

- Third-Party Summons — A third-party summons is a summons directed to a third party (e.g., an individual or an institution such as a bank) who has records pertaining to a taxpayer under audit. When a taxpayer challenges a third-party summons, the statute of limitation is tolled indefinitely until this judicial proceeding is resolved [§ 7609].

- Designated Summons — A designated summons is issued by the IRS 60 days before the assessment period expires. It suspends the statute of limitations during the judicial enforcement period (as defined in § 6503(j)(3)) [§ 6503(j)].

- Bankruptcy — In a bankruptcy case under Title 11, the statute of limitations on assessment is suspended for the period during which the IRS is prohibited from making an assessment, plus 60 days [§ 6503(h)].

- Tax Court — The mailing of a notice of deficiency suspends the running of the statutory period of limitations for the time during which assessment or collection of the deficiency is prohibited and for 60 days thereafter [§ 6503(a)].

### XXIII.C.4. Collection of Tax/Installment Payments

### XXIII.C.4.a. IRS Collection Procedures

[637 T.M., II., 638 T.M., XV.; TPS ¶3870.01.]

The IRS is required to assess all taxes (including interest, additional amounts, additions to the tax, and assessable penalties); thus, the assessment is usually the first step in the collection process. Assessment is the administrative act by which the IRS establishes that the taxpayer is liable for the tax [§ 6201(a)]. An assessment is made when an IRS official records the taxpayer's liability on the IRS books [§ 6203].

After an assessment has been made, the IRS must notify the taxpayer as soon as practicable, but no later than 60 days after the assessment, of the amount of the tax due and must demand payment. The notice must be delivered to the taxpayer's residence or usual place of business or mailed to the taxpayer's last known address [§ 6303]. The taxpayer's last known address is the address that appears on the taxpayer's most recently filed and properly processed federal tax return, unless the IRS is given clear and concise notification of a change of address [Reg. § 301.6212-2(a)].

The IRS must adhere to fair tax collection practices. The IRS may not, without prior taxpayer consent or without express court permission, communicate with a taxpayer in connection with the collection of any unpaid tax [§ 6304(a)]:

- at any unusual time or place or a time or place known or which should be known to be inconvenient to the taxpayer;

- directly with the taxpayer if the taxpayer is represented by someone authorized to practice before the IRS with respect to the unpaid tax, unless the representative fails to respond within a reasonable period of time to an IRS communication or consents to direct communication with the taxpayer; or

- at the taxpayer's place of employment if the IRS knows or has reason to know that the taxpayer's employer prohibits the taxpayer from receiving such communication.

The IRS may not engage in conduct the natural consequence of which is to harass, oppress, or abuse any person in connection with the collection of any unpaid tax, including [§ 6304(b)]:

- the use or threat of violence or other criminal means to harm the physical person, reputation, or property of any person;

- the use of obscene or profane language;

- repeated telephone calling with the intent to annoy, abuse, or harass any person at the called number; and

- the placement of telephone calls without meaningful disclosure of the caller's identity (except under rules similar to the rules of the Fair Debt Collection Practices Act).

Violations of these prohibitions may subject the government to civil actions [§ 7433].

### XXIII.C.4.b. Federal Tax Lien

[637 T.M., III.A.; TPS ¶3870.02.]

If a taxpayer, after notice and demand for payment, neglects or refuses to pay a tax assessment, the amount of the tax assessment (including any interest or penalties) becomes a lien in favor of the federal government upon all property and rights to property, whether real or personal, belonging to the taxpayer. Thus, the IRS's lien attaches to all property and rights to property, whether real or personal, belonging to the taxpayer. Once a lien arises, it attaches automatically to the property owned by the taxpayer on the assessment date and to all property subsequently acquired by the taxpayer. In other words, the tax lien attaches to virtually anything that can be considered the taxpayer's property (as defined by state law), provided that the lien is still in existence — i.e., the tax assessment has not been satisfied or collection is not barred by the expiration of the statute of limitations [§ 6321].

The federal tax lien arises automatically when the taxpayer fails to pay the tax assessed and relates back and attaches to property belonging to the taxpayer as of the date of the assessment [§ 6322]. The mere existence of a tax lien does not divest the taxpayer of his property; this is accomplished by levy and seizure of the encumbered property or by a suit to enforce the lien.

*Notice of Federal Tax Lien.* A tax lien is generally valid against third parties when the IRS files Form 668(Y), *Notice of Federal Tax Lien*, with the appropriate authority. Until the notice of federal tax lien (NFTL) is filed, the lien does not have priority over subsequent purchasers, holders of security interests, judgment creditors, or holders of mechanic's liens. Once the NFTL is properly filed, any person acquiring property from the taxpayer does so at its own peril, because the property is subject to the lien [§ 6323].

The rules for filing a NFTL are as follows [Reg. § 301.6323(f)-1(a)]:

- For real property, the notice must be filed in the office within the state, county, or other governmental subdivision as designated by state law in which the property subject to the lien is physically located.

- For personal property, the notice must be filed in the office within the state, county, or other governmental subdivision as designated by state law in which the property subject to the lien is physically located. Personal property, either tangible or intangible, is deemed to be located in the state where the taxpayer resides at the time the lien notice is filed.

- The residence of a taxpayer who resides outside the United States is deemed to be in Washington, D.C., and Notice of Federal Tax Lien against personal property is filed with the Recorder of Deeds for the District of Columbia.

- A corporation is deemed to be a resident of the state where it maintains its principal office.

- If state law does not designate an office where the notice is to be filed or provides for more than one office, the notice must be filed with the clerk of the federal district court for the judicial district in which the property is deemed situated.

*Validity and Enforceability of Lien.* The federal tax lien attaches at the time the assessment is made and, if not released, discharged, or terminated, continues to exist until the assessed tax liability is satisfied or until the lien becomes unenforceable by reason of the expiration of the 10-year statute of limitations for collection [§ 6322, § 6502].

### XXIII.C.4.c. Collection Due Process (CDP) Hearing

[638 T.M., XI.; TPS ¶3870.02.B.3.]

Within five business days after the day the NFTL is filed, the IRS must provide written notification of the lien filing to the taxpayer. The notice of lien filing, in letter form, must be provided in person, left at the taxpayer's dwelling or usual place of business, or sent to the taxpayer's last known address by certified or registered mail. The letter must inform the taxpayer of the right to request a due process (CDP) hearing. The hearing must occur during the 30-day period beginning on the day after the five business day period following the notice of lien filing date [§ 6320; Reg. § 301.6320-1].

The required notice given to the taxpayer must contain the following information [§ 6320(a)(3)]:

- the amount of the unpaid tax;

- the right to request a hearing during the 30-day period beginning on the day after the five business day notification period;

- the administrative appeals available to the taxpayer; and

- the statutory provisions and procedures relating to the release of liens.

A taxpayer must make a written request for a CDP hearing and may use IRS Form 12153, *Request for a Collection Due Process Hearing.* A taxpayer is entitled to only one hearing for the first filing of a NFTL for the tax period or periods and the unpaid tax shown on the notice. The hearing must be conducted by an impartial IRS employee who, before the first CDP hearing, had no involvement with the unpaid tax for the tax periods in issue. However, a taxpayer may waive the right to have this hearing conducted by an employee with no prior involvement [§ 6320(b)].

If a taxpayer does not timely request a hearing with respect to the first filing of an NFTL for a given tax period or periods with respect to an amount of unpaid tax, the taxpayer foregoes the right to a due process hearing with Appeals, and judicial review of the Appeals determination as to the NFTL [Reg. § 301.6320-1(b)(2)]. However, the taxpayer may request an "equivalent hearing."

A request that is deemed frivolous by the IRS is treated as if it were never submitted and is not subject to further administrative or judicial review. However, a determination that some or all portions of a request are frivolous is subject to Tax Court review [§ 6320(c), § 6330(g)].

The Appeals Officer must verify that all legal and administrative requirements for the filing of the NFTL have been met. Issues that may be raised at the hearing include [§ 6320(c)]:

- appropriate spousal defenses, unless the IRS has already made a final determination regarding those defenses in a deficiency notice or final determination letter;
- challenges to the appropriateness of collection actions;
- collection alternatives; and
- challenges to the existence or amount of the liability specified in the due process hearing notice.

A taxpayer may challenge the existence or amount of the tax liability specified in the CDP hearing notice if the taxpayer did not receive a notice of deficiency for the liability or did not otherwise have an opportunity to dispute the liability [Reg. § 301.6320-1(e)(3), Q-E2].

Following a CDP hearing, the Appeals Officer issues a Notice of Determination, which can be appealed to the Tax Court within 30 days. The Appeals Officer must consider [§ 6320(c), § 6330(d)]:

- whether the IRS met the requirements of any applicable law or administrative procedure in filing the notice of federal tax lien;
- the issues raised at the hearing;
- any offers submitted by the taxpayer for collection alternatives; and
- whether the proposed collection action balances the need for the efficient collection of taxes with the legitimate concern of the person that any collection be no more intrusive than necessary.

In a CDP appeal in which the underlying tax liability is not in issue, the Tax Court reviews the determination of the Appeals Office for abuse of discretion. If the validity of the underlying tax liability is properly at issue, the Tax Court reviews the matter de novo.

When a taxpayer timely requests a CDP hearing, the period of limitation relating to collection is suspended until the taxpayer withdraws the request or there is a final determination. The period of suspension cannot expire before the 90th day after the day on which the IRS receives the taxpayer's written withdrawal of the request for hearing or the day the determination from that hearing becomes final [§ 6320(c), § 6330(e)(1)].

During a suspension period, the IRS may continue to levy for tax periods and taxes, whether or not covered by the due process notice regarding the NFTL, provided that pre-levy due process requirements for those taxes and periods have been met. The IRS also may file NFTLs for tax periods or taxes not covered by the due process notice, file an NFTL for the same tax and tax period stated on the due process notice at another recording office, start judicial proceedings to collect the tax shown on the due process notice, or offset overpayments from other periods (or other taxes) against the tax shown on the CDP notice [Reg. § 301.6320-1(g)(2), Q-G3].

Taxpayers who fail to timely request a CDP hearing can obtain an "equivalent hearing" with Appeals that generally follows the procedures for a CDP hearing.

However, there is no right of appeal and an equivalent hearing does not trigger a suspension of any statute of limitations and does not halt any collection action [Reg. § 301.6320-1(i)].

### XXIII.C.4.d. Priority of Federal Tax Lien

[637 T.M., III.F.; TPS ¶3870.02.D.]

Where there are competing liens against the same property, the order of satisfaction must be determined. If federal tax liens and state law created liens compete for priority, state law defines the property or rights to property to which liens attach, and federal law determines the priority of federal tax liens.

The first lien to arise usually has priority, under the so-called "first in time, first in right" rule, provided that this lien is perfected (or choate) before the time the federal tax lien arises [*United States v. City of New Britain*, 347 U.S. 81 (1954)].

**Simultaneous Attachment in After-Acquired Property.** On arising, the federal tax lien encumbers all of the taxpayer's property, both real and personal, as well as property subsequently acquired by the taxpayer. For a competing state law created lien to prime the federal tax lien in the taxpayer's after-acquired property, the competing lien must be perfected before the federal tax lien arises. Otherwise, the federal tax lien is given a priority interest in the after-acquired property.

There are statutory exceptions that give priority to the federal tax lien and that, in other instances, give priority to certain special lien creditors. An NFTL must be filed for the IRS's lien to have priority against the following categories of lien holders [§ 6323(a)]:

1. purchasers (as defined in § 6323(h)(6));
2. holders of security interests (as defined in § 6323(h)(1));
3. mechanic's lienors (as defined in § 6323(h)(2)); and
4. judgment lien creditors.

**Superpriority Rules.** Even though a notice of federal tax lien is filed, holders of certain claims against a delinquent taxpayer are given interests that take priority over a filed federal tax lien. Under these rules, a qualifying claimant's interest has priority, even though its interest in the taxpayer's property arises after the IRS has filed the notice of federal tax lien. These include [§ 6323(b), § 6323(c)]:

- purchasers of securities without actual notice or knowledge of the lien's existence;
- purchasers of motor vehicles without actual notice or knowledge of the lien's existence;
- purchasers of tangible personal property from a retail store;
- purchasers of personal property purchased in a casual sale;
- personal property subject to a possessory lien;
- real property taxes and special assessments;
- residential property subject to mechanic's lien for small repairs;
- attorney's lien;
- certain insurance contracts;
- deposit-secured loans;
- certain commercial financing transactions;
- real property construction or improvement financing agreements;
- security interests arising from obligatory disbursement agreements;

- certain disbursements made within 45 days of tax lien filing; and
- certain interest and expense items.

### XXIII.C.4.e. Release of Lien, Discharge of Property, and Subordination of Lien

[637 T.M., III.G.; TPS ¶3870.02.E.]

There are various ways to eliminate or minimize the effect of a federal tax lien. The release of a tax lien completely extinguishes the lien. A discharge of property removes certain specific property from the lien but does not otherwise affect the validity of the lien filed against other property. Subordination of a tax lien indicates that the tax lien's priority in payment is subordinated to the interest of some other creditor or lienor. A foreclosure sale of the taxpayer's property by a party with a security interest that is senior to the federal tax lien can discharge the tax lien from the property.

*Release of Lien.* The IRS must release a federal tax lien within 30 days after (i) the date on which the IRS determines that the assessed tax liability and any related interest have been fully paid or have become legally unenforceable due to the expiration of the statutory period of limitations on collection, or (ii) the date on which the taxpayer offers and the IRS accepts a bond under which payment of the assessed tax liability, with interest, is guaranteed before the statute of limitations expires [§ 6325(a)].

A taxpayer may request a certificate of release; the IRS does not ordinarily initiate such action. The request must be in writing and set forth the grounds on which the release is requested, and if because of satisfaction of the tax liability, provide evidence of payment. The IRS issues a certificate of release from a tax lien when it finds that the taxpayer has satisfied the tax liability in full. A certificate of release may also be issued if the taxpayer furnishes a bond that is accepted by the IRS for guaranteed payment of the liability to be paid not later than six months before the period of limitations for collection expires [Reg. § 301.6325-1(a)].

*Discharge of Property.* The IRS has the discretion to issue a certificate of discharge for any part of the property subject to a federal tax lien in any of the following cases [§ 6325(b)]:

- The IRS determines that the fair market value of the property remaining subject to the lien (after issuance of the certificate) is at least double the amount of the tax liability.
- Partial payment of the tax liability equals the value of the government's interest in the specific property to be discharged, or the IRS determines that the government's interest in the discharged property has no value.
- The proceeds from the sale of a specific piece of property (with the IRS's consent) are substituted for the underlying property and held subject to the tax lien, in the same manner and with the same priority as the lien on the sold property.

*Subordination of Lien.* Any part of the taxpayer's property subject to a federal tax lien may be subordinated to another interest or a lien of equal or lower priority when [§ 6325(d)(1)]:

- the IRS is paid an amount that equals its subordinated tax lien;
- the amount that can be realized from the property subject to the lien has increased and that the ultimate collection of the tax is facilitated; or

- for the special lien for additional estate tax attributable to the special use valuation of a farm, the IRS determines its interests are adequately secured after subordination.

*Nonattachment of Lien.* If the IRS determines that, because of some confusion of names or for some other reason, a person (other than the taxpayer) may be injured by the appearance that a notice of tax lien refers to him, the IRS can issue a certificate stating that the lien does not attach to the property belonging to this person [§ 6325(e)].

*Effect of Certificate.* Once a certificate of release, discharge, subordination, or nonattachment is properly filed (in the same office as the NFTL to which it relates), the certificate [§ 6325(f)(1)]:

- extinguishes the lien (but not the liability for the tax), in the case of a certificate of release;

- releases the property from the lien, in the case of certificate of discharge;

- gives priority over the IRS's lien to other interest/liens, in the case of a certificate of subordination; or

- indicates that the IRS's lien does not encumber the property of the person named in the certificate, in the case of a certificate of non-attachment.

*Foreclosure Sale Discharges Federal Tax Lien.* A federal tax lien that is junior to the interest of a secured party can be discharged by the foreclosure of the senior secured interest. If the foreclosure sale is made pursuant to a judicial proceeding in which the IRS is joined as a party, the resulting judicial sale is binding on the IRS, and the IRS takes whatever interest is provided in the judgment. If, however, the IRS is not properly joined as a party in the judicial proceeding, the property remains subject to the federal tax lien, provided that the IRS files the NFTL before the judicial action begins. If the federal tax lien is not filed before the judicial proceedings commence, the tax lien still may be discharged, provided that the law of the state where the property is located would discharge other junior liens filed against the property [§ 7425(a)].

If real property is discharged from the federal tax lien, the IRS retains a right to redeem the property within the longer of 120 days or the redemption period of the state where the property is located. This redemption right allows the IRS to purchase the property from the party who bought it at the nonjudicial sale or the agent of the purchaser. The IRS must pay the amount the purchaser paid for the property at the sale plus interest and expenses incurred to maintain the property [§ 7425(d)].

*Withdrawal of Federal Tax Lien Notice.* The IRS can withdraw filed notices of tax lien and treat the taxpayer as if the lien notice had not been filed if it is determined that [§ 6323(j)]:

- the lien notice has been filed prematurely or not in accordance with IRS administrative procedures;

- the taxpayer has entered into an installment agreement for payment of the underlying tax liability (unless the installment agreement provides otherwise);

- the withdrawal of the lien notice will facilitate collection of the tax liability; or

- with the consent of the taxpayer or the Taxpayer Advocate, the withdrawal of the lien notice is determined to be in the best interests of the taxpayer (as determined by the Taxpayer Advocate) and the government.

### XXIII.C.4.f. Enforced Collection — Seizure and Sale of Property

[637 T.M., IV.; TPS ¶3870.03.]

If any person liable for any federal tax does not pay within 10 days after notice and demand by the IRS, the IRS may then collect the tax by levy upon all property and rights to property belonging to the person, unless there is an explicit statutory restriction on doing so. A levy is the seizure of the person's property or rights to property. Property that is not cash may be sold pursuant to statutory requirements. However, before the IRS can sell seized property or a right to property, it must complete a thorough investigation of the status of that property or right to property before making a levy [§ 6331].

In general, a levy does not apply to property acquired after the date of the levy, regardless of whether the property is held by the taxpayer or by a third party (such as a bank) on behalf of a taxpayer. However, a levy on salary and wages is continuous from the date it is first made until the date it is fully paid or becomes unenforceable [§ 6331(d)].

The IRS has very substantial powers to enforce collection of unpaid taxes. The property of a delinquent taxpayer subject to a federal tax lien can be levied against — whether by notice of levy or seizure — and sold to collect unpaid taxes [§ 6331]. Any person in possession of the taxpayer's property or rights to property must surrender the property to the IRS when served with a levy notice [§ 6332]. "Levy" ordinarily describes the process of reaching amounts owing to the taxpayer by a third party. Property or rights to property includes receivables, bank accounts, stocks, bonds, salary and wages, and all other property, whether real or personal, tangible or intangible.

If the IRS has made an assessment, has issued a notice and demand for payment, and has issued a notice of a right to a CDP hearing, and the taxpayer fails to pay the tax within 30 days after notice and demand, the IRS can collect the tax by levy on the taxpayer's property or rights to property. Levy can be accomplished either by issuance of a notice of levy or by seizure of the taxpayer's property to satisfy a tax liability [§ 6330, § 6331(a)].

The IRS can serve a notice of levy on the taxpayer: (i) in person, (ii) by leaving it at the taxpayer's residence or usual place of business (or at the residence or place of business of the person in possession of the property), or (iii) by sending it by certified or registered mail to the taxpayer's/possessor's last known address.

**Effect of Levy.** A levy gives the IRS full legal rights to the property seized, including the right to sell the property to collect the unpaid tax. If the taxpayer's liability is not satisfied by the initial levy, the IRS can make successive subsequent levies on any other property until the unpaid taxes are paid in full [§ 6331(c)].

### XXIII.C.4.g. Restrictions on Levy Authority

[637 T.M., IV.C.; TPS ¶3870.03.]

**Statute of Limitations.** Any tax can be collected by levy within 10 years after the assessment of the tax. The normal 10-year statute of limitations may be extended by agreement or by the rules suspending the running of the statute [§ 6502].

**Unreasonable Search and Seizure.** The Fourth Amendment restricts the levy authority of the IRS. Seizure of a taxpayer's property if in the public streets or open areas is permitted; however, seizure of property in the taxpayer's home or office is invalid unless a search warrant or writ of entry is first obtained from a court [*GM Leasing Corp. v. United States*, 429 U.S. 338 (1977)].

*Uneconomical Levy.* A levy may not be made on the taxpayer's property if the estimated amount of expenses incurred in the levy and sale of the property exceeds the fair market value of the property at the time of the levy [§ 6331(f)].

*Levy on Appearance Date of Summons.* The IRS cannot levy against property on a day when the person, or an officer or employee of that person, is required to appear in response to an IRS summons issued for the purpose of collecting any underpayment of tax. This prohibition does not apply if the IRS finds that the collection of tax is in jeopardy [§ 6331(g)].

*Levy Prohibited During Pendency of Refund Proceedings.* The IRS must withhold levy activity on liabilities during the pendency of a refund suit for taxes for which a suit may be brought without full payment of the tax (i.e., divisible taxes) [§ 6331(i)].

*Levy Prohibited During Pendency of Offer in Compromise.* The IRS must withhold levy activity while an offer in compromise is pending, during the 30-day period following rejection of an offer in compromise, and, if the taxpayer appeals the rejection of the offer, while the appeal is pending. This prohibition applies unless jeopardy exists or the IRS returns the offer to the taxpayer after determining that it was not processable or submitted solely for purposes of delay. The statute of limitations on collection is suspended during the time that the IRS is prohibited from levying [§ 6331(k)].

*Levy Prohibited During Term of Installment Agreement.* The IRS cannot engage in levy activity while the taxpayer's request for an installment agreement is pending, for 30 days after the IRS rejects a proposed agreement and, if the taxpayer appeals the rejection, while the appeal is pending. The IRS is further prohibited from levying while an installment agreement is in effect. If an installment agreement is terminated, the IRS cannot levy for 30 days after the termination and while an appeal is pending. However, the IRS is not prohibited from levying to carry out an offset of an overpayment. The IRS also can continue its levy activity if the levy was first made before the IRS accepted the installment agreement for processing [§ 6331(i)].

*Levy Prohibited Before Investigation of Status of Property.* Before making a levy, the IRS must make a thorough investigation of the status of any seized property or right to property which is to be sold. The investigation must include [§ 6331(j)]:

- verification of the taxpayer's liability;
- completion of an analysis of whether levy would be uneconomical;
- determination of the sufficiency of the equity in the property in terms of applying the net proceeds from sale to the liability; and
- thorough consideration of alternative collection methods.

### XXIII.C.4.h. Surrender of Property Subject to Levy

[637 T.M., IV.E.; TPS ¶3870.03.]

If the IRS serves a levy upon any person in possession of (or obligated with respect to) the taxpayer's property or rights to property, that person must surrender the property to the IRS on demand. Failure or refusal to surrender the property renders that person personally liable for the payment of an amount equal to the lesser of (i) the value of the property he refused to surrender, or (ii) the tax liability for which levy was made, plus costs and interest. Any payment made on account of such personal liability is credited to the delinquent taxpayer's account. In addition to the personal liability imposed, a person refusing to surrender the property on demand without reasonable cause is also subject to a penalty equal to 50% of the value of the withheld property [§ 6332(a)].

A person can properly refuse to surrender property on which levy has been made if (i) the property or rights to property are subject to attachment or execution under any prior judicial process, or (ii) the person is not in possession of any property subject to levy [§ 6332]. If the person surrenders the levied property on demand, that person is statutorily protected and discharged from any liability to the taxpayer for claims arising out of the surrender [§ 6332(e)].

### XXIII.C.4.i. Property Exempt from Levy

[637 T.M., IV.C.; TPS ¶3870.03.B.]

As a general rule, the IRS can levy on all property or rights to property belonging to a delinquent taxpayer. For these purposes, the definition of property subject to levy is the same as property that is subject to the federal tax lien. The only property or rights to property exempt from levy and seizure are those specifically exempted by statute. The exempt categories are [§ 6334]:

1. necessary wearing apparel and school books;
2. fuel, provisions, furniture, personal effects, personal firearms, livestock, and poultry not exceeding $8,940 for 2014 ($9,080 for 2015) [Rev. Proc. 2013-35, 2013-47 I.R.B. 537, Rev. Proc. 2014-61, 2014-47 I.R.B. 860]
3. books and tools of the taxpayer's trade, business, or profession that do not exceed, $4,470 for 2014 ($4,540 for 2015) [Rev. Proc. 2013-35, Rev. Proc. 2014-61];
4. a percentage of unemployment benefits;
5. undelivered mail addressed to any person;
6. certain annuity and pension payments under the Railroad Retirement Act, the Railroad Unemployment Insurance Act, special payments to congressional medal of honor holders, and annuities based on retired or retainer pay for military servicemen;
7. a percentage of worker's compensation;
8. wages or other income, to the extent required to satisfy a judgment for child support that is entered before the date of levy;
9. a minimum exemption for the taxpayer's wages or salary for personal services, or income derived from other sources;
10. certain service-connected disability benefits;
11. a percentage of certain public assistance payments;
12. any amount paid to a taxpayer under the Job Training Partnership Act;
13. any real property used as a residence by the taxpayer or any real property of the taxpayer (other than real property which is rented) used by another individual if the amount of the levy does not exceed $5,000;
14. the taxpayer's principal residence, unless court-approved; and
15. certain business assets, unless the levy is approved in writing by the area director or collection of the tax is in jeopardy.

For any federal payment for which eligibility is based on the income and/or assets of the payee, a levy is continuous from the date it is made until it is released and it attaches to up to 15% of the specified payment due to the taxpayer. However, for vendors who sell or lease property, goods or services to the federal government, the IRS may levy on up to 100% of any payment(s) to the vendor [§ 6331(h)].

***Amount of Wages Exempt from Levy.*** For a taxpayer paid on a weekly basis, the amount of wages or salary exempt from levy for each week is equal to (i) the taxpayer's standard deduction; plus (ii) the total of personal exemptions allowable for the tax year in which the levy occurs; (iii) divided by 52 weeks [§ 6334(d)(1)]. For a taxpayer who is paid on a basis other than weekly, the amount of exempt wages or salary is computed to equal an amount of wages exempt from levy as if the taxpayer were paid on a weekly basis [§ 6334(d)(3)].

### XXIII.C.4.j. Seizure and Sale of Property

[627 T.M., IV.; TPS ¶3870.03.]

A levy on property that is in the taxpayer's possession may be accomplished by seizure and public sale of the property. A levy on the taxpayer's property or rights to property in the possession of a third party is accomplished by serving a notice of levy on the third party demanding surrender of the property [§ 6332].

**Collection Due Process (CDP) Rights Related to Levy.** Before levying against wages, salary, or any other property of a delinquent taxpayer (except for certain exceptions described below), the IRS must give the taxpayer written notice of its intent to levy. The notice must be delivered personally, left at the taxpayer's dwelling or usual place of business, or sent by certified or registered mail to the taxpayer's last known address. The IRS must deliver or mail the notice of intent to levy no later than 30 days before the day of levy [§ 6331(d)].

Taxpayers also must be provided with notice and an opportunity for a hearing before an Appeals Officer, with limited exceptions, before a levy may be initiated (see XXIII.C.4.c.). The pre-levy notice must be provided no less than 30 days before the day of the first levy. A request for a hearing within the 30-day period would stay any proposed related IRS collection activity until Appeals has issued a determination [§ 6330].

Taxpayers subject to jeopardy collection proceedings, levies to collect a federal tax liability from a state tax refund, levies to collect disqualified employment taxes, and levies on federal contractors for unpaid taxes are not eligible for pre-levy hearing procedures, but are entitled to a post-levy hearing. In such cases, the IRS provides notice of the right to, and an opportunity for, a due process hearing within a reasonable period of time after the levy. A levy also is permitted when the taxpayer fails to respond to the notice, but a hearing known as an "equivalent hearing" must be provided if later requested by the taxpayer [§ 6330(f)].

### XXIII.C.4.k. Release and Return of Levied Property

[637 T.M. IV.D.2.a.; TPS ¶3870.03.E.]

The IRS must release a levy on property if any of the following criteria is present [§ 6343]:

- the tax liability, for which the levy was made, is satisfied or becomes unenforceable by reason of the expiration of the statutory period for collection;
- release of the levy facilitates collection of the tax liability;
- the taxpayer has entered into an installment payment agreement (and the agreement does not prohibit release of the levy);
- the IRS determines that the levy causes an economic hardship due to the taxpayer's financial condition; or
- the fair market value of the property exceeds the tax liability and release of the levy on a part of the property does not hinder collection of the liability.

### *XXIII.C.4.l. Transferee Liability*

[628 T.M.; TPS ¶3870.07.B.]

The liability for unpaid income, estate, or gift taxes owed by a delinquent tax-payer/transferor may be assessed, paid, and collected from the transferee in the same manner as a tax liability due from the taxpayer/transferor. If a taxpayer/transferor is liable for other types of federal taxes, this method of collection is available but only if the tax liability arises (i) on the liquidation of a partnership or a corporation, or (ii) on a corporate reorganization [§ 6901]. A transferee's liability under these provisions is either liability at law or in equity. The existence and extent of transferee liability is determined by reference to state law [*Commissioner v. Stern*, 357 U.S. 39 (1958)].

### *XXIII.C.4.m. Offer in Compromise*

[638 T.M., VI.; TPS ¶3870.08.E.]

The IRS can accept less than full payment and compromise the taxpayer's tax liability [§ 7122]. The IRS's policy is to compromise a tax liability when:

- it is unlikely that the IRS can collect the tax liability in full; and
- the amount offered by the taxpayer reasonably reflects collection potential.

There are two prerequisites for compromising a tax liability. First, the tax liability must be assessed [§ 7122(b)(1)]. Second, there must be at least one of the following: (i) doubt as to liability, (ii) doubt as to collectibility, or (iii) a situation where a compromise would promote effective tax administration [Reg. § 301.7122-1(b)].

Doubt as to collectibility exists where the taxpayer is unable to pay the assessed tax liability [Reg. § 301.7122-1(c)(2)(i)]. In determining whether the taxpayer meets the doubt as to collectibility requirement, the IRS considers the taxpayer's assets and present and future income potential. The IRS also considers the assets and income of a jointly liable spouse who submits an offer in compromise. The IRS does not consider the assets and income of a non-liable spouse in determining the amount of an adequate offer, except to the extent property has been transferred by the taxpayer to the non-liable spouse under circumstances that would permit the IRS to effect collection of the taxpayer's liability from such property — for example, if the taxpayer has made a fraudulent conveyance to the non-liable spouse or if collection from the assets and/or income of the non-liable spouse is permitted by applicable state law (e.g., under state community property laws). Regardless, the IRS may request information regarding the nonliable spouse's assets and/or income solely to verify the amount of and responsibility for expenses claimed by the taxpayer [Reg. § 301.7122-1(c)(2)(ii)].

Even if there is no doubt as to liability or doubt as to collectibility, compromise may be appropriate to promote effective tax administration when [Reg. § 301.7122-1(b)(3)]:

- full collection will create economic hardship for the taxpayer; or
- the taxpayer identifies compelling public policy or equity considerations where exceptional circumstances exist so that collection of the full liability would undermine public confidence that the tax laws are being administered in a fair and equitable manner, and the compromise would not undermine compliance with the tax laws.

***Process for Making Offer in Compromise.*** The IRS's objectives in compromising a tax liability are to resolve tax accounts that cannot be collected in full (or for which the taxpayer legitimately disputes the amount owed) and to collect what can be reasonably collected at the earliest possible time [IRS Policy Statement P-5-100 (1-30-92)].

An offer in compromise must be made in writing, must be signed by the taxpayer under penalty of perjury, must be submitted on Form 656, *Offer in Compromise*, and must be accompanied by partial payment of the compromise amount. The taxpayer must provide certain information, including [§ 7122(c)(1), § 7122(d)(1); Reg. § 301.7122-1(d)]:

- the amount, type, and period/year of taxes to be compromised;
- the amount that the taxpayer is offering to pay in order to compromise the tax liability;
- the terms of any payments to be made under the offer; and
- the basis of the offer (i.e., doubt as to liability, doubt as to collectibility, or effective tax administration) and supporting statements.

If the basis for compromising the liability is doubt as to collectibility, the taxpayer must also submit an appropriate financial statement, Form 433-A, *Collection Information Statement for Wage Earners and Self-Employed Individuals*, or Form 433-B, *Collection Information Statement for Businesses* [Rev. Proc. 2003-71, 2003-36 I.R.B. 517].

There is a $186 user fee for submitting an offer in compromise that it has accepted for processing. However, the user fee does not apply to offers based on doubt as to liability or offers made by certain low income taxpayers. In addition, the user fee is applied against the amount of the offer or, if the taxpayer prefers, refunded to the taxpayer if the IRS either accepts an offer to promote effective tax administration or accepts an offer based on doubt as to collectibility where there has also been a determination that, although an amount greater than the amount offered could be collected, collection of more than the amount offered would create economic hardship. For all other offers, the IRS includes the processing fee in the amount determined to be collectible from the taxpayer and takes the fee into account when considering whether the amount offered is acceptable. Except as indicated above, the IRS does not refund the fee if the offer is accepted, rejected, withdrawn, or returned as nonprocessible after acceptance for processing [Reg. § 300.3].

By submitting an offer in compromise, the taxpayer agrees to waive refunds or credits for any tax years/periods ending before, during, or at the end of the calendar year in which the IRS accepts the offer in compromise, and to waive the right to contest the liability after the IRS accepts the offer. The statute of limitations on collection is suspended for the time that the offer is under consideration by the IRS [Reg. § 301.7122-1].

The taxpayer must (i) in the case of a lump sum offer, pay 20% of the offer when the offer is submitted, or (ii) in the case of an offer of periodic payments, pay the amount of the first proposed installment when the offer is submitted. During the time an offer of periodic payments is being evaluated by the IRS, if the taxpayer fails to make a payment under the submitted offer, it is treated as a withdrawal of the offer. If the IRS fails to reject the offer-in-compromise within 24 months of its submission (not taking into account any period during which the subject tax liability is in dispute in a judicial proceeding), it is deemed accepted [§ 7122].

Once the IRS decides to accept the offer in compromise, the offer may be subject to review by the Treasury Department's General Counsel. If the dollar amount of unpaid taxes to be compromised is $50,000 or more, the Office of Chief Counsel must review the offer. The Chief Counsel opinion, in addition to information about the compromised tax liability, is kept on file. Because acceptance of an offer "conclusively settles" the taxpayer's liability specified in the offer, it is only set aside for fraud, concealment of assets or income, or a mutual mistake of material fact. [§ 7122(b); Reg. § 301.7122-1(e)].

The IRS may not reject an offer to compromise received from any taxpayer solely because of the amount of the offer without the evaluating whether the offer meets a ground for compromise and IRS policies and procedures regarding compromise [§ 7122(d)(3)(A)]. In addition, the IRS must conduct an internal independent administrative review of any rejection of any proposed offer in compromise before the rejection is communicated to a taxpayer. The rejection must be communicated to the taxpayer or the taxpayer's representative in a written notice that also states the reasons for the rejection and the taxpayer's right to an appeal to Appeals. The taxpayer has 30 days after the date on the rejection letter in which to request administrative review [Reg. § 301.7122-1(f)]. After administrative review, the taxpayer may appeal to Tax Court on an abuse of discretion standard.

### XXIII.C.4.n. Installment Agreements

[638 T.M., V.; TPS ¶3870.08.F.]

A taxpayer who cannot timely pay the full amount of taxes due may be allowed to pay the taxes in installments [§ 6159]. In determining if the taxpayer is a good candidate for an installment agreement, the IRS examines the taxpayer's income and expenses. The IRS considers the excess income over the taxpayer's ordinary and necessary expenses to be available for payment under the installment agreement. The taxpayer should propose to pay a specific amount each month. If the taxpayer does not make such a proposal, the IRS will request that the taxpayer specify how much can be paid each month.

***Guaranteed Installment Agreements.*** At the taxpayer's request, the IRS must enter into an installment agreement for full payment of the tax liability if [§ 6159(c)]:

1. the liability for income tax only is $10,000 or less (excluding penalties and interest);
2. within the previous five years, the taxpayer has not failed to file or pay, nor entered into a another installment agreement;
3. the taxpayer demonstrates that he is unable to pay the tax in full;
4. the installment agreement provides for full payment of the liability within three years; and
5. the taxpayer agrees to remain in full compliance with the tax laws and the terms of the agreement for the period (up to three years) that the agreement is in place.

***Streamlined Installment Agreements.*** If the taxpayer has aggregate unpaid liabilities of $50,000 or less, the taxpayer may qualify for a "streamlined" installment agreement. To qualify for a streamlined agreement, the taxpayer must be able to fully pay the aggregate unpaid balance of assessments within 60 months or before the expiration of the collection statute of limitations, whichever comes first. All tax returns that are due before entering into the agreement must have been filed.

***In-Business Trust Fund Express Agreements.*** Businesses owing employment taxes may qualify for an installment agreement if the entire liability (including accruals) does not exceed a specified amount and the taxes can be fully paid within 24 months or before the expiration of the statute of limitations on collection, whichever comes first.

***Partial Pay Installment Agreements.*** The IRS may allow for an installment agreement that does not result in full payment (Partial Payment Installment Agreement or PPIA). Taxpayers who request a PPIA must provide a full collection information statement. Only necessary expenses are permitted. The IRS also requires the taxpayer to make a good faith effort to utilize equity in assets to reduce or fully pay the amount of the outstanding liability, and may request that assets be sold or that equity be borrowed against. However, complete utilization of equity is not always required as a condition of a PPIA. If a taxpayer qualifies for a PPIA, the IRS will encourage the taxpayer to pay using the direct debit option. A taxpayer granted a PPIA is subject to financial review every two years. If the IRS determines that the taxpayer's financial condition has improved, the IRS may request an increase in the amount of the installment payments or may terminate the agreement altogether.

***Requesting an Installment Agreement.*** Proposals to enter into installment agreements may result from letters, phone contacts, voice-mail, e-mail, or other communications between a taxpayer and the IRS. The taxpayer may request an installment agreement using Form 9465, *Installment Agreement Request,* or by completing an application for on Online Payment Agreement is available online at: www.irs.gov/Individuals/Online-Payment-Agreement-Application.

The taxpayer must provide information about assets, property, and income. Generally, the taxpayer provides this information to the IRS on Form 433-D, *Installment Agreement,* and/or Form 433-A, *Collection Information Statement for Wage Earners and Self-Employed Individuals,* or Form 433-B, *Collection Information Statement for Businesses.* Alternatively, the IRS may use Form 433-F, *Collection Information Statement,* for individual taxpayers whose total tax liability is less than $100,000.

The IRS may terminate an installment agreement if (i) information provided by the taxpayer in connection with the granting of the agreement or a financial update is found to be inaccurate or incomplete in any material respect, or (ii) the IRS determines that collection is in jeopardy. The IRS may modify or terminate an installment agreement if (i) a determination is made that the taxpayer's financial condition has significantly changed, or (ii) the taxpayer fails to timely pay an installment, pay any other federal tax liability when the liability becomes due, or fails to provide a financial condition update when requested [Reg. § 301.6159-1(e)]. The IRS generally notifies the taxpayer in writing at least 30 days before modifying or terminating an installment agreement. The taxpayer may appeal the proposed modification or termination within 30 days following issuance of the modification/termination notice [§ 6159(b)(5); Reg. § 301.6159-1(e)(5)].

For proposed installment agreements, the IRS is prohibited from levying during the following periods [§ 6331(k)(2)]:

- while an offer for an installment agreement for payment of the unpaid tax in issue is pending;

- in the 30-day period following rejection of the offer and, if the rejection is appealed, during the period the appeal is pending;

- throughout the period the installment agreement is in effect; and

- if the IRS terminates the installment agreement, in the 30-day period following the termination, and if the termination is appealed, during the period the appeal is pending.

### XXIII.C.4.o. Taxpayer Assistance Orders (TAOs)

[638 T.M., XIII.; TPS ¶3870.08.J.]

The Taxpayer Advocate Service (TAS) handles taxpayers' complaints and represents taxpayers' interests and concerns within the IRS. The TAS is directed by the National Taxpayer Advocate (NTA). The NTA has the authority to issue a Taxpayer Assistance Order (TAO) when the taxpayer is suffering or is about to suffer a significant hardship as a result of the manner of the administration of the tax laws, including action or inaction on the part of the IRS. In issuing a TAO, the NTA can require the IRS to release a levy against the taxpayer's property, to stop other collection or audit actions, to take any action permitted by law, or to stop any other action, as listed in the TAO [§ 7811; Reg. § 301.7811-1(a)].

**Issuance of Taxpayer Assistance Order.** To request a TAO, a taxpayer or a taxpayer's representative must use Form 911, *Request for Taxpayer Advocate Assistance (And Application for Taxpayer Assistance Order)*, or submit a written statement containing information sufficient for TAS to determine the nature of the harm or the need for assistance [Reg. § 301.7811-1(b)].

If the NTA determines that the taxpayer is facing significant hardship and that the facts and the law support relief, the NTA may issue a TAO ordering the IRS to [Reg. § 301.7811-1(c)]:

- release levied property (to the extent permitted by law);
- cease any action, take any action, or refrain from taking any action with respect to a taxpayer involving collection, bankruptcy, receivership, title enforcement, or any other provision of the internal revenue laws; or
- expedite, reconsider, or review at a higher level an action taken on a determination or collection of a tax liability.

A TAO may be issued to any office, division, or IRS function, but not if the action ordered could reasonably be suspected to impede a criminal investigation. Once issued, a TAO cannot be modified or rescinded unless approved by the NTA or the IRS Commissioner or Deputy Commissioner [§ 7811(c)].

## XXIII.D. Penalties and Interest

### XXIII.D.1. Penalties

### XXIII.D.1.a. Delinquency Penalties

### XXIII.D.1.a.(1) Failure to File Timely Return

[634 T.M., II.B.; TPS ¶3830.01.A.]

A taxpayer who fails to file a tax return on or before the due date prescribed for filing, including any extensions, is subject to a penalty equal to 5% of the net amount of tax due for each month or fraction of a month the return is not filed, up to a maximum of 25% [§ 6651(a)(1)].

The net amount of tax due is the amount of tax required to be shown on the return, reduced by any payments made on or before the due date for payment and by the amount of any credits against the tax which may be claimed on the return [§ 6651(b)(1)]. The net amount of tax due includes any deficiency [Reg. § 301.6651-1(f), *Ex.* 1].

The failure to file penalty applies to all income tax returns (individual, corporation, estates or trusts) as well as to gift tax and estate tax returns, unless the taxpayer shows that the failure was due to reasonable cause [§ 6651(a)]. The penalty does not apply to information returns or to estimated tax payments [§ 6651(e), § 6652] In cases where the taxpayer fails to file and the IRS prepares a substitute for return, the penalty does not apply [§ 6651(g)(1)].

A minimum penalty is imposed where a taxpayer fails to file an income tax return within 60 days of the due date (including extensions). The minimum penalty in such cases is the lesser of (i) $135, or (ii) the net amount of tax owed [§ 6651(a)].

If the failure to file is fraudulent, the failure to file penalty is increased to 15% of the net amount of tax due for each month or fraction of a month the return is not filed, up to a maximum of 75% [§ 6651(f)].

If both the failure to file and the failure to pay penalties apply to the same month or portion thereof, the failure to file penalty is reduced by the 0.5% failure to pay penalty (see XXIII.D.1.a.(2)). There is, however, no reduction in the failure to file penalty if the minimum penalty is being imposed for failure to file within 60 days of the due date [§ 6651(a)(1), § 6651(c)(1)].

A return is considered late if it is not filed by the due date. The due date is the date prescribed for filing, and includes any valid extension of time for filing. If a taxpayer fails to estimate his or her tax liability properly on his extension request, the extension is considered invalid and the late filing penalty can be imposed. If the return is filed late, the late filing penalty begins to accrue on the day after the extended due date [§ 6651(a)(1)].

### XXIII.D.1.a.(2) Failure to Pay Tax Shown on Return

[634 T.M., III.A.; TPS ¶3830.01.B.]

A taxpayer who fails to pay the amount of tax shown on a tax return by the due date prescribed for payment is subject to a penalty of 0.5% of the amount of tax shown on the return for each month the amount remains unpaid, up to a maximum of 25% (50 months), unless the failure to pay was due to reasonable cause [§ 6651(a)(2); Reg. § 301.6651-1(a)(2)]. Where the taxpayer is an individual who filed the tax return in a timely manner, including extensions, the 0.5% penalty rate is reduced to 0.25% for any month in which an installment payment agreement is in effect for the payment of the tax [§ 6651(h); Reg. § 301.6651-1(a)(4)]. The 0.5% rate increases to 1% for each month or fraction thereof beginning after the earlier of (i) the date 10 days after the IRS issues a notice of levy, or (ii) the date of the notice and demand of a jeopardy assessment [§ 6651(d)].

The penalty is based on the amount shown on the tax return, not the amount required to be shown. However, if the amount required to be shown is less than the amount shown, the penalty is calculated using the lesser amount [§ 6651(c)(2)]. In calculating the failure to pay penalty for any month, the amount of tax shown on the return is reduced by any payments made on or before the beginning of such month and by any credit against the tax claimed on the return [§ 6651(b)(2); Reg. § 301.6651-1(d)(1)].

A return prepared by the IRS under substitute for return provisions is treated as a return filed by the taxpayer for purposes of determining liability for the failure to pay penalty [§ 6651(g)(2)].

### XXIII.D.1.a.(3) Failure to Pay Additional Tax After Notice and Demand

[634 T.M., III.B.; TPS ¶3830.01.C.]

A taxpayer who fails to pay any tax required to be shown on a return and that is not so shown within 21 calendar days of notice and demand (10 business days if the amount for which the notice and demand is made equals $100,000 or more) is subject to a penalty of 0.5% per month of this amount for each month it remains unpaid, up to a maximum of 25% (50 months), unless the failure to pay is due to reasonable cause [§ 6651(a)(3); Reg. § 301.6651-1(a)(3)]. The penalty rate is reduced to 0.25% for individual taxpayers who file their returns in a timely manner, including extensions, for any month in which an installment agreement is in effect for the payment of the tax [§ 6651(h); Reg. § 301.6651-1(a)(4)]. The amount stated in the notice is reduced by any payments made before the beginning of the month for which the penalty is computed [§ 6651(b)(3)].

The penalty for failure to pay additional tax after notice and demand also applies to returns prepared by the IRS under the substitute for return provisions of the Code. The substitute for return prepared by the IRS is treated as if filed by the taxpayer for purposes of determining the penalty [§ 6651(g)(2); Reg. § 301.6651-1(g)].

### XXIII.D.1.a.(4) Computation of Delinquency Penalties

[634 T.M., II.B.4.; TPS ¶3830.01.E.]

Delinquency penalties are imposed on the net amount of tax due.

*Failure to File Penalty.* The net amount due is the amount of tax required to be shown on the return, reduced by the amount of any taxes paid on or before the due date prescribed for payment and by any credits that may be claimed on the return (e.g., withheld income taxes and estimated tax payments) [§ 6651(b)(1)]. The amount of tax required to be shown on the return means the correct tax liability for the period as finally determined, including deficiency assessments [Reg. § 301.6651-1(f), *Ex.* 1]. If the taxpayer fails to file a return within 60 days of the return due date, as extended, even if there is no unpaid tax or net amount due (e.g., where the tax withheld equals or exceeds the tax owed) there is a minimum penalty of the lesser of (i) $100, or (ii) 100% of the amount required to be shown as tax on the return [§ 6651(a)].

*Penalty for Failure to Pay Tax Shown on Return.* For purposes of computing the amount of the penalty for any month, the unpaid tax liability shown on the return is reduced by any payments made before the beginning of the month, as well as any credits that may be claimed on the return [§ 6651(b)(2); Reg. § 301.6651-1(d)(2)(i)].

*Penalty for Failure to Pay Deficiency After Receipt of Notice and Demand.* For purposes of computing the amount of the penalty for any month, the amount of tax stated in the notice and demand is reduced by any payments thereof made before the beginning of the month [§ 6651(b)(3); Reg. § 301.6651-1(d)(2)(ii)].

---

**EXAMPLE:** B, an individual, filed his 2012 Year 1 calendar year tax return on July 19, 2013. B did not file an application for extension of the Apr. 15 filing date. The return shows a tax liability of $800, credits allowable for amounts withheld of $400, and estimated tax payments of $300. This totals $700 ($300 + $400) of taxes withheld or paid, leaving $100 as the balance due on the $800 liability. B paid the $100 on Aug. 23, 2013. In July 2014, the IRS determined and B agreed to a deficiency of $200, which was assessed and paid in July 2014. B is liable for a failure to file penalty of 20% (four months [three months plus a fraction of a fourth month] at 5% per month) of the net amount of tax "required to be shown." This amount is $300 (($800 + $200 deficiency) − $700 of credits). Thus, the addition to tax is $60 (20% × $300). However, because of the minimum penalty provision (no less than $100 or the net amount of tax due), the penalty imposed is $100. The failure to pay penalty applies since the tax shown to be due on the return ($100) was not paid until four months and a fraction of a fifth month after the due date of the return (i.e., from Apr. 15 through Aug. 23). The penalty is therefore $2.50 (0.5% × $100 × 5 months). Ordinarily, this $2.50 penalty for failure to pay reduces the failure to file penalty. In this case, since the minimum penalty of $100 applies, no reduction is permitted.

### XXIII.D.1.b. Accuracy Related Penalties

### XXIII.D.1.b.(1) Negligence or Disregard of Rules or Regulations Penalty

[634 T.M., IV.; TPS ¶3830.02.]

If any part of an underpayment of tax is due to negligence or disregard of rules or regulations, a penalty of 20% is imposed. The 20% rate is applied to the portion of the underpayment attributable to negligence or disregard of rules and regulations. If the fraud penalty also is asserted, the negligence penalty does not apply to the portion of the underpayment to which the fraud penalty is applied [§ 6662(a), § 6662(b)(1)]. The negligence penalty is not imposed on any portion of an underpayment to the extent the taxpayer can show that there was reasonable cause for the underpayment and that the taxpayer acted in good faith [§ 6664(c)(1)].

The amount of an underpayment is the amount by which income tax imposed under Subtitle A exceeds the following amount [§ 6664]:

- the sum of (i) the amount equal to the tax shown on the return, and (ii) amounts not so shown previously assessed or collected without assessment; less

- the amount of rebates made.

**EXAMPLE:** Taxpayer's return for Year 1 showed a tax liability of $18,000. There were no other amounts assessed or collected without assessment and there were no rebates. Taxpayer received a refund of $5,000 because of withholding of $23,000. The IRS determined that taxpayer had unreported additional income and that the correct tax for the year is $25,500. The underpayment is $7,500 ($25,500 − $18,000) [Reg. § 1.6664-2(g), *Ex. 1*].

*Negligence and Disregard of Rules or Regulations Defined.* The term "negligence" includes any failure to make a reasonable attempt to comply with the provisions of the internal revenue laws or to exercise ordinary and reasonable care in the preparation of a tax return. Negligence also includes any failure by a taxpayer to keep adequate books and records. A position with respect to an item is attributable to negligence if it lacks a reasonable basis [Reg. § 1.6662-3(b)(1)]. Negligence includes acts of omission or commission, e.g., omitting income or overstating deductions, conduct in which a reasonable person would not engage. Even if the understatement is unintentional, the negligence penalty may be imposed where an excessive deduction is claimed or income is understated as the result of inadequate or improper recordkeeping.

The penalty for disregarding rules or regulations may not be imposed on any portion of an underpayment that is attributable to a position contrary to a rule or regulation if the position is adequately disclosed and represents a good faith challenge to the validity of the regulation. The disclosure exception does not apply, however, where the position does not have a reasonable basis or where the taxpayer fails to keep adequate books and records or to substantiate items properly. [Reg. § 1.6662-3(a), § 1.6662-3(c)(1), § 1.6662-7(b)].

## XXIII.D.1.b.(2) Substantial Understatement Penalty

[634 T.M., IV.E.; TPS ¶3830.06.]

An accuracy-related penalty for underpayments is imposed at the rate of 20% (40% in the case of a gross valuation misstatement) on the portion of any underpayment of tax required to be shown on a return attributable to any of the following [§ 6662(b)]:

- negligence;
- substantial understatement of tax;
- substantial valuation misstatement;
- substantial overstatement of pension liabilities;
- substantial estate or gift tax valuation understatement;
- transactions lacking economic substance; or
- undisclosed foreign financial asset.

The accuracy-related penalty applies only when a return (other than one prepared by the IRS pursuant to § 6020(b)) has been filed [§ 6664(b)]. When no return has been filed, only the failure to file penalty applies. Thus, for example, no additional penalties are imposed as a result of a determination that the taxpayer's failure to file a return was negligent. If a return is filed late, both the accuracy-related penalty and the failure to file penalty under § 6651 may apply, but the fact that the return is filed late is not taken into account in determining whether the accuracy-related penalty should be applied [Reg. § 1.6662-2(a)]. The accuracy-related penalty also does not apply to any portion of an underpayment on which the fraud penalty is imposed nor does it apply to the portion of an underpayment on which the reportable transaction penalty under § 6662A is imposed [§ 6662(b)].

***Substantial Authority.*** The amount of any understatement is reduced by any portion of the understatement attributable to tax treatment for which there is or was substantial authority or there was adequate disclosure coupled with a reasonable basis for the taxpayer's position [§ 6662(d)(2)(B)]. The substantial authority standard is less stringent than a "more likely than not" standard (i.e., a greater than 50% likelihood of being upheld in litigation), but more stringent than a reasonable basis standard (the standard necessary to prevent imposition of the negligence penalty under § 6662(b)(1)).

***Adequate Disclosure.*** Items as to which the relevant facts are adequately disclosed on the return are treated as if they were properly reported for purposes of determining whether there was an understatement so long as there is a reasonable basis for the tax treatment on the return. Thus, properly disclosed items can reduce or eliminate the substantial understatement portion of the accuracy-related penalty. For purposes of the disclosure requirement, the reasonable basis standard is intended to be significantly higher than the "not frivolous" standard under prior law, and is not satisfied by a position that is merely arguable or merely a colorable claim. On the other hand, it is less stringent than "substantial authority" [§ 6662(d)(2)(B)(ii)].

Disclosure is adequate for an item or a position on a return if the disclosure is made on a properly completed form attached to the return, to a qualified amended return for the tax year, or on Form 8275 or 8275-R [Reg. § 1.6662-4(f)(1)]. The IRS periodically issues guidance listing the circumstances under which disclosure of information on a return in accordance with the applicable forms and instructions is deemed adequate disclosure for penalty purposes [Reg. § 1.6662-4(f)(2); Rev. Proc. 2014-15, 2014-5 I.R.B. 456].

*Disclosure of Uncertain Tax Positions.* Certain taxpayers with both uncertain tax positions and assets equal to or exceeding $10 million must report uncertain tax positions taken on their tax returns on Form 1120 Schedule UTP, *Uncertain Tax Positions Statement.* These taxpayers include [Reg. § 1.6012-2(a)(4)]:

- corporations that file Form 1120, *U.S. Corporation Income Tax Return;*
- insurance companies that file Form 1120L, *U.S. Life Insurance Company Income Tax Return,* or Form 1120PC, *U.S. Property and Casualty Insurance Company Income Tax Return;* and
- foreign corporations that file Form 1120F, *U.S. Income Tax Return of a Foreign Corporation.*

*Reasonable Cause Exception.* The accuracy-related penalty will not be imposed for a substantial understatement where the taxpayer can show reasonable cause for the underpayment and that the taxpayer acted in good faith. However, reasonable cause and good faith do not prevent the imposition of the accuracy-related penalty on understatements that are attributable to transactions lacking economic substance or failing to meet the requirements of any similar rule of law [§ 6664(c)]. Reliance on an information return or the advice of a professional constitutes reasonable cause and good faith if, under all the circumstances, that reliance was reasonable. Circumstances that may indicate reasonable cause and good faith include an honest misunderstanding of fact or law that is reasonable in light of all the facts and circumstances, including the experience, knowledge, and education of the taxpayer [Reg. § 1.6664-4(b)].

### XXIII.D.1.b.(3) Penalties for Valuation Misstatements and Understatements

[634 T.M., IV.G.; TPS ¶3830.05.]

*Substantial Valuation Misstatements.* The accuracy-related penalty may be imposed if a taxpayer has an underpayment of income tax for any tax year that is attributable to a substantial valuation misstatement [§ 6662(b)(3)]. A "substantial valuation misstatement" exists if [§ 6662(e)]:

- the value of any property or the adjusted basis of any property claimed on any tax return is 150% or more of the amount determined to be the correct amount; or
- the price for any property or services (or for the use of property) claimed on any return in connection with any transaction between persons described in § 482 is 200% or more (or 50% or less) of the amount determined under § 482 to be the correct price or the net § 482 transfer price adjustment for the tax year exceeds the lesser of $5 million or 10% of the taxpayer's gross receipts.

The penalty imposed is equal to 20% of the amount of the underpayment that is attributable to the substantial valuation misstatement [§ 6662(a)]. The penalty is increased to 40% where the claimed valuation is 200% or more of the correct value, the claimed price of property or services in a § 482 transfer is at least 400% (or 25% or less) of the amount determined to be the correct price, or the net § 482 transfer price adjustment exceeds the lesser of $20 million or 20% of the taxpayer's gross receipts [§ 6662(h)].

No penalty may be imposed unless the underpayment of tax for the tax year attributable to the valuation misstatement exceeds $5,000 ($10,000 for corporations other than S corporations and personal holding companies) [§ 6662(e)(2)].

*Pension Liabilities.* The accuracy-related penalty applies to any underpayment attributable to a substantial overstatement of pension liabilities [§ 6662(a),

§ 6662(b)(4)]. To determine whether there is such a substantial overstatement, the actuarial determination of a plan's liabilities used to compute the employer's deduction for contributions to the plan is compared to the plan's actual liabilities. If the actuarial amount is 200% or more of the actual amount, the 20% penalty applies [§ 6662(f)(1)]. Where the actuarial amount of liabilities is 400% or more of the actual valuation, the penalty increases to 40% [§ 6662(h)].

*Estate and Gift Tax.* The accuracy-related penalty applies to underpayments of estate and gift taxes that are attributable to valuation understatements of property transferred by will or gift [§ 6662(a), § 6662(b)(5); Reg. § 1.6662-1]. The penalty does not apply if the underpayment of tax is less than $5,000 [§ 6662(g)(2)]. The penalty applies if the value of any property claimed on a return is 65% or less of the amount determined to be the correct value [§ 6662(g)(1)].

The penalty imposed is 20% of the amount of underpayment attributable to the undervaluation [§ 6662(a)]. If, however, the claimed valuation is 40% or less of the correct value, the penalty increases to 40% [§ 6662(h)].

### XXIII.D.1.b.(4) Economic Substance Penalty

[634 T.M. IV.J.2.; TPS ¶3830.06.A.5.]

An understatement penalty applies to any understatement resulting from the disallowance of claimed tax benefits if the transaction lacks economic substance or fails to meet the requirements of any similar rule of law [§ 6662(b)(6)]. The penalty is equal to 20% of the underpayment but is increased to 40% if the taxpayer does not adequately disclose the relevant facts affecting the tax treatment in the return or a statement attached to the return [§ 6662(i)]. The reasonable cause exceptions for underpayments and reportable transaction understatements do not apply [§ 6664(c)(2), § 6664(d)(2)].

### XXIII.D.1.b.(5) Appraiser Penalty

[634 T.M., IV.M.; TPS ¶3830.11.]

Where an accuracy-related penalty for a substantial or gross valuation misstatement is imposed, the person who prepared an appraisal used in connection with the return or claim for refund is subject to a penalty if he knew or reasonably should have known that the appraisal would be used for this purpose. The amount of the penalty is the lesser of the following two amounts [§ 6695A]:

- the greater of 10% of the underpayment attributable to misstatement and $1,000; or

- 125% of the gross income received by the appraiser for the appraisal.

### XXIII.D.1.c. Civil Fraud Penalty

[634 T.M., V.; TPS ¶3830.03.]

If any portion of an underpayment of tax is due to fraud, a civil penalty equal to 75% of the portion of the underpayment attributable to fraud may be imposed [§ 6663(a)]. If both the accuracy-related and fraud penalties apply, the accuracy-related penalty does not apply to the fraud-induced portion of the underpayment [§ 6662(b)]. The fraud penalty applies only if a return is filed [§ 6664(b)]. If no return is filed, the fraudulent failure to file penalty may apply [§ 6651(f)]. If a late, but fraudulent return is filed, then both the regular late filing penalty and the fraud penalty can be asserted.

### XXIII.D.1.d. Penalty for Failure to Deposit Taxes

[634 T.M., III.D.; TPS ¶3830.04.]

If a taxpayer is required to deposit taxes (see XXII.C.1.b. and XXII.C.2.b.), a penalty may be is imposed if the taxpayer fails to make the deposit in the correct amount, within the prescribed time period, and/or in the required manner (e.g., by an electronic funds transfer) The penalty does not apply if the taxpayer has reasonable cause [§ 6656].

The amount of the penalty is based on the number of days a deposit is late [§ 6656(b)(1)]:

- 2% for deposits 1 – 5 days late;
- 5% for deposits 6 – 15 days late;
- 10% for all direct payments and those deposits made more than 15 days late, but paid on or before the 10th day following notice and demand; and
- 15% (i.e., a 5% addition to the 10% penalty) for all undeposited taxes still unpaid after the 10th day following the first balance due notice or the day on which notice and demand for immediate payment is given.

The deposit penalty applies to tax deposits for the following forms:

- Form 720, *Quarterly Federal Excise Tax Return*;
- Form 940, *Employer's Annual Federal Unemployment (FUTA) Tax Return*;
- Form 941, *Employer's Quarterly Federal Tax Return*;
- Form 943, *Employer's Annual Tax Return of Agricultural Employees*;
- Form 944, *Employer's Annual Federal Tax Return*;
- Form 945, *Annual Return of Withheld Federal Income Tax*;
- Form 1042, *Annual Withholding Tax Return for U.S. Source Income of Foreign Persons*; and
- Form CT-1, *Employer's Annual Railroad Retirement and Unemployment Repayment Tax Return*.

***Electronic Deposit Method (EFTPS).*** All taxpayers required to make deposits must use the Electronic Deposit Method (EFTPS). A deposit of taxes by electronic funds transfer is deemed made when the amount is withdrawn from the taxpayer's account, provided the U.S. Government is the payee and the amount is not returned or reversed [Reg. § 31.6302-1(h)(8)].

***How IRS Applies Deposits.*** For penalty purposes, in situations in which a taxpayer has not made deposits sufficient to satisfy the cumulative deposit obligations as of at least one deposit due date, the IRS generally applies a tax deposit to the most recently ended deposit period or periods within the specified tax period to which the deposit relates and will apply any excess to deposit periods that end on or after the date of the deposit in period-ending-date order [Rev. Proc. 2001-58, 2001-2 C.B. 579].

The failure to deposit penalty will not apply if [Reg. § 31.6302-1(f)]:

- the amount of any shortfall does not exceed the greater of $100 or 2% of the amount of employment taxes required to be deposited; and
- the employer deposits the shortfall on or before the shortfall makeup date.

***Special Exceptions to Penalty.*** The IRS may waive the failure-to-deposit penalty on a person's inadvertent failure to deposit any employment tax if [§ 6656(c)]:

1. the failure occurs during the first quarter that such person was required to deposit any employment tax or the person is required to change the frequency

of deposits and the failure relates to the first deposit to which the change in frequency applies;

2. the return was filed on or before the due date; and

3. the person meets the requirements of § 7430(c)(4)(A)(ii).

### XXIII.D.1.e. Information Return Reporting Penalties

[634 T.M., VI.; TPS ¶3830.07.]

Three-tiered penalties may be imposed on each failure to timely file a correct information return or to furnish a statement to the payee. The penalties apply to both failures to file/furnish on or before the required due date and reporting incomplete or inaccurate information [§ 6721(a)(2), § 6722(a)(2)]. The penalties vary based on when, if at all, the correct information return is filed or statement furnished [§ 6721(b), § 6722(b)]. Both penalties may apply to the same information return and related statement.

The amount of the penalty for each return for which a failure has occurred is as follows [§ 6721(a), § 6721(d), § 6722(a), § 6722(d)]:

- $30, up to a maximum of $250,000 per year ($75,000 for small businesses) if the person files a correct information return after the due date but on or before 30 days after the due date;

- $60, up to a maximum of $500,000 per year ($200,000 for small businesses) if the person files a correct information return after 30 days following the due date, but before August 2;

- $100, up to a maximum of $1,500,000 per year ($500,000 for small businesses) if a correct information return is not filed before August 2.

For this penalty, a small business is a person with average annual gross receipts for the most recent three tax years ending before the calendar year in question of $5 million or less.

Increased penalties are imposed if the failure is due to intentional disregard of the filing requirements, and there is no ceiling on the aggregate amount of the penalty in this situation [§ 6721(e), § 6722(e)].

Failure to timely file includes a failure to file in the required manner — for example, on magnetic media or in other machine readable form — or a failure to include information in the correct format. For persons required to file at least 250 returns during the calendar year on magnetic media, the penalty is imposed only to the extent that a failure occurs with respect to more than 250 returns. A similar waiver of the penalty applies to partnerships with more than 100 partners. Because they must file at least 100 returns, the penalty for failure to file using magnetic media is imposed only to the extent that the failure occurs with respect to more than 100 returns [§ 6724(c)].

---

**EXAMPLE:** For calendar Year 2013, X Corp. files 300 Forms 1099-MISC on paper rather than on the required magnetic media. The forms are filed with the IRS on Mar. 17, 2014, rather than the required Feb. 28, 2014, filing date. X further fails to file the returns on magnetic media by Aug. 1, 2014. X is subject to a penalty of $7,500 (250 × $30) for filing 250 returns late and $5,000 ($100 × 50) for failing to file 50 returns on magnetic media, for a total penalty of $12,500 [Reg. § 301.6721-1(b)(5), *Ex. 4*].

---

The penalties imposed for failing to file an information return, failing to furnish a correct payee statement or failing to comply with other information reporting requirements are not imposed where the filer's failure is due to reasonable cause. Reasonable cause exists if the filer establishes that either there are significant mitigating factors with respect to the failure or the failure is due to events beyond the filer's control and the filer acted in a reasonable manner both before and after the failure. Whether the filer promptly corrects an erroneous information return is one factor that the IRS considers in deciding whether the filer has shown reasonable cause [§ 6724(a); Reg. § 301.6724-1(a), § 301.6724-1(d)]. Under proposed regulations, the IRS would deem information to be promptly corrected for purposes of the penalty waiver, if corrected: (i) within 30 days of the required filing date; (ii) by August 1 following the required filing date; or (iii) after August 1, but by the deadline announced in IRS guidance for the electronic or magnetic filing of information returns, or in other published guidance.

### XXIII.D.1.f. *Frivolous Tax Submissions*

[634 T.M.; VIII.C.; TPS ¶3830.11.H.]

A $5,000 penalty may be imposed on any individual who files what purports to be an income tax return but that (i) does not contain information on which the substantial correctness of the self-assessment of taxes may be judged, or contains information that on its face indicates the self-assessment is substantially incorrect, and (ii) is based on a frivolous position as identified by the IRS in published guidance or reflects a desire to delay or impede the administration of the federal tax laws. The penalty also applies to submissions of requests for collection due process hearing, applications for installment agreements, offers in compromise, and taxpayer assistance orders if the submission is based on a frivolous position or reflects a desire to delay or impede the administration of federal tax laws [§ 6702].

Examples of frivolous submissions include claims that [Notice 2010-33, 2010-17 I.R.B. 609]:

- compliance with the internal revenue laws is voluntary or optional and not required by law;
- the Code is not law or its provisions are ineffective or inoperative;
- a taxpayer's income is excluded from tax when the taxpayer rejects or renounces U.S. citizenship;
- compensation for the performance of personal services are not taxable or are offset by an equivalent deduction for the personal services rendered;
- U.S. citizens and residents are not subject to tax on U.S. source income;
- a taxpayer has been untaxed, detaxed, or removed from the federal tax system;
- only certain types of taxpayers are subject to income and employment taxes;
- only certain types of income are taxable;
- federal income taxes are unconstitutional or a taxpayer has a constitutional right not to comply with the federal tax laws;
- a taxpayer is not a person;
- only fiduciaries are taxpayers, or only persons with a fiduciary relationship to the U.S. are obligated to pay taxes;
- Federal Reserve Notes are not taxable income;
- in a transaction using gold and silver coins, the value of the coins is excluded from income or the amount realized in the transaction is the face value of the coins;

- a taxpayer who is employed on board a ship that provides meals at no cost to the taxpayer as part of the employment may deduct the cost of such meals;
- a taxpayer may deduct personal expenses or the cost of maintaining the taxpayer's residence in connection with a home-based business;
- a "reparations" tax credit exists;
- a taxpayer who is not an employer may claim the Indian employment credit;
- a taxpayer's wages are excluded from Social Security taxes if the taxpayer waives the right to receive Social Security benefits, or may claim a charitable contribution deduction for the Social Security taxes paid;
- a taxpayer may reduce or eliminate its federal tax liability by striking out the penalty-of-perjury declaration or by attaching a statement disclaiming liability;
- a taxpayer is not obligated to pay income tax because the government has created an entity separate and distinct from the taxpayer;
- a taxpayer may use a Form 1099 as a financial or other instrument to obtain money from the government;
- a taxpayer may claim a credit for an amount withheld despite it being obviously false;
- inserting the phrase "nunc pro tunc" on a return has retroactive effect;
- a taxpayer may avoid tax on income by attributing the income to a trust;
- a taxpayer may avoid tax on income by sending the income offshore;
- a taxpayer can claim the disabled access credit by purportedly purchasing equipment or services for an inflated price;
- a taxpayer may claim a refund based on purported advance payments to employees of the earned income tax credit that reports an amount of purported compensation but does not report any other information;
- a taxpayer may claim the fuels tax credit even though the taxpayer did not purchase and use gasoline for an off-highway business use;
- a taxpayer may buy or sell the right to claim a child as a qualifying child for purposes of the earned income credit;
- a Form 23C, *Assessment Certificate*, is not a valid record of assessment, and must be signed personally by the Secretary of the Treasury or must be provided to the taxpayer;
- a tax cannot be assessed from a substitute for return under § 6020(b);
- a statutory notice of deficiency is invalid because the taxpayer did not file a tax return reporting the deficiency or because the notice was not signed by a particular official;
- a notice of the federal tax lien is invalid because it was not signed by a particular official;
- the form or content of a notice of federal tax lien is controlled by state or local law;
- a collection due process notice is invalid because it was not signed by a particular official;
- verification under § 6330 that the requirements of any applicable law or administrative procedure have been met may only be based on particular forms or documents, or that the forms or documents on which the verification was determined must be provided to the taxpayer;

- a notice and demand is invalid because it was not signed, was not on the correct form or was not accompanied by a certificate of assessment;

- the Tax Court is not a legitimate court or does not have the authority to hear or decide matters within its jurisdiction;

- federal courts may not enforce the internal revenue laws;

- IRS revenue officers are not authorized to issue levies or notices of federal tax liens, or to seize property to satisfy unpaid taxes;

- IRS employees lack the authority to carry out their duties for the IRS;

- any person may represent a taxpayer before the IRS or in a court proceeding;

- a civil action to collect taxes must be personally authorized by the Secretary of the Treasury and the Attorney General;

- a taxpayer's income is not taxable if the taxpayer assigns or attributes the income to a religious organization;

- IRS is not an agency of the U.S. government, and has no authority to administer the internal revenue laws; and

- any position described as frivolous in any revenue ruling or other published guidance before the return or submission adopting the position is filed.

### XXIII.D.1.g. Trust Fund Recovery Penalty

[639 T.M.; TPS ¶3875.]

When a business fails to remit trust fund taxes — e.g., withheld income and employment taxes or collected excise taxes — to the government, the IRS can collect the taxes from sources other than the defaulting business. The IRS may assert the Trust Fund Recovery Penalty, which is equal to the total amount of tax not paid to the government, against persons who are responsible for collecting, accounting for, and paying over the trust fund taxes but willfully fail to do so. For the Trust Fund Recovery Penalty to apply to an individual, the individual must be a responsible person, and the individual must willfully fail to pay over to the government the amount of taxes otherwise due [§ 6672].

### XXIII.D.1.h. Penalty for Aiding and Abetting an Understatement of Tax Liability

[634 T.M., VIII.B.; TPS ¶3830.09.]

A penalty of $1,000 ($10,000 where the offense relates to the returns or documents of a corporation) may be imposed on any person who [§ 6701(a), § 6701(b)]:

- aids, assists, procures or advises in the preparation or presentation of any portion of a return, claim, or other document;

- knows (or has reason to believe) that such portion will be used in connection with any material matter arising under the internal revenue laws; and

- knows that the portion, if so used, would result in an understatement of another person's tax liability.

### XXIII.D.1.i. Other Civil Penalties

[634 T.M., TPS ¶3830.11.]

***Payment of Tax with Bad Check, Bad Money Order, or Bad Electronic Payment Instrument.*** A penalty is imposed on any taxpayer who tenders a bad check, money order, or other payment instrument (including electronic payment) to the IRS. The penalty is 2% of the amount of the check (or other instrument) if the check (or other instrument) is for $1,250 or more. If the amount of the check (or other instrument) is less than $1,250, the penalty is $25 or the amount of the check (or other instrument), whichever is less [§ 6657].

*Instituting Suit for Purpose of Delay.* The Tax Court may require the taxpayer to pay to the government a penalty of up to $25,000 whenever it determines that a proceeding was instituted or maintained by the taxpayer primarily for delay, that the taxpayer's position is frivolous or groundless, or that the taxpayer unreasonably failed to pursue available administrative remedies [§ 6673(a)(1)]. In addition, the Tax Court may require counsel to pay court costs and attorneys' fees whenever it determines that counsel multiplied the proceedings unreasonably and vexatiously [§ 6673(a)(2)]. A district court may impose a penalty not in excess of $10,000 in an action for damages for unauthorized collection action where it is determined that the taxpayer's position is frivolous or groundless [§ 6673(b)(1)].

*Failure to File Returns Concerning Foreign Trusts.* Any person who does not timely file any notice or return required by § 6048(a) or (c) (relating to information reporting about foreign trusts or who fails to include any of the required information is subject to a penalty equal to the lesser of $10,000 or 35% of the gross reportable amount [§ 6677(a)]. A person who fails to file an annual return under § 6048(b) (relating to owners of any portion of a foreign trust under the grantor trust rules) is subject to a penalty of 5% of the gross reportable amount [§ 6677(b)]. If the failure to file continues for more than 90 days after the day on which the IRS mails a notice to the person required to file, the IRS may impose an additional penalty of $10,000 for each 30-day period during which the failure continues. The IRS is required to refund the penalty if a taxpayer provides sufficient information to determine that the aggregate amount of the penalties exceeds the gross reportable amount [§ 6677(a)].

*False Information on Withholding Allowances.* A $500 penalty may be imposed on individuals who file false withholding information that results in reduced withholding if, at the time of the statement, there was no reasonable basis for the statement [§ 6682].

*Failure to Provide Reports on Certain Tax-Favored Accounts and Annuities.* A penalty of $50 per failure may be imposed on trustees or issuers for each failure to make required disclosure statements [§ 6693(a)].

*Failure to File Partnership or S Corporation Information Returns.* Partnerships or S Corporations that fail to file information returns (Form 1065 or Form 1120S) on time or that file incomplete returns are liable for penalties equal to $195 times the number of months that the failures continue, up to 12 months [§ 6698, § 6699(a)].

*Fraudulent W-2 Statement, or Failure to Furnish Statement to Employee.* Employers may be liable for a penalty of $50 per failure for willfully furnishing a false or fraudulent statement or willfully failing to furnish a timely statement showing the information [§ 6674].

*Failure to Meet Disclosure Requirements for Quid Pro Quo Contributions.* Charitable organizations receiving "quid pro quo" contributions exceeding $75 that do not provide written statements to donors containing information regarding the amount of the contribution that is deductible for tax purposes and the value of goods and services provided to the donor are subject to a penalty of $10 for each contribution for which the organization fails to make the required disclosure [§ 6714].

### XXIII.D.1.j. Reasonable Cause to Excuse Penalties

[634 T.M., XI.; TPS ¶3830.12.]

Most civil penalties are not imposed or are abated if the taxpayer's failure is due to "reasonable cause." A taxpayer can request relief from (or abatement) of penalties due to reasonable cause. A taxpayer who intends to show that an underpayment was due to reasonable cause and not due to willful neglect must make an affirmative showing of all of the facts which he or she contends provide reasonable cause. This showing should be in the form of a written statement containing a declaration that it is made under penalty of perjury. The statement of reasonable cause generally should be filed with the area director or the director of the service center with whom the return is filed.

A taxpayer can prove reasonable cause by demonstrating that he or she exercised ordinary business care and prudence in his or her affairs but was nevertheless unable to comply with the requirements of the law. While there is no all-inclusive definition of reasonable cause for many of the major penalties, the following have been accepted as reasonable cause by the IRS:

- death, serious illness, or unavoidable absence of the taxpayer or a death or serious illness in the taxpayer's immediate family;
- a fire, other casualty, natural disaster, or other disturbance that destroyed tax records or prevented compliance in some other way;
- the inability of the taxpayer to obtain records necessary to comply with a tax;
- lack of funds;
- ignorance of the law;
- tax law changes and IRS form revisions;
- taxpayer or subordinate made a mistake or was forgetful; and
- reliance on the advice of a competent tax advisor.

***Penalty Abatement Based on Reliance on IRS Advice.*** The IRS must abate a penalty if [§ 6404(f)]:

- the penalty is attributable to erroneous advice that was furnished to the taxpayer by an officer or employee of the IRS;
- the officer or employee acted in that person's official capacity;
- the advice was in writing;
- the advice was reasonably relied on by the taxpayer;
- the advice was in response to a specific written request of the taxpayer; and
- the taxpayer requesting the advice provided the IRS with adequate or accurate information.

The IRS may also abate penalties due to reasonable cause if the taxpayer relied on erroneous oral advice from an IRS employee. The IRS will not abate a penalty unless the taxpayer provided the IRS with accurate and complete information and exercised ordinary business care and prudence in relying on that advice.

Taxpayers requesting an abatement should file Form 843, *Claim for Refund and Request for Abatement*, and should include the statement that "Abatement of penalty or addition to tax pursuant to § 6404(f)" on the top of the form. The claim should also indicate whether the penalty has been paid, and copies of the written request for advice, the advice furnished, and the document asserting the penalty should be attached.

*IRS's First-Time Penalty Abatement Policy.* The IRS maintains a first-time penalty abatement policy (FTA) under which a taxpayer who has incurred a failure to file, failure to pay, or failure to deposit penalty may have the policy administratively waived if:

- the taxpayer previously did not have to file a return or had no penalties for the preceding three years for the tax account under review; and
- has filed, or filed a valid extension for, all currently required returns and paid, or arranged to pay, any tax due.

If the request is being considered for two or more tax periods for the same IRS account and the earliest tax period meets the FTA criteria, relief based on FTA only applies to the earliest tax period, not all periods being considered. Relief for subsequent periods would be based on a showing of reasonable cause.

The FTA waiver does not apply to:

- returns with an event-based filing requirement (e.g., estate and gift tax returns);
- the daily delinquency penalty;
- corporate and S corporation returns, if in the prior three years, at least one S corporation return was filed late but not penalized; and
- information return reporting that is dependent on another filing, e.g., where various forms are attached.

An FTA waiver will not be granted if any of the following applies:

- any period under the tax account review for the prior three years is in collection (TDI) status;
- an un-reversed penalty for a "significant" amount is present on any tax period in the prior three years for the tax account under review and a notice was issued showing the assessed penalty; or
- there are any penalty reversals or suppressions on any tax period in the prior three years for the same tax account under review and the exceptions resulted from IRS penalty codes 018, 020, or 021.

The following additional criteria apply in the case of business taxpayers:

- an FTA waiver is not available for any portion of a failure to deposit penalty relating to a failure to use EFTPS;
- an FTA waiver is not available if there are four or more failure to deposit waiver codes present in the taxpayer's three year penalty history with respect to the tax account under review; and
- the three year penalty history under review must include both Form 941 (payroll) and Form 944 (non-payroll) accounts.

### XXIII.D.2. Interest on Underpayments and Overpayments

### XXIII.D.2.a. Interest on Underpayments

[627 T.M., III.; TPS ¶3840.01.]

Where a taxpayer pays less than the full amount of his or her tax obligation by the due date, there is an underpayment. An underpayment may arise as a result of the taxpayer's failure to pay the full amount of tax shown to be due on the tax return, failure to report the correct tax liability on the tax return, or failure to file a tax return.

---

**EXAMPLE:** T files her 2013 individual income tax return on Apr. 15, 2014. The return shows a total tax liability of $6,000, a tax credit of $5,500 (withholding) and a balance due of $500. T fails to remit the balance due with her return. There is an underpayment of $500.

---

If a taxpayer applies for, and receives, an extension of time to file a return, he or she must still pay the full amount of his tax liability by the original due date of the return. Failure to do so results in an underpayment [§ 6601(b)].

### XXIII.D.2.a.(1) Rate of Interest

[627 T.M., III.D.; TPS ¶3840.01.B.2.]

Interest on an underpayment is computed by applying a prescribed rate of interest to the amount of underpayment for the period during which the unpaid tax remains outstanding. The computation of interest involves three elements: (i) the amount of underpayment, (ii) the rate of interest, and (iii) the period of underpayment.

The interest rate charged on underpayments of tax (other than large corporate underpayments) is the federal short-term rate plus 3 percentage points. [§ 6621(a)(2)]. The federal short-term rate is determined during the first month of each quarter, and takes effect at the beginning of the following calendar quarter [§ 6621(b)(1)]. For example, the rate determined during April is effective for the calendar quarter beginning in July.

Where the prescribed annual interest rate on underpayments changes during the underpayment period, the computation is broken down into subperiods and the appropriate rate applied [Reg. § 301.6621-1(d)]. Interest on the underpayment of tax is compounded daily by dividing the prescribed annual rate by 365 (366 in leap years) and compounding the result each day. The IRS provides uniform tables for computing interest using the daily compounding rules [Rev. Proc. 95-17, 1995-1 C.B. 556].

---

**EXAMPLE:** C, a calendar year taxpayer, files his 2012 Form 1040 on Aug. 15, 2013, pursuant to an extension of time to file, and pays the $10,000 tax due with the return without paying any interest on the amount due. The IRS sends him a bill for the unpaid interest on Dec. 3, 2013. The amount of interest due is $100.85, calculated as follows: The applicable underpayment rate is 3% for the second, third, and fourth quarters of 2013. The 3% interest factor is found in Table 11 of Rev. Proc. 95-17.

- Apr. 16 through Aug. 15, 121 days, 0.009994411 × $10,000, or $99.94
- Aug. 16 through Dec. 3, 110 days, 0.009081715 × $99.94, or $0.91
- Total interest $100.85

---

In the case of a "large corporate underpayment," the underpayment rate for periods after the applicable date is equal to the federal short-term rate plus five percentage points. This rate applies only to underpayments made by C corporations when there is a threshold underpayment of tax for a tax period that exceeds $100,000, computed without regard to interest, penalties, additional amounts, and additions to tax [§ 6621(c)(3); Reg. § 301.6621-3(b)(2)(ii)].

The large corporate underpayment rate applies only to tax deficiencies and is effective after the date that is the 30th day after the earlier of the date a notice of proposed deficiency is sent that offers an Appeals conference (30-day letter) or the date on which a deficiency notice is sent or, if the deficiency procedures do not apply, the date on which the IRS notifies the taxpayer that the tax has been assessed or proposes assessment of the tax [§ 6621(c)(2)].

Another exception to the general underpayment rate of interest is the special rate for an estate with a closely held business that elects to pay the estate tax in installments [§ 6166]. For these estates, a 2% rate of interest is payable on the lesser of (a) the tax attributable to the first $1 million, indexed for inflation ($1,450,000 in 2014; $1,470,000 in 2015) in taxable value of a closely held business, after applying the unified credit and any other exclusion and (b) the deferred tax. Interest on the deferred tax that exceeds the 2% portion is payable at a rate equal to 45% of the general underpayment rate [§ 6601(j); Rev. Proc. 2013-35, 2013-47 I.R.B. 537, Rev. Proc. 2014-61, 2014-47 I.R.B. 860].

### *XXIII.D.2.a.(2) Period of Underpayment*

[627 T.M., III.B.; TPS ¶3840.01.B.3.a.]

Interest on an underpayment generally starts running on the last date prescribed for payment of tax [§ 6601(a)]. As a general rule, in a case where a taxpayer is required to file a tax return that shows a tax liability, the last date prescribed for payment of such tax liability is the due date of the return (not including extensions) [§ 6151(a)]. The fact that an underpayment for one year arises as a result of an event that takes place in a following year does not postpone the date interest starts to run on the underpayment.

---

**EXAMPLE:** Taxpayer C timely filed a return for 2012, reporting a gain of $20,000 from the involuntary conversion of investment property. C excluded this gain from gross income since C intended to reinvest the proceeds in property related in service or use within the two-year period permitted for the nonrecognition of gain on the conversion. The tax liability shown on C's return was paid in full. C failed to reinvest as intended within the two-year period, and a $5,000 tax deficiency was assessed by the IRS. Interest on the $5,000 underpayment begins on Apr. 15, 2013, the last date prescribed for payment of the 2012 tax.

---

*Underpayment Determined After Credit of an Overpayment.* Where a taxpayer overpays income tax as of the due date of the return, the taxpayer can elect to have the overpayment applied against estimated tax for the succeeding year. The IRS will apply the overpayment to unpaid installments of estimated tax due on or after the date the overpayment arose in the order in which they are required to be paid to avoid an addition to tax for failure to pay estimated income tax. If a deficiency is subsequently determined for the year of the overpayment, interest on the underpayment starts to run from the due date of the installment to which the overpayment was credited [§ 6402(b); Reg. § 301.6402-3(a)(5)].

*When the Tax Is to Be Determined by the IRS.* If an individual taxpayer does not show the tax due on his or her return and elects to have it determined by the IRS, the last date prescribed for payment is 30 days after the IRS mails the taxpayer a notice which states the amount of tax owed and makes a demand for payment [§ 6151(b)(1)].

*Interest on Penalties and Additions to Tax.* Interest on assessed penalties for failure to file, for failure to pay a stamp tax, for accuracy-related underpayments, and for fraud begins to run from the due date of the return to which the penalty relates [§ 6601(e)(2)]. In all other cases, if the IRS assesses penalties, additional amounts or additions to tax, no interest is payable on such amounts if the assessed amounts are paid within 21 calendar days of receiving notice and demand for payment from the IRS (10 business days for a tax liability of $100,000 or more). Moreover, if the taxpayer fails to pay the assessed penalties, additional amounts or additions to tax within 21 days, interest starts running on such amounts from the date of notice and demand for payment [§ 6601(e)(3)].

*Last Payment Date Not Prescribed.* In all cases of taxes payable by stamp and in all other cases in which the last date for payment is not otherwise prescribed, the underpayment period begins and interest is payable from the date the liability for tax arises, but not later than the date of notice and demand [§ 6601(b)(5)].

*Jeopardy Assessments.* If, by reason of a jeopardy assessment, notice and demand is mailed before the normal due date of the return, the last date for payment is, and interest begins to run from, the due date of the return, and not from the date of the jeopardy assessment [§ 6601(b)(3)].

*Accumulated Earnings Tax.* Interest is imposed on underpayments of the accumulated earnings tax from the due date (without regard to extensions) of the return for the tax year the tax is imposed [§ 6601(b)(4)].

*Erroneous Refunds.* Where the IRS erroneously refunds any tax, interest, or penalty that is recoverable by a suit for refund, interest at the underpayment rate begins on the date the refund check is cashed. Nevertheless, the IRS must abate all assessed interest on erroneous refunds from the date of payment until the date a demand for repayment is made. There is no abatement where the taxpayer or a related party has in any way caused the erroneous return and where the erroneous refund exceeds $50,000 [§ 6602, § 6404(e)(2)].

*Excessive Refunds.* When a taxpayer receives a refund of tax that creates or increases an underpayment of that tax for the same tax year and interest is paid on the excessive refund, the IRS charges interest on the underpayment. For the period for which the taxpayer was paid interest on the excessive tax refund, the IRS charges interest at the same rate on the portion of the tax underpayment that does not exceed the excessive tax refund. Also, for any period for which interest is not paid on the excessive tax refund, the IRS does not charge interest on the portion of the tax underpayment that does not exceed the excessive tax refund. Interest at the applicable underpayment rate is charged on the portion of the tax underpayment that exceeds the excessive tax refund from the original due date of the tax return, and on the entire tax underpayment from the date of the refund check. In computing the interest charged for any period, previously accrued interest is treated in the same manner as the portion of the tax underpayment to which such interest relates [Rev. Proc. 94-60, 1994-2 C.B. 774].

*Interest on Estate Tax Imposed by § 2032A(c).* Additional estate tax is imposed on the premature disposition or cessation of a qualifying use of real property which received its special use valuation benefit available to family farms and closely held small businesses (see XXI.B.3.). This tax becomes due and payable six months after the date of disposition or cessation of qualifying use. Interest on the tax runs only from the date that the tax becomes due and payable [§ 2032A(c)].

*Interest on Underpayments Resulting from § 482 Allocations of Income.* Where the same person or interest owns or controls, directly or indirectly, two or more trades or businesses, whether incorporated or not, the IRS has authority to allocate or apportion gross income, deductions, credits or allowances between or among such organizations, to prevent evasion of taxes or to clearly reflect income.

Interest on underpayments resulting from such allocations accrues from the due date of the original return [§ 482].

### XXIII.D.2.a.(3) End of the Period — Date Interest Stops Accruing

[627 T.M., III.B.; TPS ¶3840.01.B.3.b.]

Interest generally stops accruing on any underpayment of tax on the date the underpayment is fully paid or satisfied. Ordinarily, for purposes of computing interest, this means the date the payment is received by the IRS, not the date a check is placed in the mail for delivery [§ 6601(a); Reg. § 301.6601-1(a)(1)]. If payment of any tax or penalty is made within 21 calendar days of the date of notice and demand, interest stops on the date of notice and demand. If payment is not received within the 21-day period, interest continues to accrue from the date of notice and demand to the date of payment. If the tax liability is $100,000 or more, payment must be received within 10 business days of the date of notice and demand in order to take advantage of the interest-free period [§ 6601(e)(3)]. For example, if T receives notice and demand for tax and interest due in the amount of $95,000 dated June 4, 2014, and pays this amount in full on or before Monday, June 25, 2014, T will not owe any additional interest between June 4 and the date of payment. T has 21 calendar days to pay the $95,000 before interest accrues on this liability, because the total due is less than $100,000. However, if T were to receive notice and demand for tax and interest due in the amount of $120,000, T would have to pay this amount in full on or before Monday, June 18, 2014 (10 business days later), in order not to owe additional interest.

*Advance Payments and Deposits.* A taxpayer who has been presented with a notice of proposed changes to a tax liability (i.e., a 30-day letter) at the conclusion of an audit may pay the tax, interest, and any penalty before it is assessed to stop the running of interest. Payment of the proposed tax liability before the date the notice of deficiency is mailed will, however, deprive the taxpayer of the right to petition the Tax Court. [§ 6213(b)(4)]. To stop the running of interest and still preserve the right to petition the Tax Court, a taxpayer may pay the tax after the notice of deficiency has been mailed; make a "cash deposit" with the IRS; or make a payment of a part of the proposed tax deficiency [§ 6213(b)(4), § 6603; Rev. Proc. 2005-18, 2005-13 I.R.B. 798].

*Net Operating Loss and Capital Loss Carrybacks.* If an underpayment is reduced or satisfied by the application of a carryback of a net operating loss or capital loss incurred in a subsequent year, the carryback stops the running of interest as of the due date of the return for the year in which the loss carryback arose. The carryback is treated as a payment on the due date of the return for the year of the loss [§ 6601(d)(1)].

*Certain Credit Carrybacks.* If an underpayment is satisfied by the application of a carryback of unused credit, interest stops running on the last date for filing the return (determined without extensions) for the tax year in which the credit carryback arises. If a credit carryback used to satisfy an underpayment arises as a result of a net operating loss, capital loss carryback, or other credit carryback from a subsequent year, interest on the underpayment stops on the due date of the return for that subsequent year [§ 6601(d)(3)].

*Partial Payments.* If a taxpayer voluntarily makes partial payments of taxes, interest, and penalties covering more than one year, the payments will be applied in accordance with the specific instructions of the taxpayer. Absent allocation instructions from the taxpayer, the IRS will apply partial to periods in the order of priority that the IRS determines will serve its best interest. The payment will be applied to satisfy the liability for successive periods in descending order of priority until the payment is absorbed. If the amount applied to a period is less than the liability for the period, the amount will be applied to tax, penalty, and interest, in that order, until the amount is absorbed. The IRS will apply involuntary payments (e.g., as the result of an IRS levy) to obtain the maximum benefit for the IRS, regardless of any instructions from the taxpayer as to how to allocate the payments [Rev. Proc. 2002-26, 2002-15 I.R.B. 746].

*Tax Court Decisions*. The IRS is barred from assessing and collecting a tax deficiency until the decision of the Tax Court becomes final. A deficiency redetermined by a Tax Court decision that has become final is assessed and payable upon issuance of notice and demand by the IRS. A taxpayer is not relieved of liability for interest even if the decision omits a reference to interest on the deficiency [§ 6213(a)]. There are no special rules as to the running of interest on deficiencies assessed after a Tax Court decision. Payment within 21 days of the issuance of the notice and demand will cut off the running of interest as of the date of the notice and demand, as it does for any other amount assessed. Note that if the taxpayer waives the restrictions on assessment in a stipulation filed with the court, interest will be suspended if notice and demand is not issued within 30 days [§ 6601(c)].

*Credit of an Overpayment to Satisfy Underpayment*. Where an underpayment of tax is reduced or satisfied by credit of an overpayment, no interest is imposed on that portion of the deficiency so satisfied for any period during which interest on the overpayment would have been allowable if the credit had not been made. Thus, interest on both the underpayment and the overpayment is eliminated during the period both exist [§ 6601(f)]. For example, if an examination of B's returns for 2011 and 2012 discloses an underpayment of $800 for 2011 and an overpayment of $500 for 2012, interest would ordinarily accrue on the $800 underpayment from Apr. 15, 2012, to the date of payment. However, if the 2012 overpayment is credited against the 2011 underpayment, interest will run on the $800 underpayment from Apr. 15, 2012 (the last date prescribed for payment of the 2011 tax) to Apr. 15, 2013, the date the 2012 overpayment was made. Because interest would have been allowed on the overpayment if it had been refunded rather than credited, from Apr. 15, 2013, to a date not more than 30 days before the date of the refund check, no interest is imposed after Apr. 15, 2013, on $500, the portion of the underpayment satisfied by credit of the overpayment. Interest will continue to accrue after Apr. 15, 2013, on $300 of the underpayment (the difference between the $800 underpayment less the $500 overpayment) to the date of payment [Reg. § 301.6601-1(b)(2), *Ex.* 1].

*Carryback of Foreign Tax Credit*. There is a limit on the amount of foreign tax credits that a taxpayer can use in a particular year. Any unused foreign tax credits may be carried back one year and forward 10 years. If the taxpayer carries back a foreign tax credit to earlier years and this eliminates a deficiency, the taxpayer is still liable for interest that accrued on the deficiency until the due date for the return for the year that the credit carryback arises or, in the case where the credit carryback from a tax year is attributable to a net operating loss carryback, capital loss carryback, or other credit carryback from a subsequent tax year, the due date for the return for that subsequent tax year [§ 6601(d)(2)].

### XXIII.D.2.b. Interest on Overpayments
[627 T.M., IV.; TPS ¶3840.02.]

If the tax payments and credits exceed the taxpayer's correct tax liability, there is an overpayment of tax. An overpayment of tax can result from any number of factors (e.g., overwithholding on wages, overpayment of estimated taxes, net operating loss carrybacks, adjustments upon audit, math errors on the return) [§ 6611; Reg.

§ 301.6611-1(b)]. The IRS is required to pay interest on overpayments of tax. The interest is computed by applying the rate specified by law to the amount of overpayment for the period during which the IRS holds the funds.

### XXIII.D.2.b.(1) Amounts Treated as Overpayments

[627 T.M., IV.A.; TPS ¶3840.02.B.1.]

Overpayments generally are payments in excess of the correct tax liability. Additionally, any excess of refundable credits over the correct tax liability is an overpayment [Reg. § 301.6611-1(b)].

### XXIII.D.2.b.(2) Rate of Interest on Overpayments

[627 T.M., IV.B.; TPS ¶3840.02.B.2.]

The interest rate payable on overpayments is based on the prevailing federal short-term rate plus three percentage points (two percentage points in the case of a corporation), rounded to the nearest full percentage. To the extent that an overpayment of tax by a corporation exceeds $10,000, the overpayment interest rate is the federal short-term rate plus one-half percentage point [§ 6621(a)(1)].

Where the prescribed annual interest rate on overpayments changes during the underpayment period, the computation is broken down into subperiods and the appropriate rate applied [Reg. § 301.6621-1(d)].

Interest on an overpayment of tax is compounded daily by dividing the prescribed annual rate by 365 (366 in leap years) and compounding the result each day. The IRS publishes tables showing the daily amount of compound interest [Rev. Proc. 95-17, 1995-1 C.B. 556]. The interest rates for each calendar quarter are published in a quarterly revenue ruling [§ 6621(b)(3)]. For example, the rate determined during April is effective for the calendar quarter beginning in July.

### XXIII.D.2.b.(3) Period of Overpayment

[627 T.M., IV.C.; TPS ¶3840.01.B.3.]

Interest on an overpayment of tax begins on the date of the overpayment [§ 6611(b)]. If it is credited against another tax liability, interest ceases on the due date of the tax against which the credit is taken [§ 6611(b)(1)]. If the overpayment is refunded, interest ceases on a date that is not more than 30 days preceding the date of the refund check [§ 6611(b)(2)].

**General Rule.** The dates of overpayment of any tax are the date of payment of the first amount that (when added to previous payments) is in excess of the tax liability (including any interest, addition to the tax, or additional amount) and the dates of payment of all amounts subsequently paid with respect to that tax liability [Reg. § 301.6611-1(b)]. If the payment was in the form of a check submitted with a return or after the due date for the return, the date of payment is the date the IRS receives the taxpayer's check, not the mailing date or date of deposit. However, a payment mailed before the due date and delivered after the due date is treated as having made on the registration date or the postmark date [§ 7502]. The date of payment by credit or debit card is the date when the issuer of the card properly authorizes the transaction, provided that the payment is actually received [Reg. § 301.6311-2(b)].

---

**EXAMPLE:** Ted files his 2013 individual income tax return on Apr. 15, 2014, showing a tax liability of $900 and tax credits of $600. The balance due of $300 is paid in full with the return. Upon audit, the IRS asserts a deficiency of $1,000, plus interest. Ted signs Form 870, *Waiver of Restrictions on Assessment.* The IRS assesses the deficiency and mails a notice and demand for payment on Oct. 10, 2014, and Ted pays the entire amount due on Oct. 15, 2014. Ted files a claim for refund asserting that the deficiency determined upon audit is in error and his original return should have reflected a tax liability of $400 instead of $900. The IRS allows the claim, with the result that Ted made overpayments totaling $1,500 plus the amount of interest paid on the $1,000 deficiency: one on Apr. 15, 2014, in the amount of $500 (because on that date the "correct" tax liability had been entirely paid); and a second overpayment on Oct. 15, 2014, in the amount of $1,000 plus the interest paid.

---

***Payment After Expiration of Period of Limitations.*** If the taxpayer pays a tax assessment made after the expiration of the period of limitations, the payment constitutes an overpayment, and interest begins from the date the payment was made [§ 6401(a); Reg. § 301.6611-1(a)].

***Estimated Tax Payments and Income Tax Withholding Credits.*** For interest purposes, payments of estimated tax and income tax withholding credits are deemed paid on the last day prescribed for filing the return (without regard to extensions) to which the credits apply [§ 6513(b), § 6611(d)].

---

**EXAMPLE:** T files his individual income tax return for 2011 on Mar. 20, 2014, reporting total tax credits of $1,000, of which $500 is withholding on wages and $500 is the sum of quarterly estimated tax payments of $125 paid on Apr. 15, June 15, and Sept. 15, 2011, and Jan. 15, 2012. For purposes of determining the date of payment of any overpayment, the entire $1,000 is deemed paid on Apr. 15, 2012, the due date of the return.

---

If a taxpayer elects to apply an overpayment of income tax against the amount due as estimated tax for the succeeding tax year, the overpayment is deemed paid on account of the income tax liability for the succeeding year and taxpayer is not entitled to any overpayment interest. For example, an overpayment of 2012 income tax applied against the estimated tax due for 2013 is deemed paid on or after April 15, 2014. No interest is allowed on the amount credited. However, if an overpayment of income tax is applied against the estimated tax due for a subsequent year that is not the immediately succeeding year, then interest is allowed from the date of overpayment to the due date of the amount against which the credit is taken [§ 6513(d), § 6611(d); Reg. § 301.6402-3(a)(5), § 301.6611-1(h)(2)(vii)].

***45-Day Interest-Free Period.*** No interest is allowed if the overpayment shown on a tax return is refunded within 45 days after the due date of the return or, if the return is filed after that date, within 45 days after the date of filing the return [§ 6611(e)(1)]. However, the grace period for which IRS need not pay interest on an overpayment related to tax deducted and withheld under chapters 3 or 4 of the Code (foreign or FATCA withholding) is 180 days [§ 6611(e)(4)].

---

**EXAMPLE:** C files an individual income tax return on Mar. 15, which shows an overpayment due to tax credits in excess of the total tax liability. No interest is allowed if the refund is made on or before May 30 (within 45 days of Apr. 15). If this return is filed on June 15 no interest is allowed if the refund is made on or before July 30, (within 45 days of the date of filing, whether or not such filing was pursuant to an extension). If the refund is not made by July 30, interest is allowed only from June 15 to a date no more than 30 days before the date of the refund check [§ 6611(b)(2), § 6611(b)(3)].

---

*Claim for Credit or Refund.* If a taxpayer files a claim for a credit or refund for any overpayment of tax and the overpayment is refunded within 45 days after the claim is filed, no interest is allowed on the overpayment from the date the claim is filed until the day the refund is made [§ 6611(e)(2)]. If an adjustment initiated by the IRS results in a refund or credit of an overpayment, interest on the overpayment is computed by subtracting 45 days from the number of days interest would otherwise be allowed with respect to the overpayment [§ 6611(e)(3)].

*Advance Payments and Deposits.* Advance tax payments made on or before the due date of a return are treated in the same manner as estimated tax payments and withholding credits. They are deemed paid as of the due date of the return for the tax year to which they relate [§ 6513(a), § 6513(b), § 6611(d)].

A remittance designated as a deposit will not constitute a tax payment, and generally is not returned with interest. A remittance not designated a deposit will be treated as a tax payment and will be applied against any outstanding liability for tax, penalty, or interest [Rev. Proc. 2005-18, 2005-13 I.R.B. 798].

### XXIII.D.2.b.(4) Interest on Net Operating Loss and Capital Loss Carrybacks

[627 T.M., IV.C.2.g.; TPS ¶3840.01.B.3.]

If an overpayment results from a net operating loss or capital loss carryback, the overpayment, for interest purposes, is treated as not accruing before the due date of the return for the tax year in which the loss or credit carryback occurs. The overpayment is considered an overpayment for the loss year. The 45-day interest-free-period rule is applied by treating the return for the loss year as not filed before the claim for refund of the overpayment is filed [§ 6611(f)(1)].

---

**EXAMPLE:** X Corp. timely filed a return for calendar year 2010 showing tax due of $500,000. On Mar. 15, 2013, X Corp. timely filed its 2012 return, showing a net operating loss, the carryback of which entitles it to a refund of $300,000 for 2010. X Corp. filed a claim for refund on Feb. 15, 2014. The IRS makes the refund before Apr. 1, 2014. The 45-day interest-free period begins to run as of Feb. 15, 2014.

---

*Credit Carrybacks.* An overpayment resulting from the carryback of an unused business credit (e.g., investment credit) to the prior year begins accruing interest from the filing date of the return for the year in which the credit carryback arises. Similarly, an overpayment resulting from the carryback of unused foreign tax credits to prior tax years begins to accrue interest on the filing date for the tax year in which the foreign tax credit arises [§ 6611(f)].

*Mismatched TINs on Tax Return and Attachments.* If a Form 1040 contains the correct individual taxpayer identification number (ITIN) and claims a refund and an attached Form W-2 contains an incorrect social security number (SSN), the IRS takes the position that it will freeze the refund until the identification number problem is corrected without liability for overpayment interest [§ 6611(b)(3), § 6611(g)].

### XXIII.D.2.b.(5) End of the Period — Date Interest Stops

[627 T.M., IV.C.3.; TPS ¶3840.02.B.3.b.]

**Overpayment Credited Against Underpayments.** Where an overpayment is credited against an underpayment, interest is payable from the date of the overpayment to the due date of the underpayment against which it is credited [§ 6611(b)(1)].

---

**EXAMPLE:** The IRS, upon audit of B's timely filed returns for 2011 and 2012, determines that B has an overpayment of $500 for 2011 and deficiency of $1,000 for 2012. The overpayment was tax paid on the date the return was filed. The IRS assessed the deficiency for 2012 and on Apr. 15, 2014, credited the overpayment against the assessment. B is entitled to interest on the overpayment from Apr. 15, 2012, (the due date of the 2011 return) to Apr. 15, 2013 (the due date of the $1,000 deficiency for 2012). No interest is payable on the overpayment from Apr. 15, 2013, to Apr. 15, 2014. Similarly, no interest on $500 of the assessment is payable from Apr. 15, 2013, to Apr. 15, 2014. Interest on the remaining $500 deficiency runs from Apr. 15, 2013, until it is paid.

---

This cut-off date (due date of the underpayment satisfied) is enforced even where there is no underpayment until a credit-elect for the underpayment year is applied to the next tax year.

---

**EXAMPLE:** On its return for 2009, corporation M reported an overpayment of $12 million and elected to apply this overpayment to its 2010 tax liability. On Mar. 15, 2011, the IRS transferred the $12 million into the 2010 account. In 2014, the IRS determined that for 2009 M had an underpayment of $1 million. This amount was assessed and satisfied as of Mar. 15, 2011, by a credit of an overpayment made for 2007. No interest is allowable on the 2007 overpayment after Mar. 15, 2010, the due date of the tax for 2009, despite the fact that the account for 2009 was fully paid until the transfer of the credit elect on Mar. 15, 2011.

---

The rules for determining the due date of the tax, interest, or penalty against which an overpayment might be credited are as follows:

- Taxes: Generally, the due date is the last date fixed for payment of the tax.
- Interest: The due date of interest is as it economically accrues on a daily basis, rather than when it is assessed [Reg. § 301.6611-1(h)(2)(v)].
- Additions to tax and assessable penalties: In the case of a credit against an amount assessed as an additional amount, addition to tax, or assessable penalty, the due date is the earlier of the date of assessment or the date from which such amount would bear interest if not satisfied by payment or credit [Reg. § 301.6611-1(h)(2)(vi)].

Any credit of an overpayment against a tax liability made after the time has run for assessment or collection is void. Likewise, once the time for filing a claim for refund for an overpayment has expired, it cannot be credited or refunded [§ 6514(b), § 6401(a), § 6511(b)].

*Overpayment Refunded.* If an overpayment is refunded to the taxpayer, interest is payable from the date of overpayment to a date not more than 30 days preceding the date of the refund check. Acceptance of the refund check does not prevent the taxpayer from subsequently claiming an additional overpayment with interest thereon, provided that the claim is timely filed within the applicable period of limitations. If a taxpayer refuses to accept a tendered check, the taxpayer is not entitled to additional interest for the overpayment included in the check [§ 6611(b)(2)].

A delay in the delivery of a refund check normally does not entitle the taxpayer to interest beyond the initial date set by the IRS. Additional interest may be recovered, however, where the fault is that of the IRS. Similarly, if the IRS issues a refund check with an error in the name of the payee, the taxpayer is entitled to overpayment interest through the date of the replacement check with the correct payee.

## XXIII.E. Overpayments of Tax

### XVIII.E.1. Authority to Refund Overpayments

[627 T.M., IV.C.; TPS ¶3890.01.A.]

When taxpayers overpay their taxes (whether the overpayment results from excess withholdings, estimated payments, loss carrybacks, or credit adjustments), the IRS is authorized to refund the overpayment. The IRS also has full discretion to credit a tax overpayment against any other tax liability of the person who made the overpayment [§ 6402(a)]. In addition, any payment made with respect to any tax assessed or collected after the expiration of the statute of limitations constitutes an overpayment, as of the date of payment [§ 6401(a)].

Overpayments are applied in the following order [§ 6402]:

1. against any other tax liabilities;

2. to past due support obligations;

3. to past due debts owed to federal agencies (e.g., delinquent student loans); and

4. to past due state income tax obligations.

If there is any remaining overpayment, the taxpayer can request a refund or elect to apply it to estimated taxes for the next year, if the overpayment is shown on a tax return [§ 6402(b)].

The IRS may exercise its discretion to bypass the outstanding federal tax liability and issue an offset bypass refund (OBR) to a taxpayer experiencing economic hardship.

For purposes of determining the statute of limitations for filing a refund claim when the IRS applies an overpayment against a tax liability, the date the IRS credits the overpayment against the tax assessment is deemed to be the date of payment. Accordingly, the taxpayer has two years after this date (or three years after the date the subject return is filed, whichever is later) in which to file a refund claim with the IRS regarding the particular application of the overpayment [§ 6402(a)].

*Offsets.* The IRS may offset against a tax refund claim any additional amount the taxpayer owes for the tax shown on the return, even though the statute of limitations would bar assessing the additional tax (or interest or penalties). The rule is that before a refund is authorized, there must be an overpayment. In determining whether there is an overpayment, the IRS may re-audit a return. Therefore, a taxpayer's entire tax liability under the particular tax return is open for redetermination whenever a refund is claimed, regardless of the statute of limitations for making assessments [*Lewis v. Reynolds*, 284 U.S. 281 (1932)].

*Application of Overpayments of Tax Against Non-tax Liabilities.* The Financial Management Service (FMS) has the authority to credit a tax overpayment against other liabilities of the taxpayer in the following order [§ 6402(f)(2)]:

1. past-due child or spousal support assigned to a state;

2. past-due, legally enforceable debts (in the order they accrued) owed to federal agencies;

3. qualifying past-due child or spousal support not assigned to a state; and

4. (i) past-due, legally enforceable state income tax obligations, and (ii) state unemployment compensation debts resulting from fraud (both given equal priority, in the order they accrued).

The amount of overpayment remaining after reduction for these debts is refunded or credited against future tax liability as the taxpayer has elected.

Past-due support must be established by a court order or an administrative process established under state law and the obligation must be the subject of an assignment to the state. The amount of past due support must be at least $25. All such requirements are met if a state agency is providing support collection services, the amount of past-due support is $500 or more, and the past-due support is owed to or for the benefit of a qualified child. The notification of liability must be accompanied by a certification that the state has provided advance notification to the debtor of its intent to collect by tax refund offset, and has complied with applicable state law regarding the collection of past-due support by offsetting federal tax refunds [31 C.F.R. § 285.3(a), 31 C.F.R. § 285.3(c)].

The aggregate amount of income tax debts that an individual owes a state must be at least $25 or such greater amount as determined by FMS. A state must make reasonable efforts to collect the debt before submitting it to FMS for collection by tax refund offset [31 C.F.R. § 285.8(c)].

### XXIII.E.2. Refund Claims

[631 T.M., VI.; TPS ¶3890.01.C.]

A tax overpayment cannot be refunded after the expiration of the statute of limitations for filing a refund claim [§ 6511(b)(1)]. Taxpayers must establish that an overpayment has been made for the tax year and establish the amount of such overpayment [§ 6402(a)]. A taxpayer cannot maintain a refund suit unless a refund claim is timely filed with the IRS [§ 7422(a)].

*Forms.* The tax return itself can serve as a refund claim [Reg. § 301.6402-3(a)(5)]. An amended return can also serve as a refund claim. Individual taxpayers claiming an income tax refund must generally use Form 1040 or Form 1040X; corporate taxpayers must use Form 1120 or Form 1120X. In the case of refunds attributable to "partnership items," a partner generally will not be allowed a refund or credit of such overpayment, unless (i) the IRS conducts a partnership level proceeding, or (ii) the partner files Form 8082, *Notice of Inconsistent Treatment or Administrative Adjustment Request.* For other taxes, a taxpayer can file a Form 843, *Claim for Refund and Request for Abatement* [Reg. § 301.6402-2(c)].

If the taxpayer makes a mistake on the return and does not show that the tax has been overpaid, the IRS may issue a refund if its records indicate that the tax has been overpaid [Reg. § 301.6402-4]. If at the conclusion of an audit, the IRS determines that the taxpayer has overpaid the tax, the IRS generally requests that the taxpayer sign Form 870, *Waiver of Restrictions on Assessment and Collection of Deficiency in Tax and Acceptance of Overassessment* (or a similar waiver form). A signed Form

870 is considered to be a refund claim where there is an overpayment [Rev. Rul. 68-65, 1968-1 C.B. 555].

If a refund check is lost, stolen, or destroyed, the taxpayer should file Form 3911, *Taxpayer Statement Regarding Refund*, requesting a replacement check.

### XXIII.E.3. Basis for Refund Claim

[631 T.M., IV.D.; TPS ¶3890.01.C.]

Regardless of the form used to make a refund claim, the taxpayer must state the grounds for the refund claim and sufficient facts to inform the IRS of the exact basis for the claim. In addition, separate claims must be made for each taxable period in which a refund of tax is claimed and for each type of tax claimed [Reg. § 301.6402-2(b), § 301.6402-2(d)]. A claim for refund must identify and/or set forth [Reg. § 301.6402-2(b)]:

- the date and time of each tax payment to be refunded;
- the period for which it was paid; and
- each ground on which the claimed refund is based.

A claim that does not state grounds and/or facts supporting a refund can be amended before the statute of limitations expires. However, once the limitations period expires, the refund claim cannot be amended to include new grounds.

*Informal Claims.* Courts have found that under certain special circumstances, a timely "informal" claim may serve to toll the statute of limitations until the taxpayer can properly file a formal refund request. An informal refund claim must be subsequently amended by a formal claim since the informal refund claim doctrine is predicated on an expectation that whatever deficiencies existed in the informal claim will at some point be corrected [*United States v. Kales*, 314 U.S. 186 (1941)].

While what constitutes an adequate or valid informal refund claim is not well settled, to be valid, an informal claim must apprise the IRS that a refund is sought, give notice of the tax and year at issue, and must include a written component.

### XXIII.E.4. Person to File Refund Claim

[631 T.M., IV.D.; TPS ¶3890.01.C.4.]

In most cases, the proper party to file a refund claim is the taxpayer [§ 6402]. A refund claim can be filed by a representative of the taxpayer (e.g., an executor, administrator, guardian, trustee, receiver, or other fiduciary) [Reg. § 301.6402-2(e)]. For a deceased taxpayer, the refund claim is filed on Form 1310, *Statement of Person Claiming Refund Due to a Deceased Taxpayer*. Form 1310 is not used where there is a surviving spouse filing a joint return with the decedent for the year of death or where the personal representative files a Form 1040 on behalf of the decedent.

### XXIII.E.5. Time, Place and Manner for Filing Refund Claims

[631 T.M., III.B.; TPS ¶3890.01.C.5.]

A taxpayer generally must file the claim for refund with the IRS Submission Processing Center where the original return was filed. Alternatively, a refund claim can be hand-delivered (not mailed) to the local IRS office serving the taxpayer's legal residence or, in the case of a business or corporation, its principal place of business or principal office [Reg. § 301.6402-2(a)(2)].

*Date Considered Filed and Timely Mailed/Timely Filed Exception.* A tax return filed before its due date is deemed filed on the due date [§ 6513(a)]. A taxpayer seeking to establish that a return is timely filed can prove it by showing one of the following [§ 7502(a)]:

- physical delivery to the IRS;
- proof of the postmark on the envelope in which the return was mailed; or
- the registered or certified mail receipt of the mailed return or receipt of a designated private delivery service.

If the return is filed after the due date, the return is deemed filed when received by the IRS. This general rule also applies to refund claims. A refund claim is considered filed on the date that it is delivered to and received by the IRS. However, a return is deemed to be filed on the date of the postmark stamped on the envelope in which the return was mailed. Thus, if the envelope that contains the return has a timely postmark, the return is considered timely filed even if it is received after the last date, or the last day of the period prescribed for filing the return. The timely-mailed timely-filed rules apply to claims for credit or refund made on late filed original income tax returns [Reg. § 301.7502-1].

---

**EXAMPLE:** Thomas mailed his 2010 Form 1040 on Apr. 15, 2014, claiming a refund of amounts paid through withholding during 2010. The date of the postmark on the envelope containing the return and claim for refund is Apr. 15, 2014. The return and claim for refund are received by the IRS on Apr. 18, 2014. Amounts withheld in 2010 exceeded T's tax liability for 2010 and are treated as paid on Apr. 15, 2014. Even though the date of the postmark on the envelope is after the due date of the return, the claim for refund and the late filed return are treated as filed on the postmark date. Accordingly, the return will be treated as filed on Apr. 15, 2014. In addition, the claim for refund will be treated as timely filed on Apr. 15, 2014. Further, the entire amount of the refund attributable to withholding is allowable as a refund.

---

### XXIII.E.6. Refund Suits

[631 T.M., III.C.; TPS ¶3890.03.]

No suit for refund can be initiated before the expiration of six months from the date on which the claim for refund is filed, or after two years from the date the IRS issues a notice of claim disallowance. A taxpayer may file a written waiver of the requirement that the IRS send a notice of claim disallowance, by registered or certified mail. The waiver starts the running of the two-year period of limitations for filing suit on the claim, from the date the waiver is filed [§ 6532].

# INDEX

## A

**A REORGANIZATIONS**
Built-in gains, limitation on use,
XIII.E.5.c
Carryover of tax attributes, XIII.E.5.a
Statutory mergers, description,
XIII.E.1.a.(1)

**ABANDONMENT**
Loss deduction, VIII.H.2
Partnership losses, XIV.H.1.b

**ACCELERATED DEATH BENEFITS**
Exclusions from income, II.E.2
Information returns, XXIII.A.2.e
Sales and exchanges, III.C.6.c

**ACCIDENT INSURANCE**
Employer contributions, XVII.C.1.a
Employer-provided, II.D.1
FICA and FUTA tax exception,
XXII.B.4.b
Medical expense reimbursements,
XVII.C.1.b
S corporations, shareholder-employee deduction limit, XV.B.5.a
Withholding of tax on benefits, XXII.A.5.g

**ACCOUNTING**
Accountants, education expenses, IV.A.5
Change in method. *See* CHANGE IN AC-
COUNTING METHOD
Corporations, XIII.C.1.f; XVI.D.1.c
Depreciation deduction, V.A.4.e
Fair value. *See* FAIR VALUE
Farmers, XI.H
Installment sales, XI.F
Inventory. *See* INVENTORY
Long-term contracts
Cost allocation rules, XI.E.4
Exempt contracts, XI.E.3
Percentage-of-completion method,
XI.E.2
Methods
Overview, XI.B
Accrual method
Description, XI.B.1.d.(1)
Farmers, XI.H.1
§ 467 rental agreements, XI.G.2
Adoption of method, XI.B.2
Advance payments, XI.B.1.d.(1)
Cash method
Corporations, XI.B.1.c.(3)
Partnerships, XVI.D.1.c
Personal service corporations,
XIII.C.6.c
S corporations, XVI.D.1.c
Sole proprietorships, XVI.D.1.c

Tax shelters, XI.B.1.c.(3)
Change. *See* CHANGE IN AC-
COUNTING METHOD
Hybrid methods, XI.B.1.f
Permissible methods, XI.B.1
Special method, XI.B.1.e
Partnerships, XIV.D.4.d; XVI.D.1.c
Personal service corporations, XIII.C.6.c;
XVI.D.1.c
Regulated taxpayers, optional method,
VIII.A.2
REMICs, XIII.F.3.b
S corporations, XV.C.4.d; XVI.D.1.c
Sole proprietorship, XVI.D.1.c
Tax year. *See* TAX YEAR

**ACCOUNTS RECEIVABLE, IV.E; VIII.I**

**ACCUMULATED ADJUSTMENT AC-
COUNTS, XV.B.4.c.(2)**

**ACCUMULATED EARNINGS AND
PROFITS, XV.A.4.a**

**ACCUMULATED EARNINGS TAX**
Accumulated earnings credit, XIII.C.4.b
Affiliated groups, XIII.C.7
Burden of proof, XIII.c.4.a
Consent dividends, XIII.C.4.b
Consolidated returns, XIII.C.8.c.(2)
Corporations, XIII.C.4; XVI.D.2.a
Foreign corporations, XIII.C.4.b
Holding companies, XIII.C.4.b
Investment companies, XIII.C.4.b
Passive foreign investment companies,
XX.C.3.d
Personal service corporations, XIII.C.4.b
Reasonable needs of business exception,
XIII.C.4.a
S corporations, XV.C.2; XVI.D.2.a
Tax avoidance purpose, XIII.C.4.a

**ACQUISITION INDEBTEDNESS,
XIX.D.3.b**

**ADDRESSES, XXIII.A.1.e**

**ADMINISTRATIVE EXPENSES**
Estate income tax deduction,
XVIII.A.4.b.(19)
Estate tax deduction, XXI.B.4.a
Trust income tax deduction,
XVIII.A.4.b.(19)

**ADOPTION**
Adoption taxpayer identification numbers,
XXIII.A.1.b
Excludible fringe benefits, XVII.E.1
Expense credit, IX.B.3; IX.G.10
Medical expenses deductibility, VII.D.2.a

**ADVANCE PRICING AGREEMENTS,
XX.C.5.c**

1147

# Index

# Index

# Index

# Index

# Index

# Index

# Index

Property purchase for less, inclusion in gross income, I.B.7

S corporation distributions, reporting requirement, XVI.D.2.d

Securities inventory, XI.C.3.d

**FALSE RETURNS**

Partnerships, extension of limitations period, XXIII.C.3.b

Tax returns, XXIII.A.2.f

**FARMING**

Accounting, XI.H

Capitalization of expenses, IV.F.3

Conservation property disposition, III.C.8.e

Cooperatives, XIII.F.4.b; XIX.B.1; XIX.B.2

Discharge of indebtedness income, II.A.4
Basis reduction election, II.A.8.b
Priority, II.A.4

Estate tax, charitable remainder trust gift, XXI.B.4.c

Gross income, I.H.2

Income averaging, Form 1040, Sch. J, X.A.1.a

Inventory valuation, XI.H.2

Livestock and breeding expenses, IV.F.3.d

Loss deduction, VIII.H.5

NOLs, carryover and carryback exceptions, VIII.G.3.b

S corporations, election not to apply Uniform Capitalization Rules, XV.C.3.a

SECA tax exception, X.A.7.b.(2)

Soil and water conservation expenses, III.C.8.c

Tax shelter losses, AMT adjustments, X.A.2.b

Wetlands and croplands disposition, III.C.8.d

Withholding, reporting requirements, XXII.C.1.a

**FATCA** *See* **FOREIGN BANK ACCOUNT REPORTING**

**FDAP INCOME, XX.F.1; XX.F.1.b.(1)**

**FEDERAL HOME LOAN BANKS, XIII.C.2.b**

**FEDERAL NATIONAL MORTGAGE ASSOCIATION, IV.F.5.l**

**FICA TAX**

Compensation subject to tax, XXII.B.3

Deferred compensation plans, XVII.B.1.d.(3)

Deposit of taxes, XXII.C.1.b

Employee compensation, I.C.8

Employees subject to tax, XXII.B.5

Employer collection, XXII.B.2.a

Employer Social Security credit, IX.A.15

ESOPs, XVII.A.10.d

Exceptions, XXII.B.4

§ 401(k) plans, XVII.A.2.g; XVII.A.3.e

Government employees, XXII.B.7

Information returns, XXII.C.1.c

IRAs, XVII.A.5.g

Multiple employers, XXII.B.1.c

Nonqualified deferred compensation, XVII.B.1.e.(7)

Reporting requirements, XXII.C.1.a

Retirement plan contributions, XVII.A.2.g

Roth IRAs, XVII.A.3.b

S corporation shareholders, XVI.D.2.a

SIMPLE plans, XVII.A.9.d

Statutory nonemployee exclusion, XXII.B.6

Tax rate, XXII.B.1.a

Trust Fund Recovery Penalty, XXII.B.2.a; XXIII.D.1.g

**FILING TAX RETURNS**

Address of where to file, XXIII.A.1.e

Charitable remainder trust information returns, XVIII.C.6

Corporations
Forms, XIII.C.1.b
Mandate, XIII.C.1.a; XXIII.A.1.a.(2)

Due date, XXIII.A.1.c.(1)

Estate income tax, XVIII.D.1

Estate tax, XXI.B.6.a; XXIII.A.1a.(5)

Extension of time, XIII.A.1.d

Generation-skipping transfer tax return, XXI.D.4

Gift tax, XXI.C.7

Individuals
Decedent final return, XII.A.4
Dependents, filing threshold, XII.A.1.b
Due date, XII.A.3.a
Estimated tax, XII.F.2
Extension of time, XII.A.3.b; XXIII.A.1.d
Filing return when not required, XII.A.1.e
Filing status, XII.C
Filing threshold, XII.A.1.a
Form required, XII.A.2
Methods, XII.A.3.c
Nonresidents, XII.A.1; XXIII.A.1.a.(2)
Residents, XII.A.1; XXIII.A.1.a.(2)

Mailbox rule, XXIII.A.1.c.(2)

Partnerships, XXIII.A.1.(a).(3)

Partnerships, election to opt-out of Subchapter K, XIV.B.3.b

Recordkeeping requirement, XXIII.A.1.i

S corporations, XV.B.1.c; XV.C.4; XXIII.A.1.a.(4)

Signature requirement, XXIII.A.1.g

# Index

## H

# Index

# Index

# Index

# Index

# Index

# Index

## Z

_____

# TABLE OF INTERNAL REVENUE CODE SECTIONS

# Table of Internal Revenue Code Sections

# Table of Internal Revenue Code Sections

# Table of Internal Revenue Code Sections

# Table of Internal Revenue Code Sections

# Table of Internal Revenue Code Sections

# Table of Internal Revenue Code Sections

# Table of Internal Revenue Code Sections

# Table of Internal Revenue Code Sections

# Table of Internal Revenue Code Sections

# Table of Internal Revenue Code Sections

# Table of Internal Revenue Code Sections

# Table of Internal Revenue Code Sections

# Table of Internal Revenue Code Sections

# Table of Internal Revenue Code Sections

# Table of Internal Revenue Code Sections

# Table of Internal Revenue Code Sections

## TABLE OF TAX FORMS

1237

# Table of Tax Forms

# Table of Tax Forms